MW00576589

PARALLEL
COMMENTARY
ON THE
NEW TESTAMENT

PARALLEL
COMMENTARY
ON THE
NEW
TESTAMENT

AMG *Publishers*

Parallel Commentary on the New Testament

Published by AMG Publishers
6815 Shallowford Road
Chattanooga, Tennessee 37421

Copyright © 2003 John Hunt Publishing Ltd
Cover illustration: Nautilus Design, Basingstoke, UK
Typography: Jim Weaver Design. Basingstoke, UK

ISBN 13: 978-089957444-8
ISBN 10: 0-89957-440-0

Unless otherwise stated Scripture quotations are taken from
The Holy Bible, King James Version/Authorised (KJV, AV): Oxford University Press

Printed in Canada
14 13 12 11 10 09 08 –T– 8 7 6 5 4 3 2

Contents

Introduction

Multi New Testament Commentary brings together, for the first time, three classic Bible commentators on the whole of the New Testament in one volume.

Bible commentators

This parallel commentary consists of the commentaries and sermons of:

1. *Matthew Henry* and his New Testament commentary, abbreviated;
2. *John Wesley* and his complete New Testament commentary; and
3. *C.H. Spurgeon* and a selection of his New Testament sermons, from Matthew to Revelation.

Matthew Henry, 1662–1714

In his *Commenting & Commentaries*, C.H. Spurgeon wrote the following about this godly Non-conformist's renowned commentary on the whole Bible:

> "First among the mighty for general usefullness we are bound to mention the man whose name is a household word, Matthew Henry. He is most pious and pithy, sound and sensible, suggestive and sober, terse and trustworthy. You will find him to be glittering with metaphors, rich in analogies, overflowing with illustrations, superabundant in reflections. He delights in apposition and alliteration; he is usually plain, quaint, and full of pith.
>
> "Every minister ought to read Matthew Henry entirely and carefully through once at least. I should recommend you to get through it in the next twelve months after you leave college. Begin at the beginning, and resolve that you will traverse the goodly land from Dan to Beersheba. You will acquire a vast store of sermons if you read with your notebook close at hand; and as for thoughts, they will swarm around you like twittering swallows around an old gable towards the close of autumn. If you publicly expound the chapter you have just been reading, your people will wonder at the novelty of your remarks and the depth of your thoughts, and then you may tell them what a treasure Henry is. What more could I say in commendation of this author?"

John Wesley, 1703–1791

John Wesley, known for being the reluctant founder of Methodism, often preached six times a day and regularly rode over 10,000 miles a year. Wesley worked equally hard to provide everyone who came to accept Jesus Christ through his ministry with lasting spiritual help. Referring to this in his own *Journal*, Wesley wrote: "I determined by the grace of God not to strike one blow in any place where I cannot follow the blow."

George Whitefield acknowledged the importance of these Methodist Christian fellowships which met weekly in people's homes: "My brother Wesley acted more wisely than I. The souls that were awakened under his ministry he joined together in classes, and so preserved the fruit of his labors. I failed to do this, and as a result my people are a rope of sand."

Wesley wrote his commentary on the Bible to instruct the members of these Methodist "classes."

Wesley's commentary reflects his high view of Scripture. He spent his life in working to become "A man of one book." He wrote: "I want to know one thing, the way to heaven: how to land safe on that happy shore. God himself has condescended to teach the way; for this very end he came from heaven. He has written it down in a book! Oh, give me that book! At any price, give me the book of God! I have it: here is knowledge enough for me. Let me be *homo unius libri*: 'A man of one book.'"

Wesley had no doubts about how the Bible should be interpreted. He wrote: "The general rule of interpreting Scripture is this: the literal sense of every text is to be taken, if it be not contrary to some other texts. But in that case, the obscure text is to be interpreted by those which speak more plainly. . . . Try all things by the written word, and let all bow down before it. You are in danger of fanaticism every hour, if you depart ever so little from Scripture; yea, or from the plain, literal meaning of a text, taken in connection with the context."

C.H. Spurgeon, 1834–1892

The Baptist, Charles Haddon Spurgeon, was the greatest preacher of his day. During his 38-year long London ministry he preached twice weekly to a 5,000 strong congregation and also saw 14,000 new members join it. His sermons were very popular, yet very scholarly, and were in the Augustinian and Puritan theological tradition. During his lifetime 2,241 of his sermons were published and during the next 25 years a further 1,000 of his sermons were published. Over 100,000,000 copies of his sermons, in 23 different languages, were published by the printers Passmore and Alabaster, who were formed to print his sermons and his 135 books.

Multi New Testament Commentary includes a representative selection of Spurgeon's timeless New Testament expositions.

Spurgeon gave the following advice to would-be preachers:

"In order to be able to expound the Scriptures, and as an aid to your pulpit studies, you will need to be familiar with the commentators: a glorious army, let me tell you, whose acquaintance will be your delight and profit. Of course, you are not such wiseacres as to think or say that you can expound Scripture without assistance from the works of divines and learned men who have labored before you in the field of exposition. If you are of that opinion, pray remain so, for you are not worth the trouble of conversion, and like a little coterie who think with you, would resent the attempt as an insult to your infallibility. It seems odd, that certain men who talk so much of what the Holy Spirit reveals to themselves, should think so little of what he has revealed to others. You must be content to learn of holy men, taught of God, and mighty in the Scriptures. A respectable acquaintance with the opinions of the giants of the past, might have saved many an erratic thinker from wild interpretations and outrageous inferences."

Bible version

The King James Version, which was used by Henry, Wesley, and Spurgeon, is set out on each page of *Multi New Testament Commentary*, enabling the reader to see, at a glance, the relevant part of the Scripture as it is expounded and commentated on.

Through the centuries

Matthew Henry, John Wesley, and C.H. Spurgeon probably rank as the outstanding Bible commentators, evangelists, and Bible expositors of the seventeenth century, eighteenth century, and nineteenth century respectively. *Multi New Testament Commentary* now brings together the writings and sermons of these three spiritual giants for our own edification.

John Wesley
Notes On The New Testament

Preface

1. For many years I have had a desire of setting down and laying together, what has occurred to my mind, either in reading, thinking, or conversation, which might assist serious persons, who have not the advantage of learning, in understanding the New Testament. But I have been continually deterred from attempting any thing of this kind, by a deep sense of my own inability: of my want, not only of learning for such a work, but much more, of experience and wisdom. This has often occasioned my laying aside the thought. And when, by much importunity, I have been prevailed upon to resume it, still I determined to delay it as long as possible, that (if it should please God) I might finish my work and my life together.

2. But having lately had a loud call from God to arise and go hence, I am convinced that if I attempt any thing of this kind at all, I must not delay any longer. My day is far spent, and (even in a natural way) the shadows of the evening come on apace. And I am the rather induced to do what little I can in this way, because I can do nothing else: being prevented, by my present weakness, from either traveling or preaching. But, blessed be God, I can still read, and write, and think. O that it may be to his glory!

3. It will be easily discerned, even from what I have said already, and much more from the notes themselves, that they were not principally designed for men of learning; who are provided with many other helps: and much less for men of long and deep experience in the ways and word of God. I desire to sit at their feet, and to learn of them. But I write chiefly for plain unlettered men, who understand only their mother tongue, and yet reverence and love the word of God, and have a desire to save their souls.

4. In order to assist these in such a measure, as I am able, I design first to set down the text itself, for the most part, in the common English translation, which is, in general, (so far as I can judge) abundantly the best that I have seen. Yet I do not say it is incapable of being brought, in several places, nearer to the original. Neither will I affirm, that the Greek copies from which this translation was made, are always the most correct. And therefore I shall take the liberty, as occasion may require, making here and there a small alteration.

5. I am very sensible this will be liable to objections: nay, to objections of quite opposite kinds. Some will probably think, the text is altered too much; and others, that it is altered too little. To the former I would observe, that I never knowingly, so much as in one place, altered it for altering sake: but there, and there only, where first, the sense was made better, stronger, clearer, or more consistent with the context: secondly, where the sense being equally good, the phrase was better or nearer the original. To the latter, who think the alterations too few, and that the translation might have been nearer still, I answer, and this is true: I acknowledge it might. But what valuable end would it have answered, to multiply such trivial alterations as add neither clearness nor strength to

the text? This I could not prevail upon myself to do: so much the less because there is, to my apprehension, I know not what, peculiarly solemn and venerable in the old language of our translation. And suppose this a mistaken apprehension, and an instance of human infirmity; yet, is it not an excusable infirmity, to be unwilling to part with what we have been long accustomed to; and to love the very words by which God has often conveyed strength or comfort to our souls!

6. I have endeavored to make the notes as short as possible that the comment may not obscure or swallow up the text: and as plain as possible, in pursuance of my main design, to assist the unlearned reader: for this reason I have studiously avoided, not only all curious and critical inquiries, and all use of the learned languages, but all such methods of reasoning and modes of expression as people in common life are unacquainted with: for the same reason, as I rather endeavor to obviate than to propose and answer questions, so I purposely decline going deep into many difficulties, lest I should leave the ordinary reader behind me.

7. I once designed to write down barely what occurred, to my own mind, consulting none but the inspired writers. But no sooner was I acquainted with that great light of the Christian world, (lately gone to his reward,) Bengelius, than I entirely changed my design, being thoroughly convinced it might be of more service to the cause of religion, were I barely to translate his *Gnomon Novi Testamenti*, than to write many volumes upon it. Many of his excellent notes I have therefore translated. Many more I have abridged, omitting that part which was purely critical, and giving the substance of the rest. Those various readings likewise, which he has showed to have a vast majority of ancient copies and translations on their side, I have without scruple incorporated with the text; which, after his manner, I have divided all along (though not omitting the common division into chapters and verses, which is of use on various accounts) according to the matter it contains, making a larger or smaller pause, just as the sense requires. And even this is such a help in many places, as one who has not tried it can scarcely conceive.

8. I am likewise indebted for some useful observations to Dr. Heylin's *Theological Lectures*: and for many more to Dr. Guyse, and to the *Family Expositor* of the late pious and learned Dr. Doddridge It was a doubt with me for some time, whether I should not subjoin to every note I received from them the name of the author from whom it was taken; especially considering I had transcribed some, and abridged many more, almost in the words of the author. But upon farther consideration, I resolved to name none, that nothing might divert the mind of the reader from keeping close to the point in view, and receiving what was spoken only according to its own intrinsic value.

9. I cannot flatter myself so far (to use the words of one of the above-named writers) as to imagine that I have fallen into no mistakes in a work of so great difficulty. But my own conscience acquits me of having designedly misrepresented any single passage of Scripture, or of having written one line with a purpose of inflaming the hearts of Christians against each other. God forbid that I should make the words of the most gentle and benevolent Jesus a vehicle to convey such poison. Would to God that all the

party names, and unscriptural phrases and forms, which have divided the Christian world, were forgot: and that we might all agree to sit down together, as humble, loving disciples, at the feet of our common Master, to hear his word, to imbibe his Spirit, and to transcribe his life in our own!

10. Concerning the Scriptures in general, it may be observed, the word of the living God, which directed the first patriarchs also, was, in the time of Moses, committed to writing. To this were added, in several succeeding generations, the inspired writings of the other prophets. Afterward, what the Son of God preached, and the Holy Ghost spoke by the apostles, the apostles and evangelists wrote – This is what we now style the Holy Scripture: this is that word of God which remained forever: of which, though heaven and earth pass away, one jot or tittle shall not pass away. The Scripture therefore of the Old and New Testament, is a most solid and precious system of Divine truth. Every part thereof is worthy of God; and all together are one entire body, wherein is no defect, no excess. It is the fountain of heavenly wisdom, which they who are able to taste, prefer to all writings of men, however wise, or learned, or holy.

11. An exact knowledge of the truth was accompanied in the inspired writers with an exactly regular series of arguments, a precise expression of their meaning, and a genuine vigor of suitable affections. The chain of argument in each book is briefly exhibited in the table prefixed to it, which contains also the sum thereof, and may be of more use than prefixing the argument to each chapter; the division of the New Testament into chapters having been made in the dark ages, and very incorrectly; often separating things that are closely joined, and joining those that are entirely distinct from each other.

12. In the language of the sacred writings, we may observe the utmost depth, together with the utmost ease. All the elegancies of human composures sink into nothing before it: God speaks not as man, but as God. His thoughts are very deep: and thence his words are of inexhaustible virtue. And the language of his messengers also is exact in the highest degree: for the words which were given them accurately answered the impression made upon their minds: and hence Luther says, "Divinity is nothing but a grammar of the language of the Holy Ghost." To understand this thoroughly, we should observe the emphasis, which lies on every word; the holy affections expressed thereby, and the tempers shown by every writer. But how little are these, the latter especially, regarded? Though they are wonderfully diffused through the whole New Testament, and are in truth a continued commendation of him who acts, or speaks, or writes.

13. The New Testament is all those sacred writings in which the New Testament or covenant is described. The former part of this contains the writings of the evangelists and apostles: the latter, the Revelation of Jesus Christ. In the former is, first, the history of Jesus Christ, from his coming in the flesh to his ascension into heaven; then the institution and history of the Christian Church, from the time of his ascension. The Revelation delivers what is to be, with regard to Christ, the Church, and the universe, till the consummation of all things.

BRISTOL HOT-WELLS, January 4, 1754.

List of sermons by Charles H. Spurgeon

Matthew

MATTHEW 1

1 The book of the generation of Jesus Christ, the son of David, the son of Abraham.

2 Abraham begat Isaac; and Isaac begat Jacob; and Jacob begat Judas and his brethren;

3 And Judas begat Phares and Zara of Thamar; and Phares begat Esrom; and Esrom begat Aram;

4 And Aram begat Aminadab; and Aminadab begat Naasson; and Naasson begat Salmon;

5 And Salmon begat Booz of Rachab; and Booz begat Obed of Ruth; and Obed begat Jesse;

6 And Jesse begat David the king; and David the king begat Solomon of her that had been the wife of Urias;

7 And Solomon begat Roboam; and Roboam begat Abia; and Abia begat Asa;

8 And Asa begat Josaphat; and Josaphat begat Joram; and Joram begat Ozias;

9 And Ozias begat Joatham; and Joatham begat Achaz; and Achaz begat Ezekias;

10 And Ezekias begat Manasses; and Manasses begat Amon; and Amon begat Josias;

11 And Josias begat Jechonias and his brethren, about the time they were carried away to Babylon:

12 And after they were brought to Babylon, Jechonias begat Salathiel; and Salathiel begat Zorobabel;

13 And Zorobabel begat Abiud; and Abiud begat Eliakim; and Eliakim begat Azor;

14 And Azor begat Sadoc; and Sadoc begat Achim; and Achim begat Eliud;

15 And Eliud begat Eleazar; and Eleazar begat Matthan; and Matthan begat Jacob;

16 And Jacob begat Joseph the husband of Mary, of whom was born Jesus, who is called Christ.

17 So all the generations from Abraham to David are fourteen generations; and from David until the carrying away into Babylon are fourteen generations; and from the carrying away into Babylon unto Christ are fourteen generations.

18 Now the birth of Jesus Christ was on this wise: When as his mother Mary was espoused to Joseph, before they came together, she was found with child of the Holy Ghost.

19 Then Joseph her husband, being a just man, and not willing to make her a public example, was minded to put her away privily.

20 But while he thought on these

The Gospel (that is, good tidings) means a book containing the good tidings of our salvation by Jesus Christ. St. Mark in his Gospel presupposes that of St. Matthew, and supplies what is omitted therein. St. Luke supplies what is omitted by both the former: St. John what is omitted by all the three. St. Matthew particularly points out the fulfilling of the prophecies for the conviction of the Jews. St. Mark wrote a short compendium, and yet added many remarkable circumstances omitted by St. Matthew, particularly with regard to the apostles, immediately after they were called. St. Luke treated principally of the office of Christ, and mostly in a historical manner. St. John refuted those who denied his Godhead: each choosing to treat more largely on those things, which most suited the time when, and the persons to whom, he wrote.

MATTHEW 1

1. The book of the generation of Jesus Christ – That is, strictly speaking, the account of his birth and genealogy. The son of David, the son of Abraham – He is so called, because to these he was more peculiarly promised; and of these it was often foretold the Messiah should spring. Luke iii, 31.

3. Of Thamar – St. Matthew adds the names of those women also, that were remarkable in the sacred history.

4. Naasson – Who was prince of the tribe of Judah, when the Israelites entered into Canaan.

5. Obed begat Jesse – The providence of God was peculiarly shown in this, that Salmon, Boaz, and Obed, must each of them have been near a hundred years old, at the birth of his son here recorded.

6. David the king – Particularly mentioned under this character, because his throne is given to the Messiah.

8. Jehoram begat Uzziah – Jehoahaz, Joash, and Amaziah coming between. So that he begat him immediately, as Christ is immediately the son of David and of Abraham. So the progeny of Hezekiah, after many generations, are called the sons that should issue from him, whom he should beget, Isaiah xxxix, 7.

11. Josiah begat Jeconiah – Mediately, Jehoiakim coming between. And his brethren – That is, his uncles. The Jews term all kinsmen brethren. About the time they were carried away – Which was a little after the birth of Jeconiah.

16. The husband of Mary – Jesus was generally believed to be the son of Joseph. It was needful for all who believed this, to know, that Joseph was sprung from David. Otherwise they would not allow Jesus to be the Christ. Jesus, who is called Christ – The name Jesus respects chiefly the promise of blessing made to Abraham: the name Christ, the promise of the Messiah's kingdom, which was made to David. It may be farther observed, that the word Christ in Greek, and Messiah in Hebrews, signify anointed, and imply the prophetic, priestly, and royal characters, which were to meet in the Messiah.

17. So all the generations – Observe, in order to complete the three fourteens, David ends the first fourteen, and begins the second (which reaches to the captivity) and Jesus ends the third fourteen.

19. A just man – A strict observer of the law: therefore not thinking it right to keep her.

21. Jesus – That is, a Savior. It is the same name with Joshua (who was a type of him) which properly signifies, The Lord, Salvation. His people – Israel. And all the Israel of God.

MATTHEW HENRY

CHARLES H. SPURGEON

Matthew, surnamed Levi, before his conversion was a publican, or tax-gatherer under the Romans at Capernaum. He is generally allowed to have written his Gospel before any other of the evangelists. The contents of this Gospel, and the evidence of ancient writers, show that it was written primarily for the use of the Jewish nation. The fulfilment of prophecy was regarded by the Jews as strong evidence, therefore this is especially dwelt upon by St. Matthew. Here are particularly selected such parts of our Savior's history and discourses as were best suited to awaken the Jewish nation to a sense of their sins; to remove their erroneous expectations of an earthly kingdom; to abate their pride and self-conceit; to teach them the spiritual nature and extent of the gospel; and to prepare them for the admission of the Gentiles into the church.

MATTHEW 1

The genealogy of Jesus. (1-17)
An angel appears to Joseph. (18-25)

1-17 Concerning this genealogy of our Savior, observe the chief intention. It is not a needless genealogy. It is not a vain-glorious one, as those of great men often are. It proves that our Lord Jesus is of the nation and family out of which the Messiah was to arise. The promise of the blessing was made to Abraham and his seed; of the dominion, to David and his seed. It was promised to Abraham that Christ should descend from him, Ge 12:3; 22:18; and to David that he should descend from him, 2Sa 7:12; Ps 89:3, &c.; 132:11; and, therefore, unless Jesus is a son of David, and a son of Abraham, he is not the Messiah. Now this is here proved from well-known records. When the Son of God was pleased to take our nature, he came near to us, in our fallen, wretched condition; but he was perfectly free from sin: and while we read the names in his genealogy, we should not forget how low the Lord of glory stooped to save the human race.

18-25 Let us look to the circumstances under which the Son of God entered into this lower world, till we learn to despise the vain honors of this world, when compared with piety and holiness. The mystery of Christ's becoming man is to be adored, not curiously inquired into. It was so ordered that Christ should partake of our nature, yet that he should be pure from the defilement of original sin, which has been communicated to all the race of Adam. Observe, it is the thoughtful, not the unthinking, whom God will guide. God's time to come with instruction to his people, is when they are at a loss. Divine comforts most delight the soul when under the pressure of perplexed thoughts. Joseph is told that Mary should bring forth the Savior of the world. He was to call his name Jesus, a Savior. Jesus is the same name with Joshua. And the reason of that name is clear, for those whom Christ saves, he saves from their sins; from the guilt of sin by

THE FATHERHOOD OF GOD
Sermon number 213 delivered on Sabbath Morning, September 12, 1858, at the Music Hall, Royal Surrey Gardens.

"Our Father which art in heaven."—Matthew 6:9.

IN THE TEXT, there are several things we shall have to notice. And first, I shall dwell for a few minutes upon the double relationship mentioned: "Our Father which art in heaven." There is sonship—"Father;" there is brotherhood, for it says, "Our Father;" and if he be the common father of us, then we must be brothers; for there are two relationships, sonship and brotherhood. In the next place, I shall utter a few words upon the spirit which is necessary to help us before we are able to utter this—"The spirit of adoption," whereby we can cry, "Our Father which art in heaven." And then, thirdly, I shall conclude the double argument of the text, for it is really an argument upon which the rest of the prayer is based. "Our Father which art in heaven," is, as it were, a strong argument used before supplication itself is presented.

I. First, THE DOUBLE RELATIONSHIP IMPLIED IN THE TEXT.
We take the first one. Here is sonship—"Our Father which art in heaven." How are we to understand this, and in what sense are we the sons and daughters of God? Some say that the Fatherhood of God is universal, and that every man, from the fact of his being created by God, is necessarily God's son, and that therefore every man has a right to approach the throne of God, and say, "Our Father which art in heaven." To that I must demur. I believe that in this prayer we are to come before God, looking upon him not as our Father through creation, but as our Father through adoption and the new birth. I will very briefly state my reasons for this.

I have never been able to see that creation necessarily implies fatherhood. I believe God has made many things that are not his children. Hath he not made the heavens and the earth, the sea and the fullness thereof? and are they his children? You say these are not rational and intelligent beings; but he made the angels, who stand in an eminently high and holy position, are they his children? "Unto which of the angels said he at any time, thou art my son?" I do not find, as a rule, that angels are called the children of God; and I must demur to the idea that mere creation brings God necessarily into the relationship of a Father. Doth not the potter make vessels of clay? But is the potter the father of the vase, or of the bottle? No, beloved, it

things, behold, the angel of the Lord appeared unto him in a dream, saying, Joseph, thou son of David, fear not to take unto thee Mary thy wife: for that which is conceived in her is of the Holy Ghost.

21 And she shall bring forth a son, and thou shalt call his name JESUS: for he shall save his people from their sins.

22 Now all this was done, that it might be fulfilled which was spoken of the Lord by the prophet, saying,

23 Behold, a virgin shall be with child, and shall bring forth a son, and they shall call his name Emmanuel, which being interpreted is, God with us.

24 Then Joseph being raised from sleep did as the angel of the Lord had bidden him, and took unto him his wife:

25 And knew her not till she had brought forth her firstborn son: and he called his name JESUS.

MATTHEW 2

1 Now when Jesus was born in Bethlehem of Judea in the days of Herod the king, behold, there came wise men from the east to Jerusalem,

2 Saying, Where is he that is born King of the Jews? for we have seen his star in the east, and are come to worship him.

3 When Herod the king had heard these things, he was troubled, and all Jerusalem with him.

4 And when he had gathered all the chief priests and scribes of the people together, he demanded of them where Christ should be born.

5 And they said unto him, In Bethlehem of Judea: for thus it is written by the prophet,

6 And thou Bethlehem, in the land of Juda, art not the least among the princes of Juda: for out of thee shall come a Governor, that shall rule my people Israel.

7 Then Herod, when he had privily called the wise men, inquired of them diligently what time the star appeared.

8 And he sent them to Bethlehem, and said, Go and search diligently for the young child; and when ye have found him, bring me word again, that I may come and worship him also.

9 When they had heard the king, they departed; and, lo, the star, which they saw in the east, went before them, till it came and stood over where the young child was.

10 When they saw the star, they rejoiced with exceeding great joy.

11 And when they were come into the

23. They shall call his name Emmanuel – To be called, only means, according to the Hebrews manner of speaking, that the person spoken of shall really and effectually be what he is called, and actually fulfill that title. Thus, Unto us a child is born – and his name shall be called Wonderful, Counselor, the Mighty God, the Prince of Peace – That is, he shall be all these, though not so much nominally, as really, and in effect. And thus was he called Emmanuel; which was no common name of Christ, but points out his nature and office; as he is God incarnate, and dwells by his Spirit in the hearts of his people. It is observable, the words in Isaiah are, Thou (namely, his mother) shalt call; but here, They – that is, all his people, shall call – shall acknowledge him to be Emmanuel, God with us. Which being interpreted – This is a clear proof that St. Matthew wrote his Gospel in Greek, and not in Hebrew. Isaiah vii, 14.

25. He knew her not, till after she had brought forth – It cannot be inferred from hence, that he knew her afterward: no more than it can be inferred from that expression, 2 Sam. vi, 23, Michal had no child till the day of her death, that she had children afterward. Nor do the words that follow, the first-born son, alter the case. For there are abundance of places, wherein the term first born is used, though there were no subsequent children. Luke ii, 7.

MATTHEW 2

1. Bethlehem of Judea – There was another Bethlehem in the tribe of Zebulon.

In the days of Herod – commonly called Herod the Great, born at Ascalon. The scepter was now on the point of departing from Judah. Among his sons were Archelaus, mentioned ver. 22; Herod Antipas, mentioned chap. xiv, and Philip, mentioned Luke iii, 19. Herod Agrippa, mentioned Acts xii, 1; &c., was his grandson.

Wise men – The first fruits of the Gentiles. Probably they were Gentile philosophers, who, through the Divine assistance, had improved their knowledge of nature, as a means of leading to the knowledge of the one true God. Nor is it unreasonable to suppose, that God had favored them with some extraordinary Revelations of himself, as he did Melchisedec, Job, and several others, who were not of the family of Abraham; to which he never intended absolutely to confine his favors. The title given them in the original was anciently given to all philosophers, or men of learning; those particularly who were curious in examining the works of nature, and observing the motions of the heavenly bodies.

From the east – So Arabia is frequently called in Scripture. It lay to the east of Judea, and was famous for gold, frankincense, and myrrh.

We have seen his star – Undoubtedly they had before heard Balaam's prophecy. And probably when they saw this unusual star, it was revealed to them that this prophecy was fulfilled. In the east – That is, while we were in the east.

2. To do him homage – To pay him that honor, by bowing to the earth before him, which the eastern nations used to pay to their monarchs.

4. The chief priests – That is, not only the high priest and his deputy, with those who formerly had borne that office: but also the chief man in each of those twenty-four courses, into which the body of priests were divided, 1 Chron. xxiv, 6-19. The scribes were those whose peculiar business it was to explain the Scriptures to the people.

6. Thou art in nowise the least among the princes of Judah – That is,

the merit of his death, and from the power of sin by the Spirit of his grace. In saving them from sin, he saves them from wrath and the curse, and all misery, here and hereafter. Christ came to save his people, not in their sins, but from their sins; and so to redeem them from among men, to himself, who is separate from sinners. Joseph did as the angel of the Lord had bidden him, speedily, without delay, and cheerfully, without dispute. By applying the general rules of the written word, we should in all the steps of our lives, particularly the great turns of them, take direction from God, and we shall find this safe and comfortable.

MATTHEW 2

The wise men's search after Christ. (1-8)
The wise men worship Jesus. (9-12)
Jesus carried into Egypt. (13-15)
Herod causes the infants of Bethlehem to be massacred.
   (16-18)
Death of Herod. Jesus brought to Nazareth. (19-23)

1-8 Those who live at the greatest distance from the means of grace often use most diligence, and learn to know the most of Christ and his salvation. But no curious arts, or mere human learning, can direct men unto him. We must learn of Christ by attending to the word of God, as a light that shineth in a dark place, and by seeking the teaching of the Holy Spirit. And those in whose hearts the day-star is risen, to give them any thing of the knowledge of Christ, make it their business to worship him. Though Herod was very old, and never had shown affection for his family, and was not himself likely to live till a new-born infant had grown up to manhood, he began to be troubled with the dread of a rival. He understood not the spiritual nature of the Messiah's kingdom. Let us beware of a dead faith. A man may be persuaded of many truths, and yet may hate them, because they interfere with his ambition, or sinful indulgences. Such a belief will make him uneasy, and the more resolved to oppose the truth and the cause of God; and he may be foolish enough to hope for success therein.

9-12 What joy these wise men felt upon this sight of the star, none know so well as those who, after a long and melancholy night of temptation and desertion, under the power of a spirit of bondage, at length receive the Spirit of adoption, witnessing with their spirits that they are the children of God. We may well think what a disappointment it was to them, when they found a cottage was his palace, and his own poor mother the only attendant he had. However, these wise men did not think themselves baffled; but having found the King they sought, they presented their gifts to him. The humble inquirer after Christ will not be stumbled at finding him and his disciples in obscure cottages, after having in vain sought them in palaces and populous cities. Is a soul busy, seeking after Christ? Would it

needs something beyond creation to constitute the relationship, and those who can say, "Our Father which art in heaven," are something more than God's creatures: they have been adopted into his family. He has taken them out of the old black family in which they were born; he has washed them, and cleansed them, and given them a new name and a new spirit, and made them "heirs of God, and joint-heirs with Christ;" and all this of his own free, sovereign, unmerited, distinguishing grace.

And having adopted them to be his children, he has in the next place, regenerated them by the Spirit of the living God. He has "begotten them again unto a lively hope, by the resurrection of Jesus Christ from the dead," and no man hath a right to claim God as his Father, unless he feeleth in his soul, and believeth, solemnly, through the faith of God's election, that he has been adopted into the one family which is in heaven and earth, and that he has been regenerated or born again.

This relationship also involves love, If God be my Father, he loves me. And oh, how he loves me! When God is a Husband he is the best of husbands. Widows, somehow or other, are always well cared for. When God is a Friend, he is the best of friends, and sticketh closer than a brother; and when he is a Father he is the best of fathers. O fathers! perhaps ye do not know how much ye love your children. When they are sick ye find it out, for ye stand by their couches and ye pity them, as their little frames are writhing in pain. Well, "like as a father pitieth his children, so the Lord pitieth them that fear him." Ye know how ye love your children too, when they grieve you by their sin; anger arises, and you are ready to chasten them, but no sooner is the tear in their eye, than your hand is heavy, and you feel that you had rather smite yourself than smite them; and every time you smite them you seem to cry, "Oh that I should have thus to afflict my child for his sin! Oh that I could suffer in his stead!" And God, even our Father, "doth not afflict willingly." Is not that a sweet thing? He is, as it were, compelled to it; even the Eternal arm is not willing to do it; it is only his great love and deep wisdom that brings down the blow. But if you want to know your love to your children, you will know it most if they die. David knew that he loved his son Absalom, but he never knew how much he loved him till he heard that he had been slain, and that he had been buried by Joshua "Precious in the sight of the Lord is the death of his saints." He knows then how deep and pure is the love that death can never sever, and the terrors of eternity never can unbind. But, parents, although ye love your children much, and

house, they saw the young child with Mary his mother, and fell down, and worshiped him: and when they had opened their treasures, they presented unto him gifts; gold, and frankincense, and myrrh.

12 And being warned of God in a dream that they should not return to Herod, they departed into their own country another way.

13 And when they were departed, behold, the angel of the Lord appeareth to Joseph in a dream, saying, Arise, and take the young child and his mother, and flee into Egypt, and be thou there until I bring thee word: for Herod will seek the young child to destroy him.

14 When he arose, he took the young child and his mother by night, and departed into Egypt:

15 And was there until the death of Herod: that it might be fulfilled which was spoken of the Lord by the prophet, saying, Out of Egypt have I called my son.

16 Then Herod, when he saw that he was mocked of the wise men, was exceeding wroth, and sent forth, and slew all the children that were in Bethlehem, and in all the coasts thereof, from two years old and under, according to the time which he had diligently inquired of the wise men.

17 Then was fulfilled that which was spoken by Jeremy the prophet, saying,

18 In Rama was there a voice heard, lamentation, and weeping, and great mourning, Rachel weeping for her children, and would not be comforted, because they are not.

19 But when Herod was dead, behold, an angel of the Lord appeareth in a dream to Joseph in Egypt,

20 Saying, Arise, and take the young child and his mother, and go into the land of Israel: for they are dead which sought the young child's life.

21 And he arose, and took the young child and his mother, and came into the land of Israel.

22 But when he heard that Archelaus did reign in Judea in the room of his father Herod, he was afraid to go thither: notwithstanding, being warned of God in a dream, he turned aside into the parts of Galilee:

23 And he came and dwelt in a city called Nazareth: that it might be fulfilled which was spoken by the prophets, He shall be called a Nazarene.

MATTHEW 3

1 In those days came John the Baptist, preaching in the wilderness of Judea,

among the cities belonging to the princes or heads of thousands in Judah. When this and several other quotations from the Old Testament are compared with the original, it plainly appears, the apostles did not always think it necessary exactly to transcribe the passages they cited, but contented themselves with giving the general sense, though with some diversity of language. The words of Micah, which we render, Though thou be little, may be rendered, Art thou little? And then the difference which seems to be here between the prophet and the evangelist vanishes away. Micah v, 2.

8. And if ye find him, bring me word – Probably Herod did not believe he was born; otherwise would not so suspicious a prince have tried to make sure work at once?

10. Seeing the star – Standing over where the child was.

11. They presented to him gifts – It was customary to offer some present to any eminent person whom they visited. And so it is, as travelers observe, in the eastern countries to this day.

Gold, frankincense, and myrrh – Probably these were the best things their country afforded; and the presents ordinarily made to great persons. This was a most seasonable, providential assistance for a long and expensive journey into Egypt, a country where they were entirely strangers, and were to stay for a considerable time.

15. That it might be fulfilled – That is, whereby was fulfilled. The original word frequently signifies, not the design of an action, but barely the consequence or event of it.

Which was spoken of the Lord by the prophet – on another occasion: Out of Egypt have I called my Son – which was now fulfilled as it were anew; Christ being in a far higher sense the Son of God than Israel, of whom the words were originally spoken. Hosea xi, 1.

16. Then Herod, seeing that he was deluded by the wise men – So did his pride teach him to regard this action, as if it were intended to expose him to the derision of his subjects.

17. Then was fulfilled – A passage of Scripture, whether prophetic, historical, or poetical, is in the language of the New Testament fulfilled, when an event happens to which it may with great propriety be accommodated.

18. Rachel weeping for her children – The Benjamites, who inhabited Rama, sprung from her. She was buried near this place; and is here beautifully represented risen, as it were out of her grave, and bewailing her lost children.

22. He was afraid to go thither – into Judea; and so turned aside into the region of Galilee – a part of the land of Israel not under the jurisdiction of Archelaus.

23. He came and dwelt in Nazareth – (where he had dwelt before he went to Bethlehem) a place contemptible to a proverb. So that hereby was fulfilled what has been spoken in effect by several of the prophets, (though by none of them in express words,) He shall be called a Nazarene – that is, he shall be despised and rejected, shall be a mark of public contempt and reproach.

MATTHEW 3

1. In those days – that is, while Jesus dwelt there. In the wilderness of Judea – This was a wilderness properly so called, a wild, barren, desolate place as was that also where our Lord was tempted.

2. The kingdom of heaven, and the kingdom of God, are but two phrases for the same thing. They mean, not barely a future happy state,

worship him, and does it say, Alas! I am a foolish and poor creature, and have nothing to offer? Nothing! Hast thou not a heart, though unworthy of him, dark, hard, and foul? Give it to him as it is, and be willing that he use and dispose of it as it pleases him; he will take it, and will make it better, and thou shalt never repent having given it to him. He shall frame it to his own likeness, and will give thee himself, and be thine for ever. The gifts the wise men presented were gold, frankincense, and myrrh. Providence sent these as a seasonable relief to Joseph and Mary in their present poor condition. Thus our heavenly Father, who knows what his children need, uses some as stewards to supply the wants of others, and can provide for them, even from the ends of the earth.

13-15 Egypt had been a house of bondage to Israel, and particularly cruel to the infants of Israel; yet it is to be a place of refuge to the holy Child Jesus. God, when he pleases, can make the worst of places serve the best of purposes. This was a trial of the faith of Joseph and Mary. But their faith, being tried, was found firm. If we and our infants are at any time in trouble, let us remember the straits in which Christ was when an infant.

16-18 Herod killed all the male children, not only in Bethlehem, but in all the villages of that city. Unbridled wrath, armed with an unlawful power, often carries men to absurd cruelties. It was no unrighteous thing with God to permit this; every life is forfeited to his justice as soon as it begins. The diseases and deaths of little children are proofs of original sin. But the murder of these infants was their martyrdom. How early did persecution against Christ and his kingdom begin! Herod now thought that he had baffled the Old Testament prophecies, and the efforts of the wise men in finding Christ; but whatever crafty, cruel devices are in men's hearts, the counsel of the Lord shall stand.

19-23 Egypt may serve to sojourn in, or take shelter in, for awhile, but not to abide in. Christ was sent to the lost sheep of the house of Israel, to them he must return. Did we but look upon the world as our Egypt, the place of our bondage and banishment, and heaven only as our Canaan, our home, our rest, we should as readily arise and depart thither, when we are called for, as Joseph did out of Egypt. The family must settle in Galilee. Nazareth was a place held in bad esteem, and Christ was crucified with this accusation, Jesus the Nazarene. Wherever Providence allots the bounds of our habitation, we must expect to share the reproach of Christ; yet we may glory in being called by his name, sure that if we suffer with him, we shall also be glorified with him.

MATTHEW 3

John the Baptist, his preaching, manner of life, and baptism. (1-6)

ye know it, ye do not know, and ye cannot tell how deep is the unfathomable abyss of the love of God to you. Go out at midnight and consider the heavens, the work of God's fingers, the moon and the stars which he hath ordained; and I am sure you will say, "What is man, that thou shouldst be mindful of him?" But, more than all, you will wonder, not at your loving him, but that while he has all these treasures, he should set his heart upon so insignificant a creature as man. And the sonship that God has given us is not a mere name; there is all our Father's great heart given to us in the moment when be claims us as his sons.

But if this sonship involves the love of God to us, it involves also, the duty of love to God. Oh! heir of heaven, if thou art God's child, wilt thou not love thy Father? What son is there that loveth not his father? Is he not less than human if he loveth not his sire? Let his name be blotted from the book of remembrance that loveth not the woman that brought him forth, and the father that begat him. And we, the chosen favorites of heaven, adopted and regenerated, shall not we loose him? Shall we not say, "Whom have I in heaven but thee, and there is none upon earth that I desire in comparison with thee? My father, I will give thee my heart; thou shalt be the guide of my youth; thou dost love me, and the little heart that I have shall be all thine own for ever."

Furthermore, if we say "Our Father which art in heaven," we must recollect that our being sons involves the duty of obedience to God. When I say "My Father," it is not for me to rise up and go in rebellion against his wishes; if he be a father, let me note his commands, and let me reverentially obey; if he hath said "Do this," let me do it, not because I dread him, but because I love him; and if he forbids me to do anything, let me avoid it. There are some persons in the world who have not the spirit of adoption, and they can never be brought to do a thing unless they see some advantage to themselves in it; but with the child of God, there is no motive at all; he can boldly say, "I have never done a right thing since I have followed Christ because I hoped to get to heaven by it, nor have I ever avoided a wrong thing because I was afraid of being damned." For the child of God knows his good works do not make him acceptable to God, for he was acceptable to God by Jesus Christ long before he had any good works; and the fear of hell does not affect him, for he knows that he is delivered from that, and shall never come into condemnation, having passed from death unto life. He acts from pure love and gratitude, and until we come to that state of mind, I do not think there is such a

2 And saying, Repent ye: for the kingdom of heaven is at hand.

3 For this is he that was spoken of by the prophet Esaias, saying, The voice of one crying in the wilderness, Prepare ye the way of the Lord, make his paths straight.

4 And the same John had his raiment of camel's hair, and a leathern girdle about his loins; and his meat was locusts and wild honey.

5 Then went out to him Jerusalem, and all Judea, and all the region round about Jordan,

6 And were baptized of him in Jordan, confessing their sins.

7 But when he saw many of the Pharisees and Sadducees come to his baptism, he said unto them, O generation of vipers, who hath warned you to flee from the wrath to come?

8 Bring forth therefore fruits meet for repentance:

9 And think not to say within yourselves, We have Abraham to our father: for I say unto you, that God is able of these stones to raise up children unto Abraham.

10 And now also the axe is laid unto the root of the trees: therefore every tree which bringeth not forth good fruit is hewn down, and cast into the fire.

11 I indeed baptize you with water unto repentance: but he that cometh after me is mightier than I, whose shoes I am not worthy to bear: he shall baptize you with the Holy Ghost, and with fire:

12 Whose fan is in his hand, and he will throughly purge his floor, and gather his wheat into the garner; but he will burn up the chaff with unquenchable fire.

13 Then cometh Jesus from Galilee to Jordan unto John, to be baptized of him.

14 But John forbad him, saying, I have need to be baptized of thee, and comest thou to me?

15 And Jesus answering said unto him, Suffer it to be so now: for thus it becometh us to fulfill all righteousness. Then he suffered him.

16 And Jesus, when he was baptized, went up straightway out of the water: and, lo, the heavens were opened unto him, and he saw the Spirit of God descending like a dove, and lighting upon him:

17 And lo a voice from heaven, saying, This is my beloved Son, in whom I am well pleased.

MATTHEW 4

1 Then was Jesus led up of the Spirit into the wilderness to be tempted of the devil.

in heaven, but a state to be enjoyed on earth: the proper disposition for the glory of heaven, rather than the possession of it. Is at hand – As if he had said, God is about to erect that kingdom, spoken of by Daniel, Dan. ii, 44; vii, 13, 14; the kingdom of the God of heaven.

3. The way of the Lord – Of Christ. Make his paths straight – By removing every thing which might prove a hindrance to his gracious appearance. Isaiah xl, 3.

4. John had his raiment of camels' hair – Coarse and rough, suiting his character and doctrine. A leathern girdle – Like Elijah, in whose spirit and power he came. His food was locusts and wild honey – Locusts are ranked among clean meats, Lev. xi, 22. But these were not always to be had. So in default of those, he fed on wild honey.

6. Confessing their sins – Of their own accord; freely and openly. John, passing along before them, cast water on their heads or faces, by which means he might baptize many thousands in a day. And this way most naturally signified Christ's baptizing them with the Holy Ghost and with fire, which John spoke of, as prefigured by his baptizing with water, and which was eminently fulfilled, when the Holy Ghost sat upon the disciples in the appearance of tongues, or flames of fire.

7. The Pharisees were a very ancient sect among the Jews. They were outwardly strict observers of the law, fasted often, made long prayers, rigorously kept the Sabbath, and paid all tithe, even of mint, anise, and cummin. The Sadducees were another sect among the Jews. They denied the existence of angels, and the immortality of the soul, and by consequence the resurrection of the dead. Ye brood of vipers – It was fitting such men should be marked out, either for a caution to others, or a warning to themselves.

8. Repentance is of two sorts; that which is termed legal, and that which is styled evangelical repentance. The former (which is the same that is spoken of here) is a thorough conviction of sin. The latter is a change of heart (and consequently of life) from all sin to all holiness.

9. We have Abraham to our father – It is almost incredible, how great the presumption of the Jews was on this their relation to Abraham. One of their famous sayings was, "Abraham sits near the gates of hell, and suffers no Israelite to go down into it."

10. But the axe also already lieth – That is, there is no room for such idle pretenses. Speedy execution is determined against all that do not repent.

11. He shall baptize you with the Holy Ghost and with fire – He shall fill you with the Holy Ghost, inflaming your hearts with that fire of love, which many waters cannot quench. And this was done, even with a visible appearance as of fire, on the day of Pentecost.

12. Whose fan – That is, the word of the Gospel. His floor – That is, his Church, which is now covered with a mixture of wheat and chaff. He will gather the wheat into the garner – Will lay up those who are truly good in heaven.

15. It becometh us to fulfill all righteousness – It becometh every messenger of God to observe all his righteous ordinances.

16. And Jesus being baptized – Let our Lord's submitting to baptism teach us a holy exactness in the observance of those institutions which owe their obligation merely to a Divine command.

17. And lo, a voice – We have here a glorious manifestation of the ever-blessed Trinity: the Father speaking from heaven, the Son spoken to, the Holy Ghost descending upon him. In whom I delight – What an encomium is this! How poor to this are all other kinds of praise! To be the pleasure, the delight of God, this is praise indeed: this is true glory:

John reproves the Pharisees and Sadducees. (7-12)
The baptism of Jesus. (13-17)

1-6 After Malachi there was no prophet until John the Baptist came. He appeared first in the wilderness of Judea. This was not an uninhabited desert, but a part of the country not thickly peopled, nor much enclosed. No place is so remote as to shut us out from the visits of Divine grace. The doctrine he preached was repentance; "Repent ye." The word here used, implies a total alteration in the mind, a change in the judgment, disposition, and affections, another and a better bias of the soul. Consider your ways, change your minds: you have thought amiss; think again, and think aright. True penitents have other thoughts of God and Christ, sin and holiness, of this world and the other, than they had. The change of the mind produces a change of the way. That is gospel repentance, which flows from a sight of Christ, from a sense of his love, and from hopes of pardon and forgiveness through him.

7-12 To make application to the souls of the hearers, is the life of preaching; so it was of John's preaching. The Pharisees laid their chief stress on outward observances, neglecting the weightier matters of the moral law, and the spiritual meaning of their legal ceremonies. Others of them were detestable hypocrites, making their pretenses to holiness a cloak for iniquity. The Sadducees ran into the opposite extreme, denying the existence of spirits, and a future state. They were the scornful infidels of that time and country. There is a wrath to come. It is the great concern of every one to flee from that wrath. God, who delights not in our ruin, has warned us; he warns by the written word, by ministers, by conscience.

13-17 Christ's gracious condescensions are so surprising, that even the strongest believers at first can hardly believe them; so deep and mysterious, that even those who know his mind well, are apt to start objections against the will of Christ. And those who have much of the Spirit of God while here, see that they need to apply to Christ for more. Christ does not deny that John had need to be baptized of him, yet declares he will now be baptized of John. Christ is now in a state of humiliation. Our Lord Jesus looked upon it as well becoming him to fulfill all righteousness, to own every Divine institution, and to show his readiness to comply with all God's righteous precepts. In and through Christ, the heavens are opened to the children of men. This descent of the Spirit upon Christ, showed that he was endued with his sacred influences without measure.

MATTHEW 4

The temptation of Christ. (1-11)
The opening of Christ's ministry in Galilee. (12-17)
Call of Simon and others. (18-22)
Jesus teaches and works miracles. (23-25)

thing as virtue; for if a man has done what is called a virtuous action because he hoped to get to heaven or to avoid hell by it, whom has he served? Has he not served himself? and what is that but selfishness? But the man who has no hell to fear and no heaven to gain, because heaven is his own and hell he never can enter, that man is capable of virtue; for he says—
"Now for the love I bear his name,
What was my gain I count my loss;
I pour contempt on all my shame,
And nail my glory to his cross"—
to his cross who loved, and lived, and died for me who loved him not, but who desires now to love him with all my heart, and soul, and strength.

And now permit me to draw your attention to one encouraging thought that may help to cheer the downcast and Satan-tempted child of God. Sonship is a thing which all the infirmities of our flesh, and all the sins into which we are hurried by temptation, can never violate or weaken. A man hath a child; that child on a sudden is bereaved of its senses; it becomes an idiot. What a grief that is to a father, for a child to become a lunatic or an idiot, and to exist only as an animal, apparently without a soul! But the idiot child is a child, and the lunatic child is a child still; and if we are the fathers of such children they are ours, and all the idiocy and all the lunacy that can possibly befall them can never shake the fact that they are our sons. Oh! what a mercy, when we transfer this to God's case and ours! How foolish we are sometimes—how worse than foolish! We may say as David did, "I was as a beast before thee." God brings before us the truths of his kingdom; we cannot see their beauty, we cannot appreciate them; we seem to be as if we were totally demented, ignorant, unstable, weary, and apt to slide. But, thanks be unto God, we are his children still! And if there be anything worse that can happen to a father than his child becoming a lunatic or an idiot, it is when he grows up to be wicked. It is well said, "Children are doubtful blessings." I remember to have heard one say, and, as I thought, not very kindly, to a mother with an infant at her breast—"Woman! you may be suckling a viper there." It stung the mother to the quick, and it was not needful to have said it. But how often is it the fact, that the child that has hung upon its mother's breast, when it grows up, brings that mother's gray hairs with sorrow to the grave!
"Oh! sharper than a serpent's tooth
To have a thankless child!"
ungodly, vile, debauched—a blasphemer! But mark, brethren: if he be a child he cannot lose his childship, nor we our fatherhood, be he who

2 And when he had fasted forty days and forty nights, he was afterward an hungred.

3 And when the tempter came to him, he said, If thou be the Son of God, command that these stones be made bread.

4 But he answered and said, It is written, Man shall not live by bread alone, but by every word that proceedeth out of the mouth of God.

5 Then the devil taketh him up into the holy city, and setteth him on a pinnacle of the temple,

6 And saith unto him, If thou be the Son of God, cast thyself down: for it is written, He shall give his angels charge concerning thee: and in their hands they shall bear thee up, lest at any time thou dash thy foot against a stone.

7 Jesus said unto him, It is written again, Thou shalt not tempt the Lord thy God.

8 Again, the devil taketh him up into an exceeding high mountain, and sheweth him all the kingdoms of the world, and the glory of them;

9 And saith unto him, All these things will I give thee, if thou wilt fall down and worship me.

10 Then saith Jesus unto him, Get thee hence, Satan: for it is written, Thou shalt worship the Lord thy God, and him only shalt thou serve.

11 Then the devil leaveth him, and, behold, angels came and ministered unto him.

12 Now when Jesus had heard that John was cast into prison, he departed into Galilee;

13 And leaving Nazareth, he came and dwelt in Capernaum, which is upon the sea coast, in the borders of Zabulon and Nephthalim:

14 That it might be fulfilled which was spoken by Esaias the prophet, saying,

15 The land of Zabulon, and the land of Nephthalim, by the way of the sea, beyond Jordan, Galilee of the Gentiles;

16 The people which sat in darkness saw great light; and to them which sat in the region and shadow of death light is sprung up.

17 From that time Jesus began to preach, and to say, Repent: for the kingdom of heaven is at hand.

18 And Jesus, walking by the sea of Galilee, saw two brethren, Simon called Peter, and Andrew his brother, casting a net into the sea: for they were fishers.

19 And he saith unto them, Follow me, and I will make you fishers of men.

20 And they straightway left their nets, and followed him.

21 And going on from thence, he saw

this is the highest, the brightest light, that virtue can appear in.

MATTHEW 4

1. Then – After this glorious evidence of his Father's love, he was completely armed for the combat. Thus after the clearest light and the strongest consolation, let us expect the sharpest temptations. By the Spirit – Probably through a strong inward impulse. Mark i, 12; Luke iv, 1.

2. Having fasted – Whereby doubtless he received more abundant spiritual strength from God. Forty days and forty nights – As did Moses, the giver of the law, and Elijah, the great restorer of it. He was afterward hungry – And so prepared for the first temptation.

3. Coming to him – In a visible form; probably in a human shape, as one that desired to inquire farther into the evidences of his being the Messiah.

4. It is written – Thus Christ answered, and thus we may answer all the suggestions of the devil. By every word that proceedeth out of the mouth of God – That is, by whatever God commands to sustain him. Therefore it is not needful I should work a miracle to procure bread, without any intimation of my Father's will. Deut. viii, 3.

5. The holy city – So Jerusalem was commonly called, being the place God had peculiarly chosen for himself. On the battlement of the temple – Probably over the king's gallery, which was of such a prodigious height, that no one could look down from the top of it without making himself giddy.

6. In their hands – That is, with great care. Psalm xci, 11, 12.

7. Thou shalt not tempt the Lord thy God – By requiring farther evidence of what he hath already made sufficiently plain. Deut. vi, 16.

8. Showeth him all the kingdoms of the world – In a kind of visionary representation.

9. If thou wilt fall down and worship me – Here Satan clearly shows who he was. Accordingly Christ answering this suggestion, calls him by his own name, which he had not done before.

10. Get thee hence, Satan – Not, get thee behind me, that is, into thy proper place; as he said on a quite different occasion to Peter, speaking what was not expedient. Deut. vi, 13.

11. Angels came and waited upon him – Both to supply him with food, and to congratulate his victory.

12. He retired into Galilee – This journey was not immediately after his temptation. He first went from Judea into Galilee, John i, 43; ii, 1. Then into Judea again, and celebrated the Passover at Jerusalem, John ii, 13. He baptized in Judea while John was baptizing at Enon, John iii, 22, 23. All this time John was at liberty, John iii, 24. But the Pharisees being offended, John iv, 1; and John put in prison, he then took this journey into Galilee. Mark i, 14.

13. Leaving Nazareth – Namely, when they had wholly rejected his word, and even attempted to kill him, Luke iv, 29.

15. Galilee of the Gentiles – That part of Galilee which lay beyond Jordan was so called, because it was in a great measure inhabited by Gentiles, that is, heathens. Isaiah ix, 1, 2.

16. Here is a beautiful gradation, first, they walked, then they sat in darkness, and lastly, in the region of the shadow of death.

17. Repent, for the kingdom of heaven is at hand – Although it is the peculiar business of Christ to establish the kingdom of heaven in the hearts of men, yet it is observable, he begins his preaching in the same

1-11 Concerning Christ's temptation, observe, that directly after he was declared to be the Son of God, and the Savior of the world, he was tempted; great privileges, and special tokens of Divine favor, will not secure any from being tempted. But if the Holy Spirit witness to our being adopted as children of God, that will answer all the suggestions of the evil spirit. Christ was directed to the combat. If we presume upon our own strength, and tempt the devil to tempt us, we provoke God to leave us to ourselves. Others are tempted, when drawn aside of their own lust, and enticed, Jas 1:14; but our Lord Jesus had no corrupt nature, therefore he was tempted only by the devil. In the temptation of Christ it appears that our enemy is subtle, spiteful, and very daring; but he can be resisted. It is a comfort to us that Christ suffered, being tempted; for thus it appears that our temptations, if not yielded to, are not sins, they are afflictions only. Satan aimed in all his temptations, to bring Christ to sin against God.

12-17 It is just with God to take the gospel and the means of grace, from those that slight them and thrust them away. Christ will not stay long where he is not welcome. Those who are without Christ, are in the dark. They were sitting in this condition, a contented posture; they chose it rather than light; they were willingly ignorant. When the gospel comes, light comes; when it comes to any place, when it comes to any soul, it makes day there. Light discovers and directs; so does the gospel. The doctrine of repentance is right gospel doctrine. Not only the austere John Baptist, but the gracious Jesus, preached repentance. There is still the same reason to do so. The kingdom of heaven was not reckoned to be fully come, till the pouring out of the Holy Spirit after Christ's ascension.

18-22 When Christ began to preach, he began to gather disciples, who should be hearers, and afterwards preachers of his doctrine, who should be witnesses of his miracles, and afterwards testify concerning them. He went not to Herod's court, not to Jerusalem, among the chief priests and the elders, but to the sea of Galilee, among the fishermen. The same power which called Peter and Andrew, could have wrought upon Annas and Caiaphas, for with God nothing is impossible. But Christ chooses the foolish things of the world to confound the wise. Diligence in an honest calling is pleasing to Christ, and it is no hinderance to a holy life. Idle people are more open to the temptations of Satan than to the calls of God. It is a happy and hopeful thing to see children careful of their parents, and dutiful. When Christ comes, it is good to be found doing. Am I in Christ? is a very needful question to ask ourselves; and, next to that, Am I in my calling? They had followed Christ before, as common disciples, Joh 1:37; now they must leave their calling. Those who would follow Christ aright, must, at his command, leave all things to follow him, must be ready to part with them. This instance of the power of the Lord

or what he may. Let him be transported beyond the seas, he is still our son; let us deny him the house because his conversation might lead others of our children into sin, yet our son he is, and must be, and when the sod shall cover his head and ours, "father and son" shall still be on the tombstone. The relationship never can be severed as long as time shall last. The prodigal was his father's son, when he was amongst the harlots, and when he was feeding swine; and God's children are God's children anywhere and everywhere, and shall be even unto the end. Nothing can sever that sacred tie, or divide us from his heart.

There is yet another thought that may cheer the Little-faiths and Feeble minds. The fatherhood of God is common to all his children. Ah! Little-faith, you have often looked up to Mr. Great-heart, and you have said, "Oh that I had the courage of Great-heart, that I could wield his sword and cut old giant Grim in pieces! Oh that I could fight the dragons, and that I could overcome the lions! But I am stumbling at every straw, and a shadow makes me afraid." List thee, Little-faith. Great-heart is God's child, and you are God's child too; and Great-heart is not a whit more God's child than you are. David was the son of God, but not more the son of God than thou. Peter and Paul, the highly favored apostles, were of the family of the Most High; and so are you. You have children yourselves; one is a son grown up, and out in business, perhaps, and you have another, a little thing still in arms. Which is most your child the little one or the big one? "Both alike," you say. "This little one is my child near my heart and the big one is my child too." And so the little Christian is as much a child of God as the great one.

One may be an older child than another, but he is not more a child; one may do more mighty works, and may bring more glory to his Father, but he whose name is the least in the kingdom of heaven is as much the child of God as he who stands among the king's mighty men. Let this cheer and comfort us, when we draw near to God and say, "Our Father which art in heaven."

I will make but one more remark before I leave this point, namely, this,—that our being the children of God brings with it innumerable privileges. Time would fail me, if I were to attempt to read the long roll of the Christian's joyous privileges. I am God's child: if so, he will clothe me; my shoes shall be iron and brass; he will array me with the robe of my Savior's righteousness, for he has said, "Bring forth the best robe and put it on him," and he has also said that he will put a crown of pure gold upon my head and inasmuch as I am a king's son, I shall have a royal crown. Am I his child? Then he will

other two brethren, James the son of Zebedee, and John his brother, in a ship with Zebedee their father, mending their nets; and he called them.

22 And they immediately left the ship and their father, and followed him.

23 And Jesus went about all Galilee, teaching in their synagogues, and preaching the gospel of the kingdom, and healing all manner of sickness and all manner of disease among the people.

24 And his fame went throughout all Syria: and they brought unto him all sick people that were taken with divers diseases and torments, and those which were possessed with devils, and those which were lunatick, and those that had the palsy; and he healed them.

25 And there followed him great multitudes of people from Galilee, and from Decapolis, and from Jerusalem, and from Judea, and from beyond Jordan.

MATTHEW 5

1 And seeing the multitudes, he went up into a mountain: and when he was set, his disciples came unto him:

2 And he opened his mouth, and taught them, saying,

3 Blessed are the poor in spirit: for theirs is the kingdom of heaven.

4 Blessed are they that mourn: for they shall be comforted.

5 Blessed are the meek: for they shall inherit the earth.

6 Blessed are they which do hunger and thirst after righteousness: for they shall be filled.

7 Blessed are the merciful: for they shall obtain mercy.

8 Blessed are the pure in heart: for they shall see God.

9 Blessed are the peacemakers: for they shall be called the children of God.

10 Blessed are they which are persecuted for righteousness' sake: for theirs is the kingdom of heaven.

11 Blessed are ye, when men shall revile you, and persecute you, and shall say all manner of evil against you falsely, for my sake.

12 Rejoice, and be exceeding glad: for great is your reward in heaven: for so persecuted they the prophets which were before you.

13 Ye are the salt of the earth: but if the salt have lost his savor, wherewith shall it be salted? it is thenceforth good for nothing, but to be cast out, and to be trodden under foot of men.

14 Ye are the light of the world. A city that is set on an hill cannot be hid.

words with John the Baptist: because the repentance which John taught still was, and ever will be, the necessary preparation for that inward kingdom.

23. The Gospel of the kingdom – The Gospel, that is, the joyous message, is the proper name of our religion: as will be amply verified in all who earnestly and perseveringly embrace it.

24. Through all Syria – The whole province, of which the Jewish country was only a small part. And demoniacs – Men possessed with devils: and lunatics, and paralytics – Men ill of the palsy, whose cases were of all others most deplorable and most helpless.

25. Decapolis – A tract of land on the east side of the sea of Galilee, in which were ten cities near each other.

MATTHEW 5

1. And seeing the multitudes – At some distance, as they were coming to him from every quarter. He went up into the mountain – Which was near: where there was room for them all. His disciples – not only his twelve disciples, but all who desired to learn of him.

2. And he opened his mouth – A phrase which always denotes a set and solemn discourse; and taught them – To bless men; to make men happy, was the great business for which our Lord came into the world.

3. Happy are the poor – In the following discourse there is,

    1. A sweet invitation to true holiness and happiness, ver. 3-12.

    2. A persuasive to impart it to others, ver. 13-16.

    3. A description of true Christian holiness, ver. 17; chap.vii, 12. (in which it is easy to observe, the latter part exactly answers the former.)

    4. The conclusion: giving a sure mark of the true way, warning against false prophets, exhorting to follow after holiness. The poor in spirit – They who are unfeignedly penitent, they who are truly convinced of sin; who see and feel the state they are in by nature, being deeply sensible of their sinfulness, guiltiness, helplessness. For theirs is the kingdom of heaven – The present inward kingdom: righteousness, and peace, and joy in the Holy Ghost, as well as the eternal kingdom, if they endure to the end. Luke vi, 20.

4. They that mourn – Either for their own sins, or for other men's, and are steadily and habitually serious. They shall be comforted – More solidly and deeply even in this world, and eternally in heaven.

5. Happy are the meek – They that hold all their passions and affections evenly balanced. They shall inherit the earth – They shall have all things really necessary for life and godliness. They shall enjoy whatever portion God hath given them here, and shall hereafter possess the new earth, wherein dwelleth righteousness.

6. They that hunger and thirst after righteousness – After the holiness here described. They shall be satisfied with it.

7. The merciful – The tender-hearted: they who love all men as themselves: They shall obtain mercy – Whatever mercy therefore we desire from God, the same let us show to our brethren. He will repay us a thousand fold, the love we bear to any for his sake.

8. The pure in heart – The sanctified: they who love God with all their hearts. They shall see God – In all things here; hereafter in glory.

9. The peace makers – They that out of love to God and man do all possible good to all men. Peace in the Scripture sense implies all blessings temporal and eternal. They shall be called the children of God – Shall be acknowledged such by God and man.

10. For righteousness' sake – That is, because they have, or follow after,

MATTHEW HENRY CHARLES H. SPURGEON

Jesus encourages us to depend upon his grace. He speaks, and it is done.

23-25 Wherever Christ went, he confirmed his Divine mission by miracles, which were emblems of the healing power of his doctrine, and the influences of the Spirit which accompanied it. We do not now find the Savior's miraculous healing power in our bodies; but if we are cured by medicine, the praise is equally his. Three general words are here used. He healed every sickness or disease; none was too bad; none too hard, for Christ to heal with a word. Three diseases are named; the palsy, which is the greatest weakness of the body; lunacy, which is the greatest malady of the mind; and possession of the devil, which is the greatest misery and calamity of both; yet Christ healed all, and by thus curing bodily diseases, showed that his great errand into the world was to cure spiritual maladies. Sin is the sickness, disease, and torment of the soul: Christ came to take away sin, and so to heal the soul.

MATTHEW 5

Christ's sermon on the mount. (1,2)
Who are blessed. (3-12)
Exhortations and warnings. (13-16)
Christ came to confirm the law. (17-20)
The sixth commandment. (21-26)
The seventh commandment. (27-32)
The third commandment. (33-37)
The law of retaliation. (38-42)
The law of love explained. (43-48)

1,2 None will find happiness in this world or the next, who do not seek it from Christ by the rule of his word. He taught them what was the evil they should abhor, and what the good they should seek and abound in.

3-12 Our Savior here gives eight characters of blessed people, which represent to us the principal graces of a Christian.
1. The poor in spirit are happy. These bring their minds to their condition, when it is a low condition. They are humble and lowly in their own eyes. They see their want, bewail their guilt, and thirst after a Redeemer. The kingdom of grace is of such; the kingdom of glory is for them.
2. Those that mourn are happy. That godly sorrow which worketh true repentance, watchfulness, a humble mind, and continual dependence for acceptance on the mercy of God in Christ Jesus, with constant seeking the Holy Spirit, to cleanse away the remaining evil, seems here to be intended. Heaven is the joy of our Lord; a mountain of joy, to which our way is through a vale of tears. Such mourners shall be comforted by their God.
3. The meek are happy. The meek are those who quietly submit to God; who can bear insult; are silent, or return a soft answer; who, in their patience, keep

feed me; my bread shall be given me, and my water shall be sure; he that feeds the ravens will never let his children starve. If a good husbandman feeds the barn-door fowl, and the sheep and the bullocks, certainly his children shall not starve. Does my Father deck the lily, and shall I go naked? Does he feed the fowls of the heaven that sow not, neither do they reap, and shall I feel necessity? God forbid! My Father knoweth what things I have need of before I ask him, and he will give me all I want. If I be his child, then I have a portion in his heart here, and I shall have a portion in his house above. for "if children then heirs, heirs of God and joint heirs with Christ," "If we suffer with him we shall be also glorified together." And oh! brethren, what a prospect this opens up! The fact of our being heirs of God and joint-heirs with Christ, proves that all things are ours—the gift of God, the purchase of a Savior's blood.

Talk of princes, and kings, and potentates: Their inheritance is but a pitiful foot of land, across which the bird's wing can soon direct its flight; but the broad acres of the Christian cannot be measured by eternity. He is rich, without a limit to his wealth. he is blessed, without a boundary to his bliss. All this, and more than I can enumerate, is involved in our being able to say, "Our Father which art in heaven."

The second tie of the text is brotherhood. It does not say my Father, but our Father. Then it seems there are a great many in the family. I will be very brief on this point.

"Our Father." When you pray that prayer, remember you have a good many brothers and sisters that do not know their Father yet, and you must include them all; for all God's elect ones, though they be uncalled as yet, are still his children, though they know it not. In one of Krummacher's beautiful little parables there is a story like this: "Abraham sat one day in the grove at Mamre, leaning his head on his hand, and sorrowing. Then his son Isaac came to him, and said, 'My father, why mournest thou? what aileth thee?' Abraham answered and said, 'My soul mourneth for the people of Canaan, that they know not the Lord, but walk in their own ways, in darkness and foolishness.' 'Oh, my father,' answered the son, is it only this? Let not thy heart be sorrowful; for are not these their own ways?' Then the patriarch rose up from his seat, and said, 'Come now, follow me.' And he led the youth to a hut. and said to him, 'Behold.' There was a child which was an imbecile, and the mother sat weeping by it. Abraham asked her, 'Why weepest thou?' Then the mother said, 'Alas, this my son eateth and drinketh, and we minister unto him; but he knows not the face of his father, nor of his mother. Thus his life is lost,

15 Neither do men light a candle, and put it under a bushel, but on a candlestick; and it giveth light unto all that are in the house.

16 Let your light so shine before men, that they may see your good works, and glorify your Father which is in heaven.

17 Think not that I am come to destroy the law, or the prophets: I am not come to destroy, but to fulfill.

18 For verily I say unto you, Till heaven and earth pass, one jot or one tittle shall in no wise pass from the law, till all be fulfilled.

19 Whosoever therefore shall break one of these least commandments, and shall teach men so, he shall be called the least in the kingdom of heaven: but whosoever shall do and teach them, the same shall be called great in the kingdom of heaven.

20 For I say unto you, That except your righteousness shall exceed the righteousness of the scribes and Pharisees, ye shall in no case enter into the kingdom of heaven.

21 Ye have heard that it was said by them of old time, Thou shalt not kill; and whosoever shall kill shall be in danger of the judgment:

22 But I say unto you, That whosoever is angry with his brother without a cause shall be in danger of the judgment: and whosoever shall say to his brother, Raca, shall be in danger of the council: but whosoever shall say, Thou fool, shall be in danger of hell fire.

23 Therefore if thou bring thy gift to the altar, and there rememberest that thy brother hath ought against thee;

24 Leave there thy gift before the altar, and go thy way; first be reconciled to thy brother, and then come and offer thy gift.

25 Agree with thine adversary quickly, whiles thou art in the way with him; lest at any time the adversary deliver thee to the judge, and the judge deliver thee to the officer, and thou be cast into prison.

26 Verily I say unto thee, Thou shalt by no means come out thence, till thou hast paid the uttermost farthing.

27 Ye have heard that it was said by them of old time, Thou shalt not commit adultery:

28 But I say unto you, That whosoever looketh on a woman to lust after her hath committed adultery with her already in his heart.

29 And if thy right eye offend thee, pluck it out, and cast it from thee: for it is profitable for thee that one of thy members should perish, and not that thy whole body should be cast into hell.

the righteousness here described. He that is truly a righteous man, he that mourns, and he that is pure in heart, yea, all that will live godly in Christ Jesus, shall suffer persecution, 2 Tim. iii, 12.

11. Revile – When present: say all evil – When you are absent.

12. Your reward – Even over and above the happiness that naturally and directly results from holiness.

13. Ye – Not the apostles, not ministers only; but all ye who are thus holy, are the salt of the earth – Are to season others. Mark ix, 50; Luke xiv, 34.

14. Ye are the light of the world – If ye are thus holy, you can no more be hid than the sun in the firmament: no more than a city on a mountain – Probably pointing to that on the brow of the opposite hill.

15. Nay, the very design of God in giving you this light was, that it might shine. Mark iv, 21; Luke viii, 16; xi, 33.

16. That they may see – and glorify – That is, that seeing your good works, they may be moved to love and serve God likewise.

17. Think not – Do not imagine, fear, hope, that I am come – Like your teachers, to destroy the law or the prophets. I am not come to destroy – The moral law, but to fulfill – To establish, illustrate, and explain its highest meaning, both by my life and doctrine.

18. Till all things shall be effected – Which it either requires or foretells. For the law has its effect, when the rewards are given, and the punishments annexed to it inflicted, as well as when its precepts are obeyed. Luke xvi, 17; xxi, 33.

19. One of the least – So accounted by men; and shall teach – Either by word or example; shall be the least – That is, shall have no part therein.

20. The righteousness of the scribes and Pharisees – Described in the sequel of this discourse.

21. Ye have heard – From the scribes reciting the law; Thou shalt do no murder – And they interpreted this, as all the other commandments, barely of the outward act.

22. But I say unto you – Which of the prophets ever spake thus? Their language is, Thus saith the Lord. Who hath authority to use this language, but the one lawgiver, who is able to save and to destroy. Christ teaches, that we ought not, for any cause, to be so angry as to call any man Raca, or fool. We ought not, for any cause, to be angry at the person of the sinner, but at his sins only.

23. Thy brother hath aught against thee – On any of the preceding accounts: for any unkind thought or word: any that did not spring from love.

24. Leaving thy gift, go – For neither thy gift nor thy prayer will atone for thy want of love: but this will make them both an abomination before God.

25. Agree with thine adversary – With any against whom thou hast thus offended: while thou art in the way – Instantly, on the spot; before you part. Lest the adversary deliver thee to the judge – Lest he commit his cause to God. Luke xii, 58.

26. Till thou hast paid the last farthing – That is, for ever, since thou canst never do this. What has been hitherto said refers to meekness: what follows, to purity of heart.

27. Thou shalt not commit adultery – And this, as well as the sixth commandment, the scribes and Pharisees interpreted barely of the outward act. Exod. xx, 14.

29, 30. As if he had said, Part with any thing, however dear to you, or otherwise useful, if you cannot avoid sin while you keep it. Even cut off your right hand, if you are of so passionate a temper, that you cannot

possession of their own souls, when they can scarcely keep possession of anything else. These meek ones are happy, even in this world. Meekness promotes wealth, comfort, and safety, even in this world.

4. Those who hunger and thirst after righteousness are happy. Righteousness is here put for all spiritual blessings. These are purchased for us by the righteousness of Christ, confirmed by the faithfulness of God. Our desires of spiritual blessings must be earnest. Though all desires for grace are not grace, yet such a desire as this, is a desire of God's own raising, and he will not forsake the work of his own hands.

5. The merciful are happy. We must not only bear our own afflictions patiently, but we must do all we can to help those who are in misery. We must have compassion on the souls of others, and help them; pity those who are in sin, and seek to snatch them as brands out of the burning.

6. The pure in heart are happy; for they shall see God. Here holiness and happiness are fully described and put together. The heart must be purified by faith, and kept for God. Create in me such a clean heart, O God. None but the pure are capable of seeing God, nor would heaven be happiness to the impure. As God cannot endure to look upon their iniquity, so they cannot look upon his purity.

7. The peace-makers are happy. They love, and desire, and delight in peace; and study to be quiet. They keep the peace that it be not broken, and recover it when it is broken. If the peace-makers are blessed, woe to the peace-breakers!

8. Those who are persecuted for righteousness' sake are happy. This saying is peculiar to Christianity; and it is more largely insisted upon than any of the rest. Yet there is nothing in our sufferings that can merit of God; but God will provide that those who lose for him, though life itself, shall not lose by him in the end. Blessed Jesus! how different are thy maxims from those of men of this world! They call the proud happy, and admire the gay, the rich, the powerful, and the victorious. May we find mercy from the Lord; may we be owned as his children, and inherit his kingdom. With these enjoyments and hopes, we may cheerfully welcome low or painful circumstances.

13-16 Ye are the salt of the earth. Mankind, lying in ignorance and wickedness, were as a vast heap, ready to putrify; but Christ sent forth his disciples, by their lives and doctrines to season it with knowledge and grace. If they are not such as they should be, they are as salt that has lost its savor.

17-20 Let none suppose that Christ allows his people to trifle with any commands of God's holy law. No sinner partakes of Christ's justifying righteousness, till he repents of his evil deeds. The mercy revealed in the gospel leads the believer to still deeper self-abhorrence.

and this source of joy is sealed to him.' " Is not that a sweet little parable, to teach us how we ought to pray for the many sheep that are not yet of the fold, but which must be brought in? We ought to pray for them, because they do not know their Father. Christ has bought them, and they do not know Christ; the Father has loved them from before the foundation of the world, and yet, they know not the face of their Father. When thou sayest "Our Father," think of the many of thy brothers and sisters that are in the back streets of London, that are in the dens and caves of Satan. Think of thy poor brother that is intoxicated with the spirit of the devil; think of him, led astray to infamy, and lust, and perhaps to murder, and in thy prayer pray thou for them who know not the Lord.

"Our Father." That, then, includes those of God's children who differ from us in their doctrine. Ah! there are some that differ from us as wide as the poles; but yet they are God's children. Come, Mr. Bigot, do not kneel down, and say, "My Father," but "Our Father." "If you please, I cannot put in Sir. So-and-So, for I think he is a heretic." Put him in, sir. God has put him in, and you must put him in too, and say, "Our Father." Is it not remarkable how very much alike all God's people are upon their knees? Some time ago at a prayer-meeting I called upon two brothers in Christ to pray one after another, the one a Wesleyan and the other a strong Calvinist, and the Wesleyan prayed the most Calvinistic prayer of the two, I do believe—at least, I could not tell which was which. I listened to see if I could not discern some peculiarity even in their phraseology, but there was none. "Saints in prayer appear as one." for when they get on their knees, they are all compelled to say "Our Father," and all their language afterwards is of the same sort.

When thou prayest to God put in the poor; for is he not the Father of many of the poor, rich in faith, and heirs of the kingdom, though they be poor in this world. Come my sister, if thou bowest thy knee amid the rustling of silk and satin, yet remember the cotton and the print. My brother, is there wealth in thy hand, yet I pray thee, remember thy brethren of the horny hand and the dusty brow; remember those who could not wear what thou wearest, nor eat what thou eatest, but are as Lazarus compared with thee, while thou art as Dives. Pray for them; put them all in the same prayer and say, "Our Father."

And pray for those that are divided from us by the sea—those that are in heathen lands, scattered like precious salt in the midst of this world's putrefaction. Pray for all that name the name of Jesus, and let thy prayer be a great and

30 And if thy right hand offend thee, cut off, and cast it from thee: for it is profitable for thee that one of thy members should perish, and not that thy whole body should be cast into hell.

31 It hath been said, Whosoever shall put away his wife, let him give her a writing of divorcement:

32 But I say unto you, That whosoever shall put away his wife, saving for the cause of fornication, causeth her to commit adultery: and whosoever shall marry her that is divorced committeth adultery.

33 Again, ye have heard that it hath been said by them of old time, Thou shalt not forswear thyself, but shalt perform unto the Lord thine oaths:

34 But I say unto you, Swear not at all; neither by heaven; for it is God's throne:

35 Nor by the earth; for it is his footstool: neither by Jerusalem; for it is the city of the great King.

36 Neither shalt thou swear by thy head, because thou canst not make one hair white or black.

37 But let your communication be, Yea, yea; Nay, nay: for whatsoever is more than these cometh of evil.

38 Ye have heard that it hath been said, An eye for an eye, and a tooth for a tooth:

39 But I say unto you, That ye resist not evil: but whosoever shall smite thee on thy right cheek, turn to him the other also.

40 And if any man will sue thee at the law, and take away thy coat, let him have thy cloke also.

41 And whosoever shall compel thee to go a mile, go with him twain.

42 Give to him that asketh thee, and from him that would borrow of thee turn not thou away.

43 Ye have heard that it hath been said, Thou shalt love thy neighbor, and hate thine enemy.

44 But I say unto you, Love your enemies, bless them that curse you, do good to them that hate you, and pray for them which despitefully use you, and persecute you;

45 That ye may be the children of your Father which is in heaven: for he maketh his sun to rise on the evil and on the good, and sendeth rain on the just and on the unjust.

46 For if ye love them which love you, what reward have ye? do not even the publicans the same?

47 And if ye salute your brethren only, what do ye more than others? do not even the publicans so?

48 Be ye therefore perfect, even as your Father which is in heaven is perfect.

otherwise be restrained from hurting your brother.

31. Let him give her a writing of divorce – Which the scribes and Pharisees allowed men to do on any trifling occasion. Deut. xxiv, 1; Matt. xix, 7; Mark x, 2; Luke xvi, 18.

32. Causeth her to commit adultery – If she marry again.

33. What he forbids is, the swearing at all, 1, by any creature, 2, in our ordinary conversation: both of which the scribes and Pharisees taught to be perfectly innocent. Exod. xx, 7.

36. For thou canst not make one hair white or black – Whereby it appears, that this also is not thine but God's.

37. Let your conversation be yea, yea; nay, nay – That is, in your common discourse, barely affirm or deny.

38. Ye have heard – Our Lord proceeds to enforce such meekness and love on those who are persecuted for righteousness' sake (which he pursues to the end of the chapter) as were utterly unknown to the scribes and Pharisees.

39. But I say unto you, that ye resist not the evil man – Thus; the Greek word translated resist signifies standing in battle array, striving for victory. If a man smite thee on the right cheek – Return not evil for evil: yea, turn to him the other – Rather than revenge thyself.

40, 41. Where the damage is not great, choose rather to suffer it, though possibly it may on that account be repeated, than to demand an eye for an eye, to enter into a rigorous prosecution of the offender.

42. Give and lend to any so far, as is consistent with thy engagements to thy creditors, thy family, and the household of faith. Luke vi, 30.

43. Thou shalt love thy neighbor; And hate thy enemy – God spoke the former part; the scribes added the latter. Lev. xix, 18.

44. Bless them that curse you – Speak all the good you can to and of them, who speak all evil to and of you. Repay love in thought, word, and deed, to those who hate you, and show it both in word and deed. Luke vi, 27, 35.

45. That ye may be the children – That is, that ye may continue and appear such before men and angels. For he maketh his sun to rise – He gives them such blessings as they will receive at his hands. Spiritual blessings they will not receive.

46. The publicans – were officers of the revenue, farmers, or receivers of the public money: men employed by the Romans to gather the taxes and customs, which they exacted of the nations they had conquered.

47. And if ye salute your friends only – Our Lord probably glances at those prejudices, which different sects had against each other, and intimates, that he would not have his followers imbibe that narrow spirit.

48. Therefore ye shall be perfect; as your Father who is in heaven is perfect – So the original runs, referring to all that holiness which is described in the foregoing verses, which our Lord in the beginning of the chapter recommends as happiness, and in the close of it as perfection.

MATTHEW 6

1. In the foregoing chapter our Lord particularly described the nature of inward holiness. In this he describes that purity of intention without which none of our outward actions are holy. This chapter contains four parts,

   1. The right intention and manner of giving alms, ver. 1-4.

   2. The right intention, manner, form, and prerequisites of prayer,

MATTHEW HENRY

CHARLES H. SPURGEON

21-26 The Jewish teachers had taught, that nothing except actual murder was forbidden by the sixth commandment. Thus they explained away its spiritual meaning. Christ showed the full meaning of this commandment; according to which we must be judged hereafter, and therefore ought to be ruled now. All rash anger is heart murder. By our brother, here, we are to understand any person, though ever so much below us, for we are all made of one blood. "Raca," is a scornful word, and comes from pride: "Thou fool," is a spiteful word, and comes from hatred. Malicious slanders and censures are poison that kills secretly and slowly.

27-32 Victory over the desires of the heart, must be attended with painful exertions. But it must be done. Every thing is bestowed to save us from our sins, not in them. All our senses and powers must be kept from those things which lead to transgression. Those who lead others into temptation to sin, by dress or in other ways, or leave them in it, or expose them to it, make themselves guilty of their sin, and will be accountable for it.

33-37 There is no reason to consider that solemn oaths in a court of justice, or on other proper occasions, are wrong, provided they are taken with due reverence. But all oaths taken without necessity, or in common conversation, must be sinful, as well as all those expressions which are appeals to God, though persons think thereby to evade the guilt of swearing.

38-42 The plain instruction is, Suffer any injury that can be borne, for the sake of peace, committing your concerns to the Lord's keeping. And the sum of all is, that Christians must avoid disputing and striving. If any say, Flesh and blood cannot pass by such an affront, let them remember, that flesh and blood shall not inherit the kingdom of God; and those who act upon right principles will have most peace and comfort.

43-48 Those who promise themselves a reward above others must study to do more than others. Lastly, Our Saviour concludes this subject with this exhortation (v. 48), Be ye therefore perfect, as your Father which is in heaven is perfect. Which may be understood, 1. In general, including all those things wherein we must be followers of God as dear children. Note, It is the duty of Christians to desire, and aim at, and press toward a perfection in grace and holiness, Phil. 3:12–14. And therein we must study to conform ourselves to the example of our heavenly Father, 1 Pt. 1:15, 16. Or, 2. In this particular before mentioned, of doing good to our enemies; see Lu. 6:36. It is God's perfection to forgive injuries and to entertain strangers, and to do good to the evil and unthankful, and it will be ours to be like him. We that owe so much, that owe our all, to the divine bounty, ought to copy it out as well as we can.

comprehensive one. "Our Father, which art in heaven." And after thou hast prayed that rise up and act it. Say not "Our Father," and then look upon thy brethren with a sneer or a frown. I beseech thee, live like a brother, and act like a brother. Help the needy; cheer the sick; comfort the faint-hearted; go about doing good, minister unto the suffering people of God, wherever thou findest them, and let the world take knowledge of thee, that thou art when on thy feet what thou art upon thy knees—that thou art a brother unto all the brotherhood of Christ, a brother born for adversity, like thy Master himself.

II. Having thus expounded the double relationship, I have left myself but little time for a very important part of the subject, namely, THE SPIRIT OF ADOPTION.

I am extremely puzzled and bewildered how to explain to the ungodly what is the spirit with which we must be filled, before we can pray this prayer. If I had a foundling here, one who had never seen either father or mother, I think I should have a very great difficulty in trying to make him understand what are the feelings of a child towards its father. Poor little thing, he has been under tutors and governors; he has learned to respect them for their kindness, or to fear them for their austerity, but there never can be in that child's heart that love towards tutor or governor, however kind he may be, that there is in the heart of another child towards his own mother or father. There is a nameless charm there: we cannot describe or understand it: it is a sacred touch of nature, a throb in the breast that God has put there, and that cannot be taken away. The fatherhood is recognized by the childship of the child. And what is that spirit of a child—that sweet spirit that makes him recognize and love his father? I cannot tell you unless you are a child yourself, and then you will know. And what is "the spirit of adoption, whereby we cry Abba, Father?" I cannot tell you; but if you have felt it you will know it. It is a sweet compound of faith that knows God to be my Father, love that loves him as my Father, joy that rejoices in him as my Father, fear that trembles to disobey him because he is my Father and a confident affection and trustfulness that relies upon him, and casts itself wholly upon him, because it knows by the infallible witness of the Holy Spirit, that Jehovah, the God of earth and heaven, is the Father of my heart. Oh! have you ever felt the spirit of adoption? There is nought like it beneath the sky. Save heaven itself there is nought more blissful than to enjoy that spirit of adoption. Oh! when the wind of trouble is

MATTHEW 6

1 Take heed that ye do not your alms before men, to be seen of them: otherwise ye have no reward of your Father which is in heaven.

2 Therefore when thou doest thine alms, do not sound a trumpet before thee, as the hypocrites do in the synagogues and in the streets, that they may have glory of men. Verily I say unto you, They have their reward.

3 But when thou doest alms, let not thy left hand know what thy right hand doeth:

4 That thine alms may be in secret: and thy Father which seeth in secret himself shall reward thee openly.

5 And when thou prayest, thou shalt not be as the hypocrites are: for they love to pray standing in the synagogues and in the corners of the streets, that they may be seen of men. Verily I say unto you, They have their reward.

6 But thou, when thou prayest, enter into thy closet, and when thou hast shut thy door, pray to thy Father which is in secret; and thy Father which seeth in secret shall reward thee openly.

7 But when ye pray, use not vain repetitions, as the heathen do: for they think that they shall be heard for their much speaking.

8 Be not ye therefore like unto them: for your Father knoweth what things ye have need of, before ye ask him.

9 After this manner therefore pray ye: Our Father which art in heaven, Hallowed be thy name.

10 Thy kingdom come. Thy will be done in earth, as it is in heaven.

11 Give us this day our daily bread.

12 And forgive us our debts, as we forgive our debtors.

13 And lead us not into temptation, but deliver us from evil: For thine is the kingdom, and the power, and the glory, for ever. Amen.

14 For if ye forgive men their trespasses, your heavenly Father will also forgive you:

15 But if ye forgive not men their trespasses, neither will your Father forgive your trespasses.

16 Moreover when ye fast, be not, as the hypocrites, of a sad countenance: for they disfigure their faces, that they may appear unto men to fast. Verily I say unto you, They have their reward.

17 But thou, when thou fastest, anoint thine head, and wash thy face;

18 That thou appear not unto men to fast, but unto thy Father which is in secret: and thy Father, which seeth in secret, shall reward thee openly.

ver. 5-15.

3. The right intention, and manner of fasting, ver. 16-18.

4. The necessity of a pure intention in all things, unmixed either with the desire of riches, or worldly care, and fear of want, ver. 19-34. This verse is a general caution against vain glory, in any of our good works: All these are here summed up together, in the comprehensive word righteousness. This general caution our Lord applies in the sequel to the three principal branches of it, relating to our neighbor, ver. 2-4, to God, ver. 5, 6, and to ourselves, ver. 16-18. To be seen – Barely the being seen, while we are doing any of these things, is a circumstance purely indifferent. But the doing them with this view, to be seen and admired, this is what our Lord condemns.

2. As the hypocrites do – Many of the scribes and Pharisees did this, under a pretense of calling the poor together. They have their reward – All they will have; for they shall have none from God.

3. Let not thy left hand know what thy right hand doth – A proverbial expression for doing a thing secretly. Do it as secretly as is consistent,

1. With the doing it at all.

2. With the doing it in the most effectual manner.

5. The synagogues – These were properly the places where the people assembled for public prayer, and hearing the Scriptures read and expounded.

6. Enter into thy closet – That is, do it with as much secrecy as thou canst.

7. Use not vain repetitions – To repeat any words without meaning them, is certainly a vain repetition. Therefore we should be extremely careful in all our prayers to mean what we say; and to say only what we mean from the bottom of our hearts.

8. Your Father knoweth what things ye have need of – We do not pray to inform God of our wants. Omniscient as he is, he cannot be informed of any thing which he knew not before: and he is always willing to relieve them.

9. Thus therefore pray ye – He who best knew what we ought to pray for, and how we ought to pray, what matter of desire, what manner of address would most please himself, would best become us, has here dictated to us a most perfect and universal form of prayer, comprehending all our real wants, expressing all our lawful desires; a complete directory and full exercise of all our devotions.

10. Our Father – Who art good and gracious to all, our Creator, our Preserver; the Father of our Lord, and of us in him, thy children by adoption and grace: not my Father only, who now cry unto thee, but the Father of the universe, of angels and men: who art in heaven – Beholding all things, both in heaven and earth.

1. Hallowed be thy name – Mayest thou, O Father, be truly known by all intelligent beings, and with affections suitable to that knowledge: mayest thou be duly honored, loved, feared, by all in heaven and in earth, by all angels and all men.

2. Thy kingdom come – May thy kingdom of grace come quickly, and swallow up all the kingdoms of the earth.

3. Thy will be done on earth, as it is in heaven – May all the inhabitants of the earth do thy will as willingly as the holy angels.

4. Give us – O Father (for we claim nothing of right, but only of thy free mercy) this day – (for we take no thought for the morrow) our daily bread.

5. And forgive us our debts, as we also forgive our debtors – Give us, O Lord, redemption in thy blood, even the forgiveness of sins: as

MATTHEW HENRY   CHARLES H. SPURGEON

MATTHEW 6

Against hypocrisy in almsgiving. (1-4)
Against hypocrisy in prayer. (5-8)
How to pray. (9-15)
Respecting fasting. (16-18)
Evil of being worldly-minded. (19-24)
Trust in God commended. (25-34)

1-4 Our Lord next warned against hypocrisy and outward show in religious duties. What we do, must be done from an inward principle, that we may be approved of God, not that we may be praised of men. In these verses we are cautioned against hypocrisy in giving alms. Take heed of it. It is a subtle sin; and vain-glory creeps into what we do, before we are aware.

5-8 It is taken for granted that all who are disciples of Christ pray. You may as soon find a living man that does not breathe, as a living Christian that does not pray. If prayerless, then graceless. The Scribes and Pharisees were guilty of two great faults in prayer, vain-glory and vain repetitions. "Verily they have their reward;" if in so great a matter as is between us and God, when we are at prayer, we can look to so poor a thing as the praise of men, it is just that it should be all our reward.

9-15 Christ saw it needful to show his disciples what must commonly be the matter and method of their prayer. The petitions are six; the first three relate more expressly to God and his honor, the last three to our own concerns, both temporal and spiritual. This prayer teaches us to seek first the kingdom of God and his righteousness, and that all other things shall be added. After the things of God's glory, kingdom, and will, we pray for the needful supports and comforts of this present life. Every word here has a lesson in it. We ask for bread; that teaches us sobriety and temperance: and we ask only for bread; not for what we do not need. We are taught to hate and dread sin while we hope for mercy, to distrust ourselves, to rely on the providence and grace of God to keep us from it, to be prepared to resist the tempter, and not to become tempters of others. Here is a promise, If you forgive, your heavenly Father will also forgive. We must forgive, as we hope to be forgiven. Those who desire to find mercy with God, must show mercy to their brethren. Christ came into the world as the great Peace-maker, not only to reconcile us to God, but one to another.

16-18 Religious fasting is a duty required of the disciples of Christ, but it is not so much a duty itself, as a means to dispose us for other duties. Fasting is the humbling of the soul, Ps 35:13; that is the inside of the duty; let that, therefore, be thy principal care, and as to the outside of it, covet not to let it be seen. God sees in secret, and will reward openly.

19-24 Worldly-mindedness is a common and fatal symptom of hypocrisy, for by no sin can Satan have a

blowing and waves of adversity are rising, and the ship is reeling to the rock how sweet then to say "My Father," and to believe that his strong hand is on the helm!—when the bones are aching, and when the loins are filled with pain, and when the cup is brimming with wormwood and gall, to say "My Father," and seeing that Father's hand holding the cup to the lip, to drink it steadily to the very dregs because we can say, "My Father, not my will, but thine be done."

Well says Martin Luther, in his Exposition of the Galatians, "there is more eloquence in that word, 'Abba, Father,' than in all the orations of Demosthenes or Cicero put together." "My Father!" Oh! there is music there; there is eloquence there; there is the very essence of heaven's own bliss in that word, "My Father," when applied to God, and when said by us with an unfaltering tongue, through the inspiration of the Spirit of the living God.

My hearers, have you the spirit of adoption? If not, ye are miserable men. May God himself bring you to know him! May he teach you your need of him! May he lead you to the cross of Christ, and help you to look to your dying Brother! May he bathe you in the blood that flowed from his open wounds, and then, accepted in the beloved, may you rejoice that you have the honor to be one of that sacred family.

III. And now, in the last place, I said that there was in the title, A DOUBLE ARGUMENT. "Our Father." That is, "Lord, hear what I have got to say. Thou art my Father." If I come before a judge I have no right to expect that he shall hear me at any particular season in aught that I have to say. If I came merely to crave for some boon or benefit to myself, if the law were on my side, then I could demand an audience at his hands; but when I come as a law-breaker, and only come to crave for mercy, or for favors I deserve not, I have no right to expect to be heard. But a child, even though he is erring, always expects his father will hear what he has to say. "Lord, if I call thee King thou wilt say, 'Thou art a rebellious subject; get thee gone.' If I call thee Judge thou wilt say, 'Be still, or out of thine own mouth will I condemn thee.' If I call thee Creator thou wilt say unto me 'It repenteth me that I made man upon the earth.' If I call thee my Preserver thou wilt say unto me, 'I have preserved thee, but thou hast rebelled against me.' But if I call thee Father, all my sinfulness doth not invalidate my claim. If thou be my Father, then thou lovest me; if I be thy child, then thou wilt regard me, and poor though my language be, thou wilt not despise it." If a child

19 Lay not up for yourselves treasures upon earth, where moth and rust doth corrupt, and where thieves break through and steal:

20 But lay up for yourselves treasures in heaven, where neither moth nor rust doth corrupt, and where thieves do not break through nor steal:

21 For where your treasure is, there will your heart be also.

22 The light of the body is the eye: if therefore thine eye be single, thy whole body shall be full of light.

23 But if thine eye be evil, thy whole body shall be full of darkness. If therefore the light that is in thee be darkness, how great is that darkness!

24 No man can serve two masters: for either he will hate the one, and love the other; or else he will hold to the one, and despise the other. Ye cannot serve God and mammon.

25 Therefore I say unto you, Take no thought for your life, what ye shall eat, or what ye shall drink; nor yet for your body, what ye shall put on. Is not the life more than meat, and the body than raiment?

26 Behold the fowls of the air: for they sow not, neither do they reap, nor gather into barns; yet your heavenly Father feedeth them. Are ye not much better than they?

27 Which of you by taking thought can add one cubit unto his stature?

28 And why take ye thought for raiment? Consider the lilies of the field, how they grow; they toil not, neither do they spin:

29 And yet I say unto you, That even Solomon in all his glory was not arrayed like one of these.

30 Wherefore, if God so clothe the grass of the field, which to day is, and to morrow is cast into the oven, shall he not much more clothe you, O ye of little faith?

31 Therefore take no thought, saying, What shall we eat? or, What shall we drink? or, Wherewithal shall we be clothed?

32 (For after all these things do the Gentiles seek:) for your heavenly Father knoweth that ye have need of all these things.

33 But seek ye first the kingdom of God, and his righteousness; and all these things shall be added unto you.

34 Take therefore no thought for the morrow: for the morrow shall take thought for the things of itself. Sufficient unto the day is the evil thereof.

thou enablest us freely and fully to forgive every man, so do thou forgive all our trespasses.

6. And lead us not into temptation, but deliver us from evil – Whenever we are tempted, O thou that helpest our infirmities, suffer us not to enter into temptation; to be overcome or suffer loss thereby.

16. When ye fast? – Our Lord does not enjoin either fasting, alms-deeds, or prayer: all these being duties which were before fully established in the Church of God. Disfigure – By the dust and ashes which they put upon their heads, as was usual at the times of solemn humiliation.

17. Anoint thy head – So the Jews frequently did. Dress thyself as usual.

19. Lay not up for yourselves – Our Lord here makes a transition from religious to common actions, and warns us of another snare, the love of money, as inconsistent with purity of intention as the love of praise. 22. The eye is the lamp of the body – And what the eye is to the body, the intention is to the soul.

24. Mammon – Riches, money; any thing loved or sought, without reference to God. Luke xvi, 13.

25. And if you serve God, you need be careful for nothing. Therefore take not thought – That is, be not anxiously careful. Beware of worldly cares.

27. And which of you – If you are ever so careful, can even add a moment to your own life thereby? This seems to be far the most easy and natural sense of the words.

29. Solomon in all his glory was not arrayed like one of these – Not in garments of so pure a white. The eastern monarchs were often clothed in white robes.

30. The grass of the field – is a general expression, including both herbs and flowers. If God so clothe – The word properly implies, the putting on a complete dress, that surrounds the body on all sides. Every microscope in which a flower is viewed gives a lively comment on this text.

31. Therefore take not thought – How kind are these precepts! The substance of which is only this, Do thyself no harm! Let us not be so ungrateful to him, nor so injurious to ourselves, as to harass and oppress our minds with that burden of anxiety, which he has so graciously taken off.

33. Seek the kingdom of God and his righteousness – Singly aim at this, that God, reigning in your heart, may fill it with the righteousness above described.

34. The morrow shall take thought for itself – That is, be careful for the morrow when it comes.

surer and faster hold of the soul, under the cloak of a profession of religion. Something the soul will have, which it looks upon as the best thing; in which it has pleasure and confidence above other things. Christ counsels to make our best things the joys and glories of the other world, those things not seen which are eternal, and to place our happiness in them. There are treasures in heaven. It is our wisdom to give all diligence to make our title to eternal life sure through Jesus Christ, and to look on all things here below, as not worthy to be compared with it, and to be content with nothing short of it.

25-34 There is scarcely any sin against which our Lord Jesus more warns his disciples, than disquieting, distracting, distrustful cares about the things of this life. This often insnares the poor as much as the love of wealth does the rich. But there is a carefulness about temporal things which is a duty, though we must not carry these lawful cares too far. Take no thought for your life. Not about the length of it; but refer it to God to lengthen or shorten it as he pleases; our times are in his hand, and they are in a good hand. Not about the comforts of this life; but leave it to God to make it bitter or sweet as he pleases. Food and raiment God has promised, therefore we may expect them. Take no thought for the morrow, for the time to come. Be not anxious for the future, how you shall live next year, or when you are old, or what you shall leave behind you. As we must not boast of tomorrow, so we must not care for tomorrow, or the events of it. God has given us life, and has given us the body. And what can he not do for us, who did that? If we take care about our souls and for eternity, which are more than the body and its life, we may leave it to God to provide for us food and raiment, which are less. Improve this as an encouragement to trust in God. We must reconcile ourselves to our worldly estate, as we do to our stature. We cannot alter the disposals of Providence, therefore we must submit and resign ourselves to them. Thoughtfulness for our souls is the best cure of thoughtfulness for the world. Seek first the kingdom of God, and make religion your business: say not that this is the way to starve; no, it is the way to be well provided for, even in this world. The conclusion of the whole matter is, that it is the will and command of the Lord Jesus, that by daily prayers we may get strength to bear us up under our daily troubles, and to arm us against the temptations that attend them, and then let none of these things move us.

were called upon to speak in the presence of a number of persons, how very much alarmed he would be lest he should not use right language. I may sometimes feel when I have to address a mighty auditory, lest I should not select choice words, full well knowing that if I were to preach as I never shall, like the mightiest of orators I should always have enough of carping critics to rail at me. But if I had my Father here and if you could all stand in the relationship of father to me, I should not be very particular what language I used. When I talk to my Father I am not afraid he will misunderstand me; if I put my words a little out of place he understands my meaning somehow.

When we are little children we only prattle; still our father understands us. Our children talk a great deal more like Dutchmen than Englishmen when they begin to talk, and strangers come in and my, "Dear me, what is the child talking about?" But we know what it is and though in what they say there may not be an intelligible sound that any one could print, and a reader make it out, we know they have got certain little wants, and having a way of expressing their desires, and we can understand them. So when we come to God, our prayers are little broken things; we cannot put them together but our Father, he will hear us. Oh! what a beginning is "Our Father," to a prayer full of faults, and a foolish prayer perhaps, a prayer in which we are going to ask what we ought not to ask for! "Father, forgive the language! forgive the matter!" As one dear brother said the other day at the prayer meeting. He could not get on in prayer, and he finished up on a sudden by saying, "Lord, I cannot pray tonight as I should wish; I cannot put the words together; Lord, take the meaning, take the meaning," and sat down. That is just what David said once, "Lo, all my desire is before thee"—not my words, but my desire, and God could read it. We should say, "Our Father," because that is a reason why God should hear what we have to say.

But there is another argument. "Our Father." "Lord, give me what I want." If I come to a stranger, I have no right to expect he will give it me. He may out of his charity; but if I come to a father, I have a claim, a sacred claim. It is thy business to relieve me; I can come confidently to thee, knowing thou wilt give me all I want. If we ask our Father for anything when we are little children, we are under an obligation certainly; but it is an obligation we never feel. Now, we are all deeply under obligation to God, but it is a child's obligation—an obligation which impels us to gratitude, but which does not constrain us to feel that we have been

MATTHEW 7

1 Judge not, that ye be not judged.

2 For with what judgment ye judge, ye shall be judged: and with what measure ye mete, it shall be measured to you again.

3 And why beholdest thou the mote that is in thy brother's eye, but considerest not the beam that is in thine own eye?

4 Or how wilt thou say to thy brother, Let me pull out the mote out of thine eye; and, behold, a beam is in thine own eye?

5 Thou hypocrite, first cast out the beam out of thine own eye; and then shalt thou see clearly to cast out the mote out of thy brother's eye.

6 Give not that which is holy unto the dogs, neither cast ye your pearls before swine, lest they trample them under their feet, and turn again and rend you.

7 Ask, and it shall be given you; seek, and ye shall find; knock, and it shall be opened unto you:

8 For every one that asketh receiveth; and he that seeketh findeth; and to him that knocketh it shall be opened.

9 Or what man is there of you, whom if his son ask bread, will he give him a stone?

10 Or if he ask a fish, will he give him a serpent?

11 If ye then, being evil, know how to give good gifts unto your children, how much more shall your Father which is in heaven give good things to them that ask him?

12 Therefore all things whatsoever ye would that men should do to you, do ye even so to them: for this is the law and the prophets.

13 Enter ye in at the strait gate: for wide is the gate, and broad is the way, that leadeth to destruction, and many there be which go in thereat:

14 Because strait is the gate, and narrow is the way, which leadeth unto life, and few there be that find it.

15 Beware of false prophets, which come to you in sheep's clothing, but inwardly they are ravening wolves.

16 Ye shall know them by their fruits. Do men gather grapes of thorns, or figs of thistles?

17 Even so every good tree bringeth forth good fruit; but a corrupt tree bringeth forth evil fruit.

18 A good tree cannot bring forth evil fruit, neither can a corrupt tree bring forth good fruit.

19 Every tree that bringeth not forth good fruit is hewn down, and cast into the fire.

20 Wherefore by their fruits ye shall

MATTHEW 7

Our Lord now proceeds to warn us against the chief hindrances of holiness. And how wisely does he begin with judging? wherein all young converts are so apt to spend that zeal which is given them for better purposes.

1. Judge not – any man without full, clear, certain knowledge, without absolute necessity, without tender love. Luke vi, 37.

2. With what measure ye mete, it shall be measured to you – Awful words! So we may, as it were, choose for ourselves, whether God shall be severe or merciful to us.

3. In particular, why do you open your eyes to any fault of your brother, while you yourself are guilty of a much greater? The mote – The word properly signifies a splinter or shiver of wood. This and a beam, its opposite, were proverbially used by the Jews, to denote, the one, small infirmities, the other, gross, palpable faults. Luke vi, 41.

5. Thou hypocrite – It is mere hypocrisy to pretend zeal for the amendment of others while we have none for our own.

6. Give not – to dogs – lest turning they rend you: Cast not – to swine – lest they trample them under foot. Yet even then, when the beam is cast out of thine own eye, Give not – That is, talk not of the deep things of God to those whom you know to be wallowing in sin.

7. But ask – Pray for them, as well as for yourselves: in this there can be no such danger. Seek – Add your own diligent endeavors to your asking: and knock – Persevere importunately in that diligence. Luke xi, 9.

8. For every one that asketh receiveth – Provided he ask aright, and ask what is agreeable to God's will.

11. To them that ask him – But on this condition, that ye follow the example of his goodness, by doing to all as ye would they should do to you. For this is the law and the prophets – This is the sum of all.

13. The strait gate – The holiness described in the foregoing chapters. And this is the narrow way. Wide is the gate, and many there are that go in through it – They need not seek for this; they come to it of course. Many go in through it, because strait is the other gate – Therefore they do not care for it; they like a wider gate. Luke xiii, 24.

15. Beware of false prophets – Who in their preaching describe a broad way to heaven: it is their prophesying, their teaching the broad way, rather than their walking in it themselves, that is here chiefly spoken of. All those are false prophets, who teach any other way than that our Lord hath here marked out. In sheep's clothing – With outside religion and fair professions of love: Wolves – Not feeding, but destroying souls.

16. By their fruits ye shall know them – A short, plain, easy rule, whereby to know true from false prophets: and one that may be applied by people of the weakest capacity, who are not accustomed to deep reasoning. True prophets convert sinners to God, or at least confirm and strengthen those that are converted. False prophets do not. They also are false prophets, who though speaking the very truth, yet are not sent by the Spirit of God, but come in their own name, to declare it: their grand mark is, "Not turning men from the power of Satan to God." Luke vi, 43, 44.

18. A good tree cannot bring forth evil fruit, neither a corrupt tree good fruit – But it is certain, the goodness or badness here mentioned respects the doctrine, rather than the personal character. For a bad man preaching the good doctrine here delivered, is sometimes an instrument of converting sinners to God. Yet I do not aver, that all are true prophets who speak the truth, and thereby convert sinners. I only

MATTHEW HENRY   CHARLES H. SPURGEON

MATTHEW 7

Christ reproves rash judgment. (1-6)
Encouragements to prayer. (7-11)
The broad and narrow way. (12-14)
Against false prophets. (15-20)
To be doers of the word, not hearers only. (21-29)

1-6 We must judge ourselves, and judge of our own acts, but not make our word a law to everybody. We must not judge rashly, nor pass judgment upon our brother without any ground. We must not make the worst of people. Here is a just reproof to those who quarrel with their brethren for small faults, while they allow in themselves greater ones. Some sins are as motes, while others are as beams; some as a gnat, others as a camel. Not that there is any sin little; if it be a mote, or splinter, it is in the eye; if a gnat, it is in the throat; both are painful and dangerous, and we cannot be easy or well till they are got out. That which charity teaches us to call but a splinter in our brother's eye, true repentance and godly sorrow will teach us to call a beam in our own.

7-11 Prayer is the appointed means for obtaining what we need. Pray; pray often; make a business of prayer, and be serious and earnest in it. Ask, as a beggar asks alms. Ask, as a traveler asks the way. Seek, as for a thing of value that we have lost; or as the merchantman that seeks goodly pearls. Knock, as he that desires to enter into the house knocks at the door. Sin has shut and barred the door against us; by prayer we knock. Whatever you pray for, according to the promise, shall be given you, if God see it fit for you, and what would you have more? This is made to apply to all that pray aright; every one that asketh receiveth, whether Jew or Gentile, young or old, rich or poor, high or low, master or servant, learned or unlearned, all are alike welcome to the throne of grace, if they come in faith.

12-14 Christ came to teach us, not only what we are to know and believe, but what we are to do; not only toward God, but toward men; not only toward those of our party and persuasion, but toward men in general, all with whom we have to do. We must do that to our neighbor which we ourselves acknowledge to be fit and reasonable. We must, in our dealings with men, suppose ourselves in the same case and circumstances with those we have to do with, and act accordingly.

15-20 Nothing so much prevents men from entering the strait gate, and becoming true followers of Christ, as the carnal, soothing, flattering doctrines of those who oppose the truth. They may be known by the drift and effects of their doctrines. Some part of their temper and conduct is contrary to the mind of Christ. Those opinions come not from God that lead to sin.

21-29 Christ here shows that it will not be enough to

demeaned by it. Oh! if he were not my Father, how could I expect that he would relieve my wants? But since he is my Father, he will, he must hear my prayers, and answer the voice of my crying, and supply all my needs out of the riches of his fullness in Christ Jesus the Lord.

Has your father treated you badly lately? I have this word to you, then; your father loves you quite as much when he treats you roughly as when he treats you kindly. There is often more love in an angry father's heart than there is in the heart of a father who is too kind. I will suppose a case. Suppose there were two fathers, and their two sons went away to some remote part of the earth where idolatry is still practiced. Suppose these two sons were decoyed and deluded into idolatry. The news comes to England, and the first father is very angry. His son, his own son, has forsaken the religion of Christ and become an idolater. The second father says, "Well, if it will help him in trade I don't care, if he gets on the better by it, all well and good." Now, which loves most, the angry father, or the father who treats the matter with complacency? Why, the angry father is the best. He loves his son; therefore he cannot give away his son's soul for gold. Give me a father that is angry with my sins, and that seeks to bring me back, even though it be by chastisement. Thank God you have got a father that can be angry, but that loves you as much when he is angry as when he smiles upon you.

Go away with that upon your mind, and rejoice. But if you love not God and fear him not, go home, I beseech you, to confess your sins, and to seek mercy through the blood of Christ; and may this sermon be made useful in bringing you into the family of Christ though you have strayed from him long; and though his love has followed you long in vain, may it now find you, and bring you to his house rejoicing!

PREACHING FOR THE POOR
Sermon number 114, delivered on Sabbath Morning, January 25, 1857, at the Music Hall, Royal Surrey Gardens.

"The poor have the gospel preached to them."—Matthew 11:5.

I FIND THAT these words will bear three transla-tions; I shall, therefore, have three heads, which shall be composed of three translations of the text. The first is that of the authorized version: "The poor have the gospel preached to them;" it is also Tyndal's version. The second is the ver-sion of Cranmer, and the version of Geneva, which is the best, "The poor are evangelized,"

know them.

21 Not every one that saith unto me, Lord, Lord, shall enter into the kingdom of heaven; but he that doeth the will of my Father which is in heaven.

22 Many will say to me in that day, Lord, Lord, have we not prophesied in thy name? and in thy name have cast out devils? and in thy name done many wonderful works?

23 And then will I profess unto them, I never knew you: depart from me, ye that work iniquity.

24 Therefore whosoever heareth these sayings of mine, and doeth them, I will liken him unto a wise man, which built his house upon a rock:

25 And the rain descended, and the floods came, and the winds blew, and beat upon that house; and it fell not: for it was founded upon a rock.

26 And every one that heareth these sayings of mine, and doeth them not, shall be likened unto a foolish man, which built his house upon the sand:

27 And the rain descended, and the floods came, and the winds blew, and beat upon that house; and it fell: and great was the fall of it.

28 And it came to pass, when Jesus had ended these sayings, the people were astonished at his doctrine:

29 For he taught them as one having authority, and not as the scribes.

MATTHEW 8

1 When he was come down from the mountain, great multitudes followed him.

2 And, behold, there came a leper and worshiped him, saying, Lord, if thou wilt, thou canst make me clean.

3 And Jesus put forth his hand, and touched him, saying, I will; be thou clean. And immediately his leprosy was cleansed.

4 And Jesus saith unto him, See thou tell no man; but go thy way, shew thyself to the priest, and offer the gift that Moses commanded, for a testimony unto them.

5 And when Jesus was entered into Capernaum, there came unto him a centurion, beseeching him,

6 And saying, Lord, my servant lieth at home sick of the palsy, grievously tormented.

7 And Jesus saith unto him, I will come and heal him.

8 The centurion answered and said, Lord, I am not worthy that thou shouldest come under my roof: but speak the word only, and my servant

affirm, that none are such who do not.

19. Every tree that bringeth not forth good fruit is hewn down and cast into the fire – How dreadful then is the condition of that teacher who hath brought no sinners to God!

21. Not every one – That is, no one that saith, Lord, Lord – That makes a mere profession of me and my religion, shall enter – Whatever their false teachers may assure them to the contrary: He that doth the will of my Father – as I have now declared it. Observe: every thing short of this is only saying, Lord, Lord. Luke vi, 46.

22. We have prophesied – We have declared the mysteries of thy kingdom, wrote books; preached excellent sermons: In thy name done many wonderful works – So that even the working of miracles is no proof that a man has saving faith.

23. I never knew you – There never was a time that I approved of you: so that as many souls as they had saved, they were themselves never saved from their sins. Lord, is it my case? Luke xiii, 27.

24. Luke vi, 47.

29. He taught them – The multitudes, as one having authority – With a dignity and majesty peculiar to himself as the great Lawgiver, and with the demonstration and power of the Spirit: and not as the scribes – Who only expounded the law of another; and that in a lifeless, ineffectual manner.

MATTHEW 8

2. A leper came – Leprosies in those countries were seldom curable by natural means, any more than palsies or lunacy. Probably this leper, though he might not mix with the people, had heard our Lord at a distance. Mark i, 40; Luke v, 12.

4. See thou tell no man – Perhaps our Lord only meant here, Not till thou hast showed thyself to the priest – who was appointed to inquire into the case of leprosy. But many others he commanded, absolutely, to tell none of the miracles he had wrought upon them. And this he seems to have done, chiefly for one or more of these reasons:

1. To prevent the multitude from thronging him, in the manner related Mark i, 45.

2. To fulfill the prophecy, Isaiah xlii, 1, that he would not be vain or ostentatious. This reason St. Matthew assigns, chap. xii, 17, &c.

3. To avoid the being taken by force and made a king, John vi, 15. And,

4. That he might not enrage the chief priests, scribes, and Pharisees, who were the most bitter against him, any more than was unavoidable, Matt. xvi, 20, 21. For a testimony – That I am the Messiah; to them – The priests, who otherwise might have pleaded want of evidence. Lev. xiv, 2.

5. There came to him a centurion – A captain of a hundred Roman soldiers. Probably he came a little way toward him, and then went back. He thought himself not worthy to come in person, and therefore spoke the words that follow by his messengers. As it is not unusual in all languages, so in the Hebrew it is peculiarly frequent, to ascribe to a person himself the thing which is done, and the words which are spoken by his order. And accordingly St. Matthew relates as said by the centurion himself, what others said by order from him. An instance of the same kind we have in the case of Zebedee's children. From St. Matthew xx, 20, we learn it was their mother that spoke those words, which, Mark x, 35, 37, themselves are said to speak; because she was

own him for our Master, only in word and tongue. It is necessary to our happiness that we believe in Christ, that we repent of sin, that we live a holy life, that we love one another. This is his will, even our sanctification. Let us take heed of resting in outward privileges and doings, lest we deceive ourselves, and perish eternally, as multitudes do, with a lie in our right hand. Let every one that names the name of Christ, depart from all sin. There are others, whose religion rests in bare hearing, and it goes no further; their heads are filled with empty notions. These two sorts of hearers are represented as two builders. This parable teaches us to hear and do the sayings of the Lord Jesus: some may seem hard to flesh and blood, but they must be done. Christ is laid for a foundation, and every thing besides Christ is sand. Some build their hopes upon worldly prosperity; others upon an outward profession of religion. Upon these they venture; but they are all sand, too weak to bear such a fabric as our hopes of heaven. There is a storm coming that will try every man's work.

MATTHEW 8

Multitudes follow Christ. (1)
He heals a leper. (2-4)
A centurion's servant healed. (5-13)
Cure of Peter's wife's mother. (14-17)
The scribe's zealous proposal. (18-22)
Christ in a storm. (23-27)
He heals two possessed with devils. (28-34)

1 This verse refers to the close of the foregoing sermon. Those to whom Christ has made himself known, desire to know more of him.

2-4 In these verses we have an account of Christ's cleansing a leper, who came and worshiped him, as one clothed with Divine power. This cleansing directs us, not only to apply to Christ, who has power over bodily diseases, for the cure of them, but it also teaches us in what manner to apply to him. When we cannot be sure of God's will, we may be sure of his wisdom and mercy. No guilt is so great, but there is that in Christ's blood which atones for it; no corruption so strong, but there is that in his grace which can subdue it. To be made clean we must commend ourselves to his pity; we cannot demand it as a debt, but we must humbly request it as a favor.

5-13 This centurion was a heathen, a Roman soldier. Though he was a soldier, yet he was a godly man. No man's calling or place will be an excuse for unbelief and sin. See how he states his servant's case. We should concern ourselves for the souls of our children and servants, who are spiritually sick, who feel not spiritual evils, who know not that which is spiritually good; and we should bring them to Christ by faith and prayers. Observe his self-abasement. Humble souls are made more humble by Christ's gracious dealings

that is to say, they not only hear the gospel, but they are influenced by it;—the poor receive it. The last is a translation of some eminent writers, and above all, of Wyckliffe, which amused me when I read it, although I believe it to be as correct as any of the others. Wyckliffe translates it—"pore men ben taken to prechynge of the gospel." The verb may be equally well translated in the active as in the passive sense: "The poor have taken to the preaching of the gospel." That is to be one of the marks of the gospel dispensation in all times.

I. First, then, THE AUTHORISED VERSION, "The poor have the gospel preached to them." It was so in Christ's day; it is to be so with Christ's gospel to the end of time. Almost every impostor who has come into the world has aimed principally at the rich, and the mighty, and the respectable; very few impostors have found it to be worth their while to make it prominent in their preaching that they preach to the poor. They went before princes to promulgate their doctrines; they sought the halls of nobles where they might expatiate upon their pretended revelations. Few of them thought it worth their while to address themselves to those who have been most wickedly called "the swinish multitude," and to speak to them the glorious things of the gospel of Christ. But it is one delightful mark of Christ's dispensation, that he aims first at the poor. "The poor have the gospel preached to them." It was wise in him to do so. If we would fire a building, it is best to light it at the basement; so our Savior, when he would save a world, and convert men of all classes, and all ranks, begins at the lowest rank, that the fire may burn upwards, knowing right well that what was received by the poor, will ultimately by his grace be received by the rich also. Nevertheless, he chose this to be given to his disciples, and to be the mark of his gospel—"The poor have the gospel preached to them." Now, I have some things to say this morning, which I think are absolutely necessary, if the poor are to have the gospel preached unto them.

In the first place, let me say then, that the gospel must be preached where the poor can come and hear it. How can the poor have the gospel preached to them, if they cannot come and listen to it? And yet how many of our places of worship are there into which they cannot come, and into which, if they could come, they would only come as inferior creatures. They may sit in the back seats, but are not to be known and recognized as anything like other people. Hence the absolute necessity of having places of worship large enough to accommodate the multitude; and hence, moreover, the obligation

shall be healed.

9 For I am a man under authority, having soldiers under me: and I say to this man, Go, and he goeth; and to another, Come, and he cometh; and to my servant, Do this, and he doeth it.

10 When Jesus heard it, he marveled, and said to them that followed, Verily I say unto you, I have not found so great faith, no, not in Israel.

11 And I say unto you, That many shall come from the east and west, and shall sit down with Abraham, and Isaac, and Jacob, in the kingdom of heaven.

12 But the children of the kingdom shall be cast out into outer darkness: there shall be weeping and gnashing of teeth.

13 And Jesus said unto the centurion, Go thy way; and as thou hast believed, so be it done unto thee. And his servant was healed in the selfsame hour.

14 And when Jesus was come into Peter's house, he saw his wife's mother laid, and sick of a fever.

15 And he touched her hand, and the fever left her: and she arose, and ministered unto them.

16 When the even was come, they brought unto him many that were possessed with devils: and he cast out the spirits with his word, and healed all that were sick:

17 That it might be fulfilled which was spoken by Esaias the prophet, saying, Himself took our infirmities, and bare our sicknesses.

18 Now when Jesus saw great multitudes about him, he gave commandment to depart unto the other side.

19 And a certain scribe came, and said unto him, Master, I will follow thee whithersoever thou goest.

20 And Jesus saith unto him, The foxes have holes, and the birds of the air have nests; but the Son of man hath not where to lay his head.

21 And another of his disciples said unto him, Lord, suffer me first to go and bury my father.

22 But Jesus said unto him, Follow me; and let the dead bury their dead.

23 And when he was entered into a ship, his disciples followed him.

24 And, behold, there arose a great tempest in the sea, insomuch that the ship was covered with the waves: but he was asleep.

25 And his disciples came to him, and awoke him, saying, Lord, save us: we perish.

26 And he saith unto them, Why are ye fearful, O ye of little faith? Then he arose, and rebuked the winds and the sea; and there was a great calm.

only their mouth. Yet from ver. 13, Go thy way home, it appears he at length came in person, probably on hearing that Jesus was nearer to his house than he apprehended when he sent the second message by his friends. Luke vii, 1.

8. The centurion answered – By his second messengers.

9. For I am a man under authority – I am only an inferior officer: and what I command, is done even in my absence: how much more what thou commandest, who art Lord of all!

10. I have not found so great faith, no, not in Israel – For the centurion was not an Israelite.

11. Many from the farthest parts of the earth shall embrace the terms and enjoy the rewards of the Gospel covenant established with Abraham. But the Jews, who have the first title to them, shall be shut out from the feast; from grace here, and hereafter from glory. Luke xiii, 29.

12. The outer darkness – Our Lord here alludes to the custom the ancients had of making their feast in the night time. Probably while he was speaking this, the centurion came in person. Matt. xiii, 42, 50; xxii, 13; xxiv, 51; xxv, 30.

14. Peter's wife's mother – St. Peter was then a young man, as were all the apostles. Mark i, 29; Luke iv, 38.

16. Mark i, 32; Luke iv, 40.

17. Whereby was fulfilled what was spoken by the Prophet Isaiah – He spoke it in a more exalted sense. The evangelist here only alludes to those words, as being capable of this lower meaning also. Such instances are frequent in the sacred writings, and are elegancies rather than imperfections. He fulfilled these words in the highest sense, by bearing our sins in his own body on the tree: in a lower sense, by sympathizing with us in our sorrows, and healing us of the diseases which were the fruit of sin. Isaiah liii, 4.

18. He commanded to go to the other side – That both himself and the people might have a little rest.

19. Luke ix, 57.

20. The Son of man – The expression is borrowed from Dan. vii, 13, and is the appellation which Christ generally gives himself: which he seems to do out of humility, as having some relation to his mean appearance in this world. Hath not where to lay his head – Therefore do not follow me from any view of temporal advantage.

21. Another said – I will follow thee without any such view; but I must mind my business first. It is not certain that his father was already dead. Perhaps his son desired to stay with him, being very old, till his death.

22. But Jesus said – When God calls, leave the business of the world to them who are dead to God.

23. Mark iv, 35; Luke viii, 22.

24. The ship was covered – So man's extremity is God's opportunity.

26. Why are ye fearful – Then he rebuked the winds – First, he composed their spirits, and then the sea.

28. The country of the Gergesenes – Or of the Gadarenes – Gergesa and Gadara were towns near each other. Hence the country between them took its name, sometimes from the one, sometimes from the other. There met him two demoniacs – St. Mark and St. Luke mention only one, who was probably the fiercer of the two, and the person who spoke to our Lord first. But this is no way inconsistent with the account which St. Matthew gives. The tombs – Doubtless those malevolent spirits love such tokens of death and destruction. Tombs were usually in those days in desert places, at a distance from towns, and were often

with them. Observe his great faith. The more diffident we are of ourselves, the stronger will be our confidence in Christ. Herein the centurion owns him to have Divine power, and a full command of all the creatures and powers of nature, as a master over his servants.

14-17 Peter had a wife, yet was an apostle of Christ, who showed that he approved of the married state, by being thus kind to Peter's wife's relations. The church of Rome, which forbids ministers to marry, goes contrary to that apostle upon whom they rest so much.

18-22 One of the scribes was too hasty in promising; he proffers himself to be a close follower of Christ. He seems to be very resolute. Many resolutions for religion are produced by sudden conviction, and taken up without due consideration; these come to nothing. When this scribe offered to follow Christ, one would think he should have been encouraged; one scribe might do more credit and service than twelve fishermen; but Christ saw his heart, and answered to its thoughts, and therein teaches all how to come to Christ. His resolve seems to have been from a worldly, covetous principle; but Christ had not a place to lay his head on, and if he follows him, he must not expect to fare better than he fared. We have reason to think this scribe went away. Another was too slow. Delay in doing is as bad on the one hand, as hastiness in resolving is on the other. He asked leave to attend his father to his grave, and then he would be at Christ's service. This seemed reasonable, yet it was not right. He had not true zeal for the work. Burying the dead, especially a dead father, is a good work, but it is not thy work at this time. If Christ requires our service, affection even for the nearest and dearest relatives, and for things otherwise our duty, must give way. An unwilling mind never wants an excuse. Jesus said to him, Follow me; and, no doubt, power went with this word to him as to others; he did follow Christ, and cleaved to him. The scribe said, I will follow thee; to this man Christ said, Follow me; comparing them together, it shows that we are brought to Christ by the force of his call to us, Ro 9:16.

23-27 It is a comfort to those who go down to the sea in ships, and are often in perils there, to reflect that they have a Savior to trust in and pray to, who knows what it is to be on the water, and to be in storms there. Those who are passing with Christ over the ocean of this world, must expect storms.

28-34 The devils have nothing to do with Christ as a Savior; they neither have, nor hope for any benefit from him. Oh the depth of this mystery of Divine love; that fallen man has so much to do with Christ, when fallen angels have nothing to do with him! Heb 2:16. Surely here was torment, to be forced to own the excellence that is in Christ, and yet they had no part in him. The devils desire not to have any thing to do with Christ as

to go out into the highways and hedges. If the poor are to have the gospel preached unto them, then we must take it where they can get it. If I wanted to preach to English people, it would be of no use for me to go and stand on one of the peaks of the Himalayas, and begin preaching; they could not hear me there. And it is of little avail to build a gorgeous structure for a fashionable congregation, and then to think of preaching to the poor; they cannot come any more than the Hottentots can make their journey from Africa and listen to me here. I should not expect them to come to such a place, nor will they willingly enter it. The gospel should be preached, then, where the poor will come; and if they will not come after it, then let it be taken to them. We should have places where there is accommodation for them, and where they are regarded and respected as much as any other rank and condition of men. It is with this view alone that I have labored earnestly to be the means of building a large place of worship, because I feel that although the bulk of my congregation in New Park-street Chapel are poor, yet there are many poor who can by no possibility enter the doors, because we cannot find room for the multitudes to be received. You ask me why I do not preach in the street. I reply, I would do so, and am constantly doing so in every place except London, but here I cannot do it, since it would amount to an absolute breach of the peace, it being impossible to conceive what a multitude of people must necessarily be assembled. I trembled when I saw twelve thousand on the last occasion I preached in the open air; therefore I have thought it best, for the present at least, to desist, until happily there shall be fewer to follow me. Otherwise my heart is in the open-air movement; I practice it everywhere else, and I pray God to give to our ministers zeal and earnestness, that they may take the gospel into the streets, highways and byways, and compel the people to come in, that the house may be filled. Oh that God would give us this characteristic mark of his precious grace, that the poor might have the gospel preached unto them!

"But," you reply, "there are plenty of churches and chapels to which they might come." I answer, yes, but that is only one half of the matter. The gospel must be preached attractively before the poor will have the gospel preached unto them. Why, there is no attraction in the gospel to the great mass of our race, as it is currently preached. I confess that when I have a violent headache, and cannot sleep, I could almost wish for some droning minister to preach to me; I feel certain I could go to sleep then, for I have heard some under the soporific

27 But the men marveled, saying, What manner of man is this, that even the winds and the sea obey him!

28 And when he was come to the other side into the country of the Gergesenes, there met him two possessed with devils, coming out of the tombs, exceeding fierce, so that no man might pass by that way.

29 And, behold, they cried out, saying, What have we to do with thee, Jesus, thou Son of God? art thou come hither to torment us before the time?

30 And there was a good way off from them an herd of many swine feeding.

31 So the devils besought him, saying, If thou cast us out, suffer us to go away into the herd of swine.

32 And he said unto them, Go. And when they were come out, they went into the herd of swine: and, behold, the whole herd of swine ran violently down a steep place into the sea, and perished in the waters.

33 And they that kept them fled, and went their ways into the city, and told every thing, and what was befallen to the possessed of the devils.

34 And, behold, the whole city came out to meet Jesus: and when they saw him, they besought him that he would depart out of their coasts.

MATTHEW 9

1 And he entered into a ship, and passed over, and came into his own city.

2 And, behold, they brought to him a man sick of the palsy, lying on a bed: and Jesus seeing their faith said unto the sick of the palsy; Son, be of good cheer; thy sins be forgiven thee.

3 And, behold, certain of the scribes said within themselves, This man blasphemeth.

4 And Jesus knowing their thoughts said, Wherefore think ye evil in your hearts?

5 For whether is easier, to say, Thy sins be forgiven thee; or to say, Arise, and walk?

6 But that ye may know that the Son of man hath power on earth to forgive sins, (then saith he to the sick of the palsy,) Arise, take up thy bed, and go unto thine house.

7 And he arose, and departed to his house.

8 But when the multitudes saw it, they marveled, and glorified God, which had given such power unto men.

9 And as Jesus passed forth from thence, he saw a man, named MATTHEW , sitting at the receipt of cus-

made in the sides of caves, in the rocks and mountains. No one could pass – Safely. Mark v, 1; Luke viii, 26.

29. What have we to do with thee – This is a Hebrew phrase, which signifies. Why do you concern yourself about us? 2 Sam. xvi, 10. Before the time – The great day.

30. There was a herd of many swine – Which it was not lawful for the Jews to keep. Therefore our Lord both justly and mercifully permitted them to be destroyed.

31. He said, Go – A word of permission only, not command.

34. They besought him to depart out of their coasts – They loved their swine so much better than their souls! How many are of the same mind!

MATTHEW 9

1. His own city – Capernaum, chap. iv, 13; Mark v, 18; Luke viii, 37.

2. Seeing their faith – Both that of the paralytic, and of them that brought him. Son – A title of tenderness and condescension. Mark ii, 3; Luke v, 18.

3. This man blasphemeth – Attributing to himself a power (that of forgiving sins) which belongs to God only.

5. Which is easier – Do not both of them argue a Divine power? Therefore if I can heal his disease, I can forgive his sins: especially as his disease is the consequence of his sins. Therefore these must be taken away, if that is.

6. On earth – Even in my state of humiliation.

8. So what was to the scribes an occasion of blaspheming, was to the people an incitement to praise God.

9. He saw a man named Matthew – Modestly so called by himself. The other evangelists call him by his more honorable name, Levi. Sitting – In the very height of his business, at the receipt of custom – The custom house, or place where the customs were received. Mark ii, 14; Luke v, 27.

10. As Jesus sat at table in the house – Of Matthew, who having invited many of his old companions, made him a feast, Mark ii, 15; and that a great one, though he does not himself mention it. The publicans, or collectors of the taxes which the Jews paid the Romans, were infamous for their illegal exactions: Sinners – Open, notorious, sinners.

11. The Pharisees said to his disciples, Why eateth your Master? – Thus they commonly ask our Lord, Why do thy disciples this? And his disciples, Why doth your Master?

13. Go ye and learn – Ye that take upon you to teach others. I will have mercy and not sacrifice – That is, I will have mercy rather than sacrifice. I love acts of mercy better than sacrifice itself. Hosea vi, 6.

14. Then – While he was at table. Mark ii, 18; Luke v, 33.

15. The children of the bride chamber – The companions of the bridegroom. Mourn – Mourning and fasting usually go together. As if he had said, While I am with them, it is a festival time, a season of rejoicing, not mourning. But after I am gone, all my disciples likewise shall be in fastings often.

16. This is one reason, – It is not a proper time for them to fast. Another is, they are not ripe for it. New cloth – The words in the original properly signify cloth that hath not passed through the fuller's hands, and which is consequently much harsher than what has been washed and worn; and therefore yielding less than that, will tear away the edges to which it is sewed.

17. New – Fermenting wine will soon burst those bottles, the leather of

a Ruler. See whose language those speak, who will have nothing to do with the gospel of Christ. But it is not true that the devils have nothing to do with Christ as a Judge; for they have, and they know it, and thus it is with all the children of men. Satan and his instruments can go no further than he permits; they must quit possession when he commands. They cannot break his hedge of protection about his people; they cannot enter even a swine without his leave. They had leave. God often, for wise and holy ends, permits the efforts of Satan's rage. Thus the devil hurries people to sin; hurries them to what they have resolved against, which they know will be shame and grief to them: miserable is the condition of those who are led captive by him at his will. There are a great many who prefer their swine before the Savior, and so come short of Christ and salvation by him. They desire Christ to depart out of their hearts, and will not suffer his word to have place in them, because he and his word would destroy their brutish lusts, those swine which they give themselves up to feed. And justly will Christ forsake all that are weary of him; and say hereafter, Depart, ye cursed, to those who now say to the Almighty, Depart from us.

MATTHEW 9

Jesus returns to Capernaum, and heals a paralytic. (1-8)

Matthew called. (9)

Matthew, or Levi's feast. (10-13)

Objections of John's disciples. (14-17)

Christ raises the daughter of Jairus. He heals the issue of blood. (18-26)

He heals two blind men. (27-31)

Christ casts out a dumb spirit. (32-34)

He sends forth the apostles. (35-38)

1-8 The faith of the friends of the paralytic in bringing him to Christ, was a strong faith; they firmly believed that Jesus Christ both could and would heal him. A strong faith regards no obstacles in pressing after Christ. It was a humble faith; they brought him to attend on Christ. It was an active faith. Sin may be pardoned, yet the sickness not be removed; the sickness may be removed, yet the sin not pardoned: but if we have the comfort of peace with God, with the comfort of recovery from sickness, this makes the healing a mercy indeed. This is no encouragement to sin. If thou bring thy sins to Jesus Christ, as thy malady and misery to be cured of, and delivered from, it is well; but to come with them, as thy darlings and delight, thinking still to retain them and receive him, is a gross mistake, a miserable delusion. The great intention of the blessed Jesus in the redemption he wrought, is to separate our hearts from sin. Our Lord Jesus has perfect knowledge of all that we say within ourselves. There is a great deal of evil in sinful thoughts, which is very offensive to the Lord Jesus. Christ designed to show that his great errand to the world was, to save his people from their sins. He

influence of whose eloquence I could most comfortably snore. But it is not at all likely that the poor will ever go to hear such preachers as these. If they are preached to in fine terms—in grandiloquent language which they cannot lay hold of—the poor will not have the gospel preached to them, for they will not go to hear it. They must have something attractive to them; we must preach as Christ did; we must tell anecdotes, and stories, and parables, as he did; we must come down and make the gospel attractive. The reason why the old puritan preachers could get congregations was this— they did not give their hearers dry theology; they illustrated it; they had an anecdote from this and a quaint passage from that classic author; here a verse of poetry; here and there even a quip or pun—a thing which now-a-days is a sin above all sins, but which was constantly committed by these preachers, whom I have ever esteemed as the patterns of pulpit eloquence. Christ Jesus was an attractive preacher; he sought above all means to set the pearl in a frame of gold, that it might attract the attention of the people. He was not willing to place himself in a parish church, and preach to a large congregation of thirteen and a-half, like our good brethren in the city, but would preach in such a style that people felt they must go to hear him. Some of them gnashed their teeth in rage and left his presence in wrath, but the multitudes still thronged to him to hear and to be healed. It was no dull work to hear this King of preachers, he was too much in earnest to be dull, and too humane to be incomprehensible. I believe that until this is imitated, the poor will not have the gospel preached to them. There must be an interesting style adopted, to bring the people to hear. But if we adopt such a style they will call us clownish, vulgar, and so on. Blessed be God, we have long learnt that vulgarity is a very different thing from what some men suppose. We have been so taught, that we are willing to be even clowns for Christ's sake, and so long as we are seeing souls saved we are not likely to alter our course. During this last week I have seen, I believe, a score of persons who have been in the lowest ranks, the very meanest of sinners, the greatest of transgressors, who have, through preaching in this place, been restored and reclaimed. Do you think then I shall shear my locks to please the Philistine? Oh, no; by the grace of God, Samson knoweth where his strength lieth, and is not likely to do that to please any man or any set of men. Preaching must reach the popular ear; and to get at the people it must be interesting to them, and by the grace of God we hope it shall be.

But, in the next place, if the poor are to have

tom: and he saith unto him, Follow me. And he arose, and followed him.

10 And it came to pass, as Jesus sat at meat in the house, behold, many publicans and sinners came and sat down with him and his disciples.

11 And when the Pharisees saw it, they said unto his disciples, Why eateth your Master with publicans and sinners?

12 But when Jesus heard that, he said unto them, They that be whole need not a physician, but they that are sick.

13 But go ye and learn what that meaneth, I will have mercy, and not sacrifice: for I am not come to call the righteous, but sinners to repentance.

14 Then came to him the disciples of John, saying, Why do we and the Pharisees fast oft, but thy disciples fast not?

15 And Jesus said unto them, Can the children of the bridechamber mourn, as long as the bridegroom is with them? but the days will come, when the bridegroom shall be taken from them, and then shall they fast.

16 No man putteth a piece of new cloth unto an old garment, for that which is put in to fill it up taketh from the garment, and the rent is made worse.

17 Neither do men put new wine into old bottles: else the bottles break, and the wine runneth out, and the bottles perish: but they put new wine into new bottles, and both are preserved.

18 While he spake these things unto them, behold, there came a certain ruler, and worshiped him, saying, My daughter is even now dead: but come and lay thy hand upon her, and she shall live.

19 And Jesus arose, and followed him, and so did his disciples.

20 And, behold, a woman, which was diseased with an issue of blood twelve years, came behind him, and touched the hem of his garment:

21 For she said within herself, If I may but touch his garment, I shall be whole.

22 But Jesus turned him about, and when he saw her, he said, Daughter, be of good comfort; thy faith hath made thee whole. And the woman was made whole from that hour.

23 And when Jesus came into the ruler's house, and saw the minstrels and the people making a noise,

24 He said unto them, Give place: for the maid is not dead, but sleepeth. And they laughed him to scorn.

25 But when the people were put forth, he went in, and took her by the hand, and the maid arose.

26 And the fame hereof went abroad

which is almost worn out. The word properly means vessels made of goats' skins, wherein they formerly put wine, (and do in some countries to this day) to convey it from place to place. Put new wine into new bottles – Give harsh doctrines to such as have strength to receive them.

18. Just dead – He had left her at the point of death, Mark v, 23. Probably a messenger had now informed him she was dead. Mark v, 22; Luke viii, 41.

20. Coming behind – Out of bashfulness and humility.

22. Take courage – Probably she was struck with fear, when he turned and looked upon her, Mark v, 33; Luke viii, 47; lest she should have offended him, by touching his garment privately; and the more so, because she was unclean according to the law, Lev. xv, 25.

23. The minstrels – The musicians. The original word means flute players. Musical instruments were used by the Jews as well as the heathens, in their Lamentations for the dead, to soothe the melancholy of surviving friends, by soft and solemn notes. And there were persons who made it their business to perform this, while others sung to their music. Flutes were used especially on the death of children; louder instruments on the death of grown persons.

24. Withdraw – There is no need of you now; for the maid is not dead – Her life is not at an end; but sleepeth – This is only a temporary suspension of sense and motion, which should rather be termed sleep than death.

25. The maid arose – Christ raised three dead persons to life; this child, the widow's son, and Lazarus: one newly departed, another on the bier, the third smelling in the grave: to show us that no degree of death is so desperate as to be past his help.

32. Luke xi, 14.

33. Even in Israel – Where so many wonders have been seen.

36. Because they were faint – In soul rather than in body. As sheep having no shepherd – And yet they had many teachers; they had scribes in every city. But they had none who cared for their souls, and none that were able, if they had been willing, to have wrought any deliverance. They had no pastors after God's own heart.

37. The harvest truly is great – When Christ came into the world, it was properly the time of harvest; till then it was the seed time only. But the laborers are few – Those whom God sends; who are holy, and convert sinners. Of others there are many. Luke x, 2.

38. The Lord of the harvest – Whose peculiar work and office it is, and who alone is able to do it: that he would thrust forth – for it is an employ not pleasing to flesh and blood; so full of reproach, labor, danger, temptation of every kind, that nature may well be averse to it. Those who never felt this, never yet knew what it is to be laborers in Christ's harvest. He sends them forth, when he calls them by his Spirit, furnishes them with grace and gifts for the work, and makes a way for them to be employed therein.

MATTHEW HENRY

CHARLES H. SPURGEON

turned from disputing with the scribes, and spake healing to the sick man. Not only he had no more need to be carried upon his bed, but he had strength to carry it. God must be glorified in all the power that is given to do good.

9 Matthew was in his calling, as the rest of those whom Christ called. As Satan comes with his temptations to the idle, so Christ comes with his calls to those who are employed. We are all naturally averse from thee, O God; do thou bid us to follow thee; draw us by thy powerful word, and we shall run after thee. Speak by the word of the Spirit to our hearts, the world cannot hold us down, Satan cannot stop our way, we shall arise and follow thee. A saving change is wrought in the soul, by Christ as the author, and his word as the means. Neither Matthew's place, nor his gains by it, could detain him, when Christ called him. He left it, and though we find the disciples, who were fishers, occasionally fishing again afterwards, we never more find Matthew at his sinful gain.

10-13 Some time after his call, Matthew sought to bring his old associates to hear Christ. He knew by experience what the grace of Christ could do, and would not despair concerning them. Those who are effectually brought to Christ, cannot but desire that others also may be brought to him. Those who suppose their souls to be without disease will not welcome the spiritual Physician. This was the case with the Pharisees; they despised Christ, because they thought themselves whole; but the poor publicans and sinners felt that they wanted instruction and amendment. It is easy, and too common, to put the worst constructions upon the best words and actions. It may justly be suspected that those have not the grace of God themselves, who are not pleased with others' obtaining it. Christ's conversing with sinners is here called mercy; for to promote the conversion of souls is the greatest act of mercy. The gospel call is a call to repentance; a call to us to change our minds, and to change our ways. If the children of men had not been sinners, there had been no need for Christ to come among them. Let us examine whether we have found out our sickness, and have learned to follow the directions of our great Physician.

14-17 John was at this time in prison; his circumstances, his character, and the nature of the message he was sent to deliver, led those who were peculiarly attached to him, to keep frequent fasts. Christ referred them to John's testimony of him, Joh 3:29. Though there is no doubt that Jesus and his disciples lived in a spare and frugal manner, it would be improper for his disciples to fast while they had the comfort of his presence. When he is with them, all is well. The presence of the sun makes day, and its absence produces night. Our Lord further reminded them of common rules of prudence. It was not usual to

the gospel preached unto them, it must be preached simply. It is a waste of time to preach Latin to you, is it not? To the multitude of people it is of no use delivering a discourse in Greek. Possibly five or six of the assembly might be mightily edified, and go away delighted; but what of that? The mass would retire unedified and uninstructed. You talk about the education of the people, don't you, and about the vast extent of English refinement? For the most part it is a dream. Ignorance is not buried yet. The language of one class of Englishmen is a dead language to another class; and many a word which is very plain to many of us, is as hard and difficult a word to the multitude as if it had been culled out of Hindostani or Bengali. There are multitudes who cannot understand words composed of Latin, but must have the truth told them in round homely Saxon, if it is to reach their hearts. There is my friend the Rev. So-and-so, Doctor of Divinity; he is a great student, and whenever he finds a hard word in his books he tells it next Sunday to his congregation. He has a little intellectual circle, who think his preaching must be good, because they cannot understand it, and who think it proven that he must be an intelligent man because all the pews are empty. They believe he must be a very useful member of society; in fact, they compare him to Luther, and think he is a second Paul, because nobody will listen to him, seeing it is impossible to understand him. Well, we conceive of that good man that he may have a work to do, but we do not know what it is. There is another friend of ours, Mr. Cloudyton, who always preaches in such a style that if you should try to dissect the sermon for a week afterwards, you could by no possibility tell what he meant. If you could look at things from his point of view you might possibly discover something; but it does appear by his preaching as if he himself had lost his way in a fog, and were scattering a whole mass of mist about him everywhere. I suppose he goes so deep down into the subject that he stirs the mud at the bottom, and he cannot find his way up again. There are some such preachers, whom you cannot possibly understand. Now, we say, and say very boldly too, that while such preaching may be esteemed by some people to be good, we have no faith in it all. If ever the world is to be reclaimed, and if sinners are to be saved, we can see no likelihood in the world of its being done by such means. We think the word must be understood before it can really penetrate the conscience and the heart; and we would always be preaching such as men can understand, otherwise the poor will not "have the gospel preached to them."

Why did John Bunyan become the apostle of

into all that land.

27 And when Jesus departed thence, two blind men followed him, crying, and saying, Thou Son of David, have mercy on us.

28 And when he was come into the house, the blind men came to him: and Jesus saith unto them, Believe ye that I am able to do this? They said unto him, Yea, Lord.

29 Then touched he their eyes, saying, According to your faith be it unto you.

30 And their eyes were opened; and Jesus straitly charged them, saying, See that no man know it.

31 But they, when they were departed, spread abroad his fame in all that country.

32 As they went out, behold, they brought to him a dumb man possessed with a devil.

33 And when the devil was cast out, the dumb spake: and the multitudes marveled, saying, It was never so seen in Israel.

34 But the Pharisees said, He casteth out devils through the prince of the devils.

35 And Jesus went about all the cities and villages, teaching in their synagogues, and preaching the gospel of the kingdom, and healing every sickness and every disease among the people.

36 But when he saw the multitudes, he was moved with compassion on them, because they fainted, and were scattered abroad, as sheep having no shepherd.

37 Then saith he unto his disciples, The harvest truly is plenteous, but the laborers are few;

38 Pray ye therefore the Lord of the harvest, that he will send forth laborers into his harvest.

MATTHEW 10

1 And when he had called unto him his twelve disciples, he gave them power against unclean spirits, to cast them out, and to heal all manner of sickness and all manner of disease.

2 Now the names of the twelve apostles are these; The first, Simon, who is called Peter, and Andrew his brother; James the son of Zebedee, and John his brother;

3 Philip, and Bartholomew; Thomas, and MATTHEW the publican; James the son of Alpheus, and Lebbeus, whose surname was Thaddeus;

4 Simon the Canaanite, and Judas Iscariot, who also betrayed him.

5 These twelve Jesus sent forth, and

MATTHEW 10

1. His twelve disciples – Hence it appears that he had already chosen out of his disciples, those whom he afterward termed apostles. The number seems to have relation to the twelve patriarchs, and the twelve tribes of Israel. Mark iii, 14; vi, 7; Luke vi, 13; ix, 1.

2. The first, Simon – The first who was called to a constant attendance on Christ; although Andrew had seen him before Simon. Acts i, 13.

3. Lebbeus – Commonly called Judas, the brother of James.

4. Iscariot – So called from Iscarioth, (the place of his birth,) a town of the tribe of Ephraim, near the city of Samaria.

5. These twelve Jesus sent forth – Herein exercising his supreme authority, as God over all. None but God can give men authority to preach his word. Go not – Their commission was thus confined now, because the calling of the Gentiles was deferred till after the more plentiful effusion of the Holy Ghost on the day of Pentecost. Enter not – Not to preach; but they might to buy what they wanted, John iv, 9.

8. Cast out devils – It is a great relief to the spirits of an infidel, sinking under a dread, that possibly the Gospel may be true, to find it observed by a learned brother, that the diseases therein ascribed to the operation of the devil have the very same symptoms with the natural diseases of lunacy, epilepsy, or convulsions; whence he readily and very willingly concludes, that the devil had no hand in them. But it were well to stop and consider a little. Suppose God should suffer an evil spirit to usurp the same power over a man's body, as the man himself has naturally; and suppose him actually to exercise that power; could we conclude the devil had no hand therein, because his body was bent in the very same manner wherein the man himself might have bent it naturally? And suppose God gives an evil spirit a greater power, to effect immediately the organ of the nerves in the brain, by irritating them to produce violent motions, or so relaxing them that they can produce little or no motion; still the symptoms will be those of over tense nerves, as in madness, epilepsies, convulsions; or of relaxed nerves, as in paralytic cases. But could we conclude thence that the devil had no hand in them? Will any man affirm that God cannot or will not, on any occasion whatever, give such a power to an evil spirit? Or that effects, the like of which may be produced by natural causes, cannot possibly be produced by preternatural? If this be possible, then he who affirms it was so, in any particular case, cannot be justly charged with falsehood, merely for affirming the reality of a possible thing. Yet in this manner are the evangelists treated by those unhappy men, who above all things dread the truth of the Gospel, because, if it is true, they are of all men the most miserable. Freely ye have received – All things; in particular the power of working miracles; freely give – Exert that power wherever you come. Mark vi, 7; Luke ix, 2.

9. Provide not – The stress seems to lie on this word: they might use what they had ready; but they might not stay a moment to provide any thing more, neither take any thought about it. Nor indeed were they to take any thing with them, more than was strictly necessary.

    1. Lest it should retard them.

    2. Because they were to learn hereby to trust to God in all future exigencies.

10. Neither scrip – That is, a wallet, or bag to hold provisions: Nor yet a staff – We read, Mark vi, 8, Take nothing, save a staff only. He that had one might take it; they that had none, might not provide any. For the workman is worthy of his maintenance – The word includes all that is mentioned in the 9th and 10th verses; all that they were forbidden to

MATTHEW HENRY

CHARLES H. SPURGEON

take a piece of rough woolen cloth, which had never been prepared, to join to an old garment, for it would not join well with the soft, old garment, but would tear it further, and the rent would be made worse. Nor would men put new wine into old leathern bottles, which were going to decay, and would be liable to burst from the fermenting of the wine; but putting the new wine into strong, new, skin bottles, both would be preserved. Great caution and prudence are necessary, that young converts may not receive gloomy and forbidding ideas of the service of our Lord; but duties are to be urged as they are able to bear them.

18-26 The death of our relations should drive us to Christ, who is our life. And it is high honor to the greatest rulers to attend on the Lord Jesus; and those who would receive mercy from Christ, must honor him. The variety of methods Christ took in working his miracles, perhaps was because of the different frames and tempers of mind, which those were in who came to him, and which He who searches the heart perfectly knew. A poor woman applied herself to Christ, and received mercy from him by the way. If we do but touch, as it were, the hem of Christ's garment by living faith, our worst evils will be healed; there is no other real cure, nor need we fear his knowing things which are a grief and burden to us, but which we would not tell to any earthly friend. When Christ entered the ruler's house, he said, Give place. Sometimes, when the sorrow of the world prevails, it is difficult for Christ and his comforts to enter. The ruler's daughter was really dead, but not so to Christ. The death of the righteous is in a special manner to be looked on as only a sleep. The words and works of Christ may not at first be understood, yet they are not therefore to be despised. The people were put forth. Scorners who laugh at what they do not understand, are not proper witnesses of the wonderful works of Christ. Dead souls are not raised to spiritual life, unless Christ take them by the hand: it is done in the day of his power. If this single instance of Christ's raising one newly dead so increased his fame, what will be his glory when all that are in their graves shall hear his voice, and come forth; those that have done good to the resurrection of life, and those that have done evil to the resurrection of damnation!

27-31 At this time the Jews expected Messiah would appear; these blind men knew and proclaimed in the streets of Capernaum that he was come, and that Jesus was he. Those who, by the providence of God, have lost their bodily sight, may, by the grace of God, have the eyes of their understanding fully enlightened. And whatever our wants and burdens are, we need no more for supply and support, than to share in the mercy of our Lord Jesus. In Christ is enough for all. They followed him crying aloud. He would try their faith, and would teach us always to pray, and not to faint, though the answer does not come at once. They followed Christ,

Bedfordshire, and Huntingdonshire, and round about? It was because John Bunyan, while he had a surpassing genius, would not condescend to cull his language from the garden of flowers, but he went into the hayfield and the meadow, and plucked up his language by the roots, and spoke out in words that the people used in their cottages. Why is it that God has blessed other men to the stirring of the people, to the bringing about of spiritual revivals, to the renewal of the power of godliness? We believe it has always been owing to this—under God's Spirit—that they have adopted the phraseology of the people, and have not been ashamed to be despised because they talked as common people did.

But now we have something to say more important than this. We may preach, very simply too, and very attractively, and yet it may not be true that "the poor have the gospel preached to them," for the poor may have something else preached to them beside the gospel. It is, then, highly important that we should each of us ask what the gospel is, and that when we think we know it we should not be ashamed to say, "This is the gospel, and I will preach it boldly, though all men should deny it." Oh! I fear that there is such a thing as preaching another gospel, "which is not another, but there be some that trouble us." There is such a thing as preaching science and philosophy attractively, but not preaching the gospel. Mark, it is not preaching, but it is preaching the gospel that is the mark of Christ's dispensation and of his truth. Let us take care to preach fully the depravity of man, let us dwell thoroughly upon his lost and ruined estate under the law, and his restoration under the gospel; let us preach of these three things, for, as a good brother said, "The gospel lies in three things, the Word of God only, the blood of Christ only, and the Holy Spirit only." These three things make up the gospel. "The Bible; the Bible alone the religion of Protestants; the blood of Christ the only salvation from sin, the only means of the pardon of our guilt; and the Holy Spirit the only regenerator, the only converting power that will alone work in us to will and to do of his good pleasure." Without these three things there is no gospel. Let us take heed, then, for it is a serious matter, that when the people listen to us, it is the gospel that we preach, or else we may be as guilty as was Nero, the tyrant, who, when Rome was starving, sent his ships to Alexandria, where there was corn in plenty, not for wheat, for sand to scatter in the arena for his gladiators. Ah! there be some who seem to do so—scattering the floor of their sanctuary, not with the good corn of the kingdom, upon which the souls of God's people may

commanded them, saying, Go not into the way of the Gentiles, and into any city of the Samaritans enter ye not:

6 But go rather to the lost sheep of the house of Israel.

7 And as ye go, preach, saying, The kingdom of heaven is at hand.

8 Heal the sick, cleanse the lepers, raise the dead, cast out devils: freely ye have received, freely give.

9 Provide neither gold, nor silver, nor brass in your purses,

10 Nor scrip for your journey, neither two coats, neither shoes, nor yet staves: for the workman is worthy of his meat.

11 And into whatsoever city or town ye shall enter, inquire who in it is worthy; and there abide till ye go thence.

12 And when ye come into an house, salute it.

13 And if the house be worthy, let your peace come upon it: but if it be not worthy, let your peace return to you.

14 And whosoever shall not receive you, nor hear your words, when ye depart out of that house or city, shake off the dust of your feet.

15 Verily I say unto you, It shall be more tolerable for the land of Sodom and Gomorrha in the day of judgment, than for that city.

16 Behold, I send you forth as sheep in the midst of wolves: be ye therefore wise as serpents, and harmless as doves.

17 But beware of men: for they will deliver you up to the councils, and they will scourge you in their synagogues;

18 And ye shall be brought before governors and kings for my sake, for a testimony against them and the Gentiles.

19 But when they deliver you up, take no thought how or what ye shall speak: for it shall be given you in that same hour what ye shall speak.

20 For it is not ye that speak, but the Spirit of your Father which speaketh in you.

21 And the brother shall deliver up the brother to death, and the father the child: and the children shall rise up against their parents, and cause them to be put to death.

22 And ye shall be hated of all men for my name's sake: but he that endureth to the end shall be saved.

23 But when they persecute you in this city, flee ye into another: for verily I say unto you, Ye shall not have gone over the cities of Israel, till the Son of man be come.

24 The disciple is not above his master, nor the servant above his lord.

25 It is enough for the disciple that he be as his master, and the servant as his

provide for themselves, so far as it was needful for them. Luke x, 7.

11. Inquire who is worthy – That you should abide with him: who is disposed to receive the Gospel. There abide – In that house, till ye leave the town. Mark vi, 10; Luke ix, 4.

12. Salute it – In the usual Jewish form, "Peace (that is, all blessings) be to this house."

13. If the house be worthy – of it, God shall give them the peace you wish them. If not, he shall give you what they refuse. The same will be the case, when we pray for them that are not worthy.

14. Shake off the dust from your feet – The Jews thought the land of Israel so peculiarly holy, that when they came home from any heathen country, they stopped at the borders and shook or wiped off the dust of it from their feet, that the holy land might not be polluted with it. Therefore the action here enjoined was a lively intimation, that those Jews who had rejected the Gospel were holy no longer, but were on a level with heathens and idolaters.

16. Luke x, 3.

17. But think not that all your innocence and all your wisdom will screen you from persecution. They will scourge you in their synagogues – In these the Jews held their courts of judicature, about both civil and ecclesiastical affairs. Matt. xxiv, 9.

19. Take no thought – Neither at this time, on any sudden call, need we be careful how or what to answer. Luke xii, 11.

21. Luke xxi, 16.

22. Of all men – That know not God. Matt. xxiv, 13.

23. Ye shall not have gone over the cities of Israel – Make what haste ye will; till the Son of man be come – To destroy their temple and nation. Luke vi, 30; John xv, 20.

25. How much more – This cannot refer to the quantity of reproach and persecution: (for in this the servant cannot be above his Lord:) but only to the certainty of it. Matt. xii, 24.

26. Therefore fear them not – For ye have only the same usage with your Lord. There is nothing covered – So that however they may slander you now, your innocence will at length appear. Mark iv, 22; Luke viii, 17; xii, 2.

27. Even what I now tell you secretly is not to be kept secret long, but declared publicly. Therefore, What ye hear in the ear, publish on the house-top – Two customs of the Jews seem to be alluded to here. Their doctors used to whisper in the ear of their disciples what they were to pronounce aloud to others. And as their houses were low and flat roofed, they sometimes preached to the people from thence. Luke xii, 3.

28. And be not afraid – of any thing which ye may suffer for proclaiming it. Be afraid of him who is able to destroy both body and soul in hell – It is remarkable, that our Lord commands those who love God, still to fear him, even on this account, under this notion.

29, 30. The particular providence of God is another reason for your not fearing man. For this extends to the very smallest things. And if he has such care over the most inconsiderable creatures, how much more will he take care of you, (provided you confess him before men, before powerful enemies of the truth,) and that not only in this life, but in the other also?

32. Whosoever shall confess me – Publicly acknowledge me for the promised Messiah. But this confession implies the receiving his whole doctrine, Mark viii, 38, and obeying all his commandments. Luke ix, 26.

and followed him crying; but the great question is, Do ye believe? Nature may make us earnest, but it is only grace that can work faith. Christ touched their eyes. He gives sight to blind souls by the power of his grace going with his word, and he puts the cure upon their faith. Those who apply to Jesus Christ, shall be dealt with, not according to their fancies, nor according to their profession, but according to their faith. Christ sometimes concealed his miracles, because he would not indulge the conceit which prevailed among the Jews, that their Messiah should be a temporal prince, and so give occasion to the people to attempt tumults and seditions.

32-34 Of the two, better a dumb devil than a blaspheming one. Christ's cures strike at the root, and remove the effect by taking away the cause; they open the lips, by breaking Satan's power in the soul. Nothing can convince those who are under the power of pride. They will believe anything, however false or absurd, rather than the Holy Scriptures; thus they show the enmity of their hearts against a holy God.

35-38 Jesus visited not only the great and wealthy cities, but the poor, obscure villages; and there he preached, there he healed. The souls of the meanest in the world are as precious to Christ, and should be so to us, as the souls of those who make the greatest figure. There were priests, Levites, and scribes, all over the land; but they were idol shepherds, Zec 11:17; therefore Christ had compassion on the people as sheep scattered, as men perishing for lack of knowledge. To this day vast multitudes are as sheep not having a shepherd, and we should have compassion and do all we can to help them. The multitudes desirous of spiritual instruction formed a plenteous harvest, needing many active laborers; but few deserved that character. Christ is the Lord of the harvest. Let us pray that many may be raised up and sent forth, who will labor in bringing souls to Christ. It is a sign that God is about to bestow some special mercy upon a people, when he stirs them up to pray for it. And commissions given to laborers in answer to prayer, are most likely to be successful.

MATTHEW 10

The apostles called. (1-4)
The apostles instructed and sent forth. (5-15)
Directions to the apostles. (16-42)

1-4 The word "apostle" signifies messenger; they were Christ's messengers, sent forth to proclaim his kingdom. Christ gave them power to heal all manner of sickness. In the grace of the gospel there is a salve for every sore, a remedy for every malady. There is no spiritual disease, but there is power in Christ for the cure of it. There names are recorded, and it is their honor; yet they had more reason to rejoice that their

feed and grow thereby, but with sand of controversy, and of logic, which no child of God can ever receive to his soul's profit. "The poor have the gospel preached to them." Let us take heed that it is the gospel. Hear then, ye chief of sinners, the voice of Jesus. "This is a faithful saying, and worthy of all acceptance, that Christ Jesus came into the world to save sinners; of whom I am chief." "Him that cometh to me I will in no wise cast out." "Whosoever believeth and is baptized, shall be saved." "For the Son of man is come to seek and save that which is lost."

And just one more hint on this point, namely, this,—it must be said of us, if we would keep true to Christ's rule and apostolic practice, that "the poor have the gospel preached to them." In these days there is a growing hatred of the pulpit. The pulpit has maintained its ground full many a year, but partially by its becoming inefficient, it is losing its high position. Through a timid abuse of it, instead of a strong stiff use of the pulpit, the world has come to despise it; and now most certainly we are not a priest-ridden people one-half so much as we are a press-ridden people. By the press we are ridden indeed. Mercuries, Despatches, Journals, Gazettes and Magazines, are now the judges of pulpit eloquence and style. They thrust themselves into the censor's seat, and censure those whose office it should rather be to censure them. For my own part, I cheerfully accord to all men the liberty of abusing me; but I must protest against the lying conduct of at least one editor, who has misquoted in order to pervert my meaning, and has done more; he has, to his eternal disgrace, manufactured a quotation from his own head, which never did occur in my works or words. The pulpit has become dishonored; it is esteemed as being of very little worth and of no esteem. Ah! we must always maintain the dignity of the pulpit. I hold that it is the Thermopylae of Christendom; it is here the battle must be fought between right and wrong— not so much with the pen, valuable as that is as an assistant, as with the living voice of earnest men, "contending earnestly for the faith once delivered unto the saints." In some churches the pulpit is put away; there is a prominent altar, but the pulpit is omitted. Now, the most prominent thing under the gospel dispensation is not the altar which belonged to the Jewish dispensation, but the pulpit. "We have an altar, whereof they have no right to eat which serve the tabernacle;" that altar is Christ; but Christ has been pleased to exalt "the foolishness of preaching" to the most prominent position in his house of prayer. We must take heed that we always maintain preaching. It is this that God will bless; it is this that he has promised to

lord. If they have called the master of the house Beelzebub, how much more shall they call them of his household?

26 Fear them not therefore: for there is nothing covered, that shall not be revealed; and hid, that shall not be known.

27 What I tell you in darkness, that speak ye in light: and what ye hear in the ear, that preach ye upon the housetops.

28 And fear not them which kill the body, but are not able to kill the soul: but rather fear him which is able to destroy both soul and body in hell.

29 Are not two sparrows sold for a farthing? and one of them shall not fall on the ground without your Father.

30 But the very hairs of your head are all numbered.

31 Fear ye not therefore, ye are of more value than many sparrows.

32 Whosoever therefore shall confess me before men, him will I confess also before my Father which is in heaven.

33 But whosoever shall deny me before men, him will I also deny before my Father which is in heaven.

34 Think not that I am come to send peace on earth: I came not to send peace, but a sword.

35 For I am come to set a man at variance against his father, and the daughter against her mother, and the daughter in law against her mother in law.

36 And a man's foes shall be they of his own household.

37 He that loveth father or mother more than me is not worthy of me: and he that loveth son or daughter more than me is not worthy of me.

38 And he that taketh not his cross, and followeth after me, is not worthy of me.

39 He that findeth his life shall lose it: and he that loseth his life for my sake shall find it.

40 He that receiveth you receiveth me, and he that receiveth me receiveth him that sent me.

41 He that receiveth a prophet in the name of a prophet shall receive a prophet's reward; and he that receiveth a righteous man in the name of a righteous man shall receive a righteous man's reward.

42 And whosoever shall give to drink unto one of these little ones a cup of cold water only in the name of a disciple, verily I say unto you, he shall in no wise lose his reward.

MATTHEW 11

1 And it came to pass, when Jesus had made an end of commanding his twelve

33, 34. Whosoever shall deny me before men – To which ye will be strongly tempted. For Think not that I am come – That is, think not that universal peace will be the immediate consequence of my coming. Just the contrary. Both public and private divisions will follow, wheresoever my Gospel comes with power. Ye – this is not the design, though it be the event of his coming, through the opposition of devils and men.

36. And the foes of a man – That loves and follows me. Micah vii, 6.

37. He that loveth father or mother more than me – He that is not ready to give up all these, when they stand in competition with his duty.

38. He that taketh not his cross – That is, whatever pain or inconvenience cannot be avoided, but by doing some evil, or omitting some good. Matt. xvi, 24; Luke xiv, 27.

39. He that findeth his life shall lose it – He that saves his life by denying me, shall lose it eternally; and he that loseth his life by confessing me, shall save it eternally. And as you shall be thus rewarded, so in proportion shall they who entertain you for my sake. Matt. xvi, 25; John xii, 25.

40. Matt. xviii, 5; Luke x, 16; John xiii, 20.

41. He that entertaineth a prophet – That is, a preacher of the Gospel: In the name of a prophet – That is, because he is such, shall share in his reward.

42. One of these little ones – The very least Christian. Mark ix, 41.

MATTHEW 11

1. In their cities – The other cities of Israel.

2. He sent two of his disciples – Not because he doubted himself; but to confirm their faith. Luke vii, 18.

3. He that is to come – The Messiah.

4. Go and tell John the things that ye hear and see – Which are a stronger proof of my being the Messiah, than any bare assertion can be.

5. The poor have the Gospel preached to them – The greatest mercy of all. Isaiah xxix, 18; xxxv, 5.

6. Happy is he who shall not be offended at me – Notwithstanding all these proofs that I am the Messiah.

7. As they departed, he said concerning John – Of whom probably he would not have said so much when they were present. A reed shaken by the wind? – No; nothing could ever shake John in the testimony he gave to the truth. The expression is proverbial.

8. A man clothed in soft, delicate raiment – An effeminate courtier, accustomed to fawning and flattery? You may expect to find persons of such a character in palaces; not in a wilderness.

9. More than a prophet – For the prophets only pointed me out afar off; but John was my immediate forerunner.

10. Mal. iii, 1.

11. But he that is least in the kingdom of heaven, is greater than he – Which an ancient author explains thus: – "One perfect in the law, as John was, is inferior to one who is baptized into the death of Christ. For this is the kingdom of heaven, even to be buried with Christ, and to be raised up together with him. John was greater than all who had been then born of women, but he was cut off before the kingdom of heaven was given." [He seems to mean, that righteousness, peace, and joy, which constitute the present inward kingdom of heaven.] "He was blameless as to that righteousness which is by the law; but he fell short

names were written in heaven, while the high and mighty names of the great ones of the earth are buried in the dust.

5-15 See commentary at Mark 6:8-11; Luke 9:3-5; 10:4-12

16-42 See commentary at Mark 13:11-13; Luke 12: 2-9, 12-17, 51-53

MATTHEW 11

Christ's preaching. (1)
Christ's answer to John's disciples. (2-6)
Christ's testimony to John the Baptist. (7-15)
The perverseness of the Jews. (16-24)
The gospel revealed to the simple. The heavy-laden invited. (25-30)

1 Our Divine Redeemer never was weary of his labor of love; and we should not be weary of well-doing, for in due season we shall reap, if we faint not.

2-6 Some think that John sent this inquiry for his own satisfaction. Where there is true faith, yet there may be a mixture of unbelief. The remaining unbelief of good men may sometimes, in an hour of temptation; call in question the most important truths. But we hope that John's faith did not fail in this matter, and that he only desired to have it strengthened and confirmed. Others think that John sent his disciples to Christ for their satisfaction. Christ points them to what they heard and saw. Christ's gracious condescensions and compassions to the poor, show that it was he that should bring to the world the tender mercies of our God. Those things which men see and hear, if compared with the Scriptures, direct in what way salvation is to be found. It is difficult to conquer prejudices, and dangerous not to conquer them; but those who believe in Christ, their faith will be found so much the more to praise, and honor, and glory.

7-15 What Christ said concerning John, was not only for his praise, but for the people's profit. Those who attend on the word will be called to give an account of their improvements. Do we think when the sermon is done, the care is over? No, then the greatest of the care begins. John was a self-denying man, dead to all the pomps of the world and the pleasures of sense. It becomes people, in all their appearances, to be consistent with their character and their situation. John was a great and good man, yet not perfect; therefore he came short of glorified saints. The least in heaven knows more, loves more, and does more in praising God, and receives more from him, than the greatest in this world. But by the kingdom of heaven here, is rather to be understood the kingdom of grace, the gospel dispensation in its power and purity. What reason we have to be thankful that our lot is cast in the days of the

crown with success. "Faith cometh by hearing, and hearing by the Word of God." We must not expect to see great changes nor any great progress of the gospel until there is greater esteem for the pulpit—more said of it and thought of it. "Well," some may reply, "you speak of the dignity of the pulpit; I take it, you lower it yourself, sir, by speaking in such a style to your hearers." Ah! no doubt you think so. Some pulpits die of dignity. I take it, the greatest dignity in the world is the dignity of converts—that the glory of the pulpit is, if I may use such a metaphor, to have captives at its chariot-wheels, to see converts following it, and where there are such, and those from the very worst of men; there is a dignity in the pulpit beyond any dignity which a fine mouthing of words and a grand selection of fantastic language could ever give to it. "The poor have the gospel preached to them."

II. Now, the next translation is, THE TRANSLATION OF GENEVA, principally used by Calvin in his commentary; and it is also the translation of Thomas Cranmer, whose translation, I believe, was at least in some degree molded by the Genevan translation. He translates it thus:— "The poor receive the gospel." The Genevan translation has it, "The poor receive the glad tidings of the gospel," which is a tautology, since glad tidings mean the same thing as gospel. The Greek has it, "The poor are evangelized." Now, what is the meaning of this word "evangelized?" They talk with a sneer in these days of evangelical drawing rooms and evangelicals, and so on. It is one of the most singular sneers in the world; for to call a man an evangelical by way of joke, is the same as calling a man a gentleman by way of scoffing at him. To say a man is one of the gospelers by way of scorn, is like calling a man a king by way of contempt. It is an honorable, a great, a glorious title, and nothing is more honorable than to be ranked among the evangelicals. What is meant, then, by the people being evangelized?

Old Master Burkitt, thinking that we should not easily understand the word, says, that as a man is said to be Italianised by living among the Italians, getting their manners and customs, and becoming a citizen of the state, so a man is evangelized when he lives where the gospel is preached and gets the manners and customs of those who profess it. Now, that is one meaning of the text. One of the proofs of our Savior's mission is not only that the poor hear the Word, but are influenced by it and are gospelized. Oh! how great a work it is to gospelize any man, and to gospelize a poor man. What does it mean? It means, to make him like the gospel.

disciples, he departed thence to teach and to preach in their cities.

2 Now when John had heard in the prison the works of Christ, he sent two of his disciples,

3 And said unto him, Art thou he that should come, or do we look for another?

4 Jesus answered and said unto them, Go and shew John again those things which ye do hear and see:

5 The blind receive their sight, and the lame walk, the lepers are cleansed, and the deaf hear, the dead are raised up, and the poor have the gospel preached to them.

6 And blessed is he, whosoever shall not be offended in me.

7 And as they departed, Jesus began to say unto the multitudes concerning John, What went ye out into the wilderness to see? A reed shaken with the wind?

8 But what went ye out for to see? A man clothed in soft raiment? behold, they that wear soft clothing are in kings' houses.

9 But what went ye out for to see? A prophet? yea, I say unto you, and more than a prophet.

10 For this is he, of whom it is written, Behold, I send my messenger before thy face, which shall prepare thy way before thee.

11 Verily I say unto you, Among them that are born of women there hath not risen a greater than John the Baptist: notwithstanding he that is least in the kingdom of heaven is greater than he.

12 And from the days of John the Baptist until now the kingdom of heaven suffereth violence, and the violent take it by force.

13 For all the prophets and the law prophesied until John.

14 And if ye will receive it, this is Elias, which was for to come.

15 He that hath ears to hear, let him hear.

16 But whereunto shall I liken this generation? It is like unto children sitting in the markets, and calling unto their fellows,

17 And saying, We have piped unto you, and ye have not danced; we have mourned unto you, and ye have not lamented.

18 For John came neither eating nor drinking, and they say, He hath a devil.

19 The Son of man came eating and drinking, and they say, Behold a man gluttonous, and a winebibber, a friend of publicans and sinners. But wisdom is justified of her children.

20 Then began he to upbraid the cities

of those who are perfected by the spirit of life which is in Christ. Whosoever, therefore, is least in the kingdom of heaven, by Christian regeneration, is greater than any who has attained only the righteousness of the law, because the law maketh nothing perfect." It may farther mean, the least true Christian believer has a more perfect knowledge of Jesus Christ, of his redemption and kingdom, than John the Baptist had, who died before the full manifestation of the Gospel.

12. And from the days of John – That is, from the time that John had fulfilled his ministry, men rush into my kingdom with a violence like that of those who are taking a city by storm.

13. For all the prophets and the law prophesied until John – For all that is written in the law and the prophets only foretold as distant what is now fulfilled. In John the old dispensation expired, and the new began. Luke xvi, 16.

14. Mal. iv, 5.

15. He that hath ears to hear, let him hear – A kind of proverbial expression; requiring the deepest attention to what is spoken.

16. This generation – That is, the men of this age. They are like those froward children of whom their fellows complain, that they will be pleased no way.

18. John came neither eating nor drinking – In a rigorous austere way, like Elijah. And they say, He hath a devil – Is melancholy, from the influence of an evil spirit.

19. The Son of man came eating and drinking – Conversing in a free, familiar way. Wisdom is justified by her children – That is, my wisdom herein is acknowledged by those who are truly wise.

20. Then began he to upbraid the cities – It is observable he had never upbraided them before. Indeed at first they received him with all gladness, Capernaum in particular.

21. Woe to thee, Chorazin – That is, miserable art thou. For these are not curses or imprecations, as has been commonly supposed; but a solemn, compassionate declaration of the misery they were bringing on themselves. Chorazin and Bethsaida were cities of Galilee, standing by the lake Gennesareth. Tyre and Sidon were cities of Phenicia, lying on the sea shore. The inhabitants of them were heathens. Luke x, 13.

22, 24. Moreover I say unto you – Beside the general denunciation of woe to those stubborn unbelievers, the degree of their misery will be greater than even that of Tyre and Sidon, yea, of Sodom.

23. Thou Capernaum, who hast been exalted to heaven – That is, highly honored by my presence and miracles.

25. Jesus answering – This word does not always imply, that something had been spoken, to which an answer is now made. It often means no more than the speaking in reference to some action or circumstance preceding. The following words Christ speaks in reference to the case of the cities above mentioned: I thank thee – That is, I acknowledge and joyfully adore the justice and mercy of thy dispensations: Because thou hast hid – That is, because thou hast suffered these things to be hid from men, who are in other respects wise and prudent, while thou hast discovered them to those of the weakest understanding, to them who are only wise to Godward. Luke x, 21.

27. All things are delivered to me – Our Lord, here addressing himself to his disciples, shows why men, wise in other things, do not know this: namely, because none can know it by natural reason: none but those to whom he revealeth it.

28. Come to me – Here he shows to whom he is pleased to reveal these things to the weary and heavy laden; ye that labor – After rest in God:

MATTHEW HENRY

kingdom of heaven, under such advantages of light and love! Multitudes were wrought upon by the ministry of John, and became his disciples. And those strove for a place in this kingdom, that one would think had no right nor title to it, and so seemed to be intruders. It shows us what fervency and zeal are required of all. Self must be denied; the bent, the frame and temper of the mind must be altered. Those who will have an interest in the great salvation, will have it upon any terms, and not think them hard, nor quit their hold without a blessing. The things of God are of great and common concern. God requires no more from us than the right use of the faculties he has given us. People are ignorant, because they will not learn.

16-24 Christ reflects on the scribes and Pharisees, who had a proud conceit of themselves. He likens their behavior to children's play, who being out of temper without reason, quarrel with all the attempts of their fellows to please them, or to get them to join in the plays for which they used to assemble. The cavils of worldly men are often very trifling and show great malice. Something they have to urge against every one, however excellent and holy. Christ, who was undefiled, and separate from sinners, is here represented as in league with them, and polluted by them. The most unspotted innocence will not always be a defense against reproach. Christ knew that the hearts of the Jews were more bitter and hardened against his miracles and doctrines, than those of Tyre and Sidon would have been; therefore their condemnation would be the greater. The Lord exercises his almighty power, yet he punishes none more than they deserve, and never withholds the knowledge of the truth from those who long after it.

25-30 It becomes children to be grateful. When we come to God as a Father, we must remember that he is Lord of heaven and earth, which obliges us to come to him with reverence as to the sovereign Lord of all; yet with confidence, as one able to defend us from evil, and to supply us with all good. Our blessed Lord added a remarkable declaration, that the Father had delivered into his hands all power, authority, and judgment. We are indebted to Christ for all the revelation we have of God the Father's will and love, ever since Adam sinned. Our Savior has invited all that labor and are heavy-laden, to come unto him. In some senses all men are so. Worldly men burden themselves with fruitless cares for wealth and honors; the gay and the sensual labor in pursuit of pleasures; the slave of Satan and his own lusts, is the merest drudge on earth. Those who labor to establish their own righteousness also labor in vain. The convinced sinner is heavy-laden with guilt and terror; and the tempted and afflicted believer has labors and burdens. Christ invites all to come to him for rest to their souls. He alone gives this invitation; men come to him, when, feeling their guilt and misery, and believing his love and power to help, they seek him in

CHARLES H. SPURGEON

Now, the gospel is holy, just, and true, and loving, and honest, and benevolent, and kind, and gracious. So, then, to gospelize a man is to make a rogue honest, to make a harlot modest, to make a profane man serious, to make a grasping man liberal, to make a covetous man benevolent, to make the drunken man sober, to make the untruthful man truthful, to make the unkind man loving, to make the hater the lover of his species, and, in a word, to gospelize a man is, in his outward character, to bring him into such a condition that he labors to carry out the command of Christ, "Love thy God with all thy heart, and thy neighbor as thyself."

Gospelizing, furthermore, has something to do with an inner principle; gospelizing a man means saving him from hell and making him a heavenly character; it means blotting out his sins, writing a new name upon his heart—the new name of God. It means bringing him to know his election, to put his trust in Christ, to renounce his sins, and his good works too, and to trust solely and wholly upon Jesus Christ as his Redeemer. Oh! what a blessed thing it is to be gospelized! How many of you have been so gospelized? The Lord grant that the whole of us may feel the influence of the gospel. I contend for this, that to gospelize a man is the greatest miracle in the world. All the other miracles are wrapped up in this one. To gospelize a man, or, in other words, to convert him, is a greater work than to open the eyes of the blind; for is it not opening the eyes of the blind soul that he may see spiritual matters, and understand the things of heavenly wisdom, and is not a surgical operation easier than operation on the soul? Souls we cannot touch, although science and skill have been able to remove films and cataracts from the eyes. "The lame walk."

Gospelizing a man is more than this. It is not only making a lame man walk, but it is making a dead man who could not walk in the right way walk in the right way ever afterwards. "The lepers are cleansed." Ah! but to cleanse a sinner is greater work than cleansing a leper. "The deaf hear." Yes, and to make a man who never listened to the voice of God hear the voice of his Maker, is a miracle greater than to make the deaf hear, or even to raise the dead. Great though that be, it is not a more stupendous effort of divine power than to save a soul, since men are naturally dead in sins, and must be quickened by divine grace if they are saved. To gospelize a man is the highest instance of divine might, and remains an unparalleled miracle, a miracle of miracles. "The poor are evangelized."

Beloved, there have been some very precious specimens of poor people who have come under the influence of the gospel. I think I

wherein most of his mighty works were done, because they repented not:

21 Woe unto thee, Chorazin! woe unto thee, Bethsaida! for if the mighty works, which were done in you, had been done in Tyre and Sidon, they would have repented long ago in sackcloth and ashes.

22 But I say unto you, It shall be more tolerable for Tyre and Sidon at the day of judgment, than for you.

23 And thou, Capernaum, which art exalted unto heaven, shalt be brought down to hell: for if the mighty works, which have been done in thee, had been done in Sodom, it would have remained until this day.

24 But I say unto you, That it shall be more tolerable for the land of Sodom in the day of judgment, than for you.

25 At that time Jesus answered and said, I thank thee, O Father, Lord of heaven and earth, because thou hast hid these things from the wise and prudent, and hast revealed them unto babes.

26 Even so, Father: for so it seemed good in thy sight.

27 All things are delivered unto me of my Father: and no man knoweth the Son, but the Father; neither knoweth any man the Father, save the Son, and he to whomsoever the Son will reveal him.

28 Come unto me, all ye that labor and are heavy laden, and I will give you rest.

29 Take my yoke upon you, and learn of me; for I am meek and lowly in heart: and ye shall find rest unto your souls.

30 For my yoke is easy, and my burden is light.

MATTHEW 12

1 At that time Jesus went on the sabbath day through the corn; and his disciples were an hungred, and began to pluck the ears of corn, and to eat.

2 But when the Pharisees saw it, they said unto him, Behold, thy disciples do that which is not lawful to do upon the sabbath day.

3 But he said unto them, Have ye not read what David did, when he was an hungred, and they that were with him;

4 How he entered into the house of God, and did eat the shewbread, which was not lawful for him to eat, neither for them which were with him, but only for the priests?

5 Or have ye not read in the law, how that on the sabbath days the priests in the temple profane the sabbath, and are blameless?

and are heavy laden – With the guilt and power of sin: and I will give you rest – I alone (for none else can) will freely give you (what ye cannot purchase) rest from the guilt of sin by justification, and from the power of sin by sanctification.

29. Take my yoke upon you – Believe in me: receive me as your prophet, priest, and king. For I am meek and lowly in heart – Meek toward all men, lowly toward God: and ye shall find rest – Whoever therefore does not find rest of soul, is not meek and lowly. The fault is not in the yoke of Christ: but in thee, who hast not taken it upon thee. Nor is it possible for any one to be discontented, but through want of meekness or lowliness.

30. For my yoke is easy – Or rather gracious, sweet, benign, delightful: and my burden – Contrary to those of men, is ease, liberty, and honor.

MATTHEW 12

1. His disciples plucked the ears of corn, and ate – Just what sufficed for present necessity: dried corn was a common food among the Jews. Mark ii, 23; Luke vi, 1.

3. Have ye not read what David did – And necessity was a sufficient plea for his transgressing the law in a higher instance.

4. He entered into the house of God – Into the tabernacle. The temple was not yet built. The show bread – So they called the bread which the priest, who served that week, put every Sabbath day on the golden table that was in the holy place, before the Lord. The loaves were twelve in number, and represented the twelve tribes of Israel: when the new were brought, the stale were taken away, but were to be eaten by the priests only. 1 Sam. xxi, 6.

5. The priests in the temple profane the Sabbath – That is, do their ordinary work on this, as on a common day, cleansing all things, and preparing the sacrifices. A greater than the temple – If therefore the Sabbath must give way to the temple, much more must it give way to me.

7. I will have mercy and not sacrifice – That is, when they interfere with each other, I always prefer acts of mercy, before matters of positive institution: yea, before all ceremonial institutions whatever; because these being only means of religion, are suspended of course, if circumstances occur, wherein they clash with love, which is the end of it. Matt. ix, 13.

8. For the Son of man – Therefore they are guiltless, were it only on this account, that they act by my authority, and attend on me in my ministry, as the priests attended on God in the temple: is Lord even of the Sabbath – This certainly implies, that the Sabbath was an institution of great and distinguished importance; it may perhaps also refer to that signal act of authority which Christ afterward exerted over it, in changing it from the seventh to the first day of the week. If we suppose here is a transposition of the 7th and 8th verses, then the 8th verse is a proof of the 6th. Matt. xii, 7, 8, 6.

9. Mark iii, 1; Luke vi, 6.

12. It is lawful to do good on the Sabbath day – To save a beast, much more a man.

18. He shall show judgment to the heathens – That is, he shall publish the merciful Gospel to them also: the Hebrew word signifies either mercy or justice. Isaiah xlii, 1, &c.

19. He shall not strive, nor clamor; neither shall any man hear his voice in the streets – That is, he shall not be contentious, noisy, or

MATTHEW HENRY

CHARLES H. SPURGEON

fervent prayer. Thus it is the duty and interest of weary and heavy-laden sinners, to come to Jesus Christ. This is the gospel call; Whoever will, let him come. All who thus come will receive rest as Christ's gift, and obtain peace and comfort in their hearts. But in coming to him they must take his yoke, and submit to his authority. They must learn of him all things, as to their comfort and obedience. He accepts the willing servant, however imperfect the services. Here we may find rest for our souls, and here only. Nor need we fear his yoke. His commandments are holy, just, and good. It requires self-denial, and exposes to difficulties, but this is abundantly repaid, even in this world, by inward peace and joy. It is a yoke that is lined with love. So powerful are the assistances he gives us, so suitable the encouragements, and so strong the consolations to be found in the way of duty, that we may truly say, it is a yoke of pleasantness. The way of duty is the way of rest. The truths Christ teaches are such as we may venture our souls upon. Such is the Redeemer's mercy; and why should the laboring and burdened sinner seek for rest from any other quarter? Let us come to him daily, for deliverance from wrath and guilt, from sin and Satan, from all our cares, fears, and sorrows. But forced obedience, far from being easy and light, is a heavy burden. In vain do we draw near to Jesus with our lips, while the heart is far from him. Then come to Jesus to find rest for your souls.

MATTHEW 12

Jesus defends his disciples for plucking corn on the sabbath day. (1-8)

Jesus heals a man with a withered hand on the sabbath. (9-13)

The malice of the Pharisees. (14-21)

Jesus heals a demoniac. (22-30)

Blasphemy of the Pharisees. (31,32)

Evil words proceed from an evil heart. (33-37)

The scribes and Pharisees reproved for seeking a sign. (38-45)

The disciples of Christ are his nearest relations. (46-50)

1-8 Being in the corn-fields, the disciples began to pluck the ears of corn: the law of God allowed it, De 23:25. This was slender provision for Christ and his disciples; but they were content with it. The Pharisees did not quarrel with them for taking another man's corn, but for doing it on the sabbath day. Christ came to free his followers, not only from the corruptions of the Pharisees, but from their unscriptural rules, and justified what they did. The greatest shall not have their lusts indulged, but the meanest shall have their wants considered. Those labors are lawful on the sabbath day which are necessary, and sabbath rest is to froward, not to hinder sabbath worship. Needful provision for health and food is to be made; but when servants are kept at home, and families become a scene of hurry and confusion on the Lord's day, to furnish a feast for

appeal to the hearts of all of you who are now present, when I say there is nothing we more reverence and respect than the piety of the poor and needy. I had an engraving sent to me the other day which pleased me beyond measure. It was an engraving simply but exquisitely executed. It represented a poor girl in an upper room, with a lean-to roof. There was a post driven in the ground, on which was a piece of wood, standing on which were a candle and a Bible. She was on her knees at a chair, praying, wrestling with God. Everything in the room had on it the stamp of poverty. There was the mean coverlet to the old stump bedstead; there were the walls that had never been papered, and perhaps scarcely whitewashed. It was an upper story to which she had climbed with aching knees, and where perhaps she had worked away till her fingers were worn to the bone to earn her bread at needlework. There it was that she was wrestling with God. Some would turn away and laugh at it; but it appeals to the best feelings of man, and moves the heart far more than does the fine engraving of the monarch on his knees in the grand assembly. We have had lately a most excellent volume, the Life of Captain Hedley Vicars; it is calculated to do great good, and I pray God to bless it; but I question whether the history of Captain Hedley Vicars will last as long in the public mind as the history of the Dairyman's Daughter, or the Shepherd of Salisbury Plain. The histories of those who have come from the ranks of the poor always lay hold of the Christian mind.

Oh! we love piety anywhere; we bless God where coronets and grace go together; but if piety in any place do shine more brightly than anywhere else, it is in rags and poverty. When the poor woman in the almshouse takes her bread and her water, and blesses God for both—when the poor creature who has not where to lay his head, yet lifts his eye and says, "My Father will provide," it is then like the glow-worm in the damp leaves, a spark the more conspicuous for the blackness around it. Then religion gleams in its true brightness, and is seen in all its luster. It is a mark of Christ's gospel that the poor are gospelized—that they can receive the gospel. True it is, the gospel affects all ranks, and is equally adapted to them all; but yet we say, "If one class be more prominent than another, we believe that in Holy Scripture the poor are most of all appealed to." "Oh!" say some very often, "the converts whom God has given to such a man are all from the lower ranks; they are all people with no sense; they are all uneducated people that hear such-and-such a person." Very well, if you say so; we might deny it if we pleased, but we do not

6 But I say unto you, That in this place is one greater than the temple.

7 But if ye had known what this meaneth, I will have mercy, and not sacrifice, ye would not have condemned the guiltless.

8 For the Son of man is Lord even of the sabbath day.

9 And when he was departed thence, he went into their synagogue:

10 And, behold, there was a man which had his hand withered. And they asked him, saying, Is it lawful to heal on the sabbath days? that they might accuse him.

11 And he said unto them, What man shall there be among you, that shall have one sheep, and if it fall into a pit on the sabbath day, will he not lay hold on it, and lift it out?

12 How much then is a man better than a sheep? Wherefore it is lawful to do well on the sabbath days.

13 Then saith he to the man, Stretch forth thine hand. And he stretched it forth; and it was restored whole, like as the other.

14 Then the Pharisees went out, and held a council against him, how they might destroy him.

15 But when Jesus knew it, he withdrew himself from thence: and great multitudes followed him, and he healed them all;

16 And charged them that they should not make him known:

17 That it might be fulfilled which was spoken by Esaias the prophet, saying,

18 Behold my servant, whom I have chosen; my beloved, in whom my soul is well pleased: I will put my spirit upon him, and he shall shew judgment to the Gentiles.

19 He shall not strive, nor cry; neither shall any man hear his voice in the streets.

20 A bruised reed shall he not break, and smoking flax shall he not quench, till he send forth judgment unto victory.

21 And in his name shall the Gentiles trust.

22 Then was brought unto him one possessed with a devil, blind, and dumb: and he healed him, insomuch that the blind and dumb both spake and saw.

23 And all the people were amazed, and said, Is not this the son of David?

24 But when the Pharisees heard it, they said, This fellow doth not cast out devils, but by Beelzebub the prince of the devils.

25 And Jesus knew their thoughts, and said unto them, Every kingdom divided

ostentatious: but gentle, quiet, and lowly. We may observe each word rises above the other, expressing a still higher degree of humility and gentleness.

20. A bruised reed – A convinced sinner: one that is bruised with the weight of sin: smoking flax – One that has the least good desire, the faintest spark of grace: till he send forth judgment unto victory – That is, till he make righteousness completely victorious over all its enemies.

21. In his name – That is, in him.

22. A demoniac, blind and dumb – Many undoubtedly supposed these defects to be merely natural. But the Spirit of God saw otherwise, and gives the true account both of the disorder and the cure. How many disorders, seemingly natural, may even now be owing to the same cause? Luke xi, 14.

23. Is not this the son of David – That is, the Messiah.

24. Mark iii, 22.

25. Jesus knowing their thoughts – It seems they had as yet only said it in their hearts.

26. How shall his kingdom be established – Does not that subtle spirit know this is not the way to establish his kingdom?

27. By whom do your children – That is, disciples, cast them out – It seems, some of them really did this; although the sons of Sceva could not. Therefore shall they be your judge – Ask them, if Satan will cast out Satan: let even them be Judge in this matter. And they shall convict you of obstinacy and partiality, who impute that in me to Beelzebub, which in them you impute to God. Beside, how can I rob him of his subjects, till I have conquered him? The kingdom of God is come upon you – Unawares; before you expected: so the word implies.

29. How can one enter into the strong one's house, unless he first bind the strong one – So Christ coming into the world, which was then eminently the strong one's, Satan's house, first bound him, and then took his spoils.

30. He that is not with me is against me – For there are no neuters in this war. Every one must be either with Christ or against him; either a loyal subject or a rebel. And there are none upon earth, who neither promote nor obstruct his kingdom. For he that does not gather souls to God, scatters them from him.

31. The blasphemy against the Spirit – How much stir has been made about this? How many sermons, yea, volumes, have been written concerning it? And yet there is nothing plainer in all the Bible. It is neither more nor less than the ascribing those miracles to the power of the devil, which Christ wrought by the power of the Holy Ghost. Mark iii, 28; Luke xii, 10.

32. Whosoever speaketh against the Son of man – In any other respects: It shall be forgiven him – Upon his true repentance: But whosoever speaketh thus against the Holy Ghost, it shall not be forgiven, neither in this world nor in the world to come – This was a proverbial expression among the Jews, for a thing that would never be done. It here means farther, He shall not escape the punishment of it, either in this world, or in the world to come. The judgment of God shall overtake him, both here and hereafter.

33. Either make the tree good and its fruit good: or make the tree corrupt and its fruit corrupt – That is, you must allow, they are both good, or both bad – For if the fruit is good, so is the tree; if the fruit is evil, so is the tree also. For the tree is known by its fruit – As if he had said, Ye may therefore know me by my fruits. By my converting sinners to God, you may know that God hath sent me. Matt. vii, 16; Luke vi, 43.

visitors, or for indulgence, the case is very different. Such things as these, and many others common among professors, are to be blamed. The resting on the sabbath was ordained for man's good, De 5:14. No law must be understood so as to contradict its own end. And as Christ is the Lord of the sabbath, it is fit the day and the work of it should be dedicated to him.

9-13 Christ shows that works of mercy are lawful and proper to be done on the Lord's day. There are more ways of doing well upon sabbath days, than by the duties of worship: attending the sick, relieving the poor, helping those who need speedy relief, teaching the young to care for their souls; these are doing good: and these must be done from love and charity, with humility and self-denial, and shall be accepted, Ge 4:7. This, like other cures which Christ wrought, had a spiritual meaning. By nature our hands are withered, and we are unable of ourselves to do any thing that is good. Christ only, by the power of his grace, cures us; he heals the withered hand by putting life into the dead soul, works in us both to will and to do: for, with the command, there is a promise of grace given by the word.

14-21 The Pharisees took counsel to find some accusation, that Jesus might be condemned to death. Aware of their design, as his time was not come, he retired from that place. Face does not more exactly answer to face in water, than the character of Christ drawn by the prophet, to his temper and conduct as described by the evangelists. Let us with cheerful confidence commit our souls to so kind and faithful a Friend. Far from breaking, he will strengthen the bruised reed; far from quenching the smoking flax, or wick nearly out, he will rather blow it up into a flame. Let us lay aside contentious and angry debates; let us receive one another as Christ receives us. And while encouraged by the gracious kindness of our Lord, we should pray that his Spirit may rest upon us, and make us able to copy his example.

22-30 A soul under Satan's power, and led captive by him, is blind in the things of God, and dumb at the throne of grace; sees nothing, and says nothing to the purpose. Satan blinds the eyes by unbelief, and seals up the lips from prayer. The more people magnified Christ, the more desirous the Pharisees were to vilify him. It was evident that if Satan aided Jesus in casting out devils, the kingdom of hell was divided against itself; how then could it stand! And if they said that Jesus cast out devils by the prince of the devils, they could not prove that their children cast them out by any other power. There are two great interests in the world; and when unclean spirits are cast out by the Holy Spirit, in the conversion of sinners to a life of faith and obedience, the kingdom of God is come unto us. All who do not aid or rejoice in such a change are against Christ.

31,32 Here is a gracious assurance of the pardon of all

know that we shall take the trouble, because we think it no disgrace whatever; we think it rather to be an honor that the poor are evangelized, and that they listen to the gospel from our lips. I have never thought it a disgrace at any time. When any have said, "Look, what a mass of uneducated people they are." Yes, I have thought, and blessed be God they are, for those are the very people that want the gospel most. If you saw a physician's door surrounded by a number of ladies of the sentimental school, who are sick about three times a week, and never were ill at all—if it were said he cured them, you would say, "No great wonder too, for there never was anything the matter with them." But if you heard of another man, that people with the worst diseases have come to him, and that God has made use of him, and his medicine has been the means of healing their diseases, you would then say, "There is something in it, for the people that want it most have received it." If, then, it be true that the poor will come to hear the gospel more than others, it is no disgrace to the gospel, it is an honor to it, that those who most want it do freely receive it.

III. And now I must close up by briefly dwelling on the last point. It was the third translation, WYCKLIFFE'S TRANSLATION. To give it you in old English—"Poor men are taking to the preaching of the gospel." "Ah!" say some, "they had better remain at home, minding their plows or their blacksmith's hammer; they had better have kept on with their tinkering and tailoring, and not have turned preachers." But it is one of the honors of the gospel that poor men have taken to the preaching of it. There was a tinker once, and let the worldly-wise blush when they hear of it—there was a tinker once, a tinker of whom a great divine said he would give all his learning if he could preach like him. There was a tinker once, who never so much as brushed his back against the walls of a college, who wrote a "Pilgrim's Progress". Did ever a doctor in divinity write such a book. There was a potboy once—a boy who carried on his back the pewter pots for his mother, who kept the Old Bell. That man drove men mad, as the world had it, but led them to Christ, as we have it, all his life long, until, loaded with honors, he sank into his grave, with the good will of a multitude round about him, with an imperishable name written in the world's records, as well as in the records of the church. Did you ever hear of any mighty man, whose name stood in more esteem among God's people than the name of George Whitfield?

And yet these were poor men, who, as

against itself is brought to desolation; and every city or house divided against itself shall not stand:

26 And if Satan cast out Satan, he is divided against himself; how shall then his kingdom stand?

27 And if I by Beelzebub cast out devils, by whom do your children cast them out? therefore they shall be your judges.

28 But if I cast out devils by the Spirit of God, then the kingdom of God is come unto you.

29 Or else how can one enter into a strong man's house, and spoil his goods, except he first bind the strong man? and then he will spoil his house.

30 He that is not with me is against me; and he that gathereth not with me scattereth abroad.

31 Wherefore I say unto you, All manner of sin and blasphemy shall be forgiven unto men: but the blasphemy against the Holy Ghost shall not be forgiven unto men.

32 And whosoever speaketh a word against the Son of man, it shall be forgiven him: but whosoever speaketh against the Holy Ghost, it shall not be forgiven him, neither in this world, neither in the world to come.

33 Either make the tree good, and his fruit good; or else make the tree corrupt, and his fruit corrupt: for the tree is known by his fruit.

34 O generation of vipers, how can ye, being evil, speak good things? for out of the abundance of the heart the mouth speaketh.

35 A good man out of the good treasure of the heart bringeth forth good things: and an evil man out of the evil treasure bringeth forth evil things.

36 But I say unto you, That every idle word that men shall speak, they shall give account thereof in the day of judgment.

37 For by thy words thou shalt be justified, and by thy words thou shalt be condemned.

38 Then certain of the scribes and of the Pharisees answered, saying, Master, we would see a sign from thee.

39 But he answered and said unto them, An evil and adulterous generation seeketh after a sign; and there shall no sign be given to it, but the sign of the prophet Jonas:

40 For as Jonas was three days and three nights in the whale's belly; so shall the Son of man be three days and three nights in the heart of the earth.

41 The men of Nineveh shall rise in judgment with this generation, and shall condemn it: because they repented at

34. In another kind likewise, the tree is known by its fruit – Namely, the heart by the conversation.

36. Ye may perhaps think, God does not so much regard your words. But I say to you – That not for blasphemous and profane words only, but for every idle word which men shall speak – For want of seriousness or caution; for every discourse which is not conducive to the glory of God, they shall give account in the day of judgment.

37. For by thy words (as well as thy tempers and works) thou shalt then be either acquitted or condemned – Your words as well as actions shall be produced in evidence for or against you, to prove whether you were a true believer or not. And according to that evidence you will either be acquitted or condemned in the great day.

38. We would see a sign – Else we will not believe this. Matt. xvi, 1; Luke xi, 16, 29.

39. An adulterous generation – Whose heart wanders from God, though they profess him to be their husband. Such adulterers are all those who love the world, and all who seek the friendship of it. Seeketh a sign – After all they have had already, which were abundantly sufficient to convince them, had not their hearts been estranged from God, and consequently averse to the truth. The sign of Jonah – Who was herein a type of Christ.

40. Three days and three nights – It was customary with the eastern nations to reckon any part of a natural day of twenty-four hours, for the whole day. Accordingly they used to say a thing was done after three or seven days, if it was done on the third or seventh day, from that which was last mentioned. Instances of this may be seen, 1 Kings xx, 29; and in many other places. And as the Hebrews had no word to express a natural day, they used night and day, or day and night for it. So that to say a thing happened after three days and three nights, was with them the very same, as to say, it happened after three days, or on the third day. See Esther iv, 16; v, 1; Gen. vii, 4, 12; Exod. xxiv, 18; xxxiv, 28. Jonah ii, 1.

42. She came from the uttermost parts of the earth – That part of Arabia from which she came was the uttermost part of the earth that way, being bounded by the sea. 1 Kings x, 1.

43. But how dreadful will be the consequence of their rejecting me? When the unclean spirit goeth out – Not willingly, but being compelled by one that is stronger than he. He walketh – Wanders up and down; through dry places – Barren, dreary, desolate; or places not yet watered with the Gospel: Seeking rest, and findeth none – How can he, while he carries with him his own hell? And is it not the case of his children too? Reader, is it thy case? Luke xi, 24.

44. Whence he came out – He speaks as if he had come out of his own accord: See his pride! He findeth it empty – of God, of Christ, of his Spirit: Swept – from love, lowliness, meekness, and all the fruits of the Spirit: And garnished – With levity and security: so that there is nothing to keep him out, and much to invite him in.

45. Seven other spirits – That is, a great many; a certain number being put for an uncertain: More wicked than himself – Whence it appears, that there are degrees of wickedness among the devils themselves: They enter in and dwell – For ever in him who is forsaken of God. So shall it be to this wicked generation – Yea, and to apostates in all ages.

46. His brethren – His kinsmen: they were the sons of Mary, the wife of Cleopas, or Alpheus, his mother's sister; and came now seeking to take him, as one beside himself, Mark iii, 21. Mark iii, 31; Luke viii, 19.

MATTHEW HENRY   CHARLES H. SPURGEON

sin upon gospel terms. Christ herein has set an example to the sons of men, to be ready to forgive words spoken against them. But humble and conscientious believers, at times are tempted to think they have committed the unpardonable sin, while those who have come the nearest to it, seldom have any fear about it. We may be sure that those who indeed repent and believe the gospel, have not committed this sin, or any other of the same kind; for repentance and faith are the special gifts of God, which he would not bestow on any man, if he were determined never to pardon him; and those who fear they have committed this sin, give a good sign that they have not. The trembling, contrite sinner, has the witness in himself that this is not his case.

33-37 Men's language discovers what country they are of, likewise what manner of spirit they are of. The heart is the fountain, words are the streams. A troubled fountain, and a corrupt spring, must send forth muddy and unpleasant streams. Nothing but the salt of grace, cast into the spring, will heal the waters, season the speech, and purify the corrupt communication. An evil man has an evil treasure in his heart, and out of it brings forth evil things. Lusts and corruptions, dwelling and reigning in the heart, are an evil treasure, out of which the sinner brings forth bad words and actions, to dishonor God, and hurt others. Let us keep constant watch over ourselves, that we may speak words agreeable to the Christian character.

38-45 Though Christ is always ready to hear and answer holy desires and prayers, yet those who ask amiss, ask and have not. Signs were granted to those who desired them to confirm their faith, as Abraham and Gideon; but denied to those who demanded them to excuse their unbelief. The resurrection of Christ from the dead by his own power, called here the sign of the prophet Jonah, was the great proof of Christ's being the Messiah. As Jonah was three days and three nights in the whale, and then came out again alive, thus Christ would be so long in the grave, and then rise again. The Ninevites would shame the Jews for not repenting; the queen of Sheba, for not believing in Christ. And we have no such cares to hinder us, we come not to Christ upon such uncertainties. This parable represents the case of the Jewish church and nation. It is also applicable to all those who hear the word of God, and are in part reformed, but not truly converted. The unclean spirit leaves for a time, but when he returns, he finds Christ is not there to shut him out; the heart is swept by outward reformation, but garnished by preparation to comply with evil suggestions, and the man becomes a more decided enemy of the truth. Every heart is the residence of unclean spirits, except those which are temples of the Holy Ghost, by faith in Christ.

46-50 Christ's preaching was plain, easy, and familiar,

Wyckliffe said, were taking to the preaching of the gospel. If you will read the life of Wyckliffe, you will find him saying there, that he believed that the Reformation in England was more promoted by the labors of the poor men whom he sent out from Lutterworth than by his own. He gathered round him a number of the poor people whom he instructed in the faith, and then he sent them two and two into every village, as Jesus did. They went into the market-place, and they gathered the people around; they opened the book and read a chapter, and then they left them a manuscript of it which for months and years after the people would assemble to read, and would remember the gospelers that had come to tell them the gospel of Christ. These men went from market-place to market-place, from town to town, and from village to village, and though their names are unknown to fame, they were the real reformers. You may talk of Cranmer, and Latimer, and Ridley; they did much, but the real reformers of the English nation were people whose names have perished from the annals of time, but are written in the records of eternity. God has blessed the poor man in preaching the truth. Far be it from me to depreciate learning and wisdom. We should not have had the Bible translated without learning and the more learning a man can have, if he be a sanctified man, the better; he has so many more talents to lay out in his Master's service; but it is not absolutely necessary for preaching of the Word. Rough, untamed, untaught energy, has done much in the church.

A Boanerges has stood up in a village; he could not put three words together in grammatical English; but where the drowsy parson had for many a year lulled all his people into an unhallowed rest, this man started up, like the herdsman Amos, and brought about a great awakening. He began to preach in some cottage; people thronged around him, then a house was built, and his name is handed down to use as the Rev. So-and-so, but then he was known as Tom the plowman, or John the tinker. God has made use of men whose origin was the most obscure, who seemed to have little, except the gifts of nature, which could be made use of in God's service; and we hold that this is no disgrace, but on the contrary an honor, that poor men are taking to preaching the gospel.

I have to ask you this morning to help some poor men in preaching the gospel. We are constantly receiving letters from our poor brethren, and it is very seldom that we say "No," to their appeals for assistance, but we must do so, unless our friends, more especially those who love the gospel, really will do something towards the maintenance of God's faithful servants. I have,

the preaching of Jonas; and, behold, a greater than Jonas is here.

42 The queen of the south shall rise up in the judgment with this generation, and shall condemn it: for she came from the uttermost parts of the earth to hear the wisdom of Solomon; and, behold, a greater than Solomon is here.

43 When the unclean spirit is gone out of a man, he walketh through dry places, seeking rest, and findeth none.

44 Then he saith, I will return into my house from whence I came out; and when he is come, he findeth it empty, swept, and garnished.

45

Then goeth he, and taketh with himself seven other spirits more wicked than himself, and they enter in and dwell there: and the last state of that man is worse than the first. Even so shall it be also unto this wicked generation.

46 While he yet talked to the people, behold, his mother and his brethren stood without, desiring to speak with him.

47 Then one said unto him, Behold, thy mother and thy brethren stand without, desiring to speak with thee.

48 But he answered and said unto him that told him, Who is my mother? and who are my brethren?

49 And he stretched forth his hand toward his disciples, and said, Behold my mother and my brethren!

50 For whosoever shall do the will of my Father which is in heaven, the same is my brother, and sister, and mother.

MATTHEW 13

1 The same day went Jesus out of the house, and sat by the sea side.

2 And great multitudes were gathered together unto him, so that he went into a ship, and sat; and the whole multitude stood on the shore.

3 And he spake many things unto them in parables, saying, Behold, a sower went forth to sow;

4 And when he sowed, some seeds fell by the way side, and the fowls came and devoured them up:

5 Some fell upon stony places, where they had not much earth: and forthwith they sprung up, because they had no deepness of earth:

6 And when the sun was up, they were scorched; and because they had no root, they withered away.

7 And some fell among thorns; and the thorns sprung up, and choked them:

8 But other fell into good ground, and brought forth fruit, some an hundred-

48. And he answering, said – Our Lord's knowing why they came, sufficiently justifies his seeming disregard of them.

49, 50. See the highest severity, and the highest goodness! Severity to his natural, goodness to his spiritual relations! In a manner disclaiming the former, who opposed the will of his heavenly Father, and owning the latter, who obeyed it.

MATTHEW 13

1. Mark iv, 1; Luke viii, 4.

2. He went into the vessel – Which constantly waited upon him, while he was on the sea coast.

3. In parables – The word is here taken in its proper sense, for apt similes or comparisons. This way of speaking, extremely common in the eastern countries, drew and fixed the attention of many, and occasioned the truths delivered to sink the deeper into humble and serious hearers. At the same time, by an awful mixture of justice and mercy, it hid them from the proud and careless. In this chapter our Lord delivers seven parables; directing the four former (as being of general concern) to all the people; the three latter to his disciples. Behold the sower – How exquisitely proper is this parable to be an introduction to all the rest! In this our Lord answers a very obvious and a very important question. The same sower, Christ, and the same preachers sent by him, always sow the same seed: why has it not always the same effect? He that hath ears to hear, let him hear!

4. And while he sowed, some seeds fell by the highway side, and the birds came and devoured them – It is observable, that our Lord points out the grand hindrances of our bearing fruit, in the same order as they occur. The first danger is, that the birds will devour the seed. If it escape this, there is then another danger, namely, lest it be scorched, and wither away. It is long after this that the thorns spring up and choke the good seed. A vast majority of those who hear the word of God, receive the seed as by the highway side. Of those who do not lose it by the birds, yet many receive it as on stony places. Many of them who receive it in a better soil, yet suffer the thorns to grow up, and choke it: so that few even of these endure to the end, and bear fruit unto perfection: yet in all these cases, it is not the will of God that hinders, but their own voluntary perverseness.

8. Good ground – Soft, not like that by the highway side; deep, not like the stony ground; purged, not full of thorns.

11. To you, who have, it is given to know the mysteries of the kingdom of heaven – The deep things which flesh and blood cannot reveal, pertaining to the inward, present kingdom of heaven. But to them who have not, it is not given – Therefore speak I in parables, that ye may understand, while they do not understand.

12. Whosoever hath – That is, improves what he hath, uses the grace given according to the design of the giver; to him shall be given – More and more, in proportion to that improvement. But whosoever hath not – Improves it not, from him shall be taken even what he hath – Here is the grand rule of God's dealing with the children of men: a rule fixed as the pillars of heaven. This is the key to all his providential dispensations; as will appear to men and angels in that day. Matt. xxv, 29; Mark iv, 25; Luke viii, 18; xix, 26.

13. Therefore I speak to them in parables, because seeing, they see not – In pursuance of this general rule, I do not give more knowledge to this people, because they use not that which they have already: having

MATTHEW HENRY

CHARLES H. SPURGEON

and suited to his hearers. His mother and brethren stood without, desiring to speak with him, when they should have been standing within, desiring to hear him. Frequently, those who are nearest to the means of knowledge and grace are most negligent. We are apt to neglect that which we think we may have any day, forgetting that tomorrow is not ours. We often meet with hinderances in our work from friends about us, and are taken off by care for the things of this life, from the concerns of our souls. Christ was so intent on his work, that no natural or other duty took him from it. Not that, under pretense of religion, we may be disrespectful to parents, or unkind to relations; but the lesser duty must stand by, while the greater is done. Let us cease from men, and cleave to Christ; let us look upon every Christian, in whatever condition of life, as the brother, sister, or mother of the Lord of glory; let us love, respect, and be kind to them, for his sake, and after his example.

MATTHEW 13

The parable of the sower. (1-23)
The parable of the tares. (24-30; 36-43)
The parables of the mustard-seed and the leaven. (31-35)
The parables of the hidden treasure, the pearl of great price, the net cast into the sea, and the householder. (44-52)
Jesus is again rejected at Nazareth. (53-58)

1-23 See commentary at Mark 4:1-20; Luke 8:4-15

24-30, 36-43 This parable represents the present and future state of the gospel church; Christ's care of it, the devil's enmity against it, the mixture there is in it of good and bad in this world, and the separation between them in the other world. So prone is fallen man to sin, that if the enemy sow the tares, he may go his way, they will spring up, and do hurt; whereas, when good seed is sown, it must be tended, watered, and fenced. The servants complained to their master; Sir, didst thou not sow good seed in thy field? No doubt he did; whatever is amiss in the church, we are sure it is not from Christ. Though gross transgressors, and such as openly oppose the gospel, ought to be separated from the society of the faithful, yet no human skill can make an exact separation. Those who oppose must not be cut off, but instructed, and that with meekness. And though good and bad are together in this world, yet at the great day they shall be parted; then the righteous and the wicked shall be plainly known; here sometimes it is hard to distinguish between them. Let us, knowing the terrors of the Lord, not do iniquity. At death, believers shall shine forth to themselves; at the great day they shall shine forth before all the world. They shall shine by reflection, with light borrowed from the Fountain of light. Their sanctification will be made perfect, and their justification published. May we be found of that happy number.

during the past year, preached many times for ministers on this ground, that they could not live unless some preached a sermon and made a collection for them. In some places the population was so small that they could not maintain their minister, and in others it was a new movement, and therefore they were unable to support him.

And now, beloved, I have opened my mouth for the dumb, and pleaded the cause of the poor, let me end by entreating the poor of the flock to consider the poor man's Christ; let me urge them to give Him their thoughts, and may the Lord enable them to yield him their hearts. "He that believeth and is baptized shall be saved; but he that believeth not shall be damned."

May God bless the high and low, the rich and poor; yea, all of you, for his name's sake.

JESUS ONLY
Sermon number 924, delivered on Lord's-Day Morning, April 3rd, 1870, at the Metropolitan Tabernacle, Newington.

"And when they had lifted up their eyes, they saw no man, save Jesus only."—Matthew 17:8.

THIS MORNING, in trying to dwell upon the simple sight of "Jesus only," we shall hold it up as beyond measure important and delightful, and shall bear our witness that as it was said of Goliath's sword, "there is none like it," so may it be said of fellowship with "Jesus only." We shall first notice what might have happened to the disciples after the transfiguration; we shall then dwell on what did happen; and then, thirdly, we shall speak on what we anxiously desire may happen to those who hear us this day.

I. First, then, WHAT MIGHT HAVE HAPPENED to the three disciples after they had seen the transfiguration.

There were four things, either of which might have occurred. As a first supposition, they might have seen nobody with them on the holy mount; they might have found all gone but themselves. When the cloud had overshadowed them, and they were sore afraid, they might have lifted up their eyes and found the entire vision melted into thin air; no Moses, no Elias, and no Jesus. In such a case they would have been in a sorry plight, like those who having begun to taste of a banquet, suddenly find all the viands swept away; like thirsty men who have tasted the cooling crystal drops, and then seen the fountain dried up before their eyes. They would not have gone down the moun-

fold, some sixtyfold, some thirtyfold.

9 Who hath ears to hear, let him hear.

10 And the disciples came, and said unto him, Why speakest thou unto them in parables?

11 He answered and said unto them, Because it is given unto you to know the mysteries of the kingdom of heaven, but to them it is not given.

12 For whosoever hath, to him shall be given, and he shall have more abundance: but whosoever hath not, from him shall be taken away even that he hath.

13 Therefore speak I to them in parables: because they seeing see not; and hearing they hear not, neither do they understand.

14 And in them is fulfilled the prophecy of Esaias, which saith, By hearing ye shall hear, and shall not understand; and seeing ye shall see, and shall not perceive:

15 For this people's heart is waxed gross, and their ears are dull of hearing, and their eyes they have closed; lest at any time they should see with their eyes, and hear with their ears, and should understand with their heart, and should be converted, and I should heal them.

16 But blessed are your eyes, for they see: and your ears, for they hear.

17 For verily I say unto you, That many prophets and righteous men have desired to see those things which ye see, and have not seen them; and to hear those things which ye hear, and have not heard them.

18 Hear ye therefore the parable of the sower.

19 When any one heareth the word of the kingdom, and understandeth it not, then cometh the wicked one, and catcheth away that which was sown in his heart. This is he which received seed by the way side.

20 But he that received the seed into stony places, the same is he that heareth the word, and anon with joy receiveth it;

21 Yet hath he not root in himself, but dureth for a while: for when tribulation or persecution ariseth because of the word, by and by he is offended.

22 He also that received seed among the thorns is he that heareth the word; and the care of this world, and the deceitfulness of riches, choke the word, and he becometh unfruitful.

23 But he that received seed into the good ground is he that heareth the word, and understandeth it; which also beareth fruit, and bringeth forth, some

all the means of seeing, hearing, and understanding, they use none of them: they do not effectually see, or hear, or understand any thing.

14. Hearing ye will hear, but in nowise understand – That is, Ye will surely hear. All possible means will be given you: yet they will profit you nothing; because your heart is sensual, stupid, and insensible; your spiritual senses are shut up; yea, you have closed your eyes against the light; as being unwilling to understand the things of God, and afraid, not desirous that he should heal you. Isaiah vi, 9; John xii, 40; Acts xxviii, 26.

16. But blessed are your eyes – For you both see and understand. You know how to prize the light which is given you. Luke x, 23.

19. When any one heareth the word, and considereth it not – The first and most general cause of unfruitfulness. The wicked one cometh – Either inwardly; filling the mind with thoughts of other things; or by his agent. Such are all they that introduce other subjects, when men should be considering what they have heard.

20. The seed sown on stony places, therefore sprang up soon, because it did not sink deep, ver. 5. He receiveth it with joy – Perhaps with transport, with ecstasy: struck with the beauty of truth, and drawn by the preventing grace of God.

21. Yet hath he not root in himself – No deep work of grace: no change in the ground of his heart. Nay, he has no deep conviction; and without this, good desires soon wither away. He is offended – He finds a thousand plausible pretenses for leaving so narrow and rugged a way.

22. He that received the seed among the thorns, is he that heareth the word and considereth it – In spite of Satan and his agents: yea, hath root in himself, is deeply convinced, and in a great measure inwardly changed; so that he will not draw back, even when tribulation or persecution ariseth. And yet even in him, together with the good seed, the thorns spring up, ver. 7. (perhaps unperceived at first) till they gradually choke it, destroy all its life and power, and it becometh unfruitful. Cares are thorns to the poor: wealth to the rich; the desire of other things to all. The deceitfulness of riches – Deceitful indeed! for they smile, and betray: kiss, and smite into hell. They put out the eyes, harden the heart, steal away all the life of God; fill the soul with pride, anger, love of the world; make men enemies to the whole cross of Christ! And all the while are eagerly desired, and vehemently pursued, even by those who believe there is a God!

23. Some a hundred fold, some sixty, some thirty – That is, in various proportions; some abundantly more than others.

24. He proposed another parable – in which he farther explains the case of unfruitful hearers. The kingdom of heaven (as has been observed before) sometimes signifies eternal glory: sometimes the way to it, inward religion; sometimes, as here, the Gospel dispensation: the phrase is likewise used for a person or thing relating to any one of those: so in this place it means, Christ preaching the Gospel, who is like a man sowing good seed – The expression, is like, both here and in several other places, only means, that the thing spoken of may be illustrated by the following similitude. Who sowed good seed in his field – God sowed nothing but good in his whole creation. Christ sowed only the good seed of truth in his Church.

25. But while men slept – They ought to have watched: the Lord of the field sleepeth not. His enemy came and sowed darnel – This is very like wheat, and commonly grows among wheat rather than among other grain: but tares or vetches are of the pulse kind, and bear no resemblance to wheat.

31-35 See commentary at Mark 4:30-32; Luke 13: 18-21

44-52 Here are four parables.

1. That of the treasure hid in the field. Many slight the gospel, because they look only upon the surface of the field. But all who search the Scriptures, so as in them to find Christ and eternal life, Joh 5:39|, will discover such treasure in this field as makes it unspeakably valuable; they make it their own upon any terms. Though nothing can be given as a price for this salvation, yet much must be given up for the sake of it.

2. All the children of men are busy; one would be rich, another would be honorable, another would be learned; but most are deceived, and take up with counterfeits for pearls. Jesus Christ is a Pearl of great price; in having him, we have enough to make us happy here and for ever. A man may buy gold too dear, but not this Pearl of great price. When the convinced sinner sees Christ as the gracious Savior, all things else become worthless to his thoughts.

3. The world is a vast sea, and men, in their natural state, are like the fishes. Preaching the gospel is casting a net into this sea, to catch something out of it, for His glory who has the sovereignty of this sea. Hypocrites and true Christians shall be parted: miserable is the condition of those that shall then be cast away.

4. A skillful, faithful minister of the gospel, is a scribe, well versed in the things of the gospel, and able to teach them. Christ compares him to a good householder, who brings forth fruits of last year's growth and this year's gathering, abundance and variety, to entertain his friends. Old experiences and new observations, all have their use. Our place is at Christ's feet, and we must daily learn old lessons over again, and new ones also.

53-58 We have here Christ in his own country. He went about doing good, yet left not any place till he had finished his testimony there at that time. His own countrymen had rejected him once, yet he came to them again. Note, Christ does not take refusers at their first word, but repeats his offers to those who have often repulsed them. In this, as in other things, Christ was like his brethren; he had a natural affection to his own country; Patriam quisque amat, non quia pulchram, sed quia suam—Every one loves his country, not because it is beautiful, but because it is his own. Seneca. His treatment this time was much the same as before, scornful and spiteful. Observe, I. How they expressed their contempt of him. When he taught them in their synagogue, they were astonished; not that they were taken with his preaching, or admired his doctrine in itself, but only that it should be his; looking upon him as unlikely to be such a teacher. Two things they upbraided him with. 1. His want of academical education. They owned that he had wisdom, and did mighty works; but the question was, Whence he had

tainside that day asking questions and receiving instruction, for they would have had no teacher left them. They would have descended to face a multitude and to contend with a demon; not to conquer Satan, but to stand defeated by him before the crowd; for they would have had no champion to espouse their cause and drive out the evil spirit. They would have gone down among Scribes and Pharisees to be baffled with their knotty questions, and to be defeated by their sophistries, for they would have had no wise man, who spoke as never man spoke, to untie the knots and disentangle the snarls of controversy. They would have been like sheep without a shepherd, like orphan children left alone in the world. They would henceforth have reckoned it an unhappy day on which they saw the transfiguration; because having seen it, having been led to high thoughts by it, and excited to great expectations, all had disappeared like the foam upon the waters, and left no solid residuum behind. Alas! For those who have seen the image of the spirits of just men made perfect, and beheld the great Lord of all such spirits, and then have found themselves alone, and all the high companionship forever gone.

My dear brethren and sisters, there are some in this world and we ourselves have been among them, to whom something like this has actually occurred. You have been under a sermon, or at a gospel ordinance, or in reading the word of God, for a while delighted, exhilarated, lifted up to the sublimer regions, and then afterwards when it has all been over, there has been nothing left of joy or benefit, nothing left of all that was preached and for the moment enjoyed, nothing, at any rate, that you could take with you into the conflicts of every-day life. The whole has been a splendid vision and nothing more. There has been neither Moses not Elias, nor Jesus left. You did remember what you saw, but only with regret, because nothing remained with you. And, indeed, this which happens sometimes to us, is a general habit of that portion of this ungodly world which hears the gospel and perceives not its reality; it listens with respect to gospel histories as to legends of ancient times; it hears with reverence the stories of the days of miracles; it venerates the far-off ages and their heroic deeds, but it does not believe that anything is left of all the vision, any thing for today, for common life, and for common men. Moses it knows, and Elias it knows, and Christ it knows, as shadows that have passed across the scene and have disappeared, but it knows nothing of any one of these as abiding in permanent influence over the mind and the spirit of the present. All come and all gone, all to be reverenced, all to be respected,

an hundredfold, some sixty, some thirty.

24 Another parable put he forth unto them, saying, The kingdom of heaven is likened unto a man which sowed good seed in his field:

25 But while men slept, his enemy came and sowed tares among the wheat, and went his way.

26 But when the blade was sprung up, and brought forth fruit, then appeared the tares also.

27 So the servants of the householder came and said unto him, Sir, didst not thou sow good seed in thy field? from whence then hath it tares?

28 He said unto them, An enemy hath done this. The servants said unto him, Wilt thou then that we go and gather them up?

29 But he said, Nay; lest while ye gather up the tares, ye root up also the wheat with them.

30 Let both grow together until the harvest: and in the time of harvest I will say to the reapers, Gather ye together first the tares, and bind them in bundles to burn them: but gather the wheat into my barn.

31 Another parable put he forth unto them, saying, The kingdom of heaven is like to a grain of mustard seed, which a man took, and sowed in his field:

32 Which indeed is the least of all seeds: but when it is grown, it is the greatest among herbs, and becometh a tree, so that the birds of the air come and lodge in the branches thereof.

33 Another parable spake he unto them; The kingdom of heaven is like unto leaven, which a woman took, and hid in three measures of meal, till the whole was leavened.

34 All these things spake Jesus unto the multitude in parables; and without a parable spake he not unto them:

35 That it might be fulfilled which was spoken by the prophet, saying, I will open my mouth in parables; I will utter things which have been kept secret from the foundation of the world.

36 Then Jesus sent the multitude away, and went into the house: and his disciples came unto him, saying, Declare unto us the parable of the tares of the field.

37 He answered and said unto them, He that soweth the good seed is the Son of man;

38 The field is the world; the good seed are the children of the kingdom; but the tares are the children of the wicked one;

39 The enemy that sowed them is the devil; the harvest is the end of the world; and the reapers are the angels.

40 As therefore the tares are gathered

26. When the blade was sprung up, then appeared the darnel – It was not discerned before: it seldom appears, as soon as the good seed is sown: all at first appears to be peace, and love, and joy.

27. Didst not thou sow good seed in thy field? Whence then hath it darnel? – Not from the parent of good. Even the heathen could say, "No evil can from thee proceed: 'Tis only suffer'd, not decreed: As darkness is not from the sun, Nor mount the shades, till he is gone."

28. He said, An enemy hath done this – A plain answer to the great question concerning the origin of evil. God made men (as he did angels) intelligent creatures, and consequently free either to choose good or evil: but he implanted no evil in the human soul: An enemy (with man's concurrence) hath done this. Darnel, in the Church, is properly outside Christians, such as have the form of godliness, without the power. Open sinners, such as have neither the form nor the power, are not so properly darnel, as thistles and brambles: these ought to be rooted up without delay, and not suffered in the Christian community. Whereas should fallible men attempt to gather up the darnel, they would often root up the wheat with them.

31. He proposed to them another parable – The former parables relate chiefly to unfruitful hearers; these that follow, to those who bear good fruit. The kingdom of heaven – Both the Gospel dispensation, and the inward kingdom. Mark iv, 30; Luke xiii, 18.

32. The least – That is, one of the least: a way of speaking extremely common among the Jews. It becometh a tree – In those countries it grows exceeding large and high. So will the Christian doctrine spread in the world, and the life of Christ in the soul.

33. Three measures – This was the quantity which they usually baked at once: till the whole was leavened – Thus will the Gospel leaven the world and grace the Christian. Luke xiii, 20.

34. Without a parable spake he not unto them – That is, not at that time; at other times he did.

35. Psalm lxxviii, 2.

38. The good seed are the children of the kingdom – That is, the children of God, the righteous.

41. They shall gather all things that offend – Whatever had hindered or grieved the children of God; whatever things or persons had hindered the good seed which Christ had sown from taking root or bearing fruit. The Greek word is, All scandals.

44. The three following parables are proposed, not to the multitude, but peculiarly to the apostles: the two former of them relate to those who receive the Gospel; the third, both to those who receive, and those who preach it. The kingdom of heaven is like treasure hid in a field – The kingdom of God within us is a treasure indeed, but a treasure hid from the world, and from the most wise and prudent in it. He that finds this treasure, (perhaps when he thought it far from him,) hides it deep in his heart, and gives up all other happiness for it.

45. The kingdom of heaven – That is, one who earnestly seeks for it: in verse 47 it means, the Gospel preached, which is like a net gathering of every kind: just so the Gospel, wherever it is preached, gathers at first both good and bad, who are for a season full of approbation and warm with good desires. But Christian discipline, and strong, close exhortation, begin that separation in this world, which shall be accomplished by the angels of God in the world to come.

52. Every scribe instructed unto the kingdom of heaven – That is, every duly prepared preacher of the Gospel has a treasure of Divine knowledge, out of which he is able to bring forth all sorts of

them: for they knew that he was not brought up at the feet of the rabbin: he had never been at the university, nor taken his degree, nor was called of men, Rabbi, Rabbi. Note, Mean and prejudiced spirits are apt to judge of men by their education, and to inquire more into their rise than into their reasons. "Whence has this man these mighty works? Did he come honestly by them? Has he not been studying the black art?" Thus they turned that against him which was really for him; for if they had not been wilfully blind, they must have concluded him to be divinely assisted and commissioned, who without the help of education gave such proofs of extraordinary wisdom and power. 2. The meanness and poverty of his relations, v. 55, 56. (1.) They upbraid him with his father. Is not this the carpenter's son? Yes, it is true he was reputed so: and what harm in that? No disparagement to him to be the son of an honest tradesman. They remember not (though they might have known it) that this carpenter was of the house of David (Lu. 1:27), a son of David (ch. 1:20); though a carpenter, yet a person of honor. Those who are willing to pick quarrels will overlook that which is worthy and deserving, and fasten upon that only which seems mean. Some sordid spirits regard no branch, no not the Branch from the stem of Jesse (Isa. 11:1), if it be not the top branch. (2.) They upbraid him with his mother; and what quarrel have they with her? Why, truly, his mother is called Mary, and that was a very common name, and they all knew her, and knew her to be an ordinary person; she was called Mary, not Queen Mary, nor Lady Mary, nor so much as Mistress Mary, but plain Mary; and this is turned to his reproach, as if men had nothing to be valued by but foreign extraction, noble birth, or splendid titles; poor things to measure worth by. (3.) They upbraid him with his brethren, whose names they knew, and had them ready enough to serve this turn; James, and Joses, and Simon, and Judas, good men but poor men, and therefore despised; and Christ for their sakes. These brethren, it is probable, were Joseph's children by a former wife; or whatever their relation was to him, they seem to have been brought up with him in the same family. And therefore of the calling of three of these, who were of the twelve, to that honor (James, Simon, and Jude, the same with Thaddeus), we read not particularly, because they needed not such an express call into acquaintance with Christ who had been the companions of his youth. (4.) His sisters too are all with us; they should therefore have loved him and respected him the more, because he was one of themselves, but therefore they despised him. They were offended in him: they stumbled at these stumbling-stones, for he was set for a sign that should be spoken against, Lu. 2:34; Isa. 8:14. II. See how he resented this contempt, v. 57, 58. 1. It did not trouble his heart. It appears he was not much concerned at it; he despised the shame, Heb. 12:2. Instead of aggravating the affront, or expressing an offense at it, or returning such an answer to their foolish suggestions as they deserved, he mildly

but nothing more; there is nothing left, so far as they are concerned, to influence or bless the present hour. Jesus and his gospel have come and gone, and we may very properly recollect the fact, but according to certain sages there is nothing in the New Testament to affect this advanced age, this enlightened nineteenth century; we have got beyond all that. Ah! Brethren, let those who can be content to do so, put up with this worship of moral relics and spiritual phantoms; to us it would be wretchedness itself. We, on the other hand, say, blessing the name of the Lord that we can say it, that there abides with us our Lord Jesus. At this day he is with us, and will be with us even to the end of the world. Christ's existence is not a fact confined to antiquity or to remote distance. By his Spirit he is actually in his church; we have seen him, though not with eyes; we have heard him, though not with ears; we have grasped him, though not with hands; and we feed upon his flesh, which is meat indeed, and his blood, which is drink indeed. We have with us at this very day Jesus our friend, to whom we make known our secrets, and who beareth all our sorrows. We have Jesus our interpreting instructor, who still reveals his secrets to us, and leads us into the mind and name of God. We have Jesus still with us to supply us with strength, and in his power we still are mighty. We confess his reigning sovereignty in the church, and we receive his all-sufficient succors. The church is not decapitated, her Head abides in vital union with her; Jesus is no myth to us, whatever he may be to others; he is no departed shade, he is no heroic personification: in very deed there is a Christ, and though others see him not, and even we with these eyes see him not, yet in him believing we rejoice with joy unspeakable and full of glory. Oh, I trust it will never be so with us, that as we go about our life work our religion shall melt into fiction and become nothing but mere sentiment, nothing but thought, and dream, and vision; but may our religion be a matter of fact, a walking with the living and abiding Savior. Though Moses may be gone, and Elias may be gone, yet Jesus Christ abideth with us and in us, and we in him, and so shall it be evermore.

Now, there was a second thing that might have happened to the disciples. When they lifted up their eyes they might have seen Moses only. It would certainly have been a very sad exchange for what they did see, to have seen Moses only. The face of Moses would have shone, his person would have awed them, and it would have been no mean thing for men of humble origin like themselves to walk down the mountain with that mighty king in Jeshurun,

and burned in the fire; so shall it be in the end of this world.

41 The Son of man shall send forth his angels, and they shall gather out of his kingdom all things that offend, and them which do iniquity;

42 And shall cast them into a furnace of fire: there shall be wailing and gnashing of teeth.

43 Then shall the righteous shine forth as the sun in the kingdom of their Father. Who hath ears to hear, let him hear.

44 Again, the kingdom of heaven is like unto treasure hid in a field; the which when a man hath found, he hideth, and for joy thereof goeth and selleth all that he hath, and buyeth that field.

45 Again, the kingdom of heaven is like unto a merchant man, seeking goodly pearls:

46 Who, when he had found one pearl of great price, went and sold all that he had, and bought it.

47 Again, the kingdom of heaven is like unto a net, that was cast into the sea, and gathered of every kind:

48 Which, when it was full, they drew to shore, and sat down, and gathered the good into vessels, but cast the bad away.

49 So shall it be at the end of the world: the angels shall come forth, and sever the wicked from among the just,

50 And shall cast them into the furnace of fire: there shall be wailing and gnashing of teeth.

51 Jesus saith unto them, Have ye understood all these things? They say unto him, Yea, Lord.

52 Then said he unto them, Therefore every scribe which is instructed unto the kingdom of heaven is like unto a man that is an householder, which bringeth forth out of his treasure things new and old.

53 And it came to pass, that when Jesus had finished these parables, he departed thence.

54 And when he was come into his own country, he taught them in their synagogue, insomuch that they were astonished, and said, Whence hath this man this wisdom, and these mighty works?

55 Is not this the carpenter's son? is not his mother called Mary? and his brethren, James, and Joses, and Simon, and Judas?

56 And his sisters, are they not all with us? Whence then hath this man all these things?

57 And they were offended in him. But Jesus said unto them, A prophet is not without honor, save in his own country,

instructions. The word treasure signifies any collection of things whatsoever, and the places where such collections are kept.

53. He departed thence – He crossed the lake from Capernaum: and came once more into his own country – Nazareth: but with no better success than he had had there before.

54. Whence hath HE – Many texts are not understood, for want of knowing the proper emphasis; and others are utterly misunderstood, by placing the emphasis wrong. To prevent this in some measure, the emphatic words are here printed in capital letters. Mark vi, 1; Luke iv, 16, 22.

55. The carpenter's son – The Greek word means, one that works either in wood, iron, or stone. His brethren – Our kinsmen. They were the sons of Mary, sister to the virgin, and wife of Cleophas or Alpheus. James – Styled by St. Paul also, the Lord's brother, Gal. i, 19. Simon – Surnamed the Canaanite.

57. They were offended at him – They looked on him as a mean, ignoble man, not worthy to be regarded. John iv, 44; Luke vii, 23.

58. He wrought not many mighty works, because of their unbelief – And the reason why many mighty works are not wrought now, is not, that the faith is not every where planted; but, that unbelief every where prevails.

MATTHEW 14

1. At that time – When our Lord had spent about a year in his public ministry. Tetrarch – King of a fourth part of his father's dominions. ["And king Herod heard of him; (for his name was spread abroad:) and he said, That John the Baptist was risen from the dead, and therefore mighty works do shew forth themselves in him." Mark vi, 14.]

2. He is risen from the dead – Herod was a Sadducee: and the Sadducees denied the resurrection of the dead. But Sadduceeism staggers when conscience awakes.

3. His brother Philip's wife – Who was still alive. ["For Herod himself had sent forth and laid hold upon John, and bound him in prison for Herodias' sake, his brother Philip's wife: for he had married her." Mark vi, 17.]

4. It is not lawful for thee to have her – It was not lawful indeed for either of them to have her. For her father Aristobulus was their own brother. John's words were rough, like his raiment. He would not break the force of truth by using soft words, even to a king.

5. He would have put him to death – in his fit of passion; but he was then restrained by fear of the multitude; and afterward by the reverence he bore him.

6. The daughter of Herodias – Afterward infamous for a life suitable to this beginning.

8. Being before instructed by her mother – Both as to the matter and manner of her petition: She said, Give me here – Fearing if he had time to consider, he would not do it: John the Baptist's head in a charger – A large dish or bowl.

9. And the king was sorry – Knowing that John was a good man. Yet for the oath's sake – So he murdered an innocent man from mere tenderness of conscience.

10. And he sent and beheaded John in the prison, and his head was given to the damsel – How mysterious is the providence, which left the life of so holy a man in such infamous hands! which permitted it to be sacrificed to the malice of an abandoned harlot, the petulancy of a vain

imputes it to the common humour of the children of men, to undervalue excellences that are cheap, and common, and home-bred. It is usually so. A prophet is not without honor, save in his own country. Note, (1.) Prophets should have honor paid them, and commonly have; men of God are great men, and men of honor, and challenge respect. It is strange indeed if prophets have not honor. (2.) Notwithstanding this, they are commonly least regarded and reverenced in their own country, nay, and sometimes are most envied. Familiarity breeds contempt. 2. It did for the present (to speak with reverence), in effect, tie his hands: He did not many mighty works there, because of their unbelief. Note, Unbelief is the great obstruction to Christ's favors. All things are in general possible to God (ch. 19:26), but then it is to him that believes as to the particulars, Mk. 9:23. The gospel is the power of God unto salvation, but then it is to every one that believes, Rom. 1:16. So that if mighty works be not wrought in us, it is not for want of power or grace in Christ, but for want of faith in us. By grace ye are saved, and that is a mighty work, but it is through faith, Eph. 2:8.

MATTHEW 14

Death of John the Baptist. (1-12)
Five thousand people miraculously fed. (13-21)
Jesus walks upon the sea. (22-33)
Jesus healing the sick. (34-36)

1-12 The terror and reproach of conscience, which Herod, like other daring offenders, could not shake off, are proofs and warnings of a future judgment, and of future misery to them. But there may be the terror of convictions, where there is not the truth of conversion. When men pretend to favor the gospel, yet live in evil, we must not favor their self-delusion, but must deliver our consciences as John did. The world may call this rudeness and blind zeal. False professors, or timid Christians, may censure it as want of civility; but the most powerful enemies can go no further than the Lord sees good to permit. Herod feared that the putting of John to death might raise a rebellion among the people, which it did not; but he never feared it might stir up his own conscience against him, which it did. Men fear being hanged for what they do not fear being damned for. And times of carnal mirth and jollity are convenient times for carrying on bad designs against God's people. Herod would profusely reward a worthless dance, while imprisonment and death were the recompense of the man of God who sought the salvation of his soul. But there was real malice to John beneath his consent, or else Herod would have found ways to get clear of his promise. When the under shepherds are smitten, the sheep need not be scattered while they have the Great Shepherd to go to. And it is better to be drawn to Christ by want and loss, than not to come to him at all.

who had spoken with God face to face, and rested with him in solemn conclave by the space of forty days at a time. But yet who would exchange the sun for the moon? Who would exchange the cold moonbeams of Moses and the law for the sunny rays of the Savior's divine affection? It would have been an unhappy exchange for them to have lost their Master whose name is love, and to have found a leader in the man whose name is synonymous with law. Moses, the man of God, cannot be compared with Jesus, the Son of God. Yet dear brethren, there are some who see Moses only. After all the gospel preaching that there has been in the world, and the declaration of the precious doctrines of grace every Sabbath day; after the clear revelations of Scripture, and the work of the Holy Spirit in men's hearts; yet we have among us some who persist in seeing nothing but Moses only. I mean this, there are some who will see nothing but shadows still, mere shadows still. As I read my Bible I see there that the age of the symbolical, the typical, the pictorial, has passed away. I am glad of the symbols, and types, and pictures, for they remain instructive to me; but the age in which they were in the foreground has given way to a clearer light, and they are gone forever. There are, however, certain persons who profess to read the Bible and to see very differently, and they set up a new system of types and shadows—a system, let me say, ridiculous to men of sense, and obnoxious to men of spiritual taste. Blessed be God, we have not so learned Christ. We see something better than Moses only.

There are too many who see Moses only, inasmuch as they see nothing but law, nothing but duty and precept in the Bible. I know that some here, though we have tried to preach Christ crucified as their only hope, yet whenever they read the Bible, or hear the Gospel, feel nothing except a sense of their own sinfulness, and, arising out of that sense of sinfulness, a desire to work out a righteousness of their own. They are continually measuring themselves by the law of God, they feel their shortcomings, they mourn over their transgressions, but they go no further. I am glad that they see Moses, may the stern voice of the lawgiver drive them to the law fulfiller; but I grieve that they tarry so long in legal servitude, which can only bring them sorrow and dismay. The sight of Sinai, what is it but despair? God revealed in flaming fire, and proclaiming with thunder his fiery law, what is there here to save the soul? To see the Lord who will by no means spare the guilty, but will surely visit transgression with eternal vengeance, is a sight which never should eclipse Calvary, where love makes recompense to jus-

and in his own house.

58 And he did not many mighty works there because of their unbelief.

MATTHEW 14

1 At that time Herod the tetrarch heard of the fame of Jesus,

2 And said unto his servants, This is John the Baptist; he is risen from the dead; and therefore mighty works do shew forth themselves in him.

3 For Herod had laid hold on John, and bound him, and put him in prison for Herodias' sake, his brother Philip's wife.

4 For John said unto him, It is not lawful for thee to have her.

5 And when he would have put him to death, he feared the multitude, because they counted him as a prophet.

6 But when Herod's birthday was kept, the daughter of Herodias danced before them, and pleased Herod.

7 Whereupon he promised with an oath to give her whatsoever she would ask.

8 And she, being before instructed of her mother, said, Give me here John Baptist's head in a charger.

9 And the king was sorry: nevertheless for the oath's sake, and them which sat with him at meat, he commanded it to be given her.

10 And he sent, and beheaded John in the prison.

11 And his head was brought in a charger, and given to the damsel: and she brought it to her mother.

12 And his disciples came, and took up the body, and buried it, and went and told Jesus.

13 When Jesus heard of it, he departed thence by ship into a desert place apart: and when the people had heard thereof, they followed him on foot out of the cities.

14 And Jesus went forth, and saw a great multitude, and was moved with compassion toward them, and he healed their sick.

15 And when it was evening, his disciples came to him, saying, This is a desert place, and the time is now past; send the multitude away, that they may go into the villages, and buy themselves victuals.

16 But Jesus said unto them, They need not depart; give ye them to eat.

17 And they say unto him, We have here but five loaves, and two fishes.

18 He said, Bring them hither to me.

19 And he commanded the multitude to sit down on the grass, and took the five loaves, and the two fishes, and looking up to heaven, he blessed, and brake, and gave the loaves to his disciples, and

girl, and the rashness of a foolish, perhaps drunken prince, who made a prophet's head the reward of a dance! But we are sure the Almighty will repay his servants in another world for what ever they suffer in this.

13. Jesus withdrew into a desert place –

1. To avoid Herod:

2. Because of the multitude pressing upon him, ["And they departed into a desert place by ship privately."

Mark vi, xxxii,] and

3. To talk with his disciples, newly returned from their progress, Luke ix, x, apart – From all but his disciples. [" After these things Jesus went over the sea of Galilee, which is the sea of Tiberias." John vi, 1.]

15. The time is now past – The usual meal time. ["And when the day was now far spent, his disciples came unto him, and said, This is a desert place, and now the time is far passed:" Mark vi, 35; "And when the day began to wear away, then came the twelve, and said unto him, Send the multitude away, that they may go into the towns and country round about, and lodge, and get victuals: for we are here in a desert place." Luke ix, 12]

22. He constrained his disciples – Who were unwilling to leave him. ["And straightway he constrained his disciples to get into the ship, and to go to the other side before unto Bethsaida, while he sent away the people." And straightway he constrained his disciples to get into the ship, and to go to the other side before unto Bethsaida, while he sent away the people." And straightway he constrained his disciples to get into the ship, and to go to the other side before unto Bethsaida, while he sent away the people." Mark vi:45; "When Jesus therefore perceived that they would come and take him by force, to make him a king, he departed again into a mountain himself alone." John vi, 15.]

24. In the evening – Learned men say the Jews reckoned two evenings; the first beginning at three in the afternoon, the second, at sunset. If so, the latter is meant here.

25. The fourth watch – The Jews (as well as the Romans) usually divided the night into four watches, of three hours each. The first watch began at six, the second at nine, the third at twelve, the fourth at three in the morning. If it be thou – It is the same as, Since it is thou. The particle if frequently bears this meaning, both in ours and in all languages. So it means, [" If I then, your Lord and Master, have washed your feet; ye also ought to wash one another's feet. . . . If ye know these things, happy are ye if ye do them." John xiii, 14, 17.] St. Peter was in no doubt, or he would not have quitted the ship.

30. He was afraid – Though he had been used to the sea, and was a skillful swimmer. But so it frequently is. When grace begins to act, the natural courage and strength are withdrawn.

33. Thou art the Son of God – They mean, the Messiah.

35. Mark vi, 45.

MATTHEW 15

1. ["Then came together unto him the Pharisees, and certain of the scribes, which came from Jerusalem." Mark vii, 1.]

2. The elders – The chief doctors or, teachers among the Jews.

3. They wash not their hands when they eat bread – Food in general is termed bread in Hebrew; so that to eat bread is the same as to make a meal.

4. Honor thy father and mother – Which implies all such relief as they

13-21 See commentary at Mark 6:32-44; Luke 9: 10-17; John 6:1-13

22-33 See commentary at Mark 6:45-56; John 6: 15-21

34-36 We have here an account of miracles by wholesale, which Christ wrought on the other side of the water, in the land of Gennesaret. Whithersoever Christ went, he was doing good. Gennesaret was a tract of land that lay between Bethsaida and Capernaum, and either gave the name to, or took the name from, this sea, which is called (Lu. 5:1) The Lake of Gennesaret; it signifies the valley of branches. Observe here,

I. The forwardness and faith of the men of that place. These were more noble than the Gergesenes, their neighbors, who were borderers upon the same lake. Those besought Christ to depart from them, they had no occasion for him; these besought him to help them, they had need of him. Christ reckons it the greatest honor we can do him, to make use of him. Now here we are told,

1. How the men of that place were brought to Christ; they had knowledge of him. It is probable that his miraculous passage over the sea, which they that were in the ship would industriously spread the report of, might help to make way for his entertainment in those parts; and perhaps it was one thing Christ intended in it, for he has great reaches in what he does. This they had knowledge of, and of the other miracles Christ had wrought, and therefore they flocked to him. Note, They that know Christ's name, will make their application to him: if Christ were better known, he would not be neglected as he is; he is trusted as far as he is known. They had knowledge of him, that is, of his being among them, and that he would be put awhile among them. Note, The discerning of the day of our opportunities is a good step toward the improvement of it.

2. How they brought others to Christ, by giving notice to their neighbors of Christ's being come into those parts; They sent out into all that country. Note, those that have got the knowledge of Christ themselves, should do all they can to bring others acquainted with him too. We must not eat these spiritual morsels alone; there is in Christ enough for us all, so that there is nothing got by monopolizing. When we have opportunities of getting good to our souls, we should bring as many as we can to share with us. More than we think of would close with opportunities, if they were but called upon and invited to them. They sent into their own country, because it was their own, and they desired the welfare of it.

3. What their business was with Christ; not only, perhaps not chiefly, if at all, to be taught, but to have their sick healed; They brought unto him all that were diseased. If love to Christ and his doctrine will not bring them to him, yet self-love would. Did we but

tice. O that you may get beyond the mount that might be touched, and come to Calvary, where God in vengeance is clearly seen, but where God in mercy fills the throne. Oh how blessed is it to escape from the voice of command and threatening and come to the blood of sprinkling, where "Jesus only" speaketh better things!

Moses only, however, has become a sight very common with some of you who write bitter things against yourselves. You never read the Scriptures or hear the gospel without feeling condemned. You know your duty, and confess how short you have fallen of it, and therefore you abide under conscious condemnation, and will not come to him who is the propitiation for your sins. Alas, that there should be so many who with strange perversity of unbelief twist every promise into a threatening, and out of every gracious word that drips with honey manage to extract gall and wormwood. They see the dark shadow of Moses only; the broken tablets of the law, the smoking mount, and the terrible trumpet are ever with them, and over all an angry God. They had a better vision once, they have it sometimes now; for now and then under the preaching of the gospel they have glimpses of hope and mercy, but they relapse into darkness, they fall again into despair, because they have chosen to see Moses only. I pray that a change may come over the spirit of their dream, and that yet like the apostles they may see "Jesus only."

But, my brethren, there was a third alternative that might have happened to the disciples, they might have seen Elijah only. Instead of the gentle Savior, they might have been standing at the side of the rough clad and the stern-spirited Elias. Instead of the Lamb of God, there might have remained to them only the lion who roared like the voice of God's own majesty in the midst of sinful Israel. In such a case, with such a leader, they would have gone down from the mount, and I wot that if John had said, "Command fire from heaven," Elias would have consumed his foes; the Pharisees, like the priests of Baal, would have found a speedy end; Herod's blood, like Ahab's, would have been licked up by dogs; and Herodias, like another Jezebel, would have been devoured of the same. But all this power for vengeance would have been a poor exchange for the gracious omnipotence of the Friend of sinners. Who would prefer the slayer of the priests to the Savior of men? The top of Carmel was glorious when its intercession brought the rain for Israel, but how poor it is compared with Gethsemane, whose pleadings bring eternal life to millions! In company with Jesus we are at Elim beneath the palm tree, but with Elias we are in the

the disciples to the multitude.

20 And they did all eat, and were filled: and they took up of the fragments that remained twelve baskets full.

21 And they that had eaten were about five thousand men, beside women and children.

22 And straightway Jesus constrained his disciples to get into a ship, and to go before him unto the other side, while he sent the multitudes away.

23 And when he had sent the multitudes away, he went up into a mountain apart to pray: and when the evening was come, he was there alone.

24 But the ship was now in the midst of the sea, tossed with waves: for the wind was contrary.

25 And in the fourth watch of the night Jesus went unto them, walking on the sea.

26 And when the disciples saw him walking on the sea, they were troubled, saying, It is a spirit; and they cried out for fear.

27 But straightway Jesus spake unto them, saying, Be of good cheer; it is I; be not afraid.

28 And Peter answered him and said, Lord, if it be thou, bid me come unto thee on the water.

29 And he said, Come. And when Peter was come down out of the ship, he walked on the water, to go to Jesus.

30 But when he saw the wind boisterous, he was afraid; and beginning to sink, he cried, saying, Lord, save me.

31 And immediately Jesus stretched forth his hand, and caught him, and said unto him, O thou of little faith, wherefore didst thou doubt?

32 And when they were come into the ship, the wind ceased.

33 Then they that were in the ship came and worshiped him, saying, Of a truth thou art the Son of God.

34 And when they were gone over, they came into the land of Gennesaret.

35 And when the men of that place had knowledge of him, they sent out into all that country round about, and brought unto him all that were diseased;

36 And besought him that they might only touch the hem of his garment: and as many as touched were made perfectly whole.

MATTHEW 15

1 Then came to Jesus scribes and Pharisees, which were of Jerusalem, saying,

2 Why do thy disciples transgress the tradition of the elders? for they wash

stand in need of. ["Honor thy father and thy mother: that thy days may be long upon the land which the LORD thy God giveth thee. "Exod. xx, 12; "And he that curseth his father, or his mother, shall surely be put to death." Exod. xxi, 17.]

5. It is a gift by whatsoever thou mightest have been profited by me – That is, I have given, or at least, purpose to give to the treasury of the temple, what you might otherwise have had from me.

7. Well did Isaiah prophesy of you, saying – That is, the description which Isaiah gave of your fathers, is exactly applicable to you. The words therefore which were a description of them, are a prophecy with regard to you.

8. Their heart is far from me – And without this all outward worship is mere mockery of God. I["Wherefore the Lord said, Forasmuch as this people draw near me with their mouth, and with their lips do honor me, but have removed their heart far from me, and their fear toward me is taught by the precept of men:" Isaiah xxix, 13.]

9. Teaching the commandments of men – As equal with, nay, superior to, those of God. What can be a more heinous sin?

13. Every plant – That is, every doctrine.

14. Let them alone – If they are indeed blind leaders of the blind; let them alone: concern not yourselves about them: a plain direction how to behave with regard to all such. ["And he spake a parable unto them, Can the blind lead the blind? shall they not both fall into the ditch?" Luke vi, 39.]

17. Are ye also yet without understanding – How fair and candid are the sacred historians? Never concealing or excusing their own blemishes.

19. First evil thoughts – then murders – and the rest. Railings – The Greek word includes all reviling, backbiting, and evil speaking.

21. ["And from thence he arose, and went into the borders of Tyre and Sidon, and entered into an house, and would have no man know it: but he could not be hid." Mark vii, 24.]

22. A woman of Canaan – Canaan was also called Syrophenicia, as lying between Syria properly so called, and Phenicia, by the sea side. Cried to him – From afar, Thou Son of David – So she had some knowledge of the promised Messiah.

23. He answered her not a word – He sometimes tries our faith in like manner.

24. I am not sent – Not primarily; not yet.

25. Then came she – Into the house where he now was.

28. Thy faith – Thy reliance on the power and goodness of God.

29. The sea of Galilee – The Jews gave the name of seas to all large lakes. This was a hundred furlongs long, and forty broad. It was called also, the sea of Tiberias. It lay on the borders of Galilee, and the city of Tiberias stood on its western shore. It was likewise styled the lake of Gennesareth: perhaps a corruption of Cinnereth, the name by which it was anciently called, ["And the coast shall go down from Shepham to Riblah, on the east side of Ain; and the border shall descend, and shall reach unto the side of the sea of Chinnereth eastward: "Num. xxxiv, 11. "And again, departing from the coasts of Tyre and Sidon, he came unto the sea of Galilee, through the midst of the coasts of Decapolis." Mark vii, 31.]

32. They continue with me now three days – It was now the third day since they came. ["In those days the multitude being very great, and having nothing to eat, Jesus called his disciples unto him, and saith unto them," Mark viii, 1.]

rightly seek our own things, the things of our own peace and welfare, we should seek the things of Christ. We should do him honor, and please him, by deriving grace and righteousness from him. Note, Christ is the proper Person to bring the diseased to; whither should they go but to the Physician, to the Sun of Righteousness, that hath healing under his wings?

4. How they made their application to him; They besought him that they might only touch the hem of his garment, v. 36. They applied themselves to him, (1.) With great importunity; they besought him. Well may we beseech to be healed, when God by his ministers beseecheth us that we will be healed. (2.) With great humility; they came to him as those that were sensible of their distance, humbly beseeching him to help them; and their desiring to touch the hem of his garment, intimates that they thought themselves unworthy that he should take any particular notice of them, that he should so much as speak to their case, much less touch them for their cure; but they will look upon it as a great favor, if he will give them leave to touch the hem of his garment. The eastern nations show respect to their princes, by kissing their sleeve, or skirt. (3.) With great assurance of the all-sufficiency of his power, not doubting but that they should be healed, even by touching the hem of his garment; that they should receive abundant communications from him by the smallest token of symbol of communion with him. They did not expect the formality of striking his hand over the place or persons diseased, as Naaman did (2 Ki. 5:11); but they were sure that there was in him such an overflowing fullness of healing virtue, that they could not fail of a cure, who were but admitted near him. It was in this country and neighborhood that the woman with the bloody issue was cured by touching the hem of his garment, and was commended for her faith (ch. 9:20–22); and thence, probably, they took occasion to ask this.

II. The fruit and success of this their application to Christ. It was not in vain that these seed of Jacob sough him, for as many as touched, were made perfectly whole. It is but thus touching, and we are made whole. On such easy terms are spiritual cures offered by him, that he may truly be said to heal freely; so that if our souls die of their wounds, it is not owing to our Physician, it is not for want of skill or will in him; but it is purely owing to ourselves. He could have healed us, he would have healed us, but we would not be healed; so that our blood will lie upon our own heads.

MATTHEW 15

Jesus discourses about human traditions. (1-9)

He warns against things which really defile. (10-20)

He heals the daughter of a Syrophenician woman. (21-28)

Jesus heals the sick, and miraculously feeds four thousand. (29-39)

wilderness beneath the stunted juniper. Who would exchange the excellency of Olivet for the terrors of Horeb? Yet I fear there are many who see Elias only. Prophecies of future woe fascinate them rather than thoughts of present salvation. Their souls are rent and torn by Elijah's challenge, "If the Lord be God, follow him: but if Baal, then follow him;" but they remain still halting between two opinions, trembling before Elias and not rejoicing before the Savior. Unhappy men and women, so near the kingdom, and yet out of it; so near the feast, and yet perishing for want of the living bread. The word is near you (ah, how near!), and yet you receive it not. Remember, I pray you, that merely to prepare for a Savior is not to be saved; that to have a sense of sin is not the same thing as being pardoned. Your repentance, unless you also believe in Jesus, is a repentance that needs to be repented of. At the girdle of John the Baptist the keys of heaven did never hang; Elias is not the door of salvation; preparation for Christ is not Christ, despair is not regeneration, doubt is not repentance. Only by faith in Jesus can you be saved, but complaining of yourselves is not faith. "Jesus only" is the way, the truth, and the life. "Jesus only" is the sinner's Savior. O that your eyes may be opened, not to see Elias, not to see Moses, but to see "Jesus only."

You see, then, these three alternatives, but there was also another: a fourth thing might have happened when the disciples opened their eyes—they might have seen Moses and Elias with Jesus, even as in the transfiguration. At first sight it seems as if this would have been superior to that which they did enjoy. To walk down the mountain with that blessed trio, how great a privilege! How strong might they have been for the accomplishment of the divine purposes! Moses could preach the law and make men tremble, and then Jesus could follow with his gospel of grace and truth. Elias could flash the thunderbolt in their faces, and then Christ could have uplifted the humble spirits. Would not the contrast have been delightful, and the connection inspiriting? Would not the assemblage of such divers kinds of forces have contributed to the greatest success? I think not. It is a vastly better thing to see "Jesus only," as a matter of perpetuity, than to see Moses and Elias with Jesus. It is night, I know it, for I see the moon and stars. The morning cometh, I know it cometh, for I see no longer many stars, only one remains, and that the morning star. But the full day has arrived, I know it has, for I cannot even see the morning star; all those guardians and comforters of the night have disappeared; I see the sun only. Now, inasmuch as every man prefers the moon to midnight and to the twi-

not their hands when they eat bread.

3 But he answered and said unto them, Why do ye also transgress the commandment of God by your tradition?

4 For God commanded, saying, Honor thy father and mother: and, He that curseth father or mother, let him die the death.

5 But ye say, Whosoever shall say to his father or his mother, It is a gift, by whatsoever thou mightest be profited by me;

6 And honor not his father or his mother, he shall be free. Thus have ye made the commandment of God of none effect by your tradition.

7 Ye hypocrites, well did Esaias prophesy of you, saying,

8 This people draweth nigh unto me with their mouth, and honoreth me with their lips; but their heart is far from me.

9 But in vain they do worship me, teaching for doctrines the commandments of men.

10 And he called the multitude, and said unto them, Hear, and understand:

11 Not that which goeth into the mouth defileth a man; but that which cometh out of the mouth, this defileth a man.

12 Then came his disciples, and said unto him, Knowest thou that the Pharisees were offended, after they heard this saying?

13 But he answered and said, Every plant, which my heavenly Father hath not planted, shall be rooted up.

14 Let them alone: they be blind leaders of the blind. And if the blind lead the blind, both shall fall into the ditch.

15 Then answered Peter and said unto him, Declare unto us this parable.

16 And Jesus said, Are ye also yet without understanding?

17 Do not ye yet understand, that whatsoever entereth in at the mouth goeth into the belly, and is cast out into the draught?

18 But those things which proceed out of the mouth come forth from the heart; and they defile the man.

19 For out of the heart proceed evil thoughts, murders, adulteries, fornications, thefts, false witness, blasphemies:

20 These are the things which defile a man: but to eat with unwashen hands defileth not a man.

21 Then Jesus went thence, and departed into the coasts of Tyre and Sidon.

22 And, behold, a woman of Canaan came out of the same coasts, and cried unto him, saying, Have mercy on me, O Lord, thou Son of David; my daughter is grievously vexed with a devil.

36. He gave thanks, or blessed the food – That is, he praised God for it, and prayed for a blessing upon it.

MATTHEW 16

1. A sign from heaven – Such they imagined Satan could not counterfeit. Mark viii, 11; Matt. xii, 38.

2. Luke xii, 54.

3. The signs of the times – The signs which evidently show, that this is the time of the Messiah.

4. A wicked and adulterous generation – Ye would seek no farther sign, did not your wickedness, your love of the world, which is spiritual adultery, blind your understanding.

5. Mark viii, 14.

6. Beware of the leaven of the Pharisees – That is, of their false doctrine: this is elegantly so called; for it spreads in the soul, or the Church, as leaven does in meal. Luke xii, 1.

7. They reasoned among themselves – What must we do then for bread, since we have taken no bread with us?

8. Why reason ye – Why are you troubled about this? Am I not able, if need so require, to supply you by a word?

11. How do ye not understand – Beside, do you not understand, that I did not mean bread, by the leaven of the Pharisees and Sadducees?

13. And Jesus coming – There was a large interval of time between what has been related, and what follows. The passages that follow were but a short time before our Lord suffered. Mark viii, 27; Luke ix, 18.

14. Jeremiah, or one of the prophets – There was at that time a current tradition among the Jews, that either Jeremiah, or some other of the ancient prophets would rise again before the Messiah came.

16. Peter – Who was generally the most forward to speak.

17. Flesh and blood – That is, thy own reason, or any natural power whatsoever.

18. On this rock – Alluding to his name, which signifies a rock, namely, the faith which thou hast now professed; I will build my Church – But perhaps when our Lord uttered these words, he pointed to himself, in like manner as when he said, Destroy this temple, John ii, 19; meaning the temple of his body. And it is certain, that as he is spoken of in Scripture, as the only foundation of the Church, so this is that which the apostles and evangelists laid in their preaching. It is in respect of laying this, that the names of the twelve apostles (not of St. Peter only) were equally inscribed on the twelve foundations of the city of God, Rev. xxi, 14. The gates of hell – As gates and walls were the strength of cities, and as courts of judicature were held in their gates, this phrase properly signifies the power and policy of Satan and his instruments. Shall not prevail against it – Not against the Church universal, so as to destroy it. And they never did. There hath been a small remnant in all ages.

19. I will give thee the keys of the kingdom of heaven – Indeed not to him alone, (for they were equally given to all the apostles at the same time, John xx, 21, 22, 23;) but to him were first given the keys both of doctrine and discipline. He first, after our Lord's resurrection, exercised the apostleship, Acts i, 15. And he first by preaching opened the kingdom of heaven, both to the Jews, Acts ii, and to the Gentiles, Acts x. Under the term of binding and loosing are contained all those acts of discipline which Peter and his brethren performed as apostles: and undoubtedly what they thus performed on earth, God confirmed in

MATTHEW HENRY   CHARLES H. SPURGEON

1-9 Additions to God's laws reflect upon his wisdom, as if he had left out something which was needed, and which man could supply; in one way or other they always lead men to disobey God. How thankful ought we to be for the written word of God! Never let us think that the religion of the Bible can be improved by any human addition, either in doctrine or practice. Our blessed Lord spoke of their traditions as inventions of their own, and pointed out one instance in which this was very clear, that of their transgressing the fifth commandment. When a parent's wants called for assistance, they pleaded, that they had devoted to the temple all they could spare, even though they did not part with it, and therefore their parents must expect nothing from them. This was making the command of God of no effect. The doom of hypocrites is put in a little compass; "In vain do they worship me." It will neither please God, nor profit themselves; they trust in vanity, and vanity will be their recompense.

10-20 Christ shows that the defilement they ought to fear, was not from what entered their mouths as food, but from what came out of their mouths, which showed the wickedness of their hearts. Nothing will last in the soul but the regenerating graces of the Holy Spirit; and nothing should be admitted into the church but what is from above; therefore, whoever is offended by a plain, seasonable declaration of the truth, we should not be troubled at it. The disciples ask to be better taught as to this matter. Where a weak head doubts concerning any word of Christ, an upright heart and a willing mind seek for instruction. It is the heart that is desperately wicked, Jer 17:9, for there is no sin in word or deed, which was not first in the heart. They all come out of the man, and are fruits of that wickedness which is in the heart, and is wrought there. When Christ teaches, he will show men the deceitfulness and wickedness of their own hearts; he will teach them to humble themselves, and to seek to be cleansed in the Fountain opened for sin and uncleanness.

21-28 The dark corners of the country, the most remote, shall share Christ's influences; afterwards the ends of the earth shall see his salvation. The distress and trouble of her family brought a woman to Christ; and though it is need that drives us to Christ, yet we shall not therefore be driven from him. She did not limit Christ to any particular instance of mercy, but mercy, mercy, is what she begged for: she pleads not merit, but depends upon mercy. It is the duty of parents to pray for their children, and to be earnest in prayer for them, especially for their souls. Have you a son, a daughter, grievously vexed with a proud devil, an unclean devil, a malicious devil, led captive by him at his will? this is a case more deplorable than that of bodily possession, and you must bring them by faith and prayer to Christ, who alone is able to heal them. Many methods of Christ's providence, especially of his grace, in dealing with his people, which are dark and

light of dawn, the disappearance of Moses and Elias, indicating the full noontide of light, was the best thing that could happen. Why should we wish to see Moses? The ceremonials are all fulfilled in Jesus; the law is honored and fulfilled in him. Let Moses go, his light is already in "Jesus only." And why should I wish to retain Elias? The prophecies are all fulfilled in Jesus, and the preparation of which Elias preached Jesus brings with himself. Let, then, Elias go, his light also is in "Jesus only." It is better to see Moses and Elias in Christ, than to see Moses and Elias with Christ. The absence of some things betokens a higher state of things than their presence. In all my library I do not know that I have a Lennie's English Grammar, or a Mavor's Spelling Book, or a Henry's First Latin Exercises, nor do I regret the absence of those valuable works, because I have got beyond the need of them. So the Christian wants not the symbols of Moses, or the preparations of Elias, for Christ is all, and we are complete in him. He who is conversant with the higher walks of sacred literature and reads in the golden book of Christ's heart, may safely lay the legal schoolbook by; this was good enough for the church's infancy, but we have now put away childish things. "We, when we were children, were in bondage under the elements of the world: but when the fullness of the time was come, God sent forth his Son, made of a woman, made under the law to redeem them that were under the law, that we might receive the adoption of sons. And because ye are sons, God hath sent forth the Spirit of his Son into your hearts, crying, Abba, Father. Wherefore thou art no more a servant, but a son; and if a son, then an heir of God through Christ." My brethren, the principle may be carried still further, for even the most precious things we treasure here below will disappear when fully realized in heaven. Beautiful for situation was the temple on Mount Zion, and though we believe not in the sanctity of buildings under the gospel, we love the place of solemn meeting where we are accustomed to offer prayer and praise; but when we enter into perfection we shall find no temple in heaven. We delight in our Sabbaths, and we would not give them up. O may England never lose her Sabbaths! but when we reach the Jerusalem above, we shall not observe the first day of the week above the rest, for we shall enjoy one everlasting Sabbath. No temple, because all temple; and no Sabbath day, because all Sabbath in heaven. Thus, you see, the losing of some things is gain: it proves that we have got beyond their help. Just as we get beyond the nursery and all its appurtenances, and never regret it because we have become men, so do

23 But he answered her not a word. And his disciples came and besought him, saying, Send her away; for she crieth after us.

24 But he answered and said, I am not sent but unto the lost sheep of the house of Israel.

25 Then came she and worshiped him, saying, Lord, help me.

26 But he answered and said, It is not meet to take the children's bread, and to cast it to dogs.

27 And she said, Truth, Lord: yet the dogs eat of the crumbs which fall from their masters' table.

28 Then Jesus answered and said unto her, O woman, great is thy faith: be it unto thee even as thou wilt. And her daughter was made whole from that very hour.

29 And Jesus departed from thence, and came nigh unto the sea of Galilee; and went up into a mountain, and sat down there.

30 And great multitudes came unto him, having with them those that were lame, blind, dumb, maimed, and many others, and cast them down at Jesus' feet; and he healed them:

31 Insomuch that the multitude wondered, when they saw the dumb to speak, the maimed to be whole, the lame to walk, and the blind to see: and they glorified the God of Israel.

32 Then Jesus called his disciples unto him, and said, I have compassion on the multitude, because they continue with me now three days, and have nothing to eat: and I will not send them away fasting, lest they faint in the way.

33 And his disciples say unto him, Whence should we have so much bread in the wilderness, as to fill so great a multitude?

34 And Jesus saith unto them, How many loaves have ye? And they said, Seven, and a few little fishes.

35 And he commanded the multitude to sit down on the ground.

36 And he took the seven loaves and the fishes, and gave thanks, and brake them, and gave to his disciples, and the disciples to the multitude.

37 And they did all eat, and were filled: and they took up of the broken meat that was left seven baskets full.

38 And they that did eat were four thousand men, beside women and children.

39 And he sent away the multitude, and took ship, and came into the coasts of Magdala,

MATTHEW 16

1   The Pharisees also with the Sadducees came, and tempting desired

heaven. Matt. xviii, 18.

20. Then charged he his disciples to tell no one that he was the Christ – Jesus himself had not said it expressly even to his apostles, but left them to infer it from his doctrine and miracles. Neither was it proper the apostles should say this openly, before that grand proof of it, his resurrection. If they had, they who believed them would the more earnestly have sought to take and make him a king: and they who did not believe them would the more vehemently have rejected and opposed such a Messiah.

21. From that time Jesus began to tell his disciples, that he must suffer many things – Perhaps this expression, began, always implied his entering on a set and solemn discourse. Hitherto he had mainly taught them only one point, That he was the Christ. From this time he taught them another, That Christ must through sufferings and death enter into his glory. From the elders – The most honorable and experienced men; the chief priests – Accounted the most religious; and the scribes – The most learned body of men in the nation. Would not one have expected, that these should have been the very first to receive him? But not many wise, not many noble were called. Favor thyself – The advice of the world, the flesh, and the devil, to every one of our Lord's followers. Mark viii, 31; Luke ix, 22.

23. Get thee behind me – Out of my sight. It is not improbable, Peter might step before him, to stop him. Satan – Our Lord is not recorded to have given so sharp a reproof to any other of his apostles on any occasion. He saw it was needful for the pride of Peter's heart, puffed up with the commendation lately given him. Perhaps the term Satan may not barely mean, Thou art my enemy, while thou fanciest thyself most my friend; but also, Thou art acting the very part of Satan, both by endeavoring to hinder the redemption of mankind, and by giving me the most deadly advice that can ever spring from the pit of hell. Thou savorest not – Dost not relish or desire. We may learn from hence,

1. That whosoever says to us in such a case, favor thyself, is acting the part of the devil:

2. That the proper answer to such an adviser is, Get thee behind me:

3. That otherwise he will be an offense to us, an occasion of our stumbling, if not falling:

4. That this advice always proceeds from the not relishing the things of God, but the things of men. Yea, so far is this advice, favor thyself, from being fit for a Christian either to give or take, that if any man will come after Christ, his very first step is to deny, or renounce himself: in the room of his own will, to substitute the will of God, as his one principle of action.

24. If any man be willing to come after me – None is forced; but if any will be a Christian, it must be on these terms, Let him deny himself, and take up his cross – A rule that can never be too much observed: let him in all things deny his own will, however pleasing, and do the will of God, however painful. Should we not consider all crosses, all things grievous to flesh and blood, as what they really are, as opportunities of embracing God's will at the expense of our own? And consequently as so many steps by which we may advance toward perfection? We should make a swift progress in the spiritual life, if we were faithful in this practice. Crosses are so frequent, that whoever makes advantage of them, will soon be a great gainer. Great crosses are occasions of great improvement: and the little ones, which come daily, and even hourly, make up in number what they want in weight. We may in these daily and hourly crosses make effectual oblations of our will to God; which

perplexing, may be explained by this story, which teaches that there may be love in Christ's heart while there are frowns in his face; and it encourages us, though he seems ready to slay us, yet to trust in him. Those whom Christ intends most to honor, he humbles to feel their own unworthiness. A proud, unhumbled heart would not have borne this; but she turned it into an argument to support her request. The state of this woman is an emblem of the state of a sinner, deeply conscious of the misery of his soul. The least of Christ is precious to a believer, even the very crumbs of the Bread of life. Of all graces, faith honors Christ most; therefore of all graces Christ honors faith most. He cured her daughter. He spake, and it was done. From hence let such as seek help from the Lord, and receive no gracious answer, learn to turn even their unworthiness and discouragements into pleas for mercy.

29-39 See commentary at Mark 8:1-10

MATTHEW 16

The Pharisees and Sadducees ask a sign. (1-4)
Jesus cautions against the doctrine of the Pharisees. (5-12)
Peter's testimony that Jesus was the Christ. (13-20)
Christ foretells his sufferings, and rebukes Peter. (21-23)
The necessity of self-denial. (24-28)

1-4 The Pharisees and Sadducees were opposed to each other in principles and in conduct; yet they joined against Christ. But they desired a sign of their own choosing: they despised those signs which relieved the necessity of the sick and sorrowful, and called for something else which would gratify the curiosity of the proud. It is great hypocrisy, when we slight the signs of God's ordaining, to seek for signs of our own devising.

5-12 Christ speaks of spiritual things under a similitude, and the disciples misunderstand him of carnal things. He took it ill that they should think him as thoughtful about bread as they were; that they should be so little acquainted with his way of preaching. Then understood they what he meant. Christ teaches by the Spirit of wisdom in the heart, opening the understanding to the Spirit of revelation in the word.

13-20 Peter, for himself and his brethren, said that they were assured of our Lord's being the promised Messiah, the Son of the living God. This showed that they believed Jesus to be more than man. Our Lord declared Peter to be blessed, as the teaching of God made him differ from his unbelieving countrymen. Christ added that he had named him Peter, in allusion to his stability or firmness in professing the truth. The word translated ''rock,'' is not the same word as Peter, but is of a similar meaning. Nothing can be more wrong

Moses and Elias pass away, but we do not miss them, for "Jesus only" indicates our manhood. It is a sign of a higher growth when we can see Jesus only. My brethren, much of this sort of thing takes place with all Christians in their spiritual life. Do you remember when you were first of all convinced and awakened, what a great deal you thought of the preacher, and how much of the very style in which he spoke the gospel! But now, though you delight to listen to his voice, and find that God blesses you through him, yet you have sunk the thought of the preacher in the glory of the Master, you see no man save "Jesus only." And as you grow in grace you will find that many doctrines and points of church government which once appeared to you to be all important, though you will still value them, will seem but of small consequence compared with Christ himself. Like the traveler ascending the Alps to reach the summit of Mont Blanc; at first he observes that lord of the hills as one born among many, and often in the twistings of his upward path he sees other peaks which appear more elevated than that monarch of mountains; but when at last he is near the summit, he sees all the rest of the hills beneath his feet, and like a mighty wedge of alabaster Mount Blanc pierces the very clouds. So, as we grow in grace, other things sink and Jesus rises. They must decrease, but Christ must increase; until he alone fills the full horizon of your soul, and rises clear and bright and glorious up into the very heaven of God. O that we may thus see "Jesus only!"

II. Time hastens so rapidly, this morning, that I know not how I shall be able to compress the rest of my discourse into the allotted space. We must in the most rapid manner speak upon WHAT REALLY HAPPENED.

"They saw no man, save Jesus only." This was all they wanted to see for their comfort. They were sore afraid: Moses was gone, and he could give them no comfort; Elias was gone, he could speak no consolatory word; yet when Jesus said, "Be not afraid," their fears vanished. All the comfort, then, that any troubled heart wants, it can find in Christ. Go not to Moses, nor Elias, neither to the old covenant, not to prophecy: go straight away to Jesus only. He was all the Savior they wanted. Those three men all needed washing from sin; all needed to be kept and held on their way, but neither Moses nor Elias could have washed them from sin, nor have kept them from returning to it. But Jesus only could cleanse them, and did; Christ could lead them on, and did. Ah! brethren, all the Savior we want, we find in Jesus only. The priests of Rome and their Anglican mimics officiously offer us

KING JAMES VERSION   JOHN WESLEY

him that he would shew them a sign from heaven.

2 He answered and said unto them, When it is evening, ye say, It will be fair weather: for the sky is red.

3 And in the morning, It will be foul weather to day: for the sky is red and lowring. O ye hypocrites, ye can discern the face of the sky; but can ye not discern the signs of the times?

4 A wicked and adulterous generation seeketh after a sign; and there shall no sign be given unto it, but the sign of the prophet Jonas. And he left them, and departed.

5 And when his disciples were come to the other side, they had forgotten to take bread.

6 Then Jesus said unto them, Take heed and beware of the leaven of the Pharisees and of the Sadducees.

7 And they reasoned among themselves, saying, It is because we have taken no bread.

8 Which when Jesus perceived, he said unto them, O ye of little faith, why reason ye among yourselves, because ye have brought no bread?

9 Do ye not yet understand, neither remember the five loaves of the five thousand, and how many baskets ye took up?

10 Neither the seven loaves of the four thousand, and how many baskets ye took up?

11 How is it that ye do not understand that I spake it not to you concerning bread, that ye should beware of the leaven of the Pharisees and of the Sadducees?

12 Then understood they how that he bade them not beware of the leaven of bread, but of the doctrine of the Pharisees and of the Sadducees.

13 When Jesus came into the coasts of Cesarea Philippi, he asked his disciples, saying, Whom do men say that I the Son of man am?

14 And they said, Some say that thou art John the Baptist: some, Elias; and others, Jeremias, or one of the prophets.

15 He saith unto them, But whom say ye that I am?

16 And Simon Peter answered and said, Thou art the Christ, the Son of the living God.

17 And Jesus answered and said unto him, Blessed art thou, Simon Barjona: for flesh and blood hath not revealed it unto thee, but my Father which is in heaven.

18 And I say also unto thee, That thou art Peter, and upon this rock I will build my church; and the gates of hell shall

oblations, so frequently repeated, will soon amount to a great sum. Let us remember then (what can never be sufficiently inculcated) that God is the author of all events: that none is so small or inconsiderable, as to escape his notice and direction. Every event therefore declares to us the will of God, to which thus declared we should heartily submit. We should renounce our own to embrace it; we should approve and choose what his choice warrants as best for us. Herein should we exercise ourselves continually; this should be our practice all the day long. We should in humility accept the little crosses that are dispensed to us, as those that best suit our weakness. Let us bear these little things, at least for God's sake, and prefer his will to our own in matters of so small importance. And his goodness will accept these mean oblations; for he despiseth not the day of small things. Matt. x, 38.

25. Whosoever will save his life – At the expense of his conscience: whosoever, in the very highest instance, that of life itself, will not renounce himself, shall be lost eternally. But can any man hope he should be able thus to renounce himself, if he cannot do it in the smallest instances? And whosoever will lose his life shall find it – What he loses on earth he shall find in heaven. Matt. x, 39; Mark viii, 35; Luke ix, 24; xvii, 33; John xii, 25.

27. For the Son of man shall come – For there is no way to escape the righteous judgment of God.

28. And as an emblem of this, there are some here who shall live to see the Messiah coming to set up his mediatorial kingdom, with great power and glory, by the increase of his Church, and the destruction of the temple, city, and polity of the Jews.

MATTHEW HENRY   CHARLES H. SPURGEON

than to suppose that Christ meant the person of Peter was the rock. Without doubt Christ himself is the Rock, the tried foundation of the church; and woe to him that attempts to lay any other! Peter's confession is this rock as to doctrine. If Jesus be not the Christ, those that own him are not of the church, but deceivers and deceived. Our Lord next declared the authority with which Peter would be invested. He spoke in the name of his brethren, and this related to them as well as to him. They had no certain knowledge of the characters of men, and were liable to mistakes and sins in their own conduct; but they were kept from error in stating the way of acceptance and salvation, the rule of obedience, the believer's character and experience, and the final doom of unbelievers and hypocrites. In such matters their decision was right, and it was confirmed in heaven. But all pretensions of any man, either to absolve or retain men's sins, are blasphemous and absurd. None can forgive sins but God only. And this binding and loosing, in the common language of the Jews, signified to forbid and to allow, or to teach what is lawful or unlawful.

21-23 Christ reveals his mind to his people gradually. From that time, when the apostles had made the full confession of Christ, that he was the Son of God, he began to show them of his sufferings. He spake this to set right the mistakes of his disciples about the outward pomp and power of his kingdom. Those that follow Christ, must not expect great or high things in this world. Peter would have Christ to dread suffering as much as he did; but we mistake, if we measure Christ's love and patience by our own. We do not read of any thing said or done by any of his disciples, at any time, that Christ resented so much as this. Whoever takes us from that which is good, and would make us fear to do too much for God, speaks Satan's language. Whatever appears to be a temptation to sin, must be resisted with abhorrence, and not be parleyed with. Those that decline suffering for Christ, savor more of the things of man than of the things of God.

24-28 A true disciple of Christ is one that does follow him in duty, and shall follow him to glory. He is one that walks in the same way Christ walked in, is led by his Spirit, and treads in his steps, whithersoever he goes. "Let him deny himself." If self-denial be a hard lesson, it is no more than what our Master learned and practiced, to redeem us, and to teach us. "Let him take up his cross." The cross is here put for every trouble that befalls us. We are apt to think we could bear another's cross better than our own; but that is best which is appointed us, and we ought to make the best of it. We must not by our rashness and folly pull crosses down upon our own heads, but must take them up when they are in our way. If any man will have the name and credit of a disciple, let him follow Christ in the work and duty of a disciple. If all worldly things are worthless when compared with the life of the body, how forcible

their services. How glad they would be if we would bend our necks once again to their yoke! But we thank God we have seen "Jesus only," and if Moses has gone, and if Elias has gone, we are not likely to let the shavelings of Rome come in and fill up the vacancy. "Jesus only," is enough for our comfort, without either Anglican, Mosaic, or Roman priest craft.

He, again, was to them, as they went afterwards into the world, enough for a Master. "No man can serve two masters," and albeit, Moses and Elias might sink into the second rank, yet might there have been some difficulty in the follower's mind if the leadership were divided. But when they had no leader but Jesus, his guidance, his direction and command were quite sufficient. He, in the day of battle, was enough for their captain; in the day of difficulty, enough for their direction. They wanted none but Jesus. At this day, my brethren, we have no Master but Christ; we submit ourselves to no vicar of God; we bow down ourselves before no great leader of a sect, neither to Calvin, nor to Arminius, to Wesley, or Whitfield, "One is our Master," and that one is enough, for we have learned to see the wisdom of God and the power of God in Jesus only.

He was enough as their power for future life, as well as their Master. They needed not ask Moses to lend them official dignity, nor to ask Elias to bring them fire from heaven: Jesus would give them of his Holy Spirit, and they should be strong enough for every enterprise. And, brethren, all the power you and I want to preach the gospel, and to conquer souls to the truth, we can find in Jesus only. You want no sacred State prestige, no pretended apostolic succession, no prelatical unction; Jesus will anoint you with his Holy Spirit, and you shall be plenteously endowed with power from on high, so that you shall do great things and prevail. "Jesus only." Why, they wanted no other motive to constrain them to use their power aright. It is enough incentive to a man to be allowed to live for such a one as Christ. Only let the thought of Christ fill the enlightened intellect, and it must conquer the sanctified affections. Let but Jesus be well understood as the everlasting God who bowed the heavens, and came down and suffered shame and ignominy, that he might redeem us from the wrath to come; let us get but a sight of the thorn-crowned head, and those dear eyes all red with weeping, and those sweet cheeks bruised and battered by the scoffer's fists; let us but look into the tender heart that was broken with griefs unutterable for our sakes, and the love of Christ must constrain us, and we shall thus "judge, that if one died for all, then were we dead: and that he

not prevail against it.

19 And I will give unto thee the keys of the kingdom of heaven: and whatsoever thou shalt bind on earth shall be bound in heaven: and whatsoever thou shalt loose on earth shall be loosed in heaven.

20 Then charged he his disciples that they should tell no man that he was Jesus the Christ.

21 From that time forth began Jesus to shew unto his disciples, how that he must go unto Jerusalem, and suffer many things of the elders and chief priests and scribes, and be killed, and be raised again the third day.

22 Then Peter took him, and began to rebuke him, saying, Be it far from thee, Lord: this shall not be unto thee.

23 But he turned, and said unto Peter, Get thee behind me, Satan: thou art an offense unto me: for thou savorest not the things that be of God, but those that be of men.

24 Then said Jesus unto his disciples, If any man will come after me, let him deny himself, and take up his cross, and follow me.

25 For whosoever will save his life shall lose it: and whosoever will lose his life for my sake shall find it.

26 For what is a man profited, if he shall gain the whole world, and lose his own soul? or what shall a man give in exchange for his soul?

27 For the Son of man shall come in the glory of his Father with his angels; and then he shall reward every man according to his works.

28 Verily I say unto you, There be some standing here, which shall not taste of death, till they see the Son of man coming in his kingdom.

MATTHEW 17

1 And after six days Jesus taketh Peter, James, and John his brother, and bringeth them up into an high mountain apart,

2 And was transfigured before them: and his face did shine as the sun, and his raiment was white as the light.

3 And, behold, there appeared unto them Moses and Elias talking with him.

4 Then answered Peter, and said unto Jesus, Lord, it is good for us to be here: if thou wilt, let us make here three tabernacles; one for thee, and one for Moses, and one for Elias.

5 While he yet spake, behold, a bright cloud overshadowed them: and behold a voice out of the cloud, which said, This is my beloved Son, in whom I am well pleased; hear ye him.

MATTHEW 17

1. A high mountain – Probably Mount Tabor. ["And after six days Jesus taketh with him Peter, and James, and John, and leadeth them up into an high mountain apart by themselves: and he was transfigured before them." Mark ix, 2; ""And the LORD said unto me, They have well spoken that which they have spoken." Luke ix, 28.]

2. And was transfigured – Or transformed. The indwelling Deity darted out its rays through the veil of the flesh; and that with such transcendent splendor, that he no longer bore the form of a servant. His face shone with Divine majesty, like the sun in its strength; and all his body was so irradiated by it, that his clothes could not conceal its glory, but became white and glittering as the very light, with which he covered himself as with a garment.

3. There appeared Moses and Elijah – Here for the full confirmation of their faith in Jesus, Moses, the giver of the law, Elijah, the most zealous of all the prophets, and God speaking from heaven, all bore witness to him.

4. Let us make three tents – The words of rapturous surprise. He says three, not six: because the apostles desired to be with their Master.

5. Hear ye him – As superior even to Moses and the prophets. See Deut. xviii, 17, "And the LORD said unto me, They have well spoken that which they have spoken."

7. Be not afraid – And doubtless the same moment he gave them courage and strength.

9. Tell the vision to no man – Not to the rest of the disciples, lest they should be grieved and discouraged because they were not admitted to the sight: nor to any other persons, lest it should enrage some the more, and his approaching sufferings shall make others disbelieve it; till the Son of man be risen again – Till the resurrection should make it credible, and confirm their testimony about it.

10. Why then say the scribes, that Elijah must come first – Before the Messiah? If no man is to know of his coming? Should we not rather tell every man, that he is come, and that we have seen him, witnessing to thee as the Messiah?

11. Regulate all things – In order to the coming of Christ.

12. Elijah is come already – And yet when the Jews asked John, Art thou Elijah? He said, I am not, John i, 21. "And they asked him, What then? Art thou Elias? And he saith, I am not. Art thou that prophet? And he answered, No."

His meaning was, I am not Elijah the Tishbite, come again into the world. But he was the person of whom Malachi prophesied under that name.

14. ["And when he came to his disciples, he saw a great multitude about them, and the scribes questioning with them." Mark ix, 14; ""And as he spake, a certain Pharisee besought him to dine with him: and he went in, and sat down to meat." Luke xi, 37.]

15. He is lunatic – This word might with great propriety be used, though the case was mostly preternatural; as the evil spirit would undoubtedly take advantage of the influence which the changes of the moon have on the brain and nerves.

17. O unbelieving and perverse generation – Our Lord speaks principally this to his disciples. How long shall I be with you? – Before you steadfastly believe?

20. Because of your unbelief – Because in this particular they had not faith. If ye have faith as a grain of mustard seed – That is, the least measure of it. But it is certain, the faith which is here spoken of does

the same argument with respect to the soul and its state of never-ending happiness or misery! Thousands lose their souls for the most trifling gain, or the most worthless indulgence, nay, often from mere sloth and negligence. Whatever is the object for which men forsake Christ, that is the price at which Satan buys their souls. Yet one soul is worth more than all the world. This is Christ's judgment upon the matter; he knew the price of souls, for he redeemed them; nor would he underrate the world, for he made it. The dying transgressor cannot purchase one hour's respite to seek mercy for his perishing soul. Let us then learn rightly to value our souls, and Christ as the only Savior of them.

MATTHEW 17

The transfiguration of Christ. (1-13)
Jesus casts out a dumb and deaf spirit. (14-21)
He again foretells his sufferings. (22,23)
He works a miracle to pay the tribute money. (24-27)

1-13 Now the disciples beheld somewhat of Christ's glory, as of the only begotten of the Father. It was intended to support their faith, when they would have to witness his crucifixion; and would give them an idea of the glory prepared for them, when changed by his power and made like him. The apostles were overcome by the glorious sight. Peter thought that it was most desirable to continue there, and to go no more down to meet the sufferings of which he was so unwilling to hear. In this he knew not what he said. We are wrong, if we look for a heaven here upon earth. Whatever tabernacles we propose to make for ourselves in this world, we must always remember to ask Christ's leave. That sacrifice was not yet offered, without which the souls of sinful men could not have been saved; and important services were to be done by Peter and his brethren. While Peter spoke, a bright cloud overshadowed them, an emblem of the Divine presence and glory. Ever since man sinned, and heard God's voice in the garden, unusual appearances of God have been terrible to man. They fell prostrate to the earth, till Jesus encouraged them; when looking round, they beheld only their Lord as they commonly saw him. We must pass through varied experiences in our way to glory; and when we return to the world after an ordinance, it must be our care to take Christ with us, and then it may be our comfort that he is with us.

14-21 See commentary at Mark 9:14-28; Luke 9: 37-42

22,23 Christ perfectly knew all things that should befall him, yet undertook the work of our redemption, which strongly shows his love. What outward debasement and Divine glory was the life of the Redeemer! And all his humiliation ended in his exaltation. Let us learn to endure the cross, to despise

died for all, that they which live should not henceforth live unto themselves, but unto him which died for them and rose again." In the point of motive, believers do not need the aid of Moses. That you ought to do such a thing because otherwise you will be punished, will but little strengthen you, nor will you be much aided by the spirit of prophecy which leads you to hope that in the millennial period you will be made a ruler over many cities. It will be enough to you that you serve the Lord Christ; it suffices you if you may be enabled to honor him, to deck his crown, to magnify his name. Here is a stimulus sufficient for martyrs and confessors, "Jesus only." Brethren, it is all the gospel we have to preach—it is all the gospel we want to preach—it is the only ground of confidence which we have for ourselves; it is all the hope we have to set before others. I know that in this age there is an overweening desire for that which has the aspect of being intellectual, deep, and novel; and we are often informed that there are to be developments in religion, even as in science; and we are despised as being hardly men, certainly not thinking men, if we preach today what was preached two hundred years ago. Brethren, we preach today what was preached eighteen hundred years ago, and wherein others make alterations, they create deformities, and not improvements. We are not ashamed to avow that the old truth of Christ alone is everlasting; all else has gone or shall go, but the gospel towers above the wrecks of time: to us "Jesus only" remains as the sole topic of our ministry, and we want nothing else.

For "Jesus only" shall be our reward, to be with him where he is, to behold his glory, to be like him when we shall see him as he is, we ask no other heaven. No other bliss can our soul conceive of. The Lord grant that we may have a fullness of this, and "Jesus only" shall be throughout eternity our delight.

There was here space to have dilated at great length, but we have rather given you the heads of thought, than the thoughts themselves. Though the apostles saw "Jesus only," they saw quite sufficient, for Jesus is enough for time and eternity, enough to live by and enough to die by.

III. I must close, though I fain would linger. Brethren, let us think of WHAT WE DESIRE MAY HAPPEN to all now present.

I do desire for my fellow Christians and for myself, that more and more the great object of our thoughts, motives, and acts may be "Jesus only." I believe that whenever our religion is most vital, it is most full of Christ. Moreover, when it is most practical, downright, and com-

6 And when the disciples heard it, they fell on their face, and were sore afraid.

7 And Jesus came and touched them, and said, Arise, and be not afraid.

8 And when they had lifted up their eyes, they saw no man, save Jesus only.

9 And as they came down from the mountain, Jesus charged them, saying, Tell the vision to no man, until the Son of man be risen again from the dead.

10 And his disciples asked him, saying, Why then say the scribes that Elias must first come?

11 And Jesus answered and said unto them, Elias truly shall first come, and restore all things.

12 But I say unto you, That Elias is come already, and they knew him not, but have done unto him whatsoever they listed. Likewise shall also the Son of man suffer of them.

13 Then the disciples understood that he spake unto them of John the Baptist.

14 And when they were come to the multitude, there came to him a certain man, kneeling down to him, and saying,

15 Lord, have mercy on my son: for he is lunatick, and sore vexed: for ofttimes he falleth into the fire, and oft into the water.

16 And I brought him to thy disciples, and they could not cure him.

17 Then Jesus answered and said, O faithless and perverse generation, how long shall I be with you? how long shall I suffer you? bring him hither to me.

18 And Jesus rebuked the devil; and he departed out of him: and the child was cured from that very hour.

19 Then came the disciples to Jesus apart, and said, Why could not we cast him out?

20 And Jesus said unto them, Because of your unbelief: for verily I say unto you, If ye have faith as a grain of mustard seed, ye shall say unto this mountain, Remove hence to yonder place; and it shall remove; and nothing shall be impossible unto you.

21 Howbeit this kind goeth not out but by prayer and fasting.

22 And while they abode in Galilee, Jesus said unto them, The Son of man shall be betrayed into the hands of men:

23 And they shall kill him, and the third day he shall be raised again. And they were exceeding sorry.

24 And when they were come to Capernaum, they that received tribute money came to Peter, and said, Doth not your master pay tribute?

25 He saith, Yes. And when he was come into the house, Jesus prevented him, saying, What thinkest thou, Simon?

not always imply saving faith. Many have had it who thereby cast out devils, and yet will at last have their portion with them. It is only a supernatural persuasion given a man, that God will work thus by him at that hour. Now, though I have all this faith so as to remove mountains, yet if I have not the faith which worketh by love, I am nothing. To remove mountains was a proverbial phrase among the Jews, and is still retained in their writings, to express a thing which is very difficult, and to appearance impossible. "Jesus answered and said unto them, Verily I say unto you, If ye have faith, and doubt not, ye shall not only do this which is done to the fig tree, but also if ye shall say unto this mountain, Be thou removed, and be thou cast into the sea; it shall be done." Matt. xxi, 21; Luke xvii, 6.

21. This kind of devils – goeth not out but by prayer and fasting – What a testimony is here of the efficacy of fasting, when added to fervent prayer! Some kinds of devils the apostles had cast out before this, without fasting.

22. Mark ix, 30; Luke ix, 44.

24. When they were come to Capernaum – Where our Lord now dwelt. This was the reason why they stayed till he came thither, to ask him for the tribute. Doth not your Master pay tribute? – This was a tribute or payment of a peculiar kind, being half a shekel, (that is, about fifteen pence,) which every master of a family used to pay yearly to the service of the temple, to buy salt, and little things not otherwise provided for. It seems to have been a voluntary thing, which custom rather than any law had established.

25. Jesus prevented him – Just when St. Peter was going to ask him for it. Of their own sons, or of strangers? – That is, such as are not of their own family.

26. Then are the sons free – The sense is, This is paid for the use of the house of God. But I am the Son of God. Therefore I am free from any obligation of paying this to my own Father.

27. Yet that, we may not offend them – Even those unjust, unreasonable men, who claim what they have no manner of right to: do not contest it with them, bat rather yield to their demand, than violate peace or love. O what would not one of a loving spirit do for peace! Any thing which is not expressly forbidden in the word of God. A piece of money – The original word is a stater, which was in value two shillings and sixpence: just the sum that was wanted. Give for me and thee – Peter had a family of his own: the other apostles were the family of Jesus. How illustrious a degree of knowledge and power did our Lord here discover! Knowledge, penetrating into this animal, though beneath the waters; and power, in directing this very fish to Peter's hook, though he himself was at a distance! How must this have encouraged both him and his brethren in a firm dependence on Divine Providence.

riches and worldly honors, and to be content with his will.

24-27 Peter felt sure that his Master was ready to do what was right. Christ spoke first to give him proof that no thought can be withholden from him. We must never decline our duty for fear of giving offense; but we must sometimes deny ourselves in our worldly interests, rather than give offense. However the money was lodged in the fish, He who knows all things alone could know it, and only almighty power could bring it to Peter's hook. The power and the poverty of Christ should be mentioned together. If called by providence to be poor, like our Lord, let us trust in his power, and our God shall supply all our need, according to his riches in glory by Christ Jesus. In the way of obedience, in the course, perhaps, of our usual calling, as he helped Peter, so he will help us. And if any sudden call should occur, which we are not prepared to meet, let us not apply to others, till we first seek Christ. Christ could as easily have commanded a bag of money as a piece of money; but he would teach us not to covet superfluities, but, having enough for our present occasions, therewith to be content, and not to distrust God, though we live but from hand to mouth. Christ made the fish his cash-keeper; and why may not we make God's providence our storehouse and treasury? If we have a competency for today, let tomorrow take thought for the things of itself. Christ paid for himself and Peter, because it is probable that here he only was assessed, and of him it was at this time demanded; perhaps the rest had paid already, or were to pay elsewhere. Note, it is a desirable thing, if God so please, to have wherewithal of this world's goods, not only to be just, but to be kind; not only to be charitable to the poor, but obliging to our friends. What is a great estate good for, but that it enables a man to do so much the more good? Lastly, Observe, The evangelist records here the orders Christ gave to Peter, the warrant; the effect is not particularly mentioned, but taken for granted, and justly; for, with Christ, saying and doing are the same thing.

mon sense, it always gets nearest to Jesus. I can bear witness that whenever I am in deeps of sorrow, nothing will do for me but "Jesus only." I can rest in some degree in the externals of religion, its outward escarpments and bulwarks, when I am in health; but I retreat to the innermost citadel of our holy faith, namely, to the very heart of Christ, when my spirit is assailed by temptation, or besieged with sorrow and anguish. What is more, my witness is that whenever I have high spiritual enjoyments, enjoyments right, rare, celestial, they are always connected with Jesus only. Other religious things may give some kind of joy, and joy that is healthy too, but the sublimest, the most inebriating, the most divine of all joys, must be found in Jesus only. In fine, I find if I want to labor much, I must live on Jesus only; if I desire to suffer patiently, I must feed on Jesus only; if I wish to wrestle with God successfully, I must plead Jesus only; if I aspire to conquer sin, I must use the blood of Jesus only; if I pant to learn the mysteries of heaven, I must seek the teachings of Jesus only. I believe that any thing which we add to Christ lowers our position, and that the more elevated our soul becomes, the more nearly like what it is to be when it shall enter into the religion of the perfect, the more completely every thing else will sink, die out, and Jesus, Jesus, Jesus only, will be first and last, and midst and without end, the Alpha and Omega of every thought of head and pulse of heart. May it be so with every Christian.

There are others here who are not yet believers in Jesus, and our desire is that this may happen to them, that they may see "Jesus only." "Oh," saith one, "Sir, I want to see my sins. My heart is very hard, and very proud; I want to see my sins." Friend, I also desire that you should, but I desire that you may see them not on yourself, but on Jesus only. No sight of sin ever brings such true humiliation of spirit as when the soul sees its sins laid on the Savior. Sinner, I know you have thought of sins as lying on yourself, and you have been trying to feel their weight, but there is a happier and better view still. Sin was laid on Jesus, and it made him to be covered with a bloody sweat; it nailed him to the cross; it made him cry, "Lama Sabachthani;" it bowed him into the dust of death. Why, friend, if you see sin on Jesus you will hate it, you will bemoan it, you will abhor it. You need not look evermore to sin as burdening yourself, see Jesus only, and the best kind of repentance will follow. "Ah, but," saith another, "I want to feel my need of Christ more." You will see your need all the better if you look at Jesus only. Many a time an appetite for a thing is created by the sight of it. Why, there are some of us who

of whom do the kings of the earth take custom or tribute? of their own children, or of strangers?

26 Peter saith unto him, Of strangers. Jesus saith unto him, Then are the children free.

27 Notwithstanding, lest we should offend them, go thou to the sea, and cast an hook, and take up the fish that first cometh up; and when thou hast opened his mouth, thou shalt find a piece of money: that take, and give unto them for me and thee.

MATTHEW 18

1 At the same time came the disciples unto Jesus, saying, Who is the greatest in the kingdom of heaven?

2 And Jesus called a little child unto him, and set him in the midst of them,

3 And said, Verily I say unto you, Except ye be converted, and become as little children, ye shall not enter into the kingdom of heaven.

4 Whosoever therefore shall humble himself as this little child, the same is greatest in the kingdom of heaven.

5 And whoso shall receive one such little child in my name receiveth me.

6 But whoso shall offend one of these little ones which believe in me, it were better for him that a millstone were hanged about his neck, and that he were drowned in the depth of the sea.

7 Woe unto the world because of offenses! for it must needs be that offenses come; but woe to that man by whom the offense cometh!

8 Wherefore if thy hand or thy foot offend thee, cut them off, and cast them from thee: it is better for thee to enter into life halt or maimed, rather than having two hands or two feet to be cast into everlasting fire.

9 And if thine eye offend thee, pluck it out, and cast it from thee: it is better for thee to enter into life with one eye, rather than having two eyes to be cast into hell fire.

10 Take heed that ye despise not one of these little ones; for I say unto you, That in heaven their angels do always behold the face of my Father which is in heaven.

11 For the Son of man is come to save that which was lost.

12 How think ye? if a man have an hundred sheep, and one of them be gone astray, doth he not leave the ninety and nine, and goeth into the mountains, and seeketh that which is gone astray?

13 And if so be that he find it, verily I

MATTHEW 18

1. Who is the greatest in the kingdom of heaven? – Which of us shall be thy prime minister? They still dreamed of a temporal kingdom.

2. And Jesus calling to him a little child – This is supposed to have been the great Ignatius, whom Trajan, the wise, the good Emperor Trajan, condemned to be cast to the wild beasts at Rome! Mark ix, 36; Luke ix, 47.

3. Except ye be converted – The first step toward entering into the kingdom of grace, is to become as little children: lowly in heart, knowing yourselves utterly ignorant and helpless, and hanging wholly on your Father who is in heaven, for a supply of all your wants. We may farther assert, (though it is doubtful whether this text implies so much,) except ye be turned from darkness to light, and from the power of Satan to God:, except ye be entirely, inwardly changed, renewed in the image of God, ye cannot enter into the kingdom of glory. Thus must every man be converted in this life, or he can never enter into life eternal. Ye shall in no wise enter – So far from being great in it. Matt. xix, 14.

5, 6. And all who are in this sense little children are unspeakably dear to me. Therefore help them all you can, as if it were myself in person, and see that ye offend them not; that is, that ye turn them not out of the right way, neither hinder them in it. Matt. x, 40; Luke x, 16; John xiii, 20.

7. Woe to the world because of offenses – That is, unspeakable misery will be in the world through them; for it must needs be that offenses come – Such is the nature of things, and such the weakness, folly, and wickedness of mankind, that it cannot be but they will come; but woe to that man – That is, miserable is that man, by whom the offense cometh. Offenses are, all things whereby any one is turned out of, or hindered in the way of God.

8, 9. If thy hand, foot, eye, cause thee to offend – If the most dear enjoyment, the most beloved and useful person, turn thee out of, or hinder thee in the way Is not this a hard saying? Yes; if thou take counsel with flesh and blood. Matt. v, 29; Mark ix, 43.

10. See that ye despise not one of these little ones – As if they were beneath your notice. Be careful to receive and not to offend, the very weakest believer in Christ: for as inconsiderable as some of these may appear to thee, the very angels of God have a peculiar charge over them: even those of the highest order, who continually appear at the throne of the Most High. To behold the face of God seems to signify the waiting near his throne; and to be an allusion to the office of chief ministers in earthly courts, who daily converse with their princes.

11. Another, and yet a stronger reason for your not despising them is, that I myself came into the world to save them. Luke xix, 10.

12. Luke xv, 4.

14. So it is not the will of your Father – Neither doth my Father despise the least of them. Observe the gradation. The angels, the Son, the Father.

15. But how can we avoid giving offense to some? or being offended at others! Especially suppose they are quite in the wrong? Suppose they commit a known sin? Our Lord here teaches us how: he lays down a sure method of avoiding all offenses. Whosoever closely observes this threefold rule, will seldom offend others, and never be offended himself. If any do any thing amiss, of which thou art an eye or ear witness, thus saith the Lord, If thy brother – Any who is a member of the same religious community: Sin against thee,

MATTHEW 18

The importance of humility. (1-6)
Caution against offenses. (7-14)
The removal of offenses. (15-20)
Conduct towards brethren, The parable of the unmerciful
servant. (21-35)

1-6 As there never was a greater pattern of humility, so there never was a greater preacher of it, than Christ; he took all occasions to command it, to commend it, to his disciples and followers. The occasion of this discourse concerning humility was an unbecoming contest among the disciples for precedency; they came to him, saying, among themselves (for they were ashamed to ask him, Mk. 9:34), Who is the greatest in the kingdom of heaven? They mean not, who by character (then the question had been good, that they might know what graces and duties to excel in), but who by name. They had heard much, and preached much, of the kingdom of heaven, the kingdom of the Messiah, his church in this world; but as yet they were so far from having any clear notion of it, that they dreamt of a temporal kingdom, and the external pomp and power of it. Christ had lately foretold his sufferings, and the glory that should follow, that he should rise again, from whence they expected his kingdom would commence; and now they thought it was time to put in for their places in it; it is good, in such cases, to speak early. Upon other discourses of Christ to that purport, debates of this kind arose (ch. 20:19, 20; Lu. 22:22, 24); he spoke many words of his sufferings, but only one of his glory; yet they fasten upon that, and overlook the other; and, instead of asking how they might have strength and grace to suffer with him, they ask him, "Who shall be highest in reigning with him." Note, Many love to hear and speak of privileges and glory, who are willing to pass by the thoughts of work and trouble. They look so much at the crown, that they forget the yoke and the cross. So the disciples here did, when they asked, Who is the greatest in the kingdom of heaven?

7-14 Considering the cunning and malice of Satan, and the weakness and depravity of men's hearts, it is not possible but that there should be offenses. God permits them for wise and holy ends, that those who are sincere, and those who are not, may be made known. Being told before, that there will be seducers, tempters, persecutors, and bad examples, let us stand on our guard. We must, as far as lawfully we may, part with what we cannot keep without being entangled by it in sin. The outward occasions of sin must be avoided. If we live after the flesh, we must die. If we, through the Spirit, mortify the deeds of the body, we shall live. Christ came into the world to save souls, and he will reckon severely with those who hinder the progress of others who are setting their faces heavenward. And shall any of us refuse attention to those whom the Son of God came to seek and to save? A father takes care of all his children, but is particularly tender of the little ones.

can hardly be trusted in a bookseller's shop, because though we might have done very well at home without a certain volume, we no sooner see it than we are in urgent need of it. So often is it with some of you about other matters, so that it becomes most dangerous to let you see, because you want as soon as you see. A sight of Jesus, of what he is to sinners, of what he makes sinners, of what he is in himself, will more tend to make you feel your need of him than all your poring over your poor miserable self. You will get no further there, look to "Jesus only." "Ay," saith another, "but I want to read my title clear, I want to know that I have an interest in Jesus." You will best read your interest in Christ, by looking at him. If I want to know whether a certain estate is mine, do I look into my own heart to see if I have a right to it? No. I look into the archives of the estate, I search testaments and covenants.

Now, Christ Jesus is God's covenant with the people, a leader and commander to the people. Today, I personally can read my title clear to heaven, and shall I tell you how I read it? Not because I feel all I wish to feel, nor because I am what I hope I yet shall be, but I read in the word that "Jesus Christ came into the world to save sinners," I am a sinner, even the devil cannot tell me I am not. O precious Savior, then thou hast come to save such as I am. Then I see it written again, "He that believeth and is baptized, shall be saved." I have believed, and have been baptized; I know I trust alone in Jesus, and that is believing. As surely then as there is a God in heaven I shall be in heaven one day. It must be so, because unless God be a liar, he that believeth must be saved. You see it is not by looking within, it is by looking to Jesus only that you perceive at last your name graven on his hands. I wish to have Christ's name written on my heart, but if I want assurance, I have to look at his heart till I see my name written there. O turn your eye away from your sin and your emptiness to his righteousness and his fullness. See the sweat drops bloody as they fall in Gethsemane, see his heart pierced and pouring out blood and water for the sins of men upon Calvary! There is life in a look at him! O look to him, and though it be Jesus only, though Moses should condemn you, and Elias should alarm you, yet "Jesus only" shall be enough to comfort and enough to save you. May God grant us grace every one of us to take for our motto in life, for our hope in death, and for our joy in eternity, "Jesus only." May God bless you for the sake of "Jesus only." Amen.

say unto you, he rejoiceth more of that sheep, than of the ninety and nine which went not astray.

14 Even so it is not the will of your Father which is in heaven, that one of these little ones should perish.

15 Moreover if thy brother shall trespass against thee, go and tell him his fault between thee and him alone: if he shall hear thee, thou hast gained thy brother.

16 But if he will not hear thee, then take with thee one or two more, that in the mouth of two or three witnesses every word may be established.

17 And if he shall neglect to hear them, tell it unto the church: but if he neglect to hear the church, let him be unto thee as an heathen man and a publican.

18 Verily I say unto you, Whatsoever ye shall bind on earth shall be bound in heaven: and whatsoever ye shall loose on earth shall be loosed in heaven.

19 Again I say unto you, That if two of you shall agree on earth as touching any thing that they shall ask, it shall be done for them of my Father which is in heaven.

20 For where two or three are gathered together in my name, there am I in the midst of them.

21 Then came Peter to him, and said, Lord, how oft shall my brother sin against me, and I forgive him? till seven times?

22 Jesus saith unto him, I say not unto thee, Until seven times: but, Until seventy times seven.

23 Therefore is the kingdom of heaven likened unto a certain king, which would take account of his servants.

24 And when he had begun to reckon, one was brought unto him, which owed him ten thousand talents.

25 But forasmuch as he had not to pay, his lord commanded him to be sold, and his wife, and children, and all that he had, and payment to be made.

26 The servant therefore fell down, and worshiped him, saying, Lord, have patience with me, and I will pay thee all.

27 Then the lord of that servant was moved with compassion, and loosed him, and forgave him the debt.

28 But the same servant went out, and found one of his fellowservants, which owed him an hundred pence: and he laid hands on him, and took him by the throat, saying, Pay me that thou owest.

29 And his fellowservant fell down at his feet, and besought him, saying, Have patience with me, and I will pay thee all.

30 And he would not: but went and cast him into prison, till he should pay the debt.

1. Go and reprove him alone – If it may be in person; if that cannot so well be done, by thy messenger; or in writing. Observe, our Lord gives no liberty to omit this; or to exchange it for either of the following steps. If this do not succeed,

2. Take with thee one or two more – Men whom he esteems or loves, who may then confirm and enforce what thou sayest; and afterward, if need require, bear witness of what was spoken. If even this does not succeed, then, and not before,

3. Tell it to the elders of the Church – Lay the whole matter open before those who watch over yours and his soul. If all this avail not, have no farther intercourse with him, only such as thou hast with heathens.

Can any thing be plainer? Christ does here as expressly command all Christians who see a brother do evil, to take this way, not another, and to take these steps, in this order, as he does to honor their father and mother. But if so, in what land do the Christians live? If we proceed from the private carriage of man to man, to proceedings of a more public nature, in what Christian nation are Church censures conformed to this rule? Is this the form in which ecclesiastical judgments appear, in the popish, or even the Protestant world? Are these the methods used even by those who boast the most loudly of the authority of Christ to confirm their sentences? Let us earnestly pray, that this dishonor to the Christian name may be wiped away, and that common humanity may not, with such solemn mockery, be destroyed in the name of the Lord! Let him be to thee as the heathen – To whom thou still owest earnest good will, and all the offices of humanity. Luke xvii, 3.

18. Whatsoever ye shall bind on earth – By excommunication, pronounced in the spirit and power of Christ. Whatsoever ye shall loose – By absolution from that sentence. In the primitive Church, absolution meant no more than a discharge from Church censure. Again I say – And not only your intercession for the penitent, but all your united prayers, shall be heard. How great then is the power of joint prayer! If two of you – Suppose a man and his wife. Matt. xvi, 19.

20. Where two or three are gathered together in my name – That is, to worship me. I am in the midst of them – By my Spirit, to quicken their prayers, guide their counsels, and answer their petitions.

22. Till seventy times seven – That is, as often as there is occasion. A certain number is put for an uncertain.

23. Therefore – In this respect.

24. One was brought who owed him ten thousand talents – According to the usual computation, if these were talents of gold, this would amount to seventy-two millions sterling. If they were talents of silver, it must have been four millions, four hundred thousand pounds. Hereby our Lord intimates the vast number and weight of our offenses against God, and our utter incapacity of making him any satisfaction.

25. As he had not to pay, his Lord commanded him to be sold – Such was the power which creditors anciently had over their insolvent debtors in several countries.

30. Went with him before a magistrate, and cast him into prison, protesting he should lie there, till he should pay the whole debt.

34. His Lord delivered him to the tormentors – Imprisonment is a much severer punishment in the eastern countries than in ours. State criminals, especially when condemned to it, are not only confined to a very mean and scanty allowance, but are frequently loaded with clogs or heavy yokes, so that they can neither lie nor sit at ease: and by

15-20 If a professed Christian is wronged by another, he ought not to complain of it to others, as is often done merely upon report, but to go to the offender privately, state the matter kindly, and show him his conduct. This would generally have all the desired effect with a true Christian, and the parties would be reconciled. The principles of these rules may be practiced every where, and under all circumstances, though they are too much neglected by all. But how few try the method which Christ has expressly enjoined to all his disciples! In all our proceedings we should seek direction in prayer; we cannot too highly prize the promises of God. Wherever and whenever we meet in the name of Christ, we should consider him as present in the midst of us.

21-35 Though we live wholly on mercy and forgiveness, we are backward to forgive the offenses of our brethren. This parable shows how much provocation God has from his family on earth, and how untoward his servants are. There are three things in the parable:
1. The master's wonderful clemency. The debt of sin is so great, that we are not able to pay it. See here what every sin deserves; this is the wages of sin, to be sold as a slave. It is the folly of many who are under strong convictions of their sins, to fancy they can make God satisfaction for the wrong they have done him.
2. The servant's unreasonable severity toward his fellow-servant, notwithstanding his lord's clemency toward him. Not that we may make light of wronging our neighbor, for that is also a sin against God; but we should not aggravate our neighbor's wronging us, nor study revenge. Let our complaints, both of the wickedness of the wicked, and of the afflictions of the afflicted, be brought to God, and left with him.
3. The master reproved his servant's cruelty. The greatness of sin magnifies the riches of pardoning mercy; and the comfortable sense of pardoning mercy, does much to dispose our hearts to forgive our brethren. We are not to suppose that God actually forgives men, and afterwards reckons their guilt to them to condemn them; but this latter part of the parable shows the false conclusions many draw as to their sins being pardoned, though their after-conduct shows that they never entered into the spirit, or experienced the sanctifying grace of the gospel. We do not forgive our offending brother aright, if we do not forgive from the heart. Yet this is not enough; we must seek the welfare even of those who offend us. How justly will those be condemned, who, though they bear the Christian name, persist in unmerciful treatment of their brethren! The humbled sinner relies only on free, abounding mercy, through the ransom of the death of Christ. Let us seek more and more for the renewing grace of God, to teach us to forgive others as we hope for forgiveness from him.

THE TRIUMPHAL ENTRY INTO JERUSALEM
Sermon, number 405, delivered on Sunday Morning, August the 18th, 1861 at the Metropolitan Tabernacle, Newington.

"Tell ye the daughter of Zion, Behold, thy King cometh unto thee, meek, and sitting upon an ass, and a colt the foal of an ass."—Matthew 21:5.

CHRIST'S RIDING through the streets of Jerusalem was as plain a manifesto and proclamation of his royal rights as could possibly have been issued. I think, moreover,—and upon this I build the discourse of this morning,—I think that Christ used the popular fanaticism as an opportunity of preaching to us a living sermon, embodying great truths which are too apt to be forgotten because of their spiritual character, embodying them in the outward form and symbol of himself riding as a king, attended by hosts of followers. We come to this as the subject of our sermon. Let us see what we can learn from it.

I. One of the first things we learn is this. By thus through the streets in state, Jesus Christ claimed to be a king. That claim had been to a great extent kept in the background until now, but ere he goes to his Father, when his enemies' rage has reached its utmost fury, and when his own hour of deepest humiliation has just arrived, he makes an open claim before the eyes of all men to be called and acknowledged a king. He summonses first his heralds. Two disciples come. He sends forth his mandate—"Go ye into the village over against you, and ye shall find an ass and a colt." He gathers together his courtiers. His twelve disciples, those who usually attended him, come around him. He mounts the ass which of old had been ridden by the Jewish lawgivers, the rulers of the people. He begins to ride through the streets and the multitudes clap their hands. It is reckoned by some that no fewer than three thousand people must have been present on the occasion, some going before some following after, and others standing on either side to see the show. He rides to his capital; the streets of Jerusalem, the royal city, are open to him, like a king, he ascends to his palace. He was a spiritual king, and therefore he went not to the palace temporal but to the palace spiritual. He rides to the temple, and then, taking possession of it, he begins to teach in it as he had not done before. He had been sometimes in Solomon's porch, but he was oftener on the mountain's side than in the temple; but now, like a king, he takes possession of his palace, and there, sitting down on his

31 So when his fellowservants saw what was done, they were very sorry, and came and told unto their lord all that was done.

32 Then his lord, after that he had called him, said unto him, O thou wicked servant, I forgave thee all that debt, because thou desiredst me:

33 Shouldest not thou also have had compassion on thy fellowservant, even as I had pity on thee?

34 And his lord was wroth, and delivered him to the tormentors, till he should pay all that was due unto him.

35 So likewise shall my heavenly Father do also unto you, if ye from your hearts forgive not every one his brother their trespasses.

MATTHEW 19

1 And it came to pass, that when Jesus had finished these sayings, he departed from Galilee, and came into the coasts of Judea beyond Jordan;

2 And great multitudes followed him; and he healed them there.

3 The Pharisees also came unto him, tempting him, and saying unto him, Is it lawful for a man to put away his wife for every cause?

4 And he answered and said unto them, Have ye not read, that he which made them at the beginning made them male and female,

5 And said, For this cause shall a man leave father and mother, and shall cleave to his wife: and they twain shall be one flesh?

6 Wherefore they are no more twain, but one flesh. What therefore God hath joined together, let not man put asunder.

7 They say unto him, Why did Moses then command to give a writing of divorcement, and to put her away?

8 He saith unto them, Moses because of the hardness of your hearts suffered you to put away your wives: but from the beginning it was not so.

9 And I say unto you, Whosoever shall put away his wife, except it be for fornication, and shall marry another, committeth adultery: and whoso marrieth her which is put away doth commit adultery.

10 His disciples say unto him, If the case of the man be so with his wife, it is not good to marry.

11 But he said unto them, All men cannot receive this saying, save they to whom it is given.

12 For there are some eunuchs, which were so born from their mother's womb: and there are some eunuchs, which

frequent scourgings and sometimes rackings are brought to an untimely end. Till he should pay all that was due to him – That is, without all hope of release, for this he could never do. How observable is this whole account; as well as the great inference our Lord draws from it:

1. The debtor was freely and fully forgiven;

2. He willfully and grievously offended;

3. His pardon was retracted, the whole debt required, and the offender delivered to the tormentors for ever. And shall we still say, but when we are once freely and fully forgiven, our pardon can never be retracted? Verily, verily, I say unto you, So likewise will my heavenly Father do to you, if ye from your hearts forgive not every one his brother their trespasses.

MATTHEW 19

1. He departed – and from that time walked no more in Galilee. Mark x, 1.

2. Multitudes followed him, and he healed them there – That is, wheresoever they followed him.

3. The Pharisees came tempting him – Trying to make him contradict Moses. For every cause – That is, for any thing which he dislikes in her. This the scribes allowed.

4. He said, Have ye not read – So instead of contradicting him, our Lord confutes them by the very words of Moses. He who made them, made them male and female from the beginning – At least from the beginning of the Mosaic creation. And where do we read of any other? Does it not follow, that God's making Eve was part of his original design, and not a consequence of Adam's beginning to fall? By making them one man and one woman, he condemned polygamy: by making them one flesh, he condemned divorce.

5. And said – By the mouth of Adam, who uttered the words. Gen. ii, 24.

7. Why did Moses command – Christ replies, Moses permitted (not commanded) it, because of the hardness of your hearts – Because neither your fathers nor you could bear the more excellent way. Deut. xxiv, 1; Matt. v, 31; Mark x, 2; Luke xvi, 18.

9. And I say to you – I revoke that indulgence from this day, so that from henceforth, Whosoever, &c.

11. But he said to them – This is not universally true; it does not hold, with regard to all men, but with regard to those only to whom is given this excellent gift of God. Now this is given to three sorts of persons to some by natural constitution, without their choice: to others by violence, against their choice; and to others by grace with their choice: who steadily withstand their natural inclinations, that they may wait upon God without distraction.

12. There are eunuchs who have made themselves eunuchs for the kingdom of heaven's sake – Happy they! who have abstained from marriage (though without condemning or despising it) that they might walk more closely with God! He that is able to receive it, let him receive it – This gracious command (for such it is unquestionably, since to say, such a man may live single, is saying nothing. Who ever doubted this?) is not designed for all men: but only for those few who are able to receive it. O let these receive it joyfully!

13. That he should lay his hands on them – This was a rite which was very early used, in praying for a blessing on young persons. See Gen. xlviii, 14, 20. The disciples rebuked them – That is, them that brought

MATTHEW HENRY

CHARLES H. SPURGEON

MATTHEW 19

Jesus enters Judea. (1,2)
The Pharisees' question about divorces. (3-12)
Young children brought to Jesus. (13-15)
The rich young man's inquiry. (16-22)
The recompense of Christ's followers. (23-30)

1,2 Great multitudes followed Christ. When Christ departs, it is best for us to follow him. They found him as able and ready to help elsewhere, as he had been in Galilee; wherever the Sun of Righteousness arose, it was with healing in his wings.

3-12 The Pharisees were desirous of drawing something from Jesus which they might represent as contrary to the law of Moses. Cases about marriage have been numerous, and sometimes perplexed; made so, not by the law of God, but by the lusts and follies of men; and often people fix what they will do, before they ask for advice. Jesus replied by asking whether they had not read the account of the creation, and the first example of marriage; thus pointing out that every departure therefrom was wrong. That condition is best for us, and to be chosen and kept to accordingly, which is best for our souls, and tends most to prepare us for, and preserve us to, the kingdom of heaven. When the gospel is really embraced, it makes men kind relatives and faithful friends; it teaches them to bear the burdens, and to bear with the infirmities of those with whom they are connected, to consider their peace and happiness more than their own. As to ungodly persons, it is proper that they should be restrained by laws, from breaking the peace of society. And we learn that the married state should be entered upon with great seriousness and earnest prayer.

13-15 It is well when we come to Christ ourselves, and bring our children. Little children may be brought to Christ as needing, and being capable of receiving blessings from him, and having an interest in his intercession. We can but beg a blessing for them: Christ only can command the blessing. It is well for us, that Christ has more love and tenderness in him than the best of his disciples have. And let us learn of him not to discountenance any willing, well-meaning souls, in their seeking after Christ, though they are but weak. Those who are given to Christ, as part of his purchase, he will in no wise cast out. Therefore he takes it ill of all who forbid, and try to shut out those whom he has received. And all Christians should bring their children to the Savior that he may bless them with spiritual blessings.

16-22 Christ knew that covetousness was the sin which most easily beset this young man; though he had got honestly what he possessed, yet he could not cheerfully part with it, and by this his want of sincerity was shown. Christ's promises make his precepts easy, and his yoke pleasant and very comfortable; yet this

prophetic throne, he teaches the people in his royal courts. Ye princes of the earth, give ear, there is one who claims to be numbered with you. It is Jesus, the Son of David, the King of the Jews. Room for him, ye emperors, room for him! Room for the man who was born in a manger! Room for the man whose disciples were fishermen! Room for him whose garment was that of a peasant, without seam, woven from the top throughout! He wears no crown except the crown of thorns, yet he is more royal than you. About his loins he wears no purple, yet he is more imperial far than you. Upon his feet there are no silver sandals bedight with pearls, yet he is more glorious than you. Room for him: room for him! Hosanna! Hosanna! Let him be proclaimed again a King! a King! a King! Let him value his place upon his throne, high above the kings of the earth. This is what he then did, he proclaimed himself a King.

II. Moreover, Christ by this act showed what sort of a king he might have been if he had pleased, and what sort of a king he might be now, if he willed it. Had it been our Lord's will, those multitudes who followed him in the streets would actually have crowned him there and then, and bowing the knee, they would have accepted him as the branch that sprung out of the dried root of Jesse—him that was to come—the ruler, the Shiloh among God's people. He had only to have said a word, and they would have rushed with him at their head to Pilate's palace, and taking him by surprise, with but few soldiers in the land, Pilate might soon have been his prisoner, and have been tried for his life. Before the indomitable valor and the tremendous fury of a Jewish army, Palestine might soon have been cleared of all the Roman legions, and have become again a royal land. Nay, we aver it, with his power of working miracles, with his might by which he drove the soldiers back, when he said, "I am he;" he might have cleared not only that land but every other, he might have marched from country to country, and from kingdom to kingdom, till every royal city and every regal state would have yielded to his supremacy. He could have made those that dwelt in the isles of the sea to bow before him, and they that inhabit the wilderness could have been bidden to lick the dust. There was no reason, O ye kings of the earth, why Christ should not have been mightier than you. If his kingdom had been of this world, he might have founded a dynasty more lasting than yours, he might have gathered troops before whose might your legions would be melted like snow before the summer's sun, he might have dashed to pieces the Roman image, till, a broken mass,

were made eunuchs of men: and there be eunuchs, which have made themselves eunuchs for the kingdom of heaven's sake. He that is able to receive it, let him receive it.

13 Then were there brought unto him little children, that he should put his hands on them, and pray: and the disciples rebuked them.

14 But Jesus said, Suffer little children, and forbid them not, to come unto me: for of such is the kingdom of heaven.

15 And he laid his hands on them, and departed thence.

16 And, behold, one came and said unto him, Good Master, what good thing shall I do, that I may have eternal life?

17 And he said unto him, Why callest thou me good? there is none good but one, that is, God: but if thou wilt enter into life, keep the commandments.

18 He saith unto him, Which? Jesus said, Thou shalt do no murder, Thou shalt not commit adultery, Thou shalt not steal, Thou shalt not bear false witness,

19 Honor thy father and thy mother: and, Thou shalt love thy neighbor as thyself.

20 The young man saith unto him, All these things have I kept from my youth up: what lack I yet?

21 Jesus said unto him, If thou wilt be perfect, go and sell that thou hast, and give to the poor, and thou shalt have treasure in heaven: and come and follow me.

22 But when the young man heard that saying, he went away sorrowful: for he had great possessions.

23 Then said Jesus unto his disciples, Verily I say unto you, That a rich man shall hardly enter into the kingdom of heaven.

24 And again I say unto you, It is easier for a camel to go through the eye of a needle, than for a rich man to enter into the kingdom of God.

25 When his disciples heard it, they were exceedingly amazed, saying, Who then can be saved?

26 But Jesus beheld them, and said unto them, With men this is impossible; but with God all things are possible.

27 Then answered Peter and said unto him, Behold, we have forsaken all, and followed thee; what shall we have therefore?

28 And Jesus said unto them, Verily I say unto you, That ye which have followed me, in the regeneration when the Son of man shall sit in the throne of his glory, ye also shall sit upon twelve thrones, judging the twelve tribes of Israel.

them: probably thinking such an employ beneath the dignity of their Master. Mark x, 13; Luke xviii, 15.

14. Of such is the kingdom of heaven – Little children, either in a natural or spiritual sense, have a right to enter into my kingdom. Matt. xviii, 3.

16. And behold one came – Many of the poor had followed him from the beginning. One rich man came at last. Mark x, 17; Luke xviii, 18.

17. Why callest thou me good – Whom thou supposest to be only a man. There is none good – Supremely, originally, essentially, but God. If thou wilt enter into life, keep the commandments – From a principle of loving faith. Believe, and thence love and obey. And this undoubtedly is the way to eternal life. Our Lord therefore does not answer ironically, which had been utterly beneath his character, but gives a plain, direct, serious answer to a serious question.

19. Exod. xx, 12. &c.

20. The young man saith, All these have I kept from my childhood – So he imagined; and perhaps he had, as to the letter; but not as to the spirit, which our Lord immediately shows.

21. If thou desirest to be perfect – That is, to be a real Christian: Sell what thou hast – He who reads the heart saw his bosom sin was love of the world; and knew he could not be saved from this, but by literally renouncing it. To him therefore he gave this particular direction, which he never designed for a general rule. For him that was necessary to salvation: to us it is not. To sell all was an absolute duty to him; to many of us it would be an absolute sin. The young man went away – Not being willing to have salvation at so high a price.

24. It is easier for a camel to go through the eye of a needle, (a proverbial expression,) than for a rich man to go through the strait gate: that is, humanly speaking, it is an absolute impossibility. Rich man! tremble! feel this impossibility; else thou art lost for ever!

25. His disciples were amazed, saying, Who then can be saved? – If rich men, with all their advantages, cannot? Who? A poor man; a peasant; a beggar: ten thousand of them, sooner than one that is rich.

26. Jesus looking upon them – To compose their hurried spirits. O what a speaking look was there! Said to them – With the utmost sweetness: With men this is impossible – It is observable, he does not retract what he had said: no, nor soften it in the least degree, but rather strengthens it, by representing the salvation of a rich man as the utmost effort of Omnipotence.

28. In the renovation – In the final renovation of all things: Ye shall sit – In the beginning of the judgment they shall stand, 2 Cor. v, 10. Then being absolved, they shall sit with the Judge, 1 Cor. vi, 2, On twelve thrones – So our Lord promised, without expressing any condition: yet as absolute as the words are, it is certain there is a condition implied, as in many scriptures, where none is expressed. In consequence of this, those twelve did not sit on those twelve thrones: for the throne of Judas another took, so that he never sat thereon.

29. And every one – In every age and country; not you my apostles only; That hath forsaken houses, or brethren, or wife, or children – Either by giving any of them up, when they could not be retained with a clear conscience or by willingly refraining from acquiring them: Shall receive a hundred-fold – In value, though not in kind, even in the present world.

30. But many first – Many of those who were first called, shall be last – Shall have the lowest reward: those who came after them being preferred before them: and yet possibly both the first and the last may

MATTHEW HENRY   CHARLES H. SPURGEON

promise was as much a trial of the young man's faith, as the precept was of his charity and contempt of the world. It is required of us in following Christ, that we duly attend his ordinances, strictly follow his pattern, and cheerfully submit to his disposals; and this from love to him, and in dependence on him. To sell all, and give to the poor, will not serve, but we are to follow Christ. The gospel is the only remedy for lost sinners. Many abstain from gross vices who do not attend to their obligations to God. Thousands of instances of disobedience in thought, word, and deed, are marked against them in the book of God. Thus numbers forsake Christ, loving this present world: they feel convictions and desires, but they depart sorrowful, perhaps trembling. It behoves us to try ourselves in these matters, for the Lord will try us.

23-30 Though Christ spoke so strongly, few that have riches do not trust in them. How few that are poor are not tempted to envy! But men's earnestness in this matter is like their toiling to build a high wall to shut themselves and their children out of heaven. It should be satisfaction to those who are in a low condition, that they are not exposed to the temptations of a high and prosperous condition. If they live more hardly in this world than the rich, yet, if they get more easily to a better world, they have no reason to complain. Christ's words show that it is hard for a rich man to be a good Christian, and to be saved. The way to heaven is a narrow way to all, and the gate that leads into it, a strait gate; particularly so to rich people. More duties are expected from them than from others, and more sins easily beset them. It is hard not to be charmed with a smiling world. Rich people have a great account to make up for their opportunities above others. It is utterly impossible for a man that sets his heart upon his riches, to get to heaven. Christ used an expression, denoting a difficulty altogether unconquerable by the power of man. Nothing less than the almighty grace of God will enable a rich man to get over this difficulty. Who then can be saved? If riches hinder rich people, are not pride and sinful lusts found in those not rich, and as dangerous to them? Who can be saved? say the disciples. None, saith Christ, by any created power. The beginning, progress, and perfecting the work of salvation, depend wholly on the almighty power of God, to which all things are possible. Not that rich people can be saved in their worldliness, but that they should be saved from it. Peter said, We have forsaken all. Alas! it was but a poor all, only a few boats and nets; yet observe how Peter speaks, as if it had been some mighty thing. We are too apt to make the most of our services and sufferings, our expenses and losses, for Christ. However, Christ does not upbraid them; though it was but little that they had forsaken, yet it was their all, and as dear to them as if it had been more. Christ took it kindly that they left it to follow him; he accepts according to what a man hath. Our Lord's promise to the apostles is, that when the Son of man shall sit on the

like a potter's vessel shivered by a rod of iron, it might have been dashed to shivers.

It is even so, my brethren. If it were Christ's will, he might make his saints, everyone of them, a prince, he might make his Church rich and powerful, he might lift up his religion if he chose, and make it the most magnificent and sumptuous. If it were his will, there is no reason why all the glory we read of in the Old Testament under Solomon, might not be given to the Church under David's greater Son. But he does not come to do it, and hence the impertinence of those who think that Christ is to be worshiped with a gorgeous architecture, with magnificent vestments, with proud processions, with the alliance of states with churches, with making the bishops of God magnificent lords and rulers, with lifting up the Church herself, and attempting to put upon her shoulders those garments that will never fit her, vestments that were never meant for her. If Christ cared for this world's glory, it might soon be at his feet. If he willed to take it, who should raise a tongue against his claim, or who should lift a finger against his might! But he cares not for it. Take your gewgaws elsewhere, take your tinsel hence, he wants it not. Remove your glory, and your pomp, and your splendor, he needs it not at your hands. His kingdom is not of this world, else would his servants fight, else were his ministers clothed in robes of scarlet, and his servants would sit among princes, he cares not for it. People of God, seek not after it. What your Master would not have, do not court yourselves. Oh! Church of Christ what thine husband disdained, do thou disdain also. He might have had it, but he would not. And he read to us the lesson, that if all these things might be the Church's, it were well for he to pass by and say, "These are not for me—I was not meant to shine in these borrowed plumes."

III. But thirdly, and here lies the pith of the matter, you have seen that Christ claimed to be a king; you have seen what kind of a king he might have been and would not be, but now you see what kind of a king he is, and what kind of a king he claimed to be. What was his kingdom? What its nature? What was his royal authority? Who were to be his subjects? What his laws? What his government? Now you perceive at once from the passage taken as a whole, that Christ's kingdom is a very strange one, totally different from anything that ever has been seen or ever will be seen besides.

It is a kingdom, in the first place, in which the disciples are the courtiers. Our blessed Lord had no prince in waiting, no usher of the black rod, no gentlemen-at-arms who supplied the

29 And every one that hath forsaken houses, or brethren, or sisters, or father, or mother, or wife, or children, or lands, for my name's sake, shall receive an hundredfold, and shall inherit everlasting life.

30 But many that are first shall be last; and the last shall be first.

MATTHEW 20

1 For the kingdom of heaven is like unto a man that is an householder, which went out early in the morning to hire laborers into his vineyard.

2 And when he had agreed with the laborers for a penny a day, he sent them into his vineyard.

3 And he went out about the third hour, and saw others standing idle in the marketplace,

4 And said unto them; Go ye also into the vineyard, and whatsoever is right I will give you. And they went their way.

5 Again he went out about the sixth and ninth hour, and did likewise.

6 And about the eleventh hour he went out, and found others standing idle, and saith unto them, Why stand ye here all the day idle?

7 They say unto him, Because no man hath hired us. He saith unto them, Go ye also into the vineyard; and whatsoever is right, that shall ye receive.

8 So when even was come, the lord of the vineyard saith unto his steward, Call the laborers, and give them their hire, beginning from the last unto the first.

9 And when they came that were hired about the eleventh hour, they received every man a penny.

10 But when the first came, they supposed that they should have received more; and they likewise received every man a penny.

11 And when they had received it, they murmured against the goodman of the house,

12 Saying, These last have wrought but one hour, and thou hast made them equal unto us, which have borne the burden and heat of the day.

13 But he answered one of them, and said, Friend, I do thee no wrong: didst not thou agree with me for a penny?

14 Take that thine is, and go thy way: I will give unto this last, even as unto thee.

15 Is it not lawful for me to do what I will with mine own? Is thine eye evil, because I am good?

16 So the last shall be first, and the first last: for many be called, but few chosen.

17 And Jesus going up to Jerusalem

be saved, though with different degrees of glory. Matt. xx, 16; Mark x, 31; Luke xiii, 30.

MATTHEW 20

1. That some of those who were first called may yet be last, our Lord confirms by the following parable: of which the primary scope is, to show, That many of the Jews would be rejected, and many of the Gentiles accepted; the secondary, That of the Gentiles, many who were first converted would be last and lowest in the kingdom of glory; and many of those who were last converted would be first, and highest therein. The kingdom of heaven is like – That is, the manner of God's proceeding in his kingdom resembles that of a householder. In the morning – At six, called by the Roman and Jews, the first hour. From thence reckoning on to the evening, they called nine, the third hour; twelve, the sixth; three in the afternoon, the ninth; and five, the eleventh. To hire laborers into his vineyard – All who profess to be Christians are in this sense laborers, and are supposed during their life to be working in God's vineyard.

2. The Roman penny was about seven pence halfpenny. [About thirteen and three quarter cents, American.] This was then the usual price of a day's labor.

6. About the eleventh hour – That is, very late; long after the rest were called.

8. In the evening – Of life; or of the world.

9. Who were hired about the eleventh hour – Either the Gentiles, who were called long after the Jews into the vineyard of the Church of Christ; or those in every age who did not hear, or at least understand the Gospel call, till their day of life was drawing to a period. Some circumstances of the parable seem best to suit the former, some the latter of these senses.

10. The first supposed they should have received more – Probably the first here may mean the Jews, who supposed they should always be preferred before the Gentiles.

12. Thou hast made them equal to us – So St. Peter expressly, ["And put no difference between us and them, purifying their hearts by faith." Acts xv, 9.] God- hath put no difference between us (Jews) and them, (Gentiles,) purifying their hearts by faith. And those who were equally holy here, whenever they were called, will be equally happy hereafter.

14. It is my will to give to this last called among the heathens even as to the first called among the Jews: yea, and to the late converted publicans and sinners, even as to those who were called long before.

15. Is it not lawful for me to do what I will with my own? – Yea, doubtless, to give either to Jew or Gentile a reward infinitely greater than he deserves. But can it be inferred from hence, that it is lawful, or possible, for the merciful Father of spirits to "Consign an unborn soul to hell? Or damn him from his mother's womb?" Is thine eye evil because I am good – Art thou envious, because I am gracious? Here is an evident reference to that malignant aspect, which is generally the attendant of a selfish and envious temper.

16. So the last shall be first, and the first last – Not only with regard to the Jews and Gentiles, but in a thousand other instances. For many are called – All who hear the Gospel; but few chosen – Only those who obey it. ["But many that are first shall be last; and the last shall be first." Matt. xix, 30; "For many are called, but few are chosen. " Matt. xxii, 14.]

throne of his glory, he will make all things new, and they shall sit with him in judgment on those who will be judged according to their doctrine. This sets forth the honor, dignity, and authority of their office and ministry. Our Lord added, that every one who had forsaken possessions or comforts, for his sake and the gospel, would be recompensed at last. May God give us faith to rest our hope on this his promise; then we shall be ready for every service or sacrifice. Our Savior, in the last verse, does away a mistake of some. The heavenly inheritance is not given as earthly ones are, but according to God's pleasure. Let us not trust in promising appearances or outward profession. Others may, for aught we know, become eminent in faith and holiness.

MATTHEW 20

The parable of the laborers in the vineyard. (1-16)
Jesus again foretells his sufferings. (17-19)
The ambition of James and John. (20-28)
Jesus gives sight to two blind men near Jericho. (29-34)

1-16 The direct object of this parable seems to be, to show that though the Jews were first called into the vineyard, at length the gospel should be preached to the Gentiles, and they should be admitted to equal privileges and advantages with the Jews. Let us forego every proud claim, and seek for salvation as a free gift. Let us never envy or grudge, but rejoice and praise God for his mercy to others as well as to ourselves.

17-19 Christ is more particular here in foretelling his sufferings than before. And here, as before, he adds the mention of his resurrection and his glory, to that of his death and sufferings, to encourage his disciples, and comfort them. A believing view of our once crucified and now glorified Redeemer, is good to humble a proud, self-justifying disposition. When we consider the need of the humiliation and sufferings of the Son of God, in order to the salvation of perishing sinners, surely we must be aware of the freeness and richness of Divine grace in our salvation.

20-28 The sons of Zebedee abused what Christ said to comfort the disciples. Some cannot have comforts but they turn them to a wrong purpose. Pride is a sin that most easily besets us; it is sinful ambition to outdo others in pomp and grandeur. To put down the vanity and ambition of their request, Christ leads them to the thoughts of their sufferings. It is a bitter cup that is to be drunk of; a cup of trembling, but not the cup of the wicked. It is but a cup, it is but a draught, bitter perhaps, but soon emptied; it is a cup in the hand of a Father, Joh 18:11. Baptism is an ordinance by which we are joined to the Lord in covenant and communion; and so is suffering for Christ, Eze 20:37; Isa 48:10. Baptism is an outward and visible sign of an inward and spiritual grace; and so is suffering for Christ, for unto us it is

place of those grand officers? Why a few poor humble fishermen, who were his disciples. Learn, then, that if in Christ's kingdom you would be a peer you must be a disciple; to sit at his feet is the honor which he will give you. Hearing his words, obeying his commands, receiving of his grace—this is true dignity, this is true magnificence. The poorest man that loves Christ, or the humblest woman who is willing to accept him as her teacher, becomes at once one of the nobility that wait upon Christ Jesus. What a kingdom is this which makes fishermen nobles, and peasants princes while they remain but fishermen and peasants still! This is the kingdom of which we speak, in which discipleship is the highest degree, in which divine service is the patent of nobility.

It is a kingdom, strange to say it, in which the king's laws are none of then written upon paper. The king's laws are not promulgated by mouth of herald, but are written upon the heart. Do you not perceive that in the narrative Christ bids his servants go and take his royal steed, such as it was, and this was the law, "Loose him and let him go?" but where was the law written? It was written upon the heart of that man to whom the ass and the foal belonged, for he immediately said, "Let them go" cheerfully and with great joy; he thought it a high honor to contribute to the royal state of this great King of peace. So, brethren, in the kingdom of Christ you shall see no huge law books, no attorneys, no solicitors, no barristers who have need to expound the law. The law-book is here in the heart, the barrister is here in the conscience, the law is written no more on parchment, no more promulgated and written, as the Roman decrees were, upon steel and harass, but upon the fleshy tablets of the heart. The human will is subdued to obedience, the human heart is molded to Christ's image, his desire becomes the desire of his subjects, his glory their chief aim, and his law the very delight of their souls. Strange kingdom this, which needs no law save those which are written upon the hearts of the subjects.

Stranger still, as some will think it, this was a kingdom in which riches ensure no part whatever of its glory. There rides the King, the poorest of the whole state, for yonder King had not where to lay his head. There rides the King, the poorest of them all, upon another man's ass that he has borrowed. There rides the King, one who is soon to die; stripped of his robes to die naked and exposed. And yet he is the King of this kingdom, the First, the Prince, the Leader, the crowned One of the whole generation, simply because he had the least. He it was who had given most to others, and retained least himself.

took the twelve disciples apart in the way, and said unto them,

18 Behold, we go up to Jerusalem; and the Son of man shall be betrayed unto the chief priests and unto the scribes, and they shall condemn him to death,

19 And shall deliver him to the Gentiles to mock, and to scourge, and to crucify him: and the third day he shall rise again.

20 Then came to him the mother of Zebedee's children with her sons, worshiping him, and desiring a certain thing of him.

21 And he said unto her, What wilt thou? She saith unto him, Grant that these my two sons may sit, the one on thy right hand, and the other on the left, in thy kingdom.

22 But Jesus answered and said, Ye know not what ye ask. Are ye able to drink of the cup that I shall drink of, and to be baptized with the baptism that I am baptized with? They say unto him, We are able.

23 And he saith unto them, Ye shall drink indeed of my cup, and be baptized with the baptism that I am baptized with: but to sit on my right hand, and on my left, is not mine to give, but it shall be given to them for whom it is prepared of my Father.

24 And when the ten heard it, they were moved with indignation against the two brethren.

25 But Jesus called them unto him, and said, Ye know that the princes of the Gentiles exercise dominion over them, and they that are great exercise authority upon them.

26 But it shall not be so among you: but whosoever will be great among you, let him be your minister;

27 And whosoever will be chief among you, let him be your servant:

28 Even as the Son of man came not to be ministered unto, but to minister, and to give his life a ransom for many.

29 And as they departed from Jericho, a great multitude followed him.

30 And, behold, two blind men sitting by the way side, when they heard that Jesus passed by, cried out, saying, Have mercy on us, O Lord, thou Son of David.

31 And the multitude rebuked them, because they should hold their peace: but they cried the more, saying, Have mercy on us, O Lord, thou Son of David.

32 And Jesus stood still, and called them, and said, What will ye that I shall do unto you?

33 They say unto him, Lord, that our eyes may be opened.

34 So Jesus had compassion on them,

17. ["And they were in the way going up to Jerusalem; and Jesus went before them: and they were amazed; and as they followed, they were afraid. And he took again the twelve, and began to tell them what things should happen unto him," Mark x, 32; "Then he took unto him the twelve, and said unto them, Behold, we go up to Jerusalem, and all things that are written by the prophets concerning the Son of man shall be accomplished." Luke xviii, 31.]

20. Then came to him the mother of Zebedee's children – Considering what he had been just speaking, was ever any thing more unreasonable? Perhaps Zebedee himself was dead, or was not a follower of Christ. ["And James and John, the sons of Zebedee, come unto him, saying, Master, we would that thou shouldest do for us whatsoever we shall desire." Mark x, 35.]

21. In thy kingdom – Still they expected a temporal kingdom.

22. Ye know not what is implied in being advanced in my kingdom, and necessarily prerequired thereto. All who share in my kingdom must first share in my sufferings. Are you able and willing to do this? Both these expressions, The cup, the baptism, are to be understood of his sufferings and death. The like expressions are common among the Jews.

23. But to sit on my right hand – Christ applies to the glories of heaven, what his disciples were so stupid as to understand of the glories of earth. But he does not deny that this is his to give. It is his to give in the strictest propriety, both as God, and as the Son of man. He only asserts, that he gives it to none but those for whom it is originally prepared; namely, those who endure to the end in the faith that worketh by love.

25. Ye know that the princes of the Gentiles Lord it over them – And hence you imagine, the chief in my kingdom will do as they: but it will be quite otherwise.

26. Your minister – That is, your servant. ["But he that is greatest among you shall be your servant." Matt. xxiii; "11]

29. ["And they came to Jericho: and as he went out of Jericho with his disciples and a great number of people, blind Bartimeus, the son of Timaeus, sat by the highway side begging." Mark x, 46; "And it came to pass, that as he was come nigh unto Jericho, a certain blind man sat by the way side begging:" Luke xviii, 35.]

30. Behold two blind men cried out – St. Mark and St. Luke mention only one of them, blind Bartimeus. He was far the more eminent of the two, and, as it seems, spoke for both.

31. The multitude charged them to hold their peace – And so they will all who begin to cry after the Son of David. But let those who feel their need of him cry the more; otherwise they will come short of a cure.

given, Php 1:29. But they knew not what Christ's cup was, nor what his baptism. Those are commonly most confident, who are least acquainted with the cross. Nothing makes more mischief among brethren, than desire of greatness. And we never find Christ's disciples quarrelling, but something of this was at the bottom of it. That man who labors most diligently, and suffers most patiently, seeking to do good to his brethren, and to promote the salvation of souls, most resembles Christ, and will be most honored by him to all eternity. Our Lord speaks of his death in the terms applied to the sacrifices of old. It is a sacrifice for the sins of men, and is that true and substantial sacrifice, which those of the law faintly and imperfectly represented. It was a ransom for many, enough for all, working upon many; and, if for many, then the poor trembling soul may say, Why not for me?

29-34 It is good for those under the same trial, or infirmity of body or mind, to join in prayer to God for relief, that they may quicken and encourage one another. There is mercy enough in Christ for all that ask. They were earnest in prayer. They cried out as men in earnest. Cold desires beg denials. They were humble in prayer, casting themselves upon, and referring themselves cheerfully to, the Mediator's mercy. They showed faith in prayer, by the title they gave to Christ. Surely it was by the Holy Ghost that they called Jesus, Lord. They persevered in prayer. When they were in pursuit of such mercy, it was no time for timidity or hesitation: they cried earnestly. Christ encouraged them. The wants and burdens of the body we are soon sensible of, and can readily relate. Oh that we did as feelingly complain of our spiritual maladies, especially our spiritual blindness! Many are spiritually blind, yet say they see. Jesus cured these blind men; and when they had received sight, they followed him. None follow Christ blindly. He first by his grace opens men's eyes, and so draws their hearts after him. These miracles are our call to Jesus; may we hear it, and make it our daily prayer to grow in grace and in the knowledge of the Lord and Savior Jesus Christ. What he did was an instance, (1.) Of his pity; He had compassion on them. Misery is the object of mercy. They that are poor and blind are wretched and miserable (Rev. 3:17), and the objects of compassion. It was the tender mercy of our God, that gave light and sight to them that sat in darkness, Lu. 1:78, 79. We cannot help those that are under such calamities, as Christ did; but we may and must pity them, as Christ did, and draw out our soul to them. (2.) Of his power; He that formed the eye, can he not heal it? Yes, he can, he did, he did it easily, he touched their eyes; he did it effectually, Immediately their eyes received sight. Thus he not only proved that he was sent of God, but showed on what errand he was sent—to give sight to those that are spiritually blind, to turn them from darkness to light. Lastly, These blind men, when they had received sight, followed him.

He who was least selfish and most disinterested, he who lived most for others, was King of this kingdom. And look at the courtiers, look at the princes! they were all poor too; they had no flags to hang out from the windows, so they cast their poor clothes upon the hedges or hung them from the windows as he rode along. They had no splendid purple to make a carpet for the feet of his ass, so they cast their own toil-worn clothes in the way, they strewed along the path palm branches which they could easily reach from the trees which lined the road, because they had no money with which to bear the expense of a greater triumph. Every way it was a poor thing. No spangles of gold, no flaunting banners, no blowing of silver trumpets, no pomp, no state! It was poverty's own triumph. Poverty enthroned on Poverty's own beast rides through the streets. Strange kingdom this, brethren! I trust we recognize it—a kingdom in which he that is chief among us, is not he that is richest in gold, but he that is richest in faith; a kingdom which depends on no revenue except the revenue of divine grace; a kingdom which bids every man sit down under its shadow with delight, be he rich or be he poor.

Strange kingdom this! But, brethren, here is something perhaps yet more exceeding wonderful, it was a kingdom without armed force. Oh, prince, where are thy soldiers? Is this thine army? These thousands that attend thee? Where are their swords? They carry branches of palm. Where are their accoutrements? They have almost stripped themselves to pave thy way with their garments. Is this thine host? Are these thy battalions? Oh strange kingdom, without an army! Most strange King, who wears no sword, but rides along in this midst of his people conquering and to conquer a strange kingdom, in which there is the palm without the sword, the victory without the battle. No blood, no tears, no devastation, no burned cities, no mangled bodies! King of peace, King of peace, this is thy dominion! 'Tis even so in the kingdom over which Christ is king today, there is no force to be used. If the kings of the earth should say to the ministers of Christ, "We will lend you our soldiers," our reply would be, "What can we do with them?—as soldiers they are worthless to us." It was an ill day for the Church when she borrowed the army of that unhallowed heathen, the emperor Constantine and thought that would make her great. She gained nothing by it save pollution, degradation and shame, and that Church which asks the civil arm to help it, that Church which would make her Sabbaths binding on the people by force of law, that Church which would have her dogmas proclaimed with beat of drum, and

and touched their eyes: and immediately their eyes received sight, and they followed him.

MATTHEW 21

1   And when they drew nigh unto Jerusalem, and were come to Bethphage, unto the mount of Olives, then sent Jesus two disciples,

2   Saying unto them, Go into the village over against you, and straightway ye shall find an ass tied, and a colt with her: loose them, and bring them unto me.

3   And if any man say ought unto you, ye shall say, The Lord hath need of them; and straightway he will send them.

4   All this was done, that it might be fulfilled which was spoken by the prophet, saying,

5   Tell ye the daughter of Sion, Behold, thy King cometh unto thee, meek, and sitting upon an ass, and a colt the foal of an ass.

6   And the disciples went, and did as Jesus commanded them,

7   And brought the ass, and the colt, and put on them their clothes, and they set him thereon.

8   And a very great multitude spread their garments in the way; others cut down branches from the trees, and strawed them in the way.

9   And the multitudes that went before, and that followed, cried, saying, Hosanna to the Son of David: Blessed is he that cometh in the name of the Lord; Hosanna in the highest.

10   And when he was come into Jerusalem, all the city was moved, saying, Who is this?

11   And the multitude said, This is Jesus the prophet of Nazareth of Galilee.

12   And Jesus went into the temple of God, and cast out all them that sold and bought in the temple, and overthrew the tables of the moneychangers, and the seats of them that sold doves,

13   And said unto them, It is written, My house shall be called the house of prayer; but ye have made it a den of thieves.

14   And the blind and the lame came to him in the temple; and he healed them.

15   And when the chief priests and scribes saw the wonderful things that he did, and the children crying in the temple, and saying, Hosanna to the Son of David; they were sore displeased,

16   And said unto him, Hearest thou what these say? And Jesus saith unto them, Yea; have ye never read, Out of the mouth of babes and sucklings thou

MATTHEW 21

1. ["And when they came nigh to Jerusalem, unto Bethphage and Bethany, at the mount of Olives, he sendeth forth two of his disciples," Mark xi, 1; "And it came to pass, when he was come nigh to Bethphage and Bethany, at the mount called the mount of Olives, he sent two of his disciples,

" Luke xix, 29; "On the next day much people that were come to the feast, when they heard that Jesus was coming to Jerusalem," John xii, 12.]

5. The daughter of Sion – That is, the inhabitants of Jerusalem: the first words of the passage are cited from ["Behold, the LORD hath proclaimed unto the end of the world, Say ye to the daughter of Zion, Behold, thy salvation cometh; behold, his reward is with him, and his work before him." Isaiah lxii, 11]; the rest from ["Rejoice greatly, O daughter of Zion; shout, O daughter of Jerusalem: behold, thy King cometh unto thee: he is just, and having salvation; lowly, and riding upon an ass, and upon a colt the foal of an ass." Zech. ix, 9.] The ancient Jewish doctors were wont to apply these prophecies to the Messiah. On an ass – The Prince of Peace did not take a horse, a warlike animal. But he will ride on that by and by, ["And I saw heaven opened, and behold a white horse; and he that sat upon him was called Faithful and True, and in righteousness he doth judge and make war." Rev. xix, 11.] In the patriarchal ages, illustrious persons thought it no disgrace to make use of this animal: but it by no means appears, that this opinion prevailed, or this custom continued, till the reign of Tiberias. Was it a mean attitude wherein our Lord then appeared? Mean even to contempt! I grant it: I glory in it: it is for the comfort of my soul for the honor of his humility, and for the utter confusion of all worldly pomp and grandeur.

7. They set him thereon – That is, on the clothes.

8. A great multitude spread their garments in the way – A custom which was usual at the creation of a king, ["Then they hasted, and took every man his garment, and put it under him on the top of the stairs, and blew with trumpets, saying, Jehu is king." 2 Kings ix, 13.]

9. The multitudes cried, saying – Probably from a Divine impulse; for certainly most of them understood not the words they uttered. Hosanna – (Lord save us) was a solemn word in frequent use among the Jews. The meaning is, "We sing hosanna to the Son of David. Blessed is he, the Messiah, of the Lord. Save. Thou that art in the highest heavens." Our Lord restrained all public tokens of honor from the people till now, lest the envy of his enemies should interrupt his preaching before the time. But this reason now ceasing, he suffered their acclamations, that they might be a public testimony against their wickedness, who in four or five days after cried out, Crucify him, crucify him. The expressions recorded by the other evangelists are somewhat different from these: but all of them were undoubtedly used by some or others of the multitude.

11. This is Jesus from Nazareth – What a stumbling block was this! if he was of Nazareth, he could not be the Messiah. But they who earnestly desired to know the truth would not stumble thereat: for upon inquiry (which such would not fail to make) they would find, he was not of Nazareth, but Bethlehem.

12. He cast out all that sold and bought – Doves and oxen for sacrifice. He had cast them out three years before, ["And found in the temple those that sold oxen and sheep and doves, and the changers of money sitting:" John ii, 14]; bidding them not make that house a house of

MATTHEW 21

Christ enters Jerusalem. (1-11)
He drives out those who profaned the temple. (12-17)
The barren fig-tree cursed. (18-22)
Jesus' discourse in the temple. (23-27)
The parable of the two sons. (28-32)
The parable of the wicked husbandmen. (33-46)

1-11 This coming of Christ was described by the prophet Zechariah, Zec 9:9. When Christ would appear in his glory, it is in his meekness, not in his majesty, in mercy to work salvation. As meekness and outward poverty were fully seen in Zion's King, and marked his triumphal entrance to Jerusalem, how wrong covetousness, ambition, and the pride of life must be in Zion's citizens! They brought the ass, but Jesus did not use it without the owner's consent. The trappings were such as came to hand. We must not think the clothes on our backs too dear to part with for the service of Christ. The chief priests and the elders afterwards joined with the multitude that abused him upon the cross; but none of them joined the multitude that did him honor. Those that take Christ for their King, must lay their all under his feet. Hosanna signifies, Save now, we beseech thee! Blessed is he that cometh in the name of the Lord! But of how little value is the applause of the people! The changing multitude join the cry of the day, whether it be Hosanna, or Crucify him. Multitudes often seem to approve the gospel, but few become consistent disciples. When Jesus was come into Jerusalem all the city was moved; some perhaps were moved with joy, who waited for the Consolation of Israel; others, of the Pharisees, were moved with envy. So various are the motions in the minds of men upon the approach of Christ's kingdom.

12-17 Christ found some of the courts of the temple turned into a market for cattle and things used in the sacrifices, and partly occupied by the money-changers. Our Lord drove them from the place, as he had done at his entering upon his ministry, Joh 2:13-17. His works testified of him more than the hosannas; and his healing in the temple was the fulfilling the promise, that the glory of the latter house should be greater than the glory of the former. If Christ came now into many parts of his visible church, how many secret evils he would discover and cleanse! And how many things daily practiced under the cloak of religion, would he show to be more suitable to a den of thieves than to a house of prayer!

18-22 This cursing of the barren fig-tree represents the state of hypocrites in general, and so teaches us that Christ looks for the power of religion in those who profess it, and the savor of it from those that have the show of it. His just expectations from flourishing professors are often disappointed; he comes to many, seeking fruit, and finds leaves only. A false profession commonly withers in this world, and it is the effect of

make the fist or the sword to become her weapons, knoweth not what spirit she is of. These are carnal weapons. They are out of place in a spiritual kingdom. His armies are loving thoughts, his troops are kind words. The power by which he rules his people is not the strong hand and the stretched-out arm of police or sol-diery, but by deeds of love and words of over-flowing benediction he asserts his sovereign sway.

This was a strange kingdom too, my brethren, because it was without any pomp. If you call it pomp, what singular pomp it was! When our kings are proclaimed, three strange fellows, the like of whom one would never see at any other time, called heralds, come riding forth to proclaim the king. Strange are their dresses, romantic their costume, and with sound of trumpet the king is magnificently pro-claimed. Then comes the coronation and how the nation is moved from end to end with trans-port when the new king is about to be crowned! What multitudes crowd the street. Sometimes of old the fountains were made to flow with wine, and there was scarce a street which was not hung with tapestry throughout. But here comes the King of kings, the Prince of the kings of the earth; no mottled steed, no prancing horse which would keep at a distance the sons of poverty; he rides upon his ass, and as he rides along speaks kindly to the little chil-dren, who are crying, "Hosanna," and wishes well to the mothers and fathers of the lowest grade, who crowd around him. He is approach-able; he is not divided from them; he claims not to be their superior, but their servant so stately as a king, he was the servant of all. No trumpet sounds—he is content with the voice of men, no caparisons upon his ass, but his own disciple's garments, no pomp but the pomp which loving hearts right willingly yielded to him. Thus on he rides; his the kingdom of meek-ness, the kingdom of humiliation. Brethren, may we belong to that kingdom too; may we feel in our hearts that Christ is come in us to cast down every high and every proud thought, that every valley may be lifted up, and every hill may be abased, and the whole land exalted in that day!

Listen again, and this perhaps is a striking part of Christ's kingdom—he came to establish a kingdom without taxations. Where were the collectors of the King's revenue? You say he had not any; yes he had, but what a revenue it was! Every man took off his garments willingly; he never asked it; his revenue flowed freely from the willing gifts of his people. The first had lent his ass and his colt, the rest had given their clothes. Those who had scarce clothes to part

hast perfected praise?

17 And he left them, and went out of the city into Bethany; and he lodged there.

18 Now in the morning as he returned into the city, he hungered.

19 And when he saw a fig tree in the way, he came to it, and found nothing thereon, but leaves only, and said unto it, Let no fruit grow on thee henceforward for ever. And presently the fig tree withered away.

20 And when the disciples saw it, they marveled, saying, How soon is the fig tree withered away!

21 Jesus answered and said unto them, Verily I say unto you, If ye have faith, and doubt not, ye shall not only do this which is done to the fig tree, but also if ye shall say unto this mountain, Be thou removed, and be thou cast into the sea; it shall be done.

22 And all things, whatsoever ye shall ask in prayer, believing, ye shall receive.

23 And when he was come into the temple, the chief priests and the elders of the people came unto him as he was teaching, and said, By what authority doest thou these things? and who gave thee this authority?

24 And Jesus answered and said unto them, I also will ask you one thing, which if ye tell me, I in like wise will tell you by what authority I do these things.

25 The baptism of John, whence was it? from heaven, or of men? And they reasoned with themselves, saying, If we shall say, From heaven; he will say unto us, Why did ye not then believe him?

26 But if we shall say, Of men; we fear the people; for all hold John as a prophet.

27 And they answered Jesus, and said, We cannot tell. And he said unto them, Neither tell I you by what authority I do these things.

28 But what think ye? A certain man had two sons; and he came to the first, and said, Son, go work to day in my vineyard.

29 He answered and said, I will not: but afterward he repented, and went.

30 And he came to the second, and said likewise. And he answered and said, I go, sir: and went not.

31 Whether of them twain did the will of his father? They say unto him, The first. Jesus saith unto them, Verily I say unto you, That the publicans and the harlots go into the kingdom of God before you.

32 For John came unto you in the way of righteousness, and ye believed him not: but the publicans and the harlots believed him: and ye, when ye had seen

merchandise. Upon the repetition of the offense, he used sharper words. In the temple – That is, in the outer court of it, where the Gentiles used to worship. The money changers – The exchangers of foreign money into current coin, which those who came from distant parts might want to offer for the service of the temple. ["And Jesus entered into Jerusalem, and into the temple: and when he had looked round about upon all things, and now the eventide was come, he went out unto Bethany with the twelve. . . . And they come to Jerusalem: and Jesus went into the temple, and began to cast out them that sold and bought in the temple, and overthrew the tables of the moneychangers, and the seats of them that sold doves." Mark xi, 11, 15; "And he went into the temple, and began to cast out them that sold therein, and them that bought." Luke xix, 45.]

13. A den of thieves – A proverbial expression, for a harbor of wicked men. ["Even them will I bring to my holy mountain, and make them joyful in my house of prayer: their burnt offerings and their sacrifices shall be accepted upon mine altar; for mine house shall be called an house of prayer for all people." Isaiah lvi, 7; "Is this house, which is called by my name, become a den of robbers in your eyes? Behold, even I have seen it, saith the LORD." Jer. vii, 11.]

16. [Out of the mouth of babes and sucklings hast thou ordained strength because of thine enemies, that thou mightest still the enemy and the avenger." Psalm viii, 2.]

17. ""And Jesus entered into Jerusalem, and into the temple: and when he had looked round about upon all things, and now the eventide was come, he went out unto Bethany with the twelve. And on the morrow, when they were come from Bethany, he was hungry:" Mark xi, 11, 12.]

20. The disciples seeing it – As they went by, the next day.

21. Jesus answering, said, If ye have faith – Whence we may learn, that one great end of our Lord in this miracle was to confirm and increase their faith: another was, to warn them against unfruitfulness. [""And Jesus said unto them, Because of your unbelief: for verily I say unto you, If ye have faith as a grain of mustard seed, ye shall say unto this mountain, Remove hence to yonder place; and it shall remove; and nothing shall be impossible unto you." Matt. xvii, 20.]

23. When he was come into the temple, the chief priests came – Who thought he violated their right: and the elders of the people – Probably, members of the Sanhedrin, to whom that title most properly belonged: which is the more probable, as they were the persons under whose cognizance the late action of Christ, in purging the temple, would naturally fall. These, with the chief priests, seem purposely to have appeared in a considerable company, to give the more weight to what they said, and if need were, to bear a united testimony against him. As he was teaching – Which also they supposed he had no authority to do, being neither priest, nor Levite, nor scribe. Some of the priests (though not as priests) and all the scribes were authorized teachers. By what authority dost thou these things – Publicly teach the people! And drive out those who had our commission to traffic in the outer court? "And it came to pass, that on one of those days, as he taught the people in the temple, and preached the gospel, the chief priests and the scribes came upon him with the elders," Luke xx, 1; ""And they come again to Jerusalem: and as he was walking in the temple, there come to him the chief priests, and the scribes, and the elders," Mark xi, 27.]

24. I will ask you one thing – Who have asked me many: The baptism, that is, the whole ministry of John, was it from heaven or from men? – By what authority did he act and teach? Did man or God give him that

Christ's curse. The fig-tree that had no fruit, soon lost its leaves. This represents the state of the nation and people of the Jews in particular. Our Lord Jesus found among them nothing but leaves. And after they rejected Christ, blindness and hardness grew upon them, till they were undone, and their place and nation rooted up. The Lord was righteous in it. Let us greatly fear the doom denounced on the barren fig-tree.

23-27 As our Lord now openly appeared as the Messiah, the chief priests and scribes were much offended, especially because he exposed and removed the abuses they encouraged. Our Lord asked what they thought of John's ministry and baptism. Many are more afraid of the shame of lying than of the sin, and therefore scruple not to speak what they know to be false, as to their own thoughts, affections, and intentions, or their remembering and forgetting. Our Lord refused to answer their inquiry. It is best to shun needless disputes with wicked opposers.

28-32 As Christ instructed his disciples by parables, which made the instructions the more easy, so sometimes he convinced his adversaries by parables, which bring reproofs more close, and make men, or ever they are aware, to reprove themselves. Thus Nathan convinced David by a parable (2 Sa. 22:1), and the woman of Tekoa surprised him in like manner, 2 Sa. 14:2: Reproving parables are appeals to the offenders themselves, and judge them out of their own mouths. This Christ designs here, as appears by the first words (v. 28), But what think you? In these verses we have the parable of the two sons sent to work in the vineyard, the scope of which is to show that they who knew not John's baptism to be of God, were shamed even by the publicans and harlots, who knew it, and owned it. Here is, The parable itself, which represents two sorts of persons; some that prove better than they promise, represented by the first of those sons; others that promise better than they prove represented by the second.

1. They had both one and the same father, which signifies that God is a common Father to all mankind. There are favors which all alike receive from him, and obligations which all alike lie under to him; Have we not all one Father? Yes, and yet there is a vast difference between men's characters.

2. They had both the same command given them; Son, go work today in my vineyard. Parents should not breed up their children in idleness; nothing is more pleasing, and yet nothing more pernicious, to youth than that. Lam. 3:27. God sets his children to work, though they are all heirs. This command is given to every one of us.

3. Their conduct was very different. (1.) One of the sons did better than he said, proved better than he promised. His answer was bad, but his actions were good. [1.] Here is the untoward answer that he gave to his father; he said, flat and plain I will not. See to what a

with, plucked the branches from the trees, and here was state for once which cost no man anything, or rather for which nothing was demanded of any man, but everything spontaneously given. This is the kingdom of Christ,—a kingdom which subsists not upon tithe, Church-rate or Easter dues, but a kingdom which lives upon the free-will offering of the willing people, a kingdom which demands nothing of any man, but which comes to him with a stronger force than demand, saying to him, "Thou art not under the law, but under grace, wilt thou not, being bought with a price, consecrate thyself and all that thou hast, to the service of the King of kings! Brethren, do you think me wild and fanatical in talking of a kingdom of this sort? Indeed, 'twere fanatical if we said that any mere man could establish such a dominion. But Christ has done it, and this day there be tens of thousands of men in this world who call him King, and who feel that he is more their King than the ruler of their Dative land; that they give to him a sincerer homage than they ever give to the beg beloved sovereign, they feel that his power over them is such as they would not wish to resist—the power of love, that their gifts to him are an too little, for they wish to give themselves away, 'tis all that they can do. Marvelous and matchless kingdom! its like shall never be found on earth.

Before I leave this point, I should like to remark that apparently this was a kingdom in which all creatures were considered. Why did Christ have two beasts? There was an ass and a colt the foal of an ass; he rode on the foal of the ass because it had never been ridden before. Now I have looked at several of the commentators to see what they say about it, and one old commentator has made me laugh—I trust he will not make you laugh too—by saying, that Christ telling his disciples to bring the foal as well as the ass should teach us that infants ought to be baptized as well as their parents, which seemed to me to be an argument eminently worthy of childish baptism. Thinking the matter over, however, I consider there is a better reason to be given,—Christ would not have any pain in his kingdom, he would not have even an ass suffer by him, and if the foal had been taken away from its mother, there would have been the poor mother in the stable at home, thinking of its foal, and there would have been the foal longing to get back, like those oxen that the Philistines used when they took back the ark, and which went lowing as they went, because their calves were at home. Wondrous kingdom of Christ, in which the very beast shall have its share! "For the creature was made subject to vanity by our sin." It was the

it, repented not afterward, that ye might believe him.

33 Hear another parable: There was a certain householder, which planted a vineyard, and hedged it round about, and digged a winepress in it, and built a tower, and let it out to husbandmen, and went into a far country:

34 And when the time of the fruit drew near, he sent his servants to the husbandmen, that they might receive the fruits of it.

35
And the husbandmen took his servants, and beat one, and killed another, and stoned another.

36 Again, he sent other servants more than the first: and they did unto them likewise.

37 But last of all he sent unto them his son, saying, They will reverence my son.

38 But when the husbandmen saw the son, they said among themselves, This is the heir; come, let us kill him, and let us seize on his inheritance.

39 And they caught him, and cast him out of the vineyard, and slew him.

40
When the lord therefore of the vineyard cometh, what will he do unto those husbandmen?

41 They say unto him, He will miserably destroy those wicked men, and will let out his vineyard unto other husbandmen, which shall render him the fruits in their seasons.

42 Jesus saith unto them, Did ye never read in the scriptures, The stone which the builders rejected, the same is become the head of the corner: this is the Lord's doing, and it is marvelous in our eyes?

43
Therefore say I unto you, The kingdom of God shall be taken from you, and given to a nation bringing forth the fruits thereof.

44 And whosoever shall fall on this stone shall be broken: but on whomsoever it shall fall, it will grind him to powder.

45 And when the chief priests and Pharisees had heard his parables, they perceived that he spake of them.

46 But when they sought to lay hands on him, they feared the multitude, because they took him for a prophet.

authority? Was it not God? But if so, the consequence was clear. For John testified that Jesus was the Christ.

25. Why did ye not believe him – Testifying this.

27. Neither tell I you – Not again, in express terms: he had often told them before, and they would not believe him.

30. He answered, I go, sir: but went not – Just so did the scribes and Pharisees: they professed the greatest readiness and zeal in the service of God: but it was bare profession, contradicted by all their actions.

32. John came in a way of righteousness – Walking in it, as well as teaching it. The publicans and harlots – The most notorious sinners were reformed, though at first they said, I will not. And ye seeing the amazing change which was wrought in them, though at first ye said, I go, sir, repented not afterward – Were no more convinced than before. O how is this scripture fulfilled at this day!

33. A certain householder planted a vineyard – God planted the Church in Canaan; and hedged it round about – First with the law, then with his peculiar providence: and digged a wine press – Perhaps it may mean Jerusalem: and built a tower – The temple: and went into a far country – That is, left the keepers of his vineyard, in some measure, to behave as they should see good. ["And he began to speak unto them by parables. A certain man planted a vineyard, and set an hedge about it, and digged a place for the winefat, and built a tower, and let it out to husbandmen, and went into a far country." Mark xii, 1; "Then began he to speak to the people this parable; A certain man planted a vineyard, and let it forth to husbandmen, and went into a far country for a long time." Luke xx, 9.]

34. He sent his servants – His extraordinary messengers, the prophets: to the husbandmen – The ordinary preachers or ministers of the Jews.

41. They say – Perhaps some of the by-standers, not the chief priests or Pharisees; who, as St. Luke relates, said, God forbid, "He shall come and destroy these husbandmen, and shall give the vineyard to others. And when they heard it, they said, God forbid." Luke xx, 16.]

42. The builders – The scribes and priests, whose office it was to build up the Church. Is become the head of the corner – Or the chief corner stone: he is become the foundation of the Church, on which the whole building rests, and is the principal corner stone, for uniting the Gentiles to it, as the chief corner stone of a house supports and links its two sides together. ["The stone which the builders refused is become the head stone of the corner." Psalm cxviii, 22.]

43. Therefore – Because ye reject this corner stone. The kingdom of God – That is, the Gospel.

44. Whosoever shall fall on this stone shall be broken – Stumblers at Christ shall even then receive much hurt. He is said to fall on this stone, who hears the Gospel and does not believe. But on whomsoever it shall fall – In vengeance, it will utterly destroy him. It will fall on every unbeliever, when Christ cometh in the clouds of heaven. ["Whosoever shall fall upon that stone shall be broken; but on whomsoever it shall fall, it will grind him to powder." Luke xx, 18.]

degree of impudence the corrupt nature of man rises, to say, I will not, to the command of a Father; such a command of such a Father; they are impudent children, and stiff-hearted. Those that will not bend, surely they cannot blush; if they had any degree of modesty left them, they could not say, We will not. Jer. 2:25. Excuses are bad, but downright denials are worse; yet such peremptory refusals do the calls of the gospel often meet with. First, Some love their ease, and will not work; they would live in the world as leviathan in the waters, to play therein (Ps. 104:26); they do not love working. Secondly, Their hearts are so much upon their own fields, that they are not for working in God's vineyard. They love the business of the world better than the business of their religion. Thus some by the delights of sense, and others by the employments of the world, are kept from doing that great work which they were sent into the world about, and so stand all the day idle. [2.] Here is the happy change of his mind, and of his way, upon second thought; Afterward he repented, and went. Note, There are many who in the beginning are wicked and wilful, and very unpromising, who afterward repent and mend, and come to something. Some that God hath chosen, are suffered for a great while to run to a great excess of riot; Such were some of you, 1 Co. 6:11. These are set forth for patterns of long-suffering, 1 Tim. 1:16. Afterward he repented. Repentance is metanoia — an after-wit: and metameleia — an after-care. Better late than never. Observe, When he repented he went; that was the fruit meet for repentance. The only evidence of our repentance for our former resistance, is, immediately to comply, and set to work; and then what is past, shall be pardoned, and all shall be well. See what a kind Father God is; he resents not the affront of our refusals, as justly he might. He that told his father to his face, that he would not do as he bid him, deserved to be turned out of doors, and disinherited; but our God waits to be gracious, and, not withstanding our former follies, if we repent and mend, will favorably accept of us; blessed be God, we are under a covenant that leaves room for such a repentance. (2.) The other son said better than he did, promised better than he proved; his answer was good but his actions bad. To him the father said likewise, v. 30. The gospel call, though very different, is, in effect, the same to all, and is carried on with an even tenour. We have all the same commands, engagements, encouragements, though to some they are a savor of life unto life, to others of death unto death. Observe, [1.] How fairly this other son promised; He said, I go, sir. He gives his father a title of respect, sir. Note, It becomes children to speak respectfully to their parents. It is one branch of that honor which the fifth commandment requires. He professes a ready obedience, I go; not, "I will go by and by," but, "Ready, sir, you may depend upon it, I go just now." This answer we should give from the heart heartily to all the calls and commands of the word of God. See Jer. 3:22; Ps. 27:8. [2.] How he failed in the

beast that suffered because we sinned, and Christ intends that his kingdom should bring back the beast to its own pristine happiness. He would make us merciful men, considerate even to the beasts. I believe that when his kingdom fully comes, the animal nature will be put back to its former happiness. "Then shall the lion eat straw like the ox, the sucking child shall play on the hole of the asp, and the weaned child shall put his hand on the cockatrice den." Old Eden's peacefulness, and the familiarity between man and the lower creatures, shall come back once more. And even now, wherever the gospel is fully known in man's heart, man begins to recognize that he has no right wantonly to kill a sparrow or a worm, because it is in Christ's dominion; and he who would not ride a foal without having its mother by its side, that it might be at peace and happy, would not have any of his disciples think lightly of the meanest creature that his hands have made. Blessed kingdom this which considereth even the beasts! Doth God care for oxen? Ay, that he doth; and for the very ass itself, that heir of toil, he careth. Christ's kingdom, then, shall care for beasts as well as men.

Once more: Christ, in riding through the streets of Jerusalem, taught in a public manner, that his kingdom was to be one of joy. Brethren, when great conquerors ride through the streets, you often hear of the joy of the people; how the women throw roses on the pathway, how they crowd around the hero of the day, and wave their handkerchiefs to show their appreciation of the deliverance he has wrought. The city has been long besieged; the champion has driven away the besiegers, and the people will now have rest. Fling open wide the gates, clear the road and let the hero come, let the meanest page that is in his retinue be honored this day for the deliverer's sake. Ah! brethren, but in those triumphs how many tears there are that are hidden! There is a woman who hears the sound of the bells for victory, and she says, "Ah! victory indeed, but I am a widow, and my little ones are orphans." And from the balconies where beauty looks down and smiles, there may be a forgetfulness for the moment of friends and kindred over whom they will soon have to weep, for every battle is with blood, and every conquest is with woe, and every shout of victory hath in it weeping, and wailing, and gnashing of teeth. Every sound of trumpet because the battle is obtained, doth but cover over the cries, the sorrows, and the deep agonies of those that have been bereaved of their kinsfolk! But in thy triumph, Jesu, there were no tears! When the little children cried, "Hosanna," they had not lost their fathers in battle. When the

MATTHEW 22

1 And Jesus answered and spake unto them again by parables, and said,

2 The kingdom of heaven is like unto a certain king, which made a marriage for his son,

3 And sent forth his servants to call them that were bidden to the wedding: and they would not come.

4 Again, he sent forth other servants, saying, Tell them which are bidden, Behold, I have prepared my dinner: my oxen and my fatlings are killed, and all things are ready: come unto the marriage.

5 But they made light of it, and went their ways, one to his farm, another to his merchandise:

6 And the remnant took his servants, and entreated them spitefully, and slew them.

7 But when the king heard thereof, he was wroth: and he sent forth his armies, and destroyed those murderers, and burned up their city.

8 Then saith he to his servants, The wedding is ready, but they which were bidden were not worthy.

9 Go ye therefore into the highways, and as many as ye shall find, bid to the marriage.

10 So those servants went out into the highways, and gathered together all as many as they found, both bad and good: and the wedding was furnished with guests.

11 And when the king came in to see the guests, he saw there a man which had not on a wedding garment:

12 And he saith unto him, Friend, how camest thou in hither not having a wedding garment? And he was speechless.

13 Then said the king to the servants, Bind him hand and foot, and take him away, and cast him into outer darkness; there shall be weeping and gnashing of teeth.

14 For many are called, but few are chosen.

15 Then went the Pharisees, and took counsel how they might entangle him in his talk.

16 And they sent out unto him their disciples with the Herodians, saying, Master, we know that thou art true, and teachest the way of God in truth, neither carest thou for any man: for thou regardest not the person of men.

17 Tell us therefore, What thinkest thou? Is it lawful to give tribute unto Cesar, or not?

18 But Jesus perceived their wickedness, and said, Why tempt ye me, ye hypocrites?

MATTHEW 22

1. Jesus answering, spake – That is, spake with reference to what had just past.

2. A king, who made a marriage feast for his son – So did God, when he brought his first-begotten into the world.

3. Them that were invited – Namely, the Jews.

4. Fatlings – Fatted beasts and fowls.

5. One to his farm, another to his merchandise – One must mind what he has; another, gain what he wants. How many perish by misusing lawful things!

7. The king sending forth his troops – The Roman armies employed of God for that purpose. Destroyed those murderers – Primarily the Jews.

8. Go into the highways – The word properly signifies, the by-ways, or turnings of the road.

10. They gathered all – By preaching every where.

11. The guest – The members of the visible Church.

12. A wedding garment – The righteousness of Christ, first imputed, then implanted. It may easily be observed, this has no relation to the Lord's Supper, but to God's proceeding at the last day.

14. Many are called; few chosen – Many hear; few believe. Yea, many are members of the visible, but few of the invisible Church. ["So the last shall be first, and the first last: for many be called, but few chosen." Matt. xx, 16.]

15. ["And they send unto him certain of the Pharisees and of the Herodians, to catch him in his words." Mark xii, 13; "And they watched him, and sent forth spies, which should feign themselves just men, that they might take hold of his words, that so they might deliver him unto the power and authority of the governor."Luke xx, 20.]

16. The Herodians were a set of men peculiarly attached to Herod, and consequently zealous for the interest of the Roman government, which was the main support of the dignity and royalty of his family. Thou regardest not the person of men – Thou favor no man for his riches or greatness.

17. Is it lawful to give tribute to Cesar? – If he had said, Yes, the Pharisees would have accused him to the people, as a betrayer of the liberties of his country. If he had said, No, the Herodians would have accused him to the Roman governor.

18. Ye hypocrites – Pretending a scruple of conscience.

20. The tribute money – A Roman coin, stamped with the head of Cesar, which was usually paid in tribute.

21. They say to him, Cesar's – Plainly acknowledging, by their having received his coin, that they were under his government. And indeed this is a standing rule. The current coin of every nation shows who is the supreme governor of it. Render therefore, ye Pharisees, to Cesar the things which ye yourselves acknowledge to be Cesar's: and, ye Herodians, while ye are zealous for Cesar, see that ye render to God the things that are God's.

23. ["And they watched him, and sent forth spies, which should feign themselves just men, that they might take hold of his words, that so they might deliver him unto the power and authority of the governor." Mark xii, 18.]

24. ["If brethren dwell together, and one of them die, and have no child, the wife of the dead shall not marry without unto a stranger: her husband's brother shall go in unto her, and take her to him to wife, and perform the duty of an husband's brother unto her." Deut. xxv, 5.]

25. Now there were with us seven brethren – This story seems to have

MATTHEW HENRY

CHARLES H. SPURGEON

performance; He went not. Note, There are many that give good words, and make fair promises, in religion, and those from some good motions for the present, that rest there, and go no further, and so come to nothing. Saying and doing are two things; and many there are that say, and do not; it is particularly charged upon the Pharisees, ch. 23:3. Many with their mouth show much love, but their heart goes another way. They had a good mind to be religious, but they met with something to be done, that was too hard, or something to be parted with, that was too dear, and so their purposes are to no purpose. Buds and blossoms are not fruit.

33-46 So quick and powerful is the word of God, and such a discerner of the thoughts and intents of the heart, that it is easy for bad men (if conscience be not quite seared) to perceive that it speaks of them. 2. They sought to lay hands on him. Note, When those who hear the reproofs of the word, perceive that it speaks of them, if it do not do them a great deal of good, it will certainly do them a great deal of hurt. If they be not pricked to the heart with conviction and contrition, as they were Acts 2:37, they will be cut to the heart with rage and indignation, as they were Acts 5:33. 3. They durst not do it, for fear of the multitude, who took him for a prophet, though not for the Messiah; this served to keep the Pharisees in awe. The fear of the people restrained them from speaking ill of John (v. 26), and here from doing ill to Christ. Note, God has many ways of restraining the remainders of wrath, as he has of making that which breaks out redound to his praise, Ps. 76:10.

MATTHEW 22

The parable of the marriage feast. (1-14)
The Pharisees question Jesus as to the tribute. (15-22)
The question of the Sadducees as to the resurrection.
  (23-33)
The substance of the commandments. (34-40)
Jesus questions the Pharisees. (41-46)

1-14 See commentary at Luke 14:16-24

15-22 The Pharisees sent their disciples with the Herodians, a party among the Jews, who were for full subjection to the Roman emperor. Though opposed to each other, they joined against Christ. What they said of Christ was right; whether they knew it or not, blessed be God we know it. Jesus Christ was a faithful Teacher, and a bold reprover. Christ saw their wickedness. Whatever mask the hypocrite puts on, our Lord Jesus sees through it. Christ did not interpose as a judge in matters of this nature, for his kingdom is not of this world, but he enjoins peaceable subjection to the powers that be. His adversaries were reproved, and his disciples were taught that the Christian religion is no enemy to civil government. Christ is, and will be, the wonder, not only of his friends, but of his enemies. They

men and women shouted, "Blessed is he that cometh in the name of the Lord," they had no cause to shout with bated breath, or to mar their joys with the remembrance of misery. No, in his kingdom there is unalloyed, unmingled joy. Shout, shout, ye that are subjects of King Jesus! Sorrows ye may have, but not from him, troubles may come to you because you are in the world, but they come not from him, His service is perfect liberty. His ways are ways of pleasantness, and all his paths are peace.

"Joy to the world, the Savior comes,
  The Savior promised long;
Let every heart prepare a tune,
  And every voice a song."

He comes to wipe away your tears and not to make them flow, he comes to lift you from your dunghills and set you upon his throne, to fetch you from your dungeons and make you leap in liberty.

"Blessings abound wherein he reigns,
  The prisoner leaps to loose his chain;
The weary find eternal rest,
  And all the sons of want are blessed."

Singular kingdom this!

IV. And now I come to my fourth and last head. The Savior, in his triumphal entrance into the capital of his fathers, declared to us very plainly the practical effects of his kingdom. Now what are these? One of the first effects was that the whole city was moved. What does that mean? It means that everybody had something to say about it, and that everybody felt something because Christ rode through the street. There were some who leaned from the tops of their houses, and looked down the street and said to one another—"Aha! Did ever you see such fool's play as this? Humph! Here is Jesus of Nazareth down here riding on an ass! Surely if he meant to be king he might have chosen a horse. Look at him! They call that pomp! There is some old fisherman has just thrown down his bad-smelling garment; I dare say it had fish in it an hour or two ago? "Look," says one, "see that old beggar throwing his cap into the air for joy!" "Aha!" say they, "was there ever such a ridiculous thing as that?" I cannot put it in such terms as they would describe it; if I could, I think I would. I should like to make you see how ridiculous this must have seemed to the people. Why, if Pilate himself had heard about it he would have said—"Ah! there is nothing much to fear from that. There is no fear that that man will ever upset Cesar; there is no fear that he will ever overturn an army. Where are their swords? There is not a sword among them! They have no cries that sound like rebellion; their songs are only some religious verses taken out

19 Shew me the tribute money. And they brought unto him a penny.

20 And he saith unto them, Whose is this image and superscription?

21 They say unto him, Cesar's. Then saith he unto them, Render therefore unto Cesar the things which are Cesar's; and unto God the things that are God's.

22 When they had heard these words, they marveled, and left him, and went their way.

23 The same day came to him the Sadducees, which say that there is no resurrection, and asked him,

24 Saying, Master, Moses said, If a man die, having no children, his brother shall marry his wife, and raise up seed unto his brother.

25 Now there were with us seven brethren: and the first, when he had married a wife, deceased, and, having no issue, left his wife unto his brother:

26 Likewise the second also, and the third, unto the seventh.

27 And last of all the woman died also.

28 Therefore in the resurrection whose wife shall she be of the seven? for they all had her.

29 Jesus answered and said unto them, Ye do err, not knowing the scriptures, nor the power of God.

30 For in the resurrection they neither marry, nor are given in marriage, but are as the angels of God in heaven.

31 But as touching the resurrection of the dead, have ye not read that which was spoken unto you by God, saying,

32 I am the God of Abraham, and the God of Isaac, and the God of Jacob? God is not the God of the dead, but of the living.

33 And when the multitude heard this, they were astonished at his doctrine.

34 But when the Pharisees had heard that he had put the Sadducees to silence, they were gathered together.

35 Then one of them, which was a lawyer, asked him a question, tempting him, and saying,

36 Master, which is the great commandment in the law?

37 Jesus said unto him, Thou shalt love the Lord thy God with all thy heart, and with all thy soul, and with all thy mind.

38 This is the first and great commandment.

39 And the second is like unto it, Thou shalt love thy neighbor as thyself.

40 On these two commandments hang all the law and the prophets.

41 While the Pharisees were gathered together, Jesus asked them,

42 Saying, What think ye of Christ? whose son is he? They say unto him,

been a kind of common-place objection, which no doubt they brought upon all occasions.

29. Ye err, not knowing the Scriptures – Which plainly assert a resurrection. Nor the power of God – Which is well able to effect it. How many errors flow from the same source?

30. They are as the angels – Incorruptible and immortal. So is the power of God shown in them! So little need had they of marriage!

31. Have ye not read – The Sadducees had a peculiar value for the books of Moses. Out of these therefore our Lord argues with them.

32. I am the God of Abraham – The argument runs thus: God is not the God of the dead, but of the living: (for that expression, Thy God, implies both benefit from God to man, and duty from man to God) but he is the God of Abraham, Isaac, and Jacob: therefore, Abraham, Isaac, and Jacob are not dead, but living. Therefore, the soul does not die with the body. So indeed the Sadducees supposed, and it was on this ground that they denied the resurrection. [" Moreover he said, I am the God of thy father, the God of Abraham, the God of Isaac, and the God of Jacob. And Moses hid his face; for he was afraid to look upon God." Exod. iii, 6.]

33. At his doctrine – At the clearness and solidity of his answers.

34. ["And one of the scribes came, and having heard them reasoning together, and perceiving that he had answered them well, asked him, Which is the first commandment of all?" Mark xii, 28; "And, behold, a certain lawyer stood up, and tempted him, saying, Master, what shall I do to inherit eternal life?" Luke x, 25.]

35. A scribe asking him a question, trying him – Not, as it seems, with any ill design: but barely to make a farther trial of that wisdom, which he had shown in silencing the Sadducees.

37. ["And thou shalt love the LORD thy God with all thine heart, and with all thy soul, and with all thy might." Deut. vi, 5.]

39. ["Thou shalt not avenge, nor bear any grudge against the children of thy people, but thou shalt love thy neighbor as thyself: I am the LORD." Lev. xix, 18.]

42. ["And he said unto them, How say they that Christ is David's son?" Luke xx, 41.]

43. How doth David then by the Spirit – By inspiration, call him Lord? If he be merely the son (or descendant) of David? If he be, as you suppose, a mere man, the son of a man?

44. The Lord said to my Lord – This his dominion, to which David himself was subject, shows both the heavenly majesty of the king, and the nature of his kingdom. Sit thou on my right hand – That is, remain in the highest authority and power. ["The LORD said unto my Lord, Sit thou at my right hand, until I make thine enemies thy footstool." Psalm cx, 1.]

46. Neither durst any question him any more – Not by way of ensnaring or tempting him.

admire his wisdom, but will not be guided by it; his power, but will not submit to it.

23-33 The doctrines of Christ displeased the infidel Sadducees, as well as the Pharisees and Herodians. He carried the great truths of the resurrection and a future state, further than they had yet been revealed. There is no arguing from the state of things in this world, as to what will take place hereafter. Let truth be set in a clear light, and it appears in full strength. Having thus silenced them, our Lord proceeded to show the truth of the doctrine of the resurrection from the books of Moses. God declared to Moses that he was the God of the patriarchs, who had died long before; this shows that they were then in a state of being, capable of enjoying his favor, and proves that the doctrine of the resurrection is clearly taught in the Old Testament as well as in the New. But this doctrine was kept for a more full revelation, after the resurrection of Christ, who was the first-fruits of them that slept. All errors arise from not knowing the Scriptures and the power of God. In this world death takes away one after another, and so ends all earthly hopes, joys, sorrows, and connexions. How wretched are those who look for nothing better beyond the grave!

34-40 An interpreter of the law asked our Lord a question, to try, not so much his knowledge, as his judgment. The love of God is the first and great commandment, and the sum of all the commands of the first table. Our love of God must be sincere, not in word and tongue only. All our love is too little to bestow upon him, therefore all the powers of the soul must be engaged for him, and carried out toward him. To love our neighbor as ourselves, is the second great commandment. There is a self-love which is corrupt, and the root of the greatest sins, and it must be put off and mortified; but there is a self-love which is the rule of the greatest duty: we must have a due concern for the welfare of our own souls and bodies. And we must love our neighbor as truly and sincerely as we love ourselves; in many cases we must deny ourselves for the good of others. By these two commandments let our hearts be formed as by a mold.

41-46 When Christ baffled his enemies, he asked what thoughts they had of the promised Messiah? How he could be the Son of David and yet his Lord? He quotes Ps 110:1. If the Christ was to be a mere man, who would not exist till many ages after David's death, how could his forefather call him Lord? The Pharisees could not answer it. Nor can any solve the difficulty except he allows the Messiah to be the Son of God, and David's Lord equally with the Father. He took upon him human nature, and so became God manifested in the flesh; in this sense he is the Son of man and the Son of David. It behoves us above all things seriously to inquire, "What think we of Christ?" Is he altogether glorious in our eyes, and precious to our hearts? May Christ be our

of the Psalms." "Oh!" says he, "the whole thing is contemptible and ridiculous." And this was the opinion of a great many in Jerusalem. Perhaps that is your opinion, my friend. The kingdom of Christ, you say, is ridiculous; you do not believe perhaps that there are any people who are ruled by him though we say that we own him as our King, and that we feel the law of love to be a law which constrains us to sweet obedience. "Oh," you say, "it is cant and hypocrisy." And there are some who attend where they have golden censers, and altars, and priests, and they say, "Oh! a religion that is so simple—singing a few hymns, and offering extempore prayer!—Ah! give me a bishop with a miter—a fine fellow in lawn sleeves—that is the thing for me." "Oh," says another, "let me hear the peals of the organ; let me see the thing done scientifically, let me see a little drapery too; let the man come up clad in his proper garb to show that he is something different from other people; do not let him stand dressed as if he were an ordinary man; let me see something in the worship different from anything I have seen before." They want it clothed with a little pomp, and because if is not so they say—"Ah! Humph!" They sneer at it, and this is all that Christ gets from multitudes of men who think themselves exceeding wise. He is to them foolishness and they pass by with a sneer. Your sneers will be exchanged for tears ere long sirs! When he comes with real pomp and splendor you will weep and wail, because you disowned the King of Peace.

"The Lord shall come! a dreadful form,
With rainbow wreath and robes of storm,
With cherub voice and wings of wind,
The appointed Judge of all mankind."

Then you will find it inconvenient to have treated him with contempt. Others no doubt there were in Jerusalem who were filled with curiosity. They said—"Dear me, whatever can it be? What is the meaning of it? Who is this? I wish you would come," they said to their neighbors, "and tell us the history of this singular man, we should like to know about it." Some of them said, "He is gone to the temple, I dare say he will work a miracle;" so off they ran, and squeezed and pressed, and thronged to see a marvel. They were like Herod, they longed to see some wonder wrought by him. It was the first day of Christ's coming too, and of course the enthusiasm might last some nine days if he would keep it up, so they were very curious about it. And this is all Christ gets from thousands of people. They hear about a revival of religion. Well, they would like to know what it is and hear about it. There is something doing at such-and-such a place of worship; well, they

The Son of David.

43 He saith unto them, How then doth David in spirit call him Lord, saying,

44 The LORD said unto my Lord, Sit thou on my right hand, till I make thine enemies thy footstool?

45 If David then call him Lord, how is he his son?

46 And no man was able to answer him a word, neither durst any man from that day forth ask him any more questions.

MATTHEW 23

1 Then spake Jesus to the multitude, and to his disciples,

2 Saying, The scribes and the Pharisees sit in Moses' seat:

3 All therefore whatsoever they bid you observe, that observe and do; but do not ye after their works: for they say, and do not.

4 For they bind heavy burdens and grievous to be borne, and lay them on men's shoulders; but they themselves will not move them with one of their fingers.

5 But all their works they do for to be seen of men: they make broad their phylacteries, and enlarge the borders of their garments,

6 And love the uppermost rooms at feasts, and the chief seats in the synagogues,

7 And greetings in the markets, and to be called of men, Rabbi, Rabbi.

8 But be not ye called Rabbi: for one is your Master, even Christ; and all ye are brethren.

9 And call no man your father upon the earth: for one is your Father, which is in heaven.

10 Neither be ye called masters: for one is your Master, even Christ.

11 But he that is greatest among you shall be your servant.

12 And whosoever shall exalt himself shall be abased; and he that shall humble himself shall be exalted.

13 But woe unto you, scribes and Pharisees, hypocrites! for ye shut up the kingdom of heaven against men: for ye neither go in yourselves, neither suffer ye them that are entering to go in.

14 Woe unto you, scribes and Pharisees, hypocrites! for ye devour widows' houses, and for a pretense make long prayer: therefore ye shall receive the greater damnation.

15 Woe unto you, scribes and Pharisees, hypocrites! for ye compass sea and land to make one proselyte, and when he is made, ye make him twofold more the child of hell than yourselves.

MATTHEW 23

1. Then — Leaving all converse with his adversaries, whom he now left to the hardness of their hearts.

2. The scribes sit in the chair of Moses — That is, read and expound the law of Moses, and are their appointed teachers.

3. All things therefore — Which they read out of the law, and enforce there from.

4. ["And he said, Woe unto you also, ye lawyers! for ye lade men with burdens grievous to be borne, and ye yourselves touch not the burdens with one of your fingers." Luke xi, 46.]

5. Their phylacteries — The Jews, understanding those words literally, It shall be as a token upon thy hand, and as frontlets between thine eyes, Exod. xiii, 16. And thou shalt bind these words for a sign upon thine hand, and they shall be as frontlets between thine eyes, Deut. vi, 8; used to wear little scrolls of paper or parchment, bound on their wrist and foreheads, on which several texts of Scripture were writ. These they supposed, as a kind of charm, would preserve them from danger. And hence they seem to have been called phylacteries, or preservatives. The fringes of their garments — Which God had enjoined them to wear, to remind them of doing all the commandments, Num. xv, 38. These, as well as their phylacteries, the Pharisees affected to wear broader and larger than other men. Mark xii, 38, "And he said unto them in his doctrine, Beware of the scribes, which love to go in long clothing, and love salutations in the marketplaces."

8, 9, 10. The Jewish rabbis were also called father and master, by their several disciples, whom they required,

   1. To believe implicitly what they affirmed, without asking any farther reason;

   2. To obey implicitly what they enjoined, without seeking farther authority. Our Lord, therefore, by forbidding us either to give or receive the title of rabbi, master, or father, forbids us either to receive any such reverence, or to pay any such to any but God.

11. ["But it shall not be so among you: but whosoever will be great among you, let him be your minister." Matt. xx, 26.]

12. Whosoever shall exalt himself shall be humbled, and he that shall humble himself shall be exalted — It is observable that no one sentence of our Lord's is so often repeated as this: it occurs, with scarce any variation, at least ten times in the evangelists. Luke xiv, 11; xviii, 14.

13. Woe to you — Our Lord pronounced eight blessings upon the mount: he pronounces eight woes here; not as imprecations, but solemn, compassionate declarations of the misery, which these stubborn sinners were bringing upon themselves. Ye go not in — For ye are not poor in spirit; and ye hinder those that would be so.

14. Mark xii, 40; Luke xx, 47.

16. Woe to you, ye blind guides — Before he had styled them hypocrites, from their personal character: now he gives them another title, respecting their influence upon others. Both these appellations are severely put together in the 23rd and 25th verses; and this severity rises to the height in the 33rd verse. The gold of the temple — The treasure kept there. He is bound — To keep his oath.

20. He that sweareth by the altar, sweareth by it, and by all things thereon — Not only by the gift, but by the holy fire, and the sacrifice; and above all, by that God to whom they belong; inasmuch as every oath by a creature is an implicit appeal to God.

23. Judgment — That is, justice: Faith — The word here means fidelity.

24. Ye blind guides, who teach others to do as you do yourselves, to

joy, our confidence, our all. May we daily be made more like to him, and more devoted to his service.

MATTHEW 23

Jesus reproves the scribes and Pharisees. (1-12)
Crimes of the Pharisees. (13-33)
The guilt of Jerusalem. (34-39)

1-12 The scribes and Pharisees explained the law of Moses, and enforced obedience to it. They are charged with hypocrisy in religion. We can only judge according to outward appearance; but God searches the heart. They made phylacteries. These were scrolls of paper or parchment, wherein were written four paragraphs of the law, to be worn on their foreheads and left arms, Ex 13:2-10; 13:11-16; De 6:4-9; 11:13-21. They made these phylacteries broad, that they might be thought more zealous for the law than others. God appointed the Jews to make fringes upon their garments, Nu 15:38, to remind them of their being a peculiar people; but the Pharisees made them larger than common, as if they were thereby more religious than others. Pride was the darling, reigning sin of the Pharisees, the sin that most easily beset them, and which our Lord Jesus takes all occasions to speak against. For him that is taught in the word to give respect to him that teaches, is commendable; but for him that teaches, to demand it, to be puffed up with it, is sinful. How much is all this against the spirit of Christianity! The consistent disciple of Christ is pained by being put into chief places. But who that looks around on the visible church, would think this was the spirit required? It is plain that some measure of this antichristian spirit prevails in every religious society, and in every one of our hearts.

13-33 The scribes and Pharisees were enemies to the gospel of Christ, and therefore to the salvation of the souls of men. It is bad to keep away from Christ ourselves, but worse also to keep others from him. Yet it is no new thing for the show and form of godliness to be made a cloak to the greatest enormities. But dissembled piety will be reckoned double iniquity. They were very busy to turn souls to be of their party. Not for the glory of God and the good of souls, but that they might have the credit and advantage of making converts. Gain being their godliness, by a thousand devices they made religion give way to their worldly interests. They were very strict and precise in smaller matters of the law, but careless and loose in weightier matters. It is not the scrupling a little sin that Christ here reproves; if it be a sin, though but a gnat, it must be strained out; but the doing that, and then swallowing a camel, or, committing a greater sin. While they would seem to be godly, they were neither sober nor righteous. We are really, what we are inwardly. Outward motives may keep the outside clean, while the inside is filthy; but if the heart and spirit be made new, there will

would like to go if it were only to see the place. "There is a strange minister says queer things; let us go and hear him. We had intended to go out"—you know who I mean among yourselves—"we had intended to go out on an excursion today," said you, "but let us go there instead." Just so, curiosity, curiosity; this is all Christ gets today, and he that died upon the cross becomes a theme for an idle tale, and he that is Lord of angels and adored of men, is to be talked of as though he were a Wizard of the North or some eccentric impostor! Ah! you will find it inconvenient to have treated him thus by-and-bye; for when he comes, and when every eye shall see him, you who merely curiously inquired for him shall find that he shall inquire for you, not with animosity but with wrath, and it shall be—"Depart, ye cursed, into everlasting fire." But among the crowd there were some who were worse still, for they looked on the whole thing with envy "Ah!" said Rabbi Simeon to Rabbi Hillel, "the people were never so pleased with us. We know a great deal more than that impostor; we have read through all our religious books." "Don't you remember him," says one, "that when he was a boy he was rather precocious? You remember he came into the temple and talked with us, and since then he deceiveth the people," meaning by that he outshone them, that he had more esteem in the hearts of the multitude than they had, though they were prouder far. "Oh!" said the Pharisee, "he does not wear any phylactery, and I have made mine very large; I have made my garments almost all borders, so that they may be exceeding broad." "Ah!" says another, "I tithe my mint, my anise, and my cumin, and I stand at the corner of the street and blow a trumpet when I give away a penny, but yet people will not put me on an ass; they will not clap their hands and say, 'Hosanna' to me, but the whole earth is gone after this man like a parcel of children. Besides, think of going into the temple disturbing their betters, disturbing us who are making a show of our pretended prayers and standing in the courts!" And this is what Christ gets from a great many. They do not like to see Christ's cause get on. Nay, they would have Christ be lean that they might fatten themselves upon the plunder, they would have his Church be despicable. They like to hear of the falls of Christian ministers. If they can find a fault in a Christian man "Report it, report it, report it," say they. But if a man walk uprightly, if he glorifies Christ, if the Church increases, if souls are saved, straightway there is an uproar and the whole city is stirred, the whole uproar begins and is carried on by falsehoods, lying accusations, and slanders against the characters of

16 Woe unto you, ye blind guides, which say, Whosoever shall swear by the temple, it is nothing; but whosoever shall swear by the gold of the temple, he is a debtor!

17 Ye fools and blind: for whether is greater, the gold, or the temple that sanctifieth the gold?

18 And, Whosoever shall swear by the altar, it is nothing; but whosoever sweareth by the gift that is upon it, he is guilty.

19 Ye fools and blind: for whether is greater, the gift, or the altar that sanctifieth the gift?

20 Whoso therefore shall swear by the altar, sweareth by it, and by all things thereon.

21 And whoso shall swear by the temple, sweareth by it, and by him that dwelleth therein.

22 And he that shall swear by heaven, sweareth by the throne of God, and by him that sitteth thereon.

23 Woe unto you, scribes and Pharisees, hypocrites! for ye pay tithe of mint and anise and cummin, and have omitted the weightier matters of the law, judgment, mercy, and faith: these ought ye to have done, and not to leave the other undone.

24 Ye blind guides, which strain at a gnat, and swallow a camel.

25 Woe unto you, scribes and Pharisees, hypocrites! for ye make clean the outside of the cup and of the platter, but within they are full of extortion and excess.

26 Thou blind Pharisee, cleanse first that which is within the cup and platter, that the outside of them may be clean also.

27 Woe unto you, scribes and Pharisees, hypocrites! for ye are like unto whited sepulchers, which indeed appear beautiful outward, but are within full of dead men's bones, and of all uncleanness.

28 Even so ye also outwardly appear righteous unto men, but within ye are full of hypocrisy and iniquity.

29 Woe unto you, scribes and Pharisees, hypocrites! because ye build the tombs of the prophets, and garnish the sepulchers of the righteous,

30 And say, If we had been in the days of our fathers, we would not have been partakers with them in the blood of the prophets.

31 Wherefore ye be witnesses unto yourselves, that ye are the children of them which killed the prophets.

32 Fill ye up then the measure of your fathers.

strain out a gnat – From the liquor they are going to drink! and swallow a camel – It is strange, that glaring false print, strain at a gnat, which quite alters the sense, should run through all the editions of our English Bibles.

25. Full of rapine and intemperance – The censure is double (taking intemperance in the vulgar sense.) These miserable men procured unjustly what they used intemperately. No wonder tables so furnished prove a snare, as many find by sad experience. Thus luxury punishes fraud while it feeds disease with the fruits of injustice. But intemperance in the full sense takes in not only all kinds of outward intemperance, particularly in eating and drinking, but all intemperate or immoderate desires, whether of honor, gain, or sensual pleasure.

26. Ye build the tombs of the prophets – And that is all, for ye neither observe their sayings, nor imitate their actions.

30. We would not have been partakers – So ye make fair professions, as did your fathers.

31. Wherefore ye testify against yourselves – By your smooth words as well as devilish actions: that ye are the genuine sons of them who killed the prophets of their own times, while they professed the utmost veneration for those of past ages. From the 3rd to the 30th is exposed every thing that commonly passes in the world for religion, whereby the pretenders to it keep both themselves and others from entering into the kingdom of God; from attaining, or even seeking after those tempers, in which alone true Christianity consists. As,

1. Punctuality in attending on public and private prayer, ver. 4-14. Matt. xxiii, 4-14

2. Zeal to make proselytes to our opinion or communion, though they have less of the spirit of religion than before, ver. 15.

3. A superstitious reverence for consecrated places or things, without any for Him to whom they are consecrated, ver. 16-22.

4. A scrupulous exactness in little observances, though with the neglect of justice, mercy, and faith, ver. 23, 24.

5. A nice cautiousness to cleanse the outward behavior, but without any regard to inward purity, ver. 25, 26.

6. A specious face of virtue and piety, covering the deepest hypocrisy and villany, ver. 27, 28.

7. A professed veneration for all good men, except those among whom they live.

32. Fill ye up – A word of permission, not of command: as if he had said, I contend with you no longer: I leave you to yourselves: you have conquered: now ye may follow the devices of your own hearts. The measure of your fathers – Wickedness: ye may now be as wicked as they.

33. Ye serpents – Our Lord having now lost all hope of reclaiming these, speaks so as to affright others from the like sins.

34. Wherefore – That it may appear you are the true children of those murderers, and have a right to have their iniquities visited on you: Behold, I send – Is not this speaking as one having authority? Prophets – Men with supernatural credentials: Wise men – Such as have both natural abilities and experience; and scribes – Men of learning: but all will not avail. ["Therefore also said the wisdom of God, I will send them prophets and apostles, and some of them they shall slay and persecute:" Luke xi, 49.]

35. That upon you may come – The consequence of which will be, that upon you will come the vengeance of all the righteous blood shed on the earth – Zechariah the son of Barachiah – Termed Jehoiada, 2

be newness of life; here we must begin with ourselves. The righteousness of the scribes and Pharisees was like the ornaments of a grave, or dressing up a dead body, only for show. The deceitfulness of sinners' hearts appears in that they go down the streams of the sins of their own day, while they fancy that they should have opposed the sins of former days. We sometimes think, if we had lived when Christ was upon earth, that we should not have despised and rejected him, as men then did; yet Christ in his Spirit, in his word, in his ministers, is still no better treated. And it is just with God to give those up to their hearts' lusts, who obstinately persist in gratifying them. Christ gives men their true characters.

34-39 We have left the blind leaders fallen into the ditch, under Christ's sentence, into the damnation of hell; let us see what will become of the blind followers, of the body of the Jewish church, and particularly Jerusalem.

I. Jesus Christ designs yet to try them with the means of grace; I send unto you prophets, and wise men, and scribes. The connection is strange; "You are a generation of vipers, not likely to escape the damnation of hell;" one would think it should follow, "Therefore you shall never have a prophet sent to you any more;" but no, "Therefore I will send unto you prophets, to see if you will yet at length be wrought upon, or else to leave you inexcusable, and to justify God in your ruin." It is therefore ushered in with a note of admiration, behold! Observe that it is Christ that sends them; I send. By this he avows himself to be God, having power to gift and commission prophets. It is an act of kingly office; he sends them as ambassadors to treat with us about the concerns of our souls. After his resurrection, he made this word good, when he said, So send I you, Jn. 20:21. Though now he appeared mean, yet he was entrusted with this great authority. 2. He sends them to the Jews first; "I send them to you." They began at Jerusalem; and, wherever they went, they observed this rule, to make the first tender of gospel grace to the Jews, Acts 13:46. 3. Those he sends are called prophets, wise men, and scribes, Old-Testament names for New-Testament officers; to show that the ministers sent to them now should not be inferior to the prophets of the Old Testament, to Solomon the wise, or Ezra the scribe. The extraordinary ministers, who in the first ages were divinely inspired, were as the prophets commissioned immediately from heaven; the ordinary settled ministers, who were then, and continue in the church still, and will do to the end of time, are as the wise men and scribes, to guide and instruct the people in the things of God. Or, we may take the apostles and evangelists for the prophets and wise men, and the pastors and teachers for the scribes, instructed to the kingdom of heaven (ch. 13:52); for the office of a scribe was honorable till the men dishonored it.

Christ's people. In some way or other, men are sure to be moved, if they are not moved to laugh, if they are not moved to inquire, they are moved to envy. But blessed is it that some in Jerusalem were moved to rejoice. Oh! there were many who, like Simeon and Anna rejoiced to see that day, and many of them went home and said, "Lord, now lettest thou thy servant depart in peace, for mine eyes have seen thy salvation." There was many a bedridden woman in the back streets of Jerusalem, that sat up in the bed and said, "Hosanna," and wished that she could get down into the street, that she might throw her old mantle in the way, and might bow before him who was the King of the Jews. There were many weeping eyes that wiped away their tears that day, and many mourning believers who began from that hour to rejoice with joy unspeakable. And so there are some of you that hear of Christ the King with joy. You join in the hymn; not as we have all joined with the voice, but with the heart.

"Rejoice, the Savior reigns,
The God of peace and love
When he had purged our stains.
He took his seat above
Rejoice, rejoice!
Rejoice aloud, ye saints, rejoice!"

Such, then, the first effect of Christ's kingdom! Wherever it comes, the city is stirred. Do not believe the gospel is preached at all if it does not make a stir. Do not believe, my brethren, that the gospel is preached in Christ's way if it does not make some angry and some happy, if it does not make many enemies and some friends.

There is yet another practical effect of Christ's kingdom. He went up to the temple and there at one table sat a lot of men with baskets containing pairs of doves. "Any doves, sir, any doves!" He looked at them and said, "Take these things hence." He spoke with a holy furore. There were others changing money as the people came in to pay their half shekel; he overturned the tables and set them all a-flying, and soon emptied the whole court of all these merchants who were making a gain of godliness, and making religion a stalking-horse for their own emolument. Now this is what Christ does wherever he comes. I wish he would come in the Church of England a little more, and get rid of that accursed simony which is still tolerated by law and purge out the men that are malappropriators, who take that which belongs to the ministers of Christ, and apply it to their own uses. I would that he would come into all our places of worship, so that once for all it might be seen that they who serve God serve him because they love him, and not for what they can get by it. I would that every professor of religion

33 Ye serpents, ye generation of vipers, how can ye escape the damnation of hell?

34 Wherefore, behold, I send unto you prophets, and wise men, and scribes: and some of them ye shall kill and crucify; and some of them shall ye scourge in your synagogues, and persecute them from city to city:

35 That upon you may come all the righteous blood shed upon the earth, from the blood of righteous Abel unto the blood of Zacharias son of Barachias, whom ye slew between the temple and the altar.

36 Verily I say unto you, All these things shall come upon this generation.

37 O Jerusalem, Jerusalem, thou that killest the prophets, and stonest them which are sent unto thee, how often would I have gathered thy children together, even as a hen gathereth her chickens under her wings, and ye would not!

38 Behold, your house is left unto you desolate.

39 For I say unto you, Ye shall not see me henceforth, till ye shall say, Blessed is he that cometh in the name of the Lord.

MATTHEW 24

1 And Jesus went out, and departed from the temple: and his disciples came to him for to shew him the buildings of the temple.

2 And Jesus said unto them, See ye not all these things? verily I say unto you, There shall not be left here one stone upon another, that shall not be thrown down.

3 And as he sat upon the mount of Olives, the disciples came unto him privately, saying, Tell us, when shall these things be? and what shall be the sign of thy coming, and of the end of the world?

4 And Jesus answered and said unto them, Take heed that no man deceive you.

5 For many shall come in my name, saying, I am Christ; and shall deceive many.

6 And ye shall hear of wars and rumors of wars: see that ye be not troubled: for all these things must come to pass, but the end is not yet.

7 For nation shall rise against nation, and kingdom against kingdom: and there shall be famines, and pestilences, and earthquakes, in divers places.

8 All these are the beginning of sorrows.

9 Then shall they deliver you up to be

Chron. xxiv, 20, where the story is related: Ye slew – Ye make that murder also of your fathers your own, by imitating it: Between the temple – That is, the inner temple, and the altar – Which stood in the outer court. Our Lord seems to refer to this instance, rather than any other, because he was the last of the prophets on record that were slain by the Jews for reproving their wickedness: and because God's requiring this blood as well as that of Abel, is particularly taken notice of in Scripture.

37. Luke xiii, 34.

38. Behold your house – The temple, which is now your house, not God's: Is left unto you – Our Lord spake this as he was going out of it for the last time: Desolate – Forsaken of God and his Christ, and sentenced to utter destruction.

39. Ye – Jews in general; men of Jerusalem in particular: shall not see me from this time – Which includes the short space till his death, till, after a long interval of desolation and misery, ye say, Blessed is he that cometh in the name of the Lord – Ye receive me with joyful and thankful hearts. This also shall be accomplished in its season.

MATTHEW 24

1. Mark xiii, 1; Luke xxi, 5.

2. There shall not be left one stone upon another – This was most punctually fulfilled; for after the temple was burnt, Titus, the Roman general, ordered the very foundations of it to be dug up; after which the ground on which it stood was plowed up by Turnus Rufus.

3. As he sat on the mount of Olives – Whence they had a full view of the temple. When shall these things be? And what shall be the sign of thy coming, and of the end of the world? – The disciples inquire confusedly

   1. Concerning the time of the destruction of the temple;

   2. Concerning the signs of Christ's coming, and of the end of the world, as if they imagined these two were the same thing.

Our Lord answers distinctly concerning

   1. The destruction of the temple and city, with the signs preceding, ver. 4, &c., 15, &c.

   2. His own coming, and the end of the world, with the signs thereof, ver. 29-31.

   3. The time of the destruction of the temple, ver. 32, &c.

   4. The time of the end of the world, ver. 36.

4. Take heed that no man deceive you – The caution is more particularly designed for the succeeding Christians, whom the apostles then represented. The first sign of my coming is, the rise of false prophets. But it is highly probable, many of these things refer to more important events, which are yet to come.

5. Many shall come in my name – First, false Christs, next, false prophets, Matt. xxiv, 11. At length, both together, ver. 24. And indeed never did so many impostors appear in the world as a few years before the destruction of Jerusalem; undoubtedly because that was the time wherein the Jews in general expected the Messiah.

6. Wars – Near: Rumors of wars – At a distance. All these things must come to pass – As a foundation for lasting tranquillity. But the end – Concerning which ye inquire, is not yet – So far from it, that this is but the beginning sorrows.

9. Then shall they deliver you up to affliction – As if ye were the cause of all these evils. And ye shall be hated of all nations – Even of those

MATTHEW HENRY · CHARLES H. SPURGEON

II. He foresees and foretels the ill usage that his messengers would meet with among them; "Some of them ye shall kill and crucify, and yet I will send them." Christ knows beforehand how ill his servants will be treated, and yet sends them, and appoints them their measure of sufferings; yet he loves them never the less for his thus exposing them, for he designs to glorify himself by their sufferings, and them after them; he will counter-balance them, though not prevent them. Observe, the cruelty of these persecutors; Ye shall kill and crucify them. It is no less than the blood, the life-blood, that they thirst after; their lust is not satisfied with any thing short of their destruction, Ex. 15:9. They killed the two James's, crucified Simon the son of Cleophas, and scourged Peter and John; thus did the members partake of the sufferings of the Head, he was killed and crucified, and so were they. Christians must expect to resist unto blood. 2. Their unwearied industry; Ye shall persecute them from city to city. As the apostles went from city to city, to preach the gospel, the Jews dodged them, and haunted them, and stirred up persecution against them, Acts 14:19; 17:13. They that did not believe in Judea were more bitter enemies to the gospel than any other unbelievers, Rom. 15:31. 3. The pretense of religion in this; they scourged them in their synagogues, their place of worship, where they kept their ecclesiastical courts; so that they did it as a piece of service to the church; cast them out, and said, Let the Lord be glorified, Isa. 66:5; Jn. 16:2.

MATTHEW 24

Christ foretells the destruction of the temple. (1-3)
The troubles before the destruction of Jerusalem. (4-28)
Christ foretells other signs and miseries, to the end of the world. (29-41)
Exhortations to watchfulness. (42-51)

1-3 Christ foretells the utter ruin and destruction coming upon the temple. A believing foresight of the defacing of all worldly glory, will help to keep us from admiring it, and overvaluing it. The most beautiful body soon will be food for worms, and the most magnificent building a ruinous heap. See ye not all these things? It will do us good so to see them as to see through them, and see to the end of them. Our Lord having gone with his disciples to the Mount of Olives, he set before them the order of the times concerning the Jews, till the destruction of Jerusalem; and as to men in general till the end of the world.

4-28 The disciples had asked concerning the times, When these things should be? Christ gave them no answer to that; but they had also asked, What shall be the sign? This question he answers fully. The prophecy first respects events near at hand, the destruction of Jerusalem, the end of the Jewish church and state, the calling of the Gentiles, and the setting up of Christ's

could be quite clean in his own conscience that he never made a profession to get respectability or to get esteem, but only made it that he might honor Christ and glorify his Master. The spiritual meaning of it all is this—We have no houses of God now; bricks and mortar are not holy, the places where we worship God are places of worship, but they are not the houses of God any longer than we are in them. We believe no superstition which makes any place holy, but we are the temple of God. Men themselves are God's temples, and where Christ comes he drives out the buyers and sellers, and he expunges all selfishness. I will never believe that Christ, the King, has made your heart his palace till you are unselfish. Oh, how many professors there are who want to get so much honor, so much respect! As to giving to the poor, thinking it more blessed to give than to receive, as for feeding the hungry and clothing the naked, as for living for other people, and not for themselves—they do not think of that. O Master, come into thy temple and drive out our selfishness, now come, turn out all those things which would make it convenient to serve Mammon by serving God; help us to live unto thee, and to live for others by living to thee, and not live unto ourselves!

The last practical effect of our Lord Jesus Christ's kingdom was he held a grand levee; he had, if I may so speak, a drawing-room day; and who are the people who came to attend him? Now, ye courtiers, the disciples, show up your nobility and gentry that are come to wait upon him. Here comes one man, he has a bandage over here, and the other eye has almost failed—show him in, here comes another, his feet are all twisted and contorted—show him in, here comes another limping on two crutches, both his limbs are disabled, and another has lost his limbs. Here they come and here is the levee. The King himself comes here and holds a grand meeting, and the blind and the lame are his guests, and now he comes, he touches that blind eye and light shines in; he speaks to this man with a withered leg, he walks; he touches two eyes at once, and they both see, and to another he says, "I will take away thy crutches, stand upright and rejoice and leap with joy." This is what the King does wherever he comes. Come hither this morning, I beseech thee, thou great King! There are blind eyes here that cannot see thy beauty. Walk, Jesu, walk among this crowd and touch the eyes. Ah! then, brethren, if he should do that, you will say, "There is a beauty in him that I never saw before." Jesu, touch their eyes, they cannot take away their own blindness, do thou do it! Help them to look to thee hanging upon the cross! They cannot do it unless thou dost enable them. May they do it

afflicted, and shall kill you: and ye shall be hated of all nations for my name's sake.

10 And then shall many be offended, and shall betray one another, and shall hate one another.

11 And many false prophets shall rise, and shall deceive many.

12 And because iniquity shall abound, the love of many shall wax cold.

13 But he that shall endure unto the end, the same shall be saved.

14 And this gospel of the kingdom shall be preached in all the world for a witness unto all nations; and then shall the end come.

15 When ye therefore shall see the abomination of desolation, spoken of by Daniel the prophet, stand in the holy place, (whoso readeth, let him understand:)

16 Then let them which be in Judea flee into the mountains:

17 Let him which is on the housetop not come down to take any thing out of his house:

18 Neither let him which is in the field return back to take his clothes.

19 And woe unto them that are with child, and to them that give suck in those days!

20 But pray ye that your flight be not in the winter, neither on the sabbath day:

21 For then shall be great tribulation, such as was not since the beginning of the world to this time, no, nor ever shall be.

22 And except those days should be shortened, there should no flesh be saved: but for the elect's sake those days shall be shortened.

23 Then if any man shall say unto you, Lo, here is Christ, or there; believe it not.

24 For there shall arise false Christs, and false prophets, and shall shew great signs and wonders; insomuch that, if it were possible, they shall deceive the very elect.

25 Behold, I have told you before.

26 Wherefore if they shall say unto you, Behold, he is in the desert; go not forth: behold, he is in the secret chambers; believe it not.

27 For as the lightning cometh out of the east, and shineth even unto the west; so shall also the coming of the Son of man be.

28 For wheresoever the carcase is, there will the eagles be gathered together.

29 Immediately after the tribulation of those days shall the sun be darkened, and the moon shall not give her light,

who tolerate all other sects and parties; but in no nation will the children of the devil tolerate the children of God. Matt. x, 17.

10. Then shall many be offended – So as utterly to make shipwreck of faith and a pure conscience. But hold ye fast faith, ver. 11. in spite of false prophets: love, even when iniquity and offenses abound, ver. 12. And hope, unto the end, ver. 13. He that does so, shall be snatched out of the burning. The love of many will wax cold – The generality of those who love God will (like the Church at Ephesus, Rev. ii, 4,) leave their first love.

13. Matt. x, 22; Mark xiii, 13; Luke xxi, 17.

14. This Gospel shall be preached in all the world – Not universally: this is not done yet: but in general through the several parts of the world, and not only in Judea And this was done by St. Paul and the other apostles, before Jerusalem was destroyed. And then shall the end come – Of the city and temple. Josephus's *History of the Jewish War* is the best commentary on this chapter. it is a wonderful instance of God's providence, that he, an eye witness, and one who lived and died a Jew, should, especially in so extraordinary a manner, be preserved, to transmit to us a collection of important facts, which so exactly illustrate this glorious prophecy, in almost every circumstance. Mark xiii, 10.

15. When ye see the abomination of desolation – Daniel's term is, The abomination that maketh desolate, Dan. xi, 31; that is, the standards of the desolating legions, on which they bear the abominable images of their idols: Standing in the holy place – Not only the temple and the mountain on which it stood, but the whole city of Jerusalem, and several furlongs of land round about it, were accounted holy; particularly the mount on which our Lord now sat, and on which the Roman afterward planted their ensigns. He that readeth let him understand – Whoever reads that prophecy of Daniel, let him deeply consider it. Mark xiii, 14; Luke xxi, 20; Dan. ix, 27.

16. Then let them who are in Judea flee to the mountains – So the Christians did, and were preserved. It is remarkable that after the Romans under Cestus Gallus made their first advances toward Jerusalem, they suddenly withdrew again, in a most unexpected and indeed impolitic manner. This the Christians took as a signal to retire, which they did, some to Pella, and others to Mount Libanus.

17. Let not him that is on the house top come down to take any thing out of his house – It may be remembered that their stairs used to be on the outside of their houses.

19. Woe to them that are with child, and to them that give suck – Because they cannot so readily make their escape.

20. Pray ye that your flight be not in the winter – They did so; and their flight was in the spring. Neither on the Sabbath – Being on many accounts inconvenient; beside that many would have scrupled to travel far on that day. For the Jews thought it unlawful to walk above two thousand paces (two miles) on the Sabbath day.

21. Then shall be great tribulation – Have not many things spoken in the chapter, as well as in Mark xiii, Luke xxi. a farther and much more extensive meaning than has been yet fulfilled?

22. And unless those days were shortened – By the taking of Jerusalem sooner than could be expected: No flesh would be saved – The whole nation would be destroyed. But for the elect's sake – That is, for the sake of the Christians.

23. Mark xiii, 21; Luke xvii, 23.

24. They would deceive, if possible, the very elect – But it is not possible that God should suffer the body of Christians to be thus deceived.

kingdom in the world; but it also looks to the general judgment; and toward the close, points more particularly to the latter. What Christ here said to his disciples, tended more to promote caution than to satisfy their curiosity; more to prepare them for the events that should happen, than to give a distinct idea of the events. This is that good understanding of the times which all should covet, thence to infer what Israel ought to do. Our Savior cautions his disciples to stand on their guard against false teachers. And he foretells wars and great commotions among nations. From the time that the Jews rejected Christ, and he left their house desolate, the sword never departed from them. See what comes of refusing the gospel. Those who will not hear the messengers of peace, shall be made to hear the messengers of war. But where the heart is fixed, trusting in God, it is kept in peace, and is not afraid. It is against the mind of Christ, that his people should have troubled hearts, even in troublous times. When we looked forward to the eternity of misery that is before the obstinate refusers of Christ and his gospel, we may truly say, The greatest earthly judgments are but the beginning of sorrows. It is comforting that some shall endure even to the end. Our Lord foretells the preaching of the gospel in all the world. The end of the world shall not be till the gospel has done its work. Christ foretells the ruin coming upon the people of the Jews; and what he said here, would be of use to his disciples, for their conduct and for their comfort. If God opens a door of escape, we ought to make our escape, otherwise we do not trust God, but tempt him. It becomes Christ's disciples, in times of public trouble, to be much in prayer: that is never out of season, but in a special manner seasonable when we are distressed on every side. Though we must take what God sends, yet we may pray against sufferings; and it is very trying to a good man, to be taken by any work of necessity from the solemn service and worship of God on the sabbath day. But here is one word of comfort, that for the elect's sake these days shall be made shorter than their enemies designed, who would have cut all off, if God, who used these foes to serve his own purpose, had not set bounds to their wrath. Christ foretells the rapid spreading of the gospel in the world. It is plainly seen as the lightning. Christ preached his gospel openly. The Romans were like an eagle, and the ensign of their armies was an eagle. When a people, by their sin, make themselves as loathsome carcasses, nothing can be expected but that God should send enemies to destroy them. It is very applicable to the day of judgment, the coming of our Lord Jesus Christ in that day, 2Th 2:1. Let us give diligence to make our calling and election sure; then may we know that no enemy or deceiver shall ever prevail against us.

29-41 Christ foretells his second coming. It is usual for prophets to speak of things as near and just at hand, to express the greatness and certainty of them. Concerning Christ's second coming, it is foretold that

now, and find life in thee! O Jesu, there are some here that are lame—knees that cannot bend, they have never prayed; there are some here whose feet will not run in the way of thy commandments—feet that will not carry them up where thy name is praised, and where thou art had in honor. Walk, great King, walk thou in solemn pomp throughout this house, and make it like the temple of old! Display here thy power and hold thy grand meeting in the healing of the lame and the curing of the blind "Oh!" saith one, "I would that he would open my blind eyes." Soul, he will do it, he will do it. Breathe thy prayer out now, and it shall be done, for he is nigh thee now. He is standing by thy side, he speaks to thee, and he saith—"Look unto me and be thou saved, thou vilest of the vile." There is another, and he says—"Lord, I would be made whole." He says—"Be thou whole then." Believe on him and he will save thee. He is near you, brother, he is near you. He is not in the pulpit more than he is in the pew, nor in one pew more than in another. Say not—"Who shall go to heaven to find him, or into the depths to bring him up?" He is near you; he will hear your prayer even though you speak not; he will hear your heart speak. Oh! say unto him—"Jesus, heal me," and he will do it; he will do it now. Let us breathe the prayer, and then we will part.

Jesus, heal us! Save us, Son of David, save us! Thou seest how blind we be—oh, give us the sight of faith! Thou seest how lame we be—oh, give us the strength of grace! And now, e'en now, thou Son of David, purge out our selfishness, and come and live and reign in us as in thy temple-palaces! We ask it, O thou great King, for thine own sake. Amen. And ere we leave this place, we cry again, "Hosanna, hosanna, hosanna. Blessed is he that cometh in the name of the Lord."

THE PARABLE OF THE WEDDING FEAST
Sermon number 975 delivered on Lord's-day Morning, February 12th, 1871 at the Metropolitan Tabernacle, Newington.

"The kingdom of heaven is like unto a certain king, which made a marriage for his son, and sent forth his servants to call them that were bidden to the wedding: and they would not come. Again, he sent forth other servants, saying, Tell them which are bidden, Behold, I have prepared my dinner: my oxen and my fatlings are killed and all things are ready: come unto the marriage."—Matthew 22:2,3,4.

IN ORDER TO understand the parable before us we must first direct our attention to the design

and the stars shall fall from heaven, and the powers of the heavens shall be shaken:

30 And then shall appear the sign of the Son of man in heaven: and then shall all the tribes of the earth mourn, and they shall see the Son of man coming in the clouds of heaven with power and great glory.

31 And he shall send his angels with a great sound of a trumpet, and they shall gather together his elect from the four winds, from one end of heaven to the other.

32 Now learn a parable of the fig tree; When his branch is yet tender, and putteth forth leaves, ye know that summer is nigh:

33 So likewise ye, when ye shall see all these things, know that it is near, even at the doors.

34 Verily I say unto you, This generation shall not pass, till all these things be fulfilled.

35 Heaven and earth shall pass away, but my words shall not pass away.

36 But of that day and hour knoweth no man, no, not the angels of heaven, but my Father only.

37 But as the days of Noe were, so shall also the coming of the Son of man be.

38 For as in the days that were before the flood they were eating and drinking, marrying and giving in marriage, until the day that Noe entered into the ark,

39 And knew not until the flood came, and took them all away; so shall also the coming of the Son of man be.

40 Then shall two be in the field; the one shall be taken, and the other left.

41 Two women shall be grinding at the mill; the one shall be taken, and the other left.

42 Watch therefore: for ye know not what hour your Lord doth come.

43 But know this, that if the goodman of the house had known in what watch the thief would come, he would have watched, and would not have suffered his house to be broken up.

44 Therefore be ye also ready: for in such an hour as ye think not the Son of man cometh.

45 Who then is a faithful and wise servant, whom his lord hath made ruler over his household, to give them meat in due season?

46 Blessed is that servant, whom his lord when he cometh shall find so doing.

47 Verily I say unto you, That he shall make ruler over all his goods.

48 But and if that evil servant shall say in his heart, My lord delayeth his coming;

27. For as the lightning goeth forth – For the next coming of Christ will be as quick as lightning; so that there will not be time for any such previous warning.

28. For wheresoever the carcass is, there will the eagles be gathered together – Our Lord gives this, as a farther reason, why they should not hearken to any pretended deliverer. As if he had said, Expect not any deliverer of the Jewish nation; for it is devoted to destruction. It is already before God a dead carcass, which the Roman eagles will soon devour. Luke xvii, 37.

29. Immediately after the tribulation of those days – Here our Lord begins to speak of his last coming. But he speaks not so much in the language of man as of God, with whom a thousand years are as one day, one moment. Many of the primitive Christians not observing this, thought he would come immediately, in the common sense of the word: a mistake which St. Paul labors to remove, in his Second Epistle to the Thessalonians. The powers of the heavens – Probably the influences of the heavenly bodies. Mark xiii, 24; Luke xxi, 25.

30. Then shall appear the sign of the Son of man in heaven – It seems a little before he himself descends. The sun, moon, and stars being extinguished, (probably not those of our system only,) the sign of the Son of man (perhaps the cross) will appear in the glory of the Lord.

31. They shall gather together his elect – That is, all that have endured to the end in the faith which worketh by love.

32. Learn a parable – Our Lord having spoken of the signs preceding the two grand events, concerning which the apostles had inquired, begins here to speak of the time of them. And to the question proposed, ver. 3, concerning the time of the destruction of Jerusalem, he answers ver. 34. Concerning the time of the end of the world, he answers chap. xxiv, 36. Mark xiii, 28; Luke xxi, 29.

34. This generation of men now living shall not pass till all these things be done – The expression implies, that great part of that generation would be passed away, but not the whole. Just so it was. For the city and temple were destroyed thirty-nine or forty years after.

36. But of that day – The day of judgment; Knoweth no man – Not while our Lord was on earth. Yet it might be afterward revealed to St. John consistently with this.

37. Luke xvii, 26.

40. One is taken – Into God's immediate protection: and one is left – To share the common calamities. Our Lord speaks as having the whole transaction present before his eyes.

41. Two women shall be grinding – Which was then a common employment of women.

42. Ye know not what hour your Lord cometh – Either to require your soul of you, or to avenge himself of this nation. Mark xiii, 33; Luke xii, 35; xxi, 34.

45. Who then is the faithful and wise servant – Which of you aspires after this character? Wise – Every moment retaining the clearest conviction, that all he now has is only intrusted to him as a steward: Faithful – Thinking, speaking, and acting continually, in a manner suitable to that conviction.

48. But if that evil servant – Now evil, having put away faith and a good conscience.

51. And allot him his portion with the hypocrites – The worst of sinners, as upright and sincere as he was once. If ministers are the persons here primarily intended, there is a peculiar propriety in the expression. For no hypocrisy can be baser, than to call ourselves

there shall be a great change, in order to the making all things new. Then they shall see the Son of man coming in the clouds. At his first coming, he was set for a sign that should be spoken against, but at his second coming, a sign that should be admired. Sooner or later, all sinners will be mourners; but repenting sinners look to Christ, and mourn after a godly sort; and those who sow in those tears shall shortly reap in joy. Impenitent sinners shall see Him whom they have pierced, and, though they laugh now, shall mourn and weep in endless horror and despair. The elect of God are scattered abroad; there are some in all places, and all nations; but when that great gathering day comes, there shall not one of them be missing. Distance of place shall keep none out of heaven. Our Lord declares that the Jews should never cease to be a distinct people, until all things he had been predicting were fulfilled. His prophecy reaches to the day of final judgment; therefore he here, ver. 34, foretells that Judah shall never cease to exist as a distinct people, so long as this world shall endure. Men of the world scheme and plan for generation upon generation here, but they plan not with reference to the overwhelming, approaching, and most certain event of Christ's second coming, which shall do away every human scheme, and set aside for ever all that God forbids. That will be as surprising a day, as the deluge to the old world. Apply this, first, to temporal judgments, particularly that which was then hastening upon the nation and people of the Jews. Secondly, to the eternal judgment. Christ here shows the state of the old world when the deluge came. They were secure and careless; they knew not, until the flood came; and they believed not. Did we know aright that all earthly things must shortly pass away, we should not set our eyes and hearts so much upon them as we do. The evil day is not the further off for men's putting it far from them. What words can more strongly describe the suddenness of our Savior's coming! Men will be at their respective businesses, and suddenly the Lord of glory will appear. Women will be in their house employments, but in that moment every other work will be laid aside, and every heart will turn inward and say, It is the Lord! Am I prepared to meet him? Can I stand before him? And what, in fact, is the day of judgment to the whole world, but the day of death to every one?

42-51 To watch for Christ's coming, is to maintain that temper of mind which we would be willing that our Lord should find us in. We know we have but a little time to live, we cannot know that we have a long time to live; much less do we know the time fixed for the judgment. Our Lord's coming will be happy to those that shall be found ready, but very dreadful to those that are not. If a man, professing to be the servant of Christ, be an unbeliever, covetous, ambitious, or a lover of pleasure, he will be cut off. Those who choose the world for their portion in this life, will have hell for their portion in the other life. May our Lord, when he cometh, pronounce

of the "certain king" here spoken of. He had a grand object in view; he desired to do honor to his son upon the occasion of his marriage. We shall then notice the very generous method by which he proposed to accomplish his purpose; he made a dinner, and bade many: there were other modes of honoring his son, but the great king elected the mode which would best display his bounty. We shall then observe, with sad interest, the serious hindrance which arose to the carrying out of his generous design—those who were bidden would not come. There was nothing to hinder the magnificence of the festival in the riches of the prince—he lavished out his stores for the feast; but here was a hindrance strange and difficult to remove, they would not come. Then our thoughts will linger admiringly over the gracious rejoinder which the king made to the opposers of his design; he sent other servants to repeat the invitation, "Come ye to the marriage." If we shall drink deep into the meaning of these three verses, we shall have more than enough for one meditation.

I. A certain king of wide dominions and great power designed to give a magnificent banquet, with a GRAND OBJECT in view. The crown prince, his well beloved heir, was about to take to himself a fair bride, and therefore the royal father desired to celebrate the event with extraordinary honors. From earth, look up to heaven. The great object of God the Father is to glorify his Son. It is his will "that all men should honor the Son, even as they honor the Father." (John 5:23.) Jesus Christ, the Son of God, is glorious already in his divine person. He is ineffably blessed, and infinitely beyond needing honor. All the angels of God worship him, and his glory fills all heaven. He has appeared on the stage of action as the Creator and as such his glory is perfect, "For by him were all things created, that are in heaven, and that are in earth, visible and invisible, whether they be thrones, or dominions, or principalities, or powers: all things were created by him, and for him." He said, "Light be," and it flamed forth. He bade the mountains lift their heads, and their summits pierced the clouds. He created the water-floods, he bade them seek their channels, and he appointed their bounds. Nothing is lacking to the glory of the Word of God, who was in the beginning with God, who spoke and it was done, who commanded, and it stood forth. He is highly exalted also as the preserver, for he is before all things, and by him all things consist. He is that nail fastened in a sure place, upon which all things hang. The keys of heaven, and death, and hell, are fastened to his girdle, and the government shall be upon his shoulders, and his

49 And shall begin to smite his fellowservants, and to eat and drink with the drunken;

50 The lord of that servant shall come in a day when he looketh not for him, and in an hour that he is not aware of,

51 And shall cut him asunder, and appoint him his portion with the hypocrites: there shall be weeping and gnashing of teeth.

MATTHEW 25

1 Then shall the kingdom of heaven be likened unto ten virgins, which took their lamps, and went forth to meet the bridegroom.

2 And five of them were wise, and five were foolish.

3 They that were foolish took their lamps, and took no oil with them:

4 But the wise took oil in their vessels with their lamps.

5 While the bridegroom tarried, they all slumbered and slept.

6 And at midnight there was a cry made, Behold, the bridegroom cometh; go ye out to meet him.

7 Then all those virgins arose, and trimmed their lamps.

8 And the foolish said unto the wise, Give us of your oil; for our lamps are gone out.

9 But the wise answered, saying, Not so; lest there be not enough for us and you: but go ye rather to them that sell, and buy for yourselves.

10 And while they went to buy, the bridegroom came; and they that were ready went in with him to the marriage: and the door was shut.

11 Afterward came also the other virgins, saying, Lord, Lord, open to us.

12 But he answered and said, Verily I say unto you, I know you not.

13 Watch therefore, for ye know neither the day nor the hour wherein the Son of man cometh.

14 For the kingdom of heaven is as a man traveling into a far country, who called his own servants, and delivered unto them his goods.

15 And unto one he gave five talents, to another two, and to another one; to every man according to his several ability; and straightway took his journey.

16 Then he that had received the five talents went and traded with the same, and made them other five talents.

17 And likewise he that had received two, he also gained other two.

18 But he that had received one went and digged in the earth, and hid his lord's money.

ministers of Christ, while we are the slaves of avarice, ambition, or sensuality. Wherever such are found, may God reform them by his grace, or disarm them of that power and influence, which they continually abuse to his dishonor, and to their own aggravated damnation!

MATTHEW 25

This chapter contains the last public discourse which our Lord uttered before he was offered up. He had before frequently declared what would be the portion of all the workers of iniquity. But what will become of those who do no harm? Honest, inoffensive, good sort of people? We have here a clear and full answer to this important question.

1. Then shall the kingdom of heaven – That is, the candidates for it, be like ten virgins – The bridesmaids on the wedding night were wont to go to the house where the bride was, with burning lamps or torches in their hands, to wait for the bridegroom's coming. When he drew near, they went to meet him with their lamps, and to conduct him to the bride.

3. The foolish took no oil with them – No more than kept them burning just for the present. None to supply their future want, to recruit their lamp's decay. The lamp is faith. A lamp and oil with it, is faith working by love.

4. The wise took oil in their vessels – Love in their hearts. And they daily sought a fresh supply of spiritual strength, till their faith was made perfect.

5. While the bridegroom delayed – That is, before they were called to attend him, they all slumbered and slept – Were easy and quiet, the wise enjoying a true, the foolish a false peace.

6. At midnight – In an hour quite unthought of.

7. They trimmed their lamps – They examined themselves and prepared to meet their God.

8. Give us of your oil, for our lamps are gone out – Our faith is dead. What a time to discover this! Whether it mean the time of death, or of judgment. Unto which of the saints wilt thou then turn? Who can help thee at such a season?

9. But the wise answered, Lest there be not enough for us and you! – Beginning the sentence with a beautiful abruptness; such as showed their surprise at the state of those poor wretches, who had so long received them, as well as their own souls. Lest there be not enough – It is sure there is not; for no man has more than holiness enough for himself. Go ye rather to them that sell – Without money and without price: that is, to God, to Christ. And buy – If ye can. O no! The time is past and returns no more!

13. Watch therefore – He that watches has not only a burning lamp, but likewise oil in his vessel. And even when he sleepeth, his heart waketh. He is quiet; but not secure.

14. Our Lord proceeds by a parable still plainer (if that can be) to declare the final reward of a harmless man. May God give all such in this their day, ears to hear and hearts to understand it! The kingdom of heaven – That is, the King of heaven, Christ. Mark xiii, 34; Luke xix, 12.

15. To one he gave five talents, to another two, and to another one – And who knows whether (all circumstances considered) there be a greater disproportion than this, in the talents of those who have received the most, and those who have received the fewest? According

us blessed, and present us to the Father, washed in his blood, purified by his Spirit, and fit to be partakers of the inheritance of the saints in light.

MATTHEW 25

The parable of the ten virgins. (1-13)
The parable of the talents. (14-30)
The judgment. (31-46)

1-13 The circumstances of the parable of the ten virgins were taken from the marriage customs among the Jews, and explain the great day of Christ's coming. See the nature of Christianity. As Christians we profess to attend upon Christ, to honor him, also to be waiting for his coming. Sincere Christians are the wise virgins, and hypocrites the foolish ones. Those are the truly wise or foolish that are so in the affairs of their souls. Many have a lamp of profession in their hands, but have not, in their hearts, sound knowledge and settled resolution, which are needed to carry them through the services and trials of the present state. Their hearts are not stored with holy dispositions, by the new-creating Spirit of God. Our light must shine before men in good works; but this is not likely to be long done, unless there is a fixed, active principle in the heart, of faith in Christ, and love to God and our brethren. They all slumbered and slept. The delay represents the space between the real or apparent conversion of these professors, and the coming of Christ, to take them away by death, or to judge the world. But though Christ tarry past our time, he will not tarry past the due time. The wise virgins kept their lamps burning, but they did not keep themselves awake. Too many real Christians grow remiss, and one degree of carelessness makes way for another. Those that allow themselves to slumber, will scarcely keep from sleeping; therefore dread the beginning of spiritual decays. A startling summons was given. Go ye forth to meet him, is a call to those prepared. The notice of Christ's approach, and the call to meet him, will awaken. Even those best prepared for death have work to do to get actually ready, 2Pe 3:14. It will be a day of search and inquiry; and it concerns us to think how we shall then be found. Some wanted oil to supply their lamps when going out. Those that take up short of true grace, will certainly find the want of it one time or other. An outward profession may light a man along this world, but the damps of the valley of the shadow of death will put out such a light. Those who care not to live the life, yet would die the death of the righteous. But those that would be saved, must have grace of their own; and those that have most grace, have none to spare. The best need more from Christ. And while the poor alarmed soul addresses itself, upon a sick-bed, to repentance and prayer, in awful confusion, death comes, judgment comes, the work is undone, and the poor sinner is undone for ever. This comes of having oil to buy when we should burn it, grace to get when we should use it. Those, and those

name shall be called Wonderful. He hath a name which is above every name, before which all things shall bow, in heaven, and earth, and under the earth. He is God over all. He is blessed forever. To him that is, and was, and is to come, the universal song goeth up.

But there is another relation in which the Son of God has graciously been pleased to stand towards us. He has undertaken to be a Savior, in order that he might be a bridegroom. He had enough glory before, but in the greatness of his heart, he would magnify his compassion even above his power, and he therefore condescended to take into union with himself the nature of man, in order that he might redeem the beloved objects of his choice from the penalty due to their sins, and might enter into the nearest conceivable union with them. It is as Savior that the Father seeks to honor the Son, and the gospel feast is not for the honor of his person merely, but for the honor of his person in this new, yet anciently purposed relationship. It is for the honor of Jesus as entering into spiritual union with his church, that the gospel is prepared as a royal entertainment.

Brethren, when I said that here was a grand occasion, it certainly is so in God's esteem, and it should be so in ours; we should delight to glorify the Son of God. To all loyal subjects in any realm, the marriage of one of the royal family is a matter of great interest, and it is usual and fitting to give expression to congratulations and sympathies by suitable rejoicings. In the instance before us the occasion calls for special joy from all the subjects of the great king of kings. For the occasion in itself is a subject for great delight and thankfulness to us personally. The marriage is with whom? With angels? He took not up angels. It is a marriage with our own nature, "he took up the seed of Abraham." Shall we not rejoice when heaven's great Lord is incarnate as a man, and stoops to redeem humanity from the ruin of the fall? Angels rejoice but they have no such share in the joy as we have. It is the highest personal joy to manhood that Jesus Christ who thought it not robbery to be equal with God, was made in the likeness of men that he might be one flesh with his chosen. Arise ye who slumber! If there was ever an occasion when ye should bestir your spirits and cry "wake up my glory, awake psaltery and harp" it is now, when Jesus comes to be affianced to his church, to make himself of one flesh with her, that he may redeem her, and afterwards exalt her to sit with him upon his throne. Here were abundant reasons why the invited guests should come with joyful steps, and count themselves thrice happy to be bidden to such a banquet. There is overwhelming rea-

19 After a long time the lord of those servants cometh, and reckoneth with them.

20 And so he that had received five talents came and brought other five talents, saying, Lord, thou deliveredst unto me five talents: behold, I have gained beside them five talents more.

21 His lord said unto him, Well done, thou good and faithful servant: thou hast been faithful over a few things, I will make thee ruler over many things: enter thou into the joy of thy lord.

22 He also that had received two talents came and said, Lord, thou deliveredst unto me two talents: behold, I have gained two other talents beside them.

23 His lord said unto him, Well done, good and faithful servant; thou hast been faithful over a few things, I will make thee ruler over many things: enter thou into the joy of thy lord.

24 Then he which had received the one talent came and said, Lord, I knew thee that thou art an hard man, reaping where thou hast not sown, and gathering where thou hast not strawed:

25 And I was afraid, and went and hid thy talent in the earth: lo, there thou hast that is thine.

26 His lord answered and said unto him, Thou wicked and slothful servant, thou knewest that I reap where I sowed not, and gather where I have not strawed:

27 Thou oughtest therefore to have put my money to the exchangers, and then at my coming I should have received mine own with usury.

28 Take therefore the talent from him, and give it unto him which hath ten talents.

29 For unto every one that hath shall be given, and he shall have abundance: but from him that hath not shall be taken away even that which he hath.

30 And cast ye the unprofitable servant into outer darkness: there shall be weeping and gnashing of teeth.

31 When the Son of man shall come in his glory, and all the holy angels with him, then shall he sit upon the throne of his glory:

32 And before him shall be gathered all nations: and he shall separate them one from another, as a shepherd divideth his sheep from the goats:

33 And he shall set the sheep on his right hand, but the goats on the left.

34 Then shall the King say unto them on his right hand, Come, ye blessed of my Father, inherit the kingdom prepared for you from the foundation of the world:

to his own ability – The words may be translated more literally, according to his own mighty power. And immediately took his journey – To heaven.

18. He that had received one – Made his having fewer talents than others a pretense for not improving any. Went and hid his master's money – Reader, art thou doing the same? Art thou hiding the talent God hath lent thee?

24. I knew thou art a hard man – No. Thou knowest him not. He never knew God, who thinks him a hard master. Reaping where thou hast not sown – That is, requiring more of us than thou hast given us power to perform. So does every obstinate sinner, in one kind or other, lay the blame of his own sins on God.

25. And I was afraid – Lest if I had improved my talent, I should have had the more to answer for. So from this fear, one will not learn to read, another will not hear sermons!

26. Thou knewest – That I require impossibilities! This is not an allowing, but a strong denial of the charge.

27. Thou oughtest therefore – On that very account, on thy own supposition, to have improved my talent, as far as was possible.

29. To every one that hath shall be given – So close does God keep to this stated rule, from the beginning to the end of the world. Matt. xiii, 12.

30. Cast ye the unprofitable servant into the outer darkness – For what? what had he done? It is true he had not done good. But neither is he charged with doing any harm. Why, for this reason, for barely doing no harm, he is consigned to outer darkness. He is pronounced a wicked, because he was a slothful, an unprofitable servant. So mere harmlessness, on which many build their hope of salvation, was the cause of his damnation! There shall be the weeping – Of the careless thoughtless sinner; and the gnashing of teeth – Of the proud and stubborn. The same great truth, that there is no such thing as negative goodness, is in this chapter shown three times:

1. In the parable of the virgins;

2. In the still plainer parable of the servants, who had received the talents; and

3. In a direct unparabolical declaration of the manner wherein our Lord will proceed at the last day. The several parts of each of these exactly answers each other, only each rises above the preceding.

31. When the Son of man shall come in his glory, and all the holy angels with him – With what majesty and grandeur does our Lord here speak of himself. Giving us one of the noblest instances of the true sublime. Indeed not many descriptions in the sacred writings themselves seem to equal this. Methinks we can hardly read it without imagining ourselves before the awful tribunal it describes.

34. Inherit the kingdom – Purchased by my blood, for all who have believed in me with the faith which wrought by love. Prepared for you – On purpose for you. May it not be probably inferred from hence, that man was not created merely to fill up the places of the fallen angels?

35. I was hungry, and ye gave me meat; I was thirsty, and ye gave me drink – All these works of outward mercy suppose faith and love, and must needs be accompanied with works of spiritual mercy. But works of this kind the Judge could not mention in the same manner. He could not say, I was in error, and ye recalled me to the truth; I was in sin, and ye brought me to repentance. In prison – Prisoners need to be visited above all others, as they are commonly solitary and forsaken by the rest

only, shall go to heaven hereafter, that are made ready for heaven here. The suddenness of death and of Christ's coming to us then, will not hinder our happiness, if we have been prepared. The door was shut. Many will seek admission into heaven when it is too late. The vain confidence of hypocrites will carry them far in expectations of happiness. The unexpected summons of death may alarm the Christian; but, proceeding without delay to trim his lamp, his graces often shine more bright; while the mere professor's conduct shows that his lamp is going out. Watch therefore, attend to the business of your souls. Be in the fear of the Lord all the day long.

14-30 See commentary at Luke 19:12-27

31-46 This is a description of the last judgment. It is as an explanation of the former parables. There is a judgment to come, in which every man shall be sentenced to a state of everlasting happiness, or misery. Christ shall come, not only in the glory of his Father, but in his own glory, as Mediator. The wicked and godly here dwell together, in the same cities, churches, families, and are not always to be known the one from the other; such are the weaknesses of saints, such the hypocrisies of sinners; and death takes both: but in that day they will be parted for ever. Jesus Christ is the great Shepherd; he will shortly distinguish between those that are his, and those that are not. All other distinctions will be done away; but the great one between saints and sinners, holy and unholy, will remain for ever. The happiness the saints shall possess is very great. It is a kingdom; the most valuable possession on earth; yet this is but a faint resemblance of the blessed state of the saints in heaven. It is a kingdom prepared. The Father provided it for them in the greatness of his wisdom and power; the Son purchased it for them; and the blessed Spirit, in preparing them for the kingdom, is preparing it for them. It is prepared for them: it is in all points adapted to the new nature of a sanctified soul. It is prepared from the foundation of the world. This happiness was for the saints, and they for it, from all eternity. They shall come and inherit it. What we inherit is not got by ourselves. It is God that makes heirs of heaven. We are not to suppose that acts of bounty will entitle to eternal happiness. Good works done for God's sake, through Jesus Christ, are here noticed as marking the character of believers made holy by the Spirit of Christ, and as the effects of grace bestowed on those who do them. The wicked in this world were often called to come to Christ for life and rest, but they turned from his calls; and justly are those bid to depart from Christ, that would not come to him. Condemned sinners will in vain offer excuses. The punishment of the wicked will be an everlasting punishment; their state cannot be altered. Thus life and death, good and evil, the blessing and the curse, are set before us, that we may choose our way, and as our way so shall our end be.

son why mankind should rejoice in the glorious gospel of Jesus and hasten to avail themselves of it.

Beside that we must consider the royal descent of the Bridegroom. Remember that Jesus Christ our Savior is very God of very God. Are we asked to do him honor? It is right, for to whom else should honor be given? Surely we should glorify our Creator and Preserver! Willful must be the disobedience which will not pay reverence to one so highly exalted and so worthy of all homage. It is heaven to serve such a Lord. His glory reacheth unto the clouds; let him be adored forever and ever; O come let us worship and bow down, let us cheerfully obey those commands of God which aim at the honor of his Son.

Remember also the person of Immanuel, and you will desire his glory. This glorious Son, whose fame is to be spread abroad, is most certainly God—of that we have spoken, but he is also most assuredly man, our brother, bone of our bone, and flesh of our flesh. Do we not delight to believe that he, tempted in all points as we are, has never yet submitted to be stained by sin? Never such a man as he, head of the race, the second Adam, the everlasting Father— who among us would not do him reverence? Will we not seek his honor, seeing that now he lifts our race to be next to the throne of God.

Remember, too, his character. Was there ever such a life as his? I will not so much speak of his divine character, though that furnishes abundant reason for worship and adoration, but think of him even as a man. O beloved, what tenderness, what compassion, yet what holy boldness; what love for sinners, and yet what love for truth! Men who have not loved him have nevertheless admired him, and hearts in which we least expected to see such recognition of his excellence have nevertheless been deeply affected as they have studied his life. We must praise him, for He is "chief among ten thousand, and altogether lovely." It were treason to be silent when the hour has come to speak of him who is peerless among men and matchless among angels. Clap, clap your hands at the thought of the marriage of the King's Son, for whom his bride hath made herself ready.

Think, too, of his achievements. We take into reckoning whenever we do honor to a prince all that he may have done for the nation over which he rules. What, then, has Jesus done for us? Rather let me say what has he not done? Upon his shoulders were laid our sins; he carried them into the wilderness, and they are gone forever. Against him came forth our foes; he met them in shock of battle, and where are they

35 For I was an hungred, and ye gave me meat: I was thirsty, and ye gave me drink: I was a stranger, and ye took me in:

36 Naked, and ye clothed me: I was sick, and ye visited me: I was in prison, and ye came unto me.

37 Then shall the righteous answer him, saying, Lord, when saw we thee an hungred, and fed thee? or thirsty, and gave thee drink?

38 When saw we thee a stranger, and took thee in? or naked, and clothed thee?

39 Or when saw we thee sick, or in prison, and came unto thee?

40 And the King shall answer and say unto them, Verily I say unto you, Inasmuch as ye have done it unto one of the least of these my brethren, ye have done it unto me.

41 Then shall he say also unto them on the left hand, Depart from me, ye cursed, into everlasting fire, prepared for the devil and his angels:

42 For I was an hungred, and ye gave me no meat: I was thirsty, and ye gave me no drink:

43 I was a stranger, and ye took me not in: naked, and ye clothed me not: sick, and in prison, and ye visited me not.

44 Then shall they also answer him, saying, Lord, when saw we thee an hungred, or athirst, or a stranger, or naked, or sick, or in prison, and did not minister unto thee?

45 Then shall he answer them, saying, Verily I say unto you, Inasmuch as ye did it not to one of the least of these, ye did it not to me.

46 And these shall go away into everlasting punishment: but the righteous into life eternal.

MATTHEW 26

1 And it came to pass, when Jesus had finished all these sayings, he said unto his disciples,

2 Ye know that after two days is the feast of the passover, and the Son of man is betrayed to be crucified.

3 Then assembled together the chief priests, and the scribes, and the elders of the people, unto the palace of the high priest, who was called Caiaphas,

4 And consulted that they might take Jesus by subtilty, and kill him.

5 But they said, Not on the feast day, lest there be an uproar among the people.

6 Now when Jesus was in Bethany, in the house of Simon the leper,

7 There came unto him a woman having an alabaster box of very precious

of the world.

37. Then shall the righteous answer – It cannot be, that either the righteous or the wicked should answer in these very words. What we learn here is that neither of them have the same estimation of their own works as the Judge hath.

40. Inasmuch as ye did it to one of the least of these my brethren, ye did it to me – What encouragement is here to assist the household of faith? But let us likewise remember to do good to all men.

41. Depart into the everlasting fire, which was prepared for the devil and his angels – Not originally for you: you are intruders into everlasting fire.

44. Then will they answer – So the endeavor to justify themselves, will remain with the wicked even to that day!

46. And these shall go away into everlasting punishment, but the righteous into life everlasting – Either therefore the punishment is strictly eternal, or the reward is not: the very same expression being applied to the former as to the latter. The Judge will speak first to the righteous, in the audience of the wicked. The wicked shall then go away into everlasting fire, in the view of the righteous. Thus the damned shall see nothing of the everlasting life; but the just will see the punishment of the ungodly. It is not only particularly observable here

1. That the punishment lasts as long as the reward; but,

2. That this punishment is so far from ceasing at the end of the world, that it does not begin till then.

MATTHEW 26

1. When Jesus had finished all these discourses – When he had spoken all he had to speak. Till then he would not enter upon his passion: then he would delay it no longer. Mark xiv, 1; Luke xxii, 1.

2. After two days is the Passover – The manner wherein this was celebrated gives much light to several circumstances that follow. The master of the family began the feast with a cup of wine, which having solemnly blessed, he divided among the guests, Luke xxii, 17. Then the supper began with the unleavened bread and bitter herbs; which when they had all tasted, one of the young persons present, according to Exod. xii, 26 "And it shall come to pass, when your children shall say unto you, What mean ye by this service?", asked the reason of the solemnity. This introduced the showing forth, or declaration of it: in allusion to which we read of showing forth the Lord's death, "For as often as ye eat this bread, and drink this cup, ye do shew the Lord's death till he come." 1 Cor. xi, 26. Then the master rose up and took another cup, before the lamb was tasted. After supper, he took a thin loaf or cake, which he broke and divided to all at the table, and likewise the cup, usually called the cup of thanksgiving, of which he drank first, and then all the guests. It was this bread and this cup which our Lord consecrated to be a standing memorial of his death.

3. The chief priests and the scribes and the elders of the people – (Heads of families.) These together constituted the Sanhedrin, or great council, which had the supreme authority, both in civil and ecclesiastical affairs.

5. But they said, Not at the feast – This was the result of human wisdom. But when Judas came they changed their purpose. So the counsel of God took place, and the true paschal Lamb was offered up on the great day of the paschal solemnity.

6. ["And being in Bethany in the house of Simon the leper, as he sat at

MATTHEW 26

The rulers conspire against Christ. (1-5)
Christ anointed at Bethany. (6-13)
Judas bargains to betray Christ. (14-16)
The Passover. (17-25)
Christ institutes his holy supper. (26-30)
He warns his disciples. (31-35)
His agony in the garden. (36-46)
He is betrayed. (47-56)
Christ before Caiaphas. (57-68)
Peter denies him. (69-75)

1-5 Our Lord had often told of his sufferings as at a distance, now he speaks of them as at hand. At the same time the Jewish council consulted how they might put him to death secretly. But it pleased God to defeat their intention. Jesus, the true paschal Lamb, was to be sacrificed for us at that very time, and his death and resurrection rendered public.

6-13 The pouring ointment upon the head of Christ was a token of the highest respect. Where there is true love in the heart to Jesus Christ, nothing will be thought too good to bestow upon him. The more Christ's servants and their services are cavilled at, the more he manifests his acceptance. This act of faith and love was so remarkable, that it would be reported, as a memorial of Mary's faith and love, to all future ages, and in all places where the gospel should be preached. This prophecy is fulfilled.

14-16 There were but twelve called apostles, and one of them was like a devil; surely we must never expect any society to be quite pure on this side heaven. The greater profession men make of religion, the greater opportunity they have of doing mischief, if their hearts be not right with God. Observe, that Christ's own disciple, who knew so well his doctrine and manner of his life, and was false to him, could not charge him with any thing criminal, though it would have served to justify his treachery. What did Judas want? Was not he welcome wherever his Master was? Did he not fare as Christ fared? It is not the lack, but the love of money, that is the root of all evil. After he had made that wicked bargain, Judas had time to repent, and to revoke it; but when lesser acts of dishonesty have hardened the conscience men do without hesitation that which is more shameful.

17-25 Observe, the place for their eating the passover was pointed out by Christ to the disciples. He knows those hidden ones who favor his cause, and will graciously visit all who are willing to receive him. The disciples did as Jesus had appointed. Those who would have Christ's presence in the gospel passover, must do what he says. It well becomes the disciples of Christ always to be jealous over themselves, especially in trying times. We know not how strongly we may be tempted, nor how far God may leave us to ourselves,

now? They are cast into the depths of the sea. As for death itself, that last of foes, he has virtually overcome it, and ere long the weakest of us through him shall say "O death, where is thy sting? O grave, where is thy victory?" He is the hero of heaven. He returned to his Father's throne amidst the acclamations of the universe. Do we not, for whom he fought, for whom he conquered, do we not desire to honor him? I feel I speak with bated breath upon a theme where all our powers of speech should be let loose. Bring forth the royal diadem and crown him! Is it not the universal verdict of all who know him? Ought it not to be the cry of all the sons of men? East and west, and north and south, ought they not to ring the joy bells and hang out streamers on his marriage day, for joy of him? Is the King's Son to be married, is there a festival in his honor? O then let him be great, let him be glorious! Long live the King! Let the maidens go forth with their timbrels, and the sons of music make sweet melody—yea, let all creatures that have breath break forth with his praises. "Hosanna! Hosanna! Blessed is he that cometh in the name of the Lord."

II. Secondly, here is a GENEROUS METHOD of accomplishing the design. A king's son is to be honored on the day of his marriage, in what way shall it be done? Barbarous nations have their great festivals, and alas, that men should have sunk so low; on such occasions rivers of human blood are made to flow. To this very day, on the borders of civilization, there is found a wretched tyrant whose infernal customs, for I dare not call them by a less severe term, command the murder of hundreds of his fellow creatures in cold blood, on certain high days and festivals. Thus would the monster honor his son by acting like a fiend. No blood is poured forth to honor the Son of heaven's great King. I doubt not Jesus will have honor even in the destruction of men if they reject his mercy, but it is not so that God elects to glorify his Son. Jesus the Savior, on his wedding-day with manhood, is glorified by mercy, not by wrath. If blood be mentioned on such a day, it is his own by which he is glorified. The slaughter of mankind would bring no joy to him, he is meek and lowly, a lover of the sons of men. It has been the custom of most kings to signalize a princely wedding by levying a fresh tax, or demanding an increased subsidy from their subjects. In the case of the anticipated wedding of our beloved Queen's daughter, the dowry sought will be given with greater pleasure than upon any former occasion, and none of us would lift a whisper of complaint; but the parable shows that the King of kings deals with us

ointment, and poured it on his head, as he sat at meat.

8 But when his disciples saw it, they had indignation, saying, To what purpose is this waste?

9 For this ointment might have been sold for much, and given to the poor.

10 When Jesus understood it, he said unto them, Why trouble ye the woman? for she hath wrought a good work upon me.

11 For ye have the poor always with you; but me ye have not always.

12 For in that she hath poured this ointment on my body, she did it for my burial.

13 Verily I say unto you, Wheresoever this gospel shall be preached in the whole world, there shall also this, that this woman hath done, be told for a memorial of her.

14 Then one of the twelve, called Judas Iscariot, went unto the chief priests,

15 And said unto them, What will ye give me, and I will deliver him unto you? And they covenanted with him for thirty pieces of silver.

16 And from that time he sought opportunity to betray him.

17 Now the first day of the feast of unleavened bread the disciples came to Jesus, saying unto him, Where wilt thou that we prepare for thee to eat the passover?

18 And he said, Go into the city to such a man, and say unto him, The Master saith, My time is at hand; I will keep the passover at thy house with my disciples.

19 And the disciples did as Jesus had appointed them; and they made ready the passover.

20 Now when the even was come, he sat down with the twelve.

21 And as they did eat, he said, Verily I say unto you, that one of you shall betray me.

22 And they were exceeding sorrowful, and began every one of them to say unto him, Lord, is it I?

23 And he answered and said, He that dippeth his hand with me in the dish, the same shall betray me.

24 The Son of man goeth as it is written of him: but woe unto that man by whom the Son of man is betrayed! it had been good for that man if he had not been born.

25 Then Judas, which betrayed him, answered and said, Master, is it I? He said unto him, Thou hast said.

26 And as they were eating, Jesus took bread, and blessed it, and brake it, and gave it to the disciples, and said, Take,

meat, there came a woman having an alabaster box of ointment of spikenard very precious; and she brake the box, and poured it on his head." Mark xiv, 3.]

8. His disciples seeing it, had indignation, saying – It seems several of them were angry, and spoke, though none so warmly as Judas Iscariot.

11. Ye have the poor always with you – Such is the wise and gracious providence of God, that we may have always opportunities of relieving their wants, and so laying up for ourselves treasures in heaven.

12. She hath done it for my burial – As it were for the embalming of my body. Indeed this was not her design: but our Lord puts this construction upon it, to confirm thereby what he had before said to his disciples, concerning his approaching death.

13. This Gospel – That is, this part of the Gospel history.

14. ["And Judas Iscariot, one of the twelve, went unto the chief priests, to betray him unto them." Mark xiv, 10; "Then entered Satan into Judas surnamed Iscariot, being of the number of the twelve." Luke xxii, 3.]

15. They bargained with him for thirty pieces of silver – (About three pounds fifteen shillings sterling; or sixteen dollars sixty-seven cents,) the price of a slave, ["If the ox shall push a manservant or a maidservant; he shall give unto their master thirty shekels of silver, and the ox shall be stoned." Exod. xxi, 32.]

17. On the first day of unleavened bread – Being Thursday, the fourteenth day of the first month, ["And ye shall keep it up until the fourteenth day of the same month: and the whole assembly of the congregation of Israel shall kill it in the evening. . . . Seven days shall ye eat unleavened bread; even the first day ye shall put away leaven out of your houses: for whosoever eateth leavened bread from the first day until the seventh day, that soul shall be cut off from Israel." Exod. xii, 6, 15.] Mark xiv, 12 Luke xxii, 7

18. The Master saith, My time is at hand – That is, the time of my suffering.

20. Mark xiv, 17; Luke xxii, 14.

23. He that dippeth his hand with me in the dish – Which it seems Judas was doing at that very time. This dish was a vessel full of vinegar, wherein they dipped their bitter herbs.

24. The Son of man goeth through sufferings to glory, as it is written of him – Yet this is no excuse for him that betrayeth him: miserable will that man be: it had been good for that man if he had not been born – May not the same be said of every man that finally perishes? But who can reconcile this, if it were true of Judas alone, with the doctrine of universal salvation?

25. Thou hast said – That is, it is as thou hast said.

26. Jesus took the bread – the bread or cake, which the master of the family used to divide among them, after they had eaten the Passover. The custom our Lord now transferred to a nobler use. This bread is, that is, signifies or represents my body, according to the style of the sacred writers. Thus Gen. xl, 12, "And Joseph said unto him, This is the interpretation of it: The three branches are three days:" the three branches are three days. Thus Gal. iv, 24, "Which things are an allegory: for these are the two covenants; the one from the mount Sinai, which gendereth to bondage, which is Agar.," St. Paul speaking of Sarah and Hagar, says, These are the two covenants. Thus in the grand type of our Lord, Exod. xii, 11, God says of the paschal lamb, This is the Lord's Passover. Now Christ substituting the holy communion for the Passover, follows the style of the Old Testament, and uses the same

therefore we have reason not to be high-minded, but to fear. Heart-searching examination and fervent prayer are especially proper before the Lord's supper, that, as Christ our Passover is now sacrificed for us, we may keep this feast, renewing our repentance, our faith in his blood, and surrendering ourselves to his service.

26-30 This ordinance of the Lord's supper is to us the passover supper, by which we commemorate a much greater deliverance than that of Israel out of Egypt. Take, eat; accept of Christ as he is offered to you; receive the atonement, approve of it, submit to his grace and his government. Meat looked upon, be the dish ever so well garnished, will not nourish; it must be fed upon: so must the doctrine of Christ. This is my body; that is, spiritually, it signifies and represents his body. We partake of the sun, not by having the sun put into our hands, but the beams of it darted down upon us; so we partake of Christ by partaking of his grace, and the blessed fruits of the breaking of his body. The blood of Christ is signified and represented by the wine. He gave thanks, to teach us to look to God in every part of the ordinance. This cup he gave to the disciples with a command, Drink ye all of it. The pardon of sin is that great blessing which is, in the Lord's supper, conferred on all true believers; it is the foundation of all other blessings. He takes leave of such communion; and assures them of a happy meeting again at last; "Until that day when I drink it new with you", may be understood of the joys and glories of the future state, which the saints shall partake with the Lord Jesus. That will be the kingdom of his Father; the wine of consolation will there be always new. While we look at the outward signs of Christ's body broken and his blood shed for the remission of our sins, let us recollect that the feast cost him as much as though he had literally given his flesh to be eaten and his blood for us to drink.

31-35 Improper self-confidence, like that of Peter, is the first step to a fall. There is a proneness in all of us to be over-confident. But those fall soonest and foulest, who are the most confident in themselves. Those are least safe, who think themselves most secure. Satan is active to lead such astray; they are most off their guard: God leaves them to themselves, to humble them.

36-46 He who made atonement for the sins of mankind, submitted himself in a garden of suffering, to the will of God, from which man had revolted in a garden of pleasure. Christ took with him into that part of the garden where he suffered his agony, only those who had witnessed his glory in his transfiguration. Those are best prepared to suffer with Christ, who have by faith beheld his glory. The words used denote the most entire dejection, amazement, anguish, and horror of mind; the state of one surrounded with sorrows, overwhelmed with miseries, and almost swallowed up with terror and dismay. He now began to be sorrowful,

not after the manner of man. He asks no dowry for his Son; he makes the marriage memorable not by demands but by gifts. Nothing is sought for from the people, but much is prepared for them, gifts are lavishly bestowed, and all that is requested of the subjects is, that they for awhile merge the subject in the more honorable character of the guest, and willingly come to the palace, not to labor or serve at the table, but to feast and to rejoice.

Observe, then, the generous method by which God honors Christ is set forth here under the form of a banquet. I noted Matthew Henry's way of describing the objects of a feast, and with the alliteration of the Puritans, he says, "A feast is for love and for laughter, for fullness and for fellowship." It is even so with the gospel. It is for love; in the gospel, sinner, you are invited to be reconciled to God, you are assured that God forgives your sins, ceases to be angry, and would have you reconciled to him through his Son. Thus love is established between God and the soul. Then it is for laughter, for happiness, for joy. Those who come to God in Christ Jesus, and believe in him, have their hearts filled with overflowing peace, which calm lake of peace often lifts up itself in waves of joy, which clap their hands in exultation.

It is not to sorrow but to joy that the great King invites his subjects, when he glorifies his Son Jesus. It is not that you may be distressed, but that you may be delighted that he bids you believe in the crucified Savior and live. A feast, moreover, is for fullness. The hungry famished soul of man is satisfied with the blessings of grace. The gospel fills the whole capacity of our manhood. There is not a faculty of our nature which is not made to feel its need supplied when the soul accepts the provisions of mercy; our whole manhood is satisfied with good things and our youth is renewed like the eagles. "For I have satisfied the weary soul, and I have replenished every sorrowful soul." To crown all, the gospel brings us into fellowship with the Father and his Son Jesus Christ. In Christ Jesus we commune with the sacred Trinity. God becomes our Father, and reveals his paternal heart. Jesus manifests himself unto us as he doth not unto the world, and the communion of the Holy Ghost abides with us. Our fellowship is like that of Jonathan with David, or Jesus with John. We feast on the bread of heaven, and drink wines on the lees well refined. We are brought into the heavenly banqueting house where the secret of the Lord is revealed to us, and our heart pours itself out before the Lord. Very near is our communion with God; most intimate love and condescension does he show

eat; this is my body.

27 And he took the cup, and gave thanks, and gave it to them, saying, Drink ye all of it;

28 For this is my blood of the new testament, which is shed for many for the remission of sins.

29 But I say unto you, I will not drink henceforth of this fruit of the vine, until that day when I drink it new with you in my Father's kingdom.

30 And when they had sung an hymn, they went out into the mount of Olives.

31 Then saith Jesus unto them, All ye shall be offended because of me this night: for it is written, I will smite the shepherd, and the sheep of the flock shall be scattered abroad.

32 But after I am risen again, I will go before you into Galilee.

33 Peter answered and said unto him, Though all men shall be offended because of thee, yet will I never be offended.

34 Jesus said unto him, Verily I say unto thee, That this night, before the cock crow, thou shalt deny me thrice.

35 Peter said unto him, Though I should die with thee, yet will I not deny thee. Likewise also said all the disciples.

36 Then cometh Jesus with them unto a place called Gethsemane, and saith unto the disciples, Sit ye here, while I go and pray yonder.

37 And he took with him Peter and the two sons of Zebedee, and began to be sorrowful and very heavy.

38 Then saith he unto them, My soul is exceeding sorrowful, even unto death: tarry ye here, and watch with me.

39 And he went a little further, and fell on his face, and prayed, saying, O my Father, if it be possible, let this cup pass from me: nevertheless not as I will, but as thou wilt.

40 And he cometh unto the disciples, and findeth them asleep, and saith unto Peter, What, could ye not watch with me one hour?

41 Watch and pray, that ye enter not into temptation: the spirit indeed is willing, but the flesh is weak.

42 He went away again the second time, and prayed, saying, O my Father, if this cup may not pass away from me, except I drink it, thy will be done.

43 And he came and found them asleep again: for their eyes were heavy.

44 And he left them, and went away again, and prayed the third time, saying the same words.

45 Then cometh he to his disciples, and saith unto them, Sleep on now, and take your rest: behold, the hour is at hand,

expressions the Jews were wont to use in celebrating the Passover.

27. And he took the cup – Called by the Jews the cup of thanksgiving; which the master of the family used likewise to give to each after supper.

28. This is the sign of my blood, whereby the new testament or covenant is confirmed. Which is shed for many – As many as spring from Adam.

29. I will not drink henceforth of this fruit of the vine, till I drink it new with you in my Father's kingdom – That is, I shall taste no more wine, till I drink wine of quite another kind in the glorious kingdom of my Father. And of this you shall also partake with me.

30. And when they had sung the hymn – Which was constantly sung at the close of the Passover. It consisteth of six psalms, from the 113th to the 118th. The mount of Olives – Was over against the temple, about two miles from Jerusalem. ["And when they had sung an hymn, they went out into the mount of Olives." Mark xiv, 26; "And he came out, and went, as he was wont, to the mount of Olives; and his disciples also followed him." Luke xxii, 39; "When Jesus had spoken these words, he went forth with his disciples over the brook Cedron, where was a garden, into the which he entered, and his disciples." John xviii, 1.]

31. All ye will be offended at me – Something will happen to me, which will occasion your falling into sin by forsaking me. ["Awake, O sword, against my shepherd, and against the man that is my fellow, saith the LORD of hosts: smite the shepherd, and the sheep shall be scattered: and I will turn mine hand upon the little ones." Zech. xiii, 7.]

32. But notwithstanding this, after I am risen I will go before you (as a shepherd before his sheep) into Galilee. Though you forsake me, I will not for this forsake you.

34. Before cock crowing thou wilt deny me thrice – That is, before three in the morning, the usual time of cock crowing: although one cock was heard to crow once, after Peter's first denial of his Lord.

35. In like manner also said all the disciples – But such was the tenderness of our Lord, that he would not aggravate their sin by making any reply.

36. Then cometh Jesus to a place called Gethsemane – That is, the valley of fatness. The garden probably had its name from its soil and situation, laying in some little valley between two of those many hills, the range of which constitutes the mount of Olives. Mark xiv, 32; Luke xxii, 40.

37. And taking with him Peter and the two sons of Zebedee – To be witnesses of all; he began to be sorrowful and in deep anguish – Probably from feeling the arrows of the Almighty stick fast in his soul, while God laid on him the iniquities of us all. Who can tell what painful and dreadful sensations were then impressed on him by the immediate hand of God? The former word in the original properly signifies, to be penetrated with the most exquisite sorrow; the latter to be quite depressed, and almost overwhelmed with the load.

39. And going a little farther – About a stone's cast, Luke xxii, 41 – So that the apostles could both see and hear him still. If it be possible, let this cup pass from me – And it did pass from him quickly. When he cried unto God with strong cries and tears, he was heard in that which he feared. God did take away the terror and severity of that inward conflict.

41. The spirit – Your spirit: ye yourselves. The flesh – Your nature. How

MATTHEW HENRY   CHARLES H. SPURGEON

and never ceased to be so till he said, It is finished. He prayed that, if possible, the cup might pass from him. But he also showed his perfect readiness to bear the load of his sufferings; he was willing to submit to all for our redemption and salvation. According to this example of Christ, we must drink of the bitterest cup which God puts into our hands; though nature struggle, it must submit. It should be more our care to get troubles sanctified, and our hearts satisfied under them, than to get them taken away. It is well for us that our salvation is in the hand of One who neither slumbers nor sleeps. All are tempted, but we should be much afraid of entering into temptation. To be secured from this, we should watch and pray, and continually look unto the Lord to hold us up that we may be safe. Doubtless our Lord had a clear and full view of the sufferings he was to endure, yet he spoke with the greatest calmness till this time. Christ was a Surety, who undertook to be answerable for our sins. Accordingly he was made sin for us, and suffered for our sins, the Just for the unjust; and Scripture ascribes his heaviest sufferings to the hand of God. He had full knowledge of the infinite evil of sin, and of the immense extent of that guilt for which he was to atone; with awful views of the Divine justice and holiness, and the punishment deserved by the sins of men, such as no tongue can express, or mind conceive. At the same time, Christ suffered being tempted; probably horrible thoughts were suggested by Satan that tended to gloom and every dreadful conclusion: these would be the more hard to bear from his perfect holiness. And did the load of imputed guilt so weigh down the soul of him of whom it is said, he upholdeth all things by the word of his power? into what misery then must those sink whose sins are left upon their own heads! How will those escape who neglect so great salvation?

47-56 No enemies are so much to be abhorred as those professed disciples that betray Christ with a kiss. God has no need of our services, much less of our sins, to bring about his purposes. Though Christ was crucified through weakness, it was voluntary weakness; he submitted to death. If he had not been willing to suffer, they could not conquer him. It was a great sin for those who had left all to follow Jesus; now to leave him for they knew not what. What folly, for fear of death to flee from Him, whom they knew and acknowledged to be the Fountain of life!

57-68 Jesus was hurried into Jerusalem. It looks ill, and bodes worse, when those who are willing to be Christ's disciples, are not willing to be known to be so. Here began Peter's denying him: for to follow Christ afar off, is to begin to go back from him. It is more our concern to prepare for the end, whatever it may be, than curiously to ask what the end will be. The event is God's, but the duty is ours. Now the Scriptures were fulfilled, which said, False witnesses are risen up against me. Christ was accused, that we might not be

to us. What say you to this? Is there not here a rich repast worthy of him who prepares it. Here all your capacious powers can wish, O sinner, shall be given to you; all you want for time and for eternity God prepares in the person of his dear Son, and bids you receive it without money and without price.

How honorable, too, is the gospel to those who receive it. An invitation to a regal marriage was a high honor to those who were bidden. I do not suppose that many of us are likely to be invited to the Princess's wedding, and, if we were, we should probably be greatly elated, for we should most of us feel it to be one of the great events of our lives. So was it with these people. A king's son is not married every day, and it is not everybody that is bidden to the monarch's entertainment. All their lives long they would say, "I was at his wedding, and saw all the splendor of the marriage festival." Probably some of them had never before enjoyed such a feast as the luxurious potentate had prepared for that day, and had never before been in such good company. My brethren nothing so honors a man as for him to accept the gospel. While his faith honors Christ, Christ honors him. It is no mean thing to be a king's son, but those who come to the marriage feast of God's own Son shall become King's sons themselves—themselves participators in the glory of the great heir of all things. While I am speaking of this generous method my heart glows with sacred ardor, and my wonder rises that men do not come to the banquet of love which honors all its guests. When the banquet is so costly to the host, so free to the guests, and so honorable to all concerned, how is it that there should be found any so unwise as to refuse the favor. Surely here is an illustration of the folly of the unrenewed heart, and a proof of the deep depravity which sin has caused. If men turn their backs on Moses with his stony tables, I do not marvel, but to despise the loaded tables of grace, heaped up with oxen and fatlings—this is strange. To resist the justice of God is a crime, but to repel the generosity of heaven, what is this? We must invent a term of infamy with which to brand the base ingratitude. To resist God in majesty of terror is insanity but to spurn him in the majesty of his mercy is something more than madness. Sin reaches its climax when it resolves to starve sooner than owe anything to divine goodness. I feel I must anticipate the period for delivering my message, and as I have described to you the way in which God honors his Son, I must at once proclaim the invitation, and cry to you, "Come to the wedding feast. Come ye, and glorify Jesus by accepting the provisions of grace. Your works

and the Son of man is betrayed into the hands of sinners.

46 Rise, let us be going: behold, he is at hand that doth betray me.

47 And while he yet spake, lo, Judas, one of the twelve, came, and with him a great multitude with swords and staves, from the chief priests and elders of the people.

48 Now he that betrayed him gave them a sign, saying, Whomsoever I shall kiss, that same is he: hold him fast.

49 And forthwith he came to Jesus, and said, Hail, master; and kissed him.

50 And Jesus said unto him, Friend, wherefore art thou come? Then came they, and laid hands on Jesus, and took him.

51 And, behold, one of them which were with Jesus stretched out his hand, and drew his sword, and struck a servant of the high priest's, and smote off his ear.

52 Then said Jesus unto him, Put up again thy sword into his place: for all they that take the sword shall perish with the sword.

53 Thinkest thou that I cannot now pray to my Father, and he shall presently give me more than twelve legions of angels?

54 But how then shall the scriptures be fulfilled, that thus it must be?

55 In that same hour said Jesus to the multitudes, Are ye come out as against a thief with swords and staves for to take me? I sat daily with you teaching in the temple, and ye laid no hold on me.

56 But all this was done, that the scriptures of the prophets might be fulfilled. Then all the disciples forsook him, and fled.

57 And they that had laid hold on Jesus led him away to Caiaphas the high priest, where the scribes and the elders were assembled.

58 But Peter followed him afar off unto the high priest's palace, and went in, and sat with the servants, to see the end.

59 Now the chief priests, and elders, and all the council, sought false witness against Jesus, to put him to death;

60 But found none: yea, though many false witnesses came, yet found they none. At the last came two false witnesses,

61 And said, This fellow said, I am able to destroy the temple of God, and to build it in three days.

62 And the high priest arose, and said unto him, Answerest thou nothing? what is it which these witness against thee?

63 But Jesus held his peace. And the

gentle a rebuke was this, and how kind an apology! especially at a time when our Lord's own mind was so weighed down with sorrow.

45. Sleep on now, if you can, and take your rest – For any farther service you can be of to me.

47. ["And immediately, while he yet spake, cometh Judas, one of the twelve, and with him a great multitude with swords and staves, from the chief priests and the scribes and the elders." Mark xiv, 43; "And while he yet spake, behold a multitude, and he that was called Judas, one of the twelve, went before them, and drew near unto Jesus to kiss him." Luke xxii, 47; "And Judas also, which betrayed him, knew the place: for Jesus ofttimes resorted thither with his disciples." John xviii, 2.]

50. The heroic behavior of the blessed Jesus, in the whole period of his sufferings, will be observed by every attentive eye, and felt by every pious heart: although the sacred historians, according to their usual but wonderful simplicity, make no encomiums upon it. With what composure does he go forth to meet the traitor! With what calmness receive that malignant kiss! With what dignity does he deliver himself into the hands of his enemies! Yet plainly showing his superiority over them, and even then leading as it were captivity captive!

51. And one of them striking the servant of the high priest – Probably the person that seized Jesus first; Cut off his ear – Aiming, it seems, to cleave his head, but that by a secret providence interposing, he declined the blow. Mark xiv, 47; Luke xxii, 49; John xviii, 10.

52. All they that take the sword – Without God's giving it them: without sufficient authority.

53. He will presently give me more than twelve legions of angels – The least of whom, it is probable, could overturn the earth and destroy all the inhabitants of it.

55. ["And Jesus answered and said unto them, Are ye come out, as against a thief, with swords and with staves to take me?" Mark xiv, 48; "Then Jesus said unto the chief priests, and captains of the temple, and the elders, which were come to him, Be ye come out, as against a thief, with swords and staves?" Luke xxii, 52]

57. They led him away to Caiaphas – From the house of Annas, the father-in-law of Caiaphas, to whom they had carried him first. Mark xiv, 53; Luke xxii, 54; John xviii, 12.

58. But Peter followed him afar off – Variously agitated by conflicting passions; love constrained him to follow his Master; fear made him follow afar off. And going in, sat with the servants – Unfit companions as the event showed.

60. Yet found they none – On whose evidence they could condemn him to die. At last came two false witnesses – Such they were, although part of what they said was true; because our Lord did not speak some of those words at all; nor any of them in this sense.

64. Hereafter shall ye see the Son of man – He speaks in the third person, modestly, and yet plainly; Sitting on the right hand of power – That is, the right hand of God: And coming upon the clouds of heaven – As he is represented by Daniel, ["I saw in the night visions, and, behold, one like the Son of man came with the clouds of heaven, came to the Ancient of days, and they brought him near before him. And there was given him dominion, and glory, and a kingdom, that all people, nations, and languages, should serve him: his dominion is an everlasting dominion, which shall not pass away, and his kingdom that which shall not be destroyed." Dan. vii, 13, 14.] Our Lord looked very unlike that person now! But nothing could be more awful, more

condemned; and if at any time we suffer thus, let us remember we cannot expect to fare better than our Master. When Christ was made sin for us, he was silent, and left it to his blood to speak. Hitherto Jesus had seldom professed expressly to be the Christ, the Son of God; the tenor of his doctrine spoke it, and his miracles proved it; but now he would not omit to make an open confession of it. It would have looked like declining his sufferings. He thus confessed, as an example and encouragement to his followers, to confess him before men, whatever hazard they ran. Disdain, cruel mocking, and abhorrence, are the sure portion of the disciple as they were of the Master, from such as would buffet and deride the Lord of glory. These things were exactly foretold in the fiftieth chapter of Isaiah. Let us confess Christ's name, and bear the reproach, and he will confess us before his Father's throne.

69-75 Peter's sin is truly related, for the Scriptures deal faithfully. Bad company leads to sin: those who needlessly thrust themselves into it, may expect to be tempted and insnared, as Peter. They scarcely can come out of such company without guilt or grief, or both. It is a great fault to be shy of Christ; and to dissemble our knowledge of him, when we are called to own him, is, in effect, to deny him. Peter's sin was aggravated; but he fell into the sin by surprise, not as Judas, with design. But conscience should be to us as the crowing of the cock, to put us in mind of the sins we had forgotten. Peter was thus left to fall, to abate his self-confidence, and render him more modest, humble, compassionate, and useful to others. The event has taught believers many things ever since, and if infidels, Pharisees, and hypocrites stumble at it or abuse it, it is at their peril. Little do we know how we should act in very difficult situations, if we were left to ourselves. Let him, therefore, that thinketh he standeth, take heed lest he fall; let us all distrust our own hearts, and rely wholly on the Lord. Peter wept bitterly. Sorrow for sin must not be slight, but great and deep. Peter, who wept so bitterly for denying Christ, never denied him again, but confessed him often in the face of danger. True repentance for any sin will be shown by the contrary grace and duty; that is a sign of our sorrowing not only bitterly but sincerely. This deep sorrow is requisite, not to satisfy divine justice (a sea of tears would not do that), but to evidence that there is a real change of mind, which is the essence of repentance, to make the pardon the more welcome, and sin for the future the more loathsome. Peter, who wept so bitterly for denying Christ, never denied him again, but confessed him often and openly, and in the mouth of danger; so far from ever saying, I know not the man, that he made all the house of Israel know assuredly that this same Jesus was Lord and Christ. True repentance for any sin will be best evidenced by our abounding in the contrary grace and duty; that is a sign of our weeping, not only bitterly, but sincerely. Some of the ancients say, that as long as Peter lived, he never heard a cock crow but it

will not honor him, if you set them up as a right-eousness in competition with his righteousness. Not even your repentance can glorify him, if you think to make it a rival to his precious blood. Come, guilty sinner, as you are, and take the mercy Jesus freely presents to you, and accept the pardon which his blood secures to those who believe in him." Methinks when the messenger went out from the King and first of all marked signs of neglect among those who were bidden, and saw that they would not come, he must have been mute with astonishment. He had seen the oxen, and seen the fatlings, and all the goodly preparations, he knew the King, he knew his Son, he knew what joy it was to be at such a feast; and when the bidden ones began to turn their backs on him, and go their way to their farms, the messenger, repeated his message over and over again with eagerness, wondering all the while at the treason which dared insult so good a Being. I think I see him, at first indignant for his Master's sake, and afterwards melted to pity as he saw what would surely come of such an extravagance of ingratitude, such a superfluity of insolence. He mourned that his fellow-citizens whom he loved should be such fools as to reject so good an offer, and spurn so blessed a proclamation. I, too, am tossed to and fro in soul, with mingled but vehement feelings. O, my God, thou hast provided the gospel, let none in this house reject it, and so slight thy Son and dishonor thee, but may all rejoice in thy generous way of glorifying Jesus Christ, the Bridegroom of his church, and may they come, and willingly grace the festival of thy love.

III. We now advance to our third point, and regretfully remember THE SERIOUS HINDRANCE which for a while interfered with the joyful event.

The king had thought in his mind, "I will make a great feast, I will invite a large number. They shall enjoy all my kingdom can afford, and I shall thus show how much I love my son, and moreover all the guests will have sweet memories in connection with his marriage." When his messengers went out to intimate to those who had received previously an express invitation that the time was come, it is written, "They would not come;" not they could not, but they "would not come." Some for one reason, some for another, but without exception they would not come. Here was a very serious hindrance to the grand business. Cannot the king drag his guests to the table? Yes, but then it would not accomplish his purpose. He wants not slaves to grace his throne. Persons compelled to sit at a marriage-feast would not adorn it. What credit

high priest answered and said unto him, I adjure thee by the living God, that thou tell us whether thou be the Christ, the Son of God.

64 Jesus saith unto him, Thou hast said: nevertheless I say unto you, Hereafter shall ye see the Son of man sitting on the right hand of power, and coming in the clouds of heaven.

65 Then the high priest rent his clothes, saying, He hath spoken blasphemy; what further need have we of witnesses? behold, now ye have heard his blasphemy.

66 What think ye? They answered and said, He is guilty of death.

67 Then did they spit in his face, and buffeted him; and others smote him with the palms of their hands,

68 Saying, Prophesy unto us, thou Christ, Who is he that smote thee?

69 Now Peter sat without in the palace: and a damsel came unto him, saying, Thou also wast with Jesus of Galilee.

70 But he denied before them all, saying, I know not what thou sayest.

71 And when he was gone out into the porch, another maid saw him, and said unto them that were there, This fellow was also with Jesus of Nazareth.

72 And again he denied with an oath, I do not know the man.

73 And after a while came unto him they that stood by, and said to Peter, Surely thou also art one of them; for thy speech bewrayeth thee.

74 Then began he to curse and to swear, saying, I know not the man. And immediately the cock crew.

75 And Peter remembered the word of Jesus, which said unto him, Before the cock crow, thou shalt deny me thrice. And he went out, and wept bitterly.

MATTHEW 27

1 When the morning was come, all the chief priests and elders of the people took counsel against Jesus to put him to death:

2 And when they had bound him, they led him away, and delivered him to Pontius Pilate the governor.

3 Then Judas, which had betrayed him, when he saw that he was condemned, repented himself, and brought again the thirty pieces of silver to the chief priests and elders,

4 Saying, I have sinned in that I have betrayed the innocent blood. And they said, What is that to us? see thou to that.

5 And he cast down the pieces of silver in the temple, and departed, and went and hanged himself.

majestic and becoming, than such an admonition in such circumstances!

65. Then the high priest rent his clothes – Though the high priest was forbidden to rend his clothes (that is, his upper garment) in some cases where others were allowed to do it, ["And he that is the high priest among his brethren, upon whose head the anointing oil was poured, and that is consecrated to put on the garments, shall not uncover his head, nor rend his clothes;" Lev. xxi, 10]; yet in case of blasphemy or any public calamity, it was thought allowable. Caiaphas hereby expressed, in the most artful manner, his horror at hearing such grievous blasphemy.

67. Then – After he had declared he was the Son of God, the Sanhedrin doubtless ordered him to be carried out, while they were consulting what to do. And then it was that the soldiers who kept him began these insults upon him.

72. He denied with an oath – To which possibly he was not unaccustomed, before our Lord called him.

73. Surely thou art also one of them, for thy speech discovereth thee – Malchus might have brought a stronger proof than this. But such is the overruling providence of God, that the world, in the height of their zeal, commonly catch hold of the very weakest of all arguments against the children of God.

74. Then began he to curse and to swear – Having now quite lost the reins, the government of himself.

MATTHEW 27

1. In the morning – As the Sanhedrin used to meet in one of the courts of the temple, which was never opened in the night, they were forced to stay till the morning before they could proceed regularly, in the resolution they had taken to put him to death. ["And straightway in the morning the chief priests held a consultation with the elders and scribes and the whole council, and bound Jesus, and carried him away, and delivered him to Pilate." Mark xv, 1; "And as soon as it was day, the elders of the people and the chief priests and the scribes came together, and led him into their council, saying," Luke xxii, 66; "And the whole multitude of them arose, and led him unto Pilate." xxiii, 1; "Then led they Jesus from Caiaphas unto the hall of judgment: and it was early; and they themselves went not into the judgment hall, lest they should be defiled; but that they might eat the passover." John xviii, 28.]

2. Having bound him – They had bound him when he was first apprehended. But they did it now afresh, to secure him from any danger of an escape, as he passed through the streets of Jerusalem.

3. Then Judas seeing that he was condemned – Which probably he thought Christ would have prevented by a miracle.

4. They said, what is that to us? – How easily could they digest innocent blood! And yet they had a conscience! It is not lawful (say they) to put it into the treasury – But very lawful to slay the innocent!

5. In that part of the temple where the Sanhedrin met.

7. They bought with them the potter's field – Well known, it seems, by that name. This was a small price for a field so near Jerusalem. But the earth had probably been digged for potters' vessels, so that it was now neither fit for tillage nor pasture, and consequently of small value. Foreigners – Heathens especially, of whom there were then great numbers in Jerusalem.

9. Then was fulfilled – What was figuratively represented of old, was

set him a weeping. Those that have truly sorrowed for sin, will sorrow upon every remembrance of it; yet not so as to hinder, but rather to increase, their joy in God and in his mercy and grace.

MATTHEW 27

Christ delivered to Pilate. The despair of Judas. (1-10)
Christ before Pilate. (11-25)
Barabbas loosed, Christ mocked. (26-30)
Christ led to be crucified. (31-34)
He is crucified. (35-44)
The death of Christ. (45-50)
Events at the crucifixion. (51-56)
The burial of Christ. (57-61)
The sepulcher secured. (62-66)

1-10 Wicked men see little of the consequences of their crimes when they commit them, but they must answer for them all. In the fullest manner Judas acknowledged to the chief priests that he had sinned, and betrayed an innocent person. This was full testimony to the character of Christ; but the rulers were hardened. Casting down the money, Judas departed, and went and hanged himself, not being able to bear the terror of Divine wrath, and the anguish of despair. There is little doubt but that the death of Judas was before that of our blessed Lord. But was it nothing to them that they had thirsted after this blood, and hired Judas to betray it, and had condemned it to be shed unjustly? Thus do fools make a mock at sin. Thus many make light of Christ crucified. And it is a common instance of the deceitfulness of our hearts, to make light of our own sin by dwelling upon other people's sins. But the judgment of God is according to truth. Many apply this passage of the buying the piece of ground, with the money Judas brought back, to signify the favor intended by the blood of Christ to strangers, and sinners of the Gentiles. It fulfilled a prophecy, Zec 11:12. Judas went far toward repentance, yet it was not to salvation. He confessed, but not to God; he did not go to him, and say, I have sinned, Father, against heaven. Let none be satisfied with such partial convictions as a man may have, and yet remain full of pride, enmity, and rebellion.

11-25 Having no malice against Jesus, Pilate urged him to clear himself, and labored to get him discharged. The message from his wife was a warning. God has many ways of giving checks to sinners, in their sinful pursuits, and it is a great mercy to have such checks from Providence, from faithful friends, and from our own consciences. O do not this abominable thing which the Lord hates! is what we may hear said to us, when we are entering into temptation, if we will but regard it. Being overruled by the priests, the people made choice of Barabbas. Multitudes who choose the world, rather than God, for their ruler and portion, thus choose their own delusions. The Jews were so bent

could it be to a king to force his subjects to feast at his table? No for once, as I have said before, the subject must be merged in the guest. It was essential to the dignity of the festival that the guests should come with cheerfulness to the festival, but they would not come. Why? Why would they not come? The answer shall be such as to answer another question—Why do not you come and believe in Jesus! With many of them it was an indifference to the whole affair. They did not see what concern they had in the king or his son. Royal marriages were high things and concerned high people; they were plain-speaking men, farmers who went hedging and ditching, or tradesmen who made out bills and sold by the yard or pound. What cared they for the court, the palace, the king, the prince, his bride, or his dinner! They did not say quite that, but such was their feeling; it might be a fine thing, but it was altogether out of their line. How many run in the same groove at this hour? We have heard it said, "What has a working man to do with religion?" and we have heard others of another grade in life affirm that persons who are in business cannot afford time for religion, but had better mind the main chance. The Lord have mercy upon your folly! Here is one great obstacle to the gospel, the stolid indifference of the human mind concerning this grandest of all conceptions—God's glorifying his dear Son by having mercy upon sinners.

At the bottom the real reason for the refusal of those in the parable was that they were disloyal, they would not come to the supper because they saw an opportunity for the loyal to be glad, and not being loyal they did not wish to hear the songs and acclamations of others who were. By staying away they insulted the king, and declared that they cared not whether he was a king or not, whether his son was a prince or not. They determined to disavow their allegiance by refusing the invitation. They said in effect, "Anyhow, if he be a king and his son a prince, we will do him no honor, we will not be numbered with those who surround his board and show forth his splendor. No doubt a feast is worth having, and such a feast as there will be provided t'were well for us to participate in, but for once we will deny our appetites that we may indulge our pride. We proclaim a revolt. We declare we will not go." Ah, ye who believe not in Jesus, at the bottom of it your unbelief is enmity to your Maker, sedition against the great Ruler of the universe, who deserves your homage. "The ox knoweth his owner, and the ass his master's crib," but ye know not, neither do ye consider; ye are rebels against the Majesty of heaven.

6 And the chief priests took the silver pieces, and said, It is not lawful for to put them into the treasury, because it is the price of blood.

7 And they took counsel, and bought with them the potter's field, to bury strangers in.

8 Wherefore that field was called, The field of blood, unto this day.

9 Then was fulfilled that which was spoken by Jeremy the prophet, saying, And they took the thirty pieces of silver, the price of him that was valued, whom they of the children of Israel did value;

10 And gave them for the potter's field, as the Lord appointed me.

11 And Jesus stood before the governor: and the governor asked him, saying, Art thou the King of the Jews? And Jesus said unto him, Thou sayest.

12 And when he was accused of the chief priests and elders, he answered nothing.

13 Then said Pilate unto him, Hearest thou not how many things they witness against thee?

14 And he answered him to never a word; insomuch that the governor marveled greatly.

15 Now at that feast the governor was wont to release unto the people a prisoner, whom they would.

16 And they had then a notable prisoner, called Barabbas.

17 Therefore when they were gathered together, Pilate said unto them, Whom will ye that I release unto you? Barabbas, or Jesus which is called Christ?

18 For he knew that for envy they had delivered him.

19 When he was set down on the judgment seat, his wife sent unto him, saying, Have thou nothing to do with that just man: for I have suffered many things this day in a dream because of him.

20 But the chief priests and elders persuaded the multitude that they should ask Barabbas, and destroy Jesus.

21 The governor answered and said unto them, Whether of the twain will ye that I release unto you? They said, Barabbas.

22 Pilate saith unto them, What shall I do then with Jesus which is called Christ? They all say unto him, Let him be crucified.

23 And the governor said, Why, what evil hath he done? But they cried out the more, saying, Let him be crucified.

24 When Pilate saw that he could prevail nothing, but that rather a tumult was made, he took water, and washed

now really accomplished. What was spoken by the prophet – The word Jeremy, which was added to the text in latter copies, and thence received into many translations, is evidently a mistake: for he who spoke what St. Matthew here cites (or rather paraphrases) was not Jeremy, but Zechariah. ["And I said unto them, If ye think good, give me my price; and if not, forbear. So they weighed for my price thirty pieces of silver." Zech. xi, 12.]

10. As the Lord commanded me – To write, to record.

11. Art thou the king of the Jews? – Jesus before Caiaphas avows himself to be the Christ, before Pilate to be a king; clearly showing thereby, that his answering no more, was not owing to any fear.

15. At every feast – Every year, at the feast of the Passover. ["Now at that feast he released unto them one prisoner, whomsoever they desired." Mark xv, 6; "(For of necessity he must release one unto them at the feast.)" Luke xxiii, 17; "But ye have a custom, that I should release unto you one at the passover: will ye therefore that I release unto you the King of the Jews?" John xviii, 39.]

18. He knew that for envy they had delivered him – As well as from malice and revenge; they envied him, because the people magnified him.

22. They all say, Let him be crucified – The punishment which Barabbas had deserved: and this probably made them think of it. But in their malice they forgot with how dangerous a precedent they furnished the Roman governor. And indeed within the compass of a few years it turned dreadfully upon themselves.

24. Then Pilate took water and washed his hands – This was a custom frequently used among the heathens as well as among the Jews, in token of innocency.

25. His blood be on us and on our children – As this imprecation was dreadfully answered in the ruin so quickly brought on the Jewish nation, and the calamities which have ever since pursued that wretched people, so it was peculiarly fulfilled by Titus the Roman general, on the Jews whom he took during the siege of Jerusalem. So many, after having been scourged in a terrible manner, were crucified all round the city, that in a while there was not room near the wall for the crosses to stand by each other. Probably this befell some of those who now joined in this cry, as it certainly did many of their children: the very finger of God thus pointing out their crime in crucifying his Son.

26. He delivered him to be crucified – The person crucified was nailed to the cross as it lay on the ground, through each hand extended to the utmost stretch, and through both the feet together. Then the cross was raised up, and the foot of it thrust with a violent shock into a hole in the ground prepared for it. This shock disjointed the body, whose whole weight hung upon the nails, till the persons expired through mere dint of pain. This kind of death was used only by the Romans, and by them inflicted only on slaves and the vilest criminals.

27. The whole troop – or cohort. This was a body of foot commanded by the governor, which was appointed to prevent disorders and tumults, especially on solemn occasions. ["And the soldiers led him away into the hall, called Pretorium; and they call together the whole band." Mark xv, 16; "And the soldiers platted a crown of thorns, and put it on his head, and they put on him a purple robe." John xix, 2.]

28. They put on him a scarlet robe – Such as kings and generals wore; probably an old tattered one.

32. Him they compelled to bear his cross – He bore it himself, till he sunk under it, John xix, 17.

upon the death of Christ, that Pilate thought it would be dangerous to refuse. And this struggle shows the power of conscience even on the worst men. Yet all was so ordered to make it evident that Christ suffered for no fault of his own, but for the sins of his people. How vain for Pilate to expect to free himself from the guilt of the innocent blood of a righteous person, whom he was by his office bound to protect! The Jews' curse upon themselves has been awfully answered in the sufferings of their nation. None could bear the sin of others, except him that had no sin of his own to answer for. And are we not all concerned? Is not Barabbas preferred to Jesus, when sinners reject salvation that they may retain their darling sins, which rob God of his glory, and murder their souls? The blood of Christ is now upon us for good, through mercy, by the Jews' rejection of it. O let us flee to it for refuge!

26-30 Crucifixion was a death used only among the Romans; it was very terrible and miserable. A cross was laid on the ground, to which the hands and feet were nailed, it was then lifted up and fixed upright, so that the weight of the body hung on the nails, till the sufferer died in agony. Christ thus answered the type of the brazen serpent raised on a pole. Christ underwent all the misery and shame here related, that he might purchase for us everlasting life, and joy, and glory.

31-34 Christ was led as a Lamb to the slaughter, as a Sacrifice to the altar. Even the mercies of the wicked are really cruel. Taking the cross from him, they compelled one Simon to bear it. Make us ready, O Lord, to bear the cross thou hast appointed us, and daily to take it up with cheerfulness, following thee. Was ever sorrow like unto his sorrow? And when we behold what manner of death he died, let us in that behold with what manner of love he loved us. As if death, so painful a death, were not enough, they added to its bitterness and terror in several ways.

35-44 It was usual to put shame upon malefactors, by a writing to notify the crime for which they suffered. So they set up one over Christ's head. This they designed for his reproach, but God so overruled it, that even his accusation was to his honor. There were crucified with him at the same time, two robbers. He was, at his death, numbered among the transgressors, that we, at our death, might be numbered among the saints. The taunts and jeers he received are here recorded. The enemies of Christ labor to make others believe that of religion and of the people of God, which they themselves know to be false. The chief priests and scribes, and the elders, upbraid Jesus with being the King of Israel. Many people could like the King of Israel well enough, if he would but come down from the cross; if they could but have his kingdom without the tribulation through which they must enter into it. But if no cross, then no Christ, no crown. Those that would reign with him, must be willing to suffer with him. Thus

Moreover, the refusal was a slight to the prince as well as to his father, and in some cases the gospel is refused mainly with this intent, because the unbeliever rejects the deity of Christ, or despises his atonement. O sirs, beware of this, I know of no rock more fatal than to dishonor Christ by denying his sonship and his deity. Spit not upon it, I beseech you—"Kiss the Son, lest he be angry, and ye perish from the way when his wrath is kindled but a little." Indifference covered the refusal in the text, "they made light of it," but if you take off the film you will see that at the bottom there was treason against the majesty of the king, and distaste to the dignity of his son.

No doubt some of them despised the feast itself. They must have known that with such a king it could not be a starveling meal, but they pretended to despise the feast. How many there are who despise the gospel which they do not understand, I say which they do not understand, for almost invariably if you hear a man depreciate the gospel, you will find that he has scarcely even read the New Testament and is an utter stranger to the doctrines of grace. Listen to a man who is voluble in condemnation of the gospel, and you may rest assured that he is fond because he is empty. If he understood the subject better he would find, if he were indeed a man of candor, that he would be led at least to be silent in admiration if he did not become loyal in acceptance.

Beloved friends, the feast is such as you greatly need, let me tell you what it is. It is pardon for the past, renewal of nature for the present, and glory for the future. Here is God to be our helper, his Son to be our shepherd, the Spirit to be our instructor. Here is the love of the Father to be our delight, the blood of the Son to be our cleansing, the energy of the Holy Spirit to be life from the dead to us. You cannot want anything that you ought to want, but what is provided in the gospel, and Jesus Christ will be glorified if you accept it by faith. But here is the hindrance, men do not accept it, "they would not come." Some of us thought that if we put the gospel in a clear light, and if we were earnest in stating it our hearers must be converted, and God forbid we should ever try to do otherwise than make it plain and be earnest, but for all that the best ministry that ever was, or ever could be, will be unsuccessful in a measure; yea, and altogether so, unless the effectual work of the Spirit be present. Still will the cry go up, "Who hath believed our report?" Still will those who serve their Master best, have reason to mourn that they sow on stony ground, and cast their bread on thankless waters. Even the prince of preachers had to say, "Ye search the

his hands before the multitude, saying, I am innocent of the blood of this just person: see ye to it.

25 Then answered all the people, and said, His blood be on us, and on our children.

26 Then released he Barabbas unto them: and when he had scourged Jesus, he delivered him to be crucified.

27 Then the soldiers of the governor took Jesus into the common hall, and gathered unto him the whole band of soldiers.

28 And they stripped him, and put on him a scarlet robe.

29 And when they had platted a crown of thorns, they put it upon his head, and a reed in his right hand: and they bowed the knee before him, and mocked him, saying, Hail, King of the Jews!

30 And they spit upon him, and took the reed, and smote him on the head.

31 And after that they had mocked him, they took the robe off from him, and put his own raiment on him, and led him away to crucify him.

32 And as they came out, they found a man of Cyrene, Simon by name: him they compelled to bear his cross.

33 And when they were come unto a place called Golgotha, that is to say, a place of a skull,

34 They gave him vinegar to drink mingled with gall: and when he had tasted thereof, he would not drink.

35 And they crucified him, and parted his garments, casting lots: that it might be fulfilled which was spoken by the prophet, They parted my garments among them, and upon my vesture did they cast lots.

36 And sitting down they watched him there;

37 And set up over his head his accusation written, THIS IS JESUS THE KING OF THE JEWS.

38 Then were there two thieves crucified with him, one on the right hand, and another on the left.

39 And they that passed by reviled him, wagging their heads,

40 And saying, Thou that destroyest the temple, and buildest it in three days, save thyself. If thou be the Son of God, come down from the cross.

41 Likewise also the chief priests mocking him, with the scribes and elders, said,

42 He saved others; himself he cannot save. If he be the King of Israel, let him now come down from the cross, and we will believe him.

43 He trusted in God; let him deliver him now, if he will have him: for he said, I am the Son of God.

33. A place called Golgotha, that is, the place of a skull – Golgotha in Syriac signifies a skull or head: it was probably called so from this time; being an eminence upon Mount Calvary, not far from the king's gardens. Mark xv, 22; Luke xxiii, 33; John xix, 17

34. They gave him vinegar mingled with gall – Out of derision: which, however nauseous, he received and tasted of. St. Mark mentions also a different mixture which was given him, Wine mingled with myrrh: such as it was customary to give to dying criminals, to make them less sensible of their sufferings: but this our Lord refused to taste, determining to bear the full force of his pains.

35. They parted his garments – This was the custom of the Romans. The soldiers performed the office of executioners, and divided among them the spoils of the criminals. My vesture – That is, my inner garment. Psalm xxii, 18.

38. ["And with him they crucify two thieves; the one on his right hand, and the other on his left." Mark xv, 27; "And there were also two other, malefactors, led with him to be put to death." Luke xxiii, 32.]

44. Mark xv, 32; Luke xxiii, 33.

45. From the sixth hour, there was darkness over all the earth unto the ninth hour – Insomuch, that even a heathen philosopher seeing it, and knowing it could not be a natural eclipse, because it was at the time of the full moon, and continued three hours together, cried out, "Either the God of nature suffers, or the frame of the world is dissolved." By this darkness God testified his abhorrence of the wickedness which was then committing. It likewise intimated Christ's sore conflicts with the Divine justice, and with all the powers of darkness.

46. About the ninth hour, Jesus cried with a loud voice – Our Lord's great agony probably continued these three whole hours, at the conclusion of which he thus cried out, while he suffered from God himself what was unutterable. My God, my God, why hast thou forsaken me? – Our Lord hereby at once expresses his trust in God, and a most distressing sense of his letting loose the powers of darkness upon him, withdrawing the comfortable discoveries of his presence, and filling his soul with a terrible sense of the wrath due to the sins which he was bearing. Psalm xxii, 1.

48. One taking a sponge, filled it with vinegar – Vinegar and water was the usual drink of the Roman soldiers. It does not appear, that this was given him in derision, but rather with a friendly design, that he might not die before Elijah came. John xix, 28.

50. After he had cried with a loud voice – To show that his life was still whole in him. He dismissed his spirit – So the original expression may be literally translated: an expression admirably suited to our Lord's words, John x, xviii, No man taketh my life from me, but I lay it down of myself. He died by a voluntary act of his own, and in a way peculiar to himself. He alone of all men that ever were, could have continued alive even in the greatest tortures, as long as he pleased, or have retired from the body whenever he had thought fit. And how does it illustrate that love which he manifested in his death? Insomuch as he did not use his power to quit his body, as soon as it was fastened to the cross, leaving only an insensible corpse, to the cruelty of his murderers: but continued his abode in it, with a steady resolution, as long as it was proper. He then retired from it, with a majesty and dignity never known or to be known in any other death: dying, if one may so express it, like the Prince of life.

51. Immediately upon his death, while the sun was still darkened, the veil of the temple, which separated the holy of holies from the court of

our Lord Jesus, having undertaken to satisfy the justice of God, did it, by submitting to the punishment of the worst of men. And in every minute particular recorded about the sufferings of Christ, we find some prediction in the Prophets or the Psalms fulfilled.

45-50 During the three hours which the darkness continued, Jesus was in agony, wrestling with the powers of darkness, and suffering his Father's displeasure against the sin of man, for which he was now making his soul an offering. Never were there three such hours since the day God created man upon the earth, never such a dark and awful scene; it was the turning point of that great affair, man's redemption and salvation. Jesus uttered a complaint from Ps 22:1. Hereby he teaches of what use the word of God is to direct us in prayer, and recommends the use of Scripture expressions in prayer. The believer may have tasted some drops of bitterness, but he can only form a very feeble idea of the greatness of Christ's sufferings. Yet, hence he learns something of the Savior's love to sinners; hence he gets deeper conviction of the vileness and evil of sin, and of what he owes to Christ, who delivers him from the wrath to come. His enemies wickedly ridiculed his complaint. Many of the reproaches cast upon the word of God and the people of God, arise, as here, from gross mistakes. Christ, just before he expired, spake in his full strength, to show that his life was not forced from him, but was freely delivered into his Father's hands. He had strength to bid defiance to the powers of death: and to show that by the eternal Spirit he offered himself, being the Priest as well as the Sacrifice, he cried with a loud voice. Then he yielded up the ghost. The Son of God upon the cross, did die by the violence of the pain he was put to. His soul was separated from his body, and so his body was left really and truly dead. It was certain that Christ did die, for it was needful that he should die. He had undertaken to make himself an offering for sin, and he did it when he willingly gave up his life.

51-56 The rending of the veil signified that Christ, by his death, opened a way to God. We have an open way through Christ to the throne of grace, or mercy-seat now, and to the throne of glory hereafter. When we duly consider Christ's death, our hard and rocky hearts should be rent; the heart, and not the garments. That heart is harder than a rock that will not yield, that will not melt, where Jesus Christ is plainly set forth crucified. The graves were opened, and many bodies of saints which slept, arose. To whom they appeared, in what manner, and how they disappeared, we are not told; and we must not desire to be wise above what is written. The dreadful appearances of God in his providence, sometimes work strangely for the conviction and awakening of sinners. This was expressed in the terror that fell upon the centurion and the Roman soldiers. We may reflect with comfort on the abundant testimonies given to the character of Jesus;

scriptures, for in them ye think ye have eternal life, but ye will not come to me that ye might have life." Alas, alas, that mercy should be rejected and heaven spurned.

IV. So now we must close with the most practical matter of consideration, THE GRACIOUS REJOINDER of the king to the impertinence which interfered with his plans. What did he say? You will observe that they had been bidden, and then called; after the Oriental custom, the call intimated that the festival was now approaching, so that they were not taken unawares, but knew what they did. The second invitation they rejected in cold blood, deliberately, and with intent. What did the monarch do? Set their city in a blaze, and at once root out the rebels? No, but in the first place, he winked at their former insolent refusal. He said in himself, "Peradventure they mistook my servants, peradventure they did not understand that the hour was come. Perhaps the message that was delivered to them was too brief, and they missed its meaning. Or, if perchance, they have fallen into some temporary enmity against me, on reconsideration, they will wish that they had not been so rude, and ungenerous to me. What have I done that they should refuse my dinner? What has my son done that they should not be willing to honor him by feasting at my table. Men love feasting, my son deserves their honor—why should they not come? I will pass over the past and begin again." My hearers, there are many of you who have rejected Christ after many invitations, and this morning my Lord forgets your former unkindnesses, and sends me again with the same message, again to bid you "come to the wedding." It is no small patience which overlooks the past and perseveres in kindness, honestly desiring your good.

The King sent another invitation—"all things are ready, come ye to the marriage," but you will please to observe that he changed the messenger. "Again he sent forth other servants." Yes, and I will say it, for my soul feels it, if a change of messengers will win you, much as I love the task of speaking in my Master's name, I would gladly die now, where I am, that some other preacher might occupy this platform, if thereby you might be saved. I know my speech to some of you must be monotonous. I seek out images fresh and many, and try to vary my voice and manner, but for all that one man must grow stale to you when heard so often. Perhaps my modes are not the sort to touch your peculiarities of temperament—well, good Master, set thy servant aside, and consider him not. Send other messengers if perchance they may succeed. But to some of you I am another messen-

44 The thieves also, which were crucified with him, cast the same in his teeth.

45 Now from the sixth hour there was darkness over all the land unto the ninth hour.

46 And about the ninth hour Jesus cried with a loud voice, saying, Eli, Eli, lama sabachthani? that is to say, My God, my God, why hast thou forsaken me?

47 Some of them that stood there, when they heard that, said, This man calleth for Elias.

48 And straightway one of them ran, and took a sponge, and filled it with vinegar, and put it on a reed, and gave him to drink.

49 The rest said, Let be, let us see whether Elias will come to save him.

50 Jesus, when he had cried again with a loud voice, yielded up the ghost.

51 And, behold, the veil of the temple was rent in twain from the top to the bottom; and the earth did quake, and the rocks rent;

52 And the graves were opened; and many bodies of the saints which slept arose,

53 And came out of the graves after his resurrection, and went into the holy city, and appeared unto many.

54 Now when the centurion, and they that were with him, watching Jesus, saw the earthquake, and those things that were done, they feared greatly, saying, Truly this was the Son of God.

55 And many women were there beholding afar off, which followed Jesus from Galilee, ministering unto him:

56 Among which was Mary Magdalene, and Mary the mother of James and Joses, and the mother of Zebedee's children.

57 When the even was come, there came a rich man of Arimathea, named Joseph, who also himself was Jesus' disciple:

58 He went to Pilate, and begged the body of Jesus. Then Pilate commanded the body to be delivered.

59 And when Joseph had taken the body, he wrapped it in a clean linen cloth,

60 And laid it in his own new tomb, which he had hewn out in the rock: and he rolled a great stone to the door of the sepulcher, and departed.

61 And there was Mary Magdalene, and the other Mary, sitting over against the sepulcher.

62 Now the next day, that followed the day of the preparation, the chief priests and Pharisees came together unto Pilate,

the priests, though made of the richest and strongest tapestry, was rent in two from the top to the bottom: so that while the priest was ministering at the golden altar (it being the time of the sacrifice) the sacred oracle, by an invisible power was laid open to full view: God thereby signifying the speedy removal of the veil of the Jewish ceremonies, the casting down the partition wall, so that the Jews and Gentiles were now admitted to equal privileges, and the opening a way through the veil of his flesh for all believers into the most holy place. And the earth was shaken – There was a general earthquake through the whole globe, though chiefly near Jerusalem: God testifying thereby his wrath against the Jewish nation, for the horrid impiety they were committing.

52. Some of the tombs were shattered and laid open by the earthquake, and while they continued unclosed (and they must have stood open all the Sabbath, seeing the law would not allow any attempt to close them) many bodies of holy men were raised, (perhaps Simeon, Zacharias, John the Baptist, and others who had believed in Christ, and were known to many in Jerusalem,) And coming out of the tombs after his resurrection, went into the holy city (Jerusalem) and appeared to many – Who had probably known them before: God hereby signifying, that Christ had conquered death, and would raise all his saints in due season.

54. The centurion – The officer who commanded the guard; and they that were with him feared, saying, Truly this was the Son of God – Referring to the words of the chief priests and scribes, chap. xxvii, 43, He said, I am the Son of God.

56. James – The less: he was so called, to distinguish him from the other James, the brother of John; probably because he was less in stature.

57. When the evening was come – That is, after three o'clock; the time from three to six they termed the evening. ["And now when the even was come, because it was the preparation, that is, the day before the sabbath," Mark xv, 42; "And, behold, there was a man named Joseph, a counselor; and he was a good man, and a just:" Luke xxiii, 50; "And after this Joseph of Arimathea, being a disciple of Jesus, but secretly for fear of the Jews, besought Pilate that he might take away the body of Jesus: and Pilate gave him leave. He came therefore, and took the body of Jesus." John xix, 38]

62. On the morrow, the day that followed the day of the preparation – The day of preparation was the day before the Sabbath, whereon they were to prepare for the celebration of it. The next day then was the Sabbath according to the Jews. But the evangelist seems to express it by this circumlocution, to show the Jewish Sabbath was then abolished.

63. That impostor said, while he was yet alive, After three days I will rise again – We do not find that he had ever said this to them, unless when he spoke of the temple of his body, "Jesus answered and said unto them, Destroy this temple, and in three days I will raise it up. . . . But he spake of the temple of his body" John ii, 19, 21. And if they here refer to what he then said, how perverse and iniquitous was their construction on these words, when he was on his trial before the council? "And said, This fellow said, I am able to destroy the temple of God, and to build it in three days." Chap. xxvi, 61. Then they seemed not to understand them!

65. Ye have a guard – Of your own, in the tower of Antonia, which was stationed there for the service of the temple.

66. They went and secured the sepulcher, sealing the stone, and setting

and, seeking to give no just cause of offense, we may leave it to the Lord to clear our characters, if we live to Him. Let us, with an eye of faith, behold Christ and him crucified, and be affected with that great love wherewith he loved us. But his friends could give no more than a look; they beheld him, but could not help him. Never were the horrid nature and effects of sin so tremendously displayed, as on that day when the beloved Son of the Father hung upon the cross, suffering for sin, the Just for the unjust, that he might bring us to God. Let us yield ourselves willingly to his service.

57-61 In the burial of Christ was nothing of pomp or solemnity. As Christ had not a house of his own, wherein to lay his head, while he lived, so he had not a grave of his own, wherein to lay his body, when he was dead. Our Lord Jesus, who had no sin of his own, had no grave of his own. The Jews designed that he should have made his grave with the wicked, should have been buried with the thieves with whom he was crucified, but God overruled it, so that he should make it with the rich in his death, Isa 53:9. And although to the eye of man the beholding a funeral may cause terror, yet if we remember how Christ by his burial has changed the nature of the grave to believers, it should make us rejoice. And we are ever to imitate Christ's burial in being continually occupied in the spiritual burial of our sins.

62-66 On the Jewish sabbath, the chief priests and Pharisees, when they should have been at their devotions, were dealing with Pilate about securing the sepulcher. This was permitted that there might be certain proof of our Lord's resurrection. Pilate told them that they might secure the sepulcher as carefully as they could. They sealed the stone, and set a guard, and were satisfied that all needful care was taken. But to guard the sepulcher against the poor weak disciples was folly, because needless; while to think to guard it against the power of God, was folly, because fruitless, and to no purpose; yet they thought they dealt wisely. But the Lord took the wise in their own craftiness. Thus shall all the rage and the plans of Christ's enemies be made to promote his glory. They sealed the stone; probably with the great seal of their sanhedrim, whereby they interposed their authority, for who durst break the public seal? But not trusting too much to that, withal they set a watch, to keep his disciples from coming to steal him away, and, if possible, to hinder him from coming out of the grave. So they intended, but God brought this good out of it, that they who were set to oppose his resurrection, thereby had an opportunity to observe it, and did so, and told the chief priests what they observed, who were thereby rendered the more inexcusable. Here was all the power of earth and hell combined to keep Christ a prisoner, but all in vain, when his hour was come; death, and all those sons and heirs of death, could then no longer hold him, no longer

ger, not a better, but another, since my brethren have failed with you. Oh, then, when my voice cries, "Come unto Jesus, trust in his atonement, believe in him, look to him and live," let the new voice be successful, where former heralds have been disregarded.

You notice, too, that the message was a little changed. At first it was very short. Surely if men's hearts were right, short sermons would be enough. A very brief invitation might suffice if the heart were right, but since hearts are wrong God bids his servants enlarge, expand, and expound. "Come, for all things are ready. I have prepared my dinner, my oxen and my fatlings are killed, all things are ready, come to the marriage." One of the best ways of bringing sinners to Christ is to explain the gospel to them. If we dwell upon its preparations, if we speak of its richness and freeness, some may be attracted whom the short message which merely tells the plan of salvation might not attract. To some it is enough to say, "Believe in the Lord Jesus Christ and thou shalt be saved," for they are asking, "Sirs, what must I do to be saved?" but others need to be attracted to the wedding feast by the description of the sumptuousness of the repast. We must try to preach the gospel more fully to you, but we shall never tell you of all the richness of the grace of God. As high as the heavens are above the earth, so high are his thoughts above your thoughts, and his ways above your ways. Forsake your sins and your thoughts and turn to the Lord, for he will abundantly pardon you. He will receive you to his heart of love, and give you the kiss of his affection at this hour, if, like prodigal children, you come back, and seek your Father's face. The gospel is a river of love, it is a sea of love, it is a heaven of love, it is a universe of love, it is all love. Words there are none, fully to set forth the amazing love of God to sinners, no sin too big or too black, no crime too crimson or too cursed for pardon. If you do but look to his dear crucified Son all manner of sin and of blasphemy shall be forgiven you. There is forgiveness. Jesus gives repentance and remission. And then the happiness which will be brought to you here and hereafter are equally beyond description. You shall have heaven on earth and heaven in heaven; God shall be your God, Christ shall be your friend, and eternal bliss shall be your portion.

In this last message the "guests were pressed very delicately", but still in a way which if they had possessed any generosity of heart at all, must have touched them. You see how the evangelist puts it, he does not say, "Come, or else you will miss the feast; come, or else the king will be angry; come, come, or else you will

63 Saying, Sir, we remember that that deceiver said, while he was yet alive, After three days I will rise again.

64 Command therefore that the sepulcher be made sure until the third day, lest his disciples come by night, and steal him away, and say unto the people, He is risen from the dead: so the last error shall be worse than the first.

65 Pilate said unto them, Ye have a watch: go your way, make it as sure as ye can.

66 So they went, and made the sepulcher sure, sealing the stone, and setting a watch.

MATTHEW 28

1 In the end of the sabbath, as it began to dawn toward the first day of the week, came Mary Magdalene and the other Mary to see the sepulcher.

2 And, behold, there was a great earthquake: for the angel of the Lord descended from heaven, and came and rolled back the stone from the door, and sat upon it.

3 His countenance was like lightning, and his raiment white as snow:

4 And for fear of him the keepers did shake, and became as dead men.

5 And the angel answered and said unto the women, Fear not ye: for I know that ye seek Jesus, which was crucified.

6 He is not here: for he is risen, as he said. Come, see the place where the Lord lay.

7 And go quickly, and tell his disciples that he is risen from the dead; and, behold, he goeth before you into Galilee; there shall ye see him: lo, I have told you.

8 And they departed quickly from the sepulcher with fear and great joy; and did run to bring his disciples word.

9 And as they went to tell his disciples, behold, Jesus met them, saying, All hail. And they came and held him by the feet, and worshiped him.

10 Then said Jesus unto them, Be not afraid: go tell my brethren that they go into Galilee, and there shall they see me.

11 Now when they were going, behold, some of the watch came into the city, and shewed unto the chief priests all the things that were done.

12 And when they were assembled with the elders, and had taken counsel, they gave large money unto the soldiers,

13 Saying, Say ye, His disciples came by night, and stole him away while we slept.

a guard – They set Pilate's signet, or the public seal of the Sanhedrin upon a fastening which they had put on the stone. And all this uncommon caution was overruled by the providence of God, to give the strongest proofs of Christ's ensuing resurrection; since there could be no room for the least suspicion of deceit, when it should be found, that his body was raised out of a new tomb, where there was no other corpse, and this tomb hewn out of a rock, the mouth of which was secured by a great stone, under a seal, and a guard of soldiers.

MATTHEW 28

1. ["And when the sabbath was past, Mary Magdalene, and Mary the mother of James, and Salome, had bought sweet spices, that they might come and anoint him." Mark xvi, 1; "Now upon the first day of the week, very early in the morning, they came unto the sepulcher, bringing the spices which they had prepared, and certain others with them." Luke xxiv, 1; "The first day of the week cometh Mary Magdalene early, when it was yet dark, unto the sepulcher, and seeth the stone taken away from the sepulcher." John xx, 1]

2. An angel of the Lord had rolled away the stone and sat upon it – St. Luke and St. John speak of two angels that appeared: but it seems as if only one of them had appeared sitting on the stone without the sepulcher, and then going into it, was seen with another angel, sitting, one where the head, the other where the feet of the body had lain.

6. Come, see the place where the Lord lay – Probably in speaking he rose up, and going before the women into the sepulcher, said, Come, see the place. This clearly reconciles what St. John relates, John xx, 12, ["And seeth two angels in white sitting, the one at the head, and the other at the feet, where the body of Jesus had lain."] this being one of the two angels there mentioned.

7. There shall ye see him – In his solemn appearance to them all together. But their gracious Lord would not be absent so long: he appeared to them several times before then. Lo, I have told you – A solemn confirmation of what he had said.

9. Hail – The word in its primary sense means, "Rejoice:" in its secondary and more usual meaning, "Happiness attend you."

10. Go tell my brethren – I still own them as such, though they so lately disowned and forsook me.

13. Say, his disciples came by night, and stole him while we slept – Is it possible, that any man of sense should digest this poor, shallow inconsistency? If ye were awake, why did you let the disciples steal him? If asleep, how do you know they did?

16. To the mountain where Jesus had appointed them – This was probably Mount Tabor, where, (it is commonly supposed,) he had been before transfigured. It seems to have been here also, that he appeared to above five hundred brethren at once.

18. All power is given to me – Even as man. As God, he had all power from eternity.

19. Disciple all nations – Make them my disciples. This includes the whole design of Christ's commission. Baptizing and teaching are the two great branches of that general design. And these were to be determined by the circumstances of things; which made it necessary in baptizing adult Jews or heathens, to teach them before they were baptized; in discipling their children, to baptize them before they were taught; as the Jewish children in all ages were first circumcized, and after taught to do all God had commanded them. "And he said unto

have dominion over him. To guard the sepulcher against the poor weak disciples, was folly, because needless; but to think to guard it against the power of God was folly, because fruitless and to no purpose; and yet they thought they had dealt wisely.

MATTHEW 28

Christ's resurrection. (1-8)
He appears to the women. (9,10)
Confession of the soldiers. (11-15)
Christ's commission to his disciples. (16-20)

1-8 Christ rose the third day after his death; that was the time he had often spoken of. On the first day of the first week God commanded the light to shine out of darkness. On this day did He who is the Light of the world, shine out of the darkness of the grave; and this day is from henceforward often mentioned in the New Testament, as the day which Christians religiously observed in solemn assemblies, to the honor of Christ. Our Lord Jesus could have rolled back the stone by his own power, but he chose to have it done by an angel. The resurrection of Christ, as it is the joy of his friends, so it is the terror and confusion of his enemies. The angel encouraged the women against their fears. Let the sinners in Zion be afraid. Fear not ye, for his resurrection will be your consolation. Our communion with him must be spiritual, by faith in his word. When we are ready to make this world our home, and to say, It is good to be here, then let us remember our Lord Jesus is not here, he is risen; therefore let our hearts rise, and seek the things that are above. He is risen, as he said. Let us never think that strange which the word of Christ has told us to expect; whether the sufferings of this present time, or the glory that is to be revealed. It may have a good effect upon us, by faith to view the place where the Lord lay. Go quickly. It was good to be there, but the servants of God have other work appointed. Public usefulness must be chosen before the pleasure of secret communion with God. Tell the disciples, that they may be comforted under their present sorrows. Christ knows where his disciples dwell, and will visit them. Even to those at a distance from the plenty of the means of grace, he will graciously manifest himself. The fear and the joy together quickened their pace. The disciples of Christ should be forward to make known to each other their experiences of communion with their Lord; and should tell others what God has done for their souls.

9,10 God's gracious visits usually meet us in the way of duty; and to those who use what they have for others' benefit, more shall be given. This interview with Christ was unexpected; but Christ was nigh them, and still is nigh us in the word. The salutation speaks the good-will of Christ to man, even since he entered upon his state of exaltation. It is the will of Christ that his people should be a cheerful, joyful people, and his

be the losers." No, but—he puts it, as I read it, in a very remarkable way. I venture to say—if I be wrong, the Master forgive me so saying—the king makes himself the object of sympathy, as though he were an embarrassed host. See here, "My dinner is ready, but there is no one to eat it; my oxen and fatlings are all killed, but there are no guests." "Come, come," he seems to say, "for I am a host without guests." So sometimes in the gospel you will see God speaks as if he would represent himself as getting an advantage by our being saved. Now we know that herein he condescends in love to speak after the manner of men. What can he gain by us? If we perish what is he the loser? But he makes himself often in the gospel to be like a father who yearns over his child, longing for him to come home. He makes himself, the infinite God, turn beggar to his own creatures, and beseeches them to be reconciled. Wondrous stoop; for, like a man who sells his wares, he cries, "Ho, every one that thirsteth, come ye to the waters; and he that hath no money, let him come." Do you observe how Christ, as he wept over Jerusalem, seems to weep for himself as well as for them. "How often would I have gathered thy children together." And God, in the prophets, puts it as his own sorrow, "How can I set thee as Admah, how can I make thee as Zeboim," as if it were not the child's loss alone, but the father's loss also, if the sinner died. Do you not feel, as it were, a sympathy with God when you see his gospel rejected? Shall the cross be lifted high, and none look to it? Shall Jesus die, and men not be saved by his death? O blessed Lord, we feel, if nothing else should draw us, we must come when we see, as it were, thyself represented as a host under our embarrassment, for lack of guests. Great God, we come, we come right gladly, we come to participate of the bounties which thou hast provided, and to glorify Jesus Christ by receiving as needy sinners that which thy mercy has provided.

Brethren and sisters since Christ finds many loath to honor him, my exhortation is to you who love him, honor him the more since the world will not. You who have been constrained to come, remember to sing as you sit at his table, and rejoice and bless his name. Next go home and intercede for those who will not come, that the Lord will enlighten their understandings, and change their wills, that they may be yet constrained to believe in Jesus; and as for those of you who feel half inclined this morning by the soft touches of his grace to come and feast, let me bid you come. It is a glorious gospel—the feast is good. He is a glorious king—the Host is good. He is a blessed Savior, he who is married, he is good. It is all good, and

14 And if this come to the governor's ears, we will persuade him, and secure you.

15 So they took the money, and did as they were taught: and this saying is commonly reported among the Jews until this day.

16 Then the eleven disciples went away into Galilee, into a mountain where Jesus had appointed them.

17

And when they saw him, they worshiped him: but some doubted.

18 And Jesus came and spake unto them, saying, All power is given unto me in heaven and in earth.

19 Go ye therefore, and teach all nations, baptizing them in the name of the Father, and of the Son, and of the Holy Ghost:

20 Teaching them to observe all things whatsoever I have commanded you: and, lo, I am with you alway, even unto the end of the world. Amen.

them, Go ye into all the world, and preach the gospel to every creature." Mark xvi, 15.

resurrection furnishes abundant matter for joy. Be not afraid. Christ rose from the dead, to silence his people's fears, and there is enough in that to silence them. The disciples had just before shamefully deserted him in his sufferings; but, to show that he could forgive, and to teach us to do so, he calls them brethren. Notwithstanding his majesty and purity, and our meanness and unworthiness, he still condescends to call believers his brethren.

11-15 What wickedness is it which men will not be brought to by the love of money! Here was large money given to the soldiers for advancing that which they knew to be a lie, yet many grudge a little money for advancing what they know to be the truth. Let us never starve a good cause, when we see bad ones so liberally supported.

16-20 This evangelist passes over other appearances of Christ, recorded by Luke and John, and hastens to the most solemn; one appointed before his death, and after his resurrection. All that see the Lord Jesus with an eye of faith, will worship him. Yet the faith of the sincere may be very weak and wavering. But Christ gave such convincing proofs of his resurrection, as made their faith to triumph over doubts. He now solemnly commissioned the apostles and his ministers to go forth among all nations. The salvation they were to preach, is a common salvation; whoever will, let him come, and take the benefit; all are welcome to Christ Jesus. Christianity is the religion of a sinner who applies for salvation from deserved wrath and from sin; he applies to the mercy of the Father, through the atonement of the incarnate Son, and by the sanctification of the Holy Spirit, and gives up himself to be the worshiper and servant of God, as the Father, Son, and Holy Ghost, three Persons but one God, in all his ordinances and commandments. Baptism is an outward sign of that inward washing, or sanctification of the Spirit, which seals and evidences the believer's justification. Let us examine ourselves, whether we really possess the inward and spiritual grace of a death unto sin, and a new birth unto righteousness, by which those who were the children of wrath become the children of God. Believers shall have the constant presence of their Lord always; all days, every day. There is no day, no hour of the day, in which our Lord Jesus is not present with his churches and with his ministers; if there were, in that day, that hour, they would be undone. The God of Israel, the Savior, is sometimes a God that hideth himself, but never a God at a distance. To these precious words Amen is added. Even so, Lord Jesus, be thou with us and all thy people; cause thy face to shine upon us, that thy way may be known upon earth, thy saving health among all nations.

you shall be made good too, if your souls accept the invitation of the gospel which is given to you this day. "He that believeth and is baptized shall be saved: he that believeth not shall be damned." "Believe on the Lord Jesus Christ and thou shalt be saved." The Lord send his Spirit to make the call effectual, for his dear Son's sake. Amen.

Mark

MARK 1

1 The beginning of the gospel of Jesus Christ, the Son of God;

2 As it is written in the prophets, Behold, I send my messenger before thy face, which shall prepare thy way before thee.

3 The voice of one crying in the wilderness, Prepare ye the way of the Lord, make his paths straight.

4 John did baptize in the wilderness, and preach the baptism of repentance for the remission of sins.

5 And there went out unto him all the land of Judea, and they of Jerusalem, and were all baptized of him in the river of Jordan, confessing their sins.

6 And John was clothed with camel's hair, and with a girdle of a skin about his loins; and he did eat locusts and wild honey;

7 And preached, saying, There cometh one mightier than I after me, the latchet of whose shoes I am not worthy to stoop down and unloose.

8 I indeed have baptized you with water: but he shall baptize you with the Holy Ghost.

9 And it came to pass in those days, that Jesus came from Nazareth of Galilee, and was baptized of John in Jordan.

10 And straightway coming up out of the water, he saw the heavens opened, and the Spirit like a dove descending upon him:

11 And there came a voice from heaven, saying, Thou art my beloved Son, in whom I am well pleased.

12 And immediately the Spirit driveth him into the wilderness.

13 And he was there in the wilderness forty days, tempted of Satan; and was with the wild beasts; and the angels ministered unto him.

14 Now after that John was put in prison, Jesus came into Galilee, preaching the gospel of the kingdom of God,

15 And saying, The time is fulfilled, and the kingdom of God is at hand: repent ye, and believe the gospel.

16 Now as he walked by the sea of Galilee, he saw Simon and Andrew his brother casting a net into the sea: for they were fishers.

17 And Jesus said unto them, Come ye after me, and I will make you to become fishers of men.

18 And straightway they forsook their nets, and followed him.

19 And when he had gone a little further thence, he saw James the son of Zebedee, and John his brother, who also were in the ship mending their nets.

20 And straightway he called them: and they left their father Zebedee in the ship with the hired servants, and went after him.

21 And they went into Capernaum; and straightway on the sabbath day he entered into the synagogue, and taught.

22 And they were astonished at his doctrine: for he taught them as one that had authority, and not as the scribes.

23 And there was in their synagogue a man with an unclean spirit; and he cried out,

24 Saying, Let us alone; what have we to do with thee, thou Jesus of Nazareth? art thou come to destroy us? I know thee who thou art, the Holy One of God.

25 And Jesus rebuked him, saying, Hold thy peace, and come out of him.

26 And when the unclean spirit had torn him, and cried with a loud voice, he came out of him.

27 And they were all amazed, insomuch that they questioned among themselves, saying, What thing is this? what new doctrine is this? for with authority commandeth he even the unclean spirits, and they do obey him.

28 And immediately his fame spread abroad throughout all the region round about Galilee.

29 And forthwith, when they were come out of the synagogue, they entered into the house of Simon and Andrew, with James and John.

30 But Simon's wife's mother lay sick of a fever, and anon they tell him of her.

MARK 1

1. The beginning of the Gospel of Jesus Christ – The evangelist speaks with strict propriety: for the beginning of the Gospel is in the account of John the Baptist, contained in the first paragraph; the Gospel itself in the rest of the book. Matt. iii, 1; Luke iii, 1

2. Mal. iii, 1

3. Isaiah xl, 3.

4. Preaching the baptism of repentance – That is, preaching repentance, and baptizing as a sign and means of it.

7. The latchet of whose shoes I am not worthy to unloose – That is, to do him the very meanest service.

9. Matt. iii, 13; Luke iii, 21.

12. And immediately the Spirit thrusteth him out into the wilderness – So in all the children of God, extraordinary manifestations of his favor are wont to be followed by extraordinary temptations. Matt. iv, 1; Luke iv, 1.

13. And he was there forty days, tempted by Satan – Invisibly. After this followed the temptation by him in a visible shape, related by St. Matthew. And he was with the wild beasts – Though they had no power to hurt him. St. Mark not only gives us a compendium of St. Matthew's Gospel, but likewise several valuable particulars, which the other evangelists have omitted.

14. Matt. iv, 12.

15. The time is fulfilled – The time of my kingdom, foretold by Daniel, expected by you, is fully come.

16. Matt. iv, 18; Luke v, 1.

18. Straightway leaving their nets, they followed him – From this time they forsook their employ, and constantly attended him. Happy they who follow Christ at the first call!

21. Luke iv, 31.

26. A loud noise – For he was forbidden to speak. Christ would neither suffer those evil spirits to speak in opposition, nor yet in favor of him. He needed not their testimony, nor would encourage it, lest any should infer that he acted in concert with them.

29. Matt. viii, 14; Luke iv, 38.

32. When the sun was set – And, consequently, the Sabbath was ended, which they reckoned from sunset to sunset.

33. And the whole city was gathered together at the door – O what a fair prospect was here! Who could then have imagined that all these blossoms would die away without fruit?

34. He suffered not the devils to say that they knew him – That is, according to Dr. Mead's

MATTHEW HENRY

Mark was a sister's son to Barnabas, Col 4:10; and Ac 12:12 shows that he was the son of Mary, a pious woman of Jerusalem, at whose house the apostles and first Christians assembled. From Peter's styling him his son, 1Pe 5:13, the evangelist is supposed to have been converted by that apostle. Thus Mark was closely united with the followers of our Lord, if not himself one of the number. Mark wrote at Rome; some suppose that Peter dictated to him, though the general testimony is, that the apostle having preached at Rome, Mark, who was the apostle's companion, and had a clear understanding of what Peter delivered, was desired to commit the particulars to writing. And we may remark, that the great humility of Peter is very plain where any thing is said about himself. Scarcely an action or a work of Christ is mentioned, at which this apostle was not present, and the minuteness shows that the facts were related by an eyewitness. This Gospel records more of the miracles than of the discourses of our Lord, and though in many things it relates the same things as the Gospel according to St. Matthew, we may reap advantages from reviewing the same events, placed by each of the evangelists in that point of view which most affected his own mind.

MARK 1

The office of John the Baptist. (1-8)
The baptism and temptation of Christ. (9-13)
Christ preaches and calls disciples. (14-22)
He casts out an unclean spirit. (23-28)
He heals many diseased. (29-39)
He heals a leper. (40-45)

1-8 Isaiah and Malachi each spake concerning the beginning of the gospel of Jesus Christ, in the ministry of John. From these prophets we may observe, that Christ, in his gospel, comes among us, bringing with him a treasure of grace, and a scepter of government. Such is the corruption of the world, that there is great opposition to his progress. When God sent his Son into the world, he took care, and when he sends him into the heart, he takes care, to prepare his way before him. John thinks himself unworthy of the meanest office about Christ. The most eminent saints have always been the most humble. They feel their need of Christ's atoning blood and sanctifying Spirit, more than others. The great promise Christ makes in his gospel to those who have repented, and have had their sins forgiven them, is, they shall be baptized with the Holy Ghost; shall be purified by his graces, and refreshed by his comforts. We use the ordinances, word, and sacraments without profit and comfort, for the most part, because we have not of that Divine light within us; and we have it not because we ask it not; for we have his word that cannot fail, that our heavenly Father will give this light, his Holy Spirit, to those that ask it.

9-13 Christ's baptism was his first public appearance, after he had long lived unknown. How much hidden worth is there, which in this world is not known! But sooner or later it shall be known, as Christ was. He took upon himself the likeness of sinful flesh; and thus, for our sakes, he sanctified

CHARLES H. SPURGEON

FAITH AND REPENTANCE INSEPARABLE
Sermon number 460 delivered on Sunday Morning, July 13th, 1862, at the Metropolitan Tabernacle, Newington.

"Repent ye, and believe the gospel."— Mark 1:15.

I. I shall commence my remarking that the gospel which Christ preached was, very plainly, a command. "Repent ye, and believe the gospel." Our Lord does condescend to reason. Often his ministry graciously acted out the old text, "Come, now, and let us reason together; though your sins be as scarlet, they shall be as wool." He does persuade men by telling and forcible arguments, which should lead them to seek the salvation of their souls. He does invite men, and oh, how lovingly he woos them to be wise. "Come unto me all ye that labor and are heavy laden, and I will give you rest." He does entreat men; he condescendeth to become, as it were, a beggar to his own sinful creatures, beseeching them to come to him. Indeed, he maketh this to be the duty of his ministers, "As though God did beseech you by us, we pray you, in Christ's stead, be ye reconciled to God." Yet, remember, though he condescendeth to reason, to persuade, to invite, and to beseech, still his gospel hath in it all the dignity and force of a command; and if we would preach it in these days as Christ did, we must proclaim it as a command from God, attended with a divine sanction, and not to be neglected save at the infinite peril of the soul. When the feast was spread upon the table for the marriage-supper, there was an invitation, but it had all the obligation of a command, since those who rejected it were utterly destroyed as despisers of their king. When the builders reject Christ, he becomes a stone of stumbling to "the disobedient"; but how could they disobey if there were no command? The gospel contemplates, I say, invitations, entreaties, and beseechings, but it also takes the higher ground of authority. "Repent ye" is as much a command of God as "Thou shalt not steal." "Believe on the Lord Jesus Christ" has as fully a divine authority as "Thou shalt love the Lord thy God with all thy heart, with all thy soul, with all thy strength." Think not, O men, that the gospel is a thing left to your option to choose it or not! Dream not, O sinners, that ye may despise the Word from heav-

31 And he came and took her by the hand, and lifted her up; and immediately the fever left her, and she ministered unto them.

32 And at even, when the sun did set, they brought unto him all that were diseased, and them that were possessed with devils.

33 And all the city was gathered together at the door.

34 And he healed many that were sick of divers diseases, and cast out many devils; and suffered not the devils to speak, because they knew him.

35 And in the morning, rising up a great while before day, he went out, and departed into a solitary place, and there prayed.

36 And Simon and they that were with him followed after him.

37 And when they had found him, they said unto him, All men seek for thee.

38 And he said unto them, Let us go into the next towns, that I may preach there also: for therefore came I forth.

39 And he preached in their synagogues throughout all Galilee, and cast out devils.

40 And there came a leper to him, beseeching him, and kneeling down to him, and saying unto him, If thou wilt, thou canst make me clean.

41 And Jesus, moved with compassion, put forth his hand, and touched him, and saith unto him, I will; be thou clean.

42 And as soon as he had spoken, immediately the leprosy departed from him, and he was cleansed.

43 And he straitly charged him, and forthwith sent him away;

44 And saith unto him, See thou say nothing to any man: but go thy way, shew thyself to the priest, and offer for thy cleansing those things which Moses commanded, for a testimony unto them.

45 But he went out, and began to publish it much, and to blaze abroad the matter, insomuch that Jesus could no more openly enter into the city, but was without in desert places: and they came to him from every quarter.

MARK 2

1 And again he entered into Capernaum, after some days; and it was noised that he was in the house.

2 And straightway many were gathered together, insomuch that there was no room to receive them, no, not so much as about the door: and he preached the word unto them.

3 And they come unto him, bringing one sick of the palsy, which was borne of four.

4 And when they could not come nigh unto him for the press, they uncovered the roof where he was: and when they had broken it up, they let down the bed wherein the sick of the palsy lay.

5 When Jesus saw their faith, he said unto the sick of the palsy, Son, thy sins be forgiven thee.

6 But there were certain of the scribes sitting there, and reasoning in their hearts,

7 Why doth this man thus speak blasphemies? who can forgive sins but God only?

8 And immediately when Jesus perceived in his spirit that they so reasoned within themselves, he said unto them, Why reason ye these things in your hearts?

9 Whether is it easier to say to the sick of the palsy, Thy sins be forgiven thee; or to say, Arise, and take up thy bed, and walk?

10 But that ye may know that the Son of man hath power on earth to forgive sins, (he saith to the sick of the palsy,)

11 I say unto thee, Arise, and take up thy bed, and go thy way into thine house.

12 And immediately he arose, took up the bed, and went forth before them all; insomuch that they were all amazed, and glorified God, saying, We never saw it on this fashion.

13 And he went forth again by the sea side; and all the multitude

hypothesis, (that the Scriptural demoniacs were only diseased persons,) He suffered not the diseases to say that they knew him!

35. Rising a great while before day – So did he labor for us, both day and night. Luke iv, 42.

40. Matt. viii, 2; Luke v, 12.

44. See thou say nothing to any man – But our blessed Lord gives us no such charge to us. If he has made us clean from our leprosy of sin, we are not commanded to conceal it. On the contrary, it is our duty to publish it abroad, both for the honor of our Benefactor, and that others who are sick of sin may be encouraged to ask and hope for the same benefit. But go, show thyself to the priest, and offer for thy cleansing what Moses commanded for a testimony to them – The priests seeing him, pronouncing him clean, Lev. xiii, 17, 23, 28, 37, and accordingly allowing him to offer as Moses commanded, Lev. xiv, 2, 7, was such a proof against them, that they durst never say the leper was not cleansed; which out of envy or malice against our Savior they might have been ready to say, upon his presenting himself to be viewed, according to the law, if by the cleansed person's talking much about his cure, the account of it had reached their ears before he came in person. This is one great reason why our Lord commanded this man to say nothing.

45. So that Jesus could no more openly enter into the city – It was also to prevent this inconvenience that our Lord had enjoined him silence.

MARK 2

1. And again – After having been in desert places for some time, he returned privately to the city. In the house – In Peter's house.

2. And immediately many were gathered together – Hitherto continued the general impression on their hearts. Hitherto, even at Capernaum, all who heard received the word with joy.

3. Matt. ix, 2; Luke v, 18.

4. They uncovered the roof – Or, took up the covering, the lattice or trap door, which was on all their houses, (being flat roofed.) And finding it not wide enough, broke the passage wider, to let down the couch.

6. But certain of the scribes – See whence the first offense cometh! As yet not one of the plain unlettered people were offended. They all rejoiced in the light, till these men of learning came, to put darkness for light, and light for darkness. Woe to all such blind guides! Good had it been for these if they had never been born. O God, let me never offend one of thy simple ones! Sooner let my tongue cleave to the roof of my mouth!

MATTHEW HENRY

CHARLES H. SPURGEON

himself, that we also might be sanctified, and be baptized with him, John 17:19. See how honorably God owned him, when he submitted to John's baptism. He saw the Spirit descending upon him like a dove. We may see heaven opened to us, when we perceive the Spirit descending and working upon us. God's good work in us, is sure evidence of his good will towards us, and preparations for us. As to Christ's temptation, Mark notices his being in the wilderness and that he was with the wild beasts. It was an instance of his Father's care of him, which encouraged him the more that his Father would provide for him. Special protections are earnests of seasonable supplies. The serpent tempted the first Adam in the garden, the Second Adam in the wilderness; with different success indeed; and ever since he still tempts the children of both, in all places and conditions. Company and conversation have their temptations; and being alone, even in a wilderness, has its own also. No place or state exempts, no business, not lawful laboring, eating, or drinking, not even fasting and praying; often in these duties there are the most assaults, but in them is the sweetest victory. The ministration of the good angels is matter of great comfort in reference to the malignant designs of the evil angels; but much more does it comfort us, to have the indwelling of God the Holy Spirit in our hearts.

14-22 Jesus began to preach in Galilee, after that John was put in prison. If some be laid aside, others shall be raised up, to carry on the same work. Observe the great truths Christ preached. By repentance we give glory to our Creator whom we have offended; by faith we give glory to our Redeemer who came to save us from our sins. Christ has joined these two together, and let no man think to put them asunder. Christ puts honor upon those who, though mean in this world, are diligent in their business and kind to one another. Industry and unity are good and pleasant, and the Lord Jesus commands a blessing on them. Those whom Christ calls, must leave all to follow him; and by his grace he makes them willing to do so. Not that we must needs go out of the world, but we must sit loose to the world; forsake every thing that is against our duty to Christ, and that cannot be kept without hurt to our souls. Jesus strictly kept the Sabbath day, by applying himself unto, and abounding in the Sabbath work, in order to which the Sabbath rest was appointed. There is much in the doctrine of Christ that is astonishing; and the more we hear it, the more cause we see to admire it.

23-28 The devil is an unclean spirit, because he has lost all the purity of his nature, because he acts in direct opposition to the Holy Spirit of God, and by his suggestions defiles the spirits of men. There are many in our assemblies who quietly attend under merely formal teachers; but if the Lord come with faithful ministers and holy doctrine, and by his convincing Spirit, they are ready to say, like this man, What have we to do with thee, Jesus of Nazareth! No disorder could enable a man to know Jesus to be the Holy One of God. He desires to have nothing to do with Jesus, for he despairs of being saved by him, and dreads being destroyed by him. See whose language those speak, that

en and incur no guilt! Think not that ye may neglect it and no ill consequences shall follow! It is just this neglect and despising of yours which shall fill up the measure of your iniquity. It is this concerning which we cry aloud, "How shall we escape if we neglect so great a salvation!" God commands you to repent. The same God before whom Sinai was moved and was altogether on a smoke—that same God who proclaimed the law with sound of trumpet, with lightnings and with thunders, speaketh to us more gently, but still as divinely, through his only begotten Son, when he saith to us, "Repent ye, and believe the gospel."

Why is this, dear friends; why has the Lord made it a command to us to believe in Christ? There is a blessed reason. Many souls would never venture to believe at all if it were not made penal to refuse to do so. For this is the difficulty with many awakened sinners: may I believe? Have I a right to believe? Am I permitted to trust Christ? Now this question is put aside, once for all, and should never irritate a broken heart again. You are commanded by God to do it, therefore you may do it. Every creature under heaven is commanded to believe in the Lord Jesus, and bow the knee at his name; every creature, wherever the gospel comes, wherever the truth is preached, is commanded there and then to believe the gospel; and it is put in that shape, I say, lest any conscience-stricken sinner should question whether he may do it. Surely, you may do what God commands you to do. You may know this in the devil's teeth—"I may do it; I am bidden to do it by him who hath authority, and I am threatened if I do not with eternal damnation from his presence, for 'he that believeth not shall be damned.'" This gives the sinner such a blessed permit, that whatever he may be or may not be, whatever he may have felt or may not have felt, he has a warrant which he may use whenever he is led to approach the cross. However benighted and darkened you may be, however hard-hearted and callous you may be, you have still a warrant to look to Jesus in the words, "Look unto me and be ye saved all ye ends of the earth." He that commanded thee to believe will justify thee in believing; he cannot condemn thee for that which he himself bids thee do. But while there is this blessed reason for the gospel's being a command, there is yet another solemn

resorted unto him, and he taught them.

14 And as he passed by, he saw Levi the son of Alpheus sitting at the receipt of custom, and said unto him, Follow me. And he arose and followed him.

15 And it came to pass, that, as Jesus sat at meat in his house, many publicans and sinners sat also together with Jesus and his disciples: for there were many, and they followed him.

16 And when the scribes and Pharisees saw him eat with publicans and sinners, they said unto his disciples, How is it that he eateth and drinketh with publicans and sinners?

17 When Jesus heard it, he saith unto them, They that are whole have no need of the physician, but they that are sick: I came not to call the righteous, but sinners to repentance.

18 And the disciples of John and of the Pharisees used to fast: and they come and say unto him, Why do the disciples of John and of the Pharisees fast, but thy disciples fast not?

19 And Jesus said unto them, Can the children of the bridechamber fast, while the bridegroom is with them? as long as they have the bridegroom with them, they cannot fast.

20 But the days will come, when the bridegroom shall be taken away from them, and then shall they fast in those days.

21 No man also seweth a piece of new cloth on an old garment: else the new piece that filled it up taketh away from the old, and the rent is made worse.

22 And no man putteth new wine into old bottles: else the new wine doth burst the bottles, and the wine is spilled, and the bottles will be marred: but new wine must be put into new bottles.

23 And it came to pass, that he went through the corn fields on the sabbath day; and his disciples began, as they went, to pluck the ears of corn.

24 And the Pharisees said unto him, Behold, why do they on the sabbath day that which is not lawful?

25 And he said unto them, Have ye never read what David did, when he had need, and was an hungred, he, and they that were with him?

26 How he went into the house of God in the days of Abiathar the high priest, and did eat the shewbread, which is not lawful to eat but for the priests, and gave also to them which were with him?

27 And he said unto them, The sabbath was made for man, and not man for the sabbath:

28 Therefore the Son of man is Lord also of the sabbath.

MARK 3

1 And he entered again into the synagogue; and there was a man there which had a withered hand.

2 And they watched him, whether he would heal him on the sabbath day; that they might accuse him.

3 And he saith unto the man which had the withered hand, Stand forth.

4 And he saith unto them, Is it lawful to do good on the sabbath days, or to do evil? to save life, or to kill? But they held their peace.

5 And when he had looked round about on them with anger, being grieved for the hardness of their hearts, he saith unto the man, Stretch forth thine hand. And he stretched it out: and his hand was restored whole as the other.

6 And the Pharisees went forth, and straightway took counsel with the Herodians against him, how they might destroy him.

7 But Jesus withdrew himself with his disciples to the sea: and a great multitude from Galilee followed him, and from Judea,

8 And from Jerusalem, and from Idumea, and from beyond Jordan; and they about Tyre and Sidon, a great multitude, when they had heard what great things he did, came unto him.

9 And he spake to his disciples, that a small ship should wait on him because of the multitude, lest they should throng him.

12. They were all amazed — Even the scribes themselves for a time.

13. All the multitude came to him — Namely, by the sea side. And he as readily taught them there as if they had been in a synagogue.

14. Matt. ix, 9; Luke v, 27.

15. Many publicans and notorious sinners sat with Jesus — Some of them doubtless invited by Matthew, moved with compassion for his old companions in sin. But the next words, For there were many, and they followed him, seem to imply, that the greater part, encouraged by his gracious words and the tenderness of his behavior, and impatient to hear more, stayed for no invitation, but pressed in after him, and kept as close to him as they could.

16. And the scribes and Pharisees said — So now the wise men being joined by the saints of the world, went a little farther in raising prejudices against our Lord. In his answer he uses as yet no harshness, but only calm, dispassionate reasoning.

17. I came not to call the righteous — Therefore if these were righteous I should not call them. But now, they are the very persons I came to save.

18. Matt. ix, 14; Luke v, 33.

23. Matt. xii, 1; Luke vi, 1.

26. In the days of Abiathar the high priest — Abimelech, the father of Abiathar, was high priest then; Abiathar himself not till some time after. This phrase therefore only means, In the time of Abiathar, who was afterward the high priest. 1 Sam. xxi, 6.

27. The Sabbath was made for man — And therefore must give way to man's necessity.

28. Moreover the Son of man is Lord even of the Sabbath — Being the supreme Lawgiver, he hath power to dispense with his own laws; and with this in particular.

MARK 3

He entered again into the synagogue — At Capernaum on the same day. Matt. xii, 9; Luke vi, 6.

2. And they — The scribes and Pharisees, watched him, that they might accuse him — Pride, anger, and shame, after being so often put to silence, began now to ripen into malice.

4. Is it lawful to save life or to kill? — Which he knew they were seeking occasion to do. But they held their peace — Being confounded, though not convinced.

5. Looking round upon them with anger, being grieved — Angry at the sin, grieved at the sinner; the true standard of Christian anger. But who

MATTHEW HENRY   CHARLES H. SPURGEON

say to the Almighty, Depart from us. This unclean spirit hated and dreaded Christ, because he knew him to be a Holy One; for the carnal mind is enmity against God, especially against his holiness. When Christ by his grace delivers souls out of the hands of Satan, it is not without tumult in the soul; for that spiteful enemy will disquiet those whom he cannot destroy. This put all who saw it upon considering, What is this new doctrine? A work as great often is wrought now, yet men treat it with contempt and neglect. If this were not so, the conversion of a notorious wicked man to a sober, righteous, and godly life, by the preaching of a crucified Savior, would cause many to ask, What doctrine is this?

29-39 Wherever Christ comes, he comes to do good. He cures, that we may minister to him, and to others who are his, and for his sake. Those kept from public ordinances by sickness or other real hindrances, may expect the Savior's gracious presence; he will soothe their sorrows, and abate their pains. Observe how numerous the patients were. When others speed well with Christ, it should quicken us in seeking after him. Christ departed into a solitary place. Though he was in no danger of distraction, or of temptation to vainglory, yet he retired. Those who have the most business in public, and of the best kind, must yet sometimes be alone with God.

40-45 We have here Christ's cleansing of a leper. It teaches us to apply to the Savior with great humility, and with full submission to his will, saying, "Lord, if thou wilt," without any doubt of Christ's readiness to help the distressed. See also what to expect from Christ; that according to our faith it shall be to us. The poor leper said, If thou wilt. Christ readily wills favors to those who readily refer themselves to his will. Christ would have nothing done that looked like seeking praise of the people. But no reasons now exist why we should hesitate to spread the praises of Christ.

MARK 2

Christ heals one sick of the palsy. (1-12)
Levi's call, and the entertainment given to Jesus. (13-17)
Why Christ's disciples did not fast. (18-22)
He justifies his disciples for plucking corn on the Sabbath. (23-28)

1-12 It was this man's misery that he needed to be so carried, and shows the suffering state of human life; it was kind of those who so carried him, and teaches the compassion that should be in men, toward their fellow-creatures in distress. True faith and strong faith may work in various ways; but it shall be accepted and approved by Jesus Christ. Sin is the cause of all our pains and sicknesses. The way to remove the effect, is to take away the cause. Pardon of sin strikes at the root of all diseases. Christ proved his power to forgive sin, by showing his power to cure the man sick of the palsy. And his curing diseases was a figure of his pardoning sin, for sin is the disease of the soul; when it is pardoned, it is healed. When we see what Christ does in healing souls, we must own that we never saw the like. Most

and an awful one. It is that men may be without excuse in the day of judgment; that no man may say at the last, "Lord, I did not know that I might believe in Christ; Lord, heaven's gate was shut in my face; I was told that I might not come, that I was not the man." "Nay," saith the Lord, with tones of thunder, "the times of man's ignorance I winked at, but in the gospel I commanded all men everywhere to repent; I sent my Son, and then I sent my apostles, and afterwards my ministers, and I bade them all make this the burden of their cry, 'Repent and be converted everyone of you'; and as Peter preached at Pentecost, so bade I them preach to thee. I bade them warn, exhort, and invite with all affection, but also to command with all authority, compelling you to come in, and inasmuch as you did not come at my command, you have added sin to sin; you have added the suicide of your own soul to all your other iniquities; and now, inasmuch as you did reject my Son, you shall have the portion of unbelievers, for 'he that believeth not shall be damned.'" To all the nations of the earth, then, let us sound forth this decree from God. O men, Jehovah that made you, he who gives you the breath of your nostrils, he against whom you have offended, commands you this day to repent and believe the gospel. He gives his promise—"He that believeth and is baptized shall be saved"; and he adds the solemn threatening—"He that believeth not shall be damned." I know some brethren will not like this, but that I cannot help. The slave of systems I will never be, for the Lord has loosed this iron bondage from my neck, and now I am the joyful servant of the truth which maketh free. Offend or please, as God shall help me, I will preach every truth as I learn it from the Word; and I know if there be anything written in the Bible at all it is written as with a sunbeam, that God in Christ commandeth men to repent, and believe the gospel. It is one of the saddest proofs of man's utter depravity that he will not obey this command, but that he will despise Christ, and so make his doom worse than the doom of Sodom and Gomorrah. Without the regenerating work of God the Holy Ghost, no man ever will be obedient to this command, but still it must be published for a witness against them if they reject it; and while publishing God's command with all simplicity, we may expect that he will divinely enforce it in

10 For he had healed many; insomuch that they pressed upon him for to touch him, as many as had plagues.

11 And unclean spirits, when they saw him, fell down before him, and cried, saying, Thou art the Son of God.

12 And he straitly charged them that they should not make him known.

13 And he goeth up into a mountain, and calleth unto him whom he would: and they came unto him.

14 And he ordained twelve, that they should be with him, and that he might send them forth to preach,

15 And to have power to heal sicknesses, and to cast out devils:

16 And Simon he surnamed Peter;

17 And James the son of Zebedee, and John the brother of James; and he surnamed them Boanerges, which is, The sons of thunder:

18 And Andrew, and Philip, and Bartholomew, and Matthew, and Thomas, and James the son of Alpheus, and Thaddeus, and Simon the Canaanite,

19 And Judas Iscariot, which also betrayed him: and they went into an house.

20 And the multitude cometh together again, so that they could not so much as eat bread.

21 And when his friends heard of it, they went out to lay hold on him: for they said, He is beside himself.

22 And the scribes which came down from Jerusalem said, He hath Beelzebub, and by the prince of the devils casteth he out devils.

23 And he called them unto him, and said unto them in parables, How can Satan cast out Satan?

24 And if a kingdom be divided against itself, that kingdom cannot stand.

25 And if a house be divided against itself, that house cannot stand.

26 And if Satan rise up against himself, and be divided, he cannot stand, but hath an end.

27 No man can enter into a strong man's house, and spoil his goods, except he will first bind the strong man; and then he will spoil his house.

28 Verily I say unto you, All sins shall be forgiven unto the sons of men, and blasphemies wherewith soever they shall blaspheme:

29 But he that shall blaspheme against the Holy Ghost hath never forgiveness, but is in danger of eternal damnation:

30 Because they said, He hath an unclean spirit.

31 There came then his brethren and his mother, and, standing without, sent unto him, calling him.

32 And the multitude sat about him, and they said unto him, Behold, thy mother and thy brethren without seek for thee.

33 And he answered them, saying, Who is my mother, or my brethren?

34 And he looked round about on them which sat about him, and said, Behold my mother and my brethren!

35 For whosoever shall do the will of God, the same is my brother, and my sister, and mother.

MARK 4

1 And he began again to teach by the sea side: and there was gathered unto him a great multitude, so that he entered into a ship, and sat in the sea; and the whole multitude was by the sea on the land.

2 And he taught them many things by parables, and said unto them in his doctrine,

3 Hearken; Behold, there went out a sower to sow:

4 And it came to pass, as he sowed, some fell by the way side, and the fowls of the air came and devoured it up.

5 And some fell on stony ground, where it had not much earth; and immediately it sprang up, because it had no depth of earth:

6 But when the sun was up, it was scorched; and because it had no

can separate anger at sin from anger at the sinner? None but a true believer in Christ.

6. The Pharisees going out – Probably leaving the scribes to watch him still: took counsel with the Herodians – as bitter as they usually were against each other.

8. From Idumea – The natives of which had now professed the Jewish religion above a hundred and fifty years. They about Tyre and Sidon – The Israelites who lived in those coasts.

10. Plagues or scourges (so the Greek word properly means) seem to be those very painful or afflictive disorders which were frequently sent, or at least permitted of God, as a scourge or punishment of sin.

12. He charged them not to make him known – It was not the time: nor were they fit preachers.

13. He calleth whom he would – With regard to the eternal states of men, God always acts as just and merciful. But with regard to numberless other things, he seems to us to act as a mere sovereign. Luke vi, 12

14. Matt. x, 2; Luke vi, 13; Acts i, 13.

16. He surnamed them sons of thunder – Both with respect to the warmth and impetuosity of their spirit, their fervent manner of preaching, and the power of their word.

20. To eat bread – That is, to take any subsistence.

21. His relations – His mother and his brethren, ver. 31. But it was some time before they could come near him.

22. The scribes and Pharisees, Matt. xii, 22; who had come down from Jerusalem – Purposely on the devil's errand. And not without success. For the common people now began to drink in the poison, from these learned, good, honorable men! He hath Beelzebub – at command, is in league with him: And by the prince of the devils casteth he out devils – How easily may a man of learning elude the strongest proof of a work of God! How readily can he account for every incident without ever taking God into the question. Matt. xii, 24; Luke xi, 15.

28. Matt. xii, 31; Luke xii, 10.

30. Because they said, He hath an unclean spirit – Is it not astonishing, that men who have ever read these words, should doubt, what is the blasphemy against the Holy Ghost? Can any words declare more plainly, that it is "the ascribing those miracles to the power of the devil which Christ wrought by the power of the Holy Ghost?"

31. Then come his brethren and his mother – Having at length made their way through the crowd, so as to come to the door. His brethren

men think themselves whole; they feel no need of a physician, therefore despise or neglect Christ and his gospel. But the convinced, humbled sinner, who despairs of all help, excepting from the Savior, will show his faith by applying to him without delay.

13-17 Matthew was not a good character, or else, being a Jew, he would never have been a publican, that is, a tax-gatherer for the Romans. However, Christ called this publican to follow him. With God, through Christ, there is mercy to pardon the greatest sins, and grace to change the greatest sinners, and make them holy. A faithful, fair-dealing publican was rare. And because the Jews had a particular hatred to an office which proved that they were subject to the Romans, they gave these tax-gatherers an ill name. But such as these our blessed Lord did not hesitate to converse with, when he appeared in the likeness of sinful flesh. And it is no new thing for that which is both well done and well designed, to be slandered, and turned to the reproach of the wisest and best of men. Christ would not withdraw, though the Pharisees were offended. If the world had been righteous, there had been no occasion for his coming, either to preach repentance, or to purchase forgiveness. We must not keep company with ungodly men out of love to their vain conversation; but we are to show love to their souls, remembering that our good Physician had the power of healing in himself, and was in no danger of taking the disease; but it is not so with us. In trying to do good to others, let us be careful we do not get harm to ourselves.

18-22 Strict professors are apt to blame all that do not fully come up to their own views. Christ did not escape slanders; we should be willing to bear them, as well as careful not to deserve them; but should attend to every part of our duty in its proper order and season.

23-28 The Sabbath is a sacred and Divine institution; a privilege and benefit, not a task and drudgery. God never designed it to be a burden to us, therefore we must not make it so to ourselves. The Sabbath was instituted for the good of mankind, as living in society, having many wants and troubles, preparing for a state of happiness or misery. Man was not made for the Sabbath, as if his keeping it could be of service to God, nor was he commanded to keep its outward observances to his real hurt. Every observance respecting it, is to be interpreted by the rule of mercy.

MARK 3

The withered hand healed. (1-5)
The people resort to Christ. (6-12)
The apostles called. (13-21)
The blasphemy of the scribes. (22-30)
Christ's relatives. (31-35)

1-5 This man's case was piteous; he had a withered hand, which disabled him from working for his living; and those that are so, are the most proper objects of charity. Let those

the souls of those whom he has ordained unto eternal life.

II. While the gospel is a command, it is a two-fold command explaining itself. "Repent ye, and believe the gospel."
I know some very excellent brethren—would God there were more like them in zeal and love—who, in their zeal to preach up simple faith in Christ have felt a little difficulty about the matter of repentance; and I have known some of them who have tried to get over the difficulty by softening down the apparent hardness of the word repentance, by expounding it according to its more usual Greek equivalent, a word which occurs in the original of my text, and signifies "to change one's mind." Apparently they interpret repentance to be a somewhat slighter thing than we usually conceive it to be, a mere change of mind, in fact. Now, allow me to suggest to those dear brethren, that the Holy Ghost never preaches repentance as a trifle; and the change of mind or understanding of which the gospel speaks is a very deep and solemn work, and must not on any account be depreciated. Moreover, there is another word which is also used in the original Greek for repentance, not so often I admit, but still is used, which signifies "an after-care," a word which has in it something more of sorrow and anxiety, than that which signifies changing one's mind. There must be sorrow for sin and hatred of it in true repentance, or else I have read my Bible to little purpose.

To repent does mean a change of mind; but then it is a thorough change of the understanding and all that is in the mind, so that it includes an illumination, an illumination of the Holy Spirit; and I think it includes a discovery of iniquity and a hatred of it, without which there can hardly be a genuine repentance. We must not, I think, undervalue repentance. It is a blessed grace of God the Holy Spirit, and it is absolutely necessary unto salvation.
The command explains itself. We will take, first of all, repentance. It is quite certain that whatever the repentance here mentioned may be, it is a repentance perfectly consistent with faith; and therefore we get the explanation of what repentance must be, from its being connected with the next command, "Believe the gospel." Then, dear friends, we may be sure that that unbelief which leads a man to think that his sin is too great for Christ

root, it withered away.

7 And some fell among thorns, and the thorns grew up, and choked it, and it yielded no fruit.

8 And other fell on good ground, and did yield fruit that sprang up and increased; and brought forth, some thirty, and some sixty, and some an hundred.

9 And he said unto them, He that hath ears to hear, let him hear.

10 And when he was alone, they that were about him with the twelve asked of him the parable.

11 And he said unto them, Unto you it is given to know the mystery of the kingdom of God: but unto them that are without, all these things are done in parables:

12 That seeing they may see, and not perceive; and hearing they may hear, and not understand; lest at any time they should be converted, and their sins should be forgiven them.

13 And he said unto them, Know ye not this parable? and how then will ye know all parables?

14 The sower soweth the word.

15 And these are they by the way side, where the word is sown; but when they have heard, Satan cometh immediately, and taketh away the word that was sown in their hearts.

16 And these are they likewise which are sown on stony ground; who, when they have heard the word, immediately receive it with gladness;

17 And have no root in themselves, and so endure but for a time: afterward, when affliction or persecution ariseth for the word's sake, immediately they are offended.

18 And these are they which are sown among thorns; such as hear the word,

19 And the cares of this world, and the deceitfulness of riches, and the lusts of other things entering in, choke the word, and it becometh unfruitful.

20 And these are they which are sown on good ground; such as hear the word, and receive it, and bring forth fruit, some thirtyfold, some sixty, and some an hundred.

21 And he said unto them, Is a candle brought to be put under a bushel, or under a bed? and not to be set on a candlestick?

22 For there is nothing hid, which shall not be manifested; neither was any thing kept secret, but that it should come abroad.

23 If any man have ears to hear, let him hear.

24 And he said unto them, Take heed what ye hear: with what measure ye mete, it shall be measured to you: and unto you that hear shall more be given.

25 For he that hath, to him shall be given: and he that hath not, from him shall be taken even that which he hath.

26 And he said, So is the kingdom of God, as if a man should cast seed into the ground;

27 And should sleep, and rise night and day, and the seed should spring and grow up, he knoweth not how.

28 For the earth bringeth forth fruit of herself; first the blade, then the ear, after that the full corn in the ear.

29 But when the fruit is brought forth, immediately he putteth in the sickle, because the harvest is come.

30 And he said, Whereunto shall we liken the kingdom of God? or with what comparison shall we compare it?

31 It is like a grain of mustard seed, which, when it is sown in the earth, is less than all the seeds that be in the earth:

32 But when it is sown, it groweth up, and becometh greater than all herbs, and shooteth out great branches; so that the fowls of the air may lodge under the shadow of it.

33 And with many such parables spake he the word unto them, as they were able to hear it.

34 But without a parable spake he not unto them: and when they were alone, he expounded all things to his disciples.

35 And the same day, when the even was come, he saith unto them,

are here named first, as being first and most earnest in the design of taking him: for neither did these of his brethren believe on him. They sent to him, calling him – They sent one into the house, who called him aloud, by name. Matt. xii, 46; Luke viii, 19.

34. Looking round on them who sat about him – With the utmost sweetness; He said, Behold my mother and my brethren – In this preference of his true disciples even to the Virgin Mary, considered merely as his mother after the flesh, he not only shows his high and tender affection for them, but seems designedly to guard against those excessive and idolatrous honors, which he foresaw would in after ages be paid to her.

MARK 4

1. Matt. xiii, 1; Luke viii, 4.

2. He taught them many things by parables – After the usual manner of the eastern nations, to make his instructions more agreeable to them, and to impress them the more upon attentive hearers. A parable signifies not only a simile or comparison, and sometimes a proverb, but any kind of instructive speech, wherein spiritual things are explained and illustrated by natural, Prov. i, 6. To understand a proverb and the interpretation – The proverb is the literal sense, the interpretation is the spiritual; resting in the literal sense killeth, but the spiritual giveth life.

3. Hearken – This word he probably spoke with a loud voice, to stop the noise and hurry of the people.

10. When he was alone – That is, retired apart from the multitude.

11. To them that are without – So the Jews termed the heathens: so our Lord terms all obstinate unbelievers: for they shall not enter into his kingdom: they shall abide in outer darkness.

12. So that seeing they see and do not perceive – They would not see before now they could not, God having given them up to the blindness which they had chosen.

13. Know ye not this parable? – Which is as it were the foundation of all those that I shall speak hereafter; and is so easy to be understood?

19. The desire of other things choke the word – A deep and important truth! The desire of any thing, otherwise than as it leads to happiness in God, directly tends to barrenness of soul. Entering in – Where they were not before. Let him therefore who has received and retained the word, see that no other desire then enter in, such as perhaps till then he never knew. It becometh unfruitful – After the fruit had grown almost to

be helped that cannot help themselves. But stubborn infidels, when they can say nothing against the truth, yet will not yield. We hear what is said amiss, and see what is done amiss; but Christ looks at the root of bitterness in the heart, the blindness and hardness of that, and is grieved. Let hardhearted sinners tremble to think of the anger with which he will look upon them shortly, when the day of his wrath comes. The great healing day now is the Sabbath, and the healing place the house of prayer; but the healing power is of Christ. The gospel command is like that recorded here: though our hands are withered, yet, if we will not stretch them out, it is our own fault that we are not healed. But if we are healed, Christ, his power and grace, must have all the glory.

6-12 All our sicknesses and calamities spring from the anger of God against our sins. Their removal, or the making them blessings to us, was purchased to us by the blood of Christ. But the plagues and diseases of our souls, of our hearts, are chiefly to be dreaded; and He can heal them also by a word. May more and more press to Christ to be healed of these plagues, and to be delivered from the enemies of their souls.

13-21 Christ calls whom he will; for his grace is his own. He had called the apostles to separate themselves from the crowd, and they came unto him. He now gave them power to heal sicknesses, and to cast out devils. May the Lord send forth more and more of those who have been with him, and have learned of him to preach his gospel, to be instruments in his blessed work. Those whose hearts are enlarged in the work of God, can easily bear with what is inconvenient to themselves, and will rather lose a meal than an opportunity of doing good. Those who go on with zeal in the work of God, must expect hindrances, both from the hatred of enemies, and mistaken affections of friends, and need to guard against both.

22-30 It was plain that the doctrine of Christ had a direct tendency to break the devil's power; and it was as plain, that casting of him out of the bodies of people, confirmed that doctrine; therefore Satan could not support such a design. Christ gave an awful warning against speaking such dangerous words. It is true the gospel promises, because Christ has purchased, forgiveness for the greatest sins and sinners; but by this sin, they would oppose the gifts of the Holy Ghost after Christ's ascension. Such is the enmity of the heart, that unconverted men pretend believers are doing Satan's work, when sinners are brought to repentance and newness of life.

31-35 It is a great comfort to all true Christians, that they are dearer to Christ than mother, brother, or sister as such, merely as relations in the flesh would have been, even had they been holy. Blessed be God, this great and gracious privilege is ours even now; for though Christ's bodily presence cannot be enjoyed by us, his spiritual presence is not denied us.

to pardon it, is not the repentance meant here. Many who truly repent are tempted to believe that they are too great sinners for Christ to pardon. That, however, is not part of their repentance; it is a sin, a very great and grievous sin, for it is undervaluing the merit of Christ's blood; it is a denial of the truthfulness of God's promise; it is a detracting from the grace and favor of God who sent the gospel. Such a persuasion you must labor to get rid of, for it came from Satan, and not from the Holy Spirit. God the Holy Ghost never did teach a man that his sins were too great to be forgiven, for that would be to make God the Holy Spirit to teach a lie. If any of you have a thought of that kind this morning, be rid of it; it cometh from the powers of darkness, and not from the Holy Ghost; and if some of you are troubled because you never were haunted by that fear, be glad instead of being troubled. He can save you; be you as black as hell he can save you; and it is a wicked falsehood, and a high insult against the high majesty of divine love when you are tempted to believe that you are past the mercy of God. That is not repentance, but a foul sin against the infinite mercy of God.

Then, there is another spurious repentance which makes the sinner dwell upon the consequences of his sin, rather than upon the sin itself, and so keeps him from believing. I have known some sinners so distressed with fears of hell, and thoughts of death and of eternal judgment, that to use the words of one terrible preacher, "They have been shaken over the mouth of hell by their collar," and have felt the torments of the pit before they went thither. Dear friends, this is not repentance. Many a man has felt all that and has yet been lost. Look at many a dying man, tormented with remorse, who has had all its pangs and convictions, and yet has gone down to the grave without Christ and without hope. These things may come with repentance, but, they are not an essential part of it. That which is called law-work, in which the sinner is terrified with horrible thoughts that God's mercy is gone for ever, may be permitted by God for some special purpose, but it is not repentance; in fact, it may often be devilish rather than heavenly, for, as John Bunyan tells us, Diabolus doth often beat the great hell-drum in the ears of the men of Mansoul, to prevent their hearing the sweet trumpet of the gospel which pro-

Let us pass over unto the other side.

36 And when they had sent away the multitude, they took him even as he was in the ship. And there were also with him other little ships.

37 And there arose a great storm of wind, and the waves beat into the ship, so that it was now full.

38 And he was in the hinder part of the ship, asleep on a pillow: and they awake him, and say unto him, Master, carest thou not that we perish?

39 And he arose, and rebuked the wind, and said unto the sea, Peace, be still. And the wind ceased, and there was a great calm.

40 And he said unto them, Why are ye so fearful? how is it that ye have no faith?

41 And they feared exceedingly, and said one to another, What manner of man is this, that even the wind and the sea obey him?

MARK 5

1 And they came over unto the other side of the sea, into the country of the Gadarenes.

2 And when he was come out of the ship, immediately there met him out of the tombs a man with an unclean spirit,

3 Who had his dwelling among the tombs; and no man could bind him, no, not with chains:

4 Because that he had been often bound with fetters and chains, and the chains had been plucked asunder by him, and the fetters broken in pieces: neither could any man tame him.

5 And always, night and day, he was in the mountains, and in the tombs, crying, and cutting himself with stones.

6 But when he saw Jesus afar off, he ran and worshiped him,

7 And cried with a loud voice, and said, What have I to do with thee, Jesus, thou Son of the most high God? I adjure thee by God, that thou torment me not.

8 For he said unto him, Come out of the man, thou unclean spirit.

9 And he asked him, What is thy name? And he answered, saying, My name is Legion: for we are many.

10 And he besought him much that he would not send them away out of the country.

11 Now there was there nigh unto the mountains a great herd of swine feeding.

12 And all the devils besought him, saying, Send us into the swine, that we may enter into them.

13 And forthwith Jesus gave them leave. And the unclean spirits went out, and entered into the swine: and the herd ran violently down a steep place into the sea, (they were about two thousand;) and were choked in the sea.

14 And they that fed the swine fled, and told it in the city, and in the country. And they went out to see what it was that was done.

15 And they come to Jesus, and see him that was possessed with the devil, and had the legion, sitting, and clothed, and in his right mind: and they were afraid.

16 And they that saw it told them how it befell to him that was possessed with the devil, and also concerning the swine.

17 And they began to pray him to depart out of their coasts.

18 And when he was come into the ship, he that had been possessed with the devil prayed him that he might be with him.

19 Howbeit Jesus suffered him not, but saith unto him, Go home to thy friends, and tell them how great things the Lord hath done for thee, and hath had compassion on thee.

20 And he departed, and began to publish in Decapolis how great things Jesus had done for him: and all men did marvel.

21 And when Jesus was passed over again by ship unto the other side, much people gathered unto him: and he was nigh unto the sea.

22 And, behold, there cometh one of the rulers of the synagogue, Jairus by name; and when he saw him, he fell at his feet,

perfection.

21. And he said, Is a candle – As if he had said, I explain these things to you, I give you this light, not to conceal, but to impart it to others. And if I conceal any thing from you now, it is only that it may be more effectually manifested hereafter. Matt. v, 15; Luke viii, 16; xi, 33.

22. Matt. x, 26; Luke viii, 17.

24. Take heed what ye hear – That is, attend to what you hear, that it may have its due influence upon you. With what measure you mete – That is, according to the improvement you make of what you have heard, still farther assistance shall be given. And to you that hear – That is, with improvement.

25. He that hath – That improves whatever he has received, to the good of others, as well as of his own soul. Matt. xiii, 12; Luke viii, 18.

26. So is the kingdom of God – The inward kingdom is like seed which a man casts into the ground – This a preacher of the Gospel casts into the heart. And he sleeps and rises night and day – That is, he has it continually in his thoughts. Meantime it springs and grows up he knows not how – Even he that sowed it cannot explain how it grows. For as the earth by a curious kind of mechanism, which the greatest philosophers cannot comprehend, does as it were spontaneously bring forth first the blade, then the ear, then the full corn in the ear: so the soul, in an inexplicable manner, brings forth, first weak graces, then stronger, then full holiness: and all this of itself, as a machine, whose spring of motion is within itself. Yet observe the amazing exactness of the comparison. The earth brings forth no corn (as the soul no holiness) without both the care and toil of man, and the benign influence of heaven.

29. He putteth in the sickle – God cutteth down and gathereth the corn into his garner.

30. Matt. xiii, 31; Luke xiii, 18.

33. He spake the word as they were able to hear it – Adapting it to the capacity of his hearers; and speaking as plain as he could without offending them. A rule never to be forgotten by those who instruct others.

35. Matt. viii, 23; Luke viii, 22.

36. They take him as he was in the vessel – They carried him immediately in the same vessel from which he had been preaching to the people.

38. On the pillow – So we translate it, for want of a proper English expression, for that particular part of the vessel near the rudder, on which he lay.

39. Peace – Cease thy tossing: Be still – Cease thy roaring; literally, Be thou gagged.

MARK 4

The parable of the sower. (1-20)
Other parables. (21-34)
Christ stills the tempest. (35-41)

1-20 This parable contained instruction so important, that all capable of hearing were bound to attend to it. There are many things we are concerned to know; and if we understand not the plain truths of the gospel, how shall we learn those more difficult! It will help us to value the privileges we enjoy as disciples of Christ, if we seriously consider the deplorable state of all who have not such privileges. In the great field of the church, the word of God is dispensed to all. Of the many that hear the word of the gospel, but few receive it, so as to bring forth fruit. Many are much affected with the word for the present, who yet receive no abiding benefit. The word does not leave abiding impressions upon the minds of men, because their hearts are not duly disposed to receive it. The devil is very busy about careless hearers, as the fowls of the air go about the seed that lies above ground. Many continue in a barren, false profession, and go down to hell. Impressions that are not deep, will not last. Many do not mind heart-work, without which religion is nothing. Others are hindered from profiting by the word of God, by abundance of the world. And those who have but little of the world, may yet be ruined by indulging the body. God expects and requires fruit from those who enjoy the gospel, a temper of mind and Christian graces daily exercised, Christian duties duly performed. Let us look to the Lord, that by his new-creating grace our hearts may become good ground, and that the good seed of the word may produce in our lives those good words and works which are through Jesus Christ, to the praise and glory of God the Father.

21-34 These declarations were intended to call the attention of the disciples to the word of Christ. By his thus instructing them, they were made able to instruct others; as candles are lighted, not to be covered, but to be placed on a candlestick, that they may give light to a room. This parable of the good seed, shows the manner in which the kingdom of God makes progress in the world. Let but the word of Christ have the place it ought to have in a soul, and it will show itself in a good conversation. It grows gradually: first the blade; then the ear; after that the full corn in the ear. When it is sprung up, it will go forward. The work of grace in the soul is, at first, but the day of small things; yet it has mighty products even now, while it is in its growth; but what will there be when it is perfected in heaven!

35-41 Christ was asleep in the storm, to try the faith of his disciples, and to stir them up to pray. Their faith appeared weak, and their prayers strong. When our wicked hearts are like the troubled sea which cannot rest, when our passions are unruly, let us think we hear the law of Christ, saying, Be silent, be dumb. When without are fightings, and within are fears, and the spirits are in a tumult, if he say, "Peace, be still," there is a great calm at once. Why are ye so fearful? Though there may be cause for some fear, yet not for such

claimeth pardon to them. I tell thee, sinner, any repentance that keeps thee from believing in Christ is a repentance that needs to be repented of; any repentance that makes thee think Christ will not save thee, goes beyond the truth and against the truth, and the sooner thou are rid of it the better. God deliver thee from it, for the repentance that will save thee is quite consistent with faith in Christ.

There is, again, a false repentance which leads men to hardness of heart and despair. We have known some seared as with a hot iron by burning remorse. They have said, "I have done much evil; there is no hope for me; I will not hear the Word any more." If they hear it it is nothing to them, their hearts are hard as adamant. If they could once get the thought that God would forgive them, their hearts would flow in rivers of repentance; but no; they feel a kind of regret that they did wrong, but yet they go on in it all the same, feeling that there is no hope, and that they may as well continue to live as they were wont to do, and get the pleasures of sin since they cannot, as they think, have the pleasures of grace. Now, that is no repentance. It is a fire which hardens, and not the Lord's fire which melts; it may be a hammer, but it is a hammer used to knit the particles of your soul together, and not to break the heart. If, dear friends, you have never been the subject of these terrors do not desire them. Thank God if you have been brought to Jesus any how, but long not for needless horrors. Jesus saves you, not by what you feel, but by that finished work, that blood and righteousness which God accepted on your behalf. Do remember that no repentance is worth having which is not perfectly consistent with faith in Christ. An old saint, on his sick-bed, once used this remarkable expression; "Lord, sink me low as hell in repentance; but"—and here is the beauty of it—"lift me high as heaven in faith." Now, the repentance that sinks a man low as hell is of no use except there is faith also that lifts him as high as heaven, and the two are perfectly consistent one with the other. A man may loathe and detest himself, and all the while he may know that Christ is able to save, and has saved him. In fact, this is how true Christians live; they repent as bitterly as for sin as if they knew they should be damned for it; but they rejoice as much in Christ as if sin were nothing at all. Oh, how blessed it is to

23 And besought him greatly, saying, My little daughter lieth at the point of death: I pray thee, come and lay thy hands on her, that she may be healed; and she shall live.

24 And Jesus went with him; and much people followed him, and thronged him.

25 And a certain woman, which had an issue of blood twelve years,

26 And had suffered many things of many physicians, and had spent all that she had, and was nothing bettered, but rather grew worse,

27 When she had heard of Jesus, came in the press behind, and touched his garment.

28 For she said, If I may touch but his clothes, I shall be whole.

29 And straightway the fountain of her blood was dried up; and she felt in her body that she was healed of that plague.

30 And Jesus, immediately knowing in himself that virtue had gone out of him, turned him about in the press, and said, Who touched my clothes?

31 And his disciples said unto him, Thou seest the multitude thronging thee, and sayest thou, Who touched me?

32 And he looked round about to see her that had done this thing.

33 But the woman fearing and trembling, knowing what was done in her, came and fell down before him, and told him all the truth.

34 And he said unto her, Daughter, thy faith hath made thee whole; go in peace, and be whole of thy plague.

35 While he yet spake, there came from the ruler of the synagogue's house certain which said, Thy daughter is dead: why troublest thou the Master any further?

36 As soon as Jesus heard the word that was spoken, he saith unto the ruler of the synagogue, Be not afraid, only believe.

37 And he suffered no man to follow him, save Peter, and James, and John the brother of James.

38 And he cometh to the house of the ruler of the synagogue, and seeth the tumult, and them that wept and wailed greatly.

39 And when he was come in, he saith unto them, Why make ye this ado, and weep? the damsel is not dead, but sleepeth.

40 And they laughed him to scorn. But when he had put them all out, he taketh the father and the mother of the damsel, and them that were with him, and entereth in where the damsel was lying.

41 And he took the damsel by the hand, and said unto her, Talitha cumi; which is, being interpreted, Damsel, I say unto thee, arise.

42 And straightway the damsel arose, and walked; for she was of the age of twelve years. And they were astonished with a great astonishment.

43 And he charged them straitly that no man should know it; and commanded that something should be given her to eat.

MARK 6

1 And he went out from thence, and came into his own country; and his disciples follow him.

2 And when the sabbath day was come, he began to teach in the synagogue: and many hearing him were astonished, saying, From whence hath this man these things? and what wisdom is this which is given unto him, that even such mighty works are wrought by his hands?

3 Is not this the carpenter, the son of Mary, the brother of James, and Joses, and of Juda, and Simon? and are not his sisters here with us? And they were offended at him.

4 But Jesus said unto them, A prophet is not without honor, but in his own country, and among his own kin, and in his own house.

5 And he could there do no mighty work, save that he laid his hands upon a few sick folk, and healed them.

6 And he marveled because of their unbelief. And he went round about the villages, teaching.

7 And he called unto him the twelve, and began to send them forth by two and two; and gave them power over unclean spirits;

MARK 5

1. Matt. viii, 28; Luke viii, 26.

2. There met him a man with an unclean spirit – St. Matthew mentions two. Probably this, so particularly spoken of here, was the most remarkably fierce and ungovernable.

9. My name is Legion! for we are many – But all these seem to have been under one commander, who accordingly speaks all along, both for them and himself.

15. And they were afraid – It is not improbable they might otherwise have offered some rudeness, if not violence.

18. Matt. ix, 1; Luke viii, 37;

19. Tell them how great things the Lord hath done for thee – This was peculiarly needful there, where Christ did not go in person.

20. He published in Decapolis – Not only at home, but in all that country where Jesus himself did not come.

21. Luke viii, 40.

22. One of the rulers of the synagogue – To regulate the affairs of every synagogue, there was a council of grave men. Over these was a president, who was termed the ruler of the synagogue. Sometimes there was no more than one ruler in a synagogue. Matt. ix, 18; Luke viii, 41.

25. Matt. ix, 20; Luke viii, 43.

37. John, the brother of James – When St. Mark wrote, not long after our Lord's ascension, the memory of St. James, lately beheaded, was so fresh, that his name was more known than that of John himself.

40. Them that were with him – Peter, James, and John.

43. He charged them that no man should know it – That he might avoid every appearance of vain glory, might prevent too great a concourse of people, and might not farther enrage the scribes and Pharisees against him; the time for his death, and for the full manifestation of his glory, being not yet come. He commanded something should be given her to eat – So that when either natural or spiritual life is restored, even by immediate miracle, all proper means are to be used in order to preserve it.

MARK 6

1. Matt. xiii, 54; Luke iv, 16.

3. Is not this the carpenter? – There can be no doubt, but in his youth he wrought with his supposed father Joseph.

5. He could do no miracle there – Not consistently with his wisdom and goodness. It being inconsistent with his wisdom to work them

fear as this. Those may suspect their faith, who can have such a thought as that Jesus careth not though his people perish. How imperfect are the best of saints! Faith and fear take their turns while we are in this world; but ere long, fear will be overcome, and faith will be lost in sight.

MARK 5

The demoniac healed. (1-20)
A woman healed. (21-34)
The daughter of Jairus raised. (35-43)

1-20 Some openly willfull sinners are like this madman. The commands of the law are as chains and fetters, to restrain sinners from their wicked courses; but they break those bands in sunder; and it is an evidence of the power of the devil in them. A legion of soldiers consisted of six thousand men, or more. What multitudes of fallen spirits there must be, and all enemies to God and man, when here was a legion in one poor wretched creature! Many there are that rise up against us. We are not a match for our spiritual enemies, in our own strength; but in the Lord, and in the power of his might, we shall be able to stand against them, though there are legions of them. When the vilest transgressor is delivered by the power of Jesus from the bondage of Satan, he will gladly sit at the feet of his Deliverer, and hear his word, who delivers the wretched slaves of Satan, and numbers them among his saints and servants. When the people found that their swine were lost, they had a dislike to Christ. Long-suffering and mercy may be seen, even in the corrections by which men lose their property while their lives are saved, and warning given them to seek the salvation of their souls. The man joyfully proclaimed what great things Jesus had done for him. All men marveled, but few followed him. Many who cannot but wonder at the works of Christ, yet do not, as they ought, wonder after him.

21-34 A despised gospel will go where it will be better received. One of the rulers of a synagogue earnestly besought Christ for a little daughter, about twelve years old, who was dying. Another cure was wrought by the way. We should do good, not only when in the house, but when we walk by the way, De 6:7. It is common with people not to apply to Christ till they have tried in vain all other helpers, and find them, as certainly they will, physicians of no value. Some run to diversions and gay company; others plunge into business, or even into intemperance; others go about to establish their own righteousness, or torment themselves by vain superstitions. Many perish in these ways; but none will ever find rest to the soul by such devices; while those whom Christ heals of the disease of sin, find in themselves an entire change for the better. As secret acts of sin, so secret acts of faith, are known to the Lord Jesus. The woman told all the truth. It is the will of Christ that his people should be comforted, and he has power to command comfort to troubled spirits. The more simply we depend on Him, and expect great things from him, the more we shall find in ourselves that he is become our salvation. Those who, by faith, are healed of their spiritual diseases, have reason to go in peace.

know where these two lines meet, the stripping of repentance, and the clothing of faith! The repentance that ejects sin as an evil tenant, and the faith which admits Christ to be the sole master of the heart; the repentance which purges the soul from dead works, and the faith that fills the soul with living works; the repentance which pulls down, and the faith which builds up; the repentance that scatters stones, and the faith which puts stones together; the repentance which ordains a time to weep, and the faith that gives a time to dance— these two things together make up the work of grace within, whereby men's souls are saved. Be it, then laid down as a great truth, most plainly written in our text, that the repentance we ought to preach is one connected with faith, and thus we may preach repentance and faith together without any difficulty whatever.

Having shown you what this repentance is not, let us dwell for a moment on what it is. The repentance which is here commanded is the result of faith; it is born at the same time with faith—they are twins, and to say which is the elder-born passes my knowledge. It is a great mystery; faith is before repentance in some of its acts, and repentance before faith in another view of it; the fact being that they come into the soul together. Now, a repentance which makes me weep and abhor my past life because of the love of Christ which has pardoned it, is the right repentance. When I can say, "My sin is washed away by Jesu's blood," and then repent because I so sinned as to make it necessary that Christ should die—that dove-eyed repentance which looks at his bleeding wounds, and feels that her heart must bleed because she wounded Christ— that broken heart that breaks because Christ was nailed to the cross for it—that is the repentance which bringeth us salvation.

Again, the repentance which makes us avoid present sin because of the love of God who died for us, this also is saving repentance. If I avoid sin today because I am afraid of being lost if I commit it, I have not the repentance of a child of God; but when I avoid it and seek to lead a holy life because Christ loved me and gave himself up for me, and because I am not my own, but am bought with a price, this is the work of the Spirit of God.

And again, that change of mind, that

8 And commanded them that they should take nothing for their journey, save a staff only; no scrip, no bread, no money in their purse:

9 But be shod with sandals; and not put on two coats.

10 And he said unto them, In what place soever ye enter into an house, there abide till ye depart from that place.

11 And whosoever shall not receive you, nor hear you, when ye depart thence, shake off the dust under your feet for a testimony against them. Verily I say unto you, It shall be more tolerable for Sodom and Gomorrha in the day of judgment, than for that city.

12 And they went out, and preached that men should repent.

13 And they cast out many devils, and anointed with oil many that were sick, and healed them.

14 And king Herod heard of him; (for his name was spread abroad:) and he said, That John the Baptist was risen from the dead, and therefore mighty works do shew forth themselves in him.

15 Others said, That it is Elias. And others said, That it is a prophet, or as one of the prophets.

16 But when Herod heard thereof, he said, It is John, whom I beheaded: he is risen from the dead.

17 For Herod himself had sent forth and laid hold upon John, and bound him in prison for Herodias' sake, his brother Philip's wife: for he had married her.

18 For John had said unto Herod, It is not lawful for thee to have thy brother's wife.

19 Therefore Herodias had a quarrel against him, and would have killed him; but she could not:

20 For Herod feared John, knowing that he was a just man and an holy, and observed him; and when he heard him, he did many things, and heard him gladly.

21 And when a convenient day was come, that Herod on his birthday made a supper to his lords, high captains, and chief estates of Galilee;

22 And when the daughter of the said Herodias came in, and danced, and pleased Herod and them that sat with him, the king said unto the damsel, Ask of me whatsoever thou wilt, and I will give it thee.

23 And he sware unto her, Whatsoever thou shalt ask of me, I will give it thee, unto the half of my kingdom.

24 And she went forth, and said unto her mother, What shall I ask? And she said, The head of John the Baptist.

25 And she came in straightway with haste unto the king, and asked, saying, I will that thou give me by and by in a charger the head of John the Baptist.

26 And the king was exceeding sorry; yet for his oath's sake, and for their sakes which sat with him, he would not reject her.

27 And immediately the king sent an executioner, and commanded his head to be brought: and he went and beheaded him in the prison,

28 And brought his head in a charger, and gave it to the damsel: and the damsel gave it to her mother.

29 And when his disciples heard of it, they came and took up his corpse, and laid it in a tomb.

30 And the apostles gathered themselves together unto Jesus, and told him all things, both what they had done, and what they had taught.

31 And he said unto them, Come ye yourselves apart into a desert place, and rest a while: for there were many coming and going, and they had no leisure so much as to eat.

32 And they departed into a desert place by ship privately.

33 And the people saw them departing, and many knew him, and ran afoot thither out of all cities, and outwent them, and came together unto him.

34 And Jesus, when he came out, saw much people, and was moved with compassion toward them, because they were as sheep not having a shepherd: and he began to teach them many things.

35 And when the day was now far spent, his disciples came unto him, and said, This is a desert place, and now the time is far passed:

there, where it could not promote his great end; and with his goodness, seeing he well knew his countrymen would reject whatever evidence could be given them. And therefore to have given them more evidence, would only have increased their damnation.

6. He marveled – As man. As he was God, nothing was strange to him.

7. Matt. x, 1; Luke ix, 1.

8. He commanded them to take nothing for their journey – That they might be always unencumbered, free, ready for motion. Save a staff only – He that had one might take it; but he that had not was not to provide one, Matt. x, 9. Luke ix, 3.

9. Be shod with sandals – As you usually are. Sandals were pieces of strong leather or wood, tied under the sole of the foot by thongs, something resembling modern clogs. The shoes which they are in St. Matthew forbidden to take, were a kind of short boots, reaching a little above the mid-leg, which were then commonly used in journeys. Our Lord intended by this mission to initiate them into their apostolic work. And it was doubtless an encouragement to them all their life after, to recollect the care which God took of them, when they had left all they had, and went out quite unfurnished for such an expedition. In this view our Lord himself leads them to consider it, Luke xxii, 35, When I sent you forth without purse or scrip, lacked ye any thing?

10. Matt. x, 11; Luke ix, 4.

12. Luke ix, 6.

13. They anointed with oil many that were sick – Which St. James gives as a general direction, James v, 14, 15, adding those peremptory words, And the Lord shall heal him – He shall be restored to health: not by the natural efficacy of the oil, but by the supernatural blessing of God. And it seems this was the great standing means of healing desperate diseases in the Christian Church, long before extreme unction was used or heard of, which bears scarce any resemblance to it; the former being used only as a means of health; the latter only when life is despaired of.

14. Matt. xiv, 1; Luke ix, 7.

15. A prophet, as one of the prophets – Not inferior to one of the ancient prophets.

16. But Herod hearing thereof – Of their various judgments concerning him, still said, It is John.

20. And preserved him – Against all the malice and contrivances of Herodias. And when he heard him – Probably sending for him, at times, during his imprisonment, which continued a year and a half. He heard him gladly – Delusive

MATTHEW HENRY   CHARLES H. SPURGEON

35-43 We may suppose Jairus hesitating whether he should ask Christ to go on or not, when told that his daughter was dead. But have we not as much occasion for the grace of God, and the comfort of his Spirit, for the prayers of our ministers and Christian friends, when death is in the house, as when sickness is there? Faith is the only remedy against grief and fear at such a time. Believe the resurrection, then fear not. He raised the dead child to life by a word of power. Such is the gospel call to those who are by nature dead in trespasses and sins. It is by the word of Christ that spiritual life is given. All who saw it, and heard of it, admired the miracle, and Him that wrought it. Though we cannot now expect to have our dead children or relatives restored, we may hope to find comfort under our trials.

MARK 6

Christ despised in his own country. (1-6)
The apostles sent forth. (7-13)
John the Baptist put to death. (14-29)
The apostles return. Five thousand fed by a miracle. (30-44)
Christ walks on the sea. He heals those that touch him. (45-56)

1-6 Our Lord's countrymen tried to prejudice the minds of people against him. Is not this the carpenter? Our Lord Jesus probably had worked in that business with his father. He thus put honor upon mechanics, and encouraged all persons who eat by the labor of their hands. It becomes the followers of Christ to content themselves with the satisfaction of doing good, although they are denied the praise of it. How much did these Nazarenes lose by obstinate prejudices against Jesus! May Divine grace deliver us from that unbelief, which renders Christ a savor of death, rather than of life to the soul. Let us, like our Master, go and teach cottagers and peasants the way of salvation.

7-13 Though the apostles were conscious to themselves of great weakness, and expected no worldly advantage, yet, in obedience to their Master, and in dependence upon his strength, they went out. They did not amuse people with curious matters, but told them they must repent of their sins, and turn to God. The servants of Christ may hope to turn many from darkness unto God, and to heal souls by the power of the Holy Ghost.

14-29 Herod feared John while he lived, and feared him still more when he was dead. Herod did many of those things which John in his preaching taught him; but it is not enough to do many things, we must have respect to all the commandments. Herod respected John, till he touched him in his Herodias. Thus many love good preaching, if it keep far away from their beloved sin. But it is better that sinners persecute ministers now for faithfulness, than curse them eternally for unfaithfulness. The ways of God are unsearchable; but we may be sure he never can be at a loss to repay his servants for what they endure or lose for his sake. Death could not come so as to surprise this holy man; and the triumph of the wicked was short.

after-carefulness which leads me to resolve that in future I will live like Jesus, and will not live unto the lusts of the flesh, because he hath redeemed me, not with corruptible things as silver and gold, but with his own precious blood—that is the repentance which will save me, and the repentance he asks of me. O ye nations of the earth, he asks not the repentance of Mount Sinai, while ye do fear and shake because his lightnings are abroad; but he asks you to weep and wail because of him; to look on him whom you have pierced, and to mourn for him as a man mourneth for his only son; he bids you remember that you nailed the Savior to the tree, and asks that this argument may make you hate the murderous sins which fastened the Savior there, and put the Lord of glory to an ignominious and an accursed death. This is the only repentance we have to preach; not law and terrors; not despair; not driving men to self-murder—this is the terror of the world which worketh death; but godly sorrow is a sorrow unto salvation through Jesus Christ our Lord.

This brings me to the second half of the command, which is, "Believe the gospel." Faith means trust in Christ. Now, I must again remark that some have preached this trust in Christ so well and so fully, that I can admire their faithfulness and bless God for them; yet there is a difficulty and a danger; it may be that in preaching simple trust in Christ as being the way of salvation, that they omit to remind the sinner that no faith can be genuine but such as is perfectly consistent with repentance for past sin; for my text seems to me to put it thus: no repentance is true but that which consorts with faith; no faith is true but that which is linked with a hearty and sincere repentance on account of past sin. So then, dear friends, those people who have a faith which allows them to think lightly of past sin, have the faith of devils, and not the faith of God's elect. Those who say, "Oh, as for the past, that is nothing; Jesus Christ has washed all that away"; and can talk about all the crimes of their youth, and the iniquitous of their riper years, as if they were mere trifles, and never think of shedding a tear; never feel their souls ready to burst because they should have been such great offenders—such men who can trifle with the past, and even fight their battles o'er again when their passions are too cold for new rebellions—I say that such who think

36 Send them away, that they may go into the country round about, and into the villages, and buy themselves bread: for they have nothing to eat.

37 He answered and said unto them, Give ye them to eat. And they say unto him, Shall we go and buy two hundred pennyworth of bread, and give them to eat?

38 He saith unto them, How many loaves have ye? go and see. And when they knew, they say, Five, and two fishes.

39 And he commanded them to make all sit down by companies upon the green grass.

40 And they sat down in ranks, by hundreds, and by fifties.

41 And when he had taken the five loaves and the two fishes, he looked up to heaven, and blessed, and brake the loaves, and gave them to his disciples to set before them; and the two fishes divided he among them all.

42 And they did all eat, and were filled.

43 And they took up twelve baskets full of the fragments, and of the fishes.

44 And they that did eat of the loaves were about five thousand men.

45 And straightway he constrained his disciples to get into the ship, and to go to the other side before unto Bethsaida, while he sent away the people.

46 And when he had sent them away, he departed into a mountain to pray.

47 And when even was come, the ship was in the midst of the sea, and he alone on the land.

48 And he saw them toiling in rowing; for the wind was contrary unto them: and about the fourth watch of the night he cometh unto them, walking upon the sea, and would have passed by them.

49 But when they saw him walking upon the sea, they supposed it had been a spirit, and cried out:

50 For they all saw him, and were troubled. And immediately he talked with them, and saith unto them, Be of good cheer: it is I; be not afraid.

51 And he went up unto them into the ship; and the wind ceased: and they were sore amazed in themselves beyond measure, and wondered.

52 For they considered not the miracle of the loaves: for their heart was hardened.

53 And when they had passed over, they came into the land of Gennesaret, and drew to the shore.

54 And when they were come out of the ship, straightway they knew him,

55 And ran through that whole region round about, and began to carry about in beds those that were sick, where they heard he was.

56 And whithersoever he entered, into villages, or cities, or country, they laid the sick in the streets, and besought him that they might touch if it were but the border of his garment: and as many as touched him were made whole.

MARK 7

1 Then came together unto him the Pharisees, and certain of the scribes, which came from Jerusalem.

2 And when they saw some of his disciples eat bread with defiled, that is to say, with unwashen, hands, they found fault.

3 For the Pharisees, and all the Jews, except they wash their hands oft, eat not, holding the tradition of the elders.

4 And when they come from the market, except they wash, they eat not. And many other things there be, which they have received to hold, as the washing of cups, and pots, brasen vessels, and of tables.

5 Then the Pharisees and scribes asked him, Why walk not thy disciples according to the tradition of the elders, but eat bread with unwashen hands?

6 He answered and said unto them, Well hath Esaias prophesied of

joy! While Herodias lay in his bosom.

21. A convenient day – Convenient for her purpose. His lords, captains, and principal men of Galilee – The great men of the court, the army, and the province.

23. To the half of my kingdom – A proverbial expression.

26. Yet for his oath's sake, and for the sake of his guests – Herod's honor was like the conscience of the chief priests, Matt. xxvii, 6. To shed innocent blood wounded neither one nor the other.

30. Luke ix, 10.

31. Matt. xiv, 13; John vi, 1.

32. They departed – Across a creek or corner of the lake.

34. Coming out – of the vessel.

40. They sat down in ranks – The word properly signifies a parterre or bed in a garden; by a metaphor, a company of men ranged in order, by hundreds and by fifties – That is, fifty in rank, and a hundred in file. So a hundred multiplied by fifty, make just five thousand.

43. Full of the fragments – of the bread.

45. He constrained his disciples – Who did not care to go without him. Matt. xiv, 22.

46. Matt. xiv, 23; John vi, 15.

48. And he saw them – For the darkness could veil nothing from him. And would have passed by them – That is, walked, as if he was passing by.

52. Their heart was hardened – And yet they were not reprobates. It means only, they were slow and dull of apprehension.

53. Matt. xiv, 34; John vi, 21.

MARK 7

1. Coming from Jerusalem – Probably on purpose to find occasion against him. Matt. xv, 1.

4. Washing of cups and pots and brazen vessels and couches – The Greek word (baptisms) means indifferently either washing or sprinkling. The cups, pots, and vessels were washed; the couches sprinkled.

5. The tradition of the elders – The rule delivered down from your forefathers.

6. Isaiah xxix, 13.

10. Exod. xx, 12; Exod. xxi, 17.

15. There is nothing entering into a man from without which can defile him – Though it is very true, a man may bring guilt, which is moral defilement, upon himself by eating what hurts his health, or by excess either in meat or drink yet even here the pollution arises from the wickedness of the heart, and is just proportional to it. And this is all that our Lord asserts.

30-44 Let not ministers do any thing or teach any thing, but what they are willing should be told to their Lord. Christ notices the frights of some, and the toils of others of his disciples, and provides rest for those that are tired, and refuge for those that are terrified. The people sought the spiritual food of Christ's word, and then he took care that they should not want bodily food. If Christ and his disciples put up with mean things, surely we may. And this miracle shows that Christ came into the world, not only to restore, but to preserve and nourish spiritual life; in him there is enough for all that come. None are sent empty away from Christ but those who come to him full of themselves. Though Christ had bread enough at command, he teaches us not to waste any of God's bounties, remembering how many are in want. We may, some time, need the fragments that we now throw away.

45-56 The church is often like a ship at sea, tossed with tempests, and not comforted: we may have Christ for us, yet wind and tide against us; but it is a comfort to Christ's disciples in a storm, that their Master is in the heavenly mount, interceding for them. And no difficulties can hinder Christ's appearance for his people, when the set time is come. He silenced their fears, by making himself known to them. Our fears are soon satisfied, if our mistakes are set right, especially our mistakes as to Christ. Let the disciples have their Master with them, and all is well. It is for want of rightly understanding Christ's former works, that we view his present works as if there never were the like before. If Christ's ministers now could cure people's bodily diseases, what multitudes would flock after them! It is sad to think how much more most care about their bodies than about their souls.

MARK 7

The traditions of the elders. (1-13)
What defiles the man. (14-23)
The woman of Canaan's daughter cured. (24-30)
Christ restores a man to hearing and speech. (31-37)

1-13 One great design of Christ's coming was, to set aside the ceremonial law; and to make way for this, he rejects the ceremonies men added to the law of God's making. Those clean hands and that pure heart which Christ bestows on his disciples, and requires of them, are very different from the outward and superstitious forms of Pharisees of every age. Jesus reproves them for rejecting the commandment of God. It is clear that it is the duty of children, if their parents are poor, to relieve them as far as they are able; and if children deserve to die that curse their parents, much more those that starve them. But if a man conformed to the traditions of the Pharisees, they found a device to free him from the claim of this duty.

14-23 Our wicked thoughts and affections, words and actions, defile us, and these only. As a corrupt fountain sends forth corrupt streams, so does a corrupt heart send forth corrupt reasonings, corrupt appetites and passions,

sin a trifle and have never sorrowed on account of it, may know that their faith is not genuine. Such men as have a faith which allows them to live carelessly in the present who say, "Well, I am saved by a simple faith"; and then sit on the ale-bench with the drunkard, or stand at the bar with the spirit-drinker, or go into worldly company and enjoy the carnal pleasures and the lusts of the flesh, such men are liars; they have not the faith which will save the soul. They have a deceitful hypocrisy; they have not the faith which will bring them to heaven.

And then, there be some other people who have a faith which leads them to no hatred of sin. They do not look upon sin in others with any kind of shame. It is true they would not do as others do, but then they can laugh at what others commit. They take pleasure in the vices of others; laugh at their profane jests, and smile at their loose speeches. They do not flee from sin as from a serpent, nor detest it as the murderer of their best friend. No, they dally with it; they make excuses for it; they commit in private what in public they condemn. They call grave offenses slight faults and little defalcations; and in business they wink at departures from uprightness, and consider them to be mere matters of trade; the fact being that they have a faith which will sit down arm-in-arm with sin, and eat and drink at the same table with unrighteousness. Oh! if any of you have such a faith as this, I pray God to turn it out bag and baggage. It is of no good to you; the sooner you are cleaned out of it the better for you, for when this sandy foundation shall all be washed away, perhaps you may then begin to build upon the rock. My dear friends, I would be very faithful with your souls, and would lay the lancet at each man's heart. What is your repentance? Have you a repentance that leads you to look out of self to Christ, and to Christ only? On the other hand, have you that faith which leads you to true repentance; to hate the very thought of sin; so that the dearest idol you have known, whatever it may be, you desire to tear from its throne that you may worship Christ, and Christ only? Be assured of this, that nothing short of this will be of any use to you at the last. A repentance and a faith of any other sort may do to please you now, as children are pleased with fancies; but when you get on a death-bed, and see the reality of things, you will be

you hypocrites, as it is written, This people honoreth me with their lips, but their heart is far from me.

7 Howbeit in vain do they worship me, teaching for doctines the commandments of men.

8 For laying aside the commandment of God, ye hold the tradition of men, as the washing of pots and cups: and many other such like things ye do.

9 And he said unto them, Full well ye reject the commandment of God, that ye may keep your own tradition.

10 For Moses said, Honor thy father and thy mother; and, Whoso curseth father or mother, let him die the death:

11 But ye say, If a man shall say to his father or mother, It is Corban, that is to say, a gift, by whatsoever thou mightest be profited by me; he shall be free.

12 And ye suffer him no more to do ought for his father or his mother;

13 Making the word of God of none effect through your tradition, which ye have delivered: and many such like things do ye.

14 And when he had called all the people unto him, he said unto them, Hearken unto me every one of you, and understand:

15 There is nothing from without a man, that entering into him can defile him: but the things which come out of him, those are they that defile the man.

16 If any man have ears to hear, let him hear.

17 And when he was entered into the house from the people, his disciples asked him concerning the parable.

18 And he saith unto them, Are ye so without understanding also? Do ye not perceive, that whatsoever thing from without entereth into the man, it cannot defile him;

19 Because it entereth not into his heart, but into the belly, and goeth out into the draught, purging all meats?

20 And he said, That which cometh out of the man, that defileth the man.

21 For from within, out of the heart of men, proceed evil thoughts, adulteries, fornications, murders,

22 Thefts, covetousness, wickedness, deceit, lasciviousness, an evil eye, blasphemy, pride, foolishness:

23 All these evil things come from within, and defile the man.

24 And from thence he arose, and went into the borders of Tyre and Sidon, and entered into an house, and would have no man know it: but he could not be hid.

25 For a certain woman, whose young daughter had an unclean spirit, heard of him, and came and fell at his feet:

26 The woman was a Greek, a Syrophenician by nation; and she besought him that he would cast forth the devil out of her daughter.

27 But Jesus said unto her, Let the children first be filled: for it is not meet to take the children's bread, and to cast it unto the dogs.

28 And she answered and said unto him, Yes, Lord: yet the dogs under the table eat of the children's crumbs.

29 And he said unto her, For this saying go thy way; the devil is gone out of thy daughter.

30 And when she was come to her house, she found the devil gone out, and her daughter laid upon the bed.

31 And again, departing from the coasts of Tyre and Sidon, he came unto the sea of Galilee, through the midst of the coasts of Decapolis.

32 And they bring unto him one that was deaf, and had an impediment in his speech; and they beseech him to put his hand upon him.

33 And he took him aside from the multitude, and put his fingers into his ears, and he spit, and touched his tongue;

34 And looking up to heaven, he sighed, and saith unto him, Ephphatha, that is, Be opened.

35 And straightway his ears were opened, and the string of his tongue was loosed, and he spake plain.

36 And he charged them that they should tell no man: but the more

19. Purging all meats – Probably the seat was usually placed over running water.

22. Wickedness – The word means ill natured, cruelty, inhumanity, and all malevolent affections. Foolishness – Directly contrary to sobriety of thought and discourse: all kind of wild imaginations and extravagant passions.

24. Matt. xv, 21.

26. The woman was a Greek (that is, a Gentile, not a Jew) a Syrophenician or Canaanite. Canaan was also called Syrophenicia, as lying between Syria, properly so called, and Phoenicia.

31. Matt. xv, 29.

33. He put his fingers into his ears – Perhaps intending to teach us, that we are not to prescribe to him (as they who brought this man attempted to do) but to expect his blessing by whatsoever means he pleases: even though there should be no proportion or resemblance between the means used, and the benefit to be conveyed thereby.

34. Ephphatha – This was a word of SOVEREIGN AUTHORITY, not an address to God for power to heal: such an address was needless; for Christ had a perpetual fund of power residing in himself, to work all miracles whenever he pleased, even to the raising the dead, John v, 21, 26.

36. Them – The blind man and those that brought him.

MARK 8

1. Matt. xv, 32.

8. So they did eat – This miracle was intended to demonstrate, that Christ was the true bread which cometh down from heaven; for he who was almighty to create bread without means to support natural life, could not want power to create bread without means to support spiritual life. And this heavenly bread we stand so much in need of every moment, that we ought to be always praying, Lord, evermore give us this bread.

11. Tempting him – That is, trying to ensnare him. Matt. xvi, 1.

12. Matt. xvi, 4.

15. Beware of the leaven of the Pharisees and of Herod, or of the Sadducees; two opposite extremes.

17, 18. Our Lord here affirms of all the apostles, (for the question is equivalent to an affirmation,) That their hearts were hardened; that having eyes they saw not, having ears they heard not; that they did not consider, neither understand: the very same expressions that occur in the thir-

and all the wicked words and actions that come from them. A spiritual understanding of the law of God, and a sense of the evil of sin, will cause a man to seek for the grace of the Holy Spirit, to keep down the evil thoughts and affections that work within.

24-30 Christ never put any from him that fell at his feet, which a poor trembling soul may do. As she was a good woman, so a good mother. This sent her to Christ. His saying, Let the children first be filled, shows that there was mercy for the Gentiles, and not far off. She spoke, not as making light of the mercy, but magnifying the abundance of miraculous cures among the Jews, in comparison with which a single cure was but as a crumb. Thus, while proud Pharisees are left by the blessed Savior, he manifests his compassion to poor humbled sinners, who look to him for children's bread. He still goes about to seek and save the lost.

31-37 Here is a cure of one that was deaf and dumb. Those who brought this poor man to Christ, besought him to observe the case, and put forth his power. Our Lord used more outward actions in the doing of this cure than usual. These were only signs of Christ's power to cure the man, to encourage his faith, and theirs that brought him. Though we find great variety in the cases and manner of relief of those who applied to Christ, yet all obtained the relief they sought. Thus it still is in the great concerns of our souls.

MARK 8

Four thousand fed by a miracle. (1-10)
Christ cautions against the Pharisees and Herodians. (11-21)
A blind man healed. (22-26)
Peter's testimony to Christ. (27-33)
Christ must be followed. (34-38)

1-10 Our Lord Jesus encouraged the meanest to come to him for life and grace. Christ knows and considers our frames. The bounty of Christ is always ready; to show that, he repeated this miracle. His favors are renewed, as our wants and necessities are. And those need not fear want, who have Christ to live upon by faith, and do so with thanksgiving.

11-21 Obstinate unbelief will have something to say, though ever so unreasonable. Christ refused to answer their demand. If they will not be convinced, they shall not. Alas! what cause we have to lament for those around us, who destroy themselves and others by their perverse and obstinate unbelief, and enmity to the gospel! When we forget the works of God, and distrust him, we should chide ourselves severely, as Christ here reproves his disciples. How is it that we so often mistake his meaning, disregard his warnings, and distrust his providence?

22-26 Here is a blind man brought to Christ by his friends. Therein appeared the faith of those that brought him. If those who are spiritually blind, do not pray for themselves,

compelled to say that they are a falsehood and a refuge of lies. You will find that you have been daubed with untempered mortar; that you have said, "Peace, peace," to yourselves, when there was no peace. Again, I say, in the words of Christ, "Repent and believe the gospel." Trust Christ to save you, and lament that you need to be saved, and mourn because this need of yours has put the Savior to open shame, to frightful sufferings, and to a terrible death.

III. But we must pass on to a third remark. These commands of Christ are of the most reasonable character.

Is it an unreasonable thing to demand of a man that he should repent? You have a person who has offended you; you are ready to forgive him; do you think it is at all exacting or overbearing if you ask of him an apology; if you merely ask him, as the very least thing he can do, to acknowledge that he has done wrong? "No," say you, "I should think I showed my kindness in accepting rather than any harshness in demanding an apology from him." So God, against whom we have rebelled, who is our liege sovereign and monarch, seeth it to be inconsistent with the dignity of his kingship to absolve an offender who expresseth no contrition; and I say again, is this a harsh, exacting, unreasonable command? Doth God in this mode act like Solomon, who made the taxes of his people heavy? Rather doth he not ask of you that which your heart, if it were in a right state, would be but too willing to give, only too thankful that the Lord in his grace has said, "He that confesseth his sin shall find mercy"? Why, dear friends, do you expect to be saved while you are in your sins? Are you to be allowed to love your iniquities, and yet go to heaven? What, you think to have poison in your veins, and yet be healthy? What, man, keep the thief in doors, and yet be acquitted of dishonesty? Be stained, and yet be thought spotless? Harbor the disease and yet be in health? Ridiculous! Absurd! Repentance is founded on the necessity of things. The demand for a change of heart is absolutely necessary; it is but a reasonable service. O that men were reasonable, and they would repent; it is because they are not reasonable that it needs the Holy Spirit to teach their reason right reason before they will repent and believe the gospel.

he charged them, so much the more a great deal they published it;

37 And were beyond measure astonished, saying, He hath done all things well: he maketh both the deaf to hear, and the dumb to speak.

MARK 8

1 In those days the multitude being very great, and having nothing to eat, Jesus called his disciples unto him, and saith unto them,

2 I have compassion on the multitude, because they have now been with me three days, and have nothing to eat:

3 And if I send them away fasting to their own houses, they will faint by the way: for divers of them came from far.

4 And his disciples answered him, From whence can a man satisfy these men with bread here in the wilderness?

5 And he asked them, How many loaves have ye? And they said, Seven.

6 And he commanded the people to sit down on the ground: and he took the seven loaves, and gave thanks, and brake, and gave to his disciples to set before them; and they did set them before the people.

7 And they had a few small fishes: and he blessed, and commanded to set them also before them.

8 So they did eat, and were filled: and they took up of the broken meat that was left seven baskets.

9 And they that had eaten were about four thousand: and he sent them away.

10 And straightway he entered into a ship with his disciples, and came into the parts of Dalmanutha.

11 And the Pharisees came forth, and began to question with him, seeking of him a sign from heaven, tempting him.

12 And he sighed deeply in his spirit, and saith, Why doth this generation seek after a sign? verily I say unto you, There shall no sign be given unto this generation.

13 And he left them, and entering into the ship again departed to the other side.

14 Now the disciples had forgotten to take bread, neither had they in the ship with them more than one loaf.

15 And he charged them, saying, Take heed, beware of the leaven of the Pharisees, and of the leaven of Herod.

16 And they reasoned among themselves, saying, It is because we have no bread.

17 And when Jesus knew it, he saith unto them, Why reason ye, because ye have no bread? perceive ye not yet, neither understand? have ye your heart yet hardened?

18 Having eyes, see ye not? and having ears, hear ye not? and do ye not remember?

19 When I brake the five loaves among five thousand, how many baskets full of fragments took ye up? They say unto him, Twelve.

20 And when the seven among four thousand, how many baskets full of fragments took ye up? And they said, Seven.

21 And he said unto them, How is it that ye do not understand?

22 And he cometh to Bethsaida; and they bring a blind man unto him, and besought him to touch him.

23 And he took the blind man by the hand, and led him out of the town; and when he had spit on his eyes, and put his hands upon him, he asked him if he saw ought.

24 And he looked up, and said, I see men as trees, walking.

25 After that he put his hands again upon his eyes, and made him look up: and he was restored, and saw every man clearly.

26 And he sent him away to his house, saying, Neither go into the town, nor tell it to any in the town.

27 And Jesus went out, and his disciples, into the towns of Cesarea Philippi: and by the way he asked his disciples, saying unto them, Whom do men say that I am?

teenth of Matthew. And yet it is certain they were not judicially hardened. Therefore all these strong expressions do not necessarily import any thing more than the present want of spiritual understanding.

23. He led him out of the town – It was in just displeasure against the inhabitants of Bethsaida for their obstinate infidelity, that our Lord would work no more miracles among them, nor even suffer the person he had cured, either to go into the town, or to tell it to any therein.

24. I see men as trees walking – He distinguished men from trees only by their motion.

27. Matt. xvi, 13; Luke ix, 18.

30. He enjoined them silence for the present,

1. That he might not encourage the people to set him up for a temporal king;

2. That he might not provoke the scribes and Pharisees to destroy him before the time and,

3. That he might not forestall the bright evidence which was to be given of his Divine character after his resurrection.

31. Matt. xvi, 21; Luke ix, 22.

32. He spake that saying openly – Or in express terms. Till now he had only intimated it to them. And Peter taking hold of him – Perhaps by the arms or clothes.

33. Looking on his disciples – That they might the more observe what he said to Peter.

34. And when he called the people – To hear a truth of the last importance, and one that equally concerned them all. Let him deny himself – His own will, in all things small and great, however pleasing, and that continually: And take up his cross – Embrace the will of God, however painful, daily, hourly, continually. Thus only can he follow me in holiness to glory.

35. Matt. xvi, 25; Luke ix, 24; Luke xvii, 33; John xii, 25.

38. Whosoever shall be ashamed of me and of my words – That is, avowing whatever I have said (particularly of self denial and the daily cross) both by word and action. Matt. x, 32; Luke ix, 26; Luke xii, 8.

MARK 9

1. Till they see the kingdom of God coming with power – So it began to do at the day of Pentecost, when three thousand were converted to God at once.

2. By themselves – That is, separate from the multitude: Apart – From the other apostles: and was transfigured – The Greek word seems to refer to the form of God, and the form of a servant, {mentioned by St. Paul, Phil. ii, 6, 7, } and

yet their friends and relations should pray for them, that Christ would be pleased to touch them. The cure was wrought gradually, which was not usual in our Lord's miracles. Christ showed in what method those commonly are healed by his grace, who by nature are spiritually blind. At first, their knowledge is confused; but, like the light of the morning, it shines more and more to the perfect day, and then they see all things clearly. Slighting Christ's favors is forfeiting them; and he will make those who do so know the worth of privileges by the want of them.

27-33 These things are written, that we may believe that Jesus is the Christ, the Son of God. These miracles of our Lord assure us that he was not conquered, but a Conqueror. Now the disciples are convinced that Jesus is the Christ; they may bear to hear of his sufferings, of which Christ here begins to give them notice. He sees that amiss in what we say and do, of which we ourselves are not aware, and knows what manner of spirit we are of, when we ourselves do not. The wisdom of man is folly, when it pretends to limit the Divine counsels. Peter did not rightly understand the nature of Christ's kingdom.

34-38 Frequent notice is taken of the great flocking there was to Christ for help in various cases. All are concerned to know this, if they expect him to heal their souls. They must not indulge the ease of the body. As the happiness of heaven with Christ, is enough to make up for the loss of life itself for him, so the gain of all the world in sin, will not make up for the ruin of the soul by sin. And there is a day coming, when the cause of Christ will appear as glorious, as some now think it mean and contemptible. May we think of that season, and view every earthly object as we shall do at that great day.

MARK 9

The transfiguration. (1-13)
An evil spirit cast out. (14-29)
The apostles reproved. (30-40)
Pain to be preferred to sin. (41-50)

1-13 Here is a prediction of the near approach of Christ's kingdom. A glimpse of that kingdom was given in the transfiguration of Christ. It is good to be away from the world, and alone with Christ: and how good to be with Christ glorified in heaven with all the saints! But when it is well with us, we are apt not to care for others, and in the fullness of our enjoyments, we forget the many wants of our brethren. God owns Jesus, and accepts him as his beloved Son, and is ready to accept us in him. Therefore we must own and accept him as our beloved Savior, and must give up ourselves to be ruled by him. Christ does not leave the soul, when joys and comforts leave it. Jesus explained to the disciples the prophecy about Elias. This was very suitable to the ill usage of John Baptist.

14-29 The father of the suffering youth reflected on the

And then, again, believing; is that an unreasonable thing to ask of you? For a creature to believe its Creator is but a duty; altogether apart from the promise of salvation, I say, God has a right to demand of the creature that he has made, that he should believe what he tells him. And what is it he asks you to believe? Anything hideous, contradictory, irrational? It may be above reason, but it is not contrary to reason. He asks you to believe that through the blood of Jesus Christ, he can still be just, and yet the justifier of the ungodly. He asks you to trust in Christ to save you. Can you expect that he will save you if you will not trust him? Have you really the hardihood to think that he will carry you to heaven while all the while you declare he cannot do it? Do you think it consistent with the dignity of a Savior to save you while you say, "I do not believe thou art a Savior, and I will not trust thee"? Is it consistent with his dignity for him to save you, and suffer you to remain an unbelieving sinner, doubting his grace, mistrusting his love, slandering his character, doubting the efficacy of his blood, and of his plea? Why, man, it is the most reasonable thing in the world that he should demand of thee that thou shouldst believe in Christ. And this he doth demand of thee this morning. "Repent and believe the gospel." O friends, O friends, how sad, how sad is the state of man's soul when he will not do this! We may preach to you, but you never will repent and believe the gospel. We may lay God's command, like an axe, to the root of the tree, but, reasonable as these commands are, you will still refuse to give God his due; you will go on in your sins; you will not come unto him that you may have life; and it is here the Spirit of God must come in to work in the souls of the elect to make them willing in the day of his power. But oh! in God's name I warn you that, if, after hearing this command, you do, as I know you will do, without his Spirit, continue to refuse obedience to so reasonable a gospel, you shall find at the last it shall be more tolerable for Sodom and Gomorrah, than for you; for had the things which are preached in London been proclaimed in Sodom and Gomorrah, they would have repented long ago in sackcloth and in ashes. Woe unto you, inhabitants of London! Woe unto you, subjects of the British Empire! for if the truths which have been declared in your streets

28 And they answered, John the Baptist: but some say, Elias; and others, One of the prophets.

29 And he saith unto them, But whom say ye that I am? And Peter answereth and saith unto him, Thou art the Christ.

30 And he charged them that they should tell no man of him.

31 And he began to teach them, that the Son of man must suffer many things, and be rejected of the elders, and of the chief priests, and scribes, and be killed, and after three days rise again.

32 And he spake that saying openly. And Peter took him, and began to rebuke him.

33 But when he had turned about and looked on his disciples, he rebuked Peter, saying, Get thee behind me, Satan: for thou savorest not the things that be of God, but the things that be of men.

34 And when he had called the people unto him with his disciples also, he said unto them, Whosoever will come after me, let him deny himself, and take up his cross, and follow me.

35 For whosoever will save his life shall lose it; but whosoever shall lose his life for my sake and the gospel's, the same shall save it.

36 For what shall it profit a man, if he shall gain the whole world, and lose his own soul?

37 Or what shall a man give in exchange for his soul?

38 Whosoever therefore shall be ashamed of me and of my words in this adulterous and sinful generation; of him also shall the Son of man be ashamed, when he cometh in the glory of his Father with the holy angels.

MARK 9

1 And he said unto them, Verily I say unto you, That there be some of them that stand here, which shall not taste of death, till they have seen the kingdom of God come with power.

2 And after six days Jesus taketh with him Peter, and James, and John, and leadeth them up into an high mountain apart by themselves: and he was transfigured before them.

3 And his raiment became shining, exceeding white as snow; so as no fuller on earth can white them.

4 And there appeared unto them Elias with Moses: and they were talking with Jesus.

5 And Peter answered and said to Jesus, Master, it is good for us to be here: and let us make three tabernacles; one for thee, and one for Moses, and one for Elias.

6 For he wist not what to say; for they were sore afraid.

7 And there was a cloud that overshadowed them: and a voice came out of the cloud, saying, This is my beloved Son: hear him.

8 And suddenly, when they had looked round about, they saw no man any more, save Jesus only with themselves.

9 And as they came down from the mountain, he charged them that they should tell no man what things they had seen, till the Son of man were risen from the dead.

10 And they kept that saying with themselves, questioning one with another what the rising from the dead should mean.

11 And they asked him, saying, Why say the scribes that Elias must first come?

12 And he answered and told them, Elias verily cometh first, and restoreth all things; and how it is written of the Son of man, that he must suffer many things, and be set at nought.

13 But I say unto you, That Elias is indeed come, and they have done unto him whatsoever they listed, as it is written of him.

14 And when he came to his disciples, he saw a great multitude about them, and the scribes questioning with them.

15 And straightway all the people, when they beheld him, were greatly amazed, and running to him saluted him.

16 And he asked the scribes, What question ye with them?

17 And one of the multitude answered and said, Master, I have

may intimate, that the Divine rays, which the indwelling God let out on this occasion, made the glorious change from one of these forms into the other. Matt. xvii, 1; Luke ix, 28.

3. White as snow, such as no fuller can whiten – Such as could not be equaled either by nature or art.

4. Elijah – Whom they expected: Moses, whom they did not.

7. There came a (bright, luminous) cloud, overshadowing them – This seems to have been such a cloud of glory as accompanied Israel in the wilderness, which, as the Jewish writers observe, departed at the death of Moses. But it now appeared again, in honor of our Lord, as the great Prophet of the Church, who was prefigured by Moses. Hear ye him – Even preferably to Moses and Elijah.

12. Elijah verily coming first restoreth all things: and how it is written – That is, And he told them how it is written – As if he had said, Elijah's coming is not inconsistent with my suffering. He is come: yet I shall suffer. The first part of the verse answers their question concerning Elijah; the second refutes their error concerning the Messiah's continuing for ever.

14. Matt. xvii, 14; Luke ix, 37.

15. All the multitude seeing him were greatly amazed – At his coming so suddenly, so seasonably, so unexpectedly: perhaps also at some unusual rays of majesty and glory, which yet remained on his countenance.

17. And one of the multitude answering – The scribes gave no answer to our Lord's question. They did not care to repeat what they had said to his disciples. A dumb spirit – A spirit that takes his speech from him.

20. When he saw him – When the child saw Christ; when his deliverance was at hand. Immediately the spirit tore him – Made his last grand effort to destroy him. Is it not generally so, before Satan is cast out of a soul, of which he has long had possession?

22. If thou canst do any thing – In so desperate a case: Have compassion on us – Me as well as him.

23. If thou canst believe – As if he had said, The thing does not turn on my power, but on thy faith. I can do all things: canst thou believe?

24. Help thou mine unbelief – Although my faith be so small, that it might rather be termed unbelief, yet help me.

25. Thou deaf and dumb spirit – So termed, because he made the child so. When Jesus spake, the devil heard, though the child could not. I command thee – I myself now; not my disciples.

want of power in the disciples; but Christ will have him reckon the disappointment to the want of faith. Very much is promised to our believing. If thou canst believe, it is possible that thy hard heart may be softened, thy spiritual diseases may be cured; and, weak as thou art, thou mayest be able to hold out to the end. Those that complain of unbelief, must look up to Christ for grace to help them against it, and his grace will be sufficient for them. Whom Christ cures, he cures effectually. But Satan is unwilling to be driven from those that have been long his slaves, and, when he cannot deceive or destroy the sinner, he will cause him all the terror that he can. The disciples must not think to do their work always with the same ease; some services call for more than ordinary pains.

30-40 The time of Christ's suffering drew nigh. Had he been delivered into the hands of devils, and they had done this, it had not been so strange; but that men should thus shamefully treat the Son of man, who came to redeem and save them, is wonderful. Still observe that when Christ spake of his death, he always spake of his resurrection, which took the reproach of it from himself, and should have taken the grief of it from his disciples. Many remain ignorant because they are ashamed to inquire. Alas! that while the Savior teaches so plainly the things which belong to his love and grace, men are so blinded that they understand not his sayings. We shall be called to account about our discourses, and to account for our disputes, especially about being greater than others. Those who are most humble and self-denying, most resemble Christ, and shall be most tenderly owned by him. This Jesus taught them by a sign; whoever shall receive one like this child, receives me. Many have been like the disciples, ready to silence men who have success in preaching to sinners repentance in Christ's name, because they follow not with them. Our Lord blamed the apostles, reminding them that he who wrought miracles in his name would not be likely to hurt his cause. If sinners are brought to repent, to believe in the Savior, and to live sober, righteous, and godly lives, we then see that the Lord works by the preacher.

41-50 It is repeatedly said of the wicked, Their worm dieth not, as well as, The fire is never quenched. Doubtless, remorse of conscience and keen self-reflection are this never-dying worm. Surely it is beyond compare better to undergo all possible pain, hardship, and self-denial here, and to be happy for ever hereafter, than to enjoy all kinds of worldly pleasure for a season, and to be miserable for ever. Like the sacrifices, we must be salted with salt; our corrupt affections must be subdued and mortified by the Holy Spirit. Those that have the salt of grace, must show they have a living principle of grace in their hearts, which works out corrupt dispositions in the soul that would offend God, or our own consciences.

MARK 10

The Pharisees' question concerning divorce. (1-12)
Christ's love to little children. (13-16)

had been preached to Tyre and Sidon, they would have continued even unto this day.

IV. But still, to pass on, I have yet a fourth remark to make, and that is, this is a command which demands immediate obedience. I do not know how it is, let us preach as we may, we cannot lead others to think that there is any great alarm, that there is any reason why they should think about their souls now. Last night there was a review on Wimbledon Common, and living not very far away from it, I could hear in one perpetual roll the cracks of the rifles and the thunder of cannon. One remarked to me, "Supposing there really were war there, we should not sit quite so comfortably in our room with our window open, listening to all this noise." No; and so when people come to chapel, they hear a sermon about repentance and faith; they listen to it. "What do you think of it?" "Oh—very well." But suppose it were real; suppose they believed it to be real, would they sit quite so comfortably? Would they be quite so easy? Ah, no! But you do not think it is real. You do not think that the God who made you actually asks of you this day that you should repent and believe. Yes, sirs, but it is real, and it is your procrastination, it is your self-confidence that is the sham, the bubble that is soon to burst. God's demand is the solemn reality, and if you could but hear it as it should be heard you would escape from your lives and flee for refuge to the hope that is set before you in the gospel, and you would do this today. This is the command of Christ, I say, today. Today is God's time. "Today if ye will hear his voice, harden not your heart, as in the provocation." "Today," the gospel always cries, for if it tolerated sin a single day, it were an unholy gospel. If the gospel told men to repent of sin tomorrow, it would give them an allowance to continue in it today, and that would indeed be to pander to men's lusts. But the gospel maketh a clean sweep of sin, and demandeth of man that he should throw down the weapons of his rebellion now. Down with them, man! every one of them. Down, sir, down with them, and down with them now! You must not keep one of them; throw them down at once! The gospel challengeth him that he believe in Jesus now. So long as thou continuest in unbelief thou continuest in sin, and art increas-

brought unto thee my son, which hath a dumb spirit;

18 And wheresoever he taketh him, he teareth him: and he foameth, and gnasheth with his teeth, and pineth away: and I spake to thy disciples that they should cast him out; and they could not.

19 He answereth him, and saith, O faithless generation, how long shall I be with you? how long shall I suffer you? bring him unto me.

20 And they brought him unto him: and when he saw him, straightway the spirit tare him; and he fell on the ground, and wallowed foaming.

21 And he asked his father, How long is it ago since this came unto him? And he said, Of a child.

22 And ofttimes it hath cast him into the fire, and into the waters, to destroy him: but if thou canst do any thing, have compassion on us, and help us.

23 Jesus said unto him, If thou canst believe, all things are possible to him that believeth.

24 And straightway the father of the child cried out, and said with tears, Lord, I believe; help thou mine unbelief.

25 When Jesus saw that the people came running together, he rebuked the foul spirit, saying unto him, Thou dumb and deaf spirit, I charge thee, come out of him, and enter no more into him.

26 And the spirit cried, and rent him sore, and came out of him: and he was as one dead; insomuch that many said, He is dead.

27 But Jesus took him by the hand, and lifted him up; and he arose.

28 And when he was come into the house, his disciples asked him privately, Why could not we cast him out?

29 And he said unto them, This kind can come forth by nothing, but by prayer and fasting.

30 And they departed thence, and passed through Galilee; and he would not that any man should know it.

31 For he taught his disciples, and said unto them, The Son of man is delivered into the hands of men, and they shall kill him; and after that he is killed, he shall rise the third day.

32 But they understood not that saying, and were afraid to ask him.

33 And he came to Capernaum: and being in the house he asked them, What was it that ye disputed among yourselves by the way?

34 But they held their peace: for by the way they had disputed among themselves, who should be the greatest.

35 And he sat down, and called the twelve, and saith unto them, If any man desire to be first, the same shall be last of all, and servant of all.

36 And he took a child, and set him in the midst of them: and when he had taken him in his arms, he said unto them,

37 Whosoever shall receive one of such children in my name, receiveth me: and whosoever shall receive me, receiveth not me, but him that sent me.

38 And John answered him, saying, Master, we saw one casting out devils in thy name, and he followeth not us: and we forbad him, because he followeth not us.

39 But Jesus said, Forbid him not: for there is no man which shall do a miracle in my name, that can lightly speak evil of me.

40 For he that is not against us is on our part.

41 For whosoever shall give you a cup of water to drink in my name, because ye belong to Christ, verily I say unto you, he shall not lose his reward.

42 And whosoever shall offend one of these little ones that believe in me, it is better for him that a millstone were hanged about his neck, and he were cast into the sea.

43 And if thy hand offend thee, cut it off: it is better for thee to enter into life maimed, than having two hands to go into hell, into the fire that never shall be quenched:

44 Where their worm dieth not, and the fire is not quenched.

45 And if thy foot offend thee, cut it off: it is better for thee to enter halt into life, than having two feet to be cast into hell, into the fire that never shall be quenched:

26. Having rent him sore – So does even the body sometimes suffer, when God comes to deliver the soul from Satan.

30. They passed through Galilee – Though not through the cities, but by them, in the most private ways. He was not willing that any should know it: for he taught his disciples – He wanted to be alone with them some time, in order to instruct them fully concerning his sufferings. The Son of man is delivered – It is as sure as if it were done already. Matt. xvii, 22; Luke ix, 44.

32. They understood not the word – They did not understand how to reconcile the death of our Savior (nor consequently his resurrection, which supposed his death) with their notions of his temporal kingdom.

33. Luke ix, 46.

34. Who should be greatest – Prime minister in his kingdom.

35. Let him be the least of all – Let him abase himself the most.

36. Matt. xviii, 2; Luke ix, 47.

37. One such little child – Either in years or in heart.

38. And John answered him – As if he had said, But ought we to receive those who follow not us? Master, we saw one casting out devils in thy name – Probably this was one of John the Baptist's disciples, who believed in Jesus, though he did not yet associate with our Lord's disciples. And we forbad him, because he followeth not us – How often is the same temper found in us! How readily do we also lust to envy? But how does that spirit become a disciple, much more a minister of the benevolent Jesus! St. Paul had learnt a better temper, when he rejoiced that Christ was preached, even by those who were his personal enemies. But to confine religion to them that follow us, is a narrowness of spirit which we should avoid and abhor. Luke ix, 49.

39. Jesus said – Christ here gives us a lovely example of candor and moderation. He was willing to put the best construction on doubtful cases, and to treat as friends those who were not avowed enemies. Perhaps in this instance it was a means of conquering the remainder of prejudice, and perfecting what was wanting in the faith and obedience of these persons. Forbid him not – Neither directly nor indirectly discourage or hinder any man who brings sinners from the power of Satan to God, because he followeth not us, in opinions, modes of worship, or any thing else which does not affect the essence of religion.

40. For he that is not against you, is for you – Our Lord had formerly said, he that is not with me, is against me: thereby admonishing his hear-

Christ's discourse with the rich young man. (17-22)
The hindrance of riches. (23-31)
Christ foretells his sufferings. (32-45)
Bartimeus healed. (46-52)

1-12 Wherever Jesus was, the people flocked after him in crowds, and he taught them. Preaching was Christ's constant practice. He here shows that the reason why Moses' law allowed divorce, was such that they ought not to use the permission; it was only for the hardness of their hearts. God himself joined man and wife together; he has fitted them to be comforts and helps for each other. The bond which God has tied, is not to be lightly untied. Let those who are for putting away their wives consider what would become of themselves, if God should deal with them in like manner.

13-16 Some parents or nurses brought little children to Christ, that he should touch them, in token of his blessing them. It does not appear that they needed bodily cures, nor were they capable of being taught: but those who had the care of them believed that Christ's blessing would do their souls good; therefore they brought them to him. Jesus ordered that they should be brought to him, and that nothing should be said or done to hinder it. Children should be directed to the Savior as soon as they are able to understand his words. Also, we must receive the kingdom of God as little children; we must stand affected to Christ and his grace, as little children to their parents, nurses, and teachers.

17-22 This young ruler showed great earnestness. He asked what he should do now, that he might be happy forever. Most ask for good to be had in this world; any good, Ps 4:6; he asks for good to be done in this world, in order to enjoy the greatest good in the other world. Christ encouraged this address by assisting his faith, and by directing his practice. But here is a sorrowful parting between Jesus and this young man. He asks Christ what he shall do more than he has done, to obtain eternal life; and Christ puts it to him, whether he has indeed that firm belief of, and that high value for eternal life which he seems to have. Is he willing to bear a present cross, in expectation of a future crown? The young man was sorry he could not be a follower of Christ upon easier terms; that he could not lay hold on eternal life, and keep hold of his worldly possessions too. He went away grieved. See Mt 6:24, Ye cannot serve God and mammon.

23-31 Christ took this occasion to speak to his disciples about the difficulty of the salvation of those who have abundance of this world. Those who thus eagerly seek the wealth of the world, will never rightly prize Christ and his grace. Also, as to the greatness of the salvation of those who have but little of this world, and leave it for Christ. The greatest trial of a good man's constancy is, when love to Jesus calls him to give up love to friends and relatives. Even when gainers by Christ, let them still expect to suffer for him, till they reach heaven. Let us learn contentment in a low state, and to watch against the love of riches in a high one. Let us pray to be enabled to part with all, if required,

ing thy sin; and to give thee leave to be an unbeliever for an hour, were to pander to thy lusts; therefore it demandeth of thee faith, and faith now, for this is God's time, and the time which holiness must demand of a sinner. Besides, sinner, it is thy time. This is the only time thou canst call thine own. To-morrow! Is there such a thing? In what calendar is it written save in the almanack of the fool? To-morrow! Oh, how hast thou ruined multitudes! "To-morrow," say men; but like the hind-wheel of a chariot, they are always near to the front-wheel, always near to their duty; they still go on, and on, but never get one whit the nearer, for, travel as they may, tomorrow is still a little beyond them—but a little, and so they never come to Christ at all. This is how they speak, as an ancient poet said—

"'I will tomorrow, that I will, I will be
sure to do it';
To-morrow comes, tomorrow goes,
And still thou art 'to do it';
Thus, then, repentance is deferred
from one day to another,
Until the day of death is one, And
judgment is the other."

O sons of men, always to be blessed, to be obedient, but never obedient, when will ye learn to be wise? This is your only time; it is God's time, and this is the best time. You will never find it easier to repent than now; you will never find it easier to believe than now. It is impossible now except the Spirit of God be with you; it will be as impossible tomorrow; but if now you would believe and repent, the Spirit of God is in the gospel which I preach; and while I cry out to thee in God's name, "Repent and believe," he that bade me command you thus to do gives power with the command, that even as Christ spake to the waves and said, "Be still," and they were still, and to the winds, "Be calm,", and they were quiet, so when we speak to your proud heart it yields because of the grace that accompanies the word, and you repent and believe the gospel. So may it be, and may the message of this morning gather out the elect, and make them willing in the day of God's power.

But now, lastly, this command, while it has an immediate power, has also a continual force. "Repent ye, and believe the gospel," is advice to the young beginner, and it is advice to the old gray-headed Christian, for this is our life all the way through—"Repent ye, and believe the

46 Where their worm dieth not, and the fire is not quenched.

47 And if thine eye offend thee, pluck it out: it is better for thee to enter into the kingdom of God with one eye, than having two eyes to be cast into hell fire:

48 Where their worm dieth not, and the fire is not quenched.

49 For every one shall be salted with fire, and every sacrifice shall be salted with salt.

50 Salt is good: but if the salt have lost his saltness, wherewith will ye season it? Have salt in yourselves, and have peace one with another.

MARK 10

1 And he arose from thence, and cometh into the coasts of Judea by the farther side of Jordan: and the people resort unto him again; and, as he was wont, he taught them again.

2 And the Pharisees came to him, and asked him, Is it lawful for a man to put away his wife? tempting him.

3 And he answered and said unto them, What did Moses command you?

4 And they said, Moses suffered to write a bill of divorcement, and to put her away.

5 And Jesus answered and said unto them, For the hardness of your heart he wrote you this precept.

6 But from the beginning of the creation God made them male and female.

7 For this cause shall a man leave his father and mother, and cleave to his wife;

8 And they twain shall be one flesh: so then they are no more twain, but one flesh.

9 What therefore God hath joined together, let not man put asunder.

10
And in the house his disciples asked him again of the same matter.

11 And he saith unto them, Whosoever shall put away his wife, and marry another, committeth adultery against her.

12 And if a woman shall put away her husband, and be married to another, she committeth adultery.

13 And they brought young children to him, that he should touch them: and his disciples rebuked those that brought them.

14 But when Jesus saw it, he was much displeased, and said unto them, Suffer the little children to come unto me, and forbid them not: for of such is the kingdom of God.

15 Verily I say unto you, Whosoever shall not receive the kingdom of God as a little child, he shall not enter therein.

16 And he took them up in his arms, put his hands upon them, and blessed them.

17 And when he was gone forth into the way, there came one running, and kneeled to him, and asked him, Good Master, what shall I do that I may inherit eternal life?

18 And Jesus said unto him, Why callest thou me good? there is none good but one, that is, God.

19 Thou knowest the commandments, Do not commit adultery, Do not kill, Do not steal, Do not bear false witness, Defraud not, Honor thy father and mother.

20 And he answered and said unto him, Master, all these have I observed from my youth.

21 Then Jesus beholding him loved him, and said unto him, One thing thou lackest: go thy way, sell whatsoever thou hast, and give to the poor, and thou shalt have treasure in heaven: and come, take up the cross, and follow me.

22 And he was sad at that saying, and went away grieved: for he had great possessions.

23 And Jesus looked round about, and saith unto his disciples, How hardly shall they that have riches enter into the kingdom of God!

24 And the disciples were astonished at his words. But Jesus

ers, that the war between him and Satan admitted of no neutrality, and that those who were indifferent to him now, would finally be treated as enemies. But here in another view, he uses a very different proverb; directing his followers to judge of men's characters in the most candid manner; and charitably to hope that those who did not oppose his cause wished well to it. Upon the whole, we are to be rigorous in judging ourselves, and candid in judging each other.

41. For whosoever shall give you a cup – Having answered St. John, our Lord here resumes the discourse which was broken off at the 37th verse. Mark ix, 37. Matt. x, 42.

42. On the contrary, whosoever shall offend the very least Christian. Matt. xviii, 6; Luke xvii, 1.

43. And if a person cause thee to offend – (The discourse passes from the case of offending, to that of being offended) if one who is as useful or dear to thee as a hand or eye, hinder or slacken thee in the ways of God, renounce all intercourse with him. This primarily relates to persons, secondarily to things. Matt. v, 29; Matt. xviii, 8.

44. Where their worm – That gnaweth the soul, (pride, self will, desire, malice, envy, shame, sorrow, despair,) dieth not – No more than the soul itself: and the fire (either material, or infinitely worse!) that tormenteth the body, is not quenched for ever. Isaiah lxvi, 24.

49. Every one – Who does not cut off the offending member, and consequently is cast into hell, shall be, as it were, salted with fire, preserved, not consumed thereby whereas every acceptable sacrifice shall be salted with another kind of salt, even that of Divine grace, which purifies the soul, (though frequently with pain) and preserves it from corruption.

50. Such salt is good indeed; highly beneficial to the world, in respect of which I have termed you the salt of the earth. But if the salt which should season others, have lost its own saltiness, wherewith will ye season it? – Beware of this; see that ye retain your savor; and as a proof of it, have peace one with another. More largely this obscure text might be paraphrased thus: As every burnt offering was salted with salt, in order to its being cast into the fire of the altar, so every one who will not part with his hand or eye, shall fall a sacrifice to Divine justice, and be cast into hell fire, which will not consume, but preserve him from a cessation of being. And on the other hand, every one, who, denying himself and taking up his cross, offers up himself as a living sacrifice to God, shall be seasoned with grace, which like salt will make him savory, and preserve him from destruction for ever. As salt is good for pre-

in Christ's service, and to use all we are allowed to keep in his service.

32-45 Christ's going on with his undertaking for the salvation of mankind, was, is, and will be, the wonder of all his disciples. Worldly honor is a glittering thing, with which the eyes of Christ's own disciples have many times been dazzled. Our care must be, that we may have wisdom and grace to know how to suffer with him; and we may trust him to provide what the degrees of our glory shall be. Christ shows them that dominion was generally abused in the world. If Jesus would gratify all our desires, it would soon appear that we desire fame or authority, and are unwilling to taste of his cup, or to have his baptism; and should often be ruined by having our prayers answered. But he loves us, and will only give his people what is good for them.

46-52 Bartimeus had heard of Jesus and his miracles, and learning that he was passing by, hoped to recover his eyesight. In coming to Christ for help and healing, we should look to him as the promised Messiah. The gracious calls Christ gives us to come to him, encourage our hope, that if we come to him we shall have what we come for. Those who would come to Jesus, must cast away the garment of their own sufficiency, must free themselves from every weight, and the sin that, like long garments, most easily besets them, Heb 12:1. He begged that his eyes might be opened. It is very desirable to be able to earn our bread; and where God has given men limbs and senses, it is a shame, by foolishness and slothfulness, to make themselves, in effect, blind and lame. His eyes were opened. Thy faith has made thee whole: faith in Christ as the Son of David, and in his pity and power; not thy repeated words, but thy faith; Christ setting thy faith to work. Let sinners be exhorted to imitate blind Bartimeus. Where the gospel is preached, or the written words of truth circulated, Jesus is passing by, and this is the opportunity. It is not enough to come to Christ for spiritual healing, but, when we are healed, we must continue to follow him; that we may honor him, and receive instruction from him. Those who have spiritual eyesight, see that beauty in Christ which will draw them to run after him.

MARK 11

Christ's triumphant entry into Jerusalem. (1-11)
The barren fig tree cursed. The temple cleansed. (12-18)
Prayer in faith. (19-26)
The priests and elders questioned concerning John the Baptist. (27-33)

1-11 Christ's coming into Jerusalem thus remarkably, shows that he was not afraid of the power and malice of his enemies. This would encourage his disciples who were full of fear. Also, that he was not disquieted at the thoughts of his approaching sufferings. But all marked his humiliation; and these matters teach us not to mind high things, but to condescend to those of low estate. How ill it becomes Christians to take state, when Christ was so far from claim-

gospel." St. Anselm, who was a saint—and that is more than many of them were who were called so—St. Anselm once cried out "Oh! sinner that I have been, I will spend all the rest of my life in repenting of my whole life!" And Rowland Hill, whom I think I might call St. Rowland, when he was near death, said he had one regret, and that was that a dear friend who had lived with him for sixty years would have to leave him at the gate of heaven. "That dear friend," said he, "is repentance; repentance has been with me all my life, and I think I shall drop a tear," said the good man, "as I go through the gates, to think that I can repent no more." Repentance is the daily and hourly duty of a man who believes in Christ; and as we walk by faith from the wicket gate to the celestial city, so our right-hand companion all the journey through must be repentance. Why, dear friend, the Christian man, after he is saved, repents more than he ever did before, for now he repents not merely of overt deeds, but even of imaginations. He will take himself to task at night, and chide himself because he had tolerated one foul thought; because he has looked on vanity, though perhaps the heart had gone no further than the look of lust; because the thought of evil has flitted through the mind—for all this he will vex himself before God; and were it not that he still continues to believe the gospel, one foul imagination would be such a plague and sting to him, that he would have no peace and rest. When temptation comes to him the good man finds the use of repentance, for having hated sin and fled from it of old, he has ceased to be what he once was. One of the ancient fathers, we are told, had, before his conversion, lived with an ill woman, and some little time after, she accosted him as usual. Knowing how likely he was to fall into sin he ran away with all his might, and she ran after him, crying, "Wherefore runnest thou away? It is I." He answered, "I run away because I am not I; I am a new man." Now, it is just that, "I am not I," which keeps the Christian out of sin; that hating of the former "I," that repenting of the old sin that maketh him run from evil, abhor it, and look not upon it, lest by his eyes he should be led into sin. Dear friend, the more the Christian man knows of Christ's love, the more will he hate himself to think that he has sinned against such love. Every doctrine of the gospel will make a Christian

answereth again, and saith unto them, Children, how hard is it for them that trust in riches to enter into the kingdom of God!

25 It is easier for a camel to go through the eye of a needle, than for a rich man to enter into the kingdom of God.

26 And they were astonished out of measure, saying among themselves, Who then can be saved?

27 And Jesus looking upon them saith, With men it is impossible, but not with God: for with God all things are possible.

28 Then Peter began to say unto him, Lo, we have left all, and have followed thee.

29 And Jesus answered and said, Verily I say unto you, There is no man that hath left house, or brethren, or sisters, or father, or mother, or wife, or children, or lands, for my sake, and the gospel's,

30 But he shall receive an hundredfold now in this time, houses, and brethren, and sisters, and mothers, and children, and lands, with persecutions; and in the world to come eternal life.

31 But many that are first shall be last; and the last first.

32 And they were in the way going up to Jerusalem; and Jesus went before them: and they were amazed; and as they followed, they were afraid. And he took again the twelve, and began to tell them what things should happen unto him,

33 Saying, Behold, we go up to Jerusalem; and the Son of man shall be delivered unto the chief priests, and unto the scribes; and they shall condemn him to death, and shall deliver him to the Gentiles:

34 And they shall mock him, and shall scourge him, and shall spit upon him, and shall kill him: and the third day he shall rise again.

35 And James and John, the sons of Zebedee, come unto him, saying, Master, we would that thou shouldest do for us whatsoever we shall desire.

36 And he said unto them, What would ye that I should do for you?

37 They said unto him, Grant unto us that we may sit, one on thy right hand, and the other on thy left hand, in thy glory.

38 But Jesus said unto them, Ye know not what ye ask: can ye drink of the cup that I drink of? and be baptized with the baptism that I am baptized with?

39 And they said unto him, We can. And Jesus said unto them, Ye shall indeed drink of the cup that I drink of; and with the baptism that I am baptized withal shall ye be baptized:

40 But to sit on my right hand and on my left hand is not mine to give; but it shall be given to them for whom it is prepared.

41 And when the ten heard it, they began to be much displeased with James and John.

42 But Jesus called them to him, and saith unto them, Ye know that they which are accounted to rule over the Gentiles exercise lordship over them; and their great ones exercise authority upon them.

43 But so shall it not be among you: but whosoever will be great among you, shall be your minister:

44 And whosoever of you will be the chiefest, shall be servant of all.

45 For even the Son of man came not to be ministered unto, but to minister, and to give his life a ransom for many.

46 And they came to Jericho: and as he went out of Jericho with his disciples and a great number of people, blind Bartimeus, the son of Timaeus, sat by the highway side begging.

47 And when he heard that it was Jesus of Nazareth, he began to cry out, and say, Jesus, thou Son of David, have mercy on me.

48 And many charged him that he should hold his peace: but he cried the more a great deal, Thou Son of David, have mercy on me.

49 And Jesus stood still, and commanded him to be called. And they call the blind man, saying unto him, Be of good comfort, rise; he calleth thee.

50 And he, casting away his garment, rose, and came to Jesus.

51 And Jesus answered and said unto him, What wilt thou that I should do unto thee? The blind man said unto him, Lord, that I might receive my sight.

serving meats, and making them savory, so it is good that ye be seasoned with grace, for the purifying your hearts and lives, and for spreading the savor of my knowledge, both in your own souls, and wherever ye go. But as salt if it loses its saltiness is fit for nothing, so ye, if ye lose your faith and love, are fit for nothing but to be utterly destroyed. See therefore that grace abide in you, and that ye no more contend, Who shall be greatest. Matt. v, 13; Luke xiv, 34.

MARK 10

1. He cometh thence – From Galilee. Matt. xix, 1.

2. Matt. v, 31; Matt. xix, 7; Luke xvi, 18.

4. Deut. xxiv, 1.

6. From the beginning of the creation – Therefore Moses in the first of Genesis gives us an account of things from the beginning of the creation. Does it not clearly follow, that there was no creation previous to that which Moses describes? God made them male and female – Therefore Adam did not at first contain both sexes in himself: but God made Adam, when first created, male only; and Eve female only. And this man and woman he joined together, in a state of innocence, as husband and wife.

7. Gen. ii, 24.

11, 12. All polygamy is here totally condemned.

13. Matt. xix, 13.

14. Jesus seeing it was much displeased – At their blaming those who were not blame worthy: and endeavoring to hinder the children from receiving a blessing. Of such is the kingdom of God – The members of the kingdom which I am come to set up in the world are such as these, as well as grown persons, of a child-like temper.

15. Whosoever shall not receive the kingdom of God as a little child – As totally disclaiming all worthiness and fitness, as if he were but a week old.

17. Matt. xix, 16; Luke xviii, 18.

20. He answering, said to him, Master – He stands reproved now, and drops the epithet good.

21. Jesus looking upon him – And looking into his heart, loved him – Doubtless for the dawnings of good which he saw in him: and said to him – Out of tender love, One thing thou lackest – The love of God, without which all religion is a dead carcass. In order to this, throw away what is to thee the grand hindrance of it. Give up thy great idol, riches. Go, sell whatsoever thou hast.

24. Jesus saith to them, Children – See how he softens the harsh truth, by the manner of deliv-

ing it! They welcomed his person; Blessed is he that cometh, the "He that should come," so often promised, so long expected; he comes in the name of the Lord. Let him have our best affections; he is a blessed Savior, and brings blessings to us, and blessed be He that sent him. Praises be to our God, who is in the highest heavens, over all, God blessed forever.

12-18 Christ looked to find some fruit, for the time of gathering figs, though it was near, was not yet come; but he found none. He made this fig tree an example, not to the trees, but to the men of that generation. It was a figure of the doom upon the Jewish church, to which he came seeking fruit, but found none. Christ went to the temple, and began to reform the abuses in its courts, to show that when the Redeemer came to Zion, it was to turn away ungodliness from Jacob. The scribes and the chief priests sought, not how they might make their peace with him, but how they might destroy him. A desperate attempt, which they could not but fear was fighting against God.

19-26 The disciples could not think why that fig tree should so soon wither away; but all wither who reject Christ; it represented the state of the Jewish church. We should rest in no religion that does not make us fruitful in good works. Christ taught them from hence to pray in faith. It may be applied to that mighty faith with which all true Christians are endued, and which does wonders in spiritual things. It justifies us, and so removes mountains of guilt, never to rise up in judgment against us. It purifies the heart, and so removes mountains of corruption, and makes them plain before the grace of God. One great errand to the throne of grace is to pray for the pardon of our sins; and care about this ought to be our daily concern.

27-33 Our Savior shows how near akin his doctrine and baptism were to those of John; they had the same design and tendency, to bring in the gospel kingdom. These elders did not deserve to be taught; for it was plain that they contended not for truth, but victory: nor did he need to tell them; for the works he did, told them plainly he had authority from God; since no man could do the miracles which he did, unless God were with him.

MARK 12

The parable of the vineyard and husbandmen. (1-12)
Question about tribute. (13-17)
Concerning the resurrection. (18-27)
The great command of the law. (28-34)
Christ the Son and yet the Lord of David. (35-40)
The poor widow commended. (41-44)

1-12 Christ showed in parables, that he would lay aside the Jewish church. It is sad to think what base usage God's faithful ministers have met with in all ages, from those who have enjoyed the privileges of the church, but have not brought forth fruit answerable. God at length sent his Son, his Well beloved; and it might be expected that he whom

man repent. Election, for instance. "How could I sin," saith he. "I that was God's favorite, chosen of him from before the foundation of the world?" Final perseverance will make him repent. "How can I sin," says he, "that am loved so much and kept so surely? How can I be so villainous as to sin against everlasting mercy?" Take any doctrine you please, the Christian will make it a fount for sacred woe; and there are times when his faith in Christ will be so strong that his repentance will burst its bonds, and will cry with George Herbert—

"Oh, who will give me tears?
Come, all ye springs,
Ye clouds and rain dwell in my eyes,
My grief hath need of all the wat'ry things
That nature hath produc'd. Let ev'ry vein
Suck up a river to supply mine eyes,
My weary weeping eyes; too dry for me,
Unless they set new conduits, new supplies
To bear them out, and with my state agree."

And all this is because he murdered Christ; because his sin nailed the Savior to the tree; and therefore he weepeth and mourneth even to his life's end. Sinning, repenting, and believing—these are three things that will keep with us till we die. Sinning will stop at the river Jordan; repentance will die triumphing over the dead body of sin; and faith itself, though perhaps it may cross the stream, will cease to be so needful as it has been here, for there we shall see even as we are seen, and shall know even as we are known.

I send you away when I have once again solemnly declared my Master's will to you this morning, "Repent ye, and believe the gospel." Here are some of you come from foreign countries, and many of you are from our provincial towns in England; you came here, perhaps, to hear the preacher of whom many a strange thing has been said. Well and good, and may stranger things still be said if they will but bring men under the sound of the Word that they may be blessed. Now, this I have to say to you this morning: In that great day when a congregation ten thousand times larger than this shall be assembled, and on the great white throne the Judge shall sit, there will be not a man, or woman, or child, who is here this morning, able to make excuse and say, "I did not

52 And Jesus said unto him, Go thy way; thy faith hath made thee whole. And immediately he received his sight, and followed Jesus in the way.

MARK 11

1 And when they came nigh to Jerusalem, unto Bethphage and Bethany, at the mount of Olives, he sendeth forth two of his disciples,

2 And saith unto them, Go your way into the village over against you: and as soon as ye be entered into it, ye shall find a colt tied, whereon never man sat; loose him, and bring him.

3 And if any man say unto you, Why do ye this? say ye that the Lord hath need of him; and straightway he will send him hither.

4 And they went their way, and found the colt tied by the door without in a place where two ways met; and they loose him.

5 And certain of them that stood there said unto them, What do ye, loosing the colt?

6 And they said unto them even as Jesus had commanded: and they let them go.

7 And they brought the colt to Jesus, and cast their garments on him; and he sat upon him.

8 And many spread their garments in the way: and others cut down branches off the trees, and strawed them in the way.

9 And they that went before, and they that followed, cried, saying, Hosanna; Blessed is he that cometh in the name of the Lord:

10 Blessed be the kingdom of our father David, that cometh in the name of the Lord: Hosanna in the highest.

11 And Jesus entered into Jerusalem, and into the temple: and when he had looked round about upon all things, and now the eventide was come, he went out unto Bethany with the twelve.

12 And on the morrow, when they were come from Bethany, he was hungry:

13 And seeing a fig tree afar off having leaves, he came, if haply he might find any thing thereon: and when he came to it, he found nothing but leaves; for the time of figs was not yet.

14 And Jesus answered and said unto it, No man eat fruit of thee hereafter for ever. And his disciples heard it.

15 And they come to Jerusalem: and Jesus went into the temple, and began to cast out them that sold and bought in the temple, and overthrew the tables of the moneychangers, and the seats of them that sold doves;

16 And would not suffer that any man should carry any vessel through the temple.

17 And he taught, saying unto them, Is it not written, My house shall be called of all nations the house of prayer? but ye have made it a den of thieves.

18 And the scribes and chief priests heard it, and sought how they might destroy him: for they feared him, because all the people was astonished at his doctrine.

19 And when even was come, he went out of the city.

20 And in the morning, as they passed by, they saw the fig tree dried up from the roots.

21 And Peter calling to remembrance saith unto him, Master, behold, the fig tree which thou cursedst is withered away.

22 And Jesus answering saith unto them, Have faith in God.

23 For verily I say unto you, That whosoever shall say unto this mountain, Be thou removed, and be thou cast into the sea; and shall not doubt in his heart, but shall believe that those things which he saith shall come to pass; he shall have whatsoever he saith.

24 Therefore I say unto you, What things soever ye desire, when ye pray, believe that ye receive them, and ye shall have them.

25 And when ye stand praying, forgive, if ye have ought against any: that your Father also which is in heaven may forgive you your trespasses.

ering it! And yet without retracting or abating one tittle: How hard is it for them that trust in riches – Either for defense, or happiness, or deliverance from the thousand dangers that life is continually exposed to. That these cannot enter into God's glorious kingdom, is clear and undeniable: but it is easier for a camel to go through a needle's eye, than for a man to have riches, and not trust in them. Therefore, it is easier for a camel to go through the eye of a needle, than for a rich man to enter the kingdom.

28. Lo, we have left all – Though the young man would not.

30. He shall receive a hundred fold, houses, &c. – Not in the same kind: for it will generally be with persecutions: but in value: a hundred fold more happiness than any or all of these did or could afford. But let it be observed, none is entitled to this happiness, but he that will accept it with persecutions.

32. They were in the way to Jerusalem, and Jesus went before them: and they were amazed – At his courage and intrepidity, considering the treatment which he had himself told them he should meet with there: and as they followed, they were afraid – Both for him and themselves: nevertheless he judged it best to prepare them, by telling them more particularly what was to ensue. Matt. xx, 17; Luke xviii, 31.

35. Saying – By their mother. It was she, not they that uttered the words. Matt. xx, 20.

38. Ye know not what ye ask – Ye know not that ye ask for sufferings, which must needs pave the way to glory. The cup – Of inward; the baptism – Of outward sufferings. Our Lord was filled with sufferings within, and covered with them without.

40. Save to them for whom it is prepared – Them who by patient continuance in well doing, seek for glory, and honor, and immortality. For these only eternal life is prepared. To these, only he will give it in that day; and to every man his own reward, according to his own labor.

45. A ransom for many – Even for as many souls as needed such a ransom, 2 Cor. v, 15.

46. Matt. xx, 29; Luke xviii, 35.

50. Casting away his garment – Through joy and eagerness.

MATTHEW HENRY

CHARLES H. SPURGEON

their Master loved, they also should respect and love; but instead of honoring him because he was the Son and Heir, they therefore hated him. But the exaltation of Christ was the Lord's doing; and it is his doing to exalt him in our hearts, and to set up his throne there; and if this be done, it cannot but be marvelous in our eyes. The Scriptures, and faithful preachers, and the coming of Christ in the flesh, call on us to render due praise to God in our lives. Let sinners beware of a proud, carnal spirit; if they revile or despise the preachers of Christ, they would have done so their Master, had they lived when he was upon earth.

13-17 The enemies of Christ would be thought desirous to know their duty, when really they hoped that which soever side he took of the question, they might find occasion to accuse him. Nothing is more likely to ensnare the followers of Christ, than bringing them to meddle with disputes about worldly politics. Jesus avoided the snare, by referring to the submission they had already made as a nation; and all that heard him, marveled at the great wisdom of his answer. Many will praise the words of a sermon, who will not be commanded by the doctrines of it.

18-27 A right knowledge of the Scripture, as the fountain whence all revealed religion now flows, and the foundation on which it is built, is the best preservative against error. Christ put aside the objection of the Sadducees, who were the scoffing infidels of that day, by setting the doctrine of the future state in a true light. The relation between husband and wife, though appointed in the earthly paradise, will not be known in the heavenly one. It is no wonder if we confuse ourselves with foolish errors, when we form our ideas of the world of spirits by the affairs of this world of sense. It is absurd to think that the living God should be the portion and happiness of a man if he is forever dead; and therefore it is certain that Abraham's soul exists and acts, though now for a time separate from the body. Those that deny the resurrection greatly err, and ought to be told so. Let us seek to pass through this dying world, with a joyful hope of eternal happiness, and of a glorious resurrection.

28-34 Those who sincerely desire to be taught their duty, Christ will guide in judgment, and teach his way. He tells the scribe that the great commandment, which indeed includes all, is, that of loving God with all our hearts. Wherever this is the ruling principle in the soul, there is a disposition to every other duty. Loving God with all our heart, will engage us to every thing by which he will be pleased. The sacrifices only represented the atonements for men's transgressions of the moral law; they were of no power except as they expressed repentance and faith in the promised Savior, and as they led to moral obedience. And because we have not thus loved God and man, but the very reverse, therefore we are condemned sinners; we need repentance, and we need mercy. Christ approved what the scribe said, and encouraged him. He stood fair for further advance; for this knowledge of the law leads to conviction of sin, to repentance, to discovery of our need of mercy, and understanding the way of justification by Christ.

hear the gospel; I did not know what I must do to be saved!" You have heard it: "Repent ye, and believe the gospel." That is, trust Christ; believe that he is able and willing to save you. But there is something better. In that great day, I say, there will be some of you present—oh! let us hope all of us—who will be able to say, "Thank God that ever I yielded up the weapons of my proud rebellion by repentance; thank God that I looked to Christ, and took him to be my Savior from first to last; for here am I, a monument of grace, a sinner saved by blood, to praise him while time and eternity shall last!" God grant that we may meet each other at the last with joy and not with grief! I will be a swift witness against you to condemn you if you believe not this gospel; but if you repent and believe, then we shall praise that grace which turned our hearts, and so gave us the repentance which led us to trust Christ, and the faith which is the effectual gift of the Holy Spirit. What shall I say more unto you? Wherefore, wherefore will you reject this? If I have spoken to you of fables, of fictions, of dreams, then turn on your heel and reject my discourse. If I have spoken in my own name, who am I that you should care one whit for me? But if I have preached that which Christ preached, "Repent ye, and believe the gospel," I charge you by the living God, I charge you by the world's Redeemer, I charge you by cross of Calvary, and by the blood which stained the dust at Golgotha, obey this divine message and you shall have eternal life; but refuse it, and on your heads be your blood for ever and ever!

UNBELIEVERS UPBRAIDED

Sermon number 2890 delivered at the Metropolitan Tabernacle, Newington, on Thursday Evening, June 8th, 1876.

"He . . . upbraided them with their unbelief."—Mark 16:14.

I want, in this discourse, to upbraid myself, and you also, for any unbelief that we may have harbored, by noticing, first, the evil of unbelief in itself; and, then, the evils that surely flow out of unbelief.

I. First, then, I have to say to any of God's children who have given way to unbelief in any degree,—YOUR UNBELIEF IS AN EVIL THING IN ITSELF.

26 But if ye do not forgive, neither will your Father which is in heaven forgive your trespasses.

27 And they come again to Jerusalem: and as he was walking in the temple, there come to him the chief priests, and the scribes, and the elders,

28 And say unto him, By what authority doest thou these things? and who gave thee this authority to do these things?

29 And Jesus answered and said unto them, I will also ask of you one question, and answer me, and I will tell you by what authority I do these things.

30 The baptism of John, was it from heaven, or of men? answer me.

31 And they reasoned with themselves, saying, If we shall say, From heaven; he will say, Why then did ye not believe him?

32 But if we shall say, Of men; they feared the people: for all men counted John, that he was a prophet indeed.

33 And they answered and said unto Jesus, We cannot tell. And Jesus answering saith unto them, Neither do I tell you by what authority I do these things.

MARK 12

1 And he began to speak unto them by parables. A certain man planted a vineyard, and set an hedge about it, and digged a place for the winefat, and built a tower, and let it out to husbandmen, and went into a far country.

2 And at the season he sent to the husbandmen a servant, that he might receive from the husbandmen of the fruit of the vineyard.

3 And they caught him, and beat him, and sent him away empty.

4 And again he sent unto them another servant; and at him they cast stones, and wounded him in the head, and sent him away shamefully handled.

5 And again he sent another; and him they killed, and many others; beating some, and killing some.

6 Having yet therefore one son, his wellbeloved, he sent him also last unto them, saying, They will reverence my son.

7 But those husbandmen said among themselves, This is the heir; come, let us kill him, and the inheritance shall be ours.

8 And they took him, and killed him, and cast him out of the vineyard.

9 What shall therefore the lord of the vineyard do? he will come and destroy the husbandmen, and will give the vineyard unto others.

10 And have ye not read this scripture; The stone which the builders rejected is become the head of the corner:

11 This was the Lord's doing, and it is marvelous in our eyes?

12 And they sought to lay hold on him, but feared the people: for they knew that he had spoken the parable against them: and they left him, and went their way.

13 And they send unto him certain of the Pharisees and of the Herodians, to catch him in his words.

14 And when they were come, they say unto him, Master, we know that thou art true, and carest for no man: for thou regardest not the person of men, but teachest the way of God in truth: Is it lawful to give tribute to Cesar, or not?

15 Shall we give, or shall we not give? But he, knowing their hypocrisy, said unto them, Why tempt ye me? bring me a penny, that I may see it.

16 And they brought it. And he saith unto them, Whose is this image and superscription? And they said unto him, Cesar's.

17 And Jesus answering said unto them, Render to Cesar the things that are Cesar's, and to God the things that are God's. And they marveled at him.

18 Then come unto him the Sadducees, which say there is no resurrection; and they asked him, saying,

19 Master, Moses wrote unto us, If a man's brother die, and leave his wife behind him, and leave no children, that his brother should take his

MARK 11

1. To Bethphage and Bethany, at the mount of Olives – The limits of Bethany reached to the mount of Olives, and joined to those of Bethphage. Bethphage was part of the suburbs of Jerusalem, and reached from the mount of Olives to the walls of the city. Our Lord was now come to the place where the boundaries of Bethany and Bethphage met. Matt. xxi, 1; Luke xix, 29; John xii, 12.

11. Matt. xxi, 10, 17.

12. Matt. xxi, 18.

13. For it was not a season of figs – It was not (as we say) a good year for figs; at least not for that early sort, which alone was ripe so soon in the spring. If we render the words, It was not the season of figs, that is, the time of gathering them in, it may mean, The season was not yet: and so (inclosing the words in a parenthesis, And coming to it, he found nothing but leaves) it may refer to the former part of the sentence, and may be considered as the reason of Christ's going to see whether there were any figs on this tree. Some who also read that clause in a parenthesis, translate the following words, for where he was, it was the season of figs. And it is certain, this meaning of the words suits best with the great design of the parable, which was to reprove the Jewish Church for its unfruitfulness at that very season, when fruit might best be expected from them.

15. Matt. xxi, 12; Luke xix, 45.

16. He suffered not that any should carry a vessel through the temple – So strong notions had our Lord, of even relative holiness! And of the regard due to those places (as well as times) that are peculiarly dedicated to God.

17. Isaiah lvi, 7; Jer. vii, 11.

18. They feared him – That is, they were afraid to take him by violence, lest it should raise a tumult; because all the people was astonished at his teaching – Both at the excellence of his discourse, and at the majesty and authority with which he taught.

20. Matt. xxi, 20.

22. Have faith in God – And who could find fault, if the Creator and Proprietor of all things were to destroy, by a single word of his mouth, a thousand of his inanimate creatures, were it only to imprint this important lesson more deeply on one immortal spirit?

25. When ye stand praying – Standing was their usual posture when they prayed. Forgive – And on this condition, ye shall have whatever you ask, without wrath or doubting. Matt. vi, 14.

27. Matt. xxi, 23; Luke xx, 1.

35-40 When we attend to what the Scriptures declare, as to the person and offices of Christ, we shall be led to confess him as our Lord and God; to obey him as our exalted Redeemer. If the common people hear these things gladly, while the learned and distinguished oppose, the former are happy, and the latter to be pitied. And as sin, disguised with a show of piety, is double iniquity, so its doom will be doubly heavy.

41-44 Let us not forget that Jesus still sees the treasury. He knows how much, and from what motives, men give to his cause. He looks at the heart, and what our views are, in giving alms; and whether we do it as unto the Lord, or only to be seen of men. It is so rare to find any who would not blame this widow, that we cannot expect to find many who will do like to her; and yet our Savior commends her, therefore we are sure that she did well and wisely. The feeble efforts of the poor to honor their Savior, will be commended in that day, when the splendid actions of unbelievers will be exposed to contempt.

MARK 13

The destruction of the temple foretold. (1-4)
Christ's prophetic declaration. (5-13)
Christ's prophecy. (14-23)
His prophetic declarations. (24-27)
Watchfulness urged. (28-37)

1-4 See how little Christ values outward pomp, where there is not real purity of heart. He looks with pity upon the ruin of precious souls, and weeps over them, but we do not find him look with pity upon the ruin of a fine house. Let us then be reminded how needful it is for us to have a more lasting abode in heaven, and to be prepared for it by the influences of the Holy Spirit, sought in the earnest use of all the means of grace.

5-13 Our Lord Jesus, in reply to the disciples' question, does not so much satisfy their curiosity as direct their consciences. When many are deceived, we should thereby be awakened to look to ourselves. And the disciples of Christ, if it be not their own fault, may enjoy holy security and peace of mind, when all around is in disorder. But they must take heed that they are not drawn away from Christ and their duty to him, by the sufferings they will meet with for his sake. They shall be hated of all men: trouble enough! Yet the work they were called to should be carried on and prosper. Though they may be crushed and borne down, the gospel cannot be. The salvation promised is more than deliverance from evil, it is everlasting blessedness.

14-23 The Jews in rebelling against the Romans, and in persecuting the Christians, hastened their own ruin apace. Here we have a prediction of that ruin which came upon them within less than forty years after this. Such destruction and desolation, that the like cannot be found in any history. Promises of power to persevere, and cautions against falling away, well agree with each other. But the more we

This truth will come very closely home to you if you will just think how you would feel if others disbelieved you. If anyone were to question your veracity, you would be very vexed; and if you made a promise to any man, and he expressed a doubt as to the fulfillment of it, you would feel hurt; but if those, with whom you are most closely connected, were to disbelieve you, you would feel still more grieved, for you expect absolute confidence from them. If mutual trust were taken away from any family, how unhappy the members of that family would be;—the children suspecting the sincerity of their parents' love,—the wife doubting the reality of her husband's affection,—the husband dubious of his wife's faithfulness! Try to conceive, if you can, what it would be if those, who now call you friend, or child, or husband, or wife, or brother, or sister, should no longer accept what you say as being true. Suppose, also, that you were perfectly conscious that you had never broken your word to them,—that you had faithfully kept every promise that you had made to them, and had been in all things honest, and true, and sincere, would you not feel their doubts and suspicions most acutely? I am sure you would; they would touch the very apple of your eye, and cut you to the quick; you could not endure such treatment from them. Then, how can you mete out to the Lord Jesus Christ such treatment as would be so painful to yourself? And, further, how can you expect your child to trust you when you doubt your Savior? How can you look even to your wife for confidence in you when, if there be some little trouble, or things go somewhat awkwardly, you straightway begin to mistrust your God and Savior?

Remember, too, that the sin of your unbelief may be measured by the excellence of the person whom you mistrust. I said, just now, that, if you were conscious of your absolute sincerity, you would be the more deeply wounded by the suspicion of those who doubted you. What think you then, of the sin of doubting Christ, who cannot lie, who is "the Truth" itself? I know, beloved, that you have a very high opinion of your Lord and Savior; do you not worship him as Divine? Do you not also feel his truly human sympathy? You know that there is no clause in his everlasting covenant, ordered in all things and sure, which he has not already ful-

wife, and raise up seed unto his brother.

20 Now there were seven brethren: and the first took a wife, and dying left no seed.

21 And the second took her, and died, neither left he any seed: and the third likewise.

22 And the seven had her, and left no seed: last of all the woman died also.

23 In the resurrection therefore, when they shall rise, whose wife shall she be of them? for the seven had her to wife.

24 And Jesus answering said unto them, Do ye not therefore err, because ye know not the scriptures, neither the power of God?

25 For when they shall rise from the dead, they neither marry, nor are given in marriage; but are as the angels which are in heaven.

26 And as touching the dead, that they rise: have ye not read in the book of Moses, how in the bush God spake unto him, saying, I am the God of Abraham, and the God of Isaac, and the God of Jacob?

27 He is not the God of the dead, but the God of the living: ye therefore do greatly err.

28 And one of the scribes came, and having heard them reasoning together, and perceiving that he had answered them well, asked him, Which is the first commandment of all?

29 And Jesus answered him, The first of all the commandments is, Hear, O Israel; The Lord our God is one Lord:

30 And thou shalt love the Lord thy God with all thy heart, and with all thy soul, and with all thy mind, and with all thy strength: this is the first commandment.

31 And the second is like, namely this, Thou shalt love thy neighbor as thyself. There is none other commandment greater than these.

32 And the scribe said unto him, Well, Master, thou hast said the truth: for there is one God; and there is none other but he:

33 And to love him with all the heart, and with all the understanding, and with all the soul, and with all the strength, and to love his neighbor as himself, is more than all whole burnt offerings and sacrifices.

34 And when Jesus saw that he answered discreetly, he said unto him, Thou art not far from the kingdom of God. And no man after that durst ask him any question.

35 And Jesus answered and said, while he taught in the temple, How say the scribes that Christ is the Son of David?

36 For David himself said by the Holy Ghost, The Lord said to my Lord, Sit thou on my right hand, till I make thine enemies thy footstool.

37 David therefore himself calleth him Lord; and whence is he then his son? And the common people heard him gladly.

38 And he said unto them in his doctrine, Beware of the scribes, which love to go in long clothing, and love salutations in the marketplaces,

39 And the chief seats in the synagogues, and the uppermost rooms at feasts:

40 Which devour widows' houses, and for a pretense make long prayers: these shall receive greater damnation.

41

And Jesus sat over against the treasury, and beheld how the people cast money into the treasury: and many that were rich cast in much.

42 And there came a certain poor widow, and she threw in two mites, which make a farthing.

43 And he called unto him his disciples, and saith unto them, Verily I say unto you, That this poor widow hath cast more in, than all they which have cast into the treasury:

44 For all they did cast in of their abundance; but she of her want did cast in all that she had, even all her living.

MARK 13

1 And as he went out of the temple, one of his disciples saith unto him, Master, see what manner of stones and what buildings are here!

2 And Jesus answering said unto them, Seest thou these great build-

MARK 12

1. Matt. xxi, 43; Luke xx, 9.

10. Psalm cxviii, 22.

12. They feared the multitude – How wonderful is the providence of God, using all things for the good of his children! Generally the multitude is restrained from tearing them in pieces only by the fear of their rulers. And here the rulers themselves are restrained, through fear of the multitude!

13. Matt. xxii, 15; Luke xx, 20.

17. They marveled at him – At the wisdom of his answer.

18. Matt. xxi, 23; Luke xx, 27.

19. Deut. xxv, 5.

25. When they rise from the dead, neither men marry nor women are given in marriage.

26. Exod. iii, 6.

27. He is not the God of the dead, but the God of the living – That is, (if the argument be proposed at length,) since the character of his being the God of any persons, plainly intimates a relation to them, not as dead, but as living; and since he cannot be said to be at present their God at all, if they are utterly dead; nor to be the God of human persons, such as Abraham, Isaac, and Jacob, consisting of souls and bodies, if their bodies were to abide in everlasting death; there must needs be a future state of blessedness, and a resurrection of the body to share with the soul in it.

28. Which is the first commandment? – The principal, and most necessary to be observed. Matt. xxii, 34; Luke x, 25.

29. The Lord our God is one Lord – This is the foundation of the first commandment, yea, of all the commandments. The Lord our God, the Lord, the God of all men, is one God, essentially, though three persons. From this unity of God it follows, that we owe all our love to him alone. Deut. vi, 4.

30. With all thy strength – That is, the whole strength and capacity of thy understanding, will, and affections.

31. The second is like unto it – Of a like comprehensive nature: comprising our whole duty to man. There is no other moral, much less ceremonial commandment, greater than these. Lev. xix, 18.

33. To love him with all the heart – To love and serve him, with all the united powers of the soul in their utmost vigor; and to love his neighbor as himself – To maintain the same equitable and charitable temper and behavior toward all men, as we, in like circumstances, would wish for from them toward ourselves, is a more necessary and

consider these things, the more we shall see abundant cause to flee without delay for refuge to Christ, and to renounce every earthly object, for the salvation of our souls.

24-27 The disciples had confounded the destruction of Jerusalem and the end of the world. This mistake Christ set right, and showed that the day of Christ's coming, and the day of judgment, shall be after that tribulation. Here he foretells the final dissolution of the present frame and fabric of the world. Also, the visible appearance of the Lord Jesus coming in the clouds, and the gathering together of all the elect to him.

28-37 We have the application of this prophetic sermon. As to the destruction of Jerusalem, expect it to come very shortly. As to the end of the world, do not inquire when it will come, for of that day and that hour knoweth no man. Christ, as God, could not be ignorant of anything; but the Divine wisdom which dwelt in our Savior, communicated itself to his human soul according to the Divine pleasure. As to both, our duty is to watch and pray. Our Lord Jesus, when he ascended on high, left something for all his servants to do. We ought to be always upon our watch, in expectation of his return. This applies to Christ's coming to us at our death, as well as to the general judgment. We know not whether our Master will come in the days of youth, or middle age, or old age; but, as soon as we are born, we begin to die, and therefore we must expect death. Our great care must be, that, whenever our Lord comes, he may not find us secure, indulging in ease and sloth, mindless of our work and duty. He says to all, Watch, that you may be found in peace, without spot, and blameless.

MARK 14

Christ anointed at Bethany. (1-11)
The Passover. Jesus declares that Judas would betray him. (12-21)
The Lord's supper instituted. (22-31)
Christ's agony in the garden. (32-42)
He is betrayed and taken. (43-52)
Christ before the high priest. (53-65)
Peter denies Christ. (66-72)

1-11 Did Christ pour out his soul unto death for us, and shall we think any thing too precious for him? Do we give him the precious ointment of our best affections? Let us love him with all the heart, though it is common for zeal and affection to be misunderstood and blamed; and remember that charity to the poor will not excuse any from particular acts of piety to the Lord Jesus. Christ commended this woman's pious attention to the notice of believers in all ages. Those who honor Christ he will honor. Covetousness was Judas' master lust, and that betrayed him to the sin of betraying his Master; the devil suited his temptation to that, and so conquered him. And see what wicked contrivances many have in their sinful pursuits; but what appears to forward their plans, will prove curses in the end.

filled or which he will not fulfill at the appointed time. His incarnation, his life here below, his shameful sufferings, his vicarious death;—all these he promised to undergo, and all these he performed in due season, and he will go right through, to the end, with the great work of your eternal salvation. By the mouth of his servant Jeremiah, the Lord asked, long ago, "Have I been a wilderness unto Israel? a land of darkness?" And the Lord Jesus might well say to his professed followers, "Have I been as the barren fig tree was to me when I found on it nothing but leaves?" As he points to the long list of his favors to us, he may well ask, "For which of them do you thus misjudge and mistrust me?" And when he spreads out the whole roll of his life and work before you, he may well inquire, "Upon which part of my life or work do you base your suspicions? What is there in my nature, as Divine and human,—what is there in my character,—what is there in my life below, or in my life above,—that should lead you to question my faithfulness to you, my power to help you, my readiness to sympathize with you, my willingness to bless you!" Why, you are doubting him whom the angels adore and worship! You have felt, sometimes, as if you would like to wash his feet with your tears. How, then, can you ever insult him with your doubts? You have even said that you could die for him; and it has been your great ambition to live for him; yet you cannot trust him! If you have run with the footmen in the matter of these minor trials of your faith, and they have wearied you, what would you do if you had to contend with horsemen as many others have had to do in the day of martyrdom? And if, in the favorable circumstances in which you have been placed, you have doubted your Savior, what are you likely to do when you are in the swellings of Jordan? Ah, my brethren, when you think of unbelief as aiming her darts at Jesus Christ, the Well-beloved of our soul, surely you will say that it is a shameful sin, and a disgraceful crime against infinite love!

Then, remember, beloved in the Lord, the relationship in which Jesus Christ stands to you. You know that, the more closely we are allied to a person, the more painful any suspicion on the part of that person becomes. I have repeatedly used, in this connection, the figure of a child's trust in a parent, a husband's trust in his wife,

ings? there shall not be left one stone upon another, that shall not be thrown down.

3 And as he sat upon the mount of Olives over against the temple, Peter and James and John and Andrew asked him privately,

4 Tell us, when shall these things be? and what shall be the sign when all these things shall be fulfilled?

5 And Jesus answering them began to say, Take heed lest any man deceive you:

6 For many shall come in my name, saying, I am Christ; and shall deceive many.

7 And when ye shall hear of wars and rumors of wars, be ye not troubled: for such things must needs be; but the end shall not be yet.

8 For nation shall rise against nation, and kingdom against kingdom: and there shall be earthquakes in divers places, and there shall be famines and troubles: these are the beginnings of sorrows.

9 But take heed to yourselves: for they shall deliver you up to councils; and in the synagogues ye shall be beaten: and ye shall be brought before rulers and kings for my sake, for a testimony against them.

10 And the gospel must first be published among all nations.

11 But when they shall lead you, and deliver you up, take no thought beforehand what ye shall speak, neither do ye premeditate: but whatsoever shall be given you in that hour, that speak ye: for it is not ye that speak, but the Holy Ghost.

12 Now the brother shall betray the brother to death, and the father the son; and children shall rise up against their parents, and shall cause them to be put to death.

13 And ye shall be hated of all men for my name's sake: but he that shall endure unto the end, the same shall be saved.

14 But when ye shall see the abomination of desolation, spoken of by Daniel the prophet, standing where it ought not, (let him that readeth understand,) then let them that be in Judea flee to the mountains:

15 And let him that is on the housetop not go down into the house, neither enter therein, to take any thing out of his house:

16 And let him that is in the field not turn back again for to take up his garment.

17 But woe to them that are with child, and to them that give suck in those days!

18 And pray ye that your flight be not in the winter.

19 For in those days shall be affliction, such as was not from the beginning of the creation which God created unto this time, neither shall be.

20 And except that the Lord had shortened those days, no flesh should be saved: but for the elect's sake, whom he hath chosen, he hath shortened the days.

21 And then if any man shall say to you, Lo, here is Christ; or, lo, he is there; believe him not:

22 For false Christs and false prophets shall rise, and shall shew signs and wonders, to seduce, if it were possible, even the elect.

23 But take ye heed: behold, I have foretold you all things.

24 But in those days, after that tribulation, the sun shall be darkened, and the moon shall not give her light,

25 And the stars of heaven shall fall, and the powers that are in heaven shall be shaken.

26 And then shall they see the Son of man coming in the clouds with great power and glory.

27 And then shall he send his angels, and shall gather together his elect from the four winds, from the uttermost part of the earth to the uttermost part of heaven.

28 Now learn a parable of the fig tree; When her branch is yet tender, and putteth forth leaves, ye know that summer is near:

29 So ye in like manner, when ye shall see these things come to pass, know that it is nigh, even at the doors.

30 Verily I say unto you, that this generation shall not pass, till all these things be done.

important duty, than the offering the most noble and costly sacrifices.

34. Jesus said to him, Thou art not far from the kingdom of God – Reader, art not thou? then go on: be a real Christian: else it had been better for thee to have been afar off.

35. Matt. xxii, 41; Luke xx, 41.

36. Psalm cx, 1.

38. Beware of the scribes – There was an absolute necessity for these repeated cautions. For, considering their inveterate prejudices against Christ, it could never be supposed the common people would receive the Gospel till these incorrigible blasphemers of it were brought to just disgrace. Yet he delayed speaking in this manner till a little before his passion, as knowing what effect it would quickly produce. Nor is this any precedent for us: we are not invested with the same authority. Matt. xxiii, 5; Luke xx, 46.

41. He beheld how people cast money into the treasury – This treasury received the voluntary contributions of the worshipers who came up to the feast; which were given to buy wood for the altar, and other necessaries not provided for in any other way. Luke xxi, 1.

43. I say to you, that this poor widow hath cast in more than they all – See what judgment is cast on the most specious, outward actions by the Judge of all! And how acceptable to him is the smallest, which springs from self-denying love!

MARK 13

1. Matt. xxiv, 1; Luke xxi, 5.

4. Two questions are here asked; the one concerning the destruction of Jerusalem: the other concerning the end of the world.

9. Luke xxi, 12.

10. Matt. xxiv, 14.

11. The Holy Ghost will help you. But do not depend upon any other help. For all the nearest ties will be broken.

14. Where it ought not – That place being set apart for sacred use. Matt. xxiv, 15; Luke xxi, 20; Dan. ix, 27.

19. In those days shall be affliction, such as was not from the beginning of the creation – May it not be doubted, whether this be yet fully accomplished? Is not much of this affliction still to come?

20. The elect – The Christians: whom he hath chosen – That is, hath taken out of, or separated from, the world, through sanctification of the Spirit and belief of the truth. He hath shortened – That is, will surely shorten.

21. Matt. xxiv, 23.

MATTHEW HENRY

CHARLES H. SPURGEON

12-21 Nothing could be less the result of human foresight than the events here related. But our Lord knows all things about us before they come to pass. If we admit him, he will dwell in our hearts. The Son of man goes, as it is written of him, as a lamb to the slaughter; but woe to that man by whom he is betrayed! God's permitting the sins of men, and bringing glory to himself out of them, does not oblige them to sin; nor will this be any excuse for their guilt, or lessen their punishment.

22-31 The Lord's supper is food for the soul, therefore a very little of that which is for the body, as much as will serve for a sign, is enough. It was instituted by the example and the practice of our Master, to remain in force till his second coming. It was instituted with blessing and giving of thanks, to be a memorial of Christ's death. Frequent mention is made of his precious blood, as the price of our redemption. How comfortable is this to poor repenting sinners, that the blood of Christ is shed for many! If for many, why not for me? It was a sign of the conveyance of the benefits purchased for us by his death. Apply the doctrine of Christ crucified to yourselves; let it be meat and drink to your souls, strengthening and refreshing your spiritual life. It was to be an earnest and foretaste of the happiness of heaven, and thereby to put us out of taste for the pleasures and delights of sense. Every one that has tasted spiritual delights, straightway desires eternal ones. Though the great Shepherd passed through his sufferings without one false step, yet his followers often have been scattered by the small measure of sufferings allotted to them. How very apt we are to think well of ourselves, and to trust our own hearts! It was ill done of Peter thus to answer his Master, and not with fear and trembling. Lord, give me grace to keep me from denying thee.

32-42 Christ's sufferings began with the sorest of all, those in his soul. He began to be sorely amazed; words not used in St. Matthew, but very full of meaning. The terrors of God set themselves in array against him, and he allowed him to contemplate them. Never was sorrow like unto his at this time. Now he was made a curse for us; the curses of the law were laid upon him as our Surety. He now tasted death, in all the bitterness of it. This was that fear of which the apostle speaks, the natural fear of pain and death, at which human nature startles. Can we ever entertain favorable, or even slight thoughts of sin, when we see the painful sufferings which sin, though but reckoned to him, brought on the Lord Jesus? Shall that sit light upon our souls, which sat so heavy upon his? Was Christ in such agony for our sins, and shall we never be in agony about them? How should we look upon him whom we have pierced, and mourn! It becomes us to be exceedingly sorrowful for sin, because He was so, and never to mock at it. Christ, as Man, pleaded, that, if it were possible, his sufferings might pass from him. As Mediator, he submitted to the will of God, saying, Nevertheless, not what I will, but what thou wilt; I bid it welcome. See how the sinful weakness of Christ's disciples returns, and overpowers them. What heavy clogs these bodies of ours are to our souls! But when we see trouble at

and the wife's trust in her husband; and you have readily accepted the comparisons because you have felt that the nearness of the relationship would involve a corresponding degree of trust. How near—how very near—we are in kinship to Christ! Are we not married to him? Has he not espoused us unto himself for ever? There is a conjugal union between Christ and his Church of which the marriage bond on earth is but a feeble type. Then, can you who have been renewed in heart by the Holy Spirit, and washed in the blood of the Lamb, doubt him whom your soul loveth? Can you distrust him to whom you are so closely allied? Oh, shame, shame, shame, that want of confidence should come in to mar such a wondrous union as that!

But we are even more closely knit to Christ than the marriage union implies, for "we are members of his body, of his flesh, and of his bones." I cannot explain that secret, mystical union of which the Scripture speaks; but it is a true union, whatever mystery there may be about it. Then, shall there be such disunion amongst the members of the body that the eye shall begin to doubt the heart, and the hand to mistrust the foot? It would be pitiful if such a state of things could prevail in our bodies; then, what must it be if such a state of things prevails among the members of the mystical body of Christ? Beloved, may God render this unbelief impossible by sending such life floods of grace through all the members of Christ's body that never more shall a single thought of mistrust of our glorious covenant Head enter our minds even for a single instant!

Consider next, I pray you, dear friends, how many times some of us have doubted our Lord. The sin of unbelief becomes all the greater because it is so frequently committed. God be thanked that it is not so with all Christians: for there are some who walk in faith and dwell in faith. I suppose that, as birds fly over everybody's head, as doubts fly around all good men's minds; but our old proverb says, "You need not let birds build in your hair," although there are some people, who let doubts come and lodge in their minds, and even dwell in their hearts. We know some persons of this kind, who seem to be very easily led into despondency, and doubt, and mistrust of Christ. Well now, if a man has done this only once, I think he

31 Heaven and earth shall pass away: but my words shall not pass away.

32 But of that day and that hour knoweth no man, no, not the angels which are in heaven, neither the Son, but the Father.

33 Take ye heed, watch and pray: for ye know not when the time is.

34 For the Son of man is as a man taking a far journey, who left his house, and gave authority to his servants, and to every man his work, and commanded the porter to watch.

35 Watch ye therefore: for ye know not when the master of the house cometh, at even, or at midnight, or at the cockcrowing, or in the morning:

36 Lest coming suddenly he find you sleeping.

37 And what I say unto you I say unto all, Watch.

MARK 14

1 After two days was the feast of the passover, and of unleavened bread: and the chief priests and the scribes sought how they might take him by craft, and put him to death.

2 But they said, Not on the feast day, lest there be an uproar of the people.

3 And being in Bethany in the house of Simon the leper, as he sat at meat, there came a woman having an alabaster box of ointment of spikenard very precious; and she brake the box, and poured it on his head.

4 And there were some that had indignation within themselves, and said, Why was this waste of the ointment made?

5 For it might have been sold for more than three hundred pence, and have been given to the poor. And they murmured against her.

6 And Jesus said, Let her alone; why trouble ye her? she hath wrought a good work on me.

7 For ye have the poor with you always, and whensoever ye will ye may do them good: but me ye have not always.

8 She hath done what she could: she is come aforehand to anoint my body to the burying.

9 Verily I say unto you, Wheresoever this gospel shall be preached throughout the whole world, this also that she hath done shall be spoken of for a memorial of her.

10 And Judas Iscariot, one of the twelve, went unto the chief priests, to betray him unto them.

11 And when they heard it, they were glad, and promised to give him money. And he sought how he might conveniently betray him.

12 And the first day of unleavened bread, when they killed the passover, his disciples said unto him, Where wilt thou that we go and prepare that thou mayest eat the passover?

13 And he sendeth forth two of his disciples, and saith unto them, Go ye into the city, and there shall meet you a man bearing a pitcher of water: follow him.

14 And wheresoever he shall go in, say ye to the goodman of the house, The Master saith, Where is the guestchamber, where I shall eat the passover with my disciples?

15 And he will shew you a large upper room furnished and prepared: there make ready for us.

16 And his disciples went forth, and came into the city, and found as he had said unto them: and they made ready the passover.

17 And in the evening he cometh with the twelve.

18 And as they sat and did eat, Jesus said, Verily I say unto you, One of you which eateth with me shall betray me.

19 And they began to be sorrowful, and to say unto him one by one, Is it I? and another said, Is it I?

20 And he answered and said unto them, It is one of the twelve, that dippeth with me in the dish.

21 The Son of man indeed goeth, as it is written of him: but woe to that man by whom the Son of man is betrayed! good were it for that

24. But in those days – Which immediately precede the end of the world: after that tribulation – Above described.

28. Matt. xxiv, 32; Luke xxi, 28.

29. He is nigh – The Son of man.

30. All these things – Relating to the temple and the city.

32. Of that day – The day of judgment is often in the Scriptures emphatically called that day. Neither the Son – Not as man: as man he was no more omniscient than omnipresent. But as God he knows all the circumstances of it.

33. Matt. xxiv, 42; Luke xxi, 34.

34. The Son of man is as a man taking a far journey – Being about to leave this world and go to the Father, he appoints the services that are to be performed by all his servants, in their several stations. This seems chiefly to respect ministers at the day of judgment: but it may be applied to all men, and to the time of death. Matt. xxv, 14; Luke xix, 12.

MARK 14

1. Matt. xxvi, 1; Luke xxii, 1.

3. Matt. xxvi, 6.

4. Some had indignation – Being incited thereto by Judas: and said – Probably to the women.

10. Judas went to the chief priests – Immediately after this reproof, having anger now added to his covetousness. Matt. xxvi, 14; Luke xxii, 3.

12. Matt. xxvi, 17; Luke xxii, 7.

13. Go into the city, and there shall meet you a man – It was highly seasonable for our Lord to give them this additional proof both of his knowing all things, and of his influence over the minds of men.

15. Furnished – The word properly means, spread with carpets.

17. Matt. xxvi, 20; Luke xxii, 14.

24. This is my blood of the New Testament – That is, this I appoint to be a perpetual sign and memorial of my blood, as shed for establishing the new covenant, that all who shall believe in me may receive all its gracious promises.

25. I will drink no more of the fruit of the vine, till I drink it new in the kingdom of God – That is, I shall drink no more before I die: the next wine I drink will not be earthly, but heavenly.

26. Matt. xxvi, 30; Luke xxii, 39; John xviii, 1.

27. This night – The Jews in reckoning their days began with the evening, according to the Mosaic computation, which called the evening and the morning the first day, Gen. i, 5. And so that which after sunset is here called this night is, ver. 30, called today. The expression there is peculiar-

the door, we should get ready for it. Alas, even believers often look at the Redeemer's sufferings in a drowsy manner, and instead of being ready to die with Christ, they are not even prepared to watch with him one hour.

43-52 Because Christ appeared not as a temporal prince, but preached repentance, reformation, and a holy life, and directed men's thoughts, and affections, and aims to another world, therefore the Jewish rulers sought to destroy him. Peter wounded one of the band. It is easier to fight for Christ than to die for him. But there is a great difference between faulty disciples and hypocrites. The latter rashly and without thought call Christ Master, and express great affection for him, yet betray him to his enemies. Thus they hasten their own destruction.

53-65 We have here Christ's condemnation before the great council of the Jews. Peter followed; but the high priest's fireside was no proper place, nor his servants proper company, for Peter: it was an entrance into temptation. Great diligence was used to procure false witnesses against Jesus, yet their testimony was not equal to the charge of a capital crime, by the utmost stretch of their law. He was asked, Art thou the Son of the Blessed? that is, the Son of God. For the proof of his being the Son of God, he refers to his second coming. In these outrages we have proofs of man's enmity to God, and of God's free and unspeakable love to man.

66-72 Peter's denying Christ began by keeping at a distance from him. Those that are shy of godliness, are far in the way to deny Christ. Those who think it dangerous to be in company with Christ's disciples, because thence they may be drawn in to suffer for him, will find it much more dangerous to be in company with his enemies, because there they may be drawn in to sin against him. When Christ was admired and flocked after, Peter readily owned him; but will own no relation to him now he is deserted and despised. Yet observe, Peter's repentance was very speedy. Let him that thinketh he standeth take heed lest he fall; and let him that has fallen think of these things, and of his own offenses, and return to the Lord with weeping and supplication, seeking forgiveness, and to be raised up by the Holy Spirit.

MARK 15

Christ before Pilate. (1-14)
Christ led to be crucified. (15-21)
The crucifixion. (22-32)
The death of Christ. (33-41)
His body buried. (42-47)

1-14 They bound Christ. It is good for us often to remember the bonds of the Lord Jesus, as bound with him who was bound for us. By delivering up the King, they, in effect, delivered up the kingdom of God, which was, therefore, as by their own consent, taken from them, and given to anoth-

might well say to himself, "I did once question everlasting truth. I did once stain the spotless robe of infinite veracity with a dark blot of suspicion;" and I think that he might find it difficult to forgive himself for having done a thing so vile even once. But when it comes to many times, and when it comes to long periods of doubt and mistrust, it is still worse. I want to press this point home upon all whom it concerns, and I want your consciences to be wide awake, so that, as you recall the many times in which you have thus sinned against your Heavenly Father, and against his blessed Spirit, and against his Divine Son you may recollect that each distinct act of unbelief is a sin,—each act of mistrust is another wounding of the Lord. God grant that we may truly repent as we think of the many times in which we have been thus guilty!

Then there is this further point—some of these actions have been repetitions of former ones. For instance, a man is in trouble, and he has doubts concerning the providence of God; but he is delivered, God is gracious to him, and helps him out of his difficulty. Well, now if he falls into a similar trouble, and if he is again guilty of harboring doubt, this is far worse. If a man should doubt your word the first time you speak to him, you might say, "Well, he does not know me." The second time, you might say, "When he has proved me more, he will trust me." But what shall I say of those, whose hair has a sprinkling of gray in it, and whose Christian experience extends to a score of years, or more,—perhaps, two score,—possibly, three scores. Oh, if you doubt the Lord now, it will be a crying shame! It will not be surprising if some of us act thus, for so did Israel for forty years in the wilderness; but that does not mitigate the evil in our case. It is a desperately evil thing that God should be mistrusted over and over again, and that he should have to say, "How long will it be ere ye believe me?"

I scarcely like to linger on such a sad theme; yet it does our hearts good to be thus upbraided; so, recollect that, oftentimes our unbelief has come in the teeth of our own assurance to the contrary. Do you not sometimes catch yourself saying, after a very great mercy, "Well, I never can doubt the Lord again"? When you have had an answer to prayer of a very memorable kind, you have said, "Oh, I must believe in the power of prayer now! For

man if he had never been born.

22 And as they did eat, Jesus took bread, and blessed, and brake it, and gave to them, and said, Take, eat: this is my body.

23 And he took the cup, and when he had given thanks, he gave it to them: and they all drank of it.

24 And he said unto them, This is my blood of the new testament, which is shed for many.

25 Verily I say unto you, I will drink no more of the fruit of the vine, until that day that I drink it new in the kingdom of God.

26 And when they had sung an hymn, they went out into the mount of Olives.

27 And Jesus saith unto them, All ye shall be offended because of me this night: for it is written, I will smite the shepherd, and the sheep shall be scattered.

28 But after that I am risen, I will go before you into Galilee.

29 But Peter said unto him, Although all shall be offended, yet will not I.

30 And Jesus saith unto him, Verily I say unto thee, That this day, even in this night, before the cock crow twice, thou shalt deny me thrice.

31 But he spake the more vehemently, If I should die with thee, I will not deny thee in any wise. Likewise also said they all.

32 And they came to a place which was named Gethsemane: and he saith to his disciples, Sit ye here, while I shall pray.

33 And he taketh with him Peter and James and John, and began to be sore amazed, and to be very heavy;

34 And saith unto them, My soul is exceeding sorrowful unto death: tarry ye here, and watch.

35 And he went forward a little, and fell on the ground, and prayed that, if it were possible, the hour might pass from him.

36 And he said, Abba, Father, all things are possible unto thee; take away this cup from me: nevertheless not what I will, but what thou wilt.

37 And he cometh, and findeth them sleeping, and saith unto Peter, Simon, sleepest thou? couldest not thou watch one hour?

38 Watch ye and pray, lest ye enter into temptation. The spirit truly is ready, but the flesh is weak.

39 And again he went away, and prayed, and spake the same words.

40 And when he returned, he found them asleep again, (for their eyes were heavy,) neither wist they what to answer him.

41 And he cometh the third time, and saith unto them, Sleep on now, and take your rest: it is enough, the hour is come; behold, the Son of man is betrayed into the hands of sinners.

42 Rise up, let us go; lo, he that betrayeth me is at hand.

43 And immediately, while he yet spake, cometh Judas, one of the twelve, and with him a great multitude with swords and staves, from the chief priests and the scribes and the elders.

44 And he that betrayed him had given them a token, saying, Whomsoever I shall kiss, that same is he; take him, and lead him away safely.

45 And as soon as he was come, he goeth straightway to him, and saith, Master, master; and kissed him.

46 And they laid their hands on him, and took him.

47 And one of them that stood by drew a sword, and smote a servant of the high priest, and cut off his ear.

48 And Jesus answered and said unto them, Are ye come out, as against a thief, with swords and with staves to take me?

49 I was daily with you in the temple teaching, and ye took me not: but the scriptures must be fulfilled.

50 And they all forsook him, and fled.

51 And there followed him a certain young man, having a linen cloth cast about his naked body; and the young men laid hold on him:

52 And he left the linen cloth, and fled from them naked.

53 And they led Jesus away to the high priest: and with him were assembled all the chief priests and the elders and the scribes.

ly significant. Verily I say to thee, that thou thyself, confident as thou art, today, even within four and twenty hours; yea, this night, or ever the sun be risen, nay, before the cock crow twice, before three in the morning, wilt deny me thrice. Our Lord doubtless spoke so determinately, as knowing a cock would crow once before the usual time of cock crowing. By chap. xiii, 35, it appears, that the third watch of the night, ending at three in the morning, was commonly styled the cock crowing. Zech. xiii, 7.

32. Matt. xxvi, 36.

33. Sore amazed – The original word imports the most shocking amazement, mingled with grief: and that word in the next verse which we render sorrowful intimates, that he was surrounded with sorrow on every side, breaking in upon him with such violence, as was ready to separate his soul from his body.

36. Abba, Father – St. Mark seems to add the word Father, by way of explication.

37. Saith to Peter – The zealous, the confident Peter.

43. Matt. xxvi, 47; Luke xxii, 47; John xviii, 2.

44. Whomsoever I shall kiss – Probably our Lord, in great condescension, had used (according to the Jewish custom) to permit his disciples to do this, after they had been some time absent.

47. Matt. xxvi, 51; Luke xxii, 49; John xviii, 10.

51. A young man – It does not appear, that he was one of Christ's disciples. Probably hearing an unusual noise, he started up out of his bed, not far from the garden, and ran out with only the sheet about him, to see what was the matter. And the young men laid hold on him – Who was only suspected to be Christ's disciple: but could not touch them who really were so.

53. Matt. xxvi, 57; Luke xxii, 54; John xviii, 12.

55. All the council sought for witness and found none – What an amazing proof of the overruling providence of God, considering both their authority, and the rewards they could offer, that no two consistent witnesses could be procured, to charge him with any gross crime. Matt. xxvi, 59.

56. Their evidences were not sufficient – The Greek words literally rendered are, Were not equal: not equal to the charge of a capital crime: it is the same word in the 59th verse.

58. We heard him say – It is observable, that the words which they thus misrepresented, were spoken by Christ at least three years before, John ii, 19. Their going back so far to find matter for the charge, was a glorious, though silent attestation of the unexceptionable manner wherein he had behaved, through the whole course of his public

MATTHEW HENRY   CHARLES H. SPURGEON

er nation. Christ gave Pilate a direct answer, but would not answer the witnesses, because the things they alleged were known to be false, even Pilate himself was convinced they were so. Pilate thought that he might appeal from the priests to the people, and that they would deliver Jesus out of the priests' hands. But they were more and more urged by the priests, and cried, Crucify him! Crucify him! Let us judge of persons and things by their merits, and the standard of God's word, and not by common report. The thought that no one ever was so shamefully treated, as the only perfectly wise, holy, and excellent Person that ever appeared on earth, leads the serious mind to strong views of man's wickedness and enmity to God. Let us more and more abhor the evil dispositions which marked the conduct of these persecutors.

15-21 Christ met death in its greatest terror. It was the death of the vilest malefactors. Thus the cross and the shame are put together. God having been dishonored by the sin of man, Christ made satisfaction by submitting to the greatest disgrace human nature could be loaded with. It was a cursed death; thus it was branded by the Jewish law, De 21:23. The Roman soldiers mocked our Lord Jesus as a King; thus in the high priest's hall the servants had mocked him as a Prophet and Savior. Shall a purple or scarlet robe be matter of pride to a Christian, which was matter of reproach and shame to Christ? He wore the crown of thorns which we deserved, that we might wear the crown of glory which he merited. We were by sin liable to everlasting shame and contempt; to deliver us, our Lord Jesus submitted to shame and contempt. He was led forth with the workers of iniquity, though he did no sin. The sufferings of the meek and holy Redeemer, are ever a source of instruction to the believer, of which, in his best hours, he cannot be weary. Did Jesus thus suffer, and shall I, a vile sinner, fret or repine? Shall I indulge anger, or utter reproaches and threats because of troubles and injuries?

22-32 The place where our Lord Jesus was crucified, was called the place of a skull; it was the common place of execution; for he was in all respects numbered with the transgressors. Whenever we look unto Christ crucified, we must remember what was written over his head; he is a King, and we must give up ourselves to be his subjects, as Israelites indeed. They crucified two thieves with him, and him in the midst; they thereby intended him great dishonor. But it was foretold that he should be numbered with the transgressors, because he was made sin for us. Even those who passed by railed at him. They told him to come down from the cross, and they would believe; but they did not believe, though he gave them a more convincing sign when he came up from the grave. With what earnestness will the man who firmly believes the truth, as made known by the sufferings of Christ, seek for salvation! With what gratitude will he receive the dawning hope of forgiveness and eternal life, as purchased for him by the sufferings and death of the Son of God! and with what godly sorrow will he mourn over the sins which crucified the Lord of glory!

me ever to think that the Lord will deny me, must be impossible." Yes, in that respect also, we are just like the Israelites, who promised to keep the covenant, yet speedily broke it.

There is also this aggravation of your sin; although you do not trust the Lord as you should, you do trust your fellow-creatures. You can believe that lie of the old serpent,—

"The Lord hath forsaken thee quite;
Thy God will be gracious no more;"—
yet you cannot so readily believe the oath and promise of God. If an earthly friend were to say to you, "I will help you," how readily you would jump at his offer! If there be an arm of flesh near, how cheerfully you lean upon it; and, though, perhaps, there be nothing for you to stay yourself upon but a broken reed, you think it is a strong staff, and throw all your weight upon it. It is quite true that ungodly men, who have no faith, generally have any amount of credulity. They cannot believe the truth, but they can believe lies to any extent. So is it, alas! with God's own people when they get off the track of faith. They seem to become credulous concerning the things seen, which are temporal, in proportion as they become dubious of the things unseen, which are eternal. Is not this a sin of the greatest blackness? Thou canst not trust thy husband, but thou canst trust a flatterer who deceives thee! Thou canst not trust thy God, but thou makest idol gods unto thyself, and trustest to them. Thou canst not stay thyself on Jehovah, but thou canst stay thyself on Egypt. Thou canst stay thyself on the promise of man who is but as a moth which is soon crushed; but as for him who made the heavens and the earth, and all things that are, thou canst not rely upon him. I feel as if I could sit down and cover my face for shame, when I think of those occasions wherein I have been guilty of this sin. Perhaps the best thing we could all do would be to go home, and fall on our knees, and ask our blessed Savior to wash away all this unbelief, and not to believe us when we talk about doubting, but only to believe that, as he knows all things, he knows that, after all, we do trust him.

II. Now, with great brevity, I have to speak upon the second point, which is, THE MANY EVILS WHICH COME OUT OF UNBELIEF TO THOSE OF US WHO LOVE THE LORD.

54 And Peter followed him afar off, even into the palace of the high priest: and he sat with the servants, and warmed himself at the fire.

55 And the chief priests and all the council sought for witness against Jesus to put him to death; and found none.

56 For many bare false witness against him, but their witness agreed not together.

57

And there arose certain, and bare false witness against him, saying,

58 We heard him say, I will destroy this temple that is made with hands, and within three days I will build another made without hands.

59 But neither so did their witness agree together.

60

And the high priest stood up in the midst, and asked Jesus, saying, Answerest thou nothing? what is it which these witness against thee?

61 But he held his peace, and answered nothing. Again the high priest asked him, and said unto him, Art thou the Christ, the Son of the Blessed?

62 And Jesus said, I am: and ye shall see the Son of man sitting on the right hand of power, and coming in the clouds of heaven.

63 Then the high priest rent his clothes, and saith, What need we any further witnesses?

64 Ye have heard the blasphemy: what think ye? And they all condemned him to be guilty of death.

65 And some began to spit on him, and to cover his face, and to buffet him, and to say unto him, Prophesy: and the servants did strike him with the palms of their hands.

66 And as Peter was beneath in the palace, there cometh one of the maids of the high priest:

67 And when she saw Peter warming himself, she looked upon him, and said, And thou also wast with Jesus of Nazareth.

68 But he denied, saying, I know not, neither understand I what thou sayest. And he went out into the porch; and the cock crew.

69 And a maid saw him again, and began to say to them that stood by, This is one of them.

70 And he denied it again. And a little after, they that stood by said again to Peter, Surely thou art one of them: for thou art a Galilean, and thy speech agreeth thereto.

71 But he began to curse and to swear, saying, I know not this man of whom ye speak.

72 And the second time the cock crew. And Peter called to mind the word that Jesus said unto him, Before the cock crow twice, thou shalt deny me thrice. And when he thought thereon, he wept.

MARK 15

1 And straightway in the morning the chief priests held a consultation with the elders and scribes and the whole council, and bound Jesus, and carried him away, and delivered him to Pilate.

2 And Pilate asked him, Art thou the King of the Jews? And he answering said unto him, Thou sayest it.

3 And the chief priests accused him of many things: but he answered nothing.

4 And Pilate asked him again, saying, Answerest thou nothing? behold how many things they witness against thee.

5 But Jesus yet answered nothing; so that Pilate marveled.

6 Now at that feast he released unto them one prisoner, whomsoever they desired.

7 And there was one named Barabbas, which lay bound with them that had made insurrection with him, who had committed murder in the insurrection.

8 And the multitude crying aloud began to desire him to do as he had ever done unto them.

9 But Pilate answered them, saying, Will ye that I release unto you the

ministry.

61. Matt. xxvi, 63; Luke xxii, 67.

66. Matt. xxvi, 69; Luke xxii, 56; John xviii, 25.

72. And he covered his head – Which was a usual custom with mourners, and was fitly expressive both of grief and shame.

MARK 15

1. Matt. xxvii, 1, 2; Luke xxii, 66; Luke xxiii, 1; John xviii, 28.

3. Matt. xxvii, 12.

7. Insurrection – A crime which the Roman governors, and Pilate in particular, were more especially concerned and careful to punish.

9. Will ye that I release to you the king of the Jews – Which does this wretched man discover most? Want of justice, or courage, or common sense? The poor coward sacrifices justice to popular clamor, and enrages those whom he seeks to appease, by so unseasonably repeating that title, The king of the Jews, which he could not but know was so highly offensive to them.

16. Pretorium – The inner hall, where the pretor, a Roman magistrate, used to give judgment. But St. John calls the whole palace by this name. Matt. xxvii, 27; John xix, 2.

17. Purple – As royal robes were usually purple and scarlet, St. Mark and John term this a purple robe, St. Matthew a scarlet one. The Tyrian purple is said not to have been very different from scarlet.

20. Matt. xxvii, 31; John xix, 16.

21. The father of Alexander and Rufus – These were afterward two eminent Christians, and must have been well known when St. Mark wrote.

22. Matt. xxvii, 33; Luke xxiii, 33; John xix, 17.

24, 25. St. Mark seems to intimate, that they first nailed him to the cross, then parted his garments, and afterward reared up the cross.

28. Isaiah liii, 12.

29. Matt. xxvii, 39.

33. Matt. xxvii, 45; Luke xxiii, 44.

34. My God, my God, why hast thou forsaken me – Thereby claiming God as his God; and yet lamenting his Father's withdrawing the tokens of his love, and treating him as an enemy, while he bare our sins.

37. Matt. xxvii, 50; Luke xxiii, 46; John xix, 30.

41. Who served him – Provided him with necessaries.

42. Because it was the day before the Sabbath – And the bodies might not hang on the Sabbath day: therefore they were in haste to have them taken down.

MATTHEW HENRY

CHARLES H. SPURGEON

33-41 There was a thick darkness over the land, from noon until three in the afternoon. The Jews were doing their utmost to extinguish the Sun of Righteousness. The darkness signified the cloud which the human soul of Christ was under, when he was making it an offering for sin. He did not complain that his disciples forsook him, but that his Father forsook him. In this especially he was made sin for us. When Paul was to be offered as a sacrifice for the service of the saints, he could joy and rejoice, Php 2:17; but it is another thing to be offered as a sacrifice for the sin of sinners. At the same instant that Jesus died, the veil of the temple was rent from the top to the bottom. This spake terror to the unbelieving Jews, and was a sign of the destruction of their church and nation. It speaks comfort to all believing Christians, for it signified the laying open a new and living way into the holiest by the blood of Jesus. The confidence with which Christ had openly addressed God as his Father, and committed his soul into his hands, seems greatly to have affected the centurion. Right views of Christ crucified will reconcile the believer to the thought of death; he longs to behold, love, and praise, as he ought, that Savior who was wounded and pierced to save him from the wrath to come.

42-47 We are here attending the burial of our Lord Jesus. Oh that we may by grace be planted in the likeness of it! Joseph of Arimathea was one who waited for the kingdom of God. Those who hope for a share in its privileges, must own Christ's cause, when it seems to be crushed. This man God raised up for his service. There was a special providence, that Pilate should be so strict in his inquiry, that there might be no pretense to say Jesus was alive. Pilate gave Joseph leave to take down the body, and do what he pleased with it. Some of the women beheld where Jesus was laid, that they might come after the Sabbath to anoint the dead body, because they had not time to do it before. Special notice was taken of Christ's sepulcher, because he was to rise again. And he will not forsake those who trust in him, and call upon him. Death, deprived of its sting, will soon end the believer's sorrows, as it ended those of the Savior.

MARK 16

Christ's resurrection made known the women. (1-8)
Christ appears to Mary Magdalene and other disciples. (9-13)
His commission to the apostles. (14-18)
Christ's ascension. (19,20)

1-8 Nicodemus brought a large quantity of spices, but these good women did not think that enough. The respect others show to Christ, should not hinder us from showing our respect. And those who are carried by holy zeal, to seek Christ diligently, will find the difficulties in their way speedily vanish. When we put ourselves to trouble and expense, from love to Christ, we shall be accepted, though our endeavors are not successful. The sight of the angel might justly have encouraged them, but they were affrighted. Thus many times that which should be matter of com-

Brethren and sisters, it is enough of evil—if there were no more,—that unbelief is so cruel to Christ and grieves his Holy Spirit so much. I should but repeat myself if I reminded you how mistrust grieves you; and, speaking after the manner of men, in the same fashion it grieves the Holy Spirit. He dwells in you; shall he dwell in you to be grieved by you? He assuages your grief; will you cause him grief? Your vexations vanish because he is the Comforter; will you vex the Comforter? And what can vex him more than suspecting the ever-faithful heart of Christ? That is evil enough,—to wound Christ and the Holy Spirit.

Next, remember,—though this is a more selfish argument,—how much unrest and misery unbelief has caused to yourself. You have never had half as many trials from God as you have manufactured for yourself. Death, which you so much dread, is nothing compared with the thousand deaths that you have died through the fear of death. You make a whip for yourself, and you mix bitter cups for yourself, by your unbelief. There is quite enough trial for you to bear, and God will help you to bear it; but you put away the helping hand when you are unbelieving, and then you increase your own burden. Oh, you can sing, even by the rivers of Babylon, if you have but faith! you may lie on your sick bed, and feel great pain; yet your spirit shall not smart, but shall dance away your pangs, if your heart be but looking in simple confidence to Christ; and you shall die, as the negro said his master died,—"full of life,"—if you have true faith in Jesus. But if faith shall fail you, oh then you are distressed when there is no cause for distress, and full of fear where no fear is!

And, then, how much you lose, in other things, besides happiness! A thousand promises are missed because there is not the faith to claim them. There are the caskets, and you have the keys; yet you do not put the keys into the locks to open them. There are Joseph's granaries, and you are hungry; but you do not go unto Joseph, and show your confidence in him by asking for what you need. Ye are not straitened in God, but in yourselves. If you believe not, you shall not be established, neither shall your prayers prevail, nor shall you grow in grace. If you believe not, your experience shall not be of that high and lofty kind that otherwise it might have

King of the Jews?

10 For he knew that the chief priests had delivered him for envy.

11 But the chief priests moved the people, that he should rather release Barabbas unto them.

12 And Pilate answered and said again unto them, What will ye then that I shall do unto him whom ye call the King of the Jews?

13 And they cried out again, Crucify him.

14 Then Pilate said unto them, Why, what evil hath he done? And they cried out the more exceedingly, Crucify him.

15 And so Pilate, willing to content the people, released Barabbas unto them, and delivered Jesus, when he had scourged him, to be crucified.

16 And the soldiers led him away into the hall, called Pretorium; and they call together the whole band.

17 And they clothed him with purple, and platted a crown of thorns, and put it about his head,

18 And began to salute him, Hail, King of the Jews!

19 And they smote him on the head with a reed, and did spit upon him, and bowing their knees worshiped him.

20 And when they had mocked him, they took off the purple from him, and put his own clothes on him, and led him out to crucify him.

21 And they compel one Simon a Cyrenian, who passed by, coming out of the country, the father of Alexander and Rufus, to bear his cross.

22 And they bring him unto the place Golgotha, which is, being interpreted, The place of a skull.

23 And they gave him to drink wine mingled with myrrh: but he received it not.

24 And when they had crucified him, they parted his garments, casting lots upon them, what every man should take.

25 And it was the third hour, and they crucified him.

26 And the superscription of his accusation was written over, THE KING OF THE JEWS.

27 And with him they crucify two thieves; the one on his right hand, and the other on his left.

28 And the scripture was fulfilled, which saith, And he was numbered with the transgressors.

29 And they that passed by railed on him, wagging their heads, and saying, Ah, thou that destroyest the temple, and buildest it in three days,

30 Save thyself, and come down from the cross.

31 Likewise also the chief priests mocking said among themselves with the scribes, He saved others; himself he cannot save.

32 Let Christ the King of Israel descend now from the cross, that we may see and believe. And they that were crucified with him reviled him.

33 And when the sixth hour was come, there was darkness over the whole land until the ninth hour.

34 And at the ninth hour Jesus cried with a loud voice, saying, Eloi, Eloi, lama sabachthani? which is, being interpreted, My God, my God, why hast thou forsaken me?

35 And some of them that stood by, when they heard it, said, Behold, he calleth Elias.

36 And one ran and filled a sponge full of vinegar, and put it on a reed, and gave him to drink, saying, Let alone; let us see whether Elias will come to take him down.

37 And Jesus cried with a loud voice, and gave up the ghost.

38 And the veil of the temple was rent in twain from the top to the bottom.

39 And when the centurion, which stood over against him, saw that he so cried out, and gave up the ghost, he said, Truly this man was the Son of God.

40 There were also women looking on afar off: among whom was Mary Magdalene, and Mary the mother of James the less and of Joses, and Salome;

41 (Who also, when he was in Galilee, followed him, and ministered

43. Honorable – A man of character and reputation: A counselor – A member of the Sanhedrin. Who waited for the kingdom of God – Who expected to see it set up on earth. Matt. xxvii, 57; Luke xxiii, 50; John xix, 38.

46. He rolled a stone – By his servants. It was too large for him to roll himself.

MARK 16

1. Matt. xxviii, 1; Luke xxiv, 1; John xx, 1.

2. At the rising of the sun – They set out while it was yet dark, and came within sight of the sepulcher, for the first time, just as it grew light enough to discern that the stone was rolled away, Matt. xxviii, 1; Luke xxiv, 1; John xx, 1. But by the time Mary had called Peter and John, and they had viewed the sepulcher, the sun was rising.

3. Who shall roll us away the stone – This seems to have been the only difficulty they apprehended. So they knew nothing of Pilate's having sealed the stone, and placed a guard of soldiers there.

7. And Peter – Though he so oft denied his Lord. What amazing goodness was this!

9. John xx, 11.

10. Luke xxiv, 9; John xx, 18.

12. Luke xxiv, 13.

13. Neither believed they them – They were moved a little by the testimony of these, added to that of St. Peter, Luke xxiv, 34; but they did not yet fully believe it.

14. Luke xxiv, 36; John xx, 19.

15. Go ye into all the world, and preach the Gospel to every creature – Our Lord speaks without any limitation or restriction. If therefore every creature in every age hath not heard it, either those who should have preached, or those who should have heard it, or both, made void the counsel of God herein. Matt. xxviii, 19.

16. And is baptized – In token thereof. Every one that believed was baptized. But he that believeth not – Whether baptized or unbaptized, shall perish everlastingly.

17. And these signs shall follow them that believe – An eminent author sub-joins, "That believe with that very faith mentioned in the preceding verse." (Though it is certain that a man may work miracles, and not have saving faith, Matt. vii, 22, 23.) "It was not one faith by which St. Paul was saved, another by which he wrought miracles. Even at this day in every believer faith has a latent miraculous power; (every effect of prayer being really miraculous;) although in many, both because of their own littleness of

fort to us, through our own mistake, proves a terror to us. He was crucified, but he is glorified. He is risen, he is not here, not dead, but alive again; hereafter you will see him, but you may here see the place where he was laid. Thus seasonable comforts will be sent to those that lament after the Lord Jesus. Peter is particularly named, Tell Peter; it will be most welcome to him, for he is in sorrow for sin. A sight of Christ will be very welcome to a true penitent, and a true penitent is very welcome to a sight of Christ. The men ran with all the haste they could to the disciples; but disquieting fears often hinder us from doing that service to Christ and to the souls of men, which, if faith and the joy of faith were strong, we might do.

9-13 Better news cannot be brought to disciples in tears, than to tell them of Christ's resurrection. And we should study to comfort disciples that are mourners, by telling them whatever we have seen of Christ. It was a wise providence that the proofs of Christ's resurrection were given gradually, and admitted cautiously, that the assurance with which the apostles preached this doctrine afterwards might the more satisfy. Yet how slowly do we admit the consolations which the word of God holds forth! Therefore while Christ comforts his people, he often sees it needful to rebuke and correct them for hardness of heart in distrusting his promise, as well as in not obeying his holy precepts.

14-18 The evidences of the truth of the gospel are so full, that those who receive it not, may justly be upbraided with their unbelief. Our blessed Lord renewed his choice of the eleven as his apostles, and commissioned them to go into all the world, to preach his gospel to every creature. Only he that is a true Christian shall be saved through Christ. Simon Magus professed to believe, and was baptized, yet he was declared to be in the bonds of iniquity: see his history in Ac 8:13-25. Doubtless this is a solemn declaration of that true faith which receives Christ in all his characters and offices, and for all the purposes of salvation, and which produces its right effect on the heart and life; not a mere assent, which is a dead faith, and cannot profit. The commission of Christ's ministers extends to every creature throughout the world, and the declarations of the gospel contain not only truths, encouragements, and precepts, but also most awful warnings. Observe what power the apostles should be endued with, for confirming the doctrine they were to preach. These were miracles to confirm the truth of the gospel, and means of spreading the gospel among nations that had not heard it.

19,20 After the Lord had spoken he went up into heaven. Sitting is a posture of rest, he had finished his work; and a posture of rule, he took possession of his kingdom. He sat at the right hand of God, which denotes his sovereign dignity and universal power. Whatever God does concerning us, gives to us, or accepts from us, it is by his Son. Now he is glorified with the glory he had before the world. The apostles went forth, and preached everywhere, far and near. Though the doctrine they preached was spiritual and heavenly, and directly contrary to the spirit and temper of

been. We live down here in the marsh and the mist, when, had we faith, we might live in the everlasting sunshine. We are down below in the dungeons, fretting under imaginary chains, when the key of promise is in our bosom, which will open every door in Doubting Castle. If we will but use it, we may get away to the tops of the mountains, and see the New Jerusalem, and the land which is very far off.

Further, unbelief weakens us for all practical purposes. What can the man who is unbelieving do? O brothers and sisters in Christ, it is a terrible thing to think how much work there is that falls flat because it is not done in faith. You saw the trees when they were covered with bloom; there seemed to be a promise of much fruit; but there were chilling winds, and sharp frosts, and so, perhaps, only one in a hundred of the blossoms ever turned to fruit. The tree of the Church seems, at times, covered with beauteous blossoms; what can be more lovely to the sight? But the blossoms do not knit—faith is the bee that carries the pollen, it is faith that fructifies the whole, and makes it truly fruitful unto God. What might my sermons not have done had I believed my Master more? You, Sunday-school teacher, may say, "Had I taught in greater faith, I might have won my scholars." Or you may say, "Had I gone to my visitings of the poor and the sick in the strength of the Lord, who knows what I might have done for him?" Faith is the Nazarite lock of Samson; if it be shorn away, Samson is weak as other men. Then, as to suffering, wonderful is the power of faith there. If you are trusting your Heavenly Father, believing that all is right that seems most wrong, that everything that happens is ordered or permitted by him, and that his grace will sweeten every bitter cup, you can suffer patiently; and, as your tribulations abound, so will your consolations abound in Christ Jesus. Like the ark of Noah, as the waters deepen, you will rise upon them, and get nearer to heaven in proportion as the great floods increase.

Unbelief, in any Christian, no doubt has a very injurious effect upon other Christians. There are some, who are like sickly sheep, which—

"Infect the flock,
And poison all the rest."

Especially is it so, dear brethren, if you happen to be in office in the church, or to

unto him;) and many other women which came up with him unto Jerusalem.

42
And now when the even was come, because it was the preparation, that is, the day before the sabbath,

43 Joseph of Arimathea, and honorable counselor, which also waited for the kingdom of God, came, and went in boldly unto Pilate, and craved the body of Jesus.

44 And Pilate marveled if he were already dead: and calling unto him the centurion, he asked him whether he had been any while dead.

45 And when he knew it of the centurion, he gave the body to Joseph.

46 And he bought fine linen, and took him down, and wrapped him in the linen, and laid him in a sepulcher which was hewn out of a rock, and rolled a stone unto the door of the sepulcher.

47 And Mary Magdalene and Mary the mother of Joses beheld where he was laid.

MARK 16

1 And when the sabbath was past, Mary Magdalene, and Mary the mother of James, and Salome, had bought sweet spices, that they might come and anoint him.

2 And very early in the morning the first day of the week, they came unto the sepulcher at the rising of the sun.

3 And they said among themselves, Who shall roll us away the stone from the door of the sepulcher?

4 And when they looked, they saw that the stone was rolled away: for it was very great.

5 And entering into the sepulcher, they saw a young man sitting on the right side, clothed in a long white garment; and they were affrighted.

6 And he saith unto them, Be not affrighted: Ye seek Jesus of Nazareth, which was crucified: he is risen; he is not here: behold the place where they laid him.

7 But go your way, tell his disciples and Peter that he goeth before you into Galilee: there shall ye see him, as he said unto you.

8 And they went out quickly, and fled from the sepulcher; for they trembled and were amazed: neither said they any thing to any man; for they were afraid.

9 Now when Jesus was risen early the first day of the week, he appeared first to Mary Magdalene, out of whom he had cast seven devils.

10 And she went and told them that had been with him, as they mourned and wept.

11 And they, when they had heard that he was alive, and had been seen of her, believed not.

12 After that he appeared in another form unto two of them, as they walked, and went into the country.

13 And they went and told it unto the residue: neither believed they them.

14 Afterward he appeared unto the eleven as they sat at meat, and upbraided them with their unbelief and hardness of heart, because they believed not them which had seen him after he was risen.

15 And he said unto them, Go ye into all the world, and preach the gospel to every creature.

16 He that believeth and is baptized shall be saved; but he that believeth not shall be damned.

17 And these signs shall follow them that believe; In my name shall they cast out devils; they shall speak with new tongues;

18 They shall take up serpents; and if they drink any deadly thing, it shall not hurt them; they shall lay hands on the sick, and they shall recover.

19 So then after the Lord had spoken unto them, he was received up into heaven, and sat on the right hand of God.

20 And they went forth, and preached everywhere, the Lord working

faith, and because the world is unworthy, that power is not exerted. Miracles, in the beginning, were helps to faith; now also they are the object of it. At Leonberg, in the memory of our fathers, a cripple that could hardly move with crutches, while the dean was preaching on this very text, was in a moment made whole." Shall follow – The word and faith must go before. In my name – By my authority committed to them. Raising the dead is not mentioned. So our Lord performed even more than he promised.

18. If they drink any deadly thing – But not by their own choice. God never calls us to try any such experiments.

19. The Lord – How seasonable is he called by this title! After he had spoken to them – For forty days. Luke xxiv, 50.

20. They preached every where – At the time St. Mark wrote, the apostles had already gone into all the known world, Rom. x, 18; and each of them was there known where he preached: the name of Christ only was known throughout the world.

MATTHEW HENRY

the world; though it met with much opposition, and was wholly destitute of all worldly supports and advantages; yet in a few years the sound went forth unto the ends of the earth. Christ's ministers do not now need to work miracles to prove their message; the Scriptures are proved to be of Divine origin, and this renders those without excuse who reject or neglect them. The effects of the gospel, when faithfully preached, and truly believed, in changing the tempers and characters of mankind, form a constant proof, a miraculous proof, that the gospel is the power of God unto salvation, of all who believe.

CHARLES H. SPURGEON

be doing any prominent work for Christ. If the commander-in-chief trembles, the army is already conquered; if the captain begins to fear, fear will take possession of every soldier's heart in his company. Was it not grand of Paul, in the shipwreck, when all others were dismayed, and thought they should go to the bottom, but he said, "Have no fear, sirs," and he bade them eat, as he ate,—calmly giving thanks to God before them all? Why, Paul saved them all by his calm confidence in God. If we have but faith, we shall strengthen our brethren; and if we have it not, we shall weaken them. I am sure, too, that the influence of unbelief in Christians, upon the unconverted, is very serious indeed. If we do not play the man in times of trial,— if we do not show them what faith in God can do,—they will think that there is nothing in it. And suppose, brethren, you should make anyone think there is nothing in religion, how sad that would be! When the devil wants a friend, surely he could not find one more able to do him service than a child of God who is full of mistrust. The children say, "Our father only trusts God for bread when there is plenty in the cupboard." And the servants say, "The master is only happy in the Lord when he is in good health." And those who know our business affairs say, "Oh, yes! So-and-so is a great believer; but, then, he has a big balance at his banker's; you should see him when trade is bad; you should see him when there are bad debts; and you will find that he is not a bit more a believer in Jesus Christ than any of the rest of us. He is a fair-weather Christian; he is like the flowers that open when the sun shines; but take away the summer prosperity, and you will see but little of his religion." Let it not be so with any of us, but may God deliver us from this tremendous evil of unbelief!

Luke

LUKE 1

1 Forasmuch as many have taken in hand to set forth in order a declaration of those things which are most surely believed among us,

2 Even as they delivered them unto us, which from the beginning were eyewitnesses, and ministers of the word;

3 It seemed good to me also, having had perfect understanding of all things from the very first, to write unto thee in order, most excellent Theophilus,

4 That thou mightest know the certainty of those things, wherein thou hast been instructed.

5 There was in the days of Herod, the king of Judea, a certain priest named Zacharias, of the course of Abia: and his wife was of the daughters of Aaron, and her name was Elisabeth.

6 And they were both righteous before God, walking in all the commandments and ordinances of the Lord blameless.

7 And they had no child, because that Elisabeth was barren, and they both were now well stricken in years.

8 And it came to pass, that while he executed the priest's office before God in the order of his course,

9 According to the custom of the priest's office, his lot was to burn incense when he went into the temple of the Lord.

10 And the whole multitude of the people were praying without at the time of incense.

11 And there appeared unto him an angel of the Lord standing on the right side of the altar of incense.

12 And when Zacharias saw him, he was troubled, and fear fell upon him.

13 But the angel said unto him, Fear not, Zacharias: for thy prayer is heard; and thy wife Elisabeth shall bear thee a son, and thou shalt call his name John.

14 And thou shalt have joy and gladness; and many shall rejoice at his birth.

15 For he shall be great in the sight of the Lord, and shall drink neither wine nor strong drink; and he shall be filled with the Holy Ghost, even from his mother's womb.

16 And many of the children of Israel shall he turn to the Lord their God.

17 And he shall go before him in the spirit and power of Elias, to turn the hearts of the fathers to the children, and the disobedient to the wisdom of the just; to make ready a people prepared for the Lord.

18 And Zacharias said unto the angel, Whereby shall I know this? for I am an old man, and my wife well stricken in years.

19 And the angel answering said unto him, I am Gabriel, that stand in the presence of God; and am sent to speak unto thee, and to shew thee these glad tidings.

20 And, behold, thou shalt be dumb, and not able to speak, until the day that these things shall be performed, because thou believest not my words, which shall be fulfilled in their season.

21 And the people waited for Zacharias, and marveled that he tarried so long in the temple.

22 And when he came out, he could not speak unto them: and they perceived that he had seen a vision in the temple: for he beckoned unto them, and remained speechless.

23 And it came to pass, that, as soon as the days of his ministration were accomplished, he departed to his own house.

24 And after those days his wife Elisabeth conceived, and hid herself five months, saying,

25 Thus hath the Lord dealt with me in the days wherein he looked on me, to take away my reproach among men.

26 And in the sixth month the angel Gabriel was sent from

LUKE 1

1, 2. This short, weighty, artless, candid dedication, belongs to the Acts, as well as the Gospel of St. Luke. Many have undertaken – He does not mean St. Matthew or Mark; and St. John did not write so early. For these were eye witnesses themselves and ministers of the word.

3. To write in order – St. Luke describes in order of time; first, The Acts of Christ; his conception, birth, childhood, baptism, miracles, preaching, passion, resurrection, ascension: then, The Acts of the Apostles. But in many smaller circumstances he does not observe the order of time. Most excellent Theophilus – This was the appellation usually given to Roman governors. Theophilus (as the ancients inform us) was a person of eminent quality at Alexandria. In Acts i, 1, St. Luke does not give him that title. He was then probably a private man. After the preface St. Luke gives us the history of Christ, from his coming into the world to his ascension into heaven.

5. The course of Abia – The priests were divided into twenty-four courses, of which that of Abia was the eighth, 1 Ch xxiv, 10. Each course ministered in its turn, for seven days, from Sabbath to Sabbath. And each priest of the course or set in waiting, had his part in the temple service assigned him by lot.

6. Walking in all the moral commandments, and ceremonial ordinances, blameless – How admirable a character! May our behavior be thus unblamable, and our obedience thus sincere and universal!

10. The people were praying without, at the time of the incense – So the pious Jews constantly did. And this was the foundation of that elegant figure, by which prayer is in Scripture so often compared to incense. Perhaps one reason of ordaining incense might be, to intimate the acceptableness of the prayer that accompanied it; as well as to remind the worshipers of that sacrifice of a sweet-smelling savor, which was once to be offered to God for them, and of that incense, which is continually offered with the prayers of the saints, upon the golden altar that is before the throne, Rev. viii, 3, 4.

12. Zacharias was troubled – Although he was accustomed to converse with God, yet we see he was thrown into a great consternation, at the appearance of his angelical messenger, nature not being able to sustain the sight. Is it not then an instance of the goodness as well as of the wisdom of God, that the services, which these heavenly spirits render us, are generally invisible?

13. Thy prayer is heard – Let us observe with pleasure, that the prayers of pious worshipers come up with acceptance before God; to whom no costly perfume is so sweet, as the fragrance of an upright heart. An answer of peace was here returned, when the case seemed to be most helpless. Let us wait patiently for the Lord, and leave to his own wisdom the time and manner wherein

MATTHEW HENRY

CHARLES H. SPURGEON

This evangelist is generally supposed to have been a physician, and a companion of the apostle Paul. The style of his writings, and his acquaintance with the Jewish rites and usages, sufficiently show that he was a Jew, while his knowledge of the Greek language and his name, speak his Gentile origin. He is first mentioned Ac 16:10,11, as with Paul at Troas, whence he attended him to Jerusalem, and was with him in his voyage, and in his imprisonment at Rome. This Gospel appears to be designed to supersede many defective and unauthentic narratives in circulation, and to give a genuine and inspired account of the life, miracles, and doctrines of our Lord, learned from those who heard and witnessed his discourses and miracles.

LUKE 1

The Preface. (1-4)
Zacharias and Elisabeth. (5-25)
Christ's birth announced. (26-38)
Interview of Mary and Elisabeth. (39-56)
The birth of John the Baptist. (57-66)
The song of Zacharias. (67-80)

1-4 Luke will not write of things about which Christians may safely differ from one another, and hesitate within themselves; but the things which are, and ought to be surely believed. The doctrine of Christ is what the wisest and best of men have ventured their souls upon with confidence and satisfaction. And the great events whereon our hopes depend, have been recorded by those who were from the beginning eyewitnesses and ministers of the word, and who were perfected in their understanding of them through Divine inspiration.

5-25 The father and mother of John the Baptist were sinners as all are, and were justified and saved in the same way as others; but they were eminent for piety and integrity. They had no children, and it could not be expected that Elisabeth should have any in her old age. While Zacharias was burning incense in the temple, the whole multitude of the people were praying without. All the prayers we offer up to God, are acceptable and successful only by Christ's intercession in the temple of God above. We cannot expect an interest therein if we do not pray, and pray with our spirits, and are not earnest in prayer. Nor can we expect that the best of our prayers should gain acceptance, and bring an answer of peace, but through the mediation of Christ, who ever lives, making intercession. The prayers Zacharias often made, received an answer of peace. Prayers of faith are filed in heaven, and are not forgotten. Prayers made when we were young and entering into the world, may be answered when we are old and going out of the world. Mercies are doubly sweet that are given in answer to prayer. Zacharias shall have a son in his old

JOY BORN AT BETHLEHEM
A sermon delivered on December 24th, 1871, at the Metropolitan Tabernacle, Newington.

"And the angel said unto them, Fear not: for, behold, I bring you good tidings of great joy, which shall be to all people. For unto you is born this day in the city of David a Savior, which is Christ the Lord. And this shall be a sign unto you; Ye shall find the babe wrapped in swaddling clothes, lying in a manger."—Luke 2:10-12.

WE HAVE NO superstitious regard for times and seasons. Certainly we do not believe in the present ecclesiastical arrangement called Christmas: first, because we do not believe in the mass at all, but abhor it, whether it be said or sung in Latin or in English; and, secondly, because we find no Scriptural warrant whatever for observing any day as the birthday of the Savior; and, consequently, its observance is a superstition, because not of divine authority. Superstition has fixed most positively the day of our Savior's birth, although there is no possibility of discovering when it occurred. Fabricius gives a catalogue of 136 different learned opinions upon the matter; and various divines invent weighty arguments for advocating a date in every month in the year. It was not till the middle of the third century that any part of the church celebrated the nativity of our Lord; and it was not till very long after the Western church had set the example, that the Eastern adopted it. Because the day is not known, therefore superstition has fixed it; while, since the day of the death of our Savior might be determined with much certainty, therefore superstition shifts the date of its observance every year. Where is the method in the madness of the superstitious? Probably the fact is that the holy days were arranged to fit in with heathen festivals. We venture to assert, that if there be any day in the year, of which we may be pretty sure that it was not the day on which the Savior was born, it is the twenty-fifth of December. Nevertheless since, the current of men's thoughts is led this way just now, and I see no evil in the current itself, I shall launch the bark of our discourse upon that stream, and make use of the fact, which I shall neither justify nor condemn, by endeavoring to lead your thoughts in the same direction. Since it is lawful, and even laudable, to meditate upon the incarnation of the Lord upon any day in the year, it cannot be in the power of other men's superstitions to render such a meditation improper for today. Regarding not the day, let us, nevertheless, give God thanks for the gift of his dear son.

God unto a city of Galilee, named Nazareth,

27 To a virgin espoused to a man whose name was Joseph, of the house of David; and the virgin's name was Mary.

28 And the angel came in unto her, and said, Hail, thou that art highly favored, the Lord is with thee: blessed art thou among women.

29 And when she saw him, she was troubled at his saying, and cast in her mind what manner of salutation this should be.

30 And the angel said unto her, Fear not, Mary: for thou hast found favor with God.

31 And, behold, thou shalt conceive in thy womb, and bring forth a son, and shalt call his name JESUS.

32 He shall be great, and shall be called the Son of the Highest: and the Lord God shall give unto him the throne of his father David;

33 And he shall reign over the house of Jacob for ever; and of his kingdom there shall be no end.

34 Then said Mary unto the angel, How shall this be, seeing I know not a man?

35 And the angel answered and said unto her, The Holy Ghost shall come upon thee, and the power of the Highest shall overshadow thee: therefore also that holy thing which shall be born of thee shall be called the Son of God.

36 And, behold, thy cousin Elisabeth, she hath also conceived a son in her old age: and this is the sixth month with her, who was called barren.

37 For with God nothing shall be impossible.

38 And Mary said, Behold the handmaid of the Lord; be it unto me according to thy word. And the angel departed from her.

39 And Mary arose in those days, and went into the hill country with haste, into a city of Juda;

40 And entered into the house of Zacharias, and saluted Elisabeth.

41 And it came to pass, that, when Elisabeth heard the salutation of Mary, the babe leaped in her womb; and Elisabeth was filled with the Holy Ghost:

42 And she spake out with a loud voice, and said, Blessed art thou among women, and blessed is the fruit of thy womb.

43 And whence is this to me, that the mother of my Lord should come to me?

44 For, lo, as soon as the voice of thy salutation sounded in mine ears, the babe leaped in my womb for joy.

45 And blessed is she that believed: for there shall be a performance of those things which were told her from the Lord.

46 And Mary said, My soul doth magnify the Lord,

47 And my spirit hath rejoiced in God my Savior.

48 For he hath regarded the low estate of his handmaiden: for, behold, from henceforth all generations shall call me blessed.

49 For he that is mighty hath done to me great things; and holy is his name.

50 And his mercy is on them that fear him from generation to generation.

51 He hath shewed strength with his arm; he hath scattered the proud in the imagination of their hearts.

52 He hath put down the mighty from their seats, and exalted them of low degree.

53 He hath filled the hungry with good things; and the rich he hath sent empty away.

54 He hath holpen his servant Israel, in remembrance of his mercy;

55 As he spake to our fathers, to Abraham, and to his seed for ever.

he will appear for us. Thou shalt call his name John – John signifies the grace or favor of Jehovah. A name well suiting the person, who was afterward so highly in favor with God, and endued with abundance of grace; and who opened a way to the most glorious dispensation of grace in the Messiah's kingdom. And so Zacharias's former prayers for a child, and the prayer which he, as the representative of the people, was probably offering at this very time, for the appearing of the Messiah, were remarkably answered in the birth of his forerunner.

15. He shall be great before the Lord – God the Father: of the Holy Ghost and the Son of God mention is made immediately after. And shall drink neither wine nor strong drink – Shall be exemplary for abstemiousness and self-denial; and so much the more filled with the Holy Ghost.

16. And many of the children of Israel shall he turn – None therefore need be ashamed of "preaching like John the Baptist." To the Lord their God – To Christ.

17. He shall go before him, Christ, in the power and spirit of Elijah – With the same integrity, courage, austerity, and fervor, and the same power attending his word: to turn the hearts of the fathers to the children – To reconcile those that are at variance, to put an end to the most bitter quarrels, such as are very frequently those between the nearest relations: and the hearts of the disobedient to the wisdom of the just – And the most obstinate sinners to true wisdom, which is only found among them that are righteous before God.

18. Zacharias said, Whereby shall I know this? – In how different a spirit did the blessed virgin say, How shall this be? Zacharias disbelieved the fact: Mary had no doubt of the thing; but only inquired concerning the manner of it.

19. I am Gabriel, that stand in the presence of God – Seven angels thus stand before God, Rev. vii, 2; who seem the highest of all. There seems to be a remarkable gradation in the words, enhancing the guilt of Zacharias's unbelief. As if he had said, I am Gabriel, a holy angel of God: yea, one of the highest order. Not only so, but am now peculiarly sent from God; and that with a message to thee in particular. Nay, and to show thee glad tidings, such as ought to be received with the greatest joy and readiness.

20. Thou shalt be dumb – The Greek word signifies deaf, as well as dumb: and it seems plain, that he was as unable to hear, as he was to speak; for his friends were obliged to make signs to him, that he might understand them, ver. 62.

21. The people were waiting – For him to come and dismiss them (as usual) with the blessing.

24. Hid herself – She retired from company, that she might have the more leisure to rejoice and bless God for his wonderful mercy.

25. He looked upon me to take away my reproach –

MATTHEW HENRY   CHARLES H. SPURGEON

age, who shall be instrumental in the conversion of many souls to God, and preparing them to receive the gospel of Christ. He shall go before Him with courage, zeal, holiness, and a mind dead to earthly interests and pleasures. The disobedient and rebellious would be brought back to the wisdom of their righteous forefathers, or rather, brought to attend to the wisdom of that Just One who was coming among them. Zacharias heard all that the angel said; but his unbelief spake. In striking him dumb, God dealt justly with him, because he had objected against God's word. We may admire the patience of God towards us. God dealt kindly with him, for thus he prevented his speaking any more distrustful, unbelieving words. Thus also God confirmed his faith. If by the rebukes we are under for our sin, we are brought to give the more credit to the word of God, we have no reason to complain. Even real believers are apt to dishonor God by unbelief; and their mouths are stopped in silence and confusion, when otherwise they would have been praising God with joy and gratitude. In God's gracious dealings with us we ought to observe his gracious regards to us. He has looked on us with compassion and favor, and therefore has thus dealt with us.

26-38 We have here an account of the mother of our Lord; though we are not to pray to her, yet we ought to praise God for her. Christ must be born miraculously. The angel's address means only, Hail, thou that art the especially chosen and favored of the Most High, to attain the honor Jewish mothers have so long desired. This wondrous salutation and appearance troubled Mary. The angel then assured her that she had found favor with God, and would become the mother of a son whose name she should call Jesus, the Son of the Highest, one in a nature and perfection with the Lord God. JESUS! the name that refreshes the fainting spirits of humbled sinners; sweet to speak and sweet to hear, Jesus, a Savior! We know not his riches and our own poverty, therefore we run not to him; we perceive not that we are lost and perishing, therefore a Savior is a word of little relish. Were we convinced of the huge mass of guilt that lies upon us, and the wrath that hangs over us for it, ready to fall upon us, it would be our continual thought, Is the Savior mine? And that we might find him so, we should trample on all that hinders our way to him. Mary's reply to the angel was the language of faith and humble admiration, and she asked no sign for the confirming her faith. Without controversy, great was the mystery of godliness, God manifest in the flesh, 1Ti 3:16. Christ's human nature must be produced so, as it was fit that should be which was to be taken into union with the Divine nature. And we must, as Mary here, guide our desires by the word of God. In all conflicts, let us remember that with God nothing is impossible; and as we read and hear his promises, let us turn them into prayers, Behold the willing ser-

In our text we have before us the sermon of the first evangelist under the gospel dispensation. The preacher was an angel, and it was meet it should be so, for the grandest and last of all evangels will be proclaimed by an angel when he shall sound the trumpet of the resurrection, and the children of the regeneration shall rise into the fullness of their joy. The keynote of this angelic gospel is joy—"I bring unto you good tidings of great joy." Nature fears in the presence of God—the shepherds were sore afraid. The law itself served to deepen this natural feeling of dismay; seeing men were sinful, and the law came into the world to reveal sin, its tendency was to make men fear and tremble under any and every divine revelation. The Jews unanimously believed that if any man beheld supernatural appearances, he would be sure to die, so that what nature dictated, the law and the general beliefs of those under it also abetted. But the first word of the gospel ended all this, for the angelic evangelist said, "Fear not, behold I bring you good tidings." Henceforth, it is to be no dreadful thing for man to approach his Maker; redeemed man is not to fear when God unveils the splendor of his majesty, since he appears no more a judge upon his throne of terror, but a Father unbending in sacred familiarity before his own beloved children.

The joy which this first gospel preacher spoke of was no mean one, for he said, "I bring you good tidings"—that alone were joy: and not good tidings of joy only, but "good tidings of great joy." Every word is emphatic, as if to show that the gospel is above all things intended to promote, and will most abundantly create the greatest possible joy in the human heart wherever it is received. Man is like a harp unstrung, and the music of his soul's living strings is discordant, his whole nature wails with sorrow; but the son of David, that mighty harper, has come to restore the harmony of humanity, and where his gracious fingers move among the strings, the touch of the fingers of an incarnate God brings forth music sweet as that of the spheres, and melody rich as a seraph's canticle. Would God that all men felt that divine hand.

In trying to open up this angelic discourse this morning, we shall note three things: the joy which is spoken of; next, the persons to whom this joy comes; and then, thirdly, the sign, which is to us a sign as well as to these shepherds—a sign of the birth and source of joy.

I. First, then, THE JOY, which is mentioned in

56 And Mary abode with her about three months, and returned to her own house.

57 Now Elisabeth's full time came that she should be delivered; and she brought forth a son.

58 And her neighbors and her cousins heard how the Lord had shewed great mercy upon her; and they rejoiced with her.

59 And it came to pass, that on the eighth day they came to circumcize the child; and they called him Zacharias, after the name of his father.

60 And his mother answered and said, Not so; but he shall be called John.

61 And they said unto her, There is none of thy kindred that is called by this name.

62 And they made signs to his father, how he would have him called.

63 And he asked for a writing table, and wrote, saying, His name is John. And they marveled all.

64 And his mouth was opened immediately, and his tongue loosed, and he spake, and praised God.

65 And fear came on all that dwelt round about them: and all these sayings were noised abroad throughout all the hill country of Judea.

66 And all they that heard them laid them up in their hearts, saying, What manner of child shall this be! And the hand of the Lord was with him.

67 And his father Zacharias was filled with the Holy Ghost, and prophesied, saying,

68 Blessed be the Lord God of Israel; for he hath visited and redeemed his people,

69 And hath raised up an horn of salvation for us in the house of his servant David;

70 As he spake by the mouth of his holy prophets, which have been since the world began:

71 That we should be saved from our enemies, and from the hand of all that hate us;

72 To perform the mercy promised to our fathers, and to remember his holy covenant;

73 The oath which he sware to our father Abraham,

74 That he would grant unto us, that we being delivered out of the hand of our enemies might serve him without fear,

75 In holiness and righteousness before him, all the days of our life.

76 And thou, child, shalt be called the prophet of the Highest: for thou shalt go before the face of the Lord to prepare his ways;

77 To give knowledge of salvation unto his people by the remission of their sins,

78 Through the tender mercy of our God; whereby the dayspring from on high hath visited us,

79 To give light to them that sit in darkness and in the shadow of death, to guide our feet into the way of peace.

80 And the child grew, and waxed strong in spirit, and was in the deserts till the day of his shewing unto Israel.

LUKE 2

1 And it came to pass in those days, that there went out a decree from Cesar Augustus, that all the world should be taxed.

2 (And this taxing was first made when Cyrenius was governor of Syria.)

3 And all went to be taxed, every one into his own city.

4 And Joseph also went up from Galilee, out of the city of Nazareth, into Judea, unto the city of David, which is called

Barrenness was a great reproach among the Jews. Because fruitfulness was promised to the righteous.

26. In the sixth month – After Elisabeth had conceived.

27. Espoused – It was customary among the Jews, for persons that married to contract before witnesses some time before. And as Christ was to be born of a pure virgin, so the wisdom of God ordered it to be of one espoused, that to prevent reproach he might have a reputed father, according to the flesh.

28. Hail, thou highly favored; the Lord is with thee; blessed art thou among women – Hail is the salutation used by our Lord to the women after his resurrection: thou art highly favored, or hast found favor with God, ver. 30, is no more than was said of Noah, Moses, and David. The Lord is with thee, was said to Gideon, Judg. vi, 12; and blessed shall she be above women, of Jael, Judg. v, 24. This salutation gives no room for any pretense of paying adoration to the virgin; as having no appearance of a prayer, or of worship offered to her.

32. He shall be called the Son of the Highest – In this respect also: and that in a more eminent sense than any, either man or angel, can be called so. The Lord shall give him the throne of his father David – That is, the spiritual kingdom, of which David's was a type.

33. He shall reign over the house of Jacob – In which all true believers are included.

35. The Holy Ghost shall come upon thee, and the power of the Highest shall overshadow thee – The power of God was put forth by the Holy Ghost, as the immediate Divine agent in this work: and so he exerted the power of the Highest as his own power, who together with the Father and the Son is the most high God. Therefore also – Not only as he is God from eternity, but on this account likewise he shall be called the Son of God.

36. And behold, thy cousin Elisabeth – Though Elisabeth was of the house of Aaron, and Mary of the house of David, by the father's side, they might be related by their mothers. For the law only forbad heiresses marrying into another tribe. And so other persons continually intermarried; particularly the families of David and of Levi.

38. And Mary said, Behold the handmaid of the Lord – It is not improbable, that this time of the virgin's humble faith, consent, and expectation, might be the very time of her conceiving.

39. A city of Judah – Probably Hebron, which was situated in the hill country of Judea, and belonged to the house of Aaron.

41. When Elisabeth heard the salutation of Mary – The discourse with which she saluted her, giving an account of what the angel had said, the joy of her soul so affected her body, that the very child in her womb was moved in an uncommon manner, as if it leaped for joy.

45. Happy is she that believed – Probably she had in her

vant of the Lord; let it be unto me according to thy word.

39-56 It is very good for those who have the work of grace begun in their souls, to communicate one to another. On Mary's arrival, Elisabeth was conscious of the approach of her who was to be the mother of the great Redeemer. At the same time she was filled with the Holy Ghost, and under his influence declared that Mary and her expected child were most blessed and happy, as peculiarly honored of and dear to the Most High God. Mary, animated by Elisabeth's address, and being also under the influence of the Holy Ghost, broke out into joy, admiration, and gratitude. She knew herself to be a sinner who needed a Savior, and that she could no otherwise rejoice in God than as interested in his salvation through the promised Messiah. Those who see their need of Christ, and are desirous of righteousness and life in him, he fills with good things, with the best things; and they are abundantly satisfied with the blessings he gives. He will satisfy the desires of the poor in spirit who long for spiritual blessings, while the self-sufficient shall be sent empty away.

57-66 In these verses we have an account of the birth of John the Baptist, and the great joy among all the relations of the family. He shall be called Johanan, or "Gracious," because he shall bring in the gospel of Christ, wherein God's grace shines most bright. Zacharias recovered his speech. Unbelief closed his mouth, and believing opened it again: he believers, therefore he speaks. When God opens our lips, our mouths must show forth his praise; and better be without speech, than not use it in praising God. It is said, The hand of the Lord was working with John. God has ways of working on children in their infancy, which we cannot account for. We should observe the dealings of God, and wait the event.

67-80 Zacharias uttered a prophecy concerning the kingdom and salvation of the Messiah. The gospel brings light with it; in it the day dawns. In John the Baptist it began to break, and increased apace to the perfect day. The gospel is discovering; it shows that about which we were utterly in the dark; it is to give light to those that sit in darkness, the light of the knowledge of the glory of God in the face of Jesus Christ. It is reviving; it brings light to those that sit in the shadow of death, as condemned prisoners in the dungeon. It is directing; it is to guide our feet in the way of peace, into that way which will bring us to peace at last, Ro 3:17. John gave proofs of strong faith, vigorous and holy affections, and of being above the fear and love of the world. Thus he ripened for usefulness; but he lived a retired life, till he came forward openly as the forerunner of the Messiah. Let us follow peace with all men, as well as seek peace with God and our own consciences. And if it be the will of God

our text—whence comes it, and what is it?

We have already said it is a "great joy"— "good tidings of great joy." Earth's joy is small, her mirth is trivial, but heaven has sent us joy immeasurable, fit for immortal minds. Inasmuch as no note of time is appended, and no intimation is given that the message will ever be reversed, we may say that it is a lasting joy, a joy which will ring all down the ages, the echoes of which shall be heard until the trumpet brings the resurrection; aye, and onward for ever and for ever. For when God sent forth the angel in his brightness to say, "I bring you good tidings of great joy, which be to all people," he did as much as say, "From this time forth it shall be joy to the sons of men; there shall be peace to the human race, and goodwill towards men for ever and for ever, as long as there is glory to God in the highest." O blessed thought! the Star of Bethlehem shall never set. Jesus, the fairest among ten thousand, the most lovely among the beautiful, is a joy forever.

Since this joy is expressly associated with the glory of God, by the Words, "Glory to God in the highest," we may be quite clear that it is a pure and holy joy. No other would an angel have proclaimed, and, indeed, no other joy is joy. The wine pressed from the grapes of Sodom may sparkle and foam, but it is bitterness in the end, and the dregs thereof are death; only that which comes from the clusters of Eschol is the true wine of the kingdom, making glad the heart of God and man. Holy joy is the joy of heaven, and that, be ye sure, is the very cream of joy. The joy of sin is a fire-fountain, having its source in the burning soil of hell, maddening and consuming those who drink its firewater; of such delights we desire not to drink. It were to be worse than damned to be happy in sin, since it is the beginning of grace to be wretched in sin, and the consummation of grace to be wholly escaped from sin, and to shudder even at the thought of it. It is hell to live in sin and misery, it is a deep lower still when men could fashion a joy in sin. God save us from unholy peace and from unholy joy! The joy announced by the angel of the nativity is as pure as it is lasting, as holy as it is great. Let us then always believe concerning the Christian religion that it has its joy within itself, and holds its feasts within its own pure precincts, a feast whose viands all grow on holy ground. There are those who, tomorrow, will pretend to exhibit joy in the remembrance of our Savior's birth, but they will not seek their pleasure in the Savior: they will need many additions to the feast before they can be satis-

Bethlehem; (because he was of the house and lineage of David:)

5 To be taxed with Mary his espoused wife, being great with child.

6 And so it was, that, while they were there, the days were accomplished that she should be delivered.

7 And she brought forth her firstborn son, and wrapped him in swaddling clothes, and laid him in a manger; because there was no room for them in the inn.

8 And there were in the same country shepherds abiding in the field, keeping watch over their flock by night.

9 And, lo, the angel of the Lord came upon them, and the glory of the Lord shone round about them: and they were sore afraid.

10 And the angel said unto them, Fear not: for, behold, I bring you good tidings of great joy, which shall be to all people.

11 For unto you is born this day in the city of David a Savior, which is Christ the Lord.

12 And this shall be a sign unto you; Ye shall find the babe wrapped in swaddling clothes, lying in a manger.

13 And suddenly there was with the angel a multitude of the heavenly host praising God, and saying,

14 Glory to God in the highest, and on earth peace, good will toward men.

15 And it came to pass, as the angels were gone away from them into heaven, the shepherds said one to another, Let us now go even unto Bethlehem, and see this thing which is come to pass, which the Lord hath made known unto us.

16 And they came with haste, and found Mary, and Joseph, and the babe lying in a manger.

17 And when they had seen it, they made known abroad the saying which was told them concerning this child.

18 And all they that heard it wondered at those things which were told them by the shepherds.

19 But Mary kept all these things, and pondered them in her heart.

20 And the shepherds returned, glorifying and praising God for all the things that they had heard and seen, as it was told unto them.

21 And when eight days were accomplished for the circumcising of the child, his name was called JESUS, which was so named of the angel before he was conceived in the womb.

22 And when the days of her purification according to the law of Moses were accomplished, they brought him to Jerusalem, to present him to the Lord;

23 (As it is written in the law of the Lord, Every male that openeth the womb shall be called holy to the Lord;)

24 And to offer a sacrifice according to that which is said in the law of the Lord, A pair of turtledoves, or two young pigeons.

25 And, behold, there was a man in Jerusalem, whose name was Simeon; and the same man was just and devout, waiting for the consolation of Israel: and the Holy Ghost was upon him.

26 And it was revealed unto him by the Holy Ghost, that he should not see death, before he had seen the Lord's Christ.

27 And he came by the Spirit into the temple: and when the parents brought in the child Jesus, to do for him after the custom of the law,

28 Then took he him up in his arms, and blessed God, and said,

29 Lord, now lettest thou thy servant depart in peace, according to thy word:

30 For mine eyes have seen thy salvation,

mind the unbelief of Zacharias.

46. And Mary said – Under a prophetic impulse, several things, which perhaps she herself did not then fully understand.

47. My spirit hath rejoiced in God my Savior – She seems to turn her thoughts here to Christ himself, who was to be born of her, as the angel had told her, he should be the Son of the Highest, whose name should be Jesus, the Savior. And she rejoiced in hope of salvation through faith in him, which is a blessing common to all true believers, more than in being his mother after the flesh, which was an honor peculiar to her. And certainly she had the same reason to rejoice in God her Savior that we have: because he had regarded the low estate of his handmaid, in like manner as he regarded our low estate; and vouchsafed to come and save her and us, when we were reduced to the lowest estate of sin and misery.

51. He hath wrought strength with his arm – That is, he hath shown the exceeding greatness of his power. She speaks prophetically of those things as already done, which God was about to do by the Messiah. He hath scattered the proud – Visible and invisible.

52. He hath put down the mighty – Both angels and men.

54. He hath helped his servant Israel – By sending the Messiah.

55. To his seed – His spiritual seed: all true believers.

56. Mary returned to her own house – And thence soon after to Bethlehem.

60. His mother said – Doubtless by Revelation, or a particular impulse from God.

66. The hand of the Lord – The peculiar power and blessing of God.

67. And Zacharias prophesied – Of things immediately to follow. But it is observable, he speaks of Christ chiefly; of John only, as it were, incidentally.

69. A horn – Signifies honor, plenty, and strength. A horn of salvation – That is, a glorious and mighty Savior.

70. His prophets, who have been since the world began – For there were prophets from the very beginning.

74. To serve him without fear – Without any slavish fear. Here is the substance of the great promise. That we shall be always holy, always happy: that being delivered from Satan and sin, from every uneasy and unholy temper, we shall joyfully love and serve God, in every thought, word, and work.

76. And thou, child – He now speaks to John; yet not as a parent, but as a prophet.

77. To give knowledge of salvation by the remission of sins – The knowledge of the remission of our sins being the grand instrument of present and eternal salvation, Heb. viii, 11, 12. But the immediate sense of the words seems to be, to preach to them the Gospel doctrine of

MATTHEW HENRY

CHARLES H. SPURGEON

that we live unknown to the world, still let us diligently seek to grow strong in the grace of Jesus Christ.

LUKE 2

The birth of Christ. (1-7)
It is made known to the shepherds. (8-20)
Christ presented in the temple. (21-24)
Simeon prophesies concerning Jesus. (25-35)
Anna prophesies concerning him. (36-40)
Christ with the learned men in the temple. (41-52)

1-7 The fullness of time was now come, when God would send forth his Son, made of a woman, and made under the law. The circumstances of his birth were very mean. Christ was born at an inn; he came into the world to sojourn here for a while, as at an inn, and to teach us to do likewise. We are become by sin like an outcast infant, helpless and forlorn; and such a one was Christ. He well knew how unwilling we are to be meanly lodged, clothed, or fed; how we desire to have our children decorated and indulged; how apt the poor are to envy the rich, and how prone the rich to disdain the poor. But when we by faith view the Son of God being made man and lying in a manger, our vanity, ambition, and envy are checked. We cannot, with this object rightly before us, seek great things for ourselves or our children.

8-20 Angels were heralds of the newborn Savior, but they were only sent to some poor, humble, pious, industrious shepherds, who were in the business of their calling, keeping watch over their flock. We are not out of the way of Divine visits, when we are employed in an honest calling, and abide with God in it. Let God have the honor of this work; Glory to God in the highest. God's good will to men, manifested in sending the Messiah, redounds to his praise. Other works of God are for his glory, but the redemption of the world is for his glory in the highest. God's goodwill in sending the Messiah, brought peace into this lower world. Peace is here put for all that good which flows to us from Christ's taking our nature upon him. This is a faithful saying, attested by an innumerable company of angels, and well worthy of all acceptation, That the good will of God toward men, is glory to God in the highest, and peace on the earth. The shepherds lost no time, but came with haste to the place. They were satisfied, and made known abroad concerning this child, that he was the Savior, even Christ the Lord. Mary carefully observed and thought upon all these things, which were so suited to enliven her holy affections. We should be more delivered from errors in judgment and practice, did we more fully ponder these things in our hearts. It is still proclaimed in our ears that to us is born a Savior, Christ the Lord. These should be glad tidings to all.

21-24 Our Lord Jesus was not born in sin, and did not

fied. Joy in Immanuel would be a poor sort of mirth to them. In this country, too often, if one were unaware of the name, one might believe the Christmas festival to be a feast of Bacchus, or of Ceres, certainly not a commemoration of the Divine birth. Yet is there cause enough for holy joy in the Lord himself, and reasons for ecstasy in his birth among men. It is to be feared that most men imagine that in Christ there is only seriousness and solemnity, and to them consequently weariness, gloom, and discontent; therefore, they look out of and beyond what Christ allows, to snatch from the tables of Satan the delicacies with which to adorn the banquet held in honor of a Savior. Let it not be so among you. The joy which the gospel brings is not borrowed but blooms in its own garden. We may truly say in the language of one of our sweetest hymns—

"I need not go abroad for joy,
I have a feast at home,
My sighs are turned into songs,
My heart has ceased to roam.
Down from above the Blessed Dove
Has come into my breast,
To witness his eternal love,
And give my spirit rest."

Let our joy be living water from those sacred wells which the Lord himself has digged; may his joy abide in us, that our joy may be full. Of Christ's joy we cannot have too much; no fear of running to excess when his love is the wine we drink. Oh to be plunged in this pure stream of spiritual delights!

But why is it that the coming of Christ into the world is the occasion of joy? The answer is as follows:—First, because it is evermore a joyous fact that God should be in alliance with man, especially when the alliance is so near that God should in very deed take our manhood into union with his godhead; so that God and man should constitute one divine, mysterious person. Sin had separated between God and man; but the incarnation bridges the separation: it is a prelude to the atoning sacrifice, but it is a prelude full of the richest hope. From henceforth, when God looks upon man, he will remember that his own Son is a man. From this day forth, when he beholds the sinner, if his wrath should burn, he will remember that his own Son, as man, stood in the sinner's place, and bore the sinner's doom. As in the case of war, the feud is ended when the opposing parties intermarry, so there is no more war between God and man, because God has taken man into intimate union with himself. Herein, then, there was cause for joy.

31 Which thou hast prepared before the face of all people;

32 A light to lighten the Gentiles, and the glory of thy people Israel.

33 And Joseph and his mother marveled at those things which were spoken of him.

34 And Simeon blessed them, and said unto Mary his mother, Behold, this child is set for the fall and rising again of many in Israel; and for a sign which shall be spoken against;

35 (Yea, a sword shall pierce through thy own soul also,) that the thoughts of many hearts may be revealed.

36 And there was one Anna, a prophetess, the daughter of Phanuel, of the tribe of Aser: she was of a great age, and had lived with an husband seven years from her virginity;

37 And she was a widow of about fourscore and four years, which departed not from the temple, but served God with fastings and prayers night and day.

38 And she coming in that instant gave thanks likewise unto the Lord, and spake of him to all them that looked for redemption in Jerusalem.

39 And when they had performed all things according to the law of the Lord, they returned into Galilee, to their own city Nazareth.

40 And the child grew, and waxed strong in spirit, filled with wisdom: and the grace of God was upon him.

41 Now his parents went to Jerusalem every year at the feast of the passover.

42 And when he was twelve years old, they went up to Jerusalem after the custom of the feast.

43 And when they had fulfilled the days, as they returned, the child Jesus tarried behind in Jerusalem; and Joseph and his mother knew not of it.

44 But they, supposing him to have been in the company, went a day's journey; and they sought him among their kinsfolk and acquaintance.

45 And when they found him not, they turned back again to Jerusalem, seeking him.

46 And it came to pass, that after three days they found him in the temple, sitting in the midst of the doctors, both hearing them, and asking them questions.

47 And all that heard him were astonished at his understanding and answers.

48 And when they saw him, they were amazed: and his mother said unto him, Son, why hast thou thus dealt with us? behold, thy father and I have sought thee sorrowing.

49 And he said unto them, How is it that ye sought me? wist ye not that I must be about my Father's business?

50 And they understood not the saying which he spake unto them.

51 And he went down with them, and came to Nazareth, and was subject unto them: but his mother kept all these sayings in her heart.

52 And Jesus increased in wisdom and stature, and in favor with God and man.

LUKE 3

1 Now in the fifteenth year of the reign of Tiberius Cesar, Pontius Pilate being governor of Judea, and Herod being tetrarch of Galilee, and his brother Philip tetrarch of Iturea and of the region of Trachonitis, and Lysanias the tetrarch of Abilene,

2 Annas and Caiaphas being the high priests, the word of God came unto John the son of Zacharias in the wilderness.

3 And he came into all the country about Jordan, preaching

salvation by the remission of their sins.

78. The day spring – Or the rising sun; that is, Christ.

LUKE 2

1. That all the world should be enrolled – That all the inhabitants, male and female, of every town in the Roman empire, with their families and estates, should be registered.

2. When Cyrenius was governor of Syria – When Publius Sulpicius Quirinus governed the province of Syria, in which Judea was then included.

6. And while they were there, the days were fulfilled that she should be delivered – Mary seems not to have known that the child must have been born in Bethlehem, agreeably to the prophecy. But the providence of God took care for it.

7. She laid him in the manger – Perhaps it might rather be translated in the stall. They were lodged in the ox stall, fitted up on occasion of the great concourse, for poor guests. There was no room for them in the inn – Now also, there is seldom room for Christ in an inn. Matt. i, 25

11. To you – Shepherds; Israel; mankind.

14. Glory be to God in the highest; on earth peace; good will toward men – The shouts of the multitude are generally broken into short sentences. This rejoicing acclamation strongly represents the piety and benevolence of these heavenly spirits: as if they had said, Glory be to God in the highest heavens: let all the angelic legions resound his praises. For with the Redeemer's birth, peace, and all kind of happiness, come down to dwell on earth: yea, the overflowings of Divine good will and favor are now exercised toward men.

20. For all the things that they had heard – From Mary; as it was told them – By the angels.

21. To circumcize the child – That he might visibly be made under the law by a sacred rite, which obliged him to keep the whole law; as also that he might be owned to be the seed of Abraham, and might put an honor on the solemn dedication of children to God.

22. The days – The forty days prescribed, Lev. xii, 2, 4.

23. Exod. xiii, 2.

24. A pair of turtle doves, or two young pigeons – This offering sufficed for the poor. Lev. xii, 8.

25. The consolation of Israel – A common phrase for the Messiah, who was to be the everlasting consolation of the Israel of God. The Holy Ghost was upon him – That is, he was a prophet.

27. By the Spirit – By a particular Revelation or impulse from him.

30. Thy salvation – Thy Christ, thy Savior.

32. And the glory of thy people Israel – For after the Gentiles are enlightened, all Israel shall be saved.

33. Joseph and his mother marveled at those things

MATTHEW HENRY   CHARLES H. SPURGEON

need that mortification of a corrupt nature, or that renewal unto holiness, which were signified by circumcision. This ordinance was, in his case, a pledge of his future perfect obedience to the whole law, in the midst of sufferings and temptations, even unto death for us. At the end of forty days, Mary went up to the temple to offer the appointed sacrifices for her purification. Joseph also presented the holy child Jesus, because, as a first-born son, he was to be presented to the Lord, and redeemed according to the law. Let us present our children to the Lord who gave them to us, beseeching him to redeem them from sin and death, and make them holy to himself.

25-35 The same Spirit that provided for the support of Simeon's hope, provided for his joy. Those who would see Christ must go to his temple. Here is a confession of his faith, that this Child in his arms was the Savior, the salvation itself, the salvation of God's appointing. He bids farewell to this world. How poor does this world look to one that has Christ in his arms, and salvation in his view! See here, how comfortable is the death of a good man; he departs in peace with God, peace with his own conscience, in peace with death. Those that have welcomed Christ, may welcome death. Joseph and Mary marveled at the things which were spoken of this Child. Simeon shows them likewise, what reason they had to rejoice with trembling. And Jesus, his doctrine, and people, are still spoken against; his truth and holiness are still denied and blasphemed; his preached word is still the touchstone of men's characters. The secret good affections in the minds of some, will be revealed by their embracing Christ; the secret corruptions of others will be revealed by their enmity to Christ. Men will be judged by the thoughts of their hearts concerning Christ. He shall be a suffering Jesus; his mother shall suffer with him, because of the nearness of her relation and affection.

36-40 There was much evil then in the church, yet God left not himself without witness. Anna always dwelt in, or at least attended at, the temple. She was always in a praying spirit; gave herself to prayer, and in all things she served God. Those to whom Christ is made known, have great reason to thank the Lord. She taught others concerning him. Let the example of the venerable saints, Simeon and Anna, give courage to those whose hoary heads are, like theirs, a crown of glory, being found in the way of righteousness. The lips soon to be silent in the grave, should be showing forth the praises of the Redeemer. In all things it became Christ to be made like unto his brethren, therefore he passed through infancy and childhood as other children, yet without sin, and with manifest proofs of the Divine nature in him. By the Spirit of God all his faculties performed their offices in a manner not seen in any one else. Other children have foolishness bound in their hearts, which appears in what

But there was more than that, for the shepherds were aware that there had been promises made of old which had been the hope and comfort of believers in all ages, and these were now to be fulfilled. There was that ancient promise made on the threshold of Eden to the first sinners of our race, that the seed of the woman should bruise the serpent's head; another promise made to the Father of the faithful that in his seed should all the nations of the earth be blessed, and promises uttered by the mouths of prophets and of saints since the world began. Now, the announcement of the angel of the Lord to the shepherds was a declaration that the covenant was fulfilled, that now in the fullness of time God would redeem his word, and the Messiah, who was to be Israel's glory and the world's hope, was now really come. Be glad ye heavens, and be joyful O earth, for the Lord hath done it, and in mercy hath he visited his people. The Lord hath not suffered his word to fail, but hath fulfilled unto his people his promises. The time to favor Zion, yea the set time, is come. Now that the scepter is departed from Judah, behold the Shiloh comes, the Messenger of the covenant suddenly appears in his temple!

But the angel's song had in it yet fuller reason for joy; for our Lord who was born in Bethlehem came as a Savior. "Unto you is born this day a Savior." God had come to earth before, but not as a Savior. Remember that terrible coming when there went three angels into Sodom at night-fall, for the Lord said, "I will go now and see whether it be altogether according to the cry thereof." He had come as a spy to witness human sin, and as an avenger to lift his hand to heaven, and bid the red fire descend and burn up the accursed cities of the plain. Horror to the world when God thus descends. If Sinai smokes when the law is proclaimed, the earth itself shall melt when the breaches of the law are punished. But now not as an angel of vengeance, but as a man in mercy God has come; not to spy out our sin, but to remove it; not to punish guilt, but to forgive it. The Lord might have come with thunderbolts in both his hands; he might have come like Elias to call fire from heaven; but no, his hands are full of gifts of love, and his presence is the guarantee of grace. The babe born in the manger might have been another prophet of tears, or another son of thunder, but he was not so: he came in gentleness, his glory and his thunder alike laid aside.

"'Twas mercy filled the throne,
And wrath stood silent by,

the baptism of repentance for the remission of sins;

4 As it is written in the book of the words of Esaias the prophet, saying, The voice of one crying in the wilderness, Prepare ye the way of the Lord, make his paths straight.

5 Every valley shall be filled, and every mountain and hill shall be brought low; and the crooked shall be made straight, and the rough ways shall be made smooth;

6 And all flesh shall see the salvation of God.

7 Then said he to the multitude that came forth to be baptized of him, O generation of vipers, who hath warned you to flee from the wrath to come?

8 Bring forth therefore fruits worthy of repentance, and begin not to say within yourselves, We have Abraham to our father: for I say unto you, That God is able of these stones to raise up children unto Abraham.

9 And now also the axe is laid unto the root of the trees: every tree therefore which bringeth not forth good fruit is hewn down, and cast into the fire.

10 And the people asked him, saying, What shall we do then?

11 He answereth and saith unto them, He that hath two coats, let him impart to him that hath none; and he that hath meat, let him do likewise.

12 Then came also publicans to be baptized, and said unto him, Master, what shall we do?

13 And he said unto them, Exact no more than that which is appointed you.

14 And the soldiers likewise demanded of him, saying, And what shall we do? And he said unto them, Do violence to no man, neither accuse any falsely; and be content with your wages.

15 And as the people were in expectation, and all men mused in their hearts of John, whether he were the Christ, or not;

16 John answered, saying unto them all, I indeed baptize you with water; but one mightier than I cometh, the latchet of whose shoes I am not worthy to unloose: he shall baptize you with the Holy Ghost and with fire:

17 Whose fan is in his hand, and he will throughly purge his floor, and will gather the wheat into his garner; but the chaff he will burn with fire unquenchable.

18 And many other things in his exhortation preached he unto the people.

19 But Herod the tetrarch, being reproved by him for Herodias his brother Philip's wife, and for all the evils which Herod had done,

20 Added yet this above all, that he shut up John in prison.

21 Now when all the people were baptized, it came to pass, that Jesus also being baptized, and praying, the heaven was opened,

22 And the Holy Ghost descended in a bodily shape like a dove upon him, and a voice came from heaven, which said, Thou art my beloved Son; in thee I am well pleased.

23 And Jesus himself began to be about thirty years of age, being (as was supposed) the son of Joseph, which was the son of Heli,

24 Which was the son of Matthat, which was the son of Levi, which was the son of Melchi, which was the son of Janna, which was the son of Joseph,

25 Which was the son of Mattathias, which was the son of Amos, which was the son of Naum, which was the son of Esli, which was the son of Nagge,

26 Which was the son of Maath, which was the son of Mattathias, which was the son of Semei, which was the son of Joseph, which was the son of Juda,

27 Which was the son of Joanna, which was the son of

which were spoken – For they did not thoroughly understand them.

34. Simeon blessed them – Joseph and Mary. This child is set for the fall and rising again of many – That is, he will be a savor of death to some, to unbelievers: a savor of life to others, to believers: and for a sign which shall be spoken against – A sign from God, yet rejected of men: but the time for declaring this at large was not yet come: that the thoughts of many hearts may be revealed – The event will be, that by means of that contradiction, the inmost thoughts of many, whether good or bad, will be made manifest.

35. A sword shall pierce through thy own soul – So it did, when he suffered: particularly at his crucifixion.

37. Fourscore and four years – These were the years of her life, not her widowhood only. Who departed not from the temple – Who attended there at all the stated hours of prayer. But served God with fastings and prayers – Even at that age. Night and day – That is, spending therein a considerable part of the night, as well as of the day.

38. To all that were waiting for redemption – The scepter now appeared to be departing from Judah, though it was not actually gone: Daniel's weeks were plainly near their period. And the revival of the spirit of prophecy, together with the memorable occurrences relating to the birth of John the Baptist, and of Jesus, could not but encourage and quicken the expectation of pious persons at this time. Let the example of these aged saints animate those, whose hoary heads, like theirs, are a crown of glory, being found in the way of righteousness. Let those venerable lips, so soon to be silent in the grave, be now employed in the praises of their Redeemer. Let them labor to leave those behind, to whom Christ will be as precious as he has been to them; and who will be waiting for God's salvation, when they are gone to enjoy it.

40. And the child grew – In bodily strength and stature; and waxed strong in spirit – The powers of his human mind daily improved; filled with wisdom – By the light of the indwelling Spirit, which gradually opened itself in his soul; and the grace of God was upon him – That is, the peculiar favor of God rested upon him, even as man.

43. The child Jesus – St. Luke describes in order Jesus the fruit of the womb, chap. i, 42; an infant, chap. ii, 12; a little child, ver. 40; a child here, and afterward a man. So our Lord passed through and sanctified every stage of human life. Old age only did not become him.

44. Supposing him to have been in the company – As the men and women usually traveled in distinct companies.

46. After three days – The first day was spent in their journey, the second, in their return to Jerusalem: and the third, in searching for him there: they found him in the temple – In an apartment of it: sitting in the midst

they say or do, but he was filled with wisdom, by the influence of the Holy Ghost; every thing he said and did, was wisely said and wisely done, above his years. Other children show the corruption of their nature; nothing but the grace of God was upon him.

41-52 It is for the honor of Christ that children should attend on public worship. His parents did not return till they had stayed all the seven days of the feast. It is well to stay to the end of an ordinance, as becomes those who say, It is good to be here. Those that have lost their comforts in Christ, and the evidences of their having a part in him, must bethink themselves where, and when, and how they lost them, and must turn back again. Those that would recover their lost acquaintance with Christ, must go to the place in which he has put his name; there they may hope to meet him. They found him in some part of the temple, where the doctors of the law kept their schools; he was sitting there, hearkening to their instructions, proposing questions, and answering inquiries, with such wisdom, that those who heard were delighted with him. Young persons should seek the knowledge of Divine truth, attend the ministry of the gospel, and ask such questions of their elders and teachers as may tend to increase their knowledge. Those who seek Christ in sorrow, shall find him with the greater joy. Know ye not that I ought to be in my Father's house; at my Father's work; I must be about my Father's business. Herein is an example; for it becomes the children of God, in conformity to Christ, to attend their heavenly Father's business, and make all other concerns give way to it. Though he was the Son of God, yet he was subject to his earthly parents; how then will the foolish and weak sons of men answer it, who are disobedient to their parents? However we may neglect men's sayings, because they are obscure, yet we must not think so of God's sayings. That which at first is dark, may afterwards become plain and easy. The greatest and wisest, those most eminent, may learn of this admirable and Divine Child, that it is the truest greatness of soul to know our own place and office; to deny ourselves amusements and pleasures not consistent with our state and calling.

LUKE 3

John the Baptist's ministry. (1-14)
John the Baptist testifies concerning Christ. (15-20)
The baptism of Christ. (21,22)
The genealogy of Christ. (23-38)

1-14 The scope and design of John's ministry were, to bring the people from their sins, and to their Savior. He came preaching, not a sect, or party, but a profession; the sign or ceremony was washing with water. By the words here used John preached the necessity of repentance, in order to the remission of

When Christ on the kind errand came
To sinners doomed to die."
Rejoice, ye who feel that ye are lost; your Savior comes to seek and save you. Be of good cheer ye who are in prison, for be comes to set you free. Ye who are famished and ready to die, rejoice that he has consecrated for you a Bethlehem, a house of bread, and he has come to be the bread of life to your souls. Rejoice, O sinners, everywhere for the restorer of the castaways, the Savior of the fallen is born. Join in the joy, ye saints, for he is the preserver of the saved ones, delivering them from innumerable perils, and he is the sure perfecter of such as he preserves. Jesus is no partial Savior, beginning a work and not concluding it; but, restoring and upholding, he also perfects and presents the saved ones without spot or wrinkle, or any such thing before his Father's throne. Rejoice aloud all ye people, let your hills and valleys ring with joy, for a Savior who is mighty to save is born among you.

Nor was this all the holy mirth, for the next word has also in it a fullness of joy:—"a Savior, who is Christ," or the Anointed. Our Lord was not an amateur Savior who came down from heaven upon an unauthorized mission; but he was chosen, ordained, and anointed of God; he could truly say, "the Spirit of the Lord is upon me, because the Lord hath anointed me." Here is great comfort for all such as need a Savior; it is to them no mean consolation that God has himself authorized Christ to save. There can be no fear of a jar between the mediator and the judge, no peril of a nonacceptance of our Savior's work; because God has commissioned Christ to do what he has done, and in saving sinners he is only executing his Father's own will. Christ is here called "the anointed." All his people are anointed, and there were priests after the order of Aaron who were anointed, but he is the anointed, "anointed with the oil of gladness above his fellows;" so plenteously anointed that, like the unction upon Aaron's head, the sacred anointing of the Head of the church distils in copious streams, till we who are like the skirts of his garments are made sweet with the rich perfume. He is "the anointed" in a threefold sense: as prophet to preach the gospel with power; as priest to offer sacrifice; as king to rule and reign. In each of these he is preeminent; he is such a teacher, priest, and ruler as was never seen before. In him was a rare conjunction of glorious offices, for never did prophet, priest, and king meet in one person before among the sons of men, nor shall it ever be so again. Triple is the anointing of him

Rhesa, which was the son of Zorobabel, which was the son of Salathiel, which was the son of Neri,

28 Which was the son of Melchi, which was the son of Addi, which was the son of Cosam, which was the son of Elmodam, which was the son of Er,

29 Which was the son of Jose, which was the son of Eliezer, which was the son of Jorim, which was the son of Matthat, which was the son of Levi,

30 Which was the son of Simeon, which was the son of Juda, which was the son of Joseph, which was the son of Jonan, which was the son of Eliakim,

31 Which was the son of Melea, which was the son of Menan, which was the son of Mattatha, which was the son of Nathan, which was the son of David,

32 Which was the son of Jesse, which was the son of Obed, which was the son of Booz, which was the son of Salmon, which was the son of Naasson,

33 Which was the son of Aminadab, which was the son of Aram, which was the son of Esrom, which was the son of Phares, which was the son of Juda,

34 Which was the son of Jacob, which was the son of Isaac, which was the son of Abraham, which was the son of Thara, which was the son of Nachor,

35 Which was the son of Saruch, which was the son of Ragau, which was the son of Phalec, which was the son of Heber, which was the son of Sala,

36 Which was the son of Cainan, which was the son of Arphaxad, which was the son of Sem, which was the son of Noe, which was the son of Lamech,

37 Which was the son of Mathusala, which was the son of Enoch, which was the son of Jared, which was the son of Maleleel, which was the son of Cainan,

38 Which was the son of Enos, which was the son of Seth, which was the son of Adam, which was the son of God.

LUKE 4

1 And Jesus being full of the Holy Ghost returned from Jordan, and was led by the Spirit into the wilderness,

2 Being forty days tempted of the devil. And in those days he did eat nothing: and when they were ended, he afterward hungered.

3 And the devil said unto him, If thou be the Son of God, command this stone that it be made bread.

4 And Jesus answered him, saying, It is written, That man shall not live by bread alone, but by every word of God.

5 And the devil, taking him up into an high mountain, shewed unto him all the kingdoms of the world in a moment of time.

6 And the devil said unto him, All this power will I give thee, and the glory of them: for that is delivered unto me; and to whomsoever I will give it.

7 If thou therefore wilt worship me, all shall be thine.

8 And Jesus answered and said unto him, Get thee behind me, Satan: for it is written, Thou shalt worship the Lord thy God, and him only shalt thou serve.

9 And he brought him to Jerusalem, and set him on a pinnacle of the temple, and said unto him, If thou be the Son of God, cast thyself down from hence:

10 For it is written, He shall give his angels charge over thee, to keep thee:

11 And in their hands they shall bear thee up, lest at any time thou dash thy foot against a stone.

12 And Jesus answering said unto him, It is said, Thou shalt not tempt the Lord thy God.

of the doctors – Not one word is said of his disputing with them, but only of his asking and answering questions, which was a very usual thing in these assemblies, and indeed the very end of them. And if he was, with others, at the feet of these teachers (where learners generally sat) he might be said to be in the midst of them, as they sat on benches of a semicircular form, raised above their hearers and disciples.

49. Why sought ye me? – He does not blame them for losing, but for thinking it needful to seek him: and intimates, that he could not be lost, nor found any where, but doing the will of a higher parent.

50. It is observable that Joseph is not mentioned after this time; whence it is probable, he did not live long after.

52. Jesus increased in wisdom – As to his human nature, and in favor with God – In proportion to that increase. It plainly follows, that though a man were pure, even as Christ was pure, still he would have room to increase in holiness, and in consequence thereof to increase in the favor, as well as in the love of God.

LUKE 3

1. The fifteenth year of Tiberius – Reckoning from the time when Augustus made him his colleague in the empire. Herod being tetrarch of Galilee – The dominions of Herod the Great were, after his death, divided into four parts or tetrarchies. This Herod his son was tetrarch of Galilee, reigning over that fourth part of his dominions. His brother reigned over two other fourth parts, the region of Iturea, and that of Trachonitis (that tract of land on the other side Jordan, which had formerly belonged to the tribe of Manasseh.) And Lysanias (probably descended from a prince of that name, who was some years before governor of that country) was tetrarch of the remaining part of Abilene, which was a large city of Syria, whose territories reached to Lebanon and Damascus, and contained great numbers of Jews. Matt. iii, 1; Mark i, 1.

2. Annas being high priest, and Caiaphas – There could be but one high priest, strictly speaking, at once. Annas was the high priest at that time, and Caiaphas his sagan or deputy.

4. Isaiah xl, 3.

5. Every valley shall be filled, &c. – That is, every hindrance shall be removed.

6. The salvation of God – The Savior, the Messiah.

8. Say not within yourselves, We have Abraham to our father – That is, trust not in your being members of the visible Church, or in any external privileges whatsoever: for God now requires a change of heart; and that without delay.

10. He answereth – It is not properly John, but the Holy Ghost, who teaches us in the following answers, how to

sins, and that the baptism of water was an outward sign of that inward cleansing and renewal of heart, which attend, or are the effects of true repentance, as well as a profession of it. Here is the fulfilling of the Scriptures, Isa 40:3, in the ministry of John. When way is made for the gospel into the heart, by taking down high thoughts, and bringing them into obedience to Christ, by leveling the soul, and removing all that hinders us in the way of Christ and his grace, then preparation is made to welcome the salvation of God. Here are general warnings and exhortations which John gave. The guilty, corrupted race of mankind is become a generation of vipers; hateful to God, and hating one another. There is no way of fleeing from the wrath to come, but by repentance; and by the change of our way the change of our mind must be shown. If we are not really holy, both in heart and life, our profession of religion and relation to God and his church, will stand us in no stead at all; the sorer will our destruction be, if we do not bring forth fruits meet for repentance. John the Baptist gave instructions to several sorts of persons. Those that profess and promise repentance, must show it by reformation, according to their places and conditions. The gospel requires mercy, not sacrifice; and its design is, to engage us to do all the good we can, and to be just to all men. And the same principle which leads men to forego unjust gain, leads to restore that which is gained by wrong. John tells the soldiers their duty. Men should be cautioned against the temptations of their employments. These answers declared the present duty of the inquirers, and at once formed a test of their sincerity. As none can or will accept Christ's salvation without true repentance, so the evidence and effects of this repentance are here marked out.

15-20 John the Baptist disowned being himself the Christ, but confirmed the people in their expectations of the long-promised Messiah. He could only exhort them to repent, and assure them of forgiveness upon repentance; but he could not work repentance in them, nor confer remission on them. Thus highly does it become us to speak of Christ, and thus humbly of ourselves. John can do no more than baptize with water, in token that they ought to purify and cleanse themselves; but Christ can, and will baptize with the Holy Ghost; he can give the Spirit, to cleanse and purify the heart, not only as water washes off the dirt on the outside, but as fire clears out the dross that is within, and melts down the metal, that it may be cast into a new mold. John was an affectionate preacher; he was beseeching; he pressed things home upon his hearers. He was a practical preacher; quickening them to their duty, and directing them in it. He was a popular preacher; he addressed the people, according to their capacity. He was an evangelical preacher. In all his exhortations, he directed people to Christ. When we press duty upon people,

who is a priest after the order of Melchisedec, a prophet like unto Moses, and a king of whose dominion there is no end. In the name of Christ, the Holy Ghost is glorified, by being seen as anointing the incarnate God. Truly, dear brethren, if we did but understand all this, and receive it into our hearts, our souls would leap for joy on this Sabbath day, to think that there is born unto us a Savior who is anointed of the Lord.

One more note, and this the loudest, let us sound it well and hear it well— "which is Christ the Lord." Now the word Lord, or Kurios, here used is tantamount to Jehovah. We cannot doubt that, because it is the same word used twice in the ninth verse, and in the ninth verse none can question that it means Jehovah. Hear it, "And, lo, the angel of the Lord came upon them, and the glory of the Lord shone round about them." And if this be not enough, read the 23rd verse, "As it is written in the law of the Lord, every male that openeth the womb shall be called holy to the Lord." Now the word Lord here assuredly refers to Jehovah, the one God, and so it must do here. Our Savior is Christ, God, Jehovah. No testimony to his divinity could be plainer; it is indisputable. And what joy there is in this; for suppose an angel had been our Savior, he would not have been able to bear the load of my sin or yours; or if anything less than God had been set up as the ground of our salvation, it might have been found too frail a foundation. But if he who undertakes to save is none other than the Infinite and the Almighty, then the load of our guilt can be carried upon such shoulders, the stupendous labor of our salvation can be achieved by such a worker, and that with ease: for all things are possible with God, and he is able to save to the uttermost them that come unto God by him. Ye sons of men perceive ye here the subject of your joy. The God who made you, and against whom you have offended, has come down from heaven and taken upon himself your nature that he might save you. He has come in the fullness of his glory and the infinity of his mercy that he might redeem you. Do you not welcome this news? What! will not your hearts be thankful for this? Does this matchless love awaken no gratitude? Were it not for this divine Savior, your life here would have been wretchedness, and your future existence would have been endless woe. Oh, I pray you adore the incarnate God, and trust in him. Then will you bless the Lord for delivering you from the wrath to come, and as you lay hold of Jesus and find salvation in his

13 And when the devil had ended all the temptation, he departed from him for a season.

14 And Jesus returned in the power of the Spirit into Galilee: and there went out a fame of him through all the region round about.

15 And he taught in their synagogues, being glorified of all.

16 And he came to Nazareth, where he had been brought up: and, as his custom was, he went into the synagogue on the sabbath day, and stood up for to read.

17 And there was delivered unto him the book of the prophet Esaias. And when he had opened the book, he found the place where it was written,

18 The Spirit of the Lord is upon me, because he hath anointed me to preach the gospel to the poor; he hath sent me to heal the brokenhearted, to preach deliverance to the captives, and recovering of sight to the blind, to set at liberty them that are bruised,

19 To preach the acceptable year of the Lord.

20 And he closed the book, and he gave it again to the minister, and sat down. And the eyes of all them that were in the synagogue were fastened on him.

21 And he began to say unto them, This day is this scripture fulfilled in your ears.

22 And all bare him witness, and wondered at the gracious words which proceeded out of his mouth. And they said, Is not this Joseph's son?

23 And he said unto them, Ye will surely say unto me this proverb, Physician, heal thyself: whatsoever we have heard done in Capernaum, do also here in thy country.

24 And he said, Verily I say unto you, No prophet is accepted in his own country.

25 But I tell you of a truth, many widows were in Israel in the days of Elias, when the heaven was shut up three years and six months, when great famine was throughout all the land;

26 But unto none of them was Elias sent, save unto Sarepta, a city of Sidon, unto a woman that was a widow.

27 And many lepers were in Israel in the time of Eliseus the prophet; and none of them was cleansed, saving Naaman the Syrian.

28 And all they in the synagogue, when they heard these things, were filled with wrath,

29 And rose up, and thrust him out of the city, and led him unto the brow of the hill whereon their city was built, that they might cast him down headlong.

30 But he passing through the midst of them went his way,

31 And came down to Capernaum, a city of Galilee, and taught them on the sabbath days.

32 And they were astonished at his doctrine: for his word was with power.

33 And in the synagogue there was a man, which had a spirit of an unclean devil, and cried out with a loud voice,

34 Saying, Let us alone; what have we to do with thee, thou Jesus of Nazareth? art thou come to destroy us? I know thee who thou art; the Holy One of God.

35 And Jesus rebuked him, saying, Hold thy peace, and come out of him. And when the devil had thrown him in the midst, he came out of him, and hurt him not.

36 And they were all amazed, and spake among themselves, saying, What a word is this! for with authority and power he commandeth the unclean spirits, and they come out.

37 And the fame of him went out into every place of the country round about.

38 And he arose out of the synagogue, and entered into Simon's house. And Simon's wife's mother was taken with a

come ourselves, and how to instruct other penitent sinners to come to Christ, that he may give them rest. The sum of all this is, Cease to do evil, learn to do well. These are the fruits worthy of repentance.

20. He shut up John – This circumstance, though it happened after, is here mentioned before our Lord's baptism, that his history (that of John being concluded) may then follow without any interruption.

21. Jesus praying, the heaven was opened – It is observable, that the three voices from heaven, see chap. ix, 29, 35; John xii, 28; by which the Father bore witness to Christ, were pronounced either while he was praying, or quickly after it. Matt. iii, 13; Mark i, 9.

23. And Jesus was – John's beginning was computed by the years of princes: our Savior's by the years of his own life, as a more august era. About thirty years of age – He did not now enter upon his thirtieth year (as the common translation would induce one to think) but he now entered on his public ministry: being of such an age as the Mosaic law required. Our great Master attained not, as it seems, to the conclusion of his thirty-fourth year. Yet what glorious achievements did he accomplish within those narrow limits of time! Happy that servant, who, with any proportional zeal, despatches the great business of life; and so much the more happy, if his sun go down at noon. For the space that is taken from the labors of time, shall be added to the rewards of eternity. The son of Heli – That is, the son-in-law: for Heli was the father of Mary. So St. Matthew writes the genealogy of Joseph, descended from David by Solomon; St. Luke that of Mary, descended from David by Nathan. In the genealogy of Joseph (recited by St. Matthew) that of Mary is implied, the Jews being accustomed to marry into their own families.

38. Adam the son of God – That is, whatever the sons of Adam receive from their human parents, Adam received immediately from God, except sin and misery.

LUKE 4

1. The wilderness – Supposed by some to have been in Judea; by others to have been that great desert of Horeb or Sinai, where the children of Israel were tried for forty years, and Moses and Elijah fasted forty days. Matt. iv, 1; Mark i, 12.

4. Deut. viii, 3.

6. I give it to whomsoever I will – Not so, Satan. It is God, not thou, that putteth down one, and setteth up another: although sometimes Satan, by God's permission, may occasion great revolutions in the world.

8. Deut. vi, 13.

10. Psalm xci, 11.

12. Deut. vi, 16.

13. A convenient season – In the garden of Gethsemane, chap. xxii, 53.

MATTHEW HENRY

CHARLES H. SPURGEON

we must direct them to Christ, both for righteousness and strength. He was a copious preacher; he shunned not to declare the whole counsel of God. But a full stop was put to John's preaching when he was in the midst of his usefulness. Herod being reproved by him for many evils, shut up John in prison. Those who injure the faithful servants of God, add still greater guilt to their other sins.

21,22 Christ did not confess sin, as others did, for he had none to confess; but he prayed, as others did, and kept up communion with his Father. Observe, all the three voices from heaven, by which the Father bare witness to the Son, were pronounced while he was praying, or soon after, Lu 9:35; Joh 12:28. The Holy Ghost descended in a bodily shape like a dove upon him, and there came a voice from heaven, from God the Father, from the excellent glory. Thus was a proof of the Holy Trinity, of the Three Persons in the Godhead, given at the baptism of Christ.

23-38 Matthew's list of the forefathers of Jesus showed that Christ was the son of Abraham, in whom all the families of the earth are blessed, and heir to the throne of David; but Luke shows that Jesus was the Seed of the woman that should break the serpent's head, and traces the line up to Adam, beginning with Eli, or Heli, the father, not of Joseph, but of Mary. The seeming differences between the two evangelists in these lists of names have been removed by learned men. But our salvation does not depend upon our being able to solve these difficulties, nor is the Divine authority of the Gospels at all weakened by them. The list of names ends thus, ''Who was the son of Adam, the son of God;'' that is, the offspring of God by creation. Christ was both the son of Adam and the Son of God, that he might be a proper Mediator between God and the sons of Adam, and might bring the sons of Adam to be, through him, the sons of God. All flesh, as descended from the first Adam, is as grass, and withers as the flower of the field; but he who partakes of the Holy Spirit of life from the Second Adam, has that eternal happiness, which by the gospel is preached unto us.

LUKE 4

The temptation of Christ. (1-13)
Christ in the synagogue of Nazareth. (14-30)
He casts out an unclean spirit and heals the sick. (31-44)

1-13 Christ's being led into the wilderness gave an advantage to the tempter; for there he was alone, none were with him by whose prayers and advice he might be helped in the hour of temptation. He who knew his own strength might give Satan advantage; but we may not, who know our own weakness. Being in all things made like unto his brethren, Jesus would,

name, you will tune your songs to his praise, and exult with sacred joy. So much concerning this joy.

II. Follow me while I briefly speak of THE PEOPLE to whom this joy comes. Observe how the angel begins, "Behold, I bring you good tidings of great joy, for unto you is born this day." So, then, the joy began with the first who heard it, the shepherds. "To you," saith he; "for unto you is born." Beloved hearer, shall the joy begin with you today?—for it little avails you that Christ was born, or that Christ died, unless unto you a child is born, and for you Jesus bled. A personal interest is the main point. "But I am poor," saith one. So were the shepherds. O ye poor, to you this mysterious child is born. "The poor have the gospel preached unto them." "He shall judge the poor and needy, and break in pieces the oppressor." But I am obscure and unknown," saith one. So were the watchers on the midnight plain. Who knew the men who endured hard toil, and kept their flocks by night? But you, unknown of men, are known to God: shall it not be said, that "unto you a child is born?" The Lord regardeth not the greatness of men, but hath respect unto the lowly. But you are illiterate you say, you cannot understand much. Be it so, but unto the shepherds Christ was born, and their simplicity did not hinder their receiving him, but even helped them to it. Be it so with yourself: receive gladly the simple truth as it is in Jesus. The Lord hath exalted one chosen out of the people. No aristocratic Christ have I to preach to you, but the Savior of the people, the friend of publicans and sinners. Jesus is the true "poor men's friend;" he is "a covenant for the people," given to be "a leader and commander to the people." To you is Jesus given. O that each heart might truly say, to me is Jesus born; for if I truly believe in Jesus, unto me Christ is born, and I may be as sure of it as if an angel announced it, since the Scripture tells me that if I believe in Jesus He is mine.

After the angel had said "to you," he went on to say, "it shall be to all people." But our translation is not accurate, the Greek is, "it shall be to all the people." This refers most assuredly to the Jewish nation; there can be no question about that; if any one looks at the original, he will not find so large and wide an expression as that given by our translators. It should be rendered "to all the people." And here let us speak a word for the Jews. How long and how sinfully has the Christian church despised the most honorable amongst the nations! How barbarously

great fever; and they besought him for her.

39 And he stood over her, and rebuked the fever; and it left her: and immediately she arose and ministered unto them.

40 Now when the sun was setting, all they that had any sick with divers diseases brought them unto him; and he laid his hands on every one of them, and healed them.

41 And devils also came out of many, crying out, and saying, Thou art Christ the Son of God. And he rebuking them suffered them not to speak: for they knew that he was Christ.

42 And when it was day, he departed and went into a desert place: and the people sought him, and came unto him, and stayed him, that he should not depart from them.

43 And he said unto them, I must preach the kingdom of God to other cities also: for therefore am I sent.

44 And he preached in the synagogues of Galilee.

LUKE 5

1 And it came to pass, that, as the people pressed upon him to hear the word of God, he stood by the lake of Gennesaret,

2 And saw two ships standing by the lake: but the fishermen were gone out of them, and were washing their nets.

3 And he entered into one of the ships, which was Simon's, and prayed him that he would thrust out a little from the land. And he sat down, and taught the people out of the ship.

4 Now when he had left speaking, he said unto Simon, Launch out into the deep, and let down your nets for a draught.

5 And Simon answering said unto him, Master, we have toiled all the night, and have taken nothing: nevertheless at thy word I will let down the net.

6 And when they had this done, they inclosed a great multitude of fishes: and their net brake.

7 And they beckoned unto their partners, which were in the other ship, that they should come and help them. And they came, and filled both the ships, so that they began to sink.

8 When Simon Peter saw it, he fell down at Jesus' knees, saying, Depart from me; for I am a sinful man, O Lord.

9 For he was astonished, and all that were with him, at the draught of the fishes which they had taken:

10 And so was also James, and John, the sons of Zebedee, which were partners with Simon. And Jesus said unto Simon, Fear not; from henceforth thou shalt catch men.

11 And when they had brought their ships to land, they forsook all, and followed him.

12 And it came to pass, when he was in a certain city, behold a man full of leprosy: who seeing Jesus fell on his face, and besought him, saying, Lord, if thou wilt, thou canst make me clean.

13 And he put forth his hand, and touched him, saying, I will: be thou clean. And immediately the leprosy departed from him.

14 And he charged him to tell no man: but go, and shew thyself to the priest, and offer for thy cleansing, according as Moses commanded, for a testimony unto them.

15 But so much the more went there a fame abroad of him: and great multitudes came together to hear, and to be healed by him of their infirmities.

16 And he withdrew himself into the wilderness, and prayed.

17 And it came to pass on a certain day, as he was teaching, that there were Pharisees and doctors of the law sitting by, which were come out of every town of Galilee, and Judea, and Jerusalem: and the power of the Lord was present to heal them.

14. Jesus returned in the power of the Spirit – Being more abundantly strengthened after his conflict.

15. Being glorified of all – So God usually gives strong cordials after strong temptations. But neither their approbation continued long, nor the outward calm which he now enjoyed.

16. He stood up – Showing thereby that he had a desire to read the Scripture to the congregation: on which the book was given to him. It was the Jewish custom to read standing, but to preach sitting. Matt. xiii, 54; Mark vi, 1.

17. He found – It seems, opening upon it, by the particular providence of God.

18. He hath anointed me – With the Spirit. He hath by the power of his Spirit which dwelleth in me, set me apart for these offices. To preach the Gospel to the poor – Literally and spiritually. How is the doctrine of the ever-blessed trinity interwoven, even in those scriptures where one would least expect it? How clear a declaration of the great Three-One is there in those very words, The Spirit – of the Lord is upon me! To proclaim deliverance to the captives, and recovery of sight to the blind, to set at liberty them that are bruised – Here is a beautiful gradation, in comparing the spiritual state of men to the miserable state of those captives, who are not only cast into prison, but, like Zedekiah, had their eyes put out, and were laden and bruised with chains of iron. Isaiah lxi, 1.

19. The acceptable year – Plainly alluding to the year of jubilee, when all, both debtors and servants, were set free.

21. Today is this scripture fulfilled in your ears – By what you hear me speak.

22. The gracious words which proceeded out of his mouth – A person of spiritual discernment may find in all the discourses of our Lord a peculiar sweetness, gravity, and becomingness, such as is not to be found in the same degree, not even in those of the apostles.

23. Ye will surely say – That is, your approbation now outweighs your prejudices. But it will not be so long. You will soon ask, why my love does not begin at home? Why I do not work miracles here, rather than at Capernaum? It is because of your unbelief. Nor is it any new thing for me to be despised in my own country. So were both Elijah and Elisha, and thereby driven to work miracles among heathens, rather than in Israel.

24. No prophet is acceptable in his own country – That is, in his own neighborhood. It generally holds, that a teacher sent from God is not so acceptable to his neighbors as he is to strangers. The meanness of his family, or lowness of his circumstances, bring his office into contempt: nor can they suffer that he, who was before equal with, or below themselves, should now bear a superior character.

25. When the heaven was shut up three years and six

like the other children of God, live in dependence upon the Divine Providence and promise. The word of God is our sword, and faith in that word is our shield. God has many ways of providing for his people, and therefore is at all times to be depended upon in the way of duty. All Satan's promises are deceitful; and if he is permitted to have any influence in disposing of the kingdoms of the world and the glory of them, he uses them as baits to ensnare men to destruction. We should reject at once and with abhorrence, every opportunity of sinful gain or advancement, as a price offered for our souls; we should seek riches, honors, and happiness in the worship and service of God only. Christ will not worship Satan; nor, when he has the kingdoms of the world delivered to him by his Father, will he suffer any remains of the worship of the devil to continue in them. Satan also tempted Jesus to be his own murderer, by unfitting confidence in his Father's protection, such as he had no warrant for. Let not any abuse of Scripture by Satan or by men abate our esteem, or cause us to abandon its use; but let us study it still, seek to know it, and seek our defense from it in all kinds of assaults. Let this word dwell richly in us, for it is our life. Our victorious Redeemer conquered, not for himself only, but for us also. The devil ended all the temptation. Christ let him try all his force, and defeated him. Satan saw it was to no purpose to attack Christ, who had nothing in him for his fiery darts to fasten upon. And if we resist the devil, he will flee from us. Yet he departed but till the season when he was again to be let loose upon Jesus, not as a tempter, to draw him to sin, and so to strike at his head, at which he now aimed and was wholly defeated in; but as a persecutor, to bring Christ to suffer, and so to bruise his heel, which it was told him, he should have to do, and would do, though it would be the breaking of his own head, Ge 3:15. Though Satan depart for a season, we shall never be out of his reach till removed from this present evil world.

14-30 Christ taught in their synagogues, their places of public worship, where they met to read, expound, and apply the word, to pray and praise. All the gifts and graces of the Spirit were upon him and on him, without measure. By Christ, sinners may be loosed from the bonds of guilt, and by his Spirit and grace from the bondage of corruption. He came by the word of his gospel, to bring light to those that sat in the dark, and by the power of his grace, to give sight to those that were blind. And he preached the acceptable year of the Lord. Let sinners attend to the Savior's invitation when liberty is thus proclaimed. Christ's name was Wonderful; in nothing was he more so than in the word of his grace, and the power that went along with it. We may well wonder that he should speak such words of grace to such graceless wretches as mankind. Some prejudice often furnishes an objection against the humbling doctrine of the

has Israel been handled by the so-called church! I felt my spirit burn indignantly within me in Rome when I stood in the Jew's quarter, and heard of the cruel indignities which Popery has heaped upon the Jews, even until recently. At this hour there stands in the Jew's quarter a church built right in front of the entrance to it, and into this the unhappy Jews were driven forcibly on certain occasions. To this church they were compelled to subscribe—subscribe, mark you, as worshipers of the one invisible God, to the support of a system which is as leprous with idolatry as were the Canaanites whom the Lord abhorred. Paganism is not more degrading than Romanism. Over the door of this church is placed, in their own tongue in the Hebrew, these words: —"All day long have I stretched out my hands to a disobedient and gainsaying generation;" how, by such an insult as that, could they hope to convert the Jew. The Jew saw everywhere idols which his soul abhorred, and he loathed the name of Christ, because he associated it with idol worship, and I do not wonder that he did. I praise the Jew that he could not give up his own simple theism, and the worship of the true God, for such a base, degrading superstition as that which Rome presented to him. Instead of thinking it a wonder of unbelief that the Jew is not a Christian, I honor him for his faith and his courageous resistance of a fascinating heathenism. If Romanism be Christianity I am not, neither could I be, a Christian. It were a more manly thing to be a simple believer in one God, or even an honest doubter upon all religion, than worship such crowds of gods and goddesses as Popery has set up, and to bow, as she does, before rotten bones and dead men's winding sheets. Let the true Christian church think lovingly of the Jew, and with respectful earnestness tell him the true gospel; let her sweep away superstition, and set before him the one gracious God in the Trinity of his divine Unity; and the day shall yet come when the Jews, who were the first apostles to the Gentiles, the first missionaries to us who were afar off; shall be gathered in again. Until that shall be, the fullness of the church's glory can never come. Matchless benefits to the world are bound up with the restoration of Israel; their gathering in shall be as life from the dead. Jesus the Savior is the joy of all nations, but let not the chosen race be denied their peculiar share of whatever promise holy writ has recorded with a special view to them. The woes which their sins brought upon them have fallen thick and heavily; and even so let the richest blessings distil upon them. Although our translation is not literally cor-

18 And, behold, men brought in a bed a man which was taken with a palsy: and they sought means to bring him in, and to lay him before him.

19 And when they could not find by what way they might bring him in because of the multitude, they went upon the housetop, and let him down through the tiling with his couch into the midst before Jesus.

20 And when he saw their faith, he said unto him, Man, thy sins are forgiven thee.

21 And the scribes and the Pharisees began to reason, saying, Who is this which speaketh blasphemies? Who can forgive sins, but God alone?

22 But when Jesus perceived their thoughts, he answering said unto them, What reason ye in your hearts?

23 Whether is easier, to say, Thy sins be forgiven thee; or to say, Rise up and walk?

24 But that ye may know that the Son of man hath power upon earth to forgive sins, (he said unto the sick of the palsy,) I say unto thee, Arise, and take up thy couch, and go into thine house.

25 And immediately he rose up before them, and took up that whereon he lay, and departed to his own house, glorifying God.

26 And they were all amazed, and they glorified God, and were filled with fear, saying, We have seen strange things to day.

27 And after these things he went forth, and saw a publican, named Levi, sitting at the receipt of custom: and he said unto him, Follow me.

28 And he left all, rose up, and followed him.

29 And Levi made him a great feast in his own house: and there was a great company of publicans and of others that sat down with them.

30 But their scribes and Pharisees murmured against his disciples, saying, Why do ye eat and drink with publicans and sinners?

31 And Jesus answering said unto them, They that are whole need not a physician; but they that are sick.

32 I came not to call the righteous, but sinners to repentance.

33 And they said unto him, Why do the disciples of John fast often, and make prayers, and likewise the disciples of the Pharisees; but thine eat and drink?

34 And he said unto them, Can ye make the children of the bridechamber fast, while the bridegroom is with them?

35 But the days will come, when the bridegroom shall be taken away from them, and then shall they fast in those days.

36 And he spake also a parable unto them; No man putteth a piece of a new garment upon an old; if otherwise, then both the new maketh a rent, and the piece that was taken out of the new agreeth not with the old.

37 And no man putteth new wine into old bottles; else the new wine will burst the bottles, and be spilled, and the bottles shall perish.

38 But new wine must be put into new bottles; and both are preserved.

39 No man also having drunk old wine straightway desireth new: for he saith, The old is better.

LUKE 6

1 And it came to pass on the second sabbath after the first, that he went through the corn fields; and his disciples plucked the ears of corn, and did eat, rubbing them in their hands.

2 And certain of the Pharisees said unto them, Why do ye that

months – Such a proof had they that God had sent him. In 1 Kings xviii, 1, it is said, The word of the Lord came to Elijah in the third year: namely, reckoning not from the beginning of the drought, but from the time when he began to sojourn with the widow of Sarepta. A year of drought had preceded this, while he dwelt at the brook Cherith. So that the whole time of the drought was (as St. James likewise observes) three years and six months. 1 Kings xvii, 19; xviii, 44.

27. 2 Kings v, 14.

28. And all in the synagogue were filled with fury – Perceiving the purport of his discourse, namely, that the blessing which they despised, would be offered to, and accepted by, the Gentiles. So changeable are the hearts of wicked men! So little are their starts of love to be depended on! So unable are they to bear the close application, even of a discourse which they most admire!

30. Passing through the midst of them – Perhaps invisibly; or perhaps they were overawed; so that though they saw, they could not touch him.

31. He came down to Capernaum – And dwelt there, entirely quitting his abode at Nazareth. Mark i, 21.

34. What have we to do with thee – Thy present business is with men, not with devils. I know thee who thou art – But surely he did not know a little before, that he was God over all, blessed for ever; or he would not have dared to tell him, All this power is delivered to me, and I give it to whomsoever I will. The Holy One of God – Either this confession was extorted from him by terror, (for the devils believe and tremble,) or he made it with a design to render the character of Christ suspected. Possibly it was from hence the Pharisees took occasion to say, He casteth out devils by the prince of the devils.

38. Matt. viii, 14; Mark i, 29.

40. When the sun was set – And consequently the Sabbath ended, which they reckoned from sunset to sunset. Matt. viii, 16; Mark i, 32.

42. Mark i, 35.

LUKE 5

1. Matt. iv, 18; Mark i, 16.

6. Their net brake – Began to tear.

8. Depart from me, for I am a sinful man – And therefore not worthy to be in thy presence.

11. They forsook all and followed him – They had followed him before, John i, 43, but not so as to forsake all. Till now, they wrought at their ordinary calling.

12. Matt. viii, 2; Mark i, 40.

14. Lev. xiv, 2.

16. He withdrew – The expression in the original implies, that he did so frequently.

17. Sitting by – As being more honorable than the bulk of the congregation, who stood. And the power of the Lord was present to heal them – To heal the sickness of

cross; and while it is the word of God that stirs up men's enmity, they will blame the conduct or manner of the speaker. The doctrine of God's sovereignty, his right to do his will, provokes proud men. They will not seek his favor in his own way; and are angry when others have the favors they neglect. Still is Jesus rejected by multitudes who hear the same message from his words. While they crucify him afresh by their sins, may we honor him as the Son of God, the Savior of men, and seek to show we do so by our obedience.

31-44 Christ's preaching much affected the people; and a working power went with it to the consciences of men. These miracles showed Christ to be a controller and conqueror of Satan, a healer of diseases. Where Christ gives a new life, in recovery from sickness, it should be a new life, spent more than ever in his service, to his glory. Our business should be to spread abroad Christ's fame in every place, to beseech him in behalf of those diseased in body or mind, and to use our influence in bringing sinners to him, that his hands may be laid upon them for their healing. He cast the devils out of many who were possessed. We were not sent into this world to live to ourselves only, but to glorify God, and to do good in our generation. The people sought him, and came unto him. A desert is no desert, if we are with Christ there. He will continue with us, by his word and Spirit, and extend the same blessings to other nations, till, throughout the earth, the servants and worshipers of Satan are brought to acknowledge him as the Christ, the Son of God, and to find redemption through his blood, even the forgiveness of sins.

LUKE 5

The miraculous draught of fishes. Peter, James, and John called. (1-11)
A leper cleansed. (12-16)
A paralytic cured. (17-26)
Levi called. Christ's answer to the Pharisees. (27-39)

1-11 When Christ had done preaching, he told Peter to apply to the business of his calling. Time spent on week days in public exercises of religion, need be but little hindrance in time, and may be great furtherance to us in temper of mind, as to our worldly business. With what cheerfulness may we go about the duties of our calling, when we have been with God, and thus have our worldly employments sanctified to us by the word and prayer! Though they had taken nothing, yet Christ told them to let down their nets again. We must not abruptly quit our callings because we have not the success in them we desire. We are likely to speed well, when we follow the guidance of Christ's word. The draught of fishes was by a miracle. We must all, like Peter, own ourselves to be sinful men, therefore Jesus Christ might justly depart from

rect, it, nevertheless, expresses a great truth, taught plainly in the context; and, therefore, we will advance another step. The coming of Christ is a joy to all people. It is so, for the fourteenth verse says: "On earth peace," which is a wide and even unlimited expression. It adds, "Good will towards"—not Jews, but "men" — all men. The word is the generic name of the entire race, and there is no doubt that the coming of Christ does bring joy to all sorts of people. It brings a measure of joy even to those who are not Christians. Christ does not bless them in the highest and truest sense, but the influence of his teaching imparts benefits of an inferior sort, such as they are capable of receiving; for wherever the gospel is proclaimed, it is no small blessing to all the population. Note this fact: there is no land beneath the sun where there is an open Bible and a preached gospel, where a tyrant long can hold his peace. It matters not who he be, whether pope or king; let the pulpit be used properly for the preaching of Christ crucified, let the Bible be opened to be read by all men, and no tyrant can long rule in peace. England owes her freedom to the Bible; and France will never possess liberty, lasting and well-established, till she comes to reverence the gospel, which too long she has rejected. There is joy to all mankind where Christ comes. The religion of Jesus makes men think, and to make men think is always dangerous to a despot's power. The religion of Jesus Christ sets a man free from superstition; when he believes in Jesus, what cares he for Papal excommunications, or whether priests give or withhold their absolution? The man no longer cringes and bows down; he is no more willing, like a beast, to be led by the nose; but, learning to think for himself and becoming a man, he disdains the childish fears which once held him in slavery. Hence, where Jesus comes, even if men do not receive him as the Savior, and so miss the fullest joy, yet they get a measure of benefit; and I pray God that everywhere his gospel may be so proclaimed, and that so many may be actuated by the spirit of it, that it may be better for all mankind. If men receive Christ, there will be no more oppression: the true Christian does to others as he would that they should do to him, and there is no more contention of classes, nor grinding of the faces of the poor. Slavery must go down where Christianity rules, and mark you, if Romanism be once destroyed, and pure Christianity shall govern all nations, war itself must come to an end; for if there be anything which this book denounces and counts the hugest of all crimes,

which is not lawful to do on the sabbath days?

3 And Jesus answering them said, Have ye not read so much as this, what David did, when himself was an hungred, and they which were with him;

4 How he went into the house of God, and did take and eat the shewbread, and gave also to them that were with him; which it is not lawful to eat but for the priests alone?

5 And he said unto them, That the Son of man is Lord also of the sabbath.

6 And it came to pass also on another sabbath, that he entered into the synagogue and taught: and there was a man whose right hand was withered.

7 And the scribes and Pharisees watched him, whether he would heal on the sabbath day; that they might find an accusation against him.

8 But he knew their thoughts, and said to the man which had the withered hand, Rise up, and stand forth in the midst. And he arose and stood forth.

9 Then said Jesus unto them, I will ask you one thing; Is it lawful on the sabbath days to do good, or to do evil? to save life, or to destroy it?

10 And looking round about upon them all, he said unto the man, Stretch forth thy hand. And he did so: and his hand was restored whole as the other.

11 And they were filled with madness; and communed one with another what they might do to Jesus.

12 And it came to pass in those days, that he went out into a mountain to pray, and continued all night in prayer to God.

13 And when it was day, he called unto him his disciples: and of them he chose twelve, whom also he named apostles;

14 Simon, (whom he also named Peter,) and Andrew his brother, James and John, Philip and Bartholomew,

15 Matthew and Thomas, James the son of Alpheus, and Simon called Zelotes,

16 And Judas the brother of James, and Judas Iscariot, which also was the traitor.

17 And he came down with them, and stood in the plain, and the company of his disciples, and a great multitude of people out of all Judea and Jerusalem, and from the sea coast of Tyre and Sidon, which came to hear him, and to be healed of their diseases;

18 And they that were vexed with unclean spirits: and they were healed.

19 And the whole multitude sought to touch him: for there went virtue out of him, and healed them all.

20 And he lifted up his eyes on his disciples, and said, Blessed be ye poor: for yours is the kingdom of God.

21 Blessed are ye that hunger now: for ye shall be filled. Blessed are ye that weep now: for ye shall laugh.

22 Blessed are ye, when men shall hate you, and when they shall separate you from their company, and shall reproach you, and cast out your name as evil, for the Son of man's sake.

23 Rejoice ye in that day, and leap for joy: for, behold, your reward is great in heaven: for in the like manner did their fathers unto the prophets.

24 But woe unto you that are rich! for ye have received your consolation.

25 Woe unto you that are full! for ye shall hunger. Woe unto you that laugh now! for ye shall mourn and weep.

26 Woe unto you, when all men shall speak well of you! for so did their fathers to the false prophets.

27 But I say unto you which hear, Love your enemies, do good to them which hate you,

their souls, as well as all bodily diseases.

18. Matt. ix, 2; Mark ii, 3.

19. Not being able to bring him in through the multitude, they went round about by a back passage, and going up the stairs on the outside, they came upon the flat-roofed house, and let him down through the trap door, such as was on the top of most of the Jewish houses: doubtless, with such circumspection as the circumstances plainly required.

26. We have seen strange things today – Sins forgiven, miracles wrought.

27. Matt. ix, 9; Mark ii, 14.

28. Leaving all – His business and gain.

29. And Levi made him a great entertainment – It was necessarily great, because of the great number of guests.

33. Make prayers – Long and solemn. Matt. ix, 14; Mark ii, 18.

34. Can ye make – That is, is it proper to make men fast and mourn, during a festival solemnity?

36. He spake also a parable – Taken from clothes and wine; therefore peculiarly proper at a feast.

39. And no man having drunk old wine – And beside, men are not wont to be immediately freed from old prejudices.

LUKE 6

1. The first Sabbath – So the Jews reckoned their Sabbaths, from the Passover to Pentecost; the first, second, third, and so on, till the seventh Sabbath (after the second day.) This immediately preceded Pentecost, which was the fiftieth day after the second day of unleavened bread. Matt. xii, 1; Mark ii, 23.

2. Why do ye – St. Matthew and Mark represent the Pharisees as proposing the question to our Lord himself. It was afterward, probably, they proposed it to his disciples.

4. 1 Sam. xxi, 6.

6. Matt. xii, 9; Mark iii, 1.

9. To save life or to kill – He just then probably saw the design to kill him rising in their hearts.

12. In the prayer of God – The phrase is singular and emphatic, to imply an extraordinary and sublime devotion. Mark iii, 13.

13. Matt. x, 2; Mark iii, 14; Acts i, 13.

15. Simon called Zelotes – Full of zeal; otherwise called Simon the Canaanite.

17. On a plain – At the foot of the mountain.

20. In the following verses our Lord, in the audience of his newly- chosen disciples, and of the multitude, repeats, standing on the plain, many remarkable passages of the sermon he had before delivered, sitting on the mount. He here again pronounces the poor and the hungry, the mourners, and the persecuted, happy; and represents as miserable those who are rich, and full, and

us. But we must beseech him that he would not depart; for woe unto us if the Savior depart from sinners! Rather let us entreat him to come and dwell in our hearts by faith, that he may transform and cleanse them. These fishermen forsook all, and followed Jesus, when their calling prospered. When riches increase, and we are tempted to set our hearts upon them, then to quit them for Christ is thankworthy.

12-16 This man is said to be full of leprosy; he had that distemper in a high degree, which represents our natural pollution by sin; we are full of that leprosy; from the crown of the head to the sole of the foot there is no soundness in us. Strong confidence and deep humility are united in the words of this leper. And if any sinner, from a deep sense of vileness, says, I know the Lord can cleanse, but will he look upon such a one as me? will he apply his own precious blood for my cleansing and healing? Yes, he will. Speak not as doubting, but as humbly referring the matter to Christ. And being saved from the guilt and power of our sins, let us spread abroad Christ's fame, and bring others to hear him and to be healed.

17-26 How many are there in our assemblies, where the gospel is preached, who do not sit under the word, but sit by! It is to them as a tale that is told them, not as a message that is sent to them. Observe the duties taught and recommended to us by the history of the paralytic. In applying to Christ, we must be very pressing and urgent; that is an evidence of faith, and is very pleasing to Christ, and prevailing with him. Give us, Lord, the same kind of faith with respect to thy ability and willingness to heal our souls. Give us to desire the pardon of sin more than any earthly blessing, or life itself. Enable us to believe thy power to forgive sins; then will our souls cheerfully arise and go where thou pleasest.

27-39 It was a wonder of Christ's grace, that he would call a publican to be his disciple and follower. It was a wonder of his grace, that the call was made so effectual. It was a wonder of his grace, that he came to call sinners to repentance, and to assure them of pardon. It was a wonder of his grace, that he so patiently bore the contradiction of sinners against himself and his disciples. It was a wonder of his grace, that he fixed the services of his disciples according to their strength and standing. The Lord trains up his people gradually for the trials allotted them; we should copy his example in dealing with the weak in faith, or the tempted believer.

LUKE 5

The disciples pluck corn on the Sabbath. (1-5)
Works of mercy suitable to the Sabbath day. (6-11)
The apostles chosen. (12-19)
Blessings and woes declared. (20-26)

it is the crime of war. Put up thy sword into thy sheath, for hath not he said, "Thou shalt not kill," and he meant not that it was a sin to kill one but a glory to kill a million, but he meant that bloodshed on the smallest or largest scale was sinful. Let Christ govern, and men shall break the bow and cut the spear in sunder, and burn the chariot in the fire. It is joy to all nations that Christ is born, the Prince of Peace, the King who rules in righteousness.

But, beloved, the greatest joy is to those who know Christ as a Savior. Here the song rises to a higher and sublimer note. Unto us indeed a child is born, if we can say that he is our "Savior who is Christ the Lord." Let me ask each of you a few personal questions. Are your sins forgiven you for his name's sake? Is the head of the serpent bruised in your soul? Does the seed of the woman reign in sanctifying power over your nature? Oh then, you have the joy that is to all the people in the truest form of it; and, dear brother, dear sister, the further you submit yourself to Christ the Lord, the more completely you know him, and are like him, the fuller will your happiness become. Surface joy is to those who live where the Savior is preached; but the great deeps, the great fathomless deeps of solemn joy which glisten and sparkle with delight, are for such as know the Savior, obey the anointed one, and have communion with the Lord himself. He is the most joyful man who is the most Christly man. I wish that some Christians were more truly Christians: they are Christians and something else; it were much better if they were altogether Christians. Perhaps you know the legend, or perhaps true history of the awakening of St. Augustine. He dreamed that he died, and went to the gates of heaven, and the keeper of the gates said to him, "Who are you?" And he answered, "Christianus sum," I am a Christian. But the porter replied, "No, you are not a Christian, you are a Ciceronian, for your thoughts and studies were most of all directed to the works of Cicero and the classics, and you neglected the teaching of Jesus. We judge men here by that which most engrossed their thoughts, and you are judged not to be a Christian but a Ciceronian." When Augustine awoke, he put aside the classics which he had studied, and the eloquence at which he had aimed, and he said, "I will be a Christian and a theologian;" and from that time he devoted his thoughts to the word of God, and his pen and his tongue to the instruction of others in the truth. Oh I would not have it said of any of you, "Well, he may be somewhat Christian, but he is far more a keen

28 Bless them that curse you, and pray for them which despitefully use you.

29 And unto him that smiteth thee on the one cheek offer also the other; and him that taketh away thy cloke forbid not to take thy coat also.

30 Give to every man that asketh of thee; and of him that taketh away thy goods ask them not again.

31 And as ye would that men should do to you, do ye also to them likewise.

32 For if ye love them which love you, what thank have ye? for sinners also love those that love them.

33 And if ye do good to them which do good to you, what thank have ye? for sinners also do even the same.

34 And if ye lend to them of whom ye hope to receive, what thank have ye? for sinners also lend to sinners, to receive as much again.

35 But love ye your enemies, and do good, and lend, hoping for nothing again; and your reward shall be great, and ye shall be the children of the Highest: for he is kind unto the unthankful and to the evil.

36 Be ye therefore merciful, as your Father also is merciful.

37 Judge not, and ye shall not be judged: condemn not, and ye shall not be condemned: forgive, and ye shall be forgiven:

38 Give, and it shall be given unto you; good measure, pressed down, and shaken together, and running over, shall men give into your bosom. For with the same measure that ye mete withal it shall be measured to you again.

39 And he spake a parable unto them, Can the blind lead the blind? shall they not both fall into the ditch?

40 The disciple is not above his master: but every one that is perfect shall be as his master.

41 And why beholdest thou the mote that is in thy brother's eye, but perceivest not the beam that is in thine own eye?

42 Either how canst thou say to thy brother, Brother, let me pull out the mote that is in thine eye, when thou thyself beholdest not the beam that is in thine own eye? Thou hypocrite, cast out first the beam out of thine own eye, and then shalt thou see clearly to pull out the mote that is in thy brother's eye.

43 For a good tree bringeth not forth corrupt fruit; neither doth a corrupt tree bring forth good fruit.

44 For every tree is known by his own fruit. For of thorns men do not gather figs, nor of a bramble bush gather they grapes.

45 A good man out of the good treasure of his heart bringeth forth that which is good; and an evil man out of the evil treasure of his heart bringeth forth that which is evil: for of the abundance of the heart his mouth speaketh.

46 And why call ye me, Lord, Lord, and do not the things which I say?

47 Whosoever cometh to me, and heareth my sayings, and doeth them, I will shew you to whom he is like:

48 He is like a man which built an house, and digged deep, and laid the foundation on a rock: and when the flood arose, the stream beat vehemently upon that house, and could not shake it: for it was founded upon a rock.

49 But he that heareth, and doeth not, is like a man that without a foundation built an house upon the earth; against which the stream did beat vehemently, and immediately it fell; and the ruin of that house was great.

LUKE 7

1 Now when he had ended all his sayings in the audience of the people, he entered into Capernaum.

joyous, and applauded: because generally prosperity is a sweet poison, and affliction a healing, though bitter medicine. Let the thought reconcile us to adversity, and awaken our caution when the world smiles upon us; when a plentiful table is spread before us, and our cup is running over; when our spirits are gay; and we hear (what nature loves) our own praise from men. Happy are ye poor – The word seems here to be taken literally: ye who have left all for me. Matt. v, 3.

24. Miserable are ye rich – If ye have received or sought your consolation or happiness therein.

25. Full – Of meat and drink, and worldly goods. That laugh – That are of a light trifling spirit.

26. Woe to you when all men shall speak well of you – But who will believe this?

27. But I say to you that hear – Hitherto our Lord had spoken only to particular sorts of persons: now he begins speaking to all in general. Matt. v, 44.

29. To him that smiteth thee on the cheek – Taketh away thy cloak – These seem to be proverbial expressions, to signify an invasion of the tenderest points of honor and property. Offer the other – Forbid not thy coat – That is, rather yield to his repeating the affront or injury, than gratify resentment in righting your self; in any method not becoming Christian love. Matt. v, 39.

30. Give to every one – Friend or enemy, what thou canst spare, and he really wants: and of him that taketh away thy goods – By borrowing, if he be insolvent, ask them not again. Matt. v, 42.

31. Matt. vii, 12.

32. It is greatly observable, our Lord has so little regard for one of the highest instances of natural virtue, namely, the returning love for love, that he does not account it even to deserve thanks. For even sinners, saith he, do the same: men who do not regard God at all. Therefore he may do this, who has not taken one step in Christianity.

37. Matt. vii, 1.

38. Into your bosom – Alluding to the mantles the Jews wore, into which a large quantity of corn might be received. With the same measure that ye mete with, it shall be measured to you again – Amazing goodness! So we are permitted even to carve for ourselves! We ourselves are, as it were, to tell God how much mercy he shall show us! And can we be content with less than the very largest measure? Give then to man, what thou designest to receive of God.

39. He spake a parable – Our Lord sometimes used parables when he knew plain and open declarations would too much inflame the passions of his hearers. It is for this reason he uses this parable, Can the blind lead the blind? – Can the scribes teach this way, which they know not themselves? Will not they and their scholars perish together? Can they make their disciples any better than themselves? But as for those who will be my dis-

MATTHEW HENRY

CHARLES H. SPURGEON

Christ exhorts to mercy. (27-36)
And to justice and sincerity. (37-49)

1-5 Christ justifies his disciples in a work of necessity for themselves on the Sabbath day, and that was plucking the ears of corn when they were hungry. But we must take heed that we mistake not this liberty for leave to commit sin. Christ will have us to know and remember that it is his day, therefore to be spent in his service, and to his honor.

6-11 Christ was neither ashamed nor afraid to own the purposes of his grace. He healed the poor man, though he knew that his enemies would take advantage against him for it. Let us not be drawn either from our duty or from our usefulness by any opposition. We may well be amazed, that the sons of men should be so wicked.

12-19 We often think one half hour a great deal to spend in meditation and secret prayer, but Christ was whole nights engaged in these duties. In serving God, our great care should be not to lose time, but to make the end of one good duty the beginning of another. The twelve apostles are here named; never were men so privileged, yet one of them had a devil, and proved a traitor. Those who have not faithful preaching near them, had better travel far than be without it. It is indeed worthwhile to go a great way to hear the word of Christ, and to go out of the way of other business for it. They came to be cured by him, and he healed them. There is a fullness of grace in Christ, and healing virtue in him, ready to go out from him, that is enough for all, enough for each. Men regard the diseases of the body as greater evils than those of their souls; but the Scripture teaches us differently.

20-26 Here begins a discourse of Christ, most of which is also found in Mt 5; 7. But some think that this was preached at another time and place. All believers that take the precepts of the gospel to themselves, and live by them, may take the promises of the gospel to themselves, and live upon them. Woes are denounced against prosperous sinners as miserable people, though the world envies them. Those are blessed indeed whom Christ blesses, but those must be dreadfully miserable who fall under his woe and curse! What a vast advantage will the saint have over the sinner in the other world! and what a wide difference will there be in their rewards, how much soever the sinner may prosper, and the saint be afflicted here!

27-36 These are hard lessons to flesh and blood. But if we are thoroughly grounded in the faith of Christ's love, this will make his commands easy to us. Every one that comes to him for washing in his blood, and knows the greatness of the mercy and the love there

money-getting tradesman." I would not have it said, "Well, he may be a believer in Christ, but he is a good deal more a politician." Perhaps he is a Christian, but he is most at home when he is talking about science, farming, engineering, horses, mining, navigation, or pleasure-taking. No, no, you will never know the fullness of the joy which Jesus brings to the soul, unless under the power of the Holy Spirit you take the Lord your Master to be your All in all, and make him the fountain of your intensest delight. "He is my Savior, my Christ, my Lord," be this your loudest boast. Then will you know the joy which the angel's song predicts for men.

III. But I must pass on. The last thing in the text is The SIGN. The shepherds did not ask for a sign, but one was graciously given. Sometimes it is sinful for us to require as an evidence what God's tenderness may nevertheless see fit to give as an aid to faith. Willful unbelief shall have no sign, but weak faith shall have compassionate aid. The sign that the joy of the world had come was this,—they were to go to the manger to find the Christ in it, and he was to be the sign. Every circumstance is therefore instructive. The babe was found "wrapped in swaddling clothes." Now, observe, as you look at this infant, that there is not the remotest appearance of temporal power here. Mark the two little puny arms of a little babe that must be carried if it go. Alas, the nations of the earth look for joy in military power. By what means can we make a nation of soldiers? The Prussian method is admirable; we must have thousands upon thousands of armed men and big cannon and ironclad vessels to kill and destroy by wholesale. Is it not a nation's pride to be gigantic in arms? What pride flushes the patriot's cheek when he remembers that his nation can murder faster than any other people. Ah, foolish generation, ye are groping in the flames of hell to find your heaven, raking amid blood and bones for the foul thing which ye call glory. A nation's joy can never lie in the misery of others. Killing is not the path to prosperity; huge armaments are a curse to the nation itself as well as to its neighbors. The joy of a nation is a golden sand over which no stream of blood has ever rippled. It is only found in that river, the streams whereof make glad the city of God. The weakness of submissive gentleness is true power. Jesus founds his eternal empire not on force but on love. Here, O ye people, see your hope; the mild pacific prince, whose glory is his self-sacrifice, is our true benefactor.

But look again, and you shall observe no

2 And a certain centurion's servant, who was dear unto him, was sick, and ready to die.

3 And when he heard of Jesus, he sent unto him the elders of the Jews, beseeching him that he would come and heal his servant.

4 And when they came to Jesus, they besought him instantly, saying, That he was worthy for whom he should do this:

5 For he loveth our nation, and he hath built us a synagogue.

6 Then Jesus went with them. And when he was now not far from the house, the centurion sent friends to him, saying unto him, Lord, trouble not thyself: for I am not worthy that thou shouldest enter under my roof:

7 Wherefore neither thought I myself worthy to come unto thee: but say in a word, and my servant shall be healed.

8 For I also am a man set under authority, having under me soldiers, and I say unto one, Go, and he goeth; and to another, Come, and he cometh; and to my servant, Do this, and he doeth it.

9 When Jesus heard these things, he marveled at him, and turned him about, and said unto the people that followed him, I say unto you, I have not found so great faith, no, not in Israel.

10 And they that were sent, returning to the house, found the servant whole that had been sick.

11 And it came to pass the day after, that he went into a city called Nain; and many of his disciples went with him, and much people.

12 Now when he came nigh to the gate of the city, behold, there was a dead man carried out, the only son of his mother, and she was a widow: and much people of the city was with her.

13 And when the Lord saw her, he had compassion on her, and said unto her, Weep not.

14 And he came and touched the bier: and they that bare him stood still. And he said, Young man, I say unto thee, Arise.

15 And he that was dead sat up, and began to speak. And he delivered him to his mother.

16 And there came a fear on all: and they glorified God, saying, That a great prophet is risen up among us; and, That God hath visited his people.

17 And this rumor of him went forth throughout all Judea, and throughout all the region round about.

18 And the disciples of John shewed him of all these things.

19 And John calling unto him two of his disciples sent them to Jesus, saying, Art thou he that should come? or look we for another?

20 When the men were come unto him, they said, John Baptist hath sent us unto thee, saying, Art thou he that should come? or look we for another?

21 And in that same hour he cured many of their infirmities and plagues, and of evil spirits; and unto many that were blind he gave sight.

22 Then Jesus answering said unto them, Go your way, and tell John what things ye have seen and heard; how that the blind see, the lame walk, the lepers are cleansed, the deaf hear, the dead are raised, to the poor the gospel is preached.

23 And blessed is he, whosoever shall not be offended in me.

24 And when the messengers of John were departed, he began to speak unto the people concerning John, What went ye out into the wilderness for to see? A reed shaken with the wind?

25 But what went ye out for to see? A man clothed in soft raiment? Behold, they which are gorgeously apparelled, and live delicately, are in kings' courts.

26 But what went ye out for to see? A prophet? Yea, I say

ciples, they shall be all taught of God; who will enable them to come to the measure of the stature of the fullness of their Master. Be not ye like their disciples, censuring others, and not amending yourselves. Matt. xv, 14.

40. Matt. x, 24; John xv, 20.

41. Matt. vii, 3.

46. And why call ye me Lord, Lord – What will fair professions avail, without a life answerable thereto? Matt. vii, 21.

47. Matt. vii, 24.

LUKE 7

1. Matt. viii, 5.

3. Hearing of Jesus – Of his miracles, and of his arrival at Capernaum.

18. Matt. xi, 2.

22. To the poor the Gospel is preached – Which is the greatest mercy, and the greatest miracle of all.

24. When the messengers were departed – He did not speak the following things in the hearing of John's disciples, lest he should seem to flatter John, or to compliment him into an adherence to his former testimony. To avoid all suspicion of this kind, he deferred his commendation of him, till the messengers were gone; and then delivered it to the people, to prevent all imaginations, as if John were wavering in his judgment, and had sent the two disciples for his own, rather than their satisfaction.

27. Mal. iii, 1.

28. There is not a greater prophet than John – A greater teacher. But he that is least in the kingdom of God – The least teacher whom I send forth.

29. And all the people – Our Lord continues his discourse: justified God – Owned his wisdom and mercy in thus calling them to repentance, and preparing them for Him that was to come.

30. But the Pharisees and scribes – The good, learned, honorable men: made void the counsel, the gracious design, of God toward them – They disappointed all these methods of his love, and would receive no benefit from them.

32. They are like children sitting in the market place – So froward and perverse, that no contrivance can be found to please them. It is plain our Lord means, that they were like the children complained of, not like those that made the complaint.

34. But wisdom is justified by all her children – The children of wisdom are those who are truly wise unto salvation. The wisdom of God in all these dispensations, these various methods of calling sinners to repentance, is owned and heartily approved by all these.

36. And one of the Pharisees asked him to eat with him – Let the candor with which our Lord accepted this

MATTHEW HENRY

CHARLES H. SPURGEON

is in him, can say, in truth and sincerity, Lord, what wilt thou have me to do? Let us then aim to be merciful, even according to the mercy of our heavenly Father to us.

37-49 All these sayings Christ often used; it was easy to apply them. We ought to be very careful when we blame others; for we need allowance ourselves. If we are of a giving and a forgiving spirit, we shall ourselves reap the benefit. Though full and exact returns are made in another world, not in this world, yet Providence does what should encourage us in doing good. Those who follow the multitude to do evil, follow in the broad way that leads to destruction. The tree is known by its fruits; may the word of Christ be so grafted in our hearts, that we may be fruitful in every good word and work. And what the mouth commonly speaks, generally agrees with what is most in the heart. Those only make sure work for their souls and eternity, and take the course that will profit in a trying time, who think, speak, and act according to the words of Christ. Those who take pains in religion, found their hope upon Christ, who is the Rock of Ages, and other foundation can no man lay. In death and judgment they are safe, being kept by the power of Christ through faith unto salvation, and they shall never perish.

LUKE 7

The centurion's servant healed. (1-10)
The widow's son raised. (11-18)
John the Baptist's inquiry concerning Jesus. (19-35)
Christ anointed in the house of the Pharisee. The parable of the two debtors. (36-50)

1-10 Servants should study to endear themselves to their masters. Masters ought to take particular care of their servants when they are sick. We may still, by faithful and fervent prayer, apply to Christ, and ought to do so when sickness is in our families. The building places for religious worship is a good work, and an instance of love to God and his people. Our Lord Jesus was pleased with the centurion's faith; and he never fails to answer the expectations of that faith which honors his power and love. The cure soon wrought and perfect.

11-18 When the Lord saw the poor widow following her son to the grave, he had compassion on her. See Christ's power over death itself. The gospel call to all people, to young people particularly, is, Arise from the dead, and Christ shall give you light and life. When Christ put life into him, it appeared by the youth's sitting up. Have we grace from Christ? Let us show it. He began to speak: whenever Christ gives us spiritual life, he opens the lips in prayer and praise. When dead souls are raised to spiritual life, by Divine power going with the gospel, we must glorify God,

pomp to dazzle you. Is the child wrapped in purple and fine linen? Ah, no. Sleeps he in a cradle of gold? The manger alone is his shelter. No crown is upon the babe's head, neither does a coronet surround the mother's brow. A simple maiden of Galilee, and a little child in ordinary swaddling bands, it is all you see.

"Bask not in courtly bower,
Or sunbright hall of power,
Pass Babel quick,
and seek the holy land.
From robes of Tyrian dye,
Turn with undazzled eye
To Bethlehem's glade, and by the manger stand."

Alas, the nations are dazzled with a vain show. The pomp of empires, the pageants of kings are their delight. How can they admire those gaudy courts, in which too often glorious apparel, decorations, and rank stand in the stead of virtue, chastity, and truth. When will the people cease to be children? Must they for ever crave for martial music which stimulates to violence, and delight in a lavish expenditure which burdens them with taxation? These make not a nation great or joyous. Bah! how has the bubble burst across yon narrow sea. A bubble empire has collapsed. Ten thousand bayonets and millions of gold proved but a sandy foundation for a Babel throne. Vain are the men who look for joy in pomp; it lies in truth and righteousness, in peace and salvation, of which yonder new-born prince in the garments of a peasant child is the true symbol.

Neither was there wealth to be seen at Bethlehem. Here in this quiet island, the bulk of men are comfortably seeking to acquire their thousands by commerce and manufactures. We are the sensible people who follow the main chance, and are not to be deluded by ideas of glory; we are making all the money we can, and wondering that other nations waste so much in fight. The main prop and pillar of England's joy is to be found, as some tell us, in the Three per Cents., in the possession of colonies, in the progress of machinery, in steadily increasing our capital. Is not Mammon a smiling deity? But, here, in the cradle of the world's hope at Bethlehem, I see far more of poverty than wealth; I perceive no glitter of gold, or spangle of silver. I perceive only a poor babe, so poor, so very poor, that he is in a manger laid; and his mother is a mechanic's wife, a woman who wears neither silk nor gem. Not in your gold, O Britons, will ever lie your joy, but in the gospel enjoyed by all classes, the gospel freely preached and joyfully received.

unto you, and much more than a prophet.

27

This is he, of whom it is written, Behold, I send my messenger before thy face, which shall prepare thy way before thee.

28 For I say unto you, Among those that are born of women there is not a greater prophet than John the Baptist: but he that is least in the kingdom of God is greater than he.

29

And all the people that heard him, and the publicans, justified God, being baptized with the baptism of John.

30 But the Pharisees and lawyers rejected the counsel of God against themselves, being not baptized of him.

31 And the Lord said, Whereunto then shall I liken the men of this generation? and to what are they like?

32 They are like unto children sitting in the marketplace, and calling one to another, and saying, We have piped unto you, and ye have not danced; we have mourned to you, and ye have not wept.

33 For John the Baptist came neither eating bread nor drinking wine; and ye say, He hath a devil.

34 The Son of man is come eating and drinking; and ye say, Behold a gluttonous man, and a winebibber, a friend of publicans and sinners!

35 But wisdom is justified of all her children.

36 And one of the Pharisees desired him that he would eat with him. And he went into the Pharisee's house, and sat down to meat.

37 And, behold, a woman in the city, which was a sinner, when she knew that Jesus sat at meat in the Pharisee's house, brought an alabaster box of ointment,

38 And stood at his feet behind him weeping, and began to wash his feet with tears, and did wipe them with the hairs of her head, and kissed his feet, and anointed them with the ointment.

39 Now when the Pharisee which had bidden him saw it, he spake within himself, saying, This man, if he were a prophet, would have known who and what manner of woman this is that toucheth him: for she is a sinner.

40

And Jesus answering said unto him, Simon, I have somewhat to say unto thee. And he saith, Master, say on.

41 There was a certain creditor which had two debtors: the one owed five hundred pence, and the other fifty.

42 And when they had nothing to pay, he frankly forgave them both. Tell me therefore, which of them will love him most?

43 Simon answered and said, I suppose that he, to whom he forgave most. And he said unto him, Thou hast rightly judged.

44 And he turned to the woman, and said unto Simon, Seest thou this woman? I entered into thine house, thou gavest me no water for my feet: but she hath washed my feet with tears, and wiped them with the hairs of her head.

45 Thou gavest me no kiss: but this woman since the time I came in hath not ceased to kiss my feet.

46 My head with oil thou didst not anoint: but this woman hath anointed my feet with ointment.

47 Wherefore I say unto thee, Her sins, which are many, are forgiven; for she loved much: but to whom little is forgiven, the same loveth little.

48 And he said unto her, Thy sins are forgiven.

49 And they that sat at meat with him began to say within themselves, Who is this that forgiveth sins also?

50 And he said to the woman, Thy faith hath saved thee; go in peace.

invitation, and his gentleness and prudence at this ensnaring entertainment, teach us to mingle the wisdom of the serpent, with the innocence and sweetness of the dove. Let us neither absolutely refuse all favors, nor resent all neglects, from those whose friendship is at best very doubtful, and their intimacy by no means safe.

37. A woman – Not the same with Mary of Bethany, who anointed him six days before his last Passover.

40. And Jesus said, Simon, I have somewhat to say to thee – So tender and courteous an address does our Lord use even to a proud, censorious Pharisee!

43. Which of them will love him most? – Neither of them will love him at all, before he has forgiven them. An insolvent debtor, till he is forgiven, does not love, but fly his creditor.

44. Thou gavest me no water – It was customary with the Jews to show respect and kindness to their welcome guests, by saluting them with a kiss, by washing their feet, and anointing their heads with oil, or some fine ointment.

47. Those many sins of hers are forgiven; therefore she loveth much – The fruit of her having had much forgiven. It should carefully be observed here, that her love is mentioned as the effect and evidence, not the cause of her pardon. She knew that much had been forgiven her, and therefore she loved much.

50. Thy faith hath saved thee – Not thy love. Love is salvation.

MATTHEW HENRY

CHARLES H. SPURGEON

and look upon it as a gracious visit to his people. Let us seek for such an interest in our compassionate Savior, that we may look forward with joy to the time when the Redeemer's voice shall call forth all that are in their graves. May we be called to the resurrection of life, not to that of damnation.

19-35 To his miracles in the kingdom of nature, Christ adds this in the kingdom of grace, To the poor the gospel is preached. It clearly pointed out the spiritual nature of Christ's kingdom, that the messenger he sent before him to prepare his way, did it by preaching repentance and reformation of heart and life. We have here the just blame of those who were not wrought upon by the ministry of John Baptist or of Jesus Christ himself. They made a jest of the methods God took to do them good. This is the ruin of multitudes; they are not serious in the concerns of their souls. Let us study to prove ourselves children of Wisdom, by attending the instructions of God's word, and adoring those mysteries and glad tidings which infidels and Pharisees deride and blaspheme.

36-50 None can truly perceive how precious Christ is, and the glory of the gospel, except the brokenhearted. But while they feel they cannot enough express self-abhorrence on account of sin, and admiration of his mercy, the self-sufficient will be disgusted, because the gospel encourages such repenting sinners. The Pharisee, instead of rejoicing in the tokens of the woman's repentance, confined his thoughts to her former bad character. But without free forgiveness none of us can escape the wrath to come; this our gracious Savior has purchased with his blood, that he may freely bestow it on every one that believes in him. Christ, by a parable, forced Simon to acknowledge that the greater sinner this woman had been, the greater love she ought to show to him when her sins were pardoned. Learn here, that sin is a debt; and all are sinners, are debtors to Almighty God. Some sinners are greater debtors; but whether our debt be more or less, it is more than we are able to pay. God is ready to forgive; and his Son having purchased pardon for those who believe in him, his gospel promises it to them, and his Spirit seals it to repenting sinners, and gives them the comfort. Let us keep far from the proud spirit of the Pharisee, simply depending upon and rejoicing in Christ alone, and so be prepared to obey him more zealously, and more strongly to recommend him unto all around us. The more we express our sorrow for sin, and our love to Christ, the clearer evidence we have of the forgiveness of our sins. What a wonderful change does grace make upon a sinner's heart and life, as well as upon his state before God, by the full remission of all his sins through faith in the Lord Jesus!

Jesus, by raising us to spiritual wealth, redeems us from the chains of Mammon, and in that liberty gives us joy.

And here, too, I see no superstition. I know the artist paints angels in the skies, and surrounds the scene with a mysterious light, of which tradition's tongue of falsehood has said that it made midnight as bright as noon. This is fiction merely; there was nothing more there than the stable, the straw the oxen ate, and perhaps the beasts themselves, and the child in the plainest, simplest manner, wrapped as other children are; the cherubs were invisible and of haloes there were none. Around this birth of joy was no sign of superstition: that demon dared not intrude its tricks and posturings into the sublime spectacle: it would have been there as much out of place as a harlequin in the holy of holies. A simple gospel, a plain gospel, as plain as that babe wrapped in the commonest garments, is this day the only hope for men. Be ye wise and believe in Jesus, and abhor all the lies of Rome, and inventions of those who ape her detestable abominations.

Nor does the joy of the world lie in philosophy. You could not have made a schoolmen's puzzle of Bethlehem if you had tried to do so; it was just a child in the manger and a Jewish woman looking on and nursing it, and a carpenter standing by. There was no metaphysical difficulty there, of which men could say, "A doctor of divinity is needed to explain it, and an assembly of divines must expound it." It is true the wise men came there, but it was only to adore and offer gifts; would that all the wise had been as wise as they. Alas, human subtlety has disputed over the manger, and logic has darkened counsel with its words. But this is one of man's many inventions; God's work was sublimely simple. Here was "The Word made flesh" to dwell among us, a mystery for faith, but not a football for argument. Mysterious, yet the greatest simplicity that was ever spoken to human ears, and seen by mortal eyes. And such is the gospel, in the preaching of which our apostle said, "we use great plainness of speech." Away, away, away with your learned sermons, and your fine talk, and your pretentious philosophies; these never created a jot of happiness in this world. Fine-spun theories are fair to gaze on, and to bewilder fools, but they are of no use to practical men, they comfort not the sons of toil, nor cheer the daughters of sorrow. The man of common sense, who feels the daily rub and tear of this poor world, needs richer consolation than your novel theologies, or neologies, can give him. In a simple Christ,

LUKE 8

1 And it came to pass afterward, that he went throughout every city and village, preaching and shewing the glad tidings of the kingdom of God: and the twelve were with him,

2 And certain women, which had been healed of evil spirits and infirmities, Mary called Magdalene, out of whom went seven devils,

3 And Joanna the wife of Chuza Herod's steward, and Susanna, and many others, which ministered unto him of their substance.

4 And when much people were gathered together, and were come to him out of every city, he spake by a parable:

5 A sower went out to sow his seed: and as he sowed, some fell by the way side; and it was trodden down, and the fowls of the air devoured it.

6 And some fell upon a rock; and as soon as it was sprung up, it withered away, because it lacked moisture.

7 And some fell among thorns; and the thorns sprang up with it, and choked it.

8 And other fell on good ground, and sprang up, and bare fruit an hundredfold. And when he had said these things, he cried, He that hath ears to hear, let him hear.

9 And his disciples asked him, saying, What might this parable be?

10 And he said, Unto you it is given to know the mysteries of the kingdom of God: but to others in parables; that seeing they might not see, and hearing they might not understand.

11 Now the parable is this: The seed is the word of God.

12 Those by the way side are they that hear; then cometh the devil, and taketh away the word out of their hearts, lest they should believe and be saved.

13 They on the rock are they, which, when they hear, receive the word with joy; and these have no root, which for a while believe, and in time of temptation fall away.

14 And that which fell among thorns are they, which, when they have heard, go forth, and are choked with cares and riches and pleasures of this life, and bring no fruit to perfection.

15 But that on the good ground are they, which in an honest and good heart, having heard the word, keep it, and bring forth fruit with patience.

16 No man, when he hath lighted a candle, covereth it with a vessel, or putteth it under a bed; but setteth it on a candlestick, that they which enter in may see the light.

17 For nothing is secret, that shall not be made manifest; neither any thing hid, that shall not be known and come abroad.

18 Take heed therefore how ye hear: for whosoever hath, to him shall be given; and whosoever hath not, from him shall be taken even that which he seemeth to have.

19 Then came to him his mother and his brethren, and could not come at him for the press.

20 And it was told him by certain which said, Thy mother and thy brethren stand without, desiring to see thee.

21 And he answered and said unto them, My mother and my brethren are these which hear the word of God, and do it.

22 Now it came to pass on a certain day, that he went into a ship with his disciples: and he said unto them, Let us go over unto the other side of the lake. And they launched forth.

23 But as they sailed he fell asleep: and there came down a storm of wind on the lake; and they were filled with water, and were in jeopardy.

24 And they came to him, and awoke him, saying, Master, master, we perish. Then he arose, and rebuked the wind and

LUKE 8

2. Mary Magdalene – Or Mary of Magdala, a town in Galilee: probably the person mentioned in the last chapter.

4. Matt. xiii, 1; Mark iv, 1.

15. Who – keep it – Not like the highway side: And bring forth fruit – Not like the thorny ground: With perseverance – Not like the stony.

16. No man having lighted a candle – As if he had said, And let your good fruit appear openly. Matt. v, 15; Mark iv, 21; Luke xi, 33.

17. For nothing is hid – Strive not to conceal it at all; for you can conceal nothing long. Matt. x, 26; Mark iv, 22; Luke xii, 2.

18. The word commonly translated seemeth, wherever it occurs, does not weaken, but greatly strengthens the sense. Matt. xiii, 12; Mark iv, 25; Luke xix, 26.

19. Matt. xii, 46; Mark iii, 31.

22. Matt. viii, 23; Mark iv, 35.

26. Matt. viii, 28; Mark v, 1.

29. For many times it had caught him – Therefore our compassionate Lord made the more haste to cast him out.

31. The abyss – That is, the bottomless pit.

32. To enter into the swine – Not that they were any easier in the swine than out of them. Had it been so, they would not so soon have dislodged themselves, by destroying the herd.

37. Matt. ix, 1; Mark v, 18.

40. Mark v, 21.

52. She is not dead but sleepeth – Her soul is not separated finally from the body; and this short separation is rather to be called sleep than death.

LUKE 9

1. Matt. x, 1; Mark vi, 7.

4. There abide and thence depart – That is, stay in that house till ye leave the city.

7. It was said by some – And soon after by Herod himself. Matt. xiv, 1; Mark vi, 14.

8. That Elijah had appeared – He could not rise again, because he did not die.

10. Mark vi, 30.

12. Matt. xiv, 15; Mark vi, 35; John vi, 3.

18. Apart – From the multitude. And he asked them – When he had done praying, during which they probably stayed at a distance. Matt. xiv, 13; Mark viii, 27.

22. Saying – Ye must prepare for a scene far different from this.

23. Let him deny himself, and take up his cross – The necessity of this duty has been shown in many places: the extent of it is specified here, daily – Therefore that day is lost wherein no cross is taken up.

24. Matt. xvi, 25; Mark viii, 35; John xii, 25.

LUKE 8

The ministry of Christ. (1-3)
The parable of the sower. (4-21)
Christ stilleth the tempest and casteth out devils. (22-40)
The daughter of Jairus restored to life. (41-56)

1-3 We are here told what Christ made the constant business of his life, it was teaching the gospel. Tidings of the kingdom of God are glad tidings, and what Christ came to bring. Certain women attended upon him who ministered to him of their substance. It showed the mean condition to which the Savior humbled himself, that he needed their kindness, and his great humility, that he accepted it. Though rich, yet for our sakes he became poor.

4-21 There are many very needful and excellent rules and cautions for hearing the word, in the parable of the sower, and the application of it. Happy are we, and forever indebted to free grace, if the same thing that is a parable to others, with which they are only amused, is a plain truth to us, by which we are taught and governed. We ought to take heed of the things that will hinder our profiting by the word we hear; to take heed lest we hear carelessly and slightly, lest we entertain prejudices against the word we hear; and to take heed to our spirits after we have heard the word, lest we lose what we have gained. The gifts we have, will be continued to us or not, as we use them for the glory of God, and the good of our brethren. Nor is it enough not to hold the truth in unrighteousness; we should desire to hold forth the word of life, and to shine, giving light to all around. Great encouragement is given to those who prove themselves faithful hearers of the word, by being doers of the work. Christ owns them as his relations.

22-40 Those that put to sea in a calm, even at Christ's word, must yet prepare for a storm, and for great peril in that storm. There is no relief for souls under a sense of guilt, and fear of wrath, but to go to Christ, and call him Master, and say, I am undone, if thou dost not help me. When our dangers are over, it becomes us to take to ourselves the shame of our own fears, and to give Christ the glory of our deliverance. We may learn much out of this history concerning the world of infernal, malignant spirits, which though not working now exactly in the same way as then, yet all must at all times carefully guard against. And these malignant spirits are very numerous. They have enmity to man and all his comforts. Those under Christ's government are sweetly led with the bands of love; those under the devil's government are furiously driven. Oh what a comfort it is to the believer, that all the powers of darkness are under the control of the Lord Jesus! It is a miracle of mercy, if those whom Satan possesses, are not brought to destruction and eternal ruin. Christ will not stay with those who slight

and in a simple faith in that Christ, there is a peace deep and lasting; in a plain, poor man's gospel there is a joy and a bliss unspeakable, of which thousands can speak, and speak with confidence, too, for they declare what they do know, and testify what they have seen.

I say, then, to you who would know the only true peace and lasting joy, come ye to the babe of Bethlehem, in after days the Man of Sorrows, the substitutionary sacrifice for sinners. Come, ye little children, ye boys and girls, come ye; for he also was a boy. "The holy child Jesus" is the children's Savior, and saith still, "Suffer the little children to come unto me, and forbid them not. Come hither, ye maidens, ye who are still in the morning of your beauty, and, like Mary, rejoice in God your Savior. The virgin bore him on her bosom, so come ye and bear him in your hearts, saying, "Unto us a child is born, onto us a son is given." And you, ye men in the plenitude of your strength, remember how Joseph cared for him, and watched with reverent solicitude his tender years; be you to his cause as a Father and a helper; sanctify your strength to his service. And ye women advanced in years, ye matrons and widows, come like Anna and bless the Lord that you have seen the salvation of Israel, and ye hoar heads, who like Simeon are ready to depart, come ye and take the Savior in your arms, adoring him as your Savior and your all. Ye shepherds, ye simple hearted, ye who toil for your daily bread, come and adore the Savior; and stand not back ye wise men, ye who know by experience and who by meditation peer into deep truth, come ye, and like the sages of the East bow low before his presence, and make it your honor to pay honor to Christ the Lord. For my own part, the incarnate God is all my hope and trust. I have seen the world's religion at the fountain head, and my heart has sickened within me; I come back to preach, by God's help, yet more earnestly the gospel, the simple gospel of the Son of Man. Jesus, Master, I take thee to be mine for ever! May all in this house, through the rich grace of God, be led to do the same, and may they all be thine, great Son of God, in the day of thine appearing, for thy love's sake. Amen.

CARRIED BY FOUR

Sermon number 981 delivered on March 19th, 1871 at the Metropolitan Tabernacle, Newington.

"And he withdrew himself into the wilderness,

the raging of the water: and they ceased, and there was a calm.

25 And he said unto them, Where is your faith? And they being afraid wondered, saying one to another, What manner of man is this! for he commandeth even the winds and water, and they obey him.

26 And they arrived at the country of the Gadarenes, which is over against Galilee.

27 And when he went forth to land, there met him out of the city a certain man, which had devils long time, and ware no clothes, neither abode in any house, but in the tombs.

28 When he saw Jesus, he cried out, and fell down before him, and with a loud voice said, What have I to do with thee, Jesus, thou Son of God most high? I beseech thee, torment me not.

29 (For he had commanded the unclean spirit to come out of the man. For oftentimes it had caught him: and he was kept bound with chains and in fetters; and he brake the bands, and was driven of the devil into the wilderness.)

30 And Jesus asked him, saying, What is thy name? And he said, Legion: because many devils were entered into him.

31 And they besought him that he would not command them to go out into the deep.

32 And there was there an herd of many swine feeding on the mountain: and they besought him that he would suffer them to enter into them. And he suffered them.

33 Then went the devils out of the man, and entered into the swine: and the herd ran violently down a steep place into the lake, and were choked.

34 When they that fed them saw what was done, they fled, and went and told it in the city and in the country.

35 Then they went out to see what was done; and came to Jesus, and found the man, out of whom the devils were departed, sitting at the feet of Jesus, clothed, and in his right mind: and they were afraid.

36 They also which saw it told them by what means he that was possessed of the devils was healed.

37 Then the whole multitude of the country of the Gadarenes round about besought him to depart from them; for they were taken with great fear: and he went up into the ship, and returned back again.

38 Now the man out of whom the devils were departed besought him that he might be with him: but Jesus sent him away, saying,

39 Return to thine own house, and shew how great things God hath done unto thee. And he went his way, and published throughout the whole city how great things Jesus had done unto him.

40 And it came to pass, that, when Jesus was returned, the people gladly received him: for they were all waiting for him.

41 And, behold, there came a man named Jairus, and he was a ruler of the synagogue: and he fell down at Jesus' feet, and besought him that he would come into his house:

42 For he had one only daughter, about twelve years of age, and she lay a dying. But as he went the people thronged him.

43 And a woman having an issue of blood twelve years, which had spent all her living upon physicians, neither could be healed of any,

44 Came behind him, and touched the border of his garment: and immediately her issue of blood stanched.

45 And Jesus said, Who touched me? When all denied, Peter and they that were with him said, Master, the multitude throng thee and press thee, and sayest thou, Who touched me?

28. Matt. xvii, 1; Mark ix, 2.

31. In glory – Like Christ with whom they talked.

32. They saw his glory – The very same expression in which it is described by St. John, John i, 14; and by St. Peter, 2 Pet. i, 16.

34. A cloud came and overshadowed them all. And they, the apostles, feared, while they (Moses and Elijah) entered into the cloud, which took them away.

37. Matt. xvii, 14; Mark ix, 14.

44. Let these sayings sink down into your ears – That is, consider them deeply. In joy remember the cross. So wisely does our Lord balance praise with sufferings. Matt. xvii, 22; Mark ix, 31.

46. And there arose a reasoning among them – This kind of reasoning always arose at the most improper times that could be imagined.

47. Matt. xviii, 2; Mark ix, 37.

48. And said to them – If ye would be truly great, humble yourselves to the meanest offices. He that is least in his own eyes shall be great indeed.

49. Mark ix, 38.

51. The days are fulfilled that he should be received up – That is, the time of his passion was now at hand. St. Luke looks through this, to the glory which was to follow. He steadfastly set his face – Without fear of his enemies, or shame of the cross, Heb. xii, 2.

52. He sent messengers to make ready – A lodging and needful entertainment for him and those with him.

53. His face was as though he would go to Jerusalem – It plainly appeared, he was going to worship at the temple, and thereby, in effect, to condemn the Samaritan worship at Mount Gerizim.

54. As Elisha did – At or near this very place, which might put it into the minds of the apostles to make the motion now, rather than at any other time or place, where Christ had received the like affront.

55. Ye know not what manner of spirit – The spirit of Christianity is. It is not a spirit of wrath and vengeance, but of peace, and gentleness, and love.

57. Matt. viii, 19.

58. But Jesus said to him – First understand the terms: consider on what conditions thou art to follow me.

61. Suffer me first to bid them farewell that are in my house – As Elisha did after Elijah had called him from the plow, 1 Kings xix, 19; to which our Lord's answer seems to allude.

62. Is fit for the kingdom of God – Either to propagate or to receive it.

LUKE 10

2. Pray ye the Lord of the harvest, that he would thrust forth laborers – For God alone can do this: he alone can qualify and commission men for this work. Matt. ix, 37.

3. Matt. x, 16.

MATTHEW HENRY

CHARLES H. SPURGEON

him; perhaps he may no more return to them, while others are waiting for him, and glad to receive him.

41-56 Let us not complain of a crowd, and a throng, and a hurry, as long as we are in the way of our duty, and doing good; but otherwise every wise man will keep himself out of it as much as he can. And many a poor soul is healed, and helped, and saved by Christ, that is hidden in a crowd, and nobody notices it. This woman came trembling, yet her faith saved her. There may be trembling, where yet there is saving faith. Observe Christ's comfortable words to Jairus, Fear not, believe only, and thy daughter shall be made whole. No less hard was it not to grieve for the loss of an only child, than not to fear the continuance of that grief. But in perfect faith there is no fear; the more we fear, the less we believe. The hand of Christ's grace goes with the calls of his word, to make them effectual. Christ commanded to give her meat. As babes new born, so those newly raised from sin, desire spiritual food, that they may grow thereby.

LUKE 9

The apostles sent forth. (1-9)
The multitude miraculously fed. (10-17)
Peter's testimony to Christ. Self-denial enjoined. (18-27)
The transfiguration. (28-36)
An evil spirit cast out. (37-42)
Christ checks the ambition of his disciples. (43-50)
He reproves their mistaken zeal. (51-56)
Every thing to be given up for Christ. (57-62)

1-9 Christ sent his twelve disciples abroad, who by this time were able to teach others what they had received from the Lord. They must not be anxious to commend themselves to people's esteem by outward appearance. They must go as they were. The Lord Jesus is the fountain of power and authority, to whom all creatures must, in one way or another, be subject; and if he goes with the word of his ministers in power, to deliver sinners from Satan's bondage, they may be sure that he will care for their wants. When truth and love thus go together, and yet the message of God is rejected and despised, it leaves men without excuse, and turns to a testimony against them. Herod's guilty conscience was ready to conclude that John was risen from the dead. He desired to see Jesus; and why did he not go and see him? Probably, because he thought it below him, or because he wished not to have any more reprovers of sin. Delaying it now, his heart was hardened, and when he did see Jesus, he was as much prejudiced against him as others, Lu 23:11.

10-17 The people followed Jesus, and though they came unseasonably, yet he gave them what they came for. He spake unto them of the kingdom of God.

and prayed. And it came to pass on a certain day, as he was teaching, that there were Pharisees and doctors of the law sitting by, which were come out of every town of Galilee, and Judea, and Jerusalem: and the power of the Lord was present to heal them. And, behold, men brought in a bed a man which was taken with a palsy: and they sought means to bring him in, and to lay him before him. And when they could not find by what way they might bring him in because of the multitude, they went upon the housetop, and let him down through the tiling with his couch into the midst before Jesus. And when he saw their faith, he said unto him, Man, thy sins are forgiven thee. And the scribes and the Pharisees began to reason, saying, Who is this which speaketh blasphemies? Who can forgive sins, but God alone? But when Jesus perceived their thoughts, he answering said unto them, What reason ye in your hearts? Whether is easier, to say, Thy sins be forgiven thee; or to say, Rise up and walk? But that ye may know that the Son of man hath power upon earth to forgive sins (he said unto the sick of the palsy), I say unto thee, Arise, and take up thy couch, and go into thine house. And immediately he rose up before them, and took up that whereon he lay, and departed to his own house, glorifying God. And they were all amazed, and they glorified God, and were filled with fear, saying, We have seen strange things today."—Luke 5:16-26.

YOU HAVE THIS SAME NARRATIVE in the ninth chapter of Matthew, and in the second chapter of Mark. What is three times recorded by inspired pens must be regarded as trebly important, and well worthy of our earnest consideration. Observe the instructive fact, that our Savior retired and spent a special time in prayer when he saw an unusual crowd assembling. He withdrew into the wilderness to hold communion with his Father, and, as a consequence, to come forth clothed with an abundance of healing and saving power. Not but that in himself as God he always had that power without measure; but for our sakes he did it, that we might learn that the power of God will only rest upon us in proportion as we draw near to God. Neglect of private prayer is the locust which devours the strength of the church.

When our Lord left his retirement he found the crowd around him exceeding great, and it was as motley as it was great; for while here were many sincere believers, there were still more skeptical observers; some were anxious to receive his healing power, others equally

46 And Jesus said, Somebody hath touched me: for I perceive that virtue is gone out of me.

47 And when the woman saw that she was not hid, she came trembling, and falling down before him, she declared unto him before all the people for what cause she had touched him and how she was healed immediately.

48 And he said unto her, Daughter, be of good comfort: thy faith hath made thee whole; go in peace.

49 While he yet spake, there cometh one from the ruler of the synagogue's house, saying to him, Thy daughter is dead; trouble not the Master.

50 But when Jesus heard it, he answered him, saying, Fear not: believe only, and she shall be made whole.

51 And when he came into the house, he suffered no man to go in, save Peter, and James, and John, and the father and the mother of the maiden.

52 And all wept, and bewailed her: but he said, Weep not; she is not dead, but sleepeth.

53 And they laughed him to scorn, knowing that she was dead.

54 And he put them all out, and took her by the hand, and called, saying, Maid, arise.

55 And her spirit came again, and she arose straightway: and he commanded to give her meat.

56 And her parents were astonished: but he charged them that they should tell no man what was done.

LUKE 9

1 Then he called his twelve disciples together, and gave them power and authority over all devils, and to cure diseases.

2 And he sent them to preach the kingdom of God, and to heal the sick.

3 And he said unto them, Take nothing for your journey, neither staves, nor scrip, neither bread, neither money; neither have two coats apiece.

4 And whatsoever house ye enter into, there abide, and thence depart.

5 And whosoever will not receive you, when ye go out of that city, shake off the very dust from your feet for a testimony against them.

6 And they departed, and went through the towns, preaching the gospel, and healing every where.

7 Now Herod the tetrarch heard of all that was done by him: and he was perplexed, because that it was said of some, that John was risen from the dead;

8 And of some, that Elias had appeared; and of others, that one of the old prophets was risen again.

9 And Herod said, John have I beheaded: but who is this, of whom I hear such things? And he desired to see him.

10 And the apostles, when they were returned, told him all that they had done. And he took them, and went aside privately into a desert place belonging to the city called Bethsaida.

11 And the people, when they knew it, followed him: and he received them, and spake unto them of the kingdom of God, and healed them that had need of healing.

12 And when the day began to wear away, then came the twelve, and said unto him, Send the multitude away, that they may go into the towns and country round about, and lodge, and get victuals: for we are here in a desert place.

13 But he said unto them, Give ye them to eat. And they said, We have no more but five loaves and two fishes; except we should go and buy meat for all this people.

4. Salute no man by the way – The salutations usual among the Jews took up much time. But these had so much work to do in so short a space, that they had not a moment to spare.

6. A son of peace – That is, one worthy of it.

7. Matt. x, 11.

11. The kingdom of God is at hand – Though ye will not receive it.

13. Woe to thee, Chorazin – The same declaration Christ had made some time before. By repeating it now, he warns the seventy not to lose time by going to those cities. Matt. xi, 21.

16. Matt. x, 40; John xiii, 20.

18. I beheld Satan – That is, when ye went forth, I saw the kingdom of Satan, which was highly exalted, swiftly and suddenly cast down.

19. I give you power – That is, I continue it to you: and nothing shall hurt you – Neither the power, nor the subtlety of Satan.

20. Rejoice not so much that the devils are subject to you, as that your names are written in heaven – Reader, so is thine, if thou art a true believer. God grant it may never be blotted out!

21. Lord of heaven and earth – In both of which thy kingdom stands, and that of Satan is destroyed. That thou hast hid these things – He rejoiced not in the destruction of the wise and prudent, but in the display of the riches of God's grace to others, in such a manner as reserves to Him the entire glory of our salvation, and hides pride from man. Matt. xi, 25.

22. Who the Son is – Essentially one with the Father: who the Father is – How great, how wise, how good!

23. Matt. xiii, 16.

25. Matt. xxii, 35; Mark xii, 28.

27. Thou shalt love the Lord thy God – That is, thou shalt unite all the faculties of thy soul to render him the most intelligent and sincere, the most affectionate and resolute service. We may safely rest in this general sense of these important words, if we are not able to fix the particular meaning of every single word. If we desire to do this, perhaps the heart, which is a general expression, may be explained by the three following, With all thy soul, with the warmest affection, with all thy strength, the most vigorous efforts of thy will, and with all thy mind or understanding, in the most wise and reasonable manner thou canst; thy understanding guiding thy will and affections. Deut. vi, 5; Lev. xix, 18.

28. Thou hast answered right; this do, and thou shalt live – Here is no irony, but a deep and weighty truth. He, and he alone, shall live for ever, who thus loves God and his neighbor in the present life.

29. To justify himself – That is, to show he had done this. Lev. xviii, 5.

30. From Jerusalem to Jericho – The road from Jerusalem to Jericho (about eighteen miles from it) lay

MATTHEW HENRY

CHARLES H. SPURGEON

He healed those who had need of healing. And with five loaves of bread and two fishes, Christ fed five thousand men. He will not see those that fear him, and serve him faithfully, want any good thing. When we receive creature comforts, we must acknowledge that we receive them from God, and that we are unworthy to receive them; that we owe them all, and all the comfort we have in them, to the mediation of Christ, by whom the curse is taken away. The blessing of Christ will make a little go a great way. He fills every hungry soul, abundantly satisfies it with the goodness of his house. Here were fragments taken up: in our Father's house there is bread enough, and to spare. We are not straitened, nor stinted in Christ.

18-27 It is an unspeakable comfort that our Lord Jesus is God's Anointed; this signifies that he was both appointed to be the Messiah, and qualified for it. Jesus discourses concerning his own sufferings and death. And so far must his disciples be from thinking how to prevent his sufferings, that they must prepare for their own. We often meet with crosses in the way of duty; and though we must not pull them upon our own heads, yet, when they are laid for us, we must take them up, and carry them after Christ. It is well or ill with us, according as it is well or ill with our souls. The body cannot be happy, if the soul be miserable in the other world; but the soul may be happy, though the body is greatly afflicted and oppressed in this world. We must never be ashamed of Christ and his gospel.

28-36 Christ's transfiguration was a specimen of that glory in which he will come to judge the world; and was an encouragement to his disciples to suffer for him. Prayer is a transfiguring, transforming duty, which makes the face to shine. Our Lord Jesus, even in his transfiguration, was willing to speak concerning his death and sufferings. In our greatest glories on earth, let us remember that in this world we have no continuing city. What need we have to pray to God for quickening grace, to make us lively! Yet that the disciples might be witnesses of this sign from heaven, after awhile they became awake, so that they were able to give a full account of what passed. But those know not what they say, that talk of making tabernacles on earth for glorified saints in heaven.

37-42 How deplorable the case of this child! He was under the power of an evil spirit. Diseases of that nature are more frightful than such as arise merely from natural causes. What mischief Satan does where he gets possession! But happy those that have access to Christ! He can do that for us which his disciples cannot. A word from Christ healed the child; and when our children recover from sickness, it is comfortable to receive them as healed by the hand of Christ.

desirous to find occasion against him. So in all congregations, however the preacher may be clothed with his Master's spirit and his Master's might, there will be a mixed gathering; there will come together your Pharisees and doctors of the law, your sharp critics ready to pick holes, your cold-blooded cavilers searching for faults; at the same time, chosen of God and drawn by his grace, there will be present some devout believers who rejoice in the power that is revealed among men, and earnest seekers who wish to feel in themselves the healing energy. It seems to have been a rule with our Savior to supply each hearer with food after his kind. The Pharisees soon found the matters to cavil at for which they were looking; the Savior so worded his expressions that they caught at them eagerly, and charged him with blasphemy; the enmity of their hearts was thus thrown out upon the surface that the Lord might have an opportunity of rebuking it; and had they been but willing, the power of the Lord was present to heal even them. Meanwhile, those poor tremblers who were praying for healing were not disappointed; the Good Physician passed not by a single case, and at the same time his disciples who were looking for opportunities of praising him anew, were also fully gratified, for with glad eyes they saw the paralytic restored, and heard sins forgiven.

The case which the narrative brings before us, is that of a man stricken down with paralysis. This sad disease may have been of long continuance. There is a paralysis which gradually kills the body, binding it more and more surely in utter helplessness. The nerve power is almost destroyed; the power of motion is entirely suspended; and yet the faculties of the mind remain, though greatly weakened, and some of them almost extinguished. Some have thought that this man may have been stricken with what is called the universal paralysis, which very speedily brings on death, which may account for the extreme haste of the four bearers to bring him near the Savior. We do not know the details of his case, but certain is it that he was paralyzed; and, as I look at the case, and study the three records, I think I perceive with equal clearness that this paralysis was in some way or other, at least in the man's own judgment, connected with his sin. He was evidently penitent, as well as paralytic. His mind was as much oppressed as his bodily frame. I do not know that he could be altogether called a believer, but it is most probable that being burdened with a sense of sin he had a feeble hope in divine mercy, which, like a

14 For they were about five thousand men. And he said to his disciples, Make them sit down by fifties in a company.

15 And they did so, and made them all sit down.

16 Then he took the five loaves and the two fishes, and looking up to heaven, he blessed them, and brake, and gave to the disciples to set before the multitude.

17 And they did eat, and were all filled: and there was taken up of fragments that remained to them twelve baskets.

18 And it came to pass, as he was alone praying, his disciples were with him: and he asked them, saying, Whom say the people that I am?

19 They answering said, John the Baptist; but some say, Elias; and others say, that one of the old prophets is risen again.

20 He said unto them, But whom say ye that I am? Peter answering said, The Christ of God.

21 And he straitly charged them, and commanded them to tell no man that thing;

22 Saying, The Son of man must suffer many things, and be rejected of the elders and chief priests and scribes, and be slain, and be raised the third day.

23 And he said to them all, If any man will come after me, let him deny himself, and take up his cross daily, and follow me.

24 For whosoever will save his life shall lose it: but whosoever will lose his life for my sake, the same shall save it.

25 For what is a man advantaged, if he gain the whole world, and lose himself, or be cast away?

26 For whosoever shall be ashamed of me and of my words, of him shall the Son of man be ashamed, when he shall come in his own glory, and in his Father's, and of the holy angels.

27 But I tell you of a truth, there be some standing here, which shall not taste of death, till they see the kingdom of God.

28 And it came to pass about an eight days after these sayings, he took Peter and John and James, and went up into a mountain to pray.

29 And as he prayed, the fashion of his countenance was altered, and his raiment was white and glistering.

30 And, behold, there talked with him two men, which were Moses and Elias:

31 Who appeared in glory, and spake of his decease which he should accomplish at Jerusalem.

32 But Peter and they that were with him were heavy with sleep: and when they were awake, they saw his glory, and the two men that stood with him.

33 And it came to pass, as they departed from him, Peter said unto Jesus, Master, it is good for us to be here: and let us make three tabernacles; one for thee, and one for Moses, and one for Elias: not knowing what he said.

34 While he thus spake, there came a cloud, and overshadowed them: and they feared as they entered into the cloud.

35 And there came a voice out of the cloud, saying, This is my beloved Son: hear him.

36 And when the voice was past, Jesus was found alone. And they kept it close, and told no man in those days any of those things which they had seen.

37 And it came to pass, that on the next day, when they were come down from the hill, much people met him.

38 And, behold, a man of the company cried out, saying, Master, I beseech thee, look upon my son: for he is mine only child.

39 And, lo, a spirit taketh him, and he suddenly crieth out; and it teareth him that he foameth again, and bruising him hardly departeth from him.

through desert and rocky places: so many robberies and murders were committed therein, that it was called the bloody way. Jericho was situated in the valley: hence the phrase of going down to it. About twelve thousand priests and Levites dwelt there, who all attended the service of the temple.

31. The common translation is, by chance – Which is full of gross improprieties. For if we speak strictly, there is no such thing in the universe as either chance or fortune. A certain priest came down that way, and passed by on the other side – And both he and the Levite no doubt could find an excuse for passing over on the other side, and might perhaps gravely thank God for their own deliverance, while they left their brother bleeding to death. Is it not an emblem of many living characters, perhaps of some who bear the sacred office? O house of Levi and of Aaron, is not the day coming, when the virtues of heathens and Samaritans will rise up in judgment against you?

33. But a certain Samaritan came where he was – It was admirably well judged to represent the distress on the side of the Jew, and the mercy on that of the Samaritan. For the case being thus proposed, self interest would make the very scribe sensible, how amiable such a conduct was, and would lay him open to our Lord's inference. Had it been put the other way, prejudice might more easily have interposed, before the heart could have been affected.

34. Pouring in oil and wine – Which when well beaten together are one of the best balsams that can be applied to a fresh wound.

36. Which of these was the neighbor to him that fell among the robbers – Which acted the part of a neighbor?

37. And he said, He that showed mercy on him – He could not for shame say otherwise, though he thereby condemned himself and overthrew his own false notion of the neighbor to whom our love is due. Go and do thou in like manner – Let us go and do likewise, regarding every man as our neighbor who needs our assistance. Let us renounce that bigotry and party zeal which would contract our hearts into an insensibility for all the human race, but a small number whose sentiments and practices are so much our own, that our love to them is but self love reflected. With an honest openness of mind let us always remember that kindred between man and man, and cultivate that happy instinct whereby, in the original constitution of our nature, God has strongly bound us to each other.

40. Martha was encumbered – The Greek word properly signifies to be drawn different ways at the same time, and admirably expresses the situation of a mind, surrounded (as Martha's then was) with so many objects of care, that it hardly knows which to attend to first.

41. Martha, Martha – There is a peculiar spirit and ten-

43-50 This prediction of Christ's sufferings was plain enough, but the disciples would not understand it, because it agreed not with their notions. A little child is the emblem by which Christ teaches us simplicity and humility. What greater honor can any man attain to in this world, than to be received by men as a messenger of God and Christ; and to have God and Christ own themselves received and welcomed in him! If ever any society of Christians in this world, had reason to silence those not of their own communion, the twelve disciples at this time had; yet Christ warned them not to do the like again. Those may be found faithful followers of Christ, and may be accepted of him, who do not follow with us.

51-56 The disciples did not consider that the conduct of the Samaritans was rather the effect of national prejudices and bigotry, than of enmity to the word and worship of God; and through they refused to receive Christ and his disciples, they did not ill use or injure them, so that the case was widely different from that of Ahaziah and Elijah. Nor were they aware that the gospel dispensation was to be marked by miracles of mercy. But above all, they were ignorant of the prevailing motives of their own hearts, which were pride and carnal ambition. Of this our Lord warned them. It is easy for us to say, Come, see our zeal for the Lord! and to think we are very faithful in his cause, when we are seeking our own objects, and even doing harm instead of good to others.

57-62 Here is one that is forward to follow Christ, but seems to have been hasty and rash, and not to have counted the cost. If we mean to follow Christ, we must lay aside the thoughts of great things in the world. Let us not try to join the profession of Christianity, with seeking after worldly advantages. Here is another that seems resolved to follow Christ, but he begs a short delay. To this man Christ first gave the call; he said to him, Follow me. Religion teaches us to be kind and good, to show piety at home, and to requite our parents; but we must not make these an excuse for neglecting our duty to God. Here is another that is willing to follow Christ, but he must have a little time to talk with his friends about it, and to set in order his household affairs, and give directions concerning them. He seemed to have worldly concerns more upon his heart than he ought to have, and he was willing to enter into a temptation leading him from his purpose of following Christ. No one can do any business in a proper manner, if he is attending to other things. Those who begin with the work of God, must resolve to go on, or they will make nothing of it. Looking back, leads to drawing back, and drawing back is to perdition. He only that endures to the end shall be saved.

spark in smoking flax, had hard work to exist, but yet was truly there. The affliction for which his friends pitied him was in his body, but he himself felt a far severer trouble in his soul, and probably it was not so much with the view of being healed bodily, as in the hope of spiritual blessing, that he was willing to be subjected to any process by which he might come under the Savior's eye. I gather that from the fact that our Savior addressed him in these words, "Be of good cheer;" intimating that he was desponding, that his spirit sunk within him, and, therefore, instead of saying to him at once, "Rise, take up thy bed," our tender-hearted Lord said, "Son, thy sins be forgiven thee." He gave him at the outset a blessing for which the patient's friends had not asked, but which the man, though speechless, was seeking for in the silence of his soul. He was a "son," though an afflicted one: he was ready to obey the Lord's bidding when power was given, though as yet he could neither lift hand nor foot. He was longing for the pardon of sin, yet could not stretch out his hand to lay hold upon the Savior.

I intend to use this narrative for practical purposes; may the Holy Spirit make it really useful. Our first remark will be this:

I. THERE ARE CASES WHICH WILL NEED THE AID OF A LITTLE BAND OF WORKERS BEFORE THEY WILL BE FULLY SAVED.

This man must needs be borne of four, so the evangelist, Mark, tells us; there must be a bearer at each corner of the couch whereon he lay. The great mass of persons who are brought into the kingdom of Christ are converted through the general prayers of the church by the means of her ministry. Probably three out of four of the members of any church will owe their conversion to the church's regular teaching in some form or other; her school, her pulpit, her press have been the nets in which they were taken. Private personal prayer has, of course, in many instances been mingled with all this; but still the most of cases could not be so distinctly traced out as to be attributable mainly to individual prayers or exertions. This is the rule, I think, that the Lord will have the many brought to himself by the sounding of the great trumpet of jubilee in the dispensation of the gospel by his ministers. There are some, again, who are led to Jesus by the individual efforts of one person; just as Andrew found his own brother Simon, so one believer by his private communication of the truth to another person becomes instrumental, by the power of God's Spirit, in his conversion. One convert will

40 And I besought thy disciples to cast him out; and they could not.

41 And Jesus answering said, O faithless and perverse generation, how long shall I be with you, and suffer you? Bring thy son hither.

42 And as he was yet a coming, the devil threw him down, and tare him. And Jesus rebuked the unclean spirit, and healed the child, and delivered him again to his father.

43 And they were all amazed at the mighty power of God. But while they wondered every one at all things which Jesus did, he said unto his disciples,

44 Let these sayings sink down into your ears: for the Son of man shall be delivered into the hands of men.

45 But they understood not this saying, and it was hid from them, that they perceived it not: and they feared to ask him of that saying.

46 Then there arose a reasoning among them, which of them should be greatest.

47 And Jesus, perceiving the thought of their heart, took a child, and set him by him,

48 And said unto them, Whosoever shall receive this child in my name receiveth me: and whosoever shall receive me receiveth him that sent me: for he that is least among you all, the same shall be great.

49 And John answered and said, Master, we saw one casting out devils in thy name; and we forbad him, because he followeth not with us.

50 And Jesus said unto him, Forbid him not: for he that is not against us is for us.

51 And it came to pass, when the time was come that he should be received up, he stedfastly set his face to go to Jerusalem,

52 And sent messengers before his face: and they went, and entered into a village of the Samaritans, to make ready for him.

53 And they did not receive him, because his face was as though he would go to Jerusalem.

54 And when his disciples James and John saw this, they said, Lord, wilt thou that we command fire to come down from heaven, and consume them, even as Elias did?

55 But he turned, and rebuked them, and said, Ye know not what manner of spirit ye are of.

56 For the Son of man is not come to destroy men's lives, but to save them. And they went to another village.

57 And it came to pass, that, as they went in the way, a certain man said unto him, Lord, I will follow thee whithersoever thou goest.

58 And Jesus said unto him, Foxes have holes, and birds of the air have nests; but the Son of man hath not where to lay his head.

59 And he said unto another, Follow me. But he said, Lord, suffer me first to go and bury my father.

60 Jesus said unto him, Let the dead bury their dead: but go thou and preach the kingdom of God.

61 And another also said, Lord, I will follow thee; but let me first go bid them farewell, which are at home at my house.

62 And Jesus said unto him, No man, having put his hand to the plow, and looking back, is fit for the kingdom of God.

LUKE 10

1 After these things the Lord appointed other seventy also, and sent them two and two before his face into every city and place, whither he himself would come.

derness in the repetition of the word: thou art careful, inwardly, and hurried, outwardly.

42. Mary hath chosen the good part – To save her soul. Reader, hast thou?

LUKE 11

1. Lord, teach us to pray, as John also taught his disciples – The Jewish masters used to give their followers some short form of prayer, as a peculiar badge of their relation to them. This it is probable John the Baptist had done. And in this sense it seems to be that the disciples now asked Jesus, to teach them to pray. Accordingly he here repeats that form, which he had before given them in his sermon on the mount, and likewise enlarges on the same head, though still speaking the same things in substance. And this prayer uttered from the heart, and in its true and full meaning, is indeed the badge of a real Christian: for is not he such whose first and most ardent desire is the glory of God, and the happiness of man by the coming of his kingdom? Who asks for no more of this world than his daily bread, longing meantime for the bread that came down from heaven? And whose only desires for himself are forgiveness of sins, (as he heartily forgives others,) and sanctification.

2. When ye pray, say – And what he said to them is undoubtedly said to us also. We are therefore here directed, not only to imitate this in all our prayers, but to use this very form of prayer. Matt. vi, 9.

4. Forgive us; for we forgive them – Not once, but continually. This does not denote the meritorious cause of our pardon; but the removal of that hindrance which otherwise would render it impossible.

5. At midnight – The most unseasonable time: but no time is unseasonable with God, either for hearing or answering prayer.

9. Matt. vii, 7.

13. How much more shall your heavenly Father – How beautiful is the gradation! A friend: a father: God! Give the Holy Spirit – The best of gifts, and that which includes every good gift.

14. It was dumb – That is, it made the man so. Matt. xii, 22.

15. But some said, He casteth out devils by Beelzebub – These he answers, ver. 17. Others, to try whether it were so or no, sought a sign from heaven. These he reproves in ver. 29 and following verses. Beelzebub signifies the Lord of flies, a title which the heathens gave to Jupiter, whom they accounted the chief of their gods, and yet supposed him to be employed in driving away flies from their temple and sacrifices. The Philistines worshiped a deity under this name, as the God of Ekron: from hence the Jews took the name, and applied it to the chief of the devils. Mark iii, 22.

MATTHEW HENRY

CHARLES H. SPURGEON

LUKE 10

Seventy disciples sent forth. (1-16)
The blessedness of Christ's disciples. (17-24)
The good Samaritan. (25-37)
Jesus at the house of Martha and Mary. (38-42)

1-16 Christ sent the seventy disciples, two and two, that they might strengthen and encourage one another. The ministry of the gospel calls men to receive Christ as a Prince and a Savior; and he will surely come in the power of his Spirit to all places whither he sends his faithful servants. But the doom of those who receive the grace of God in vain, will be very fearful. Those who despise the faithful ministers of Christ, who think meanly of them, and look scornfully upon them, will be reckoned as despisers of God and Christ.

17-24 All our victories over Satan, are obtained by power derived from Jesus Christ, and he must have all the praise. But let us beware of spiritual pride, which has been the destruction of many. Our Lord rejoiced at the prospect of the salvation of many souls. It was fit that particular notice should be taken of that hour of joy; there were few such, for He was a man of sorrows: in that hour in which he saw Satan fall, and heard of the good success of his ministers, in that hour he rejoiced. He has ever resisted the proud, and given grace to the humble. The more simply dependent we are on the teaching, help, and blessing of the Son of God, the more we shall know both of the Father and of the Son; the more blessed we shall be in seeing the glory, and hearing the words of the Divine Savior; and the more useful we shall be made in promoting his cause.

25-37 If we speak of eternal life, and the way to it, in a careless manner, we take the name of God in vain. No one will ever love God and his neighbor with any measure of pure, spiritual love, who is not made a partaker of converting grace. But the proud heart of man strives hard against these convictions. Christ gave an instance of a poor Jew in distress, relieved by a good Samaritan. This poor man fell among thieves, who left him about to die of his wounds. He was slighted by those who should have been his friends, and was cared for by a stranger, a Samaritan, of the nation which the Jews most despised and detested, and would have no dealings with. It is lamentable to observe how selfishness governs all ranks; how many excuses men will make to avoid trouble or expense in relieving others. But the true Christian has the law of love written in his heart. The Spirit of Christ dwells in him; Christ's image is renewed in his soul. The parable is a beautiful explanation of the law of loving our neighbor as ourselves, without regard to nation, party, or any other distinction. It also sets forth the kindness and love of God our Savior toward sinful, miserable men. We were like this poor, distressed

bring another, and that other a third. But this narrative seems to show that there are cases which will neither be brought by the general preaching of the word, nor yet by the instrumentality of one; they require that there should be two, or three, or four in holy combination, who, with one consent, feeling one common agony of soul, shall resolve to band themselves together as a company for this one object, and never to cease from their holy confederation until this object is gained and their friend is saved. This man could not be brought to Christ by one, he must have four to lend their strength for his carrying, or he cannot reach the place of healing. Let us apply the principle. Yonder is a householder as yet unsaved: his wife has prayed for him long; her prayers are yet unanswered. Good wife, God has blessed thee with a son who with thee rejoices in the fear of God. Hast thou not two Christian daughters also? O ye four, take each a corner of this sick man's coach and bring your husband, bring your father, to the Savior. A husband and a wife are here, both happily brought to Christ; you are praying for your children; never cease from that supplication: pray on. Perhaps one of your beloved family is unusually stubborn. Extra help is needed. Well, to you the Sabbath school teacher will make a third; he will take one corner of the bed; and happy shall I be if I may join the blessed quaternion, and make the fourth. Perhaps, when home discipline, the school's teaching, and the minister's preaching shall go together, the Lord will look down in love and save your child. Dear brother, you are thinking of one whom you have long prayed for; you have spoken to him also, and used all proper means, but as yet without effect. Perhaps you speak too comfortingly to him: it may be you have not brought that precise truth to bear upon him which his conscience requires. Seek yet more help. It may possibly be that a second brother will speak instructively, where you have only spoken consolingly; perhaps the instruction may be the means of grace. Yet may it possibly happen that even instruction will not suffice any more than consolation, and it may be needful for you to call in a third, who perhaps will speak impressively with exhortation, and with warning, which may possibly be the great requisite. You two, already in the field, may balance his exhortation, which might have been too pungent by itself, and might have raised prejudice in the person's mind if it had come alone. All three of you together may prove the fit instruments in the Lord's hand. Yet when you three

2 Therefore said he unto them, The harvest truly is great, but the laborers are few: pray ye therefore the Lord of the harvest, that he would send forth laborers into his harvest.

3 Go your ways: behold, I send you forth as lambs among wolves.

4 Carry neither purse, nor scrip, nor shoes: and salute no man by the way.

5 And into whatsoever house ye enter, first say, Peace be to this house.

6 And if the son of peace be there, your peace shall rest upon it: if not, it shall turn to you again.

7 And in the same house remain, eating and drinking such things as they give: for the laborer is worthy of his hire. Go not from house to house.

8 And into whatsoever city ye enter, and they receive you, eat such things as are set before you:

9 And heal the sick that are therein, and say unto them, The kingdom of God is come nigh unto you.

10 But into whatsoever city ye enter, and they receive you not, go your ways out into the streets of the same, and say,

11 Even the very dust of your city, which cleaveth on us, we do wipe off against you: notwithstanding be ye sure of this, that the kingdom of God is come nigh unto you.

12 But I say unto you, that it shall be more tolerable in that day for Sodom, than for that city.

13 Woe unto thee, Chorazin! woe unto thee, Bethsaida! for if the mighty works had been done in Tyre and Sidon, which have been done in you, they had a great while ago repented, sitting in sackcloth and ashes.

14 But it shall be more tolerable for Tyre and Sidon at the judgment, than for you.

15 And thou, Capernaum, which art exalted to heaven, shalt be thrust down to hell.

16 He that heareth you heareth me; and he that despiseth you despiseth me; and he that despiseth me despiseth him that sent me.

17 And the seventy returned again with joy, saying, Lord, even the devils are subject unto us through thy name.

18 And he said unto them, I beheld Satan as lightning fall from heaven.

19 Behold, I give unto you power to tread on serpents and scorpions, and over all the power of the enemy: and nothing shall by any means hurt you.

20 Notwithstanding in this rejoice not, that the spirits are subject unto you; but rather rejoice, because your names are written in heaven.

21 In that hour Jesus rejoiced in spirit, and said, I thank thee, O Father, Lord of heaven and earth, that thou hast hid these things from the wise and prudent, and hast revealed them unto babes: even so, Father; for so it seemed good in thy sight.

22 All things are delivered to me of my Father: and no man knoweth who the Son is, but the Father; and who the Father is, but the Son, and he to whom the Son will reveal him.

23 And he turned him unto his disciples, and said privately, Blessed are the eyes which see the things that ye see:

24 For I tell you, that many prophets and kings have desired to see those things which ye see, and have not seen them; and to hear those things which ye hear, and have not heard them.

25 And, behold, a certain lawyer stood up, and tempted him, saying, Master, what shall I do to inherit eternal life?

26 He said unto him, What is written in the law? how readest thou?

16. Matt. xii, 38.

17. A house – That is, a family.

20. If I cast out devils by the finger of God – That is, by a power manifestly Divine. Perhaps the expression intimates farther, that it was done without any labor: then the kingdom of God is come upon you – Unawares, unexpected: so the Greek word implies.

21. The strong one armed – The devil, strong in himself, and armed with the pride, obstinacy, and security of him in whom he dwells.

26. The last state of that man becometh worse than the first – Whoever reads the sad account Josephus gives of the temple and conduct of the Jews, after the ascension of Christ and before their final destruction by the Romans, must acknowledge that no emblem could have been more proper to describe them. Their characters were the vilest that can be conceived, and they pressed on to their own ruin, as if they had been possessed by legions of devils, and wrought up to the last degree of madness. But this also is fulfilled in all who totally and finally apostatize from true faith.

27. Blessed is the womb that bare thee, and the paps which thou hast sucked! – How natural was the thought for a woman! And how gently does our Lord reprove her!

28. Yea, rather blessed are they that hear the word of God and keep it – For if even she that bare him had not done this, she would have forfeited all her blessedness.

29. It seeketh – The original word implies seeking more, or over and above what one has already.

32. They repented at the preaching of Jonah – But it was only for a season. Afterward they relapsed into wickedness, till (after about forty years) they were destroyed. It is remarkable, that in this also the comparison held. God reprieved the Jews for about forty years; but they still advanced in wickedness, till having filled up their measure, they were destroyed with an utter destruction.

33. The meaning is, God gives you this Gospel light, that you may repent. Let your eye be singly fixed on him, aim only at pleasing God; and while you do this, your whole soul will be full of wisdom, holiness, and happiness. Matt. v, 15; Mark iv, 21; Luke viii, 16.

34. But when thine eye is evil – When thou aimest at any thing else, thou wilt be full of folly, sin, and misery. On the contrary, Matt. vi, 22.

36. If thy whole body be full of light – If thou art filled with holy wisdom, having no part dark, giving way to no sin or folly, then that heavenly principle will, like the clear flame of a lamp in a room that was dark before, shed its light into all thy powers and faculties.

39. Now ye Pharisees – Probably many of them were present at the Pharisee's house. Matt. xxiii, 25.

41. Give what is in them – The vessels which ye clean, in alms, and all things are clean to you. As if he had said, By acts directly contrary to rapine and wickedness, show

MATTHEW HENRY

CHARLES H. SPURGEON

traveler. Satan, our enemy, has robbed us, and wounded us: such is the mischief sin has done us. The blessed Jesus had compassion on us. The believer considers that Jesus loved him, and gave his life for him, when an enemy and a rebel; and having shown him mercy, he bids him go and do likewise. It is the duty of us all, in our places, and according to our ability, to succor, help, and relieve all that are in distress and necessity.

38-42 A good sermon is not the worse for being preached in a house; and the visits of our friends should be so managed, as to make them turn to the good of their souls. Sitting at Christ's feet, signifies readiness to receive his word, and submission to the guidance of it. Martha was providing for the entertainment of Christ, and those that came with him. Here were respect to our Lord Jesus and right care of her household affairs. But there was something to be blamed. She was for much serving; plenty, variety, and exactness. Worldly business is a snare to us, when it hinders us from serving God, and getting good to our souls. What needless time is wasted, and expense often laid out, even in entertaining professors of the gospel! Though Martha was on this occasion faulty, yet she was a true believer, and in her general conduct did not neglect the one thing needful. The favor of God is needful to our happiness; the salvation of Christ is needful to our safety. Where this is attended to, all other things will be rightly pursued. Christ declared, Mary hath chosen the good part. For one thing is needful, this one thing that she has done, to give up herself to the guidance of Christ. The things of this life will be taken away from us, at the furthest, when we shall be taken away from them; but nothing shall separate from the love of Christ, and a part in that love. Men and devils cannot take it away from us, and God and Christ will not. Let us mind the one thing needful more diligently.

LUKE 11

The disciples taught to pray. (1-4)
Christ encourages being earnest in prayer. (5-13)
Christ casts out a devil. The blasphemy of the Pharisees. (14-26)
True happiness. (27,28)
Christ reproves the Jews. (29-36)
He reproves the Pharisees. (37-54)

1-4 "Lord, teach us to pray," is a good prayer, and a very needful one, for Jesus Christ only can teach us, by his word and Spirit, how to pray. Lord, teach me what it is to pray; Lord, stir up and quicken me to the duty; Lord, direct me what to pray for; teach me what I should say. Christ taught them a prayer, much the same that he had given before in his sermon upon the mount. There are some differences in the words of the Lord's prayer in Matthew and in Luke, but they are of

have happily combined, it may be the poor paralyzed one is not yet affected savingly; a fourth may be needed, who, with deeper affection than all three of you, and perhaps with an experience more suited to the case than yours, may come in, and working with you, the result may be secured. The four fellow-helpers together may accomplish, by the power of the Spirit, what neither one, nor two, nor three were competent to have done. It may sometimes happen that a man has heard Paul preach, but his clear doctrine, though it has enlightened his intellect, has not yet convinced his conscience. He has heard Apollos, and the glow of the orator's eloquent appeals has warmed his heart, but not humbled his pride. He has later still listened to Cephas, whose rough cutting sentences have hewn him down, and convinced him of sin; but ere he can find joy and peace in believing, he will require to hear the sweet affectionate words of John. Only when the fourth shall grasp the bed and give a hearty lift will the paralyzed person he laid in mercy's path. I anxiously desire to see in this church little bands of men and women bound to each other by zealous love to souls. I would have you say to one another, "This is a case in which we feel a common interest: we will pledge each other to pray for this person; we will unitedly seek his salvation." It may be that one of our seat holders, after listening to my voice these ten or fifteen years, is not impressed; it may be that another has left the Sabbath school unsaved. Let brotherly quaternions look after these by God's help. Moved by one impulse, form a square about these persons, beset them behind and before, and let them not say, "No man careth for my soul." Meet together in prayer with the definite object before you, and then seek that object by the most likely ways. I do not know, my brethren, how much of blessing might come to us through this, but I feel certain that until we have tried it we cannot pronounce a verdict upon it; nor can we be quite sure that we are free from all responsibility to men's souls until we have tested every possible and probable method for doing them good.

I am afraid that there are not many, even in a large church, who will become sick-bearers. Many will say the plan is admirable, but they will leave it to others to carry it out. Remember that the four persons who join in such a labor of love ought all of them to be filled with intense affection to the persons whose salvation they seek. They must be men who will not shrink because of difficulty; who will put forth

27 And he answering said, Thou shalt love the Lord thy God with all thy heart, and with all thy soul, and with all thy strength, and with all thy mind; and thy neighbor as thyself.

28 And he said unto him, Thou hast answered right: this do, and thou shalt live.

29 But he, willing to justify himself, said unto Jesus, And who is my neighbor?

30 And Jesus answering said, A certain man went down from Jerusalem to Jericho, and fell among thieves, which stripped him of his raiment, and wounded him, and departed, leaving him half dead.

31 And by chance there came down a certain priest that way: and when he saw him, he passed by on the other side.

32 And likewise a Levite, when he was at the place, came and looked on him, and passed by on the other side.

33 But a certain Samaritan, as he journeyed, came where he was: and when he saw him, he had compassion on him,

34 And went to him, and bound up his wounds, pouring in oil and wine, and set him on his own beast, and brought him to an inn, and took care of him.

35 And on the morrow when he departed, he took out two pence, and gave them to the host, and said unto him, Take care of him; and whatsoever thou spendest more, when I come again, I will repay thee.

36 Which now of these three, thinkest thou, was neighbor unto him that fell among the thieves?

37 And he said, He that shewed mercy on him. Then said Jesus unto him, Go, and do thou likewise.

38 Now it came to pass, as they went, that he entered into a certain village: and a certain woman named Martha received him into her house.

39 And she had a sister called Mary, which also sat at Jesus' feet, and heard his word.

40 But Martha was cumbered about much serving, and came to him, and said, Lord, dost thou not care that my sister hath left me to serve alone? bid her therefore that she help me.

41 And Jesus answered and said unto her, Martha, Martha, thou art careful and troubled about many things:

42 But one thing is needful: and Mary hath chosen that good part, which shall not be taken away from her.

LUKE 11

1 And it came to pass, that, as he was praying in a certain place, when he ceased, one of his disciples said unto him, Lord, teach us to pray, as John also taught his disciples.

2 And he said unto them, When ye pray, say, Our Father which art in heaven, Hallowed be thy name. Thy kingdom come. Thy will be done, as in heaven, so in earth.

3 Give us day by day our daily bread.

4 And forgive us our sins; for we also forgive every one that is indebted to us. And lead us not into temptation; but deliver us from evil.

5 And he said unto them, Which of you shall have a friend, and shall go unto him at midnight, and say unto him, Friend, lend me three loaves;

6 For a friend of mine in his journey is come to me, and I have nothing to set before him?

7 And he from within shall answer and say, Trouble me not: the door is now shut, and my children are with me in bed; I cannot rise and give thee.

8 I say unto you, Though he will not rise and give him, because he is his friend, yet because of his importunity he will rise and give him as many as he needeth.

that your hearts are cleansed, and these outward washings are needless.

42. Woe to you – That is, miserable are you. In the same manner is the phrase to be understood throughout the chapter.

44. For ye are as graves which appear not – Probably in speaking this our Lord fixed his eyes on the scribes. As graves which appear not, being overgrown with grass, so that men are not aware, till they stumble upon them, and either hurt themselves, or at least are defiled by touching them. On another occasion Christ compared them to white sepulchers, fair without, but foul within; Matt. xxiii, 27.

45. One of the lawyers – That is scribes; expounders of the law.

48. Whom they killed, ye build their sepulchers – Just like them pretending great reverence for the ancient prophets, while ye destroy those whom God sends to yourselves. Ye therefore bear witness by this deep hypocrisy that ye are of the very same spirit with them.

49. The wisdom of God, agreeably to this, hath said – In many places of Scripture, though not in these very words, I will send them prophets – Chiefly under the Old Testament: and apostles – Under the New. Matt. xxiii, 34.

50. The blood of all shall be required of this generation – That is, shall be visibly and terribly punished upon it.

51. And so it was within forty years, in a most astonishing manner, by the dreadful destruction of the temple, the city, and the whole nation. Between the temple and the altar – In the court of the temple.

52. Ye have taken away the key of knowledge – Ye have obscured and destroyed the knowledge of the Messiah, which is the key of both the present and the future kingdom of heaven; the kingdom of grace and glory. Ye have not entered in – Into the present kingdom of heaven.

LUKE 12

1. He said to his disciples first – But afterward ver. 54 to all the people. Matt. xvi, 6.

3. Matt. x, 27.

4. But I say to you, Fear not – Let not the fear of man make you act the hypocrite, or conceal any thing which I have commissioned you to publish.

5. Fear him who hath power to cast into hell – Even to his peculiar friends, Christ gives this direction. Therefore the fearing of God as having power to cast into hell, is to be pressed even on true believers.

6. Are not five sparrows – But trust as well as fear him.

7. Matt. x, 30.

8. And I say to you – If you avoid all hypocrisy, and openly avow my Gospel: The Son of man shall confess you – before the angels – At the last day. Mark viii, 38; Luke ix, 26.

MATTHEW HENRY

CHARLES H. SPURGEON

no moment. Let us in our requests, both for others and for ourselves, come to our heavenly Father, confiding in his power and goodness.

5-13 Christ encourages fervency and constancy in prayer. We must come for what we need, as a man does to his neighbor or friend, who is kind to him. We must come for bread; for that which is needful. If God does not answer our prayers speedily, yet he will in due time, if we continue to pray. Observe what to pray for; we must ask for the Holy Spirit, not only as necessary in order to our praying well, but as all spiritual blessings are included in that one. For by the influences of the Holy Spirit we are brought to know God and ourselves, to repent, believe in, and love Christ, and so are made comfortable in this world, and meet for happiness in the next. All these blessings our heavenly Father is more ready to bestow on every one that asks for them, than an indulgent parent is to give food to a hungry child. And this is the advantage of the prayer of faith, that it quiets and establishes the heart in God.

14-26 Christ's thus casting out the devils, was really the destroying of their power. The heart of every unconverted sinner is the devil's palace, where he dwells, and where he rules. There is a kind of peace in the heart of an unconverted soul, while the devil, as a strong man armed, keeps it. The sinner is secure, has no doubt concerning the goodness of his state, nor any dread of the judgment to come. But observe the wonderful change made in conversion. The conversion of a soul to God, is Christ's victory over the devil and his power in that soul, restoring the soul to its liberty, and recovering his own interest in it and power over it. All the endowments of mind or body are now employed for Christ. Here is the condition of a hypocrite. The house is swept from common sins, by a forced confession, as Pharaoh's; by a feigned contrition, as Ahab's; or by a partial reformation, as Herod's. The house is swept, but it is not washed; the heart is not made holy. Sweeping takes off only the loose dirt, while the sin that besets the sinner, the beloved sin, is untouched. The house is garnished with common gifts and graces. It is not furnished with any true grace; it is all paint and varnish, not real nor lasting. It was never given up to Christ, nor dwelt in by the Spirit. Let us take heed of resting in that which a man may have, and yet come short of heaven. The wicked spirits enter in without any difficulty; they are welcomed, and they dwell there; there they work, there they rule. From such an awful state let all earnestly pray to be delivered.

27,28 While the scribes and Pharisees despised and blasphemed the discourses of our Lord Jesus, this good woman admired them, and the wisdom and power with which he spake. Christ led the woman to a higher consideration. Though it is a great privilege

their whole strength to shoulder the beloved burden, and will persevere until they succeed. They need be strong, for the burden is heavy; they need be resolute, for the work will try their faith; they need be prayerful, for otherwise they labor in vain; they must be believing, or they will be utterly useless,—Jesus saw their faith, and therefore accepted their service; but without faith it is impossible to please him. Where shall we find quartets such as these? May the Lord find them, and may he send them to some of you poor dying sinners who lie paralyzed here today.

II. We now pass on to the second observation, that SOME CASES THUS TAKEN UP WILL NEED MUCH THOUGHT BEFORE THE DESIGN IS ACCOMPLISHED.

The essential means by which a soul is saved is clear enough. The four bearers had no question with each other as to what was the way to effect this man's cure: they were unanimous in this—that they must bring him to Jesus; by some means or other, by hook or by crook, they must place him in the Savior's way. That was undoubted fact. The question was, how to do this? There is an old worldly proverb, that "where there's a will there's a way;" and that proverb, I believe, may be safely imported into spiritual things, almost without a caution or grain of salt. "Where there's a will there's a way;" and if men be called of God's grace to a deep anxiety for any particular soul, there is a way by which that soul may be brought to Jesus; but that way may not suggest itself till after much consideration. In some cases the way to impress the heart may be an out-of-the-way way, an extraordinary way—a way which ordinarily should not be used and would not be successful. I dare say the four bearers in the narrative thought early in the morning, "We will carry this poor paralytic to the Savior, passing into the house by the ordinary door;" but when they attempted to do so the multitudes so blocked up the road that they could not even reach the threshold. "Make way; make way for the sick! Stand aside there, and give room for a poor paralyzed man. For mercy's sake, give a little space, and let the sick man reach the healing prophet!" In vain their entreaties and commands. Here and there a few compassionate persons back out of the crowd, but the many neither can nor will remove; besides, many of them are engaged upon a similar business, and have equal reasons for pressing in. "See," cries one of the four, "I will make way;" and he pushes and elbows himself a little dis-

9 And I say unto you, Ask, and it shall be given you; seek, and ye shall find; knock, and it shall be opened unto you.

10 For every one that asketh receiveth; and he that seeketh findeth; and to him that knocketh it shall be opened.

11 If a son shall ask bread of any of you that is a father, will he give him a stone? or if he ask a fish, will he for a fish give him a serpent?

12 Or if he shall ask an egg, will he offer him a scorpion?

13 If ye then, being evil, know how to give good gifts unto your children: how much more shall your heavenly Father give the Holy Spirit to them that ask him?

14 And he was casting out a devil, and it was dumb. And it came to pass, when the devil was gone out, the dumb spake; and the people wondered.

15 But some of them said, He casteth out devils through Beelzebub the chief of the devils.

16

And others, tempting him, sought of him a sign from heaven.

17 But he, knowing their thoughts, said unto them, Every kingdom divided against itself is brought to desolation; and a house divided against a house falleth.

18 If Satan also be divided against himself, how shall his kingdom stand? because ye say that I cast out devils through Beelzebub.

19 And if I by Beelzebub cast out devils, by whom do your sons cast them out? therefore shall they be your judges.

20 But if I with the finger of God cast out devils, no doubt the kingdom of God is come upon you.

21 When a strong man armed keepeth his palace, his goods are in peace:

22 But when a stronger than he shall come upon him, and overcome him, he taketh from him all his armor wherein he trusted, and divideth his spoils.

23 He that is not with me is against me: and he that gathereth not with me scattereth.

24 When the unclean spirit is gone out of a man, he walketh through dry places, seeking rest; and finding none, he saith, I will return unto my house whence I came out.

25 And when he cometh, he findeth it swept and garnished.

26 Then goeth he, and taketh to him seven other spirits more wicked than himself; and they enter in, and dwell there: and the last state of that man is worse than the first.

27 And it came to pass, as he spake these things, a certain woman of the company lifted up her voice, and said unto him, Blessed is the womb that bare thee, and the paps which thou hast sucked.

28 But he said, Yea rather, blessed are they that hear the word of God, and keep it.

29 And when the people were gathered thick together, he began to say, This is an evil generation: they seek a sign; and there shall no sign be given it, but the sign of Jonas the prophet.

30 For as Jonas was a sign unto the Ninevites, so shall also the Son of man be to this generation.

31 The queen of the south shall rise up in the judgment with the men of this generation, and condemn them: for she came from the utmost parts of the earth to hear the wisdom of Solomon; and, behold, a greater than Solomon is here.

32 The men of Nineve shall rise up in the judgment with this generation, and shall condemn it: for they repented at the preaching of Jonas; and, behold, a greater than Jonas is here.

33 No man, when he hath lighted a candle, putteth it in a secret place, neither under a bushel, but on a candlestick, that they which come in may see the light.

10. And whosoever – As if he had said, Yet the denying me in some degree, may, upon true repentance, be forgiven; but if it rise so high as that of the blasphemy against the Holy Ghost, it shall never be forgiven, neither is there place for repentance. Matt. xii, 31; Mark iii, 28.

11. Take no thought – Be not solicitous about the matter or manner of your defense; nor how to express yourselves. Matt. x, 19; Luke xxi, 12.

14. Who made me a judge? – In worldly things. His kingdom is not of this world.

15. He said to them – Perhaps to the two brothers, and through them to the people. A man's life – That is, the comfort or happiness of it.

17. What shall I do? – The very language of want! Do? Why, lay up treasure in heaven.

20. Thou fool – To think of satisfying thy soul with earthly goods! To depend on living many years! Yea, one day! They – The messengers of death, commissioned by God, require thy soul of thee!

21. Rich toward God – Namely, in faith, and love, and good works.

22. Matt. vi, 25.

25. Which of you can add the least measure – It seems, to add one cubit to a thing (which is the phrase in the original) was a kind of proverbial expression for making the least addition to it.

28. The grass – The Greek word means all sorts of herbs and flowers.

29. Neither be ye of a doubtful mind – The word in the original signifies, any speculations or musings in which the mind fluctuates, or is suspended (like meteors in the air) in an uneasy hesitation.

32. It is your Father's good pleasure to give you the kingdom – How much more food and raiment? And since ye have such an inheritance, regard not your earthly possessions.

33. Sell what ye have – This is a direction, not given to all the multitude: (much less is it a standing rule for all Christians:) neither to the apostles; for they had nothing to sell, having left all before: but to his other disciples, (mentioned Luke xii, 22, and Acts i, 15,) especially to the seventy, that they might be free from all worldly entanglements. Matt. vi, 19.

35. Let your loins be girt – An allusion to the long garments, worn by the eastern nations, which they girded or tucked up about their loins, when they journeyed or were employed in any labor: as also to the lights that servants used to carry at weddings, which were generally in the night.

37. He will come and serve them – The meaning is, he will show them his love, in the most condescending and tender manner.

38. The Jews frequently divided the night into three watches, to which our Lord seems here to allude.

to hear the word of God, yet those only are truly blessed, that is, blessed of the Lord, that hear it, keep it in memory, and keep to it as their way and rule.

29-36 Christ promised that there should be one sign more given, even the sign of Jonah the prophet; which in Matthew is explained, as meaning the resurrection of Christ; and he warned them to improve this sign. But though Christ himself were the constant preacher in any congregation, and worked miracles daily among them, yet unless his grace humbled their hearts, they would not profit by his word. Let us not desire more evidence and fuller teaching than the Lord is pleased to afford us. We should pray without ceasing that our hearts and understandings may be opened, that we may profit by the light we enjoy. And especially take heed that the light which is in us be not darkness; for if our leading principles be wrong, our judgment and practice must become more so.

37-54 We should all look to our hearts, that they may be cleansed and new created; and while we attend to the great things of the law and of the gospel, we must not neglect the smallest matter God has appointed. When any wait to catch something out of our mouths, that they may ensnare us, O Lord, give us thy prudence and thy patience, and disappoint their evil purposes. Furnish us with such meekness and patience that we may glory in reproaches, for Christ's sake, and that thy Holy Spirit may rest upon us.

LUKE 12

Christ reproves the interpreters of the law. (1-12)
A caution against covetousness. The parable of the rich
*   man. (13-21)*
Worldly care reproved. (22-40)
Watchfulness enforced. (41-53)
A warning to be reconciled to God. (54-59)

1-12 A firm belief of the doctrine of God's universal providence, and the extent of it, would satisfy us when in peril, and encourage us to trust God in the way of duty. Providence takes notice of the meanest creatures, even of the sparrows, and therefore of the smallest interests of the disciples of Christ. Those who confess Christ now, shall be owned by him in the great day, before the angels of God. To deter us from denying Christ, and deserting his truths and ways, we are here assured that those who deny Christ, though they may thus save life itself, and though they may gain a kingdom by it, will be great losers at last; for Christ will not know them, will not own them, nor show them favor. But let no trembling, penitent backslider doubt of obtaining forgiveness. This is far different from the determined enmity that is blasphemy against the Holy Ghost, which shall never be forgiven, because it will never be repented of.

tance into the passage. "Come on you three!" he cries: "follow up, and fight for it, inch by inch." But they cannot do it; it is impossible; the poor patient is ready to die for fear; the bed is tossed about by the throng like a cockleshell boat on the sea-waves, the patient's alarm increases, the bearers are distressed, and they are quite glad to get outside again and consider. It is evidently quite impossible by ordinary means to get him in. What then? "We cannot burrow under the ground: can we not go over the heads of the people, and let the man down from above? Where is the staircase?" Frequently there is an external staircase to the top of an eastern house; we cannot be sure that there was one in this case; but if not, the next door house may have had such a convenience, and so the resolute bearers reached the top and passed from one roof to another. Where we have no definite information much may be left to conjecture; but this much is clear: by some means they elevated their unhappy burden to the housetop, and provided themselves with the necessary tackle with which to let him down. The Savior was probably preaching in one of the upper rooms, unless the house was a poor one without an upper story. Perhaps the room was open to the courtyard, which was crowded. At any rate, the Lord Jesus was under cover of a roof, and a substantial roof too. No one who carefully reads the original will fail to see that there was real roofing to be broken through. It has been suggested as a difficulty, that the breaking up of a roof might involve danger to those below, and would probably make a great smother of dust; and to avoid this, there have been various suppositions—such as that the Savior was standing under an awning, and the men rolled up the canvas; or that our Lord stood under a verandah with a very light covering, which the men could readily uncover; others have even invented a trap-door for the occasion. But with all due deference to eminent travelers, the words of the evangelists cannot be so readily disposed of. According to our text, the man was let down through "tiling," not canvas, or any light material; whatever sort of tiling it was, it was certainly made of burnt clay, for that enters into the essence of the word. Moreover, according to Mark, after they had uncovered the roof, which, I suppose, means the removal of the "tiling," they broke it up, which looks exceedingly like breaking through a ceiling. The Greek word used by Mark, which is interpreted "breaking up," is a very emphatic word, and signifies digging through, or scooping up,

34 The light of the body is the eye: therefore when thine eye is single, thy whole body also is full of light; but when thine eye is evil, thy body also is full of darkness.

35 Take heed therefore that the light which is in thee be not darkness.

36 If thy whole body therefore be full of light, having no part dark, the whole shall be full of light, as when the bright shining of a candle doth give thee light.

37 And as he spake, a certain Pharisee besought him to dine with him: and he went in, and sat down to meat.

38 And when the Pharisee saw it, he marveled that he had not first washed before dinner.

39 And the Lord said unto him, Now do ye Pharisees make clean the outside of the cup and the platter; but your inward part is full of ravening and wickedness.

40 Ye fools, did not he that made that which is without make that which is within also?

41 But rather give alms of such things as ye have; and, behold, all things are clean unto you.

42 But woe unto you, Pharisees! for ye tithe mint and rue and all manner of herbs, and pass over judgment and the love of God: these ought ye to have done, and not to leave the other undone.

43 Woe unto you, Pharisees! for ye love the uppermost seats in the synagogues, and greetings in the markets.

44 Woe unto you, scribes and Pharisees, hypocrites! for ye are as graves which appear not, and the men that walk over them are not aware of them.

45 Then answered one of the lawyers, and said unto him, Master, thus saying thou reproachest us also.

46 And he said, Woe unto you also, ye lawyers! for ye lade men with burdens grievous to be borne, and ye yourselves touch not the burdens with one of your fingers.

47 Woe unto you! for ye build the sepulchers of the prophets, and your fathers killed them.

48 Truly ye bear witness that ye allow the deeds of your fathers: for they indeed killed them, and ye build their sepulchers.

49 Therefore also said the wisdom of God, I will send them prophets and apostles, and some of them they shall slay and persecute:

50 That the blood of all the prophets, which was shed from the foundation of the world, may be required of this generation;

51 From the blood of Abel unto the blood of Zacharias, which perished between the altar and the temple: verily I say unto you, It shall be required of this generation.

52 Woe unto you, lawyers! for ye have taken away the key of knowledge: ye entered not in yourselves, and them that were entering in ye hindered.

53 And as he said these things unto them, the scribes and the Pharisees began to urge him vehemently, and to provoke him to speak of many things:

54 Laying wait for him, and seeking to catch something out of his mouth, that they might accuse him.

LUKE 12

1 In the mean time, when there were gathered together an innumerable multitude of people, insomuch that they trode one upon another, he began to say unto his disciples first of all, Beware ye of the leaven of the Pharisees, which is hypocrisy.

41. Speakest thou this parable to us – Apostles and disciples: Or to all – The people? Does it concern us alone? Or all men?

42. Who is that faithful and wise steward – Our Lord's answer manifestly implies, that he had spoken this parable primarily (though not wholly) to the ministers of his word: Whom his Lord shall make ruler over his household – For his wisdom and faithfulness.

43. Happy is that servant – God himself pronounces him wise, faithful, happy! Yet we see, he might fall from all, and perish for ever.

46. The Lord will appoint him his portion – His everlasting portion, with the unfaithful – As faithful as he was once, God himself being the Judge!

47. And that servant who knew his Lord's will shall be beaten with many stripes – And his having much knowledge will increase, not lessen, his punishment.

49. I am come to send fire – To spread the fire of heavenly love over all the earth.

50. But I have a baptism to be baptized with – I must suffer first, before I can set up my kingdom. And how I long to fight my way through all!

51. Suppose ye that I am come to send peace upon earth – That universal peace will be the immediate effect of my coming? Not so, but quite the contrary. Matt. x, 34.

52. There shall be five in one house, three against two, and two against three – There being an irreconcilable enmity between the Spirit of Christ and the spirit of the world.

53. The father against the son – For those who reject me will be implacable toward their very nearest relations who receive me. At this day also is this scripture fulfilled. Now likewise there is no concord between Christ and Belial.

54. And he said to the people also – In the preceding verses he speaks only to his disciples. From the west – In Judea, the west wind, blowing from the sea, usually brought rain: the south wind, blowing from the deserts of Arabia, occasioned sultry heat. Matt. xvi, 2.

56. How do ye not discern this season – Of the Messiah's coming, distinguishable by so many surer signs.

57. Why even of yourselves, without any external sign, judge ye not what is right? – Why do ye not discern and acknowledge the intrinsic excellence of my doctrine?

58. When thou art going – As if he had said, And ye have not a moment to lose. For the executioners of God's vengeance are at hand. And when he hath once delivered you over to them, ye are undone for ever. Matt. v, 25.

59. A mite – was about the third part of a farthing sterling.

13-21 Christ's kingdom is spiritual, and not of this world. Christianity does not meddle with politics; it obliges all to do justly, but worldly dominion is not founded in grace. It does not encourage expectations of worldly advantages by religion. The rewards of Christ's disciples are of another nature. Covetousness is a sin we need constantly to be warned against; for happiness and comfort do not depend on the wealth of this world. The things of the world will not satisfy the desires of a soul. Here is a parable, which shows the folly of carnal worldlings while they live, and their misery when they die. The character drawn is exactly that of a prudent, worldly man, who has no grateful regard to the providence of God, nor any right thought of the uncertainty of human affairs, the worth of his soul, or the importance of eternity. How many, even among professed Christians, point out similar characters as models for imitation, and proper persons to form connexions with! We mistake if we think that thoughts are hid, and thoughts are free. When he saw a great crop upon his ground, instead of thanking God for it, or rejoicing to be able to do more good, he afflicts himself. What shall I do now? The poorest beggar in the country could not have said a more anxious word. The more men have, the more perplexity they have with it. It was folly for him to think of making no other use of his plenty, than to indulge the flesh and gratify the sensual appetites, without any thought of doing good to others. Carnal worldlings are fools; and the day is coming when God will call them by their own name, and they will call themselves so. The death of such persons is miserable in itself, and terrible to them. Thy soul shall be required. He is loath to part with it; but God shall require it, shall require an account of it, require it as a guilty soul to be punished without delay. It is the folly of most men, to mind and pursue that which is for the body and for time only, more than that for the soul and eternity.

22-40 Christ largely insisted upon this caution not to give way to disquieting, perplexing cares, Mt 6:25-34. The arguments here used are for our encouragement to cast our care upon God, which is the right way to get ease. As in our stature, so in our state, it is our wisdom to take it as it is. An eager, anxious pursuit of the things of this world, even necessary things, ill becomes the disciples of Christ. Fears must not prevail; when we frighten ourselves with thoughts of evil to come, and put upon ourselves needless cares how to avoid it. If we value the beauty of holiness, we shall not crave the luxuries of life. Let us then examine whether we belong to this little flock. Christ is our Master, and we are his servants; not only working servants, but waiting servants. We must be as men that wait for their lord, that sit up while he stays out late, to be ready to receive him. In this Christ alluded to his own ascension to heaven, his coming to call his people to him by death, and his return to judge the world. We are uncertain as to the time of his coming to us,

which evidently conveys the idea of considerable labor for the removal of material. We are told that the roofs of Oriental houses are often made of big stones; that may be true as a general rule, but not in this case, for the house was covered with tiles; and as to the dust and falling rubbish, that may or may not be a necessary conclusion; but as clear as noonday is it that a substantial housetop, which required untiling and digging through, had a hole made in it, and through the aperture the man in his bed was let down. Perhaps there was dust, and possibly there was danger too, but the bearers were prepared to accomplish their purpose at all risks. They must get the sick man in somehow. There is no need, however, to suppose either, for no doubt the four men would be careful not to incommode the Savior or his hearers. The tiles or plaster might be removed to another part of the flat roof, and the boards likewise, as they were broken up; and as for the spars, they might be sufficiently wide to admit the narrow couch of the sick man without moving any of them from their places. Mr. Hartley, in his Travels, says: "When I lived at Aegina I used to look up not infrequently at the roof above my head, and contemplate how easily the whole transaction of the paralytic might take place. The roof was made in the following manner:—A layer of reeds, of a large species, was placed upon the rafters, on these a quantity of heather was strewed; on the heather earth was deposited, and beaten down into a solid mass. Now, what difficulty would there be in removing first the earth, next the heather, and then the reeds? Nor would the difficulty be increased, if the earth had a pavement of tiling laid upon it. No inconvenience could result to the persons in the house, from the removal of the tiles and earth; for the heather and reeds would stop anything that might otherwise fall down, and would be removed last of all." To let a man down through the roof was a device most strange and striking, but it only gives point to the remark which we have now to make here. If we want to have souls saved, we must not be too squeamish and delicate about conventionalities, rules, and proprieties, for the kingdom of heaven suffereth violence. We must make up our minds to this: "Smash or crash, everything shall go to pieces which stands between the soul and its God: it matters not what tiles are to be taken off, what plaster is to be digged up, or what boards are to be torn away, or what labor, or trouble, or expense we may be at; the soul is too precious for us to stand upon nice questions. If by any means we

2 For there is nothing covered, that shall not be revealed; neither hid, that shall not be known.

3 Therefore whatsoever ye have spoken in darkness shall be heard in the light; and that which ye have spoken in the ear in closets shall be proclaimed upon the housetops.

4 And I say unto you my friends, Be not afraid of them that kill the body, and after that have no more that they can do.

5 But I will forewarn you whom ye shall fear: Fear him, which after he hath killed hath power to cast into hell; yea, I say unto you, Fear him.

6 Are not five sparrows sold for two farthings, and not one of them is forgotten before God?

7 But even the very hairs of your head are all numbered. Fear not therefore: ye are of more value than many sparrows.

8 Also I say unto you, Whosoever shall confess me before men, him shall the Son of man also confess before the angels of God:

9 But he that denieth me before men shall be denied before the angels of God.

10 And whosoever shall speak a word against the Son of man, it shall be forgiven him: but unto him that blasphemeth against the Holy Ghost it shall not be forgiven.

11 And when they bring you unto the synagogues, and unto magistrates, and powers, take ye no thought how or what thing ye shall answer, or what ye shall say:

12 For the Holy Ghost shall teach you in the same hour what ye ought to say.

13 And one of the company said unto him, Master, speak to my brother, that he divide the inheritance with me.

14 And he said unto him, Man, who made me a judge or a divider over you?

15 And he said unto them, Take heed, and beware of covetousness: for a man's life consisteth not in the abundance of the things which he possesseth.

16 And he spake a parable unto them, saying, The ground of a certain rich man brought forth plentifully:

17 And he thought within himself, saying, What shall I do, because I have no room where to bestow my fruits?

18 And he said, This will I do: I will pull down my barns, and build greater; and there will I bestow all my fruits and my goods.

19 And I will say to my soul, Soul, thou hast much goods laid up for many years; take thine ease, eat, drink, and be merry.

20 But God said unto him, Thou fool, this night thy soul shall be required of thee: then whose shall those things be, which thou hast provided?

21 So is he that layeth up treasure for himself, and is not rich toward God.

22 And he said unto his disciples, Therefore I say unto you, Take no thought for your life, what ye shall eat; neither for the body, what ye shall put on.

23 The life is more than meat, and the body is more than raiment.

24 Consider the ravens: for they neither sow nor reap; which neither have storehouse nor barn; and God feedeth them: how much more are ye better than the fowls?

25 And which of you with taking thought can add to his stature one cubit?

26 If ye then be not able to do that thing which is least, why take ye thought for the rest?

27 Consider the lilies how they grow: they toil not, they spin not; and yet I say unto you, that Solomon in all his glory was not arrayed like one of these.

28 If then God so clothe the grass, which is to day in the field,

LUKE 13

1. The Galileans, whose blood Pilate had mingled with their sacrifices – Some of the followers of Judas Gaulonites. They absolutely refused to own the Roman authority. Pilate surrounded and slew them, while they were worshiping in the temple, at a public feast.

3. Ye shall all likewise perish – All ye of Galilee and of Jerusalem shall perish in the very same manner. So the Greek word implies. And so they did. There was a remarkable resemblance between the fate of these Galileans and of the main body of the Jewish nation; the flower of which was slain at Jerusalem by the Roman sword, while they were assembled at one of their great festivals. And many thousands of them perished in the temple itself, and were literally buried under its ruins.

6. A man had a fig tree – Either we may understand God the Father by him that had the vineyard, and Christ by him that kept it: or Christ himself is he that hath it, and his ministers they that keep it. Psalm lxxx, 8. &c.

7. Three years – Christ was then in the third year of his ministry. But it may mean only several years; a certain number being put for an uncertain. Why doth it also cumber the ground? – That is, not only bear no fruit itself, but take up the ground of another tree that would.

11. She was bowed together, and utterly unable to lift up herself – The evil spirit which possessed her afflicted her in this manner. To many doubtless it appeared a natural distemper. Would not a modern physician have termed it a nervous case?

15. Thou hypocrite – For the real motive of his speaking was envy, not (as he pretended) pure zeal for the glory of God.

16. And ought not this woman? – Ought not any human creature, which is so far better than an ox or an ass? Much more, this daughter of Abraham – probably in a spiritual as well as natural sense, to be loosed?

18. Matt. xiii, 31; Mark iv, 30.

20. Matt. xiii, 33.

21. Covered up – So that, for a time, nothing of it appeared.

24. Strive to enter in – Agonize. Strive as in an agony. So the word signifies. Otherwise none shall enter in. Barely seeking will not avail. Matt. vii, 13.

25. And even agonizing will not avail, after the door is shut. Agonize, therefore, now by faith, prayer, holiness, patience. And ye begin to stand without – Till then they had no thought of it! O how new will that sense of their misery be? How late? How lasting? I know not whence ye are – I know not, that is, I approve not of your ways.

27. Matt. vii, 23.

28. Matt. viii, 11.

29. They shall sit down in the kingdom of God – Both the kingdom of grace and of glory.

30. But there are last – Many of the Gentiles who were

MATTHEW HENRY

CHARLES H. SPURGEON

we should therefore be always ready. If men thus take care of their houses, let us be thus wise for our souls. Be ye therefore ready also; as ready as the good man of the house would be, if he knew at what hour the thief would come.

41-53 All are to take to themselves what Christ says in his word, and to inquire concerning it. No one is left so ignorant as not to know many things to be wrong which he does, and many things to be right which he neglects; therefore all are without excuse in their sin. The bringing in the gospel dispensation would occasion desolations. Not that this would be the tendency of Christ's religion, which is pure, peaceable, and loving; but the effect of its being contrary to men's pride and lusts. There was to be a wide publication of the gospel. But before that took place, Christ had a baptism to be baptized with, far different from that of water and the Holy Spirit. He must endure sufferings and death. It agreed not with his plan to preach the gospel more widely, till this baptism was completed. We should be zealous in making known the truth, for though divisions will be stirred up, and a man's own household may be his foes, yet sinners will be converted, and God will be glorified.

54-59 Christ would have the people to be as wise in the concerns of their souls as they are in outward affairs. Let them hasten to obtain peace with God before it is too late. If any man has found that God has set himself against him concerning his sins, let him apply to him as God in Christ reconciling the world to himself. While we are alive, we are in the way, and now is our time.

LUKE 13

*Christ exhorts to repentance from the case of the
    Galileans and others. (1-5)*
Parable of the barren fig tree. (6-9)
The infirm woman strengthened. (10-17)
The parables of the mustard seed, and leaven. (18-22)
Exhortation to enter at the strait gate. (23-30)
*Christ's reproof to Herod, and to the people of
    Jerusalem. (31-35)*

1-5 Mention was made to Christ of the death of some Galileans. This tragic story is briefly related here, and is not met with in any historians. In Christ's reply he spoke of another event, which, like it, gave an instance of people taken away by sudden death. Towers, that are built for safety, often prove to be men's destruction. He cautioned his hearers not to blame great sufferers, as if they were therefore to be accounted great sinners. As no place or employment can secure from the stroke of death, we should consider the sudden removals of others as warnings to ourselves. On these accounts Christ founded a call to repentance. The same Jesus that bids us repent, for

may save some, is our policy. Skin for skin, yea, all that we have is nothing comparable to a man's soul." When four true hearts are set upon the spiritual good of a sinner, their holy hunger will break through stone walls or house roofs.

I have no doubt it was a difficult task to carry the paralyzed man upstairs; the breaking up of the roof, the removing the tiling with all due care, must have been a laborious task, and have required much skill, but the work was done, and the end was gained. We must never stop at difficulties; however stern the task, it must always be more difficult to us to let a soul perish than to labor in the most self-denying form for its deliverance.

It was a very singular action which the bearers performed. Who would have thought of breaking up a roof? Nobody but those who loved much, and much desired to benefit the sick. O that God would make us attempt singular things to save souls. May a holy ingenuity be excited in the church; a sacred inventiveness set at work for winning men's hearts. It appeared to his generation a singular thing when John Wesley stood on his father's tombstone and preached at Epworth. Glory be to God that he had the courage to preach in the open air. It seemed an extraordinary thing when certain ministers delivered sermons in the theaters; but it is matter of joy that sinners have been reached by such irregularities who might have escaped all other means. Let us but feel our hearts full of zeal for God, and love for souls, and we shall soon be led to adopt means which others may criticize, but which Jesus Christ will accept.

After all, the method which the four friends followed was one most suitable to their abilities. They were, I suppose, four strong fellows, to whom the load was no great weight, and the work of digging was comparatively easy. The method suited their capacity exactly. And what did they do when they had let the sick man down? Look at the scene and admire? I do not read that they said a single word, yet what they did was enough: abilities for lifting and carrying did the needful work. Some of you say, "Ah, we cannot be of any use; we wish we could preach." These men could not preach: they did not need to preach. They lowered the paralytic, and their work was done. They could not preach, but they could hold a rope. We want in the Christian church not only preachers, but soul-winners, who can bear souls on their hearts, and feel the solemn burden; men who, it may be, cannot talk, but who

and to morrow is cast into the oven; how much more will he clothe you, O ye of little faith?

29 And seek not ye what ye shall eat, or what ye shall drink, neither be ye of doubtful mind.

30 For all these things do the nations of the world seek after: and your Father knoweth that ye have need of these things.

31 But rather seek ye the kingdom of God; and all these things shall be added unto you.

32 Fear not, little flock; for it is your Father's good pleasure to give you the kingdom.

33 Sell that ye have, and give alms; provide yourselves bags which wax not old, a treasure in the heavens that faileth not, where no thief approacheth, neither moth corrupteth.

34 For where your treasure is, there will your heart be also.

35 Let your loins be girded about, and your lights burning;

36 And ye yourselves like unto men that wait for their lord, when he will return from the wedding; that when he cometh and knocketh, they may open unto him immediately.

37 Blessed are those servants, whom the lord when he cometh shall find watching: verily I say unto you, that he shall gird himself, and make them to sit down to meat, and will come forth and serve them.

38 And if he shall come in the second watch, or come in the third watch, and find them so, blessed are those servants.

39 And this know, that if the goodman of the house had known what hour the thief would come, he would have watched, and not have suffered his house to be broken through.

40 Be ye therefore ready also: for the Son of man cometh at an hour when ye think not.

41 Then Peter said unto him, Lord, speakest thou this parable unto us, or even to all?

42 And the Lord said, Who then is that faithful and wise steward, whom his lord shall make ruler over his household, to give them their portion of meat in due season?

43 Blessed is that servant, whom his lord when he cometh shall find so doing.

44 Of a truth I say unto you, that he will make him ruler over all that he hath.

45 But and if that servant say in his heart, My lord delayeth his coming; and shall begin to beat the menservants and maidens, and to eat and drink, and to be drunken;

46 The lord of that servant will come in a day when he looketh not for him, and at an hour when he is not aware, and will cut him in sunder, and will appoint him his portion with the unbelievers.

47 And that servant, which knew his lord's will, and prepared not himself, neither did according to his will, shall be beaten with many stripes.

48 But he that knew not, and did commit things worthy of stripes, shall be beaten with few stripes. For unto whomsoever much is given, of him shall be much required: and to whom men have committed much, of him they will ask the more.

49 I am come to send fire on the earth; and what will I if it be already kindled?

50 But I have a baptism to be baptized with; and how am I straitened till it be accomplished!

51 Suppose ye that I am come to give peace on earth? I tell you, Nay; but rather division:

52 For from henceforth there shall be five in one house divided, three against two, and two against three.

53 The father shall be divided against the son, and the son against the father; the mother against the daughter, and the daughter against the mother; the mother in law against her

latest called, shall be most highly rewarded; and many of the Jews who were first called, shall have no reward at all. Matt. xix, 30.

31. Herod is minded to kill thee – Possibly they gave him the caution out of good will.

32. And he said, Go and tell that fox – With great propriety so called, for his subtlety and cowardice. The meaning of our Lord's answer is, Notwithstanding all that he can do, I shall for the short time I have left, do the works of him that sent me. When that time is fulfilled, I shall be offered up. Yet not here, but in the bloody city. Behold, I cast out devils – With what majesty does he speak to his enemies! With what tenderness to his friends! The third day I am perfected – On the third day he left Galilee, and set out for Jerusalem, to die there. But let us carefully distinguish between those things wherein Christ is our pattern, and those which were peculiar to his office. His extraordinary office justified him in using that severity of language, when speaking of wicked princes, and corrupt teachers, to which we have no call; and by which we should only bring scandal on religion, and ruin on ourselves, while we irritated rather than convinced or reformed those whom we so indecently rebuked.

33. It cannot be, that a prophet perish out of Jerusalem – Which claims prescription for murdering the messengers of God. Such cruelty and malice cannot be found elsewhere.

34. How often would I have gathered thy children together – Three solemn visits he had made to Jerusalem since his baptism for this very purpose. Matt. xxiii, 37.

35. Your house is left to you desolate – Is now irrecoverably consigned to desolation and destruction: And verily I say to you, after a very short space, ye shall not see me till the time come, when taught by your calamities, ye shall be ready and disposed to say, Blessed is he that cometh in the name of the Lord. It does not imply, that they should then see Jesus at all; but only that they would earnestly wish for the Messiah, and in their extremity be ready to entertain any who should assume that character.

the kingdom of heaven is at hand, bids us repent, for otherwise we shall perish.

6-9 This parable of the barren fig tree is intended to enforce the warning given just before: the barren tree, except it brings forth fruit, will be cut down. This parable in the first place refers to the nation and people of the Jews. Yet it is, without doubt, for awakening all that enjoy the means of grace, and the privileges of the visible church. When God has borne long, we may hope that he will bear with us yet a little longer, but we cannot expect that he will bear always.

10-17 Our Lord Jesus attended upon public worship on the Sabbaths. Even bodily infirmities, unless very grievous, should not keep us from public worship on Sabbath days. This woman came to Christ to be taught, and to get good to her soul, and then he relieved her bodily infirmity. This cure represents the work of Christ's grace upon the soul. And when crooked souls are made straight, they will show it by glorifying God. Christ knew that this ruler had a real enmity to him and to his gospel, and that he did but cloak it with a pretended zeal for the Sabbath day; he really would not have them be healed any day; but if Jesus speaks the word, and puts forth his healing power, sinners are set free. This deliverance is often wrought on the Lord's day; and whatever labor tends to put men in the way of receiving the blessing, agrees with the design of that day.

18-22 Here is the progress of the gospel foretold in two parables, as in Mt 13. The kingdom of the Messiah is the kingdom of God. May grace grow in our hearts; may our faith and love grow exceedingly, so as to give undoubted evidence of their reality. May the example of God's saints be blessed to those among whom they live; and may his grace flow from heart to heart, until the little one becomes a thousand.

23-30 Our Savior came to guide men's consciences, not to gratify their curiosity. Ask not, How many shall be saved? But, Shall I be one of them? Not, What shall become of such and such? But, What shall I do, and what will become of me? Strive to enter in at the strait gate. This is directed to each of us; it is, Strive ye. All that will be saved, must enter in at the strait gate, must undergo a change of the whole man. Those that would enter in, must strive to enter. Here are awakening considerations, to enforce this exhortation. Oh that we may be all awakened by them! They answer the question, Are there few that shall be saved? But let none despond either as to themselves or others, for there are last who shall be first, and first who shall be last. If we reach heaven, we shall meet many there whom we little thought to meet, and miss many whom we expected to find.

31-35 Christ, in calling Herod a fox, gave him his true

can weep; men who cannot break other men's hearts with their language, but who break their own hearts with their compassion. In the case before us there was no need to plead "Jesus, thou son of David, look up, for a man is coming down who needs thee." There was no need to urge that the patient had been so many years sick. We do not know that the man himself uttered a word. Helpless and paralyzed, he had not the vigor to become a suppliant. They placed his almost lifeless form before the Savior's eye, and that was appeal enough; his sad condition was more eloquent than words. O hearts that love sinners lay their lost estate before Jesus; bring their cases as they are before the Savior; if your tongues stammer, your hearts will prevail; if you cannot speak even to Christ himself, as you would desire, because you have not the gift of prayer, yet if your strong desires spring from the spirit of prayer you cannot fail. God help us to make use of such means as are within our power, and not to sit down idly to regret the powers we do not possess. Perhaps it would be dangerous for us to possess the abilities we covet; it is always safe to consecrate those we have.

III. Now we must pass on to an important truth. We may safely gather from the narrative THAT THE ROOT OF SPIRITUAL PARALYSIS GENERALLY LIES IN UNPARDONED SIN.

Jesus intended to heal the paralyzed man, but he did so by first of all saying, "Thy sins are forgiven thee." There are some in this house of prayer this morning who are spiritually paralyzed; they have eyes and they see the gospel; they have ears and they have heard it, and heard it attentively too; but they are so paralyzed that they will tell you, and honestly tell you, that they cannot lay hold upon the promise of God; they cannot believe in Jesus to the saving of their souls. If you urge them to pray, they say: "We try to pray, but it is not acceptable prayer." If you bid them have confidence, they will tell you, though not in so many words perhaps, that they are given up to despair. Their mournful ditty is:—

"I would, but cannot sing;
I would, but cannot pray
For Satan meets me when I try,
And frights my soul away.
I would, but can't repeat,
Though I endeavor oft;
This stony heart can never relent
Till Jesus makes it soft.
I would, but cannot love,

daughter in law, and the daughter in law against her mother in law.

54 And he said also to the people, When ye see a cloud rise out of the west, straightway ye say, There cometh a shower; and so it is.

55 And when ye see the south wind blow, ye say, There will be heat; and it cometh to pass.

56 Ye hypocrites, ye can discern the face of the sky and of the earth; but how is it that ye do not discern this time?

57 Yea, and why even of yourselves judge ye not what is right?

58 When thou goest with thine adversary to the magistrate, as thou art in the way, give diligence that thou mayest be delivered from him; lest he hale thee to the judge, and the judge deliver thee to the officer, and the officer cast thee into prison.

59 I tell thee, thou shalt not depart thence, till thou hast paid the very last mite.

LUKE 13

1 There were present at that season some that told him of the Galileans, whose blood Pilate had mingled with their sacrifices.

2 And Jesus answering said unto them, Suppose ye that these Galileans were sinners above all the Galileans, because they suffered such things?

3 I tell you, Nay: but, except ye repent, ye shall all likewise perish.

4 Or those eighteen, upon whom the tower in Siloam fell, and slew them, think ye that they were sinners above all men that dwelt in Jerusalem?

5 I tell you, Nay: but, except ye repent, ye shall all likewise perish.

6 He spake also this parable; A certain man had a fig tree planted in his vineyard; and he came and sought fruit thereon, and found none.

7 Then said he unto the dresser of his vineyard, Behold, these three years I come seeking fruit on this fig tree, and find none: cut it down; why cumbereth it the ground?

8 And he answering said unto him, Lord, let it alone this year also, till I shall dig about it, and dung it:

9 And if it bear fruit, well: and if not, then after that thou shalt cut it down.

10 And he was teaching in one of the synagogues on the sabbath.

11 And, behold, there was a woman which had a spirit of infirmity eighteen years, and was bowed together, and could in no wise lift up herself.

12 And when Jesus saw her, he called her to him, and said unto her, Woman, thou art loosed from thine infirmity.

13 And he laid his hands on her: and immediately she was made straight, and glorified God.

14 And the ruler of the synagogue answered with indignation, because that Jesus had healed on the sabbath day, and said unto the people, There are six days in which men ought to work: in them therefore come and be healed, and not on the sabbath day.

15 The Lord then answered him, and said, Thou hypocrite, doth not each one of you on the sabbath loose his ox or his ass from the stall, and lead him away to watering?

16 And ought not this woman, being a daughter of Abraham, whom Satan hath bound, lo, these eighteen years, be loosed from this bond on the sabbath day?

LUKE 14

2. There was a certain man before him – It does not appear that he was come thither with any insidious design. Probably he came, hoping for a cure, or perhaps was one of the family.

3. And Jesus answering, spake – Answering the thoughts which he saw rising in their hearts.

7. He spake a parable – The ensuing discourse is so termed, because several parts are not to be understood literally. The general scope of it is, Not only at a marriage feast, but on every occasion, he that exalteth himself shall be abased, and he that abaseth himself shall be exalted.

11. Matt. xxiii, 12.

12. Call not thy friends – That is, I do not bid thee call thy friends or thy neighbors. Our Lord leaves these offices of humanity and courtesy as they were, and teaches a higher duty. But is it not implied herein, that we should be sparing in entertaining those that need it not, in order to assist those that do need, with all that is saved from those needless entertainments? Lest a recompense be made – This fear is as much unknown to the world, as even the fear of riches.

14. One of them that sat at table hearing these things – And being touched therewith, said, Happy is he that shall eat bread in the kingdom of God – Alluding to what had just been spoken. It means, he that shall have a part in the resurrection of the just.

16. Then said he – Continuing the allusion. A certain man made a great supper – As if he had said, All men are not sensible of this happiness. Many might have a part in it, and will not.

18. They all began to make excuse – One of them pleads only his own will, I go: another, a pretended necessity, I must needs go: the third, impossibility, I cannot come: all of them want the holy hatred mentioned ver. 26. All of them perish by things in themselves lawful. I must needs go – The most urgent worldly affairs frequently fall out just at the time when God makes the freest offers of salvation.

21. The servant came and showed his Lord these things – So ministers ought to lay before the Lord in prayer the obedience or disobedience of their hearers.

23. Compel them to come in – With all the violence of love, and the force of God's word. Such compulsion, and such only, in matters of religion, was used by Christ and his apostles.

24. For refers to Go out, ver. 23.

26. If any man come to me, and hate not his father – Comparatively to Christ: yea, so as actually to renounce his field, oxen, wife, all things, and act as if he hated them, when they stand in competition with him. Matt. x, 37.

28. And which of you intending to build a tower – That is, and whoever of you intends to follow me, let him first

MATTHEW HENRY

CHARLES H. SPURGEON

character. The greatest of men were accountable to God, therefore it became him to call this proud king by his own name; but it is not an example for us. I know, said our Lord, that I must die very shortly; when I die, I shall be perfected, I shall have completed my undertaking. It is good for us to look upon the time we have before us as but little, that we may thereby be quickened to do the work of the day in its day. The wickedness of persons and places which more than others profess religion and relation to God, especially displeases and grieves the Lord Jesus. The judgment of the great day will convince unbelievers; but let us learn thankfully to welcome, and to profit by all who come in the name of the Lord, to call us to partake of his great salvation.

LUKE 14

Christ heals a man on the Sabbath. (1-6)
He teaches humility. (7-14)
Parable of the great supper. (15-24)
The necessity of consideration and self-denial. (25-35)

1-6 This Pharisee, as well as others, seems to have had an ill design in entertaining Jesus at his house. But our Lord would not be hindered from healing a man, though he knew a clamor would be raised at his doing it on the Sabbath. It requires care to understand the proper connexion between piety and charity in observing the Sabbath, and the distinction between works of real necessity and habits of self-indulgence. Wisdom from above, teaches patient perseverance in well doing.

7-14 Even in the common actions of life, Christ marks what we do, not only in our religious assemblies, but at our tables. We see in many cases, that a man's pride will bring him low, and before honor is humility. Our Savior here teaches, that works of charity are better than works of show. But our Lord did not mean that a proud and unbelieving liberality should be rewarded, but that his precept of doing good to the poor and afflicted should be observed from love to him.

15-24 In this parable observe the free grace and mercy of God shining in the gospel of Christ, which will be food and a feast for the soul of a man that knows its own wants and miseries. All found some pretense to put off their attendance. This reproves the Jewish nation for their neglect of the offers of Christ's grace. It shows also the backwardness there is to close with the gospel call. The want of gratitude in those who slight gospel offers, and the contempt put upon the God of heaven thereby, justly provoke him. The apostles were to turn to the Gentiles, when the Jews refused the offer; and with them the church was filled. The provision made for precious souls in the gospel of Christ, has not been made in vain; for if

Though wooed by love divine;
No arguments have power to move
A soul so base as mine.
O could I but believe!
Then all would easy be;
I would, but cannot—Lord, relieve:
My help must come from thee."

The bottom of this paralysis is sin upon the conscience, working death in them. They are sensible of their guilt, but powerless to believe that the crimson fountain can remove it: they are alive only to sorrow, despondency, and agony. Sin paralyses them with despair. I grant you that into this despair there enters largely the element of unbelief, which is sinful; but I hope there is also in it a measure of sincere repentance, which bears in it the hope of something better. Our poor, awakened paralytics sometimes hope that they may be forgiven, but they cannot believe it; they cannot rejoice; they cannot cast themselves on Jesus; they are utterly without strength. Now, the bottom of it, I say again, lies in unpardoned sin, and I earnestly entreat you who love the Savior to be earnest in seeking the pardon of these paralyzed persons. You tell me that I should be earnest; so I should; and so I desire to be: but, brethren, their cases appear to be beyond the minister's sphere of action; the Holy Spirit determines to use other agencies in their salvation. They have heard the public word; they now need private consolation and aid, and that from three or four. Lend us your help, ye earnest brethren; form your parties of four; grasp the couches of these who wish to be saved, but who feel they cannot believe. The Lord, the Holy Spirit, make you the means of leading them into forgiveness and eternal salvation. They have been lying a long time waiting; their sin, however, still keeps them where they are; their guilt prevents their laying hold on Christ; there is the point, and it is for such cases that I earnestly invoke my brethren's aid.

IV. Let us proceed to notice, fourthly, that JESUS CAN REMOVE BOTH THE SIN AND THE PARALYSIS IN A SINGLE MOMENT. It was the business of the four bearers to bring the man to Christ; but there their power ended. It is our part to bring the guilty sinner to the Savior: there our power ends. Thank God, when we end, Christ begins, and works right gloriously. Observe that he began by saying: "Thy sins be forgiven thee." He laid the axe at the root; he did not desire that the man's sins might be forgiven, or express a good wish in that direction, but he pronounced an absolution by virtue of that authority with which he was clothed as the Savior. The

17 And when he had said these things, all his adversaries were ashamed: and all the people rejoiced for all the glorious things that were done by him.

18 Then said he, Unto what is the kingdom of God like? and whereunto shall I resemble it?

19 It is like a grain of mustard seed, which a man took, and cast into his garden; and it grew, and waxed a great tree; and the fowls of the air lodged in the branches of it.

20 And again he said, Whereunto shall I liken the kingdom of God?

21 It is like leaven, which a woman took and hid in three measures of meal, till the whole was leavened.

22 And he went through the cities and villages, teaching, and journeying toward Jerusalem.

23 Then said one unto him, Lord, are there few that be saved? And he said unto them,

24 Strive to enter in at the strait gate: for many, I say unto you, will seek to enter in, and shall not be able.

25 When once the master of the house is risen up, and hath shut to the door, and ye begin to stand without, and to knock at the door, saying, Lord, Lord, open unto us; and he shall answer and say unto you, I know you not whence ye are:

26 Then shall ye begin to say, We have eaten and drunk in thy presence, and thou hast taught in our streets.

27 But he shall say, I tell you, I know you not whence ye are; depart from me, all ye workers of iniquity.

28 There shall be weeping and gnashing of teeth, when ye shall see Abraham, and Isaac, and Jacob, and all the prophets, in the kingdom of God, and you yourselves thrust out.

29 And they shall come from the east, and from the west, and from the north, and from the south, and shall sit down in the kingdom of God.

30 And, behold, there are last which shall be first, and there are first which shall be last.

31 The same day there came certain of the Pharisees, saying unto him, Get thee out, and depart hence: for Herod will kill thee.

32 And he said unto them, Go ye, and tell that fox, Behold, I cast out devils, and I do cures to day and to morrow, and the third day I shall be perfected.

33 Nevertheless I must walk to day, and to morrow, and the day following: for it cannot be that a prophet perish out of Jerusalem.

34 O Jerusalem, Jerusalem, which killest the prophets, and stonest them that are sent unto thee; how often would I have gathered thy children together, as a hen doth gather her brood under her wings, and ye would not!

35 Behold, your house is left unto you desolate: and verily I say unto you, Ye shall not see me, until the time come when ye shall say, Blessed is he that cometh in the name of the Lord.

LUKE 14

1 And it came to pass, as he went into the house of one of the chief Pharisees to eat bread on the sabbath day, that they watched him.

2 And, behold, there was a certain man before him which had the dropsy.

3 And Jesus answering spake unto the lawyers and Pharisees, saying, Is it lawful to heal on the sabbath day?

4 And they held their peace. And he took him, and healed him, and let him go;

seriously weigh these things.

31. Another king – Does this mean, the prince of this world? Certainly he has greater numbers on his side. How numerous are his children and servants!

33. So – Like this man, who, being afraid to face his enemy, sends to make peace with him, every one who forsaketh not all that he hath –

1. By withdrawing his affections from all the creatures;

2. By enjoying them only in and for God, only in such a measure and manner as leads to him;

3. By hating them all, in the sense above mentioned, cannot be my disciple – But will surely desist from building that tower, neither can he persevere in fighting the good fight of faith.

34. Salt – Every Christian, but more eminently every minister. Matt. v, 13; Mark ix, 50.

LUKE 15

1. All the publicans – That is, all who were in that place. It seems our Lord was in some town of Galilee of the Gentiles, from whence he afterward went to Jerusalem, chap. xvii, 11.

3. He spake – Three parables of the same import: for the sheep, the piece of silver, and the lost son, all declare (in direct contrariety to the Pharisees and scribes) in what manner God receiveth sinners.

4. Leave the ninety and nine in the wilderness – Where they used to feed: all uncultivated ground, like our commons, was by the Jews termed wilderness or desert. And go after – In recovering a lost soul, God as it were labors. May we not learn hence, that to let them alone who are in sin, is both unchristian and inhuman! Matt. xviii, 12.

7. Joy shall be – Solemn and festal joy, in heaven – First, in our blessed Lord himself, and then among the angels and spirits of just men, perhaps informed thereof by God himself, or by the angels who ministered to them. Over one sinner – One gross, open, notorious sinner, that repenteth – That is, thoroughly changed in heart and life; more than over ninety and nine just persons – Comparatively just, outwardly blameless: that need not such a repentance – For they need not, cannot repent of the sins which they never committed. The sum is, as a father peculiarly rejoices when an extravagant child, supposed to be utterly lost, comes to a thorough sense of his duty; or as any other person who has recovered what he had given up for gone, has a more sensible satisfaction in it, than in several other things equally valuable, but not in such danger: so do the angels in heaven peculiarly rejoice in the conversion of the most abandoned sinners. Yea, and God himself so readily forgives and receives them, that he may be represented as having part in the joy.

12. Give me the part of goods that falleth to me – See

some reject, others will thankfully accept the offer. The very poor and low in the world, shall be as welcome to Christ as the rich and great; and many times the gospel has the greatest success among those that labor under worldly disadvantages and bodily infirmities. Christ's house shall at last be filled; it will be so when the number of the elect is completed.

25-35 Though the disciples of Christ are not all crucified, yet they all bear their cross, and must bear it in the way of duty. Jesus bids them count upon it, and then consider of it. Our Savior explains this by two similitudes; the former showing that we must consider the expenses of our religion; the latter, that we must consider the perils of it. Sit down and count the cost; consider it will cost the mortifying of sin, even the most beloved lusts. The proudest and most daring sinner cannot stand against God, for who knows the power of his anger? It is our interest to seek peace with him, and we need not send to ask conditions of peace, they are offered to us, and are highly to our advantage. In some way a disciple of Christ will be put to the trial. May we seek to be disciples indeed, and be careful not to grow slack in our profession, or afraid of the cross; that we may be the good salt of the earth, to season those around us with the savor of Christ.

LUKE 15

Parables of the lost sheep, and the piece of silver. (1-10)
The prodigal son, his wickedness and distress. (11-16)
His repentance and pardon. (17-24)
The elder brother offended. (25-32)

1-10 The parable of the lost sheep is very applicable to the great work of man's redemption. The lost sheep represents the sinner as departed from God, and exposed to certain ruin if not brought back to him, yet not desirous to return. Christ is earnest in bringing sinners home. In the parable of the lost piece of silver, that which is lost, is one piece, of small value compared with the rest. Yet the woman seeks diligently till she finds it. This represents the various means and methods God makes use of to bring lost souls home to himself, and the Savior's joy on their return to him. How careful then should we be that our repentance is unto salvation!

11-16 The parable of the prodigal son shows the nature of repentance, and the Lord's readiness to welcome and bless all who return to him. It fully sets forth the riches of gospel grace; and it has been, and will be, while the world stands, of unspeakable use to poor sinners, to direct and to encourage them in repenting and returning to God. It is bad, and the beginning of worse, when men look upon God's gifts as debts due to them. The great folly of sinners, and

poor man's sins there and then ceased to be, and he was justified in the sight of God. Believest thou this, my hearer, that Christ did thus for the paralytic man? Then I charge you believe something more, that if on earth Christ had power to forgive sins before he had offered an atonement, much more hath he power to do this, now that he hath poured out his blood, and hath said, "It is finished," and hath gone into his glory, and is at the right hand of the Father. He is exalted on high, to give repentance and remission of sin. Should he send his Spirit into thy soul to reveal himself in thee, thou wouldst in an instant be entirely absolved. Does blasphemy blacken thee? Does a long life of infidelity pollute thee? Hast thou been licentious? Hast thou been abominably wicked? A word can absolve thee—a word from those dear lips which said, "Father forgive them, for they know not what they do." I charge thee ask for that absolving word. No earthly priest can give it thee; but the great High Priest, the Lord Jesus, can utter it at once. Ye twos and fours who are seeking the salvation of men, here is encouragement for you. Pray for them now, while the gospel is being preached in their hearing; pray for them day and night, and bring the glad tidings constantly before them, for Jesus is still able "to save to the uttermost them that come unto God by him."

After our blessed Lord had taken away the root of the evil, you observe he then took away the paralysis itself. It was gone in a single moment. Every limb in the man's body was restored to a healthy state; he could stand, could walk, could lift his bed, both nerve and muscle were restored to vigor. One moment will suffice, if Jesus speaks, to make the despairing happy, and the unbelieving full of confidence. What we cannot do with our reasoning, persuadings, and entreaties, nor even with the letter of God's promise, Christ can do in a single instant by his Holy Spirit, and it has been our joy to see it done. This is the standing miracle of the church, performed by Christ today even as aforetime. Paralyzed souls who could neither do nor will, have been able to do valiantly, and to will with solemn resolution. The Lord has poured power into the faint, and to them that had no might he hath increased strength. He can do it still. I say again to loving spirits who are seeking the good of others, let this encourage you. You may not have to wait long for the conversions you aim at; it may be ere another Sabbath ends, the person you pray for may be brought to Jesus; or if you have to wait a little, the waiting shall well repay you, and mean-

5 And answered them, saying, Which of you shall have an ass or an ox fallen into a pit, and will not straightway pull him out on the sabbath day?

6 And they could not answer him again to these things.

7 And he put forth a parable to those which were bidden, when he marked how they chose out the chief rooms; saying unto them,

8 When thou art bidden of any man to a wedding, sit not down in the highest room; lest a more honorable man than thou be bidden of him;

9 And he that bade thee and him come and say to thee, Give this man place; and thou begin with shame to take the lowest room.

10 But when thou art bidden, go and sit down in the lowest room; that when he that bade thee cometh, he may say unto thee, Friend, go up higher: then shalt thou have worship in the presence of them that sit at meat with thee.

11 For whosoever exalteth himself shall be abased; and he that humbleth himself shall be exalted.

12 Then said he also to him that bade him, When thou makest a dinner or a supper, call not thy friends, nor thy brethren, neither thy kinsmen, nor thy rich neighbors; lest they also bid thee again, and a recompense be made thee.

13 But when thou makest a feast, call the poor, the maimed, the lame, the blind:

14 And thou shalt be blessed; for they cannot recompense thee: for thou shalt be recompensed at the resurrection of the just.

15 And when one of them that sat at meat with him heard these things, he said unto him, Blessed is he that shall eat bread in the kingdom of God.

16 Then said he unto him, A certain man made a great supper, and bade many:

17 And sent his servant at supper time to say to them that were bidden, Come; for all things are now ready.

18 And they all with one consent began to make excuse. The first said unto him, I have bought a piece of ground, and I must needs go and see it: I pray thee have me excused.

19 And another said, I have bought five yoke of oxen, and I go to prove them: I pray thee have me excused.

20 And another said, I have married a wife, and therefore I cannot come.

21 So that servant came, and shewed his lord these things. Then the master of the house being angry said to his servant, Go out quickly into the streets and lanes of the city, and bring in hither the poor, and the maimed, and the halt, and the blind.

22 And the servant said, Lord, it is done as thou hast commanded, and yet there is room.

23 And the lord said unto the servant, Go out into the highways and hedges, and compel them to come in, that my house may be filled.

24 For I say unto you, That none of those men which were bidden shall taste of my supper.

25 And there went great multitudes with him: and he turned, and said unto them,

26 If any man come to me, and hate not his father, and mother, and wife, and children, and brethren, and sisters, yea, and his own life also, he cannot be my disciple.

27 And whosoever doth not bear his cross, and come after me, cannot be my disciple.

28 For which of you, intending to build a tower, sitteth not down first, and counteth the cost, whether he have sufficient to finish it?

the root of all sin! A desire of disposing of ourselves; of independency on God!

13. He took a journey into a far country – Far from God: God was not in all his thoughts: And squandered away his substance – All the grace he had received.

14. He began to be in want – All his worldly pleasures failing, he grew conscious of his want of real good.

15. And he joined himself to a citizen of that country – Either the devil or one of his children, the genuine citizens of that country which is far from God. He sent him to feed swine – He employed him in the base drudgery of sin.

16. He would fain have filled his belly with the husks – He would fain have satisfied himself with worldly comforts. Vain, fruitless endeavor!

17. And coming to himself – For till then he was beside himself, as all men are, so long as they are without God in the world.

18. I will arise and go to my father – How accurately are the first steps of true repentance here pointed out! Against Heaven – Against God.

20. And he arose and came to his father – The moment he had resolved, he began to execute his resolution. While he was yet a great way off, his father saw him – Returning, starved, naked.

22. But the father said – Interrupting him before he had finished what he intended to say. So does God frequently cut an earnest confession short by a display of his pardoning love.

23. Let us be merry – Both here, and wherever else this word occurs, whether in the Old or New Testament, it implies nothing of levity, but a solid, serious, religious, heartfelt joy: indeed this was the ordinary meaning of the word two hundred years ago, when our translation was made.

25. The elder son seems to represent the Pharisees and scribes, mentioned chap. xv, 2.

27. Thy father hath killed the fatted calf – Perhaps he mentions this rather than the robe or ring, as having a nearer connection with the music and dancing.

28. He was angry, and would not go in – How natural to us is this kind of resentment!

29. Lo, so many years do I serve thee – So he was one of the instances mentioned ver. 7. How admirably therefore does this parable confirm that assertion! Yet thou never gavest me a kid, that I might make merry with my friends – Perhaps God does not usually give much joy to those who never felt the sorrows of repentance.

31. Thou art ever with me, and all that I have is thine – This suggests a strong reason against murmuring at the indulgence shown to the greatest of sinners. As the father's receiving the younger son did not cause him to disinherit the elder; so God's receiving notorious sinners will be no loss to those who have always served him; neither will he raise these to a state of glory equal to that of

that which ruins them, is, being content in their lifetime to receive their good things. Our first parents ruined themselves and all their race, by a foolish ambition to be independent, and this is at the bottom of sinners' persisting in their sin. We may all discern some features of our own characters in that of the prodigal son. A sinful state is of departure and distance from God. A sinful state is a spending state: willfull sinners misemploy their thoughts and the powers of their souls, misspend their time and all their opportunities. A sinful state is a wanting state. Sinners want necessaries for their souls; they have neither food nor raiment for them, nor any provision for hereafter. A sinful state is a vile, slavish state. The business of the devil's servants is to make provision for the flesh, to fulfill the lusts thereof, and that is no better than feeding swine. A sinful state is a state of constant discontent. The wealth of the world and the pleasures of the senses will not even satisfy our bodies; but what are they to precious souls! A sinful state is a state which cannot look for relief from any creature. In vain do we cry to the world and to the flesh; they have that which will poison a soul, but have nothing to give which will feed and nourish it. A sinful state is a state of death. A sinner is dead in trespasses and sins, destitute of spiritual life. A sinful state is a lost state. Souls that are separated from God, if his mercy prevent not, will soon be lost forever. The prodigal's wretched state, only faintly shadows forth the awful ruin of man by sin. Yet how few are sensible of their own state and character!

17-24 Having viewed the prodigal in his abject state of misery, we are next to consider his recovery from it. This begins by his coming to himself. That is a turning point in the sinner's conversion. The Lord opens his eyes, and convinces him of sin; then he views himself and every object, in a different light from what he did before. Thus the convinced sinner perceives that the meanest servant of God is happier than he is. To look unto God as a Father, and our Father, will be of great use in our repentance and return to him. The prodigal arose, nor stopped till he reached his home. Thus the repenting sinner resolutely quits the bondage of Satan and his lusts, and returns to God by prayer, notwithstanding fears and discouragements. The Lord meets him with unexpected tokens of his forgiving love. Again; the reception of the humbled sinner is like that of the prodigal. He is clothed in the robe of the Redeemer's righteousness, made partaker of the Spirit of adoption, prepared by peace of conscience and gospel grace to walk in the ways of holiness, and feasted with Divine consolations. Principles of grace and holiness are wrought in him, to do, as well as to will.

25-32 In the latter part of this parable we have the character of the Pharisees, though not of them alone. It sets forth the kindness of the Lord, and the proud

while remember he has never spoken in secret in the dark places of the earth; he has not said to the seed of Jacob, "Seek ye my face in vain."

V. Passing on, and drawing to a conclusion: WHEREVER OUR LORD WORKS THE DOUBLE MIRACLE IT WILL BE APPARENT. He forgave the man's sin and took away his disease at the same time. How was this apparent? I have no doubt the pardon of the man's sin was best known to himself; but possibly those who saw that gleaming countenance which had been so sad before, might have noticed that the word of absolution sunk into his soul as the rain into the thirsty earth. "Thy sins be forgiven thee," fell on him as a dew from heaven; he believed the sacred declaration, and his eyes sparkled. He might almost have felt indifferent whether he remained paralyzed or not, it was such joy to be forgiven, forgiven by the Lord himself. That was enough, quite enough for him; but it was not enough for the Savior, and therefore he bade him take up his couch and walk, for he had given him strength to do so. The man's healing was proved by his obedience. Openly to all onlookers an active obedience became indisputable proof of the poor creature's restoration. Notice, our Lord bade him rise—he rose; he had no power to do so except that power which comes with divine commands. He rose, for Christ said "Rise." Then he folded up that miserable palliasse—the Greek word used shows us that it was a very poor, mean, miserable affair—he rolled it up as the Savior bade him, he shouldered it, and went to his home. His first impulse must have been to throw himself down at the Savior's feet, and say, "Blessed be thy name;" but the Master said, "Go to thy house;" and I do not find that he stayed to make one grateful obeisance, but elbowing the crowd, jostling the throng with his load on his back, he proceeded to his house just as he was told, and that without deliberation, or questioning. He did his Lord's bidding, and he did it accurately, in detail, at once, and most cheerfully. Oh! how cheerfully; none can tell but those in like case restored. So, the true sign of pardoned sin, and of paralysis removed from the heart, is obedience. If thou art really saved thou wilt do what Jesus bids thee; thy request will be, "Lord, what wilt thou have me to do?" and that once ascertained, thou wilt be sure to do it. You tell me Christ has forgiven you, and yet you live in rebellion to his commands; how can I believe you? You say you are a saved man, and yet you willfully set up your own will against Christ's will; what evidence have I of what you say? Have I not, rather, clear

29 Lest haply, after he hath laid the foundation, and is not able to finish it, all that behold it begin to mock him,

30 Saying, This man began to build, and was not able to finish.

31 Or what king, going to make war against another king, sitteth not down first, and consulteth whether he be able with ten thousand to meet him that cometh against him with twenty thousand?

32 Or else, while the other is yet a great way off, he sendeth an ambassage, and desireth conditions of peace.

33 So likewise, whosoever he be of you that forsaketh not all that he hath, he cannot be my disciple.

34 Salt is good: but if the salt have lost his savor, wherewith shall it be seasoned?

35 It is neither fit for the land, nor yet for the dunghill; but men cast it out. He that hath ears to hear, let him hear.

LUKE 15

1 Then drew near unto him all the publicans and sinners for to hear him.

2 And the Pharisees and scribes murmured, saying, This man receiveth sinners, and eateth with them.

3 And he spake this parable unto them, saying,

4 What man of you, having an hundred sheep, if he lose one of them, doth not leave the ninety and nine in the wilderness, and go after that which is lost, until he find it?

5 And when he hath found it, he layeth it on his shoulders, rejoicing.

6 And when he cometh home, he calleth together his friends and neighbors, saying unto them, Rejoice with me; for I have found my sheep which was lost.

7 I say unto you, that likewise joy shall be in heaven over one sinner that repenteth, more than over ninety and nine just persons, which need no repentance.

8 Either what woman having ten pieces of silver, if she lose one piece, doth not light a candle, and sweep the house, and seek diligently till she find it?

9 And when she hath found it, she calleth her friends and her neighbors together, saying, Rejoice with me; for I have found the piece which I had lost.

10 Likewise, I say unto you, there is joy in the presence of the angels of God over one sinner that repenteth.

11 And he said, A certain man had two sons:

12 And the younger of them said to his father, Father, give me the portion of goods that falleth to me. And he divided unto them his living.

13 And not many days after the younger son gathered all together, and took his journey into a far country, and there wasted his substance with riotous living.

14 And when he had spent all, there arose a mighty famine in that land; and he began to be in want.

15 And he went and joined himself to a citizen of that country; and he sent him into his fields to feed swine.

16 And he would fain have filled his belly with the husks that the swine did eat: and no man gave unto him.

17 And when he came to himself, he said, How many hired servants of my father's have bread enough and to spare, and I perish with hunger!

18 I will arise and go to my father, and will say unto him, Father, I have sinned against heaven, and before thee,

19 And am no more worthy to be called thy son: make me as one of thy hired servants.

20 And he arose, and came to his father. But when he was

those who have always served him, if they have, upon the whole, made a greater progress in inward as well as outward holiness.

32. This thy brother was dead, and is alive – A thousand of these delicate touches in the inspired writings escape an inattentive reader. In ver. 30, the elder son had unkindly and indecently said, This thy son. The father in his reply mildly reproves him, and tenderly says, This thy brother – Amazing intimation, that the best of men ought to account the worst sinners their brethren still; and should especially remember this relation, when they show any inclination to return. Our Lord in this whole parable shows, not only that the Jews had no cause to murmur at the reception of the Gentiles, (a point which did not at that time so directly fall under consideration,) but that if the Pharisees were indeed as good as they fancied themselves to be, still they had no reason to murmur at the kind treatment of any sincere penitent. Thus does he condemn them, even on their own principles, and so leaves them without excuse. We have in this parable a lively emblem of the condition and behavior of sinners in their natural state. Thus, when enriched by the bounty of the great common Father, do they ungratefully run from him, ver. 12. Sensual pleasures are eagerly pursued, till they have squandered away all the grace of God, ver. 13. And while these continue, not a serious thought of God can find a place in their minds. And even when afflictions come upon them, ver. 14, still they will make hard shifts before they will let the grace of God, concurring with his providence, persuade them to think of a return, ver. 15, 16. When they see themselves naked, indigent, and undone, then they recover the exercise of their reason, ver. 17. Then they remember the blessings they have thrown away, and attend to the misery they have incurred. And hereupon they resolve to return to their father, and put the resolution immediately in practice, ver. 18, 19. Behold with wonder and pleasure the gracious reception they find from Divine, injured goodness! When such a prodigal comes to his father, he sees him afar off, ver. 20. He pities, meets, embraces him, and interrupts his acknowledgments with the tokens of his returning favor, ver. 21. He arrays him with the robe of a Redeemer's righteousness, with inward and outward holiness; adorns him with all his sanctifying graces, and honors him with the tokens of adopting love, ver. 22. And all this he does with unutterable delight, in that he who was lost is now found, ver. 23, 24. Let no elder brother murmur at this indulgence, but rather welcome the prodigal back into the family. And let those who have been thus received, wander no more, but emulate the strictest piety of those who for many years have served their heavenly Father, and not transgressed his commandments.

manner in which his gracious kindness is often received. The Jews, in general, showed the same spirit towards the converted Gentiles; and numbers in every age object to the gospel and its preachers, on the same ground. What must that temper be, which stirs up a man to despise and abhor those for whom the Savior shed his precious blood, who are objects of the Father's choice, and temples of the Holy Ghost! This springs from pride, self-preference, and ignorance of a man's own heart. The mercy and grace of our God in Christ, shine almost as bright in his tender and gentle bearing with peevish saints, as his receiving prodigal sinners upon their repentance. It is the unspeakable happiness of all the children of God, who keep close to their Father's house, that they are, and shall be ever with him. Happy will it be for those who thankfully accept Christ's invitation.

LUKE 16

The parable of the unjust steward. (1-12)
Christ reproves the hypocrisy of the covetous
Pharisees. (13-18)
The rich man and Lazarus. (19-31)

1-12 Whatever we have, the property of it is God's; we have only the use of it, according to the direction of our great Lord, and for his honor. This steward wasted his lord's goods. And we are all liable to the same charge; we have not made due improvement of what God has trusted us with. The steward cannot deny it; he must make up his accounts, and be gone. This may teach us that death will come, and deprive us of the opportunities we now have. The steward will make friends of his lord's debtors or tenants, by striking off a considerable part of their debt to his lord. The lord referred to in this parable commended not the fraud, but the policy of the steward. In that respect alone is it so noticed. Worldly men, in the choice of their object, are foolish; but in their activity, and perseverance, they are often wiser than believers. The unjust steward is not set before us as an example in cheating his master, or to justify any dishonesty, but to point out the careful ways of worldly men. It would be well if the children of light would learn wisdom from the men of the world, and would as earnestly pursue their better object. The true riches signify spiritual blessings; and if a man spends upon himself, or hoards up what God has trusted to him, as to outward things, what evidence can he have, that he is an heir of God through Christ? The riches of this world are deceitful and uncertain. Let us be convinced that those are truly rich, and very rich, who are rich in faith, and rich toward God, rich in Christ, in the promises; let us then lay up our treasure in heaven, and expect our portion from thence.

13-18 To this parable our Lord added a solemn warning. Ye cannot serve God and the world, so

evidence that you speak not the truth? Open, careful, prompt, cheerful obedience to Christ, becomes the test of the wonderful work which Jesus works in the soul.

VI. Lastly, ALL THIS TENDS TO GLORIFY GOD.

Those four men had been the indirect means of bringing much honor to God and much glory to Jesus, and they, I doubt not, glorified God in their very hearts on the housetop. Happy men to have been of so much service to their bedridden friend! Who else united in glorifying God? Why, first the man who was restored. Did not every part of his body glorify God? I think I see him! He sets one foot down to God's glory, he plants the other to the same note, he walks to God's glory, he carries his bed to God's glory, he moves his whole body to the glory of God, he speaks, he shouts, he sings, he leaps to the glory of God. When a man is saved his whole manhood glorifies God; he becomes instinct with a new-born life which glows in every part of him, spirit, soul and body. As an heir of heaven, he brings glory to the Great Father who has adopted him into the family, he breathes and eats and drinks to God's praise. When a sinner is brought into the church of God we are all glad, but we are none of us so joyous and thankful as he; we would all praise God, but he must praise him the loudest, and he will.

But who next glorified God! The text does not say so, but we feel sure that his family did, for he went to his own house. We will suppose that he had a wife. That morning when the four friends came and put him on the bed, and carried him out, it may be she shook her head in loving anxiety, and I dare say she said, "I am half afraid to trust him with you. Poor, poor creature, I dread his encountering the throng. I am afraid it is madness to hope for success. I wish you Godspeed in it, but I tremble. Hold well the bed; be sure you do not let him fall. If you do let him down through the roof hold fast the ropes, be careful that no accident occurs to my poor bedridden husband; he is bad enough as he is, do not cause him more misery." But when she saw him coming home, walking with the bed on his back, can you picture her delight? How she would begin to sing, and praise and bless the Lord Jehovah Rophi, who had healed her beloved one. If there were little children about, playing before the house, how they would shout for glee, "Here's father; here's father walking again, and come home with the bed on his back; he is made whole

yet a great way off, his father saw him, and had compassion, and ran, and fell on his neck, and kissed him.

21 And the son said unto him, Father, I have sinned against heaven, and in thy sight, and am no more worthy to be called thy son.

22 But the father said to his servants, Bring forth the best robe, and put it on him; and put a ring on his hand, and shoes on his feet:

23 And bring hither the fatted calf, and kill it; and let us eat, and be merry:

24 For this my son was dead, and is alive again; he was lost, and is found. And they began to be merry.

25 Now his elder son was in the field: and as he came and drew nigh to the house, he heard musick and dancing.

26 And he called one of the servants, and asked what these things meant.

27 And he said unto him, Thy brother is come; and thy father hath killed the fatted calf, because he hath received him safe and sound.

28 And he was angry, and would not go in: therefore came his father out, and intreated him.

29 And he answering said to his father, Lo, these many years do I serve thee, neither transgressed I at any time thy commandment: and yet thou never gavest me a kid, that I might make merry with my friends:

30 But as soon as this thy son was come, which hath devoured thy living with harlots, thou hast killed for him the fatted calf.

31 And he said unto him, Son, thou art ever with me, and all that I have is thine.

32 It was meet that we should make merry, and be glad: for this thy brother was dead, and is alive again; and was lost, and is found.

LUKE 16

1 And he said also unto his disciples, There was a certain rich man, which had a steward; and the same was accused unto him that he had wasted his goods.

2 And he called him, and said unto him, How is it that I hear this of thee? give an account of thy stewardship; for thou mayest be no longer steward.

3 Then the steward said within himself, What shall I do? for my lord taketh away from me the stewardship: I cannot dig; to beg I am ashamed.

4 I am resolved what to do, that, when I am put out of the stewardship, they may receive me into their houses.

5 So he called every one of his lord's debtors unto him, and said unto the first, How much owest thou unto my lord?

6 And he said, An hundred measures of oil. And he said unto him, Take thy bill, and sit down quickly, and write fifty.

7 Then said he to another, And how much owest thou? And he said, An hundred measures of wheat. And he said unto him, Take thy bill, and write fourscore.

8 And the lord commended the unjust steward, because he had done wisely: for the children of this world are in their generation wiser than the children of light.

9 And I say unto you, Make to yourselves friends of the mammon of unrighteousness; that, when ye fail, they may receive you into everlasting habitations.

10 He that is faithful in that which is least is faithful also in much: and he that is unjust in the least is unjust also in much.

11 If therefore ye have not been faithful in the unrighteous mammon, who will commit to your trust the true riches?

LUKE 16

1. And he said also to his disciples – Not only to the scribes and Pharisees to whom he had hitherto been speaking, but to all the younger as well as the elder brethren: to the returning prodigals who were now his disciples. A certain rich man had a steward – Christ here teaches all that are now in favor with God, particularly pardoned penitents, to behave wisely in what is committed to them.

3. To beg I am ashamed – But not ashamed to cheat! This was likewise a sense of honor! "By men called honor, but by angels pride."

4. I know – That is, I am resolved, what to do.

8. And the Lord commended the unjust steward – Namely, in this respect, because he had used timely precaution: so that though the dishonesty of such a servant be detestable, yet his foresight, care, and contrivance, about the interests of this life, deserve our imitation, with regard to the more important affairs of another. The children of this world – Those who seek no other portion than this world: Are wiser – Not absolutely, for they are, one and all, egregious fools; but they are more consistent with themselves; they are truer to their principles; they more steadily pursue their end; they are wiser in their generation – That is, in their own way, than the children of light – The children of God, whose light shines on their hearts.

9. And I say to you – Be good stewards even of the lowest talents wherewith God hath entrusted you. Mammon means riches or money. It is termed the mammon of unrighteousness, because of the manner wherein it is commonly either procured or employed. Make yourselves friends of this, by doing all possible good, particularly to the children of God: that when ye fail, when your flesh and your heart faileth, when this earthly tabernacle is dissolved, those of them who have gone before may receive, may welcome you into the everlasting habitations.

10. And whether ye have more or less, see that ye be faithful as well as wise stewards. He that is faithful in what is meanest of all, worldly substance, is also faithful in things of a higher nature; and he that uses these lowest gifts unfaithfully, is likewise unfaithful in spiritual things.

11. Who will entrust you with the true riches? – How should God entrust you with spiritual and eternal, which alone are true riches?

12. If ye have not been faithful in that which was another's – None of these temporal things are yours: you are only stewards of them, not proprietors: God is the proprietor of all; he lodges them in your hands for a season: but still they are his property. Rich men, understand and consider this. If your steward uses any part of your estate (so called in the language of men) any farther or any otherwise than you direct, he is a knave: he has nei-

divided are the two interests. When our Lord spoke thus, the covetous Pharisees treated his instructions with contempt. But he warned them, that what they contended for as the law, was a wresting of its meaning: this our Lord showed in a case respecting divorce. There are many covetous sticklers for the forms of godliness, who are the bitterest enemies to its power, and try to set others against the truth.

19-31 Here the spiritual things are represented, in a description of the different state of good and bad, in this world and in the other. We are not told that the rich man got his estate by fraud, or oppression; but Christ shows, that a man may have a great deal of the wealth, pomp, and pleasure of this world, yet perish for ever under God's wrath and curse. The sin of this rich man was his providing for himself only. Here is a godly man, and one that will hereafter be happy forever, in the depth of adversity and distress. It is often the lot of some of the dearest of God's saints and servants to be greatly afflicted in this world. We are not told that the rich man did him any harm, but we do not find that he had any care for him. Here is the different condition of this godly poor man, and this wicked rich man, at and after death. The rich man in hell lifted up his eyes, being in torment. It is not probable that there are discourses between glorified saints and damned sinners, but this dialogue shows the hopeless misery and fruitless desires, to which condemned spirits are brought. There is a day coming, when those who now hate and despise the people of God, would gladly receive kindness from them. But the damned in hell shall not have the least abatement of their torment. Sinners are now called upon to remember; but they do not, they will not, they find ways to avoid it. As wicked people have good things only in this life, and at death are forever separated from all good, so godly people have evil things only in this life, and at death they are forever put from them. In this world, blessed be God, there is no gulf between a state of nature and grace, we may pass from sin to God; but if we die in our sins, there is no coming out. The rich man had five brethren, and would have them stopped in their sinful course; their coming to that place of torment, would make his misery the worse, who had helped to show them the way thither. How many would now desire to recall or to undo what they have written or done! Those who would make the rich man's praying to Abraham justify praying to saints departed, go far to seek for proofs, when the mistake of a damned sinner is all they can find for an example. And surely there is no encouragement to follow the example, when all his prayers were made in vain. A messenger from the dead could say no more than what is said in the Scriptures. The same strength of corruption that breaks through the convictions of the written word, would triumph over a witness from the dead. Let us seek to the law and to the testimony, Isa 8:19,20, for

again, as he used to be when we were very little." What a glad house! They would gather round him, all of them, wife and children, and friends and neighbors, and they would begin to sing, "Bless the Lord, O my soul: and all that is within me, bless his holy name. Bless the Lord, O my soul, and forget not all his benefits: who forgiveth all thine iniquities: who healeth all thy diseases." How the man would sing those verses, rejoicing in the forgiveness first, and the healing next, and wondering how it was that David knew so much about it, and had put his case into such fit words.

Well, but it did not end there. A wife and family utter but a part of the glad chorus of praise, though a very melodious part. There are other adoring hearts who unite in glorifying the healing Lord. The disciples who were around the Savior, they glorified God, too. They rejoiced, and said one to another, "We have seen strange things today." The whole Christian church is full of sacred praise when a sinner is saved; even heaven itself is glad.

But there was glory brought to God, even by the common people who stood around. They had not yet entered into that sympathy with Christ which the disciples felt, but they were struck by the sight of this great wonder, and they, too, could not help saying that God had wrought great marvels. I pray that onlookers, strangers from the commonwealth of Israel, when they see the desponding comforted, and lost ones brought in, may be compelled to bear their witness to the power of divine grace, and be led themselves to be partakers in it. There is "Glory to God in the highest, and on earth peace, good-will towards men," when a paralyzed soul is filled with gracious strength.

Now, shall I need to stand here, and entreat for the four to carry poor souls to Jesus? Shall I need to appeal to my brethren who love their Lord, and say, band yourselves together to win souls? Your humanity to the paralytic soul claims it, but your desire to bring glory to God compels it. If you are indeed what you profess to be, to glorify God must be the fondest wish and the loftiest ambition of your souls. Unless ye be traitors to my Lord as well as inhuman to your fellow-men, you will catch the practical thought which I have striven to bring before you, and you will seek out some fellow Christians, and say, "Come, let us pray together, for such an one," and if you know a desperate case you will make up a sacred quaternion, to resolve upon its salvation. May the power of the Highest abide upon you, and who knoweth what glory the Lord may gain through you?

12 And if ye have not been faithful in that which is another man's, who shall give you that which is your own?

13 No servant can serve two masters: for either he will hate the one, and love the other; or else he will hold to the one, and despise the other. Ye cannot serve God and mammon.

14 And the Pharisees also, who were covetous, heard all these things: and they derided him.

15 And he said unto them, Ye are they which justify yourselves before men; but God knoweth your hearts: for that which is highly esteemed among men is abomination in the sight of God.

16 The law and the prophets were until John: since that time the kingdom of God is preached, and every man presseth into it.

17 And it is easier for heaven and earth to pass, than one tittle of the law to fail.

18 Whosoever putteth away his wife, and marrieth another, committeth adultery: and whosoever marrieth her that is put away from her husband committeth adultery.

19 There was a certain rich man, which was clothed in purple and fine linen, and fared sumptuously every day:

20 And there was a certain beggar named Lazarus, which was laid at his gate, full of sores,

21 And desiring to be fed with the crumbs which fell from the rich man's table: moreover the dogs came and licked his sores.

22 And it came to pass, that the beggar died, and was carried by the angels into Abraham's bosom: the rich man also died, and was buried;

23 And in hell he lift up his eyes, being in torments, and seeth Abraham afar off, and Lazarus in his bosom.

24 And he cried and said, Father Abraham, have mercy on me, and send Lazarus, that he may dip the tip of his finger in water, and cool my tongue; for I am tormented in this flame.

25 But Abraham said, Son, remember that thou in thy lifetime receivedst thy good things, and likewise Lazarus evil things: but now he is comforted, and thou art tormented.

26 And beside all this, between us and you there is a great gulf fixed: so that they which would pass from hence to you cannot; neither can they pass to us, that would come from thence.

27 Then he said, I pray thee therefore, father, that thou wouldest send him to my father's house:

28 For I have five brethren; that he may testify unto them, lest they also come into this place of torment.

29 Abraham saith unto him, They have Moses and the prophets; let them hear them.

30 And he said, Nay, father Abraham: but if one went unto them from the dead, they will repent.

31 And he said unto him, If they hear not Moses and the prophets, neither will they be persuaded, though one rose from the dead.

LUKE 17

1 Then said he unto the disciples, It is impossible but that offenses will come: but woe unto him, through whom they come!

2 It were better for him that a millstone were hanged about his neck, and he cast into the sea, than that he should offend one of these little ones.

3 Take heed to yourselves: If thy brother trespass against thee, rebuke him; and if he repent, forgive him.

4 And if he trespass against thee seven times in a day, and

ther conscience nor honor. Neither have you either one or the other, if you use any part of that estate, which is in truth God's, not yours, any otherwise than he directs. That which is your own – Heaven, which when you have it, will be your own for ever.

13. And you cannot be faithful to God, if you trim between God and the world, if you do not serve him alone. Matt. vi, 24.

15. And he said to them, Ye are they who justify yourselves before men – The sense of the whole passage is, that pride, wherewith you justify yourselves, feeds covetousness, derides the Gospel, ver. 14, and destroys the law, ver. 18. All which is illustrated by a terrible example. Ye justify yourselves before men – Ye think yourselves righteous, and persuade others to think you so.

16. The law and the prophets were in force until John: from that time the Gospel takes place; and humble upright men receive it with inexpressible earnestness. Matt. xi, 13.

17. Not that the Gospel at all destroys the law. Matt. v, 18.

18. But ye do; particularly in this notorious instance. Matt. v, 31; xix, 7.

19. There was a certain rich man – Very probably a Pharisee, and one that justified himself before men; a very honest, as well as honorable gentleman: though it was not proper to mention his name on this occasion: who was clothed in purple and fine linen – and doubtless esteemed on this account, (perhaps not only by those who sold it, but by most that knew him,) as encouraging trade, and acting according to his quality: And feasted splendidly every day – And consequently was esteemed yet more, for his generosity and hospitality in keeping so good a table.

20. And there was a certain beggar named Lazarus, (according to the Greek pronunciation) or Eleazer. By his name it may be conjectured, he was of no mean family, though it was thus reduced. There was no reason for our Lord to conceal his name, which probably was then well known. Theophylact observes, from the tradition of the Hebrews, that he lived at Jerusalem. Yea, the dogs also came and licked his sores – It seems this circumstance is recorded to show that all his ulcers lay bare, and were not closed or bound up.

22. And the beggar – Worn out with hunger, and pain, and want of all things, died: and was carried by angels (amazing change of the scene!) into Abraham's bosom – So the Jews styled paradise; the place where the souls of good men remain from death to the resurrection. The rich man also died, and was buried – Doubtless with pomp enough, though we do not read of his lying in state; that stupid, senseless pageantry, that shocking insult on a poor, putrefying carcass, was reserved for our enlightened age!

23. He seeth Abraham afar off – And yet knew him at

MATTHEW HENRY

CHARLES H. SPURGEON

that is the sure word of prophecy, upon which we may rest, 2Pe 1:19. Circumstances in every age show that no terrors, or arguments, can give true repentance without the special grace of God renewing the sinner's heart.

LUKE 17

To avoid offenses. To pray for increase of faith. Humility taught. (11-19). Ten lepers cleansed. (11-19) Christ's kingdom. (20-37)

1-10 It is no abatement of their guilt by whom an offense comes, nor will it lessen their punishment that offenses will come. Faith in God's pardoning mercy, will enable us to get over the greatest difficulties in the way of forgiving our brethren. As with God nothing is impossible, so all things are possible to him that can believe. Our Lord showed his disciples their need of deep humility. The Lord has such a property in every creature, as no man can have in another; he cannot be in debt to them for their services, nor do they deserve any return from him.

11-19 A sense of our spiritual leprosy should make us very humble whenever we draw near to Christ. It is enough to refer ourselves to the compassions of Christ, for they fail not. We may look for God to meet us with mercy, when we are found in the way of obedience. Only one of those who were healed returned to give thanks. It becomes us, like him, to be very humble in thanksgivings, as well as in prayers. Christ noticed the one who thus distinguished himself, he was a Samaritan. The others only got the outward cure, he alone got the spiritual blessing.

20-37 The kingdom of God was among the Jews, or rather within some of them. It was a spiritual kingdom, set up in the heart by the power of Divine grace. Observe how it had been with sinners formerly, and in what state the judgments of God, which they had been warned of, found them. Here is shown what a dreadful surprise this destruction will be to the secure and sensual. Thus shall it be in the day when the Son of man is revealed. When Christ came to destroy the Jewish nation by the Roman armies, that nation was found in such a state of false security as is here spoken of. In like manner, when Jesus Christ shall come to judge the world, sinners will be found altogether regardless; for in like manner the sinners of every age go on securely in their evil ways, and remember not their latter end. But wherever the wicked are, who are marked for eternal ruin, they shall be found by the judgments of God.

LUKE 18

The parable of the importunate widow. (1-8) The Pharisee and the publican. (9-14)

Never forget this strange story of the bed which carried the man, and the man who carried his bed.

THE ONE THING NEEDFUL
Sermon number 1015 delivered on October 15th, 1871 at the Metropolitan Tabernacle, Newington.

"But one thing is needful."—Luke 10:42.

WE HAVE no difficulty whatever in deciding what the one thing is. We are not allowed to say that it is the Savior, for he is not a thing; and we are not permitted to say that it is attention to our own salvation, for although that would be true, it is not mentioned in the context. The one thing needful evidently is that which Mary chose—that good part which should not be taken away from her. Very clearly this was to sit at Jesus' feet and hear his word. This and nothing less, this and nothing more.

The mere posture of sitting down and listening to the Savior's word was nothing in itself: it was that which it indicated. It indicated, in Mary's case, a readiness to believe what the Savior taught, to accept and to obey—nay to delight in, the precepts which fell from his lips. And this is the one thing needful—absolutely needful; for no rebel can enter the kingdom of heaven with the weapons of rebellion in his hands. We cannot know Christ while we resist Christ: we must be reconciled to his gentle sway, and confess that he is Lord, to the glory of God the Father.

To sit at Jesus' feet implies faith as well as submission. Mary believed in what Jesus said, and, therefore, sat there to be taught by him. It is absolutely necessary that we have faith in the Lord Jesus Christ, in his power as God and man, in his death as being expiatory, in his crucifixion as being a sacrifice for our sins. We must trust him for time and eternity, in all his relationships as Prophet, Priest, and King. We must rely on him; he must be our hope, our salvation, our all in all. This one thing is absolutely necessary: without it we are undone. A believing submission, and a submissive faith in Jesus we must have, or perish.

But sitting at Jesus' feet implies, also, that having submitted and believed, we now desire to be his disciples. Discipleship is too often forgotten; it is as needful as faith. We are to go into all the world and disciple all nations, baptizing them in the name of the Father, the Son and of the Holy Ghost. A man cannot be saved

seven times in a day turn again to thee, saying, I repent; thou shalt forgive him.

5 And the apostles said unto the Lord, Increase our faith.

6 And the Lord said, If ye had faith as a grain of mustard seed, ye might say unto this sycamine tree, Be thou plucked up by the root, and be thou planted in the sea; and it should obey you.

7 But which of you, having a servant plowing or feeding cattle, will say unto him by and by, when he is come from the field, Go and sit down to meat?

8 And will not rather say unto him, Make ready wherewith I may sup, and gird thyself, and serve me, till I have eaten and drunken; and afterward thou shalt eat and drink?

9 Doth he thank that servant because he did the things that were commanded him? I trow not.

10 So likewise ye, when ye shall have done all those things which are commanded you, say, We are unprofitable servants: we have done that which was our duty to do.

11 And it came to pass, as he went to Jerusalem, that he passed through the midst of Samaria and Galilee.

12 And as he entered into a certain village, there met him ten men that were lepers, which stood afar off:

13 And they lifted up their voices, and said, Jesus, Master, have mercy on us.

14 And when he saw them, he said unto them, Go shew yourselves unto the priests. And it came to pass, that, as they went, they were cleansed.

15 And one of them, when he saw that he was healed, turned back, and with a loud voice glorified God,

16 And fell down on his face at his feet, giving him thanks: and he was a Samaritan.

17 And Jesus answering said, Were there not ten cleansed? but where are the nine?

18 There are not found that returned to give glory to God, save this stranger.

19 And he said unto him, Arise, go thy way: thy faith hath made thee whole.

20 And when he was demanded of the Pharisees, when the kingdom of God should come, he answered them and said, The kingdom of God cometh not with observation:

21 Neither shall they say, Lo here! or, lo there! for, behold, the kingdom of God is within you.

22 And he said unto the disciples, The days will come, when ye shall desire to see one of the days of the Son of man, and ye shall not see it.

23 And they shall say to you, See here; or, see there: go not after them, nor follow them.

24 For as the lightning, that lighteneth out of the one part under heaven, shineth unto the other part under heaven; so shall also the Son of man be in his day.

25 But first must he suffer many things, and be rejected of this generation.

26 And as it was in the days of Noe, so shall it be also in the days of the Son of man.

27 They did eat, they drank, they married wives, they were given in marriage, until the day that Noe entered into the ark, and the flood came, and destroyed them all.

28 Likewise also as it was in the days of Lot; they did eat, they drank, they bought, they sold, they planted, they builded;

29 But the same day that Lot went out of Sodom it rained fire and brimstone from heaven, and destroyed them all.

30 Even thus shall it be in the day when the Son of man is revealed.

31 In that day, he which shall be upon the housetop, and his

that distance: and shall not Abraham's children, when they are together in paradise, know each other!

24. Father Abraham, have mercy on me – It cannot be denied, but here is one precedent in Scripture of praying to departed saints: but who is it that prays, and with what success? Will any, who considers this, be fond of copying after him?

25. But Abraham said, Son – According to the flesh. Is it not worthy of observation, that Abraham will not revile even a damned soul? and shall living men revile one another? Thou in thy lifetime receivedst thy good things – Thou didst choose and accept of worldly things as thy good, thy happiness. And can any be at a loss to know why he was in torments? This damnable idolatry, had there been nothing more, was enough to sink him to the nethermost hell.

26. Beside this there is a great gulf fixed – Reader, to which side of it wilt thou go?

28. Lest they also come into this place – He might justly fear lest their reproaches should add to his own torment.

31. Neither will they be persuaded – Truly to repent: for this implies an entire change of heart: but a thousand apparitions cannot effect this. God only can, applying his word.

LUKE 17

1. It is impossible but offenses will come – And they ever did and do come chiefly by Pharisees, that is, men who trust in themselves that they are righteous, and despise others. Matt. xviii, 6; Mark ix, 42.

2. Little ones – Weak believers.

3. Take heed to yourselves – That ye neither offend others, nor be offended by others. Matt. xviii, 15.

4. If he sin against thee seven times in a day, and seven times in a day return, saying, I repent – That is, if he give sufficient proof that he does really repent, after having sinned ever so often, receive him just as if he had never sinned against thee. But this forgiveness is due only to real penitents. In a lower sense we are to forgive all, penitent or impenitent; (so as to bear them the sincerest good will, and to do them all the good we can;) and that not seven times only, but seventy times seven.

5. Lord, increase our faith – That we may thus forgive, and may neither offend nor be offended. Matt. xvii, 20.

6. And he said, If ye had faith as a grain of mustard seed – If ye had the least measure of true faith, no instance of duty would be too hard for you. Ye would say to this sycamore tree – This seems to have been a kind of proverbial expression.

7. But which of you – But is it not meet that you should first obey, and then triumph? Though still with a deep sense of your utter unprofitableness.

9. Doth he thank that servant – Does he account him-

MATTHEW HENRY

CHARLES H. SPURGEON

Children brought to Christ. (15-17)
The ruler hindered by his riches. (18-30)
Christ foreshows his death. (31-34)
A blind man restored to sight. (35-43)

1-8 All God's people are praying people. Here earnest steadiness in prayer for spiritual mercies is taught. The widow's earnestness prevailed even with the unjust judge: she might fear lest it should set him more against her; but our earnest prayer is pleasing to our God. Even to the end there will still be ground for the same complaint of weakness of faith.

9-14 This parable was to convince some who trusted in themselves that they were righteous, and despised others. God sees with what disposition and design we come to him in holy ordinances. What the Pharisee said, shows that he trusted to himself that he was righteous. We may suppose he was free from gross and scandalous sins. All this was very well and commendable. Miserable is the condition of those who come short of the righteousness of this Pharisee, yet he was not accepted; and why not? He went up to the temple to pray, but was full of himself and his own goodness; the favor and grace of God he did not think worth asking. Let us beware of presenting proud devotions to the Lord, and of despising others. The publican's address to God was full of humility, and of repentance for sin, and desire toward God. His prayer was short, but to the purpose; God be merciful to me a sinner. Blessed be God, that we have this short prayer upon record, as an answered prayer; and that we are sure that he who prayed it, went to his house justified; for so shall we be, if we pray it, as he did, through Jesus Christ. He owned himself a sinner by nature, by practice, guilty before God. He had no dependence but upon the mercy of God; upon that alone he relied. And God's glory is to resist the proud, and give grace to the humble. Justification is of God in Christ; therefore the self-condemned, and not the self-righteous, are justified before God.

15-17 None are too little, too young, to be brought to Christ, who knows how to show kindness to those not capable of doing service to him. It is the mind of Christ, that little children should be brought to him. The promise is to us, and to our seed; therefore He will bid them welcome to him with us. And we must receive his kingdom as children, not by purchase, and must call it our Father's gift.

18-30 Many have a great deal in them very commendable, yet perish for lack of some one thing; so this ruler could not bear Christ's terms, which would part between him and his estate. Many who are loathed to leave Christ, yet do leave him. After a long struggle between their convictions and their corruptions, their corruptions carry the day. They are very sorry that they cannot serve both; but if one must be

unless he has become a learner in the school of Christ, and a learner, too, in a practical sense, being willing to practice what he learns. Only he who does the Master's will knows his doctrines. We are, if we have chosen the good part, sitters at the feet of Jesus, just as Saul of Tarsus sat at the feet of Gamaliel; Christ is to us our great Instructor, and we take the law from his lips. The believer's position is that of a pupil, and the Lord Jesus is his teacher. Except we be converted and become as little children, we can in no wise enter the kingdom of heaven. Sitting at the feet of Jesus indicates the child-like spirit of true discipleship; and this is the one thing needful: there is no salvation apart from it.

It meant, also, service, for though Mary was not apparently engaged in waiting upon Christ as Martha was, yet she was, in very truth, ministering unto him in a deeper and truer sense. No one gives greater joy to a public speaker than an attentive listener; no one serves a teacher better than he who is an apt and attentive scholar. The first duty, indeed, of the student to the tutor is that he be cheerful in accepting, and diligent in retaining, what is taught: in this sense, Mary was really waiting upon Christ in one of his loftiest capacities, namely—that of a teacher and prophet in the midst of Israel. In that same spirit, had the Master only intimated it, she would have risen to wash his feet, or anoint his head, or wait at table, as Martha did; but she would, while she was performing these active duties, have continued spiritually in her first posture; she could not, of course, have continued literally sitting at the feet of the Savior, but her heart would have remained in the condition which that posture indicates. She was in the fittest position for service, for she waited to hear what her Lord would have her to do. We must all be servants, too; as we have been servants of unrighteousness, we must by grace submit ourselves unto the rules of Jesus, and become servants of righteousness, or, else, we miss the one thing that is indispensable for entrance into heaven.

Sitting at the feet of Jesus, also, signifies love. She would not have been sitting there at ease and happy in mind, if she had not loved him. There was a charm in the very tone of his words to her. She knew how he had loved her, and, therefore, each syllable was music to her soul. She looked up again and again, I doubt not, into that dear face, and often caught the meaning of the words more readily as she read his countenance, marked his eyes ofttimes suffused with tears, and ever bright with holy sympathy. Her love to his person made her a willing

stuff in the house, let him not come down to take it away: and he that is in the field, let him likewise not return back.

32 Remember Lot's wife.

33 Whosoever shall seek to save his life shall lose it; and whosoever shall lose his life shall preserve it.

34 I tell you, in that night there shall be two men in one bed; the one shall be taken, and the other shall be left.

35 Two women shall be grinding together; the one shall be taken, and the other left.

36 Two men shall be in the field; the one shall be taken, and the other left.

37 And they answered and said unto him, Where, Lord? And he said unto them, Wheresoever the body is, thither will the eagles be gathered together.

LUKE 18

1 And he spake a parable unto them to this end, that men ought always to pray, and not to faint;

2 Saying, There was in a city a judge, which feared not God, neither regarded man:

3 And there was a widow in that city; and she came unto him, saying, Avenge me of mine adversary.

4 And he would not for a while: but afterward he said within himself, Though I fear not God, nor regard man;

5 Yet because this widow troubleth me, I will avenge her, lest by her continual coming she weary me.

6 And the Lord said, Hear what the unjust judge saith.

7 And shall not God avenge his own elect, which cry day and night unto him, though he bear long with them?

8 I tell you that he will avenge them speedily. Nevertheless when the Son of man cometh, shall he find faith on the earth?

9 And he spake this parable unto certain which trusted in themselves that they were righteous, and despised others:

10 Two men went up into the temple to pray; the one a Pharisee, and the other a publican.

11 The Pharisee stood and prayed thus with himself, God, I thank thee, that I am not as other men are, extortioners, unjust, adulterers, or even as this publican.

12 I fast twice in the week, I give tithes of all that I possess.

13 And the publican, standing afar off, would not lift up so much as his eyes unto heaven, but smote upon his breast, saying, God be merciful to me a sinner.

14 I tell you, this man went down to his house justified rather than the other: for every one that exalteth himself shall be abased; and he that humbleth himself shall be exalted.

15 And they brought unto him also infants, that he would touch them: but when his disciples saw it, they rebuked them.

16 But Jesus called them unto him, and said, Suffer little children to come unto me, and forbid them not: for of such is the kingdom of God.

17 Verily I say unto you, Whosoever shall not receive the kingdom of God as a little child shall in no wise enter therein.

18 And a certain ruler asked him, saying, Good Master, what shall I do to inherit eternal life?

19 And Jesus said unto him, Why callest thou me good? none is good, save one, that is, God.

20 Thou knowest the commandments, Do not commit adultery, Do not kill, Do not steal, Do not bear false witness, Honor thy father and thy mother.

21 And he said, All these have I kept from my youth up.

22 Now when Jesus heard these things, he said unto him, Yet lackest thou one thing: sell all that thou hast, and distribute unto the poor, and thou shalt have treasure in heaven: and

self obliged to him?

10. When ye have done all, say, We are unprofitable servants – For a man cannot profit God. Happy is he who judges himself an unprofitable servant: miserable is he whom God pronounces such. But though we are unprofitable to him, our serving him is not unprofitable to us. For he is pleased to give by his grace a value to our good works, which in consequence of his promise entitles us to an eternal reward.

20. The kingdom of God cometh not with observation – With such outward pomp as draws the observation of every one.

21. Neither shall they say, Lo here, or lo there – This shall not be the language of those who are, or shall be sent by me, to declare the coming of my kingdom. For behold the kingdom of God is within or among you – Look not for it in distant times or remote places: it is now in the midst of you: it is come: it is present in the soul of every true believer: it is a spiritual kingdom, an internal principle. Wherever it exists, it exists in the heart.

22. Ye shall desire to see one of the days of the Son of man – One day of mercy, or one day wherein you might converse with me, as you do now.

23. They shall say, See, Christ is here, or there – Limiting his presence to this or that place. Matt. xxiv, 23.

24. So shall also the Son of man be – So swift, so wide, shall his appearing be: In his day – The last day.

26. The days of the Son of man – Those which immediately follow that which is eminently styled his day. Matt. xxiv, 37.

31. In that day – (Which will be the grand type of the last day) when ye shall see Jerusalem encompassed with armies.

32. Remember Lot's wife – And escape with all speed, without ever looking behind you. Luke ix, 24; John xii, 25.

33. The sense of this and the following verses is, Yet as great as the danger will be, do not seek to save your life by violating your conscience: if you do, you will surely lose it: whereas if you should lose it for my sake, you shall be paid with life everlasting. But the most probable way of preserving it now, is to be always ready to give it up: a peculiar Providence shall then watch over you, and put a difference between you and other men.

37. Matt. xxiv, 28.

LUKE 18

1. He spake a parable to them – This and the following parable warn us against two fatal extremes, with regard to prayer: the former against faintness and weariness, the latter against self confidence.

7. And shall not God – The most just Judge, vindicate

quitted, it shall be their God, not their worldly gain. Their boasted obedience will be found mere outside show; the love of the world in some form or other lies at the root. Men are apt to speak too much of what they have left and lost, of what they have done and suffered for Christ, as Peter did. But we should rather be ashamed that there has been any regret or difficulty in doing it.

31-34 The Spirit of Christ, in the Old Testament prophets, testified beforehand his sufferings, and the glory that should follow, 1Pe 1:11. The disciples' prejudices were so strong, that they would not understand these things literally. They were so intent upon the prophecies which spake of Christ's glory, that they overlooked those which spake of his sufferings. People run into mistakes, because they read their Bibles by halves, and are only for the smooth things. We are as backward to learn the proper lessons from the sufferings, crucifixion, and resurrection of Christ, as the disciples were to what he told them as to those events; and for the same reason; self-love, and a desire of worldly objects, close our understandings.

35-43 This poor blind man sat by the wayside, begging. He was not only blind, but poor, the fitter emblem of the world of mankind which Christ came to heal and save. The prayer of faith, guided by Christ's encouraging promises, and grounded on them, shall not be in vain. The grace of Christ ought to be thankfully acknowledged, to the glory of God. It is for the glory of God if we follow Jesus, as those will do whose eyes are opened. We must praise God for his mercies to others, as well as for mercies to ourselves. Would we rightly understand these things, we must come to Christ, like the blind man, earnestly beseeching him to open our eyes, and to show us clearly the excellence of his precepts, and the value of his salvation.

LUKE 19

The conversion of Zaccheus. (1-10)
The parable of the nobleman and his servants. (11-27)
Christ enters Jerusalem. (28-40)
Christ laments over Jerusalem. (41-48)

1-10 Those who sincerely desire a sight of Christ, like Zaccheus, will break through opposition, and take pains to see him. Christ invited himself to Zaccheus' house. Wherever Christ comes he opens the heart, and inclines it to receive him. He that has a mind to know Christ, shall be known of him. Those whom Christ calls, must humble themselves, and come down. We may well receive him joyfully, who brings all good with him. Zaccheus gave proofs publicly that he was become a true convert. He does not look to be justified by his works, as the Pharisee; but by his good works he will, through the grace of God,

learner, and we must be the same. We must not learn of Christ like unwilling truant boys, who go to school and must needs have learning flogged into them; we must be eager to learn; we must open our mouth wide that he may fill it, like the thirsty earth when it needs the shower, our soul must break for the longing it hath towards his commandments at all times. We must rejoice in his statutes more than gold, yea, than much fine gold. When we are moved by this spirit, we have found the one thing needful.

Having laid before you the meaning of the text, that to sit at Jesus' feet is the one thing necessary, for a literal translation of the text would be—"of one thing there is a necessity;" let us take the text as it stands and notice in it four things. The first is a word of consideration: the disjunctive conjunction, "but." The Savior bids us to make a pause. He says, "but one thing is needful." Then there comes a word of necessity: "one thing is needful." thirdly, a word of concentration: "one thing is needful;" and then a word of immediateness "one thing is needful"—needful now, at once.

I.—To begin, then, here is a word of CONSIDERATION, which, as I have already said, is interjected into the middle of our Lord's brief word to Martha. Martha is very busy; she is rather quick tempered also, and so she speaks to the Savior somewhat shortly; and the Master says, "Martha, Martha,"—very tenderly, kindly, gently, with only the slightest tinge of rebuke in his tone—"Martha, Martha, thou art careful and troubled about many things—but, but, but, but, but, wait a while and hear." That wise and warning but may be very useful to many here. You are engaged today in business; very diligent you are in it. You throw your whole energy into your trading, as you must, if you would succeed. You rise up wearily, and you sit up late. Shall I say a word that should discourage your industry? I will not; but, but is there nothing else?—is this life all? Is making money everything? Is wealth worth gaining merely for the sake of having it said, "He died worth fifty thousand pounds?" Is it so?

Perhaps, you are a very hard-working man. You have very little rest during the week, and in order to bring up your family comfortably, you strain every nerve; you live as you should, economically, and you work diligently; from morning to night the thought with you is, "How shall I fill these many little mouths? How shall I bring them up properly? How shall I, as a working man, pay my way?" Very right; I wish

come, follow me.

23 And when he heard this, he was very sorrowful: for he was very rich.

24 And when Jesus saw that he was very sorrowful, he said, How hardly shall they that have riches enter into the kingdom of God!

25 For it is easier for a camel to go through a needle's eye, than for a rich man to enter into the kingdom of God.

26 And they that heard it said, Who then can be saved?

27 And he said, The things which are impossible with men are possible with God.

28 Then Peter said, Lo, we have left all, and followed thee.

29 And he said unto them, Verily I say unto you, There is no man that hath left house, or parents, or brethren, or wife, or children, for the kingdom of God's sake,

30 Who shall not receive manifold more in this present time, and in the world to come life everlasting.

31 Then he took unto him the twelve, and said unto them, Behold, we go up to Jerusalem, and all things that are written by the prophets concerning the Son of man shall be accomplished.

32 For he shall be delivered unto the Gentiles, and shall be mocked, and spitefully entreated, and spitted on:

33 And they shall scourge him, and put him to death: and the third day he shall rise again.

34 And they understood none of these things: and this saying was hid from them, neither knew they the things which were spoken.

35 And it came to pass, that as he was come nigh unto Jericho, a certain blind man sat by the way side begging:

36 And hearing the multitude pass by, he asked what it meant.

37 And they told him, that Jesus of Nazareth passeth by.

38 And he cried, saying, Jesus, thou Son of David, have mercy on me.

39 And they which went before rebuked him, that he should hold his peace: but he cried so much the more, Thou Son of David, have mercy on me.

40 And Jesus stood, and commanded him to be brought unto him: and when he was come near, he asked him,

41 Saying, What wilt thou that I shall do unto thee? And he said, Lord, that I may receive my sight.

42 And Jesus said unto him, Receive thy sight: thy faith hath saved thee.

43 And immediately he received his sight, and followed him, glorifying God: and all the people, when they saw it, gave praise unto God.

LUKE 19

1 And Jesus entered and passed through Jericho.

2 And, behold, there was a man named Zaccheus, which was the chief among the publicans, and he was rich.

3 And he sought to see Jesus who he was; and could not for the press, because he was little of stature.

4 And he ran before, and climbed up into a sycomore tree to see him: for he was to pass that way.

5 And when Jesus came to the place, he looked up, and saw him, and said unto him, Zaccheus, make haste, and come down; for to day I must abide at thy house.

6 And he made haste, and came down, and received him joyfully.

7 And when they saw it, they all murmured, saying, That he was gone to be guest with a man that is a sinner.

his own elect – Preserve the Christians from all their adversaries, and in particular save them out of the general destruction, and avenge them of the Jews? Though he bear long with them – Though he does not immediately put an end, either to the wrongs of the wicked, or the sufferings of good men.

8. Yet when the Son of man cometh, will he find faith upon earth – Yet notwithstanding all the instances both of his long suffering and of his justice, whenever he shall remarkably appear, against their enemies in this age or in after ages, how few true believers will be found upon earth!

9. He spake this parable – Not to hypocrites; the Pharisee here mentioned was no hypocrite, no more than an outward adulterer: but he sincerely trusted in himself that he was righteous, and accordingly told God so, in the prayer which none but God heard.

12. I fast twice in the week – So did all the strict Pharisees: every Monday and Thursday. I give tithes of all that I possess – Many of them gave one full tenth of their income in tithes, and another tenth in alms. the sum of this plea is, I do no harm: I use all the means of grace: I do all the good I can.

13. The publican standing afar off – From the holy of holies, would not so much as lift up his eyes to heaven – Touched with shame, which is more ingenuous than fear.

14. This man went down – From the hill on which the temple stood, justified rather than the other – That is, and not the other.

15. Matt. xix, 13; Mark x, 13.

16. Calling them – Those that brought the children: of such is the kingdom of God – Such are subjects of the Messiah's kingdom. And such as these it properly belongs to.

18. Matt. xix, 16; Mark x, 17.

20. Exod. xx, 12, &c.

22. Yet lackest thou one thing – Namely, to love God more than mammon. Our Savior knew his heart, and presently put him upon a trial which laid it open to the ruler himself. And to cure his love of the world, which could not in him be cured otherwise, Christ commanded him to sell all that he had. But he does not command us to do this; but to use all to the glory of God.

31. Matt. xx, 17; Mark x, 32.

34. They understood none of these things – The literal meaning they could not but understand. But as they could not reconcile this to their preconceived opinion of the Messiah, they were utterly at a loss in what parabolic or figurative sense to take what he said concerning his sufferings; having their thoughts still taken up with the temporal kingdom.

35. Matt. xx, 29; Mark x, 46.

MATTHEW HENRY

CHARLES H. SPURGEON

show the sincerity of his faith and repentance. Zaccheus is declared to be a happy man, now he is turned from sin to God. Now that he is saved from his sins, from the guilt of them, from the power of them, all the benefits of salvation are his. Christ is come to his house, and where Christ comes he brings salvation with him. He came into this lost world to seek and to save it. His design was to save, when there was no salvation in any other. He seeks those that sought him not, and asked not for him.

11-27 This parable is like that of the talents, Mt 25. Those that are called to Christ, he furnishes with gifts needful for their business; and from those to whom he gives power, he expects service. The manifestation of the Spirit is given to every man to profit withal, 1Co 12:7. And as every one has received the gift, so let him minister the same, 1Pe 4:10. The account required, resembles that in the parable of the talents; and the punishment of the avowed enemies of Christ, as well as of false professors, is shown. The principal difference is, that the pound given to each seems to point out the gift of the gospel, which is the same to all who hear it; but the talents, distributed more or less, seem to mean that God gives different capacities and advantages to men, by which this one gift of the gospel may be differently improved.

28-40 Christ has dominion over all creatures, and may use them as he pleases. He has all men's hearts both under his eye and in his hand. Christ's triumphs, and his disciples' joyful praises, vex proud Pharisees, who are enemies to him and to his kingdom. But Christ, as he despises the contempt of the proud, so he accepts the praises of the humble. Pharisees would silence the praises of Christ, but they cannot; for as God can out of stones raise up children unto Abraham, and turn the stony heart to himself, so he can bring praise out of the mouths of children. And what will be the feelings of men when the Lord returns in glory to judge the world!

41-48 Who can behold the holy Jesus, looking forward to the miseries that awaited his murderers, weeping over the city where his precious blood was about to be shed, without seeing that the likeness of God in the believer, consists much in good-will and compassion? Surely those cannot be right who take up any doctrines of truth, so as to be hardened towards their fellow-sinners. But let every one remember, that though Jesus wept over Jerusalem, he executed awful vengeance upon it. Though he delights not in the death of a sinner, yet he will surely bring to pass his awful threatenings on those who neglect his salvation. The Son of God did not weep vain and causeless tears, nor for a light matter, nor for himself. He knows the value of souls, the weight of guilt, and how low it will press and sink mankind. May he then come and cleanse our hearts by his Spirit,

all working men would be equally thoughtful and economical, and that there were fewer of those foolish spendthrifts who waste their substance when they have it, and who, the moment there is a frost, or they are out of employ, become paupers, loafing upon the charity of others. I commend your industry, but, but, but, at the same time, is that all? Were you made only to be a machine for digging holes, laying bricks, or cutting out pieces of wood? Were you created only to stand at a counter and measure or weigh out goods? do you think your God made you for that and that only? Is this the chief end of man—to earn shillings a week, and try to make ends meet therewith? is that all immortal men were made for? As an animal like a dog, nor a machine like a steam engine, can you stand up and look at yourself, and say, "I believe I am perfectly fulfilling my destiny"? I beg this morning to interject that quiet "but," right into the middle of your busy life, and ask from you space for consideration, a pause for the voice of wisdom, that a hearing may be granted her. Business? Labor? Yes, but there is a higher bread to be earned, and there is a higher life to be considered. Hence the Lord puts it, "Labor not for the meat that perisheth," that is to say, not for that first and foremost; "but for that which endureth unto life eternal." God hath made man that he may glorify him; and whatever else man accomplishes, if he fail to reach that end, and make eternal shipwreck, unless he comes to sit at Jesus' feet; there and there only can he learn how to sanctify his business and to consecrate his labor, and so bring forth unto God; through his grace, that which is due to him.

Now, I have spoken thus to the busy, but I might speak, and I should have certainly as good a claim to do so, to those who are lovers of pleasure. They are not cumbered with much serving; rather, they laugh at those who cumber themselves about anything. They are merry as the birds, their life is as the flight of a butterfly, which lightly floats from flower to flower, according to its own sweet will; with neither comb to make, nor hive to guard. Now, thou gay young man, what doth Solomon say to thee? "Rejoice, O young man, in thy youth; and let thy heart cheer thee in the days of thy youth; but"—there comes in a pause, and the cool hand of wisdom is laid upon the hot brow of folly, and the youth is asked to think awhile—"but know thou, that for all these things, God will bring thee into judgment." It cannot be that an immortal spirit was made of frivolities; a soul immortal spending all her fires

8 And Zaccheus stood, and said unto the Lord; Behold, Lord, the half of my goods I give to the poor; and if I have taken any thing from any man by false accusation, I restore him fourfold.

9 And Jesus said unto him, This day is salvation come to this house, forsomuch as he also is a son of Abraham.

10 For the Son of man is come to seek and to save that which was lost.

11 And as they heard these things, he added and spake a parable, because he was nigh to Jerusalem, and because they thought that the kingdom of God should immediately appear.

12 He said therefore, A certain nobleman went into a far country to receive for himself a kingdom, and to return.

13 And he called his ten servants, and delivered them ten pounds, and said unto them, Occupy till I come.

14 But his citizens hated him, and sent a message after him, saying, We will not have this man to reign over us.

15 And it came to pass, that when he was returned, having received the kingdom, then he commanded these servants to be called unto him, to whom he had given the money, that he might know how much every man had gained by trading.

16 Then came the first, saying, Lord, thy pound hath gained ten pounds.

17 And he said unto him, Well, thou good servant: because thou hast been faithful in a very little, have thou authority over ten cities.

18 And the second came, saying, Lord, thy pound hath gained five pounds.

19 And he said likewise to him, Be thou also over five cities.

20 And another came, saying, Lord, behold, here is thy pound, which I have kept laid up in a napkin:

21 For I feared thee, because thou art an austere man: thou takest up that thou layedst not down, and reapest that thou didst not sow.

22 And he saith unto him, Out of thine own mouth will I judge thee, thou wicked servant. Thou knewest that I was an austere man, taking up that I laid not down, and reaping that I did not sow:

23 Wherefore then gavest not thou my money into the bank, that at my coming I might have required mine own with usury?

24 And he said unto them that stood by, Take from him the pound, and give it to him that hath ten pounds.

25 (And they said unto him, Lord, he hath ten pounds.)

26 For I say unto you, That unto every one which hath shall be given; and from him that hath not, even that he hath shall be taken away from him.

27 But those mine enemies, which would not that I should reign over them, bring hither, and slay them before me.

28 And when he had thus spoken, he went before, ascending up to Jerusalem.

29 And it came to pass, when he was come nigh to Bethphage and Bethany, at the mount called the mount of Olives, he sent two of his disciples,

30 Saying, Go ye into the village over against you; in the which at your entering ye shall find a colt tied, whereon yet never man sat: loose him, and bring him hither.

31 And if any man ask you, Why do ye loose him? thus shall ye say unto him, Because the Lord hath need of him.

32 And they that were sent went their way, and found even as he had said unto them.

33 And as they were loosing the colt, the owners thereof said unto them, Why loose ye the colt?

LUKE 19

1. He passed through Jericho – So that Zaccheus must have lived near the end of the town: the tree was in the town itself. And he was rich – These words seem to refer to the discourse in the last chapter, ver. 24, particularly to ver. 27. Zaccheus is a proof, that it is possible by the power of God for even a rich man to enter into the kingdom of heaven.

2. The chief of the publicans – What we would term, commissioner of the customs. A very honorable as well as profitable place.

4. And running before – With great earnestness. He climbed up – Notwithstanding his quality: desire conquering honor and shame.

5. Jesus said, Zaccheus, make haste and come down – What a strange mixture of passions must Zaccheus have now felt, hearing one speak, as knowing both his name and his heart!

7. They all murmured – All who were near: though most of them rather out of surprise than indignation.

8. And Zaccheus stood – Showing by his posture, his deliberate, purpose and ready mind, and said, Behold, Lord, I give – I determine to do it immediately.

9. He also is a son of Abraham – A Jew born, and as such has a right to the first offer of salvation.

10. Matt. xviii, 11.

11. They thought the kingdom of God – A glorious temporal kingdom, would immediately appear.

12. He went into a far country to receive a kingdom – Christ went to heaven, to receive his sovereign power as man, even all authority in heaven and earth. Matt. xxv, 14; Mark xiii, 34.

13. Trade till I come – To visit the nation, to destroy Jerusalem, to judge the world: or, in a more particular sense, to require thy soul of thee.

14. But his citizens – Such were those of Jerusalem, hated him, and sent an embassy after him – The word seems to imply, their sending ambassadors to a superior court, to enter their protest against his being admitted to the regal power. In such a solemn manner did the Jews protest, as it were, before God, that Christ should not reign over them: this man – So they call him in contempt.

15. When he was returned – In his glory.

23. With interest – Which does not appear to be contrary to any law of God or man. But this is no plea for usury, that is, the taking such interest as implies any degree of oppression or extortion.

25. They said – With admiration, not envy.

26. Matt. xxv, 29; Luke viii, 18.

27. He went before – The foremost of the company, showing his readiness to suffer.

29. He drew nigh to the place where the borders of Bethphage and Bethany met, which was at the foot of the mount of Olives. Matt. xxi, 1; Mark xi, 1.

MATTHEW HENRY

CHARLES H. SPURGEON

from all that defiles. May sinners, on every side, become attentive to the words of truth and salvation.

LUKE 20

The priests and scribes question Christ's authority. (1-8)
The parable of the vineyard and husbandmen. (9-19)
Of giving tribute. (20-26)
Concerning the resurrection. (27-38)
The scribes silenced. (39-47)

1-8 Men often pretend to examine the evidences of revelation, and the truth of the gospel, when only seeking excuses for their own unbelief and disobedience. Christ answered these priests and scribes with a plain question about the baptism of John, which the common people could answer. They all knew it was from heaven, nothing in it had an earthly tendency. Those that bury the knowledge they have, are justly denied further knowledge. It was just with Christ to refuse to give account of his authority, to those who knew the baptism of John to be from heaven, yet would not believe in him, nor own their knowledge.

9-19 Christ spake this parable against those who resolved not to own his authority, though the evidence of it was so full. How many resemble the Jews who murdered the prophets and crucified Christ, in their enmity to God, and aversion to his service, desiring to live according to their lusts, without control! Let all who are favored with God's word, look to it that they make proper use of their advantages. Awful will be the doom, both of those who reject the Son, and of those who profess to reverence Him, yet render not the fruits in due season. Though they could not but own that for such a sin, such a punishment was just, yet they could not bear to hear of it. It is the folly of sinners, that they persevere in sinful ways, though they dread the destruction at the end of those ways.

20-26 Those who are most crafty in their designs against Christ and his gospel, cannot hide them. He did not give a direct answer, but reproved them for offering to impose upon him; and they could not fasten upon any thing wherewith to stir up either the governor or the people against him. The wisdom which is from above, will direct all who teach the way of God truly, to avoid the snares laid for them by wicked men; and will teach our duty to God, to our rulers, and to all men, so clearly, that opposers will have no evil to say of us.

27-38 It is common for those who design to undermine any truth of God, to load it with difficulties. But we wrong ourselves, and wrong the truth of Christ, when we form our notions of the world of spirits by this world of sense. There are more worlds than one; a present visible world, and a future unseen world;

on the playthings of the world, "resembles ocean into tempest toss'd, to waft a feather, or to drown a fly." So great a thing as an immortal soul could not have been made by God with no higher object than to spend itself upon trifles light as air. Oh, pause a while, thou careless, godless one, and hear the voice that saith unto thee, "but." There is something more than the fool's hell; and should not life be? The charms of music, the merriment of the gay assembly, the beauties of art, and the delights of banqueting—there must be something more for thee than these; and something more must be required of thee than that thou shouldst waste from morn to night thy precious time upon nothing but to please thyself. Stop, stop, and let this admonitory "but" sound in thine ears.

I take liberty, moreover, to address the same word to religious people, who, perhaps, need it as much as the others. They will, of course, agree with anything I can say about the mere worldling or the profligate; but, will they listen to me when I say to them, "You are very diligent in your religion, you are attentive to all its outward rites and ceremonies, you believe the articles of your church, you practice the ceremonies ordained by its rulers; but, but, do you know that all this is nothing, unless you sit at Jesus' feet?" We may do what the church tells us, and never do what Christ tells us, for these may be different things; and the church is not our Savior, but Christ. We may believe what a certain creed tells us, but not believe what Jesus teaches; for our creed and Christ may be two very different things. Ay, and we may believe even what the Bible itself teaches to us, or think we believe it; but, if our heart has never made submission to the Teacher himself, so as to sit at his feet, and receive the truth obediently from him, our religion is altogether vain. Traditional religion is not submission to Christ, but to custom. Obedience to a denomination is not obedience to Jesus himself. How I wish that all professing Christians would bring themselves to an examination and inquire, "Do I really believe in the person of my Lord, and accept him as my Teacher? Do I study the Word of God to learn the truth from him, and not accept it blindly and at second hand from my minister, or my parents, or the church of the nation, or the creed of my family?" We go to Jesus for teaching, desiring in our hearts to be taught by his book and his Spirit, cheerfully agreeing in all things to shape our faith to his declaration, and our life to his rule. For us, there must be no spiritual law-giver, and no infallible Rabbi, but the Blessed One, whom

34 And they said, The Lord hath need of him.

35 And they brought him to Jesus: and they cast their garments upon the colt, and they set Jesus thereon.

36 And as he went, they spread their clothes in the way.

37 And when he was come nigh, even now at the descent of the mount of Olives, the whole multitude of the disciples began to rejoice and praise God with a loud voice for all the mighty works that they had seen;

38 Saying, Blessed be the King that cometh in the name of the Lord: peace in heaven, and glory in the highest.

39 And some of the Pharisees from among the multitude said unto him, Master, rebuke thy disciples.

40 And he answered and said unto them, I tell you that, if these should hold their peace, the stones would immediately cry out.

41 And when he was come near, he beheld the city, and wept over it,

42 Saying, If thou hadst known, even thou, at least in this thy day, the things which belong unto thy peace! but now they are hid from thine eyes.

43 For the days shall come upon thee, that thine enemies shall cast a trench about thee, and compass thee round, and keep thee in on every side,

44 And shall lay thee even with the ground, and thy children within thee; and they shall not leave in thee one stone upon another; because thou knewest not the time of thy visitation.

45 And he went into the temple, and began to cast out them that sold therein, and them that bought;

46 Saying unto them, It is written, My house is the house of prayer: but ye have made it a den of thieves.

47 And he taught daily in the temple. But the chief priests and the scribes and the chief of the people sought to destroy him,

48 And could not find what they might do: for all the people were very attentive to hear him.

LUKE 20

1 And it came to pass, that on one of those days, as he taught the people in the temple, and preached the gospel, the chief priests and the scribes came upon him with the elders,

2 And spake unto him, saying, Tell us, by what authority doest thou these things? or who is he that gave thee this authority?

3 And he answered and said unto them, I will also ask you one thing; and answer me:

4 The baptism of John, was it from heaven, or of men?

5 And they reasoned with themselves, saying, If we shall say, From heaven; he will say, Why then believed ye him not?

6 But and if we say, Of men; all the people will stone us: for they be persuaded that John was a prophet.

7 And they answered, that they could not tell whence it was.

8 And Jesus said unto them, Neither tell I you by what authority I do these things.

9 Then began he to speak to the people this parable; A certain man planted a vineyard, and let it forth to husbandmen, and went into a far country for a long time.

10 And at the season he sent a servant to the husbandmen, that they should give him of the fruit of the vineyard: but the husbandmen beat him, and sent him away empty.

11 And again he sent another servant: and they beat him also, and entreated him shamefully, and sent him away empty.

12 And again he sent a third: and they wounded him also,

37. The whole multitude began to praise God – Speaking at once, as it seems, from a Divine impulse, words which most of them did not understand.

38. Peace in heaven – God being reconciled to man.

39. Rebuke thy disciples – Paying thee this immoderate honor.

40. If these should hold their peace, the stones, which lie before you, would cry out – That is, God would raise up some still more unlikely instruments to declare his praise. For the power of God will not return empty.

42. O that thou hadst known, at least in this thy day – After thou hast neglected so many. Thy day – The day wherein God still offers thee his blessings.

43. Thine enemies shall cast a trench about thee, and compass thee around – All this was exactly performed by Titus, the Roman general.

44. And thy children within thee – All the Jews were at that time gathered together, it being the time of the Passover. They shall not leave in thee one stone upon another – Only three towers were left standing for a time, to show the former strength and magnificence of the place. But these likewise were afterward leveled with the ground.

45. Matt. xxi, 12; Mark xi, 11.

46. Isaiah lvi, 7.

LUKE 20

1. Matt. xxi, 23; Mark xi, 27.

9. A long time – It was a long time from the entrance of the Israelites into Canaan to the birth of Christ. Matt. xxi, 33; Mark xii, 1.

16. He will destroy these husbandmen – Probably he pointed to the scribes, chief priests, and elders: who allowed, he will miserably destroy those wicked men, Matt. xxi, 41; but could not bear that this should be applied to themselves. They might also mean, God forbid that we should be guilty of such a crime as your parable seems to charge us with, namely, rejecting and killing the heir. Our Savior answers, But yet will ye do it, as is prophesied of you.

17. He looked on them – To sharpen their attention. Psalm cxviii, 22.

18. Matt. xxi, 45.

20. Just men – Men of a tender conscience. To take hold of his discourse – If he answered as they hoped he would. Matt. xxii, 16; Mark xii, 12.

21. Thou speakest – In private, and teachest – In public.

24. Show me a penny – A Roman penny, which was the money that was usually paid on that occasion.

26. They could not take hold of his words before the people – As they did afterward before the Sanhedrin, in the absence of the people, chap. xxii, 67.

27. Matt. xxii, 23; Mark xii, 18.

and let every one compare this world and that world, and give the preference in his thoughts and cares to that which deserves them. Believers shall obtain the resurrection from the dead, that is the blessed resurrection. What shall be the happy state of the inhabitants of that world, we cannot express or conceive, 1Co 2:9. Those that are entered into the joy of their Lord, are entirely taken up therewith; when there is perfection of holiness there will be no occasion for preservatives from sin. And when God called himself the God of these patriarchs, he meant that he was a God all-sufficient to them, Ge 17:1, their exceeding great Reward, Ge 15:1. He never did that for them in this world, which answered the full extent of his undertaking; therefore there must be another life, in which he will do that for them, which will completely fulfill the promise.

39-47 The scribes commended the reply Christ made to the Sadducees about the resurrection, but they were silenced by a question concerning the Messiah. Christ, as God, was David's Lord; but Christ, as man, was David's son. The scribes would receive the severest judgment for defrauding the poor widows, and for their abuse of religion, particularly of prayer, which they used as a pretense for carrying on worldly and wicked plans. Dissembled piety is double sin. Then let us beg of God to keep us from pride, ambition, covetousness, and every evil thing; and to teach us to seek that honor which comes from him alone.

LUKE 21

Christ commends a poor widow. (1-4)
His prophecy. (5-28)
Christ exhorts to watchfulness. (29-38)

1-4 From the offering of this poor widow, learn that what we rightly give for the relief of the poor, and the support of God's worship, is given unto God; and our Savior sees with pleasure whatever we have in our hearts to give for the relief of his members, or for his service. Blessed Lord! the poorest of thy servants have two mites, they have a soul and a body; persuade and enable us to offer both unto thee; how happy shall we be in thine accepting of them!

5-28 With much curiosity those about Christ ask as to the time when the great desolation should be. He answers with clearness and fullness, as far as was necessary to teach them their duty; for all knowledge is desirable as far as it is in order to practice. Though spiritual judgments are the most common in gospel times, yet God makes use of temporal judgments also. Christ tells them what hard things they should suffer for his name's sake, and encourages them to bear up under their trials, and to go on in their work, notwithstanding the opposition they would meet with.

Magdalene called "Rabboni," and whom Thomas saluted as, "My Lord and my God."

Yes, and let me say, even to those of you who can honestly declare that Christ is your sole confidence, it is possible for you to forget the necessity of sitting at his feet. You, dear brethren, are looking to his precious blood alone for your salvation, and his name is sweet to you, and you desire all things to be conformed to his will. So far it is well with you, for in this you have a measure of sitting at his feet; but so had Martha; she loved her Lord, and she knew his word, and she was a saved soul, for "Jesus loved Mary, and Martha, and Lazarus;" but you have not perhaps so much of this needful thing as Mary had, and as you ought to have. You have been very busy this week, and have been drifted from your moorings; you have not lived with your Lord in conscious fellowship; you have been full of care and empty of prayer; you have not committed your sorrows to your loving friend; you have blundered on in duty without asking his guidance or assistance, you have not maintained, in your Christian service, the communion of your spirit with the Well-Beloved, and, if such has been the case, let me say "but" to you, and ask you, as you sit here this morning, to make a little stop in your Sunday-school teaching or your street preaching, or whatever else it is that you are so laudably engaged in, and say to yourself: "To me, as a worker, the one thing needful is to keep near my Lord, and I must not so suffer the watering of others to occupy me, as to neglect my own heart, lest I should have to say 'woe is me, they made me keeper in the vineyards, but my own vineyard have I not kept.'" To the saints, as well as to others, the one thing needful is to sit at Jesus' feet. We are to be always learners and lovers of Jesus. Departure from him, and independence of him, let them not once be named among you. It is weakness, sickness, sin, and sorrow for a believer to leave his Lord and become either his own leader or reliance. We are only safe while we remain humbly and gladly subservient to him. You see, then, that this word "but" suggests a very useful and salutary pause to us all. May God help us to benefit thereby.

II. Secondly, our text speaks of NECESSITY—one thing is a necessity. If this be proven, it overrides all other considerations. We are nearly right when we say proverbially, "Necessity has no law." If a man steal, and it be found that he was dying of hunger, he is always half forgiven, and charity has been known to excuse him alto-

and cast him out.

13 Then said the lord of the vineyard, What shall I do? I will send my beloved son: it may be they will reverence him when they see him.

14 But when the husbandmen saw him, they reasoned among themselves, saying, This is the heir: come, let us kill him, that the inheritance may be ours.

15 So they cast him out of the vineyard, and killed him. What therefore shall the lord of the vineyard do unto them?

16 He shall come and destroy these husbandmen, and shall give the vineyard to others. And when they heard it, they said, God forbid.

17 And he beheld them, and said, What is this then that is written, The stone which the builders rejected, the same is become the head of the corner?

18 Whosoever shall fall upon that stone shall be broken; but on whomsoever it shall fall, it will grind him to powder.

19 And the chief priests and the scribes the same hour sought to lay hands on him; and they feared the people: for they perceived that he had spoken this parable against them.

20 And they watched him, and sent forth spies, which should feign themselves just men, that they might take hold of his words, that so they might deliver him unto the power and authority of the governor.

21 And they asked him, saying, Master, we know that thou sayest and teachest rightly, neither acceptest thou the person of any, but teachest the way of God truly:

22 Is it lawful for us to give tribute unto Cesar, or no?

23 But he perceived their craftiness, and said unto them, Why tempt ye me?

24 Shew me a penny. Whose image and superscription hath it? They answered and said, Cesar's.

25 And he said unto them, Render therefore unto Cesar the things which be Cesar's, and unto God the things which be God's.

26 And they could not take hold of his words before the people: and they marveled at his answer, and held their peace.

27 Then came to him certain of the Sadducees, which deny that there is any resurrection; and they asked him,

28 Saying, Master, Moses wrote unto us, If any man's brother die, having a wife, and he die without children, that his brother should take his wife, and raise up seed unto his brother.

29 There were therefore seven brethren: and the first took a wife, and died without children.

30 And the second took her to wife, and he died childless.

31 And the third took her; and in like manner the seven also: and they left no children, and died.

32 Last of all the woman died also.

33 Therefore in the resurrection whose wife of them is she? for seven had her to wife.

34 And Jesus answering said unto them, The children of this world marry, and are given in marriage:

35 But they which shall be accounted worthy to obtain that world, and the resurrection from the dead, neither marry, nor are given in marriage:

36 Neither can they die any more: for they are equal unto the angels; and are the children of God, being the children of the resurrection.

37 Now that the dead are raised, even Moses shewed at the bush, when he calleth the Lord the God of Abraham, and the God of Isaac, and the God of Jacob.

38 For he is not a God of the dead, but of the living: for all live unto him.

28. Deut. xxv, 5.

34. The children of this world – The inhabitants of earth, marry and are given in marriage – As being all subject to the law of mortality; so that the species is in need of being continually repaired.

35. But they who obtain that world – Which they enter into, before the resurrection of the dead.

36. They are the children of God – In a more eminent sense when they rise again.

37. That the dead are raised, even Moses, as well as the other prophets showed, when he calleth – That is, when he recites the words which God spoke of himself, I am the God of Abraham, &c. It cannot properly be said, that God is the God of any who are totally perished. Exod. iii, 6.

38. He is not a God of the dead, or, there is no God of the dead – That is, though the term God implies such a relation, as cannot possibly subsist between him and the dead; who in the Sadducees' sense are extinguished spirits; who could neither worship him, nor receive good from him. So that all live to him – All who have him for their God, live to and enjoy him. This sentence is not an argument for what went before; but the proposition which was to be proved. And the consequence is apparently just. For as all the faithful are the children of Abraham, and the Divine promise of being a God to him and his seed is entailed upon them, it implies their continued existence and happiness in a future state as much as Abraham's. And as the body is an essential part of man, it implies both his resurrection and theirs; and so overthrows the entire scheme of the Saducean doctrine.

40. They durst not ask him any question – The Sadducees durst not. One of the scribes did, presently after.

41. Matt. xxii, 41; Mark xii, 35.

42. Psalm cx, 1.

46. Matt. xxiii, 5.

47. Matt. xxiii, 14.

LUKE 21

1. He looked up – From those on whom his eyes were fixed before. Mark xii, 41.

5. Goodly stones – Such as no engines now in use could have brought, or even set upon each other. Some of them (as an eye witness who lately measured them writes) were forty-fifty cubits long, five high, and six broad; yet brought thither from another country. And gifts – Which persons delivered from imminent dangers had, in accomplishment of their vows, hung on the walls and pillars. The marble of the temple was so white, that it appeared like a mountain of snow at a distance. And the gilding of many parts made it, especially when the sun shone, a most splendid and beautiful spectacle.

God will stand by you, and own you, and assist you. This was remarkably fulfilled after the pouring out of the Spirit, by whom Christ gave his disciples wisdom and utterance. Though we may be losers for Christ, we shall not, we cannot be losers by him, in the end. It is our duty and interest at all times, especially in perilous, trying times, to secure the safety of our own souls. It is by Christian patience we keep possession of our own souls, and keep out all those impressions which would put us out of temper. We may view the prophecy before us much as those Old Testament prophecies, which, together with their great object, embrace, or glance at some nearer object of importance to the church. Having given an idea of the times for about thirty-eight years next to come, Christ shows what all those things would end in, namely, the destruction of Jerusalem, and the utter dispersion of the Jewish nation; which would be a type and figure of Christ's second coming. The scattered Jews around us preach the truth of Christianity; and prove, that though heaven and earth shall pass away, the words of Jesus shall not pass away. They also remind us to pray for those times when neither the real, nor the spiritual Jerusalem, shall any longer be trodden down by the Gentiles, and when both Jews and Gentiles shall be turned to the Lord. When Christ came to destroy the Jews, he came to redeem the Christians that were persecuted and oppressed by them; and then had the churches rest. When he comes to judge the world, he will redeem all that are his from their troubles. So fully did the Divine judgments come upon the Jews, that their city is set as an example before us, to show that sins will not pass unpunished; and that the terrors of the Lord, and his threatenings against impenitent sinners, will all come to pass, even as his word was true, and his wrath great upon Jerusalem.

29-38 Christ tells his disciples to observe the signs of the times, which they might judge by. He charges them to look upon the ruin of the Jewish nation as near. Yet this race and family of Abraham shall not be rooted out; it shall survive as a nation, and be found as prophesied, when the Son of man shall be revealed. He cautions them against being secure and sensual. This command is given to all Christ's disciples, Take heed to yourselves, that ye be not overpowered by temptations, nor betrayed by your own corruptions. We cannot be safe, if we are carnally secure. Our danger is, lest the day of death and of judgment should come upon us when we are not prepared. Lest, when we are called to meet our Lord, that be the furthest from our thoughts, which ought to be nearest our hearts. For so it will come upon the most of men, who dwell upon the earth, and mind earthly things only, and have no converse with heaven. It will be a terror and a destruction to them. Here see what should be our aim, that we may be accounted worthy to escape all those things; that when the judgments of

gether. Necessity has been frequently accepted as a good excuse for what else might not have been tolerated; and when a thing is right, and necessity backs it, then indeed the right become imperative, and pushes to the front to force its way. Necessity, like hunger breaks through stone walls. The text claims for sitting at Jesus' feet that it is the first and only necessity. Now, I see all around me a crowd of things alluring and fascinating. Pleasure calls to me, I hear her syren song—but I reply, "I cannot regard thee, for necessity presses upon me to hearken to another voice." Philosophy and learning charm me, fain would I yield my heart to them; but, while I am yet unsaved, the one thing needful demands my first care, and wisdom bids me give it. Not that we love human learning less, but eternal wisdom more. Pearls? Yes. Emeralds? Yes; but bread, in God's name— bread at once, when I am starving in the desert! What is the use of ingots of gold, or bars of silver, or caskets of jewels, when food is wanting? If one thing be needful, it devours, like Aaron's rod, all the matters which are merely pleasurable. All the fascinating things on earth may go, but the needful things we must have. If you are wise, you will evermore prefer the necessary to the dazzling.

About us are a thousand things entangling. This world is very much like the pools we have heard of in India, in which grows a long grass of so clinging a character that, if a man once falls into the water, it is almost certain to be his death, for only with the utmost difficulty could he be rescued from the meshes of the deadly, weedy net, which immediately wraps itself around him. This world is even thus entangling. All the efforts of grace are needed to preserve men from being ensnared with the deceitfulness of riches and the cares of this life. The ledger demands you, the day-book wants you, the shop requires you, the warehouse bell rings for you; the theater invites, the ball-room calls: you must live, you say, and you must have a little enjoyment, and, consequently, you give your heart to the world. These things, I say, are very entangling; but we must be disentangled from them, for we cannot afford to lose our souls. "What shall it profit a man if he gain the whole world and lose his own soul?" If a ship is going down, and a passenger has his gold in a bag about him, and he has upon him a costly cloak, see how he acts. Off goes the garment when he knows that he cannot possibly swim with it upon him. No matter though it be lined with miniver and be made of costliest stuff, off he throws it; and, as for his bag of treasure,

39 Then certain of the scribes answering said, Master, thou hast well said.

40 And after that they durst not ask him any question at all.

41 And he said unto them, How say they that Christ is David's son?

42 And David himself saith in the book of Psalms, The LORD said unto my Lord, Sit thou on my right hand,

43 Till I make thine enemies thy footstool.

44 David therefore calleth him Lord, how is he then his son?

45 Then in the audience of all the people he said unto his disciples,

46 Beware of the scribes, which desire to walk in long robes, and love greetings in the markets, and the highest seats in the synagogues, and the chief rooms at feasts;

47 Which devour widows' houses, and for a shew make long prayers: the same shall receive greater damnation.

LUKE 21

1 And he looked up, and saw the rich men casting their gifts into the treasury.

2 And he saw also a certain poor widow casting in thither two mites.

3 And he said, Of a truth I say unto you, that this poor widow hath cast in more than they all:

4 For all these have of their abundance cast in unto the offerings of God: but she of her penury hath cast in all the living that she had.

5 And as some spake of the temple, how it was adorned with goodly stones and gifts, he said,

6 As for these things which ye behold, the days will come, in the which there shall not be left one stone upon another, that shall not be thrown down.

7 And they asked him, saying, Master, but when shall these things be? and what sign will there be when these things shall come to pass?

8 And he said, Take heed that ye be not deceived: for many shall come in my name, saying, I am Christ; and the time draweth near: go ye not therefore after them.

9 But when ye shall hear of wars and commotions, be not terrified: for these things must first come to pass; but the end is not by and by.

10 Then said he unto them, Nation shall rise against nation, and kingdom against kingdom:

11 And great earthquakes shall be in divers places, and famines, and pestilences; and fearful sights and great signs shall there be from heaven.

12 But before all these, they shall lay their hands on you, and persecute you, delivering you up to the synagogues, and into prisons, being brought before kings and rulers for my name's sake.

13 And it shall turn to you for a testimony.

14 Settle it therefore in your hearts, not to meditate before what ye shall answer:

15 For I will give you a mouth and wisdom, which all your adversaries shall not be able to gainsay nor resist.

16 And ye shall be betrayed both by parents, and brethren, and kinsfolks, and friends; and some of you shall they cause to be put to death.

17 And ye shall be hated of all men for my name's sake.

18 But there shall not an hair of your head perish.

19 In your patience possess ye your souls.

20 And when ye shall see Jerusalem compassed with armies, then know that the desolation thereof is nigh.

Matt. xxiv, 1; Mark xiii, 1.

8. I am the Christ; and the time is near – When I will deliver you from all your enemies. They are the words of the seducers.

9. Commotions – Intestine broils; civil wars.

11. Fearful sights and signs from heaven – Of which Josephus gives a circumstantial account.

12. Mark xiii, 9.

13. It shall turn to you for a testimony – Of your having delivered your own souls, and of their being without excuse.

16. Matt. x, 21.

17. Matt. xxiv, 13; Mark xiii, 13.

18. Not a hair of your head – A proverbial expression, shall perish – Without the special providence of God. And then, not before the time, nor without A full reward.

19. In your patience possess ye your souls – Be calm and serene, masters of yourselves, and superior to all irrational and disquieting passions. By keeping the government of your spirits, you will both avoid much misery, and guard the better against all dangers.

21. Let them that are in the midst of it – Where Jerusalem stands (that is, they that are in Jerusalem) depart out of it, before their retreat is cut off by the uniting of the forces near the city, and let not them that are in the adjacent countries by any means enter into it.

22. And things which are written – Particularly in Daniel.

24. They shall fall by the edge of the sword, and shall be led away captive – Eleven hundred thousand perished in the siege of Jerusalem, and above ninety thousand were sold for slaves. So terribly was this prophecy fulfilled! And Jerusalem shall be trodden by the Gentiles – That is, inhabited. So it was indeed. The land was sold, and no Jew suffered even to come within sight of Jerusalem. The very foundations of the city were plowed up, and a heathen temple built where the temple of God had stood. The times of the Gentiles – That is, the times limited for their treading the city; which shall terminate in the full conversion of the Gentiles.

25. And there shall be – Before the great day, which was typified by the destruction of Jerusalem: signs – Different from those mentioned in ver. 11. Matt. xxiv, 29; Mark xiii, 24.

28. Now when these things – Mentioned ver. 8, 10, &c., begin to come to pass, look up with firm faith, and lift up your heads with joy: for your redemption out of many troubles draweth nigh, by God's destroying your implacable enemies.

29. Behold the fig tree and all the trees – Christ spake this in the spring, just before the Passover; when all the trees were budding on the mount of Olives, where they then were.

30. Ye know of yourselves – Though none teach you.

God are abroad, we may not be in the common calamity, or it may not be that to us which it is to others. Do you ask how you may be found worthy to stand before Christ at that day? Those who never yet sought Christ, let them now go unto him; those who never yet were humbled for their sins, let them now begin; those who have already begun, let them go forward and be kept humbled. Watch therefore, and pray always. Watch against sin; watch in every duty, and make the most of every opportunity to do good. Pray always: those shall be accounted worthy to live a life of praise in the other world, who live a life of prayer in this world. May we begin, employ, and conclude each day attending to Christ's word, obeying his precepts, and following his example, that whenever he comes we may be found watching.

LUKE 22

The treachery of Judas. (1-6)
The Passover. (7-18)
The Lord's supper instituted. (19,20)
Christ admonishes the disciples. (21-38)
Christ's agony in the garden. (39-46)
Christ betrayed. (47-53)
The fall of Peter. (54-62)
Christ confesses himself to be the Son of God. (63-71)

1-6 Christ knew all men, and had wise and holy ends in taking Judas to be a disciple. How he who knew Christ so well, came to betray him, we are here told; Satan entered into Judas. It is hard to say whether more mischief is done to Christ's kingdom, by the power of its open enemies, or by the treachery of its pretended friends; but without the latter, its enemies could not do so much evil as they do.

7-18 Christ kept the ordinances of the law, particularly that of the Passover, to teach us to observe his gospel institutions, and most of all that of the Lord's supper. Those who go upon Christ's word, need not fear disappointment. According to the orders given them, the disciples got all ready for the Passover. Jesus bids this Passover welcome. He desired it, though he knew his sufferings would follow, because it was in order to his Father's glory and man's redemption. He takes his leave of all Passovers, signifying thereby his doing away all the ordinances of the ceremonial law, of which the Passover was one of the earliest and chief. That type was laid aside, because now in the kingdom of God the substance was come.

19,20 The Lord's supper is a sign or memorial of Christ already come, who by dying delivered us; his death is in special manner set before us in that ordinance, by which we are reminded of it. The breaking of Christ's body as a sacrifice for us, is therein brought to our remembrance by the breaking of bread. Nothing can be more nourishing and satisfy-

with many a regret he flings them down upon the deck, for his life is dearer than they. If he may but save his life, he is willing to lose all beside. Oh sirs! for the one thing needful, all entangling things must be give up. You must lay aside every weight, and the sin that doth so easily beset you, if by any means the one thing needful may be yours.

There are many things very puzzling, and some people have a strange delight in being bewildered. It is astonishing the many letters I receive and interviews I am asked to give, in order to adjust in people's minds the doctrine of predestination and the fact of free agency; and equally remarkable is the way in which young people, and old people too, will pick out extremely difficult texts, perhaps relating to the Second Advent, or to the battle of Armageddon, and they must needs have these opened up to them before they will believe the gospel. I think it utterly useless to begin upon such things with those who are unsaved. One thing is needful, sir, and that is by no means a puzzling matter; it is plainly this, that thou submit thyself to Jesus Christ and sit at his feet. That is needful: as for the doctrines of election and the second advent, they are important, but they are neither the most essential nor the most pressing. The one thing needful for a seeking soul is that it receives Jesus and become submissive to him, sitting as a disciple at his feet and as a servant doing his will. It is true there is the ninth chapter of Romans in the Bible, and a precious chapter it is: but the seeking sinner should take care to read first the third chapter of John, and till he has mastered that, he had better let the Romans alone. Go first to the business which concerns your salvation; attend to that, and when all is right with you, then, at Jesus' feet, you will be in the best possible position to learn all that can be learned of the higher mysteries and the deeper truths.

Moreover, there is much that is desirable, very desirable—desirable in the highest spiritual sense; but it must be second to that which is needful. If I read the experience of men who have known their own hearts and mourned before the Lord, I wish that I had as deep a sense of sin as they had; or, I read the story of saints who have lived the angelic life, and even here on earth have dwelt with Christ and walked the golden streets in fellowship with him, I wish I could rise to all their heights; but for all that, if my soul is still polluted with sin, for me the one thing needful is cleansing by the Redeemer's blood; I must at once believingly yield to Jesus, for this is of necessity, and the

21 Then let them which are in Judea flee to the mountains; and let them which are in the midst of it depart out; and let not them that are in the countries enter thereinto.

22 For these be the days of vengeance, that all things which are written may be fulfilled.

23 But woe unto them that are with child, and to them that give suck, in those days! for there shall be great distress in the land, and wrath upon this people.

24 And they shall fall by the edge of the sword, and shall be led away captive into all nations: and Jerusalem shall be trodden down of the Gentiles, until the times of the Gentiles be fulfilled.

25 And there shall be signs in the sun, and in the moon, and in the stars; and upon the earth distress of nations, with perplexity; the sea and the waves roaring;

26 Men's hearts failing them for fear, and for looking after those things which are coming on the earth: for the powers of heaven shall be shaken.

27 And then shall they see the Son of man coming in a cloud with power and great glory.

28 And when these things begin to come to pass, then look up, and lift up your heads; for your redemption draweth nigh.

29 And he spake to them a parable; Behold the fig tree, and all the trees;

30 When they now shoot forth, ye see and know of your own selves that summer is now nigh at hand.

31 So likewise ye, when ye see these things come to pass, know ye that the kingdom of God is nigh at hand.

32 Verily I say unto you, This generation shall not pass away, till all be fulfilled.

33 Heaven and earth shall pass away: but my words shall not pass away.

34 And take heed to yourselves, lest at any time your hearts be overcharged with surfeiting, and drunkenness, and cares of this life, and so that day come upon you unawares.

35 For as a snare shall it come on all them that dwell on the face of the whole earth.

36 Watch ye therefore, and pray always, that ye may be accounted worthy to escape all these things that shall come to pass, and to stand before the Son of man.

37 And in the day time he was teaching in the temple; and at night he went out, and abode in the mount that is called the mount of Olives.

38 And all the people came early in the morning to him in the temple, for to hear him.

LUKE 22

1 Now the feast of unleavened bread drew nigh, which is called the Passover.

2 And the chief priests and scribes sought how they might kill him; for they feared the people.

3 Then entered Satan into Judas surnamed Iscariot, being of the number of the twelve.

4 And he went his way, and communed with the chief priests and captains, how he might betray him unto them.

5 And they were glad, and covenanted to give him money.

6 And he promised, and sought opportunity to betray him unto them in the absence of the multitude.

7 Then came the day of unleavened bread, when the passover must be killed.

8 And he sent Peter and John, saying, Go and prepare us the passover, that we may eat.

9 And they said unto him, Where wilt thou that we prepare?

31. The kingdom of God is nigh – The destruction of the Jewish city, temple, and religion, to make way for the advancement of my kingdom.

32. Till all things be effected – All that has been spoken of the destruction of Jerusalem, to which the question, ver. 7, relates: and which is treated of from ver. 8-24.

34. Take heed, lest at any time your hearts be overloaded with gluttony and drunkenness – And was there need to warn the apostles themselves against such sins as these? Then surely there is reason to warn even strong Christians against the very grossest sins. Neither are we wise, if we think ourselves out of the reach of any sin: and so that day – Of judgment or of death, come upon you, even you that are not of this world – Unawares. Matt. xxiv, 42; Mark xiii, 33; Luke xii, 35.

35. That sit – Careless and at ease.

36. Watch ye therefore – This is the general conclusion of all that precedes. That ye may be counted worthy – This word sometimes signifies an honor conferred on a person, as when the apostles are said to be counted worthy to suffer shame for Christ, Acts v, 41. Sometimes meet or becoming: as when John the Baptist exhorts, to bring fruits worthy of repentance, chap. iii, 8. And so to be counted worthy to escape, is to have the honor of it, and to be fitted or prepared for it. To stand – With joy and triumph: not to fall before him as his enemies.

37. Now by day – In the day time, he was teaching in the temple – This shows how our Lord employed his time after coming to Jerusalem: but it is not said, he was this day in the temple, and next morning the people came. It does not therefore by any means imply, that he came any more after this into the temple.

38. And all the people came early in the morning to hear him – How much happier were his disciples in these early lectures, than the slumbers of the morning could have made them on their beds! Let us not scruple to deny ourselves the indulgence of unnecessary sleep, that we may morning after morning place ourselves at his feet, receiving the instructions of his word, and seeking those of his Spirit.

LUKE 22

1. Matt. xxvi, 1; Mark xiv, 1.

3. Then entered Satan – Who is never wanting to assist those whose heart is bent upon mischief.

4. Captains – Called captains of the temple, ver. 52. They were Jewish officers, who presided over the guards which kept watch every night in the temple.

7. Matt. xxvi, 17; Mark xiv, 12.

14. Matt. xxvi, 20; Mark xiv, 17.

15. With desire have I desired – That is, I have earnestly desired it. He desired it, both for the sake of his disciples, to whom he desired to manifest himself farther, at this solemn parting: and for the sake of his whole

ing to the soul, than the doctrine of Christ's making atonement for sin, and the assurance of an interest in that atonement. Therefore we do this in remembrance of what He did for us, when he died for us; and for a memorial of what we do, in joining ourselves to him in an everlasting covenant. The shedding of Christ's blood, by which the atonement was made, is represented by the wine in the cup.

21-38 How unbecoming is the worldly ambition of being the greatest, to the character of a follower of Jesus, who took upon him the form of a servant, and humbled himself to the death of the cross! In the way to eternal happiness, we must expect to be assaulted and sifted by Satan. If he cannot destroy, he will try to disgrace or distress us. Nothing more certainly forebodes a fall, in a professed follower of Christ, than self-confidence, with disregard to warnings, and contempt of danger. Unless we watch and pray always, we may be drawn in the course of the day into those sins which we were in the morning most resolved against. If believers were left to themselves, they would fall; but they are kept by the power of God, and the prayer of Christ. Our Lord gave notice of a very great change of circumstances now approaching. The disciples must not expect that their friends would be kind to them as they had been. Therefore, he that has a purse, let him take it, for he may need it. They must now expect that their enemies would be more fierce than they had been, and they would need weapons. At the time the apostles understood Christ to mean real weapons, but he spake only of the weapons of the spiritual warfare. The sword of the Spirit is the sword with which the disciples of Christ must furnish themselves.

39-46 Every description which the evangelists give of the state of mind in which our Lord entered upon this conflict, proves the tremendous nature of the assault, and the perfect foreknowledge of its terrors possessed by the meek and lowly Jesus. Here are three things not in the other evangelists.
1. When Christ was in his agony, there appeared to him an angel from heaven, strengthening him. It was a part of his humiliation that he was thus strengthened by a ministering spirit.
2. Being in agony, he prayed more earnestly. Prayer, though never out of season, is in a special manner seasonable when we are in an agony.
3. In this agony his sweat was as it were great drops of blood falling down. This showed the travail of his soul. We should pray also to be enabled to resist unto the shedding of our blood, striving against sin, if ever called to it. When next you dwell in imagination upon the delights of some favorite sin, think of its effects as you behold them here! See its fearful effects in the garden of Gethsemane, and desire, by the help of God, deeply to hate and to forsake that enemy, to ransom sinners from whom the Redeemer prayed, agonized, and bled.

desirable things will come to me afterwards, if I sit down at Jesus' feet. So near the source of all good things, it will be easy to be enriched with all knowledge and grace, but our first business is to get there, and by the Holy Spirit's blessing we may come there without either the deep experience or the elevated feelings we have described; we may come just as we are, all guilty and lost, and submit ourselves to the Savior. Having done that, we are in the best position for spiritual attainments—yea, they shall surely be ours. Let the heart yield itself to our sole reliance and sure confidence, it is well with us: we have all that is needful, and the pledge of all that is desirable.

Tell us it is a necessity, and everything else must give way: necessity overrules all else. Now, what is it that sitting at Jesus' feet is a necessity? It is so, because it is needful for us to have our sins forgiven; but Jesus will never forgive the unhumbled rebel. If he will not take Jesus to be a Master, the sinner cannot have him to be a Savior. As long as we rebel against him, we cannot be saved by him. Submission, by repentance and faith, we must have, or our transgressions will remain upon us to our everlasting ruin. It is necessary, because we must have our inbred sins overcome; but none can stay corruption in a many but Christ, who has come to destroy the work of the devil, and to save his people from their sins. Jesus, the seed of the woman, is the only power that can crush the serpent's head. Only at the feet of Jesus can the divine power be gained which works in us holiness and sanctifies us practically; therefore, as you must be purified or you cannot enter heaven, you must come to Jesus' feet. Moreover, it is at the feet of Jesus that the soul's ignorance is removed; and since ignorance concerning ourselves and our God must be taken from us, we must be taught of him. God is "our light and our salvation;" our light first, and our salvation in consequence. We must have the light. The spiritually blind man cannot enter heaven, he must have his eyes opened, but Jesus alone can work that miracle of grace. Neither can we receive true light except from him, for he is "the true light, that lighteth every man that cometh into the world;" none are ever enlightened, except by him. "In him is light—all light; and the light is the light of men." As God is the mind of the world, he who has not God is demented; and as Christ is the light of the world, he that believes not in him abideth in darkness even until now. We must come, then, and yield ourselves unreservedly to Jesus, worshiping him,

10 And he said unto them, Behold, when ye are entered into the city, there shall a man meet you, bearing a pitcher of water; follow him into the house where he entereth in.

11 And ye shall say unto the goodman of the house, The Master saith unto thee, Where is the guestchamber, where I shall eat the passover with my disciples?

12 And he shall shew you a large upper room furnished: there make ready.

13 And they went, and found as he had said unto them: and they made ready the passover.

14 And when the hour was come, he sat down, and the twelve apostles with him.

15 And he said unto them, With desire I have desired to eat this passover with you before I suffer:

16 For I say unto you, I will not any more eat thereof, until it be fulfilled in the kingdom of God.

17 And he took the cup, and gave thanks, and said, Take this, and divide it among yourselves:

18 For I say unto you, I will not drink of the fruit of the vine, until the kingdom of God shall come.

19 And he took bread, and gave thanks, and brake it, and gave unto them, saying, This is my body which is given for you: this do in remembrance of me.

20 Likewise also the cup after supper, saying, This cup is the new testament in my blood, which is shed for you.

21 But, behold, the hand of him that betrayeth me is with me on the table.

22 And truly the Son of man goeth, as it was determined: but woe unto that man by whom he is betrayed!

23 And they began to inquire among themselves, which of them it was that should do this thing.

24 And there was also a strife among them, which of them should be accounted the greatest.

25 And he said unto them, The kings of the Gentiles exercise lordship over them; and they that exercise authority upon them are called benefactors.

26 But ye shall not be so: but he that is greatest among you, let him be as the younger; and he that is chief, as he that doth serve.

27 For whether is greater, he that sitteth at meat, or he that serveth? is not he that sitteth at meat? but I am among you as he that serveth.

28 Ye are they which have continued with me in my temptations.

29 And I appoint unto you a kingdom, as my Father hath appointed unto me;

30 That ye may eat and drink at my table in my kingdom, and sit on thrones judging the twelve tribes of Israel.

31 And the Lord said, Simon, Simon, behold, Satan hath desired to have you, that he may sift you as wheat:

32 But I have prayed for thee, that thy faith fail not: and when thou art converted, strengthen thy brethren.

33 And he said unto him, Lord, I am ready to go with thee, both into prison, and to death.

34 And he said, I tell thee, Peter, the cock shall not crow this day, before that thou shalt thrice deny that thou knowest me.

35 And he said unto them, When I sent you without purse, and scrip, and shoes, lacked ye any thing? And they said, Nothing.

36 Then said he unto them, But now, he that hath a purse, let him take it, and likewise his scrip: and he that hath no sword, let him sell his garment, and buy one.

37 For I say unto you, that this that is written must yet be accomplished in me, And he was reckoned among the trans-

Church, that he might institute the grand memorial of his death.

16. For I will not eat thereof any more – That is, it will be the last I shall eat with you before I die. The kingdom of God did not properly commence till his resurrection. Then was fulfilled what was typified by the Passover.

17. And he took the cup – That cup which used to be brought at the beginning of the paschal solemnity, and said, Take this and divide it among yourselves; for I will not drink – As if he had said, Do not expect me to drink of it: I will drink no more before I die.

19. And he took bread – Namely, some time after, when supper was ended, wherein they had eaten the paschal lamb. This is my body – As he had just now celebrated the paschal supper, which was called the Passover, so in like figurative language, he calls this bread his body. And this circumstance of itself was sufficient to prevent any mistake, as if this bread was his real body, any more than the paschal lamb was really the Passover.

20. This cup is the New Testament – Here is an undeniable figure, whereby the cup is put for the wine in the cup. And this is called, The New Testament in Christ's blood, which could not possibly mean, that it was the New Testament itself, but only the seal of it, and the sign of that blood which was shed to confirm it.

21. The hand of him that betrayeth me is with me on the table – It is evident Christ spake these words before he instituted the Lord's Supper: for all the other evangelists mention the sop, immediately after receiving which he went out: John xiii, 30. Nor did he return any more, till he came into the garden to betray his Master. Now this could not be dipped or given, but while the meat was on the table. But this was all removed before that bread and cup were brought.

24. There was also a contention among them – It is highly probable, this was the same dispute which is mentioned by St. Matthew and St. Mark: and consequently, though it is related here, it happened some time before.

25. They that exercise the most arbitrary authority over them, have from their flatterers the vain title of benefactors.

26. But ye are to be benefactors to mankind, not by governing, but by serving.

27. For – This he proves by his own example. I am in the midst of you – Just now: see with your eyes. I take no state upon me, but sit in the midst, on a level with the lowest of you.

28. Ye have continued with me in my temptations – And all his life was nothing else, particularly from his entering on his public ministry.

29. And I – Will preserve you in all your temptations, till ye enter into the kingdom of glory: appoint to you – By these very words. Not a primacy to one, but a kingdom to every one: on the same terms: as my Father hath

47-53 Nothing can be a greater affront or grief to the Lord Jesus, than to be betrayed by those who profess to be his followers, and say that they love him. Many instances there are, of Christ's being betrayed by those who, under the form of godliness, fight against the power of it. Jesus here gave an illustrious example of his own rule of doing good to those that hate us, as afterwards he did of praying for those that despitefully use us. Corrupt nature warps our conduct to extremes; we should seek for the Lord's direction before we act in difficult circumstances. Christ was willing to wait for his triumphs till his warfare was accomplished, and we must be so too. But the hour and the power of darkness were short, and such the triumphs of the wicked always will be.

54-62 Peter's fall was his denying that he knew Christ, and was his disciple; disowning him because of distress and danger. He that has once told a lie, is strongly tempted to persist: the beginning of that sin, like strife, is as the letting forth of water. The Lord turned and looked upon Peter.
1. It was a convincing look. Jesus turned and looked upon him, as if he should say, Dost thou not know me, Peter?
2. It was a chiding look. Let us think with what a rebuking countenance Christ may justly look upon us when we have sinned.
3. It was an expostulating look. Thou who wast the most forward to confess me to be the Son of God, and didst solemnly promise thou wouldest never disown me!
4. It was a compassionate look. Peter, how art thou fallen and undone if I do not help thee!
5. It was a directing look, to go and bethink himself.
6. It was a significant look; it signified the conveying of grace to Peter's heart, to enable him to repent. The grace of God works in and by the word of God, brings that to mind, and sets that home upon the conscience, and so gives the soul the happy turn. Christ looked upon the chief priests, and made no impression upon them as he did on Peter. It was not the mere look from Christ, but the Divine grace with it, that restored Peter.

63-71 Those that condemned Jesus for a blasphemer, were the vilest blasphemers. He referred them to his second coming, for the full proof of his being the Christ, to their confusion, since they would not admit the proof of it to their conviction. He owns himself to be the Son of God, though he knew he should suffer for it. Upon this they ground his condemnation. Their eyes being blinded, they rush on. Let us meditate on this amazing transaction, and consider Him who endured such contradiction of sinners against himself.

trusting him, and obeying him—in a word, we must sit at his feet, and hear his word; otherwise, we shall abide in darkness and death.

In order to enter heaven, it is necessary that our nature should become like the nature of Christ. This earth is for those who bear the image of the first Adam; but the new heaven and the new earth are for those who bear the image of the second Adam.. We must, by some means, acquire the nature of the second and heavenly Adam, and this must be wrought in us by regeneration, and developed by acquaintance with him. By sitting at his feet, and beholding him, we become changed into the same image from glory to glory even as by the Spirit of the Lord. If we reject the Lord Jesus as our trust, teacher, and exemplar, we have no new life, we are not new creatures in Christ, and we can never be admitted within the holy gates where those alone dwell who are fashioned after his likeness. We must, then, sit at his feet; it is absolutely necessary, and, without it, our whole life will be a complete failure; we may make money, but we shall lose our souls; we may gain honor, but shall have come short of the glory of God; we may enjoy pleasure, but we shall forfeit the pleasures which are at God's right hand for evermore; we may have done our country some service, but to our God, and the higher country, we shall have rendered no service, for we cannot serve God if we will not obey Christ. "He that honored not the Son, honored not the Father which hath sent him." This life is a blank, a long rebellion, to the man who submits not to Jesus, and the life for ever hereafter will be darkness and confusion; as darkness itself, a land of sorrow, and of weeping, and of wailing, and of gnashing of teeth, a land of despair, upon which no star shall ever shine, or sun shall ever rise. Woe, woe, woe, woe to the Godless, Christless spirit that passeth across the river of death without a hope. Woe, woe, woe, woe eternally to the soul that will not sit at the feet of Jesus! he shall be trodden beneath his feet in his anger, and crushed in his hot displeasure. God grant that may never be our portion. To sit at Jesus' feet is the one thing needful then.

And, brethren, let me just say, and leave this point, it is needful to every one of you. It is not some of us who must be there, but all. The wisest must become fools to learn of him, or fools they are; the most educated and cultured mind must submit to this further culture, or else it is nothing but a barren waste in his sight. One thing is a necessity to you all, high or low, rich or poor, queen or beggar—you

gressors: for the things concerning me have an end.

38 And they said, Lord, behold, here are two swords. And he said unto them, It is enough.

39 And he came out, and went, as he was wont, to the mount of Olives; and his disciples also followed him.

40 And when he was at the place, he said unto them, Pray that ye enter not into temptation.

41 And he was withdrawn from them about a stone's cast, and kneeled down, and prayed,

42 Saying, Father, if thou be willing, remove this cup from me: nevertheless not my will, but thine, be done.

43 And there appeared an angel unto him from heaven, strengthening him.

44 And being in an agony he prayed more earnestly: and his sweat was as it were great drops of blood falling down to the ground.

45 And when he rose up from prayer, and was come to his disciples, he found them sleeping for sorrow,

46 And said unto them, Why sleep ye? rise and pray, lest ye enter into temptation.

47 And while he yet spake, behold a multitude, and he that was called Judas, one of the twelve, went before them, and drew near unto Jesus to kiss him.

48 But Jesus said unto him, Judas, betrayest thou the Son of man with a kiss?

49 When they which were about him saw what would follow, they said unto him, Lord, shall we smite with the sword?

50 And one of them smote the servant of the high priest, and cut off his right ear.

51 And Jesus answered and said, Suffer ye thus far. And he touched his ear, and healed him.

52 Then Jesus said unto the chief priests, and captains of the temple, and the elders, which were come to him, Be ye come out, as against a thief, with swords and staves?

53 When I was daily with you in the temple, ye stretched forth no hands against me: but this is your hour, and the power of darkness.

54 Then took they him, and led him, and brought him into the high priest's house. And Peter followed afar off.

55 And when they had kindled a fire in the midst of the hall, and were set down together, Peter sat down among them.

56 But a certain maid beheld him as he sat by the fire, and earnestly looked upon him, and said, This man was also with him.

57 And he denied him, saying, Woman, I know him not.

58 And after a little while another saw him, and said, Thou art also of them. And Peter said, Man, I am not.

59 And about the space of one hour after another confidently affirmed, saying, Of a truth this fellow also was with him: for he is a Galilean.

60 And Peter said, Man, I know not what thou sayest. And immediately, while he yet spake, the cock crew.

61 And the Lord turned, and looked upon Peter. And Peter remembered the word of the Lord, how he had said unto him, Before the cock crow, thou shalt deny me thrice.

62 And Peter went out, and wept bitterly.

63 And the men that held Jesus mocked him, and smote him.

64 And when they had blindfolded him, they struck him on the face, and asked him, saying, Prophesy, who is it that smote thee?

65 And many other things blasphemously spake they against him.

66 And as soon as it was day, the elders of the people and the chief priests and the scribes came together, and led him

appointed to me – Who have fought and conquered.

30. That ye may eat and drink at my table – That is, that ye may enjoy the highest happiness, as guests, not as servants. These expressions seem to be primarily applicable to the twelve apostles, and secondarily, to all Christ's servants and disciples, whose spiritual powers, honors, and delights, are here represented in figurative terms, with respect to their advancement both in the kingdom of grace and of glory.

31. Satan hath desired to have you – My apostles, that he might sift you as wheat – Try you to the uttermost.

32. But I have prayed for thee – Who wilt be in the greatest danger of all: that thy faith fail not – Altogether: and when thou art returned – From thy flight, strengthen thy brethren – All that are weak in faith; perhaps scandalized at thy fall.

34. It shall not be the time of cock crowing this day – The common time of cock crowing (which is usually about three in the morning) probably did not come till after the cock which Peter heard had crowed twice, if not oftener.

35. When I sent you – lacked ye any thing – Were ye not born above all want and danger?

36. But now – You will be quite in another situation. You will want every thing. He that hath no sword, let him sell his garment and buy one – It is plain, this is not to be taken literally. It only means, This will be a time of extreme danger.

37. The things which are written concerning me have an end – Are now drawing to a period; are upon the point of being accomplished. Isaiah liii, 12.

38. Here are two swords – Many of Galilee carried them when they traveled, to defend themselves against robbers and assassins, who much infested their roads. But did the apostles need to seek such defense? And he said; It is enough – I did not mean literally, that every one of you must have a sword.

39. Matt. xxvi, 30.

40. The place – The garden of Gethsemane.

43. Strengthening him – Lest his body should sink and die before the time.

44. And being in an agony – Probably just now grappling with the powers of darkness: feeling the weight of the wrath of God, and at the same time surrounded with a mighty host of devils, who exercised all their force and malice to persecute and distract his wounded spirit. He prayed more earnestly – Even with stronger cries and tears: and his sweat – As cold as the weather was, was as it were great drops of blood – Which, by the vehement distress of his soul, were forced out of the pores, in so great a quantity as afterward united in large, thick, grumous drops, and even fell to the ground.

48. Betrayest thou the Son of man – He whom thou knowest to be the Son of man, the Christ?

49. Seeing what would follow – That they were just

LUKE 23

Christ before Pilate. (1-5)
Christ before Herod. (6-12)
Barabbas preferred to Christ. (13-25)
Christ speaks of the destruction of Jerusalem. (26-31)
The crucifixion, The repentant malefactor. (32-43)
The death of Christ. (44-49)
The burial of Christ. (50-56)

1-5 Pilate well understood the difference between armed forces and our Lord's followers. But instead of being softened by Pilate's declaration of his innocence, and considering whether they were not bringing the guilt of innocent blood upon themselves, the Jews were the more angry. The Lord brings his designs to a glorious end, even by means of those who follow the devices of their own hearts. Thus all parties joined, so as to prove the innocence of Jesus, who was the atoning sacrifice for our sins.

6-12 Herod had heard many things of Jesus in Galilee, and out of curiosity longed to see him. The poorest beggar that asked a miracle for the relief of his necessity, was never denied; but this proud prince, who asked for a miracle only to gratify his curiosity, is refused. He might have seen Christ and his wondrous works in Galilee, and would not, therefore it is justly said, Now he would see them, and shall not. Herod sent Christ again to Pilate: the friendships of wicked men are often formed by union in wickedness. They agree in little, except in enmity to God, and contempt of Christ.

13-25 The fear of man brings many into this snare, that they will do an unjust thing, against their consciences, rather than get into trouble. Pilate declares Jesus innocent, and has a mind to release him; yet, to please the people, he would punish him as an evildoer. If no fault be found in him, why chastise him? Pilate yielded at length; he had not courage to go against so strong a stream. He delivered Jesus to their will, to be crucified.

26-31 We have here the blessed Jesus, the Lamb of God, led as a lamb to the slaughter, to the sacrifice. Though many reproached and reviled him, yet some pitied him. But the death of Christ was his victory and triumph over his enemies: it was our deliverance, the purchase of eternal life for us. Therefore weep not for him, but let us weep for our own sins, and the sins of our children, which caused his death; and weep for fear of the miseries we shall bring upon ourselves, if we slight his love, and reject his grace. If God delivered him up to such sufferings as these, because he was made a sacrifice for sin, what will he do with sinners themselves, who make themselves a dry tree, a corrupt and wicked generation, and good for nothing! The bitter sufferings of our Lord Jesus should make us stand in awe of the justice of God. The best

must sit at Jesus' feet; and all alike must accept his teaching, or you know nothing that can save you.

Some things in this world are necessary, after a measure, but this is necessary without measure; infinitely needful is it that you sit at Jesus' feet, needful now, needful in life; needful in life for peace, in death for rest, and in eternity for bliss. This is needful always. Many things have their uses for youth, others come not into value till old age; but one thing, the one thing, is needful for childhood, and needful for palsied age; it is needful for the ruddy cheek, and the active limb, and needful everywhere and always. In the highest and most emphatic sense, "one thing is needful."

III. Thus much about the necessity, the next word is CONCENTRATION: "One thing is needful." I am glad it says "one thing," because a division of ends and objects is always weakening. A man cannot follow two things well. Our life-flood suffices not to fill two streams or three; there is only enough water, as it were, in our life's brooklet, to turn one wheel. It is a great pity when a man fritters away his energies by being "everything by turns, and nothing long;" trying all things, and mastering nothing. Oh soul, it is well for thee that there is only one thing in this world that is absolutely necessary, give thy whole soul to that. If other things are necessary in a secondary place, "Seek first the kingdom of God and his righteousness, and all these shall be added unto you."

One thing is needful, and this is well arranged, for we cannot follow two things. If Christ be one of them, we cannot follow another. Is it not written, "No man can serve two masters, either he will hate the one and love the other, or cleave to the one and despise the other. Ye cannot serve God and mammon." Not only would it be very weakening to you to attempt to serve both, but it is absolutely impossible that you should do so. Jesus Christ is a monopolizer of human hearts, he will never accept a portion of our manhood. He bought us altogether, and he will have the whole of our personality. Christ must be everything, or he will be nothing. He does not love Christ who loves anything as well as Christ, neither does he trust him who trusts in anything besides. Christ must reign alone. "Jesus only," must be the motto of our spirits. It is well for us, therefore, that only one thing is necessary, for only one thing is possible.

It is an unspeakable mercy that the one

into their council, saying,

67 Art thou the Christ? tell us. And he said unto them, If I tell you, ye will not believe:

68 And if I also ask you, ye will not answer me, nor let me go.

69 Hereafter shall the Son of man sit on the right hand of the power of God.

70 Then said they all, Art thou then the Son of God? And he said unto them, Ye say that I am.

71 And they said, What need we any further witness? for we ourselves have heard of his own mouth.

LUKE 23

1 And the whole multitude of them arose, and led him unto Pilate.

2 And they began to accuse him, saying, We found this fellow perverting the nation, and forbidding to give tribute to Cesar, saying that he himself is Christ a King.

3 And Pilate asked him, saying, Art thou the King of the Jews? And he answered him and said, Thou sayest it.

4 Then said Pilate to the chief priests and to the people, I find no fault in this man.

5 And they were the more fierce, saying, He stirreth up the people, teaching throughout all Jewry, beginning from Galilee to this place.

6 When Pilate heard of Galilee, he asked whether the man were a Galilean.

7 And as soon as he knew that he belonged unto Herod's jurisdiction, he sent him to Herod, who himself also was at Jerusalem at that time.

8 And when Herod saw Jesus, he was exceeding glad: for he was desirous to see him of a long season, because he had heard many things of him; and he hoped to have seen some miracle done by him.

9 Then he questioned with him in many words; but he answered him nothing.

10 And the chief priests and scribes stood and vehemently accused him.

11 And Herod with his men of war set him at nought, and mocked him, and arrayed him in a gorgeous robe, and sent him again to Pilate.

12 And the same day Pilate and Herod were made friends together: for before they were at enmity between themselves.

13 And Pilate, when he had called together the chief priests and the rulers and the people,

14 Said unto them, Ye have brought this man unto me, as one that perverteth the people: and, behold, I, having examined him before you, have found no fault in this man touching those things whereof ye accuse him:

15 No, nor yet Herod: for I sent you to him; and, lo, nothing worthy of death is done unto him.

16 I will therefore chastise him, and release him.

17 (For of necessity he must release one unto them at the feast.)

18 And they cried out all at once, saying, Away with this man, and release unto us Barabbas:

19 (Who for a certain sedition made in the city, and for murder, was cast into prison.)

20 Pilate therefore, willing to release Jesus, spake again to them.

21 But they cried, saying, Crucify him, crucify him.

22 And he said unto them the third time, Why, what evil hath he done? I have found no cause of death in him: I will there-

going to seize him. Matt. xxvi, 51; Mark xiv, 47.

51. Suffer me at least to have my hands at liberty thus far, while I do one more act of mercy.

52. Jesus said to the chief priests, and captains, and the elders who were come – And all these came of their own accord: the soldiers and servants were sent.

53. This is your hour – Before which ye could not take me: and the power of darkness – The time when Satan has power.

54. Matt. xxvi, 57; Mark xiv, 53; John xviii, 12.

58. Another man saw him and said – Observe here, in order to reconcile the four evangelists, that divers persons concurred in charging Peter with belonging to Christ.

1. The maid that led him in, afterward seeing him at the fire, first put the question to him, and then positively affirmed, that he was with Christ.

2. Another maid accused him to the standers by, and gave occasion to the man here mentioned, to renew the charge against him, which caused the second denial.

3. Others of the company took notice of his being a Galilean, and were seconded by the kinsman of Malchus, who affirmed he had seen him in the garden. And this drew on the third denial.

59. And about one hour after – So he did not recollect himself in all that time.

63. Matt. xxvi, 67; Mark xiv, 65.

64. And having blindfolded him, they struck him on the face – This is placed by St. Matthew and Mark, after the council's condemning him. Probably he was abused in the same manner, both before and after his condemnation.

65. Many other things blasphemously spake they against him – The expression is remarkable. They charged him with blasphemy, because he said he was the Son of God: but the evangelist fixes that charge on them, because he really was so.

66. Matt. xxvi, 63; Mark xiv, 61.

70. They all said, Art thou then the Son of God? – Both these, the Son of God, and the Son of man, were known titles of the Messiah; the one taken from his Divine, and the other from his human nature.

LUKE 23

1. Matt. xxvii, 1; Mark xv, 1; John xviii, 28.

4. Then said Pilate – After having heard his defense – I find no fault in this man – I do not find that he either asserts or attempts any thing seditious or injurious to Cesar.

5. He stirreth up the people, beginning from Galilee – Probably they mentioned Galilee to alarm Pilate, because the Galileans were notorious for sedition and rebellion.

7. He sent him to Herod – As his proper judge.

MATTHEW HENRY

CHARLES H. SPURGEON

saints, compared with Christ, are dry trees; if he suffer, why may not they expect to suffer? And what then shall the damnation of sinners be! Even the sufferings of Christ preach terror to obstinate transgressors.

32-43 As soon as Christ was fastened to the cross, he prayed for those who crucified him. The great thing he died to purchase and procure for us, is the forgiveness of sin. This he prays for. Jesus was crucified between two thieves; in them were shown the different effects the cross of Christ would have upon the children of men in the preaching the gospel. One malefactor was hardened to the last. No troubles of themselves will change a wicked heart. The other was softened at the last: he was snatched as a brand out of the burning, and made a monument of Divine mercy. This gives no encouragement to any to put off repentance to their deathbeds, or to hope that they shall then find mercy. It is certain that true repentance is never too late; but it is as certain that late repentance is seldom true. None can be sure they shall have time to repent at death, but every man may be sure he cannot have the advantages this penitent thief had. We shall see the case to be singular, if we observe the uncommon effects of God's grace upon this man. He reproved the other for railing on Christ. He owned that he deserved what was done to him. He believed Jesus to have suffered wrongfully. Observe his faith in this prayer. Christ was in the depth of disgrace, suffering as a deceiver, and not delivered by his Father. He made this profession before the wonders were displayed which put honor on Christ's sufferings, and startled the centurion. He believed in a life to come, and desired to be happy in that life; not like the other thief, to be only saved from the cross. Observe his humility in this prayer. All his request is, Lord, remember me; quite referring it to Jesus in what way to remember him. Thus he was humbled in true repentance, and he brought forth all the fruits for repentance his circumstances would admit. Christ upon the cross, is gracious like Christ upon the throne. Though he was in the greatest struggle and agony, yet he had pity for a poor penitent. By this act of grace we are to understand that Jesus Christ died to open the kingdom of heaven to all penitent, obedient believers. It is a single instance in Scripture; it should teach us to despair of none, and that none should despair of themselves; but lest it should be abused, it is contrasted with the awful state of the other thief, who died hardened in unbelief, though a crucified Savior was so near him. Be sure that in general men die as they live.

44-49 We have here the death of Christ magnified by the wonders that attended it, and his death explained by the words with which he breathed out his soul. He was willing to offer himself. Let us seek to glorify God by true repentance and conversion; by protesting against those who crucify the Savior; by a sober,

thing needful is a very simple one. Little child, thou couldst not climb the mountain, but thou canst sit down at Jesus' feet; thou canst not understand hard doctrine, but thou canst love him who said, "Suffer the little children to come unto me, and forbid them not, for of such is the kingdom of heaven." Unlearned man, thou who hast no time to acquire earthly lore, if the one thing needful were something that belonged only to the learned, alas for thee; but if thou canst not teach, it is not needful that thou shouldst, it is only needful that thou shouldst learn. Take the Incarnate Wisdom to be thy Master, and sit as a little child at his feet to learn with all thine heart. That is all he asks of thee. Men will have it that they must do something to be saved. They must fret and worry like Martha, but after all, the right way is to end your doing and fretting by sitting down content with Jesus' doing, satisfied with his righteousness and with the merit of his precious blood. The one thing needful is very easy, except to proud hearts, which cannot brook to accept everything gratis, and to be beholden to sovereign mercy. To the poor in spirit it is not only simple but sweet to sit at Jesus' feet. I would be nothing but what he makes me, I would have nothing but what he gives me, I would ask nothing but what he promises me, I would trust in nothing but what he has done for me, and I would desire nothing but what he has prepared for me. To sit at Jesus' feet in humble submission and quiet rest, he the master and I the little child, I the vessel waiting to be filled, and he my fullness, I the mown grass, and he the falling dew, I the rain drop, and he the sun that makes me glisten in life with diamond brilliance, and then exhales me in death to be absorbed in him; this is all in all to me.

Let us remark that, though this is only one thing, and so concentrated, yet it is also comprehensive and contains many things. Imagine not that to sit at Jesus' feet is a very small, unmeaning thing. It means peace, for they who submit to Jesus find peace through his precious blood. It means holiness, for those who learn of Jesus learn no sin, but are instructed in things lovely and of good repute. It means strength, for they that sit with Jesus, and feed upon him, are girded with his strength; the joy of the Lord is their strength. It means wisdom, for they that learn of the Son of God understand more than the ancients because they keep his statutes. It means zeal, for the love of Christ fires hearts that live upon it, and they that are much with Jesus become

fore chastise him, and let him go.

23 And they were instant with loud voices, requiring that he might be crucified. And the voices of them and of the chief priests prevailed.

24 And Pilate gave sentence that it should be as they required.

25 And he released unto them him that for sedition and murder was cast into prison, whom they had desired; but he delivered Jesus to their will.

26 And as they led him away, they laid hold upon one Simon, a Cyrenian, coming out of the country, and on him they laid the cross, that he might bear it after Jesus.

27 And there followed him a great company of people, and of women, which also bewailed and lamented him.

28 But Jesus turning unto them said, Daughters of Jerusalem, weep not for me, but weep for yourselves, and for your children.

29 For, behold, the days are coming, in the which they shall say, Blessed are the barren, and the wombs that never bare, and the paps which never gave suck.

30 Then shall they begin to say to the mountains, Fall on us; and to the hills, Cover us.

31 For if they do these things in a green tree, what shall be done in the dry?

32 And there were also two other, malefactors, led with him to be put to death.

33 And when they were come to the place, which is called Calvary, there they crucified him, and the malefactors, one on the right hand, and the other on the left.

34 Then said Jesus, Father, forgive them; for they know not what they do. And they parted his raiment, and cast lots.

35 And the people stood beholding. And the rulers also with them derided him, saying, He saved others; let him save himself, if he be Christ, the chosen of God.

36 And the soldiers also mocked him, coming to him, and offering him vinegar,

37 And saying, If thou be the king of the Jews, save thyself.

38 And a superscription also was written over him in letters of Greek, and Latin, and Hebrew, THIS IS THE KING OF THE JEWS.

39 And one of the malefactors which were hanged railed on him, saying, If thou be Christ, save thyself and us.

40 But the other answering rebuked him, saying, Dost not thou fear God, seeing thou art in the same condemnation?

41 And we indeed justly; for we receive the due reward of our deeds: but this man hath done nothing amiss.

42 And he said unto Jesus, Lord, remember me when thou comest into thy kingdom.

43 And Jesus said unto him, Verily I say unto thee, To day shalt thou be with me in paradise.

44 And it was about the sixth hour, and there was a darkness over all the earth until the ninth hour.

45 And the sun was darkened, and the veil of the temple was rent in the midst.

46 And when Jesus had cried with a loud voice, he said, Father, into thy hands I commend my spirit: and having said thus, he gave up the ghost.

47 Now when the centurion saw what was done, he glorified God, saying, Certainly this was a righteous man.

48 And all the people that came together to that sight, beholding the things which were done, smote their breasts, and returned.

49 And all his acquaintance, and the women that followed him from Galilee, stood afar off, beholding these things.

8. He had been long desirous to see him – Out of mere curiosity.

9. He questioned him – Probably concerning the miracles which were reported to have been wrought by him.

11. Herod set him at nought – Probably judging him to be a fool, because he answered nothing. In a splendid robe – In royal apparel; intimating that he feared nothing from this king.

15. He hath done nothing worthy of death – According to the judgment of Herod also.

16. I will therefore chastise him – Here Pilate began to give ground, which only encouraged them to press on. Matt. xxvii, 15; Mark xv, 6; John xviii, 39.

22. He said to them the third time, Why, what evil hath he done? – As Peter, a disciple of Christ, dishonored him by denying him thrice, so Pilate, a heathen, honored Christ, by thrice owning him to be innocent.

26. Matt. xxvii, 31; Mark xv, 21; John xix, 16.

30. Hosea x, 8.

31. If they do these things in the green tree, what shall be done in the dry? – Our Lord makes use of a proverbial expression, frequent among the Jews, who compare a good man to a green tree, and a bad man to a dead one: as if he had said, If an innocent person suffer thus, what will become of the wicked? Of those who are as ready for destruction as dry wood for the fire?

34. Then said Jesus – Our Lord passed most of the time on the cross in silence: yet seven sentences which he spoke thereon are recorded by the four evangelists, though no one evangelist has recorded them all. Hence it appears that the four Gospels are, as it were, four parts, which, joined together, make one symphony. Sometimes one of these only, sometimes two or three, sometimes all sound together. Father – So he speaks both in the beginning and at the end of his sufferings on the cross: Forgive them – How striking is this passage! While they are actually nailing him to the cross, he seems to feel the injury they did to their own souls more than the wounds they gave him; and as it were to forget his own anguish out of a concern for their own salvation. And how eminently was his prayer heard! It procured forgiveness for all that were penitent, and a suspension of vengeance even for the impenitent.

35. If thou be the Christ; ver. 37. If thou be the king – The priests deride the name of Messiah: the soldiers the name of king.

38. Matt. xxvii, 37; Mark xv, 26; John xix, 19.

39. And one of the malefactors reviled him – St. Matthew says, the robbers: St. Mark, they that were crucified with him, reviled him. Either therefore St. Matthew and Mark put the plural for the singular (as the best authors sometimes do) or both reviled him at the first, till one of them felt "the overwhelming power of saving grace."

40. The other rebuked him – What a surprising degree

righteous, and godly life; and by employing our talents in the service of Him who died for us and rose again.

50-56 Many, though they do not make any show in outward profession, yet, like Joseph of Arimathea, will be far more ready to do real service, when there is occasion, than others who make a greater noise. Christ was buried in haste, because the Sabbath drew on. Weeping must not hinder sowing. Though they were in tears for the death of their Lord, yet they must prepare to keep holy the Sabbath. When the Sabbath draws on, there must be preparation. Our worldly affairs must be so ordered, that they may not hinder us from our Sabbath work; and our holy affections so stirred up, that they may carry us on in it. In whatever business we engage, or however our hearts may be affected, let us never fail to get ready for, and to keep holy, the day of sacred rest, which is the Lord's day.

LUKE 24

The resurrection of Christ. (1-12)
He appears to two disciples on the way to Emmaus. (13-27)
And makes himself known to them. (28-35)
Christ appears to the other disciples. (36-49)
His ascension. (50-53)

1-12 See the affection and respect the women showed to Christ, after he was dead and buried. Observe their surprise when they found the stone rolled away, and the grave empty. Christians often perplex themselves about that with which they should comfort and encourage themselves. They look rather to find their Master in his grave-clothes, than angels in their shining garments. The angels assure them that he is risen from the dead; is risen by his own power. These angels from heaven bring not any new gospel, but remind the women of Christ's words, and teach them how to apply them. We may wonder that these disciples, who believed Jesus to be the Son of God and the true Messiah, who had been so often told that he must die, and rise again, and then enter into his glory, who had seen him more than once raise the dead, yet should be so backward to believe his raising himself. But all our mistakes in religion spring from ignorance or forgetfulness of the words Christ has spoken. Peter now ran to the sepulcher, who so lately ran from his Master. He was amazed. There are many things puzzling and perplexing to us, which would be plain and profitable, if we rightly understood the words of Christ.

13-27 This appearance of Jesus to the two disciples going to Emmaus, happened the same day that he rose from the dead. It well becomes the disciples of

like Jesus, so that the zeal of the Lord's house eats them up. If we say that in an army the one thing needful is loyalty to the sovereign, we know what that means; for the loyal solider will be sure to be obedient to his officers, and if attached to his queen, he will be brave in the day of battle, and do his duty well. If we said that the one thing needful in a family was love, we should not have required a small thing; for love will place husband and wife in their true position; love will produce obedience in children, and diligence in servants. Let love permeate everything, and other virtues will grow out of it, as flowers spring from the soil. So when we say that sitting at Jesus' feet is the one thing needful, we have not uttered a mere truism: it comprehends a world of blessings.

And here would I address a word to the church of God in this country at this present time. She, too, is as Martha, cumbered with much serving. It were her wisdom, and her strength, if she would become more like Mary, and sit at Jesus' feet. Just now we need revival. Oh that God would send it! Oh for a mighty flood of spiritual influences, that would bear the stranded churches right out into a sea of usefulness. But how can we get revival? We shall have it, brethren, when we commune with Christ. When the saints habitually sit at Jesus' feet they will be revived, and of necessity the revival will spread from them, and the hearts of sinners will be touched.

There is great talk now-a-days of union; the walls of the various churches are to be broken down, and the denominations are to be blended. Think not of it in such a fashion; the only union possible, or desirable, is that we all unite to sit at Jesus' feet. It is not allowable that we concede one truth and you another; that is not natural charity, but common treason to Christ. We have no right to yield an atom of the truth of God, under the pretense of charity. Truth is no property of ours; we are only God's stewards, and it behooves us to be faithful to our trust. Neither one church nor another has any right to bate its testimony one jot, if it be true. To alter the statute-book of Christ is blasphemy. True union will come when all the churches learn of Christ, for Christ does not teach two things opposed to each other. There are not two baptisms in the Bible; we shall not find two sets of dogmas diametrically opposite to each other. If we give up the various things that are of man, and hold fast each of us only that which is of God, we shall be united in principle and in doctrine; and "One Lord, one

50 And, behold, there was a man named Joseph, a counselor; and he was a good man, and a just:

51 (The same had not consented to the counsel and deed of them;) he was of Arimathea, a city of the Jews: who also himself waited for the kingdom of God.

52 This man went unto Pilate, and begged the body of Jesus.

53 And he took it down, and wrapped it in linen, and laid it in a sepulcher that was hewn in stone, wherein never man before was laid.

54 And that day was the preparation, and the sabbath drew on.

55 And the women also, which came with him from Galilee, followed after, and beheld the sepulcher, and how his body was laid.

56 And they returned, and prepared spices and ointments; and rested the sabbath day according to the commandment.

LUKE 24

1 Now upon the first day of the week, very early in the morning, they came unto the sepulcher, bringing the spices which they had prepared, and certain others with them.

2 And they found the stone rolled away from the sepulcher.

3 And they entered in, and found not the body of the Lord Jesus.

4 And it came to pass, as they were much perplexed thereabout, behold, two men stood by them in shining garments:

5 And as they were afraid, and bowed down their faces to the earth, they said unto them, Why seek ye the living among the dead?

6 He is not here, but is risen: remember how he spake unto you when he was yet in Galilee,

7 Saying, The Son of man must be delivered into the hands of sinful men, and be crucified, and the third day rise again.

8 And they remembered his words,

9 And returned from the sepulcher, and told all these things unto the eleven, and to all the rest.

10 It was Mary Magdalene, and Joanna, and Mary the mother of James, and other women that were with them, which told these things unto the apostles.

11 And their words seemed to them as idle tales, and they believed them not.

12 Then arose Peter, and ran unto the sepulcher; and stooping down, he beheld the linen clothes laid by themselves, and departed, wondering in himself at that which was come to pass.

13 And, behold, two of them went that same day to a village called Emmaus, which was from Jerusalem about threescore furlongs.

14 And they talked together of all these things which had happened.

15 And it came to pass, that, while they communed together and reasoned, Jesus himself drew near, and went with them.

16 But their eyes were holden that they should not know him.

17 And he said unto them, What manner of communications are these that ye have one to another, as ye walk, and are sad?

18 And the one of them, whose name was Cleopas, answering said unto him, Art thou only a stranger in Jerusalem, and hast not known the things which are come to pass therein these days?

19 And he said unto them, What things? And they said unto him, Concerning Jesus of Nazareth, which was a prophet mighty in deed and word before God and all the people:

was here of repentance, faith, and other graces! And what abundance of good works, in his public confession of his sin, reproof of his fellow criminal, his honorable testimony to Christ, and profession of faith in him, while he was in so disgraceful circumstances as were stumbling even to his disciples! This shows the power of Divine grace. But it encourages none to put off their repentance to the last hour; since, as far as appears, this was the first time this criminal had an opportunity of knowing any thing of Christ, and his conversion was designed to put a peculiar glory on our Savior in his lowest state, while his enemies derided him, and his own disciples either denied or forsook him.

42. Remember me when thou comest – From heaven, in thy kingdom – He acknowledges him a king, and such a king, as after he is dead, can profit the dead. The apostles themselves had not then so clear conceptions of the kingdom of Christ.

43. In paradise – The place where the souls of the righteous remain from death till the resurrection. As if he had said, I will not only remember thee then, but this very day.

44. There was darkness over all the earth – The noontide darkness, covering the sun, obscured all the upper hemisphere. And the lower was equally darkened, the moon being in opposition to the sun, and so receiving no light from it. Matt. xxvii, 45.

45. Mark xv, 38.

46. Father, into thy hands – The Father receives the Spirit of Jesus: Jesus himself the spirits of the faithful.

47. Certainly this was a righteous man – Which implies an approbation of all he had done and taught.

48. All the people – Who had not been actors therein, returned smiting their breasts – In testimony of sorrow.

50. Matt. xxvii, 57; Mark xv, 43; John xix, 38.

LUKE 24

1. Certain others with them – Who had not come from Galilee. Matt. xxviii, 1; Mark xvi, 1; John xx, 1.

4. Behold two – Angels in the form of men. Mary had seen them a little before. They had disappeared on these women's coming to the sepulcher, but now appeared again. St. Matthew and Mark mention only one of them, appearing like a young man.

6. Remember how he spake to you, saying, The Son of man must be delivered – This is only a repetition of the words which our Lord had spoken to them before his passion but it is observable, he never styles himself the Son of man after his resurrection.

13. Mark xvi, 12.

21. Today is the third day – The day he should have risen again, if at all.

25. O foolish – Not understanding the designs and works of God: And slow of heart – Unready to believe

Christ to talk together of his death and resurrection; thus they may improve one another's knowledge, refresh one another's memory, and stir up each other's devout affections. And where but two together are well employed in work of that kind, he will come to them, and make a third. Those who seek Christ, shall find him: he will manifest himself to those that inquire after him; and give knowledge to those who use the helps for knowledge which they have. No matter how it was, but so it was, they did not know him; he so ordering it, that they might the more freely discourse with him. Christ's disciples are often sad and sorrowful, even when they have reason to rejoice; but through the weakness of their faith, they cannot take the comfort offered to them. Though Christ is entered into his state of exaltation, yet he notices the sorrows of his disciples, and is afflicted in their afflictions. Those are strangers in Jerusalem, that know not of the death and sufferings of Jesus. Those who have the knowledge of Christ crucified, should seek to spread that knowledge. Our Lord Jesus reproved them for the weakness of their faith in the Scriptures of the Old Testament. Did we know more of the Divine counsels as far as they are made known in the Scriptures, we should not be subject to the perplexities we often entangle ourselves in. He shows them that the sufferings of Christ were really the appointed way to his glory; but the cross of Christ was that to which they could not reconcile themselves. Beginning at Moses, the first inspired writer of the Old Testament, Jesus expounded to them the things concerning himself. There are many passages throughout all the Scriptures concerning Christ, which it is of great advantage to put together. We cannot go far in any part, but we meet with something that has reference to Christ, some prophecy, some promise, some prayer, some type or other. A golden thread of gospel grace runs through the whole web of the Old Testament. Christ is the best expositor of Scripture; and even after his resurrection, he led people to know the mystery concerning himself, not by advancing new notions, but by showing how the Scripture was fulfilled, and turning them to the earnest study of it.

28-35 If we would have Christ dwell with us, we must be earnest with him. Those that have experienced the pleasure and profit of communion with him, cannot but desire more of his company. He took bread, and blessed it, and brake, and gave to them. This he did with his usual authority and affection, with the same manner, perhaps with the same words. He here teaches us to crave a blessing on every meal. See how Christ by his Spirit and grace makes himself known to the souls of his people. He opens the Scriptures to them. He meets them at his table, in the ordinance of the Lord's supper; is known to them in breaking of bread. But the work is completed by the opening of the eyes of their mind; yet it is but short

faith, one baptism" will once again be emblazoned upon the banners of the church of God. Sit at Jesus' feet, O thou church of Christ, and true unity will come to thee.

We hear a great deal about the necessity of controversy. We ought to be ready to answer all that infidels object, so wise men say. Every absurdity of every fool we are to sit down and reply to, and when this labor of Hercules is accomplished, we are to begin again, for by that time new whimsies will be in men's brains, and new lies will have been begotten. Is this so? Am I to do nothing in winning souls and glorifying God, but to spend all my time in finding wind for the nostrils of the wild asses of the desert? Well, let those do it who please, we believe that the settlement of all controversy in the church and for the church would come from the Lord himself, if we believed more fully in him, and waited more upon him for guidance, and if we preached the gospel more in his own strength, and in his own Spirit.

And, as for missions: we appoint our committees, we amend our plans, and suggest schemes. All very well and good; but missions will never flourish till the church, with regard to missions, sits at Jesus' feet. She will never convert the heathen in her own way: God will give success only when we work in his way. It may be very useful to make translations, and exceedingly beneficial to keep schools; but if I read my Bible right, it is not Christ's way. "Go ye into all the world, and preach the gospel to every creature," is the law of Jesus Christ, and when the church everywhere, at home and abroad, takes more earnestly to preaching, when the testimony of the truth is perpetual and incessant, in simple language, and popular speech, then Christ the Lord will look upon the church that, like Mary, sits at his feet, and say "Thou hast done thy part," and blessing shall follow. "Thy work is done, and I will give thee thy reward."

For us all, beloved, saints and sinners, one thing is needful: that we always sit, like Mary, at the Master's feet.

IV. The last word is IMMEDIATENESS, and there is no need that we say much upon it. One thing is a necessity, a necessity not of the future only, but of today. It is not written, "it shall be needful," on certain coming days, to sit at Jesus' feet; but it is so now. Young man, one thing is necessary to you while yet young; do not postpone it till advanced years. Christian, it is needful for thee today to have communion with Christ; do not think of it as indispensable

20 And how the chief priests and our rulers delivered him to be condemned to death, and have crucified him.

21 But we trusted that it had been he which should have redeemed Israel: and beside all this, to day is the third day since these things were done.

22 Yea, and certain women also of our company made us astonished, which were early at the sepulcher;

23 And when they found not his body, they came, saying, that they had also seen a vision of angels, which said that he was alive.

24 And certain of them which were with us went to the sepulcher, and found it even so as the women had said: but him they saw not.

25 Then he said unto them, O fools, and slow of heart to believe all that the prophets have spoken:

26 Ought not Christ to have suffered these things, and to enter into his glory?

27 And beginning at Moses and all the prophets, he expounded unto them in all the scriptures the things concerning himself.

28 And they drew nigh unto the village, whither they went: and he made as though he would have gone further.

29 But they constrained him, saying, Abide with us: for it is toward evening, and the day is far spent. And he went in to tarry with them.

30 And it came to pass, as he sat at meat with them, he took bread, and blessed it, and brake, and gave to them.

31 And their eyes were opened, and they knew him; and he vanished out of their sight.

32 And they said one to another, Did not our heart burn within us, while he talked with us by the way, and while he opened to us the scriptures?

33 And they rose up the same hour, and returned to Jerusalem, and found the eleven gathered together, and them that were with them,

34 Saying, The Lord is risen indeed, and hath appeared to Simon.

35 And they told what things were done in the way, and how he was known of them in breaking of bread.

36 And as they thus spake, Jesus himself stood in the midst of them, and saith unto them, Peace be unto you.

37 But they were terrified and affrighted, and supposed that they had seen a spirit.

38 And he said unto them, Why are ye troubled? and why do thoughts arise in your hearts?

39 Behold my hands and my feet, that it is I myself: handle me, and see; for a spirit hath not flesh and bones, as ye see me have.

40 And when he had thus spoken, he shewed them his hands and his feet.

41 And while they yet believed not for joy, and wondered, he said unto them, Have ye here any meat?

42 And they gave him a piece of a broiled fish, and of an honeycomb.

43 And he took it, and did eat before them.

44 And he said unto them, These are the words which I spake unto you, while I was yet with you, that all things must be fulfilled, which were written in the law of Moses, and in the prophets, and in the psalms, concerning me.

45 Then opened he their understanding, that they might understand the scriptures,

46 And said unto them, Thus it is written, and thus it behoved Christ to suffer, and to rise from the dead the third day:

47 And that repentance and remission of sins should be

what the prophets have so largely spoken.

26. Ought not Christ – If he would redeem man, and fulfill the prophecies concerning him, to have suffered these things? – These very sufferings which occasion your doubts, are the proofs of his being the Messiah. And to enter into his glory – Which could be done no other way.

28. He made as though he would go farther – Walking forward, as if he was going on; and he would have done it, had they not pressed him to stay.

29. They constrained him – By their importunate entreaties.

30. He took the bread, and blessed, and brake – Just in the same manner as when he instituted his last supper.

31. Their eyes were opened – That is, the supernatural cloud was removed: And he vanished – Went away insensibly.

32. Did not our heart burn within us – Did not we feel an unusual warmth of love! Was not our heart burning, &c.

33. The same hour – Late as it was.

34. The Lord hath appeared to Simon – Before he was seen of the twelve apostles, 1 Cor. xv, 5. He had, in his wonderful condescension and grace, taken an opportunity on the former part of that day (though where, or in what manner, is not recorded) to show himself to Peter, that he might early relieve his distresses and fears, on account of having so shamefully denied his Master.

35. In the breaking of bread – The Lord's Supper.

36. Jesus stood in the midst of them – It was just as easy to his Divine power to open a door undiscernibly, as it was to come in at a door opened by some other hand. Mark xvi, 14, 19; John xx, 19.

40. He showed them his hands and his feet – That they might either see or feel the prints of the nails.

41. While they believed not for joy – They did in some sense believe: otherwise they would not have rejoiced. But their excess of joy prevented a clear, rational belief.

43. He took it and ate before them – Not that he had any need of food; but to give them still farther evidence.

44. And he said – On the day of his ascension. In the law, and the prophets, and the psalms – The prophecies as well as types, relating to the Messiah, are contained either in the books of Moses (usually called the law) in the Psalms, or in the writings of the prophets; little being said directly concerning him in the historical books.

45. Then opened he their understanding, to understand the Scriptures – He had explained them before to the two as they went to Emmaus. But still they understood them not, till he took off the veil from their hearts, by the illumination of his Spirit.

47. Beginning at Jerusalem – This was appointed most graciously and wisely: graciously, as it encouraged the greatest sinners to repent, when they saw that even the

MATTHEW HENRY   CHARLES H. SPURGEON

views we have of Christ in this world, but when we enter heaven, we shall see him forever. They had found the preaching powerful, even when they knew not the preacher. Those Scriptures which speak of Christ, will warm the hearts of his true disciples. That is likely to do most good, which affects us with the love of Jesus in dying for us. It is the duty of those to whom he has shown himself, to let others know what he has done for their souls. It is of great use for the disciples of Christ to compare their experiences, and tell them to each other.

36-49 Jesus appeared in a miraculous manner, assuring the disciples of his peace, though they had so lately forsaken him, and promising spiritual peace with every blessing. Many troublesome thoughts which disquiet our minds, rise from mistakes concerning Christ. All the troublesome thoughts which rise in our hearts at any time, are known to the Lord Jesus, and are displeasing to him. He spake with them on their unreasonable unbelief. Nothing had passed but what was foretold by the prophets, and necessary for the salvation of sinners. And now all men should be taught the nature and necessity of repentance, in order to the forgiveness of their sins. And these blessings were to be sought for, by faith in the name of Jesus. Christ by his Spirit works on the minds of men. Even good men need to have their understandings opened. But that we may have right thoughts of Christ, there needs no more than to be made to understand the Scriptures.

50-53 Christ ascended from Bethany, near the Mount of Olives. There was the garden in which his sufferings began; there he was in his agony. Those that would go to heaven, must ascend thither from the house of sufferings and sorrows. The disciples did not see him rise out of the grave; his resurrection could be proved by their seeing him alive afterwards: but they saw him ascend into heaven; they could not otherwise have a proof of his ascension. He lifted up his hands, and blessed them. He did not go away in displeasure, but in love, he left a blessing behind him. As he arose, so he ascended, by his own power. They worshiped him. This fresh display of Christ's glory drew from them fresh acknowledgments. They returned to Jerusalem with great joy. The glory of Christ is the joy of all true believers, even while they are here in this world. While waiting for God's promises, we must go forth to meet them with our praises. And nothing better prepares the mind for receiving the Holy Ghost. Fears are silenced, sorrows sweetened and allayed, and hopes kept up. And this is the ground of a Christian's boldness at the throne of grace; yea, the Father's throne is the throne of grace to us, because it is also the throne of our Mediator, Jesus Christ. Let us rely on his promises, and plead them. Let us attend his ordinances, praise and bless God for his mercies, set our affections on things

tomorrow or tonight at the communion table; it is needful now. There are dangers thou canst not see, which can only be warded off by present and immediate fellowship with Christ. "One thing is needful." It is not that it was needful in the past, indeed it was so; but it is needful now. It was needful for me in the days of my sinfulness to submit to Christ, it is equally needful for me now. However much you advance, O believer, you never advance beyond this; whatever your experience, or your information, or your ripeness for glory, it is needful still to sit at Jesus' feet. You shall never get into a higher class in the school of wisdom than is the class which Christ teaches; his is the infant class in the school, but it is the highest class also. It is always needful, every moment needful, that we sit at Jesus' feet.

It is needful, I have already said, to the sinner. Life, and health, and peace will come to him when he becomes a disciple of the Crucified. Would God that he might be made so this very morning. There is life in a look at the Crucified One. To depend entirely upon the sinner's Savior is the sinner's salvation. God bring you to his feet, dear hearers.

But it is equally needful for the saint. Covered with the fruits of righteousness, his root must still cling to the riven rock. You must never imagine, whatever you have done or whatever you have attained, that you are to leave Mary's seat; still must you abide there.

It is the one thing needful for the backslider. If you have fallen never so much, you will rise again if you come to the Master submissively and abide with him. It was the mark of the man who had the devil cast out of him, that he was clothed and in his right mind, sitting at the feet of Jesus; it shall show that you, too, are restored when you learn of your Lord. A seat at Jesus' feet is the place for all Christians to die in, they shall sleep sweetly with their heads in Jesus' bosom: it is the place for them to live in, for joy and bliss are there.

Beloved, I desire for myself never again to be worried with the cares of this church, but to take them all to my Master, and wait at his feet. I desire not to be troubled about my preaching, nor to be cumbered about anything beneath the sun, but to leave all these, as he would have me leave them, in his hands. You who are working in the classes, in the school, or anywhere else, I pray you look well to your fellowship with Jesus. You cannot slay the enemy by throwing away your sword, and nearness to Christ is your battle-axe and weapons of war; you have lost your power

preached in his name among all nations, beginning at Jerusalem.

48 And ye are witnesses of these things.

49 And, behold, I send the promise of my Father upon you: but tarry ye in the city of Jerusalem, until ye be endued with power from on high.

50 And he led them out as far as to Bethany, and he lifted up his hands, and blessed them.

51

 And it came to pass, while he blessed them, he was parted from them, and carried up into heaven.

52 And they worshiped him, and returned to Jerusalem with great joy:

53 And were continually in the temple, praising and blessing God. Amen.

murderers of Christ were not excepted from mercy: and wisely, as hereby Christianity was more abundantly attested; the facts being published first on the very spot where they happened.

49. Behold I send the promise – Emphatically so called; the Holy Ghost.

50. He led them out as far as Bethany – Not the town, but the district: to the mount of Olives, Acts i, 12, which stood within the boundaries of Bethany.

51. And while he was blessing them, he was parted from them – It was much more proper that our Lord should ascend into heaven, than that he should rise from the dead, in the sight of the apostles. For his resurrection was proved when they saw him alive after his passion: but they could not see him in heaven while they continued on earth. Please see Notes at Matt. i, 1.

above, and expect the Redeemer's return to complete our happiness. Amen. Even so, Lord Jesus, come quickly.

when you have left your Lord. One thing is needful—let the rest go. What if we have not learning?—what if we have not eloquence? If we live near to Christ, we have something better than all these; if we abide in him, and he abides in us, we shall go and bring forth fruit, and our fruit shall remain; if he abides in us, we shall enjoy heaven on earth, and be daily preparing of that eternal heaven which is to be our portion. "One thing is needful." God grant it to every one of us!—Amen.

John

JOHN 1

1 In the beginning was the Word, and the Word was with God, and the Word was God.

2 The same was in the beginning with God.

3 All things were made by him; and without him was not any thing made that was made.

4 In him was life; and the life was the light of men.

5 And the light shineth in darkness; and the darkness comprehended it not.

6 There was a man sent from God, whose name was John.

7 The same came for a witness, to bear witness of the Light, that all men through him might believe.

8 He was not that Light, but was sent to bear witness of that Light.

9 That was the true Light, which lighteth every man that cometh into the world.

10 He was in the world, and the world was made by him, and the world knew him not.

11 He came unto his own, and his own received him not.

12 But as many as received him, to them gave he power to become the sons of God, even to them that believe on his name:

13 Which were born, not of blood, nor of the will of the flesh, nor of the will of man, but of God.

14 And the Word was made flesh, and dwelt among us, (and we beheld his glory, the glory as of the only begotten of the Father,) full of grace and truth.

15 John bare witness of him, and cried, saying, This was he of whom I spake, He that cometh after me is preferred before me: for he was before me.

16 And of his fullness have all we received, and grace for grace.

17 For the law was given by Moses, but grace and truth came by Jesus Christ.

18 No man hath seen God at any time; the only begotten Son, which is in the bosom of the Father, he hath declared him.

19 And this is the record of John, when the Jews sent priests and Levites from Jerusalem to ask him, Who art thou?

20 And he confessed, and denied not; but confessed, I am not the Christ.

21 And they asked him, What then? Art thou Elias? And he saith, I am not. Art thou that prophet? And he answered, No.

22 Then said they unto him, Who art thou? that we may give an answer to them that sent us. What sayest thou of thyself?

23 He said, I am the voice of one crying in the wilderness, Make straight the way of the Lord, as said the prophet Esaias.

24 And they which were sent were of the Pharisees.

25 And they asked him, and said unto him, Why baptizest thou then, if thou be not that Christ, nor Elias, neither that prophet?

26 John answered them, saying, I baptize with

JOHN 1

1. In the beginning – (Referring to Gen. i, 1, and Prov. viii, 23.) When all things began to be made by the Word: in the beginning of heaven and earth, and this whole frame of created beings, the Word existed, without any beginning. He was when all things began to be, whatsoever had a beginning. The Word – So termed Psalm xxxiii, 6, and frequently by the seventy, and in the Chaldee paraphrase. So that St. John did not borrow this expression from Philo, or any heathen writer. He was not yet named Jesus, or Christ. He is the Word whom the Father begat or spoke from eternity; by whom the Father speaking, maketh all things; who speaketh the Father to us. We have, in the 18th verse, both a real description of the Word, and the reason why he is so called. He is the only begotten Son of the Father, who is in the bosom of the Father, and hath declared him. And the Word was with God – Therefore distinct from God the Father. The word rendered with, denotes a perpetual tendency as it were of the Son to the Father, in unity of essence. He was with God alone; because nothing beside God had then any being. And the Word was God – Supreme, eternal, independent. There was no creature, in respect of which he could be styled God in a relative sense. Therefore he is styled so in the absolute sense. The Godhead of the Messiah being clearly revealed in the Old Testament, (Jer. xxiii, 7; Hosea i, 6; Psalm xxiii, 1,) the other evangelists aim at this, to prove that Jesus, a true man, was the Messiah. But when, at length, some from hence began to doubt of his Godhead, then St. John expressly asserted it, and wrote in this book as it were a supplement to the Gospels, as in the Revelation to the prophets.

2. The same was in the beginning with God – This verse repeats and contracts into one the three points mentioned before. As if he had said, This Word, who was God, was in the beginning, and was with God.

3. All things beside God were made, and all things which were made, were made by the Word. In the first and second verse is described the state of things before the creation: verse 3, In the creation: verse 4, In the time of man's innocency: verse 5, In the time of man's corruption.

4. In him was life – He was the foundation of life to every living thing, as well as of being to all that is. And the life was the light of men – He who is essential life, and the giver of life to all that liveth, was also the light of men; the fountain of wisdom, holiness, and happiness, to man in his original state.

5. And the light shineth in darkness – Shines even on fallen man; but the darkness – Dark, sinful man, perceiveth it not.

6. There was a man – The evangelist now proceeds to him who testified of the light, which he had spoken of in the five preceding verses.

7. The same came for (that is, in order to give) a testimony – The evangelist, with the most strong and tender affection, interweaves his own testimony with that of John, by noble digressions, wherein he explains the office of the Baptist; partly premises and partly subjoins a farther explication to his short sentences. What St. Matthew, Mark, and Luke term the Gospel, in respect of the promise going before, St. John usually terms the testimony, intimating the certain knowledge of the relator; to testify of the light – Of Christ.

MATTHEW HENRY

CHARLES H. SPURGEON

The apostle and evangelist, John, seems to have been the youngest of the twelve. He was especially favored with our Lord's regard and confidence, so as to be spoken of as the disciple whom Jesus loved. He was very sincerely attached to his Master. He exercised his ministry at Jerusalem with much success, and outlived the destruction of that city, agreeably to Christ's prediction, ch. 21:22. History relates that after the death of Christ's mother, John resided chiefly at Ephesus. Towards the close of Domitian's reign he was banished to the isle of Patmos, where he wrote his Revelation. On the accession of Nerva, he was set at liberty, and returned to Ephesus, where it is thought he wrote his Gospel and Epistles, about A. D. 97, and died soon after. The design of this Gospel appears to be to convey to the Christian world, just notions of the real nature, office, and character of that Divine Teacher, who came to instruct and to redeem mankind. For this purpose, John was directed to select for his narrative, those passages of our Savior's life, which most clearly displayed his Divine power and authority; and those of his discourses, in which he spake most plainly of his own nature, and of the power of his death, as an atonement for the sins of the world. By omitting, or only briefly mentioning, the events recorded by the other evangelists, John gave testimony that their narratives are true, and left room for the doctrinal statements already mentioned, and for particulars omitted in the other Gospels, many of which are exceedingly important.

JOHN 1

The Divinity of Christ. (1-5)
His Divine and human nature. (6-14)
John the Baptist's testimony to Christ. (15-18)
John's public testimony concerning Christ. (19-28)
Other testimonies of John concerning Christ. (29-36)
Andrew and another disciple follow Jesus. (37-42)
Philip and Nathanael called. (43-51)

1-5 The plainest reason why the Son of God is called the Word, seems to be, that as our words explain our minds to others, so was the Son of God sent in order to reveal his Father's mind to the world. What the evangelist says of Christ proves that he is God. He asserts his existence in the beginning; His coexistence with the Father. The Word was with God. All things were made by him, and not as an instrument. Without him was not any thing made that was made, from the highest angel to the meanest worm. This shows how well qualified he was for the work of our redemption and salvation. The light of reason, as well as the life of sense, is derived from him, and depends upon him. This eternal Word, this true Light shines, but the darkness comprehends it not. Let us pray without ceasing, that our eyes may be opened to behold this Light, that we may walk in it; and thus be made wise unto salvation, by faith in Jesus Christ.

THE WATERPOTS AT CANA
Sermon number 1556 delivered at the Metropolitan Tabernacle, Newington.

"Jesus saith unto them, Fill the waterpots with water. And they filled them up to the brim."— John 2:7.

YOU KNOW THE NARRATIVE. Jesus was at a wedding feast, and when the wine ran short, he provided for it right bountifully. I do not think that I should do any good if I were to enter upon the discussion as to what sort of wine our Lord Jesus made on this occasion. It was wine, and I am sure it was very good wine, for he would produce nothing quite but the best. Was it wine such as men understand by that word now? It was wine; but there are very few people in this country who ever see, much less drink, any of that beverage. That which goes under the name of wine is not true wine, but a fiery, brandied concoction of which I feel sure that Jesus would not have tasted a drop. The fire-waters and blazing spirits of modern wine manufacturers are very different articles from the juice of the grape, mildly exhilarating, which was the usual wine of more sober centuries. As to the wine such as is commonly used in the East, a person must drink inordinately before he would become intoxicated with it. It would be possible, for there were cases in which men were intoxicated with wine; but, as a rule, intoxication was a rare vice in the Savior's times and in the preceding ages. Had our great Exemplar lived under our present circumstances, surrounded by a sea of deadly drink, which is ruining tens of thousands, I know how he would have acted. I am sure he would not have contributed by word or deed to the rivers of poisonous beverages in which bodies and souls are now being destroyed wholesale. The kind of wine which he made was such that, if there had been no stronger drink in the world, nobody might have thought it necessary to enter any protest against drinking it. It would have done nobody any hurt, be sure of that, or else Jesus our loving Savior would not have made it.

Some have raised a question about the great quantity of wine, for I suppose there must have been no less than one hundred and twenty gallons, and probably more. "They did not want all that," says one, "and even of the weakest kind of wine it would be a deal too much." But you are thinking of an ordinary wedding here, are you not, when there are ten or a dozen, or a score or two, met together in a parlor? An oriental wedding is quite another affair. Even if it be only a village, like Cana of

water: but there standeth one among you, whom ye know not;

27 He it is, who coming after me is preferred before me, whose shoe's latchet I am not worthy to unloose.

28 These things were done in Bethabara beyond Jordan, where John was baptizing.

29 The next day John seeth Jesus coming unto him, and saith, Behold the Lamb of God, which taketh away the sin of the world.

30 This is he of whom I said, After me cometh a man which is preferred before me: for he was before me.

31 And I knew him not: but that he should be made manifest to Israel, therefore am I come baptizing with water.

32 And John bare record, saying, I saw the Spirit descending from heaven like a dove, and it abode upon him.

33 And I knew him not: but he that sent me to baptize with water, the same said unto me, Upon whom thou shalt see the Spirit descending, and remaining on him, the same is he which baptizeth with the Holy Ghost.

34 And I saw, and bare record that this is the Son of God.

35 Again the next day after John stood, and two of his disciples;

36 And looking upon Jesus as he walked, he saith, Behold the Lamb of God!

37 And the two disciples heard him speak, and they followed Jesus.

38 Then Jesus turned, and saw them following, and saith unto them, What seek ye? They said unto him, Rabbi, (which is to say, being interpreted, Master,) where dwellest thou?

39 He saith unto them, Come and see. They came and saw where he dwelt, and abode with him that day: for it was about the tenth hour.

40 One of the two which heard John speak, and followed him, was Andrew, Simon Peter's brother.

41 He first findeth his own brother Simon, and saith unto him, We have found the Messias, which is, being interpreted, the Christ.

42 And he brought him to Jesus. And when Jesus beheld him, he said, Thou art Simon the son of Jona: thou shalt be called Cephas, which is by interpretation, A stone.

43 The day following Jesus would go forth into Galilee, and findeth Philip, and saith unto him, Follow me.

44 Now Philip was of Bethsaida, the city of Andrew and Peter.

45 Philip findeth Nathanael, and saith unto him, We have found him, of whom Moses in the law, and the prophets, did write, Jesus of Nazareth, the son of Joseph.

46 And Nathanael said unto him, Can there any good thing come out of Nazareth? Philip saith unto him, Come and see.

47 Jesus saw Nathanael coming to him, and saith of him, Behold an Israelite indeed, in whom is no guile!

9. Who lighteth every man – By what is vulgarly termed natural conscience, pointing out at least the general lines of good and evil. And this light, if man did not hinder, would shine more and more to the perfect day.

10. He was in the world – Even from the creation.

11. He came – In the fullness of time, to his own – Country, city, temple: And his own – People, received him not.

12. But as many as received him – Jews or Gentiles; that believe on his name – That is, on him. The moment they believe, they are sons; and because they are sons, God sendeth forth the Spirit of his Son into their hearts, crying, Abba, Father.

13. Who were born – Who became the sons of God, not of blood – Not by descent from Abraham, nor by the will of the flesh – By natural generation, nor by the will of man – Adopting them, but of God – By his Spirit.

14. Flesh sometimes signifies corrupt nature; sometimes the body; sometimes, as here, the whole man. We beheld his glory – We his apostles, particularly Peter, James, and John, Luke ix, 32. Grace and truth – We are all by nature liars and children of wrath, to whom both grace and truth are unknown. But we are made partakers of them, when we are accepted through the Beloved. The whole verse might be paraphrased thus: And in order to raise us to this dignity and happiness, the eternal Word, by a most amazing condescension, was made flesh, united himself to our miserable nature, with all its innocent infirmities. And he did not make us a transient visit, but tabernacled among us on earth, displaying his glory in a more eminent manner, than even of old in the tabernacle of Moses. And we who are now recording these things beheld his glory with so strict an attention, that we can testify, it was in every respect such a glory as became the only begotten of the Father. For it shone forth not only in his transfiguration, and in his continual miracles, but in all his tempers, ministrations, and conduct through the whole series of his life. In all he appeared full of grace and truth: he was himself most benevolent and upright; made those ample discoveries of pardon to sinners, which the Mosaic dispensation could not do: and really exhibited the most substantial blessings, whereas that was but a shadow of good things to come.

15. John cried – With joy and confidence; This is he of whom I said – John had said this before our Lord's baptism, although he then knew him not in person: he knew him first at his baptism, and afterward cried, This is he of whom I said. &c. He is preferred before me – in his office: for he was before me – in his nature.

16. And – Here the apostle confirms the Baptist's words: as if he had said, He is indeed preferred before thee: so we have experienced: We all – That believe: have received – All that we enjoy out of his fullness: and in the particular, grace upon grace – One blessing upon another, immeasurable grace and love.

17. The law – Working wrath and containing shadows: was given – No philosopher, poet, or orator, ever chose his words so accurately as St. John. The law, saith he, was given by Moses: grace was by Jesus Christ. Observe the reason for placing each word thus: The law of Moses was not his own. The grace of Christ was. His grace was opposite to the wrath, his truth to the shadowy ceremonies of the law. Jesus – St. John having once mentioned the incarnation (ver. 14,) no more uses that name, the Word, in all his

6-14 John the Baptist came to bear witness concerning Jesus. Nothing more fully shows the darkness of men's minds, than that when the Light had appeared, there needed a witness to call attention to it. Christ was the true Light; that great Light which deserves to be called so. By his Spirit and grace he enlightens all that are enlightened to salvation; and those that are not enlightened by him, perish in darkness. Christ was in the world when he took our nature upon him, and dwelt among us. The Son of the Highest was here in this lower world. He was in the world, but not of it. He came to save a lost world, because it was a world of his own making. Yet the world knew him not. When he comes as a Judge, the world shall know him. Many say that they are Christ's own, yet do not receive him, because they will not part with their sins, nor have him to reign over them. All the children of God are born again. This new birth is through the word of God as the means, 1Pe 1:23, and by the Spirit of God as the Author. By his Divine presence Christ always was in the world. But now that the fullness of time was come, he was, after another manner, God manifested in the flesh. But observe the beams of his Divine glory, which darted through this veil of flesh. Men discover their weaknesses to those most familiar with them, but it was not so with Christ; those most intimate with him saw most of his glory. Although he was in the form of a servant, as to outward circumstances, yet, in respect of graces, his form was like the Son of God His Divine glory appeared in the holiness of his doctrine, and in his miracles. He was full of grace, fully acceptable to his Father, therefore qualified to plead for us; and full of truth, fully aware of the things he was to reveal.

15-18 As to the order of time and entrance on his work, Christ came after John, but in every other way he was before him. The expression clearly shows that Jesus had existence before he appeared on earth as man. All fullness dwells in him, from which alone fallen sinners have, and shall receive, by faith, all that renders them wise, strong, holy, useful, and happy. Our receivings by Christ are all summed up in this one word, grace; we have received "even grace," a gift so great, so rich, so invaluable; the good will of God towards us, and the good work of God in us. The law of God is holy, just, and good; and we should make the proper use of it. But we cannot derive from it pardon, righteousness, or strength. It teaches us to adorn the doctrine of God our Savior, but it cannot supply the place of that doctrine. As no mercy comes from God to sinners but through Jesus Christ, no man can come to the Father but by him; no man can know God, except as he is made known in the only begotten and beloved Son.

19-28 John disowns himself to be the Christ, who was now expected and waited for. He came in the spirit and power of Elias, but he was not the person of Elias. John was not that Prophet whom Moses said the Lord

Galilee, everybody comes to eat and drink, and the feast lasts on for a week or a fortnight. Hundreds of people must be fed, for often open house is kept. Nobody is refused, and consequently a great quantity of provision is required. Besides, they may not have consumed all the wine at once. When the Lord multiplied loaves and fishes, they must eat the loaves and fishes directly, or else the bread would grow moldy, and the fish would be putrid; but wine could be stored and used months afterward. I have no doubt that such wine as Jesus Christ made was as good for keeping as it was for using. And why not set the family up with a store in hand? They were not very rich people. They might sell it if they liked. At any rate, that is not my subject, and I do not intend getting into hot water over the question of cold water. I abstain myself from alcoholic drink in every form, and I think others would be wise to do the same; but of this each one must be a guide unto himself.

Jesus Christ commenced the gospel dispensation, not with a miracle of vengeance, like that of Moses, who turned water into blood, but with a miracle of liberality, turning water into wine. He does not only supply necessaries, but gives luxuries, and this is highly significant of the kingdom of his grace. Here he not only gives sinners enough to save them, but he gives abundantly, grace upon grace. The gifts of the covenant are not stinted or stunted, they are neither small in quantity nor in quality. He gives to men not only the water of life that they may drink and be refreshed, but "wines on the lees well refined" that they may rejoice exceedingly. And he gives like a king, who gives lavishly, without counting the cups and bottles. As to one hundred and twenty gallons, how little is that in comparison with the rivers of love and mercy which he is pleased to bestow freely out of his bountiful heart upon the most needy souls. You may forget all about the wine question, and all about wine, bad, good, or indifferent. The less we have to do with it the better, I am quite sure. And now let us think about our Lord's mercy, and let the wine stand as a type of his grace, and the abundance of it as the type of the abundance of his grace which he doth so liberally bestow.

Now, concerning this miracle, it may well be remarked how simple and unostentatious it was. One might have expected that when the great Lord of all came here in human form he would commence his miraculous career by summoning the scribes and Pharisees at least, if not the kings and princes of the earth, to see the marks of his calling and the guarantees and warrants of his commission; gathering them all

48 Nathanael saith unto him, Whence knowest thou me? Jesus answered and said unto him, Before that Philip called thee, when thou wast under the fig tree, I saw thee.

49 Nathanael answered and saith unto him, Rabbi, thou art the Son of God; thou art the King of Israel.

50 Jesus answered and said unto him, Because I said unto thee, I saw thee under the fig tree, believest thou? thou shalt see greater things than these.

51 And he saith unto him, Verily, verily, I say unto you, Hereafter ye shall see heaven open, and the angels of God ascending and descending upon the Son of man.

JOHN 2

1 And the third day there was a marriage in Cana of Galilee; and the mother of Jesus was there:

2 And both Jesus was called, and his disciples, to the marriage.

3 And when they wanted wine, the mother of Jesus saith unto him, They have no wine.

4 Jesus saith unto her, Woman, what have I to do with thee? mine hour is not yet come.

5 His mother saith unto the servants, Whatsoever he saith unto you, do it.

6 And there were set there six waterpots of stone, after the manner of the purifying of the Jews, containing two or three firkins apiece.

7 Jesus saith unto them, Fill the waterpots with water. And they filled them up to the brim.

8 And he saith unto them, Draw out now, and bear unto the governor of the feast. And they bare it.

9 When the ruler of the feast had tasted the water that was made wine, and knew not whence it was: (but the servants which drew the water knew;) the governor of the feast called the bridegroom,

10 And saith unto him, Every man at the beginning doth set forth good wine; and when men have well drunk, then that which is worse: but thou hast kept the good wine until now.

11 This beginning of miracles did Jesus in Cana of Galilee, and manifested forth his glory; and his disciples believed on him.

12 After this he went down to Capernaum, he, and his mother, and his brethren, and his disciples: and they continued there not many days.

13 And the Jews' passover was at hand, and Jesus went up to Jerusalem,

14 And found in the temple those that sold oxen and sheep and doves, and the changers of money sitting:

15 And when he had made a scourge of small cords, he drove them all out of the temple, and the sheep, and the oxen; and poured out the changers' money, and overthrew the tables;

16 And said unto them that sold doves, Take these things hence; make not my Father's house an house of merchandise.

book.

18. No man hath seen God – With bodily eyes: yet believers see him with the eye of faith. Who is in the bosom of the Father – The expression denotes the highest unity, and the most intimate knowledge.

19. The Jews – Probably the great council sent.

20. I am not the Christ – For many supposed he was.

21. Art thou Elijah? – He was not that Elijah (the Tishbite) of whom they spoke. Art thou the prophet – Of whom Moses speaks, Deut. xviii, 15.

23. He said – I am that forerunner of Christ of whom Isaiah speaks. I am the voice – As if he had said, Far from being Christ, or even Elijah, I am nothing but a voice: a sound that so soon as it has expressed the thought of which it is the sign, dies into air, and is known no more. Isaiah xl, 3.

24. They who were sent were of the Pharisees – Who were peculiarly tenacious of old customs, and jealous of any innovation (except those brought in by their own scribes) unless the innovator had unquestionable proofs of Divine authority.

25. They asked him, Why baptizest thou then? – Without any commission from the Sanhedrin? And not only heathens (who were always baptized before they were admitted to circumcision) but Jews also?

26. John answered, I baptize – To prepare for the Messiah; and indeed to show that Jews, as well as Gentiles, must be proselytes to Christ, and that these as well as those stand in need of being washed from their sins.

28. Where John was baptizing – That is, used to baptize.

29. He seeth Jesus coming and saith, Behold the Lamb – Innocent; to be offered up; prophesied of by Isaiah, Isaiah liii, 7, typified by the paschal lamb, and by the daily sacrifice: The Lamb of God – Whom God gave, approves, accepts of; who taketh away – Atoneth for; the sin – That is, all the sins: of the world – Of all mankind. Sin and the world are of equal extent.

31. I knew him not – Till he came to be baptized. How surprising is this; considering how nearly they were related, and how remarkable the conception and birth of both had been. But there was a peculiar providence visible in our Savior's living, from his infancy to his baptism, at Nazareth: John all the time living the life of a hermit in the deserts of Judea, Luke i, 80, ninety or more miles from Nazareth: hereby that acquaintance was prevented which might have made John's testimony of Christ suspected.

34. I saw it – That is, the Spirit so descending and abiding on him. And testified – From that time.

37. They followed Jesus – They walked after him, but had not the courage to speak to him.

41. He first findeth his own brother Simon – Probably both of them sought him: Which is, being interpreted, the Christ – This the evangelist adds, as likewise those words in ver. 38, that is, being interpreted, Master.

42. Jesus said, Thou art Simon, the son of Jonah – As none had told our Lord these names, this could not but strike Peter. Cephas, which is Peter – Meaning the same in Syriac which Peter does in Greek, namely, a rock.

45. Jesus of Nazareth – So Philip thought, not knowing he was born in Bethlehem. Nathanael was probably the same with

MATTHEW HENRY

CHARLES H. SPURGEON

would raise up to them of their brethren, like unto him. He was not such a prophet as they expected, who would rescue them from the Romans. He gave such an account of himself, as might excite and awaken them to hearken to him. He baptized the people with water as a profession of repentance, and as an outward sign of the spiritual blessings to be conferred on them by the Messiah, who was in the midst of them, though they knew him not, and to whom he was unworthy to render the meanest service.

29-36 John saw Jesus coming to him, and pointed him out as the Lamb of God. The paschal lamb, in the shedding and sprinkling of its blood, the roasting and eating of its flesh, and all the other circumstances of the ordinance, represented the salvation of sinners by faith in Christ. And the lambs sacrificed every morning and evening, can only refer to Christ slain as a sacrifice to redeem us to God by his blood. John came as a preacher of repentance, yet he told his followers that they were to look for the pardon of their sins to Jesus only, and to his death. It agrees with God's glory to pardon all who depend on the atoning sacrifice of Christ. He takes away the sin of the world; purchases pardon for all that repent and believe the gospel.

37-42 The strongest and most prevailing argument with an awakened soul to follow Christ, is, that it is he only who takes away sin. Whatever communion there is between our souls and Christ, it is he who begins the discourse. He asked, What seek ye? The question Jesus put to them, we should all put to ourselves when we begin to follow Him, What do we design and desire? In following Christ, do we seek the favor of God and eternal life? He invites them to come without delay. Now is the accepted time, 2Co 6:2. It is good for us to be where Christ is, wherever it be. We ought to labor for the spiritual welfare of those related to us, and seek to bring them to Him. Those who come to Christ, must come with a fixed resolution to be firm and constant to him, like a stone, solid and steadfast; and it is by his grace that they are so.

43-51 See the nature of true Christianity; it is following Jesus; devoting ourselves to him, and treading in his steps. Observe the objection Nathanael made. All who desire to profit by the word of God, must beware of prejudices against places, or denominations of men. They should examine for themselves, and they will sometimes find good where they looked for none. Many people are kept from the ways of religion by the unreasonable prejudices they conceive. The best way to remove false notions of religion, is to make trial of it. In Nathanael there was no guile. His profession was not hypocritical. He was not a dissembler, nor dishonest; he was a sound character, a really upright, godly man. Christ knows what men are indeed. Does He know us? Let us desire to know him. Let us seek and pray to be Israelites indeed, in whom is no guile; truly Christians,

together to work some miracle before them, as Moses and Aaron did before Pharaoh, that they might be convinced of his Messiahship. He does nothing of the kind. He goes to a simple wedding among poor people, and there in the simplest and most natural way he displays his glory. When the water is to be turned into wine, when he selects that as the first miracle, he does not call for the master of the feast even, or for the bridegroom himself or for any of the guests, and begin to say, "You clearly perceive that your wine is all gone. Now, I am about to show you a great marvel, to turn water into wine." No, he does it quietly with the servants: he tells them to fill the waterpots: he uses the baths: he does not ask for any new vessels, but uses what were there, making no fuss or parade. He uses water, too, of which they had abundance, and works the miracle, if I may so speak, in the most commonplace and natural style; and that is just the style of Jesus Christ. Now, if it had been a Romish miracle it would have been done in a very mysterious, theatrical, sensational way, with no end of paraphernalia; but, being a genuine miracle, it is done just as nearly after the course of nature as the supernatural can go. Jesus does not have the waterpots emptied and then fill them with wine, but he goes as far with nature as nature will go, and uses water to make the wine from; therein following the processes of his providence which are at work every day. When the water drops from heaven, and flows into the earth to the roots of the vine, and so swells out the clusters with ruddy juice, it is through water that wine is produced. There is only a difference as to time whether the wine is created in the cluster, or in the waterpots. Our Lord does not call for any strangers to do it, but the ordinary servants shall bring ordinary water; and while they are drawing out the water, or what appears to them to be water, the servants shall perceive that the water has been turned into wine.

Now, whenever you try to serve Jesus Christ do not make a fuss about it, because he never made any fuss in what he did, even when he was working amazing miracles. If you want to do a good thing, go and do it as naturally as ever you can. Be simple hearted and simple minded. Be yourself. Do not be affected in your piety, as if you were going to walk to heaven on stilts: walk on your own feet, and bring religion to your own door and to your own fireside. If you have a grand work to do, do it with that genuine simplicity which is next akin to sublimity; for affectation, and everything that is gaudy and ostentatious, is, after all, mean and beggarly. Nothing but simple naturalness

17 And his disciples remembered that it was written, The zeal of thine house hath eaten me up.

18 Then answered the Jews and said unto him, What sign shewest thou unto us, seeing that thou doest these things?

19 Jesus answered and said unto them, Destroy this temple, and in three days I will raise it up.

20 Then said the Jews, Forty and six years was this temple in building, and wilt thou rear it up in three days?

21 But he spake of the temple of his body.

22 When therefore he was risen from the dead, his disciples remembered that he had said this unto them; and they believed the scripture, and the word which Jesus had said.

23 Now when he was in Jerusalem at the passover, in the feast day, many believed in his name, when they saw the miracles which he did.

24 But Jesus did not commit himself unto them, because he knew all men,

25 And needed not that any should testify of man: for he knew what was in man.

JOHN 3

1 There was a man of the Pharisees, named Nicodemus, a ruler of the Jews:

2 The same came to Jesus by night, and said unto him, Rabbi, we know that thou art a teacher come from God: for no man can do these miracles that thou doest, except God be with him.

3 Jesus answered and said unto him, Verily, verily, I say unto thee, Except a man be born again, he cannot see the kingdom of God.

4 Nicodemus saith unto him, How can a man be born when he is old? can he enter the second time into his mother's womb, and be born?

5 Jesus answered, Verily, verily, I say unto thee, Except a man be born of water and of the Spirit, he cannot enter into the kingdom of God.

6 That which is born of the flesh is flesh; and that which is born of the Spirit is spirit.

7 Marvel not that I said unto thee, Ye must be born again.

8 The wind bloweth where it listeth, and thou hearest the sound thereof, but canst not tell whence it cometh, and whither it goeth: so is every one that is born of the Spirit.

9 Nicodemus answered and said unto him, How can these things be?

10 Jesus answered and said unto him, Art thou a master of Israel, and knowest not these things?

11 Verily, verily, I say unto thee, We speak that we do know, and testify that we have seen; and ye receive not our witness.

12 If I have told you earthly things, and ye believe not, how shall ye believe, if I tell you of heavenly things?

13 And no man hath ascended up to heaven,

Bartholomew, that is, the son of Tholomew. St. Matthew joins Bartholomew with Philip, Matt. x, 3, and St. John places Nathanael in the midst of the apostles, immediately after Thomas, chap. xxi, 2, just as Bartholomew is placed, Acts i, 13.

46. Can any good thing come out of Nazareth? – How cautiously should we guard against popular prejudices! When these had once possessed so honest a heart as that of Nathanael, they led him to suspect the blessed Jesus himself for an impostor, because he had been brought up at Nazareth. But his integrity prevailed over that foolish bias, and laid him open to the force of evidence, which a candid inquirer will always be glad to admit, even when it brings the most unexpected discoveries. Can any good thing – That is, have we ground from Scripture to expect the Messiah, or any eminent prophet from Nazareth? Philip saith, Come and see – The same answer which he had received himself from our Lord the day before.

48. Under the fig tree I saw thee – Perhaps at prayer.

49. Nathanael answered – Happy are they that are ready to believe, swift to receive the truth and grace of God. Thou art the Son of God – So he acknowledges now more than he had heard from Philip: The Son of God, the king of Israel – A confession both of the person and office of Christ.

51. Hereafter ye shall see – All of these, as well as thou, who believe on me now in my state of humiliation, shall hereafter see me come in my glory, and all the angels of God with me. This seems the most natural sense of the words, though they may also refer to his ascension.

JOHN 2

1. And the third day – After he had said this. In Cana of Galilee – There were two other towns of the same name, one in the tribe of Ephraim, the other in Caelosyria.

2. Jesus and his disciples were invited to the marriage – Christ does not take away human society, but sanctifies it. Water might have quenched thirst; yet our Lord allows wine; especially at a festival solemnity. Such was his facility in drawing his disciples at first, who were afterward to go through rougher ways.

3. And wine falling short – How many days the solemnity had lasted, and on which day our Lord came, or how many disciples might follow him, does not appear. His mother saith to him, They have not wine – Either she might mean, supply them by miracle; or, Go away, that others may go also, before the want appears.

4. Jesus saith to her, Woman – So our Lord speaks also, chap. xix, 26. It is probable this was the constant appellation which he used to her. He regarded his Father above all, not knowing even his mother after the flesh. What is it to me and thee? A mild reproof of her inordinate concern and untimely interposal. Mine hour is not yet come – The time of my working this miracle, or of my going away. May we not learn hence, if his mother was rebuked for attempting to direct him in the days of his flesh, how absurd it is to address her as if she had a right to command him, on the throne of his glory? Likewise how indecent it is for us to direct his supreme wisdom, as to the time or manner in which he shall appear for us in any of the exigencies of life!

5. His mother saith to the servants – Gathering from his answer he

MATTHEW HENRY

CHARLES H. SPURGEON

approved of Christ himself. Some things weak, imperfect, and sinful, are found in all, but hypocrisy belongs not to a believer's character. Jesus witnessed what passed when Nathanael was under the fig tree. Probably he was then in fervent prayer, seeking direction as to the Hope and Consolation of Israel, where no human eye observed him. This showed him that our Lord knew the secrets of his heart. Through Christ we commune with, and benefit by the holy angels; and things in heaven and things on earth are reconciled and united together.

JOHN 2

The miracle at Cana. (1-11)
Christ casts the buyers and sellers out of the temple. (12-22)
Many believe in Christ. (23-25)

1-11 It is very desirable when there is a marriage, to have Christ own and bless it. Those that would have Christ with them at their marriage, must invite him by prayer, and he will come. Christ showed that he improves creature comforts to all true believers, and make them comforts indeed. And Christ's works are all for use. Has he turned thy water into wine, given thee knowledge and grace? it is to profit withal; therefore draw out now, and use it. It was the best wine. Christ's works commend themselves even to those who know not their Author. What was produced by miracles, always was the best in its kind. Though Christ hereby allows a right use of wine, he does not in the least do away his own caution, which is, that our hearts be not at any time overcharged with surfeiting and drunkenness, Lu 21:34. Though we need not scruple to feast with our friends on proper occasions, yet every social interview should be so conducted, that we might invite the Redeemer to join with us, if he were now on earth; and all levity, luxury, and excess offend him.

12-22 The first public work in which we find Christ engaged, was driving from the temple the traders whom the covetous priests and rulers encouraged to make a market-place of its courts. Those now make God's house a house of merchandise, whose minds are filled with cares about worldly business when attending religious exercises, or who perform Divine offices for love of gain. Christ, having thus cleansed the temple, gave a sign to those who demanded it, to prove his authority for so doing. He foretells his death by the Jews' malice, Destroy ye this temple; I will permit you to destroy it. He foretells his resurrection by his own power; In three days I will raise it up. Christ took again his own life. Men mistake by understanding that according to the letter, which the Scripture speaks by way of figure. When Jesus was risen from the dead, his disciples remembered he has said this. It helps

has about it a genuine beauty; and such a beauty there is about this miracle of the Savior.

Let all these remarks stand as a kind of preface; for now I want to draw out the principles which are hidden in my text; and then, secondly, when I have displayed those principles, I want to show how they should be carried out.

I. "Jesus saith unto them, Fill the waterpots with water." WHAT ARE THE PRINCIPLES INVOLVED IN OUR LORD'S MODE OF PROCEDURE?

First, that, as a rule, when Christ is about to bestow a blessing he gives a command. This is a fact which your memories will help you to establish in a moment. It is not always so; but, as a general rule, a word of command goes before a word of power, or else with it. He is about to give wine, and the process does not consist in saying, "Let wine be," but it begins by a command addressed to men,—"Fill the waterpots with water." Here is a blind man: Christ is about to give him sight. He puts clay on his eyes, and then says, "Go to the pool of Siloam and wash." There is a man with his arm swinging at his side, useless to him: Christ is going to restore it, and he says, "Stretch forth thine hand." Ay, and the principle goes so far that it holds good in cases where it would seem to be quite inapplicable, for if it be a child that is dead he says, "Maid, arise;" or if it be Lazarus, who by this time stinks, being four days buried, yet he cries, "Lazarus, come forth." And thus he bestows a benefit by a command. Gospel benefits come with a gospel precept.

Do you wonder that this principle which is seen in the miracles is seen in the wonders of his divine grace? Here is a sinner to be saved. What does Christ say to that sinner? "Believe in the Lord Jesus Christ, and thou shalt be saved." Can he believe of himself? Is he not dead in sin? Brethren, raise no such questions, but learn that Jesus Christ has bidden men believe, and has commissioned his disciples to cry, "Repent ye, for the kingdom of heaven is at hand." "The times of this ignorance God winked at; but now commandeth all men everywhere to repent." And he bids us go and preach this word—"Believe in the Lord Jesus Christ, and thou shalt be saved." But why command them? It is his will to do so, and that should be enough for you who call yourself his disciple. It was so even in the olden times, when the Lord set forth in vision his way of dealing with a dead nation. There lay the dry bones of the valley, exceeding many, and exceeding dry, and Ezekiel was sent to prophesy to them. What said the prophet? "O ye dry

but he that came down from heaven, even the Son of man which is in heaven.

14 And as Moses lifted up the serpent in the wilderness, even so must the Son of man be lifted up:

15 That whosoever believeth in him should not perish, but have eternal life.

16 For God so loved the world, that he gave his only begotten Son, that whosoever believeth in him should not perish, but have everlasting life.

17 For God sent not his Son into the world to condemn the world; but that the world through him might be saved.

18 He that believeth on him is not condemned: but he that believeth not is condemned already, because he hath not believed in the name of the only begotten Son of God.

19 And this is the condemnation, that light is come into the world, and men loved darkness rather than light, because their deeds were evil.

20 For every one that doeth evil hateth the light, neither cometh to the light, lest his deeds should be reproved.

21 But he that doeth truth cometh to the light, that his deeds may be made manifest, that they are wrought in God.

22 After these things came Jesus and his disciples into the land of Judea; and there he tarried with them, and baptized.

23 And John also was baptizing in Aenon near to Salim, because there was much water there: and they came, and were baptized.

24 For John was not yet cast into prison.

25 Then there arose a question between some of John's disciples and the Jews about purifying.

26 And they came unto John, and said unto him, Rabbi, he that was with thee beyond Jordan, to whom thou barest witness, behold, the same baptizeth, and all men come to him.

27 John answered and said, A man can receive nothing, except it be given him from heaven.

28 Ye yourselves bear me witness, that I said, I am not the Christ, but that I am sent before him.

29 He that hath the bride is the bridegroom: but the friend of the bridegroom, which standeth and heareth him, rejoiceth greatly because of the bridegroom's voice: this my joy therefore is fulfilled.

30 He must increase, but I must decrease.

31 He that cometh from above is above all: he that is of the earth is earthly, and speaketh of the earth: he that cometh from heaven is above all.

32 And what he hath seen and heard, that he testifieth; and no man receiveth his testimony.

33 He that hath received his testimony hath set to his seal that God is true.

34 For he whom God hath sent speaketh the words of God: for God giveth not the Spirit by measure unto him.

35 The Father loveth the Son, and hath given all things into his hand.

36 He that believeth on the Son hath everlast-

was about to do something extraordinary.

6. The purifying of the Jews – Who purified themselves by frequent washings particularly before eating.

9. The governor of the feast – The bridegroom generally procured some friend to order all things at the entertainment.

10. And saith – St. John barely relates the words he spoke, which does not imply his approving them. When they have well drunk – does not mean any more than toward the close of the entertainment.

11. And his disciples believed – More steadfastly.

14. Oxen, and sheep, and doves – Used for sacrifice: And the changers of money – Those who changed foreign money for that which was current at Jerusalem, for the convenience of them that came from distant countries.

15. Having made a scourge of rushes – (Which were strewed on the ground,) he drove all out of the temple, (that is, the court of it,) both the sheep and the oxen – Though it does not appear that he struck even them; and much less, any of the men. But a terror from God, it is evident, fell upon them.

17. Psalm lxix, 9.

18. Then answered the Jews – Either some of those whom he had just driven out, or their friends: What sign showest thou? – So they require a miracle, to confirm a miracle!

19. This temple – Doubtless pointing, while he spoke, to his body, the temple and habitation of the Godhead.

20. Forty and six years – Just so many years before the time of this conversation, Herod the Great had begun his most magnificent reparation of the temple, (one part after another,) which he continued all his life, and which was now going on, and was continued thirty-six years longer, till within six or seven years of the destruction of the state, city, and temple by the Romans.

22. They believed the scripture, and the word which Jesus had said – Concerning his resurrection.

23. Many believed – That he was a teacher sent from God.

24. He did not trust himself to them – Let us learn hence not rashly to put ourselves into the power of others. Let us study a wise and happy medium between universal suspiciousness and that easiness which would make us the property of every pretender to kindness and respect.

25. He – To whom all things are naked, knew what was in man – Namely, a desperately deceitful heart.

JOHN 3

1. A ruler – One of the great council.

2. The same came – Through desire; but by night – Through shame: We know – Even we rulers and Pharisees.

3. Jesus answered – That knowledge will not avail thee unless thou be born again – Otherwise thou canst not see, that is, experience and enjoy, either the inward or the glorious kingdom of God. In this solemn discourse our Lord shows, that no external profession, no ceremonial ordinances or privileges of birth, could entitle any to the blessings of the Messiah's kingdom: that an entire change of heart as well as of life was necessary for that purpose: that this could only be wrought in man by the almighty power of God: that every man born into the world was by nature in a state of sin, condem-

much in understanding the Divine word, to observe the fulfilling of the Scriptures.

23-25 Our Lord knew all men, their nature, dispositions, affections, designs, so as we do not know any man, not even ourselves. He knows his crafty enemies, and all their secret projects; his false friends, and their true characters. He knows who are truly his, knows their uprightness, and knows their weaknesses. We know what is done by men; Christ knows what is in them, he tries the heart. Beware of a dead faith, or a formal profession: carnal, empty professors are not to be trusted, and however men impose on others or themselves, they cannot impose on the heart-searching God.

JOHN 3

Christ's discourse with Nicodemus. (1-21)
The baptism of John. John's testimony of Christ. (22-36)

1-21 Nicodemus was afraid, or ashamed to be seen with Christ, therefore came in the night. When religion is out of fashion, there are many Nicodemites. But though he came by night, Jesus bid him welcome, and hereby taught us to encourage good beginnings, although weak. And though now he came by night, yet afterward he owned Christ publicly. He did not talk with Christ about state affairs, though he was a ruler, but about the concerns of his own soul and its salvation, and went at once to them. Our Savior spoke of the necessity and nature of regeneration or the new birth, and at once directed Nicodemus to the source of holiness of the heart. Christ's discourse of gospel truths, ver. 11-13, shows the folly of those who make these things strange unto them; and it recommends us to search them out. Jesus Christ is every way able to reveal the will of God to us; for he came down from heaven, and yet is in heaven. We have here a notice of Christ's two distinct natures in one person, so that while he is the Son of man, yet he is in heaven. God is the "HE THAT IS," and heaven is the dwelling-place of his holiness. The knowledge of this must be from above, and can be received by faith alone. Jesus Christ came to save us by healing us, as the children of Israel, stung with fiery serpents, were cured and lived by looking up to the brazen serpent, Nu 21:6-9. In this observe the deadly and destructive nature of sin. Ask awakened consciences, ask damned sinners, they will tell you, that how charming soever the allurements of sin may be, at the last it bites like a serpent. See the powerful remedy against this fatal malady. Christ is plainly set forth to us in the gospel. He has said, Look and be saved, look and live; lift up the eyes of your faith to Christ crucified. And until we have grace to do this, we shall not be cured, but still are wounded with the stings of Satan, and in a dying state. Jesus Christ came to save us by pardoning us, that we might not die by the sentence of the law. Here is gospel, good news indeed. Here is God's love in giving his Son for the world. God

bones, hear the word of the Lord." Is that his way of making them alive? Yes, by a command to hear; a thing which dry bones cannot do. He issues his command to the dead, the dry, the helpless, and by its power life comes. I pray you, be not disobedient to the gospel, for faith is a duty, or we should not read of "the obedience of faith." Jesus Christ, when he is about to bless, challenges men's obedience by issuing his royal orders.

The same thing is true when we come away from the unconverted to believers. When God means to bless his people and make them blessings it is by issuing a command to them. We have been praying to the Lord that he would arise and make bare his arm. His answer is, "Awake, awake, O Zion." We ask that the world may be brought to his feet, and his reply is, "All power is given unto me in heaven and in earth. Go ye therefore, and teach all nations, baptizing them." The command is to us the vehicle of the blessing. If we are to have the blessing of converts multiplied, and churches built up, Christ must give us the boon: it is altogether his gift, as much as it was his to turn the water into wine; yet first of all he says to us, "Go ye and proclaim my salvation unto the ends of the earth," for thus are we to fill the waterpots with water. If we be obedient to his command we shall see how he will work—how mightily he will be with us, and how our prayers shall be heard.

That is the first principle that I see here: Christ issues commands to those whom he will bless.

Secondly, Christ's commands are not to be questioned, but to be obeyed. The people want wine, and Christ says, "Fill the waterpots with water." Well, now, if these servants had been of the mind of the captious critics of modern times, they would have looked at our Lord a long while, and objected boldly: "We do not want any water; it is not the feast of purifications; it is a wedding feast. We do not require water at a wedding. We shall want water when we are going up to the synagogue, or to the temple, that we may purify our hands according to our custom: but we do not want water just now: the hour, the occasion, and the fitness of things, call for wine." But Mary's advice to them was sound—"Whatsoever he saith to you, do it." Thus, too, let us neither question nor cavil, but do his bidding straight away.

It may sometimes seem that Christ's command is not pertinent to the point in hand. The sinner, for instance, says, "Lord, save me: conquer in me my sin." Our Lord cries, "Believe," and the sinner cannot see how believing in Jesus will enable him to get the mastery over a

ing life: and he that believeth not the Son shall not see life; but the wrath of God abideth on him.

JOHN 4

1 When therefore the Lord knew how the Pharisees had heard that Jesus made and baptized more disciples than John,

2 (Though Jesus himself baptized not, but his disciples,)

3 He left Judea, and departed again into Galilee.

4 And he must needs go through Samaria.

5 Then cometh he to a city of Samaria, which is called Sychar, near to the parcel of ground that Jacob gave to his son Joseph.

6 Now Jacob's well was there. Jesus therefore, being wearied with his journey, sat thus on the well: and it was about the sixth hour.

7 There cometh a woman of Samaria to draw water: Jesus saith unto her, Give me to drink.

8 (For his disciples were gone away unto the city to buy meat.)

9 Then saith the woman of Samaria unto him, How is it that thou, being a Jew, askest drink of me, which am a woman of Samaria? for the Jews have no dealings with the Samaritans.

10 Jesus answered and said unto her, If thou knewest the gift of God, and who it is that saith to thee, Give me to drink; thou wouldest have asked of him, and he would have given thee living water.

11 The woman saith unto him, Sir, thou hast nothing to draw with, and the well is deep: from whence then hast thou that living water?

12 Art thou greater than our father Jacob, which gave us the well, and drank thereof himself, and his children, and his cattle?

13 Jesus answered and said unto her, Whosoever drinketh of this water shall thirst again:

14 But whosoever drinketh of the water that I shall give him shall never thirst; but the water that I shall give him shall be in him a well of water springing up into everlasting life.

15 The woman saith unto him, Sir, give me this water, that I thirst not, neither come hither to draw.

16 Jesus saith unto her, Go, call thy husband, and come hither.

17 The woman answered and said, I have no husband. Jesus said unto her, Thou hast well said, I have no husband:

18 For thou hast had five husbands; and he whom thou now hast is not thy husband: in that saidst thou truly.

19 The woman saith unto him, Sir, I perceive that thou art a prophet.

20 Our fathers worshiped in this mountain; and ye say, that in Jerusalem is the place where men ought to worship.

21 Jesus saith unto her, Woman, believe me, the hour cometh, when ye shall neither in this

nation, and misery: that the free mercy of God had given his Son to deliver them from it, and to raise them to a blessed immortality: that all mankind, Gentiles as well as Jews, might share in these benefits, procured by his being lifted up on the cross, and to be received by faith in him: but that if they rejected him, their eternal, aggravated condemnation, would be the certain consequence. Except a man be born again – If our Lord by being born again means only reformation of life, instead of making any new discovery, he has only thrown a great deal of obscurity on what was before plain and obvious.

4. When he is old – As Nicodemus himself was.

5. Except a man be born of water and of the Spirit – Except he experience that great inward change by the Spirit, and be baptized (wherever baptism can be had) as the outward sign and means of it.

6. That which is born of the flesh is flesh – Mere flesh, void of the Spirit, yea, at enmity with it; And that which is born of the Spirit is spirit – Is spiritual, heavenly, divine, like its Author.

7. Ye must be born again – To be born again, is to be inwardly changed from all sinfulness to all holiness. It is fitly so called, because as great a change then passes on the soul as passes on the body when it is born into the world.

8. The wind bloweth – According to its own nature, not thy will, and thou hearest the sound thereof – Thou art sure it doth blow, but canst not explain the particular manner of its acting. So is every one that is born of the Spirit – The fact is plain, the manner of his operations inexplicable.

11. We speak what we know – I and all that believe in me.

12. Earthly things – Things done on earth; such as the new birth, and the present privileges of the children of God. Heavenly things – Such as the eternity of the Son, and the unity of the Father, Son, and Spirit.

13. For no one – For here you must rely on my single testimony, whereas there you have a cloud of witnesses: Hath gone up to heaven, but he that came down from heaven. Who is in heaven – Therefore he is omnipresent; else he could not be in heaven and on earth at once. This is a plain instance of what is usually termed the communication of properties between the Divine and human nature; whereby what is proper to the Divine nature is spoken concerning the human, and what is proper to the human is, as here, spoken of the Divine.

14. And as Moses – And even this single witness will soon be taken from you; yea, and in a most ignominious manner. Num. xxi, 8, 9.

15. That whosoever – He must be lifted up, that hereby he may purchase salvation for all believers: all those who look to him by faith recover spiritual health, even as all that looked at that serpent recovered bodily health.

16. Yea, and this was the very design of God's love in sending him into the world. Whosoever believeth on him – With that faith which worketh by love, and hold fast the beginning of his confidence steadfast to the end. God so loved the world – That is, all men under heaven; even those that despise his love, and will for that cause finally perish. Otherwise not to believe would be no sin to them. For what should they believe? Ought they to believe that Christ was given for them? Then he was given for them. He gave his only Son – Truly and seriously. And the Son of God gave him-

MATTHEW HENRY   CHARLES H. SPURGEON

so loved the world; so really, so richly. Behold and wonder, that the great God should love such a worthless
world! Here, also, is the great gospel duty, to believe in
Jesus Christ. God having given him to be our Prophet,
Priest, and King, we must give up ourselves to be ruled,
and taught, and saved by him. And here is the great
gospel benefit, that whoever believes in Christ, shall not
perish, but shall have everlasting life. God was in Christ
reconciling the world to himself, and so saving it. It
could not be saved, but through him; there is no salvation in any other. From all this is shown the happiness of
true believers; he that believeth in Christ is not condemned. Though he has been a great sinner, yet he is
not dealt with according to what his sins deserve. How
great is the sin of unbelievers! God sent One to save us,
that was dearest to himself; and shall he not be dearest
to us? How great is the misery of unbelievers! they are
condemned already; which speaks a certain condemnation; a present condemnation. The wrath of God now
fastens upon them; and their own hearts condemn
them. There is also a condemnation grounded on their
former guilt; they are open to the law for all their sins;
because they are not by faith interested in the gospel
pardon. Unbelief is a sin against the remedy. It springs
from the enmity of the heart of man to God, from love of
sin in some form. Read also the doom of those that
would not know Christ. Sinful works are works of darkness. The wicked world keep as far from this light as
they can, lest their deeds should be reproved. Christ is
hated, because sin is loved. If they had not hated saving
knowledge, they would not sit down contentedly in condemning ignorance. On the other hand, renewed hearts
bid this light welcome. A good man acts truly and sincerely in all he does. He desires to know what the will of
God is, and to do it, though against his own worldly
interest. A change in his whole character and conduct
has taken place. The love of God is shed abroad in his
heart by the Holy Ghost, and is become the commanding principle of his actions. So long as he continues
under a load of unforgiven guilt, there can be little else
than slavish fear of God; but when his doubts are done
away, when he sees the righteous ground whereon this
forgiveness is built, he rests on it as his own, and is united to God by unfeigned love. Our works are good when
the will of God is the rule of them, and the glory of God
the end of them; when they are done in his strength, and
for his sake; to him, and not to men. Regeneration, or the
new birth, is a subject to which the world is very averse;
it is, however, the grand concern, in comparison with
which every thing else is but trifling. What does it signify though we have food to eat in plenty, and variety of
raiment to put on, if we are not born again? if after a few
mornings and evenings spent in unthinking mirth, carnal pleasure, and riot, we die in our sins, and lie down
in sorrow? What does it signify though we are well able
to act our parts in life, in every other respect, if at last we
hear from the Supreme Judge, "Depart from me, I know
you not, ye workers of iniquity?"

besetting sin. There does not at first sight
appear to be any connection between the simple trusting of the Savior and the conquest of a
bad temper, or the getting rid of a bad habit,
such as intemperance, passion, covetousness,
or falsehood. There is such a connection, but
recollect, whether you can see the connection
or not, it is yours "not to reason why," but
yours to do what Jesus bids you do; for it is in
the way of the command that the miracle of
mercy will be wrought. "Fill the waterpots with
water," though what you want is wine. Christ
sees a connection between the water and the
wine, though you do not. He has a reason for
the pots being filled with water, which reason,
as yet, you do not know: it is not yours to ask
an explanation, but to yield obedience. You
are, in the first instance, just to do what Jesus
bids you, as he bids you, now that he bids you,
and because he bids you, and you shall find
that his commandments are not grievous, and
in keeping of them there is a great reward.

Sometimes these commands may even
seem to be trivial. They may look as if he trifled
with us. The family were in need of wine; Jesus
says, "Fill the waterpots with water." The servants might have said, "This is clearly a mere
putting of us off and playing with us. Why, we
should be better employed in going round to
these poor people's friends, and asking them to
contribute another skin of wine. We should be
much better employed in finding out some
shop where we could purchase more: but to
send us to the well to fill those great waterpots
that hold so much water does seem altogether
a piece of child's play." I know, brethren, that
sometimes the path of duty seems as if it could
not lead to the desired result. We want to be
doing something more; that something more
might be wrong, but it looks as if we could
thereby compass our design more easily and
directly, and so we hanker after this uncom-
manded and perhaps forbidden course. And I
know that many a troubled conscience thinks
that simply to believe in Jesus is too little a
thing. The deceitful heart suggests a course
which looks to be more effectual. "Do some
penance: feel some bitterness; weep a certain
amount of tears. Goad your mind, or break
your heart": so cries carnal self. Jesus simply
commands, "Believe." It does appear to be too
little a thing to be done, as if it could not be
that eternal life should be given upon putting
your trust in Jesus Christ: but this is the principle we want to teach you—that when Jesus
Christ is about to give a blessing he issues a
command which is not to be questioned, but to
be at once obeyed. If ye will not believe, neither shall ye be established; but if ye be willing

mountain, nor yet at Jerusalem, worship the Father.

22 Ye worship ye know not what: we know what we worship: for salvation is of the Jews.

23 But the hour cometh, and now is, when the true worshipers shall worship the Father in spirit and in truth: for the Father seeketh such to worship him.

24 God is a Spirit: and they that worship him must worship him in spirit and in truth.

25 The woman saith unto him, I know that Messias cometh, which is called Christ: when he is come, he will tell us all things.

26 Jesus saith unto her, I that speak unto thee am he.

27 And upon this came his disciples, and marveled that he talked with the woman: yet no man said, What seekest thou? or, Why talkest thou with her?

28 The woman then left her waterpot, and went her way into the city, and saith to the men,

29 Come, see a man, which told me all things that ever I did: is not this the Christ?

30 Then they went out of the city, and came unto him.

31 In the mean while his disciples prayed him, saying, Master, eat.

32 But he said unto them, I have meat to eat that ye know not of.

33 Therefore said the disciples one to another, Hath any man brought him ought to eat?

34 Jesus saith unto them, My meat is to do the will of him that sent me, and to finish his work.

35 Say not ye, There are yet four months, and then cometh harvest? behold, I say unto you, Lift up your eyes, and look on the fields; for they are white already to harvest.

36 And he that reapeth receiveth wages, and gathereth fruit unto life eternal: that both he that soweth and he that reapeth may rejoice together.

37 And herein is that saying true, One soweth, and another reapeth.

38 I sent you to reap that whereon ye bestowed no labor: other men labored, and ye are entered into their labors.

39 And many of the Samaritans of that city believed on him for the saying of the woman, which testified, He told me all that ever I did.

40 So when the Samaritans were come unto him, they besought him that he would tarry with them: and he abode there two days.

41 And many more believed because of his own word;

42 And said unto the woman, Now we believe, not because of thy saying: for we have heard him ourselves, and know that this is indeed the Christ, the Savior of the world.

43 Now after two days he departed thence, and went into Galilee.

44 For Jesus himself testified, that a prophet hath no honor in his own country.

45 Then when he was come into Galilee, the Galileans received him, having seen all the

self, Gal. iv, 4, truly and seriously.

17. God sent not his Son into the world to condemn the world – Although many accuse him of it.

18. He that believeth on him is not condemned – Is acquitted, is justified before God. The name of the only-begotten Son of God – The name of a person is often put for the person himself. But perhaps it is farther intimated in that expression, that the person spoken of is great and magnificent. And therefore it is generally used to express either God the Father or the Son.

19. This is the condemnation – That is, the cause of it. So God is clear.

21. He that practiceth the truth (that is, true religion) cometh to the light – So even Nicodemus, afterward did. Are wrought in God – That is, in the light, power, and love of God.

22. Jesus went – From the capital city, Jerusalem, into the land of Judea – That is, into the country. There he baptized – Not himself; but his disciples by his order, chap. iv, 2.

23. John also was baptizing – He did not repel them that offered, but he more willingly referred them to Jesus.

25. The Jews – Those men of Judea, who now went to be baptized by Jesus; and John's disciples, who were mostly of Galilee: about purifying – That is, baptism. They disputed, which they should be baptized by.

27. A man can receive nothing – Neither he nor I. Neither could he do this, unless God had sent him: nor can I receive the title of Christ, or any honor comparable to that which he hath received from heaven. They seem to have spoken with jealousy and resentment; John answers with sweet composure of spirit.

29. He that hath the bride is the bridegroom – He whom the bride follows. But all men now come to Jesus. Hence it is plain he is the bridegroom. The friend who heareth him – Talk with the bride; rejoiceth greatly – So far from envying or resenting it.

30. He must increase, but I must decrease – So they who are now, like John, burning and shining lights, must (if not suddenly eclipsed) like him gradually decrease, while others are increasing about them; as they in their turns grew up, amidst the decays of the former generation. Let us know how to set, as well as how to rise; and let it comfort our declining days to trace, in those who are likely to succeed us in our work, the openings of yet greater usefulness.

31. It is not improbable, that what is added, to the end of the chapter, are the words of the evangelist, not the Baptist. He that is of the earth – A mere man; of earthly original, has a spirit and speech answerable to it.

32. No man – None comparatively, exceeding few; receiveth his testimony – With true faith.

33. Hath set to his seal – It was customary among the Jews for the witness to set his seal to the testimony he had given. That God is true – Whose words the Messiah speaks.

34. God giveth not him the Spirit by measure – As he did to the prophets, but immeasurably. Hence he speaketh the words of God in the most perfect manner.

36. He that believeth on the Son hath everlasting life – He hath it already. For he loves God. And love is the essence of heaven. He that obeyeth not – A consequence of not believing.

MATTHEW HENRY   CHARLES H. SPURGEON

22-36 John was fully satisfied with the place and work assigned him; but Jesus came on a more important work. He also knew that Jesus would increase in honor and influence, for of his government and peace there would be no end, while he himself would be less followed. John knew that Jesus came from heaven as the Son of God, while he was a sinful, mortal man, who could only speak about the more plain subjects of religion. The words of Jesus were the words of God; he had the Spirit, not by measure, as the prophets, but in all fullness. Everlasting life could only be had by faith in Him, and might be thus obtained; whereas all those, who believe not in the Son of God, cannot partake of salvation, but the wrath of God forever rests upon them.

JOHN 4

Christ's departure into Galilee. (1-3)
His discourse with the Samaritan woman. (4-26)
The effects of Christ's conversation with the woman of
*   Samaria. (27-42)*
Christ heals the nobleman's son. (43-54)

1-3 Jesus applied himself more to preaching, which was the more excellent, 1Co 1:17, than to baptism. He would put honor upon his disciples, by employing them to baptize. He teaches us that the benefit of sacraments depends not on the hand that administers them.

4-26 There was great hatred between the Samaritans and the Jews. Christ's road from Judea to Galilee lay through Samaria. We should not go into places of temptation but when we needs must; and then must not dwell in them, but hasten through them. We have here our Lord Jesus under the common fatigue of travelers. Thus we see that he was truly a man. Toil came in with sin; therefore Christ, having made himself a curse for us, submitted to it. Also, he was a poor man, and went all his journeys on foot. Being wearied, he sat thus on the well; he had no couch to rest upon. He sat thus, as people wearied with traveling sit. Surely, we ought readily to submit to be like the Son of God in such things as these. Christ asked a woman for water. She was surprised because he did not show the anger of his own nation against the Samaritans. Moderate men of all sides are men wondered at. Christ took the occasion to teach her Divine things: he converted this woman, by showing her ignorance and sinfulness, and her need of a Savior. By this living water is meant the Spirit. Under this comparison the blessing of the Messiah had been promised in the Old Testament. The graces of the Spirit, and his comforts, satisfy the thirsting soul, that knows its own nature and necessity. What Jesus spake figuratively, she took literally. Christ shows that the water of Jacob's well yielded a very short satisfaction. Of whatever waters of comfort we drink, we

and obedient, ye shall eat the good of the land. "Whatsoever he saith unto you, do it."

The third principle is this—that whenever we get a command from Christ it is always wisdom to carry it out zealously. He said, "Fill the waterpots with water," and they filled them up to the brim. You know there is a way of filling a waterpot, and there is another way of filling it. It is full, and you cannot heap it up; but still you can fill it up till it begins almost to run over: the liquid trembles as if it must surely fall in a crystal cascade. It is a filling fullness. In fulfilling Christ's commands, my dear brethren and sisters, let us go to their widest extent: let us fill them up to the brim. If it is "Believe," oh, believe him with all your might; trust him with your whole heart. If it is "Preach the gospel," preach it in season and out of season; and preach the gospel—the whole of it. Fill it up to the brim. Do not give the people a half gospel. Give them a brimming-over gospel. Fill the vessels up to the very brim. If you are to repent, ask to have a hearty and a deep repentance—full to the brim. If you are to believe, ask to have an intense, absolute, childlike dependence, that your faith may be full to the brim. If you are bidden pray, pray mightily: fill the vessel of prayer up to the brim. If you are to search the Scriptures for blessing, search them from end to end: fill the Bible-reading vessel up to the brim. Christ's commands are never meant to be done in a half-hearted manner. Let us throw our whole soul into whatever he commands us, even though, as yet, we cannot see the reason why he has set us the task. Christ's commands should be fulfilled with enthusiasm, and carried out to the extreme, if extreme be possible.

The fourth principle is that our earnest action in obedience to Christ is not contrary to our dependence upon him, but it is necessary to our dependence upon him. I will show you that in a moment. There are some brethren I know who say, "Hem! you hold what you call revival services, and you try to arouse men by earnest appeals and exciting addresses. Do you not see that God will do his own work? These efforts are just your trying to take the work out of God's hands. The proper way is to trust in him, and do nothing." All right, brother. We have your word for it—that you trust in him and do nothing. I take the liberty not to be so very certain that you do trust him, for if I remember who you are, and I think I have been to your house, you are about the most miserable, desponding, unbelieving person that I know. You do not even know whether you are saved yourself nine times out of ten. Well now, I think you should hardly come and cry yourself

things that he did at Jerusalem at the feast: for they also went unto the feast.

46 So Jesus came again into Cana of Galilee, where he made the water wine. And there was a certain nobleman, whose son was sick at Capernaum.

47 When he heard that Jesus was come out of Judea into Galilee, he went unto him, and besought him that he would come down, and heal his son: for he was at the point of death.

48 Then said Jesus unto him, Except ye see signs and wonders, ye will not believe.

49 The nobleman saith unto him, Sir, come down ere my child die.

50 Jesus saith unto him, Go thy way; thy son liveth. And the man believed the word that Jesus had spoken unto him, and he went his way.

51

And as he was now going down, his servants met him, and told him, saying, Thy son liveth.

52 Then inquired he of them the hour when he began to amend. And they said unto him, Yesterday at the seventh hour the fever left him.

53 So the father knew that it was at the same hour, in the which Jesus said unto him, Thy son liveth: and himself believed, and his whole house.

54 This is again the second miracle that Jesus did, when he was come out of Judea into Galilee.

JOHN 5

1 After this there was a feast of the Jews; and Jesus went up to Jerusalem.

2 Now there is at Jerusalem by the sheep market a pool, which is called in the Hebrew tongue Bethesda, having five porches.

3 In these lay a great multitude of impotent folk, of blind, halt, withered, waiting for the moving of the water.

4 For an angel went down at a certain season into the pool, and troubled the water: whosoever then first after the troubling of the water stepped in was made whole of whatsoever disease he had.

5 And a certain man was there, which had an infirmity thirty and eight years.

6 When Jesus saw him lie, and knew that he had been now a long time in that case, he saith unto him, Wilt thou be made whole?

7 The impotent man answered him, Sir, I have no man, when the water is troubled, to put me into the pool: but while I am coming, another steppeth down before me.

8 Jesus saith unto him, Rise, take up thy bed, and walk.

9 And immediately the man was made whole, and took up his bed, and walked: and on the same day was the sabbath.

10 The Jews therefore said unto him that was cured, It is the sabbath day: it is not lawful for thee to carry thy bed.

JOHN 4

1. The Lord knew – Though none informed him of it.

3. He left Judea – To shun the effects of their resentment.

4. And he must needs go through Samaria – The road lying directly through it.

5. Sychar – Formerly called Sichem or Shechem. Jacob gave – On his death bed, Gen. xlviii, 22.

6. Jesus sat down – Weary as he was. It was the sixth hour – Noon; the heat of the day.

7. Give me to drink – In this one conversation he brought her to that knowledge which the apostles were so long in attaining.

8. For his disciples were gone – Else he needed not have asked her.

9. How dost thou – Her open simplicity appears from her very first words. The Jews have no dealings – None by way of friendship. They would receive no kind of favor from them.

10. If thou hadst known the gift – The living water; and who it is – He who alone is able to give it: thou wouldst have asked of him – On those words the stress lies. Water – In like manner he draws the allegory from bread, chap. vi, 27, and from light, viii, 12; the first, the most simple, necessary, common, and salutary things in nature. Living water – The Spirit and its fruits. But she might the more easily mistake his meaning, because living water was a common phrase among the Jews for spring water.

12. Our father Jacob – So they fancied he was; whereas they were, in truth, a mixture of many nations, placed there by the king of Assyria, in the room of the Israelites whom he had carried away captive, 2 Kings xvii, 24. Who gave us the well – In Joseph their supposed forefather: and drank thereof – So even he had no better water than this.

14. Will never thirst – Will never (provided he continue to drink thereof) be miserable, dissatisfied, without refreshment. If ever that thirst returns, it will be the fault of the man, not the water. But the water that I shall give him – The spirit of faith working by love, shall become in him – An inward living principle, a fountain – Not barely a well, which is soon exhausted, springing up into everlasting life – Which is a confluence, or rather an ocean of streams arising from this fountain.

15. That I thirst not – She takes him still in a gross sense.

16. Jesus saith to her – He now clears the way that he might give her a better kind of water than she asked for. Go, call thy husband – He strikes directly at her bosom sin.

17. Thou hast well said – We may observe in all our Lord's discourses the utmost weightiness, and yet the utmost courtesy.

18. Thou hast had five husbands – Whether they were all dead or not, her own conscience now awakened would tell her.

19. Sir, I perceive – So soon was her heart touched.

20. The instant she perceived this, she proposes what she thought the most important of all questions. This mountain – Pointing to Mount Gerizim. Sanballat, by the permission of Alexander the Great, had built a temple upon Mount Gerizim, for Manasseh, who for marrying Sanballat's daughter had been expelled from the priesthood and from Jerusalem, Neh. xiii, 28. This was the place where the Samaritans used to worship in opposition to Jerusalem. And it was so near Sychar, that a man's voice might be heard from the one to the other. Our fathers worshiped – This plainly refers to Abraham and Jacob (from whom the Samaritans pretended to

MATTHEW HENRY   CHARLES H. SPURGEON

shall thirst again. But whoever partakes of the Spirit of grace, and the comforts of the gospel, shall never want that which will abundantly satisfy his soul. Carnal hearts look no higher than carnal ends. Give it me, saith she, not that I may have everlasting life, which Christ proposed, but that I come not hither to draw. The carnal mind is very ingenious in shifting off convictions, and keeping them from fastening. But how closely our Lord Jesus brings home the conviction to her conscience! He severely reproved her present state of life. The woman acknowledged Christ to be a prophet. The power of his word in searching the heart, and convincing the conscience of secret things, is a proof of Divine authority. It should cool our contests, to think that the things we are striving about are passing away. The object of worship will continue still the same, God, as a Father; but an end shall be put to all differences about the place of worship. Reason teaches us to consult decency and convenience in the places of our worship; but religion gives no preference to one place above another, in respect of holiness and approval with God. The Jews were certainly in the right. Those who by the Scriptures have obtained some knowledge of God, know whom they worship. The word of salvation was of the Jews. It came to other nations through them. Christ justly preferred the Jewish worship before the Samaritan, yet here he speaks of the former as soon to be done away. God was about to be revealed as the Father of all believers in every nation. The spirit or the soul of man, as influenced by the Holy Spirit, must worship God, and have communion with him. Spiritual affections, as shown in fervent prayers, supplications, and thanksgivings, form the worship of an upright heart, in which God delights and is glorified. The woman was disposed to leave the matter undecided, till the coming of the Messiah. But Christ told her, I that speak to thee, am he. She was an alien and a hostile Samaritan, merely speaking to her was thought to disgrace our Lord Jesus. Yet to this woman did our Lord reveal himself more fully than as yet he had done to any of his disciples. No past sins can bar our acceptance with him, if we humble ourselves before him, believing in him as the Christ, the Savior of the world.

27-42 The disciples wondered that Christ talked thus with a Samaritan. Yet they knew it was for some good reason, and for some good end. Thus when particular difficulties occur in the word and providence of God, it is good to satisfy ourselves that all is well that Jesus Christ says and does. Two things affected the woman. The extent of his knowledge. Christ knows all the thoughts, words, and actions, of all the children of men. And the power of his word. He told her secret sins with power. She fastened upon that part of Christ's discourse, many would think she would have been most shy of repeating; but the knowledge of Christ, into which we are led by conviction of sin, is most likely to be sound and saving. They came to him: those who would know Christ, must meet him where he records

up for your faith. If you had such a wonderfully great faith, there is no doubt whatever that according to your faith it would be unto you. How many have been added to your church through your doing nothing this year—that blessed church of yours, where you exercise this blessed faith without works? How many have been brought in? "Well, we do not have very many additions." No, and I think you are not likely to have. If you go about the extension of the Redeemer's kingdom by inaction, I do not think that you go the way to work which Jesus Christ approves of. But we venture to say to you that we who go in for working for Christ with all our heart and soul, using any means within our reach to bring men in to hear the gospel, feel as much as ever you do that we cannot do anything at all in the matter apart from the Holy Spirit, and we trust in God, I think, almost as much as you do, because our faith has produced rather more results than yours has done. I should not wonder if it turns out that your faith without works is dead, being alone, and that our faith having works with it has been living faith after all. I will put the case thus: Jesus Christ says, "Fill the waterpots with water." The orthodox servant says, "My Lord, I fully believe that thou canst make wine for these people without any water, and by thy leave I will bring no water. I am not going to interfere with the work of God. I am quite certain that thou dost not want our help, gracious Lord. Thou canst make these waterpots to be full of wine without our bringing a single bucket of water, and so we will not rob thee of the glory of it. We will just stand back, and wait for thee. When the wine is made we will drink some of it and bless thy name; but meanwhile we pray thee have us excused, for pails are heavy carrying, and a good many must needs be brought to fill all those waterpots. It would be interfering with the divine work, and so we would rather take our ease." Do you not think that servants who talked so would prove that they had no faith in Jesus at all? We will not say that it would prove their unbelief, but we will say that it looks very like it. But look at the servant there who, as soon as ever Jesus commands "Fill the waterpots with water," says, "I do not know what he is at. I do not see the connection between fetching this water and providing the feast with wine, but I am off to the well: here, hand me a couple of pails. Come along, brother; come along and help fill the baths." There they go, and soon come joyfully back with the water, pouring it into the troughs till they are full up to the brim. Those seem to me to be the believing servants who obey the command, not understanding it, but

11 He answered them, He that made me whole, the same said unto me, Take up thy bed, and walk.

12 Then asked they him, What man is that which said unto thee, Take up thy bed, and walk?

13 And he that was healed wist not who it was: for Jesus had conveyed himself away, a multitude being in that place.

14 Afterward Jesus findeth him in the temple, and said unto him, Behold, thou art made whole: sin no more, lest a worse thing come unto thee.

15 The man departed, and told the Jews that it was Jesus, which had made him whole.

16 And therefore did the Jews persecute Jesus, and sought to slay him, because he had done these things on the sabbath day.

17 But Jesus answered them, My Father worketh hitherto, and I work.

18 Therefore the Jews sought the more to kill him, because he not only had broken the sabbath, but said also that God was his Father, making himself equal with God.

19 Then answered Jesus and said unto them, Verily, verily, I say unto you, The Son can do nothing of himself, but what he seeth the Father do: for what things soever he doeth, these also doeth the Son likewise.

20 For the Father loveth the Son, and sheweth him all things that himself doeth: and he will shew him greater works than these, that ye may marvel.

21 For as the Father raiseth up the dead, and quickeneth them; even so the Son quickeneth whom he will.

22 For the Father judgeth no man, but hath committed all judgment unto the Son:

23 That all men should honor the Son, even as they honor the Father. He that honoreth not the Son honoreth not the Father which hath sent him.

24 Verily, verily, I say unto you, He that heareth my word, and believeth on him that sent me, hath everlasting life, and shall not come into condemnation; but is passed from death unto life.

25 Verily, verily, I say unto you, The hour is coming, and now is, when the dead shall hear the voice of the Son of God: and they that hear shall live.

26 For as the Father hath life in himself; so hath he given to the Son to have life in himself;

27 And hath given him authority to execute judgment also, because he is the Son of man.

28 Marvel not at this: for the hour is coming, in the which all that are in the graves shall hear his voice,

29 And shall come forth; they that have done good, unto the resurrection of life; and they that have done evil, unto the resurrection of damnation.

30 I can of mine own self do nothing: as I hear, I judge: and my judgment is just; because I seek

deduce their genealogy) who erected altars in this place: Gen. xii, 6, 7, and Gen. xxxiii, 18, 20. And possibly to the whole congregation, who were directed when they came into the land of Canaan to put the blessing upon Mount Gerizim, Deut. xi, 29. Ye Jews say, In Jerusalem is the place – Namely, the temple.

21. Believe me – Our Lord uses this expression in this manner but once; and that to a Samaritan. To his own people, the Jews, his usual language is, I say unto you. The hour cometh when ye – Both Samaritans and Jews, shall worship neither in this mountain, nor at Jerusalem – As preferable to any other place. True worship shall be no longer confined to any one place or nation.

22. Ye worship ye know not what – Ye Samaritans are ignorant, not only of the place, but of the very object of worship. Indeed, they feared the Lord after a fashion; but at the same time served their own gods, 2 Kings xvii, 33. Salvation is from the Jews – So spake all the prophets, that the Savior should arise out of the Jewish nation: and that from thence the knowledge of him should spread to all nations under heaven.

23. The true worshipers shall worship the Father – Not here or there only, but at all times and in all places.

24. God is a Spirit – Not only remote from the body, and all the properties of it, but likewise full of all spiritual perfections, power, wisdom, love, holiness. And our worship should be suitable to his nature. We should worship him with the truly spiritual worship of faith, love, and holiness, animating all our tempers, thoughts, words, and actions.

25. The woman saith – With joy for what she had already learned, and desire of fuller instruction.

26. Jesus saith – Hasting to satisfy her desire before his disciples came. l am He – Our Lord did not speak this so plainly to the Jews who were so full of the Messiah's temporal kingdom. If he had, many would doubtless have taken up arms in his favor, and others have accused him to the Roman governor. Yet he did in effect declare the thing, though he denied the particular title. For in a multitude of places he represented himself, both as the Son of man, and as the Son of God: both which expressions were generally understood by the Jews as peculiarly applicable to the Messiah.

27. His disciples marveled that he talked with a woman – Which the Jewish rabbis reckoned scandalous for a man of distinction to do. They marveled likewise at his talking with a woman of that nation, which was so peculiarly hateful to the Jews. Yet none said – To the woman, What seekest thou? – Or to Christ, Why talkest thou with her?

28. The woman left her water pot – Forgetting smaller things.

29. A man who told me all things that ever I did – Our Lord had told her but a few things. But his words awakened her conscience, which soon told her all the rest. Is not this the Christ? – She does not doubt of it herself, but incites them to make the inquiry.

31. In the meantime – Before the people came.

34. My meat – That which satisfies the strongest appetite of my soul.

35. The fields are white already – As if he had said, The spiritual harvest is ripe already. The Samaritans, ripe for the Gospel, covered the ground round about them.

36. He that reapeth – Whoever saves souls, receiveth wages – A peculiar blessing to himself, and gathereth fruit – Many souls: that

his name. Our Master has left us an example, that we may learn to do the will of God as he did; with diligence, as those that make a business of it; with delight and pleasure in it. Christ compares his work to harvest-work. The harvest is appointed and looked for before it comes; so was the gospel. Harvest-time is busy time; all must be then at work. Harvest-time is a short time, and harvest-work must be done then, or not at all; so the time of the gospel is a season, which if once past, cannot be recalled. God sometimes uses very weak and unlikely instruments for beginning and carrying on a good work. Our Savior, by teaching one poor woman, spread knowledge to a whole town. Blessed are those who are not offended at Christ. Those taught of God, are truly desirous to learn more. It adds much to the praise of our love to Christ and his word, if it conquers prejudices. Their faith grew. In the matter of it: they believed him to be the Savior, not only of the Jews but of the world. In the certainty of it: we know that this is indeed the Christ. And in the ground of it, for we have heard him ourselves.

43-54 The father was a nobleman, yet the son was sick. Honors and titles are no security from sickness and death. The greatest men must go themselves to God, must become beggars. The nobleman did not stop from his request till he prevailed. But at first he discovered the weakness of his faith in the power of Christ. It is hard to persuade ourselves that distance of time and place, are no hindrance to the knowledge, mercy, and power of our Lord Jesus. Christ gave an answer of peace. Christ's saying that the soul lives, makes it alive. The father went his way, which showed the sincerity of his faith. Being satisfied, he did not hurry home that night, but returned as one easy in his own mind. His servants met him with the news of the child's recovery. Good news will meet those that hope in God's word. Diligent comparing the works of Jesus with his word, will confirm our faith. And the bringing the cure to the family brought salvation to it. Thus an experience of the power of one word of Christ, may settle the authority of Christ in the soul. The whole family believed likewise. The miracle made Jesus dear to them. The knowledge of Christ still spreads through families, and men find health and salvation to their souls.

JOHN 5

The cure at the pool of Bethesda. (1-9)
The Jews' displeasure. (10-16)
Christ reproves the Jews. (17-23)
Christ's discourse. (24-47)

1-9 We are all by nature impotent folk in spiritual things, blind, halt, and withered; but full provision is made for our cure, if we attend to it. An angel went down, and troubled the water; and what disease soever it was, this water cured it, but only he that first stepped in had benefit. This teaches us to be careful,

expecting that, somehow or other, Jesus Christ knows the way to work his own miracle. By our earnest exertions we are not interfering with him, dear friends; far from it. We are proving our faith in him if we work for him as he bids us work, and trust in him alone with undivided faith.

The next principle I must lay equal stress upon is this,—our action alone is not sufficient. That we know, but let me remind you of it yet again. There are these waterpots, these troughs, these baths: they are full, and could not be fuller. What a spilling of water there is! You see that in their trying to fill them the water runs over here and there. Well, all these six great baths are full of water. Is there any more wine for all that? Not a drop. It is water that they brought, nothing but water, and it remains water still. Suppose that they should take that water into the feast; I am half afraid that the guests would not have thought cold water quite the proper liquid to drink at a wedding. They ought to have done so; but I am afraid they were not educated in the school of total abstinence. They would have said to the master of the feast, "Thou hast given us good wine, and water is a poor finish for the feast." I am sure it would not have done. And yet water it was, depend upon it, and nothing else but water, when the servants poured it into the pots. Even so, after all that sinners can. do, and all that saints can do, there is nothing in any human effort which can avail for the saving of a soul till Christ speaks the word of power. When Paul has planted and Apollos watered, there is no increase till God gives it. Preach the gospel, labor with souls, persuade, entreat, exhort; but there is no power in anything that you do until Jesus Christ displays his divine might. His presence is our power. Blessed be his name, he will come; and if we fill the waterpots with water, he will turn it into wine. He alone can do it, and those servants who show the most alacrity in filling up the waterpots are among the first to confess that it is he alone who can perform the deed.

And now the last principle here is that although human action in itself falls short of the desired end, yet it has its place, and God has made it necessary by his appointment. Why did our Lord have these waterpots filled with water? I do not say that it was necessary that it should have been done. It was not absolutely necessary in itself; but in order that the miracle might be all open and above board, it was necessary; for suppose he had said, "Go to those waterpots and draw out wine," those who watched him might have said that there was wine there before, and that no miracle was

not mine own will, but the will of the Father which hath sent me.

31 If I bear witness of myself, my witness is not true.

32 There is another that beareth witness of me; and I know that the witness which he witnesseth of me is true.

33 Ye sent unto John, and he bare witness unto the truth.

34 But I receive not testimony from man: but these things I say, that ye might be saved.

35 He was a burning and a shining light: and ye were willing for a season to rejoice in his light.

36 But I have greater witness than that of John: for the works which the Father hath given me to finish, the same works that I do, bear witness of me, that the Father hath sent me.

37 And the Father himself, which hath sent me, hath borne witness of me. Ye have neither heard his voice at any time, nor seen his shape.

38 And ye have not his word abiding in you: for whom he hath sent, him ye believe not.

39 Search the scriptures; for in them ye think ye have eternal life: and they are they which testify of me.

40 And ye will not come to me, that ye might have life.

41 I receive not honor from men.

42 But I know you, that ye have not the love of God in you.

43 I am come in my Father's name, and ye receive me not: if another shall come in his own name, him ye will receive.

44 How can ye believe, which receive honor one of another, and seek not the honor that cometh from God only?

45 Do not think that I will accuse you to the Father: there is one that accuseth you, even Moses, in whom ye trust.

46 For had ye believed Moses, ye would have believed me: for he wrote of me.

47 But if ye believe not his writings, how shall ye believe my words?

JOHN 6

1 After these things Jesus went over the sea of Galilee, which is the sea of Tiberias.

2 And a great multitude followed him, because they saw his miracles which he did on them that were diseased.

3 And Jesus went up into a mountain, and there he sat with his disciples.

4 And the passover, a feast of the Jews, was nigh.

5 When Jesus then lifted up his eyes, and saw a great company come unto him, he saith unto Philip, Whence shall we buy bread, that these may eat?

6 And this he said to prove him: for he himself knew what he would do.

7 Philip answered him, Two hundred pennyworth of bread is not sufficient for them, that every one of them may take a little.

he that soweth – Christ the great sower of the seed, and he that reapeth may rejoice together – In heaven.

37. That saying – A common proverb; One soweth – The prophets and Christ; another reapeth – The apostles and succeeding ministers.

38. I – The Lord of the whole harvest, have sent you – He had employed them already in baptizing, ver. 2.

42. We know that this is the Savior of the world – And not of the Jews only.

43. He went into Galilee – That is, into the country of Galilee: but not to Nazareth. It was at that town only that he had no honor. Therefore he went to other towns.

44. Matt. xiii, 57.

47. To come down – For Cana stood much higher than Capernaum.

48. Unless ye see signs and wonders – Although the Samaritans believed without them.

52. He asked the hour when he amended – The more exactly the works of God are considered, the more faith is increased.

JOHN 5

1. A feast – Pentecost.

2. There is in Jerusalem – Hence it appears, that St. John wrote his Gospel before Jerusalem was destroyed: it is supposed about thirty years after the ascension. Having five porticos – Built for the use of the sick. Probably the basin had five sides! Bethesda signifies the house of mercy.

4. An angel – Yet many undoubtedly thought the whole thing to be purely natural. At certain times – Perhaps at a certain hour of the day, during this paschal week, went down – The Greek word implies that he had ceased going down, before the time of St. John's writing this. God might design this to raise expectation of the acceptable time approaching, to add a greater luster to his Son's miracles, and to show that his ancient people were not entirely forgotten of him. The first – Whereas the Son of God healed every day not one only, but whole multitudes that resorted to him.

7. The sick man answered – Giving the reason why he was not made whole, notwithstanding his desire.

14. Sin no more – It seems his former illness was the effect or punishment of sin.

15. The man went and told the Jews, that it was Jesus who had made him whole – One might have expected, that when he had published the name of his benefactor, crowds would have thronged about Jesus, to have heard the words of his mouth, and to have received the blessings of the Gospel. Instead of this, they surround him with a hostile intent: they even conspire against his life, and for an imagined transgression in point of ceremony, would have put out this light of Israel. Let us not wonder then, if our good be evil spoken of: if even candor, benevolence, and usefulness, do not disarm the enmity of those who have been taught to prefer sacrifice to mercy; and who, disrelishing the genuine Gospel, naturally seek to slander and persecute the professors, but especially the defenders of it.

17. My Father worketh until now, and I work – From the creation

that we let not a season slip which may never return. The man had lost the use of his limbs thirty-eight years. Shall we, who perhaps for many years have scarcely known what it has been to be a day sick, complain of one wearisome night, when many others, better than we, have scarcely known what it has been to be a day well? Christ singled this one out from the rest. Those long in affliction, may comfort themselves that God keeps account how long. Observe, this man speaks of the unkindness of those about him, without any peevish reflections. As we should be thankful, so we should be patient. Our Lord Jesus cures him, though he neither asked nor thought of it. Arise, and walk. God's command, Turn and live; Make ye a new heart; no more supposes power in us without the grace of God, his distinguishing grace, than this command supposed such power in the impotent man: it was by the power of Christ, and he must have all the glory. What a joyful surprise to the poor cripple, to find himself of a sudden so easy, so strong, so able to help himself! The proof of spiritual cure, is our rising and walking. Has Christ healed our spiritual diseases, let us go wherever he sends us, and take up whatever he lays upon us; and walk before him.

10-16 Those eased of the punishment of sin, are in danger of returning to sin, when the terror and restraint are over, unless Divine grace dries up the fountain. The misery believers are made whole from, warns us to sin no more, having felt the smart of sin. This is the voice of every providence, Go, and sin no more. Christ saw it necessary to give this caution; for it is common for people, when sick, to promise much; when newly recovered, to perform only something; but after awhile to forget all. Christ spoke of the wrath to come, which is beyond compare worse than the many hours, nay, weeks and years of pain, some wicked men have to suffer in consequence of their unlawful indulgences. And if such afflictions are severe, how dreadful will be the everlasting punishment of the wicked!

17-23 The Divine power of the miracle proved Jesus to be the Son of God, and he declared that he worked with, and like unto his Father, as he saw good. These ancient enemies of Christ understood him, and became more violent, charging him not only with breaking, but blasphemy, in calling God his own Father, and making himself equal with God. But all things now, and at the final judgment, are committed to the Son, purposely that all men might honor the Son, as they honor the Father; and every one who does not thus honor the Son, whatever he may think or pretend, does not honor the Father who sent him.

24-29 Our Lord declared his authority and character, as the Messiah. The time was come when the dead should hear his voice, as the Son of God, and live. Our Lord first refers to his raising those who were dead in

wrought. When our Lord had them filled up with water, there remained no room for any wine to be hidden away. It was just the same as with Elijah, when, in order to prove that there was no concealed fire upon the altar at Carmel, he bade them go down to the sea, and bring water, and pour it upon the altar, and upon the victim, till the trenches were filled. He said, "Do it a second time," and they did it a second time; and he said. "Do it a third time," and they did it a third time, and no possibility of imposture remained. And so, when the Lord Jesus bade the servants fill the waterpots with water, he put it beyond all possibility that he should be charged with imposture; and thus we see why it was necessary that they should be filled with water.

Moreover, it was necessary, because it was so instructive to the servants. Did you notice when I was reading it that the master of the feast, when he tasted the good wine, did not know where it came from. He could not make it out, and he uttered an expression which showed his surprise, mingled with his ignorance. But it is written, "The servants which drew the water knew." Now, when souls are converted in a church, it happens much in the same way with certain of the members, who are good people, but they do not know much about the conversion of sinners. They do not feel much joy in revivals; in fact, like the elder brother, they are rather suspicious of these wild characters being brought in: they consider themselves to be very respectable, and they would rather not have the lowest of people sitting in the pew with them: they feel awkward in coming so near them. They know little about what is going on. "But the servants which drew the water knew": that is to say, the earnest believers who do the work, and try to fill the waterpots, know all about it. Jesus bade them fill the vessels with water on purpose that the men who drew the water might know that it was a miracle. I warrant you, if you bring souls to Christ you will know his power. It will make you leap for joy to hear the cry of the penitent, and mark the bright flash of delight that passes over the new-born believer's face when his sins are washed away, and he feels himself renewed. If you want to know Jesus Christ's miraculous power you must go and—not work miracles, but just draw the water and fill the waterpots. Do the ordinary duties of Christian men and women—things in which there is no power of themselves, but which Jesus Christ makes to be connected with his divine working, and it shall be for your instruction, and your comfort, that you had such work to do. "The servants which drew the water knew."

8 One of his disciples, Andrew, Simon Peter's brother, saith unto him,

9 There is a lad here, which hath five barley loaves, and two small fishes: but what are they among so many?

10 And Jesus said, Make the men sit down. Now there was much grass in the place. So the men sat down, in number about five thousand.

11 And Jesus took the loaves; and when he had given thanks, he distributed to the disciples, and the disciples to them that were set down; and likewise of the fishes as much as they would.

12 When they were filled, he said unto his disciples, Gather up the fragments that remain, that nothing be lost.

13 Therefore they gathered them together, and filled twelve baskets with the fragments of the five barley loaves, which remained over and above unto them that had eaten.

14 Then those men, when they had seen the miracle that Jesus did, said, This is of a truth that prophet that should come into the world.

15 When Jesus therefore perceived that they would come and take him by force, to make him a king, he departed again into a mountain himself alone.

16 And when even was now come, his disciples went down unto the sea,

17 And entered into a ship, and went over the sea toward Capernaum. And it was now dark, and Jesus was not come to them.

18 And the sea arose by reason of a great wind that blew.

19 So when they had rowed about five and twenty or thirty furlongs, they see Jesus walking on the sea, and drawing nigh unto the ship: and they were afraid.

20 But he saith unto them, It is I; be not afraid.

21 Then they willingly received him into the ship: and immediately the ship was at the land whither they went.

22 The day following, when the people which stood on the other side of the sea saw that there was none other boat there, save that one whereinto his disciples were entered, and that Jesus went not with his disciples into the boat, but that his disciples were gone away alone;

23 (Howbeit there came other boats from Tiberias nigh unto the place where they did eat bread, after that the Lord had given thanks:)

24 When the people therefore saw that Jesus was not there, neither his disciples, they also took shipping, and came to Capernaum, seeking for Jesus.

25 And when they had found him on the other side of the sea, they said unto him, Rabbi, when camest thou hither?

26 Jesus answered them and said, Verily, verily, I say unto you, Ye seek me, not because ye saw the miracles, but because ye did eat of the loaves, and were filled.

27 Labour not for the meat which perisheth, but for that meat which endureth unto everlast-

till now he hath been working without intermission. I do likewise. This is the proposition which is explained ver. 19-30, confirmed and vindicated in ver. 31 and following verses.

18. His own Father – The Greek word means his own Father in such a sense as no creature can speak. Making himself equal with God – It is evident all the hearers so understood him, and that our Lord never contradicted, but confirmed it.

19. The Son can do nothing of himself – This is not his imperfection, but his glory, resulting from his eternal, intimate, indissoluble unity with the Father. Hence it is absolutely impossible, that the Son should judge, will, testify, or teach any thing without the Father, ver. 30, &c.; chap. vi, 38; chap. vii, 16; or that he should be known or believed on, separately from the Father. And he here defends his doing good every day, without intermission, by the example of his Father, from which he cannot depart: these doth the Son likewise – All these, and only these; seeing he and the Father are one.

20. The Father showeth him all things that himself doth – A proof of the most intimate unity. And he will show him – By doing them. At the same time (not at different times) the Father showeth and doth, and the Son seeth and doth. Greater works – Jesus oftener terms them works, than signs or wonders, because they were not wonders in his eyes. Ye will marvel – So they did, when he raised Lazarus.

21. For – He declares which are those greater works, raising the dead, and judging the world. The power of quickening whom he will follows from the power of judging. These two, quickening and judging, are proposed ver. 21, 22. The acquittal of believers, which presupposes judgment, is treated of ver. 24; the quickening some of the dead, ver. 25; and the general resurrection, ver. 28.

22. For neither doth the Father judge – Not without the Son: but he doth judge by that man whom he hath ordained, Acts xvii, 31.

23. That all men may honor the Son, even as they honor the Father – Either willingly, and so escaping condemnation, by faith: or unwillingly, when feeling the wrath of the Judge. This demonstrates the EQUALITY of the Son with the Father. If our Lord were God only by office or investiture, and not in the unity of the Divine essence, and in all respects equal in Godhead with the Father, he could not be honored even as, that is, with the same honor that they honored the Father. He that honored not the Son – With the same equal honor, greatly dishonored the Father that sent him.

24. And cometh not into condemnation – Unless he make shipwreck of the faith.

25. The dead shall hear the voice of the Son of God – So did Jairus's daughter, the widow's son, Lazarus.

26. He hath given to the Son – By eternal generation, to have life in himself – Absolute, independent.

27. Because he is the Son of man – He is appointed to judge mankind because he was made man.

28. The time is coming – When not two or three, but all shall rise.

29. The resurrection of life – That resurrection which leads to life everlasting.

30. I can do nothing of myself – It is impossible I should do any thing separately from my Father. As I hear – Of the Father, and see, so I judge and do; A because I am essentially united to him. See

MATTHEW HENRY

CHARLES H. SPURGEON

sin, to newness of life, by the power of the Spirit, and then to his raising the dead in their graves. The office of Judge of all men, can only be exercised by one who has all knowledge, and almighty power. May we believe His testimony; thus our faith and hope will be in God, and we shall not come into condemnation. And may His voice reach the hearts of those dead in sin; that they may do works meet for repentance, and prepare for the solemn day.

30-38 Our Lord returns to his declaration of the entire agreement between the Father and the Son, and declared himself the Son of God. He had higher testimony than that of John; his works bore witness to all he had said. But the Divine word had no abiding-place in their hearts, as they refused to believe in Him whom the Father had sent, according to his ancient promises. The voice of God, accompanied by the power of the Holy Ghost, thus made effectual to the conversion of sinners, still proclaims that this is the beloved Son, in whom the Father is well pleased. But when the hearts of men are full of pride, ambition, and the love of the world, there is no room for the word of God to abide in them.

39-44 The Jews considered that eternal life was revealed to them in their Scriptures, and that they had it, because they had the word of God in their hands. Jesus urged them to search those Scriptures with more diligence and attention. "Ye do search the Scriptures," and ye do well to do so. They did indeed search the Scriptures, but it was with a view to their own glory. It is possible for men to be very studious in the letter of the Scriptures, yet to be strangers to its power. Or, "Search the Scriptures," and so it was spoken to them in the nature of an appeal. Ye profess to receive and believe the Scripture, let that be the judge. It is spoken to us as advising or commanding all Christians to search the Scriptures. Not only read them, and hear them, but search them; which denotes diligence in examining and studying them. We must search the Scriptures for heaven as our great end; For in them ye think ye have eternal life. We must search the Scriptures for Christ, as the new and living Way, that leads to this end. To this testimony Christ adds reproofs of their unbelief and wickedness; their neglect of him and his doctrine. Also he reproves their want of the love of God. But there is life with Jesus Christ for poor souls. Many who make a great profession of religion, yet show they want the love of God, by their neglect of Christ and contempt of his commandments. It is the love of God in us, the love that is a living, active principle in the heart, which God will accept. They slighted and undervalued Christ, because they admired and overvalued themselves. How can those believe, who make the praise and applause of men their idol! When Christ and his followers are men wondered at, how can those believe, the utmost of whose ambition is to make a fair show in the flesh!

I think that I have said enough upon the principles which lie concealed within my text.

II. You must have patience with me while I try to apply these principles to practical purposes. LET US SEE HOW TO CARRY OUT THIS DIVINE COMMAND, "Fill the waterpots with water."

First, use in the service of Christ such abilities as you have. There stood the waterpots, six of them, and Jesus used what he found ready to his hand. There was water in the well; our Lord used that also. Our Lord is accustomed to employ his own people, and such abilities as they have, rather than angels or a novel class of beings created fresh for the purpose. Now, dear brothers and sisters, if you have no golden chalices, fill your earthen vessels. If you cannot consider yourselves to be goblets of rarest workmanship in silver, or if you could not liken yourselves to the best Sevres ware, it does not matter; fill the vessels which you have. If you cannot, with Elias, bring fire from heaven, and if you cannot work miracles with the apostles, do what you can. If silver and gold you have none, yet such as you have dedicate to Christ. Bring water at his bidding, and it will be better than wine. The commonest gifts can be made to serve Christ's purpose. Just as he took a few loaves and fishes, and fed the crowd with them, so will he take your six waterpots and the water, and do his wine-making therewith.

Thus, you see, they improved what they had; for the waterpots were empty, but they filled them. There are a good many brethren here from the College tonight, and they are trying to improve their gifts and their abilities. I think you do right, my brethren. But I have heard some people say, "The Lord Jesus does not want your learning." No, it is very likely that he does not, any more than he needed the water: but then he certainly does not want your stupidity and your ignorance, and he does not want your rough, uncultivated ways of speaking. He did not seek for empty pitchers on this occasion; he would have them full, and the servants did well to fill them. Our Lord today does not want empty heads in his ministers, nor empty hearts; so, my brethren, fill your waterpots with water. Work away, and study away, and learn all you can, and fill the waterpots with water. "Oh," somebody will say, "but how are such studies to lead to the conversion of men? Conversion is like wine, and all that these young fellows will learn will be like water." You are right; but still I bid these students fill the waterpots with water, and expect the Lord Jesus to turn the water into wine. He can sanctify human knowledge so that it shall be useful to the setting forth of

ing life, which the Son of man shall give unto you: for him hath God the Father sealed.

28 Then said they unto him, What shall we do, that we might work the works of God?

29 Jesus answered and said unto them, This is the work of God, that ye believe on him whom he hath sent.

30 They said therefore unto him, What sign shewest thou then, that we may see, and believe thee? what dost thou work?

31 Our fathers did eat manna in the desert; as it is written, He gave them bread from heaven to eat.

32 Then Jesus said unto them, Verily, verily, I say unto you, Moses gave you not that bread from heaven; but my Father giveth you the true bread from heaven.

33 For the bread of God is he which cometh down from heaven, and giveth life unto the world.

34 Then said they unto him, Lord, evermore give us this bread.

35 And Jesus said unto them, I am the bread of life: he that cometh to me shall never hunger; and he that believeth on me shall never thirst.

36 But I said unto you, That ye also have seen me, and believe not.

37 All that the Father giveth me shall come to me; and him that cometh to me I will in no wise cast out.

38 For I came down from heaven, not to do mine own will, but the will of him that sent me.

39 And this is the Father's will which hath sent me, that of all which he hath given me I should lose nothing, but should raise it up again at the last day.

40 And this is the will of him that sent me, that every one which seeth the Son, and believeth on him, may have everlasting life: and I will raise him up at the last day.

41 The Jews then murmured at him, because he said, I am the bread which came down from heaven.

42 And they said, Is not this Jesus, the son of Joseph, whose father and mother we know? how is it then that he saith, I came down from heaven?

43 Jesus therefore answered and said unto them, Murmur not among yourselves.

44 No man can come to me, except the Father which hath sent me draw him: and I will raise him up at the last day.

45 It is written in the prophets, And they shall be all taught of God. Every man therefore that hath heard, and hath learned of the Father, cometh unto me.

46 Not that any man hath seen the Father, save he which is of God, he hath seen the Father.

47 Verily, verily, I say unto you, He that believeth on me hath everlasting life.

48 I am that bread of life.

49 Your fathers did eat manna in the wilderness, and are dead.

50 This is the bread which cometh down from

ver. 19.

31. If I testify of myself – That is, if I alone, (which indeed is impossible,) my testimony is not valid.

32. There is another – The Father, ver. 37, and I know that, even in your judgment, his testimony in beyond exception.

33. He bare testimony – That I am the Christ.

34. But I have no need to receive, &c. But these things – Concerning John, whom ye yourselves reverence, I say, that ye may be saved – So really and seriously did he will their salvation. Yet they were not saved. Most, if not all of them, died in their sins.

35. He was a burning and a shining light – Inwardly burning with love and zeal, outwardly shining in all holiness. And even ye were willing for a season – A short time only.

37. He hath testified of me – Namely at my baptism. I speak not of my supposed father Joseph. Ye are utter strangers to him of whom I speak.

38. Ye have not his word – All who believe have the word of the Father (the same with the word of the Son) abiding in them, that is, deeply ingrafted in their hearts.

39. Search the Scriptures – A plain command to all men. In them ye are assured ye have eternal life – Ye know they show you the way to eternal life. And these very Scriptures testify of me.

40. Yet ye will not come unto me – As they direct you.

41. I receive not honor from men – I need it not. I seek it not from you for my own sake.

42. But I know you – With this ray he pierces the hearts of the hearers. And this doubtless he spake with the tenderest compassion.

43. If another shall come – Any false Christ.

44. While ye receive honor – That is, while ye seek the praise of men rather than the praise of God. At the feast of Pentecost, kept in commemoration of the giving the law from Mount Sinai, their sermons used to be full of the praises of the law, and of the people to whom it was given. How mortifying then must the following words of our Lord be to them, while they were thus exulting in Moses and his law!

45. There is one that accuseth you – By his writings.

46. He wrote of me – Every where; in all his writings; particularly Deut. xviii, 15, 18.

JOHN 6

1. After these things – The history of between ten and eleven months is to be supplied here from the other evangelists. Matt. xiv, 13; Mark vi, 32; Luke ix, 10.

3. Jesus went up – Before the people overtook him.

5. Jesus saith to Philip – Perhaps he had the care of providing victuals for the family of the apostles.

15. He retired to the mountain alone – Having ordered his disciples to cross over the lake.

45-47 Many trust in some form of doctrines or some parties, who no more enter into the real meaning of those doctrines, or the views of the persons whose names they bear, than the Jews did into those of Moses. Let us search and pray over the Scriptures, as intent on finding eternal life; let us observe how Christ is the great subject of them, and daily apply to him for the life he bestows.

JOHN 6

Five thousand miraculously fed. (1-14)
Jesus walks on the sea. (15-21)
He directs to spiritual food. (22-27)
His discourse with the multitude. (28-65)
Many of the disciples go back. (66-71)

1-14 John relates the miracle of feeding the multitude, for its reference to the following discourse. Observe the effect this miracle had upon the people. Even the common Jews expected the Messiah to come into the world, and to be a great Prophet. The Pharisees despised them as not knowing the law; but they knew most of Him who is the end of the law. Yet men may acknowledge Christ as that Prophet, and still turn a deaf ear to him.

15-21 Here were Christ's disciples in the way of duty, and Christ was praying for them; yet they were in distress. There may be perils and afflictions of this present time, where there is an interest in Christ. Clouds and darkness often surround the children of the light and of the day. They see Jesus walking on the sea. Even the approaches of comfort and deliverance often are so mistaken, as to become the occasions of fear. Nothing is more powerful to convince sinners than that word, "I am Jesus whom thou persecutest;" nothing more powerful to comfort saints than this, "I am Jesus whom thou lovest." If we have received Christ Jesus the Lord, though the night be dark, and the wind high, yet we may comfort ourselves, we shall be at the shore before long.

22-27 Instead of answering the inquiry how he came there, Jesus blamed their asking. The utmost earnestness should be employed in seeking salvation, in the use of appointed means; yet it is to be sought only as the gift of the Son of man. Him the Father has sealed, proved to be God. He declared the Son of man to be the Son of God with power.

28-35 Constant exercise of faith in Christ, is the most important and difficult part of the obedience required from us, as sinners seeking salvation. When by his grace we are enabled to live a life of faith in the Son of God, holy tempers follow, and acceptable services may be done. God, even his Father, who gave their fathers that food from heaven to support their natural lives, now gave them the true Bread for the salvation of

the knowledge of Jesus Christ. I hope that the day has gone by when it is so much as dreamed that ignorance and coarseness are helpful to the kingdom of Christ. The great Teacher would have his people know all that they can know, and especially know himself and the Scriptures, that they may set him forth, and proclaim his gospel. "Fill the waterpots with water."

Next, to apply this principle, let us all use such means of blessing as God appoints. What are they? First, there is the reading of the Scriptures. "Search the Scriptures." Search them all you can. Try to understand them. "But if I know the Bible, shall I be therefore saved." No, you must know Christ himself by the Spirit. Still, "fill the waterpots with water." While you are studying the Scriptures you may expect the Savior will bless his own word, and turn the water into wine.

Then there is attendance upon the means of grace, and hearing a gospel ministry. Mind you fill that waterpot with water. "But I may hear thousands of sermons and not be saved." I know it is so, but your business is to fill this waterpot with water, and while you are listening to the gospel God will bless it, for "faith cometh by hearing, and hearing by the word of God." Take care to use the means which God appoints. Since our Lord has appointed to save men by the preaching of the word, I pray that he will raise up those who will preach without ceasing, in season and out of season, indoors and in the streets. "But they won't be saved by our preaching." I know that. Preaching is the water: and while we are preaching, God will bless it, and turn the water into wine. Let us distribute religious books and tracts. "Oh, but people won't be saved by reading them." Very likely not, but while they are reading them God may bring his truth to remembrance and impress their hearts. "Fill the waterpots with water." Give away abundance of tracts. Scatter religious literature everywhere. "Fill the waterpots with water," and the Lord will turn the water into wine.

Remember the prayer-meeting. What a blessed means of grace it is for it brings down power for all the works of the church: fill that waterpot with water. I have not to complain of your attendance at prayer-meetings; but oh, keep it up, dear brethren! You can pray. Blessed be his name, you have the spirit of prayer. Pray on! "Fill the waterpots with water," and in answer to prayer Jesus will turn it into wine. Sunday-school teachers, do not neglect your blessed means of usefulness. "Fill the waterpots with water." Work the Sunday-school system with all your might. "But it will

heaven, that a man may eat thereof, and not die.

51 I am the living bread which came down from heaven: if any man eat of this bread, he shall live for ever: and the bread that I will give is my flesh, which I will give for the life of the world.

52

The Jews therefore strove among themselves, saying, How can this man give us his flesh to eat?

53 Then Jesus said unto them, Verily, verily, I say unto you, Except ye eat the flesh of the Son of man, and drink his blood, ye have no life in you.

54 Whoso eateth my flesh, and drinketh my blood, hath eternal life; and I will raise him up at the last day.

55 For my flesh is meat indeed, and my blood is drink indeed.

56 He that eateth my flesh, and drinketh my blood, dwelleth in me, and I in him.

57 As the living Father hath sent me, and I live by the Father: so he that eateth me, even he shall live by me.

58 This is that bread which came down from heaven: not as your fathers did eat manna, and are dead: he that eateth of this bread shall live for ever.

59 These things said he in the synagogue, as he taught in Capernaum.

60 Many therefore of his disciples, when they had heard this, said, This is an hard saying; who can hear it?

61

When Jesus knew in himself that his disciples murmured at it, he said unto them, Doth this offend you?

62 What and if ye shall see the Son of man ascend up where he was before?

63 It is the spirit that quickeneth; the flesh profiteth nothing: the words that I speak unto you, they are spirit, and they are life.

64 But there are some of you that believe not. For Jesus knew from the beginning who they were that believed not, and who should betray him.

65 And he said, Therefore said I unto you, that no man can come unto me, except it were given unto him of my Father.

66 From that time many of his disciples went back, and walked no more with him.

67 Then said Jesus unto the twelve, Will ye also go away?

68 Then Simon Peter answered him, Lord, to whom shall we go? thou hast the words of eternal life.

69 And we believe and are sure that thou art that Christ, the Son of the living God.

70 Jesus answered them, Have not I chosen you twelve, and one of you is a devil?

71 He spake of Judas Iscariot the son of Simon: for he it was that should betray him, being one of the twelve.

16. Matt. xiv, 22; Mark vi, 45.

22. Who had stood on the other side – They were forced to stay a while, because there were then no other vessels; and they stayed the less unwillingly, because they saw that Jesus was not embarked.

26. Our Lord does not satisfy their curiosity, but corrects the wrong motive they had in seeking him: because ye did eat – Merely for temporal advantage. Hitherto Christ had been gathering hearers: he now begins to try their sincerity, by a figurative discourse concerning his passion, and the fruit of it, to be received by faith.

27. Labor not for the meat which perisheth – For bodily food: not for that only nor chiefly: not at all, but in subordination to grace, faith, love, the meat which endureth to everlasting life. Labor, work for this; for everlasting life. So our Lord expressly commands, work for life, as well as from life: from a principle of faith and love. Him hath the Father sealed – By this very miracle, as well as by his whole testimony concerning him. See chap. iii, 33. Sealing is a mark of the authenticity of a writing.

28. The works of God – Works pleasing to God.

29. This is the work of God – The work most pleasing to God, and the foundation of all others: that ye believe – He expresses it first properly, afterward figuratively.

30. What sign dost thou? – Amazing, after what they had just seen!

31. Our fathers ate manna – This sign Moses gave them. He gave them bread from heaven – From the lower sublunary heaven; to which Jesus opposes the highest heaven: in which sense he says seven times, ver. 32, 33, 38, 50, 58, 62, that he himself came down from heaven.

32. Moses gave you not bread from heaven – It was not Moses who gave the manna to your fathers; but my Father who now giveth the true bread from heaven. Psalm lxxviii, 24.

33. He that giveth life to the world – Not (like the manna) to one people only: and that from generation to generation. Our Lord does not yet say, I am that bread; else the Jews would not have given him so respectful an answer, ver. 34.

34. Give us this bread – Meaning it still, in a literal sense: yet they seem now to be not far from believing.

35. I am the bread of life – Having and giving life: he that cometh – He that believeth – Equivalent expressions: shall never hunger, thirst – Shall be satisfied, happy, for ever.

36. I have told you – Namely, ver. 26.

37. All that the Father giveth me – All that feel themselves lost, and follow the drawings of the Father, he in a peculiar manner giveth to the Son: will come to me – By faith. And him that thus cometh to me, I will in nowise cast out – I will give him pardon, holiness, and heaven, if he endure to the end – To rejoice in his light.

39. Of all which he hath already given me – See chap. xvii, 6, 12. If they endure to the end. But Judas did not.

40. Here is the sum of the three foregoing verses. This is the will of him that sent me – This is the whole of what I have said: this is the eternal, unchangeable will of God. Every one who truly believeth, shall have everlasting life. Every one that seeth and believeth – The Jews saw, and yet believed not. And I will raise him up – As this is the will of him that sent me, I will perform it effectually.

44. Christ having checked their murmuring, continues what he was saying, ver. 40. No man comes to me, unless my Father draw him – No man can believe in Christ, unless God give him power:

MATTHEW HENRY

CHARLES H. SPURGEON

their souls. Coming to Jesus, and believing on him, signify the same. Christ shows that he is the true Bread; he is to the soul what bread is to the body, nourishes and supports the spiritual life. He is the Bread of God. Bread which the Father gives, which he has made to be the food of our souls. Bread nourishes only by the powers of a living body; but Christ is himself living Bread, and nourishes by his own power. The doctrine of Christ crucified is now as strengthening and comforting to a believer as ever it was. He is the Bread which came down from heaven. It denotes the Divinity of Christ's person and his authority; also, the Divine origin of all the good which flows to us through him. May we with understanding and earnestness say, Lord, evermore give us this Bread.

36-46 The discovery of their guilt, danger, and remedy, by the teaching of the Holy Spirit, makes men willing and glad to come, and to give up every thing which hinders applying to him for salvation. The Father's will is, that not one of those who were given to the Son, should be rejected or lost by him. No one will come, till Divine grace has subdued, and in part changed his heart; therefore no one who comes will ever be cast out. The gospel finds none willing to be saved in the humbling, holy manner, made known therein; but God draws with his word and the Holy Ghost; and man's duty is to hear and learn; that is to say, to receive the grace offered, and consent to the promise. None had seen the Father but his beloved Son; and the Jews must expect to be taught by his inward power upon their minds, and by his word, and the ministers whom he sent among them.

47-51 The advantage of the manna was small, it only referred to this life; but the living Bread is so excellent, that the man who feedeth on it shall never die. This bread is Christ's human nature, which he took to present to the Father, as a sacrifice for the sins of the world; to purchase all things pertaining to life and godliness, for sinners of every nation, who repent and believe in him.

52-59 The flesh and blood of the Son of man, denote the Redeemer in the nature of man; Christ and him crucified, and the redemption wrought out by him, with all the precious benefits of redemption; pardon of sin, acceptance with God, the way to the throne of grace, the promises of the covenant, and eternal life. These are called the flesh and blood of Christ, because they are purchased by the breaking his body, and the shedding of his blood. Also, because they are meat and drink to our souls. Eating this flesh and drinking this blood mean believing in Christ. We partake of Christ and his benefits by faith. The soul that rightly knows its state and wants, finds whatever can calm the conscience, and promote true holiness, in the redeemer, God manifest in the flesh. Meditating upon the cross of Christ gives life to our repentance, love,

not save the children merely to get them together, and teach them of Jesus. We cannot give them new hearts." Who said that you could? "Fill the waterpots with water." Jesus Christ knows how to turn it into wine, and he does not fail to do it when we are obedient to his commands.

Use all the means, but take care that you use those means right heartily. I come back to that part of the text—"And they filled them up to the brim." When you teach the young ones in the Sunday-school, teach them well. Fill them to the brim. When you preach, dear sir, do not preach as if you were only half awake; stir yourself up; fill your ministry to the brim. When you are trying to evangelize the community, do not attempt it in a half-hearted way, as if you did not care whether their souls were saved or not; fill them to the brim; preach the gospel with all your might, and beg for power from on high. Fill every vessel to the brim. Whatever is worth doing is worth doing well. Nobody ever yet served Christ too well. I have heard that in some services there may be too much zeal, but in the service of Christ you may have as much zeal as ever you will and yet not exceed, if prudence be joined therewith. "Fill the waterpots with water," and fill them to the brim. Go in for doing good with all your heart and soul and strength.

Further, in order to apply this principle, be sure to remember when you have done all that you can do, that there is a great deficiency in all that you have done. It is well to come away from tract-distributing and Sunday-school teaching and preaching, and go home and get to your knees, and cry, "Lord, I have done all that thou hast commanded me, and yet there is nothing done unless thou givest the finishing touch. Lord, I have filled the waterpots, and though I could only fill them with water, yet I have filled them to the brim. Lord, to the best of my ability, I have sought to win men for thyself. There cannot be a soul saved, a child converted, or any glory brought to thy name by what I have done, in and of itself; but, my Master, speak the miracle-working word, and let the water which fills the vessels blush into wine. Thou canst do it, though I cannot. I cast the burden upon thee."

And this leads me to the last application of the principle, which is—trust in your Lord to do the work. You see, there are two ways of filling waterpots. Suppose these people had never been commanded to fill the waterpots, and their doing it had had no reference to Christ whatever; suppose that it had been a freak of their own imagination, and they had said, "These people have no wine, but they shall

JOHN 7

1 After these things Jesus walked in Galilee: for he would not walk in Jewry, because the Jews sought to kill him.

2 Now the Jews' feast of tabernacles was at hand.

3 His brethren therefore said unto him, Depart hence, and go into Judea, that thy disciples also may see the works that thou doest.

4 For there is no man that doeth any thing in secret, and he himself seeketh to be known openly. If thou do these things, shew thyself to the world.

5 For neither did his brethren believe in him.

6 Then Jesus said unto them, My time is not yet come: but your time is alway ready.

7 The world cannot hate you; but me it hateth, because I testify of it, that the works thereof are evil.

8 Go ye up unto this feast: I go not up yet unto this feast; for my time is not yet full come.

9 When he had said these words unto them, he abode still in Galilee.

10 But when his brethren were gone up, then went he also up unto the feast, not openly, but as it were in secret.

11 Then the Jews sought him at the feast, and said, Where is he?

12 And there was much murmuring among the people concerning him: for some said, He is a good man: others said, Nay; but he deceiveth the people.

13 Howbeit no man spake openly of him for fear of the Jews.

14 Now about the midst of the feast Jesus went up into the temple, and taught.

15 And the Jews marveled, saying, How knoweth this man letters, having never learned?

16 Jesus answered them, and said, My doctrine is not mine, but his that sent me.

17 If any man will do his will, he shall know of the doctrine, whether it be of God, or whether I speak of myself.

18 He that speaketh of himself seeketh his own glory: but he that seeketh his glory that sent him, the same is true, and no unrighteousness is in him.

19 Did not Moses give you the law, and yet none of you keepeth the law? Why go ye about to kill me?

20 The people answered and said, Thou hast a devil: who goeth about to kill thee?

21 Jesus answered and said unto them, I have done one work, and ye all marvel.

22 Moses therefore gave unto you circumcision; (not because it is of Moses, but of the fathers;) and ye on the sabbath day circumcize a man.

23 If a man on the sabbath day receive circumcision, that the law of Moses should not be broken; are ye angry at me, because I have made a man every whit whole on the sabbath day?

he draws us first, by good desires. Not by compulsion, not by laying the will under any necessity; but by the strong and sweet, yet still resistible, motions of his heavenly grace.

45. Every man that hath heard – The secret voice of God, he, and he only believeth. Isaiah liv, 13.

46. Not that any one – Must expect him to appear in a visible shape. He who is from or with God – In a more eminent manner than any creature.

50. Not die – Not spiritually; not eternally.

51. If any eat of this bread – That is, believe in me: he shall live for ever – In other words, he that believeth to the end shall be saved. My flesh which I will give you – This whole discourse concerning his flesh and blood refers directly to his passion, and but remotely, if at all, to the Lord's Supper.

52. Observe the degrees: the Jews are tried here; the disciples, ver. 60-66, the apostles, ver. 67.

53. Unless ye eat the flesh of the Son of man – Spiritually: unless ye draw continual virtue from him by faith. Eating his flesh is only another expression for believing.

55. Meat – Drink indeed – With which the soul of a believer is as truly fed, as his body with meat and drink.

57. I live by the Father – Being one with him. He shall live by me – Being one with me. Amazing union!

58. This is – That is, I am the bread – Which is not like the manna your fathers ate, who died notwithstanding.

60. This is a hard saying – Hard to the children of the world, but sweet to the children of God. Scarce ever did our Lord speak more sublimely, even to the apostles in private. Who can hear – Endure it?

62. What if ye shall see the Son of man ascend where he was before? – How much more incredible will it then appear to you, that he should give you his flesh to eat?

63. It is the Spirit – The spiritual meaning of these words, by which God giveth life. The flesh – The bare, carnal, literal meaning, profiteth nothing. The words which I have spoken, they are spirit – Are to be taken in a spiritual sense and, when they are so understood, they are life – That is, a means of spiritual life to the hearers.

64. But there are some of you who believe not – And so receive no life by them, because you take them in a gross literal sense. For Jesus knew from the beginning – Of his ministry: who would betray him – Therefore it is plain, God does foresee future contingencies:- "But his foreknowledge causes not the fault, Which had no less proved certain unforeknown."

65. Unless it be given – And it is given to those only who will receive it on God's own terms.

66. From this time many of his disciples went back – So our Lord now began to purge his floor: the proud and careless were driven away, and those remained who were meet for the Master's use.

68. Thou hast the words of eternal life – Thou, and thou alone, speakest the words which show the way to life everlasting.

69. And we – Who have been with thee from the beginning, whatever others do, have known – Are absolutely assured, that thou art the Christ.

70. Jesus answered them – And yet even ye have not all acted suitable to this knowledge. Have I not chosen or elected you twelve? – But they might fall even from that election. Yet one of you – On

MATTHEW HENRY

CHARLES H. SPURGEON

and gratitude. We live by him, as our bodies live by our food. We live by him, as the members by the head, the branches by the root: because he lives we shall live also.

60-65 The human nature of Christ had not before been in heaven, but being God and man, that wondrous Person was truly said to have come down from heaven. The Messiah's kingdom was not of this world; and they were to understand by faith, what he had said of a spiritual living upon him, and his fullness. As without the soul of man the flesh is of no value, so without the quickening Spirit of God all forms of religion are dead and worthless. He who made this provision for our souls, alone can teach us these things, and draw us unto Christ, that we may live by faith in him. Let us apply to Christ, thankful that it is declared that every one who is willing to come unto him shall be made welcome.

66-71 When we admit into our minds hard thoughts of the words and works of Jesus, we enter into temptation, which, if the Lord in mercy prevent not, will end in drawing back. The corrupt and wicked heart of man often makes that an occasion for offense, which is matter of the greatest comfort. Our Lord had, in the foregoing discourse, promised eternal life to his followers; the disciples fastened on that plain saying, and resolved to cleave to him, when others fastened on hard sayings, and forsook him. Christ's doctrine is the word of eternal life, therefore we must live and die by it. If we forsake Christ, we forsake our own mercies. They believed that this Jesus was the Messiah promised to their fathers, the Son of the living God. When we are tempted to backslide or turn away, it is good to remember first principles, and to keep to them. And let us ever remember our Lord's searching question; Shall we go away and forsake our Redeemer? To whom can we go? He alone can give salvation by the forgiveness of sins. And this alone brings confidence, comfort, and joy, and bids fear and despondency flee away. It gains the only solid happiness in this world, and opens a way to the happiness of the next.

JOHN 7

Christ goes to the feast of tabernacles. (1-13)
His discourse at the feast. (14-39)
The people dispute concerning Christ. (40-53)

1-13 The brethren or kinsmen of Jesus were disgusted, when they found there was no prospect of worldly advantages from him. Ungodly men sometimes undertake to counsel those employed in the work of God; but they only advise what appears likely to promote present advantages. The people differed about his doctrine and miracles, while those who favored him, dared not openly to avow their sentiments. Those who count the preachers of the gospel to be

have a bath if they like, and so we will fill the six waterpots with water." Nothing would have come of such a proceeding. There would have stood the water. The Eton school-boy said, "The conscious water saw its God and blushed," a truly poetic expression; but the conscious water would have seen the servants, and would not have blushed. It would have reflected their faces upon its shining surface, but nothing more would have happened. Jesus Christ himself must come, and in present power must work the miracle. It was because he had commanded the servants to fill the waterpots with water that therefore he was bound, if I may use such an expression of our free King, bound to turn it into wine, for otherwise he would have been making fools of them, and they also might have turned round and said, "Why didst thou give us such a command as this?" If, after we have filled the waterpots with water, Jesus does not work by us, we shall have done what he bade us; but if we believe in him, I make bold to say that he is bound to come; for though we should be losers, and dreadful losers too, if he did not display his power, for we should have to lament, "I have labored in vain, and spent my strength for nought," yet we should not be such losers as he would be, for straightway the world would affirm that Christ's commands are empty, fruitless, idle. It would be declared that obedience to his word brings no result. The world would say, "You have filled the waterpots with water because he told you to do it. You expected him to turn the water into wine, but he did not do it. Your faith is vain; your whole obedience is vain; and he is not a fit Master to be served." We should be losers, but he would be a greater loser still, for he would lose his glory. For my part, I do not believe that a good word for Christ is ever spoken in vain. I am sure that no sermon with Christ in it is ever preached without result. Something will come of it, if not tonight, nor tomorrow; something will come of it. When I have printed a sermon, and seen it fairly in the volume, I have before long been delighted to hear of souls saved by its means. And when I have not printed, but only preached, a discourse, I have still thought, something will come of it. I preached Christ. I put his saving truth into that sermon, and that seed cannot die. If it shall lie in the volume for years, like the grains of wheat in the mummy's hand, it will live, and grow, and bear fruit. Consequently, I have heard but lately of a soul brought to Christ by a sermon that I preached twenty-five years ago. I hear almost every week of souls having been brought to Christ by sermons preached at Park Street, and Exeter Hall,

24 Judge not according to the appearance, but judge righteous judgment.

25 Then said some of them of Jerusalem, Is not this he, whom they seek to kill?

26 But, lo, he speaketh boldly, and they say nothing unto him. Do the rulers know indeed that this is the very Christ?

27 Howbeit we know this man whence he is: but when Christ cometh, no man knoweth whence he is.

28 Then cried Jesus in the temple as he taught, saying, Ye both know me, and ye know whence I am: and I am not come of myself, but he that sent me is true, whom ye know not.

29 But I know him: for I am from him, and he hath sent me.

30 Then they sought to take him: but no man laid hands on him, because his hour was not yet come.

31 And many of the people believed on him, and said, When Christ cometh, will he do more miracles than these which this man hath done?

32 The Pharisees heard that the people murmured such things concerning him; and the Pharisees and the chief priests sent officers to take him.

33 Then said Jesus unto them, Yet a little while am I with you, and then I go unto him that sent me.

34 Ye shall seek me, and shall not find me: and where I am, thither ye cannot come.

35 Then said the Jews among themselves, Whither will he go, that we shall not find him? will he go unto the dispersed among the Gentiles, and teach the Gentiles?

36 What manner of saying is this that he said, Ye shall seek me, and shall not find me: and where I am, thither ye cannot come?

37 In the last day, that great day of the feast, Jesus stood and cried, saying, If any man thirst, let him come unto me, and drink.

38 He that believeth on me, as the scripture hath said, out of his belly shall flow rivers of living water.

39 (But this spake he of the Spirit, which they that believe on him should receive: for the Holy Ghost was not yet given; because that Jesus was not yet glorified.)

40 Many of the people therefore, when they heard this saying, said, Of a truth this is the Prophet.

41 Others said, This is the Christ. But some said, Shall Christ come out of Galilee?

42 Hath not the scripture said, That Christ cometh of the seed of David, and out of the town of Bethlehem, where David was?

43 So there was a division among the people because of him.

44 And some of them would have taken him; but no man laid hands on him.

45 Then came the officers to the chief priests and Pharisees; and they said unto them, Why have ye not brought him?

46 The officers answered, Never man spake

this gracious warning, Judas ought to have repented; is a devil – Is now influenced by one.

JOHN 7

1. After these things Jesus walked in Galilee – That is, continued there, for some months after the second Passover. For he would not walk – Continue in Judea; because the Jews – Those of them who did not believe; and in particular the chief priests, scribes, and Pharisees, sought an opportunity to kill him.

2. The feast of tabernacles – The time, manner, and reason of this feast may be seen, Lev. xxiii, 34, &c.

3. His brethren – So called according to the Jewish way of speaking. They were his cousins, the sons of his mother's sister. Depart hence – From this obscure place.

4. For no man doth any thing – Of this kind, in secret; but rather desireth to be of public use. If thou really dost these things – These miracles which are reported; show thyself to the world – To all men.

6. Jesus saith, Your time is always ready – This or any time will suit you.

7. The world cannot hate you – Because ye are of the world. But me it hateth – And all that bear the same testimony.

10. He also went up to the feast – This was his last journey but one to Jerusalem. The next time he went up he suffered.

11. The Jews – The men of Judea, particularly of Jerusalem.

12. There was much murmuring among the multitude – Much whispering; many private debates with each other, among those who were come from distant parts.

13. However no man spake openly of him – Not in favor of him: for fear of the Jews – Those that were in authority.

14. Now at the middle of the feast – Which lasted eight days. It is probable this was on the Sabbath day. Jesus went up into the temple – Directly, without stopping any where else.

15. How does this man know letters, having never learned? – How comes he to be so well acquainted with sacred literature as to be able thus to expound the Scripture, with such propriety and gracefulness, seeing he has never learned this, at any place of education?

16. My doctrine is not mine – Acquired by any labor of learning; but his that sent me – Immediately infused by him.

17. If any man be willing to do his will, he shall know of the doctrine, whether it be of God – This is a universal rule, with regard to all persons and doctrines. He that is thoroughly willing to do it, shall certainly know what the will of God is.

18. There is no unrighteousness in him – No deceit or falsehood.

19. But ye are unrighteous; for ye violate the very law which ye profess so much zeal for.

20. The people answered, Thou hast a devil – A lying spirit. Who seeketh to kill thee? – These, coming from distant parts, probably did not know the design of the priests and rulers.

21. I did – At the pool of Bethesda: one work – Out of many: and ye all marveled at it – Are amazed, because I did it on the Sabbath day.

22. Moses gave you circumcision – The sense is, because Moses enjoined you circumcision (though indeed it was far more ancient than him) you think it no harm to circumcise a man on the

deceivers, speak out, while many who favor them, fear to get reproach by avowing regard for them.

14-24 Every faithful minister may humbly adopt Christ's words. His doctrine is not his own finding out, but is from God's word, through the teaching of his Spirit. And amidst the disputes which disturb the world, if any man, of any nation, seeks to do the will of God, he shall know whether the doctrine is of God, or whether men speak of themselves. Only those who hate the truth shall be given up to errors which will be fatal. Surely it was as agreeable to the design of the Sabbath to restore health to the afflicted, as to administer an outward rite. Jesus told them to decide on his conduct according to the spiritual import of the Divine law. We must not judge concerning any by their outward appearance, but by their worth, and by the gifts and graces of God's Spirit in them.

25-30 Christ proclaimed aloud, that they were in error in their thoughts about his origin. He was sent of God, who showed himself true to his promises. This declaration, that they knew not God, with his claim to peculiar knowledge, provoked the hearers; and they sought to take him, but God can tie men's hands, though he does not turn their hearts.

31-36 The discourses of Jesus convinced many that he was the Messiah; but they had not courage to own it. It is comfort to those who are in the world, but not of it, and therefore are hated by it and weary of it, that they shall not be in it always, that they shall not be in it long. Our days being evil, it is well they are few. The days of life and of grace do not last long; and sinners, when in misery, will be glad of the help they now despise. Men dispute about such sayings, but the event will explain them.

37-39 On the last day of the feast of tabernacles, the Jews drew water and poured it out before the Lord. It is supposed that Christ alluded to this. If any man desires to be truly and forever happy, let him apply to Christ, and be ruled by him. This thirst means strong desires after spiritual blessings, which nothing else can satisfy; so the sanctifying and comforting influences of the Holy Spirit, were intended by the waters which Jesus called on them to come to him and drink. The comfort flows plentifully and constantly as a river; strong as a stream to bear down the opposition of doubts and fears. There is a fullness in Christ, of grace for grace. The Spirit dwelling and working in believers, is as a fountain of living, running water, out of which plentiful streams flow, cooling and cleansing as water. The miraculous gifts of the Holy Spirit we do not expect, but for his more common and more valuable influences we may apply. These streams have flowed from our glorified Redeemer, down to this age, and to the remote corners of the earth. May we be anxious to make them known to others.

and the Surrey Gardens, and therefore I feel that God will not let a single faithful testimony fall to the ground. Go on, brethren. Go on filling the waterpots with water. Do not believe that you are doing much when you have done your utmost. Do not begin to congratulate yourselves on your past success. All must come from Christ; and it will come from Christ. Do not go to the prayer-meeting and say, "Paul may plant and Apollos may water, but "—and so on. That is not how the passage runs. It says just the contrary, and runs thus,—"Paul planteth, Apollos watereth, but God giveth the increase." The increase is surely given by God where the planting and sowing are rightly done. The servants fill the waterpots: the Master turns the water into wine.

The Lord grant us grace to be obedient to his command, especially to that command, "Believe and live!" and may we meet him in the marriage-feast above to drink of the new wine with him for ever and ever. Amen and amen.

THE SHEEP AND THEIR SHEPHERD
Sermon number 995 delivered at the Metropolitan Tabernacle, Newington.

"My sheep hear my voice, and I know them, and they follow me."—John 10:27.

CHRISTIANS ARE HERE compared to sheep. Not a very flattering comparison you may say; but then we do not wish to be flattered, nor would our Lord deem it good to flatter us, While far from flattering, it is, however, eminently consoling, for of all creatures there are not any more compassed about with infirmity than sheep. In this frailty of their nature they are a fit emblem of ourselves; at least, of so many of us as have believed in Jesus and become his disciples. Let others boast how strong they are; yet if there be strong ones anywhere, certainly we are weak. We have proved our weakness, and day by day we lament it. We do confess our weakness; yet may we not repine at it, for, as Paul said, so we find, when we are weak then are we strong. Sheep have many wants, yet they are very helpless, and quite unable to provide for themselves. But for the shepherd's cure they would soon perish. This, too, is our case. Our spiritual needs are numerous and pressing, Yet we cannot supply any of them. We are travelers through a wilderness that yields us neither food nor water. Unless our bread drop down from heaven, and our water flow out of the living rock, we must die. Our weakness and our want we keenly feel: still we

like this man.

47 Then answered them the Pharisees, Are ye also deceived?

48 Have any of the rulers or of the Pharisees believed on him?

49 But this people who knoweth not the law are cursed.

50 Nicodemus saith unto them, (he that came to Jesus by night, being one of them,)

51 Doth our law judge any man, before it hear him, and know what he doeth?

52 They answered and said unto him, Art thou also of Galilee? Search, and look: for out of Galilee ariseth no prophet.

53 And every man went unto his own house.

JOHN 8

1 Jesus went unto the mount of Olives.

2 And early in the morning he came again into the temple, and all the people came unto him; and he sat down, and taught them.

3 And the scribes and Pharisees brought unto him a woman taken in adultery; and when they had set her in the midst,

4 They say unto him, Master, this woman was taken in adultery, in the very act.

5 Now Moses in the law commanded us, that such should be stoned: but what sayest thou?

6 This they said, tempting him, that they might have to accuse him. But Jesus stooped down, and with his finger wrote on the ground, as though he heard them not.

7 So when they continued asking him, he lifted up himself, and said unto them, He that is without sin among you, let him first cast a stone at her.

8 And again he stooped down, and wrote on the ground.

9 And they which heard it, being convicted by their own conscience, went out one by one, beginning at the eldest, even unto the last: and Jesus was left alone, and the woman standing in the midst.

10 When Jesus had lifted up himself, and saw none but the woman, he said unto her, Woman, where are those thine accusers? hath no man condemned thee?

11 She said, No man, Lord. And Jesus said unto her, Neither do I condemn thee: go, and sin no more.

12 Then spake Jesus again unto them, saying, I am the light of the world: he that followeth me shall not walk in darkness, but shall have the light of life.

13 The Pharisees therefore said unto him, Thou bearest record of thyself; thy record is not true.

14 Jesus answered and said unto them, Though I bear record of myself, yet my record is true: for I know whence I came, and whither I go; but ye cannot tell whence I come, and whither I go.

15 Ye judge after the flesh; I judge no man.

Sabbath: and are ye angry at me (which anger had now continued sixteen months) for doing so much greater a good, for healing a man, body and soul, on the Sabbath?

27. When Christ cometh, none knoweth whence he is – This Jewish tradition was true, with regard to his Divine nature: in that respect none could declare his generation. But it was not true with regard to his human nature, for both his family and the place of his birth were plainly foretold.

28. Then cried Jesus – With a loud and earnest voice. Do ye both know me, and know whence I am? – Ye do indeed know whence I am as a man. But ye know not my Divine nature, nor that I am sent from God.

29. I am from him – By eternal generation: and he hath sent me – His mission follows from his generation. These two points answer those: Do ye know me? Do ye know whence I am?

30. His hour – The time of his suffering.

33. Then said Jesus – Continuing his discourse (from ver. 29) which they had interrupted.

34. Ye shall seek me – Whom ye now despise. These words are, as it were, the text which is commented upon in this and the following chapter. Where I am – Christ's so frequently saying while on earth, where I am, when he spake of his being in heaven, intimates his perpetual presence there in his Divine nature: though his going thither was a future thing, with regard to his human nature.

35. Will he go to the dispersed among the Greeks – The Jews scattered abroad in heathen nations, Greece particularly. Or, Will he teach the Greeks? – The heathens themselves.

37. On the last, the great day of the feast – On this day there was the greatest concourse of people, and they were then wont to fetch water from the fountain of Siloam, which the priests poured out on the great altar, singing one to another, With joy shall ye draw water from the wells of salvation. On this day likewise they commemorated God's miraculously giving water out of the rock, and offered up solemn prayers for seasonable rains.

38. He that believeth – This answers to let him come to me. And whosoever doth come to him by faith, his inmost soul shall be filled with living water, with abundance of peace, joy, and love, which shall likewise flow from him to others. As the Scripture hath said – Not expressly in any one particular place. But here is a general reference to all those scriptures which speak of the effusion of the Spirit by the Messiah, under the similitude of pouring out water. Zech. xiv. 8.

39. The Holy Ghost was not yet given – That is, those fruits of the Spirit were not yet given even to true believers, in that full measure.

40. The prophet – Whom we expect to be the forerunner of the Messiah.

42. From Bethlehem – And how could they forget that Jesus was born there? Had not Herod given them terrible reason to remember it? Micah v, 2.

48. Hath any of the rulers – Men of rank or eminence, or of the Pharisees – Men of learning or religion, believed on him?

49. But this populace, who know not the law – This ignorant rabble; are accursed – Are by that ignorance exposed to the curse of being thus seduced.

50. Nicodemus, he that came to him by night – Having now a lit-

MATTHEW HENRY

CHARLES H. SPURGEON

40-53 The malice of Christ's enemies is always against reason, and sometimes the staying of it cannot be accounted for. Never any man spake with that wisdom, and power, and grace, that convincing clearness, and that sweetness, wherewith Christ spake. Alas, that many, who are for a time restrained, and who speak highly of the word of Jesus, speedily lose their convictions, and go on in their sins! People are foolishly swayed by outward motives in matters of eternal moment, are willing even to be damned for fashion's sake. As the wisdom of God often chooses things which men despise, so the folly of men commonly despises those whom God has chosen. The Lord brings forward his weak and timid disciples, and sometimes uses them to defeat the designs of his enemies.

JOHN 8

The Pharisees and the adulteress. (1-11)
Christ's discourse with the Pharisees. (12-59)

1-11 Christ neither found fault with the law, nor excused the prisoner's guilt; nor did he countenance the pretended zeal of the Pharisees. Those are self-condemned who judge others, and yet do the same thing. All who are any way called to blame the faults of others, are especially concerned to look to themselves, and keep themselves pure. In this matter Christ attended to the great work about which he came into the world, that was, to bring sinners to repentance; not to destroy, but to save. He aimed to bring, not only the accused to repentance, by showing her his mercy, but the prosecutors also, by showing them their sins; they thought to ensnare him, he sought to convince and convert them. He declined to meddle with the magistrate's office. Many crimes merit far more severe punishment than they meet with; but we should not leave our own work, to take that upon ourselves to which we are not called. When Christ sent her away, it was with this caution, Go, and sin no more. Those who help to save the life of a criminal, should help to save the soul with the same caution. Those are truly happy, whom Christ does not condemn. Christ's favor to us in the forgiveness of past sins should prevail with us, Go then, and sin no more.

12-16 Christ is the Light of the world. God is light, and Christ is the image of the invisible God. One sun enlightens the whole world; so does one Christ, and there needs no more. What a dark dungeon would the world be without the sun! So would it be without Jesus, by whom light came into the world. Those who follow Christ shall not walk in darkness. They shall not be left without the truths which are necessary to keep them from destroying error, and the directions in the way of duty, necessary to keep them from condemning sin.

17-20 If we knew Christ better, we should know the

have no cause to murmur, since the Lord knows our poor estate, and succors us with the tenderest care. Sheep, too, are silly creatures, and in this respect likewise we are very sheepish. We meekly own it to him who is ready to guide us. We say, as David said, "O God, thou knowest my foolishness;" and he says to us as he said to David, "I will instruct thee and teach thee in the way which thou shalt go." If Christ were not our wisdom, we should soon fall a prey to the destroyer. Every grain of true wisdom that we possess we have derived from him; of ourselves we are dull and giddy; folly is bound up in our heart. The more conscious you are, dear brethren, of your own deficiencies, your lack of stamina, discretion, sagacity, and all the instincts of self-preservation, the more delighted you will be to see that the Lord accepts you under these conditions, and calls you the people of his pasture and the sheep of his hand. He discerns you as you are, claims you as his own, foresees all the ills to which you are exposed, yet tends you as his flock, sets store by every lamb of the fold, and so feeds you according to the integrity of his heart, and guides you by the skillfulness of his hands. "I will feed my flock, and I will cause them to lie down, saith the Lord God." Oh, what sweet music there is to us in the name which is given to our Lord Jesus Christ of "the good Shepherd"! It not only describes the office he holds, but it sets forth the sympathy he feels, the aptness he shows, and the responsibility he bears to promote our well-being. What if the sheep be weak, yet is the shepherd strong to guard his flock from the prowling wolf or the roaring lion. If the sheep suffer privation because the soil is barren, yet is the shepherd able to lead them into pasturage suitable for them. If they be foolish, yet he goes before them, cheers them with his voice, and rules them with the rod of his command. There cannot be a flock without a shepherd; neither is there a shepherd truly without a flock. The two must go together. They are the fullness of each other. As the church is the fullness of him that filleth all in all, so we rejoice to remember that "of his fullness have all we received, and grace for grace." That I am like a sheep is a sorry reflection; but that I have a shepherd charms away the sorrow and creates a new joy. It even becomes a gladsome thing to be weak, that I may rely on his strength; to be full of wants, that I may draw from his fullness; to be shallow and often at my wit's end, that I may be always regulated by his wisdom. Even so doth my shame redound to his praise. Not to you, ye great and mighty, who lift your heads high, and claim for yourselves honor: not for you is

16 And yet if I judge, my judgment is true: for I am not alone, but I and the Father that sent me.
17 It is also written in your law, that the testimony of two men is true.
18 I am one that bear witness of myself, and the Father that sent me beareth witness of me.
19 Then said they unto him, Where is thy Father? Jesus answered, Ye neither know me, nor my Father: if ye had known me, ye should have known my Father also.
20 These words spake Jesus in the treasury, as he taught in the temple: and no man laid hands on him; for his hour was not yet come.
21 Then said Jesus again unto them, I go my way, and ye shall seek me, and shall die in your sins: whither I go, ye cannot come.
22 Then said the Jews, Will he kill himself? because he saith, Whither I go, ye cannot come.
23 And he said unto them, Ye are from beneath; I am from above: ye are of this world; I am not of this world.
24 I said therefore unto you, that ye shall die in your sins: for if ye believe not that I am he, ye shall die in your sins.
25 Then said they unto him, Who art thou? And Jesus saith unto them, Even the same that I said unto you from the beginning.
26 I have many things to say and to judge of you: but he that sent me is true; and I speak to the world those things which I have heard of him.
27 They understood not that he spake to them of the Father.
28 Then said Jesus unto them, When ye have lifted up the Son of man, then shall ye know that I am he, and that I do nothing of myself; but as my Father hath taught me, I speak these things.
29 And he that sent me is with me: the Father hath not left me alone; for I do always those things that please him.
30 As he spake these words, many believed on him.
31 Then said Jesus to those Jews which believed on him, If ye continue in my word, then are ye my disciples indeed;
32 And ye shall know the truth, and the truth shall make you free.
33 They answered him, We be Abraham's seed, and were never in bondage to any man: how sayest thou, Ye shall be made free?
34 Jesus answered them, Verily, verily, I say unto you, Whosoever committeth sin is the servant of sin.
35 And the servant abideth not in the house for ever: but the Son abideth ever.
36 If the Son therefore shall make you free, ye shall be free indeed.
37 I know that ye are Abraham's seed; but ye seek to kill me, because my word hath no place in you.
38 I speak that which I have seen with my Father: and ye do that which ye have seen with your father.

tle more courage, being one of them – Being present as a member of the great council, saith to them – Do not we ourselves act as if we knew not the law, if we pass sentence on a man before we hear him?
52. They answered – By personal reflection; the argument they could not answer, and therefore did not attempt it. Art thou also a Galilean? – One of his party? Out of Galilee ariseth no prophet – They could not but know the contrary. They knew Jonah arose out of Gethhepher; and Nahum from another village in Galilee. Yea, and Thisbe, the town of Elijah, the Tishbite, was in Galilee also. They might likewise have known that Jesus was not born in Galilee, but at Bethlehem, even from the public register there, and from the genealogies of the family of David. They were conscious this poor answer would not bear examination, and so took care to prevent a reply.
53. And every man went to his own house – So that short plain question of Nicodemus spoiled all their measures, and broke up the council! A word spoken in season, how good it is! Especially when God gives it his blessing.

JOHN 8

5. Moses hath commanded us to stone such – If they spoke accurately, this must have been a woman, who, having been betrothed to a husband, had been guilty of this crime before the marriage was completed; for such only Moses commanded to be stoned. He commanded indeed that other adulteresses should be put to death; but the manner of death was not specified. Deut. xxii, 23.
6. That they might have to accuse him – Either of usurping the office of a judge, if he condemned her, or of being an enemy to the law, if he acquitted her. Jesus stooping down, wrote with his finger on the ground – God wrote once in the Old Testament; Christ once in the New: perhaps the words which he afterward spoke, when they continued asking him. By this silent action, he, 1, fixed their wandering, hurrying thoughts, in order to awaken their consciences: and, 2, signified that he was not then come to condemn but to save the world.
7. He that is without sin – He that is not guilty: his own conscience being the judge, either of the same sin, or of some nearly resembling it; let him – As a witness, cast the first stone at her.
9. Beginning at the eldest – Or the elders. Jesus was left alone – By all those scribes and Pharisees who proposed the question. But many others remained, to whom our Lord directed his discourse presently after.
10. Hath no man condemned thee? – Hath no judicial sentence been passed upon thee?
11. Neither do I condemn thee – Neither do I take upon me to pass any such sentence. Let this deliverance lead thee to repentance.
12. He that followeth me shall in nowise walk in darkness – In ignorance, wickedness, misery: but shall have the light of life – He that closely, humbly, steadily follows me, shall have the Divine light continually shining upon him, diffusing over his soul knowledge, holiness, joy, till he is guided by it to life everlasting.
13. Thou testifiest of thyself; thy testimony is not valid – They

Father better. Those become vain in their imaginations concerning God, who will not learn of Christ. Those who know not his glory and grace, know not the Father that sent him. The time of our departure out of the world, depends upon God. Our enemies cannot hasten it any sooner, nor can our friends delay it any longer, than the time appointed of the Father. Every true believer can look up and say with pleasure, My times are in thy hand, and better there than in my own. To all God's purposes there is a time.

21-29 Those that live in unbelief, are for ever undone, if they die in unbelief. The Jews belonged to this present evil world, but Jesus was of a heavenly and Divine nature, so that his doctrine, kingdom, and blessings, would not suit their taste. But the curse of the law is done away to all that submit to the grace of the gospel. Nothing but the doctrine of Christ's grace will be an argument powerful enough, and none but the Spirit of Christ's grace will be an agent powerful enough, to turn us from sin to God; and that Spirit is given, and that doctrine is given, to work upon those only who believe in Christ. Some say, Who is this Jesus? They allow him to have been a Prophet, an excellent Teacher, and even more than a creature; but cannot acknowledge him as over all, God blessed for evermore. Will not this suffice? Jesus here answers the question. Is this to honor him as the Father? Does this admit his being the Light of the world, and the Life of men, one with the Father? All shall know by their conversion, or in their condemnation, that he always spake and did what pleased the Father, even when he claimed the highest honors to himself.

30-36 Such power attended our Lord's words, that many were convinced, and professed to believe in him. He encouraged them to attend his teaching, rely on his promises, and obey his commands, notwithstanding all temptations to evil. Thus doing, they would be his disciples truly; and by the teaching of his word and Spirit, they would learn where their hope and strength lay. Christ spoke of spiritual liberty; but carnal hearts feel no other grievances than those that molest the body, and distress their worldly affairs. Talk to them of their liberty and property, tell them of waste committed upon their lands, or damage done to their houses, and they understand you very well; but speak of the bondage of sin, captivity to Satan, and liberty by Christ; tell of wrong done to their precious souls, and the hazard of their eternal welfare, then you bring strange things to their ears. Jesus plainly reminded them, that the man who practiced any sin, was, in fact, a slave to that sin, which was the case with most of them. Christ in the gospel offers us freedom, he has power to do this, and those whom Christ makes free are really so. But often we see persons disputing about liberty of every kind, while they are slaves to some sinful lust.

peace, not to you is rest; but unto you, ye lowly ones, who delight in the valley of humiliation, and feel yourselves to be taken down in your own esteem—to you it is that the Shepherd becomes dear; and to you will he give to lie down in green pastures beside the still waters.

In a very simple way, we shall speak about the proprietor of the sheep. "My sheep," says Christ. Then, we shall have a little to say about the marks of the sheep. After that I propose to talk awhile about the privileges of the sheep. "I know my sheep:" they are privileged to be known of Christ. "My sheep hear my voice."

I. Who is the proprietor of the sheep? They are all Christ's. "My sheep hear my voice." How came the saints to be Christ's?

They are his, first of all, because he chose them. Ere the worlds were made, out of all the rest of mankind he selected them. He knew the race would fall, and become unworthy of the faculties with which he had endowed them, and the inheritance he had assigned them. To him belonged the sovereign prerogative that he might have mercy on whom he would have mercy; and he, out of his own absolute will, and according to the counsel of his own good pleasure, made choice severally and individually of certain persons, and he said, "These are mine." Their names were written in his book: they became his portion and his heritage. Having chosen them of old so many ages ago, rest assured he will not lose them now. Men prize that which they have long had. If there is a thing that was mine but yesterday, and it is lost today, I might not fret about it; but if I have long possessed it, and called it my patrimony, I would not willingly part with it. Sheep of Christ, ye shall be his for ever, because ye have been his from ever. They are Christ's sheep, because his Father gave them to him. They were the gift of the Father to Christ. He often speaks of them in this way. "As many as thou hast given me:" "Thou hast given me," saith he, over and over again. Of old, the Father gave his people to Christ. Separating them from among men, he presented them to him as a gift, committed them into his hand as a trust, and ordained them for him as the lot of his inheritance. Thus they become a token of the Father's love to his only begotten Son, a proof of the confidence he reposed in him, and a pledge of the honor that shall be done unto him. Now, I suppose we most of us know how to value a gift for the donor's sake. If presented to us by one whom we love, we set great store by it. If it has been designed to be a love-token, it awakens in our minds many sweet memories. Though the intrinsic worth may be

39 They answered and said unto him, Abraham is our father. Jesus saith unto them, If ye were Abraham's children, ye would do the works of Abraham.

40 But now ye seek to kill me, a man that hath told you the truth, which I have heard of God: this did not Abraham.

41 Ye do the deeds of your father. Then said they to him, We be not born of fornication; we have one Father, even God.

42 Jesus said unto them, If God were your Father, ye would love me: for I proceeded forth and came from God; neither came I of myself, but he sent me.

43 Why do ye not understand my speech? even because ye cannot hear my word.

44 Ye are of your father the devil, and the lusts of your father ye will do. He was a murderer from the beginning, and abode not in the truth, because there is no truth in him. When he speaketh a lie, he speaketh of his own: for he is a liar, and the father of it.

45 And because I tell you the truth, ye believe me not.

46 Which of you convinceth me of sin? And if I say the truth, why do ye not believe me?

47 He that is of God heareth God's words: ye therefore hear them not, because ye are not of God.

48 Then answered the Jews, and said unto him, Say we not well that thou art a Samaritan, and hast a devil?

49 Jesus answered, I have not a devil; but I honor my Father, and ye do dishonor me.

50 And I seek not mine own glory: there is one that seeketh and judgeth.

51 Verily, verily, I say unto you, If a man keep my saying, he shall never see death.

52 Then said the Jews unto him, Now we know that thou hast a devil. Abraham is dead, and the prophets; and thou sayest, If a man keep my saying, he shall never taste of death.

53 Art thou greater than our father Abraham, which is dead? and the prophets are dead: whom makest thou thyself?

54 Jesus answered, If I honor myself, my honor is nothing: it is my Father that honoreth me; of whom ye say, that he is your God:

55 Yet ye have not known him; but I know him: and if I should say, I know him not, I shall be a liar like unto you: but I know him, and keep his saying.

56 Your father Abraham rejoiced to see my day: and he saw it, and was glad.

57 Then said the Jews unto him, Thou art not yet fifty years old, and hast thou seen Abraham?

58 Jesus said unto them, Verily, verily, I say unto you, Before Abraham was, I am.

59 Then took they up stones to cast at him: but Jesus hid himself, and went out of the temple, going through the midst of them, and so passed by.

retort upon our Lord his own words, chap. v, 31; if I testify of myself, my testimony is not valid. He had then added, There is another who testifieth of me. To the same effect he replies here, verse 14, Though I testify of myself, yet my testimony is valid; for I am inseparably united to the Father. I know – And from firm and certain knowledge proceeds the most unexceptionable testimony: whence I came, and whither I go – To these two heads may be referred all the doctrine concerning Christ. The former is treated of verse 16, &c., the latter ver. 21, &c. For I know whence I came – That is, For I came from God, both as God and as man. And I know it, though ye do not.

15. Ye judge after the flesh – As the flesh, that is, corrupt nature dictates. I judge no man – Not thus; not now; not at my first coming.

16. I am not alone – No more in judging, than in testifying: but I and the Father that sent me – His Father is in him, and he is in the Father, chap. xiv, 10, 11; and so the Father is no more alone without the Son, than the Son is without the Father, Prov. viii, 22, 23, 30. His Father and he are not one and another God, but one God, (though distinct persons,) and so inseparable from each other. And though the Son came from the Father, to assume human nature, and perform his office as the Messiah upon earth, as God is sometimes said to come from heaven, for particular manifestations of himself; yet Christ did not leave the Father, nor the Father leave him, any more than God leaves heaven when he is said to come down to the earth.

17. Deut. xix, 15.

19. Then said they to him, Where is thy Father? Jesus answered – Showing the perverseness of their question; and teaching that they ought first to know the Son, if they would know the Father. Where the Father is – He shows, ver. 23. Meantime he plainly intimates that the Father and he were distinct persons, as they were two witnesses; and yet one in essence, as the knowledge of him includes the knowledge of the Father.

23. Ye are – Again he passes over their interruption, and proves what he advanced, ver. 21. Of them that are beneath – From the earth. I am of them that are above – Here he directly shows whence he came, even from heaven, and whither he goes.

24. If ye believe not that I AM – Here (as in ver. 58) our Lord claims the Divine name, I AM, Exod. iii, 14. But the Jews, as if he had stopped short, and not finished the sentence, answered, Who art thou?

25. Even what I say to you from the beginning – The same which I say to you, as it were in one discourse, with one even tenor from the time I first spake to you.

26. I have many things to say and to judge of you – I have much to say concerning your inexcusable unbelief: but he that sent me is true – Whether ye believe or no. And I speak the things which I have heard from him – I deliver truly what he hath given me in charge.

27. They understood not – That by him that sent him he meant God the Father. Therefore in ver. 28, 29 he speaks plainly of the Father, and again claims the Divine name, I AM.

28. When ye shall have lifted up – On the cross, ye shall know – And so many of them did, that I AM – God over all; and that I do nothing of myself – Being one with the Father.

37-40 Our Lord opposed the proud and vain confidence of these Jews, showing that their descent from Abraham could not profit those of a contrary spirit to him. Where the word of God has no place, no good is to be expected; room is left there for all wickedness. A sick person who turns from his physician, and will take neither remedies nor food, is past hope of recovery. The truth both heals and nourishes the hearts of those who receive it. The truth taught by philosophers has not this power and effect, but only the truth of God. Those who claim the privileges of Abraham, must do Abraham's works; must be strangers and sojourners in this world; keep up the worship of God in their families, and always walk before God.

41-47 Satan prompts men to excesses by which they murder themselves and others, while what he puts into the mind tends to ruin men's souls. He is the great promoter of falsehood of every kind. He is a liar, all his temptations are carried on by his calling evil good, and good evil, and promising freedom in sin. He is the author of all lies; whom liars resemble and obey, with whom all liars shall have their portion forever. The special lusts of the devil are spiritual wickedness, the lusts of the mind, and corrupt reasonings, pride and envy, wrath and malice, enmity to good, and enticing others to evil. By the truth, here understand the revealed will of God as to the salvation of men by Jesus Christ, the truth Christ was now preaching, and which the Jews opposed.

48-53 Observe Christ's disregard of the applause of men. Those who are dead to the praises of men can bear their contempt. God will seek the honor of all who do not seek their own. In these verses we have the doctrine of the everlasting happiness of believers. We have the character of a believer; he is one that keeps the sayings of the Lord Jesus. And the privilege of a believer; he shall by no means see death forever. Though now they cannot avoid seeing death, and tasting it also, yet they shall shortly be where it will be no more forever, Ex 14:13.

54-59 Christ and all that are his, depend upon God for honor. Men may be able to dispute about God, yet may not know him. Such as know not God, and obey not the gospel of Christ, are put together, 2Th 1:8. All who rightly know anything of Christ, earnestly desire to know more of him. Those who discern the dawn of the light of the Sun of Righteousness, wish to see his rising. "Before Abraham was, I AM." This speaks Abraham a creature, and our Lord the Creator; well, therefore, might he make himself greater than Abraham. I AM, is the name of God, Ex 3:14; it speaks his self-existence; he is the First and the Last, ever the same, Re 1:8. Thus he was not only before Abraham, but before all worlds, Pr 8:23; Joh 1:1. As Mediator, he was the appointed Messiah, long before Abraham; the Lamb slain from the foundation of the world, Re 13:8.

of small account, the associations make it exceedingly precious. We might be content to lose something of far greater value in itself rather than that which is the gift of a friend, the offering of his love. I like the delicate sentiment of the poet, as it is expressed in that pretty verse—

"I never cast a flower away,
The gift of one who cared for me;
A little flower—a faded flower,
But it was done reluctantly."

Yet, oh, how weak the words of human passion! but, oh, how strong the expressions of divine ardor, when Jesus speaks to the Father of "the men whom thou gavest me out of the world"! "Thine they were," he says, "and thou gavest them me; and those that thou gavest me I have kept." Ye sheep of Christ, rest safely; let not your soul be disturbed with fear. The Father gave you to his Son, and he will not lightly lose what God himself has given him. The infernal lions shall not rend the meanest lamb that is a love-token from the Father to his best Beloved. While Christ stands defending his own, he will protect them from the lion and the bear, that would take the lambs of his flock; he will not suffer the least of them to perish.

"My sheep," says Christ. They are his, furthermore, because, in addition to his choice and to the gift, he has bought them with a price. They had sold themselves for nought; but he has redeemed them, not with corruptible things as with silver and gold, but with his precious blood. A man always esteems that to be exceedingly valuable which he procured with risk—with risk of life and limb. David felt he could not drink the water that the brave warriors who broke through the host of the Philistines brought to him from the well at Bethlehem, because it seemed to him as though it were the blood of the men that went in jeopardy of their lives; and he poured it out before the Lord. It was too precious a draught for him, when men's lives had been hazarded for it. But the good Shepherd not only hazarded his life, but even laid it down for his sheep. Jacob exceedingly valued one part of his possessions, and he gave it to Joseph: he gave him one portion above his brethren. Now, you may be sure he would give Joseph that which he thought most precious. But why did he give him that particular portion? Because, he says, "I took it out of the hand of the Amorite with my sword and with my bow." Now, our blessed Shepherd esteems his sheep because they cost him his blood. They cost him his blood—I may say, he took them out of the hand of the Amorite with his sword and with his bow in

JOHN 9

1 And as Jesus passed by, he saw a man which was blind from his birth.

2 And his disciples asked him, saying, Master, who did sin, this man, or his parents, that he was born blind?

3 Jesus answered, Neither hath this man sinned, nor his parents: but that the works of God should be made manifest in him.

4 I must work the works of him that sent me, while it is day: the night cometh, when no man can work.

5 As long as I am in the world, I am the light of the world.

6 When he had thus spoken, he spat on the ground, and made clay of the spittle, and he anointed the eyes of the blind man with the clay,

7 And said unto him, Go, wash in the pool of Siloam, (which is by interpretation, Sent.) He went his way therefore, and washed, and came seeing.

8 The neighbors therefore, and they which before had seen him that he was blind, said, Is not this he that sat and begged?

9 Some said, This is he: others said, He is like him: but he said, I am he.

10 Therefore said they unto him, How were thine eyes opened?

11 He answered and said, A man that is called Jesus made clay, and anointed mine eyes, and said unto me, Go to the pool of Siloam, and wash: and I went and washed, and I received sight.

12 Then said they unto him, Where is he? He said, I know not.

13 They brought to the Pharisees him that aforetime was blind.

14 And it was the sabbath day when Jesus made the clay, and opened his eyes.

15 Then again the Pharisees also asked him how he had received his sight. He said unto them, He put clay upon mine eyes, and I washed, and do see.

16 Therefore said some of the Pharisees, This man is not of God, because he keepeth not the sabbath day. Others said, How can a man that is a sinner do such miracles? And there was a division among them.

17 They say unto the blind man again, What sayest thou of him, that he hath opened thine eyes? He said, He is a prophet.

18 But the Jews did not believe concerning him, that he had been blind, and received his sight, until they called the parents of him that had received his sight.

19 And they asked them, saying, Is this your son, who ye say was born blind? how then doth he now see?

20 His parents answered them and said, We know that this is our son, and that he was born blind:

21 But by what means he now seeth, we know not; or who hath opened his eyes, we know not:

29. The Father hath not left me alone – Never from the moment I came into the world.

32. The truth – Written in your hearts by the Spirit of God, shall make you free – From guilt, sin, misery, Satan.

33. They – The other Jews that were by, (not those that believed,) as appears by the whole tenor of the conversation. We were never enslaved to any man – A bold, notorious untruth. At that very time they were enslaved to the Romans.

34. Jesus answered – Each branch of their objection, first concerning freedom, then concerning their being Abraham's offspring, ver. 37, &c. He that committeth sin, is, in fact, the slave of sin.

35. And the slave abideth not in the house – All sinners shall be cast out of God's house, as the slave was out of Abraham's: but I, the Son, abide therein for ever.

36. If I therefore make you free, ye – Shall partake of the same privilege: being made free from all guilt and sin, ye shall abide in the house of God for ever.

37. I know that ye are Abraham's offspring – As to the other branch of your objection, I know that, ye are Abraham's offspring, after the flesh; but not in a spiritual sense. Ye are not followers of the faith of Abraham: my word hath no place in your hearts.

41. Ye do the deeds of your father – He is not named yet. But when they presumed to call God their Father, then he is expressly called the devil, ver. 44.

42. I proceeded forth – As God, and come – As Christ.

43. Ye cannot – Such is your stubbornness and pride, hear – Receive, obey my word. Not being desirous to do my will, ye cannot understand my doctrine, chap. vii, 17.

44. He was a murderer – In inclination, from the beginning – Of his becoming a devil; and abode not in the truth – Commencing murderer and liar at the same time. And certainly he was a killer of men (as the Greek word properly signifies) from the beginning of the world: for from the very creation he designed and contrived the ruin of men. When he speaketh a lie, he speaketh of his own – For he is the proper parent, and, as it were, creator of it. See the origin not only of lies, but of evil in general!

45. Because I speak the truth – Which liars hate.

46. Which of you convicteth me of sin? – And is not my life as unreprovable as my doctrine? Does not my whole behavior confirm the truth of what I teach?

47. He that is of God – That either loves or fears him, heareth – With joy and reverence, God's words – Which I preach.

48. Say we not well – Have we not just cause to say, Thou art, a Samaritan – An enemy to our Church and nation; and hast a devil? – Art possessed by a proud and lying spirit?

49. I honor my Father – I seek his honor only.

50. I seek not my own glory – That is, as I am the Messiah, I consult not my own glory. I need not. For my Father consulteth it, and will pass sentence on you accordingly.

51. If a man keep my word – So will my Father consult my glory. We keep his doctrine by believing, his promises by hoping, his command by obeying. He shall never see death – That is, death eternal. He shall live for ever. Hereby he proves that he was no Samaritan; for the Samaritans in general were Sadducees.

54. If I honor myself – Referring to their words, Whom makest thou thyself?

MATTHEW HENRY

CHARLES H. SPURGEON

The Lord Jesus was made of God Wisdom, Righteousness, Sanctification, and Redemption, to Adam, and Abel, and all that lived and died by faith in him, before Abraham. The Jews were about to stone Jesus for blasphemy, but he withdrew; by his miraculous power he passed through them unhurt. Let us steadfastly profess what we know and believe concerning God; and if heirs of Abraham's faith, we shall rejoice in looking forward to that day when the Savior shall appear in glory, to the confusion of his enemies, and to complete the salvation of all who believe in him.

JOHN 9

Christ gives sight to one born blind. (1-7)
The account given by the blind man. (8-12)
The Pharisees question the man that had been blind. (13-17)
They ask concerning him. (18-23)
They cast him out. (24-34)
Christ's words to the man that had been blind. (35-38)
He reproves the Pharisees. (39-41)

1-7 Christ cured many who were blind by disease or accident; here he cured one born blind. Thus he showed his power to help in the most desperate cases, and the work of his grace upon the souls of sinners, which gives sight to those blind by nature. This poor man could not see Christ, but Christ saw him. And if we know or apprehend anything of Christ, it is because we were first known of him. Christ says of uncommon calamities, that they are not always to be looked on as special punishments of sin; sometimes they are for the glory of God, and to manifest his works. Our life is our day, in which it concerns us to do the work of the day. We must be busy, and not waste daytime; it will be time to rest when our day is done, for it is but a day. The approach of death should quicken us to improve all our opportunities of doing and getting good. What good we have an opportunity to do, we should do quickly. And he that will never do a good work till there is nothing to be objected against, will leave many a good work for ever undone, Ec 11:4. Christ magnified his power, in making a blind man to see, doing that which one would think more likely to make a seeing man blind. Human reason cannot judge of the Lord's methods; he uses means and instruments that men despise. Those that would be healed by Christ must be ruled by him. He came back from the pool wondering and wondered at; he came seeing. This represents the benefits in attending on ordinances of Christ's appointment; souls go weak, and come away strengthened; go doubting, and come away satisfied; go mourning, and come away rejoicing; go blind, and come away seeing.

8-12 Those whose eyes are opened, and whose hearts are cleansed by grace, being known to be the

bloody conflict, where he was victor, but yet was slain. There is not one sheep of all his flock but what he can see the mark of his blood on him. In the face of every saint the Savior sees, as in a glass, the memorial of his bloody sweat in Gethsemane, and his agonies at Golgotha. "Ye are not your own, for ye are bought with a price." That stands as a call to duty, but it is at the same time a consolation, for if he has bought me, he will have me. Bought with such a price, he will not like to lose me, nor suffer any foe to take me out of his hand. Think not that Christ will suffer those to perish for whom he died. To me the very suggestion seems to draw near to the verge of blasphemy. If he has bought me with his blood, I cannot conceive he cares nothing for me, will take no further concern about me, or will suffer my soul to be cast into the pit. If he has suffered in my stead, where is justice gone that the substitute should bear my guilt, and I should bear it too? and where is mercy fled, that God should execute twice the punishment for one offense! Nay, beloved, those whom he hath bought with blood are his, and he will keep them.

"My sheep," says Christ. They are his, or in due time they shall become so, through his capturing them by sacred power. As well by power are we redeemed as by price, for the blood-bought sheep had gone astray even as others. "All we like sheep have gone astray; we have turned every one to his own way," but, my brethren, the good shepherd has brought many of us back with infinite condescension: with boundless mercy he followed us when we went astray. Oh, what blind slaves we were when we sported with death! We did not know then what his love had ordained for us: it never entered our poor, silly heads that there was a crown for us; we did not know that the Father's love had settled itself on us, or ever the day-star knew its place. We know it now, and it is he that has taught us; for he followed us over mountains of vanity, through bogs and miry places of foul transgression; tracked our devious footsteps on and on, through youth and manhood, till at last, with mighty grace, he grasped us in his arms and laid us on his shoulder, and is this day carrying us home to the great fold above, rejoicing as he bears all our weight and finds us in all we need. Oh, that blessed work of effectual grace! He has made us his own, he has defeated the enemy, the prey has been taken from the mighty, and the lawful captive has been delivered. "He hath broken the gates of brass, and cut the bars of iron asunder," to set his people free. "O that men would praise the Lord for his goodness, and for his wonderful works to the children of men!"

he is of age; ask him: he shall speak for himself.

22 These words spake his parents, because they feared the Jews: for the Jews had agreed already, that if any man did confess that he was Christ, he should be put out of the synagogue.

23 Therefore said his parents, He is of age; ask him.

24 Then again called they the man that was blind, and said unto him, Give God the praise: we know that this man is a sinner.

25 He answered and said, Whether he be a sinner or no, I know not: one thing I know, that, whereas I was blind, now I see.

26 Then said they to him again, What did he to thee? how opened he thine eyes?

27 He answered them, I have told you already, and ye did not hear: wherefore would ye hear it again? will ye also be his disciples?

28 Then they reviled him, and said, Thou art his disciple; but we are Moses' disciples.

29 We know that God spake unto Moses: as for this fellow, we know not from whence he is.

30 The man answered and said unto them, Why herein is a marvelous thing, that ye know not from whence he is, and yet he hath opened mine eyes.

31 Now we know that God heareth not sinners: but if any man be a worshiper of God, and doeth his will, him he heareth.

32 Since the world began was it not heard that any man opened the eyes of one that was born blind.

33 If this man were not of God, he could do nothing.

34 They answered and said unto him, Thou wast altogether born in sins, and dost thou teach us? And they cast him out.

35 Jesus heard that they had cast him out; and when he had found him, he said unto him, Dost thou believe on the Son of God?

36 He answered and said, Who is he, Lord, that I might believe on him?

37 And Jesus said unto him, Thou hast both seen him, and it is he that talketh with thee.

38 And he said, Lord, I believe. And he worshiped him.

39 And Jesus said, For judgment I am come into this world, that they which see not might see; and that they which see might be made blind.

40 And some of the Pharisees which were with him heard these words, and said unto him, Are we blind also?

41 Jesus said unto them, If ye were blind, ye should have no sin: but now ye say, We see; therefore your sin remaineth.

JOHN 10

1 Verily, verily, I say unto you, He that entereth not by the door into the sheepfold, but climbeth up some other way, the same is a thief and a robber.

56. He saw it – By faith in types, figures, and promises; as particularly in Melchisedec; in the appearance of Jehovah to him in the plains of Mamre, Gen. xviii, 1; and in the promise that in his seed all the nations of the earth shall be blessed. Possibly he had likewise a peculiar Revelation either of Christ's first or second coming.

57. Thou art not yet fifty years old – At the most. Perhaps the gravity of our Lord's countenance, together with his afflictions and labors, might make him appear older than he really was. Hast thou seen Abraham – Which they justly supposed must have been, if Abraham had seen him.

58. Before Abraham was I AM – Even from everlasting to everlasting. This is a direct answer to the objection of the Jews, and shows how much greater he was than Abraham.

59. Then they took up stones – To stone him as a blasphemer; but Jesus concealed himself – Probably by becoming invisible; and so passed on – With the same ease as if none had been there.

JOHN 9

2. Who sinned, this man or his parents, that he was born blind? – That is, was it for his own sins, or the sins of his parents? They suppose (as many of the Jews did, though without any ground from Scripture) that he might have sinned in a pre-existent state, before he came into the world.

3. Jesus answered, Neither hath this man sinned, nor his parents – It was not the manner of our Lord to answer any questions that were of no use, but to gratify an idle curiosity. Therefore he determines nothing concerning this. The scope of his answer is, It was neither for any sins of his own, nor yet of his parents; but that the power of God might be displayed.

4. The night is coming – Christ is the light. When the light is withdrawn night comes, when no man can work – No man can do any thing toward working out his salvation after this life is ended. Yet Christ can work always. But he was not to work upon earth, only during the day, or season which was appointed for him.

5. I am the light of the world – I teach men inwardly by my Spirit, and outwardly by my preaching, what is the will of God; and I show them, by my example, how they must do it.

6. He anointed the eyes of the blind man with the clay – This might almost have blinded a man that had sight. But what could it do toward curing the blind? It reminds us that God is no farther from the event, when he works either with, or without means, and that all the creatures are only that which his almighty operation makes them.

7. Go, wash at the pool of Siloam – Perhaps our Lord intended to make the miracle more taken notice of. For a crowd of people would naturally gather round him to observe the event of so strange a prescription, and it is exceeding probable, the guide who must have led him in traversing a great part of the city, would mention the errand he was going upon, and so call all those who saw him to a greater attention. From the fountain of Siloam, which was without the walls of Jerusalem, a little stream flowed into the city, and was received in a kind of basin, near the temple, and called the pool of Siloam. Which is, by interpretation, Sent – And so was a type of the Messiah, who was sent of God. He went and washed,

same person, but widely different in character, live as monuments to the Redeemer's glory, and recommend his grace to all who desire the same precious salvation. It is good to observe the way and method of God's works, and they will appear the more wonderful. Apply this spiritually. In the work of grace wrought upon the soul we see the change, but we see not the hand that makes it: the way of the Spirit is like that of the wind, which thou hearest the sound of, but canst not tell whence it comes, nor whither it goes.

13-17 Christ not only worked miracles on the Sabbath, but in such a manner as would give offense to the Jews, for he would not seem to yield to the scribes and Pharisees. Their zeal for mere rites consumed the substantial matters of religion; therefore Christ would not give place to them. Also, works of necessity and mercy are allowed, and the Sabbath rest is to be kept, in order to the Sabbath work. How many blind eyes have been opened by the preaching of the gospel on the Lord's day! how many impotent souls cured on that day! Much unrighteous and uncharitable judging comes from men's adding their own fancies to God's appointments. How perfect in wisdom and holiness was our Redeemer, when his enemies could find nothing against him, but the oft refuted charge of breaking the Sabbath! May we be enabled, by well doing, to silence the ignorance of foolish men.

18-23 The Pharisees vainly hoped to disprove this notable miracle. They expected a Messiah, but could not bear to think that this Jesus should be he, because his precepts were all contrary to their traditions, and because they expected a Messiah in outward pomp and splendor. The fear of man brings a snare, Pr 29:25, and often makes people deny and disown Christ and his truths and ways, and act against their consciences. The unlearned and poor, who are simple-hearted, readily draw proper inferences from the evidences of the light of the gospel; but those whose desires are another way, though ever learning, never come to the knowledge of the truth.

24-34 As Christ's mercies are most valued by those who have felt the want of them, that have been blind, and now see; so the most powerful and lasting affections to Christ, arise from actual knowledge of him. In the work of grace in the soul, though we cannot tell when, and how, and by what steps the blessed change was wrought, yet we may take the comfort, if we can say, through grace, Whereas I was blind, now I see. I did live a worldly, sensual life, but, thanks be to God, it is now otherwise with me, Eph 5:8. The unbelief of those who enjoy the means of knowledge and conviction, is indeed marvelous. All who have felt the power and grace of the Lord Jesus, wonder at the willfulness of others who reject him. He argues strongly against them, not only that Jesus was not a sinner, but that he was of God. We may each of us know by this, whether

"My SHEEP," saith Christ, as he stands in the midst of his disciples. "My Shepherd," let us one and all reply. All the sheep of Christ who have been redeemed by his power, become his by their own willing and cheerful surrender of themselves to him. We would not belong to another if we might; nor would we wish to belong to ourselves if we could; nor, I trust, do we want any part of ourselves to be our own property. Judge ye whether this be true of you or not. In that day when I surrendered my soul to my Savior, I gave him my body, my soul, my spirit; I gave him all I had, and all I shall have for time and for eternity. I gave him all my talents, my powers, my faculties, my eyes, my ears, my limbs, my emotions, my judgment, my whole manhood, and all that could come of it, whatever fresh capacity or new capability I may be endowed with. Were I at this good hour to change the note of gladness for one of sadness, it should be to wail out my penitent confession of the times and circumstances in which I have failed to observe the strict and unwavering allegiance I owe to my Lord. So far from regretting, I would fain renew my vows and make them over again. In this I think every Christian would join.

"'Tis done!
the great transaction's done:
I am my Lord's, and he is mine:
He drew me, and I follow'd on,
Charm'd to confess the voice divine.
Now rest, my long-divided heart;
Fix'd on this blissful center, rest:
With ashes who would grudge to part,
When call'd on angels' bread to feast?
High heaven, that heard the solemn vow,
That vow renew'd shall daily hear:
Till in life's latest hour I bow,
And bless in death a bond so dear."

And yet, brethren, though our hearts may now be all in a glow, lest they should presently grow cold, or the bleak atmosphere of this evil world should chill our devotion, let us never cease to think of the good Shepherd in that great, good act, which most of all showed his love when he laid down his life for the sheep. You have heard the story told by Francis de Sales. He saw a girl carrying a pail of water on her head, in the midst of which she had placed a piece of wood. On asking her why she did this, she told him it was to prevent the motion of the water, for fear it might be spilt. And so, said he, let us place the cross of Christ in the midst of our hearts to check the movement of our affections, that they may not be spilt in restless cares or grievous troubles.

"My sheep," says Christ, and thus he describes his people. They are Christ's, his own,

2 But he that entereth in by the door is the shepherd of the sheep.

3 To him the porter openeth; and the sheep hear his voice: and he calleth his own sheep by name, and leadeth them out.

4 And when he putteth forth his own sheep, he goeth before them, and the sheep follow him: for they know his voice.

5 And a stranger will they not follow, but will flee from him: for they know not the voice of strangers.

6 This parable spake Jesus unto them: but they understood not what things they were which he spake unto them.

7 Then said Jesus unto them again, Verily, verily, I say unto you, I am the door of the sheep.

8 All that ever came before me are thieves and robbers: but the sheep did not hear them.

9 I am the door: by me if any man enter in, he shall be saved, and shall go in and out, and find pasture.

10 The thief cometh not, but for to steal, and to kill, and to destroy: I am come that they might have life, and that they might have it more abundantly.

11 I am the good shepherd: the good shepherd giveth his life for the sheep.

12 But he that is an hireling, and not the shepherd, whose own the sheep are not, seeth the wolf coming, and leaveth the sheep, and fleeth: and the wolf catcheth them, and scattereth the sheep.

13 The hireling fleeth, because he is an hireling, and careth not for the sheep.

14 I am the good shepherd, and know my sheep, and am known of mine.

15 As the Father knoweth me, even so know I the Father: and I lay down my life for the sheep.

16 And other sheep I have, which are not of this fold: them also I must bring, and they shall hear my voice; and there shall be one fold, and one shepherd.

17 Therefore doth my Father love me, because I lay down my life, that I might take it again.

18 No man taketh it from me, but I lay it down of myself. I have power to lay it down, and I have power to take it again. This commandment have I received of my Father.

19 There was a division therefore again among the Jews for these sayings.

20 And many of them said, He hath a devil, and is mad; why hear ye him?

21 Others said, These are not the words of him that hath a devil. Can a devil open the eyes of the blind?

22 And it was at Jerusalem the feast of the dedication, and it was winter.

23 And Jesus walked in the temple in Solomon's porch.

24 Then came the Jews round about him, and said unto him, How long dost thou make us to doubt? If thou be the Christ, tell us plainly.

25 Jesus answered them, I told you, and ye believed not: the works that I do in my Father's

and came seeing – He believed, and obeyed, and found a blessing. Had he been wise in his own eyes, and reasoned, like Naaman, on the impropriety of the means, he had justly been left in darkness. Lord, may our proud hearts be subdued to the methods of thy recovering grace! May we leave thee to choose how thou wilt bestow favors, which it is our highest interest to receive on any terms.

11. A man called Jesus – He seems to have been before totally ignorant of him.

14. Anointing the eyes – With any kind of medicine on the Sabbath, was particularly forbidden by the tradition of the elders.

16. This man is not of God – Not sent of God. How can a man that is a sinner – That is, one living in wilful sin, do such miracles?

17. What sayest thou of him, for that he hath opened thine eyes? – What inference dost thou draw herefrom?

22. He should be put out of the synagogue – That is be excommunicated.

27. Are ye also – As well as I, at length convinced and willing to be his disciples?

29. We know not whence he is – By what power and authority he does things.

30. The man answered – Utterly illiterate as he was. And with what strength and clearness of reason! So had God opened the eyes of his understanding, as well as his bodily eyes. Why, herein is a marvelous thing, that ye – The teachers and guides of the people, should not know, that a man who has wrought a miracle, the like of which was never heard of before, must be from heaven, sent by God.

31. We – Even we of the populace, know that God heareth not sinners – Not impenitent sinners, so as to answer their prayers in this manner. The honest courage of this man in adhering to the truth, though he knew the consequence, ver. 22, gives him claim to the title of a confessor.

33. He could do nothing – Of this kind; nothing miraculous.

34. Born in sin – And therefore, they supposed, born blind. They cast him out – Of the synagogue; excommunicated him.

35. Having found him – For he had sought him.

36. Who is he, that I may believe? – This implies some degree of faith already. He was ready to receive whatever Jesus said.

37. Lord, I believe – What an excellent spirit was this man of! Of so deep and strong an understanding; (as he had just shown to the confusion of the Pharisees,) and yet of so teachable a temper!

39. For judgment am I come into the world – That is, the consequence of my coming will be, that by the just judgment of God, while the blind in body and soul receive their sight, they who boast they see, will be given up to still greater blindness than before.

41. If ye had been blind – Invincibly ignorant; if ye had not had so many means of knowing: ye would have had no sin – Comparatively to what ye have now. But now ye say – Ye yourselves acknowledge, Ye see, therefore your sin remaineth – Without excuse, without remedy.

JOHN 10

1. He that entereth not by the door – By Christ. He is the only law-

MATTHEW HENRY

CHARLES H. SPURGEON

we are of God or not. What do we? What do we for God? What do we for our souls? What do we more than others?

35-38 Christ owns those who own him and his truth and ways. There is particular notice taken of such as suffer in the cause of Christ, and for the testimony of a good conscience. Our Lord Jesus graciously reveals himself to the man. Now he was made sensible what an unspeakable mercy it was, to be cured of his blindness, that he might see the Son of God. None but God is to be worshiped; so that in worshiping Jesus, he owned him to be God. All who believe in him, will worship him.

39-41 Christ came into the world to give sight to those who were spiritually blind. Also, that those who see might be made blind; that those who have a high conceit of their own wisdom, might be sealed up in ignorance. The preaching of the cross was thought to be folly by such as by carnal wisdom knew not God. Nothing fortifies men's corrupt hearts against the convictions of the word, more than the high opinion which others have of them; as if all that gained applause with men, must obtain acceptance with God. Christ silenced them. But the sin of the self-conceited and self-confident remains; they reject the gospel of grace, therefore the guilt of their sin remains unpardoned, and the power of their sin remains unbroken.

JOHN 10

The parable of the good shepherd. (1-5)
Christ the Door. (6-9)
Christ the good Shepherd. (10-18)
The Jews' opinion concerning Jesus. (19-21)
His discourse at the feast of dedication. (22-30)
The Jews attempt to stone Jesus. (31-38)
He departs from Jerusalem. (39-42)

1-5 Here is a parable or similitude, taken from the customs of the East, in the management of sheep. Men, as creatures depending on their Creator, are called the sheep of his pasture. The church of God in the world is as a sheepfold, exposed to deceivers and persecutors. The great Shepherd of the sheep knows all that are his, guards them by his providence, guides them by his Spirit and word, and goes before them, as the Eastern shepherds went before their sheep, to set them in the way of his steps. Ministers must serve the sheep in their spiritual concerns. The Spirit of Christ will set before them an open door. The sheep of Christ will observe their Shepherd, and be cautious and shy of strangers, who would draw them from faith in him to fancies about him.

6-9 Many who hear the word of Christ, do not understand it, because they will not. But we shall find one scripture expounding another, and the blessed Spirit

a peculiar property. May I hope that this truth will be henceforth treasured up in your soul! It is a common truth, certainly; but when it is laid home by the Holy Spirit it shines, it beams, not merely as a lamp in a dark chamber, but as the day-star rising in your hearts. Remember this is no more our shame that we are sheep, but it is our honor that we are Christ's sheep. To belong to a king carries some measure of distinction. We are the sheep of the imperial pastures. This is our safety: he will not suffer the enemy to destroy his sheep. This is our sanctity: we are separated, the sheep of the pasture of the Lord's Christ. This is sanctification in one aspect of it: for it is the making of us holy, by setting us apart to be the Lord's own portion for ever. And this is the key to our duty: we are his sheep: then let us live to him, and consecrate ourselves to him who loved us and gave himself for us. Christ is the proprietor of the sheep; and we are the property of the good Shepherd.

II. Now, let us commune together awhile upon the marks of the sheep. When there are so many flocks of sheep, it is necessary to mark them. Our Savior marks us. It has been very properly observed, that there are two marks on Christ's sheep. One is on their ear, the other is on their foot. These are two marks of Christ's sheep not to be found on any other; but they are to be found on all his own—the mark on the ear: "My sheep hear my voice."—the mark on the foot: "I know them, and they follow me."

Think of this mark on their ear. "My sheep hear my voice." They hear spiritually. A great many people in Christ's day heard his voice who did not hear it in the way and with the perception that is here intended. They would not hear; that is to say, they would not hearken or give heed, neither would they obey his call or come unto him that they might have life. These were not always the worst sort of people: there were some of the best that would not hear Christ, of whom he said, according to the original, as translated by some, "Ye search the Scriptures; for in them ye think ye have eternal life: and they are they which testify of me. And ye will not come to me, that ye might have life." They would get as far as curiosity or criticism might allure them; but they would not go any farther: they would not believe in Jesus. Now, the spiritual ear listens to God. The opening of it is the work of the Holy Spirit, and this is a mark of Christ's chosen blood-bought people, that they hear not only the hollow sound, but the hidden sense; not the bare letter, but the spiritual lesson; and that too not merely with the outward

name, they bear witness of me.

26 But ye believe not, because ye are not of my sheep, as I said unto you.

27 My sheep hear my voice, and I know them, and they follow me:

28 And I give unto them eternal life; and they shall never perish, neither shall any man pluck them out of my hand.

29 My Father, which gave them me, is greater than all; and no man is able to pluck them out of my Father's hand.

30 I and my Father are one.

31 Then the Jews took up stones again to stone him.

32 Jesus answered them, Many good works have I shewed you from my Father; for which of those works do ye stone me?

33 The Jews answered him, saying, For a good work we stone thee not; but for blasphemy; and because that thou, being a man, makest thyself God.

34 Jesus answered them, Is it not written in your law, I said, Ye are gods?

35 If he called them gods, unto whom the word of God came, and the scripture cannot be broken;

36 Say ye of him, whom the Father hath sanctified, and sent into the world, Thou blasphemest; because I said, I am the Son of God?

37 If I do not the works of my Father, believe me not.

38 But if I do, though ye believe not me, believe the works: that ye may know, and believe, that the Father is in me, and I in him.

39 Therefore they sought again to take him: but he escaped out of their hand,

40 And went away again beyond Jordan into the place where John at first baptized; and there he abode.

41 And many resorted unto him, and said, John did no miracle: but all things that John spake of this man were true.

42 And many believed on him there.

JOHN 11

1 Now a certain man was sick, named Lazarus, of Bethany, the town of Mary and her sister Martha.

2 (It was that Mary which anointed the Lord with ointment, and wiped his feet with her hair, whose brother Lazarus was sick.)

3 Therefore his sisters sent unto him, saying, Lord, behold, he whom thou lovest is sick.

4 When Jesus heard that, he said, This sickness is not unto death, but for the glory of God, that the Son of God might be glorified thereby.

5 Now Jesus loved Martha, and her sister, and Lazarus.

6 When he had heard therefore that he was sick, he abode two days still in the same place where he was.

7 Then after that saith he to his disciples, Let us go into Judea again.

ful entrance. Into the sheepfold – The Church. He is a thief and a robber – In God's account. Such were all those teachers, to whom our Lord had just been speaking.

3. To him the door keeper openeth – Christ is considered as the shepherd, ver. 11. As the door in the first and following verses. And as it is not unworthy of Christ to be styled the door, by which both the sheep and the true pastor enter, so neither is it unworthy of God the Father to be styled the door keeper. See Acts xiv, 27; Colossians iv, 3; Rev. iii, 8; Acts xvi, 14. And the sheep hear his voice – The circumstances that follow, exactly agree with the customs of the ancient eastern shepherds. They called their sheep by name, went before them and the sheep followed them. So real Christians hear, listen to, understand, and obey the voice of the shepherd whom Christ hath sent. And he counteth them his own, dearer than any friend or brother: calleth, advises, directs each by name, and leadeth them out, in the paths of righteousness, beside the waters of comfort.

4. He goeth before them – In all the ways of God, teaching them in every point, by example as well as by precept; and the sheep follow him – They tread in his steps: for they know his voice – Having the witness in themselves that his words are the wisdom and the power of God. Reader, art thou a shepherd of souls? Then answer to God. Is it thus with thee and thy flock?

5. They will not follow a stranger – One whom Christ hath not sent, who doth not answer the preceding description. Him they will not follow – And who can constrain them to it? But will flee from him – As from the plague. For they know not the voice of strangers – They cannot relish it; it is harsh and grating to them. They find nothing of God therein.

6. They – The Pharisees, to whom our Lord more immediately spake, as appears from the close of the foregoing chapter.

7. I am the door – Christ is both the Door and the Shepherd, and all things.

8. Whosoever are come – Independently of me, assuming any part of my character, pretending, like your elders and rabbis, to a power over the consciences of men, attempting to make laws in the Church, and to teach their own traditions as the way of salvation: all those prophets and expounders of God's word, that enter not by the door of the sheepfold, but run before I have sent them by my Spirit. Our Lord seems in particular to speak of those that had undertaken this office since he began his ministry, are thieves – Stealing temporal profit to themselves, and robbers – Plundering and murdering the sheep.

9. If any one – As a sheep, enter in by me – Through faith, he shall be safe – From the wolf, and from those murdering shepherds. And shall go in and out – Shall continually attend on the shepherds whom I have sent; and shall find pasture – Food for his soul in all circumstances.

10. The thief cometh not but to steal, and to kill, and to destroy – That is, nothing else can be the consequence of a shepherd's coming, who does not enter in by me.

12. But the hireling – It is not the bare receiving hire, which denominates a man a hireling: (for the laborer is worthy of his hire; Jesus Christ himself being the Judge: yea, and the Lord hath ordained, that they who preach the Gospel, should live of the Gospel:) but the loving hire: the loving the hire more than the

MATTHEW HENRY

CHARLES H. SPURGEON

making known the blessed Jesus. Christ is the Door. And what greater security has the church of God than that the Lord Jesus is between it and all its enemies? He is a door open for passage and communication. Here are plain directions how to come into the fold; we must come in by Jesus Christ as the Door. By faith in him as the great Mediator between God and man. Also, we have precious promises to those that observe this direction. Christ has all that care of his church, and every believer, which a good shepherd has of his flock; and he expects the church, and every believer, to wait on him, and to keep in his pasture.

10-18 Christ is a good Shepherd; many who were not thieves, yet were careless in their duty, and by their neglect the flock was much hurt. Bad principles are the root of bad practices. The Lord Jesus knows whom he has chosen, and is sure of them; they also know whom they have trusted, and are sure of him. See here the grace of Christ; since none could demand his life of him, he laid it down of himself for our redemption. He offered himself to be the Savior; Lo, I come. And the necessity of our case calling for it, he offered himself for the Sacrifice. He was both the offerer and the offering, so that his laying down his life was his offering up himself. From hence it is plain, that he died in the place and stead of men; to obtain their being set free from the punishment of sin, to obtain the pardon of their sin; and that his death should obtain that pardon. Our Lord laid not his life down for his doctrine, but for his sheep.

19-21 Satan ruins many, by putting them out of conceit with the word and ordinances. Men would not be laughed out of their necessary food, yet suffer themselves thus to be laughed out of what is far more necessary. If our zeal and earnestness in the cause of Christ, especially in the blessed work of bringing his sheep into his fold, bring upon us evil names, let us not heed it, but remember our Master was thus reproached before us.

22-30 All who have any thing to say to Christ, may find him in the temple. Christ would make us to believe; we make ourselves doubt. The Jews understood his meaning, but could not form his words into a full charge against him. He described the gracious disposition and happy state of his sheep; they heard and believed his word, followed him as his faithful disciples, and none of them should perish; for the Son and the Father were one. Thus he was able to defend his sheep against all their enemies, which proves that he claimed Divine power and perfection equally with the Father.

31-38 Christ's works of power and mercy proclaim him to be over all, God blessed for evermore, that all may know and believe He is in the Father, and the Father in him. Whom the Father sends, he sanctifies.

organ, but with the inward heart. The chief point is that they hear his voice. Oh, if all that heard my voice heard Christ's voice, how would I wander down every street in this city to proclaim the gospel of Jesus Christ; but, alas! the voice of the minister is utterly ineffectual to save a soul, unless the voice of Christ reach the conscience and rouse its dormant powers. "My sheep hear my voice;" the voice of Jesus, his counsel, his command, clothed with the authority of his own sacred sovereign utterance. When the gospel comes to you as Christ's gospel, with demonstration of the Spirit, the invitation is addressed to you by him. You can look upon it in no other light; so you must accept and receive it. When his princely power comes with it—being mighty to save, he puts saving power into the word—then you hear Christ's voice as a fiat that must be obeyed, as a summons that must be attended to, as a call to which there must be a quick response. O beloved, do not ever rest satisfied with hearing the voice of the preacher. We are only Christ's speaking-trumpets: there is nothing in us: it is only his speaking through us that can do any good. O children of God, some of you do not always listen to Christ's voice in the preaching. While we comment on the word, you make your comments on us. Our style, or our tone, or even our gesture, is enough to absorb—I might rather say, to distract—your thoughts. "Why look ye so earnestly on us?" I beseech you, give less heed to the livery of the servant, and give more care to the message of the Master. Listen warily, if you please; but judge wisely, if you can. See how much pure grain, and how much of Christ, there is in the sermon. Use your sieve; put away all the chaff; take only the good wheat; hear Christ's voice. Well were it if we could obscure ourselves that we might manifest him. I could wish so to preach that you could not see even my little finger; might I but so preach that you could get a full view of Jesus only. O that you could hear his voice drowning ours! This is the mark, the peculiar mark of those who are Christ's peculiar people: they hear his voice. Sometimes, truly it sounds in the ministry; sometimes it thrills forth from that book of books, which is often grossly neglected; sometimes it comes in the night watches. His voice may speak to us in the street. Silent as to vocal utterance, but like familiar tones that sometimes greet us in our dreams, the voice of Christ is distinctly audible to the soul. It will come to you in sweet or in bitter providences; yea, there is such a thing as hearing Christ's voice in the rustling of every leaf upon the tree, in the moaning of every wind, in the rippling of every wave. And there be those that have

8 His disciples say unto him, Master, the Jews of late sought to stone thee; and goest thou thither again?

9 Jesus answered, Are there not twelve hours in the day? If any man walk in the day, he stumbleth not, because he seeth the light of this world.

10 But if a man walk in the night, he stumbleth, because there is no light in him.

11 These things said he: and after that he saith unto them, Our friend Lazarus sleepeth; but I go, that I may awake him out of sleep.

12 Then said his disciples, Lord, if he sleep, he shall do well.

13 Howbeit Jesus spake of his death: but they thought that he had spoken of taking of rest in sleep.

14 Then said Jesus unto them plainly, Lazarus is dead.

15 And I am glad for your sakes that I was not there, to the intent ye may believe; nevertheless let us go unto him.

16 Then said Thomas, which is called Didymus, unto his fellowdisciples, Let us also go, that we may die with him.

17 Then when Jesus came, he found that he had lain in the grave four days already.

18 Now Bethany was nigh unto Jerusalem, about fifteen furlongs off:

19 And many of the Jews came to Martha and Mary, to comfort them concerning their brother.

20 Then Martha, as soon as she heard that Jesus was coming, went and met him: but Mary sat still in the house.

21 Then said Martha unto Jesus, Lord, if thou hadst been here, my brother had not died.

22 But I know, that even now, whatsoever thou wilt ask of God, God will give it thee.

23 Jesus saith unto her, Thy brother shall rise again.

24 Martha saith unto him, I know that he shall rise again in the resurrection at the last day.

25 Jesus said unto her, I am the resurrection, and the life: he that believeth in me, though he were dead, yet shall he live:

26 And whosoever liveth and believeth in me shall never die. Believest thou this?

27 She saith unto him, Yea, Lord: I believe that thou art the Christ, the Son of God, which should come into the world.

28 And when she had so said, she went her way, and called Mary her sister secretly, saying, The Master is come, and calleth for thee.

29 As soon as she heard that, she arose quickly, and came unto him.

30 Now Jesus was not yet come into the town, but was in that place where Martha met him.

31 The Jews then which were with her in the house, and comforted her, when they saw Mary, that she rose up hastily and went out, followed her, saying, She goeth unto the grave to weep there.

32 Then when Mary was come where Jesus was, and saw him, she fell down at his feet,

work: the working for the sake of the hire. He is a hireling, who would not work, were it not for the hire; to whom this is the great (if not only) motive of working. O God! If a man who works only for hire is such a wretch, a mere thief and a robber, what is he who continually takes the hire, and yet does not work at all? The wolf – signifies any enemy who, by force or fraud, attacks the Christian's faith, liberty, or life. So the wolf seizeth and scattereth the flock – He seizeth some, and scattereth the rest; the two ways of hurting the flock of Christ.

13. The hireling fleeth because he is a hireling – Because he loves the hire, not the sheep.

14. I know my sheep – With a tender regard and special care: and am known of mine – With a holy confidence and affection.

15. As the Father knoweth me, and I know the Father – With such a knowledge as implies an inexpressible union: and I lay down my life – Speaking of the present time. For his whole life was only a going unto death.

16. I have also other sheep – Which he foreknew; which are not of this fold – Not of the Jewish Church or nation, but Gentiles. I must bring them likewise – Into my Church, the general assembly of those whose names are written in heaven. And there shall be one flock – (Not one fold, a plain false print) no corrupt or divided flocks remaining. And one shepherd – Who laid down his life for the sheep, and will leave no hireling among them. The unity both of the flock and the shepherd shall be completed in its season. The shepherd shall bring all into one flock: and the whole flock shall hear the one shepherd.

17. I lay down my life that I may take it again – I cheerfully die to expiate the sins of men, to the end I may rise again for their justification.

18. I lay it down of myself – By my own free act and deed. I have power to lay it down, and I have power to take it again – I have an original power and right of myself, both to lay it down as a ransom, and to take it again, after full satisfaction is made, for the sins of the whole world. This commission have I received of my Father – Which I readily execute. He chiefly spoke of the Father, before his suffering: of his own glory, after it. Our Lord's receiving this commission as mediator is not to be considered as the ground of his power to lay down and resume his life. For this he had in himself, as having an original right to dispose thereof, antecedent to the Father's commission. But this commission was the reason why he thus used his power in laying down his life. He did it in obedience to his Father.

21. These are not the words – The word in the original takes in actions too.

22. It was the feast of the dedication – Instituted by Judas Maccabeus, 1 Macc. iv, 59, when he purged and dedicated the altar and temple after they had been polluted. So our Lord observed festivals even of human appointment. Is it not, at least, innocent for us to do the same?

23. In Solomon's portico – Josephus informs us, that when Solomon built the temple, he filled up a part of the adjacent valley, and built a portico over it toward the east. This was a noble structure, supported by a wall four hundred cubits high: and continued even to the time of Albinus and Agrippa, which was several years after the death of Christ.

The holy God will reward, and therefore will employ, none but such as he makes holy. The Father was in the Son, so that by Divine power he wrought his miracles; the Son was so in the Father, that he knew the whole of his mind. This we cannot by searching find out to perfection, but we may know and believe these declarations of Christ.

39-42 No weapon formed against our Lord Jesus shall prosper. He escaped, not because he was afraid to suffer, but because his hour was not come. And he who knew how to deliver himself, knows how to deliver the godly out of their temptations, and to make a way for them to escape. Persecutors may drive Christ and his gospel out of their own city or country, but they cannot drive him or it out of the world. When we know Christ by faith in our hearts, we find all that the Scripture saith of him is true.

JOHN 11

The sickness of Lazarus. (1-6)
Christ returns to Judea. (7-10)
The death of Lazarus. (11-16)
Christ arrives at Bethany. (17-32)
He raises Lazarus. (33-46)
The Pharisees consult against Jesus. (47-53)
The Jews seek for him. (54-57)

1-6 God has gracious intentions, even when he seems to delay. When the work of deliverance, temporal or spiritual, public or personal, is delayed, it does but stay for the right time.

7-10 Christ never brings his people into any danger but he goes with them in it.

11-16 Since we are sure to rise again at the last, why should not the believing hope of that resurrection to eternal life, make it as easy for us to put off the body and die, as it is to put off our clothes and go to sleep? A true Christian, when he dies, does but sleep; he rests from the labors of the past day. Nay, herein death is better than sleep, that sleep is only a short rest, but death is the end of earthly cares and toils. The disciples thought that it was now needless for Christ to go to Lazarus, and expose himself and them. Thus we often hope that the good work we are called to do, will be done by some other hand, if there be peril in the doing of it. But when Christ raised Lazarus from the dead, many were brought to believe on him; and there was much done to make perfect the faith of those that believed. Let us go to him; death cannot separate from the love of Christ, nor put us out of the reach of his call. Like Thomas, in difficult times Christians should encourage one another. The dying of the Lord Jesus should make us willing to die whenever God calls us.

17-32 Here was a house where the fear of God was,

learned to lean on Christ's bosom, till they have looked for all the world as though they were a shell that lay in the ocean of Christ's love, listening for ever to the sonorous cadence of that deep, unfathomed, all-mysterious main. The billows of his love never cease to swell. The billowy anthem still peals on with solemn grandeur in the ear of the Christian. O may we hear Christ's voice each one of us for ourselves! I find that language fails me, and metaphors are weak to describe its potent spell.

One point is worth noticing, however. I think our Lord meant here that his sheep, when they hear his voice, know it so well that they can tell it at once from the voice of strangers. The true child of God knows the gospel from the law. It is not by learning catechisms, reading theological books, or listening to endless controversies, that he finds this out. There is an instinct of his regenerate nature far more trustworthy than any lessons he has been taught. The voice of Jesus! Why there is no music like it. If you have once heard it, you cannot mistake it for another, or another for it. Some are babes in grace: others are of full age, and by reason of use, have their senses exercised; but one sense is quickly brought out— the sense of hearing. It is so easy to tell the joy-bells of the gospel from the death-knell of the law; for the letter killeth, but the Spirit giveth life. "Do, or die," says Moses. "Believe, and live," says Christ: you must know which is which. Yes; and I think they are equally shrewd and quick to discriminate between the flesh and the Spirit. Let some of the very feeblest of God's people sit down under a fluent ministry, with all the beauties of rhetoric, and let the minister preach up the dignity of human nature, and the sufficiency of man's reason to find out the way of righteousness, and you will hear them say: "It is very clever; but there is no food for me in it." Bring, however, the best and most instructed, and most learned Christian man, and set him down under a ministry that is very faulty as to the gift of utterance, and incorrect even in grammar; but if it is full of Jesus Christ, I know what he will say: "Ah! never mind the man, and never mind the platter on which he brought the meat; it was food to my soul that I fed upon with a hearty relish; it was marrow and fatness, for I could hear Christ's voice in it." I am not going to follow out these tests; but certain it is, that the sheep know Christ's voice, and can easily distinguish it. I saw hundreds of lambs the other day together, and there were also their mothers; and I am sure if I had had the task of allotting the proper lamb to each, or to any of them, it would have kept me till now to have done it.

saying unto him, Lord, if thou hadst been here, my brother had not died.

33 When Jesus therefore saw her weeping, and the Jews also weeping which came with her, he groaned in the spirit, and was troubled,

34 And said, Where have ye laid him? They said unto him, Lord, come and see.

35 Jesus wept.

36 Then said the Jews, Behold how he loved him!

37 And some of them said, Could not this man, which opened the eyes of the blind, have caused that even this man should not have died?

38 Jesus therefore again groaning in himself cometh to the grave. It was a cave, and a stone lay upon it.

39 Jesus said, Take ye away the stone. Martha, the sister of him that was dead, saith unto him, Lord, by this time he stinketh: for he hath been dead four days.

40 Jesus saith unto her, Said I not unto thee, that, if thou wouldest believe, thou shouldest see the glory of God?

41 Then they took away the stone from the place where the dead was laid. And Jesus lifted up his eyes, and said, Father, I thank thee that thou hast heard me.

42 And I knew that thou hearest me always: but because of the people which stand by I said it, that they may believe that thou hast sent me.

43 And when he thus had spoken, he cried with a loud voice, Lazarus, come forth.

44 And he that was dead came forth, bound hand and foot with graveclothes: and his face was bound about with a napkin. Jesus saith unto them, Loose him, and let him go.

45 Then many of the Jews which came to Mary, and had seen the things which Jesus did, believed on him.

46 But some of them went their ways to the Pharisees, and told them what things Jesus had done.

47 Then gathered the chief priests and the Pharisees a council, and said, What do we? for this man doeth many miracles.

48 If we let him thus alone, all men will believe on him: and the Romans shall come and take away both our place and nation.

49 And one of them, named Caiaphas, being the high priest that same year, said unto them, Ye know nothing at all,

50 Nor consider that it is expedient for us, that one man should die for the people, and that the whole nation perish not.

51 And this spake he not of himself: but being high priest that year, he prophesied that Jesus should die for that nation;

52 And not for that nation only, but that also he should gather together in one the children of God that were scattered abroad.

53 Then from that day forth they took counsel together for to put him to death.

54 Jesus therefore walked no more openly

26. Ye do not believe, because ye are not of my sheep – Because ye do not, will not follow me: because ye are proud, unholy, lovers of praise, lovers of the world, lovers of pleasure, not of God.

27, 28, 29. My sheep hear my voice, and I know them, and they follow me, &c – Our Lord still alludes to the discourse he had before this festival. As if he had said, My sheep are they who,

1. Hear my voice by faith;

2. Are known (that is, approved) by me, as loving me; and

3. Follow me, keep my commandments, with a believing, loving heart. And to those who,

1. Truly believe (observe three promises annexed to three conditions) I give eternal life. He does not say, I will, but I give. For he that believeth hath everlasting life. Those whom,

2. I know truly to love me, shall never perish, provided they abide in my love.

3. Those who follow me, neither men nor devils can pluck out of my hand. My Father who hath, by an unchangeable decree, given me all that believe, love, and obey, is greater than all in heaven or earth, and none is able to pluck them out of his hand.

30. I and the Father are one – Not by consent of will only, but by unity of power, and consequently of nature. Are – This word confutes Sabellius, proving the plurality of persons: one – This word confutes Arius, proving the unity of nature in God. Never did any prophet before, from the beginning of the world, use any one expression of himself, which could possibly be so interpreted as this and other expressions were, by all that heard our Lord speak. Therefore if he was not God he must have been the vilest of men.

34. Psalm lxxxii, 6.

35. If he (God) called them gods unto whom the word of God came, (that is, to whom God was then speaking,) and the Scripture cannot be broken – That is, nothing which is written therein can be censured or rejected.

36. Say ye of him whom the Father hath sanctified, and sent into the world – This sanctification (whereby he is essentially the Holy One of God) is mentioned as prior to his mission, and together with it implies, Christ was God in the highest sense, infinitely superior to that wherein those Judges were so called.

38. That ye may know and believe – In some a more exact knowledge precedes, in others it follows faith. I am in the Father and the Father in me. I and the Father are one – These two sentences illustrate each other.

40. To the desert place where John baptized, and gave so honorable a testimony of him.

41. John did no miracle – An honor reserved for him, whose forerunner he was.

JOHN 11

1. One Lazarus – It is probable, Lazarus was younger than his sisters. Bethany is named, the town of Mary and Martha, and Lazarus is mentioned after them, ver. 5. Ecclesiastical history informs us, that Lazarus was now thirty years old, and that he lived thirty years after Christ's ascension.

2. It was that Mary who afterward anointed, &c. She was more known than her elder sister Martha, and as such is named before her.

and on which his blessing rested; yet it was made a house of mourning. Grace will keep sorrow from the heart, but not from the house. When God, by his grace and providence, is coming towards us in ways of mercy and comfort, we should, like Martha, go forth by faith, hope, and prayer, to meet him. When Martha went to meet Jesus, Mary sat still in the house; this temper formerly had been an advantage to her, when it put her at Christ's feet to hear his word; but in the day of affliction, the same temper disposed her to melancholy. It is our wisdom to watch against the temptations, and to make use of the advantages of our natural tempers. When we know not what in particular to ask or expect, let us refer ourselves to God; let him do as seemeth him good. To enlarge Martha's expectations, our Lord declared himself to be the Resurrection and the Life. In every sense he is the Resurrection; the source, the substance, the first fruits, the cause of it. The redeemed soul lives after death in happiness; and after the resurrection, both body and soul are kept from all evil forever. When we have read or heard the word of Christ, about the great things of the other world, we should put it to ourselves, Do we believe this truth? The crosses and comforts of this present time would not make such a deep impression upon us as they do, if we believed the things of eternity as we ought. When Christ our Master comes, he calls for us. He comes in his word and ordinances, and calls us to them, calls us by them, calls us to himself. Those who, in a day of peace, set themselves at Christ's feet to be taught by him, may with comfort, in a day of trouble, cast themselves at his feet, to find favor with him.

33-46 Christ's tender sympathy with these afflicted friends, appeared by the troubles of his spirit. In all the afflictions of believers he is afflicted. His concern for them was shown by his kind inquiry after the remains of his deceased friend. Being found in fashion as a man, he acts in the way and manner of the sons of men. It was shown by his tears. He was a man of sorrows, and acquainted with grief. Tears of compassion resemble those of Christ. But Christ never approved that sensibility of which many are proud, while they weep at mere tales of distress, but are hardened to real woe. He sets us an example to withdraw from scenes of giddy mirth, that we may comfort the afflicted. And we have not a High Priest who cannot be touched with a feeling of our infirmities. It is a good step toward raising a soul to spiritual life, when the stone is taken away, when prejudices are removed, and got over, and way is made for the word to enter the heart. If we take Christ's word, and rely on his power and faithfulness, we shall see the glory of God, and be happy in the sight. Our Lord Jesus has taught us, by his own example, to call God Father, in prayer, and to draw nigh to him as children to a father, with humble reverence, yet with holy boldness. He openly made this address to God, with uplifted eyes and loud

But somehow the lambs knew the mothers, and the mothers knew the lambs; and they were all happy enough in each other's company.

Every saint here, mixed up as he may be at times with parties and professors of all sorts, knows Christ, and Christ knows him, and he is therefore bound to his owner. That is the mark on the ear. You have seen sometimes in the country two flocks together on the road, and you say: "I wonder how the shepherds will manage to keep them distinct? They will get mixed up." They do not; they go this way and that way; and after a little commingling they separate, for they know their master's voice; "and a stranger will they not follow." You will go tomorrow, many of you, out into the world, some to the Exchange, others to the market, and others again into the factory: you are all mixed. Yes; but the seeming confusion of your company is temporary, not real and permanent. You will come right again, and you will go to your own home and your own fellowship. And at the last, when we shall have ended our pilgrimage, the one shall wend his way to the glory land, and the other to the abyss of woe. There will be no mistake. You will hear the Master's call, and obey. There is a mark on the ear which identifies every saint.

Christ's sheep hear his voice obediently. This is an important proof of discipleship. Indeed, it may serve as a reproof to many. Oh, I would that you were more careful about this! "He that hath my commandments, and keepeth them," said Jesus, "he it is that loveth me." "He that loveth me not keepeth not my sayings." How comes it to pass, then, that there are certain commands of Christ which some Christians will suffer to lie in abeyance? They will say, "The Lord commands this, but it is not essential." Oh, unloving spirit, that can think anything unessential that thy Bridegroom bids thee do! They that love, think little things of great moment, especially when they are looked upon as tokens of the strength or the tenderness of one's regard. It may not be essential, in order to prove the relation in which a wife stands to her husband, that she should study his tastes, consult his wishes, or attend to his comfort. But will she the less strive to please, because love, not fear, constrains her? I know not. And can it be that any of you, my brethren, would harbor such a thought as your negligence implies? Do you really suppose that after the choice of Christ has been fixed on you, and the love of Christ has been plighted to you, you may now be as remiss or careless as you like? Nay, rather, might we not expect that a sacred passion, an ardent zeal, a touch of

among the Jews; but went thence unto a country near to the wilderness, into a city called Ephraim, and there continued with his disciples.

55 And the Jews' passover was nigh at hand: and many went out of the country up to Jerusalem before the passover, to purify themselves.

56 Then sought they for Jesus, and spake among themselves, as they stood in the temple, What think ye, that he will not come to the feast?

57 Now both the chief priests and the Pharisees had given a commandment, that, if any man knew where he were, he should shew it, that they might take him.

JOHN 12

1 Then Jesus six days before the passover came to Bethany, where Lazarus was which had been dead, whom he raised from the dead.

2 There they made him a supper; and Martha served: but Lazarus was one of them that sat at the table with him.

3 Then took Mary a pound of ointment of spikenard, very costly, and anointed the feet of Jesus, and wiped his feet with her hair: and the house was filled with the odor of the ointment.

4 Then saith one of his disciples, Judas Iscariot, Simon's son, which should betray him,

5 Why was not this ointment sold for three hundred pence, and given to the poor?

6 This he said, not that he cared for the poor; but because he was a thief, and had the bag, and bare what was put therein.

7 Then said Jesus, Let her alone: against the day of my burying hath she kept this.

8 For the poor always ye have with you; but me ye have not always.

9 Much people of the Jews therefore knew that he was there: and they came not for Jesus' sake only, but that they might see Lazarus also, whom he had raised from the dead.

10 But the chief priests consulted that they might put Lazarus also to death;

11 Because that by reason of him many of the Jews went away, and believed on Jesus.

12 On the next day much people that were come to the feast, when they heard that Jesus was coming to Jerusalem,

13 Took branches of palm trees, and went forth to meet him, and cried, Hosanna: Blessed is the King of Israel that cometh in the name of the Lord.

14 And Jesus, when he had found a young ass, sat thereon; as it is written,

15 Fear not, daughter of Sion: behold, thy King cometh, sitting on an ass's colt.

16 These things understood not his disciples at the first: but when Jesus was glorified, then remembered they that these things were written of him, and that they had done these things unto him.

17 The people therefore that was with him

4. This sickness is not to death, but for the glory of God – The event of this sickness will not be death, in the usual sense of the word, a final separation of his soul and body; but a manifestation of the glorious power of God.

7. Let us go into Judea – From the country east of Jordan, whither he had retired some time before, when the Jews sought to stone him, chap. x, 39, 40.

9. Are there not twelve hours in the day? – The Jews always divided the space from sunrise to sunset, were the days longer or shorter, into twelve parts: so that the hours of their day were all the year the same in number, though much shorter in winter than in summer. If any man walk in the day he stumbleth not – As if he had said, So there is such a space, a determined time, which God has allotted me. During that time I stumble not, amidst all the snares that are laid for me. Because he seeth the light of this world – And so I see the light of God surrounding me.

10. But if a man walk in the night – If he have not light from God; if his providence does no longer protect him.

11. Our friend Lazarus sleepeth – This he spoke, just when he died. Sleepeth – Such is the death of good men in the language of heaven. But the disciples did not yet understand this language. And the slowness of our understanding makes the Scripture often descend to our barbarous manner of speaking.

16. Thomas in Hebrew, as Didymus in Greek, signifies a twin. With him – With Jesus, whom he supposed the Jews would kill. It seems to be the language of despair.

20. Mary sat in the house – Probably not hearing what was said.

22. Whatsoever thou wilt ask, God will give it thee – So that she already believed he could raise him from the dead.

25. I am the resurrection – Of the dead. And the life – Of the living. He that believeth in me, though he die, yet shall he live – In life everlasting.

32. She fell at his feet – This Martha had not done. So she makes amends for her slowness in coming.

33. He groaned – So he restrained his tears. So he stopped them soon after, ver. 38. He troubled himself – An expression amazingly elegant, and full of the highest propriety. For the affections of Jesus were not properly passions, but voluntary emotions, which were wholly in his own power. And this tender trouble which he now voluntarily sustained, was full of the highest order and reason.

35. Jesus wept – Out of sympathy with those who were in tears all around him, as well as from a deep sense of the misery sin had brought upon human nature.

37. Could not this person have even caused, that this man should not have died? – Yet they never dreamed that he could raise him again! What a strange mixture of faith and unbelief.

38. It was a cave – So Abraham, Isaac, and Jacob, and their wives, except Rachel, were buried in the cave of Machpelah, Gen. xlix, 29-31. These caves were commonly in rocks, which abounded in that country, either hollowed by nature or hewn by art. And the entrance was shut up with a great stone, which sometimes had a monumental inscription.

39. Lord, by this time he stinketh – Thus did reason and faith struggle together.

40. Said I not – It appears by this, that Christ had said more to Martha than is before recorded.

voice, that they might be convinced the Father had sent him as his beloved Son into the world. He could have raised Lazarus by the silent exertion of his power and will, and the unseen working of the Spirit of life; but he did it by a loud call. This was a figure of the gospel call, by which dead souls are brought out of the grave of sin: and of the sound of the archangel's trumpet at the last day, with which all that sleep in the dust shall be awakened, and summoned before the great tribunal. The grave of sin and this world, is no place for those whom Christ has quickened; they must come forth. Lazarus was thoroughly revived, and returned not only to life, but to health. The sinner cannot quicken his own soul, but he is to use the means of grace; the believer cannot sanctify himself, but he is to lay aside every weight and hindrance. We cannot convert our relatives and friends, but we should instruct, warn, and invite them.

47-53 There can hardly be a more clear discovery of the madness that is in man's heart, and of its desperate enmity against God, than what is here recorded. Words of prophecy in the mouth, are not clear evidence of a principle of grace in the heart. The calamity we seek to escape by sin, we take the most effectual course to bring upon our own heads; as those do who think by opposing Christ's kingdom, to advance their own worldly interest. The fear of the wicked shall come upon them. The conversion of souls is the gathering of them to Christ as their ruler and refuge; and he died to effect this. By dying he purchased them to himself, and the gift of the Holy Ghost for them: his love in dying for believers should unite them closely together.

54-57 Before our gospel Passover we must renew our repentance. Thus by a voluntary purification, and by religious exercises, many, more devout than their neighbors, spent some time before the Passover at Jerusalem. When we expect to meet God, we must solemnly prepare. No devices of man can alter the purposes of God: and while hypocrites amuse themselves with forms and disputes, and worldly men pursue their own plans, Jesus still orders all things for his own glory and the salvation of his people.

JOHN 12

Christ anointed by Mary. (1-11)
He enters Jerusalem. (12-19)
Greeks apply to see Jesus. (20-26)
A voice from heaven bears testimony to Christ. (27-33)
His discourse with the people. (34-36)
Unbelief of the Jews. (37-43)
Christ's address to them. (44-50)

1-11 Christ had formerly blamed Martha for being troubled with much serving. But she did not leave off serving, as some, who when found fault with for going

inspiration would stir you up, put you on the alert, make you wake at the faintest sound of his voice, or keep you listening to do his will? Be it ours, then, to act out with fidelity that verse we have often sung with enthusiasm:—

"In all my Lord's appointed ways
My journey I'll pursue."

However little the precept may appear in the eyes of others; however insignificant as compared with our salvation, yet—doth the Lord command it?—then his sheep hear his voice, and they follow him.

Christ has marked his sheep on their feet as well as their ears. They follow him: they are gently led, not harshly driven. They follow him as the Captain of their salvation; they trust in the power of his arm to clear the way for them. All their trust on him is stayed; all their hope on him they lean. They follow him as their teacher; they call no man "Rabbi" under heaven, but Christ alone. He is the infallible source of their creeds; neither will they allow their minds to be ruled by conclaves, councils, nor decrees. Hath a Christ said it? It is enough. If not, it is no more for me than the whistling of the wind. They follow a Christ as their teacher.

And the sheep of Christ follow him as their example; they desire to be in this world as he was. It is one of their marks, that to a greater or less degree they have a Christ-like spirit; and if they could they would be altogether like their Lord.

They follow him, too, as their Commander, and Lawgiver, and Prince. "Whatsoever he saith unto you, do it," was his mother's wise speech; and it is the children's wise speech: "Whatsoever he saith unto you, do it." Oh, blessed shall they be above many of whom it shall be said, "These are they that have not defiled their garments." "These are they which follow the Lamb whithersoever he goeth." Some of his followers are not very scrupulous. They love him. It is not for us to judge them. Rather we place ourselves among them and share in the censure. But happiest of all the happy are they who see the footprint—the print of that foot that once was pierced with the nail—and put their foot down where he placed it, and then again, in the selfsame mark, follow where he trod, till they climb at last to the throne. Keep close to Christ; take care of his little precepts unto the end. Remember, "Whosoever shall break one of these least commandments, and shall teach men so, he shall be called the least in the kingdom of heaven." Do not peril being least in the heavenly kingdom though it is better to be that than to be greatest in the kingdom of darkness. O seek to be very near him, to be a choice

when he called Lazarus out of his grave, and raised him from the dead, bare record.

18 For this cause the people also met him, for that they heard that he had done this miracle.

19 The Pharisees therefore said among themselves, Perceive ye how ye prevail nothing? behold, the world is gone after him.

20 And there were certain Greeks among them that came up to worship at the feast:

21 The same came therefore to Philip, which was of Bethsaida of Galilee, and desired him, saying, Sir, we would see Jesus.

22 Philip cometh and telleth Andrew: and again Andrew and Philip tell Jesus.

23 And Jesus answered them, saying, The hour is come, that the Son of man should be glorified.

24 Verily, verily, I say unto you, Except a corn of wheat fall into the ground and die, it abideth alone: but if it die, it bringeth forth much fruit.

25 He that loveth his life shall lose it; and he that hateth his life in this world shall keep it unto life eternal.

26 If any man serve me, let him follow me; and where I am, there shall also my servant be: if any man serve me, him will my Father honor.

27 Now is my soul troubled; and what shall I say? Father, save me from this hour: but for this cause came I unto this hour.

28 Father, glorify thy name. Then came there a voice from heaven, saying, I have both glorified it, and will glorify it again.

29 The people therefore, that stood by, and heard it, said that it thundered: others said, An angel spake to him.

30 Jesus answered and said, This voice came not because of me, but for your sakes.

31 Now is the judgment of this world: now shall the prince of this world be cast out.

32 And I, if I be lifted up from the earth, will draw all men unto me.

33 This he said, signifying what death he should die.

34 The people answered him, We have heard out of the law that Christ abideth for ever: and how sayest thou, The Son of man must be lifted up? who is this Son of man?

35 Then Jesus said unto them, Yet a little while is the light with you. Walk while ye have the light, lest darkness come upon you: for he that walketh in darkness knoweth not whither he goeth.

36 While ye have light, believe in the light, that ye may be the children of light. These things spake Jesus, and departed, and did hide himself from them.

37 But though he had done so many miracles before them, yet they believed not on him:

38 That the saying of Esaias the prophet might be fulfilled, which he spake, Lord, who hath believed our report? and to whom hath the arm of the Lord been revealed?

39 Therefore they could not believe, because that Esaias said again,

41. Jesus lifted up his eyes – Not as if he applied to his Father for assistance. There is not the least show of this. He wrought the miracle with an air of absolute sovereignty, as the Lord of life and death. But it was as if he had said, I thank thee, that by the disposal of thy providence, thou hast granted my desire, in this remarkable opportunity of exerting my power, and showing forth thy praise.

43. He cried with a loud voice – That all who were present might hear. Lazarus, come forth – Jesus called him out of the tomb as easily as if he had been not only alive, but awake also.

44. And he came forth bound hand and foot with grave clothes – Which were wrapt round each hand and each foot, and his face was wrapt about with a napkin – If the Jews buried as the Egyptians did, the face was not covered with it, but it only went round the forehead, and under the chin; so that he might easily see his way.

45. Many believed on Him – And so the Son of God was glorified, according to what our Lord had said, ver. 4.

46. But some of them went to the Pharisees – What a dreadful confirmation of that weighty truth, If they hear not Moses and the prophets, neither will they be persuaded though one rose from the dead!

47. What do we? – What? Believe. Yea, but death yields to the power of Christ sooner than infidelity.

48. All men will believe – And receive him as the Messiah. And this will give such umbrage to the Romans that they will come and subvert both our place – Temple; and nation – Both our Church and state. Were they really afraid of this? Or was it a fair color only? Certainly it was no more. For they could not but know, that he that raised the dead was able to conquer the Romans.

49. That year – That memorable year, in which Christ was to die. It was the last and chief of Daniel's seventy weeks, the fortieth year before the destruction of Jerusalem, and was celebrated for various causes, in the Jewish history. Therefore that year is so peculiarly mentioned: Caiaphas was the high priest both before and after it. Ye know nothing – He reproves their slow deliberations in so clear a case.

50. It is expedient that one man should die for the people – So God overruled his tongue, for he spake not of himself, by his own spirit only, but by the spirit of prophecy. And thus he gave unawares as clear a testimony to the priestly, as Pilate did to the kingly office of Christ.

52. But that, he might gather into one – Church, all the children of God that were scattered abroad – Through all ages and nations.

55. Many went up to purify themselves – That they might remove all hindrances to their eating the Passover.

JOHN 12

1. Six days before the Passover – Namely, on the Sabbath: that which was called by the Jews, "The Great Sabbath." This whole week was anciently termed "The great and holy week." Jesus came – From Ephraim, chap. xi, 54.

2. It seems Martha was a person of some figure, from the great respect which was paid to her and her sister, in visits and condolences on Lazarus's death, as well as from the costly ointment men-

MATTHEW HENRY   CHARLES H. SPURGEON

too far in one way, peevishly run too far another way; she still served, but within hearing of Christ's gracious words. Mary gave a token of love to Christ, who had given real tokens of his love to her and her family. God's Anointed should be our Anointed. Has God poured on him the oil of gladness above his fellows, let us pour on him the ointment of our best affections. In Judas a foul sin is gilded over with a plausible pretense. We must not think that those do no acceptable service, who do it not in our way. The reigning love of money is heart-theft. The grace of Christ puts kind comments on pious words and actions, makes the best of what is amiss, and the most of what is good. Opportunities are to be improved; and those first and most vigorously, which are likely to be the shortest. To consult to hinder the further effect of the miracle, by putting Lazarus to death, is such wickedness, malice, and folly, as cannot be explained, except by the desperate enmity of the human heart against God. They resolved that the man should die whom the Lord had raised to life. The success of the gospel often makes wicked men so angry, that they speak and act as if they hoped to obtain a victory over the Almighty himself.

12-19 Christ's riding in triumph to Jerusalem is recorded by all the evangelists. Many excellent things, both in the word and providence of God, disciples do not understand at their first acquaintance with the things of God. The right understanding of the spiritual nature of Christ's kingdom, prevents our misapplying the Scriptures which speak of it.

20-26 In attendance upon holy ordinances, particularly the gospel Passover, the great desire of our souls should be to see Jesus; to see him as ours, to keep up communion with him, and derive grace from him. The calling of the Gentiles magnified the Redeemer. A corn of wheat yields no increase unless it is cast into the ground. Thus Christ might have possessed his heavenly glory alone, without becoming man. Or, after he had taken man's nature, he might have entered heaven alone, by his own perfect righteousness, without suffering or death; but then no sinner of the human race could have been saved. The salvation of souls hitherto, and henceforward to the end of time, is owing to the dying of this corn of wheat. Let us search whether Christ be in us the hope of glory; let us beg him to make us indifferent to the trifling concerns of this life, that we may serve the Lord Jesus with a willing mind, and follow his holy example.

27-33 The sin of our souls was the trouble of Christ's soul, when he undertook to redeem and save us, and to make his soul an offering for our sin. Christ was willing to suffer, yet prayed to be saved from suffering. Prayer against trouble may well agree with patience under it, and submission to the will of God in it. Our Lord Jesus undertook to satisfy God's injured honor,

sheep in his chosen flock, and to have the mark distinctly upon your foot!

I will not stay to apply these truths, but leave each one of you to make such self-searching enquiries as the text suggests. Have I the ear mark? Have I the foot mark? "My sheep hear my voice," "and they follow me." I hope that I am among the number.

III. The last point, with which we now proceed to close, is—THE PRIVILEGE OF CHRIST'S SHEEP. It does not look very large, but if we open it we shall see an amazing degree of blessedness in it. "I know them," "I know them." What does it mean?

I have not time now to tell you all it means. "I know them." What is the reverse of this but one of the most dreadful things that is reserved for the day of judgment? There will be some who will say, "Lord, Lord, have we not prophesied in thy name, and in thy name cast out devils?" And he shall say, "Verily, verily, I say unto you, I never knew you; depart from me, ye cursed." Now measure the height of that privilege by the depth of this misery. "I never knew you." What a volume of scorn it implies! What a stigma of infamy it conveys! Change the picture. The Redeemer says, "I know them," "I know them." How his eyes flash with kindness; how their cheeks burn with gratitude, as he says, "I know them"! Why, if a man had a friend and acquaintance that he used to know, and some years after he found him a disreputable, abandoned, wicked, guilty criminal, I feel pretty sure he would not say much about having known such a fellow, though he might be driven to confess that he had some years ago a passing acquaintance with him. But our Lord Jesus Christ, though he knows what poor, unworthy ones we are, yet when we shall be brought up before the Lord, before the great white throne, he will confess he knew us. He does know us, we are old acquaintances of his, and he has known us from before the foundation of the world, "For whom he did foreknow, he also did predestinate to be conformed to the image of his Son, that he might be the firstborn among many brethren. Moreover whom he did predestinate, them he also called." There are riches of grace in this; but we will consider it in another way. Our Savior knows us, our Shepherd knows us. Beloved, he knows your person and all about you. You, with that sick body, that aching head, he knows you and he knows your sin with all its sensitiveness; that timidity, that anxiety, that constitutional depression—he knows it all. A physician may come to see you, and be unable to detect what the disease is that pains or prostrates you, but

40 He hath blinded their eyes, and hardened their heart; that they should not see with their eyes, nor understand with their heart, and be converted, and I should heal them.

41 These things said Esaias, when he saw his glory, and spake of him.

42 Nevertheless among the chief rulers also many believed on him; but because of the Pharisees they did not confess him, lest they should be put out of the synagogue:

43 For they loved the praise of men more than the praise of God.

44 Jesus cried and said, He that believeth on me, believeth not on me, but on him that sent me.

45 And he that seeth me seeth him that sent me.

46 I am come a light into the world, that whosoever believeth on me should not abide in darkness.

47 And if any man hear my words, and believe not, I judge him not: for I came not to judge the world, but to save the world.

48 He that rejecteth me, and receiveth not my words, hath one that judgeth him: the word that I have spoken, the same shall judge him in the last day.

49 For I have not spoken of myself; but the Father which sent me, he gave me a commandment, what I should say, and what I should speak.

50 And I know that his commandment is life everlasting: whatsoever I speak therefore, even as the Father said unto me, so I speak.

JOHN 13

1 Now before the feast of the passover, when Jesus knew that his hour was come that he should depart out of this world unto the Father, having loved his own which were in the world, he loved them unto the end.

2 And supper being ended, the devil having now put into the heart of Judas Iscariot, Simon's son, to betray him;

3 Jesus knowing that the Father had given all things into his hands, and that he was come from God, and went to God;

4 He riseth from supper, and laid aside his garments; and took a towel, and girded himself.

5 After that he poureth water into a bason, and began to wash the disciples' feet, and to wipe them with the towel wherewith he was girded.

6 Then cometh he to Simon Peter: and Peter saith unto him, Lord, dost thou wash my feet?

7 Jesus answered and said unto him, What I do thou knowest not now; but thou shalt know hereafter.

8 Peter saith unto him, Thou shalt never wash my feet. Jesus answered him, If I wash thee not, thou hast no part with me.

9 Simon Peter saith unto him, Lord, not my feet only, but also my hands and my head.

10 Jesus saith to him, He that is washed

tioned in the next verse. And probably it was at their house our Lord and his disciples lodged, when he returned from Jerusalem to Bethany, every evening of the last week of his life, upon which he was now entered.

3. Then Mary, taking a pound of ointment – There were two persons who poured ointment on Christ. One toward the beginning of his ministry, at or near Nain, Luke vii, 37, &c. The other six days before his last Passover, at Bethany; the account of whom is given here, as well as by St. Matthew and Mark.

7. Against the day of my burial – Which now draws nigh.

10. The chief priests consulted, how to kill Lazarus also – Here is the plain reason why the other evangelists, who wrote while Lazarus was living, did not relate his story.

12. The next day – On Sunday. Who were come to the feast – So that this multitude consisted chiefly of Galileans, not men of Jerusalem. Matt. xxi, 8.

13. Psalm cxviii, 26; Mark xi, 8; Luke xix, 36.

15. Fear not – For his meekness forbids fear, as well as the end of his coming. Zech. ix, 9.

16. These things his disciples understood not at first – The design of God's providential dispensations is seldom understood at first. We ought therefore to believe, though we understand not, and to give ourselves up to the Divine disposal. The great work of faith is, to embrace those things which we knew not now, but shall know hereafter. When he had been glorified – At his ascension.

17. When he called Lazarus out of the tomb – How admirably does the apostle express, as well the greatness of the miracle, as the facility with which it was wrought! The easiness of the Scripture style on the most grand occurrences, is more sublime than all the pomp of orators.

18. The multitude went to meet him, because they heard – From those who had seen the miracle. So in a little time both joined together, to go before and to follow him.

20. Certain Greeks – A prelude of the Gentile Church. That these were circumcized does not appear. But they came up on purpose to worship the God of Israel.

21. These came to Philip of Bethsaida in Galilee – Perhaps they used to lodge there, in their journey to Jerusalem. Or they might believe, a Galilean would be more ready to serve them herein, than a Jew. Sir – They spake to him, as to one they were little acquainted with. We would see Jesus – A modest request. They could scarce expect that he would now have time to talk with them.

23. The hour is come that the Son of man should be glorified – With the Father and in the sight of every creature. But he must suffer first.

24. Unless a grain of wheat die – The late resurrection of Lazarus gave our Lord a natural occasion of speaking on this subject. And agreeable to his infinite knowledge, he singles out, from among so many thousands of seeds, almost the only one that dies in the earth: and which therefore was an exceeding proper similitude, peculiarly adapted to the purpose for which he uses it. The like is not to be found in any other grain, except millet, and the large bean.

25. He that loveth his life – More than the will of God; shall lose it eternally: and he that hateth his life – In comparison of the will of God, shall preserve it. Matt. x, 39.

MATTHEW HENRY

CHARLES H. SPURGEON

and he did it by humbling himself. The voice of the Father from heaven, which had declared him to be his beloved Son, at his baptism, and when he was transfigured, was heard proclaiming that he had both glorified his name, and would glorify it. Christ, reconciling the world to God by the merit of his death, broke the power of death, and cast out Satan as a destroyer. Christ, bringing the world to God by the doctrine of his cross, broke the power of sin, and cast out Satan as a deceiver. The soul that was at a distance from Christ, is brought to love him and trust him. Jesus was now going to heaven, and he would draw men's hearts thither. There is power in the death of Christ to draw souls to him. We have heard from the gospel that which exalts free grace, and we have heard also that which enjoins duty; we must from the heart embrace both, and not separate them.

34-36 The people drew false notions from the Scriptures, because they overlooked the prophecies that spoke of Christ's sufferings and death. Our Lord warned them that the light would not long continue with them, and exhorted them to walk in it, before the darkness overtook them. Those who would walk in the light must believe in it, and follow Christ's directions. But those who have not faith, cannot behold what is set forth in Jesus, lifted up on the cross, and must be strangers to its influence as made known by the Holy Spirit; they find a thousand objections to excuse their unbelief.

37-43 Observe the method of conversion implied here. Sinners are brought to see the reality of Divine things, and to have some knowledge of them. To be converted, and truly turned from sin to Christ, is their Happiness and Portion. God will heal them, will justify and sanctify them; will pardon their sins, which are as bleeding wounds, and mortify their corruptions, which are as lurking diseases. See the power of the world in smothering convictions, from regard to the applause or censure of men. Love of the praise of men, as a by-end in that which is good, will make a man a hypocrite when religion is in fashion, and credit is to be got by it; and love of the praise of men, as a base principle in that which is evil, will make a man an apostate, when religion is in disgrace, and credit is to be lost for it.

44-50 Our Lord publicly proclaimed, that every one who believed on him, as his true disciple, did not believe on him only, but on the Father who sent him. Beholding in Jesus the glory of the Father, we learn to obey, love, and trust in him. By daily looking to Him, who came a Light into the world, we are more and more freed from the darkness of ignorance, error, sin, and misery; we learn that the command of God our Savior is everlasting life. But the same word will seal the condemnation of all who despise it, or neglect it.

Christ knows you through and through; all the parts of your nature he understands. "I know them," saith he; he can therefore prescribe for you. He knows your sins. Do not let that dismay you, because he has blotted them all out; and he only knows them to forgive them, to cover them with his righteousness. He knows your corruptions; he will help you to overcome them; he will deal with you in providence and in grace, so that they shall be rooted up. He knows your temptations. Perhaps you are living away from your parents and Christian friends, and you have had an extraordinary temptation, and you wish you could go home and tell your mother. Oh, he knows it, he knows it; he can help you better than your mother can. You say: "I wish the minister knew the temptation I have passed through." Do not tell it; God knows it. As Daniel did not want Nebuchadnezzar to tell him the nature of his dream, but gave him the dream and the interpretation at the same time, so God can send you comfort. There will be a word as plainly suited to your case as though it were all printed and the preacher had known it all. It must be so. Depend upon it, the Lord knows your temptation, and watches your trial; or be it a sick child, or be it a bad matter of business that has lately occurred; or be it a slander that has wounded your heart, there is not a pang you feel but God as surely sees it as the weaver sees the shuttle which he throws with his own hand. He knows your trial, and he knows the meaning of your groans: he can read the secret desire of your heart, you need not write it nor speak it: he has understood it all. You were saying: "O that my child were converted! O that I grew in grace!" He knows it: he knows it every whit. There is not a word on your tongue, nor a wish in your heart, but he knoweth it altogether. O dear heart, he knows your sincerity! Perhaps you want to join the church, and your proposal has been declined, because you could not give satisfactory testimony. If you are sincere, he knows it; he knows, moreover, what your anxiety is. You cannot tell another what it is that is bitter to you—the heart knoweth its own bitterness—he knows it. As his secret is with you, so your secret is with him. He knows you: he knows what you have been trying to do. That secret gift—that offering dropped so quietly where none could see it—he knows it. And he knows that you love him. "Yes," you are saying in your soul, "if ever I loved thee, my Jesus, 'tis now." No, you cannot tell him, nor tell others; but he knows it all.

So, now, in closing, let us say that in the text there is mutual knowledge. "I know them, but they also know me, because they hear my

needeth not save to wash his feet, but is clean every whit: and ye are clean, but not all.

11 For he knew who should betray him; therefore said he, Ye are not all clean.

12 So after he had washed their feet, and had taken his garments, and was set down again, he said unto them, Know ye what I have done to you?

13 Ye call me Master and Lord: and ye say well; for so I am.

14 If I then, your Lord and Master, have washed your feet; ye also ought to wash one another's feet.

15 For I have given you an example, that ye should do as I have done to you.

16 Verily, verily, I say unto you, The servant is not greater than his lord; neither he that is sent greater than he that sent him.

17 If ye know these things, happy are ye if ye do them.

18 I speak not of you all: I know whom I have chosen: but that the scripture may be fulfilled, He that eateth bread with me hath lifted up his heel against me.

19 Now I tell you before it come, that, when it is come to pass, ye may believe that I am he.

20 Verily, verily, I say unto you, He that receiveth whomsoever I send receiveth me; and he that receiveth me receiveth him that sent me.

21 When Jesus had thus said, he was troubled in spirit, and testified, and said, Verily, verily, I say unto you, that one of you shall betray me.

22 Then the disciples looked one on another, doubting of whom he spake.

23 Now there was leaning on Jesus' bosom one of his disciples, whom Jesus loved.

24 Simon Peter therefore beckoned to him, that he should ask who it should be of whom he spake.

25 He then lying on Jesus' breast saith unto him, Lord, who is it?

26 Jesus answered, He it is, to whom I shall give a sop, when I have dipped it. And when he had dipped the sop, he gave it to Judas Iscariot, the son of Simon.

27 And after the sop Satan entered into him. Then said Jesus unto him, That thou doest, do quickly.

28 Now no man at the table knew for what intent he spake this unto him.

29 For some of them thought, because Judas had the bag, that Jesus had said unto him, Buy those things that we have need of against the feast; or, that he should give something to the poor.

30 He then having received the sop went immediately out: and it was night.

31 Therefore, when he was gone out, Jesus said, Now is the Son of man glorified, and God is glorified in him.

32 If God be glorified in him, God shall also glorify him in himself, and shall straightway glorify him.

26. Let him follow me – By hating his life: and where I am – In heaven. If any man serve me – Thus, him will the Father honor.

27. Now is my soul troubled – He had various foretastes of his passion. And what shall I say? – Not what shall I choose? For his heart was fixed in choosing the will of his Father: but he labored for utterance. The two following clauses, Save me from this hour – For this cause I came – Into the world; for the sake of this hour (of suffering) seem to have glanced through his mind in one moment. But human language could not so express it.

28. Father, glorify thy name – Whatever I suffer. Now the trouble was over. I have glorified it – By thy entrance into this hour. And I will glorify it – By thy passing through it.

29. The multitude who stood and heard – A sound, but not the distinct words – In the most glorious Revelations there may remain something obscure, to exercise our faith. Said, It thundered – Thunder did frequently attend a voice from heaven. Perhaps it did so now.

31. Now – This moment. And from this moment Christ thirsted more than ever, till his baptism was accomplished. Is the judgment of this world – That is, now is the judgment given concerning it, whose it shall be. Now shall the prince of this world – Satan, who had gained possession of it by sin and death, be cast out – That is, judged, condemned, cast out of his possession, and out of the bounds of Christ's kingdom.

32. Lifted up from the earth – This is a Hebraism which signifies dying. Death in general is all that is usually imported. But our Lord made use of this phrase, rather than others that were equivalent, because it so well suited the particular manner of his death. I will draw all men – Gentiles as well as Jews. And those who follow my drawings, Satan shall not be able to keep.

34. How sayest thou, The Son of man must be lifted up? – How can these things be reconciled? Very easily. He first dies, and then abideth for ever. Who is this Son of man? – Is he the Christ? Psalm cx, 4.

35. Then Jesus said to them – Not answering them directly, but exhorting them to improve what they had heard already. The light – I and my doctrine.

36. The children of light – The children of God, wise, holy, happy.

37. Though he had done so many miracles before them – So that they could not but see them.

38. The arm of the Lord – The power of God manifested by Christ, in his preaching, miracles, and work of redemption. Isaiah liii, 1.

39. Therefore now they could not believe – That is, by the just judgment of God, for their obstinacy and wilful resistance of the truth, they were at length so left to the hardness of their hearts, that neither the miracles nor doctrines of our Lord could make any impression upon them.

40. Isaiah vi, 10; Matt. xiii, 14; Acts xxviii, 26.

41. When he saw his glory – Christ's, Isaiah vi, 1, &c. And it is there expressly said to be the glory of the Lord, Jehovah, the Supreme God.

44. Jesus said with a loud voice – This which follows to the end of the chapter, is with St. John the epilogue of our Lord's public discourses, and a kind of recapitulation of them. Believeth not on me – Not on me alone, but also on him that sent me: because the

JOHN 13

Christ washes the disciples' feet. (1-17)
The treachery of Judas foretold. (18-30)
Christ commands the disciples to love one another. (31-38)

1-17 We must address ourselves to duty, and must lay aside every thing that would hinder us in what we have to do. Christ washed his disciples' feet, that he might signify to them the value of spiritual washing, and the cleansing of the soul from the pollutions of sin. Our Lord Jesus does many things of which even his own disciples do not for the present know the meaning, but they shall know afterward. We see in the end what was the kindness from events which seemed most cross. And it is not humility, but unbelief, to put away the offers of the gospel, as if too rich to be made to us, or too good news to be true. All those, and those only, who are spiritually washed by Christ, have a part in Christ. All whom Christ owns and saves, he justifies and sanctifies. Peter more than submits; he begs to be washed by Christ. How earnest he is for the purifying grace of the Lord Jesus, and the full effect of it, even upon his hands and head! Those who truly desire to be sanctified, desire to be sanctified throughout, to have the whole man, with all its parts and powers, made pure. The true believer is thus washed when he receives Christ for his salvation. See then what ought to be the daily care of those who through grace are in a justified state, and that is, to wash their feet; to cleanse themselves from daily guilt, and to watch against everything defiling. This should make us the more cautious. From yesterday's pardon, we should be strengthened against this day's temptation. And when hypocrites are discovered, it should be no surprise or cause of stumbling to us. Observe the lesson Christ here taught. Duties are mutual; we must both accept help from our brethren, and afford help to our brethren. When we see our Master serving, we cannot but see how ill it becomes us to domineer. And the same love which led Christ to ransom and reconcile his disciples when enemies, still influences him.

18-30 Our Lord had often spoken of his own sufferings and death, without such trouble of spirit as he now discovered when he spake of Judas. The sins of Christians are the grief of Christ. We are not to confine our attention to Judas. The prophecy of his treachery may apply to all who partake of God's mercies, and meet them with ingratitude. See the infidel, who only looks at the Scriptures with a desire to do away their authority and destroy their influence; the hypocrite, who professes to believe the Scriptures, but will not govern himself by them; and the apostate, who turns aside from Christ for a thing of naught. Thus mankind, supported by God's providence, after eating bread with him, lift up the heel against him! Judas went out as one weary of Jesus and his apostles. Those whose deeds are evil, love darkness rather than light.

voice, and recognize it." Here is mutual confession. Christ speaks, else there would be no voice: they hear, else were the voice not useful. "I know them;" that is his thoughts go towards them. "They follow me;" that is, their thoughts go towards him. He leads the way, else they could not follow. They follow, wherever he leads them. They are like partners in that, what the one does the other returns through grace; and what grace puts into the sheep the shepherd recognizes, and makes a return to them. Christ and his church become an echo of each other: his the voice, theirs is but a faint echo of it; still it is a true echo, and you shall know who are Christ's by this. Do they echo what Christ saith? Oh, how I wish we were all sheep! How my soul longs that we may many of us who are not of his fold be brought in. The Lord bring you in, my dear hearers. The Lord give you his grace, and make you his own, comfort you, and make you to follow him. And if you are his, show it. These, dear brethren and sisters, here at this time, desire to confess Christ in your presence. If they are doing right, and you are not doing as they do, then you are doing wrong. If it is the duty of one, it is the duty of all; and if one Christian may neglect making a profession, all may do so, and then there will be no visible church whatever, and the visible ordinances must die out. If you know him, own him, for he hath said: "Whosoever therefore shall confess me before men, him will I confess also before my Father which is in heaven. But whosoever shall deny me before men, him will I also deny before my Father which is in heaven." God bless you, for Christ's sake. Amen.

THOUGH HE WERE DEAD

Sermon number 1799 delivered on September 14th, 1884, at the Metropolitan Tabernacle, Newington.

"Martha saith unto him, I know that he shall rise again in the resurrection at the last day. Jesus said unto her, I am the resurrection, and the life: he that believeth in me, though he were dead, yet shall he live: and whosoever liveth and believeth in me shall never die. Believest thou this?"—John 11:24-26.

MARTHA is a very accurate type of a class of anxious believers. They do believe truly, but not with such confidence as to lay aside their care. They do not distrust the Lord, or question the truth of what He says, yet they puzzle their brain about "How shall this thing be?" and so they miss the major part of the present comfort

33 Little children, yet a little while I am with you. Ye shall seek me: and as I said unto the Jews, Whither I go, ye cannot come; so now I say to you.

34 A new commandment I give unto you, That ye love one another; as I have loved you, that ye also love one another.

35 By this shall all men know that ye are my disciples, if ye have love one to another.

36 Simon Peter said unto him, Lord, whither goest thou? Jesus answered him, Whither I go, thou canst not follow me now; but thou shalt follow me afterwards.

37 Peter said unto him, Lord, why cannot I follow thee now? I will lay down my life for thy sake.

38 Jesus answered him, Wilt thou lay down thy life for my sake? Verily, verily, I say unto thee, The cock shall not crow, till thou hast denied me thrice.

JOHN 14

1 Let not your heart be troubled: ye believe in God, believe also in me.

2 In my Father's house are many mansions: if it were not so, I would have told you. I go to prepare a place for you.

3 And if I go and prepare a place for you, I will come again, and receive you unto myself; that where I am, there ye may be also.

4 And whither I go ye know, and the way ye know.

5 Thomas saith unto him, Lord, we know not whither thou goest; and how can we know the way?

6 Jesus saith unto him, I am the way, the truth, and the life: no man cometh unto the Father, but by me.

7 If ye had known me, ye should have known my Father also: and from henceforth ye know him, and have seen him.

8 Philip saith unto him, Lord, shew us the Father, and it sufficeth us.

9 Jesus saith unto him, Have I been so long time with you, and yet hast thou not known me, Philip? he that hath seen me hath seen the Father; and how sayest thou then, Shew us the Father?

10 Believest thou not that I am in the Father, and the Father in me? the words that I speak unto you I speak not of myself: but the Father that dwelleth in me, he doeth the works.

11 Believe me that I am in the Father, and the Father in me: or else believe me for the very works' sake.

12 Verily, verily, I say unto you, He that believeth on me, the works that I do shall he do also; and greater works than these shall he do; because I go unto my Father.

13 And whatsoever ye shall ask in my name, that will I do, that the Father may be glorified in the Son.

Father hath sent the Son, and because he and the Father are one.

45. And he that seeth me – By the eye of faith.

47. I judge him not – Not now: for I am not come to judge the world. See, Christ came to save even them that finally perish! Even these are a part of that world, which he lived and died to save.

50. His commandment – Kept, is life everlasting – That is the way to it, and the beginning of it.

JOHN 13

1. Before the feast – Namely, on Wednesday, in the paschal week. Having loved his own – His apostles, he loved them to the end – Of his life.

2. Having now – Probably now first.

3. Jesus knowing – Though conscious of his own greatness, thus humbled himself.

4. Layeth aside his garments – That part of them which would have hindered him.

5. Into the basin – A large vessel was usually placed for this very purpose, wherever the Jews supped.

7. What I do thou knowest not now; but thou shalt know hereafter – We do not now know perfectly any of his works, either of creation, providence, or grace. It is enough that we can love and obey now, and that we shall know hereafter.

8. If I wash thee not – If thou dost not submit to my will, thou hast no part with me – Thou art not my disciple. In a more general sense it may mean, If I do not wash thee in my blood, and purify thee by my Spirit, thou canst have no communion with me, nor any share in the blessings of my kingdom.

9. Lord, not my feet only – How fain would man be wiser than God! Yet this was well meant, though ignorant earnestness.

10. And so ye, having been already cleansed, need only to wash your feet – That is, to walk holy and undefiled.

14. Ye ought also to wash one another's feet – And why did they not? Why do we not read of any one apostle ever washing the feet of any other? Because they understood the Lord better. They knew he never designed that this should be literally taken. He designed to teach them the great lesson of humble love, as well as to confer inward purity upon them. And hereby he teaches us,

    1. In every possible way to assist each other in attaining that purity;

    2. To wash each other's feet, by performing all sorts of good offices to each other, even those of the lowest kind, when opportunity serves, and the necessity of any calls for them.

16. The servant is not greater than his Lord – Nor therefore ought to think much of either doing or suffering the same things.

18. I speak not of you all – When I call you happy, I know one of you twelve whom I have chosen, will betray me; whereby that scripture will be fulfilled. Psalm xli, 9.

20. And I put my own honor upon you, my ambassadors. Matt. x, 40.

21. One of you – The speaking thus indefinitely at first was profitable to them all.

23. There was lying in the bosom of Jesus – That is, sitting next to him at table. This phrase only expresses the then customary posture at meals, where the guests all leaned sidewise on couches. And

31-35 Christ had been glorified in many miracles he wrought, yet he speaks of his being glorified now in his sufferings, as if that were more than all his other glories in his humbled state. Satisfaction was thereby made for the wrong done to God by the sin of man. We cannot now follow our Lord to his heavenly happiness, but if we truly believe in him, we shall follow him hereafter; meanwhile we must wait his time, and do his work. Before Christ left the disciples, he would give them a new commandment. They were to love each other for Christ's sake, and according to his example, seeking what might benefit others, and promoting the cause of the gospel, as one body, animated by one soul. But this commandment still appears new to many professors. Men in general notice any of Christ's words rather than these. By this it appears, that if the followers of Christ do not show love one to another, they give cause to suspect their sincerity.

36-38 What Christ had said concerning brotherly love, Peter overlooked, but spoke of that about which Christ kept them ignorant. It is common to be more eager to know about secret things, which belong to God only, than about things revealed, which belong to us and our children; to be more desirous to have our curiosity gratified, than our consciences directed; to know what is done in heaven, than what we may do to get thither. How soon discourse as to what is plain and edifying is dropped, while a doubtful dispute runs on into endless strife of words! We are apt to take it amiss to be told we cannot do this and the other, whereas, without Christ we can do nothing. Christ knows us better than we know ourselves, and has many ways of discovering those to themselves, whom he loves, and he will hide pride from them. May we endeavor to keep the unity of the Spirit in the bond of peace, to love one another with a pure heart fervently, and to walk humbly with our God.

JOHN 14

Christ comforts his disciples. (1-11)
He further comforts his disciples. (12-17)
He still further comforts his disciples. (18-31)

1-11 Here are three words, upon any of which stress may be laid. Upon the word troubled. Be not cast down and disquieted. The word heart. Let your heart be kept with full trust in God. The word your. However others are overwhelmed with the sorrows of this present time, be not you so. Christ's disciples, more than others, should keep their minds quiet, when everything else is unquiet. Here is the remedy against this trouble of mind, "Believe." By believing in Christ as the Mediator between God and man, we gain comfort. The happiness of heaven is spoken of as in a father's house.

12-17 Whatever we ask in Christ's name, that shall be

which the word of the Lord would minister to their hearts if they received it more simply. How? and why? belong unto the Lord. It is his business to arrange matters so as to fulfill his own promises. If we would sit at our Lord's feet with Mary, and consider what he has promised, we should choose a better part than if we ran about with Martha, crying, "How can these things be?"

Martha, you see, in this case, when the Lord Jesus Christ told her that her brother would rise again, replied, "I know that he shall rise again in the resurrection at the last day." She was a type, I say, of certain anxious believers, for she set a practical bound to the Savior's words. "Of course there will be a resurrection, and then my brother will rise with the rest." She concluded that the Savior could not mean anything beyond that. The first meaning and the commonest meaning that suggests itself to her must be what Jesus means. Is not that the way with many of us? We had a statesman once, and a good man too, who loved reform; but whenever he had accomplished a little progress, he considered that all was done. We called him at last "Finality John," for he was always coming to an ultimatum, and taking for his motto "Rest, and be thankful." Into that style Christian people too frequently drop with regard to the promises of God. We limit the Holy one of Israel as to the meaning of His words. Of course they mean so much, but we cannot allow that they intend more. It were well if the spirit of progress would enter into our faith, so that we felt within our souls that we had never beheld the innermost glory of the Lord's words of grace. We often wonder that the disciples put such poor meanings upon our Lord's words, but I fear we are almost as far off as they were from fully comprehending all his gracious teachings. Are we not still as little children, making little out of great words? Have we grasped as yet a tithe of our Lord's full meaning, in many of his sayings of love? When he is talking of bright and sparkling gems of benediction, we are thinking of common pebble-stones in the brook of mercy; when he speaketh of stars and heavenly crowns, we think of sparks and childish coronals of fading flowers. Oh that we could but have our intellect cleared; better still, could have our understanding expanded, or, best of all, our faith increased, so as to reach to the height or our Lord's great arguments of love!

Martha also had another fault in which she was very like ourselves: she laid the words of Jesus on the shelf, as things so trite and sure that they were of small practical importance. "Thy brother shall rise again." Now, if she had

14 If ye shall ask any thing in my name, I will do it.

15 If ye love me, keep my commandments.

16 And I will pray the Father, and he shall give you another Comforter, that he may abide with you for ever;

17 Even the Spirit of truth; whom the world cannot receive, because it seeth him not, neither knoweth him: but ye know him; for he dwelleth with you, and shall be in you.

18 I will not leave you comfortless: I will come to you.

19 Yet a little while, and the world seeth me no more; but ye see me: because I live, ye shall live also.

20 At that day ye shall know that I am in my Father, and ye in me, and I in you.

21 He that hath my commandments, and keepeth them, he it is that loveth me: and he that loveth me shall be loved of my Father, and I will love him, and will manifest myself to him.

22 Judas saith unto him, not Iscariot, Lord, how is it that thou wilt manifest thyself unto us, and not unto the world?

23 Jesus answered and said unto him, If a man love me, he will keep my words: and my Father will love him, and we will come unto him, and make our abode with him.

24 He that loveth me not keepeth not my sayings: and the word which ye hear is not mine, but the Father's which sent me.

25 These things have I spoken unto you, being yet present with you.

26 But the Comforter, which is the Holy Ghost, whom the Father will send in my name, he shall teach you all things, and bring all things to your remembrance, whatsoever I have said unto you.

27 Peace I leave with you, my peace I give unto you: not as the world giveth, give I unto you. Let not your heart be troubled, neither let it be afraid.

28 Ye have heard how I said unto you, I go away, and come again unto you. If ye loved me, ye would rejoice, because I said, I go unto the Father: for my Father is greater than I.

29 And now I have told you before it come to pass, that, when it is come to pass, ye might believe.

30 Hereafter I will not talk much with you: for the prince of this world cometh, and hath nothing in me.

31 But that the world may know that I love the Father; and as the Father gave me commandment, even so I do. Arise, let us go hence.

JOHN 15

1 I am the true vine, and my Father is the husbandman.

2 Every branch in me that beareth not fruit he taketh away: and every branch that beareth fruit, he purgeth it, that it may bring forth more fruit.

each was said to lie in the bosom of him who was placed next above him. One of the disciples whom Jesus loved – St. John avoids with great care the expressly naming himself. Perhaps our Lord now gave him the first proof of his peculiar love, by disclosing this secret to him.

24. Simon Peter – Behind Jesus, who lay between them.

25. Leaning down, and so asking him privately.

26. Jesus answered – In his ear. So careful was he not to offend (if it had been possible) even Judas himself. The sop – Which he took up while he was speaking. He giveth it to Judas – And probably the other disciples thought Judas peculiarly happy! But when even this instance of our Lord's tenderness could not move him, then Satan took full possession.

27. What thou doest, do quickly – This is not a permission, much less a command. It is only as if he had said, If thou art determined to do it, why dost thou delay? Hereby showing Judas, that he could not be hid, and expressing his own readiness to suffer.

28. None knew why he said this – Save John and Judas.

30. He went out – To the chief priests. But he returned afterward, and was with them when they ate the Passover, Matt. xxvi, 20, though not at the Lord's Supper.

31. Jesus saith – Namely, the next day; on Thursday, in the morning. Here the scene, as it were, is opened, for the discourse which is continued in the following chapters. Now – While I speak this, the Son of man is glorified – Being fully entered into his glorious work of redemption. This evidently relates to the glory which belongs to his suffering in so holy and victorious a manner.

33. Ye cannot come – Not yet; being not yet ripe for it. John vii, 34.

34. A new commandment – Not new in itself; but new in the school of Christ: for he had never before taught it them expressly. Likewise new, as to the degree of it, as I have loved you.

36. Peter saith, Lord, whither goest thou? – St. Peter seems to have thought, that Christ, being rejected by the Jews, would go to some other part of the earth to erect his throne, where he might reign without disturbance, according to the gross notions he had of Christ's kingdom. Thou canst not follow me now – But Peter would not believe him. And he did follow him, chap. xviii, 15. But it was afar off. And not without great loss.

38. The cock shall not have crowed – That is, cock crowing shall not be over, till thou hast denied me thrice – His three-fold denial was thrice foretold; first, at the time mentioned here; secondly, at that mentioned by St. Luke; lastly, at that recorded by St. Matthew and Mark.

JOHN 14

1. Let not your heart be troubled – At my departure. Believe – This is the sum of all his discourse, which is urged till they did believe, chap. xvi, 30. And then our Lord prays and departs.

2. In my Father's house are many mansions – Enough to receive both the holy angels, and your predecessors in the faith, and all that now believe, and a great multitude, which no man can number.

4. The way – Of faith, holiness, sufferings.

5. Thomas saith – Taking him in a gross sense.

for our good, and suitable to our state, he shall give it to us. To ask in Christ's name, is to plead his merit and intercession, and to depend upon that plea. The gift of the Spirit is a fruit of Christ's mediation, bought by his merit, and received by his intercession. The word used here, signifies an advocate, counselor, monitor, and comforter. He would abide with the disciples to the end of time; his gifts and graces would encourage their hearts. The expressions used here and elsewhere, plainly denote a person, and the office itself includes all the Divine perfections. The gift of the Holy Ghost is bestowed upon the disciples of Christ, and not on the world. This is the favor God bears to his chosen. As the source of holiness and happiness, the Holy Spirit will abide with every believer forever.

18-24 Christ promises that he would continue his care of his disciples. I will not leave you orphans, or fatherless, for though I leave you, yet I leave you this comfort, I will come to you. I will come speedily to you at my resurrection. I will come daily to you in my Spirit; in the tokens of his love, and visits of his grace. I will come certainly at the end of time. Those only that see Christ with an eye of faith, shall see him forever: the world sees him no more till his second coming; but his disciples have communion with him in his absence. These mysteries will be fully known in heaven. It is a further act of grace, that they should know it, and have the comfort of it. Having Christ's commands, we must keep them. And having them in our heads, we must keep them in our hearts and lives. The surest evidence of our love to Christ is, obedience to the laws of Christ. There are spiritual tokens of Christ and his love given to all believers. Where sincere love to Christ is in the heart, there will be obedience. Love will be a commanding, constraining principle; and where love is, duty follows from a principle of gratitude. God will not only love obedient believers, but he will take pleasure in loving them, will rest in love to them. He will be with them as his home. These privileges are confined to those whose faith worketh by love, and whose love to Jesus leads them to keep his commandments. Such are partakers of the Holy Spirit's new-creating grace.

25-27 Would we know these things for our good, we must pray for, and depend on the teaching of the Holy Ghost; thus the words of Jesus will be brought to our remembrance, and many difficulties be cleared up which are not plain to others. To all the saints, the Spirit of grace is given to be a remembrance, and to him, by faith and prayer, we should commit the keeping of what we hear and know. Peace is put for all good, and Christ has left us all that is really and truly good, all the promised good; peace of mind from our justification before God. This Christ calls his peace, for he is himself our Peace. The peace of God widely differs from that of Pharisees or hypocrites, as is shown by its humbling and holy effects.

possessed faith enough, she might truthfully have said, "Lord, I thank thee for that word! I expect within a short space to see him sitting at the table with thee. I put the best meaning possible upon thy words, for I know that thou art always better than I can think thee to be; and therefore I expect to see my beloved Lazarus walk home from the sepulcher before the sun sets again." But no, she lays the truth aside as a matter past all dispute, and says, "I know that my brother shall rise again in the resurrection at the last day." A great many precious truths are laid up by us like the old hulks in the Medway, never to see service any more, or like aged pensioners at Chelsea, as relics of the past. We say "Yes, quite true, we fully believe that doctrine." Somehow it is almost as bad to lay up a doctrine in lavender as it is to throw it out of the window. When you so believe a truth as to put it to bed and smother it with the bolster of neglect, it is much the same as if you did not believe it at all. An official belief is very much akin to infidelity. Some persons never question a doctrine: that is not their line of temptation; they accept the gospel as true, but then they never expect to see its promises practically carried out; it is a proper thing to believe, but by no means a prominent, practical factor in actual life. It is true but it is mysterious, misty, mythical, far removed from the realm of practical common sense. We do with the promises often as a poor old couple did with a precious document, which might have cheered their old age had they used it according to its real value. A gentleman stepping into a poor woman's house saw framed and glazed upon the wall a French note for a thousand francs. He said to the old folks, "How came you by this?" They informed him that a poor French soldier had been taken in by them and nursed until he died, and he had given them that little picture when he was dying as a memorial of him. They thought it such a pretty souvenir that they had framed it, and there it was adorning the cottage wall. They were greatly surprised when they were told that it was worth a sum which would be quite a little fortune for them if they would but turn it into money. Are we not equally unpractical with far more precious things? Have you not certain of the words of your great Lord framed and glazed in your hearts, and do you not say to yourselves, "They are so sweet and precious"? and yet you have never turned them into actual blessing—never used them in the hour of need. You have done as Martha did when she took the words, "Thy brother shall rise again," and put round about them this handsome frame, "in the resurrection at the last day." Oh

KING JAMES VERSION

JOHN WESLEY

3 Now ye are clean through the word which I have spoken unto you.

4 Abide in me, and I in you. As the branch cannot bear fruit of itself, except it abide in the vine; no more can ye, except ye abide in me.

5 I am the vine, ye are the branches: He that abideth in me, and I in him, the same bringeth forth much fruit: for without me ye can do nothing.

6 If a man abide not in me, he is cast forth as a branch, and is withered; and men gather them, and cast them into the fire, and they are burned.

7 If ye abide in me, and my words abide in you, ye shall ask what ye will, and it shall be done unto you.

8 Herein is my Father glorified, that ye bear much fruit; so shall ye be my disciples.

9 As the Father hath loved me, so have I loved you: continue ye in my love.

10 If ye keep my commandments, ye shall abide in my love; even as I have kept my Father's commandments, and abide in his love.

11 These things have I spoken unto you, that my joy might remain in you, and that your joy might be full.

12 This is my commandment, That ye love one another, as I have loved you.

13 Greater love hath no man than this, that a man lay down his life for his friends.

14 Ye are my friends, if ye do whatsoever I command you.

15 Henceforth I call you not servants; for the servant knoweth not what his lord doeth: but I have called you friends; for all things that I have heard of my Father I have made known unto you.

16 Ye have not chosen me, but I have chosen you, and ordained you, that ye should go and bring forth fruit, and that your fruit should remain: that whatsoever ye shall ask of the Father in my name, he may give it you.

17 These things I command you, that ye love one another.

18 If the world hate you, ye know that it hated me before it hated you.

19 If ye were of the world, the world would love his own: but because ye are not of the world, but I have chosen you out of the world, therefore the world hateth you.

20 Remember the word that I said unto you, The servant is not greater than his lord. If they have persecuted me, they will also persecute you; if they have kept my saying, they will keep yours also.

21 But all these things will they do unto you for my name's sake, because they know not him that sent me.

22 If I had not come and spoken unto them, they had not had sin: but now they have no cloke for their sin.

23 He that hateth me hateth my Father also.

24 If I had not done among them the works which none other man did, they had not had sin:

6. To the question concerning the way, he answers, I am the way. To the question concerning knowledge, he answers, I am the truth. To the question whither, I am the life. The first is treated of in this verse; the second, ver. 7-17; the third, xiv, 18, &c.

7. Ye have known – Ye have begun to know him.

10. I am in the Father – The words that I speak, &c. – That is, I am one with the Father, in essence, in speaking, and in acting.

11. Believe me – On my own word, because I am God. The works – This respects not merely the miracles themselves, but his sovereign, Godlike way of performing them.

12. Greater works than these shall he do – So one apostle wrought miracles merely by his shadow, Acts v, 15; another by handkerchiefs carried from his body, Acts xix, 12; and all spake with various tongues. But the converting one sinner is a greater work than all these. Because I go to my Father – To send you the Holy Ghost.

15. If ye love me, keep my commandments – Immediately after faith he exhorts to love and good works.

16. And I will ask the Father – The 21st verse, ver. 21, shows the connection between this and the preceding verses. And he will give you another Comforter – The Greek word signifies also an advocate, instructer, or encourager. Another – For Christ himself was one. To remain with you for ever – With you, and your followers in faith, to the end of the world.

17. The Spirit of truth – Who has, reveals, testifies, and defends the truth as it is in Jesus. Whom the world – All who do not love or fear God, cannot receive, because it seeth him not – Having no spiritual senses, no internal eye to discern him; nor consequently knoweth him. He shall be in you – As a constant guest. Your bodies and souls shall be temples of the Holy Ghost dwelling in you.

18. I will not leave you orphans – A word that is elegantly applied to those who have lost any dear friend. I come to you – What was certainly and speedily to be, our Lord speaks of as if it were already.

19. But ye see me – That is, ye shall certainly see me. Because I live, ye shall live also – Because I am the living One in my Divine nature, and shall rise again in my human nature, and live for ever in heaven: therefore ye shall live the life of faith and love on earth, and hereafter the life of glory.

20. At that day – When ye see me after my resurrection; but more eminently at the day of Pentecost.

21. He that hath my commandments – Written in his heart. I will manifest myself to him – More abundantly.

23. Jesus answered – Because ye love and obey me, and they do not, therefore I will reveal myself to you, and not to them. My Father will love him – The more any man loves and obeys, the more God will love him. And we will come to him, and make our abode with him – Which implies such a large manifestation of the Divine presence and love, that the former in justification is as nothing in comparison of it.

26. In my name – For my sake, in my room, and as my agent. He will teach you all things – Necessary for you to know. Here is a clear promise to the apostles, and their successors in the faith, that the Holy Ghost will teach them all that truth which is needful for their salvation.

27. Peace I leave with you – Peace in general; peace with God and with your own consciences. My peace – In particular; that peace which I enjoy, and which I create, I give – At this instant. Not as

28-31 Christ raises the expectations of his disciples to something beyond what they thought was their greatest happiness. His time was now short, he therefore spake largely to them. When we come to be sick, and to die, we may not be capable of talking much to those about us; such good counsel as we have to give, let us give while in health. Observe the prospect Christ had of an approaching conflict, not only with men, but with the powers of darkness. Satan has something in us to perplex us with, for we have all sinned; but when he would disturb Christ, he found nothing sinful to help him. The best evidence of our love to the Father is, our doing as he has commanded us. Let us rejoice in the Savior's victories over Satan the prince of this world. Let us copy the example of his love and obedience.

JOHN 15

Christ the true Vine. (1-8)
His love for his disciples. (9-17)
The world hates the disciples. (18-25)
The Comforter promised. (26,27)

1-8 Jesus Christ is the Vine, the true Vine. The union of the human and Divine natures, and the fullness of the Spirit that is in him, resemble the root of the vine made fruitful by the moisture from a rich soil. Believers are branches of this Vine. The root is unseen, and our life is hid with Christ; the root bears the tree, diffuses sap to it, and in Christ are all supports and supplies. The branches of the vine are many, yet, meeting in the root, are all but one vine; thus all true Christians, though in place and opinion distant from each other, meet in Christ.

9-17 Those whom God loves as a Father, may despise the hatred of all the world. As the Father loved Christ, who was most worthy, so he loved his disciples, who were unworthy. All that love the Savior should continue in their love to him, and take all occasions to show it. The joy of the hypocrite is but for a moment, but the joy of those who abide in Christ's love is a continual feast. They are to show their love to him by keeping his commandments. If the same power that first shed abroad the love of Christ's in our hearts, did not keep us in that love, we should not long abide in it. Christ's love to us should direct us to love each other. He speaks as about to give many things in charge, yet names this only; it includes many duties.

18-25 How little do many persons think, that in opposing the doctrine of Christ as our Prophet, Priest, and King, they prove themselves ignorant of the one living and true God, whom they profess to worship! The name into which Christ's disciples were baptized, is that which they will live and die by. It is a comfort to the greatest sufferers, if they suffer for Christ's name's sake. The world's ignorance is the true cause of its hatred to the disciples of Jesus. The clearer and fuller

that we had grace to turn God's bullion of gospel into current coin, and use them as our present spending money.

Moreover, Martha made another blunder, and that was setting the promise in the remote distance. This is a common folly, this distancing the promises of the Most High. "In the resurrection at the last day"—no doubt she thought it a very long way off, and therefore she did not get much comfort out of it. Telescopes are meant to bring objects near to the eye, but I have known people use the mental telescope in the wrong way: they always put the big end of it to their eye, and then the glass sends the object further away. Her brother was to be raised that very day: she might so have understood the Savior, but instead of it she looked at his words through the wrong end of the glass, and said, "I know that he will rise again in the resurrection at the last day." Brethren, do not refuse the present blessing. Death and heaven, or the advent and the glory, are at your doors. A little while and he that will come shall come, and will not tarry. Think not that the Lord is slack concerning his promise. Do not say in your heart, "My Lord delayeth his coming"; or dream that his words of love are only for the dim future. In the ages to come marvels shall be revealed, but even the present hour is bejewelled with loving-kindness. Today the Lord has rest, and peace, and joy to give to you. Lose not these treasures by unbelief.

Martha also appears to me to have made the promise unreal and impersonal. "Thy brother shall rise again"; to have realized that would have been a great comfort to her, but she mixes Lazarus up with all the rest of the dead. "Yes, he will rise in the resurrection at the last day; when thousands of millions shall be rising from their graves, no doubt Lazarus will rise with the rest." That is the way with us; we take the promise and say, "This is true to all the children of God." If so it is true to us; but we miss that point. What a blessing God has bestowed upon the covenanted people! Yes, and you are one of them; but you shake your head, as if the word was not for you. It is a fine feast, and yet you are hungry; it is a full and flowing stream, but you remain thirsty. Why is this? Somehow the generality of your apprehension misses the sweetness which comes of personal appropriation. There is such a thing as speaking of the promises in a magnificent style, and yet being in deep spiritual poverty; as if a man should boast of the wealth of old England, and the vast amount of treasure in the Bank, while he does not possess a penny wherewith to bless himself. In your case you know it is your own fault that you are poor and

but now have they both seen and hated both me and my Father.

25 But this cometh to pass, that the word might be fulfilled that is written in their law, They hated me without a cause.

26 But when the Comforter is come, whom I will send unto you from the Father, even the Spirit of truth, which proceedeth from the Father, he shall testify of me:

27 And ye also shall bear witness, because ye have been with me from the beginning.

JOHN 16

1 These things have I spoken unto you, that ye should not be offended.

2 They shall put you out of the synagogues: yea, the time cometh, that whosoever killeth you will think that he doeth God service.

3 And these things will they do unto you, because they have not known the Father, nor me.

4 But these things have I told you, that when the time shall come, ye may remember that I told you of them. And these things I said not unto you at the beginning, because I was with you.

5 But now I go my way to him that sent me; and none of you asketh me, Whither goest thou?

6 But because I have said these things unto you, sorrow hath filled your heart.

7 Nevertheless I tell you the truth; It is expedient for you that I go away: for if I go not away, the Comforter will not come unto you; but if I depart, I will send him unto you.

8 And when he is come, he will reprove the world of sin, and of righteousness, and of judgment:

9 Of sin, because they believe not on me;

10 Of righteousness, because I go to my Father, and ye see me no more;

11 Of judgment, because the prince of this world is judged.

12 I have yet many things to say unto you, but ye cannot bear them now.

13 Howbeit when he, the Spirit of truth, is come, he will guide you into all truth: for he shall not speak of himself; but whatsoever he shall hear, that shall he speak: and he will shew you things to come.

14 He shall glorify me: for he shall receive of mine, and shall shew it unto you.

15 All things that the Father hath are mine: therefore said I, that he shall take of mine, and shall shew it unto you.

16 A little while, and ye shall not see me: and again, a little while, and ye shall see me, because I go to the Father.

17 Then said some of his disciples among themselves, What is this that he saith unto us, A little while, and ye shall not see me: and again, a little while, and ye shall see me: and, Because I go to the Father?

18 They said therefore, What is this that he

the world giveth – Unsatisfying unsettled, transient; but filling the soul with constant, even tranquillity. Lord, evermore give us this peace! How serenely may we pass through the most turbulent scenes of life, when all is quiet and harmonious within! Thou hast made peace through the blood of thy cross. May we give all diligence to preserve the inestimable gift inviolate, till it issue in everlasting peace!

28. God the Father is greater than I – As he was man. As God, neither is greater nor less than the other.

29. I have told you – Of my going and return.

30. The prince of this world is coming – To make his grand assault. But he hath nothing in me – No right, no claim, or power. There is no guilt in me, to give him power over me; no corruption to take part with his temptation.

31. But I suffer him thus to assault me,

1. Because it is the Father's commission to me, chap. x, 18.

2. To convince the world of my love to the Father, in being obedient unto death, Phil. ii, 8. Arise, let us go hence – Into the city, to the Passover. All that has been related from chap. xii, 31, was done and said on Thursday, without the city. But what follows in the fifteenth, sixteenth, and seventeenth chapters, was said in the city, on the very evening of the Passover just before he went over the brook Kedron.

JOHN 15

1. I am the true vine – So the true bread, chap. vi, 32; that is, the most excellent.

2. Every one that beareth fruit, he purifieth – by obeying the truth, 1 Pet. i, 22; and by inward or outward sufferings, Heb. xii, 10, 11. So purity and fruitfulness help each other. That it may bear more fruit – For this is one of the noblest rewards God can bestow on former acts of obedience, to make us yet more holy, and fit for farther and more eminent service.

3. Ye are clean – All of you, to whom I now speak, are purged from the guilt and power of sin; by the word – Which, applied by the Spirit, is the grand instrument of purifying the soul.

4. Abide in me – Ye who are now pure by living faith, producing all holiness; by which alone ye can be in me.

5. I am the vine, ye are the branches – Our Lord in this whole passage speaks of no branches but such as are, or at least were once, united to him by living faith.

6. If any one abide not in me – By living faith; not by Church communion only. He may thus abide in Christ, and be withered all the time, and cast into the fire at last. He is cast out – Of the vineyard, the invisible Church. Therefore he was in it once.

7. If ye abide in me, ye shall ask – Prayers themselves are a fruit of faith, and they produce more fruit.

8. So shall ye be my disciples – Worthy of the name. To be a disciple of Christ is both the foundation and height of Christianity.

9. Abide ye in my love – Keep your place in my affection. See that ye do not forfeit that invaluable blessing. How needless a caution, if it were impossible for them not to abide therein?

10. If ye keep my commandments, ye shall abide in my love – On these terms, and no other, ye shall remain the objects of my special affection.

MATTHEW HENRY

CHARLES H. SPURGEON

the discoveries of the grace and truth of Christ, the greater is our sin if we do not love him and believe in him.

26,27 The blessed Spirit will maintain the cause of Christ in the world, notwithstanding the opposition it meets with. Believers taught and encouraged by his influences, would bear testimony to Christ and his salvation.

JOHN 16

Persecution foretold. (1-6)
The promise of the Holy Spirit, and his office. (7-15)
Christ's departure and return. (16-22)
Encouragement to prayer. (23-27)
Christ's discoveries of himself. (28-33)

1-6 Our Lord Jesus, by giving his disciples notice of trouble, designed that the terror might not be a surprise to them. It is possible for those who are real enemies to God's service, to pretend zeal for it. This does not lessen the sin of the persecutors; villainies will never be changed by putting the name of God to them.

7-15 Christ's departure was necessary to the Comforter's coming. Sending the Spirit was to be the fruit of Christ's death, which was his going away. His bodily presence could be only in one place at one time, but his Spirit is everywhere, in all places, at all times, wherever two or three are gathered together in his name. See here the office of the Spirit, first to reprove, or to convince. Convincing work is the Spirit's work; he can do it effectually, and none but he. It is the method the Holy Spirit takes, first to convince, and then to comfort. The Spirit shall convince the world, of sin; not merely tell them of it. The Spirit convinces of the fact of sin; of the fault of sin; of the folly of sin; of the filth of sin, that by it we are become hateful to God; of the fountain of sin, the corrupt nature; and lastly, of the fruit of sin, that the end thereof is death.

16-22 It is good to consider how near our seasons of grace are to an end, that we may be quickened to improve them. But the sorrows of the disciples would soon be turned into joy; as those of a mother, at the sight of her infant. The Holy Spirit would be their Comforter, and neither men nor devils, neither sufferings in life nor in death, would ever deprive them of their joy. Believers have joy or sorrow, according to their sight of Christ, and the tokens of his presence. Sorrow is coming on the ungodly, which nothing can lessen; the believer is an heir to joy which no one can take away. Where now is the joy of the murderers of our Lord, and the sorrow of his friends?

23-27 Asking of the Father shows a sense of spiritual wants, and a desire of spiritual blessings, with convic-

miserable, for if you would but exercise an appropriating faith you might possess a boundless heritage. If you are a child of God all things are yours, and you may help yourself. If you are hungry at this banquet it is for want of faith: if you are thirsty by the brink of this river it is because you do not stoop down and drink. Behold, God is your portion: the Father is your shepherd, the Son of God is your food, and the Spirit of God is your comforter. Rejoice and be glad, and grasp with the firm hand of a personal faith that royal boon which Jesus sets before you in his promises.

I beg you to observe how the Lord Jesus Christ in great wisdom dealt with Martha. In the first place, he did not grow angry with her. There is not a trace of petulance in his speech. He did not say to her, "Martha, I am ashamed of you that you should have such low thoughts of me." She thought that she was honoring Jesus when she said,—"I know, that even now, whatsoever thou wilt ask of God, God will give it thee." Her idea of Jesus was that He was a great prophet who would ask of God and obtain answers to his prayers; she has not grasped the truth of his own personal power to give and sustain life. But the Savior did not say, "Martha, these are low and groveling ideas of your Lord and Savior." He did not chide her, though she lacked wisdom,—wisdom which she ought to have possessed. I do not think God's people learn much by being scolded; it is not the habit of the great Lord to scold his disciples, and therefore they do not take it well when his servants take upon themselves to rate them. If ever you meet with one of the Lord's own who falls far short of the true ideal of the gospel, do not bluster and upbraid. Who taught you what you know? He that has taught you did it of his infinite love and grace and pity, and he was very tender with you, for you were doltish enough; therefore be tender with others, and give them line upon line, even as your Lord was gentle towards you. It ill becomes a servant to lose patience where his Master shows so much.

The Lord Jesus, with gentle spirit, proceeded to teach her more of the things concerning himself. More of Jesus! More of Jesus! That is the sovereign cure for our faults. He revealed himself to her, that in him she might behold reasons for a clearer hope and a more substantial faith. How sweetly fell those words upon her ear: "I am the resurrection and the life"! Not "I can get resurrection by my prayers," but "I am, myself, the resurrection." God's people need to know more of what Jesus is, more of the fullness which it has pleased the Father to place in him. Some of them know quite

saith, A little while? we cannot tell what he saith.

19 Now Jesus knew that they were desirous to ask him, and said unto them, Do ye inquire among yourselves of that I said, A little while, and ye shall not see me: and again, a little while, and ye shall see me?

20 Verily, verily, I say unto you, That ye shall weep and lament, but the world shall rejoice: and ye shall be sorrowful, but your sorrow shall be turned into joy.

21 A woman when she is in travail hath sorrow, because her hour is come: but as soon as she is delivered of the child, she remembereth no more the anguish, for joy that a man is born into the world.

22 And ye now therefore have sorrow: but I will see you again, and your heart shall rejoice, and your joy no man taketh from you.

23 And in that day ye shall ask me nothing. Verily, verily, I say unto you, Whatsoever ye shall ask the Father in my name, he will give it you.

24 Hitherto have ye asked nothing in my name: ask, and ye shall receive, that your joy may be full.

25 These things have I spoken unto you in proverbs: but the time cometh, when I shall no more speak unto you in proverbs, but I shall shew you plainly of the Father.

26 At that day ye shall ask in my name: and I say not unto you, that I will pray the Father for you:

27 For the Father himself loveth you, because ye have loved me, and have believed that I came out from God.

28 I came forth from the Father, and am come into the world: again, I leave the world, and go to the Father.

29 His disciples said unto him, Lo, now speakest thou plainly, and speakest no proverb.

30 Now are we sure that thou knowest all things, and needest not that any man should ask thee: by this we believe that thou camest forth from God.

31 Jesus answered them, Do ye now believe?

32 Behold, the hour cometh, yea, is now come, that ye shall be scattered, every man to his own, and shall leave me alone: and yet I am not alone, because the Father is with me.

33 These things I have spoken unto you, that in me ye might have peace. In the world ye shall have tribulation: but be of good cheer; I have overcome the world.

JOHN 17

1 These words spake Jesus, and lifted up his eyes to heaven, and said, Father, the hour is come; glorify thy Son, that thy Son also may glorify thee:

2 As thou hast given him power over all flesh, that he should give eternal life to as many as thou hast given him.

3 And this is life eternal, that they might know

11. That my joy might remain in you – The same joy which I feel in loving the Father, and keeping his commandments.

12. Your joy will be full, if ye so love one another.

13. Greater love – To his friends. He here speaks of them only.

14. Ye are my friends, if ye do whatsoever I command you – On this condition, not otherwise. A thunderbolt for Antinomianism! Who then dares assert that God's love does not at all depend on man's works?

15. All things – Which might be of service to you.

16. Ye – My apostles, have not chosen me, but I have chosen you – As clearly appears from the sacred history: and appointed you, that ye may go and bear fruit – I have chosen and appointed you for this end, that ye may go and convert sinners: and that your fruit may remain – That the fruit of your labors may remain to the end of the world; yea, to eternity; that whatsoever ye shall ask – The consequence of your going and bearing fruit will be, that all your prayers will be heard.

19. Because ye are not of the world, therefore the world hateth you – Because your maxims, tempers, actions, are quite opposite to theirs. For the very same reason must the world in all ages hate those who are not of the world.

20. John xiii, 16; Matt. x, 24; Luke vi, 40.

21. All these things will they do to you, because they know not him that sent me – And in all ages and nations they who know not God will, for this cause, hate and persecute those that do.

22. They had not had sin – Not in this respect.

23. He that hateth me – As every unbeliever doth, For as the love of God is inseparable from faith, so is the hatred of God from unbelief.

25. Psalm lxix, 4.

26. When the Comforter is come, whom I will send from the Father, the Spirit of truth, who proceedeth from the Father, he shall testify of me – The Spirit's coming, and being sent by our Lord from the Father, to testify of him, are personal characters, and plainly distinguish him from the Father and the Son; and his title as the Spirit of truth, together with his proceeding from the Father, can agree to none but a Divine person. And that he proceeds from the Son, as well as from the Father, may be fairly argued from his being called the Spirit of Christ, 1 Pet. i, 11; and from his being here said to be sent by Christ from the Father, as well as sent by the Father in his name.

JOHN 16

2. The time cometh, that whosoever killeth you will think he doth God service – But, blessed be God, the time is so far past, that those who bear the name of Christ do not now generally suppose they do him service by killing each other for a difference in opinion or mode of worship.

3. They have not known the Father nor me – This is the true root of persecution in all its forms.

4. I did not tell you these things at the beginning, because I was with you – To bear the chief shock in my own person, and to screen you from it.

5. None of you asketh me – Now when it is most seasonable. Peter did ask this before, chap. xiii, 36.

tion that they are to be had from God only. Asking in Christ's name, is acknowledging our unworthiness to receive any favors from God, and shows full dependence upon Christ as the Lord our Righteousness. Our Lord had hitherto spoken in short and weighty sentences, or in parables, the import of which the disciples did not fully understand, but after his resurrection he intended plainly to teach them such things as related to the Father and the way to him, through his intercession. And the frequency with which our Lord enforces offering up petitions in his name, shows that the great end of the mediation of Christ is to impress us with a deep sense of our sinfulness, and of the merit and power of his death, whereby we have access to God. And let us ever remember, that to address the Father in the name of Christ, or to address the Son as God dwelling in human nature, and reconciling the world to himself, are the same, as the Father and Son are one.

28-33 Here is a plain declaration of Christ's coming from the Father, and his return to him. The Redeemer, in his entrance, was God manifest in the flesh, and in his departure was received up into glory. By this saying the disciples improved in knowledge. Also in faith; "Now are we sure." Alas! they knew not their own weakness. The Divine nature did not desert the human nature, but supported it, and put comfort and value into Christ's sufferings. And while we have God's favorable presence, we are happy, and ought to be easy, though all the world forsake us. Peace in Christ is the only true peace, in him alone believers have it. Through him we have peace with God, and so in him we have peace in our own minds. We ought to be encouraged, because Christ has overcome the world before us. But while we think we stand, let us take heed lest we fall. We know not how we should act if brought into temptation; let us watch and pray without ceasing, that we may not be left to ourselves.

JOHN 17
Christ's prayer for himself. (1-5)
His prayer for his disciples. (6-10)
His prayer. (11-26)

1-5 Our Lord prayed as a man, and as the Mediator of his people; yet he spoke with majesty and authority, as one with and equal to the Father. Eternal life could not be given to believers, unless Christ, their Surety, both glorified the Father, and was glorified of him. This is the sinner's way to eternal life, and when this knowledge shall be made perfect, holiness and happiness will be fully enjoyed. The holiness and happiness of the redeemed, are especially that glory of Christ, and of his Father, which was the joy set before him, for which he endured the cross and despised the shame; this glory was the end of the sorrow of his soul, and in obtaining it he was fully satisfied. Thus we are taught

enough of what they are themselves, and they will break their hearts if they go on reading much longer in that black-letter book: they need, I say, to rest their eyes upon the person of their Lord, and to spy out all the riches of grace which lie hidden in him; then they will pluck up courage, and look forward with surer expectancy. When our Lord said, "I am the resurrection and the life," He indicated to Martha that resurrection and life were not gifts which he must seek, nor even boons which he must create; but that he himself was the resurrection and the life: these things were wherever he was. He was the author, and giver, and maintainer of life, and that life was himself. He would have her to know that he was himself precisely what she wanted for her brother. She did know a little of the Lord's power, for she said, "If Thou hadst been here, my brother had not died," which being very kindly interpreted might mean, "Lord, Thou art the life." "Ah, but," saith Jesus, "you must also learn that I am the resurrection! You already admit that if I had been here Lazarus would not have died; I would have you further learn that I being here your brother shall live though he has died; and that when I am with my people none of them shall die for ever, for I am to them the resurrection and the life." Poor Martha was looking up into the sky for life, or gazing down into the deeps for resurrection, when the Resurrection and the Life stood before her, smiling upon her, and cheering her heavy heart. She had thought of what Jesus might have done if he had been there before; now he let her know what he is at the present moment.

Thus I have introduced the text to you, and I pray God the Holy Spirit to bless these prefatory observations; for if we learn only these first lessons we shall not have been here in vain. Let us construe promises in their largest sense, let us regard them as real, and set them down as facts. Let us look to the Promisor, even to Jesus the Lord, and not so much to the difficulties which surround the accomplishment of the promise. In beginning the divine life let us look to Jesus, and in afterwards running the heavenly race let us still be looking unto Jesus, till we see in him our all in all. When both eyes look on Jesus we are in the light; but when we have one eye for him, and one eye for self, all is darkness. Oh, to see him with all our soul's eyes!

Now, I am going to speak as I am helped of the Spirit; and I shall proceed thus—first, by asking you to view the text as a stream of comfort to Martha and other bereaved persons; and, secondly, to view it as a great deep of comfort to all believers.

thee the only true God, and Jesus Christ, whom thou hast sent.

4 I have glorified thee on the earth: I have finished the work which thou gavest me to do.

5 And now, O Father, glorify thou me with thine own self with the glory which I had with thee before the world was.

6 I have manifested thy name unto the men which thou gavest me out of the world: thine they were, and thou gavest them me; and they have kept thy word.

7 Now they have known that all things whatsoever thou hast given me are of thee.

8 For I have given unto them the words which thou gavest me; and they have received them, and have known surely that I came out from thee, and they have believed that thou didst send me.

9 I pray for them: I pray not for the world, but for them which thou hast given me; for they are thine.

10 And all mine are thine, and thine are mine; and I am glorified in them.

11 And now I am no more in the world, but these are in the world, and I come to thee. Holy Father, keep through thine own name those whom thou hast given me, that they may be one, as we are.

12 While I was with them in the world, I kept them in thy name: those that thou gavest me I have kept, and none of them is lost, but the son of perdition; that the scripture might be fulfilled.

13 And now come I to thee; and these things I speak in the world, that they might have my joy fulfilled in themselves.

14 I have given them thy word; and the world hath hated them, because they are not of the world, even as I am not of the world.

15 I pray not that thou shouldest take them out of the world, but that thou shouldest keep them from the evil.

16 They are not of the world, even as I am not of the world.

17 Sanctify them through thy truth: thy word is truth.

18 As thou hast sent me into the world, even so have I also sent them into the world.

19 And for their sakes I sanctify myself, that they also might be sanctified through the truth.

20 Neither pray I for these alone, but for them also which shall believe on me through their word;

21 That they all may be one; as thou, Father, art in me, and I in thee, that they also may be one in us: that the world may believe that thou hast sent me.

22 And the glory which thou gavest me I have given them; that they may be one, even as we are one:

23 I in them, and thou in me, that they may be made perfect in one; and that the world may know that thou hast sent me, and hast loved them, as thou hast loved me.

24 Father, I will that they also, whom thou hast

7. It is expedient for you – In respect of the Comforter, ver. 7, &c., and of me, ver. 16, &c., and of the Father, ver. 23, &c.

8. He – Observe his twofold office; toward the world, ver. 8, &c.; toward believers, ver. 12, &c.: will convince – All of the world – Who do not obstinately resist, by your preaching and miracles, of sin, and of righteousness, and of judgment – He who is convinced of sin either accepts the righteousness of Christ, or is judged with Satan. An abundant accomplishment of this we find in the Acts of the Apostles.

9. Of sin – Particularly of unbelief, which is the confluence of all sins, and binds them all down upon us.

10. Of righteousness, because I go to my Father – Which the Spirit will testify, though ye do not then see me. But I could not go to him if I were not righteous.

11. The prince of this world is judged – And in consequence thereof dethroned, deprived of the power he had so long usurped over men. Yet those who reject the deliverance offered them will remain slaves of Satan still.

12. I have yet many things to say – Concerning my passion, death, resurrection, and the consequences of it. These things we have, not in uncertain traditions, but in the Acts, the Epistles, and the Revelation. But ye cannot bear them now – Both because of your littleness of faith, and your immoderate sorrow.

13. When he is come – It is universally allowed that the Father, Son, and Holy Ghost dwell in all believers. And the internal agency of the Holy Ghost is generally admitted. That of the Father and the Son, as represented in this Gospel, deserves our deepest consideration.

15. All things that the Father hath are mine – Could any creature say this?

16. A little while and ye shall not see me – When I am buried: and again, a little while, and ye shall see me – When I am risen: because I go to my Father – I die and rise again, in order to ascend to my Father.

19. Jesus said to them – Preventing their question.

20. Ye will weep and lament – When ye see me dead; but your sorrow will be turned into joy – When ye see me risen.

22. Ye now therefore have sorrow – This gives us no manner of authority to assert all believers must come into a state of darkness. They never need lose either their peace, or love, or the witness that they are the children of God. They never can lose these, but either through sin, or ignorance, or vehement temptation, or bodily disorder.

23. Ye shall not question me about any thing – Which you do not now understand. You will not need to inquire of me; for you will know all things clearly. Whatsoever ye shall ask – Knowledge, love, or any thing else, he will give it – Our Lord here gives us a carte blanche. Believer, write down what thou wilt. He had said, chap. xiv, 13, I will do it, where the discourse was of glorifying the Father through the Son. Here, speaking of the love of the Father to believers, he saith, He will give it.

24. Hitherto ye have asked nothing in my name – For they had asked him directly for all they wanted.

26. At that day ye shall ask – For true knowledge begets prayer. And I say not that I will pray – This in nowise implies that he will not: it means only, The Father himself now loves you, not only

MATTHEW HENRY

CHARLES H. SPURGEON

that our glorifying God is needed as an evidence of our interest in Christ, through whom eternal life is God's free gift.

6-10 Christ prays for those that are his. Thou gavest them me, as sheep to the shepherd, to be kept; as a patient to the physician, to be cured; as children to a tutor, to be taught: thus he will deliver up his charge. It is a great satisfaction to us, in our reliance upon Christ, that he, all he is and has, and all he said and did, all he is doing and will do, are of God. Christ offered this prayer for his people alone as believers; not for the world at large. Yet no one who desires to come to the Father, and is conscious that he is unworthy to come in his own name, need be discouraged by the Savior's declaration, for he is both able and willing to save to the uttermost, all that come unto God by him. Earnest convictions and desires, are hopeful tokens of a work already wrought in a man; they begin to evidence that he has been chosen unto salvation, through sanctification of the Spirit and belief of the truth. They are thine; wilt thou not provide for thine own? Wilt thou not secure them? Observe the foundation on which this plea is grounded, All mine are thine, and thine are mine. This speaks the Father and Son to be one. All mine are thine. The Son owns none for his, that are not devoted to the service of the Father.

11-16 Christ does not pray that they might be rich and great in the world, but that they might be kept from sin, strengthened for their duty, and brought safe to heaven. The prosperity of the soul is the best prosperity. He pleaded with his holy Father, that he would keep them by his power and for his glory, that they might be united in affection and labors, even according to the union of the Father and the Son. He did not pray that his disciples should be removed out of the world, that they might escape the rage of men, for they had a great work to do for the glory of God, and the benefit of mankind. But he prayed that the Father would keep them from the evil, from being corrupted by the world, the remains of sin in their hearts, and from the power and craft of Satan. So that they might pass through the world as through an enemy's country, as he had done. They are not left here to pursue the same objects as the men around them, but to glorify God, and to serve their generation. The Spirit of God in true Christians is opposed to the spirit of the world.

17-19 Christ next prayed for the disciples, that they might not only be kept from evil, but made good. It is the prayer of Jesus for all that are his, that they may be made holy. Even disciples must pray for sanctifying grace. The means of giving this grace is, "through thy truth, thy word is truth." Sanctify them, set them apart for thyself and thy service. Own them in the office; let thy hand go with them. Jesus entirely devoted himself to his undertaking, and all the parts of it, especially the offering up himself without spot unto God, by the eter-

I. First, I long for you to VIEW THE TEXT AS A STREAM OF COMFORT TO MARTHA AND OTHER BEREAVED PERSONS.

Observe, in the beginning, that the presence of Jesus Christ means life and resurrection. It meant that to Lazarus. If Jesus comes to Lazarus, Lazarus must live. Had Martha taken the Savior's words literally, as she should have done, as I have already told you, she would have had immediate comfort from them; and the Savior intended her to understand them in that sense. He virtually says, "I am to Lazarus the Power that can make him live again; and I am the Power that can keep him in life. Yea, I am the resurrection and the life." A statement so understood would have been very comfortable to her. Nothing could have been more so. It would there and then have abolished death so far as her brother was concerned. Somebody says, "But I do not see that this is any comfort to us, for if Jesus be here, yet it is only a spiritual presence, and we cannot expect to see our dear mother, or child, or husband raised from the dead thereby." I answer that our Lord Jesus is able at this moment to give us back our departed ones, for he is still the resurrection and the life. But let me ask you whether you really wish that Jesus would raise your departed ones from the dead. You say at first, "Of course I do wish it"; but I would ask you to reconsider that decision; for I believe that upon further thought you will say, "No, I could not wish it." Do you really desire to see your glorified husband sent back again to this world of care and pain? Would you have your father or mother deprived of the glories which they are now enjoying in order that they might help you in the struggles of this mortal life? Would you discrown the saints? You are not so cruel. That dear child, would you have it back from among the angels, and from the inner glory, to come here and suffer again? You would not have it so. And to my mind it is a comfort to you, or should be, that it is not within your power to have it so; because you might be tempted in some selfish moment to accept the doubtful boon. Lazarus could return, and fit into his place again, but scarcely one in ten thousand could do so. There would be serious drawbacks in the return of those whom we have loved best. Do you cry, "Give back my father! Give me back my friend"? You know not what you ask. It might be a cause of regret to you as long as they lingered here, for you would each morning think to yourself, "Beloved one, I have brought you out of heaven by my wish. I have robbed you of infinite felicity to gratify myself." For my own part, I had rather that the Lord Jesus should keep the

given me, be with me where I am; that they may behold my glory, which thou hast given me: for thou lovedst me before the foundation of the world.

25 O righteous Father, the world hath not known thee: but I have known thee, and these have known that thou hast sent me.

26 And I have declared unto them thy name, and will declare it: that the love wherewith thou hast loved me may be in them, and I in them.

JOHN 18

1 When Jesus had spoken these words, he went forth with his disciples over the brook Cedron, where was a garden, into the which he entered, and his disciples.

2 And Judas also, which betrayed him, knew the place: for Jesus ofttimes resorted thither with his disciples.

3 Judas then, having received a band of men and officers from the chief priests and Pharisees, cometh thither with lanterns and torches and weapons.

4 Jesus therefore, knowing all things that should come upon him, went forth, and said unto them, Whom seek ye?

5 They answered him, Jesus of Nazareth. Jesus saith unto them, I am he. And Judas also, which betrayed him, stood with them.

6 As soon then as he had said unto them, I am he, they went backward, and fell to the ground.

7 Then asked he them again, Whom seek ye? And they said, Jesus of Nazareth.

8 Jesus answered, I have told you that I am he: if therefore ye seek me, let these go their way:

9 That the saying might be fulfilled, which he spake, Of them which thou gavest me have I lost none.

10 Then Simon Peter having a sword drew it, and smote the high priest's servant, and cut off his right ear. The servant's name was Malchus.

11 Then said Jesus unto Peter, Put up thy sword into the sheath: the cup which my Father hath given me, shall I not drink it?

12 Then the band and the captain and officers of the Jews took Jesus, and bound him,

13 And led him away to Annas first; for he was father in law to Caiaphas, which was the high priest that same year.

14 Now Caiaphas was he, which gave counsel to the Jews, that it was expedient that one man should die for the people.

15 And Simon Peter followed Jesus, and so did another disciple: that disciple was known unto the high priest, and went in with Jesus into the palace of the high priest.

16 But Peter stood at the door without. Then went out that other disciple, which was known unto the high priest, and spake unto her that kept the door, and brought in Peter.

17 Then saith the damsel that kept the door unto Peter, Art not thou also one of this man's disciples? He saith, I am not.

because of my intercession, but also because of the faith and love which he hath wrought in you.

30. Thou knowest all things – Even our hearts. Although no question is asked thee, yet thou answerest the thoughts of every one. By this we believe that thou camest forth from God – They, as it were, echo back the words which he had spoken in ver. 27, implying, We believe in God; we believe also in thee.

JOHN 17

In this chapter our Lord prays,
1. For himself, ver. 1-5.
2. For the apostles, ver. 6-19; and again, ver. 24-26.
3. For all believers, ver. 20-23. And
4. For the world, ver. 21-23.

In his prayer he comprises all he had said from chap. xiii, 31, and seals, as it were, all he had hitherto done, beholding things past, present, and to come. This chapter contains the easiest words, and the deepest sense of any in all the Scripture: yet is here no incoherent rhapsody, but the whole is closely and exactly connected.

1. Father – This simplicity of appellation highly became the only-begotten Son of God; to which a believer then makes the nearest approach, when he is fullest of love and humble confidence. The hour is come – The appointed time for it; glorify thy Son – The Son glorified the Father, both before and after his own glorification. When he speaks to the Father he does not style himself the Son of man.

2. As thou hast given him power over all flesh – This answers to glorify thy Son. That he may give eternal life, &c. – This answers to that thy Son may glorify thee. To all whom thou hast given him – To all believers. This is a clear proof that Christ designed his sacrifice should avail for all: yea, that all flesh, every man, should partake of everlasting life. For as the Father had given him power over all flesh, so he gave himself a ransom for all.

3. To know – By loving, holy faith, thee the only true God – The only cause and end of all things; not excluding the Son and the Holy Ghost, no more than the Father is excluded from being Lord, 1 Cor. viii, 6; but the false gods of the heathens; and Jesus Christ – As their prophet, priest, and king: this is life eternal – It is both the way to, and the essence of, everlasting happiness.

4. I have finished the work – Thus have I glorified thee, laying the foundation of thy kingdom on earth.

5. The glory which I had – He does not say received – He always had it, till he emptied himself of it in the days of his flesh.

6. I have manifested thy name – All thy attributes; and in particular thy paternal relation to believers; to the men whom thou hast given me – The apostles, and so ver. 12. They were thine – By creation, and by descent from Abraham. And thou hast given them me – By giving them faith in what I have spoken. So ver. 9.

7. Now they know that all things – Which I have done and spoken, are of thee – And consequently right and true.

8. They have received them – By faith.

9. I pray not for the world – Not in these petitions, which are adapted to the state of believers only. (He prays for the world at ver. 21, 23, that they may believe – That they may know God hath sent him.) This no more proves that our Lord did not pray for the

MATTHEW HENRY

CHARLES H. SPURGEON

nal Spirit. The real holiness of all true Christians is the fruit of Christ's death, by which the gift of the Holy Ghost was purchased; he gave himself for his church, to sanctify it. If our views have not this effect on us, they are not Divine truth, or we do not receive them by a living and a working faith, but as mere notions.

20-23 Our Lord especially prayed, that all believers might be as one body under one head, animated by one soul, by their union with Christ and the Father in him, through the Holy Spirit dwelling in them. The more they dispute about lesser things, the more they throw doubts upon Christianity. Let us endeavor to keep the unity of the Spirit in the bond of peace, praying that all believers may be more and more united in one mind and one judgment. Thus shall we convince the world of the truth and excellence of our religion, and find more sweet communion with God and his saints.

24-26 Christ, as one with the Father, claimed on behalf of all that had been given to him, and should in due time believe on him, that they should be brought to heaven; and that there the whole company of the redeemed might behold his glory as their beloved Friend and Brother, and therein find happiness. He had declared and would further declare the name or character of God, by his doctrine and his Spirit, that, being one with him, the love of the Father to him might abide with them also. Thus, being joined to him by one Spirit, they might be filled with all the fullness of God, and enjoy a blessedness of which we can form no right idea in our present state.

JOHN 18

Christ taken in the garden. (1-12)
Christ before Annas and Caiaphas. (13-27)
Christ before Pilate. (28-40)

1-12 Sin began in the garden of Eden, there the curse was pronounced, there the Redeemer was promised; and in a garden that promised Seed entered into conflict with the old serpent. Christ was buried also in a garden. Let us, when we walk in our gardens, take occasion from thence to mediate on Christ's sufferings in a garden.

13-27 Simon Peter denied his Master. The particulars have been noticed in the remarks on the other Gospels. The beginning of sin is as the letting forth of water. The sin of lying is a fruitful sin; one lie needs another to support it, and that another. If a call to expose ourselves to danger be clear, we may hope God will enable us to honor him; if it be not, we may fear that God will leave us to shame ourselves. They said nothing concerning the miracles of Jesus, by which he had done so much good, and which proved his doctrine. Thus the enemies of Christ, whilst they

keys of death than that he should lend them to me. It would be too dreadful a privilege to be empowered to rob heaven of the perfected merely to give pleasure to imperfect ones below. Jesus would raise them now if he knew it to be right; I do not wish to take the government from his shoulder. It is more comfortable to me to think that Jesus Christ could give them back to me, and would if it were for his glory and my good. My dear ones that lie asleep could be awakened in an instant if the Master thought it best; but it would not be best, and therefore even I would hold his skirt, and say, "Tread softly, Master! Do not arouse them! I shall go to them, but they shall not return to me. It is not my wish they should return: it is better that they should be with thee where Thou art, to behold thy glory." It does not seem to me, then, dear friend, that you are one whit behind Martha: and you ought to be comforted while Jesus says to you, "I am even now the resurrection and the life."

Furthermore, here is comfort which we may each one safely take, namely, that when Jesus comes the dead shall live. The Revised Version has it, "He that believeth on me, though he die, yet shall he live." We do not know when our Lord will descend from heaven, but we do know the message of the angel, "This same Jesus, which is taken up from you into heaven, shall so come in like manner as ye have seen him go into heaven." The Lord will come; we may not question the certainty of his appearing. When he cometh, all his redeemed shall live with him. The trump of the archangel shall startle the happy sleepers, and they shall wake to put on their beauteous array; the body transformed and made like unto Christ's glorious body shall be once more wrapt about them as the vesture of their perfected and emancipated spirits. Then our brother shall rise again, and all our dear ones who have fallen asleep in Jesus the Lord will bring with him. This is the glorious hope of the church, wherein we see the death of death, and the destruction of the grave. Wherefore comfort one another with these words.

Then we are also told that when Jesus comes, living believers shall not die. After the coming of Christ there shall be no more death for his people. What does Paul say? "Behold, I show you a mystery. We shall not all die, but we shall all be changed." Did I see a little school-girl put up her finger? Did I hear her say, "Please, sir, you made a mistake." So I did; I made it on purpose. Paul did not say, "We shall not all die," for the Lord had already said, "Whosoever liveth and believeth in me shall never die"; Paul would not say that any of us

18 And the servants and officers stood there, who had made a fire of coals; for it was cold: and they warmed themselves: and Peter stood with them, and warmed himself.

19 The high priest then asked Jesus of his disciples, and of his doctrine.

20 Jesus answered him, I spake openly to the world; I ever taught in the synagogue, and in the temple, whither the Jews always resort; and in secret have I said nothing.

21 Why askest thou me? ask them which heard me, what I have said unto them: behold, they know what I said.

22 And when he had thus spoken, one of the officers which stood by struck Jesus with the palm of his hand, saying, Answerest thou the high priest so?

23 Jesus answered him, If I have spoken evil, bear witness of the evil: but if well, why smitest thou me?

24 Now Annas had sent him bound unto Caiaphas the high priest.

25 And Simon Peter stood and warmed himself. They said therefore unto him, Art not thou also one of his disciples? He denied it, and said, I am not.

26 One of the servants of the high priest, being his kinsman whose ear Peter cut off, saith, Did not I see thee in the garden with him?

27 Peter then denied again: and immediately the cock crew.

28 Then led they Jesus from Caiaphas unto the hall of judgment: and it was early; and they themselves went not into the judgment hall, lest they should be defiled; but that they might eat the passover.

29 Pilate then went out unto them, and said, What accusation bring ye against this man?

30 They answered and said unto him, If he were not a malefactor, we would not have delivered him up unto thee.

31 Then said Pilate unto them, Take ye him, and judge him according to your law. The Jews therefore said unto him, It is not lawful for us to put any man to death:

32 That the saying of Jesus might be fulfilled, which he spake, signifying what death he should die.

33 Then Pilate entered into the judgment hall again, and called Jesus, and said unto him, Art thou the King of the Jews?

34 Jesus answered him, Sayest thou this thing of thyself, or did others tell it thee of me?

35 Pilate answered, Am I a Jew? Thine own nation and the chief priests have delivered thee unto me: what hast thou done?

36 Jesus answered, My kingdom is not of this world: if my kingdom were of this world, then would my servants fight, that I should not be delivered to the Jews: but now is my kingdom not from hence.

37 Pilate therefore said unto him, Art thou a king then? Jesus answered, Thou sayest that I am a king. To this end was I born, and for this

world, both before and afterward, than his praying for the apostles alone, ver. 6-19, proves that he did not pray for them also which shall believe through their word, ver. 20.

10. All things that are mine are thine, and that are thine are mine – These are very high and strong expressions, too grand for any mere creature to use; as implying that all things whatsoever, inclusive of the Divine nature, perfections, and operations, are the common property of the Father and the Son. And this is the original ground of that peculiar property, which both the Father and the Son have in the persons who were given to Christ as Mediator; according to what is said in the close of the verse, of his being glorified by them; namely, believing in him, and so acknowledging his glory.

11. Keep them through thy name – Thy power, mercy, wisdom, that they may be one – with us and with each other; one body, separate from the world: as we are – By resemblance to us, though not equality.

12. Those whom thou hast given me I have guarded, and none of them is lost, but the son of perdition – So one even of them whom God had given him is lost. So far was even that decree from being unchangeable! That the Scripture might be fulfilled – That is, whereby the Scripture was fulfilled. The son of perdition signifies one that deservedly perishes; as a son of death, 2 Sam. xii, 5; children of hell, Matt. xxiii, 15, and children of wrath, Eph. ii, 3, signify persons justly obnoxious to death, hell, wrath. Psalm cix, 8.

13. In the world – That is, before I leave the world. My joy – The joy I feel at going to the Father.

15. That thou wouldest take them out of the world – Not yet: but that thou wouldest keep them from the evil one – Who reigns therein.

17. Sanctify – Consecrate them by the anointing of thy Spirit to their office, and perfect them in holiness, by means of thy word.

19. I sanctify myself – I devote myself as a victim, to be sacrificed.

20. For them who will believe – In all ages.

21. As thou art in me – This also is to be understood in a way of similitude, and not of sameness or equality. That the world may believe – Here Christ prays for the world. Observe the sum of his whole prayer,

    1. Receive me into thy own and my glory;

    2. Let my apostles share therein;

    3. And all other believers;

    4. And let all the world believe.

22. The glory which thou hast given me, I have given them – The glory of the only begotten shines in all the sons of God. How great is the majesty of Christians.

24. Here he returns to the apostles. I will – He asks, as having a right to be heard, and prays, not as a servant, but a Son: that they may behold my glory – Herein Is the happiness of heaven, 1 John iii, 2.

25. Righteous Father – The admission of believers to God through Christ, flows even from the justice of God.

26. I have declared to them thy name – Thy new, best name of love; that the love wherewith thou hast loved me – That thou and thy love, and I and my love, may be in them – That they may love me with that love.

quarrel with his truth, willfully shut their eyes against it. He appeals to those who heard him. The doctrine of Christ may safely appeal to all that know it, and those who judge in truth bear witness to it. Our resentment of injuries must never be passionate. He reasoned with the man that did him the injury, and so may we.

28-32 It was unjust to put one to death who had done so much good, therefore the Jews were willing to save themselves from reproach. Many fear the scandal of an ill thing, more than the sin of it. Christ had said he should be delivered to the Gentiles, and they should put him to death; hereby that saying was fulfilled. He had said that he should be crucified, lifted up. If the Jews had judged him by their law, he had been stoned; crucifying never was used among the Jews. It is determined concerning us, though not discovered to us, what death we shall die: this should free us from disquiet about that matter. Lord, what, when, and how, thou hast appointed.

33-40 Art thou the King of the Jews? that King of the Jews who has been so long expected? Messiah the Prince; art thou he? Dost thou call thyself so, and wouldest thou be thought so? Christ answered this question with another; not for evasion, but that Pilate might consider what he did. He never took upon him any earthly power, never were any traitorous principles or practices laid to him. Christ gave an account of the nature of his kingdom. Its nature is not worldly; it is a kingdom within men, set up in their hearts and consciences; its riches spiritual, its power spiritual, and its glory within. Its supports are not worldly; its weapons are spiritual; it needed not, nor used, force to maintain and advance it, nor opposed any kingdom but that of sin and Satan. Its object and design are not worldly. When Christ said, I am the Truth, he said, in effect, I am a King. He conquers by the convincing evidence of truth; he rules by the commanding power of truth. The subjects of this kingdom are those that are of the truth. Pilate put a good question, he said, What is truth? When we search the Scriptures, and attend the ministry of the word, it must be with this inquiry, What is truth? and with this prayer, Lead me in thy truth; into all truth. But many put this question, who have not patience to preserve in their search after truth; or not humility enough to receive it. By this solemn declaration of Christ's innocence, it appears, that though the Lord Jesus was treated as the worst of evildoers, he never deserved such treatment. But it unfolds the design of his death; that he died as a Sacrifice for our sins. Pilate was willing to please all sides; and was governed more by worldly wisdom than by the rules of justice. Sin is a robber, yet is foolishly chosen by many rather than Christ, who would truly enrich us. Let us endeavor to make our accusers ashamed as Christ did; and let us beware of crucifying Christ afresh.

should die, but he used his Master's own term, and said, "We shall not all sleep, but we shall all be changed." When the Lord comes there will be no more death; we who are alive and remain (as some of us may be—we cannot tell) will undergo a sudden transformation—for flesh and blood, as they are, cannot inherit the kingdom of God—and by that transformation our bodies shall be made meet to be "partakers of the inheritance of the saints in light." There shall be no more death then. Here, then, we have two sacred handkerchiefs with which to wipe the eyes of mourners: when Christ cometh the dead shall live; when Christ cometh those that live shall never die. Like Enoch, or Elias, we shall pass into the glory state without wading through the black stream, while those who have already forded it shall prove to have been no losers thereby. All this is in connection with Jesus. Resurrection with Jesus is resurrection indeed. Life in Jesus is life indeed. It endears to us resurrection, glory, eternal life, and ultimate perfection, when we see them all coming to us in Jesus. He is the golden pot which hath this manna, the rod which beareth these almonds, the life whereby we live.

But further, I have not made you drink deep enough of this stream yet,—I think our Savior meant that even now his dead are alive. "He that believeth on me, though he die, but yet they live. They are not in the grave, they are for ever with the Lord. They are not unconscious, they are with their Lord in Paradise. Death cannot kill a believer, it can only usher him into a freer form of life. Because Jesus lives, his people live. God is not the God of the dead but of the living: those who have departed have not perished. We laid the precious body in the cemetery, and we set up stones at the head and foot; but we might engrave on them the Lord's words, "She is not dead, but sleepeth." True, an unbelieving generation may laugh us to scorn, but we scorn their laughing.

Again, even now his living do not die. There is an essential difference between the decease of the godly and the death of the ungodly. Death comes to the ungodly man as a penal infliction, but to the righteous as a summons to his Father's palace: to the sinner it is an execution, to the saint an undressing. Death to the wicked is the King of terrors: death to the saint is the end of terrors, the commencement of glory. To die in the Lord is a covenant blessing. Death is ours; it is set down in the list of our possessions among the "all things", and it follows life in the list as if it were an equal favor. No longer is it death to die. The name remains, but the thing itself is changed. Wherefore, then, are we in bondage through fear of

cause came I into the world, that I should bear witness unto the truth. Every one that is of the truth heareth my voice.

38 Pilate saith unto him, What is truth? And when he had said this, he went out again unto the Jews, and saith unto them, I find in him no fault at all.

39 But ye have a custom, that I should release unto you one at the passover: will ye therefore that I release unto you the King of the Jews?

40 Then cried they all again, saying, Not this man, but Barabbas. Now Barabbas was a robber.

JOHN 19

1 Then Pilate therefore took Jesus, and scourged him.

2 And the soldiers platted a crown of thorns, and put it on his head, and they put on him a purple robe,

3 And said, Hail, King of the Jews! and they smote him with their hands.

4 Pilate therefore went forth again, and saith unto them, Behold, I bring him forth to you, that ye may know that I find no fault in him.

5 Then came Jesus forth, wearing the crown of thorns, and the purple robe. And Pilate saith unto them, Behold the man!

6 When the chief priests therefore and officers saw him, they cried out, saying, Crucify him, crucify him. Pilate saith unto them, Take ye him, and crucify him: for I find no fault in him.

7 The Jews answered him, We have a law, and by our law he ought to die, because he made himself the Son of God.

8 When Pilate therefore heard that saying, he was the more afraid;

9 And went again into the judgment hall, and saith unto Jesus, Whence art thou? But Jesus gave him no answer.

10 Then saith Pilate unto him, Speakest thou not unto me? knowest thou not that I have power to crucify thee, and have power to release thee?

11 Jesus answered, Thou couldest have no power at all against me, except it were given thee from above: therefore he that delivered me unto thee hath the greater sin.

12 And from thenceforth Pilate sought to release him: but the Jews cried out, saying, If thou let this man go, thou art not Cesar's friend: whosoever maketh himself a king speaketh against Cesar.

13 When Pilate therefore heard that saying, he brought Jesus forth, and sat down in the judgment seat in a place that is called the Pavement, but in the Hebrew, Gabbatha.

14 And it was the preparation of the passover, and about the sixth hour: and he saith unto the Jews, Behold your King!

15 But they cried out, Away with him, away with him, crucify him. Pilate saith unto them, Shall I crucify your King? The chief priest

JOHN 18

1. A garden – Probably belonging to one of his friends. He might retire to this private place, not only for the advantage of secret devotion, but also that the people might not be alarmed at his apprehension, nor attempt, in the first sallies of their zeal, to rescue him in a tumultuous manner. Kedron was (as the name signifies) a dark shady valley, on the east side of Jerusalem, between the city and the mount of Olives, through which a little brook ran, which took its name from it. It was this brook, which David, a type of Christ, went over with the people, weeping in his flight from Absalom. Matt. xxvi, 30; Mark xiv, 26; Luke xxii, 39.

2. Mark xiv, 43; Luke xxii, 47.

3. A troop of soldiers – A cohort of Roman foot.

6. As soon as he said, I am he, they went backward and fell to the ground – How amazing is it, that they should renew the assault, after so sensible an experience both of his power and mercy! But probably the priests among them might persuade themselves and their attendants, that this also was done by Beelzebub; and that it was through the providence of God, not the indulgence of Jesus, that they received no farther damage.

8. If ye seek me, let these (my disciples) go – It was an eminent instance of his power over the spirits of men, that they so far obeyed this word, as not to seize even Peter, when he had cut off the ear of Malchus.

9. John xvii, 12.

10. Then Simon Peter – No other evangelist names him. Nor could they safely. But St. John, writing after his death, might do it without any such inconvenience.

13. Annas had been high priest before his son-in-law Caiaphas. And though he had for some time resigned that office, yet they paid so much regard to his age and experience, that they brought Christ to Annas first. But we do not read of any thing remarkable which passed at the house of Annas; for which reason, his being carried thither is omitted by the other evangelists. Matt. xxvi, 57; Mark xiv, 53; Luke xxii, 54.

17. Art thou also – As well as the others, one of this man's disciples – She does not appear to have asked with any design to hurt him.

20. I spake openly – As to the manner: continually – As to the time: in the synagogue and temple – As to the place. In secret have I said nothing – No point of doctrine which I have not taught in public.

21. Why askest thou me – Whom thou wilt not believe?

22. Answerest thou the high priest so? – With so little reverence?

24. Now Annas had sent him to Caiaphas – As is implied ver. 13. Bound – Being still bound, ver. 12.

28. They went not into the palace themselves, lest they should be defiled – By going into a house which was not purged from leaven, Deut. xvi, 4. Matt. xxvii, 2; Mark xv, 1; Luke xxiii, 1.

31. It is not lawful for us to put any man to death – The power of inflicting capital punishment had been taken from them that very year. So the scepter was departed from Judah, and transferred to the Romans.

32. Signifying what death he should die – For crucifixion was not a Jewish, but a Roman punishment. So that had he not been condemned by the Roman governor, he could not have been crucified. chap. iii, 14.

JOHN 19

Christ condemned and crucified. (1-18)
Christ on the cross. (19-30)
His side pierced. (31-37)
The burial of Jesus. (38-42)

1-18 Little did Pilate think with what holy regard these sufferings of Christ would, in after-ages, be thought upon and spoken of by the best and greatest of men. Our Lord Jesus came forth, willing to be exposed to their scorn. It is good for every one with faith, to behold Christ Jesus in his sufferings. Behold him, and love him; be still looking unto Jesus. Did their hatred sharpen their endeavors against him? and shall not our love for him quicken our endeavors for him and his kingdom? Pilate seems to have thought that Jesus might be some person above the common order. Even natural conscience makes men afraid of being found fighting against God. As our Lord suffered for the sins both of Jews and Gentiles, it was a special part of the counsel of Divine Wisdom, that the Jews should first purpose his death, and the Gentiles carry that purpose into effect. Had not Christ been thus rejected of men, we had been forever rejected of God. Now was the Son of man delivered into the hands of wicked and unreasonable men. He was led forth for us, that we might escape. He was nailed to the cross, as a Sacrifice bound to the altar. The Scripture was fulfilled; he did not die at the altar among the sacrifices, but among criminals sacrificed to public justice. And now let us pause, and with faith look upon Jesus. Was ever sorrow like unto his sorrow? See him bleeding, see him dying, see him and love him! love him, and live to him!

19-30 Here are some remarkable circumstances of Jesus' death, more fully related than before. Pilate would not gratify the chief priests by allowing the writing to be altered; which was doubtless owing to a secret power of God upon his heart, that this statement of our Lord's character and authority might continue. Many things done by the Roman soldiers were fulfillments of the prophecies of the Old Testament. All things therein written shall be fulfilled. Christ tenderly provided for his mother at his death. Sometimes, when God removes one comfort from us, he raises up another for us, where we looked not for it. Christ's example teaches all men to honor their parents in life and death; to provide for their wants, and to promote their comfort by every means in their power. Especially observe the dying word wherewith Jesus breathed out his soul. It is finished; that is, the counsels of the Father concerning his sufferings were now fulfilled. It is finished; all the types and prophecies of the Old Testament, which pointed at the sufferings of the Messiah, were accomplished. It is finished; the ceremonial law is abolished; the substance is now come, and all the shadows are done away. It is finished; an end is made of transgression by bringing in an ever-

death? Why do we dread the process which gives us liberty? I am told that persons who in the cruel ages had lain in prison for years suffered much more in the moment of the knocking off of their fetters than they had endured for months in wearing the hard iron; and yet I suppose that no man languishing in a dungeon would have been unwilling to stretch out his arm or leg, that the heavy chains might be beaten off by the smith. We should all be content to endure that little inconvenience to obtain lasting liberty. Now, such is death—the knocking off of the fetters; yet the iron may never seem to be so truly iron as when that last liberating blow of grace is about to fall. Let us not mind the harsh grating of the key as it turns in the lock; if we understand it aright it will be as music to our ears. Imagine that your last hour is come! The key turns with pain for a moment; but, lo, the bolt is shot! The iron gate is open! The spirit is free! Glory be unto the Lord for ever and ever!

II. I leave the text now as a stream of comfort for the bereaved, for I wish you to VIEW IT AS A GREAT DEEP OF COMFORT FOR ALL BELIEVERS. I cannot fathom it, any more than I could measure the abyss, but I can invite you to survey it by the help of the Holy Ghost.

Methinks, first, this text plainly teaches that the Lord Jesus Christ is the life of his people. We are dead by nature, and you can never produce life out of death: the essential elements are wanting. Should a spark be lingering among the ashes, you may yet fan it to a flame; but from human nature the last spark of heavenly life is gone, and it is vain to seek for life among the dead. The life of every Christian is Christ. He is the beginning of life, being the Resurrection: when he comes to us we live. Regeneration is the result of contact with Christ: we are begotten again unto living hope by his resurrection from the dead. The life of the Christian in its commencement is in Christ alone; not a fragment of it is from himself, and the continuance of that life is equally the same; Jesus is not only the resurrection to begin with, but the life to go on with. "I have life in myself," saith one. I answer—not otherwise than as you are one with Christ: your spiritual life in every breath it draws is in Christ. If you are regarded for a moment as separated from Christ, you are cast forth as a branch and are withered. A member severed from the head is dead flesh and no more. In union to Christ is your life. Oh that our hearers would understand this! I see a poor sinner look into himself, and look again, and then cry, "I cannot see any life within!" Of course you cannot; you have no

answered, We have no king but Cesar.

16 Then delivered he him therefore unto them to be crucified. And they took Jesus, and led him away.

17 And he bearing his cross went forth into a place called the place of a skull, which is called in the Hebrew Golgotha:

18 Where they crucified him, and two other with him, on either side one, and Jesus in the midst.

19 And Pilate wrote a title, and put it on the cross. And the writing was, JESUS OF NAZARETH THE KING OF THE JEWS.

20 This title then read many of the Jews: for the place where Jesus was crucified was nigh to the city: and it was written in Hebrew, and Greek, and Latin.

21 Then said the chief priests of the Jews to Pilate, Write not, The King of the Jews; but that he said, I am King of the Jews.

22 Pilate answered, What I have written I have written.

23 Then the soldiers, when they had crucified Jesus, took his garments, and made four parts, to every soldier a part; and also his coat: now the coat was without seam, woven from the top throughout.

24 They said therefore among themselves, Let us not rend it, but cast lots for it, whose it shall be: that the scripture might be fulfilled, which saith, They parted my raiment among them, and for my vesture they did cast lots. These things therefore the soldiers did.

25 Now there stood by the cross of Jesus his mother, and his mother's sister, Mary the wife of Cleophas, and Mary Magdalene.

26 When Jesus therefore saw his mother, and the disciple standing by, whom he loved, he saith unto his mother, Woman, behold thy son!

27 Then saith he to the disciple, Behold thy mother! And from that hour that disciple took her unto his own home.

28 After this, Jesus knowing that all things were now accomplished, that the scripture might be fulfilled, saith, I thirst.

29 Now there was set a vessel full of vinegar: and they filled a sponge with vinegar, and put it upon hyssop, and put it to his mouth.

30 When Jesus therefore had received the vinegar, he said, It is finished: and he bowed his head, and gave up the ghost.

31 The Jews therefore, because it was the preparation, that the bodies should not remain upon the cross on the sabbath day, (for that sabbath day was an high day,) besought Pilate that their legs might be broken, and that they might be taken away.

32 Then came the soldiers, and brake the legs of the first, and of the other which was crucified with him.

33 But when they came to Jesus, and saw that he was dead already, they brake not his legs:

34 But one of the soldiers with a spear pierced his side, and forthwith came there out blood

36. My kingdom is not of this world – Is not an external, but a spiritual kingdom; that I might not be delivered to the Jews – Which Pilate had already attempted to do, ver. 31, and afterward actually did, chap. xix, 16.

37. Thou sayest – The truth. To this end was I born – Speaking of his human origin: his Divine was above Pilate's comprehension. Yet it is intimated in the following words, I came into the world, that I might witness to the truth – Which was both declared to the Jews, and in the process of his passion to the princes of the Gentiles also. Every one that is of the truth – That is, a lover of it, heareth my voice – A universal maxim. Every sincere lover of truth will hear him, so as to understand and practice what he saith.

38. What is truth? – Said Pilate, a courtier; perhaps meaning what signifies truth? Is that a thing worth hazarding your life for? So he left him presently, to plead with the Jews for him, looking upon him as an innocent but weak man.

JOHN 19

1. Matt. xxvii, 26; Mark xv, 15.

7. By our law he ought to die, because he made himself the Son of God – Which they understood in the highest sense, and therefore accounted blasphemy.

8. He was the more afraid – He seems to have been afraid before of shedding innocent blood.

9. Whence art thou? – That is, whose son art thou?

11. Thou couldst have no power over me – For I have done nothing to expose me to the power of any magistrate. Therefore he that delivered me to thee, namely, Caiaphas, knowing this, is more blamable than thou.

13. Pilate sat down on the judgment seat – Which was then without the palace, in a place called, in Greek, the pavement, on account of a beautiful piece of Mosaic work, with which the floor was adorned: but in Hebrew, Gabbatha – Or the high place, because it stood on an eminence, so that the judge sitting on his throne might be seen and heard by a considerable number of people.

14. It was the preparation of the Passover – For this reason both the Jews and Pilate were desirous to bring the matter to a conclusion. Every Friday was called the preparation, (namely, for the Sabbath.) And as often as the Passover fell on a Friday, that day was called the preparation of the Passover.

17. Bearing his cross – Not the whole cross, (for that was too large and heavy,) but the transverse beam of it, to which his hands were afterward fastened. This they used to make the person to be executed carry. Matt. xxvii, 31; Mark xv, 20; Luke xxiii, 26.

19. Jesus of Nazareth, the king of the Jews – Undoubtedly these were the very words, although the other evangelists do not express them at large.

20. It was written in Latin – For the majesty of the Roman empire; in Hebrew – Because it was the language of the nation; and in Greek – For the information of the Hellenists, who spoke that language, and came in great numbers to the feast.

22. What I have written, I have written – That shall stand.

23. The vesture – The upper garment.

24. They parted my garments among them – No circumstance of David's life bore any resemblance to this, or to several other passages

lasting righteousness. His sufferings were now finished, both those of his soul, and those of his body. It is finished; the work of man's redemption and salvation is now completed. His life was not taken from him by force, but freely given up.

31-37 A trial was made whether Jesus was dead. He died in less time than persons crucified commonly did. It showed that he had laid down his life of himself. The spear broke up the very fountains of life; no human body could survive such a wound. But its being so solemnly attested, shows there was something peculiar in it. The blood and water that flowed out, signified those two great benefits which all believers partake of through Christ, justification and sanctification; blood for atonement, water for purification. They both flow from the pierced side of our Redeemer. To Christ crucified we owe merit for our justification, and Spirit and grace for our sanctification. Let this silence the fears of weak Christians, and encourage their hopes; there came both water and blood out of Jesus' pierced side, both to justify and sanctify them. The Scripture was fulfilled, in Pilate's not allowing his legs to be broken, Ps 34:20. There was a type of this in the paschal lamb, Ex 12:46. May we ever look to him, whom, by our sins, we have ignorantly and heedlessly pierced, nay, sometimes against convictions and mercies; and who shed from his wounded side both water and blood, that we might be justified and sanctified in his name.

38-42 Joseph of Arimathea was a disciple of Christ in secret. Disciples should openly own themselves; yet some, who in lesser trials have been fearful, in greater have been courageous. When God has work to do, he can find out such as are proper to do it. The embalming was done by Nicodemus, a secret friend to Christ, though not his constant follower. That grace which at first is like a bruised reed, may afterward resemble a strong cedar. Hereby these two rich men showed the value they had for Christ's person and doctrine, and that it was not lessened by the reproach of the cross. We must do our duty as the present day and opportunity are, and leave it to God to fulfill his promises in his own way and his own time. The grave of Jesus was appointed with the wicked, as was the case of those who suffered as criminals; but he was with the rich in his death, as prophesied, Isa 53:9; these two circumstances it was very unlikely should ever be united in the same person. He was buried in a new sepulcher; therefore it could not be said that it was not he, but some other that rose. We also are here taught not to be particular as to the place of our burial. He was buried in the sepulcher next at hand. Here is the Sun of Righteousness set for a while, to rise again in greater glory, and then to set no more.

life of your own. "Alas," cries a Christian, "I cannot find anything within to feed my soul with!" Do you expect to feed upon yourself? Must not Israel look up for the manna? Did one of all the tribes find it in his own bosom? To look to self is to turn to a broken cistern which can hold no water. I tell you you must learn that Jesus is the resurrection and the life. Hearken to that great "I"—that infinite EGO! This must cover over and swallow up your little ego. "I live; yet not I, but Christ liveth in me." What are you? Less than nothing, and vanity; but over all springs up that divine, all-sufficient personality, "I am the resurrection and the life." Take the two first words together, and they seem to me to have a wondrous majesty about them—"I AM!" Here is Self-Existence. Life in himself! Even as the Mediator, the Lord Jesus tells us that it is given him to have life in himself, even as the Father hath life in himself (John 5:26). I am fills the yawning mouth of the sepulcher. He that liveth and was dead and is alive for evermore, the Alpha and the Omega, the beginning and the end, declares, "I am the resurrection and the life." If, then, I want to live unto God, I must have Christ; and if I desire to continue to live unto God I must continue to have Christ; and if I aspire to have that life developed to the utmost fullness of which it is capable, I must find it all in Christ. He has come not only that we may have life, but that we may have it more abundantly. Anything that is beyond the circle of Christ is death. If I conjure up an experience over which I foolishly dote, which puffs me up as so perfect that I need not come to Christ now as a poor empty-handed sinner, I have entered into the realm of death, I have introduced into my soul a damning leaven. Away with it! Away with it! Everything of life is put into this golden casket of Christ Jesus: all else is death. We have not a breath of life anywhere but in Jesus, who ever liveth to give life. He saith, "Because I live, ye shall live also," and this is true. We live not for any other reason—not because of anything in us or connected with us, but only because of Jesus. "For ye are dead, and your life is hid with Christ in God."

Now, further, in this great deep to which we would conduct you, faith is the only channel by which we can draw from Jesus our life. "I am the resurrection, and the life: he that believeth in Me": that is it. He does not say, "He that loves me," though love is a bright grace, and very sweet to God: he does not say, "He that serves me," though every one that believes in Christ will endeavor to serve him: but it is not put so: he does not even say, "He that imitates me," though every one that

and water.

35 And he that saw it bare record, and his record is true: and he knoweth that he saith true, that ye might believe.

36 For these things were done, that the scripture should be fulfilled, A bone of him shall not be broken.

37 And again another scripture saith, They shall look on him whom they pierced.

38 And after this Joseph of Arimathea, being a disciple of Jesus, but secretly for fear of the Jews, besought Pilate that he might take away the body of Jesus: and Pilate gave him leave. He came therefore, and took the body of Jesus.

39 And there came also Nicodemus, which at the first came to Jesus by night, and brought a mixture of myrrh and aloes, about an hundred pound weight.

40 Then took they the body of Jesus, and wound it in linen clothes with the spices, as the manner of the Jews is to bury.

41 Now in the place where he was crucified there was a garden; and in the garden a new sepulcher, wherein was never man yet laid.

42 There laid they Jesus therefore because of the Jews' preparation day; for the sepulcher was nigh at hand.

JOHN 20

1 The first day of the week cometh Mary Magdalene early, when it was yet dark, unto the sepulcher, and seeth the stone taken away from the sepulcher.

2 Then she runneth, and cometh to Simon Peter, and to the other disciple, whom Jesus loved, and saith unto them, They have taken away the Lord out of the sepulcher, and we know not where they have laid him.

3 Peter therefore went forth, and that other disciple, and came to the sepulcher.

4 So they ran both together: and the other disciple did outrun Peter, and came first to the sepulcher.

5 And he stooping down, and looking in, saw the linen clothes lying; yet went he not in.

6 Then cometh Simon Peter following him, and went into the sepulcher, and seeth the linen clothes lie,

7 And the napkin, that was about his head, not lying with the linen clothes, but wrapped together in a place by itself.

8 Then went in also that other disciple, which came first to the sepulcher, and he saw, and believed.

9 For as yet they knew not the scripture, that he must rise again from the dead.

10 Then the disciples went away again unto their own home.

11 But Mary stood without at the sepulcher weeping: and as she wept, she stooped down, and looked into the sepulcher,

12 And seeth two angels in white sitting, the one at the head, and the other at the feet,

in the 22nd Psalm. So that in this scripture, as in some others, the prophet seems to have been thrown into a preternatural ecstasy, wherein, personating the Messiah, he spoke barely what the Spirit dictated, without any regard to himself. Psalm xxii, 18.

25. His mother's sister – But we do not read she had any brother. She was her father's heir, and as such transmitted the right of the kingdom of David to Jesus: Mary, the wife of Cleopas – Called likewise Alpheus, the father, as Mary was the mother of James, and Joses, and Simon, and Judas.

27. Behold thy mother – To whom thou art now to perform the part of a son in my place, a peculiar honor which Christ conferred on him. From that hour – From the time of our Lord's death.

29. A stalk of hyssop – Which in those countries grows exceeding large and strong. Psalm lxix, 21.

30. It is finished – My suffering: the purchase of man's redemption. He delivered up his spirit – To God, Matt. xxvii, 50.

31. Lest the bodies should remain on the cross on the Sabbath – Which they would have accounted a profanation of any Sabbath, but of that in particular. For that Sabbath was a great day – Being not only a Sabbath, but the second day of the feast of unleavened bread (from whence they reckoned the weeks to Pentecost:) and also the day for presenting and offering the sheaf of new corn: so that it was a treble solemnity.

34. Forthwith there came out blood and water – It was strange, seeing he was dead, that blood should come out; more strange, that water also; and most strange of all, that both should come out immediately, at one time, and yet distinctly. It was pure and true water, as well as pure and true blood. The asseveration of the beholder and testifier of it, shows both the truth and greatness of the miracle and mystery.

35. His testimony is true – Valid, unexceptionable. And he knoweth – And his conscience beareth him witness, that he testifieth this for no other end, than that ye may believe.

36. A bone of it shall not be broken – This was originally spoken of the paschal lamb, an eminent type of Christ. Exod. xii, 46.

37. They shall look on him whom they have pierced – He was pierced by the soldier's spear. They who have occasioned his sufferings by their sins (and who has not?) shall either look upon him in this world with penitential sorrow: or with terror, when he cometh in the clouds of heaven, Rev. i, 7. Zech. xii, 10.

38. Joseph of Arimathea asked Pilate – And Nicodemus also came – Acknowledging Christ, when even his chosen disciples forsook him. In that extremity Joseph was no longer afraid, Nicodemus no longer ashamed.

41. In the place where he was crucified – There was a garden in the same tract of land: but the cross did not stand in the garden.

42. Because of the preparation – That is, they chose the rather to lay him in that sepulcher which was nigh, because it was the day before the Sabbath, which also was drawing to an end, so that they had no time to carry him far.

JOHN 20

1. Matt. xxviii, 1; Mark xvi, 1; Luke xxiv, 1.

3. Peter went out – Of the city.

6. Peter seeth the linen clothes lie – and the napkin folded up –

MATTHEW HENRY

CHARLES H. SPURGEON

JOHN 20

The sepulcher found to be empty. (1-10)
Christ appears to Mary. (11-18)
He appears to the disciples. (19-25)
The unbelief of Thomas. (26-29)
Conclusion. (30,31)

1-10 If Christ gave his life a ransom, and had not taken it again, it would not have appeared that his giving it was accepted as satisfaction. It was a great trial to Mary, that the body was gone. Weak believers often make that the matter of complaint, which is really just ground of hope, and matter of joy. It is well when those more honored than others with the privileges of disciples, are more active than others in the duty of disciples; more willing to take pains, and run hazards, in a good work. We must do our best, and neither envy those who can do better, nor despise those who do as well as they can, though they come behind. The disciple whom Jesus loved in a special manner, and who therefore in a special manner loved Jesus, was foremost. The love of Christ will make us to abound in every duty more than any thing else. He that was behind was Peter, who had denied Christ. A sense of guilt hinders us in the service of God. As yet the disciples knew not the Scripture; that Christ must rise again from the dead.

11-18 We are likely to seek and find, when we seek with affection, and seek in tears. But many believers complain of the clouds and darkness they are under, which are methods of grace for humbling their souls, mortifying their sins, and endearing Christ to them. A sight of angels and their smiles, will not suffice, without a sight of Jesus, and God's smiles in him. None know, but those who have tasted it, the sorrows of a deserted soul, which has had comfortable evidences of the love of God in Christ, and hopes of heaven, but has now lost them, and walks in darkness; such a wounded spirit who can bear? Christ, in manifesting himself to those that seek him, often outdoes their expectations. See how Mary's heart was in earnest to find Jesus. Christ's way of making himself known to his people is by his word; his word applied to their souls, speaking to them in particular.

19-25 This was the first day of the week, and this day is afterwards often mentioned by the sacred writers; for it was evidently set apart as the Christian Sabbath, in remembrance of Christ's resurrection. The disciples had shut the doors for fear of the Jews; and when they had no such expectation, Jesus himself came and stood in the midst of them, having miraculously, though silently, opened the doors. It is a comfort to Christ's disciples, when their assemblies can only be held in private, that no doors can shut out Christ's presence. When he manifests his love to believers by the comforts of his Spirit, he assures them that because he lives, they shall live also. A sight of Christ

believes in Christ must and will imitate Him; but it is put, "He that believeth in me." Why is that? Why doth the Lord so continually make faith to be the only link between himself and the soul? I take it, because faith is a grace which arrogates nothing to itself, and has not operation apart from Jesus, to whom it unites us. You want to conduct the electric fluid, and, in order to this, you find a metal which will not create any action of its own; if it did so, it would disturb the current which you wish to send along it. If it set up an action of its own, how would you know the difference between what came of the metal and what came of the battery? Now, faith is an empty-handed receiver and communicator; it is nothing apart from that upon which it relies, and therefore it is suitable to be a conductor for grace. When an auditorium has to be erected for a speaker in which he may be plainly heard, the essential thing is to get rid of all echo. When you have no echo, then you have a perfect building: faith makes no noise of its own, it allows the Word to speak. Faith cries, "Non nobis Domine! Not unto us! Not unto us! Christ puts his crown on faith's head, exclaiming, "Thy faith hath saved thee;" but faith hastens to ascribe all the glory of salvation to Jesus only. So you see why the Lord selects faith rather than any other grace, because it is a self-forgetting thing. It is best adapted to be the tubing through which the water of life runs, because it will not communicate a flavor of its own, but will just convey the stream purely and simply from Christ to the soul. "He that believeth in me."

Now notice, to the reception of Christ by faith there is no limit. "He that believeth in me, though he were dead, yet shall he live: and whosoever"—I am deeply in love with that word "whosoever." It is a splendid word. A person who kept many animals had some great dogs and some little ones, and in his eagerness to let them enter his house freely he had two holes cut in the door, one for the big dogs and another for the little dogs. You may well laugh, for the little dogs could surely have come in wherever there was room for the larger ones. This "whosoever" is the great opening, suitable for sinners of every size. "Whosoever liveth and believeth in me shall never die." Has any man a right to believe in Christ? The gospel gives every creature the right to believe in Christ, for we are bidden to preach it to every creature, with this command, "Hear, and your soul shall live." Every man has a right to believe in Christ, because he will be damned if he does not, and he must have a right to do that which will bring him into condemnation if he does it not. It is written, "He that believeth and is bap-

where the body of Jesus had lain.

13 And they say unto her, Woman, why weepest thou? She saith unto them, Because they have taken away my Lord, and I know not where they have laid him.

14 And when she had thus said, she turned herself back, and saw Jesus standing, and knew not that it was Jesus.

15 Jesus saith unto her, Woman, why weepest thou? whom seekest thou? She, supposing him to be the gardener, saith unto him, Sir, if thou have borne him hence, tell me where thou hast laid him, and I will take him away.

16 Jesus saith unto her, Mary. She turned herself, and saith unto him, Rabboni; which is to say, Master.

17 Jesus saith unto her, Touch me not; for I am not yet ascended to my Father: but go to my brethren, and say unto them, I ascend unto my Father, and your Father; and to my God, and your God.

18 Mary Magdalene came and told the disciples that she had seen the Lord, and that he had spoken these things unto her.

19 Then the same day at evening, being the first day of the week, when the doors were shut where the disciples were assembled for fear of the Jews, came Jesus and stood in the midst, and saith unto them, Peace be unto you.

20 And when he had so said, he shewed unto them his hands and his side. Then were the disciples glad, when they saw the Lord.

21 Then said Jesus to them again, Peace be unto you: as my Father hath sent me, even so send I you.

22 And when he had said this, he breathed on them, and saith unto them, Receive ye the Holy Ghost:

23 Whose soever sins ye remit, they are remitted unto them; and whose soever sins ye retain, they are retained.

24 But Thomas, one of the twelve, called Didymus, was not with them when Jesus came.

25 The other disciples therefore said unto him, We have seen the Lord. But he said unto them, Except I shall see in his hands the print of the nails, and put my finger into the print of the nails, and thrust my hand into his side, I will not believe.

26 And after eight days again his disciples were within, and Thomas with them: then came Jesus, the doors being shut, and stood in the midst, and said, Peace be unto you.

27 Then saith he to Thomas, reach hither thy finger, and behold my hands; and reach hither thy hand, and thrust it into my side: and be not faithless, but believing.

28 And Thomas answered and said unto him, My Lord and my God.

29 Jesus saith unto him, Thomas, because thou hast seen me, thou hast believed: blessed are they that have not seen, and yet have believed.

30 And many other signs truly did Jesus in the

The angels who ministered to him when he rose, undoubtedly folded up the napkin and linen clothes.

8. He saw – That the body was not there, and believed – That they had taken it away as Mary said.

9. For as yet – They had no thought of his rising again.

10. They went home – Not seeing what they could do farther.

11. But Mary stood – With more constancy. Mark xvi, 9.

16. Jesus saith to her, Mary – With his usual voice and accent.

17. Touch me not – Or rather, Do not cling to me (for she held him by the feet,) Matt. xxviii, 9. Detain me not now. You will have other opportunities of conversing with me. For I am not ascended to my Father – I have not yet left the world. But go immediately to my brethren – Thus does he intimate in the strongest manner the forgiveness of their fault, even without ever mentioning it. These exquisite touches, which every where abound in the evangelical writings, show how perfectly Christ knew our frame. I ascend – He anticipates it in his thoughts, and so speaks of it as a thing already present. To my Father and your Father, to my God and your God – This uncommon expression shows that the only-begotten Son has all kind of fellowship with God. And a fellowship with God the Father, some way resembling his own, he bestows upon his brethren. Yet he does not say, Our God: for no creature can be raised to an equality with him: but my God and your God: intimating that the Father is his in a singular and incommunicable manner; and ours through him, in such a kind as a creature is capable of.

19. Mark xvi, 14 Luke xxiv, 36.

21. Peace be unto you – This is the foundation of the mission of a true Gospel minister, peace in his own soul, 2 Cor. iv, 1. As the Father hath sent me, so send I you – Christ was the apostle of the Father, Heb. iii, 1. Peter and the rest, the apostles of Christ.

22. He breathed on them – New life and vigor, and saith, as ye receive this breath out of my mouth, so receive ye the Spirit out of my fullness: the Holy Ghost influencing you in a peculiar manner, to fit you for your great embassy. This was an earnest of Pentecost.

23. Whose soever sins ye remit – (According to the tenor of the Gospel, that is, supposing them to repent and believe) they are remitted, and whose soever sins ye retain (supposing them to remain impenitent) they are retained. So far is plain. But here arises a difficulty. Are not the sins of one who truly repents, and unfeignedly believes in Christ, remitted, without sacerdotal absolution? And are not the sins of one who does not repent or believe, retained even with it? What then does this commission imply? Can it imply any more than,

1. A power of declaring with authority the Christian terms of pardon; whose sins are remitted and whose retained? As in our daily form of absolution; and

2. A power of inflicting and remitting ecclesiastical censures? That is, of excluding from, and re-admitting into, a Christian congregation.

26. After eight days – On the next Sunday.

28. And Thomas said, My Lord and my God – The disciples had said, We have seen the Lord. Thomas now not only acknowledges him to be the Lord, as he had done before, and to be risen, as his fellow disciples had affirmed, but also confesses his Godhead, and that more explicitly than any other had yet done. And all this he

will gladden the heart of a disciple at any time; and the more we see of Jesus, the more we shall rejoice. He said, Receive ye the Holy Ghost, thus showing that their spiritual life, as well as all their ability for their work, would be derived from him, and depended upon him.

26-29 That one day in seven should be religiously observed, was an appointment from the beginning. And that, in the kingdom of the Messiah, the first day of the week should be that solemn day, was pointed out, in that Christ on that day once and again met his disciples in a religious assembly. The religious observance of that day has come down to us through every age of the church. There is not an unbelieving word in our tongues, nor thought in our minds, but it is known to the Lord Jesus; and he was pleased to accommodate himself even to Thomas, rather than leave him in his unbelief. We ought thus to bear with the weak, Ro 15:1,2. This warning is given to all. If we are faithless, we are Christless and graceless, hopeless and joyless. Thomas was ashamed of his unbelief, and cried out, My Lord and my God. He spoke with affection, as one that took hold of Christ with all his might; "My Lord and my God." Sound and sincere believers, though slow and weak, shall be graciously accepted of the Lord Jesus. It is the duty of those who read and hear the gospel, to believe, to embrace the doctrine of Christ, and that record concerning him, 1Jo 5:11.

30,31 There were other signs and proofs of our Lord's resurrection, but these were committed to writing, that all might believe that Jesus was the promised Messiah, the Savior of sinners, and the Son of God; that, by this faith, they might obtain eternal life, by his mercy, truth, and power. May we believe that Jesus is the Christ, and believing may we have life through his name.

JOHN 21

Christ appears to his disciples. (1-14)
His discourse with Peter. (15-19)
Christ's declaration concerning John. (20-24)
The conclusion. (25)

1-14 Christ makes himself known to his people, usually in his ordinances; but sometimes by his Spirit he visits them when employed in their business. It is good for the disciples of Christ to be together in common conversation, and common business. The hour for their entering upon action was not come. They would help to maintain themselves, and not be burdensome to any. Christ's time of making himself known to his people, is when they are most at a loss. He knows the temporal wants of his people, and has promised them not only grace sufficient, but food convenient. Divine Providence extends itself to things most minute, and

tized shall be saved; but he that believeth not shall be damned," and that makes it clear that I, whoever I may be, as I have a right to endeavor to escape from damnation, have a right to avail myself of the blessed command, "Believe in the Lord Jesus Christ, and live." Oh that "whosoever," that hole in the door for the big dog! Do not forget it! Come along with you, and put your trust in Christ. If you can only get linked with Christ you are a living man; if but a finger touches his garment's hem you are made whole. Only the touch of faith, and the virtue flows from him to you, and he is to you the resurrection and the life.

I desire you to notice that there is no limit to this power. Before I was ill this time, and even since, I have had to deal with such a swarm of despairing sinners, that if I have not pulled them up they have pulled me down. I have been trying to speak very large words for Christ when I have met with those disconsolate ones. I hear one say, "How far can Christ be life to a sinner? I feel myself to be utterly wrong, I am altogether wrong; there is nothing right about me: though I have eyes I cannot see, though I have ears I do not hear; if I have a hand I cannot use it, if I have a foot I cannot run with it—I seem altogether wrong." Yes, but if you believe in Christ, though you were still more wrong—that is to say, though you were dead, which is the wrongest state in which a man's body can be,—though you were dead yet shall you live. You look at the spiritual thermometer, and you say, "How low will the grace of God go? will it descend to summer heat? will it touch the freezing point? will it go to zero?" Yes, it will go below the lowest conceivable point,—lower than any instrument can indicate: it will go below the zero of death. If you believe in Jesus, though you are not only wrong, but dead, yet shall you live.

But, says another, "I feel so weak. I cannot understand, I cannot lay hold of things; I cannot pray. I cannot do anything. All I can do is feebly to trust in Jesus." All right! Though you had gone further than that, and were so weak as to be dead, yet should you live. Though the weakness had turned to a dire paralysis, that left you altogether without strength, yet it is written, "He that believeth in me, though he were dead, yet shall he live." "Oh, Sir," says one, "I am so unfeeling." Mark you, these generally are the most feeling people in the world. "I am sorry every day because I cannot be sorry for my sin"—that is the way they talk; it is very absurd, but still very real to them. "Oh," cries one, "the earth shook, the sun was darkened, the rocks rent, the very dead came out of their graves at the death of Christ.

presence of his disciples, which are not written in this book:

31 But these are written, that ye might believe that Jesus is the Christ, the Son of God; and that believing ye might have life through his name.

JOHN 21

1 After these things Jesus shewed himself again to the disciples at the sea of Tiberias; and on this wise shewed he himself.

2 There were together Simon Peter, and Thomas called Didymus, and Nathanael of Cana in Galilee, and the sons of Zebedee, and two other of his disciples.

3 Simon Peter saith unto them, I go a fishing. They say unto him, We also go with thee. They went forth, and entered into a ship immediately; and that night they caught nothing.

4 But when the morning was now come, Jesus stood on the shore: but the disciples knew not that it was Jesus.

5 Then Jesus saith unto them, Children, have ye any meat? They answered him, No.

6 And he said unto them, Cast the net on the right side of the ship, and ye shall find. They cast therefore, and now they were not able to draw it for the multitude of fishes.

7 Therefore that disciple whom Jesus loved saith unto Peter, It is the Lord. Now when Simon Peter heard that it was the Lord, he girt his fisher's coat unto him, (for he was naked,) and did cast himself into the sea.

8 And the other disciples came in a little ship; (for they were not far from land, but as it were two hundred cubits,) dragging the net with fishes.

9 As soon then as they were come to land, they saw a fire of coals there, and fish laid thereon, and bread.

10 Jesus saith unto them, Bring of the fish which ye have now caught.

11 Simon Peter went up, and drew the net to land full of great fishes, an hundred and fifty and three: and for all there were so many, yet was not the net broken.

12 Jesus saith unto them, Come and dine. And none of the disciples durst ask him, Who art thou? knowing that it was the Lord.

13 Jesus then cometh, and taketh bread, and giveth them, and fish likewise.

14 This is now the third time that Jesus shewed himself to his disciples, after that he was risen from the dead.

15 So when they had dined, Jesus saith to Simon Peter, Simon, son of Jonas, lovest thou me more than these? He saith unto him, Yea, Lord; thou knowest that I love thee. He saith unto him, Feed my lambs.

16 He saith to him again the second time, Simon, son of Jonas, lovest thou me? He saith unto him, Yea, Lord; thou knowest that I love thee. He saith unto him, Feed my sheep.

did without putting his hand upon his side.

30. Jesus wrought many miracles, which are not written in this book – Of St. John, nor indeed of the other evangelists.

31. But these things are written that ye may believe – That ye may be confirmed in believing. Faith cometh sometimes by reading; though ordinarily by hearing.

JOHN 21

2. There were together – At home, in one house.

4. They knew not that it was Jesus – Probably their eyes were holden.

6. They were not able to draw it for the multitude of fishes – This was not only a demonstration of the power of our Lord, but a kind supply for them and their families, and such as might be of service to them, when they waited afterward in Jerusalem. It was likewise an emblem of the great success which should attend them as fishers of men.

7. Peter girt on his upper coat (for he was stript of it before) – Reverencing the presence of his Lord: and threw himself into the sea – To swim to him immediately. The love of Christ draws men through fire and water.

12. Come ye and dine – Our Lord needed not food. And none presumed – To ask a needless question.

14. The third time – That he appeared to so many of the apostles together.

15. Simon, son of Jonah – The appellation Christ had given him, when be made that glorious confession, Matt. xvi, 16, the remembrance of which might make him more deeply sensible of his late denial of him whom he had so confessed. Lovest thou me? – Thrice our Lord asks him, who had denied him thrice: more than these – Thy fellow disciples do? – Peter thought so once, Matt. xxvi, 33, but he now answers only – I love thee, without adding more than these. Thou knowest – He had now learnt by sad experience that Jesus knew his heart. My lambs – The weakest and tenderest of the flock.

17. Because he said the third time – As if he did not believe him.

18. When thou art old – He lived about thirty-six years after this: another shall gird thee – They were tied to the cross till the nails were driven in; and shall carry thee – With the cross: whither thou wouldest not – According to nature; to the place where the cross was set up.

19. By what death he should glorify God – It is not only by acting, but chiefly by suffering, that the saints glorify God. Follow me – Showing hereby likewise what death he should die.

20. Peter turning – As he was walking after Christ. Seeth the disciple whom Jesus loved following him – There is a peculiar spirit and tenderness in this plain passage. Christ orders St. Peter to follow him in token of his readiness to be crucified in his cause. St. John stays not for the call; he rises and follows him too; but says not one word of his own love or zeal. He chose that the action only should speak this; and even when he records the circumstance, he tells us not what that action meant, but with great simplicity relates the fact only. If here and there a generous heart sees and emulates it, be it so; but he is not solicitous that men should admire it. It was addressed to his beloved Master, and it was enough that he

MATTHEW HENRY

CHARLES H. SPURGEON

those are happy who acknowledge God in all their ways. Those who are humble, diligent, and patient, though their labors may be crossed, shall be crowned; they sometimes live to see their affairs take a happy turn, after many struggles. And there is nothing lost by observing Christ's orders; it is casting the net on the right side of the ship. Jesus manifests himself to his people by doing that for them which none else can do, and things which they looked not for. He would take care that those who left all for him, should not want any good thing. And latter favors are to bring to mind former favors, that eaten bread may not be forgotten. He whom Jesus loved was the first that said, It is the Lord. John had cleaved most closely to his Master in his sufferings, and knew him soonest. Peter was the most zealous, and reached Christ the first. How variously God dispenses his gifts, and what difference there may be between some believers and others in the way of their honoring Christ, yet they all may be accepted of him! Others continue in the ship, drag the net, and bring the fish to shore, and such persons ought not to be blamed as worldly; for they, in their places, are as truly serving Christ as the others. The Lord Jesus had provision ready for them. We need not be curious in inquiring whence this came; but we may be comforted at Christ's care for his disciples. Although there were so many, and such great fishes, yet they lost none, nor damaged their net. The net of the gospel has enclosed multitudes, yet it is as strong as ever to bring souls to God.

15-19 Our Lord addressed Peter by his original name, as if he had forfeited that of Peter through his denying him. He now answered, Thou knowest that I love thee; but without professing to love Jesus more than others. We must not be surprised to have our sincerity called into question, when we ourselves have done that which makes it doubtful. Every remembrance of past sins, even pardoned sins, renews the sorrow of a true penitent. Conscious of integrity, Peter solemnly appealed to Christ, as knowing all things, even the secrets of his heart. It is well when our falls and mistakes make us more humble and watchful. The sincerity of our love to God must be brought to the test; and it behoves us to inquire with earnest, preserving prayer to the heart-searching God, to examine and prove us, whether we are able to stand this test. No one can be qualified to feed the sheep and lambs of Christ, who does not love the good Shepherd more than any earthly advantage or object. It is the great concern of every good man, whatever death he dies, to glorify God in it; for what is our chief end but this, to die to the Lord, at the word of the Lord?

20-24 Sufferings, pains, and death, will appear formidable even to the experienced Christian; but in the hope to glorify God, to leave a sinful world, and to be present with his Lord, he becomes ready to obey the Redeemer's call, and to follow him through death to

"Of feeling all things show some sign
But this unfeeling heart of mine."

Yet if thou believest, unfeeling as thou art, thou livest; for if thou wert gone further than numb-ness to deadness, yet if thou believest in him thou shalt live.

But the poor creature fetches a sigh, and cries, "Sir, it is not only that I have no feeling, but I am become objectionable and obnoxious to everybody. I am a weariness to myself and to others. I am sure when I come to tell you my troubles you must wish me at Jericho, or somewhere else far away." Now, I admit that such a thought has occurred to us sometimes when we have been very busy, and some poor soul has grown prosy with rehearsing his seven-times-repeated miseries; but if you were to get more wearisome still, if you were to become so bad that people would as soon see a corpse as see you, yet remember Jesus says, "He that believeth in me, though he were dead, yet shall he live."

"Oh, sir, I have no hope; my case is quite hopeless!" Very well; but if you had got beyond that, so that you were dead, and could not even know you had no hope, yet if you believed in him you should live. "Oh, but I have tried everything, and there is nothing more for me to attempt. I have read books, I have spoken to Christians, and I am nothing bettered." No doubt it is quite so; but if you had even passed beyond that stage, so that you could not try anything more, yet if you did believe in Jesus you should live. Oh, the blessed power of faith! Nay, rather say the matchless power of him who is the resurrection and the life; for though the poor believer were dead, yet shall he live! Glory be to the Lord who works so wonderfully.

To conclude, if you once do believe in Christ, and come to live, there is this sweet reflection for you, "Whosoever liveth and believeth in me shall never die." Our Arminian friends say that you may be a child of God today and a child of the devil tomorrow. Write out that statement, and place at the bottom of it the name "Arminius," and then put the scrap of paper into the fire: it is the best thing you can do with it, for there is no truth in it. Jesus says, "Whosoever liveth and believeth in me shall never die." Here is a very literal translation—"And every one who lives and believes on me, in no wise shall die forever." This is from "The Englishman's Greek New Testament," and nothing can be better. The believer may pass through the natural change called death, as far as his body is concerned; but as for his soul it cannot die, for it is written, "I give unto my sheep eternal life; and they shall never perish,

17 He saith unto him the third time, Simon, son of Jonas, lovest thou me? Peter was grieved because he said unto him the third time, Lovest thou me? And he said unto him, Lord, thou knowest all things; thou knowest that I love thee. Jesus saith unto him, Feed my sheep.

18 Verily, verily, I say unto thee, When thou wast young, thou girdedst thyself, and walkedst whither thou wouldest: but when thou shalt be old, thou shalt stretch forth thy hands, and another shall gird thee, and carry thee whither thou wouldest not.

19 This spake he, signifying by what death he should glorify God. And when he had spoken this, he saith unto him, Follow me.

20 Then Peter, turning about, seeth the disciple whom Jesus loved following; which also leaned on his breast at supper, and said, Lord, which is he that betrayeth thee?

21 Peter seeing him saith to Jesus, Lord, and what shall this man do?

22 Jesus saith unto him, If I will that he tarry till I come, what is that to thee? follow thou me.

23 Then went this saying abroad among the brethren, that that disciple should not die: yet Jesus said not unto him, He shall not die; but, If I will that he tarry till I come, what is that to thee?

24 This is the disciple which testifieth of these things, and wrote these things: and we know that his testimony is true.

25 And there are also many other things which Jesus did, the which, if they should be written every one, I suppose that even the world itself could not contain the books that should be written. Amen.

understood it.

22. If I will that he tarry – Without dying, till I come – To judgment. Certainly he did tarry, till Christ came to destroy Jerusalem. And who can tell, when or how he died? What is that to thee? – Who art to follow me long before.

23. The brethren – That is, the Christians. Our Lord himself taught them that appellation, chap. xx, 17. Yet Jesus did not say to him, that he should not die – Not expressly. And St. John himself, at the time of writing his Gospel, seems not to have known clearly, whether he should die or not.

24. This is the disciple who testifieth – Being still alive after he had wrote. And we know that his testimony is true – The Church added these words to St. John's Gospel, as Tertius did those to St. Paul's Epistle to the Romans, Rom. xvi, 22.

25. If they were to be written particularly – Every fact, and all the circumstances of it. I suppose – This expression, which softens the hyperbole, shows that St. John wrote this verse.

glory. It is the will of Christ that his disciples should mind their own duty, and not be curious about future events, either as to themselves or others. Many things we are apt to be anxious about, which are nothing to us. Other people's affairs are nothing to us, to intermeddle in; we must quietly work, and mind our own business. Many curious questions are put about the counsels of God, and the state of the unseen world, as to which we may say, What is this to us? And if we attend to the duty of following Christ, we shall find neither heart nor time to meddle with that which does not belong to us. How little are any unwritten traditions to be relied upon! Let the Scripture be its own interpreter, and explain itself; as it is, in a great measure, its own evidence, and proves itself, for it is light. See the easy setting right such mistakes by the word of Christ. Scripture language is the safest channel for Scripture truth; the words which the Holy Ghost teaches, 1 Co 2:13. Those who cannot agree in the same terms of art, and the application of them, may yet agree in the same Scripture terms, and to love one another.

25 Only a small part of the actions of Jesus had been written. But let us bless God for all that is in the Scriptures, and be thankful that there is so much in so small a space. Enough is recorded to direct our faith, and regulate our practice; more would have been unnecessary. Much of what is written is overlooked, much forgotten, and much made the matter of doubtful disputes. We may, however, look forward to the joy we shall receive in heaven, from a more complete knowledge of all Jesus did and said, as well as of the conduct of his providence and grace in his dealings with each of us. May this be our happiness. These are written that ye might believe that Jesus is the Christ, the Son of God; and that believing ye might have life through his name, ch. 20:31.

neither shall any man pluck them out of my hand." "He that believeth in me hath everlasting life." "The water that I shall give him shall be in him a well of water springing up into everlasting life." "He that believeth and is baptized shall be saved." These are not "ifs" and "buts," and faint hopes; but they are dead certainties, nay, living certainties, out of the mouth of the living Lord himself. You get the life of God in your soul, and you shall never die. "Do you mean that I may do as I like, and live in sin?" No, man, I mean nothing of the sort; what right have you to impute such teaching as that to me? I mean that you shall not love sin and live in it, for that is death; but you shall live unto God. Your likes shall be so radically changed that you shall abhor evil all your days, and long to be holy as God is holy; and you shall be kept from transgression, and shall not go back to wallow in sin. If in some evil hour you back-slide, yet shall you be restored; and the main current of your life shall be from the hour of your regeneration towards God, and holiness, and heaven. The angels that rejoiced over you when you repented made no mistake; they shall go on to rejoice till they welcome you amidst the everlasting songs and Hallelujahs of the blessed at the right hand of God. Believest thou this? Come, poor soul, believest thou this? Who are you? That does not matter, you can get into the "whosoever." That ark will hold all God's Noahs. What is any man that he should have the filth of another man's drains poured into his ear? No, no: confess to God, but not to man unless you have wronged him, and confession of the wrong is due to him.

"Ah," saith one, "you don't know what I am." No, and I don't want to know what you are; but if you are so far gone that there seems to be not even a ghost of a shade of a shadow of a hope anywhere about you, yet if you believe in Jesus you shall live. Trust the Lord Jesus Christ, for he is worthy to be trusted. Throw yourself upon him, and he will carry you in his bosom. Cast your whole weight upon his atonement; it will bear the strain. Hang on him as the vessel hangs on the nail, and seek no other support. Depend upon Christ with all your might just as you now are, and as the Lord liveth you shall live, and as Christ reigneth you shall reign over sin, and as Christ cometh to glory you shall partake of that glory for ever and ever. Amen.

Acts

ACTS 1

1 The former treatise have I made, O Theophilus, of all that Jesus began both to do and teach,

2 Until the day in which he was taken up, after that he through the Holy Ghost had given commandments unto the apostles whom he had chosen:

3 To whom also he shewed himself alive after his passion by many infallible proofs, being seen of them forty days, and speaking of the things pertaining to the kingdom of God:

4 And, being assembled together with them, commanded them that they should not depart from Jerusalem, but wait for the promise of the Father, which, saith he, ye have heard of me.

5 For John truly baptized with water; but ye shall be baptized with the Holy Ghost not many days hence.

6 When they therefore were come together, they asked of him, saying, Lord, wilt thou at this time restore again the kingdom to Israel?

7 And he said unto them, It is not for you to know the times or the seasons, which the Father hath put in his own power.

8 But ye shall receive power, after that the Holy Ghost is come upon you: and ye shall be witnesses unto me both in Jerusalem, and in all Judea, and in Samaria, and unto the uttermost part of the earth.

9 And when he had spoken these things, while they beheld, he was taken up; and a cloud received him out of their sight.

10 And while they looked stedfastly toward heaven as he went up, behold, two men stood by them in white apparel;

11 Which also said, Ye men of Galilee, why stand ye gazing up into heaven? this same Jesus, which is taken up from you into heaven, shall so come in like manner as ye have seen him go into heaven.

12 Then returned they unto Jerusalem from the mount called Olivet, which is from Jerusalem a sabbath day's journey.

13 And when they were come in, they went up into an upper room, where abode both Peter, and James, and John, and Andrew, Philip, and Thomas, Bartholomew, and Matthew, James the son of Alpheus, and Simon Zelotes, and Judas the brother of James.

14 These all continued with one accord in prayer and supplication, with the women, and Mary the mother of Jesus, and with his brethren.

15 And in those days Peter stood up in the midst of the disciples, and said, (the number of names together were about an hundred and twenty,)

16 Men and brethren, this scripture must needs have been fulfilled, which the Holy Ghost by the mouth of David spake before concerning Judas, which was guide to them that took Jesus.

THIS book, in which St. Luke records the actions of the apostles, particularly of St. Peter and St. Paul, (whose companion in travel he was,) is as it were the center between the Gospel and the Epistles. It contains, after a very brief recapitulation of the evangelical history, a continuation of the history of Christ, the event of his predictions, and a kind of supplement to what he had before spoken to his disciples, by the Holy Ghost now given unto them. It contains also the seeds, and first stamina of all those things, which are enlarged upon in the epistles. The Gospels treat of Christ the head. The Acts show that the same things befell his body; which is animated by his Spirit, persecuted by the world, defended and exalted by God. In this book is shown the Christian doctrine, and the method of applying it to Jews, heathens, and believers; that is, to those who are to be converted, and those who are converted: the hindrances of it in particular men, in several kinds of men, in different ranks and nations: the propagation of the Gospel, and that grand revolution among both Jews and heathens: the victory thereof, in spite of all opposition, from all the power, malice, and wisdom of the whole world, spreading from one chamber into temples, houses, streets, markets, fields, inns, prisons, camps, courts, chariots, ships, villages, cities, islands: to Jews, heathens, magistrates, generals, soldiers, eunuchs, captives, slaves, women, children, sailors: to Athens, and at length to Rome.

ACTS 1

1. The former treatise – In that important season which reached from the resurrection of Christ to his ascension, the former treatise ends, and this begins: this describing the Acts of the Holy Ghost, (by the apostles,) as that does the acts of Jesus Christ. Of all things – In a summary manner: which Jesus began to do – until the day – That is, of all things which Jesus did from the beginning till that day.

2. After having given commandment – In the 3rd verse St. Luke expresses in general terms what Christ said to his apostles during those forty days. But in the 4th and following verses he declares what he said on the day of his ascension. He had brought his former account down to that day; and from that day begins the Acts of the Apostles.

3. Being seen by them forty days – That is, many times during that space. And speaking of the things pertaining to the kingdom of God – Which was the sum of all his discourses with them before his passion also.

4. Wait for the promise of the Father, which ye have heard from me – When he was with them a little before, as it is recorded, Luke xxiv, 49.

5. Ye shall be baptized with the Holy Ghost – And so are all true believers to the end of the world. But the extraordinary gifts of the Holy Ghost also are here promised.

6. Dost thou at this time – At the time thou now speakest of? not many days hence? restore the kingdom to Israel? – They still seemed to dream of an outward, temporal kingdom, in which the Jews should have dominion over all nations. It seems they came in a body, having before concerted the design, to ask when this kingdom would come.

7. The times or the seasons – Times, in the language of the Scriptures, denote a longer; seasons, a shorter space. Which the Father hath put in his own power – To be revealed when and to whom it pleaseth him.

MATTHEW HENRY   CHARLES H. SPURGEON

This book unites the Gospels to the Epistles. It contains many particulars concerning the apostles Peter and Paul, and of the Christian church from the ascension of our Savior to the arrival of St. Paul at Rome, a space of about thirty years. St. Luke was the writer of this book; he was present at many of the events he relates, and attended Paul to Rome. But the narrative does not afford a complete history of the church during the time to which it refers, nor even of St. Paul's life. The object of the book has been considered to be, 1. To relate in what manner the gifts of the Holy Spirit were communicated on the day of Pentecost, and the miracles performed by the apostles, to confirm the truth of Christianity, as showing that Christ's declarations were really fulfilled. 2. To prove the claim of the Gentiles to be admitted into the church of Christ. This is shown by much of the contents of the book. A large portion of the Acts is occupied by the discourses or sermons of various persons, the language and manner of which differ, and all of which will be found according to the persons by whom they were delivered, and the occasions on which they were spoken. It seems that most of these discourses are only the substance of what was actually delivered. They relate nevertheless fully to Jesus as the Christ, the anointed Messiah.

ACTS 1

Proofs of Christ's resurrection. (1-5)
Christ's ascension. (6-11)
The apostles unite in prayer. (12-14)
Matthias chosen in the place of Judas. (15-26)

1-5 Our Lord told the disciples the work they were to do. The apostles met together at Jerusalem; Christ having ordered them not to depart thence, but to wait for the pouring out of the Holy Spirit. This would be a baptism by the Holy Ghost, giving them power to work miracles, and enlightening and sanctifying their souls. This confirms the Divine promise, and encourages us to depend upon it, that we have heard it from Christ; for in Him all the promises of God are yea and amen.

6-11 They were earnest in asking about that which their Master never had directed or encouraged them to seek. Our Lord knew that his ascension and the teaching of the Holy Spirit would soon end these expectations, and therefore only gave them a rebuke; but it is a caution to his church in all ages, to take heed of a desire of forbidden knowledge. He had given his disciples instructions for the discharge of their duty, both before his death and since his resurrection, and this knowledge is enough for a Christian. It is enough that He has engaged to give believers strength equal to their

WITNESSING BETTER THAN KNOWING THE FUTURE
Sermon number 2330 delivered at the Metropolitan Tabernacle, Newington on Thursday Evening, August 29th, 1889.

"When they therefore were come together, they asked of him, saying, Lord, wilt thou at this time restore again the kingdom to Israel? And he said unto them, It is not for you to know the times or the seasons, which the Father hath put in his own power. But ye shall receive power, after that the Holy Ghost is come upon you: and ye shall be witnesses unto me both in Jerusalem, and in all Judea, and in Samaria, and unto the uttermost part of the earth."—Acts 1:6-8.

THESE ARE AMONG THE LAST WORDS of our Lord. We greatly prize the last words of good men. Let us set high store by these later words of our ascending Lord. It is very curious to my mind that Jesus should make mention of John the Baptist and of John's baptism in these last words. Read the fifth verse: "John truly baptized with water; but ye shall be baptized with the Holy Ghost not many days hence." It is very usual for good men's memories, in their last hours, to go back to their first hours. I trust that some of us will think of our baptism even when we are dying.

"High heaven, that heard the solemn vow,
That vow renew'd shall daily hear;
Till in life's latest hour I bow,
And bless in death a bond so dear."

Our Lord began in such a way that he could afford to look back on his beginning. Some do not commence so; their beginning is so undecided, so imperfect, so hesitating, that they may well wish to have it forgotten. But our Lord, at the close of his sojourn on earth, thinks of John the Baptist, and pays him a dying word of respect just before he is taken up into glory. I like to notice that interesting fact.

But, now, to come more to the text, a question was put to our Lord. Many questions were asked of him by his disciples, some of them not very wise ones. We are very glad that they asked them, for they have extracted from the Savior a great amount of instruction; and although this question about restoring the kingdom to Israel may have been a mistaken one, and they may have meant a more material and carnal kingdom than our Savior intended to establish (of that I am not sure), yet the question brought to us a reply which we may well store up in our memories and hearts: "It is not for you to know the times or the seasons, which the Father hath put in his own power. But ye shall receive power after that the Holy Ghost is come upon you: and ye shall be witnesses unto me both in Jerusalem, and in all Judea, and in Samaria, and

17 For he was numbered with us, and had obtained part of this ministry.

18 Now this man purchased a field with the reward of iniquity; and falling headlong, he burst asunder in the midst, and all his bowels gushed out.

19 And it was known unto all the dwellers at Jerusalem; insomuch as that field is called in their proper tongue, Aceldama, that is to say, The field of blood.

20 For it is written in the book of Psalms, Let his habitation be desolate, and let no man dwell therein: and his bishoprick let another take.

21 Wherefore of these men which have companied with us all the time that the Lord Jesus went in and out among us,

22 Beginning from the baptism of John, unto that same day that he was taken up from us, must one be ordained to be a witness with us of his resurrection.

23 And they appointed two, Joseph called Barsabas, who was surnamed Justus, and Matthias.

24 And they prayed, and said, Thou, Lord, which knowest the hearts of all men, shew whether of these two thou hast chosen,

25 That he may take part of this ministry and apostleship, from which Judas by transgression fell, that he might go to his own place.

26 And they gave forth their lots; and the lot fell upon Matthias; and he was numbered with the eleven apostles.

ACTS 2

1 And when the day of Pentecost was fully come, they were all with one accord in one place.

2 And suddenly there came a sound from heaven as of a rushing mighty wind, and it filled all the house where they were sitting.

3 And there appeared unto them cloven tongues like as of fire, and it sat upon each of them.

4 And they were all filled with the Holy Ghost, and began to speak with other tongues, as the Spirit gave them utterance.

5 And there were dwelling at Jerusalem Jews, devout men, out of every nation under heaven.

6 Now when this was noised abroad, the multitude came together, and were confounded, because that every man heard them speak in his own language.

7 And they were all amazed and marveled, saying one to another, Behold, are not all these which speak Galileans?

8 And how hear we every man in our own tongue, wherein we were born?

9 Parthians, and Medes, and Elamites, and the dwellers in Mesopotamia, and in Judea, and Cappadocia, in Pontus, and Asia,

10 Phrygia, and Pamphylia, in Egypt, and in

8. But ye shall receive power – and shall be witnesses to me – That is, ye shall be empowered to witness my Gospel, both by your preaching and suffering.

12. A Sabbath-day's journey – The Jews generally fix this to two thousand cubits, which is not a mile.

13. They went up into the upper room – The upper rooms, so frequently mentioned in Scripture, were chambers in the highest part of the house, set apart by the Jews for private prayer. These, on account of their being so retired and convenient, the apostles now used for all the offices of religion. Matt. x, 2; Mark iii, 14; Luke vi, 13.

14. His brethren – His near kinsmen, who for some time did not believe; it seems not till near his death.

15. The number of persons together – Who were together in the upper room were a hundred and twenty – But he had undoubtedly many more in other places; of whom more than five hundred saw him at once after his resurrection, 1 Cor. xv, 6.

16. Psalm xli, 9.

18. This man purchased a field with the reward of iniquity – That is, a field was purchased with the reward of his iniquity; though very possibly Judas might design the purchase. And falling down on his face – It seems the rope broke before, or as he died.

19. In their own tongue – This expression, That is, the field of blood, St. Luke seems to have added to the words of St. Peter, for the use of Theophilus and other readers who did not understand Hebrew.

20. His bishopric – That is, his apostleship. Psalm lxix, 25.

21. All the time that the Lord Jesus was going in and out – That is, conversing familiarly: over us – as our Master. Psalm cix, 8.

22. To be a witness with us of his resurrection – And of the circumstances which preceded and followed it.

23. And they appointed two – So far the faithful could go by consulting together, but no further. Therefore here commenced the proper use of the lot, whereby a matter of importance, which cannot be determined by any ordinary method, is committed to the Divine decision.

25. Fell – By his transgression – Some time before his death: to go to his own place – That which his crimes had deserved, and which he had chosen for himself, far from the other apostles, in the region of death.

ACTS 2

1. At the Pentecost of Sinai, in the Old Testament, and the Pentecost of Jerusalem, in the New, where the two grand manifestations of God, the legal and the evangelical; the one from the mountain, and the other from heaven; the terrible, and the merciful one. They were all with one accord in one place – So here was a conjunction of company, minds, and place; the whole hundred and twenty being present.

2. And suddenly there came a sound from heaven – So will the Son of man come to judgment. And it filled all the house – That is, all that part of the temple where they were sitting.

3. And there appeared distinct tongues, as of fire – That is, small flames of fire. This is all which the phrase, tongues of fire, means in the language of the seventy. Yet it might intimate God's touching their tongues as it were (together with their hearts) with Divine fire: his giving them such words as were active and penetrating, even as

trials and services; that under the influence of the Holy Spirit they may, in one way or other, be witnesses for Christ on earth, while in heaven he manages their concerns with perfect wisdom, truth, and love. When we stand gazing and trifling, the thoughts of our Master's second coming should quicken and awaken us: when we stand gazing and trembling, they should comfort and encourage us. May our expectation of it be steadfast and joyful, giving diligence to be found of him blameless.

12-14 God can find hiding-places for his people. They made supplication. All God's people are praying people. It was now a time of trouble and danger with the disciples of Christ; but if any is afflicted, let him pray; that will silence cares and fears. They had now a great work to do, and before they entered upon it, they were earnest in prayer to God for his presence. They were waiting for the descent of the Spirit, and abounded in prayer. Those are in the best frame to receive spiritual blessings, who are in a praying frame. Christ had promised shortly to send the Holy Ghost; that promise was not to do away prayer, but to quicken and encourage it. A little company united in love, exemplary in their conduct, fervent in prayer, and wisely zealous to promote the cause of Christ, are likely to increase rapidly.

15-26 The great thing the apostles were to attest to the world, was, Christ's resurrection; for that was the great proof of his being the Messiah, and the foundation of our hope in him. The apostles were ordained, not to worldly dignity and dominion, but to preach Christ, and the power of his resurrection. An appeal was made to God; "Thou, Lord, who knowest the hearts of all men," which we do not; and better than they know their own. It is fit that God should choose his own servants; and so far as he, by the disposals of his providence, or the gifts of his Spirit, shows whom he has chosen, or what he has chosen for us, we ought to fall in with his will. Let us own his hand in the determining everything which befalls us, especially in those by which any trust may be committed to us.

ACTS 2

The descent of the Holy Spirit at the day of Pentecost. (1-4)
The apostles speak in divers languages. (5-13)
Peter's address to the Jews. (14-36)
Three thousand souls converted. (37-41)
The piety and affection of the disciples. (42-47)

1-4 We cannot forget how often, while their Master was with them there were strifes among the disci-

unto the uttermost part of the earth."

We have three things to talk about tonight; first, some things which are not for us; secondly, some things for us to receive; and thirdly, something for us to be.

I. First, then, let us consider SOME THINGS WHICH ARE NOT FOR US. It is not for us to know the times and the seasons, and to be able to make a map of the future. There are some great events of the future very clearly revealed. The prophecy is not at all indistinct about the facts that will occur; but as to when they will occur, we have no data. Some think that they have; but our Lord here seems to say that we do not know the times and the seasons, and that it is not for us to know them. I pass no censure upon brethren who think that, by elaborate calculations, they find out what is to be in the future; I say that I pass no censure, but time has passed censure of the strongest kind upon all their predecessors. I forget how many miles of books interpreting prophecy there are in the British Museum; but I believe it amounts to miles, all of which have been disproved by the lapse of time. Some of the writers were wonderfully definite; they knew within half-an-hour when the Lord would come. Some of them were very distinct about all the events; they had mapped them all within a few years. The men who wrote the books, happily for themselves, had mostly died before the time appointed came. It is always wise to pitch on a long period of prophecy, that you may be out of the way if the thing does not come off; and they mostly did so. There were very few of them who lived to suffer the disappointment which would certainly have come to them through having fixed the wrong date. I let time censure their mistake. God forgave it, for they did it with a desire for his glory. The bulk of them were most sincere students of the Word, and herein are a lesson to us, even though they were mistaken in their calculations; but, beloved, it is not for you to know the times and the seasons.

First, it is not proper for you. It is not your work. You are not sent into the world to be prophets; you are sent into the world to be witnesses. You do not come here to be prognosticators of the events of tomorrow about yourself, or about your children, or about your friends, or about the nations of the earth. A veil hangs between you and the future. Your prayer is to be, "Thy kingdom come. Thy will be done in earth, as it is in heaven." You are told to look for the coming of your Lord, and to stand in perpetual expectation of his return; but to know the time when he will come, is no part of your office. You are servants who are to look for your Lord, who may come at cock-crowing, or at midday, or at midnight. Keep you always on the tiptoe of expecta-

the parts of Libya about Cyrene, and strangers of Rome, Jews and proselytes,

11 Cretes and Arabians, we do hear them speak in our tongues the wonderful works of God.

12 And they were all amazed, and were in doubt, saying one to another, What meaneth this?

13 Others mocking said, These men are full of new wine.

14 But Peter, standing up with the eleven, lifted up his voice, and said unto them, Ye men of Judea, and all ye that dwell at Jerusalem, be this known unto you, and hearken to my words:

15 For these are not drunken, as ye suppose, seeing it is but the third hour of the day.

16 But this is that which was spoken by the prophet Joel;

17 And it shall come to pass in the last days, saith God, I will pour out of my Spirit upon all flesh: and your sons and your daughters shall prophesy, and your young men shall see visions, and your old men shall dream dreams:

18 And on my servants and on my handmaidens I will pour out in those days of my Spirit; and they shall prophesy:

19 And I will shew wonders in heaven above, and signs in the earth beneath; blood, and fire, and vapour of smoke:

20 The sun shall be turned into darkness, and the moon into blood, before that great and notable day of the Lord come:

21 And it shall come to pass, that whosoever shall call on the name of the Lord shall be saved.

22 Ye men of Israel, hear these words; Jesus of Nazareth, a man approved of God among you by miracles and wonders and signs, which God did by him in the midst of you, as ye yourselves also know:

23 Him, being delivered by the determinate counsel and foreknowledge of God, ye have taken, and by wicked hands have crucified and slain:

24 Whom God hath raised up, having loosed the pains of death: because it was not possible that he should be holden of it.

25 For David speaketh concerning him, I foresaw the Lord always before my face, for he is on my right hand, that I should not be moved:

26 Therefore did my heart rejoice, and my tongue was glad; moreover also my flesh shall rest in hope:

27 Because thou wilt not leave my soul in hell, neither wilt thou suffer thine Holy One to see corruption.

28 Thou hast made known to me the ways of life; thou shalt make me full of joy with thy countenance.

29 Men and brethren, let me freely speak unto you of the patriarch David, that he is both dead and buried, and his sepulcher is with us unto this day.

flaming fire.

4. And they began to speak with other tongues – The miracle was not in the ears of the hearers, (as some have unaccountably supposed,) but in the mouth of the speakers. And this family praising God together, with the tongues of all the world, was an earnest that the whole world should in due time praise God in their various tongues. As the Spirit gave them utterance – Moses, the type of the law, was of a slow tongue; but the Gospel speaks with a fiery and flaming one.

5. And there were dwelling in Jerusalem Jews – Gathered from all parts by the peculiar providence of God.

6. The multitude came together, and were confounded – The motions of their minds were swift and various.

9. Judea – The dialect of which greatly differed from that of Galilee. Asia – The country strictly so called.

10. Roman sojourners – Born at Rome, but now living at Jerusalem. These seem to have come to Jerusalem after those who are above mentioned. All of them were partly Jews by birth, and partly proselytes.

11. Cretans – One island seems to be mentioned for all. The wonderful works of God – Probably those which related to the miracles, death, resurrection, and ascension of Christ, together with the effusion of his Spirit, as a fulfillment of his promises, and the glorious dispensations of Gospel grace.

12. They were all amazed – All the devout men.

13. But others mocking – The world begins with mocking, thence proceeds to caviling, chap. iv, 7; to threats, iv, 17; to imprisoning, chap. v, 18; blows, v, 40; to slaughter, chap. vii, 58. These mockers appear to have been some of the natives of Judea, and inhabitants of Jerusalem, (who understood only the dialect of the country,) by the apostle's immediately directing his discourse to them in the next verse. They are full of sweet wine – So the Greek word properly signifies. There was no new wine so early in the year as Pentecost. Thus natural men are wont to ascribe supernatural things to mere natural causes; and many times as impudently and unskillfully as in the present case.

14. Then Peter standing up – All the gestures, all the words of Peter, show the utmost sobriety; lifted up his voice – With cheerfulness and boldness; and said to them – This discourse has three parts; each of which, ver. 14, 22, 29, begins with the same appellation, men: only to the last part he prefixes with more familiarity the additional word brethren. Men of Judea – That is, ye that are born in Judea. St. Peter spoke in Hebrew, which they all understood.

15. It is but the third hour of the day – That is, nine in the morning. And on the solemn festivals the Jews rarely ate or drank any thing till noon.

16. But this is that which was spoken of by the prophet – But there is another and better way of accounting for this. Joel ii, 28.

17. The times of the Messiah are frequently called the last days, the Gospel being the last dispensation of Divine grace. I will pour out of my Spirit – Not on the day of Pentecost only, upon all flesh – On persons of every age, sex, and rank. And your young men shall see visions – In young men the outward sense, are most vigorous, and the bodily strength is entire, whereby they are best qualified to sustain the shock which usually attends the visions of God. In old men the internal senses are most vigorous, suited to divine dreams. Not that the old are wholly excluded from the former, nor the young from the latter.

MATTHEW HENRY   CHARLES H. SPURGEON

ples which should be the greatest; but now all these strifes were at an end. They had prayed more together of late. Would we have the Spirit poured out upon us from on high, let us be all of one accord. And notwithstanding differences of sentiments and interests, as there were among those disciples, let us agree to love one another; for where brethren dwell together in unity, there the Lord commands his blessing. A rushing mighty wind came with great force. This was to signify the powerful influences and working of the Spirit of God upon the minds of men, and thereby upon the world. Thus the convictions of the Spirit make way for his comforts; and the rough blasts of that blessed wind, prepare the soul for its soft and gentle gales. There was an appearance of something like flaming fire, lighting on every one of them, according to John Baptist's saying concerning Christ; He shall baptize you with the Holy Ghost, and with fire. The Spirit, like fire, melts the heart, burns up the dross, and kindles pious and devout affections in the soul; in which, as in the fire on the altar, the spiritual sacrifices are offered up. They were all filled with the Holy Ghost, more than before. They were filled with the graces of the Spirit, and more than ever under his sanctifying influences; more weaned from this world, and better acquainted with the other. They were more filled with the comforts of the Spirit, rejoiced more than ever in the love of Christ and the hope of heaven: in it all their griefs and fears were swallowed up. They were filled with the gifts of the Holy Ghost; they had miraculous powers for the furtherance of the gospel. They spake, not from previous thought or meditation, but as the Spirit gave them utterance.

5-13 The difference in languages which arose at Babel, has much hindered the spread of knowledge and religion. The instruments whom the Lord first employed in spreading the Christian religion, could have made no progress without this gift, which proved that their authority was from God.

14-21 Peter's sermon shows that he was thoroughly recovered from his fall, and thoroughly restored to the Divine favor; for he who had denied Christ, now boldly confessed him. His account of the miraculous pouring forth of the Spirit, was designed to awaken the hearers to embrace the faith of Christ, and to join themselves to his church. It was the fulfilling the Scripture, and the fruit of Christ's resurrection and ascension, and proof of both. Though Peter was filled with the Holy Ghost, and spake with tongues as the Spirit gave him utterance, yet he did not think to set aside the Scriptures. Christ's scholars never learn above their Bible; and the Spirit is given, not to do away the Scriptures, but to enable us to understand,

tion. It would be wrong for you to profess that you need not watch until such and such a time, for he would not come until such a date arrived.

As it is not proper for you, so it is not profitable for you. What would you be the better if you could make a map of all that is yet to be? Suppose it were revealed to yon tonight, by an angel, in what respect would it alter your conduct for tomorrow? In what way would it help you to perform the duties which your Master has enjoined upon you? I believe that it would be to you a very dangerous gift; you would be tempted to set yourself up as an interpreter of the future. If men believed in you, you would become eminent and notable, and you would be looked upon with awe. The temptation would be to become a prophet on your own account, to head a new sect, to lead a new company of men to believe in yourself. I say that that would be the temptation. For my part, I would rather not know any more than my Lord pleases to reveal to me; and if he did reveal all the future to me, I should feel like the prophets who spake of "the burden of the Lord." Neither would it ensure your salvation to be able to foretell the future, for Balaam was a great prophet, but he was a great sinner; he was an arch-rebel although he was an arch-divine. Nor do I know that, by foretelling the future, you would convince your fellow-men; for Noah told them that the world would be destroyed by the flood, he could give them a very accurate account of the time when the rain would descend, and yet they were not converted by his preaching, neither did they come into the ark. Those truths which God has revealed, you must accept for yourselves and proclaim to others; they are profitable for all purposes, and sufficient for your work; but the future is known only to God.

And as it is not proper or profitable, so it is not possible for you to know the times and the seasons. You may study as you will, and pray as you please; but the times and the seasons are not committed to you. Our Lord, as man, spoke of one great event of which he did not know the time: "Of that day and that hour knoweth no man, no, not the angels which are in heaven, neither the Son, but the Father." He does not say that now that he has risen from the dead, but he seems to hint that he did not know so as to tell his disciples; he must keep secret, even from them, that, which the Father hath put in his own power.

Notice, next, dear friends, that it is not good for you to know the times and the seasons. That is what the Savior means when he says, "It is not for you to know." For, first, it would distract your attention from the great things of which you have to think. It is enough for your mind to dwell upon the cross and the coming glory of your Lord. Keep these two things distinctly before you, and you need not puzzle your brains about the future. If

30 Therefore being a prophet, and knowing that God had sworn with an oath to him, that of the fruit of his loins, according to the flesh, he would raise up Christ to sit on his throne;

31 He seeing this before spake of the resurrection of Christ, that his soul was not left in hell, neither his flesh did see corruption.

32 This Jesus hath God raised up, whereof we all are witnesses.

33 Therefore being by the right hand of God exalted, and having received of the Father the promise of the Holy Ghost, he hath shed forth this, which ye now see and hear.

34 For David is not ascended into the heavens: but he saith himself, The LORD said unto my Lord, Sit thou on my right hand,

35 Until I make thy foes thy footstool.

36 Therefore let all the house of Israel know assuredly, that God hath made that same Jesus, whom ye have crucified, both Lord and Christ.

37 Now when they heard this, they were pricked in their heart, and said unto Peter and to the rest of the apostles, Men and brethren, what shall we do?

38 Then Peter said unto them, Repent, and be baptized every one of you in the name of Jesus Christ for the remission of sins, and ye shall receive the gift of the Holy Ghost.

39 For the promise is unto you, and to your children, and to all that are afar off, even as many as the Lord our God shall call.

40 And with many other words did he testify and exhort, saying, Save yourselves from this untoward generation.

41 Then they that gladly received his word were baptized: and the same day there were added unto them about three thousand souls.

42 And they continued stedfastly in the apostles' doctrine and fellowship, and in breaking of bread, and in prayers.

43 And fear came upon every soul: and many wonders and signs were done by the apostles.

44 And all that believed were together, and had all things common;

45 And sold their possessions and goods, and parted them to all men, as every man had need.

46 And they, continuing daily with one accord in the temple, and breaking bread from house to house, did eat their meat with gladness and singleness of heart,

47 Praising God, and having favor with all the people. And the Lord added to the church daily such as should be saved.

ACTS 3

1 Now Peter and John went up together into the temple at the hour of prayer, being the ninth hour.

2 And a certain man lame from his mother's womb was carried, whom they laid daily at the gate of the temple which is called Beautiful, to

18. And upon my servants – On those who are literally in a state of servitude.

19. And I will show prodigies in heaven above, and signs on earth beneath – Great Revelations of grace are usually attended with great judgments on those who reject it. In heaven – Treated of, ver. 20. On earth – Described in this verse. Such signs were those mentioned, ver. 22, before the passion of Christ; which are so mentioned as to include also those at the very time of the passion and resurrection, at the destruction of Jerusalem, and at the end of the world. Terrible indeed were those prodigies in particular which preceded the destruction of Jerusalem: such as the flaming sword hanging over the city, and the fiery comet pointing down upon it for a year; the light that shone upon the temple and the altar in the night, as if it had been noon-day; the opening of the great and heavy gate of the temple without hands; the voice heard from the most holy place, Let us depart hence; the admonition of Jesus the son of Ananus, crying for seven years together, Woe, woe, woe; the vision of contending armies in the air, and of entrenchments thrown up against a city there represented; the terrible thunders and lightnings, and dreadful earthquakes, which every one considered as portending some great evil: all which, through the singular providence of God, are particularly recorded by Josephus. Blood – War and slaughter. Fire – Burnings of houses and towns, involving all in clouds of smoke.

20. The moon shall be turned into blood – A bloody color: before the day of the Lord – Eminently the last day; though not excluding any other day or season, wherein the Lord shall manifest his glory, in taking vengeance of his adversaries.

21. But – whosoever shall call on the name of the Lord – This expression implies the whole of religion, and particularly prayer uttered in faith; shall be saved – From all those plagues; from sin and hell.

23. Him, being delivered by the determinate counsel and foreknowledge of God – The apostle here anticipates an objection, Why did God suffer such a person to be so treated? Did he not know what wicked men intended to do? And had he not power to prevent it? Yea. He knew all that those wicked men intended to do. And he had power to blast all their designs in a moment. But he did not exert that power, because he so loved the world! Because it was the determined counsel of his love, to redeem mankind from eternal death, by the death of his only-begotten Son.

24. Having loosed the pains of death – The word properly means, the pains of a woman in travail. As it was not possible that he should be held under it – Because the Scripture must needs be fulfilled.

25. Psalm xvi, 8.

27. Thou wilt not leave my soul in hades – The invisible world. But it does not appear, that ever our Lord went into hell. His soul, when it was separated from the body, did not go thither, but to paradise, Luke xxiii, 43. The meaning is, Thou wilt not leave my soul in its separate state, nor suffer my body to be corrupted.

28. Thou hast made known to me the ways of life – That is, Thou hast raised me from the dead. Thou wilt fill me with joy by thy countenance – When I ascend to thy right hand.

29. The patriarch – A more honorable title than king.

30. Psalm lxxxix, 4, &c.

32. He foreseeing this, spake of the resurrection of Christ – St. Peter argues thus: It is plain, David did not speak this of himself. Therefore he spake of Christ's rising. But how does that promise of a kingdom imply his resurrection? Because he did not receive it

approve, and obey them. Assuredly none will escape the condemnation of the great day, except those who call upon the name of the Lord, in and through his Son Jesus Christ, as the Savior of sinners, and the Judge of all mankind.

22-36 From this gift of the Holy Ghost, Peter preaches unto them Jesus: and here is the history of Christ. Here is an account of his death and sufferings, which they witnessed but a few weeks before. His death is considered as God's act; and of wonderful grace and wisdom. Thus Divine justice must be satisfied, God and man brought together again, and Christ himself glorified, according to an eternal counsel, which could not be altered. And as the people's act; in them it was an act of awful sin and folly. Christ's resurrection did away the reproach of his death; Peter speaks largely upon this. Christ was God's Holy One, sanctified and set apart to his service in the work of redemption. His death and sufferings should be, not to him only, but to all his, the entrance to a blessed life for evermore. This event had taken place as foretold, and the apostles were witnesses. Nor did the resurrection rest upon this alone; Christ had poured upon his disciples the miraculous gifts and Divine influences, of which they witnessed the effects. Through the Savior, the ways of life are made known; and we are encouraged to expect God's presence, and his favor for evermore. All this springs from assured belief that Jesus is the Lord, and the anointed Savior.

37-41 From the first delivery of that Divine message, it appeared that there was Divine power going with it; and thousands were brought to the obedience of faith. But neither Peter's words, nor the miracle they witnessed, could have produced such effects, had not the Holy Spirit been given. Sinners, when their eyes are opened, cannot but be pricked to the heart for sin, cannot but feel an inward uneasiness. The apostle exhorted them to repent of their sins, and openly to avow their belief in Jesus as the Messiah, by being baptized in his name. Thus professing their faith in Him, they would receive remission of their sins, and partake of the gifts and graces of the Holy Spirit. To separate from wicked people, is the only way to save ourselves from them. Those who repent of their sins, and give up themselves to Jesus Christ, must prove their sincerity by breaking off from the wicked. We must save ourselves from them; which denotes avoiding them with dread and holy fear. By God's grace three thousand persons accepted the gospel invitation. There can be no doubt that the gift of the Holy Ghost, which they all received, and from which no true believer has ever been shut out, was that Spirit of adoption, that converting, guiding, sanctifying grace, which is bestowed

you did know that something important was going to happen very speedily, you might be full of consternation, and do your work in a great hurry. You might be worked up into a frenzy that would spoil all your service. Or, if there was a long time to elapse before the great event, you might feel the indifference of distance. If our Lord were not to come for another hundred years, and he may not, we cannot tell,—then we might say, "My Lord delayeth his coming," and so we might begin to sleep, or to play the wanton. It is for our good to stand ever in this condition, knowing that he is coming, knowing that he will reign, knowing that certain great events will certainly transpire; but not knowing the exact times and seasons when those events are to be expected.

But there is something better than knowing the times or the seasons; it is good for us to know that they are in the Father's power: "which the Father hath put in his own power." The events will come to pass, then, in due time. The future is all in God's hand. No prophecy will lack its mate. No word of God will fall unfulfilled to the ground. Possess your souls in patience: the things that are foretold are sure to happen. "Though the vision tarry, wait for it; because it will surely come, it will not tarry." I am persuaded that God never is before his time, but he never is too late. He never failed to keep tryst with his people to the tick of the clock. The future is in the Father's power.

And especially let it be remembered that it is in his power as our Father. He must arrange it rightly; he must arrange it in infinite love to us. It cannot be that, in some dark hour yet to come, he will forget us. He is our Father; will he forget his children? If the times could be in my hand, how earnestly would I pray that Christ would take them into his hand, or that the Father would take away from me the dangerous power, and wield it all himself! Did we not sing just now,—

"All my times are in thy hand,
All events at thy command"?

The time of birth, the time of the new birth, the time of a sore trial, the time of the death of your beloved one, the time of your sickness, and how long it shall last, all these times must come, and last, and end, as shall please your Father. It is for you to know that your Father is at the helm of the ship, and therefore it cannot be wrecked. It may rock and reel to and fro; but, since he rules the waves, the vessel will not have one more tossing than his infinite love permits. Let us, then, not seek to unroll the map of the future, but calmly say,—

"My God, I would not long to see
My fate with curious eyes,
What gloomy lines are writ for me,
Or what bright scenes arise;"

but just leave it all with God. The Father hath it in his own hands, and there we wish it to be.

ask alms of them that entered into the temple;

3 Who seeing Peter and John about to go into the temple asked an alms.

4 And Peter, fastening his eyes upon him with John, said, Look on us.

5 And he gave heed unto them, expecting to receive something of them.

6 Then Peter said, Silver and gold have I none; but such as I have give I thee: In the name of Jesus Christ of Nazareth rise up and walk.

7 And he took him by the right hand, and lifted him up: and immediately his feet and ankle bones received strength.

8 And he leaping up stood, and walked, and entered with them into the temple, walking, and leaping, and praising God.

9 And all the people saw him walking and praising God:

10 And they knew that it was he which sat for alms at the Beautiful gate of the temple: and they were filled with wonder and amazement at that which had happened unto him.

11 And as the lame man which was healed held Peter and John, all the people ran together unto them in the porch that is called Solomon's, greatly wondering.

12 And when Peter saw it, he answered unto the people, Ye men of Israel, why marvel ye at this? or why look ye so earnestly on us, as though by our own power or holiness we had made this man to walk?

13 The God of Abraham, and of Isaac, and of Jacob, the God of our fathers, hath glorified his Son Jesus; whom ye delivered up, and denied him in the presence of Pilate, when he was determined to let him go.

14 But ye denied the Holy One and the Just, and desired a murderer to be granted unto you;

15 And killed the Prince of life, whom God hath raised from the dead; whereof we are witnesses.

16 And his name through faith in his name hath made this man strong, whom ye see and know: yea, the faith which is by him hath given him this perfect soundness in the presence of you all.

17 And now, brethren, I wot that through ignorance ye did it, as did also your rulers.

18 But those things, which God before had shewed by the mouth of all his prophets, that Christ should suffer, he hath so fulfilled.

19 Repent ye therefore, and be converted, that your sins may be blotted out, when the times of refreshing shall come from the presence of the Lord;

20 And he shall send Jesus Christ, which before was preached unto you:

21 Whom the heaven must receive until the times of restitution of all things, which God hath spoken by the mouth of all his holy prophets since the world began.

22 For Moses truly said unto the fathers, A prophet shall the Lord your God raise up unto

before he died, and because his kingdom was to endure for ever, 2 Sam. vii, 13.

33. Being exalted by the right hand of God – By the right hand; that is, the mighty power of God. Our Lord was exalted at his ascension to God's right hand in heaven.

34. Sit thou on my right hand – In this and the following verse is an allusion to two ancient customs; one, to the highest honor that used to be paid to persons by placing them on the right hand, as Solomon did Bathsheba, when sitting on his throne, 1 Kings ii, 19; and the other, to the custom of conquerors, who used to tread on the necks of their vanquished enemies, as a token of their entire victory and triumph over them.

35. Until I make thine enemies thy footstool – This text is here quoted with the greatest address, as suggesting in the words of David, their great prophetic monarch, how certain their own ruin must be, if they went on to oppose Christ. Psalm cx, 1.

36. Lord – Jesus, after his exaltation, is constantly meant by this word in the New Testament, unless sometimes where it occurs, in a text quoted from the Old Testament.

37. They said to the apostles, Brethren – They did not style them so before.

38. Repent – And hereby return to God: be baptized – Believing in the name of Jesus – And ye shall receive the gift of the Holy Ghost – See the three-one God clearly proved. See chap. xxvi, 20. The gift of the Holy Ghost does not mean in this place the power of speaking with tongues. For the promise of this was not given to all that were afar off, in distant ages and nations. But rather the constant fruits of faith, even righteousness, and peace, and joy in the Holy Ghost. Whomsoever the Lord our God shall call – (Whether they are Jews or Gentiles) by his word and by his Spirit: and who are not disobedient to the heavenly calling. But it is observable St. Peter did not yet understand the very words he spoke.

40. And with many other words did he testify and exhort – In such an accepted time we should add line upon line, and not leave off, till the thing is done. Save yourselves from this perverse generation – Many of whom were probably mocking still.

41. And there were added – To the hundred and twenty.

42. And they continued steadfast – So their daily Church communion consisted in these four particulars:

    1. Hearing the word;

    2. Having all things common;

    3. Receiving the Lord's Supper;

    4. Prayer. Ye diff'rent sects, who all declare, Lo here is Christ, and Christ is there; Your stronger proofs divinely give, And show me where the Christians live!

43. And fear came upon every soul – Of those who did not join with them: whereby persecution was prevented, till it was needful for them.

45. And sold their possessions – Their lands and houses; and goods – Their movables. And parted them to all as any one had need – To say the Christians did this only till the destruction of Jerusalem, is not true; for many did it long after. Not that there was any positive command for so doing: it needed not; for love constrained them. It was a natural fruit of that love wherewith each member of the community loved every other as his own soul. And if the whole Christian Church had continued in this spirit, this usage must have continued through all ages. To affirm therefore that Christ did not design it should continue, is neither more nor less than to affirm, that Christ

upon all the members of the family of our heavenly Father. Repentance and remission of sins are still preached to the chief of sinners, in the Redeemer's name; still the Holy Spirit seals the blessing on the believer's heart; still the encouraging promises are to us and our children; and still the blessings are offered to all that are afar off.

42-47 In these verses we have the history of the truly primitive church, of the first days of it; its state of infancy indeed, but, like that, the state of its greatest innocence. They kept close to holy ordinances, and abounded in piety and devotion; for Christianity, when admitted in the power of it, will dispose the soul to communion with God in all those ways wherein he has appointed us to meet him, and has promised to meet us. The greatness of the event raised them above the world, and the Holy Ghost filled them with such love, as made every one to be to another as to himself, and so made all things common, not by destroying property, but doing away selfishness, and causing charity. And God who moved them to it, knew that they were quickly to be driven from their possessions in Judea. The Lord, from day to day, inclined the hearts of more to embrace the gospel; not merely professors, but such as were actually brought into a state of acceptance with God, being made partakers of regenerating grace. Those whom God has designed for eternal salvation, shall be effectually brought to Christ, till the earth is filled with the knowledge of his glory.

ACTS 3

A lame man healed by Peter and John. (1-11)
Peter's address to the Jews. (12-26)

1-11 The apostles and the first believers attended the temple worship at the hours of prayer. Peter and John seem to have been led by a Divine direction, to work a miracle on a man above forty years old, who had been a cripple from his birth. Peter, in the name of Jesus of Nazareth, bade him rise up and walk. Thus, if we would attempt to good purpose the healing of men's souls, we must go forth in the name and power of Jesus Christ, calling on helpless sinners to arise and walk in the way of holiness, by faith in him. How sweet the thought to our souls, that in respect to all the crippled faculties of our fallen nature, the name of Jesus Christ of Nazareth can make us whole! With what holy joy and rapture shall we tread the holy courts, when God the Spirit causes us to enter therein by his strength!

12-18 Observe the difference in the manner of working the miracles. Our Lord always spoke as

So much concerning some things which are not for us.

II. And now, secondly, there are SOME THINGS FOR US TO RECEIVE. The Savior said to the eleven that they were to wait at Jerusalem till they had received power by the Holy Ghost coming upon them. This is what we want; we want the Holy Ghost. We often speak about this; but, in truth, it is unspeakable, the power of the Holy Ghost, mysterious, divine. When it comes upon a man, he is bathed in the very essence of the Deity. The atmosphere about him becomes the life and power of God. There is an old proverb that knowledge is power; Christ has taken away the knowledge that is not power. He said, "It is not for you, child; it is not for you." But he gives you the knowledge that is power; or, rather, that power which is better than all knowledge, the power of the Holy Spirit. Gotthold, in his parables, speaks of his little child who wanted to come into his room; but he was doing something there which he did not wish the child to see, and so he went on with his work, when, to his horror and surprise, he found that his child had in some way climbed up outside the window, and was standing on the sill trying to look in to see what his father was doing hazarding his life in the attempt. You may guess that it was not long before that child was taken down with a pat, and something more, to teach him not to pry into his father's secrets. It is so with some of us; we need just a little pat, and perhaps more than that, to keep us from looking into things that do not belong to us. We may be comforted even if we do not know the times and the seasons, for we may get something vastly better, namely, the Holy Spirit to give us real power for our life-work.

The Holy Spirit gives to his people power which may be looked at from different points. He gave to some of them in the olden times miraculous power, and they went forth, having received the Spirit of God, to do great signs and wonders in the name of Christ. If you have not that, you may hope to have mental power. The Holy Spirit does not educate us, or give us culture after the common method of men, and yet there is an inner education and a higher culture which is much more to be desired, which comes from him. He leads us into all truth; he makes us feel the force of truth; he gives us a grip of truth; he writes truth upon the heart; he applies it to the understanding. Many a man has become quick of understanding in the fear of the Lord, who was very slow of understanding in other respects. The Holy Spirit takes the fool, and makes him know the wonders of redeeming love. It is amazing how persons, of very scanty gifts, and very small attainments, have, nevertheless, become wise toward God, their mental faculties

you of your brethren, like unto me; him shall ye hear in all things whatsoever he shall say unto you.

23 And it shall come to pass, that every soul, which will not hear that prophet, shall be destroyed from among the people.

24 Yea, and all the prophets from Samuel and those that follow after, as many as have spoken, have likewise foretold of these days.

25 Ye are the children of the prophets, and of the covenant which God made with our fathers, saying unto Abraham, And in thy seed shall all the kindreds of the earth be blessed.

26 Unto you first God, having raised up his Son Jesus, sent him to bless you, in turning away every one of you from his iniquities.

ACTS 4

1 And as they spake unto the people, the priests, and the captain of the temple, and the Sadducees, came upon them,

2 Being grieved that they taught the people, and preached through Jesus the resurrection from the dead.

3 And they laid hands on them, and put them in hold unto the next day: for it was now eventide.

4 Howbeit many of them which heard the word believed; and the number of the men was about five thousand.

5 And it came to pass on the morrow, that their rulers, and elders, and scribes,

6 And Annas the high priest, and Caiaphas, and John, and Alexander, and as many as were of the kindred of the high priest, were gathered together at Jerusalem.

7 And when they had set them in the midst, they asked, By what power, or by what name, have ye done this?

8 Then Peter, filled with the Holy Ghost, said unto them, Ye rulers of the people, and elders of Israel,

9 If we this day be examined of the good deed done to the impotent man, by what means he is made whole;

10 Be it known unto you all, and to all the people of Israel, that by the name of Jesus Christ of Nazareth, whom ye crucified, whom God raised from the dead, even by him doth this man stand here before you whole.

11 This is the stone which was set at nought of you builders, which is become the head of the corner.

12 Neither is there salvation in any other: for there is none other name under heaven given among men, whereby we must be saved.

13 Now when they saw the boldness of Peter and John, and perceived that they were unlearned and ignorant men, they marveled; and they took knowledge of them, that they had been with Jesus.

14 And beholding the man which was healed standing with them, they could say nothing against it.

did not design this measure of love should continue. I see no proof of this.

46. Continuing daily – breaking the bread – in the Lord's Supper, as did many Churches for some ages. They partook of their food with gladness and singleness of heart – They carried the same happy and holy temper through all their common actions: eating and working with the same spirit wherewith they prayed and received the Lord's Supper.

47. The Lord added daily such as were saved – From their sins: from the guilt and power of them.

ACTS 3

1. The ninth hour – The Jews divided the time from sunrise to sunset into twelve hours; which were consequently of unequal length at different times of the year, as the days were longer or shorter. The third hour therefore was nine in the morning; the ninth, three in the afternoon; but not exactly. For the third hour was the middle space between sunrise and noon; which, if the sun rose at five, (the earliest hour of its rising in that climate,) was half an hour after eight: if at seven (the latest hour of its rising there) was half an hour after nine. The chief hours of prayer were the third and ninth; at which seasons the morning and evening sacrifices were offered, and incense (a kind of emblem representing prayer) burnt on the golden altar.

2. At the gate of the temple, called Beautiful – This gate was added by Herod the Great, between the court of the Gentiles and that of Israel. It was thirty cubits high, and fifteen broad, and made of Corinthian brass, more pompous in its workmanship and splendor than those that were covered with silver and gold.

6. Then said Peter, Silver and gold have I none – How unlike his supposed successor! Can the bishop of Rome either say or do the same?

12. Peter answered the people – Who were running together, and inquiring into the circumstances of the fact.

13. The God of our fathers – This was wisely introduced in the beginning of his discourse, that it might appear they taught no new religion, inconsistent with that of Moses, and were far from having the least design to divert their regards from the God of Israel. Hath glorified his Son – By this miracle, whom ye delivered up – When God had given him to you, and when ye ought to have received him as a most precious treasure, and to have preserved him with all your power.

14. Ye renounced the Holy One – Whom God had marked out as such; and the Just One – Even in the judgment of Pilate.

16. His name – Himself: his power and love. The faith which is by him – Of which he is the giver, as well as the object.

17. And now, brethren – A word full of courtesy and compassion, I know – He speaks to their heart, that through ignorance ye did it – which lessened, though it could not take away, the guilt. As did also your rulers – The prejudice lying from the authority of the chief priests and elders, he here removes, but with great tenderness. He does not call them our, but your rulers. For as the Jewish dispensation ceased at the death of Christ, consequently so did the authority of its rulers.

18. But God – Who was not ignorant, permitted this which he had foretold, to bring good out of it.

19. Be converted – Be turned from sin and Satan unto God. See chap. xxvi, 20. But this term, so common in modern writings, very

MATTHEW HENRY

CHARLES H. SPURGEON

having Almighty power, never hesitated to receive the greatest honor that was given to him on account of his Divine miracles. But the apostles referred all to their Lord, and refused to receive any honor, except as his undeserving instruments. This shows that Jesus was one with the Father, and co-equal with him; while the apostles knew that they were weak, sinful men, and dependent for every thing on Jesus, whose power effected the cure. Useful men must be very humble. Not unto us, O Lord, not unto us, but to thy name, give glory. Every crown must be cast at the feet of Christ. The apostle showed the Jews the greatness of their crime, but would not anger or drive them to despair. Assuredly, those who reject, refuse, or deny Christ, do it through ignorance; but this can in no case be an excuse.

19-21 The absolute necessity of repentance is to be solemnly charged upon the consciences of all who desire that their sins may be blotted out, and that they may share in the refreshment which nothing but a sense of Christ's pardoning love can afford. Blessed are those who have felt this. It was not needful for the Holy Spirit to make known the times and seasons of these dispensations. These subjects are still left obscure. But when sinners are convinced of their sins, they will cry to the Lord for pardon; and to the penitent, converted, and believing, times of refreshment will come from the presence of the Lord. In a state of trial and probation, the glorified Redeemer will be out of sight, because we must live by faith in him.

22-26 Here is a powerful address to warn the Jews of the dreadful consequences of their unbelief, in the very words of Moses, their favorite prophet, out of pretended zeal for whom they were ready to reject Christianity, and to try to destroy it. Christ came into the world to bring a blessing with him. And he sent his Spirit to be the great blessing. Christ came to bless us, by turning us from our iniquities, and saving us from our sins. We, by nature cleave to sin; the design of Divine grace is to turn us from it, that we may not only forsake, but hate it. Let none think that they can be happy by continuing in sin, when God declares that the blessing is in being turned from all iniquity. Let none think that they understand or believe the gospel, who only seek deliverance from the punishment of sin, but do not expect happiness in being delivered from sin itself. And let none expect to be turned from their sin, except by believing in, and receiving Christ the Son of God, as their wisdom, righteousness, sanctification, and redemption.

being quickened with regard to heavenly things in a very remarkable manner.

The power of the Spirit is also, in part, moral power. He gives to men qualities that make them strong and influential over their fellow-men, he imparts dauntless courage, calm confidence, intense affection, burning zeal, deep patience, much-enduring perseverance. Many other hallowed influences besides these are graces of the Spirit of God, which form in men a moral power exceedingly useful and exceedingly forcible. I have known men who have been slow of speech, and who have exhibited very few gifts, who have, nevertheless, been very strong men in our assemblies, true pillars of the church, for piety is power, and grace is power.

Besides that, there is a more secret, subtle power still, spiritual power, wherein, in the spiritual world, a man is made a prince with God, and hath power with God; and learning how to prevail with God for men, he catches the art of prevailing with men for God. He is first a wrestler alone by Jabbok; then he becomes a wrestler in the midst of the host of sinners, conquering them for Christ, taking them captive in the name of the Most High. Power in prayer is the highest form of power; and. communion with God is power; and holiness, above all things, is a great power among the sons of men.

This spiritual power makes a man influential, in a sense very different from that in which the world uses the word "influential"—a disgraceful use of the word. We want men who have influence in the divinest sense, men who, somehow or other, cast a spell over their fellow-men. In their presence men cannot do what they are accustomed to do elsewhere; when these men are in any company, they check sin without a word, they incite to righteousness almost without a sentence. They carry everything before them, not by might, nor by power, but by the Spirit of the Lord who dwells in them. Have I not seen some, decrepit and bedridden, yet ruling a house, and influencing a parish? Have I not seen some tottering old woman who, nevertheless, has been a very queen in the circle in which she moved? Have I not seen some poor, humble rustic from the plow who, nevertheless, has worn a coronet in the midst of his fellow-men by the holiness of his life, and the spiritual power that God the Holy Ghost had imparted to him?

Now, beloved, I have not time fully to describe this endowment; I have only mentioned one or two points in which it is seen, but this endowment is what we need before we can do anything for Christ. Do you always think enough of this? The teacher prepares her lesson; but does she also prepare herself by seeking the power of the Holy Spirit? The minister studies his text; but does he ask for a baptism of the Holy Ghost? I am afraid

15 But when they had commanded them to go aside out of the council, they conferred among themselves,

16 Saying, What shall we do to these men? for that indeed a notable miracle hath been done by them is manifest to all them that dwell in Jerusalem; and we cannot deny it.

17 But that it spread no further among the people, let us straitly threaten them, that they speak henceforth to no man in this name.

18 And they called them, and commanded them not to speak at all nor teach in the name of Jesus.

19 But Peter and John answered and said unto them, Whether it be right in the sight of God to hearken unto you more than unto God, judge ye.

20 For we cannot but speak the things which we have seen and heard.

21 So when they had further threatened them, they let them go, finding nothing how they might punish them, because of the people: for all men glorified God for that which was done.

22 For the man was above forty years old, on whom this miracle of healing was shewed.

23 And being let go, they went to their own company, and reported all that the chief priests and elders had said unto them.

24 And when they heard that, they lifted up their voice to God with one accord, and said, Lord, thou art God, which hast made heaven, and earth, and the sea, and all that in them is:

25 Who by the mouth of thy servant David hast said, Why did the heathen rage, and the people imagine vain things?

26 The kings of the earth stood up, and the rulers were gathered together against the Lord, and against his Christ.

27 For of a truth against thy holy child Jesus, whom thou hast anointed, both Herod, and Pontius Pilate, with the Gentiles, and the people of Israel, were gathered together,

28 For to do whatsoever thy hand and thy counsel determined before to be done.

29 And now, Lord, behold their threatenings: and grant unto thy servants, that with all boldness they may speak thy word,

30 By stretching forth thine hand to heal; and that signs and wonders may be done by the name of thy holy child Jesus.

31 And when they had prayed, the place was shaken where they were assembled together; and they were all filled with the Holy Ghost, and they spake the word of God with boldness.

32 And the multitude of them that believed were of one heart and of one soul: neither said any of them that ought of the things which he possessed was his own; but they had all things common.

33 And with great power gave the apostles witness of the resurrection of the Lord Jesus: and great grace was upon them all.

rarely occurs in Scripture: perhaps not once in the sense we now use it, for an entire change from vice to holiness. That the times of refreshing – Wherein God largely bestows his refreshing grace, may come – To you also. To others they will assuredly come, whether ye repent or no.

20. And he may send – The apostles generally speak of our Lord's second coming, as being just at hand. Who was before appointed – Before the foundation of the world.

21. Till the times of the restitution of all things – The apostle here comprises at once the whole course of the times of the New Testament, between our Lord's ascension and his coming in glory. The most eminent of these are the apostolic age, and that of the spotless Church, which will consist of all the Jews and Gentiles united, after all persecutions and apostacies are at an end.

22. The Lord shall raise you up a prophet like unto me – And that in many particulars. Moses instituted the Jewish Church: Christ instituted the Christian. With the prophesying of Moses was soon joined the effect, the deliverance of Israel from Egypt: with the prophesying of Christ that grand effect, the deliverance of his people from sin and death. Those who could not bear the voice of God, yet desired to hear that of Moses. Much more do those who are wearied with the law, desire to hear the voice of Christ. Moses spake to the people all, and only those things, which God had commanded him: so did Christ. But though he was like Moses, yet he was infinitely superior to him, in person, as well as in office. Deut. xviii, 15.

23. Every soul who will not hear that prophet, shall be destroyed from among the people – One cannot imagine a more masterly address than this, to warn the Jews of the dreadful consequence of their infidelity, in the very words of their favorite prophet, out of a pretended zeal for whom they rejected Christ.

24. These days – The days of the Messiah.

25. Ye are the sons of the prophets and of the covenant – That is, heirs of the prophecies. To you properly, as the first heirs, belong the prophecies and the covenant. Gen. xii, 3.

26. To bless you, by turning you from your iniquities – Which is the great Gospel blessing.

ACTS 4

1. And as they were speaking to the people, the priests – came upon them – So wisely did God order, that they should first bear a full testimony to the truth in the temple, and then in the great council; to which they could have had no access, had they not been brought before it as criminals.

2. The priests being grieved – That the name of Jesus was preached to the people; especially they were offended at the doctrine of his resurrection; for as they had put him to death, his rising again proved him to be the Just One, and so brought his blood upon their heads. The priests were grieved, lest their office and temple services should decline, and Christianity take root, through the preaching of the apostles, and their power of working miracles: the captain of the temple – Being concerned to prevent all sedition and disorder, the Sadducees – Being displeased at the overturning of all their doctrines, particularly with regard to the resurrection.

4. The number of the men – Beside women and children, were about five thousand – So many did our Lord now feed at once with the bread from heaven!

5. Rulers, and elders, and scribes – Who were eminent for power, for

MATTHEW HENRY CHARLES H. SPURGEON

ACTS 4

Peter and John imprisoned. (1-4)
The apostles boldly testify to Christ. (5-14)
Peter and John refuse to be silenced. (15-22)
The believers unite in prayer and praise. (23-31)
The holy charity of the Christians. (32-37)

1-4 The apostles preached through Jesus the resurrection from the dead. It includes all the happiness of the future state; this they preached through Jesus Christ, to be had through him only. Miserable is their case, to whom the glory of Christ's kingdom is a grief; for since the glory of that kingdom is everlasting, their grief will be everlasting also. The harmless and useful servants of Christ, like the apostles, have often been troubled for their work of faith and labor of love, when wicked men have escaped. And to this day instances are not wanting, in which reading the Scriptures, social prayer, and religious conversation meet with frowns and checks. But if we obey the precepts of Christ, he will support us.

5-14 Peter being filled with the Holy Ghost, would have all to understand, that the miracle had been wrought by the name, or power, of Jesus of Nazareth, the Messiah, whom they had crucified; and this confirmed their testimony to his resurrection from the dead, which proved him to be the Messiah. These rulers must either be saved by that Jesus whom they had crucified, or they must perish for ever. The name of Jesus is given to men of every age and nation, as that whereby alone believers are saved from the wrath to come. But when covetousness, pride, or any corrupt passion, rules within, men shut their eyes, and close their hearts, in enmity against the light; considering all as ignorant and unlearned, who desire to know nothing in comparison with Christ crucified. And the followers of Christ should act so that all who converse with them, may take knowledge that they have been with Jesus. That makes them holy, heavenly, spiritual, and cheerful, and raises them above this world.

15-22 All the care of the rulers is, that the doctrine of Christ spread not among the people, yet they cannot say it is false or dangerous, or of any ill tendency; and they are ashamed to own the true reason; that it testifies against their hypocrisy, wickedness, and tyranny. Those who know how to put a just value upon Christ's promises, know how to put just contempt upon the world's threatenings. The apostles look with concern on perishing souls, and know they cannot escape eternal ruin but by Jesus Christ, therefore they are faithful in warning, and showing the right way. None will enjoy peace of mind, nor act uprightly, till they have learned to guide their conduct by the fixed standard of truth,

that this spiritual qualification, the most essential of all, is frequently overlooked. Then, the Lord have mercy upon us! The soldier had better go to battle without sword or rifle, the artilleryman had better wheel up his gun without powder or shot, than that we should attempt to win a soul until first of all the Holy Spirit has given us power. Power must go with the word that is preached or taught if any large result is to follow; and that power must first be in the man who speaks that word.

For this power the disciples were to wait. The world was dying, hell was raging, yet they must tarry at Jerusalem till they had that power. Impetuous Peter must hold his tongue, and loving John must be quiet and must commune in secret with his Master. None of them must go out into the street or stand in the temple to proclaim the words of this life. They must stop till God should see fit to pour out his Spirit upon them; and I would to God that sometimes we could be quiet, too. It were better to be dumb than to speak only in the power of our own spirit. It were better to lay the finger on the lip than to begin to talk before our message has been burnt into us by the Holy Ghost. Wait for the live coal from off the altar to blister thy lip, for then only canst thou speak with power when thou thyself hast felt the fire of the Spirit.

III. Now we pass on to the third point, which is a very important practical one, SOMETHING FOR US TO BE. If you are a disciple of Christ, you are not to look into the times and the seasons which the Father hath put in his own power; you are to receive the Spirit of God, and then there is something for you to be. Did you expect me to say that then there is something for you to do? Well, there is a great deal for you to do; but the text says, "Ye shall be witnesses"; not "Ye shall act as witnesses" only, but "Ye shall be witnesses." Every true Christian should, in his own proper person, be a witness for his Lord. "Here I stand," says he, "myself a proof of what my Lord can do. I, his servant, saved by him, and renewed by him, washed in his blood, it is I who, while I live, whether I speak or not, am a monument of his love, a trophy of his grace." "Ye shall be witnesses unto me."

Dear friends, we are to be witnesses of what Christ has done. If we have seen Christ, if we believe in Christ, let us tell it honestly. These apostles had a great deal to tell. They had been with Christ in private; they had seen his miracles; they had heard his choicest and more secret words; they had to go and bear witness to it all. And you, who have been let into the secrets of Christ, you who have communed with him more closely than others, you have much to tell. Tell it all, for whatever he has said to you in the closet you are to proclaim

34 Neither was there any among them that lacked: for as many as were possessors of lands or houses sold them, and brought the prices of the things that were sold,

35 And laid them down at the apostles' feet: and distribution was made unto every man according as he had need.

36 And Joses, who by the apostles was surnamed Barnabas, (which is, being interpreted, The son of consolation,) a Levite, and of the country of Cyprus,

37 Having land, sold it, and brought the money, and laid it at the apostles' feet.

ACTS 5

1 But a certain man named Ananias, with Sapphira his wife, sold a possession,

2 And kept back part of the price, his wife also being privy to it, and brought a certain part, and laid it at the apostles' feet.

3 But Peter said, Ananias, why hath Satan filled thine heart to lie to the Holy Ghost, and to keep back part of the price of the land?

4 Whiles it remained, was it not thine own? and after it was sold, was it not in thine own power? why hast thou conceived this thing in thine heart? thou hast not lied unto men, but unto God.

5 And Ananias hearing these words fell down, and gave up the ghost: and great fear came on all them that heard these things.

6 And the young men arose, wound him up, and carried him out, and buried him.

7 And it was about the space of three hours after, when his wife, not knowing what was done, came in.

8 And Peter answered unto her, Tell me whether ye sold the land for so much? And she said, Yea, for so much.

9 Then Peter said unto her, How is it that ye have agreed together to tempt the Spirit of the Lord? behold, the feet of them which have buried thy husband are at the door, and shall carry thee out.

10 Then fell she down straightway at his feet, and yielded up the ghost: and the young men came in, and found her dead, and, carrying her forth, buried her by her husband.

11 And great fear came upon all the church, and upon as many as heard these things.

12 And by the hands of the apostles were many signs and wonders wrought among the people; (and they were all with one accord in Solomon's porch.

13 And of the rest durst no man join himself to them: but the people magnified them.

14 And believers were the more added to the Lord, multitudes both of men and women.)

15 Insomuch that they brought forth the sick into the streets, and laid them on beds and couches, that at the least the shadow of Peter passing by might overshadow some of them.

wisdom, and for learning.

6. Annas, who had been the high priest, and Caiaphas, who was so then.

7. By what name – By what authority, have ye done this? – They seem to speak ambiguously on purpose.

8. Then Peter, filled with the Holy Ghost – That moment. God moves his instruments, not when they please, but just when he sees it needful. Ye rulers – He gives them the honor due to their office.

10. Be it known to you all – Probably the herald of God proclaimed this with a loud voice. Whom God hath raised from the dead – They knew in their own consciences that it was so. And though they had hired the soldiers to tell a most senseless and incredible tale to the contrary, Matt. xxviii, 12, 15, yet it is observable, they did not, so far as we can learn, dare to plead it before Peter and John.

11. Psalm cxviii, 22.

12. There is no other name whereby we must be saved – The apostle uses a beautiful gradation, from the temporal deliverance which had been wrought for the poor cripple, by the power of Christ, to that of a much nobler and more important kind, which is wrought by Christ for impotent and sinful souls. He therein follows the admirable custom of his great Lord and Master, who continually took occasion from earthly to speak of spiritual things.

13. Illiterate and uneducated men – Even by such men (though not by such only) hath God in all ages caused his word to be preached before the world.

17. Yet that it spread no farther – For they look upon it as a mere gangrene. So do all the world upon genuine Christianity. Let us severely threaten them – Great men, ye do nothing. They have a greater than you to flee to.

18. They charged them not to speak – Privately; nor teach – Publicly.

19. Whether it be just to obey you rather than God, judge ye – Was it not by the same spirit, that Socrates, when they were condemning him to death, for teaching the people, said, "O ye Athenians, I embrace and love you; but I will obey God rather than you. And if you would spare my life on condition I should cease to teach my fellow citizens, I would die a thousand times rather than accept the proposal."

21. They all glorified God – So much wiser were the people than those who were over them.

24. The sense is, Lord, thou hast all power. And thy word is fulfilled. Men do rage against thee: but it is in vain.

25. Psalm ii, 1.

27. Whom thou hast anointed – To be king of Israel.

28. The sense is, but they could do no more than thou wast pleased to permit, according to thy determinate counsel, to save mankind by the sufferings of thy Son. And what was needful for this end, thou didst before determine to permit to be done.

30. Thou stretchest forth thy hand – Exertest thy power.

31. They were all filled – Afresh; and spake the word with boldness – So their petition was granted.

32. And the multitude of them that believed – Every individual person were of one heart and one soul – Their love, their hopes, their passions joined: and not so much as one – In so great a multitude: this was a necessary consequence of that union of heart; said that aught of the things which he had was his own – It is impossible any one should, while all were of one soul. So long as that truly Christian love continued, they could not but have all things common.

MATTHEW HENRY

CHARLES H. SPURGEON

and not by the shifting opinions and fancies of men. Especially beware of a vain attempt to serve two masters, God and the world; the end will be, you can serve neither fully.

23-31 Christ's followers do best in company, provided it is their own company. It encourages God's servants, both in doing work, and suffering work, that they serve the God who made all things, and therefore has the disposal of all events; and the Scriptures must be fulfilled. Jesus was anointed to be a Savior, therefore it was determined he should be a sacrifice, to make atonement for sin. But sin is not the less evil for God's bringing good out of it. In threatening times, our care should not be so much that troubles may be prevented, as that we may go on with cheerfulness and courage in our work and duty. They do not pray, Lord let us go away from our work, now that it is become dangerous, but, Lord, give us thy grace to go on steadfastly in our work, and not to fear the face of man. Those who desire Divine aid and encouragement, may depend upon having them, and they ought to go forth, and go on, in the strength of the Lord God. God gave a sign of acceptance of their prayers. The place was shaken, that their faith might be established and unshaken. God gave them greater degrees of his Spirit; and they were all filled with the Holy Ghost, more than ever; by which they were not only encouraged, but enabled to speak the word of God with boldness. When they find the Lord God helps them by his Spirit, they know they shall not be confounded, Isa 1.7.

32-37 The disciples loved one another. This was the blessed fruit of Christ's dying precept to his disciples, and his dying prayer for them. Thus it was then, and it will be so again, when the Spirit shall be poured upon us from on high. The doctrine preached was the resurrection of Christ; a matter of fact, which being duly explained, was a summary of all the duties, privileges, and comforts of Christians. There were evident fruits of Christ's grace in all they said and did. They were dead to this world. This was a great evidence of the grace of God in them. They did not take away others' property, but they were indifferent to it. They did not call it their own; because they had, in affection, forsaken all for Christ, and were expecting to be stripped of all for cleaving to him. No marvel that they were of one heart and soul, when they sat so loose to the wealth of this world. In effect, they had all things common; for there was not any among them who lacked, care was taken for their supply. The money was laid at the apostles' feet. Great care ought to be taken in the distribution of public charity, that it be given to such as have need, such as are not able to procure a maintenance for themselves; those who are reduced to want for well-

upon the housetop. You are to witness what you have seen, and tasted, and handled, concerning your Lord.

You are to witness to what he has revealed, to make known to others the doctrine that he preached, or taught by his apostles. Mind that you do not tell any other. You are not sent to be "an original thinker", to make up a gospel as you go along; you are a witness, that is all, a retailer of Christ's truth, and you miss the end of your life unless you perpetually witness, and witness, and witness to what you know of him, and to what you have learnt from him. Let this be your prayer and your resolve,—

"Give me thy strength, O God of power!
Then let winds blow, or thunders roar,
Thy faithful witness will I be:
'Tis fixed: I can do all through thee."

You are to witness to what you have experienced concerning Christ. Now, what is that? I will just run over this witness, feeling that there are many hundreds of dear friends here tonight who could bear the same testimony, and who will do so as they have opportunity.

First, I beg to say to all present here, tonight, that the Lord Jesus Christ can remove despair, and every form of spiritual distress. He did so to me. I was full of darkness, the shadow of death was upon me, and I found no comfort till I heard that blessed text, "Look unto me, and be ye saved, all the ends of the earth." I looked unto him, and was lightened, and my face was not ashamed; and I am here tonight to bear witness that its load was thus taken from me, which I could not get rid of in any other way, and my midnight was, in a single moment, turned into the blaze of midday. Neither have I ever gone back to that darkness, nor have I again had reason to cry, "Woe is me that ever I was born." Nay, there is in the name of Jesus a balm for every mental wound, a relief for all the agony of a tortured spirit. I am sure of it; I am not saying to you what I have merely heard from other people, but what I have myself felt, and there are many here who can endorse my testimony that there is no relief for a sinner's aching heart like that which Jesus brings. I wish that you would all prove this truth for yourselves; but, at any rate, we are witnesses that it is so.

And, next, our Lord Jesus is a great transformer of character. I do not like to speak of myself, but I will speak of many a man whom I know. He came into this Tabernacle a drunkard, a swearer, a lover of unholy pleasures, and while the Word was preached, the Lord broke him down, and melted his heart. Now he hates what once he loved; and as to those pursuits which were once distasteful to him, so that he cursed and swore at the very mention of them, or at least poured ridicule upon others who loved them, he now loves them himself,

16 There came also a multitude out of the cities round about unto Jerusalem, bringing sick folks, and them which were vexed with unclean spirits: and they were healed every one.

17 Then the high priest rose up, and all they that were with him, (which is the sect of the Sadducees,) and were filled with indignation,

18 And laid their hands on the apostles, and put them in the common prison.

19 But the angel of the Lord by night opened the prison doors, and brought them forth, and said,

20 Go, stand and speak in the temple to the people all the words of this life.

21 And when they heard that, they entered into the temple early in the morning, and taught. But the high priest came, and they that were with him, and called the council together, and all the senate of the children of Israel and sent to the prison to have them brought.

22 But when the officers came, and found them not in the prison, they returned, and told,

23 Saying, The prison truly found we shut with all safety, and the keepers standing without before the doors: but when we had opened, we found no man within.

24 Now when the high priest and the captain of the temple and the chief priests heard these things, they doubted of them whereunto this would grow.

25 Then came one and told them, saying, Behold, the men whom ye put in prison are standing in the temple, and teaching the people.

26 Then went the captain with the officers, and brought them without violence: for they feared the people, lest they should have been stoned.

27 And when they had brought them, they set them before the council: and the high priest asked them,

28 Saying, Did not we straitly command you that ye should not teach in this name? and, behold, ye have filled Jerusalem with your doctrine, and intend to bring this man's blood upon us.

29 Then Peter and the other apostles answered and said, We ought to obey God rather than men.

30 The God of our fathers raised up Jesus, whom ye slew and hanged on a tree.

31 Him hath God exalted with his right hand to be a Prince and a Savior, for to give repentance to Israel, and forgiveness of sins.

32 And we are his witnesses of these things; and so is also the Holy Ghost, whom God hath given to them that obey him.

33 When they heard that, they were cut to the heart, and took counsel to slay them.

34 Then stood there up one in the council, a Pharisee, named Gamaliel, a doctor of the law, had in reputation among all the people, and commanded to put the apostles forth a little space;

33. And great grace – A large measure of the inward power of the Holy Ghost, was upon them all – Directing all their thoughts, words, and actions.

34. For neither was there any one among them that wanted – We may observe, this is added as the proof that great grace was upon them all. And it was the immediate, necessary consequence of it: yea, and must be to the end of the world. In all ages and nations, the same cause, the same degree of grace, could not but in like circumstances produce the same effect. For whosoever were possessors of houses and lands sold them – Not that there was any particular command for this; but there was great grace and great love: of which this was the natural fruit.

35. And distribution was made – At first by the apostles themselves, afterward by them whom they appointed.

36. A son of consolation – Not only on account of his so largely assisting the poor with his fortune; but also of those peculiar gifts of the Spirit, whereby he was so well qualified both to comfort and to exhort.

37. Having an estate – Probably of considerable value. It is not unlikely that it was in Cyprus. Being a Levite, he had no portion, no distinct inheritance in Israel.

ACTS 5

1. But a certain man named Ananias – It is certain, not a believer, for all that believed were of one heart and of one soul: probably not baptized; but intending now to offer himself for baptism.

2. And bringing a certain part – As if it had been the whole: perhaps saying it was so.

3. To lie to the Holy Ghost – Who is in us. And to keep back – Here was the first instance of it. This was the first attempt to bring propriety of goods into the Christian Church.

4. While it remained, did it not remain thine? – It is true, whosoever among the Christians (not one excepted) had houses or lands, sold them, and laid the price at the feet of the apostles. But it was in his own choice to be a Christian or not: and consequently either to sell his land, or keep it. And when it was sold, was it not in thy power? – For it does not appear that he professed himself a Christian when he sold it. Why hast thou conceived this thing in thy heart? – So profanely to dissemble on so solemn an occasion? Thou hast not lied to men only, but to God also. Hence the Godhead of the Holy Ghost evidently appears: since lying to him, ver. 3, is lying to God.

5. And Ananias fell down and expired – And this severity was not only just, considering that complication of vain glory, covetousness, fraud, and impiety, which this action contained: but it was also wise and gracious, as it would effectually deter any others from following his example. It was likewise a convincing proof of the upright conduct of the apostles, in managing the sums with which they were intrusted; and in general of their Divine mission. For none can imagine that Peter would have had the assurance to pronounce, and much less the power to execute such a sentence, if he had been guilty himself of a fraud of the same kind; or had been belying the Holy Ghost in the whole of his pretensions to be under his immediate direction.

7. About the space of three hours – How precious a space! The woman had a longer time for repentance.

8. If ye sold the land for so much – Naming the sum.

10. The Church – This is the first time it is mentioned: and here is

MATTHEW HENRY   CHARLES H. SPURGEON

doing, and for the testimony of a good conscience, ought to be provided for. Here is one in particular mentioned, remarkable for this generous charity; it was Barnabas. As one designed to be a preacher of the gospel, he disentangled himself from the affairs of this life. When such dispositions prevail, and are exercised according to the circumstances of the times, the testimony will have very great power upon others.

ACTS 5

The death of Ananias and Sapphira. (1-11)
The power which accompanied the preaching of the gospel. (12-16)
The apostles imprisoned, but set free by an angel. (17-25)
The apostles testify to Christ before the council. (26-33)
The advice of Gamaliel. The council let the apostles go. (34-42)

1-11 The sin of Ananias and Sapphira was, that they were ambitious of being thought eminent disciples, when they were not true disciples. Hypocrites may deny themselves, may forego their worldly advantage in one instance, with a prospect of finding their account in something else. They were covetous of the wealth of the world, and distrustful of God and his providence. They thought they might serve both God and mammon. They thought to deceive the apostles. The Spirit of God in Peter discerned the principle of unbelief reigning in the heart of Ananias. But whatever Satan might suggest, he could not have filled the heart of Ananias with this wickedness had he not been consenting. The falsehood was an attempt to deceive the Spirit of truth, who so manifestly spoke and acted by the apostles. The crime of Ananias was not his retaining part of the price of the land; he might have kept it all, had he pleased; but his endeavoring to impose upon the apostles with an awful lie, from a desire to make a vain show, joined with covetousness. But if we think to put a cheat upon God, we shall put a fatal cheat upon our own souls. How sad to see those relations who should quicken one another to that which is good, hardening one another in that which is evil! And this punishment was in reality mercy to vast numbers. It would cause strict self-examination, prayer, and dread of hypocrisy, covetousness, and vain-glory, and it should still do so. It would prevent the increase of false professors. Let us learn hence how hateful falsehood is to the God of truth, and not only shun a direct lie, but all advantages from the use of doubtful expressions, and double meaning in our speech.

12-16 The separation of hypocrites by distin-

and it is a wonder to himself to find himself where he now is. He never dreamt of being what he is. Ask his wife whether there is a change in him; ask his little children whether there is a change in him; ask his workmates, ask his employer, ask anybody, and they will all say, "He is not the same man." The Lord Jesus Christ has turned everything upside down with him. It was the wrong way up before, and so he has put it all right. He can turn the lion into a lamb, the raven into a dove; and he has done so to many of our friends who are sitting in this house tonight, as they would willingly bear witness. Oh, if there are any here, tonight, who would learn the way of righteousness, and quit the paths of sin, let them believe my testimony, which comes not out of feigned lips! "I speak the truth in Christ, and lie not." The Lord is able to transform character in a very wonderful way; he has done it for many of us, and if thou believest in him, he will do it for thee also.

Next, we should like to bear witness to the sustaining power of Christ under temptation. After being saved, we have been tempted, and we are men of like passions with others. I speak for my sisters as well as for my brothers here. We have all been tempted, and we have been well nigh thrown back to our old condition; but when we have fled to Christ, and trusted in him, our feet have stood firm even upon the brink of the precipice. We have passed through fire and water by way of trial and temptation, and yet we stand, for Christ is able to guard us even from stumbling, and to present us faultless before the presence of his glory with an exceeding joy. We are not talking to you of things that we have dreamt. O sirs, we would not like to tell some of you how we have been tempted, how hard it has gone with us, how we have been saved by the skin of our teeth; but saved we have been, to the praise of God's mighty grace. Let his name be praised for ever and ever. That is our witness. If you would be kept from temptation, come and trust him, too.

We wish also to say that the Spirit of God coming from Christ moves men to high and noble thoughts. Selfishness no longer rules the man who believes in Christ; he loves his fellow-men, he desires their good, he can forgive them if they persecute him, he can lay down his life for them. Have we not had many who have gone forth among the heathen, and laid down their lives for Christ? I was speaking with a brother from the Congo on Monday, and I spoke of the many deaths there, and he said, "Yes, it looks a sad thing that so many missionaries should die; but, sir," he added, "that is the first thing that we have done in Africa that is really hopeful. I have often heard the natives say to me, 'These men must believe a true religion, or else they would not come here to die for us poor black men.' Men begin to believe this new kind of

35 And said unto them, Ye men of Israel, take heed to yourselves what ye intend to do as touching these men.

36 For before these days rose up Theudas, boasting himself to be somebody; to whom a number of men, about four hundred, joined themselves: who was slain; and all, as many as obeyed him, were scattered, and brought to nought.

37 After this man rose up Judas of Galilee in the days of the taxing, and drew away much people after him: he also perished; and all, even as many as obeyed him, were dispersed.

38 And now I say unto you, Refrain from these men, and let them alone: for if this counsel or this work be of men, it will come to nought:

39 But if it be of God, ye cannot overthrow it; lest haply ye be found even to fight against God.

40 And to him they agreed: and when they had called the apostles, and beaten them, they commanded that they should not speak in the name of Jesus, and let them go.

41 And they departed from the presence of the council, rejoicing that they were counted worthy to suffer shame for his name.

42 And daily in the temple, and in every house, they ceased not to teach and preach Jesus Christ.

ACTS 6

1 And in those days, when the number of the disciples was multiplied, there arose a murmuring of the Grecians against the Hebrews, because their widows were neglected in the daily ministration.

2 Then the twelve called the multitude of the disciples unto them, and said, It is not reason that we should leave the word of God, and serve tables.

3 Wherefore, brethren, look ye out among you seven men of honest report, full of the Holy Ghost and wisdom, whom we may appoint over this business.

4 But we will give ourselves continually to prayer, and to the ministry of the word.

5 And the saying pleased the whole multitude: and they chose Stephen, a man full of faith and of the Holy Ghost, and Philip, and Prochorus, and Nicanor, and Timon, and Parmenas, and Nicolas a proselyte of Antioch:

6 Whom they set before the apostles: and when they had prayed, they laid their hands on them.

7 And the word of God increased; and the number of the disciples multiplied in Jerusalem greatly; and a great company of the priests were obedient to the faith.

8 And Stephen, full of faith and power, did great wonders and miracles among the people.

9 Then there arose certain of the synagogue, which is called the synagogue of the

a native specimen of a New Testament Church; which is a company of men, called by the Gospel, grafted into Christ by baptism, animated by love, united by all kind of fellowship, and disciplined by the death of Ananias and Sapphira.

12. And they were all – All the believers.

13. None of the rest – No formalists or hypocrites, durst join themselves – In an outward show only, like Ananias and Sapphira.

14. But so much the more were true believers added, because unbelievers kept at a distance.

17. The high priest – and the sect of the Sadducees – A goodly company for the priest! He, and these deniers of any angel or resurrection, were filled with zeal – Angry, bitter, persecuting zeal.

20. The words of this – That is, these words of life: words which show the way to life everlasting.

23. We found the prison shut – The angel probably had shut the doors again.

24. They doubted what this should be – They were even at their wits' end. The world, in persecuting the children of God, entangles themselves in numberless difficulties.

28. Did not we strictly command you, not to teach? – See the poor cunning of the enemies of the Gospel. They make laws and interdicts at their pleasure, which those who obey God cannot but break; and then take occasion thereby to censure and punish the innocent, as guilty. Ye would bring the blood of this man upon us – An artful and invidious word. The apostles did not desire to accuse any man. They simply declared the naked truth.

29. Then Peter – In the name of all the apostles, said – He does not now give them the titles of honor, which he did before, chap. iv, 8; but enters directly upon the subject, and justifies what he had done. This is, as it were, a continuation of that discourse, but with an increase of severity.

30. Hath raised up Jesus – Of the seed of David, according to the promises made to our fathers.

31. Him hath God exalted – From the grave to heaven; to give repentance – Whereby Jesus is received as a Prince; and forgiveness of sins – Whereby he is received as a Savior. Hence some infer, that repentance and faith are as mere gifts as remission of sins. Not so: for man co-operates in the former, but not in the latter. God alone forgives sins.

32. And also the Holy Ghost – A much greater witness.

34. But a certain Pharisee – And as such believing the resurrection of the dead; a doctor, or teacher of the law – That is, a scribe, and indeed one of the highest rank; had in honor by all the people – Except the Sadducees; rising up in the council – So God can raise defenders of his servants, whensoever and wheresoever he pleases.

36. Before these days – He prudently mentions the facts first, and then makes the inference.

38. Let them alone – In a cause which is manifestly good, we should immediately join. In a cause, on the other hand, which is manifestly evil, we should immediately oppose. But in a sudden, new, doubtful occurrence, this advice is eminently useful. If this counsel or this work – He seems to correct himself, as if it were some sudden work, rather than a counsel or design. And so it was. For the apostles had no counsel, plan, or design of their own; but were mere instruments in the hand of God, working just as he led them from day to day.

41. Rejoicing – to suffer shame – This is a sure mark of the truth, joy in affliction, such is true, deep, pure.

guishing judgments, should make the sincere cleave closer to each other and to the gospel ministry. Whatever tends to the purity and reputation of the church, promotes its enlargement; but that power alone which wrought such miracles by the apostles, can rescue sinners from the power of sin and Satan, and add believers to His worshipers. Christ will work by all his faithful servants; and every one who applies to him shall be healed.

17-25 There is no prison so dark, so strong, but God can visit his people in it, and, if he pleases, fetch them out. Recoveries from sickness, releases out of trouble, are granted, not that we may enjoy the comforts of life, but that God may be honored with the services of our life. It is not for the preachers of Christ's gospel to retire into corners, as long as they can have any opportunity of preaching in the great congregation. They must preach to the lowest, whose souls are as precious to Christ as the souls of the greatest. Speak to all, for all are concerned. Speak as those who resolve to stand to it, to live and die by it. Speak all the words of this heavenly, divine life, in comparison with which the present earthly life does not deserve the name. These words of life, which the Holy Ghost puts into your mouth. The words of the gospel are the words of life; words whereby we may be saved. How wretched are those who are vexed at the success of the gospel! They cannot but see that the word and power of the Lord are against them; and they tremble for the consequences, yet they will go on.

26-33 Many will do an evil thing with daring, yet cannot bear to hear of it afterward, or to have it charged upon them. We cannot expect to be redeemed and healed by Christ, unless we give up ourselves to be ruled by him. Faith takes the Savior in all his offices, who came, not to save us in our sins, but to save us from our sins. Had Christ been exalted to give dominion to Israel, the chief priests would have welcomed him. But repentance and remission of sins are blessings they neither valued nor saw their need of; therefore they, by no means, admitted his doctrine. Wherever repentance is wrought, remission is granted without fail. None are freed from the guilt and punishment of sin, but those who are freed from the power and dominion of sin; who are turned from it, and turned against it. Christ gives repentance, by his Spirit working with the word, to awaken the conscience, to work sorrow for sin, and an effectual change in the heart and life. The giving of the Holy Ghost, is plain evidence that it is the will of God that Christ should be obeyed. And he will surely destroy those who will not have him to reign over them.

34-42 The Lord still has all hearts in his hands, and sometimes directs the prudence of the worldly

evidence. The blood of the missionary becomes the seed of the Church." I do not doubt that it is so and, beloved, if you and I can live wholly and alone for Christ, if we can live nobly, if we can get out of ourselves, if we can rise superior to worldly advantages, and prove that we believe all we say, we shall convince our fellow-men of the truth of our religion. This is what the Holy Spirit would have us to be, and we desire to obey his promptings more and more.

"Holy Spirit, dwell in me;
I, myself, would holy be."

I will not detain you many minutes more; but I must bear my testimony to the supporting power of Christ in the time of trouble. There are many here, who would have been in the asylum, in their time of trial, if it had not been that they could carry their grief to Christ. There are some of us who are not strangers to very acute pain, and to a long continuance of it, too; and we have found no comfort in the world like going to our Lord when racked with anguish, and torn with pain. There is a power about him to charm us into joy; when everything would drive us to distress, and almost to despair.

And, specially, I want to bear my witness, not of course a personal one, but that of an observer, as to the power of our holy religion in the hour of death. I have been at many death-beds; I have seen many Christians just about to die. There it is that the power of our holy religion comes in. How calm, how resigned, sometimes how triumphant, how ecstatic, is the frame of mind of the departing believer! I never heard one of them regret that he was a Christian. In times when men sift what they have done and believed, and when they tell no lies, for the naked truth comes up before them, I have heard them glory in belonging to Christ, and in resting in him; but I have never heard them regret that they did so. Our religion is not all of the future; it is not a thing that dreams concerning the world to come. It gives us present joy, present strength, present comfort, and we commend it to you most heartily, for this is our duty, to be witnesses for Christ. There are some who can give their evidence-in-chief, but the pity is that, when they come to be cross-examined, when they get among the ungodly in the world, they make a mess of it. The Lord have mercy upon some who come in among us, and even profess to know Christ, and do not; it is their lie that taints the testimony of the true in the judgment of mankind! Be you the more zealous to overbear their treachery by your consistency. Be you the more full of integrity, and stern truthfulness, and boundless love, to make up for these wounds which your Lord receives so often in the house of his friends.

May the Spirit of God rest upon you, beloved in the Lord, and may you hear your Master say to you, Ye shall be witnesses unto me"! Amen.

Libertines, and Cyrenians, and Alexandrians, and of them of Cilicia and of Asia, disputing with Stephen.

10 And they were not able to resist the wisdom and the spirit by which he spake.

11 Then they suborned men, which said, We have heard him speak blasphemous words against Moses, and against God.

12 And they stirred up the people, and the elders, and the scribes, and came upon him, and caught him, and brought him to the council,

13 And set up false witnesses, which said, This man ceaseth not to speak blasphemous words against this holy place, and the law:

14 For we have heard him say, that this Jesus of Nazareth shall destroy this place, and shall change the customs which Moses delivered us.

15 And all that sat in the council, looking stedfastly on him, saw his face as it had been the face of an angel.

ACTS 7

1 Then said the high priest, Are these things so?

2 And he said, Men, brethren, and fathers, hearken; The God of glory appeared unto our father Abraham, when he was in Mesopotamia, before he dwelt in Charran,

3 And said unto him, Get thee out of thy country, and from thy kindred, and come into the land which I shall shew thee.

4 Then came he out of the land of the Chaldeans, and dwelt in Charran: and from thence, when his father was dead, he removed him into this land, wherein ye now dwell.

5 And he gave him none inheritance in it, no, not so much as to set his foot on: yet he promised that he would give it to him for a possession, and to his seed after him, when as yet he had no child.

6 And God spake on this wise, That his seed should sojourn in a strange land; and that they should bring them into bondage, and entreat them evil four hundred years.

7 And the nation to whom they shall be in bondage will I judge, said God: and after that shall they come forth, and serve me in this place.

8 And he gave him the covenant of circumcision: and so Abraham begat Isaac, and circumcized him the eighth day; and Isaac begat Jacob; and Jacob begat the twelve patriarchs.

9 And the patriarchs, moved with envy, sold Joseph into Egypt: but God was with him,

10 And delivered him out of all his afflictions, and gave him favor and wisdom in the sight of Pharaoh king of Egypt; and he made him governor over Egypt and all his house.

11 Now there came a dearth over all the land of Egypt and Chanaan, and great affliction:

ACTS 6

1. There arose a murmuring – Here was the first breach made on those who were before of one heart and of one soul. Partiality crept in unawares on some; and murmuring on others. Ah Lord! how short a time did pure, genuine, undefiled Christianity remain in the world! O the depth! How unsearchable are thy counsels! marvelous are thy ways, O King of saints! The Hellenists were Jews born out of Palestine. They were so called, because they spoke Greek as their second language. In this partiality of the Hebrews, and murmuring of the Hellenists, were the needs of a general persecution sown. Did God ever, in any age or country, withdraw his restraining providence, and let loose the world upon the Christians, till there was a cause among themselves? Is not an open, general persecution, always both penal and medicinal? A punishment of those that will not accept of milder reproofs, as well as a medicine to heal their sickness? And at the same time a means both of purifying and strengthening those whose heart is still right with God.

2. It is not right that we should leave the word of God and serve tables – In the first Church, the primary business of apostles, evangelists, and bishops, was to preach the word of God; the secondary, to take a kind of paternal care (the Church being then like a family,) for the food, especially of the poor, the strangers, and the widows. Afterward, the deacons of both sexes were constituted for this latter business. And whatever time they had to spare from this, they employed in works of spiritual mercy. But their proper office was, to take care of the poor. And when some of them afterward preached the Gospel, they did this not by virtue of their deaconship, but of another commission, that of evangelists, which they probably received, not before, but after they were appointed deacons. And it is not unlikely that others were chosen deacons, or stewards, in their room, when any of these commenced evangelists.

3. Of good report – That there may be no room to suspect them of partiality or injustice. Full of the Holy Ghost and wisdom – For it is not a light matter to dispense even the temporal goods of the Church. To do even this well, a large measure both of the gifts and grace of God is requisite. Whom we will set over this business – It would have been happy for the Church, had its ordinary ministers in every age taken the same care to act in concert with the people committed to their charge, which the apostles themselves, extraordinary as their office was, did on this and other occasions.

4. We will constantly attend to prayer, and to the ministry of the word – This is doubtless the proper business of a Christian bishop: to speak to God in prayer; to men in preaching his word, as an ambassador for Christ.

5. And they chose – It seems seven Hellenists, as their names show. And Nicholas a proselyte – To whom the proselytes would the more readily apply.

7. And the word of God grew – The hindrances being removed.

9. There arose certain of the synagogue which is called – It was one and the same synagogue which consisted of these several nations. Saul of Cilicia was doubtless a member of it; whence it is not at all improbable, that Gamaliel presided over it. Libertines – So they were styled, whose fathers were once slaves, and afterward made free. This was the case of many Jews who had been taken captive by the Romans.

14. We have heard him say – So they might. But yet the consequence they drew would not follow.

15. As the face of an angel – Covered with supernatural luster. They

MATTHEW HENRY

wise, so as to restrain the persecutors. Common sense tells us to be cautious, while experience and observation show that the success of frauds in matters of religion has been very short. Reproach for Christ is true preferment, as it makes us conformable to his pattern, and serviceable to his interest. They rejoiced in it. If we suffer ill for doing well, provided we suffer it well, and as we should, we ought to rejoice in that grace which enabled us so to do. The apostles did not preach themselves, but Christ. This was the preaching that most offended the priests. But it ought to be the constant business of gospel ministers to preach Christ: Christ, and him crucified; Christ, and him glorified; nothing beside this, but what has reference to it. And whatever is our station or rank in life, we should seek to make Him known, and to glorify his name.

ACTS 6

The appointment of deacons. (1-7)
Stephen falsely accused of blasphemy. (8-15)

1-7 Hitherto the disciples had been of one accord; this often had been noticed to their honor; but now they were multiplied, they began to murmur. The word of God was enough to take up all the thoughts, cares, and time of the apostles. The persons chosen to serve tables must be duly qualified. They must be filled with gifts and graces of the Holy Ghost, necessary to rightly managing this trust; men of truth, and hating covetousness. All who are employed in the service of the church, ought to be commended to the Divine grace by the prayers of the church. They blessed them in the name of the Lord. The word and grace of God are greatly magnified, when those are wrought upon by it, who were least likely.

8-15 When they could not answer Stephen's arguments as a disputant, they prosecuted him as a criminal, and brought false witnesses against him. And it is next to a miracle of providence, that no greater number of religious persons have been murdered in the world, by the way of perjury and pretense of law, when so many thousands hate them, who make no conscience of false oaths. Wisdom and holiness make a man's face to shine, yet will not secure men from being treated badly. What shall we say of man, a rational being, yet attempting to uphold a religious system by false witness and murder! And this has been done in numberless instances. But the blame rests not so much upon the understanding, as upon the heart of a fallen creature, which is deceitful above all things and desperately wicked. Yet the servant of the Lord, possessing a clear conscience, cheerful hope, and Divine consolations, may smile in the midst of danger and death.

CHARLES H. SPURGEON

PRICKED IN THEIR HEART
Sermon number 2102 delivered on September 1st, 1889, at the Metropolitan Tabernacle, Newington.

"Therefore let all the house of Israel know assuredly, that God hath made that same Jesus, whom ye have crucified, both Lord and Christ. Now when they heard this, they were pricked in their heart, and said unto Peter and to the rest of the apostles, Men and brethren, what shall we do?"—Acts 2:36-37.

THIS WAS THE FIRST public preaching of the gospel after our Lord was taken up into glory. It was thus a very memorable sermon, a kind of first-fruits of the great harvest of gospel testimony. It is very encouraging to those who are engaged in preaching that the first sermon should have been so successful. Three thousand made up a grand take of fish at that first cast of the net. We are serving a great and growing cause in the way chosen of God, and we hope in the future to see still larger results produced by that same undying and unchanging power which helped Peter to preach such a heart-piercing sermon.

Peter's discourse was not distinguished by any special rhetorical display: he used not the words of man's wisdom or eloquence. It was not an oration, but it was a heart-moving argument, entreaty, and exhortation. He gave his hearers a simple, well-reasoned, Scriptural discourse, sustained by the facts of experience; and every passage of it pointed to the Lord Jesus. It was in these respects a model of what a sermon ought to be as to its contents. His plea was personally addressed to the people who stood before him, and it had a practical and pressing relation to them and to their conduct. It was aimed, not at the head, but at the heart. Every word of it was directed to the conscience and the affections. It was plain, practical, personal, and persuasive; and in this it was a model of what a sermon ought to be as to its aim and style. Yet Peter could not have spoken otherwise under the impression of the divine Spirit: his speech was as the oracles of God, a true product of a divine inspiration. Under the circumstances, any other kind of address would have been sadly out of place. A flashy, dazzling oration would have been a piece of horrible irreverence to the Holy Ghost; and Peter would have been guilty of the blood of souls if he had attempted it. In sober earnestness he kept to the plain facts of the case, setting them in the light of God's Word; and then with all his might he pressed home the truth upon those for whose salvation he was laboring. May it ever be the preacher's one desire to win men to repentance towards God and faith in our Lord Jesus Christ! May no minister wish to be admired, but may he long that his Lord and Master may be

and our fathers found no sustenance.

12 But when Jacob heard that there was corn in Egypt, he sent out our fathers first.

13 And at the second time Joseph was made known to his brethren; and Joseph's kindred was made known unto Pharaoh.

14 Then sent Joseph, and called his father Jacob to him, and all his kindred, threescore and fifteen souls.

15 So Jacob went down into Egypt, and died, he, and our fathers,

16 And were carried over into Sychem, and laid in the sepulcher that Abraham bought for a sum of money of the sons of Emmor the father of Sychem.

17 But when the time of the promise drew nigh, which God had sworn to Abraham, the people grew and multiplied in Egypt,

18 Till another king arose, which knew not Joseph.

19 The same dealt subtilly with our kindred, and evil entreated our fathers, so that they cast out their young children, to the end they might not live.

20 In which time Moses was born, and was exceeding fair, and nourished up in his father's house three months:

21 And when he was cast out, Pharaoh's daughter took him up, and nourished him for her own son.

22 And Moses was learned in all the wisdom of the Egyptians, and was mighty in words and in deeds.

23 And when he was full forty years old, it came into his heart to visit his brethren the children of Israel.

24 And seeing one of them suffer wrong, he defended him, and avenged him that was oppressed, and smote the Egyptian:

25 For he supposed his brethren would have understood how that God by his hand would deliver them: but they understood not.

26 And the next day he shewed himself unto them as they strove, and would have set them at one again, saying, Sirs, ye are brethren; why do ye wrong one to another?

27 But he that did his neighbor wrong thrust him away, saying, Who made thee a ruler and a judge over us?

28 Wilt thou kill me, as thou diddest the Egyptian yesterday?

29 Then fled Moses at this saying, and was a stranger in the land of Madian, where he begat two sons.

30 And when forty years were expired, there appeared to him in the wilderness of mount Sina an angel of the Lord in a flame of fire in a bush.

31 When Moses saw it, he wondered at the sight: and as he drew near to behold it, the voice of the Lord came unto him,

32 Saying, I am the God of thy fathers, the God of Abrham, and the God of Isaac, and the God of Jacob. Then Moses trembled, and durst

reckoned his preaching of Jesus to be the Christ was destroying Moses and the law; and God bears witness to him, with the same glory as he did to Moses, when he gave the law by him.

ACTS 7

2. And he said – St. Stephen had been accused of blasphemy against Moses, and even against God; and of speaking against the temple and the law, threatening that Jesus would destroy the one, and change the other. In answer to this accusation, rehearsing as it were the articles of his historical creed, he speaks of God with high reverence, and a grateful sense of a long series of acts of goodness to the Israelites, and of Moses with great respect, on account of his important and honorable employments under God: of the temple with regard, as being built to the honor of God; yet not with such superstition as the Jews; putting them in mind, that no temple could comprehend God. And he was going on, no doubt, when he was interrupted by their clamor, to speak to the last point, the destruction of the temple, and the change of the law by Christ. Men, brethren, and fathers, hearken – The sum of his discourse is this: I acknowledge the glory of God revealed to the fathers, ver. 2; the calling of Moses, ver. 34, &c.; the dignity of the law, verses 8, 38, 44; the holiness of this place, verses 7, 45, 47. And indeed the law is more ancient than the temple; the promise more ancient than the law. For God showed himself the God of Abraham, Isaac, Jacob, and their children freely, ver. 2, &c.; 9, &c.; 17,&c.; 32, 34, 35; and they showed faith and obedience to God, ver. 4, 20, &c., 23, particularly by their regard for the law, ver. 8, and the promised land, ver. 16. Meantime, God never confined his presence to this one place or to the observers of the law. For he hath been acceptably worshiped before the law was given, or the temple built, and out of this land, ver. 2, 9, 33, 44. And that our fathers and their posterity were not tied down to this land, their various sojourning, ver. 4, &c.; 14, 29, 44, and exile, ver. 43, show. But you and your fathers have always been evil, ver. 9; have withstood Moses, ver. 25, &c., 39, &c.; have despised the land, ver. 39, forsaken God, ver. 40, &c., superstitiously honored the temple, ver. 48, resisted God and his Spirit, ver 50, killed the prophets and the Messiah himself, ver. 51, and kept not the law for which ye contend, ver. 53. Therefore God is not bound to you; much less to you alone. And truly this solemn testimony of Stephen is most worthy of his character, as a man full of the Holy Ghost, and of faith and power: in which, though he does not advance so many regular propositions, contradictory to those of his adversaries, yet he closely and nervously answers them all. Nor can we doubt but he would, from these premises, have drawn inferences touching the destruction of the temple, the abrogation of the Mosaic law, the punishment of that rebellious people; and above all, touching Jesus of Nazareth, the true Messiah, had not his discourse been interrupted by the clamors of the multitude, stopping their ears, and rushing upon him. Men, brethren, and fathers – All who are here present, whether ye are my equals in years, or of more advanced age. The word which in this and in many other places is rendered men is a mere expletive. The God of glory – The glorious God, appeared to Abraham before he dwelt in Haran – Therefore Abraham knew God, long before he was in this land. Gen. xii, 1.

3. Which I will show thee – Abraham knew not where he went.

4. After his father was dead – While Terah lived, Abraham lived partly with him, partly in Canaan: but after he died, altogether in

ACTS 7

Stephen's defense. (1-50)

Stephen reproves the Jews for the death of Christ. (51-53)

The martyrdom of Stephen. (54-60)

1-16 Stephen was charged as a blasphemer of God, and an apostate from the church; therefore he shows that he is a son of Abraham, and values himself on it. The slow steps by which the promise made to Abraham advanced toward performance, plainly show that it had a spiritual meaning, and that the land intended was the heavenly. God owned Joseph in his troubles, and was with him by the power of his Spirit, both on his own mind by giving him comfort, and on those he was concerned with, by giving him favor in their eyes. Stephen reminds the Jews of their mean beginning as a check to priding themselves in the glories of that nation. Likewise of the wickedness of the patriarchs of their tribes, in envying their brother Joseph; and the same spirit was still working in them toward Christ and his ministers. The faith of the patriarchs, in desiring to be buried in the land of Canaan, plainly showed they had regard to the heavenly country. It is well to recur to the first rise of usages, or sentiments, which have been perverted. Would we know the nature and effects of justifying faith, we should study the character of the father of the faithful. His calling shows the power and freeness of Divine grace, and the nature of conversion. Here also we see that outward forms and distinctions are as nothing, compared with separation from the world, and devotedness to God.

17-29 Let us not be discouraged at the slowness of the fulfilling of God's promises. Suffering times often are growing times with the church. God is preparing for his people's deliverance, when their day is darkest, and their distress deepest. Moses was exceeding fair, "fair toward God;" it is the beauty of holiness which is in God's sight of great price. He was wonderfully preserved in his infancy; for God will take special care of those of whom he designs to make special use. And did he thus protect the child Moses? Much more will he secure the interests of his holy child Jesus, from the enemies who are gathered together against him. They persecuted Stephen for disputing in defense of Christ and his gospel: in opposition to these they set up Moses and his law. They may understand, if they do not willfully shut their eyes against the light, that God will, by this Jesus, deliver them out of a worse slavery than that of Egypt. Although men prolong their own miseries, yet the Lord will take care of his servants, and effect his own designs of mercy.

sought after! May none bewilder their people with the clouds of theoretic philosophy, but refresh them with the rain of revealed truth? Oh, that we could so preach that our hearers should be at once pricked in their hearts, and so be led at once to believe in our Lord Jesus, and immediately to come forward and confess their faith in his name!

We must not forget, however, to trace the special success of the sermon on the day of Pentecost to the outpouring of the Holy Ghost, in which Peter had shared. This it is which is the making of the preacher. Immersed into the Holy Spirit, the preacher will think rightly, and speak wisely; his word will be with power to those who hear. We must not forget, also, that there had been a long season of earnest, united, believing prayer on the part of the whole church. Peter was not alone: he was the voice of a praying company, and the believers had been with one accord in one place crying for a blessing; and thus not only was the Spirit resting upon the preacher, but on all who were with him. What a difference this makes to a preacher of the gospel, when all his comrades are as much anointed of the Spirit as himself! His power is enhanced a hundredfold. We shall seldom see the very greatest wonders wrought when the preacher stands by himself; but when Peter is described as standing up "with the eleven," then is there a twelve-man ministry concentrated in one; and when the inner circle is further sustained by a company of men and women who have entered into the same truth, and are of one heart and one soul, then is the power increased beyond measure. A lonely ministry may sometimes effect great things, as Jonah did in Nineveh; but if we look for the greatest and most desirable result of all, it must come from one who is not alone, but is the mouthpiece of many. Peter had the one hundred and twenty registered brethren for a loving body-guard, and this tended to make him strong for his Lord. How greatly I value the loving co-operation of the friends around me! I have no word, to express my gratitude to God for the army of true men and women who surround me with their love, and support me with their faith. I pray you, never cease to sustain me by your prayers, your sympathy, and your co-operation, until some other preacher shall take my place when increasing years shall warn me to stand aside.

Yet much responsibility must rest with the preacher himself; and there was much about Peter's own self that is well worthy of imitation. The sermon was born of the occasion, and it used the event of the hour as God intended it to be used. It was earnest without a trace of passion, and prudent without a suspicion of fear. The preacher himself was self-collected, calm, courteous, and gentle. He aired no theories, but went on

not behold.

33 Then said the Lord to him, Put off thy shoes from thy feet: for the place where thou standest is holy ground.

34 I have seen, I have seen the affliction of my people which is in Egypt, and I have heard their groaning, and am come down to deliver them. And now come, I will send thee into Egypt.

35 This Moses whom they refused, saying, Who made thee a ruler and a judge? the same did God send to be a ruler and a deliverer by the hand of the angel which appeared to him in the bush.

36 He brought them out, after that he had shewed wonders and signs in the land of Egypt, and in the Red sea, and in the wilderness forty years.

37 This is that Moses, which said unto the children of Israel, A prophet shall the Lord your God raise up unto you of your brethren, like unto me; him shall ye hear.

38 This is he, that was in the church in the wilderness with the angel which spake to him in the mount Sina, and with our fathers: who received the lively oracles to give unto us:

39 To whom our fathers would not obey, but thrust him from them, and in their hearts turned back again into Egypt,

40 Saying unto Aaron, Make us gods to go before us: for as for this Moses, which brought us out of the land of Egypt, we wot not what is become of him.

41 And they made a calf in those days, and offered sacrifice unto the idol, and rejoiced in the works of their own hands.

42 Then God turned, and gave them up to worship the host of heaven; as it is written in the book of the prophets, O ye house of Israel, have ye offered to me slain beasts and sacrifices by the space of forty years in the wilderness?

43 Yea, ye took up the tabernacle of Moloch, and the star of your god Remphan, figures which ye made to worship them: and I will carry you away beyond Babylon.

44 Our fathers had the tabernacle of witness in the wilderness, as he had appointed, speaking unto Moses, that he should make it according to the fashion that he had seen.

45 Which also our fathers that came after brought in with Jesus into the possession of the Gentiles, whom God drave out before the face of our fathers, unto the days of David;

46 Who found favor before God, and desired to find a tabernacle for the God of Jacob.

47 But Solomon built him an house.

48 Howbeit the most High dwelleth not in temples made with hands; as saith the prophet,

49 Heaven is my throne, and earth is my footstool: what house will ye build me? saith the Lord: or what is the place of my rest?

50 Hath not my hand made all these things?

Canaan.

5. No, not to set his foot on – For the field mentioned, ver. 16, he did not receive by a Divine donation, but bought it; even thereby showing that he was a stranger in the land.

6. Gen. xv, 13.

7. They shall serve me – Not the Egyptians.

8. And so he begat Isaac – After the covenant was given, of which circumcision was the seal. Gen. xvii, 10.

9. But God was with him – Though he was not in this land. Gen. xxxvii, 28.

12. Sent our fathers first – Without Benjamin.

14. Seventy-five souls – So the seventy interpreters, (whom St. Stephen follows,) one son and a grandson of Manasseh, and three children of Ephraim, being added to the seventy persons mentioned Gen. xlvi, 27.

16. And were carried over to Shechem – It seems that St. Stephen, rapidly running over so many circumstances of history, has not leisure (nor was it needful where they were so well known) to recite them all distinctly. Therefore he here contracts into one, two different sepulchers, places, and purchases, so as in the former history, to name the buyer, omitting the seller, in the latter, to name the seller, omitting the buyer. Abraham bought a burying place of the children of Heth, Gen. xxiii. Gen. xxiii, 1-20 There Jacob was buried. Jacob bought a field of the children of Hamor. There Joseph was buried. You see here, how St. Stephen contracts these two purchases into one. This concise manner of speaking, strange as it seems to us, was common among the Hebrews; particularly, when in a case notoriously known, the speaker mentioned but part of the story, and left the rest, which would have interrupted the current of his discourse, to be supplied in the mind of the hearer. And laid in the sepulcher that Abraham bought – The first land which these strangers bought was for a sepulcher. They sought for a country in heaven. Perhaps the whole sentence might be rendered thus: So Jacob went down into Egypt and died, he and our fathers, and were carried over to Shechem, and laid by the sons (that is, descendants) of Hamor, the father of Shechem, in the sepulcher that Abraham bought for a sum of money.

17. Exod. i, 7.

18. Another king – Probably of another family.

19. Exposed – Cast out to perish by hunger or wild beasts.

20. In which time – A sad but a seasonable time. Exod. ii, 2.

21. Pharaoh's daughter took him up – By which means, being designed for a kingdom, he had all those advantages of education, which he could not have had, if he had not been exposed.

22. In all the wisdom of the Egyptians – Which was then celebrated in all the world, and for many ages after. And mighty in words – Deep, solid, weighty, though not of a ready utterance.

23. It came into his heart – Probably by an impulse from God.

24. Seeing one wronged – Probably by one of the task masters.

25. They understood it not – Such was their stupidity and sloth; which made him afterward unwilling to go to them.

26. He showed himself – Of his own accord, unexpectedly.

27. Who appointed thee – "Under the presence of the want of a call by man, the instruments of God are often rejected."

30. The angel – The Son of God; as appears from his styling himself Jehovah. In a flame of fire – Signifying the majesty of God then present. Exod. iii, 2.

33. Then said the Lord, Loose thy shoes – An ancient token of rev-

30-41 Men deceive themselves, if they think God cannot do what he sees to be good any where; he can bring his people into a wilderness, and there speak comfortably to them. He appeared to Moses in a flame of fire, yet the bush was not consumed; which represented the state of Israel in Egypt, where, though they were in the fire of affliction, yet they were not consumed. It may also be looked upon as a type of Christ's taking upon him the nature of man, and the union between the Divine and human nature. The death of Abraham, Isaac, and Jacob, cannot break the covenant relation between God and them. Our Savior by this proves the future state, Mt 22:31. Abraham is dead, yet God is still his God, therefore Abraham is still alive. Now, this is that life and immortality which are brought to light by the gospel. Stephen here shows that Moses was an eminent type of Christ, as he was Israel's deliverer. God has compassion for the troubles of his church, and the groans of his persecuted people; and their deliverance takes rise from his pity. And that deliverance was typical of what Christ did, when, for us men, and for our salvation, he came down from heaven. This Jesus, whom they now refused, as their fathers did Moses, even this same has God advanced to be a Prince and Savior. It does not at all take from the just honor of Moses to say, that he was but an instrument, and that he is infinitely outshone by Jesus. In asserting that Jesus should change the customs of the ceremonial law, Stephen was so far from blaspheming Moses, that really he honored him, by showing how the prophecy of Moses was come to pass, which was so clear. God who gave them those customs by his servant Moses, might, no doubt, change the custom by his Son Jesus. But Israel thrust Moses from them, and would have returned to their bondage; so men in general will not obey Jesus, because they love this present evil world, and rejoice in their own works and devices.

42-50 Stephen upbraids the Jews with the idolatry of their fathers, to which God gave them up as a punishment for their early forsaking him. It was no dishonor, but an honor to God, that the tabernacle gave way to the temple; so it is now, that the earthly temple gives way to the spiritual one; and so it will be when, at last, the spiritual shall give way to the eternal one. The whole world is God's temple, in which he is every where present, and fills it with his glory; what occasion has he then for a temple to manifest himself in? And these things show his eternal power and Godhead. But as heaven is his throne, and the earth his footstool, so none of our services can profit Him who made all things. Next to the human nature of Christ, the broken and spiritual heart is his most valued temple.

51-53 Stephen was going on, it seems, to show

firm ground, stepping from fact to fact, from Scripture to Scripture, from plain truth to plain truth. He was patient at the beginning, argumentative all along, and conclusive at the end. He fought his way through the doubts and prejudices of his hearers; and when he came to the end, he stated the inevitable conclusion with clearness and certainty. All along he spake very boldly, without mincing the truth—Ye with wicked hands have crucified and slain him whom God has highly exalted. He boldly accused them of the murder of the Lord of glory, doing his duty in the sight of God, and for the good of their souls, with great firmness and fearlessness. Yet there is great tenderness in his discourse. Impulsive and hot-headed Peter, who, a little while before, had drawn his sword to fight for his Lord, does not, in this instance, use a harsh word; but speaks with great gentleness and meekness of spirit, using words and terms all through the address which indicate a desire to conciliate, and then to convince. Though he was as faithful as an Elijah, yet he used terms so courteous and kindly that, if men took offense, it would not be because of any offensiveness of tone on the speaker's part. Peter was gentle in his manner, but forceful in his matter. This art he had learned from his Lord; and we shall never have master-preachers among us till we see men who have been with Jesus, and have learned of him. Oh, that we could become partakers of our Lord's Spirit, and echoes of his tone! Then may we hope to attain to Pentecostal results, when we have preachers like Peter, surrounded by a band of earnest witnesses, and all baptized with the Holy Ghost and with fire.

When we follow the run of Peter's argument, we do not wonder that his hearers were pricked in their hearts. We ascribe that deep compunction to the Spirit of God; and yet it was a very reasonable thing that it should be so. When it was clearly shown to them that they had really crucified the Messiah, the great hope of their nation, it was not wonderful that they should be smitten with horror. Looking as they were for Israel's King, and finding that he had been among them, and they had despitefully used him, and crucified him, they might well be smitten at the heart. Though for the result of our ministry we depend wholly upon the Spirit of God, yet we must adapt our discourse to the end we aim at; or, say rather, we must leave ourselves in the Spirit's hand as to the sermon itself as well as in reference to the result of the sermon. The Holy Ghost uses means which are adapted to the end designed. Because, beloved, I do desire beyond all things that many in this congregation may be pricked in the heart, I have taken this concluding part of Peter's discourse to be the text of my sermon this morning. Yet my trust is not in the Word itself, but in the quickening Spirit who works by it. May the Spirit of God use the rapier of his

51 Ye stiffnecked and uncircumcized in heart and ears, ye do always resist the Holy Ghost: as your fathers did, so do ye.

52 Which of the prophets have not your fathers persecuted? and they have slain them which shewed before of the coming of the Just One; of whom ye have been now the betrayers and murderers:

53 Who have received the law by the disposition of angels, and have not kept it.

54 When they heard these things, they were cut to the heart, and they gnashed on him with their teeth.

55 But he, being full of the Holy Ghost, looked up stedfastly into heaven, and saw the glory of God, and Jesus standing on the right hand of God,

56 And said, Behold, I see the heavens opened, and the Son of man standing on the right hand of God.

57 Then they cried out with a loud voice, and stopped their ears, and ran upon him with one accord,

58 And cast him out of the city, and stoned him: and the witnesses laid down their clothes at a young man's feet, whose name was Saul.

59 And they stoned Stephen, calling upon God, and saying, Lord Jesus, receive my spirit.

60 And he kneeled down, and cried with a loud voice, Lord, lay not this sin to their charge. And when he had said this, he fell asleep.

ACTS 8

1 And Saul was consenting unto his death. And at that time there was a great persecution against the church which was at Jerusalem; and they were all scattered abroad throughout the regions of Judea and Samaria, except the apostles.

2 And devout men carried Stephen to his burial, and made great lamentation over him.

3 As for Saul, he made havoc of the church, entering into every house, and haling men and women committed them to prison.

4 Therefore they that were scattered abroad went every where preaching the word.

5 Then Philip went down to the city of Samaria, and preached Christ unto them.

6 And the people with one accord gave heed unto those things which Philip spake, hearing and seeing the miracles which he did.

7 For unclean spirits, crying with loud voice, came out of many that were possessed with them: and many taken with palsies, and that were lame, were healed.

8 And there was great joy in that city.

9 But there was a certain man, called Simon, which beforetime in the same city used sorcery, and bewitched the people of Samaria, giving out that himself was some great one:

10 To whom they all gave heed, from the least

erence; for the place is holy ground – The holiness of places depends on the peculiar presence of God there.

35. This Moses whom they refused – Namely, forty years before. Probably, not they, but their fathers did it, and God imputes it to them. So God frequently imputes the sins of the fathers to those of their children who are of the same spirit. Him did God send to be a deliverer – Which is much more than a judge; by the hand of – That is, by means of the angel – This angel who spoke to Moses on Mount Sinai expressly called himself Jehovah, a name which cannot, without the highest presumption, be assumed by any created angel, since he whose name alone is Jehovah, is the Most High over all the earth, Psalm lxxxiii, 18. Psalm lxxxiii, 18. It was therefore the Son of God who delivered the law to Moses, under the character of Jehovah, and who is here spoken of as the angel of the covenant, in respect of his mediatorial office.

37. The Lord will raise you up a prophet – St. Stephen here shows that there is no opposition between Moses and Christ. Deut. xviii, 15

38. This is he – Moses. With the angel, and with our fathers – As a mediator between them. Who received the living oracles – Every period beginning with, And the Lord said unto Moses, is properly an oracle. But the oracles here intended are chiefly the ten commandments. These are termed living, because all the word of God, applied by his Spirit, is living and powerful, Heb. iv, 12, enlightening the eyes, rejoicing the heart, converting the soul, raising the dead. Exod. xix, 3.

40. Make us gods to go before us – Back into Egypt. Exod. xxxii, 1.

41. And they made a calf – In imitation of Apis, the Egyptian God: and rejoiced in the works of their hands – In the God they had made.

42. God turned – From them in anger; and gave them up – Frequently from the time of the golden calf, to the time of Amos, and afterward. The host of heaven – The stars are called an army or host, because of their number, order, and powerful influence. In the book of the prophets – Of the twelve prophets, which the Jews always wrote together in one book. Have ye offered – The passage of Amos referred to, chap. v, 25, &c., Amos v, 25 consists of two parts; of which the former confirms ver. 41, of the sin of the people; the latter the beginning of ver. 42, concerning their punishment. Have ye offered to me – They had offered many sacrifices; but God did not accept them as offered to him, because they sacrificed to idols also; and did not sacrifice to him with an upright heart. Amos v, 25.

43. Ye took up – Probably not long after the golden calf: but secretly; else Moses would have mentioned it. The shrine – A small, portable chapel, in which was the image of their God. Moloch was the planet Mars, which they worshiped under a human shape. Remphan, that is, Saturn, they represented by a star. And I will carry you beyond Babylon – That is, beyond Damascus (which is the word in Amos) and Babylon. This was fulfilled by the king of Assyria, 2 Kings xvii, 6.

44. Our fathers had the tabernacle of the testimony – The testimony was properly the two tables of stone, on which the ten commandments were written. Hence the ark which contained them is frequently called the ark of the testimony; and the whole tabernacle in this place. The tabernacle of the testimony – according to the model which he had seen – When he was caught up in the visions of God on the mount.

45. Which our fathers having received – From their ancestors;

that the temple and the temple service must come to an end, and it would be the glory of both to give way to the worship of the Father in spirit and in truth; but he perceived they would not bear it. Therefore he broke off, and by the Spirit of wisdom, courage, and power, sharply rebuked his persecutors. When plain arguments and truths provoke the opposers of the gospel, they should be shown their guilt and danger. They, like their fathers, were stubborn and willfull. There is that in our sinful hearts, which always resists the Holy Ghost, a flesh that lusts against the Spirit, and wars against his motions; but in the hearts of God's elect, when the fullness of time comes, this resistance is overcome. The gospel was offered now, not by angels, but from the Holy Ghost; yet they did not embrace it, for they were resolved not to comply with God, either in his law or in his gospel. Their guilt stung them to the heart, and they sought relief in murdering their reprover, instead of sorrow and supplication for mercy.

54-60 Nothing is so comfortable to dying saints, or so encouraging to suffering saints, as to see Jesus at the right hand of God: blessed be God, by faith we may see him there. Stephen offered up two short prayers in his dying moments. Our Lord Jesus is God, to whom we are to seek, and in whom we are to trust and comfort ourselves, living and dying. And if this has been our care while we live, it will be our comfort when we die. Here is a prayer for his persecutors. Though the sin was very great, yet if they would lay it to their hearts, God would not lay it to their charge. Stephen died as much in a hurry as ever any man did, yet, when he died, the words used are, he fell asleep; he applied himself to his dying work with as much composure as if he had been going to sleep. He shall awake again in the morning of the resurrection, to be received into the presence of the Lord, where is fullness of joy, and to share the pleasures that are at his right hand, for evermore.

ACTS 8

Saul persecutes the church. (1-4)
Philip's success at Samaria. Simon the sorcerer baptized. (5-13)
The hypocrisy of Simon detected. (14-25)
Philip and the Ethiopian. (26-40)

1-4 Though persecution must not drive us from our work, yet it may send us to work elsewhere. Wherever the established believer is driven, he carries the knowledge of the gospel, and makes known the preciousness of Christ in every place. Where a simple desire of doing good influences the heart, it will be found impossible to shut a man out from all opportunities of usefulness.

Word to pierce the hearts of my hearers!

First, note that Peter speaks to his hearers upon their evil conduct to the Lord Jesus; and, secondly, he declares to them the exaltation that God has bestowed upon him. When we have dwelt on these two things, we will notice, in the third place, the result of knowing this grand fact—"Let all the house of Israel know assuredly, that God hath made that same Jesus, whom ye have crucified, both Lord and Christ."

I. First, then, Peter dwelt tenderly, but very plainly, upon THEIR EVIL CONDUCT TOWARDS THE LORD JESUS. "He came unto his own, and his own received him not." As a nation, Israel had rejected him whom God had sent. The inhabitants of Jerusalem had gone further, and had consented unto his death; nay, had even clamored for it, crying, "Crucify him, crucify him." Solemnly had the Jews exclaimed, "His blood be on us, and on our children." None of them had protested against the murder of the innocent One; but many of them had been eager to make an end of him. This Peter, in plain words, charged upon them, and they could not deny it; nor did they pretend to do so. It is well when a sense of guilt compels a man to stand silent under the rebuke of God. We then have hope of him that he will seek for pardon.

Men and brethren, we are not in Jerusalem, and the death of our Lord happened more than eighteen hundred years ago; therefore we need not dwell upon the sin of those long since dead. It will be more profitable for us practically to consider how far we have been guilty of similar sins against the Lord Jesus Christ. Let us look at home. Let each one consider his own case. I may be addressing some today who have blasphemed the name of the Lord Jesus. I do not suppose that you have been guilty of the vulgar language of blasphemy, which is coarse and revolting, as well as profane; but there are politer methods of committing the self-same crime. Some, with their elaborate criticisms of Christianity, wound it far more seriously than atheists with their profanities. In these days, wiseacres, with their philosophy, derogate from the glory of our Lord's nature, and, with their novel doctrines, undermine his gospel. Denying the atonement, or teaching it as something other than a substitutionary sacrifice, they try to make away with that which is the very heart and soul of the Redeemer's work. Men nowadays drink in opinions which lessen the guilt of sin, and, of course, lower the value of the atoning blood. The cross is still a stone of stumbling, and a rock of offense. Men do not now accept the words of the Bible as authoritative, nor the teaching of the apostles as final; they set themselves up to be teachers of the great Teacher, reformers of the divine gospel. They do not accept the teaching of

to the greatest, saying, This man is the great power of God.

11 And to him they had regard, because that of long time he had bewitched them with sorceries.

12 But when they believed Philip preaching the things concerning the kingdom of God, and the name of Jesus Christ, they were baptized, both men and women.

13 Then Simon himself believed also: and when he was baptized, he continued with Philip, and wondered, beholding the miracles and signs which were done.

14 Now when the apostles which were at Jerusalem heard that Samaria had received the word of God, they sent unto them Peter and John:

15 Who, when they were come down, prayed for them, that they might receive the Holy Ghost:

16 (For as yet he was fallen upon none of them: only they were baptized in the name of the Lord Jesus.)

17 Then laid they their hands on them, and they received the Holy Ghost.

18 And when Simon saw that through laying on of the apostles' hands the Holy Ghost was given, he offered them money,

19 Saying, Give me also this power, that on whomsoever I lay hands, he may receive the Holy Ghost.

20 But Peter said unto him, Thy money perish with thee, because thou hast thought that the gift of God may be purchased with money.

21 Thou hast neither part nor lot in this matter: for thy heart is not right in the sight of God.

22 Repent therefore of this thy wickedness, and pray God, if perhaps the thought of thine heart may be forgiven thee.

23 For I perceive that thou art in the gall of bitterness, and in the bond of iniquity.

24 Then answered Simon, and said, Pray ye to the Lord for me, that none of these things which ye have spoken come upon me.

25 And they, when they had testified and preached the word of the Lord, returned to Jerusalem, and preached the gospel in many villages of the Samaritans.

26 And the angel of the Lord spake unto Philip, saying, Arise, and go toward the south unto the way that goeth down from Jerusalem unto Gaza, which is desert.

27 And he arose and went: and, behold, a man of Ethiopia, an eunuch of great authority under Candace queen of the Ethiopians, who had the charge of all her treasure, and had come to Jerusalem for to worship,

28 Was returning, and sitting in his chariot read Esaias the prophet.

29 Then the Spirit said unto Philip, Go near, and join thyself to this chariot.

30 And Philip ran thither to him, and heard him read the prophet Esaias, and said, Understandest thou what thou readest?

brought into the possession of the Gentiles – Into the land which the Gentiles possessed before. So that God's favor is not a necessary consequence of inhabiting this land. All along St. Stephen intimates two things:

1. That God always loved good men in every land:

2. That he never loved bad men even in this. Josh iii, 14.

46. Who petitioned to find a habitation for the God of Jacob – But he did not obtain his petition: for God remained without any temple till Solomon built him a house. Observe how wisely the word is chosen with respect to what follows.

48. Yet the Most High inhabiteth not temples made with hands – As Solomon declared at the very dedication of the temple, 1 Kings viii, 27. The Most High – Whom as such no building can contain. Isaiah lxvi, 1.

49. What is the place of my rest? – Have I need to rest?

51. Ye stiff necked – Not bowing the neck to God's yoke; and uncircumcised in heart – So they showed themselves, ver. 54; Act vii, 54 and ears – As they showed, ver. 57. Act vii, 57. So far were they from receiving the word of God into their hearts, that they would not hear it even with their ears. Ye – And your fathers, always – As often as ever ye are called, resist the Holy Ghost – Testifying by the prophets of Jesus, and the whole truth. This is the sum of what he had shown at large.

53. Who have received the law by the administration of angels – God, when he gave the law on Mount Sinai, was attended with thousands of his angels, Gal. iii, 19; Psalm lxviii, 17.

55. But he looking steadfastly up to heaven, saw the glory of God – Doubtless he saw such a glorious representation, God miraculously operating on his imagination, as on Ezekiel's, when he sat in his house at Babylon, and saw Jerusalem, and seemed to himself transported thither, chap. viii, 1-4. And probably other martyrs, when called to suffer the last extremity, have had extraordinary assistance of some similar kind.

56. I see the Son of man standing – As if it were just ready to receive him. Otherwise he is said to sit at the right hand of God.

57. They rushed upon him – Before any sentence passed.

58. The witnesses laid down their clothes at the feet of a young man, whose name was Saul – O Saul, couldst thou have believed, if one had told thee, that thou thyself shouldst be stoned in the same cause? and shouldst triumph in committing thy soul likewise to that Jesus whom thou art now blaspheming? His dying prayer reached thee, as well as many others. And the martyr Stephen, and Saul the persecutor, (afterward his brother both in faith and martyrdom,) are now joined in everlasting friendship, and dwell together in the happy company of those who have made their robes white in the blood of the Lamb.

59. And they stoned Stephen, invoking and saying, Lord Jesus, receive my spirit – This is the literal translation of the words, the name of God not being in the original. Nevertheless such a solemn prayer to Christ, in which a departing soul is thus committed into his hands, is such an act of worship, as no good man could have paid to a mere creature; Stephen here worshiping Christ in the very same manner in which Christ worshiped the Father on the cross.

ACTS 8

1. At that time there was great persecution against the Church – Their adversaries having tasted blood, were the more eager. And they

5-13 As far as the gospel prevails, evil spirits are dislodged, particularly unclean spirits. All inclinations to the lusts of the flesh which war against the soul are such. Distempers are here named, the most difficult to be cured by the course of nature, and most expressive of the disease of sin. Pride, ambition, and desire after grandeur have always caused abundance of mischief, both to the world and to the church. The people said of Simon, This man is the great power of God. See how ignorant and thoughtless people mistake. But how strong is the power of Divine grace, by which they were brought to Christ, who is Truth itself! The people not only gave heed to what Philip said, but were fully convinced that it was of God, and not of men, and gave up themselves to be directed thereby. Even bad men, and those whose hearts still go after covetousness, may come before God as his people come, and for a time continue with them. And many wonder at the proofs of Divine truths, who never experience their power. The gospel preached may have a common operation upon a soul, where it never produced inward holiness. All are not savingly converted who profess to believe the gospel.

14-25 The Holy Ghost was as yet fallen upon none of these coverts, in the extraordinary powers conveyed by the descent of the Spirit upon the day of Pentecost. We may take encouragement from this example, in praying to God to give the renewing graces of the Holy Ghost to all for whose spiritual welfare we are concerned; for that includes all blessings. No man can give the Holy Spirit by the laying on of his hands; but we should use our best endeavors to instruct those for whom we pray. Simon Magus was ambitious to have the honor of an apostle, but cared not at all to have the spirit and disposition of a Christian. He was more desirous to gain honor to himself, than to do good to others. Peter shows him his crime. He esteemed the wealth of this world, as if it would answer for things relating to the other life, and would purchase the pardon of sin, the gift of the Holy Ghost, and eternal life. This was such a condemning error as could by no means consist with a state of grace. Our hearts are what they are in the sight of God, who cannot be deceived. And if they are not right in his sight, our religion is vain, and will stand us in no stead. A proud and covetous heart cannot be right with God. It is possible for a man to continue under the power of sin, yet to put on a form of godliness. When tempted with money to do evil, see what a perishing thing money is, and scorn it. Think not that Christianity is a trade to live by in this world. There is much wickedness in the thought of the heart, its false notions, and corrupt affections, and wicked projects, which must be repented of, or we are undone. But it shall be forgiven, upon our

the Lord Jesus one half so much as they criticize it. If any here present have been thus guilty, may the Holy Spirit convince them of their sin! Since the Lord God hath made this atoning Jesus both Lord and Christ, and set him on his right hand, any teaching which does despite to him, however learned, however advanced, however cultured it may seem to be, is a grievous sin against the Lord God himself. By such conduct we are, as far as in us lies, again putting the Lord Jesus to death; we are attempting to make away with that which is the very life and glory of Christ. O my hearer, if you have denied his Deity, rejected his atoning blood, ridiculed his imputed righteousness, or scoffed at salvation by faith in him, may you be pricked in the heart as you see that God hath made that same Jesus to be Lord of all!

Much more common, however, is another sin against our Lord Jesus—namely, neglecting him, ignoring his claims, and postponing the day of faith in him. I trust that none here are willing to die unconverted, or would even dare to think of passing away without being washed in the precious blood; yet, my hearers, you have lived to manhood; to ripe years; perhaps even to old age, without yielding your hearts to the Lord Jesus, and accepting him as your Savior. To say the least of it, this is a very sad piece of neglect. To ignore a man altogether is, in a certain sense, as far as you are concerned, to kill that man.

If you put him out of your reckoning, if you treat him as if he were nothing, if your estimate of life is made as if he were a cipher, you have put your Lord out of existence in reference to yourself. You treat him with empty compliment by observing his day, and hearing his Word; but you have no real regard for him. Is not this a cruel fault? From morning till night your Lord is not in all your thoughts; he never affects your dealings with your fellow-men; you never endeavor to catch his spirit of love, and considerateness, and meekness; and thus, as a Leader and Exemplar, he is dead to you. You have never confessed your sin before him, nor sought for pardon at his hands, nor have you looked to see whether he hath borne your sins in his own body on the tree. O soul, this is base neglect—ungrateful contempt! God thinks so much of his Son that he cannot set him too high; he has placed him at his own right hand, and yet you will not spare him a thought! The great God thinks heaven and earth too little for him, and magnifies him exceedingly above all, as King of kings, and Lord of lords; and yet you treat him as if he were of no account, and might be safely made to wait your time and leisure. Is this right? Will you treat your Savior thus? May this prick you in the heart, and may you cease from this base ingratitude!

There are others who have done more than this, for they have rejected Christ. I now allude to

31 And he said, How can I, except some man should guide me? And he desired Philip that he would come up and sit with him.

32 The place of the scripture which he read was this, He was led as a sheep to the slaughter; and like a lamb dumb before his shearer, so opened he not his mouth:

33 In his humiliation his judgment was taken away: and who shall declare his generation? for his life is taken from the earth.

34 And the eunuch answered Philip, and said, I pray thee, of whom speaketh the prophet this? of himself, or of some other man?

35 Then Philip opened his mouth, and began at the same scripture, and preached unto him Jesus.

36 And as they went on their way, they came unto a certain water: and the eunuch said, See, here is water; what doth hinder me to be baptized?

37 And Philip said, If thou believest with all thine heart, thou mayest. And he answered and said, I believe that Jesus Christ is the Son of God.

38 And he commanded the chariot to stand still: and they went down both into the water, both Philip and the eunuch; and he baptized him.

39 And when they were come up out of the water, the Spirit of the Lord caught away Philip, that the eunuch saw him no more: and he went on his way rejoicing.

40 But Philip was found at Azotus: and passing through he preached in all the cities, till he came to Cesarea.

ACTS 9

1 And Saul, yet breathing out threatenings and slaughter against the disciples of the Lord, went unto the high priest,

2 And desired of him letters to Damascus to the synagogues, that if he found any of this way, whether they were men or women, he might bring them bound unto Jerusalem.

3 And as he journeyed, he came near Damascus: and suddenly there shined round about him a light from heaven:

4 And he fell to the earth, and heard a voice saying unto him, Saul, Saul, why persecutest thou me?

5 And he said, Who art thou, Lord? And the Lord said, I am Jesus whom thou persecutest: it is hard for thee to kick against the pricks.

6 And he trembling and astonished said, Lord, what wilt thou have me to do? And the Lord said unto him, Arise, and go into the city, and it shall be told thee what thou must do.

7 And the men which journeyed with him stood speechless, hearing a voice, but seeing no man.

8 And Saul arose from the earth; and when his eyes were opened, he saw no man: but they led him by the hand, and brought him into Damascus.

were all dispersed – Not all the Church: if so, who would have remained for the apostles to teach, or Saul to persecute? But all the teachers except the apostles, who, though in the most danger, stayed with the flock.

2. Devout men – Who feared God more than persecution. And yet were they not of little faith? Else they would not have made so great lamentation.

3. Saul made havoc of the Church – Like some furious beast of prey. So the Greek word properly signifies. Men and women – Regarding neither age nor sex.

4. Therefore they that were dispersed went every where – These very words are reassumed, after as it were a long parenthesis, chap. xi, 19, and the thread of the story continued.

5. Stephen – Being taken away, Philip, his next colleague, (not the apostle,) rises in his place.

9. A certain man – using magic – So there was such a thing as witchcraft once! In Asia at least, if not in Europe or America.

12. But when they believed – What Philip preached, then they saw and felt the real power of God, and submitted thereto.

13. And Simon believed – That is, was convinced of the truth.

14. And the apostles hearing that Samaria – The inhabitants of that country, had received the word of God – By faith, sent Peter and John – He that sends must be either superior, or at least equal, to him that is sent. It follows that the college of the apostles was equal if not superior to Peter.

15. The Holy Ghost – In his miraculous gifts? Or his sanctifying graces? Probably in both.

18. Simon offered them money – And hence the procuring any ministerial function, or ecclesiastical benefice by money, is termed Simony.

21. Thou hast neither part – By purchase, nor lot – Given gratis, in this matter – This gift of God. For thy heart is not right before God – Probably St. Peter discerned this long before he had declared it; although it does not appear that God gave to any of the apostles a universal power of discerning the hearts of all they conversed with; any more than a universal power of healing all the sick they came near. This we are sure St. Paul had not; though he was not inferior to the chief of the apostles. Otherwise he would not have suffered the illness of Epaphroditus to have brought him so near to death, Phil. ii, 25-27; nor have left so useful a fellow laborer as Trophimus sick at Miletus, 2 Tim. iv, 20.

22. Repent – if perhaps the thought of thy heart may be forgiven thee – Without all doubt if he had repented, he would have been forgiven. The doubt was, whether he would repent. Thou art in the gall of bitterness – In the highest degree of wickedness, which is bitterness, that is, misery to the soul; and in the bond of iniquity – Fast bound therewith.

26. The way which is desert – There were two ways from Jerusalem to Gaza, one desert, the other through a more populous country.

27. An eunuch – Chief officers were anciently called eunuchs, though not always literally such; because such used to be chief ministers in the eastern courts. Candace, queen of the Ethiopians – So all the queens of Ethiopia were called.

28. Sitting in his chariot, he read the Prophet Isaiah – God meeteth those that remember him in his ways. It is good to read, hear, seek information even in a journey. Why should we not redeem all our time?

30. And Philip running to him, said, Understandest thou what thou

repentance. The doubt here is of the sincerity of Simon's repentance, not of his pardon, if his repentance was sincere. Grant us, Lord, another sort of faith than that which made Simon wonder only, and did not sanctify his heart. May we abhor all thoughts of making religion serve the purposes of pride or ambition. And keep us from that subtle poison of spiritual pride, which seeks glory to itself even from humility. May we seek only the honor which cometh from God.

26-40 Philip was directed to go to a desert. Sometimes God opens a door of opportunity to his ministers in very unlikely places. We should study to do good to those we come into company with by traveling. We should not be so shy of all strangers as some affect to be. As to those of whom we know nothing else, we know this, that they have souls. It is wisdom for men of business to redeem time for holy duties; to fill up every minute with something which will turn to a good account. In reading the word of God, we should often pause, to inquire of whom and of what the sacred writers spake; but especially our thoughts should be employed about the Redeemer. The Ethiopian was convinced by the teaching of the Holy Spirit, of the exact fulfillment of the Scripture, was made to understand the nature of the Messiah's kingdom and salvation, and desired to be numbered among the disciples of Christ. Those who seek the truth, and employ their time in searching the Scriptures, will be sure to reap advantages. The avowal of the Ethiopian must be understood as expressing simple reliance on Christ for salvation, and unreserved devotion to him. Let us not be satisfied till we get faith, as the Ethiopian did, by diligent study of the Holy Scriptures, and the teaching of the Spirit of God; let us not be satisfied till we get it fixed as a principle in our hearts. As soon as he was baptized, the Spirit of God took Philip from him, so that he saw him no more; but this tended to confirm his faith. When the inquirer after salvation becomes acquainted with Jesus and his gospel, he will go on his way rejoicing, and will fill up his station in society, and discharge his duties, from other motives, and in another manner than heretofore. Though baptized in the name of the Father, Son, and Holy Ghost, with water, it is not enough without the baptism of the Holy Ghost. Lord, grant this to every one of us; then shall we go on our way rejoicing.

ACTS 9

The conversion of Saul. (1-9)

Saul converted preaches Christ. (10-22)

Saul is persecuted at Damascus, and goes to Jerusalem. (23-31)

Cure of Eneas. (32-35)

Dorcas raised to life. (36-43)

those of you who have not been able to resist the appeals made to you by the Lord's ministers. You have felt a good deal—felt more than you would like to confess. You have been so inclined to seek the Savior that you have almost done so; sin has flashed in your face like the flames of Tophet, and in alarm you have resolved to seek salvation; you have gone home to bend the knee in prayer, you have read the Scriptures to learn the way of eternal life; but, alas! an evil companion crossed your path, and the question came, "Shall it be this man or Christ?" You chose the man: I had almost said, you chose Barabbas, and rejected Jesus. A sinful pleasure came before you when you had begun to be serious, and the question arose, "Shall I give up this pleasure, or shall I renounce all hope of Christ?" You snatched at the pleasure, and you let your Savior go. Do you not remember when you did violence to your conscience? There was an effort about it, as you stifled conviction. You had to put forth a decided act of the will to quench the Spirit of God, and to escape from the strivings of your awakened conscience. I know not to whom this may apply; but I am certain, as certain as Peter was when he spoke to the crucifiers of Christ, that I am speaking to some who have been rejecters of the Lord Jesus Christ, not once nor twice. Some of you have distinctly rejected him almost every Sabbath-day; but especially when the Word of the Lord has been with extraordinary power, and you have felt it shake you, as a lion shakes his prey. Thank God, you are not past feeling yet! I pray you, do not presume upon the continuance of your tenderness. You will not always feel as you have felt: the day may come when even the thunders of God may not be heard by your deafened ear, and the love of Christ will not affect the heart which you have made callous by willfull obstinacy. Woe to the man when his heart is turned to stone! When flesh turns to stone, it is a conversion unto eternal death; just as the turning of stone to flesh is conversion to eternal life. God have mercy upon you, and prick you in the heart this morning, while you yet have tenderness enough to feel that you have rejected him whom you ought to embrace with all your heart!

I must come a little closer to certain of you, who have forsaken the Lord Jesus Christ. There are a few unhappy persons here this morning, over whom I greatly grieve, because of their wanderings; and yet I am glad that they have not quite forsaken the courts of the Lord's house. These once professed to be disciples of Christ; but they have gone back, and walk no more with him. They were once numbered with us, and went in and out of our solemn assemblies for prayer and breaking of bread; but now we know them not. They were not backward to confess themselves Christians, but now they deny their Lord. In former days they

9 And he was three days without sight, and neither did eat nor drink.

10 And there was a certain disciple at Damascus, named Ananias; and to him said the Lord in a vision, Ananias. And he said, Behold, I am here, Lord.

11 And the Lord said unto him, Arise, and go into the street which is called Straight, and inquire in the house of Judas for one called Saul, of Tarsus: for, behold, he prayeth,

12 And hath seen in a vision a man named Ananias coming in, and putting his hand on him, that he might receive his sight.

13 Then Ananias answered, Lord, I have heard by many of this man, how much evil he hath done to thy saints at Jerusalem:

14 And here he hath authority from the chief priests to bind all that call on thy name.

15 But the Lord said unto him, Go thy way: for he is a chosen vessel unto me, to bear my name before the Gentiles, and kings, and the children of Israel:

16 For I will shew him how great things he must suffer for my name's sake.

17 And Ananias went his way, and entered into the house; and putting his hands on him said, Brother Saul, the Lord, even Jesus, that appeared unto thee in the way as thou camest, hath sent me, that thou mightest receive thy sight, and be filled with the Holy Ghost.

18 And immediately there fell from his eyes as it had been scales: and he received sight forthwith, and arose, and was baptized.

19 And when he had received meat, he was strengthened. Then was Saul certain days with the disciples which were at Damascus.

20 And straightway he preached Christ in the synagogues, that he is the Son of God.

21 But all that heard him were amazed, and said; Is not this he that destroyed them which called on this name in Jerusalem, and came hither for that intent, that he might bring them bound unto the chief priests?

22 But Saul increased the more in strength, and confounded the Jews which dwelt at Damascus, proving that this is very Christ.

23 And after that many days were fulfilled, the Jews took counsel to kill him:

24 But their laying await was known of Saul. And they watched the gates day and night to kill him.

25 Then the disciples took him by night, and let him down by the wall in a basket.

26 And when Saul was come to Jerusalem, he assayed to join himself to the disciples: but they were all afraid of him, and believed not that he was a disciple.

27 But Barnabas took him, and brought him to the apostles, and declared unto them how he had seen the Lord in the way, and that he had spoken to him, and how he had preached boldly at Damascus in the name of Jesus.

28 And he was with them coming in and

readest? – He did not begin about the weather, news, or the like. In speaking for God, we may frequently come to the point at once, without circumlocution.

31. He desired Philip to come up and sit with him – Such was his modesty, and thirst after instruction.

32. The portion of Scripture – By reading that very chapter, the fifty-third of Isaiah, many Jews, yea, and atheists, have been converted. Some of them history records. God knoweth them all. Isaiah liii, 7

33. In his humiliation his judgment was taken away – That is, when he was a man, he had no justice shown him. To take away a person's judgment, is a proverbial phrase for oppressing him. And who shall declare, or count his generation – That is, who can number his seed, Isaiah liii, 10; which he hath purchased by laying down his life?

36. And as they went on the way they came to a certain water – Thus, even the circumstances of the journey were under the direction of God. The kingdom of God suits itself to external circumstances, without any violence, as air yields to all bodies, and yet pervades all. What hindereth me to be baptized? – Probably he had been circumcised: otherwise Cornelius would not have been the first fruits of the Gentiles.

38. And they both went down – Out of the chariot. It does not follow that he was baptized by immersion. The text neither affirms nor intimates any thing concerning it.

39. The Spirit of the Lord caught away Philip – Carried him away with a miraculous swiftness, without any action or labor of his own. This had befallen several of the prophets.

40. But Philip was found at Azotus – Probably none saw him, from his leaving the eunuch, till he was there.

ACTS 9

1. Acts xxii, 3, &c.; Acts xxvi, 9, &c.

2. Bound – By the connivance, if not authority, of the governor, under Aretas the king. See Acts ix, 14, 24.

3. And suddenly – When God suddenly and vehemently attacks a sinner, it is the highest act of mercy. So Saul, when his rage was come to the height, is taught not to breathe slaughter. And what was wanting in time to confirm him in his discipleship, is compensated by the inexpressible terror he sustained. By his also the suddenly constituted apostle was guarded against the grand snare into which novices are apt to fall.

4. He heard a voice – Severe, yet full of grace.

5. To kick against the goads – is a Syriac proverb, expressing an attempt that brings nothing but pain.

6. It shall be told thee – So God himself sends Saul to be taught by a man, as the angel does Cornelius, chap. x, 5. Admirable condescension! that the Lord deals with us by men, like ourselves.

7. The men – stood – Having risen before Saul; for they also fell to the ground, chap. xxvi, 14. It is probable they all journeyed on foot. Hearing the noise – But not an articulate voice. And seeing the light, but not Jesus himself, chap. xxvi, 13, &c.

9. And he was three days – An important season! So long he seems to have been in the pangs of the new birth. Without sight – By scales growing over his eyes, to intimate to him the blindness of the state he had been in, to impress him with a deeper sense of the almighty power of Christ, and to turn his thoughts inward, while he was less capable of conversing with outward objects. This was likewise a manifest token to others, of what had happened to him in his jour-

1-9 So ill informed was Saul, that he thought he ought to do all he could against the name of Christ, and that he did God service thereby; he seemed to breathe in this as in his element. Let us not despair of renewing grace for the conversion of the greatest sinners, nor let such despair of the pardoning mercy of God for the greatest sin. It is a signal token of Divine favor, if God, by the inward working of his grace, or the outward events of his providence, stops us from prosecuting or executing sinful purposes. Saul saw that Just One, ch. 22:14; 26:13. How near to us is the unseen world! It is but for God to draw aside the veil, and objects are presented to the view, compared with which, whatever is most admired on earth is mean and contemptible. Saul submitted without reserve, desirous to know what the Lord Jesus would have him to do. Christ's discoveries of himself to poor souls are humbling; they lay them very low, in mean thoughts of themselves. For three days Saul took no food, and it pleased God to leave him for that time without relief. His sins were now set in order before him; he was in the dark concerning his own spiritual state, and wounded in spirit for sin. When a sinner is brought to a proper sense of his own state and conduct, he will cast himself wholly on the mercy of the Savior, asking what he would have him to do. God will direct the humbled sinner, and though he does not often bring transgressors to joy and peace in believing, without sorrows and distress of conscience, under which the soul is deeply engaged as to eternal things, yet happy are those who sow in tears, for they shall reap in joy.

10-22 A good work was begun in Saul, when he was brought to Christ's feet with those words, Lord, what wilt thou have me to do? And never did Christ leave any who were brought to that. Behold, the proud Pharisee, the unmerciful oppressor, the daring blasphemer, prayeth! And thus it is even now, and with the proud infidel, or the abandoned sinner. What happy tidings are these to all who understand the nature and power of prayer, of such prayer as the humbled sinner presents for the blessings of free salvation! Now he began to pray after another manner than he had done; before, he said his prayers, now, he prayed them. Regenerating grace sets people on praying; you may as well find a living man without breath, as a living Christian without prayer. Yet even eminent disciples, like Ananias, sometimes stagger at the commands of the Lord. But it is the Lord's glory to surpass our scanty expectations, and show that those are vessels of his mercy whom we are apt to consider as objects of his vengeance. The teaching of the Holy Spirit takes away the scales of ignorance and pride from the understanding; then the sinner becomes a new creature, and endeavors to

were zealous, and apparently devout; they were quick in the service of God, and sound in their creed. But there came a day—I need not describe the circumstances, for they differ in different cases—when two roads were before them, and they must go either to the right or to the left; and they took the road by which they turned their back upon Christ, and upon the vitality of godliness. They went off into sin, and apostatized from the faith. We fear "they went out from us, but they were not of us; for if they had been of us, they would no doubt have continued with us." They have gone aside unto crooked ways, and we fear that the Lord will lead them forth with the workers of iniquity. O my backsliding hearer, I hope you are not a Judas; my trust is that you may be a Peter! You have denied your Master, but I hope you will yet weep bitterly, and be restored to your Lord's service. For your good I must bring home your wanderings to you; may the Lord prick you in the heart about them! Why have you left your Lord? Wherein has he wearied you? There may be present persons from the country, or friends from America, who were once glad to be numbered with the children of God, but now they care nothing for God, or his people. Alas! they take part with the adversaries of Christ, and the despisers of his precious blood! Friend, you are here this morning that I may bring your sin to remembrance, and ask you why you have done this thing! Were you a hypocrite? If not, why have you turned aside? God has exalted to his throne the Savior, on whom you have turned your back; have you not acted madly in what you have done? The Most High God is on the side of Jesus, and you are avowedly on the other side; is this right, or wise? It is painful to me to speak of these things. I hope it is far more painful for you to hear of them. I want you to feel as David did, when his heart smote him. What have you been doing? Has the Lord Jesus deserved this at your hands? Turn, I pray you, from your evil way, and turn unto the Lord with full purpose of heart.

II. After Peter had dwelt upon the sin of his hearers in treating the Lord so ill, he declared to them THE EXALTATION BESTOWED ON HIM BY GOD. The great God loved, and honored, and exalted that same Jesus whom they had crucified. O my hearers, whatever you may think of the Lord Jesus, God thinks everything of him! To you he may be dead and buried, but God hath raised him from the dead. To God he is the ever-living, the ever well-beloved Christ. You cannot destroy the Lord Jesus, or his cause. If you could do all that the most malicious heart could suggest, you could not really defeat him. Men wreaked their vengeance on him: once they put him to a felon's death, they laid him in the grave, and sealed the stone; but he rose

going out at Jerusalem.

29 And he spake boldly in the name of the Lord Jesus, and disputed against the Grecians: but they went about to slay him.

30 Which when the brethren knew, they brought him down to Cesarea, and sent him forth to Tarsus.

31 Then had the churches rest throughout all Judea and Galilee and Samaria, and were edified; and walking in the fear of the Lord, and in the comfort of the Holy Ghost, were multiplied.

32 And it came to pass, as Peter passed throughout all quarters, he came down also to the saints which dwelt at Lydda.

33 And there he found a certain man named Eneas, which had kept his bed eight years, and was sick of the palsy.

34 And Peter said to him, Eneas, Jesus Christ maketh thee whole: arise, and make thy bed. And he arose immediately.

35 And all that dwelt at Lydda and Saron saw him, and turned to the Lord.

36 Now there was at Joppa a certain disciple named Tabitha, which by interpretation is called Dorcas: this woman was full of good works and almsdeeds which she did.

37 And it came to pass in those days, that she was sick, and died: whom when they had washed, they laid her in an upper chamber.

38 And forasmuch as Lydda was nigh to Joppa, and the disciples had heard that Peter was there, they sent unto him two men, desiring him that he would not delay to come to them.

39 Then Peter arose and went with them. When he was come, they brought him into the upper chamber: and all the widows stood by him weeping, and shewing the coats and garments which Dorcas made, while she was with them.

40 But Peter put them all forth, and kneeled down, and prayed; and turning him to the body said, Tabitha, arise. And she opened her eyes: and when she saw Peter, she sat up.

41 And he gave her his hand, and lifted her up, and when he had called the saints and widows, presented her alive.

42 And it was known throughout all Joppa; and many believed in the Lord.

43 And it came to pass, that he tarried many days in Joppa with one Simon a tanner.

ACTS 10

1 There was a certain man in Cesarea called Cornelius, a centurion of the band called the Italian band,

2 A devout man, and one that feared God with all his house, which gave much alms to the people, and prayed to God alway.

3 He saw in a vision evidently about the ninth hour of the day an angel of God coming in to him, and saying unto him, Cornelius.

ney, and ought to have humbled and convinced those bigoted Jews, to whom he had been sent from the Sanhedrin.

11. Behold he is praying – He was shown thus to Ananias.

12. A man called Ananias – His name also was revealed to Saul.

13. But he answered – How natural it is to reason against God.

14. All that call on thy name – That is, all Christians.

15. He is a chosen vessel to bear my name – That is, to testify of me. It is undeniable, that some men are unconditionally chosen or elected, to do some works for God

16. For I – Do thou as thou art commanded. I will take care of the rest; will show him – In fact, through the whole course of his ministry. How great things he must suffer – So far will he be now from persecuting others.

17. The Lord hath sent me – Ananias does not tell Saul all which Christ had said concerning him. It was not expedient that he should know yet to how great a dignity he was called.

24. They guarded the gates day and night – That is, the governor did, at their request, 2 Cor. xi, 32.

26. And coming to Jerusalem – Three years after, Gal. i, 18. These three years St. Paul passes over, chap. xxii, 17, likewise.

27. To the apostles – Peter and James, Gal. i, 18, 19. Gal. i, 18,

19 And declared – He who has been an enemy to the truth ought not to be trusted till he gives proof that he is changed.

31. Then the Church – The whole body of Christian believers, had peace – Their bitterest persecutor being converted. And being built up – In holy, loving faith, continually increasing, and walking in – That is, speaking and acting only from this principle, the fear of God and the comfort of the Holy Ghost – An excellent mixture of inward and outward peace, tempered with filial fear.

35. Lydda was a large town, one day's journey from Jerusalem. It stood in the plain or valley of Sharon, which extended from Cesarea to Joppa, and was noted for its fruitfulness.

36. Tabitha, which is by interpretation Dorcas – She was probably a Hellenist Jew, known among the Hebrews by the Syriac name Tabitha, while the Greeks called her in their own language, Dorcas. They are both words of the same import, and signify a roe or fawn.

38. The disciples sent to him – Probably none of those at Joppa had the gift of miracles. Nor is it certain that they expected a miracle from him.

39. While she was with them – That is, before she died.

40. Peter having put them all out – That he might have the better opportunity of wrestling with God in prayer, said, Tabitha, arise. And she opened her eyes, and seeing Peter, sat up – Who can imagine the surprise of Dorcas, when called back to life? Or of her friends, when they saw her alive? For the sake of themselves, and of the poor, there was cause of rejoicing, and much more, for such a confirmation of the Gospel. Yet to herself it was matter of resignation, not joy, to be called back to these scenes of vanity: but doubtless, her remaining days were still more zealously spent in the service of her Savior and her God. Thus was a richer treasure laid up for her in heaven, and she afterward returned to a more exceeding weight of glory, than that from which so astonishing a providence had recalled her for a season.

ACTS 10

1. And there was a certain man – The first fruits of the Gentiles, in Cesarea – Where Philip had been before, chap. viii, 40; so that the

recommend the anointed Savior, the Son of God, to his former companions.

23-31 When we enter into the way of God, we must look for trials; but the Lord knows how to deliver the godly, and will, with the temptation, also make a way to escape. Though Saul's conversion was and is a proof of the truth of Christianity, yet it could not, of itself, convert one soul at enmity with the truth; for nothing can produce true faith, but that power which new-creates the heart. Believers are apt to be too suspicious of those against whom they have prejudices. The world is full of deceit, and it is necessary to be cautious, but we must exercise charity, 1Co 13:5. The Lord will clear up the characters of true believers; and he will bring them to his people, and often gives them opportunities of bearing testimony to his truth, before those who once witnessed their hatred to it. Christ now appeared to Saul, and ordered him to go quickly out of Jerusalem, for he must be sent to the Gentiles: see ch. 22:21. Christ's witnesses cannot be slain till they have finished their testimony. The persecutions were stayed. The professors of the gospel walked uprightly, and enjoyed much comfort from the Holy Ghost, in the hope and peace of the gospel, and others were won over to them. They lived upon the comfort of the Holy Ghost, not only in the days of trouble and affliction, but in days of rest and prosperity. Those are most likely to walk cheerfully, who walk circumspectly.

32-35 Christians are saints, or holy people; not only the eminent ones, as Saint Peter and Saint Paul, but every sincere professor of the faith of Christ. Christ chose patients whose diseases were incurable in the course of nature, to show how desperate was the case of fallen mankind. When we were wholly without strength, as this poor man, he sent his word to heal us. Peter does not pretend to heal by any power of his own, but directs Eneas to look up to Christ for help. Let none say, that because it is Christ, who, by the power of his grace, works all our works in us, therefore we have no work, no duty to do; for though Jesus Christ makes thee whole, yet thou must arise, and use the power he gives thee.

36-43 Many are full of good words, who are empty and barren in good works; but Tabitha was a great doer, no great talker. Christians who have not property to give in charity, may yet be able to do acts of charity, working with their hands, or walking with their feet, for the good of others. Those are certainly best praised whose own works praise them, whether the words of others do so or not. But such are ungrateful indeed, who have kindness shown them, and will not acknowledge it, by showing the kindness that is done them. While we live

again, for God was on his side. My hearer, whatever you do, you cannot shake the truth of the gospel, nor rob the Lord Jesus of a single beam of his glory. He lives and reigns, and he will live and reign, whatever becomes of you. You may refuse his salvation but he is still a Savior, and a great one. His gospel chariot rolls on, and every stone which is placed to hinder it is crushed into the earth, and compelled to make a road for him. If you resist the Lord, you do it at your peril; but you do it in vain. You might as well hope to reverse the laws of nature, quench the sun, and snatch the moon from her orbit, as hope to overthrow the cause and kingdom of the Lord Jesus; for God is on his side, and his throne is established for ever. God hath raised his Son from the dead, and taken him up to sit at his right hand, and there he will remain while his enemies shall be made his footstool. By this you may see what evil you have done through rejecting Christ, and may know who he is whom you have neglected, refused, and forsaken.

Let me remind you that, when we read of our Lord as being at the right hand of God, we perceive that he enjoys infinite felicity. At the right hand of God there are pleasures for evermore; and David said, as the representative of our Lord, "Thou hast made known to me the ways of life; thou shalt make me full of joy with thy countenance." He who was the Man of sorrows now overflows with gladness. All his work and warfare done, he rests in boundless blessedness. His priestly work being finished, he sits down. No more does be feel the cross and nails, no more does he endure the mockery of cruel eyes and ribald lips. He is full of joy, that joy which be bids his people share when he says, "Enter thou into the joy of thy Lord." His portion is measureless, infinite, inconceivable delight. Can it be that you are opposed to him, and neglect him, while God lavishes upon him more than all the bliss of heaven, and makes him to be the fountain of unspeakable delight to all his redeemed ones? Grieve that you should grieve him whom God thus loads with blessedness.

Moreover, remember that at the right hand of God our Lord sits in infinite majesty. Jesus, whom you think little of, Jesus, from whom you turn aside, is today adored of angels, obeyed by seraphs, worshiped by just men made perfect. He is the highest in the highest heavens. Do you not hear the blast of heaven's trumpets, which proclaims him head over principalities and powers? Do you not hear the song which ascribes to him honor, and glory, and power, and dominion, and might? My faith anticipates the happy day when I shall stand a courtier in his unrivalled courts, and behold him, the Lamb upon the throne, reigning high over all, with every knee in heaven and in earth gladly bowing before him. Can it be that you have neglected him whom God hath exalted? Can

4 And when he looked on him, he was afraid, and said, What is it, Lord? And he said unto him, Thy prayers and thine alms are come up for a memorial before God.

5 And now send men to Joppa, and call for one Simon, whose surname is Peter:

6 He lodgeth with one Simon a tanner, whose house is by the sea side: he shall tell thee what thou oughtest to do.

7 And when the angel which spake unto Cornelius was departed, he called two of his household servants, and a devout soldier of them that waited on him continually;

8 And when he had declared all these things unto them, he sent them to Joppa.

9 On the morrow, as they went on their journey, and drew nigh unto the city, Peter went up upon the housetop to pray about the sixth hour:

10 And he became very hungry, and would have eaten: but while they made ready, he fell into a trance,

11 And saw heaven opened, and a certain vessel descending unto him, as it had been a great sheet knit at the four corners, and let down to the earth:

12 Wherein were all manner of fourfooted beasts of the earth, and wild beasts, and creeping things, and fowls of the air.

13 And there came a voice to him, Rise, Peter; kill, and eat.

14 But Peter said, Not so, Lord; for I have never eaten any thing that is common or unclean.

15 And the voice spake unto him again the second time, What God hath cleansed, that call not thou common.

16 This was done thrice: and the vessel was received up again into heaven.

17 Now while Peter doubted in himself what this vision which he had seen should mean, behold, the men which were sent from Cornelius had made inquiry for Simon's house, and stood before the gate,

18 And called, and asked whether Simon, which was surnamed Peter, were lodged there.

19 While Peter thought on the vision, the Spirit said unto him, Behold, three men seek thee.

20 Arise therefore, and get thee down, and go with them, doubting nothing: for I have sent them.

21 Then Peter went down to the men which were sent unto him from Cornelius; and said, Behold, I am he whom ye seek: what is the cause wherefore ye are come?

22 And they said, Cornelius the centurion, a just man, and one that feareth God, and of good report among all the nation of the Jews, was warned from God by an holy angel to send for thee into his house, and to hear words of thee.

23 Then called he them in, and lodged them. And on the morrow Peter went away with

doctrine of salvation by faith in Jesus was not unknown there. Cesarea was the seat of the civil government, as Jerusalem was of the ecclesiastical. It is observable, that the Gospel made its way first through the metropolitan cities. So it first seized Jerusalem and Cesarea: afterward Philippi, Athens, Corinth, Ephesus, Rome itself. A centurion, or captain, of that called the Italian band – That is, troop or company.

2. Who gave much alms to the people – That is, to the Jews, many of whom were at that time extremely poor.

3. He saw in a vision – Not in a trance, like Peter: plainly, so as to leave one not accustomed to things of this kind no room to suspect any imposition.

4. Thy prayers and thine alms are come up for a memorial before God – Dare any man say, These were only splendid sins? Or that they were an abomination before God? And yet it is certain, in the Christian sense Cornelius was then an unbeliever. He had not then faith in Christ. So certain it is, that every one who seeks faith in Christ, should seek it in prayer, and doing good to all men: though in strictness what is not exactly according to the Divine rule must stand in need of Divine favor and indulgence.

8. A devout soldier – How many such attendants have our modern officers? A devout soldier would now be looked upon as little better than a deserter from his colors.

10. And he became very hungry – At the usual meal time. The symbols in visions and trances, it is easy to observe, are generally suited to the state of the natural faculties.

11. Tied at the corners – Not all in one knot, but each fastened as it were up to heaven.

14. But Peter said, In nowise, Lord – When God commands a strange or seemingly improper thing, the first objection frequently finds pardon. But it ought not to be repeated. This doubt and delay of St. Peter had several good effects. Hereby the will of God in this important point was made more evident and incontestable. And Peter also, having been so slow of belief himself, could the more easily bear the doubting of his brethren, chap. xi, 2, &c.

15. What God hath purified – Hath made and declared clean. Nothing but what is clean can come down from heaven. St. Peter well remembered this saying in the council at Jerusalem, chap. xv, 9.

16. This was done thrice – To make the deeper impression.

17. While Peter doubted in himself, behold the men – Frequently the things which befall us within and from without at the same time, are a key to each other. The things which thus concur and agree together, ought to be diligently attended to.

19. Behold three men seek thee, arise therefore and go down, and go with them, doubting nothing – How gradually was St. Peter prepared to receive this new admonition of the Spirit! Thus God is wont to lead on his children by degrees, always giving them light for the present hour.

24. Cornelius was waiting for them – Not engaging himself in any secular business during that solemn time, but being altogether intent on this one thing.

26. I myself also am a man – And not God, who alone ought to be worshipped, Matt. iv, 10. Have all his pretended successors attended to this?

28. But God hath showed me – He speaks sparingly to them of his former doubt, and his late vision.

29. I ask for what intent ye have sent for me? – St. Peter knew this already. But he puts Cornelius on telling the story, both that the rest

upon the fullness of Christ for our whole salvation, we should desire to be full of good works, for the honor of his name, and for the benefit of his saints. Such characters as Dorcas are useful where they dwell, as showing the excellency of the word of truth by their lives. How mean then the cares of the numerous females who seek no distinction but outward decoration, and who waste their lives in the trifling pursuits of dress and vanity! Power went along with the word, and Dorcas came to life. Thus in the raising of dead souls to spiritual life, the first sign of life is the opening of the eyes of the mind. Here we see that the Lord can make up every loss; that he overrules every event for the good of those who trust in him, and for the glory of his name.

ACTS 10

Cornelius directed to send for Peter. (1-8)
Peter's vision. (9-18)
He goes to Cornelius. (19-33)
His discourse to Cornelius. (34-43)
The gifts of the Holy Spirit poured out. (44-48)

1-8 Hitherto none had been baptized into the Christian church but Jews, Samaritans, and those converts who had been circumcized and observed the ceremonial law; but now the Gentiles were to be called to partake all the privileges of God's people, without first becoming Jews. Pure and undefiled religion is sometimes found where we least expect it. Wherever the fear of God rules in the heart, it will appear both in works of charity and of piety, neither will excuse from the other. Doubtless Cornelius had true faith in God's word, as far as he understood it, though not as yet clear faith in Christ. This was the work of the Spirit of God, through the mediation of Jesus, even before Cornelius knew him, as is the case with us all when we, who before were dead in sin, are made alive. Through Christ also his prayers and alms were accepted, which otherwise would have been rejected. Without dispute or delay Cornelius was obedient to the heavenly vision. In the affairs of our souls, let us not lose time.

9-18 The prejudices of Peter against the Gentiles, would have prevented his going to Cornelius, unless the Lord had prepared him for this service. To tell a Jew that God had directed those animals to be reckoned clean which were hitherto deemed unclean, was in effect saying, that the law of Moses was done away. Peter was soon made to know the meaning of it. God knows what services are before us, and how to prepare us; and we know the meaning of what he has taught us, when we find what occasion we have to make use of it.

19-33 When we see our call clear to any service,

it be that you have refused him, that you have done despite to him, that you have, as far as you could, put him to death whom Jehovah has made Lord of all?

Nor is this all: for the place at the right hand of God, to which he is now exalted, is the place of power. There sits the Mediator, the Son of God, the man Christ Jesus, while his enemies are being subdued under him. Do not believe it, O proudest of doubters, that thou canst take away from Christ any measure of his power! He overrules all mortal things; he directs the movements of the stars; he rules the armies of heaven. He restrains the rage of his adversaries, and what he suffers to be let loose he turns to his glory. All power is given to him in heaven and earth; he reigns in the three realms of nature, providence, and grace. His kingdom ruleth over all, and of his dominion there shall be no end. O sirs, what do our hearts suggest but that we bow at his feet? that we worship him with loving reverence? that we yield to that supreme power which is used for purposes of love? Yet it is this Christ, this mighty Christ, who is set at nought by some of you, so that you run the risk of perishing because you have no heart for him and his great salvation.

Learn, next, that he is at the right hand of the Majesty in the heavens, seated as our Judge. If we refuse him as a Savior, we shall not be able to escape from him as Judge in the last great day. All the acts of men are being recorded, and in that day, when the great white throne shall be set in the heavens, all things shall be made manifest, and we must stand unveiled in his presence. You have often heard and sung of him whose face was more marred than that of any man, when he was here as a sacrifice for guilty men. If you refuse him, you will have to stand before his bar to answer for it. The most awful sight for the impenitent in the day of judgment will be the face of the Lord Jesus Christ. I do not find that they cry, "Hide us from the tempest," nor "Hide us from the angel-guards," nor "Hide us from their swords of fire," but, "Hide us from the face of him that sitteth on the throne, and from the wrath of the Lamb." Love, when once it turns to wrath, is terrible beyond compare. As oil when set on fire blazes with great force, so the meek and loving Jesus, when finally rejected, will exhibit a wrath more terrible than death.

> "Ye sinners, seek his grace,
> Whose wrath ye cannot bear;
> Fly to the shelter of his cross,
> And find salvation there."

Perhaps through ignorance you have rebelled; repent, and take another course. You supposed that when you kicked against a sermon, you had only put down the minister's words; but in reality you resisted the Savior's love. You thought that

them, and certain brethren from Joppa accompanied him.

24 And the morrow after they entered into Cesarea. And Cornelius waited for them, and had called together his kinsmen and near friends.

25 And as Peter was coming in, Cornelius met him, and fell down at his feet, and worshiped him.

26 But Peter took him up, saying, Stand up; I myself also am a man.

27 And as he talked with him, he went in, and found many that were come together.

28 And he said unto them, Ye know how that it is an unlawful thing for a man that is a Jew to keep company, or come unto one of another nation; but God hath shewed me that I should not call any man common or unclean.

29 Therefore came I unto you without gainsaying, as soon as I was sent for: I ask therefore for what intent ye have sent for me?

30 And Cornelius said, Four days ago I was fasting until this hour; and at the ninth hour I prayed in my house, and, behold, a man stood before me in bright clothing,

31 And said, Cornelius, thy prayer is heard, and thine alms are had in remembrance in the sight of God.

32 Send therefore to Joppa, and call hither Simon, whose surname is Peter; he is lodged in the house of one Simon a tanner by the sea side: who, when he cometh, shall speak unto thee.

33 Immediately therefore I sent to thee; and thou hast well done that thou art come. Now therefore are we all here present before God, to hear all things that are commanded thee of God.

34 Then Peter opened his mouth, and said, Of a truth I perceive that God is no respecter of persons:

35 But in every nation he that feareth him, and worketh righteousness, is accepted with him.

36 The word which God sent unto the children of Israel, preaching peace by Jesus Christ: (he is Lord of all:)

37 That word, I say, ye know, which was published throughout all Judea, and began from Galilee, after the baptism which John preached;

38 How God anointed Jesus of Nazareth with the Holy Ghost and with power: who went about doing good, and healing all that were oppressed of the devil; for God was with him.

39 And we are witnesses of all things which he did both in the land of the Jews, and in Jerusalem; whom they slew and hanged on a tree:

40 Him God raised up the third day, and shewed him openly;

41 Not to all the people, but unto witnesses chosen before of God, even to us, who did eat and drink with him after he rose from the dead.

might be informed, and Cornelius himself more impressed by the narration: the repetition of which, even as we read it, gives a new dignity and spirit to Peter's succeeding discourse,

30. Four days ago I was fasting – The first of these days he had the vision; the second his messengers came to Joppa; on the third, St. Peter set out; and on the fourth, came to Cesarea.

31. Thy prayer is heard – Doubtless he had been praying for instruction, how to worship God in the most acceptable manner.

33. Now therefore we are all present before God – The language of every truly Christian congregation.

34. I perceive of a truth – More clearly than ever, from such a concurrence of circumstances. That God is not a respecter of persons – Is not partial in his love. The words mean, in a particular sense, that he does not confine his love to one nation; in a general, that he is loving to every man, and willeth all men should be saved.

35. But in every nation he that feareth God and worketh righteousness – He that, first, reverences God, as great, wise, good, the cause, end, and governor of all things; and secondly, from this awful regard to him, not only avoids all known evil, but endeavors, according to the best light he has, to do all things well; is accepted of him – Through Christ, though he knows him not. The assertion is express, and admits of no exception. He is in the favor of God, whether enjoying his written word and ordinances or not. Nevertheless the addition of these is an unspeakable blessing to those who were before in some measure accepted. Otherwise God would never have sent an angel from heaven to direct Cornelius to St. Peter.

36. This is the word which God sent – When he sent his Son into the world, preaching – Proclaiming by him – peace between God and man, whether Jew or Gentile, by the God-man. He is Lord of both; yea, Lord of and over all.

37. Ye know the word which was published – You know the facts in general, the meaning of which I shall now more particularly explain and confirm to you. The baptism which John preached – To which he invited them by his preaching, in token of their repentance. This began in Galilee, which is near Cesarea.

38. How God anointed Jesus – Particularly at his baptism, thereby inaugurating him to his office: with the Holy Ghost and with power – It is worthy our remark, that frequently when the Holy Ghost is mentioned there is added a word particularly adapted to the present circumstance. So the deacons were to be full of the Holy Ghost and wisdom, chap. vi, 3. Barnabas was full of the Holy Ghost and faith, chap. xi, 24. The disciples were filled with joy, and with the Holy Ghost, chap. xiii, 52. And here, where his mighty works are mentioned, Christ himself is said to be anointed with the Holy Ghost and with power. For God was with him – He speaks sparingly here of the majesty of Christ, as considering the state of his hearers.

41. Not now to all the people – As before his death; to us who did eat and drink with him – That is, conversed familiarly and continually with him, in the time of his ministry.

42. It is he who is ordained by God the Judge of the living and the dead – Of all men, whether they are alive at his coming, or had died before it. This was declaring to them, in the strongest terms, how entirely their happiness depended on a timely and humble subjection to him who was to be their final Judge.

43. To him give all the prophets witness – Speaking to heathens he does not quote any in particular; that every one who believeth in him – Whether he be Jew or Gentile; receiveth remission of sins – Though he had not before either feared God, or worked righteousness.

we should not be perplexed with doubts and scruples arising from prejudices or former ideas. Cornelius had called together his friends, to partake with him of the heavenly wisdom he expected from Peter. We should not covet to eat our spiritual morsels alone. It ought to be both given and taken as kindness and respect to our kindred and friends, to invite them to join us in religious exercises. Cornelius declared the direction God gave him to send for Peter. We are right in our aims in attending a gospel ministry, when we do it with regard to the Divine appointment requiring us to make use of that ordinance. How seldom ministers are called to speak to such companies, however small, in which it may be said that they are all present in the sight of God, to hear all things that are commanded of God! But these were ready to hear what Peter was commanded of God to say.

34-43 Acceptance cannot be obtained on any other ground than that of the covenant of mercy, through the atonement of Christ; but wherever true religion is found, God will accept it without regarding names or sects. The fear of God and works of righteousness are the substance of true religion, the effects of special grace. Though these are not the cause of a man's acceptance, yet they show it; and whatever may be wanting in knowledge or faith, will in due time be given by him who has begun it. They knew in general the word, that is, the gospel, which God sent to the children of Israel. The purport of this word was, that God by it published the good tidings of peace by Jesus Christ. They knew the several matters of fact relating to the gospel. They knew the baptism of repentance which John preached. Let them know that this Jesus Christ, by whom peace is made between God and man, is Lord of all; not only as over all, God blessed for evermore, but as Mediator. All power, both in heaven and in earth, is put into his hand, and all judgment committed to him. God will go with those whom he anoints; he will be with those to whom he has given his Spirit. Peter then declares Christ's resurrection from the dead, and the proofs of it. Faith has reference to a testimony, and the Christian faith is built upon the foundation of the apostles and prophets, on the testimony given by them. See what must be believed concerning him. That we are all accountable to Christ as our Judge; so every one must seek his favor, and to have him as our Friend. And if we believe in him, we shall all be justified by him as our Righteousness. The remission of sins lays a foundation for all other favors and blessings, by taking that out of the way which hinders the bestowing of them. If sin be pardoned, all is well, and shall end well for ever.

44-48 The Holy Ghost fell upon others after they were baptized, to confirm them in the faith; but

when you turned away from Christ and his people, it was only leaving a church, and having your name crossed out of a book. Ah, sirs! take heed, for I fear you have left the Lamb of God, and renounced your part in his Book of Life! At the last it may turn out to have been an awful thing to have been put forth from the Church of Christ on earth; for when we, as a church, do our Lord's bidding, that which we bind on earth is bound in heaven. In refusing the Lord's Word, you refuse him who speaks from heaven: you refuse not only his words, but himself, and he shall be your Judge—your Judge most just, most holy. Oh, how will you bear it? How will you bear to stand at the bar of the despised Savior?

Peter also showed his hearers that the Lord was greatly exalted in heaven as the Head over all things to his church, for he had that day shed abroad the Holy Spirit. When the Holy Spirit comes, he comes from Christ, and as the witness of his power. He proceedeth from the Father and the Son, and he bears witness with both. Christ's power was marvelously proved when, after he had been but a little while in heaven, he was able to bestow such gifts upon men, and specially to send the tongues of fire, and the rushing mighty wind, which betoken the energy of the Holy Ghost. He is such a Lord that he can save or destroy. The Christ that died upon the cross hath all things committed into his hands. He can this morning send forth salvation to the ends of the earth, so that multitudes shall believe and live; for him hath God exalted with his right hand to be a Prince and a Savior, to give repentance and forgiveness of sins. Or, he can turn the key the other way, and shut the door against this untoward generation; for he openeth, and no man shutteth; and he shutteth, and no man openeth. In any case, be ye sure of this, ye Gentiles, even as Peter would have the house of Israel be sure of it, that "God hath made that same Jesus, whom ye have crucified, both Lord and Christ."

I notice that, at this time, few writers or preachers use the expression, "Our Lord Jesus Christ." We have lives of Christ, and lives of Jesus; but, brethren, he is THE LORD. Jesus is both Lord and Christ: we need to acknowledge his Deity, his dominion, and his divine anointing. He is "God over all, blessed for ever," and we can never praise him too much. A great and grievous error of the times is a want of reverence for our Lord and his sacrifice. To sit in judgment on his sacred teaching, is to spit in his face; to deny his miracles, is to strip him of his own clothes; to make him out to be a mere teacher of ethics, is to mock him with a purple robe; and to deny his atonement, in philosophical phraseology, is to crown him with thorns, and crucify him afresh, and put him to an open shame. Be not guilty of this, my hearers, for God

42 And he commanded us to preach unto the people, and to testify that it is he which was ordained of God to be the Judge of quick and dead.

43 To him give all the prophets witness, that through his name whosoever believeth in him shall receive remission of sins.

44 While Peter yet spake these words, the Holy Ghost fell on all them which heard the word.

45 And they of the circumcision which believed were astonished, as many as came with Peter, because that on the Gentiles also was poured out the gift of the Holy Ghost.

46 For they heard them speak with tongues, and magnify God. Then answered Peter,

47 Can any man forbid water, that these should not be baptized, which have received the Holy Ghost as well as we?

48 And he commanded them to be baptized in the name of the Lord. Then prayed they him to tarry certain days.

ACTS 11

1 And the apostles and brethren that were in Judea heard that the Gentiles had also received the word of God.

2 And when Peter was come up to Jerusalem, they that were of the circumcision contended with him,

3 Saying, Thou wentest in to men uncircumcised, and didst eat with them.

4 But Peter rehearsed the matter from the beginning, and expounded it by order unto them, saying,

5 I was in the city of Joppa praying: and in a trance I saw a vision, A certain vessel descend, as it had been a great sheet, let down from heaven by four corners; and it came even to me:

6 Upon the which when I had fastened mine eyes, I considered, and saw fourfooted beasts of the earth, and wild beasts, and creeping things, and fowls of the air.

7 And I heard a voice saying unto me, Arise, Peter; slay and eat.

8 But I said, Not so, Lord: for nothing common or unclean hath at any time entered into my mouth.

9 But the voice answered me again from heaven, What God hath cleansed, that call not thou common.

10 And this was done three times: and all were drawn up again into heaven.

11 And, behold, immediately there were three men already come unto the house where I was, sent from Cesarea unto me.

12 And the spirit bade me go with them, nothing doubting. Moreover these six brethren accompanied me, and we entered into the man's house:

13 And he shewed us how he had seen an

44. The Holy Ghost fell on all that were hearing the word – Thus were they consecrated to God, as the first fruits of the Gentiles. And thus did God give a clear and satisfactory evidence, that he had accepted them as well as the Jews.

45. The believers of the circumcision – The believing Jews.

47. Can any man forbid water, that these should not be baptized, who have received the Holy Ghost? – He does not say they have the baptism of the Spirit; therefore they do not need baptism with water. But just the contrary: if they have received the Spirit, then baptize them with water. How easily is this question decided, if we will take the word of God for our rule! Either men have received the Holy Ghost or not. If they have not, Repent, saith God, and be baptized, and ye shall receive the gift of the Holy Ghost. If they have, if they are already baptized with the Holy Ghost, then who can forbid water?

48. In the name of the Lord – Which implies the Father who anointed him, and the Spirit with which he was anointed to his office. But as the Gentiles had before believed in God the Father, and could not but now believe in the Holy Ghost, under whose powerful influence they were at this very time, there was the less need of taking notice, that they were baptized into the belief and profession of the sacred Three: though doubtless the apostle administered the ordinances in that very form which Christ himself had prescribed.

ACTS 11

4. Peter laid all things before them – So he did not take it ill to be questioned, nor desire to be treated as infallible. And he answers the more mildly because it related to a point which he had not readily believed himself.

5. Being in a trance – Which suspends the use of the outward senses.

14. Saved – With the full Christian salvation, in this world and the world to come.

17. To us, when we believed – The sense is, because we believed, not because we were circumcised, was the Holy Ghost given to us. What was I – A mere instrument in God's hand. They had inquired only concerning his eating with the Gentiles. He satisfies them likewise concerning his baptizing them, and shows that he had done right in going to Cornelius, not only by the command of God, but also by the event, the descent of the Holy Ghost. And who are we that we should withstand God? Particularly by laying down rules of Christian communion which exclude any whom he has admitted into the Church of the first born, from worshiping God together. O that all Church governors would consider how bold an usurpation this is of the authority of the supreme Lord of the Church! O that the sin of thus withstanding God may not be laid to the charge of those, who perhaps with a good intention, but in an over fondness for their own forms, have done it, and are continually doing it.

18. They glorified God – Being thoroughly satisfied. Repentance unto life – True repentance is a change from spiritual death to spiritual life, and leads to life everlasting.

19. They who had been dispersed – St. Luke here resumes the thread of his narration, in the very words wherewith he broke it off, chap. viii, 6. As far as Phoenicia to the north, Cyprus to the west, and Antioch to the east.

20. Some of them were men of Cyprus and Cyrene – Who were more accustomed to converse with the Gentiles. Who coming into Antioch – Then the capital of Syria, and, next to Rome and

upon these Gentiles before they were baptized, to show that God does not confine himself to outward signs. The Holy Ghost fell upon those who were neither circumcized nor baptized; it is the Spirit that quickeneth, the flesh profiteth nothing. They magnified God, and spake of Christ and the benefits of redemption. Whatever gift we are endued with, we ought to honor God with it. The believing Jews who were present, were astonished that the gift of the Holy Ghost was poured out upon the Gentiles also. By mistaken notions of things, we make difficult for ourselves as to the methods of Divine providence and grace. As they were undeniably baptized with the Holy Ghost, Peter concluded they were not to be refused the baptism of water, and the ordinance was administered. The argument is conclusive; can we deny the sign to those who have received the things signified? Those who have some acquaintance with Christ, cannot but desire more. Even those who have received the Holy Ghost, must see their need of daily learning more of the truth.

ACTS 11

Peter's defense. (1-18)
The success of the gospel at Antioch. (19-24)
The disciples named Christians. Relief sent to Judea. (25-30)

1-18 The imperfect state of human nature strongly appears, when godly persons are displeased even to hear that the word of God has been received, because their own system has not been attended to. And we are too apt to despair of doing good to those who yet, when tried, prove very teachable. It is the bane and damage of the church, to shut out those from it, and from the benefit of the means of grace, who are not in every thing as we are. Peter stated the whole affair. We should at all times bear with the infirmities of our brethren; and instead of taking offense, or answering with warmth, we should explain our motives, and show the nature of our proceedings. That preaching is certainly right, with which the Holy Ghost is given. While men are very zealous for their own regulations, they should take care that they do not withstand God; and those who love the Lord will glorify him, when made sure that he has given repentance to life to any fellow-sinners. Repentance is God's gift; not only his free grace accepts it, but his mighty grace works it in us, grace takes away the heart of stone, and gives us a heart of flesh. The sacrifice of God is a broken spirit.

19-24 The first preachers of the gospel at Antioch, were dispersed from Jerusalem by persecution; thus what was meant to hurt the church, was made to work for its good. The wrath of man is made to

hath made this same Jesus "both Lord and Christ"; let us worship him as Lord, and trust him as Christ.

III. Now I come to my closing point, which is, THE RESULT OF KNOWING THIS ASSUREDLY. May I here pause to ask—do you know this assuredly? I hope all of you believe that God hath made Jesus Christ, the Mediator, in his complex person, as God-and-man, to be " both Lord and Christ." He was Lord, as God, always; but as God-and-man, he is now Lord and Christ. Manhood and Godhead are in him united in one wondrous Person, and this Person is "both Lord and Christ." You believe it. But do you so believe it that it is a fact of the utmost importance to you? Will you assuredly believe it, that the man of Nazareth, who died on Calvary, is today both Lord and Christ? If you do now believe this, what are your feelings as you review your past misconduct towards him? Does not your past neglect prick you in the heart? If you do not so believe, it is of little use for me to describe what the result of such belief would be, for that result will not take place in you; but if you have so believed, and Jesus is to you Lord and Christ, you will look on him whom you have pierced, and mourn for him. As you recollect your negligence of him, your rejection of him, your backsliding from him, and all your ungrateful acts which show contempt of him, your heart will be ready to break, and you will be seized with a great sorrow, and a hearty repentance. The Lord work it in you, for his Son's sake!

Observe, that as the result of Peter's sermon, his hearers felt a mortal sting. "They were pricked in their heart." The truth had pierced their souls. When a man finds out that he has done a fearful wrong to one who loved him, he grows sick at heart, and views his own conduct with abhorrence. We all remember the story of Llewellyn and his faithful dog. The prince came back from the hunt, and missed his infant child, but saw marks of blood everywhere. Suspecting his dog Gelert of having killed the child he drove his vengeful sword into the faithful hound, which had bravely defending his child against a huge wolf, which lay there, all torn and dead, "tremendous still in death." Yes, he had slain the faithful creature which had preserved his child. Poor Gelert's dying yell pierced the prince to the heart; and well it might. If such emotions fitly arise when we discover that we have, in error, been ungenerous and cruel to a dog, how ought we to feel towards the Lord Jesus, who laid down his life that we, who were his enemies, might live?

I recall an awfully tragic story of an evil couple, who kept an inn of base repute. A young man called one night to lodge. They noticed that he had gold in his purse, and they murdered him in the night. It was their own son, who had come back to gladden their old age, and wished to see

angel in his house, which stood and said unto him, Send men to Joppa, and call for Simon, whose surname is Peter;

14 Who shall tell thee words, whereby thou and all thy house shall be saved.

15 And as I began to speak, the Holy Ghost fell on them, as on us at the beginning.

16 Then remembered I the word of the Lord, how that he said, John indeed baptized with water; but ye shall be baptized with the Holy Ghost.

17 Forasmuch then as God gave them the like gift as he did unto us, who believed on the Lord Jesus Christ; what was I, that I could withstand God?

18 When they heard these things, they held their peace, and glorified God, saying, Then hath God also to the Gentiles granted repentance unto life.

19 Now they which were scattered abroad upon the persecution that arose about Stephen traveled as far as Phenice, and Cyprus, and Antioch, preaching the word to none but unto the Jews only.

20 And some of them were men of Cyprus and Cyrene, which, when they were come to Antioch, spake unto the Grecians, preaching the Lord Jesus.

21 And the hand of the Lord was with them: and a great number believed, and turned unto the Lord.

22 Then tidings of these things came unto the ears of the church which was in Jerusalem: and they sent forth Barnabas, that he should go as far as Antioch.

23 Who, when he came, and had seen the grace of God, was glad, and exhorted them all, that with purpose of heart they would cleave unto the Lord.

24 For he was a good man, and full of the Holy Ghost and of faith: and much people was added unto the Lord.

25 Then departed Barnabas to Tarsus, for to seek Saul:

26 And when he had found him, he brought him unto Antioch. And it came to pass, that a whole year they assembled themselves with the church, and taught much people. And the disciples were called Christians first in Antioch.

27 And in these days came prophets from Jerusalem unto Antioch.

28 And there stood up one of them named Agabus, and signified by the spirit that there should be great dearth throughout all the world: which came to pass in the days of Claudius Cesar.

29 Then the disciples, every man according to his ability, determined to send relief unto the brethren which dwelt in Judea:

30 Which also they did, and sent it to the elders by the hands of Barnabas and Saul.

Alexandria, the most considerable city of the empire. Spake to the Greeks – As the Greeks were the most celebrated of the Gentile nations near Judea, the Jews called all the Gentiles by that name. Here we have the first account of the preaching the Gospel to the idolatrous Gentiles. All those to whom it had been preached before, did at least worship one God, the God of Israel.

21. And the hand of the Lord – That is, the power of his Spirit.

26. And the disciples were first called Christians at Antioch – Here it was that they first received this standing appellation. They were before termed Nazarenes and Galileans.

28. Agabus rising up – In the congregation. All the world – The word frequently signifies all the Roman empire. And so it is doubtless to be taken here.

29. Then – Understanding the distress they would otherwise be in on that account, the disciples determined to send relief to the brethren in Judea – Who herein received a manifest proof of the reality of their conversion.

30. Sending it to the elders – Who gave it to the deacons, to be distributed by them, as every one had need.

ACTS 12

1. About that time – So wisely did God mix rest and persecution in due time and measure succeeding each other. Herod – Agrippa; the latter was his Roman, the former his Syrian name. He was the grandson of Herod the Great, nephew to Herod Antipas, who beheaded John the Baptist; brother to Herodias, and father to that Agrippa before whom St. Paul afterward made his defense. Caligula made him king of the tetrarchy of his uncle Philip, to which he afterward added the territories of Antipas. Claudius made him also king of Judea, and added thereto the dominions of Lysanias.

2. James the brother of John – So one of the brothers went to God the first, the other the last of the apostles.

3. Then were the days of unleavened bread – At which the Jews came together from all parts.

4. Four quaternions – Sixteen men, who watched by turns day and night.

5. Continual prayer was made for him – Yet when their prayer was answered, they could scarce believe it, ver. 15. But why had they not prayed for St. James also? Because he was put to death as soon as apprehended.

6. Peter was sleeping – Easy and void of fear; between two soldiers – Sufficiently secured to human appearance.

7. His chains – With which his right arm was bound to one of the soldiers, and his left arm to the other.

8. Gird thyself – Probably he had put off his girdle, sandals, and upper garment, before he lay down to sleep.

10. The first and second ward – At each of which doubtless was a guard of soldiers. The gate opened of its own accord – Without either Peter or the angel touching it. And they went on through one street – That Peter might know which way to go. And the angel departed from him – Being himself sufficient for what remained to be done.

11. Now I know of a truth – That this is not a vision, ver. 9.

12. And having considered – What was best to be done. Many were gathered together – At midnight.

13. The gate – At some distance from the house; to hearken – If any knocked.

praise God. What should the ministers of Christ preach, but Christ? Christ, and him crucified? Christ, and him glorified? And their preaching was accompanied with the Divine power. The hand of the Lord was with them, to bring that home to the hearts and consciences of men, which they could but speak to the outward ear. They believed; they were convinced of the truth of the gospel. They turned from a careless, carnal way of living, to live a holy, heavenly, spiritual life. They turned from worshiping God in show and ceremony, to worship him in the Spirit and in truth. They turned to the Lord Jesus, and he became all in all with them. This was the work of conversion wrought upon them, and it must be wrought upon every one of us. It was the fruit of their faith; all who sincerely believe, will turn to the Lord, When the Lord Jesus is preached in simplicity, and according to the Scriptures, he will give success; and when sinners are thus brought to the Lord, really good men, who are full of faith and of the Holy Ghost, will admire and rejoice in the grace of God bestowed on them. Barnabas was full of faith; full of the grace of faith, and full of the fruits of the faith that works by love.

25-30 Hitherto the followers of Christ were called disciples, that is, learners, scholars; but from that time they were called Christians. The proper meaning of this name is, a follower of Christ; it denotes one who, from serious thought, embraces the religion of Christ, believes his promises, and makes it his chief care to shape his life by Christ's precepts and example. Hence it is plain that multitudes take the name of Christian to whom it does not rightly belong. But the name without the reality will only add to our guilt. While the bare profession will bestow neither profit nor delight, the possession of it will give both the promise of the life that now is, and of that which is to come. Grant, Lord, that Christians may forget other names and distinctions, and love one another as the followers of Christ ought to do. True Christians will feel for their brethren under afflictions. Thus will fruit be brought forth to the praise and glory of God. If all mankind were true Christians, how cheerfully would they help one another! The whole earth would be like one large family, every member of which would strive to be dutiful and kind.

ACTS 12

The martyrdom of James, and the imprisonment of Peter. (1-5)
He is delivered from prison by an angel. (6-11)
Peter departs. Herod's rage. (12-19)
The death of Herod. (20-25)

1-5 James was one of the sons of Zebedee, whom

whether his parents would remember him. Oh, the bitterness of their lamentation when they found that through the lust of gold they had murdered their own son!

Take out of such amazing grief its better portion, and then add to it a spiritual conviction of the sin of evil—entreating the Son of God, the perfect One, the Lover of our souls, and you come near the meaning of being "pricked in the heart." Oh, to think that we should despise him who loved us, and gave himself for us, and should rebel against him that bought us with his own blood while we were his enemies! I would to God everyone here, that has not come to Christ, would feel a sting in his conscience now; and would mourn that he has done this exceeding evil thing against the ever-blessed Son of God, who became man, and died for love of guilty men.

When we read "they were pricked in their heart," we may see in it the meaning, that they felt a movement of love to him—a relenting of heart, a stirring of emotion towards him. They said to themselves, "Have we treated him thus? What can we do to show our horror of our own conduct?" They were not merely convinced of their fault so as to be grieved, but their desires and affections went out towards the offended One, and they cried, "What shall we do? In what way can we acknowledge our wrong? Is there any way of undoing this ill towards him whom we now love?" To this point I would have you all come. I would have you know the meaning of Newton's hymn:—

"I saw One hanging on a tree,
In agonies and blood,
Who fix'd his languid eyes on me,
As near his cross I stood.
Sure never till my latest breath
Can I forget that look;
It seem'd to charge me with his death,
Though not a word he spoke.
My conscience felt and own'd the guilt,
And plunged me in despair;
I saw my sins his blood had spilt,
And help'd to nail him there.
Alas! I knew not what I did;
But now my tears are vain;
Where shall my trembling soul be hid?
For I the Lord have slain."

Let us tearfully inquire how we can end our opposition, and prove ourselves to be his friends and humble servants.

As a consequence of Peter's sermon, preached in the power of the Holy Spirit, these people exhibited obedient faith. They were roused to action, and they said, "Men and brethren, what shall we do?" They believed that the same Jesus whom they had crucified was now Lord of all, and they hastened to be obedient unto him. When

Acts

KING JAMES VERSION
ACTS 12
1 Now about that time Herod the king stretched forth his hands to vex certain of the church.

2 And he killed James the brother of John with the sword.

3 And because he saw it pleased the Jews, he proceeded further to take Peter also. (Then were the days of unleavened bread.)

4 And when he had apprehended him, he put him in prison, and delivered him to four quaternions of soldiers to keep him; intending after Easter to bring him forth to the people.

5 Peter therefore was kept in prison: but prayer was made without ceasing of the church unto God for him.

6 And when Herod would have brought him forth, the same night Peter was sleeping between two soldiers, bound with two chains: and the keepers before the door kept the prison.

7 And, behold, the angel of the Lord came upon him, and a light shined in the prison: and he smote Peter on the side, and raised him up, saying, Arise up quickly. And his chains fell off from his hands.

8 And the angel said unto him, Gird thyself, and bind on thy sandals. And so he did. And he saith unto him, Cast thy garment about thee, and follow me.

9 And he went out, and followed him; and wist not that it was true which was done by the angel; but thought he saw a vision.

10 When they were past the first and the second ward, they came unto the iron gate that leadeth unto the city; which opened to them of his own accord: and they went out, and passed on through one street; and forthwith the angel departed from him.

11 And when Peter was come to himself, he said, Now I know of a surety, that the Lord hath sent his angel, and hath delivered me out of the hand of Herod, and from all the expectation of the people of the Jews.

12 And when he had considered the thing, he came to the house of Mary the mother of John, whose surname was Mark; where many were gathered together praying.

13 And as Peter knocked at the door of the gate, a damsel came to hearken, named Rhoda.

14 And when she knew Peter's voice, she opened not the gate for gladness, but ran in, and told how Peter stood before the gate.

15 And they said unto her, Thou art mad. But she constantly affirmed that it was even so. Then said they, It is his angel.

16 But Peter continued knocking: and when they had opened the door, and saw him, they were astonished.

17 But he, beckoning unto them with the hand to hold their peace, declared unto them how the Lord had brought him out of the prison. And he said, Go shew these things unto

JOHN WESLEY

14. And knowing Peter's voice – Bidding her open the door.

15. They said, Thou art mad – As we say, Sure you are not in your senses to talk so. It is his angel – It was a common opinion among the Jews, that every man had his particular guardian angel, who frequently assumed both his shape and voice. But this is a point on which the Scriptures are silent.

17. Beckoning to them – Many of whom being amazed, were talking together. And he said, Show these things to James – The brother or kinsman of our Lord, and author of the epistle which bears his name. He appears to have been a person of considerable weight and importance, probably the chief overseer of that province, and of the Church in Jerusalem in particular. He went into another place – Where he might be better concealed till the storm was over.

19. Herod commanded them to be put to death – And thus the wicked suffered in the room of the righteous. And going down from Judea – With shame, for not having brought forth Peter, according to his promise.

20. Having gained Blastus – To their side, they sued for, and obtained peace – Reconciliation with Herod. And so the Christians of those parts were, by the providence of God, delivered from scarcity. Their country was nourished – Was provided with, corn, by the king's country – Thus Hiram also, king of Tyre, desired of Solomon food or corn for his household, 1 Kings v, 9.

21. And on a set day – Which was solemnized yearly, in honor of Claudius Cesar; Herod, arrayed in royal apparel – In a garment so wrought with silver, that the rays of the rising sun striking upon, and being reflected from it, dazzled the eyes of the beholders. The people shouted, It is the voice of a God – Such profane flattery they frequently paid to princes. But the commonness of a wicked custom rather increases than lessens the guilt of it.

23. And immediately – God does not delay to vindicate his injured honor; an angel of the Lord smote him – Of this other historians say nothing: so wide a difference there is between Divine and human history! An angel of the Lord brought out Peter; an angel smote Herod. Men did not see the instruments in either case. These were only known to the people of God. Because he gave not glory to God – He willingly received it to himself, and by this sacrilege filled up the measure of his iniquities. So then vengeance tarried not. And he was eaten by worms, or vermin – How changed! And on the fifth day expired in exquisite torture. Such was the event! The persecutor perished, and the Gospel grew and multiplied.

25. Saul returned – To Antioch; taking John, surnamed Mark – The son of Mary, (at whose house the disciples met, to pray for Peter,) who was sister to Barnabas.

Christ told that they should drink of the cup that he was to drink of, and be baptized with the baptism that he was to be baptized with, Mt 20:23. Now the words of Christ were made good in him; and if we suffer with Christ, we shall reign with him. Herod imprisoned Peter: the way of persecution, as of other sins, is downhill; when men are in it, they cannot easily stop. Those make themselves an easy prey to Satan, who make it their business to please men. Thus James finished his course. But Peter, being designed for further services, was safe; though he seemed now marked out for a speedy sacrifice. We that live in a cold, prayerless generation, can hardly form an idea of the earnestness of these holy men of old. But if the Lord should bring on the church an awful persecution like this of Herod, the faithful in Christ would learn what soul-felt prayer is.

6-11 A peaceful conscience, a lively hope, and the consolations of the Holy Spirit, can keep men calm in the full prospect of death; even those very persons who have been most distracted with terrors on that account. God's time to help, is when things are brought to the last extremity. Peter was assured that the Lord would cause this trial to end in the way that should be most for his glory. Those who are delivered out of spiritual imprisonment must follow their Deliverer, like the Israelites when they went out of the house of bondage. They knew not whither they went, but knew whom they followed. When God will work salvation for his people, all difficulties in their way will be overcome, even gates of iron are made to open of their own accord. This deliverance of Peter represents our redemption by Christ, which not only proclaims liberty to the captives, but brings them out of the prison-house. Peter, when he recollected himself, perceived what great things God had done for him. Thus souls delivered out of spiritual bondage, are not at first aware what God has wrought in them; many have the truth of grace, that want evidence of it. But when the Comforter comes, whom the Father will send, sooner or later, he will let them know what a blessed change is wrought.

12-19 God's providence leaves room for the use of our prudence, though he has undertaken to perform and perfect what he has begun. These Christians continued in prayer for Peter, for they were truly in earnest. Thus men ought always to pray, and not to faint. As long as we are kept waiting for a mercy, we must continue praying for it. But sometimes that which we most earnestly wish for, we are most backward to believe. The Christian law of self-denial and of suffering for Christ, has not done away the natural law of caring for our own safety by lawful means. In times of public danger, all believers have God for their hiding-place;

Peter said, "Repent!" they did indeed repent. If repentance be grief, they grieved at their hearts. If repentance be a change of mind and life, they were indeed altered men. Then Peter said, "Be baptized every one of you in the name of Jesus Christ for the remission of sins." Take the open and decisive step: stand forth as believers in Jesus, and confess him by that outward and visible sign which he has ordained. Be buried with him in whom your sin is buried. You slew him in error; be buried with him in truth. They did it gladly, they repented of the sin; they were baptized into the sacred name. And then Peter could tell them—"You have remission of sins: the wrong you have done to your Lord is cancelled: the Lord hath put away your sin for ever. Remission of sins comes to you through Jesus, whom you slew, whom the Father has raised up. You shall not be summoned before the bar of God to account even for the hideous crime of murdering the Lord, for by his death you are forgiven. In proof of forgiveness you shall now be made partakers of the great gift which marks his ascending power. The Holy Spirit shall come upon you, even upon you his murderers, and you shall go forth, and be witnesses for him."

O my hearers, to what a place have I brought you now! If indeed the Holy Spirit has helped you to follow me in my discourse, see where we have climbed! However black your crime, however vile your character, if you have seen the wrong that you have done, if you have repented of having done it because you see that you have sinned against your loving Lord, and if you will now come to him repenting and believing, and will confess him as he bids you confess him in baptism; then you have full remission, and you shall be partakers of the gifts and graces of his Holy Spirit, and henceforth you shall be chosen witnesses for the Christ whom God hath raised from the dead. Beloved, you need no choice speech from me: pure gold needs no gilding, and as I have told you the most wonderful of all facts in heaven or in earth, I let it remain in all its simple grandeur.

May God write out this old, old story on your hearts! Oh, that he would issue a new edition of his gospel of love, printed on your hearts! Every man's conversion is a freshly printed copy of the poem of salvation. May the Lord issue you hot from the press this morning, a living epistle to be known and read of all men; and specially to be read by your children at home, and your neighbors in the same street! The Lord grant that hearts may be pricked by this sermon, for his name's sake! Amen.

James, and to the brethren. And he departed, and went into another place.

18 Now as soon as it was day, there was no small stir among the soldiers, what was become of Peter.

19 And when Herod had sought for him, and found him not, he examined the keepers, and commanded that they should be put to death. And he went down from Judea to Cesarea, and there abode.

20 And Herod was highly displeased with them of Tyre and Sidon: but they came with one accord to him, and, having made Blastus the king's chamberlain their friend, desired peace; because their country was nourished by the king's country.

21 And upon a set day Herod, arrayed in royal apparel, sat upon his throne, and made an oration unto them.

22 And the people gave a shout, saying, It is the voice of a god, and not of a man.

23 And immediately the angel of the Lord smote him, because he gave not God the glory: and he was eaten of worms, and gave up the ghost.

24 But the word of God grew and multiplied.

25 And Barnabas and Saul returned from Jerusalem, when they had fulfilled their ministry, and took with them John, whose surname was Mark.

ACTS 13

1 Now there were in the church that was at Antioch certain prophets and teachers; as Barnabas, and Simeon that was called Niger, and Lucius of Cyrene, and Manaen, which had been brought up with Herod the tetrarch, and Saul.

2 As they ministered to the Lord, and fasted, the Holy Ghost said, Separate me Barnabas and Saul for the work whereunto I have called them.

3 And when they had fasted and prayed, and laid their hands on them, they sent them away.

4 So they, being sent forth by the Holy Ghost, departed unto Seleucia; and from thence they sailed to Cyprus.

5 And when they were at Salamis, they preached the word of God in the synagogues of the Jews: and they had also John to their minister.

6 And when they had gone through the isle unto Paphos, they found a certain sorcerer, a false prophet, a Jew, whose name was Barjesus:

7 Which was with the deputy of the country, Sergius Paulus, a prudent man; who called for Barnabas and Saul, and desired to hear the word of God.

8 But Elymas the sorcerer (for so is his name by interpretation) withstood them, seeking to turn away the deputy from the faith.

9 Then Saul, (who also is called Paul,) filled

ACTS 13

1. Manaen, who had been brought up with Herod – His foster brother, now freed from the temptations of a court.

2. Separate me Barnabas and Saul for the work to which I have called them – This was not ordaining them. St. Paul was ordained long before, and that not of men, neither by man: it was only inducting him to the province for which our Lord had appointed him from the beginning, and which was now revealed to the prophets and teachers. In consequence of this they fasted, prayed, and laid their hands on them, a rite which was used not in ordination only, but in blessing, and on many other occasions.

3. Then having fasted – Again. Thus they did also, chap. xiv, 23.

5. In the synagogues – Using all opportunities that offered.

6. Paphos was on the western, Salamis on the eastern part of the island.

7. The proconsul – The Roman governor of Cyprus, a prudent man – And therefore not overswayed by Elymas, but desirous to inquire farther.

9. Then Saul, who was also called Paul – It is not improbable, that coming now among the Romans, they would naturally adapt his name to their own language, and so called him Paul instead of Saul. Perhaps the family of the proconsul might be the first who addressed to or spoke of him by this name. And from this time, being the apostle of the Gentiles, he himself used the name which was more familiar to them.

10. O full of all guile – As a false prophet, and all mischief – As a magician. Thou son of the devil – A title well suited to a magician; and one who not only was himself unrighteous, but labored to keep others from all goodness. Wilt thou not cease to pervert the right ways of the Lord? – Even now thou hast heard the truth of the Gospel.

11. And immediately a mist – Or dimness within, and darkness without, fell upon him.

12. Being astonished at the doctrine of the Lord – Confirmed by such a miracle.

13. John withdrawing from them returned – Tired with the fatigue, or shrinking from danger.

14. Antioch in Pisidia – Different from the Antioch mentioned ver. 1.

15. And after the reading of the law and the prophets, the chief of the synagogue sent to them – The law was read over once every year, a portion of it every Sabbath: to which was added a lesson taken out of the prophets. After this was over, any one might speak to the people, on any subject he thought convenient. Yet it was a circumstance of decency which Paul and Barnabas would hardly omit, to acquaint the rulers with their desire of doing it: probably by some message before the service began.

16. Ye that fear God – Whether proselytes or heathens.

17. The God – By such a commemoration of God's favors to their fathers, at once their minds were conciliated to the speaker, they were convinced of their duty to God, and invited to believe his promise, and the accomplishment of it. The six verses 17-22, contain the whole sum of the Old Testament. Of this people – Paul here chiefly addresses himself to those whom he styles, Ye that fear God: he speaks of Israel first; and ver. 26, speaks more directly to the Israelites themselves. Chose – And this exalted the people; not any merit or goodness of their own, Ezek. xx, 5. Our fathers – Abraham and his posterity. Isaiah i, 2.

18. Deut. i, 31.

MATTHEW HENRY   CHARLES H. SPURGEON

which is so secret, that the world cannot find them. Also, the instruments of persecution are themselves exposed to danger; the wrath of God hangs over all that engage in this hateful work. And the range of persecutors often vents itself on all in its way.

20-25 Many heathen princes claimed and received Divine honors, but it was far more horrible impiety in Herod, who knew the word and worship of the living God, to accept such idolatrous honors without rebuking the blasphemy. And such men as Herod, when puffed with pride and vanity, are ripening fast for signal vengeance. God is very jealous for his own honor, and will be glorified upon those whom he is not glorified by. See what vile bodies we carry about with us; they have in them the seeds of their own dissolution, by which they will soon be destroyed, whenever God does but speak the word. We may learn wisdom from the people of Tyre and Sidon, for we have offended the Lord with our sins. We depend on him for life, and breath, and all things; it surely then behoves us to humble ourselves before him, that through the appointed Mediator, who is ever ready to befriend us, we may be reconciled to him, lest wrath come upon us to the utmost.

ACTS 13

The mission of Paul and Barnabas. (1-3)
Elymas the sorcerer. (4-13)
Paul's discourse at Antioch. (14-41)
He preaches to the Gentiles, and is persecuted by the Jews. (42-52)

1-3 What an assemblage was here! In these names we see that the Lord raises up instruments for his work, from various places and stations in life; and zeal for his glory induces men to give up flattering connexions and prospects to promote his cause. It is by the Spirit of Christ that his ministers are made both able and willing for his service, and taken from other cares that would hinder in it. Christ's ministers are to be employed in Christ's work, and, under the Spirit's guidance, to act for the glory of God the Father. They are separated to take pains, and not to take state. A blessing upon Barnabas and Saul in their present undertaking was sought for, and that they might be filled with the Holy Ghost in their work. Whatever means are used, or rules observed, the Holy Ghost alone can fit ministers for their important work, and call them to it.

4-13 Satan is in a special manner busy with great men and men in power, to keep them from being religious, for their example will influence many. Saul is here for the first time called Paul, and never

THE WAY OF SALVATION
Sermon number 209 delivered on Sabbath Morning, August 15, 1858, at the Music Hall, Royal Surrey Gardens.

"Neither is there salvation in any other: for there is none other name under heaven given among men, whereby we must be saved."—Acts 4:12.

IT IS A VERY HAPPY CIRCUMSTANCE when the servants of God are able to turn everything to account in their ministry. Now, the apostle Peter was summoned before the priests and Sadducees, the chief of his nation, to answer for having restored a man who was lame from his mother's womb. Whilst accounting for this case of cure, or, if I may use the expression, for this case of temporal salvation, the apostle Peter had this thought suggested to him, "While I am accounting for the salvation of this man from lameness, I have now a fine opportunity of showing to these people, who otherwise will not listen to us, the way of the salvation of the soul." So he proceeds from the less to the greater, from the healing of a man's limb to the healing of a man's spirit; and having informed them once that it was through the name of Jesus Christ that the impotent man had been made whole, he now announces that salvation,—the great salvation, must be wrought by the selfsame means; "Neither is there salvation in any other: for there is none other name under heaven given among men, whereby we must be saved."

What a great word that word "salvation" is! It includes the cleansing of our conscience from all past guilt, the delivery of our soul from all those propensities to evil which now so strongly predominate in us; it takes in, in fact, the undoing of all that Adam did. Salvation is the total restoration of man from his fallen estate; and yet it is something more than that, for God's salvation fixes our standing more secure than it was before we fell. It finds us broken in pieces by the sin of our first parent, defiled, stained, accursed: it first heals our wounds, it removes our diseases, it takes away our curse, it puts our feet upon the rock Christ Jesus, and having thus done, at last it lifts our heads far above all principalities. and powers, to be crowned for ever with Jesus Christ, the King of heaven. Some people, when they use the word "salvation," understand nothing more by it than deliverance from hell and admittance into heaven. Now, that is not salvation: those two things are the effects of salvation. We are redeemed from hell because we are saved, and we enter heaven because we have been saved beforehand. Our everlasting state is the effect of salvation in this life. Salvation, it is true, includes all that, because salvation is the mother of it, and carrieth it within its bowels; but still it were wrong for us to imagine that that is all

with the Holy Ghost, set his eyes on him,

10 And said, O full of all subtilty and all mischief, thou child of the devil, thou enemy of all righteousness, wilt thou not cease to pervert the right ways of the Lord?

11 And now, behold, the hand of the Lord is upon thee, and thou shalt be blind, not seeing the sun for a season. And immediately there fell on him a mist and a darkness; and he went about seeking some to lead him by the hand.

12 Then the deputy, when he saw what was done, believed, being astonished at the doctrine of the Lord.

13 Now when Paul and his company loosed from Paphos, they came to Perga in Pamphylia: and John departing from them returned to Jerusalem.

14 But when they departed from Perga, they came to Antioch in Pisidia, and went into the synagogue on the sabbath day, and sat down.

15 And after the reading of the law and the prophets the rulers of the synagogue sent unto them, saying, Ye men and brethren, if ye have any word of exhortation for the people, say on.

16 Then Paul stood up, and beckoning with his hand said, Men of Israel, and ye that fear God, give audience.

17 The God of this people of Israel chose our fathers, and exalted the people when they dwelt as strangers in the land of Egypt, and with an high arm brought he them out of it.

18 And about the time of forty years suffered he their manners in the wilderness.

19 And when he had destroyed seven nations in the land of Chanaan, he divided their land to them by lot.

20 And after that he gave unto them judges about the space of four hundred and fifty years, until Samuel the prophet.

21 And afterward they desired a king: and God gave unto them Saul the son of Cis, a man of the tribe of Benjamin, by the space of forty years.

22 And when he had removed him, he raised up unto them David to be their king; to whom also he gave testimony, and said, I have found David the son of Jesse, a man after mine own heart, which shall fulfill all my will.

23 Of this man's seed hath God according to his promise raised unto Israel a Savior, Jesus:

24 When John had first preached before his coming the baptism of repentance to all the people of Israel.

25 And as John fulfilled his course, he said, Whom think ye that I am? I am not he. But, behold, there cometh one after me, whose shoes of his feet I am not worthy to loose.

26 Men and brethren, children of the stock of Abraham, and whosoever among you feareth God, to you is the word of this salvation sent.

27 For they that dwell at Jerusalem, and their rulers, because they knew him not, nor yet the voices of the prophets which are read every sabbath day, they have fulfilled them in condemning him.

19. Seven nations – Enumerated Deut. vii, 1; about four hundred and fifty years – That is, from the choice of the fathers to the dividing of the land; it was about four hundred and fifty years.

21. He gave them Saul forty years – Including the time wherein Samuel judged Israel.

22. Having removed him – Hence they might understand that the dispensations of God admit of various changes. I have found David, a man after my own heart – This expression is to be taken in a limited sense. David was such at that time, but not at all times. And he was so, in that respect, as he performed all God's will, in the particulars there mentioned: But he was not a man after God's own heart, in other respects, wherein he performed his own will. In the matter of Uriah, for instance, he was as far from being a man after God's own heart as Saul himself was. It is therefore a very gross, as well as dangerous mistake, to suppose this is the character of David in every part of his behavior. We must beware of this, unless we would recommend adultery and murder as things after God's own heart. 1 Sam. xvi, 12, 13.

24. John having first preached – He mentions this, as a thing already known to them. And so doubtless it was. For it gave so loud an alarm to the whole Jewish nation, as could not but be heard of in foreign countries, at least as remote as Pisidia.

25. His course – His work was quickly finished, and might therefore well be termed a course or race. Luke iii, 16.

27. For they that dwell at Jerusalem, and their rulers – He here anticipates a strong objection, "Why did not they at Jerusalem, and especially their rulers, believe?" They know not him, because they understood not those very prophets whom they read or heard continually. Their very condemning him, innocent as he was, proves that they understood not the prophecies concerning him.

29. They fulfilled all things that were written of him – So far could they go, but no farther.

31. He was seen many days by them who came up with him from Galilee to Jerusalem – This last journey both presupposes all the rest, and was the most important of all.

33. Thou art my Son, this day have I begotten thee – It is true, he was the Son of God from eternity. The meaning therefore is, I have this day declared thee to be my Son. As St. Paul elsewhere, declared to be the Son of God with power, by the resurrection from the dead, Rom. i, 4. And it is with peculiar propriety and beauty that God is said to have begotten him, on the day when he raised him from the dead, as he seemed then to be born out of the earth anew. Psalm ii, 7.

34. No more to return to corruption – That is, to die no more. I will give you the sure mercies of David – The blessings promised to David in Christ. These are sure, certain, firm, solid, to every true believer in him. And hence the resurrection of Christ necessarily follows; for without this, those blessings could not be given. Isaiah lv, 3.

35. He saith – David in the name of the Messiah. Psalm xvi, 10.

36. David, having served the will of God in his generation, fell asleep – So his service extended not itself beyond the bounds of the common age of man: but the service of the Messiah to all generations, as his kingdom to all ages. Served the will of God – Why art thou here thou who art yet in the world? Is it not that thou also mayest serve the will of God? Art thou serving it now? Doing all his will? And was added to his fathers – Not only in body. This expression refers to the soul also, and supposes the immortality of it.

MATTHEW HENRY   CHARLES H. SPURGEON

after Saul. Saul was his name as he was a Hebrew; Paul was his name as he was a citizen of Rome. Under the direct influence of the Holy Ghost, he gave Elymas his true character, but not in passion. A fullness of deceit and mischief together, make a man indeed a child of the devil. And those who are enemies to the doctrine of Jesus, are enemies to all righteousness; for in it all righteousness is fulfilled. The ways of the Lord Jesus are the only right ways to heaven and happiness. There are many who not only wander from these ways themselves, but set others against these ways. They commonly are so hardened, that they will not cease to do evil. The proconsul was astonished at the force of the doctrine upon his own heart and conscience, and at the power of God by which it was confirmed. The doctrine of Christ astonishes; and the more we know of it, the more reason we shall see to wonder at it. Those who put their hand to the plow and look back, are not fit for the kingdom of God. Those who are not prepared to face opposition, and to endure hardship, are not fitted for the work of the ministry.

14-31 When we come together to worship God, we must do it, not only by prayer and praise, but by the reading and hearing of the word of God. The bare reading of the Scriptures in public assemblies is not enough; they should be expounded, and the people exhorted out of them. This is helping people in doing that which is necessary to make the word profitable, to apply it to themselves. Every thing is touched upon in this sermon, which might best prevail with Jews to receive and embrace Christ as the promised Messiah. And every view, however short or faint, of the Lord's dealings with his church, reminds us of his mercy and long-suffering, and of man's ingratitude and perverseness. Paul passes from David to the Son of David, and shows that this Jesus is his promised Seed; a Savior to do that for them, which the judges of old could not do, to save them from their sins, their worst enemies. When the apostles preached Christ as the Savior, they were so far from concealing his death, that they always preached Christ crucified. Our complete separation from sin, is represented by our being buried with Christ. But he rose again from the dead, and saw no corruption: this was the great truth to be preached.

32-37 The resurrection of Christ was the great proof of his being the Son of God. It was not possible he should be held by death, because he was the Son of God, and therefore had life in himself, which he could not lay down but with a design to take it again. The sure mercies of David are that everlasting life, of which the resurrection was a sure pledge; and the blessings of redemption in Christ are a certain earnest, even in this world. David was a great blessing to the age wherein he

the meaning of the word. Salvation begins with us as wandering sheep; it follows us through all our mazy wanderings; it puts us on the shoulders of the shepherd; it carries us into the fold; it calls together the friends and the neighbors; it rejoices over us; it preserves us in that fold through life; and then at last it brings us to the green pastures of heaven, beside the still waters of bliss, where we lie down for ever, in the presence of the Chief Shepherd, never more to be disturbed.

Now our text tells us there is only one way of salvation. "Neither is there salvation in any other: for there is none other name under heaven given among men, whereby we must be saved." I shall take first of all a negative truth taught here, namely, that there is no salvation out of Christ; and then, secondly, a positive truth inferred, namely, that there is salvation in Jesus Christ whereby we must be saved.

I. First, then, A NEGATIVE FACT. "Neither is there salvation in any other." Did you ever notice the intolerance of God's religion? In olden times the heathen, who had different gods, all of them respected the gods of their neighbors. For instance, the king of Egypt would confess that the gods of Nineveh were true and real gods, and the prince of Babylon would acknowledge that the gods of the Philistines were true and real gods: but Jehovah, the God of Israel, put this as one of his first commandments, "Thou shalt have none other gods besides me;" and he would not allow them to pay the slightest possible respect to the gods of any other nation: "Thou shalt hew them in pieces, thou shalt break down their temples, and cut down their groves." All other nations were tolerant the one to the other, but the Jew could not be so. One part of his religion was, "Hear, O Israel, the Lord thy God is one God;" and as the consequence of his belief that there was but one God, and that that one God was Jehovah, he felt it his bounden duty to call all pretended gods by nicknames, to spit upon them, to treat them with contumely and contempt. Now the Christian religion, you observe, is just as intolerant as this. If you apply to a Brahmin to know the way of salvation, he will very likely tell you at once, that all persons who follow out their sincere religious convictions will undoubtedly be saved. "There," says he, "are the Mohammedans; if they obey Mohammed, and sincerely believe what he has taught without doubt, Alla will glorify them at last." And the Brahmin turns round upon the Christian missionary, and says, "What is the use of your bringing your Christianity here to disturb us? I tell you our religion is quite capable of carrying us to heaven, if we are faithful to it." Now just hear the text: how intolerant is the Christian religion! "Neither is there salvation in any other." The Brahmin may

28 And though they found no cause of death in him, yet desired they Pilate that he should be slain.

29 And when they had fulfilled all that was written of him, they took him down from the tree, and laid him in a sepulcher.

30 But God raised him from the dead:

31 And he was seen many days of them which came up with him from Galilee to Jerusalem, who are his witnesses unto the people.

32 And we declare unto you glad tidings, how that the promise which was made unto the fathers,

33 God hath fulfilled the same unto us their children, in that he hath raised up Jesus again; as it is also written in the second psalm, Thou art my Son, this day have I begotten thee.

34 And as concerning that he raised him up from the dead, now no more to return to corruption, he said on this wise, I will give you the sure mercies of David.

35 Wherefore he saith also in another psalm, Thou shalt not suffer thine Holy One to see corruption.

36 For David, after he had served his own generation by the will of God, fell on sleep, and was laid unto his fathers, and saw corruption:

37 But he, whom God raised again, saw no corruption.

38 Be it known unto you therefore, men and brethren, that through this man is preached unto you the forgiveness of sins:

39 And by him all that believe are justified from all things, from which ye could not be justified by the law of Moses.

40 Beware therefore, lest that come upon you, which is spoken of in the prophets;

41 Behold, ye despisers, and wonder, and perish: for I work a work in your days, a work which ye shall in no wise believe, though a man declare it unto you.

42 And when the Jews were gone out of the synagogue, the Gentiles besought that these words might be preached to them the next sabbath.

43 Now when the congregation was broken up, many of the Jews and religious proselytes followed Paul and Barnabas: who, speaking to them, persuaded them to continue in the grace of God.

44 And the next sabbath day came almost the whole city together to hear the word of God.

45 But when the Jews saw the multitudes, they were filled with envy, and spake against those things which were spoken by Paul, contradicting and blaspheming.

46 Then Paul and Barnabas waxed bold, and said, It was necessary that the word of God should first have been spoken to you: but seeing ye put it from you, and judge yourselves unworthy of everlasting life, lo, we turn to the Gentiles.

39. Every one that believeth is justified from all things – Has the actual forgiveness of all his sins, at the very time of his believing; from which ye could not be justified – Not only ye cannot now; but ye never could. For it afforded no expiation for presumptuous sins. By the law of Moses – The whole Mosaic institution! The division of the law into moral and ceremonial was not so common among the Jews, as it is among us. Nor does the apostle here consider it at all: but Moses and Christ are opposed to each other.

40. Beware – A weighty and seasonable admonition. No reproof is as yet added to it.

41. I work a work which ye will in nowise believe – This was originally spoken to those, who would not believe that God would ever deliver them from the power of the Chaldeans. But it is applicable to any who will not believe the promises, or the works of God. Hab. i, 5.

42. When the Jews were going out – Probably many of them, not bearing to hear him, went out before he had done. The Sabbath between – So the Jews call to this day the Sabbath between the first day of the month Tisri (on which the civil year begins) and the tenth of the same month, which is the solemn day of expiation.

43. Who speaking to them – More familiarly, persuaded them to continue – For trials were at hand, in the grace of God – That is, to adhere to the Gospel or Christian faith.

46. Then Paul and Barnabas speaking boldly, said – Those who hinder others must be publicly reproved. It was necessary – Though ye are not worthy: he shows that he had not preached to them, from any confidence of their believing, but seeing ye judge yourselves unworthy of eternal life – They indeed judged none but themselves worthy of it. Yet their rejecting of the Gospel was the same as saying, "We are unworthy of eternal life." Behold! – A thing now present! An astonishing revolution! We turn to the Gentiles – Not that they left off preaching to the Jews in other places. But they now determined to lose no more time at Antioch on their ungrateful countrymen, but to employ themselves wholly in doing what they could for the conversion of the Gentiles there.

47. For so hath the Lord commanded us – By sending us forth, and giving us an opportunity of fulfilling what he had foretold. I have set thee – The Father speaks to Christ. Isaiah xlix, 6.

48. As many as were ordained to eternal life – St. Luke does not say fore-ordained. He is not speaking of what was done from eternity, but of what was then done, through the preaching of the Gospel. He is describing that ordination, and that only, which was at the very time of hearing it. During this sermon those believed, says the apostle, to whom God then gave power to believe. It is as if he had said, "They believed, whose hearts the Lord opened;" as he expresses it in a clearly parallel place, speaking of the same kind of ordination, chap. xvi, 14, &c. It is observable, the original word is not once used in Scripture to express eternal predestination of any kind. The sum is, all those and those only, who were now ordained, now believed. Not that God rejected the rest: it was his will that they also should have been saved: but they thrust salvation from them. Nor were they who then believed constrained to believe. But grace was then first copiously offered them. And they did not thrust it away, so that a great multitude even of Gentiles were converted. In a word, the expression properly implies, a present operation of Divine grace working faith in the hearers.

lived. We were not born for ourselves, but there are those living around us, to whom we must study to be serviceable. Yet here is the difference; Christ was to serve all generations. May we look to him who is declared to be the Son of God by his resurrection from the dead, that by faith in him we may walk with God, and serve our generation according to his will; and when death comes, may we fall asleep in him, with a joyful hope of a blessed resurrection.

38-41 Let all that hear the gospel of Christ, know these two things: 1. That through this Man, who died and rose again, is preached unto you the forgiveness of sins. Your sins, though many and great, may be forgiven, and they may be so without any injury to God's honor. 2. It is by Christ only that those who believe in him, and none else, are justified from all things; from all the guilt and stain of sin, from which they could not be justified by the law of Moses. The great concern of convinced sinners is, to be justified, to be acquitted from all their guilt, and accepted as righteous in God's sight, for if any is left charged upon the sinner, he is undone. By Jesus Christ we obtain a complete justification; for by him a complete atonement was made for sin. We are justified, not only by him as our Judge but by him as the Lord our Righteousness. What the law could not do for us, in that it was weak, the gospel of Christ does. This is the most needful blessing, bringing in every other. The threatenings are warnings; what we are told will come upon impenitent sinners, is designed to awaken us to beware lest it come upon us. It ruins many, that they despise religion. Those that will not wonder and be saved, shall wonder and perish.

42-52 The Jews opposed the doctrine the apostles preached; and when they could find no objection, they blasphemed Christ and his gospel. Commonly those who begin with contradicting, end with blaspheming. But when adversaries of Christ's cause are daring, its advocates should be the bolder. And while many judge themselves unworthy of eternal life, others, who appear less likely, desire to hear more of the glad tidings of salvation. This is according to what was foretold in the Old Testament. What light, what power, what a treasure does this gospel bring with it! How excellent are its truths, its precepts, its promises! Those came to Christ whom the Father drew, and to whom the Spirit made the gospel call effectual, Ro 8:30. As many as were disposed to eternal life, as many as had concern about their eternal state, and aimed to make sure of eternal life, believed in Christ, in whom God has treasured up that life, and who is the only Way to it; and it was the grace of God that wrought it in them. It is good to see honorable women devout; the less they have to do in

admit, that there is salvation in fifty religions besides his own; but we admit no such thing. There is no true salvation out of Jesus Christ. The gods of the heathens may approach us with their mock charity, and tell us that every man may follow out his own conscientious conviction and be saved. We reply—No such thing: there is no salvation in any other; "for there is none other name under heaven given among men, whereby we must be saved."

Now, what do you suppose is the reason of this intolerance—if I may use the word again? I believe it is just because there is the truth both with the Jew and with the Christian. A thousand errors may live in peace with one another, but truth is the hammer that breaks them all in pieces. A hundred lying religions may sleep peaceably in one bed, but wherever the Christian religion goes as the truth, it is like a fire-brand, and it abideth nothing that is not more substantial than the wood, the hay, and the stubble of carnal error. All the gods of the heathen, and all other religions are born of hell, and therefore, being children of the same father, it would seem amiss that they should fall out, and chide, and fight; but the religion of Christ is a thing of God's—its pedigree is from on high, and, therefore, when once it is thrust into the midst of an ungodly and gainsaying generation, it hath neither peace, nor parley, nor treaty with them, for it is truth, and cannot afford to be yoked with error: it stands upon its own rights, and gives to error its due, declaring that it hath no salvation, but that in the truth, and in the truth alone, is salvation to be found.

Again, it is because we have here the sanction of God. It would be improper in any man who had invented a creed of his own, to state that all others must be damned who do not believe it; that would be an overweening censoriousness and bigotry, at which we might afford to smile; but since this religion of Christ is revealed from heaven itself, God, who is the author of all truth, hath a right to append to this truth the dreadful condition, that who so rejecteth it shall perish without mercy; and in proclaiming that, apart from Christ, no man can be saved. We are not really intolerant, for we are but echoing the words of him that speaketh from heaven, and who declares, that cursed is the man who rejects this religion of Christ, seeing that there is no salvation out of him. "Neither is there salvation in any other: for there is none other name under heaven given among men, whereby we must be saved."

Now I hear one or two persons saying, "Do you imagine then, sir, that none are saved apart from Christ?" I reply, I don't imagine it, but I have it here in my text plainly taught. "Well but," saith one, 'how is it concerning the death of infants? Do not infants die without actual sin? Are they saved? and

47 For so hath the Lord commanded us, saying, I have set thee to be a light of the Gentiles, that thou shouldest be for salvation unto the ends of the earth.

48 And when the Gentiles heard this, they were glad, and glorified the word of the Lord: and as many as were ordained to eternal life believed.

49 And the word of the Lord was published throughout all the region.

50 But the Jews stirred up the devout and honorable women, and the chief men of the city, and raised persecution against Paul and Barnabas, and expelled them out of their coasts.

51 But they shook off the dust of their feet against them, and came unto Iconium.

52 And the disciples were filled with joy, and with the Holy Ghost.

ACTS 14

1 And it came to pass in Iconium, that they went both together into the synagogue of the Jews, and so spake, that a great multitude both of the Jews and also of the Greeks believed.

2 But the unbelieving Jews stirred up the Gentiles, and made their minds evil affected against the brethren.

3 Long time therefore abode they speaking boldly in the Lord, which gave testimony unto the word of his grace, and granted signs and wonders to be done by their hands.

4 But the multitude of the city was divided: and part held with the Jews, and part with the apostles.

5 And when there was an assault made both of the Gentiles, and also of the Jews with their rulers, to use them despitefully, and to stone them,

6 They were ware of it, and fled unto Lystra and Derbe, cities of Lycaonia, and unto the region that lieth round about:

7 And there they preached the gospel.

8 And there sat a certain man at Lystra, impotent in his feet, being a cripple from his mother's womb, who never had walked:

9 The same heard Paul speak: who stedfastly beholding him, and perceiving that he had faith to be healed,

10 Said with a loud voice, Stand upright on thy feet. And he leaped and walked.

11 And when the people saw what Paul had done, they lifted up their voices, saying in the speech of Lycaonia, The gods are come down to us in the likeness of men.

12 And they called Barnabas, Jupiter; and Paul, Mercurius, because he was the chief speaker.

13 Then the priest of Jupiter, which was before their city, brought oxen and garlands unto the gates, and would have done sacrifice with the people.

ACTS 14

1. They so spake – Persecution having increased their strength.

9. He had faith to be healed – He felt the power of God in his soul; and thence knew it was sufficient to heal his body also.

11. The gods are come down – Which the heathens supposed they frequently did; Jupiter especially. But how amazingly does the prince of darkness blind the minds of them that believe not! The Jews would not own Christ's Godhead, though they saw him work numberless miracles. On the other hand, the heathens seeing mere men work one miracle, were for deifying them immediately.

13. The priest of Jupiter – Whose temple and image were just without the gate of the city, brought garlands – To put on the victims, and bulls – The usual offerings to Jupiter.

14. They sprang in among the people, crying out – As in a fire, or other sudden and great danger.

15. To turn from these vanities – From worshiping any but the true God. He does not deign to call them gods; unto the living God – Not like these dead idols; who made the heaven and the earth, the sea – Each of which they supposed to have its own gods.

16. Who in times past – He prevents their objection, "But if these things are so, we should have heard them from our fathers." Suffered – An awful judgment, all nations – The multitude of them that err does not turn error into truth, to walk in their own ways – The idolatries which they had chosen.

17. He left not himself without witness – For the heathens had always from God himself a testimony both of his existence and of his providence; in that he did good – Even by punishments he testifies of himself; but more peculiarly by benefits; giving rain – By which air, earth, and sea, are, as it were, all joined together; from heaven – The seat of God; to which St. Paul probably pointed while he spoke, filling the body with food, the soul with gladness.

19. Who persuaded the multitude – Moved with equal ease either to adore or murder him.

20. But as the disciples stood round – Probably after sunset. The enraged multitude would scarce have suffered it in the day time: he rose and went into the city – That he should be able to do this, just after he had been left for dead, was a miracle little less than a resurrection from the dead. Especially considering the manner wherein the Jewish malefactors were stoned. The witnesses first threw as large a stone as they could lift, with all possible violence upon his head, which alone was sufficient to dash the skull in pieces. All the people then joined, as long as any motion or token of life remained.

23. When they had ordained them presbyters in every Church – Out of those who were themselves but newly converted. So soon can God enable even a babe in Christ to build up others in the common faith: they commended them to the Lord – An expression implying faith in Christ, as well as love to the brethren.

25. Perga and Attalia were cities of Pamphylia.

26. Recommended to the grace – Or favor, of God, for the work which they had fulfilled – This shows the nature and design of that laying on of hands, which was mentioned chap. xiii, 3.

MATTHEW HENRY

CHARLES H. SPURGEON

the world, the more they should do for their own souls, and the souls of others: but it is sad, when, under color of devotion to God, they try to show hatred to Christ. And the more we relish the comforts and encouragements we meet with in the power of godliness, and the fuller our hearts are of them, the better prepared we are to face difficulties in the profession of godliness.

ACTS 14

Paul and Barnabas at Iconium. (1-7)

A cripple healed at Lystra. The people would have sacrificed to Paul and Barnabas. (8-18)

Paul stoned at Lystra. The churches visited again. (19-28)

1-7 The apostles spake so plainly, with such evidence and proof of the Spirit, and with such power; so warmly, and with such concern for the souls of men; that those who heard them could not but say, God was with them of a truth. Yet the success was not to be reckoned to the manner of their preaching, but to the Spirit of God who used that means. Perseverance in doing good, amidst dangers and hardships, is a blessed evidence of grace. Wherever God's servants are driven, they should seek to declare the truth. When they went on in Christ's name and strength, he failed not to give testimony to the word of his grace. He has assured us it is the word of God, and that we may venture our souls upon it. The Gentiles and Jews were at enmity with one another, yet united against Christians. If the church's enemies join to destroy it, shall not its friends unite for its preservation? God has a shelter for his people in a storm; he is, and will be their Hiding-place. In times of persecution, believers may see cause to quit a spot, though they do not quit their Master's work.

8-18 All things are possible to those that believe. When we have faith, that most precious gift of God, we shall be delivered from the spiritual helplessness in which we were born, and from the dominion of sinful habits since formed; we shall be made able to stand upright and walk cheerfully in the ways of the Lord. When Christ, the Son of God, appeared in the likeness of men, and did many miracles, men were so far from doing sacrifice to him, that they made him a sacrifice to their pride and malice; but Paul and Barnabas, upon their working one miracle, were treated as gods. The same power of the god of this world, which closes the carnal mind against truth, makes errors and mistakes find easy admission. We do not learn that they rent their clothes when the people spake of stoning them; but when they spake of worshiping them; they could not bear it, being more concerned for God's honor than their own. God's truth

if so, how?" I answer, saved they are beyond a doubt; all children dying in infancy are caught away to dwell in the third heaven of bliss for ever. But mark this—no infant was ever saved apart from the death of Christ. Christ Jesus hath with his blood bought all those who die in infancy; they are all regenerated, not in sprinkling, but probably in the instant of their death a marvelous change passes over them by the breathing of the Holy Spirit, the blood of Jesus is applied to them, and they are washed from all original corruption which they had inherited from their parents, and thus washed and cleansed they enter into the kingdom of heaven. Otherwise, beloved, infants would be unable to join in the everlasting song, "Unto him that loved us and washed us from our sins in his blood." If infants were not washed in the blood of Christ, they could not join in that universal song which perpetually surrounds the throne of God. We believe that they are all saved—every one of them without exception—but not apart from the one great sacrifice of the Lord Jesus Christ. Another says, "But how about the heathen? They know not Christ; are any of the heathen saved?" Mark, Holy Scripture saith but very little concerning the salvation of the heathen. There are many texts in Scripture which would lead us to infer that all the heathen perish; but there are some texts which, on the other hand, lead us to believe that there are some out of the heathen race who, led by God's secret spirit, are seeking after him in the dark, endeavoring to find out something they cannot discover in nature; and it may be that the God of infinite mercy who loves his creatures, is pleased to make to them these revelations in their own heart—dark and mysterious revelations concerning the things of heaven—so that even they may be made partakers of the blood of Jesus Christ, without having such an open vision as we have received, without beholding the cross visibly elevated, and Christ set forth crucified among them. It has been observed in many heathen lands, that before the missionaries have gone there, there has been a strong desire after the religion of Christ. In the Sandwich Islands, before our missionaries went there, there was a strange commotion in the minds of those poor barbarians; they did not know what it was, but they were all on a sudden discontented with their idolatries, and had a longing desire after something higher, better, and purer, than anything they had hitherto discovered; and no sooner was Jesus Christ preached, than they willingly renounced all their idolatries, and laid hold upon him to be their strength and their salvation. Now, we believe this was the Work of God's Spirit secretly inclining these poor creatures to seek after him; and we cannot tell but that in some sequestered spots where we had thought the gospel never has been preached, there may be

14 Which when the apostles, Barnabas and Paul, heard of, they rent their clothes, and ran in among the people, crying out,

15 And saying, Sirs, why do ye these things? We also are men of like passions with you, and preach unto you that ye should turn from these vanities unto the living God, which made heaven, and earth, and the sea, and all things that are therein:

16 Who in times past suffered all nations to walk in their own ways.

17 Nevertheless he left not himself without witness, in that he did good, and gave us rain from heaven, and fruitful seasons, filling our hearts with food and gladness.

18 And with these sayings scarce restrained they the people, that they had not done sacrifice unto them.

19 And there came thither certain Jews from Antioch and Iconium, who persuaded the people, and, having stoned Paul, drew him out of the city, supposing he had been dead.

20 Howbeit, as the disciples stood round about him, he rose up, and came into the city: and the next day he departed with Barnabas to Derbe.

21 And when they had preached the gospel to that city, and had taught many, they returned again to Lystra, and to Iconium, and Antioch,

22 Confirming the souls of the disciples, and exhorting them to continue in the faith, and that we must through much tribulation enter into the kingdom of God.

23 And when they had ordained them elders in every church, and had prayed with fasting, they commended them to the Lord, on whom they believed.

24 And after they had passed throughout Pisidia, they came to Pamphylia.

25 And when they had preached the word in Perga, they went down into Attalia:

26 And thence sailed to Antioch, from whence they had been recommended to the grace of God for the work which they fulfilled.

27 And when they were come, and had gathered the church together, they rehearsed all that God had done with them, and how he had opened the door of faith unto the Gentiles.

28 And there they abode long time with the disciples.

ACTS 15

1 And certain men which came down from Judea taught the brethren, and said, Except ye be circumcized after the manner of Moses, ye cannot be saved.

2 When therefore Paul and Barnabas had no small dissension and disputation with them, they determined that Paul and Barnabas, and certain other of them, should go up to Jerusalem unto the apostles and elders about this question.

3 And being brought on their way by the

ACTS 15

1. Coming down from Judea – Perhaps to supply what they thought Paul and Barnabas had omitted.

2. They (the brethren) determined that Paul and Barnabas, and certain others should go up to Jerusalem about this question – This is the journey to which St. Paul refers, Gal. ii, 1, 2, when he says he went up by Revelation: which is very consistent with this; for the Church in sending them might be directed by a Revelation made either immediately to St. Paul, or to some other person, relating to so important an affair. Important indeed it was, that these Jewish impositions should be solemnly opposed in time; because multitudes of converts were still zealous for the law, and ready to contend for the observance of it. Indeed many of the Christians of Antioch would have acquiesced in the determination of Paul alone. But as many others might have prejudices against him, for his having been so much concerned for the Gentiles, it was highly expedient to take the concurrent judgment of all the apostles on this occasion.

4. They were received – That is solemnly welcomed.

5. But certain Pharisees – For even believers are apt to retain their former turn of mind, and prejudices derived therefrom. The law of Moses – The whole law, both moral and ritual.

7. After much debate – It does not appear that this was among the apostles themselves. But if it had, if they themselves had debated at first, yet might their final decision be from an unerring direction. For how really soever they were inspired, we need not suppose their inspiration was always so instantaneous and express, as to supersede any deliberation in their own minds, or any consultation with each other. Peter rose up – This is the last time he is mentioned in the Acts.

8. God bare them witness – That he had accepted them, by giving them the Holy Ghost.

9. Purifying – This word is repeated from chap. x, 15; their hearts – The heart is the proper seat of purity; by faith – Without concerning themselves with the Mosaic law.

10. Now therefore – Seeing these things are so: why tempt ye God? – Why do ye provoke him to anger, by putting so heavy a yoke on their neck?

11. The Lord Jesus – He does not here say our Lord; because in this solemn place he means the Lord of all, we – Jews, shall be saved even as they – Gentiles, namely, through the grace of the Lord Jesus, not by our observance of the ceremonial law.

12. Miracles and wonders – By which also what St. Peter had said was confirmed.

14. Simon hath declared – James, the apostle of the Hebrews, calls Peter by his Hebrew name. To take out of them a people for his name – That is to believe in him, to be called by his name.

15. To this agree – St. Peter had urged the plain fact, which St. James confirms by Scripture prophecy. The words of the prophets – One of whom is immediately cited.

16. After this – After the Jewish dispensation expires. I will build again the fallen tabernacle of David – By raising from his seed the Christ, who shall build on the ruins of his fallen tabernacle a spiritual and eternal kingdom. Amos ix, 11.

17. The Gentiles on whom my name is called – That is, who are called by my name; who are my people.

18. Known unto God are all his works from eternity – Which the apostle infers from the prophecy itself, and the accomplishment of it. And this conversion of the Gentiles being known to him from

needs not the services of man's falsehood. The servants of God might easily obtain undue honors if they would wink at men's errors and vices; but they must dread and detest such respect more than any reproach. When the apostles preached to the Jews, who hated idolatry, they had only to preach the grace of God in Christ; but when they had to do with the Gentiles, they must set right their mistakes in natural religion. Compare their conduct and declaration with the false opinions of those who think the worship of a God, under any name, or in any manner, is equally acceptable to the Lord Almighty. The most powerful arguments, the most earnest and affectionate addresses, even with miracles, are scarcely enough to keep men from absurdities and abominations; much less can they, without special grace, turn the hearts of sinners to God and to holiness.

19-28 See how restless the rage of the Jews was against the gospel of Christ. The people stoned Paul, in a popular tumult. So strong is the bent of the corrupt and carnal heart, that as it is with great difficulty that men are kept back from evil on one side, so it is with great ease they are persuaded to evil on the other side. If Paul would have been Mercury, he might have been worshiped; but if he will be a faithful minister of Christ, he shall be stoned, and thrown out of the city. Thus men who easily submit to strong delusions, hate to receive the truth in the love of it. All who are converted need to be confirmed in the faith; all who are planted need to be rooted. Ministers' work is to establish saints as well as to awaken sinners. The grace of God, and nothing less, effectually establishes the souls of the disciples. It is true, we must count upon much tribulation, but it is encouragement that we shall not be lost and perish in it. The Person to whose power and grace the converts and the newly established churches are commended, clearly was the Lord Jesus, "on whom they had believed." It was an act of worship. The praise of all the little good we do at any time, must be ascribed to God; for it is he who not only worketh in us both to will and to do, but also worketh with us to make what we do successful. All who love the Lord Jesus, will rejoice to hear that he has opened the door of faith wide, to those who were strangers to him and to his salvation. And let us, like the apostles, abide with those who know and love the Lord.

ACTS 15

The dispute raised by Judaizing teachers. (1-6)
The council at Jerusalem. (7-21)
The letter from the council. (22-35)
Paul and Barnabas separate. (36-41)

1-6 Some from Judea taught the Gentile converts

some lone tract, some chapter of the Bible, some solitary verse of Holy Writ remembered, which may be sufficient to open blind eyes, and to guide poor benighted hearts to the foot of the cross of Christ. But this much is certain; no heathen, however moral—whether in the days of their old philosophy, or in the present time of their barbarism—ever did or ever could enter the kingdom of heaven apart from the name of Jesus Christ. "Neither is their salvation in any other." A man may seek after it and labor after it in his own way, but there he cannot possibly find it, "for there is none other name under heaven given among men, whereby we must be saved."

But after all, my dear friends, it is a great deal better, when we are dealing with these subjects, not to talk upon speculative matters, but to come home personally to ourselves. And let me now ask you this question, have you ever proved by experience the truth of this great negative fact, that there is no salvation in any other? I can speak what I do know, and testify what I have seen, when I solemnly declare in the presence of this congregation, that it is even so. Once I thought there was salvation in good works, and I labored hard, and strove diligently to preserve a character for integrity and uprightness; but when the Spirit of God came into my heart, "sin revived and I died," that which I thought had been good proved to be evil; wherein I thought I had been holy I found myself to be unholy. I discovered that my very best actions were sinful. that my tears needed to be wept over, and that my very prayers needed God's forgiveness. I discovered that I was seeking after salvation by the works of the law, that I was doing all my good works from a selfish motive, namely to save myself, and therefore they could not be acceptable to God. I found out that I could not be saved by good works for two very good reasons: first, I had not got any and secondly, if I had any, they could not save me. After that I thought, surely salvation might be obtained, partly by reformation, and partly by trusting in Christ; so I labored hard again, and thought if I added a few prayers here and there, a few tears of penitence, and a few vows of improvement, all would be well. But after forging on for many a weary day, like a poor blind horse toiling round the mill, I found I had got no farther, for there was still the curse of God hanging over me: "Cursed is every one that continueth not in all things that are written in the book of the law to do them;" and there was still an aching void in my heart the world could never fill—a void of distress and care, for I was sorely troubled because I could not attain unto the rest which my soul desired. Have you tried those two ways of getting to heaven? If you have, I trust the Lord, the Holy Spirit, has made you heartily sick of them, for you shall never enter the kingdom of heaven by the

church, they passed through Phenice and Samaria, declaring the conversion of the Gentiles: and they caused great joy unto all the brethren.

4 And when they were come to Jerusalem, they were received of the church, and of the apostles and elders, and they declared all things that God had done with them.

5 But there rose up certain of the sect of the Pharisees which believed, saying, That it was needful to circumcize them, and to command them to keep the law of Moses.

6 And the apostles and elders came together for to consider of this matter.

7 And when there had been much disputing, Peter rose up, and said unto them, Men and brethren, ye know how that a good while ago God made choice among us, that the Gentiles by my mouth should hear the word of the gospel, and believe.

8 And God, which knoweth the hearts, bare them witness, giving them the Holy Ghost, even as he did unto us;

9 And put no difference between us and them, purifying their hearts by faith.

10 Now therefore why tempt ye God, to put a yoke upon the neck of the disciples, which neither our fathers nor we were able to bear?

11 But we believe that through the grace of the Lord Jesus Christ we shall be saved, even as they.

12 Then all the multitude kept silence, and gave audience to Barnabas and Paul, declaring what miracles and wonders God had wrought among the Gentiles by them.

13 And after they had held their peace, James answered, saying, Men and brethren, hearken unto me:

14 Simeon hath declared how God at the first did visit the Gentiles, to take out of them a people for his name.

15 And to this agree the words of the prophets; as it is written,

16 After this I will return, and will build again the tabernacle of David, which is fallen down; and I will build again the ruins thereof, and I will set it up:

17 That the residue of men might seek after the Lord, and all the Gentiles, upon whom my name is called, saith the Lord, who doeth all these things.

18 Known unto God are all his works from the beginning of the world.

19 Wherefore my sentence is, that we trouble not them, which from among the Gentiles are turned to God:

20 But that we write unto them, that they abstain from pollutions of idols, and from fornication, and from things strangled, and from blood.

21 For Moses of old time hath in every city them that preach him, being read in the synagogues every sabbath day.

22 Then pleased it the apostles and elders,

eternity, we ought not to think a new or strange thing. It is observable, he does not speak of God's works in the natural world, (which had been nothing to his present purpose,) but of his dealing with the children of men. Now he could not know these, without knowing the characters and actions of particular persons, on a correspondence with which the wisdom and goodness of his providential dispensations is founded. For instance, he could not know how he would deal with heathen idolaters (whom he was now calling into his Church) without knowing there would be heathen idolaters: and yet this was a thing purely contingent, a thing as dependent on the freedom of the human mind, as any we can imagine. This text, therefore, among a thousand more, is an unanswerable proof, that God foreknows future contingencies, though there are difficulties relating hereto which men cannot solve.

20. To abstain from fornication – Which even the philosophers among the heathens did not account any fault. It was particularly frequent in the worship of their idols, on which account they are here named together. And from things strangled – That is, from whatever had been killed, without pouring out the blood. When God first permitted man to eat flesh, he commanded Noah, and in him all his posterity, whenever they killed any creature for food, to abstain from the blood thereof. It was to be poured upon the ground as water: doubtless in honor of that blood which was in due time poured out for the sin of the world.

21. Perhaps the connection is, To the Jews we need write nothing on these heads; for they hear the law continually.

22. With the whole Church – Which therefore had a part therein; to send chosen men – Who might put it beyond all dispute, that this was the judgment of the apostles and all the brethren.

23. Writing thus, and sending it by their hand – The whole conduct of this affair plainly shows that the Church in those days had no conception of St. Peter's primacy, or of his being the chief judge in controversies. For the decree is drawn up, not according to his, but the Apostle James's proposal and direction: and that in the name, not of St. Peter, but of all the apostles and elders, and of the whole Church. Nay, St. Peter's name is not mentioned at all, either in the order for sending to Jerusalem on the question, ver. 2, or in the address of the messengers concerning it, ver. 4, or in the letter which was written in answer.

24. Forasmuch as, &c. – The simplicity, weightiness, and conciseness of this letter are highly observable.

26. Men that have hazarded their lives – This is spoken of Paul and Barnabas.

27. Who will tell you the same things – Which we have written.

28. These necessary things – All of these were necessary for that time. But the first of them was not necessary long; and the direction concerning it was therefore repealed by the same Spirit, as we read in the former Epistle to the Corinthians.

29. Blood – The eating which was never permitted the children of God from the beginning of the world. Nothing can be clearer than this. For,

1. From Adam to Noah no man ate flesh at all; consequently no man then ate blood.

2. When God allowed Noah and his posterity to eat flesh, he absolutely forbade them to eat blood; and accordingly this, with the other six precepts of Noah, was delivered down from Noah to Moses.

3. God renewed this prohibition by Moses, which was not

at Antioch, that they could not be saved, unless they observed the whole ceremonial law as given by Moses; and thus they sought to destroy Christian liberty. There is a strange proneness in us to think that all do wrong who do not just as we do. Their doctrine was very discouraging. Wise and good men desire to avoid contests and disputes as far as they can; yet when false teachers oppose the main truths of the gospel, or bring in hurtful doctrines, we must not decline to oppose them.

7-21 We see from the words "purifying their hearts by faith," and the address of St. Peter, that justification by faith, and sanctification by the Holy Ghost, cannot be separated; and that both are the gift of God. We have great cause to bless God that we have heard the gospel. May we have that faith which the great Searcher of hearts approves, and attests by the seal of the Holy Spirit. Then our hearts and consciences will be purified from the guilt of sin, and we shall be freed from the burdens some try to lay upon the disciples of Christ. Paul and Barnabas showed by plain matters of fact, that God owned the preaching of the pure gospel to the Gentiles without the law of Moses; therefore to press that law upon them, was to undo what God had done. The opinion of James was, that the Gentile converts ought not to be troubled about Jewish rites, but that they should abstain from meats offered to idols, so that they might show their hatred of idolatry. Also, that they should be cautioned against fornication, which was not abhorred by the Gentiles as it should be, and even formed a part of some of their rites. They were counseled to abstain from things strangled, and from eating blood; this was forbidden by the law of Moses, and also here, from reverence to the blood of the sacrifices, which being then still offered, it would needlessly grieve the Jewish converts, and further prejudice the unconverted Jews. But as the reason has long ceased, we are left free in this, as in the like matters. Let converts be warned to avoid all appearances of the evils which they formerly practiced, or are likely to be tempted to; and caution them to use Christian liberty with moderation and prudence.

22-35 Being warranted to declare themselves directed by the immediate influence of the Holy Ghost, the apostles and disciples were assured that it seemed good unto God the Holy Spirit, as well as to them, to lay upon the converts no other burden than the things before mentioned, which were necessary, either on their own account, or from present circumstances. It was a comfort to hear that carnal ordinances were no longer imposed on them, which perplexed the conscience, but could not purify or pacify it; and that

right door, until you have first of all been led to confess that all the other doors are barred in your teeth. No man ever will come to God through the straight and narrow way until he has tried all the other ways; and when we find ourselves beaten, and foiled, and defeated, then it is, that pressed by sore necessity, we betake ourselves to the one open fountain, and there wash ourselves, and are made clean.

Perhaps I have in my presence this morning some who are trying to gain salvation by ceremonies. You have been baptized in your infancy; you regularly take the Lord's Supper; you attend your church or chapel; and if you knew any other ceremonies you would attend to them. Ah! my dear friends, all these things are as the chaff before the wind in the matter of salvation; they cannot help you one step towards acceptance in the person of Christ. As well might you labor to build your house with water, as to build salvation with such poor things as these. These are good enough for you when you are saved, but if you seek salvation in them, they shall be to your soul as wells without water, clouds without rain, and withered trees, twice dead, plucked up by the roots. Whatever is your way of salvation—for there are a thousand different inventions of men whereby they seek to save themselves—whatever it may be, hear thou its death knell tolled from this verse: "Neither is there salvation in any other: for there is none other name under heaven given among men, whereby we must be saved."

II. Now, this brings me to the POSITIVE FACT which is inferred in the text, namely, that there is salvation in Jesus Christ. Surely, when I make that simple statement I might burst forth with the song of the angels, and say—"Glory to God in the highest, and on earth peace, good will towards men." Here are a thousand mercies all bound up in one bundle, in this sweet, sweet fact, that there is salvation in Jesus Christ. I shall endeavor now merely to deal with any soul here present who entertains a doubt as to his own salvation in Jesus Christ; I shall single him out, and address him affectionately and earnestly, and endeavor to show him that he may yet be saved, and that in Christ there is salvation for him.

I know thee, sinner! Thou hast long been trying to find the road to heaven, and thou hast missed it. Hitherto thou hast had a thousand dazzling cheats to deceive thee, and never yet one solid ground of comfort for thy poor weary foot; and now, encompassed about by thy sins, thou art not able to look up. Guilt, like a heavy burden, is on thy back, and thy finger is on thy lip, for thou darest not yet cry for pardon; thou art afraid to speak, lest out of thine own mouth thou shouldest be condemned. Satan whispers in thine ear, "It is

with the whole church, to send chosen men of their own company to Antioch with Paul and Barnabas; namely, Judas surnamed Barsabas, and Silas, chief men among the brethren:

23 And they wrote letters by them after this manner; The apostles and elders and brethren send greeting unto the brethren which are of the Gentiles in Antioch and Syria and Cilicia:

24 Forasmuch as we have heard, that certain which went out from us have troubled you with words, subverting your souls, saying, Ye must be circumcized, and keep the law: to whom we gave no such commandment:

25 It seemed good unto us, being assembled with one accord, to send chosen men unto you with our beloved Barnabas and Paul,

26 Men that have hazarded their lives for the name of our Lord Jesus Christ.

27 We have sent therefore Judas and Silas, who shall also tell you the same things by mouth.

28 For it seemed good to the Holy Ghost, and to us, to lay upon you no greater burden than these necessary things;

29 That ye abstain from meats offered to idols, and from blood, and from things strangled, and from fornication: from which if ye keep yourselves, ye shall do well. Fare ye well.

30 So when they were dismissed, they came to Antioch: and when they had gathered the multitude together, they delivered the epistle:

31 Which when they had read, they rejoiced for the consolation.

32 And Judas and Silas, being prophets also themselves, exhorted the brethren with many words, and confirmed them.

33 And after they had tarried there a space, they were let go in peace from the brethren unto the apostles.

34 Notwithstanding it pleased Silas to abide there still.

35 Paul also and Barnabas continued in Antioch, teaching and preaching the word of the Lord, with many others also.

36 And some days after Paul said unto Barnabas, Let us go again and visit our brethren in every city where we have preached the word of the Lord, and see how they do.

37 And Barnabas determined to take with them John, whose surname was Mark.

38 But Paul thought not good to take him with them, who departed from them from Pamphylia, and went not with them to the work.

39 And the contention was so sharp between them, that they departed asunder one from the other: and so Barnabas took Mark, and sailed unto Cyprus;

40 And Paul chose Silas, and departed, being recommended by the brethren unto the grace of God.

41 And he went through Syria and Cilicia, confirming the churches.

repealed from the time of Moses till Christ came.

4. Neither after his coming did any presume to repeal this decree of the Holy Ghost, till it seemed good to the bishop of Rome so to do, about the middle of the eighth century.

5. From that time those Churches which acknowledged his authority held the eating of blood to be an indifferent thing. But,

6. In all those Churches which never did acknowledge the bishop of Rome's authority, it never was allowed to eat blood; nor is it allowed at this day. This is the plain fact; let men reason as plausibly as they please on one side or the other. From which keeping yourselves ye will do well – That is, ye will find a blessing. This gentle manner of concluding was worthy the apostolic wisdom and goodness. But how soon did succeeding councils of inferior authority change it into the style of anathemas! Forms which have proved an occasion of consecrating some of the most devilish passions under the most sacred names; and like some ill-adjusted weapons of war, are most likely to hurt the hand from which they are thrown.

35. Paul and Barnabas abode in Antioch – And it was during this time that Peter came down from Jerusalem, and that St. Paul withstood him to the face, for separating himself from the Gentiles, Gal. ii, 11, &c.

36. Let us go and visit the brethren in every city where we have preached – This was all that St. Paul designed at first; but it was not all that God designed by his journey, whose providence carried him much farther than he intended. And see how they do – How their souls prosper: how they grow in faith, hope love: what else ought to be the grand and constant inquiry in every ecclesiastical visitation? Reader, how dost thou do?

37. Barnabas counseled to take John – His kinsman.

38. But Paul thought it not right – To trust him again, who had deserted them before: who had shrunk from the labor and danger of converting those they were now going to confirm.

39. And there was a sharp contention – Literally, a paroxysm, or fit of a fever. But nothing in the text implies that the sharpness was on both sides. It is far more probable that it was not; that St. Paul, who had the right on his side, as he undoubtedly had,) maintained it with love. And Barnabas taking Mark with him, sailed away to Cyprus – Forsaking the work in which he was engaged, he went away to his own country.

40. But Paul departed – Held on his intended course: being recommended by the brethren to the grace of God – We do not find that Barnabas stayed for this. O how mighty is the grace of God! which in the midst of the world, in the midst of sin, among so many snares of Satan, and in spite of the incredible weakness and depravity of nature, yet overcomes all opposition, sanctifies, sustains, and preserves us to the end! It appears not only that Paul and Barnabas were afterward thoroughly reconciled, 1 Cor. ix, 6; Gal. ii, 9; but also that John was again admitted by St. Paul as a companion in his labors, Colossians iv, 10; Phil. i, 24; 2 Tim. iv, 11.

ACTS 16

3. He took and circumcized him because of the Jews – The unbelieving Jews, to whom he designed he should preach. For they would not have conversed with him at all, so long as he was uncircumcized.

6. And having gone through Phrygia – And spoken there what was

those who troubled their minds were silenced, so that the peace of the church was restored, and that which threatened division was removed. All this was consolation for which they blessed God. Many others were at Antioch. Where many labor in the word and doctrine, yet there may be opportunity for us: the zeal and usefulness of others should stir us up, not lay us asleep.

36-41 Here we have a private quarrel between two ministers, no less than Paul and Barnabas, yet made to end well. Barnabas wished his nephew John Mark to go with them. We should suspect ourselves of being partial, and guard against this in putting our relations forward. Paul did not think him worthy of the honor, nor fit for the service, who had departed from them without their knowledge, or without their consent: see ch. 13:13. Neither would yield, therefore there was no remedy but they must part. We see that the best of men are but men, subject to like passions as we are. Perhaps there were faults on both sides, as usual in such contentions. Christ's example alone, is a copy without a blot. Yet we are not to think it strange, if there are differences among wise and good men. It will be so while we are in this imperfect state; we shall never be all of one mind till we come to heaven. But what mischief the remainders of pride and passion which are found even in good men, do in the world, and do in the church! Many who dwelt at Antioch, who had heard but little of the devotedness and piety of Paul and Barnabas, heard of their dispute and separation; and thus it will be with ourselves, if we give way to contention. Believers must be constant in prayer, that they may never be led by the allowance of unholy tempers, to hurt the cause they really desire to serve. Paul speaks with esteem and affection both of Barnabas and Mark, in his epistles, written after this event. May all who profess thy name, O loving Savior, be thoroughly reconciled by that love derived from thee which is not easily provoked, and which soon forgets and buries injuries.

ACTS 16

Paul takes Timothy to be his assistant. (1-5)
Paul proceeds to Macedonia. The conversion of Lydia. (6-15)
An evil spirit cast out. Paul and Silas scourged and imprisoned. (16-24)
The conversion of the jailer at Philippi. (25-34)
Paul and Silas released. (35-40)

1-5 Well may the church look for much service from youthful ministers who set out in the same spirit as Timothy. But when men will submit in nothing, and oblige in nothing, the first elements of the

all over with thee; there is no mercy for such as thou art: thou art condemned, and condemned thou must be; Christ is able to save many, but not to save thee." Poor soul! what shall I say unto thee but this—Come with me to the cross of Christ, and thou shalt there see something which shall remove thine unbelief. Seest thou that man nailed to yonder tree? Dost thou know his character? He is without spot or blemish, or any such thing: he was no thief, that he should die a felon's death: he was no murderer and no assassin, that he should be crucified between two malefactors. No; his original was pure, without a sin; and his life was holy, without a flaw. Out of his mouth there proceeded only blessing; his hands were full of good deeds, and his feet were swift for acts of mercy; his heart was white with holiness. There was nought in him that man could blame; even his enemies, when they sought to accuse him, found false witnesses, but even they "agreed not together." Dost thou see him dying? Sinner, there must be merit in the death of such a man as that; for without sin himself, when he is put to grief, it must be for other men's sins. God would not afflict and grieve him when he deserved it not. God is no tyrant that he should crush the innocent; he is not unholy that he should punish the righteous. He suffered, then, for the sins of others.

"For sins, not his own, he died to atone."

Think of the purity of Christ, and then see whether there is not salvation in him. Come now With thy blackness about thee, and look at his whiteness; come with thy defilement, and look at his purity; and as thou lookest at that purity, like the lily, and thou seest the crimson of his blood overflowing it, let this whisper be heard in thine ear,—he is able to save thee, sinner, inasmuch as though he was "tempted in all points like as we are," yet he was "without sin;" therefore, the merit of his blood must be great. Oh, may God help thee to believe on him!

But this is not the grand thing which should recommend him to thee. Remember, he who died upon the cross, was no less than the everlasting Son of God. Dost see him there? Come, turn thine eye once more to him. Seest thou his hands and feet trickling with streamlets of gore? That man is Almighty God. Those hands that are nailed to the tree, are hands that could shake the world; those feet that are there pierced have in them, if he willed to put it forth, a potency of strength that might make the mountains melt beneath their tread. That head, now bowed in anguish and in weakness, has in it the wisdom of the Godhead, and with its nod it could make the universe tremble. He who hangs upon the cross yonder, is he without whom was not anything made that was made: by him all things consist—Maker, Creator, Preserver, God of providence, and God of grace—

ACTS 16

1 Then came he to Derbe and Lystra: and, behold, a certain disciple was there, named Timotheus, the son of a certain woman, which was a Jewess, and believed; but his father was a Greek:

2 Which was well reported of by the brethren that were at Lystra and Iconium.

3 Him would Paul have to go forth with him; and took and circumcized him because of the Jews which were in those quarters: for they knew all that his father was a Greek.

4 And as they went through the cities, they delivered them the decrees for to keep, that were ordained of the apostles and elders which were at Jerusalem.

5 And so were the churches established in the faith, and increased in number daily.

6 Now when they had gone throughout Phrygia and the region of Galatia, and were forbidden of the Holy Ghost to preach the word in Asia,

7 After they were come to Mysia, they assayed to go into Bithynia: but the Spirit suffered them not.

8 And they passing by Mysia came down to Troas.

9 And a vision appeared to Paul in the night; There stood a man of Macedonia, and prayed him, saying, Come over into Macedonia, and help us.

10 And after he had seen the vision, immediately we endeavored to go into Macedonia, assuredly gathering that the Lord had called us for to preach the gospel unto them.

11 Therefore loosing from Troas, we came with a straight course to Samothracia, and the next day to Neapolis;

12 And from thence to Philippi, which is the chief city of that part of Macedonia, and a colony: and we were in that city abiding certain days.

13 And on the sabbath we went out of the city by a river side, where prayer was wont to be made; and we sat down, and spake unto the women which resorted thither.

14 And a certain woman named Lydia, a seller of purple, of the city of Thyatira, which worshiped God, heard us: whose heart the Lord opened, that she attended unto the things which were spoken of Paul.

15 And when she was baptized, and her household, she besought us, saying, If ye have judged me to be faithful to the Lord, come into my house, and abide there. And she constrained us.

16 And it came to pass, as we went to prayer, a certain damsel possessed with a spirit of divination met us, which brought her masters much gain by soothsaying:

17 The same followed Paul and us, and cried, saying, These men are the servants of the most high God, which shew unto us the way of salvation.

sufficient, as well as in the region of Galatia, being forbid by the Spirit (probably by an inward dictate) to speak as yet in the proconsular Asia, the time for it not being come.

7. Coming to Mysia, and passing it by, as being a part of Asia, they attempted to go into Bithynia; but the Spirit suffered them not – Forbidding them as before. Sometimes a strong impression, for which we are not able to give any account, is not altogether to be despised.

9. A vision appeared to Paul by night – It was not a dream, though it was by night. No other dream is mentioned in the New Testament than that of Joseph and of Pilate's wife. A man of Macedonia – Probably an angel clothed in the Macedonian habit, or using the language of the country, and representing the inhabitants of it. Help us – Against Satan, ignorance, and sin.

10. We sought to go into Macedonia – This is the first place in which St. Luke intimates his attendance on the apostle. And here he does it only in an oblique manner. Nor does he throughout the history once mention his own name, or any one thing which he did or said for the service of Christianity; though Paul speaks of him in the most honorable terms, Colossians iv, 14; 2 Tim. iv, 11; and probably as the brother whose praise in the Gospel went through all the Churches, 2 Cor. viii, 18. The same remark may be made on the rest of the sacred historians, who every one of them show the like amiable modesty.

11. We ran with a straight course – Which increased their confidence that God had called them.

12. The first city – Neapolis was the first city they came to in that part of Macedonia which was nearest to Asia: in that part which was farthest from it, Philippi. The river Strymon ran between them. Philippi was a Roman colony.

13. We went out of the gate – The Jews usually held their religious assemblies (either by choice or constraint) at a distance from the heathens: by a river side – Which was also convenient for purifying themselves. Where prayer was wont to be made – Though it does not appear there was any house built there. We spake – At first in a familiar manner. Paul did not immediately begin to preach.

14. A worshiper of God – Probably acquainted with the prophetic writings whose heart the Lord opened – The Greek word properly refers to the opening of the eyes: and the heart has its eyes, Eph. i, 18. These are closed by nature and to open them is the peculiar work of God.

15. She was baptized and her family – Who can believe that in so many families there was no infant? Or that the Jews, who were so long accustomed to circumcize their children, would not now devote them to God by baptism? She entreated us – The souls of the faithful cleave to those by whom they were gained to God. She constrained us – By her importunity. They did not immediately comply, lest any should imagine they sought their own profit by coming into Macedonia.

17. These men are – A great truth: but St. Paul did not need, nor would accept, of such testimony.

19. The magistrates – The supreme magistrates of the city. In the next verse they are called by a title which often signifies pretors. These officers exercised both the military and civil authority.

20. Being Jews – A nation peculiarly despised by the Romans.

21. And teach customs which it is not lawful for us to receive – The world has received all the rules and doctrines of all the philosophers that ever were. But this is a property of Gospel truth: it has some-

Christian temper seem to be wanting; and there is great reason to believe that the doctrines and precepts of the gospel will not be successfully taught. The design of the decree being to set aside the ceremonial law, and its carnal ordinances, believers were confirmed in the Christian faith, because it set up a spiritual way of serving God, as suited to the nature both of God and man. Thus the church increased in numbers daily.

6-15 The removals of ministers, and the dispensing the means of grace by them, are in particular under Divine conduct and direction. We must follow Providence: and whatever we seek to do, if that suffer us not, we ought to submit and believe to be for the best. People greatly need help for their souls, it is their duty to look out for it, and to invite those among them who can help them. And God's calls must be complied with readily. A solemn assembly the worshipers of God must have, if possible, upon the Sabbath day. If we have not synagogues, we must be thankful for more private places, and resort to them; not forsaking the assembling together, as our opportunities are. Among the hearers of Paul was a woman, named Lydia. She had an honest calling, which the historian notices to her praise. Yet though she had a calling to mind, she found time to improve advantages for her soul. It will not excuse us from religious duties, to say, We have a trade to mind; for have not we also a God to serve, and souls to look after? Religion does not call us from our business in the world, but directs us in it. Pride, prejudice, and sin shut out the truths of God, till his grace makes way for them into the understanding and affections; and the Lord alone can open the heart to receive and believe his word. We must believe in Jesus Christ; there is no coming to God as a Father, but by the Son as Mediator.

16-24 Satan, though the father of lies, will declare the most important truths, when he can thereby serve his purposes. But much mischief is done to the real servants of Christ, by unholy and false preachers of the gospel, who are confounded with them by careless observers. Those who do good by drawing men from sin, may expect to be reviled as troublers of the city. While they teach men to fear God, to believe in Christ, to forsake sin, and to live godly lives, they will be accused of teaching bad customs.

25-34 The consolations of God to his suffering servants are neither few nor small. How much more happy are true Christians than their prosperous enemies! As in the dark, so out of the depths, we may cry unto God. No place, no time is amiss for prayer, if the heart be lifted up to God. No trouble, however grievous, should hinder us from

he who died for thee is God over all, blessed for ever. And now, sinner, is there any power to save in such a Savior as this? If he were a mere man, a Socinian's Christ, or an Arian's Christ, I would not bid thee trust him; but since he is none other than God himself incarnate in human flesh, I beseech thee cast thyself upon him;

"He is able,
He is willing, doubt no more."
"He is able to save unto the uttermost, them
that come unto God by him."

Will you recollect again, as a further consolation for your faith that you may believe that God the Father has accepted the sacrifice of Christ. It is the Father's anger that you have the most cause to dread. The Father is angry with you, for you have sinned, and he has sworn with an oath that he will punish you for your offenses. Now, Jesus Christ was punished in the room, place, and stead of every sinner who hath repented. or ever shall repent. Jesus Christ stood as his substitute and scapegoat. God the Father hath accepted Christ in the stead of sinners. Oh, ought not this to lead you to accept him? If the Judge has accepted the sacrifice, sure you may accept it too; and if he be satisfied, sure you may be content also. If the creditor has written a full and free discharge; you, the poor debtor, may rejoice and believe that that discharge is satisfactory to you, because it is satisfactory to God. But do you ask me how I know that God has accepted Christ's atonement? I remind you that Christ rose again from the dead. Christ was put into the prison-house of the tomb after he died, and there he waited until God should have accepted the atonement.

"If Jesus ne'er had paid the debt,
He ne'er had been at freedom set."

Christ would have been in the tomb at this very day, if God had not accepted his atonement for our justification; but the Lord looked down from heaven, and he surveyed the work of Christ, and said within himself, "It is very good; it is enough;" and turning to an angel, he said, "Angel, my Son is confined in prison, a hostage for my elect; he has paid the price; I know he will not break the prison down himself; go, angel, go and roll away the stone from the door of the sepulcher, and set him at liberty." Down flew the angel, and rolled away the massive stone; and rising from the shades of death the Savior lived. "He died and rose again for our justification." Now, poor soul, thou seest God has accepted Christ; surely then, thou mayest accept him and believe on him.

Another argument, which may perhaps come nearer to thine own soul is this—many have been saved who were as vile as thou art. and therefore there is salvation. "No," sayest thou, "none are so vile as I am." It is a mercy that thou thinkest so, but nevertheless it is quite certain that others have

18 And this did she many days. But Paul, being grieved, turned and said to the spirit, I command thee in the name of Jesus Christ to come out of her. And he came out the same hour.

19 And when her masters saw that the hope of their gains was gone, they caught Paul and Silas, and drew them into the marketplace unto the rulers,

20 And brought them to the magistrates, saying, These men, being Jews, do exceedingly trouble our city,

21 And teach customs, which are not lawful for us to receive, neither to observe, being Romans.

22 And the multitude rose up together against them: and the magistrates rent off their clothes, and commanded to beat them.

23 And when they had laid many stripes upon them, they cast them into prison, charging the jailor to keep them safely:

24 Who, having received such a charge, thrust them into the inner prison, and made their feet fast in the stocks.

25 And at midnight Paul and Silas prayed, and sang praises unto God: and the prisoners heard them.

26 And suddenly there was a great earthquake, so that the foundations of the prison were shaken: and immediately all the doors were opened, and every one's bands were loosed.

27 And the keeper of the prison awaking out of his sleep, and seeing the prison doors open, he drew out his sword, and would have killed himself, supposing that the prisoners had been fled.

28 But Paul cried with a loud voice, saying, Do thyself no harm: for we are all here.

29 Then he called for a light, and sprang in, and came trembling, and fell down before Paul and Silas,

30 And brought them out, and said, Sirs, what must I do to be saved?

31 And they said, Believe on the Lord Jesus Christ, and thou shalt be saved, and thy house.

32 And they spake unto him the word of the Lord, and to all that were in his house.

33 And he took them the same hour of the night, and washed their stripes; and was baptized, he and all his, straightway.

34 And when he had brought them into his house, he set meat before them, and rejoiced, believing in God with all his house.

35 And when it was day, the magistrates sent the serjeants, saying, Let those men go.

36 And the keeper of the prison told this saying to Paul, The magistrates have sent to let you go: now therefore depart, and go in peace.

37 But Paul said unto them, They have beaten us openly uncondemned, being Romans, and have cast us into prison; and now do they thrust us out privily? nay verily; but let them come themselves and fetch us out.

thing in it peculiarly intolerable to the world.

23. They laid many stripes upon them – Either they did not immediately say they were Romans, or in the tumult it was not regarded. Charging the jailer – Perhaps rather to quiet the people than because they thought them criminal.

24. Secured their feet in the stocks – These were probably those large pieces of wood, in use among the Romans, which not only loaded the legs of the prisoner, but also kept them extended in a very painful manner.

25. Paul and Silas sung a hymn to God – Notwithstanding weariness, hunger, stripes, and blood. And the prisoners heard – A song to which they were not accustomed.

28. But Paul cried – As they were all then in the dark, it is not easy to say, how Paul knew of the jailer's purpose; unless it were by some immediate notice from God, which is by no means incredible. With a loud voice – Through earnestness, and because he was at some distance. Do thyself no harm – Although the Christian faith opens the prospect into another life, yet it absolutely forbids and effectually prevents a man's discharging himself from this.

30. Sirs – He did not style them so the day before. What must I do to be saved? – From the guilt I feel and the vengeance I fear? Undoubtedly God then set his sins in array before him, and convinced him in the clearest and strongest manner that the wrath of God abode upon him.

31. Thou shalt be saved and thy household – If ye believe. They did so, and were saved.

33. He washed their stripes – It should not be forgot, that the apostles had not the power of working miraculous cures when they pleased, either on themselves, or their dearest friends. Nor was it expedient they should, since it would have frustrated many wise designs of God, which were answered by their sufferings.

34. He set a table before them and rejoiced – Faith makes a man joyful, prudent, liberal.

35. The pretors sent – Being probably terrified by the earthquake; saying, Let those men go – How different from the charge given a few hours before! And how great an ease of mind to the jailer!

37. They have beaten us publicly, being Roman – St. Paul does not always plead this privilege. But in a country where they were entire strangers, such treatment might have brought upon them a suspicion of having been guilty of some uncommon crime, and so have hindered the course of the Gospel.

40. When they had seen the brethren, they comforted them and departed – Though many circumstances now invited their stay, yet they wisely complied with the request of the magistrates, that they might not seem to express any degree of obstinacy or revenge, or give any suspicion of a design to stir up the people.

ACTS 17

1. And taking their journey through Amphipolis and Apollonia – St. Luke seems to have been left at Philippi; and to have continued in those parts, traveling from place to place among the Churches, till St. Paul returned thither. For here he leaves off speaking of himself as one of St. Paul's company; neither does he resume that style, till we find them together there, chap. xx, 5, 6. After this he constantly uses it to the end of the history. Amphipolis and Apollonia were cities of Macedonia.

2. And Paul, according to his custom – Of doing all things, as far as

MATTHEW HENRY   CHARLES H. SPURGEON

praise. Christianity proves itself to be of God, in that it obliges us to be just to our own lives. Paul cried aloud to make the jailer hear, and to make him heed, saying, Do thyself no harm. All the cautions of the word of God against sin, and all appearances of it, and approaches to it, have this tendency. Man, woman, do not ruin thyself; hurt not thyself, and then none else can hurt thee; do not sin, for nothing but that can hurt thee. Even as to the body, we are cautioned against the sins which do harm to that. Converting grace changes people's language of and to good people and good ministers. How serious the jailer's inquiry! His salvation becomes his great concern; that lies nearest his heart, which before was furthest from his thoughts. It is his own precious soul that he is concerned about. Those who are thoroughly convinced of sin, and truly concerned about their salvation, will give themselves up to Christ. Here is the sum of the whole gospel, the covenant of grace in a few words; Believe in the Lord Jesus Christ, and thou shalt be saved, and thy house. The Lord so blessed the word, that the jailer was at once softened and humbled. He treated them with kindness and compassion, and, professing faith in Christ, was baptized in that name, with his family. The Spirit of grace worked such a strong faith in them, as did away further doubt; and Paul and Silas knew by the Spirit, that a work of God was wrought in them. When sinners are thus converted, they will love and honor those whom they before despised and hated, and will seek to lessen the suffering they before desired to increase. When the fruits of faith begin to appear, terrors will be followed by confidence and joy in God.

35-40 Paul, though willing to suffer for the cause of Christ, and without any desire to avenge himself, did not choose to depart under the charge of having deserved wrongful punishment, and therefore required to be dismissed in an honorable manner. It was not a mere point of honor that the apostle stood upon, but justice, and not to himself so much as to his cause. And when proper apology is made, Christians should never express personal anger, nor insist too strictly upon personal amends. The Lord will make them more than conquerors in every conflict; instead of being cast down by their sufferings, they will become comforters of their brethren.

ACTS 17

been saved, who have been as filthy as thyself. Have you been a persecutor? "Yes," you say. Ay, but you have not been more blood-thirsty than Saul! And yet that chief of sinners became the chief of saints. Have you been a swearer? Have you cursed the Almighty to his face? Ay; and such were some of us who now lift up our voices in prayer, and approach his throne with acceptance. Have you been a drunkard? Ay, and so have many of God's people been for many a day and many a year; but they have forsaken their filthiness, and they have turned unto the Lord with full purpose of heart. However great thy sin, I tell thee, man, there have been some saved as deep in sin as thou art. And if even none have been saved, who are such great sinners as thou art, so much the more reason why God should save thee, that he may go beyond all that he ever has done. The Lord always delights to be doing wonders; and if thou standest the chief of sinners, a little ahead of all the rest, I believe he will delight to save thee, that the wonders of his love and his grace may be the more manifestly known. Do you still say that you are the chief of sinners? I tell you I do not think it. The chief of sinners was saved years ago; that was the Apostle Paul: but even if you should exceed him, still that word "uttermost" goes a little beyond you. "He is able to save them to the uttermost that come unto God by him." Recollect, sinner, if thou dost not find salvation in Christ it will be because thou dost not look for it, for it certainly is there. If thou shalt perish without being saved through the blood of Christ, it will not be through a want of power in that blood to save thee, but entirely through a want of will on thy part—even that thou wilt not believe on him, but dost wantonly and willfully reject his blood to thine own destruction. Take heed to thyself, for as surely as there is salvation in none other, so surely there is salvation in him.

I could turn to you myself, and tell you that surely there must be salvation in Christ for you, since I have found salvation in Christ for myself. Often have I said, I will never doubt the salvation of any one, so long as I can but know that Christ has accepted me. Oh! how dark was my despair when I first sought his mercy seat, I thought then that if he had mercy on all the world, yet he would never have mercy on me; the sins of my childhood and my youth haunted me; I sought to get rid of them one by one, but I was caught as in an iron net of evil habits, and I could not overthrow them; and even when I could renounce my sin, yet the guilt still did cling to my garments—I could not wash myself clean; I prayed for three long years, I bent my knees in vain, and sought, but found no mercy. But, at last, blessed be his name, when I had given up all hope, and thought, that his swift anger would destroy me, and that the pit would

38 And the serjeants told these words unto the magistrates: and they feared, when they heard that they were Romans.

39 And they came and besought them, and brought them out, and desired them to depart out of the city.

40 And they went out of the prison, and entered into the house of Lydia and when they had seen the brethren, they comforted them, and departed.

ACTS 17

1 Now when they had passed through Amphipolis and Apollonia, they came to Thessalonica, where was a synagogue of the Jews:

2 And Paul, as his manner was, went in unto them, and three sabbath days reasoned with them out of the scriptures,

3 Opening and alleging, that Christ must needs have suffered, and risen again from the dead; and that this Jesus, whom I preach unto you, is Christ.

4 And some of them believed, and consorted with Paul and Silas; and of the devout Greeks a great multitude, and of the chief women not a few.

5 But the Jews which believed not, moved with envy, took unto them certain lewd fellows of the baser sort, and gathered a company, and set all the city on an uproar, and assaulted the house of Jason, and sought to bring them out to the people.

6 And when they found them not, they drew Jason and certain brethren unto the rulers of the city, crying, These that have turned the world upside down are come hither also;

7 Whom Jason hath received: and these all do contrary to the decrees of Cesar, saying that there is another king, one Jesus.

8 And they troubled the people and the rulers of the city, when they heard these things.

9 And when they had taken security of Jason, and of the other, they let them go.

10 And the brethren immediately sent away Paul and Silas by night unto Berea: who coming thither went into the synagogue of the Jews.

11 These were more noble than those in Thessalonica, in that they received the word with all readiness of mind, and searched the scriptures daily, whether those things were so.

12 Therefore many of them believed; also of honorable women which were Greeks, and of men, not a few.

13 But when the Jews of Thessalonica had knowledge that the word of God was preached of Paul at Berea, they came thither also, and stirred up the people.

14 And then immediately the brethren sent away Paul to go as it were to the sea: but Silas and Timotheus abode there still.

15 And they that conducted Paul brought him

might be, in a regular manner, went in to them three Sabbath days – Not excluding the days between.

4. Of the principal women, not a few – Our free thinkers pique themselves upon observing, that women are more religious than men; and this, in compliment both to religion and good manners, they impute to the weakness of their understandings. And indeed as far as nature can go, in imitating religion by performing the outward acts of it, this picture of religion may make a fairer show in women than in men, both by reason of their more tender passions, and their modesty, which will make those actions appear to more advantage. But in the case of true religion, which always implies taking up the cross, especially in time of persecution, women lie naturally under a great disadvantage, as having less courage than men. So that their embracing the Gospel was a stronger evidence of the power of him whose strength is perfected in weakness, as a stronger assistance of the Holy Spirit was needful for them to overcome their natural fearfulness.

11. These were more ingenuous – Or generous. To be teachable in the things of God is true generosity of soul. The receiving the word with all readiness of mind, and the most accurate search into the truth, are well consistent.

12. Many of them – Of the Jews. And of the Grecian women – Who were followed by their husbands.

16. While Paul was waiting for them – Having no design, as it seems, to preach at Athens, but his zeal for God drew him into it unawares, without staying till his companions came.

18. Some of the Epicurean and Stoic philosophers – The Epicureans entirely denied a providence, and held the world to be the effect of mere chance; asserting sensual pleasure to be man's chief good, and that the soul and body died together. The Stoics held, that matter was eternal; that all things were governed by irresistible fate; that virtue was its own sufficient reward, and vice its own sufficient punishment. It is easy to see, how happily the apostle levels his discourse at some of the most important errors of each, while, without expressly attacking either, he gives a plain summary of his own religious principles. What would this babbler say? – Such is the language of natural reason, full of, and satisfied with itself. Yet even here St. Paul had some fruit; though nowhere less than at Athens. And no wonder, since this city was a seminary of philosophers, who have ever been the pest of true religion. He seemeth to be a proclaimer – This he returns upon them at the 23rd verse; of strange gods – Such as are not known even at Athens. Because he preached to them Jesus and the resurrection – A God and a goddess. And as stupid as this mistake was, it is the less to be wondered at, since the Athenians might as well count the resurrection a deity, as shame, famine, and many others.

19. The Areopagus, or hill of Mars, (dedicated to Mars, the heathen God of war,) was the place where the Athenians held their supreme court of judicature. But it does not appear he was carried thither as a criminal. The original number of its Judges was twelve; but afterward it increased to three hundred. These were generally men of the greatest families in Athens, and were famed for justice and integrity.

21. And the strangers sojourning there – And catching the distemper of them. Some new thing – The Greek word signifies some newer thing. New things quickly grew cheap, and they wanted those that were newer still.

22. Then Paul standing in the midst of the Areopagus – An ample theater; said – Giving them a lecture of natural divinity, with

MATTHEW HENRY

CHARLES H. SPURGEON

1-9 The drift and scope of Paul's preaching and arguing, was to prove that Jesus is the Christ. He must needs suffer for us, because he could not otherwise purchase our redemption for us; and he must needs have risen again, because he could not otherwise apply the redemption to us. We are to preach concerning Jesus that he is Christ; therefore we may hope to be saved by him, and are bound to be ruled by him. The unbelieving Jews were angry, because the apostles preached to the Gentiles, that they might be saved. How strange it is, that men should grudge others the privileges they will not themselves accept! Neither rulers nor people need be troubled at the increase of real Christians, even though turbulent spirits should make religion the pretext for evil designs. Of such let us beware, from such let us withdraw, that we may show a desire to act aright in society, while we claim our right to worship God according to our consciences.

10-15 The Jews in Berea applied seriously to the study of the word preached unto them. They not only heard Paul preach on the Sabbath, but daily searched the Scriptures, and compared what they read with the facts related to them. The doctrine of Christ does not fear inquiry; advocates for his cause desire no more than that people will fully and fairly examine whether things are so or not. Those are truly noble, and likely to be more and more so, who make the Scriptures their rule, and consult them accordingly. May all the hearers of the gospel become like those of Berea, receiving the word with readiness of mind, and searching the Scriptures daily, whether the things preached to them are so.

16-21 Athens was then famed for polite learning, philosophy, and the fine arts; but none are more childish and superstitious, more impious, or more credulous, than some persons, deemed eminent for learning and ability. It was wholly given to idolatry. The zealous advocate for the cause of Christ will be ready to plead for it in all companies, as occasion offers. Most of these learned men took no notice of Paul; but some, whose principles were the most directly contrary to Christianity, made remarks upon him. The apostle ever dwelt upon two points, which are indeed the principal doctrines of Christianity, Christ and a future state; Christ our way, and heaven our end. They looked on this as very different from the knowledge for many ages taught and professed at Athens; they desire to know more of it, but only because it was new and strange. They led him to the place where judges sat who inquired into such matters. They asked about Paul's doctrine, not because it was good, but because it was new. Great talkers are always busy-bodies. They spend their time in noth-

open its mouth and swallow me up, then in the hour of my extremity did he manifest himself to me, and teach me to cast myself simply and wholly upon him. So shall it be with thee, only trust him, for there is salvation in him—rest assured of that.

To quicken thy diligence, however, I will conclude by noting that if you do not find salvation in Christ, remember you will never find it elsewhere. What a dreadful thing it will be for you if you should lose the salvation provided by Christ! For "how shall you escape if you neglect so great salvation?" Today, very probably I am not speaking to very many of the grossest of sinners, yet I know I am speaking to some even of that class; but whether we are gross sinners or not, how fearful a thing it will be for us to die without first having found an interest in the Savior! Oh sinner! this should quicken thee in going to the mercy seat; this thought, that if thou findest no mercy at the feet of Jesus, thou canst never find it any where else. If the gates of heaven shall never open to thee, remember there is no other gate that ever can be opened for thy salvation. If Christ refuse thee thou art refused; if his blood be not sprinkled on thee thou art lost indeed. Oh! if he keeps thee waiting a little while, still continue in prayer; it is worth waiting for, especially when thou hast this thought to keep thee waiting, namely, that there is none other, no other way, no other hope, no other ground of trust, no other refuge. There I see the gate of heaven, and if I must enter it, I must creep on my hands and knees, for it is a low gate; there I see it, it is a strait and narrow one, I must leave my sins behind me, and my proud righteousness, and I must creep in through that wicket. Come sinner, what sayest thou? Wilt thou go beyond this strait and narrow gate, or wilt thou despise eternal life and risk eternal bliss? Or wilt thou go through it humbly hoping that he who gave himself for thee will accept thee in himself, and save thee now, and save thee everlastingly?

May these few words have power to draw some to Christ, and I am content. "Believe on the Lord Jesus Christ, and thou shalt be saved." "For there is none other name under heaven given among men, whereby we must be saved."

THE OUTPOURING OF THE HOLY SPIRIT
Sermon number 201 delivered on June 20, 1858, at the Music Hall, Royal Surrey Gardens.

"While Peter yet spake these words, the Holy Ghost fell on all them which heard the Word"—Acts 10:44.

THE BIBLE IS A BOOK of the Revelation of God. The God after whom the heathen blindly

unto Athens: and receiving a commandment unto Silas and Timotheus for to come to him with all speed, they departed.

16 Now while Paul waited for them at Athens, his spirit was stirred in him, when he saw the city wholly given to idolatry.

17 Therefore disputed he in the synagogue with the Jews, and with the devout persons, and in the market daily with them that met with him.

18 Then certain philosophers of the Epicureans, and of the Stoics, encountered him. And some said, What will this babbler say? other some, He seemeth to be a setter forth of strange gods: because he preached unto them Jesus, and the resurrection.

19 And they took him, and brought him unto Areopagus, saying, May we know what this new doctrine, whereof thou speakest, is?

20 For thou bringest certain strange things to our ears: we would know therefore what these things mean.

21 (For all the Athenians and strangers which were there spent their time in nothing else, but either to tell, or to hear some new thing.)

22 Then Paul stood in the midst of Mars' hill, and said, Ye men of Athens, I perceive that in all things ye are too superstitious.

23 For as I passed by, and beheld your devotions, I found an altar with this inscription, TO THE UNKNOWN GOD. Whom therefore ye ignorantly worship, him declare I unto you.

24 God that made the world and all things therein, seeing that he is Lord of heaven and earth, dwelleth not in temples made with hands;

25 Neither is worshiped with men's hands, as though he needed any thing, seeing he giveth to all life, and breath, and all things;

26 And hath made of one blood all nations of men for to dwell on all the face of the earth, and hath determined the times before appointed, and the bounds of their habitation;

27 That they should seek the Lord, if haply they might feel after him, and find him, though he be not far from every one of us:

28 For in him we live, and move, and have our being; as certain also of your own poets have said, For we are also his offspring.

29 Forasmuch then as we are the offspring of God, we ought not to think that the Godhead is like unto gold, or silver, or stone, graven by art and man's device.

30 And the times of this ignorance God winked at; but now commandeth all men every where to repent:

31 Because he hath appointed a day, in the which he will judge the world in righteousness by that man whom he hath ordained; whereof he hath given assurance unto all men, in that he hath raised him from the dead.

32 And when they heard of the resurrection of the dead, some mocked: and others said, We will hear thee again of this matter.

admirable wisdom, acuteness, fullness, and courtesy. They inquire after new things: Paul in his divinely philosophical discourse, begins with the first, and goes on to the last things, both which were new things to them. He points out the origin and the end of all things, concerning which they had so many disputes, and equally refutes both the Epicurean and Stoic. I perceive – With what clearness and freedom does he speak! Paul against Athens!

23. I found an altar – Some suppose this was set up by Socrates, to express in a covert way his devotion to the only true God, while he derided the plurality of the heathen gods, for which he was condemned to death: and others, that whoever erected this altar, did it in honor to the God of Israel, of whom there was no image, and whose name Jehovah was never made known to the idolatrous Gentiles. Him proclaim I unto you – Thus he fixes the wandering attention of these blind philosophers; proclaiming to them an unknown, and yet not a new God.

24. God who made the world – Thus is demonstrated even to reason, the one true, good God; absolutely different from the creatures, from every part of the visible creation.

25. Neither is he served as though he needed any thing – or person – The Greek word equally takes in both. To all – That live and breathe; – in him we live; and breathe – In him we move. By breathing life is continued. I breathe this moment: the next is not in my power: and all things – For in him we are. So exactly do the parts of this discourse answer each other.

26. He hath made of one blood the whole nation of men – By this expression the apostle showed them in the most unaffected manner, that though he was a Jew, he was not enslaved to any narrow views, but looked on all mankind as his brethren: having determined the times – That it is God who gave men the earth to inhabit, Paul proves from the order of times and places, showing the highest wisdom of the Disposer, superior to all human counsels. And the bounds of their habitation – By mountains, seas, rivers, and the like.

27. If haply – The way is open; God is ready to be found. But he will lay no force upon man; they might feel after him – This is in the midst between seeking and finding. Feeling being the lowest and grossest of all our senses, is fitly applied to the low knowledge of God; though he be not far from every one of us – We need not go far to seek or find him. He is very near us; in us. It is only perverse reason which thinks he is afar off.

28. In him – Not in ourselves, we live, and move, and have our being – This denotes his necessary, intimate, and most efficacious presence. No words can better express the continual and necessary dependence of all created beings, in their existence and all their operations, on the first and almighty cause, which the truest philosophy as well as divinity teaches. As certain also of your own poets have said – Aratus, whose words these are, was an Athenian, who lived almost three hundred years before this time. They are likewise to be found, with the alteration of one letter only, in the hymn of Cleanthes to Jupiter or the supreme being, one of the purest and finest pieces of natural religion in the whole world of Pagan antiquity.

29. We ought not to think – A tender expression especially in the first person plural. As if he had said, Can God himself be a less noble being than we who are his offspring? Nor does he only here deny, that these are like God, but that they have any analogy to him at all, so as to be capable of representing him.

30. The times of ignorance – What! does he object ignorance to the knowing Athenians? Yes, and they acknowledge it by this very altar.

MATTHEW HENRY   CHARLES H. SPURGEON

ing else, and a very uncomfortable account they have to give of their time who thus spend it. Time is precious, and we are concerned to employ it well, because eternity depends upon it, but much is wasted in unprofitable conversation.

22-31 Here we have a sermon to heathens, who worshiped false gods, and were without the true God in the world; and to them the scope of the discourse was different from what the apostle preached to the Jews. In the latter case, his business was to lead his hearers by prophecies and miracles to the knowledge of the Redeemer, and faith in him; in the former, it was to lead them, by the common works of providence, to know the Creator, and worship Him. The apostle spoke of an altar he had seen, with the inscription, "TO THE UNKNOWN GOD." This fact is stated by many writers. After multiplying their idols to the utmost, some at Athens thought there was another god of whom they had no knowledge. And are there not many now called Christians, who are zealous in their devotions, yet the great object of their worship is to them an unknown God? Observe what glorious things Paul here says of that God whom he served, and would have them to serve. The Lord had long borne with idolatry, but the times of this ignorance were now ending, and by his servants he now commanded all men every where to repent of their idolatry. Each sect of the learned men would feel themselves powerfully affected by the apostle's discourse, which tended to show the emptiness or falsity of their doctrines.

32-34 The apostle was treated with more outward civility at Athens than in some other places; but none more despised his doctrine, or treated it with more indifference. Of all subjects, that which deserves the most attention gains the least. But those who scorn, will have to bear the consequences, and the word will never be useless. Some will be found, who cleave to the Lord, and listen to his faithful servants. Considering the judgment to come, and Christ as our Judge, should urge all to repent of sin, and turn to him. Whatever matter is used, all discourses must lead to him, and show his authority; our salvation, and resurrection, come from and by him.

ACTS 18

Paul at Corinth, with Aquila and Priscilla. (1-6)
He continues to preach at Corinth. (7-11)
Paul before Gallio. (12-17)
He visits Jerusalem. (18-23)
Apollos teaches at Ephesus and in Achaia. (24-28)

1-6 Though Paul was entitled to support from the churches he planted, and from the people to whom

searched, and for whom reason gropes in darkness, is here plainly revealed to us in the pages of divine authorship, so that he who is willing to understand as much of Godhead as man can know, may here learn it if he be not willingly ignorant and willfully obstinate. The doctrine of the Trinity is specially taught in Holy Scripture. The word certainly does not occur, but the three divine persons of the One God are frequently and constantly mentioned, and Holy Scripture is exceedingly careful that we should all receive and believe that great truth of the Christian religion, that the Father is God, that the Son is God, that the Spirit is God, and yet there are not three Gods but one God: though they be each of them very God of very God, yet three in one and one in three is the Jehovah whom we worship. You will notice in the works of Creation how carefully the Scriptures assure us that all the three divine persons took their share. "In the beginning Jehovah created the heavens and the earth;" and in another place we are told that God said "Let us make man"—not one person, but all three taking counsel with each other with regard to the making of mankind. We know that the Father hath laid the foundations and fixed those solid beams of light on which the blue arches of the sky are sustained; but we know with equal certainty that Jesus Christ, the eternal Logos, was with the Father in the beginning, and "without him was not anything made that was made:" moreover we have equal certainty that the Holy Spirit had a hand in Creation, for we are told that "the earth was without form and void, and darkness was upon the face of the earth; and the spirit of the Lord moved upon the face of the waters;" and brooding with his dove-like wing, he brought out of the egg of chaos this mighty thing, the fair round world. We have the like proof of the three persons in the Godhead in the matter of Salvation. We know that God the Father gave his Son; we have abundant proof that God the Father chose his people from before the foundations of the world, that he did invent the plan of salvation, and hath always given his free, willing, and joyous consent to the salvation of his people. With regard to the share that the Son had in salvation, that is apparent enough to all. For us men and for our salvation he came down from heaven; he was incarnate in a mortal body; he was crucified, dead, and buried; he descended into Hades; the third day he rose again from the dead; he ascended into heaven; he sitteth at the right hand of God, where also he maketh intercession for us. As to the Holy Spirit, we have equally sure proof that the Spirit of God worketh in conversion; for everywhere we are said to be begotten of the Holy Spirit; continually it is declared, that unless a man be born again from above, he cannot see the kingdom of God; while all the virtues and the graces of Christianity are

33 So Paul departed from among them.

34 Howbeit certain men clave unto him, and believed: among the which was Dionysius the Areopagite, and a woman named Damaris, and others with them.

ACTS 18

1 After these things Paul departed from Athens, and came to Corinth;

2 And found a certain Jew named Aquila, born in Pontus, lately come from Italy, with his wife Priscilla; (because that Claudius had commanded all Jews to depart from Rome:) and came unto them.

3 And because he was of the same craft, he abode with them, and wrought: for by their occupation they were tentmakers.

4 And he reasoned in the synagogue every sabbath, and persuaded the Jews and the Greeks.

5 And when Silas and Timotheus were come from Macedonia, Paul was pressed in the spirit, and testified to the Jews that Jesus was Christ.

6 And when they opposed themselves, and blasphemed, he shook his raiment, and said unto them, Your blood be upon your own heads; I am clean: from henceforth I will go unto the Gentiles.

7 And he departed thence, and entered into a certain man's house, named Justus, one that worshiped God, whose house joined hard to the synagogue.

8 And Crispus, the chief ruler of the synagogue, believed on the Lord with all his house; and many of the Corinthians hearing believed, and were baptized.

9 Then spake the Lord to Paul in the night by a vision, Be not afraid, but speak, and hold not thy peace:

10 For I am with thee, and no man shall set on thee to hurt thee: for I have much people in this city.

11 And he continued there a year and six months, teaching the word of God among them.

12 And when Gallio was the deputy of Achaia, the Jews made insurrection with one accord against Paul, and brought him to the judgment seat,

13 Saying, This fellow persuadeth men to worship God contrary to the law.

14 And when Paul was now about to open his mouth, Gallio said unto the Jews, If it were a matter of wrong or wicked lewdness, O ye Jews, reason would that I should bear with you:

15 But if it be a question of words and names, and of your law, look ye to it; for I will be no judge of such matters.

16 And he drave them from the judgment seat.

17 Then all the Greeks took Sosthenes, the

God overlooked – As one paraphrases, "The beams of his eye did in a manner shoot over it." He did not appear to take notice of them, by sending express messages to them as he did to the Jews. But now – This day, this hour, saith Paul, puts an end to the Divine forbearance, and brings either greater mercy or punishment. Now he commandeth all men every where to repent – There is a dignity and grandeur in this expression, becoming an ambassador from the King of heaven. And this universal demand of repentance declared universal guilt in the strongest manner, and admirably confronted the pride of the haughtiest Stoic of them all. At the same time it bore down the idle plea of fatality. For how could any one repent of doing what he could not but have done?

31. He hath appointed a day in which he will judge the world – How fitly does he speak this, in their supreme court of justice? By the man – So he speaks, suiting himself to the capacity of his hearers. Whereof he hath given assurance to all men, in that he hath raised him from the dead – God raising Jesus demonstrated hereby, that he was to be the glorious Judge of all. We are by no means to imagine that this was all which the apostle intended to have said, but the indolence of some of his hearers and the petulancy of others cut him short.

32. Some mocked – Interrupting him thereby. They took offense at that which is the principal motive of faith, from the pride of reason. And having once stumbled at this, they rejected all the rest.

33. So Paul departed – Leaving his hearers divided in their judgment.

34. Among whom was even Dionysius the Areopagite – One of the Judges of that court: on whom some spurious writings have been fathered in later ages, by those who are fond of high sounding nonsense.

ACTS 18

1. Paul departing from Athens – He did not stay there long. The philosophers there were too easy, too indolent, and too wise in their own eyes to receive the Gospel.

2. Claudius, the Roman emperor, had commanded all the Jews to depart from Rome – All who were Jews by birth. Whether they were Jews or Christians by religion, the Romans were too stately to regard.

3. They were tent makers by trade – For it was a rule among the Jews (and why is it not among the Christians?) to bring up all their children to some trade, were they ever so rich or noble.

5. And when Silas and Timotheus were come from Macedonia – Silas seems to have stayed a considerable time at Berea: but Timotheus had come to the apostle while he was at Athens, and been sent by him to comfort and confirm the Church at Thessalonica, 1 Thess. iii, 1-5. But now at length both Silas and Timotheus came to the apostle at Corinth. Paul was pressed in spirit – The more probably from what Silas and Timotheus related. Every Christian ought diligently to observe any such pressure in his own spirit, and if it agree with Scripture, to follow it: if he does not he will feel great heaviness.

6. He shook his raiment – To signify he would from that time refrain from them: and to intimate, that God would soon shake them off as unworthy to be numbered among his people. I am pure – None can say this but he that has born a full testimony against sin. From henceforth I will go to the Gentiles – But not to them altogether. He did not break off all intercourse with the Jews even at Corinth. Only

he preached, yet he worked at his calling. An honest trade, by which a man may get his bread, is not to be looked upon with contempt by any. It was the custom of the Jews to bring up their children to some trade, though they gave them learning or estates. Paul was careful to prevent prejudices, even the most unreasonable. The love of Christ is the best bond of the saints; and the communing of the saints with each other, sweeten labor, contempt, and even persecution. Most of the Jews persisted in contradicting the gospel of Christ, and blasphemed. They would not believe themselves, and did all they could to keep others from believing. Paul hereupon left them. He did not give over his work; for though Israel be not gathered, Christ and his gospel shall be glorious. The Jews could not complain, for they had the first offer. When some oppose the gospel, we must turn to others. Grief that many persist in unbelief should not prevent gratitude for the conversion of some to Christ.

7-11 The Lord knows those that are his, yea, and those that shall be his; for it is by his work upon them that they become his. Let us not despair concerning any place, when even in wicked Corinth Christ had much people. He will gather in his chosen flock from the places where they are scattered. Thus encouraged, the apostle continued at Corinth, and a numerous and flourishing church grew up.

12-17 Paul was about to show that he did not teach men to worship God contrary to law; but the judge would not allow the Jews to complain to him of what was not within his office. It was right in Gallio that he left the Jews to themselves in matters relating to their religion, but yet would not let them, under pretense of that, persecute another. But it was wrong to speak slightly of a law and religion which he might have known to be of God, and which he ought to have acquainted himself with. In what way God is to be worshiped, whether Jesus be the Messiah, and whether the gospel be a Divine revelation, are not questions of words and names, they are questions of vast importance. Gallio spoke as if he boasted of his ignorance of the Scriptures, as if the law of God was beneath his notice. Gallio cared for none of these things. If he cared not for the affronts of bad men, it was commendable; but if he concerned not himself for the abuses done to good men, his indifference was carried too far. And those who see and hear of the sufferings of God's people, and have no feeling with them, or care for them, who do not pity and pray for them, are of the same spirit as Gallio, who cared for none of these things.

18-23 While Paul found he labored not in vain, he continued laboring. Our times are in God's hand;

described as being the fruits of the Spirit, because the Holy Spirit doth from first to last work in us and carry out that which Jesus Christ hath beforehand worked for us in his great redemption, which also God the Father hath designed for us in his great predestinating scheme of salvation.

Now, it is to the work of the Holy Spirit that I shall this morning specially direct your attention; and I may as well mention the reason why I do so. It is this. We have received continually fresh confirmations of the good news from a far country, which has already made glad the hearts of many of God's people. In the United States of America there is certainly a great awakening. No sane man living there could think of denying it. There may be something of spurious excitement mixed up with it, but that good, lasting good, has been accomplished, no rational man can deny. Two hundred and fifty thousand persons—that is a quarter of a million—profess to have been regenerated since December last, have made a profession of their faith, and have united themselves with different sections of God's church. The work still progresses, if anything, at a more rapid rate than before, and that which makes me believe the work to be genuine is just this—that the enemies of Christ's holy gospel are exceedingly wroth at it. When the devil roars at anything, you may rest assured there is some good in it. The devil is not like some dogs we know of; he never barks unless there is something to bark at. When Satan howls we may rest assured he is afraid his kingdom is in danger. Now this great work in America has been manifestly caused by the outpouring of the Spirit, for no one minister has been a leader in it. All the ministers of the gospel have co-operated in it, but none of them have stood in the van. God himself has been the leader of his own hosts. It began with a desire for prayer. God's people began to pray; the prayer-meetings were better attended than before. it was then proposed to hold meetings at times that had never been set apart for prayer; these also were well attended; and now, in the city of Philadelphia, at the hour of noon, every day in the week, three thousand persons can always be seen assembled together for prayer in one place. Men of business, in the midst of their toil and labor, find an opportunity of running in there and offering a word of prayer, and then return to their occupations. And so, throughout all the States, prayer-meetings, larger or smaller in number, have been convened. And there has been real prayer. Sinners beyond all count, have risen up in the prayer-meeting, and have requested the people of God to pray for them; thus making public to the world that they had a desire after Christ; they have been prayed for, and the church has seen that God verily doth hear and answer prayer. I find that the Unitarian ministers for a little while took no notice

chief ruler of the synagogue, and beat him before the judgment seat. And Gallio cared for none of those things.

18 And Paul after this tarried there yet a good while, and then took his leave of the brethren, and sailed thence into Syria, and with him Priscilla and Aquila; having shorn his head in Cenchrea: for he had a vow.

19 And he came to Ephesus, and left them there: but he himself entered into the synagogue, and reasoned with the Jews.

20 When they desired him to tarry longer time with them, he consented not;

21 But bade them farewell, saying, I must by all means keep this feast that cometh in Jerusalem: but I will return again unto you, if God will. And he sailed from Ephesus.

22 And when he had landed at Cesarea, and gone up, and saluted the church, he went down to Antioch.

23 And after he had spent some time there, he departed, and went over all the country of Galatia and Phrygia in order, strengthening all the disciples.

24 And a certain Jew named Apollos, born at Alexandria, an eloquent man, and mighty in the scriptures, came to Ephesus.

25 This man was instructed in the way of the Lord; and being fervent in the spirit, he spake and taught diligently the things of the Lord, knowing only the baptism of John.

26 And he began to speak boldly in the synagogue: whom when Aquila and Priscilla had heard, they took him unto them, and expounded unto him the way of God more perfectly.

27 And when he was disposed to pass into Achaia, the brethren wrote, exhorting the disciples to receive him: who, when he was come, helped them much which had believed through grace:

28 For he mightily convinced the Jews, and that publicly, shewing by the scriptures that Jesus was Christ.

ACTS 19

1 And it came to pass, that, while Apollos was at Corinth, Paul having passed through the upper coasts came to Ephesus: and finding certain disciples,

2 He said unto them, Have ye received the Holy Ghost since ye believed? And they said unto him, We have not so much as heard whether there be any Holy Ghost.

3 And he said unto them, Unto what then were ye baptized? And they said, Unto John's baptism.

4 Then said Paul, John verily baptized with the baptism of repentance, saying unto the people, that they should believe on him which should come after him, that is, on Christ Jesus.

5 When they heard this, they were baptized in

he preached no more in their synagogue.

7. He went into the house of one named Justus – A Gentile, and preached there, though probably he still lodged with Aquila.

8. And many hearing – The conversation of Crispus, and the preaching of Paul.

10. I am with thee: therefore fear not all the learning, politeness, grandeur, or power of the inhabitants of this city. Speak and hold not thy peace – For thy labor shall not be in vain. For I have much people in this city – So he prophetically calls them that afterward believed.

11. He continued there a year and six months – A long time! But how few souls are now gained in a longer time than this? Who is in the fault? Generally both teachers and hearers.

12. When Gallio was proconsul of Achaia – Of which Corinth was the chief city. This Gallio, the brother of the famous Seneca, is much commended both by him and by other writers, for the sweetness and generosity of his temper, and easiness of his behavior. Yet one thing he lacked! But he knew it not and had no concern about it.

15. But if it be – He speaks with the utmost coolness and contempt, a question of names – The names of the heathen gods were fables and shadows. But the question concerning the name of Jesus is of more importance than all things else under heaven. Yet there is this singularity (among a thousand others) in the Christian religion, that human reason, curious as it is in all other things, abhors to inquire into it.

17. Then they all took Sosthenes – The successor of Crispus, and probably Paul's chief accuser, and beat him – It seems because he had occasioned them so much trouble to no purpose, before the judgment seat – One can hardly think in the sight of Gallio, though at no great distance from him. And it seems to have had a happy effect. For Sosthenes himself was afterward a Christian, 1 Cor. i, 1.

18. Paul continued many days – After the year and six months, to confirm the brethren. Aquila having shaved his head – As was the custom in a vow, chap. xxi, 24; Num. vi, 18. At Cenchrea – A seaport town, at a small distance from Corinth.

21. I must by all means keep the feast at Jerusalem – This was not from any apprehension that he was obliged in conscience to keep the Jewish feasts; but to take the opportunity of meeting a great number of his countrymen to whom he might preach Christ, or whom he might farther instruct, or free from the prejudices they had imbibed against him. But I will return to you – So he did, chap. xix, 1.

22. And landing at Cesarea, he went up – Immediately to Jerusalem; and saluted the Church – Eminently so called, being the mother Church of Christian believers: and having kept the feast there, he went down from thence to Antioch.

23. He went over the country of Galatia and Phrygia – It is supposed, spending about four years therein, including the time he stayed at Ephesus.

24. An eloquent man, mighty in the Scriptures – Of the Old Testament. Every talent may be of use in the kingdom of God, if joined with the knowledge of the Scriptures and fervor of spirit.

25. This man had been instructed – Though not perfectly, in the way of the Lord – In the doctrine of Christ. Knowing only the baptism of John – Only what John taught those whom he baptized, namely, to repent and believe in a Messiah shortly to appear.

26. He spake – Privately; and taught publicly. Probably he returned to live at Alexandria, soon after he had been baptized by John; and so had no opportunity of being fully acquainted with the doctrines

MATTHEW HENRY

CHARLES H. SPURGEON

we purpose, but he disposes; therefore we must make all promises with submission to the will of God; not only if providence permits, but if God does not otherwise direct our motions. A very good refreshment it is to a faithful minister, to have for awhile the society of his brethren. Disciples are compassed about with infirmity; ministers must do what they can to strengthen them, by directing them to Christ, who is their Strength. Let us earnestly seek, in our several places, to promote the cause of Christ, forming plans that appear to us most proper, but relying on the Lord to bring them to pass if he sees good.

24-28 Apollos taught in the gospel of Christ, as far as John's ministry would carry him, and no further. We cannot but think he had heard of Christ's death and resurrection, but he was not informed as to the mystery of them. Though he had not the miraculous gifts of the Spirit, as the apostles, he made use of the gifts he had. The dispensation of the Spirit, whatever the measure of it may be, is given to every man to profit withal. He was a lively, affectionate preacher; fervent in spirit. He was full of zeal for the glory of God and the salvation of precious souls. Here was a complete man of God, thoroughly furnished for his work. Aquila and Priscilla encouraged his ministry, by attendance upon it. They did not despise Apollos themselves, or undervalue him to others; but considered the disadvantages he had labored under. And having themselves got knowledge in the truths of the gospel by their long intercourse with Paul, they told what they knew to him. Young scholars may gain a great deal by converse with old Christians. Those who do believe through grace, yet still need help. As long as they are in this world, there are remainders of unbelief, and something lacking in their faith to be perfected, and the work of faith to be fulfilled. If the Jews were convinced that Jesus is Christ, even their own law would teach them to hear him. The business of ministers is to preach Christ. Not only to preach the truth, but to prove and defend it, with meekness, yet with power.

ACTS 19

Paul instructs the disciples of John at Ephesus. (1-7)
He teaches there. (8-12)
The Jewish exorcists disgraced. Some Ephesians burn their evil books. (13-20)
The tumult at Ephesus. (21-31)
The tumult appeased. (32-41)

1-7 Paul, at Ephesus, found some religious persons, who looked to Jesus as the Messiah. They had not been led to expect the miraculous powers of the Holy Ghost, nor were they informed that the gospel was especially the ministration of the Spirit.

of it. Theodore Parker snarls and raves tremendously at it, but he is evidently in a maze; he does not understand the mystery, and acts with regard to it as swine are said to do with pearls. While the church was found asleep, and doing very little, the Socinian could afford to stand in his pulpit and sneer at anything like evangelical religion, but now that there has been an awakening, he looks like a man that has just awakened out of sleep. He sees something; he does not know what it is. The power of religion is just that which will always puzzle the Unitarian, for he knows but little about that. At the form of religion he is not much amazed, for he can to an extent endorse that himself, but the supernaturalism of the gospel—the mystery—the miracle—the power—the demonstration of the Spirit that comes with the preaching, is what such men cannot comprehend, and they gaze and wonder, and then become filled with wrath, but still they have to confess there is something there they cannot understand, a mental phenomenon that is far beyond their philosophy—a thing which they cannot reach by all their science nor understand by all their reason.

Now, if we have the like effect produced in this land, the one thing we must seek is the outpouring of the Holy Spirit, and I thought, perhaps, this morning in preaching upon the work of the Holy Spirit, that text might be fulfilled—"Him that honored me I will honor." My sincere desire is to honor the Holy Spirit this morning, and if he will be pleased to honor his church in return, unto him shall be the glory for ever.

"While Peter yet spake these words, the Holy Ghost fell on all them which heard the word." In the first place, I shall endeavor to describe the method of the Spirit's operation, secondly, the absolute necessity of the Holy Spirit's influence, if we could see men converted, and then, in the third place, I shall suggest the ways and means by which under divine grace we may obtain a like falling down of the Spirit upon our churches.

1. In the first place, then, I will endeavor to explain THE METHOD OF THE HOLY SPIRIT'S OPERATIONS. But let me guard myself against being misunderstood. We can explain what the Spirit does, but how he does it, no man must pretend to know. The work of the Holy Spirit is the peculiar mystery of the Christian religion. Almost any other thing is plain, but this must remain an inscrutable secret into which it were wrong for us to attempt to pry. Who knoweth where the winds are begotten? Who knoweth, therefore, how the Spirit worketh, for he is like the wind? "The wind bloweth where it listeth, and thou hearest the sound thereof but canst not tell whence it cometh, and whither it goeth: so is every one that is born of the Spirit." In Holy Scripture certain great secrets of nature are

the name of the Lord Jesus.

6 And when Paul had laid his hands upon them, the Holy Ghost came on them; and they spake with tongues, and prophesied.

7 And all the men were about twelve.

8 And he went into the synagogue, and spake boldly for the space of three months, disputing and persuading the things concerning the kingdom of God.

9 But when divers were hardened, and believed not, but spake evil of that way before the multitude, he departed from them, and separated the disciples, disputing daily in the school of one Tyrannus.

10 And this continued by the space of two years; so that all they which dwelt in Asia heard the word of the Lord Jesus, both Jews and Greeks.

11 And God wrought special miracles by the hands of Paul:

12 So that from his body were brought unto the sick handkerchiefs or aprons, and the diseases departed from them, and the evil spirits went out of them.

13 Then certain of the vagabond Jews, exorcists, took upon them to call over them which had evil spirits the name of the Lord Jesus, saying, We adjure you by Jesus whom Paul preacheth.

14 And there were seven sons of one Sceva, a Jew, and chief of the priests, which did so.

15 And the evil spirit answered and said, Jesus I know, and Paul I know; but who are ye?

16 And the man in whom the evil spirit was leaped on them, and overcame them, and prevailed against them, so that they fled out of that house naked and wounded.

17 And this was known to all the Jews and Greeks also dwelling at Ephesus; and fear fell on them all, and the name of the Lord Jesus was magnified.

18 And many that believed came, and confessed, and shewed their deeds.

19 Many of them also which used curious arts brought their books together, and burned them before all men: and they counted the price of them, and found it fifty thousand pieces of silver.

20 So mightily grew the word of God and prevailed.

21 After these things were ended, Paul purposed in the spirit, when he had passed through Macedonia and Achaia, to go to Jerusalem, saying, After I have been there, I must also see Rome.

22 So he sent into Macedonia two of them that ministered unto him, Timotheus and Erastus; but he himself stayed in Asia for a season.

23 And the same time there arose no small stir about that way.

24 For a certain man named Demetrius, a silversmith, which made silver shrines for Diana,

of the Gospel, as delivered by Christ and his apostles. And explained to him the way of God more perfectly – He who knows Christ, is able to instruct even those that are mighty in the Scriptures.

27. Who greatly helped through grace – It is through grace only that any gift of any one is profitable to another. Them that had believed – Apollos did not plant, but water. This was the peculiar gift which he had received. And he was better able to convince the Jews, than to convert the heathens.

ACTS 19

1. Having passed through – Galatia and Phrygia, which were termed the upper parts of Asia Minor. Certain disciples – Who had been formerly baptized by John the Baptist, and since imperfectly instructed in Christianity.

2. Have ye received the Holy Ghost? – The extraordinary gifts of the Spirit, as well as his sanctifying graces? We have not so much as heard – Whether there be any such gifts.

3. Into what were ye baptized – Into what dispensation? To the sealing of what doctrine? Into John's baptism – We were baptized by John and believe what he taught.

4. John baptized – That is, the whole baptism and preaching of John pointed at Christ. After this John is mentioned no more in the New Testament. Here he gives way to Christ altogether.

5. And hearing this, they were baptized – By some other. Paul only laid his hands upon them. They were baptized – They were baptized twice; but not with the same baptism. John did not administer that baptism which Christ afterward commanded, that is, in the name of the Father, Son, and Holy Ghost.

9. The way – The Christian way of worshiping God. He departed – Leaving them their synagogue to themselves. Discoursing daily – Not on the Sabbath only, in the school of one Tyrannus – Which we do not find was any otherwise consecrated, than by preaching the Gospel there.

10. All who desired it among the inhabitants of the proconsular Asia, now heard the word: St. Paul had been forbidden to preach it in Asia before, chap. xvi, 6. But now the time was come.

11. Special miracles – Wrought in a very uncommon manner.

12. Evil spirits – Who also occasioned many of those diseases, which yet might appear to be purely natural.

13. Exorcists – Several of the Jews about this time pretended to a power of casting out devils, particularly by certain arts or charms, supposed to be derived from Solomon. Undertook to name – Vain undertaking! Satan laughs at all those who attempt to expel him either out of the bodies or the souls of men but by Divine faith. All the light of reason is nothing to the craft or strength of that subtle spirit. His craft cannot be known but by the Spirit of God nor can his strength be conquered but by the power of faith.

17. And the name of the Lord Jesus was magnified – So that even the malice of the devil wrought for the furtherance of the Gospel.

18. Many came confessing – Of their own accord, and openly declaring their deeds – The efficacy of God's word, penetrating the inmost recesses of their soul, wrought that free and open confession to which perhaps even torments would not have compelled them.

19. Curious arts – Magical arts, to which that soft appellation was given by those who practiced them. Ephesus was peculiarly famous for these. And as these practices were of so much reputation there, it

But they spake as ready to welcome the notice of it. Paul shows them that John never designed that those he baptized should rest there, but told them that they should believe on him who should come after him, that is, on Christ Jesus. They thankfully accepted the discovery, and were baptized in the name of the Lord Jesus. The Holy Ghost came upon them in a surprising, overpowering manner; they spake with tongues, and prophesied, as the apostles and the first Gentile converts did. Though we do not now expect miraculous powers, yet all who profess to be disciples of Christ, should be called on to examine whether they have received the seal of the Holy Ghost, in his sanctifying influences, to the sincerity of their faith. Many seem not to have heard that there is a Holy Ghost, and many deem all that is spoken concerning his graces and comforts, to be delusion. Of such it may properly be inquired, "Unto what, then, were ye baptized?" for they evidently know not the meaning of that outward sign on which they place great dependence.

8-12 When arguments and persuasions only harden men in unbelief and blasphemy, we must separate ourselves and others from such unholy company. God was pleased to confirm the teaching of these holy men of old, that if their hearers believed them not, they might believe the works.

13-20 It was common, especially among the Jews, for persons to profess or to try to cast out evil spirits. If we resist the devil by faith in Christ, he will flee from us; but if we think to resist him by the using of Christ's name, or his works, as a spell or charm, Satan will prevail against us. Where there is true sorrow for sin, there will be free confession of sin to God in every prayer and to man whom we have offended, when the case requires it. Surely if the word of God prevailed among us, many lewd, infidel, and wicked books would be burned by their possessors. Will not these Ephesian converts rise up in judgment against professors, who traffic in such works for the sake of gain, or allow themselves to possess them? If we desire to be in earnest in the great work of salvation, every pursuit and enjoyment must be given up which hinders the effect of the gospel upon the mind, or loosens its hold upon the heart.

21-31 Persons who came from afar to pay their devotions at the temple of Ephesus, bought little silver shrines, or models of the temple, to carry home with them. See how craftsmen make advantage to themselves of people's superstition, and serve their worldly ends by it. Men are jealous for that by which they get their wealth; and many set themselves against the gospel of Christ, because it calls men from all unlawful crafts, however much wealth is to be gotten by them. There are persons

mentioned as being parallel with the secret working of the Spirit. The procreation of children is instanced as a parallel wonder, for we know not the mystery thereof; how much less, therefore, shall we expect to know that more secret and hidden mystery of the new birth and new creation of man in Christ Jesus. But let no man be staggered at this, for they are mysteries in nature: the wisest man will tell you there are depths in nature into which he cannot dive, and heights into which he cannot soar. He who pretends to have unraveled the knot of creation hath made a mistake, he may have cut the knot by his rough ignorance, and by his foolish conjectures, but the knot itself must remain beyond the power of man's unraveling, until God himself shall explain the secret. There are marvelous things, that, as yet, men have sought to know in vain. They may, perhaps, discover many of them, but how the Spirit works, no man can know. But now I wish to explain what the Holy Spirit does, although we cannot tell how he does it. I take it that the Holy Spirit's work in conversion is two-fold. First it is an awakening of the powers that man already has, and secondly, it is an implantation of powers which he never had at all.

In the great work of the new birth, the Holy Spirit first of all awakens the mental powers; for be it remembered that, the Holy Spirit never gives any man new mental powers. Take for instance reason—the Holy Spirit does not give men reason, for they have reason prior to their conversion. What the Holy Spirit does is to teach our reason, right reason—to set our reason in the right track, so that he can use it for the high purpose of discerning between good and evil; between the precious and vile. The Holy Spirit does not give man a will, for man has a will before; but he makes the will that was in bondage to Satan free to the service of God. The Holy Spirit gives no man the power to think, or the organ of belief—for man has power to believe or think as far as the mental act is concerned; but he gives that belief which is already there a tendency to believe the right thing, and he gives to the power of thought the propensity to think in the right way so that instead of thinking irregularly, we begin to think as God would have us think, and our mind desireth to walk in the steps of God's revealed truth. There may be here, this morning, a man of enlarged understanding in things political—but his understanding is darkened with regard to spiritual things—he sees no beauty in the person of Christ—he sees nothing desirable in the way of holiness—he chooses the evil and forsakes the good. Now the Holy Spirit will not give him a new understanding, but he will cleanse his old understanding so that he will discern between things that differ, and shall discover that it is but a poor thing to enjoy "the pleasures of sin for a season,"

brought no small gain unto the craftsmen;

25 Whom he called together with the workmen of like occupation, and said, Sirs, ye know that by this craft we have our wealth.

26 Moreover ye see and hear, that not alone at Ephesus, but almost throughout all Asia, this Paul hath persuaded and turned away much people, saying that they be no gods, which are made with hands:

27 So that not only this our craft is in danger to be set at nought; but also that the temple of the great goddess Diana should be despised, and her magnificence should be destroyed, whom all Asia and the world worshipeth.

28 And when they heard these sayings, they were full of wrath, and cried out, saying, Great is Diana of the Ephesians.

29 And the whole city was filled with confusion: and having caught Gaius and Aristarchus, men of Macedonia, Paul's companions in travel, they rushed with one accord into the theater.

30 And when Paul would have entered in unto the people, the disciples suffered him not.

31 And certain of the chief of Asia, which were his friends, sent unto him, desiring him that he would not adventure himself into the theater.

32 Some therefore cried one thing, and some another: for the assembly was confused; and the more part knew not wherefore they were come together.

33 And they drew Alexander out of the multitude, the Jews putting him forward. And Alexander beckoned with the hand, and would have made his defense unto the people.

34 But when they knew that he was a Jew, all with one voice about the space of two hours cried out, Great is Diana of the Ephesians.

35 And when the townclerk had appeased the people, he said, Ye men of Ephesus, what man is there that knoweth not how that the city of the Ephesians is a worshiper of the great goddess Diana, and of the image which fell down from Jupiter?

36 Seeing then that these things cannot be spoken against, ye ought to be quiet, and to do nothing rashly.

37 For ye have brought hither these men, which are neither robbers of churches, nor yet blasphemers of your goddess.

38 Wherefore if Demetrius, and the craftsmen which are with him, have a matter against any man, the law is open, and there are deputies: let them implead one another.

39 But if ye inquire any thing concerning other matters, it shall be determined in a lawful assembly.

40 For we are in danger to be called in question for this day's uproar, there being no cause whereby we may give an account of this concourse.

41 And when he had thus spoken, he dismissed the assembly.

is no wonder the books which taught them should bear a great price. Bringing their books together — As it were by common consent, burnt them — Which was far better than selling them, even though the money had been given to the poor. Fifty thousand pieces of silver — If these pieces of silver be taken for Jewish shekels, the sum will amount to six thousand two hundred and fifty pounds.

20. So powerfully did the word of God grow — In extent, and prevail — In power and efficacy.

21. After these things were ended — Paul sought not to rest, but pressed on, as if he had yet done nothing. He is already possessed of Ephesus and Asia. He purposes for Macedonia and Achaia. He has his eye upon Jerusalem, then upon Rome; afterward on Spain, Rom. xv, 28. No Cesar, no Alexander the Great, no other hero, comes up to the magnanimity of this little Benjamite. Faith and love to God and man had enlarged his heart, even as the sand of the sea.

24. Silver shrines — Silver models of that famous temple, which were bought not only by the citizens, but by strangers from all parts. The artificers — The other silversmiths.

25. The workmen — Employed by him and them.

26. Saying, that they are not gods which are made with hands — This manifestly shows, that the contrary opinion did then generally prevail, namely, that there was a real Divinity in their sacred images. Though some of the later heathens spoke of them just as the Romanists do now.

27. There is danger, not only that this our craft [trade] should come into disgrace, but also that the temple of the great goddess Diana should be despised — No wonder a discourse should make so deep an impression, which was edged both by interest and superstition. The great goddess was one of the standing titles of Diana. Her majesty destroyed — Miserable majesty, which was capable of being thus destroyed! Whom all Asia and the world — That is, the Roman empire, worshiped — Although under a great variety of titles and characters. But the multitude of those that err does not turn error into truth.

29. They rushed with one accord — Demetrius and his company, into the theater — Where criminals were wont to be thrown to the wild beasts, dragging with them Gaius and Aristarchus — When they could not find Paul. Probably they hoped to oblige them to fight with the wild beasts, as some think St. Paul had done before.

30. When Paul would have gone in to the people — Being above all fear, to plead the cause of his companions, and prove they are not gods which are made with hands.

31. The principal officers of Asia — The Asian priests, who presided over the public games, which they were then celebrating in honor of Diana.

32. The greater part did not know for what they were come together — Which is commonly the case in such an assembly.

33. And they thrust forward — Namely, the artificers and workmen, Alexander — Probably some well-known Christian whom they saw in the crowd: the Jews pushing him on — To expose him to the more danger. And Alexander waving with his hand — In token of desiring silence, would have made a defense — For himself and his brethren.

34. But when they knew that he was a Jew — And consequently an enemy to their worship of images; they prevented him, by crying, Great is Diana of the Ephesians.

35. The register — Probably the chief governor of the public games. The image which fell down from Jupiter — They believed that very image of Diana, which stood in her temple, fell down from Jupiter

MATTHEW HENRY   CHARLES H. SPURGEON

who will stickle for what is most grossly absurd, unreasonable, and false; as this, that those are gods which are made with hands, if it has but worldly interest on its side. The whole city was full of confusion, the common and natural effect of zeal for false religion. Zeal for the honor of Christ, and love to the brethren, encourage zealous believers to venture into danger. Friends will often be raised up among those who are strangers to true religion, but have observed the honest and consistent behavior of Christians.

32-41 The Jews came forward in this tumult. Those who are thus careful to distinguish themselves from the servants of Christ now, and are afraid of being taken for them, shall have their doom accordingly in the great day. One, having authority, at length stilled the noise. It is a very good rule at all times, both in private and public affairs, not to be hasty and rash in our motions, but to take time to consider; and always to keep our passions under check. We ought to be quiet, and to do nothing rashly; to do nothing in haste, of which we may repent at leisure. The regular methods of the law ought always to stop popular tumults, and in well-governed nations will do so. Most people stand in awe of men's judgments more than of the judgment of God. How well it were if we would thus quiet our disorderly appetites and passions, by considering the account we must shortly give to the Judge of heaven and earth! And see how the overruling providence of God keeps the public peace, by an unaccountable power over the spirits of men. Thus the world is kept in some order, and men are held back from devouring each other. We can scarcely look around but we see men act like Demetrius and the workmen. It is as safe to contend with wild beasts as with men enraged by party zeal and disappointed covetousness, who think that all arguments are answered, when they have shown that they grow rich by the practices which are opposed. Whatever side in religious disputes, or whatever name this spirit assumes, it is worldly, and should be discountenanced by all who regard truth and piety. And let us not be dismayed; the Lord on high is mightier than the noise of many waters; he can still the rage of the people.

ACTS 20

Paul's journeys. (1-6)
Eutychus restored to life. (7-12)
Paul travels towards Jerusalem. (13-16)
Paul's discourse to the elders of Ephesus. (17-27)
Their farewell. (28-38)

1-6 Tumults or opposition may constrain a Christian to remove from his station or alter his

and let go an "eternal weight of glory." There shall be a man here too who is desperately set against religion, and willeth not to come to God, and do what we will, we are not able to persuade him to change his mind and turn to God. The Holy Spirit will not make a new will in that man, but he will turn his old will, and instead of willing to do evil he will make him will to do right—he will make him will to be saved by Christ—he will make him "willing in the day of his power." Remember, there is no power in man so fallen but that the Holy Spirit can raise it up. However debased a man may be, in one instant, by the miraculous power of the Spirit, all his faculties may be cleansed and purged. Ill-judging reason may be made to judge rightly; stout, obstinate wills may be made to run willingly in the ways of God's commandments; evil and depraved affections may in an instant be turned to Christ, and old desires that are tainted with vice, may be replaced by heavenly aspirations. The work of the Spirit on the mind is the re-modeling of it; the new forming of it. He doth not bring new material to the mind—it is in another part of the man that he puts up a new structure—but he puts the mind that had fallen out of order into its proper shape. He builds up pillars that had fallen down, and erects the palaces that had crumbled to the earth. This is the first work of the Holy Spirit upon the mind of man.

Besides this, the Holy Spirit gives to men powers which they never had before. According to Scripture, I believe man is constituted in a threefold manner. He has a body; by the Holy Spirit that body is made the temple of the Lord. He has a mind; by the Holy Spirit that mind is made like an altar in the temple. But man by nature is nothing higher than that; he is mere body and soul. When the Spirit comes, he breathes into him a third higher principle which we call the spirit. The apostle describes man as man, "body, soul and spirit." Now if you search all the mental writers through, you will find they all declare there are only two parts—body and mind; and they are quite right, for they deal with unregenerate man; but in regenerate man there is a third principle as much superior to mere mind as mind is superior to dead animal matter—that third principle is that with which a man prays; it is that with which he lovingly believes; or rather it is that which compels the mind to perform their acts. It is that which, operating upon the mind, makes the same use of the mind as the mind does of the body. When, after desiring to walk I make my legs move, it is my mind that compels them; and so my Spirit, when I desire to pray, compels my mind to think the thought of prayer and compels my soul also, if I desire to praise, to think the thought of praise, and lift itself upward towards God. As the body without the soul is dead, so the soul without the Spirit is dead,

ACTS 20

1 And after the uproar was ceased, Paul called unto him the disciples, and embraced them, and departed for to go into Macedonia.

2 And when he had gone over those parts, and had given them much exhortation, he came into Greece,

3 And there abode three months. And when the Jews laid wait for him, as he was about to sail into Syria, he purposed to return through Macedonia.

4 And there accompanied him into Asia Sopater of Berea; and of the Thessalonians, Aristarchus and Secundus; and Gaius of Derbe, and Timotheus; and of Asia, Tychicus and Trophimus.

5 These going before tarried for us at Troas.

6 And we sailed away from Philippi after the days of unleavened bread, and came unto them to Troas in five days; where we abode seven days.

7 And upon the first day of the week, when the disciples came together to break bread, Paul preached unto them, ready to depart on the morrow; and continued his speech until midnight.

8 And there were many lights in the upper chamber, where they were gathered together.

9 And there sat in a window a certain young man named Eutychus, being fallen into a deep sleep: and as Paul was long preaching, he sunk down with sleep, and fell down from the third loft, and was taken up dead.

10 And Paul went down, and fell on him, and embracing him said, Trouble not yourselves; for his life is in him.

11 When he therefore was come up again, and had broken bread, and eaten, and talked a long while, even till break of day, so he departed.

12 And they brought the young man alive, and were not a little comforted.

13 And we went before to ship, and sailed unto Assos, there intending to take in Paul: for so had he appointed, minding himself to go afoot.

14 And when he met with us at Assos, we took him in, and came to Mitylene.

15 And we sailed thence, and came the next day over against Chios; and the next day we arrived at Samos, and tarried at Trogyllium; and the next day we came to Miletus.

16 For Paul had determined to sail by Ephesus, because he would not spend the time in Asia: for he hasted, if it were possible for him, to be at Jerusalem the day of Pentecost.

17 And from Miletus he sent to Ephesus, and called the elders of the church.

18 And when they were come to him, he said unto them, Ye know, from the first day that I came into Asia, after what manner I have been with you at all seasons,

19 Serving the Lord with all humility of mind,

in heaven. Perhaps he designed to insinuate, as if falling down from Jupiter, it was not made with hands, and so was not that sort of idols which Paul had said were no gods.

37. Nor blasphemers of your goddess – They simply declared the one God, and the vanity of idols in general.

38. There are proconsuls – One in every province. There was one at Ephesus.

39. In a lawful assembly – In such a regular assembly as has authority to judge of religious and political affairs.

40. This concourse – He wisely calls it by an inoffensive name.

ACTS 20

1. After the tumult was ceased – So Demetrius gained nothing. Paul remained there till all was quiet.

2. He came into Greece – That part of it which lay between Macedonia and Achaia.

3. An ambush being laid for him – In his way to the ship.

4. To Asia – There some of them left him. But Trophimus went with him to Jerusalem, chap. xxi, 29. Aristarchus, even to Rome, chap. xxvii, 2.

6. We set sail – St. Luke was now with St. Paul again, as we learn from his manner of expressing himself.

7. To break bread – That is, to celebrate the Lord's Supper; continued his discourse – Through uncommon fervor of spirit.

8. There were many lamps in the room where they were assembled – To prevent any possible scandal.

9. In the window – Doubtless kept open, to prevent heat, both from the lamps and the number of people.

10. Paul fell on him – It is observable, our Lord never used this gesture. But Elijah and Elisha did as well as Paul. His life is in him – He is alive again.

11. So departed – Without taking any rest at all.

12. And they brought the young man alive – But alas! How many of those who have allowed themselves to sleep under sermons, or as it were to dream awake, have slept the sleep of eternal death, and fallen to rise no more!

13. Being himself to go on foot – That he might enjoy the company of his Christian brethren a little longer, although he had passed the night without sleep, and though Assos was of difficult and dangerous access by land.

14. Mitylene – Was a city and part of the isle of Lesbos, about seven miles distant from the Asiatic coast.

16. For Paul had determined to sail by Ephesus – Which lay on the other side of the bay. He hasted to be at Jerusalem on the day of Pentecost – Because then was the greatest concourse of people.

17. Sending to Ephesus, he called the elders of the Church – These are called bishops in the 28th verse, (rendered overseers in our translation.) Perhaps elders and bishops were then the same; or no otherwise different than are the rector of a parish and his curates.

18. Ye know – Happy is he who can thus appeal to the conscience of his hearers.

19. Serving – See the picture of a faithful servant! The Lord – Whose the church is, with all humility, and with tears, and trials – These are the concomitants of it. The service itself is described more particularly in the following verse. This humility he recommends to the Ephesians themselves, Eph. iv, 2. His tears are mentioned again,

purpose, but his work and his pleasure will be the same, wherever he goes. Paul thought it worth while to bestow five days in going to Troas, though it was but for seven days' stay there; but he knew, and so should we, how to redeem even journeying time, and to make it turn to some good account.

7-12 Though the disciples read, and meditated, and prayed, and sung apart, and thereby kept up communion with God, yet they came together to worship God, and so kept up their communion with one another. They came together on the first day of the week, the Lord's day. It is to be religiously observed by all disciples of Christ. In the breaking of the bread, not only the breaking of Christ's body for us, to be a sacrifice for our sins, is remembered, but the breaking of Christ's body to us, to be food and a feast for our souls, is signified. In the early times it was the custom to receive the Lord's supper every Lord's day, thus celebrating the memorial of Christ's death. In this assembly Paul preached. The preaching of the gospel ought to go with the sacraments. They were willing to hear, he saw they were so, and continued his speech till midnight. Sleeping when hearing the word, is an evil thing, a sign of low esteem of the word of God. We must do what we can to prevent being sleepy; not put ourselves to sleep, but get our hearts affected with the word we hear, so as to drive sleep far away. Infirmity requires tenderness; but contempt requires severity. It interrupted the apostle's preaching; but was made to confirm his preaching. Eutychus was brought to life again. And as they knew not when they should have Paul's company again, they made the best use of it they could, and reckoned a night's sleep well lost for that purpose. How seldom are hours of repose broken for the purposes of devotion! but how often for mere amusement or sinful revelry! So hard is it for spiritual life to thrive in the heart of man! so naturally do carnal practices flourish there!

13-16 Paul hastened to Jerusalem, but tried to do good by the way, when going from place to place, as every good man should do. In doing God's work, our own wills and those of our friends must often be crossed; we must not spend time with them when duty calls us another way.

17-27 The elders knew that Paul was no designing, self-seeking man. Those who would in any office serve the Lord acceptably, and profitably to others, must do it with humility. He was a plain preacher, one that spoke his message so as to be understood. He was a powerful preacher; he preached the gospel as a testimony to them if they received it; but as a testimony against them if they rejected it. He was a profitable preacher; one that aimed to inform their judgments, and reform their

and one work of the Spirit is to quicken the dead soul by breathing into it the firing Spirit; as it is written, "The first man, Adam, was made a living soul, but the second Adam was made a quickening Spirit"—and, "as we have borne the image of the earthy, so must we bear the image of the heavenly;" that is, we must have in us, if we would be converted, the quickening Spirit, which is put into us by God the Holy Ghost. I say again, the spirit has powers which the mind never has. It has the power of communion with Christ, which to a degree is a mental act, but it can no more be performed by man without the Spirit, than the act of walking could be performed by man, if he were destitute of a soul to suggest the idea of walking. The Spirit suggests the thoughts of communion which the mind obeys and carries out. Nay, there are times, I think, when the spirit leaves the mind altogether, times when we forget everything of earth and one almost ceases to think, to reason, to judge, to weigh, or to will. Our souls are like the chariots of Amminadib, drawn swiftly onwards without any powers of volition. We lean upon the breast of Jesus, and in rhapsody divine, and in ecstasy celestial, we enjoy the fruits of the land of the blessed, and pluck the clusters of Eschol before entering into the land of promise.

I think I have clearly put these two points before you. The work of the Spirit consists, first, in awakening powers already possessed by man, but which were asleep and out of order; and in the next place in putting into man powers which he had not before. And to make this simple to the humblest mind, let me suppose man to be something like a machine; all the wheels are out of order, the cogs do not strike upon each other, the wheels do not turn regularly, the rods will not act, the order is gone. Now, the first work of the Spirit is to put these wheels in the right place, to fit the wheels upon the axles, to put the right axle to the right wheel, then to put wheel to wheel, so that they may act upon each other. But that is not all his work. The next thing is to put fire and steam so that these things shall go to work. He does not put fresh wheels, he puts old wheels into order, and then he puts the motive power which is to move the whole. First he puts our mental powers into their proper order and condition, and then he puts a living quickening spirit, so that all these shall move according to the holy will and law of God.

But, mark you, this is not all the Holy Spirit does. For if he were to do this, and then leave us, none of us should ever get to heaven. If any of you should be so near to heaven that you could hear the angels singing over the walls—if you could almost see within the pearly gates still, if the Holy Spirit did not help you the last step, you would never enter there. All the work is through his divine operation. Hence it is the Spirit who keeps

and with many tears, and temptations, which befell me by the lying in wait of the Jews:

20 And how I kept back nothing that was profitable unto you, but have shewed you, and have taught you publicly, and from house to house,

21 Testifying both to the Jews, and also to the Greeks, repentance toward God, and faith toward our Lord Jesus Christ.

22 And now, behold, I go bound in the spirit unto Jerusalem, not knowing the things that shall befall me there:

23 Save that the Holy Ghost witnesseth in every city, saying that bonds and afflictions abide me.

24 But none of these things move me, neither count I my life dear unto myself, so that I might finish my course with joy, and the ministry, which I have received of the Lord Jesus, to testify the gospel of the grace of God.

25 And now, behold, I know that ye all, among whom I have gone preaching the kingdom of God, shall see my face no more.

26 Wherefore I take you to record this day, that I am pure from the blood of all men.

27 For I have not shunned to declare unto you all the counsel of God.

28 Take heed therefore unto yourselves, and to all the flock, over the which the Holy Ghost hath made you overseers, to feed the church of God, which he hath purchased with his own blood.

29 For I know this, that after my departing shall grievous wolves enter in among you, not sparing the flock.

30 Also of your own selves shall men arise, speaking perverse things, to draw away disciples after them.

31 Therefore watch, and remember, that by the space of three years I ceased not to warn every one night and day with tears.

32 And now, brethren, I commend you to God, and to the word of his grace, which is able to build you up, and to give you an inheritance among all them which are sanctified.

33 I have coveted no man's silver, or gold, or apparel.

34 Yea, ye yourselves know, that these hands have ministered unto my necessities, and to them that were with me.

35 I have shewed you all things, how that so laboring ye ought to support the weak, and to remember the words of the Lord Jesus, how he said, It is more blessed to give than to receive.

36 And when he had thus spoken, he kneeled down, and prayed with them all.

37 And they all wept sore, and fell on Paul's neck, and kissed him,

38 Sorrowing most of all for the words which he spake, that they should see his face no more. And they accompanied him unto the ship.

verse 31, as also 2 Cor. ii, 4; Phil. iii, 18. These passages laid together supply us with the genuine character of St. Paul. Holy tears, from those who seldom weep on account of natural occurrences, are no mean specimen of the efficacy and proof of the truth of Christianity. Yet joy is well consistent therewith, ver. 24. The same person may be sorrowful, yet always rejoicing.

20. I have preached – Publicly; and taught – From house to house. Else he had not been pure from their blood. For even an apostle could not discharge his duty by public preaching only. How much less can an ordinary pastor!

21. Repentance toward God – The very first motion of the soul toward God is a kind of repentance.

22. Bound by the Spirit – Strongly impelled by him.

23. Save that – Only this I know in general; the Holy Ghost witnesseth – By other persons. Such was God's good pleasure to reveal these things to him, not immediately, but by the ministry of others.

24. Nor do I count my life precious – It adds great force to this and all the other passages of Scripture, in which the apostles express their contempt of the world, that they were not uttered by persons like Seneca and Antoninus, who talked elegantly of despising the world in the full affluence of all its enjoyments; but by men who daily underwent the greatest calamities, and exposed their lives in proof of their assertions.

25. Ye shall see my face no more – He wisely inserts this, that what follows might make the deeper impression.

27. For I have not shunned – Otherwise if any had perished, their blood would have been on his head.

28. Take heed therefore – I now devolve my care upon you; first to yourselves; then to the flock over which the Holy Ghost hath made you overseers – For no man, or number of men upon earth, can constitute an overseer, bishop, or any other Christian minister. To do this is the peculiar work of the Holy Ghost: to feed the Church of God – That is, the believing, loving, holy children of God; which he hath purchased – How precious is it then in his sight! with his own blood – For it is the blood of the only begotten Son of God, 1 John i, 7.

29. Grievous wolves – From without, namely, false apostles. They had, not yet broke in on the Church at Ephesus.

30. Yea, from among yourselves men will arise – Such were the Nicolaitans, of whom Christ complains, Rev. ii, 6; to draw away disciples – From the purity of the Gospel and the unity of the body.

31. I ceased not to warn every one night and day – This was watching indeed! Who copies after this example?

32. The word of his grace – It is the grand channel of it, to believers as well as unbelievers. Who is able to build you up – To confirm and increase your faith, love, holiness. God can thus build us up, without any instrument. But he does build us up by them. O beware of dreaming that you have less need of human teachers after you know Christ than before! And to give you an inheritance – Of eternal glory, among them that are sanctified – And so made meet for it. A large number of these Paul doubtless knew, and remembered before God.

33. I have coveted – Here the apostle begins the other branch of his farewell discourse, like old Samuel, 1 Sam. xii, 3, taking his leave of the children of Israel.

34. These hands – Callous, as you see, with labor. Who is he that envies such a bishop or archbishop as this?

35. I have showed you – Bishops, by my example, all things – And

hearts and lives. He was a painful preacher, very industrious in his work. He was a faithful preacher; he did not keep back reproofs when necessary, nor keep back the preaching of the cross. He was a truly Christian, evangelical preacher; he did not preach notions or doubtful matters; nor affairs of state or the civil government; but he preached faith and repentance. A better summary of these things, without which there is no salvation, cannot be given: even repentance towards God, and faith towards our Lord Jesus Christ, with their fruits and effects. Without these no sinner can escape, and with these none will come short of eternal life. Let them not think that Paul left Asia for fear of persecution; he was in full expectation of trouble, yet resolved to go on, well assured that it was by Divine direction. Thanks be to God that we know not the things which shall befall us during the year, the week, the day which has begun. It is enough for the child of God to know that his strength shall be equal to his day. He knows not, he would not know, what the day before him shall bring forth. The powerful influences of the Holy Spirit bind the true Christian to his duty. Even when he expects persecution and affliction, the love of Christ constrains him to proceed. None of these things moved Paul from his work; they did not deprive him of his comfort. It is the business of our life to provide for a joyful death. Believing that this was the last time they should see him, he appeals concerning his integrity. He had preached to them the whole counsel of God. As he had preached to them the gospel purely, so he had preached it to them entire; he faithfully did his work, whether men would bear or forbear.

28-38 If the Holy Ghost has made ministers overseers of the flock, that is, shepherds, they must be true to their trust. Let them consider their Master's concern for the flock committed to their charge. It is the church he has purchased with his own blood. The blood was his as Man; yet so close is the union between the Divine and human nature, that it is there called the blood of God, for it was the blood of him who is God. This put such dignity and worth into it, as to ransom believers from all evil, and purchase all good. Paul spake about their souls with affection and concern. They were full of care what would become of them. Paul directs them to look up to God with faith, and commends them to the word of God's grace, not only as the foundation of their hope and the fountain of their joy, but as the rule of their walking. The most advanced Christians are capable of growing, and will find the word of grace helps their growth. As those cannot be welcome guests to the holy God who are unsanctified; so heaven would be no heaven to them; but to all who are born again, and on whom the image of God is renewed, it is sure, as almighty

the wheels in motion, and who takes away that defilement which, naturally engendered by our original sin, falls upon the machine and puts it out of order. He takes this away, and keeps the machine constantly going without injury, until at last he removes man from the place of defilement to the land of the blessed, a perfect creature, as perfect as he was when he came from the mold of his Maker.

And I must say, before I leave this point, that all the former part of what I have mentioned is done instantaneously. When a man is converted to God, it is done in a moment. Regeneration is an instantaneous work. Conversion to God, the fruit of regeneration, occupies all our life, but regeneration itself is effected in an instant. A man hates God; the Holy Spirit makes him love God. A man is opposed to Christ, he hates his gospel, does not understand it and will not receive it: the Holy Spirit comes, puts light into his darkened understanding, takes the chain from his bandaged will, gives liberty to his conscience, gives life to his dead soul, so that the voice of conscience is heard, and the man becomes a new creature in Christ Jesus. And all this is done, mark you, by the instantaneous supernatural influence of God the Holy Ghost working as he willeth among the sons of men.

II. Having thus dwelt upon the method of the Holy Spirit's work, I shall now turn to the second point, THE ABSOLUTE NECESSITY OF THE SPIRIT'S WORK IN ORDER TO CONVERSION. In our text we are told that "while Peter spake these words, the Holy Ghost fell on all them which heard the word." Beloved, the Holy Ghost fell on Peter first, or else it would not have fallen on his hearers. There is a necessity that the preacher himself, if we are to have souls saved, should be under the influence of the Spirit. I have constantly made it my prayer that I might be guided by the Spirit even in the smallest and least important parts of the service; for you cannot tell but that the salvation of a soul may depend upon the reading of a hymn, or upon the selection of a chapter. Two persons have joined our church and made a profession of being converted simply through my reading a hymn—

"Jesus, lover of my soul"

They did not remember anything else in the hymn, but those words made such a deep impression upon their mind, that they could not help repeating them for days afterwards, and then the thought arose, "Do I love Jesus?" And then they considered what strange ingratitude it was that he should be the lover of their souls, and yet they should not love him. Now I believe the Holy Spirit led me to read that hymn. And many persons have been converted by some striking saying of the preacher. But why was it the preacher uttered that saying? Simply because he was led thereunto by

ACTS 21

1 And it came to pass, that after we were gotten from them, and had launched, we came with a straight course unto Coos, and the day following unto Rhodes, and from thence unto Patara:

2 And finding a ship sailing over unto Phenicia, we went aboard, and set forth.

3 Now when we had discovered Cyprus, we left it on the left hand, and sailed into Syria, and landed at Tyre: for there the ship was to unlade her burden.

4 And finding disciples, we tarried there seven days: who said to Paul through the Spirit, that he should not go up to Jerusalem.

5 And when we had accomplished those days, we departed and went our way; and they all brought us on our way, with wives and children, till we were out of the city: and we kneeled down on the shore, and prayed.

6 And when we had taken our leave one of another, we took ship; and they returned home again.

7 And when we had finished our course from Tyre, we came to Ptolemais, and saluted the brethren, and abode with them one day.

8 And the next day we that were of Paul's company departed, and came unto Cesarea: and we entered into the house of Philip the evangelist, which was one of the seven; and abode with him.

9 And the same man had four daughters, virgins, which did prophesy.

10 And as we tarried there many days, there came down from Judea a certain prophet, named Agabus.

11 And when he was come unto us, he took Paul's girdle, and bound his own hands and feet, and said, Thus saith the Holy Ghost, So shall the Jews at Jerusalem bind the man that owneth this girdle, and shall deliver him into the hands of the Gentiles.

12 And when we heard these things, both we, and they of that place, besought him not to go up to Jerusalem.

13 Then Paul answered, What mean ye to weep and to break mine heart? for I am ready not to be bound only, but also to die at Jerusalem for the name of the Lord Jesus.

14 And when he would not be persuaded, we ceased, saying, The will of the Lord be done.

15 And after those days we took up our carriages, and went up to Jerusalem.

16 There went with us also certain of the disciples of Cesarea, and brought with them one Mnason of Cyprus, an old disciple, with whom we should lodge.

17 And when we were come to Jerusalem, the brethren received us gladly.

18 And the day following Paul went in with us unto James; and all the elders were present.

19 And when he had saluted them, he declared particularly what things God had wrought among the Gentiles by his ministry.

this among the rest; that thus laboring – So far as the labors of your office allow you time; ye ought to help the weak – Those who are disabled by sickness, or any bodily infirmity, from maintaining themselves by their own labor. And to remember – Effectually, so as to follow it; the word which he himself said – Without doubt his disciples remembered many of his words which are not recorded. It is happier to give – To imitate God, and have him, as it were, indebted to us.

37. They all wept – Of old, men, yea, the best and bravest of men, were easily melted into tears; a thousand instances of which might be produced from profane as well as sacred writers. But now, notwithstanding the effeminacy which almost universally prevails, we leave those tears to women and children.

38. Sorrowing most for that word which he spake, that they should see his face no more – What sorrow will be in the great day, when God shall speak that word to all who are found on the left hand, that they shall see his face no more!

ACTS 21

1. And when we were torn away from them – Not without doing violence both to ourselves and them.

3. We landed at Tyre – That there should be Christians there was foretold, Psalm lxxxvii, 4. What we read in that psalm of the Philistines and Ethiopians also may be compared with chap. viii, 40; xxvii, 4.

4. And finding disciples, we tarried there seven days – in order to spend a Sabbath with them. Who told Paul by the Spirit – That afflictions awaited him at Jerusalem. This was properly what they said by the Spirit. They themselves advised him not to go up. The disciples seemed to understand their prophetic impulse to be an intimation from the Spirit, that Paul, if he were so minded, might avoid the danger, by not going to Jerusalem.

7. Having finished our voyage – From Macedonia, chap. xx, 6, we came to Ptolemais – A celebrated city on the sea coast, anciently called Accos. It is now, like many other once noble cities, only a heap of ruins.

8. We came to Cesarea – So called from a stately temple which Herod the Great dedicated there to Augustus Cesar. It was the place where the Roman governor of Judea generally resided and kept his court. The evangelist, who was one of the seven deacons – An evangelist is a preacher of the Gospel to those who had never heard it, as Philip had done to the Samaritans, to the Ethiopian eunuch, and to all the towns from Azotus to Cesarea, chap. viii, 5, 26, 40. It is not unlikely he spent the following years preaching in Tyre and Sidon, and the other heathen cities in the neighborhood of Galilee, his house being at Cesarea, a convenient situation for that purpose. We abode with him – We lodged at his house during our stay at Cesarea.

10. A certain prophet came – The nearer the event was, the more express were the predictions which prepared Paul for it.

11. Binding his own feet and hands – In the manner that malefactors were wont to be bound when apprehended. So shall the Jews bind the man whose girdle this is – St. Paul's bonds were first particularly foretold at Cesarea, to which he afterward came in bonds, chap. xxiii, 33.

12. Both we, (his fellow travelers,) and they of the place, besought him not to go up to Jerusalem – St. Paul knew that this prediction had the force of a command. They did not know this.

MATTHEW HENRY   CHARLES H. SPURGEON

power and eternal truth make it so. He recommends himself to them as an example of not caring as to things of the present world; this they would find help forward their comfortable passage through it. It might seem a hard saying, therefore Paul adds to it a saying of their Master's, which he would have them always remember; "It is more blessed to give than to receive:" it seems they were words often used to his disciples. The opinion of the children of this world, is contrary to this; they are afraid of giving, unless in hope of getting. Clear gain, is with them the most blessed thing that can be; but Christ tell us what is more blessed, more excellent. It makes us more like to God, who gives to all, and receives from none; and to the Lord Jesus, who went about doing good. This mind was in Christ Jesus, may it be in us also. It is good for friends, when they part, to part with prayer. Those who exhort and pray for one another, may have many weeping seasons and painful separations, but they will meet before the throne of God, to part no more. It was a comfort to all, that the presence of Christ both went with him and stayed with them.

ACTS 21

Paul's voyage towards Jerusalem. (1-7)
Paul at Cesarea. The prophecy of Agabus. Paul at Jerusalem. (8-18)
He is persuaded to join in ceremonial observances. (19-26)
Being in danger from the Jews, he is rescued by the Romans. (27-40)

1-7 Providence must be acknowledged when our affairs go on well. Wherever Paul came, he inquired what disciples were there, and found them out. Foreseeing his troubles, from love to him, and concern for the church, they wrongly thought it would be most for the glory of God that he should continue at liberty; but their earnestness to dissuade him from it, renders his pious resolution the more illustrious. He has taught us by example, as well as by rule, to pray always, to pray without ceasing. Their last farewell was sweetened with prayer.

8-18 Paul had express warning of his troubles, that when they came, they might be no surprise or terror to him. The general notice given us, that through much tribulation we must enter into the kingdom of God, should be of the same use to us. Their weeping began to weaken and slacken his resolution. Has not our Master told us to take up our cross? It was a trouble to him, that they should so earnestly press him to do that in which he could not gratify them without wronging his conscience. When we see trouble coming, it becomes us to say, not only, The will of the Lord must be done, and there is no remedy; but, Let the will of the Lord be

the Holy Spirit. Rest assured, beloved, that when any part of the sermon is blessed to your heart, the minister said it because he was ordered to say it by his Master. I might preach today a sermon which I preached on Friday, and which was useful then, and there might be no good whatever come from it now, because it might not be the sermon which the Holy Ghost would have delivered today. But if with sincerity of heart I have sought God's guidance in selecting the topic, and he rests upon me in the preaching of the Word, there is no fear but that it shall be found adapted to your immediate wants. The Holy Spirit must rest upon your preachers. Let them have all the learning of the wisest men, and all the eloquence of such men as Desmosthenes and Cicero, still the Word cannot be blessed to you, unless first of all the Spirit of God hath guided the minister's mind in the selection of his subject, and in the discussion of it.

But if Peter himself were under the hand of the Spirit, that would fail unless the Spirit of God, then, did fall upon our hearers; and I shall endeavor now to show the absolute necessity of the Spirit's work in the conversion of men.

Let us remember what kind of thing the work is, and we shall see that other means are altogether out of the question. It is quite certain that men cannot be converted by physical means. The Church of Rome thought that she could convert men by means of armies; so she invaded countries, and threatened them with war and bloodshed unless they would repent and embrace her religion. However, it availed but little, and men were prepared to die rather than leave their faith; she therefore tried those beautiful things—stakes, racks, dungeons, axes, swords, fire; and by these things she hoped to convert men. You have heard of the man who tried to wind up his watch with a pick-axe. That man was extremely wise, compared with the man who thought to touch mind through matter. All the machines you like to invent cannot touch mind. Talk about tying angel's wings with green withes, or manacling the cherubim with iron chains, and then talk about meddling with the minds of men through physical means. Why, the things don't set; they cannot act. All the king's armies that ever were, and all the warriors clothed with mail, with all their ammunition, could never touch the mind of man. That is an impregnable castle which is not to be reached by physical agency.

Nor, again, can man be converted by moral argument. "Well," says one, "I think he may. Let a minister preach earnestly, and he may persuade men to be converted." Ah! beloved, it is for want of knowing better that you say so. Melancthon thought so, but you know what he said after he tried it—"Old Adam is too strong for young Melancthon." So will every preacher find it, if he

20 And when they heard it, they glorified the Lord, and said unto him, Thou seest, brother, how many thousands of Jews there are which believe; and they are all zealous of the law:

21 And they are informed of thee, that thou teachest all the Jews which are among the Gentiles to forsake Moses, saying that they ought not to circumcize their children, neither to walk after the customs.

22 What is it therefore? the multitude must needs come together: for they will hear that thou art come.

23 Do therefore this that we say to thee: We have four men which have a vow on them;

24 Them take, and purify thyself with them, and be at charges with them, that they may shave their heads: and all may know that those things, whereof they were informed concerning thee, are nothing; but that thou thyself also walkest orderly, and keepest the law.

25 As touching the Gentiles which believe, we have written and concluded that they observe no such thing, save only that they keep themselves from things offered to idols, and from blood, and from strangled, and from fornication.

26 Then Paul took the men, and the next day purifying himself with them entered into the temple, to signify the accomplishment of the days of purifcation, until that an offering should be offered for every one of them.

27 And when the seven days were almost ended, the Jews which were of Asia, when they saw him in the temple, stirred up all the people, and laid hands on him,

28 Crying out, Men of Israel, help: This is the man, that teacheth all men every where against the people, and the law, and this place: and further brought Greeks also into the temple, and hath polluted this holy place.

29 (For they had seen before with him in the city Trophimus an Ephesian, whom they supposed that Paul had brought into the temple.)

30 And all the city was moved, and the people ran together: and they took Paul, and drew him out of the temple: and forthwith the doors were shut.

31 And as they went about to kill him, tidings came unto the chief captain of the band, that all Jerusalem was in an uproar.

32 Who immediately took soldiers and centurions, and ran down unto them: and when they saw the chief captain and the soldiers, they left beating of Paul.

33 Then the chief captain came near, and took him, and commanded him to be bound with two chains; and demanded who he was, and what he had done.

34 And some cried one thing, some another, among the multitude: and when he could not know the certainty for the tumult, he commanded him to be carried into the castle.

35 And when he came upon the stairs, so it

13. Breaking my heart – For the apostles themselves were not void of human affections. I am ready not only to be bound, but to die – And to him that is ready for it, the burden is light.

14. And when he would not be persuaded – This was not obstinacy, but true Christian resolution. We should never be persuaded, either to do evil, or to omit doing any good which is in our power; saying, the will of the Lord be done – Which they were satisfied Paul knew.

15. We took up our carriages – Our baggage; which probably went by sea before. What they took with them now in particular was the alms they were carrying to Jerusalem, chap. xxiv, 17.

16. The disciples brought us to one Mnason, a Cyprian, an old disciple – He was a native of Cyprus, but an inhabitant of Jerusalem, and probably one of the first converts there.

18. Paul went in with us – That it might appear we are all of one mind, to James – Commonly called the Lord's brother; the only apostle then presiding over the Churches in Judea.

20. They are all zealous for the law – For the whole Mosaic dispensation. How astonishing is this! Did none of the apostles, beside St. Paul, know that this dispensation was now abolished? And if they did both know and testify this, how came their hearers not to believe them?

21. They have been informed concerning thee, that thou teachest the Jews – not to circumcize their children, nor to walk after the customs – Of the Mosaic law. And so undoubtedly he did. And so he wrote to all the Churches in Galatia, among whom were many Jews. Yea, and James himself had long before assented to Peter, affirming before all the apostles and all the brethren, chap. xv, 10, that this very law was a yoke which (said he) neither our fathers nor we were able to bear – Amazing! that they did not know this! Or, that if they did, they did not openly testify it at all hazards, to every Jewish convert in Jerusalem!

22. What is it therefore – What is to be done? The multitude must needs come together – They will certainly gather together in a tumultuous manner, unless they be some way pacified.

23. Therefore – To obviate their prejudice against thee: do this that we say to thee – Doubtless they meant this advice well: but could Paul follow it in godly sincerity? Was not the yielding so far to the judgment of others too great a deference to be paid to any mere men?

24. And all will know – that thou thyself walkest orderly, keeping the law – Ought he not, without any reverence to man, where the truth of God was so deeply concerned, to have answered plainly, I do not keep the Mosaic law; neither need any of you. Yea, Peter doth not keep the law. And God himself expressly commanded him not to keep it; ordering him to go in to men uncircumcized, and to eat with them, chap. xi, 3, which the law utterly forbids.

26. Then Paul took the men – Yielding his own judgment to their advice, which seemed to flow not out of spiritual but carnal wisdom; seeming to be what he really was not: making as if he believed the law still in force. Declaring – Giving notice to the priests in waiting, that he designed to accomplish the days of purification, till all the sacrifice should be offered, as the Mosaic law required, Num. vi, 13.

27. And when the seven days were about to be accomplished – When after giving notice to the priests, they were entering upon the accomplishment of those days. It was toward the beginning of them that Paul was seized. The Jews that were from Asia – Some of those Jews who came from Asia to the feast.

28. Against the people – The Jewish nation; and the law – Of Moses;

done; for his will is his wisdom, and he doeth all according to the counsel of it. When a trouble is come, this must allay our griefs, that the will of the Lord is done; when we see it coming, this must silence our fears, that the will of the Lord shall be done; and we ought to say, Amen, let it be done. It is honorable to be an old disciple of Jesus Christ, to have been enabled by the grace of God to continue long in a course of duty, steadfast in the faith, growing more and more experienced, to a good old age. And with these old disciples one would choose to lodge; for the multitude of their years shall teach wisdom. Many brethren at Jerusalem received Paul gladly. We think, perhaps, that if we had him among us, we should gladly receive him; but we should not, if, having his doctrine, we do not gladly receive that.

19-26 Paul ascribed all his success to God, and to God they gave the praise. God had honored him more than any of the apostles, yet they did not envy him; but on the contrary, glorified the Lord. They could not do more to encourage Paul to go on cheerfully in his work. James and the elders of the church at Jerusalem, asked Paul to gratify the believing Jews, by some compliance with the ceremonial law. They thought it was prudent in him to conform thus far. It was great weakness to be so fond of the shadows, when the substance was come. The religion Paul preached, tended not to destroy the law, but to fulfill it. He preached Christ, the end of the law for righteousness, and repentance and faith, in which we are to make great use of the law. The weakness and evil of the human heart strongly appear, when we consider how many, even of the disciples of Christ, had not due regard to the most eminent minister that even lived. Not the excellence of his character, nor the success with which God blessed his labors, could gain their esteem and affection, seeing that he did not render the same respect as themselves to mere ceremonial observances. How watchful should we be against prejudices! The apostles were not free from blame in all they did; and it would be hard to defend Paul from the charge of giving way too much in this matter. It is vain to attempt to court the favor of zealots, or bigots to a party. This compliance of Paul did not answer, for the very thing by which he hoped to pacify the Jews, provoked them, and brought him into trouble. But the all-wise God overruled both their advice and Paul's compliance with it, to serve a better purpose than was intended. It was in vain to think of pleasing men who would be pleased with nothing but the rooting out of Christianity. Integrity and uprightness will be more likely to preserve us than insincere compliances. And it should warn us not to press men to doing what is contrary to their own judgment to oblige us.

thinks his arguments can ever convert man. Let me give you a parallel case. Where is the logic that can persuade an Ethiopian to change his skin? By what argument can you induce a leopard to renounce his spots? Even so may he that is accustomed to do evil learn to do well. But if the Ethiopian's skin be changed it must be by a supernatural process and if the leopard's spots be removed, he that made the leopard must do it. Even so is it with the heart of man. If sin were a thing and extra and external, we could induce man to change it. For instance, you may induce a man to leave off drunkenness or swearing, because those things are not a part of his nature—he has added that vice to his original depravity. But the hidden evil at the heart is beyond all moral change. I dare say a man might have enough argument to induce him to hang himself, but I am certain no argument will ever induce him to hang his sins, to hang his self-righteousness, and to come and humble himself at the foot of the cross; for the religion of Christ is so contrary to all the propensities of man, that it is like swimming against the stream to approach it, for the stream of man's will and man's desire is exactly the opposite of the religion of Jesus Christ. If you wanted a proof of that, at the lifting of my finger, there are thousands in this hall who would rise to prove it, for they would say, "I have found it so sir, in my experience; I hated religion as much as any man; I despised Christ, and his people, and I know not to this day how it is that I am what I am, unless it be the work of God." I have seen the tears run down a man's cheeks when he has come to me in order to be united to the church of Christ, and he has said, "Sir, I wonder how it is I am here today, if anyone had told me a year ago that I should think as I now think, and feel as I now feel, I should have called him a born fool for his pains; I used to say I never would be one of those canting Methodists, I liked to spend my Sunday in pleasure, and I did not see why I was to be cooping myself up in the house of God listening to a man talk. I pray, sir? No, not I. I said the best providence in all the world was a good strong pair of hands, and to take care of what you got. If any man talked to me about religion, why I would slam the door in his face, and pretty soon put him out; but the things that I loved then, I now hate, and the things that then I hated, now I love, I cannot do or say enough to show how total is the change that has been wrought in me. It must have been the work of God; it could not have been wrought by me, I feel assured; it must be some one greater than myself, who could thus turn my heart." I think these two things are proofs that we want something more than nature, and since physical agency will not do, and mere moral suasion will never accomplish it, that there must be an absolute necessity for the Holy Spirit.

But again, if you will just think a minute what

was, that he was borne of the soldiers for the violence of the people.

36 For the multitude of the people followed after, crying, Away with him.

37 And as Paul was to be led into the castle, he said unto the chief captain, May I speak unto thee? Who said, Canst thou speak Greek?

38 Art not thou that Egyptian, which before these days madest an uproar, and leddest out into the wilderness four thousand men that were murderers?

39 But Paul said, I am a man which am a Jew of Tarsus, a city in Cilicia, a citizen of no mean city: and, I beseech thee, suffer me to speak unto the people.

40 And when he had given him license, Paul stood on the stairs, and beckoned with the hand unto the people. And when there was made a great silence, he spake unto them in the Hebrew tongue, saying,

ACTS 22

1 Men, brethren, and fathers, hear ye my defense which I make now unto you.

2 (And when they heard that he spake in the Hebrew tongue to them, they kept the more silence: and he saith,)

3 I am verily a man which am a Jew, born in Tarsus, a city in Cilicia, yet brought up in this city at the feet of Gamaliel, and taught according to the perfect manner of the law of the fathers, and was zealous toward God, as ye all are this day.

4 And I persecuted this way unto the death, binding and delivering into prisons both men and women.

5 As also the high priest doth bear me witness, and all the estate of the elders: from whom also I received letters unto the brethren, and went to Damascus, to bring them which were there bound unto Jerusalem, for to be punished.

6 And it came to pass, that, as I made my journey, and was come nigh unto Damascus about noon, suddenly there shone from heaven a great light round about me.

7 And I fell unto the ground, and heard a voice saying unto me, Saul, Saul, why persecutest thou me?

8 And I answered, Who art thou, Lord? And he said unto me, I am Jesus of Nazareth, whom thou persecutest.

9 And they that were with me saw indeed the light, and were afraid; but they heard not the voice of him that spake to me.

10 And I said, What shall I do, Lord? And the Lord said unto me, Arise, and go into Damascus; and there it shall be told thee of all things which are appointed for thee to do.

11 And when I could not see for the glory of that light, being led by the hand of them that were with me, I came into Damascus.

12 And one Ananias, a devout man according

and this place – The temple. Yea, and hath even brought Greeks into the temple – They might come into the outer court. But they imagined Paul had brought them into the inner temple, and had thereby polluted it.

30. And immediately the gates were shut – Both to prevent any farther violation of the temple; and to prevent Paul's taking sanctuary at the horns of the altar.

31. And as they went about to kill him – It was a rule among the Jews, that any uncircumcized person who came into the inner temple, might be stoned without farther process. And they seemed to think Paul, who brought such in thither, deserved no better treatment. Word came to the tribune – A cohort or detachment of soldiers, belonging to the Roman legion, which lodged in the adjacent castle of Antonia, were stationed on feast days near the temple, to prevent disorders. It is evident, Lysias himself was not present, when the tumult began. Probably he was the oldest Roman tribune (or colonel) then at Jerusalem. And as such he was the commanding officer of the legion quartered at the castle.

33. Then the tribune – Having made his way through the multitude, came near and took him – And how many great ends of providence were answered by this imprisonment? This was not only a means of preserving his life, (after he had suffered severely for worldly prudence,) but gave him an opportunity of preaching the Gospel safely, in spite of all tumult, chap. xxii, 22, yea, and that in those places to which otherwise he could have had no access, verse 40. And commanded him to be bound with two chains – Taking it for granted he was some notorious offender. And thus the prophecy of Agabus was fulfilled, though by the hands of a Roman.

35. When he came upon the stairs – The castle of Antonia was situate on a rock fifty cubits high, at that corner of the outward temple, where the western and northern porticos joined, to each of which there were stairs descending from it.

37. As Paul was about to be brought into the castle – The wisdom of God taught to make use of that very time and place.

38. Art not thou that Egyptian – Who came into Judea when Felix had been some years governor there! Calling himself a prophet, he drew much people after him; and having brought them through the wilderness, led them to Mount Olivet, promising that the walls of the city should fall down before them. But Felix marching out of Jerusalem against him, his followers quickly dispersed, many of whom were taken or slain; but he himself made his escape.

40. In the Hebrew tongue – That dialect of it, which was then commonly spoken at Jerusalem.

ACTS 22

1. Hear ye now my defense – Which they could not hear before for the tumult.

3. I am verily – This defense answers all that is objected, chap. xxi, 28. As there, so here also mention is made of the person of Paul, ver. 3, of the people and the law, ver. 3, 5, 12; of the temple, ver. 17; of teaching all men, ver. 15-17, 21; and of the truth of his doctrine, ver. 6. But he speaks closely and nervously, in few words, because the time was short. But brought up at the feet of Gamaliel – The scholars usually sat on low seats, or upon mats on the floor, at the feet of their masters, whose seats were raised to a considerable height. Accurately instructed – The learned education which Paul had

MATTHEW HENRY

CHARLES H. SPURGEON

27-40 In the temple, where Paul should have been protected as in a place of safety, he was violently set upon. They falsely charged him with ill doctrine and ill practice against the Mosaic ceremonies. It is no new thing for those who mean honestly and act regularly, to have things laid to their charge which they know not and never thought of. It is common for the wise and good to have that charged against them by malicious people, with which they thought to have obliged them. God often makes those a protection to his people, who have no affection to them, but only have compassion for sufferers, and regard to the public peace. And here see what false, mistaken notions of good people and good ministers, many run away with. But God seasonably interposes for the safety of his servants, from wicked and unreasonable men; and gives them opportunities to speak for themselves, to plead for the Redeemer, and to spread abroad his glorious gospel.

ACTS 22

Paul's account of his conversion. (1-11)
Paul directed to preach to the Gentiles. (12-21)
The rage of the Jews. Paul pleads that he is a Roman citizen. (22-30)

1-11 The apostle addressed the enraged multitude, in the customary style of respect and goodwill. Paul relates the history of his early life very particularly; he notices that his conversion was wholly the act of God. Condemned sinners are struck blind by the power of darkness, and it is a lasting blindness, like that of the unbelieving Jews. Convinced sinners are struck blind as Paul was, not by darkness, but by light. They are for a time brought to be at a loss within themselves, but it is in order to their being enlightened. A simple relation of the Lord's dealings with us, in bringing us, from opposing, to profess and promote his gospel, when delivered in a right spirit and manner, will sometimes make more impression than labored speeches, even though it amounts not to the full proof of the truth, such as was shown in the change wrought in the apostle.

12-21 The apostle goes on to relate how he was confirmed in the change he had made. The Lord having chosen the sinner, that he should know his will, he is humbled, enlightened, and brought to the knowledge of Christ and his blessed gospel. Christ is here called that Just One; for he is Jesus Christ the righteous. Those whom God has chosen to know his will, must look to Jesus, for by him God has made known his good-will to us. The great gospel privilege, sealed to us by baptism, is the pardon of sins. Be baptized, and wash away thy sins; that is, receive the comfort of the pardon of thy

the work is, you will soon see that none but God can accomplish it. In the Holy Scripture, conversion is often spoken of as being a new creation. If you talk about creating yourselves, I should feel obliged if you would create a fly first. Create a gnat, create a grain of sand, and when you have created that, you may talk about creating a new heart. Both are alike, impossible, for creation is the work of God. But still, if you could create a grain of dust, or create even a world, it would not be half the miracle, for you must first find a thing which has created itself. Could that be? Suppose you had no existence, how could you create yourself? Nothing cannot produce anything. Now, how can man re-create himself. A man cannot create himself into a new condition, when he has no being in that condition, but is, as yet, a thing that is not.

Then, again, the work of creation is said to be like the resurrection. "We are alive from the dead." Now, can the dead in the grave raise themselves. Let any minister who thinks he can convert souls, go and raise a corpse let him go and stand in one of the cemeteries, and bid the tombs open wide their mouths, and make room for those once buried there to awaken, and he will have to preach in vain. But if he could do it, that is not the miracle: it is for the dead to raise themselves, for an inanimate corpse; to kindle in its own breast the spark of life anew. If the work be a resurrection, a creation, does it not strike you that it must be beyond the power of man? It must be wrought in him by no one less than God himself.

And there is yet one more consideration, and I shall have concluded this point. Beloved, even if man could save himself, I would have you recollect how averse he is to it? If we could make our hearers all willing, the battle would be accomplished. "Well," says one, "If I am willing to be saved, can I not be saved?" Assuredly you can, but the difficulty is, we cannot bring men to be willing. That shows, therefore, that there must be a constraint put upon their will. There must be an influence exerted upon them, which they have not in themselves, in order to make them willing in the day of God's power. And this is the glory of the Christian religion. The Christian religion has within its own bowels power to spread itself. We do not ask you to be willing first. We come and tell you the news, and we believe that the Spirit of God working with us, will make you willing. If the progress of the Christian religion depended upon the voluntary assent of mankind it would never go an inch further but because the Christian religion has within an omnipotent influence, constraining men to believe it, it is therefore that it is and must be triumphant, "till like a sea of glory it spreads from shore to shore."

to the law, having a good report of all the Jews which dwelt there,

13 Came unto me, and stood, and said unto me, Brother Saul, receive thy sight. And the same hour I looked up upon him.

14 And he said, The God of our fathers hath chosen thee, that thou shouldest know his will, and see that Just One, and shouldest hear the voice of his mouth.

15 For thou shalt be his witness unto all men of what thou hast seen and heard.

16 And now why tarriest thou? arise, and be baptized, and wash away thy sins, calling on the name of the Lord.

17 And it came to pass, that, when I was come again to Jerusalem, even while I prayed in the temple, I was in a trance;

18 And saw him saying unto me, Make haste, and get thee quickly out of Jerusalem: for they will not receive thy testimony concerning me.

19 And I said, Lord, they know that I imprisoned and beat in every synagogue them that believed on thee:

20 And when the blood of thy martyr Stephen was shed, I also was standing by, and consenting unto his death, and kept the raiment of them that slew him.

21 And he said unto me, Depart: for I will send thee far hence unto the Gentiles.

22 And they gave him audience unto this word, and then lifted up their voices, and said, Away with such a fellow from the earth: for it is not fit that he should live.

23 And as they cried out, and cast off their clothes, and threw dust into the air,

24 The chief captain commanded him to be brought into the castle, and bade that he should be examined by scourging; that he might know wherefore they cried so against him.

25 And as they bound him with thongs, Paul said unto the centurion that stood by, Is it lawful for you to scourge a man that is a Roman, and uncondemned?

26 When the centurion heard that, he went and told the chief captain, saying, Take heed what thou doest: for this man is a Roman.

27 Then the chief captain came, and said unto him, Tell me, art thou a Roman? He said, Yea.

28 And the chief captain answered, With a great sum obtained I this freedom. And Paul said, But I was free born.

29 Then straightway they departed from him which should have examined him: and the chief captain also was afraid, after he knew that he was a Roman, and because he had bound him.

30 On the morrow, because he would have known the certainty wherefore he was accused of the Jews, he loosed him from his bands, and commanded the chief priests and all their council to appear, and brought Paul down, and set him before them.

received was once no doubt the matter of his boasting and confidence. Unsanctified learning made his bonds strong, and furnished him with numerous arguments against the Gospel. Yet when the grace of God had changed his heart, and turned his accomplishments into another channel, he was the fitter instrument to serve God's wise and merciful purposes, in the defense and propagation of Christianity.

4. And persecuted this way – With the same zeal that you do now. Binding both men and women – How much better was his condition, now he was bound himself.

5. The high priest is my witness – Is able to testify. The brethren – Jews: so this title was not peculiar to the Christians.

6. About noon – All was done in the face of the sun. A great light shone – By whatever method God reveals himself to us, we shall have everlasting cause to recollect it with pleasure. Especially when he has gone in any remarkable manner out of his common way for this gracious purpose. If so, we should often dwell on the particular circumstances, and be ready, on every proper occasion, to recount those wonders of power and love, for the encouragement and instruction of others.

9. They did not hear the voice – Distinctly; but only a confused noise.

12. A devout man according to the law – A truly religious person, and though a believer in Christ, yet a strict observer of the law of Moses.

16. Be baptized, and wash away thy sins – Baptism administered to real penitents, is both a means and seal of pardon. Nor did God ordinarily in the primitive Church bestow this on any, unless through this means.

17. When I was returned to Jerusalem – From Damascus, and was praying in the temple – Whereby he shows that he still paid the temple its due honor, as the house of prayer. I was in a trance – Perhaps he might continue standing all the while, so that any who were near him would hardly discern it.

18. And I saw him – Jesus, saying to me, Depart quickly out of Jerusalem – Because of the snares laid for thee: and in order to preach where they will hear.

19. And I said – It is not easy for a servant of Christ, who is himself deeply impressed with Divine truths, to imagine to what a degree men are capable of hardening their hearts against thee. He is often ready to think with Paul, It is impossible for any to resist such evidence. But experience makes him wiser and shows that willfull unbelief is proof against all truth and reason.

20. When the blood of thy martyr Stephen was shed, I also was standing by – A real convert still retains the remembrance of his former sins. He confesses them and is humbled for them, all the days of his life.

22. And they heard him to this word – Till he began to speak of his mission to the Gentiles, and this too in such a manner as implied that the Jews were in danger of being cast off.

23. They rent their garments – In token of indignation and horror at this pretended blasphemy, and cast dust into the air – Through vehemence of rage, which they knew not how to vent.

25. And as they – The soldiers ordered by the tribune, were binding him with thongs – A freeman of Rome might be bound with a chain and beaten with a staff: but he might not be bound with thongs, neither scourged, or beaten with rods: Paul said to the centurion – The captain, who stood by to see the orders of the tribune executed.

MATTHEW HENRY

CHARLES H. SPURGEON

sins in and through Jesus Christ, and lay hold on his righteousness for that purpose; and receive power against sin, for the mortifying of thy corruptions. Be baptized, and rest not in the sign, but make sure of the thing signified, the putting away of the filth of sin. The great gospel duty, to which by our baptism we are bound, is, to seek for the pardon of our sins in Christ's name, and in dependence on him and his righteousness. God appoints his laborers their day and their place, and it is fit they should follow his appointment, though it may cross their own will. Providence contrives better for us than we do for ourselves; we must refer ourselves to God's guidance. If Christ send any one, his Spirit shall go along with him, and give him to see the fruit of his labors. But nothing can reconcile man's heart to the gospel, except the special grace of God.

22-30 The Jews listened to Paul's account of his conversion, but the mention of his being sent to the Gentiles, was so contrary to all their national prejudices, that they would hear no more. Their frantic conduct astonished the Roman officer, who supposed that Paul must have committed some great crime. Paul pleaded his privilege as a Roman citizen, by which he was exempted from all trials and punishments which might force him to confess himself guilty. The manner of his speaking plainly shows what holy security and serenity of mind he enjoyed. As Paul was a Jew, in low circumstances, the Roman officer questioned how he obtained so valuable a distinction; but the apostle told him he was free born. Let us value that freedom to which all the children of God are born; which no sum of money, however large, can purchase for those who remain unregenerate. This at once put a stop to his trouble. Thus many are kept from evil practices by the fear of man, who would not be held back from them by the fear of God. The apostle asks, simply, Is it lawful? He knew that the God whom he served would support him under all sufferings for his name's sake. But if it were not lawful, the apostle's religion directed him, if possible, to avoid it. He never shrunk from a cross which his Divine Master laid upon his onward road; and he never stepped aside out of that road to take one up.

ACTS 23

Paul's defense before the council of the Jews. (1-5)
Paul's defense. He receives a Divine assurance that he shall go to Rome. (6-11)
The Jews conspire to kill Paul. Lysias sends him to Cesarea. (12-24)
Lysias's letter to Felix. (25-35)

1-5 See here the character of an honest man. He sets God before him, and lives as in his sight. He

III. Now I shall conclude by bringing one or two thoughts forward, with regard to WHAT MUST BE DONE AT THIS TIME IN ORDER TO BRING DOWN THE HOLY SPIRIT. It is quite certain, beloved, if the Holy Spirit willed to do it, that every man, woman, and child in this place might be converted now. If God, the Sovereign Judge of all, would be pleased now to send out his Spirit, every inhabitant of this million-peopled city might be brought at once to turn unto the living God. Without instrumentality, without the preacher, without books, without anything, God has it in his power to convert men. We have known persons about their business, not thinking about religion at all, who have had a thought injected into their heart, and that thought has been the prolific mother of a thousand meditations and through these meditations they have been brought to Christ. Without the aid of the minister, the Holy Spirit has thus worked, and today he is not restrained. There may be some men, great in infidelity, staunch in opposition to the cross of Christ, but, without asking their consent, the Holy Spirit can pull down the strong man, and make the mighty man bow himself. For when we talk of the Omnipotent God, there is nothing too great for him to do. But, beloved, God has been pleased to put great honor upon instrumentality; he could work without it if he pleased but he does not do so. However, this is the first thought I want to give you; if you would have the Holy Spirit exert himself in our midst, you must first of all look to him and not to instrumentality. When Jesus Christ preached, there were very few converted under him, and the reason was, because the Holy Spirit was not abundantly poured forth. He had the Holy Spirit without measure himself, but on others the Holy Spirit was not as yet poured out. Jesus Christ said, "Greater works than these shall ye do because I go to my Father, in order to send the Holy Spirit;" and recollect that those few who were converted under Christ's ministry, were not converted by him, but by the Holy Spirit that rested upon him at that time. Jesus of Nazareth was anointed of the Holy Spirit. Now then, if Jesus Christ, the great founder of our religion, needed to be anointed of the Holy Spirit, how much more our ministers? And if God would always make the distinction even between his own Son as an instrument, and the Holy Spirit as the agent, how much more ought we to be careful to do that between poor puny men and the Holy Spirit? Never let us hear you say again, "So many persons were converted by So-and so." They were not. If converted they were not converted by man. Instrumentality is to be used, but the Spirit is to have the honor of it. Pay no more a superstitious reverence to man, think no more that God is tied to your plans, and to your agencies. Do not imagine that so many city missionaries, so much good will be done. Do not

ACTS 23

1 And Paul, earnestly beholding the council, said, Men and brethren, I have lived in all good conscience before God until this day.

2 And the high priest Ananias commanded them that stood by him to smite him on the mouth.

3 Then said Paul unto him, God shall smite thee, thou whited wall: for sittest thou to judge me after the law, and commandest me to be smitten contrary to the law?

4 And they that stood by said, Revilest thou God's high priest?

5 Then said Paul, I wist not, brethren, that he was the high priest: for it is written, Thou shalt not speak evil of the ruler of thy people.

6 But when Paul perceived that the one part were Sadducees, and the other Pharisees, he cried out in the council, Men and brethren, I am a Pharisee, the son of a Pharisee: of the hope and resurrection of the dead I am called in question.

7 And when he had so said, there arose a dissension between the Pharisees and the Sadducees: and the multitude was divided.

8 For the Sadducees say that there is no resurrection, neither angel, nor spirit: but the Pharisees confess both.

9 And there arose a great cry: and the scribes that were of the Pharisees' part arose, and strove, saying, We find no evil in this man: but if a spirit or an angel hath spoken to him, let us not fight against God.

10 And when there arose a great dissension, the chief captain, fearing lest Paul should have been pulled in pieces of them, commanded the soldiers to go down, and to take him by force from among them, and to bring him into the castle.

11 And the night following the Lord stood by him, and said, Be of good cheer, Paul: for as thou hast testified of me in Jerusalem, so must thou bear witness also at Rome.

12 And when it was day, certain of the Jews banded together, and bound themselves under a curse, saying that they would neither eat nor drink till they had killed Paul.

13 And they were more than forty which had made this conspiracy.

14 And they came to the chief priests and elders, and said, We have bound ourselves under a great curse, that we will eat nothing until we have slain Paul.

15 Now therefore ye with the council signify to the chief captain that he bring him down unto you to morrow, as though ye would inquire something more perfectly concerning him: and we, or ever he come near, are ready to kill him.

16 And when Paul's sister's son heard of their lying in wait, he went and entered into the castle, and told Paul.

17 Then Paul called one of the centurions unto him, and said, Bring this young man unto

26. Consider what thou art about to do; for this man is a Roman – Yea, there was a stronger reason to consider. For this man was a servant of God.

28. But I was free born – Not barely as being born at Tarsus; for this was not Roman colony. But probably either his father, or some of his ancestors, had been made free of Rome, for some military service. We learn hence, that we are under no obligation as Christians to give up our civil privileges (which we are to receive and prize as the gift of God) to every insolent invader. In a thousand circumstances, gratitude to God, and duty to men, will oblige us to insist upon them; and engage us to strive to transmit them improved, rather than impaired to posterity.

ACTS 23

1. And Paul earnestly beholding the council – Professing a clear conscience by his very countenance; and likewise waiting to see whether any of them was minded to ask him any question, said, I have lived in all good conscience before God till this day – He speaks chiefly of the time since he became a Christian. For none questioned him concerning what he had been before. And yet even in his unconverted state, although he was in an error, yet he had acted from conscience, before God – Whatever men may think or say of me.

3. Then said Paul – Being carried away by a sudden and prophetic impulse. God is about to smite thee, thou white wall – Fair without; full of dirt and rubbish within. And he might well be so termed, not only as he committed this outrage, while gravely sitting on the tribunal of justice but also as, at the same time that he stood high in the esteem of the citizens, he cruelly defrauded the priests of their legal subsistence, so that some of them even perished for want. And God did remarkably smite him; for about five years after this, his house being reduced to ashes, in a tumult begun by his own son, he was besieged in the royal palace; where having hid himself in an old aqueduct, he was dragged out and miserably slain.

5. I was not aware, brethren, that it was the high priest – He seems to mean, I did not advert to it, in the prophetic transport of my mind: but he does not add, that his not adverting to it proceeded from the power of the Spirit coming upon him; as knowing they were not able to bear it. This answer admirably shows the situation of mind he was then in, partly with regard to the bystanders, whom he thus softens, adding also the title of brethren, and justifying their reproof by the prohibition of Moses; partly with regard to himself, who, after that singular transport subsided, was again under the direction of the general command. Exod. xxii, 28.

6. I am a Pharisee, the son of a Pharisee: for the hope of the resurrection of the dead am I called in question – So he was in effect; although not formally, or explicitly.

8. The Pharisees confess both – Both the resurrection, and the existence of angels and separate spirits.

9. And the scribes of the Pharisees' side arising – Every sect contains both learned and unlearned. The former used to be the mouth of the party. If a spirit – St. Paul in his speech from the stairs had affirmed, that Jesus, whom they knew to have been dead, was alive, and that he had spoken to him from heaven, and again in a vision. So they add nothing, only they construe it in their own way, putting an angel or spirit for Jesus.

11. And the night following, the Lord Jesus – What Paul had before purposed in spirit, chap. xix, 21, God now in due time confirms.

makes conscience of what he says and does, and, according to the best of his knowledge, he keeps from whatever is evil, and cleaves to what is good. He is conscientious in all his words and conduct. Those who thus live before God, may, like Paul, have confidence both toward God and man. Though the answer of Paul contained a just rebuke and prediction, he seems to have been too angry at the treatment he received in uttering them. Great men may be told of their faults, and public complaints may be made in a proper manner; but the law of God requires respect for those in authority.

6-11 The Pharisees were correct in the faith of the Jewish church. The Sadducees were no friends to the Scripture or Divine revelation; they denied a future state; they had neither hope of eternal happiness, nor dread of eternal misery. When called in question for his being a Christian, Paul might truly say he was called in question for the hope of the resurrection of the dead. It was justifiable in him, by this profession of his opinion on that disputed point, to draw off the Pharisees from persecuting him, and to lead them to protect him from this unlawful violence. How easily can God defend his own cause! Though the Jews seemed to be perfectly agreed in their conspiracy against religion, yet they were influenced by very different motives. There is no true friendship among the wicked, and in a moment, and with the utmost ease, God can turn their union into open enmity. Divine consolations stood Paul in the most stead; the chief captain rescued him out of the hands of cruel men, but the event he could not tell. Whoever is against us, we need not fear, if the Lord stand by us. It is the will of Christ, that his servants who are faithful, should be always cheerful. He might think he should never see Rome; but God tells him, even in that he should be gratified, since he desired to go there only for the honor of Christ, and to do good.

12-24 False religious principles, adopted by carnal men, urge on to such wickedness, as human nature would hardly be supposed capable of. Yet the Lord readily disappoints the best concerted schemes of iniquity. Paul knew that the Divine providence acts by reasonable and prudent means; and that, if he neglected to use the means in his power, he could not expect God's providence to work on his behalf. He who will not help himself according to his means and power, has neither reason nor revelation to assure him that he shall receive help from God. Believing in the Lord, we and ours shall be kept from every evil work, and kept to his kingdom. Heavenly Father, give us by thy Holy Spirit, for Christ's sake, this precious faith.

25-35 God has instruments for every work. The natural abilities and moral virtues of the heathens

say, "So many preachers; so many sermons, so many souls saved." Do not say, "So many Bibles, so many tracts; so much good done." Not so, use these, but remember it is not in that proportion the blessing comes; it is, so much Holy Spirit, so many souls in-gathered.

And now another thought. If we would have the Spirit, beloved, we must each of us try to honor him. There are some chapels into which if you were to enter, you would never know there was a Holy Spirit. Mary Magdalen said of old, "They have taken away my Lord, and I know not where they have laid him," and the Christian might often say so, for there is nothing said about the Lord until they come to the end, and then there is just the benediction, or else you would not know that there were three persons in one God at all. Until our churches honor the Holy Spirit, we shall never see it abundantly manifested in our midst. Let the preacher always confess before he preaches that he relies upon the Holy Spirit. Let him burn his manuscript and depend upon the Holy Spirit. If the Spirit does not come to help him, let him be still and let the people go home and pray that the Spirit will help him next Sunday.

And do you also, in the use of all your agencies, always honor the Spirit? We often begin our religious meetings without prayer; it is all wrong. We must honor the Spirit; unless we put him first, he will never make crowns for us to wear. He will get victories, but he will have the honor of them, and if we do not give to him the honor, he will never give to us the privilege and success. And best of all, if you would have the Holy Spirit, let us meet together earnestly to pray for him. Remember, the Holy Spirit will not come to us as a church, unless we seek him. "For this thing will I be inquired of by the house of Israel to do it for them." We purpose during the coming week to hold meetings of special prayer, to supplicate for a revival of religion. On the Friday morning I opened the first prayer meeting at Trinity Chapel, Brixton; and, I think, at seven o'clock, we had as many as two hundred and fifty persons gathered together. It was a pleasant sight. During the hour, nine brethren prayed, one after the other; and I am sure there was the spirit of prayer there. Some persons present sent up their names, asking that we would offer special petitions for them; and I doubt not the prayers will be answered; At Park Street, on Monday morning, we shall have a prayer. meeting from eight to nine; then during the rest of the week there will be a prayer meeting in the morning from seven to eight. On Monday evening we shall have the usual prayer-meeting at seven, when I hope there will be a large number attending. I find that my brother, Baptist Noel, has commenced morning and evening prayer-meetings, and they have done the same thing in Norwich and many provincial towns,

the chief captain: for he hath a certain thing to tell him.

18 So he took him, and brought him to the chief captain, and said, Paul the prisoner called me unto him, and prayed me to bring this young man unto thee, who hath something to say unto thee.

19 Then the chief captain took him by the hand, and went with him aside privately, and asked him, What is that thou hast to tell me?

20 And he said, The Jews have agreed to desire thee that thou wouldest bring down Paul to morrow into the council, as though they would inquire somewhat of him more perfectly.

21 But do not thou yield unto them: for there lie in wait for him of them more than forty men, which have bound themselves with an oath, that they will neither eat nor drink till they have killed him: and now are they ready, looking for a promise from thee.

22 So the chief captain then let the young man depart, and charged him, See thou tell no man that thou hast shewed these things to me.

23 And he called unto him two centurions, saying, Make ready two hundred soldiers to go to Cesarea, and horsemen threescore and ten, and spearmen two hundred, at the third hour of the night;

24 And provide them beasts, that they may set Paul on, and bring him safe unto Felix the governor.

25 And he wrote a letter after this manner:

26 Claudius Lysias unto the most excellent governor Felix sendeth greeting.

27 This man was taken of the Jews, and should have been killed of them: then came I with an army, and rescued him, having understood that he was a Roman.

28 And when I would have known the cause wherefore they accused him, I brought him forth into their council:

29 Whom I perceived to be accused of questions of their law, but to have nothing laid to his charge worthy of death or of bonds.

30 And when it was told me how that the Jews laid wait for the man, I sent straightway to thee, and gave commandment to his accusers also to say before thee what they had against him. Farewell.

31 Then the soldiers, as it was commanded them, took Paul, and brought him by night to Antipatris.

32 On the morrow they left the horsemen to go with him, and returned to the castle:

33 Who, when they came to Cesarea, and delivered the epistle to the governor, presented Paul also before him.

34 And when the governor had read the letter, he asked of what province he was. And when he understood that he was of Cilicia;

35 I will hear thee, said he, when thine accusers are also come. And he commanded him to be kept in Herod's judgment hall.

Another declaration to the same effect is made by an angel of God, chap. xxvii, 23. And from the 23rd chapter the sum of this book turns on the testimony of Paul to the Romans. How would the defenders of St. Peter's supremacy triumph, could they find out half as much ascribed to him! Be of good courage, Paul – As he labored under singular distresses and persecutions, so he was favored with extraordinary assurances of the Divine assistance. Thou must testify – Particular promises are usually given when all things appear desperate. At Rome also – Danger is nothing in the eyes of God: all hindrances farther his work. A promise of what is afar off, implies all that necessarily lies between. Paul shall testify at Rome: therefore he shall come to Rome; therefore he shall escape the Jews, the sea, the viper.

12. Some of the Jews bound themselves – Such execrable vows were not uncommon among the Jews. And if they were prevented from accomplishing what they had vowed, it was an easy matter to obtain absolution from their rabbis.

15. Now therefore ye – Which they never scrupled at all, as not doubting but they were doing God service.

17. And Paul – Though he had an express promise of it from Christ, was not to neglect any proper means of safety.

19. And the tribune taking him by the hand – In a mild, condescending way. Lysias seems to have conducted this whole affair with great integrity, humanity, and prudence.

24. Provide beasts – If a change should be necessary, to set Paul on – So we read of his riding once; but not by choice.

27. Having learned that he was a Roman – True; but not before he rescued him. Here he uses art.

31. The soldiers brought him by night to Antipatris – But not the same night they set out. For Antipatris was about thirty-eight of our miles northwest of Jerusalem. Herod the Great rebuilt it, and gave it this name in honor of his father Antipater: Cesarea was near seventy miles from Jerusalem, and about thirty from Antipatris.

35. In Herod's palace – This was a palace and a court built by Herod the Great. Probably some tower belonging to it might be used for a kind of state prison.

often have been employed to protect his persecuted servants. Even the men of the world can discern between the conscientious conduct of upright believers, and the zeal of false professors, though they disregard or understand not their doctrinal principles. All hearts are in God's hand, and those are blessed who put their trust in him, and commit their ways unto him.

ACTS 24

The speech of Tertullus against Paul. (1-9)
Paul's defense before Felix. (10-21)
Felix trembles at the reasoning of Paul. (22-27)

1-9 See here the unhappiness of great men, and a great unhappiness it is, to have their services praised beyond measure, and never to be faithfully told of their faults; hereby they are hardened and encouraged in evil, like Felix. God's prophets were charged with being troublers of the land, and our Lord Jesus Christ, that he perverted the nation; the very same charges were brought against Paul. The selfish and evil passions of men urge them forward, and the graces and power of speech, too often have been used to mislead and prejudice men against the truth. How different will the characters of Paul and Felix appear at the day of judgment, from what they are represented in the speech of Tertullus! Let not Christians value the applause, or be troubled at the reviling of ungodly men, who represent the vilest of the human race almost as gods, and the excellent of the earth as pestilences and movers of sedition.

10-21 Paul gives a just account of himself, which clears him from crime, and likewise shows the true reason of the violence against him. Let us never be driven from any good way by its having an ill name. It is very comfortable, in worshiping God, to look to him as the God of our fathers, and to set up no other rule of faith or practice but the Scriptures. This shows there will be a resurrection to a final judgment. Prophets and their doctrines were to be tried by their fruits. Paul's aim was to have a conscience void of offense. His care and endeavor was to abstain from many things, and to abound in the exercises of religion at all times; both towards God, and towards man. If blamed for being more earnest in the things of God than our neighbors, what is our reply? Do we shrink from the accusation? How many in the world would rather be accused of any weakness, nay, even of wickedness, than of an earnest, fervent feeling of love to the Lord Jesus Christ, and of devotedness to his service! Can such think that he will confess them when he comes in his glory, and before the angels of God? If there is any sight pleasing to the God of our salvation, and a sight at which the angels

where, without any pressure, the people are found willing to come. I certainly did not expect to see so many as two hundred and fifty persons at an early hour in the morning meet together for prayer. I believe it was a good sign The Lord hath put prayer into their hearts and therefore they were willing to come, "Prove me now here, saith the Lord of host, and see if I do not pour you out a blessing so that there shall not be room enough to receive it." Let us meet and pray, and if God doth not hear us, it will be the first time he has broken his promise. Come, let us go up to the sanctuary; let us meet together in the house of the Lord, and offer solemn supplication; and I say again, if the Lord doth not make bare his arm in the sight of all the people, it will be the reverse of all his previous actions, it will be the contrary of all his promises, and contradictory to himself. We have only to try him, and the result is certain. In dependence on his Spirit, if we only meet for prayer, the Lord shall bless us, and all the ends of the earth shall fear him. O Lord, lift up thyself because of thine enemies; pluck thy right hand out of thy bosom, O Lord our God, for Christ's sake, Amen.

LYDIA, THE FIRST EUROPEAN CONVERT
Sermon number 2222 intended for Reading on September 20th, 1891, delivered at the Metropolitan Tabernacle, Newington.

"And a certain woman named Lydia, a seller of purple, of the city of Thyatira, which worshiped God, heard us: whose hearts the Lord opened, that she attended unto the things which were spoken of Paul."—Acts 16:14.

I. First, notice THE WORKING OF PROVIDENCE. When I was in Amsterdam, I visited the works of a diamond-cutter, where I saw many large wheels and much powerful machinery at work; and I must confess that it seemed very odd that all that great array of apparatus should be brought to bear upon a tiny bit of crystal, which looked like a fragment of glass. Was that diamond worth so much that a whole factory should be set to work to cut its facets, and cause it to sparkle? So the diamond-cutter believed. Within that small space lay a gem which was thought worthy of all this care and labor. That diamond may be at this time glistening upon the finger or brow of royalty! Now, when I look abroad upon providence, it seems preposterous to believe that kingdoms, dynasties, and great events should all be co-operating and working together for the accomplishment of the divine purpose in the salvation of God's people. But they are so working. It might have seemed preposterous, but it was not so, that these great wheels

ACTS 24

1 And after five days Ananias the high priest descended with the elders, and with a certain orator named Tertullus, who informed the governor against Paul.

2 And when he was called forth, Tertullus began to accuse him, saying, Seeing that by thee we enjoy great quietness, and that very worthy deeds are done unto this nation by thy providence,

3 We accept it always, and in all places, most noble Felix, with all thankfulness.

4 Notwithstanding, that I be not further tedious unto thee, I pray thee that thou wouldest hear us of thy clemency a few words.

5 For we have found this man a pestilent fellow, and a mover of sedition among all the Jews throughout the world, and a ringleader of the sect of the Nazarenes:

6 Who also hath gone about to profane the temple: whom we took, and would have judged according to our law.

7 But the chief captain Lysias came upon us, and with great violence took him away out of our hands,

8 Commanding his accusers to come unto thee: by examining of whom thyself mayest take knowledge of all these things, whereof we accuse him.

9 And the Jews also assented, saying that these things were so.

10 Then Paul, after that the governor had beckoned unto him to speak, answered, Forasmuch as I know that thou hast been of many years a judge unto this nation, I do the more cheerfully answer for myself:

11 Because that thou mayest understand, that there are yet but twelve days since I went up to Jerusalem for to worship.

12 And they neither found me in the temple disputing with any man, neither raising up the people, neither in the synagogues, nor in the city:

13 Neither can they prove the things whereof they now accuse me.

14 But this I confess unto thee, that after the way which they call heresy, so worship I the God of my fathers, believing all things which are written in the law and in the prophets:

15 And have hope toward God, which they themselves also allow, that there shall be a resurrection of the dead, both of the just and unjust.

16 And herein do I exercise myself, to have always a conscience void of offense toward God, and toward men.

17 Now after many years I came to bring alms to my nation, and offerings.

18 Whereupon certain Jews from Asia found me purified in the temple, neither with multitude, nor with tumult.

19 Who ought to have been here before thee, and object, if they had ought against me.

ACTS 24

1. Ananias – Who would spare no trouble on the occasion, with several of the elders, members of the Sanhedrin.

2. Tertullus began – A speech how different from St. Paul's; which is true, modest, solid, and without paint. Felix was a man of the most infamous character, and a plague to all the provinces over which he presided.

4. But that I may not trouble thee any farther – By trespassing either on thy patience or modesty. The eloquence of Tertullus was as bad as his cause: a lame introduction, a lame transition, and a lame conclusion. Did not God confound the orator's language?

10. Knowing – for several years thou hast been a judge over this nation – And so not unacquainted with our religious rites and customs, and consequently more capable of understanding and deciding a cause of this nature. There was no flattery in this. It was a plain fact. He governed Judea six or seven years. I answer for myself – As it may be observed, his answer exactly corresponds with the three articles of Tertullus's charge: sedition, heresy, and profanation of the temple. As to the first, he suggests, that he had not been long enough at Jerusalem to form a party and attempt an insurrection: (for it was about twelve days since he came up thither; five of which he had been at Cesarea, ver. 1; one or two were spent in his journey thither, and most of the rest he had been confined at Jerusalem.) And he challenges them, in fact, to produce any evidence of such practices, ver. 11-13. As to the second, he confesses himself to be a Christian; but maintains this to be a religion perfectly agreeable to the law and the prophets, and therefore deserving a fair reception, ver. 14, 16. And as for profaning the temple, he observes that he behaved there in a most peaceful and regular manner, so that his innocence had been manifest even before the Sanhedrin, where the authors of the tumult did not dare to appear against him.

14. After the way which they call heresy – This appellation St. Paul corrects. Not that it was then an odious word; but it was not honorable enough. A party or sect (so that word signifies) is formed by men. This way was prescribed by God. The apostle had now said what was sufficient for his defense; but having a fair occasion, he makes an ingenuous confession of his faith in this verse, his hope in the next, his love in the 17th. ver. 14, 15, 17. So worship I the God of my fathers – This was a very proper plea before a Roman magistrate; as it proved that he was under the protection of the Roman laws, since the Jews were so: whereas had he introduced the worship of new gods he would have forfeited that protection. Believing all things which are written – Concerning the Messiah.

15. Both of the just and of the unjust – In a public court this was peculiarly proper to be observed.

16. For this cause – With a view to this, I also exercise myself – As well as they.

19. Who ought to have been present before thee – But the world never commits greater blunders, even against its own laws, than when it is persecuting the children of God.

21. Unless they think me blamable for this one word – Which nevertheless was the real truth. chap. xxiii, 6.

22. After I have been more accurately informed – Which he afterward was; and he doubtless (as well as Festus and Agrippa) transmitted a full account of these things to Rome.

23. He commanded the centurion to let him have liberty – To be only a prisoner at large. Hereby the Gospel was spread more and more; not to the satisfaction of the Jews. But they could not hinder it.

rejoice, it is, to behold a devoted follower of the Lord, here upon earth, acknowledging that he is guilty, if it be a crime, of loving the Lord who died for him, with all his heart, and soul, and mind, and strength. And that he will not in silence see God's word despised, or hear his name profaned; he will rather risk the ridicule and the hatred of the world, than one frown from that gracious Being whose love is better than life.

22-27 The apostle reasoned concerning the nature and obligations of righteousness, temperance, and of a judgment to come; thus showing the oppressive judge and his profligate mistress, their need of repentance, forgiveness, and of the grace of the gospel. Justice respects our conduct in life, particularly in reference to others; temperance, the state and government of our souls, in reference to God. He who does not exercise himself in these, has neither the form nor the power of godliness, and must be overwhelmed with the Divine wrath in the day of God's appearing. A prospect of the judgment to come, is enough to make the stoutest heart to tremble. Felix trembled, but that was all. Many are startled by the word of God, who are not changed by it. Many fear the consequences of sin, yet continue in the love and practice of sin. In the affairs of our souls, delays are dangerous. Felix put off this matter to a more convenient season, but we do not find that the more convenient season ever came. Behold now is the accepted time; hear the voice of the Lord today. He was in haste to turn from hearing the truth. Was any business more urgent than for him to reform his conduct, or more important than the salvation of his soul! Sinners often start up like a man roused from his sleep by a loud noise, but soon sink again into their usual drowsiness. Be not deceived by occasional appearances of religion in ourselves or in others. Above all, let us not trifle with the word of God. Do we expect that as we advance in life our hearts will grow softer, or that the influence of the world will decline? Are we not at this moment in danger of being lost for ever? Now is the day of salvation; tomorrow may be too late.

ACTS 25

Paul before Festus, he appeals to Cesar. (1-12)
Festus confers with Agrippa respecting Paul. (13-27)

1-12 See how restless malice is. Persecutors deem it a peculiar favor to have their malice gratified. Preaching Christ, the end of the law, was no offense against the law. In suffering times the prudence of the Lord's people is tried, as well as their patience; they need wisdom. It becomes those who are innocent, to insist upon their innocence. Paul was willing to abide by the rules of the law, and to let that

should all be working for the cutting of a single diamond; and it is not preposterous, however it may seem so, to say that all the events of providence are being ordered by God to effect the salvation of his own people, the perfecting of the precious jewels which are to adorn the crown of Christ for ever and ever.

In the case before us, the working of God's providence is seen, first of all, in bringing Paul to Philippi. Lydia is there. I do not know how long she had been there, nor exactly what brought her there; but there she is, selling her purple, her Turkey-red cloth. Paul must come there, too, but he does not want to come; he has not, indeed, had any desire to come there. He has a kind of prejudice hanging about him still, so that, though he is willing to preach to the Gentiles, he scarcely likes to go out of Asia among those Gentiles of the Gentiles over in Europe. He wants to preach the word in Asia. Very singularly, the Spirit suffers him not, and he seems to have a cold hand laid on him to stop him when his heart is warmest. He is gagged; he cannot speak. "Then I will go into Bithynia," he says; but when he starts on the journey, he is distinctly told that there is no work for him to do there. He must not speak for his Master in that region, at least not yet: "the Spirit suffered him not." He feels himself to be a silenced man. What is he to do? He gets down to Troas on the verge of the sea, and there comes to him the vision of a man of Macedonia, who prayed him, saying, "Come over into Macedonia, and help us." He infers that he must go across to Macedonia. A ship is ready for him; he has a free course, a favorable passage, and he soon arrives at Philippi. God brings Paul to the spot where Lydia was, in this strange and singular manner.

But the working of providence was quite as much manifested in bringing Lydia there; for Lydia was not originally at Philippi. She was a seller of purple, of Thyatira. Thyatira was a city famous for its dyers. They made a peculiar purple, which was much prized by the Romans. Lydia appears to have carried on this business. She was either a widow, or perhaps had had no husband, though she may have gathered a household of servants about her. She comes over to Philippi across the sea. I think I see them bringing the great rolls of red cloth up the hill, that she may sell at Philippi the cloth which she has made and dyed at Thyatira. Why does she come just at this season? Why does she come just when Paul is coming? Why does she come to Philippi? Why not to Neapolis? Why not press on to Athens? Why not sell her cloth over at Corinth? Whatever reason she might have given for her choice, there was one cause, of which she was ignorant, which shaped her action, and brought her to Philippi at that time. God had a surprise in store for her. She and Paul have to meet. It

20 Or else let these same here say, if they have found any evil doing in me, while I stood before the council,

21 Except it be for this one voice, that I cried standing among them, Touching the resurrection of the dead I am called in question by you this day.

22 And when Felix heard these things, having more perfect knowledge of that way, he deferred them, and said, When Lysias the chief captain shall come down, I will know the uttermost of your matter.

23 And he commanded a centurion to keep Paul, and to let him have liberty, and that he should forbid none of his acquaintance to minister or come unto him.

24 And after certain days, when Felix came with his wife Drusilla, which was a Jewess, he sent for Paul, and heard him concerning the faith in Christ.

25 And as he reasoned of righteousness, temperance, and judgment to come Felix trembled, and answered, Go thy way for this time; when I have a convenient season, I will call for thee.

26 He hoped also that money should have been given him of Paul, that he might loose him: wherefore he sent for him the oftener, and communed with him.

27 But after two years Porcius Festus came into Felix' room: and Felix, willing to shew the Jews a pleasure, left Paul bound.

ACTS 25

1 Now when Festus was come into the province, after three days he ascended from Cesarea to Jerusalem.

2 Then the high priest and the chief of the Jews informed him against Paul, and besought him,

3 And desired favor against him, that he would send for him to Jerusalem, laying wait in the way to kill him.

4 But Festus answered, that Paul should be kept at Cesarea, and that he himself would depart shortly thither.

5 Let them therefore, said he, which among you are able, go down with me, and accuse this man, if there be any wickedness in him.

6 And when he had tarried among them more than ten days, he went down unto Cesarea; and the next day sitting on the judgment seat commanded Paul to be brought.

7 And when he was come, the Jews which came down from Jerusalem stood round about, and laid many and grievous complaints against Paul, which they could not prove.

8 While he answered for himself, Neither against the law of the Jews, neither against the temple, nor yet against Cesar, have I offended any thing at all.

9 But Festus, willing to do the Jews a pleas-

24. And after Paul had been kept some days in this gentle confinement at Cesarea, Felix, who had been absent for a short time, coming thither again, with Drusilla, his wife – The daughter of Herod Agrippa, one of the finest women of that age. Felix persuaded her to forsake her husband, Azizus, king of Emessa, and to be married to himself, though a heathen. She was afterward, with a son she had by Felix, consumed in an eruption of Mount Vesuvius. Concerning the faith in Christ – That is, the doctrine of Christ.

25. And as he reasoned of justice, temperance, and judgment to come – This was the only effectual way of preaching Christ to an unjust, lewd judge. Felix being terrified – How happily might this conviction have ended, had he been careful to pursue the views which were then opening upon his mind! But, like thousands, he deferred the consideration of these things to a more convenient season. A season which, alas! never came. For though he heard again, he was terrified no more. In the meantime we do not find Drusilla, though a Jewess, was thus alarmed. She had been used to hear of a future judgment: perhaps too she trusted to the being a daughter of Abraham, or to the expiation of the law, and so was proof against the convictions which seized on her husband, though a heathen. Let this teach us to guard against all such false dependencies as tend to elude those convictions that might otherwise be produced in us by the faithful preaching of the word of God. Let us stop our ears against those messengers of Satan, who appear as angels of light; who would teach us to reconcile the hope of salvation with a corrupt heart or an unholy life. Go thy way for this time – O how will every damned soul one day lament his having neglected such a time as this!

26. He hoped also – An evil hope: so when he heard his eye was not single. No marvel then that he profited nothing by all St. Paul's discourses: that money would be given – By the Christians for the liberty of so able a minister. And waiting for this, unhappy Felix fell short of the treasure of the Gospel.

27. But after two years – After St. Paul had been two years a prisoner, Felix desiring to gratify the Jews, left Paul bound – Thus men of the world, to gratify one another, stretch forth their hands to the things of God! Yet the wisdom of Felix did not profit him, did not satisfy the Jews at all. Their accusations followed him to Rome, and had utterly ruined him, but for the interest which his brother Pallas had with Nero.

ACTS 25

2. Then the high priest and the chief of the Jews appeared against Paul – In so long a time their rage was not cooled. So much louder a call had Paul to the Gentiles.

4. But Festus answered – So Festus's care to preserve the imperial privileges was the means of preserving Paul's life. By what invisible springs does God govern the world! With what silence, and yet with what wisdom and energy!

5. Let those of you who are able – Who are best able to undertake the journey, and to manage the cause. If there be any wickedness in him – So he does not pass sentence before he hears the cause.

6. Not more than ten days – A short space for a new governor to stay at such a city as Jerusalem. He could not with any convenience have heard and decided the cause of Paul within that time.

7. Bringing many accusations – When many accusations are heaped together, frequently not one of them is true.

8. While he answered – To a general charge a general answer was suf-

take its course. If he deserved death, he would accept the punishment. But if none of the things whereof they accused him were true, no man could deliver him unto them, with justice. Paul is neither released nor condemned. It is an instance of the slow steps which Providence takes; by which we are often made ashamed, both of our hopes and of our fears, and are kept waiting on God.

13-27 Agrippa had the government of Galilee. How many unjust and hasty judgments the Roman maxim, ver. 16 condemn! This heathen, guided only by the light of nature, followed law and custom exactly, yet how many Christians will not follow the rules of truth, justice, and charity, in judging their brethren! The questions about God's worship, the way of salvation, and the truths of the gospel, may appear doubtful and without interest, to worldly men and mere politicians. See how slightly this Roman speaks of Christ, and of the great controversy between the Jews and the Christians. But the day is at hand when Festus and the whole world will see, that all the concerns of the Roman empire were but trifles and of no consequence, compared with this question of Christ's resurrection. Those who have had means of instruction, and have despised them, will be awfully convinced of their sin and folly. Here was a noble assembly brought together to hear the truths of the gospel, though they only meant to gratify their curiosity by attending to the defense of a prisoner. Many, even now, attend at the places of hearing the word of God with "great pomp," and too often with no better motive than curiosity. And though ministers do not now stand as prisoners to make a defense for their lives, yet numbers affect to sit in judgment upon them, desirous to make them offenders for a word, rather than to learn from them the truth and will of God, for the salvation of their souls. But the pomp of this appearance was outshone by the real glory of the poor prisoner at the bar. What was the honor of their fine appearance, compared with that of Paul's wisdom, and grace, and holiness; his courage and constancy in suffering for Christ! It is no small mercy to have God clear up our righteousness as the light, and our just dealing as the noon-day; to have nothing certain laid to our charge. And God makes even the enemies of his people to do them right.

ACTS 26

Paul's defense before Agrippa. (1-11)

His conversion and preaching to the Gentiles. (12-23)

Festus and Agrippa convinced of Paul's innocence. (24-32)

does not matter what their will is; their wills shall be so moved and actuated by the providence of God that they shall cross each other's path, and Paul shall preach the gospel to Lydia. I wot it never entered into Lydia's heart, when she left Thyatira with her purple bales, that she was going to find Jesus Christ over at Philippi; neither did Paul guess, when he saw, in a vision, a man of Macedonia, and heard him say, "Come over into Macedonia, and help us," that the first person he would have to help would not be a man of Macedonia at all, but a woman of Thyatira and that the congregation he should preach to would be just a handful of women gathered by the side of the little stream that runs through Philippi. Neither Paul nor Lydia knew what God was about to do; but God knew. He understands the end from the beginning, and times his acts of providence to meet our deepest needs in the wisest way.

"His wisdom is sublime,
His heart profoundly kind;
God never is before his time,
And never is behind."

What an odd thing it seemed that this woman should be a woman of Thyatira in Asia, and Paul must not go and preach in Asia; and yet, when he comes to Macedonia, the first person who hears him is a woman of Asia! Why, you and I would have said, "If the woman belongs to Thyatira, let her stop at home, and let Paul go there; that is the shortest cut." Not so. The woman of Thyatira must go to Philippi, and Paul must go to Philippi too. This is God's plan; and if we knew all the circumstances as God knows them, we should doubtless admire the wisdom of it. Perhaps the very peculiarity of the circumstances made Paul more alert to seize the opportunity at Philippi than he would have been had he gone on to Thyatira; perhaps the isolation of the strange city made Lydia yearn more after spiritual things. God can answer a dozen ends by one act. One of our evangelists tells of a man who was converted in a small Irish town, and it was afterwards discovered that he, and the preacher who led him to Christ, resided but a few hundred yards from each other in London. They had never met in this great city, where neighbors are strangers to each other; nor was it likely that they ever would have been brought into contact with one another here; for the man, who was a commercial traveler, was too careless ever to attend a place of worship in London. But to sell his goods he went to Ireland, where, also, went the evangelist to preach the gospel; and being somewhat at a loss to know what to do with his time, he no sooner saw the name of a preacher from London announced, than he determined to attend the service, and there he met with Christ. We can see how natural this was in the case of which we know all the particulars, and it was doubtless as

ure, answered Paul, and said, Wilt thou go up to Jerusalem, and there be judged of these things before me?

10 Then said Paul, I stand at Cesar's judgment seat, where I ought to be judged: to the Jews have I done no wrong, as thou very well knowest.

11 For if I be an offender, or have committed any thing worthy of death, I refuse not to die: but if there be none of these things whereof these accuse me, no man may deliver me unto them. I appeal unto Cesar.

12 Then Festus, when he had conferred with the council, answered, Hast thou appealed unto Cesar? unto Cesar shalt thou go.

13 And after certain days king Agrippa and Bernice came unto Cesarea to salute Festus.

14 And when they had been there many days, Festus declared Paul's cause unto the king, saying, There is a certain man left in bonds by Felix:

15 About whom, when I was at Jerusalem, the chief priests and the elders of the Jews informed me, desiring to have judgment against him.

16 To whom I answered, It is not the manner of the Romans to deliver any man to die, before that he which is accused have the accusers face to face, and have license to answer for himself concerning the crime laid against him.

17 Therefore, when they were come hither, without any delay on the morrow I sat on the judgment seat, and commanded the man to be brought forth.

18 Against whom when the accusers stood up, they brought none accusation of such things as I supposed:

19 But had certain questions against him of their own superstition, and of one Jesus, which was dead, whom Paul affirmed to be alive.

20 And because I doubted of such manner of questions, I asked him whether he would go to Jerusalem, and there be judged of these matters.

21 But when Paul had appealed to be reserved unto the hearing of Augustus, I commanded him to be kept till I might send him to Cesar.

22 Then Agrippa said unto Festus, I would also hear the man myself. To morrow, said he, thou shalt hear him.

23 And on the morrow, when Agrippa was come, and Bernice, with great pomp, and was entered into the place of hearing, with the chief captains, and principal men of the city, at Festus' commandment Paul was brought forth.

24 And Festus said, King Agrippa, and all men which are here present with us, ye see this man, about whom all the multitude of the Jews have dealt with me, both at Jerusalem, and also here, crying that he ought not to live any longer.

ficient.

9. Art thou willing to go up to Jerusalem – Festus could have ordered this without asking Paul. But God secretly overruled the whole, that he might have an occasion of appealing to Rome.

10. I am standing at Cesar's judgment seat – For all the courts of the Roman governors were held in the name of the emperor, and by commission from him. No man can give me up – He expresses it modestly: the meaning is, Thou canst not. I appeal to Cesar – Which any Roman citizen might do before sentence was passed.

12. The council – It was customary for a considerable number of persons of distinction to attend the Roman governors. These constituted a kind of council, with whom they frequently advised.

13. Agrippa – The son of Herod Agrippa, chap. xii, 1; and Bernice – His sister, with whom he lived in a scandalous familiarity. This was the person whom Titus Vespasian so passionately loved, that he would have made her empress, had not the clamors of the Roman prevented it.

15. Desiring judgment against him – As upon a previous conviction, which they falsely pretended.

16. It is not the custom of the Romans – How excellent a rule, to condemn no one unheard! A rule, which as it is common to all nations, (courts of inquisition only excepted,) so it ought to direct our proceedings in all affairs, not only in public, but private life.

18. Such things as I supposed – From their passion and vehemence.

19. But had certain questions – How coldly does he mention the things of the last importance! And about one Jesus – Thus does Festus speak of him, to whom every knee shall bow! Whom Paul affirmed to be alive – And was this a doubtful question? But why, O Festus, didst thou doubt concerning it? Only because thou didst not search into the evidence of it. Otherwise that evidence might have opened to thee, till it had grown up into full conviction; and thy illustrious prisoner have led thee into the glorious liberty of the children of God.

23. With the tribunes and principal men of the city – The chief officers, both military and civil.

1-11 Christianity teaches us to give a reason of the hope that is in us, and also to give honor to whom honor is due, without flattery or fear of man. Agrippa was well versed in the Scriptures of the Old Testament, therefore could the better judge as to the controversy about Jesus being the Messiah. Surely ministers may expect, when they preach the faith of Christ, to be heard patiently. Paul professes that he still kept to all the good in which he was first educated and trained up. See here what his religion was. He was a moralist, a man of virtue, and had not learned the arts of the crafty, covetous Pharisees; he was not chargeable with any open vice and profaneness. He was sound in the faith. He always had a holy regard for the ancient promise made of God unto the fathers, and built his hope upon it. The apostle knew very well that all this would not justify him before God, yet he knew it was for his reputation among the Jews, and an argument that he was not such a man as they represented him to be. Though he counted this but loss, that he might win Christ, yet he mentioned it when it might serve to honor Christ. See here what Paul's religion is; he has not such zeal for the ceremonial law as he had in his youth; the sacrifices and offerings appointed by that, are done away by the great Sacrifice which they typified. Of the ceremonial cleansings he makes no conscience, and thinks the Levitical priesthood is done away in the priesthood of Christ; but, as to the main principles of his religion, he is as zealous as ever. Christ and heaven, are the two great doctrines of the gospel; that God has given to us eternal life, and this life is in his Son. These are the matter of the promise made unto the fathers. The temple service, or continual course of religious duties, day and night, was kept up as the profession of faith in the promise of eternal life, and in expectation of it. The prospect of eternal life should engage us to be diligent and steadfast in all religious exercises. Yet the Sadducees hated Paul for preaching the resurrection; and the other Jews joined them, because he testified that Jesus was risen, and was the promised Redeemer of Israel. Many things are thought to be beyond belief, only because the infinite nature and perfections of Him that has revealed, performed, or promised them, are overlooked. Paul acknowledged, that while he continued a Pharisee, he was a bitter enemy to Christianity. This was his character and manner of life in the beginning of his time; and there was every thing to hinder his being a Christian. Those who have been most strict in their conduct before conversion, will afterwards see abundant reason for humbling themselves, even on account of things which they then thought ought to have been done.

12-23 Paul was made a Christian by Divine power; by a revelation of Christ both to him and in him;

well arranged in the case of Lydia and Paul.

Now, I should not wonder tonight if there are a number of providences that have worked together to bring some of my hearers into their places at this time. What brought you to London, friend? It was not your intention to be in this city. Coming to London, what brought you to this part of it? What led you to be at this service? And why was it that you did not come on one of the Sundays when the preacher would have been here if he could, but could not be here by reason of his weakness? Because, it may be, that only from these lips can the word come to you, and only tonight, and you must come to this place. Perhaps there is some one who preaches the gospel much better in the town where you live; or, peradventure, you have had opportunities of hearing the same preacher near your own door, and you did not avail yourself of them; and yet God has brought you here. I wish we watched providences more. "Whoso is wise, and will observe these things, even they shall understand the loving kindness of the Lord." If the Lord should meet with you, and convert you tonight, I will warrant you that you will be a believer in providence, and say, "Yes, God guided my steps. He directed my path, and he brought me to the spot where Jesus met with me, and opened my heart that I might receive the gospel of his grace." Be of good courage, you ministers of the gospel! Providence is always working with you while you are working for God. I have often admired the language of Mahomet, when in the battle of Ohod he said to his followers, pointing to their foes, "Charge them! I can hear the wings of the angels as they hasten to our help." That was a delusion on his part, for he and his men were badly beaten; but it is no delusion in the case of the servants of Christ. We can hear the wings of the angels. We may hear the grinding of the great wheels of providence as they revolve for the help of the preacher of the gospel. Everything is with us when we are with God. Who can be against us? The stars in their courses fight for the servants of God; and all things, great and small, shall bow before the feet of him who trod the waves of the Sea of Galilee, and still is Master of all things, and ruleth all things to the accomplishment of his diving purposes.

So much, then, for the working of providence.

II. The next thing is, THE WORKING OF LYDIA. God's intention is that Lydia shall be saved. Yet, you know, no woman was ever saved against her will. God makes us willing in the day of his power, and it is the way of his grace not to violate the will, but sweetly to overcome it. Never will there be anybody dragged to heaven by the ears: depend upon that. We shall go there with all our hearts and all our desires. What, then, was Lydia doing?

25 But when I found that he had committed nothing worthy of death, and that he himself hath appealed to Augustus, I have determined to send him.

26 Of whom I have no certain thing to write unto my lord. Wherefore I have brought him forth before you, and specially before thee, O king Agrippa, that, after examination had, I might have somewhat to write.

27 For it seemeth to me unreasonable to send a prisoner, and not withal to signify the crimes laid against him.

ACTS 26

1 Then Agrippa said unto Paul, Thou art permitted to speak for thyself. Then Paul stretched forth the hand, and answered for himself:

2 I think myself happy, king Agrippa, because I shall answer for myself this day before thee touching all the things whereof I am accused of the Jews:

3 Especially because I know thee to be expert in all customs and questions which are among the Jews: wherefore I beseech thee to hear me patiently.

4 My manner of life from my youth, which was at the first among mine own nation at Jerusalem, know all the Jews;

5 Which knew me from the beginning, if they would testify, that after the most straitest sect of our religion I lived a Pharisee.

6 And now I stand and am judged for the hope of the promise made of God unto our fathers:

7 Unto which promise our twelve tribes, instantly serving God day and night, hope to come. For which hope's sake, king Agrippa, I am accused of the Jews.

8 Why should it be thought a thing incredible with you, that God should raise the dead?

9 I verily thought with myself, that I ought to do many things contrary to the name of Jesus of Nazareth.

10 Which thing I also did in Jerusalem: and many of the saints did I shut up in prison, having received authority from the chief priests; and when they were put to death, I gave my voice against them.

11 And I punished them oft in every synagogue, and compelled them to blaspheme; and being exceedingly mad against them, I persecuted them even unto strange cities.

12 Whereupon as I went to Damascus with authority and commission from the chief priests,

13 At midday, O king, I saw in the way a light from heaven, above the brightness of the sun, shining round about me and them which journeyed with me.

14 And when we were all fallen to the earth, I heard a voice speaking unto me, and saying in the Hebrew tongue, Saul, Saul, why persecutest thou me? it is hard for thee to kick

ACTS 26

And Paul stretching forth his hand – Chained as it was: a decent expression of his own earnestness, and proper to engage the attention of his hearers; answered for himself – Not only refuting the accusations of the Jews, but enlarging upon the faith of the Gospel.

2. King Agrippa – There is a peculiar force in thus addressing a person by name. Agrippa felt this.

3. Who art accurately acquainted – Which Festus was not; with the customs – In practical matters; and questions – In speculative. This word Festus had used in the absence of Paul, chap. xxv, 19, who, by the Divine leading, repeats and explains it. Agrippa had had peculiar advantages for an accurate knowledge of the Jewish customs and questions, from his education under his father Herod, and his long abode at Jerusalem. Nothing can be imagined more suitable or more graceful, than this whole discourse of Paul before Agrippa; in which the seriousness of the Christian, the boldness of the apostle, and the politeness of the gentleman and the scholar, appear in a most beautiful contrast, or rather a most happy union.

4. From my youth, which was from the beginning – That is, which was from the beginning of my youth.

5. If they would testify – But they would not, for they well knew what weight his former life must add to his present testimony.

6. And now – This and the two following verses are in a kind of ver. 6, 7, 8 parenthesis, and show that what the Pharisees rightly taught concerning the resurrection, Paul likewise asserted at this day. The ninth verse is connected with the fifth. For Pharisaism ver. 9, 5 impelled him to persecute. I stand in judgment for the hope of the promise – Of the resurrection. So it was in effect. For unless Christ had risen, there could have been no resurrection of the dead. And it was chiefly for testifying the resurrection of Christ, that the Jews still persecuted him.

7. Our twelve tribes – For a great part of the ten tribes also had at various times returned from the east to their own country, James i, 1; 1 Pet. i, 1. Worshipping continually night and day – That is, this is what they aim at in all their public and private worship.

8. Is it judged by you an incredible thing – It was by Festus, chap. xxv, 19, to whom Paul answers as if he had heard him discourse.

9. I thought – When I was a Pharisee: that I ought to do many things – Which he now enumerates.

10. I shut up many of the saints – Men not only innocent, but good, just, holy. I gave my vote against them – That is, I joined with those who condemned them. Perhaps the chief priests did also give him power to vote on these occasions.

11. I compelled them – That is, some of them; to blaspheme – This is the most dreadful of all! Repent, ye enemies of the Gospel. If Spira, who was compelled, suffered so terribly, what will become of those who compel, like Saul, but do not repent like him.

12. Acts ix, 2.

13. O King – Most seasonably, in the height of the narration, does he thus fix the king's attention. Above the brightness of the sun – And no marvel. For what is the brightness of this created sun, to the Sun of righteousness, the brightness of the Father's glory?

14. In the Hebrew tongue – St. Paul was not now speaking in Hebrew: when he was, chap. xxiii, 7, he did not add, In the Hebrew tongue. Christ used this tongue both on earth and from heaven.

17. Delivering thee from the people – The Jews and the Gentiles, to whom, both Jews and Gentiles, I now send thee – Paul gives them to know, that the liberty he enjoys even in bonds, was promised to

MATTHEW HENRY   CHARLES H. SPURGEON

when in the full career of his sin. He was made a minister by Divine authority: the same Jesus who appeared to him in that glorious light, ordered him to preach the gospel to the Gentiles. A world that sits in darkness must be enlightened; those must be brought to know the things that belong to their everlasting peace, who are yet ignorant of them. A world that lies in wickedness must be sanctified and reformed; it is not enough for them to have their eyes opened, they must have their hearts renewed; not enough to be turned from darkness to light, but they must be turned from the power of Satan unto God. All who are turned from sin to God, are not only pardoned, but have a grant of a rich inheritance. The forgiveness of sins makes way for this. None can be happy who are not holy; and to be saints in heaven we must be first saints on earth. We are made holy, and saved by faith in Christ; by which we rely upon Christ as the Lord our Righteousness, and give up ourselves to him as the Lord our Ruler; by this we receive the remission of sins, the gift of the Holy Ghost, and eternal life. The cross of Christ was a stumbling-block to the Jews, and they were in a rage at Paul's preaching the fulfilling of the Old Testament predictions. Christ should be the first that should rise from the dead; the Head or principal One. Also, it was foretold by the prophets, that the Gentiles should be brought to the knowledge of God by the Messiah; and what in this could the Jews justly be displeased at? Thus the true convert can give a reason of his hope, and a good account of the change manifest in him. Yet for going about and calling on men thus to repent and to be converted, vast numbers have been blamed and persecuted.

24-32 It becomes us, on all occasions, to speak the words of truth and soberness, and then we need not be troubled at the unjust censures of men. Active and laborious followers of the gospel often have been despised as dreamers or madmen, for believing such doctrines and such wonderful facts; and for attesting that the same faith and diligence, and an experience like their own, are necessary to all men, whatever their rank, in order to their salvation. But apostles and prophets, and the Son of God himself, were exposed to this charge; and none need be moved thereby, when Divine grace has made them wise unto salvation. Agrippa saw a great deal of reason for Christianity. His understanding and judgment were for the time convinced, but his heart was not changed. And his conduct and temper were widely different from the humility and spirituality of the gospel. Many are almost persuaded to be religious, who are not quite persuaded; they are under strong convictions of their duty, and of the excellence of the ways of God, yet do not pursue their convictions. Paul urged that it was the concern of every one to

Having by God's grace been made willing, the first thing was that she kept the Sabbath. She was a proselyte, and she kept the seventh day. She was away from Thyatira, and nobody would know what she would do, yet she observed the Lord's-day carefully. She was abroad when she was at Philippi, but she had not left God behind her. I have known some English people, when they once reached the Continent, go rattling along, Sundays and week-days, as if God did not live on the Continent, and as if at home they only observed the Sabbath because they happened to be in England, which is very probably the case with a good many. When they get away they say, "When you are at Rome, you must do as Rome does;" and so they take their pleasure on God's day. It was not so with Lydia. There was no selling of purple that day; she regarded the Sabbath. Oh, I would to God that every one would regard the Sabbath! May God grant that it may never be taken away from us! There is a plot now to make some of you work all the seven days of the week, and you will not get any more pay for seven days than you get for six. Stand out against it, and preserve your right to rest upon God's day. The observance of one day in seven as a day of rest materially helps towards the conversion of men, because then they are inclined to think. They have the opportunity to hear, and, if they choose to avail themselves of it, the probabilities are that God will bless the hearing, and they will be saved.

Now, notice next that, not only did Lydia observe the Sabbath, but she went up to the place of worship. It was not a very fine place. I do not suppose there was any building. It may have been a little temporary oratory put up by the river side; but very probably it was just on the bank of the river that they met together. It does not appear that there were any men, but only a few women. They only held a prayer-meeting: "where prayer was wont to be made." But Lydia did not stop away from the gathering. She might easily have excused herself after her long journey, and the wearying work of setting up a new establishment; but her heart was in this matter, and so she found it no drudgery to meet where prayer was offered. She did not say "I can read a sermon at home," or, "I can read in the Book of the Law indoors." She wished to be where God's people were, however few, or however poor they might be. She did not go to the gorgeous heathen temple at Philippi, but she sought out the few faithful ones that met to worship the true God. Now, dear friends, do the same. You that are not converted, still attend the means of grace, and do not go to a place simply because it is a fine building, and because there is a crowd, but go where they are truly worshiping God in spirit and in truth. If they should happen to be very few and very poor, yet go with them, for

against the pricks.

15 And I said, Who art thou, Lord? And he said, I am Jesus whom thou persecutest.

16 But rise, and stand upon thy feet: for I have appeared unto thee for this purpose, to make thee a minister and a witness both of these things which thou hast seen, and of those things in the which I will appear unto thee;

17 Delivering thee from the people, and from the Gentiles, unto whom now I send thee,

18 To open their eyes, and to turn them from darkness to light, and from the power of Satan unto God, that they may receive forgiveness of sins, and inheritance among them which are sanctified by faith that is in me.

19 Whereupon, O king Agrippa, I was not disobedient unto the heavenly vision:

20 But shewed first unto them of Damascus, and at Jerusalem, and throughout all the coasts of Judea, and then to the Gentiles, that they should repent and turn to God, and do works meet for repentance.

21 For these causes the Jews caught me in the temple, and went about to kill me.

22 Having therefore obtained help of God, I continue unto this day, witnessing both to small and great, saying none other things than those which the prophets and Moses did say should come:

23 That Christ should suffer, and that he should be the first that should rise from the dead, and should shew light unto the people, and to the Gentiles.

24 And as he thus spake for himself, Festus said with a loud voice, Paul, thou art beside thyself; much learning doth make thee mad.

25 But he said, I am not mad, most noble Festus; but speak forth the words of truth and soberness.

26 For the king knoweth of these things, before whom also I speak freely: for I am persuaded that none of these things are hidden from him; for this thing was not done in a corner.

27 King Agrippa, believest thou the prophets? I know that thou believest.

28 Then Agrippa said unto Paul, Almost thou persuadest me to be a Christian.

29 And Paul said, I would to God, that not only thou, but also all that hear me this day, were both almost, and altogether such as I am, except these bonds.

30 And when he had thus spoken, the king rose up, and the governor, and Bernice, and they that sat with them:

31 And when they were gone aside, they talked between themselves, saying, This man doeth nothing worthy of death or of bonds.

32 Then said Agrippa unto Festus, This man might have been set at liberty, if he had not appealed unto Cesar.

him, as well as his preaching to the Gentiles. I, denotes the authority of the sender. Now, the time whence his mission was dated. For his apostleship, as well as his conversion, commenced at this moment.

18. To open – He opens them, who sends Paul; and he does it by Paul who is sent; their eyes – Both of the Jews and Gentiles: that they may turn – Through the power of the Almighty, from the spiritual darkness wherein they were involved, to the light of Divine knowledge and holiness, and from the power of Satan, who now holds them in sin, guilt, and misery, to the love and happy service of God: that they may receive through faith – (He seems to place the same blessings in a fuller light,) pardon, holiness, and glory.

19. From that time – Having received power to obey, I was not disobedient – I did obey, I used that power, Gal. i, 16. So that even this grace whereby St Paul was influenced was not irresistible.

20. I declared – From that hour to this, both to Jew and Gentile, that they should repent – This repentance, we may observe, is previous both to inward and outward holiness.

21. For these things – The apostle now applies all that he had said.

22. Having obtained help from God – When all other help failed, God sent the Romans from the castle, and so fulfilled the promise he had made, ver. 17.

24. Festus said, Paul, thou art beside thyself – To talk of men's rising from the dead! And of a Jew's enlightening not only his own nation, but the polite and learned Greeks and Romans! Nay, Festus, it is thou that art beside thyself. That strikest quite wide of the mark. And no wonder: he saw that nature did not act in Paul; but the grace that acted in him he did not see. And therefore he took all this ardor which animated the apostle for a mere start of learned frenzy.

25. I am not mad, most excellent Festus – The style properly belonging to a Roman propretor. How inexpressibly beautiful is this reply! How strong! yet how decent and respectful! Mad men seldom call men by their names, and titles of honor. Thus also St. Paul refutes the charge. But utter the words of truth (confirmed in the next verse) and sobriety – The very reverse of madness. And both these remain, even when the men of God act with the utmost vehemence.

26. For the king knoweth of these things – St. Paul having refuted Festus, pursues his purpose, returning naturally, and as it were, step by step, from Festus to Agrippa. To whom I speak with freedom – This freedom was probably one circumstance which Festus accounted madness.

27. King Agrippa, believest thou the prophets? – He that believes these, believes Paul, yea, and Christ. The apostle now comes close to his heart. What did Agrippa feel when he heard this? I know that thou believest! – Here Paul lays so fast hold on the king that he can scarce make any resistance.

28. Then Agrippa said unto Paul, Almost thou persuadest me to be a Christian! – See here, Festus altogether a heathen, Paul altogether a Christian, Agrippa halting between both. Poor Agrippa! But almost persuaded! So near the mark, and yet fall short! Another step, and thou art within the veil. Reader, stop not with Agrippa; but go on with Paul.

29. I would to God – Agrippa had spoke of being a Christian, as a thing wholly in his own power. Paul gently corrects this mistake; intimating, it is the gift and the work of God; that all that hear me – It was modesty in St. Paul, not to apply directly to them all; yet he looks upon them and observes them; were such as I am – Christians indeed; full of righteousness, peace, and joy in the Holy Ghost. He

become a true Christian; that there is grace enough in Christ for all. He expressed his full conviction of the truth of the gospel, the absolute necessity of faith in Christ in order to salvation. Such salvation from such bondage, the gospel of Christ offers to the Gentiles; to a lost world. Yet it is with much difficulty that any person can be persuaded he needs a work of grace on his heart, like that which was needful for the conversion of the Gentiles. Let us beware of fatal hesitation in our own conduct; and recollect how far the being almost persuaded to be a Christian, is from being altogether such a one as every true believer is.

ACTS 27

Paul's voyage towards Rome. (1-11)
Paul and his companions endangered by a tempest.
(12-20)
He receives a Divine assurance of safety. (21-29)
Paul encourages those with him. (30-38)
They are shipwrecked. (39-44)

1-11 It was determined by the counsel of God, before it was determined by the counsel of Festus, that Paul should go to Rome; for God had work for him to do there. The course they steered, and the places they touched at, are here set down. And God here encourages those who suffer for him, to trust in him; for he can put it into the hearts of those to befriend them, from whom they least expect it. Sailors must make the best of the wind: and so must we all in our passage over the ocean of this world. When the winds are contrary, yet we must be getting forward as well as we can. Many who are not driven backward by cross providences, do not get forward by favorable providences. And many real Christians complain as to the concerns of their souls, that they have much ado to keep their ground. Every fair haven is not a safe haven. Many show respect to good ministers, who will not take their advice. But the event will convince sinners of the vanity of their hopes, and the folly of their conduct.

12-20 Those who launch forth on the ocean of this world, with a fair gale, know not what storms they may meet with; and therefore must not easily take it for granted that they have obtained their purpose. Let us never expect to be quite safe till we enter heaven. They saw neither sun nor stars for many days. Thus melancholy sometimes is the condition of the people of God as to their spiritual matters; they walk in darkness, and have no light. See what the wealth of this world is: though coveted as a blessing, the time may come when it will be a burden; not only too heavy to be carried safely, but heavy enough to sink him that has it. The children of this world can be prodigal of their

in so doing you are in the way of blessing. I think you will yet have to say, "Being in the way, God met with me." If it is what some call "only a prayer-meeting", you will do well to go. Some of the best blessings that men have ever gained have been received at prayer-meetings. If we would meet with God, let us seek him diligently, "not forsaking the assembling of ourselves together, as the manner of some is." Though you cannot save yourself, or open your own heart, you can at least do what Lydia did: observe the Sabbath, and gather together with God's people.

Lydia being there with the assembly, when Paul began to speak, we find that she attended to the things that were spoken, which is another thing that we can do. It is very ill when people come up to the house of God, and do not attend. I have never had to complain of people not attending in this house since the day I first preached in it; but I have been in places of worship where there seemed to be anything but attention. How can it be expected that there will be a blessing when the pew becomes a place to slumber in, or when the mind is active over the farm, or in the kitchen, or in the shop, forgetting altogether the gospel which is being preached to the outward ear? If you want a blessing, attend with all your might to the word that is preached; but of that we will speak more by-and-by.

So far we have spoken upon the working of providence and the working of Lydia.

III. Now, next, THE WORKING OF PAUL; for this was necessary too. In order to the conversion of men, it is necessary that the person who aims at their conversion should work as if it all depended upon him, though he knows that he cannot accomplish the work. We are to seek to win souls with as much earnestness, and prudence, and zeal, as if everything depended upon ourselves; and then we are to leave all with God, knowing that none but the Lord can save a single soul.

Now, notice, Paul, wishing for converts, is judicious in the choice of the place where he will go to look after them. He goes to the spot where there should be a synagogue. He thinks that where people have a desire to pray, there he will find the kind of people who will be ready to hear the word. So he selects devout people, devout worshipers of the one God, that he may go and speak to them about Christ. It is sometimes our plain duty to publish the word from the housetop to the careless crowd; but I think you will generally find that more success comes when those, on whose hearts the Spirit of God has already begun to work, are sought out and instructed. When Christ sent out his disciples on their first journey, he told them, when they entered a town, to "Inquire who in it is worthy; and there abide till ye go thence;" evi-

ACTS 27

1 And when it was determined that we should sail into Italy, they delivered Paul and certain other prisoners unto one named Julius, a centurion of Augustus' band.

2 And entering into a ship of Adramyttium, we launched, meaning to sail by the coasts of Asia; one Aristarchus, a Macedonian of Thessalonica, being with us.

3 And the next day we touched at Sidon. And Julius courteously entreated Paul, and gave him liberty to go unto his friends to refresh himself.

4 And when we had launched from thence, we sailed under Cyprus, because the winds were contrary.

5 And when we had sailed over the sea of Cilicia and Pamphylia, we came to Myra, a city of Lycia.

6 And there the centurion found a ship of Alexandria sailing into Italy; and he put us therein.

7 And when we had sailed slowly many days, and scarce were come over against Cnidus, the wind not suffering us, we sailed under Crete, over against Salmone;

8 And, hardly passing it, came unto a place which is called The fair havens; nigh whereunto was the city of Lasea.

9 Now when much time was spent, and when sailing was now dangerous, because the fast was now already past, Paul admonished them,

10 And said unto them, Sirs, I perceive that this voyage will be with hurt and much damage, not only of the lading and ship, but also of our lives.

11 Nevertheless the centurion believed the master and the owner of the ship, more than those things which were spoken by Paul.

12 And because the haven was not commodious to winter in, the more part advised to depart thence also, if by any means they might attain to Phenice, and there to winter; which is an haven of Crete, and lieth toward the south west and north west.

13 And when the south wind blew softly, supposing that they had obtained their purpose, loosing thence, they sailed close by Crete.

14 But not long after there arose against it a tempestuous wind, called Euroclydon.

15 And when the ship was caught, and could not bear up into the wind, we let her drive.

16 And running under a certain island which is called Clauda, we had much work to come by the boat:

17 Which when they had taken up, they used helps, undergirding the ship; and, fearing lest they should fall into the quicksands, strake sail, and so were driven.

18 And we being exceedingly tossed with a tempest, the next day they lightened the ship;

19 And the third day we cast out with our own hands the tackling of the ship.

20 And when neither sun nor stars in many

speaks from a full sense of his own happiness, and an overflowing love to all.

30. And as he said this, the king rose up – An unspeakably precious moment to Agrippa. Whether he duly improved it or no, we shall see in that day.

31. This man doth nothing worthy of death, or of bonds – They speak of his whole life, not of one action only. And could ye learn nothing more than this from that discourse? A favorable judgment of such a preacher, is not all that God requires.

ACTS 27

1. As soon as it was determined to sail – As being a shorter and less expensive passage to Rome.

2. Adramyttium – was a sea port of Mysia. Aristarchus and Luke went with Paul by choice, not being ashamed of his bonds.

3. Julius treating Paul courteously – Perhaps he had heard him make his defense.

4. We sailed under Cyprus – Leaving it on the left hand.

7. Cnidus – was a cape and city of Caria.

8. The Fair Havens still retain the name. But the city of Lasea is now utterly lost, together with many more of the hundred cities for which Crete was once so renowned.

9. The fast, or day of atonement, was kept on the tenth of Tisri, that is, the 25th of September. This was to them an ill time of sailing; not only because winter was approaching, but also because of the sudden storms, which are still common in the Mediterranean at that time of the year. Paul exhorted them – Not to leave Crete. Even in external things, faith exerts itself with the greatest presence of mind, and readiness of advice.

10. Saying to them – To the centurion and other officers.

11. The centurion regarded the master – And indeed it is a general rule, believe an artificer in his own art. Yet when there is the greatest need, a real Christian will often advise even better than him.

12. Which is a haven – Having a double opening, one to the southwest, the other to the northwest.

14. There arose against it – The south wind; a tempestuous wind, called in those parts Euroclydon. This was a kind of hurricane, not carrying them any one way, but tossing them backward and forward. These furious winds are now called levanters, and blow in all directions from the northeast to the southeast.

16. We were hardly able to get masters of the boat – To prevent its being staved.

18. They lightened the ship – Casting the heavy goods into the sea.

19. We cast out the tackling of the ship – Cutting away even those masts that were not absolutely necessary.

20. Neither sun nor stars appeared for many days – Which they could the less spare, before the compass was found out.

21. This loss – Which is before your eyes.

23. The God whose I am, and whom I serve – How short a compendium of religion! Yet how full! Comprehending both faith, hope, and love.

24. God hath given – Paul had prayed for them. And God gave him their lives; perhaps their souls also. And the centurion, subserving the providence of God, gave to Paul the lives of the prisoners. How wonderfully does his providence reign in the most contingent things! And rather will many bad men be preserved with a few good,

goods for the saving their lives, yet are sparing of them in works of piety and charity, and in suffering for Christ. Any man will rather make shipwreck of his goods than of his life; but many rather make shipwreck of faith and a good conscience, than of their goods. The means the sailors used did not succeed; but when sinners give up all hope of saving themselves, they are prepared to understand God's word, and to trust in his mercy through Jesus Christ.

21-29 They did not hearken to the apostle when he warned them of their danger; yet if they acknowledge their folly, and repent of it, he will speak comfort and relief to them when in danger. Most people bring themselves into trouble, because they do not know when they are well off; they come to harm and loss by aiming to mend their condition, often against advice. Observe the solemn profession Paul made of relation to God. No storms or tempests can hinder God's favor to his people, for he is a Help always at hand. It is a comfort to the faithful servants of God when in difficulties, that as long as the Lord has any work for them to do, their lives shall be prolonged. If Paul had thrust himself needlessly into bad company, he might justly have been cast away with them; but God calling him into it, they are preserved with him. They are given thee; there is no greater satisfaction to a good man than to know he is a public blessing. He comforts them with the same comforts wherewith he himself was comforted. God is ever faithful, therefore let all who have an interest in his promises be ever cheerful. As, with God, saying and doing are not two things, believing and enjoying should not be so with us. Hope is an anchor of the soul, sure and steadfast, entering into that within the veil. Let those who are in spiritual darkness hold fast by that, and think not of putting to sea again, but abide by Christ, and wait till the day break, and the shadows flee away.

30-38 God, who appointed the end, that they should be saved, appointed the means, that they should be saved by the help of these shipmen. Duty is ours, events are God's; we do not trust God, but tempt him, when we say we put ourselves under his protection, if we do not use proper means, such as are within our power, for our safety. But how selfish are men in general, often even ready to seek their own safety by the destruction of others! Happy those who have such a one as Paul in their company, who not only had intercourse with Heaven, but was of an enlivening spirit to those about him. The sorrow of the world works death, while joy in God is life and peace in the greatest distresses and dangers. The comfort of God's promises can only be ours by believing dependence on him, to fulfill his word to us; and

dently showing that, even amongst those who do not know the truth, there are some whose hearts are prepared to receive it, who are of a devout spirit, and in that sense are worthy. These are the people who should first be sought after. In the same limited sense was Cornelius, to whom Peter was sent, worthy to hear the glad tidings of great joy. His reverent spirit was well pleasing to God; for we read, "Thy prayer is heard, and thine alms are had in remembrance in the sight of God." We must not, of course, think that these things give any claim to salvation; but rather that they are the expression of hearts prepared to receive the message of salvation, seeking the Lord, "if haply they might feel after him, and find him." One of our greatest difficulties in these days is, that so many have lost all reverence for authority of any kind, even God's: having risen against human despotism, they also foolishly try to break God's bands asunder. We are cast back on the infinite power of God when we come to deal with such people; but when we meet with others who are willing to listen and pray, we know that God has already begun to work. Now, dear worker, choose the person who is evidently pointed out to you by God's gracious providence. Choose judiciously, and try to speak with those with whom you may hopefully speak, and trust that God will bless the word.

I am sure Paul's talk would aim straight at the center of the target: it was evidently addressed to the heart, for we are told that it was with the heart Lydia heard it. There would be sure to be many such that day in that earnest simple talk by the river side. Let us multiply such conversations, if we would win more Lydias for the church.

IV. But, now, fourthly—and here is the main point—let us notice THE WORKING OF THE SPIRIT OF GOD. Providence brings Paul and Lydia together. Lydia comes there because she observes the Sabbath, and loves the place of worship. Paul comes there because he loves to win souls, and, like his Master, is on the watch for stray sheep. But it would have been a poor meeting for them if the Spirit of God had not been there also. So we next read of Lydia: "Whose heart the Lord opened, that she attended unto the things which were spoken of Paul." It is not wonderful that the Lord can open a human heart; for he who made the lock knows well what key will fit it. What means he made use of in the case of Lydia, I do not know; but I will tell you what might have happened. Perhaps she had lost her husband; many a woman's heart has been opened by that great gash. The joy of her soul has been taken away, and she has turned to God. Perhaps her husband was spared to her; but she had lost a child. Oh, how many a babe has been sent here on purpose to entice its mother to the skies; a lamb taken away

days appeared, and no small tempest lay on us, all hope that we should be saved was then taken away.

21 But after long abstinence Paul stood forth in the midst of them, and said, Sirs, ye should have hearkened unto me, and not have loosed from Crete, and to have gained this harm and loss.

22 And now I exhort you to be of good cheer: for there shall be no loss of any man's life among you, but of the ship.

23 For there stood by me this night the angel of God, whose I am, and whom I serve,

24 Saying, Fear not, Paul; thou must be brought before Cesar: and, lo, God hath given thee all them that sail with thee.

25 Wherefore, sirs, be of good cheer: for I believe God, that it shall be even as it was told me.

26 Howbeit we must be cast upon a certain island.

27 But when the fourteenth night was come, as we were driven up and down in Adria, about midnight the shipmen deemed that they drew near to some country;

28 And sounded, and found it twenty fathoms: and when they had gone a little further, they sounded again, and found it fifteen fathoms.

29 Then fearing lest we should have fallen upon rocks, they cast four anchors out of the stern, and wished for the day.

30 And as the shipmen were about to flee out of the ship, when they had let down the boat into the sea, under color as though they would have cast anchors out of the foreship,

31 Paul said to the centurion and to the soldiers, Except these abide in the ship, ye cannot be saved.

32 Then the soldiers cut off the ropes of the boat, and let her fall off.

33 And while the day was coming on, Paul besought them all to take meat, saying, This day is the fourteenth day that ye have tarried and continued fasting, having taken nothing.

34 Wherefore I pray you to take some meat: for this is for your health: for there shall not an hair fall from the head of any of you.

35 And when he had thus spoken, he took bread, and gave thanks to God in presence of them all: and when he had broken it, he began to eat.

36 Then were they all of good cheer, and they also took some meat.

37 And we were in all in the ship two hundred threescore and sixteen souls.

38 And when they had eaten enough, they lightened the ship, and cast out the wheat into the sea.

39 And when it was day, they knew not the land: but they discovered a certain creek with a shore, into the which they were minded, if it were possible, to thrust in the ship.

40 And when they had taken up the anchors, they committed themselves unto the sea, and loosed the rudder bands, and hoised up the

(so it frequently happens,) than one good man perish with many bad. So it was in this ship: so it is in the world. Thee – At such a time as this, there was not the same danger, which might otherwise have been, of St. Paul's seeming to speak out of vanity, what he really spoke out of necessity. All the souls – Not only all the prisoners, as Julius afterward did, ver. 43; ask for souls, they shall be given thee: yea, more than thou hopest for, that sail with thee – So that Paul, in the sight of God, was the master and pilot of the ship.

27. The fourteenth night – Since they left Crete, ver. 18, 19. In the Adriatic sea – So the ancients called all that part of the Mediterranean, which lay south of Italy.

30. The sailors were attempting to flee out of the ship – Supposing the boat would go more safely over the shallows.

31. Unless these mariners abide in the ship – Without them ye know not how to manage her, ye cannot be saved – He does not say we. That they would not have regarded. The soldiers were not careful for the lives of the prisoners: nor was Paul careful for his own. We may learn hence, to use the most proper means for security and success, even while we depend on Divine Providence, and wait for the accomplishment of God's own promise. He never designed any promise should encourage rational creatures to act in an irrational manner; or to remain inactive, when he has given them natural capacities of doing something, at least, for their own benefit. To expect the accomplishment of any promise, without exerting these, is at best vain and dangerous presumption, if all pretense of relying upon it be not profane hypocrisy.

33. Ye continue fasting, having taken nothing – No regular meal, through a deep sense of their extreme danger. Let us not wonder then, if men who have a deep sense of their extreme danger of everlasting death, for a time forget even to eat their bread, or to attend to their worldly affairs. Much less let us censure that as madness, which may be the beginning of true wisdom.

34. This is for your preservation – That ye may be the better able to swim to shore.

36. Then they were all encouraged – By his example, as well as words.

38. Casting out the wheat – So firmly did they now depend on what St. Paul had said.

39. They did not know the land – Which they saw near them: having a level shore.

40. Loosing the rudder bands – Their ships had frequently two rudders, one on each side. They were fastened while they let the ship drive; but were now loosened, when they had need of them to steer her into the creek.

41. A place where two seas met – Probably by reason of a sand bank running parallel with the shore.

42. The counsel – Cruel, unjust, ungrateful.

44. They all escaped safe to land – And some of them doubtless received the apostle as a teacher sent from God. These would find their deliverance from the fury of the sea, but an earnest of an infinitely greater deliverance, and are long ere this lodged with him in a more peaceful harbor than Malta, or than the earth could afford.

ACTS 28

1. Melita or Malta, is about twelve miles broad, twenty long, and sixty distant from Sicily to the south. It yields abundance of honey,

the salvation he reveals must be waited for in use of the means he appoints. If God has chosen us to salvation, he has also appointed that we shall obtain it by repentance, faith, prayer, and persevering obedience; it is fatal presumption to expect it in any other way. It is an encouragement to people to commit themselves to Christ as their Savior, when those who invite them, clearly show that they do so themselves.

39-44 The ship that had weathered the storm in the open sea, where it had room, is dashed to pieces when it sticks fast. Thus, if the heart fixes in the world in affection, and cleaving to it, it is lost. Satan's temptations beat against it, and it is gone; but as long as it keeps above the world, though tossed with cares and tumults, there is hope for it. They had the shore in view, yet suffered shipwreck in the harbor; thus we are taught never to be secure. Though there is great difficulty in the way of the promised salvation, it shall, without fail, be brought to pass. It will come to pass that whatever the trials and dangers may be, in due time all believers will get safely to heaven. Lord Jesus, thou hast assured us that none of thine shall perish. Thou wilt bring them all safe to the heavenly shore. And what a pleasing landing will that be! Thou wilt present them to thy Father, and give thy Holy Spirit full possession of them for ever.

ACTS 28

Paul kindly received at Melita. (1-10)
He arrives at Rome. (11-16)
His conference with the Jews. (17-22)
Paul preaches to the Jews, and abides at Rome a prisoner. (23-31)

1-10 God can make strangers to be friends; friends in distress. Those who are despised for homely manners, are often more friendly than the more polished; and the conduct of heathens, or persons called barbarians, condemns many in civilized nations, professing to be Christians. The people thought that Paul was a murderer, and that the viper was sent by Divine justice, to be the avenger of blood. They knew that there is a God who governs the world, so that things do not come to pass by chance, no, not the smallest event, but all by Divine direction; and that evil pursues sinners; that there are good works which God will reward, and wicked works which he will punish. Also, that murder is a dreadful crime, one which shall not long go unpunished. But they thought all wicked people were punished in this life. Though some are made examples in this world, to prove that there is a God and a Providence, yet many are left unpunished, to prove that there is a judgment to come. They also thought all who were remarkably afflict-

that the sheep might follow the Shepherd! Perhaps she had had bad trade; the price of purple may have fallen. She may have been half afraid she would fail in business. I have known such trouble open some people's hearts. Perhaps she had had prosperity; possibly the purple had gone up in price. I have known some so impressed with God's temporal blessings that they have been ready to think of him, and to turn to him. I do not know; I cannot guess, and I have no right to guess what it was. But I know that God has very wonderful plows, with which he breaks up the hard soil of human hearts. When I have been through the Britannia Iron Works, at Bedford, I have wondered at the strange clod-crushers, clod-breakers, and plows, made there by the Messrs. Howard; and God has some marvelous machines in his providence for turning up the soil of our hearts. I cannot tell what he has done to you, dear friend, but I do trust that whatever has happened has been opening the soil, so that the good seed may drop in. It was the Spirit of God who did it, whatever the instrument may have been, and Lydia's heart was "opened." Opened to what? To attend. "She attended unto the things which were spoken of Paul."

So, first, her heart was opened to listen very intently. She wanted to catch every word. She did as some of you do, put her hand to her ear, for fear she should not hear all that was spoken. There are many ways of listening. Some people listen with both their ears, allowing it to go in at one ear and out at the other; like that wit, who, when he was being seriously spoken to, and yet seemed very inattentive, at length wearied the friend who was discoursing. "I am afraid it is not doing you much good," he said. "No," came the reply; "but I think it will do this gentleman some good," pointing to one who sat beside him, "for as it has gone in at this side it has gone out at the other." Oh, how I wish that you had only one ear, so that the truth you hear could never get out again after it had once got in! Well did the Lord speak through Isaiah the prophet unto the people, "Hearken diligently unto me, and eat ye that which is good." Many people can listen for an hour or two to a scientific lecture, or a political speech, without feeling in the least weary; they can even go to the theater, and sit there a whole evening without dreaming of being tired; yet they complain if the sermon is a minute beyond the appointed time. They seem to endure the preaching as a sort of penance, scarcely hearing the words, or, at least, never imagining that the message can have any application to their own case.

Lydia's heart was so opened "that she attended", that is, she listened to the word of salvation until she began to desire it. It is always a pleasure to entertain guests who relish the food placed

mainsail to the wind, and made toward shore.

41 And falling into a place where two seas met, they ran the ship aground; and the forepart stuck fast, and remained unmoveable, but the hinder part was broken with the violence of the waves.

42 And the soldiers' counsel was to kill the prisoners, lest any of them should swim out, and escape.

43 But the centurion, willing to save Paul, kept them from their purpose; and commanded that they which could swim should cast themselves first into the sea, and get to land:

44 And the rest, some on boards, and some on broken pieces of the ship. And so it came to pass, that they escaped all safe to land.

ACTS 28

1 And when they were escaped, then they knew that the island was called Melita.

2 And the barbarous people shewed us no little kindness: for they kindled a fire, and received us every one, because of the present rain, and because of the cold.

3 And when Paul had gathered a bundle of sticks, and laid them on the fire, there came a viper out of the heat, and fastened on his hand.

4 And when the barbarians saw the venomous beast hang on his hand, they said among themselves, No doubt this man is a murderer, whom, though he hath escaped the sea, yet vengeance suffereth not to live.

5 And he shook off the beast into the fire, and felt no harm.

6 Howbeit they looked when he should have swollen, or fallen down dead suddenly: but after they had looked a great while, and saw no harm come to him, they changed their minds, and said that he was a god.

7 In the same quarters were possessions of the chief man of the island, whose name was Publius; who received us, and lodged us three days courteously.

8 And it came to pass, that the father of Publius lay sick of a fever and of a bloody flux: to whom Paul entered in, and prayed, and laid his hands on him, and healed him.

9 So when this was done, others also, which had diseases in the island, came, and were healed:

. 10 Who also honored us with many honors; and when we departed, they laded us with such things as were necessary.

11 And after three months we departed in a ship of Alexandria, which had wintered in the isle, whose sign was Castor and Pollux.

12 And landing at Syracuse, we tarried there three days.

13 And from thence we fetched a compass, and came to Rhegium: and after one day the south wind blew, and we came the next day to Puteoli:

(whence its name was taken,) with much cotton, and is very fruitful, though it has only three feet depth of earth above the solid rock. The Emperor Charles the Fifth gave it, in 1530, to the knights of Rhodes, driven out of Rhodes by the Turks. They are a thousand in number, of whom five hundred always reside on the island.

2. And the barbarians – So the Roman and Greeks termed all nations but their own. But surely the generosity shown by these uncultivated inhabitants of Malta, was far more valuable than all the varnish which the politest education could give, where it taught not humanity and compassion.

4. And when the barbarians saw – they said – Seeing also his chains, Doubtless this man is a murderer – Such rarely go unpunished even in this life; whom vengeance hath not suffered to live – They look upon him as a dead man already. It is with pleasure that we trace among these barbarians the force of conscience, and the belief of a particular providence: which some people of more learning have stupidly thought it philosophy to despise. But they erred in imagining, that calamities must always be interpreted as judgments. Let us guard against this, lest, like them, we condemn not only the innocent, but the excellent of the earth.

5. Having shaken off the venomous animal, he suffered no harm – The words of an eminent modern historian are, "No venomous kind of serpent now breeds in Malta, neither hurts if it be brought thither from another place. Children are seen there handling and playing even with scorpions; I have seen one eating them." If this be so, it seems to be fixed by the wisdom of God, as an eternal memorial of what he once wrought there.

6. They changed their minds, and said he was a God – Such is the stability of human reason! A little before he was a murderer; and presently he is a God: (just as the people of Lystra; one hour sacrificing, and the next stoning:) nay, but there is a medium. He is neither a murderer nor a God, but a man of God. But natural men never run into greater mistakes, than in judging of the children of God.

7. The chief man of the island – In wealth if not in power also. Three days – The first three days of our stay on the island.

11. Whose sign was – It was the custom of the ancients to have images on the head of their ships, from which they took their names. Castor and Pollux – Two heathen gods who were thought favorable to mariners.

15. The brethren – That is, the Christians, came out thence to meet us – It is remarkable that there is no certain account by whom Christianity was planted at Rome. Probably some inhabitants of that city were at Jerusalem on the day of Pentecost, chap. ii, 10; and being then converted themselves, carried the Gospel thither at their return. Appii-Forum was a town fifty-one miles from Rome; the Three Taverns about thirty. He took courage – He saw Christ was at Rome also, and now forgot all the troubles of his journey.

16. With the soldier – To whom he was chained, as the Roman custom was.

17. And after three days – Given to rest and prayer, Paul called the chief of the Jews together – He always sought the Jews first; but being now bound, he could not so conveniently go round to them. Though I have done nothing – Seeing him chained, they might have suspected he had. Therefore he first obviates this suspicion.

19. When the Jews opposed it – He speaks tenderly of them, not mentioning their repeated attempts to murder him. Not that I had any thing to accuse my nation of – Not that I had any design to

MATTHEW HENRY   CHARLES H. SPURGEON

ed in this life were wicked people. Divine revelation sets this matter in a true light. Good men often are greatly afflicted in this life, for the trial and increase of their faith and patience. Observe Paul's deliverance from the danger. And thus in the strength of the grace of Christ, believers shake off the temptations of Satan, with holy resolution. When we despise the censures and reproaches of men, and look upon them with holy contempt, having the testimony of our consciences for us, then, like Paul, we shake off the viper into the fire. It does us no harm, except we are kept by it from our duty. God hereby made Paul remarkable among these people, and so made way for the receiving of the gospel. The Lord raises up friends for his people in every place whither he leads them, and makes them blessings to those in affliction.

11-16 The common events of traveling are seldom worthy of being told; but the comfort of communion with the saints, and kindness shown by friends, deserve particular mention. The Christians at Rome were so far from being ashamed of Paul, or afraid of owning him, because he was a prisoner, that they were the more careful to show him respect. He had great comfort in this. And if our friends are kind to us, God puts it into their hearts, and we must give him the glory. When we see those even in strange places, who bear Christ's name, fear God, and serve him, we should lift up our hearts to heaven in thanksgiving. How many great men have made their entry into Rome, crowned and in triumph, who really were plagues to the world! But here a good man makes his entry into Rome, chained as a poor captive, who was a greater blessing to the world than any other merely a man. Is not this enough to put us for ever out of conceit with worldly favor? This may encourage God's prisoners, that he can give them favor in the eyes of those that carry them captives. When God does not soon deliver his people out of bondage, yet makes it easy to them, or them easy under it, they have reason to be thankful.

17-22 It was for the honor of Paul that those who examined his case, acquitted him. In his appeal he sought not to accuse his nation, but only to clear himself. True Christianity settles what is of common concern to all mankind, and is not built upon narrow opinions and private interests. It aims at no worldly benefit or advantage, but all its gains are spiritual and eternal. It is, and always has been, the lot of Christ's holy religion, to be every where spoken against. Look through every town and village where Christ is exalted as the only Savior of mankind, and where the people are called to follow him in newness of life, and we see those who give themselves up to Christ, still called a sect, a party, and reproached. And this is the treatment they are

before them; and it is a great joy to preach to those who are eagerly hungering after the truth. But how heart-breaking a task it is to keep continually praising the pearl of great price to those who know not its value, nor desire its beauty! Daniel was a man "greatly beloved"; the Hebrew word there employed means "a man of desires." He was not one of your conceited, self-satisfied individuals. He longed and yearned for better things than he had yet attained, and hence was "greatly beloved." God loves people to thirst after him, and to desire to know his love and power. Let us explain the gospel as we may, if there is no desire in the heart, our plainest messages are lost. A man said, about something he wished to make clear, "Why, it is as plain as A B C!" "Yes," said a third party, "but the man you are talking to is D E F." So, some of our hearers seem to turn away from the Word of God. But when a person says, "I want to find salvation; I want to get Christ this very day; and I am going to listen with the determination that I will find out the way of salvation;" surely, if the things spoken are the same things that Paul spoke of, few in that condition will go out of the house without finding salvation. Lydia's heart was opened to attend to the gospel, that is, to desire it.

But, next, her heart was opened to understand it. It is wonderful how little even well-educated people sometimes understand of the gospel when it is preached in the simplest manner. One is constantly being astounded by the misapprehensions that persons have as to the way of salvation. But Lydia had grasped the truth. "Thanks be to God," she said, "I see it. Jesus Christ suffered in our stead; and we, by an act of faith, accept him as our Substitute, and we are saved thereby. I have it. I never saw it before. I read about a paschal lamb, and the sprinkling of the blood, and the passing over of the houses where the blood was sprinkled. I could not quite make it out. Now I see, if the blood be sprinkled upon me, God will pass over me, according to his word, 'When I see the blood, I will pass over you.'" She attended unto the things which were spoken of Paul, so as to understand them.

But more than that; her heart was so opened that she attended to the gospel so as to accept it. "Ah!" she said, "now I understand it, I will have it. Christ for me! Christ for me! That blessed Substitute for sinners! Is that all I have to do, simply to trust him? Then I will trust him. Sink or swim, I will cast myself upon him now." She did so there and then. There was no hesitating. She believed what Paul said; that Jesus was the Son of God, the appointed propitiation for sin, and that whosoever believed on him should then and there be justified; and she did believe in him, and she was justified; as you will be, my friend, if you will

14 Where we found brethren, and were desired to tarry with them seven days: and so we went toward Rome.

15 And from thence, when the brethren heard of us, they came to meet us as far as Appiiforum, and The three taverns: whom when Paul saw, he thanked God, and took courage.

16 And when we came to Rome, the centurion delivered the prisoners to the captain of the guard: but Paul was suffered to dwell by himself with a soldier that kept him.

17 And it came to pass, that after three days Paul called the chief of the Jews together: and when they were come together, he said unto them, Men and brethren, though I have committed nothing against the people, or customs of our fathers, yet was I delivered prisoner from Jerusalem into the hands of the Romans.

18 Who, when they had examined me, would have let me go, because there was no cause of death in me.

19 But when the Jews spake against it, I was constrained to appeal unto Cesar; not that I had ought to accuse my nation of.

20 For this cause therefore have I called for you, to see you, and to speak with you: because that for the hope of Israel I am bound with this chain.

21 And they said unto him, We neither received letters out of Judea concerning thee, neither any of the brethren that came shewed or spake any harm of thee.

22 But we desire to hear of thee what thou thinkest: for as concerning this sect, we know that every where it is spoken against.

23 And when they had appointed him a day, there came many to him into his lodging; to whom he expounded and testified the kingdom of God, persuading them concerning Jesus, both out of the law of Moses, and out of the prophets, from morning till evening.

24 And some believed the things which were spoken, and some believed not.

25 And when they agreed not among themselves, they departed, after that Paul had spoken one word, Well spake the Holy Ghost by Esaias the prophet unto our fathers,

26 Saying, Go unto this people, and say, Hearing ye shall hear, and shall not understand; and seeing ye shall see, and not perceive:

27 For the heart of this people is waxed gross, and their ears are dull of hearing, and their eyes have they closed; lest they should see with their eyes, and hear with their ears, and understand with their heart, and should be converted, and I should heal them.

28 Be it known therefore unto you, that the salvation of God is sent unto the Gentiles, and that they will hear it.

29 And when he had said these words, the Jews departed, and had great reasoning among themselves.

accuse others, but merely to defend myself.

20. The hope of Israel – What Israel hopes for, namely, the Messiah and the resurrection.

21. We have neither received letters concerning thee – There must have been a peculiar providence in this, nor has any of the brethren – The Jews, related – Professedly, in a set discourse, or spoke – Occasionally, in conversation, any evil of thee – How must the bridle then have been in their mouth!

22. This sect we know is every where spoken against – This is no proof at all of a bad cause, but a very probable mark of a good one.

23. To whom he expounded, testifying the kingdom of God, and persuading them concerning Jesus – These were his two grand topics,

1. That the kingdom of the Messiah was of a spiritual, not temporal nature:

2. That Jesus of Nazareth was the very person foretold, as the Lord of that kingdom. On this head he had as much need to persuade as to convince, their will making as strong a resistance as their understanding.

24. And some believed the things that were spoken – With the heart, as well as understanding.

25. Well spake the Holy Ghost to your fathers – Which is equally applicable to you.

26. Hearing ye shall hear – That is, ye shall most surely hear, and shall not understand – The words manifestly denote a judicial blindness, consequent upon a willfull and obstinate resistance of the truth. First they would not, afterward they could not, believe. Isaiah vi, 9, &c.; Matt. xiii, 14; John xii, 40.

28. The salvation of God is sent to the Gentiles – Namely, from this time. Before this no apostle had been at Rome. St. Paul was the first.

30. And Paul continued two whole years – After which this book was written, long before St. Paul's death, and was undoubtedly published with his approbation by St. Luke, who continued with him to the last, 2 Tim. iv, 11. And received all that came to him – Whether they were Jews or Gentiles. These two years completed twenty-five years after our Savior's passion. Such progress had the Gospel made by that time, in the parts of the world which lay west of Jerusalem, by the ministry of St. Paul among the Gentiles. How far eastward the other apostles had carried it in the same time, history does not inform us.

31. No man forbidding him – Such was the victory of the word of God. While Paul was preaching at Rome, the Gospel shone with its highest luster. Here therefore the Acts of the Apostles end; and end with great advantage. Otherwise St. Luke could easily have continued his narrative to the apostle's death.

sure to receive, so long as there shall continue an ungodly man upon earth.

23-31 Paul persuaded the Jews concerning Jesus. Some were wrought upon by the word, and others hardened; some received the light, and others shut their eyes against it. And the same has always been the effect of the gospel. Paul parted with them, observing that the Holy Ghost had well described their state. Let all that hear the gospel, and do not heed it, tremble at their doom; for who shall heal them, if God does not? The Jews had afterwards much reasoning among themselves. Many have great reasoning, who do not reason aright. They find fault with one another's opinions, yet will not yield to truth. Nor will men's reasoning among themselves convince them, without the grace of God to open their understandings. While we mourn on account of such despisers, we should rejoice that the salvation of God is sent to others, who will receive it; and if we are of that number, we should be thankful to him who hath made us to differ. The apostle kept to his principle, to know and preach nothing but Christ and him crucified. Christians, when tempted from their main business, should bring themselves back with this question, What does this concern the Lord Jesus? What tendency has it to bring us to him, and to keep us walking in him? The apostle preached not himself, but Christ, and he was not ashamed of the gospel of Christ. Though Paul was placed in a very narrow opportunity for being useful, he was not disturbed in it. Though it was not a wide door that was opened to him, yet no man was suffered to shut it; and to many it was an effectual door, so that there were saints even in Nero's household, Php 4:22. We learn also from Php 1:13, how God overruled Paul's imprisonment for the furtherance of the gospel. And not the residents at Rome only, but all the church of Christ, to the present day, and in the most remote corner of the globe, have abundant reason to bless God, that during the most mature period of his Christian life and experience, he was detained a prisoner. It was from his prison, probably chained hand to hand to the soldier who kept him, that the apostle wrote the epistles to the Ephesians, Philippians, Colossians, and Hebrews; epistles showing, perhaps more than any others, the Christian love with which his heart overflowed, and the Christian experience with which his soul was filled. The believer of the present time may have less of triumph, and less of heavenly joy, than the apostle, but every follower of the same Savior, is equally sure of safety and peace at the last. Let us seek to live more and more in the love of the Savior; to labor to glorify him by every action of our lives; and we shall assuredly, by his strength, be among the number of those who now overcome our enemies; and by his free grace and mercy, be

believe in him at this moment. You, too, shall have immediate salvation, my dear sister sitting yonder, if you will come, like this Lydia of old, and just take Christ to be yours, and trust him now. She attended unto the things which were spoken of Paul, so that she accepted Christ.

Having done that, she went further: her heart was so won, that she was, by the Spirit, led to obey the word, and avow her faith. Paul told her that the gospel was this—"He that believeth and is baptized shall be saved." He said to her, "My commission is, 'Go ye into all the world, and preach the gospel to every creature. He that believeth and is baptized shall be saved.'" Perhaps she said, "But why must I be baptized?" He said, "As a testimony of your obedience to Christ, whom you take to be your Master and your Lord; and as a type of your being one with him in his burial. You are to be buried in water as he was buried in the tomb of Joseph; and you are to be raised up out of the water even as he rose again from the dead. This act is to be a token and type to you of your oneness with him in his death and burial and resurrection." What did Lydia say? Did she say, "Well, I think I must wait a little while: the water is cold"? Did she say, "I think I must ask about it; I must consider it"? No, not at all. Paul tells her that this is Christ's ordinance, and she at once replies, "Here am I, Paul, let me be baptized, and my servants, too, and all that belong to my household, for they also believe in Jesus Christ. Let us have the baptism at once." There and then "she was baptized, and her household." She did at once obey the heavenly message, and she became a baptized believer. She was not ashamed to confess Christ. She had not known him long; but what she did know of him was so blessed and joyous to her soul, that she would have said, if she had known the hymn—

"Through floods and flames, if Jesus lead,
I'll follow where he goes;
'Hinder me not,' shall be my cry,
Though earth and hell oppose."

You can imagine her saying, "Did he go down into the Jordan, and say, 'Thus it becometh us to fulfill all righteousness'? Then I will go where he leads the way, and be obedient to him, and say to all the world, 'I, too, am a follower of the crucified Christ.'"

Now, lastly, after Lydia was baptized, she became an enthusiastic Christian. She said to Paul, "You must come home with me. I know you have not anywhere to go. Come along; and there is your friend Silas. I have plenty of room for him; and Timothy too; and Luke also. We can make room for the four of you among the purple bales, or somewhere; but, at any rate, I have house-room for you four, and I have heart-room for forty thousand of you. I wish I could take in the whole church of God." Dear good woman that she was, she felt

30 And Paul dwelt two whole years in his own hired house, and received all that came in unto him,

31 Preaching the kingdom of God, and teaching those things which concern the Lord Jesus Christ, with all confidence, no man forbidding him.

MATTHEW HENRY

hereafter among the blessed company who shall sit with him upon his throne, even as he also has overcome, and is sitting on his Father's throne, at God's right hand for evermore.

CHARLES H. SPURGEON

that she could not do too much for the men who had been made a blessing to her; for she regarded what she did to them as done to their Lord and Master. They might have said, "No, really, we cannot trouble you. You have the household. You have all this business to look after." "Yes," she would answer, "I know that. It is very kind of you to excuse yourselves; but you must come." "No," Paul might urge, "my dear good woman, I am going to find out some tent-makers, and make tents with them. We will find a lodging where we have been." "Ah!" she would say, "but I mean to have you. You must come to my home." "She constrained us." She would probably put it thus: "Now, I shall not think that you fully believe in me if you do not come home with me. Come, you baptized me, and by that very act you professed that you considered that I was a true believer. If you do really believe it, come and stay in my house as long as you like, and I will make you as comfortable as ever I can." So at last Paul yields to her constraint, and goes to her home. How glad they would all be, and what praise to Christ would rise from that household! I hope that the generous spirit, which glowed in the heart of the first convert in Europe, will always continue amongst the converts of Europe till the last day. I trust that when they are called not merely to entertain God's ministers, but to help all God's people of every sort, they may be ready and willing to do it for Christ's sake; for love shall fill them with a holy hospitality, and an earnest desire to bless the children of God. Love one another, brothers and sisters, and do good to one another, as you have opportunity; for so will you be worthy followers of Lydia, the first European convert, whose heart the Lord opened.

The Lord open your hearts, for his name's sake! Amen.

Romans

ROMANS 1

1 Paul, a servant of Jesus Christ, called to be an apostle, separated unto the gospel of God,

2 (Which he had promised afore by his prophets in the holy scriptures,)

3 Concerning his Son Jesus Christ our Lord, which was made of the seed of David according to the flesh;

4 And declared to be the Son of God with power, according to the spirit of holiness, by the resurrection from the dead:

5 By whom we have received grace and apostleship, for obedience to the faith among all nations, for his name:

6 Among whom are ye also the called of Jesus Christ:

7 To all that be in Rome, beloved of God, called to be saints: Grace to you and peace from God our Father, and the Lord Jesus Christ.

8 First, I thank my God through Jesus Christ for you all, that your faith is spoken of throughout the whole world.

9 For God is my witness, whom I serve with my spirit in the gospel of his Son, that without ceasing I make mention of you always in my prayers;

10 Making request, if by any means now at length I might have a prosperous journey by the will of God to come unto you.

11 For I long to see you, that I may impart unto you some spiritual gift, to the end ye may be established;

12 That is, that I may be comforted together with you by the mutual faith both of you and me.

13 Now I would not have you ignorant, brethren, that oftentimes I purposed to come unto you, (but was let hitherto,) that I might have some fruit among you also, even as among other Gentiles.

14 I am debtor both to the Greeks, and to the Barbarians; both to the wise, and to the unwise.

15 So, as much as in me is, I am ready to preach the gospel to you that are at Rome also.

16 For I am not ashamed of the gospel of Christ: for it is the

Paul's chief design herein is to show,

1. That neither the Gentiles by the law of nature, nor the Jews by the law of Moses, could obtain justification before God; and that therefore it was necessary for both to seek it from the free mercy of God by faith.

2. That God has an absolute right to show mercy on what terms he pleases, and to withhold it from those who will not accept it on his own terms.

ROMANS 1

1. Paul, a servant of Jesus Christ – To this introduction the conclusion answers, chap. xv, 15, &c. Called to be an apostle – And made an apostle by that calling. While God calls, he makes what he calls. As the Judaizing teachers disputed his claim to the apostolic office, it is with great propriety that he asserts it in the very entrance of an epistle wherein their principles are entirely overthrown. And various other proper and important thoughts are suggested in this short introduction; particularly the prophecies concerning the gospel, the descent of Jesus from David, the great doctrines of his Godhead and resurrection, the sending the gospel to the Gentiles, the privileges of Christians, and the obedience and holiness to which they were obliged in virtue of their profession. Separated – By God, not only from the bulk of other men, from other Jews, from other disciples, but even from other Christian teachers, to be a peculiar instrument of God in spreading the gospel.

2. Which he promised before – Of old time, frequently, solemnly. And the promise and accomplishment confirm each other. Deut. xviii, 18; Isa. ix, 6, 7; Chapter liii; lxi; Jer. xxiii, 5.

3. Who was of the seed of David according to the flesh – That is, with regard to his human nature. Both the natures of our Savior are here mentioned; but the human is mentioned first, because the divine was not manifested in its full evidence till after his resurrection.

4. But powerfully declared to be the Son of God, according to the Spirit of Holiness – That is, according to his divine nature. By the resurrection from the dead – For this is both the fountain and the object of our faith; and the preaching of the apostles was the consequence of Christ's resurrection.

5. By whom we have received – I and the other apostles. Grace and apostleship – The favor to be an apostle, and qualifications for it. For obedience to the faith in all nations – That is, that all nations may embrace the faith of Christ. For his name – For his sake; out of regard to him.

6. Among whom – The nations brought to the obedience of faith. Are ye also – But St. Paul gives them no preeminence above others.

7. To all that are in Rome – Most of these were heathens by birth, ver. 13, though with Jews mixed among them. They were scattered up and down in that large city, and not yet reduced into the form of a church. Only some had begun to meet in the house of Aquila and Priscilla. Beloved of God – And from his free love, not from any merit of yours, called by his word and his Spirit to believe in him, and now through faith holy as he is holy. Grace – The peculiar favor of God. And peace – All manner of blessings, temporal, spiritual, and eternal. This is both a Christian salutation and an apostolic benediction. From God our Father, and the Lord Jesus Christ – This is the usual way wherein the apostles speak, "God the Father," "God our Father." Nor do they often, in speaking of him, use the word Lord, as it implies the proper name of God, Jehovah. In the Old Testament, indeed, the holy men generally said, "The Lord our God;" for they were then, as it were, servants; whereas now they are sons: and sons so well know their father, that they need not frequently mention his proper name. It is one and the same peace, and one and the same grace, which is from God and from Jesus Christ. Our trust and prayer fix on God, as he is the Father of Christ; and on Christ, as he presents us to the Father.

MATTHEW HENRY   CHARLES H. SPURGEON

The scope or design of the apostle in writing to the Romans appears to have been, to answer the unbelieving, and to teach the believing Jew; to confirm the Christian and to convert the idolatrous Gentile; and to show the Gentile convert as equal with the Jewish, in respect of his religious condition, and his rank in the Divine favor. These several designs are brought into one view, by opposing or arguing with the infidel or unbelieving Jew, in favor of the Christian or believing Gentile. The way of a sinner's acceptance with God, or justification in his sight, merely by grace, through faith in the righteousness of Christ, without distinction of nations, is plainly stated. This doctrine is cleared from the objections raised by Judaizing Christians, who were for making terms of acceptance with God by a mixture of the law and the gospel, and for shutting out the Gentiles from any share in the blessings of salvation brought in by the Messiah. In the conclusion, holiness is further enforced by practical exhortations.

ROMANS 1

The apostle's commission. (1-7)
Prays for the saints at Rome, and expresses his desire to see them. (8-15)
The gospel way of justification by faith, for Jews and Gentiles. (16,17)
The sins of the Gentiles set forth. (18-32)

1-7 The doctrine of which the apostle Paul wrote, set forth the fulfillment of the promises by the prophets. It spoke of the Son of God, even Jesus the Savior, the promised Messiah, who came from David as to his human nature, but was also declared to be the Son of God, by the Divine power which raised him from the dead. The Christian profession does not consist in a notional knowledge or a bare assent, much less in perverse disputing, but in obedience. And all those, and those only, are brought to obedience of the faith, who are effectually called of Jesus Christ. Here is, 1. The privilege of Christians; they are beloved of God, and are members of that body which is beloved. 2. The duty of Christians; to be holy, hereunto are they called, called to be saints. These the apostle saluted, by wishing them grace to sanctify their souls, and peace to comfort their hearts, as springing from the free mercy of God, the reconciled Father of all believers, and coming to them through the Lord Jesus Christ.

8-15 We must show love for our friends, not only by praying for them, but by praising God for them. As in our purposes, so in our desires, we must remember to say, If the Lord will, Jas 4:15. Our journeys are made prosperous or otherwise, according to the will of God. We should readily impart to others what God has trusted to us, rejoicing to make others joyful, especially taking pleasure in communing with those who believe the same things with us. If redeemed by the blood, and converted by the grace of the Lord Jesus, we are altogether his; and

THE HOLY SPIRIT'S INTERCESSION
Sermon number 1532 delivered on April 11th, 1880, at the Metropolitan Tabernacle, Newington.

"Likewise the Spirit also helpeth our infirmities: for we know not what we should pray for as we ought: but the Spirit itself maketh intercession for us with groanings which cannot be uttered. And he that searcheth the hearts knoweth what is the mind of the Spirit, because he maketh intercession for the saints according to the will of God."—Romans 8:26,27.

THE APOSTLE PAUL was writing to a tried and afflicted people, and one of his objects was to remind them of the rivers of comfort which were flowing near at hand. He first of all stirred up their pure minds by way of remembrance as to their sonship,—for saith he "as many as are led by the Spirit of God, they are the sons of God." They were, therefore, encouraged to take part and lot with Christ, the elder brother, with whom they had become joint heirs; and they were exhorted to suffer with him, that they might afterwards be glorified with him. All that they endured came from a Father's hand, and this should comfort them. A thousand sources of joy are opened in that one blessing of adoption. Blessed be the God and Father of our Lord Jesus Christ, by whom we have been begotten into the family of grace.

When Paul had alluded to that consoling subject he turned to the next ground of comfort—namely, that we are to be sustained under present trial by hope. There is an amazing glory in reserve for us, and though as yet we cannot enter upon it, but in harmony with the whole creation must continue to groan and travail, yet the hope itself should minister strength to us, and enable us patiently to bear "these light afflictions, which are but for a moment." This also is a truth full of sacred refreshment: hope sees a crown in reserve, mansions in readiness, and Jesus himself preparing a place for us, and by the rapturous sight she sustains the soul under the sorrows of the hour. Hope is the grand anchor by whose means we ride out the present storm.

The apostle then turns to a third source of comfort, namely, the abiding of the Holy Spirit in and with the Lord's people. He uses the word "likewise" to intimate that in the same manner as hope sustains the soul, so does the Holy Spirit strengthen us under trial. Hope operated spiritually upon our spiritual

power of God unto salvation to every one that believeth; to the Jew first, and also to the Greek.

17 For therein is the righteousness of God revealed from faith to faith: as it is written, The just shall live by faith.

18 For the wrath of God is revealed from heaven against all ungodliness and unrighteousness of men, who hold the truth in unrighteousness;

19 Because that which may be known of God is manifest in them; for God hath shewed it unto them.

20 For the invisible things of him from the creation of the world are clearly seen, being understood by the things that are made, even his eternal power and Godhead; so that they are without excuse:

21 Because that, when they knew God, they glorified him not as God, neither were thankful; but became vain in their imaginations, and their foolish heart was darkened.

22 Professing themselves to be wise, they became fools,

23 And changed the glory of the uncorruptible God into an image made like to corruptible man, and to birds, and fourfooted beasts, and creeping things.

24 Wherefore God also gave them up to uncleanness through the lusts of their own hearts, to dishonor their own bodies between themselves:

25 Who changed the truth of God into a lie, and worshiped and served the creature more than the Creator, who is blessed for ever. Amen.

26 For this cause God gave them up unto vile affections: for even their women did change the natural use into that which is against nature:

27 And likewise also the men, leaving the natural use of the woman, burned in their lust one toward another; men with men working that which is unseemly, and receiving in themselves that recompense of their error which was meet.

28 And even as they did not like to retain God in their knowledge, God gave them over to a reprobate mind, to do those things which are not convenient;

8. I thank – In the very entrance of this one epistle are the traces of all spiritual affections; but of thankfulness above all, with the expression of which almost all St. Paul's epistles begin. He here particularly thanks God, that what otherwise himself should have done, was done at Rome already. My God – This very word expresses faith, hope, love, and consequently all true religion. Through Jesus Christ – The gifts of God all pass through Christ to us; and all our petitions and thanksgivings pass through Christ to God. That your faith is spoken of – In this kind of congratulations St. Paul describes either the whole of Christianity, as Colossians i, 3, &c.; or some part of it, as 1 Cor. i, 5. Accordingly here he mentions the faith of the Romans, suitably to his design, ver. 12, 17. Through the whole world – This joyful news spreading everywhere, that there were Christians also in the imperial city. And the goodness and wisdom of God established faith in the chief cities; in Jerusalem and Rome particularly; that from thence it might be diffused to all nations.

9. God, whom I serve – As an apostle. In my spirit – Not only with my body, but with my inmost soul. In the gospel – By preaching it.

10. Always – In all my solemn addresses to God. If by any means now at length – This accumulation of particles declares the strength of his desire.

11. That I may impart to you – Face to face, by laying on of hands, prayer, preaching the gospel, private conversation. Some spiritual gift – With such gifts the Corinthians, who had enjoyed the presence of St. Paul, abounded, 1 Cor. i, 7; xii, 1; xiv, 1. So did the Galatians likewise, Gal. iii, 5; and, indeed, all those churches which had had the presence of any of the apostles had peculiar advantages in this kind, from the laying on of their hands, Acts xix, 6; viii, 17, &c., 2 Tim. i, 6. But as yet the Romans were greatly inferior to them in this respect; for which reason the apostle, in the twelfth chapter also, says little, if any thing, of their spiritual gifts. He therefore desires to impart some, that they might be established; for by these was the testimony of Christ confirmed among them. That St. Peter had no more been at Rome than St. Paul, at the time when this epistle was written, appears from the general tenor thereof, and from this place in particular: for, otherwise, what St. Paul wishes to impart to the Romans would have been imparted already by St. Peter.

12. That is, I long to be comforted by the mutual faith both of you and me – He not only associates the Romans with, but even prefers them before, himself. How different is this style of the apostle from that of the modern court of Rome!

13. Brethren – A frequent, holy, simple, sweet, and yet grand, appellation. The apostles but rarely address persons by their names; "O ye Corinthians," "O Timotheus." St. Paul generally uses this appellation, " Brethren;" sometimes in exhortation, "My beloved," or, "My beloved brethren;" St. James, "Brethren," "My brethren," My beloved brethren;" St. Peter and Jude always, "Beloved;" St. John frequently, "Beloved;" once, "Brethren;" oftener than once, "My little children." Though I have been hindered hitherto – Either by business, see chap. xv, 22; or persecution, 1 Thess. ii, 2; or the Spirit, Acts xvi, 7. That I might have some fruit – Of my ministerial labors. Even as I have already had from the many churches I have planted and watered among the other Gentiles.

14. To the Greeks and the barbarians – He includes the Roman under the Greeks; so that this division comprises all nations. Both to the wise, and the unwise – For there were unwise even among the Greeks, and wise even among the barbarians. I am a debtor to all – I am bound by my divine mission to preach the gospel to them.

16. For I am not ashamed of the gospel – To the world, indeed, it is folly and weakness, 1 Cor. i, 18; therefore, in the judgment of the world, he ought to be ashamed of it; especially at Rome, the head and theater of the world. But Paul is not ashamed, knowing it is the power of God unto salvation to every one that believeth – The great and gloriously powerful means of saving all who accept salvation in God's own way. As St. Paul comprises the sum of the gospel in this

MATTHEW HENRY

CHARLES H. SPURGEON

for his sake we are debtors to all men, to do all the good we can. Such services are our duty.

16,17 In these verses the apostle opens the design of the whole epistle, in which he brings forward a charge of sinfulness against all flesh; declares the only method of deliverance from condemnation, by faith in the mercy of God, through Jesus Christ; and then builds upon it purity of heart, grateful obedience, and earnest desires to improve in all those Christian graces and tempers, which nothing but a lively faith in Christ can bring forth. God is a just and holy God, and we are guilty sinners. It is necessary that we have a righteousness to appear in before him: there is such a righteousness brought in by the Messiah, and made known in the gospel; a gracious method of acceptance, notwithstanding the guilt of our sins. It is the righteousness of Christ, who is God, coming from a satisfaction of infinite value. Faith is all in all, both in the beginning and progress of Christian life. It is not from faith to works, as if faith put us into a justified state, and then works kept us in it; but it is all along from faith to faith; it is faith pressing forward, and gaining the victory over unbelief.

18-25 The apostle begins to show that all mankind need the salvation of the gospel, because none could obtain the favor of God, or escape his wrath by their own works. For no man can plead that he has fulfilled all his obligations to God and to his neighbor; nor can any truly say that he has fully acted up to the light afforded him. The sinfulness of man is described as ungodliness against the laws of the first table, and unrighteousness against those of the second. The cause of that sinfulness is holding the truth in unrighteousness. All, more or less, do what they know to be wrong, and omit what they know to be right, so that the plea of ignorance cannot be allowed from any. Our Creator's invisible power and Godhead are so clearly shown in the works he has made, that even idolaters and wicked Gentiles are left without excuse. They foolishly followed idolatry; and rational creatures changed the worship of the glorious Creator, for that of brutes, reptiles, and senseless images. They wandered from God, till all traces of true religion must have been lost, had not the revelation of the gospel prevented it. For whatever may be pretended, as to the sufficiency of man's reason to discover Divine truth and moral obligation, or to govern the practice aright, facts cannot be denied. And these plainly show that men have dishonored God by the most absurd idolatries and superstitions; and have degraded themselves by the vilest affections and most abominable deeds.

26-32 In the horrid depravity of the heathen, the truth of our Lord's words was shown: "Light was come into the world, but men loved darkness rather than light, because their deeds were evil; for he that doeth evil hateth the light." The truth was not to their taste. And we all know how soon a man will contrive, against the strongest evidence, to reason himself out of the belief of what he dis-

faculties, and so does the Holy Spirit, in some mysterious way, divinely operate upon the new-born faculties of the believer, so that he is sustained under his infirmities. In his light shall we see light: I pray, therefore, that we may be helped of the Spirit while we consider his mysterious operations, that we may not fall into error or miss precious truth through blindness of heart.

The text speaks of "our infirmities," or as many translators put it in the singular—of "our infirmity." By this is intended our affliction, and the weakness which trouble discovers in us. The Holy Spirit helps us to bear the infirmity of our body and of our mind; he helps us to bear our cross, whether it be physical pain, or mental depression, or spiritual conflict, or slander, or poverty, or persecution. He helps our infirmity; and with a helper so divinely strong we need not fear for the result. God's grace will be sufficient for us; his strength will be made perfect in weakness.

I think, dear friends, you will all admit that if a man can pray, his trouble is at once lightened. When we feel that we have power with God and can obtain anything we ask for at his hands, then our difficulties cease to oppress us. We take our burden to our heavenly Father and tell it out in the accents of childlike confidence, and we come away quite content to bear whatever his holy will may lay upon us. Prayer is a great outlet for grief; it draws up the sluices, and abates the swelling flood, which else might be too strong for us. We bathe our wound in the lotion of prayer, and the pain is lulled, the fever is removed. We may be brought into such perturbation of mind, and perplexity of heart, that we do not know how to pray. We see the mercy-seat, and we perceive that God will hear us: we have no doubt about that, for we know that we are his own favored children, and yet we hardly know what to desire. We fall into such heaviness of spirit, and entanglement of thought, that the one remedy of prayer, which we have always found to be unfailing, appears to be taken from us. Here, then, in the nick of time, as a very present help in time of trouble, comes in the Holy Spirit. He draws near to teach us how to pray, and in this way he helps our infirmity, relieves our suffering, and enables us to bear the heavy burden without fainting under the load.

At this time our subjects for consideration shall be, firstly, the help which the Holy Spirit gives; secondly, the prayers which he inspires; and thirdly, the success which such prayers are certain to obtain.

29 Being filled with all unrighteousness, fornication, wickedness, covetousness, maliciousness; full of envy, murder, debate, deceit, malignity; whisperers,

30 Backbiters, haters of God, despiteful, proud, boasters, inventors of evil things, disobedient to parents,

31 Without understanding, covenantbreakers, without natural affection, implacable, unmerciful:

32 Who knowing the judgment of God, that they which commit such things are worthy of death, not only do the same, but have pleasure in them that do them.

ROMANS 2

1 Therefore thou art inexcusable, O man, whosoever thou art that judgest: for wherein thou judgest another, thou condemnest thyself; for thou that judgest doest the same things.

2 But we are sure that the judgment of God is according to truth against them which commit such things.

3 And thinkest thou this, O man, that judgest them which do such things, and doest the same, that thou shalt escape the judgment of God?

4 Or despisest thou the riches of his goodness and forbearance and longsuffering; not knowing that the goodness of God leadeth thee to repentance?

5 But after thy hardness and impenitent heart treasurest up unto thyself wrath against the day of wrath and revelation of the righteous judgment of God;

6 Who will render to every man according to his deeds:

7 To them who by patient continuance in well doing seek for glory and honor and immortality, eternal life:

8 But unto them that are contentious, and do not obey the truth, but obey unrighteousness, indignation and wrath,

9 Tribulation and anguish, upon every soul of man that doeth evil, of the Jew first, and also of the Gentile;

10 But glory, honor, and peace, to every man that worketh good,

epistle, so he does the sum of the epistle in this and the following verse. Both to the Jew, and to the Gentile – There is a noble frankness, as well as a comprehensive sense, in these words, by which he, on the one hand, shows the Jews their absolute need of the gospel; and, on the other, tells the politest and greatest nation in the world both that their salvation depended on receiving it, and that the first offers of it were in every place to be made to the despised Jews.

17. The righteousness of God – This expression sometimes means God's eternal, essential righteousness, which includes both justice and mercy, and is eminently shown in condemning sin, and yet justifying the sinner. Sometimes it means that righteousness by which a man, through the gift of God, is made and is righteous; and that, both by receiving Christ through faith, and by a conformity to the essential righteousness of God. St. Paul, when treating of justification, means hereby the righteousness of faith; therefore called the righteousness of God, because God found out and prepared, reveals and gives, approves and crowns it. In this verse the expression means, the whole benefit of God through Christ for the salvation of a sinner. Is revealed – Mention is made here, and ver. 18, of a twofold Revelation, – of wrath and of righteousness: the former, little known to nature, is revealed by the law; the latter, wholly unknown to nature, by the gospel. That goes before, and prepares the way; this follows. Each, the apostle says, is revealed at the present time, in opposition to the times of ignorance. From faith to faith – By a gradual series of still clearer and clearer promises. As it is written – St. Paul had just laid down three propositions:

1. Righteousness is by faith, ver. xvii,

2. Salvation is by righteousness, ver. xvi,

3. Both to the Jews and to the Gentiles, ver. 16. Now all these are confirmed by that single sentence, The just shall live by faith – Which was primarily spoken of those who preserved their lives, when the Chaldeans besieged Jerusalem, by believing the declarations of God, and acting according to them. Here it means, He shall obtain the favor of God, and continue therein by believing. Hab. ii, 4.

18. For – There is no other way of obtaining life and salvation. Having laid down his proposition, the apostle now enters upon the proof of it. His first argument is, The law condemns all men, as being under sin. None therefore is justified by the works of the law. This is treated of chap. iii, 20. And hence he infers, Therefore justification is by faith. The wrath of God is revealed – Not only by frequent and signal interpositions of divine providence, but likewise in the sacred oracles, and by us, his messengers. From heaven – This speaks the majesty of him whose wrath is revealed, his all-seeing eye, and the extent of his wrath: whatever is under heaven is under the effects of his wrath, believers in Christ excepted. Against all ungodliness and unrighteousness – These two are treated of, ver. 23, &c. Of men – He is speaking here of the Gentiles, and chiefly the wisest of them. Who detain the truth – For it struggles against their wickedness. In unrighteousness – The word here includes ungodliness also.

19. For what is to be known of God – Those great principles which are indispensably necessary to be known. Is manifest in them; for God hath showed it to them – By the light which enlightens every man that cometh into the world.

20. For those things of him which are invisible, are seen – By the eye of the mind. Being understood – They are seen by them, and them only, who use their understanding.

21. Because, knowing God – For the wiser heathens did know that there was one supreme God; yet from low and base considerations they conformed to the idolatry of the vulgar. They did not glorify him as God, neither were thankful – They neither thanked him for his benefits, nor glorified him for his divine perfection. But became vain – Like the idols they worshiped. In their reasonings – Various, uncertain, foolish. What a terrible instance have we of this in the writ-

likes. But a man cannot be brought to greater slavery than to be given up to his own lusts. As the Gentiles did not like to keep God in their knowledge, they committed crimes wholly against reason and their own welfare. The nature of man, whether pagan or Christian, is still the same; and the charges of the apostle apply more or less to the state and character of men at all times, till they are brought to full submission to the faith of Christ, and renewed by Divine power. There never yet was a man, who had not reason to lament his strong corruptions, and his secret dislike to the will of God. Therefore this chapter is a call to self-examination, the end of which should be, a deep conviction of sin, and of the necessity of deliverance from a state of condemnation.

ROMANS 2

The Jews could not be justified by the law of Moses, any more than the Gentiles by the law of nature. (1-16)
The sins of the Jews confuted all their vain confidence in their outward privileges. (17-29)

1-16 The Jews thought themselves a holy people, entitled to their privileges by right, while they were unthankful, rebellious, and unrighteous. But all who act thus, of every nation, age, and description, must be reminded that the judgment of God will be according to their real character. The case is so plain, that we may appeal to the sinner's own thoughts. In every willfull sin, there is contempt of the goodness of God. And though the branches of man's disobedience are very various, all spring from the same root. But in true repentance, there must be hatred of former sinfulness, from a change wrought in the state of the mind, which disposes it to choose the good and to refuse the evil. It shows also a sense of inward wretchedness. Such is the great change wrought in repentance, it is conversion, and is needed by every human being. The ruin of sinners is their walking after a hard and impenitent heart. Their sinful doings are expressed by the strong words, "treasuring up wrath." In the description of the just man, notice the full demand of the law. It demands that the motives shall be pure, and rejects all actions from earthly ambition or ends. In the description of the unrighteous, contention is held forth as the principle of all evil. The human will is in a state of enmity against God. Even Gentiles, who had not the written law, had that within, which directed them what to do by the light of nature. Conscience is a witness, and first or last will bear witness. As they kept or broke these natural laws and dictates, their consciences either acquitted or condemned them. Nothing speaks more terror to sinners, and more comfort to saints, than that Christ shall be the Judge. Secret services shall be rewarded, secret sins shall be then punished, and brought to light.

17-24 The apostle directs his discourse to the Jews, and shows of what sins they were guilty, notwithstanding their profession and vain pretensions. A believing, humble, thankful glorying in God, is the root and sum of all reli-

I. First, then, let us consider THE HELP WHICH THE HOLY GHOST GIVES.

The help which the Holy Ghost renders to us meets the weakness which we deplore. As I have already said, if in time of trouble a man can pray, his burden loses its weight. If the believer can take anything and everything to God, then he learns to glory in infirmity, and to rejoice in tribulation; but sometimes we are in such confusion of mind that we know not what we should pray for as we ought. In a measure, through our ignorance, we never know what we should pray for until we are taught of the Spirit of God, but there are times when this beclouding of the soul is dense indeed, and we do not even know what would help us out of our trouble if we could obtain it. He see the disease, but the name of the medicine is not known to us. We look over the many things which we might ask for of the Lord, and we feel that each of them would be helpful, but that none of them would precisely meet our case. For spiritual blessings which we know to be according to the divine will we could ask with confidence, but perhaps these would not meet our peculiar circumstances. There are other things for which we are allowed to ask, but we scarcely know whether, if we had them, they would really serve our turn, and we also feel a diffidence as to praying for them. In praying for temporal things we plead with measured voices, ever referring our petition for revision to the will of the Lord. Moses prayed that he might enter Canaan, but God denied him; and the man that was healed asked our Lord that he might be with him, but he received for answer, "Go home to thy friends." We pray evermore on such matters with this reserve, "Nevertheless, not as I will, but as thou wilt." At times this very spirit of resignation appears to increase our spiritual difficulty, for we do not wish to ask for anything that would be contrary to the mind of God and yet we must ask for something. We are reduced to such straits that we must pray, but what shall be the particular subject of prayer we cannot for a while make out. Even when ignorance and perplexity are removed, we know not what we should pray for "as we ought." When we know the matter of prayer, we yet fail to pray in a right manner. We ask, but we are afraid that we shall not have, because we do not exercise the thought, or the faith, which we judge to be essential to prayer. We cannot at times command even the earnestness which is the life of supplication: a torpor steals over us, our

to the Jew first, and also to the Gentile:

11 For there is no respect of persons with God.

12 For as many as have sinned without law shall also perish without law: and as many as have sinned in the law shall be judged by the law;

13 (For not the hearers of the law are just before God, but the doers of the law shall be justified.

14 For when the Gentiles, which have not the law, do by nature the things contained in the law, these, having not the law, are a law unto themselves:

15 Which shew the work of the law written in their hearts, their conscience also bearing witness, and their thoughts the mean while accusing or else excusing one another;)

16 In the day when God shall judge the secrets of men by Jesus Christ according to my gospel.

17 Behold, thou art called a Jew, and restest in the law, and makest thy boast of God,

18 And knowest his will, and approvest the things that are more excellent, being instructed out of the law;

19 And art confident that thou thyself art a guide of the blind, a light of them which are in darkness,

20 An instructor of the foolish, a teacher of babes, which hast the form of knowledge and of the truth in the law.

21 Thou therefore which teachest another, teachest thou not thyself? thou that preachest a man should not steal, dost thou steal?

22 Thou that sayest a man should not commit adultery, dost thou commit adultery? thou that abhorrest idols, dost thou commit sacrilege?

23 Thou that makest thy boast of the law, through breaking the law dishonorest thou God?

24 For the name of God is blasphemed among the Gentiles through you, as it is written.

25 For circumcision verily profiteth, if thou keep the law: but if thou be a breaker of the law, thy circumcision is made uncircumcision.

ings of Lucretius! What vain reasonings, and how dark a heart, amidst so pompous professions of wisdom!

23. And changed – With the utmost folly. Here are three degrees of ungodliness and of punishment: the first is described, ver. 21-24; the second, ver. 25-27; the third, in ver. 28, and following verses. The punishment in each case is expressed by God gave them up. If a man will not worship God as God, he is so left to himself that he throws away his very manhood. Reptiles – Or creeping things; as beetles, and various kinds of serpents.

24. Wherefore – One punishment of sin is from the very nature of it, as ver. 27; another, as here, is from vindictive justice. Uncleanness – Ungodliness and uncleanness are frequently joined, 1 Thess. iv, 5 as are the knowledge of God and purity. God gave them up – By withdrawing his restraining grace.

25. Who changed the truth – The true worship of God. Into a lie – False, abominable idolatries. And worshiped – Inwardly. And served – Outwardly.

26. Therefore God gave them up to vile affections – To which the heathen Romans were then abandoned to the last degree; and none more than the emperors themselves.

27. Receiving the just recompense of their error – Their idolatry being punished with that unnatural lust, which was as horrible a dishonor to the body, as their idolatry was to God.

28. God gave them up to an undiscerning mind – Treated of, ver. 32. To do things not expedient – Even the vilest abominations, treated of verses ver. 29-31.

29. Filled with all injustice – This stands in the first place; unmercifulness, in the last. Fornication – Includes here every species of uncleanness. Maliciousness – The Greek word properly implies a temper which delights in hurting another, even without any advantage to itself.

30. Whisperers – Such as secretly defame others. Backbiters – Such as speak against others behind their back. Haters of God – That is, rebels against him, deniers of his providence, or accusers of his justice in their adversities; yea, having an inward heart – enmity to his justice and holiness. Inventors of evil things – Of new pleasures, new ways of gain, new arts of hurting, particularly in war.

31. Covenant-breakers – It is well known, the Romans, as a nation, from the very beginning of their commonwealth, never made any scruple of vacating altogether the most solemn engagement, if they did not like it, though made by their supreme magistrate, in the name of the whole people. They only gave up the general who had made it, and then supposed themselves to be at full liberty. Without natural affection – The custom of exposing their own newborn children to perish by cold, hunger, or wild beasts, which so generally prevailed in the heathen world, particularly among the Greeks and Romans, was an amazing instance of this; as is also that of killing their aged and helpless parents, now common among the American heathens.

32. Not only do the same, but have pleasure in those that practice them – This is the highest degree of wickedness. A man may be hurried by his passions to do the thing he hates; but he that has pleasure in those that do evil, loves wickedness for wickedness' sake. And hereby he encourages them in sin, and heaps the guilt of others upon his own head.

ROMANS 2

1. Therefore – The apostle now makes a transition from the Gentiles to the Jews, till, at ver. 6, he comprises both. Thou art inexcusable – Seeing knowledge without practice only increases guilt. O man – Having before spoken of the Gentile in the third person, he addresses the Jew in the second person. But he calls him by a common appellation, as not acknowledging him to be a Jew. See verses 17, 28. Whosoever thou art that Judgest – Censurest, condemnest. For in

MATTHEW HENRY   CHARLES H. SPURGEON

gion. But proud, vain-glorious boasting in God, and in the outward profession of his name, is the root and sum of all hypocrisy. Spiritual pride is the most dangerous of all kinds of pride. A great evil of the sins of professors is, the dishonor done to God and religion, by their not living according to their profession. Many despise their more ignorant neighbors who rest in a dead form of godliness; yet themselves trust in a form of knowledge, equally void of life and power, while some glory in the gospel, whose unholy lives dishonor God, and cause his name to be blasphemed.

25-29 No forms, ordinances, or notions can profit, without regenerating grace, which will always lead to seeking an interest in the righteousness of God by faith. For he is no more a Christian now, than he was really a Jew of old, who is only one outwardly: neither is that baptism, which is outward in the flesh: but he is the real Christian, who is inwardly a true believer, with an obedient faith. And the true baptism is that of the heart, by the washing of regeneration and the renewal of the Holy Ghost; bringing a spiritual frame of mind, and a willing following of truth in its holy ways. Let us pray that we may be made real Christians, not outwardly, but inwardly; in the heart and spirit, not in the letter; baptized, not with water only, but with the Holy Ghost; and let our praise be, not of men, but of God.

ROMANS 3

Objections answered. (1-8)
All mankind are sinners. (9-18)
Both Jews and Gentiles cannot be justified by their own deeds. (19,20)
It is owing to the free grace of God, through faith in the righteousness of Christ, yet the law is not done away. (21-31)

1-8 The law could not save in or from sins, yet it gave the Jews advantages for obtaining salvation. Their stated ordinances, education in the knowledge of the true God and his service, and many favors shown to the children of Abraham, all were means of grace, and doubtless were made useful to the conversion of many. But especially the Scriptures were committed to them. Enjoyment of God's word and ordinances, is the chief happiness of a people. But God's promises are made only to believers; therefore the unbelief of some, or of many professors, cannot make this faithfulness of no effect. He will fulfill his promises to his people, and bring his threatened vengeance upon unbelievers. God's judging the world, should for ever silence all doubting and reflections upon his justice. The wickedness and obstinate unbelief of the Jews, proved man's need of the righteousness of God by faith, and also his justice in punishing for sin. Let us do evil, that good may come, is oftener in the heart than in the mouth of sinners; for few thus justify themselves in their wicked ways. The believer knows that duty belongs to him, and events to God; and that he must not commit any sin, or speak

heart is chilled, our hand is numbed, and we cannot wrestle with the angel. We know what to pray for as to objects, but we do not know what to pray for "as we ought"; it is the manner of the prayer which perplexes us, even when the matter is decided upon. How can I pray? My mind wanders: I chatter like a crane; I roar like a beast in pain; I moan in the brokenness of my heart, but oh, my God, I know not what it is my inmost spirit needs; or if I know it, I know not how to frame my petition aright before thee. I know not how to open my lips in thy majestic presence: I am so troubled that I cannot speak. My spiritual distress robs me of the power to pour out my heart before my God. Now, beloved, it is in such a plight as this that the Holy Ghost aids us with his divine help. and hence he is "a very present help in time of trouble."

Coming to our aid in our bewilderment he instructs us. This is one of his frequent operations upon the mind of the believer: "he shall teach you all things." He instructs us as to our need, and as to the promises of God which refer to that need. He shows us where our deficiencies are, what our sins are, and what our necessities are; he sheds a light upon our condition, and makes us feel deeply our helplessness, sinfulness, and dire poverty; and then he casts the same light upon the promises of the Word, and lays home to the heart that very text which was intended to meet the occasion—the precise promise which was framed with foresight of our present distress. In that light he makes the promise shine in all its truthfulness, certainty, sweetness, and suitability, so that we, poor trembling sons of men, dare take that word into our mouth which first came out of God's mouth, and then come with it as an argument, and plead it before the throne of the heavenly grace. Our prevalence in prayer lies in the plea, "Lord, do as thou hast said." How greatly we ought to value the Holy Spirit, because when we are in the dark he gives us light, and when our perplexed spirit is so befogged and beclouded that it cannot see its own need, and cannot find out the appropriate promise in the Scriptures, the Spirit of God comes in and teaches us all things, and brings all things to our remembrance, whatsoever our Lord has told us. He guides us in prayer, and thus he helps our infirmity.

But the blessed Spirit does more than this, he will often direct the mind to the special subject of prayer. He dwells within us as a counselor, and points out to us what it is we should seek at the hands of God. We do not

26 Therefore if the uncircumcision keep the righteousness of the law, shall not his uncircumcision be counted for circumcision?

27 And shall not uncircumcision which is by nature, if it fulfill the law, judge thee, who by the letter and circumcision dost transgress the law?

28 For he is not a Jew, which is one outwardly; neither is that circumcision, which is outward in the flesh:

29 But he is a Jew, which is one inwardly; and circumcision is that of the heart, in the spirit, and not in the letter; whose praise is not of men, but of God.

ROMANS 3

1 What advantage then hath the Jew? or what profit is there of circumcision?

2 Much every way: chiefly, because that unto them were committed the oracles of God.

3 For what if some did not believe? shall their unbelief make the faith of God without effect?

4 God forbid: yea, let God be true, but every man a liar; as it is written, That thou mightest be justified in thy sayings, and mightest overcome when thou art judged.

5 But if our unrighteousness commend the righteousness of God, what shall we say? Is God unrighteous who taketh vengeance? (I speak as a man)

6 God forbid: for then how shall God judge the world?

7 For if the truth of God hath more abounded through my lie unto his glory; why yet am I also judged as a sinner?

8 And not rather, (as we be slanderously reported, and as some affirm that we say,) Let us do evil, that good may come? whose damnation is just.

9 What then? are we better than they? No, in no wise: for we have before proved both Jews and Gentiles, that they are all under sin;

10 As it is written, There is none righteous, no, not one:

11 There is none that understandeth, there is none that seeketh after God.

that thou Judgest the other – The heathen. Thou condemnest thyself; for thou doest the same things – In effect; in many instances.

2. For we know – Without thy teaching. That the judgment of God – Not thine, who exceptest thyself from its sentence. Is according to truth – Is just, making no exception, ver. 5, 6, 11; and reaches the heart as well as the life, ver. 16.

3. That thou shalt escape – Rather than the Gentile.

4. Or despisest thou – Dost thou go farther still, – from hoping to escape his wrath, to the abuse of his love?. The riches – The abundance. Of his goodness, forbearance, and longsuffering – Seeing thou both hast sinned, dost sin, and wilt sin. All these are afterwards comprised in the single word goodness. Leadeth thee – That is, is designed of God to lead or encourage thee to it.

5. Treasurest up wrath – Although thou thinkest thou art treasuring up all good things. O what a treasure may a man lay up either way, in this short day of life! To thyself – Not to him whom thou Judgest. In the day of wrath, and Revelation, and righteous judgment of God – Just opposite to "the goodness and forbearance and longsuffering" of God. When God shall be revealed, then shall also be "revealed" the secrets of men's hearts, ver. 16. Forbearance and Revelation respect God, and are opposed to each other; longsuffering and righteous judgment respect the sinner; goodness and wrath are words of a more general import.

6. Prov. xxiv, 12.

7. To them that seek for glory – For pure love does not exclude faith, hope, desire, 1 Cor. xv, 58.

8. But to them that are contentious – Like thee, O Jew, who thus fightest against God. The character of a false Jew is disobedience, stubbornness, impatience. Indignation and wrath, tribulation and anguish – Alluding to Psalm lxxviii, xlix, "He cast upon them," the Egyptians. "the fierceness of his anger, wrath, and indignation, and trouble;" and finely intimating, that the Jews would in the day of vengeance be more severely punished than even the Egyptians were when God made their plagues so wonderful.

9. Of the Jew first – Here we have the first express mention of the Jews in this chapter. And it is introduced with great propriety. Their having been trained up in the true religion, and having had Christ and his apostles first sent to them, will place them in the foremost rank of the criminals that obey not the truth.

10. But glory – Just opposite to "wrath," from the divine approbation. Honor – Opposite to "indignation," by the divine appointment; and peace now and for ever, opposed to tribulation and anguish.

11. For there is no respect of persons with God – He will reward every one according to his works. But this is well consistent with his distributing advantages and opportunities of improvement, according to his own good pleasure.

12. For as many as have sinned – He speaks as of the time past, for all time will be past at the day of judgment. Without the law – Without having any written law. Shall also perish without the law – Without regard had to any outward law; being condemned by the law written in their hearts. The word also shows the agreement of the manner of sinning, with the manner of suffering. Perish – He could not so properly say, Shall be judged without the law.

13. For not the hearers of the law are, even now, just before God, but the doers of the law shall be justified – Finally acquitted and rewarded a most sure and important truth, which respects the Gentiles also, though principally the Jews. St. Paul speaks of the former, ver. 14, &c.; of the latter, ver. 17, &c. Here is therefore no parenthesis; for the sixteenth verse also depends on the fifteenth, not on the twelfth. Rom. ii, 16, 15, 12.

14. For when the Gentiles – That is, any of them.

15. Who show – To themselves, to other men, and, in a sense, to God himself. The work of the law – The substance, though not the letter, of it. Written on their hearts – By the same hand which wrote the commandments on the tables

one falsehood, upon the hope, or even assurance, that God may thereby glorify himself. If any speak and act thus, their condemnation is just.

9-18 Here again is shown that all mankind are under the guilt of sin, as a burden; and under the government and dominion of sin, as enslaved to it, to work wickedness. This is made plain by several passages of Scripture from the Old Testament, which describe the corrupt and depraved state of all men, till grace restrain or change them. Great as our advantages are, these texts describe multitudes who call themselves Christians. Their principles and conduct prove that there is no fear of God before their eyes. And where no fear of God is, no good is to be looked for.

19,20 It is in vain to seek for justification by the works of the law. All must plead guilty. Guilty before God, is a dreadful word; but no man can be justified by a law which condemns him for breaking it. The corruption in our nature, will for ever stop any justification by our own works.

21-26 Must guilty man remain under wrath? Is the wound for ever incurable? No; blessed be God, there is another way laid open for us. This is the righteousness of God; righteousness of his ordaining, and providing, and accepting. It is by that faith which has Jesus Christ for its object; an anointed Savior, so Jesus Christ signifies. Justifying faith respects Christ as a Savior, in all his three anointed offices, as Prophet, Priest, and King; trusting in him, accepting him, and cleaving to him: in all these, Jews and Gentiles are alike welcome to God through Christ. There is no difference, his righteousness is upon all that believe; not only offered to them, but put upon them as a crown, as a robe. It is free grace, mere mercy; there is nothing in us to deserve such favors. It comes freely unto us, but Christ bought it, and paid the price. And faith has special regard to the blood of Christ, as that which made the atonement. God, in all this, declares his righteousness. It is plain that he hates sin, when nothing less than the blood of Christ would satisfy for it. And it would not agree with his justice to demand the debt, when the Surety has paid it, and he has accepted that payment in full satisfaction.

27-31 God will have the great work of the justification and salvation of sinners carried on from first to last, so as to shut out boasting. Now, if we were saved by our own works, boasting would not be excluded. But the way of justification by faith for ever shuts out boasting. Yet believers are not left to be lawless; faith is a law, it is a working grace, wherever it is in truth. By faith, not in this matter an act of obedience, or a good work, but forming the relation between Christ and the sinner, which renders it proper that the believer should be pardoned and justified for the sake of the Savior, and that the unbeliever who is not thus united or related to him, should remain under condemnation. The law is still of use to convince us of what is past,

know why it is so, but we sometimes find our minds carried as by a strong under current into a particular line of prayer for some one definite object. It is not merely that our judgment leads us in that direction, though usually the Spirit of God acts upon us by enlightening our judgment, but we often feel an unaccountable and irresistible desire rising again and again within our heart, and this so presses upon us, that we not only utter the desire before God at our ordinary times for prayer, but we feel it crying in our hearts all the day long, almost to the supplanting of all other considerations. At such times we should thank God for direction and give our desire a clear road: the Holy Spirit is granting us inward direction as to how we should reckon upon good success in our pleadings. Such guidance will the Spirit give to each of you if you will ask him to illuminate you. He will guide you both negatively and positively. Negatively, he will forbid you to pray for such and such a thing, even as Paul essayed to go into Bithynia, but the Spirit suffered him not: and, on other hand, he will cause you to hear a cry within your soul which shall guide your petitions, even as he made Paul hear the cry from Macedonia, saying, "Come over and help us." The Spirit teaches wisely, as no other teacher can do. Those who obey his promptings shall not walk in darkness. He leads the spiritual eye to take good and steady aim at the very center of the target, and thus we hit the mark in our pleadings.

Nor is this all, for the spirit of God is not sent merely to guide and help our devotion, but he himself "maketh intercession for us" according to the will of God. By this expression it cannot be meant that the Holy Spirit ever groans or personally prays; but that he excites intense desire and creates unutterable groanings in us, and these are ascribed to him. Even as Solomon built the temple because he superintended and ordained all, and yet I know not that he ever fashioned a timber or prepared a stone, so doth the Holy Spirit pray and plead within us by leading us to pray and plead. This he does by arousing our desires. The Holy Spirit has a wonderful power over renewed hearts, as much power as the skillful minstrel hath over the strings among which he lays his accustomed hand. The influences of the Holy Ghost at times pass through the soul like winds through an Eolian harp, creating and inspiring sweet notes of gratitude and tones of desire, to which we should have been strangers if it had not been for his divine visitation. He can

12 They are all gone out of the way, they are together become unprofitable; there is none that doeth good, no, not one.

13 Their throat is an open sepulcher; with their tongues have used deceit; the poison of asps is under their lips:

14 Whose mouth is full of cursing and bitterness:

15 Their feet are swift to shed blood:

16 Destruction and misery are in their ways:

17 And the way of peace have they not known:

18 There is no fear of God before their eyes.

19 Now we know that what things soever the law saith, it saith to them who are under the law: that every mouth may be stopped, and all the world may become guilty before God.

20 Therefore by the deeds of the law there shall no flesh be justified in his sight: for by the law is the knowledge of sin.

21 But now the righteousness of God without the law is manifested, being witnessed by the law and the prophets;

22 Even the righteousness of God which is by faith of Jesus Christ unto all and upon all them that believe: for there is no difference:

23 For all have sinned, and come short of the glory of God;

24 Being justified freely by his grace through the redemption that is in Christ Jesus:

25 Whom God hath set forth to be a propitiation through faith in his blood, to declare his righteousness for the remission of sins that are past, through the forbearance of God;

26 To declare, I say, at this time his righteousness: that he might be just, and the justifier of him which believeth in Jesus.

27 Where is boasting then? It is excluded. By what law? of works? Nay: but by the law of faith.

28 Therefore we conclude that a man is justified by faith without the deeds of the law.

29 Is he the God of the Jews only? is he not also of the Gentiles? Yes, of the Gentiles also:

30 Seeing it is one God, which

of stone. Their conscience – There is none of all its faculties which the soul has less in its power than this. Bearing witness – In a trial there are the plaintiff, the defendant, and the witnesses. Conscience and sin itself are witnesses against the heathens. Their thoughts sometimes excuse, sometimes condemn, them. Among themselves – Alternately, like plaintiff and defendant. Accusing or even defending them – The very manner of speaking shows that they have far more room to accuse than to defend.

16. In the day – That is, who show this in the day. Everything will then be shown to be what it really is. In that day will appear the law written in their hearts as it often does in the present life. When God shall judge the secrets of men – On secret circumstances depends the real quality of actions, frequently unknown to the actors themselves, ver. 29. Men generally form their judgments, even of themselves merely from what is apparent. According to my gospel – According to the tenor of that gospel which is committed to my care. Hence it appears that the gospel also is a law.

17. But if thou art called a Jew – This highest point of Jewish glorying, after a farther description of it interposed, ver. 17-20, and refuted, ver. 21-24, is itself refuted, ver. 25, &c. The description consists of twice five articles; of which the former five, ver. 17, 18, show what he boasts of in himself; the other five, ver. 19, 20, what he glories in with respect to others. The first particular of the former five answers to the first of the latter; the second, to the second, and so on. And restest in the law – Dependest on it, though it can only condemn thee. And gloriest in God – As thy God; and that, too, to the exclusion of others.

19. Blind, in darkness, ignorant, babes – These were the titles which the Jews generally gave the Gentiles.

20. Having the form of knowledge and truth – That is, the most accurate knowledge of the truth.

21. Thou dost not teach thyself – He does not teach himself who does not practice what he teaches. Dost thou steal, commit adultery, commit sacrilege – Sin grievously against thy neighbor, thyself, God. St. Paul had shown the Gentiles, first their sins against God, then against themselves, then against their neighbors. He now inverts the order: for sins against God are the most glaring in an heathen, but not in a Jew. Thou that abhorrest idols – Which all the Jews did, from the time of the Babylonish captivity. Thou committest sacrilege – Doest what is worse, robbing him "who is God over all" of the glory which is due to him. None of these charges were rashly advanced against the Jews of that age; for, as their own historian relates, some even of the priests lived by rapine, and others in gross uncleanness. And as for sacrilegiously robbing God and his altar, it had been complained of ever since Malachi; so that the instances are given with great propriety and judgment.

24. Isaiah lii, 5.

25. Circumcision indeed profiteth – He does not say, justifies. How far it profited is shown in the third and fourth chapters. Thy circumcision is become uncircumcision – is so already in effect. Thou wilt have no more benefit by it than if thou hadst never received it. The very same observation holds with regard to baptism.

26. If the uncircumcision – That is, a person uncircumcized. Keep the law – Walk agreeably to it. Shall not his uncircumcision be counted for circumcision – In the sight of God?

27. Yea, the uncircumcision that is by nature – Those who are, literally speaking, uncircumcized. Fulfilling the law – As to the substance of it. Shall judge thee – Shall condemn thee in that day. Who by the letter and circumcision – Who having the bare, literal, external circumcision, transgressest the law.

28. For he is not a Jew – In the most important sense, that is, one of God's beloved people. Who is one in outward show only; neither is that the true, acceptable circumcision, which is apparent in the flesh.

and to direct us for the future. Though we cannot be saved by it as a covenant, yet we own and submit to it, as a rule in the hand of the Mediator.

ROMANS 4

The doctrine of justification by faith is shown by the case of Abraham. (1-12)

He received the promise through the righteousness of faith. (13-22)

And we are justified in the same way of believing. (23-25)

1-12 To meet the views of the Jews, the apostle first refers to the example of Abraham, in whom the Jews gloried as their most renowned forefather. However exalted in various respects, he had nothing to boast in the presence of God, being saved by grace, through faith, even as others. Without noticing the years which passed before his call, and the failures at times in his obedience, and even in his faith, it was expressly stated in Scripture that "he believed God, and it was counted to him for righteousness," Ge 15:6. From this example it is observed, that if any man could work the full measure required by the law, the reward must be reckoned as a debt, which evidently was not the case even of Abraham, seeing faith was reckoned to him for righteousness. When believers are justified by faith, "their faith being counted for righteousness," their faith does not justify them as a part, small or great, of their righteousness; but as the appointed means of uniting them to him who has chosen as the name whereby he shall be called, "the Lord our Righteousness." Pardoned people are the only blessed people. It clearly appears from the Scripture, that Abraham was justified several years before his circumcision. It is, therefore, plain that this rite was not necessary in order to justification. It was a sign of the original corruption of human nature. And it was such a sign as was also an outward seal, appointed not only to confirm God's promises to him and to his seed, and their obligation to be the Lord's, but likewise to assure him of his being already a real partaker of the righteousness of faith. Thus Abraham was the spiritual forefather of all believers, who walked after the example of his obedient faith. The seal of the Holy Spirit in our sanctification, making us new creatures, is the inward evidence of the righteousness of faith.

13-22 The promise was made to Abraham long before the law. It points at Christ, and it refers to the promise, Ge 12:3. In thee shall all families of the earth be blessed. The law worketh wrath, by showing that every transgressor is exposed to the Divine displeasure. As God intended to give men a title to the promised blessings, so he appointed it to be by faith, that it might be wholly of grace, to make it sure to all who were of the like precious faith with Abraham, whether Jews or Gentiles, in all ages. The justification and salvation of sinners, the taking to himself the Gentiles who had not been a people, were a gracious calling of things which are not, as though they were; and

arouse us from our lethargy, he can warm us out of our lukewarmness, he can enable us when we are on our knees to rise above the ordinary routine of prayer into that victorious importunity against which nothing can stand. He can lay certain desires so pressingly upon our hearts that we can never rest till they are fulfilled. He can make the zeal for God's house to eat us up, and the passion for God's glory to be like a fire within our bones; and this is one part of that process by which in inspiring our prayers he helps our infirmity. True Advocate is he, and Comforter most effectual. Blessed be his name.

The Holy Spirit also divinely operates in the strengthening of the faith of believers. That faith is at first of his creating, and afterwards it is of his sustaining and increasing: and oh, brothers and sisters, have you not often felt your faith rise in proportion to your trials? Have you not, like Noah's ark, mounted towards heaven as the flood deepened around you? You have felt as sure about the promise as you felt about the trial. The affliction was, as it were, in your very bones, but the promise was also in your very heart. You could not doubt the affliction, for you smarted under it, but you might almost as soon have doubted the divine help, for your confidence was firm and unmoved. The greatest faith is only what God has a right to expect from us, yet do we never exhibit it except as the Holy Ghost strengthens our confidence, and opens up before us the covenant with all its seals and securities. He it is that leads our soul to cry, "though my house be not so with God, yet hath he made with me an everlasting covenant ordered in all things and sure." Blessed be the Divine Spirit then, that since faith is essential to prevailing prayer, he helps us in supplication by increasing our faith. Without faith prayer cannot speed, for he that wavereth is like a wave of the sea driven with the wind and tossed, and such an one may not expect anything of the Lord; happy are we when the Holy Spirit removes our wavering, and enables us like Abraham to believe without staggering, knowing full well that he who has promised is able also to perform.

By three figures I will endeavor to describe the work of the Spirit of God in this matter, though they all fall short, and indeed all that I can say must fall infinitely short of the glory of his work. The actual mode of his working upon the mind we may not attempt to explain; it remains a mystery, and it would be an unholy intrusion to attempt to remove the veil. There is no difficulty in our believing

shall justify the circumcision by faith, and uncircumcision through faith.

31 Do we then make void the law through faith? God forbid: yea, we establish the law.

ROMANS 4

1 What shall we say then that Abraham our father, as pertaining to the flesh, hath found?

2 For if Abraham were justified by works, he hath whereof to glory; but not before God.

3 For what saith the scripture? Abraham believed God, and it was counted unto him for righteousness.

4 Now to him that worketh is the reward not reckoned of grace, but of debt.

5 But to him that worketh not, but believeth on him that justifieth the ungodly, his faith is counted for righteousness.

6 Even as David also describeth the blessedness of the man, unto whom God imputeth righteousness without works,

7 Saying, Blessed are they whose iniquities are forgiven, and whose sins are covered.

8 Blessed is the man to whom the Lord will not impute sin.

9 Cometh this blessedness then upon the circumcision only, or upon the uncircumcision also? for we say that faith was reckoned to Abraham for righteousness.

10 How was it then reckoned? when he was in circumcision, or in uncircumcision? Not in circumcision, but in uncircumcision.

11 And he received the sign of circumcision, a seal of the righteousness of the faith which he had yet being uncircumcized: that he might be the father of all them that believe, though they be not circumcized; that righteousness might be imputed unto them also:

12 And the father of circumcision to them who are not of the circumcision only, but who also walk in the steps of that faith of our father Abraham, which he had being yet uncircumcized.

13 For the promise, that he should be the heir of the world, was not to Abraham, or to his

29. But he is a Jew – That is, one of God's people. Who is one inwardly – In the secret recesses of his soul. And the acceptable circumcision is that of the heart – Referring to Deut. xxx, 6; the putting away all inward impurity. This is seated in the spirit, the inmost soul, renewed by the Spirit of God. And not in the letter – Not in the external ceremony. Whose praise is not from men, but from God – The only searcher of the heart.

ROMANS 3

1. What then, may some say, is the advantage of the Jew, or of the circumcision – That is, those that are circumcized, above the Gentiles?

2. Chiefly in that they were intrusted with the oracles of God – The scriptures, in which are so great and precious promises. Other prerogatives will follow, chap. ix, 4-5. St. Paul here singles out this by which, after removing the objection, he will convict them so much the more.

3. Shall their unbelief disannul the faithfulness of God – Will he not still make good his promises to them that do believe?

4. Psalm ii, 4.

5. But, it may be farther objected, if our unrighteousness be subservient to God's glory, is it not unjust in him to punish us for it? I speak as a man – As human weakness would be apt to speak.

6. God forbid – By no means. If it were unjust in God to punish that unrighteousness which is subservient to his own glory, how should God judge the world – Since all the unrighteousness in the world will then commend the righteousness of God.

7. But, may the objector reply, if the truth of God hath abounded – Has been more abundantly shown. Through my lie – If my lie, that is, practice contrary to truth, conduces to the glory of God, by making his truth shine with superior advantage. Why am I still judged as a sinner – Can this be said to be any sin at all? Ought I not to do what would otherwise be evil, that so much "good may come?" To this the apostle does not deign to give a direct answer, but cuts the objector short with a severe reproof.

8. Whose condemnation is just – The condemnation of all who either speak or act in this manner. So the apostle absolutely denies the lawfulness of "doing evil," any evil, "that good may come."

9. What then – Here he resumes what he said, verse 1. Rom. iii, 1. Under sin – Under the guilt and power of it: the Jews, by transgressing the written law; the Gentiles, by transgressing the law of nature.

10. As it is written – That all men are under sin appears from the vices which have raged in all ages. St. Paul therefore rightly cites David and Isaiah, though they spoke primarily of their own age, and expressed what manner of men God sees, when he "looks down from heaven;" not what he makes them by his grace. There is none righteous – This is the general proposition. The particulars follow: their dispositions and designs, ver. 11, 12; their discourse, ver. 13, 14; their actions, ver. 16-18. Psalm xiv, 1, &c.

11. There is none that understandeth – The things of God.

12. They have all turned aside – From the good way. They are become unprofitable – Helpless impotent, unable to profit either themselves or others.

14. Cursing – Against God. Bitterness – Against their neighbor. Psalm x, 7.

15. Isaiah lix, 7, 8.

17. Of peace – Which can only spring from righteousness.

18. The fear of God is not before their eyes – Much less is the love of God in their heart. Psalm xxxvi, 1.

20. No flesh shall be justified – None shall be forgiven and accepted of God. By the works of the law – On this ground, that he hath kept the law. St. Paul means chiefly the moral part of it, ver. 9, 19; chap. ii, 21, 26; &c. which alone is not

this giving a being to things that were not, proves the almighty power of God. The nature and power of Abraham's faith are shown. He believed God's testimony, and looked for the performance of his promise, firmly hoping when the case seemed hopeless. It is weakness of faith, that makes a man lie poring on the difficulties in the way of a promise. Abraham took it not for a point that would admit of argument or debate. Unbelief is at the bottom of all our staggering at God's promises. The strength of faith appeared in its victory over fears. God honors faith; and great faith honors God. It was imputed to him for righteousness. Faith is a grace that of all others gives glory to God. Faith clearly is the instrument by which we receive the righteousness of God, the redemption which is by Christ; and that which is the instrument whereby we take or receive it, cannot be the thing itself, nor can it be the gift thereby taken and received. Abraham's faith did not justify him by its own merit or value, but as giving him a part in Christ.

23-25 The history of Abraham, and of his justification, was recorded to teach men of after-ages; those especially to whom the gospel was then made known. It is plain, that we are not justified by the merit of our own works, but by faith in Jesus Christ and his righteousness; which is the truth urged in this and the foregoing chapter, as the great spring and foundation of all comfort. Christ did meritoriously work our justification and salvation by his death and passion, but the power and perfection thereof, with respect to us, depend on his resurrection. By his death he paid our debt, in his resurrection he received our acquittance, Isa 53:8. When he was discharged, we, in him and together with him, received the discharge from the guilt and punishment of all our sins. This last verse is an abridgement or summary of the whole gospel.

ROMANS 5

The happy effects of justification through faith in the righteousness of Christ. (1-5)
That we are reconciled by his blood. (6-11)
The fall of Adam brought all mankind into sin and death. (12-14)
The grace of God, through the righteousness of Christ, has more power to bring salvation, than Adam's sin had to bring misery. (15-19)
As grace did superabound. (20,21)

1-5 A blessed change takes place in the sinner's state, when he becomes a true believer, whatever he has been. Being justified by faith he has peace with God. The holy, righteous God, cannot be at peace with a sinner, while under the guilt of sin. Justification takes away the guilt, and so makes way for peace. This is through our Lord Jesus Christ; through him as the great Peace-maker, the Mediator between God and man. The saints' happy state is a state of grace. Into this grace we are brought, which teaches that we were not born in this state. We could not

that as one human mind operates upon another mind, so does the Holy Spirit influence our spirits. We are forced to use words if we would influence our fellow-men, but the Spirit of God can operate upon the human mind more directly, and communicate with it in silence. Into that matter, however, we will not dive lest we intrude where our knowledge would be drowned by our presumption.

My illustrations do not touch the mystery, but set forth the grace. The Holy Spirit acts to his people somewhat as a prompter to a reciter. A man has to deliver a piece which he has learned; but his memory is treacherous, and therefore somewhere out of sight there is a prompter, so that when the speaker is at a loss and might use a wrong word, a whisper is heard, which suggests the right one. When the speaker has almost lost the thread of his discourse he turns his ear, and the prompter gives him the catch-word and aids his memory. If I may be allowed the simile, I would say that this represents in part the work of the Spirit of God in us,—suggesting to us the right desire, and bringing all things to our remembrance whatsoever Christ has told us. In prayer we should often come to a dead stand, but he incites, suggests, and inspires, and so we go onward. In prayer we might grow weary, but the Comforter encourages and refreshes us with cheering thoughts. When, indeed, we are in our bewilderment almost driven to give up prayer, the whisper of his love drops a live coal from off the altar into our soul, and our hearts glow with greater ardor than before. Regard the Holy Spirit as your prompter, and let your ear be opened to his voice.

But he is much more than this. Let me attempt a second simile: he is as an advocate to one in peril at law. Suppose that a poor man had a great law-suit, touching his whole estate, and he was forced personally to go into court and plead his own cause, and speak up for his rights. If he were an uneducated man he would be in a poor plight. An adversary in the court might plead against him, and overthrow him, for he could not answer him. This poor man knows very little about law, and is quite unable to meet his cunning opponent. Suppose one who was perfect in the law should take up his cause warmly, and come and live with him, and use all his knowledge so as to prepare his case for him, draw up his petitions for him, and fill his mouth with arguments,—would not that be a grand relief? This counselor would suggest the line of pleading, arrange the arguments, and put

seed, through the law, but through the righteousness of faith.

14 For if they which are of the law be heirs, faith is made void, and the promise made of none effect:

15 Because the law worketh wrath: for where no law is, there is no transgression.

16 Therefore it is of faith, that it might be by grace; to the end the promise might be sure to all the seed; not to that only which is of the law, but to that also which is of the faith of Abraham; who is the father of us all,

17 (As it is written, I have made thee a father of many nations,) before him whom he believed, even God, who quickeneth the dead, and calleth those things which be not as though they were.

18 Who against hope believed in hope, that he might become the father of many nations; according to that which was spoken, So shall thy seed be.

19 And being not weak in faith, he considered not his own body now dead, when he was about an hundred years old, neither yet the deadness of Sara's womb:

20 He staggered not at the promise of God through unbelief; but was strong in faith, giving glory to God;

21 And being fully persuaded that, what he had promised, he was able also to perform.

22 And therefore it was imputed to him for righteousness.

23 Now it was not written for his sake alone, that it was imputed to him;

24 But for us also, to whom it shall be imputed, if we believe on him that raised up Jesus our Lord from the dead;

25 Who was delivered for our offenses, and was raised again for our justification.

ROMANS 5

1 Therefore being justified by faith, we have peace with God through our Lord Jesus Christ:

2 By whom also we have access by faith into this grace wherein we stand, and rejoice in hope of the glory of God.

abolished, ver. 31. And it is not without reason, that he so often mentions the works of the law, whether ceremonial or moral; for it was on these only the Jews relied, being wholly ignorant of those that spring from faith. For by the law is only the knowledge of sin – But no deliverance either from the guilt or power of it.

21. But now the righteousness of God – That is, the manner of becoming righteous which God hath appointed. Without the law – Without that previous obedience which the law requires; without reference to the law, or dependence on it. Is manifested – In the gospel. Being attested by the Law itself, and by the Prophets – By all the promises in the Old Testament.

22. To all – The Jews. And upon all – The Gentiles. That believe: for there is no difference – Either as to the need of justification, or the manner of it.

23. For all have sinned – In Adam, and in their own persons; by a sinful nature, sinful tempers, and sinful actions. And are fallen short of the glory of God – The supreme end of man; short of his image on earth, and the enjoyment of him in heaven.

24. And are justified – Pardoned and accepted. Freely – Without any merit of their own. By his grace – Not their own righteousness or works. Through the redemption – The price Christ has paid. Freely by his grace – One of these expressions might have served to convey the apostle's meaning; but he doubles his assertion, in order to give us the fullest conviction of the truth, and to impress us with a sense of its peculiar importance. It is not possible to find words that should more absolutely exclude all consideration of our own works and obedience, or more emphatically ascribe the whole of our justification to free, unmerited goodness.

25. Whom God hath set forth – Before angels and men. A propitiation – To appease an offended God. But if, as some teach, God never was offended, there was no need of this propitiation. And, if so, Christ died in vain. To declare his righteousness – To demonstrate not only his clemency, but his justice; even that vindictive justice whose essential character and principal office is, to punish sin. By the remission of past sins – All the sins antecedent to their believing.

27. Where is the boasting then of the Jew against the Gentile? It is excluded. By what law? of works? Nay – This would have left room for boasting. But by the law of faith – Since this requires all, without distinction, to apply as guilty and helpless sinners, to the free mercy of God in Christ. The law of faith is that divine constitution which makes faith, not works, the condition of acceptance.

28. We conclude then that a man is justified by faith – And even by this, not as it is a work, but as it receives Christ; and, consequently, has something essentially different from all our works whatsoever.

29. Surely of the Gentiles also – As both nature and the scriptures show.

30. Seeing it is one God who – Shows mercy to both, and by the very same means.

31. We establish the law – Both the authority, purity, and the end of it; by defending that which the law attests; by pointing out Christ, the end of it; and by showing how it may be fulfilled in its purity.

ROMANS 4

Having proved it by argument, he now proves by example, and such example as must have greater weight with the Jews than any other.

    1. That justification is by faith:

    2. That it is free for the Gentiles.

1. That our father Abraham hath found – Acceptance with God. According to the flesh – That is, by works.

2. The meaning is, If Abraham had been justified by works, he would have had room to glory. But he had not room to glory. Therefore he was not justified by

have got into it of ourselves, but we are led into it, as pardoned offenders. Therein we stand, a posture that denotes perseverance; we stand firm and safe, upheld by the power of the enemy. And those who have hope for the glory of God hereafter, have enough to rejoice in now. Tribulation worketh patience, not in and of itself, but the powerful grace of God working in and with the tribulation. Patient sufferers have most of the Divine consolations, which abound as afflictions abound. It works needful experience of ourselves. This hope will not disappoint, because it is sealed with the Holy Spirit as a Spirit of love. It is the gracious work of the blessed Spirit to shed abroad the love of God in the hearts of all the saints. A right sense of God's love to us, will make us not ashamed, either of our hope, or of our sufferings for him.

6-11 Christ died for sinners; not only such as were useless, but such as were guilty and hateful; such that their everlasting destruction would be to the glory of God's justice. The living Lord of all, will complete the purpose of his dying love, by saving all true believers to the uttermost. Having such a pledge of salvation in the love of God through Christ, the apostle declared that believers not only rejoiced in the hope of heaven, and even in their tribulations for Christ's sake, but they gloried in God also, as their unchangeable Friend and all-sufficient Portion, through Christ only.

12-14 The design of what follows is plain. It is to exalt our views respecting the blessings Christ has procured for us, by comparing them with the evil which followed upon the fall of our first father; and by showing that these blessings not only extend to the removal of these evils, but far beyond. Adam sinning, his nature became guilty and corrupted, and so came to his children. Thus in him all have sinned. And death is by sin; for death is the wages of sin. Then entered all that misery which is the due desert of sin; temporal, spiritual, eternal death. If Adam had not sinned, he had not died; but a sentence of death was passed, as upon a criminal; it passed through all men, as an infectious disease that none escape. In proof of our union with Adam, and our part in his first transgression, observe, that sin prevailed in the world, for many ages before the giving of the law by Moses. And death reigned in that long time, not only over adults who willfully sinned, but also over multitudes of infants, which shows that they had fallen in Adam under condemnation, and that the sin of Adam extended to all his posterity. He was a figure or type of him that was to come as Surety of a new covenant, for all who are related to him.

15-19 Through one man's offense, all mankind are exposed to eternal condemnation. But the grace and mercy of God, and the free gift of righteousness and salvation, are through Jesus Christ, as man: yet the Lord from heaven has brought the multitude of believers into a more safe and exalted state than that from which they fell in Adam. This free gift did not place them anew in a state of trial, but fixed them in a state of justification, as Adam

them into right courtly language. When the poor man was baffled by a question asked in court, he would run home and ask his adviser, and he would tell him exactly how to meet the objector. Suppose, too, that when he had to plead with the judge himself, this advocate at home should teach him how to behave and what to urge, and encourage him to hope that he would prevail,—would not this be a great boon? Who would be the pleader in such a case? The poor client would plead, but still, when he won the suit, he would trace it all to the advocate who lived at home, and gave him counsel: indeed, it would be the advocate pleading for him, even while he pleaded himself. This is an instructive emblem of a great fact. Within this narrow house of my body, this tenement of clay, if I be a true believer, there dwells the Holy Ghost, and when I desire to pray I may ask him what I should pray for as I ought, and he will help me. He will write the prayers which I ought to offer upon the tablets of my heart, and I shall see them there, and so I shall be taught how to plead. It will be the Spirit's own self pleading in me, and by me, and through me, before the throne of grace. What a happy man in his law-suit would such a poor man be, and how happy are you and I that we have the Holy Ghost to be our Counselor!

Yet one more illustration: it is that of a father aiding his boy. Suppose it to be a time of war centuries back. Old English warfare was then conducted by bowmen to a great extent. Here is a youth who is to be initiated in the art of archery, and therefore he carries a bow. It is a strong bow, and therefore very hard to draw; indeed, it requires more strength than the urchin can summon to bend it. See how his father teaches him. "Put your right hand here, my boy, and place your left hand so. Now pull;" and as the youth pulls, his father's hands are on his hands, and the bow is drawn. The lad draws the bow: ay, but it is quite as much his father, too. We cannot draw the bow of prayer alone. Sometimes a bow of steel is not broken by our hands, for we cannot even bend it; and then the Holy Ghost puts his mighty hand over ours, and covers our weakness so that we draw; and lo, what splendid drawing of the bow it is then! The bow bends so easily we wonder how it is; away flies the arrow, and it pierces the very center of the target, for he who giveth have won the day, but it was his secret might that made us strong, and to him be the glory of it.

Thus have I tried to set forth the cheering fact that the Spirit helps the people of God.

3 And not only so, but we glory in tribulations also: knowing that tribulation worketh patience;

4 And patience, experience; and experience, hope:

5 And hope maketh not ashamed; because the love of God is shed abroad in our hearts by the Holy Ghost which is given unto us.

6 For when we were yet without strength, in due time Christ died for the ungodly.

7 For scarcely for a righteous man will one die: yet peradventure for a good man some would even dare to die.

8 But God commendeth his love toward us, in that, while we were yet sinners, Christ died for us.

9 Much more then, being now justified by his blood, we shall be saved from wrath through him.

10 For if, when we were enemies, we were reconciled to God by the death of his Son, much more, being reconciled, we shall be saved by his life.

11 And not only so, but we also joy in God through our Lord Jesus Christ, by whom we have now received the atonement.

12 Wherefore, as by one man sin entered into the world, and death by sin; and so death passed upon all men, for that all have sinned:

13 (For until the law sin was in the world: but sin is not imputed when there is no law.

14 Nevertheless death reigned from Adam to Moses, even over them that had not sinned after the similitude of Adam's transgression, who is the figure of him that was to come.

15 But not as the offense, so also is the free gift. For if through the offense of one many be dead, much more the grace of God, and the gift by grace, which is by one man, Jesus Christ, hath abounded unto many.

16 And not as it was by one that sinned, so is the gift: for the judgment was by one to condemnation, but the free gift is of many offenses unto justification.

17 For if by one man's offense

works.

3. Abraham believed God – That promise of God concerning the numerousness of his seed, Gen. xv, 5, 7; but especially the promise concerning Christ, Gen. xii, 3, through whom all nations should be blessed. And it was imputed to him for righteousness – God accepted him as if he had been altogether righteous. Gen. xv, 6.

5. But to him that worketh not – It being impossible he should without faith. But believeth, his faith is imputed to him for righteousness – Therefore God's affirming of Abraham, that faith was imputed to him for righteousness, plainly shows that he worked not; or, in other words, that he was not justified by works, but by faith only.

6. So David also – David is fitly introduced after Abraham, because he also received and delivered down the promise. Affirmeth – A man is justified by faith alone, and not by works. Without works – That is, without regard to any former good works supposed to have been done by him.

7. Happy are they whose sins are covered – With the veil of divine mercy. If there be indeed such a thing as happiness on earth, it is the portion of that man whose iniquities are forgiven, and who enjoys the manifestation of that pardon. Well may he endure all the afflictions of life with cheerfulness, and look upon death with comfort. O let us not contend against it, but earnestly pray that this happiness may be ours! Psalm xxxii, 1, 2.

9. This happiness – Mentioned by Abraham and David. On the circumcision – Those that are circumcized only. Faith was imputed to Abraham for righteousness – This is fully consistent with our being justified, that is, pardoned and accepted by God upon our believing, for the sake of what Christ hath done and suffered. For though this, and this alone, be the meritorious cause of our acceptance with God, yet faith may be said to be "imputed to us for righteousness," as it is the sole condition of our acceptance. We may observe here, forgiveness, not imputing sin, and imputing righteousness, are all one.

10. Not in circumcision – Not after he was circumcized; for he was justified before Ishmael was born, Gen. xv, 1-21; but he was not circumcized till Ishmael was thirteen years old, Gen. xvii, 25.

11. And – After he was justified. He received the sign of circumcision – Circumcision, which was a sign or token of his being in covenant with God. A seal – An assurance on God's part, that he accounted him righteous, upon his believing, before he was circumcized. Who believe in uncircumcision – That is, though they are not circumcized.

12. And the father of the circumcision – Of those who are circumcized, and believe as Abraham did. To those who believe not, Abraham is not a father, neither are they his seed.

13. The promise, that he should be the heir of the world – Is the same as that he should be "the father of all nations," namely, of those in all nations who receive the blessing. The whole world was promised to him and them conjointly. Christ is the heir of the world, and of all things; and so are all Abraham's seed, all that believe in him with the faith of Abraham

14. If they only who are of the law – Who have kept the whole law. Are heirs, faith is made void – No blessing being to be obtained by it; and so the promise is of no effect.

15. Because the law – Considered apart from that grace, which though it was in fact mingled with it, yet is no part of the legal dispensation, is so difficult, and we so weak and sinful, that, instead of bringing us a blessing, it only worketh wrath; it becomes to us an occasion of wrath, and exposes us to punishment as transgressors. Where there is no law in force, there can be no transgression of it.

16. Therefore it – The blessing. Is of faith, that it might be of grace – That it might appear to flow from the free love of God, and that the promise might be firm, sure, and effectual, to all the spiritual seed of Abraham; not only Jews, but

would have been placed, had he stood. Notwithstanding the differences, there is a striking similarity. As by the offense of one, sin and death prevailed to the condemnation of all men, so by the righteousness of one, grace prevailed to the justification of all related to Christ by faith. Through the grace of God, the gift by grace has abounded to many through Christ; yet multitudes choose to remain under the dominion of sin and death, rather than to apply for the blessings of the reign of grace. But Christ will in nowise cast out any who are willing to come to him.

20,21 By Christ and his righteousness, we have more and greater privileges than we lost by the offense of Adam. The moral law showed that many thoughts, tempers, words, and actions, were sinful, thus transgressions were multiplied. Not making sin to abound the more, but discovering the sinfulness of it, even as the letting in a clearer light into a room, discovers the dust and filth which were there before, but were not seen. The sin of Adam, and the effect of corruption in us, are the abounding of that offense which appeared on the entrance of the law. And the terrors of the law make gospel comforts the more sweet. Thus God the Holy Spirit has, by the blessed apostle, delivered to us a most important truth, full of consolation, suited to our need as sinners. Whatever one may have above another, every man is a sinner against God, stands condemned by the law, and needs pardon. A righteousness that is to justify cannot be made up of a mixture of sin and holiness. There can be no title to an eternal reward without a pure and spotless righteousness: let us look for it, even to the righteousness of Christ.

ROMANS 6

Believers must die to sin, and live to God. (1,2)
This is urged by their Christian baptism and union with Christ. (3-10)
They are made alive to God. (11-15)
And are freed from the dominion of sin. (16-20)
The end of sin is death, and of holiness everlasting life. (21-23)

1,2 The apostle is very full in pressing the necessity of holiness. He does not explain away the free grace of the gospel, but he shows that connexion between justification and holiness are inseparable. Let the thought be abhorred, of continuing in sin that grace may abound. True believers are dead to sin, therefore they ought not to follow it. No man can at the same time be both dead and alive. He is a fool who, desiring to be dead unto sin, thinks he may live in it.

3-10 Baptism teaches the necessity of dying to sin, and being as it were buried from all ungodly and unholy pursuits, and of rising to walk with God in newness of life. Unholy professors may have had the outward sign of a death unto sin, and a new birth unto righteousness, but they never passed from the family of Satan to that of God.

II. Our second subject is THE PRAYER WHICH THE HOLY SPIRIT INSPIRES, or that part of prayer which is especially and peculiarly the work of the Spirit of God. The text says, "The Spirit itself maketh intercession for us with groanings which cannot be uttered." It is not the Spirit that groans, but we that groan; but as I have shown you, the Spirit excited the emotion which causes us to groan.

It is clear then the prayers which are indicted in us by the spirit of God are those which arise from our inmost soul. A man's heart is moved when he groans. A groan is a matter about which there is no hypocrisy. A groan cometh not from the lips, but from the heart. A groan then is a part of prayer which we owe to the Holy Ghost, and the same is true of all the prayer which wells up from the deep fountains of our inner life. The prophet cried, "My bowels, my bowels, I am pained at my very heart: my heart maketh a noise in me." This deep ground-swell of desire, this tidal motion of the life-floods is caused by the Holy Spirit. His work is never superficial, but always deep and inward.

Such prayers will rise within us when the mind is far too troubled to let us speak. We know not what we should pray for as we ought, and then it is that we groan, or utter some other inarticulate sound. Hezekiah said, "like a crane or a swallow did I chatter." The psalmist said, "I am troubled; I have roared by reason of the disquietness of my heart"; but he added, "Lord, all my desire is before thee; and my groaning is not hid from thee." The sighing of the prisoner surely cometh up into the ears of the Lord. There is real prayer in these "groanings that cannot be uttered." It is the power of the Holy Ghost in us which creates all real prayer, even that which takes the form of a groan because the mind is incapable, by reason of its bewilderment and grief, of clothing its emotion in words. I pray you never think lightly of the supplications of your anguish. Rather judge that such prayers are like Jabez, of whom it is written, that "he was more honorable than his brethren, because his mother bare him with sorrow." That which is thrown up from the depth of the soul, when it is stirred with a terrible tempest, is more precious than pearl or coral, for it is the intercession of the Holy Spirit.

These prayers are sometimes "groanings that cannot be uttered," because they concern such great things that they cannot be spoken. I want, my Lord! I want, I want; I cannot tell thee what I want: but I seem to want all things. If it were some little thing, my nar-

death reigned by one; much more they which receive abundance of grace and of the gift of righteousness shall reign in life by one, Jesus Christ.)

18 Therefore as by the offense of one judgment came upon all men to condemnation; even so by the righteousness of one the free gift came upon all men unto justification of life.

19 For as by one man's disobedience many were made sinners, so by the obedience of one shall many be made righteous.

20 Moreover the law entered, that the offense might abound. But where sin abounded, grace did much more abound:

21 That as sin hath reigned unto death, even so might grace reign through righteousness unto eternal life by Jesus Christ our Lord.

ROMANS 6

1 What shall we say then? Shall we continue in sin, that grace may abound?

2 God forbid. How shall we, that are dead to sin, live any longer therein?

3 Know ye not, that so many of us as were baptized into Jesus Christ were baptized into his death?

4 Therefore we are buried with him by baptism into death: that like as Christ was raised up from the dead by the glory of the Father, even so we also should walk in newness of life.

5 For if we have been planted together in the likeness of his death, we shall be also in the likeness of his resurrection:

6 Knowing this, that our old man is crucified with him, that the body of sin might be destroyed, that henceforth we should not serve sin.

7 For he that is dead is freed from sin.

8 Now if we be dead with Christ, we believe that we shall also live with him:

9 Knowing that Christ being raised from the dead dieth no more; death hath no more dominion over him.

10 For in that he died, he died unto sin once: but in that he liveth, he liveth unto God.

Gentiles also, if they follow his faith.

23. On his account only – To do personal honor to him.

24. But on ours also – To establish us in seeking justification by faith, and not by works; and to afford a full answer to those who say that, "to be justified by works means only, by Judaism; to be justified by faith means, by embracing Christianity, that is, the system of doctrines so called."

25. Who was delivered – To death. For our offenses – As an atonement for them. And raised for our justification – To empower us to receive that atonement by faith.

ROMANS 5

1. Being justified by faith – This is the sum of the preceding chapters. We have peace with God – Being enemies to God no longer, ver. 10; neither fearing his wrath, ver. 9. We have peace, hope, love, and power over sin, the sum of the fifth, sixth, seventh, and eighth chapters. These are the fruits of justifying faith: where these are not, that faith is not.

2. Into this grace – This state of favor.

3. We glory in tribulations also – Which we are so far from esteeming a mark of God's displeasure, that we receive them as tokens of his fatherly love, whereby we are prepared for a more exalted happiness. The Jews objected to the persecuted state of the Christians as inconsistent with the people of the Messiah. It is therefore with great propriety that the apostle so often mentions the blessings arising from this very thing.

4. And patience works more experience of the sincerity of our grace, and of God's power and faithfulness.

5. Hope shameth us not – That is, gives us the highest glorying. We glory in this our hope, because the love of God is shed abroad in our hearts – The divine conviction of God's love to us, and that love to God which is both the earnest and the beginning of heaven. By the Holy Ghost – The efficient cause of all these present blessings, and the earnest of those to come.

6. How can we now doubt of God's love? For when we were without strength – Either to think, will, or do anything good. In due time – Neither too soon nor too late; but in that very point of time which the wisdom of God knew to be more proper than any other. Christ died for the ungodly – Not only to set them a pattern, or to procure them power to follow it. It does not appear that this expression, of dying for any one, has any other signification than that of rescuing the life of another by laying down our own.

7. A just man – One who gives to all what is strictly their due The good man – One who is eminently holy; full of love, of compassion, kindness, mildness, of every heavenly and amiable temper. Perhaps one would even dare to die – Every word increases the strangeness of the thing, and declares even this to be something great and unusual.

8. But God recommendeth – A most elegant expression. Those are wont to be recommended to us, who were before either unknown to, or alienated from, us. While we were sinners – So far from being good, that we were not even just.

9. By his blood – By his blood shedding. We shall be saved from wrath through him – That is, from all the effects of the wrath of God. But is there then wrath in God? Is not wrath a human passion? And how can this human passion be in God? We may answer this by another question: Is not love a human passion? And how can this human passion be in God? But to answer directly: wrath in man, and so love in man, is a human passion. But wrath in God is not a human passion; nor is love, as it is in God. Therefore the inspired writers ascribe both the one and the other to God only in an analogical sense.

10. If – As sure as; so the word frequently signifies; particularly in this and the eighth chapter. We shalt be saved – Sanctified and glorified. Through his life –

The corrupt nature, called the old man, because derived from our first father Adam, is crucified with Christ, in every true believer, by the grace derived from the cross. It is weakened and in a dying state, though it yet struggles for life, and even for victory. But the whole body of sin, whatever is not according to the holy law of God, must be done away, so that the believer may no more be the slave of sin, but live to God, and find happiness in his service.

11-15 The strongest motives against sin, and to enforce holiness, are here stated. Being made free from the reign of sin, alive unto God, and having the prospect of eternal life, it becomes believers to be greatly concerned to advance thereto. But, as unholy lusts are not quite rooted out in this life, it must be the care of the Christian to resist their motions, earnestly striving, that, through Divine grace, they may not prevail in this mortal state. Let the thought that this state will soon be at an end, encourage the true Christian, as to the motions of lusts, which so often perplex and distress him. Let us present all our powers to God, as weapons or tools ready for the warfare, and work of righteousness, in his service. There is strength in the covenant of grace for us. Sin shall not have dominion. God's promises to us are more powerful and effectual for mortifying sin, than our promises to God. Sin may struggle in a real believer, and create him a great deal of trouble, but it shall not have dominion; it may vex him, but it shall not rule over him. Shall any take occasion from this encouraging doctrine to allow themselves in the practice of any sin? Far be such abominable thoughts, so contrary to the perfections of God, and the design of his gospel, so opposed to being under grace. What can be a stronger motive against sin than the love of Christ? Shall we sin against so much goodness, and such love?

16-20 Every man is the servant of the master to whose commands he yields himself; whether it be the sinful dispositions of his heart, in actions which lead to death, or the new and spiritual obedience implanted by regeneration. The apostle rejoiced now they obeyed from the heart the gospel, into which they were delivered as into a mold. As the same metal becomes a new vessel, when melted and recast in another mold, so the believer has become a new creature. And there is great difference in the liberty of mind and spirit, so opposite to the state of slavery, which the true Christian has in the service of his rightful Lord, whom he is enabled to consider as his Father, and himself as his son and heir, by the adoption of grace. The dominion of sin consists in being willingly slaves thereto, not in being harassed by it as a hated power, struggling for victory. Those who now are the servants of God, once were the slaves of sin.

21-23 The pleasure and profit of sin do not deserve to be called fruit. Sinners are but plowing iniquity, sowing vanity, and reaping the same. Shame came into the world with sin, and is still the certain effect of it. The end of sin

row capacity could comprehend and describe it, but I need all covenant blessings. Thou knowest what I have need of before I ask thee, and though I cannot go into each item of my need, I know it to be very great, and such as I myself can never estimate. I groan, for I can do no more. Prayers which are the offspring of great desires, sublime aspirations, and elevated designs are surely the work of the Holy Spirit, and their power within a man is frequently so great that he cannot find expression for them. Words fail, and even the sighs which try to embody them cannot be uttered.

But it may be, beloved, that we groan because we are conscious of the littleness of our desire, and the narrowness of our faith. The trial, too, may seem too mean to pray about. I have known what it is to feel as if I could not pray about a certain matter, and yet I have been obliged to groan about it. A thorn in the flesh may be as painful a thing as a sword in the bones, and yet we may go and beseech the Lord thrice about it, and getting no answer we may feel that we know not what to pray for as we ought; and yet it makes us groan. Yes, and with that natural groan there may go up an unutterable groaning of the Holy Spirit. Beloved, what a different view of prayer God has from that which men think to be the correct one. You may have seen very beautiful prayers in print, and you may have heard very charming compositions from the pulpit, but I trust you have not fallen in love with them. Judge these things rightly. I pray you never think well of fine prayers, for before the thrice holy God it ill becomes a sinful suppliant to play the orator. We heard of a certain clergyman who was said to have given forth "the finest prayer ever offered to a Boston audience." Just so! The Boston audience received the prayer, and there it ended. We want the mind of the spirit in prayer, and not the mind of the flesh. The tail feathers of pride should be pulled out of our prayers, for they need only the wing feathers of faith; the peacock feathers of poetical expression are out of place before the throne of God. Hear me, what remarkably beautiful language he used in prayer!" "What an intellectual treat his prayer was!" Yes, yes; but God looks at the heart. To him fine language is as sounding brass or tinkling cymbal, but a groan has music in it. We do not like groans: our ears are much too delicate to tolerate such dreary sounds; but not so the great Father of spirits. A Methodist brother cries, "Amen," and you say, "I cannot bear such Methodistic noise";

11 Likewise reckon ye also yourselves to be dead indeed unto sin, but alive unto God through Jesus Christ our Lord.

12 Let not sin therefore reign in your mortal body, that ye should obey it in the lusts thereof.

13 Neither yield ye your members as instruments of unrighteousness unto sin: but yield yourselves unto God, as those that are alive from the dead, and your members as instruments of righteousness unto God.

14 For sin shall not have dominion over you: for ye are not under the law, but under grace.

15 What then? shall we sin, because we are not under the law, but under grace? God forbid.

16 Know ye not, that to whom ye yield yourselves servants to obey, his servants ye are to whom ye obey; whether of sin unto death, or of obedience unto righteousness?

17 But God be thanked, that ye were the servants of sin, but ye have obeyed from the heart that form of doctrine which was delivered you.

18 Being then made free from sin, ye became the servants of righteousness.

19 I speak after the manner of men because of the infirmity of your flesh: for as ye have yielded your members servants to uncleanness and to iniquity unto iniquity; even so now yield your members servants to righteousness unto holiness.

20 For when ye were the servants of sin, ye were free from righteousness.

21 What fruit had ye then in those things whereof ye are now ashamed? for the end of those things is death.

22 But now being made free from sin, and become servants to God, ye have your fruit unto holiness, and the end everlasting life.

23 For the wages of sin is death; but the gift of God is eternal life through Jesus Christ our Lord.

ROMANS 7

1 Know ye not, brethren, (for I speak to them that know the

Who "ever liveth to make intercession for us."

11. And not only so, but we also glory – The whole sentence, from the third to the eleventh verse, may be taken together thus: We not only "rejoice in hope of the glory of God," but also in the midst of tribulations we glory in God himself through our Lord Jesus Christ, by whom we have now received the reconciliation.

13. For until the law sin was in the world – All, I say, had sinned, for sin was in the world long before the written law; but, I grant, sin is not so much imputed, nor so severely punished by God, where there is no express law to convince men of it. Yet that all had sinned, even then, appears in that all died.

14. Death reigned – And how vast is his kingdom! Scarce can we find any king who has as many subjects, as are the kings whom he hath conquered. Even over them that had not sinned after the likeness of Adam's transgression – Even over infants who had never sinned, as Adam did, in their own persons; and over others who had not, like him, sinned against an express law. Who is the figure of him that was to come – Each of them being a public person, and a federal head of mankind. The one, the fountain of sin and death to mankind by his offense; the other, of righteousness and life by his free gift.

16. The sentence was by one offense to Adam's condemnation – Occasioning the sentence of death to pass upon him, which, by consequence, overwhelmed his posterity. But the free gift is of many offenses unto justification – Unto the purchasing it for all men, notwithstanding many offenses.

17. There is a difference between grace and the gift. Grace is opposed to the offense; the gift, to death, being the gift of life.

18. Justification of life – Is that sentence of God, by which a sinner under sentence of death is adjudged to life.

19. As by the disobedience of one man many (that is, all men) were constituted sinners – Being then in the loins of their first parent, the common head and representative of them all. So by the obedience of one – By his obedience unto death; by his dying for us. Many – All that believe. Shall be constituted righteous – Justified, pardoned.

20. The law came in between – The offense and the free gift. That the offense might abound – That is, the consequence (not the design) of the law's coming in was, not the taking away of sin, but the increase of it. Yet where sin abounded, grace did much more abound – Not only in the remission of that sin which Adam brought on us, but of all our own; not only in remission of sins, but infusion of holiness; not only in deliverance from death, but admission to everlasting life, a far more noble and excellent life than that which we lost by Adam's fall.

21. That as sin had reigned – so grace also might reign – Which could not reign before the fall; before man had sinned. Through righteousness to eternal life by Jesus Christ our Lord – Here is pointed out the source of all our blessings, the rich and free grace of God. The meritorious cause; not any works of righteousness of man, but the alone merits of our Lord Jesus Christ. The effect or end of all; not only pardon, but life; divine life, leading to glory.

ROMANS 6

1. The apostle here sets himself more fully to vindicate his doctrine from the consequence above suggested, chap. iii, 7, 8. He had then only in strong terms denied and renounced it: here he removes the very foundation thereof.

2. Dead to sin – Freed both from the guilt and from the power of it.

3. As many as have been baptized into Jesus Christ have been baptized into his death – In baptism we, through faith, are ingrafted into Christ; and we draw new spiritual life from this new root, through his Spirit, who fashions us like unto him, and particularly with regard to his death and resurrection.

is death. Though the way may seem pleasant and inviting, yet it will be bitterness in the latter end. From this condemnation the believer is set at liberty, when made free from sin. If the fruit is unto holiness, if there is an active principle of true and growing grace, the end will be everlasting life; a very happy end! Though the way is up-hill, though it is narrow, thorny, and beset, yet everlasting life at the end of it is sure. The gift of God is eternal life. And this gift is through Jesus Christ our Lord. Christ purchased it, prepared it, prepares us for it, preserves us to it; he is the All in all in our salvation.

ROMANS 7

Believers are united to Christ, that they may bring forth
*   fruit unto God. (1-6)*
The use and excellence of the law. (7-13)
The spiritual conflicts between corruption and grace in a
*   believer. (14-25)*

1-6 So long as a man continues under the law as a covenant, and seeks justification by his own obedience, he continues the slave of sin in some form. Nothing but the Spirit of life in Christ Jesus, can make any sinner free from the law of sin and death. Believers are delivered from that power of the law, which condemns for the sins committed by them. And they are delivered from that power of the law which stirs up and provokes the sin that dwells in them. Understand this not of the law as a rule, but as a covenant of works.

7-13 There is no way of coming to that knowledge of sin, which is necessary to repentance, and therefore to peace and pardon, but by trying our hearts and lives by the law. In his own case the apostle would not have known the sinfulness of his thoughts, motives, and actions, but by the law. That perfect standard showed how wrong his heart and life were, proving his sins to be more numerous than he had before thought, but it did not contain any provision of mercy or grace for his relief. He is ignorant of human nature and the perverseness of his own heart, who does not perceive in himself a readiness to fancy there is something desirable in what is out of reach. We may perceive this in our children, though self-love makes us blind to it in ourselves. The more humble and spiritual any Christian is, the more clearly will he perceive that the apostle describes the true believer, from his first convictions of sin to his greatest progress in grace, during this present imperfect state. St. Paul was once a Pharisee, ignorant of the spirituality of the law, having some correctness of character, without knowing his inward depravity. When the commandment came to his conscience by the convictions of the Holy Spirit, and he saw what it demanded, he found his sinful mind rise against it. He felt at the same time the evil of sin, his own sinful state, that he was unable to fulfill the law, and was like a criminal when condemned. But though the evil principle in the human heart produces sinful motions, and the more by taking occasion of the commandment;

no, but if it comes from the man's heart God can bear it. When you get upstairs into your chamber this evening to pray, and find you cannot pray, but have to moan out, "Lord, I am too full of anguish and too perplexed to pray, hear thou the voice of my roaring," though you reach to nothing else you will be really praying. When like David we can say, "I opened my mouth and panted," we are by no means in an ill state of mind. All fine language in prayer, and especially all intoning or performing of prayers, must be abhorrent to God; it is little short of profanity to offer solemn supplication to God after the manner called "intoning." The sighing of a true heart is infinitely more acceptable, for it is the work of the Spirit of God.

We may say of the prayers which the Holy Spirit works in us that they are prayers of knowledge. Notice, our difficulty is that we know not what we should pray for; but the Holy Spirit does know, and therefore he helps us by enabling us to pray intelligently, knowing what we are asking for, so far as this knowledge is needful to valid prayer. The text speaks "of the mind of the Spirit." What a mind that must be!—the mind of that Spirit who arranged all the order which now pervades this earth! There once was chaos and confusion, but the Holy Spirit brooded over all, and his mind is the originator of that beautiful arrangement which we so admire in the visible creation. What a mind his must be! What the Holy Spirit's mind is seen in our intercessions when under his sacred influence we order our case before the Lord, and plead with holy wisdom for things convenient and necessary. What wise and admirable desires must those be which the Spirit of Wisdom himself works in us!

Moreover, the Holy Spirit's intercession creates prayers offered in a proper manner. I showed you that the difficulty is that we know not what we should pray for "as we ought," and the Spirit meets that difficulty by making intercession for us in a right manner. The Holy Spirit works in us humility, earnestness, intensity, importunity, faith, and resignation, and all else that is acceptable to God in our supplications. We know not how to mingle these sacred spices in the incense of prayer. We, if left to ourselves at our very best, get too much of one ingredient or another, and spoil the sacred compound, but the Holy Spirit's intercessions have in them such a blessed blending of all that is good that they come up as a sweet perfume before the Lord. Spirit-taught prayers are offered as they ought to be. They are his own interces-

law,) how that the law hath dominion over a man as long as he liveth?

2 For the woman which hath an husband is bound by the law to her husband so long as he liveth; but if the husband be dead, she is loosed from the law of her husband.

3 So then if, while her husband liveth, she be married to another man, she shall be called an adulteress: but if her husband be dead, she is free from that law; so that she is no adulteress, though she be married to another man.

4 Wherefore, my brethren, ye also are become dead to the law by the body of Christ; that ye should be married to another, even to him who is raised from the dead, that we should bring forth fruit unto God.

5 For when we were in the flesh, the motions of sins, which were by the law, did work in our members to bring forth fruit unto death.

6 But now we are delivered from the law, that being dead wherein we were held; that we should serve in newness of spirit, and not in the oldness of the letter.

7 What shall we say then? Is the law sin? God forbid. Nay, I had not known sin, but by the law: for I had not known lust, except the law had said, Thou shalt not covet.

8 But sin, taking occasion by the commandment, wrought in me all manner of concupiscence. For without the law sin was dead.

9 For I was alive without the law once: but when the commandment came, sin revived, and I died.

10 And the commandment, which was ordained to life, I found to be unto death.

11 For sin, taking occasion by the commandment, deceived me, and by it slew me.

12 Wherefore the law is holy, and the commandment holy, and just, and good.

13 Was then that which is good made death unto me? God forbid. But sin, that it might appear sin, working death in me by that which is good; that sin by the

4. We are buried with him – Alluding to the ancient manner of baptizing by immersion. That as Christ was raised from the dead by the glory – Glorious power. Of the Father, so we also, by the same power, should rise again; and as he lives a new life in heaven, so we should walk in newness of life. This, says the apostle, our very baptism represents to us.

5. For – Surely these two must go together; so that if we are indeed made conformable to his death, we shall also know the power of his resurrection.

6. Our old man – Coeval with our being, and as old as the fall; our evil nature; a strong and beautiful expression for that entire depravity and corruption which by nature spreads itself over the whole man, leaving no part uninfected. This in a believer is crucified with Christ, mortified, gradually killed, by virtue of our union with him. That the body of sin – All evil tempers, words, and actions, which are the "members" of the "old man," Colossians iii, 5, might be destroyed.

7. For he that is dead – With Christ. Is freed from the guilt of past, and from the power of present, sin, as dead men from the commands of their former masters.

8. Dead with Christ – Conformed to his death, by dying to sin.

10. He died to sin – To atone for and abolish it. He liveth unto God – A glorious eternal life, such as we shall live also.

12. Let not sin reign even in your mortal body – It must be subject to death, but it need not be subject to sin.

13. Neither present your members to sin – To corrupt nature, a mere tyrant. But to God – Your lawful King.

14. Sin shall not have dominion over you – It has neither right nor power. For ye are not under the law – A dispensation of terror and bondage, which only shows sin, without enabling you to conquer it. But under grace – Under the merciful dispensation of the gospel, which brings complete victory over it to every one who is under the powerful influences of the Spirit of Christ.

17. The form of doctrine into which ye have been delivered – Literally it is, The mold into which ye have been delivered; which, as it contains a beautiful allusion, conveys also a very instructive admonition; intimating that our minds, all pliant and ductile, should be conformed to the gospel precepts, as liquid metal take the figure of the mold into which they are cast.

19. I speak after the manner of men – Thus it is necessary that the scripture should let itself down to the language of men. Because of the weakness of your flesh – Slowness of understanding flows from the weakness of the flesh, that is, of human nature. As ye have presented your members servants to uncleanness and iniquity unto iniquity, so now present your members servants of righteousness unto holiness – Iniquity (whereof uncleanness is an eminent part) is here opposed to righteousness; and unto iniquity is the opposite of unto holiness. Righteousness here is a conformity to the divine will; holiness, to the whole divine nature. Observe, they who are servants of righteousness go on to holiness; but they who are servants to iniquity get no farther. Righteousness is service, because we live according to the will of another; but liberty, because of our inclination to it, and delight in it.

20. When ye were the servants of sin, ye were free from righteousness – In all reason, therefore, ye ought now to be free from unrighteousness; to be as uniform and zealous in serving God as ye were in serving the devil.

21. Those things – He speaks of them as afar off.

23. Death – Temporal, spiritual, and eternal. Is the due wages of sin; but eternal life is the gift of God – The difference is remarkable. Evil works merit the reward they receive: good works do not. The former demand wages: the latter accept a free gift.

yet the law is holy, and the commandment holy, just, and good. It is not favorable to sin, which it pursues into the heart, and discovers and reproves in the inward motions thereof. Nothing is so good but a corrupt and vicious nature will pervert it. The same heat that softens wax, hardens clay. Food or medicine when taken wrong, may cause death, though its nature is to nourish or to heal. The law may cause death through man's depravity, but sin is the poison that brings death. Not the law, but sin discovered by the law, was made death to the apostle. The ruinous nature of sin, and the sinfulness of the human heart, are here clearly shown.

14-17 Compared with the holy rule of conduct in the law of God, the apostle found himself so very far short of perfection, that he seemed to be carnal; like a man who is sold against his will to a hated master, from whom he cannot set himself at liberty. A real Christian unwillingly serves this hated master, yet cannot shake off the galling chain, till his powerful and gracious Friend above, rescues him. The remaining evil of his heart is a real and humbling hindrance to his serving God as angels do and the spirits of just made perfect. This strong language was the result of St. Paul's great advance in holiness, and the depth of his self-abasement and hatred of sin. If we do not understand this language, it is because we are so far beneath him in holiness, knowledge of the spirituality of God's law, and the evil of our own hearts, and hatred of moral evil. And many believers have adopted the apostle's language, showing that it is suitable to their deep feelings of abhorrence of sin, and self-abasement. The apostle enlarges on the conflict he daily maintained with the remainder of his original depravity. He was frequently led into tempers, words, or actions, which he did not approve or allow in his renewed judgment and affections. By distinguishing his real self, his spiritual part, from the self, or flesh, in which sin dwelt, and by observing that the evil actions were done, not by him, but by sin dwelling in him, the apostle did not mean that men are not accountable for their sins, but he teaches the evil of their sins, by showing that they are all done against reason and conscience. Sin dwelling in a man, does not prove its ruling, or having dominion over him. If a man dwells in a city, or in a country, still he may not rule there.

18-22 The more pure and holy the heart is, it will have the more quick feeling as to the sin that remains in it. The believer sees more of the beauty of holiness and the excellence of the law. His earnest desires to obey, increase as he grows in grace. But the whole good on which his will is fully bent, he does not do; sin ever springing up in him, through remaining corruption, he often does evil, though against the fixed determination of his will. The motions of sin within grieved the apostle. If by the striving of the flesh against the Spirit, was meant that he could not do or perform as the Spirit suggested, so also, by the effectual opposition of the Spirit, he could not do what the flesh prompted him to do. How different this case from that of those who make themselves easy

sion in some respects, for we read that the Holy Spirit not only helps us to intercede but "maketh intercession." It is twice over declared in our text that he maketh intercession for us; and the meaning of this I tried to show when I described a father as putting his hands upon his child's hands. This is something more than helping us to pray, something more than encouraging us or directing us,—but I venture no further, except to say that he puts such force of his own mind into our poor weak thoughts and desires and hopes, that he himself maketh intercession for us, working in us to will and to pray according to his good pleasure.

I want you to notice, however, that these intercessions of the Spirit are only in the saints. "He maketh intercession for us," and "He maketh intercession for the saints." Does he do nothing for sinners, then? Yes, he quickens sinners into spiritual life, and he strives with them to overcome their sinfulness and turn them into the right way; but in the saints he works with us and enables us to pray after his mind and according to the will of God. His intercession is not in or for the unregenerate. O, unbelievers you must first be made saints or you cannot feel the Spirit's intercession within you. What need we have to go to Christ for the blessing of the Holy Ghost, which is peculiar to the children of God, and can only be ours by faith in Christ Jesus! "To as many as received him to them gave he power to become the sons of God"; and to the sons of God alone cometh the Spirit of adoption, and all his helping grace. Unless we are the sons of God the Holy Spirit's indwelling shall not be ours: we are shut out from the intercession of the Holy Ghost, ay, and from the intercession of Jesus too, for he hath said, "I pray not for the world, but for them which thou hast given me."

Thus I have tried to show you the kind of prayer which the Spirit inspires.

III. Our third and last point is THE SURE SUCCESS OF ALL SUCH PRAYERS.

All the prayers which the Spirit of God inspires in us must succeed, because, first, there is a meaning in them which God reads and approves. When the Spirit of God writes a prayer upon a man's heart, the man himself may be in such a state of mind that he does not altogether know what it is. His interpretation of it is a groan, and that is all. Perhaps he does not even get so far as that in expressing the mind of the Spirit, but he feels groanings which he cannot utter, he cannot find a door of utterance for his inward grief. Yet

commandment might become exceeding sinful.

14 For we know that the law is spiritual: but I am carnal, sold under sin.

15 For that which I do I allow not: for what I would, that do I not; but what I hate, that do I.

16 If then I do that which I would not, I consent unto the law that it is good.

17 Now then it is no more I that do it, but sin that dwelleth in me.

18 For I know that in me (that is, in my flesh,) dwelleth no good thing: for to will is present with me; but how to perform that which is good I find not.

19 For the good that I would I do not: but the evil which I would not, that I do.

20 Now if I do that I would not, it is no more I that do it, but sin that dwelleth in me.

21 I find then a law, that, when I would do good, evil is present with me.

22 For I delight in the law of God after the inward man:

23 But I see another law in my members, warring against the law of my mind, and bringing me into captivity to the law of sin which is in my members.

24 O wretched man that I am! who shall deliver me from the body of this death?

25 I thank God through Jesus Christ our Lord. So then with the mind I myself serve the law of God; but with the flesh the law of sin.

ROMANS 8

1 There is therefore now no condemnation to them which are in Christ Jesus, who walk not after the flesh, but after the Spirit.

2 For the law of the Spirit of life in Christ Jesus hath made me free from the law of sin and death.

3 For what the law could not do, in that it was weak through the flesh, God sending his own Son in the likeness of sinful flesh, and for sin, condemned sin in the flesh:

4 That the righteousness of the law might be fulfilled in us, who

ROMANS 7

1. The apostle continues the comparison between the former and the present state of a believer, and at the same time endeavors to wean the Jewish believers from their fondness for the Mosaic law. I speak to them that know the law – To the Jews chiefly here. As long – So long, and no longer. As it liveth – The law is here spoken of, by a common figure, as a person, to which, as to an husband, life and death are ascribed. But he speaks indifferently of the law being dead to us, or we to it, the sense being the same.

2. She is freed from the law of her husband – From that law which gave him a peculiar property in her.

4. Thus ye also – Are now as free from the Mosaic law as an husband is, when his wife is dead. By the body of Christ – Offered up; that is, by the merits of his death, that law expiring with him.

5. When ye were in the flesh – Carnally minded, in a state of nature; before we believed in Christ. Our sins which were by the law – Accidentally occasioned, or irritated thereby. Wrought in our members – Spread themselves all over the whole man.

6. Being dead to that whereby we were held – To our old husband, the law. That we might serve in newness of spirit – In a new, spiritual manner. And not in the oldness of the letter – Not in a bare literal, external way, as we did before.

8. But sin – My inbred corruption. Taking occasion by the commandment – Forbidding, but not subduing it, was only fretted, and wrought in me so much the more all manner of evil desire. For while I was without the knowledge of the law, sin was dead – Neither so apparent, nor so active; nor was I under the least apprehensions of any danger from it.

9. And I was once alive without the law – Without the close application of it. I had much life, wisdom, virtue, strength: so I thought. But when the commandment – That is, the law, a part put for the whole; but this expression particularly intimates its compulsive force, which restrains, enjoins, urges, forbids, threatens. Came – In its spiritual meaning, to my heart, with the power of God. Sin revived, and I died – My inbred sin took fire, and all my virtue and strength died away; and I then saw myself to be dead in sin, and liable to death eternal.

10. The commandment which was intended for life – Doubtless it was originally intended by God as a grand means of preserving and increasing spiritual life, and leading to life everlasting.

11. Deceived me – While I expected life by the law, sin came upon me unawares and slew all my hopes.

12. The commandment – That is, every branch of the law. Is holy, and just, and good – It springs from, and partakes of, the holy nature of God; it is every way just and right in itself; it is designed wholly for the good of man.

13. Was then that which is good made the cause of evil to me; yea, of death, which is the greatest of evil? Not so. But it was sin, which was made death to me, inasmuch as it wrought death in me even by that which is good – By the good law. So that sin by the commandment became exceeding sinful – The consequence of which was, that inbred sin, thus driving furiously in spite of the commandment, became exceeding sinful; the guilt thereof being greatly aggravated.

14. I am carnal – St. Paul, having compared together the past and present state of believers, that "in the flesh," ver. 5, and that "in the spirit," ver. 6, in answering two objections, (Is then the law sin? ver. 7, and, Is the law death? ver. 13,) interweaves the whole process of a man reasoning, groaning, striving, and escaping from the legal to the evangelical state. This he does from ver. 7, to the end of this chapter. Sold under sin – Totally enslaved; slaves bought with money were absolutely at their master's disposal.

16. It is good – This single word implies all the three that were used before, ver. 12, "holy, just, and good."

with regard to the inward motions of the flesh prompting them to evil; who, against the light and warning of conscience, go on, even in outward practice, to do evil, and thus, with forethought, go on in the road to perdition! For as the believer is under grace, and his will is for the way of holiness, he sincerely delights in the law of God, and in the holiness which it demands, according to his inward man; that new man in him, which after God is created in true holiness.

23-25 This passage does not represent the apostle as one that walked after the flesh, but as one that had it greatly at heart, not to walk so. And if there are those who abuse this passage, as they also do the other Scriptures, to their own destruction, yet serious Christians find cause to bless God for having thus provided for their support and comfort. We are not, because of the abuse of such as are blinded by their own lusts, to find fault with the scripture, or any just and well warranted interpretation of it. And no man who is not engaged in this conflict, can clearly understand the meaning of these words, or rightly judge concerning this painful conflict, which led the apostle to bemoan himself as a wretched man, constrained to what he abhorred. He could not deliver himself; and this made him the more fervently thank God for the way of salvation revealed through Jesus Christ, which promised him, in the end, deliverance from this enemy. So then, says he, I myself, with my mind, my prevailing judgment, affections, and purposes, as a regenerate man, by Divine grace, serve and obey the law of God; but with the flesh, the carnal nature, the remains of depravity, I serve the law of sin, which wars against the law of my mind. Not serving it so as to live in it, or to allow it, but as unable to free himself from it, even in his very best state, and needing to look for help and deliverance out of himself. It is evident that he thanks God for Christ, as our deliverer, as our atonement and righteousness in himself, and not because of any holiness wrought in us. He knew of no such salvation, and disowned any such title to it. He was willing to act in all points agreeable to the law, in his mind and conscience, but was hindered by indwelling sin, and never attained the perfection the law requires. What can be deliverance for a man always sinful, but the free grace of God, as offered in Christ Jesus? The power of Divine grace, and of the Holy Spirit, could root out sin from our hearts even in this life, if Divine wisdom had not otherwise thought fit. But it is suffered, that Christians might constantly feel, and understand thoroughly, the wretched state from which Divine grace saves them; might be kept from trusting in themselves; and might ever hold all their consolation and hope, from the rich and free grace of God in Christ.

ROMANS 8

The freedom of believers from condemnation. (1-9)
Their privileges as being the children of God. (10-17)
Their hopeful prospects under tribulations. (18-25)
Their assistance from the Spirit in prayer. (26,27)

our heavenly Father, who looks immediately upon the heart, reads what the Spirit of God has indicted there, and does not need even our groans to explain the meaning. He reads the heart itself: "he knoweth," says the text, "what is the mind of the Spirit." The Spirit is one with the Father, and the Father knows what the Spirit means. The desires which the Spirit prompts may be too spiritual for such babes in grace as we are actually to describe or to express, and yet the Spirit writes the desire on the renewed mind, and the Father sees it. Now that which God reads in the heart and approves of—for the word to "know" in this case includes approval as well as the mere act of omniscience—what God sees and approves of in the heart must succeed. Did not Jesus say, "Your heavenly Father knoweth that you have need of these things before you ask them"? Did he not tell us this as an encouragement to believe that we shall receive all needful blessings? So it is with those prayers which are all broken up, wet with tears, and discordant with those sighs and inarticulate expressions and heavings of the bosom, and sobbings of the heart and anguish and bitterness of spirit, our gracious Lord reads them as a man reads a book, and they are written in a character which he fully understands. To give a simple figure: if I were to come into your house I might find there a little child that cannot yet speak plainly. It cries for something, and it makes very odd and objectionable noises, combined with signs and movements, which are almost meaningless to a stranger, but his mother understands him, and attends to his little pleadings. A mother can translate baby-talk: she comprehends incomprehensible noises. Even so doth our Father in heaven know all about our poor baby talk, for our prayer is not much better. He knows and comprehends the cryings, and moanings, and sighings, and chatterings of his bewildered children. Yea, a tender mother knows her child's needs before the child knows what it wants. Perhaps the little one stutters, stammers, and cannot get its words out, but the mother sees what he would say, and takes the meaning. Even so we know concerning our great Father:—

"He knows the thoughts we mean to speak,
Ere from our opening lips they break."

Do you therefore rejoice in this, that because the prayers of the Spirit are known and understood of God, therefore they will be sure to speed.

The next argument for making us sure

walk not after the flesh, but after the Spirit.

5 For they that are after the flesh do mind the things of the flesh; but they that are after the Spirit the things of the Spirit.

6 For to be carnally minded is death; but to be spiritually minded is life and peace.

7 Because the carnal mind is enmity against God: for it is not subject to the law of God, neither indeed can be.

8 So then they that are in the flesh cannot please God.

9 But ye are not in the flesh, but in the Spirit, if so be that the Spirit of God dwell in you. Now if any man have not the Spirit of Christ, he is none of his.

10 And if Christ be in you, the body is dead because of sin; but the Spirit is life because of righteousness.

11 But if the Spirit of him that raised up Jesus from the dead dwell in you, he that raised up Christ from the dead shall also quicken your mortal bodies by his Spirit that dwelleth in you.

12 Therefore, brethren, we are debtors, not to the flesh, to live after the flesh.

13 For if ye live after the flesh, ye shall die: but if ye through the Spirit do mortify the deeds of the body, ye shall live.

14 For as many as are led by the Spirit of God, they are the sons of God.

15 For ye have not received the spirit of bondage again to fear; but ye have received the Spirit of adoption, whereby we cry, Abba, Father.

16 The Spirit itself beareth witness with our spirit, that we are the children of God:

17 And if children, then heirs; heirs of God, and joint-heirs with Christ; if so be that we suffer with him, that we may be also glorified together.

18 For I reckon that the sufferings of this present time are not worthy to be compared with the glory which shall be revealed in us.

19 For the earnest expectation of the creature waiteth for the manifestation of the sons of God.

20 For the creature was made subject to vanity, not willingly,

17. It is no more I that can properly be said to do it, but rather sin that dwelleth in me – That makes, as it were, another person, and tyrannizes over me.

18. In my flesh – The flesh here signifies the whole man as he is by nature.

21. I find then a law – An inward constraining power, flowing from the dictate of corrupt nature.

22. For I delight in the law of God – This is more than "I consent to," ver. 16. The day of liberty draws near. The inward man – Called the mind, ver. 23, 25.

23. But I see another law in my members – Another inward constraining power of evil inclinations and bodily appetites. Warring against the law of my mind – The dictate of my mind, which delights in the law of God. And captivating me – In spite of all my resistance

24. Wretched man that I am – The struggle is now come to the height; and the man, finding there is no help in himself, begins almost unawares to pray, Who shall deliver me? He then seeks and looks for deliverance, till God in Christ appears to answer his question. The word which we translate deliver, implies force. And indeed without this there can be no deliverance. The body of this death – That is, this body of death; this mass of sin, leading to death eternal, and cleaving as close to me as my body to my soul. We may observe, the deliverance is not wrought yet.

25. I thank God through Jesus Christ our Lord – That is, God will deliver me through Christ. But the apostle, as his frequent manner is, beautifully interweaves his assertion with thanksgiving; the hymn of praise answering in a manner to the voice of sorrow, "Wretched man that I am!" So then – He here sums up the whole, and concludes what he began, ver. 7. I myself – Or rather that I, the person whom I am personating, till this deliverance is wrought. Serve the law of God with my mind – My reason and conscience declare for God. But with my flesh the law of sin – But my corrupt passions and appetites still rebel. The man is now utterly weary of his bondage, and upon the brink of liberty.

ROMANS 8

1. There is therefore now no condemnation – Either for things present or past. Now he comes to deliverance and liberty. The apostle here resumes the thread of his discourse, which was interrupted, chap. vii, 7.

2. The law of the Spirit – That is, the gospel. Hath freed me from the law of sin and death – That is, the Mosaic dispensation.

3. For what the law – Of Moses. Could not do, in that it was weak through the flesh – Incapable of conquering our evil nature. If it could, God needed not to have sent his own Son in the likeness of sinful flesh – We with our sinful flesh were devoted to death. But God sending his own Son, in the likeness of that flesh, though pure from sin, condemned that sin which was in our flesh; gave sentence, that sin should be destroyed, and the believer wholly delivered from it.

4. That the righteousness of the law – The holiness it required, described, ver. 11. Might be fulfilled in us, who walk not after the flesh, but after the Spirit – Who are guided in all our thoughts, words, and actions, not by corrupt nature, but by the Spirit of God. From this place St. Paul describes primarily the state of believers, and that of unbelievers only to illustrate this.

5. They that are after the flesh – Who remain under the guidance of corrupt nature. Mind the things of the flesh – Have their thoughts and affections fixed on such things as gratify corrupt nature; namely, on things visible and temporal; on things of the earth, on pleasure, (of sense or imagination,) praise, or riches. But they who are after the Spirit – Who are under his guidance. Mind the things of the Spirit – Think of, relish, love things invisible, eternal; the things which the Spirit hath revealed, which he works in us, moves us to, and promises to give us.

MATTHEW HENRY   CHARLES H. SPURGEON

Their interest in the love of God. (28-31)
Their final triumph, through Christ. (32-39)

1-9 Believers may be chastened of the Lord, but will not be condemned with the world. By their union with Christ through faith, they are thus secured. What is the principle of their walk; the flesh or the Spirit, the old or the new nature, corruption or grace? For which of these do we make provision, by which are we governed? The unrenewed will is unable to keep any commandment fully. And the law, besides outward duties, requires inward obedience. God showed abhorrence of sin by the sufferings of his Son in the flesh, that the believer's person might be pardoned and justified.

10-17 If the Spirit be in us, Christ is in us. He dwells in the heart by faith. Grace in the soul is its new nature; the soul is alive to God, and has begun its holy happiness which shall endure for ever. The righteousness of Christ imputed, secures the soul, the better part, from death. From hence we see how much it is our duty to walk, not after the flesh, but after the Spirit. If any habitually live according to corrupt lusting, they will certainly perish in their sins, whatever they profess. And what can a worldly life present, worthy for a moment to be put against this noble prize of our high calling? Let us then, by the Spirit, endeavor more and more to mortify the flesh. Regeneration by the Holy Spirit brings a new and Divine life to the soul, though in a feeble state. And the sons of God have the Spirit to work in them the disposition of children; they have not the spirit of bondage, which the Old Testament church was under, through the darkness of that dispensation. The Spirit of adoption was not then plentifully poured out. Also it refers to that spirit of bondage, under which many saints were at their conversion. Many speak peace to themselves, to whom God does not speak peace. But those who are sanctified, have God's Spirit witnessing with their spirits, in and by his speaking peace to the soul. Though we may now seem to be losers for Christ, we shall not, we cannot, be losers by him in the end.

18-25 The sufferings of the saints strike no deeper than the things of time, last no longer than the present time, are light afflictions, and but for a moment. How vastly different are the sentence of the word and the sentiment of the world, concerning the sufferings of this present time! Indeed the whole creation seems to wait with earnest expectation for the period when the children of God shall be manifested in the glory prepared for them. There is an impurity, deformity, and infirmity, which has come upon the creature by the fall of man. There is an enmity of one creature to another. And they are used, or abused rather, by men as instruments of sin. Yet this deplorable state of the creation is in hope. God will deliver it from thus being held in bondage to man's depravity. The miseries of the human race, through their own and each other's wickedness, declare that the world is not always to continue as it is. Our having received the first-

that they will speed is this—that they are "the mind of the Spirit." God the ever blessed is one, and there can be no division between the Father, the Son, and the Holy Ghost. These divine persons always work together, and there is a common desire for the glory of each blessed Person of the Divine Unity, and therefore it cannot be conceived without profanity, that anything could be the mind of the Holy Spirit and not be the mind of the Father and the mind of the Son. The mind of God is one and harmonious; if, therefore, the Holy Spirit dwells in you, and he move you to any desire, then his mind is in your prayer, and it is not possible that the eternal Father should reject your petitions. That prayer which came from heaven will certainly go back to heaven. If the Holy Ghost prompts it, the Father must and will accept it, for it is not possible that he should put a slight upon the ever blessed and adorable Spirit.

But one more word, and that circles the argument, namely, that the work of the Spirit in the heart is not only the mind of the Spirit which God knows, but it is also according to the will or mind of God, for he never maketh intercession in us other than is consistent with the divine will. Now, the divine will or mind may be viewed two ways. First, there is the will declared in the proclamations of holiness by the Ten Commandments. The Spirit of God never prompts us to ask for anything that is unholy or inconsistent with the precepts of the Lord. Then secondly, there is the secret mind of God, the will of his eternal predestination and decree, of which we know nothing; but we do know this, that the Spirit of God never prompts us to ask anything which is contrary to the eternal purpose of God. Reflect for a moment: the Holy Spirit knows all the purposes of God, and when they are about to be fulfilled, he moves the children of God to pray about them, and so their prayers keep touch and tally with the divine decrees. Oh would you not pray confidently if you knew that your prayer corresponded with the sealed book of destiny? We may safely entreat the Lord to do what he has ordained to do. A carnal man draws the inference that if God has ordained an event we need not pray about it, but faith obediently draws the inference that the God who secretly ordained to give the blessing has openly commanded that we should pray for it, and therefore faith obediently prays. Coming events cast their shadows before them, and when God is about to bless his people his coming favor casts the shadow of

but by reason of him who hath subjected the same in hope,

21 Because the creature itself also shall be delivered from the bondage of corruption into the glorious liberty of the children of God.

22 For we know that the whole creation groaneth and travaileth in pain together until now.

23

And not only they, but ourselves also, which have the firstfruits of the Spirit, even we ourselves groan within ourselves, waiting for the adoption, to wit, the redemption of our body.

24 For we are saved by hope: but hope that is seen is not hope: for what a man seeth, why doth he yet hope for?

25 But if we hope for that we see not, then do we with patience wait for it.

26 Likewise the Spirit also helpeth our infirmities: for we know not what we should pray for as we ought: but the Spirit itself maketh intercession for us with groanings which cannot be uttered.

27 And he that searcheth the hearts knoweth what is the mind of the Spirit, because he maketh intercession for the saints according to the will of God.

28 And we know that all things work together for good to them that love God, to them who are the called according to his purpose.

29 For whom he did foreknow, he also did predestinate to be conformed to the image of his Son, that he might be the first-born among many brethren.

30 Moreover whom he did pre-destinate, them he also called: and whom he called, them he also justified: and whom he jus-tified, them he also glorified.

31 What shall we then say to these things? If God be for us, who can be against us?

32 He that spared not his own Son, but delivered him up for us all, how shall he not with him also freely give us all things?

33 Who shall lay any thing to the charge of God's elect? It is God that justifieth.

34 Who is he that condemneth? It is Christ that died, yea rather,

6. For to be carnally minded – That is, to mind the things of the flesh. Is death – The sure mark of spiritual death, and the way to death everlasting. But to be spiritually minded – That is, to mind the things of the Spirit. Is life – A sure mark of spiritual life, and the way to life everlasting. And attended with peace – The peace of God, which is the foretaste of life everlasting; and peace with God, opposite to the enmity mentioned in the next verse.

7. Enmity against God – His existence, power, and providence.

8. They who are in the flesh – Under the government of it.

9. In the Spirit – Under his government. If any man have not the Spirit of Christ – Dwelling and governing in him. He is none of his – He is not a member of Christ; not a Christian; not in a state of salvation. A plain, express declaration, which admits of no exception. He that hath ears to hear, let him hear!

10. Now if Christ be in you – Where the Spirit of Christ is, there is Christ. The body indeed is dead – Devoted to death. Because of sin – Heretofore commit-ted. But the Spirit is life – Already truly alive. Because of righteousness – Now attained. From ver. 13, St. Paul, having finished what he had begun, chap. vi, 1, describes purely the state of believers.

12. We are not debtors to the flesh – We ought not to follow it.

13. The deeds of the flesh – Not only evil actions, but evil desires, tempers, thoughts. If ye mortify – Kill, destroy these. Ye shall live – The life of faith more abundantly here, and hereafter the life of glory.

14. For as many as are led by the Spirit of God – In all the ways of righteous-ness. They are the sons of God – Here St. Paul enters upon the description of those blessings which he comprises, ver. 30, in the word glorified; though, indeed, he does not describe mere glory, but that which is still mingled with the cross. The sum is, through sufferings to glory.

16. The same Spirit beareth witness with our spirit – With the spirit of every true believer, by a testimony distinct from that of his own spirit, or the testi-mony of a good conscience. Happy they who enjoy this clear and constant.

17. Joint heirs – That we may know it is a great inheritance which God will give us for he hath given a great one to his Son. If we suffer with him – Willingly and cheerfully, for righteousness' sake. This is a new proposition, referring to what follows.

18. For I reckon – This verse gives the reason why he but now mentioned suf-ferings and glory. When that glory "shall be revealed in us," then the sons of God will be revealed also.

19. For the earnest expectation – The word denotes a lively hope of something drawing near, and a vehement longing after it. Of the creation – Of all visible creatures, believers excepted, who are spoken of apart; each kind, according as it is capable. All these have been sufferers through sin; and to all these (the final-ly impenitent excepted) shall refreshment redound from the glory of the chil-dren of God. Upright heathens are by no means to be excluded from this earnest expectation: nay, perhaps something of it may at some times be found even in the vainest of men; who (although in the hurry of life they mistake vanity for liberty, and partly stifle, partly dissemble, their groans, yet) in their sober, quiet, sleepless, afflicted hours, pour forth many sighs in the ear of God.

20. The creation was made subject to vanity – Abuse, misery, and corruption. By him who subjected it – Namely, God, Gen. iii, 17, v, 29. Adam only made it liable to the sentence which God pronounced; yet not without hope.

21. The creation itself shall be delivered – Destruction is not deliverance: there-fore whatsoever is destroyed, or ceases to be, is not delivered at all. Will, then, any part of the creation be destroyed? Into the glorious liberty – The excellent state wherein they were created.

22. For the whole creation groaneth together – With joint groans, as it were with one voice. And travaileth – Literally, is in the pains of childbirth, to be delivered of the burden of the curse. Until now – To this very hour; and so on

fruits of the Spirit, quickens our desires, encourages our hopes, and raises our expectations. Sin has been, and is, the guilty cause of all the suffering that exists in the creation of God. It has brought on the woes of earth; it has kindled the flames of hell. As to man, not a tear has been shed, not a groan has been uttered, not a pang has been felt, in body or mind, that has not come from sin. This is not all; sin is to be looked at as it affects the glory of God. Of this how fearfully regardless are the bulk of mankind! Believers have been brought into a state of safety; but their comfort consists rather in hope than in enjoyment. From this hope they cannot be turned by the vain expectation of finding satisfaction in the things of time and sense. We need patience, our way is rough and long; but he that shall come, will come, though he seems to tarry.

26,27 Though the infirmities of Christians are many and great, so that they would be overpowered if left to themselves, yet the Holy Spirit supports them. The Spirit, as an enlightening Spirit, teaches us what to pray for; as a sanctifying Spirit, works and stirs up praying graces; as a comforting Spirit, silences our fears, and helps us over all discouragements. The Holy Spirit is the spring of all desires toward God, which are often more than words can utter. The Spirit who searches the hearts, can perceive the mind and will of the spirit, the renewed mind, and advocates his cause. The Spirit makes intercession to God, and the enemy prevails not.

28-31 That is good for the saints which does their souls good. Every providence tends to the spiritual good of those that love God; in breaking them off from sin, bringing them nearer to God, weaning them from the world, and fitting them for heaven. When the saints act out of character, corrections will be employed to bring them back again.

32-39 All things whatever, in heaven and earth, are not so great a display of God's free love, as the gift of his coequal Son to be the atonement on the cross for the sin of man; and all the rest follows upon union with him, and interest in him. All things, all which can be the causes or means of any real good to the faithful Christian. He that has prepared a crown and a kingdom for us, will give us what we need in the way to it. Men may justify themselves, though the accusations are in full force against them; but if God justifies, that answers all. By Christ we are thus secured. By the merit of his death he paid our debt. Yea, rather that is risen again. This is convincing evidence that Divine justice was satisfied. We have such a Friend at the right hand of God; all power is given to him. He is there, making intercession. Believer! does your soul say within you, Oh that he were mine! and oh that I were his; that I could please him and live to him! Then do not toss your spirit and perplex your thoughts in fruitless, endless doubting, but as you are convinced of ungodliness, believe on him who justifies the ungodly. You are condemned, yet Christ is dead and risen. Flee to him as such. God having manifested his love in giving his own Son for us, can we think

prayer over the church. When he is about to favor an individual he casts the shadow of hopeful expectation over his soul. Our prayers, let men laugh at them as they will, and say there is no power in them, are the indicators of the movement of the wheels of Providence. Believing supplications are forecasts of the future. He who prayeth in faith is like the seer of old, he sees that which is to be: his holy expectancy, like a telescope, brings distant objects near to him. He is bold to declare that he has the petition which he has asked of God, and he therefore begins to rejoice and to praise God, even before the blessing has actually arrived. So it is: prayer prompted by the Holy Spirit is the footfall of the divine decree.

I conclude by saying, see, my dear hearers, the absolute necessity of the Holy Spirit, for if the saints know not what they should pray for as they ought; if consecrated men and women, with Christ suffering in them, still feel their need of the instruction of the Holy Spirit, how much more do you who are not saints, and have never given yourselves up to God, require divine teaching! Oh, that you would know and feel your dependence upon the Holy Ghost that he may prompt the once crucified but now ascended Redeemer that this gift of the Spirit, this promise of the Father, is shed abroad upon men. May he who comes from Jesus lead you to Jesus.

And, then O ye people of God, let this last thought abide with you,—what condescension is this that Divine Person should dwell in you for ever, and that he should be with you to help your prayers. Listen to me for a moment. If I read in the Scriptures that in the most heroic acts of faith God the Holy Ghost helpeth his people, I can understand it; if I read that in the sweetest music of their songs when they worship best, and chant their loftiest strains before the Most High God, the Spirit helpeth them, I can understand it; and even if I hear that in their wrestling prayers and prevalent intercessions God the Holy Spirit helpeth them, I can understand it: but I bow with reverent amazement, my heart sinking into the dust with adoration, when I reflect that God the Holy Ghost helps us when we cannot speak, but only groan. Yea, and when we cannot even utter our groanings, he doth not only help us but he claims as his own particular creation the "groanings that cannot be uttered." This is condescension indeed! In deigning to help us in the grief that cannot even vent itself in groaning, he proves himself to be a true Comforter. O God, my God, thou hast not forsaken me:

that is risen again, who is even at the right hand of God, who also maketh intercession for us.

35 Who shall separate us from the love of Christ? shall tribulation, or distress, or persecution, or famine, or nakedness, or peril, or sword?

36 As it is written, For thy sake we are killed all the day long; we are accounted as sheep for the slaughter.

37 Nay, in all these things we are more than conquerors through him that loved us.

38 For I am persuaded, that neither death, nor life, nor angels, nor principalities, nor powers, nor things present, nor things to come,

39 Nor height, nor depth, nor any other creature, shall be able to separate us from the love of God, which is in Christ Jesus our Lord.

ROMANS 9

1 I say the truth in Christ, I lie not, my conscience also bearing me witness in the Holy Ghost,

2 That I have great heaviness and continual sorrow in my heart.

3 For I could wish that myself were accursed from Christ for my brethren, my kinsmen according to the flesh:

4 Who are Israelites; to whom pertaineth the adoption, and the glory, and the covenants, and the giving of the law, and the service of God, and the promises;

5 Whose are the fathers, and of whom as concerning the flesh Christ came, who is over all, God blessed for ever. Amen.

6 Not as though the word of God hath taken none effect. For they are not all Israel, which are of Israel:

7 Neither, because they are the seed of Abraham, are they all children: but, In Isaac shall thy seed be called.

8 That is, They which are the children of the flesh, these are not the children of God: but the children of the promise are counted for the seed.

9 For this is the word of promise, At this time will I come, and Sara shall have a son.

till the time of deliverance.

23. And even we, who have the first-fruits of the Spirit – That is, the Spirit, who is the first-fruits of our inheritance. The adoption – Persons who had been privately adopted among the Romans were often brought forth into the forum, and there publicly owned as their sons by those who adopted them. So at the general resurrection, when the body itself is redeemed from death, the sons of God shall be publicly owned by him in the great assembly of men and angels. The redemption of our body – From corruption to glory and immortality.

24. For we are saved by hope – Our salvation is now only in hope. We do not yet possess this full salvation.

27. But he who searcheth the hearts – Wherein the Spirit dwells and intercedes. Knoweth – Though man cannot utter it. What is the mind of the Spirit, for he maketh intercession for the saints – Who are near to God. According to God – According to his will, as is worthy of God, and acceptable to him.

28. And we know – This in general; though we do not always know particularly what to pray for. That all things – Ease or pain, poverty or riches, and the ten thousand changes of life. Work together for good – Strongly and sweetly for spiritual and eternal good. To them that are called according to his purpose – His gracious design of saving a lost world by the death of his Son. This is a new proposition. St. Paul, being about to recapitulate the whole blessing contained in justification, (termed "glorification," ver. 30,) first goes back to the purpose or decree of God, which is frequently mentioned in holy writ. To explain this (nearly in the words of an eminent writer) a little more at large: When a man has a work of time and importance before him, he pauses, consults, and contrives; and when he has laid a plan, resolves or decrees to proceed accordingly. Having observed this in ourselves, we are ready to apply it to God also; and he, in condescension to us has applied it to himself. The works of providence and redemption are vast and stupendous, and therefore we are apt to conceive of God as deliberating and consulting on them, and then decreeing to act according to "the counsel of his own will;" as if, long before the world was made, he had been concerting measures both as to the making and governing of it, and had then writ down his decrees, which altered not, any more than the laws of the Medes and Persians.

29. Whom he foreknew, he also predestinated conformable to the image of his Son – Here the apostle declares who those are whom he foreknew and predestinated to glory; namely, those who are conformable to the image of his Son. This is the mark of those who are foreknown and will be glorified, 2 Tim. ii, 19. Phil. iii, 10, 21.

30. Them he – In due time. Called – By his gospel and his Spirit. And whom he called – When obedient to the heavenly calling, Acts xxvi, 19. He also justified – Forgave and accepted. And whom he justified – Provided they "continued in his goodness," chap. xi, 22, he in the end glorified – St. Paul does not affirm, either here or in any other part of his writings, that precisely the same number of men are called, justified, and glorified. He does not deny that a believer may fall away and be cut off between his special calling and his glorification, chap. xi, 22. Neither does he deny that many are called who never are justified. He only affirms that this is the method whereby God leads us step by step toward heaven.

32. He that – This period contains four sentences: He spared not his own Son; therefore he will freely give us all things. He delivered him up for us all; therefore, none can lay anything to our charge. Freely – For all that follows justification is a free gift also. All things – Needful or profitable for us.

33. God's elect – It does not appear that even good men were ever termed God's elect till above two thousand years from the creation. God's electing or choosing the nation of Israel, and separating them from the other nations, who were sunk in idolatry and all wickedness, gave the first occasion to this sort of lan-

that any thing should turn aside or do away that love? Troubles neither cause nor show any abatement of his love. Whatever believers may be separated from, enough remains. None can take Christ from the believer: none can take the believer from him; and that is enough. All other hazards signify nothing. Alas, poor sinners! though you abound with the possessions of this world, what vain things are they! Can you say of any of them, Who shall separate us? You may be removed from pleasant dwellings, and friends, and estates. You may even live to see and seek your parting. At last you must part, for you must die. Then farewell, all this world accounts most valuable. And what hast thou left, poor soul, who hast not Christ, but that which thou wouldest gladly part with, and canst not; the condemning guilt of all thy sins! But the soul that is in Christ, when other things are pulled away, cleaves to Christ, and these separations pain him not. Yea, when death comes, that breaks all other unions, even that of the soul and body, it carries the believer's soul into the nearest union with its beloved Lord Jesus, and the full enjoyment of him for ever.

ROMANS 9

The apostle's concern that his countrymen were strangers to the gospel. (1-5)

The promises are made good to the spiritual seed of Abraham. (6-13)

Answers to objections against God's sovereign conduct, in exercising mercy and justice. (14-24)

This sovereignty is in God's dealing both with Jews and Gentiles. (25-29)

The falling short of the Jews is owing to their seeking justification, not by faith, but by the works of the law. (30-33)

1-5 Being about to discuss the rejection of the Jews and the calling of the Gentiles, and to show that the whole agrees with the sovereign electing love of God, the apostle expresses strongly his affection for his people. He solemnly appeals to Christ; and his conscience, enlightened and directed by the Holy Spirit, bore witness to his sincerity. He would submit to be treated as "accursed," to be disgraced, crucified; and even for a time be in the deepest horror and distress; if he could rescue his nation from the destruction about to come upon them for their obstinate unbelief. To be insensible to the eternal condition of our fellow-creatures, is contrary both to the love required by the law, and the mercy of the gospel. They had long been professed worshipers of Jehovah. The law, and the national covenant which was grounded thereon, belonged to them. The temple worship was typical of salvation by the Messiah, and the means of communion with God. All the promises concerning Christ and his salvation were given to them. He is not only over all, as Mediator, but he is God blessed for ever.

6-13 The rejection of the Jews by the gospel dispensation, did not break God's promise to the patriarchs. The promises and threatenings shall be fulfilled. Grace does

thou art not far from me, nor from the voice of my roaring. Thou didst for awhile leave the Firstborn when he was made a curse for us, so that he cried in agony, "Why hast thou forsaken me?" but thou wilt not leave one of the "many brethren" for whom he died: the Spirit shall be with them, and when they cannot so much as groan he will make intercession for them with groanings that cannot be uttered. God bless you, my beloved brethren, and may you feel the Spirit of the Lord thus working in you and with you. Amen and amen.

SOVEREIGN GRACE AND MAN'S RESPONSIBILITY
Sermon number 207 delivered on August 1, 1858, at the Music Hall, Royal Surrey Gardens.

"But Esaias is very bold, and saith, I was found of them that sought me not; I was made manifest unto them that asked not after me. But to Israel he saith, all day long I have stretched forth my hands unto a disobedient and gainsaying people."—Romans 10:20-21.

DOUBTLESS THESE WORDS primarily refer to the casting away of the Jews, and to the choosing of the Gentiles. The Gentiles were a people who sought not after God, but lived in idolatry; nevertheless, Jehovah was pleased in these latter times to send the gospel of his grace to them: while the Jews who had long enjoyed the privileges of the Word of God, on account of their disobedience and rebellion were cast away. I believe, however, that while this is the primary object of the words of our text, yet, as Calvin says, the truth taught in the text is a type of a universal fact. As God did choose the people who knew him not, so hath he chosen, in the abundance of his grace, to manifest his salvation to men who are out of the way; while, on the other hand, the men who are lost, after having heard the Word, are lost because of their willfull sin; for God doth all the day long "stretch forth his hands unto a disobedient and gainsaying people."

The system of truth is not one straight line, but two. No man will ever get a right view of the gospel until he knows how to look at the two lines at once. I am taught in one book to believe that what I sow I shall reap: I am taught in another place, that "it is not of him that willeth nor of him that runneth, but of God that showeth mercy." I see

10 And not only this; but when Rebecca also had conceived by one, even by our father Isaac;

11 (For the children being not yet born, neither having done any good or evil, that the purpose of God according to election might stand, not of works, but of him that calleth;)

12 It was said unto her, The elder shall serve the younger.

13 As it is written, Jacob have I loved, but Esau have I hated.

14 What shall we say then? Is there unrighteousness with God? God forbid.

15 For he saith to Moses, I will have mercy on whom I will have mercy, and I will have compassion on whom I will have compassion.

16 So then it is not of him that willeth, nor of him that runneth, but of God that sheweth mercy.

17 For the scripture saith unto Pharaoh, Even for this same purpose have I raised thee up, that I might shew my power in thee, and that my name might be declared throughout all the earth.

18 Therefore hath he mercy on whom he will have mercy, and whom he will he hardeneth.

19 Thou wilt say then unto me, Why doth he yet find fault? For who hath resisted his will?

20 Nay but, O man, who art thou that repliest against God? Shall the thing formed say to him that formed it, Why hast thou made me thus?

21 Hath not the potter power over the clay, of the same lump to make one vessel unto honor, and another unto dishonor?

22 What if God, willing to shew his wrath, and to make his power known, endured with much longsuffering the vessels of wrath fitted to destruction:

23 And that he might make known the riches of his glory on the vessels of mercy, which he had afore prepared unto glory,

24 Even us, whom he hath called, not of the Jews only, but also of the Gentiles?

25 As he saith also in Osee, I will call them my people, which were not my people; and her beloved, which was not beloved.

26 And it shall come to pass, that in the place where it was

guage. And as the separating the Christians from the Jews was a like event, no wonder it was expressed in like words and phrases only with this difference, the term elect was of old applied to all the members of the visible church; whereas in the New Testament it is applied only to the members of the invisible.

34. Yea rather, that is risen – Our faith should not stop at his death, but be exercised farther on his resurrection, kingdom, second coming. Who maketh intercession for us – Presenting there his obedience, his sufferings, his prayers, and our prayers sanctified through him.

35. Who shall separate us from the love of Christ – Toward us? Shall affliction or distress – He proceeds in order, from less troubles to greater: can any of these separate us from his protection in it; and, if he sees good, deliverance from it?

36. All the day – That is, every day, continually. We are accounted – By our enemies; by ourselves. Psalm xliv, 22.

37. We more than conquer – We are not only no losers, but abundant gainers, by all these trials. This period seems to describe the full assurance of hope.

38. I am persuaded – This is inferred from the thirty-fourth verse, in an admirable order: – "Neither death" shall hurt us; For "Christ is dead:" "Nor life;" is risen "Nor angels, nor principalities, nor powers; nor things pre- sent, nor things to come;" "is at the right hand of God:" "Nor height, nor depth, nor any other creature;" "maketh intercession for us." Neither death – Terrible as it is to natural men; a violent death in particular, ver. 36. Nor life – With all the affliction and distress it can bring, ver. 35; or a long, easy life; or all living men. Nor angels – Whether good (if it were possible they should attempt it) or bad, with all their wisdom and strength. Nor principalities, nor powers – Not even those of the highest rank, or the most eminent power. Nor things present – Which may befall us during our pilgrimage; or the whole world, till it passeth away. Nor things to come – Which may occur either when our time on earth is past, or when time itself is at an end, as the final judgment, the general conflagration, the everlasting fire. Nor height, nor depth – The former sentence respected the differences of times; this, the differences of places. How many great and various things are contained in these words, we do not, need not, cannot know yet. The height – In St. Paul's sublime style, is put for heaven. The depth – For the great abyss: that is, neither the heights, I will not say of walls, mountains, seas, but, of heaven itself, can move us; nor the abyss itself, the very thought of which might astonish the boldest creature. Nor any creature – Nothing beneath the Almighty; visible enemies he does not even deign to name. Shall be able – Either by force, ver. 35; or by any legal claim, ver. 33, &c.

ROMANS 9

1. In Christ – This seems to imply an appeal to him. In the Holy Ghost – Through his grace.

2. I have great sorrow – A high degree of spiritual sorrow and of spiritual Joy may consist together, chap. viii, 39. By declaring his sorrow for the unbelieving Jews, who excluded themselves from all the blessings he had enumerated, he shows that what he was now about to speak, he did not speak from any prejudice to them.

3. I could wish – Human words cannot fully describe the motions of souls that are full of God. As if he had said, I could wish to suffer in their stead; yea, to be an anathema from Christ in their place. In how high a sense he wished this, who can tell, unless himself had been asked and had resolved the question? Certainly he did not then consider himself at all, but only others and the glory of God. The thing could not be; yet the wish was pious and solid; though with a tacit condition, if it were right and possible.

4. Whose is the adoption, &c. – He enumerates six prerogatives, of which the first pair respect God the Father, the second Christ, the third the Holy Ghost.

not run in the blood; nor are saving benefits always found with outward church privileges. Not only some of Abraham's seed were chosen, and others not, but God therein wrought according to the counsel of his own will. God foresaw both Esau and Jacob as born in sin, by nature children of wrath even as others. If left to themselves they would have continued in sin through life; but for wise and holy reasons, not made known to us, he purposed to change Jacob's heart, and to leave Esau to his perverseness. This instance of Esau and Jacob throws light upon the Divine conduct to the fallen race of man. The whole Scripture shows the difference between the professed Christian and the real believer. Outward privileges are bestowed on many who are not the children of God. There is, however, full encouragement to diligent use of the means of grace which God has appointed.

14-24 Whatever God does, must be just. Wherein the holy, happy people of God differ from others, God's grace alone makes them differ. In this preventing, effectual, distinguishing grace, he acts as a benefactor, whose grace is his own. None have deserved it; so that those who are saved, must thank God only; and those who perish, must blame themselves only, Hos 13:9. God is bound no further than he has been pleased to bind himself by his own covenant and promise, which is his revealed will. And this is, that he will receive, and not cast out, those that come to Christ; but the drawing of souls in order to that coming, is an anticipating, distinguishing favor to whom he will. Why does he yet find fault? This is not an objection to be made by the creature against his Creator, by man against God. The truth, as it is in Jesus, abases man as nothing, as less than nothing, and advances God as sovereign Lord of all. Who art thou that art so foolish, so feeble, so unable to judge the Divine counsels? It becomes us to submit to him, not to reply against him. Would not men allow the infinite God the same sovereign right to manage the affairs of the creation, as the potter exercises in disposing of his clay, when of the same lump he makes one vessel to a more honorable, and one to a meaner use? God could do no wrong, however it might appear to men. God will make it appear that he hates sin. Also, he formed vessels filled with mercy. Sanctification is the preparation of the soul for glory. This is God's work. Sinners fit themselves for hell, but it is God who prepares saints for heaven; and all whom God designs for heaven hereafter, he fits for heaven now. Would we know who these vessels of mercy are? Those whom God has called; and these not of the Jews only, but of the Gentiles. Surely there can be no unrighteousness in any of these Divine dispensations. Nor in God's exercising long-suffering, patience, and forbearance towards sinners under increasing guilt, before he brings utter destruction upon them. The fault is in the hardened sinner himself. As to all who love and fear God, however such truths appear beyond their reason to fathom, yet they should keep silence before him. It is the Lord alone who made us to differ; we should adore his pardoning mercy and new-creating grace, and give diligence to make our calling and election sure.

in one place, God presiding over all in providence; and yet I see, and I cannot help seeing, that man acts as he pleases, and that God has left his actions to his own will, in a great measure. Now, if I were to declare that man was so free to act, that there was no presidence of God over his actions, I should be driven very near to Atheism; and if, on the other hand, I declare that God so overrules all things, as that man is not free enough to be responsible, I am driven at once into Antinomianism or fatalism. That God predestines, and that man is responsible, are two things that few can see. They are believed to be inconsistent and contradictory; but they are not. It is just the fault of our weak judgment. Two truths cannot be contradictory to each other. If, then, I find taught in one place that everything is fore-ordained, that is true; and if I find in another place that man is responsible for all his actions, that is true; and it is my folly that leads me to imagine that two truths can ever contradict each other. These two truths, I do not believe, can ever be welded into one upon any human anvil, but one they shall be in eternity: they are two lines that are so nearly parallel, that the mind that shall pursue them farthest, will never discover that they converge; but they do converge, and they will meet somewhere in eternity, close to the throne of God, whence all truth doth spring.

Now, this morning I am about to consider the two doctrines. In the 20th verse, we have taught us the doctrines of sovereign grace—"But Esaias is very bold, and saith, I was found of them that sought me not; I was made manifest unto them that asked not after me." In the next verse, we have the doctrine of man's guilt in rejecting God. "To Israel he saith, all day long I have stretched forth my hands unto a disobedient and gainsaying people."

I. First, then, DIVINE SOVEREIGNTY AS EXEMPLIFIED IN SALVATION. If any man be saved, he is saved by Divine grace, and by Divine grace alone; and the reason of his salvation is not to be found in him, but in God. We are not saved as the result of anything that we do or that we will; but we will and do as the result of God's good pleasure, and the work of his grace in our hearts. No sinner can prevent God; that is, he cannot go before him, cannot anticipate him; God is always first in the matter of salvation. He is before our convictions, before our desires, before our fears, before our hopes. All that is good or ever will be good in us, is preceded by the grace of

said unto them, Ye are not my people; there shall they be called the children of the living God.

27 Esaias also crieth concerning Israel, Though the number of the children of Israel be as the sand of the sea, a remnant shall be saved:

28 For he will finish the work, and cut it short in righteousness: because a short work will the Lord make upon the earth.

29 And as Esaias said before, Except the Lord of Sabaoth had left us a seed, we had been as Sodoma, and been made like unto Gomorrha.

30 What shall we say then? That the Gentiles, which followed not after righteousness, have attained to righteousness, even the righteousness which is of faith.

31 But Israel, which followed after the law of righteousness, hath not attained to the law of righteousness.

32 Wherefore? Because they sought it not by faith, but as it were by the works of the law. For they stumbled at that stumblingstone;

33 As it is written, Behold, I lay in Sion a stumblingstone and rock of offense: and whosoever believeth on him shall not be ashamed.

ROMANS 10

1 Brethren, my heart's desire and prayer to God for Israel is, that they might be saved.

2 For I bear them record that they have a zeal of God, but not according to knowledge.

3 For they being ignorant of God's righteousness, and going about to establish their own righteousness, have not submitted themselves unto the righteousness of God.

4 For Christ is the end of the law for righteousness to every one that believeth.

5 For Moses describeth the righteousness which is of the law, That the man which doeth those things shall live by them.

6 But the righteousness which is of faith speaketh on this wise, Say not in thine heart, Who shall ascend into heaven? (that is, to bring Christ down from above:)

The adoption and the glory – That is, Israel is the first-born child of God, and the God of glory is their God, Deut. iv, 7; Psalm cvi, 20. These are relative to each other. At once God is the Father of Israel, and Israel are the people of God. He speaks not here of the ark, or any corporeal thing. God himself is "the glory of his people Israel." And the covenants, and the giving of the law – The covenant was given long before the law. It is termed covenants, in the plural, because it was so often and so variously repeated, and because there were two dispositions of it, Gal. iv, 24, frequently called two covenants; the one promising, the other exhibiting the promise. And the worship, and the promises – The true way of worshiping God; and all the promises made to the fathers.

5. To the preceding, St. Paul now adds two more prerogatives. Theirs are the fathers – The patriarchs and holy men of old, yea, the Messiah himself. Who is over all, God blessed for ever – The original words imply the self-existent, independent Being, who was, is, and is to come. Over all – The supreme; as being God, and consequently blessed for ever. No words can more clearly express his divine, supreme majesty, and his gracious sovereignty both over Jews and Gentiles.

6. Not as if – The Jews imagined that the word of God must fail if all their nation were not saved. This St. Paul now refutes, and proves that the word itself had foretold their falling away. The word of God – The promises of God to Israel. Had fallen to the ground – This could not be. Even now, says the apostle, some enjoy the promises; and hereafter "all Israel shall be saved." This is the sum of the ninth, tenth, and eleventh chapters. For – Here he enters upon the proof of it. All are not Israel, who are of Israel – The Jews vehemently maintained the contrary; namely, that all who were born Israelites, and they only, were the people of God. The former part of this assertion is refuted here, the latter, ver. 24, &c. The sum is, God accepts all believers, and them only; and this is no way contrary to his word. Nay, he hath declared in his word, both by types and by express testimonies, that believers are accepted as the "children of the promise," while unbelievers are rejected, though they are "children after the flesh." All are not Israel – Not in the favor of God. Who are lineally descended of Israel.

7. Neither because they are lineally the seed of Abraham, will it follow that they are all children of God – This did not hold even in Abraham's own family; and much less in his remote descendants. But God then said, In Isaac shall thy seed be called – That is, Isaac, not Ishmael, shall be called thy seed; that seed to which the promise is made.

8. That is, Not the children, &c. – As if he had said, This is a clear type of things to come; showing us, that in all succeeding generations, not the children of the flesh, the lineal descendants of Abraham, but the children of the promise, they to whom the promise is made, that is, believers, are the children of God. Gen. xxi, 12

9. For this is the word of the promise – By the power of which Isaac was conceived, and not by the power of nature. Not, Whosoever is born of thee shall be blessed, but, At this time – Which I now appoint. I will come, and Sarah shall have a son – And he shall inherit the blessing. Gen. xviii, 10.

12. The elder – Esau. Shall serve the younger – Not in person, for he never did; but in his posterity. Accordingly the Edomites were often brought into subjection by the Israelites. Gen. xxv, 23.

13. As it is written – With which word in Genesis, spoken so long before, that of Malachi agrees. I have loved Jacob – With a peculiar love; that is, the Israelites, the posterity of Jacob. And I have, comparatively, hated Esau – That is, the Edomites, the posterity of Esau. But observe,

　　1. This does not relate to the person of Jacob or Esau

　　2. Nor does it relate to the eternal state either of them or their posterity. Thus far the apostle has been proving his proposition, namely, that the exclusion

25-29 The rejecting of the Jews, and the taking in the Gentiles, were foretold in the Old Testament. It tends very much to the clearing of a truth, to observe how the Scripture is fulfilled in it. It is a wonder of Divine power and mercy that there are any saved: for even those left to be a seed, if God had dealt with them according to their sins, had perished with the rest. This great truth this Scripture teaches us. Even among the vast number of professing Christians it is to be feared that only a remnant will be saved.

30-33 The Gentiles knew not their guilt and misery, therefore were not careful to procure a remedy. Yet they attained to righteousness by faith. Not by becoming proselytes to the Jewish religion, and submitting to the ceremonial law; but by embracing Christ, and believing in him, and submitting to the gospel. The Jews talked much of justification and holiness, and seemed very ambitious to be the favorites of God. They sought, but not in the right way, not in the humbling way, not in the appointed way. Not by faith, not by embracing Christ, depending upon Christ, and submitting to the gospel. They expected justification by observing the precepts and ceremonies of the law of Moses. The unbelieving Jews had a fair offer of righteousness, life, and salvation, made them upon gospel terms, which they did not like, and would not accept. Have we sought to know how we may be justified before God, seeking that blessing in the way here pointed out, by faith in Christ, as the Lord our Righteousness? Then we shall not be ashamed in that awful day, when all refuges of lies shall be swept away, and the Divine wrath shall overflow every hiding-place but that which God hath prepared in his own Son.

ROMANS 10

The apostle's earnest desire for the salvation of the Jews. (1-4)
The difference between the righteousness of the law, and the righteousness of faith. (5-11)
The Gentiles stand on a level with the Jews, in justification and salvation. (12-17)
The Jews might know this from Old Testament prophecies. (18-21)

1-4 The Jews built on a false foundation, and refused to come to Christ for free salvation by faith, and numbers in every age do the same in various ways. The strictness of the law showed men their need of salvation by grace, through faith. And the ceremonies shadowed forth Christ as fulfilling the righteousness, and bearing the curse of the law. So that even under the law, all who were justified before God, obtained that blessing by faith, whereby they were made partakers of the perfect righteousness of the promised Redeemer. The law is not destroyed, nor the intention of the Lawgiver disappointed; but full satisfaction being made by the death of Christ for our breach of the law, the end is gained. That is, Christ has fulfilled the whole law, therefore whoever believeth in him, is

God, and is the effect of a Divine cause within.

Now in speaking of God's gracious acts of salvation, this morning, I notice first, that they are entirely unmerited. You will see that the people here mentioned certainly did not merit God's grace. They found him, but they never sought for him; he was made manifest to them, but they never asked for him. There never was a man saved yet who merited it. Ask all the saints of God, and they will tell you that their former life was spent in the lusts of the flesh; that in the days of their ignorance, they revolted against God and turned back from his ways, that when they were invited to come to him they despised the invitation, and, when warned, cast the warning behind their back. They will tell you that their being drawn by God, was not the result of any merit before conversion; for some of them, so far from having any merit, were the very vilest of the vile: they plunged into the very kennel of sin; they were not ashamed of all the things of which it would be a shame for us to speak; they were ringleaders in crime, very princes in the ranks of the enemy; and yet sovereign grace came to them, and they were brought to know the Lord. They will tell you that it was not the result of anything good in their disposition, for although they trust that there is now something excellent implanted in them, yet in the days of their flesh they could see no one quality which was not perverted to the service of Satan. Ask them whether they think they were chosen of God because of their courage; they will tell you, no; if they had courage it was defaced, for they were courageous to do evil. Question them whether they were chosen of God because of their talent; they will tell you, no; they had that talent, but they prostituted it to the service of Satan. Question them whether they were chosen because of the openness and generosity of their disposition; they will tell you that that very openness of temper, and that very generosity of disposition, led them to plunge deeper into the depths of sin, than they otherwise would have done, for they were "hail fellow, well met," with every evil man, and ready to drink and join every jovial party which should come in their way. There was in them no reason whatever why God should have mercy upon them, and the wonder to them is that he did not cut them down in the midst of their sins, blot out their names from the book of life, and sweep them into the gulf where the fire burneth. that shall devour the wicked. But some have

7 Or, Who shall descend into the deep? (that is, to bring up Christ again from the dead.)

8 But what saith it? The word is nigh thee, even in thy mouth, and in thy heart: that is, the word of faith, which we preach;

9 That if thou shalt confess with thy mouth the Lord Jesus, and shalt believe in thine heart that God hath raised him from the dead, thou shalt be saved.

10 For with the heart man believeth unto righteousness; and with the mouth confession is made unto salvation.

11 For the scripture saith, Whosoever believeth on him shall not be ashamed.

12 For there is no difference between the Jew and the Greek: for the same Lord over all is rich unto all that call upon him.

13 For whosoever shall call upon the name of the Lord shall be saved.

14 How then shall they call on him in whom they have not believed? and how shall they believe in him of whom they have not heard? and how shall they hear without a preacher?

15 And how shall they preach, except they be sent? as it is written, How beautiful are the feet of them that preach the gospel of peace, and bring glad tidings of good things!

16 But they have not all obeyed the gospel. For Esaias saith, Lord, who hath believed our report?

17 So then faith cometh by hearing, and hearing by the word of God.

18 But I say, Have they not heard? Yes verily, their sound went into all the earth, and their words unto the ends of the world.

19 But I say, Did not Israel know? First Moses saith, I will provoke you to jealousy by them that are no people, and by a foolish nation I will anger you.

20 But Esaias is very bold, and saith, I was found of them that sought me not; I was made manifest unto them that asked not after me.

21 But to Israel he saith, All day long I have stretched forth my hands unto a disobedient and gainsaying people.

of a great part of the seed of Abraham, yea, and of Isaac, from the special promises of God, was so far from being impossible, that, according to the scriptures themselves, it had actually happened. He now introduces and refutes an objection. Mal. i, 2, 3.

14. Is there injustice with God – Is it unjust in God to give Jacob the blessing rather than Esau? or to accept believers, and them only. God forbid – In no wise. This is well consistent with justice; for he has a right to fix the terms on which he will show mercy, according to his declaration to Moses, petitioning for all the people, after they had committed idolatry with the golden calf. I will have mercy on whom I will have mercy – According to the terms I myself have fixed. And I will have compassion on whom I will have compassion – Namely, on those only who submit to my terms, who accept of it in the way that I have appointed.

15. Exod. xxxiii, 19.

18. So then – That is, accordingly he does show mercy on his own terms, namely, on them that believe. And whom he willeth – Namely, them that believe not. He hardeneth – Leaves to the hardness of their hearts.

19. Why doth he still find fault – The particle still is strongly expressive of the objector's sour, morose murmuring. For who hath resisted his will – The word his likewise expresses his surliness and aversion to God, whom he does not even deign to name.

20. Nay, but who art thou, O man – Little, impotent, ignorant man. That repliest against God – That accusest God of injustice, for himself fixing the terms on which he will show mercy? Shall the thing formed say to him that formed it, Why hast thou made me thus – Why hast thou made me capable of honor and immortality, only by believing?

21. Hath not the potter power over the clay – And much more hath not God power over his creatures, to appoint one vessel, namely, the believer, to honor, and another, the unbeliever, to dishonor? If we survey the right which God has over us, in a more general way, with regard to his intelligent creatures, God may be considered in two different views, as Creator, Proprietor, and Lord of all; or, as their moral Governor, and Judge. God, as sovereign Lord and Proprietor of all, dispenses his gifts or favors to his creatures with perfect wisdom, but by no rules or methods of proceeding that we are acquainted with. The time when we shall exist, the country where we shall live, our parents, our constitution of body and turn of mind; these, and numberless other circumstances, are doubtless ordered with perfect wisdom, but by rules that lie quite out of our sight. But God's methods of dealing with us, as our Governor and Judge, are clearly revealed and perfectly known; namely, that he will finally reward every man according to his works: "He that believeth shalt be saved, and he that believeth not shall be damned." Therefore, though "He hath mercy on whom he willeth, and whom he willeth he hardeneth," that is, suffers to be hardened in consequence of their obstinate wickedness; yet his is not the will of an arbitrary, capricious, or tyrannical being. He wills nothing but what is infinitely wise and good; and therefore his will is a most proper rule of judgment. He will show mercy, as he hath assured us, to none but true believers, nor harden any but such as obstinately refuse his mercy. Jer. xviii, 6, 7

22. What if God, being willing – Referring to ver. 18, 19. That is, although it was now his will, because of their obstinate unbelief, To show his wrath – Which necessarily presupposes sin. And to make his power known – This is repeated from the seventeenth verse. Yet endured – As he did Pharaoh. With much long-suffering – Which should have led them to repentance. The vessels of wrath – Those who had moved his wrath by still rejecting his mercy. Fitted for destruction – By their own willfull and final impenitence. Is there any injustice in this?

23. That he might make known – What if by showing such longsuffering even to "the vessels of wrath," he did the more abundantly show the greatness of his

MATTHEW HENRY

CHARLES H. SPURGEON

counted just before God, as much as though he had fulfilled the whole law himself. Sinners never could go on in vain fancies of their own righteousness, if they knew the justice of God as a Governor, or his righteousness as a Savior.

5-11 The self-condemned sinner need not perplex himself how this righteousness may be found. When we speak of looking upon Christ, and receiving, and feeding upon him, it is not Christ in heaven, nor Christ in the deep, that we mean; but Christ in the promise, Christ offered in the word. Justification by faith in Christ is a plain doctrine. It is brought before the mind and heart of every one, thus leaving him without excuse for unbelief. If a man confessed faith in Jesus, as the Lord and Savior of lost sinners, and really believed in his heart that God had raised him from the dead, thus showing that he had accepted the atonement, he should be saved by the righteousness of Christ, imputed to him through faith. But no faith is justifying which is not powerful in sanctifying the heart, and regulating all its affections by the love of Christ. We must devote and give up to God our souls and our bodies: our souls in believing with the heart, and our bodies in confessing with the mouth. The believer shall never have cause to repent his confident trust in the Lord Jesus. Of such faith no sinner shall be ashamed before God; and he ought to glory in it before men.

12-17 There is not one God to the Jews, more kind, and another to the Gentiles, who is less kind; the Lord is a Father to all men. The promise is the same to all, who call on the name of the Lord Jesus as the Son of God, as God manifest in the flesh. All believers thus call upon the Lord Jesus, and none else will do so humbly or sincerely. But how should any call on the Lord Jesus, the Divine Savior, who had not heard of him? And what is the life of a Christian but a life of prayer? It shows that we feel our dependence on him, and are ready to give up ourselves to him, and have a believing expectation of our all from him. It was necessary that the gospel should be preached to the Gentiles. Somebody must show them what they are to believe. How welcome the gospel ought to be to those to whom it was preached! The gospel is given, not only to be known and believed, but to be obeyed. It is not a system of notions, but a rule of practice. The beginning, progress, and strength of faith is by hearing. But it is only hearing the word, as the word of God that will strengthen faith.

18-21 Did not the Jews know that the Gentiles were to be called in? They might have known it from Moses and Isaiah. Isaiah speaks plainly of the grace and favor of God, as going before in the receiving of the Gentiles. Was not this our own case? Did not God begin in love, and make himself known to us when we did not ask after him? The patience of God towards provoking sinners is wonderful. The time of God's patience is called a day, light as day, and fit for work and business; but limited as a day, and there is a night at the end of it. God's patience

said that God chooses his people because he foresees that after he chooses them, they will do this, that, and the other, which shall be meritorious and excellent. Refer again to the people of God, and they will tell you that since their conversion they have had much to weep over. Although they can rejoice that God has begun the good work in them, they often tremble lest it should not be God's work at all. They will tell you that if they are abundant in faith yet there are times when they are superabundant in unbelief; that if sometimes they are full of works of holiness, yet there are times when they weep many tears to think that those very acts of holiness were stained with sin. The Christian will tell you that he weeps over his very tears; he feels that there is filth even in the best of desires; that he has to pray to God to forgive his prayers, for there is sin in the midst of his supplications, and that he has to sprinkle even his best offerings with the atoning blood, for he never else can bring an offering without spot or blemish. You shall appeal to the brightest saint, to the man whose presence in the midst of society is like the presence of an angel, and he will tell you that he is still ashamed of himself. "Ah!" he will say, "you may praise me, but I cannot praise myself, you speak well of me, you applaud me, but if you knew my heart you would see abundant reason to think of me as a poor sinner saved by grace, who hath nothing whereof to glory, and must bow his head and confess his iniquities in the sight of God." Grace, then is entirely unmerited.

Again, the grace of God is sovereign. By that word we mean that God has an absolute right to give that grace where he chooses, and to withhold it when he pleases. He is not bound to give it to any man, much less to all men; and if he chooses to give it to one man and not to another, his answer is, "Is thine eye evil because mine eye is good? Can I not do as I will with mine own? I will have mercy on whom I will have mercy." Now, I want you to notice the sovereignty of Divine grace as illustrated in the text: "I was found of them that sought me not, I was made manifest to them that asked not after thee." You would imagine that if God gave his grace to any he would wait until he found them earnestly seeking him. You would imagine that God in the highest heavens would say, "I have mercies, but I will leave men alone, and when they feel their need of these mercies and seek me diligently with their whole heart, day and night, with tears, and vows, and supplications, then will I bless them, but not

ROMANS 11

1 I say then, Hath God cast away his people? God forbid. For I also am an Israelite, of the seed of Abraham, of the tribe of Benjamin.

2 God hath not cast away his people which he foreknew. Wot ye not what the scripture saith of Elias? how he maketh intercession to God against Israel, saying,

3 Lord, they have killed thy prophets, and digged down thine altars; and I am left alone, and they seek my life.

4 But what saith the answer of God unto him? I have reserved to myself seven thousand men, who have not bowed the knee to the image of Baal.

5 Even so then at this present time also there is a remnant according to the election of grace.

6 And if by grace, then is it no more of works: otherwise grace is no more grace. But if it be of works, then is it no more grace: otherwise work is no more work.

7 What then? Israel hath not obtained that which he seeketh for; but the election hath obtained it, and the rest were blinded

8 (According as it is written, God hath given them the spirit of slumber, eyes that they should not see, and ears that they should not hear;) unto this day.

9 And David saith, Let their table be made a snare, and a trap, and a stumblingblock, and a recompense unto them:

10 Let their eyes be darkened, that they may not see, and bow down their back alway.

11 I say then, Have they stumbled that they should fall? God forbid: but rather through their fall salvation is come unto the Gentiles, for to provoke them to jealousy.

12 Now if the fall of them be the riches of the world, and the diminishing of them the riches of the Gentiles; how much more their fullness?

13 For I speak to you Gentiles, inasmuch as I am the apostle of the Gentiles, I magnify mine office:

glorious goodness, wisdom, and power, on the vessels of mercy; on those whom he had himself, by his grace, prepared for glory. Is this any injustice?

24. Even us – Here the apostle comes to the other proposition, of grace free for all, whether Jew or Gentile. Of the Jews – This he treats of, ver. 25. Of the Gentiles – Treated of in the same verse.

25. Beloved – As a spouse. Who once was not beloved – Consequently, not unconditionally elected. This relates directly to the final restoration of the Jews. Hosea ii, 23

26. There shall they be called the sons of God – So that they need not leave their own country and come to Judea. Hosea i, 10.

27. But Isaiah testifies, that (as many Gentiles will be accepted, so) many Jews will be rejected; that out of all the thousands of Israel, a remnant only shall be saved. This was spoken originally of the few that were saved from the ravage of Sennacherib's army. Isaiah x, 22, 23.

28. For he is finishing or cutting short his account – In rigorous justice, will leave but a small remnant. There will be so general a destruction, that but a small number will escape.

29. As Isaiah had said before – Namely, Isaiah i, 9, concerning those who were besieged in Jerusalem by Rezin and Pekah. Unless the Lord had left us a seed – Which denotes,

1. The present paucity:

2. The future abundance. We had been as Sodom – So that it is no unexampled thing for the main body of the Jewish nation to revolt from God, and perish in their sin.

30. What shall we say then – What is to be concluded from all that has been said but this, That the Gentiles, who followed not after righteousness – Who a while ago had no knowledge of, no care or thought about, it. Have attained to righteousness – Or justification. Even the righteousness which is by faith. This is the first conclusion we may draw from the preceding observations. The second is, that Israel – The Jews. Although following after the law of righteousness – That law which, duly used, would have led them to faith, and thereby to righteousness. Have not attained to the law of righteousness – To that righteousness or justification which is one great end of the law.

32. And wherefore have they not? Is it because God eternally decreed they should not? There is nothing like this to be met with but agreeable to his argument the apostle gives us this good reason for it, Because they sought it not by faith – Whereby alone it could be attained. But as it were – In effect, if not professedly, by works. For they stumbled at that stumbling stone – Christ crucified.

33. As it is written – Foretold by their own prophet. Behold, I lay in Sion – I exhibit in my church, what, though it is in truth the only sure foundation of happiness, yet will be in fact a stumbling stone and rock of offense – An occasion of ruin to many, through their obstinate unbelief. Isaiah viii, 14; Isaiah xxviii, 16.

ROMANS 10

1. My prayer to God is, that they may be saved – He would not have prayed for this, had they been absolutely reprobated.

2. They have a zeal, but not according to knowledge – They had zeal without knowledge; we have knowledge without zeal.

3. For they being ignorant of the righteousness of God – Of the method God has established for the justification of a sinner. And seeking to establish their own righteousness – Their own method of acceptance with God. Have not submitted to the righteousness of God – The way of justification which he hath fixed.

4. For Christ is the end of the law – The scope and aim of it. It is the very design

makes man's disobedience worse, and renders that the more sinful. We may wonder at the mercy of God, that his goodness is not overcome by man's badness; we may wonder at the wickedness of man, that his badness is not overcome by God's goodness. And it is a matter of joy to think that God has sent the message of grace to so many millions, by the wide spread of his gospel.

ROMANS 11

The rejection of the Jews is not universal. (1-10)
God overruled their unbelief for making the Gentiles partakers of gospel privileges. (11-21)
The Gentiles cautioned against pride and unbelief. The Jews shall be called as a nation, and brought into God's visible covenant again. (22-32)
A solemn adoring of the wisdom, goodness, and justice of God. (33-36)

1-10 There was a chosen remnant of believing Jews, who had righteousness and life by faith in Jesus Christ. These were kept according to the election of grace. If then this election was of grace, it could not be of works, either performed or foreseen. Every truly good disposition in a fallen creature must be the effect, therefore it cannot be the cause, of the grace of God bestowed on him. Salvation from the first to the last must be either of grace or of debt. These things are so directly contrary to each other that they cannot be blended together. God glorifies his grace by changing the hearts and tempers of the rebellious. How then should they wonder and praise him! The Jewish nation were as in a deep sleep, without knowledge of their danger, or concern about it; having no sense of their need of the Savior, or of their being upon the borders of eternal ruin. David, having by the Spirit foretold the sufferings of Christ from his own people, the Jews, foretells the dreadful judgments of God upon them for it, Ps 69. This teaches us how to understand other prayers of David against his enemies; they are prophecies of the judgments of God, not expressions of his own anger. Divine curses will work long; and we have our eyes darkened, if we are bowed down in worldly-mindedness.

11-21 The gospel is the greatest riches of every place where it is. As therefore the righteous rejection of the unbelieving Jews, was the occasion of so large a multitude of the Gentiles being reconciled to God, and at peace with him; the future receiving of the Jews into the church would be such a change, as would resemble a general resurrection of the dead in sin to a life of righteousness. Abraham was as the root of the church. The Jews continued branches of this tree till, as a nation, they rejected the Messiah; after that, their relation to Abraham and to God was, as it were, cut off. The Gentiles were grafted into this tree in their room; being admitted into the church of God. Multitudes were made heirs of Abraham's faith, holiness and blessedness. It is the natural state of every one of us, to be wild by nature.

before." But, beloved, God saith no such thing. It is true he doth bless them that cry unto him, but he blesses them before they cry, for their cries are not their own cries, but cries which he has put into their lips; their desires are not of their own growth, but desires which he has cast like good seed into the soil of their hearts. God saves the men that do not seek him. Oh, wonder of wonders! It is mercy indeed when God saves a seeker; but how much greater mercy when he seeks the lost himself! Mark the parable of Jesus Christ concerning the lost sheep; it does not run thus: "A certain man had a hundred sheep, and one of them did go astray. And he tarried at home, and lo, the sheep came back, and he received it joyfully and said to his friends, rejoice, for the sheep that I have lost is come back." No; he went after the sheep: it never would have come after him; it would have wandered farther and farther away. He went after it; over hills of difficulty, down valleys of despondency he pursued its wandering feet, and at last he laid hold of it; he did not drive it before him, he did not lead it, but he carried it himself all the way, and when he brought it home he did not say, "the sheep is come back," but, "I have found the sheep which was lost." Men do not seek God first; God seeks them first; and if any of you are seeking him today it is because he has first sought you. If you are desiring him he desired you first, and your good desires and earnest seeking will not be the cause of your salvation, but the effects of previous grace given to you. "Well," says another, "I should have thought that although the Savior might not require an earnest seeking and sighing and groaning, and a continuous searching, after him, yet certainly he would have desired and demanded that every man, before he had grace, should ask for it." That, indeed, beloved, seems natural, and God will give grace to them that ask for it; but mark, the text says that he was manifested "to them that asked not for him." That is to say, before we ask, God gives us grace. The only reason why any man ever begins to pray is because God has put previous grace in his heart which leads him to pray. I remember, when I was converted to God, I was an Arminian thoroughly. I thought I had begun the good work myself, and I used sometimes to sit down and think, "Well, I sought the Lord four years before I found him," and I think I began to compliment myself upon the fact that I had perseveringly entreated of him in the midst of much discouragement. But one day the

14 If by any means I may provoke to emulation them which are my flesh, and might save some of them.

15 For if the casting away of them be the reconciling of the world, what shall the receiving of them be, but life from the dead?

16 For if the firstfruit be holy, the lump is also holy: and if the root be holy, so are the branches.

17 And if some of the branches be broken off, and thou, being a wild olive tree, wert graffed in among them, and with them partakest of the root and fatness of the olive tree;

18 Boast not against the branches. But if thou boast, thou bearest not the root, but the root thee.

19 Thou wilt say then, The branches were broken off, that I might be graffed in.

20 Well; because of unbelief they were broken off, and thou standest by faith. Be not highminded, but fear:

21 For if God spared not the natural branches, take heed lest he also spare not thee.

22 Behold therefore the goodness and severity of God: on them which fell, severity; but toward thee, goodness, if thou continue in his goodness: otherwise thou also shalt be cut off.

23 And they also, if they abide not still in unbelief, shall be graffed in: for God is able to graff them in again.

24 For if thou wert cut out of the olive tree which is wild by nature, and wert graffed contrary to nature into a good olive tree: how much more shall these, which be the natural branches, be graffed into their own olive tree?

25 For I would not, brethren, that ye should be ignorant of this mystery, lest ye should be wise in your own conceits; that blindness in part is happened to Israel, until the fullness of the Gentiles be come in.

26 And so all Israel shall be saved: as it is written, There shall come out of Sion the Deliverer, and shall turn away ungodliness from Jacob:

27 For this is my covenant unto

---

of the law, to bring men to believe in Christ for justification and salvation. And he alone gives that pardon and life which the law shows the want of, but cannot give. To every one – Whether Jew or Gentile, treated of, ver. 11, &c. That believeth – Treated of, ver. 5.

5. For Moses describeth the only righteousness which is attainable by the law, when he saith, The man who doeth these things shall live by them – That is, he that perfectly keeps all these precepts in every point, he alone may claim life and salvation by them. But this way of justification is impossible to any who have ever transgressed any one law in any point. Lev. xviii, 5.

6. But the righteousness which is by faith – The method of becoming righteous by believing. Speaketh a very different language, and may be considered as expressing itself thus: (to accommodate to our present subject the words which Moses spake, touching the plainness of his law:) Say not in thy heart, Who shall ascend into heaven, as if it were to bring Christ down: or, Who shall descend into the grave, as if it were to bring him again from the dead – Do not imagine that these things are to be done now, in order to procure thy pardon and salvation. Deut. xxx, 14.

8. But what saith he – Moses. Even these words, so remarkably applicable to the subject before us. All is done ready to thy hand. The word is nigh thee – Within thy reach; easy to be understood, remembered, practiced. This is eminently true of the word of faith – The gospel. Which we preach – The sum of which is, If thy heart believe in Christ, and thy life confess him, thou shalt be saved.

9. If thou confess with thy mouth – Even in time of persecution, when such a confession may send thee to the lions.

10. For with the heart – Not the understanding only. Man believeth to righteousness – So as to obtain justification. And with the mouth confession is made – So as to obtain final salvation. Confession here implies the whole of outward, as believing does the root of all inward, religion.

11. Isaiah xxviii, 16.

12. The same Lord of all is rich – So that his blessings are never to be exhausted, nor is he ever constrained to hold his hand. The great truth proposed in ver. 11 is so repeated here, and in ver. 13, and farther confirmed, ver. 14, 15, as not only to imply, that "whosoever calleth upon him shall be saved;" but also that the will of God is, that all should savingly call upon him.

13. Joel ii, 32.

15. But how shall they preach, unless they be sent – Thus by a chain of reasoning, from God's will that the Gentiles also should "call upon him," St. Paul infers that the apostles were sent by God to preach to the Gentiles also. The feet – Their very footsteps; their coming. Isaiah lii, 7.

16. Isaiah liii, 1.

17. Faith, indeed, ordinarily cometh by hearing; even by hearing the word of God.

18. But their unbelief was not owing to the want of hearing. For they have heard. Yes verily – So many nations have already heard the preachers of the gospel, that I may in some sense say of them as David did of the lights of heaven. Psalm xxix, 4.

19. But hath not Israel known – They might have known, even from Moses and Isaiah, that many of the Gentiles would be received, and many of the Jews rejected. I will provoke you to jealousy by them that are not a nation – As they followed gods that were not gods, so he accepted in their stead a nation that was not a nation; that is, a nation that was not in covenant with God. A foolish nation – Such are all which know not God. Deut. xxxii, 21.

20. But Isaiah is very bold – And speaks plainly what Moses but intimated. Isaiah lxv, 1, 2.

21. An unbelieving and gainsaying people – Just opposite to those who believed with their hearts, and made confession with their mouths.

MATTHEW HENRY   CHARLES H. SPURGEON

Conversion is as the grafting in of wild branches into the good olive. The wild olive was often engrafted into the fruitful one when it began to decay, and this not only brought forth fruit, but caused the decaying olive to revive and flourish.

22-32 Of all judgments, spiritual judgments are the sorest; of these the apostle is here speaking. The restoration of the Jews is, in the course of things, far less improbable than the call of the Gentiles to be the children of Abraham; and though others now possess these privileges, it will not hinder their being admitted again. By rejecting the gospel, and by their indignation at its being preached to the Gentiles, the Jews were become enemies to God; yet they are still to be favored for the sake of their pious fathers. Though at present they are enemies to the gospel, for their hatred to the Gentiles; yet, when God's time is come, that will no longer exist, and God's love to their fathers will be remembered. True grace seeks not to confine God's favor. Those who find mercy themselves, should endeavor that through their mercy others also may obtain mercy. Not that the Jews will be restored to have their priesthood, and temple, and ceremonies again; an end is put to all these; but they are to be brought to believe in Christ, the true become one sheep-fold with the Gentiles, under Christ the Great Shepherd. The captivities of Israel, their dispersion, and their being shut out from the church, are emblems of the believer's corrections for doing wrong; and the continued care of the Lord towards that people, and the final mercy and blessed restoration intended for them, show the patience and love of God.

33-36 The apostle Paul knew the mysteries of the kingdom of God as well as ever any man; yet he confesses himself at a loss; and despairing to find the bottom, he humbly sits down at the brink, and adores the depth. Those who know most in this imperfect state, feel their own weakness most. There is not only depth in the Divine counsels, but riches; abundance of that which is precious and valuable. The Divine counsels are complete; they have not only depth and height, but breadth and length, Eph 3:18, and that passing knowledge. There is that vast distance and disproportion between God and man, between the Creator and the creature, which for ever shuts us from knowledge of his ways. What man shall teach God how to govern the world? The apostle adores the sovereignty of the Divine counsels. All things in heaven and earth, especially those which relate to our salvation, that belong to our peace, are all of him by way of creation, through him by way of providence, that they may be to him in their end. Of God, as the Spring and Fountain of all; through Christ, to God, as the end. These include all God's relations to his creatures; if all are of him, and through him, all should be to him, and for him. Whatever begins, let God's glory be the end: especially let us adore him when we talk of the Divine counsels and acting. The saints in heaven never dispute, but always praise.

thought struck me, "How was it you came to seek God?" and in an instant the answer came from my soul, "Why, because he led me to do it; he must first have shown me my need of him, or else I should never have sought him; he must have shown me his preciousness, or I never should have thought him worth seeking;" and at once I saw the doctrines of grace as clear as possible. God must begin. Nature can never rise above itself. You put water into a reservoir, and it will rise as high as that, but no higher if let alone. Now, it is not in human nature to seek the Lord. Human nature is depraved, and therefore, there must be the extraordinary pressure of the Holy Spirit put upon the heart to lead us first to ask for mercy. But mark, we do not know anything about that, while the Spirit is operating; we find that out afterwards. We ask as much as if we were asking all of ourselves. Our business is to seek the Lord as if there were no Holy Spirit at all. But although we do not know it, there must always be a previous motion of the Spirit in our heart, before there will be a motion of our heart towards him.

"No sinner can be beforehand with thee,
Thy grace is most sovereign, most rich,
and most free."

Let me give you an illustration. You see that man on his horse surrounded by a body of troopers. How proud he is, and how he reins up his horse with conscious dignity. Sir, what have you got there? What are those despatches you treasure up with so much care? "Oh, sir, I have that in my hand that will vex the church of God in Damascus. I have dragged the fellows into the synagogue, both men and women; I have scourged them, and compelled them to blaspheme; and I have this commission from the high priest to drag them to Jerusalem, that I may put them to death." Saul! Saul! have you no love for Christ? "Love to him! No. When they stoned Stephen, I took care of the witnesses' clothes, and I rejoiced to do it. I wish I had had the crucifying of their Master, for I hate them with perfect hatred, and I breathe out threatenings and slaughter against them." What do you say of this man? If he be saved, will you not grant that it must be some Divine sovereignty that converts him? Look at poor Pilate, how much there was that was hopeful in him. He was willing to save the Master, but he feared and trembled. If we had had our choice, we should have said, "Lord, save Pilate, he does not want to kill Christ, he labors to let him escape; but slay the bloodthirsty Saul, he is the very chief of

them, when I shall take away their sins.

28 As concerning the gospel, they are enemies for your sakes: but as touching the election, they are beloved for the fathers' sakes.

29 For the gifts and calling of God are without repentance.

30 For as ye in times past have not believed God, yet have now obtained mercy through their unbelief:

31 Even so have these also now not believed, that through your mercy they also may obtain mercy.

32 For God hath concluded them all in unbelief, that he might have mercy upon all.

33 0 the depth of the riches both of the wisdom and knowledge of God! how unsearchable are his judgments, and his ways past finding out!

34 For who hath known the mind of the Lord? or who hath been his counselor?

35 Or who hath first given to him, and it shall be recompensed unto him again?

36 For of him, and through him, and to him, are all things: to whom be glory for ever. Amen.

ROMANS 12

1 I beseech you therefore, brethren, by the mercies of God, that ye present your bodies a living sacrifice, holy, acceptable unto God, which is your reasonable service.

2 And be not conformed to this world: but be ye transformed by the renewing of your mind, that ye may prove what is that good, and acceptable, and perfect, will of God.

3 For I say, through the grace given unto me, to every man that is among you, not to think of himself more highly than he ought to think; but to think soberly, according as God hath dealt to every man the measure of faith.

4 For as we have many members in one body, and all members have not the same office:

5 So we, being many, are one body in Christ, and every one members one of another.

6 Having then gifts differing

ROMANS 11

1. Hath God rejected his whole people – All Israel? In no wise. Now there is "a remnant" who believe, ver. 5; and hereafter "all Israel will be saved," ver. 26.

2. God hath not rejected that part of his people whom he foreknew – Speaking after the manner of men. For, in fact, knowing and foreknowing are the same thing with God, who knows or sees all things at once, from everlasting to everlasting. Know ye not – That in a parallel case, amidst a general apostasy, when Elijah thought the whole nation was fallen into idolatry, God "knew" there was "a remnant" of true worshipers.

3. 1 Kings xix, 10.

4. To Baal – Nor to the golden calves.

5. According to the election of grace – According to that gracious purpose of God, "He that believeth shall be saved."

6. And if by grace, then it is no more of works – Whether ceremonial or moral. Else grace is no longer grace – The very nature of grace is lost. And if it be of works, then it is no more grace: else work is no longer work – But the very nature of it is destroyed. There is something so absolutely inconsistent between the being justified by grace, and the being justified by works, that, if you suppose either, you of necessity exclude the other. For what is given to works is the payment of a debt; whereas grace implies an unmerited favor. So that the same benefit cannot, in the very nature of things, be derived from both.

7. What then – What is the conclusion from the whole? It is this: that Israel in general hath not obtained justification; but those of them only who believe. And the rest were blinded – By their own willfull prejudice.

8. God hath at length withdrawn his Spirit, and so given them up to a spirit of slumber; which is fulfilled unto this day. Isaiah xxix, 10.

9. And David saith – In that prophetic imprecation, which is applicable to them, as well as to Judas. A recompense – Of their preceding wickedness. So sin is punished by sin; and thus the gospel, which should have fed and strengthened their souls, is become a means of destroying them. Psalm lxix, 22, 23.

11. Have they stumbled so as to fall – Totally and finally? No But by their fall – Or slip: it is a very soft word in the original. Salvation is come to the Gentiles – See an instance of this, Acts xiii, 46. To provoke them – The Jews themselves, to jealousy.

12. The first part of this verse is treated of, ver. 13, &c.; the latter, How much more their fullness, (that is, their full conversion,) ver. 23, &c. So many prophecies refer to this grand event, that it is surprising any Christian can doubt of it. And these are greatly confirmed by the wonderful preservation of the Jews as a distinct people to this day. When it is accomplished, it will be so strong a demonstration, both of the Old and New Testament Revelation, as will doubtless convince many thousand Deists, in countries nominally Christian; of whom there will, of course, be increasing multitudes among merely nominal Christians. And this will be a means of swiftly propagating the gospel among Mahometans and Pagans; who would probably have received it long ago, had they conversed only with real Christians.

13. I magnify my office – Far from being ashamed of ministering to the Gentiles, I glory therein; the rather, as it may be a means of provoking my brethren to jealousy.

14. My flesh – My kinsmen.

15. Life from the dead – Overflowing life to the world, which was dead.

16. And this will surely come to pass. For if the first fruits be holy, so is the lump – The consecration of them was esteemed the consecration of all and so the conversion of a few Jews is an earnest of the conversion of all the rest. And if the root be holy – The patriarchs from whom they spring, surely God will at length make their descendants also holy.

17. Thou – O Gentile. Being a wild olive tree – Had the graft been nobler than

ROMANS 12

Believers are to dedicate themselves to God. (1,2)

To be humble, and faithfully to use their spiritual gifts, in their respective stations. (3-8)

Exhortations to various duties. (9-16)

And to peaceable conduct towards all men, with forbearance and benevolence. (17-21)

1,2 The apostle having closed the part of his epistle wherein he argues and proves various doctrines which are practically applied, here urges important duties from gospel principles. He entreated the Romans, as his brethren in Christ, by the mercies of God, to present their bodies as a living sacrifice to him. This is a powerful appeal. We receive from the Lord every day the fruits of his mercy. Let us render ourselves; all we are, all we have, all we can do: and after all, what return is it for such very rich receivings? It is acceptable to God: a reasonable service, which we are able and ready to give a reason for, and which we understand. Conversion and sanctification are the renewing of the mind; a change, not of the substance, but of the qualities of the soul. The progress of sanctification, dying to sin more and more, and living to righteousness more and more, is the carrying on this renewing work, till it is perfected in glory. The great enemy to this renewal is, conformity to this world. Take heed of forming plans for happiness, as though it lay in the things of this world, which soon pass away. Do not fall in with the customs of those who walk in the lusts of the flesh, and mind earthly things. The work of the Holy Ghost first begins in the understanding, and is carried on to the will, affections, and conversation, till there is a change of the whole man into the likeness of God, in knowledge, righteousness, and true holiness. Thus, to be godly, is to give up ourselves to God.

3-8 Pride is a sin in us by nature; we need to be cautioned and armed against it. All the saints make up one body in Christ, who is the Head of the body, and the common Center of their unity. In the spiritual body, some are fitted for and called to one sort of work; others for another sort of work. We are to do all the good we can, one to another, and for the common benefit. If we duly thought about the powers we have, and how far we fail properly to improve them, it would humble us. But as we must not be proud of our talents, so we must take heed lest, under a pretense of humility and self-denial, we are slothful in laying out ourselves for the good of others. We must not say, I am nothing, therefore I will sit still, and do nothing; but, I am nothing in myself, and therefore I will lay out myself to the utmost, in the strength of the grace of Christ. Whatever our gifts or situations may be, let us try to employ ourselves humbly, diligently, cheerfully, and in simplicity; not seeking our own credit or profit, but the good of many, for this world and that which is to come.

9-16 The professed love of Christians to each other should be sincere, free from deceit, and unmeaning and deceitful compliments. Depending on Divine grace, they

sinners." "No," says God, "I will do as I will with mine own." The heavens open, and the brightness of glory descends—brighter than the noon-day sun. Stunned with the light he falls to the ground, and a voice is heard addressing him, "Saul, Saul, why persecutest thou me? it is hard for thee to kick against the pricks." He rises up; God appears to him: "Lo, I have made thee a chosen vessel to bear my name among the Gentiles." Is not that sovereignty—sovereign grace, without any previous seeking? God was found of him that sought not for him; he manifested himself to one that asked him not. Some will say, that was it miracle; but it is one that is repeated every day in the week. I knew a man once, who had not been to the house of God for a long time; and one Sunday morning, having been to market to buy a pair of ducks for his Sunday dinner, he happened to see a house of God opened as he was passing by. "Well," he thought, "I will hear what these fellows are up to." He went inside; the hymn that was being sung struck his attention; he listened to the sermon, forgot his ducks, discovered his own character, went home, and threw himself upon his knees before God, and after a short time it pleased God to give him joy and peace in believing. That man had nothing in him to begin with, nothing that could have led you to imagine he ever would be saved, but simply because God would have it so, he struck the effectual blow of grace, and the man was brought to himself. But we are, each of us who are saved, the very people who are the best illustrations of the matter. To this day, my wonder is, that ever the Lord should have chosen thee. I cannot make it out; and my only answer to the question is, "Even so, Father, for so it seemed good in thy sight."

I have now, I think, stated the doctrine pretty plainly. Let me only say a few words about it. Some people are very much afraid of this truth. They say, "It is true, I dare say, but still you ought not to preach it before a mixed assembly; it is very well for the comfort of God's people, but it is to be very carefully handled, and not to be publicly preached upon." Very well, sir, I leave you to settle that matter with my Master. He gave me this great book to preach from, and I cannot preach from anything else. If he has put anything in it you think is not fit, go and complain to him, and not to me. I am simply his servant, and if his errand that I am to tell is objectionable, I cannot help it. If I send my servant to the door with a message, and he delivers it faithfully, he does not deserve to

according to the grace that is given to us, whether prophecy, let us prophesy according to the proportion of faith;

7 Or ministry, let us wait on our ministering: or he that teacheth, on teaching;

8 Or he that exhorteth, on exhortation: he that giveth, let him do it with simplicity; he that ruleth, with diligence; he that sheweth mercy, with cheerfulness.

9 Let love be without dissimulation. Abhor that which is evil; cleave to that which is good.

10 Be kindly affectioned one to another with brotherly love; in honor preferring one another;

11 Not slothful in business; fervent in spirit; serving the Lord;

12 Rejoicing in hope; patient in tribulation; continuing instant in prayer;

13 Distributing to the necessity of saints; given to hospitality.

14 Bless them which persecute you: bless, and curse not.

15 Rejoice with them that do rejoice, and weep with them that weep.

16 Be of the same mind one toward another. Mind not high things, but condescend to men of low estate. Be not wise in your own conceits.

17 Recompense to no man evil for evil. Provide things honest in the sight of all men.

18 If it be possible, as much as lieth in you, live peaceably with all men.

19 Dearly beloved, avenge not yourselves, but rather give place unto wrath: for it is written, Vengeance is mine; I will repay, saith the Lord.

20 Therefore if thine enemy hunger, feed him; if he thirst, give him drink: for in so doing thou shalt heap coals of fire on his head.

21 Be not overcome of evil, but overcome evil with good.

ROMANS 13

1 Let every soul be subject unto the higher powers. For there is no power but of God: the powers that be are ordained of God.

2 Whosoever therefore resisteth the power, resisteth the ordinance of God: and they that

the stock, yet its dependence on it for life and nourishment would leave it no room to boast against it. How much less, when, contrary to what is practiced among men, the wild olive tree is engrafted on the good!

18. Boast not against the branches – Do not they do this who despise the Jews? or deny their future conversion?

20. They were broken off for unbelief, and thou standest by faith – Both conditionally, not absolutely: if absolutely, there might have been room to boast. By faith – The free gift of God, which therefore ought to humble thee.

21. Be not highminded, but fear – We may observe, this fear is not opposed to trust, but to pride and security.

22. Else shalt thou – Also, who now "standest by faith," be both totally and finally cut off.

24. Contrary to nature – For according to nature, we graft the fruitful branch into the wild stock; but here the wild branch is grafted into the fruitful stock.

25. St. Paul calls any truth known but to a few, a mystery. Such had been the calling of the Gentiles: such was now the conversion of the Jews. Lest ye should be wise in your own conceits – Puffed up with your present advantages; dreaming that ye are the only church; or that the church of Rome cannot fail. Hardness in part is happened to Israel, till – Israel therefore is neither totally nor finally rejected. The fullness of the Gentiles be come in – Till there be a vast harvest amongst the heathens.

26. And so all Israel shall be saved – Being convinced by the coming of the Gentiles. But there will be a still larger harvest among the Gentiles, when all Israel is come in. The deliverer shall come – Yea, the deliverer is come; but not the full fruit of his coming. Isaiah lix, 20.

28. They are now enemies – To the gospel, to God, and to themselves, which God permits. For your sake: but as for the election – That part of them who believe, they are beloved.

29. For the gifts and the calling of God are without repentance – God does not repent of his gifts to the Jews, or his calling of the Gentiles.

32. For God hath shut up all together in disobedience – Suffering each in their turn to revolt from him. First, God suffered the Gentiles in the early age to revolt, and took the family of Abraham as a peculiar seed to himself. Afterwards he permitted them to fall through unbelief, and took in the believing Gentiles. And he did even this to provoke the Jews to jealousy, and so bring them also in the end to faith. This was truly a mystery in the divine conduct, which the apostle adores with such holy astonishment.

33. O the depth of the riches, and wisdom, and knowledge of God – In the ninth chapter, St. Paul had sailed but in a narrow sea: now he is in the ocean. The depth of the riches is described, ver. 35; the depth of wisdom, ver. 34; the depth of knowledge, in the latter part of this verse. Wisdom directs all things to the best end; knowledge sees that end. How unsearchable are his judgments – With regard to unbelievers. His ways – With regard to believers. His ways are more upon a level; His judgments "a great deep." But even his ways we cannot trace.

34. Who hath known the mind of the Lord – Before or any farther than he has revealed it. Isaiah xl, 13.

35. Given to him – Either wisdom or power?

36. Of him – As the Creator. Through him – As the Preserver. To him – As the ultimate end, are all things. To him be the glory of his riches, wisdom, knowledge. Amen – A concluding word, in which the affection of the apostle, when it is come to the height, shuts up all.

ROMANS 12

1. I exhort you – St. Paul uses to suit his exhortations to the doctrines he has

MATTHEW HENRY

CHARLES H. SPURGEON

must detest and dread all evil, and love and delight in whatever is kind and useful. We must not only do that which is good, but we must cleave to it. All our duty towards one another is summed up in one word, love. This denotes the love of parents to their children; which is more tender and natural than any other; unforced, unconstrained. And love to God and man, with zeal for the gospel, will make the wise Christian diligent in all his worldly business, and in gaining superior skill. God must be served with the spirit, under the influences of the Holy Spirit. He is honored by our hope and trust in him, especially when we rejoice in that hope. He is served, not only by working for him, but by sitting still quietly, when he calls us to suffer. Patience for God's sake, is true piety. Those that rejoice in hope, are likely to be patient in tribulation. We should not be cold in the duty of prayer, nor soon weary of it. Not only must there be kindness to friends and brethren, but Christians must not harbor anger against enemies. It is but mock love, which rests in words of kindness, while our brethren need real supplies, and it is in our power to furnish them. Be ready to entertain those who do good: as there is occasion, we must welcome strangers. Bless, and curse not. It means thorough good will; not, bless them when at prayer, and curse them at other times; but bless them always, and curse not at all.

17-21 Since men became enemies to God, they have been very ready to be enemies one to another. And those that embrace religion, must expect to meet with enemies in a world whose smiles seldom agree with Christ's. Recompense to no man evil for evil. That is a brutish recompense, befitting only animals, which are not conscious of any being above them, or of any existence hereafter. And not only do, but study and take care to do, that which is amiable and creditable, and recommends religion to all with whom you converse. Study the things that make for peace; if it be possible, without offending God and wounding conscience. Avenge not yourselves. This is a hard lesson to corrupt nature, therefore a remedy against it is added. Give place unto wrath. When a man's passion is up, and the stream is strong, let it pass off; lest it be made to rage the more against us. The line of our duty is clearly marked out, and if our enemies are not melted by persevering kindness, we are not to seek vengeance; they will be consumed by the fiery wrath of that God to whom vengeance belongeth. The last verse suggests what is not easily understood by the world; that in all strife and contention, those that revenge are conquered, and those that forgive are conquerors. Be not overcome of evil. Learn to defeat ill designs against you, either to change them, or to preserve your own peace. He that has this rule over his spirit, is better than the mighty. God's children may be asked whether it is not more sweet unto them than all earthly good, that God so enables them by his Spirit, thus to feel and act.

be scolded. Let me have the blame, not the servant. So I say; blame my Master, and not me, for I do but proclaim his message. "No," says one, "it is not to be preached." But it is to be preached. Every word of God is given by inspiration, and it is profitable for some good end. Does not the Bible say so? Let me tell you, the reason why many of our churches are declining is just because this doctrine has not been preached. Wherever this doctrine has been upheld. it has always been "Down with Popery." The first reformers held this doctrine and preached it. Well said a Church of England divine to some who railed at him, "Look at your own Luther. Do you not consider him to be the teacher of the Church of England? What Calvin and the other reformers taught is to be found in his book upon the freedom of the will." Besides, we can point you to a string of ministers from the beginning even until now. Talk of apostolic succession! The man who preaches the doctrines of grace has an apostolic succession indeed. Can we not trace our pedigree through a whole line of men like Newton, and Whitfield, and Owen, and Bunyan, straight away on till we come to Calvin, Luther, and Zwingle; and then we can go back from them to Savonarola, to Jerome of Prague, to Huss, and then back to Augustine, the mighty preacher of Christianity; and from St. Augustine to Paul is but one step. We need not be ashamed of our pedigree; although Calvinists are now considered to be heterodox, we are and ever must be orthodox. It is the old doctrine. Go and buy any puritanical book, and see if you can find Arminianism in it. Search all the book stalls over, and see if you can find one large folio book of olden times that has anything in it but the doctrine of the free grace of God. Let this once be brought to bear upon the minds of men, and away go the doctrines of penance and confession, away goes paying for the pardon of your sin. If grace be free and sovereign in the hand of God, down goes the doctrine of priest craft, away go buying and selling indulgences and such like things; they are swept to the four winds of heaven, and the efficacy of good works is dashed in pieces like Dagon before the ark of the Lord. "Well," says one, "I like the doctrine; still there are very few that preach it, and those that do are very high." Very likely; but I care little what anybody calls me. It signifies very little what men call you. Suppose they call you a "hyper," that does not make you anything wicked, does it? Suppose they call you an Antinomian, that

resist shall receive to themselves damnation.

3 For rulers are not a terror to good works, but to the evil. Wilt thou then not be afraid of the power? do that which is good, and thou shalt have praise of the same:

4 For he is the minister of God to thee for good. But if thou do that which is evil, be afraid; for he beareth not the sword in vain: for he is the minister of God, a revenger to execute wrath upon him that doeth evil.

5 Wherefore ye must needs be subject, not only for wrath, but also for conscience sake.

6 For for this cause pay ye tribute also: for they are God's ministers, attending continually upon this very thing.

7 Render therefore to all their dues: tribute to whom tribute is due; custom to whom custom; fear to whom fear; honor to whom honor.

8 Owe no man any thing, but to love one another: for he that loveth another hath fulfilled the law.

9 For this, Thou shalt not commit adultery, Thou shalt not kill, Thou shalt not steal, Thou shalt not bear false witness, Thou shalt not covet; and if there be any other commandment, it is briefly comprehended in this saying, namely, Thou shalt love thy neighbor as thyself.

10 Love worketh no ill to his neighbor: therefore love is the fulfilling of the law.

11 And that, knowing the time, that now it is high time to awake out of sleep: for now is our salvation nearer than when we believed.

12 The night is far spent, the day is at hand: let us therefore cast off the works of darkness, and let us put on the armor of light.

13 Let us walk honestly, as in the day; not in rioting and drunkenness, not in chambering and wantonness, not in strife and envying.

14 But put ye on the Lord Jesus Christ, and make not provision for the flesh, to fulfill the lusts thereof.

been delivering. So here the general use from the whole is contained in the first and second verses. The particular uses follow, from the third verse to the end of the Epistle. By the tender mercies of God – The whole sentiment is derived from Romans. The expression itself is particularly opposed to "the wrath of God," chap. i, 18. It has a reference here to the entire gospel, to the whole economy of grace or mercy, delivering us from "the wrath of God," and exciting us to all duty. To present – So chap. vi, 13; xvi, 19; now actually to exhibit before God. Your bodies – That is, yourselves; a part is put for the whole; the rather, as in the ancient sacrifices of beasts, the body was the whole. These also are particularly named in opposition to that vile abuse of their bodies mentioned, chap. i, 24. Several expressions follow, which have likewise a direct reference to other expressions in the same chapter. A sacrifice – Dead to sin and living – By that life which is mentioned, chap. i, 17; vi, 4, &c. Holy – Such as the holy law requires, chap. vii, 12. Acceptable – chap. viii, 8. Which is your reasonable service – The worship of the heathens was utterly unreasonable, chap. i, 18, &c.; so was the glorying of the Jews, chap. ii, 3, &c. But a Christian acts in all things by the highest reason, from the mercy of God inferring his own duty.

2. And be not conformed – Neither in judgment, spirit, nor behavior. To this world – Which, neglecting the will of God, entirely follows its own. That ye may prove – Know by sure trial; which is easily done by him who has thus presented himself to God. What is that good, and acceptable, and perfect will of God – The will of God is here to be understood of all the preceptive part of Christianity, which is in itself so excellently good, so acceptable to God, and so perfective of our natures.

5. So we – All believers. Are one body – Closely connected together in Christ, and consequently ought to be helpful to each other.

6. Having then gifts differing according to the grace which is given us – Gifts are various: grace is one. Whether it be prophecy – This, considered as an extraordinary gift, is that whereby heavenly mysteries are declared to men, or things to come foretold. But it seems here to mean the ordinary gift of expounding scripture. Let us prophesy according to the analogy of faith – St. Peter expresses it, "as the oracles of God;" according to the general tenor of them; according to that grand scheme of doctrine which is delivered therein, touching original sin, justification by faith, and present, inward salvation. There is a wonderful analogy between all these; and a close and intimate connection between the chief heads of that faith "which was once delivered to the saints." Every article therefore concerning which there is any question should be determined by this rule; every doubtful scripture interpreted according to the grand truths which run through the whole.

7. Ministering – As deacons. He that teacheth – Catechumens; for whom particular instructors were appointed. He that exhorteth – Whose peculiar business it was to urge Christians to duty, and to comfort them in trials.

8. He that presideth – That hath the care of a flock. He that showeth mercy – In any instance. With cheerfulness – Rejoicing that he hath such an opportunity.

9. Having spoken of faith and its fruit, ver. 3, &c., he comes now to love. The ninth, tenth, and eleventh verses refer to chapter the seventh; the twelfth verse to chapter the eighth; the thirteenth verse, of communicating to the saints, whether Jews or Gentiles, to chapter the ninth, &c. Part of the sixteenth verse is repeated from chap. xi, 25. Abhor that which is evil; cleave to that which is good – Both inwardly and outwardly, whatever ill-will or danger may follow.

10. In honor preferring one another – Which you will do, if you habitually consider what is good in others, and what is evil in yourselves.

11. Whatsoever ye do, do it with your might. In every business diligently and fervently serving the Lord – Doing all to God, not to man.

12. Rejoicing in hope – Of perfect holiness and everlasting happiness. Hitherto

MATTHEW HENRY

CHARLES H. SPURGEON

ROMANS 13

The duty of subjection to governors. (1-7)
Exhortations to mutual love. (8-10)
To temperance and sobriety. (11-14)

1-7 The grace of the gospel teaches us submission and quiet, where pride and the carnal mind only see causes for murmuring and discontent. Whatever the persons in authority over us themselves may be, yet the just power they have, must be submitted to and obeyed. In the general course of human affairs, rulers are not a terror to honest, quiet, and good subjects, but to evil-doers. Such is the power of sin and corruption, that many will be kept back from crimes only by the fear of punishment. Thou hast the benefit of the government, therefore do what thou canst to preserve it, and nothing to disturb it. This directs private persons to behave quietly and peaceably where God has set them, 1Ti 2:1,2. Christians must not use any trick or fraud. All smuggling, dealing in contraband goods, withholding or evading duties, is rebellion against the express command of God. Thus honest neighbors are robbed, who will have to pay the more; and the crimes of smugglers, and others who join with them, are abetted. It is painful that some professors of the gospel should countenance such dishonest practices. The lesson here taught it becomes all Christians to learn and practice, that the godly in the land will always be found the quiet and the peaceable in the land, whatever others are.

8-10 Christians must avoid useless expense, and be careful not to contract any debts they have not the power to discharge. They are also to stand aloof from all venturesome speculations and rash engagements, and whatever may expose them to the danger of not rendering to all their due. Do not keep in any one's debt. Give every one his own. Do not spend that on yourselves, which you owe to others. But many who are very sensible of the trouble, think little of the sin, of being in debt. Love to others includes all the duties of the second table. The last five of the ten commandments are all summed up in this royal law, Thou shalt love thy neighbor as thyself; with the same sincerity that thou lovest thyself, though not in the same measure and degree. He that loves his neighbor as himself, will desire the welfare of his neighbor. On this is built that golden rule, of doing as we would be done by. Love is a living, active principle of obedience to the whole law. Let us not only avoid injuries to the persons, connexions, property, and characters of men; but do no kind or degree of evil to any man, and study to be useful in every station of life.

11-14 Four things are here taught, as a Christian's directory for his day's work. When to awake; Now; and to awake out of the sleep of carnal security, sloth, and negligence; out of the sleep of spiritual death, and out of the sleep of spiritual deadness. Considering the time; a busy time; a perilous time. Also the salvation nigh at hand. Let us mind our way, and mend our pace, we are nearer our

will not make you one. I must confess, however, that there are some men who preach this doctrine who are doing ten thousand times more harm than good, because they don't preach the next doctrine I am going to proclaim, which is just as true. They have this to be the sail, but they have not the other to be the ballast. They can preach one side but not the other. They can go along with the high doctrine, but they will not preach the whole of the Word. Such men caricature the Word of God. And just let me say here, that it is the custom of a certain body of Ultra-Calvinists, to call those of us who teach that it is the duty of man to repent and believe, "Mongrel Calvinists." If you hear any of them say so, give them my most respectful compliments, and ask them whether they ever read Calvin's works in their lives. Not that I care what Calvin said or did not say; but ask them whether they ever read his works; and if they say "No," as they must say, for there are forty-eight large volumes, you can tell them, that the man whom they call "a Mongrel Calvinist," though he has not read them all, has read a very good share of them, and knows their spirit; and he knows that he preaches substantially what Calvin preached—that every doctrine he preaches may be found in Calvin's Commentaries on some part of Scripture or other. We are TRUE Calvinists, however. Calvin is nobody to us. Jesus Christ and him crucified, and the old fashioned Bible, are our standards. Beloved, let us take God's Word as it stands. If we find high doctrine there, let it be high; if we find low doctrine, let it be low; let us set up no other standard than the Bible affords.

II. Now then for the second point. "There now," says my ultra friend, "he is going to contradict himself." No, my friend, I am not, I am only going to contradict you. The second point is MAN'S RESPONSIBILITY. "But to Israel he saith, All day long I have stretched forth my hands unto a disobedient and gainsaying people." Now, these people whom God had cast away had been wooed, had been sought, had been entreated to be saved; but they would not, and inasmuch as they were not saved, it was the effect of their disobedience and their gainsaying. That lies clearly enough in the text. When God sent the prophets to Israel, and stretched forth his hands, what was it for? What did he wish them to come to him for? Why, to be saved. "No," says one, "it was for temporal mercies." Not so, my friend; the verse before is concerning spiritual mercies, and so is this

ROMANS 14

1 Him that is weak in the faith receive ye, but not to doubtful disputations.

2 For one believeth that he may eat all things: another, who is weak, eateth herbs.

3 Let not him that eateth despise him that eateth not; and let not him which eateth not judge him that eateth: for God hath received him.

4 Who art thou that judgest another man's servant? to his own master he standeth or falleth. Yea, he shall be holden up: for God is able to make him stand.

5 One man esteemeth one day above another: another esteemeth every day alike. Let every man be fully persuaded in his own mind.

6 He that regardeth the day, regardeth it unto the Lord; and he that regardeth not the day, to the Lord he doth not regard it. He that eateth, eateth to the Lord, for he giveth God thanks; and he that eateth not, to the Lord he eateth not, and giveth God thanks.

7 For none of us liveth to himself, and no man dieth to himself.

8 For whether we live, we live unto the Lord; and whether we die, we die unto the Lord: whether we live therefore, or die, we are the Lord's.

9 For to this end Christ both died, and rose, and revived, that he might be Lord both of the dead and living.

10 But why dost thou judge thy brother? or why dost thou set at nought thy brother? for we shall all stand before the judgment seat of Christ.

11 For it is written, As I live, saith the Lord, every knee shall bow to me, and every tongue shall confess to God.

12 So then every one of us shall give account of himself to God.

13 Let us not therefore judge one another any more: but judge this rather, that no man put a stumblingblock or an occasion to fall in his brother's way.

14 I know, and am persuaded by the Lord Jesus, that there is nothing unclean of itself: but to him that esteemeth any thing to

of faith and love; now of hope also, see the fifth and eighth chapters; afterwards of duties toward others; saints, ver. 13 persecutors, ver. 14 friends, strangers, enemies, ver. 15, &c.

13. Communicate to the necessities of the saints – Relieve all Christians that are in want. It is remarkable, that the apostle, treating expressly of the duties flowing from the communion of saints, yet never says one word about the dead. Pursue hospitality – Not only embracing those that offer, but seeking opportunities to exercise it.

14. Curse not – No, not in your heart.

15. Rejoice – The direct opposite to weeping is laughter; but this does not so well suit a Christian.

16. Mind not high things – Desire not riches, honor, or the company of the great.

17. Provide – Think beforehand; contrive to give as little offense as may be to any.

19. Dearly beloved – So he softens the rugged spirit. Revenge not yourselves, but leave that to God. Perhaps it might more properly be rendered, leave room for wrath; that is, the wrath of God, to whom vengeance properly belongs. Deut. xxxii, 35.

20. Feed him – With your own hand: if it be needful, even put bread into his mouth. Heap coals of fire upon his head – That part which is most sensible. "So artists melt the sullen ore of lead, By heaping coals of fire upon its head; In the kind warmth the metal learns to glow, And pure from dross the silver runs below." Prov. xxv, 21, &c.

21. And if you see no present fruit, yet persevere. Be not overcome with evil – As all are who avenge themselves. But overcome evil with good. Conquer your enemies by kindness and patience.

ROMANS 13

1. St. Paul, writing to the Romans, whose city was the seat of the empire, speaks largely of obedience to magistrates: and this was also, in effect, a public apology for the Christian religion. Let every soul be subject to the supreme powers – An admonition peculiarly needful for the Jews. Power, in the singular number, is the supreme authority; powers are they who are invested with it. That is more readily acknowledged to be from God than these. The apostle affirms it of both. They are all from God, who constituted all in general, and permits each in particular by his providence. The powers that be are appointed by God – It might be rendered, are subordinate to, or, orderly disposed under, God; implying, that they are God's deputies or vicegerents and consequently, their authority being, in effect, his, demands our conscientious obedience.

2. Whosoever resisteth the power – In any other manner than the laws of the community direct. Shall receive condemnation – Not only from the magistrate, but from God also.

3. For rulers are – In the general, notwithstanding some particular exceptions. A terror to evil works – Only. Wouldest thou then not be afraid – There is one fear which precedes evil actions, and deters from them: this should always remain. There is another fear which follows evil actions: they who do well are free from this.

4. The sword – The instrument of capital punishment, which God authorizes him to inflict.

5. Not only for fear of wrath – That is, punishment from man. But for conscience' sake – Out of obedience to God.

6. For this cause – Because they are the ministers (officers) of God for the public good. This very thing – The public good.

7. To all – Magistrates. Tribute – Taxes on your persons or estates. Custom – For

MATTHEW HENRY

CHARLES H. SPURGEON

journey's end. Also to make ourselves ready. The night is far spent, the day is at hand; therefore it is time to dress ourselves. Observe what we must put off; clothes worn in the night. Cast off the sinful works of darkness. Observe what we must put on; how we should dress our souls. Put on the Armor of light. A Christian must reckon himself undressed, if unarmed. The graces of the Spirit are this Armor, to secure the soul from Satan's temptations, and the assaults of this present evil world. Put on Christ; that includes all. Put on righteousness of Christ, for justification. Put on the Spirit and grace of Christ, for sanctification. The Lord Jesus Christ must be put on as Lord to rule you as Jesus to save you; and in both, as Christ anointed and appointed by the Father to this ruling, saving work. And how to walk. When we are up and ready, we are not to sit still, but to appear abroad; let us walk. Christianity teaches us how to walk so as to please God, who ever sees us. Walk honestly as in the day; avoiding the works of darkness. Where there are riot and drunkenness, there usually are chambering and wantonness, and strife and envy. Solomon puts these all together, Pr 23:29-35. See what provision to make. Our great care must be to provide for our souls: but must we take no care about our bodies? Yes; but two things are forbidden. Perplexing ourselves with anxious, encumbering care; and indulging ourselves in irregular desires. Natural wants are to be answered, but evil appetites must be checked and denied. To ask meat for our necessities, is our duty, we are taught to pray for daily bread; but to ask meat for our lusts, is provoking God, Ps 78:18.

ROMANS 14

The Jewish converts cautioned against judging, and Gentile believers against despising one the other. (1-13)
And the Gentiles exhorted to take heed of giving offense in their use of indifferent things. (14-23)

1-6 Differences of opinion prevailed even among the immediate followers of Christ and their disciples. Nor did St. Paul attempt to end them. Compelled assent to any doctrine, or conformity to outward observances without being convinced, would be hypocritical and of no avail. Attempts for producing absolute oneness of mind among Christians would be useless. Let not Christian fellowship be disturbed with strifes of words. It will be good for us to ask ourselves, when tempted to disdain and blame our brethren; Has not God owned them? and if he has, dare I disown them? Let not the Christian who uses his liberty, despise his weak brother as ignorant and superstitious. Let not the scrupulous believer find fault with his brother, for God accepted him, without regarding the distinctions of meats. We usurp the place of God, when we take upon us thus to judge the thoughts and intentions of others, which are out of our view. The case as to the observance of days was much the same. Those who knew that all these things were done away by Christ's coming, took no notice of the festivals of the Jews. But it is not enough that our con-

one, for they refer to the same thing. Now, was God sincere in his offer? God forgive the man that dares to say he was not. God is undoubtedly sincere in every act he did. He sent his prophets, he entreated the people of Israel to lay hold on spiritual things, but they would not, and though he stretched out his hands all the day long, yet they were "a disobedient and gainsaying people," and would not have his love; and on their head rests their blood.

Now let me notice the wooing of God and of what sort it is. First, it was the most affectionate wooing in the world. Lost sinners who sit under the sound of the gospel are not lost for the want of the most affectionate invitation. God says he stretched out his hands. You know what that means. You have seen the child who is disobedient and will not come to his father. The father puts out his hands, and says, "Come, my child, come; I am ready to forgive you." The tear is in his eye, and his bowels move with compassion, and he says, "Come, come." God says this is what he did—"he stretched out his hands." That is what he has done to some of you. You that are not saved today are without excuse, for God stretched out his hands to you, and he said, "Come, come." Long have you sat beneath the sound of the ministry, and it has been a faithful one, I trust, and a weeping one. Your minister has not forgotten to pray for your souls in secret or to weep over you when no eye saw him, and he has endeavored to persuade you as an ambassador from God. God is my witness, I have sometimes stood in this pulpit, and I could not have pleaded harder for my own life than I have pleaded with you. In Christ's name, I have cried, "Come unto me all ye that labor and are heavy laden, and I will give you rest." I have wept over you as the Savior did, and used his words on his behalf, "O Jerusalem, Jerusalem, how often would I have gathered thy children together as a hen gathereth her chickens under her wings, and ye would not." And you know that your conscience has often been touched; you have often been moved; you could not resist it. God was so kind to you; he invited you so affectionately by the Word; he dealt so gently with you by his providence; his hands were stretched out, and you could hear his voice speaking in your ears, "Come unto me, come: come now, let us reason together; though your sins be as scarlet they shall be as wool; though they be red like crimson they shall be whiter than snow." You have heard him cry, "Ho every one that thirsteth, come

be unclean, to him it is unclean.

15 But if thy brother be grieved with thy meat, now walkest thou not charitably. Destroy not him with thy meat, for whom Christ died.

16 Let not then your good be evil spoken of:

17 For the kingdom of God is not meat and drink; but righteousness, and peace, and joy in the Holy Ghost.

18 For he that in these things serveth Christ is acceptable to God, and approved of men.

19 Let us therefore follow after the things which make for peace, and things wherewith one may edify another.

20 For meat destroy not the work of God. All things indeed are pure; but it is evil for that man who eateth with offense.

21 It is good neither to eat flesh, nor to drink wine, nor any thing whereby thy brother stumbleth, or is offended, or is made weak.

22 Hast thou faith? have it to thyself before God. Happy is he that condemneth not himself in that thing which he alloweth.

23 And he that doubteth is damned if he eat, because he eateth not of faith: for whatsoever is not of faith is sin.

ROMANS 15

1 We then that are strong ought to bear the infirmities of the weak, and not to please ourselves.

2 Let every one of us please his neighbor for his good to edification.

3 For even Christ pleased not himself; but, as it is written, The reproaches of them that reproached thee fell on me.

4 For whatsoever things were written aforetime were written for our learning, that we through patience and comfort of the scriptures might have hope.

5 Now the God of patience and consolation grant you to be likeminded one toward another according to Christ Jesus:

6 That ye may with one mind and one mouth glorify God, even the Father of our Lord Jesus Christ.

7 Wherefore receive ye one

goods exported or imported. Fear – Obedience. Honor – Reverence. All these are due to the supreme power.

8. From our duty to magistrates he passes on to general duties. To love one another – An eternal debt, which can never be sufficiently discharged; but yet if this be rightly performed, it discharges all the rest. For he that loveth another – As he ought. Hath fulfilled the whole law – Toward his neighbor.

9. If there be any other – More particular. Commandment – Toward our neighbor; as there are many in the law. It is summed up in this – So that if you was not thinking of it, yet if your heart was full of love, you would fulfill it.

10. Therefore love is the fulfilling of the law – For the same love which restrains from all evil, incites us to all good.

11. And do this – Fulfill the law of love in all the instances above mentioned. Knowing the season – Full of grace, but hasting away. That it is high time to awake out of sleep – How beautifully is the metaphor carried on! This life, a night; the resurrection, the day; the gospel shining on the heart, the dawn of this day; we are to awake out of sleep; to rise up and throw away our night-clothes, fit only for darkness, and put on new; and, being soldiers, we are to arm, and prepare for fight, who are encompassed with so many enemies.

13. Banqueting – Luxurious, elegant feasts.

14. But put ye on the Lord Jesus Christ – Herein is contained the whole of our salvation. It is a strong and beautiful expression for the most intimate union with him, and being clothed with all the graces which were in him. The apostle does not say, Put on purity and sobriety, peacefulness and benevolence; but he says all this and a thousand times more at once, in saying, Put on Christ. And make not provision – To raise foolish desires, or, when they are raised already, to satisfy them.

ROMANS 14

1. Him that is weak – Through needless scruples. Receive – With all love and courtesy into Christian fellowship. But not to doubtful disputations – About questionable points.

2. All things – All sorts of food, though forbidden by the law.

3. Despise him that eateth not – As over-scrupulous or superstitious. Judge him that eateth – As profane, or taking undue liberties. For God hath received him – Into the number of his children, notwithstanding this.

5. One day above another – As new moons, and other Jewish festivals. Let every man be fully persuaded – That a thing is lawful, before he does it.

6. Regardeth it to the Lord – That is, out of a principle of conscience toward God. To the Lord he doth not regard it – He also acts from a principle of conscience. He that eateth not – Flesh. Giveth God thanks – For his herbs.

7. None of us – Christians, in the things we do. Liveth to himself – Is at his own disposal; doeth his own will.

10. Or why dost thou despise thy brother – Hitherto the apostle as addressed the weak brother: now he speaks to the stronger.

13. But judge this rather – Concerning ourselves. Not to lay a stumbling block – By moving him to do as thou doest, though against his conscience. Or a scandal – Moving him to hate or judge thee.

14. I am assured by the Lord Jesus – Perhaps by a particular Revelation. That there is nothing – Neither flesh nor herbs. Unclean of itself – Unlawful under the gospel.

15. If thy brother is grieved – That is, wounded, led into sin. Destroy not him for whom Christ died – So we see, he for whom Christ died may be destroyed. With thy meat – Do not value thy meat more than Christ valued his life.

16. Let not then your good and lawful liberty be evil spoken of – By being offensive to others.

MATTHEW HENRY   CHARLES H. SPURGEON

sciences consent to what we do; it is necessary that it be certified from the word of God. Take heed of acting against a doubting conscience. We are all apt to make our own views the standard of truth, to deem things certain which to others appear doubtful. Thus Christians often despise or condemn each other, about doubtful matters of no moment. A thankful regard to God, the Author and Giver of all our mercies, sanctifies and sweetens them.

7-13 Though some are weak, and others are strong, yet all must agree not to live to themselves. No one who has given up his name to Christ, is allowedly a self-seeker; that is against true Christianity. The business of our lives is not to please ourselves, but to please God. That is true Christianity, which makes Christ all in all. Though Christians are of different strength, capacities, and practices in lesser things, yet they are all the Lord's; all are looking and serving, and approving themselves to Christ. He is Lord of those that are living, to rule them; of those that are dead, to revive them, and raise them up. Christians should not judge or despise one another, because both the one and the other must shortly give an account. A believing regard to the judgment of the great day, would silence rash judging. Let every man search his own heart and life; he that is strict in judging and humbling himself, will not be apt to judge and despise his brother. We must take heed of saying or doing things which may cause others to stumble or to fall. The one signifies a lesser, the other a greater degree of offense; that which may be an occasion of grief or of guilt to our brother.

14-18 Christ deals gently with those who have true grace, though they are weak in it. Consider the design of Christ's death: also that drawing a soul to sin, threatens the destruction of that soul. Did Christ deny himself for our brethren, so as to die for them, and shall not we deny ourselves for them, so as to keep from any indulgence? We cannot hinder ungoverned tongues from speaking evil; but we must not give them any occasion. We must deny ourselves in many cases what we may lawfully do, when our doing it may hurt our good name. Our good often comes to be evil spoken of, because we use lawful things in an uncharitable and selfish manner. As we value the reputation of the good we profess and practice, let us seek that it may not be evil-spoken of. Righteousness, peace, and joy, are words that mean a great deal. As to God, our great concern is to appear before him justified by Christ's death, sanctified by the Spirit of his grace; for the righteous Lord loveth righteousness. As to our brethren, it is to live in peace, and love, and charity with them; following peace with all men. As to ourselves, it is joy in the Holy Ghost; that spiritual joy wrought by the blessed Spirit in the hearts of believers, which respects God as their reconciled Father, and heaven as their expected home. Regard to Christ in doing our duties, alone can make them acceptable. Those are most pleasing to God that are best pleased with him; and they

ye to the waters." You have heard him say with all the affection of a father's heart, "Let the wicked forsake his way, and the unrighteous man his thoughts, and let him turn unto the Lord, and he will have mercy upon him, and unto our God, for he will abundantly pardon." Oh! God does plead with men that they would be saved, and this day he says to every one of you, "Repent, and be converted for the remission of your sins. Turn ye unto me. Thus saith the Lord of hosts; consider your ways." And with love divine he woos you as a father woos his child, putting out his hands and crying, "Come unto me, come unto me." "No," says one strong-doctrine man, "God never invites all men to himself; he invites none but certain characters." Stop, sir, that is all you know about it. Did you ever read that parable where it is said, "My oxen and my fatlings are killed, and all things are ready; come unto the marriage." And they that were bidden would not come. And did you never read that they all began to make excuse, and that they were punished because they did not accept the invitations. Now, if the invitation is not to be made to anybody, but to the man who will accept it, how can that parable be true? The fact is, the oxen and fatlings are killed; the wedding feast is ready, and the trumpet sounds, "Ho every one that thirsteth, come and eat, come and drink." Here are the provisions spread, here is an all-sufficiency; the invitation is free; it is a great invitation. "Whosoever will, let him come and take of the water of life freely." And that invitation is couched in tender words, "Come to me, my child, come to me." "All day long I have stretched forth my hands."

And note again, this invitation was very frequent. The words, "all the day long," may be translated "daily"—"Daily have I stretched forth my hands." Sinner, God has not called you once to come, and then let you alone, but every day has he been at you; every day has conscience spoken to you; every day has providence warned you, and every Sabbath has the Word of God wooed you. Oh! how much some of you will have to account for at God's great bar! I cannot now read your characters, but I know there are some of you who will have a terrible account at last. All the day long has God been wooing you. From the first dawn of your life, he wooed you through your mother, and she used to put your little hands together, and teach you to say,

"Gentle Jesus meek and mild,
Look upon a little child,

another, as Christ also received us to the glory of God.

8 Now I say that Jesus Christ was a minister of the circumcision for the truth of God, to confirm the promises made unto the fathers:

9 And that the Gentiles might glorify God for his mercy; as it is written, For this cause I will confess to thee among the Gentiles, and sing unto thy name.

10 And again he saith, Rejoice, ye Gentiles, with his people.

11 And again, Praise the Lord, all ye Gentiles; and laud him, all ye people.

12 And again, Esaias saith, There shall be a root of Jesse, and he that shall rise to reign over the Gentiles; in him shall the Gentiles trust.

13 Now the God of hope fill you with all joy and peace in believing, that ye may abound in hope, through the power of the Holy Ghost.

14 And I myself also am persuaded of you, my brethren, that ye also are full of goodness, filled with all knowledge, able also to admonish one another.

15 Nevertheless, brethren, I have written the more boldly unto you in some sort, as putting you in mind, because of the grace that is given to me of God,

16 That I should be the minister of Jesus Christ to the Gentiles, ministering the gospel of God, that the offering up of the Gentiles might be acceptable, being sanctified by the Holy Ghost.

17 I have therefore whereof I may glory through Jesus Christ in those things which pertain to God.

18 For I will not dare to speak of any of those things which Christ hath not wrought by me, to make the Gentiles obedient, by word and deed,

19 Through mighty signs and wonders, by the power of the Spirit of God; so that from Jerusalem, and round about unto Illyricum, I have fully preached the gospel of Christ.

20 Yea, so have I strived to preach the gospel, not where Christ was named, lest I should build upon another man's foundation:

17. For the kingdom of God – That is, true religion, does not consist in external observances. But in righteousness – The image of God stamped on the heart; the love of God and man, accompanied with the peace that passeth all understanding, and joy in the Holy Ghost.

18. In these – Righteousness, peace, and joy. Men – Wise and good men.

19. Peace and edification are closely joined. Practical divinity tends equally to peace and to edification. Controversial divinity less directly tends to edification, although sometimes, as they of old, we cannot build without it, Neh. iv, 17.

20. The work of God – Which he builds in the soul by faith, and in the church by concord. It is evil to that man who eateth with offense – So as to offend another thereby.

21. Thy brother stumbleth – By imitating thee against his conscience, contrary to righteousness. Or is offended – At what thou doest to the loss of his peace. Or made weak – Hesitating between imitation and abhorrence, to the loss of that joy in the Lord which was his strength.

22. Hast thou faith – That all things are pure? Have it to thyself before God – In circumstances like these, keep it to thyself, and do not offend others by it. Happy is he that condemneth not himself – By an improper use of even innocent things! and happy he who is free from a doubting conscience! He that has this may allow the thing, yet condemn himself for it.

ROMANS 15

1. We who are strong – Of a clearer judgment, and free from these scruples. And not to please ourselves – Without any regard to others.

2. For his good – This is a general word: edification is one species of good.

3. But bore not only the infirmities, but reproaches, of his brethren; and so fulfilled that scripture. Psalm lxix, 9.

4. Aforetime – In the Old Testament. That we through patience and consolation of the scriptures may have hope – That through the consolation which God gives us by these, we may have patience and a joyful hope.

5. According to the power of Christ Jesus.

6. That ye – Both Jews and Gentiles, believing with one mind, and confessing with one mouth.

7. Receive ye one another – Weak and strong, with mutual love.

8. Now I say – The apostle here shows how Christ received us. Christ Jesus-Jesus is the name, Christ the surname. The latter was first known to the Jews; the former, to the Gentiles.

9. As it is written – In the eighteenth psalm, here the Gentiles and Jews are spoken of as joining in the worship of the God of Israel. Psalm xviii, 49.

10. Deut. xxxii, 43.

11. Psalm cxvii, 1.

12. There shall be the root of Jesse – That kings and the Messiah should spring from his house, was promised to Jesse before it was to David. In him shall the Gentiles hope – Who before had been "without hope," Eph. ii, 12. Isaiah xi, 10.

13. Now the God of hope – A glorious title of God, but till now unknown to the heathens; for their goddess Hope, like their other idols, was nothing; whose temple at Rome was burned by lightning. It was, indeed, built again not long after, but was again burned to the ground.

14. There are several conclusions of this Epistle. The first begins at this verse; the second, chap. xvi, 1; the third, chap. xvi, 17; the fourth, chap. xvi, 21; and the fifth, chap. xvi, 25; Ye are full of goodness – By being created anew. And filled with all knowledge – By long experience of the things of God. To admonish – To instruct and confirm.

15. Because of the grace – That is, because I am an apostle of the Gentiles.

16. The offering up of the Gentiles – As living sacrifices.

MATTHEW HENRY   CHARLES H. SPURGEON

abound most in peace and joy in the Holy Ghost. They are approved by wise and good men; and the opinion of others is not to be regarded.

19-23 Many wish for peace, and talk loudly for it, who do not follow the things that make for peace. Meekness, humility, self-denial, and love, make for peace. We cannot edify one another, while quarrelling and contending. Many, for meat and drink, destroy the work of God in themselves; nothing more destroys the soul than pampering and pleasing the flesh, and fulfilling the lusts of it; so others are hurt, by willfull offense given. Lawful things may be done unlawfully, by giving offense to brethren. This takes in all indifferent things, whereby a brother is drawn into sin or trouble; or has his graces, his comforts, or his resolutions weakened. Hast thou faith? It is meant of knowledge and clearness as to our Christian liberty. Enjoy the comfort of it, but do not trouble others by a wrong use of it. Nor may we act against a doubting conscience. How excellent are the blessings of Christ's kingdom, which consists not in outward rites and ceremonies, but in righteousness, peace, and joy in the Holy Ghost! How preferable is the service of God to all other services! and in serving him we are not called to live and die to ourselves, but unto Christ, whose we are, and whom we ought to serve.

ROMANS 15

Directions how to behave towards the weak. (1-7)
All to receive one another as brethren. (8-13)
The writing and preaching of the apostle. (14-21)
His purposed journeys. (22-29)
He requests their prayers. (30-33)

1-7 Christian liberty was allowed, not for our pleasure, but for the glory of God, and the good of others. We must please our neighbor, for the good of his soul; not by serving his wicked will, and humoring him in a sinful way; if we thus seek to please men, we are not the servants of Christ. Christ's whole life was a self-denying, self-displeasing life. And he is the most advanced Christian, who is the most conformed to Christ. Considering his spotless purity and holiness, nothing could be more contrary to him, than to be made sin and a curse for us, and to have the reproaches of God fall upon him; the just for the unjust. He bore the guilt of sin, and the curse for it; we are only called to bear a little of the trouble of it. He bore the presumptuous sins of the wicked; we are called only to bear the failings of the weak. And should not we be humble, self-denying, and ready to consider one another, who are members one of another? The Scriptures are written for our use and benefit, as much as for those to whom they were first given. Those are most learned who are most mighty in the Scriptures. That comfort which springs from the word of God, is the surest and sweetest, and the greatest stay to hope. The Spirit as a Comforter, is the earnest of our inheritance. This like-mindedness must be according to

Pity my simplicity;
Suffer me to come to thee."
And in your boyhood God was still stretching out his hands after you. How your Sunday-school teacher endeavored to bring you to the Savior! How often your youthful heart was affected; but you put all that away, and you are still untouched by it. How often did your mother speak to you, and your father warn you; and you have forgotten the prayer in that bedroom when you were sick, when your mother kissed your burning forehead, knelt down and prayed to God to spare your life, and then added that prayer, "Lord, save my boy's soul!" And you recollect the Bible she gave you, when you first went out apprentice, and the prayer she wrote on that yellow front leaf. When she gave it, you did not perhaps know, but you may now; how earnestly she longed after you, that you might be formed anew in Christ Jesus; how she followed you with her prayers, and how she entreated with her God for you. And you have not yet surely forgotten how many Sabbaths you have spent, and how many times you have been warned. Why you have had waggon-loads of sermons wasted on you. A hundred and four sermons you have heard every year, and some of you more, and yet you are still just what you were.

But sinners, sermon hearing is an awful thing unless it is blessed to our souls. If God has kept on stretching out his hands every day and all the day, it will be a hard thing for you when you shall be justly condemned not only for your breaches of the law, but for your willfull rejection of the gospel. It is probable that God will keep on stretching out his hands to you until your hairs grow gray, still continually inviting you: and perhaps when you are nearing death he will still say, "Come unto me, come unto me." But if you still persist in hardening your heart, if still you reject Christ, I beseech you let nothing make you imagine that you shall go unpunished. Oh! I do tremble sometimes when I think of that class of ministers who tell sinners that they are not guilty if they do not seek the Savior. How they shall be found innocent at God's great day I do not know. It seems to be a fearful thing that they should be lulling poor souls into sleep by telling them it is not their duty to seek Christ and repent, but that they may do as they like about that, and that when they perish they will be none the more guilty for having heard the Word. My Master did not say that. Remember how he said, "And thou, Capernaum, which art exalted unto heaven,

21 But as it is written, To whom he was not spoken of, they shall see: and they that have not heard shall understand.

22 For which cause also I have been much hindered from coming to you.

23 But now having no more place in these parts, and having a great desire these many years to come unto you;

24 Whensoever I take my journey into Spain, I will come to you: for I trust to see you in my journey, and to be brought on my way thitherward by you, if first I be somewhat filled with your company.

25 But now I go unto Jerusalem to minister unto the saints.

26 For it hath pleased them of Macedonia and Achaia to make a certain contribution for the poor saints which are at Jerusalem.

27 It hath pleased them verily; and their debtors they are. For if the Gentiles have been made partakers of their spiritual things, their duty is also to minister unto them in carnal things.

28 When therefore I have performed this, and have sealed to them this fruit, I will come by you into Spain.

29 And I am sure that, when I come unto you, I shall come in the fullness of the blessing of the gospel of Christ.

30 Now I beseech you, brethren, for the Lord Jesus Christ's sake, and for the love of the Spirit, that ye strive together with me in your prayers to God for me;

31 That I may be delivered from them that do not believe in Judea; and that my service which I have for Jerusalem may be accepted of the saints;

32 That I may come unto you with joy by the will of God, and may with you be refreshed.

33 Now the God of peace be with you all. Amen.

ROMANS 16

1 I commend unto you Phebe our sister, which is a servant of the church which is at Cenchrea:

2 That ye receive her in the Lord, as becometh saints, and

17. I have whereof to glory through Jesus Christ – All my glorying is in and through him.

18. By word – By the power of the Spirit. By deed – Namely, through "mighty signs and wonders."

21. Isaiah lii, 15.

22. Therefore I have been long hindered from coming to you – Among whom Christ had been named.

23. Having no longer place in these parts – Where Christ has now been preached in every city.

24. Into Spain – Where the gospel had not yet been preached. If first I may be somewhat satisfied with your company – How remarkable is the modesty with which he speaks! They might rather desire to be satisfied with his. Somewhat satisfied – Intimating the shortness of his stay; or, perhaps, that Christ alone can thoroughly satisfy the soul.

26. The poor of the saints that are in Jerusalem – It can by no means be inferred from this expression, that the community of goods among the Christians was then ceased. All that can be gathered from it is, that in this time of extreme dearth, Acts xi, 28, 29, some of the church in Jerusalem were in want; the rest being barely able to subsist themselves, but not to supply the necessities of their brethren.

27. It hath pleased them; and they are their debtors – That is, they are bound to it, in justice as well as mercy. Spiritual things – By the preaching of the gospel. Carnal things – Things needful for the body.

28. When I have sealed to them this fruit – When I have safely delivered to them, as under seal, this fruit of their brethren's love. I will go by you into Spain – Such was his design; but it does not appear that Paul went into Spain. There are often holy purposes in the minds of good men, which are overruled by the providence of God so as never to take effect. And yet they are precious in the sight of God.

30. I beseech you by the love of the Spirit – That is, by the love which is the genuine fruit of the Spirit. To strive together with me in your prayers – He must pray himself, who would have others strive together with him in prayer. Of all the apostles, St. Paul alone is recorded to desire the prayers of the faithful for himself. And this he generally does in the conclusions of his Epistles; yet not without making a difference. For he speaks in one manner to them whom he treats as his children, with the gravity or even severity of a father, such as Timothy, Titus, the Corinthians, and Galatians; in another, to them whom he treats rather like equals, such as the Romans, Ephesians, Thessalonians, Colossians, Hebrews.

31. That I may be delivered – He is thus urgent from a sense of the importance of his life to the church. Otherwise he would have rejoiced "to depart, and to be with Christ." And that my service may be acceptable – In spite of all their prejudices; to the end the Jewish and Gentile believers may be knit together in tender love.

32. That I may come to you – This refers to the former, With joy – To the latter, part of the preceding verse.

ROMANS 16

1. I commend unto you Phebe – The bearer of this letter. A servant – The Greek word is a deaconess. Of the church in Cenchrea – In the apostolic age, some grave and pious women were appointed deaconesses in every church. It was their office, not to teach publicly, but to visit the sick, the women in particular, and to minister to them both in their temporal and spiritual necessities.

2. In the Lord – That is, for the Lord's sake, and in a Christian manner. St. Paul seems fond of this expression.

the precept of Christ, according to his pattern and example. It is the gift of God; and a precious gift it is, for which we must earnestly seek unto him. Our Divine Master invites his disciples, and encourages them by showing himself as meek and lowly in spirit. The same disposition ought to mark the conduct of his servants, especially of the strong towards the weak. The great end in all our actions must be, that God may be glorified; nothing more forwards this, than the mutual love and kindness of those who profess religion. Those that agree in Christ may well agree among themselves.

8-13 Christ fulfilled the prophecies and promises relating to the Jews, and the Gentile converts could have no excuse for despising them. The Gentiles, being brought into the church, are companions in patience and tribulation. They should praise God. Calling upon all the nations to praise the Lord, shows that they shall have knowledge of him. We shall never seek to Christ till we trust in him. And the whole plan of redemption is suited to reconcile us to one another, as well as to our gracious God, so that an abiding hope of eternal life, through the sanctifying and comforting power of the Holy Spirit, may be attained. Our own power will never reach this; therefore where this hope is, and is abounding, the blessed Spirit must have all the glory. "All joy and peace;" all sorts of true joy and peace, so as to suppress doubts and fears, through the powerful working of the Holy Spirit.

14-21 The apostle was persuaded that the Roman Christians were filled with a kind and affectionate spirit, as well as with knowledge. He had written to remind them of their duties and their dangers, because God had appointed him the minister of Christ to the Gentiles. Paul preached to them; but what made them sacrifices to God, was, their sanctification; not his work, but the work of the Holy Ghost: unholy things can never be pleasing to the holy God. The conversion of souls pertains unto God; therefore it is the matter of Paul's glorying, not the things of the flesh. But though a great preacher, he could not make one soul obedient, further than the Spirit of God accompanied his labors. He principally sought the good of those that sat in darkness. Whatever good we do, it is Christ who does it by us.

22-29 The apostle sought the things of Christ more than his own will, and would not leave his work of planting churches to go to Rome. It concerns all to do that first which is most needful. We must not take it ill if our friends prefer work which is pleasing to God, before visits and compliments, which may please us. It is justly expected from all Christians, that they should promote every good work, especially that blessed work, the conversion of souls. Christian society is a heaven upon earth, an earnest of our gathering together unto Christ at the great day. Yet it is but partial, compared with our communion with Christ; for that only will satisfy the soul. The apostle was going to Jerusalem, as the messenger of charity. God loves a cheerful giver. Every thing that passes

shalt be brought down to hell: for if the mighty works, which have been done in thee, had been done in Sodom, it would have remained until this day. But I say unto you, That it shall be more tolerable for the land of Sodom in the day of judgment, than for thee." Jesus did not talk thus when he spoke to Chorazin and Bethsaida; for he said, "Woe unto thee, Chorazin! woe unto thee, Bethsaida! for if the mighty works, which were done in you, had been done in Tyre and Sidon, they would have repented long ago in sackcloth and ashes. But I say unto you, It shall be more tolerable for Tyre and Sidon at the day of judgment, than for you." It was not the way Paul preached. He did not tell sinners that there was no guilt in despising the cross. Hear the apostle's words once more: "For if the word spoken by angels was steadfast, and every transgression and disobedience received a just recompense of reward, how shall we escape, if we neglect so great salvation, which at the first began to be spoken by the Lord, and was confirmed unto us by them that heard him." Sinner, at the great day of God thou must give an account for every warning thou hast ever had, for every time thou hast read thy Bible, ay, and for every time thou hast neglected to read it; for every Sunday when the house of God was open and thou didst neglect to avail thyself of the opportunity of hearing the Word, and for every time thou didst hear it and didst not improve it. Ye who are careless hearers, are tying faggots for your own burning for ever. Ye that hear and straightway forget, or hear with levity, are digging for yourselves a pit into which ye must be cast. Remember, no one will be responsible for your damnation but yourself, at the last great day. God will not be responsible for it. "As I live saith the Lord"—and that is a great oath—"I have no pleasure in the death of him that dieth, but had rather that he should turn unto me and live." God has done much for you. He sent you his gospel. You are not born in a heathen land; he has given you the Book of Books; he has given you an enlightened conscience; and if you perish under the sound of the ministry, you perish more fearfully and terribly, than if you had perished anywhere else.

This doctrine is as much God's Word as the other. You ask me to reconcile the two. I answer, they do not want any reconcilement; I never tried to reconcile them to myself, because I could never see a discrepancy. If you begin to put fifty or sixty quibbles to me, I cannot give any answer. Both are true; no

that ye assist her in whatsoever business she hath need of you: for she hath been a succorer of many, and of myself also.

3 Greet Priscilla and Aquila my helpers in Christ Jesus:

4 Who have for my life laid down their own necks: unto whom not only I give thanks, but also all the churches of the Gentiles.

5 Likewise greet the church that is in their house. Salute my wellbeloved Epenetus, who is the firstfruits of Achaia unto Christ.

6 Greet Mary, who bestowed much labor on us.

7 Salute Andronicus and Junia, my kinsmen, and my fellowprisoners, who are of note among the apostles, who also were in Christ before me.

8 Greet Amplias my beloved in the Lord.

9 Salute Urbane, our helper in Christ, and Stachys my beloved.

10 Salute Apelles approved in Christ. Salute them which are of Aristobulus' household.

11 Salute Herodion my kinsman. Greet them that be of the household of Narcissus, which are in the Lord.

12 Salute Tryphena and Tryphosa, who labor in the Lord. Salute the beloved Persis, which labored much in the Lord.

13 Salute Rufus chosen in the Lord, and his mother and mine.

14 Salute Asyncritus, Phlegon, Hermas, Patrobas, Hermes, and the brethren which are with them.

15 Salute Philologus, and Julia, Nereus, and his sister, and Olympas, and all the saints which are with them.

16 Salute one another with an holy kiss. The churches of Christ salute you.

17 Now I beseech you, brethren, mark them which cause divisions and offenses contrary to the doctrine which ye have learned; and avoid them.

18 For they that are such serve not our Lord Jesus Christ, but their own belly; and by good words and fair speeches deceive the hearts of the simple.

19 For your obedience is come

4. Who have for my life, as it were, laid down their own necks – That is, exposed themselves to the utmost danger. But likewise all the churches of the Gentiles – Even that at Rome, for preserving so valuable a life.

5. Salute the church that is in their house – Aquila had been driven from Rome in the reign of Claudius, but was now returned, and performed the same part there which Caius did at Corinth, ver. 23. Where any Christian had a large house, there they all assembled together though as yet the Christians at Rome had neither bishops nor deacons. So far were they from any shadow of papal power. Nay, there does not appear to have been then in the whole city any more than one of these domestic churches. Otherwise there can be no doubt but St. Paul would have saluted them also. Epenetus – Although the apostle had never been at Rome, yet had he many acquaintance there. But here is no mention of Linus or Cemens; whence it appears, they did not come to Rome till after this. The first fruits of Asia – The first convert in the proconsular Asia.

7. Who are of note among the apostles – They seem to have been some of the most early converts. Fellow prisoners – For the gospel's sake.

9. Our fellow laborer – Mine and Timothy's, verse 21.

11. Those of the family of Aristobulus and Narcissus, who are in the Lord – It seems only part of their families were converted. Probably, some of them were not known to St. Paul by face, but only by character. Faith does not create moroseness, but courtesy, which even the gravity of an apostle did not hinder.

12. Salute Tryphena and Tryphosa – Probably they were two sisters.

13. Salute Rufus – Perhaps the same that is mentioned, Mark xv, 21. And his mother and mine – This expression may only denote the tender care which Rufus's mother had taken of him.

14. Salute Asyncritus, Phlegon, &c. – He seems to join those together, who were joined by kindred, nearness of habitation, or any other circumstance. It could not but encourage the poor especially, to be saluted by name, who perhaps did not know that the apostle had ever heard of them. It is observable, that whilst the apostle forgets none who are worthy, yet he adjusts the nature of his salutation to the degrees of worth in those whom he salutes.

15. Salute all the saints – Had St. Peter been then at Rome, St. Paul would doubtless have saluted him by name; since no one in this numerous catalogue was of an eminence comparable to his. But if he was not then at Rome, the whole Roman tradition, with regard to the succession of their bishops, fails in the most fundamental article.

16. Salute one another with an holy kiss – Termed by St. Peter, "the kiss of love," 1 Pet. v, 14. So the ancient Christians concluded all their solemn offices; the men saluting the men, and the women the women. And this apostolic custom seems to have continued for some ages in all Christian churches.

17. Mark them who cause divisions – Such there were, therefore, at Rome also. Avoid them – Avoid all unnecessary intercourse with them.

18. By good words – Concerning themselves, making great promises. And fair speeches – Concerning you, praising and flattering you. The harmless – Who, doing no ill themselves, are not upon their guard against them that do.

19. But I would have you – Not only obedient, but discreet also. Wise with regard to that which is good – As knowing in this as possible. And simple with regard to that which is evil – As ignorant of this as possible.

20. And the God of peace – The Author and Lover of it, giving a blessing to your discretion. Shall bruise Satan under your feet – Shall defeat all the artifices of that sower of tares, and unite you more and more together in love.

21. Timotheus my fellow laborer – Here he is named even before St. Paul's kinsmen. But as he had never been at Rome, he is not named in the beginning of the epistle.

22. I Tertius, who wrote this epistle, salute you – Tertius, who wrote what the apostle dictated, inserted this, either by St. Paul's exhortation or ready permis-

between Christians should be a proof and instance of the union they have in Jesus Christ. The Gentiles received the gospel of salvation from the Jews; therefore were bound to minister to them in what was needed for the body. Concerning what he expected from them he speaks doubtfully; but concerning what he expected from God he speaks confidently. We cannot expect too little from man, nor too much from God. And how delightful and advantageous it is to have the gospel with the fullness of its blessings! What wonderful and happy effects does it produce, when attended with the power of the Spirit!

30-33 Let us learn to value the effectual fervent prayers of the righteous. How careful should we be, lest we forfeit our interest in the love and prayers of God's praying people! If we have experienced the Spirit's love, let us not be wanting in this office of kindness for others. Those that would prevail in prayer, must strive in prayer. Those who beg the prayers of others, must not neglect to pray for themselves. And though Christ knows our state and wants perfectly, he will know them from us. As God must be sought, for restraining the ill-will of our enemies, so also for preserving and increasing the good-will of our friends. All our joy depends upon the will of God. Let us be earnest in prayer with and for each other, that for Christ's sake, and by the love of the Holy Spirit, great blessings may come upon the souls of Christians, and the labors of ministers.

ROMANS 16

The apostle recommends Phebe to the church at Rome, and greets several friends there. (1-16)
Cautions the church against such as made divisions. (17-20)
Christian salutations. (21-24)
The epistle concludes with ascribing glory to God. (25-27)

1-16 Paul recommends Phebe to the Christians at Rome. It becomes Christians to help one another in their affairs, especially strangers; we know not what help we may need ourselves. Paul asks help for one that had been helpful to many; he that watereth shall be watered also himself. Though the care of all the churches came upon him daily, yet he could remember many persons, and send salutations to each, with particular characters of them, and express concern for them. Lest any should feel themselves hurt, as if Paul had forgotten them, he sends his remembrances to the rest, as brethren and saints, though not named. He adds, in the close, a general salutation to them all, in the name of the churches of Christ.

17-20 How earnest, how endearing are these exhortations! Whatever differs from the sound doctrine of the Scriptures, opens a door to divisions and offenses. If truth be forsaken, unity and peace will not last long. Many call Christ, Master and Lord, who are far from serving him.

two truths can be inconsistent with each other; and what you have to do is to believe them both. With the first one, the saint has most to do. Let him praise the free and sovereign grace of God, and bless his name. With the second, the sinner has the most to do. O sinner, humble thyself under the mighty hand of God, when thou thinkest of how often he hath shown his love to thee, by bidding thee come to himself, and yet how often thou hast spurned his Word and refused his mercy, and turned a deaf ear to every invitation, and hast gone thy way to rebel against a God of love, and violate the commands of him that loved thee.

And now, how shall I conclude? My first exhortation shall be to Christian people. My dear friends, I beseech you do not in any way give yourselves up to any system of faith apart from the Word of God. The Bible, and the Bible alone, is the religion of Protestants; I am the successor of the great and venerated Dr. Gill, whose theology is almost universally received among the stronger Calvinistic churches; but although I venerate his memory, and believe his teachings, yet he is not my Rabbi. What you find in God's Word is for you to believe and to receive. Never be frightened at a doctrine; and above all, never be frightened at a name. Some one said to me the other day, that he thought the truth lay somewhere between the two extremes. He meant right, but I think he was wrong, I do not think the truth lies between the two extremes, but in them both. I believe the higher a man goes the better, when he is preaching the matter of salvation. The reason why a man is saved is grace, grace, grace; and you may go as high as you like there. But when you come to the question as to why men are damned, then the Arminian is far more right than the Antinomian. I care not for any denomination or party, I am as high as Huntingdon upon the matter of salvation, but question me about damnation, and you will get a very different answer. By the grace of God I ask no man's applause, I preach the Bible as I find it. Where we get wrong is where the Calvinist begins to meddle with the question of damnation, and interferes with the justice of God; or when the Arminian denies the doctrine of grace.

My second exhortation is,—Sinners, I beseech every one of you who are unconverted and ungodly, this morning to put away every form and fashion of excuse that the devil would have you make concerning your being unconverted. Remember, that all the teaching in the world can never excuse

abroad unto all men. I am glad therefore on your behalf: but yet I would have you wise unto that which is good, and simple concerning evil.

20 And the God of peace shall bruise Satan under your feet shortly. The grace of our Lord Jesus Christ be with you. Amen.

21 Timotheus my workfellow, and Lucius, and Jason, and Sosipater, my kinsmen, salute you.

22 I Tertius, who wrote this epistle, salute you in the Lord.

23 Gaius mine host, and of the whole church, saluteth you. Erastus the chamberlain of the city saluteth you, and Quartus a brother.

24 The grace of our Lord Jesus Christ be with you all. Amen.

25 Now to him that is of power to stablish you according to my gospel, and the preaching of Jesus Christ, according to the revelation of the mystery, which was kept secret since the world began,

26 But now is made manifest, and by the scriptures of the prophets, according to the commandment of the everlasting God, made known to all nations for the obedience of faith:

27 To God only wise, be glory through Jesus Christ for ever. Amen.

sion. Caius – The Corinthian, 1 Cor. i, 14. My host, and of the whole church – Who probably met for some time in his house.

23. The chamberlain of the city – Of Corinth.

25. Now to him who is able – The last words of this epistle exactly answer the first, chapter i, 1-v, chap. i, 1-v, in particular, concerning the power of God, the gospel, Jesus Christ, the scriptures, the obedience of faith, all nations. To establish you – Both Jews and Gentiles. According to my gospel, and the preaching of Jesus Christ – That is, according to the tenor of the gospel of Jesus Christ, which I preach. According to the Revelation of the mystery – Of the calling of the Gentiles, which, as plainly as it was foretold in the Prophets, was still hid from many even of the believing Jews.

26. According to the commandment – The foundation of the apostolic office. Of the eternal God – A more proper epithet could not be. A new dispensation infers no change in God. Known unto him are all his works, and every variation of them, from eternity. Made known to all nations – Not barely that they might know, but enjoy it also, through obeying the faith.

27. To the only wise God – Whose manifold wisdom is known in the church through the gospel, Eph. iii, 10. "To him who is able," and, "to the wise God," are joined, as 1 Cor. i, 24, where Christ is styled "the wisdom of God," and "the power of God." To him be glory through Christ Jesus for ever – And let every believer say, Amen!

MATTHEW HENRY

CHARLES H. SPURGEON

But they serve their carnal, sensual, worldly interests. They corrupt the head by deceiving the heart; perverting the judgments by winding themselves into the affections. We have great need to keep our hearts with all diligence. It has been the common policy of seducers to set upon those who are softened by convictions. A pliable temper is good when under good guidance, otherwise it may be easily led astray. Be so wise as not to be deceived, yet so simple as not to be deceivers. The blessing the apostle expects from God, is victory over Satan. This includes all designs and devices of Satan against souls, to defile, disturb, and destroy them; all his attempts to keep us from the peace of heaven here, and the possession of heaven hereafter. When Satan seems to prevail, and we are ready to give up all as lost, then will the God of peace interpose in our behalf. Hold out therefore, faith and patience, yet a little while. If the grace of Christ be with us, who can prevail against us?

21-24 The apostle adds affectionate remembrances from persons with him, known to the Roman Christians. It is a great comfort to see the holiness and usefulness of our kindred. Not many mighty, not many noble are called, but some are. It is lawful for believers to bear civil offices; and it were to be wished that all offices in Christian states, and in the church, were bestowed upon prudent and steady Christians.

25-27 That which establishes souls, is, the plain preaching of Jesus Christ. Our redemption and salvation by our Lord Jesus Christ, are, without controversy, a great mystery of godliness. And yet, blessed be God, there is as much of this mystery made plain as will bring us to heaven, if we do not willfully neglect so great salvation. Life and immortality are brought to light by the gospel, and the Sun of Righteousness is risen on the world. The Scriptures of the prophets, what they left in writing, is not only made plain in itself, but by it this mystery is made known to all nations. Christ is salvation to all nations. And the gospel is revealed, not to be talked of and disputed about, but to be submitted to. The obedience of faith is that obedience which is paid to the word of faith, and which comes by the grace of faith. All the glory that passes from fallen man to God, so as to be accepted of him, must go through the Lord Jesus, in whom alone our persons and doings are, or can be, pleasing to God. Of his righteousness we must make mention, even of his only; who, as he is the Mediator of all our prayers, so he is, and will be, to eternity, the Mediator of all our praises. Remembering that we are called to the obedience of faith, and that every degree of wisdom is from the only wise God, we should, by word and deed, render glory to him through Jesus Christ; that so the grace of our Lord Jesus Christ may be with us for ever.

you for being enemies to God by wicked works. When we beseech you to be reconciled to him, it is because we know you will never be in your proper place until you are reconciled. God has made you; can it be right that you should disobey him? God feeds you every day: can it be right that you should still live in disobedience to him? Remember, when the heavens shall be on a blaze, when Christ shall come to judge the earth in righteousness and his people with equity, there will not be one excuse that you can make which will be valid at the last great day. If you should attempt to say, "Lord, I have never heard the word;" his answer would be, "Thou didst hear it; thou heardest it plainly." "But Lord, I had an evil will." "Out of thine own mouth will I condemn thee; thou hadst that evil will, and I condemn thee for it. This is the condemnation, that light is come into the world, and men love darkness rather than light, because their deeds are evil." "But Lord," some will say, "I was not predestinated." "What hadst thou to do with that? Thou didst do according to thine own will when thou didst rebel. Thou wouldest not come unto me, and now I destroy thee for ever. Thou hast broken my law—on thine own head be the guilt." If a sinner could say at the great day, "Lord, I could not be saved" anyhow his torment in hell would be mitigated by that thought: but this shall be the very edge of the sword, and the very burning of the fire "Ye knew your duty and ye did it not: ye trampled on everything that was holy; ye neglected the Savior, and how shall ye escape if ye neglect so great salvation?"

Now, with regard to myself; you may some of you go away and say, that I was Antinomian in the first part of the sermon and Arminian at the end. I care not. I beg of you to search the Bible for yourselves. To the law and to the testimony; if I speak not according to this Word, it is because there is no light in me. I am willing to come to that test. Have nothing to do with me where I have nothing to do with Christ. Where I separate from the truth, cast my words away. But if what I say be God's teaching, I charge you, by him that sent me, give these things your thoughts, and turn unto the Lord with all your hearts.

1 Corinthians

1 CORINTHIANS 1

1 Paul, called to be an apostle of Jesus Christ through the will of God, and Sosthenes our brother,

2 Unto the church of God which is at Corinth, to them that are sanctified in Christ Jesus, called to be saints, with all that in every place call upon the name of Jesus Christ our Lord, both theirs and ours:

3 Grace be unto you, and peace, from God our Father, and from the Lord Jesus Christ.

4 I thank my God always on your behalf, for the grace of God which is given you by Jesus Christ;

5 That in every thing ye are enriched by him, in all utterance, and in all knowledge;

6 Even as the testimony of Christ was confirmed in you:

7 So that ye come behind in no gift; waiting for the coming of our Lord Jesus Christ:

8 Who shall also confirm you unto the end, that ye may be blameless in the day of our Lord Jesus Christ.

9 God is faithful, by whom ye were called unto the fellowship of his Son Jesus Christ our Lord.

10 Now I beseech you, brethren, by the name of our Lord Jesus Christ, that ye all speak the same thing, and that there be no divisions among you; but that ye be perfectly joined together in the same mind and in the same judgment.

11 For it hath been declared unto me of you, my brethren, by them which are of the house of Chloe, that there are contentions among you.

12 Now this I say, that every one of you saith, I am of Paul; and I of Apollos; and I of Cephas; and I of Christ.

13 Is Christ divided? was Paul crucified for you? or were ye baptized in the name of Paul?

14 I thank God that I baptized none of you, but Crispus and Gaius;

15 Lest any should say that I had baptized in mine own name.

16 And I baptized also the household of Stephanas: besides, I know not whether I baptized any other.

17 For Christ sent me not to baptize, but to preach the

CORINTH was a city of Achaia, situate on the isthmus which joins Peloponnesus, now called the Morea, to the rest of Greece. Being so advantageously situated for trade, the inhabitants of it abounded in riches, which, by too natural a consequence, led them into luxury, lewdness, and all manner of vice. Yet even here St. Paul planted a numerous church, chiefly of heathen converts; to whom, about three years after he had left Corinth, he wrote this epistle from Ephesus; as well to correct various disorders of which they were guilty, as to answer some questions which they had proposed to him.

1 CORINTHIANS 1

1. Paul, called to be an apostle – There is great propriety in every clause of the salutation, particularly in this, as there were some in the church of Corinth who called the authority of his mission in question. Through the will of God – Called "the commandment of God," 1 Tim. i, 1. This was to the churches the ground of his authority; to Paul himself, of an humble and ready mind. By the mention of God, the authority of man is excluded, Gal. i, 1; by the mention of the will of God, the merit of Paul, chap. xv, 8, &c. And Sosthenes – A Corinthian, St. Paul's companion in travel. It was both humility and prudence in the apostle, thus to join his name with his own, in an epistle wherein he was to reprove so many irregularities. Sosthenes the brother – Probably this word is emphatic; as if he had said, Who, from a Jewish opposer of the gospel, became a faithful brother.

2. To the church of God which is in Corinth – St. Paul, writing in a familiar manner to the Corinthians, as also to the Thessalonians and Galatians, uses this plain appellation. To the other churches he uses a more solemn address. Sanctified through Jesus Christ – And so undoubtedly they were in general, notwithstanding some exceptions. Called – Of Jesus Christ, Rom. i, 6. And – As the fruit of that calling made holy. With all that in every place – Nothing could better suit that catholic love which St. Paul labors to promote in this epistle, than such a declaration of his good wishes for every true Christian upon earth. Call upon the name of our Lord Jesus Christ – This plainly implies that all Christians pray to Christ, as well as to the Father through him.

4. Always – Whenever I mention you to God in prayer.

5. In all utterance and knowledge – Of divine things. These gifts the Corinthians particularly admired. Therefore this congratulation naturally tended to soften their spirits, and make way for the reproofs which follow.

6. The testimony of Christ – The gospel. Was confirmed among you – By these gifts attending it. They knew they had received these by the hand of Paul: and this consideration was highly proper, to revive in them their former reverence and affection for their spiritual father.

7. Waiting – With earnest desire. For the glorious Revelation of our Lord Jesus Christ – A sure mark of a true or false Christian, to long for, or dread, this Revelation.

8. Who will also – if you faithfully apply to him. Confirm you to the end – In the day of Christ – Now it is our day, wherein we are to work out our salvation; then it will be eminently the day of Christ, and of his glory in the saints.

9. God is faithful – To all his promises; and therefore "to him that hath shall be given." By whom ye are called – A pledge of his willingness to save you unto the uttermost.

10. Now I exhort you – Ye have faith and hope; secure love also. By the endearing name of our Lord Jesus Christ – infinitely preferable to all the human names in which ye glory. That ye all speak the same thing – They now spoke different things, ver. 12 .And that there be no schisms among you – No alienation of affection from each other. Is this word ever taken in any other sense in scripture? But that ye be joined in the same mind – Affections, desires. And judgment –

The Corinthian church contained some Jews, but more Gentiles, and the apostle had to contend with the superstition of the one, and the sinful conduct of the other. The peace of this church was disturbed by false teachers, who undermined the influence of the apostle. Two parties were the result; one contending earnestly for the Jewish ceremonies, the other indulging in excesses contrary to the gospel, to which they were especially led by the luxury and the sins which prevailed around them. This epistle was written to rebuke some disorderly conduct, of which the apostle had been apprized, and to give advice as to some points whereon his judgment was requested by the Corinthians. Thus the scope was twofold. 1. To apply suitable remedies to the disorders and abuses which prevailed among them. 2. To give satisfactory answers on all the points upon which his advice had been desired. The address, and Christian mildness, yet firmness, with which the apostle writes, and goes on from general truths directly to oppose the errors and evil conduct of the Corinthians, is very remarkable. He states the truth and the will of God, as to various matters, with great force of argument and animation of style.

1 CORINTHIANS 1

A salutation and thanksgiving. (1-9)
Exhortation to brotherly love, and reproof for divisions. (10-16)
The doctrine of a crucified Savior, as advancing the glory of God. (17-25)
And humbling the creature before him. (26-31)

1-9 All Christians are by baptism dedicated and devoted to Christ, and are under strict obligations to be holy. But in the true church of God are all who are sanctified in Christ Jesus, called to be saints, and who call upon him as God manifest in the flesh, for all the blessings of salvation; who acknowledge and obey him as their Lord, and as Lord of all; it includes no other persons. Christians are distinguished from the profane and atheists, that they dare not live without prayer; and they are distinguished from Jews and pagans, that they call on the name of Christ. Observe how often in these verses the apostle repeats the words, Our Lord Jesus Christ. He feared not to make too frequent or too honorable mention of him. To all who called upon Christ, the apostle gave his usual salutation, desiring, in their behalf, the pardoning mercy, sanctifying grace, and comforting peace of God, through Jesus Christ. Sinners can have no peace with God, nor any from him, but through Christ. He gives thanks for their conversion to the faith of Christ; that grace was given them by Jesus Christ. They had been enriched by him with all spiritual gifts. He speaks of utterance and knowledge. And

HEAVEN
Sermon number 56 delivered on December 16th, 1855, at New Park Street Chapel, Southwark.

"As it is written, Eye hath not seen, nor ear heard, neither have entered into the heart of man, the things which God hath prepared for them that love him. But God hath revealed them unto us by his Spirit; for the Spirit searcheth all things, yea, the deep things of God."—1 Corinthians 2:9-10.

First of all, we think a Christian gets a gaze of what heaven is, when in the midst of trials and troubles he is able to cast all his care upon the Lord, because he careth for him. When waves of distress, and billows of affliction pass over the Christian, there are times when his faith is so strong that he lies down and sleeps, though the hurricane is thundering in his ears, and though billows are rocking him like a child in its cradle, though the earth is removed, and the mountains are carried into the midst of the sea, he says, "God is our refuge and strength, a very present help in trouble." Famine and desolation come; but he says, "Though the fig tree shall not blossom, neither shall there be fruit on the vine, though the labor of the olive shall fail, and the field shall yield no increase, yet will I trust in the Lord, and stay myself on the God of Jacob." Affliction smites him to the ground; he looks up, and says, "Though he slay me, yet will I trust in him." The blows that are given to him are like the lashing of a whip upon the water, covered up immediately, and he seems to feel nothing. It is not stoicism; it is the peculiar sleep of the beloved. "So he giveth his beloved sleep." Persecution surrounds him; but he is unmoved. Heaven is something like that—a place of holy calm and trust—

"That holy calm, that sweet repose,
Which none but he who feels it knows.
This heavenly calm within the breast
Is the dear pledge of glorious rest,
Which for the church of God remains,
The end of cares, the end of pains."

But there is another season in which the Christian has heaven revealed to him; and that is, the season of quiet contemplation. There are precious hours, blessed be God, when we forget the world—times and seasons when we get quite away from it, when our weary spirit wings its way far, far, from scenes of toil and strife. There are precious moments when the angel of contemplation gives us a vision. He comes and puts his finger on the lip of the noisy world; he bids the wheels that are continually rattling in our ears be still; and we sit down, and there is a solemn silence of the mind. We find our heaven and our God; we engage ourselves in contemplating the glories of Jesus, or mounting upwards towards the bliss of heaven—in going backward to the great secrets of electing love, in considering the

gospel: not with wisdom of words, lest the cross of Christ should be made of none effect.

18 For the preaching of the cross is to them that perish foolishness; but unto us which are saved it is the power of God.

19 For it is written, I will destroy the wisdom of the wise, and will bring to nothing the understanding of the prudent.

20 Where is the wise? where is the scribe? where is the disputer of this world? hath not God made foolish the wisdom of this world?

21 For after that in the wisdom of God the world by wisdom knew not God, it pleased God by the foolishness of preaching to save them that believe.

22 For the Jews require a sign, and the Greeks seek after wisdom:

23 But we preach Christ crucified, unto the Jews a stumblingblock, and unto the Greeks foolishness;

24 But unto them which are called, both Jews and Greeks, Christ the power of God, and the wisdom of God.

25 Because the foolishness of God is wiser than men; and the weakness of God is stronger than men.

26 For ye see your calling, brethren, how that not many wise men after the flesh, not many mighty, not many noble, are called:

27 But God hath chosen the foolish things of the world to confound the wise; and God hath chosen the weak things of the world to confound the things which are mighty;

28 And base things of the world, and things which are despised, hath God chosen, yea, and things which are not, to bring to nought things that are:

29 That no flesh should glory in his presence.

30 But of him are ye in Christ Jesus, who of God is made unto us wisdom, and righteousness, and sanctification, and redemption:

31

That, according as it is written, He that glorieth, let him glory in the Lord.

Touching all the grand truths of the gospel.

11. It hath been declared to me by them of the family of Chloe – Whom some suppose to have been the wife of Stephanas, and the mother of Fortunatus and Achaicus. By these three the Corinthians had sent their letter to St. Paul, chap. xvi, 17. That there are contentions – A word equivalent with schisms in the preceding verse.

12. Now this I say – That is, what I mean is this: there are various parties among you, who set themselves, one against an other, in behalf of the several teachers they admire. And I of Christ – They spoke well, if they had not on this pretense despised their teachers, chap. iv, 8 .Perhaps they valued themselves on having heard Christ preach in his own person.

13. Is Christ divided – Are not all the members still under one head? Was not he alone crucified for you all; and were ye not all baptized in his name? The glory of Christ then is not to be divided between him and his servants; neither is the unity of the body to be torn asunder, seeing Christ is one still.

14. I thank God – (A pious phrase for the common one, "I rejoice,") that, in the course of his providence, I baptized none of you, but Crispus, once the ruler of the synagogue, and Caius.

15. Lest any should say that I had baptized in my own name – In order to attach them to myself.

16. I know not – That is, it does not at present occur to my memory, that I baptized any other.

17. For God did not send me to baptize – That was not my chief errand: those of inferior rank and abilities could do it: though all the apostles were sent to baptize also, Matt. xxviii, 19. But to preach the gospel – So the apostle slides into his general proposition: but not with wisdom of speech – With the artificial ornaments of discourse, invented by human wisdom. Lest the cross of Christ should be made of none effect – The whole effect of St. Paul's preaching was owing to the power of God accompanying the plain declaration of that great truth, "Christ bore our sins upon the cross." But this effect might have been imputed to another cause, had he come with that wisdom of speech which they admired.

18. To them that perish – By obstinately rejecting the only name whereby they can be saved. But to us who are saved – Now saved from our sins, and in the way to everlasting salvation, it is the great instrument of the power of God.

19. For it is written – And the words are remarkably applicable to this great event. Isaiah xxix, 14.

20. Where is the wise? &c. – The deliverance of Judea from Sennacherib is what Isaiah refers to in these words; in a bold and beautiful allusion to which, the apostle in the clause that follows triumphs over all the opposition of human wisdom to the victorious gospel of Christ. What could the wise men of the Gentiles do against this? or the Jewish scribes? or the disputers of this world? – Those among both, who, proud of their acuteness, were fond of controversy, and thought they could confute all opponents. Hath not God made foolish the wisdom of this world – That is, shown it to be very foolishness. Isaiah xxxiii, 18.

21. For since in the wisdom of God – According to his wise disposals, leaving them to make the trial. The world – Whether Jewish or Gentile, by all its boasted wisdom knew not God – Though the whole creation declared its Creator, and though he declared himself by all the prophets; it pleased God, by a way which those who perish count mere foolishness, to save them that believe.

22. For whereas the Jews demand of the apostles, as they did of their Lord, more signs still, after all they have seen already; and the Greeks, or Gentiles, seek wisdom – The depths of philosophy, and the charms of eloquence.

23. We go on to preach, in a plain and historical, not rhetorical or philosophical, manner, Christ crucified, to the Jews a stumbling block – Just opposite to the "signs" they demand. And to the Greeks foolishness – A silly tale, just oppo-

where God has given these two gifts, he has given great power for usefulness. These were gifts of the Holy Ghost, by which God bore witness to the apostles. Those that wait for the coming of our Lord Jesus Christ, will be kept by him to the end; and those that are so, will be blameless in the day of Christ, made so by rich and free grace. How glorious are the hopes of such a privilege; to be kept by the power of Christ, from the power of our corruptions and Satan's temptations!

10-16 In the great things of religion be of one mind; and where there is not unity of sentiment, still let there be union of affection. Agreement in the greater things should extinguish divisions about the lesser. There will be perfect union in heaven, and the nearer we approach it on earth, the nearer we come to perfection. Paul and Apollos both were faithful ministers of Jesus Christ, and helpers of their faith and joy; but those disposed to be contentious, broke into parties. So liable are the best things to be corrupted, and the gospel and its institutions made engines of discord and contention. Satan has always endeavored to stir up strife among Christians, as one of his chief devices against the gospel. The apostle left it to other ministers to baptize, while he preached the gospel, as a more useful work.

17-25 Paul had been bred up in Jewish learning; but the plain preaching of a crucified Jesus, was more powerful than all the oratory and philosophy of the heathen world. This is the sum and substance of the gospel. Christ crucified is the foundation of all our hopes, the fountain of all our joys. And by his death we live. The preaching of salvation for lost sinners by the sufferings and death of the Son of God, if explained and faithfully applied, appears foolishness to those in the way to destruction. The sensual, the covetous, the proud, and ambitious, alike see that the gospel opposes their favorite pursuits. But those who receive the gospel, and are enlightened by the Spirit of God, see more of God's wisdom and power in the doctrine of Christ crucified, than in all his other works. God left a great part of the world to follow the dictates of man's boasted reason, and the event has shown that human wisdom is folly, and is unable to find or retain the knowledge of God as the Creator. It pleased him, by the foolishness of preaching, to save them that believe. By the foolishness of preaching; not by what could justly be called foolish preaching. But the thing preached was foolishness to wise-wise men. The gospel ever was, and ever will be, foolishness to all in the road to destruction. The message of Christ, plainly delivered, ever has been a sure touchstone by which men may learn what road they are traveling. But the despised doctrine of salvation by faith

immutability of the blessed covenant, in thinking of that wind which "bloweth where it listeth," in remembering our own participation of that life which cometh from God, in thinking of our blood-bought union with the Lamb, of the consummation of our marriage with him in realms of light and bliss, or any such kindred topics. Then it is that we know a little about heaven. Have ye never found, O ye sons and daughters of gaiety, a holy calm come over you at times, in reading the thoughts of your fellowmen? But oh! how blessed to come and read the thoughts of God, and work, and weave them out in contemplation. Then we have a web of contemplation that we wrap around us like an enchanted garment, and we open our eyes and see heaven. Christian! when you are enabled by the Spirit to hold a season of sweet contemplation, then you can say—"But he hath revealed them unto us by his Spirit;" for the joys of heaven are akin to the joys of contemplation, and the joys of a holy calm in God. But there are times with me—I dare say there may be with some of you—when we do something more than contemplate—when we arise by meditation above thought itself, and when our soul, after having touched the Pisgah of contemplation by the way, flies positively into the heavenly places in Christ Jesus. There are seasons when the Spirit not only stands and flaps his wings o'er the gulf, but positively crosses the Jordan and dwells with Christ, holds fellowship with angels, and talks with spirits—gets up there with Jesus, clasps him in his arms, and cries, "My beloved is mine, and I am his; I will hold him, and will not let him go." I know what it is at times to lay my beating head on the bosom of Christ with something more than faith—actually and positively to get hold of him; not only to take him by faith, but actually and positively to feed on him; to feel a vital union with him, to grasp his arm, and feel his very pulse beating. You say. "Tell it not to unbelievers; they will laugh!" Laugh ye may; but when we are there we care not for your laughter, if ye should laugh as loud as devils; for one moment's fellowship with Jesus would recompense us for it all. Picture not fairy lands; this is heaven, this is bliss. "He hath revealed it unto us by his Spirit."

And let not the Christian, who says he has very little of this enjoyment be discouraged. Do not think you cannot have heaven revealed to you by the Spirit; I tell you, you can, if you are one of the Lord's people. And let me tell some of you, that one of the places where you may most of all expect to see heaven is at the Lord's Table. There are some of you, my dearly beloved, who absent yourselves from the supper of the Lord on earth; let me tell you in God's name, that you are not only sinning against God, but robbing yourselves of a most inestimable privilege. If there is one season in which the soul gets into closer communion with Christ than

1 CORINTHIANS 2

1 And I, brethren, when I came to you, came not with excellency of speech or of wisdom, declaring unto you the testimony of God.

2 For I determined not to know any thing among you, save Jesus Christ, and him crucified.

3 And I was with you in weakness, and in fear, and in much trembling.

4 And my speech and my preaching was not with enticing words of man's wisdom, but in demonstration of the Spirit and of power:

5 That your faith should not stand in the wisdom of men, but in the power of God.

6 Howbeit we speak wisdom among them that are perfect: yet not the wisdom of this world, nor of the princes of this world, that come to nought:

7 But we speak the wisdom of God in a mystery, even the hidden wisdom, which God ordained before the world unto our glory:

8 Which none of the princes of this world knew: for had they known it, they would not have crucified the Lord of glory.

9 But as it is written, Eye hath not seen, nor ear heard, neither have entered into the heart of man, the things which God hath prepared for them that love him.

10 But God hath revealed them unto us by his Spirit: for the Spirit searcheth all things, yea, the deep things of God.

11 For what man knoweth the things of a man, save the spirit of man which is in him? even so the things of God knoweth no man, but the Spirit of God.

12 Now we have received, not the spirit of the world, but the spirit which is of God; that we might know the things that are freely given to us of God.

13 Which things also we speak, not in the words which man's wisdom teacheth, but which the Holy Ghost teacheth; comparing spiritual things with spiritual.

14 But the natural man receiveth not the things of the Spirit of God: for they are foolishness unto him: neither can he know them, because they are spiritually discerned.

site to the wisdom they seek.

24. But to them that are called – And obey the heavenly calling. Christ – With his cross, his death, his life, his kingdom. And they experience, first, that he is the power, then, that he is the wisdom, of God.

25. Because the foolishness of God – The gospel scheme, which the world judge to be mere foolishness, is wiser than the wisdom of men; and, weak as they account it, stronger than all the strength of men.

26. Behold your calling – What manner of men they are whom God calls. That not many wise men after the flesh – In the account of the world. Not many mighty – Men of power and authority.

28. Things that are not – The Jews frequently called the Gentiles, "Them that are not," 2 Esdras vi, 56, 57. In so supreme contempt did they hold them. The things that are – In high esteem.

29. That no flesh – A fit appellation. Flesh is fair, but withering as grass. May glory before God – In God we ought to glory.

30. Of him – Out of his free grace and mercy. Are ye engrafted into Christ Jesus, who is made unto us that believe wisdom, who were before utterly foolish and ignorant. Righteousness – The sole ground of our justification, who were before under the wrath and curse of God. Sanctification – A principle of universal holiness, whereas before we were altogether dead in sin. And redemption – That is, complete deliverance from all evil, and eternal bliss both of soul and body.

31. Let him glory in the Lord – Not in himself, not in the flesh, not in the world. Jer. ix, 23, 24.

1 CORINTHIANS 2

1. And I accordingly came to you, not with loftiness of speech or of wisdom – I did not affect either deep wisdom or eloquence. Declaring the testimony of God – What God gave me to testify concerning his Son.

2. I determined not to know anything – To wave all my other knowledge, and not to preach anything, save Jesus Christ, and him crucified – That is, what he did, suffered, taught. A part is put for the whole.

3. And I was with you – At my first entrance. In weakness – Of body, 2 Cor. xii, 7. And in fear – Lest I should offend any. And in much trembling – The emotion of my mind affecting my very body.

4. And my speech in private, as well as my public preaching, was not with the persuasive words of human wisdom, such as the wise men of the world use; but with the demonstration of the Spirit and of power – With that powerful kind of demonstration, which flows from the Holy Spirit; which works on the conscience with the most convincing light, and the most persuasive evidence.

5. That your faith might not be built on the wisdom or power of man, but on the wisdom and power of God.

6. Yet we speak wisdom – Yea, the truest and most excellent wisdom. Among the perfect – Adult, experienced Christians. By wisdom here he seems to mean, not the whole Christian doctrine, but the most sublime and abstruse parts of it. But not the wisdom admired and taught by the men of this world, nor of the rulers of this world, Jewish or heathen, that come to nought – Both they and their wisdom, and the world itself.

7. But we speak the mysterious wisdom of God, which was hidden for many ages from all the world, and is still hidden even from "babes in Christ;" much more from all unbelievers. Which God ordained before the world – So far is this from coming to nought, like worldly wisdom. For our glory – Arising from the glory of our Lord, and then to be revealed when all worldly glory vanishes.

8. Had they known it – That wisdom. They would not have crucified – Punished as a slave. The Lord of glory – The giving Christ this august title, peculiar to the great Jehovah, plainly shows him to be the supreme God. In like

in a crucified Savior, God in human nature, purchasing the church with his own blood, to save multitudes, even all that believe, from ignorance, delusion, and vice, has been blessed in every age. And the weakest instruments God uses, are stronger in their effects, than the strongest men can use. Not that there is foolishness or weakness in God, but what men consider as such, overcomes all their admired wisdom and strength.

26-31 God did not choose philosophers, nor orators, nor statesmen, nor men of wealth, and power, and interest in the world, to publish the gospel of grace and peace. He best judges what men and what measures serve the purposes of his glory. Though not many noble are usually called by Divine grace, there have been some such in every age, who have not been ashamed of the gospel of Christ; and persons of every rank stand in need of pardoning grace. Often, a humble Christian, though poor as to this world, has more true knowledge of the gospel, than those who have made the letter of Scripture the study of their lives, but who have studied it rather as the witness of men, than as the word of God. And even young children have gained such knowledge of Divine truth as to silence infidels. The reason is, they are taught of God; the design is, that no flesh should glory in his presence. That distinction, in which alone they might glory, was not of themselves. It was by the sovereign choice and regenerating grace of God, that they were in Jesus Christ by faith. He is made of God to us wisdom, righteousness, sanctification, and redemption; all we need, or can desire. And he is made wisdom to us, that by his word and Spirit, and from his fullness and treasures of wisdom and knowledge, we may receive all that will make us wise unto salvation, and fit for every service to which we are called. We are guilty, liable to just punishment; and he is made righteousness, our great atonement and sacrifice. We are depraved and corrupt, and he is made sanctification, that he may in the end be made complete redemption; may free the soul from the being of sin, and loose the body from the bonds of the grave. And this is, that all flesh, according to the prophecy by Jeremiah, Jer 9:23-24, may glory in the special favor, all-sufficient grace, and precious salvation of Jehovah.

1 CORINTHIANS 2

The plain manner in which the apostle preached Christ crucified. (1-5)
The wisdom contained in this doctrine. (6-9)
It cannot be duly known but by the Holy Spirit. (10-16)

1-5 Christ, in his person, and offices, and suffer-

another, it is at the Lord's Table.

O my erring brethren, ye who live on, unbaptized, and who receive not this sacred supper, I tell you not that they will save you—most assuredly they will not, and if you are not saved before you receive them they will be an injury to you;—but if you are the Lord's people, why need you stay away? I tell you, the Lord's Table is so high a place that you can see heaven from it very often. You get so near the cross there, you breathe so near the cross, that your sight becomes clearer, and the air brighter, and you see more of heaven there than anywhere else. Christian, do not neglect the supper of thy Lord; for if thou dost, he will hide heaven from thee, in a measure.

Again, how sweetly do we realize heaven, when we assemble in our meetings for prayer. I do not know how my brethren feel at prayer meetings; but they are so much akin to what heaven is, as a place of devotion, that I really think we get more ideas of heaven by the Spirit there, than in hearing a sermon preached, because the sermon necessarily appeals somewhat to the intellect and the imagination. But if we enter into the vitality of prayer at our prayer meetings, then it is the Spirit that reveals heaven to us. I remember two texts that I preached from lately at our Monday evening meeting, which were very sweet to some of our souls. "Abide with us, for the day is far spent," and another, "By night on my bed I sought him whom my soul loveth: I sought him and found him." Then indeed we held some foretaste of heaven. Master Thomas would not believe that his Lord was risen. Why? Because he was not at the last prayer-meeting; for we are told that Thomas was not there. And those who are often away from devotional meetings are very apt to have doubting frames; they do not get sights of heaven, for they get their eye-sight spoiled by stopping away.

Another time when we get sights of heaven is in extraordinary closet seasons. Ordinary closet prayer will only make ordinary Christians of us. It is in extraordinary seasons, when we are led by God to devote, say an hour, to earnest prayer—when we feel an impulse, we scarce know why, to cut off a portion of our time during the day to go alone. Then, beloved, we kneel down, and begin to pray in earnest. It may be that we are attacked by the devil; for when the enemy knows we are going to have a great blessing, he always makes a great noise to drive us away; but if we keep at it, we shall soon get into a quiet frame of mind, and hear him roaring at a distance.

Go away and say these things; but be it known unto you, that what ye style madness is to us wisdom and what ye count folly "is the wisdom of God in a mystery, even the hidden wisdom." And if there is a poor penitent here this morning, saying, "Ah! sir, I get visions enough of hell, but I do not

15 But he that is spiritual judgeth all things, yet he himself is judged of no man.

16 For who hath known the mind of the Lord, that he may instruct him? But we have the mind of Christ.

1 CORINTHIANS 3

1 And I, brethren, could not speak unto you as unto spiritual, but as unto carnal, even as unto babes in Christ.

2 I have fed you with milk, and not with meat: for hitherto ye were not able to bear it, neither yet now are ye able.

3 For ye are yet carnal: for whereas there is among you envying, and strife, and divisions, are ye not carnal, and walk as men?

4 For while one saith, I am of Paul; and another, I am of Apollos; are ye not carnal?

5 Who then is Paul, and who is Apollos, but ministers by whom ye believed, even as the Lord gave to every man?

6 I have planted, Apollos watered; but God gave the increase.

7 So then neither is he that planteth any thing, neither he that watereth; but God that giveth the increase.

8 Now he that planteth and he that watereth are one: and every man shall receive his own reward according to his own labor.

9 For we are laborers together with God: ye are God's husbandry, ye are God's building.

10 According to the grace of God which is given unto me, as a wise masterbuilder, I have laid the foundation, and another buildeth thereon. But let every man take heed how he buildeth thereupon.

11 For other foundation can no man lay than that is laid, which is Jesus Christ.

12 Now if any man build upon this foundation gold, silver, precious stones, wood, hay, stubble;

13 Every man's work shall be made manifest: for the day shall declare it, because it shall be revealed by fire; and the fire shall try every man's work of what sort it is.

manner the Father is styled, "the Father of glory," Eph. i, 17; and the Holy Ghost, "the Spirit of glory," 1 Pet. iv, 14. The application of this title to all the three, shows that the Father, Son, and Holy Ghost are "the God of glory;" as the only true God is called, Psalm xxix, 3, and Acts vii, 2.

9. But this ignorance of theirs fulfills what is written concerning the blessings of the Messiah's kingdom. No natural man hath either seen, heard, or known, the things which God hath prepared, saith the prophet, for them that love him. Isaiah lxiv, 4.

10. But God hath revealed – Yea, and "freely given," ver. 12. Them to us – Even inconceivable peace, and joy unspeakable. By his Spirit – Who intimately and fully knows them. For the Spirit searcheth even the deep things of God – Be they ever so hidden and mysterious; the depths both of his nature and his kingdom.

11. For what man knoweth the things of a man – All the inmost recesses of his mind; although men are all of one nature, and so may the more easily know one another. So the things of God knoweth no one but the Spirit – Who, consequently, is God.

12. Now we have received, not the spirit of the world – This spirit is not properly received; for the men of the world always had it. But Christians receive the Spirit of God, which before they had not.

13. Which also we speak – As well as know. In words taught by the Holy Spirit – Such are all the words of scripture. How high a regard ought we, then, to retain for them! Explaining spiritual things by spiritual words; or, adapting spiritual words to spiritual things – Being taught of the Spirit to express the things of the Spirit.

14. But the natural man – That is, every man who hath not the Spirit; who has no other way of obtaining knowledge, but by his senses and natural understanding. Receiveth not – Does not understand or conceive. The things of the Spirit – The things revealed by the Spirit of God, whether relating to his nature or his kingdom. For they are foolishness to him – He is so far from understanding, that he utterly despises, them. Neither can he know them – As he has not the will, so neither has he the power. Because they are spiritually discerned – They can only be discerned by the aid of that Spirit, and by those spiritual senses, which he has not.

15. But the spiritual man – He that hath the Spirit. Discerneth all the things of God whereof we have been speaking. Yet he himself is discerned by no man – No natural men. They neither understand what he is, nor what he says.

16. Who – What natural man. We – Spiritual men; apostles in particular. Have – Know, understand. The mind of Christ – Concerning the whole plan of gospel salvation. Isaiah xl, 13.

1 CORINTHIANS 3

1. And I, brethren – He spoke before, ver. 1, of his entrance, now of his progress, among them. Could not speak to you as unto spiritual – Adult, experienced Christians. But as unto men who were still in great measure carnal, as unto babes in Christ – Still weak in grace, though eminent in gifts, chap. i, 5.

2. I fed you, as babes, with milk – The first and plainest truths of the gospel. So should every preacher suit his doctrine to his hearers.

3. For while there is among you emulation in your hearts, strife in your words, and actual divisions, are ye not carnal, and walk according to men – As mere men; not as Christians, according to God.

4. I am of Apollos – St. Paul named himself and Apollos, to show that he would condemn any division among them, even though it were in favor of himself, or the dearest friend he had in the world. Are ye not carnal – For the Spirit of God allows no party zeal.

MATTHEW HENRY

CHARLES H. SPURGEON

ings, is the sum and substance of the gospel, and ought to be the great subject of a gospel minister's preaching, but not so as to leave out other parts of God's revealed truth and will. Paul preached the whole counsel of God. Few know the fear and trembling of faithful ministers, from a deep sense of their own weakness. They know how insufficient they are, and are fearful for themselves. When nothing but Christ crucified is plainly preached, the success must be entirely from Divine power accompanying the word, and thus men are brought to believe, to the salvation of their souls.

6-9 Those who receive the doctrine of Christ as Divine, and, having been enlightened by the Holy Spirit, have looked well into it, see not only the plain history of Christ, and him crucified, but the deep and admirable designs of Divine wisdom therein. It is the mystery made manifest to the saints, Col 1:26, though formerly hid from the heathen world; it was only shown in dark types and distant prophecies, but now is revealed and made known by the Spirit of God. Jesus Christ is the Lord of glory; a title much too great for any creature. There are many things which people would not do, if they knew the wisdom of God in the great work of redemption. There are things God hath prepared for those that love him, and wait for him, which sense cannot discover, no teaching can convey to our ears, nor can it yet enter our hearts. We must take them as they stand in the Scriptures, as God hath been pleased to reveal them to us.

10-16 God has revealed true wisdom to us by his Spirit. Here is a proof of the Divine authority of the Holy Scriptures, 2Pe 1:21. In proof of the Divinity of the Holy Ghost, observe, that he knows all things, and he searches all things, even the deep things of God. No one can know the things of God, but his Holy Spirit, who is one with the Father and the Son, and who makes known Divine mysteries to his church. This is most clear testimony, both to the real Godhead and the distinct person of the Holy Spirit. The apostles were not guided by worldly principles. They had the revelation of these things from the Spirit of God, and the saving impression of them from the same Spirit. These things they declared in plain, simple language, taught by the Holy Spirit, totally different from the affected oratory or enticing words of man's wisdom. The natural man, the wise man of the world, receives not the things of the Spirit of God. The pride of carnal reasoning is really as much opposed to spirituality, as the basest sensuality. The sanctified mind discerns the real beauties of holiness, but the power of discerning and judging about common and natural things is not lost. But

get visions of heaven;" poor penitent sinner, thou canst not have any visions of heaven, unless thou lookest through the hands of Christ. The only glass through which a poor sinner can see bliss is that formed by the holes in Jesus' hands. Dost thou not know, that all grace and mercy was put into the hand of Christ, and that it never could have run out to thee unless his hand had been bored through in crucifixion. He cannot hold it from thee, for it will run through; and he cannot hold it in his heart, for he has got a rent in it made by the spear. Go and confess your sin to him, and he will wash you, and make you whiter than snow. If you feel you cannot repent, go to him and tell him so, for he is exalted to give repentance, as well as remission of sins. Oh! that the spirit of God might give you true repentance and true faith; and then saint and sinner shall meet together, and both shall not only know what "eye hath not seen, nor ear heard."

PREACH THE GOSPEL
Sermon number 34 delivered on August 5, 1855, at New Park Street Chapel, Southwark.

"For though I preach the gospel, I have nothing to glory of; for necessity is laid upon me; yea woe is unto me, if I preach not the gospel."—1 Corinthians 9:16.

THE greatest man of Apostolic times was the apostle Paul. He was always great in everything. If you consider him as a sinner, he was exceeding sinful; if you regard him as a persecutor, he was exceeding mad against the Christians, and persecuted them even unto strange cities. If you take him as a convert, his conversion was the most notable one of which we read, worked by miraculous power, and by the direct voice of Jesus speaking from heaven— "Saul, Saul, why persecutest thou me?"—If we take him simply as a Christian, he was an extraordinary one, loving his Master more than others, and seeking more than others to exemplify the grace of God in his life. But if you take him as an apostle, and as a preacher of the Word, he stands out pre-eminent as the prince of preachers, and a preacher to kings—for he preached before Agrippa, he preached before Nero Cesar—he stood before emperors and kings for Christ's name's sake. It was the characteristic of Paul, that whatever he did, he did with all his heart. He was one of the men who could not allow one half of his frame to be exercised, while the other half was indolent but, when he set to work, the whole of his energies—every nerve, every sinew—were strained in the work to be done, be it bad work or be it good. Paul, therefore, could speak from experience concerning his ministry; because he was the chief of ministers. There is no nonsense in what he speaks; it is all

14 If any man's work abide which he hath built thereupon, he shall receive a reward.

15 If any man's work shall be burned, he shall suffer loss: but he himself shall be saved; yet so as by fire.

16 Know ye not that ye are the temple of God, and that the Spirit of God dwelleth in you?

17 If any man defile the temple of God, him shall God destroy; for the temple of God is holy, which temple ye are.

18 Let no man deceive himself. If any man among you seemeth to be wise in this world, let him become a fool, that he may be wise.

19 For the wisdom of this world is foolishness with God. For it is written, He taketh the wise in their own craftiness.

20 And again, The Lord knoweth the thoughts of the wise, that they are vain.

21 Therefore let no man glory in men. For all things are yours;

22 Whether Paul, or Apollos, or Cephas, or the world, or life, or death, or things present, or things to come; all are yours;

23 And ye are Christ's; and Christ is God's.

1 CORINTHIANS 4

1 Let a man so account of us, as of the ministers of Christ, and stewards of the mysteries of God.

2 Moreover it is required in stewards, that a man be found faithful.

3 But with me it is a very small thing that I should be judged of you, or of man's judgment: yea, I judge not mine own self.

4 For I know nothing by myself; yet am I not hereby justified: but he that judgeth me is the Lord.

5 Therefore judge nothing before the time, until the Lord come, who both will bring to light the hidden things of darkness, and will make manifest the counsels of the hearts: and then shall every man have praise of God.

6 And these things, brethren, I have in a figure transferred to myself and to Apollos for your sakes; that ye might learn in us not to think of men above that

5. Ministers – Or servants. By whom ye believed, as the Lord, the Master of those servants, gave to every man.

7. God that giveth the increase – Is all in all: without him neither planting nor watering avails.

8. But he that planteth and he that watereth are one – Which is another argument against division. Though their labors are different, they are all employed in one general work, – the saving souls. Hence he takes occasion to speak of the reward of them that labor faithfully, and the awful account to be given by all. Every man shall receive his own peculiar reward according to his own peculiar labor – Not according to his success; but he who labors much, though with small success, shall have a great reward. Has not all this reasoning the same force still? The ministers are still surely instruments in God's hand, and depend as entirely as ever on his blessing, to give the increase to their labors. Without this, they are nothing: with it, their part is so small, that they hardly deserve to be mentioned. May their hearts and hands be more united; and, retaining a due sense of the honor God doeth them in employing them, may they faithfully labor, not as for themselves, but for the great Proprietor of all, till the day come when he will reward them in full proportion to their fidelity and diligence!

9. For we are all – God's laborers, and fellow laborers with each other. Ye are God's husbandry – This is the sum of what went before: it is a comprehensive word, taking in both a field, a garden, and a vineyard. Ye are God's building – This is the sum of what follows.

10. According to the grace of God given to me – This he premises, lest he should seem to ascribe it to himself. Let every one take heed how he buildeth thereon – That all his doctrines may be consistent with the foundation.

11. For other foundation – On which the whole church: and all its doctrines, duties, and blessings may be built. Can no man lay than what is laid – In the counsels of divine wisdom, in the promises and prophecies of the Old Testament, in the preaching of the apostles, St. Paul in particular. Which is Jesus Christ – Who, in his person and offices, is the firm, immovable Rock of Ages, every way sufficient to bear all the weight that God himself, or the sinner, when he believes, can lay upon him.

12. If any one build gold, silver, costly stones – Three sorts of materials which will bear the fire; true and solid doctrines. Wood, hay, stubble – Three which will not bear the fire. Such are all doctrines, ceremonies, and forms of human invention; all but the substantial, vital truths of Christianity.

13. The time is coming when every one's work shall be made manifest: for the day of the Lord, that great and final day, shall declare it – To all the world. For it is revealed – What faith beholds as so certain and so near is spoken of as already present. By fire; yea, the fire shall try every one's work, of what sort it is – The strict process of that day will try every man's doctrines, whether they come up to the scripture standard or not. Here is a plain allusion to the flaming light and consuming heat of the general conflagration. But the expression, when applied to the trying of doctrines, and consuming those that are wrong, is evidently figurative; because no material fire can have such an effect on what is of a moral nature. And therefore it is added, he who builds wood, hay, or stubble, shall be saved as through the fire – Or, as narrowly as a man escapes through the fire, when his house is all in flames about him. This text, then, is so far from establishing the Romanish purgatory, that it utterly overthrows it. For the fire here mentioned does not exist till the day of judgment: therefore, if this be the fire of purgatory, it follows that purgatory does not exist before the day of judgment.

14. He shall receive a reward – A peculiar degree of glory. Some degree even the other will receive, seeing he held the foundation; though through ignorance he built thereon what would not abide the fire.

15. He shall suffer loss – The loss of that peculiar degree of glory.

the carnal man is a stranger to the principles, and pleasures, and acting of the Divine life. The spiritual man only, is the person to whom God gives the knowledge of his will. How little have any known of the mind of God by natural power! And the apostles were enabled by his Spirit to make known his mind. In the Holy Scriptures, the mind of Christ, and the mind of God in Christ, are fully made known to us. It is the great privilege of Christians, that they have the mind of Christ revealed to them by his Spirit. They experience his sanctifying power in their hearts, and bring forth good fruits in their lives.

1 CORINTHIANS 3

The Corinthians reproved for their contentions. (1-4)

The true servants of Christ can do nothing without him. (5-9)

He is the only foundation, and every one should take heed what he builds thereon. (10-15)

The churches of Christ ought to be kept pure, and to be humble. (16,17)

And they should not glory in men, because ministers and all things else are theirs through Christ. (18-23)

1-4 The most simple truths of the gospel, as to man's sinfulness and God's mercy, repentance towards God, and faith in our Lord Jesus Christ, stated in the plainest language, suit the people better than deeper mysteries. Men may have much doctrinal knowledge, yet be mere beginners in the life of faith and experience. Contentions and quarrels about religion are sad evidences of carnality. True religion makes men peaceable, not contentious. But it is to be lamented, that many who should walk as Christians, live and act too much like other men. Many professors, and preachers also, show themselves to be yet carnal, by vain-glorious strife, eagerness for dispute, and readiness to despise and speak evil of others.

5-9 The ministers about whom the Corinthians contended, were only instruments used by God. We should not put ministers into the place of God. He that planteth and he that watereth are one, employed by one Master, trusted with the same revelation, busied in one work, and engaged in one design. They have their different gifts from one and the same Spirit, for the very same purposes; and should carry on the same design heartily. Those who work hardest shall fare best. Those who are most faithful shall have the greatest reward. They work together with God, in promoting the purposes of his glory, and the salvation of

from the depth of his soul. And we may be sure that when he wrote this, he wrote it with a strong unpalsied hand—"Though I preach the gospel, I have nothing to glory of, for necessity is laid upon me, yea, woe is me if I preach not the gospel."

Now, these words of Paul, I trust, are applicable to many ministers in the present day; to all those who are especially called, who are directed by the inward impulse of the Holy Spirit to occupy the position of gospel ministers. In trying to consider this verse, we shall have three inquiries this morning:—First, What is it to preach the gospel? Secondly, Why is it that a minister has nothing to glorify of? And thirdly, What is that necessity and that woe, of which it is written, "Necessity is laid upon me, yea, woe is unto me, if I preach not the gospel?"

I. The first enquiry is, WHAT IS IT TO PREACH THE GOSPEL? There are a variety of opinions concerning this question, and possibly amongst my own audience—though I believe we are very uniform in our doctrinal sentiments—there might be found two or three very ready answers to this question: What is it to preach the gospel? I shall therefore attempt to answer it myself according to my own judgment, if God will help me; and if it does not happen to be the correct answer, you are at liberty to supply a better to yourselves at home.

1. The first answer I shall give to the question is this: To preach the gospel is to state every doctrine contained in God's Word, and to give every truth its proper prominence. Men may preach a part of the gospel; they may only preach one single doctrine of it; and I would not say that a man did not preach the gospel at all if he did but maintain the doctrine of justification by faith—"By grace are ye saved through faith." I should put him down for a gospel minister, but not for one who preached the whole gospel. No man can be said to preach the whole gospel of God if he leaves out, knowingly and intentionally, one single truth of the blessed God. This remark of mine must be a very cutting one, and ought to strike into the consciences of many who make it almost a matter of principle to keep back certain truths from the people, because they are afraid of them. In conversation, a week or two ago, with an eminent professor, he said to me, "Sir, we know that we ought not to preach the doctrine of election, because it is not calculated to convert sinners." "But," said I to him, "who is the man that dares to find fault with the truth of God? You admit, with me, that it is a truth, and yet you say it must not be preached. I dare not have said that thing. I should reckon it supreme arrogance to have ventured to say that a doctrine ought not to be preached when the all-wise God has seen fit to reveal it. Besides, is the whole gospel intended to convert sinners? There are some truths which God

which is written, that no one of you be puffed up for one against another.

7 For who maketh thee to differ from another? and what hast thou that thou didst not receive? now if thou didst receive it, why dost thou glory, as if thou hadst not received it?

8 Now ye are full, now ye are rich, ye have reigned as kings without us: and I would to God ye did reign, that we also might reign with you.

9 For I think that God hath set forth us the apostles last, as it were appointed to death: for we are made a spectacle unto the world, and to angels, and to men.

10 We are fools for Christ's sake, but ye are wise in Christ; we are weak, but ye are strong; ye are honorable, but we are despised.

11 Even unto this present hour we both hunger, and thirst, and are naked, and are buffeted, and have no certain dwellingplace;

12 And labor, working with our own hands: being reviled, we bless; being persecuted, we suffer it:

13 Being defamed, we intreat: we are made as the filth of the world, and are the offscouring of all things unto this day.

14 I write not these things to shame you, but as my beloved sons I warn you.

15 For though ye have ten thousand instructors in Christ, yet have ye not many fathers: for in Christ Jesus I have begotten you through the gospel.

16 Wherefore I beseech you, be ye followers of me.

17 For this cause have I sent unto you Timotheus, who is my beloved son, and faithful in the Lord, who shall bring you into remembrance of my ways which be in Christ, as I teach every where in every church.

18 Now some are puffed up, as though I would not come to you.

19 But I will come to you shortly, if the Lord will, and will know, not the speech of them which are puffed up, but the power.

20 For the kingdom of God is not in word, but in power.

21 What will ye? shall I come unto you with a rod, or in love, and in the spirit of meekness?

16. Ye – All Christians. Are the temple of God – The most noble kind of building, ver. 9.

17. If any man destroy the temple of God – Destroy a real Christian, by schisms, or doctrines fundamentally wrong. Him shall God destroy – He shall not be saved at all; not even as through the fire.

18. Let him become a fool in this world – Such as the world accounts so. That he may become wise – In God's account.

19. For all the boasted wisdom of the world is mere foolishness in the sight of God. He taketh the wise in their own craftiness – Not only while they think they are acting wisely, but by their very wisdom, which itself is their snare, and the occasion of their destruction. Job v, 13.

20. That they are but vain – Empty, foolish; they and all their thoughts. Psalm xciv, 11.

21. Therefore – Upon the whole. Let none glory in men – So as to divide into parties on their account. For all things are yours – and we in particular. We are not your lords, but rather your servants.

22. Whether Paul or Apollos, or Cephas – We are all equally yours, to serve you for Christ's sake. Or the world – This leap from Peter to the world greatly enlarges the thought, and argues a kind of impatience of enumerating the rest. Peter and every one in the whole world, however excellent in gifts, or grace, or office, are also your servants for Christ's sake. Or life, or death – These, with all their various circumstances, are disposed as will be most for your advantage. Or things present – On earth. Or things to come – In heaven. Contend, therefore, no more about these little things; but be ye united in love, as ye are in blessings.

23. And ye are Christ's – His property, his subjects. his members. And Christ is God's – As Mediator, he refers all his services to his Father's glory.

1 CORINTHIANS 4

1. Let a man account us, as servants of Christ – The original word properly signifies such servants as labored at the oar in rowing vessels; and, accordingly, intimates the pains which every faithful minister takes in his Lord's work. O God, where are these ministers to be found? Lord, thou knowest. And stewards of the mysteries of God – Dispenseth of the mysterious truths of the gospel.

3. Yea, I judge not myself – My final state is not to be determined by my own judgment.

4. I am not conscious to myself of anything evil; yet am I not hereby justified – I depend not on this, as a sufficient justification of myself in God's account. But he that judgeth me is the Lord – By his sentence I am to stand or fall.

5. Therefore judge nothing before the time – Appointed for judging all men. Until the Lord come, who, in order to pass a righteous judgment, which otherwise would be impossible, will both bring to light the things which are now covered with impenetrable darkness, and manifest the most secret springs of action, the principles and intentions of every heart. And then shall every one – Every faithful steward, have praise of God.

6. These things – Mentioned, chap. i, 10, &c. I have by a very obvious figure transferred to myself and Apollos – And Cephas, instead of naming those particular preachers at Corinth, to whom ye are so fondly attached. That ye may learn by us – From what has been said concerning us, who, however eminent we are, are mere instruments in God's hand. Not to think of any man above what is here written – Or above what scripture warrants. chap. iii, 7.

7. Who maketh thee to differ – Either in gifts or graces. As if thou hadst not received it – As if thou hadst it originally from thyself.

8. Now ye are full – The Corinthians abounded with spiritual gifts; and so did the apostles: but the apostles, by continual want and sufferings, were kept from self-complacency. The Corinthians suffering nothing, and having plenty of all

MATTHEW HENRY

CHARLES H. SPURGEON

precious souls; and he who knows their work, will take care they do not labor in vain. They are employed in his husbandry and building; and he will carefully look over them.

10-15 The apostle was a wise master-builder; but the grace of God made him such. Spiritual pride is abominable; it is using the greatest favors of God, to feed our own vanity, and make idols of ourselves. But let every man take heed; there may be bad building on a good foundation. Nothing must be laid upon it, but what the foundation will bear, and what is of a piece with it. Let us not dare to join a merely human or a carnal life with a Divine faith, the corruption of sin with the profession of Christianity. Christ is a firm, abiding, and immovable Rock of ages, every way able to bear all the weight that God himself or the sinner can lay upon him; neither is there salvation in any other. Leave out the doctrine of his atonement, and there is no foundation for our hopes. But of those who rest on this foundation, there are two sorts. Some hold nothing but the truth as it is in Jesus, and preach nothing else. Others build on the good foundation what will not abide the test, when the day of trail comes. We may be mistaken in ourselves and others; but there is a day coming that will show our actions in the true light, without covering or disguise. Those who spread true and pure religion in all its branches, and whose work will abide in the great day, shall receive a reward. And how great! how much exceeding their deserts! There are others, whose corrupt opinions and doctrines, or vain inventions and usages in the worship of God, shall be made known, disowned, and rejected, in that day. This is plainly meant of a figurative fire, not of a real one; for what real fire can consume religious rites or doctrines? And it is to try every man's works, those of Paul and Apollos, as well as others. Let us consider the tendency of our undertakings, compare them with God's word, and judge ourselves, that we be not judged of the Lord.

16,17 From other parts of the epistle, it appears that the false teachers among the Corinthians taught unholy doctrines. Such teaching tended to corrupt, to pollute, and destroy the building, which should be kept pure and holy for God. Those who spread loose principles, which render the church of God unholy, bring destruction upon themselves. Christ by his Spirit dwells in all true believers. Christians are holy by profession, and should be pure and clean, both in heart and conversation. He is deceived who deems himself the temple of the Holy Ghost, yet is unconcerned about personal holiness, or the peace and purity of the church.

blesses to the conversion of sinners; but are there not other portions which were intended for the comfort of the saint? and ought not these to be a subject of gospel ministry as well as the others? And shall I look at one and disregard the other? No: if God says, 'Comfort ye, comfort ye, my people;' if election comforts God's people, then must I preach it." But I am not quite so sure, that after all, that doctrine is not calculated to convert sinners. For the great Jonathan Edwards tells us, that in the greatest excitement of one of his revivals, he preached the sovereignty of God in the salvation or condemnation of man, and showed that God was infinitely just if he sent men to hell! that he was infinitely merciful if he saved any; and that it was all of his own free grace, and he said, "I found no doctrine caused more thought, nothing entered more deeply into the heart than the proclamation of that truth." The same might be said of other doctrines. There are certain truths in God's word which are condemned to silence; they, forsooth, are not to be uttered, because, according to the theories of certain persons, looking at these doctrines, they are not calculated to promote certain ends. But is it for me to judge God's truth? Am I to put his words in the scale, and say, "This is good, and that is evil?' Am I to take God's Bible, and sever it and say, "this is husk, and this is wheat?" Am I to cast away any one truth, and say, "I dare not preach it?" No: God forbid. Whatsoever is written in God's Word is written for our instruction: and the whole of it is profitable, either for reproof, or for consolation, or for edification in righteousness. No truth of God's Word ought to be withheld, but every portion of it preached in its own proper order.

Some men purposely confine themselves to four or five topics continually. Should you step into their chapel, you would naturally expect to hear them preaching, either from this, "Not of the will of the flesh, but of the will of God," or else, "Elect according to the foreknowledge of God the Father." You know that the moment you step in you are sure to hear nothing but election and high doctrine that day. Such men err also, quite as much as others, if they give too great prominence to one truth to the neglect of the others. Whatsoever is here to be preached, call it whatever name you please, write it high, write it low—the Bible, the whole Bible, and nothing but the Bible, is the standard of the true Christian. Alas! alas! many make an iron ring of their doctrines, and he who dares to step beyond that narrow circle, is not reckoned orthodox. God bless heretics, then! God send us more of them! Many make theology into a kind of treadwheel, consisting of five doctrines, which are everlastingly rotated; for they never go on to anything else. There ought to be every truth preached. And if God has written in his word that "he that believeth not is condemned already," that is as much to be

1 CORINTHIANS 5

1 It is reported commonly that there is fornication among you, and such fornication as is not so much as named among the Gentiles, that one should have his father's wife.

2 And ye are puffed up, and have not rather mourned, that he that hath done this deed might be taken away from among you.

3 For I verily, as absent in body, but present in spirit, have judged already, as though I were present, concerning him that hath so done this deed,

4 In the name of our Lord Jesus Christ, when ye are gathered together, and my spirit, with the power of our Lord Jesus Christ,

5 To deliver such an one unto Satan for the destruction of the flesh, that the spirit may be saved in the day of the Lord Jesus.

6 Your glorying is not good. Know ye not that a little leaven leaveneth the whole lump?

7 Purge out therefore the old leaven, that ye may be a new lump, as ye are unleavened. For even Christ our passover is sacrificed for us:

8 Therefore let us keep the feast, not with old leaven, neither with the leaven of malice and wickedness; but with the unleavened bread of sincerity and truth.

9 I wrote unto you in an epistle not to company with fornicators:

10 Yet not altogether with the fornicators of this world, or with the covetous, or extortioners, or with idolaters; for then must ye needs go out of the world.

11 But now I have written unto you not to keep company, if any man that is called a brother be a fornicator, or covetous, or an idolater, or a railer, or a drunkard, or an extortioner; with such an one no not to eat.

12 For what have I to do to judge them also that are without? do not ye judge them that are within?

13 But them that are without God judgeth. Therefore put away from among yourselves that wicked person.

things, were pleased with and applauded themselves; and they were like children who, being raised in the world, disregard their poor parents. Now ye are full, says the apostle, in a beautiful gradation, ye are rich, ye have reigned as kings – A proverbial expression, denoting the most splendid and plentiful circumstances. Without any thought of us. And I would ye did reign – In the best sense: I would ye had attained the height of holiness. That we might reign with you – Having no more sorrow on your account, but sharing in your happiness.

9. God hath set forth us last, as appointed to death – Alluding to the Roman custom of bringing forth those persons last on the stage, either to fight with each other, or with wild beasts, who were devoted to death; so that, if they escaped one day, they were brought out again and again, till they were killed.

10. We are fools, in the account of the world, for Christ's sake, but ye are wise in Christ – Though ye are Christians, ye think yourselves wise; and ye have found means to make the world think you so too. We are weak – In presence, in infirmities, in sufferings. But ye are strong – In just opposite circumstances.

11. And are naked – Who can imagine a more glorious triumph of the truth, than that which is gained in these circumstances when St. Paul, with an impediment in his speech, and a person rather contemptible than graceful, appeared in a mean, perhaps tattered, dress before persons of the highest distinction, and yet commanded such attention. and made such deep impressions upon them!

12. We bless, suffer it, entreat – We do not return reviling, persecution, defamation; nothing but blessing.

13. We are made as the filth of the world, and off scouring of all things – Such were those poor wretches among the heathens, who were taken from the dregs of the people, to be offered as expiatory sacrifices to the infernal gods. They were loaded with curses, affronts, and injuries, all the way they went to the altars; and when the ashes of those unhappy men were thrown into the sea, these very names were given them in the ceremony.

14. I do not write these things to shame you, but as my beloved children I warn you – It is with admirable prudence and sweetness the apostle adds this, to prevent any unkind construction of his words.

15. I have begotten you – This excludes not only Apollos, his successor, but also Silas and Timothy, his companions; and the relation between a spiritual father and his children brings with it an inexpressible nearness and affection.

16. Be ye followers of me – In that spirit and behavior which I have so largely declared.

17. My beloved son – Elsewhere he styles him "brother," 2 Cor. i, 1; but here paternal affection takes place. As I teach – No less by example than precept.

18. Now some are puffed up – St. Paul saw, by a divine light, the thoughts which would arise in their hearts. As if I would not come – Because I send Timothy.

19. I will know – He here shows his fatherly authority. Not the big, empty speech of these vain boasters, but how much of the power of God attends them.

20. For the kingdom of God – Real religion, does not consist in words, but in the power of God ruling the heart.

21. With a rod – That is, with severity.

1 CORINTHIANS 5

1. Fornication – The original word implies criminal conversation of any kind whatever. His father's wife – While his father was alive.

2. Are ye puffed up? Should ye not rather have mourned – Have solemnly humbled yourselves, and at that time of solemn mourning have expelled that notorious sinner from your communion?

3. I verily, as present in spirit – Having a full (it seems, a miraculous) view of the whole fact. Have already, as if I were actually present, judged him who hath so scandalously done this.

MATTHEW HENRY   CHARLES H. SPURGEON

18-23 To have a high opinion of our own wisdom, is but to flatter ourselves; and self-flattery is the next step to self-deceit. The wisdom that worldly men esteem, is foolishness with God. How justly does he despise, and how easily can he baffle and confound it! The thoughts of the wisest men in the world, have vanity, weakness, and folly in them. All this should teach us to be humble, and make us willing to be taught of God, so as not to be led away, by pretenses to human wisdom and skill, from the simple truths revealed by Christ. Mankind are very apt to oppose the design of the mercies of God. Observe the spiritual riches of a true believer; "All are yours," even ministers and ordinances. Nay, the world itself is yours. Saints have as much of it as Infinite Wisdom sees fit for them, and they have it with the Divine blessing. Life is yours, that you may have a season and opportunity to prepare for the life of heaven; and death is yours, that you may go to the possession of it. It is the kind messenger to take you from sin and sorrow, and to guide you to your Father's house. Things present are yours, for your support on the road; things to come are yours, to delight you for ever at your journey's end. If we belong to Christ, and are true to him, all good belongs to us, and is sure to us. Believers are the subjects of his kingdom. He is Lord over us, we must own his dominion, and cheerfully submit to his command. God in Christ, reconciling a sinful world to himself, and pouring the riches of his grace on a reconciled world, is the sum and substance of the gospel.

1 CORINTHIANS 4

The true character of gospel ministers. (1-6)
Cautions against despising the apostle. (7-13)
He claims their regard as their spiritual father in Christ, and shows his concern for them. (14-21)

1-6 Apostles were no more than servants of Christ, but they were not to be undervalued. They had a great trust, and for that reason, had an honorable office. Paul had a just concern for his own reputation, but he knew that he who chiefly aimed to please men, would not prove himself a faithful servant of Christ. It is a comfort that men are not to be our final judges. And it is not judging well of ourselves, or justifying ourselves, that will prove us safe and happy. Our own judgment is not to be depended upon as to our faithfulness, any more than our own works for our justification. There is a day coming, that will bring men's secret sins into open day, and discover the secrets of their hearts. Then every slandered believer will be justified, and every faithful servant approved and rewarded. The word of God is the best rule by which to judge as to men. Pride commonly is at the bottom

preached as the truth that "there is no condemnation to them that are in Jesus Christ." If I find it written, "O Israel, thou hast destroyed thyself," that man's condemnation is his own fault, I am to preach that as well as the next clause, "In me is thy help found." We ought, each of us who are entrusted with the ministry, to seek to preach all truth. I know it may be impossible to tell you all of it. That high hill of truth hath mists upon its summit. No mortal eye can see its pinnacle; nor hath the foot of man ever trodden it. But yet let us paint the mist, if we cannot paint the summit. Let us depict the difficulty itself if we cannot unravel it. Let us not hide anything, but if the mountain of truth be cloudy at the top, let us say, "Clouds and darkness are around him," Let us not deny it; and let us not think of cutting down the mountain to our own standard, because we cannot see its summit or cannot reach its pinnacle. He who would preach the gospel must preach all the gospel. He who would have it said he is a faithful minister, must not keep back any part of revelation.

2. Again, am I asked what it is to preach the gospel? I answer to preach the gospel is to exalt Jesus Christ. Perhaps this is the best answer that I could give. I am very sorry to see very often how little the gospel is understood even by some of the best Christians. Some time ago there was a young woman under great distress of soul; she came to a very pious Christian man, who said "My dear girl, you must go home and pray." Well I thought within myself, that is not the Bible way at all. It never says, "Go home and pray." The poor girl went home; she did pray, and she still continued in distress. Said he, "You must wait, you must read the Scriptures and study them." That is not the Bible way; that is not exalting Christ; I find a great many preachers are preaching that kind of doctrine. They tell a poor convinced sinner, "You must go home and pray, and read the Scriptures; you must attend the ministry;" and so on. Works, works, works— instead of "By grace are ye saved through faith," If a penitent should come and ask me, "What must I do to be saved?" I would say, "Christ must save you—believe on the name of the Lord Jesus Christ." I would neither direct to prayer, nor reading of the Scriptures nor attending God's house; but simply direct to faith, naked faith on God's gospel. Not that I despise prayer—that must come after faith. Not that I speak a word against the searching of the Scriptures—that is an infallible mark of God's children. Not that I find fault with attendance on God's word—God forbid! I love to see people there. But none of those things are the way of salvation. It is nowhere written—"He that attendeth chapel shall be saved," or, "He that readeth the Bible shall be saved." Nor do I read—"He that prayeth and is baptized shall be saved;" but, "He that believeth,"—he that has a naked faith on the "Man Christ Jesus,"—

KING JAMES VERSION   JOHN WESLEY

1 CORINTHIANS 6

1 Dare any of you, having a matter against another, go to law before the unjust, and not before the saints?

2 Do ye not know that the saints shall judge the world? and if the world shall be judged by you, are ye unworthy to judge the smallest matters?

3 Know ye not that we shall judge angels? how much more things that pertain to this life?

4 If then ye have judgments of things pertaining to this life, set them to judge who are least esteemed in the church.

5 I speak to your shame. Is it so, that there is not a wise man among you? no, not one that shall be able to judge between his brethren?

6 But brother goeth to law with brother, and that before the unbelievers.

7 Now therefore there is utterly a fault among you, because ye go to law one with another. Why do ye not rather take wrong? why do ye not rather suffer yourselves to be defrauded?

8 Nay, ye do wrong, and defraud, and that your brethren.

9 Know ye not that the unrighteous shall not inherit the kingdom of God? Be not deceived: neither fornicators, nor idolaters, nor adulterers, nor effeminate, nor abusers of themselves with mankind,

10 Nor thieves, nor covetous, nor drunkards, nor revilers, nor extortioners, shall inherit the kingdom of God.

11 And such were some of you: but ye are washed, but ye are sanctified, but ye are justified in the name of the Lord Jesus, and by the Spirit of our God.

12 All things are lawful unto me, but all things are not expedient: all things are lawful for me, but I will not be brought under the power of any.

13 Meats for the belly, and the belly for meats: but God shall destroy both it and them. Now the body is not for fornication, but for the Lord; and the Lord for the body.

14 And God hath both raised up the Lord, and will also raise up us by his own power.

15 Know ye not that your bodies

4. And my spirit – Present with you. With the power of the Lord Jesus Christ – To confirm my sentence.

5. To deliver such an one – This was the highest degree of punishment in the Christian church; and we may observe, the passing this sentence was the act of the apostle, not of the Corinthians. To Satan – Who was usually permitted, in such cases, to inflict pain or sickness on the offender. For the destruction – Though slowly and gradually. Of the flesh – Unless prevented by speedy repentance.

6. Your glorying – Either in your gifts or prosperity, at such a time as this, is not good. Know ye not that a little leaven – One sin, or one sinner. Leaveneth the whole lump – Diffuses guilt and infection through the whole congregation.

7. Purge out therefore the old leaven – Both of sinners and of sin. That ye may be a new lump, as ye are unleavened – That is, that being unleavened ye may be a new lump, holy unto the Lord. For our Passover is slain for us – The Jewish Passover, about the time of which this epistle was wrote, ver. 11, was only a type of this. What exquisite skill both here and everywhere conducts the zeal of the inspired writer! How surprising a transition is here, and yet how perfectly natural! The apostle, speaking of the incestuous criminal, slides into his darling topic, – crucified Savior. Who would have expected it on such an occasion. Yet, when it is thus brought in, who does not see and admire both the propriety of the subject, and the delicacy of its introduction?

8. Therefore let us keep the feast – Let us feed on him by faith. Here is a plain allusion to the Lord's supper, which was instituted in the room of the Passover. Not with the old leaven – Of heathenism or Judaism. Malignity is stubbornness in evil. Sincerity and truth seem to be put here for the whole of true, inward religion.

9. I wrote to you in a former epistle – And, doubtless, both St. Paul and the other apostles wrote many things which are not extant now. Not to converse – Familiarly; not to contract any intimacy or acquaintance with them, more than is absolutely necessary.

10. But I did not mean that you should altogether refrain from conversing with heathens, though they are guilty in some of these respects. Covetous, rapacious, idolaters – Sinners against themselves, their neighbor, God. For then ye must go out of the world – Then all civil commerce must cease. So that going out of the world, which some account a perfection, St. Paul accounts an utter absurdity.

11. Who is named a brother – That is, a Christian; especially if a member of the same congregation. Rapacious – Guilty of oppression, extortion, or any open injustice. No, not to eat with him – Which is the lowest degree of familiarity.

12. I speak of Christians only. For what have I to do to judge heathens? But ye, as well as I, judge those of your own community.

13. Them that are without God will judge – The passing sentence on these he hath reserved to himself. And ye will take away that wicked person – This properly belongs to you.

1 CORINTHIANS 6

1. The unjust – The heathens. A Christian could expect no justice from these. The saints – Who might easily decide these smaller differences in a private and friendly manner.

2. Know ye not – This expression occurs six times in this single chapter, and that with a peculiar force; for the Corinthians knew and gloried in it, but they did not practice. That the saints – After having been judged themselves. Shall judge the world – Shall be assessors with Christ in the judgment wherein he shall condemn all the wicked, as well angels as men, Matt. xix, 28; Rev. xx, 4.

4. Them who are of no esteem in the church – That is, heathens, who, as such, could be in no esteem with the Christians.

5. Is there not one among you, who are such admirers of wisdom, that is wise

MATTHEW HENRY   CHARLES H. SPURGEON

of quarrels. Self-conceit contributes to produce undue esteem of our teachers, as well as of ourselves. We shall not be puffed up for one against another, if we remember that all are instruments, employed by God, and endowed by him with various talents.

7-13 We have no reason to be proud; all we have, or are, or do, that is good, is owing to the free and rich grace of God. A sinner snatched from destruction by sovereign grace alone, must be very absurd and inconsistent, if proud of the free gifts of God. St. Paul sets forth his own circumstances, ver. 9. Allusion is made to the cruel spectacles in the Roman games; where men were forced to cut one another to pieces, to divert the people; and where the victor did not escape with his life, though he should destroy his adversary, but was only kept for another combat, and must be killed at last. The thought that many eyes are upon believers, when struggling with difficulties or temptations, should encourage constancy and patience. "We are weak, but ye are strong." All Christians are not alike exposed. Some suffer greater hardships than others. The apostle enters into particulars of their sufferings. And how glorious the charity and devotion that carried them through all these hardships! They suffered in their persons and characters as the worst and vilest of men; as the very dirt of the world, that was to be swept away: nay, as the off scouring of all things, the dross of all things. And every one who would be faithful in Christ Jesus, must be prepared for poverty and contempt. Whatever the disciples of Christ suffer from men, they must follow the example, and fulfill the will and precepts of their Lord. They must be content, with him and for him, to be despised and abused. It is much better to be rejected, despised, and ill used, as St. Paul was, than to have the good opinion and favor of the world. Though cast off by the world as vile, yet we may be precious to God, gathered up with his own hand, and placed upon his throne.

14-21 In reproving for sin, we should distinguish between sinners and their sins. Reproofs that kindly and affectionately warn, are likely to reform. Though the apostle spoke with authority as a parent, he would rather beseech them in love. And as ministers are to set an example, others must follow them, as far as they follow Christ in faith and practice. Christians may mistake and differ in their views, but Christ and Christian truth are the same yesterday, today, and for ever. Whenever the gospel is effectual, it comes not in word only, but also in power, by the Holy Spirit, quickening dead sinners, delivering persons from the slavery of sin and Satan, renewing them both inwardly and outwardly, and comforting, strength-

on his Godhead, on his manhood, is delivered from sin. To preach that faith alone saves, is to preach God's truth. Nor will I for one moment concede to any man the name of a gospel minister, if he preaches anything as the plan of salvation except faith in Jesus Christ, faith, faith, nothing but faith in his name. But we are, most of us, very much muddled in our ideas. We get so much work stored into our brain, such an idea of merit and of doing, wrought into our hearts, that it is almost impossible for us to preach justification by faith clearly and fully; and when we do, our people won't receive it. We tell them, "Believe on the name of the Lord Jesus Christ and thou shalt be saved." But they have a notion that faith is something so wonderful, so mysterious, that it is quite impossible that without doing something else they can ever get it. Now, that faith which unites to the Lamb is an instantaneous gift of God, and he who believes on the Lord Jesus is that moment saved, without anything else whatsoever. Ah! my friends, do we not want more exalting Christ in our preaching, and more exalting Christ in our living? Poor Mary said, "They have taken away my Lord and I know not where they have laid him," And she might say so now-a-days if she could rise from the grave. Oh! to have a Christ-exalting ministry! Oh! to have preaching that magnifies Christ in his person, that extols his divinity, that loves his humanity; to have preaching that shows him as prophet, priest, and king to his people! to have preaching whereby the spirit manifests the Son of God unto his children: to have preaching that says, "Look unto him and be ye saved all the ends of the earth,"—Calvary preaching, Calvary theology, Calvary books, Calvary sermons! These are the things we want, and in proportion as we have Calvary exalted and Christ magnified, the gospel is preached in our midst.

3. The third answer to the question is: to preach the gospel is to give every class of character his due. "You are only to preach to God's dear people, if you go into that pulpit," said a deacon once to a minister. Said the minister, "Have you marked them all on the back, that I may know them?" What is the good of this large chapel if I am only to preach to God's dear people? They are few enough. God's dear people might be held in the vestry. We have many more here besides God's dear people, and how am I to be sure, if I am told to preach only to God's dear people, that somebody else wont take it to himself? At another time some one might say, "Now, be sure you preach to sinners. If you do not preach to sinners this morning, you won't preach the gospel. We shall only hear you once; and we shall be sure you are not right if you do not happen to preach to sinners this particular morning, in this particular sermon." What nonsense, my friends! There are times when the children must be fed, and there are times when the sinner must be warned.

are the members of Christ? shall I then take the members of Christ, and make them the members of an harlot? God forbid.

16 What? know ye not that he which is joined to an harlot is one body? for two, saith he, shall be one flesh.

17 But he that is joined unto the Lord is one spirit.

18 Flee fornication. Every sin that a man doeth is without the body; but he that committeth fornication sinneth against his own body.

19 What? know ye not that your body is the temple of the Holy Ghost which is in you, which ye have of God, and ye are not your own?

20 For ye are bought with a price: therefore glorify God in your body, and in your spirit, which are God's.

1 CORINTHIANS 7

1 Now concerning the things whereof ye wrote unto me: It is good for a man not to touch a woman.

2 Nevertheless, to avoid fornication, let every man have his own wife, and let every woman have her own husband.

3 Let the husband render unto the wife due benevolence: and likewise also the wife unto the husband.

4 The wife hath not power of her own body, but the husband: and likewise also the husband hath not power of his own body, but the wife.

5 Defraud ye not one the other, except it be with consent for a time, that ye may give yourselves to fasting and prayer; and come together again, that Satan tempt you not for your incontinency.

6 But I speak this by permission, and not of commandment.

7 For I would that all men were even as I myself. But every man hath his proper gift of God, one after this manner, and another after that.

8 I say therefore to the unmarried and widows, It is good for them if they abide even as I.

9 But if they cannot contain, let them marry: for it is better to

enough to decide such causes?

7. Indeed there is a fault, that ye quarrel with each other at all, whether ye go to law or no. Why do ye not rather suffer wrong – All men cannot or will not receive this saying. Many aim only at this, "I will neither do wrong, nor suffer it." These are honest heathens, but no Christians.

8. Nay, ye do wrong – Openly. And defraud – Privately. O how powerfully did the mystery of iniquity already work!

9. Idolatry is here placed between fornication and adultery, because they generally accompanied it. Nor the effeminate – Who live in an easy, indolent way; taking up no cross, enduring no hardship. But how is this? These good-natured, harmless people are ranked with idolaters and sodomites! We may learn hence, that we are never secure from the greatest sins, till we guard against those which are thought the least; nor, indeed, till we think no sin is little, since every one is a step toward hell.

11. And such were some of you: but ye are washed – From those gross abominations; nay, and ye are inwardly sanctified; not before, but in consequence of, your being justified in the name – That is, by the merits, of the Lord Jesus, through which your sins are forgiven. And by the Spirit of our God – By whom ye are thus washed and sanctified.

12. All things – Which are lawful for you. Are lawful for me, but all things are not always expedient – Particularly when anything would offend my weak brother; or when it would enslave my own soul. For though all things are lawful for me, yet I will not be brought under the power of any – So as to be uneasy when I abstain from it; for, if so, then I am under the power of it.

13. As if he had said, I speak this chiefly with regard to meats; (and would to God all Christians would consider it!) particularly with regard to those offered to idols, and those forbidden in the Mosaic law. These, I grant, are all indifferent, and have their use, though it is only for a time: then meats, and the organs which receive them, will together molder into dust. But the case is quite otherwise with fornication. This is not indifferent, but at all times evil. For the body is for the Lord – Designed only for his service. And the Lord, in an important sense, for the body – Being the Savior of this, as well as of the soul; in proof of which God hath already raised him from the dead.

16. Gen. ii, 24.

17. But he that is joined to the Lord – By faith. Is one spirit with him – And shall he make himself one flesh with an harlot?

18. Flee fornication – All unlawful commerce with women, with speed, with abhorrence, with all your might. Every sin that a man commits against his neighbor terminates upon an object out of himself, and does not so immediately pollute his body, though it does his soul. But he that committeth fornication, sinneth against his own body – Pollutes, dishonors, and degrades it to a level with brute beasts.

19. And even your body is not, strictly speaking, your own; even this is the temple of the Holy Ghost – Dedicated to him, and inhabited by him. What the apostle calls elsewhere "the temple of God," chap. iii, 16, 17, and "the temple of the living God," 2 Cor. vi, 16, he here styles the temple of the Holy Ghost; plainly showing that the Holy Ghost is the living God.

20. Glorify God with your body, and your spirit – Yield your bodies and all their members, as well as your souls and all their faculties, as instruments of righteousness to God. Devote and employ all ye have, and all ye are, entirely, unreservedly, and for ever, to his glory.

1 CORINTHIANS 7

1. It is good for a man – Who is master of himself. Not to touch a woman – That is, not to marry. So great and many are the advantages of a single life.

MATTHEW HENRY   CHARLES H. SPURGEON

ening, and establishing the saints, which cannot be done by the persuasive language of men, but by the power of God. And it is a happy temper, to have the spirit of love and meekness bear the rule, yet to maintain just authority.

1 CORINTHIANS 5

The apostle blames the Corinthians for connivance
*   at an incestuous person. (1-8)*
And directs their behavior towards those guilty of
*   scandalous crimes. (9-13)*

1-8 The apostle notices a flagrant abuse, winked at by the Corinthians. Party spirit, and a false notion of Christian liberty, seem to have saved the offender from censure. Grievous indeed is it that crimes should sometimes be committed by professors of the gospel, of which even heathens would be ashamed. Spiritual pride and false doctrines tend to bring in, and to spread such scandals. How dreadful the effects of sin! The devil reigns where Christ does not. And a man is in his kingdom, and under his power, when not in Christ. The bad example of a man of influence is very mischievous; it spreads far and wide. Corrupt principles and examples, if not corrected, would hurt the whole church. Believers must have new hearts, and lead new lives. Their common conversation and religious deeds must be holy. So far is the sacrifice of Christ our Passover for us, from rendering personal and public holiness unnecessary, that it furnishes powerful reasons and motives for it. Without holiness we can neither live by faith in him, nor join in his ordinances with comfort and profit.

9-13 Christians are to avoid familiar converse with all who disgrace the Christian name. Such are only fit companions for their brethren in sin, and to such company they should be left, whenever it is possible to do so. Alas, that there are many called Christians, whose conversation is more dangerous than that of heathens!

1 CORINTHIANS 6

Cautions against going to law in heathen courts.
*   (1-8)*
Sins which, if lived and died in, shut out from the
*   kingdom of God. (9-11)*
Our bodies, which are the members of Christ, and
*   temples of the Holy Ghost, must not be defiled.*
*   (12-20)*

1-8 Christians should not contend with one another, for they are brethren. This, if duly attended to, would prevent many law-suits, and end many quarrels and disputes. In matters of great

There are different times for different objects. If a man is preaching to God's saints if it so happen that little is said to sinners, is he to be blamed for it, provided that at another time when he is not comforting the saints, he directs his attention specially to the ungodly? I heard a good remark from an intelligent friend of mine the other day. A person was finding fault with "Dr. Hawker's Morning and Evening Portions" because they were not calculated to convert sinners. He said to the gentleman, "Did you ever read; 'Grote's History of Greece?'" "Yes." Well, that is a shocking book, is it not? for it is not calculated to convert sinners. "Yes, but," said the other, "'Grote's History of Greece' was never meant to convert sinners." "No," said my friend, "and if you had read the preface to 'Dr. Hawker's Morning and Evening Portion,' you would see that it was never meant to convert sinners, but to feed God's people, and if it answers its end the man has been wise, though he has not aimed at some other end." Every class of person is to have his due. He who preaches solely to saints at all times does not preach the gospel; he who preaches solely and only to the sinner, and never to the saint, does not preach the whole of the gospel. We have amalgamation here. We have the saint who is full of assurance and strong; we have the saint who is weak and low in faith; we have the young convert; we have the man halting between two opinions; we have the moral man; we have the sinner; we have the reprobate; we have the outcast. Let each have a word. Let each have a portion of meat in due season; not at every season, but in due season. He who omits one class of character does not know how to preach the entire gospel. What! Am I to be put into the pulpit and to be told that I am to confine myself to certain truths only, to comfort God's saints? I will not have it so. God gives men hearts to love their fellow-creatures, and are they to have no development for that heart? If I love the ungodly am I to have no means of speaking to them? May I not tell them of judgment to come, of righteousness, and of their sin? God forbid I should so stultify my nature and so brutalize myself, as to have a tearless eye when I consider the loss of my fellow creatures, and to stand and say "Ye are dead, I have nothing to say to you!" and to preach in effect if not in words that most damnable heresy, that if men are to be saved they will be saved—that if they are not to be saved they will not be saved; that necessarily, they must sit still and do nothing whatever; and that it matters not whether they live in sin or in righteousness—some strong fate has bound them down with adamantine chains; and their destiny is so certain that they may live on in sin. I believe their destiny is certain—that as elect, they will be saved, and if not elect they are damned for ever. But I do not believe the heresy that follows as an inference that therefore men are irresponsible and may sit

marry than to burn.

10 And unto the married I command, yet not I, but the Lord, Let not the wife depart from her husband:

11 But and if she depart, let her remain unmarried, or be reconciled to her husband: and let not the husband put away his wife.

12 But to the rest speak I, not the Lord: If any brother hath a wife that believeth not, and she be pleased to dwell with him, let him not put her away.

13 And the woman which hath an husband that believeth not, and if he be pleased to dwell with her, let her not leave him.

14 For the unbelieving husband is sanctified by the wife, and the unbelieving wife is sanctified by the husband: else were your children unclean; but now are they holy.

15 But if the unbelieving depart, let him depart. A brother or a sister is not under bondage in such cases: but God hath called us to peace.

16 For what knowest thou, O wife, whether thou shalt save thy husband? or how knowest thou, O man, whether thou shalt save thy wife?

17 But as God hath distributed to every man, as the Lord hath called every one, so let him walk. And so ordain I in all churches.

18 Is any man called being circumcized? let him not become uncircumcized. Is any called in uncircumcision? let him not be circumcized.

19 Circumcision is nothing, and uncircumcision is nothing, but the keeping of the commandments of God.

20 Let every man abide in the same calling wherein he was called.

21 Art thou called being a servant? care not for it: but if thou mayest be made free, use it rather.

22 For he that is called in the Lord, being a servant, is the Lord's freeman: likewise also he that is called, being free, is Christ's servant.

23 Ye are bought with a price; be not ye the servants of men.

24 Brethren, let every man, wherein he is called, therein

2. Yet, when it is needful, in order to avoid fornication, let every man have his own wife. His own – For Christianity allows no polygamy.

3. Let not married persons fancy that there is any perfection in living with each other, as if they were unmarried. The debt – This ancient reading seems far more natural than the common one.

4. The wife, the husband – Let no one forget this, on pretense of greater purity.

5. Unless it be by consent for a time – That on those special and solemn occasions ye may entirely give yourselves up to the exercises of devotion. Lest – If ye should long remain separate. Satan tempt you – To unclean thoughts, if not actions too.

6. But I say this – Concerning your separating for a time and coming together again. Perhaps he refers also to ver. 2.

7. For I would that all men were herein even as I – I would that all believers who are now unmarried would remain "eunuchs for the kingdom of heaven's sake" St. Paul, having tasted the sweetness of this liberty, wished others to enjoy it, as well as himself. But every one hath his proper gift from God – According to our Lord's declaration, "All men cannot receive this saying, save they," the happy few, "to whom it is given," Matt. xix, 11.

8. It is good for them if they remain even as I – That St. Paul was then single is certain and from Acts vii, 58, compared with the following parts of the history, it seems probable that he always was so. It does not appear that this declaration, any more than ver. 1, hath any reference at all to a state of persecution.

10. Not I – Only. But the Lord – Christ; by his express command, Matt. v, 32.

11. But if she depart – Contrary to this express prohibition. And let not the husband put away his wife – Except for the cause of adultery.

12. To the rest – Who are married to unbelievers. Speak I – By Revelation from God, though our Lord hath not left any commandment concerning it. Let him not put her away – The Jews, indeed, were obliged of old to put away their idolatrous wives, Ezra x, 3; but their case was quite different. They were absolutely forbid to marry idolatrous women; but the persons here spoken of were married while they were both in a state of heathenism.

14. For the unbelieving husband hath, in many instances, been sanctified by the wife – Else your children would have been brought up heathens; whereas now they are Christians. As if he had said, Ye see the proof of it before your eyes.

15. A brother or a sister – A Christian man or woman. Is not enslaved – is at full liberty. In such cases: but God hath called us to peace – To live peaceably with them, if it be possible.

17. But as God hath distributed – The various stations of life, and various relations, to every one, let him take care to discharge his duty therein. The gospel disannuls none of these. And thus I ordain in all the churches – As a point of the highest concern.

19. Circumcision is nothing, and uncircumcision is nothing – Will neither promote nor obstruct our salvation. The one point is, keeping the commandments of God; "faith working by love."

20. In the calling – The outward state. Wherein he is – When God calls him. Let him not seek to change this, without a clear direction from Providence.

21. Care not for it – Do not anxiously seek liberty. But if thou canst be free, use it rather – Embrace the opportunity.

22. Is the Lord's freeman – Is free in this respect. The Greek word implies one that was a slave, but now is free. Is the bondman of Christ – Not free in this respect; not at liberty to do his own will.

23. Ye are bought with a price – Ye belong to God; therefore, where it can be avoided, do not become the bond slaves of men – Which may expose you to many temptations.

24. Therein abide with God – Doing all things as unto God, and as in his

damage to ourselves or families, we may use lawful means to right ourselves, but Christians should be of a forgiving temper. Refer the matters in dispute, rather than go to law about them. They are trifles, and may easily be settled, if you first conquer your own spirits. Bear and forbear, and the men of least skill among you may end your quarrels. It is a shame that little quarrels should grow to such a head among Christians, that they cannot be determined by the brethren. The peace of a man's own mind, and the calm of his neighborhood, are worth more than victory. Lawsuits could not take place among brethren, unless there were faults among them.

9-11 The Corinthians are warned against many great evils, of which they had formerly been guilty. There is much force in these inquiries, when we consider that they were addressed to a people puffed up with a fancy of their being above others in wisdom and knowledge. All unrighteousness is sin; all reigning sin, nay, every actual sin, committed with design, and not repented of, shuts out of the kingdom of heaven. Be not deceived. Men are very much inclined to flatter themselves that they may live in sin, yet die in Christ, and go to heaven. But we cannot hope to sow to the flesh, and reap everlasting life. They are reminded what a change the gospel and grace of God had made in them. The blood of Christ, and the washing of regeneration, can take away all guilt. Our justification is owing to the suffering and merit of Christ; our sanctification to the working of the Holy Spirit; but both go together. All who are made righteous in the sight of God, are made holy by the grace of God.

12-20 Some among the Corinthians seem to have been ready to say, All things are lawful for me. This dangerous conceit St. Paul opposes. There is a liberty wherewith Christ has made us free, in which we must stand fast. But surely a Christian would never put himself into the power of any bodily appetite. The body is for the Lord; is to be an instrument of righteousness to holiness, therefore is never to be made an instrument of sin. It is an honor to the body, that Jesus Christ was raised from the dead; and it will be an honor to our bodies, that they will be raised. The hope of a resurrection to glory, should keep Christians from dishonoring their bodies by fleshly lusts. And if the soul be united to Christ by faith, the whole man is become a member of his spiritual body. Other vices may be conquered in fight; that here cautioned against, only by flight. And vast multitudes are cut off by this vice in its various forms and consequences. Its effects fall not only directly upon the body, but often upon the mind. Our bodies have been redeemed from deserved con-

still. That is a heresy against which I have ever protested, as being a doctrine of the devil and not of God at all. We believe in destiny; we believe in predestination; we believe in election and non-election: but, notwithstanding that, we believe that we must preach to men, "Believe on the Lord Jesus Christ and ye shall be saved," but believe not on him and ye are damned.

4. I had thought of giving one more answer to this question, but time fails me. The answer would have been somewhat like this—that to preach the gospel is not to preach certain truths about the gospel, not to preach about the people, but to preach to the people. To preach the gospel is not to talk about what the gospel is, but to preach it into the heart, not by your own might, but by the influence of the Holy Ghost—not to stand and talk as if we were speaking to the angel Gabriel, and telling him certain things, but to speak as man to man and pour our heart in to our fellow's heart. This I take it, is to preach the gospel, and not to mumble some dry manuscript over on Sunday morning or Sunday evening. To preach the gospel is not to send a curate to do your duty for you; it is not to put on your fine gown and then stand and give out some lofty speculation. To preach the gospel is not, with the hands of a bishop, to turn over some beautiful specimen of prayer, and then to go down again and leave it to some humbler person to speak. Nay; to preach the gospel is to proclaim with trumpet tongue and flaming zeal the unsearchable riches of Christ Jesus, so that men may hear, and understanding, may turn to God with full purpose of heart. This is to preach the gospel.

II. The second question is—How IS IT THAT MINISTERS ARE NOT ALLOWED TO GLORY? "For though I preach the gospel I have nothing to glorify it." There are some weeds that will grow anywhere; and one of them is Pride. Pride will grow on a rock as well as in a garden. Pride will grow in the heart of a shoe-black as well as in the heart of an alderman. Pride will grow in the heart of a servant girl and equally as well in the heart of her mistress. And pride will grow in the pulpit. It is a weed that is dreadfully rampant. It wants cutting down every week, or else we should stand up to our knees in it. This pulpit is a shocking bad soil for pride. It grows terribly; and I scarcely know whether you ever find a preacher of the gospel who will not confess that he has the greatest temptation to pride. I suppose that even those ministers of whom nothing is said, but that they are very good people, and who have a City church, with some six people attending it, have a temptation to pride. But whether that is so or not, I am quite sure wherever there is a large assembly, and wherever a great deal of noise and stir is made concerning any man there is a great danger of pride. And, mark you, the more proud a

abide with God.

25 Now concerning virgins I have no commandment of the Lord: yet I give my judgment, as one that hath obtained mercy of the Lord to be faithful.

26 I suppose therefore that this is good for the present distress, I say, that it is good for a man so to be.

27 Art thou bound unto a wife? seek not to be loosed. Art thou loosed from a wife? seek not a wife.

28 But and if thou marry, thou hast not sinned; and if a virgin marry, she hath not sinned. Nevertheless such shall have trouble in the flesh: but I spare you.

29 But this I say, brethren, the time is short: it remaineth, that both they that have wives be as though they had none;

30 And they that weep, as though they wept not; and they that rejoice, as though they rejoiced not; and they that buy, as though they possessed not;

31 And they that use this world, as not abusing it: for the fashion of this world passeth away.

32 But I would have you without carefulness. He that is unmarried careth for the things that belong to the Lord, how he may please the Lord:

33 But he that is married careth for the things that are of the world, how he may please his wife.

34 There is difference also between a wife and a virgin. The unmarried woman careth for the things of the Lord, that she may be holy both in body and in spirit: but she that is married careth for the things of the world, how she may please her husband.

35 And this I speak for your own profit; not that I may cast a snare upon you, but for that which is comely, and that ye may attend upon the Lord without distraction.

36 But if any man think that he behaveth himself uncomely toward his virgin, if she pass the flower of her age, and need so require, let him do what he will, he sinneth not: let them marry.

37 Nevertheless he that standeth stedfast in his heart, having no necessity, but hath

immediate presence. They who thus abide with God preserve an holy indifference with regard to outward things.

25. Now concerning virgins – Of either sex. I have no commandment from the Lord – By a particular Revelation. Nor was it necessary he should; for the apostles wrote nothing which was not divinely inspired: but with this difference, sometimes they had a particular Revelation, and a special commandment; at other times they wrote from the divine light which abode with them, the standing treasure of the Spirit of God. And this, also, was not their private opinion, but a divine rule of faith and practice. As one whom God hath made faithful in my apostolic office; who therefore faithfully deliver what I receive from him.

26, 27. This is good for the present distress – While any church is under persecution. For a man to continue as he is – Whether married or unmarried. St. Paul does not here urge the present distress as a reason for celibacy, any more than for marriage; but for a man's not seeking to alter his state, whatever it be, but making the best of it.

28. Such will have trouble in the flesh – Many outward troubles. But I spare you – I speak as little and as tenderly as possible.

29. But this I say, brethren – With great confidence. The time of our abode here is short. It plainly follows, that even they who have wives be as serious, zealous, active, dead to the world, as devoted to God, as holy in all manner of conversation, as if they had none – By so easy a transition does the apostle slide from every thing else to the one thing needful; and, forgetting whatever is temporal, is swallowed up in eternity.

30. And they that weep, as if they wept not – "Though sorrowful, yet always rejoicing." They that rejoice, as if they rejoiced not – Tempering their joy with godly fear. They that buy, as if they possessed not – Knowing themselves to be only stewards, not proprietors.

31. And they that use this world, as not abusing it – Not seeking happiness in it, but in God: using every thing therein only in such a manner and degree as most tends to the knowledge and love of God. For the whole scheme and fashion of this world – This marrying, weeping, rejoicing, and all the rest, not only will pass, but now passeth away, is this moment flying off like a shadow.

32. Now I would have you – For this flying moment. Without carefulness – Without any encumbrance of your thoughts. The unmarried man – If he understand and use the advantage he enjoys – Careth only for the things of the Lord, how he may please the Lord.

33. But the married careth for the things of the world – And it is his duty so to do, so far as becomes a Christian. How he may please his wife – And provide all things needful for her and his family.

34. There is a difference also between a wife and a virgin – Whether the church be under persecution or not. The unmarried woman – If she know and use her privilege. Careth only for the things of the Lord – All her time, care, and thoughts center in this, how she may be holy both in body and spirit. This is the standing advantage of a single life, in all ages and nations. But who makes a suitable use of it?

35. Not that I may cast a snare upon you – Who are not able to receive this saying. But for your profit – Who are able. That ye may resolutely and perseveringly wait upon the Lord – The word translated wait signifies sitting close by a person, in a good posture to hear. So Mary sat at the feet of Jesus, Luke x, 39. Without distraction – Without having the mind drawn any way from its center; from its close attention to God; by any person, or thing, or care, or encumbrance whatsoever.

36. But if any parent think he should otherwise act indecently – Unbecoming his character. Toward his virgin daughter, if she be above age, (or of full age,) and need so require, ver. 9, let them marry – Her suitor and she.

37. Having no necessity – Where there is no such need. But having power over

demnation and hopeless slavery by the atoning sacrifice of Christ. We are to be clean, as vessels fitted for our Master's use. Being united to Christ as one spirit, and bought with a price of unspeakable value, the believer should consider himself as wholly the Lord's, by the strongest ties. May we make it our business, to the latest day and hour of our lives, to glorify God with our bodies, and with our spirits which are his.

1 CORINTHIANS 7

The apostle answers several questions about marriage. (1-9)

Married Christians should not seek to part from their unbelieving consorts. (10-16)

Persons, in any fixed station, should usually abide in that. (17-24)

It was most desirable, on account of the then perilous days, for people to sit loose to this world. (25-35)

Great prudence be used in marriage; it should be only in the Lord. (36-40)

1-9 The apostle tells the Corinthians that it was good, in that juncture of time, for Christians to keep themselves single. Yet he says that marriage, and the comforts of that state, are settled by Divine wisdom. Though none may break the law of God, yet that perfect rule leaves men at liberty to serve him in the way most suited to their powers and circumstances, of which others often are very unfit judges. All must determine for themselves, seeking counsel from God how they ought to act.

10-16 Man and wife must not separate for any other cause than what Christ allows. Divorce, at that time, was very common among both Jews and Gentiles, on very slight pretexts. Marriage is a Divine institution; and is an engagement for life, by God's appointment. We are bound, as much as in us lies, to live peaceably with all men, Ro 12:18, therefore to promote the peace and comfort of our nearest relatives, though unbelievers. It should be the labor and study of those who are married, to make each other as easy and happy as possible. Should a Christian desert a husband or wife, when there is opportunity to give the greatest proof of love? Stay, and labor heartily for the conversion of thy relative. In every state and relation the Lord has called us to peace; and every thing should be done to promote harmony, as far as truth and holiness will permit.

17-24 The rules of Christianity reach every condition; and in every state a man may live so as to be a credit to it. It is the duty of every Christian to be content with his lot, and to conduct himself in

man is the greater will be his fall at last. If people will hold a minister up in their hands and do not keep hold of him, but let him go, what a fall he will have, poor fellow, when it is all over. It has been so with many. Many men have been held up by the arms of men, they have been held up by the arms of praise, and not of prayer; these arms have become weak, and down they have fallen. I say there is temptation to pride in the pulpit; but there is no ground for it in the pulpit; there is no soil for pride to grow on; but it will grow without any. "I have nothing to glorify of." But, notwithstanding, there often comes in some reason why we should glory, not real, but apparent to our own selves.

1. Now, how is it that a true minister feels he has "nothing to glorify of." First, because he is very conscious of his own imperfections. I think no man will ever form a more just opinion of himself than he who is called constantly and incessantly to preach. Some man once thought he could preach, and on being allowed to enter the pulpit, he found his words did not come quite so freely as he expected, and in the utmost trepidation and fear, he leaned over the front of the pulpit and said "My friends, if you would come up here, it would take the conceit out of you all." I verily believe it would out of a great many, could they once try themselves whether they could preach. It would take their critical conceit out of them, and make them think that after all it was not such easy work. He who preaches best feels that he preaches worst. He who has set up some lofty model in his own mind of what eloquence should be, and what earnest appeal ought to be, will know how much he falls below it. He, best of all, can reprove himself when he knows his own deficiency. I do not believe when a man does a thing well, that therefore he will glory in it. On the other hand, I think that he will be the best judge of his own imperfections, and will see them most clearly. He knows what he ought to be: other men do not. They stare, and gaze, and think it is wonderful, when he thinks it is wonderfully absurd and retires wondering that he has not done better. Every true minister will feel that he is deficient. He will compare himself with such men as Whitfield, with such preachers as those of puritanical times, and he will say, "What am I? Like a dwarf beside a giant, an ant-hill by the side of the mountain." When he retires to rest on Sabbath-night, he will toss from side to side on his bed, because he feels that he has missed the mark, that he has not had that earnestness, that solemnity, that death-like intenseness of purpose which became his position. He will accuse himself of not having dwelt enough on this point, or for having shunned the other, or not having been explicit enough on some certain subject, or expanded another too much. He will see his own faults, for God always chastises his own children at night-time when they have done some-

power over his own will, and hath so decreed in his heart that he will keep his virgin, doeth well.

38 So then he that giveth her in marriage doeth well; but he that giveth her not in marriage doeth better.

39 The wife is bound by the law as long as her husband liveth; but if her husband be dead, she is at liberty to be married to whom she will; only in the Lord.

40 But she is happier if she so abide, after my judgment: and I think also that I have the Spirit of God.

1 CORINTHIANS 8

1 Now as touching things offered unto idols, we know that we all have knowledge. Knowledge puffeth up, but charity edifieth.

2 And if any man think that he knoweth anything, he knoweth nothing yet as he ought to know.

3 But if any man love God, the same is known of him.

4 As concerning therefore the eating of those things which are offered in sacrifice unto idols, we know that an idol is nothing in the world, and that there is none other God but one.

5 For though there be that are called gods, whether in heaven or in earth, (as there be gods many, and lords many,)

6 But to us there is but one God, the Father, of whom are all things, and we in him; and one Lord Jesus Christ, by whom are all things, and we by him.

7 Howbeit there is not in every man that knowledge: for some with conscience of the idol unto this hour eat it as a thing offered unto an idol; and their conscience weak is defiled.

8 But meat commendeth us not to God: for neither, if we eat, are we the better; neither, if we eat not, are we the worse.

9 But take heed lest by any means this liberty of yours become a stumblingblock to them that are weak.

10 For if any man see thee which hast knowledge sit at meat in the idol's temple, shall not the conscience of him which is weak be emboldened to eat

his own will – Which would incline him to desire the increase of his family, and the strengthening it by new relations.

38. Doeth better – If there be no necessity.

39. Only in the Lord – That is, only if Christians marry Christians: a standing direction, and one of the utmost importance.

40. I also – As well as any of you. Have the Spirit of God – Teaching me all things. This does not imply any doubt; but the strongest certainty of it, together with a reproof of them for calling it in question. Whoever, therefore, would conclude from hence, that St. Paul was not certain he had the Spirit of Christ, neither understands the true import of the words, nor considers how expressly he lays claim to the Spirit, both in this epistle, chap. ii, 16, xiv, 37, and the other. 2 Cor. xiii, 3. Indeed, it may be doubted whether the word here and elsewhere translated think, does not always imply the fullest and strongest assurance. See chap. x, 12.

1 CORINTHIANS 8

1. Now concerning the next question you proposed. All of us have knowledge – A gentle reproof of their self-conceit. Knowledge without love always puffeth up. Love alone edifies – Builds us up in holiness.

2. If any man think he knoweth any thing – Aright, unless so far he is taught by God. He knoweth nothing yet as he ought to know – Seeing there is no true knowledge without divine love.

3. He is known – That is, approved, by him. Psalm i, 6.

4. We know that an idol is nothing – A mere nominal God, having no divinity, virtue, or power.

5. For though there be that are called gods – By the heathens both celestial, (as they style them,) terrestrial, and infernal deities.

6. Yet to us – Christians. There is but one God – This is exclusive, not of the One Lord, as if he were an inferior deity; but only of the idols to which the One God is opposed. From whom are all things – By creation, providence, and grace. And we for him – The end of all we are, have, and do. And one Lord – Equally the object of divine worship. By whom are all things – Created, sustained, and governed. And we by him – Have access to the Father, and all spiritual blessings.

7. Some eat, with consciousness of the idol – That is, fancying it is something, and that it makes the meat unlawful to be eaten. And their conscience, being weak – Not rightly informed. Is defiled – contracts guilt by doing it.

8. But meat commendeth us not to God – Neither by eating, nor by refraining from it. Eating and not eating are in themselves things merely indifferent.

10. For if any one see thee who hast knowledge – Whom he believes to have more knowledge than himself, and who really hast this knowledge, that an idol is nothing, sitting down to an entertainment in an idol temple. The heathens frequently made entertainments in their temples, on what hath been sacrificed to their idols. Will not the conscience of him that is weak – Scrupulous. Be encouraged – By thy example. To eat – Though with a doubting conscience.

11. And through thy knowledge shall the weak brother perish, for whom Christ died? – And for whom thou wilt not lose a meal's meat, so far from dying for him! We see, Christ died even for them that perish.

12. Ye sin against Christ – Whose members they are.

13. If meat – Of any kind. Who will follow this example? What preacher or private Christian will abstain from any thing lawful in itself, when it offends a weak brother?

MATTHEW HENRY   CHARLES H. SPURGEON

his rank and place as becomes a Christian. Our comfort and happiness depend on what we are to Christ, not what we are in the world. No man should think to make his faith or religion, an argument to break through any natural or civil obligations. He should quietly and contentedly abide in the condition in which he is placed by Divine Providence.

25-35 Considering the distress of those times, the unmarried state was best. Notwithstanding, the apostle does not condemn marriage. How opposite are those to the apostle Paul who forbid many to marry, and entangle them with vows to remain single, whether they ought to do so or not! He exhorts all Christians to holy indifference toward the world. As to relations; they must not set their hearts on the comforts of the state. As to afflictions; they must not indulge the sorrow of the world: even in sorrow the heart may be joyful. As to worldly enjoyments; here is not their rest. As to worldly employment; those that prosper in trade, and increase in wealth, should hold their possessions as though they held them not. As to all worldly concerns; they must keep the world out of their hearts, that they may not abuse it when they have it in their hands. All worldly things are show; nothing solid. All will be quickly gone. Wise concern about worldly interests is a duty; but to be full of care, to have anxious and perplexing care, is a sin. By this maxim the apostle solves the case whether it were advisable to marry. That condition of life is best for every man, which is best for his soul, and keeps him most clear of the cares and snares of the world. Let us reflect on the advantages and snares of our own condition in life; that we may improve the one, and escape as far as possible all injury from the other. And whatever cares press upon the mind, let time still be kept for the things of the Lord.

36-40 The apostle is thought to give advice here about the disposal of children in marriage. In this view, the general meaning is plain. Children should seek and follow the directions of their parents as to marriage. And parents should consult their children's wishes; and not reckon they have power to do with them, and dictate just as they please, without reason. The whole is closed with advice to widows. Second marriages are not unlawful, so that it is kept in mind, to marry in the Lord. In our choice of relations, and change of conditions, we should always be guided by the fear of God, and the laws of God, and act in dependence on the providence of God. Change of condition ought only to be made after careful consideration, and on probable grounds, that it will be to advantage in our spiritual concerns.

thing wrong. We need not others to reprove us; God himself takes us in hand, The most highly honored before God will often feel himself dishonored in his own esteem.

2. Again, another means of causing us to cease from all glory is the fact that God reminds us that all our gifts are borrowed. And strikingly have I this morning been reminded of that great truth—that all our gifts are borrowed, by reading in a newspaper to the following effect:—

"Last week, the quiet neighborhood of New Town was much disturbed by an occurrence which has thrown a gloom over the entire neighborhood. A gentleman of considerable attainment, who has won an honorable degree at the university has for some months been deranged. He had kept an academy for young gentlemen, but his insanity had obliged him to desist from his occupation, and he has for some time lived alone in a house in the neighborhood. The landlord obtained a warrant of ejectment; and it being found necessary to handcuff him, he was, by sad mismanagement, compelled to remain on the steps, exposed to the gaze of a great crowd, until at last a vehicle arrived, which conveyed him to the asylum. One of his pupils (says the paper) is Mr. Spurgeon."

The man from whom I learned whatever of human learning I have, has now become a raving lunatic in the Asylum! When I saw that, I felt I could bend my knee with humble gratitude and thank my God that not yet had my reason reeled, not yet had those powers departed. Oh! how thankful we ought to be that our talents are preserved to us, and that our mind is not gone! Nothing came nearer and closer to me than that. There was one who had taken all pains with me—a man of genius and of ability; and yet there he is! how fallen! how fallen! How speedily does human nature come from its high estate and sink below the level of the brutes? Bless God my friends, for your talents! thank him for your reason! thank him for your intellect! Simple as it may be, it is enough for you, and if you lost it you would soon mark the difference. Take heed to yourself lest in aught you say. "This is Babylon that I have builded;" for, remember, both trowel and mortar must come from him. The life, the voice, the talent, the imagination, the eloquence—all are the gift of God; and he who has the greatest gifts must feel that unto God belong the shield of the mighty, for he has given might to his people, and strength unto his servants.

3. One more answer to this question. Another means whereby God preserves his ministers from glorying is this: He makes them feel their constant dependence upon the Holy Ghost. Some do not feel it, I confess. Some will venture to preach without the Spirit of God, or without entreating it. But I think that no man, who is really commissioned from on high, will ever venture to do so, but he will

those things which are offered to idols;

11 And through thy knowledge shall the weak brother perish, for whom Christ died?

12 But when ye sin so against the brethren, and wound their weak conscience, ye sin against Christ.

13 Wherefore, if meat make my brother to offend, I will eat no flesh while the world standeth, lest I make my brother to offend.

1 CORINTHIANS 9

1 Am I not an apostle? am I not free? have I not seen Jesus Christ our Lord? are not ye my work in the Lord?

2 If I be not an apostle unto others, yet doubtless I am to you: for the seal of mine apostleship are ye in the Lord.

3 Mine answer to them that do examine me is this,

4 Have we not power to eat and to drink?

5 Have we not power to lead about a sister, a wife, as well as other apostles, and as the brethren of the Lord, and Cephas?

6 Or I only and Barnabas, have not we power to forbear working?

7 Who goeth a warfare any time at his own charges? who planteth a vineyard, and eateth not of the fruit thereof? or who feedeth a flock, and eateth not of the milk of the flock?

8 Say I these things as a man? or saith not the law the same also?

9 For it is written in the law of Moses, Thou shalt not muzzle the mouth of the ox that treadeth out the corn. Doth God take care for oxen?

10 Or saith he it altogether for our sakes? For our sakes, no doubt, this is written: that he that ploweth should plow in hope; and that he that thresheth in hope should be partaker of his hope.

11 If we have sown unto you spiritual things, is it a great thing if we shall reap your carnal things?

12 If others be partakers of this power over you, are not we rather? Nevertheless we have

1 CORINTHIANS 9

1. Am I not free? am I not an apostle? – That is, Have not I the liberty of a common Christian? yea, that of an apostle? He vindicates his apostleship, chap. ix, 1-iii, his apostolic liberty, chap. ix, 4-19. Have I not seen Jesus Christ? – Without this he could not have been one of those first grand witnesses. Are not ye my work in the Lord – A full evidence that God hath sent me? And yet some, it seems, objected to his being an apostle, because he had not asserted his privilege in demanding and receiving such maintenance from the churches as was due to that office.

2. Ye are the seal of my apostleship – Who have received not only faith by my mouth, but all the gifts of the Spirit by my hands.

3. My answer to them who examine me – Concerning my apostleship. Is this – Which I have now given.

4. Have we not power – I and my fellow laborers. To eat and to drink – At the expense of those among whom we labor.

5. Have we not power to lead about with us a sister, a wife – And to demand sustenance for her also? As well as the other apostles – Who therefore, it is plain, did this. And Peter – Hence we learn,

　　1. That St. Peter continued to live with his wife after he became an apostle:

　　2. That he had no rights as an apostle which were not common to St. Paul.

6. To forbear working – With our hands.

8. Do I speak as a man – Barely on the authority of human reason? Does not God also say, in effect, the same thing? The ox that treadeth out the corn – This was the custom in Judea, and many eastern nations. In several of them it is retained still. And at this day, horses tread out the corn in some parts of Germany.

9. Doth God – In this direction. Take care for oxen – Only? Hath he not a farther meaning? And so undoubtedly he hath in all the other Mosaic laws of this kind.

10. He who ploweth ought to plow in hope – Of reaping. This seems to be a proverbial expression. And he that thresheth in hope – Ought not to be disappointed, ought to eat the fruit of his labors. And ought they who labor in God's husbandry. Deut. xxv, 4.

11. Is it a great matter if we shall reap as much of your carnal things – As is needful for our sustenance? Do you give us things of greater value than those you receive from us?

12. If others – Whether true or false apostles. Partake of this power – Have a right to be maintained. Do not we rather – On account of our having labored so much more? Lest we should give any hindrance to the gospel – By giving an occasion of cavil or reproach.

14. Matt. x, 10.

15. It were better for me to die than – To give occasion to them that seek occasion against me, 2 Cor. xi, 12.

17. Willingly – He seems to mean, without receiving anything. St. Paul here speaks in a manner peculiar to himself. Another might have preached willingly, and yet have received a maintenance from the Corinthians. But if he had received anything from them, he would have termed it preaching unwillingly. And so, in the next verse, another might have used that power without abusing it. But his own using it at all, he would have termed abusing it. A dispensation is intrusted to me – Therefore I dare not refrain.

18. What then is my reward – That circumstance in my conduct for which I expect a peculiar reward from my great Master? That I abuse not – Make not an unseasonable use of my power which I have in preaching the gospel.

19. I made myself the servant of all – I acted with as self-denying a regard to their interest, and as much caution not to offend them, as if I had been literally their servant or slave. Where is the preacher of the gospel who treads in the

1 CORINTHIANS 8

The danger of having a high conceit of knowledge.
(1-6)
The mischief of offending weak brethren. (7-13)

1-6 There is no proof of ignorance more common than conceit of knowledge. Much may be known, when nothing is known to good purpose. And those who think they know any thing, and grow vain thereon, are the least likely to make good use of their knowledge. Satan hurts some as much by tempting them to be proud of mental powers, as others, by alluring to sensuality. Knowledge which puffs up the possessor, and renders him confident, is as dangerous as self-righteous pride, though what he knows may be right. Without holy affections all human knowledge is worthless. The heathens had gods of higher and lower degree; gods many, and lords many; so called, but not such in truth. Christians know better. One God made all, and has power over all. The one God, even the Father, signifies the Godhead as the sole object of all religious worship; and the Lord Jesus Christ denotes the person of Emmanuel, God manifest in the flesh, One with the Father, and with us; the appointed Mediator, and Lord of all; through whom we come to the Father, and through whom the Father sends all blessings to us, by the influence and working of the Holy Spirit. While we refuse all worship to the many who are called gods and lords, and to saints and angels, let us try whether we really come to God by faith in Christ.

7-13 Eating one kind of food, and abstaining from another, have nothing in them to recommend a person to God. But the apostle cautions against putting a stumbling-block in the way of the weak; lest they be made bold to eat what was offered to the idol, not as common food, but as a sacrifice, and thereby be guilty of idolatry. He who has the Spirit of Christ in him, will love those whom Christ loved so as to die for them. Injuries done to Christians, are done to Christ; but most of all, the entangling them in guilt: wounding their consciences, is wounding him. We should be very tender of doing any thing that may occasion stumbling to others, though it may be innocent in itself. And if we must not endanger other men's souls, how much should we take care not to destroy our own! Let Christians beware of approaching the brink of evil, or the appearance of it, though many do this in public matters, for which perhaps they plead plausibly. Men cannot thus sin against their brethren, without offending Christ, and endangering their own souls.

feel that he needs the Spirit. Once, while preaching in Scotland, the Spirit of God was pleased to desert me, I could not speak as usually I have done. I was obliged to tell the people that the chariot wheels were taken off; and that the chariot dragged very heavily along. I have felt the benefit of that ever since. It humbled me bitterly, for I could have crept into a nut-shell, and I would have hidden myself in any obscure corner of the earth. I felt as if I should speak no more in the name of the Lord, and then the thought came "Oh! thou art an ungrateful creature: hath not God spoken by thee hundreds of times? And this once, when he would not do so wilt thou upbraid him for it? Nay, rather thank him, that a hundred times he hath stood by thee; and, if once he hath forsaken thee, admire his goodness, that thus he would keep thee humble." Some may imagine that want of study brought me into that condition, but I can honestly affirm, that it was not so. I think that I am bound to give myself unto reading, and not tempt the Spirit by unthought-of effusions. Usually, I deem it a duty to seek a sermon of my Master and implore him to impress it on my mind, but on that occasion, I think I had even prepared more carefully then than I ordinarily do, so that unpreparedness was not the reason. The simple fact was this—"The wind bloweth where it listeth;" and winds do not always blow hurricanes. Sometimes the winds themselves are still. And, therefore, if I rest on the Spirit, I cannot expect I should always feel its power alike. What could I do without the celestial influence, for to that I owe everything. By this thought God humbles his servants. God will teach us how much we want it. He will not let us think we are doing anything ourselves. "Nay," says he, "thou shalt have none of the glory. I will take thee down. Art thou thinking 'I am doing this?' I will show thee what thou art without me." Out goes Samson. He attacks the Philistines. He fancies he can slay them; but they are on him. His eyes are out. His glory is gone, because he trusted not in his God, but rested in himself. Every minister will be made to feel his dependence upon the Spirit; and then will he, with emphasis, say, as Paul did, "If I preach the gospel, I have nothing to glorify of."

III. Now comes the third question, with which we are to finish WHAT IS THAT NECESSITY WHICH IS LAID UPON US TO PREACH THY GOSPEL?

1. First, a very great part of that necessity springs from the call itself: If a man be truly called of God to the ministry, I will defy him to withhold himself from it. A man who has really within him the inspiration of the Holy Ghost calling him to preach cannot help it. He must preach. As fire within the bones, so will that influence be until it blazes forth. Friends may check him, foes criticize him, despisers sneer at him, the man is indomitable; he

not used this power; but suffer all things, lest we should hinder the gospel of Christ.

13 Do ye not know that they which minister about holy things live of the things of the temple? and they which wait at the altar are partakers with the altar?

14 Even so hath the Lord ordained that they which preach the gospel should live of the gospel.

15 But I have used none of these things: neither have I written these things, that it should be so done unto me: for it were better for me to die, than that any man should make my glorying void.

16 For though I preach the gospel, I have nothing to glory of: for necessity is laid upon me; yea, woe is unto me, if I preach not the gospel!

17 For if I do this thing willingly, I have a reward: but if against my will, a dispensation of the gospel is committed unto me.

18 What is my reward then? Verily that, when I preach the gospel, I may make the gospel of Christ without charge, that I abuse not my power in the gospel.

19 For though I be free from all men, yet have I made myself servant unto all, that I might gain the more.

20 And unto the Jews I became as a Jew, that I might gain the Jews; to them that are under the law, as under the law, that I might gain them that are under the law;

21 To them that are without law, as without law, (being not without law to God, but under the law to Christ,) that I might gain them that are without law.

22 To the weak became I as weak, that I might gain the weak: I am made all things to all men, that I might by all means save some.

23 And this I do for the gospel's sake, that I might be partaker thereof with you.

24 Know ye not that they which run in a race run all, but one receiveth the prize? So run, that ye may obtain.

25 And every man that striveth for the mastery is temperate in all things. Now they do it to

same steps?

20. To the Jews I became as a Jew – Conforming myself in all things to their manner of thinking and living, so far as I could with innocence. To them that are under the law – Who apprehend themselves to be still bound by the Mosaic law. As under the law – Observing it myself, while I am among them. Not that he declared this to be necessary, or refused to converse with those who did not observe it. This was the very thing which he condemned in St. Peter, Gal. ii, 14.

21. To them that are without the law – The heathens. As without the law – Neglecting its ceremonies. Being not without the law to God – But as much as ever under its moral precepts. Under the law to Christ – And in this sense all Christians will be under the law for ever.

22. I became as weak – As if I had been scrupulous too. I became all things to all men – Accommodating myself to all, so far as I could consistent with truth and sincerity.

24. Know ye not that – In those famous games which are kept at the isthmus, near your city. They who run in the foot race all run, though but one receiveth the prize – How much greater encouragement have you to run; since ye may all receive the prize of your high calling!

25. And every one that there contendeth is temperate in all things – To an almost incredible degree; using the most rigorous self denial in food, sleep, and every other sensual indulgence. A corruptible crown – A garland of leaves, which must soon wither. The moderns only have discovered that it is "legal" to do all this and more for an eternal crown than they did for a corruptible!

26. I so run, not as uncertainly – I look straight to the goal; I run straight toward it. I cast away every weight, regard not any that stand by. I fight not as one that beateth the air – This is a proverbial expression for a man's missing his blow, and spending his strength, not on his enemy, but on empty air.

27. But I keep under my body – By all kinds of self denial. And bring it into subjection – To my spirit and to God. The words are strongly figurative, and signify the mortification of the body of sin, "by an allusion to the natural bodies of those who were bruised or subdued in combat. Lest by any means after having preached – The Greek word means, after having discharged the office of an herald, (still carrying on the allusion,) whose office it was to proclaim the conditions, and to display the prizes. I myself should become a reprobate – Disapproved by the Judge, and so falling short of the prize. This single text may give us a just notion of the scriptural doctrine of election and reprobation; and clearly shows us, that particular persons are not in holy writ represented as elected absolutely and unconditionally to eternal life, or predestinated absolutely and unconditionally to eternal death; but that believers in general are elected to enjoy the Christian privileges on earth; which if they abuse, those very elect persons will become reprobate. St. Paul was certainly an elect person, if ever there was one; and yet he declares it was possible he himself might become a reprobate. Nay, he actually would have become such, if he had not thus kept his body under, even though he had been so long an elect person, a Christian, and an apostle.

1 CORINTHIANS 9

The apostle shows his authority, and asserts his right to be maintained. (1-14)

He waived this part of his Christian liberty, for the good of others. (15-23)

He did all this, with care and diligence, in view of an unfading crown. (24-27)

1-14 It is not new for a minister to meet with unkind returns for good-will to a people, and diligent and successful services among them. To the cavils of some, the apostle answers, so as to set forth himself as an example of self-denial, for the good of others. He had a right to marry as well as other apostles, and to claim what was needful for his wife, and his children if he had any, from the churches, without laboring with his own hands to get it. Those who seek to do our souls good, should have food provided for them. But he renounced his right, rather than hinder his success by claiming it. It is the people's duty to maintain their minister. He may waive his right, as Paul did; but those transgress a precept of Christ, who deny or withhold due support.

15-23 It is the glory of a minister to deny himself, that he may serve Christ and save souls. But when a minister gives up his right for the sake of the gospel, he does more than his charge and office demands. By preaching the gospel, freely, the apostle showed that he acted from principles of zeal and love, and thus enjoyed much comfort and hope in his soul. And though he looked on the ceremonial law as a yoke taken off by Christ, yet he submitted to it, that he might work upon the Jews, do away their prejudices, prevail with them to hear the gospel, and win them over to Christ. Though he would transgress no laws of Christ, to please any man, yet he would accommodate himself to all men, where he might do it lawfully, to gain some. Doing good was the study and business of his life; and, that he might reach this end, he did not stand on privileges. We must carefully watch against extremes, and against relying on any thing but trust in Christ alone. We must not allow errors or faults, so as to hurt others, or disgrace the gospel.

24-27 The apostle compares himself to the racers and combatants in the Isthmian games, well known by the Corinthians. But in the Christian race all may run so as to obtain. There is the greatest encouragement, therefore, to persevere with all our strength, in this course. Those who ran in these games were kept to a spare diet. They used themselves to hardships. They practiced the exercises. And those who pursue the interests of their souls, must combat hard with fleshly lusts. The body must not be suffered to rule. The apostle

must preach if he has the call of heaven. All earth might forsake him; but he would preach to the barren mountain-tops. If he has the call of heaven, if he has no congregation, he would preach to the rippling waterfalls, and let the brooks hear his voice. He could not be silent. He would become a voice crying in the wilderness, "Prepare ye the way of the Lord." I no more believe it possible to stop ministers, than to stop the stars of heaven. I think it no more possible to make a man cease from preaching, if he is really called, than to stop some mighty cataract, by seeking, with an infant's cup, to drink its waters. The man has been moved of heaven, who shall stop him? He has been touched of God, who shall impede him? With an eagle's wing he must fly; who shall chain him to the earth? With seraph's voice he must speak, who shall stop his lips? Is not his word like a fire within me? Must I not speak if God has placed it there? And when a man does speak as the Spirit gives him utterance, he will feel a holy joy akin to heaven; and when it is over he wishes to be at his work again, and longs to be once more preaching. I do not think young men are called of God to any great work who preach once a week, and think they have done their duty. I think if God has called a man, he will impel him to be more or less constantly at it, and he will feel that he must preach among the nations the unsearchable riches of Christ.

2. But another thing will make us preach: we shall feel that woe is unto us if we preach not the gospel; and that is the sad destitution of this poor fallen world. Oh, minister of the gospel! stand for one moment and bethink thyself of thy poor fellow creatures! See them like a stream, rushing to eternity—ten thousand to their endless home each solemn moment fly! See the termination of that stream, that tremendous cataract which dashes streams of souls into the pit! Oh, minister, bethink thyself that men are being damned each hour by thousands, and that each time thy pulse beats another soul lifts up its eyes in hell, being in torments; bethink thyself how men are speeding on their way to destruction, how "the love of many waxeth cold" and "iniquity doth abound." I say, is there not a necessity laid upon thee? Is it not woe unto thee if thou preachest not the gospel? Take thy walk one evening through the streets of London when the dusk has gathered, and darkness veils the people. Mark you not yon profligate hurrying on to her accursed work? See you not thousands and tens of thousands annually ruined? Up from the hospital and the asylum there comes a voice, "Woe is unto you if ye preach not the gospel." Go to that huge place built around with massive walls, enter the dungeons, and see the thieves who have for years spent their lives in sin. Wend your way sometimes to that sad square of Newgate, and see the murderer hanged. A voice

obtain a corruptible crown; but we an incorruptible.

26 I therefore so run, not as uncertainly; so fight I, not as one that beateth the air:

27 But I keep under my body, and bring it into subjection: lest that by any means, when I have preached to others, I myself should be a castaway.

1 CORINTHIANS 10

1 Moreover, brethren, I would not that ye should be ignorant, how that all our fathers were under the cloud, and all passed through the sea;

2 And were all baptized unto Moses in the cloud and in the sea;

3 And did all eat the same spiritual meat;

4 And did all drink the same spiritual drink: for they drank of that spiritual Rock that followed them: and that Rock was Christ.

5 But with many of them God was not well pleased: for they were overthrown in the wilderness.

6 Now these things were our examples, to the intent we should not lust after evil things, as they also lusted.

7 Neither be ye idolaters, as were some of them; as it is written, The people sat down to eat and drink, and rose up to play.

8 Neither let us commit fornication, as some of them committed, and fell in one day three and twenty thousand.

9 Neither let us tempt Christ, as some of them also tempted, and were destroyed of serpents.

10 Neither murmur ye, as some of them also murmured, and were destroyed of the destroyer.

11 Now all these things happened unto them for ensamples: and they are written for our admonition, upon whom the ends of the world are come.

12 Wherefore let him that thinketh he standeth take heed lest he fall.

13 There hath no temptation taken you but such as is common to man: but God is faithful, who will not suffer you to be tempted above that ye are able; but will with the temptation also make a way to escape, that ye

1 CORINTHIANS 10

1. Now – That ye may not become reprobates, consider how highly favored your fathers were, who were God's elect and peculiar people, and nevertheless were rejected by him. They were all under the cloud – That eminent token of God's gracious presence, which screened them from the heat of the sun by day, and gave them light by night. And all passed through the sea – God opening a way through the midst of the waters. Exod. xiii, 21; Exod. xiv, 22.

2. And were all, as it were, baptized unto Moses – Initiated into the religion which he taught them. In the cloud and in the sea – Perhaps sprinkled here and there with drops of water from the sea or the cloud, by which baptism might be the more evidently signified.

3. And all ate the same manna, termed spiritual meat, as it was typical,

    1. Of Christ and his spiritual benefits:

    2. Of the sacred bread which we eat at his table. Exod. xvi, 15.

4. And all drank the same spiritual drink – Typical of Christ, and of that cup which we drink. For they drank out of the spiritual or mysterious rock, the wonderful streams of which followed them in their several journeyings, for many years, through the wilderness. And that rock was a manifest type of Christ – The Rock of Eternity, from whom his people derive those streams of blessings which follow them through all this wilderness. Exod. xvii, 6.

5. Yet – Although they had so many tokens of the divine presence. They were overthrown – With the most terrible marks of his displeasure.

6. Now these things were our examples – Showing what we are to expect if, enjoying the like benefits, we commit the like sins. The benefits are set down in the same order as by Moses in Exodus; the sins and punishments in a different order; evil desire first, as being the foundation of all; next, idolatry, ver. 7, 14; then fornication, which usually accompanied it, ver. 8; the tempting and murmuring against God, in the following verses. As they desired – Flesh, in contempt of manna. Num. xi, 4.

7. Neither be ye idolaters – And so, "neither murmur ye," ver. 10. The other cautions are given in the first person; but these in the second. And with what exquisite propriety does he vary the person! It would have been improper to say, Neither let us be idolaters; for he was himself in no danger of idolatry; nor probably of murmuring against Christ, or the divine providence. To play – That is, to dance, in honor of their idol. Exod. xxxii, 6.

8. And fell in one day three and twenty thousand – Beside the princes who were afterwards hanged, and those whom the Judges slew so that there died in all four and twenty thousand. Num. xxv, 1, 9.

9. Neither let us tempt Christ – By our unbelief. St. Paul enumerates five benefits, ver. 1-4; of which the fourth and fifth were closely connected together; and five sins, the fourth and fifth of which were likewise closely connected. In speaking of the fifth benefit, he expressly mentions Christ; and in speaking of the fourth sin, he shows it was committed against Christ. As some of them tempted him – This sin of the people was peculiarly against Christ; for when they had so long drank of that rock, yet they murmured for want of water. Num. xxi, 4, &c.

10. The destroyer – The destroying angel. Num. xiv, 1, 36.

11. On whom the ends of the ages are come – The expression has great force. All things meet together, and come to a crisis, under the last, the gospel, dispensation; both benefits and dangers, punishments and rewards. It remains, that Christ come as an avenger and judge. And even these ends include various periods, succeeding each other.

12. The common translation runs, Let him that thinketh he standeth; but the word translated thinketh, most certainly strengthens, rather than weakens, the sense.

13. Common to man – Or, as the Greek word imports, proportioned to human

presses this advice on the Corinthians. He sets before himself and them the danger of yielding to fleshly desires, pampering the body, and its lusts and appetites. Holy fear of himself was needed to keep an apostle faithful: how much more is it needful for our preservation! Let us learn from hence humility and caution, and to watch against dangers which surround us while in the body.

1 CORINTHIANS 10

The great privileges, and yet terrible overthrow of the Israelites in the wilderness. (1-5)
Cautions against all idolatrous, and other sinful practices. (6-14)
The partaking in idolatry cannot exist with having communion with Christ. (15-22)
All we do to be to the glory of God, and without offense to the consciences of others. (23-33)

1-5 To dissuade the Corinthians from communion with idolaters, and security in any sinful course, the apostle sets before them the example of the Jewish nation of old. They were, by a miracle, led through the Red Sea, where the pursuing Egyptians were drowned. It was to them a typical baptism. The manna on which they fed was a type of Christ crucified, the Bread which came down from heaven, which whoso eateth shall live for ever. Christ is the Rock on which the Christian church is built; and of the streams that issue therefrom, all believers drink, and are refreshed. It typified the sacred influences of the Holy Spirit, as given to believers through Christ. But let none presume upon their great privileges, or profession of the truth; these will not secure heavenly happiness.

6-14 Carnal desires gain strength by indulgence, therefore should be checked in their first rise. Let us fear the sins of Israel, if we would shun their plagues. And it is but just to fear, that such as tempt Christ, will be left by him in the power of the old serpent. Murmuring against God's disposals and commands, greatly provokes him. Nothing in Scripture is written in vain; and it is our wisdom and duty to learn from it. Others have fallen, and so may we. The Christian's security against sin is distrust of himself. God has not promised to keep us from falling, if we do not look to ourselves. To this word of caution, a word of comfort is added. Others have the like burdens, and the like temptations: what they bear up under, and break through, we may also. God is wise as well as faithful, and will make our burdens according to our strength. He knows what we can bear. He will make a way to escape; he will deliver either from the trial itself, or at least the mischief of it. We have full encouragement to flee from sin, and to be

shall come from each house of correction, from each prison, from each gallows, saying, "Woe is unto thee if thou preachest not the gospel." Go thou to the thousand death-beds, and mark how men are perishing in ignorance, not knowing the ways of God. See their terror as they approach their Judge, never having known what it was to be saved, not even knowing the way; and as you see them quivering before their Maker, hear a voice, "Minister, woe is unto thee if thou preachest not the gospel." Or take another course. Travel round this great metropolis, and stop at the door of some place where there is heard the tinkling of bells, chanting and music, but where the whore of Babylon hath her sway, and lies are preached for truth; and when thou comest home and thinkest of Popery and Puseyism, let a voice come to thee, "Minister woe is unto thee if thou preachest not the gospel." Or step into the hall of the infidel where he blasphemes thy Maker's name; or sit in the theater where plays, libidinous and loose are acted, and from all these haunts of vice there comes the voice, "Minister, woe is unto thee if thou preachest not the gospel." And take thy last solemn walk down to the chambers of the lost; let the abyss of hell be visited, and stand thou and hear

"The sullen groans, the hollow moans,
And shrieks of tortured ghosts."

Put thine ear at hell's gate, and for a little while list to the commingled screams and shrieks of agony and fell despair that shall lend thine ear; and as thou comest from that sad place with that doleful music still affrighting thee, thou wilt hear the voice, "Minister! minister! woe is unto thee if thou preachest not the gospel." Only let us have these things before our eyes, and we must preach. Stop preaching! Stop preaching! Let the sun stop shining, and we will preach in darkness. Let the waves stop their ebb and flow, and still our voice shall preach the gospel, let the world stop its revolutions, let the planets stay their motion; we will still preach the gospel. Until the fiery center of this earth shall burst through the thick ribs of her brazen mountains, we shall still preach the gospel; till the universal conflagration shall dissolve the earth, and matter shall be swept away, these lips, or the lips of some others called of God, shall still thunder forth the voice of Jehovah. We cannot help it. Necessity is laid upon us, yea woe is unto us if we preach not the gospel.

Now, my dear hearers, one word with you. There are some persons in this audience who are verily guilty in the sight of God because they do not preach the gospel. I cannot think out of the fifteen hundred or two thousand persons now present, within the reach of my voice, there are none who are qualified to preach the gospel besides myself. I have not so bad an opinion of you as to conceive myself to be superior in intellect to one half of you,

may be able to bear it.

14   Wherefore, my dearly beloved, flee from idolatry.

15   I speak as to wise men; judge ye what I say.

16   The cup of blessing which we bless, is it not the communion of the blood of Christ? The bread which we break, is it not the communion of the body of Christ?

17   For we being many are one bread, and one body: for we are all partakers of that one bread.

18   Behold Israel after the flesh: are not they which eat of the sacrifices partakers of the altar?

19   What say I then? that the idol is any thing, or that which is offered in sacrifice to idols is any thing?

20   But I say, that the things which the Gentiles sacrifice, they sacrifice to devils, and not to God: and I would not that ye should have fellowship with devils.

21   Ye cannot drink the cup of the Lord, and the cup of devils: ye cannot be partakers of the Lord's table, and of the table of devils.

22   Do we provoke the Lord to jealousy? are we stronger than he?

23   All things are lawful for me, but all things are not expedient: all things are lawful for me, but all things edify not.

24   Let no man seek his own, but every man another's wealth.

25   Whatsoever is sold in the shambles, that eat, asking no question for conscience sake:

26   For the earth is the Lord's, and the fullness thereof.

27   If any of them that believe not bid you to a feast, and ye be disposed to go; whatsoever is set before you, eat, asking no question for conscience sake.

28   But if any man say unto you, This is offered in sacrifice unto idols, eat not for his sake that shewed it, and for conscience sake: for the earth is the Lord's, and the fullness thereof:

29   Conscience, I say, not thine own, but of the other: for why is my liberty judged of another man's conscience?

30   For if I by grace be a partaker, why am I evil spoken of for that for which I give thanks?

strength. God is faithful – In giving the help which he hath promised. And he will with the temptation – Provide for your deliverance.

14. Flee from idolatry – And from all approaches to it.

16. The cup which we bless – By setting it apart to a sacred use, and solemnly invoking the blessing of God upon it. Is it not the communion of the blood of Christ – The means of our partaking of those invaluable benefits, which are the purchase of the blood of Christ. The communion of the body of Christ – The means of our partaking of those benefits which were purchased by the body of Christ – offered for us.

17. For it is this communion which makes us all one. We being many are yet, as it were, but different parts of one and the same broken bread, which we receive to unite us in one body.

18. Consider Israel after the flesh – Christians are the spiritual "Israel of God." Are not they who eat of the sacrifices partakers of the altar – Is not this an act of communion with that God to whom they are offered? And is not the case the same with those who eat of the sacrifices which have been offered to idols?

19. What say I then – Do I in saying this allow that an idol is anything divine? I aver, on the contrary, that what the heathens sacrifice, they sacrifice to devils. Such in reality are the gods of the heathens; and with such only can you hold communion in those sacrifices.

21. Ye cannot drink the cup of the Lord, and the cup of devils – You cannot have communion with both.

22. Do we provoke the Lord to jealousy – By thus caressing his rivals? Are we stronger than he – Are we able to resist, or to bear his wrath?

23. Supposing this were lawful in itself, yet it is not expedient, it is not edifying to my neighbor.

24. His own only, but another's welfare also.

25. The apostle now applies this principle to the point in question. Asking no questions – Whether it has been sacrificed or not.

26. For God, who is the Creator, Proprietor, and Disposer of the earth and all that is therein, hath given the produce of it to the children of men, to be used without scruple. Psalm xxiv, 1.

28. For his sake that showed thee, and for conscience' sake – That is, for the sake of his weak conscience, lest it should be wounded.

29. Conscience I say, not thy own – I speak of his conscience, not thine. For why is my liberty judged by another's conscience – Another's conscience is not the standard of mine, nor is another's persuasion the measure of my liberty.

30. If I by grace am a partaker – If I thankfully use the common blessings of God.

31. Therefore – To close the present point with a general rule, applicable not only in this, but in all cases, Whatsoever ye do – In all things whatsoever, whether of a religious or civil nature, in all the common, as well as sacred, actions of life, keep the glory of God in view, and steadily pursue in all this one end of your being, the planting or advancing the vital knowledge and love of God, first in your own soul, then in all mankind.

32. Give no offense – If, and as far as, it is possible.

33. Even as I, as much as lieth in me, please all men.

MATTHEW HENRY   CHARLES H. SPURGEON

faithful to God. We cannot fall by temptation, if we cleave fast to him. Whether the world smiles or frowns, it is an enemy; but believers shall be strengthened to overcome it, with all its terrors and enticements. The fear of the Lord, put into their hearts, will be the great means of safety.

15-22 Did not the joining in the Lord's supper show a profession of faith in Christ crucified, and of adoring gratitude to him for his salvation? Christians, by this ordinance, and the faith therein professed, were united as the grains of wheat in one loaf of bread, or as the members in the human body, seeing they were all united to Christ, and had fellowship with him and one another. This is confirmed from the Jewish worship and customs in sacrifice. The apostle applies this to feasting with idolaters. Eating food as part of a heathen sacrifice, was worshiping the idol to whom it was made, and having fellowship or communion with it; just as he who eats the Lord's supper, is accounted to partake in the Christian sacrifice, or as they who ate the Jewish sacrifices partook of what was offered on their altar. It was denying Christianity; for communion with Christ, and communion with devils, could never be had at once. If Christians venture into places, and join in sacrifices to the lust of the flesh, the lust of the eye, and the pride of life, they will provoke God.

23-33 There were cases wherein Christians might eat what had been offered to idols, without sin. Such as when the flesh was sold in the market as common food, for the priest to whom it had been given. But a Christian must not merely consider what is lawful, but what is expedient, and to edify others. Christianity by no means forbids the common offices of kindness, or allows uncourteous behavior to any, however they may differ from us in religious sentiments or practices. But this is not to be understood of religious festivals, partaking in idolatrous worship. According to this advice of the apostle, Christians should take care not to use their liberty to the hurt of others, or to their own reproach. In eating and drinking, and in all we do, we should aim at the glory of God, at pleasing and honoring him. This is the great end of all religion, and directs us where express rules are wanting. A holy, peaceable, and benevolent spirit, will disarm the greatest enemies.

1 CORINTHIANS 11

or even in the power of preaching God's Word: and even supposing I should be, I cannot believe that I have such a congregation that there are not among you many who have gifts and talents that qualify you to preach the Word. Among the Scotch Baptists it is the custom to call upon all the brethren to exhort on the Sabbath morning; they have no regular minister to preach on that occasion, but every man preaches who likes to get up and speak. That is all very well, only, I fear, many unqualified brethren would be the greatest speakers, since it is a known fact, that men who have little to say will often keep on the longest; and if I were chairman, I should say, "Brother, it is written, 'Speak to edification.' I am sure you would not edify yourself and your wife, you had better go and try that first, and if you cannot succeed, don't waste our precious time."

But still I say, I cannot conceive but what there are some here this morning who are flowers "wasting their sweetness in the desert air," "gems of purest ray serene," lying in the dark caverns of ocean's oblivion. This is a very serious question. If there be any talent in the Church at Park Street, let it be developed. If there be any preachers in my congregation let them preach. Many ministers make it a point to check young men in this respect. There is my hand, such as it is, to help any one of you if you think you can tell to sinners round what a dear Savior you have found. I would like to find scores of preachers among you; would to God that all the Lord's servants were prophets. There are some here who ought to be prophets, only they are half afraid—well, we must devise some scheme of getting rid of their bashfulness. I cannot bear to think that while the devil sets all his servants to work there should be one servant of Jesus Christ asleep. Young man, go home and examine thyself, see what thy abilities are, and if thou findest that thou hast ability, then try in some poor humble room to tell to a dozen poor people what they must do to be saved. You need not aspire to become absolutely and solely dependent upon the ministry, but if it should please God, even desire it. He that desireth a bishopric desireth a good thing. At any rate seek in some way to be preaching the gospel of God. I have preached this sermon especially, because I want to commence a movement from this place which shall reach others. I want to find some in my church, if it be possible, who will preach the gospel. And mark you, if you have talent and power, woe is unto you if you preach not the gospel.

But oh! my friends, if it is woe unto us if we preach not the gospel, what is the woe unto you if ye hear and receive not the gospel? May God give us both to escape from that woe! May the gospel of God be unto us the savor of life unto life, and not of death unto death.

31 Whether therefore ye eat, or drink, or whatsoever ye do, do all to the glory of God.

32 Give none offense, neither to the Jews, nor to the Gentiles, nor to the church of God:

33 Even as I please all men in all things, not seeking mine own profit, but the profit of many, that they may be saved.

1 CORINTHIANS 11

1 Be ye followers of me, even as I also am of Christ.

2 Now I praise you, brethren, that ye remember me in all things, and keep the ordinances, as I delivered them to you.

3 But I would have you know, that the head of every man is Christ; and the head of the woman is the man; and the head of Christ is God.

4 Every man praying or prophesying, having his head covered, dishonoreth his head.

5 But every woman that prayeth or prophesieth with her head uncovered dishonoreth her head: for that is even all one as if she were shaven.

6 For if the woman be not covered, let her also be shorn: but if it be a shame for a woman to be shorn or shaven, let her be covered.

7 For a man indeed ought not to cover his head, forasmuch as he is the image and glory of God: but the woman is the glory of the man.

8 For the man is not of the woman; but the woman of the man.

9 Neither was the man created for the woman; but the woman for the man.

10 For this cause ought the woman to have power on her head because of the angels.

11 Nevertheless neither is the man without the woman, neither the woman without the man, in the Lord.

12 For as the woman is of the man, even so is the man also by the woman; but all things of god.

13 Judge in yourselves: is it comely that a woman pray unto God uncovered?

14 Doth not even nature itself teach you, that, if a man have long hair, it is a shame unto him?

1 CORINTHIANS 11

2. I praise you – The greater part of you.

3. I would have you know – He does not seem to have given them any order before concerning this. The head of every man – Particularly every believer. Is Christ, and the head of Christ is God – Christ, as he is Mediator, acts in all things subordinately to his Father. But we can no more infer that they are not of the same divine nature, because God is said to be the head of Christ, than that man and woman are not of the same human nature, because the man is said to be the head of the woman.

4. Every man praying or prophesying – Speaking by the immediate power of God. With his head – And face. Covered – Either with a veil or with long hair. Dishonored his head – St. Paul seems to mean, As in these eastern nations veiling the head is a badge of subjection, so a man who prays or prophesies with a veil on his head, reflects a dishonor on Christ, whose representative he is.

5. But every woman – Who, under an immediate impulse of the Spirit, (for then only was a woman suffered to speak in the church,) prays or prophesies without a veil on her face, as it were disclaims subjection, and reflects dishonor on man, her head. For it is the same, in effect, as if she cut her hair short, and wore it in the distinguishing form of the men. In those ages, men wore their hair exceeding short, as appears from the ancient statues and pictures.

6. Therefore if a woman is not covered – If she will throw off the badge of subjection, let her appear with her hair cut like a man's. But if it be shameful for a woman to appear thus in public, especially in a religious assembly, let her, for the same reason, keep on her veil.

7. A man indeed ought not to veil his head, because he is the image of God – In the dominion he bears over the creation, representing the supreme dominion of God, which is his glory. But the woman is only matter of glory to the man, who has a becoming dominion over her. Therefore she ought not to appear, but with her head veiled, as a tacit acknowledgment of it.

8. The man is not – In the first production of nature.

10. For this cause also a woman ought to be veiled in the public assemblies, because of the angels – Who attend there, and before whom they should be careful not to do any thing indecent or irregular.

11. Nevertheless in the Lord Jesus, there is neither male nor female – Neither is excluded; neither is preferred before the other in his kingdom.

12. And as the woman was at first taken out of the man, so also the man is now, in the ordinary course of nature, by the woman; but all things are of God – The man, the woman, and their dependence on each other.

13. Judge of yourselves – For what need of more arguments if so plain a case? Is it decent for a woman to pray to God – The Most High, with that bold and undaunted air which she must have, when, contrary to universal custom, she appears in public with her head uncovered?

14. For a man to have long hair, carefully adjusted, is such a mark of effeminacy as is a disgrace to him.

15. Given her – Originally, before the arts of dress were in being.

16. We have no such custom here, nor any of the other churches of God – The several churches that were in the apostles' time had different customs in things that were not essential; and that under one and the same apostle, as circumstances, in different places, made it convenient. And in all things merely indifferent the custom of each place was of sufficient weight to determine prudent and peaceable men. Yet even this cannot overrule a scrupulous conscience, which really doubts whether the thing be indifferent or no. But those who are referred to here by the apostle were contentious, not conscientious, persons.

18. In the church – In the public assembly. I hear there are schisms among you; and I partly believe it – That is, I believe it of some of you. It is plain that by schisms is not meant any separation from the church, but uncharitable divisions

MATTHEW HENRY

CHARLES H. SPURGEON

And directs how to attend upon it in a due manner.
(27-34)

1 The first verse of this chapter seems properly to be the close to the last. The apostle not only preached such doctrine as they ought to believe, but led such a life as they ought to live. Yet Christ being our perfect example, the actions and conduct of men, as related in the Scriptures, should be followed only so far as they are like to his.

2-16 Here begin particulars respecting the public assemblies. In the abundance of spiritual gifts bestowed on the Corinthians, some abuses had crept in; but as Christ did the will, and sought the honor of God, so the Christian should avow his subjection to Christ, doing his will and seeking his glory. We should, even in our dress and habit, avoid every thing that may dishonor Christ. The woman was made subject to man, because made for his help and comfort. And she should do nothing, in Christian assemblies, which looked like a claim of being equal. She ought to have "power," that is, a veil, on her head, because of the angels. Their presence should keep Christians from all that is wrong while in the worship of God. Nevertheless, the man and the woman were made for one another. They were to be mutual comforts and blessings, not one a slave, and the other a tyrant. God has so settled matters, both in the kingdom of providence and that of grace, that the authority and subjection of each party should be for mutual help and benefit. It was the common usage of the churches, for women to appear in public assemblies, and join in public worship, veiled; and it was right that they should do so. The Christian religion sanctions national customs wherever these are not against the great principles of truth and holiness; affected singularities receive no countenance from any thing in the Bible.

17-22 The apostle rebukes the disorders in their partaking of the Lord's supper. The ordinances of Christ, if they do not make us better, will be apt to make us worse. If the use of them does not mend, it will harden. Upon coming together, they fell into divisions, schisms. Christians may separate from each other's communion, yet be charitable one towards another; they may continue in the same communion, yet be uncharitable. This last is schism, rather than the former. There is a careless and irregular eating of the Lord's supper, which adds to guilt. Many rich Corinthians seem to have acted very wrong at the Lord's table, or at the love-feasts, which took place at the same time as the supper. The rich despised the poor, and ate and drank up the provisions they brought, before the poor were allowed to partake; thus some

THOUGHTS ON THE LAST BATTLE
Sermon number 23 delivered on May 13, 1855, at Exeter Hall, Strand.

"The sting of death is sin; and the strength of sin is the law. But, thanks be unto God, which giveth us the victory through our Lord Jesus Christ."—1 Corinthians 15:56-57.

While the Bible is one of the most poetical of books, though its language is unutterably sublime, yet we must remark how constantly it is true to nature. There is no straining of a fact, no glossing over a truth. However dark may be the subject, while it lights it up with brilliance, yet it does not deny the gloom connected with it. If you will read this chapter of Paul's epistle, so justly celebrated as a master-piece of language, you will find him speaking of that which is to come after death with such exultation and glory that you feel, "If this be to die, then it were well to depart at once." Who has not rejoiced, and whose heart has not been lifted up or filled with a holy fire, while he has read such sentences as these: "In a moment, in the twinkling of an eye, at the last trump; for the trumpet shall sound, and the dead shall be raised incorruptible, and we shall be changed. For this corruptible must put on incorruption, and this mortal must put on immortality. So, when this corruptible shall have put on incorruption, and this mortal shall have put on immortality, then shall be brought to pass the saying that is written, Death is swallowed up in victory. O death, where is thy sting? O grave, where is thy victory?" Yet, with all that majestic language, with all that bold flight of eloquence, he does not deny that death is a gloomy thing. Even his very figures imply it. He does not laugh at it; he does not say, "Oh, it is nothing to die;" he describes death as a monster; he speaks of it as having a sting; he tells us wherein the strength of that sting lies; and even in the exclamation of triumph, he imputes that victory not to unaided flesh, but he says, "Thanks be to God, who giveth us the victory through our Lord Jesus Christ."

When I select such a text as this, I feel that I cannot preach from it. The thought o'ermasters me; my words do stagger; there are no utterances that are great enough to convey the mighty meaning of this wondrous text. If I had the eloquence of all men united in one, if I could speak as never man spake (with the exception of that one godlike man of Nazareth), I could not compass so vast a subject as this. I will not therefore pretend to do so, but offer you such thoughts as my mind is capable of producing.

Tonight we shall speak of three things: first, the sting of death; secondly, the strength of sin; and thirdly, the victory of faith.

15 But if a woman have long hair, it is a glory to her: for her hair is given her for a covering.

16 But if any man seem to be contentious, we have no such custom, neither the churches of God.

17 Now in this that I declare unto you I praise you not, that ye come together not for the better, but for the worse.

18 For first of all, when ye come together in the church, I hear that there be divisions among you; and I partly believe it.

19 For there must be also heresies among you, that they which are approved may be made manifest among you.

20 When ye come together therefore into one place, this is not to eat the Lord's supper.

21 For in eating every one taketh before other his own supper: and one is hungry, and another is drunken.

22 What? have ye not houses to eat and to drink in? or despise ye the church of God, and shame them that have not? What shall I say to you? shall I praise you in this? I praise you not.

23 For I have received of the Lord that which also I delivered unto you, That the Lord Jesus the same night in which he was betrayed took bread:

24 And when he had given thanks, he brake it, and said, Take, eat: this is my body, which is broken for you: this do in remembrance of me.

25 After the same manner also he took the cup, when he had supped, saying, This cup is the new testament in my blood: this do ye, as oft as ye drink it, in remembrance of me.

26 For as often as ye eat this bread, and drink this cup, ye do shew the Lord's death till he come.

27 Wherefore whosoever shall eat this bread, and drink this cup of the Lord, unworthily, shall be guilty of the body and blood of the Lord.

28 But let a man examine himself, and so let him eat of that bread, and drink of that cup.

29 For he that eateth and drinketh unworthily, eateth and drinketh damnation to himself, not discerning the Lord's body.

in it; for the Corinthians continued to be one church; and, notwithstanding all their strife and contention, there was no separation of any one party from the rest, with regard to external communion. And it is in the same sense that the word is used, chap. i, 10; chap. xii, 25; which are the only places in the New Testament, beside this, where church schisms are mentioned. Therefore, the indulging any temper contrary to this tender care of each other is the true scriptural schism. This is, therefore, a quite different thing from that orderly separation from corrupt churches which later ages have stigmatized as schisms; and have made a pretense for the vilest cruelties, oppressions, and murders, that have troubled the Christian world. Both heresies and schisms are here mentioned in very near the same sense; unless by schisms be meant, rather, those inward animosities which occasion heresies; that is, outward divisions or parties: so that whilst one said, "I am of Paul," another, "I am of Apollos," this implied both schism and heresy. So wonderfully have later ages distorted the words heresy and schism from their scriptural meaning. Heresy is not, in all the Bible, taken for "an error in fundamentals," or in anything else; nor schism, for any separation made from the outward communion of others. Therefore, both heresy and schism, in the modern sense of the words, are sins that the scripture knows nothing of; but were invented merely to deprive mankind of the benefit of private judgment, and liberty of conscience.

19. There must be heresies – Divisions. Among you – In the ordinary course of things; and God permits them, that it may appear who among you are, and who are not, upright of heart.

20. Therefore – That is, in consequence of those schisms. It is not eating the Lord's supper – That solemn memorial of his death; but quite another thing.

21. For in eating what ye call the Lord's supper, instead of all partaking of one bread, each person brings his own supper, and eats it without staying for the rest. And hereby the poor, who cannot provide for themselves, have nothing; while the rich eat and drink to the full just as the heathens use to do at the feasts on their sacrifices.

22. Have ye not houses to eat and drink your common meals in? or do ye despise the church of God – Of which the poor are both the larger and the better part. Do ye act thus in designed contempt of them?

23. I received – By an immediate Revelation.

24. This is my body, which is broken for you – That is, this broken bread is the sign of my body, which is even now to be pierced and wounded for your iniquities. Take then, and eat of, this bread, in an humble, thankful, obedient remembrance of my dying love; of the extremity of my sufferings on your behalf, of the blessings I have thereby procured for you, and of the obligations to love and duty which I have by all this laid upon you.

25. After supper – Therefore ye ought not to confound this with a common meal. Do this in remembrance of me – The ancient sacrifices were in remembrance of sin: this sacrifice, once offered, is still represented in remembrance of the remission of sins.

26. Ye show forth the Lord's death – Ye proclaim, as it were, and openly avow it to God, and to all the world. Till he come – In glory.

27. Whosoever shall eat this bread unworthily – That is, in an unworthy, irreverent manner; without regarding either him that appointed it, or the design of its appointment. Shall be guilty of profaning that which represents the body and blood of the Lord.

28. But let a man examine himself – Whether he know the nature and the design of the institution, and whether it be his own desire and purpose thoroughly to comply therewith.

29. For he that eateth and drinketh so unworthily as those Corinthians did, eateth and drinketh judgment to himself – Temporal judgments of various kinds, ver. 30. Not distinguishing the sacred tokens of the Lord's body – From

MATTHEW HENRY

CHARLES H. SPURGEON

wanted, while others had more than enough. What should have been a bond of mutual love and affection, was made an instrument of discord and disunion. We should be careful that nothing in our behavior at the Lord's table, appears to make light of that sacred institution. The Lord's supper is not now made an occasion for gluttony or reveling, but is it not often made the support of self-righteous pride, or a cloak for hypocrisy? Let us never rest in the outward forms of worship; but look to our hearts.

23-34 The apostle describes the sacred ordinance, of which he had the knowledge by revelation from Christ. As to the visible signs, these are the bread and wine. What is eaten is called bread, though at the same time it is said to be the body of the Lord, plainly showing that the apostle did not mean that the bread was changed into flesh. St. Matthew tells us, our Lord bid them all drink of the cup, ch. Mt 26:27, as if he would, by this expression, provide against any believer being deprived of the cup. The things signified by these outward signs, are Christ's body and blood, his body broken, his blood shed, together with all the benefits which flow from his death and sacrifice. Our Savior's actions were, taking the bread and cup, giving thanks, breaking the bread, and giving both the one and the other. The actions of the communicants were, to take the bread and eat, to take the cup and drink, and to do both in remembrance of Christ. But the outward acts are not the whole, or the principal part, of what is to be done at this holy ordinance. Those who partake of it, are to take him as their Lord and Life, yield themselves up to him, and live upon him. Here is an account of the ends of this ordinance. It is to be done in remembrance of Christ, to keep fresh in our minds his dying for us, as well as to remember Christ pleading for us, in virtue of his death, at God's right hand. It is not merely in remembrance of Christ, of what he has done and suffered; but to celebrate his grace in our redemption. We declare his death to be our life, the spring of all our comforts and hopes. And we glory in such a declaration; we show forth his death, and plead it as our accepted sacrifice and ransom. The Lord's supper is not an ordinance to be observed merely for a time, but to be continued. The apostle lays before the Corinthians the danger of receiving it with an unsuitable temper of mind; or keeping up the covenant with sin and death, while professing to renew and confirm the covenant with God. No doubt such incur great guilt, and so render themselves liable to spiritual judgments. But fearful believers should not be discouraged from attending at this holy ordinance. The Holy Spirit never caused this scripture to be written to deter serious Christians from their duty,

I. First, THE STING OF DEATH. The apostle pictures death as a terrible dragon, or monster, which, coming upon all men, must be fought with by each one for himself. He gives us no hopes whatever that any of us can avoid it. He tells us of no bridge across the river Death; he does not give us the faintest hope that it is possible to emerge from this state of existence into another without dying; he describes the monster as being exactly in our path, and with it we must fight, each man personally, separately, and alone; each man must die; we all must cross the black stream; each one of us must go through the iron gate. There is no passage from this world into another without death. Having told us, then, that there is no hope of our escape, he braces up our nerves for the combat; but he gives us no hope that we shall be able to slay the monster; he does not tell us that we can strike our sword into his heart, and so overturn and overwhelm death; but, pointing to the dragon, he seems to say, "Thou canst not slay it, man; there is no hope that thou shouldst ever put thy foot upon its neck and crush its head; but one thing can be done—it has a sting which thou mayest extract; thou canst not crush death under foot, but thou mayest pull out the sting which is deadly; and then thou need not fear the monster, for monster it shall be no longer, but rather it shall be a swift-winged angel to waft thee aloft to heaven." Where, then, is the sting of this dragon? Where must I strike? What is the sting? The apostle tells us, "that the sting of death is sin." Once let me cut off that, and then, though death may be dreary and solemn, I shall not dread it; but, holding up the monster's sting, I shall exclaim, "O death, where is thy sting? O grave, where is thy victory?" Let us now dwell upon the fact, that "the sting of death is sin."

1. First, sin puts a sting into death, from the fact that sin brought death into the world. Men could be more content to die if they did not know it was a punishment. I suppose if we had never sinned, there would have been some means for us to go from this world to another. It cannot be supposed that so huge a population would have existed, that all the myriads who have lived from Adam down till now could ever have inhabited so small a globe as this; there would not have been space enough for them. But there might have been provided some means for taking us off when the proper time should come, and bearing us safely to heaven. God might have furnished horses and chariots of fire for each of his Elijahs; or, as it was said of Enoch, so it might have been declared of each of us, "He is not, for God hath taken him." Thus to die, if we may call it death to depart from this body and to be with God, would have been no disgrace; in fact, it would have been the highest honor; fitting the loftiest aspiration of the soul, to live quickly its little time in this world, then to mount and be with its God; and

30 For this cause many are weak and sickly among you, and many sleep.

31 For if we would judge ourselves, we should not be judged.

32 But when we are judged, we are chastened of the Lord, that we should not be condemned with the world.

33 Wherefore, my brethren, when ye come together to eat, tarry one for another.

34 And if any man hunger, let him eat at home; that ye come not together unto condemnation. And the rest will I set in order when I come.

1 CORINTHIANS 12

1 Now concerning spiritual gifts, brethren, I would not have you ignorant.

2 Ye know that ye were Gentiles, carried away unto these dumb idols, even as ye were led.

3 Wherefore I give you to understand, that no man speaking by the Spirit of God calleth Jesus accursed: and that no man can say that Jesus is the Lord, but by the Holy Ghost.

4 Now there are diversities of gifts, but the same Spirit.

5 And there are differences of administrations, but the same Lord.

6 And there are diversities of operations, but it is the same God which worketh all in all.

7 But the manifestation of the Spirit is given to every man to profit withal.

8 For to one is given by the Spirit the word of wisdom; to another the word of knowledge by the same Spirit;

9 To another faith by the same Spirit; to another the gifts of healing by the same Spirit;

10 To another the working of miracles; to another prophecy; to another discerning of spirits; to another divers kinds of tongues; to another the interpretation of tongues:

11 But all these worketh that one and the selfsame Spirit, dividing to every man severally as he will.

12 For as the body is one, and hath many members, and all the members of that one body, being

his common food.

30. For this cause – Which they had not observed. Many sleep – In death.

31. If we would judge ourselves – As to our knowledge, and the design with which we approach the Lord's table. We should not be thus judged – That is, punished by God.

32. When we are thus judged, it is with this merciful design, that we may not be finally condemned with the world.

33. The rest – The other circumstances relating to the Lord's supper.

1 CORINTHIANS 12

1. Now concerning spiritual gifts – The abundance of these in the churches of Greece strongly refuted the idle learning of the Greek philosophers. But the Corinthians did not use them wisely, which occasioned St. Paul's writing concerning them. He describes,

    1. The unity of the body, ver. 1-xxvii,

    2. The variety of members and offices, ver. 27-30,

    3. The way of exercising gifts rightly, namely, by love, ver. 31, chap. xiii, 1. throughout: and adds,

    4. A comparison of several gifts with each other, in the fourteenth chapter.

2. Ye were heathens – Therefore, whatever gifts ye have received, it is from the free grace of God. Carried away – By a blind credulity. After dumb idols – The blind to the dumb; idols of wood and stone, unable to speak themselves, and much more to open your mouths, as God has done. As ye were led – By the subtlety of your priests.

3. Therefore – Since the heathen idols cannot speak themselves, much less give spiritual gifts to others, these must necessarily be among Christians only. As no one speaking by the Spirit of God calleth Jesus accursed – That is, as none who does this, (which all the Jews and heathens did,) speaketh by the Spirit of God – Is actuated by that Spirit, so as to speak with tongues, heal diseases, or cast out devils. So no one can say, Jesus is the Lord – None can receive him as such; for, in the scripture language, to say, or to believe, implies an experimental assurance. But by the Holy Ghost – The sum is, None have the Holy Spirit but Christians: all Christians have this Spirit.

4. There are diversities of gifts, but the same Spirit – Divers streams, but all from one fountain. This verse speaks of the Holy Ghost, the next of Christ, the sixth of God the Father. The apostle treats of the Spirit, ver. 7, &c.; of Christ, ver. 12, &c.; of God, ver. 28, &c.

5. Administrations – Offices. But the same Lord appoints them all.

6. Operations – Effects produced. This word is of a larger extent than either of the former. But it is the same God who worketh all these effects in all the persons concerned.

7. The manifestation – The gift whereby the Spirit manifests itself. Is given to each – For the profit of the whole body.

8. The word of wisdom – A power of understanding and explaining the manifold wisdom of God in the grand scheme of gospel salvation. The word of knowledge – Perhaps an extraordinary ability to understand and explain the Old Testament types and prophecies.

9. Faith may here mean an extraordinary trust in God under the most difficult or dangerous circumstances. The gift of healing need not be wholly confined to the healing diseases with a word or a touch. It may exert itself also, though in a lower degree, where natural remedies are applied; and it may often be this, not superior skill, which makes some physicians more successful than others. And thus it may be with regard to other gifts likewise. As, after the golden shields were lost, the king of Judah put brazen in their place, so, after the pure gifts were

MATTHEW HENRY   CHARLES H. SPURGEON

though the devil has often made this use of it. The apostle was addressing Christians, and warning them to beware of the temporal judgments with which God chastised his offending servants. And in the midst of judgment, God remembers mercy: he many times punishes those whom he loves. It is better to bear trouble in this world, than to be miserable for ever. The apostle points our the duty of those who come to the Lord's table. Self-examination is necessary to right attendance at this holy ordinance. If we would thoroughly search ourselves, to condemn and set right what we find wrong, we should stop Divine judgments. The apostle closes all with a caution against the irregularities of which the Corinthians were guilty at the Lord's table. Let all look to it, that they do not come together to God's worship, so as to provoke him, and bring down vengeance on themselves.

1 CORINTHIANS 12

The variety of use of spiritual gifts are shown. (1-11)
In the human body every member has its place and use. (12-26)
This is applied to the church of Christ. (27-30)
And there is something more excellent than spiritual gifts. (31)

1-11 Spiritual gifts were extraordinary powers bestowed in the first ages, to convince unbelievers, and to spread the gospel. Gifts and graces greatly differ. Both were freely given of God. But where grace is given, it is for the salvation of those who have it. Gifts are for the advantage and salvation of others; and there may be great gifts where there is no grace. The extraordinary gifts of the Holy Spirit were chiefly exercised in the public assemblies, where the Corinthians seem to have made displays of them, wanting in the spirit of piety, and of Christian love. While heathens, they had not been influenced by the Spirit of Christ. No man can call Christ Lord, with believing dependence upon him, unless that faith is wrought by the Holy Ghost. No man could believe with his heart, or prove by a miracle, that Jesus was Christ, unless by the Holy Ghost. There are various gifts, and various offices to perform, but all proceed from one God, one Lord, one Spirit; that is, from the Father, Son, and Holy Ghost, the origin of all spiritual blessings. No man has them merely for himself. The more he profits others, the more will they turn to his own account. The gifts mentioned appear to mean exact understanding, and uttering the doctrines of the Christian religion; the knowledge of mysteries, and skill to give advice and counsel. Also the gift of healing the sick, the working of miracles, and to explain Scripture by a peculiar gift of the Spirit, and ability to speak and

in the prayers of the most pious and devout man, one of his sublimest petitions would be, "O God, hasten the time of my departure, when I shall be with thee." When such sinless beings thought of their departure, they would not tremble, for the gate would be one of ivory and pearl—not as now, of iron—the stream would be as nectar, far different from the present "bitterness of death." But alas! how different! Death is now the punishment of sin. "In the day thou eatest there of thou shalt surely die." "In Adam all die." By his sin every one of us becomes subject to the penalty of death, and thus, being a punishment, death has its sting. To the best man, the holiest Christian, the most sanctified intellect, the soul that has the nearest and dearest intercourse with God, death must appear to have a sting, because sin was its mother. O fatal offspring of sin, I only dread thee because of they parentage! If thou didst come to me as an honor, I could wade through Jordan even now, and, when its chilling billows were around me, I would smile amidst its surges; and in the swellings of Jordan my song should swell too, and the liquid music of my voice should join with the liquid swellings of the floods, "Hallelujah! It is blessed to cross to the land of the glorified." This is one reason why the sting of sin is death.

2. But I must take it in another sense. "The sting of death is sin:"—that is to say, that which shall make death most terrible to man will be sin, if it is not forgiven. If that be not the exact meaning of the apostle, still it is a great truth, and I may find it here. If sin lay heavy on me and were not forgiven—if my transgressions were unpardoned—if such were the fact (though I rejoice to know it is not so) it would be the very sting of death to me. Let us consider a man dying, and looking back on his past life: he will find in death a sting, and that sting will be his past sin. Imagine a conqueror's deathbed. He has been a man of blood from his youth up. Bred in the camp, his lips were early set to the bugle, and his hand, even in infancy, struck the drum. He had a martial spirit; he delighted in the fame and applause of men; he loved the dust of battle and the garment rolled in blood. He has lived a life of what men call glory. He has stormed cities, conquered countries, ravaged continents, overrun the world. See his banners hanging in the hall, and the marks of glory on his escutcheon. He is one of earth's proudest warriors. But now he comes to die, and when he lies down to expire, what shall invest his death with horror? It shall be his sin. Methinks I see the monarch dying; he lies in state; around him are his nobles and his councilors; but there is somewhat else there. Hard by his side there stands a spirit from Hades; it is a soul of a departed woman. She looks on him and says, "Monster! my husband was slain in battle through thy ambition: I was made a widow, and my helpless orphans and myself were

many, are one body: so also is Christ.

13 For by one Spirit are we all baptized into one body, whether we be Jews or Gentiles, whether we be bond or free; and have been all made to drink into one Spirit.

14 For the body is not one member, but many.

15 If the foot shall say, Because I am not the hand, I am not of the body; is it therefore not of the body?

16 And if the ear shall say, Because I am not the eye, I am not of the body; is it therefore not of the body?

17 If the whole body were an eye, where were the hearing? If the whole were hearing, where were the smelling?

18 But now hath God set the members every one of them in the body, as it hath pleased him.

19 And if they were all one member, where were the body?

20 But now are they many members, yet but one body.

21 And the eye cannot say unto the hand, I have no need of thee: nor again the head to the feet, I have no need of you.

22 Nay, much more those members of the body, which seem to be more feeble, are necessary:

23 And those members of the body, which we think to be less honorable, upon these we bestow more abundant honor; and our uncomely parts have more abundant comeliness.

24 For our comely parts have no need: but God hath tempered the body together, having given more abundant honor to that part which lacked:

25 That there should be no schism in the body; but that the members should have the same care one for another.

26 And whether one member suffer, all the members suffer with it; or one member be honored, all the members rejoice with it.

27 Now ye are the body of Christ, and members in particular.

28 And God hath set some in the church, first apostles, secondarily prophets, thirdly teachers, after that miracles, then gifts of healings, helps, govern-

lost, the power of God exerts itself in a more covert manner, under human studies and helps; and that the more plentifully, according as there is the more room given for it.

10. The working of other miracles. Prophecy – Foretelling things to come. The discerning – Whether men be of an upright spirit or no; whether they have natural or supernatural gifts for offices in the church; and whether they who profess to speak by inspiration speak from a divine, a natural, or a diabolical spirit.

11. As he willeth – The Greek word does not so much imply arbitrary pleasure, as a determination founded on wise counsel.

12. So is Christ – That is, the body of Christ, the church.

13. For by that one Spirit, which we received in baptism, we are all united in one body. Whether Jews or Gentiles – Who are at the greatest distance from each other by nature. Whether slaves or freemen – Who are at the greatest distance by law and custom. We have all drank of one Spirit – In that cup, received by faith, we all imbibed one Spirit, who first inspired, and still preserves, the life of God in our souls.

15. The foot is elegantly introduced as speaking of the hand; the ear, of the eye; each, of a part that has some resemblance to it. So among men each is apt to compare himself with those whose gifts some way resemble his own, rather than with those who are at a distance, either above or beneath him. Is it therefore not of the body – Is the inference good? Perhaps the foot may represent private Christians; the hand, officers in the church; the eye, teachers; the ear, hearers.

16. The ear – A less noble part. The eye – The most noble.

18. As it hath pleased him – With the most exquisite wisdom and goodness.

20. But one body – And it is a necessary consequence of this unity, that the several members need one another.

21. Nor the head – The highest part of all. To the foot – The very lowest.

22. The members which appear to be weaker – Being of a more delicate and tender structure; perhaps the brains and bowels, or the veins, arteries, and other minute channels in the body.

23. We surround with more abundant honor – By so carefully covering them. More abundant comeliness – By the help of dress.

24. Giving more abundant honor to that which lacked – As being cared for and served by the noblest parts.

27. Now ye – Corinthians. Are the body and members of Christ – part of them, I mean, not the whole body.

28. First apostles – Who plant the gospel in the heathen nations. Secondly prophets – Who either foretell things to come, or speak by extra-ordinary inspiration, for the edification of the church. Thirdly teachers – Who precede even those that work miracles. Under prophets and teachers are comprised evangelists and pastors, Eph. iv, 11. Helps, governments – It does not appear that these mean distinct offices: rather, any persons might be called helps, from a peculiar dexterity in helping the distressed; and governments, from a peculiar talent for governing or presiding in assemblies.

31. Ye covet earnestly the best gifts – And they are worth your pursuit, though but few of you can attain them. But there is a far more excellent gift than all these; and one which all may, yea, must attain or perish.

MATTHEW HENRY   CHARLES H. SPURGEON

interpret languages. If we have any knowledge of the truth, or any power to make it known, we must give all the glory of God. The greater the gifts are, the more the possessor is exposed to temptations, and the larger is the measure of grace needed to keep him humble and spiritual; and he will meet with more painful experiences and humbling dispensations. We have little cause to glory in any gifts bestowed on us, or to despise those who have them not.

12-26 Christ and his church form one body, as Head and members. Christians become members of this body by baptism. The outward rite is of Divine institution; it is a sign of the new birth, and is called therefore the washing of regeneration, Tit 3:5. But it is by the Spirit, only by the renewing of the Holy Ghost, that we are made members of Christ's body. And by communion with Christ at the Lord's supper, we are strengthened, not by drinking the wine, but by drinking into one Spirit. Each member has its form, place, and use. The meanest makes a part of the body. There must be a distinction of members in the body. So Christ's members have different powers and different places. We should do the duties of our own place, and not murmur, or quarrel with others. All the members of the body are useful and necessary to each other. Nor is there a member of the body of Christ, but may and ought to be useful to fellow-members. As in the natural body of man, the members should be closely united by the strongest bonds of love; the good of the whole should be the object of all. All Christians are dependent one upon another; each is to expect and receive help from the rest. Let us then have more of the spirit of union in our religion.

27-31 Contempt, hatred, envy, and strife, are very unnatural in Christians. It is like the members of the same body being without concern for one another, or quarrelling with each other. The proud, contentious spirit that prevailed, as to spiritual gifts, was thus condemned. The offices and gifts, or favors, dispensed by the Holy Spirit, are noticed. Chief ministers; persons enabled to interpret Scripture; those who labored in word and doctrine; those who had power to heal diseases; such as helped the sick and weak; such as disposed of the money given in charity by the church, and managed the affairs of the church; and such as could speak divers languages. What holds the last and lowest rank in this list, is the power to speak languages; how vain, if a man does so merely to amuse or to exalt himself! See the distribution of these gifts, not to every one alike, ver. 29,30. This were to make the church all one, as if the body were all ear, or all eye. The Spirit distributes to every one as he will. We must

starved." And she passes by. Her husband comes, and opening wide his bloody wounds, he cries, "Once I called thee monarch; but, by thy vile covetousness thou didst provoke an unjust war. See here these wounds—I gained them in the siege. For thy sake I mounted first the scaling ladder; this foot stood upon the top of the wall, and I waved my sword in triumph, but in hell I lifted up my eyes in torment. Base wretch, thine ambition hurried me thither!" Turning his horrid eyes upon him, he passes by. Then up comes another, and another, and another yet; waking from their tombs, they stalk around his bed and haunt him; the dreary procession still marches on, looking at the dying tyrant. He shuts his eyes, but he feels the cold and bony hand upon his forehead; he quivers, for the sting of death is in his heart. "O Death!" says he; "to leave this large estate, this mighty realm, this pomp and power—this were somewhat; but to meet those men, those women, and those orphan children, face to face; to hear them saying, 'Art thou become like one of us?' while kings whom I have dethroned, and monarchs whom I have cast down shall rattle their chains in my ears, and say, 'Thou wast our destroyer, but how art thou fallen from heaven, O Lucifer, son of the morning! How art thou brought down as in a moment from thy glory and thy pride!'" There, you see, the sting of death would be the man's sin. It would not sting him that he had to die, but that he had sinned, that he had been a bloody man, that his hands were red with wholesale murder—this would plague him indeed, for "the sting of death is sin."

Or, suppose another character—a minister. He has stood before the world, proclaiming something which he called the gospel. He has been a noted preacher; the multitude have been hanging on his lips; they have listened to his words; before his eloquence a nation stood amazed, and thousands trembled at his voice. But his preaching is over; the time when he can mount the pulpit is gone; another standing-place awaits him, another congregation, and he must hear another and a better preacher than himself. There he lies. He has been unfaithful to his charge. He preached philosophy to charm his people, instead of preaching truth and aiming at their hearts. And, as he pants upon his bed, that worst and most accursed of men—for surely none can be worse than he—there comes up one, a soul from the pit, and looking him in the face, says, "I came to thee once, trembling on account of sin; I asked thee the road to heaven, and thou didst say, 'Do such and such good works,' and I did them, and am damned. Thou didst tell me an untruth; thou didst not declare plainly the word of God." He vanishes only to be followed by another; he has been an irreligious character, and as he sees the minister upon his deathbed, he says, "Ah! and art thou here? Once I strolled into thy house of

ments, diversities of tongues.

29 Are all apostles? are all prophets? are all teachers? are all workers of miracles?

30 Have all the gifts of healing? do all speak with tongues? do all interpret?

31 But covet earnestly the best gifts: and yet shew I unto you a more excellent way.

1 CORINTHIANS 13

1 Though I speak with the tongues of men and of angels, and have not charity, I am become as sounding brass, or a tinkling cymbal.

2 And though I have the gift of prophecy, and understand all mysteries, and all knowledge; and though I have all faith, so that I could remove mountains, and have not charity, I am nothing.

3 And though I bestow all my goods to feed the poor, and though I give my body to be burned, and have not charity, it profiteth me nothing.

4 Charity suffereth long, and is kind; charity envieth not; charity vaunteth not itself, is not puffed up,

5 Doth not behave itself unseemly, seeketh not her own, is not easily provoked, thinketh no evil;

6 Rejoiceth not in iniquity, but rejoiceth in the truth;

7 Beareth all things, believeth all things, hopeth all things, endureth all things.

8 Charity never faileth: but whether there be prophecies, they shall fail; whether there be tongues, they shall cease; whether there be knowledge, it shall vanish away.

9 For we know in part, and we prophesy in part.

10 But when that which is perfect is come, then that which is in part shall be done away.

11 When I was a child, I spake as a child, I understood as a child, I thought as a child: but when I became a man, I put away childish things.

12 For now we see through a glass, darkly; but then face to face: now I know in part; but then shall I know even as also I am known.

1 CORINTHIANS 13

The necessity of love is shown, ver. 1-3. The nature and properties, ver. 4-7. The duration of it, ver. 8-13.

1. Though I speak with all the tongues – Which are upon earth, and with the eloquence of an angel. And have not love – The love of God, and of all mankind for his sake, I am no better before God than the sounding instruments of brass, used in the worship of some of the heathen gods. Or a tinkling cymbal – This was made of two pieces of hollow brass, which, being struck together, made a tinkling, but very little variety of sound.

2. And though I have the gift of prophecy – Of foretelling future events. And understand all the mysteries – Both of God's word and providence. And all knowledge – Of things divine and human, that ever any mortal attained to. And though I have the highest degree of miracle working faith, and have not this love, I am nothing.

3. And though I – Deliberately, piece by piece. Give all my goods to feed the poor, yea, though I deliver up my body to be burned – Rather than I would renounce my religion. And have not the love – Hereafter described. It profiteth me nothing – Without this, whatever I speak, whatever I have, whatever I know, whatever I do, whatever I suffer, is nothing.

4. The love of God, and of our neighbor for God's sake, is patient toward, all men. It suffers all the weakness, ignorance, errors, and infirmities of the children of God; all the malice and wickedness of the children of the world: and all this, not only for a time, but to the end. And in every step toward overcoming evil with good, it is kind, soft, mild, benign. It inspires the sufferer at once with the most amiable sweetness, and the most fervent and tender affection. Love acteth not rashly – Does not hastily condemn any one; never passes a severe sentence on a slight or sudden view of things. Nor does it ever act or behave in a violent, headstrong, or precipitate manner. Is not puffed up – Yea, humbles the soul to the dust.

5. It doth not behave indecently – Is not rude, or willingly offensive, to any. It renders to all their due – Suitable to time, person, and all other circumstances. Seeketh not her own – Ease, pleasure, honor, or temporal advantage. Nay, sometimes the lover of mankind seeketh not, in some sense, even his own spiritual advantage; does not think of himself, so long as a zeal for the glory of God and the souls of men swallows him up. But, though he is all on fire for these ends, yet he is not provoked to sharpness or unkindness toward any one. Outward provocations indeed will frequently occur; but he triumphs over all. Love thinketh no evil – Indeed it cannot but see and hear evil things, and know that they are so; but it does not willingly think evil of any; neither infer evil where it does not appear. It tears up, root and branch, all imagining of what we have not proof. It casts out all jealousies, all evil surmises, all readiness to believe evil.

6. Rejoiceth not in iniquity – Yea, weeps at either the sin or folly of even an enemy; takes no pleasure in hearing or in repeating it, but desires it may be forgotten for ever. But rejoiceth in the truth – Bringing forth its proper fruit, holiness of heart and life. Good in general is its glory and joy, wherever diffused in all the world.

7. Love covereth all things – Whatever evil the lover of mankind sees, hears, or knows of any one, he mentions it to none; it never goes out of his lips, unless where absolute duty constrains to speak. Believeth all things – Puts the most favorable construction on everything, and is ever ready to believe whatever may tend to the advantage of any one character. And when it can no longer believe well, it hopes whatever may excuse or extenuate the fault which cannot be denied. Where it cannot even excuse, it hopes God will at length give repentance unto life. Meantime it endureth all things – Whatever the injustice, the malice, the cruelty of men can inflict. He can not only do, but likewise suffer, all things, through Christ who strengtheneth him.

MATTHEW HENRY

CHARLES H. SPURGEON

be content though we are lower and less than others. We must not despise others, if we have greater gifts. How blessed the Christian church, if all the members did their duty! Instead of coveting the highest stations, or the most splendid gifts, let us leave the appointment of his instruments to God, and those in whom he works by his providence. Remember, those will not be approved hereafter who seek the chief places, but those who are most faithful to the trust placed in them, and most diligent in their Master's work.

1 CORINTHIANS 13

The necessity and advantage of the grace of love. (1-3)

Its excellency represented by its properties and effects. (4-7)

And by its abiding, and its superiority. (8-13)

1-3 The excellent way had in view in the close of the former chapter, is not what is meant by charity in our common use of the word, almsgiving, but love in its fullest meaning; true love to God and man. Without this, the most glorious gifts are of no account to us, of no esteem in the sight of God. A clear head and a deep understanding, are of no value without a benevolent and charitable heart. There may be an open and lavish hand, where there is not a liberal and charitable heart. Doing good to others will do none to us, if it be not done from love to God, and good-will to men. If we give away all we have, while we withhold the heart from God, it will not profit. Nor even the most painful sufferings. How are those deluded who look for acceptance and reward for their good works, which are as scanty and defective as they are corrupt and selfish!

4-7 Some of the effects of charity are stated, that we may know whether we have this grace; and that if we have not, we may not rest till we have it. This love is a clear proof of regeneration, and is a touchstone of our professed faith in Christ. In this beautiful description of the nature and effects of love, it is meant to show the Corinthians that their conduct had, in many respects, been a contrast to it. Charity is an utter enemy to selfishness; it does not desire or seek its own praise, or honor, or profit, or pleasure. Not that charity destroys all regard to ourselves, or that the charitable man should neglect himself and all his interests. But charity never seeks its own to the hurt of others, or to neglect others. It ever prefers the welfare of others to its private advantage. How good-natured and amiable is Christian charity! How excellent would Christianity appear to the world, if those who profess it were more under this Divine principle, and paid due regard to the command on

prayer, but thou hadst such a sermon that I could not understand. I listened; I wanted to hear something from thy lips, some truth that might burn my soul and make me repent; but I knew not what thou saidst; and here I am." The ghost stamps his foot, and the man quivers like an aspen leaf, because he knows it is all true. Then the whole congregation arise before him as he lies upon his bed; he looks upon the motley group; he beholds the snowy heads of the old, and glittering eyes of the young; and lying there upon his pillow, he pictures all the sins of his past life, and he hears it said, "Go thou! unfaithful to thy charge; thou didst not divest thyself of thy love of pomp and dignity; thou didst not speak

'As though thou ne'er might'st speak again,

A dying man to dying men.'"

Oh! it may be something for that minister to leave his charge, somewhat for him to die; but worst of all, the sting of death will be his sin: to hear his parish come howling after him to hell; to see his congregation following behind him in one mingled herd, he having led them astray, having been a false prophet instead of a true one, speaking peace, peace, where there was no peace, deluding them with lies, charming them with music, when he ought rather to have told them in rough and rugged accents the Word of God. Verily, it is true, it is true, the sting of death to such a man shall be his great, his enormous, his heinous sin of having deluded others.

Thus, then having painted two full-length pictures, I might give each one of you miniatures of yourselves. I might picture thee, O drunkard, when thy cups are drained, and when thy liquor shall no longer be sweet to thy taste, when worse than gall shall be the dainties that thou drinkest, when, within an hour, the worms shall make a carnival upon thy flesh; I might picture thee as thou lookest back upon they misspent life. And thou, O swearer, methinks I see thee there, with thine oaths echoed back by memory to thine own dismay. And thou, man of lust and wickedness, thou who hast debauched and seduced others, I see thee there; and the sting of death to thee, how horrible, how dreadful! It shall not be that thou art groaning with pain, it shall not be that thou art racked with agony, it shall not be that thy heart and flesh faileth, but the sting, the sting, shall be thy sin. How many in this place can spell the word "remorse?" I pray you may never know its awful meaning. Remorse, remorse! You know its derivation; it signifies to bite. Ah! now we dance with our sins—it is a merry life with us—we take their hands, and, sporting in the noontide sun, we dance, we dance, and live in joy. But then those sins shall bite us. The young lions we have stroked and played with shall bite; the young adder, the serpent, whose azure hues have well delighted us, shall bite,

KING JAMES VERSION

JOHN WESLEY

13 And now abideth faith, hope, charity, these three; but the greatest of these is charity.

1 CORINTHIANS 14

1 Follow after charity, and desire spiritual gifts, but rather that ye may prophesy.
2 For he that speaketh in an unknown tongue speaketh not unto men, but unto God: for no man understandeth him; howbeit in the spirit he speaketh mysteries.
3 But he that prophesieth speaketh unto men to edification, and exhortation, and comfort.
4 He that speaketh in an unknown tongue edifieth himself; but he that prophesieth edifieth the church.
5 I would that ye all spake with tongues, but rather that ye prophesied: for greater is he that prophesieth than he that speaketh with tongues, except he interpret, that the church may receive edifying.
6 Now, brethren, if I come unto you speaking with tongues, what shall I profit you, except I shall speak to you either by revelation, or by knowledge, or by prophesying, or by doctrine?
7 And even things without life giving sound, whether pipe or harp, except they give a distinction in the sounds, how shall it be known what is piped or harped?
8 For if the trumpet give an uncertain sound, who shall prepare himself to the battle?
9 So likewise ye, except ye utter by the tongue words easy to be understood, how shall it be known what is spoken? for ye shall speak into the air.
10 There are, it may be, so many kinds of voices in the world, and none of them is without signification.
11 Therefore if I know not the meaning of the voice, I shall be unto him that speaketh a barbarian, and he that speaketh shall be a barbarian unto me.
12 Even so ye, forasmuch as ye are zealous of spiritual gifts, seek that ye may excel to the edifying of the church.
13 Wherefore let him that

8. Love never faileth – It accompanies to, and adorns us in, eternity; it prepares us for, and constitutes, heaven. But whether there be prophecies, they shall fail – When all things are fulfilled, and God is all in all. Whether there be tongues, they shall cease – One language shall prevail among all the inhabitants of heaven, and the low and imperfect languages of earth be forgotten. The knowledge likewise which we now so eagerly pursue, shall then vanish away – As starlight is lost in that of the midday sun, so our present knowledge in the light of eternity.

9. For we know in part, and we prophesy in part – The wisest of men have here but short, narrow, imperfect conceptions, even of the things round about them, and much more of the deep things of God. And even the prophecies which men deliver from God are far from taking in the whole of future events, or of that wisdom and knowledge of God which is treasured up in the scripture Revelation.

10. But when that which is perfect is come – At death and in the last day. That which is in part shall vanish away – Both that poor, low, imperfect, glimmering light, which is all the knowledge we now can attain to; and these slow and unsatisfactory methods of attaining, as well as of imparting it to others.

11. In our present state we are mere infants in point of knowledge, compared to what we shall be hereafter. I put away childish things – Of my own accord, willingly, without trouble.

12. Now we see – Even the things that surround us. But by means of a glass – Or mirror, which reflects only their imperfect forms, in a dim, faint, obscure manner; so that our thoughts about them are puzzling and intricate, and everything is a kind of riddle to us. But then – We shall see, not a faint reflection, but the objects themselves. Face to face – Distinctly. Now I know in part – Even when God himself reveals things to me, great part of them is still kept under the veil. But then I shall know even as also I am known – In a clear, full, comprehensive manner; in some measure like God, who penetrates the center of every object, and sees at one glance through my soul and all things.

13. Faith, hope, love – Are the sum of perfection on earth; love alone is the sum of perfection in heaven.

1 CORINTHIANS 14

1. Follow after love – With zeal, vigor, courage, patience; else you can neither attain nor keep it. And – In their place, as subservient to this. Desire spiritual gifts; but especially that ye may prophesy – The word here does not mean foretelling things to come; but rather opening and applying the scripture.

2. He that speaketh in an unknown tongue speaks, in effect, not to men, but to God – Who alone understands him.

4. Edifieth himself – Only, on the most favorable supposition. The church – The whole congregation.

5. Greater – That is, more useful. By this alone are we to estimate all our gifts and talents.

6. Revelation – Of some gospel mystery. Knowledge – Explaining the ancient types and prophecies. Prophecy – Foretelling some future event. Doctrine – To regulate your tempers and lives. Perhaps this may be the sense of these obscure words.

7. How shall it be known what is piped or harped – What music can be made, or what end answered?

8. Who will prepare himself for the battle – Unless he understand what the trumpet sounds? suppose a retreat or a march.

9. Unless ye utter by the tongue – Which is miraculously given you. Words easy to be understood – By your hearers. Ye will speak to the air – A proverbial expression. Will utterly lose your labor.

which its blessed Author laid the chief stress! Let us ask whether this Divine love dwells in our hearts. Has this principle guided us into becoming behavior to all men? Are we willing to lay aside selfish objects and aims? Here is a call to watchfulness, diligence, and prayer.

8-13 Charity is much to be preferred to the gifts on which the Corinthians prided themselves. From its longer continuance. It is a grace, lasting as eternity. The present state is a state of childhood, the future that of manhood. Such is the difference between earth and heaven. What narrow views, what confused notions of things, have children when compared with grown men! Thus shall we think of our most valued gifts of this world, when we come to heaven. All things are dark and confused now, compared with what they will be hereafter. They can only be seen as by the reflection in a mirror, or in the description of a riddle; but hereafter our knowledge will be free from all obscurity and error. It is the light of heaven only, that will remove all clouds and darkness that hide the face of God from us. To sum up the excellences of charity, it is preferred not only to gifts, but to other graces, to faith and hope. Faith fixes on the Divine revelation, and assents thereto, relying on the Divine Redeemer. Hope fastens on future happiness, and waits for that; but in heaven, faith will be swallowed up in actual sight, and hope in enjoyment. There is no room to believe and hope, when we see and enjoy. But there, love will be made perfect. There we shall perfectly love God. And there we shall perfectly love one another. Blessed state! how much surpassing the best below! God is love, 1Jo 4:8,16. Where God is to be seen as he is, and face to face, there charity is in its greatest height; there only will it be perfected.

1 CORINTHIANS 14

Prophecy preferred to the gift of tongues. (1-5)
The unprofitableness of speaking in unknown languages. (6-14)
Exhortations to worship that can be understood. (15-25)
Disorders from vain display of gifts. (26-33)
And from women speaking in the church. (34-40)

1-5 Prophesying, that is, explaining Scripture, is compared with speaking with tongues. This drew attention, more than the plain interpretation of Scripture; it gratified pride more, but promoted the purposes of Christian charity less; it would not equally do good to the souls of men. What cannot be understood, never can edify. No advantage can be reaped from the most excellent discourses, if

shall sting, when remorse shall occupy our souls. I might, but I will not, tell you a few stories of the awful power of remorse; it is the first pang of hell; it is the ante-chamber of the pit. To have remorse is to feel the sparks that blaze upwards from the fire of the bottomless Gehenna; to feel remorse is to have eternal torment commenced within the soul. The sting of death shall be unforgiven, unrepented sin.

3. But if sin in the retrospect be the sting of death, what must sin in the prospect be? My friends, we do not often enough look at what sin is to be. We see what it is; first the seed, then the blade, then the ear, and then the full corn in the ear. It is the wish, the imagination, the desire, the sight, the taste, the deed; but what is sin in its next development? We have observed sin as it grows; we have seen it, at first, a very little thing, but expanding itself until it has swelled into a mountain. We have seen it like "a little cloud, the size of a man's hand," but we have beheld it gather until it covered the skies with blackness, and sent down drops of bitter rain. But what is sin to be in the next state? We have gone so far, but sin is a thing that cannot stop. We have seen whereunto it has grown, but whereunto will it grow? for it is not ripe when we die; it has to go on still; it is set going, but it has to unfold itself forever. The moment we die, the voice of justice cries, "Seal up the fountain of blood; stop the stream of forgiveness; he that is holy, let him be holy still; he that is filthy, let him be filthy still." And after that, the man goes on growing filthier and filthier still; his lust develops itself, his vice increases; all those evil passions blaze with tenfold more fury, and, amidst the companionship of others like himself, without the restraints of grace, without the preached word, the man becomes worse and worse; and who can tell whereunto his sin may grow? I have sometimes likened the hour of our death to that celebrated picture, which I think you have seen in the National Gallery, of Perseus holding up the head of Medusa. That head turned all persons into stone who looked upon it. There is a warrior there with a dart in his hand; he stands stiffened, turned into stone, with the javelin even in his fist. There is another, with a poniard beneath his robe, about to stab; he is now the statue of an assassin, motionless and cold. Another is creeping along stealthily, like a man in ambuscade, and there he stands a consolidated rock; he has looked only upon that head, and he is frozen into stone. Well, such is death. What I am when death is held before me, that I must be forever. When my spirit goes, if God finds me hymning his praise, I shall hymn it in heaven; doth he find me breathing out oaths, I shall follow up those oaths in hell. Where death leaves me, judgment finds me. As I die, so shall I live eternally.

"There are no acts of pardon passed

speaketh in an unknown tongue pray that he may interpret.

14 For if I pray in an unknown tongue, my spirit prayeth, but my understanding is unfruitful.

15 What is it then? I will pray with the spirit, and I will pray with the understanding also: I will sing with the spirit, and I will sing with the understanding also.

16 Else when thou shalt bless with the spirit, how shall he that occupieth the room of the unlearned say Amen at thy giving of thanks, seeing he understandeth not what thou sayest?

17 For thou verily givest thanks well, but the other is not edified.

18 I thank my God, I speak with tongues more than ye all:

19 Yet in the church I had rather speak five words with my understanding, that by my voice I might teach others also, than ten thousand words in an unknown tongue.

20 Brethren, be not children in understanding: howbeit in malice be ye children, but in understanding be men.

21 In the law it is written, With men of other tongues and other lips will I speak unto this people; and yet for all that will they not hear me, saith the Lord.

22 Wherefore tongues are for a sign, not to them that believe, but to them that believe not: but prophesying serveth not for them that believe not, but for them which believe.

23 If therefore the whole church be come together into one place, and all speak with tongues, and there come in those that are unlearned, or unbelievers, will they not say that ye are mad?

24 But if all prophesy, and there come in one that believeth not, or one unlearned, he is convinced of all, he is judged of all:

25 And thus are the secrets of his heart made manifest; and so falling down on his face he will worship God, and report that God is in you of a truth.

26 How is it then, brethren? when ye come together, every-one of you hath a psalm, hath a doctrine, hath a tongue, hath a revelation, hath an interpretation. Let all things be done unto edifying.

11. I shall be a barbarian to him – Shall seem to talk unintelligible gibberish.

13. That he may be able to interpret – Which was a distinct gift.

14. If I pray in an unknown tongue – The apostle, as he did at ver. 6, transfers it to himself. My spirit prayeth – By the power of the Spirit I understand the words myself. But my understanding is unfruitful – The knowledge I have is no benefit to others.

15. I will pray with the spirit, but I will pray with the understanding also – I will use my own understanding, as well as the power of the Spirit. I will not act so absurdly, as to utter in a congregation what can edify none but myself.

16. Otherwise how shall he that filleth the place of a private person – That is, any private hearer. Say Amen – Assenting and confirming your words, as it was even then usual for the whole congregation to do.

19. With my understanding – In a rational manner; so as not only to understand myself, but to be understood by others.

20. Be not children in understanding – This is an admirable stroke of true oratory! to bring down the height of their spirits, by representing that wherein they prided themselves most, as mere folly and childishness. In wickedness be ye infants – Have all the innocence of that tender age. But in understanding be ye grown men – Knowing religion was not designed to destroy any of our natural faculties, but to exalt and improve them, our reason in particular.

21. It is written in the Law – The word here, as frequently, means the Old Testament. In foreign tongues will I speak to this people – And so he did. He spake terribly to them by the Babylonians, when they had set at nought what he had spoken by the prophets, who used their own language. These words received a farther accomplishment on the day of Pentecost. Isaiah xxviii, 11.

22. Tongues are intended for a sign to unbelievers – To engage their attention, and convince them the message is of God. Whereas prophecy is not so much for unbelievers, as for the confirmation of them that already believe.

23. Yet – Sometimes prophecy is of more use, even to unbelievers, than speaking with tongues. For instance: If the whole church be met together – On some extraordinary occasion. It is probable, in so large a city, they ordinarily met in several places. And there come in ignorant persons – Men of learning might have understood the tongues in which they spoke. It is observable, St. Paul says here, ignorant persons or unbelievers; but in the next verse, an unbeliever or an ignorant person. Several bad men met together hinder each other by evil discourse. Single persons are more easily gained.

24. He is convicted by all – who speak in their turns, and speak to the heart of the hearers. He is judged by all – Every one says something to which his conscience bears witness.

25. The secrets of his heart are made manifest – Laid open, clearly described; in a manner which to him is most astonishing and utterly unaccountable. How many instances of it are seen at this day! So does God still point his word.

26. What a thing is it, brethren – This was another disorder among them. Every one hath a psalm – That is, at the same time one begins to sing a psalm; another to deliver a doctrine; another to speak in an unknown tongue; another to declare what has been revealed to him; another to interpret what the former is speaking; every one probably gathering a little company about him, just as they did in the schools of the philosophers. Let all be done to edification – So as to profit the hearers.

27. By two or three at most – Let not above two or three speak at one meeting. And that by course – That is, one after another. And let one interpret – Either himself, ver. 13; or, if he have not the gift, some other, into the vulgar tongue. It seems, the gift of tongues was an instantaneous knowledge of a tongue till then unknown, which he that received it could afterwards speak when he thought fit, without any new miracle.

28. Let him speak – That tongue, if he find it profitable to himself in his pri-

MATTHEW HENRY   CHARLES H. SPURGEON

delivered in language such as the hearers cannot speak or understand. Every ability or possession is valuable in proportion to its usefulness. Even fervent, spiritual affection must be governed by the exercise of the understanding, else men will disgrace the truths they profess to promote.

6-14 Even an apostle could not edify, unless he spoke so as to be understood by his hearers. To speak words that have no meaning to those who hear them, is but speaking into the air. That cannot answer the end of speaking, which has no meaning; in this case, speaker and hearers are barbarians to each other. All religious services should be so performed in Christian assemblies, that all may join in, and profit by them. Language plain and easy to be understood, is the most proper for public worship, and other religious exercises. Every true follower of Christ will rather desire to do good to others, than to get a name for learning or fine speaking.

15-25 There can be no assent to prayers that are not understood. A truly Christian minister will seek much more to do spiritual good to men's souls, than to get the greatest applause to himself. This is proving himself the servant of Christ. Children are apt to be struck with novelty; but do not act like them. Christians should be like children, void of guile and malice; yet they should not be unskillful as to the word of righteousness, but only as to the arts of mischief. It is a proof that a people are forsaken of God, when he gives them up to the rule of those who teach them to worship in another language. They can never be benefited by such teaching. Yet thus the preachers did who delivered their instructions in an unknown tongue. Would it not make Christianity ridiculous to a heathen, to hear the ministers pray or preach in a language which neither he nor the assembly understood? But if those who minister, plainly interpret Scripture, or preach the great truths and rules of the gospel, a heathen or unlearned person might become a convert to Christianity. His conscience might be touched, the secrets of his heart might be revealed to him, and so he might be brought to confess his guilt, and to own that God was present in the assembly. Scripture truth, plainly and duly taught, has a wonderful power to awaken the conscience and touch the heart.

26-33 Religious exercises in public assemblies should have this view; Let all be done to edifying. As to the speaking in an unknown tongue, if another were present who could interpret, two miraculous gifts might be exercised at once, and thereby the church be edified, and the faith of the hearers confirmed at the same time. As to prophesying, two or three only should speak at one meeting,

In the cold grave to which we haste."
It is forever, forever, forever! Ah! there are a set of heretics in these days who talk of short punishment, and preach about God's transporting souls for a term of years, and then letting them die. Where did such men learn their doctrine, I wonder? I read in God's word that the angel shall plant one foot upon the earth, and the other upon the sea, and shall swear by him that liveth and was dead, that time shall be no longer. But, if a soul could die in a thousand years, it would die in time; if a million of years could elapse, and then the soul could be extinguished, there would be such a thing as time; for, talk to me of years, and there is time. But, sirs, when that angel has spoken the word, "Time shall be no longer," things will then be eternal; the spirit shall proceed in its ceaseless revolution of weal or woe, never to be stayed, for there is no time to stop it; the fact of its stopping would imply time; but everything shall be eternal, for time shall cease to be. It well becomes you, then, to consider where ye are and what ye are. Oh! stand and tremble on the narrow neck of land 'twixt the two unbounded seas, for God in heaven alone can tell how soon thou mayest be launched upon the eternal future. May God grant that, when that last hour may come, we may be prepared for it! Like the thief, unheard, unseen, it steals through night's dark shade. Perhaps, as here I stand, and rudely speak of these dark, hidden things, soon may the hand be stretched, and dumb the mouth that lisps the faltering strain. Oh! thou that dwellest in heaven, thou power supreme, thou everlasting King, let not that hour intrude upon me in an ill spent season; but may it find me rapt in meditation high, hymning my great Creator. So, in the last moment of my life, I will hasten beyond the azure, to bathe the wings of this my spirit in their native element, and then to dwell with thee for ever—

"Far from a world of grief and sin,
With God eternally shut in."

II. "THE STRENGTH OF SIN is the law."
I have attempted to show how to fight this monster—it is by extracting and destroying its sting. I prepare myself for the battle. It is true I have sinned, and therefore I have put a sting into death, but I will endeavor to take it away. I attempt it, but the monster laughs me in the face, and cries, "The strength of sin is the law. Before thou canst destroy sin thou must in some way satisfy the law. Sin cannot be removed by thy tears or by thy deeds, for the law is its strength; and until thou hast satisfied the vengeance of the law, until thou hast paid the uttermost farthing of its demands, my sting cannot be taken away, for the very strength of sin is the law." Now, I must try and explain this doctrine that the strength of sin is the law. Most men think that sin has no strength at all. "Oh," say many, "we may

27 If any man speak in an unknown tongue, let it be by two, or at the most by three, and that by course; and let one interpret.

28 But if there be no interpreter, let him keep silence in the church; and let him speak to himself, and to God.

29 Let the prophets speak two or three, and let the other judge.

30 If any thing be revealed to another that sitteth by, let the first hold his peace.

31 For ye may all prophesy one by one, that all may learn, and all may be comforted.

32 And the spirits of the prophets are subject to the prophets.

33 For God is not the author of confusion, but of peace, as in all churches of the saints.

34 Let your women keep silence in the churches: for it is not permitted unto them to speak; but they are commanded to be under obedience, as also saith the law.

35 And if they will learn any thing, let them ask their husbands at home: for it is a shame for women to speak in the church.

36 What? came the word of God out from you? or came it unto you only?

37 If any man think himself to be a prophet, or spiritual, let him acknowledge that the things that I write unto you are the commandments of the Lord.

38 But if any man be ignorant, let him be ignorant.

39 Wherefore, brethren, covet to prophesy, and forbid not to speak with tongues.

40 Let all things be done decently and in order.

1 CORINTHIANS 15

1 Moreover, brethren, I declare unto you the gospel which I preached unto you, which also ye have received, and wherein ye stand;

2 By which also ye are saved, if ye keep in memory what I preached unto you, unless ye have believed in vain.

3 For I delivered unto you first of all that which I also received, how that Christ died for our sins

vate devotions.

29. Let two or three of the prophets – Not more, at one meeting. Speak – One after another, expounding the scripture.

31. All – Who have that gift. That all may learn – Both by speaking and by hearing.

32. For the spirits of the prophets are subject to the prophets – But what enthusiast considers this? The impulses of the Holy Spirit, even in men really inspired, so suit themselves to their rational faculties, as not to divest them of the government of themselves, like the heathen priests under their diabolical possession. Evil spirits threw their prophets into such ungovernable ecstasies, as forced them to speak and act like madmen. But the Spirit of God left his prophets the clear use of their judgment, when, and how long, it was fit for them to speak, and never hurried them into any improprieties either as to the matter, manner, or time of their speaking.

34. Let your women be silent in the churches – Unless they are under an extraordinary impulse of the Spirit. For, in other cases, it is not permitted them to speak – By way of teaching in public assemblies. But to be in subjection – To the man whose proper office it is to lead and to instruct the congregation. Gen. iii, 16.

35. And even if they desire to learn anything – Still they are not to speak in public, but to ask their own husbands at home – That is the place, and those the persons to inquire of.

36. Are ye of Corinth either the first or the only Christians? If not, conform herein to the custom of all the churches.

37. Or spiritual – Endowed with any extraordinary gift of the Spirit. Let him – Prove it, by acknowledging that I now write by the Spirit.

38. Let him be ignorant – Be it at his own peril.

39. Therefore – To sum up the whole.

40. Decently – By every individual. In order – By the whole church.

1 CORINTHIANS 15

2. Ye are saved, if ye hold fast – Your salvation is begun, and will be perfected, if ye continue in the faith. Unless ye have believed in vain – Unless indeed your faith was only a delusion.

3. I received – From Christ himself. It was not a fiction of my own. Isaiah liii, 8, 9.

4. According to the scriptures – He proves it first from scripture, then from the testimony of a cloud of witnesses. Psalm xvi, 10.

5. By the twelve – This was their standing appellation; but their full number was not then present.

6. Above five hundred – Probably in Galilee. A glorious and incontestable proof! The greater part remain – Alive.

7. Then by all the apostles – The twelve were mentioned ver. 5. This title here, therefore, seems to include the seventy; if not all those, likewise, whom God afterwards sent to plant the gospel in heathen nations.

8. An untimely birth – It was impossible to abase himself more than he does by this single appellation. As an abortion is not worthy the name of a man, so he affirms himself to be not worthy the name of an apostle.

9. I persecuted the church – True believers are humbled all their lives, even for the sins they committed before they believed.

10. I labored more than they all – That is, more than any of them, from a deep sense of the peculiar love God had shown me. Yet, to speak more properly, it is not I, but the grace of God that is with me – This it is which at first qualified me for the work, and still excites me to zeal and diligence in it.

11. Whether I or they, so we preach – All of us speak the same thing.

and this one after the other, not all at once. The man who is inspired by the Spirit of God will observe order and decency in delivering his revelations. God never teaches men to neglect their duties, or to act in any way unbecoming their age or station.

34-40 When the apostle exhorts Christian women to seek information on religious subjects from their husbands at home, it shows that believing families ought to assemble for promoting spiritual knowledge. The Spirit of Christ can never contradict itself; and if their revelations are against those of the apostle, they do not come from the same Spirit. The way to keep peace, truth, and order in the church, is to seek that which is good for it, to bear with that which is not hurtful to its welfare, and to keep up good behavior, order, and decency.

1 CORINTHIANS 15

The apostle proves the resurrection of Christ from the dead. (1-11)

Those answered who deny the resurrection of the body. (12-19)

The resurrection of believers to eternal life. (20-34)

Objections against it answered. (35-50)

The mystery of the change that will be made on those living at Christ's second coming. (51-54)

The believer's triumph over death and the grave. An exhortation to diligence. (55-58)

1-11 The word resurrection, usually points out our existence beyond the grave. Of the apostle's doctrine not a trace can be found in all the teaching of philosophers. The doctrine of Christ's death and resurrection, is the foundation of Christianity. Remove this, and all our hopes for eternity sink at once. And it is by holding this truth firm, that Christians stand in the day of trial, and are kept faithful to God. We believe in vain, unless we keep in the faith of the gospel. This truth is confirmed by Old Testament prophecies; and many saw Christ after he was risen. This apostle was highly favored, but he always had a low opinion of himself, and expressed it. When sinners are, by Divine grace, turned into saints, God causes the remembrance of former sins to make them humble, diligent, and faithful. He ascribes to Divine grace all that was valuable in him. True believers, though not ignorant of what the Lord has done for, in, and by them, yet when they look at their whole conduct and their obligations, they are led to feel that none are so worthless as they are. All true Christians believe that Jesus Christ, and him crucified, and then risen from the dead, is the sum and substance of Christianity. All the apostles agreed in this testimony; by this faith they lived, and in this faith they died.

have sinned very much, but we will repent, and we will be better for the rest of our lives; no doubt God is merciful, and he will forgive us." And we hear many divines often speak of sin as if it were a very venial thing. Inquire of them what is a man to do? There is no deep repentance required, no real inward workings of divine grace, no casting himself upon the blood of Christ. They never tell us about a complete atonement having been made. They have, indeed, some shadowy idea of an atonement, that Christ died just as a matter of form to satisfy justice; but as to any literal taking away of our sins, and suffering the actual penalty for us, they do not consider that God's law requires any such thing. I suppose they do not, for I never hear them assert the positive satisfaction and substitution of our Lord Jesus Christ. But without that, how can we take away the strength of sin?

1. The strength of sin is in the law, first, in this respect, that the law being spiritual, it is quite impossible for us to live without sin. If the law were merely carnal, and referred to the flesh; if it simply related to open and overt actions, I question, even then, whether we could live without sin; but when I turn over the ten commandments and read, "Thou shalt not covet," I know it refers even to the wish of my heart. It is said, "Thou shalt not commit adultery;" but it is said, also that whosoever looketh on a woman to lust after her hath already committed that sin. So that it is not merely the act, it is the thought; it is not the deed simply, it is the very imagination, that is a sin. Oh now, sinner, how canst thou get rid of sin? Thy very thoughts, the inward workings of thy mind, these are crimes—this is guilt and desperate wickedness. Is there not, now, strength in sin? Hath not the law put a potency in it? Has it not nerved sin with such a power that all thy strength cannot hope to wipe away the black enormity of thy transgression?

2. Then, again, the law puts strength into sin in this respect—that it will not abate one tittle of its stern demands. It says to every man who breaks it, "I will not forgive you." You hear persons talk about God's mercy. Now, if they do not believe in the gospel, they must be under the law; but where in the law do we read of mercy? If you will read the commandments through, there is a curse after them, but there is no provision made for pardon. The law itself speaks not of that; it thunders out without the slightest mitigation, "The soul that sinneth it shall die." If any of you desire to be saved by works, remember one sin will spoil your righteousness; one dust of this earth's dross will spoil the beauty of that perfect righteousness which God requires at your hands. If ye would be saved by works, men and brethren, ye must be as holy as the angels, ye must be as pure and as immaculate as Jesus; for the law requires perfection, and nothing short of it; and God, with unflinching vengeance,

according to the scriptures;

4 And that he was buried, and that he rose again the third day according to the scriptures:

5 And that he was seen of Cephas, then of the twelve:

6 After that, he was seen of above five hundred brethren at once; of whom the greater part remain unto this present, but some are fallen asleep.

7 After that, he was seen of James; then of all the apostles.

8 And last of all he was seen of me also, as of one born out of due time.

9 For I am the least of the apostles, that am not meet to be called an apostle, because I persecuted the church of God.

10 But by the grace of God I am what I am: and his grace which was bestowed upon me was not in vain; but I labored more abundantly than they all: yet not I, but the grace of God which was with me.

11 Therefore whether it were I or they, so we preach, and so ye believed.

12 Now if Christ be preached that he rose from the dead, how say some among you that there is no resurrection of the dead?

13 But if there be no resurrection of the dead, then is Christ not risen:

14 And if Christ be not risen, then is our preaching vain, and your faith is also vain.

15 Yea, and we are found false witnesses of God; because we have testified of God that he raised up Christ: whom he raised not up, if so be that the dead rise not.

16 For if the dead rise not, then is not Christ raised:

17 And if Christ be not raised, your faith is vain; ye are yet in your sins.

18 Then they also which are fallen asleep in Christ are perished.

19 If in this life only we have hope in Christ, we are of all men most miserable.

20 But now is Christ risen from the dead, and become the firstfruits of them that slept.

21 For since by man came death, by man came also the resurrection of the dead.

22 For as in Adam all die, even

12. How say some – Who probably had been heathen philosophers.

13. If there be no resurrection – If it be a thing flatly impossible.

14. Then is our preaching – From a commission supposed to be given after the resurrection. Vain – Without any real foundation.

15. If the dead rise not – If the very notion of a resurrection be, as they say, absurd and impossible.

17. Ye are still in your sins – That is, under the guilt of them. So that there needed something more than reformation, (which was plainly wrought,) in order to their being delivered from the guilt of sin, even that atonement, the sufficiency of which God attested by raising our great Surety from the grave.

18. They who sleep in Christ – Who have died for him, or believing in him. Are perished – Have lost their life and being together.

19. If in this life only we have hope – If we look for nothing beyond the grave. But if we have a divine evidence of things not seen, if we have "a hope full of immortality," if we now taste of "the powers of the world to come," and see "the crown that fadeth not away," then, notwithstanding all our present trials, we are more happy than all men.

20. But now – St. Paul declares that Christians "have hope," not "in this life only." His proof of the resurrection lies in a narrow compass, ver. 12-19. Almost all the rest of the chapter is taken up in illustrating, vindicating, and applying it. The proof is short, but solid and convincing, that which arose from Christ's resurrection. Now this not only proved a resurrection possible, but, as it proved him to be a divine teacher, proved the certainty of a general resurrection, which he so expressly taught. The first fruit of them that slept – The earnest, pledge, and insurance of their resurrection who slept in him: even of all the righteous. It is of the resurrection of these, and these only, that the apostle speaks throughout the chapter.

22. As through Adam all, even the righteous, die, so through Christ all these shall be made alive – He does not say, "shall revive," (as naturally as they die,) but shall be made alive, by a power not their own.

23. Afterward – The whole harvest. At the same time the wicked shall rise also. But they are not here taken into the account.

24. Then – After the resurrection and the general judgment. Cometh the end – Of the world; the grand period of all those wonderful scenes that have appeared for so many succeeding generations. When he shall have delivered up the kingdom to the Father, and he (the Father) shall have abolished all adverse rule, authority, and power – Not that the Father will then begin to reign without the Son, nor will the Son then cease to reign. For the divine reign both of the Father and Son is from everlasting to everlasting. But this is spoken of the Son's mediatorial kingdom, which will then be delivered up, and of the immediate kingdom or reign of the Father, which will then commence. Till then the Son transacts the business which the Father hath given him, for those who are his, and by them as well as by the angels, with the Father, and against their enemies. So far as the Father gave the kingdom to the Son, the Son shall deliver it up to the Father, John xiii, 3. Nor does the Father cease to reign, when he gives it to the Son; neither the Son, when he delivers it to the Father: but the glory which he had before the world began, John xvii, 5; Heb. i, 8, will remain even after this is delivered up. Nor will he cease to be a king even in his human nature, Luke i, 33. If the citizens of the new Jerusalem "shall reign for ever," Rev. xxii, 5, how much more shall he?

25. He must reign – Because so it is written. Till he – the Father hath put all his enemies under his feet. Psalm cx, 1.

26. The last enemy that is destroyed is death – Namely, after Satan, Heb. ii, 14, and sin, ver. 56, are destroyed. In the same order they prevailed. Satan brought in sin, and sin brought forth death. And Christ, when he of old engaged with these enemies, first conquered Satan, then sin, in his death; and, lastly, death, in

MATTHEW HENRY   CHARLES H. SPURGEON

12-19 Having shown that Christ was risen, the apostle answers those who said there would be no resurrection. There had been no justification, or salvation, if Christ had not risen. And must not faith in Christ be vain, and of no use, if he is still among the dead? The proof of the resurrection of the body is the resurrection of our Lord. Even those who died in the faith, had perished in their sins, if Christ had not risen. All who believe in Christ, have hope in him, as a Redeemer; hope for redemption and salvation by him; but if there is no resurrection, or future recompense, their hope in him can only be as to this life. And they must be in a worse condition than the rest of mankind, especially at the time, and under the circumstances, in which the apostles wrote; for then Christians were hated and persecuted by all men. But it is not so; they, of all men, enjoy solid comforts amidst all their difficulties and trials, even in the times of the sharpest persecution.

20-34 All that are by faith united to Christ, are by his resurrection assured of their own. As through the sin of the first Adam, all men became mortal, because all had from him the same sinful nature, so, through the resurrection of Christ, shall all who are made to partake of the Spirit, and the spiritual nature, revive, and live forever. There will be an order in the resurrection. Christ himself has been the first fruits; at his coming, his redeemed people will be raised before others; at the last the wicked will rise also. Then will be the end of this present state of things. Would we triumph in that solemn and important season, we must now submit to his rule, accept his salvation, and live to his glory. Then shall we rejoice in the completion of his undertaking, that God may receive the whole glory of our salvation, that we may forever serve him, and enjoy his favor. What shall those do, who are baptized for the dead, if the dead rise not at all? Perhaps baptism is used here in a figure, for afflictions, sufferings, and martyrdom, as Mt 20:22,23. What is, or will become of those who have suffered many and great injuries, and have even lost their lives, for this doctrine of the resurrection, if the dead rise not at all? Whatever the meaning may be, doubtless the apostle's argument was understood by the Corinthians. And it is as plain to us that Christianity would be a foolish profession, if it proposed advantage to themselves by their faithfulness to God; and to have our fruit to holiness, that our end may be everlasting life. But we must not live like beasts, as we do not die like them. It must be ignorance of God that leads any to disbelieve the resurrection and future life. Those who own a God and a providence, and observe how unequal things are in the present life, how frequently the best men fare worst, cannot doubt as to an after-state, where every thing will be set to rights. Let us not be

will smite every man low who cannot bring him a perfect obedience. If I cannot, when I come before his throne, plead a perfect righteousness as being mine, God will say, "you have not fulfilled the demands of my law; depart, accursed one! You have sinned, and you must die." "Ah," says one, "can we ever have a perfect righteousness, then?" Yes, I will tell you of that in the third point; thanks be unto Christ, who giveth us the victory through his blood and through his righteousness, who adorns us as a bride in her jewels as a husband arrays his wife with ornaments.

3. Yet again; the law gives strength to sin from the fact that, for every transgression it will exact a punishment. The law never remits a farthing of debt: it says, "Sin—punishment." They are linked together with adamantine chains; they are tied, and cannot be severed. The law speaks not of sin and mercy; mercy comes in the gospel. The law says, "Sin—die; transgress—be chastised; sin—hell." Thus are they linked together. Once let me sin, and I may go to the foot of stern Justice, and as, with blind eyes, she holds the scales, I may say, "O Justice, remember, I was holy once; remember that on such and such an occasion I did keep the law." "Yes," saith Justice, "all I owe thee thou shalt have; I will not punish thee for what thou hast not done; but remember you this crime, O sinner?" and she puts in the heavy weight. The sinner trembles, and he cries, "But canst thou not forget that? Wilt thou not cast it away?" "Nay," saith Justice, and she puts in another weight. "Sinner, dost thou recollect this crime?" "Oh!" says the sinner, "wilt thou not for mercy's sake?" "I will not have mercy," says Justice; "Mercy has its own palace, but I have naught to do with forgiveness here; mercy belongs to Christ. If you will be saved by Justice, you shall have your fill of it. If you come to me for salvation, I will not have mercy brought in to help me; she is not my vicegerent; I stand here alone without her." And again, as she holds the scales, she puts in another iniquity, another crime, another enormous transgression; and each time the man begs and prays that he may have that passed by. Says Justice, "Nay, I must exact the penalty; I have sworn I will, and I will. Canst thou find a substitute for thyself? If thou canst, there is the only room I have for mercy. I will exact it of that substitute, but even at his hands I will have the utmost jot and tittle; I will abate nothing; I am God's Justice, stern and unflinching, I will not alter, I will not mitigate the penalty." She still holds the scales. The plea is in vain. "Never will I change!" she cries; "bring me the blood, bring me the price to its utmost; count it down, or else, sinner, thou shalt die."

Now, my friends, I ask you, if ye consider the spirituality of the law, the perfection it requires, and its unflinching severity, are you prepared to take away the sting of death in your own persons?

so in Christ shall all be made alive.

23 But every man in his own order: Christ the firstfruits; afterward they that are Christ's at his coming.

24 Then cometh the end, when he shall have delivered up the kingdom to God, even the Father; when he shall have put down all rule and all authority and power.

25 For he must reign, till he hath put all enemies under his feet.

26 The last enemy that shall be destroyed is death.

27 For he hath put all things under his feet. But when he saith, all things are put under him, it is manifest that he is excepted, which did put all things under him.

28 And when all things shall be subdued unto him, then shall the Son also himself be subject unto him that put all things under him, that God may be all in all.

29 Else what shall they do which are baptized for the dead, if the dead rise not at all? why are they then baptized for the dead?

30 And why stand we in jeopardy every hour?

31 I protest by your rejoicing which I have in Christ Jesus our Lord, I die daily.

32 If after the manner of men I have fought with beasts at Ephesus, what advantageth it me, if the dead rise not? let us eat and drink; for to morrow we die.

33 Be not deceived: evil communications corrupt good manners.

34 Awake to righteousness, and sin not; for some have not the knowledge of God: I speak this to your shame.

35 But some man will say, How are the dead raised up? and with what body do they come?

36 Thou fool, that which thou sowest is not quickened, except it die:

37 And that which thou sowest, thou sowest not that body that shall be, but bare grain, it may chance of wheat, or of some other grain:

38 But God giveth it a body as it hath pleased him, and to every seed his own body.

his resurrection. In the same order he delivers all the faithful from them, yea, and destroys these enemies themselves. Death he so destroys that it shall be no more; sin and Satan, so that they shall no more hurt his people.

27. Under him – Under the Son. Psalm viii, 6, 7.

28. The Son also shall be subject – Shall deliver up the mediatorial kingdom. That the three-one God may be all in all – All things, (consequently all persons,) without any interruption, without the intervention of any creature, without the opposition of any enemy, shall be subordinate to God. All shall say, "My God, and my all." This is the end. Even an inspired apostle can see nothing beyond this.

29. Who are baptized for the dead – Perhaps baptized in hope of blessings to be received after they are numbered with the dead. Or, "baptized in the room of the dead" – Of them that are just fallen in the cause of Christ: like soldiers who advance in the room of their companions that fell just before their face.

30. Why are we – The apostles. Also in danger every hour – It is plain we can expect no amends in this life.

31. I protest by your rejoicing, which I have – Which love makes my own. I die daily – I am daily in the very jaws of death. Beside that I live, as it were, in a daily martyrdom.

32. If to speak after the manner of men – That is, to use a proverbial phrase, expressive of the most imminent danger I have fought with wild beasts at Ephesus – With the savage fury of a lawless multitude, Acts xix, 29, &c. This seems to have been but just before. Let us eat, &c. – We might, on that supposition, as well say, with the Epicureans, Let us make the best of this short life, seeing we have no other portion.

33. Be not deceived – By such pernicious counsels as this. Evil communications corrupt good manners – He opposes to the Epicurean saying, a wellknown verse of the poet Menander. Evil communications – Discourse contrary to faith, hope, or love, naturally tends to destroy all holiness.

34. Awake – An exclamation full of apostolic majesty. Shake off your lethargy! To righteousness – Which flows from the true knowledge of God, and implies that your whole soul be broad awake. And sin not – That is, and ye will not sin. Sin supposes drowsiness of soul. There is need to press this. For some among you have not the knowledge of God – With all their boasted knowledge, they are totally ignorant of what it most concerns them to know. I speak this to your shame – For nothing is more shameful, than sleepy ignorance of God, and of the word and works of God; in these especially, considering the advantages they had enjoyed.

35. But some one possibly will say, How are the dead raised up, after their whole frame is dissolved? And with what kind of bodies do they come again, after these are moldered into dust?

36. To the inquiry concerning the manner of rising, and the quality of the bodies that rise, the Apostle answers first by a similitude, ver. 36-42, and then plainly and directly, ver. 42, 43. That which thou sowest, is not quickened into new life and verdure, except it die – Undergo a dissolution of its parts, a change analogous to death. Thus St. Paul inverts the objection; as if he had said, Death is so far from hindering life, that it necessarily goes before it.

37. Thou sowest not the body that shall be – Produced from the seed committed to the ground, but a bare, naked grain, widely different from that which will afterward rise out of the earth.

38. But God – Not thou, O man, not the grain itself, giveth it a body as it hath pleased him, from the time he distinguished the various species of beings; and to each of the seeds, not only of the fruits, but animals also, (to which the Apostle rises in the following verse,) its own body; not only peculiar to that species, but proper to that individual, and arising out of the substance of that very grain.

MATTHEW HENRY

CHARLES H. SPURGEON

joined with ungodly men; but warn all around us, especially children and young persons, to shun them as a pestilence. Let us awake to righteousness, and not sin.

35-50 1. How are the dead raised up? that is, by what means? How can they be raised? 2. As to the bodies which shall rise. Will it be with the like shape, and form, and stature, and members, and qualities? The former objection is that of those who opposed the doctrine, the latter of curious doubters. To the first the answer is, This was to be brought about by Divine power; that power which all may see does somewhat like it, year after year, in the death and revival of the corn. It is foolish to question the Almighty power of God to raise the dead, when we see it every day quickening and reviving things that are dead. To the second inquiry; The grain undergoes a great change; and so will the dead, when they rise and live again. The seed dies, though a part of it springs into new life, though how it is we cannot fully understand. The works of creation and providence daily teach us to be humble, as well as to admire the Creator's wisdom and goodness. There is a great variety among other bodies, as there is among plants. There is a variety of glory among heavenly bodies. The bodies of the dead, when they rise, will be fitted for the heavenly state; and there will be a variety of glories among them. Burying the dead, is like committing seed to the earth, that it may spring out of it again. Nothing is more loathsome than a dead body. But believers shall at the resurrection have bodies, made fit to be forever united with spirits made perfect. To God all things are possible. He is the Author and Source of spiritual life and holiness, unto all his people, by the supply of his Holy Spirit to the soul; and he will also quicken and change the body by his Spirit. The dead in Christ shall not only rise, but shall rise thus gloriously changed. The bodies of the saints, when they rise again, will be changed. They will be then glorious and spiritual bodies, fitted to the heavenly world and state, where they are ever afterwards to dwell. The human body in its present form, and with its wants and weaknesses, cannot enter or enjoy the kingdom of God. Then let us not sow to the flesh, of which we can only reap corruption. And the body follows the state of the soul. He, therefore, who neglects the life of the soul, casts away his present good; he who refuses to live to God, squanders all he has.

51-58 All the saints should not die, but all would be changed. In the gospel, many truths, before hidden in mystery, are made known. Death never shall appear in the regions to which our Lord will bear his risen saints. Therefore let us seek the full assurance of faith and hope, that in the midst of

Can you hope to overcome sin yourselves? Can you trust that, by some righteous works, you may yet cancel your guilt? If you think so, go, O foolish one, go! O madman, go! work out thine own salvation with fear and trembling, without the God that worketh in thee; go, twist thy rope of sand; go, build a pyramid of air; go, prepare a house with bubbles, and think it is to last forever; but know it will be a dream with an awful awakening, for as a dream when one awaketh will he despise alike your image and your righteousness. "The strength of sin is the law."

III. But now, in the last place, we have before us THE VICTORY OF FAITH. The Christian is the only champion who can smite the dragon of death, and even he cannot do it of himself; but when he has done it, he shall cry, "Thanks be to God who giveth us the victory through our Lord Jesus Christ." One moment, and I will show you how the Christian can look upon death with complacency, through the merits of Jesus Christ.

First, Christ has taken away the strength of sin in this respect, that he has removed the law. We are not under bondage, but under grace. Law is not our directing principle, grace is. Do not misunderstand me. The principle that I must do a thing—that is to say, the principle of law, "do, or be punished; do, or be rewarded," is not the motive of the Christian's life; his principle is grace: "God has done so much for me, what ought I to do for him?" We are not under the law in that sense, but under grace.

Then Christ has removed the law in this sense, that he has completely satisfied it. The law demands a perfect righteousness; Christ says, "Law, thou hast it; find fault with me; I am the sinner's substitute; have I not kept thy commandments? Wherein have I violated thy statutes?" "Come here, my beloved," he says, and then he cries to Justice, "Find a fault in this man; I have put my robe upon him; I have washed him in my blood; I have cleansed him from his sin. All the past is gone; as for the future, I have secured it by sanctification; as for the penalty, I have borne it myself; at one tremendous draught of love I have drunk that man's destruction dry; I have borne what he should have suffered; I have endured the agonies he ought to have endured. Justice, have I not satisfied thee? Did I not say upon the tree, and didst thou not coincide with it, 'It is finished; it is finished?' Have I not made so complete an atonement that there is now no need for that man to die and expiate his guilt? Do I not complete the perfect righteousness of this poor, once condemned, but now justified spirit?" "Yes" saith Justice, "I am well satisfied, and even more content, if possible, than if the sinner had brought a spotless righteousness of his own." And now, what saith the Christian after this? Boldly he

39 All flesh is not the same flesh: but there is one kind of flesh of men, another flesh of beasts, another of fishes, and another of birds.

40 There are also celestial bodies, and bodies terrestrial: but the glory of the celestial is one, and the glory of the terrestrial is another.

41 There is one glory of the sun, and another glory of the moon, and another glory of the stars: for one star differeth from another star in glory.

42 So also is the resurrection of the dead. It is sown in corruption; it is raised in incorruption:

43 It is sown in dishonor; it is raised in glory: it is sown in weakness; it is raised in power:

44 It is sown a natural body; it is raised a spiritual body. There is a natural body, and there is a spiritual body.

45 And so it is written, The first man Adam was made a living soul; the last Adam was made a quickening spirit.

46 Howbeit that was not first which is spiritual, but that which is natural; and afterward that which is spiritual.

47 The first man is of the earth, earthy: the second man is the Lord from heaven.

48 As is the earthy, such are they also that are earthy: and as is the heavenly, such are they also that are heavenly.

49 And as we have borne the image of the earthy, we shall also bear the image of the heavenly.

50 Now this I say, brethren, that flesh and blood cannot inherit the kingdom of God; neither doth corruption inherit incorruption.

51 Behold, I shew you a mystery; We shall not all sleep, but we shall all be changed,

52 In a moment, in the twinkling of an eye, at the last trump: for the trumpet shall sound, and the dead shall be raised incorruptible, and we shall be changed.

53 For this corruptible must put on incorruption, and this mortal must put on immortality.

54 So when this corruptible shall have put on incorruption, and this mortal shall have put on immortality, then shall be brought to pass the saying that

39. All flesh – As if he had said, Even earthy bodies differ from earthy, and heavenly bodies from heavenly. What wonder then, if heavenly bodies differ from earthy? or the bodies which rise from those that lay in the grave?

40. There are also heavenly bodies – As the sun, moon, and stars; and there are earthy – as vegetables and animals. But the brightest luster which the latter can have is widely different from that of the former.

41. Yea, and the heavenly bodies themselves differ from each other.

42. So also is the resurrection of the dead – So great is the difference between the body which fell, and that which rises. It is sown – A beautiful word; committed, as seed, to the ground. In corruption – Just ready to putrefy, and, by various degrees of corruption and decay, to return to the dust from whence it came. It is raised in incorruption – Utterly incapable of either dissolution or decay.

43. It is sown in dishonor – Shocking to those who loved it best, human nature in disgrace! It is raised in glory – Clothed with robes of light, fit for those whom the King of heaven delights to honor. It is sown in weakness – Deprived even of that feeble strength which it once enjoyed. It is raised in power – Endued with vigor, strength, and activity, such as we cannot now conceive.

44. It is sown in this world a merely animal body – Maintained by food, sleep, and air, like the bodies of brutes: but it is raised of a more refined contexture, needing none of these animal refreshments, and endued with qualities of a spiritual nature, like the angels of God.

45. The first Adam was made a living soul – God gave him such life as other animals enjoy: but the last Adam, Christ, is a quickening spirit – As he hath life in himself, so he quickeneth whom he will; giving a more refined life to their very bodies at the resurrection. Gen. ii, 7.

47. The first man was from the earth, earthy; the second man is the Lord from heaven – The first man, being from the earth, is subject to corruption and dissolution, like the earth from which he came. The second man – St. Paul could not so well say, "Is from heaven, heavenly:" because, though man owes it to the earth that he is earthy, yet the Lord does not owe his glory to heaven. He himself made the heavens, and by descending from thence showed himself to us as the Lord. Christ was not the second man in order of time; but in this respect, that as Adam was a public person, who acted in the stead of all mankind, so was Christ. As Adam was the first general representative of men, Christ was the second and the last. And what they severally did, terminated not in themselves, but affected all whom they represented.

48. They that are earthy – Who continue without any higher principle. They that are heavenly – Who receive a divine principle from heaven.

49. The image of the heavenly – Holiness and glory.

50. But first we must be entirely changed; for such flesh and blood as we are clothed with now, cannot enter into that kingdom which is wholly spiritual: neither doth this corruptible body inherit that incorruptible kingdom.

51. A mystery – A truth hitherto unknown; and not yet fully known to any of the sons of men. We – Christians. The Apostle considers them all as one, in their succeeding generations. Shall not all die – Suffer a separation of soul and body. But we shall all – Who do not die, be changed – So that this animal body shall become spiritual.

52. In a moment – Amazing work of omnipotence! And cannot the same power now change us into saints in a moment? The trumpet shall sound – To awaken all that sleep in the dust of the earth.

54. Death is swallowed up in victory – That is, totally conquered, abolished for ever.

55. O death, where is thy sting? – Which once was full of hellish poison. O hades, the receptacle of separate souls, where is thy victory – Thou art now robbed of all thy spoils; all thy captives are set at liberty. Hades literally means the invisible world, and relates to the soul; death, to the body. The Greek words

MATTHEW HENRY

pain, and in the prospect of death, we may think calmly on the horrors of the tomb; assured that our bodies will there sleep, and in the mean time our souls will be present with the Redeemer. Sin gives death all its hurtful power. The sting of death is sin; but Christ, by dying, has taken out this sting; he has made atonement for sin, he has obtained remission of it. The strength of sin is the law. None can answer its demands, endure its curse, or do away his own transgressions. Hence terror and anguish. And hence death is terrible to the unbelieving and the impenitent. Death may seize a believer, but it cannot hold him in its power. How many springs of joy to the saints, and of thanksgiving to God, are opened by the death and resurrection, the sufferings and conquests of the Redeemer! In verse 58 we have an exhortation, that believers should be steadfast, firm in the faith of that gospel which the apostle preached, and they received. Also, to be unmovable in their hope and expectation of this great privilege, of being raised incorruptible and immortal. And to abound in the work of the Lord, always doing the Lord's service, and obeying the Lord's commands. May Christ give us faith, and increase our faith, that we may not only be safe, but joyful and triumphant.

1 CORINTHIANS 16

A collection for the poor at Jerusalem. (1-9)
Timothy and Apollos commended. (10-12)
Exhortation to watchfulness in faith and love. (13-18)
Christian salutations. (19-24)

1-9 The good examples of other Christians and churches should rouse us. It is good to lay up in store for good uses. Those who are rich in this world, should be rich in good works, 1Ti 6:17,18. The diligent hand will not make rich, without the Divine blessing, Pr 10:4,22. And what more proper to stir us up to charity to the people and children of God, than to look at all we have as his gift? Works of mercy are real fruits of true love to God, and are therefore proper services on his own day. Ministers are doing their proper business, when putting forward, or helping works of charity. The heart of a Christian minister must be towards the people among whom he has labored long, and with success. All our purposes must be made with submission to the Divine providence, Jas 4:15. Adversaries and opposition do not break the spirits of faithful and successful ministers, but warm their zeal, and inspire them with fresh courage. A faithful minister is more discouraged by the hardness of his hearers' hearts, and the backslidings of professors, than by the enemies' attempts.

CHARLES H. SPURGEON

comes to the realms of death, and entering the gates there, he cries, "Who shall lay anything to the charge of God's elect?" And when he had said it, the dragon drops his sting. He descends into the grave; he passes by the place where fiends lie down in fetters of iron; he sees their chains, and looks into the dungeon where they dwell, and as he passes by the prison door, he shouts, "Who shall lay anything to the charge of God's elect?" They growl and bite their iron bonds, and hiss in secret, but they cannot lay aught to his charge. Now see him mount aloft. He approaches God's heaven, he come against the gates, and Faith still triumphantly shouts, "Who shall lay anything to the charge of God's elect?" And a voice comes from within: "Not Christ, for he hath died; not God, for he hath justified." Received by Jesus, Faith enters heaven, and again she cries, "Who even here amongst the spotless and ransomed, shall lay anything to the charge of God's elect?" Now the law is satisfied, sin is gone; and now surely we need not fear the sting of the dragon, but we may say, as Paul did, when he rose into the majesty of poetry—such beautiful poetry that Pope himself borrowed his words, only transposing the sentences, "O grave, where is thy victory? O death, where is thy sting?"

If it were necessary tonight, I might speak to you concerning the resurrection, and I might tell you how much that takes away the sting of death, but I will confine myself to the simple fact, that the sting of death is sin, that the strength of sin is the law, and that Christ gives us the victory by taking the sting away, and removing the strength of sin by his perfect obedience.

And now, sirs, how many are there here who have any hope that for them Christ Jesus died? Am I coming too close home, when most solemnly I put the question to each one of you, as I stand in God's presence this night, to free my head of your blood; as I stand and appeal with all the earnestness this heart is capable of? Are you prepared to die? Is sin pardoned? Is the law satisfied? Can you view the flowing

"Of Christ's soul-redeeming blood,
With divine assurance knowing,
That he hath made your peace with God?"

O! can ye now put one hand upon your heart, and the other upon the Bible, and say, "God's word and I agree; the witness of the Spirit here and the witness there are one. I have renounced my sins, I have given up my evil practices; I have abhorred my own righteousness; I trust in naught but Jesus' doings; simply do I depend on him.

'Nothing in my hand I bring,
Simply to thy cross I cling.'"

If so, should you die where you are—sudden death were sudden glory.

But, my hearers, shall I be faithful with you? or shall I belie my soul? Which shall it be? Are there

is written, Death is swallowed up in victory.

55 O death, where is thy sting? O grave, where is thy victory?

56 The sting of death is sin; and the strength of sin is the law.

57 But thanks be to God, which giveth us the victory through our Lord Jesus Christ.

58 Therefore, my beloved brethren, be ye stedfast, unmoveable, always abounding in the work of the Lord, forasmuch as ye know that your labor is not in vain in the Lord.

are found in the Septuagint translation of Hosea xiii, 14; Isaiah xxv, 8.

56. The sting of death is sin – Without which it could have no power. But this sting none can resist by his own strength. And the strength of sin is the law – As is largely declared, Rom. vii, 7, &c.

57. But thanks be to God, who hath given us the victory – Over sin, death, and hades.

58. Be ye steadfast – In yourselves. Unmovable – By others; continually increasing in the work of faith and labor of love. Knowing your labor is not in vain in the Lord – Whatever ye do for his sake shall have its full reward in that day. Let us also endeavor, by cultivating holiness in all its branches, to maintain this hope in its full energy; longing for that glorious day, when, in the utmost extent of the expression, death shall be swallowed up for ever, and millions of voices, after the long silence of the grave, shall burst out at once into that triumphant song, O death, where is thy sting? O hades, where is thy victory?

1 CORINTHIANS 16

1 Now concerning the collection for the saints, as I have given order to the churches of Galatia, even so do ye.

2 Upon the first day of the week let every one of you lay by him in store, as God hath prospered him, that there be no gatherings when I come.

3 And when I come, whomsoever ye shall approve by your letters, them will I send to bring your liberality unto Jerusalem.

4 And if it be meet that I go also, they shall go with me.

5 Now I will come unto you, when I shall pass through Macedonia: for I do pass through Macedonia.

6 And it may be that I will abide, yea, and winter with you, that ye may bring me on my journey whithersoever I go.

7 For I will not see you now by the way; but I trust to tarry a while with you, if the Lord permit.

8 But I will tarry at Ephesus until Pentecost.

9 For a great door and effectual is opened unto me, and there are many adversaries.

10 Now if Timotheus come, see that he may be with you without fear: for he worketh the work of the Lord, as I also do.

11 Let no man therefore despise him: but conduct him forth in peace, that he may come unto me: for I look for him with the brethren.

12 As touching our brother Apollos, I greatly desired him to come unto you with the brethren: but his will was not at all to come at this time; but he

1 CORINTHIANS 16

1. The saints – A more solemn and a more affecting word, than if he had said, the poor.

2. Let every one – Not the rich only: let him also that hath little, gladly give of that little. According as he hath been prospered – Increasing his alms as God increases his substance. According to this lowest rule of Christian prudence, if a man when he has or gains one pound give a tenth to God, when he has or gains an hundred he will give the tenth of this also. And yet I show unto you a more excellent way. He that hath ears to hear, let him hear. Stint yourself to no proportion at all. But lend to God all you can.

4. They shall go with me – To remove any possible suspicion.

5. I pass through Macedonia – I purpose going that way.

7. I will not see you now – Not till I have been in Macedonia.

8. I will stay at Ephesus – Where he was at this time.

9. A great door – As to the number of hearers. And effectual – As to the effects wrought upon them. And there are many adversaries – As there must always be where Satan's kingdom shakes. This was another reason for his staying there.

10. Without fear – Of any one's despising him for his youth. For he worketh the work of the Lord – The true ground of reverence to pastors. Those who do so, none ought to despise.

11. I look for him with the brethren – That accompany him.

12. I besought him much – To come to you. With the brethren – Who were then going to Corinth. Yet he was by no means willing to come now – Perhaps lest his coming should increase the divisions among them.

13. To conclude. Watch ye – Against all your seen and unseen enemies. Stand fast in the faith – Seeing and trusting him that is invisible. Acquit yourselves like men – With courage and patience. Be strong – To do and suffer all his will.

15. The first fruits of Achaia – The first converts in that province.

16. That ye also – In your turn. Submit to such – So repaying their free service. And to every one that worketh with us and labored – That labors in the gospel either with or without a fellow-laborer.

17. I rejoice at the coming of Stephanas, and Fortunatus, and Achaicus – Who were now returned to Corinth but the joy which their arrival had occasioned remained still in his heart. They have supplied what was wanting on your part – They have performed the offices of love, which you could not, by reason of your absence.

18. For they have refreshed my spirit and yours – Inasmuch as you share in my comfort. Such therefore acknowledge – With suitable love and respect.

19. Aquila and Priscilla had formerly made some abode at Corinth, and there St. Paul's acquaintance with them began, Acts xviii, 1, 2.

MATTHEW HENRY CHARLES H. SPURGEON

10-12 Timothy came to do the work of the Lord. Therefore to vex his spirit, would be to grieve the Holy Spirit; to despise him, would be to despise him that sent him. Those who work the work of the Lord, should be treated with tenderness and respect. Faithful ministers will not be jealous of each other. It becomes the ministers of the gospel to show concern for each other's reputation and usefulness.

13-18 A Christian is always in danger, therefore should ever be on the watch. He should be fixed in the faith of the gospel, and never desert or give it up. By this faith alone he will be able to keep his ground in an hour of temptation. Christians should be careful that charity not only reigns in their hearts, but shines in their lives. There is a great difference between Christian firmness and fever-ish warmth and transport. The apostle gave par-ticular directions as to some who served the cause of Christ among them. Those who serve the saints, those who desire the honor of the church-es, and to remove reproaches from them, are to be thought much of, and loved. They should will-ingly acknowledge the worth of such, and all who labored with or helped the apostle.

19-24 Christianity by no means destroys civility. Religion should promote a courteous and oblig-ing temper towards all. Those give a false idea of religion, and reproach it, who would take encour-agement from it to be sour and morose. And Christian salutations are not mere empty compli-ments; but are real expressions of good will to others, and commend them to the Divine grace and blessing. Every Christian family should be as a Christian church. Wherever two or three are gathered together in the name of Christ, and he is among them, there is a church. Here is a solemn warning. Many who have Christ's name much in their mouths, have no true love to him in their hearts. None love him in truth, who do not love his laws, and keep his commandments. Many are Christians in name, who do not love Christ Jesus the Lord in sincerity. Such are separated from the people of God, and the favor of God. Those who love not the Lord Jesus Christ, must perish without remedy. Let us not rest in any religious profession where there is not the love of Christ, earnest desires for his salvation, gratitude for his mercies, and obedience to his commandments. The grace of our Lord Jesus Christ has in it all that is good, for time and for eternity. To wish that our friends may have this grace with them, is wishing them the utmost good. And this we should wish all our friends and brethren in Christ. We can wish them nothing greater, and we should wish them nothing less. True Christianity makes us wish those whom we love, the blessings of both worlds; this is meant

not many here who, each time the bell tolls the departure of a soul, might well ask the question, "Am I prepared?" and they must say, "No." I shall not turn prophet tonight; but were it right for me to say so, I fear not one-half of you are prepared to die. Is that true? Yea, let the speaker ask himself the question, "Am I prepared to meet my Maker face to face?" Oh, sit in your seat and catechize your souls with that solemn question. Let each one ask him-self, "Am I prepared, should I be called, to die?" Methinks I hear one say with confidence, "I know that my Redeemer liveth." "Let him that thinketh he standeth take heed lest he fall." I hear another say with trembling accents—

"Ah! guilty, weak, and helpless worm,
On Christ's kind arms I fall;
He is my strength and righteousness,
My Jesus and my all."

Yes, sweet words! I would rather have written that one verse than Milton's "Paradise Lost." It is such a matchless picture of the true condition of the believing soul. But I hear another say, "I shall not answer such a question as that. I am not going to be dull today. It may be gloomy weather outside today, but I do not want to be made melancholy." Young man, young man, go thy way. Let thine heart cheer thee in the days of thy youth; but for all this the Lord shall bring thee to judgment. What wilt thou do, careless spirit, when thy friends have forsaken thee, when thou art alone with God? Thou dost not like to be alone, young man, now, dost thou? A falling leaf will startle thee. To be alone an hour will bring on an insufferable feeling of melancholy. But thou wilt be alone—and a drea-ry alone it will be—with God an enemy! How wilt thou do in the swellings of Jordan? What wilt thou do when he taketh thee by the hand at eventide, and asketh thee for an account; when he says, "What didst thou do in the beginning of thy days? how didst thou spend thy life?" When he asks thee, "Where are the years of thy manhood?" When he questions thee about thy wasted Sabbaths, and inquires how thy latter years were spent, what wilt thou say then? Speechless, without an answer, thou wilt stand. Oh, I beseech you, as ye love yourselves, take care! Even now, begin to weigh the solemn matters of eternal life. Oh! say not, "Why so earnest? why in such haste?" Sirs, if I saw you lying in your bed, and your house was on fire, the fire might be at the bottom of the house, and you might slumber safely for the next five minutes; but with all my might I would pull you from your bed, or I would shout, "Awake! awake! the flame is under thee." So with some of you who are sleeping over hell's mouth, slumbering over the pit of perdi-tion, may I not awake you? may I not depart a little from clerical rules, and speak to you as one speaketh to his fellow whom he loves? Ah! if I loved you not, I need not be here. It is because I

will come when he shall have convenient time.

13 Watch ye, stand fast in the faith, quit you like men, be strong.

14 Let all your things be done with charity.

15 I beseech you, brethren, (ye know the house of Stephanas, that it is the firstfruits of Achaia, and that they have addicted themselves to the ministry of the saints,)

16 That ye submit yourselves unto such, and to every one that helpeth with us, and laboreth.

17 I am glad of the coming of Stephanas and Fortunatus and Achaicus: for that which was lacking on your part they have supplied.

18 For they have refreshed my spirit and yours: therefore acknowledge ye them that are such.

19 The churches of Asia salute you. Aquila and Priscilla salute you much in the Lord, with the church that is in their house.

20 All the brethren greet you. Greet ye one another with an holy kiss.

21 The salutation of me Paul with mine own hand.

22 If any man love not the Lord Jesus Christ, let him be Anathema Maranatha.

23 The grace of our Lord Jesus Christ be with you.

24 My love be with you all in Christ Jesus. Amen.

21. With my own hand – What precedes having been wrote by an amanuensis.

22. If any man love not the Lord Jesus Christ – If any be an enemy to his person, offices, doctrines, or commands. Let him be Anathema Maranatha–Anathema signifies a thing devoted to destruction. It seems to have been customary with the Jews of that age, when they had pronounced any man an Anathema, to add the Syriac expression, Maran-atha, that is, "The Lord cometh;" namely, to execute vengeance upon him. This weighty sentence the apostle chose to write with his own hand; and to insert it between his salutation and solemn benediction, that it might be the more attentively regarded.

in wishing the grace of Christ to be with them. The apostle had dealt plainly with the Corinthians, and told them of their faults with just severity; but he parts in love, and with a solemn profession of his love to them for Christ's sake. May our love be with all who are in Christ Jesus. Let us try whether all things appear worthless to us, when compared with Christ and his righteousness. Do we allow ourselves in any known sin, or in the neglect of any known duty? By such inquiries, faithfully made, we may judge of the state of our souls.

wish to win your souls, and, if it be possible, to win for my Master some honor, that I would thus pour out my heart before you. As the Lord liveth, sinner, thou standest on a single plank over the mouth of hell, and that plank is rotten. Thou hangest over the pit by a solitary rope, and the strands of that rope are breaking. Thou art like that man of old, whom Dionysius placed at the head of the table; before him was a dainty feast, but the man ate not, for directly over his head was a sword suspended by a hair. So art thou, sinner. Let thy cup be full, let thy pleasures be high, let thy soul be elevated, seest thou that sword? The next time thou sittest in the theater, look up and see that sword: when next in thy business thou scornest the rules of God's gospel, look at that sword. Though thou seest it not, it is there. Even now, ye may hear God saying to Gabriel, "Gabriel, that man is sitting in his seat in the hall; he is hearing, but is as though he heard not; unsheathe thy blade; let the glittering sword cut through that hair; let the weapon fall upon him and divide his soul and body." Stop, thou Gabriel, stop! Save the man a little while. Give him yet an hour, that he may repent. Oh, let him not die. True, he has been here these ten or dozen nights, and he has listened without a tear; but stop, and peradventure he may repent yet. Jesus backs up my entreaty, and he cries, "Spare him yet another year, till I dig about him and dung him, and though he now cumbers the ground, he may yet bring forth fruit, that he may not be hewn down and cast into the fire." I thank thee, O God; thou wilt not cut him down tonight; but tomorrow may be his last day. Ye may never see the sun rise, though you have seen it set. Take heed. Hear the word of God's gospel, and depart with God's blessing. "Whosoever believeth on the name of the Lord Jesus Christ shall be saved." "He that believeth and is baptized shall be saved." "He is able to save to the uttermost, all that come unto him." "Whosoever cometh unto him, he will in no wise cast out." Let every one that heareth say, "Come; whosoever is athirst, let him come and take of the water of life, freely."

2 Corinthians

2 CORINTHIANS 1

1 Paul, an apostle of Jesus Christ by the will of God, and Timothy our brother, unto the church of God which is at Corinth, with all the saints which are in all Achaia:

2 Grace be to you and peace from God our Father, and from the Lord Jesus Christ.

3 Blessed be God, even the Father of our Lord Jesus Christ, the Father of mercies, and the God of all comfort;

4 Who comforteth us in all our tribulation, that we may be able to comfort them which are in any trouble, by the comfort wherewith we ourselves are comforted of God.

5 For as the sufferings of Christ abound in us, so our consolation also aboundeth by Christ.

6 And whether we be afflicted, it is for your consolation and salvation, which is effectual in the enduring of the same sufferings which we also suffer: or whether we be comforted, it is for your consolation and salvation.

7 And our hope of you is stedfast, knowing, that as ye are partakers of the sufferings, so shall ye be also of the consolation.

8 For we would not, brethren, have you ignorant of our trouble which came to us in Asia, that we were pressed out of measure, above strength, insomuch that we despaired even of life:

9 But we had the sentence of death in ourselves, that we should not trust in ourselves, but in God which raiseth the dead:

10 Who delivered us from so great a death, and doth deliver: in whom we trust that he will yet deliver us;

11 Ye also helping together by prayer for us, that for the gift bestowed upon us by the means of many persons thanks may be given by many on our behalf.

12 For our rejoicing is this, the testimony of our conscience, that in simplicity and godly sincerity, not with fleshly wisdom, but by the grace of God, we have had our conversation in the world, and more abundantly to you-ward.

13 For we write none other things unto you, than what ye read or acknowledge; and I trust ye shall acknowledge even to the end;

14 As also ye have acknowledged us in part, that we are your rejoicing, even as ye also are ours in the day of

IN this epistle, written from Macedonia, within a year after the former, St. Paul beautifully displays his tender affection toward the Corinthians, who were greatly moved by the seasonable severity of the former, and repeats several of the admonitions he had there given them. In that he had written concerning the affairs of the Corinthians: in this he writes chiefly concerning his own; but in such a manner as to direct all he mentions of himself to their spiritual profit. The thread and connection of the whole epistle is historical: other things are interwoven only by way of digression.

2 CORINTHIANS 1

1. Timotheus our brother – St. Paul writing to Timotheus styled him his son; writing of him, his brother.

3. Blessed be the God and Father of our Lord Jesus Christ – A solemn and beautiful introduction, highly suitable to the apostolic spirit. The Father of mercies, and God of all comfort – Mercies are the fountain of comfort; comfort is the outward expression of mercy. God shows mercy in the affliction itself. He gives comfort both in and after the affliction. Therefore is he termed, the God of all comfort. Blessed be this God!

4. Who comforteth us in all our affliction, that we may be able to comfort them who are in any affliction – He that has experienced one kind of affliction is able to comfort others in that affliction. He that has experienced all kinds of affliction is able to comfort them in all.

5. For as the sufferings of Christ abound in us – The sufferings endured on his account. So our comfort also aboundeth through Christ – The sufferings were many, the comfort one; and yet not only equal to, but overbalancing, them all.

6. And whether we are afflicted, it is for your comfort and salvation – For your present comfort, your present and future salvation. Or whether we are comforted, it is for your comfort – That we may be the better able to comfort you. Which is effectual in the patient enduring the same sufferings which we also suffer – Through the efficacy of which you patiently endure the same kind of sufferings with us.

7. And our hope concerning you – Grounded on your patience in suffering for Christ's sake, is steadfast.

8. We would not have you ignorant, brethren, of the trouble which befell us in Asia – Probably the same which is described in the nineteenth chapter of the Acts. The Corinthians knew before that he had been in trouble: he now declares the greatness and the fruit of it. We were exceedingly pressed, above our strength – Above the ordinary strength even of an apostle.

9. Yea, we had the sentence of death in ourselves – We ourselves expected nothing but death.

10. We trust that he will still deliver – That we may at length be able to come to you.

11. You likewise – As well as other churches. Helping us by prayer, that for the gift – Namely, my deliverance. Bestowed upon us by means of many persons – Praying for it, thanks may be given by many.

12. For I am the more emboldened to look for this, because I am conscious of my integrity; seeing this is our rejoicing – Even in the deepest adversity. The testimony of our conscience – Whatever others think of us. That in simplicity – Having one end in view, aiming singly at the glory of God. And godly sincerity – Without any tincture of guile, dissimulation, or disguise. Not with carnal wisdom, but by the grace of God – Not by natural, but divine, wisdom. We have had our conversation in the world – In the whole world; in every circumstance.

MATTHEW HENRY

CHARLES H. SPURGEON

The second epistle to the Corinthians probably was written about a year after the first. Its contents are closely connected with those of the former epistle. The manner in which the letter St. Paul formerly wrote had been received, is particularly noticed; this was such as to fill his heart with gratitude to God, who enabled him fully to discharge his duty towards them. Many had shown marks of repentance, and amended their conduct, but others still followed their false teachers; and as the apostle delayed his visit, from his unwillingness to treat them with severity, they charged him with levity and change of conduct. Also, with pride, vainglory, and severity, and they spake of him with contempt. In this epistle we find the same ardent affection towards the disciples at Corinth, as in the former, the same zeal for the honor of the gospel, and the same boldness in giving Christian reproof. The first six chapters are chiefly practical: the rest have more reference to the state of the Corinthian church, but they contain many rules of general application.

2 CORINTHIANS 1

The apostle blesses God for comfort in, and deliverance out of troubles. (1-11)
He professes his own and his fellow-laborers' integrity. (12-14)
Gives reasons for his not coming to them. (15-24)

1-11 We are encouraged to come boldly to the throne of grace, that we may obtain mercy, and find grace to help in time of need. The Lord is able to give peace to the troubled conscience, and to calm the raging passions of the soul. These blessings are given by him, as the Father of his redeemed family. It is our Savior who says, Let not your heart be troubled. All comforts come from God, and our sweetest comforts are in him. He speaks peace to souls by granting the free remission of sins; and he comforts them by the enlivening influences of the Holy Spirit, and by the rich mercies of his grace. He is able to bind up the broken-hearted, to heal the most painful wounds, and also to give hope and joy under the heaviest sorrows. The favors God bestows on us, are not only to make us cheerful, but also that we may be useful to others. He sends comforts enough to support such as simply trust in and serve him. If we should be brought so low as to despair even of life, yet we may then trust God, who can bring back even from death. Their hope and trust were not in vain; nor shall any be ashamed who trust in the Lord. Past experiences encourage faith and hope, and lay us under obligation to trust in God for time to come. And it is our duty, not only to help one another with prayer, but in praise and thanksgiving, and thereby to make

CHRIST—OUR SUBSTITUTE
Sermon number 310 delivered on April 15th, 1860, at New Park Street, Southwark.

"For he hath made him to be sin for us, who knew no sin; that we might be made the righteousness of God in him."—2 Corinthians 5:21.

SOMETIME AGO an excellent lady sought an interview with me, with the object as she said, of enlisting my sympathy upon the question of "Anti-Capital Punishment." I heard the excellent reasons she urged against hanging men who had committed murder, and though they did not convince me, I did not seek to answer them. She proposed that when a man committed murder, he should be confined for life. My remark was, that a great many men who had been confined half their lives were not a bit the better for it, and as for her belief that they would necessarily be brought to repentance, I was afraid it was but a dream. "Ah," she said, good soul as she was, "that is because we have been all wrong about punishments. We punish people because we think they deserve to be punished. Now, we ought to show them," said she, "that we love them; that we only punish them to make them better." "Indeed, madam," I said, "I have heard that theory a great many times, and I have seen much fine writing upon the matter, but I am no believer in it. The design of punishment should be amendment, but the ground of punishment lies in the positive guilt of the offender. I believe that when a man does wrong, he ought to be punished for it, and that there is a guilt in sin which justly merits punishment." Oh no; she could not see that. Sin was a very wrong thing, but punishment was not a proper idea. She thought that people were treated too cruelly in prison, and that they ought to be taught that we love them. If they were treated kindly in prison, and tenderly dealt with, they would grow so much better, she was sure. With a view of interpreting her own theory, I said, "I suppose, then, you would give criminals all sorts of indulgences in prison. Some great vagabond who has committed burglary dozens of times—I suppose you would let him sit in an easy chair in the evening before a nice fire, and mix him a glass of spirits and water, and give him his pipe, and make him happy, to show him how much we love him." "Well, no, she would not give him the spirits, but, still, all the rest would do him good." I thought that was a delightful picture certainly. It seemed to me to be the most prolific method of cultivating rogues which ingenuity could invent. I imagine

the Lord Jesus.

15 And in this confidence I was minded to come unto you before, that ye might have a second benefit;

16 And to pass by you into Macedonia, and to come again out of Macedonia unto you, and of you to be brought on my way toward Judea.

17 When I therefore was thus minded, did I use lightness? or the things that I purpose, do I purpose according to the flesh, that with me there should be yea yea, and nay nay?

18 But as God is true, our word toward you was not yea and nay.

19 For the Son of God, Jesus Christ, who was preached among you by us, even by me and Silvanus and Timotheus, was not yea and nay, but in him was yea.

20 For all the promises of God in him are yea, and in him Amen, unto the glory of God by us.

21 Now he which stablisheth us with you in Christ, and hath anointed us, is God;

22 Who hath also sealed us, and given the earnest of the Spirit in our hearts.

23 Moreover I call God for a record upon my soul, that to spare you I came not as yet unto Corinth.

24 Not for that we have dominion over your faith, but are helpers of your joy: for by faith ye stand.

2 CORINTHIANS 2

1 But I determined this with myself, that I would not come again to you in heaviness.

2 For if I make you sorry, who is he then that maketh me glad, but the same which is made sorry by me?

3 And I wrote this same unto you, lest, when I came, I should have sorrow from them of whom I ought to rejoice; having confidence in you all, that my joy is the joy of you all.

4 For out of much affliction and anguish of heart I wrote unto you with many tears; not that ye should be grieved, but that ye might know the love which I have more abundantly unto you.

5 But if any have caused grief, he hath not grieved me, but in part: that I may not overcharge you all.

6 Sufficient to such a man is this punishment, which was inflicted of many.

7 So that contrariwise ye ought rather to forgive him, and comfort him, lest

14. Ye have acknowledged us in part – Though not so fully as ye will do. That ye are our rejoicing – That ye rejoice in having known us. As ye also are ours – As we also rejoice in the success of our labors among you; and we trust shall rejoice therein in the day of the Lord Jesus.

15. In this confidence – That is, being confident of this.

17. Did I use levity – Did I lightly change my purpose? Do I purpose according to the flesh – Are my purposes grounded on carnal or worldly considerations? So that there should be with me yea and nay – Sometimes one, sometimes the other; that is, variableness and inconstancy.

18. Our word to you – The whole tenor of our doctrine. Hath not been yea and nay – Wavering and uncertain.

19. For Jesus Christ, who was preached by us – That is, our preaching concerning him. Was not yea and nay – Was not variable and inconsistent with itself. But was yea in him – Always one and the same, centering in him.

20. For all the promises of God are yea and amen in him – Are surely established in and through him. They are yea with respect to God promising; amen, with respect to men believing; yea, with respect to the apostles; amen, with respect to their hearers.

21. I say, to the glory of God – For it is God alone that is able to fulfill these promises. That establisheth us – Apostles and teachers. With you – All true believers. In the faith of Christ; and hath anointed us – With the oil of gladness, with joy in the Holy Ghost, thereby giving us strength both to do and suffer his will.

22. Who also hath sealed us – Stamping his image on our hearts, thus marking and sealing us as his own property. And given us the earnest of his Spirit – There is a difference between an earnest and a pledge. A pledge is to be restored when the debt is paid; but an earnest is not taken away, but completed. Such an earnest is the Spirit. The first fruits of it we have Rom. viii, 23; and we wait for all the fullness.

23. I call God for a record upon my soul – Was not St. Paul now speaking by the Spirit? And can a more solemn oath be conceived? Who then can imagine that Christ ever designed to forbid all swearing? That to spare you I came not yet to Corinth – Lest I should be obliged to use severity. He says elegantly to Corinth, not to you, when he is intimating his power to punish.

24. Not that we have dominion over your faith – This is the prerogative of God alone. But are helpers of your joy – And faith from which it springs. For by faith ye have stood – To this day. We see the light in which ministers should always consider themselves, and in which they are to be considered by others. Not as having dominion over the faith of their people, and having a right to dictate by their own authority what they shall believe, or what they shall do; but as helpers of their joy, by helping them forward in faith and holiness. In this view, how amiable does their office appear! and how friendly to the happiness of mankind! How far, then, are they from true benevolence, who would expose it to ridicule and contempt!

2 CORINTHIANS 2

1. In grief – Either on account of the particular offender, or of the church in general.

2. For if I grieve you, who is he that cheereth me, but he that is grieved by me – That is, I cannot be comforted myself till his grief is removed.

3. And I wrote thus to you – I wrote to you before in this determination, not to come to you in grief.

4. From much anguish I wrote to you, not so much that ye might be grieved, as that ye might know by my faithful admonition my abundant

suitable returns for benefits received. Thus both trials and mercies will end in good to ourselves and others.

12-14 Though, as a sinner, the apostle could only rejoice and glory in Christ Jesus, yet, as a believer, he might rejoice and glory in being really what he professed. Conscience witnesses concerning the steady course and tenor of the life. Thereby we may judge ourselves, and not by this or by that single act. Our conversation will be well ordered, when we live and act under such a gracious principle in the heart. Having this, we may leave our characters in the Lord's hands, but using proper means to clear them, when the credit of the gospel, or our usefulness, calls for it.

15-24 The apostle clears himself from the charge of levity and inconstancy, in not coming to Corinth. Good men should be careful to keep the reputation of sincerity and constancy; they should not resolve, but on careful thought; and they will not change unless for weighty reasons. Nothing can render God's promises more certain: his giving them through Christ, assures us they are his promises; as the wonders God wrought in the life, resurrection, and ascension of his Son, confirm faith. The Holy Spirit makes Christians firm in the faith of the gospel: the quickening of the Spirit is an earnest of everlasting life; and the comforts of the Spirit are an earnest of everlasting joy. The apostle desired to spare the blame he feared would be unavoidable, if he had gone to Corinth before he learned what effect his former letter produced. Our strength and ability are owing to faith; and our comfort and joy must flow from faith. The holy tempers and gracious fruits which attend faith, secure from delusion in so important a matter.

2 CORINTHIANS 2

Reasons for the apostle not coming to Corinth. (1-4)
Directions about restoring the repentant offender. (5-11)
An account of his labors and success in spreading the gospel of Christ. (12-17)

1-4 The apostle desired to have a cheerful meeting with them; and he had written in confidence of their doing what was to their benefit and his comfort; and that therefore they would be glad to remove every cause of disquiet from him. We should always give pain unwillingly, even when duty requires that it must be given.

5-11 The apostle desires them to receive the person who had done wrong, again into their communion; for he was aware of his fault, and much afflicted under his punishment. Even sorrow for sin should not unfit for other duties, and drive to despair. Not only was there

that you could grow any number of thieves in that way; for it would be a special means of propagating all manner of roguery and wickedness. These very delightful theories to such a simple mind as mine, were the source of much amusement, the idea of fondling villains, and treating their crimes as if they were the tumbles and falls of children, made me laugh heartily. I fancied I saw the government resigning its functions to these excellent persons, and the grand results of their marvelously kind experiments. The sword of the magistrate transformed into a gruel-spoon, and the jail become a sweet retreat for injured reputations.

Little however, did I think I should live to see this kind of stuff taught in pulpits; I had no idea that there would come out a divinity, which would bring down God's moral government from the solemn aspect in which Scripture reveals it, to a namby-pamby sentimentalism, which adores a Deity destitute of every masculine virtue. But we never know today what may occur tomorrow. We have lived to see a certain sort of men—thank God they are not Baptists—though I am sorry to say there are a great many Baptists who are beginning to follow in their trail—who seek to teach now-a-days, that God is a universal Father, and that our ideas of his dealing with the impenitent as a Judge, and not as a Father, are remnants of antiquated error. Sin, according to these men, is a disorder rather than an offense, an error rather than a crime. Love is the only attribute they can discern, and the full-orbed Deity they have not known. Some of these men push their way very far into the bogs and mire of falsehood, until they inform us that eternal punishment is ridiculed as a dream. In fact, books now appear, which teach us that there is no such thing as the Vicarious Sacrifice of our Lord Jesus Christ. They use the word Atonement it is true, but in regard to its meaning, they have removed the ancient landmark. They acknowledge that the Father has shown his great love to poor sinful man by sending his Son, but not that God was inflexibly just in the exhibition of his mercy, not that he punished Christ on the behalf of his people, nor that indeed God ever will punish anybody in his wrath, or that there is such a thing as justice apart from discipline. Even sin and hell are but old words employed henceforth in a new and altered sense. Those are old-fashioned notions, and we poor souls who go on talking about election and imputed righteousness, are behind our time. Ay, and the gentlemen who bring out books on this subject, applaud Mr. Maurice, and Professor Scott, and the like, but are too cow-

perhaps such a one should be swallowed up with overmuch sorrow.

8 Wherefore I beseech you that ye would confirm your love toward him.

9 For to this end also did I write, that I might know the proof of you, whether ye be obedient in all things.

10 To whom ye forgive any thing, I forgive also: for if I forgave any thing, to whom I forgave it, for your sakes forgave I it in the person of Christ;

11 Lest Satan should get an advantage of us: for we are not ignorant of his devices.

12 Furthermore, when I came to Troas to preach Christ's gospel, and a door was opened unto me of the Lord,

13 I had no rest in my spirit, because I found not Titus my brother: but taking my leave of them, I went from thence into Macedonia.

14 Now thanks be unto God, which always causeth us to triumph in Christ, and maketh manifest the savor of his knowledge by us in every place.

15 For we are unto God a sweet savor of Christ, in them that are saved, and in them that perish:

16 To the one we are the savor of death unto death; and to the other the savor of life unto life. And who is sufficient for these things?

17 For we are not as many, which corrupt the word of God: but as of sincerity, but as of God, in the sight of God speak we in Christ.

2 CORINTHIANS 3

1 Do we begin again to commend ourselves? or need we, as some others, epistles of commendation to you, or letters of commendation from you?

2 Ye are our epistle written in our hearts, known and read of all men:

3 Forasmuch as ye are manifestly declared to be the epistle of Christ ministered by us, written not with ink, but with the Spirit of the living God; not in tables of stone, but in fleshy tables of the heart.

4 And such trust have we through Christ to God-ward:

5 Not that we are sufficient of ourselves to think any thing as of ourselves; but our sufficiency is of God;

6 Who also hath made us able ministers of the new testament; not of the letter, but of the spirit: for the letter killeth, but the spirit giveth life.

7 But if the ministration of death, written and engraven in stones, was

love toward you.

5. He hath grieved me but in part – Who still rejoice over the greater part of you. Otherwise I might burden you all.

6. Sufficient for such an one – With what a remarkable tenderness does St. Paul treat this offender! He never once mentions his name. Nor does he here so much as mention his crime. By many – Not only by the rulers of the church: the whole congregation acquiesced in the sentence.

10. To whom ye forgive – He makes no question of their complying with his direction. Anything – So mildly does he speak even of that heinous sin, after it was repented of. In the person of Christ – By the authority wherewith he has invested me.

11. Lest Satan – To whom he had been delivered, and who sought to destroy not only his flesh, but his soul also. Get an advantage over us – For the loss of one soul is a common loss.

12. Now when I came to Troas – It seems, in that passage from Asia to Macedonia, of which a short account is given, Acts xx, 1, 2. Even though a door was opened to me – That is, there was free liberty to speak, and many were willing to hear: yet,

13. I had no rest in my spirit – From an earnest desire to know how my letter had been received. Because I did not find Titus – In his return from you. So I went forth into Macedonia – Where being much nearer, I might more easily be informed concerning you. The apostle resumes the thread of his discourse, chap. vii, 2, interposing an admirable digression concerning what he had done and suffered elsewhere, the profit of which he by this means derives to the Corinthians also; and as a prelude to his apology against the false apostles.

14. To triumph, implies not only victory, but an open manifestation of it. And as in triumphal processions, especially in the east, incense and perfumes were burned near the conqueror, the apostle beautifully alludes to this circumstance in the following verse: as likewise to the different effects which strong perfumes have upon different persons; some of whom they revive, while they throw others into the most violent disorders.

15. For we – The preachers of the gospel. Are to God a sweet odor of Christ – God is well-pleased with this perfume diffused by us, both in them that believe and are saved, treated of, chap. iii, 1; chap. iv, 2; and in them that obstinately disbelieve and, consequently, perish, treated of, chap. iv, 3-6.

16. And who is sufficient for these things – No man living, but by the power of God's Spirit.

17. For we are not as many, who adulterate the word of God – Like those vintners (so the Greek word implies) who mix their wines with baser liquors. But as of sincerity – Without any mixture. But as from God – This rises higher still; transmitting his pure word, not our own. In the sight of God – Whom we regard as always present, and noting every word of our tongue. Speak we – The tongue is ours, but the power is God's. In Christ – Words which he gives, approves, and blesses.

2 CORINTHIANS 3

1. Do we begin again to recommend ourselves – Is it needful? Have I nothing but my own word to recommend me? St. Paul chiefly here intends himself; though not excluding Timotheus, Titus, and Silvanus. Unless we need – As if he had said, Do I indeed want such recommendation?

2. Ye are our recommendatory letter – More convincing than bare words could be. Written on our hearts – Deeply engraved there, and plainly legible to all around us.

3. Manifestly declared to be the letter of Christ – Which he has formed and

danger last Satan should get advantage, by tempting the penitent to hard thoughts of God and religion, and so drive him to despair; but against the churches and the ministers of Christ, by bringing an evil report upon Christians as unforgiving; thus making divisions, and hindering the success of the ministry. In this, as in other things, wisdom is to be used, that the ministry may not be blamed for indulging sin on the one hand, or for too great severity towards sinners on the other hand. Satan has many plans to deceive, and knows how to make a bad use of our mistakes.

12-17 A believer's triumphs are all in Christ. To him be the praise and glory of all, while the success of the gospel is a good reason for a Christian's joy and rejoicing. In ancient triumphs, abundance of perfumes and sweet odors were used; so the name and salvation of Jesus, as ointment poured out, was a sweet savor diffused in every place. Unto some, the gospel is a savor of death unto death. They reject it to their ruin. Unto others, the gospel is a savor of life unto life: as it quickened them at first when they were dead in trespasses and sins, so it makes them more lively, and will end in eternal life. Observe the awful impressions this matter made upon the apostle, and should also make upon us. The work is great, and of ourselves we have no strength at all; all our sufficiency is of God. But what we do in religion, unless it is done in sincerity, as in the sight of God, is not of God, does not come from him, and will not reach to him. May we carefully watch ourselves in this matter; and seek the testimony of our consciences, under the teaching of the Holy Spirit, that as of sincerity, so speak we in Christ and of Christ.

2 CORINTHIANS 3

The preference of the gospel to the law given by Moses. (1-11)

The preaching of the apostle was suitable to the excellency and evidence of the gospel, through the power of the Holy Ghost. (12-18)

1-11 Even the appearance of self-praise and courting human applause, is painful to the humble and spiritual mind. Nothing is more delightful to faithful ministers, or more to their praise, than the success of their ministry, as shown in the spirits and lives of those among whom they labor. The law of Christ was written in their hearts, and the love of Christ shed abroad there. Nor was it written in tables of stone, as the law of God given to Moses, but on the fleshy (not fleshly, as fleshliness denotes sensuality) tables of the heart, Eze 36:26. Their hearts were humbled and softened to receive this impression, by the new-creating power of the Holy Spirit. He ascribes all the glory to God.

ardly to follow them, and boldly propound these sentiments. These are the new men whom God has sent down from heaven, to tell us that the apostle Paul was all wrong, that our faith is vain, that we have been quite mistaken, that there was no need for propitiating blood to wash away our sins; that the fact was, our sins needed discipline, but penal vengeance and righteous wrath are quite out of the question. When I thus speak, I am free to confess that such ideas are not boldly taught by a certain individual whose volume excites these remarks, but as he puffs the books of gross perverters of the truth, I am compelled to believe that he endorses such theology.

Well, brethren, I am happy to say that sort of stuff has not gained entrance into this pulpit. I dare say the worms will eat the wood before there will be anything of that sort sounded in this place; and may these bones be picked by vultures, and this flesh be rent in sunder by lions, and may every nerve in this body suffer pangs and tortures, ere these lips shall give utterance to any such doctrines or sentiments. We are content to remain among the vulgar souls who believe the old doctrines of grace. We are willing still to be behind in the great march of intellect, and stand by that unmoving cross, which, like the pole star, never advances, because it never stirs, but always abides in its place, the guide of the soul to heaven, the one foundation other than which no man can lay, and without building upon which, no man shall ever see the face of God and live.

Thus much have I said upon a matter which just now is exciting controversy. It has been my high privilege to be associated with six of our ablest brethren in the ministry, in a letter of protest against the countenance which a certain newspaper seemed willing to lend to this modern heresy. We trust it may be the means, in the hands of God, of helping to check that downward march—that wandering from truth which seems by some singular infatuation, to have unsettled the minds of some brethren in our denomination. Now I come to address you upon the topic which is most continually assailed by those who preach another gospel "which is not another—but there be some that trouble you, and would pervert the gospel of Christ," namely, the doctrine of the substitution of Christ on our behalf, his actual atonement for our sins, and our positive and actual justification through his sufferings and righteousness. It seems to me that until language can mean the very reverse of what it says, until by some strange logic, God's Word can be contradicted

glorious, so that the children of Israel could not stedfastly behold the face of Moses for the glory of his countenance; which glory was to be done away:

8 How shall not the ministration of the spirit be rather glorious?

9 For if the ministration of condemnation be glory, much more doth the ministration of righteousness exceed in glory.

10 For even that which was made glorious had no glory in this respect, by reason of the glory that excelleth.

11 For if that which is done away was glorious, much more that which remaineth is glorious.

12 Seeing then that we have such hope, we use great plainness of speech:

13 And not as Moses, which put a veil over his face, that the children of Israel could not stedfastly look to the end of that which is abolished:

14 But their minds were blinded: for until this day remaineth the same veil untaken away in the reading of the old testament; which veil is done away in Christ.

15 But even unto this day, when Moses is read, the veil is upon their heart.

16 Nevertheless when it shall turn to the Lord, the veil shall be taken away.

17 Now the Lord is that Spirit: and where the Spirit of the Lord is, there is liberty.

18 But we all, with open face beholding as in a glass the glory of the Lord, are changed into the same image from glory to glory, even as by the Spirit of the Lord.

2 CORINTHIANS 4

1 Therefore seeing we have this ministry, as we have received mercy, we faint not;

2 But have renounced the hidden things of dishonesty, not walking in craftiness, nor handling the word of God deceitfully; but by manifestation of the truth commending ourselves to every man's conscience in the sight of God.

3 But if our gospel be hid, it is hid to them that are lost:

4 In whom the god of this world hath blinded the minds of them which believe not, lest the light of the glorious gospel of Christ, who is the image of God, should shine unto them.

published to the world. Ministered by us – Whom he has used herein as his instruments, therefore ye are our letter also. Written not in tables of stone – Like the ten commandments. But in the tender, living tables of their hearts – God having taken away the hearts of stone and given them hearts of flesh.

4. Such trust have we in God – That is, we trust in God that this is so.

5. Not that we are sufficient of ourselves – So much as to think one good thought; much less, to convert sinners.

6. Who also hath made us able ministers of the new covenant – Of the new, evangelical dispensation. Not of the law, fitly called the letter, from God's literally writing it on the two tables. But of the Spirit – Of the gospel dispensation, which is written on the tables of our hearts by the Spirit. For the letter – The law, the Mosaic dispensation. Killeth – Seals in death those who still cleave to it. But the Spirit – The gospel, conveying the Spirit to those who receive it. Giveth life – Both spiritual and eternal: yea, if we adhere to the literal sense even of the moral law, if we regard only the precept and the sanction as they stand in themselves, not as they lead us to Christ, they are doubtless a killing ordinance, and bind us down under the sentence of death.

7. And if the ministration of death – That is, the Mosaic dispensation, which proves such to those who prefer it to the gospel, the most considerable part of which was engraved on those two stones, was attended with so great glory.

8. The ministration of the Spirit – That is, the Christian dispensation.

9. The ministration of condemnation – Such the Mosaic dispensation proved to all the Jews who rejected the gospel whereas through the gospel (hence called the ministration of righteousness) God both imputed and imparted righteousness to all believers. But how can the moral law (which alone was engraved on stone) be the ministration of condemnation, if it requires no more than a sincere obedience, such as is proportioned to our infirm state? If this is sufficient to justify us, then the law ceases to be a ministration of condemnation. It becomes (flatly contrary to the apostle's doctrine) the ministration of righteousness.

10. It hath no glory in this respect, because of the glory that excelleth – That is, none in comparison of this more excellent glory. The greater light swallows up the less.

11. That which remaineth – That dispensation which remains to the end of the world; that spirit and life which remain for ever.

12. Having therefore this hope – Being fully persuaded of this.

13. And we do not act as Moses did, who put a veil over his face – Which is to be understood with regard to his writings also. So that the children of Israel could not look steadfastly to the end of that dispensation which is now abolished – The end of this was Christ. The whole Mosaic dispensation tended to, and terminated in, him; but the Israelites had only a dim, wavering sight of him, of whom Moses spake in an obscure, covert manner.

14. The same veil remaineth on their understanding unremoved – Not so much as folded back, (so the word implies,) so as to admit a little, glimmering light. On the public reading of the Old Testament – The veil is not now on the face of Moses or of his writings, but on the reading of them, and on the heart of them that believe not. Which is taken away in Christ – That is, from the heart of them that truly believe on him.

16. When it – Their heart. Shall turn to the Lord – To Christ, by living faith. The veil is taken away – That very moment; and they see, with the utmost clearness, how all the types and prophecies of the law are fully accomplished in him.

And remember, as our whole dependence is upon the Lord, so the whole glory belongs to him alone. The letter killeth: the letter of the law is the ministration of death; and if we rest only in the letter of the gospel, we shall not be the better for so doing: but the Holy Spirit gives life spiritual, and life eternal. The Old Testament dispensation was the ministration of death, but the New Testament of life. The law made known sin, and the wrath and curse of God; it showed us a God above us, and a God against us; but the gospel makes known grace, and Emmanuel, God with us. Therein the righteousness of God by faith is revealed; and this shows us that the just shall live by his faith; this makes known the grace and mercy of God through Jesus Christ, for obtaining the forgiveness of sins and eternal life. The gospel so much exceeds the law in glory, that it eclipses the glory of the legal dispensation. But even the New Testament will be a killing letter, if shown as a mere system or form, and without dependence on God the Holy Spirit, to give it a quickening power.

12-18 It is the duty of the ministers of the gospel to use great plainness, or clearness, of speech. The Old Testament believers had only cloudy and passing glimpses of that glorious Savior, and unbelievers looked no further than to the outward institution. But the great precepts of the gospel, believe, love, obey, are truths stated as clearly as possible. And the whole doctrine of Christ crucified, is made as plain as human language can make it. Those who lived under the law, had a veil upon their hearts. This veil is taken away by the doctrines of the Bible about Christ. When any person is converted to God, then the veil of ignorance is taken away. The condition of those who enjoy and believe the gospel is happy, for the heart is set at liberty to run the ways of God's commandments. They have light, and with open face they behold the glory of the Lord. Christians should prize and improve these privileges. We should not rest contented without knowing the transforming power of the gospel, by the working of the Spirit, bringing us to seek to be like the temper and tendency of the glorious gospel of our Lord and Savior Jesus Christ, and into union with him. We behold Christ, as in the glass of his word; and as the reflection from a mirror causes the face to shine, the faces of Christians shine also.

2 CORINTHIANS 4

The apostles labored with much diligence, sincerity, and faithfulness. (1-7)

Their sufferings for the gospel were great, yet with rich supports. (8-12)

Prospects of eternal glory keep believers from fainting under troubles. (13-18)

and can be made to belief itself, the doctrine of substitution can never be rooted out of the words which I have selected for my text "He hath made him to be sin for us, who knew no sin, that we might be made the righteousness of God in him."

First, then, the sinlessness of the substitute; secondly, the reality of the imputation of sin to him; and thirdly, the glorious reality of the imputation of righteousness to us.

I. First, THE SINLESSNESS OF THE SUBSTITUTE.

The doctrine of Holy Scripture is this, that inasmuch as man could not keep God's law, having fallen in Adam, Christ came and fulfilled the law on the behalf of his people; and that inasmuch as man had already broken the divine law and incurred the penalty of the wrath of God, Christ came and suffered in the room, place, and stead of his elect ones, that so by his enduring the full vials of wrath, they might be emptied out and not a drop might ever fall upon the heads of his blood-bought people. Now, you will readily perceive that if one is to be a substitute for another before God, either to work out a righteousness or to suffer a penalty, that substitute must himself be free from sin. If he hath sin of his own, all that he can suffer will but be the due reward of his own iniquity. If he hath himself transgressed, he cannot suffer for another, because all his sufferings are already due on his own personal account. On the other hand, it is quite clear that none but a perfect man could ever work out a spotless righteousness for us, and keep the law in our stead, for if he hath dishonored the commandment in his thought, there must be a corresponding flaw in his service. If the warp and woof be speckled, how shall he bring forth the robe of milk-white purity, and wrap it about our loins? He must be a spotless one who shall become the representative of his people, either to give them a passive or active righteousness, either to offer a satisfaction as the penalty of their sins, or a righteousness as the fulfillment of God's demand.

It is satisfactory for us to know, and to believe beyond a doubt, that our Lord Jesus was without sin. Of course, in his divine nature he could not know iniquity; and as for his human nature, it never knew the original taint of depravity. He was of the seed of the woman, but not of the tainted and infected seed of Adam. Overshadowed as was the virgin by the Holy Ghost, no corruption entered into his nativity. That holy thing which was born of her was neither conceived in sin nor shapen in iniq-

5 For we preach not ourselves, but Christ Jesus the Lord; and ourselves your servants for Jesus' sake.

6 For God, who commanded the light to shine out of darkness, hath shined in our hearts, to give the light of the knowledge of the glory of God in the face of Jesus Christ.

7 But we have this treasure in earthen vessels, that the excellency of the power may be of God, and not of us.

8 We are troubled on every side, yet not distressed; we are perplexed, but not in despair;

9 Persecuted, but not forsaken; cast down, but not destroyed;

10 Always bearing about in the body the dying of the Lord Jesus, that the life also of Jesus might be made manifest in our body.

11 For we which live are alway delivered unto death for Jesus' sake, that the life also of Jesus might be made manifest in our mortal flesh.

12 So then death worketh in us, but life in you.

13 We having the same spirit of faith, according as it is written, I believed, and therefore have I spoken; we also believe, and therefore speak;

14 Knowing that he which raised up the Lord Jesus shall raise up us also by Jesus, and shall present us with you.

15 For all things are for your sakes, that the abundant grace might through the thanksgiving of many redound to the glory of God.

16 For which cause we faint not; but though our outward man perish, yet the inward man is renewed day by day.

17 For our light affliction, which is but for a moment, worketh for us a far more exceeding and eternal weight of glory;

18 While we look not at the things which are seen, but at the things which are not seen: for the things which are seen are temporal; but the things which are not seen are eternal.

2 CORINTHIANS 5

1 For we know that if our earthly house of this tabernacle were dissolved, we have a building of God, an house not made with hands, eternal in the heavens.

2 For in this we groan, earnestly desiring to be clothed upon with our house which is from heaven:

17. Now the Lord – Christ is that Spirit of the law whereof I speak, to which the letter was intended to lead. And where the Spirit of the Lord, Christ, is, there is liberty – Not the veil, the emblem of slavery. There is liberty from servile fear, liberty from the guilt and from the power of sin, liberty to behold with open face the glory of the Lord.

18. And, accordingly, all we that believe in him, beholding as in a glass – In the mirror of the gospel. The glory of the Lord – His glorious love. Are transformed into the same image – Into the same love. From one degree of this glory to another, in a manner worthy of his almighty Spirit. What a beautiful contrast is here! Moses saw the glory of the Lord, and it rendered his face so bright, that he covered it with a veil; Israel not being able to bear the reflected light. We behold his glory in the glass of his word, and our faces shine too; yet we veil them not, but diffuse the luster which is continually increasing, as we fix the eye of our mind more and more steadfastly on his glory displayed in the gospel.

2 CORINTHIANS 4

1. Therefore having this ministry – Spoken of, chap. iii, 6. As we have received mercy – Have been mercifully supported in all our trials. We faint not – We desist not in any degree from our glorious enterprise.

2. But have renounced – Set at open defiance. The hidden things of shame – All things which men need to hide, or to be ashamed of. Not walking in craftiness – Using no disguise, subtlety, guile. Nor privily corrupting the pure word of God – By any additions or alterations, or by attempting to accommodate it to the taste of the hearers.

3. But if our gospel also – As well as the law of Moses.

4. The God of this world – What a sublime and horrible description of Satan! He is indeed the God of all that believe not, and works in them with inconceivable energy. Hath blinded – Not only veiled, the eye of their understanding. Illumination – Is properly the reflection or propagation of light, from those who are already enlightened, to others. Who is the image of God – Hence also we may understand how great is the glory of Christ. He that sees the Son, sees the Father in the face of Christ. The Son exactly exhibits the Father to us.

5. For – The fault is not in us, neither in the doctrine they hear from us. We preach not ourselves – As able either to enlighten, or pardon, or sanctify you. But Jesus Christ – As your only wisdom, righteousness, sanctification. And ourselves your servants – Ready to do the meanest offices. For Jesus' sake – Not for honor, interest, or pleasure.

6. For God hath shined in our hearts – The hearts of all those whom the God of this world no longer blinds. God who is himself our light; not only the author of light, but also the fountain of it. To enlighten us with the knowledge of the glory of God – Of his glorious love, and of his glorious image. In the face of Jesus Christ – Which reflects his glory in another manner than the face of Moses did.

7. But we – Not only the apostles, but all true believers. Have this treasure – Of divine light, love, glory. In earthen vessels – In frail, feeble, perishing bodies. He proceeds to show, that afflictions, yea, death itself, are so far from hindering the ministration of the Spirit, that they even further it, sharpen the ministers, and increase the fruit. That the excellence of the power, which works these in us, may undeniably appear to be of God.

8. We are troubled, &c. – The four articles in this verse respect inward, the four in the next outward, afflictions. In each clause the former part shows the "earthen vessels;" the latter, "the excellence of the power." Not crushed – Not swallowed up in care and anxiety. Perplexed – What course to take,

MATTHEW HENRY   CHARLES H. SPURGEON

1-7 The best of men would faint, if they did not receive mercy from God. And that mercy which has helped us out, and helped us on, hitherto, we may rely upon to help us even to the end. The apostles had no base and wicked designs, covered with fair and specious pretenses. They did not try to make their ministry serve a turn. Sincerity or uprightness will keep the favorable opinion of wise and good men. Christ by his gospel makes a glorious discovery to the minds of men. But the design of the devil is, to keep men in ignorance; and when he cannot keep the light of the gospel of Christ out of the world, he spares no pains to keep men from the gospel, or to set them against it. The rejection of the gospel is here traced to the willfull blindness and wickedness of the human heart. Self was not the matter or the end of the apostles' preaching; they preached Christ as Jesus, the Savior and Deliverer, who saves to the uttermost all that come to God through him. Ministers are servants to the souls of men; they must avoid becoming servants to the humors or the lusts of men. It is pleasant to behold the sun in the firmament; but it is more pleasant and profitable for the gospel to shine in the heart. As light was the beginning of the first creation; so, in the new creation, the light of the Spirit is his first work upon the soul. The treasure of gospel light and grace is put into earthen vessels. The ministers of the gospel are subject to the same passions and weaknesses as other men. God could have sent angels to make known the glorious doctrine of the gospel, or could have sent the most admired sons of men to teach the nations, but he chose humbler, weaker vessels, that his power might be more glorified in upholding them, and in the blessed change wrought by their ministry.

8-12 The apostles were great sufferers, yet they met with wonderful support. Believers may be forsaken of their friends, as well as persecuted by enemies; but their God will never leave them nor forsake them. There may be fears within, as well as fighting without; yet we are not destroyed. The apostle speaks of their sufferings as a counterpart of the sufferings of Christ, that people might see the power of Christ's resurrection, and of grace in and from the living Jesus. In comparison with them, other Christians were, even at that time, in prosperous circumstances.

13-18 The grace of faith is an effectual remedy against fainting in times of trouble. They knew that Christ was raised, and that his resurrection was an earnest and assurance of theirs. The hope of this resurrection will encourage in a suffering day, and set us above the fear of death. Also, their sufferings were for the advantage of the church, and to God's glory. The sufferings of Christ's ministers, as well as their preaching and conversation, are for the good of the

uity. He was brought into this world immaculate. He was immaculately conceived and immaculately born. In him that natural black blood which we have inherited from Adam never dwelt. His heart was upright within him; his soul was without any bias to evil; his imagination had never been darkened. He had no infatuated mind. There was no tendency whatever in him than to do that which was good, holy, and honorable. And as he did not share in the original depravity, so he did not share in the imputed sin of Adam which we have inherited—not, I mean, in himself personally, though he took the consequences of that, as he stood as our representative. The sin of Adam had never passed over the head of the second Adam. All that were in the loins of Adam sinned in him when he touched the fruit; but Jesus was not in the loins of Adam. Though he might be conceived of as being in the womb of the woman—"a new thing which the Lord created in the earth,"—he lay not in Adam when he sinned, and consequently no guilt from Adam, either of depravity of nature, or of distance from God, ever fell upon Jesus as the result of anything that Adam did. I mean upon Jesus as considered in himself though he certainly took the sin of Adam as he was the representative of his people.

Again, as in his nature he was free from the corruption and condemnation of the sin of Adam, so also in his life, no sin ever corrupted his way. His eye never flashed with unhallowed anger; his lip never uttered a treacherous or deceitful word; his heart never harbored an evil imagination. Never did he wander after lust; no covetousness ever so much as glanced into his soul. He was "holy, harmless, undefiled, separate from sinners." From the beginning of his life to the end, you cannot put your finger even upon a mistake, much less upon a willfull error. So perfect was he, that no virtue seems to preponderate, or by an opposing quality give a bias to the scale of absolute rectitude. John is distinguished for his love, Peter for his courage; but Jesus Christ is distinguished for neither one above the another, because he possesses all in such sublime unison, such heavenly harmony, that no one virtue stands out above the rest. He is meek, but he is courageous. He is loving, but he is decided; he is bold as a lion, yet he is quiet and peaceful as a lamb. He was like that fine flour which was offered before God in the burnt offering; a flour without grit, so smooth, that when you rubbed it, it was soft and pure, no particles could be discerned: so was his character fully ground, fully compounded. There was

3 If so be that being clothed we shall not be found naked.

4 For we that are in this tabernacle do groan, being burdened: not for that we would be unclothed, but clothed upon, that mortality might be swallowed up of life.

5 Now he that hath wrought us for the selfsame thing is God, who also hath given unto us the earnest of the Spirit.

6 Therefore we are always confident, knowing that, whilst we are at home in the body, we are absent from the Lord:

7 (For we walk by faith, not by sight:)

8 We are confident, I say, and willing rather to be absent from the body, and to be present with the Lord.

9 Wherefore we labor, that, whether present or absent, we may be accepted of him.

10 For we must all appear before the judgment seat of Christ; that every one may receive the things done in his body, according to that he hath done, whether it be good or bad.

11 Knowing therefore the terror of the Lord, we persuade men; but we are made manifest unto God; and I trust also are made manifest in your consciences.

12 For we commend not ourselves again unto you, but give you occasion to glory on our behalf, that ye may have somewhat to answer them which glory in appearance, and not in heart.

13 For whether we be beside ourselves, it is to God: or whether we be sober, it is for your cause.

14 For the love of Christ constraineth us; because we thus judge, that if one died for all, then were all dead:

15 And that he died for all, that they which live should not henceforth live unto themselves, but unto him which died for them, and rose again.

16 Wherefore henceforth know we no man after the flesh: yea, though we have known Christ after the flesh, yet now henceforth know we him no more.

17 Therefore if any man be in Christ, he is a new creature: old things are passed away; behold, all things are become new.

18 And all things are of God, who hath reconciled us to himself by Jesus Christ, and hath given to us the ministry of reconciliation;

19 To wit, that God was in Christ, reconciling the world unto himself, not

but never despairing of his power and love to carry us through.

10. Always – Wherever we go. Bearing about in the body the dying of the Lord Jesus – Continually expecting to lay down our lives like him. That the life also of Jesus might be manifested in our body – That we may also rise and be glorified like him.

11. For we who yet live – Who are not yet killed for the testimony of Jesus. Are always delivered unto death – Are perpetually in the very jaws of destruction; which we willingly submit to, that we may "obtain a better resurrection."

12. So then death worketh in us, but life in you – You live in peace; we die daily. Yet – Living or dying, so long as we believe, we cannot but speak.

13. Having the same spirit of faith – Which animated the saints of old; David, in particular, when he said, I believed, and therefore have I spoken – That is, I trusted in God, and therefore he hath put this song of praise in my mouth. We also speak – We preach the gospel, even in the midst of affliction and death, because we believe that God will raise us up from the dead, and will present us, ministers, with you, all his members, "faultless before his presence with exceeding joy." Psalm cxvi, 10.

15. For all things – Whether adverse or prosperous. Are for your sakes – For the profit of all that believe, as well as all that preach. That the overflowing grace – Which continues you alive both in soul and body. Might abound yet more through the thanksgiving of many – For thanksgiving invites more: abundant grace.

16. Therefore – Because of this grace, we faint not. The outward man – The body. The inward man – The soul.

17. Our light affliction – The beauty and sublimity of St. Paul's expressions here, as descriptive of heavenly glory, opposed to temporal afflictions, surpass all imagination, and cannot be preserved in any translation or paraphrase, which after all must sink infinitely below the astonishing original.

18. The things that are seen – Men, money, things of earth. The things that are not seen – God, grace, heaven.

2 CORINTHIANS 5

1. Our earthly house – Which is only a tabernacle, or tent, not designed for a lasting habitation.

2. Desiring to be clothed upon – This body, which is now covered with flesh and blood, with the glorious house which is from heaven. Instead of flesh and blood, which cannot enter heaven, the rising body will be clothed or covered with what is analogous thereto, but incorruptible and immortal. Macarius speaks largely of this.

3. If being clothed – That is, with the image of God, while we are in the body. We shall not be found naked – Of the wedding garment.

4. We groan being burdened – The apostle speaks with exact propriety. A burden naturally expresses groans. And we are here burdened with numberless afflictions, infirmities, temptations. Not that we would be unclothed – Not that we desire to remain without a body. Faith does not understand that philosophical contempt of what the wise Creator has given. But clothed upon – With the glorious, immortal, incorruptible, spiritual body. That what is mortal – This present mortal body. May be swallowed up of life – Covered with that which lives for ever.

5. Now he that hath wrought us to this very thing – This longing for immortality. Is God – For none but God, none less than the Almighty, could have wrought this in us.

6. Therefore we behave undauntedly – But most of all when we have death in view; knowing that our greatest happiness lies beyond the grave.

MATTHEW HENRY   CHARLES H. SPURGEON

church and the glory of God. The prospect of eternal life and happiness was their support and comfort. What sense was ready to pronounce heavy and long, grievous and tedious, faith perceived to be light and short, and but for a moment. The weight of all temporal afflictions was lightness itself, while the glory to come was a substance, weighty, and lasting beyond description. If the apostle could call his heavy and long-continued trials light, and but for a moment, what must our trifling difficulties be! Faith enables to make this right judgment of things. There are unseen things, as well as things that are seen. And there is this vast difference between them; unseen things are eternal, seen things but temporal, or temporary only. Let us then look off from the things which are seen; let us cease to seek for worldly advantages, or to fear present distresses. Let us give diligence to make our future happiness sure.

2 CORINTHIANS 5

The apostle's hope and desire of heavenly glory. (1-8)
This excited to diligence. The reasons of his being affected with zeal for the Corinthians. (9-15)
The necessity of regeneration, and of reconciliation with God through Christ. (16-21)

1-8 The believer not only is well assured by faith that there is another and a happy life after this is ended, but he has good hope, through grace, of heaven as a dwelling-place, a resting-place, a hiding-place. In our Father's house there are many mansions, whose Builder and Maker is God. The happiness of the future state is what God has prepared for those that love him: everlasting habitations, not like the earthly tabernacles, the poor cottages of clay, in which our souls now dwell; that are moldering and decaying, whose foundations are in the dust. The body of flesh is a heavy burden, the calamities of life are a heavy load. But believers groan, being burdened with a body of sin, and because of the many corruptions remaining and raging within them. Death will strip us of the clothing of flesh, and all the comforts of life, as well as end all our troubles here below. But believing souls shall be clothed with garments of praise, with robes of righteousness and glory. The present graces and comforts of the Spirit are earnests of everlasting grace and comfort. And though God is with us here, by his Spirit, and in his ordinances, yet we are not with him as we hope to be. Faith is for this world, and sight is for the other world. It is our duty, and it will be our interest, to walk by faith, till we live by sight. This shows clearly the happiness to be enjoyed by the souls of believers when absent from the body, and where Jesus makes known his glorious presence. We are related to the body and to the Lord; each claims a part in us. But how much more powerfully the Lord pleads for having the

not one feature in his moral countenance which had undue preponderance above the other; but he was replete in everything that was virtuous and good. Tempted he was, it is true, but sinned he never. The whirlwind came from the wilderness, and smote upon the four corners of that house, but it fell not, for it was founded upon a rock. The rains descended, heaven afflicted him; the winds blew, the mysterious agency of hell assailed him; the floods came, all earth was in arms against him, but yet he stood firm in the midst of all. Never once did he even seem to bend before the tempest; but buffeting the fury of the blast, bearing all the temptations that could ever happen to man, which summed themselves up and consummated their fury on him, he stood to the end, without a single flaw in his life, or a stain upon his spotless robe. Let us rejoice, then, in this, my beloved brothers and sisters, that we have such a substitute—one who is fit and proper to stand in our place, and to suffer in our stead, seeing he has no need to offer a sacrifice for himself; no need to cry for himself, "Father, I have sinned;" no need to bend the knee of the penitent and confess his own iniquities, for he is without spot or blemish, the perfect lamb of God's Passover.

I would have you carefully notice the particular expression of the text, for it struck me as being very beautiful and significant,—"who knew no sin." It does not merely say did none, but knew none. Sin was no acquaintance of his; he was acquainted with grief, but no acquaintance of sin. He had to walk in the midst of its most frequented haunts, but did not know it; not that he was ignorant of its nature, or did not know its penalty, but he did not know it; he was a stranger to it, he never gave it the wink or nod of familiar recognition. Of course he knew what sin was, for he was very God, but with the sin he had no communion, no fellowship, no brotherhood. He was a perfect stranger in the presence of sin; he was a foreigner; he was not an inhabitant of that land where sin is acknowledged. He passed through the wilderness of suffering, but into the wilderness of sin he could never go. "He knew no sin;" mark that expression and treasure it up, and when you are thinking of your substitute, and see him hang bleeding upon the cross, think that you see written in those lines of blood written along his blessed body, "He knew no sin." Mingled with the redness of his blood—that Rose of Sharon; behold the purity of his nature, the Lily of the Valley—"He knew no sin."

II. Let us pass on to notice the second and most

imputing their trespasses unto them; and hath committed unto us the word of reconciliation.

20 Now then we are ambassadors for Christ, as though God did beseech you by us: we pray you in Christ's stead, be ye reconciled to God.

21 For he hath made him to be sin for us, who knew no sin; that we might be made the righteousness of God in him.

2 CORINTHIANS 6

1 We then, as workers together with him, beseech you also that ye receive not the grace of God in vain.

2 (For he saith, I have heard thee in a time accepted, and in the day of salvation have I succoured thee: behold, now is the accepted time; behold, now is the day of salvation.)

3 Giving no offense in any thing, that the ministry be not blamed:

4 But in all things approving ourselves as the ministers of God, in much patience, in afflictions, in necessities, in distresses,

5 In stripes, in imprisonments, in tumults, in labors, in watchings, in fastings;

6 By pureness, by knowledge, by longsuffering, by kindness, by the Holy Ghost, by love unfeigned,

7 By the word of truth, by the power of God, by the armor of righteousness on the right hand and on the left,

8 By honor and dishonor, by evil report and good report: as deceivers, and yet true;

9 As unknown, and yet well known; as dying, and, behold, we live; as chastened, and not killed;

10 As sorrowful, yet alway rejoicing; as poor, yet making many rich; as having nothing, and yet possessing all things.

11 O ye Corinthians, our mouth is open unto you, our heart is enlarged.

12 Ye are not straitened in us, but ye are straitened in your own bowels.

13 Now for a recompense in the same, (I speak as unto my children,) be ye also enlarged.

14 Be ye not unequally yoked together with unbelievers: for what fellowship hath righteousness with unrighteousness? and what communion hath light with darkness?

15 And what concord hath Christ with Belial? or what part hath he that believeth with an infidel?

16 And what agreement hath the

7. For we cannot clearly see him in this life, wherein we walk by faith only: an evidence, indeed, that necessarily implies a kind of "seeing him who is invisible;" yet as far beneath what we shall have in eternity, as it is above that of bare, unassisted reason.

8. Present with the Lord – This demonstrates that the happiness of the saints is not deferred till the resurrection.

9. Therefore we are ambitious – The only ambition which has place in a Christian. Whether present – In the body. Or absent – From it.

10. For we all – Apostles as well as other men, whether now present in the body, or absent from it. Must appear – Openly, without covering, where all hidden things will be revealed; probably the sins, even of the faithful, which were forgiven long before. For many of their good works, as their repentance, their revenge against sin, cannot other wise appear. But this will be done at their own desire, without grief, and without shame. According to what he hath done in the body, whether good or evil – In the body he did either good or evil; in the body he is recompensed accordingly.

11. Knowing therefore the terror of the Lord, we the more earnestly persuade men to seek his favor; and as God knoweth this, so, I trust, ye know it in your own consciences.

12. We do not say this, as if we thought there was any need of again recommending ourselves to you, but to give you an occasion of rejoicing and praising God, and to furnish you with an answer to those false apostles who glory in appearance, but not in heart, being condemned by their own conscience.

13. For if we are transported beyond ourselves – Or at least, appear so to others, treated of, 2 Cor. v, 15-21, speaking or writing with uncommon vehemence. It is to God – He understands (if men do not) the emotion which himself inspires. If we be sober – Treated of, chap. vi, 1-10. If I proceed in a more calm, sedate manner. It is for your sakes – Even good men bear this, rather than the other method, in their teachers. But these must obey God, whoever is offended by it.

14. For the love of Christ – To us, and our love to him. Constraineth us – Both to the one and the other; beareth us on with such a strong, steady, prevailing influence, as winds and tides exert when they waft the vessel to its destined harbor. While we thus judge, that if Christ died for all, then are all, even the best of men, naturally dead – In a state of spiritual death, and liable to death eternal. For had any man been otherwise, Christ had not needed to have died for him.

15. And that he died for all – That all might be saved. That they who live – That all who live upon the earth. Should not henceforth – From the moment they know him. Live unto themselves – Seek their own honor, profit, pleasure. But unto him – In all righteousness and true holiness.

16. So that we from this time – That we knew the love of Christ. Know no one – Neither ourselves, nor you, neither the rest of the apostles, Gal. ii, 6, nor any other person. After the flesh – According to his former state, country, descent, nobility, riches, power, wisdom. We fear not the great. We regard not the rich or wise. We account not the least less than ourselves. We consider all, only in order to save all. Who is he that knows no one after the flesh? In what land do these Christians live? Yea, if we have known even Christ after the flesh – So as to love him barely with a natural love, so as to glory in having conversed with him on earth, so as to expect only temporal benefits from him.

17. Therefore if any one be in Christ – A true believer in him. There is a new creation – Only the power that makes a world can make a Christian. And when he is so created, the old things are passed away – Of their own

soul of the believer closely united with himself! Thou art one of the souls I have loved and chosen; one of those given to me. What is death, as an object of fear, compared with being absent from the Lord!

9-15 The apostle quickens himself and others to acts of duty. Well-grounded hopes of heaven will not encourage sloth and sinful security. Let all consider the judgment to come, which is called, The terror of the Lord. Knowing what terrible vengeance the Lord would execute upon the workers of iniquity, the apostle and his brethren used every argument and persuasion, to lead men to believe in the Lord Jesus, and to act as his disciples. Their zeal and diligence were for the glory of God and the good of the church. Christ's love to us will have a like effect upon us, if duly considered and rightly judged. All were lost and undone, dead and ruined, slaves to sin, having no power to deliver themselves, and must have remained thus miserable forever, if Christ had not died. We should not make ourselves, but Christ, the end of our living and actions. A Christian's life should be devoted to Christ. Alas, how many show the worthlessness of their professed faith and love, by living to themselves and to the world!

16-21 The renewed man acts upon new principles, by new rules, with new ends, and in new company. The believer is created anew; his heart is not merely set right, but a new heart is given him. He is the workmanship of God, created in Christ Jesus unto good works. Though the same as a man, he is changed in his character and conduct. These words must and do mean more than an outward reformation. The man who formerly saw no beauty in the Savior that he should desire him, now loves him above all things. The heart of the unregenerate is filled with enmity against God, and God is justly offended with him. Yet there may be reconciliation. Our offended God has reconciled us to himself by Jesus Christ. By the inspiration of God, the Scriptures were written, which are the word of reconciliation; showing that peace has been made by the cross, and how we may be interested therein. Though God cannot lose by the quarrel, nor gain by the peace, yet he beseeches sinners to lay aside their enmity, and accept the salvation he offers. Christ knew no sin. He was made Sin; not a sinner, but Sin, a Sin-offering, a Sacrifice for sin. The end and design of all this was, that we might be made the righteousness of God in him, might be justified freely by the grace of God through the redemption which is in Christ Jesus. Can any lose, labor, or suffer too much for him, who gave his beloved Son to be the Sacrifice for their sins, that they might be made the righteousness of God in him?

important point; THE ACTUAL SUBSTITUTION OF CHRIST, AND THE REAL IMPUTATION OF SIN TO HIM. "He made him to be sin for us."

Here be careful to observe who transferred the sin. God the Father laid on Jesus the iniquities of us all. Man could not make Christ sin. Man could not transfer his guilt to another. It is not for us to say whether Christ could or could not have made himself sin for us; that certain it is, he did not take this priesthood upon himself, but he was called of God, as was Aaron. The Redeemer's vicarious position is warranted, nay ordained by divine authority. "He hath made him to be sin for us." I must now beg you to notice how very explicit the term is. Some of our expositors will have it that the word here used must mean "sin-offering." "He made him to be a sin-offering for us." I thought it well to look to my Greek Testament to see whether it could be so. Of course we all know that the word here translated "sin," is very often translated "sin-offering," but it is always useful, when you have a disputed passage, to look it through, and see whether in this case the word would bear such a meaning. These commentators say it means a sin-offering,—well, I will read it: "He hath made him to be a sin-offering for us who knew no sin-offering." Does not that strike you as being ridiculous? But they are precisely the same words; and if it be fair to translate it "sin-offering" in one place, it must, in all reason, be fair to translate it so in the other. The fact is, while in some passages it may be rendered "sin-offering," in this passage it cannot be so, because it would be to run counter to all honesty to translate the same word in the same sentence two different ways. No; we must take them as they stand. "He hath made him to be sin for us," not merely an offering, but sin for us.

My predecessor, Dr. Gill, edited the works of Tobias Crisp, but Tobias Crisp went further than Dr. Gill or any of us can approve; for in one place Crisp calls Christ a sinner, though he does not mean that he ever sinned himself. He actually calls Christ a transgressor, and justifies himself by that passage, "He was numbered with the transgressors." Martin Luther is reputed to have broadly said that, although Jesus Christ was sinless, yet he was the greatest sinner that ever lived, because all the sins of his people lay upon him. Now, such expressions I think to be unguarded, if not profane. Certainly Christian men should take care that they use not language which, by the ignorant and uninstructed, may be translated to mean what they never intended to teach. The fact is, brethren, that in no sense whatever—take that as I say it—in no

temple of God with idols? for ye are the temple of the living God; as God hath said, I will dwell in them, and walk in them; and I will be their God, and they shall be my people.

17 Wherefore come out from among them, and be ye separate, saith the Lord, and touch not the unclean thing; and I will receive you,

18 And will be a Father unto you, and ye shall be my sons and daughters, saith the Lord Almighty.

2 CORINTHIANS 7

1 Having therefore these promises, dearly beloved, let us cleanse ourselves from all filthiness of the flesh and spirit, perfecting holiness in the fear of God.

2 Receive us; we have wronged no man, we have corrupted no man, we have defrauded no man.

3 I speak not this to condemn you: for I have said before, that ye are in our hearts to die and live with you.

4 Great is my boldness of speech toward you, great is my glorying of you: I am filled with comfort, I am exceeding joyful in all our tribulation.

5 For, when we were come into Macedonia, our flesh had no rest, but we were troubled on every side; without were fightings, within were fears.

6 Nevertheless God, that comforteth those that are cast down, comforted us by the coming of Titus;

7 And not by his coming only, but by the consolation wherewith he was comforted in you, when he told us your earnest desire, your mourning, your fervent mind toward me; so that I rejoiced the more.

8 For though I made you sorry with a letter, I do not repent, though I did repent: for I perceive that the same epistle hath made you sorry, though it were but for a season.

9 Now I rejoice, not that ye were made sorry, but that ye sorrowed to repentance: for ye were made sorry after a godly manner, that ye might receive damage by us in nothing.

10 For godly sorrow worketh repentance to salvation not to be repented of: but the sorrow of the world worketh death.

11 For behold this selfsame thing, that ye sorrowed after a godly sort, what carefulness it wrought in you, yea, what clearing of yourselves, yea, what indignation, yea, what fear, yea,

accord, even as snow in spring. Behold – The present, visible, undeniable change! All things are become new – He has new life, new senses, new faculties, new affections, new appetites, new ideas and conceptions. His whole tenor of action and conversation is new, and he lives, as it were, in a new world. God, men, the whole creation, heaven, earth, and all therein, appear in a new light, and stand related to him in a new manner, since he was created anew in Christ Jesus.

18. And all these new things are from God, considered under this very notion, as reconciling us – The world, 2 Cor. v, 19, to himself.

19. Namely – The sum of which is, God – The whole Godhead, but more eminently God the Father. Was in Christ, reconciling the world – Which was before at enmity with God. To himself – So taking away that enmity, which could not otherwise be removed than by the blood of the Son of God.

20. Therefore we are ambassadors for Christ – we beseech you in Christ's stead – Herein the apostle might appear to some "transported beyond himself." In general he uses a more calm, sedate kind of exhortation, as in the beginning of the next chapter. What unparalleled condescension and divinely tender mercies are displayed in this verse! Did the judge ever beseech a condemned criminal to accept of pardon? Does the creditor ever beseech a ruined debtor to receive an acquittance in full? Yet our almighty Lord, and our eternal Judge, not only vouchsafes to offer these blessings, but invites us, entreats us, and, with the most tender importunity, solicits us, not to reject them.

21. He made him a sin offering, who knew no sin – A commendation peculiar to Christ. For us – Who knew no righteousness, who were inwardly and outwardly nothing but sin; who must have been consumed by the divine justice, had not this atonement been made for our sins. That we might be made the righteousness of God through him – Might through him be invested with that righteousness, first imputed to us, then implanted in us, which is in every sense the righteousness of God.

2 CORINTHIANS 6

1. We then not only beseech, but as fellow-laborers with you, who are working out your own salvation, do also exhort you, not to receive the grace of God – Which we have been now describing. In vain – We receive it by faith; and not in vain, if we add to this, persevering holiness.

2. For he saith – The sense is, As of old there was a particular time wherein God was pleased to pour out his peculiar blessing, so there is now. And this is the particular time: this is a time of peculiar blessing. Isaiah xlix, 8.

3. Giving, as far as in us lies, no offense, that the ministry be not blamed on our account.

4. But approving ourselves as the ministers of God – Such as his ministers ought to be. In much patience – Shown,

1. In afflictions, necessities, distresses – All which are general terms.

2. In stripes, imprisonments, tumults – Which are particular sorts of affliction, necessity, distress.

3. In labors, watchings, fastings – Voluntarily endured. All these are expressed in the plural number, to denote a variety of them. In afflictions, several ways to escape may appear, though none without difficulty; in necessities, one only, and that a difficult one; in distresses, none at all appears.

5. In tumults – The Greek word implies such attacks as a man cannot stand against, but which bear him hither and thither by violence.

6. By prudence – Spiritual divine; not what the world terms so. Worldly

2 CORINTHIANS 6

The apostle, with others, proved themselves faithful
ministers of Christ, by their unblamable life and
behavior. (1-10)

By affection for them. And by earnest concern, that
they might have no fellowship with unbelievers and
idolaters. (11-18)

1-10 The gospel is a word of grace sounding in our
ears. The gospel day is a day of salvation, the means
of grace the means of salvation, the offers of the
gospel the offers of salvation, and the present time the
proper time to accept these offers. The morrow is
none of ours: we know not what will be on the morrow,
nor where we shall be. We now enjoy a day of grace;
then let all be careful not to neglect it. Ministers of the
gospel should look upon themselves as God's servants, and act in every thing suitably to that character.
The apostle did so, by much patience in afflictions, by
acting from good principles, and by due temper and
behavior. Believers, in this world, need the grace of
God, to arm them against temptations, so as to bear
the good report of men without pride; and so as to
bear their reproaches with patience. They have nothing in themselves, but possess all things in Christ. Of
such differences is a Christian's life made up, and
through such a variety of conditions and reports, is
our way to heaven; and we should be careful in all
things to approve ourselves to God. The gospel,
when faithfully preached, and fully received, betters
the condition even of the poorest. They save what
before they riotously spent, and diligently employ
their time to useful purposes. They save and gain by
religion, and thus are made rich, both for the world to
come and for this, when compared with their sinful,
profligate state, before they received the gospel.

11-18 It is wrong for believers to join with the wicked
and profane. The word unbeliever applies to all destitute of true faith. True pastors will caution their
beloved children in the gospel, not to be unequally
yoked. The fatal effects of neglecting Scripture precepts as to marriages clearly appear. Instead of a
helpmeet, the union brings a snare. Those whose
cross it is to be unequally united, without their willfull
fault, may expect consolation under it; but when
believers enter into such unions, against the express
warnings of God's word, they must expect much distress. The caution also extends to common conversation. We should not join in friendship and
acquaintance with wicked men and unbelievers.
Though we cannot wholly avoid seeing and hearing,
and being with such, yet we should never choose
them for friends. We must not defile ourselves by converse with those who defile themselves with sin.
Come out from the workers of iniquity, and separate
from their vain and sinful pleasures and pursuits; from

sense whatever can Jesus Christ ever be conceived of as having been guilty. "He knew no
sin." Not only was he not guilty of any sin which
he committed himself, but he was not guilty of
our sins. No guilt can possibly attach to a man
who has not been guilty. He must have had
complicity in the deed itself, or else no guilt can
possibly be laid on him. Jesus Christ stands in the
midst of all the divine thunders, and suffers all
the punishment, but not a drop of sin ever
stained him. In no sense is he ever a guilty man,
but always is he an accepted and a holy one.
What, then, is the meaning of that very forcible
expression of my text? We must interpret
Scriptural modes of expression by the verbage
of the speakers. We know that our Master once
said himself, "This cup is the new covenant in
my blood;" he did not mean that the cup was
the covenant. He said, "Take, eat, this is my
body"—no one of us conceives that the bread is
the literal flesh and blood of Christ. We take
that bread as if it were the body, and it actually
represents it. Now, we are to read a passage like
this, according to the analogy of faith. Jesus
Christ was made by his Father sin for us, that is,
he was treated as if he had himself been sin. He
was not sin; he was not sinful; he was not guilty;
but, he was treated by his Father, as if he had
not only been sinful, but as if he had been sin
itself. That is a strong expression used here. Not
only hath he made him to be the substitute for
sin, but to be sin. God looked on Christ as if
Christ had been sin; not as if he had taken up
the sins of his people, or as if they were laid on
him, though that were true, but as if he himself
had positively been that noxious—that God-
hating—that soul-damning thing, called sin.
When the Judge of all the earth said, "Where is
Sin?" Christ presented himself. He stood before
his Father as if he had been the accumulation of
all human guilt; as if he himself were that thing
which God cannot endure, but which he must
drive from his presence for ever. And now see
how this making of Jesus to be sin was enacted
to the fullest extent. The righteous Lord looked
on Christ as being sin, and therefore Christ must
be taken without the camp. Sin cannot be
borne in God's Zion, cannot be allowed to dwell
in God's Jerusalem; it must be taken without the
camp, it is a leprous thing, put it away. Cast out
from fellowship, from love, from pity, sin must
ever be. Take him away, take him away, ye
crowd! Hurry him through the streets and bear
him to Calvary. Take him without the camp—as
was the beast which was offered for sin without
the camp, so must Christ be, who was made sin
for us. And now, God looks on him as being sin,

what vehement desire, yea, what zeal, yea, what revenge! In all things ye have approved yourselves to be clear in this matter.

12 Wherefore, though I wrote unto you, I did it not for his cause that had done the wrong, nor for his cause that suffered wrong, but that our care for you in the sight of God might appear unto you.

13 Therefore we were comforted in your comfort: yea, and exceedingly the more joyed we for the joy of Titus, because his spirit was refreshed by you all.

14 For if I have boasted any thing to him of you, I am not ashamed; but as we spake all things to you in truth, even so our boasting, which I made before Titus, is found a truth.

15 And his inward affection is more abundant toward you, whilst he remembereth the obedience of you all, how with fear and trembling ye received him.

16 I rejoice therefore that I have confidence in you in all things.

2 CORINTHIANS 8

1 Moreover, brethren, we do you to wit of the grace of God bestowed on the churches of Macedonia;

2 How that in a great trial of affliction the abundance of their joy and their deep poverty abounded unto the riches of their liberality.

3 For to their power, I bear record, yea, and beyond their power they were willing of themselves;

4 Praying us with much intreaty that we would receive the gift, and take upon us the fellowship of the ministering to the saints.

5 And this they did, not as we hoped, but first gave their own selves to the Lord, and unto us by the will of God.

6 Insomuch that we desired Titus, that as he had begun, so he would also finish in you the same grace also.

7 Therefore, as ye abound in every thing, in faith, and utterance, and knowledge, and in all diligence, and in your love to us, see that ye abound in this grace also.

8 I speak not by commandment, but by occasion of the forwardness of others, and to prove the sincerity of your love.

9 For ye know the grace of our Lord Jesus Christ, that, though he was rich, yet for your sakes he became poor,

prudence is the practical use of worldly wisdom: divine prudence is the due exercise of grace, making spiritual understanding go as far as possible. By love unfeigned – The chief fruit of the Spirit.

7. By the convincing and converting power of God – Accompanying his word; and also attesting it by divers miracles. By the Armor of righteousness on the right hand and the left – That is, on all sides; the panoply or whole Armor of God.

8. By honor and dishonor – When we are present. By evil report and good report – When we are absent. Who could bear honor and good report, were it not balanced by dishonor? As deceivers – Artful, designing men. So the world represents all true ministers of Christ. Yet true – Upright, sincere, in the sight of God.

9. As unknown – For the world knoweth us not, as it knew him not. Yet well known – To God, and to those who are the seals of our ministry. As dying, yet behold – Suddenly, unexpectedly, God interposes, and we live.

10. As sorrowing – For our own manifold imperfections, and for the sins and sufferings of our brethren. Yet always rejoicing – In present peace, love, power, and a sure hope of future glory. As having nothing, yet possessing all things – For all things are ours, if we are Christ's. What a magnificence of thought is this!

11. From the praise of the Christian ministry, which he began chap. ii, 14, he now draws his affectionate exhortation. O ye Corinthians – He seldom uses this appellation. But it has here a peculiar force. Our mouth is opened toward you – With uncommon freedom, because our heart is enlarged – In tenderness.

12. Ye are not straitened in us – Our heart is wide enough to receive you all. But ye are straitened in your own bowels – Your hearts are shut up, and so not capable of the blessings ye might enjoy.

13. Now for a recompense of the same – Of my parental tenderness. I speak as to my children – I ask nothing hard or grievous. Be ye also enlarged – Open your hearts, first to God, and then to us, so chap. viii, 5, that God may "dwell in you," 2 Cor. vi, 16; vii, 1; and that ye may "receive us," chap. vii, 2.

14. Be not unequally yoked with unbelievers – Christians with Jews or heathens. The apostle particularly speaks of marriage. But the reasons he urges equally hold against any needless intimacy with them. Of the five questions that follow, the three former contain the argument; the two latter, the conclusion.

15. What concord hath Christ – Whom ye serve. With Belial – To whom they belong.

16. What agreement hath the temple of God with idols – If God would not endure idols in any part of the land wherein he dwelt, how much less, under his own roof! He does not say, with the temple of idols, for idols do not dwell in their worshipers. As God hath said – To his ancient church, and in them to all the Israel of God. I will dwell in them, and walk in them – The former signifying his perpetual presence; the latter, his operation. And I will be to them a God, and they shall be to me a people – The sum of the whole gospel covenant. Lev. xxvi, 11, &c.

17. Touch not the unclean person – Keep at the utmost distance from him. And I will receive you – Into my house and family. Isaiah lii, 11; Zephaniah iii, 19, 20.

18. And ye shall be to me for sons and for daughters, saith the Lord Almighty – The promise made to Solomon, 1 Chr xxviii, 6, is here applied to all believers; as the promise made particularly to Joshua is applied to them, Heb. xiii, 5. Who can express the worth, who can conceive the dignity, of this divine adoption? Yet it belongs to all who believe the gospel,

all conformity to the corruptions of this present evil world. If it be an envied privilege to be the son or daughter of an earthly prince, who can express the dignity and happiness of being sons and daughters of the Almighty?

2 CORINTHIANS 7

An exhortation to holiness, and the whole church entreated to bear affection to the apostle. (1-4)
He rejoiced in their sorrowing to repentance. (5-11)
And in the comfort they and Titus had together. (12-16)

1-4 The promises of God are strong reasons for us to follow after holiness; we must cleanse ourselves from all filthiness of flesh and spirit. If we hope in God as our Father, we must seek to be holy as he is holy, and perfect as our Father in heaven. His grace, by the influences of his Spirit, alone can purify, but holiness should be the object of our constant prayers. If the ministers of the gospel are thought contemptible, there is danger lest the gospel itself be despised also; and though ministers must flatter none, yet they must be gentle towards all. Ministers may look for esteem and favor, when they can safely appeal to the people, that they have corrupted no man by false doctrines or flattering speeches; that they have defrauded no man; nor sought to promote their own interests so as to hurt any. It was affection to them made the apostle speak so freely to them, and caused him to glory of them, in all places, and upon all occasions.

5-11 There were fighting without, or continual contentions with, and opposition from Jews and Gentiles; and there were fears within, and great concern for such as had embraced the Christian faith. But God comforts those who are cast down. We should look above and beyond all means and instruments, to God, as the author of all the consolation and good we enjoy. Sorrow according to the will of God, tending to the glory of God, and wrought by the Spirit of God, renders the heart humble, contrite, submissive, disposed to mortify every sin, and to walk in newness of life. And this repentance is connected with saving faith in Christ, and an interest in his atonement. There is a great difference between this sorrow of a godly sort, and the sorrow of the world. The happy fruits of true repentance are mentioned. Where the heart is changed, the life and actions will be changed. It wrought indignation at sin, at themselves, at the tempter and his instruments. It wrought a fear of watchfulness, and a cautious fear of sin. It wrought desire to be reconciled with God. It wrought zeal for duty, and against sin. It wrought revenge against sin and their own folly, by endeavors to make satisfaction for injuries done thereby. Deep humility before God,

and sin must bear punishment. Christ is punished. The most fearful of deaths is exacted at his hand, and God has no pity for him. How should he have pity on sin? God hates it. No tongue can tell, no soul can divine the terrible hatred of God to that which is evil, and he treats Christ as if he were sin. He prays, but heaven shuts out his prayer; he cries for water, but heaven and earth refuse to wet his lips except with vinegar. He turns his eye to heaven, he sees nothing there. How should he? God cannot look on sin, and sin can have no claim on God: "My God, my God," he cries, "why hast thou forsaken me?" O solemn necessity, how could God do anything with sin but forsake it? How could iniquity have fellowship with God? Shall divine smiles rest on sin? Nay, nay, it must not be. Therefore is it that he who is made sin must bemoan desertion and terror. God cannot touch him, cannot dwell with him, cannot come near him. He is abhorred, cast away; it hath pleased the Father to bruise him; he hath put him to grief. At last he dies. God will not keep him in life—how should he? Is it not the meetest thing in the world that sin should be buried? "Bury it out of my sight, hide this corruption," and lo! Jesus, as if he were sin, is put away out of the sight of God and man as a thing obnoxious. I do not know whether I have clearly uttered what I want to state, but what a grim picture that is, to conceive of sin gathered up into one mass— murder, lust and rapine, and adultery, and all manner of crime, all piled together in one hideous heap. We ourselves, brethren, impure though we be, could not bear this; how much less should God with his pure and holy eyes bear with that mass of sin, and yet there it is, and God looked upon Christ as if he were that mass of sin. He was not sin, but he looked upon him as made sin for us. He stands in our place, assumes our guilt, takes on him our iniquity, and God treats him as if he had been sin. Now, my dear brothers and sisters, let us just lift up our hearts with gratitude for a few moments. Here we are tonight; we know that we are guilty, but our sins have all been punished years ago. Before my soul believed in Christ, the punishment of my sin had all been endured. We are not to think that Christ's blood derives its efficacy from our faith. Fact precedes faith. Christ hath redeemed us; faith discovers his; but it was a fact of that finished sacrifice. Though still defiled by sin, yet who can lay anything to the charge of the man whose guilt is gone, lifted bodily from off him, and put upon Christ? How can any punishment fall on that man who ceases to possess sins, because his sin has eighteen

that ye through his poverty might be rich.

10 And herein I give my advice: for this is expedient for you, who have begun before, not only to do, but also to be forward a year ago.

11 Now therefore perform the doing of it; that as there was a readiness to will, so there may be a performance also out of that which ye have.

12 For if there be first a willing mind, it is accepted according to that a man hath, and not according to that he hath not.

13 For I mean not that other men be eased, and ye burdened:

14 But by an equality, that now at this time your abundance may be a supply for their want, that their abundance also may be a supply for your want: that there may be equality:

15

As it is written, He that had gathered much had nothing over; and he that had gathered little had no lack.

16 But thanks be to God, which put the same earnest care into the heart of Titus for you.

17 For indeed he accepted the exhortation; but being more forward, of his own accord he went unto you.

18 And we have sent with him the brother, whose praise is in the gospel throughout all the churches;

19 And not that only, but who was also chosen of the churches to travel with us with this grace, which is administered by us to the glory of the same Lord, and declaration of your ready mind:

20 Avoiding this, that no man should blame us in this abundance which is administered by us:

21 Providing for honest things, not only in the sight of the Lord, but also in the sight of men.

22 And we have sent with them our brother, whom we have oftentimes proved diligent in many things, but now much more diligent, upon the great confidence which I have in you.

23 Whether any do inquire of Titus, he is my partner and fellowhelper concerning you: or our brethren be inquired of, they are the messengers of the churches, and the glory of Christ.

24 Wherefore shew ye to them, and before the churches, the proof of your love, and of our boasting on your behalf.

who have faith in Christ. They have access to the Almighty; such free and welcome access, as a beloved child to an indulgent father. To him they may fly for aid in every difficulty, and from him obtain a supply in all their wants. Isaiah xliii, 6.

2 CORINTHIANS 7

1. Let us cleanse ourselves – This is the latter part of the exhortation, which was proposed, chap. vi, 1, and resumed, chap. vi, 14. From all pollution of the flesh – All outward sin. And of the spirit – All inward. Yet let us not rest in negative religion, but perfect holiness – Carrying it to the height in all its branches, and enduring to the end in the loving fear of God, the sure foundation of all holiness.

2. Receive us – The sum of what is said in this, as well as in the tenth and following chapters. We have hurt no man – In his person. We have corrupted no man – In his principles. We have defrauded no man – Of his property. In this he intimates likewise the good he had done them, but with the utmost modesty, as it were not looking upon it.

3. I speak not to condemn you – Not as if I accused you of laying this to my charge. I am so far from thinking so unkindly of you, that ye are in our hearts, to live and die with you – That is, I could rejoice to spend all my days with you.

4. I am filled with comfort – Of this he treats, 2 Cor. vii, 6, &c.; of his joy, 2 Cor. vii, 7, &c.; of both, 2 Cor. vii, 13.

5. Our flesh – That is, we ourselves. Had no rest from without – From the heathens. Were fightings – Furious and cruel oppositions. From within – From our brethren. Were fears – Lest they should be seduced.

7. Your earnest desire – To rectify what had been amiss. Your grief – For what had offended God, and troubled me.

8. I did repent – That is, I felt a tender sorrow for having grieved you, till I saw the happy effect of it.

10. The sorrow of the world – Sorrow that arises from worldly considerations. Worketh death – Naturally tends to work or occasion death, temporal, spiritual, and eternal.

11. How great diligence it wrought in you – Shown in all the following particulars. Yea, clearing of yourselves – Some had been more, some less, faulty; whence arose these various affections. Hence their apologizing and indignation, with respect to themselves; their fear and desire, with respect to the apostle; their zeal and revenge, with respect to the offender, yea, and themselves also. Clearing of yourselves – From either sharing in, or approving of, his sin. Indignation – That ye had not immediately corrected the offender. Fear – Of God's displeasure, or lest I should come with a rod. Vehement desire – To see me again. Zeal – For the glory of God, and the soul of that sinner. Yea, revenge – Ye took a kind of holy revenge upon yourselves, being scarce able to forgive yourselves. In all things ye – As a church. Have approved yourselves to be pure – That is, free from blame, since ye received my letter.

12. It was not only, or chiefly, for the sake of the incestuous person, or of his father; but to show my care over you.

2 CORINTHIANS 8

1. We declare to you the grace of God – Which evidently appeared by this happy effect.

2. In a great trial of affliction – Being continually persecuted, harassed, and plundered.

hatred of all sin, with faith in Christ, a new heart and a new life, make repentance unto salvation. May the Lord bestow it on every one of us.

12-16 The apostle was not disappointed concerning them, which he signified to Titus; and he could with joy declare the confidence he had in them for the time to come. Here see the duties of a pastor and of his flock; the latter must lighten the troubles of the pastoral office, by respect and obedience; the former make a due return by his care of them, and cherish the flock by testimonies of satisfaction, joy, and tenderness.

2 CORINTHIANS 8

The apostle reminds them of charitable contributions for the poor saints. (1-6)

Enforces this by their gifts, and by the love and grace of Christ. (7-9)

By the willingness they had shown to this good work. (10-15)

He recommends Titus to them. (16-24)

1-6 The grace of God must be owned as the root and fountain of all the good in us, or done by us, at any time. It is great grace and favor from God, if we are made useful to others, and forward to any good work. He commends the charity of the Macedonians. So far from needing that Paul should urge them, they prayed him to receive the gift. Whatever we use or lay out for God, it is only giving him what is his own. All we give for charitable uses, will not be accepted of God, nor turn to our advantage, unless we first give ourselves to the Lord. By ascribing all really good works to the grace of God, we not only give the glory to him whose due it is, but also show men where their strength is. Abundant spiritual joy enlarges men's hearts in the work and labor of love. How different this from the conduct of those who will not join in any good work, unless urged into it!

7-9 Faith is the root; and as without faith it is not possible to please God, Heb 11:6, so those who abound in faith, will abound in other graces and good works also; and this will work and show itself by love. Great talkers are not always the best doers; but these Corinthians were diligent to do, as well as to know and talk well. To all these good things the apostle desires them to add this grace also, to abound in charity to the poor. The best arguments for Christian duties, are drawn from the grace and love of Christ. Though he was rich, as being God, equal in power and glory with the Father, yet he not only became man for us, but became poor also. At length he emptied himself, as it were, to ransom their souls by his sacrifice on the cross. From what riches, blessed

hundred years ago been cast upon Christ, and Christ has suffered in his place and stead? Oh, glorious triumph of faith to be able to say, whenever I feel the guilt of sin, whenever conscience pricks me, "Yes, it is true, but my Lord is answerable for it all, for he has taken it all upon himself, and suffered in my room, and place, and stead." How precious when I see my debts, to be able to say, "Yes, but the blood of Christ, God's dear Son, hath cleansed me from all sin!" How precious, not only to see my sin dying when I believe, but to know that it was dead, it was gone, it ceased to be, eighteen hundred years ago. All the sins that you and I have ever committed, or ever shall commit, if we be heirs of mercy, and children of God, are all dead things.

"Our Jesus nailed them to his cross,
And sung the triumph when he rose."

These cannot rise in judgment to condemn us; they have all been slain, shrouded, buried; they are removed from us as far as the east is from the west, because "He hath made him to be sin for us who knew no sin."

III. You see then the reality of the imputation of sin to Christ from the amazing doctrine that Christ is made sin for us. But now notice the concluding thought, upon which I must dwell a moment, but it must be very briefly, for two reasons, my time has gone, and my strength has gone too. "THAT WE MIGHT BE MADE THE RIGHTEOUSNESS OF GOD IN HIM." Now, here I beg you to notice, that it does not simply say that we might be made righteous, but "that we might be made the righteousness of God in him;" as if righteousness, that lovely, glorious, God-honoring, God-delighting thing—as if we were actually made that. God looks on his people as being abstract righteousness, not only righteous, but righteousness. To be righteous, is as if a man should have a box covered with gold, the box would then be golden; but to be righteousness is to have a box of solid gold. To be a righteous man is to have righteousness cast over me; but to be made righteousness, that is to be made solid essential righteousness in the sight of God. Well now, this is a glorious fact and a most wonderful privilege, that we poor sinners are made "the righteousness of God in him." God sees no sin in any one of his people, no iniquity in Jacob, when he looks upon them in Christ. In themselves he sees nothing but filth and abomination, in Christ nothing but purity and righteousness. Is it not, and must it not ever be to the Christian, one of his most delightful privileges to know that altogether apart from

2 CORINTHIANS 9

1 For as touching the ministering to the saints, it is superfluous for me to write to you:

2 For I know the forwardness of your mind, for which I boast of you to them of Macedonia, that Achaia was ready a year ago; and your zeal hath provoked very many.

3 Yet have I sent the brethren, lest our boasting of you should be in vain in this behalf; that, as I said, ye may be ready:

4 Lest haply if they of Macedonia come with me, and find you unprepared, we (that we say not, ye) should be ashamed in this same confident boasting.

5 Therefore I thought it necessary to exhort the brethren, that they would go before unto you, and make up beforehand your bounty, whereof ye had notice before, that the same might be ready, as a matter of bounty, and not as of covetousness.

6 But this I say, He which soweth sparingly shall reap also sparingly; and he which soweth bountifully shall reap also bountifully.

7 Every man according as he purposeth in his heart, so let him give; not grudgingly, or of necessity: for God loveth a cheerful giver.

8 And God is able to make all grace abound toward you; that ye, always having all sufficiency in all things, may abound to every good work:

9 (As it is written, He hath dispersed abroad; he hath given to the poor: his righteousness remaineth for ever.

10 Now he that ministereth seed to the sower both minister bread for your food, and multiply your seed sown, and increase the fruits of your righteousness;)

11 Being enriched in every thing to all bountifulness, which causeth through us thanksgiving to God.

12 For the administration of this service not only supplieth the want of the saints, but is abundant also by many thanksgivings unto God;

13 Whiles by the experiment of this ministration they glorify God for your professed subjection unto the gospel of Christ, and for your liberal distribution unto them, and unto all men;

14 And by their prayer for you, which long after you for the exceeding grace of God in you.

15 Thanks be unto God for his unspeakable gift.

4. Praying us with much entreaty – Probably St. Paul had lovingly admonished them not to do beyond their power.

5. And not as we hoped – That is, beyond all we could hope. They gave themselves to us, by the will of God – In obedience to his will, to be wholly directed by us.

6. As he had begun – When he was with you before.

9. For ye know – And this knowledge is the true source of love. The grace – The most sincere, most free, and most abundant love. He became poor – In becoming man, in all his life; in his death. Rich – In the favor and image of God.

12. A man – Every believer. Is accepted – With God. According to what he hath – And the same rule holds universally. Whoever acknowledges himself to be a vile, guilty sinner, and, in consequence of this acknowledgment, flies for refuge to the wounds of a crucified Savior, and relies on his merits alone for salvation, may in every circumstance of life apply this indulgent declaration to himself.

14. That their abundance – If need should so require. May be – At another time. A supply to your want: that there may be an equality – No want on one side, no superfluity on the other. It may likewise have a further meaning: that as the temporal bounty of the Corinthians did now supply the temporal wants of their poor brethren in Judea, so the prayers of these might be a means of bringing down many spiritual blessings on their benefactors: so that all the spiritual wants of the one might be amply supplied; all the temporal of the other.

15. As it is written, He that had gathered the most had nothing over; and he that had gathered the least did not lack – That is, in which that scripture is in another sense fulfilled. Exod. xvi, 18.

17. Being more forward – Than to need it, though he received it well.

18. We – I and Timothy. The brother – The ancients generally supposed this was St. Luke. Whose praise – For faithfully dispensing the gospel, is through all the churches.

19. He was appointed by the churches – Of Macedonia. With this gift – Which they were carrying from Macedonia to Jerusalem. For the declaration of our ready mind – That of Paul and his fellow-traveler, ready to be the servants of all.

22. With them – With Titus and Luke. Our brother – Perhaps Apollos.

23. My partner – In my cares and labors. The glory of Christ – Signal instruments of advancing his glory.

24. Before the churches – Present by their messengers.

2 CORINTHIANS 9

1. To write to you – Largely.

2. I boast to them of Macedonia – With whom he then was.

3. I have sent the above mentioned brethren before me.

5. Spoken of before – By me, to the Macedonians. Not as a matter of covetousness – As wrung by importunity from covetous persons.

6. He that soweth sparingly shall reap sparingly; he that soweth bountifully shall reap bountifully – A general rule. God will proportion the reward to the work, and the temper whence it proceeds.

7. Of necessity – Because he cannot tell how to refuse.

8. How remarkable are these words! Each is loaded with matter and increases all the way it goes. All grace – Every kind of blessing. That ye may abound to every good work – God gives us everything, that we may do good therewith, and so receive more blessings. All things in this life, even rewards, are, to the faithful, seeds in order to a future harvest. Prov. xxii, 9.

Lord, to what poverty didst thou descend for our sakes! and to what riches hast thou advanced us through thy poverty! It is our happiness to be wholly at thy disposal.

10-15 Good purposes are like buds and blossoms, pleasant to behold, and give hopes of good fruit; but they are lost, and signify nothing without good deeds. Good beginnings are well; but we lose the benefit, unless there is perseverance. When men purpose that which is good, and endeavor, according to their ability, to perform also, God will not reject them for what it is not in their power to do. But this scripture will not justify those who think good meanings are enough, or that good purposes, and the mere profession of a willing mind, are enough to save. Providence gives to some more of the good things of this world, and to some less, that those who have abundance might supply others who are in want. It is the will of God, that by our mutual supplying one another, there should be some sort of equality; not such a leveling as would destroy property, for in such a case there could be no exercise of charity. All should think themselves concerned to relieve those in want. This is shown from the gathering and giving out the manna in the wilderness, Ex 16:18. Those who have most of this world, have no more than food and raiment; and those who have but little of this world, seldom are quite without them.

16-24 The apostle commends the brethren sent to collect their charity, that it might be known who they were, and how safely they might be trusted. It is the duty of all Christians to act prudently; to hinder, as far as we can, all unjust suspicions. It is needful, in the first place, to act uprightly in the sight of God, but things honest in the sight of men should also be attended to. A clear character, as well as a pure conscience, is requisite for usefulness. They brought glory to Christ as instruments, and had obtained honor from Christ to be counted faithful, and employed in his service. The good opinion others have of us, should be an argument with us to do well.

2 CORINTHIANS 9

The reason for sending Titus to collect their alms. (1-5) The Corinthians to be liberal and cheerful. The apostle thanks God for his unspeakable gift. (6-15)

1-5 When we would have others do good, we must act toward them prudently and tenderly, and give them time. Christians should consider what is for the credit of their profession, and endeavor to adorn the doctrine of God their Savior in all things. The duty of ministering to the saints is so plain, that there would seem no need to exhort Christians to it; yet self-love

anything that we have ever done, or can do, God looks upon his people as being righteous, nay, as being righteousness, and that despite all of the sins they have ever committed, they are accepted in him as if they had been Christ, while Christ was punished for them as if he had been sin. Why, when I stand in my own place, I am lost and ruined; my place is the place where Judas stood, the place where the devil lies in everlasting shame. But when I stand in Christ's place—and I fail to stand where faith has put me till I stand there—when I stand in Christ's place, the Father's everlastingly beloved one, the Father's accepted one, him whom the Father delighteth to honor—when I stand there, I stand where faith hath a right to put me, and I am in the most joyous spot that a creature of God can occupy. Oh, Christian, get thee up, get thee up into the high mountain, and stand where thy Savior stands, for that is thy place. Lie not there on the dunghill of fallen humanity, that is not thy place now; Christ has once taken it on thy behalf. "He made him to be sin for us." Thy place is yonder there, above the starry hosts, where he hath raised us up together, and made us sit together in heavenly places in him. Not there, at the day of judgment, where the wicked shriek for shelter, and beg for the hills to cover them, but there, where Jesus sits upon his throne—there is thy place, my soul. He will make thee to sit upon his throne, even as he has overcome, and has sat down with his Father upon his throne. Oh! That I could mount to the heights of this argument tonight; it needs a seraphic preacher to picture the saint in Christ, robed in Christ's righteousness, wearing Christ's nature, bearing Christ's palm of victory, sitting on Christ's throne, wearing Christ's crown. And yet this is our privilege! He wore my crown, the crown of thorns; I wear his crown, the crown of glory. He wore my dress, nay, rather, he wore my nakedness when he died upon the cross; I wear his robes, the royal robes of the King of kings. He bore my shame; I bear his honor. He endured my sufferings to this end that my joy may be full, and that his joy may be fulfilled in me. He laid in the grave that I might rise from the dead and that I may dwell in him, and all this he comes again to give me, to make it sure to me and to all that love his appearing, to show that all his people shall enter into their inheritance.

Now, my brothers and sisters, Mr. Maurice, McLeod, Campbell, and their great admirer, Mr. Brown, may go on with their preaching as long as they like, but they will never make a convert of a man who knows what the vitality of religion is; for he who knows what substitution

2 CORINTHIANS 10

1 Now I Paul myself beseech you by the meekness and gentleness of Christ, who in presence am base among you, but being absent am bold toward you:

2 But I beseech you, that I may not be bold when I am present with that confidence, wherewith I think to be bold against some, which think of us as if we walked according to the flesh.

3 For though we walk in the flesh, we do not war after the flesh:

4 (For the weapons of our warfare are not carnal, but mighty through God to the pulling down of strong holds;)

5 Casting down imaginations, and every high thing that exalteth itself against the knowledge of God, and bringing into captivity every thought to the obedience of Christ;

6 And having in a readiness to revenge all disobedience, when your obedience is fulfilled.

7 Do ye look on things after the outward appearance? If any man trust to himself that he is Christ's, let him of himself think this again, that, as he is Christ's, even so are we Christ's.

8 For though I should boast somewhat more of our authority, which the Lord hath given us for edification, and not for your destruction, I should not be ashamed:

9 That I may not seem as if I would terrify you by letters.

10 For his letters, say they, are weighty and powerful; but his bodily presence is weak, and his speech contemptible.

11 Let such an one think this, that, such as we are in word by letters when we are absent, such will we be also in deed when we are present.

12 For we dare not make ourselves of the number, or compare ourselves with some that commend themselves: but they measuring themselves by themselves, and comparing themselves among themselves, are not wise.

13 But we will not boast of things without our measure, but according to the measure of the rule which God hath distributed to us, a measure to reach even unto you.

14 For we stretch not ourselves beyond our measure, as though we reached not unto you: for we are come as far as to you also in preaching the gospel of Christ:

15 Not boasting of things without our

9. He hath scattered abroad – (A generous word.) With a full hand, without any anxious thought which way each grain falls. His righteousness – His beneficence, with the blessed effects of it. Remaineth for ever – Unexhausted, God still renewing his store. Psalm cxii, 9.

10. And he who supplieth seed – Opportunity and ability to help others. And bread – All things needful for your own souls and bodies. Will continually supply you with that seed, yea, multiply it to you more and more. And increase the fruits of your righteousness – The happy effects of your love to God and man. Isaiah lv, 10.

11. Which worketh by us thanksgiving to God – Both from us who distribute, and them who receive, your bounty.

13. Your avowed subjection – Openly testified by your actions. To all men – Who stand in need of it.

15. His unspeakable gift – His outward and inward blessings, the number and excellence of which cannot be uttered.

2 CORINTHIANS 10

1. Now I Paul myself – A strongly emphatic expression. Who when present am base among you – So, probably, some of the false teachers affirmed. Copying after the meekness and gentleness of Christ, entreat – Though I might command you.

2. Do not constrain me when present to be bold – To exert my apostolic authority. Who think of us as walking after the flesh – As acting in a cowardly or crafty manner.

3. Though we walk in the flesh – In mortal bodies, and, consequently, are not free from human weakness. Yet we do not war – Against the world and the devil. After the flesh – By any carnal or worldly methods. Though the apostle here, and in several other parts of this epistle, speaks in the plural number, for the sake of modesty and decency, yet he principally means himself. On him were these reflections thrown, and it is his own authority which he is vindicating.

4. For the weapons of our warfare – Those we use in this war. Are not carnal – But spiritual, and therefore mighty to the throwing down of strong holds – Of all the difficulties which men or devils can raise in our way. Though faith and prayer belong also to the Christian Armor, Eph. vi, 15, &c., yet the word of God seems to be here chiefly intended.

5. Destroying all vain reasonings, and every high thing which exalteth itself – As a wall or rampart. Against the knowledge of God, and bringing every thought – Or, rather, faculty of the mind. Into captivity to the obedience of Christ – Those evil reasonings are destroyed. The mind itself, being overcome and taken captive, lays down all authority of its own, and entirely gives itself up to perform, for the time to come, to Christ its conqueror the obedience of faith.

6. Being in readiness to avenge all disobedience – Not only by spiritual censure, but miraculous punishments. When your obedience is fulfilled – When the sound part of you have given proof of your obedience, so that I am in no danger of punishing the innocent with the guilty.

7. Do ye look at the outward appearance of things – Does any of you judge of a minister of Christ by his person, or any outward circumstance? Let him again think this of himself – Let him learn it from his own reflection, before I convince him by a severer method.

8. I should not be ashamed – As having said more than I could make good.

9. I say this, that I may not seem to terrify you by letters – Threatening more than I can perform.

10. His bodily presence is weak – His stature, says St. Chrysostom, was

MATTHEW HENRY

CHARLES H. SPURGEON

contends so powerfully against the love of Christ, that it is often necessary to stir up their minds by way of remembrance.

6-15 Money bestowed in charity, may to the carnal mind seem thrown away, but when given from proper principles, it is seed sown, from which a valuable increase may be expected. It should be given carefully. Works of charity, like other good works, should be done with thought and design. Due thought, as to our circumstances, and those we are about to relieve, will direct our gifts for charitable uses. Help should be given freely, be it more or less; not grudgingly, but cheerfully. While some scatter, and yet increase; others withhold more than is meet, and it tends to poverty. If we had more faith and love, we should waste less on ourselves, and sow more in hope of a plentiful increase. Can a man lose by doing that with which God is pleased? He is able to make all grace abound towards us, and to abound in us; to give a large increase of spiritual and of temporal good things. He can make us to have enough in all things; and to be content with what we have. God gives not only enough for ourselves, but that also wherewith we may supply the wants of others, and this should be as seed to be sown. We must show the reality of our subjection to the gospel, by works of charity. This will be for the credit of our profession, and to the praise and glory of God. Let us endeavor to copy the example of Christ, being unwearied in doing good, and deeming it more blessed to give than to receive. Blessed be God for the unspeakable gift of his grace, whereby he enables and inclines some of his people to bestow upon others, and others to be grateful for it; and blessed be his glorious name to all eternity, for Jesus Christ, that inestimable gift of his love, through whom this and every other good thing, pertaining to life and godliness, are freely given unto us, beyond all expression, measure, or bounds.

2 CORINTHIANS 10

The apostle states his authority with meekness and humility. (1-6)

Reasons with the Corinthians. (7-11)

Seeks the glory of God, and to be approved of him. (12-18)

1-6 While others thought meanly, and spake scornfully of the apostle, he had low thoughts, and spake humbly of himself. We should be aware of our own infirmities, and think humbly of ourselves, even when men reproach us. The work of the ministry is a spiritual warfare with spiritual enemies, and for spiritual purposes. Outward force is not the method of the gospel, but strong persuasions, by the power of truth and the meekness of wisdom. Conscience is

means, he who knows what it is to stand where Christ stands, will never care to occupy the ground on which Mr. Maurice stands. He who has ever been made to sit together with Christ, and once to enjoy the real preciousness of a transfer of Christ's righteousness to him and his sin to Christ, that man has eaten the bread of heaven, and will never renounce it for husks. No, my brethren, we could lay down our lives for this truth rather than give it up. No, we cannot by any means turn aside from this glorious stability of faith, and for this good reason, that there is nothing for us in the doctrine which these men teach. It may suit intellectual gentlefolk, I dare say it does; but it will not suit us. We are poor sinners and nothing at all, and if Christ is not our all in all, there is nothing for us. I have often thought the best answer for all these new ideas is, that the true gospel was always preached to the poor;—"The poor have the gospel preached to them."—I am sure that the poor will never learn the gospel of these new divines, for they cannot make head or tail of it, nor the rich either; for after you have read through one of their volumes, you have not the least idea of what the book is about, until you have read it through eight or nine times, and then you begin to think you are a very stupid being for ever having read such inflated heresy, for it sours your temper and makes you feel angry, to see the precious truths of God trodden under foot. Some of us must stand out against these attacks on truth, although we love not controversy. We rejoice in the liberty of our fellow-men, and would have them proclaim their convictions; but if they touch these precious things, they touch the apple of our eye. We can allow a thousand opinions in the world, but that which infringes upon the precious doctrine of a covenant salvation, through the imputed righteousness of our Lord Jesus Christ,—against that we must, and will, enter our hearty and solemn protest, as long as God spares us. Take away once from us those glorious doctrines, and where are we brethren? We may lay us down and die, for nothing remains that is worth living for. We have come to the valley of the shadow of death, when we find these doctrines to be untrue. If these things which I speak to you tonight be not the verities of Christ; if they be not true, there is no comfort left for any poor man under God's sky, and it were better for us never to have been born. I may say what Jonathan Edwards says at the end of his book, "If any man could disprove the doctrines of the gospel, he should then sit down and weep to think they were not true, for," says he, "it

measure, that is, of other men's labors; but having hope, when your faith is increased, that we shall be enlarged by you according to our rule abundantly,

16 To preach the gospel in the regions beyond you, and not to boast in another man's line of things made ready to our hand.

17 But he that glorieth, let him glory in the Lord.

18 For not he that commendeth himself is approved, but whom the Lord commendeth.

2 CORINTHIANS 11

1 Would to God ye could bear with me a little in my folly: and indeed bear with me.

2 For I am jealous over you with godly jealousy: for I have espoused you to one husband, that I may present you as a chaste virgin to Christ.

3 But I fear, lest by any means, as the serpent beguiled Eve through his subtilty, so your minds should be corrupted from the simplicity that is in Christ.

4 For if he that cometh preacheth another Jesus, whom we have not preached, or if ye receive another spirit, which ye have not received, or another gospel, which ye have not accepted, ye might well bear with him.

5 For I suppose I was not a whit behind the very chiefest apostles.

6 But though I be rude in speech, yet not in knowledge; but we have been throughly made manifest among you in all things.

7 Have I committed an offense in abasing myself that ye might be exalted, because I have preached to you the gospel of God freely?

8 I robbed other churches, taking wages of them, to do you service.

9 And when I was present with you, and wanted, I was chargeable to no man: for that which was lacking to me the brethren which came from Macedonia supplied: and in all things I have kept myself from being burdensome unto you, and so will I keep myself.

10 As the truth of Christ is in me, no man shall stop me of this boasting in the regions of Achaia.

11 Wherefore? because I love you not? God knoweth.

12 But what I do, that I will do, that I may cut off occasion from them which

low, his body crooked, and his head bald.

12. For we presume not – A strong irony. To equal ourselves – As partners of the same office. Or to compare ourselves – As partakers of the same labor. They among themselves limiting themselves – Choosing and limiting their provinces according to their own fancy.

13. But we will not, like them, boastingly extend ourselves beyond our measure, but according to the measure of the province which God hath allotted us – To me, in particular, as the apostle of the Gentiles. A measure which reaches even unto you – God allotted to each apostle his province, and the measure or bounds thereof.

14. We are come even to you – By a gradual, regular process, having taken the intermediate places in our way, in preaching the gospel of Christ.

15. Having hope, now your faith is increased – So that you can the better spare us. To be enlarged by you abundantly – That is, enabled by you to go still further.

16. In the regions beyond you – To the west and south, where the gospel had not yet been preached.

2 CORINTHIANS 11

1. I wish ye would bear – So does he pave the way for what might otherwise have given offense. With my folly – Of commending myself; which to many may appear folly; and really would be so, were it not on this occasion absolutely necessary.

2. For – The cause of his seeming folly is expressed in this and the following verse; the cause why they should bear with him, 2 Cor. xi, 4.

3. But I fear – Love is full of these fears. Lest as the serpent – A most apposite comparison. Deceived Eve – Simple, ignorant of evil. By his subtlety – Which is in the highest degree dangerous to such a disposition. So your minds – We might therefore be tempted, even if there were no sin in us. Might be corrupted – Losing their virginal purity. From the simplicity that is in Christ – That simplicity which is lovingly intent on him alone, seeking no other person or thing.

4. If indeed – Any could show you another Savior, a more powerful Spirit, a better gospel. Ye might well bear with him – But this is impossible.

6. If I am unskillful in speech – If I speak in a plain, unadorned way, like an unlearned person. So the Greek word properly signifies.

7. Have I committed an offense – Will any turn this into an objection? In humbling myself – To work at my trade. That ye might be exalted – To be children of God.

8. I spoiled other churches – I, as it were, took the spoils of them: it is a military term. Taking wages (or pay, another military word) of them – When I came to you at first. And when I was present with you, and wanted – My work not quite supplying my necessities. I was chargeable to no man – Of Corinth.

9. For – I choose to receive help from the poor Macedonians, rather than the rich Corinthians! Were the poor in all ages more generous than the rich?

10. This my boasting shall not be stopped – For I will receive nothing from you.

11. Do I refuse to receive anything of you, because I love you not? God knoweth that is not the case.

12. Who desire any occasion – To censure me. That wherein they boast, they may be found even as we – They boasted of being "burdensome to no man." But it was a vain boast in them, though not in the apostle.

14. Satan himself is transformed – Uses to transform himself; to put on the

MATTHEW HENRY

accountable to God only; and people must be persuaded to God and their duty, not driven by force. Thus the weapons of our warfare are very powerful; the evidence of truth is convincing. What opposition is made against the gospel, by the powers of sin and Satan in the hearts of men! But observe the conquest the word of God gains. The appointed means, however feeble they appear to some, will be mighty through God. And the preaching of the cross, by men of faith and prayer, has always been fatal to idolatry, impiety, and wickedness.

7-11 In outward appearance, Paul was mean and despised in the eyes of some, but this was a false rule to judge by. We must not think that lack of outward appearance, as if the want of such things proved a man not to be a real Christian, or an able, faithful minister of the lowly Savior.

12-18 If we would compare ourselves with others who excel us, this would be a good method to keep us humble. The apostle fixes a good rule for his conduct; namely, not to boast of things without his measure, which was the measure God had distributed to him. There is not a more fruitful source of error, than to judge of persons and opinions by our own prejudices. How common is it for persons to judge of their own religious character, by the opinions and maxims of the world around them! But how different is the rule of God's word! And of all flattery, self-flattery is the worst. Therefore, instead of praising ourselves, we should strive to approve ourselves to God. In a word, let us glory in the Lord our salvation, and in all other things only as evidences of his love, or means of promoting his glory. Instead of praising ourselves, or seeking the praise of men, let us desire that honor which cometh from God only.

2 CORINTHIANS 11

The apostle gives the reasons for speaking in his own commendation. (1-14)
Shows that he had freely preached the gospel. (5-15)
Explains what he was going to add in defense of his own character. (16-21)
He gives an account of his labors, cares, sufferings, dangers, and deliverances. (22-33)

1-4 The apostle desired to preserve the Corinthians from being corrupted by the false apostles. There is but one Jesus, one Spirit, and one gospel, to be preached to them, and received by them; and why should any be prejudiced, by the devices of an adversary, against him who first taught them in faith? They should not listen to men, who, without cause, would draw them away from those who were the means of their conversion.

CHARLES H. SPURGEON

would be the most dreadful calamity that could happen to the world, to have a glimpse of such truths, and then for them to melt away in the thin air of fiction, as having no substantiality in them." Stand up for the truth of Christ; I would not have you be bigoted, but I would have you be decided. Do not give countenance to any of this trash and error, which is going abroad, but stand firm. Be not turned away from your steadfastness by any pretense of intellectuality and high philosophy, but earnestly contend for the faith once delivered to he saints, and hold fast the form of sound words which you have heard of us, and have been taught, even as ye have read in this sacred Book, which is the way of everlasting life.

Thus then, beloved, without gathering up my strength for the fray, or attempting to analyze the subtleties of those who would pervert the simple gospel, I speak out my mind and utter the kindling of my heart among you. Little enough will ye reck, over whom the Holy Ghost hath given me the oversight, what the grievous wolves may design, if ye keep within the fold. Break not the sacred bounds wherein God hath enclosed his Church. He hath encircled us in the arms of covenant love. He hath united us in indissoluble bonds to the Lord Jesus. He hath fortified us with the assurance that the Holy Spirit shall guide us into all truth. God grant that those beyond the pale of visible fellowship with us in this eternal gospel may see their danger and escape from the fowler's snare!

PRAISE FOR THE GIFT OF GIFTS
Sermon delivered by C. H. Spurgeon at the Metropolitan Tabernacle, Newington, on July 27th, 1890.

"Thanks be unto God for his unspeakable gift."—2 Corinthians 9:15.

In the chapter from which my text is taken, Paul is stirring up the Christians at Corinth to be ready with liberal gifts for the poor saints at Jerusalem. He finishes by reminding them of a greater gift than any they could bring, and by this one short word of praise, "Thanks be unto God for his unspeakable gift," he sets all their hearts a-singing. Let men give as liberally as they may, you can always proclaim the value of their gift; you can cast it up, and reckon its worth; but God's gift is unspeakable, unreckonable. You cannot fully estimate the value of what God gives. The gospel is a gospel of giving and forgiving. We may sum it up in those two

desire occasion; that wherein they glory, they may be found even as we.

13 For such are false apostles, deceitful workers, transforming themselves into the apostles of Christ.

14 And no marvel; for Satan himself is transformed into an angel of light.

15 Therefore it is no great thing if his ministers also be transformed as the ministers of righteousness; whose end shall be according to their works.

16 I say again, Let no man think me a fool; if otherwise, yet as a fool receive me, that I may boast myself a little.

17 That which I speak, I speak it not after the Lord, but as it were foolishly, in this confidence of boasting.

18 Seeing that many glory after the flesh, I will glory also.

19 For ye suffer fools gladly, seeing ye yourselves are wise.

20 For ye suffer, if a man bring you into bondage, if a man devour you, if a man take of you, if a man exalt himself, if a man smite you on the face.

21 I speak as concerning reproach, as though we had been weak. Howbeit whereinsoever any is bold, (I speak foolishly,) I am bold also.

22 Are they Hebrews? so am I. Are they Israelites? so am I. Are they the seed of Abraham? so am I.

23 Are they ministers of Christ? (I speak as a fool) I am more; in labors more abundant, in stripes above measure, in prisons more frequent, in deaths oft.

24 Of the Jews five times received I forty stripes save one.

25 Thrice was I beaten with rods, once was I stoned, thrice I suffered shipwreck, a night and a day I have been in the deep;

26 In journeyings often, in perils of waters, in perils of robbers, in perils by mine own countrymen, in perils by the heathen, in perils in the city, in perils in the wilderness, in perils in the sea, in perils among false brethren;

27 In weariness and painfulness, in watchings often, in hunger and thirst, in fastings often, in cold and nakedness.

28 Beside those things that are without, that which cometh upon me daily, the care of all the churches.

29 Who is weak, and I am not weak? who is offended, and I burn not?

30 If I must needs glory, I will glory of the things which concern mine infirmities.

31 The God and Father of our Lord

fairest appearances.

15. Therefore it is no great, no strange, thing; whose end, notwithstanding all their disguises, shall be according to their works.

16. I say again – He premises a new apology to this new commendation of himself. Let no man think me a fool – Let none think I do this without the utmost necessity. But if any do think me foolish herein, yet bear with my folly.

17. I speak not after the Lord – Not by an express command from him; though still under the direction of his Spirit. But as it were foolishly – In such a manner as many may think foolish.

18. After the flesh – That is, in external things.

19. Being wise – A beautiful irony.

20. For ye suffer – Not only the folly, but the gross abuses, of those false apostles. If a man enslave you – Lord it over you in the most arbitrary manner. If he devour you – By his exorbitant demands; not withstanding his boast of not being burdensome. If he take from you – By open violence. If he exalt himself – By the most unbounded self-commendation. If he smite you on the face – (A very possible case,) under pretense of divine zeal.

21. I speak with regard to reproach, as though we had been weak – I say, "Bear with me," even on supposition that the weakness be real which they reproach me with.

22. Are they Hebrews, Israelites, the seed of Abraham – These were the heads on which they boasted.

23. I am more so than they. In deaths often – Surrounding me in the most dreadful forms.

24. Five times I received from the Jews forty stripes save one – Which was the utmost that the law allowed. With the Romans he sometimes pleaded his privilege as a Roman; but from the Jews he suffered all things.

25. Thrice I have been shipwrecked – Before his voyage to Rome. In the deep – Probably floating on some part of the vessel.

27. In cold and nakedness – Having no place where to lay my head; no convenient raiment to cover me; yet appearing before noble-men, governors, kings; and not being ashamed.

28. Beside the things which are from without – Which I suffer on the account of others; namely, the care of all the churches – A more modest expression than if he had said, the care of the whole church. All – Even those I have not seen in the flesh. St. Peter himself could not have said this in so strong a sense.

29. Who – So he had not only the care of the churches, but of every person therein. Is weak, and I am not weak – By sympathy, as well as by condescension. Who is offended – Hindered in, or turned out of, the good way. And I burn not – Being pained as though I had fire in my bosom.

30. I will glory of the things that concern my infirmities – Of what shows my weakness, rather than my strength.

32. The governor under Aretas – King of Arabia and Syria of which Damascus was a chief city, willing to oblige the Jews, kept the city – Setting guards at all the gates day and night.

33. Through a window – Of an house which stood on the city wall.

MATTHEW HENRY

5-15 It is far better to be plain in speech, yet walking openly and consistently with the gospel, than to be admired by thousands, and be lifted up in pride, so as to disgrace the gospel by evil tempers and unholy lives. The apostle would not give room for any to accuse him of worldly designs in preaching the gospel, that others who opposed him at Corinth, might not in this respect gain advantage against him. Hypocrisy may be looked for, especially when we consider the great power which Satan, who rules in the hearts of the children of disobedience, has upon the minds of many. And as there are temptations to evil conduct, so there is equal danger on the other side. It serves Satan's purposes as well, to set up good works against the atonement of Christ, and salvation by faith and grace. But the end will discover those who are deceitful workers; their work will end in ruin. Satan will allow his ministers to preach either the law or the gospel separately; but the law as established by faith in Christ's righteousness and atonement, and the partaking of his Spirit, is the test of every false system.

16-21 It is the duty and practice of Christians to humble themselves, in obedience to the command and example of the Lord; yet prudence must direct in what it is needful to do things which we may do lawfully, even the speaking of what God has wrought for us, and in us, and by us. Doubtless here is reference to facts in which the character of the false apostles had been shown. It is astonishing to see how such men bring their followers into bondage, and how they take from them and insult them.

22-33 The apostle gives an account of his labors and sufferings; not out of pride or vain-glory, but to the honor of God, who enabled him to do and suffer so much for the cause of Christ; and shows wherein he excelled the false apostles, who tried to lessen his character and usefulness. It astonishes us to reflect on this account of his dangers, hardships, and sufferings, and to observe his patience, perseverance, diligence, cheerfulness, and usefulness, in the midst of all these trials. See what little reason we have to love the pomp and plenty of this world, when this blessed apostle felt so much hardship in it. Our utmost diligence and services appear unworthy of notice when compared with his, and our difficulties and trials scarcely can be perceived. It may well lead us to inquire whether or not we really are followers of Christ. Here we may study patience, courage, and firm trust in God. Here we may learn to think less of ourselves; and we should ever strictly keep to truth, as in God's presence; and should refer all to his glory, as the Father of our Lord Jesus Christ, who is blessed for evermore.

CHARLES H. SPURGEON

words; and hence, when the true spirit of it works upon the Christian, he forgives freely, and he also gives freely. The large heart of God breeds large hearts in men, and they who live upon his bounty are led by his Spirit to imitate that bounty, according to their power.

However, I am not going, on the present occasion, to say anything upon the subject of liberality. I must get straight away to the text, hoping that we may really drink in the spirit of it, and out of full hearts use the apostle's language with intenser meaning than ever as we repeat his words: "Thanks be unto God for his unspeakable gift." I shall commence by saying that salvation is altogether the gift of God, and as such is to be received by us freely. Then I shall try to show that this gift is unspeakable; and, in the third place, that for this gift thanks should be rendered to God. Though it is unspeakable, yet we should speak our praise of it. In this way you will see, as of old preachers used to say, the text naturally falls apart.

I. We begin with the thought that SALVATION IS ALTOGETHER THE GIFT OF GOD. Paul said, "Thanks be unto God for his unspeakable gift." Over and over and over again, have we to proclaim that salvation is wholly of grace: not of works nor of wages, but it is the gift of God's great bounty to undeserving men. Often as we have preached this truth, we shall have to keep on doing so as long as there are men in the world who are self-righteous, and as long as there are minds in the world so slow to grasp the meaning of the word "grace," that is, "free favor," and as long as there are memories that find it difficult to retain the idea of salvation being God's free gift.

Let us say simply and plainly, that salvation must come to us as a gift from God, for salvation comes to us by the Lord Jesus, and what else could Jesus be? The essence of salvation is the gift of God's Only-begotten Son to die for us, that we might live through him. I think you will agree with me that it is inconceivable that men should ever have merited that God should give his Only-begotten Son to them. To give Christ to us, in any sense, must have been an act of divine charity; but to give him up to die on yonder cruel and bloody tree, to yield him up as a sacrifice for sin, must be a free favor, passing the limits of thought. It is not supposable that any man could deserve such love. It is plain that if man's sins needed a sacrifice, he did not deserve that a sacrifice should be found for him. The fact is that his need proves his demerit and his guiltiness. He deserves to die; he may be res-

Jesus Christ, which is blessed for evermore, knoweth that I lie not.

32 In Damascus the governor under Aretas the king kept the city of the Damascenes with a garrison, desirous to apprehend me:

33 And through a window in a basket was I let down by the wall, and escaped his hands.

2 CORINTHIANS 12

1 It is not expedient for me doubtless to glory. I will come to visions and revelations of the Lord.

2 I knew a man in Christ above fourteen years ago, (whether in the body, I cannot tell; or whether out of the body, I cannot tell: God knoweth;) such an one caught up to the third heaven.

3 And I knew such a man, (whether in the body, or out of the body, I cannot tell: God knoweth;)

4 How that he was caught up into paradise, and heard unspeakable words, which it is not lawful for a man to utter.

5 Of such an one will I glory: yet of myself I will not glory, but in mine infirmities.

6 For though I would desire to glory, I shall not be a fool; for I will say the truth: but now I forbear, lest any man should think of me above that which he seeth me to be, or that he heareth of me.

7 And lest I should be exalted above measure through the abundance of the revelations, there was given to me a thorn in the flesh, the messenger of Satan to buffet me, lest I should be exalted above measure.

8 For this thing I besought the Lord thrice, that it might depart from me.

9 And he said unto me, My grace is sufficient for thee: for my strength is made perfect in weakness. Most gladly therefore will I rather glory in my infirmities, that the power of Christ may rest upon me.

10 Therefore I take pleasure in infirmities, in reproaches, in necessities, in persecutions, in distresses for Christ's sake: for when I am weak, then am I strong.

11 I am become a fool in glorying; ye have compelled me: for I ought to have been commended of you: for in nothing am I behind the very chiefest apostles, though I be nothing.

12 Truly the signs of an apostle were wrought among you in all patience, in

2 CORINTHIANS 12

1. It is not expedient – Unless on so pressing occasion. Visions are seen; Revelations, heard.

2. I knew a man in Christ – That is, a Christian. It is plain from 2 Cor. xii, 6, 7, that he means himself, though in modesty he speaks as of a third person. Whether in the body or out of the body I know not – It is equally possible with God to present distant things to the imagination in the body, as if the soul were absent from it, and present with them; or to transport both soul and body for what time he pleases to heaven; or to transport the soul only thither for a season, and in the mean time to preserve the body fit for its re-entrance. But since the apostle himself did not know whether his soul was in the body, or whether one or both were actually in heaven, it would be vain curiosity for us to attempt determining it. The third heaven – Where God is; far above the aerial and the starry heaven. Some suppose it was here the apostle was let into the mystery of the future state of the church; and received his orders to turn from the Jews and go to the Gentiles.

3. Yea, I knew such a man – That at another time.

4. He was caught up into paradise – The seat of happy spirits in their separate state, between death and the resurrection. Things which it is not possible for man to utter – Human language being incapable of expressing them. Here he anticipated the joyous rest of the righteous that die in the Lord. But this rapture did not precede, but follow after, his being caught up to the third heaven: a strong intimation that he must first discharge his mission, and then enter into glory. And beyond all doubt, such a foretaste of it served to strengthen him in all his after trials, when he could call to mind the very joy that was prepared for him.

5. Of such an one I will – I might, glory; but I will not glory of myself – As considered in myself.

6. For if I should resolve to glory – Referring to, I might glory of such a glorious Revelation. I should not be a fool – That is, it could not justly be accounted folly to relate the naked truth. But I forbear – I speak sparingly of these things, for fear any one should think too highly of me – O where is this fear now to be found? Who is afraid of this?

7. There was given me – By the wise and gracious providence of God. A thorn in the flesh – A visitation more painful than any thorn sticking in the flesh. A messenger or angel of Satan to buffet me – Perhaps both visibly and invisibly; and the word in the original expresses the present, as well as the past, time. All kinds of affliction had befallen the apostle. Yet none of those did he deprecate. But here he speaks of one, as above all the rest, one that macerated him with weakness, and by the pain and ignominy of it prevented his being lifted up more, or, at least, not less, than the most vehement head ache could have done; which many of the ancients say he labored under. St. Paul seems to have had a fresh fear of these buffetings every moment, when he so frequently represses himself in his boasting, though it was extorted from him by the utmost necessity.

8. Concerning this – He had now forgot his being lifted up. I besought the Lord thrice – As our Lord besought his Father.

9. But he said to me – In answer to my third request. My grace is sufficient for thee – How tender a repulse! We see there may be grace where there is the quickest sense of pain. My strength is more illustriously displayed by the weakness of the instrument. Therefore I will glory in my weaknesses rather than my Revelations, that the strength of Christ may rest upon me – The Greek word properly means, may cover me all over like a tent. We ought most willingly to accept whatever tends to this end, however contrary to flesh and blood.

MATTHEW HENRY

CHARLES H. SPURGEON

2 CORINTHIANS 12

The apostle's revelations. (1-6)

Which were improved to his spiritual advantage. (7-10)

The signs of an apostle were in him. His purpose of making them a visit; but he expresses his fear lest he should have to be severe with some. (11-21)

1-6 There can be no doubt the apostle speaks of himself. Whether heavenly things were brought down to him, while his body was in a trance, as in the case of ancient prophets; or whether his soul was dislodged from the body for a time, and taken up into heaven, or whether he was taken up, body and soul together, he knew not. We are not capable, nor is it fit we should yet know, the particulars of that glorious place and state. He did not attempt to publish to the world what he had heard there, but he set forth the doctrine of Christ. On that foundation the church is built, and on that we must build our faith and hope. And while this teaches us to enlarge our expectations of the glory that shall be revealed, it should render us contented with the usual methods of learning the truth and will of God.

7-10 The apostle gives an account of the method God took to keep him humble, and to prevent his being lifted up above measure, on account of the visions and revelations he had. We are not told what this thorn in the flesh was, whether some great trouble, or some great temptation. But God often brings this good out of evil, that the reproaches of our enemies help to hide pride from us. If God loves us, he will keep us from being exalted above measure; and spiritual burdens are ordered to cure spiritual pride. This thorn in the flesh is said to be a messenger of Satan which he sent for evil; but God designed it, and overruled it for good. Prayer is a salve for every sore, a remedy for every malady; and when we are afflicted with thorns in the flesh, we should give ourselves to prayer. If an answer be not given to the first prayer, nor to the second, we are to continue praying. Troubles are sent to teach us to pray; and are continued, to teach us to continue instant in prayer. Though God accepts the prayer of faith, yet he does not always give what is asked for: as he sometimes grants in wrath, so he sometimes denies in love. When God does not take away our troubles and temptations, yet, if he gives grace enough for us, we have no reason to complain. Grace signifies the good will of God towards us, and that is enough to enlighten and enliven us, sufficient to strengthen and comfort in all afflictions and distresses. His strength is made perfect in our weakness. Thus his grace is manifested and magnified. When we are weak in ourselves, then we are strong in the grace of our Lord Jesus Christ; when we feel that we are weak in ourselves, then we go to

cued by Another dying for him; but he certainly cannot claim that the eternal God should take from his bosom his Only-begotten and Well-beloved Son, and put him to death. The more you look that thought in the face, the more you will reject the idea that, by any possible sorrow, or by any possible labor, or by any possible promise, a man could put himself into the position of deserving to have Christ to die for him. If Christ is to come to save sinners, it must be as a gift, a free gift of God. The argument, to my mind, is conclusive.

II. Now I would try to lead your thoughts in another direction as we consider that THIS GIFT IS UNSPEAKABLE. Do not think it means that we cannot speak about this gift. Ah, how many times have I, for one, spoken upon this gift during the last forty years! I have spoken of little else. I heard of one who said, "I suppose Spurgeon is preaching that old story over again." Yes, that is what he is doing; and if he lives another twenty years, and you come here, it will be "the old, old story" still, for there is nothing like it. It is inexhaustible; it is like an Artesian well that springeth up for ever and ever. We can speak about it; yet it is unspeakable. What mean we, then, by saying it is unspeakable? Well, as I have said already, Christ Jesus our Lord is the sum and substance of salvation, and of God's gift. O God, this gift of thine is unspeakable, and it includes all other gifts beside!

> "Thou didst not spare thine only Son,
> But gav'st him for a world undone,
> And freely with that Blessed One—
> Thou givest all."

Consider, first, that Christ is unspeakable in his person. He is perfect man, and glorious God. No tongue of seraph, or of cherub, can ever describe the full nature of him whose name is "Wonderful, Counselor, the mighty God, the everlasting Father, the Prince of peace." This is he whom the Father gave "for us men, and for our sakes." He was the Creator of all things, for "without him was not anything made that was made," yet he was "made of flesh and dwelt among us." He filleth all things by his omnipresence; yet he came and tabernacled on the earth. This is that Jesus, who was born of Mary, yet who lived before all worlds. He was that Word, who "was in the beginning with God, and the Word was God." He is unspeakable. It is not possible to put into human language the divine mystery of his sacred being, truly man and yet truly God. But how great the wonder of it! Soul, God gave God for thee! Dost thou hear it? To

signs, and wonders, and mighty deeds.

13 For what is it wherein ye were inferior to other churches, except it be that I myself was not burdensome to you? forgive me this wrong.

14 Behold, the third time I am ready to come to you; and I will not be burdensome to you: for I seek not yours, but you: for the children ought not to lay up for the parents, but the parents for the children.

15 And I will very gladly spend and be spent for you; though the more abundantly I love you, the less I be loved.

16 But be it so, I did not burden you: nevertheless, being crafty, I caught you with guile.

17 Did I make a gain of you by any of them whom I sent unto you?

18 I desired Titus, and with him I sent a brother. Did Titus make a gain of you? walked we not in the same spirit? walked we not in the same steps?

19 Again, think ye that we excuse ourselves unto you? we speak before God in Christ: but we do all things, dearly beloved, for your edifying.

20 For I fear, lest, when I come, I shall not find you such as I would, and that I shall be found unto you such as ye would not: lest there be debates, envyings, wraths, strifes, backbitings, whisperings, swellings, tumults:

21 And lest, when I come again, my God will humble me among you, and that I shall bewail many which have sinned already, and have not repented of the uncleanness and fornication and lasciviousness which they have committed.

2 CORINTHIANS 13

1 This is the third time I am coming to you. In the mouth of two or three witnesses shall every word be established.

2 I told you before, and foretell you, as if I were present, the second time; and being absent now I write to them which heretofore have sinned, and to all other, that, if I come again, I will not spare:

3 Since ye seek a proof of Christ speaking in me, which to you-ward is not weak, but is mighty in you.

4 For though he was crucified through weakness, yet he liveth by the power of God. For we also are weak in him, but we shall live with him by the power of God toward you.

10. Weaknesses – Whether proceeding from Satan or men. For when I am weak – Deeply conscious of my weakness, then does the strength of Christ rest upon me.

11. Though I am nothing – Of myself.

14. The third time – Having been disappointed twice. I seek not yours – Your goods. But you – Your souls.

15. I will gladly spend – All I have. And be spent – Myself.

16. But some may object, though I did not burden you, though I did not take anything of you myself, yet being crafty I caught you with guile – I did secretly by my messengers what I would not do openly, or in person.

17. I answer this lying accusation by appealing to plain fact. Did I make a gain of you by Titus – Or any other of my messengers? You know the contrary. It should be carefully observed, that St. Paul does not allow, but absolutely denies, that he had caught them with guile; so that the common plea for guile, which has been often drawn from this text, is utterly without foundation.

18. I desired Titus – To go to you.

19. Think ye that we again excuse ourselves – That I speak this for my own sake? No. I speak all this for your sakes.

21. Who had sinned before – My last coming to Corinth. Uncleanness – Of married persons. Lasciviousness – Against nature.

2 CORINTHIANS 13

1. I am coming this third time – He had been coming twice before, though he did not actually come.

2. All the rest – Who have since then sinned in any of these kinds. I will not spare – I will severely punish them.

4. He was crucified through weakness – Through the impotence of human nature. We also are weak with him – We appear weak and despicable by partaking of the same sufferings for his sake. But we shall live with him – Being raised from the dead. By the power of God in you – By that divine energy which is now in every believer, 2 Cor. xiii, 5.

5. Prove yourselves – Whether ye are such as can, or such as cannot, bear the test – This is the proper meaning of the word which we translate, reprobates. Know ye not yourselves, that Jesus Christ is in you – All Christian believers know this, by the witness and by the fruit of his Spirit. Some translate the words, Jesus Christ is among you; that is, in the church of Corinth; and understand them of the miraculous gifts and the power of Christ which attended the censures of the apostle.

6. And I trust ye shall know – By proving yourselves, not by putting my authority to the proof.

7. I pray God that ye may do no evil – To give me occasion of showing my apostolic power. I do not desire to appear approved – By miraculously punishing you. But that ye may do that which is good, though we should be as reprobates – Having no occasion to give that proof of our apostleship.

8. For we can do nothing against the truth – Neither against that which is just and right, nor against those who walk according to the truth of the gospel.

9. For we rejoice when we are weak – When we appear so, having no occasion to show our apostolic power. And this we wish, even your perfection – In the faith that worketh by love.

11. Be perfect – Aspire to the highest degree of holiness. Be of good comfort – Filled with divine consolation. Be of one mind – Desire, labor, pray for it, to the utmost degree that is possible.

13. The grace – Or favor. Of our Lord Jesus Christ – By which alone we

Christ, receive strength from him, and enjoy most the supplies of Divine strength and grace.

11-21 We owe it to good men, to stand up in the defense of their reputation; and we are under special obligations to those from whom we have received benefit, especially spiritual benefit, to own them as instruments in God's hand of good to us. Here is an account of the apostle's behavior and kind intentions; in which see the character of a faithful minister of the gospel. This was his great aim and design, to do good. Here are noticed several sins commonly found among professors of religion. Falls and misdeeds are humbling to a minister; and God sometimes takes this way to humble those who might be tempted to be lifted up. These last verses show to what excesses the false teachers had drawn aside their deluded followers. How grievous it is that such evils should be found among professors of the gospel! Yet thus it is, and has been too often, and it was so even in the days of the apostles.

2 CORINTHIANS 13

The apostle threatens obstinate offenders. (1-6)
He prays for their reformation. (7-10)
And ends the epistle with a salutation and blessing. (11-14)

1-6 Though it is God's gracious method to bear long with sinners, yet he will not bear always; at length he will come, and will not spare those who remain obstinate and impenitent. Christ at his crucifixion, appeared as only a weak and helpless man, but his resurrection and life showed his Divine power. So the apostles, how mean and contemptible soever they appeared to the world, yet, as instruments, they manifested the power of God. Let them prove their tempers, conduct, and experience, as gold is assayed or proved by the touchstone. If they could prove themselves not to be reprobates, not to be rejected of Christ, he trusted they would know that he was not a reprobate, not disowned by Christ. They ought to know if Christ Jesus was in them, by the influences, graces, and indwelling of his Spirit, by his kingdom set up in their hearts. Let us question our own souls; either we are true Christians, or we are deceivers. Unless Christ be in us by his Spirit, and power of his love, our faith is dead, and we are yet disapproved by our Judge.

7-10 The most desirable thing we can ask of God, for ourselves and our friends, is to be kept from sin, that we and they may not do evil. We have far more need to pray that we may not do evil, than that we may not suffer evil. The apostle not only desired that they might be kept from sin, but also that they might grow

redeem thee, O believing man, God gave himself to be thy Savior; surely, that is an unspeakable gift.

Christ is unspeakable, next, in his condescension. Can any one measure or describe how far Christ stooped, when, from the throne of splendor, he came to a manger to be swaddled and lie where the horned oxen fed. Oh, what a stoop of condescension was that! The Infinite becomes an infant. The Eternal is dandled on a woman's knee. He is there in the carpenter's shop, obedient to his parents; there in the temple sitting among the doctors, hearing them and asking them questions; there in poverty, crying, "The Son of man hath not where to lay his head;" and there, in thirst, asking of a guilty woman a drink of water. It is unspeakable. That he, before whom all the hosts of heaven veiled their faces, should come here among men, and among the poorest of the poor—that he who dwelt amidst the glory and the bliss of the land of light, should deign to be a Man of sorrows and acquainted with grief, passes human thought! Such a Savior is a gift unspeakable.

III. Now, lastly, I come to this point, that FOR THIS GIFT THANKS SHOULD BE RENDERED. The text says, "Thanks be unto God for his unspeakable gift." By this the apostle not only meant that he gave thanks for Christ; but he thus calls upon the church, and upon every individual believer, to join him in his praise. Here do I adopt his language, and praise God on my own behalf, calling upon all of you who know the preciousness of Christ, the gift of God, to unite with me in thanksgiving. Let us as with one heart say it now, "Thanks be unto God for his unspeakable gift."

Some cannot say this, for they never think of the gift of God. You who never think of God, how can you thank God? There must be "think" at the bottom of "thank." Whenever we think, we ought to thank. But some never think, and therefore never thank. Beloved friend, what are you at? That Christ should die; is it nothing to you? That God "gave his Only-begotten Son, that whosoever believeth in him should not perish, but have everlasting life;" is that nothing to you? Let the question drop into your heart. Press it home upon yourself. Will you say that you have no share in this gift? Will you deliberately give up any hope you may have of ever partaking of the grace of God? Are you determined now to say, "I do not care about Christ"? Well, you would hardly like to say that; but why do you practically declare this to be your intention, if you do not want to say it? Oh, that you might now so think of Christ as to trust him at

5 Examine yourselves, whether ye be in the faith; prove your own selves. Know ye not your own selves, how that Jesus Christ is in you, except ye be reprobates?

6 But I trust that ye shall know that we are not reprobates.

7 Now I pray to God that ye do no evil; not that we should appear approved, but that ye should do that which is honest, though we be as reprobates.

8 For we can do nothing against the truth, but for the truth.

9 For we are glad, when we are weak, and ye are strong: and this also we wish, even your perfection.

10 Therefore I write these things being absent, lest being present I should use sharpness, according to the power which the Lord hath given me to edification, and not to destruction.

11 Finally, brethren, farewell. Be perfect, be of good comfort, be of one mind, live in peace; and the God of love and peace shall be with you.

12 Greet one another with an holy kiss.

13 All the saints salute you.

14 The grace of the Lord Jesus Christ, and the love of God, and the communion of the Holy Ghost, be with you all. Amen.

can come to the Father. And the love of God – Manifested to you, and abiding in you. And the communion – Or fellowship. Of the Holy Ghost – In all his gifts and graces. It is with great reason that this comprehensive and instructive blessing is pronounced at the close of our solemn assemblies; and it is a very indecent thing to see so many quitting them, or getting into postures of remove, before this short sentence can be ended. How often have we heard this awful benediction pronounced! Let us study it more and more, that we may value it proportionally; that we may either deliver or receive it with a becoming reverence, with eyes and hearts lifted up to God, "who giveth the blessing out of Sion, and life for evermore."

MATTHEW HENRY

CHARLES H. SPURGEON

in grace, and increase in holiness. We are earnestly to pray to God for those we caution, that they may cease to do evil, and learn to do well; and we should be glad for others to be strong in the grace of Christ, though it may be the means of showing our own weakness. let us also pray that we may be enabled to make a proper use of all our talents.

11-14 Here are several good exhortations. God is the Author of peace and Lover of concord; he hath loved us, and is willing to be at peace with us. And let it be our constant aim so to walk, that separation from our friends may be only for a time, and that we may meet in that happy world where parting will be unknown. He wishes that they may partake all the benefits which Christ of his free grace and favor has purchased; the Father out of his free love has purposed; and the Holy Ghost applies and bestows.

once, and begin to raise this note of praise!

Some, on the other hand, do not thank God because they are always delaying. Have I not hearers here tonight who were here ten years ago, and were rather more hopeful then than they are now? "There is plenty of time," say you; but you do not say this about other matters. I admired the children, the other day, when the teacher said, "Dear children, the weather is unsettled. You can go out next Wednesday; but do you not think it would be better to stop a month, so that we could go when the weather is more settled?" There was not a child that voted for stopping a month. All the hands we up for going next Wednesday. Now, imitate the children in that. Do not make it seem as if you were in no hurry to be happy; for as he that believeth in Christ hath eternal life, to postpone having it is an unworthy as well as unwise thing to do. No, you will have it, I hope, at once. There is a man here who is going to be a very rich man when his old aunt dies. You do not wish that she should die, I am sure; but you sometimes wonder why some people are spared to be ninety, do you not? You are very poor now, and you wish that some of this money could come to you at once; you are not for putting that off. Why should you put off heavenly riches and eternal life? I beseech you to believe in Christ now; then you will be filled with thankfulness and joy.

Beloved, may God help you thus to magnify his Son; and to him shall be all the praise! Let us again lift up our glad hallelujah: "Thanks be unto God for his unspeakable gift." Amen.

Galatians

GALATIANS 1

1 Paul, an apostle, (not of men, neither by man, but by Jesus Christ, and God the Father, who raised him from the dead;)
2 And all the brethren which are with me, unto the churches of Galatia:
3 Grace be to you and peace from God the Father, and from our Lord Jesus Christ,
4 Who gave himself for our sins, that he might deliver us from this present evil world, according to the will of God and our Father:
5 To whom be glory for ever and ever. Amen.
6 I marvel that ye are so soon removed from him that called you into the grace of Christ unto another gospel:
7 Which is not another; but there be some that trouble you, and would pervert the gospel of Christ.
8 But though we, or an angel from heaven, preach any other gospel unto you than that which we have preached unto you, let him be accursed.
9 As we said before, so say I now again, If any man preach any other gospel unto you than that ye have received, let him be accursed.
10 For do I now persuade men, or God? or do I seek to please men? for if I yet pleased men, I should not be the servant of Christ.
11 But I certify you, brethren, that the gospel which was preached of me is not after man.
12 For I neither received it of man, neither was I taught it, but by the revelation of Jesus Christ.
13 For ye have heard of my conversation in time past in the Jews' religion, how that beyond measure I persecuted the church of God, and wasted it:
14 And profited in the Jews' religion above many my equals in mine own nation, being more exceedingly zealous of the traditions of my fathers.
15 But when it pleased God, who separated me from my mother's womb, and called me by his grace,
16 To reveal his Son in me, that

THIS epistle is not written, as most of St. Paul's are, to the Christians of a particular city, but to those of a whole country in Asia Minor, the metropolis of which was Ancyra. These readily embraced the gospel; but, after St. Paul had left them, certain men came among them, who (like those mentioned, Acts xv, 1,) taught that it was necessary to be circumcized, and to keep the Mosaic law. They affirmed, that all the other apostles taught thus; that St. Paul was inferior to them; and that even he sometimes practiced and recommended the law, though at other times he opposed it. The first part, therefore, of this epistle is spent in vindicating himself and his doctrine; proving,

1. That he had it immediately from Christ himself; and that he was not inferior to the other apostles.
2. That it was the very same which the other apostles preached. And,
3. That his practice was consistent with his doctrine. The second contains proofs, drawn from the Old Testament, that the law and all its ceremonies were abolished by Christ. The third contains practical inferences, closed with his usual benediction. To be a little more distinct.

GALATIANS 1

1. Paul, an apostle – Here it was necessary for St. Paul to assert his authority; otherwise he is very modest in the use of this title. He seldom mentions it when he mentions others in the salutations with himself, as in the Epistles to the Philippians and Thessalonians; or when he writes about secular affairs, as in that to Philemon; nor yet in writing to the Hebrews because he was not properly their apostle. Not of men – Not commissioned from them, but from God the Father. Neither by man – Neither by any man as an instrument, but by Jesus Christ. Who raised him from the dead – Of which it was the peculiar business of an apostle to bear witness.
2. And all the brethren – Who agree with me in what I now write.
4. That he might deliver us from the present evil world – From the guilt, wickedness, and misery wherein it is involved, and from its vain and foolish customs and pleasures. According to the will of God – Without any merit of ours. St. Paul begins most of his epistles with thanksgiving; but, writing to the Galatians, he alters his style, and first sets down his main proposition, That by the merits of Christ alone, giving himself for our sins, we are justified: neither does he term them, as he does others, either saints, "elect," or "churches of God."
5. To whom be glory – For this his gracious will.
6. I marvel that ye are removed so soon – After my leaving you. From him who called you by the grace of Christ – His gracious gospel, and his gracious power.
7. Which, indeed, is not properly another gospel. For what ye have now received is no gospel at all; it is not glad, but heavy, tidings, as setting your acceptance with God upon terms impossible to be performed. But there are some that trouble you – The same word occurs, Acts xv, 24. And would – If they were able. Subvert or overthrow the gospel of Christ – The better to effect which, they suggest, that the other apostles, yea, and I myself, insist upon the observance of the law.
8. But if we – I and all the apostles. Or an angel from heaven – If it were possible. Preach another gospel, let him be accursed – Cut off from Christ and God.
9. As – He speaks upon mature deliberation; after pausing, it seems, between the two verses. We – I and the brethren who are with me. Have said before – Many times, in effect, if not in terms. So I say – All those brethren knew the truth of the gospel. St. Paul knew the Galatians had received the true gospel.
10. For – He adds the reason why he speaks so confidently. Do I now satisfy men – Is this what I aim at in preaching or writing? If I still – Since I was an apostle. Pleased men – Studied to please them; if this were my motive of action; nay, if I did in fact please the men who know not God. I should not be the servant of Christ – Hear this, all ye who vainly hope to keep in favor both with God and

The churches in Galatia were formed partly of converted Jews, and partly of Gentile converts, as was generally the case. St. Paul asserts his apostolic character and the doctrines he taught, that he might confirm the Galatian churches in the faith of Christ, especially with respect to the important point of justification by faith alone. Thus the subject is mainly the same as that which is discussed in the epistle to the Romans, that is, justification by faith alone. In this epistle, however, attention is particularly directed to the point, that men are justified by faith without the works of the law of Moses. Of the importance of the doctrines prominently set forth in this epistle, Luther thus speaks: "We have to fear as the greatest and nearest danger, lest Satan take from us this doctrine of faith, and bring into the church again the doctrine of works and of men's traditions. Wherefore it is very necessary that this doctrine be kept in continual practice and public exercise, both of reading and hearing. If this doctrine be lost, then is also the doctrine of truth, life and salvation, lost and gone."

GALATIANS 1

The apostle Paul asserts his apostolic character against such as lessened it. (1-5)

He reproves the Galatians for revolting from the gospel of Christ under the influence of evil teachers. (6-9)

He proves the Divine authority of his doctrine and mission; and declares what he was before his conversion and calling. (10-14)

And how he proceeded after it. (15-24)

1-5 St. Paul was an apostle of Jesus Christ; he was expressly appointed by him, consequently by God the Father, who is one with him in respect of his Divine nature, and who appointed Christ as Mediator. Grace, includes God's good will towards us, and his good work upon us; and peace, all that inward comfort, or outward prosperity, which is really needful for us. They come from God the Father, as the Fountain, through Jesus Christ. But observe, first grace, and then peace; there can be no true peace without grace. Christ gave himself for our sins, to make atonement for us: this the justice of God required, and to this he freely submitted. Here is to be observed the infinite greatness of the price bestowed, and then it will appear plainly, that the power of sin is so great, that it could by no means be put away except the Son of God be given for it. He that considers these things well, understands that sin is a thing the most horrible that can be expressed; which ought to move us, and make us afraid indeed. Especially mark well the words, "for our sins." For here our weak nature starts back, and would first be made worthy by her own works. It would bring him that is whole, and not him that has need of a physician. Not only to redeem us from the wrath of God, and the curse of the law; but also to recover us from wicked practices and customs, to which we are naturally enslaved. But it

THE CURSE REMOVED
Sermon number 3254 published on Thursday, June 15th, 1911.

"Christ hath redeemed us from the curse of the law, being made a curse for us; for it is written, Cursed is every one that hangeth on a tree."— Galatians 3:13.

THE law of God is a divine law, holy, heavenly, perfect. Those who find fault with the law, or in the least degree depreciate it, do not understand its design, and have no right idea of the law itself. Paul says, "the law is holy, but I am carnal; sold under sin." In all we ever say concerning justification by faith, we never intend to lower the opinion which our hearers have of the law, for the law is one of the most sublime of God's works. There is not a commandment too many; there is not one too few; but it is so incomparable, that its perfection is a proof of its divinity. No human lawgiver could have given forth such a law as that which we find in the Decalogue. It is a perfect law; for all human laws that are right are to be found in that brief compendium and epitome of all that is good and excellent toward God, or between man and man.

But while the law is glorious, it is never more misapplied than when it is used as a means of salvation. God never intended men to be saved by the law. When he proclaimed it on Sinai, it was with thunder, fire, and smoke; as if he would say, "O man, hear my law; but thou shalt tremble while thou hearest it." Hear it! It is a law which hath the blast of a terrible trumpet, even like the day of destruction, of which it is but the herald, if thou offendest it, and findest none to bear the doom for thee. It was written on stone; as if to teach us that it was a hard, cold, stony law—one which would have no mercy upon us, but which, if we break it, would fall upon us, and dash us into a thousand pieces. O ye who trust in the law for your salvation! ye have erred from the faith; ye do not understand God's designs; ye are ignorant of every one of God's truths. The law was given by Moses to make men feel themselves condemned, but never to save them; its very intention was to "conclude us all in unbelief, and to condemn us all, that he might have mercy upon all." It was intended by its thunders to crush every hope of self-righteousness, by its lightning to scathe and demolish every tower of our own works, that we might be brought humbly and simply to accept a finished salvation through the one mighty Mediator who has "finished the law, and made it honorable, and brought in an everlasting righteousness," whereby we stand,

I might preach him among the heathen; immediately I conferred not with flesh and blood:

17   Neither went I up to Jerusalem to them which were apostles before me; but I went into Arabia, and returned again unto Damascus.

18 Then after three years I went up to Jerusalem to see Peter, and abode with him fifteen days.

19 But other of the apostles saw I none, save James the Lord's brother.

20 Now the things which I write unto you, behold, before God, I lie not.

21 Afterwards I came into the regions of Syria and Cilicia;

22 And was unknown by face unto the churches of Judea which were in Christ:

23 But they had heard only, That he which persecuted us in times past now preacheth the faith which once he destroyed.

24 And they glorified God in me.

GALATIANS 2

1 Then fourteen years after I went up again to Jerusalem with Barnabas, and took Titus with me also.

2 And I went up by revelation, and communicated unto them that gospel which I preach among the Gentiles, but privately to them which were of reputation, lest by any means I should run, or had run, in vain.

3 But neither Titus, who was with me, being a Greek, was compelled to be circumcized:

4 And that because of false brethren unawares brought in, who came in privily to spy out our liberty which we have in Christ Jesus, that they might bring us into bondage:

5 To whom we gave place by subjection, no, not for an hour; that the truth of the gospel might continue with you.

6 But of these who seemed to be somewhat, (whatsoever they were, it maketh no matter to me: God accepteth no man's person:) for they who seemed to be somewhat in conference added nothing to me:

7 But contrariwise, when they saw that the gospel of the uncir-

with the world!

11. But I certify you, brethren – He does not till now give them even this appellation. That the gospel which was preached by me among you is not according to man – Not from man, not by man, not suited to the taste of man.

12. For neither did I receive it – At once. Nor was I taught it – Slowly and gradually, by any man. But by the Revelation of Jesus Christ – Our Lord revealed to him at first, his resurrection, ascension, and the calling of the Gentiles, and his own apostleship; and told him then, there were other things for which he would appear to him.

13. I Persecuted the church of God – That is, the believers in Christ.

14. Being zealous of the unwritten traditions – Over and above those written in the law.

16. To reveal his Son in me – By the powerful operation of his Spirit, chap. iv, 6; as well as to me, by the heavenly vision. That I might preach him to others – Which I should have been ill qualified to do, had I not first known him myself. I did not confer with flesh and blood – Being fully satisfied of the divine will, and determined to obey, I took no counsel with any man, neither with my own reason or inclinations, which might have raised numberless objections.

17. Neither did I go up to Jerusalem – The residence of the apostles. But I immediately went again into Arabia, and returned again to Damascus – He presupposes the journey to Damascus, in which he was converted, as being known to them all.

18. Then after three years – Wherein I had given full proof of my apostleship. I went to visit Peter – To converse with him.

19. But other of the apostles I saw none, save James the brother (that is, the kinsman) of the Lord – Therefore when Barnabas is said to have "brought him into the apostles," Acts ix, 27, only St. Peter and St James are meant.

24. In me – That is, on my account.

GALATIANS 2

1. Then fourteen years after – My first journey thither. I went up again to Jerusalem – This seems to be the journey mentioned Acts xv, 2; several passages here referring to that great council, wherein all the apostles showed that they were of the same judgment with him.

2. I went up – Not by any command from them, but by an express Revelation from God. And laid before them – The chief of the church in Jerusalem. The gospel which I preach among the Gentiles – Acts xv, 4, touching justification by faith alone; not that they might confirm me therein, but that I might remove prejudice from them. Yet not publicly at first, but severally to those of eminence – Speaking to them one by one. Lest I should run, or should have run, in vain – Lest I should lose the fruit either of my present or past labors. For they might have greatly hindered this, had they not been fully satisfied both of his mission and doctrine. The word run beautifully expresses the swift progress of the gospel.

3. But neither was Titus who was with me – When I conversed with them. Compelled to be circumcized – A clear proof that none of the apostles insisted on the circumcising Gentile believers. The sense is, And it is true, some of those false brethren would fain have compelled Titus to be circumcized; but I utterly refused it.

4. Because of false brethren – Who seem to have urged it. Introduced unawares – Into some of those private conferences at Jerusalem. Who had slipped in to spy out our liberty – From the ceremonial law. That they might, if possible, bring us into that bondage again.

5. To whom we did not yield by submission – Although in love he would have yielded to any. With such wonderful prudence did the apostle use his Christian liberty! circumcising Timothy, Acts xvi, 3, because of weak brethren, but not

MATTHEW HENRY   CHARLES H. SPURGEON

is in vain for those who are not delivered from this present evil world by the sanctification of the Spirit, to expect that they are freed from its condemnation by the blood of Jesus.

6-9 Those who would establish any other way to heaven than what the gospel of Christ reveals, will find themselves wretchedly mistaken. The apostle presses upon the Galatians a due sense of their guilt in forsaking the gospel way of justification; yet he reproves with tenderness, and represents them as drawn into it by the arts of some that troubled them. In reproving others, we should be faithful, and yet endeavor to restore them in the spirit of meekness. Some would set up the works of the law in the place of Christ's righteousness, and thus they corrupted Christianity. The apostle solemnly denounces, as accursed, every one who attempts to lay so false a foundation. All other gospels than that of the grace of Christ, whether more flattering to self-righteous pride, or more favorable to worldly lusts, are devices of Satan. And while we declare that to reject the moral law as a rule of life, tends to dishonor Christ, and destroy true religion, we must also declare, that all dependence for justification on good works, whether real or supposed, is as fatal to those who persist in it. While we are zealous for good works, let us be careful not to put them in the place of Christ's righteousness, and not to advance any thing which may betray others into so dreadful a delusion.

10-14 In preaching the gospel, the apostle sought to bring persons to the obedience, not of men, but of God. But Paul would not attempt to alter the doctrine of Christ, either to gain their favor, or to avoid their fury. In so important a matter we must not fear the frowns of men, nor seek their favor, by using words of men's wisdom. Concerning the manner wherein he received the gospel, he had it by revelation from Heaven. He was not led to Christianity, as many are, merely by education.

15-24 St. Paul was wonderfully brought to the knowledge and faith of Christ. All who are savingly converted, are called by the grace of God; their conversion is wrought by his power and grace working in them. It will but little avail us to have Christ revealed to us, if he is not also revealed in us. He instantly prepared to obey, without hesitating as to his worldly interest, credit, ease, or life itself. And what matter of thanksgiving and joy is it to the churches of Christ, when they hear of such instances to the praise of the glory of his grace, whether they have ever seen them or not!

GALATIANS 2

The apostle declares his being owned as an apostle of the Gentiles. (1-10)
He had publicly opposed Peter for judaizing. (11-14)

stand complete before our Maker at last, if we be in Christ. All that the law doth, you will observe, is to curse; it can not bless. In all the pages of revelation you will find no blessings that the law ever gave to one that offended it. There were blessings, and those were comparatively small, which might be gained by those who kept it thoroughly; but no blessing is ever written for one offender. Blessings we find in the gospel; curses we find in the law.

This afternoon we shall briefly consider, first, the curse of the law; secondly, the curse removed; thirdly, the great Substitute who removed it—"He was made a curse for us." And then we shall come, in the last place, solemnly to ask each other, whether we are included in the mighty number for whom Christ did bear iniquities, and for whom "He was made a curse."

I. First, then, THE CURSE OF THE LAW. All who sin against the law are cursed by the law; all who rebel against its commands are cursed—cursed instantly, cursed terribly.

1. We shall regard that curse, first as being a universal curse, resting upon every one of the seed of Adam. Perhaps some here will be inclined to say, "Of course the law of God will curse all those who are loose in their lives, or profane in their conversation. We can all of us imagine that the swearer is a cursed man, cursed by God. We can suppose that the wrath of God rests upon the head of the man who is filthy in his life, and whose conversation is not upright, or who is a degraded man, under the ban of society." But ah! my friend, it is not quite so easy to get at the real truth, which is this, that the curse of God rests upon every one of us, as by nature we stand before him. Thou mayest be the most moral in the world, but yet the curse of God is upon thee; thou mayest be lovely in thy life, modest in thy carriage, upright in thy behavior, almost Christlike in thy conduct, yet, if thou hast not been born again, and regenerated by sovereign grace, the curse of God still rests upon thine head. If thou hast but committed one sin in thy life, God's justice is so inexorable, that it condemns a man for one solitary offense; and though thy life should henceforth be one continued career of holiness, if thou hast sinned but once, unless thou hast an interest in the blood of Christ, the thunders of Sinai are launched at thee, and the lightning of terrible vengeance flash all around thee.

Ah! my hearers, how humbling is this doctrine to our pride, that the curse of God is on every man of the seed of Adam; that every child born in this world is born under the curse, since it is born under the law; and that the moment I

cumcision was committed unto me, as the gospel of the circumcision was unto Peter;

8 (For he that wrought effectually in Peter to the apostleship of the circumcision, the same was mighty in me toward the Gentiles:)

9 And when James, Cephas, and John, who seemed to be pillars, perceived the grace that was given unto me, they gave to me and Barnabas the right hands of fellowship; that we should go unto the heathen, and they unto the circumcision.

10 Only they would that we should remember the poor; the same which I also was forward to do.

11 But when Peter was come to Antioch, I withstood him to the face, because he was to be blamed.

12 For before that certain came from James, he did eat with the Gentiles: but when they were come, he withdrew and separated himself, fearing them which were of the circumcision.

13 And the other Jews dissembled likewise with him; insomuch that Barnabas also was carried away with their dissimulation.

14 But when I saw that they walked not uprightly according to the truth of the gospel, I said unto Peter before them all, If thou, being a Jew, livest after the manner of Gentiles, and not as do the Jews, why compellest thou the Gentiles to live as do the Jews?

15 We who are Jews by nature, and not sinners of the Gentiles,

16 Knowing that a man is not justified by the works of the law, but by the faith of Jesus Christ, even we have believed in Jesus Christ, that we might be justified by the faith of Christ, and not by the works of the law: for by the works of the law shall no flesh be justified.

17 But if, while we seek to be justified by Christ, we ourselves also are found sinners, is therefore Christ the minister of sin? God forbid.

18 For if I build again the things which I destroyed, I make myself a transgressor.

19 For I through the law am

Titus, because of false brethren. That the truth of the gospel – That is, the true genuine gospel. Might continue with you – With you Gentiles. So we defend, for your sakes, the privilege which you would give up.

6. And they who undoubtedly were something – Above all others. What they were – How eminent soever. It is no difference to me – So that I should alter either my doctrine or my practice. God accepteth no man's person – For any eminence in gifts or outward prerogatives. In that conference added nothing to me – Neither as to doctrine nor mission.

7. But when they saw – By the effects which I laid before them, ver. 8; Acts xv, 12. That I was intrusted with the gospel of the uncircumcision – That is, with the charge of preaching it to the uncircumcized heathens.

8. For he that wrought effectually in Peter for the apostleship of the circumcision – To qualify him for, and support him in, the discharge of that office to the Jews. Wrought likewise effectually in and by me – For and in the discharge of my office toward the Gentiles.

9. And when James – Probably named first because he was bishop of the church in Jerusalem. And Cephas – Speaking of him at Jerusalem he calls him by his Hebrew name. And John – Hence it appears that he also was at the council, though he is not particularly named in the Acts. Who undoubtedly were pillars – The principal supporters and defenders of the gospel.

10. Of the poor – The poor Christians in Judea, who had lost all they had for Christ's sake.

11. But – The argument here comes to the height. Paul reproves Peter himself. So far was he from receiving his doctrine from man, or from being inferior to the chief of the apostles. When Peter – Afterwards. Came to Antioch – Then the chief of all the Gentile churches. I withstood him to the face, because he was to be blamed – For fear of man, ver. 12; for dissimulation, ver. 13; and for not walking uprightly. ver. 14.

13. And the other believing Jews – Who were at Antioch. Dissembled with him, so that even Barnabas was carried away with their dissimulation – Was born away, as with a torrent, into the same ill practice.

14. I said to Cephas before them all – See Paul single against Peter and all the Jews! If thou being a Jew, yet livest, in thy ordinary conversation, after the manner of the Gentiles – Not observing the ceremonial law, which thou knowest to be now abolished. Why compellest thou the Gentiles – By withdrawing thyself and all the ministers from them; either to judaize, to keep the ceremonial law, or to be excluded from church communion?

16. Knowing that a man is not justified by the works of the law – Not even of the moral, much less the ceremonial, law. But by the faith of Jesus Christ – That is, by faith in him. The name Jesus was first known by the Gentiles; the name Christ by the Jews.

17. But if while we seek to be justified by Christ, we ourselves are still found sinners – If we continue in sin, will it therefore follow, that Christ is the minister or countenancer of sin?

18. By no means. For if I build again – By my sinful practice. The things which I destroyed – By my preaching. I only make myself – Or show myself, not Christ, to be a transgressor; the whole blame lies on me, not him or his gospel. As if he had said, The objection were just, if the gospel promised justification to men continuing in sin. But it does not. Therefore if any who profess the gospel do not live according to it, they are sinners, it is certain, but not justified, and so the gospel is clear.

19. For I through the law – Applied by the Spirit to my heart, and deeply convincing me of my utter sinfulness and helplessness. Am dead to the law – To all hope of justification from it. That I may live to God – Not continue in sin. For this very end am I, in this sense, freed from the law, that I may be freed from sin.

20. The Apostle goes on to describe how he is freed from sin; how far he is from

MATTHEW HENRY CHARLES H. SPURGEON

And from thence he enters upon the doctrine of justification by faith in Christ, without the works of the law. (15-21)

1-10 Observe the apostle's faithfulness in giving a full account of the doctrine he had preached among the Gentiles, and was still resolved to preach, that of Christianity, free from all mixture of Judaism. This doctrine would be ungrateful to many, yet he was not afraid to own it. His care was, lest the success of his past labors should be lessened, or his future usefulness be hindered. While we simply depend upon God for success to our labors, we should use every proper caution to remove mistakes, and against opposers. There are things which may lawfully be complied with, yet, when they cannot be done without betraying the truth, they ought to be refused. We must not give place to any conduct, whereby the truth of the gospel would be reflected upon. Though Paul conversed with the other apostles, yet he did not receive any addition to his knowledge, or authority, from them. Perceiving the grace given to him, they gave unto him and Barnabas the right hand of fellowship, whereby they acknowledged that he was designed to the honor and office of an apostle as well as themselves. They agreed that these two should go to the heathen, while they continued to preach to the Jews; judging it agreeable to the mind of Christ, so to divide their work. Here we learn that the gospel is not ours, but God's; and that men are but the keepers of it; for this we are to praise God.

11-14 Notwithstanding Peter's character, yet, when Paul saw him acting so as to hurt the truth of the gospel and the peace of the church, he was not afraid to reprove him. When he saw that Peter and the others did not live up to that principle which the gospel taught, and which they professed, namely, That by the death of Christ the partition wall between Jew and Gentile was taken down, and the observance of the law of Moses was no longer in force; as Peter's offense was public, he publicly reproved him. There is a very great difference between the prudence of St. Paul, who bore with, and used for a time, the ceremonies of the law as not sinful, and the timid conduct of St. Peter, who, by withdrawing from the Gentiles, led others to think that these ceremonies were necessary.

15-19 Paul, having thus shown he was not inferior to any apostle, not to Peter himself, speaks of the great foundation doctrine of the gospel. For what did we believe in Christ? Was it not that we might be justified by the faith of Christ? If so, is it not foolish to go back to the law, and to expect to be justified by the merit of moral works, or sacrifices, or ceremonies? The occasion of this declaration doubtless arose from the ceremonial law; but the argument is quite as strong against all dependence upon the works of the moral law, as respects justification. To give the greater weight to

sin, though I transgress but once, I am from that moment condemned already; for "cursed is every one that continueth not in all things which are written in the book of the law to do them."—cursed without a single hope of mercy, unless he find that mercy in the Substitute "who was made a curse for us." It is an awful thought, that the trail of the serpent is on the whole earth; that the poison is in the fountain of every heart; that the stream of the blood in all our veins is corrupt; that we are all condemned; that each one of us, without a single exception, whether he be philanthropist, senator, philosopher, divine, prince, or monarch, is under the curse unless he has been redeemed from it by Christ.

2. The curse, too, we must remark, while universal, is also just. This is the great difficulty. There are many persons who think that the curse of God upon those who are undeniably wicked is, of course, right; but that the curse of God upon those who for the most part appear to be excellent, and who may have sinned but once, is an act of injustice. We answer, "Nay, when God pronounces the curse, he doth it justly; he is a God of justice; 'just and right is he.'" And mark thee, man, if thou art condemned, it shall be by the strictest justice; and if thou hast sinned but once, the curse is righteous when it lights upon thy head. Dost thou ask me how this is? I answer, Thou sayest thy sin is little; then, if the sin be little, how little trouble it might have taken thee to have avoided it! If thy transgression be but small, at how small an expense thou mightest have refrained from it! Some have said, "Surely the sin of Adam was but little; he did but take an apple." Ay, but in its littleness was its greatness. If it was a little thing to take the fruit, with how little trouble might it have been avoided! And because it was so small an act, there was couched within it the greater malignity of guilt. So, too, thou mayest never have blasphemed thy God, thou mayest never have desecrated his Sabbath; yet, insomuch as thou hast committed a little sin, thou art justly condemned, for a little sin hath in it the essence of all sin; and I know not but that what we call little sins may be greater in God's sight than those which the world universally condemns, and against which the hiss of the execration of humanity continually rises. I say, God is just, although from his lips should rush thunders to blast the entire universe; God is just, although he curses all. Tremble, man, and "kiss the Son, lest he be angry, and ye perish by the way, when his wrath is kindled but a little. Blessed are all they that put their trust in him."

So the curse is universal, and it is just.

3. But let us notice, next, the curse is also

dead to the law, that I might live unto God.

20　I am crucified with Christ: nevertheless I live; yet not I, but Christ liveth in me: and the life which I now live in the flesh I live by the faith of the Son of God, who loved me, and gave himself for me.

21　I do not frustrate the grace of God: for if righteousness come by the law, then Christ is dead in vain.

GALATIANS 3

1　O foolish Galatians, who hath bewitched you, that ye should not obey the truth, before whose eyes Jesus Christ hath been evidently set forth, crucified among you?

2　This only would I learn of you, Received ye the Spirit by the works of the law, or by the hearing of faith?

3　Are ye so foolish? having begun in the Spirit, are ye now made perfect by the flesh?

4　Have ye suffered so many things in vain? if it be yet in vain.

5　He therefore that ministereth to you the Spirit, and worketh miracles among you, doeth he it by the works of the law, or by the hearing of faith?

6　Even as Abraham believed God, and it was accounted to him for righteousness.

7　Know ye therefore that they which are of faith, the same are the children of Abraham.

8　And the scripture, foreseeing that God would justify the heathen through faith, preached before the gospel unto Abraham, saying, In thee shall all nations be blessed.

9　So then they which be of faith are blessed with faithful Abraham.

10　For as many as are of the works of the law are under the curse: for it is written, Cursed is every one that continueth not in all things which are written in the book of the law to do them.

11　But that no man is justified by the law in the sight of God, it is evident: for, The just shall live by faith.

12　And the law is not of faith: but, The man that doeth them

continuing therein. I am crucified with Christ – Made conformable to his death; "the body of sin is destroyed." Rom. vi, 6. And I – As to my corrupt nature. Live no longer – Being dead to sin. But Christ liveth in me – Is a fountain of life in my inmost soul, from which all my tempers, words, and actions flow. And the life that I now live in the flesh – Even in this mortal body, I live by faith in the Son of God – I derive every moment from that supernatural principle; from a divine evidence and conviction, that "he loved me, and delivered up himself for me."

21. Meantime I do not make void – In seeking to be justified by my own works. The grace of God – The free love of God in Christ Jesus. But they do, who seek justification by the law. For if righteousness is by the law – If men might be justified by their obedience to the law, moral or ceremonial. Then Christ died in vain – Without any necessity for it, since men might have been saved without his death; might by their own obedience have been both discharged from condemnation, and entitled to eternal life.

GALATIANS 3

1. O thoughtless Galatians – He breaks in upon them with a beautiful abruptness. Who hath bewitched you – Thus to contradict both your own reason and experience. Before whose eyes Jesus Christ hath been as evidently set forth – By our preaching, as if he had been crucified among you.

2. This only would I learn of you – That is, this one argument might convince you. Did ye receive the witness and the fruit of the Spirit by performing the works of the law, or by hearing of and receiving faith?

3. Are ye so thoughtless – As not to consider what you have yourselves experienced? Having begun in the Spirit – Having set out under the light and power of the Spirit by faith, do ye now, when ye ought to be more spiritual, and more acquainted with the power of faith, expect to be made perfect by the flesh? Do you think to complete either your justification or sanctification, by giving up that faith, and depending on the law, which is a gross and carnal thing when opposed to the gospel?

4. Have ye suffered – Both from the zealous Jews and from the heathens. So many things – For adhering to the gospel. In vain – So as to lose all the blessings which ye might have obtained, by enduring to the end. If it be yet in vain – As if he had said, I hope better things, even that ye will endure to the end.

5. And, at the present time, Doth he that ministereth the gift of the Spirit to you, and worketh miracles among you, do it by the works of the law – That is, in confirmation of his preaching justification by works, or of his preaching justification by faith?

6. Doubtless in confirmation of that grand doctrine, that we are justified by faith, even as Abraham was. The Apostle, both in this and in the epistle to the Romans, makes great use of the instance of Abraham: the rather, because from Abraham the Jews drew their great argument, as they do this day, both for their own continuance in Judaism, and for denying the Gentiles to be the church of God. Gen. xv, 6.

7. Know then that they who are partakers of his faith, these, and these only, are the sons of Abraham, and therefore heirs of the promises made to him.

9. So then all they, and they only, who are of faith – Who truly believe. Are blessed with faithful Abraham – Receive the blessing as he did, namely, by faith.

10. They only receive it. For as many as are of the works of the law – As God deals with on that footing, only on the terms the law proposes, are under a curse; for it is written, Cursed is every one who continueth not in all the things which are written in the law. Who continueth not in all the things – So it requires what no man can perform, namely, perfect, uninterrupted, and perpetual obedience. Deut. xxvii, 26.

MATTHEW HENRY   CHARLES H. SPURGEON

this, it is added, But if, while we seek to be justified by Christ, we ourselves also are found sinners, is Christ the minister of sin? This would be very dishonorable to Christ, and also very hurtful to them. By considering the law itself, he saw that justification was not to be expected by the works of it, and that there was now no further need of the sacrifices and cleansings of it, since they were done away in Christ, by his offering up himself a sacrifice for us. He did not hope or fear any thing from it; any more than a dead man from enemies.

20,21 Here, in his own person, the apostle describes the spiritual or hidden life of a believer. The old man is crucified, Ro 6:6, but the new man is living; sin is mortified, and grace is quickened. He has the comforts and the triumphs of grace; yet that grace is not from himself, but from another. Believers see themselves living in a state of dependence on Christ. Hence it is, that though he lives in the flesh, yet he does not live after the flesh. Those who have true faith, live by that faith; and faith fastens upon Christ's giving himself for us. He loved me, and gave himself for me. As if the apostle said, The Lord saw me fleeing from him more and more. Such wickedness, error, and ignorance were in my will and understanding, that it was not possible for me to be ransomed by any other means than by such a price. Consider well this price. Here notice the false faith of many. And their profession is accordingly; they have the form of godliness without the power of it. They think they believe the articles of faith aright, but they are deceived. For to believe in Christ crucified, is not only to believe that he was crucified, but also to believe that I am crucified with him. And this is to know Christ crucified. Hence we learn what is the nature of grace. God's grace cannot stand with man's merit. Grace is no grace unless it is freely given every way.

GALATIANS 3

The Galatians reproved for departing from the great doctrine of justification alone, through faith in Christ. (1-5)

This doctrine established from the example of Abraham. (6-9)

From the tenor of the law and the severity of its curse. (10-14)

From the covenant of promises, which the law could not disannul. (15-18)

The law was a schoolmaster to lead them to Christ. (19-25)

Under the gospel state true believers are all one in Christ. (26-29)

1-5 Several things made the folly of the Galatian Christians worse. They had the doctrine of the cross preached, and the Lord's supper administered among them, in both which Christ crucified, and the nature of his sufferings, had been fully and clearly set forth. Had

fearful. Some there be who think it little to be cursed of God; but O! if they knew the fearful consequences of that curse; they would think it terrible indeed. It were enough to make our knees knock together, to chill our blood, and start each individual hair of our head upon its end, if we did but know what it is to be under the curse of God. What does that curse include? It involves death, the death of this body; that is by no means an insignificant portion of its sentence. It includes spiritual death, a death of that inner life which Adam had—the life of the spirit, which hath now fled, and can only be restored by that holy Spirit who "quickeneth whom he will." And it includes, last of all, and worst of all, that death eternal, a dwelling forever in the place

"Where solemn groans, and hollow moans,
And shrieks of tortured ghosts,"

make up the only music. Death eternal includes all that can be gathered in that terrible, that awful—we had almost said unutterable—word "hell." This is a curse which rests on every man by nature. We make no exception of rank or degree; for God has made none. We offer no hope of exception of character or reputation; for God has made none. The whole of us are shut up to this, that (so far as the law is concerned) we must die—die here and die in the next world, and die a death which never dies; feel a worm which shall gnaw forever, and a fire which never can be extinguished, even by a fold of tears of future penitence. There we must be forever, O! forever lost. Could we estimate that curse, I say again, the torments that tyrants could inflict we might well afford to ridicule, the injuries that this body can sustain we might well afford to despise, compared with that awful avalanche of threatening which rushes down with fearful force from the mountain of God's truth. Condemnation—that curse of God—abideth on us all.

4. We hasten from this point, beloved, for it is fearful work to speak upon it; but yet we must not depart from it entirely, till we have hinted at one thought more; and that is, that the curse of God which comes upon sinful men is a present curse. O! my dear hearers, could I lay hold of your hands, if ye be not converted, I would labor with tears and groans to get you to grasp this thought. It is not so much a condemnation in the future that you have to dread as a damnation now. Yes, sitting where thou art, my hearer, if thou art out of Christ, thou art condemned now; thy condemnation is sealed; thy death-warrant has been stamped by the great seal of the Majesty of heaven; the angel's sword of vengeance is already unsheathed, and over thy head this afternoon. Whosoever thou

shall live in them.

13 Christ hath redeemed us from the curse of the law, being made a curse for us: for it is written, Cursed is every one that hangeth on a tree:

14 That the blessing of Abraham might come on the Gentiles through Jesus Christ; that we might receive the promise of the Spirit through faith.

15 Brethren, I speak after the manner of men; Though it be but a man's covenant, yet if it be confirmed, no man disannulleth, or addeth thereto.

16 Now to Abraham and his seed were the promises made. He saith not, And to seeds, as of many; but as of one, And to thy seed, which is Christ.

17 And this I say, that the covenant, that was confirmed before of God in Christ, the law, which was four hundred and thirty years after, cannot disannul, that it should make the promise of none effect.

18 For if the inheritance be of the law, it is no more of promise: but God gave it to Abraham by promise.

19 Wherefore then serveth the law? It was added because of transgressions, till the seed should come to whom the promise was made; and it was ordained by angels in the hand of a mediator.

20 Now a mediator is not a mediator of one, but God is one.

21 Is the law then against the promises of God? God forbid: for if there had been a law given which could have given life, verily righteousness should have been by the law.

22 But the scripture hath concluded all under sin, that the promise by faith of Jesus Christ might be given to them that believe.

23 But before faith came, we were kept under the law, shut up unto the faith which should afterwards be revealed.

24 Wherefore the law was our schoolmaster to bring us unto Christ, that we might be justified by faith.

25 But after that faith is come, we are no longer under a schoolmaster.

26 For ye are all the children of

11. But that none is justified by his obedience to the law in the sight of God – Whatever may be done in the sight of man, is farther evident from the words of Habakkuk, The just shall live by faith – That is, the man who is accounted just or righteous before God, shall continue in a state of acceptance, life, and salvation, by faith. This is the way God hath chosen. Hab. ii, 4.

12. And the law is not of faith – But quite opposite to it: it does not say, Believe; but, Do. Lev. xviii, 5.

13. Christ – Christ alone. The abruptness of the sentence shows an holy indignation at those who reject so great a blessing. Hath redeemed us – Whether Jews or Gentiles, at an high price. From the curse of the law – The curse of God, which the law denounces against all transgressors of it. Being made a curse for us – Taking the curse upon himself, that we might be delivered from it, willingly submitting to that death which the law pronounces peculiarly accursed. Deut. xxi, 23.

14. That the blessing of Abraham – The blessing promised to him. Might come on the Gentiles – Also. That we – Who believe, whether Jews or Gentiles. Might receive the promise of the Spirit – Which includes all the other promises. Through faith – Not by works; for faith looks wholly to the promise.

15. I speak after the manner of men – I illustrate this by a familiar instance, taken from the practice of men. Though it be but a man's covenant, yet, if it be once legally confirmed, none – No, not the covenanter himself, unless something unforeseen occur, which cannot be the case with God. Disannulleth, or addeth thereto – Any new conditions.

16. Now the promises were made to Abraham and his seed – Several promises were made to Abraham; but the chief of all, and which was several times repeated, was that of the blessing through Christ. He – That is, God. Saith not, And to seeds, as of many – As if the promise were made to several kinds of seed. But as of one – That is, one kind of seed, one posterity, one kind of sons. And to all these the blessing belonged by promise. Which is Christ – including all that believe in him. Gen. xxii, 18.

17. And this I say – What I mean is this. The covenant which was before confirmed of God – By the promise itself, by the repetition of it, and by a solemn oath, concerning the blessing all nations. Through Christ, the law which was four hundred and thirty years after – Counting from the time when the promise was first made to Abraham, Gen. xii, 2, 3. Doth not disannul, so as to make the promise of no effect – With regard to all nations, if only the Jewish were to receive it; yea, with regard to them also, if it was by works, so as to supersede it, and introduce another way of obtaining the blessing.

19. It – The ceremonial law. Was added – To the promise.

20. Now the mediator is not a mediator of one – There must be two parties, or there can be no mediator between them; but God who made the free promise to Abraham is only one of the parties. The other, Abraham, was not present at the time of Moses. Therefore in the promise Moses had nothing to do. The law, wherein he was concerned, was a transaction of quite another nature.

21. Will it follow from hence that the law is against, opposite to, the promises of God? By no means. They are well consistent. But yet the law cannot give life, as the promise doth. If there had been a law which could have given life – Which could have entitled a sinner to life, God would have spared his own Son, and righteousness, or justification. with all the blessings consequent upon it, would have been by that law.

22. But, on the contrary, the scripture wherein that law is written hath concluded all under sin – Hath shut them up together, (so the word properly signifies,) as in a prison, under sentence of death, to the end that all being cut off from expecting justification by the law, the promise might be freely given to them that believe.

23. But before faith – That is, the gospel dispensation. Came, we were kept – As

they been made partakers of the Holy Spirit, by the ministration of the law, or on account of any works done by them in obedience thereto? Was it not by their hearing and embracing the doctrine of faith in Christ alone for justification? Which of these had God owned with tokens of his favor and acceptance? It was not by the first, but the last. And those must be very unwise, who suffer themselves to be turned away from the ministry and doctrine which have been blessed to their spiritual advantage. Alas, that men should turn from the all-important doctrine of Christ crucified, to listen to useless distinctions, mere moral preaching, or wild fancies! The god of this world, by various men and means, has blinded men's eyes, lest they should learn to trust in a crucified Savior.

6-14 The apostle proves the doctrine he had blamed the Galatians for rejecting; namely, that of justification by faith without the works of the law. This he does from the example of Abraham, whose faith fastened upon the word and promise of God, and upon his believing he was owned and accepted of God as a righteous man. The Scripture is said to foresee, because the Holy Spirit that indicted the Scripture did foresee. Through faith in the promise of God he was blessed; and it is only in the same way that others obtain this privilege. Let us then study the object, nature, and effects of Abraham's faith; for who can in any other way escape the curse of the holy law? The curse is against all sinners, therefore against all men; for all have sinned, and are become guilty before God: and if, as transgressors of the law, we are under its curse, it must be vain to look for justification by it. Those only are just or righteous who are freed from death and wrath, and restored into a state of life in the favor of God; and it is only through faith that persons become righteous. Thus we see that justification by faith is no new doctrine, but was taught in the church of God, long before the times of the gospel.

15-18 The covenant God made with Abraham, was not done away by the giving the law to Moses. The covenant was made with Abraham and his Seed. It is still in force; Christ abideth forever in his person, and his spiritual seed, who are his by faith. By this we learn the difference between the promises of the law and those of the gospel. The promises of the law are made to the person of every man; the promises of the gospel are first made to Christ, then by him to those who are by faith engrafted into Christ. Rightly to divide the word of truth, a great difference must be put between the promise and the law, as to the inward affections, and the whole practice of life. When the promise is mingled with the law, it is made nothing but the law.

19-22 If that promise was enough for salvation, wherefore then serveth the law? The Israelites, though chosen to be God's peculiar people, were sinners as well as others. The law was not intended to discover a

mayest be, if thou art out of Christ, there hangeth a sword over thee, a sword suspended by a hair, which death shall cut; and then that sword shall descend, dividing thy soul from thy body, and sending both of them to pains eternal. O! ye might start up from your seats with fear, if ye did but know this, some of you. Ye are reputable, ye are respectable, ye are honorable, perhaps right honorable, and yet condemned men, condemned women. On the walls of heaven ye are proscribed, written up there as deicides, who have slain the Savior—as rebels against God's government, who have committed high treason against him; and perhaps even now the dark-winged angel of death is spreading his pinions upon the blast, hastening to hurry you down to destruction. Say not, O sinner, that I would affright thee; say, rather, that I would bring thee to the Savior; for whether thou hearest this or not, or believest it or not, thou canst not alter the truth thereof—that thou art now, if thou hast not given thyself to Christ, "condemned already;" and wherever thou sittest, thou art but still in thy condemned cell; for this whole earth is but one huge prison-house, wherein the condemned one doth drag along a chain of condemnation, till death takes him to the scaffold, where the fearful execution of terrific woe must take place upon him. Now condemned and forever condemned; hear that word. "The curse of the law!"

II. But now I must speak, in the second place, of THE REMOVAL OF THAT CURSE. This is a sweet and pleasant duty. Some of you, my dear friends, will be able to follow me in your experience, while I just remind you how it was, that in your salvation Christ removed the curse.

1. First, you will agree with me when I say that the removal of the curse from us is done in a moment. It is an instantaneous thing. I may stand here one moment under the curse; and if the Spirit look upon me, and I breathe a prayer to heaven—if by faith I cast myself on Jesus—in one solitary second, ere the clock hath ticked, my sins may be all forgiven. Hart sung truly, when he said—

"The moment a sinner believes,
And trusts in his crucified God,
His pardon at once he receives,
Salvation in full, through his blood."

You will remember in Christ's life, that most of the cures he wrought—yea, I believe all—were instantaneous cures. See! there lies a man stretched on his couch, from which he hath not risen for years. "Take up thy bed, and walk," said Christ in majesty. The man takes up that bed, and without the intervention of weeks of convalescence at once carries it, leaping like a

God by faith in Christ Jesus.

27 For as many of you as have been baptized into Christ have put on Christ.

28 There is neither Jew nor Greek, there is neither bond nor free, there is neither male nor female: for ye are all one in Christ Jesus.

29 And if ye be Christ's, then are ye Abraham's seed, and heirs according to the promise.

GALATIANS 4

1 Now I say, That the heir, as long as he is a child, differeth nothing from a servant, though he be lord of all;

2 But is under tutors and governors until the time appointed of the father.

3 Even so we, when we were children, were in bondage under the elements of the world:

4 But when the fullness of the time was come, God sent forth his Son, made of a woman, made under the law,

5 To redeem them that were under the law, that we might receive the adoption of sons.

6 And because ye are sons, God hath sent forth the Spirit of his Son into your hearts, crying, Abba, Father.

7 Wherefore thou art no more a servant, but a son; and if a son, then an heir of God through Christ.

8 Howbeit then, when ye knew not God, ye did service unto them which by nature are no gods.

9 But now, after that ye have known God, or rather are known of God, how turn ye again to the weak and beggarly elements, whereunto ye desire again to be in bondage?

10 Ye observe days, and months, and times, and years.

11 I am afraid of you, lest I have bestowed upon you labor in vain.

12 Brethren, I beseech you, be as I am; for I am as ye are: ye have not injured me at all.

13 Ye know how through infirmity of the flesh I preached the gospel unto you at the first.

14 And my temptation which was in my flesh ye despised not, nor rejected; but received me as

in close custody. Under the law – The Mosaic dispensation. Shut up unto the faith which was to be revealed – Reserved and prepared for the gospel dispensation.

24. Wherefore the law was our schoolmaster unto Christ – It was designed to train us up for Christ. And this it did both by its commands, which showed the need we had of his atonement; and its ceremonies, which all pointed us to him.

25. But faith – That is, the gospel dispensation. Being come, we are no longer under that schoolmaster – The Mosaic dispensation.

26. For ye – Christians. Are all adult sons of God – And so need a schoolmaster no longer.

27. For as many of you as have testified your faith by being baptized in the name of Christ, have put on Christ – Have received him as your righteousness, and are therefore sons of God through him.

28. There is neither Jew nor Greek – That is, there is no difference between them; they are equally accepted through faith. There is neither male nor female – Circumcision being laid aside, which was peculiar to males, and was designed to put a difference, during that dispensation, between Jews and Gentiles.

29. If ye are Christ's – That is, believers in him.

GALATIANS 4

1. Now – To illustrate by a plain similitude the preeminence of the Christian, over the legal, dispensation. The heir, as long as he is a child – As he is under age. Differeth nothing from a servant – Not being at liberty either to use or enjoy his estate. Though he be Lord – Proprietor of it all.

2. But is under tutors – As to his person. And stewards – As to his substance.

3. So we – The church of God. When we were children – In our minority, under the legal dispensation. Were in bondage – In a kind of servile state. Under the elements of the world – Under the typical observances of the law, which were like the first elements of grammar, the A B C of children; and were of so gross a nature, as hardly to carry our thoughts beyond this world.

4. But when the fullness of the time – Appointed by the Father, ver. 2. Was come, God sent forth – From his own bosom. His Son, miraculously made of the substance of a woman – A virgin, without the concurrence of a man. Made under the law – Both under the precept, and under the curse, of it.

5. To redeem those under the law – From the curse of it, and from that low, servile state. That we – Jews who believe. Might receive the adoption – All the privileges of adult sons.

6. And because ye – Gentiles who believe, are also thus made his adult sons, God hath sent forth the Spirit of his Son into your hearts likewise, crying, Abba, Father – Enabling you to call upon God both with the confidence, and the tempers, of dutiful children. The Hebrew and Greek word are joined together, to express the joint cry of the Jews and Gentiles.

7. Wherefore thou – Who believest in Christ. Art no more a servant – Like those who are under the law. But a son – Of mature age. And if a son, then an heir of all the promises, and of the all-sufficient God himself.

8. Indeed then when ye knew not God, ye served them that by nature – That is, in reality. Are no gods – And so were under a far worse bondage than even that of the Jews. For they did serve the true God, though in a low, slavish manner.

way of justification, different from that made known by the promise, but to lead men to see their need of the promise, by showing the sinfulness of sin, and to point to Christ, through whom alone they could be pardoned and justified. The promise was given by God himself; the law was given by the ministry of angels, and the hand of a mediator, even Moses. Hence the law could not be designed to set aside the promise.

23-25 The law did not teach a living, saving knowledge; but, by its rites and ceremonies, especially by its sacrifices, it pointed to Christ, that they might be justified by faith. And thus it was, as the word properly signifies, a servant, to lead to Christ, as children are led to school by servants who have the care of them, that they might be more fully taught by him the true way of justification and salvation, which is only by faith in Christ. And the vastly greater advantage of the gospel state is shown, under which we enjoy a clearer discovery of Divine grace and mercy than the Jews of old. Most men continue shut up as in a dark dungeon, in love with their sins, being blinded and lulled asleep by Satan, through worldly pleasures, interests, and pursuits. But the awakened sinner discovers his dreadful condition. Then he feels that the mercy and grace of God form his only hope.

26-29 Real Christians enjoy great privileges under the gospel; and are no longer accounted servants, but sons; not now kept at such a distance, and under such restraints as the Jews were. Having accepted Christ Jesus as their Lord and Savior, and relying on him alone for justification and salvation, they become the sons of God. But no outward forms or profession can secure these blessings; for if any man have not the Spirit of Christ, he is none of his. In baptism we put on Christ; therein we profess to be his disciples. Being baptized into Christ, we are baptized into his death, that as he died and rose again, so we should die unto sin, and walk in newness and holiness of life. The putting on of Christ according to the gospel, consists not in outward imitation, but in a new birth, an entire change.

GALATIANS 4

The folly of returning to legal observances for justification. (1-7)

The happy change made in the Gentile believers. (8-11)

The apostle reasons against following false teachers. (12-18)

He expresses his earnest concern for them. (19,20)

And then explains the difference between what is to be expected from the law, and from the gospel. (21-31)

1-7 The apostle deals plainly with those who urged the law of Moses together with the gospel of Christ,

hart. There is another. From his closed lips a sound hath scarcely ever escaped; he is dumb; Christ toucheth his lips; "Ephphatha, be opened;" and he sings at once. He does not barely speak, but he speaks plain; the tongue of the dumb sings. Ay, and even in the cases where Christ healed death itself, he did it instantaneously. When that beautiful creature lay asleep in death upon the bed, Jesus went to her; and though her dark ringlets covered up her eyes, which were now glazed in death, Jesus did but take her clay-cold hand in his, and say, "Talitha cumi! damsel, I say unto thee, Arise;" and no sooner had he said it, than she sat up, and opened her eyes; and to show that she was not merely half alive, or half restored, she rose up, and ministered to him. We do not say that the great work of conversion is instantaneous; that may take some time; for Christ commences in the heart a work, which is to be carried on through life in sanctification; but the justification, the taking away the curse, is done in a single moment. "Unwrite the curse," says God. It is done. The acquittal is signed and sealed; it taketh not long.

"Fully discharged by Christ I am,
From sin's tremendous curse and blame."

I may stand here at this moment, and I may have believed in Christ but five minutes ago; still, if I have believed in Christ but that short space of time, I am as justified, in God's sight, as I would be should I live until these hairs are whitened by the sunlight of heaven, or as I shall be when I walk among the golden lamps of the city of palaces. God justifieth his people at once; the curse is removed in a single moment. Sinner, hear that! Thou mayest now be under condemnation; but ere thou canst say "now" again, thou mayest be able to say—"There is, therefore, now no condemnation to me, for I am in Christ Jesus." We may be fully absolved in a moment.

2. Mark, beloved, in the next place, that this removal of the curse from us, when it does take place, is an entire removal. It is not a part of the curse which is taken away. Christ doth not stand at the foot of Sinai, and say, "Thunders! diminish your force;" he doth not catch here and there a lightning, and bind its wings; nay, but when he cometh he bloweth away all the smoke, he putteth aside all the thunder, he quencheth all the lightning; he removeth it all. When Christ pardoneth, he pardoneth all sin; the sins of twice ten thousand years he pardons in an hour. Thou mayest be old and gray-headed, and hitherto unpardoned; but though thy sins exceed in number the stars spread in the sky, one moment takes them all away. Mark that "all!" That sin of midnight; that black sin which,

an angel of God, even as Christ Jesus.

15 Where is then the blessedness ye spake of? for I bear you record, that, if it had been possible, ye would have plucked out your own eyes, and have given them to me.

16 Am I therefore become your enemy, because I tell you the truth?

17 They zealously affect you, but not well; yea, they would exclude you, that ye might affect them.

18 But it is good to be zealously affected always in a good thing, and not only when I am present with you.

19 My little children, of whom I travail in birth again until Christ be formed in you,

20 I desire to be present with you now, and to change my voice; for I stand in doubt of you.

21 Tell me, ye that desire to be under the law, do ye not hear the law?

22 For it is written, that Abraham had two sons, the one by a bondmaid, the other by a freewoman.

23 But he who was of the bondwoman was born after the flesh; but he of the freewoman was by promise.

24 Which things are an allegory: for these are the two covenants; the one from the mount Sinai, which gendereth to bondage, which is Agar.

25 For this Agar is mount Sinai in Arabia, and answereth to Jerusalem which now is, and is in bondage with her children.

26 But Jerusalem which is above is free, which is the mother of us all.

27 For it is written, Rejoice, thou barren that bearest not; break forth and cry, thou that travailest not: for the desolate hath many more children than she which hath an husband.

28 Now we, brethren, as Isaac was, are the children of promise.

29 But as then he that was born after the flesh persecuted him that was born after the Spirit, even so it is now.

30 Nevertheless what saith the scripture? Cast out the bondwoman and her son: for the son

9. But now being known of God – As his beloved children. How turn ye back to the weak and poor elements – Weak, utterly unable to purge your conscience from guilt, or to give that filial confidence in God. Poor – incapable of enriching the soul with such holiness and happiness as ye are heirs to. Ye desire to be again in bondage – Though of another kind; now to these elements, as before to those idols.

10. Ye observe days – Jewish Sabbaths. And months – New moons. And times – As that of the Passover, Pentecost, and the feast of tabernacles. And years – Annual solemnities. it does not mean sabbatical years. These were not to be observed out of the land of Canaan.

11. The apostle here, dropping the argument, applies to the affections, ver. 11-20, and humbles himself to the Galatians, with an inexpressible tenderness.

12. Brethren, I beseech you, be as I am – Meet me in mutual love. For I am as ye were – I still love you as affectionately as ye once loved me. Why should I not? Ye have not injured me at all – I have received no personal injury from you.

13. I preached to you, notwithstanding infirmity of the flesh – That is, notwithstanding bodily weakness, and under great disadvantage from the despicableness of my outward appearance.

14. And ye did not slight my temptation – That is, ye did not slight or disdain me for my temptation, my "thorn in the flesh."

15. What was then the blessedness ye spake of – On which ye so congratulated one another.

18. In a good thing – In what is really worthy our zeal. True zeal is only fervent love.

19. My little children – He speaks as a parent, both with authority, and the most tender sympathy, toward weak and sickly children. Of whom I travail in birth again – As I did before, ver. 13, in vehement pain, sorrow, desire, prayer. Till Christ be formed in you – Till there be in you all the mind that was in him.

20. I could wish to be present with you now – Particularly in this exigence. And to change – Variously to attempt. My voice – He writes with much softness; but he would speak with more. The voice may more easily be varied according to the occasion than a letter can. For I stand in doubt of you – So that I am at a loss how to speak at this distance.

21. Do ye not hear the law – Regard what it says.

22. Gen. xxi, 2, 9.

23. Was born after the flesh – In a natural way. By promise – Through that supernatural strength which was given Abraham in consequence of the promise.

25. For this is mount Sinai in Arabia – That is, the type of mount Sinai. And answereth to – Resembles Jerusalem that now is, and is in bondage – Like Agar, both to the law and to the Romans.

26. But the other covenant is derived from Jerusalem that is above, which is free – Like Sarah from all inward and outward bondage, and is the mother of us all – That is, all who believe in Christ, are free citizens of the New Jerusalem.

27. For it is written – Those words in the primary sense promise a flourishing state to Judea, after its desolation by the Chaldeans. Rejoice. thou barren, that bearest not – Ye heathen nations, who, like a barren woman, were destitute, for many ages, of a seed to serve the Lord. Break forth and cry aloud for joy, thou that, in former time, travailedst not: for the desolate hath many more children than she that hath an husband – For ye that were so long utterly desolate shall at length bear more children than the Jewish church, which was of old espoused to God. Isaiah liv, 1.

28. Now we – Who believe, whether Jews or Gentiles. Are children of the promise – Not born in a natural way, but by the supernatural power of God. And as such we are heirs of the promise made to believing Abraham.

29. But as then, he that was born after the flesh persecuted him that was born after the Spirit, so it is now also – And so it will be in all ages and nations to the

and endeavored to bring believers under its bondage. They could not fully understand the meaning of the law as given by Moses. And as that was a dispensation of darkness, so of bondage; they were tied to many burdensome rites and observances, by which they were taught and kept subject like a child under tutors and governors. We learn the happier state of Christians under the gospel dispensation. From these verses see the wonders of Divine love and mercy; particularly of God the Father, in sending his Son into the world to redeem and save us; of the Son of God, in submitting so low, and suffering so much for us; and of the Holy Spirit, in condescending to dwell in the hearts of believers, for such gracious purposes.

8-11 The happy change whereby the Galatians were turned from idols to the living God, and through Christ had received the adoption of sons, was the effect of his free and rich grace; they were laid under the greater obligation to keep to the liberty wherewith he had made them free. All our knowledge of God begins on his part; we know him because we are known of him. Though our religion forbids idolatry, yet many practice spiritual idolatry in their hearts. For what a man loves most, and cares most for, that is his god: some have their riches for their god, some their pleasures, and some their lusts. And many ignorantly worship a god of their own making; a god made all of mercy and no justice.

12-18 The apostle desires that they would be of one mind with him respecting the law of Moses, as well as united with him in love. In reproving others, we should take care to convince them that our reproofs are from sincere regard to the honor of God and religion and their welfare. The apostle reminds the Galatians of the difficulty under which he labored when he first came among them. But he notices, that he was a welcome messenger to them. Yet how very uncertain are the favor and respect of men! Let us labor to be accepted of God.

19,20 The Galatians were ready to account the apostle their enemy, but he assures them he was their friend; he had the feelings of a parent toward them. He was in doubt as to their state, and was anxious to know the result of their present delusions. Nothing is so sure a proof that a sinner has passed into a state of justification, as Christ being formed in him by the renewal of the Holy Spirit; but this cannot be hoped for, while men depend on the law for acceptance with God.

21-27 The difference between believers who rested in Christ only, and those who trusted in the law, is explained by the histories of Isaac and Ishmael. These things are an allegory, wherein, beside the literal and historical sense of the words, the Spirit of God points out something further. Hagar and Sarah were apt emblems of the two different dispensations of the

like a ghost, has haunted thee all thy life; that hideous crime; that unknown act of blackness which hath darkened thy character; that awful stain upon thy conscience—they shall be all taken away. And though thou hast a stain upon that hand—a stain which thou hast often sought to wash out by all the mixtures that Moses can give thee—thou shalt find, when thou art bathed in Jesus' blood, that thou shalt be able to say, "All clean, my Lord, all clean; not a spot now; all is gone; I am completely washed from head to foot; the stains are all removed." It is the glory of this removal of the curse that it is all taken away; there is not a single atom left. Hushed now is the law's loud thunder; the sentence is entirely reversed, and there is no fear left.

3. We must say again upon this point, that when Christ removes the curse, it is an irreversible removal. Once let me be acquitted, who is he that condemns me? There be some in these modern times who teach that God justifieth, and yet, after that, condemns the same person whom he has justified. We have heard it asserted pretty boldly, that a man may be a child of God today—hear it, ye heavens, and be astonished—and be a child of the devil tomorrow; we have heard it said, but we know it is untrue, for we find nothing in Scripture to warrant it. We have often asked ourselves, Can men really believe that, after having been "begotten again to a lively hope," that birth in God, through Christ, and by his Spirit, can yet fail? We have asked ourselves, Can men imagine that, after God hath once broken our chains, and set us free, he will call us back, and bind us once again, like Prometheus, to the great rocks of despair? Will he once blot out the handwriting that is against us, and then record the charge again? Once pardoned, then condemned? We trow, that had Paul been in the way of such men, he would have said, "Who is he that condemneth? It is Christ that died; yea, rather, that is risen again. Who shall lay anything to the charge of God's elect?" There is no condemnation to us, being in Christ Jesus; we "walk not after the flesh, but after the Spirit." It is a sweet thought, that Satan himself can never rob me of my pardon. I may lose my copy of it, and lose my comfort; but the original pardon is filed in heaven. It may be that gloomy doubts may arise, and I may fear to think myself forgiven: but

"Did Jesus upon me shine?
Then Jesus is for ever mine."
"O! my distrustful heart!
How small thy faith appears.
Far greater, Lord, thou art,
Than all my doubts and fears.
'Midst all my sin, and fear, and woe,

of the bondwoman shall not be heir with the son of the free-woman.

31 So then, brethren, we are not children of the bondwoman, but of the free.

GALATIANS 5

1 Stand fast therefore in the liberty wherewith Christ hath made us free, and be not entangled again with the yoke of bondage.

2 Behold, I Paul say unto you, that if ye be circumcized, Christ shall profit you nothing.

3 For I testify again to every man that is circumcized, that he is a debtor to do the whole law.

4 Christ is become of no effect unto you, whosoever of you are justified by the law; ye are fallen from grace.

5 For we through the Spirit wait for the hope of righteousness by faith.

6 For in Jesus Christ neither circumcision availeth anything, nor uncircumcision; but faith which worketh by love.

7 Ye did run well; who did hinder you that ye should not obey the truth?

8 This persuasion cometh not of him that calleth you.

9 A little leaven leaveneth the whole lump.

10 I have confidence in you through the Lord, that ye will be none otherwise minded: but he that troubleth you shall bear his judgment, whosoever he be.

11 And I, brethren, if I yet preach circumcision, why do I yet suffer persecution? then is the offense of the cross ceased.

12 I would they were even cut off which trouble you.

13 For, brethren, ye have been called unto liberty; only use not liberty for an occasion to the flesh, but by love serve one another.

14 For all the law is fulfilled in one word, even in this; Thou shalt love thy neighbor as thyself.

15 But if ye bite and devour one another, take heed that ye be not consumed one of another.

16 This I say then, Walk in the Spirit, and ye shall not fulfill the lust of the flesh.

end of the world.

31. So then – To sum up all. We – Who believe. Are not children of the bond-woman – Have nothing to do with the servile Mosaic dispensation. But of the free – Being free from the curse and the bond of that law, and from the power of sin and Satan.

GALATIANS 5

1. Stand fast therefore in the liberty – From the ceremonial law. Wherewith Christ hath made us – And all believers, free; and be not entangled again with the yoke of legal bondage.

2. If ye be circumcized – And seek to be justified thereby. Christ – The Christian institution. Will profit you nothing – For you hereby disclaim Christ, and all the blessings which are through faith in him.

3. I testify to every man – Every Gentile. That is circumcized – He thereby makes himself a debtor – Obliges.

4. Therefore Christ is become of no effect to you – Who seek to be justified by the law. Ye are fallen from grace – Ye renounce the new covenant. Ye disclaim the benefit of this gracious dispensation.

6. For in Christ Jesus – According to the institution which he hath established, according to the tenor of the Christian covenant. Neither circumcision – With the most punctual observance of the law. Nor uncircumcision – With the most exact heathen morality. Availeth anything – Toward present justification or eternal salvation. But faith – Alone; even that faith which worketh by love – All inward and outward holiness.

7. Ye did run well – In the race of faith. Who hath hindered you in your course, that ye should not still obey the truth?

8. This your present persuasion cometh not from God, who called you – to his kingdom and glory.

9. A little leaven leaveneth the whole lump – One troubler, ver. 10, troubles all.

10. Yet I have confidence that – After ye have read this. Ye will be no otherwise minded – Than I am, and ye were. But he that troubleth you – It seems to have been one person chiefly who endeavored to seduce them. Shall bear his judgment – A heavy burden, already hanging over his head.

12. I would they were even cut off – From your communion; cast out of your church, that thus trouble you.

13. Ye have been called to liberty – From sin and misery, as well as from the ceremonial law. Only use not liberty for an occasion to the flesh – Take not occasion from hence to gratify corrupt nature. But by love serve one another – And hereby show that Christ has made you free.

14. For all the law is fulfilled in this, Thou shalt love thy neighbor as thyself – inasmuch as none can do this without loving God, 1 John iv, 12; and the love of God and man includes all perfection. Lev. xix, 18.

15. But if – On the contrary, in consequence of the divisions which those troublers have occasioned among you, ye bite one another by evil speaking. And devour one another – By railing and clamor. Take heed ye be not consumed one of another – By bitterness, strife, and contention, our health and strength, both of body and soul, are consumed, as well as our substance and reputation.

16. I say then – He now explains what he proposed, ver. 13. Walk by the Spirit – Follow his guidance in all things. And fulfill not – In anything. The desire of the flesh – Of corrupt nature.

17. For the flesh desireth against the Spirit – Nature desires what is quite contrary to the Spirit of God. But the Spirit against the flesh – But the Holy Spirit on his part opposes your evil nature. These are contrary to each other – The flesh and the Spirit; there can be no agreement between them. That ye may not do the things which ye would – That, being thus strengthened by the Spirit, ye may not

covenant. The heavenly Jerusalem, the true church from above, represented by Sarah, is in a state of freedom, and is the mother of all believers, who are born of the Holy Spirit. They were by regeneration and true faith, made a part of the true seed of Abraham, according to the promise made to him.

28-31 The history thus explained is applied. So then, brethren, we are not children of the bondwoman, but of the free. If the privileges of all believers were so great, according to the new covenant, how absurd for the Gentile converts to be under that law, which could not deliver the unbelieving Jews from bondage or condemnation! We should not have found out this allegory in the history of Sarah and Hagar, if it had not been shown to us, yet we cannot doubt it was intended by the Holy Spirit. It is an explanation of the subject, not an argument in proof of it. The two covenants of works and grace, and legal and evangelical professors, are shadowed forth. Works and fruits brought forth in a man's own strength, are legal. But if arising from faith in Christ, they are evangelical. The first covenant spirit is of bondage unto sin and death. The second covenant spirit is of liberty and freedom; not liberty to sin, but in and unto duty. The first is a spirit of persecution; the second is a spirit of love.

GALATIANS 5

An earnest exhortation to stand fast in the liberty of the gospel. (1-12)
To take heed of indulging a sinful temper. (13-15)
And to walk in the Spirit, and not to fulfill the lusts of the flesh: the works of both are described. (16-26)

1-6 Christ will not be the Savior of any who will not own and rely upon him as their only Savior. Let us take heed to the warnings and persuasions of the apostle to steadfastness in the doctrine and liberty of the gospel. All true Christians, being taught by the Holy Spirit, wait for eternal life, the reward of righteousness, and the object of their hope, as the gift of God by faith in Christ; and not for the sake of their own works. The Jewish convert might observe the ceremonies or assert his liberty, the Gentile might disregard them or might attend to them, provided he did not depend upon them. No outward privileges or profession will avail to acceptance with God, without sincere faith in our Lord Jesus.

7-12 The life of a Christian is a race, wherein he must run, and hold on, if he would obtain the prize. It is not enough that we profess Christianity, but we must run well, by living up to that profession. Many who set out fairly in religion, are hindered in their progress, or turn out of the way. It concerns those who begin to turn out of the way, or to tire in it, seriously to inquire what hinders them. The opinion or persuasion, ver. 8, was, no doubt, that of mixing the works of the law with faith in

Thy Spirit will not let me go."
I love, at times, to go back to the hour when I hope I was forgiven through a Savior's blood. There is much comfort in it to remember that blessed hour when first we knew the Lord.

Perhaps thou dost; perhaps thou canst look back to the very place where Jesus whispered thou wast his. Canst thou do so? O! how much comfort it will give thee! for, remember, once acquitted, acquitted forever. So saith God's word. Once pardoned, thou art clear; once set at liberty, thou shalt never be a slave again; once hath Sinai been appeased, it shall never roar twice. Blessed be God's name! we are brought to Calvary, and we shall be brought to Zion too. At last shall we stand before God; and even there we shall be able to say—

"Great God! I am clean;
Through Jesus' blood I'm clean."

III. And now we are brought, in the third place, to observe THE GREAT SUBSTITUTE by whom the curse is removed.

The curse of God is not easily taken away; in fact, there was but one method whereby it could be removed. The lightning were in God's hand; they must be launched; he said they must. The sword was unsheathed; it must be satisfied; God vowed it must. How, then, was the sinner to be saved? The only answer was this. The Son of God appears; and he says, "Father! launch thy thunderbolts at me; here is my breast—plunge that sword in here; here are my shoulders—let the lash of vengeance fall on them;" and Christ, the Substitute, came forth and stood for us, "the just for the unjust, that he might bring us to God." It is our delight to preach the doctrine of substitution, because we are fully persuaded that no gospel is preached where substitution is omitted. Unless men are told positively and plainly that Christ did stand in their room and stead, to bear their guilt and carry their sorrows, they never can see how God is to be "just, and yet the justifier of the ungodly."

We have heard some preach a gospel, something after this order—that though God is angry with men, yet out of his great mercy, for the sake of something that Christ has done, he does not punish them, but remits the penalty. Now, we hold, that this is not of God's gospel; for it is neither just to God, nor safe to man. We believe that God never remitted the penalty, that he did not forgive the sin without punishing it, but that there was blood for blood, and stroke for stroke, and death for death, and punishment for punishment, without the abatement of a solitary jot or tittle; that Jesus Christ, the Savior, did drink the veritable cup of our redemption to its very dregs; that he did suffer beneath the

17 For the flesh lusteth against the Spirit, and the Spirit against the flesh: and these are contrary the one to the other: so that ye cannot do the things that ye would.

18 But if ye be led of the Spirit, ye are not under the law.

19 Now the works of the flesh are manifest, which are these; Adultery, fornication, uncleanness, lasciviousness,

20 Idolatry, witchcraft, hatred, variance, emulations, wrath, strife, seditions, heresies,

21 Envyings, murders, drunkenness, revelings, and such like: of the which I tell you before, as I have also told you in time past, that they which do such things shall not inherit the kingdom of God.

22 But the fruit of the Spirit is love, joy, peace, longsuffering, gentleness, goodness, faith,

23 Meekness, temperance: against such there is no law.

24 And they that are Christ's have crucified the flesh with the affections and lusts.

25 If we live in the Spirit, let us also walk in the Spirit.

26 Let us not be desirous of vain glory, provoking one another, envying one another.

GALATIANS 6

1 Brethren, if a man be overtaken in a fault, ye which are spiritual, restore such an one in the spirit of meekness; considering thyself, lest thou also be tempted.

2 Bear ye one another's burdens, and so fulfill the law of Christ.

3 For if a man think himself to be something, when he is nothing, he deceiveth himself.

4 But let every man prove his own work, and then shall he have rejoicing in himself alone, and not in another.

5 For every man shall bear his own burden.

6 Let him that is taught in the word communicate unto him that teacheth in all good things.

7 Be not deceived; God is not mocked: for whatsoever a man soweth, that shall he also reap.

8 For he that soweth to his flesh shall of the flesh reap corrup-

fulfill the desire of the flesh, as otherwise ye would do.

18. But if ye are led by the Spirit – Of liberty and love, into all holiness. Ye are not under the law – Not under the curse or bondage of it; not under the guilt or the power of sin.

19. Now the works of the flesh – By which that inward principle is discovered. Are manifest – Plain and undeniable. Works are mentioned in the plural because they are distinct from, and often inconsistent with, each other. But "the fruit of the Spirit" is mentioned in the singular, ver. 22, as being all consistent and connected together. Which are these – He enumerates those "works of the flesh" to which the Galatians were most inclined; and those parts of "the fruit of the Spirit" of which they stood in the greatest need. Lasciviousness – The Greek word means anything inward or outward that is contrary to chastity, and yet short of actual uncleanness.

20. Idolatry, witchcraft – That this means witchcraft, strictly speaking, (not poisoning,) appears from its being joined with the worship of devil-gods, and not with murder. This is frequently and solemnly forbidden in the Old Testament. To deny therefore that there is, or ever was, any such thing, is, by plain consequence, to deny the authority both of the Old and New Testament. Divisions – In domestic or civil matters. Heresies are divisions in religious communities.

22. Love – The root of all the rest. Gentleness – Toward all men; ignorant and wicked men in particular. Goodness – The Greek word means all that is benign, soft, winning, tender, either in temper or behavior.

23. Meekness – Holding all the affections and passions in even balance.

24. And they that are Christ's – True believers in him. Have thus crucified the flesh – Nailed it, as it were, to a cross whence it has no power to break loose, but is continually weaker and weaker. With its affections and desires – All its evil passions, appetites, and inclinations.

25. If we live by the Spirit – If we are indeed raised from the dead, and are alive to God, by the operation of his Spirit. Let us walk by the Spirit – Let us follow his guidance, in all our tempers, thoughts, words, and actions.

26. Be not desirous of vain glory – Of the praise or esteem of men. They who do not carefully and closely follow the Spirit, easily slide into this: the natural effects of which are, provoking to envy them that are beneath us, and envying them that are above us.

GALATIANS 6

1. Brethren, if a man be overtaken in any fault – By surprise, ignorance, or stress of temptation. Ye who are spiritual – Who continue to live and walk by the Spirit. Restore such an one – By reproof, instruction, or exhortation. Every one who can, ought to help herein; only in the spirit of meekness – This is essential to a spiritual man; and in this lies the whole force of the cure.

2. Bear ye one another's burdens – Sympathize with, and assist, each other, in all your weaknesses, grievances, trials. And so fulfill the law of Christ – The law of Christ (an uncommon expression) is the law of love: this our Lord peculiarly recommends; this he makes the distinguishing mark of his disciples.

3. If any one think himself to be something – Above his brethren, or by any strength of his own. When he is nothing, he deceiveth himself – He alone will bear their burdens, who knows himself to be nothing.

4. But let every man try his own work – Narrowly examine all he is, and all he doeth. And then he shall have rejoicing in himself – He will find in himself matter of rejoicing, if his works are right before God. And not in another – Not in glorying over others.

5. For every one shall bear his own burden – In that day shall give an account of himself to God.

6. Let him that is taught impart to him that teacheth all such temporal good

Christ in justification. The apostle leaves them to judge whence it must arise, but sufficiently shows that it could be owing to none but Satan.

13-15 The gospel is a doctrine according to godliness, 1Ti 6:3, and is so far from giving the least countenance to sin, that it lays us under the strongest obligation to avoid and subdue it. The apostle urges that all the law is fulfilled in one word, even in this, Thou shalt love thy neighbor as thyself.

16-26 If it be our care to act under the guidance and power of the blessed Spirit, though we may not be freed from the stirrings and oppositions of the corrupt nature which remains in us, it shall not have dominion over us. Believers are engaged in a conflict, in which they earnestly desire that grace may obtain full and speedy victory. And those who desire thus to give themselves up to be led by the Holy Spirit, are not under the law as a covenant of works, nor exposed to its awful curse. Their hatred of sin, and desires after holiness, show that they have a part in the salvation of the gospel. The works of the flesh are many and manifest. And these sins will shut men out of heaven. Yet what numbers, calling themselves Christians, live in these, and say they hope for heaven! The fruits of the Spirit, or of the renewed nature, which we are to do, are named.

GALATIANS 6

*Exhortations to meekness, gentleness, and humility.
(1-5)
To kindness towards all men, especially believers.
(6-11)
The Galatians guarded against the judaizing teachers.
(12-15)
A solemn blessing. (16-18)*

1-5 We are to bear one another's burdens. So we shall fulfill the law of Christ. This obliges to mutual forbearance and compassion towards each other, agreeably to his example. It becomes us to bear one another's burdens, as fellow travelers. It is very common for a man to look upon himself as wiser and better than other men, and as fit to dictate to them. Such a one deceives himself; by pretending to what he has not, he puts a cheat upon himself, and sooner or later will find the sad effects. This will never gain esteem, either with God or men. Every one is advised to prove his own work. The better we know our own hearts and ways, the less shall we despise others, and the more be disposed to help them under infirmities and afflictions.

6-11 Many excuse themselves from the work of religion, though they may make a show, and profess it. They may impose upon others, yet they deceive themselves if they think to impose upon God, who knows

awful crushing wheels of divine vengeance, the self-same pains and sufferings which we ought to have endured. O! the glorious doctrine of substitution! When it is preached fully and rightly, what a charm and what power it hath. O! how sweet to tell sinners, that though God hath said, "Thou must die," their Maker stoops his head to die for them and Christ incarnate breathes his last upon a tree, that God might execute his vengeance, and yet might pardon all believers in Jesus because he has met all the claims of divine justice on their account.

Should there be one here who does not understand substitution, let me repeat what I have said. Sinner, the only way thou canst be saved is this. God must punish sin; if he did not, he would undeify himself; but if he has punished sin in the person of Christ for thee, thou art fully absolved, thou art quite clear; Christ hath suffered what thou oughtest to have suffered, and thou mayest rejoice in that. "Well," sayest thou, "I ought to have died." Christ hath died! "I ought to have been sent to hell." Christ did not go there to endure that torment forever; but he suffered an equivalent for it, something which satisfied God. The whole of hell was distilled into his cup of sorrows; he drank it. The cup which his father gave him, he drank to its dregs.

"At one tremendous draught of love,
He drank destruction dry."

for all who believe in him. All the punishment, all the curse, on him was laid. Vengeance now was satisfied; all was gone, and gone for ever; but not gone without having been taken away by the Savior. The thunders have not been reserved, they have been launched at him, and vengeance is satisfied, because Christ has endured the full penalty of all his people's guilt.

To close: have I one here who is saying, "What must I do to be saved, for I feel myself condemned?" Hear thou Christ's own words— "He that believeth and is baptized shall be saved; but he that believeth not shall be damned." Dost thou ask me what it is to believe? Hear, then, the answer. To believe is to look to Jesus. that little word "look" expresses beautifully what a sinner is to do. There is little in its appearance, but there is much in its meaning. Believing is letting the hands lie still, and turning the eyes to Christ. We can not be saved by our hands; but we are saved through our eyes, when they look to Jesus. Sinner! it is no use for thee to try and save thyself; but to believe in Christ is the only way of salvation; and that is, throwing self behind your back, and putting Christ right before thee.

I never can find a better figure than the Negro's one: to believe is to fall flat down upon

tion; but he that soweth to the Spirit shall of the Spirit reap life everlasting.

9 And let us not be weary in well doing: for in due season we shall reap, if we faint not.

10 As we have therefore opportunity, let us do good unto all men, especially unto them who are of the household of faith.

11 Ye see how large a letter I have written unto you with mine own hand.

12 As many as desire to make a fair shew in the flesh, they constrain you to be circumcized; only lest they should suffer persecution for the cross of Christ.

13 For neither they themselves who are circumcized keep the law; but desire to have you circumcized, that they may glory in your flesh.

14 But God forbid that I should glory, save in the cross of our Lord Jesus Christ, by whom the world is crucified unto me, and I unto the world.

15 For in Christ Jesus neither circumcision availeth anything, nor uncircumcision, but a new creature.

16 And as many as walk according to this rule, peace be on them, and mercy, and upon the Israel of God.

17 From henceforth let no man trouble me: for I bear in my body the marks of the Lord Jesus.

18 Brethren, the grace of our Lord Jesus Christ be with your spirit. Amen.

things as he stands in need of.

7. God is not mocked – Although they attempt to mock him, who think to reap otherwise than they sow.

8. For he that now soweth to the flesh – That follows the desires of corrupt nature. Shall hereafter of the flesh – Out of this very seed. Reap corruption – Death everlasting. But he that soweth to the Spirit – That follows his guidance in all his tempers and conversation. Shall of the Spirit – By the free grace and power of God, reap life everlasting.

9. But let us not be weary in well doing – Let us persevere in sowing to the Spirit. For in due season – When the harvest is come, we shall reap, if we faint not.

10. Therefore as we have opportunity – At whatever time or place, and in whatever manner we can. The opportunity in general is our lifetime; but there are also many particular opportunities. Satan is quickened in doing hurt, by the shortness of the time, Rev. xii, 12. By the same consideration let us be quickened in doing good. Let us do good – In every possible kind, and in every possible degree. Unto all men – neighbors or strangers, good or evil, friends or enemies. But especially to them who are of the household of faith. For all believers are but one family.

11. Ye see how large a letter – St. Paul had not yet wrote a larger to any church. I have written with my own hand – He generally wrote by an amanuensis.

12. As many as desire to make a fair appearance in the flesh – To preserve a fair character. These constrain you – Both by their example and importunity. To be circumcized – Not so much from a principle of conscience, as lest they should suffer persecution – From the unbelieving Jews. For the cross of Christ – For maintaining that faith in a crucified Savior is alone sufficient for justification.

13. For neither they themselves keep the whole law – So far are they from a real zeal for it. But yet they desire to have you circumcized, that they may glory in your flesh – That they may boast of you as their proselytes, and make a merit of this with the other Jews.

14. But God forbid that I should glory – Should boast of anything I have, am, or do; or rely on anything for my acceptance with God, but what Christ hath done and suffered for me. By means of which the world is crucified to me – All the things and persons in it are to me as nothing. And I unto the world – I am dead to all worldly pursuits, cares, desires, and enjoyments.

15. For neither circumcision is anything, nor uncircumcision – Neither of these is of any account. But a new creation – Whereby all things in us become new.

16. And as many as walk according to this rule –

1. Glorying only in the cross of Christ.

2. Being crucified to the world. And,

3. Created anew. Peace and mercy be upon them, and upon the Israel, that is, the Church, of God – Which consists of all those, and those only, of every nation and kindred, who walk by this rule.

17. From henceforth let none trouble me – By quarrels and disputes. For I bear – And afflictions should not be added to the afflicted. In my body the marks of the Lord Jesus – The scars, marks, and brands of my sufferings for him.

MATTHEW HENRY   CHARLES H. SPURGEON

their hearts as well as actions; and as he cannot be deceived, so he will not be mocked. Our present time is seedtime; in the other world we shall reap as we sow now. As there are two sorts of sowing, one to the flesh, and the other to the Spirit, so will the reckoning be hereafter. Those who live a carnal, sensual life, must expect no other fruit from such a course than misery and ruin. But those who, under the guidance and influences of the Holy Spirit, live a life of faith in Christ, and abound in Christian graces, shall of the Spirit reap life everlasting. We are all very apt to tire in duty, particularly in doing good. This we should carefully watch and guard against. Only to perseverance in well doing is the reward promised. Here is an exhortation to all to do good in their places. We should take care to do good in our lifetime, and make this the business of our lives. Especially when fresh occasions offer, and as far as our power reaches.

12-15 Proud, vain, and carnal hearts, are content with just so much religion as will help to keep up a fair show. But the apostle professes his own faith, hope, and joy; and that his principal glory was in the cross of Christ. By which is here meant, his sufferings and death on the cross, the doctrine of salvation by a crucified Redeemer. By Christ, or by the cross of Christ, the world is crucified to the believer, and he to the world.

16-18 A new creation to the image of Christ, as showing faith in him, is the greatest distinction between one man and another, and a blessing is declared on all who walk according this rule. The blessings are, peace and mercy. Peace with God and our conscience, and all the comforts of this life, as far as they are needful. And mercy, an interest in the free love and favor of God in Christ, the spring and fountain of all other blessings. The written word of God is the rule we are to go by, both in its doctrines and precepts. May his grace ever be with our spirit, to sanctify, quicken, and cheer us, and may we always be ready to maintain the honor of that which is indeed our life. The apostle had in his body the marks of the Lord Jesus, the scars of wounds from persecuting enemies, for his cleaving to Christ, and the doctrine of the gospel. The apostle calls the Galatians his brethren, therein he shows his humility and his tender affection for them; and he takes his leave with a very serious prayer, that they might enjoy the favor of Christ Jesus, both in its effects and in its evidences. We need desire no more to make us happy than the grace of our Lord Jesus Christ. The apostle does not pray that the law of Moses, or the righteousness of works, but that the grace of Christ, might be with them; that it might be in their hearts and with their spirits, quickening, comforting, and strengthening them: to all which he sets his Amen; signifying his desire that so it might be, and his faith that so it would be.

the promise, and there to lie. To believe is as a man would do in a stream. It is said, that if we were to fold our arms, and lie motionless, we could not sink. To believe is to float upon the stream of grace. I grant you, you shall do afterward; but you must live before you can do. The gospel is the reverse of the law. The law says, "Do and live;" the gospel says, "Live first, then do." The way to do, poor sinner, is to say, "Here, Jesus, here I am; I give myself to thee." I never had a better idea of believing than I once had from a poor countryman. I may have mentioned this before; but it struck me very forcibly at the time, and I can not help repeating it. Speaking about faith he said, "The old enemy has been troubling me very much lately; but I told him that he must not say any thing to me about my sins, he must go to my Master, for I had transferred the whole concern to him, bad debts and all." That is believing. Believing is giving up all we have to Christ, and taking all Christ has to ourselves. It is changing houses with Christ, changing clothes with Christ, changing our unrighteousness for his righteousness, changing our sins for his merits. Execute the transfer, sinner; rather, may God's grace execute it, and give thee faith in it; and then the law will be no longer thy condemnation, but it shall acquit thee. May Christ add his blessing! May the Holy Spirit rest upon us! And may we meet at last in heaven! Then will we "sing to the praise of the glory of his grace, wherein he hath made us accepted in the Beloved."

Ephesians

EPHESIANS 1

1 Paul, an apostle of Jesus Christ by the will of God, to the saints which are at Ephesus, and to the faithful in Christ Jesus:

2 Grace be to you, and peace, from God our Father, and from the Lord Jesus Christ.

3 Blessed be the God and Father of our Lord Jesus Christ, who hath blessed us with all spiritual blessings in heavenly places in Christ:

4 According as he hath chosen us in him before the foundation of the world, that we should be holy and without blame before him in love:

5 Having predestinated us unto the adoption of children by Jesus Christ to himself, according to the good pleasure of his will,

6 To the praise of the glory of his grace, wherein he hath made us accepted in the beloved.

7 In whom we have redemption through his blood, the forgiveness of sins, according to the riches of his grace;

8 Wherein he hath abounded toward us in all wisdom and prudence;

9 Having made known unto us the mystery of his will, according to his good pleasure which he hath purposed in himself:

10 That in the dispensation of the fullness of times he might gather together in one all things in Christ, both which are in heaven, and which are on earth; even in him:

11 In whom also we have obtained an inheritance, being predestinated according to the purpose of him who worketh all things after the counsel of his own will:

12 That we should be to the praise of his glory, who first trusted in Christ.

13 In whom ye also trusted, after that ye heard the word of truth, the gospel of your salvation: in whom also after that ye believed, ye were sealed with that holy Spirit of promise,

14 Which is the earnest of our inheritance until the redemption of the purchased possession, unto the praise of his glory.

EPHESUS was the chief city of that part of Asia, which was a Roman province. Here St. Paul preached for three years, Acts xx, 31; and from hence the gospel was spread throughout the whole province, Acts xix, 10. At his taking leave of the church there, he forewarned them both of great persecutions from without, and of divers heresies and schisms which would arise among themselves. And accordingly he writes this epistle, nearly resembling that to the Colossians, written about the same time, to establish them in the doctrine he had delivered, to arm them against false teachers, and to build them up in love and holiness, both of heart and conversation. He begins this, as most of his epistles, with thanksgiving to God for their embracing and adhering to the gospel. He shows the inestimable blessings and advantages they received thereby, as far above all the Jewish privileges, as all the wisdom and philosophy of the heathens. He proves that our Lord is the Head of the whole church; of angels and spirits, the church triumphant, and of Jews and Gentiles, now equally members of the church militant. In the three last chapters he exhorts them to various duties, civil and religious, personal and relative, suitable to their Christian character, privileges, assistances, and obligations.

EPHESIANS 1

1. By the will of God – Not by any merit of my own. To the saints who are at Ephesus – And in all the adjacent places. For this epistle is not directed to the Ephesians only, but likewise to all the other churches of Asia.

3. Blessed be the God and Father of our Lord Jesus Christ, who hath blessed us – God's blessing us is his bestowing all spiritual and heavenly blessings upon us. Our blessing God is the paying him our solemn and grateful acknowledgments, both on account of his own essential blessedness, and of the blessings which he bestows upon us. He is the God of our Lord Jesus Christ, as man and Mediator: he is his Father, primarily, with respect to his divine nature, as his only begotten Son; and, secondarily, with respect to his human nature, as that is personally united to the divine. With all spiritual blessings in heavenly things – With all manner of spiritual blessings, which are heavenly in their nature, origin, and tendency, and shall be completed in heaven: far different from the external privileges of the Jews, and the earthly blessings they expected from the Messiah.

4. As he hath chosen us – Both Jews and Gentiles, whom he foreknew as believing in Christ, 1 Pet. i, 2.

5. Having predestinated us to the adoption of sons – Having foreordained that all who afterwards believed should enjoy the dignity of being sons of God, and joint-heirs with Christ. According to the good pleasure of his will – According to his free, fixed, unalterable purpose to confer this blessing on all those who should believe in Christ, and those only.

6. To the praise of the glory of his grace – His glorious, free love without any desert on our part.

7. By whom we – Who believe. Have – From the moment we believe. Redemption – From the guilt and power of sin. Through his blood – Through what he hath done and suffered for us. According to the riches of his grace – According to the abundant overflowings of his free mercy and favor.

8. In all wisdom – Manifested by God in the whole scheme of our salvation. And prudence – Which he hath wrought in us, that we may know and do all his acceptable and perfect will.

9. Having made known to us – By his word and by his Spirit. The mystery of his will – The gracious scheme of salvation by faith, which depends on his own sovereign will alone. This was but darkly discovered under the law; is now totally hid from unbelievers; and has heights and depths which surpass all the knowledge even of true believers.

10. That in the dispensation of the fullness of the times – In this last adminis-

MATTHEW HENRY

CHARLES H. SPURGEON

This epistle was written when St. Paul was a prisoner at Rome. The design appears to be to strengthen the Ephesians in the faith of Christ, and to give exalted views of the love of God, and of the dignity and excellence of Christ, fortifying their minds against the scandal of the cross. He shows that they were saved by grace, and that however wretched they once were, they now had equal privileges with the Jews. He encourages them to persevere in their Christian calling, and urges them to walk in a manner becoming their profession, faithfully discharging the general and common duties of religion, and the special duties of particular relations.

EPHESIANS 1

A salutation, and an account of saving blessings, as prepared in God's eternal election, as purchased by Christ's blood. (1-8)

And as conveyed in effectual calling: this is applied to the believing Jews, and to the believing Gentiles. (9-14)

The apostle thanks God for their faith and love, and prays for the continuance of their knowledge and hope, with respect to the heavenly inheritance, and to God's powerful working in them. (15-23)

1,2 All Christians must be saints; if they come not under that character on earth, they will never be saints in glory. Those are not saints, who are not faithful, believing in Christ, and true to the profession they make of relation to their Lord. By grace, understand the free and undeserved love and favor of God, and those graces of the Spirit which come from it; by peace, all other blessings, spiritual and temporal, the fruits of the former. No peace without grace. No peace, nor grace, but from God the Father, and from the Lord Jesus Christ; and the best saints need fresh supplies of the graces of the Spirit, and desire to grow.

3-8 Spiritual and heavenly blessings are the best blessings; with which we cannot be miserable, and without which we cannot but be so. This was from the choice of them in Christ, before the foundation of the world, that they should be made holy by separation from sin, being set apart to God, and sanctified by the Holy Spirit, in consequence of their election in Christ. All who are chosen to happiness as the end, are chosen to holiness as the means. In love they were predestinated, or foreordained, to be adopted as children of God by faith in Christ Jesus, and to be openly admitted to the privileges of that high relation to himself. The reconciled and adopted believer, the pardoned sinner, gives all the praise of his salvation to his gracious Father. His love appointed this method of redemption, spared not his own Son, and brought believers to hear and embrace this salvation. It was rich grace to provide such a surety as his own Son, and freely to deliver him up.

GRIEVING THE HOLY SPIRIT
Sermon number 278, delivered on October 9th, 1859, at the Music Hall, Royal Surrey Gardens.

"And grieve not the Holy Spirit of God, whereby ye are sealed unto the day of redemption."—Ephesians 4:30.

The few words I have to say UPON THE LOVE OF THE SPIRIT will all be pressing forward to my great mark, stirring you up not to grieve the Spirit; for when we are persuaded that another loves us, we find at once a very potent reason why we should not grieve him. The love of the Spirit!—how shall I tell it forth? Surely it needs a songster to sing it, for love is only to be spoken of in words of song. The love of the Spirit!—let me tell you of his early love to us. He loved us without beginning. In the eternal covenant of grace, as I told you last Sabbath, he was one of the high contracting parties in the divine contract, whereby we are saved. All that can be said of the love of the Father, of the love of the Son, may be said of the love of the Spirit—it is eternal, it is infinite, it is sovereign, it is everlasting, it is a love which cannot be dissolved, which cannot be decreased, a love which cannot be removed from those who are the objects of it. Permit me, however, to refer you to his acts, rather than his attributes. Let me tell you of the love of the Spirit to you and to me. Oh how early was that love which he manifested towards us, even in our childhood! My brethren, we can well remember how the Spirit was wont to strive with us. We went astray from the womb speaking lies, but how early did the Spirit of God stir up our conscience, and solemnly correct us on account of our youthful sins. How frequently since then has the Spirit wooed us! How often under the ministry has he compelled our hearts to melt, and the tear has run down our cheeks, and he has sweetly whispered in our ear, "My son, give me thy heart; go to thy chamber, shut thy door about thee, confess thy sins, and seek a Savior's love and blood." Oh,— but let us blush to tell it—how often have we done despite to him! When we were in a state of unregeneracy, how we were wont to resist him! We quenched the Spirit; he strove with us but we strove against him. But blessed be his dear name, and let him have everlasting songs for it, he would not let us go! We would not be saved, but he would save us. We sought to thrust ourselves into the fire, but he sought to pluck us from the burning. We would dash ourselves from the precipice, but he wrestled with us and held us fast; he would not let us destroy our souls. Oh, how we ill-treated him, how we did set at nought his counsel! How did we scorn

15 Wherefore I also, after I heard of your faith in the Lord Jesus, and love unto all the saints,

16 Cease not to give thanks for you, making mention of you in my prayers;

17 That the God of our Lord Jesus Christ, the Father of glory, may give unto you the spirit of wisdom and revelation in the knowledge of him:

18 The eyes of your understanding being enlightened; that ye may know what is the hope of his calling, and what the riches of the glory of his inheritance in the saints,

19 And what is the exceeding greatness of his power to usward who believe, according to the working of his mighty power,

20 Which he wrought in Christ, when he raised him from the dead, and set him at his own right hand in the heavenly places,

21 Far above all principality, and power, and might, and dominion, and every name that is named, not only in this world, but also in that which is to come:

22 And hath put all things under his feet, and gave him to be the head over all things to the church,

23 Which is his body, the fullness of him that filleth all in all.

EPHESIANS 2

1 And you hath he quickened, who were dead in trespasses and sins;

2 Wherein in time past ye walked according to the course of this world, according to the prince of the power of the air, the spirit that now worketh in the children of disobedience:

3 Among whom also we all had our conversation in times past in the lusts of our flesh, fulfilling the desires of the flesh and of the mind; and were by nature the children of wrath, even as others.

4 But God, who is rich in mercy, for his great love wherewith he loved us,

5 Even when we were dead in sins, hath quickened us togeth-

tration of God's fullest grace, which took place when the time appointed was fully come. He might gather together into one in Christ – Might recapitulate, re-unite, and place in order again under Christ, their common Head. All things which are in heaven, and on earth – All angels and men, whether living or dead, in the Lord.

12. That we – Jews. Who first believed – Before the Gentiles. So did some of them in every place. Here is another branch of the true gospel predestination: he that believes is not only elected to salvation, (if he endures to the end,) but is fore-appointed of God to walk in holiness, to the praise of his glory.

13. In whom ye – Gentiles. Likewise believed, after ye had heard the gospel – Which God made the means of your salvation; in whom after ye had believed – Probably some time after their first believing. Ye were sealed by that Holy Spirit of promise – Holy both in his nature and in his operations, and promised to all the children of God. The sealing seems to imply,

    1. A full impression of the image of God on their souls.

    2. A full assurance of receiving all the promises, whether relating to time or eternity.

14. Who, thus sealing us, is an earnest – Both a pledge and a foretaste of our inheritance. Till the redemption of the purchased possession – Till the church, which he has purchased with his own blood, shall be fully delivered from all sin and sorrow, and advanced to everlasting glory. To the praise of his glory – Of his glorious wisdom, power, and mercy.

15. Since I heard of your faith and love – That is, of their perseverance and increase therein.

16. I cease not – In all my solemn addresses to God. To give thanks for you, making mention of you in my prayers – So he did of all the churches, Col. i, 9.

17. That the Father of that infinite glory which shines in the face of Christ, from whom also we receive the glorious inheritance, ver. 18, may give you the Spirit of wisdom and Revelation – The same who is the Spirit of promise is also, in the progress of the faithful, the Spirit of wisdom and Revelation; making them wise unto salvation, and revealing to them the deep things of God. He is here speaking of that wisdom and Revelation which are common to all real Christians.

18. The eyes of your understanding – It is with these alone that we discern the things of God. Being first opened, and then enlightened – By his Spirit. That ye may know what is the hope of his calling – That ye may experimentally and delightfully know what are the blessings which God has called you to hope for by his word and his Spirit. And what is the riches of the glory of his inheritance in the saints – What an immense treasure of blessedness he hath provided as an inheritance for holy souls.

19. And what the exceeding greatness of his power toward us who believe – Both in quickening our dead souls, and preserving them in spiritual life. According to the power which he exerted in Christ, raising him from the dead – By the very same almighty power whereby he raised Christ; for no less would suffice.

20. And he hath seated him at his own right hand – That is, he hath exalted him in his human nature, as a recompense for his sufferings, to a quiet, everlasting possession of all possible blessedness, majesty, and glory.

22. And he hath given him to be head over all things to the church – An head both of guidance and government, and likewise of life and influence, to the whole and every member of it. All these stand in the nearest union with him, and have as continual and effectual a communication of activity, growth, and strength from him, as the natural body from its head.

23. The fullness of him that filleth all in all – It is hard to say in what sense this can be spoken of the church; but the sense is easy and natural, if we refer it to Christ, who is the fullness of the Father.

MATTHEW HENRY

CHARLES H. SPURGEON

9-14 Blessings were made known to believers, by the Lord's showing to them the mystery of his sovereign will, and the method of redemption and salvation. But these must have been forever hidden from us, if God had not made them known by his written word, preached gospel, and Spirit of truth. Christ united the two differing parties, God and man, in his own person, and satisfied for that wrong which caused the separation. He wrought, by his Spirit, those graces of faith and love, whereby we are made one with God, and among ourselves. He dispenses all his blessings, according to his good pleasure. His Divine teaching led whom he pleased to see the glory of those truths, which others were left to blaspheme. What a gracious promise that is, which secures the gift of the Holy Ghost to those who ask him!

15-23 God has laid up spiritual blessings for us in his Son the Lord Jesus; but requires us to draw them out and fetch them in by prayer. Even the best Christians need to be prayed for: and while we hear of the welfare of Christian friends, we should pray for them. Even true believers greatly want heavenly wisdom. Are not the best of us unwilling to come under God's yoke, though there is no other way to find rest for the soul? Do we not for a little pleasure often part with our peace? And if we dispute less, and prayed more with and for each other, we should daily see more and more what is the hope of our calling, and the riches of the Divine glory in this inheritance. It is desirable to feel the mighty power of Divine grace, beginning and carrying on the work of faith in our souls. But it is difficult to bring a soul to believe fully in Christ, and to venture its all, and the hope of eternal life, upon his righteousness. Nothing less than Almighty power will work this in us. Here is signified that it is Christ the Savior, who supplies all the necessities of those who trust in him, and gives them all blessings in the richest abundance. And by being partakers of Christ himself, we come to be filled with the fullness of grace and glory in him. How then do those forget themselves who seek for righteousness out of him!

EPHESIANS 2

The riches of God's grace towards men, shown from their deplorable state by nature, and the happy change Divine grace makes in them. (1-10)
The Ephesians called to reflect on their state of heathenism. (11-13)
And the privileges and blessings of the gospel. (14-22)

1-10 Sin is the death of the soul. A man dead in trespasses and sins has no desire for spiritual pleasures. When we look upon a corpse, it gives an awful feeling. A never-dying spirit is now fled, and has left nothing but the ruins of a man. But if we viewed things aright, we should be far more affected by the thought of a dead soul, a lost, fallen spirit. A state of sin is a

and scoff him; how did we despise the ordinance which would lead us to Christ! How did we violate that holy cord which was gently drawing us to Jesus and his cross! I am sure, my brethen, at the recollections of the persevering struggles of the Spirit with you, you must be stirred up to love him. How often did he restrain you from sin, when you were about to plunge headlong into a course of vice! How often did he constrain you to good, when you would have neglected it! You, perhaps, would not have been in the way at all, and the Lord would not have met you, if it had not been for that sweet Spirit, who would not let you become a blasphemer, who would not suffer you to forsake the house of God, and would not permit you to become a regular attendant at the haunts of vice, but checked you, and held you in, as it were, with bit and bridle. Though you were like a bullock, unaccustomed to the yoke, yet he would not let you have your way. Though you struggled against him, yet he would not throw the reins upon your necks, but he said, "I will have him, I will have him against his will; I will change his heart, I will not let him go till I have made him a trophy of my mighty power to save."

Ah, then, in that blest hour, to memory dear, was it not the Holy Spirit who guided you to Jesus? Do you remember the love of the Spirit, when, after having quickened you, he took you aside, and showed you Jesus on the tree? Who was it that opened our blind eye to see a dying Savior? Who was it that opened your deaf ear to hear the voice of pardoning love? Who opened your clasped and palsied hand to receive the tokens of a Savior's grace? Who was it that brake your hard heart and made a way for the Savior to enter and dwell therein? Oh! it was that precious Spirit, that self-same Spirit, to whom you had done so much despite, whom in the days of your flesh you had resisted! What a mercy it was that he did not say, "I will swear in my wrath that they shall not enter into my rest, for they have vexed me, and I will take my everlasting flight from them;" or thus, "Ephraim is joined unto idols, I will let him alone!" And since that time, my brethren, how sweetly has the Spirit proved his love to you and to me. It is not only in his first strivings, and then his divine quickenings; but in all the sequel, how much have we owed to his instruction. We have been dull scholars with the word before us, plain and simple, so that he that reads may read, and he that reads may understand, yet how small a portion of his Word has our memory retained, how little progress have we made in the school of God's grace! We are but learners yet, unstable, weak, and apt to slide, but what a blessed

er with Christ, (by grace ye are saved;)

6 And hath raised us up together, and made us sit together in heavenly places in Christ Jesus:

7 That in the ages to come he might shew the exceeding riches of his grace in his kindness toward us through Christ Jesus.

8 For by grace are ye saved through faith; and that not of yourselves: it is the gift of God:

9 Not of works, lest any man should boast.

10 For we are his workmanship, created in Christ Jesus unto good works, which God hath before ordained that we should walk in them.

11 Wherefore remember, that ye being in time past Gentiles in the flesh, who are called Uncircumcision by that which is called the Circumcision in the flesh made by hands;

12 That at that time ye were without Christ, being aliens from the commonwealth of Israel, and strangers from the covenants of promise, having no hope, and without God in the world:

13 But now in Christ Jesus ye who sometimes were far off are made nigh by the blood of Christ.

14 For he is our peace, who hath made both one, and hath broken down the middle wall of partition between us;

15 Having abolished in his flesh the enmity, even the law of commandments contained in ordinances; for to make in himself of twain one new man, so making peace;

16 And that he might reconcile both unto God in one body by the cross, having slain the enmity thereby:

17 And came and preached peace to you which were afar off, and to them that were nigh.

18 For through him we both have access by one Spirit unto the Father.

19 Now therefore ye are no more strangers and foreigners, but fellowcitizens with the saints, and of the household of God;

20 And are built upon the foundation of the apostles and prophets, Jesus Christ himself

EPHESIANS 2

1. And he hath quickened you – In the nineteenth and twentieth verses of the preceding chapter, St. Paul spoke of God's working in them by the same almighty power whereby he raised Christ from the dead. On the mention of this he, in the fullness of his heart, runs into a flow of thought concerning the glory of Christ's exaltation in the three following verses. He here resumes the thread of his discourse. Who were dead – Not only diseased, but dead; absolutely void of all spiritual life; and as incapable of quickening yourselves, as persons literally dead. In trespasses and sins – Sins seem to be spoken chiefly of the Gentiles, who knew not God; trespasses, of the Jews, who had his law, and yet regarded it not, ver. 5. The latter herein obeyed the flesh; the former, the prince of the power of the air.

2. According to the course of this world – The word translated course properly means a long series of times, wherein one corrupt age follows another. According to the prince of the power of the air – The effect of which power all may perceive, though all do not understand the cause of it: a power unspeakably penetrating and widely diffused; but yet, as to its baneful influences, beneath the orb of believers. The evil spirits are united under one head, the seat of whose dominion is in the air. Here he sometimes raises storms, sometimes makes visionary representations, and is continually roving to and fro. The spirit that now worketh – With mighty power; and so he did, and doth in all ages. In the sons of disobedience – In all who do not believe and obey the gospel.

4. Mercy removes misery: love confers salvation.

5. He hath quickened us together with Christ – In conformity to him, and by virtue of our union with him. By grace ye are saved – Grace is both the beginning and end. The apostle speaks indifferently either in the first or second person; the Jews and Gentiles being in the same circumstance, both by nature and by grace. This text lays the axe to the very root of spiritual pride, and all glorying in ourselves. Therefore St. Paul, foreseeing the backwardness of mankind to receive it, yet knowing the absolute necessity of its being received, again asserts the very same truth, ver. 8, in the very same words.

6. And hath raised us up together – Both Jews and Gentiles already in spirit; and ere long our bodies too will be raised. And made us all sit together in heavenly places – This is spoken by way of anticipation. Believers are not yet possessed of their seats in heaven; but each of them has a place prepared for him.

7. The ages to come – That is, all succeeding ages.

8. By grace ye are saved through faith – Grace, without any respect to human worthiness, confers the glorious gift. Faith, with an empty hand, and without any pretense to personal desert, receives the heavenly blessing. And this is not of yourselves – This refers to the whole preceding clause, That ye are saved through faith, is the gift of God.

9. Not by works – Neither this faith nor this salvation is owing to any works you ever did, will, or can do.

10. For we are his workmanship – Which proves both that salvation is by faith, and that faith is the gift of God. Created unto good works – That afterwards we might give ourselves to them. Which God had before prepared – The occasions of them: so we must still ascribe the whole to God. That we might walk in them – Though not be justified by them.

11. Wherefore remember – Such a remembrance strengthens faith, and increases gratitude. That ye being formerly Gentiles in the flesh – Neither circumcized in body nor in spirit. Who were accordingly called the uncircumcision – By way of reproach. By that which is called the circumcision – By those who call themselves the circumcized, and think this a proof that they are the people of God; and who indeed have that outward circumcision which is performed by hands in the flesh.

12. Were at that time without Christ – Having no faith in, or knowledge of,

state of conformity to this world. Wicked men are slaves to Satan. Satan is the author of that proud, carnal disposition which there is in ungodly men; he rules in the hearts of men. From Scripture it is clear, that whether men have been most prone to sensual or to spiritual wickedness, all men, being naturally children of disobedience, are also by nature children of wrath. What reason have sinners, then, to seek earnestly for that grace which will make them, of children of wrath, children of God and heirs of glory! God's eternal love or good-will toward his creatures, is the fountain whence all his mercies flow to us; and that love of God is great love, and that mercy is rich mercy. And every converted sinner is a saved sinner; delivered from sin and wrath. The grace that saves is the free, undeserved goodness and favor of God; and he saves, not by the works of the law, but through faith in Christ Jesus. Grace in the soul is a new life in the soul. A regenerated sinner becomes a living soul; he lives a life of holiness, being born of God: he lives, being delivered from the guilt of sin, by pardoning and justifying grace. Sinners roll themselves in the dust; sanctified souls sit in heavenly places, are raised above this world, by Christ's grace.

11-13 Christ and his covenant are the foundation of all the Christian's hopes. A sad and terrible description is here; but who is able to remove himself out of it? Would that this were not a true description of many baptized in the name of Christ. Who can, without trembling, reflect upon the misery of a person, separated for ever from the people of God, cut off from the body of Christ, fallen from the covenant of promise, having no hope, no Savior, and without any God but a God of vengeance, to all eternity? To have no part in Christ! What true Christian can hear this without horror? Salvation is far from the wicked; but God is a help at hand to his people; and this is by the sufferings and death of Christ.

14-18 Jesus Christ made peace by the sacrifice of himself; in every sense Christ was their Peace, the author, center, and substance of their being at peace with God, and of their union with the Jewish believers in one church. Through the person, sacrifice, and mediation of Christ, sinners are allowed to draw near to God as a Father, and are brought with acceptance into his presence, with their worship and services, under the teaching of the Holy Spirit, as one with the Father and the Son. Christ purchased leave for us to come to God; and the Spirit gives a heart to come, and strength to come, and then grace to serve God acceptably.

19-22 The church is compared to a city, and every converted sinner is free of it. It is also compared to a house, and every converted sinner is one of the family; a servant, and a child in God's house. The church is also compared to a building, founded on the doc-

instructor we have had! Has he not led us into many a truth, and taken of the things of Christ and applied them unto us? Oh! When I think how stupid I have been, I wonder that he has not given me up. When I think what a dolt I have been, when he would have taught me the things of the kingdom of God, I marvel that he should have had such patience with me. Is it a wonder that Jesus should become a babe? Is it not an equal wonder that the Spirit of the living God, should become a teacher of babes? It is a marvel that Jesus should lie in a manger; is it not an equal marvel that the Holy Spirit should become an usher in the sacred school, to teach fools, and make them wise? It was condescension that brought the Savior to the cross, but is it not equal condescension that brings the mighty Spirit of grace down to dwell with stubborn unruly, wild asses' colts, to teach them the mystery of the kingdom, and make them know the wonders of a Savior's love?

Another token of the Spirit's love remains, namely, his indwelling in the saints. We ask a question which can have but one answer. He does dwell in the heart of all God's redeemed and blood-washed people. And what a condescension is this, that he whom the heaven of heavens cannot contain, dwells in thy breast my brother. That breast often covered with rags, may be a breast often agitated with anxious care and thought, a breast too often defiled with sin, and yet he dwells there. The little narrow heart of man the Holy Spirit hath made his palace. Though it is but a cottage, a very hovel, and all unholy and unclean yet doth the Holy Spirit condescend to make the heart of his people his continual abode. Oh my friends, when I think how often you and I have let the devil in, I wonder the Spirit has not withdrawn from us. The final perseverance of the saints, is one of the greatest miracles on record; in fact, it is the sum total of miracles. The perseverance of a saint for a single day, is a multitude of miracles of mercy. When you consider that the Spirit is of purer eyes than to behold iniquity, and yet he dwells in the heart where sin often intrudes, a heart out of which comes blasphemies, and murders, and all manner of evil thoughts and concupiscence, what if sometimes he is grieved, and retires and leaves us to ourselves for a season? It is a marvel that he is there at all, for he must be daily grieved with these evil guests, these false traitors, these base intruders who thrust themselves into that little temple which he has honored with his presence, the temple of the heart of man. I am afraid, dear friends, we are too much in the habit of talking of the love of Jesus, without thinking of the love of the Holy Spirit. Now I would not wish to exalt one

being the chief corner stone;

21 In whom all the building fitly framed together groweth unto an holy temple in the Lord:

22 In whom ye also are builded together for an habitation of God through the Spirit.

EPHESIANS 3

1 For this cause I Paul, the prisoner of Jesus Christ for you Gentiles,

2 If ye have heard of the dispensation of the grace of God which is given me to youward:

3 How that by revelation he made known unto me the mystery; (as I wrote afore in few words,

4 Whereby, when ye read, ye may understand my knowledge in the mystery of Christ)

5 Which in other ages was not made known unto the sons of men, as it is now revealed unto his holy apostles and prophets by the Spirit;

6 That the Gentiles should be fellowheirs, and of the same body, and partakers of his promise in Christ by the gospel:

7 Whereof I was made a minister, according to the gift of the grace of God given unto me by the effectual working of his power.

8 Unto me, who am less than the least of all saints, is this grace given, that I should preach among the Gentiles the unsearchable riches of Christ;

9 And to make all men see what is the fellowship of the mystery, which from the beginning of the world hath been hid in God, who created all things by Jesus Christ:

10 To the intent that now unto the principalities and powers in heavenly places might be known by the church the manifold wisdom of God,

11 According to the eternal purpose which he purposed in Christ Jesus our Lord:

12 In whom we have boldness and access with confidence by the faith of him.

13 Wherefore I desire that ye faint not at my tribulations for you, which is your glory.

14 For this cause I bow my knees unto the Father of our

him. Being aliens from the commonwealth of Israel – Both as to their temporal privileges and spiritual blessings. And strangers to the covenants of promise – The great promise in both the Jewish and Christian covenant was the Messiah. Having no hope – Because they had no promise whereon to ground their hope. And being without God – Wholly ignorant of the true God, and so in effect atheists. Such in truth are, more or less, all men, in all ages, till they know God by the teaching of his own Spirit. In the world – The wide, vain world, wherein ye wandered up and down, unholy and unhappy.

13. Far off – From God and his people. Nigh – Intimately united to both.

15. Having abolished by his suffering in the flesh the cause of enmity between the Jews and Gentiles, even the law of ceremonial commandments, through his decrees – Which offer mercy to all; see Colossians ii, 14. That he might form the two – Jew and Gentile. Into one new man – one mystical body.

16. In one body – One church. Having slain – By his own death on the cross. The enmity – Which had been between sinners and God.

17. And he came – After his resurrection. And preached peace – By his ministers and his Spirit. To you – Gentiles. That were afar off – At the utmost distance from God. And to them that were nigh – To the Jews, who were comparatively nigh, being his visible church.

18. For through him, we both – Jews and Gentiles. Have access – Liberty of approaching, by the guidance and aid of one Spirit to God as our Father. Christ, the Spirit, and the Father, the three-one God, stand frequently in the same order.

19. Therefore ye are no longer strangers, but citizens of the heavenly Jerusalem; no longer foreigners, but received into the very family of God.

20. And are built upon the foundation of the apostles and prophets – As the foundation sustains the building, so the word of God, declared by the apostles and prophets, sustains the faith of all believers. God laid the foundation by them; but Christ himself is the chief corner-stone of the foundation. Elsewhere he is termed the foundation itself, 1 Cor. iii, 11.

21. On whom all the building fitly framed together – The whole fabric of the universal church rises up like a great pile of living materials. Into an holy temple in the Lord – Dedicated to Christ, and inhabited by him, in which he displays his presence, and is worshiped and glorified. What is the temple of Diana of the Ephesians, whom ye formerly worshiped, to this?

EPHESIANS 3

1. For this cause – That ye may be so "built together," I am a prisoner for you Gentiles – For your advantage, and for asserting your right to these blessings. This it was which so enraged the Jews against him.

2. The dispensation of the grace of God given me in your behalf – That is, the commission to dispense the gracious gospel; to you Gentiles in particular. This they had heard from his own mouth.

3. The mystery – Of salvation by Christ alone, and that both to Jews and Gentiles. As I wrote before – Namely, chap. i, 9, 10; the very words of which passage he here repeats.

5. Which in other – In former, ages was not so clearly or fully made known to the sons of men – To any man, no, not to Ezekiel, so often styled, "son of man;" nor to any of the ancient prophets. Those here spoken of are New Testament prophets.

6. That the Gentiles are joint-heirs – Of God. And of the same body – Under Christ the head. And joint-partakers of his promise – The communion of the Holy Ghost.

7. According to the gift of the grace of God – That is, the apostle-ship which he hath graciously given me, and which he hath qualified me for. By the effectual

MATTHEW HENRY

CHARLES H. SPURGEON

trine of Christ; delivered by the prophets of the Old Testament, and the apostles of the New. God dwells in all believers now; they become the temple of God through the working of the blessed Spirit.

EPHESIANS 3

The apostle sets forth his office, and his qualifications
for it, and his call to it. (1-7)
Also the noble purposes answered by it. (8-12)
He prays for the Ephesians. (13-19)
And adds a thanksgiving. (20,21)

1-7 For having preached the doctrine of truth, the apostle was a prisoner, but a prisoner of Jesus Christ; the object of special protection and care, while thus suffering for him. All the gracious offers of the gospel, and the joyful tidings it contains, come from the rich grace of God; it is the great means by which the Spirit works grace in the souls of men. The mystery, is that secret, hidden purpose of salvation through Christ. This was not so fully and clearly shown in the ages before Christ, as unto the prophets of the New Testament. This was the great truth made known to the apostle, that God would call the Gentiles to salvation by faith in Christ. An effectual working of Divine power attends the gifts of Divine grace. As God appointed Paul to the office, so he qualified him for it.

8-12 Those whom God advances to honorable employments, he makes low in their own eyes; and where God gives grace to be humble, there he gives all other needful grace. How highly he speaks of Jesus Christ; the unsearchable riches of Christ! Though many are not enriched with these riches; yet how great a favor to have them preached among us, and to have an offer of them! And if we are not enriched with them it is our own fault. The first creation, when God made all things out of nothing, and the new creation, whereby sinners are made new creatures by converting grace, are of God by Jesus Christ. His riches are as unsearchable and as sure as ever, yet while angels adore the wisdom of God in the redemption of his church, the ignorance of self-wise and carnal men deems the whole to be foolishness.

13-19 The apostle seems to be more anxious lest the believers should be discouraged and faint upon his tribulations, than for what he himself had to bear. He asks for spiritual blessings, which are the best blessings. Strength from the Spirit of God in the inner man; strength in the soul; the strength of faith, to serve God, and to do our duty. If the law of Christ is written in our hearts, and the love of Christ is shed abroad there, then Christ dwells there. Where his Spirit dwells, there he dwells. We should desire that good affections may be fixed in us. And how desirable to have a fixed sense of the love of God in Christ to our souls! How powerfully the apostle speaks of the love of

person of the Trinity above another, but I do feel this, that because Jesus Christ was a man, bone of our bone, and flesh of our flesh, and therefore there was something tangible in him that can be seen with the eyes, and handled with the hands, therefore we more readily think of him, and fix our love on him, than we do upon the Spirit. But why should it be? Let us love Jesus with all our hearts, and let us love the Holy Spirit too. Let us have songs for him, gratitude for him. We do not forget Christ's cross, let us not forget the Spirit's operations. We do not forget what Jesus has done for us, let us always remember what the Spirit does in us. Why you talk of the love, and grace, and tenderness, and faithfulness of Christ, why do you not say the like of the Spirit? Was ever love like his, that he should visit us? Was ever mercy like his, that he should bear with our ill manners, though constantly repeated by us? Was ever faithfulness like his, that multitudes of sins cannot drive him away? Was ever power like his, that overcometh all our iniquities?

And unto his name be glory for ever and ever.

II. This brings me to the second point. Here we have another reason why we should not grieve the Spirit. IT IS BY THE HOLY SPIRIT WE ARE SEALED. "BY whom we are sealed unto the day of redemption." I shall be very brief here. The Spirit himself is expressed as the seal, even as he himself is directly said to be the pledge of our inheritance. The sealing, I think, has a three-fold meaning. It is a sealing of attestation or confirmation. I want to know whether I am truly a child of God. The Spirit itself also beareth witness with my spirit that I am born of God. I have the writings, the title-deeds of the inheritance that is to come—I want to know whether those are valid, whether they are true, or whether they are mere counterfeits written out by that old scribe of hell, Master Presumption and Carnal Security. How am I to know? I look for the seal. After that we have believed on the Son of God, the Father seals us as his children, by the gift of the Holy Ghost. "Now he which hath anointed us is God, who also hath sealed us, and given the earnest of the Spirit in our hearts." No faith is genuine which does not bear the seal of the Spirit. No love, no hope can ever save us, except it be sealed with the Spirit of God, for whatever hath not his seal upon it is spurious. Faith that is unsealed may be a poison, it may be presumption; but faith that is sealed by the Spirit is true, real, genuine faith. Never be content, my dear hearers, unless you are sealed, unless you are sure, by the inward witness and testimony of the Holy Ghost, that you have

Lord Jesus Christ,

15 Of whom the whole family in heaven and earth is named,

16 That he would grant you, according to the riches of his glory, to be strengthened with might by his Spirit in the inner man;

17 That Christ may dwell in your hearts by faith; that ye, being rooted and grounded in love,

18 May be able to comprehend with all saints what is the breadth, and length, and depth, and height;

19 And to know the love of Christ, which passeth knowledge, that ye might be filled with all the fullness of God.

20 Now unto him that is able to do exceeding abundantly above all that we ask or think, according to the power that worketh in us,

21 Unto him be glory in the church by Christ Jesus throughout all ages, world without end. Amen.

EPHESIANS 4

1 I therefore, the prisoner of the Lord, beseech you that ye walk worthy of the vocation wherewith ye are called,

2 With all lowliness and meekness, with longsuffering, forbearing one another in love;

3 Endeavoring to keep the unity of the Spirit in the bond of peace.

4 There is one body, and one Spirit, even as ye are called in one hope of your calling;

5 One Lord, one faith, one baptism,

6 One God and Father of all, who is above all, and through all, and in you all.

7 But unto every one of us is given grace according to the measure of the gift of Christ.

8 Wherefore he saith, When he ascended up on high, he led captivity captive, and gave gifts unto men.

9 (Now that he ascended, what is it but that he also descended first into the lower parts of the earth?

10 He that descended is the same also that ascended up far above all heavens, that he might fill all things.)

working of his power – In me and by me.

8. Unto me, who am less than the least of all saints, is this grace given – Here are the noblest strains of eloquence to paint the exceeding low opinion the apostle had of himself, and the fullness of unfathomable blessings which are treasured up in Christ.

9. What is the fellowship of the mystery – What those mysterious blessings are whereof all believers jointly partake. Which was, in a great measure, hidden from eternity by God, who, to make way for the free exercise of his love, created all things – This is the foundation of all his dispensations.

10. That the manifold wisdom of God might be made known by the church – By what is done in the church, which is the theater of the divine wisdom.

12. By whom we have free access – Such as those petitioners have, who are introduced to the royal presence by some distinguished favorite. And boldness – Unrestrained liberty of speech, such as children use in addressing an indulgent father, when, without fear of offending, they disclose all their wants, and make known all their requests.

13. The not fainting is your glory.

15. Of whom – The Father. The whole family of angels in heaven, saints in paradise, and believers on earth is named. Being the "children of God," (a more honorable title than "children of Abraham,") and depending on him as the Father of the family.

16. The riches of his glory – The immense fullness of his glorious wisdom, power, and mercy. The inner man – The soul.

17. Dwell – That is, constantly and sensibly abide.

18. That being rooted and grounded – That is, deeply fixed and firmly established, in love. Ye may comprehend – So far as a human mind is capable. What is the breadth of the love of Christ – Embracing all mankind. And length – From everlasting to everlasting. And depth – Not to be fathomed by any creature. And height – Not to be reached by any enemy.

19. And to know – But the apostle corrects himself, and immediately observes, it cannot be fully known. This only we know, that the love of Christ surpasses all knowledge. That ye may be filled – Which is the sum of all. With all the fullness of God – With all his light, love, wisdom, holiness, power, and glory. A perfection far beyond a bare freedom from sin.

20. Now to him – This doxology is admirably adapted to strengthen our faith, that we may not stagger at the great things the apostle has been praying for, as if they were too much for God to give, or for us to expect from him. That is able – Here is a most beautiful gradation. When he has given us exceeding, yea, abundant blessings, still we may ask for more. And he is able to do it. But we may think of more than we have asked. He is able to do this also. Yea, and above all this. Above all we ask – Above all we can think. Nay, exceedingly, abundantly above all that we can either ask or think.

21. In the church – On earth and in heaven.

EPHESIANS 4

1. I therefore, the prisoner of the Lord – Imprisoned for his sake and for your sakes; for the sake of the gospel which he had preached amongst them. This was therefore a powerful motive to them to comfort him under it by their obedience.

3. Endeavoring to keep the unity of the Spirit – That mutual union and harmony, which is a fruit of the Spirit. The bond of peace is love.

4. There is one body – The universal church, all believers throughout the world. One Spirit, one Lord, one God and Father – The ever-blessed Trinity. One hope – Of heaven.

5. One outward baptism.

MATTHEW HENRY

CHARLES H. SPURGEON

Christ! The breadth shows its extent to all nations and ranks; the length, that it continues from everlasting to everlasting; the depth, its saving those who are sunk into the depths of sin and misery; the height, its raising them up to heavenly happiness and glory.

20,21 It is proper always to end prayers with praises. Let us expect more, and ask for more, encouraged by what Christ has already done for our souls, being assured that the conversion of sinners, and the comfort of believers, will be to his glory, forever and ever.

EPHESIANS 4

Exhortations to mutual forbearance and union. (1-6)
To a due use of spiritual gifts and graces. (7-16)
To purity and holiness. (17-24)
And to take heed of the sins practiced among the heathen. (25-32)

1-6 Nothing is pressed more earnestly in the Scriptures, than to walk as becomes those called to Christ's kingdom and glory. By lowliness, understand humility, which is opposed to pride. By meekness, that excellent disposition of soul, which makes men unwilling to provoke, and not easily to be provoked or offended. We find much in ourselves for which we can hardly forgive ourselves; therefore we must not be surprised if we find in others that which we think it hard to forgive. There is one Christ in whom all believers hope, and one heaven they are all hoping for; therefore they should be of one heart. They had all one faith, as to its object, Author, nature, and power. They all believed the same as to the great truths of religion; they had all been admitted into the church by one baptism, with water, in the name of the Father, and of the Son, and of the Holy Ghost, as the sign of regeneration. In all believers God the Father dwells, as in his holy temple, by his Spirit and special grace.

7-16 Unto every believer is given some gift of grace, for their mutual help. All is given as seems best to Christ to bestow upon every one. He received for them, that he might give to them, a large measure of gifts and graces; particularly the gift of the Holy Ghost. Not a mere head knowledge, or bare acknowledging Christ to be the Son of God, but such as brings trust and obedience. There is a fullness in Christ, and a measure of that fullness given in the counsel of God to every believer; but we never come to the perfect measure till we come to heaven.

17-24 The apostle charged the Ephesians in the name and by the authority of the Lord Jesus, that having professed the gospel, they should not be as the unconverted Gentiles, who walked in vain fancies and carnal affections. Do not men, on every side, walk in the vanity of their minds? Must not we then urge the distinction between real and nominal Christians?

been begotten again unto a lively hope by the resurrection of Jesus Christ from the dead. It is possible for a man to know infallibly that he is secure of heaven. He may not only hope so, but he may know it beyond a doubt, and he may know it thus,—by being able with the eye of faith to see the seal, the broad stamp of the Holy Spirit set upon his own character and experience. It is a seal of attestation.

In the next place, it is a sealing of appropriation. When men put their mark upon an article, it is to show that it is their own. The farmer brands his tools that they may not be stolen. They are his. The shepherd marks his sheep that they may be recognized as belonging to his flock. The king himself puts his broad arrow upon everything that is his property. So the Holy Spirit puts the broad arm of God upon the hearts of all his people. He seals us. "Thou shalt be mine," saith the Lord, "in the day when I take up my jewels." And then the Spirit puts God's seal upon us to signify that we are God's reserved inheritance—his peculiar people, the portion in which his soul delighteth.

But, again, by sealing is meant preservation. Men seal up that which they wish to have preserved, and when a document is sealed it becomes valid henceforth. Now, it is by the Spirit of God that the Christian is sealed, that he is kept, he is preserved, sealed unto the day of redemption—sealed until Christ comes fully to redeem the bodies of his saints by raising them from the death, and fully to redeem the world by purging it from sin, and making it a kingdom unto himself in righteousness. We shall hold on our way, we shall be saved. The chosen seed cannot be lost, they must be brought home at last, but how? By the sealing of the Spirit. Apart from that they perish, they are undone. When the last general fire shall blaze out, everything that has not the seal of the Spirit on it, shall be burned up. But the men upon whose forehead is the seal shall be preserved. They shall be safe "amid the wreck of matter and the crash of worlds." Their spirits, mounting above the flames shall dwell with Christ eternally, and with that same seal in their forehead upon Mount Zion, they shall sing the everlasting song of gratitude and praise. I say this is the second reason why we should love the Spirit and why we should not grieve him.

III. I come now to the third part of my discourse, namely, THE GRIEVING OF THE SPIRIT. How may we grieve him,—what will be the sad result of grieving him—if we have grieved him, how may we bring him back again? How may we grieve the Spirit? I am now, mark you, speaking of those who love the Lord Jesus Christ. The Spirit

11 And he gave some, apostles; and some, prophets; and some, evangelists; and some, pastors and teachers;

12 For the perfecting of the saints, for the work of the ministry, for the edifying of the body of Christ:

13 Till we all come in the unity of the faith, and of the knowledge of the Son of God, unto a perfect man, unto the measure of the stature of the fullness of Christ:

14 That we henceforth be no more children, tossed to and fro, and carried about with every wind of doctrine, by the sleight of men, and cunning craftiness, whereby they lie in wait to deceive;

15 But speaking the truth in love, may grow up into him in all things, which is the head, even Christ:

16 From whom the whole body fitly joined together and compacted by that which every joint supplieth, according to the effectual working in the measure of every part, maketh increase of the body unto the edifying of itself in love.

17 This I say therefore, and testify in the Lord, that ye henceforth walk not as other Gentiles walk, in the vanity of their mind,

18 Having the understanding darkened, being alienated from the life of God through the ignorance that is in them, because of the blindness of their heart:

19 Who being past feeling have given themselves over unto lasciviousness, to work all uncleanness with greediness.

20 But ye have not so learned Christ;

21 If so be that ye have heard him, and have been taught by him, as the truth is in Jesus:

22 That ye put off concerning the former conversation the old man, which is corrupt according to the deceitful lusts;

23 And be renewed in the spirit of your mind;

24 And that ye put on the new man, which after God is created in righteousness and true holiness.

25 Wherefore putting away lying, speak every man truth with his neighbor: for we are

6. One God and Father of all – That believe. Who is above all – Presiding over all his children, operating through them all by Christ, and dwelling in all by his Spirit.

7. According to the measure of the gift of Christ – According as Christ is pleased to give to each.

9. Now this expression, He ascended, what is it, but that he descended – That is, does it not imply, that he descended first? Certainly it does, on the supposition of his being God. Otherwise it would not: since all the saints will ascend to heaven, though none of them descended thence. Into the lower parts of the earth – So the womb is called, Psalm cxxxix, 5; the grave, Psalm lxiii, 9.

10. He that descended – That thus amazingly humbled himself. Is the same that ascended – That was so highly exalted. That he might fill all things – The whole church, with his Spirit, presence, and operations.

11. And, among other his free gifts, he gave some apostles – His chief ministers and special witnesses, as having seen him after his resurrection, and received their commission immediately from him. And same prophets, and some evangelists – A prophet testifies of things to come; an evangelist of things past: and that chiefly by preaching the gospel before or after any of the apostles. All these were extraordinary officers. The ordinary were: Some pastors – Watching over their several flocks. And some teachers – Whether of the same or a lower order, to assist them, as occasion might require.

12. In this verse is noted the office of ministers; in the next, the aim of the saints; in the 14th, 15th, 16th, the way of growing in grace. And each of these has three parts, standing in the same order. For the perfecting the saints – The completing them both in number and their various gifts and graces. To the work of the ministry – The serving God and his church in their various ministrations. To the edifying of the body of Christ – The building up this his mystical body in faith, love, holiness.

13. Till we all – And every one of us. Come to the unity of the faith, and knowledge of the Son of God – To both an exact agreement in the Christian doctrine, and an experimental knowledge of Christ as the Son of God. To a perfect man – To a state of spiritual manhood both in understanding and strength. To the measure of the stature of the fullness of Christ – To that maturity of age and spiritual stature wherein we shall be filled with Christ, so that he will be all in all.

14. Fluctuating to and fro – From within, even when there is no wind. And carried about with every wind – From without; when we are assaulted by others, who are unstable as the wind. By the sleight of men – By their "cogging the dice;" so the original word implies.

15. Into him – Into his image and Spirit, and into a full union with him.

16. From whom the whole mystical body fitly joined together – All the parts being fitted for and adapted to each other, and most exactly harmonizing with the whole. And compacted – Knit and cemented together with the utmost firmness. Maketh increase by that which every joint supplieth – Or by the mutual help of every joint. According to the effectual working in the measure of every member – According as every member in its measure effectually works for the support and growth of the whole. A beautiful allusion to the human body, composed of different joints and members, knit together by various ligaments, and furnished with vessels of communication from the head to every part.

17. This therefore I say – He returns thither where he begun, ver. 1. And testify in the Lord – In the name and by the authority of the Lord Jesus. In the vanity of their mind – Having lost the knowledge of the true God, Rom. i, 21. This is the root of all evil walking.

18. Having their understanding darkened, through the ignorance that is in them – So that they are totally void of the light of God, neither have they any knowledge of his will. Being alienated from the life of God – Utter strangers to

MATTHEW HENRY

CHARLES H. SPURGEON

They were void of all saving knowledge; they sat in darkness, and loved it rather than light. They had a dislike and hatred to a life of holiness, which is not only the way of life God requires and approves, and by which we live to him, but which has some likeness to God himself in his purity, righteousness, truth, and goodness. The truth of Christ appears in its beauty and power, when it appears as in Jesus.

25-28 Notice the particulars wherewith we should adorn our Christian profession. Take heed of every thing contrary to truth. No longer flatter or deceive others. God's people are children who will not lie, who dare not lie, who hate and abhor lying. Take heed of anger and ungoverned passions. If there is just occasion to express displeasure at what is wrong, and to reprove, see that it be without sin. We give place to the devil, when the first motions of sin are not grievous to our souls; when we consent to them; and when we repeat an evil deed. This teaches that as sin, if yielded unto, lets in the devil upon us, we are to resist it, keeping from all appearance of evil. Idleness makes thieves.

29-32 Filthy words proceed from corruption in the speaker, and they corrupt the minds and manners of those who hear them: Christians should beware of all such discourse. It is the duty of Christians to seek, by the blessing of God, to bring persons to think seriously, and to encourage and warn believers by their conversation. Be ye kind one to another. This sets forth the principle of love in the heart, and the outward expression of it, in a humble, courteous behavior. Mark how God's forgiveness causes us to forgive. God forgives us, though we had no cause to sin against him. We must forgive, as he has forgiven us. All lying, and corrupt communications, that stir up evil desires and lusts, grieve the Spirit of God. Corrupt passions of bitterness, wrath, anger, clamor, evil speaking, and malice, grieve the Holy Spirit. Provoke not the holy, blessed Spirit of God to withdraw his presence and his gracious influences.

EPHESIANS 5
Exhortation to brotherly love. (1,2)
Cautions against several sins. (3-14)
Directions to a contrary behavior, and to relative duties. (15-21)
The duties of wives and husbands are enforced by the spiritual relation between Christ and the church. (22-33)

1,2 Because God, for Christ's sake, has forgiven you, therefore be ye followers of God, imitators of God. Resemble him especially in his love and pardoning goodness, as becomes those beloved by their heavenly Father. In Christ's sacrifice his love triumphs, and we are to consider it fully.

of God is in your hearts, and it is very, very easy indeed to grieve him. Sin is as easy as it is wicked. You may grieve him by impure thoughts. He cannot bear sin. If you indulge in lascivious expressions, or if even you allow imagination to coat upon any lascivious act, or if your heart goes after covetousness, if you set your heart upon anything that is evil, the Spirit of God will be grieved, for thus I hear him speaking of himself. "I love this man, I want to have his heart, and yet he is entertaining these filthy lusts. His thoughts, instead of running after me, and after Christ, and after the Father, are running after the temptations that are in the world through lust." And then his Spirit is grieved. He sorrows in his soul because he knows what sorrow these things must bring to our souls. We grieve him yet more if we indulge in outward acts of sin. Then is he sometimes so grieved that he takes his flight for a season, for the dove will not dwell in our hearts if we take loathsome carrion in there. A cleanly being is the dove, and we must not strew the place which the dove frequents with filth and mire, if we do he will fly elsewhere. If we commit sin, if we openly bring disgrace upon our religion, if we tempt others to go into iniquity by our evil example, it is not long before the Holy Spirit will begin to grieve. Again, if we neglect prayer, if our closet door is cob-webbed, if we forget to read the Scriptures, if the leaves of our Bible are almost stuck together by neglect, if we never seek to do any good in the world, if we live merely for ourselves and not to Christ, then the Holy Spirit will be grieved, for thus he saith, "They have forsaken me, they have left the fountain of waters, they have hewn unto themselves broken cisterns." I think I now see the Spirit of God grieving, when you are sitting down to read a novel and there is your Bible unread. Perhaps you take down some book of travels, and you forget that you have got a more precious book of travels in the Acts of the Apostles, and in the story of your blessed Lord and Master. You have no time for prayer, but the Spirit sees you very active about worldly things, and having many hours to spare for relaxation and amusement. And then he is grieved because he sees that you love worldly things better than you love him. His spirit is grieved within him; take care that he does not go away from you, for it will be a pitiful thing for you if he leaves you to yourself. Again, ingratitude tends to grieve him. Nothing cuts a man to the heart more than after having done his utmost for another, he turns round and repays him with ingratitude or insult. If we do not want to be thanked, at least we do love to know that there is thankfulness in the heart

members one of another.

26 Be ye angry, and sin not: let not the sun go down upon your wrath:

27 Neither give place to the devil.

28 Let him that stole steal no more: but rather let him labor, working with his hands the thing which is good, that he may have to give to him that needeth.

29 Let no corrupt communication proceed out of your mouth, but that which is good to the use of edifying, that it may minister grace unto the hearers.

30 And grieve not the holy Spirit of God, whereby ye are sealed unto the day of redemption.

31 Let all bitterness, and wrath, and anger, and clamor, and evil speaking, be put away from you, with all malice:

32 And be ye kind one to another, tenderhearted, forgiving one another, even as God for Christ's sake hath forgiven you.

EPHESIANS 5

1 Be ye therefore followers of God, as dear children;

2 And walk in love, as Christ also hath loved us, and hath given himself for us an offering and a sacrifice to God for a sweetsmelling savor.

3 But fornication, and all uncleanness, or covetousness, let it not be once named among you, as becometh saints;

4 Neither filthiness, nor foolish talking, nor jesting, which are not convenient: but rather giving of thanks.

5 For this ye know, that no whoremonger, nor unclean person, nor covetous man, who is an idolater, hath any inheritance in the kingdom of Christ and of God.

6 Let no man deceive you with vain words: for because of these things cometh the wrath of God upon the children of disobedience.

7 Be not ye therefore partakers with them.

8 For ye were sometimes darkness, but now are ye light in the Lord: walk as children of light:

9 (For the fruit of the Spirit is in all goodness and righteousness and truth;)

the divine, the spiritual life. Through the hardness of their hearts – Callous and senseless. And where there is no sense, there can be no life.

19. Who being past feeling – The original word is peculiarly significant. It properly means, past feeling pain. Pain urges the sick to seek a remedy, which, where there is no pain, is little thought of. Have given themselves up – Freely, of their own accord. Lasciviousness is but one branch of uncleanness, which implies impurity of every kind.

20. But ye have not so learned Christ – That is, ye cannot act thus, now ye know him, since you know the Christian dispensation allows of no sin.

21. Seeing ye have heard him – Teaching you inwardly by his Spirit. As the truth is in Jesus – According to his own gospel.

22. The old man – That is, the whole body of sin. All sinful desires are deceitful; promising the happiness which they cannot give.

23. The spirit of your mind – The very ground of your heart.

24. The new man – Universal holiness. After – In the very image of God.

25. Wherefore – Seeing ye are thus created anew, walk accordingly, in every particular. For we are members one of another – To which intimate union all deceit is quite repugnant.

26. Be ye angry, and sin not – That is, if ye are angry, take heed ye sin not. Anger at sin is not evil; but we should feel only pity to the sinner.

27. Neither give place to the devil – By any delay.

28. But rather let him labor – Lest idleness lead him to steal again. And whoever has sinned in any kind ought the more zealously to practice the opposite virtue. That he may have to give – And so be no longer a burden and nuisance, but a blessing, to his neighbors.

29. But that which is good – Profitable to the speaker and hearers. To the use of edifying – To forward them in repentance, faith, or holiness. That it may minister grace – Be a means of conveying more grace into their hearts. Hence we learn, what discourse is corrupt, as it were stinking in the nostrils of God; namely, all that is not profitable, not edifying, not apt to minister grace to the hearers.

30. Grieve not the Holy Spirit – By any disobedience. Particularly by corrupt discourse; or by any of the following sins. Do not force him to withdraw from you, as a friend does whom you grieve by unkind behavior. The day of redemption – That is, the day of judgment, in which our redemption will be completed.

31. Let all bitterness – The height of settled anger, opposite to kindness, ver. 32. And wrath – Lasting displeasure toward the ignorant, and them that are out of the way, opposite to tenderheartedness. And anger – The very first risings of disgust at those that injure you, opposite to forgiving one another. And clamor – Or bawling. "I am not angry," says one; "but it is my way to speak so." Then unlearn that way: it is the way to hell. And evil speaking – Be it in ever so mild and soft a tone, or with ever such professions of kindness. Here is a beautiful retrogradation, beginning with the highest, and descending to the lowest, degree of the want of love.

32. As God, showing himself kind and tenderhearted in the highest degree, hath forgiven you.

EPHESIANS 5

1. Be ye therefore followers – Imitators. Of God – In forgiving and loving. O how much more honorable and more happy, to be an imitator of God, than of Homer, Virgil, or Alexander the Great!

3. But let not any impure love be even named or heard of among you – Keep at the utmost distance from it, as becometh saints.

4. Nor foolish talking – Tittle tattle, talking of nothing, the weather, fashions,

MATTHEW HENRY

CHARLES H. SPURGEON

3-14 Filthy lusts must be rooted out. These sins must be dreaded and detested. Here are not only cautions against gross acts of sin, but against what some may make light of. But these things are so far from being profitable, that they pollute and poison the hearers. Our cheerfulness should show itself as becomes Christians, in what may tend to God's glory. A covetous man makes a god of his money; places that hope, confidence, and delight, in worldly good, which should be in God only. Those who allow themselves, either in the lusts of the flesh or the love of the world, belong not to the kingdom of grace, nor shall they come to the kingdom of glory. When the vilest transgressors repent and believe the gospel, they become children of obedience, from whom God's wrath is turned away. Dare we make light of that which brings down the wrath of God?

15-21 Another remedy against sin, is care, or caution, it being impossible else to maintain purity of heart and life. Time is a talent given us by God, and it is misspent and lost when not employed according to his design. If we have lost our time heretofore, we must double our diligence for the future. Of that time which thousands on a dying bed would gladly redeem at the price of the whole world, how little do men think, and to what trifles they daily sacrifice it! People are very apt to complain of bad times; it were well if that stirred them more to redeem time. Be not unwise. Ignorance of our duty, and neglect of our souls, show the greatest folly. Drunkenness is a sin that never goes alone, but carries men into other evils; it is a sin very provoking to God. The drunkard holds out to his family and to the world the sad spectacle of a sinner hardened beyond what is common, and hastening to perdition. When afflicted or weary, let us not seek to raise our spirits by strong drink, which is hateful and hurtful, and only ends in making sorrows more felt. But by fervent prayer let us seek to be filled with the Spirit, and to avoid whatever may grieve our gracious Comforter. All God's people have reason to sing for joy.

22-33 The duty of wives is, submission to their husbands in the Lord, which includes honoring and obeying them, from a principle of love to them. The duty of husbands is to love their wives. The love of Christ to the church is an example, which is sincere, pure, and constant, notwithstanding her failures. Christ gave himself for the church, that he might sanctify it in this world, and glorify it in the next, that he might bestow on all his members a principle of holiness, and deliver them from the guilt, the pollution, and the dominion of sin, by those influences of the Holy Spirit, of which baptismal water was the outward sign. The church and believers will not be without spot or wrinkle till they come to glory. But those only who are sanctified now, shall be glorified hereafter. The words of Adam, mentioned by the apostle, are spoken literally of mar-

upon which we have conferred a boon, and when the Holy Spirit looks into our soul and sees little love to Christ, no gratitude to him for all he has done for us, then is he grieved.

Again, the Holy Spirit is exceedingly grieved by our unbelief. When we distrust the promise he hath given and applied, when we doubt the power or the affection of our blessed Lord. Then the Spirit saith within himself—"They doubt my fidelity, they distrust my power, they say Jesus is not able to save unto the uttermost," thus again is the Spirit grieved. Oh, I wish the Spirit had an advocate here this morning, that could speak in better terms than I can. I have a theme that overmasters me, I seem to grieve for him; but I cannot make you grieve, nor tell out the grief I feel. In my own soul I keep saying, "Oh, this is just what you have done—you have grieved him." Let me make a full and frank confession even before you all. I know that too often, I as well as you have grieved the Holy Spirit. Much within us has made that sacred dove to mourn, and my marvel is, that he has not taken his flight from us and left us utterly to ourselves.

Now suppose the Holy Spirit is grieved, what is the effect produced upon us? When the Spirit is grieved first, he bears with us. He is grieved again and again, and again and again, and still he bears with it all. But at last, his grief becomes so excessive, that he says, "I will suspend my operations; I will be gone; I will leave life behind me, but my own actual presence I will take away. And when the Spirit of God goes away from the soul and suspends all his operations what a miserable state we are in. He suspends his instructions; we read the word, we cannot understand it; we go to our commentaries, they cannot tell us the meaning; we fall on our knees and ask to be taught, but we get no answer, we learn nothing. He suspends his comfort; we used to dance, like David before the ark, and now we sit like Job in the ash-pit, and scrape our ulcers with a potsherd. There was a time when his candle shone round about us, but now he is gone; he has left us in the blackness of darkness. Now, he takes from us all spiritual power. Once we could do all things; now we can do nothing. We could slay the Philistines, and lay them heaps upon heaps, but now Delilah can deceive us, and our eyes are put out and we are made to grind in the mill. We go preaching, and there is no pleasure in preaching, and no good follows it. We go to our tract distributing, and our Sunday-school, we might almost as well be at home. There is the machinery there, but there is no love. There is the intention to do good, or perhaps not even that, but alas! there is no power to accomplish the intention. The Lord has

10 Proving what is acceptable unto the Lord.

11 And have no fellowship with the unfruitful works of darkness, but rather reprove them.

12 For it is a shame even to speak of those things which are done of them in secret.

13 But all things that are reproved are made manifest by the light: for whatsoever doth make manifest is light.

14 Wherefore he saith, Awake thou that sleepest, and arise from the dead, and Christ shall give thee light.

15 See then that ye walk circumspectly, not as fools, but as wise,

16 Redeeming the time, because the days are evil.

17 Wherefore be ye not unwise, but understanding what the will of the Lord is.

18 And be not drunk with wine, wherein is excess; but be filled with the Spirit;

19 Speaking to yourselves in psalms and hymns and spiritual songs, singing and making melody in your heart to the Lord;

20 Giving thanks always for all things unto God and the Father in the name of our Lord Jesus Christ;

21 Submitting yourselves one to another in the fear of God.

22 Wives, submit yourselves unto your own husbands, as unto the Lord.

23 For the husband is the head of the wife, even as Christ is the head of the church: and he is the savior of the body.

24 Therefore as the church is subject unto Christ, so let the wives be to their own husbands in every thing.

25 Husbands, love your wives, even as Christ also loved the church, and gave himself for it;

26 That he might sanctify and cleanse it with the washing of water by the word,

27 That he might present it to himself a glorious church, not having spot, or wrinkle, or any such thing; but that it should be holy and without blemish.

28 So ought men to love their wives as their own bodies. He that loveth his wife loveth himself.

29 For no man ever yet hated

meat and drink. Or jesting – The word properly means, wittiness, facetiousness, esteemed by the heathens an half-virtue. But how frequently even this quenches the Spirit, those who are tender of conscience know. Which are not convenient – For a Christian; as neither increasing his faith nor holiness.

6. Because of these things – As innocent as the heathens esteem them, and as those dealers in vain words would persuade you to think them.

8. Ye were once darkness – Total blindness and ignorance. Walk as children of light – Suitably to your present knowledge.

9. The fruit of the light – Opposite to "the unfruitful works of darkness," chap. iv, 11. Is in – That is, consists in. Goodness and righteousness and truth – Opposite to the sins spoken of, chap. iv, 25,&c.

11. Reprove them – To avoid them is not enough.

12. In secret – As flying the light.

13. But all things which are reproved, are thereby dragged out into the light, and made manifest – Shown in their proper colors, by the light. For whatsoever doth make manifest is light – That is, for nothing but light, yea, light from heaven, can make anything manifest.

14. Wherefore he – God. Saith – In the general tenor of his word, to all who are still in darkness. Awake thou that sleepest – In ignorance of God and thyself; in stupid insensibility. And arise from the dead – From the death of sin. And Christ shall give thee light – Knowledge, holiness, happiness.

15. Circumspectly – Exactly, with the utmost accuracy, getting to the highest pitch of every point of holiness. Not as fools – Who think not where they are going, or do not make the best of their way.

17. What the will of the Lord is – In every time, place, and circumstance.

18. Wherein is excess – That is, which leads to debauchery of every kind. But be ye filled with the Spirit – In all his graces, who gives a more noble pleasure than wine can do.

19. Speaking to each other – By the Spirit. In the Psalms – Of David. And hymns – Of praise. And spiritual songs – On any divine subject. By there being no inspired songs, peculiarly adapted to the Christian dispensation, as there were to the Jewish, it is evident that the promise of the Holy Ghost to believers, in the last days, was by his larger effusion to supply the lack of it. Singing with your hearts – As well as your voice. To the Lord – Jesus, who searcheth the heart.

20. Giving thanks – At all times and places. And for all things – Prosperous or adverse, since all work together for good. In the name of, or through, our Lord Jesus Christ – By whom we receive all good things.

23. The head – The governor, guide, and guardian of the wife. And he is the Savior of the body – The church, from all sin and misery.

24. In everything – Which is not contrary to any command of God.

25. Even as Christ loved the church – Here is the true model of conjugal affection. With this kind of affection, with this degree of it, and to this end, should husbands love their wives.

26. That he might sanctify it through the word – The ordinary channel of all blessings. Having cleansed it – From the guilt and power of sin. By the washing of water – In baptism; if, with "the outward and visible sign," we receive the "inward and spiritual grace."

27. That he might present it – Even in this world. To himself – As his spouse. A glorious church – All glorious within. Not having spot – Of impurity from any sin. Or wrinkle – Of deformity from any decay.

28. As their own bodies – That is, as themselves. He that loveth his wife loveth himself – Which is not a sin, but an indisputable duty.

29. His own flesh – That is, himself. Nourisheth and cherisheth – That is, feeds and clothes it.

31. For this cause – Because of this intimate union. Gen. ii, 24.

riage; but they have also a hidden sense in them, relating to the union between Christ and his church. It was a kind of type, as having resemblance. There will be failures and defects on both sides, in the present state of human nature, yet this does not alter the relation. All the duties of marriage are included in unity and love. And while we adore and rejoice in the condescending love of Christ, let husbands and wives learn hence their duties to each other. Thus the worst evils would be prevented, and many painful effects would be avoided.

EPHESIANS 6

The duties of children and parents. (1-4)

Of servants and masters. (5-9)

All Christians are to put on spiritual Armor against the enemies of their souls. (10-18)

The apostle desires their prayers, and ends with his apostolic blessing. (19-24)

1-4 The great duty of children is, to obey their parents. That obedience includes inward reverence, as well as outward acts, and in every age prosperity has attended those distinguished for obedience to parents. The duty of parents. Be not impatient; use no unreasonable severities. Deal prudently and wisely with children; convince their judgments and work upon their reason. Bring them up well; under proper and compassionate correction; and in the knowledge of the duty God requires. Often is this duty neglected, even among professors of the gospel. Many set their children against religion; but this does not excuse the children's disobedience, though it may be awfully occasion it.

5-9 The duty of servants is summed up in one word, obedience. The servants of old were generally slaves. The apostles were to teach servants and masters their duties, in doing which evils would be lessened, till slavery should be rooted out by the influence of Christianity. Servants are to reverence those over them. They are to be sincere; not pretending obedience when they mean to disobey, but serving faithfully. And they must serve their masters not only when their master's eye is upon them; but must be strict in the discharge of their duty, when he is absent and out of the way. Steady regard to the Lord Jesus Christ will make men faithful and sincere in every station, not grudgingly or by constraint, but from a principle of love to the masters and their concerns. This makes service easy to them, pleasing to their masters, and acceptable to the Lord Christ. God will reward even the meanest drudgery done from a sense of duty, and with a view to glorify him. Here is the duty of masters. Act after the same manner. Be just to servants, as you expect they should be to you; show the like good will and concern for them, and be careful herein to approve yourselves to God. Be not tyrannical and

withdrawn himself, his light, his joy, his comfort, his spiritual power, all are gone. And then all our graces flag. Our graces are much like the flower called the Hydrangea, when it has plenty of water it blooms, but as soon as moisture fails, the leaves drop down at once. And so when the Spirit goes away, faith shuts up its flowers; no perfume is exhaled. Then the fruit of our love begins to rot and drops from the tree; then the sweet buds of our hope become frostbitten, and they die. Oh, what a sad thing it is to lose the Spirit. Have you never, my brethren, been on your knees and been conscious that the Spirit of God was not with you, and what awful work it has been to groan, and cry, and sigh, and yet go away again, and no light to shine upon the promises, not so much as a ray of light through the chink of the dungeon. All forsaken, forgotten, and forlorn, you are almost driven to despair. You sing with Cowper:—

"What peaceful hours I once enjoyed,
How sweet their memory still!
But they have left an aching void,
The world can never fill.
Return, thou sacred dove, return,
Sweet messenger of rest,
I hate the sins that made thee mourn,
And drove thee from my breast.
The dearest idol I have known,
Whate'er that idol be,
Help me to tear it from its throne,
And worship only thee."

Ah! sad enough it is to have the Spirit drawn from us. But, my brethren, I am about to say something, with the utmost charity, which, perhaps, may look severe, but, nevertheless, I must say it. The churches of the present day are very much in the position of those who have grieved the Spirit of God; for the Spirit deals with churches just as it does with individuals. Of these late years how little has God wrought in the midst of his churches. Throughout England, at least some four or five years ago, an almost universal torpor had fallen upon the visible body of Christ. There was a little action, but it was spasmodic; there was no real vitality. Oh! how few sinners were brought to Christ, how empty had our places of worship become; our prayer-meetings were dwindling away to nothing, and our church meetings were mere matters of farce. You know right well that this is the case with many London churches to this day; and there be some that do not mourn about it. They go up to their accustomed place, and the minister prays, and the people either sleep with their eyes or else with their hearts, and they go out, and there is never a soul saved. The pool of baptism is seldom stirred; but the saddest part

his own flesh; but nourisheth and cherisheth it, even as the Lord the church:

30 For we are members of his body, of his flesh, and of his bones.

31 For this cause shall a man leave his father and mother, and shall be joined unto his wife, and they two shall be one flesh.

32 This is a great mystery: but I speak concerning Christ and the church.

33 Nevertheless let every one of you in particular so love his wife even as himself; and the wife see that she reverence her husband.

EPHESIANS 6

1 Children, obey your parents in the Lord: for this is right.

2 Honor thy father and mother; (which is the first command-ment with promise;)

3 That it may be well with thee, and thou mayest live long on the earth.

4 And, ye fathers, provoke not your children to wrath: but bring them up in the nurture and admonition of the Lord.

5 Servants, be obedient to them that are your masters according to the flesh, with fear and trem-bling, in singleness of your heart, as unto Christ;

6 Not with eyeservice, as men-pleasers; but as the servants of Christ, doing the will of God from the heart;

7 With good will doing service, as to the Lord, and not to men:

8 Knowing that whatsoever good thing any man doeth, the same shall he receive of the Lord, whether he be bond or free.

9 And, ye masters, do the same things unto them, forbearing threatening: knowing that your Master also is in heaven; neither is there respect of persons with him.

10 Finally, my brethren, be strong in the Lord, and in the power of his might.

11 Put on the whole armor of God, that ye may be able to stand against the wiles of the devil.

12 For we wrestle not against flesh and blood, but against

EPHESIANS 6

1. Children, obey your parents – In all things lawful. The will of the parent is a law to the child. In the Lord – For his sake. For this is right – Manifestly just and reasonable.

2. Honor – That is, love, reverence, obey, assist, in all things. The mother is par-ticularly mentioned, as being more liable to be slighted than the father. Which is the first commandment with a promise – For the promise implied in the sec-ond commandment does not belong to the keeping that command in particu-lar, but the whole law. Exod. xx, 12.

3. That thou mayest live long upon the earth – This is usually fulfilled to emi-nently dutiful children; and he who lives long and well has a long seed-time for the eternal harvest. But this promise, in the Christian dispensation, is to be understood chiefly in a more exalted and Spiritual sense.

4. And, ye fathers – Mothers are included; but fathers are named, as being more apt to be stern and severe. Provoke not your children to wrath – Do not need-lessly fret or exasperate them. But bring them up – With all tenderness and mildness. In the instruction and discipline of the Lord – Both in Christian knowledge and practice.

5. Your masters according to the flesh – According to the present state of things: afterward the servant is free from his master. With fear and trembling – A proverbial expression, implying the utmost care and diligence. In singleness of heart – With a single eye to the providence and will of God.

6. Not with eye-service – Serving them better when under their eye than at other times. But doing the will of God from the heart – Doing whatever you do, as the will of God, and with your might.

7. Unto the Lord, and not to men – That is, rather than to men; and by mak-ing every action of common life a sacrifice to God; having an eye to him in all things, even as if there were no other master.

8. He shall receive the same – That is, a full and adequate recompense for it.

9. Do the same things to them – That is, act toward them from the same prin-ciple. Forbearing threatening – Behaving with gentleness and humanity, not in a harsh or domineering way.

11. Put on the whole Armor of God – The Greek word means a complete suit of Armor. Believers are said to put on the girdle, breastplate, shoes; to take the shield of faith, and sword of the Spirit. The whole Armor – As if the Armor would scarce do, it must be the whole Armor. This is repeated, ver. 13, because of the strength and subtlety of our adversaries, and because of an "evil day" of sore trial being at hand.

13. In the evil day – The war is perpetual; but the fight is one day less, another more, violent. The evil day is either at the approach of death, or in life; may be longer or shorter and admits of numberless varieties. And having done all, to stand – That ye may still keep on your Armor, still stand upon your guard, still watch and pray; and thus ye will be enabled to endure unto the end, and stand with joy before the face of the Son of Man.

14. Having your loins girt about – That ye may be ready for every motion. With truth – Not only with the truths of the gospel, but with "truth in the inward parts;" for without this all our knowledge of divine truth will prove but a poor girdle "in the evil day." So our Lord is described, Isaiah xi, 5. And as a girded man is always ready to go on, so this seems to intimate an obedient heart, a ready will. Our Lord adds to the loins girded, the lights burning, Luke xii, 35; showing that watching and ready obedience are the inseparable companions of faith and love. And having on the breastplate of righteousness – The righteousness of a spotless purity, in which Christ will present us faultless before God, through the merit of his own blood. With this breastplate our Lord is described, Isaiah lix, 17. In the breast is the seat of conscience, which is guarded by righteousness. No Armor for the back is mentioned. We are always to face our enemies.

overbearing. You have a Master to obey, and you and they are but fellow servants in respect to Christ Jesus. If masters and servants would consider their duties to God, and the account they must shortly give to him, they would be more mindful of their duty to each other, and thus families would be more orderly and happy.

10-18 Spiritual strength and courage are needed for our spiritual warfare and suffering. Those who would prove themselves to have true grace, must aim at all grace; and put on the whole Armor of God, which he prepares and bestows. The Christian Armor is made to be worn; and there is no putting off our Armor till we have done our warfare, and finished our course. The combat is not against human enemies, nor against our own corrupt nature only; we have to do with an enemy who has a thousand ways of beguiling unstable souls. The devils assault us in the things that belong to our souls, and labor to deface the heavenly image in our hearts. We must resolve by God's grace, not to yield to Satan. Resist him, and he will flee. If we give way, he will get ground. If we distrust either our cause, or our Leader, or our Armor, we give him advantage. The different parts of the armor of heavy-armed soldiers, who had to sustain the fiercest assaults of the enemy, are here described. There is none for the back; nothing to defend those who turn back in the Christian warfare. Truth, or sincerity, is the girdle. This girds on all the other pieces of our Armor, and is first mentioned. There can be no religion without sincerity. The righteousness of Christ, imputed to us, is a breastplate against the arrows of Divine wrath. The righteousness of Christ implanted in us, fortifies the heart against the attacks of Satan. Resolution must be as greaves, or Armor to our legs; and to stand their ground or to march forward in rugged paths, the feet must be shod with the preparation of the gospel of peace. Motives to obedience, amidst trials, must be drawn from a clear knowledge of the gospel. Faith is all in all in an hour of temptation. Faith, as relying on unseen objects, receiving Christ and the benefits of redemption, and so deriving grace from him, is like a shield, a defense every way. The devil is the wicked one. Violent temptations, by which the soul is set on fire of hell, are darts Satan shoots at us. Also, hard thoughts of God, and as to ourselves. Faith applying the word of God and the grace of Christ, quenches the darts of temptation. Salvation must be our helmet. A good hope of salvation, a Scriptural expectation of victory, will purify the soul, and keep it from being defiled by Satan. To the Christian armed for defense in battle, the apostle recommends only one weapon of attack; but it is enough, the sword of the Spirit, which is the word of God. It subdues and mortifies evil desires and blasphemous thoughts as they rise within; and answers unbelief and error as they assault from without. A single text, well understood, and rightly

of all is this, the churches are willing to have it so. They are not earnest to get a revival of religion. We have been doing something, the church at large has been doing something. I will not just now put my finger upon what the sin is, but there has been something done which has driven the Spirit of God from us. He is grieved, and he is gone. He is present with us here, I thank his name, he is still visible in our midst. He has not left us. Though we have been as unworthy as others, yet has he given us a long outpouring of his presence. These five years or more, we have had a revival which is not to be exceeded by any revival upon the face of the earth. Without cries or shoutings, without fallings down or swooning, steadily God adds to this church numbers upon numbers, so that your minister's heart is ready to break with very joy when he thinks how manifestly the Spirit of God is with us. But brethren, we must not be content with this, we want to see the Spirit poured out on all churches. Look at the great gatherings that there were in St. Paul's, and Westminster Abbey, and Exeter Hall, and other places, how was it that no good was done, or so very little? I have watched with anxious eye, and I have never from that day forth heard but of one conversion, and that in St. James' Hall, from all these services. Strange it seems. The blessing may have come in larger measure than we know, but not in so large a measure as we might have expected, if the Spirit of God had been present with all the ministers. Oh would that we may live to see greater things than we have ever seen yet. Go home to your houses, humble yourselves before God, ye members of Christ's church, and cry aloud that he will visit his church, and that he would open the windows of heaven and pour out his grace upon his thirsty hill of Zion, that nations may be born in a day, that sinners may be saved by thousands—that Zion may travail and may bring forth children. Oh! there are signs and tokens of a coming revival. We have heard but lately of a good work among the Ragged School boys of St. Giles's, and our soul has been glad on account of that; and the news from Ireland comes to us like good tidings, not from a far country, but from a sister province of the kingdom. Let us cry aloud to the Holy Spirit, who is certainly grieved with his church, and let us purge our churches of everything that is contrary to his Word and to sound doctrine, and then the Spirit will return, and his power shall be manifest.

And now, in conclusion, there may be some of you here who have lost the visible presence of Christ with you; who have in fact so grieved the Spirit that he has gone. It is a mercy for you to know that the Spirit of God never leaves his

principalities, against powers, against the rulers of the darkness of this world, against spiritual wickedness in high places.

13 Wherefore take unto you the whole armor of God, that ye may be able to withstand in the evil day, and having done all, to stand.

14 Stand therefore, having your loins girt about with truth, and having on the breastplate of righteousness;

15 And your feet shod with the preparation of the gospel of peace;

16 Above all, taking the shield of faith, wherewith ye shall be able to quench all the fiery darts of the wicked.

17

And take the helmet of salvation, and the sword of the Spirit, which is the word of God:

18 Praying always with all prayer and supplication in the Spirit, and watching thereunto with all perseverance and supplication for all saints;

19 And for me, that utterance may be given unto me, that I may open my mouth boldly, to make known the mystery of the gospel,

20 For which I am an ambassador in bonds: that therein I may speak boldly, as I ought to speak.

21 But that ye also may know my affairs, and how I do, Tychicus, a beloved brother and faithful minister in the Lord, shall make known to you all things:

22 Whom I have sent unto you for the same purpose, that ye might know our affairs, and that he might comfort your hearts.

23 Peace be to the brethren, and love with faith, from God the Father and the Lord Jesus Christ.

24 Grace be with all them that love our Lord Jesus Christ in sincerity. Amen.

15. And your feet shod with the preparation of the gospel – Let this be always ready to direct and confirm you in every step. This part of the Armor, for the feet, is needful, considering what a journey we have to go; what a race to run. Our feet must be so shod, that our footsteps slip not. To order our life and conversation aright, we are prepared by the gospel blessing, the peace and love of God ruling in the heart, Colossians iii, 14, 15. By this only can we tread the rough ways, surmount our difficulties, and hold out to the end.

16. Above or over all – As a sort of universal covering to every other part of the Armor itself, continually exercise a strong and lively faith. This you may use as a shield, which will quench all the fiery darts, the furious temptations, violent and sudden injections of the devil.

17. And take for an helmet the hope of salvation – 1 Thess. v, 8. The head is that part which is most carefully to be defended. One stroke here may prove fatal. The Armor for this is the hope of salvation.

18. Praying always – At all times, and on every occasion, in midst of all employments, inwardly praying without ceasing. By the Spirit – Through the influence of the Holy Spirit. With all prayer – With all sort of prayer, public, private, mental, vocal. Some are careful in respect of one kind of prayer, and negligent in others. If we would have the petitions we ask, let us use all. Some there are who use only mental prayer or ejaculations, and think they are in a state of grace, and use a way of worship, far superior to any other: but such only fancy themselves to be above what is really above them; it requiring far more grace to be enabled to pour out a fervent and continued prayer, than to offer up mental aspirations. And supplication – Repeating and urging our prayer, as Christ did in the garden. And watching – Inwardly attending on God, to know his will, to gain power to do it, and to attain to the blessings we desire. With all perseverance – Continuing to the end in this holy exercise. And supplication for all the saints – Wrestling in fervent, continued intercession for others, especially for the faithful, that they may do all the will of God, and be steadfast to the end. Perhaps we receive few answers to prayer, because we do not intercede enough for others.

19. By the opening my mouth – Removing every inward and every outward hindrance.

20. An ambassador in bonds – The ambassadors of men usually appear in great pomp. How differently does the ambassador of Christ appear!

21. Ye also – As well as others.

22. That he might comfort your hearts – By relating the supports I find from God, and the success of the gospel.

23. Peace – This verse recapitulates the whole epistle.

24. In sincerity – Or in incorruption; without corrupting his genuine gospel, without any mixture of corrupt affections. And that with continuance, till grace issue in glory.

applied, at once destroys a temptation or an objection, and subdues the most formidable adversary. Prayer must fasten all the other parts of our Christian Armor. There are other duties of religion, and of our stations in the world, but we must keep up times of prayer. Though set and solemn prayer may not be seasonable when other duties are to be done, yet short pious prayers darted out, always are so. We must use holy thoughts in our ordinary course. A vain heart will be vain in prayer. We must pray with all kinds of prayer, public, private, and secret; social and solitary; solemn and sudden: with all the parts of prayer; confession of sin, petition for mercy, and thanksgiving for favors received. And we must do it by the grace of God the Holy Spirit, in dependence on, and according to, his teaching. We must preserve in particular requests, notwithstanding discouragements. We must pray, not for ourselves only, but for all saints. Our enemies are mighty, and we are without strength, but our Redeemer is almighty, and in the power of his might we may overcome. Wherefore we must stir up ourselves. Have not we, when God has called, often neglected to answer? Let us think upon these things, and continue our prayers with patience.

19-24 The gospel was a mystery till made known by Divine revelation; and it is the work of Christ's ministers to declare it. The best and most eminent ministers need the prayers of believers. Those particularly should be prayed for, who are exposed to great hardships and perils in their work. Peace be to the brethren, and love with faith. By peace, understand all manner of peace; peace with God, peace of conscience, peace among themselves. And the grace of the Spirit, producing faith and love, and every grace. These he desires for those in whom they were already begun. And all grace and blessings come to the saints from God, through Jesus Christ our Lord. Grace, that is, the favor of God; and all good, spiritual and temporal, which is from it, is and shall be with all those who thus love our Lord Jesus Christ in sincerity, and with them only.

people finally; he leaves them for chastisement, but not for damnation. He sometimes leaves them that they may get good by knowing their own weakness, but be will not leave them finally to perish. Are you in a state of backsliding, declension, and coldness? Hearken to me for a moment, and God bless the words. Brother, stay not a moment in a condition so perilous; be not easy for a single second in the absence of the Holy Ghost. I beseech you use every means by which that Spirit may be brought back to you. Once more, let me tell you distinctly what the means are. Search out for the sin that has grieved the Spirit, give it up, slay that sin upon the spot; repent with tears and sighs; continue in prayer, and never rest satisfied until the Holy Ghost comes back to you. Frequent an earnest ministry, get much with earnest saints, but above all, be much in prayer to God, and let your daily cry be, "Return, return, O Holy Spirit return, and dwell in my soul." Oh, I beseech you be not content till that prayer is heard, for you have become weak as water, and faint and empty while the Spirit has been away from you. Oh! it may be there are some here this morning with whom the Spirit has been striving during the past week. Oh yield to him, resist him not; grieve him not, but yield to him. Is he saying to you now "Turn to Christ?" Listen to him, obey him, he moves you. Oh I beseech you do not despise him. Have you resisted him many a time, then take care you do not again, for there may come a last time when the Spirit may say, "I will go unto my rest, I will not return unto him, the ground is accursed, it shall be given up to barrenness." Oh I hear the word of the gospel, ere ye separate, for the Spirit speaketh effectually to you now in this short sentence—"Repent and be converted everyone of you, that your sins may be blotted out when the times of refreshing shall come from the presence of the Lord," and hear this solemn sentence, "He that believeth in the Lord Jesus and is baptized, shall be saved; but he that believeth not shall be damned." May the Lord grant that we may not grieve the Holy Spirit. Amen.

Philippians

PHILIPPIANS 1

1 Paul and Timotheus, the servants of Jesus Christ, to all the saints in Christ Jesus which are at Philippi, with the bishops and deacons:

2 Grace be unto you, and peace, from God our Father, and from the Lord Jesus Christ.

3 I thank my God upon every remembrance of you,

4 Always in every prayer of mine for you all making request with joy,

5 For your fellowship in the gospel from the first day until now;

6 Being confident of this very thing, that he which hath begun a good work in you will perform it until the day of Jesus Christ:

7 Even as it is meet for me to think this of you all, because I have you in my heart; inasmuch as both in my bonds, and in the defense and confirmation of the gospel, ye all are partakers of my grace.

8 For God is my record, how greatly I long after you all in the bowels of Jesus Christ.

9 And this I pray, that your love may abound yet more and more in knowledge and in all judgment;

10 That ye may approve things that are excellent; that ye may be sincere and without offense till the day of Christ;

11 Being filled with the fruits of righteousness, which are by Jesus Christ, unto the glory and praise of God.

12 But I would ye should understand, brethren, that the things which happened unto me have fallen out rather unto the furtherance of the gospel;

13 So that my bonds in Christ are manifest in all the palace, and in all other places;

14 And many of the brethren in the Lord, waxing confident by my bonds, are much more bold to speak the word without fear.

15 Some indeed preach Christ even of envy and strife; and some also of good will:

16 The one preach Christ of contention, not sincerely, supposing to add affliction to my bonds:

17 But the other of love, knowing that I am set for the defense of the gospel.

18 What then? notwithstanding, every way, whether in pretense, or in truth, Christ is preached; and I therein do rejoice, yea, and will rejoice.

19 For I know that this shall turn to my salvation through your prayer, and the supply of the Spirit of Jesus Christ,

PHILIPPI was so called from Philip, king of Macedonia, who much enlarged and beautified it. Afterwards it became a Roman colony, and the chief city of that part of Macedonia. Hither St. Paul was sent by a vision to preach and here, not long after his coming, he was shamefully entreated. Nevertheless many were converted by him, during the short time of his abode there; by whose liberality he was more assisted than by any other church of his planting. And they had now sent large assistance to him by Epaphroditus; by whom he returns them this epistle.

PHILIPPIANS 1

1. Servants – St. Paul, writing familiarly to the Philippians, does not style himself an apostle. And under the common title of servants, he tenderly and modestly joins with himself his son Timotheus, who had come to Philippi not long after St. Paul had received him, Acts xvi, 3, 12. To all the saints – The apostolic epistles were sent more directly to the churches, than to the pastors of them. With the bishops and deacons – The former properly took care of the internal state, the latter, of the externals, of the church, 1 Tim. iii, 2-8; although these were not wholly confined to the one, neither those to the other. The word bishops here includes all the presbyters at Philippi, as well as the ruling presbyters: the names bishop and presbyter, or elder, being promiscuously used in the first ages.

4. With joy – After the epistle to the Ephesians, wherein love reigns, follows this, wherein there is perpetual mention of joy. "The fruit of the Spirit is love, joy." And joy peculiarly enlivens prayer. The sum of the whole epistle is, I rejoice. Rejoice ye.

5. The sense is, I thank God for your fellowship with us in all the blessings of the gospel, which I have done from the first day of your receiving it until now.

6. Being persuaded – The grounds of which persuasion are set down in the following verse. That he who hath begun a good work in you, will perfect it until the day of Christ – That he who having justified, hath begun to sanctify you, will carry on this work, till it issue in glory.

7. As it is right for me to think this of you all – Why? He does not say, "Because of an eternal decree;" or, "Because a saint must persevere;" but, because I have you in my heart, who were all partakers of my grace – That is, because ye were all (for which I have you in my heart, I bear you the most grateful and tender affection) partakers of my grace – That is, sharers in the afflictions which God vouchsafed me as a grace or favor, ver. 29, 30; both in my bonds, and when I was called forth to answer for myself, and to confirm the gospel. It is not improbable that, after they had endured that great trial of affliction, God had sealed them unto full victory, of which the apostle had a prophetic sight.

8. I long for you with the bowels of Jesus Christ – In Paul, not Paul lives, but Jesus Christ. Therefore he longs for them with the bowels, the tenderness, not of Paul, but of Jesus Christ.

9. And this I pray, that your love – Which they had already shown. May abound yet more and more – The fire which burned in the apostle never says, It is enough. In knowledge and in all spiritual sense – Which is the ground of all spiritual knowledge. We must be inwardly sensible of divine peace, joy, love; otherwise, we cannot know what they are.

10. That ye may try – By that spiritual sense. The things that are excellent – Not only good, but the very best; the superior excellence of which is hardly discerned, but by the adult Christian. That ye may be inwardly sincere – Having a single eye to the very best things, and a pure heart. And outwardly without offense – Holy, unblamable in all things.

MATTHEW HENRY

CHARLES H. SPURGEON

The Philippians felt a very deep interest for the apostle. The scope of the epistle is to confirm them in the faith, to encourage them to walk as becomes the gospel of Christ, to caution them against judaizing teachers, and to express gratitude for their Christian bounty. This epistle is the only one, among those written by St. Paul, in which no censures are implied or expressed. Full commendation and confidence are in every part, and the Philippians are addressed with a peculiar affection, which every serious reader will perceive.

PHILIPPIANS 1

The apostle offers up thanksgivings and prayers, for the good work of grace in the Philippians. (1-7)
He expresses affection, and prays for them. (8-11)
Fortifies them against being cast down at his sufferings. (12-20)
He stood prepared for glorifying Christ by life, or death. (21-26)
Exhortations to zeal, and constancy in professing the gospel. (27-30)

1-7 The highest honor of the most eminent ministers is, to be servants of Christ. And those who are not really saints on earth, never will be saints in heaven. Out of Christ, the best saints are sinners, and unable to stand before God. There is no peace without grace. Inward peace springs from a sense of Divine favor. And there is no grace and peace but from God our Father, the fountain and origin of all blessings.

8-11 Shall not we pity and love those souls whom Christ loves and pities? Those who abound in any grace, need to abound more. Try things which differ; that we may approve the things which are excellent. The truths and laws of Christ are excellent; and they recommend themselves as such to any attentive mind. Sincerity is that in which we should have our conversation in the world, and it is the glory of all our graces. Christians should not be apt to take offense, and should be very careful not to offend God or the brethren. The things which most honor God will most benefit us. Let us not leave it doubtful whether any good fruit is found in us or not. A small measure of Christian love, knowledge, and fruitfulness should not satisfy any.

12-20 The apostle was a prisoner at Rome; and to take off the offense of the cross, he shows the wisdom and goodness of God in his sufferings. These things made him known, where he would never have otherwise been known; and led some to inquire after the gospel. He suffered from false friends, as well as from enemies. How wretched the temper of those who preached Christ out of envy and contention, and to add affliction to the bonds that oppressed this best of men! The apostle was easy in the midst of all. Since

JOY, A DUTY
Sermon number 2405 delivered at the Metropolitan Tabernacle, Newington, on March 20th, 1887.

"Rejoice in the Lord alway: and again I say, Rejoice."—Philippians 4:4.

I. It will be our first business at this time to consider THE GRACE COMMANDED, this grace of joy; "Rejoice in the Lord," says the apostle.

In the first place, this is a very delightful thing. What a gracious God we serve, who makes delight to be a duty, and who commands us to rejoice! Should we not at once be obedient to such a command as this? It is intended that we should be happy. That is the meaning of the precept, that we should be cheerful; more than that, that we should be thankful; more than that, that we should rejoice. I think this word "rejoice" is almost a French word; it is not only joy, but it is joy over again, re-joice. You know re usually signifies the reduplication of a thing, the taking of it over again. We are to joy, and then we are to re-joy. We are to chew the cud of delight; we are to roll the dainty morsel under our tongue till we get the very essence out of it. "Rejoice." Joy is a delightful thing. You cannot be too happy, brother. Nay, do not suspect yourself of being wrong because you are full of delight. You know it is said of the divine wisdom, "Her ways are ways of pleasantness, and all her paths are peace." Provided that it is joy in the Lord, you cannot have too much of it. The fly is drowned in the honey, or the sweet syrup into which he plunges himself; but this heavenly syrup of delight will not drown your soul, or intoxicate your heart. It will do you good, and not evil, all the days of your life. God never commanded us to do a thing that would really harm us; and when he bids us rejoice, we may be sure that this is as delightful as it is safe, and as safe as it is delightful. Come, brothers and sisters, I am inviting you now to no distasteful duty when, in the name of my Master, I say to you, as Paul said to the Philippians under the teaching of the Holy Spirit, "Rejoice in the Lord alway: and again I say, Rejoice."

But, next, this is a demonstrative duty: "Rejoice in the Lord." There may be such a thing as a dumb joy, but I hardly think that it can keep dumb long. Joy! Joy! Why, it speaks for itself! It is like a candle lighted in a dark chamber; you need not sound a trumpet, and say, "Now light has come." The candle proclaims itself by its own brilliance; and when joy comes into a man, it shines out of his eyes, it sparkles in his countenance. There is a something about every limb of the man that betokens that his body, like a

20 According to my earnest expectation and my hope, that in nothing I shall be ashamed, but that with all boldness, as always, so now also Christ shall be magnified in my body, whether it be by life, or by death.

21 For to me to live is Christ, and to die is gain.

22 But if I live in the flesh, this is the fruit of my labor: yet what I shall choose I wot not.

23 For I am in a strait betwixt two, having a desire to depart, and to be with Christ; which is far better:

24 Nevertheless to abide in the flesh is more needful for you.

25 And having this confidence, I know that I shall abide and continue with you all for your furtherance and joy of faith;

26 That your rejoicing may be more abundant in Jesus Christ for me by my coming to you again.

27 Only let your conversation be as it becometh the gospel of Christ: that whether I come and see you, or else be absent, I may hear of your affairs, that ye stand fast in one spirit, with one mind striving together for the faith of the gospel;

28 And in nothing terrified by your adversaries: which is to them an evident token of perdition, but to you of salvation, and that of God.

29 For unto you it is given in the behalf of Christ, not only to believe on him, but also to suffer for his sake;

30 Having the same conflict which ye saw in me, and now hear to be in me.

PHILIPPIANS 2

1 If there be therefore any consolation in Christ, if any comfort of love, if any fellowship of the Spirit, if any bowels and mercies,

2 Fulfill ye my joy, that ye be likeminded, having the same love, being of one accord, of one mind.

3 Let nothing be done through strife or vainglory; but in lowliness of mind let each esteem other better than themselves.

4 Look not every man on his own things, but every man also on the things of others.

5 Let this mind be in you, which was also in Christ Jesus:

6 Who, being in the form of God, thought it not robbery to be equal with God:

7 But made himself of no reputation, and took upon him the form of a ser-

11. Being filled with the fruits of righteousness, which are through Jesus Christ, to the glory and praise of God – Here are three properties of that sincerity which is acceptable to God:

1. It must bear fruits, the fruits of righteousness, all inward and outward holiness, all good tempers, words, and works; and that so abundantly, that we may be filled with them.

2. The branch and the fruits must derive both their virtue and their very being from the all – supporting, all – supplying root, Jesus Christ.

3. As all these flow from the grace of Christ, so they must issue in the glory and praise of God.

12. The things concerning me – My sufferings. Have fallen out rather to the furtherance, than, as you feared, the hindrance, of the gospel.

13. My bonds in Christ – Endured for his sake. Have been made manifest – Much taken notice of. In the whole palace – Of the Roman emperor.

14. And many – Who were before afraid. Trusting in the Lord through my bonds – When they observed my constancy, and safety not withstanding, are more bold.

15, 16. Some indeed preach Christ out of contention – Envying St. Paul's success, and striving to hurt him thereby. Not sincerely – From a real desire to glorify God. But supposing – Though they were disappointed. To add more affliction to my bonds – By enraging the Roman against me.

17. But the others out of love – To Christ and me. Knowing – Not barely, supposing. That I am set – Literally, I lie; yet still going forward in his work. He remained at Rome as an ambassador in a place where he is employed on an important embassy.

18. In pretense – Under color of propagating the gospel. In truth – With a real design so to do.

19. This shall turn to my salvation – Shall procure me an higher degree of glory. Through your prayer – Obtaining for me a larger supply of the Spirit.

20. As always – Since my call to the apostleship. In my body – however it may be disposed of. How that might be, he did not yet know. For the apostles did not know all things; particularly in things pertaining to themselves, they had room to exercise faith and patience.

21. To me to live is Christ – To know, to love, to follow Christ, is my life, my glory, my joy.

22. Here he begins to treat of the former clause of the preceding verse. Of the latter he treats, chap. ii, 17. But if I am to live is the flesh, this is the fruit of my labor – This is the fruit of my living longer, that I can labor more. Glorious labor! desirable fruit! in this view, long life is indeed a blessing. And what I should choose I know not – That is, if it were left to my choice.

23. To depart – Out of bonds, flesh, the world. And to be with Christ – In a nearer and fuller union. It is better to depart; it is far better to be with Christ.

25. I know – By a prophetic notice given him while he was writing this. That I shall continue some time longer with you – And doubtless he did see them after this confinement.

27. Only – Be careful for this, and nothing else. Stand fast in one spirit – With the most perfect unanimity. Striving together – With united strength and endeavors. For the faith of the gospel – For all the blessings revealed and promised therein.

28. Which – Namely, their being adversaries to the word of God, and to you the messengers of God. Is an evident token – That they are in the high road to perdition; and you, in the way of salvation.

29. For to you it is given – As a special token of God's love, and of your being in the way of salvation.

MATTHEW HENRY

CHARLES H. SPURGEON

our troubles may tend to the good of many, we ought to rejoice. Whatever turns to our salvation, is by the Spirit of Christ; and prayer is the appointed means of seeking for it. Our earnest expectation and hope should not be to be honored of men, or to escape the cross, but to be upheld amidst temptation, contempt, and affliction. Let us leave it to Christ, which way he will make us serviceable to his glory, whether by labor or suffering, by diligence or patience, by living to his honor in working for him, or dying to his honor in suffering for him.

21-26 Death is a great loss to a carnal, worldly man, for he loses all his earthly comforts and all his hopes; but to a true believer it is gain, for it is the end of all his weakness and misery. It delivers him from all the evils of life, and brings him to possess the chief good. The apostle's difficulty was not between living in this world and living in heaven; between these two there is no comparison; but between serving Christ in this world and enjoying him in another. Not between two evil things, but between two good things; living to Christ and being with him. See the power of faith and of Divine grace; it can make us willing to die. In this world we are compassed with sin; but when with Christ, we shall escape sin and temptation, sorrow and death, forever. But those who have most reason to desire to depart, should be willing to remain in the world as long as God has any work for them to do. And the more unexpected mercies are before they come, the more of God will be seen in them.

27-30 Those who profess the gospel of Christ, should live as becomes those who believe gospel truths, submit to gospel laws, and depend upon gospel promises. The original word "conversation" denotes the conduct of citizens who seek the credit, safety, peace, and prosperity of their city. There is that in the faith of the gospel, which is worth striving for; there is much opposition, and there is need of striving.

PHILIPPIANS 2

Exhortations to a kind, humble spirit and behavior.
  (1-4)
The example of Christ. (5-11)
Diligence in the affairs of salvation, and to be examples to the world. (12-18)
The apostle's purpose of visiting Philippi. (19-30)

1-4 Here are further exhortations to Christian duties; to like-mindedness and lowly-mindedness, according to the example of the Lord Jesus. Kindness is the law of Christ's kingdom, the lesson of his school, the livery of his family.

5-11 The example of our Lord Jesus Christ is set before us. We must resemble him in his life, if we

well-tuned harp, has had its strings put in order. Joy—it refreshes the marrow of the bones; it quickens the flowing of the blood in the veins; it is a healthy thing in all respects. It is a speaking thing, a demonstrative thing; and I am sure that joy in the Lord ought to have a tongue. When the Lord sends you affliction, sister, you generally grumble loudly enough; when the Lord tries you, my dear brother, you generally speak fast enough about that. Now when, on the other hand, the Lord multiplies his mercies to you, do speak about it, do sing about it. I cannot recollect, since I was a boy, ever seeing in the newspapers columns of thankfulness and expressions of delight about the prosperity of business in England. It is a long, long time since I was first able to read newspapers—a great many years now; but I do not recollect the paragraphs in which it was said that everybody was getting on in the world, and growing rich; but as soon as there was any depression in business, what lugubrious articles appeared concerning the dreadful times which had fallen upon the agricultural interest and every other interest! Oh, my dear brethren, from the way some of you grumble, I might imagine you were all ruined if I did not know better! I knew some of you when you were not worth two pence, and you are pretty well-to-do now; you have got on uncommonly well for men who are being ruined! From the way some people talk, you might imagine that everybody is bankrupt, and that we are all going to the dogs together; but it is not so, and what a pity it is that we do not give the Lord some of our praises when we have better times! If we are so loud and so eloquent over our present woes, why could we not have been as eloquent and as loud in thanksgiving for the blessings that God formerly vouchsafed to us? Perhaps the mercies buried in oblivion have been to heaven, and accused us to the Lord, and therefore he has sent us the sorrows of today. True joy, when it is joy in the Lord, must speak; it cannot hold its tongue, it must praise the name of the Lord.

Further, this blessed grace of joy is very contagious. It is a great privilege, I think, to meet a truly happy man, a graciously happy man. My mind goes back at this moment to that dear man of God who used to be with us, years ago, whom we called "Old Father Dransfield." What a lump of sunshine that man was! I think that I never came into this place with a heavy heart, but the very sight of him seemed to fill me with exhilaration, for his joy was wholly in his God! An old man and full of years, but as full of happiness as he was full of days; always having something to tell you to encourage you. He constantly made a discovery of some fresh mercy

vant, and was made in the likeness of men:

8 And being found in fashion as a man, he humbled himself, and became obedient unto death, even the death of the cross.

9 Wherefore God also hath highly exalted him, and given him a name which is above every name:

10 That at the name of Jesus every knee should bow, of things in heaven, and things in earth, and things under the earth;

11 And that every tongue should confess that Jesus Christ is Lord, to the glory of God the Father.

12 Wherefore, my beloved, as ye have always obeyed, not as in my presence only, but now much more in my absence, work out your own salvation with fear and trembling.

13 For it is God which worketh in you both to will and to do of his good pleasure.

14 Do all things without murmurings and disputings:

15 That ye may be blameless and harmless, the sons of God, without rebuke, in the midst of a crooked and perverse nation, among whom ye shine as lights in the world;

16 Holding forth the word of life; that I may rejoice in the day of Christ, that I have not run in vain, neither labored in vain.

17 Yea, and if I be offered upon the sacrifice and service of your faith, I joy, and rejoice with you all.

18 For the same cause also do ye joy, and rejoice with me.

19 But I trust in the Lord Jesus to send Timotheus shortly unto you, that I also may be of good comfort, when I know your state.

20 For I have no man likeminded, who will naturally care for your state.

21 For all seek their own, not the things which are Jesus Christ's.

22 But ye know the proof of him, that, as a son with the father, he hath served with me in the gospel.

23 Him therefore I hope to send presently, so soon as I shall see how it will go with me.

24 But I trust in the Lord that I also myself shall come shortly.

25 Yet I supposed it necessary to send to you Epaphroditus, my brother, and companion in labor, and fellowsoldier, but your messenger, and he that ministered to my wants.

26 For he longed after you all, and was full of heaviness, because that ye had heard that he had been sick.

30. Having the same kind of conflict with your adversaries, which ye saw in me – When I was with you, Acts xvi, 12, 19, &c.

PHILIPPIANS 2

1. If there be therefore any consolation – In the grace of Christ. If any comfort – In the love of God. If any fellowship of the Holy Ghost; if any bowels of mercies – Resulting therefrom; any tender affection towards each other.

2. Think the same thing – Seeing Christ is your common Head. Having the same love – To God, your common Father. Being of one soul – Animated with the same affections and tempers, as ye have all drank ill to one spirit. Of one mind – Tenderly rejoicing and grieving together.

3. Do nothing through contention – Which is inconsistent with your thinking the same thing. Or vainglory – Desire of praise, which is directly opposite to the love of God. But esteem each the others better than themselves – (For every one knows more evil of himself than he can of another:) Which is a glorious fruit of the Spirit, and an admirable help to your continuing "of one soul."

4. Aim not every one at his own things – Only. If so, ye have not bowels of mercies.

6. Who being in the essential form – The incommunicable nature. Of God – From eternity, as he was afterward in the form of man; real God, as real man. Counted it no act of robbery – That is the precise meaning of the words, – no invasion of another's prerogative, but his own strict and unquestionable right. To be equal with God – the word here translated equal, occurs in the adjective form five or six times in the New Testament, Matt. xx, 12; Luke vi, 34; John v, 18; Acts xi, 17; Rev. xxi, 16. In all which places it expresses not a bare resemblance, but a real and proper equality. It here implies both the fullness and the supreme height of the Godhead; to which are opposed, he emptied and he humbled himself.

7. Yet – He was so far from tenaciously insisting upon, that he willingly relinquished, his claim.

8. And being found in fashion as a man – A common man, without any peculiar excellence or comeliness. He humbled himself – To a still greater depth. Becoming obedient – To God, though equal with him. Even unto death – The greatest instance both of humiliation and obedience. Yea, the death of the cross – Inflicted on few but servants or slaves.

9. Wherefore – Because of his voluntary humiliation and obedience. He humbled himself; but God hath exalted him – So recompensing his humiliation. And hath given him – So recompensing his emptying himself. A name which is above every name – Dignity and majesty superior to every creature.

10. That every knee – That divine honor might be paid in every possible manner by every creature. Might bow – Either with love or trembling. Of those in heaven, earth, under the earth – That is, through the whole universe.

11. And every tongue – Even of his enemies. Confess that Jesus Christ is Lord – Jehovah; not now "in the form of a servant," but enthroned in the glory of God the Father.

12. Wherefore – Having proposed Christ's example, he exhorts them to secure the salvation which Christ has purchased. As ye have always – Hitherto. Obeyed – Both God, and me his minister. Now in my absence – When ye have not me to instruct, assist, and direct you. Work out your own salvation – Herein let every man aim at his own things.

13. For it is God – God alone, who is with you, though I am not.

would have the benefit of his death. Notice the two natures of Christ; his Divine nature, and human nature. Who being in the form of God, partaking the Divine nature, as the eternal and only-begotten Son of God, Joh 1:1, had not thought it a robbery to be equal with God, and to receive Divine worship from men. His human nature; herein he became like us in all things except sin. Thus low, of his own will, he stooped from the glory he had with the Father before the world was. Christ's two states, of humiliation and exaltation, are noticed.

12-18 We must be diligent in the use of all the means which lead to our salvation, persevering therein to the end. With great care, lest, with all our advantages, we should come short. Work out your salvation, for it is God who worketh in you. This encourages us to do our utmost, because our labor shall not be in vain: we must still depend on the grace of God. The working of God's grace in us, is to quicken and engage our endeavors. God's good will to us, is the cause of his good work in us. Do your duty without murmurings. Do it, and do not find fault with it. Mind your work, and do not quarrel with it. By peaceableness; give no just occasion of offense. The children of God should differ from the sons of men. The more perverse others are, the more careful we should be to keep ourselves blameless and harmless. The doctrine and example of consistent believers will enlighten others, and direct their way to Christ and holiness, even as the light-house warns mariners to avoid rocks, and directs their course into the harbor. Let us try thus to shine. The gospel is the word of life, it makes known to us eternal life through Jesus Christ. Running, denotes earnestness and vigor, continual pressing forward; laboring, denotes constancy, and close application. It is the will of God that believers should be much in rejoicing; and those who are so happy as to have good ministers, have great reason to rejoice with them.

19-30 It is best with us, when our duty becomes natural to us. Naturally, that is, sincerely, and not in pretense only; with a willing heart and upright views. We are apt to prefer our own credit, ease, and safety, before truth, holiness, and duty; but Timothy did not so. Paul desired liberty, not that he might take pleasure, but that he might do good. Epaphroditus was willing to go to the Philippians, that he might be comforted with those who had sorrowed for him when he was sick. It seems, his illness was caused by the work of God. The apostle urges them to love him the more on that account. It is doubly pleasant to have our mercies restored by God, after great danger of their removal; and this should make them more valued. What is given in answer to prayer, should be received with great thankfulness and joy.

for which we were again to praise God. O dear brethren, let us rejoice in the Lord, that we may set others rejoicing! One dolorous spirit brings a kind of plague into the house; one person who is always wretched seems to stop all the birds singing wherever he goes; but, as the birds pipe to each other, and one morning songster quickens all the rest, and sets the groves ringing with harmony, so will it be with the happy cheerful spirit of a man who obeys the command of the text, "Rejoice in the Lord alway." This grace of joy is contagious.

Besides, dear brethren, joy in the Lord is influential for good. I am sure that there is a mighty influence wielded by a consistently joyous spirit. See how little children are affected by the presence of a happy person. There is much more in the tone of the life than there is in the particular fashion of the life. It may be the life of one who is very poor, but oh, how poverty is gilded by a cheerful spirit! It may be the life of one who is well read and deeply instructed; but, oh, if there be a beauty of holiness, and a beauty of happiness added to the learning, nobody talks about "the blue stocking," or "the bookworm" being dull and heavy. Oh, no, there is a charm about holy joy! I wish we had more of it! There are many more flies caught with honey than with vinegar; and there are many more sinners brought to Christ by happy Christians than by doleful Christians. Let us sing unto the Lord as long as we live; and, mayhap, some weary sinner, who has discovered the emptiness of sinful pleasure, will say to himself, "Why, after all, there must be something real about the lives of these Christians; let me go and learn how I may have it." And when he comes and sees it in the light of your gladsome countenance, he will be likely to learn it, God helping him, so as never to forget it. "Rejoice in the Lord alway," says the apostle, for joy is a most influential grace, and every child of God ought to possess it in a high degree.

II. Now we come to the second head, on which I will speak but briefly; that is, THE JOY DISCRIMINATED: "Rejoice in the Lord."

Notice the sphere of this joy: "Rejoice in the Lord." We read in Scripture that children are to obey their parents "in the Lord." We read of men and women being married "only in the Lord." Now, dear friends, no child of God must go outside that ring, "in the Lord." There is where you are, where you ought to be, where you must be. You cannot truly rejoice if you get outside that ring; therefore, see that you do nothing which you cannot do "in the Lord." Mind that you seek no joy which is not joy in the Lord; if you go after the poisonous sweets of

27 For indeed he was sick nigh unto death: but God had mercy on him; and not on him only, but on me also, lest I should have sorrow upon sorrow.

28 I sent him therefore the more carefully, that, when ye see him again, ye may rejoice, and that I may be the less sorrowful.

29 Receive him therefore in the Lord with all gladness; and hold such in reputation:

30 Because for the work of Christ he was nigh unto death, not regarding his life, to supply your lack of service toward me.

PHILIPPIANS 3

1 Finally, my brethren, rejoice in the Lord. To write the same things to you, to me indeed is not grievous, but for you it is safe.

2 Beware of dogs, beware of evil workers, beware of the concision.

3 For we are the circumcision, which worship God in the spirit, and rejoice in Christ Jesus, and have no confidence in the flesh.

4 Though I might also have confidence in the flesh. If any other man thinketh that he hath whereof he might trust in the flesh, I more:

5 Circumcised the eighth day, of the stock of Israel, of the tribe of Benjamin, an Hebrew of the Hebrews; as touching the law, a Pharisee;

6 Concerning zeal, persecuting the church; touching the righteousness which is in the law, blameless.

7 But what things were gain to me, those I counted loss for Christ.

8 Yea doubtless, and I count all things but loss for the excellency of the knowledge of Christ Jesus my Lord: for whom I have suffered the loss of all things, and do count them but dung, that I may win Christ,

9 And be found in him, not having mine own righteousness, which is of the law, but that which is through the faith of Christ, the righteousness which is of God by faith:

10 That I may know him, and the power of his resurrection, and the fellowship of his sufferings, being made conformable unto his death;

11 If by any means I might attain unto the resurrection of the dead.

12 Not as though I had already attained, either were already perfect: but I follow after, if that I may apprehend that for which also I am apprehended of Christ Jesus.

15. That ye may be blameless – Before men.

17. Here he begins to treat of the latter clause of chap. i, 22.

18. Congratulate me – When I am offered up.

19. When I know – Upon my return, that ye stand steadfast.

20. I have none – Of those who are now with me.

21. For all – But Timotheus. Seek their own – Ease, safety, pleasure, or profit.

22. As a son with his father – He uses an elegant peculiarity of phrase, speaking partly as of a son, partly as of a fellow laborer.

25. To send Epaphroditus – Back immediately. Your messenger – The Philippians had sent him to St. Paul with their liberal contribution.

26. He was full of heaviness – Because he supposed you would be afflicted at hearing that he was sick.

27. God had compassion on him – Restoring him to health.

28. That I may be the less sorrowful – When I know you are rejoicing.

30. To supply your deficiency of service – To do what you could not do in person.

PHILIPPIANS 3

1. The same things – Which you have heard before.

2. Beware of dogs – Unclean, unholy, rapacious men.

3. For we – Christians. Are the only true circumcision – The people now in covenant with God. Who worship God in spirit – Not barely in the letter, but with the spiritual worship of inward holiness. And glory in Christ Jesus – As the only cause of all our blessings. And have no confidence in the flesh – In any outward advantage or prerogative.

4. Though I – He subjoins this in the singular number, because the Philippians could not say thus.

5. Circumcised the eighth day – Not at ripe age, as a proselyte. Of the tribe of Benjamin – Sprung from the wife, not the handmaid. An Hebrew of Hebrews – By both my parents; in everything, nation, religion, language. Touching the law, a Pharisee – One of that sect who most accurately observe it.

6. Having such a zeal for it as to persecute to the death those who did not observe it. Touching the righteousness which is described and enjoined by the Law – That is, external observances, blameless.

7. But all these things, which I then accounted gain, which were once my confidence, my glory, and joy, those, ever since I have believed, I have accounted loss, nothing worth in comparison of Christ.

8. Yea, I still account both all these and all things else to be mere loss, compared to the inward, experimental knowledge of Christ, as my Lord, as my prophet, priest, and king, as teaching me wisdom, atoning for my sins, and reigning in my heart.

9. And be found by God ingrafted in him, not having my own righteousness, which is of the law – That merely outward righteousness prescribed by the law, and performed by my own strength. But that inward righteousness which is through faith – Which can flow from no other fountain. The righteousness which is from God – From his almighty Spirit, not by my own strength, but by faith alone. Here also the apostle is far from speaking of justification only.

10. The knowledge of Christ, mentioned in the eighth verse, is here more largely explained. That I may know him – As my complete Savior. And the power of his resurrection – Raising me from the death of sin, into all the life of love. And the fellowship of his sufferings – Being crucified with him. And made conformable to his death – So as to be dead to all things here below.

PHILIPPIANS 3

The apostle cautions the Philippians against judaizing false teachers, and renounces his own former privileges. (1-11)

Expresses earnest desire to be found in Christ; also his pressing on toward perfection; and recommends his own example to other believers. (12-21)

1-11 Sincere Christians rejoice in Christ Jesus. The prophet calls the false prophets dumb dogs, Isa 56:10; to which the apostle seems to refer. Dogs, for their malice against faithful professors of the gospel of Christ, barking at them and biting them. They urged human works in opposition to the faith of Christ; but Paul calls them evil-workers. None can have benefit by it, who trust in themselves. Faith is the appointed means of applying the saving benefit. It is by faith in Christ's blood. We are made conformable to Christ's death, when we die to sin, as he died for sin; and the world is crucified to us, and we to the world, by the cross of Christ. The apostle was willing to do or to suffer any thing, to attain the glorious resurrection of saints. This hope and prospect carried him through all difficulties in his work. He did not hope to attain it through his own merit and righteousness, but through the merit and righteousness of Jesus Christ.

12-21 This simple dependence and earnestness of soul, were not mentioned as if the apostle had gained the prize, or were already made perfect in the Savior's likeness. He forgot the things which were behind, so as not to be content with past labors or present measures of grace. He reached forth, stretched himself forward towards his point; expressions showing great concern to become more and more like unto Christ. He who runs a race, must never stop short of the end, but press forward as fast as he can; so those who have heaven in their view, must still press forward to it, in holy desires and hopes, and constant endeavors. Eternal life is the gift of God, but it is in Christ Jesus; through his hand it must come to us, as it is procured for us by him. There is no getting to heaven as our home, but by Christ as our Way. True believers, in seeking this assurance, as well as to glorify him, will seek more nearly to resemble his sufferings and death, by dying to sin, and by crucifying the flesh with its affections and lusts. In these things there is a great difference among real Christians, but all know something of them. Believers make Christ all in all, and set their hearts upon another world. If they differ from one another, and are not of the same judgment in lesser matters, yet they must not judge one another; while they all meet now in Christ, and hope to meet shortly in heaven. Let them join in all the great things in which they are agreed, and wait for further light as to lesser things wherein they differ. The enemies of the cross of Christ mind nothing but their sensual appetites. Sin is the sinner's shame, especially

this world, woe be to you. Never rejoice in that which is sinful, for all such rejoicing is evil. Flee from it; it can do you no good. That joy which you cannot share with God is not a right joy for you. No; "in the Lord" is the sphere of your joy.

But I think that the apostle also means that God is to be the great object of your joy: "Rejoice in the Lord." Rejoice in the Father, your Father who is in heaven, your loving, tender, unchangeable God. Rejoice, too, in the Son, your Redeemer, your Brother, the Husband of you soul, your Prophet, Priest, and King. Rejoice also in the Holy Ghost, your Quickener, your Comforter, in him who shall abide with you for ever. Rejoice in the one God of Abraham, of Isaac, and of Jacob; in him delight yourselves, as it is written, "Delight thyself also in the Lord; and he shall give thee the desires of thine heart." We cannot have too much of this joy in the Lord, for the great Jehovah is our exceeding joy. Or if, by "the Lord" is meant the Lord Jesus, then let me invite, persuade, command you to delight in the Lord Jesus, incarnate in your flesh, dead for your sins, risen for your justification, gone into the glory claiming victory for you, sitting at the right hand of God interceding for you, reigning over all worlds on your behalf, and soon to come to take you up into his glory that you may be with him for ever. Rejoice in the Lord Jesus. This is a sea of delight; blessed are they that dive into its utmost depths.

Sometimes, brethren and sisters, you cannot rejoice in anything else, but you can rejoice in the Lord; then, rejoice in him to the full. Do not rejoice in your temporal prosperity, for riches take to themselves wings, and fly away. Do not rejoice even in your great successes in the work of God. Remember how the seventy disciples came back to Jesus, and said, "Lord, even the devils are subject unto us through thy name," and he answered, "Notwithstanding in this rejoice not, that the spirits are subject unto you; but rather rejoice, because your names are written in heaven." Do not rejoice in your privileges; I mean, do not make the great joy of your life to be the fact that you are favored with this and that external privilege or ordinance, but rejoice in God. He changes not. If the Lord be your joy, your joy will never dry up. All other things are but for a season; but God is for ever and ever. Make him your joy, the whole of your joy, and then let this joy absorb your every thought. Be baptized into this joy; plunge into the deeps of this unutterable bliss of joy in God.

III. Thirdly, let us think of THE TIME APPOINTED for this rejoicing: "Rejoice in the Lord alway."

"Alway." Well, then, that begins at once, certainly; so let us now begin to rejoice in the

13 Brethren, I count not myself to have apprehended: but this one thing I do, forgetting those things which are behind, and reaching forth unto those things which are before,

14 I press toward the mark for the prize of the high calling of God in Christ Jesus.

15 Let us therefore, as many as be perfect, be thus minded: and if in any thing ye be otherwise minded, God shall reveal even this unto you.

16 Nevertheless, whereto we have already attained, let us walk by the same rule, let us mind the same thing.

17 Brethren, be followers together of me, and mark them which walk so as ye have us for an ensample.

18 (For many walk, of whom I have told you often, and now tell you even weeping, that they are the enemies of the cross of Christ:

19 Whose end is destruction, whose God is their belly, and whose glory is in their shame, who mind earthly things.)

20 For our conversation is in heaven; from whence also we look for the Savior, the Lord Jesus Christ:

21 Who shall change our vile body, that it may be fashioned like unto his glorious body, according to the working whereby he is able even to subdue all things unto himself.

PHILIPPIANS 4

1 Therefore, my brethren dearly beloved and longed for, my joy and crown, so stand fast in the Lord, my dearly beloved.

2 I beseech Euodias, and beseech Syntyche, that they be of the same mind in the Lord.

3 And I intreat thee also, true yoke-fellow, help those women which labored with me in the gospel, with Clement also, and with other my fellowlaborers, whose names are in the book of life.

4 Rejoice in the Lord alway: and again I say, Rejoice.

5 Let your moderation be known unto all men. The Lord is at hand.

6 Be careful for nothing; but in every thing by prayer and supplication with thanksgiving let your requests be made known unto God.

7 And the peace of God, which passeth all understanding, shall keep your hearts and minds through Christ Jesus.

8 Finally, brethren, whatsoever things

11. The resurrection of the dead – That is, the resurrection to glory.

12. Not that I have already attained – The prize. He here enters on a new set of metaphors, taken from a race.

13. I do not account myself to have apprehended this already; to be already possessed of perfect holiness.

14. Forgetting the things that are behind – Even that part of the race which is already run. And reaching forth unto – Literally, stretched out over the things that are before – Pursuing with the whole bent and vigor of my soul, perfect holiness and eternal glory. In Christ Jesus – The author and finisher of every good thing.

15. Let us, as many as are perfect – Fit for the race, strong in faith; so it means here.

16. But let us take care not to lose the ground we have already gained. Let us walk by the same rule we have done hitherto.

17. Mark them – For your imitation.

18. Weeping – As he wrote. Enemies of the cross of Christ – Such are all cowardly, all shamefaced, all delicate Christians.

19. Whose end is destruction – This is placed in the front, that what follows may be read with the greater horror. Whose God is their belly – Whose supreme happiness lies in gratifying their sensual appetites. Who mind – Relish, desire, seek, earthly things.

20. Our conversation – The Greek word is of a very extensive meaning: our citizenship, our thoughts, our affections, are already in heaven.

21. Who will transform our vile body – Into the most perfect state, and the most beauteous form. It will then be purer than the unspotted firmament, brighter than the luster of the stars and, which exceeds all parallel, which comprehends all perfection, like unto his glorious body – Like that wonderfully glorious body which he wears in his heavenly kingdom, and on his triumphant throne.

PHILIPPIANS 4

1. So stand – As ye have done hitherto.

2. I beseech – He repeats this twice, as if speaking to each face to face, and that with the utmost tenderness.

3. And I entreat thee also, true yokefellow – St. Paul had many fellowlaborers, but not many yokefellows.

5. Let your gentleness – Yieldingness, sweetness of temper, the result of joy in the Lord. Be known – By your whole behavior. To all men – Good and bad, gentle and froward. Those of the roughest tempers are good natured to some, from natural sympathy and various motives; a Christian, to all. The Lord – The judge, the rewarder, the avenger. Is at hand – Standeth at the door.

6. Be anxiously careful for nothing – If men are not gentle towards you, yet neither on this, nor any other account, be careful, but pray. Carefulness and prayer cannot stand together.

7. And the peace of God – That calm, heavenly repose, that tranquillity of spirit, which God only can give.

8. Finally – To sum up all. Whatsoever things are true – Here are eight particulars placed in two fourfold rows; the former containing their duty; the latter, the commendation of it.

9. The things which ye have learned – As catechumens. And received – By continual instructions. And heard and seen – In my life and conversation. These do, and the God of peace shall be with you – Not only the peace of God, but God himself, the fountain of peace.

10. I rejoiced greatly – St. Paul was no Stoic: he had strong passions, but all

MATTHEW HENRY

CHARLES H. SPURGEON

when gloried in. The way of those who mind earthly things, may seem pleasant, but death and hell are at the end of it. If we choose their way, we shall share their end. The life of a Christian is in heaven, where his Head and his home are, and where he hopes to be shortly; he sets his affections upon things above; and where his heart is, there will his conversation be. There is glory kept for the bodies of the saints, in which they will appear at the resurrection. Then the body will be made glorious; not only raised again to life, but raised to great advantage. Observe the power by which this change will be wrought. May we be always prepared for the coming of our Judge; looking to have our vile bodies changed by his Almighty power, and applying to him daily to new-create our souls unto holiness; to deliver us from our enemies, and to employ our bodies and souls as instruments of righteousness in his service.

PHILIPPIANS 4

The apostle exhorts the Philippians to stand fast in the Lord. (1)

Gives directions to some, and to all in general. (2-9)

Expresses contentment in every condition of life. (10-19)

He concludes with prayer to God the Father, and his usual blessing. (20-23)

1 The believing hope and prospect of eternal life, should make us steady and constant in our Christian course. There is difference of gifts and graces, yet, being renewed by the same Spirit, we are brethren. To stand fast in the Lord, is to stand fast in his strength, and by his grace.

2-9 Let believers be of one mind, and ready to help each other. As the apostle had found the benefit of their assistance, he knew how comfortable it would be to his fellow-laborers to have the help of others. Let us seek to give assurance that our names are written in the book of life. Joy in God is of great consequence in the Christian life; and Christians need to be again and again called to it. It more than outweighs all causes for sorrow. Let their enemies perceive how moderate they were as to outward things, and how composedly they suffered loss and hardships. The day of judgment will soon arrive, with full redemption to believers, and destruction to ungodly men. There is a care of diligence which is our duty, and agrees with a wise forecast and due concern; but there is a care of fear and distrust, which is sin and folly, and only perplexes and distracts the mind. As a remedy against perplexing care, constant prayer is recommended. Not only stated times for prayer, but in every thing by prayer. We must join thanksgivings with prayers and supplications; not only seek supplies of good, but own the mercies we have received. God needs not to be told our wants or desires; he

Lord. If any of you have taken a gloomy view of religion, I beseech you to throw that gloomy view away at once. "Rejoice in the Lord alway," therefore, rejoice in the Lord now. I recollect what a damper I had, as a young Christian, when I had but lately believed in Jesus Christ. I felt that, as the Lord had said, "He that believeth in me hath everlasting life," I, having believed in him, had everlasting life, and I said so, with the greatest joy and delight and enthusiasm, to an old Christian man; and he said to me, "Beware of presumption! There are a great many who think they have eternal life, but who have not got it," which was quite true; but, for all that, is there not more presumption in doubting God's promise than there is in believing it? Is there any presumption in taking God at his word? Is there not gross presumption in hesitating and questioning as to whether these things are so or not? If God says that they are so, then they are so, whether I feel that they are so or not; and it is my place, as a believer, to accept God's bare word, and rest on it. "We count cheques as cash," said one who was making up accounts. Good cheques are to be counted as cash, and the promises of God, though as yet unfulfilled, are as good as the blessings themselves, for God cannot lie, or make a promise that he will not perform. Let us, therefore, not be afraid of being glad, but begin to be glad at once if we have hitherto taken a gloomy view of true religion, and have been afraid to rejoice.

When are we to be glad? "Rejoice in the Lord alway;" that is, when you cannot rejoice in anything or anyone but God. When the fig-tree does not blossom, when there is no fruit on the vine and no herd in the stall, when everything withers and decays and perishes, when the worm at the root of the gourd has made it to die, then rejoice in the Lord. When the day darkens into evening, and the evening into midnight, and the midnight into a seven fold horror of great darkness, rejoice in the Lord; and when that darkness does not clear, but becomes more dense and Egyptian, when night succeedeth night, and neither sun nor moon nor stars appear, still rejoice in the Lord alway. He who uttered these words had been a night and a day in the deep, he had been stoned, he had suffered from false brethren, he had been in peril of his life, and yet most fittingly do those lips cry out to us, "Rejoice in the Lord alway." Ay, at the stake itself have martyrs fulfilled this word; they clapped their hands amid the fire that was consuming them. Therefore, rejoice in the Lord when you cannot rejoice in any other.

But also take care that you rejoice in the Lord when you have other things to rejoice in. When he loads your table with good things, and

are true, whatsoever things are honest, whatsoever things are just, whatsoever things are pure, whatsoever things are lovely, whatsoever things are of good report; if there be any virtue, and if there be any praise, think on these things.

9 Those things, which ye have both learned, and received, and heard, and seen in me, do: and the God of peace shall be with you.

10 But I rejoiced in the Lord greatly, that now at the last your care of me hath flourished again; wherein ye were also careful, but ye lacked opportunity.

11 Not that I speak in respect of want: for I have learned, in whatsoever state I am, therewith to be content.

12 I know both how to be abased, and I know how to abound: every where and in all things I am instructed both to be full and to be hungry, both to abound and to suffer need.

13 I can do all things through Christ which strengtheneth me.

14 Notwithstanding ye have well done, that ye did communicate with my affliction.

15 Now ye Philippians know also, that in the beginning of the gospel, when I departed from Macedonia, no church communicated with me as concerning giving and receiving, but ye only.

16 For even in Thessalonica ye sent once and again unto my necessity.

17 Not because I desire a gift: but I desire fruit that may abound to your account.

18 But I have all, and abound: I am full, having received of Epaphroditus the things which were sent from you, an odor of a sweet smell, a sacrifice acceptable, wellpleasing to God.

19 But my God shall supply all your need according to his riches in glory by Christ Jesus.

20 Now unto God and our Father be glory for ever and ever. Amen.

21 Salute every saint in Christ Jesus. The brethren which are with me greet you.

22 All the saints salute you, chiefly they that are of Cesar's household.

23 The grace of our Lord Jesus Christ be with you all. Amen.

devoted to God. That your care of me hath flourished again – As a tree blossoms after the winter. Ye wanted opportunity – Either ye had not plenty yourselves, or you wanted a proper messenger.

11. I have learned – From God. He only can teach this. In everything, therewith to be content – Joyfully and thankfully patient. Nothing less is Christian content. We may observe a beautiful gradation in the expressions, I have learned; I know; I am instructed; I can.

12. I know how to be abased – Having scarce what is needful for my body.

13. I can do all things – Even fulfill all the will of God.

15. In the beginning of the gospel – When it was first preached at Philippi. In respect of giving – On your part. And receiving – On mine.

17. Not that I desire – For my own sake, the very gift which I receive of you.

18. An odor of a sweet smell – More pleasing to God than the sweetest perfumes to men.

19. All your need – As ye have mine. According to his riches in glory – In his abundant, eternal glory.

knows them better than we do; but he will have us show that we value the mercy, and feel our dependence on him. The peace of God, the comfortable sense of being reconciled to God, and having a part in his favor, and the hope of the heavenly blessedness, are a greater good than can be fully expressed. This peace will keep our hearts and minds through Christ Jesus; it will keep us from sinning under troubles, and from sinking under them; keep us calm and with inward satisfaction. Believers are to get and to keep a good name; a name for good things with God and good men. We should walk in all the ways of virtue, and abide therein; then, whether our praise is of men or not, it will be of God. The apostle is for an example. His doctrine and life agreed together. The way to have the God of peace with us, is to keep close to our duty. All our privileges and salvation arise in the free mercy of God; yet the enjoyment of them depends on our sincere and holy conduct. These are works of God, pertaining to God, and to him only are they to be ascribed, and to no other, neither men, words, nor deeds.

10-19 It is a good work to succor and help a good minister in trouble. The nature of true Christian sympathy, is not only to feel concern for our friends in their troubles, but to do what we can to help them. The apostle was often in bonds, imprisonments, and necessities; but in all, he learned to be content, to bring his mind to his condition, and make the best of it. Pride, unbelief, vain hankering after something we have not got, and fickle disrelish of present things, make men discontented even under favorable circumstances. Let us pray for patient submission and hope when we are abased; for humility and a heavenly mind when exalted. It is a special grace to have an equal temper of mind always. And in a low state not to lose our comfort in God, nor distrust his providence, nor take any wrong course for our own supply. In a prosperous condition not to be proud, or secure, or worldly. This is a harder lesson than the other; for the temptations of fullness and prosperity are more than those of affliction and want. The apostle had no design to urge them to give more, but to encourage such kindness as will meet a glorious reward hereafter. Through Christ we have grace to do what is good, and through him we must expect the reward; and as we have all things by him, let us do all things for him, and to his glory.

20-23 The apostle ends with praises to God. We should look upon God, under all our weakness and fears, not as an enemy, but as a Father, disposed to pity us and help us. We must give glory to God as a Father. God's grace and favor, which reconciled souls enjoy, with the whole of the graces in us, which flow from it, are all purchased for us by Christ's merit, and applied by his pleading for us; and therefore are justly called the grace of our Lord Jesus Christ.

your cup is overflowing with blessings, rejoice in him more than in them. Forget not that the Lord your Shepherd is better than the green pastures and the still waters, and rejoice not in the pastures or in the waters in comparison with your joy in the Shepherd who gives you all. Let us never make gods out of our goods; let us never allow what God gives us to supplant the Giver. Shall the wife love the jewels that her husband gave her better than she loves him who gave them to her? That were an evil love, or no love at all. So, let us love God first, and rejoice in the Lord alway when the day is brightest, and multiplied are the other joys that he permits us to have.

When you cannot get anybody else to rejoice with you, still continue to rejoice. There is a way of looking at everything which will show you that the blackest cloud has a silver lining. There is a way of looking at all things in the light of God, which will turn into sweetness that which otherwise had been bitter as gall. I do not know whether any of you keep a quassia cup at home. If you do, you know that it is made of wood, and you pour water into the bowl, and the water turns bitter directly before you drink it. You may keep this cup as long as you like, but it always embitters the water that is put into it. I think that I know some dear brethren and sisters who always seem to have one of these cups handy. Now instead of that, I want you to buy a cup of another kind that shall make everything sweet, whatever it is. Whatever God pleases to pour out of the bowl of providence shall come into your cup, and your contentment, your delight in God, shall sweeten it all. God bless you, dear friends, with much of this holy joy!

Be happy. If the present be dreary, it will soon be over. Come, then, let us make a solemn league and covenant together in the name of God, and let it be called, "The Guild of the Happy"; for the—

"Favorites of the Heavenly King
May speak their joys abroad;"

nay, they must speak their joys abroad; let us endeavor to do so always, by the help of the Holy Spirit. Amen and Amen.

Colossians

COLOSSIANS 1

1 Paul, an apostle of Jesus Christ by the will of God, and Timotheus our brother,

2 To the saints and faithful brethren in Christ which are at Colosse: Grace be unto you, and peace, from God our Father and the Lord Jesus Christ.

3 We give thanks to God and the Father of our Lord Jesus Christ, praying always for you,

4 Since we heard of your faith in Christ Jesus, and of the love which ye have to all the saints,

5 For the hope which is laid up for you in heaven, whereof ye heard before in the word of the truth of the gospel;

6 Which is come unto you, as it is in all the world; and bringeth forth fruit, as it doth also in you, since the day ye heard of it, and knew the grace of God in truth:

7 As ye also learned of Epaphras our dear fellowservant, who is for you a faithful minister of Christ;

8 Who also declared unto us your love in the Spirit.

9 For this cause we also, since the day we heard it, do not cease to pray for you, and to desire that ye might be filled with the knowledge of his will in all wisdom and spiritual understanding;

10 That ye might walk worthy of the Lord unto all pleasing, being fruitful in every good work, and increasing in the knowledge of God;

11 Strengthened with all might, according to his glorious power, unto all patience and longsuffering with joyfulness;

12 Giving thanks unto the Father, which hath made us meet to be partakers of the inheritance of the saints in light:

13 Who hath delivered us from the power of darkness, and hath translated us into the kingdom of his dear Son:

14 In whom we have redemption through his blood, even the forgiveness of sins:

15 Who is the image of the invisible God, the firstborn of every creature:

16 For by him were all things created, that are in heaven, and that are in earth, visible and invisible, whether they be thrones, or dominions, or principalities, or powers: all things were created by him, and for him:

17 And he is before all things, and by him all things consist.

18 And he is the head of the body, the church: who is the beginning, the firstborn from the dead; that in all things he might have the preeminence.

COLOSSE was a city of the Greater Phrygia, not far from Ladies and Hierapolis. Though St. Paul preached in many parts of Phrygia, yet he never had been at this city. It had received the gospel by the preaching of Epaphras, who was with St. Paul when he wrote this epistle. It seems the Colossians were now in danger of being seduced by those who strove to blend Judaism, or heathen superstitions, with Christianity; pretending that God, because of his great majesty, was not to be approached but by the mediation of angels; and that there were certain rites and observances, chiefly borrowed from the law, whereby these angels might be made our friends. In opposition to them, the apostle,

1. Commends the knowledge of Christ, as more excellent than all other, and so entire and perfect that no other knowledge was necessary for a Christian. He shows,

2. That Christ is above all angels, who are only his servants; and that, being reconciled to God through him, we have free access to him in all our necessities.

COLOSSIANS 1

2. The saints – This word expresses their union with God. And brethren – This, their union with their fellow-Christians.

3. We give thanks – There is a near resemblance between this epistle, and those to the Ephesians and Philippians.

5. Ye heard before – I wrote to you. In the word of truth, of the gospel – The true gospel preached to you.

6. It bringeth forth fruit in all the world – That is, in every place where it is preached. Ye knew the grace of God in truth – Truly experienced the gracious power of God.

7. The fellow servant – Of Paul and Timotheus.

8. Your love in the Spirit – Your love wrought in you by the Spirit.

9. We pray for you – This was mentioned in general, Colossians i, 3, but now more particularly. That ye may be filled with the knowledge of his will – Of his revealed will. In all wisdom – With all the wisdom from above. And spiritual understanding – To discern by that light whatever agrees with, or differs from, his will.

10. That, knowing his whole will, ye may walk worthy of the Lord, unto all pleasing – So as actually to please him in all things; daily increasing in the living, experimental knowledge of God, our Father, Savior, Sanctifier.

11. Strengthened unto all patience and longsuffering with joyfulness – This is the highest point: not only to know, to do, to suffer, the whole will of God; but to suffer it to the end, not barely with patience, but with thankful joy.

12. Who, by justifying and sanctifying us, hath made us meet for glory.

13. Power detains reluctant captives, a kingdom cherishes willing subjects. His beloved Son – This is treated of in the fifteenth and following verses.

14. In whom we have redemption – This is treated of from the middle of Colossians i, 18. The voluntary passion of our Lord appeased the Father's wrath, obtained pardon and acceptance for us, and, consequently, dissolved the dominion and power which Satan had over us through our sins. So that forgiveness is the beginning of redemption, as the resurrection is the completion of it.

15. Who is – By describing the glory of Christ, and his pre-eminence over the highest angels, the apostle here lays a foundation for the reproof of all worshipers of angels. The image of the invisible God – Whom none can represent, but his only begotten Son; in his divine nature the invisi-

MATTHEW HENRY

CHARLES H. SPURGEON

This epistle was sent because of some difficulties which arose among the Colossians, probably from false teachers, in consequence of which they sent to the apostle. The scope of the epistle is to show, that all hope of man's redemption is founded on Christ, in whom alone are all complete fullness, perfections, and sufficiency. The Colossians are cautioned against the devices of judaizing teachers, and also against the notions of carnal wisdom, and human inventions and traditions, as not consistent with full reliance on Christ. In the first two chapters the apostle tells them what they must believe, and in the two last what they must do; the doctrine of faith, and the precepts of life for salvation.

COLOSSIANS 1

The apostle Paul salutes the Colossians, and blesses God for their faith, love, and hope. (1-8)
Prays for their fruitfulness in spiritual knowledge. (9-14)
Gives a glorious view of Christ. (15-23)
And sets out his own character, as the apostle of the Gentiles. (24-29)

1-8 All true Christians are brethren one to another. Faithfulness runs through every character and relation of the Christian life. Faith, hope, and love, are the three principal graces in the Christian life, and proper matter for prayer and thanksgiving. The more we fix our hopes on the reward in the other world, the more free shall we be in doing good with our earthly treasure. It was treasured up for them, no enemy could deprive them of it. The gospel is the word of truth, and we may safely venture our souls upon it. And all who hear the word of the gospel, ought to bring forth the fruit of the gospel, obey it, and have their principles and lives formed according to it. Worldly love arises, either from views of interest or from likeness in manners; carnal love, from the appetite for pleasure. To these, something corrupt, selfish, and base always cleaves. But Christian love arises from the Holy Spirit, and is full of holiness.

9-14 The apostle was constant in prayer, that the believers might be filled with the knowledge of God's will, in all wisdom. Good words will not do without good works. He who undertakes to give strength to his people, is a God of power, and of glorious power. The blessed Spirit is the author of this. In praying for spiritual strength, we are not straitened, or confined in the promises, and should not be so in our hopes and desires. The grace of God in the hearts of believers is the power of God; and there is glory in this power. The special use of this strength was for sufferings. There is work to be done, even when we are suffering. Amidst all their trials they gave thanks to the Father of our Lord Jesus, whose special grace fitted them to partake of the inheritance provided for the saints. To bring about this change, those were made willing subjects of Christ, who were slaves of Satan. All who are designed for heaven hereafter, are prepared for heaven now. Those who have the inheritance of sons, have the education of sons,

ALL FULLNESS IN CHRIST
Sermon number 978 delivered on February 26th, 1871 at the Metropolitan Tabernacle, Newington.

"For it pleased the Father that in him should all fullness dwell."—Colossians 1:19.

I. First, then, let us consider the subject before us, or WHAT—"It pleased the Father that in him should all fullness dwell." Two mighty words; "fullness" a substantial, comprehensive, expressive word in itself, and "all," a great little word including everything. When combined in the expression, "all fullness," we have before us a superlative wealth of meaning.

Blessed be God for those two words. Our hearts rejoice to think that there is such a thing in the universe as "all fullness," for in the most of mortal pursuits utter barrenness is found. "Vanity of vanity all is vanity." Blessed be the Lord for ever that he has provided a fullness for us, for in us by nature there is all emptiness and utter vanity. "In me, that is, in my flesh, there dwelleth no good thing." In us there is a lack of all merit, an absence of all power to procure any, and even an absence of will to procure it if we could. In these respects human nature is a desert, empty, and void, and waste, inhabited only by the dragon of sin, and the bittern of sorrow. Sinner, saint, to you both alike these words, "all fullness," sound like a holy hymn. The accents are sweet as those of the angel-messenger when he sang, "Behold, I bring you glad tidings of great joy." Are they not stray notes from celestial sonnets? "All fullness." You, sinner, are all emptiness and death, you, saint, would be so if it were not for the "all fullness" of Christ of which you have received; therefore both to saint and sinner the words are full of hope. There is joy in these words to every soul conscious of its sad estate, and humbled before God.

I must return to the words of the text again, for I perceive more honey dropping from the honeycomb. "All fullness" is a wide, far-reaching, all-comprehending term, and in its abundant store it offers another source of delight. What joy these words give to us when we remember that our vast necessities demand a fullness, yea,

19 For it pleased the Father that in him should all fullness dwell;

20 And, having made peace through the blood of his cross, by him to reconcile all things unto himself; by him, I say, whether they be things in earth, or things in heaven.

21
And you, that were sometime alienated and enemies in your mind by wicked works, yet now hath he reconciled

22 In the body of his flesh through death, to present you holy and unblameable and unreproveable in his sight:

23 If ye continue in the faith grounded and settled, and be not moved away from the hope of the gospel, which ye have heard, and which was preached to every creature which is under heaven; whereof I Paul am made a minister;

24 Who now rejoice in my sufferings for you, and fill up that which is behind of the afflictions of Christ in my flesh for his body's sake, which is the church:

25 Whereof I am made a minister, according to the dispensation of God which is given to me for you, to fulfill the word of God;

26 Even the mystery which hath been hid from ages and from generations, but now is made manifest to his saints:

27 To whom God would make known what is the riches of the glory of this mystery among the Gentiles; which is Christ in you, the hope of glory:

28 Whom we preach, warning every man, and teaching every man in all wisdom; that we may present every man perfect in Christ Jesus:

29 Whereunto I also labor, striving according to his working, which worketh in me mightily.

COLOSSIANS 2

1 For I would that ye knew what great conflict I have for you, and for them at Laodicea, and for as many as have not seen my face in the flesh;

2 That their hearts might be comforted, being knit together in love, and unto all riches of the full assurance of understanding, to the acknowledgment of the mystery of God, and of the Father, and of Christ;

3 In whom are hid all the treasures of wisdom and knowledge.

4 And this I say, lest any man should beguile you with enticing words.

5 For though I be absent in the flesh, yet am I with you in the spirit, joying and

ble image, in his human the visible image, of the Father. The first begotten of every creature – That is, begotten before every creature; subsisting before all worlds, before all time, from all eternity.

16. For – This explains the latter part of the preceding verse. Through implies something prior to the particles by and for; so denoting the beginning, the progress, and the end. Him – This word, frequently repeated, signifies his supreme majesty, and excludes every creature. Were created all things that are in heaven – And heaven itself. But the inhabitants are named, because more noble than the house. Invisible – The several species of which are subjoined. Thrones are superior to dominions; principalities, to powers. Perhaps the two latter may express their office with regard to other creatures: the two former may refer to God, who maketh them his chariots, and, as it were, rideth upon their wings.

17. And he is before all things – It is not said, he was: he is from everlasting to everlasting. And by him all things consist – The original expression not only implies, that he sustains all things in being, but more directly, All things were and are compacted in him into one system. He is the cement, as well as support, of the universe. And is he less than the supreme God?

18. And – From the whole he now descends to the most eminent part, the church. He is the head of the church – Universal; the supreme and only head both of influence and of government to the whole body of believers. Who is – The repetition of the expression (Colossians i, 15) points out the entrance on a new paragraph. The beginning – Absolutely, the Eternal. The first begotten from the dead – From whose resurrection flows all the life, spiritual and eternal, of all his brethren. That in all things – Whether of nature or grace. He might have the pre-eminence – Who can sound this depth?

19. For it pleased the Father that all fullness – All the fullness of God. Should dwell in him – Constantly, as in a temple; and always ready for our approach to him.

20. Through the blood of the cross – The blood shed thereon. Whether things on earth – Here the enmity began: therefore this is mentioned first. Or things in heaven – Those who are now in paradise; the saints who died before Christ came.

21. And you that were alienated, and enemies – Actual alienation of affection makes habitual enmity. In your mind – Both your understanding and your affections. By wicked works – Which continually feed and increase inward alienation from, and enmity to, God. He hath now reconciled – From the moment ye believed.

22. By the body of his flesh – So distinguished from his body, the church. The body here denotes his entire manhood. Through death – Whereby he purchased the reconciliation which we receive by faith. To present you – The very end of that reconciliation. Holy – Toward God. Spotless – In yourselves. Unreprovable – As to your neighbor.

23. If ye continue in the faith – Otherwise, ye will lose all the blessings which ye have already begun to enjoy. And be not removed from the hope of the gospel – The glorious hope of perfect love. Which is preached – Is already begun to be preached to every creature under heaven.

24. Now I rejoice in my sufferings for you, and fill up – That is, whereby I fill up. That which is behind of the sufferings of Christ – That which remains to be suffered by his members. These are termed the sufferings of Christ,

1. Because the suffering of any member is the suffering of the whole; and of the head especially, which supplies strength, spirits, sense, and motion to all.

and the disposition of sons. By faith in Christ they enjoyed this redemption, as the purchase of his atoning blood, whereby forgiveness of sins, and all other spiritual blessings were bestowed

15-23 Christ in his human nature, is the visible discovery of the invisible God, and he that hath seen him hath seen the Father. Let us adore these mysteries in humble faith, and behold the glory of the Lord in Christ Jesus. He was born or begotten before all the creation, before any creature was made; which is the Scripture way of representing eternity, and by which the eternity of God is represented to us. All things being created by him, were created for him; being made by his power, they were made according to his pleasure, and for his praise and glory. He not only created them all at first, but it is by the word of his power that they are upheld. Christ as Mediator is the Head of the body, the church; all grace and strength are from him; and the church is his body. All fullness dwells in him; a fullness of merit and righteousness, of strength and grace for us. God showed his justice in requiring full satisfaction. This mode of redeeming mankind by the death of Christ was most suitable. Here is presented to our view the method of being reconciled. And that, notwithstanding the hatred of sin on God's part, it pleased God to reconcile fallen man to himself. If convinced that we were enemies in our minds by wicked works, and that we are now reconciled to God by the sacrifice and death of Christ in our nature, we shall not attempt to explain away, nor yet think fully to comprehend these mysteries; but we shall see the glory of this plan of redemption, and rejoice in the hope set before us.

24-29 Both the sufferings of the Head and of the members are called the sufferings of Christ, and make up, as it were, one body of sufferings. But he suffered for the redemption of the church; we suffer on other accounts; for we do but slightly taste that cup of afflictions of which Christ first drank deeply. A Christian may be said to fill up that which remains of the sufferings of Christ, when he takes up his cross, and after the pattern of Christ, bears patiently the afflictions God allots to him. Let us be thankful that God has made known to us mysteries hidden from ages and generations, and has showed the riches of his glory among us. As Christ is preached among us, let us seriously inquire, whether he dwells and reigns in us; for this alone can warrant our assured hope of his glory. We must be faithful to death, through all trials, that we may receive the crown of life, and obtain the end of our faith, the salvation of our souls.

COLOSSIANS 2

The apostle expresses his love to, and joy in believers. (1-7)
He cautions against the errors of heathen philosophy; also against Jewish traditions, and rites which had been ful-filled in Christ. (8-17)
Against worshiping angels; and against legal ordinances. (18-23)

1-7 The soul prospers when we have clear knowledge of

"all fullness," before they can be supplied! A little help will be of no use to us, for we are altogether without strength. A limited measure of mercy will only mock our misery. A low degree of grace will never be enough to bring us to heaven, defiled as we are with sin, beset with dangers, encompassed with infirmities, assailed by temptations, molested with afflictions, and all the while bearing about with us "the body of this death." But "all fullness," ay, that will suit us. Here is exactly what our desperate estate demands for its recovery. Had the Savior only put out his finger to help our exertions, or had he only stretched out his hand to perform a measure of salvation's work, while he left us to complete it, our soul had for ever dwelt in darkness. In these words, "all fullness," we hear the echo of his death-cry, "It is finished." We are to bring nothing, but to find all in him, yea, the fullness of all in him: we are simply to receive out of his fullness grace for grace. We are not asked to contribute, nor required to make up deficiencies, for there are none to make up—all, all is laid up in Christ. All that we shall want between this place and heaven, all we could need between the gates of hell, where we lay in our blood, to the gates of heaven, where we shall find welcome admission, is treasured up for us in the Lord Christ Jesus.

Let doubts and fears vanish at the sight of the mediatorial fullness. Jesus must be able to save to the uttermost, since all fullness dwells in him. Come, sinner; come and receive him. Believe thou in him and thou shalt find thyself made perfect in Christ Jesus.

"The moment a sinner believes,
And trusts in his crucified God,
His pardon at once he receives,
Redemption in full through his blood."

II. Having thus spoken of what, we now turn to consider WHERE.

"It pleased the Father that in him should all fullness dwell." Where else could all fullness have been placed? There was wanted a vast capacity to contain "all fullness." Where dwells there a being with nature capacious enough to compass within himself all fullness? As well might we ask, "Who hath measured the waters in the hollow of his hand, and meted out

beholding your order, and the stedfast-ness of your faith in Christ.

6 As ye have therefore received Christ Jesus the Lord, so walk ye in him:

7 Rooted and built up in him, and stab-lished in the faith, as ye have been taught, abounding therein with thanks-giving.

8 Beware lest any man spoil you through philosophy and vain deceit, after the tradition of men, after the rudiments of the world, and not after Christ.

9 For in him dwelleth all the fullness of the Godhead bodily.

10 And ye are complete in him, which is the head of all principality and power:

11 In whom also ye are circumcized with the circumcision made without hands, in putting off the body of the sins of the flesh by the circumcision of Christ:

12 Buried with him in baptism, wherein also ye are risen with him through the faith of the operation of God, who hath raised him from the dead.

13 And you, being dead in your sins and the uncircumcision of your flesh, hath he quickened together with him, having for-given you all trespasses;

14 Blotting out the handwriting of ordi-nances that was against us, which was contrary to us, and took it out of the way, nailing it to his cross;

15 And having spoiled principalities and powers, he made a shew of them open-ly, triumphing over them in it.

16 Let no man therefore judge you in meat, or in drink, or in respect of an holyday, or of the new moon, or of the sabbath days:

17 Which are a shadow of things to come; but the body is of Christ.

18 Let no man beguile you of your reward in a voluntary humility and wor-shiping of angels, intruding into those things which he hath not seen, vainly puffed up by his fleshly mind,

19 And not holding the Head, from which all the body by joints and bands having nourishment ministered, and knit together, increaseth with the increase of God.

20 Wherefore if ye be dead with Christ from the rudiments of the world, why, as though living in the world, are ye subject to ordinances,

21 (Touch not; taste not; handle not;

22 Which all are to perish with the using;) after the commandments and doctrines of men?

23 Which things have indeed a shew of wisdom in will worship, and humility,

2. Because they are for his sake, for the testimony of his truth. And these also are necessary for the church; not to reconcile it to God, or satisfy for sin, (for that Christ did perfectly,) but for example to oth-ers, perfecting of the saints, and increasing their reward.

25. According to the dispensation of God which is given me – Or, the stewardship with which I am intrusted.

26. The mystery – Namely, Christ both justifying and sanctifying Gentiles, as well as Jews. Which hath been comparatively hid from for-mer ages and past generations of men.

27. Christ dwelling and reigning in you, The hope of glory – The ground of your hope.

28. We teach the ignorant, and admonish them that are already taught.

COLOSSIANS 2

1. How great a conflict – Of care, desire, prayer. As many as have not seen my face – Therefore, in writing to the Colossians, he refrains from those familiar appellations, "Brethren," "Beloved."

2. Unto all riches of the full assurance of understanding, unto the acknowledgment of the mystery of God – That is, unto the fullest and clearest understanding and knowledge of the gospel.

6. So walk in him – In the same faith, love, holiness.

7. Rooted in him – As the vine. Built – On the sure foundation.

8. Through philosophy and empty deceit – That is, through the empty deceit of philosophy blended with Christianity. This the apostle con-demns,

1. Because it was empty and deceitful, promising happiness, but giv-ing none.

2. Because it was grounded, not on solid reason, but the traditions of men, Zeno, Epicurus, and the rest. And,

3. Because it was so shallow and superficial, not advancing beyond the knowledge of sensible things; no, not beyond the first rudiments of them.

9. For in him dwelleth – Inhabiteth, continually abideth, all the fullness of the Godhead. Believers are "filled with all the fullness of God," Eph. iii, 19. But in Christ dwelleth all the fullness of the Godhead; the most full Godhead; not only divine powers, but divine nature, Colossians i, 19. Bodily – Personally, really, substantially. The very substance of God, if one might so speak, dwells in Christ in the most full sense.

10. And ye – Who believe. Are filled with him – John i, 16. Christ is filled with God, and ye are filled with Christ. And ye are filled by him. The fullness of Christ overflows his church, Psalm cxxxiii, 3. He is orig-inally full. We are filled by him with wisdom and holiness. Who is the head of all principality and power – Of angels as well as men. Not from angels therefore, but from their head, are we to ask whatever we stand in need of.

11. By whom also ye have been circumcized – Ye have received the spir-itual blessings typified of old by circumcision. With a circumcision not performed with hands – By an inward, spiritual operation. In putting off, not a little skin, but the whole body of the sins of the flesh – All the sins of your evil nature. By the circumcision of Christ – By that spiritual cir-cumcision which Christ works in your heart.

12. Which he wrought in you, when ye were as it were buried with him in baptism – The ancient manner of baptizing by immersion is as mani-festly alluded to here, as the other manner of baptizing by sprinkling or pouring of water is, Heb. x, 22. But no stress is laid on the age of the bap-

the truth as it is in Jesus. When we not only believe with the heart, but are ready, when called, to make confession with the mouth. Knowledge and faith make a soul rich. The stronger our faith, and the warmer our love, the more will our comfort be. The treasures of wisdom are hid, not from us, but for us, in Christ. These were hid from proud unbelievers, but displayed in the person and redemption of Christ. See the danger of enticing words; how many are ruined by the false disguises and fair appearances of evil principles and wicked practices! Be aware and afraid of those who would entice to any evil; for they aim to spoil you. All Christians have, in profession at least, received Jesus Christ the Lord, consented to him, and taken him for theirs. We cannot be built up in Christ, or grow in him, unless we are first rooted in him, or founded upon him. Being established in the faith, we must abound therein, and improve in it more and more. God justly withdraws this benefit from those who do not receive it with thanksgiving; and gratitude for his mercies is justly required by God.

8-17 There is a philosophy which rightly exercises our reasonable faculties; a study of the works of God, which leads us to the knowledge of God, and confirms our faith in him. But there is a philosophy which is vain and deceitful; and while it pleases men's fancies, hinders their faith: such are curious speculations about things above us, or no concern to us. Those who walk in the way of the world, are turned from following Christ. We have in him the substance of all the shadows of the ceremonial law. All the defects of it are made up in the gospel of Christ, by his complete sacrifice for sin, and by the revelation of the will of God. To be complete, is to be furnished with all things necessary for salvation. By this one word "complete," is shown that we have in Christ whatever is required. "In him," not when we look to Christ, as though he were distant from us, but we are in him, when, by the power of the Spirit, we have faith wrought in our hearts by the Spirit, and we are united to our Head. The circumcision of the heart, the crucifixion of the flesh, the death and burial to sin and to the world, and the resurrection to newness of life, set forth in baptism, and by faith wrought in our hearts, prove that our sins are forgiven, and that we are fully delivered from the curse of the law. Through Christ, we, who were dead in sins, are quickened. Christ's death was the death of our sins; Christ's resurrection is the quickening of our souls. The law of ordinances, which was a yoke to the Jews, and a partition-wall to the Gentiles, the Lord Jesus took out of the way. When the substance was come, the shadows fled. Since every mortal man is, through the handwriting of the law, guilty of death, how very dreadful is the condition of the ungodly and unholy, who trample under foot that blood of the Son of God, whereby alone this deadly handwriting can be blotted out! Let not any be troubled about bigoted judgments which related to meats, or the Jewish solemnities. The setting apart a portion of our time for the worship and service of God, is a moral and unchangeable duty, but had no necessary dependence upon the seventh day of the week, the Sabbath of the Jews. The first day of the week, or the Lord's day, is the time kept

heaven with the span, and comprehended the dust of the earth in a measure, and weighed the mountains in scales, and the hills in a balance?" To him only could it belong to contain "all fullness," for he must be equal with God, the Infinite. How suitable was the Son of the Highest, who "was by him, as one brought up with him," to become the grand storehouse of all the treasures of wisdom, and knowledge and grace, and salvation. Moreover, there was wanted not only capacity to contain, but immutability to retain the fullness, for the text says, "It pleased the Father that in him should all fullness dwell" that is, abide, and remain, for ever. Now if any kind of fullness could be put into us mutable creatures, yet by reason of our frailty we should prove but broken cisterns that can hold no water. The Redeemer is Jesus Christ, the same yesterday, today, and for ever: therefore was it meet that all fullness should be placed in him. "The Son abideth ever." "He is a priest for ever after the order of Melchisedec." "Being made perfect he became the author of eternal salvation unto all they that obey him." "His name shall endure for ever: his name shall be continued as long as the sun: and men shall be blessed in him: all nations shall call him blessed."

Perhaps the sweetest thought is, that the "all fullness" is fitly placed in Christ Jesus, because in him there is a suitability to distribute it, so that we may obtain it from him. How could we come to God himself for grace? for "even our God is a consuming fire." But Jesus Christ while God is also man like ourselves, truly man, of a meek lowly spirit, and therefore easily approachable. They who know him, delight in nearness to him. Is it not sweet that all fullness should be treasured up in him who was the friend of publicans and sinners: and who came into the world to seek and to save that which was lost? The Man who took the child up on his knee and said, "Suffer the little children to come unto me," the Man who was tempted in all points like as we are, the Man who touched the sick, nay, who "bore their sicknesses," the Man who gave his hands to the nails, and his heart to the spear; that blessed Man, into the print of whose nails his disciple Thomas put his finger, and into whose side he thrust his hand; it is he, the

and neglecting of the body; not in any honor to the satisfying of the flesh.

COLOSSIANS 3

1 If ye then be risen with Christ, seek those things which are above, where Christ sitteth on the right hand of God.
2 Set your affection on things above, not on things on the earth.
3 For ye are dead, and your life is hid with Christ in God.
4 When Christ, who is our life, shall appear, then shall ye also appear with him in glory.
5 Mortify therefore your members which are upon the earth; fornication, uncleanness, inordinate affection, evil concupiscence, and covetousness, which is idolatry:
6 For which things' sake the wrath of God cometh on the children of disobedience:
7 In the which ye also walked some time, when ye lived in them.
8 But now ye also put off all these; anger, wrath, malice, blasphemy, filthy communication out of your mouth.
9 Lie not one to another, seeing that ye have put off the old man with his deeds;
10 And have put on the new man, which is renewed in knowledge after the image of him that created him:
11 Where there is neither Greek nor Jew, circumcision nor uncircumcision, Barbarian, Scythian, bond nor free: but Christ is all, and in all.
12 Put on therefore, as the elect of God, holy and beloved, bowels of mercies, kindness, humbleness of mind, meekness, longsuffering;
13 Forbearing one another, and forgiving one another, if any man have a quarrel against any: even as Christ forgave you, so also do ye.
14 And above all these things put on charity, which is the bond of perfectness.
15 And let the peace of God rule in your hearts, to the which also ye are called in one body; and be ye thankful.
16 Let the word of Christ dwell in you richly in all wisdom; teaching and admonishing one another in psalms and hymns and spiritual songs, singing with grace in your hearts to the Lord.
17 And whatsoever ye do in word or deed, do all in the name of the Lord Jesus, giving thanks to God and the Father by him.
18 Wives, submit yourselves unto your

tized, or the manner of performing it, in one or the other; but only on our being risen with Christ, through the powerful operation of God in the soul; which we cannot but know assuredly, if it really is so: and if we do not experience this, our baptism has not answered the end of its institution. By which ye are also risen with him – From the death of sin to the life of holiness. It does not appear, that in all this St. Paul speaks of justification at all, but of sanctification altogether.

13. And you who were dead – Doubly dead to God, not only wallowing in trespasses, outward sins, but also in the uncircumcision of your flesh – A beautiful expression for original sin, the inbred corruption of your nature, your uncircumcized heart and affections. Hath he – God the Father. Quickened together with him – Making you partakers of the power of his resurrection. It is evident the apostle thus far speaks, not of justification, but of sanctification only.

14. Having blotted out – in consequence of his gracious decrees, that Christ should come into the world to save sinners, and that whosoever believeth on him should have everlasting life. The handwriting against us – Where a debt is contracted, it is usually testified by some handwriting; and when the debt is forgiven, the handwriting is destroyed, either by blotting it out, by taking it away, or by tearing it. The apostle expresses in all these three ways, God's destroying the handwriting which was contrary to us, or at enmity with us. This was not properly our sins themselves, (they were the debt,) but their guilt and cry before God.

15. And having spoiled the principalities and powers – The evil angels, of their usurped dominion. He – God the Father. Exposed them openly – Before all the hosts of hell and heaven. Triumphing over them in or by him – By Christ. Thus the paragraph begins with Christ, goes on with him, and ends with him.

16. Therefore – Seeing these things are so. Let none judge you – That is, regard none who judge you. In meat or drink – For not observing the ceremonial law in these or any other particulars. Or in respect of a yearly feast, the new moon, or the weekly Jewish Sabbaths.

17. Which are but a lifeless shadow; but the body, the substance, is of Christ.

18. Out of pretended humility, they worshiped angels, as not daring to apply immediately to God. Yet this really sprung from their being puffed up: (the constant forerunner of a fall, (Prov. xvi, 18) so far was it from being an instance of true humility.

19. And not holding the head – He does not hold Christ, who does not trust in him alone. All the members are nourished by faith, and knit together by love and mutual sympathy.

20. Therefore – The inference begun, Colossians ii, 16; is continued. A new inference follows, Colossians iii, 1. If ye are dead with Christ from the rudiments of the world – That is, If ye are dead with Christ, and so freed from them, why receive ye ordinances – Which Christ hath not enjoined, from which he hath made you free.

21. Touch not – An unclean thing. Taste not – Any forbidden meat. Handle not – Any consecrated vessel.

22. Perish in the using – Have no farther use, no influence on the mind.

23. Not sparing the body – Denying it many gratifications, and putting it to many inconveniences. Yet they are not of any real value before God, nor do they, upon the whole, mortify, but satisfy, the flesh. They indulge our corrupt nature, our self-will, pride, and desire of being distinguished from others.

MATTHEW HENRY

CHARLES H. SPURGEON

holy by Christians, in remembrance of Christ's resurrection. All the Jewish rites were shadows of gospel blessings.

18-23 It looked like humility to apply to angels, as if men were conscious of their unworthiness to speak directly to God. But it is not warrantable; it is taking that honor which is due to Christ only, and giving it to a creature. There really was pride in this seeming humility. Those who worship angels, disclaim Christ, who is the only Mediator between God and man. It is an insult to Christ, who is the Head of the church, to use any intercessors but him. When men let go their hold of Christ, they catch at what will stand them in no stead. The body of Christ is a growing body. And true believers cannot live in the fashions of the world. True wisdom is, to keep close to the appointments of the gospel; in entire subjection to Christ, who is the only Head of his church. Self-imposed sufferings and fastings, might have a show of uncommon spirituality and willingness for suffering, but this was not "in any honor" to God. The whole tended, in a wrong manner, to satisfy the carnal mind, by gratifying self-will, self-wisdom, self-righteousness, and contempt of others. The things being such as carry not with them so much as the show of wisdom; or so faint a show that they do the soul no good, and provide not for the satisfying of the flesh. What the Lord has left indifferent, let us regard as such, and leave others to the like freedom; and remembering the passing nature of earthly things, let us seek to glorify God in the use of them.

COLOSSIANS 3

The Colossians exhorted to be heavenly-minded. (1-4)
To mortify all corrupt affections. (5-11)
To live in mutual love, forbearance, and forgiveness. (12-17)
And to practice the duties of wives and husbands, children,
*   parents, and servants. (18-25)*

1-4 As Christians are freed from the ceremonial law, they must walk the more closely with God in gospel obedience. As heaven and earth are contrary one to the other, both cannot be followed together; and affection to the one will weaken and abate affection to the other. Those that are born again are dead to sin, because its dominion is broken, its power gradually subdued by the operation of grace, and it shall at length be extinguished by the perfection of glory. To be dead, then, means this, that those who have the Holy Spirit, mortifying within them the lusts of the flesh, are able to despise earthly things, and to desire those that are heavenly. Christ is, at present, one whom we have not seen; but our comfort is, that our life is safe with him. The streams of this living water flow into the soul by the influences of the Holy Spirit, through faith. Christ lives in the believer by his Spirit, and the believer lives to him in all he does. At the second coming of Christ, there will be a general assembling of all the redeemed; and those whose life is now hid with Christ, shall then appear with him in his glory. Do we look for such happiness, and should we not set our affections upon that world, and live above this?

incarnate God, in whom all fullness dwells. Come, then, and receive of him, you who are the weakest, the most mean, and most sinful of men. Come at once, O sinner, and fear not. Who would not be reconciled unto God by such a one as this, in whom all fullness of grace is made to dwell?

III. The third question is, WHY? "It pleased the Father." That is answer enough. He is a sovereign, let him do as he wills. Ask the reason for election, you shall receive no other than this, "Even so, Father, for so it seemed good in thy sight." That one answer may reply to ten thousand questions, "It is the Lord, let him do what seemeth him good." Once "it pleased the Father to bruise him," and now "it pleased the Father that in him should all fullness dwell." Sovereignty may answer the question sufficiently, but hearken! I hear justice speak, it should not be silent. Justice saith there was no person in heaven or under heaven so meet to contain the fullness of grace as Jesus.

None so meet to be glorified as the Savior, who "made himself of no reputation, and took upon himself the form of a servant, and being found in fashion as a man, humbled himself, and became obedient to death, even the death of the cross." It is but justice that the grace which he has brought to us should be treasured up in him. And while justice speaks wisdom will not withhold her voice. Wise art thou, O Jehovah, to treasure up grace in Christ, for to him men can come; and to him coming, as unto a living stone, chosen of God and precious, men find him precious also to their souls. The Lord has laid our hell, in the right place, for he has laid it upon one that is mighty, and who is as loving as he is mighty, as ready as he is able to save. Moreover, in the fitness of things the Father's pleasure is the first point to be considered, for all things ought to be to the good pleasure of God. It is a great underlying rule of the universe that all things were created for God's pleasure. God is the source and fountain of eternal love, and it is but meet that he should convey it to us by what channel he may elect. Bowing, therefore, in lowly worship at his throne, we are glad that in this matter the fullness dwells where it perpetually satisfies the decree of heaven. It is well that "it

own husbands, as it is fit in the Lord.

19 Husbands, love your wives, and be not bitter against them.

20 Children, obey your parents in all things: for this is well pleasing unto the Lord.

21 Fathers, provoke not your children to anger, lest they be discouraged.

22 Servants, obey in all things your masters according to the flesh; not with eyeservice, as menpleasers; but in singleness of heart, fearing God:

23 And whatsoever ye do, do it heartily, as to the Lord, and not unto men;

24 Knowing that of the Lord ye shall receive the reward of the inheritance: for ye serve the Lord Christ.

25 But he that doeth wrong shall receive for the wrong which he hath done: and there is no respect of persons.

COLOSSIANS 4

1 Masters, give unto your servants that which is just and equal; knowing that ye also have a Master in heaven.

2 Continue in prayer, and watch in the same with thanksgiving;

3 Withal praying also for us, that God would open unto us a door of utterance, to speak the mystery of Christ, for which I am also in bonds:

4 That I may make it manifest, as I ought to speak.

5 Walk in wisdom toward them that are without, redeeming the time.

6 Let your speech be alway with grace, seasoned with salt, that ye may know how ye ought to answer every man.

7 All my state shall Tychicus declare unto you, who is a beloved brother, and a faithful minister and fellowservant in the Lord:

8 Whom I have sent unto you for the same purpose, that he might know your estate, and comfort your hearts;

9 With Onesimus, a faithful and beloved brother, who is one of you. They shall make known unto you all things which are done here.

10 Aristarchus my fellowprisoner saluteth you, and Marcus, sister's son to Barnabas, (touching whom ye received commandments: if he come unto you, receive him;)

11 And Jesus, which is called Justus, who are of the circumcision. These only are my fellowworkers unto the kingdom of God, which have been a comfort unto me.

12 Epaphras, who is one of you, a ser-

COLOSSIANS 3

1. If ye are risen, seek the things above – As Christ being risen, immediately went to heaven.

3. For ye are dead – To the things on earth. And your real, spiritual life is hid from the world, and laid up in God, with Christ – Who hath merited, promised, prepared it for us, and gives us the earnest and foretaste of it in our hearts.

4. When Christ – The abruptness of the sentence surrounds us with sudden light. Our life – The fountain of holiness and glory. Shall appear – In the clouds of heaven.

5. Mortify therefore – Put to death, slay with a continued stroke. Your members – Which together make up the body of sin. Which are upon the earth – Where they find their nourishment. Uncleanness – In act, word, or thought. Inordinate affection – Every passion which does not flow from and lead to the love of God. Evil desire – The desire of the flesh, the desire of the eye, and the pride of life. Covetousness – According to the derivation of the word, means the desire of having more, or of any thing independent of God. Which is idolatry – Properly and directly; for it is giving the heart to a creature.

6. For which – Though the heathens lightly regarded them.

7. Living denotes the inward principle; walking, the outward acts.

8. Wrath – Is lasting anger. Filthy discourse – And was there need to warn even these saints of God against so gross and palpable a sin as this? O what is man, till perfect love casts out both fear and sin.

10. In knowledge – The knowledge of God, his will, his word.

11. Where – In which case, it matters not what a man is externally, whether Jew or Gentile, circumcized, or uncircumcized, barbarian, void of all the advantages of education, yea, Scythian, of all barbarians most barbarous. But Christ is in all that are thus renewed, and is all things in them and to them.

12. All who are thus renewed are elected of God, holy, and therefore the more beloved of him. Holiness is the consequence of their election, and God's superior love, of their holiness.

13. Forbearing one another – If anything is now wrong. And forgiving one another – What is past.

14. The love of God contains the whole of Christian perfection, and connects all the parts of it together.

15. And then the peace of God shall rule in your hearts – Shall sway every temper, affection, thought, as the reward (so the Greek word implies) of your preceding love and obedience.

16. Let the word of Christ – So the apostle calls the whole scripture, and thereby asserts the divinity of his Master. Dwell – Not make a short stay, or an occasional visit, but take up its stated residence. Richly – In the largest measure, and with the greatest efficacy; so as to fill and govern the whole soul.

17. In the name – In the power and Spirit of the Lord Jesus. Giving thanks unto God – The Holy Ghost. And the Father through him – Christ.

18. Wives, submit – Or be subject to. It is properly a military term, alluding to that entire submission that soldiers pay to their general. Eph. v, 22, &c.

19. Be not bitter – (Which may be without any appearance of anger) either in word or spirit.

21. Lest they be discouraged – Which may occasion their turning either desperate or stupid.

22. Eyeservice – Being more diligent under their eye than at other times.

MATTHEW HENRY

CHARLES H. SPURGEON

5-11 It is our duty to mortify our members which incline to the things of the world. Mortify them, kill them, suppress them, as weeds or vermin which spread and destroy all about them. Continual opposition must be made to all corrupt workings, and no provision made for carnal indulgences. Occasions of sin must be avoided: the lusts of the flesh, and the love of the world; and covetousness, which is idolatry; love of present good, and of outward enjoyments. It is necessary to mortify sins, because if we do not kill them, they will kill us. The gospel changes the higher as well as the lower powers of the soul, and supports the rule of right reason and conscience, over appetite and passion.

12-17 We must not only do no hurt to any, but do what good we can to all. Those who are the elect of God, holy and beloved, ought to be lowly and compassionate towards all. While in this world, where there is so much corruption in our hearts, quarrels will sometimes arise. But it is our duty to forgive one another, imitating the forgiveness through which we are saved. Let the peace of God rule in your hearts; it is of his working in all who are his. Thanksgiving to God, helps to make us agreeable to all men. The gospel is the word of Christ. Many have the word, but it dwells in them poorly; it has no power over them. The soul prospers, when we are full of the Scriptures and of the grace of Christ. But when we sing psalms, we must be affected with what we sing.

18-25 The epistles most taken up in displaying the glory of the Divine grace, and magnifying the Lord Jesus, are the most particular in pressing the duties of the Christian life. We must never separate the privileges and duties of the gospel. Submission is the duty of wives. But it is submission, not to a severe lord or stern tyrant, but to her own husband, who is engaged to affectionate duty. And husbands must love their wives with tender and faithful affection. Dutiful children are the most likely to prosper. And parents must be tender, as well as children obedient. Servants are to do their duty, and obey their masters' commands, in all things consistent with duty to God their heavenly Master. They must be both just and diligent; without selfish designs, or hypocrisy and disguise. Those who fear God, will be just and faithful when from under their master's eye, because they know they are under the eye of God. And do all with diligence, not idly and slothfully; cheerfully, not discontented at the providence of God which put them in that relation. And for servants' encouragement, let them know, that in serving their masters according to the command of Christ, they serve Christ, and he will give them a glorious reward at last. But, on the other hand, he who doeth wrong, shall receive for the wrong which he hath done. God will punish the unjust, as well as reward the faithful servant; and the same if masters wrong their servants. For the righteous Judge of the earth will deal justly between master and servant. Both will stand upon a level at his tribunal.

pleased the Father."

Now, brethren, if it pleased the Father to place all grace in Christ, let us praise the elect Savior. What pleases God pleases us. Where would you desire to have grace placed, my brethren, but in the Wellbeloved? The whole church of God is unanimous about this. If I could save myself I would not; I would think salvation to be no salvation if it did not glorify Jesus. This is the very crown and glory of being saved, that our being saved will bring honor to Christ. It is delightful to think that Christ will have the glory of all God's grace; it were shocking if it were not so. Who could bear to see Jesus robbed of his reward? We are indignant that any should usurp his place, and ashamed of ourselves that we do not glorify him more. No joy ever visits my soul like that of knowing that Jesus is highly exalted, and that to him "every knee shall bow and every tongue confess that Jesus Christ is Lord, to the glory of God the Father." A sister in Christ, in her kindness and gratitude, used language to me the other day which brought a blush to my cheek, for I felt ashamed to be so undeserving of the praise. She said, "Your ministry profits me because you glorify Christ so much." Ah, I thought, if you knew how I would glorify him if I could, and how far I fall below what I fain would do for him, you would not commend me. I could weep over the best sermons I have ever preached because I cannot extol my Lord enough, and my conceptions are so low, and my words so poor. Oh, if one could but attain really to honor him, and put another crown upon his head, it were heaven indeed! We are in this agreed with the Father, for if it pleases him to glorify his Son, we sincerely feel that it pleases us.

And surely if all fullness abides perpetually in Christ, there is good reason why the unreconciled should this morning, avail themselves of it. May the blessed Spirit show thee, O sinner, that there is enough in Jesus Christ to meet thy wants, that thy weakness need not keep thee back, nor even the hardness of thy heart, nor the inveteracy of thy will; for Christ is able even to subdue all things to himself. If you seek him he will be found of you. Seek him while he may be found. Leave not the seat until your soul is bowed at his feet. I think I see him; cannot your hearts picture

vant of Christ, saluteth you, always laboring fervently for you in prayers, that ye may stand perfect and complete in all the will of God.

13 For I bear him record, that he hath a great zeal for you, and them that are in Laodicea, and them in Hierapolis.

14 Luke, the beloved physician, and Demas, greet you.

15 Salute the brethren which are in Laodicea, and Nymphas, and the church which is in his house.

16 And when this epistle is read among you, cause that it be read also in the church of the Laodiceans; and that ye likewise read the epistle from Laodicea.

17 And say to Archippus, Take heed to the ministry which thou hast received in the Lord, that thou fulfill it.

18 The salutation by the hand of me Paul. Remember my bonds. Grace be with you. Amen.

Singleness of heart – A simple intention of doing right, without looking any farther. Fearing God – That is, acting from this principle.

23. Heartily – Cheerfully, diligently. Menpleasers are soon dejected and made angry: the single-hearted are never displeased or disappointed; because they have another aim, which the good or evil treatment of those they serve cannot disappoint.

COLOSSIANS 4

1. Just – According to your contract. Equitable – Even beyond the letter of your contract.

3. That God would open to us a door of utterance – That is, give us utterance, that we "may open our mouth boldly," Eph. vi, 19, and give us an opportunity of speaking, so that none may be able to hinder.

6. Let your speech be always with grace – Seasoned with the grace of God, as flesh is with salt.

10. Aristarchus my fellowprisoner – Such was Epaphras likewise for a time, Phil. i, 23. Ye have received directions – Namely, by Tychicus, bringing this letter. The ancients adapted their language to the time of reading the letter; not, as we do, to the time when it was written. It is not improbable, they might have scrupled to receive him, without this fresh direction, after he had left St. Paul, and "departed from the work."

11. These – Three, Aristarchus, Marcus, and Justus. Of all the circumcision – That is, of all my Jewish fellowlaborers. Are the only fellowworkers unto the kingdom of God – That is, in preaching the gospel. Who have been a comfort to me – What, then, can we expect? that all our fellowworkers should be a comfort to us?

12. Perfect – Endued with every Christian grace. Filled – As no longer being babes, but grown up to the measure of the stature of Christ; being full of his light, grace, wisdom, holiness.

14. Luke, the physician – Such he had been, at least, if he was not then.

15. Nymphas – Probably an eminent Christian at Ladies.

16. The epistle from Ladies – Not to Ladies. Perhaps some letter had been written to St. Paul from thence.

17. And say to Archippus – One of the pastors of that church. Take heed – It is the duty of the flock to try them that say they are apostles to reject the false, and to warn, as well as to receive, the real. The ministry – Not a lordship, but a service; a laborious and painful work; an obligation to do and suffer all things; to be the least, and the servant, of all. In the Lord – Christ by whom, and for whose sake, we receive the various gifts of the Holy Spirit.

COLOSSIANS 4

Masters to do their duty towards servants. (1)

Persons of all ranks to persevere in prayer, and Christian prudence. (2-6)

The apostle refers to others for an account of his affairs. (7-9)

Sends greetings; and concludes with a blessing. (10-18)

1 The apostle proceeds with the duty of masters to their servants. Not only justice is required of them, but strict equity and kindness. Let them deal with servants as they expect God should deal with themselves.

2-6 No duties can be done aright, unless we persevere in fervent prayer, and watch therein with thanksgiving. The people are to pray particularly for their ministers. Believers are exhorted to right conduct towards unbelievers. Be careful in all converse with them, to do them good, and recommend religion by all fit means. Diligence in redeeming time, commends religion to the good opinion of others. Even what is only carelessness may cause a lasting prejudice against the truth. Let all discourse be discreet and seasonable, as becomes Christians. Though it be not always of grace, it must always be with grace.

7-9 Ministers are servants to Christ, and fellow servants to one another. They have one Lord, though they have different stations and powers for service. It is a great comfort under the troubles and difficulties of life, to have fellow Christians caring for us. Circumstances of life make no difference in the spiritual relation among sincere Christians; they partake of the same privileges, and are entitled to the same regards.

10-18 Paul had differed with Barnabas, on the account of this Mark, yet he is not only reconciled, but recommends him to the churches; an example of a truly Christian and forgiving spirit. If men have been guilty of a fault, it must not always be remembered against them. We must forget as well as forgive. The apostle had comfort in the communion of saints and ministers. One is his fellow servant, another his fellow-prisoner, and all his fellow-workers, working out their own salvation, and endeavoring to promote the salvation of others. The effectual, fervent prayer is the prevailing prayer, and availeth much.

him, glorious today, but yet the same Savior who was nailed like a felon to the cross for guilty ones? Reach forth thy hand and touch the silver scepter of mercy which he holds out to thee, for those who touch it live. Look into that dear face where tears once made their furrows, and grief its lines; look, I say, and live. Look at that brow radiant with many a glittering gem, it once wore a crown of thorns; let his love melt you to repentance. Throw yourself into his arms now feeling, "If I perish I will perish there. He shall be my only hope." As the Lord liveth, before whom I stand, there shall never be a soul of you lost who will come and trust in Jesus. Heaven and earth shall pass away but this word of God shall never pass away. "He that believeth and is baptized shall be saved." God has said it; will he not do it? He has declared it, it must stand fast. "Whosoever believeth in him shall not perish, but have everlasting life." O trust ye him! I implore you by the mercy of God, and by the fullness of Jesus, trust him now, this day! God grant you may, for Christ's sake. Amen.

1 Thessalonians

1 THESSALONIANS 1

1 Paul, and Silvanus, and Timotheus, unto the church of the Thessalonians which is in God the Father and in the Lord Jesus Christ: Grace be unto you, and peace, from God our Father, and the Lord Jesus Christ.

2 We give thanks to God always for you all, making mention of you in our prayers;

3 Remembering without ceasing your work of faith, and labor of love, and patience of hope in our Lord Jesus Christ, in the sight of God and our Father;

4 Knowing, brethren beloved, your election of God.

5 For our gospel came not unto you in word only, but also in power, and in the Holy Ghost, and in much assurance; as ye know what manner of men we were among you for your sake.

6 And ye became followers of us, and of the Lord, having received the word in much affliction, with joy of the Holy Ghost:

7 So that ye were ensamples to all that believe in Macedonia and Achaia.

8 For from you sounded out the word of the Lord not only in Macedonia and Achaia, but also in every place your faith to God-ward is spread abroad; so that we need not to speak any thing.

9 For they themselves shew of us what manner of entering in we had unto you, and how ye turned to God from idols to serve the living and true God;

10 And to wait for his Son from heaven, whom he raised from the dead, even Jesus, which delivered us from the wrath to come.

1 THESSALONIANS 2

1 For yourselves, brethren, know our entrance in unto you, that it was not in vain:

2 But even after that we had suffered before, and were shamefully entreated, as ye know, at Philippi, we were bold in our God to speak unto you the gospel of God with much contention.

3 For our exhortation was not of deceit, nor of uncleanness, nor in guile:

4 But as we were allowed of God to be put in trust with the gospel, even so we speak; not as pleasing men, but God, which trieth our hearts.

5 For neither at any time used we flattering words, as ye know, nor a cloke of covetousness; God is witness:

6 Nor of men sought we glory, neither of you, nor yet of others, when we might have been burdensome, as the apostles of Christ.

THIS is the first of all the epistles which St. Paul wrote. Thessalonica was one of the chief cities of Macedonia. Hither St. Paul went after the persecution at Philippi: but he had not preached here long before the unbelieving Jews raised a tumult against him and Silvanus and Timotheus. On this the brethren sent them away to Berea. Thence St. Paul went by sea to Athens, and sent for Silvanus and Timotheus to come speedily to him. But being in fear, lest the Thessalonian converts should be moved from their steadfastness, after a short time he sends Timotheus to them, to know the state of their church. Timotheus returning found the apostle at Corinth from whence he sent them this epistle, about a year after he had been at Thessalonica.

1 THESSALONIANS 1

1. Paul – In this epistle St. Paul neither uses the title of an apostle, nor any other, as writing to pious and simple-hearted men, with the utmost familiarity. There is a peculiar sweetness in this epistle, unmixed with any sharpness or reproof: those evils which the apostles afterward reproved having not yet crept into the church.

3. Remembering in the sight of God – That is, praising him for it. Your work of faith – Your active, ever-working faith. And labor of love – Love continually laboring for the bodies or souls of men. They who do not thus labor, do not love. Faith works, love labors, hope patiently suffers all things.

4. Knowing your election – Which is through faith, by these plain proofs.

5. With power – Piercing the very heart with a sense of sin and deeply convincing you of your want of a Savior from guilt, misery, and eternal ruin. With the Holy Ghost – Bearing an outward testimony, by miracles, to the truth of what we preached, and you felt: also by his descent through laying on of hands. With much assurance – Literally, with full assurance, and much of it: the Spirit bearing witness by shedding the love of God abroad in your hearts, which is the highest testimony that can be given. And these signs, if not the miraculous gifts, always attend the preaching of the gospel, unless it be in vain: neither are the extraordinary operations of the Holy Ghost ever wholly withheld, where the gospel is preached with power, and men are alive to God. For your sake – Seeking your advantage, not our own.

6. Though in much affliction, yet with much joy.

8. For from you the word sounded forth – (Thessalonica being a city of great commerce.) Being echoed, as it were, from you. And your conversion was divulged far beyond Macedonia and Achaia. So that we need not speak anything – Concerning it.

9. For they themselves – The people wherever we come.

10. Whom he hath raised from the dead – In proof of his future coming to judgment. Who delivereth us – He redeemed us once; he delivers us continually; and will deliver all that believe from the wrath, the eternal vengeance, which will then come upon the ungodly.

1 THESSALONIANS 2

1. What was proposed, chap. i, 5, 6, is now more largely treated of: concerning Paul and his fellowlaborers, ver. 1-12; concerning the Thessalonians, ver. 13-16.

2. We had suffered – In several places. We are bold – Notwithstanding. With much contention – Notwithstanding both inward and outward conflicts of all kinds.

This epistle is generally considered to have been the first of those written by St. Paul. The occasion seems to have been the good report of the steadfastness of the church at Thessalonica in the faith of the gospel. It is full of affection and confidence, and more consolatory and practical, and less doctrinal, than some of the other epistles.

1 THESSALONIANS 1

The faith, love, and patience of the Thessalonians, are evident tokens of their election which was manifested in the power with which the gospel came to them. (1-5)

Its powerful and exemplary effects upon their hearts and lives. (6-10)

1-5 As all good comes from God, so no good can be hoped for by sinners, but from God in Christ. And the best good may be expected from God, as our Father, for the sake of Christ. We should pray, not only for ourselves, but for others also; remembering them without ceasing. Wherever there is a true faith, it will work; it will affect both the heart and life. Faith works by love; it shows itself in love to God, and love to our neighbor. And wherever there is a well-grounded hope of eternal life, this will appear by the exercise of patience; and it is a sign of sincerity, when in all we do, we seek to approve ourselves to God. By this we may know our election, if we not only speak of the things of God with out lips, but feel their power in our hearts, mortifying our lusts, weaning us from the world, and raising us up to heavenly things.

6-10 When careless, ignorant, and immoral persons are turned from their carnal pursuits and connexions, to believe in and obey the Lord Jesus, to live soberly, righteously, and godly, the matter speaks for itself. The believers under the Old Testament waited for the coming of the Messiah, and believers now wait for his second coming. He is yet to come. And God had raised him from the dead, which is a full assurance unto all men that he will come to judgment. He came to purchase salvation, and will, when he comes again, bring salvation with him, full and final deliverance from that wrath which is yet to come.

1 THESSALONIANS 2

The apostle reminds the Thessalonians of his preaching and behavior. (1-12)

And of their receiving the gospel as the word of God. (13-16)

His joy on their account. (17-20)

1-6 The apostle had no worldly design in his preaching. Suffering in a good cause should sharpen holy resolution. The gospel of Christ at first met with much opposition; and it was preached with contention, with

SLEEP NOT

Sermon 1022 delivered at the Metropolitan Tabernacle, Newington.

"Let us not sleep, as do others."—
1 Thessalonians 5:6.

I. To those of you who are THE PEOPLE OF GOD, let me say, "Let us not sleep, as do others."

1. First, let us not sleep as those disciples did who went with their Lord to the garden, and fell a slumbering while he was agonizing. Let us not be as the eight who slept at a distance, nor as the highly-favored three, who were admitted into the more secret chamber of our Lord's woes, and were allowed to tread the precincts of the most holy place where he poured out his soul, and sweat as it were great drops of blood. He found them sleeping, and though he awakened them, they slept again and again. "What, could ye not watch with me one hour?" was his gentle expostulation. They were slumbering for sorrow. Though our Lord might in our case make an excuse for us as he did for them—"The spirit truly is willing, but the flesh is weak,"—let us endeavor by his grace not to need such an apology, by avoiding their fault. "Let us not sleep, as do others." But, beloved fellow Christians, are not the most of us sleeping as the apostles did? Behold our Master's zeal for the salvation of the sons of men! Throughout all his life, he seemed to have no rest. From the moment when his ministry began he was ever toiling, laboring, denying himself. It was his meat and his drink to do the will of him that sent him. Truly he might have taken for his life's motto,—"Wist ye not that I must be about my Father's business?" So intent was he on saving souls, that he counted not his life dear unto him. He would lay it down, and that amidst circumstances of the greatest pain and ignominy; anything and everything would he do to seek and to save that which was lost. Zeal for his chosen church, which was God's house, had eaten him up: for his people's sakes he could bear all the reproaches of them that reproached God, and though that reproach broke his heart, yet still he persevered and ceased not till salvation's work was done. He was incessant in toil and suffering, but, what are we?

There is our Lord, our great Exemplar, before us now. Behold him in Gethsemane! imagination readily sees him amid the olives. I might say, that his whole life was pictured in that agony in the garden, for in a certain sense it was all an agony. It was all a sweating, not such as distils from those who purchase the staff of life by the sweat of their face, but such as he must feel who purchased life itself with the agony of his

7 But we were gentle among you, even as a nurse cherisheth her children:

8 So being affectionately desirous of you, we were willing to have imparted unto you, not the gospel of God only, but also our own souls, because ye were dear unto us.

9 For ye remember, brethren, our labor and travail: for laboring night and day, because we would not be chargeable unto any of you, we preached unto you the gospel of God.

10 Ye are witnesses, and God also, how holily and justly and unblameably we behaved ourselves among you that believe:

11 As ye know how we exhorted and comforted and charged every one of you, as a father doth his children,

12 That ye would walk worthy of God, who hath called you unto his kingdom and glory.

13 For this cause also thank we God without ceasing, because, when ye received the word of God which ye heard of us, ye received it not as the word of men, but as it is in truth, the word of God, which effectually worketh also in you that believe.

14 For ye, brethren, became followers of the churches of God which in Judea are in Christ Jesus: for ye also have suffered like things of your own countrymen, even as they have of the Jews:

15 Who both killed the Lord Jesus, and their own prophets, and have persecuted us; and they please not God, and are contrary to all men:

16 Forbidding us to speak to the Gentiles that they might be saved, to fill up their sins alway: for the wrath is come upon them to the uttermost.

17 But we, brethren, being taken from you for a short time in presence, not in heart, endeavored the more abundantly to see your face with great desire.

18 Wherefore we would have come unto you, even I Paul, once and again; but Satan hindered us.

19 For what is our hope, or joy, or crown of rejoicing? Are not even ye in the presence of our Lord Jesus Christ at his coming?

20 For ye are our glory and joy.

1 THESSALONIANS 3

1 Wherefore when we could no longer forbear, we thought it good to be left at Athens alone;

2 And sent Timotheus, our brother, and minister of God, and our fellowlaborer in the gospel of Christ, to establish you,

3. For our exhortation – That is, our preaching. A part is put for the whole. Is not, at any time, of deceit – We preach not a lie, but the truth of God. Nor of uncleanness – With any unholy or selfish view. This expression is not always appropriated to lust, although it is sometimes emphatically applied thereto. Nor in guile – But with great plainness of speech.

5. Flattering words – This ye know. Nor a cloak of covetousness – Of this God is witness. He calls men to witness an open fact; God, the secret intentions of the heart. In a point of a mixed nature, ver. 10, he appeals both to God and man.

6. Nor from others – Who would have honored us more, if we had been burdensome – That is, taken state upon ourselves.

7. But we were gentle – Mild, tender. In the midst of you – Like a hen surrounded with her young. Even as a nurse cherisheth her own children – The offspring of her own womb.

8. To impart our own souls – To lay down our lives for your sake.

10. Holily – In the things of God. Justly – With regard to men. Unblammable – In respect of ourselves. Among you that believe – Who were the constant observers of our behavior.

11. By exhorting, we are moved to do a thing willingly; by comforting, to do it joyfully; by charging, to do it carefully.

12. To his kingdom here, and glory hereafter.

14. Ye suffered the same things – The same fruit, the same afflictions, and the same experience, at all times, and in all places, are an excellent criterion of evangelical truth. As they from the Jews – Their countrymen.

15. Us – Apostles and preachers of the gospel. They please not God – Nor are they even careful to please him, notwithstanding their fair professions. And are contrary to all men – Are common enemies of mankind; not only by their continual seditions and insurrections, and by their utter contempt of all other nations; but in particular, by their endeavoring to hinder their hearing or receiving the gospel.

16. To fill up – The measure of their sins always, as they have ever done. But the vengeance of God is come upon them – Hath overtaken them unawares, whilst they were seeking to destroy others, and will speedily complete their destruction.

17. In this verse we have a remarkable instance, not so much of the transient affections of holy grief, desire, or joy, as of that abiding tenderness, that loving temper, which is so apparent in all St. Paul's writings, towards those he styles his children in the faith. This is the more carefully to be observed, because the passions occasionally exercising themselves, and flowing like a torrent, in the apostle, are observable to every reader; whereas it requires a nicer attention to discern those calm standing tempers, that fixed posture of his soul, from whence the others only flow out, and which more peculiarly distinguish his character.

18. Satan – By those persecuting Jews, Acts xvii, 13.

19. Ye also – As well as our other children.

1 THESSALONIANS 3

1. We – Paul and Silvanus. Could bear no longer – Our desire and fear for you.

3. We are appointed hereto – Are in every respect laid in a fit posture for it, by the very design and contrivance of God himself for the trial and increase of our faith and all other graces. He gives riches to the world; but stores up his treasure of wholesome afflictions for his children.

6. But now when Timotheus was come to us from you – Immediately

MATTHEW HENRY

CHARLES H. SPURGEON

striving in preaching, and against opposition. And as the matter of the apostle's exhortation was true and pure, the manner of his speaking was without guile. The gospel of Christ is designed for mortifying corrupt affections, and that men may be brought under the power of faith.

7-12 Mildness and tenderness greatly recommend religion, and are most conformable to God's gracious dealing with sinners, in and by the gospel. This is the way to win people. We should not only be faithful to our calling as Christians, but in our particular callings and relations. Our great gospel privilege is, that God has called us to his kingdom and glory. The great gospel duty is, that we walk worthy of God.

13-16 We should receive the word of God with affections suitable to its holiness, wisdom, truth, and goodness. The words of men are frail and perishing, like themselves, and sometimes false, foolish, and fickle; but God's word is holy, wise, just, and faithful. Let us receive and regard it accordingly. The word wrought in them, to make them examples to others in faith and good works, and in patience under sufferings, and in trials for the sake of the gospel. Murder and persecution are hateful to God, and no zeal for any thing in religion can excuse it. Nothing tends more to any person or people's filling up the measure of their sins, than opposing the gospel, and hindering the salvation of souls.

17-20 This world is not a place where we are to be always, or long together. In heaven holy souls shall meet, and never part more. And though the apostle could not come to them yet, and thought he might never be able to come, yet our Lord Jesus Christ will come; nothing shall hinder that.

1 THESSALONIANS 3

The apostle sent Timothy to establish and comfort the Thessalonians (1-5)

He rejoiced at the good tidings of their faith and love. (6-10)

And for their increase in grace. (11-13)

1-5 The more we find pleasure in the ways of God, the more we shall desire to persevere therein. The apostle's design was to establish and comfort the Thessalonians as to the object of their faith, that Jesus Christ was the Savior of the world; and as to the recompense of faith, which was more than enough to make up all their losses, and to reward all their labors. But he feared his labors would be in vain. If the devil cannot hinder ministers from laboring in the word and doctrine, he will, if possible, hinder the success of their labors. No one would willingly labor in vain. It is the will and purpose of God, that we enter into his kingdom through many afflictions.

heart. The Savior, as I see him throughout the whole of his ministry, appears to me on his knees pleading, and before his God agonizing— laying out his life for the sons of men. But, brethren, do I speak harshly when I say that the disciples asleep are a fit emblem of our usual life? As compared or rather contrasted with our Master, I fear it is so. Where is our zeal for God? Where is our compassion for men? Do we ever feel the weight of souls as we ought to feel it? Do we ever melt in the presence of the terrors of God which we know to be coming upon others? Have we realized the passing away of an immortal spirit to the judgment bar of God? Have we felt pangs and throes of sympathy when we have remembered that multitudes of our fellow creatures have received, as their eternal sentence, the words— "Depart ye cursed into everlasting fire in hell, prepared for the devil and his angels?" Why, if these thoughts really possessed us, we should scarce sleep; if they became as real to us as they were to him, we should wrestle with God for souls as he did, and become willing to lay down our lives, if by any means we might save some. I see by the eye of faith, at this moment, Jesus pleading at the mercy-seat. "For Zion's sake," he saith, "I will not hold my peace, and for Jerusalem's sake I will not rest;" and yet, we around him lie asleep, without self-denying activity, and almost without prayer, missing opportunities, or, when opportunities for doing good have been seized, using them with but a slothful hand, and doing the work of the Lord, if not deceitfully, yet most sluggishly. Brethren, "let us not sleep, as do others." If it be true that the Christian Church is to a great extent asleep, the more reason why we should be awake; and, if it be true, as I fear it is, that we have ourselves slumbered and slept, the more reason now that we should arise and trim our lamps, and go forth to meet the Bridegroom. Let us from this moment begin to serve our Master and his church more nearly after the example which he himself has set us in his consecrated life and blessed death. Let us not sleep then, as did the disciples at Gethsemane.

> "O thou, who in the garden's shade,
> Didst wake thy weary ones again,
> Who slumbered at that fearful hour,
> Forgetful of thy pain;
> Bend o'er us now, as over them
> And set our sleep-bound spirits free;
> Nor leave us slumbering in the watch
> Our souls should keep with thee!"

Will you cease from the importunities of prayer? Will you pause in the labors of zeal? Will you bring dishonor upon Christ and upon his cross? By the living God who sleepeth not, neither is

and to comfort you concerning your faith:

3 That no man should be moved by these afflictions: for yourselves know that we are appointed thereunto.

4 For verily, when we were with you, we told you before that we should suffer tribulation; even as it came to pass, and ye know.

5 For this cause, when I could no longer forbear, I sent to know your faith, lest by some means the tempter have tempted you, and our labor be in vain.

6 But now when Timotheus came from you unto us, and brought us good tidings of your faith and charity, and that ye have good remembrance of us always, desiring greatly to see us, as we also to see you:

7 Therefore, brethren, we were comforted over you in all our affliction and distress by your faith:

8 For now we live, if ye stand fast in the Lord.

9 For what thanks can we render to God again for you, for all the joy wherewith we joy for your sakes before our God;

10 Night and day praying exceedingly that we might see your face, and might perfect that which is lacking in your faith?

11 Now God himself and our Father, and our Lord Jesus Christ, direct our way unto you.

12 And the Lord make you to increase and abound in love one toward another, and toward all men, even as we do toward you:

13 To the end he may stablish your hearts unblameable in holiness before God, even our Father, at the coming of our Lord Jesus Christ with all his saints.

1 THESSALONIANS 4

1 Furthermore then we beseech you, brethren, and exhort you by the Lord Jesus, that as ye have received of us how ye ought to walk and to please God, so ye would abound more and more.

2 For ye know what commandments we gave you by the Lord Jesus.

3 For this is the will of God, even your sanctification, that ye should abstain from fornication:

4 That every one of you should know how to possess his vessel in sanctification and honor;

5 Not in the lust of concupiscence, even as the Gentiles which know not God:

6 That no man go beyond and defraud his brother in any matter: because that the Lord is the avenger of all such, as we also have forewarned you and testified.

after his return, St. Paul wrote; while his joy was fresh, and his tenderness at the height.

8. Now we live – Indeed; we enjoy life: so great is our affection for you.

10. And perfect that which is wanting in your faith – So St. Paul did not know that "they who are once upon the rock no longer need to be taught by man."

11. Direct our way – This prayer is addressed to Christ, as well as to the Father.

13. With all his, Christ's, saints – Both angels and men.

1 THESSALONIANS 4

1. More and more – It is not enough to have faith, even so as to please God, unless we abound more and more therein.

3. Sanctification – Entire holiness of heart and life: particular branches of it are subjoined. That ye abstain from fornication – A beautiful transition from sanctification to a single branch of the contrary; and this shows that nothing is so seemingly distant, or below our thoughts, but we have need to guard against it.

4. That every one know – For this requires knowledge, as well as chastity. To possess his vessel – His wife. In sanctification and honor – So as neither to dishonor God or himself, nor to obstruct, but further, holiness; remembering, marriage is not designed to inflame, but to conquer, natural desires.

5. Not in passionate desire – Which had no place in man when in a state of innocence. Who know not God – And so may naturally seek happiness in a creature. What seemingly accidental words slide in; and yet how fine, and how vastly important!

6. In this matter – By violating his bed. The things forbidden, here are three: fornication, ver. 3; the passion of desire, or inordinate affection in the married state, ver. 5; and the breach of the marriage contract.

8. He that despiseth – The commandments we gave. Despiseth God – Himself. Who hath also given you his Holy Spirit – To convince you of the truth, and enable you to be holy. What naked majesty of words! How oratorical, and yet with what great simplicity! a simplicity that does not impair, but improve, the understanding to the utmost; that, like the rays of heat through a glass, collects all the powers of reason into one orderly point, from being scattered abroad in utter confusion.

9. We need not write – Largely. For ye are taught of God – By his Spirit.

11. That ye study – Literally, that ye be ambitious: an ambition worthy of a Christian. To work with your hands – Not a needless caution; for temporal concerns are often a cross to them who are newly filled with the love of God.

12. Decently – That they may have no pretense to say, (but they will say it still,) "This religion makes men idle, and brings them to beggary." And may want nothing – Needful for life and godliness. What Christian desires more?

13. Now – Herein the efficacy of Christianity greatly appears, – that it neither takes away nor embitters, but sweetly tempers, that most refined of all affections, our desire of or love to the dead.

14. So – As God raised him. With him – With their living head.

15. By the word of the Lord – By a particular Revelation. We who are left – This intimates the fewness of those who will be then alive, compared to the multitude of the dead. Believers of all ages and nations make up, as it were, one body; in consideration of which, the believers of that age might put themselves in the place, and speak in the person, of them who

MATTHEW HENRY

CHARLES H. SPURGEON

6-10 Thankfulness to God is very imperfect in the present state; but one great end of the ministry of the word is to help faith forward. That which was the instrument to obtain faith, is also the means of increasing and confirming it.

11-13 Prayer is religious worship, and all religious worship is due unto God only. Prayer is to be offered to God as our Father. Prayer is not only to be offered in the name of Christ, but offered up to Christ himself, as our Lord and our Savior. Let us acknowledge God in all our ways, and he will direct our paths.

1 THESSALONIANS 4

Exhortations to purity and holiness. (1-8)
To brotherly love, peaceable behavior, and diligence. (9-12)
Not to sorrow unduly for the death of godly relations and friends, considering the glorious resurrection of their bodies at Christ's second coming. (13-18)

1-8 To abide in the faith of the gospel is not enough, we must abound in the work of faith. The rule according to which all ought to walk and act, is the commandments given by the Lord Jesus Christ. Sanctification, in the renewal of their souls under the influences of the Holy Spirit, and attention to appointed duties, constituted the will of God respecting them. In aspiring after this renewal of the soul unto holiness, strict restraint must be put upon the appetites and senses of the body, and on the thoughts and inclinations of the will, which lead to wrong uses of them.

9-12 We should notice in others what is good, to their praise, that we may engage them to abound therein more and more. All who are savingly taught of God, are taught to love one another. The teaching of the Spirit exceeds the teachings of men; and men's teaching is vain and useless, unless God teach.

13-18 Here is comfort for the relations and friends of those who die in the Lord. Grief for the death of friends is lawful; we may weep for our own loss, though it may be their gain. Christianity does not forbid, and grace does not do away, our natural affections. Yet we must not be excessive in our sorrows; this is too much like those who have no hope of a better life. Death is an unknown thing, and we know little about the state after death; yet the doctrines of the resurrection and the second coming of Christ, are a remedy against the fear of death, and undue sorrow for the death of our Christian friends; and of these doctrines we have full assurance. It will be some happiness that all the saints shall meet, and remain together forever; but the principal happiness of heaven is to be with the Lord, to see him, live with him, and enjoy him for ever.

weary in his deeds of love, I beseech you, slumber not, and be not weary nor faint in your mind. "Be ye steadfast, immovable, always abounding in the work of the Lord.'

II. But I must pass on to the second part of our subject. I have now to speak TO THOSE OF YOU WHO ARE NOT CONVERTED; and if I felt as I ought to feel, it would be sorrowful work even to remember that any of you are yet unsaved. I like to see these little children here. I pray God they may grow up to fear and love him, and that their young hearts may be given to our dear Lord and Master while they are yet boys and girls. But I overlook them just now, and speak to some of you who have had many years of intelligent hearing of the word, and are still unsaved. Pitiable objects! You do not think so; but I repeat the word, Pitiable objects! The tears which flood my eyes almost prevent my seeing you. You fancy you are very merry and happy, but you are to be pitied, for "the wrath of God abideth on you." "He that believeth not is condemned already, because he hath not believed on the Son of God." You will soon be where no pity can help you, and where the Lord himself will not help you. May God give you ears to hear the words of affectionate warning which I address to you now! "Let us not sleep, as do others."

I beg you not to sleep, as did Jonah. He was in the vessel, you remember, when it was tossed with the tempest, and all the rest in the vessel were praying, but Jonah was asleep. Every man called upon his God except the man who had caused the storm. He was the most in danger, but he was the most careless. The ship-master and mate, and crew, all prayed, every man to his god, but Jonah carelessly slept on. Now, do not some of you here live in houses where they all pray but you? You have a godly mother, but are yourself godless. John, you have a Christian father, and brothers and sisters, too, whom Christ has looked upon in love, and they pray for you continually. But the strange thing is, that your soul is the only one in the house which remains unblest, and yet you are the only one who feels no anxiety or fear about the matter. There are many of us in this house who can honestly say that we would give anything we have, if we could save your souls; we do not know what we would not do, but we know we would do all in our power, if we could but reach your consciences and your hearts. I stand often in this pulpit almost wishing that I had never been born, because of the burden and distress it brings upon my soul to think of some of you who will die and be lost for ever. Lost, though you love to listen to the preacher! Lost, though

7 For God hath not called us unto uncleanness, but unto holiness.

8 He therefore that despiseth, despiseth not man, but God, who hath also given unto us his holy Spirit.

9 But as touching brotherly love ye need not that I write unto you: for ye yourselves are taught of God to love one another.

10 And indeed ye do it toward all the brethren which are in all Macedonia: but we beseech you, brethren, that ye increase more and more;

11 And that ye study to be quiet, and to do your own business, and to work with your own hands, as we commanded you;

12 That ye may walk honestly toward them that are without, and that ye may have lack of nothing.

13 But I would not have you to be ignorant, brethren, concerning them which are asleep, that ye sorrow not, even as others which have no hope.

14 For if we believe that Jesus died and rose again, even so them also which sleep in Jesus will God bring with him.

15 For this we say unto you by the word of the Lord, that we which are alive and remain unto the coming of the Lord shall not prevent them which are asleep.

16 For the Lord himself shall descend from heaven with a shout, with the voice of the archangel, and with the trump of God: and the dead in Christ shall rise first:

17 Then we which are alive and remain shall be caught up together with them in the clouds, to meet the Lord in the air: and so shall we ever be with the Lord.

18 Wherefore comfort one another with these words.

1 THESSALONIANS 5

1 But of the times and the seasons, brethren, ye have no need that I write unto you.

2 For yourselves know perfectly that the day of the Lord so cometh as a thief in the night.

3 For when they shall say, Peace and safety; then sudden destruction cometh upon them, as travail upon a woman with child; and they shall not escape.

4 But ye, brethren, are not in darkness, that that day should overtake you as a thief.

5 Ye are all the children of light, and the children of the day: we are not of the night, nor of darkness.

6 Therefore let us not sleep, as do others; but let us watch and be sober.

7 For they that sleep sleep in the night;

were to live till the coming of the Lord. Not that St. Paul hereby asserted (though some seem to have imagined so) that the day of the Lord was at hand.

16. With a shout – Properly, a proclamation made to a great multitude. Above this is, the voice of the archangel; above both, the trumpet of God; the voice of God, somewhat analogous to the sound of a trumpet.

17. Together – In the same moment. In the air – The wicked will remain beneath, while the righteous, being absolved, shall be assessors with their Lord in the judgment. With the Lord – In heaven.

1 THESSALONIANS 5

1. But of the precise times when this shall be.

2. For this in general ye do know; and ye can and need know no more.

3. When they – The men of the world say.

4. Ye are not in darkness – Sleeping secure in sin.

6. Awake, and keep awake – Being awakened, let us have all our spiritual senses about us.

7. They usually sleep and are drunken in the night – These things do not love the light.

9. God hath not appointed us to wrath – As he hath the obstinately impenitent.

10. Whether we wake or sleep – Be alive or dead at his coming.

12. Know them that,

1. Labor among you:

2. Are over you in the Lord:

3. Admonish you. Know – See, mark, take knowledge of them and their work. Sometimes the same person may both labor, that is, preach; be over, or govern; and admonish the flock by particular application to each: sometimes two or more different persons, according as God variously dispenses his gifts. But O, what a misery is it when a man undertakes this whole work without either gifts or graces for any part of it! Why, then, will he undertake it? for pay? What! will he sell both his own soul and all the souls of the flock? What words can describe such a wretch as this? And yet even this may be "an honorable man!"

13. Esteem them very highly – Literally, more than abundantly, in love – The inexpressible sympathy that is between true pastors and their flock is intimated, not only here, but also in divers other places of this epistle. See chap. ii, 7, 8. For their work's sake – The principal ground of their vast regard for them. But how are we to esteem them who do not work at all?

14. Warn the disorderly – Them that stand, as it were, out of their rank in the spiritual warfare. Some such were even in that church. The feebleminded – Literally, them of little soul; such as have no spiritual courage.

15. See that none – Watch over both yourselves and each other. Follow that which is good – Do it resolutely and perseveringly.

16. Rejoice evermore – In uninterrupted happiness in God. Pray without ceasing – Which is the fruit of always rejoicing in the Lord. In everything give thanks – Which is the fruit of both the former. This is Christian perfection. Farther than this we cannot go; and we need not stop short of it. Our Lord has purchased joy, as well as righteousness, for us. It is the very design of the gospel that, being saved from guilt, we should be happy in the love of Christ. Prayer may be said to be the breath of our spiritual life. He that lives cannot possibly cease breathing. So much as we really enjoy

MATTHEW HENRY   CHARLES H. SPURGEON

1 THESSALONIANS 5

The apostle exhorts to be always ready for the coming of Christ to judgment, which will be with suddenness and surprise. (1-11)

He directs to several particular duties. (12-22)

And concludes with prayer, greetings, and a blessing. (23-28)

1-5 It is needless or useless to ask about the particular time of Christ's coming. Christ did not reveal this to the apostles. There are times and seasons for us to work in, and these are our duty and interest to know and observe; but as to the time when we must give up our account, we know it not, nor is it needful that we should. The coming of Christ will be a great surprise to men. Our Lord himself said so. As the hour of death is the same to each person that the judgment will be to mankind in general, so the same remarks answer for both. Christ's coming will be terrible to the ungodly. Their destruction will overtake them while they dream of happiness, and please themselves with vain amusements. There will be no means to escape the terror or the punishment of that day. This day will be a happy day to the righteous. They are not in darkness; they are the children of the light.

6-11 Most of mankind do not consider the things of another world at all, because they are asleep; or they do not consider them aright, because they sleep and dream. Our moderation as to all earthly things should be known to all men. Shall Christians, who have the light of the blessed gospel shining in their faces, be careless about their souls, and unmindful of another world? We need the spiritual Armor, or the three Christian graces, faith, love, and hope. Faith; if we believe that the eye of God is always upon us, that there is another world to prepare for, we shall see reason to watch and be sober. True and fervent love to God, and the things of God, will keep us watchful and sober.

12-15 The ministers of the gospel are described by the work of their office, which is to serve and honor the Lord. It is their duty not only to give good counsel, but also to warn the flock of dangers, and reprove for whatever may be amiss. The people should honor and love their ministers, because their business is the welfare of men's souls. And the people should be at peace among themselves, doing all they can to guard against any differences. But love of peace must not make us wink at sin.

16-22 We are to rejoice in creature comforts, as if we rejoiced not, and must not expect to live many years, and rejoice in them all; but if we do rejoice in God, we may do that evermore. A truly religious life is a life of constant joy. And we should rejoice more, if we prayed more. Prayer will help forward all lawful business, and every good work. If we pray without ceas-

you sometimes resolve to be saved! We are praying for you daily, but you,—you are asleep! What do you, while we are preaching but criticize our words, as if we discoursed to you as a piece of display, and did not mean to plead as for life and death with you, that you would escape from the wrath to come. Observations will be made by the frivolous among you during the most solemn words, about someone's dress or personal appearance. Vain minds will be gadding upon the mountains of folly, while those, who are not, by far, so immediately concerned, are troubled and have deep searchings of heart about those very souls. I believe God is going to send a revival into this place; I have that conviction growing upon me, but it may be that though the gracious wave may sweep over the congregation, it will miss you. It has missed you up to this hour. Around you all the floor is wet, but you, like Gideon's fleece, are dry, and you sleep though the blessing comes not upon you,—sleep though sleep involves a certain and approaching curse. O slumbering Jonah, in the name of the Host High, I would say to thee, "Awake thou that sleepest, and call upon thy God. Peradventure, he shall deliver thee, and this great tempest shall yet be stayed." Yea, I would put it above a peradventure, for they that seek the Lord shall find him, if they seek him with full purpose of heart.

Another picture is this (may it never be seen in you)—there went once into a tent, which he thought to be friendly, a mighty man who had fought a battle and lost the day. Hot of foot and full of fear, Sisera came into the tent of Jael to ask for water, and she gave him milk; she brought forth butter in a lordly dish. He drank, and then, all weary, he threw himself along in the tent. He is a photograph of many ungodly men who have gone where they thought they had friends; for sinners think sinners their friends, and think sin their friend, and they have asked for pleasure, and they have had it; and, now, after having had their fill, and eaten butter in a lordly dish, they are tonight in contentment, sleeping in supposed security. They have gone into the house of the evil one to find pleasure, and they are going there again tonight, and they will continue there, and try to find rest in the house of their enemies. Sometimes it is the house of the strange woman, often the settle of the drunkard, or the chair of the scorner, where men think to rest in peace, Oh, hark thee, man, and beware! Fly the ways of the destroyer: fly the haunt of the strange woman, as for thy very life every den of sin; for, lo! she cometh stealthily, the tent pin is in her left hand, and in her right hand the workman's hammer. Many mighty has she slain

and they that be drunken are drunken in the night.

8 But let us, who are of the day, be sober, putting on the breastplate of faith and love; and for an helmet, the hope of salvation.

9 For God hath not appointed us to wrath, but to obtain salvation by our Lord Jesus Christ,

10 Who died for us, that, whether we wake or sleep, we should live together with him.

11   Wherefore comfort yourselves together, and edify one another, even as also ye do.

12 And we beseech you, brethren, to know them which labor among you, and are over you in the Lord, and admonish you;

13 And to esteem them very highly in love for their work's sake. And be at peace among yourselves.

14 Now we exhort you, brethren, warn them that are unruly, comfort the feeble-minded, support the weak, be patient toward all men.

15   See that none render evil for evil unto any man; but ever follow that which is good, both among yourselves, and to all men.

16 Rejoice evermore.

17 Pray without ceasing.

18 In every thing give thanks: for this is the will of God in Christ Jesus concerning you.

19 Quench not the Spirit.

20 Despise not prophesyings.

21 Prove all things; hold fast that which is good.

22 Abstain from all appearance of evil.

23 And the very God of peace sanctify you wholly; and I pray God your whole spirit and soul and body be preserved blameless unto the coming of our Lord Jesus Christ.

24 Faithful is he that calleth you, who also will do it.

25 Brethren, pray for us.

26 Greet all the brethren with an holy kiss.

27 I charge you by the Lord that this epistle be read unto all the holy brethren.

28 The grace of our Lord Jesus Christ be with you. Amen.

of the presence of God, so much prayer and praise do we offer up without ceasing; else our rejoicing is but delusion. Thanksgiving is inseparable from true prayer: it is almost essentially connected with it. He that always prays is ever giving praise, whether in ease or pain, both for prosperity and for the greatest adversity. He blesses God for all things, looks on them as coming from him, and receives them only for his sake; not choosing nor refusing, liking nor disliking, anything, but only as it is agreeable or disagreeable to his perfect will.

18. For this – That you should thus rejoice, pray, give thanks. Is the will of God – Always good, always pointing at our salvation.

19. Quench not the Spirit – Wherever it is, it burns; it flames in holy love, in joy, prayer, thanksgiving. O quench it not, damp it not in yourself or others, either by neglecting to do good, or by doing evil!

20. Despise not prophesyings – That is, preaching; for the apostle is not here speaking of extraordinary gifts. It seems, one means of grace is put for all; and whoever despises any of these, under whatever pretense, will surely (though perhaps gradually and almost insensibly) quench the Spirit.

21. Meantime, prove all things – Which any preacher recommends. (He speaks of practice, not of doctrines.) Try every advice by the touchstone of scripture, and hold fast that which is good – Zealously, resolutely, diligently practice it, in spite of all opposition.

22. And be equally zealous and careful to abstain from all appearance of evil – Observe, those who "heap to themselves teachers, having itching ears," under pretense of proving all things, have no countenance or excuse from this scripture.

23. And may the God of peace sanctify you – By the peace he works in you, which is a great means of sanctification. Wholly – The word signifies wholly and perfectly; every part and all that concerns you; all that is of or about you. And may the whole of you, the spirit and the soul and the body – Just before he said you; now he denominates them from their spiritual state. The spirit – Gal. vi, 8; wishing that it may be preserved whole and entire: then from their natural state, the soul and the body; (for these two make up the whole nature of man, Matt. x, 28;) wishing it may be preserved blameless till the coming of Christ. To explain this a little further: of the three here mentioned, only the two last are the natural constituent parts of man. The first is adventitious, and the supernatural gift of God, to be found in Christians only. That man cannot possibly consist of three parts, appears hence: The soul is either matter or not matter: there is no medium. But if it is matter, it is part of the body: if not matter, it coincides with the Spirit.

24. Who also will do it – Unless you quench the Spirit.

27. I charge you by the Lord – Christ, to whom proper divine worship is here paid. That this epistle – The first he wrote. Be read to all the brethren – That is, in all the churches. They might have concealed it out of modesty, had not this been so solemnly enjoined: but what Paul commands under so strong an adjuration, Rome forbids under pain of excommunication.

ing, we shall not want matter for thanksgiving in every thing. We shall see cause to give thanks for sparing and preventing, for common and uncommon, past and present, temporal and spiritual mercies. Not only for prosperous and pleasing, but also for afflicting providences, for chastisements and corrections; for God designs all for our good, though we at present see not how they tend to it. Quench not the Spirit. Christians are said to be baptized with the Holy Ghost and with fire. He worketh as fire, by enlightening, enlivening, and purifying the souls of men. As fire is put out by taking away fuel, and as it is quenched by pouring water, or putting a great deal of earth upon it; so we must be careful not to quench the Holy Spirit, by indulging carnal lusts and affections, minding only earthly things. Believers often hinder their growth in grace, by not giving themselves up to the spiritual affections raised in their hearts by the Holy Spirit. By prophesyings, here understand the preaching of the word, the interpreting and applying the Scriptures. We must not despise preaching, though it is plain, and we are told no more than what we knew before.

23-28 The apostle prays that they might be sanctified more perfectly, for the best are sanctified but in part while in this world; therefore we should pray for, and press toward, complete holiness. And as we must fall, if God did not carry on his good work in the soul, we should pray to God to perfect his work, till we are presented faultless before the throne of his glory. We should pray for one another; and brethren should thus express brotherly love. This epistle was to be read to all the brethren. The Scriptures should be read in all public congregations, for the benefit of the unlearned especially. We need no more to make us happy, than to know the grace of our Lord Jesus Christ. He is an ever flowing and an over-flowing fountain of grace to supply all our wants.

aforetime, for she hunts for the precious life, and her chambers lead down to death. If thou sleepest on but another night, or even another hour, the destroyer may have done the deed, and thou mayst be fastened to the earth for ever, the victim of thine own delusions. I may be in error, but I think I spear; to some man tonight who must now immediately change his ways, or else the jaws of hell will close upon him.

Ere long, Jael's tent-pin shall have passed through Sisera's skull; the sin shall have destroyed the sinner: the sin that is unto death shall have shut up the spirit in despair. Oh, may God, who is mighty to save, turn you to himself at this moment.

"Sound the trumpet in Zion: sound an alarm in my holy mountain," seems to ring in my ears; and I would fain sound that alarm to God's saints, and to sinners too. May he call many by his grace, and awaken us all; and his shall be the glory for ever and ever! Amen.

2 Thessalonians

2 THESSALONIANS 1

1 Paul, and Silvanus, and Timotheus, unto the church of the Thessalonians in God our Father and the Lord Jesus Christ:

2 Grace unto you, and peace, from God our Father and the Lord Jesus Christ.

3 We are bound to thank God always for you, brethren, as it is meet, because that your faith groweth exceedingly, and the charity of every one of you all toward each other aboundeth;

4 So that we ourselves glory in you in the churches of God for your patience and faith in all your persecutions and tribulations that ye endure:

5 Which is a manifest token of the righteous judgment of God, that ye may be counted worthy of the kingdom of God, for which ye also suffer:

6 Seeing it is a righteous thing with God to recompense tribulation to them that trouble you;

7 And to you who are troubled rest with us, when the Lord Jesus shall be revealed from heaven with his mighty angels,

8 In flaming fire taking vengeance on them that know not God, and that obey not the gospel of our Lord Jesus Christ:

9 Who shall be punished with everlasting destruction from the presence of the Lord, and from the glory of his power;

10 When he shall come to be glorified in his saints, and to be admired in all them that believe (because our testimony among you was believed) in that day.

11 Wherefore also we pray always for you, that our God would count you worthy of this calling, and fulfill all the good pleasure of his goodness, and the work of faith with power:

12 That the name of our Lord Jesus Christ may be glorified in you, and ye in him, according to the grace of our God and the Lord Jesus Christ.

2 THESSALONIANS 2

1 Now we beseech you, brethren, by the coming of our Lord Jesus Christ, and by our gathering together unto him,

2 That ye be not soon shaken in mind, or be troubled, neither by spirit, nor by word, nor by letter as from us, as that the day of Christ is at hand.

3 Let no man deceive you by any means: for that day shall not come, except there come a falling away first, and that man of sin be revealed, the son of perdition;

4 Who opposeth and exalteth himself above all that is called God, or that is worshiped; so that he as God sitteth in

---

THIS epistle seems to have been written soon after the former, chiefly on occasion of some things therein which had been misunderstood. Herein he,

1. Congratulates their constancy in the faith, and exhorts them to advance daily in grace and wisdom.

2. Reforms their mistake concerning the coming of our Lord And,

3. Recommends several Christian duties.

2 THESSALONIANS 1

3. It is highly observable, that the apostle wraps up his praise of men in praise to God; giving him the glory. Your faith groweth – Probably he had heard from them since his sending the former letter. Aboundeth – Like water that overflows its banks, and yet increaseth still.

4. Which ye endure – "That ye may be accounted worthy of the kingdom."

5. A manifest token – This is treated of in the sixth and following verses.

6. It is a righteous thing with God – (However men may judge) to transfer the pressure from you to them. And it is remarkable that about this time, at the Passover, the Jews raising a tumult, a great number (some say thirty thousand) of them were slain. St. Paul seems to allude to this beginning of sorrows, 1 Thess. ii, 16, which did not end but with their destruction.

8. Taking vengeance – Does God barely permit this, or (as "the Lord" once "rained brimstone and fire from the Lord out of heaven," Gen. xix, 24) does a fiery stream go forth from him for ever? Who know not God – (The root of all wickedness and misery) who remain in heathen ignorance. And who obey not – This refers chiefly to the Jews, who had heard the gospel.

9. From the glory of his power – Tremble, ye stout-hearted. Everlasting destruction – As there can be no end of their sins, (the same enmity against God continuing,) so neither of their punishment; sin and its punishment running parallel throughout eternity itself. They must of necessity, therefore, be cut off from all good, and all possibility of it. From the presence of the Lord – Wherein chiefly consists the salvation of the righteous. What unspeakable punishment is implied even in falling short of this, supposing that nothing more were implied in his taking vengeance!

10. To be glorified in his saints – For the wonderful glory of Christ shall shine in them.

11. All the good pleasure of his goodness – Which is no less than perfect holiness.

12. That the name – The love and power of our Lord may be glorified – Gloriously displayed in you.

2 THESSALONIANS 2

1. Our gathering together to him – In the clouds.

2. Be not shaken in mind – In judgment. Or terrified – As those easily are who are immoderately fond of knowing future things. Neither by any pretended Revelation from the Spirit, nor by pretense of any word spoken by me.

3. Unless the falling away – From the pure faith of the gospel, come first. This began even in the apostolic age. But the man of sin, the son of perdition – Eminently so called, is not come yet. However, in many respects, the Pope has an indisputable claim to those titles. He is, in an emphatical sense, the man of sin, as he increases all manner of sin above measure.

MATTHEW HENRY   CHARLES H. SPURGEON

The second epistle to the Thessalonians was written soon after the first. The apostle was told that, from some expressions in his first letter, many expected the second coming of Christ was at hand, and that the day of judgment would arrive in their time. Some of these neglected their worldly duties. St. Paul wrote again to correct their error, which hindered the spread of the gospel. He had written agreeably to the words of the prophets of the Old Testament; and he tells them there were many counsels of the Most High yet to be fulfilled, before that day of the Lord should come, though, because it is sure, he had spoken of it as near. The subject led to a remarkable foretelling, of some of the future events which were to take place in the after-ages of the Christian church, and which show the prophetic spirit the apostle possessed.

2 THESSALONIANS 1

The apostle blesses God for the growing state of the love and patience of the Thessalonians. (1-4)
And encourages them to persevere under all their sufferings for Christ, considering his coming at the great day of account. (5-12)

1-4 Where there is the truth of grace, there will be an increase of it. The path of the just is as the shining light, which shines more and more unto the perfect day. And where there is the increase of grace, God must have all the glory. Where faith grows, love will abound, for faith works by love. It shows faith and patience, such as may be proposed as a pattern for others, when trials from God, and persecutions from men, quicken the exercise of those graces; for the patience and faith of which the apostle gloried, bore them up, and enabled them to endure all their tribulations.

5-10 Religion, if worth anything, is worth every thing; and those have no religion, or none worth having, or know not how to value it, cannot find their hearts to suffer for it. We cannot by all our sufferings, any more than by our services, merit heaven; but by our patience under sufferings, we are prepared for the promised joy. Nothing more strongly marks a man for eternal ruin, than a spirit of persecution and enmity to the name and people of God. God will trouble those that trouble his people. And there is a rest for the people of God; a rest from sin and sorrow. The certainty of future recompense is proved by the righteousness of God. The thoughts of this should be terrible to wicked men, and support the righteous. Faith, looking to the great day, is enabled partly to understand the book of providence, which appears confused to unbelievers. The Lord Jesus will in that day appear from heaven. He will come in the glory and power of the upper world. His light will be piercing, and his power consuming, to all who in that day shall be found as chaff.

ELECTION
Sermon number 41 delivered on September 2, 1855, at New Park Street Chapel, Southwark.

"But we are bound to give thanks always to God for you, brethren beloved of the Lord, because God hath from the beginning chosen you to salvation through sanctification of the Spirit and belief of the truth: Whereunto he called you by our gospel, to the obtaining of the glory of our Lord Jesus Christ."—2 Thessalonians 2:13-14.

I. First, I must try and prove that the doctrine is TRUE. And let me begin with an argumentum ad hominem; I will speak to you according to your different positions and stations. There are some of you who belong to the Church of England, and I am happy to see so many of you here. Though now and then I certainly say some very hard things about Church and State, yet I love the old Church, for she has in her communion many godly ministers and eminent saints. Now, I know you are great believers in what the Articles declare to be sound doctrine. I will give you a specimen of what they utter concerning election, so that if you believe them, you cannot avoid receiving election. I will read a portion of the 17th Article upon Predestination and Election:—

"Predestination to life is the everlasting purpose of God, whereby (before the foundations of the world were laid) he hast continually decreed by his counsel secret to us, to deliver from curse and damnation those whom he hath chosen in Christ out of mankind, and to bring them by Christ to everlasting salvation, as vessels made to honor. Wherefore they which be endued with so excellent a benefit of God be called according to God's purpose by his Spirit working in due season: they through grace obey the calling: they be justified freely: they be made sons of God by adoption: they be made like the image of his only-begotten Son Jesus Christ: they walk religiously in good works, and at length, by God's mercy, they attain to everlasting felicity."

It is no novelty, then, that I am preaching; no new doctrine. I love to proclaim these strong old doctrines, which are called by nickname Calvinism, but which are surely and verily the revealed truth of God as it is in Christ Jesus. By this truth I make a pilgrimage into the past, and as I go, I see father after father, confessor after confessor, martyr after martyr, standing up to shake hands with me. Were I a Pelagian, or a believer in the doctrine of free-will, I should have to walk for centuries all alone. Here and there a heretic of no very honorable character might rise up and call me brother. But taking these things to be the standard of my faith, I see the land of the ancients peopled with my brethren—I

the temple of God, shewing himself that he is God.

5 Remember ye not, that, when I was yet with you, I told you these things?

6 And now ye know what withholdeth that he might be revealed in his time.

7 For the mystery of iniquity doth already work: only he who now letteth will let, until he be taken out of the way.

8 And then shall that Wicked be revealed, whom the Lord shall consume with the spirit of his mouth, and shall destroy with the brightness of his coming:

9 Even him, whose coming is after the working of Satan with all power and signs and lying wonders,

10 And with all deceivableness of unrighteousness in them that perish; because they received not the love of the truth, that they might be saved.

11 And for this cause God shall send them strong delusion, that they should believe a lie:

12 That they all might be damned who believed not the truth, but had pleasure in unrighteousness.

13 But we are bound to give thanks alway to God for you, brethren beloved of the Lord, because God hath from the beginning chosen you to salvation through sanctification of the Spirit and belief of the truth:

14 Whereunto he called you by our gospel, to the obtaining of the glory of our Lord Jesus Christ.

15 Therefore, brethren, stand fast, and hold the traditions which ye have been taught, whether by word, or our epistle.

16 Now our Lord Jesus Christ himself, and God, even our Father, which hath loved us, and hath given us everlasting consolation and good hope through grace,

17 Comfort your hearts, and stablish you in every good word and work.

2 THESSALONIANS 3

1 Finally, brethren, pray for us, that the word of the Lord may have free course, and be glorified, even as it is with you:

2 And that we may be delivered from unreasonable and wicked men: for all men have not faith.

3 But the Lord is faithful, who shall stablish you, and keep you from evil.

4 And we have confidence in the Lord touching you, that ye both do and will do the things which we command you.

5 And the Lord direct your hearts into the love of God, and into the patient waiting for Christ.

6 Now we command you, brethren, in

And he is, too, properly styled, the son of perdition, as he has caused the death of numberless multitudes, both of his opposers and followers, destroyed innumerable souls, and will himself perish everlastingly. He it is that opposeth himself to the emperor, once his rightful sovereign; and that exalteth himself above all that is called God, or that is worshiped – Commanding angels, and putting kings under his feet, both of whom are called gods in scripture; claiming the highest power, the highest honor; suffering himself, not once only, to be styled God or vice-God. Indeed no less is implied in his ordinary title, "Most Holy Lord," or, "Most Holy Father." So that he sitteth – Enthroned. In the temple of God – Mentioned Rev. xi, 1. Declaring himself that he is God – Claiming the prerogatives which belong to God alone.

6. And now ye know – By what I told you when I was with you. That which restraineth – The power of the Roman emperors. When this is taken away, the wicked one will be revealed. In his time – His appointed season, and not before.

7. He will surely be revealed; for the mystery – The deep, secret power of iniquity, just opposite to the power of godliness, already worketh. It began with the love of honor, and the desire of power; and is completed in the entire subversion of the gospel of Christ. This mystery of iniquity is not wholly confined to the Romish church, but extends itself to others also. It seems to consist of,

1. Human inventions added to the written word.

2. Mere outside performances put in the room of faith and love.

3. Other mediators besides the man Christ Jesus. The two last branches, together with idolatry and bloodshed, are the direct consequences of the former; namely, the adding to the word of God. Already worketh – In the church. Only he that restraineth – That is, the potentate who successively has Rome in his power. The emperors, heathen or Christian; the kings, Goths or Lombards; the Carolingian or German emperors.

8. And then – When every prince and power that restrains is taken away. Will that wicked one – Emphatically so called, be revealed. Whom the Lord will soon consume with the spirit of his mouth – His immediate power. And destroy – With the very first appearance of his glory.

10. Because they received not the love of the truth – Therefore God suffered them to fall into that "strong delusion."

11. Therefore God shall send them – That is, judicially permit to come upon them, strong delusion.

12. That they all may be condemned – That is, the consequence of which will be, that they all will be condemned who believed not the truth, but had pleasure in unrighteousness – That is, who believed not the truth, because they loved sin.

13. God hath from the beginning – Of your hearing the gospel. Chosen you to salvation – Taken you out of the world, and placed you in the way to glory.

14. To which – Faith and holiness. He hath called you by our gospel – That which we preached, accompanied with the power of his Spirit.

15. Hold – Without adding to, or diminishing from, the traditions which ye have been taught – The truths which I have delivered to you. Whether by word or by our epistle – He preached before he wrote. And he had written concerning this in his former epistle.

MATTHEW HENRY

CHARLES H. SPURGEON

11,12 Believing thoughts and expectations of the second coming of Christ should lead us to pray to God more, for ourselves and others. If there is any good in us, it is owing to the good pleasure of his goodness, and therefore it is called grace.

2 THESSALONIANS 2

Cautions against the error that the time of Christ's coming was just at hand. There would first be a general apostasy from the faith, and a revealing of the antichristian man of sin. (1-4)
His destruction, and that of those who obey him. (5-12)
The security of the Thessalonians from apostasy; an exhortation to steadfastness, and prayer for them. (13-17)

1-4 If errors arise among Christians, we should set them right; and good men will be careful to suppress errors which rise from mistaking their words and actions. We have a cunning adversary, who watches to do mischief, and will promote errors, even by the words of Scripture. Whatever uncertainty we are in, or whatever mistakes may arise about the time of Christ's coming, that coming itself is certain.

5-12 Something hindered or withheld the man of sin. It is supposed to be the power of the Roman empire, which the apostle did not mention more plainly at that time. Corruption of doctrine and worship came in by degrees, and the usurping of power was gradual; thus the mystery of iniquity prevailed. Superstition and idolatry were advanced by pretended devotion, and bigotry and persecution were promoted by pretended zeal for God and his glory.

13-15 When we hear of the apostasy of many, it is a great comfort and joy, that there is a remnant according to the election of grace, which does and shall persevere; especially we should rejoice, if we have reason to hope that we are of that number. The preservation of the saints, is because God loved them with an everlasting love, from the beginning of the world. The end and the means must not be separated. Faith and holiness must be joined together as well as holiness and happiness. The outward call of God is by the gospel; and this is rendered effectual by the inward working of the Spirit.

16,17 We may and should direct our prayers, not only to God the Father, through our Lord Jesus Christ, but also to our Lord Jesus Christ himself. And we should pray in his name unto God, not only as his Father, but as our Father in and through him. The love of God in Christ Jesus, is the spring and fountain of all the good we have or hope for. There is good reason for strong consolations, because the saints have good hope through grace.

behold multitudes who confess the same as I do, and acknowledge that this is the religion of God's own church.

II. Thus I have tried to say something with regard to the truth of the doctrine of election. And now, briefly, let me say that election is ABSOLUTE: that is, it does not depend upon what we are. The text says, "God hath from the beginning chosen us unto salvation"; but our opponents say that God chooses people because they are good, that he chooses them on account of sundry works which they have done. Now, we ask in reply to this, what works are those on account of which God elects his people? Are they what we commonly call "works of law,"—works of obedience which the creature can render? If so, we reply to you— If men cannot be justified by the works of the law, it seems to us pretty clear that they cannot be elected by the works of the law: if they cannot be justified by their good deeds, they cannot be saved by them. Then the decree of election could not have been formed upon good works. "But," say others, "God elected them on the foresight of their faith." Now, God gives faith, therefore he could not have elected them on account of faith, which he foresaw. Faith is the gift of God. Every virtue comes from him. Therefore it cannot have caused him to elect men, because it is his gift. Election, we are sure, is absolute, and altogether apart from the virtues which the saints have afterwards. What though a saint should be as holy and devout as Paul; what though he should be as bold as Peter, or as loving as John, yet he would claim nothing from his Maker. I never knew a saint yet of any denomination, who thought that God saved him because he foresaw that he would have these virtues and merits. Now, my brethren, the best jewels that the saint ever wears, if they be jewels of his own fashioning, are not of the first water. There is something of earth mixed with them. The highest grace we ever possess has something of earthliness about it. We feel this when we are most refined, when we are most sanctified, and our language must always be—
"I the chief of sinners am;
Jesus died for me."
Our only hope, our only plea, still hangs on grace as exhibited in the person of Jesus Christ. And I am sure we must utterly reject and disregard all thought that our graces, which are gifts of our Lord, which are his right-hand planting, could have ever caused his love.

III. Then, thirdly, this election is ETERNAL. "God hath from the beginning chosen you unto eternal life." Can any man tell me when the beginning was? Years ago we thought the beginning of this world was when Adam came upon it; but

the name of our Lord Jesus Christ, that ye withdraw yourselves from every brother that walketh disorderly, and not after the tradition which he received of us.

7 For yourselves know how ye ought to follow us: for we behaved not ourselves disorderly among you;

8 Neither did we eat any man's bread for nought; but wrought with labor and travail night and day, that we might not be chargeable to any of you:

9 Not because we have not power, but to make ourselves an ensample unto you to follow us.

10 For even when we were with you, this we commanded you, that if any would not work, neither should he eat.

11 For we hear that there are some which walk among you disorderly, working not at all, but are busybodies.

12 Now them that are such we command and exhort by our Lord Jesus Christ, that with quietness they work, and eat their own bread.

13 But ye, brethren, be not weary in well doing.

14 And if any man obey not our word by this epistle, note that man, and have no company with him, that he may be ashamed.

15 Yet count him not as an enemy, but admonish him as a brother.

16 Now the Lord of peace himself give you peace always by all means. The Lord be with you all.

17 The salutation of Paul with mine own hand, which is the token in every epistle: so I write.

18 The grace of our Lord Jesus Christ be with you all. Amen.

2 THESSALONIANS 3

1. May run – Go on swiftly, without any interruption. And be glorified – Acknowledged as divine, and bring forth much fruit.

2. All men have not faith – And all men who have not are more or less unreasonable and wicked men.

3. Who will establish you – That cleave to him by faith. And guard you from the evil one – And all his instruments.

4. We trust in the Lord concerning you – Thus only should we trust in any man.

5. Now the Lord – The Spirit, whose proper work this is. Direct – Lead you straight forward. Into the patience of Christ – Of which he set you a pattern.

6. That walketh disorderly – Particularly by not working. Not according to the tradition he received of us – The admonition we gave, both by word of mouth, and in our former epistle.

10. Neither let him eat – Do not maintain him in idleness.

11. Doing nothing, but being busybodies – To which idleness naturally disposes.

12. Work quietly – Letting the concerns of other people alone.

14. Have no company with him – No intimacy, no familiarity, no needless correspondence.

15. Admonish him as a brother – Tell him lovingly of the reason why you shun him.

16. The Lord of peace – Christ. Give you peace by all means – In every way and manner.

2 THESSALONIANS 3

The apostle expresses confidence in the Thess-
alonians, and prays for them. (1-5)
He charges them to withdraw from disorderly walkers,
particularly from the lazy and busybodies. (6-15)
And concludes with a prayer for them, and a greeting.
(16-18)

1-5 Those who are far apart still may meet together
at the throne of grace; and those not able to do or
receive any other kindness, may in this way do and
receive real and very great kindness. Enemies to the
preaching of the gospel, and persecutors of its faithful preachers, are unreasonable and wicked men.
Many do not believe the gospel; and no wonder if
such are restless and show malice in their endeavors
to oppose it. The evil of sin is the greatest evil, but
there are other evils we need to be preserved from,
and we have encouragement to depend upon the
grace of God. When once the promise is made, the
performance is sure and certain.

6-15 Those who have received the gospel, are to live
according to the gospel. Such as could work, and
would not, were not to be maintained in idleness.
Christianity is not to countenance slothfulness, which
would consume what is meant to encourage the
industrious, and to support the sick and afflicted.
Industry in our callings as men, is a duty required by
our calling as Christians. But some expected to be
maintained in idleness, and indulged a curious and
conceited temper. They meddled with the concerns
of others, and did much harm. It is a great error and
abuse of religion, to make it a cloak for idleness or
any other sin. The servant who waits for the coming
of his Lord aright, must be working as his Lord has
commanded.

16-18 The apostle prays for the Thessalonians. And
let us desire the same blessings for ourselves and
our friends. Peace with God. This peace is desired for
them always, or in every thing. Peace by all means; in
every way; that, as they enjoyed the means of grace,
they might use all methods to secure peace.

we have discovered that thousands of years
before that God was preparing chaotic matter to
make it a fit abode for man, putting races of
creatures upon it, who might die and leave
behind the marks of his handiwork and marvelous skill, before he tried his hand on man. But
that was not the beginning, for revelation points
us to a period long ere this world was fashioned,
to the days when the morning stars were begotten; when, like drops of dew, from the fingers of
the morning, stars and constellations fell trickling
from the hand of God; when, by his own lips, he
launched forth ponderous orbs; when with his
own hand he sent comets, like thunderbolts,
wandering through the sky, to find one day their
proper sphere. We go back to years gone by,
when worlds were made and systems fashioned,
but we have not even approached the beginning
yet. Until we go to the time when all the universe
slept in the mind of God as yet unborn, until we
enter the eternity where God the Creator lived
alone, everything sleeping within him, all creation resting in his mighty gigantic thought, we
have not guessed the beginning.

Our election then is eternal. I will not stop to
prove it, I only just run over these thoughts for
the benefit of young beginners, that they may
understand what we mean by eternal, absolute
election.

IV. And, next, the election is PERSONAL. Here
again, our opponents have tried to overthrow
election by telling us that it is an election of
nations, and not of people. But here the Apostle
says, "God hath from the beginning chosen you."

Election then is personal: it must be so. Every
one who reads this text, and others like it, will
see that Scripture continually speaks of God's
people one by one and speaks of them as having
been the special subjects of election.

Dost thou say, "I feel that I am lost; I deserve
it; and that if my brother is saved I cannot murmur. If God destroy me, I deserve it, but if he
saves the person sitting beside me, he has a right
to do what he will with his own, and I have lost
nothing by it." Can you say that honestly from
your heart? If so, then the doctrine of election
has had its right effect on your spirit, and you are
not far from the kingdom of heaven. You are
brought where you ought to be, where the Spirit
wants you to be; and being so this morning,
depart in peace; God has forgiven your sins. You
would not feel that if you were not pardoned;
you would not feel that if the Spirit of God were
not working in you. Rejoice, then, in this. Let
your hope rest on the cross of Christ. Think not
on election but on Christ Jesus. Rest on Jesus—
Jesus first, midst, and without end.

1 Timothy

1 TIMOTHY 1

1 Paul, an apostle of Jesus Christ by the commandment of God our Savior, and Lord Jesus Christ, which is our hope;

2 Unto Timothy, my own son in the faith: Grace, mercy, and peace, from God our Father and Jesus Christ our Lord.

3 As I besought thee to abide still at Ephesus, when I went into Macedonia, that thou mightest charge some that they teach no other doctrine,

4 Neither give heed to fables and endless genealogies, which minister questions, rather than godly edifying which is in faith: so do.

5 Now the end of the commandment is charity out of a pure heart, and of a good conscience, and of faith unfeigned:

6 From which some having swerved have turned aside unto vain jangling;

7 Desiring to be teachers of the law; understanding neither what they say, nor whereof they affirm.

8 But we know that the law is good, if a man use it lawfully;

9 Knowing this, that the law is not made for a righteous man, but for the lawless and disobedient, for the ungodly and for sinners, for unholy and profane, for murderers of fathers and murderers of mothers, for manslayers,

10 For whoremongers, for them that defile themselves with mankind, for menstealers, for liars, for perjured persons, and if there be any other thing that is contrary to sound doctrine;

11 According to the glorious gospel of the blessed God, which was committed to my trust.

12 And I thank Christ Jesus our Lord, who hath enabled me, for that he counted me faithful, putting me into the ministry;

13 Who was before a blasphemer, and a persecutor, and injurious: but I obtained mercy, because I did it ignorantly in unbelief.

14 And the grace of our Lord was exceeding abundant with faith and love which is in Christ Jesus.

15 This is a faithful saying, and worthy of all acceptation, that Christ Jesus came into the world to save sinners; of whom I am chief.

16 Howbeit for this cause I obtained mercy, that in me first Jesus Christ might shew forth all longsuffering, for a pattern to them which should

THE mother of Timothy was a Jewess, but his father was a Gentile. He was converted to Christianity very early; and while he was yet but a youth, was taken by St. Paul to assist him in the work of the gospel, chiefly in watering the churches which he had planted. Though St. Paul styles him his "own son in the faith," yet he does not appear to have been converted by the apostle; but only to have been exceeding dear to him, who had established him therein; and whom he had diligently and faithfully served, like a son with his father in the gospel. Phil. ii, 22.

1 TIMOTHY 1

1. Paul an apostle – Familiarity is to be set aside where the things of God are concerned. According to the commandment of God – The authoritative appointment of God the Father. Our Savior – So styled in many other places likewise, as being the grand orderer of the whole scheme of our salvation. And Christ our hope – That is, the author, object, and ground, of all our hope.

2. Grace, mercy, peace – St. Paul wishes grace and peace in his epistles to the churches. To Timotheus he adds mercy, the most tender grace towards those who stand in need of it. The experience of this prepares a man to be a minister of the gospel.

3. Charge some to teach no other doctrine – Than I have taught. Let them put nothing in the place of it, add nothing to it.

4. Neither give heed – So as either to teach or regard them. To fables – Fabulous Jewish traditions. And endless genealogies – Not those delivered in scripture, but the long intricate pedigrees whereby they strove to prove their descent from such or such a person. Which afford questions – Which lead only to useless and endless controversies.

5. Whereas the end of the commandment – of the whole Christian institution. Is love – And this was particularly the end of the commandment which Timotheus was to enforce at Ephesus, ver. 3, 18. The foundation is faith; the end, love. But this can only subsist in an heart purified by faith, and is always attended with a good conscience.

6. From which – Love and a good conscience. Some are turned aside – An affectation of high and extensive knowledge sets a man at the greatest distance from faith, and all sense of divine things. To vain jangling – And of all vanities, none are more vain than dry, empty disputes on the things of God.

7. Understanding neither the very things they speak, nor the subject they speak of.

8. We grant the whole Mosaic law is good, answers excellent purposes, if a man use it in a proper manner. Even the ceremonial is good, as it points to Christ; and the moral law is holy, just, and good, on its own nature; and of admirable use both to convince unbelievers, and to guide believers in all holiness.

9. The law doth not lie against a righteous man – Doth not strike or condemn him. But against the lawless and disobedient – They who despise the authority of the lawgiver violate the first commandment, which is the foundation of the law, and the ground of all obedience.

10. Manstealers – The worst of all thieves, in comparison of whom, highwaymen and housebreakers are innocent. What then are most traders in Negroes, procurers of servants for America, and all who list soldiers by lies, tricks, or enticements?

11. According to the glorious gospel – Which, far from "making void," does effectually "establish, the law."

12. I thank Christ, who hath enabled me, in that he accounted me faithful, having put me into the ministry – The meaning is, I thank him for putting

MATTHEW HENRY

CHARLES H. SPURGEON

The design of the epistle appears to be, that Timothy having been left at Ephesus, St. Paul wrote to instruct him in the choice of proper officers in the church, as well as in the exercise of a regular ministry. Also, to caution against the influence of false teachers, who by subtle distinctions and endless disputes, corrupted the purity and simplicity of the gospel. He presses upon him constant regard to the greatest diligence, faithfulness, and zeal. These subjects occupy the first four chapters; the fifth chapter instructs respecting particular classes; in the latter part, controversies and disputes are condemned, the love of money blamed, and the rich exhorted to good works.

1 TIMOTHY 1

The apostle salutes Timothy. (1-4)
The design of the law as given by Moses. (5-11)
Of his own conversion and call to the apostleship. (12-17)
The obligation to maintain faith and a good conscience. (18-20)

1-4 Jesus Christ is a Christian's hope; all our hopes of eternal life are built upon him; and Christ is in us the hope of glory. The apostle seems to have been the means of Timothy's conversion; who served with him in his ministry, as a dutiful son with a loving father. That which raises questions, is not for edifying; that which gives occasion for doubtful disputes, pulls down the church rather than builds it up. Godliness of heart and life can only be kept up and increased, by the exercise of faith in the truths and promises of God, through Jesus Christ.

5-11 Whatever tends to weaken love to God, or love to the brethren, tends to defeat the end of the commandment. The design of the gospel is answered, when sinners, through repentance towards God and faith in Jesus Christ, are brought to exercise Christian love. And as believers were righteous persons in God's appointed way, the law was not against them. But unless we are made righteous by faith in Christ, really repenting and forsaking sin, we are yet under the curse of the law, even according to the gospel of the blessed God, and are unfit to share the holy happiness of heaven.

12-17 The apostle knew that he would justly have perished, if the Lord had been extreme to mark what was amiss; and also if his grace and mercy had not been abundant to him when dead in sin, working faith and love to Christ in his heart. This is a faithful saying; these are true and faithful words, which may be depended on, That the Son of God came into the world, willingly and purposely to save sinners. No man, with Paul's example before him, can question the love and power of Christ to save him, if he really desires to trust in him as the Son of God, who once

SALVATION BY KNOWING THE TRUTH
Sermon number 1516 delivered at the Metropolitan Tabernacle, Newington.

"God our Savior; who will have all men to be saved, and to come unto the knowledge of the truth."—1 Timothy 2:3, 4.

Here is our proposition: IT IS BY A KNOWLEDGE OF THE TRUTH THAT MEN ARE SAVED.

Observe that stress is laid upon the article: it is the truth, and not every truth. Though it is a good thing to know the truth about anything, and we ought not to be satisfied to take up with a falsehood upon any point, yet it is not every truth that will save us. We are not saved by knowing any one theological truth we may choose to think of, for there are some theological truths which are comparatively of inferior value. They are not vital or essential, and a man may know them, and yet may not be saved. It is the truth which saves. Jesus Christ is the truth: the whole testimony of God about Christ is the truth. The work of the Holy Ghost in the heart is to work in us the truth. The knowledge of the truth is a large knowledge. It is not always so at the first: it may begin with but a little knowledge, but it is a large knowledge when it is further developed, and the soul is fully instructed in the whole range of the truth.

This knowledge of the grand facts which are here called the truth saves men, and we will notice its mode of operation. Very often it begins its work in a man by arousing him, and thus it saves him from carelessness. He did not know anything about the truth which God has revealed, and so he lived like a brute beast. If he had enough to eat and to drink he was satisfied. If he laid by a little money he was delighted. So long as the days passed pretty merrily, and he was free from aches and pains, he was satisfied. He heard about religion, but he thought it did not concern him. He supposed that there were some people who might be the better for thinking about it, but as far as he was concerned, he thought no more about God or godliness than the ox of the stall or the ostrich of the desert. Well, the truth came to him, and he received a knowledge of it. He knew only a part, and that a very dark and gloomy part of it, but it stirred him out of his carelessness, for he suddenly discovered that he was under the wrath of God. Perhaps he heard a sermon, or read a tract, or had a practical word addressed to him by some Christian friend, and he found out enough to know that "he that believeth not is condemned already, because he hath not believed on the Son of God." That startled him. "God is angry with the wicked every day:"—that amazed him.

hereafter believe on him to life everlasting.

17 Now unto the King eternal, immortal, invisible, the only wise God, be honor and glory for ever and ever. Amen.

18 This charge I commit unto thee, son Timothy, according to the prophecies which went before on thee, that thou by them mightest war a good warfare;

19 Holding faith, and a good conscience; which some having put away concerning faith have made shipwreck:

20 Of whom is Hymeneus and Alexander; whom I have delivered unto Satan, that they may learn not to blaspheme.

1 TIMOTHY 2

1 I exhort therefore, that, first of all, supplications, prayers, intercessions, and giving of thanks, be made for all men;

2 For kings, and for all that are in authority; that we may lead a quiet and peaceable life in all godliness and honesty.

3 For this is good and acceptable in the sight of God our Savior;

4 Who will have all men to be saved, and to come unto the knowledge of the truth.

5 For there is one God, and one mediator between God and men, the man Christ Jesus;

6 Who gave himself a ransom for all, to be testified in due time.

7 Whereunto I am ordained a preacher, and an apostle, (I speak the truth in Christ, and lie not;) a teacher of the Gentiles in faith and verity.

8 I will therefore that men pray every where, lifting up holy hands, without wrath and doubting.

9 In like manner also, that women adorn themselves in modest apparel, with shamefacedness and sobriety; not with braided hair, or gold, or pearls, or costly array;

10 But (which becometh women professing godliness) with good works.

11 Let the woman learn in silence with all subjection.

12 But I suffer not a woman to teach, nor to usurp authority over the man, but to be in silence.

13 For Adam was first formed, then Eve.

14 And Adam was not deceived, but

me into the ministry, and enabling me to be faithful therein.

13. A blasphemer – Of Christ. A persecutor – Of his church. A reviler – Of his doctrine and people. But I obtained mercy – He does not say, because I was unconditionally elected; but because I did it in ignorance. Not that his ignorance took away his sin; but it left him capable of mercy; which he would hardly have been, had he acted thus contrary to his own conviction.

14. And the grace – Whereby I obtained mercy. Was exceeding abundant with faith – Opposite to my preceding unbelief. And love – Opposite to my blasphemy, persecution, and oppression.

15. This is a faithful saying – A most solemn preface. And worthy of all acceptation – Well deserving to be accepted, received, embraced, with all the faculties of our whole soul. That Christ – Promised. Jesus – Exhibited. Came into the world to save sinners – All sinners, without exception.

16. For this cause God showed me mercy, that all his longsuffering might be shown, and that none might hereafter despair.

17. The King of eternity – A phrase frequent with the Hebrews. How unspeakably sweet is the thought of eternity to believers!

18. This charge I commit to thee – That thou mayest deliver it to the church. According to the prophecies concerning thee – Uttered when thou wast received as an evangelist, chap. iv, 14; probably by many persons, chap. vi, 12; that, being encouraged by them, thou mightest war the good warfare.

19. Holding fast faith – Which is as a most precious liquor. And a good conscience – Which is as a clean glass. Which – Namely, a good conscience. Some having thrust away – It goes away unwillingly it always says, "Do not hurt me." And they who retain this do not make shipwreck of their faith.

20. Whom – Though absent. I have delivered to Satan, that they may learn not to blaspheme – That by what they suffer they may be in some measure restrained, if they will not repent.

1 TIMOTHY 2

1. I exhort therefore – Seeing God is so gracious. In this chapter he gives directions,

1. With regard to public prayers.

2. With regard to doctrine. Supplication is here the imploring help in time of need: prayer is any kind of offering up our desires to God. But true prayer is the vehemence of holy zeal, the ardor of divine love, arising from a calm, undisturbed soul, moved upon by the Spirit of God.

2. For all that are in authority – Seeing even the lowest country magistrates frequently do much good or much harm. God supports the power of magistracy for the sake of his own people, when, in the present state of men, it could not otherwise be kept up in any nation whatever.

3. For this – That we pray for all men. Do you ask, "Why are not more converted?" We do not pray enough. Is acceptable in the sight of God our Savior – Who has actually saved us that believe, and willeth all men to be saved. It is strange that any whom he has actually saved should doubt the universality of his grace!

4. Who willeth seriously all men – Not a part only, much less the smallest part. To be saved – Eternally. This is treated of, ver. 5, 6. And, in order thereto, to come – They are not compelled. To the knowledge of the truth – Which brings salvation. This is treated of, ver. 6, 7.

5. For – The fourth verse is proved by the fifth; the first, by the fourth. There is one God – And they who have not him, through the one Mediator, have no God. One mediator also – We could not rejoice that there is a God, were there not a mediator also; one who stands between God and men, to reconcile man to God, and to transact the whole affair of our salvation.

MATTHEW HENRY

CHARLES H. SPURGEON

died on the cross, and now reigns upon the throne of glory, to save all that come to God through him. Let us then admire and praise the grace of God our Savior; and ascribe to the Father, Son, and Holy Ghost, three Persons in the unity of the Godhead, the glory of all done in, by, and for us.

18-20 The ministry is a warfare against sin and Satan; carried on under the Lord Jesus, who is the Captain of our salvation. The good hopes others have had of us, should stir us up to duty. And let us be upright in our conduct in all things. The design of the highest censures in the primitive church, was, to prevent further sin, and to reclaim the sinner. May all who are tempted to put away a good conscience, and to abuse the gospel, remember that this is the way to make shipwreck of faith also.

1 TIMOTHY 2

Prayer to be made for all persons, since the grace of the gospel makes no difference of ranks or stations. (1-7)
How men and women ought to behave, both in their religious and common life. (8-15)

1-7 The disciples of Christ must be praying people; all, without distinction of nation, sect, rank, or party. Our duty as Christians, is summed up in two words; godliness, that is, the right worshiping of God; and honesty, that is, good conduct toward all men. These must go together: we are not truly honest, if we are not godly, and do not render to God his due; and we are not truly godly, if not honest. What is acceptable in the sight of God our Savior, we should abound in. There is one Mediator, and that Mediator gave himself a ransom for all. And this appointment has been made for the benefit of the Jews and the Gentiles of every nation; that all who are willing may come in this way, to the mercy-seat of a pardoning God, to seek reconciliation with him.

8-15 Under the gospel, prayer is not to be confined to any one particular house of prayer, but men must pray every where. We must pray in our closets, pray in our families, pray at our meals, pray when we are on journeys, and pray in the solemn assemblies, whether more public or private. We must pray in charity; without wrath, or malice, or anger at any person. We must pray in faith, without doubting, and without disputing.

1 TIMOTHY 3

The qualifications and behavior of gospel bishops. (1-7)
And of deacons and their wives. (8-13)
The reason of writing about these, and other church affairs. (14-16)

He had not thought of it, perhaps had not known it, but when he did know it, he could rest no longer. Then he came to a knowledge of this farther truth, that after death there would be a judgment, that he would rise again, and that, being risen, he would have to stand before the judgment-seat of God to give an account of the things which he had done in the body. This came home very strikingly to him. Perhaps, also, such a text as this flamed forth before him,— "For every idle word that man shall speak he must give an account in the day of judgment." His mind began to foresee that last tremendous day, when on the clouds of heaven Christ will come and summon quick and dead, to answer at his judgment-seat for the whole of their lives. He did not know that before, but, knowing it, it startled and aroused him. I have known men, when first they have come to a knowledge of this truth, become unable to sleep. They have started up in the night. They have asked those who were with them to help them to pray. The next day they have been scarcely able to mind their business, for a dreadful sound has been in their ears. They feared lest they should stumble into the grave and into hell. Thus they were saved from carelessness. They could not go back to be the mere brute beasts they were before. Their eyes had been opened to futurity and eternity. Their spirits had been quickened—at least so much that they could not rest in that doltish, dull, dead carelessness in which they had formerly been found. They were shaken out of their deadly lethargy by a knowledge of the truth.

The truth is useful to a man in another way: it saves him from prejudice. Often when men are awakened to know something about the wrath of God they begin to plunge about to discover divers methods by which they may escape from that wrath. Consulting, first of all, with themselves, they think that, if they can reform— give up their grosser sins, and if they can join with religious people, they will make it all right. And there are some who go and listen to a kind of religious teacher, who says, "You must do good works. You must earn a good character. You must add to all this the ceremonies of our church. You must be particular and precise in receiving blessing only through the appointed channel of the apostolic succession." Of the aforesaid mystical succession this teacher has the effrontery to assure his dupe that he is a legitimate instrument; and that sacraments received at his hands are means of grace. Under such untruthful notions we have known people who were somewhat aroused sit down again in a false peace. They have done all that they judged right and attended to all that they were

the woman being deceived was in the transgression.

15 Notwithstanding she shall be saved in childbearing, if they continue in faith and charity and holiness with sobriety.

1 TIMOTHY 3

1 This is a true saying, If a man desire the office of a bishop, he desireth a good work.

2 A bishop then must be blameless, the husband of one wife, vigilant, sober, of good behavior, given to hospitality, apt to teach;

3 Not given to wine, no striker, not greedy of filthy lucre; but patient, not a brawler, not covetous;

4 One that ruleth well his own house, having his children in subjection with all gravity;

5 (For if a man know not how to rule his own house, how shall he take care of the church of God?)

6 Not a novice, lest being lifted up with pride he fall into the condemnation of the devil.

7 Moreover he must have a good report of them which are without; lest he fall into reproach and the snare of the devil.

8 Likewise must the deacons be grave, not doubletongued, not given to much wine, not greedy of filthy lucre;

9 Holding the mystery of the faith in a pure conscience.

10 And let these also first be proved; then let them use the office of a deacon, being found blameless.

11 Even so must their wives be grave, not slanderers, sober, faithful in all things.

12 Let the deacons be the husbands of one wife, ruling their children and their own houses well.

13 For they that have used the office of a deacon well purchase to themselves a good degree, and great boldness in the faith which is in Christ Jesus.

14 These things write I unto thee, hoping to come unto thee shortly:

15 But if I tarry long, that thou mayest know how thou oughtest to behave thyself in the house of God, which is the church of the living God, the pillar and ground of the truth.

16 And without controversy great is the mystery of godliness: God was manifest in the flesh, justified in the Spirit, seen of angels, preached unto

6. Who gave himself a ransom for all – Such a ransom, the word signifies, wherein a like or equal is given; as an eye for an eye, or life for life: and this ransom, from the dignity of the person redeeming, was more than equivalent to all mankind. To be testified of in due season – Literally, in his own seasons; those chosen by his own wisdom.

8. I will – A word strongly expressing his apostolic authority.

9. With sobriety – Which, in St. Paul's sense, is the virtue which governs our whole life according to true wisdom.

12. To usurp authority over the man – By public teaching.

13. First – So that woman was originally the inferior.

14. And Adam was not deceived – The serpent deceived Eve: Eve did not deceive Adam, but persuaded him. "Thou hast hearkened unto the voice of thy wife," Gen. iii, 17. The preceding verse showed why a woman should not "usurp authority over the man." this shows why she ought not "to teach." She is more easily deceived, and more easily deceives.

15. Yet she – That is, women in general, who were all involved with Eve in the sentence pronounced, Gen. iii, 16. Shall be saved in childbearing – Carried safe through the pain and danger which that sentence entails upon them for the transgression; yea, and finally saved, if they continue in loving faith and holy wisdom.

1 TIMOTHY 3

1. He desireth a good work – An excellent, but laborious, employment.

2. Therefore – That he may be capable of it. A bishop – Or pastor of a congregation. Must be blameless – Without fault or just suspicion. The husband of one wife – This neither means that a bishop must be married, nor that he may not marry a second wife; which it is just as lawful for him to do as to marry a first, and may in some cases be his bounden duty. But whereas polygamy and divorce on slight occasions were common both among the Jews and heathens, it teaches us that ministers, of all others, ought to stand clear of those sins.

4. Having his children in subjection with all seriousness – For levity undermines all domestic authority; and this direction, by a parity of reason, belongs to all parents.

6. Lest being puffed up – With this new honor, or with the applause which frequently follows it. He fall into the condemnation of the devil – The same into which the devil fell.

7. He ought also to have a good report – To have had a fair character in time past. From them that are without – That are not Christians. Lest he fall into reproach – By their rehearsing his former life, which might discourage and prove a snare to him.

8. Likewise the deacons must be serious – Men of a grave, decent, venerable behavior. But where are presbyters? Were this order essentially distinct from that of bishops, could the apostle have passed it over in silence? Not desirous of filthy gain – With what abhorrence does he everywhere speak of this!

9. Holding fast the faith in a pure conscience – Steadfast in faith, holy in heart and life.

10. Let these be proved first – Let a trial be made how they believe. Then let them minister – Let them be fixed in that office.

11. Faithful in all things – Both to God, their husbands, and the poor.

13. They purchase a good degree – Or step, toward some higher office. And much boldness – From the testimony of a good conscience.

15. That thou mayest know how to behave – This is the scope of the epistle. In the house of God – Who is the master of the family. Which is – As if he had said, By the house of God, I mean the church.

MATTHEW HENRY

CHARLES H. SPURGEON

1-7 If a man desired the pastoral office, and from love to Christ, and the souls of men, was ready to deny himself, and undergo hardships by devoting himself to that service, he sought to be employed in a good work, and his desire should be approved, provided he was qualified for the office. A minister must give as little occasion for blame as can be, lest he bring reproach upon his office. He must be sober, temperate, moderate in all his actions, and in the use of all creature-comforts. Sobriety and watchfulness are put together in Scripture, they assist one the other.

8-13 The deacons were at first appointed to distribute the charity of the church, and to manage its concerns, yet pastors and evangelists were among them. The deacons had a great trust reposed in them. They must be grave, serious, prudent men. It is not fit that public trusts should be lodged in the hands of any, till they are found fit for the business with which they are to be trusted. All who are related to ministers, must take great care to walk as becomes the gospel of Christ.

14-16 The church is the house of God; he dwells there. The church holds forth the Scripture and the doctrine of Christ, as a pillar holds forth a proclamation. When a church ceases to be the pillar and ground of truth, we may and ought to forsake her; for our regard to truth should be first and greatest. The mystery of godliness is Christ. He is God, who was made flesh, and was manifest in the flesh. God was pleased to manifest himself to man, by his own Son taking the nature of man. Though reproached as a sinner, and put to death as a malefactor, Christ was raised again by the Spirit, and so was justified from all the false charges with which he was loaded. Angels ministered to him, for he is the Lord of angels. The Gentiles welcomed the gospel which the Jews rejected. Let us remember that God was manifest in the flesh, to take away our sins, to redeem us from all iniquity, and to purify unto himself a peculiar people, zealous of good works. These doctrines must be shown forth by the fruits of the Spirit in our lives.

1 TIMOTHY 4

Of departures from the faith that began already to appear. (1-5)

Several directions, with motives for due discharge of duties. (6-16)

1-5 The Holy Spirit, both in the Old and the New Testament, spoke of a general turning from the faith of Christ, and the pure worship of God. This should come during the Christian dispensation, for those are called the latter days. False teachers forbid as evil what God has allowed, and command as a duty what he has left indifferent. We find exercise for watchfulness and self-denial, in attending to the requirements

told. Suddenly, by God's grace, they come to a knowledge of another truth, and that is that by the deeds of the law there shall no flesh be justified in the sight of God. They discover that salvation is not by works of the law or by ceremonies, and that if any man be under the law he is also under the curse. Such a text as the following comes home, "Not of blood, nor of the will of the flesh, nor of the will of man, but of God"; and such another text as this, "Ye must be born again," and then this at the back of it—"that which is born of the flesh is flesh, and that which is born of the Spirit is spirit." When they also find out that there is necessary a righteousness better than their own—a perfect righteousness to justify them before God, and when they discover that they must be made new creatures in Christ Jesus, or else they must utterly perish, then they are saved from false confidences, saved from crying, "Peace, peace," when there is no peace. It is a grand thing when a knowledge of the truth stops us from trusting in a lie. I am addressing some who remember when they were saved in that way. What an opening of the eyes it was to you! You had a great prejudice against the gospel of grace and the plan of salvation by faith; but when the Lord took you in hand and made you see your beautiful righteousness to be a moth-eaten mass of rags, and when the gold that you had accumulated suddenly turned into so much brass, cankered, and good for nothing,—when you stood stripped naked before God, and the poor cobwebs of ceremonies suddenly dropped from off you, oh, then the Lord was working his salvation in your soul, and you were being saved from false confidences by a knowledge of the truth.

Moreover, it often happens that a knowledge of the truth stands a man in good stead for another purpose; it saves him from despair. Unable to be careless, and unable to find comfort in false confidences, some poor agitated minds are driven into a wide and stormy sea without rudder or compass, with nothing but wreck before them. "There is no hope for me," says the man. "I perceive I cannot save myself. I see that I am lost. I am dead in trespasses and sins, and cannot stir hand or foot. Surely now I may as well go on in sin, and even multiply my transgressions. The gate of mercy is shut against me; what is the use of fear where there is no room for hope?" At such a time, if the Lord leads the man to a knowledge of the truth, he perceives that though his sins be as scarlet they shalt be as wool, and though they be red like crimson they shall be as white as snow. That precious doctrine of substitution comes in—that Christ stood in the stead of the sinner, that the

the Gentiles, believed on in the world, received up into glory.

1 TIMOTHY 4

1 Now the Spirit speaketh expressly, that in the latter times some shall depart from the faith, giving heed to seducing spirits, and doctrines of devils;

2 Speaking lies in hypocrisy; having their conscience seared with a hot iron;

3 Forbidding to marry, and commanding to abstain from meats, which God hath created to be received with thanksgiving of them which believe and know the truth.

4 For every creature of God is good, and nothing to be refused, if it be received with thanksgiving:

5 For it is sanctified by the word of God and prayer.

6 If thou put the brethren in remembrance of these things, thou shalt be a good minister of Jesus Christ, nourished up in the words of faith and of good doctrine, whereunto thou hast attained.

7 But refuse profane and old wives' fables, and exercise thyself rather unto godliness.

8 For bodily exercise profiteth little: but godliness is profitable unto all things, having promise of the life that now is, and of that which is to come.

9 This is a faithful saying and worthy of all acceptation.

10 For therefore we both labor and suffer reproach, because we trust in the living God, who is the Savior of all men, specially of those that believe.

11 These things command and teach.

12 Let no man despise thy youth; but be thou an example of the believers, in word, in conversation, in charity, in spirit, in faith, in purity.

13 Till I come, give attendance to reading, to exhortation, to doctrine.

14 Neglect not the gift that is in thee, which was given thee by prophecy, with the laying on of the hands of the presbytery.

15 Meditate upon these things; give thyself wholly to them; that thy profiting may appear to all.

16 Take heed unto thyself, and unto the doctrine; continue in them: for in doing this thou shalt both save thyself, and them that hear thee.

16. The mystery of godliness – Afterwards specified in six articles, which sum up the whole economy of Christ upon earth.

1 TIMOTHY 4

1. But the Spirit saith – By St. Paul himself to the Thessalonians, and probably by other contemporary prophets. Expressly – As concerning a thing of great moment, and soon to be fulfilled. That in the latter times – These extend from our Lord's ascension till his coming to judgment. Some – Yea, many, and by degrees the far greater part. Will depart from the faith – The doctrine once delivered to the saints. Giving heed to seducing spirits – Who inspire false prophets.

2. These will depart from the faith, by the hypocrisy of them that speak lies, having their own consciences as senseless and unfeeling as flesh that is seared with an hot iron.

3. Forbidding priests, monks, and nuns to marry, and commanding all men to abstain from such and such meats at such and such times. Which God hath created to be received by them that know the truth – That all meats are now clean. With thanksgiving – Which supposes a pure conscience.

5. It is sanctified by the word of God – Creating all, and giving it to man for food. And by prayer – The children of God are to pray for the sanctification of all the creatures which they use. And not only the Christians, but even the Jews, yea, the very heathens used to consecrate their table by prayer.

7. Like those who were to contend in the Grecian games, exercise thyself unto godliness – Train thyself up in holiness of heart and life, with the utmost labor, vigor, and diligence.

8. Bodily exercise profiteth a little – Increases the health and strength of the body.

10. Therefore – Animated by this promise. We both labor and suffer reproach – We regard neither pleasure, ease, nor honor. Because we trust – For this very thing the world will hate us. In the living God – Who will give us the life he has promised. Who is the Savior of all men – Preserving them in this life, and willing to save them eternally. But especially – In a more eminent manner. Of them that believe – And so are saved everlastingly.

12. Let no one have reason to despise thee for thy youth. To prevent this, Be a pattern in word – Public and private. In spirit – In your whole temper. In faith – When this is placed in the midst of several other Christian graces, it generally means a particular branch of it; fidelity or faithfulness.

13. Give thyself to reading – Both publicly and privately. Enthusiasts, observe this! Expect no end without the means.

14. Neglect not – They neglect it who do not exercise it to the full. The gift – Of feeding the flock, of power, and love, and sobriety. Which was given thee by prophecy – By immediate direction from God. By the laying on of my hands – 2 Tim. i, 6; while the elders joined also in the solemnity. This presbytery probably consisted of some others, together with Paul and Silas.

15. Meditate – The Bible makes no distinction between this and to contemplate, whatever others do.

16. Continue in them – In all the preceding advices.

1 TIMOTHY 5

1. Rebuke not – Considering your own youth, with such a severity as would otherwise be proper.

3. Honor – That is, maintain out of the public stock.

4. Let these learn to requite their parents – For all their former care, trouble, and expense.

of God's law, without being tasked to imaginary duties, which reject what he has allowed. But nothing justifies an intemperate or improper use of things; and nothing will be good to us, unless we seek by prayer for the Lord's blessing upon it.

6-10 Outward acts of self-denial profit little. What will it avail us to mortify the body, if we do not mortify sin? No diligence in mere outward things could be of much use. The gain of godliness lies much in the promise; and the promises to godly people relate partly to the life that now is, but especially to the life which is to come: though we lose for Christ, we shall not lose by him. If Christ be thus the Savior of all men, then much more will he be the Rewarder of those who seek and serve him; he will provide well for those whom he has made new creatures.

11-16 Men's youth will not be despised, if they keep from vanities and follies. Those who teach by their doctrine, must teach by their life. Their discourse must be edifying; their conversation must be holy; they must be examples of love to God and all good men, examples of spiritual-mindedness. Ministers must mind these things as their principal work and business. By this means their profiting will appear in all things, as well as to all persons; this is the way to profit in knowledge and grace, and also to profit others. The doctrine of a minister of Christ must be scriptural, clear, evangelical, and practical; well stated, explained, defended, and applied. But these duties leave no leisure for wordly pleasures, trifling visits, or idle conversation, and but little for what is mere amusement, and only ornamental. May every believer be enabled to let his profiting appear unto all men; seeking to experience the power of the gospel in his own soul, and to bring forth its fruits in his life.

1 TIMOTHY 5

Directions as to the elder and younger men and women. (1,2)
And as to poor widows. (3-8)
Concerning widows. (9-16)
The respect to be paid to elders. Timothy is to take care in rebuking offenders, in ordaining ministers, and as to his own health. (17-25)

1-2 Respect must be paid to the dignity of years and place. The younger, if faulty, must be rebuked, not as desirous to find fault with them, but as willing to make the best of them. There is need of much meekness and care in reproving those who deserve reproof.

3-8 Honor widows that are widows indeed, relieve them, and maintain them. It is the duty of children, if their parents are in need, and they are able to relieve them, to do it to the utmost of their power.

transgression of his people was laid upon him, and that God, by thus avenging sin in the person of his dear Son, and honoring his law by the suffering of the Savior, is now able to declare pardon to the penitent and grace to the believing. Now, when the soul comes to know that sin is put away by the atoning blood; when the heart discovers that it is not our life that saves us, but the life of God that comes to dwell in us; that we are not to be regenerated by our own actions, but are regenerated by the Holy Ghost who comes to us through the precious death of Jesus, then despair flies away, and the soul cries exultingly, "There is hope. There is hope. Christ died for sinners: why should I not have a part in that precious death? He came like a physician to heal the sick: why should he not heal me? Now I perceive that he does not want my goodness, but my badness; he does not need my righteousness, but my unrighteousness: for he came to save the ungodly and to redeem his people from their sins. I say, when the heart comes to a knowledge of this truth, then it is saved from despair; and this is no small part of the salvation of Jesus Christ.

But I do know that there is real salvation by believing in Christ. Know it? I have never preached to you concerning that subject what I do not know by experience. In a moment, when I believed in Christ I leaped from despair to fullness of delight. Since I have believed in Jesus I have found myself totally new—changed altogether from what I was; and I find now that, in proportion as I trust in Jesus, I love God and try to serve him; but if at any time I begin to trust in myself, I forget my God, and I become selfish and sinful. Just as I keep on being nothing and taking Christ to be everything, so am I led in the paths of righteousness. I am merely talking of myself, because a man cannot bear witness about other people so thoroughly as he can about himself. I am sure that all of you who have tried my Master can bear the same witness. You have been saved, and you have come to a knowledge of the truth experimentally; and every soul here that would be saved must in the same way believe the truth, appropriate the truth, act upon the truth, and experimentally know the truth, which is summed up in few words:—"Man lost: Christ his Savior. Man nothing: God all in all. The heart depraved: the Spirit working the new life by faith." The Lord grant that these truths may come home to your hearts with power.

I am now going to draw two inferences which are to be practical. The first one is this: in regard TO YOU THAT ARE SEEKING SALVATION. Does not the text show you that it is very possible that the reason why you have not found sal-

1 TIMOTHY 5

1 Rebuke not an elder, but intreat him as a father; and the younger men as brethren;

2 The elder women as mothers; the younger as sisters, with all purity.

3 Honor widows that are widows indeed.

4 But if any widow have children or nephews, let them learn first to shew piety at home, and to requite their parents: for that is good and acceptable before God.

5 Now she that is a widow indeed, and desolate, trusteth in God, and continueth in supplications and prayers night and day.

6 But she that liveth in pleasure is dead while she liveth.

7 And these things give in charge, that they may be blameless.

8 But if any provide not for his own, and specially for those of his own house, he hath denied the faith, and is worse than an infidel.

9 Let not a widow be taken into the number under threescore years old, having been the wife of one man,

10 Well reported of for good works; if she have brought up children, if she have lodged strangers, if she have washed the saints' feet, if she have relieved the afflicted, if she have diligently followed every good work.

11 But the younger widows refuse: for when they have begun to wax wanton against Christ, they will marry;

12 Having damnation, because they have cast off their first faith.

13 And withal they learn to be idle, wandering about from house to house; and not only idle, but tattlers also and busybodies, speaking things which they ought not.

14 I will therefore that the younger women marry, bear children, guide the house, give none occasion to the adversary to speak reproachfully.

15 For some are already turned aside after Satan.

16 If any man or woman that believeth have widows, let them relieve them, and let not the church be charged; that it may relieve them that are widows indeed.

17 Let the elders that rule well be counted worthy of double honor, especially they who labor in the word and doctrine.

18 For the scripture saith, Thou shalt not muzzle the ox that treadeth out the corn. And, The laborer is wor-

5. Widows indeed – Who have no near relations to provide for them; and who are wholly devoted to God. Desolate – Having neither children, nor grandchildren to relieve her.

6. She that liveth in pleasure – Delicately, voluptuously, in elegant, regular sensuality, though not in the use of any such pleasures as are unlawful in themselves.

7. That they – That is, the widows.

8. If any provide not – Food and raiment. For his own – Mother and grandmother, being desolate widows. He hath – Virtually. Denied the faith – Which does not destroy, but perfect, natural duties. What has this to do with heaping up money for our children, for which it is often so impertinently alleged? But all men have their reasons for laying up money. One will go to hell for fear of want; another acts like a heathen, lest he should be worse than an infidel.

9. Let not a widow be chosen – Into the number of deaconesses, who attended sick women or traveling preachers. Under threescore – Afterwards they were admitted at forty, if they were eminent for holiness. Having been the wife of one husband – That is, having lived in lawful marriage, whether with one or more persons successively.

10. If she hath washed the feet of the saints – Has been ready to do the meanest offices for them.

11. Refuse – Do not choose. For when they are waxed wanton against Christ – To whose more immediate service they had addicted themselves. They want to marry – And not with a single eye to the glory of God; and so withdraw themselves from that entire service of the church to which they were before engaged.

12. They have rejected their first faith – Have deserted their trust in God, and have acted contrary to the first conviction, namely, that wholly to devote themselves to his service was the most excellent way. When we first receive power to believe, does not the Spirit of God generally point out what are the most excellent things; and at the same time, give us an holy resolution to walk in the highest degree of Christian severity? And how unwise are we ever to sink into anything below it!

14. I counsel therefore the younger women – Widows or virgins, such as are not disposed to live single. To marry, to bear children, to guide the family – Then will they have sufficient employment of their own. And give no occasion of reproach to the adversary – Whether Jew or heathen.

15. Some – Widows. Have turned aside after Satan – Who has drawn them from Christ.

17. Let the elders that rule well – Who approve themselves faithful stewards of all that is committed to their charge. Be counted worthy of double honor – A more abundant provision, seeing that such will employ it all to the glory of God. As it was the most laborious and disinterested men who were put into these offices, so whatever any one had to bestow, in his life or death, was generally lodged in their hands for the poor. By this means the churchmen became very rich in after ages, but as the design of the donors was something else, there is the highest reason why it should be disposed of according to their pious intent. Especially those – Of them. Who labor – Diligently and painfully. In the word and teaching – In teaching the word.

18. Deut. xxv, 4.

19. Against an elder – Or presbyter. Do not even receive an accusation, unless by two or three witnesses – By the Mosaic law, a private person might be cited (though not condemned) on the testimony of one witness; but St. Paul forbids an elder to be even cited on such evidence, his reputation being of more importance than that of others.

20. Those – Elders. That sin – Scandalously, and are duly convicted. Rebuke

Widowhood is a desolate state; but let widows trust in the Lord, and continue in prayer. All who live in pleasure, are dead while they live, spiritually dead, dead in trespasses and sins. Alas, what numbers there are of this description among nominal Christians, even to the latest period of life! If any men or women do not maintain their poor relations, they in effect deny the faith. If they spend upon their lusts and pleasures, what should maintain their families, they have denied the faith, and are worse than infidels. If professors of the gospel give way to any corrupt principle or conduct, they are worse than those who do not profess to believe the doctrines of grace.

9-16 Every one brought into any office in the church, should be free from just censure; and many are proper objects of charity, yet ought not to be employed in public services. Those who would find mercy when they are in distress, must show mercy when they are in prosperity; and those who show most readiness for every good work, are most likely to be faithful in whatever is trusted to them. Those who are idle, very seldom are only idle, they make mischief among neighbors, and sow discord among brethren. All believers are required to relieve those belonging to their families who are destitute, that the church may not be prevented from relieving such as are entirely destitute and friendless.

17-25 Care must be taken that ministers are maintained. And those who are laborious in this work are worthy of double honor and esteem. It is their just due, as much as the reward of the laborer. The apostle charges Timothy solemnly to guard against partiality. We have great need to watch at all times, that we do not partake of other men's sins. Keep thyself pure, not only from doing the like thyself, but from countenancing it, or any way helping to it in others. The apostle also charges Timothy to take care of his health. As we are not to make our bodies masters, so neither slaves; but to use them so that they may be most helpful to us in the service of God. There are secret, and there are open sins: some men's sins are open before-hand, and going before unto judgment; some they follow after. God will bring to light the hidden things of darkness, and make known the counsels of all hearts. Looking forward to the judgment-day, let us all attend to our proper offices, whether in higher or lower stations, studying that the name and doctrine of God may never be blasphemed on our account.

1 TIMOTHY 6

The duty of Christians towards believing, as well as other masters. (1-5)

The advantage of godliness with contentment. (6-10)

A solemn charge to Timothy to be faithful. (11-16)

vation is because you do not know the truth? Hence, I do most earnestly entreat the many of you young people who cannot get rest to be very diligent searchers of your Bibles. The first thing and the main thing is to believe in the Lord Jesus Christ, but if you say, "I do not understand it," or "I cannot believe," or if there be any such doubt rising in your mind, then it may be because you have not gained complete knowledge of the truth. It is very possible that somebody will say to you, "Believe, believe, believe." I would say the same to you, but I should like you to act upon the common-sense principle of knowing what is to be believed and in whom you are to believe. I explained this to one who came to me a few evenings ago. She said that she could not believe. "Well," I said, "now suppose as you sit in that chair I say to you, 'Young friend, I cannot believe in you': you would say to me, 'I think you should.' Suppose I then replied, 'I wish I could.' What would you bid me do? Should I sit still and look at you till I said, 'I think I can believe in you'? That would be ridiculous. No, I should go and inquire, 'Who is this young person? What kind of character does she bear? What are her connections?' and when I knew all about you, then I have no doubt that I should say, 'I have made examination into this young woman's character, and I cannot help believing in her.'" Now, it is just so with Jesus Christ. If you say, "I cannot believe in him," read those four blessed testimonies of Matthew, Mark, Luke, and John, and especially linger much over those parts where they tell you of his death. Do you know that many, while they have been sitting, as it were, at the foot of the cross, viewing the Son of God dying for men, have cried out, "I cannot help believing. I cannot help believing. When I see my sin, it seems too great; but when I see my Savior my iniquity vanishes away." I think I have put it to you sometimes like this: if you take a ride through London, from end to end, it will take you many days to get an idea of its vastness; for probably none of us know the size of London. After your long ride of inspection you will say, "I wonder how those people can all be fed. I cannot make it out. Where does all the bread come from, and all the butter, and all the cheese, and all the meat, and everything else? Why, these people will be starved. It is not possible that Lebanon with all its beasts, and the vast plains of Europe and America should ever supply food sufficient for all this multitude." That is your feeling. And then, tomorrow morning you get up, and you go to Covent Garden, you go to the great meat-markets, and to other sources of supply, and when you come home you say, "I feel quite different now, for now I cannot make out where

thy of his reward.

19 Against an elder receive not an accusation, but before two or three witnesses.

20 Them that sin rebuke before all, that others also may fear.

21 I charge thee before God, and the Lord Jesus Christ, and the elect angels, that thou observe these things without preferring one before another, doing nothing by partiality.

22 Lay hands suddenly on no man, neither be partaker of other men's sins: keep thyself pure.

23 Drink no longer water, but use a little wine for thy stomach's sake and thine often infirmities.

24 Some men's sins are open beforehand, going before to judgment; and some men they follow after.

25 Likewise also the good works of some are manifest beforehand; and they that are otherwise cannot be hid.

1 TIMOTHY 6

1 Let as many servants as are under the yoke count their own masters worthy of all honor, that the name of God and his doctrine be not blasphemed.

2 And they that have believing masters, let them not despise them, because they are brethren; but rather do them service, because they are faithful and beloved, partakers of the benefit. These things teach and exhort.

3 If any man teach otherwise, and consent not to wholesome words, even the words of our Lord Jesus Christ, and to the doctrine which is according to godliness;

4 He is proud, knowing nothing, but doting about questions and strifes of words, whereof cometh envy, strife, railings, evil surmisings,

5 Perverse disputings of men of corrupt minds, and destitute of the truth, supposing that gain is godliness: from such withdraw thyself.

6 But godliness with contentment is great gain.

7 For we brought nothing into this world, and it is certain we can carry nothing out.

8 And having food and raiment let us be therewith content.

9 But they that will be rich fall into temptation and a snare, and into many foolish and hurtful lusts, which

before all – The church.

21. I charge thee before God – Referring to the last judgment, in which we shall stand before God and Christ, with his elect, that is, holy, angels, who are the witnesses of our conversation. The apostle looks through his own labors, and even through time itself, and seems to stand as one already in eternity. That thou observe these things without prejudging – Passing no sentence till the cause is fully heard. Or partiality – For or against any one.

22. Lay hands suddenly on no man – That is, appoint no man to church offices without full trial and examination; else thou wilt be accessory to, and accountable for, his misbehavior in his office. Keep thy self pure – From the blood of all men.

24. Some men's sins are manifest beforehand – Before any strict inquiry be made. Going before to judgment – So that you may immediately judge them unworthy of any spiritual office. And some they – Their sins. Follow after – More covertly.

25. They that are otherwise – Not so manifest. Cannot be long hid – From thy knowledge. On this account, also, be not hasty in laying on of hands.

1 TIMOTHY 6

1. Let servants under the yoke – Of heathen masters. Account them worthy of all honor – All the honor due from a servant to a master. Lest the name of God and his doctrine be blasphemed – As it surely will, if they do otherwise.

2. Let them not despise them – Pay them the less honor or obedience. Because they are brethren – And in that respect on a level with them. They that live in a religious community know the danger of this; and that greater grace is requisite to bear with the faults of a brother, than of an infidel, or man of the world. But rather do them service – Serve them so much the more diligently.

3. If any teach otherwise – Than strict practical holiness in all its branches. And consent not to sound words – Literally, healthful words; words that have no taint of falsehood, or tendency to encourage sin. And the doctrine which is after godliness – Exquisitely contrived to answer all the ends, and secure every interest, of real piety.

4. He is puffed up – Which is the cause of his not consenting to the doctrine which is after inward, practical religion. By this mark we may know them. Knowing nothing – As he ought to know..

5. Supposing that gain is godliness – Thinking the best religion is the getting of money: a far more common case than is usually supposed.

6. But godliness with content – The inseparable companion of true, vital religion. Is great gain – Brings unspeakable profit in time, as well as eternity.

7. Neither can we carry anything out – To what purpose, then, do we heap together so many things? O, give me one thing, – a safe and ready passage to my own country!

8. Covering – That is, raiment and an house to cover us. This is all that a Christian needs, and all that his religion allows him to desire.

9. They that desire to be rich – To have more than these; for then they would be so far rich; and the very desire banishes content, and exposes them to ruin. Fall – plunge – A sad gradation! Into temptation – Miserable food for the soul! And a snare – Or trap. Dreadful "covering!" And into many foolish and hurtful desires – Which are sown and fed by having more than we need. Then farewell all hope of content! What then remains, but destruction for the body, and perdition for the soul?

10. Love of money – Commonly called "prudent care" of what a man has.

The apostle repeats his warning to the rich, and closes with a blessing. (17-21)

1-5 Christians were not to suppose that religious knowledge, or Christian privileges, gave them any right to despise heathen masters, or to disobey lawful commands, or to expose their faults to others. And such as enjoyed the privilege of living with believing masters, were not to withhold due respect and reverence, because they were equal in respect to religious privileges, but were to serve with double diligence and cheerfulness, because of their faith in Christ, and as partakers of his free salvation. We are not to consent to any words as wholesome, except the words of our Lord Jesus Christ; to these we must give unfeigned consent. Commonly those are most proud who know least; for they do not know themselves. Hence come envy, strife, railings, evil-surmisings, disputes that are all subtlety, and of no solidity, between men of corrupt and carnal minds, ignorant of the truth and its sanctifying power, and seeking their worldly advantage.

6-10 Those that make a trade of Christianity to serve their turn for this world, will be disappointed; but those who mind it as their calling, will find it has the promise of the life that now is, as well as of that which is to come. He that is godly, is sure to be happy in another world; and if contented with his condition in this world, he has enough; and all truly godly people are content. When brought into the greatest straits, we cannot be poorer than when we came into this world; a shroud, a coffin, and a grave, are all that the richest man in the world can have from all his wealth.

11-16 It ill becomes any men, but especially men of God, to set their hearts upon the things of this world; men of God should be taken up with the things of God. There must be a conflict with corruption, and temptations, and the powers of darkness. Eternal life is the crown proposed for our encouragement. We are called to lay hold thereon. To the rich must especially be pointed out their dangers and duties, as to the proper use of wealth. But who can give such a charge, that is not himself above the love of things that wealth can buy? The appearing of Christ is certain, but it is not for us to know the time. Mortal eyes cannot bear the brightness of the Divine glory. None can approach him except as he is made known unto sinners in and by Christ. The Godhead is here adored without distinction of Persons, as all these things are properly spoken, whether of the Father, the Son, or the Holy Ghost. God is revealed to us, only in and through the human nature of Christ, as the only begotten Son of the Father.

17-21 Being rich in this world is wholly different from being rich towards God. Nothing is more uncertain than worldly wealth. Those who are rich, must see

all the people come from to eat all this provision: I never saw such store of food in all my life. Why, if there were two Londons, surely there is enough here to feed them." Just so—when you think about your sins and your wants you get saying, "How can I be saved?" Now, turn your thoughts the other way; think that Christ is the Son of God: think of what the merit must be of the incarnate God's hearing human guilt; and instead of saying, "My sin is too great," you will almost think the atoning sacrifice too great. Therefore I do urge you to try and know more of Christ; and I am only giving you the advice of Isaiah, "Incline your ear, and come unto me; hear, and your soul shall live." Know, hear, read, and believe more about these precious things, always with this wish—"I am not hearing for hearing's sake, and I am not wishing to know for knowing's sake, but I am wanting to hear and to know that I may be saved." I want you to be like the woman that lost her piece of silver. She did not light a candle and then say, "Bravo, I have lit a candle, this is enough." She did not take her broom and then sit down content, crying, "What a splendid broom." When she raised a dust she did not exclaim, "What a dust I am making! I am surely making progress now." Some poor sinners, when they have been seeking, get into a dust of soul-trouble, and think it to be a comfortable sign. No, I'll warrant you, the woman wanted her groat: she did not mind the broom, or the dust, or the candle; she looked for the silver. So it must be with you. Never content yourself with the reading, the hearing, or the feeling. It is Christ you want. It is the precious piece of money that you must find; and you must sweep until you find it. Why, there it is! There is Jesus! Take him! Take him! Believe him now, even now, and you are saved.

The last inference is for YOU WHO DESIRE TO SAVE SINNERS. You must, dear friends, bring the truth before them when you want to bring them to Jesus Christ. I believe that exciting meetings do good to some. Men are so dead and careless that almost anything is to be tolerated that wakes them up; but for real solid soul-work before God telling men the truth is the main thing. What truth? It is gospel truth, truth about Christ that they want. Tell it in a loving, earnest, affectionate manner, for God wills that they should be saved, not in any other way, but in this way—by a knowledge of the truth. He wills that all men should be saved in this way—not by keeping them in ignorance, but by bringing the truth before them. That is God's way of saving them. Have your Bible handy when you are reasoning with a soul. Just say, "Let me call your attention to this passage." It has a wonderful power over a poor staggering soul to

drown men in destruction and perdition.

10 For the love of money is the root of all evil: which while some coveted after, they have erred from the faith, and pierced themselves through with many sorrows.

11 But thou, O man of God, flee these things; and follow after righteousness, godliness, faith, love, patience, meekness.

12 Fight the good fight of faith, lay hold on eternal life, whereunto thou art also called, and hast professed a good profession before many witnesses.

13 I give thee charge in the sight of God, who quickeneth all things, and before Christ Jesus, who before Pontius Pilate witnessed a good confession;

14 That thou keep this commandment without spot, unrebukeable, until the appearing of our Lord Jesus Christ:

15 Which in his times he shall shew, who is the blessed and only Potentate, the King of kings, and Lord of lords;

16 Who only hath immortality, dwelling in the light which no man can approach unto; whom no man hath seen, nor can see: to whom be honor and power everlasting. Amen.

17 Charge them that are rich in this world, that they be not highminded, nor trust in uncertain riches, but in the living God, who giveth us richly all things to enjoy;

18 That they do good, that they be rich in good works, ready to distribute, willing to communicate;

19 Laying up in store for themselves a good foundation against the time to come, that they may lay hold on eternal life.

20 O Timothy, keep that which is committed to thy trust, avoiding profane and vain babblings, and oppositions of science falsely so called:

21 Which some professing have erred concerning the faith. Grace be with thee. Amen.

Is the root – The parent of all manner of evils. Which some coveting have erred – Literally, missed the mark. They aimed not at faith, but at something else. And pierced themselves with many sorrows – From a guilty conscience, tormenting passions, desires contrary to reason, religion, and one another. How cruel are worldly men to themselves!

11. But thou, O man of God – Whatever all the world else do. A man of God is either a prophet, a messenger of God, or a man devoted to God; a man of another world. Flee – As from a serpent, instead of coveting these things.

12. Fight the good fight of faith – Not about words. Lay hold on eternal life – Just before thee. Thou hast confessed the good confession – Perhaps at his baptism: so likewise, ver. 13; but with a remarkable variation of the expression. Thou hast confessed the good confession before many witnesses – To which they all assented. He witnessed the good confession; but Pilate did not assent to it.

13. I charge thee before God, who quickeneth all things – Who hath quickened thee, and will quicken thee at the great day.

15. Which – Appearing. In his own times – The power, the knowledge, and the Revelation of which, remain in his eternal mind.

16. Who only hath underived, independent immortality. Dwelling in light unapproachable – To the highest angel. Whom no man hath seen, or can see – With bodily eyes. Yet "we shall see him as he is."

17. What follows seems to be a kind of a postscript. Charge the rich in this world – Rich in such beggarly riches as this world affords.

18. To do good – To make this their daily employ, that they may be rich – May abound in all good works. Ready to distribute – Singly to particular persons. Willing to communicate – To join in all public works of charity.

19. Treasuring up for themselves a good foundation – Of an abundant reward, by the free mercy of God. That they may lay hold on eternal life – This cannot be done by alms-deeds; yet they "come up for a memorial before God," Acts x, 4. And the lack even of this may be the cause why God will withhold grace and salvation from us.

20. Keep that which is committed to thy trust – The charge I have given thee, chap. i, 18. Avoid profane empty babblings – How weary of controversy was this acute disputant! And knowledge falsely so called – Most of the ancient heretics were great pretenders to knowledge.

MATTHEW HENRY

that God gives them their riches; and he only can give to enjoy them richly; for many have riches, but enjoy them poorly, not having a heart to use them. What is the best estate worth, more than as it gives opportunity of doing the more good? Showing faith in Christ by fruits of love, let us lay hold on eternal life, when the self-indulgent, covetous, and ungodly around, lift up their eyes in torment. That learning which opposes the truth of the gospel, is not true science, or real knowledge, or it would approve the gospel, and consent to it. Those who advance reason above faith, are in danger of leaving faith. Grace includes all that is good, and grace is an earnest, a beginning of glory; wherever God gives grace, he will give glory.

CHARLES H. SPURGEON

point to the Book itself. Say, "Did you notice this promise, my dear friend? And have you seen that passage?" Have the Scriptures handy. There is a dear brother of mine here whom God blesses to many souls, and I have seen him talking to some, and turning to the texts very handily. I wondered how he did it so quickly, till I looked in his Bible, and found that he had the choice texts printed on two leaves and inserted into the book, so that he could always open upon them. That is a capital plan, to get the cheering words ready to hand, the very ones that you know have comforted you and have comforted others. It sometimes happens that one single verse of God's word will make the light to break into a soul, when fifty days of reasoning would not do it. I notice that when souls are saved it is by our texts rather than by our sermons. God the Holy Ghost loves to use his own sword. It is God's word, not man's comment on God's word, that God usually blesses. Therefore, stick to the quotation of the Scripture itself, and rely upon the truth. If a man could be saved by a lie it would be a lying salvation. Truth alone can work results that are true. Therefore, keep on teaching the truth. God help you to proclaim the precious truth about the bleeding, dying, risen, exalted, coming Savior; and God will bless it.

2 Timothy

2 TIMOTHY 1

1 Paul, an apostle of Jesus Christ by the will of God, according to the promise of life which is in Christ Jesus,

2 To Timothy, my dearly beloved son: Grace, mercy, and peace, from God the Father and Christ Jesus our Lord.

3 I thank God, whom I serve from my forefathers with pure conscience, that without ceasing I have remembrance of thee in my prayers night and day;

4 Greatly desiring to see thee, being mindful of thy tears, that I may be filled with joy;

5 When I call to remembrance the unfeigned faith that is in thee, which dwelt first in thy grandmother Lois, and thy mother Eunice; and I am persuaded that in thee also.

6 Wherefore I put thee in remembrance that thou stir up the gift of God, which is in thee by the putting on of my hands.

7 For God hath not given us the spirit of fear; but of power, and of love, and of a sound mind.

8 Be not thou therefore ashamed of the testimony of our Lord, nor of me his prisoner: but be thou partaker of the afflictions of the gospel according to the power of God;

9 Who hath saved us, and called us with an holy calling, not according to our works, but according to his own purpose and grace, which was given us in Christ Jesus before the world began,

10 But is now made manifest by the appearing of our Savior Jesus Christ, who hath abolished death, and hath brought life and immortality to light through the gospel:

11 Whereunto I am appointed a preacher, and an apostle, and a teacher of the Gentiles.

12 For the which cause I also suffer these things: nevertheless I am not ashamed: for I know whom I have believed, and am persuaded that he is able to keep that which I have committed unto him against that day.

13 Hold fast the form of sound words, which thou hast heard of me, in faith and love which is in Christ Jesus.

14 That good thing which was committed unto thee keep by the Holy Ghost which dwelleth in us.

15 This thou knowest, that all they which are in Asia be turned away from me; of whom are Phygellus and Hermogenes.

16 The Lord give mercy unto the house of Onesiphorus; for he oft refreshed me, and was not ashamed of my chain:

17 But, when he was in Rome, he sought me out very diligently, and found me.

THIS epistle was probably wrote by St. Paul, during his second confinement at Rome, not long before his martyrdom. It is, as it were, the swan's dying song. But though it was wrote many years after the former, yet they are both of the same kind, and nearly resemble each other.

2 TIMOTHY 1

3. Whom I serve from my forefathers – That is, whom both I and my ancestors served, with a pure conscience – He always worshiped God according to his conscience, both before and after his conversion. One who stands on the verge of life is much refreshed by the remembrance of his predecessors, to whom he is going.

4. Being mindful of thy tears – Perhaps frequently shed, as well as at the apostle's last parting with him.

5. Which dwelt – A word not applied to a transient guest, but only to a settled inhabitant. First – Probably this was before Timothy was born, yet not beyond St. Paul's memory.

6. Wherefore – Because I remember this. I remind thee of stirring up – Literally, blowing up the coals into a flame. The gift of God – All the spiritual gifts, which the grace of God has given thee.

7. And let nothing discourage thee, for God hath not given us – That is, the spirit which God hath given us Christians, is not the spirit of fear – Or cowardice. But of power – Banishing fear. And love and sobriety – These animate us in our duties to God, our brethren, and ourselves. Power and sobriety are two good extremes. Love is between, the tie and temperament of both; preventing the two bad extremes of fearfulness and rashness. More is said concerning power, ver. 8; concerning love, chap. ii, 14, &c.; concerning sobriety, chap. iii, 1, &c.

8. Therefore be not thou ashamed – When fear is banished, evil shame also flees away. Of the testimony of our Lord – The gospel, and of testifying the truth of it to all men. Nor of me – The cause of the servants of God doing his work, cannot be separated from the cause of God himself. But be thou partaker of the afflictions – Which I endure for the gospel's sake. According to the power of God – This which overcomes all things is nervously described in the two next verses.

9. Who hath saved us – By faith. The love of the Father, the grace of our Savior, and the whole economy of salvation, are here admirably described. Having called us with an holy calling – Which is all from God, and claims us all for God. According to his own purpose and grace – That is, his own gracious purpose. Which was given us – Fixed for our advantage, before the world began.

10. By the appearing of our Savior – This implies his whole abode upon earth. Who hath abolished death – Taken away its sting, and turned it into a blessing. And hath brought life and immortality to light – Hath clearly revealed by the gospel that immortal life which he hath purchased for us.

12. That which I have committed to him – My soul. Until that day – Of his final appearing.

13. The pattern of sound words – The model of pure, wholesome doctrine.

14. The good thing – This wholesome doctrine.

15. All who are in Asia – Who had attended me at Rome for a while. Are turned away from me – What, from Paul the aged, the faithful soldier, and now prisoner of Christ! This was a glorious trial, and wisely reserved for that time, when he was on the borders of immortality. Perhaps a little measure of the same spirit might remain with him under whose pic-

The first design of this epistle seems to have been, to apprize Timothy of what had occurred during the imprisonment of the apostle, and to request him to come to Rome. But being uncertain whether he should be suffered to live to see him, Paul gives a variety of advices and encouragements, for the faithful discharge of his ministerial duties. As this was a private epistle written to St. Paul's most intimate friend, under the miseries of imprisonment, and in the near prospect of death, it shows the temper and character of the apostle, and contains convincing proofs that he sincerely believed the doctrines he preached.

2 TIMOTHY 1

Paul expresses great affection for Timothy. (1-5)
Exhorts him to improve his spiritual gifts. (6-14)
Tells of many who basely deserted him; but speaks
*   with affection of Onesiphorus. (15-18)*

1-5 The promise of eternal life to believers in Christ Jesus, is the leading subject of ministers who are employed according to the will of God. The blessings here named, are the best we can ask for our beloved friends, that they may have peace with God the Father and Christ Jesus our Lord. Whatever good we do, God must have the glory. True believers have in every age the same religion as to substance. Their faith is unfeigned; it will stand the trial, and it dwells in them as a living principle. Thus pious women may take encouragement from the success of Lois and Eunice with Timothy, who proved so excellent and useful a minister.

6-14 God has not given us the spirit of fear, but the spirit of power, of courage and resolution, to meet difficulties and dangers; the spirit of love to him, which will carry us through opposition. And the spirit of a sound mind, quietness of mind. The Holy Spirit is not the author of a timid or cowardly disposition, or of slavish fears. We are likely to bear afflictions well, when we have strength and power from God to enable us to bear them. As is usual with Paul, when he mentions Christ and his redemption, he enlarges upon them; so full was he of that which is all our salvation, and ought to be all our desire. The call of the gospel is a holy call, making holy. Salvation is of free grace. This is said to be given us before the world began, that is, in the purpose of God from all eternity; in Christ Jesus, for all the gifts that come from God to sinful man, come in and through Christ Jesus alone. And as there is so clear a prospect of eternal happiness by faith in him, who is the Resurrection and the Life, let us give more diligence in making his salvation sure to our souls. The hope of the lowest real Christian rests on the same foundation as that of the great apostle. He also has learned the value and the danger of his soul; he also has believed in Christ; and

FAITH ILLUSTRATED
Sermon number 271, delivered on August 21st, 1859, by C.H. Spurgeon at the Music Hall, Royal Surrey Gardens.

"For the which cause I also suffer these things: nevertheless I am not ashamed: for I know whom I have believed, and am persuaded that he is able to keep that which I have committed unto him against that day."—2 Timothy, 1:12.

I. First, I am to describe THE GRANDEST ACTION OF THE CHRISTIAN'S LIFE.

With all our preaching, I am afraid that we too much omit the simple explanation of the essential act in salvation. I have feared that the anxious inquirer might visit many of our churches and chapels, month after month, and yet he would not get a clear idea of what he must do to be saved. He would come away with an indistinct notion that he was to believe, but what he was to believe he would not know. He would, perhaps, obtain some glimmering of the fact that he must be saved through the merits of Christ, but how those merits can become available to him, he would still be left to guess. I know at least that this was my case—that when sincere and anxious to do or be anything which might save my soul, I was utterly in the dark as to the way in which my salvation might be rendered thoroughly secure. Now, this morning, I hope I shall be able to put it into such a light that even he who passes by quickly may read, and that the wayfaring man, though a fool, may not err therein.

The apostle says, he committed himself into the hands of Christ. His soul with all its eternal interests; his soul with all its sins, with all its hopes, and all its fears, he had put into the hands of Christ, as the grandest and most precious deposit which man could ever make. He had taken himself just as he was and had surrendered himself to Christ, saying—"Lord save me, for I cannot save myself; I give myself up to thee, freely relying upon thy power, and believing in thy love. I give my soul up to thee to be washed, cleansed, saved, and preserved, and at last brought home to heaven." This act of committing himself to Christ was the first act which ever brought real comfort to his spirit; it was the act which he must continue to perform whenever he would escape from a painful sense of sin; the act with which he must enter heaven itself, if he would die in peace and see God's face with acceptance. He must still continue to commit himself into the keeping of Christ. I take it that when the apostle committed himself to Christ, he meant these three things. He meant first, that from that good hour he renounced all

18 The Lord grant unto him that he may find mercy of the Lord in that day: and in how many things he ministered unto me at Ephesus, thou knowest very well.

2 TIMOTHY 2

1 Thou therefore, my son, be strong in the grace that is in Christ Jesus.

2 And the things that thou hast heard of me among many witnesses, the same commit thou to faithful men, who shall be able to teach others also.

3 Thou therefore endure hardness, as a good soldier of Jesus Christ.

4 No man that warreth entangleth himself with the affairs of this life; that he may please him who hath chosen him to be a soldier.

5 And if a man also strive for masteries, yet is he not crowned, except he strive lawfully.

6 The husbandman that laboreth must be first partaker of the fruits.

7 Consider what I say; and the Lord give thee understanding in all things.

8 Remember that Jesus Christ of the seed of David was raised from the dead according to my gospel:

9 Wherein I suffer trouble, as an evil doer, even unto bonds; but the word of God is not bound.

10 Therefore I endure all things for the elect's sakes, that they may also obtain the salvation which is in Christ Jesus with eternal glory.

11 It is a faithful saying: For if we be dead with him, we shall also live with him:

12 If we suffer, we shall also reign with him: if we deny him, he also will deny us:

13 If we believe not, yet he abideth faithful: he cannot deny himself.

14 Of these things put them in remembrance, charging them before the Lord that they strive not about words to no profit, but to the subverting of the hearers.

15 Study to shew thyself approved unto God, a workman that needeth not to be ashamed, rightly dividing the word of truth.

16 But shun profane and vain babblings: for they will increase unto more ungodliness.

17 And their word will eat as doth a canker: of whom is Hymeneus and Philetus;

18 Who concerning the truth have erred, saying that the resurrection is past already; and overthrow the faith of some.

19 Nevertheless the foundation of God

ture are those affecting words, "The true effigy of Francis Xavier, apostle of the Indies, forsaken of all men, dying in a cottage."

16. The family of Onesiphorus – As well as himself. Hath often refreshed me – Both at Ephesus and Rome.

2 TIMOTHY 2

2. The things – The wholesome doctrine, ver. 13. Commit – Before thou leavest Ephesus. To faithful men, who will be able, after thou art gone, to teach others.

4. No man that warreth entangleth himself – Any more than is unavoidable. In the affairs of this life – With worldly business or cares. That – Minding war only, he may please his captain. In this and the next verse there is a plain allusion to the Roman law of arms, and to that of the Grecian games. According to the former, no soldier was to engage in any civil employment; according to the latter, none could be crowned as conqueror, who did not keep strictly to the rules of the game.

6. Unless he labor first, he will reap no fruit.

8. Of the seed of David – This one genealogy attend to.

9. Is not bound – Not hindered in its course.

10. Therefore – Encouraged by this, that "the word of God be not bound." I endure all things – See the spirit of a real Christian? Who would not wish to be likeminded? Salvation is deliverance from all evil; glory, the enjoyment of all good.

11. Dead with him – Dead to sin, and ready to die for him.

12. If we deny him – To escape suffering for him.

13. If we believe not – That is, though some believe not, God will make good all his promises to them that do believe. He cannot deny himself – His word cannot fail.

14. Remind them – Who are under thy charge. O how many unnecessary things are thus unprofitably, nay hurtfully, contended for.

15. A workman that needeth not to be ashamed – Either of unfaithfulness or unskillfullness. Rightly dividing the word of truth – Duly explaining and applying the whole scripture, so as to give each hearer his due portion. But they that give one part of the gospel to all (the promises and comforts to unawakened, hardened, scoffing men) have real need to be ashamed.

16. They – Who babble thus will grow worse and worse.

17. And their word – If they go on, will be mischievous as well as vain, and will eat as a gangrene.

18. Saying the resurrection is already past – Perhaps asserting that it is only the spiritual passing from death unto life.

19. But the foundation of God – His truth and faithfulness. Standeth fast – Can never be overthrown; being as it were sealed with a seal, which has an inscription on each side: on the one, The Lord knoweth those that are his; on the other, Let every one who nameth the name of the Lord, as his Lord, depart from iniquity. Indeed, they only are his who depart from iniquity. To all others he will say, "I know you not." Matt. vii, 22, 23.

20. But in a great house – Such as the church, it is not strange that there are not only vessels of gold and silver, designed for honorable uses, but also of wood and of earth – For less honorable purposes. Yet a vessel even of gold may be put to the vilest use, though it was not the design of him that made it.

21. If a man purge himself from these – Vessels of dishonor, so as to have no fellowship with them.

22. Flee youthful desires – Those peculiarly incident to youth. Follow

MATTHEW HENRY

CHARLES H. SPURGEON

the change wrought in his soul, convinces the believer that the Lord Jesus will keep him to his heavenly kingdom. Paul exhorts Timothy to hold fast the Holy Scriptures, the substance of solid gospel truth in them. It is not enough to assent to the sound words, but we must love them.

15-18 The apostle mentions the constancy of Onesiphorus; he oft refreshed him with his letters, and counsels, and comforts, and was not ashamed of him. A good man will seek to do good. The day of death and judgment is an awful day. And if we would have mercy then, we must seek for it now of the Lord. The best we can ask, for ourselves or our friends, is, that the Lord will grant that we and they may find mercy of the Lord, when called to pass out of time into eternity, and to appear before the judgment seat of Christ.

2 TIMOTHY 2

The apostle exhorts Timothy to persevere with diligence, like a soldier, a combatant, and a husbandman. (1-7)
Encouraging him by assurances of a happy end of his faithfulness. (8-13)
Warnings to shun vain babblings and dangerous errors. (14-21)
Charges to flee youthful lusts, and to minister with zeal against error, but with meekness of spirit. (22-26)

1-7 As our trials increase, we need to grow stronger in that which is good; our faith stronger, our resolution stronger, our love to God and Christ stronger. This is opposed to our being strong in our own strength. All Christians, but especially ministers, must be faithful to their Captain, and resolute in his cause. The great care of a Christian must be to please Christ. We are to strive to get the mastery of our lusts and corruptions, but we cannot expect the prize unless we observe the laws. We must take care that we do good in a right manner, that our good may not be spoken evil of. Some who are active, spend their zeal about outward forms and doubtful disputations. But those who strive lawfully shall be crowned at last. If we would partake the fruits, we must labor; if we would gain the prize, we must run the race. We must do the will of God, before we receive the promises, for which reason we have need of patience.

8-13 Let suffering saints remember, and look to Jesus, the Author and Finisher of their faith, who for the joy that was set before him, endured the cross, despised the shame, and is now set down at the right hand of the throne of God. We must not think it strange if the best men meet with the worst treatment; but this is cheering, that the word of God is not bound. Here we see the real and true cause of the apostle's suffering trouble in, or for, the sake of the

dependence upon his own efforts to save himself. The apostle had done very much, after a fashion, towards his own salvation. He commenced with all the advantages of ancestry. He was a Hebrew of the Hebrews, of the tribe of Benjamin, as touching the law a Pharisee. He was one of the very straightest of the straightest sect of his religion. So anxious was he to obtain salvation by his own efforts, that he left no stone unturned. Whatever Pharisee might be a hypocrite, Paul was none. Though he tithed his anise, and his mint, and his cummin, he did not neglect the weightier matters of the law. He might have united with truth, in the affirmation of the young man, "All these things have I kept from my youth up." Hear ye his own testimony: "Though I might also have confidence in the flesh. If any other man thinketh that he hath whereof he might trust in the flesh, I more." Being exceedingly desirous to serve God, he sought to put down what he thought was the pestilent heresy of Christ. Being exceeding hot in his endeavors against every thing that he thought to be wrong, he persecuted the professors of the new religion, hunted them in every city, brought them into the synagogue, and compelled them to blaspheme; when he had emptied his own country, he must needs take a journey to another, that he might there show his zeal in the cause of his God, by bringing out those whom he thought to be the deluded followers of an impostor. But suddenly Paul's mind is changed. Almighty grace leads him to see that he is working in a wrong direction, that his toil is lost, that as well might Sisyphus seek to roll his stone up hill, as for him to find a road to heaven up the steeps of Sinai; that as well might the daughters of Danaus hope to fill the bottomless cauldron with a bucket full of holes, as Paul indulge the idea that he could fill up the measure of the laws' demands. Consequently he feels that all he has done is nothing worth, and coming to Christ he cries, "But what things were gain to me, those I counted loss for Christ. Yea doubtless, and I count all things but loss for the excellency of the knowledge of Christ Jesus my Lord: for whom I have suffered the loss of all things, and do count them but dung, that I may win Christ, and be found in him, not having mine own righteousness, which is of the law, but that which is through the faith of Christ, the righteousness which is of God by faith."

I must add, however, that this act of faith must not be performed once only, but it must be continued as long as you live. As long as you live you must have no other confidence but "Jesus only." You must take him now today, to have and to hold through life and in death, in tempest and in sunshine, in poverty and in

standeth sure, having this seal, The Lord knoweth them that are his. And, Let every one that nameth the name of Christ depart from iniquity.

20 But in a great house there are not only vessels of gold and of silver, but also of wood and of earth; and some to honor, and some to dishonor.

21 If a man therefore purge himself from these, he shall be a vessel unto honor, sanctified, and meet for the master's use, and prepared unto every good work.

22 Flee also youthful lusts: but follow righteousness, faith, charity, peace, with them that call on the Lord out of a pure heart.

23 But foolish and unlearned questions avoid, knowing that they do gender strifes.

24 And the servant of the Lord must not strive; but be gentle unto all men, apt to teach, patient,

25 In meekness instructing those that oppose themselves; if God peradventure will give them repentance to the acknowledging of the truth;

26 And that they may recover themselves out of the snare of the devil, who are taken captive by him at his will.

2 TIMOTHY 3

1 This know also, that in the last days perilous times shall come.

2 For men shall be lovers of their own selves, covetous, boasters, proud, blasphemers, disobedient to parents, unthankful, unholy,

3 Without natural affection, trucebreakers, false accusers, incontinent, fierce, despisers of those that are good,

4 Traitors, heady, highminded, lovers of pleasures more than lovers of God;

5 Having a form of godliness, but denying the power thereof: from such turn away.

6 For of this sort are they which creep into houses, and lead captive silly women laden with sins, led away with divers lusts,

7 Ever learning, and never able to come to the knowledge of the truth.

8 Now as Jannes and Jambres withstood Moses, so do these also resist the truth: men of corrupt minds, reprobate concerning the faith.

9 But they shall proceed no further: for their folly shall be manifest unto all men, as theirs also was.

10 But thou hast fully known my doctrine, manner of life, purpose, faith, longsuffering, charity, patience,

11 Persecutions, afflictions, which

peace with them – Unity with all true believers. Out of a pure heart – Youthful desires, destroy this purity: righteousness, faith, love, peace, accompany it.

24. A servant of the Lord must not – Eagerly or passionately. Strive – As do the vain wranglers spoken of, verse 23. But be apt to teach – Chiefly by patience and unwearied assiduity.

25. In meekness – He has often need of zeal, always of meekness. If haply God – For it is wholly his work. May give them repentance – The acknowledging of the truth would then quickly follow.

26. Who – At present are not only captives, but asleep; utterly insensible of their captivity.

2 TIMOTHY 3

1. In the last days – The time of the gospel dispensation, commencing at the time of our Lord's death, is peculiarly styled the last days. Grievous – Troublesome and dangerous.

2. For men – Even in the church. Will be – In great numbers, and to an higher degree than ever. Lovers of themselves – Only, not their neighbors, the first root of evil. Lovers of money – The second.

3. Without natural affection – To their own children. Intemperate, fierce – Both too soft, and too hard.

4. Lovers of sensual pleasure – Which naturally extinguishes all love and sense of God.

5. Having a form – An appearance of godliness, but not regarding, nay, even denying and blaspheming, the inward power and reality of it. Is not this eminently fulfilled at this day?

6. Of these – That is, mere formalists.

7. Ever learning – New things. But not the truth of God.

8. Several ancient writers speak of Jannes and Jambres, as the chief of the Egyptian magicians. Men of corrupt minds – Impure notions and wicked inclinations. Void of judgment – Quite ignorant, as well as careless, of true, spiritual religion.

9. They shall proceed no farther – In gaining proselytes.

12. All that are resolved to live godly – Therefore count the cost. Art thou resolved? In Christ – Out of Christ there is no godliness. Shall suffer persecution – More or less. There is no exception. Either the truth of scripture fails, or those that think they are religious, and are not persecuted, in some shape or other, on that very account, deceive themselves.

13. Deceiving and being deceived – He who has once begun to deceive others is both the less likely to recover from his own error, and the more ready to embrace the errors of other men.

14. From whom – Even from me a teacher approved of God.

15. From an infant thou hast known the holy scriptures – Of the Old Testament. These only were extant when Timothy was an infant. Which are able to make thee wise unto salvation, through faith in the Messiah that was to come. How much more are the Old and New Testament together able, in God's hand, to make us more abundantly wise unto salvation! Even such a measure of present salvation as was not known before Jesus was glorified.

16. All scripture is inspired of God – The Spirit of God not only once inspired those who wrote it, but continually inspires, supernaturally assists, those that read it with earnest prayer. Hence it is so profitable for doctrine, for instruction of the ignorant, for the reproof or conviction of them that are in error or sin, for the correction or amendment of whatever is amiss, and for instructing or training up the children of God in all

gospel. If we are dead to this world, its pleasures, profits, and honors, we shall be forever with Christ in a better world.

14-21 Those disposed to strive, commonly strive about matters of small moment. But strifes of words destroy the things of God. The apostle mentions some who erred. They did not deny the resurrection, but they corrupted that true doctrine. Yet nothing can be so foolish or erroneous, but it will overturn the temporary faith of some professors. This foundation has two writings on it. One speaks our comfort. None can overthrow the faith of any whom God hath chosen. The other speaks our duty. Those who would have the comfort of the privilege, must make conscience of the duty Christ gave himself for us, that he might redeem us from all iniquity, Tit 2:14. The church of Christ is like a dwelling: some furniture is of great value; some of smaller value, and put to meaner uses. Some professors of religion are like vessels of wood and earth. When the vessels of dishonor are cast out to be destroyed, the others will be filled with all the fullness of God. We must see to it that we are holy vessels. Every one in the church whom God approves, will be devoted to his Master's service, and thus fitted for his use.

22-26 The more we follow that which is good, the faster and the further we shall flee from that which is evil. The keeping up the communion of saints, will take us from fellowship with unfruitful works of darkness. See how often the apostle cautions against disputes in religion; which surely shows that religion consists more in believing and practicing what God requires, than in subtle disputes. Those are unapt to teach, who are apt to strive, and are fierce and froward. Teaching, not persecution, is the Scripture method of dealing with those in error.

2 TIMOTHY 3

The apostle foretells the rise of dangerous enemies to the gospel. (1-9)

Proposes his own example to Timothy. (10-13)

And exhorts him to continue in the doctrine he had learned from the Holy Scriptures. (14-17)

1-9 Even in gospel times there would be perilous times; on account of persecution from without, still more on account of corruptions within. Men love to gratify their own lusts, more than to please God and do their duty. When every man is eager for what he can get, and anxious to keep what he has, this makes men dangerous to one another. When men do not fear God, they will not regard man. When children are disobedient to their parents, that makes the times perilous. Men are unholy and without the fear of God, because unthankful for the mercies of God. We abuse God's gifts, if we make them the food and fuel of our

wealth, never to part or sunder from him. You must take him to be your only prop, your only pillar from this day forth and for ever. What sayest thou sinner? Does God the Holy Ghost lead thee to say "Ay?" Does thy heart now confide in Jesus? If so, let the angels sing, for a soul is born to God, and a brand is plucked from the eternal fire. I have thus described faith in Christ—the committing of the soul to him.

II. This brings us to our second point—THE JUSTIFICATION OF THIS GRAND ACT OF TRUST.

Confidence is sometimes folly; trusting in man is always so. When I exhort you, then, to put your entire confidence in Christ, am I justified in so doing? and when the apostle could say that he trusted alone in Jesus, and had committed himself to him, was he a wise man or a fool? What saith the apostle? "I am no fool," said he, "for I know whom I have believed. I have not trusted to an unknown and untried pretender. I have not relied upon one whose character I could suspect. I have confidence in one whose power, whose willingness, whose love, whose truthfulness I know. I know whom I have believed." When silly women put their trust in yet more silly and wicked priests, they may say possibly that they know whom they have believed. But we may tell them that their knowledge must be ignorance indeed—that they are greatly deluded in imagining that any man, be he who he may, or what he may, can have any power in the salvation of his fellow's soul. You come sneaking up to me and ask me to repose my soul in you; and who are you? "I am an ordained priest of the Church of Rome." And who ordained you? "I was ordained by such a one." And who ordained him? "It cometh after all," saith he, "from the Pope." And who is he, and what is he more than any other man, or any other imposter? What ordination can he confer? "He obtained it directly from Peter." Did he? Let the link be proved; and if he did, what was Peter, and where has God given Peter power to forgive sin—a power which he should transmit to all generations? Begone! The thick pollutions of thine abominable church forbid the idea of descent from any apostle but the traitor Judas. Upon the Papal throne men worse than devils have had their seat, and even a woman big with her adulteries once reigned as head of thine accursed church. Go purge the filthiness of thy priesthood, the debauchery of thy nunneries and the stygian filth of thy mother city, the old harlot Rome. Talk not of pardoning others, while fornication is licensed in Rome itself, and her ministers are steeped to the throat in iniquity. But to return. I rest no more on Peter than Peter

came unto me at Antioch, at Iconium, at Lystra; what persecutions I endured: but out of them all the Lord delivered me.

12 Yea, and all that will live godly in Christ Jesus shall suffer persecution.

13 But evil men and seducers shall wax worse and worse, deceiving, and being deceived.

14 But continue thou in the things which thou hast learned and hast been assured of, knowing of whom thou hast learned them;

15 And that from a child thou hast known the holy scriptures, which are able to make thee wise unto salvation through faith which is in Christ Jesus.

16 All scripture is given by inspiration of God, and is profitable for doctrine, for reproof, for correction, for instruction in righteousness:

17 That the man of God may be perfect, throughly furnished unto all good works.

2 TIMOTHY 4

1 I charge thee therefore before God, and the Lord Jesus Christ, who shall judge the quick and the dead at his appearing and his kingdom;

2 Preach the word; be instant in season, out of season; reprove, rebuke, exhort with all longsuffering and doctrine.

3 For the time will come when they will not endure sound doctrine; but after their own lusts shall they heap to themselves teachers, having itching ears;

4 And they shall turn away their ears from the truth, and shall be turned unto fables.

5 But watch thou in all things, endure afflictions, do the work of an evangelist, make full proof of thy ministry.

6 For I am now ready to be offered, and the time of my departure is at hand.

7 I have fought a good fight, I have finished my course, I have kept the faith:

8 Henceforth there is laid up for me a crown of righteousness, which the Lord, the righteous judge, shall give me at that day: and not to me only, but unto all them also that love his appearing.

9 Do thy diligence to come shortly unto me:

10 For Demas hath forsaken me, having loved this present world, and is departed unto Thessalonica; Crescens to Galatia, Titus unto Dalmatia.

11 Only Luke is with me. Take Mark, and bring him with thee: for he is profitable to me for the ministry.

12 And Tychicus have I sent to Ephesus.

13 The cloke that I left at Troas with Carpus, when thou comest, bring with

righteousness.

17. That the man of God – He that is united to and approved of God. May be perfect – Blameless himself, and thoroughly furnished – By the scripture, either to teach, reprove, correct, or train up others.

2 TIMOTHY 4

1. I charge thee therefore – This is deduced from the whole preceding chapter. At his appearing and his kingdom – That is, at his appearing in the kingdom of glory.

2. Be instant – Insist on, urge these things in season, out of season – That is, continually, at all times and places. It might be translated, with and without opportunity – Not only when a fair occasion is given: even when there is none, one must be made.

3. For they will heap up teachers – Therefore thou hast need of "all longsuffering." According to their own desires – Smooth as they can wish. Having itching ears – Fond of novelty and variety, which the number of new teachers, as well as their empty, soft, or philosophical discourses, pleased. Such teachers, and such hearers, seldom are much concerned with what is strict or to the purpose. Heap to themselves – Not enduring sound doctrine, they will reject the sound preachers, and gather together all that suit their own taste. Probably they send out one another as teachers, and so are never at a loss for numbers.

5. Watch – An earnest, constant, persevering exercise. The scripture watching, or waiting, implies steadfast faith, patient hope, laboring love, unceasing prayer; yea, the mighty exertion of all the affections of the soul that a man is capable of. In all things – Whatever you are doing, yet in that, and in all things, watch. Do the work of an evangelist – Which was next to that of an apostle.

6. The time of my departure is at hand – So undoubtedly God had shown him. I am ready to be offered up – Literally, to be poured out, as the wine and oil were on the ancient sacrifices.

8. The crown of that righteousness – Which God has imputed to me and wrought in me. Will render to all – This increases the joy of Paul, and encourages Timotheus. Many of these St. Paul himself had gained. That have loved his appearing – Which only a real Christian can do. I say a real Christian, to comply with the mode of the times: else they would not understand, although the word Christian necessarily implies whatsoever is holy, as God is holy. Strictly speaking, to join real or sincere to a word of so complete an import, is grievously to debase its noble signification, and is like adding long to eternity or wide to immensity.

9. Come to me – Both that he might comfort him, and be strengthened by him. Timotheus himself is said to have suffered at Ephesus.

10. Demas – Once my fellowlaborer, Phil. i, 24. Hath forsaken me. Crescens, probably a preacher also, is gone, with my consent, to Galatia, Titus to Dalmatia, having now left Crete. These either went with him to Rome, or visited him there.

11. Only Luke – Of my fellowlaborers, is with me – But God is with me; and it is enough. Take Mark – Who, though he once "departed from the work," is now again profitable to me.

13. The cloak – Either the toga, which belonged to him as a Roman citizen, or an upper garment, which might be needful as winter came on. Which I left at Troas with Carpus – Who was probably his host there. Especially the parchments – The books written on parchment.

14. The Lord will reward him – This he spoke prophetically.

16. All – My friends and companions. Forsook me – And do we expect

lusts. Times are perilous also, when parents are without natural affection to children. And when men have no rule over their own spirits, but despise that which is good and to be honored. God is to be loved above all; but a carnal mind, full of enmity against him, prefers any thing before him, especially carnal pleasure. A form of godliness is very different from the power; from such as are found to be hypocrites, real Christians must withdraw.

10-13 The more fully we know the doctrine of Christ, as taught by the apostles, the more closely we shall cleave to it. When we know the afflictions of believers only in part, they tempt us to decline the cause for which they suffer. A form of godliness, a profession of Christian faith without a godly life, often is allowed to pass, while open profession of the truth as it is in Jesus, and resolute attention to the duties of godliness, stir up the scorn and enmity of the world. As good men, by the grace of God, grow better, so bad men, through the craft of Satan, and the power of their own corruptions, grow worse. The way of sin is downhill; such go on from bad to worse, deceiving and being deceived. Those who deceive others, deceive themselves, as they will find at last, to their cost. The history of the outward church, awfully shows that the apostle spake this as he was moved by the Holy Ghost.

14-17 Those who would learn the things of God, and be assured of them, must know the Holy Scriptures, for they are the Divine revelation. The age of children is the age to learn; and those who would get true learning, must get it out of the Scriptures. They must not lie by us neglected, seldom or never looked into. The Bible is a sure guide to eternal life. The prophets and apostles did not speak from themselves, but delivered what they received of God, 2Pe 1:21. It is profitable for all purposes of the Christian life. It is of use to all, for all need to be taught, corrected, and reproved. There is something in the Scriptures suitable for every case.

2 TIMOTHY 4

The apostle solemnly charges Timothy to be diligent, though many will not bear sound doctrine. (1-5)

Enforces the charge from his own martyrdom, then at hand. (6-8)

Desires him to come speedily. (9-13)

He cautions, and complains of such as had deserted him; and expresses his faith as to his own preservation to the heavenly kingdom. (14-18)

Friendly greetings and his usual blessing. (19-22)

1-5 People will turn away from the truth, they will grow weary of the plain gospel of Christ, they will be greedy of fables, and take pleasure in them. People do so when they will not endure that preaching which

could rest in himself, Peter must rest on Christ as a poor guilty sinner himself, an imperfect man who denied his Master with oaths and curses. He must rest where I must rest, and we must stand together on the same great rock on which Christ doth build his church, even his blood and his ever-lasting merits. I marvel that any should be found to have such confidence in men, that they should put their souls in their hands. If however any of you wish to trust in a priest, let me advise you if you do trust him, to do it wholly and fully. Trust him with your cash-box, trust him with your gold and silver. Perhaps you object to that. You don't feel at all inclined to go that length. But, my friend, if you cannot trust the man with your gold and silver, pray don't trust him with your soul. I only suggested this because I thought you might smile and at once detect your error. If you could not trust such a fox with your business; if you would as soon commit your flocks to the custody of a wolf, why will you be fool enough to lay your soul at the feet of some base priest who, likely enough, is ten thousand times more wicked than your self.

Was Paul then justified in his confidence in Christ? He says he was because he knew Christ. Paul not only knew these things by faith, but he knew much of them by experience. Our knowledge of Christ is somewhat like climbing one of our Welsh mountains. When you are at the base you see but little, the mountain itself appears to be but one half as high as it really is. Confined in a little valley you discover scarcely anything but the rippling brooks as they descend into the stream at the base of the mountain. Climb the first rising knoll, and the valley lengthens and widens beneath your feet. Go up higher, and higher still, till you stand upon the summit of one of the great roots that start out as spurs from the sides of the mountain you see the country for some four or five miles round, and you are delighted with the widening prospect. But go onward, and onward, and onward, and how the scene enlarges, till at last, when you are on the summit, and look east, west, north, and south, you see almost all England lying before you. Yonder is a forest in some distant country, perhaps two hundred miles away, and yonder the sea, and there a shining river and the smoking chimneys of a manufacturing town, or there the masts of the ships in some well known port. All these things please and delight you, and you say, "I could not have imagined that so much could be seen at this elevation." Now, the Christian life is of the same order. When we first believe in Christ we see but little of him. The higher we climb the more we discover of his excellencies and his beauties. But

thee, and the books, but especially the parchments.

14 Alexander the coppersmith did me much evil: the Lord reward him according to his works:

15 Of whom be thou ware also; for he hath greatly withstood our words.

16 At my first answer no man stood with me, but all men forsook me: I pray God that it may not be laid to their charge.

17 Notwithstanding the Lord stood with me, and strengthened me; that by me the preaching might be fully known, and that all the Gentiles might hear: and I was delivered out of the mouth of the lion.

18 And the Lord shall deliver me from every evil work, and will preserve me unto his heavenly kingdom: to whom be glory for ever and ever. Amen.

19 Salute Prisca and Aquila, and the household of Onesiphorus.

20 Erastus abode at Corinth: but Trophimus have I left at Miletum sick.

21 Do thy diligence to come before winter. Eubulus greeteth thee, and Pudens, and Linus, and Claudia, and all the brethren.

22 The Lord Jesus Christ be with thy spirit. Grace be with you. Amen.

to find such as will not forsake us? My first defense – Before the savage emperor Nero.

17. The preaching – The gospel which we preach.

18. And the Lord will deliver me from every evil work – Which is far more than delivering me from death. Yea, and, over and above, preserve me unto his heavenly kingdom – Far better than that of Nero.

20. When I came on, Erastus abode at Corinth – Being chamberlain of the city, Rom. xvi, 23. But Trophimus I have left sick – Not having power (as neither had any of the apostles) to work miracles when he pleased, but only when God pleased.

is searching, plain, and to the purpose. Those who love souls must be ever watchful, must venture and bear all the painful effects of their faithfulness, and take all opportunities of making known the pure gospel.

6-8 The blood of the martyrs, though not a sacrifice of atonement, yet was a sacrifice of acknowledgment to the grace of God and his truth. Death to a good man, is his release from the imprisonment of this world, and his departure to the enjoyments of another world. As a Christian, and a minister, Paul had kept the faith, kept the doctrines of the gospel. What comfort will it afford, to be able to speak in this manner toward the end of our days! The crown of believers is a crown of righteousness, purchased by the righteousness of Christ. Believers have it not at present, yet it is sure, for it is laid up for them.

9-13 The love of this world, is often the cause of turning back from the truths and ways of Jesus Christ. Paul was guided by Divine inspiration, yet he would have his books. As long as we live, we must still learn. The apostles did not neglect human means, in seeking the necessaries of life, or their own instruction. Let us thank the Divine goodness in having given us so many writings of wise and pious men in all ages; and let us seek that by reading them our profiting may appear to all.

14-18 There is as much danger from false brethren, as from open enemies. It is dangerous having to do with those who would be enemies to such a man as Paul. The Christians at Rome were forward to meet him, Ac 28, but when there seemed to be a danger of suffering with him, then all forsook him. God might justly be angry with them, but he prays God to forgive them. The apostle was delivered out of the mouth of the lion, that is, of Nero, or some of his judges. If the Lord stands by us, he will strengthen us in difficulties and dangers, and his presence will more than supply every one's absence.

19-22 We need no more to make us happy, than to have the Lord Jesus Christ with our spirits; for in him all spiritual blessings are summed up. It is the best prayer we can offer for our friends, that the Lord Jesus Christ may be with their spirits, to sanctify and save them, and at last to receive them to himself. Many who believed as Paul, are now before the throne, giving glory to their Lord: may we be followers of them.

who has ever gained the summit? Who has ever known all the fullness of the heights, and depths, and lengths, and breadths of the love of Christ which passeth knowledge. Paul now grown old, sitting, gray hair'd, shivering in a dungeon in Rome—he could say, with greater power than we can, "I know whom I have believed"—for each experience had been like the climbing of a hill, each trial had been like the ascending to another summit, and his death seemed like the gaining of the very top of the mountain from which he could see the whole of the faithfulness and the love of him to whom he had committed his soul.

III. And now, I close by noticing THE APOSTLE'S CONFIDENCE. The apostle said, "I am persuaded that he is able to keep that which I have committed to him." See this man. He is sure he shall be saved. But why? Paul! art thou sure that thou canst keep thyself? "No," says he, "I have nothing to do with that:" and yet thou art sure of thy salvation! "Yes," saith he, "I am!" How is it, then? "Why, I am persuaded that he is able to keep me. Christ, to whom I commit myself, I know hath power enough to hold me to the end." Martin Luther was bold enough to exclaim "Let him that died for my soul, see to the salvation of it." Let us catechize the apostle for a few minutes, and see if we cannot shake his confidence.

Paul, Paul, suppose the world should tempt you. If a kingdom were offered you—if the pomps and pleasures of this world should be laid at your feet, provided you would deny your Master, would your faith maintain its hold then? "Yea," saith the apostle, "Jesus would even then uphold my faith for my soul is not in my keeping, but in his, and empires upon empires could not tempt him to renounce that soul of which he has become the guardian and the keeper. Temptation might soon overcome me, but it could not overcome him. The world's blandishments might soon move me to renounce my own soul; but they could not for one moment move Jesus to give me up." And so the apostle continues his confidence. But Paul, when thou shalt come to die, will thou not then fear and tremble? "Nay," saith he, "he will be with me there, for my soul shall not die, that will be still in the hand of him who is immortality and life."

O poor sinner! come and put thy soul into the hands of Jesus. Attempt not to take care of it thyself; and then thy life shall be hidden in heaven, where none can destroy it and none can rob thee of it. "Whosoever believeth on the Lord Jesus Christ shall be saved."

Titus

TITUS 1

1 Paul, a servant of God, and an apostle of Jesus Christ, according to the faith of God's elect, and the acknowledging of the truth which is after godliness;

2 In hope of eternal life, which God, that cannot lie, promised before the world began;

3 But hath in due times manifested his word through preaching, which is committed unto me according to the commandment of God our Savior;

4 To Titus, mine own son after the common faith: Grace, mercy, and peace, from God the Father and the Lord Jesus Christ our Savior.

5 For this cause left I thee in Crete, that thou shouldest set in order the things that are wanting, and ordain elders in every city, as I had appointed thee:

6 If any be blameless, the husband of one wife, having faithful children not accused of riot or unruly.

7 For a bishop must be blameless, as the steward of God; not selfwilled, not soon angry, not given to wine, no striker, not given to filthy lucre;

8 But a lover of hospitality, a lover of good men, sober, just, holy, temperate;

9 Holding fast the faithful word as he hath been taught, that he may be able by sound doctrine both to exhort and to convince the gainsayers.

10 For there are many unruly and vain talkers and deceivers, specially they of the circumcision:

11 Whose mouths must be stopped, who subvert whole houses, teaching things which they ought not, for filthy lucre's sake.

12 One of themselves, even a prophet of their own, said, The Cretians are alway liars, evil beasts, slow bellies.

13 This witness is true. Wherefore rebuke them sharply, that they may be sound in the faith;

14 Not giving heed to Jewish fables, and commandments of men, that turn from the truth.

TITUS was converted from heathenism by St. Paul, and, as it seems, very early; since the apostle accounted him as his brother at his first going into Macedonia: and he managed and settled the churches there, when St. Paul thought not good to go thither himself. He had now left him at Crete, to regulate the churches; to assist him wherein, he wrote this epistle, as is generally believed, after the First, and before the Second, to Timothy. The tenor and style are much alike in this and in those; and they cast much light on each other, and are worthy the serious attention of all Christian ministers and churches in all ages.

TITUS 1

1. Paul, a servant of God, and an apostle of Jesus Christ – Titles suitable to the person of Paul, and the office he was assigning to Titus. According to the faith – The propagating of which is the proper business of an apostle. A servant of God – According to the faith of the elect. An apostle of Jesus Christ – According to the knowledge of the truth. We serve God according to the measure of our faith: we fulfill our public office according to the measure of our knowledge. The truth that is after godliness – Which in every point runs parallel with and supports the vital, spiritual worship of God; and, indeed, has no other end or scope. These two verses contain the sum of Christianity, which Titus was always to have in his eye. Of the elect of God – Of all real Christians

2. In hope of eternal life – The grand motive and encouragement of every apostle and every servant of God. Which God promised before the world began – To Christ, our Head.

3. And he hath in his own times – At sundry times; and his own times are fittest for his own work. What creature dares ask, "Why no sooner?" Manifested his word – Containing that promise, and the whole "truth which is after godliness." Through the preaching wherewith I am intrusted according to the commandment of God our Savior – And who dares exercise this office on any less authority?

4. My own son – Begot in the same image of God, and repaying a paternal with a filial affection. The common faith – Common to me and all my spiritual children.

5. The things which are wanting – Which I had not time to settle myself. Ordain elders – Appoint the most faithful, zealous men to watch over the rest. Their character follows, Tit i, 6-9. These were the elders, or bishops, that Paul approved of: men that had living faith, a pure conscience, a blameless life.

6. The husband of one wife – Surely the Holy Ghost, by repeating this so often, designed to leave the Romanists without excuse.

7. As the steward of God – To whom he entrusts immortal souls. Not self-willed – Literally, pleasing himself; but all men "for their good to edification." Not passionate – But mild, yielding, tender.

9. As he hath been taught – Perhaps it might be more literally rendered, according to the teaching, or doctrine, of the apostles; alluding to Acts ii, 42.

10. They of the circumcision – The Jewish converts.

11. Stopped – The word properly means, to put a bit into the mouth of an unruly horse.

12. A prophet – So all poets were anciently called; but, besides, Diogenes Laertius says that Epimenides, the Cretan poet, foretold many things. Evil wild beasts – Fierce and savage.

14. Commandments of men – The Jewish or other teachers, whoever they were that turned from the truth.

15. To the pure – Those whose hearts are purified by faith this we allow. All things are pure – All kinds of meat; the Mosaic distinction between clean and unclean meats being now taken away. But to the defiled and unbelieving nothing is pure – The apostle joins defiled and unbelieving, to intimate that noth-

MATTHEW HENRY

This epistle chiefly contains directions to Titus concerning the elders of the Church, and the manner in which he should give instruction; and the latter part tells him to urge obedience to magistrates, to enforce good works, avoid foolish questions, and shun heresies. The instructions the apostle gave are all plain and simple. The Christian religion was not formed to answer worldly or selfish views, but it is the wisdom of God and the power of God.

TITUS 1

The apostle salutes Titus. (1-4)
The qualifications of a faithful pastor. (5-9)
The evil temper and practices of false teachers. (10-16)

1-4 All are the servants of God who are not slaves of sin and Satan. All gospel truth is according to godliness, teaching the fear of God. The intent of the gospel is to raise up hope as well as faith; to take off the mind and heart from the world, and to raise them to heaven and the things above. How excellent then is the gospel, which was the matter of Divine promise so early, and what thanks are due for our privileges! Faith comes by hearing, and hearing by the word of God; and whoso is appointed and called, must preach the word. Grace is the free favor of God, and acceptance with him. Mercy, the fruits of the favor, in the pardon of sin, and freedom from all miseries both here and hereafter. And peace is the effect and fruit of mercy. Peace with God through Christ who is our Peace, and with the creatures and ourselves. Grace is the fountain of all blessings. Mercy, and peace, and all good, spring out of this.

5-9 The character and qualification of pastors, here called elders and bishops, agree with what the apostle wrote to Timothy. Being such bishops and overseers of the flock, to be examples to them, and God's stewards to take care of the affairs of his household, there is great reason that they should be blameless. What they are not to be, is plainly shown, as well as what they are to be, as servants of Christ, and able ministers of the letter and practice of the gospel.

10-16 False teachers are described. Faithful ministers must oppose such in good time, that their folly being made manifest, they may go no further. They had a base end in what they did; serving a worldly interest under pretense of religion: for the love of money is the root of all evil. Such should be resisted, and put to shame, by sound doctrine from the Scriptures. Shameful actions, the reproach of heathens, should be far from Christians; falsehood and lying, envious craft and cruelty, brutal and sensual practices, and idleness and sloth, are sins condemned even by the light of nature. But Christian meekness is as far from cowardly passing over sin and error, as from anger and impatience. And though there may be national differences of character, yet the heart of man in every age and place is deceitful and desperately

CHARLES H. SPURGEON

GOOD WORKS
Sermon number 70 delivered on March 16, 1856, at New Park Street Chapel, Southwark.

"Zealous of good works."—Titus 2:14.

First, we are about to answer the question, WHAT ARE GOOD WORKS? Now, I dare say we shall offend many here when we tell them what good works are; for in our opinion good works are the rarest things in the world, and we believe we might walk for many a mile before we should see a good work at all. We use the word good now in its proper sense. There are many works which are good enough between man and man, but we shall use the word good in a higher sense today as regards God. We think we shall be able to show you that there are very few good works anywhere, and that there are none out of the pale of Christ's church. We think, if we read Scripture rightly, that no work can be good unless it is commanded of God. How this cuts off a large portion of what men will do in order to win salvation! The Pharisee said he tithed mint, anise, and cummin; could he prove that God commanded him to tithe his mint, his anise, and his cummin? Perhaps not. He said he fasted so many times a week; could he prove that God told him to fast? If not, his fasting was no obedience. If I do a thing that I am not commanded to do, I do not obey in doing it. Vain, then, are all the pretenses of men, that by mortifying their bodies, by denying their flesh, by doing this, that, or the other, they shall therefore win the favor of God. No work is good unless God has commanded it. A man may build a long row of almshouses, but if he build without reference to the commandment, he has performed no good work.

Again: nothing is a good work unless it is done with a good motive; and there is no motive which can be said to be good but the glory of God. He who performs good works with a view to save himself, does not do them from a good motive, because his motive is selfish. He who does them also to gain the esteem of his fellows and for the good of society, has a laudable motive, so far as man is concerned; but it is, after all, an inferior motive.—What end had we in view? If for the benefit of our fellow-creatures, then let our fellow-creatures pay us; but that has nought to do with God. Work is not good, unless a man does it with a

15 Unto the pure all things are pure: but unto them that are defiled and unbelieving is nothing pure; but even their mind and conscience is defiled.

16 They profess that they know God; but in works they deny him, being abominable, and disobedient, and unto every good work reprobate.

TITUS 2

1 But speak thou the things which become sound doctrine:

2 That the aged men be sober, grave, temperate, sound in faith, in charity, in patience.

3 The aged women likewise, that they be in behavior as becometh holiness, not false accusers, not given to much wine, teachers of good things;

4 That they may teach the young women to be sober, to love their husbands, to love their children,

5 To be discreet, chaste, keepers at home, good, obedient to their own husbands, that the word of God be not blasphemed.

6 Young men likewise exhort to be sober minded.

7 In all things shewing thyself a pattern of good works: in doctrine shewing uncorruptness, gravity, sincerity,

8 Sound speech, that cannot be condemned; that he that is of the contrary part may be ashamed, having no evil thing to say of you.

9 Exhort servants to be obedient unto their own masters, and to please them well in all things; not answering again;

10 Not purloining, but shewing all good fidelity; that they may adorn the doctrine of God our Savior in all things.

11 For the grace of God that bringeth salvation hath appeared to all men,

12 Teaching us that, denying ungodliness and worldly lusts, we should live soberly, righteously, and godly, in this present world;

13 Looking for that blessed hope, and the glorious appearing of the great God and our

ing can be clean without a true faith: for both the understanding and conscience, those leading powers of the soul, are polluted; consequently, so is the man and all he does.

TITUS 2

1. Wholesome – Restoring and preserving spiritual health.

2. Vigilant – As veteran soldiers, not easily to be surprised. Patience – A virtue particularly needful for and becoming them. Serious – Not diverting on the brink of eternity.

3. In behavior – The particulars whereof follow. As becometh holiness – Literally, observing an holy decorum. Not slanderers – Or evil-speakers. Not given to much wine – If they use a little for their often infirmities. Teachers – Age and experience call them so to be. Let them teach good only.

4. That they instruct the young women – These Timothy was to instruct himself; Titus, by the elder women. To love their husbands, their children – With a tender, temperate, holy, wise affection. O how hard a lesson.

5. Discreet – Particularly in the love of their children. Chaste – Particularly in the love of their husbands. Keepers at home – Whenever they are not called out by works of necessity, piety, and mercy. Good – Well tempered, sweet, soft, obliging. Obedient to their husbands – Whose will, in all things lawful, is a rule to the wife. That the word of God be not blasphemed – Or evil spoken of; particularly by unbelieving husbands, who lay all the blame on the religion of their wives.

6. To be discreet – A virtue rarely found in youth.

7. Showing thyself a pattern – Titus himself was then young. In the doctrine which thou teachest in public: as to matter, uncorruptable; as to the manner of delivering it, seriousness – Weightiness, solemnity.

8. Wholesome speech – In private conversation.

9. Please them in all things – Wherein it can be done without sin. Not answering again – Though blamed unjustly. This honest servants are most apt to do. Not stealing – Not taking or giving any thing without their master's leave: this fair-spoken servants are apt to do.

10. Showing all good fidelity – Soft, obliging faithfulness That they may adorn the doctrine of God our Savior – More than St. Paul says of kings. How he raises the lowness of his subject! So may they, the lowness of their condition.

11. The saving grace of God – So it is in its nature, tendency, and design. Hath appeared to all men – High and low.

12. Instructing us – All who do not reject it. That, having renounced ungodliness – Whatever is contrary to the fear and love of God. And worldly desires – Which are opposite to sobriety and righteousness. We should live soberly – In all purity and holiness. Sobriety, in the scripture sense, is rather the whole temper of a man, than a single virtue in him. It comprehends all that is opposite to the drowsiness of sin, the folly of ignorance, the ungodliness of disorderly passions. Sobriety is no less than all the powers of the soul being consistently and constantly awake, duly governed by heavenly prudence, and entirely conformable to holy affections. And righteously – Doing to all as we would they should do to us. And godly – As those who are consecrated to God both in heart and life.

13. Looking – With eager desire. For that glorious appearing – Which we hope for. Of the great God, even our Savior Jesus Christ – So that, if there be (according to the Arian scheme) a great God and a little God, Christ is not the little God, but the great one.

14. Who gave himself for us – To die in our stead. That he might redeem us – Miserable bond slaves, as well from the power and the very being, as from the guilt, of all our sins.

wicked. But the sharpest reproofs must aim at the good of the reproved; and soundness in the faith is most desirable and necessary.

TITUS 2

The duties which become sound doctrine. (1-8)
Believing servants must be obedient. (9,10)
All is enforced from the holy design of the gospel, which concerns all believers. (11-15)

1-8 Old disciples of Christ must behave in every thing agreeably to the Christian doctrine. That the aged men be sober; not thinking that the decays of nature will justify any excess; but seeking comfort from nearer communion with God, not from any undue indulgence. Faith works by, and must be seen in love, of God for himself, and of men for God's sake. Aged persons are apt to be peevish and fretful; therefore need to be on their guard. Though there is not express Scripture for every word, or look, yet there are general rules, according to which all must be ordered. Young women must be sober and discreet; for many expose themselves to fatal temptations by what at first might be only want of discretion. The reason is added, that the word of God may not be blasphemed. Failures in duties greatly reproach Christianity. Young men are apt to be eager and thoughtless, therefore must be earnestly called upon to be sober-minded: there are more young people ruined by pride than by any other sin.

9,10 Servants must know and do their duty to their earthly masters, with a reference to their heavenly one. In serving an earthly master according to Christ's will, he is served; such shall be rewarded by him. Not giving disrespectful or provoking language; but to take a check or reproof with silence, not making confident or bold replies. When conscious of a fault, to excuse or justify it, doubles it.

11-15 The doctrine of grace and salvation by the gospel, is for all ranks and conditions of men. It teaches to forsake sin; to have no more to do with it. An earthly, sensual conversation suits not a heavenly calling. It teaches to make conscience of that which is good. We must look to God in Christ, as the object of our hope and worship. A gospel conversation must be a godly conversation. See our duty in a very few words; denying ungodliness and worldly lusts, living soberly, righteously, and godly, notwithstanding all snares, temptations, corrupt examples, ill usage, and what remains of sin in the believer's heart, with all their hindrances. It teaches to look for the glories of another world. At, and in, the glorious appearing of Christ, the blessed hope of Christians will be complete: To bring us to holiness and happiness was the end of Christ's death. Jesus Christ, that great God and our Savior, who saves not only as God, much less as Man alone; but as God-man, two natures in one person. He loved us, and gave himself for us; and what can we do less

view to God's glory, and he has been brought into subjection to God's divine will, so that in everything he has an eye to the Most High, and works in order to promote his glory and honor in the world. And even, beloved, when our works are done from the best motives, nothing is a good work unless it is done with faith; for "without faith it is impossible to please God." Like Cain, we may build the altar, and lay the first fruits of the salt of faith, there it will lie—it will not be accepted by God, for without faith it is impossible to please him. Bring me a man who all his life long has been spending his health and strength for his fellow-creatures; fetch me some public officer, who has fully discharged his trust, who has labored night and day, even to the wearing down of his constitution, because he believed that England expected every man to do his duty, and he wished to do it; bring me that man; let me see all his charitable works; let me witness the most lavish benevolence, the most profuse bounty; tell me that he has always, with a consistent motive, labored for his country; and then, if he cannot answer this question. "Dost thou believe in the Son of God?" I shall be bound in all honesty to tell him that he has not done a solitary good work in all his life, so far as God is concerned.

Augustine well said, "Good works, as they are called, in sinners, are nothing but splendid sins." This is true of the best works of the best man, who is out of Christ, they are nothing but splendid sins—vanished sins. God forgive you, dear friends, for your good works! You have as great need to be forgiven for your good works as you have for your bad ones, if you are out of Christ; for I reckon they are both alike, bad, if they come to be sifted.

II. And now, secondly, WHERE DO GOOD WORKS COME FROM?

It is an old maxim, that nature can never rise above itself. Water, coming from the top of a hill, will rise as high as its source; but unless there is some extraordinary pressure put upon it, it will never rise higher. So of human nature, Scripture says it is exceedingly vile; we cannot expect good works out of an evil nature. Can a bitter well send forth sweet water? As poison groweth not on healthful trees, with healthful fruit, so cannot healthy fruit grow on poisonous trees. We must not look for good works in an evil nature any more than we should look for the grapes of Sorek on the vines of

Savior Jesus Christ;

14 Who gave himself for us, that he might redeem us from all iniquity, and purify unto himself a peculiar people, zealous of good works.

15 These things speak, and exhort, and rebuke with all authority. Let no man despise thee.

TITUS 3

1 Put them in mind to be subject to principalities and powers, to obey magistrates, to be ready to every good work,

2 To speak evil of no man, to be no brawlers, but gentle, shewing all meekness unto all men.

3 For we ourselves also were sometimes foolish, disobedient, deceived, serving divers lusts and pleasures, living in malice and envy, hateful, and hating one another.

4 But after that the kindness and love of God our Savior toward man appeared,

5 Not by works of righteousness which we have done, but according to his mercy he saved us, by the washing of regeneration, and renewing of the Holy Ghost;

6 Which he shed on us abundantly through Jesus Christ our Savior;

7 That being justified by his grace, we should be made heirs according to the hope of eternal life.

8 This is a faithful saying, and these things I will that thou affirm constantly, that they which have believed in God might be careful to maintain good works. These things are good and profitable unto men.

9 But avoid foolish questions, and genealogies, and contentions, and strivings about the law; for they are unprofitable and vain.

10 A man that is an heretic after the first and second admonition reject;

11 Knowing that he that is such is subverted, and sinneth, being condemned of himself.

12 When I shall send Artemas

15. Let no man despise thee – That is, let none have any just cause to despise thee. Yet they surely will. Men who know not God will despise a true minister of his word.

TITUS 3

1. Remind them – All the Cretan Christians. To be subject – Passively, not resisting. To principalities – Supreme. And powers – Subordinate governors. And to obey – Them actively, so far as conscience permits.

2. To speak evil – Neither of them nor any man. Not to be quarrelsome – To assault none. To be gentle – When assaulted. Toward all men – Even those who are such as we were.

3. For we – And as God hath dealt with us, so ought we to deal with our neighbor. Were without understanding – Wholly ignorant of God. And disobedient – When he was declared to us.

4. When the love of God appeared – By the light of his Spirit to our inmost soul.

5. Not by works – In this important passage the apostle presents us with a delightful view of our redemption. Herein we have,

1. The cause of it; not our works or righteousness, but "the kindness and love of God our Savior."

2. The effects; which are, (1.) Justification; "being justified," pardoned and accepted through the alone merits of Christ, not from any desert in us, but according to his own mercy, "by his grace," his free, unmerited goodness. (2.) Sanctification, expressed by the laver of regeneration, (that is, baptism, the thing signified, as well as the outward sign,) and the renewal of the Holy Ghost; which purifies the soul, as water cleanses the body, and renews it in the whole image of God.

3. The consummation of all; – that we might become heirs of eternal life, and live now in the joyful hope of it.

8. Be careful to excel in good works – Though the apostle does not lay these for the foundation, yet he brings them in at their proper place, and then mentions them, not slightly, but as affairs of great importance. He desires that all believers should be careful – Have their thoughts upon them: use their best contrivance, their utmost endeavors, not barely to practice, but to excel, to be eminent and distinguished in them: because, though they are not the ground of our reconciliation with God, yet they are amiable and honorable to the Christian profession. And profitable to men – Means of increasing the everlasting happiness both of ourselves and others.

10. An heretic (after a first and second admonition) reject – Avoid, leave to himself. This is the only place, in the whole scripture, where this word heretic occurs; and here it evidently means, a man that obstinately persists in contending about "foolish questions," and thereby occasions strife and animosities, schisms and parties in the church. This, and this alone, is an heretic in the scripture sense; and his punishment likewise is here fixed. Shun, avoid him, leave him to himself. As for the Popish sense, "A man that errs in fundamentals," although it crept, with many other things, early into the church, yet it has no shadow of foundation either in the Old or New Testament.

11. Such an one is perverted – In his heart, at least. And sinneth, being self-condemned – Being convinced in his own conscience that he acts wrong.

12. When I shall send Artemas or Tychicus – To succeed thee in thy office. Titus was properly an evangelist, who, according to the nature of that office, had no fixed residence; but presided over other elders, wherever he traveled from place to place, assisting each of the apostles according to the measure of his abilities. Come to me to Nicopolis – Very probably not the Nicopolis in Macedonia, as the vulgar subscription asserts: (indeed, none of those subscriptions at the end

than love and give up ourselves to him! Redemption from sin and sanctification of the nature go together, and make a peculiar people unto God, free from guilt and condemnation, and purified by the Holy Spirit. All Scripture is profitable. Here is what will furnish for all parts of duty, and the right discharge of them.

TITUS 3

Obedience to magistrates, and becoming behavior towards all, are enforced from what believers were before conversion, and what they are made, through Christ. (1-7)
Good works to be done, and useless disputes avoided. (8-11)
Directions and exhortations. (12-15)

1-7 Spiritual privileges do not make void or weaken, but confirm civil duties. Mere good words and good meanings are not enough without good works. They were not to be quarrelsome, but to show meekness on all occasions, not toward friends only, but to all men, though with wisdom, Jas 3:13. And let this text teach us how wrong it is for a Christian to be churlish to the worst, weakest, and most abject. The servants of sin have many masters, their lusts hurry them different ways; pride commands one thing, covetousness another. Thus they are hateful, deserving to be hated. It is the misery of sinners, that they hate one another; and it is the duty and happiness of saints to love one another. And we are delivered out of our miserable condition, only by the mercy and free grace of God, the merit and sufferings of Christ, and the working of his Spirit. God the Father is God our Savior. He is the fountain from which the Holy Spirit flows, to teach, regenerate, and save his fallen creatures; and this blessing comes to mankind through Christ. The spring and rise of it, is the kindness and love of God to man. Love and grace have, through the Spirit, great power to change and turn the heart to God. Works must be in the saved, but are not among the causes of their salvation. A new principle of grace and holiness is wrought, which sways, and governs, and makes the man a new creature. Most pretend they would have heaven at last, yet they care not for holiness now; they would have the end without the beginning. Here is the outward sign and seal thereof in baptism, called therefore the washing of regeneration. The work is inward and spiritual; this is outwardly signified and sealed in this ordinance. Slight not this outward sign and seal; yet rest not in the outward washing, but look to the answer of a good conscience, without which the outward washing will avail nothing. The worker therein is the Spirit of God; it is the renewing of the Holy Ghost. Through him we mortify sin, perform duty, walk in God's ways; all the working of the Divine life in us, and the fruits of righteousness without, are through this blessed and holy Spirit. The Spirit and his saving gifts and graces, come through Christ, as a Savior, whose undertaking and work are to bring us to grace and glory. Justification, in the gospel sense, is the free forgiveness of a sinner; accepting him as righteous through the righteousness of Christ received by faith.

Gomorrah. We cannot expect to find good works coming from nature; truly it is vain and idle to think that good works can arise from the natural man. "Where, then," you ask, "do they come from?" We answer, good works come from a real conversion, brought about by the Spirit of God. Until our conversion, there is not the shadow of goodness about us. In the eye of the world we may be reputable and respectable, but in the eye of God we are nothing of the sort. Could we look into our hearts, as we sometimes look into other people's faces, we should see very much there which would drive out of our souls the very imagination of good works before our heart is changed.

Our good works, if we have any, spring from a real conversion; yet more, they spring also from a constant spiritual influence exercised upon us, from the time of conversion even until the hour of death. Ah! Christian, thou wouldst have no good works if thou hadst no fresh influence day by day. Thou wouldst not find the grace given thee at the first hour sufficient to produce fruit today. It is not like the planting of a tree in our hearts, which naturally of itself bringeth forth fruit; but the sap cometh up from the root of Jesus Christ. We are not trees by ourselves, but we are branches fixed on the living vine. Good works, I know whence you come! Ye come floating down on the stream of grace, and if I did not have that stream of grace always flowing, I should never find good works coming from me. Good works from the creature? Impossible! Good works are the gifts of God, his choice pearls, which he sendeth down with his grace.

III. We have thus tried to trace good works to their origin and foundation. And now we come to the third point, which is, WHAT IS THE USE OF GOOD WORKS?

I am rather fond of being called an Antinomian, for this reason, that the term generally applied to those who hold truth very firmly and will not let it go. But I should not be fond of being an Antinomian. We are not against the law of God. We believe it is no longer binding on us as the covenant of salvation; but we have nothing to say against the law of God. "The law is holy; we are carnal, sold under sin." None shall charge us truthfully with being Antinomians. We do quarrel with Antinomians; but as for some poor souls, who are so inconsistent as to say the law is

unto thee, or Tychicus, be diligent to come unto me to Nicopolis: for I have determined there to winter.

13 Bring Zenas the lawyer and Apollos on their journey diligently, that nothing be wanting unto them.

14 And let ours also learn to maintain good works for necessary uses, that they be not unfruitful.

15 All that are with me salute thee. Greet them that love us in the faith. Grace be with you all. Amen.

of St. Paul's epistles are of any authority:) rather it was a town of the same name which lay upon the sea-coast of Epirus. For I have determined to winter there – Hence it appears, he was not there yet; if so, he would have said, to winter here. Consequently, this letter was not written from thence.

13. Send forward Zenas the lawyer – Either a Roman lawyer or an expounder of the Jewish law.

14. And let ours – All our brethren at Crete. Learn – Both by thy admonition and example. Perhaps they had not before assisted Zenas and Apollos as they ought to have done.

God, in justifying a sinner in the way of the gospel, is gracious to him, yet just to himself and his law. As forgiveness is through a perfect righteousness, and satisfaction is made to justice by Christ, it cannot be merited by the sinner himself. Eternal life is set before us in the promise; the Spirit works faith in us, and hope of that life; faith and hope bring it near, and fill with joy in expectation of it.

8-11 When the grace of God towards mankind has been declared, the necessity of good works is pressed. Those who believe in God, must make it their care to maintain good works, to seek opportunities for doing them, being influenced by love and gratitude. Trifling, foolish questions must be avoided, and subtle distinctions and vain inquiries; nor should people be eager after novelties, but love sound doctrine which tends most to edifying. Though we may now think some sins light and little, if the Lord awaken the conscience, we shall feel even the smallest sin heavy upon our souls.

12-15 Christianity is not a fruitless profession; and its professors must be filled with the fruits of righteousness, which are by Jesus Christ, to the glory and praise of God. They must be doing good, as well as keeping away from evil. Let "ours" follow some honest labor and employment, to provide for themselves and their families. Christianity obliges all to seek some honest work and calling, and therein to abide with God. The apostle concludes with expressions of kind regard and fervent prayer. Grace be with you all; the love and favor of God, with the fruits and effects thereof, according to need; and the increase and feeling of them more and more in your souls. This is the apostle's wish and prayer, showing his affection to them, and desire for their good, and would be a means of obtaining for them, and bringing down on them, the thing requested. Grace is the chief thing to be wished and prayed for.

not binding, and yet try to keep it with all their might, we do not quarrel with them! they will never do much mischief; but we think they might learn to distinguish between the law as a covenant of life and a direction after we have obtained life.

Well, we do love good works. Do you ask, of what use are they? I reply, first: Good works are useful as evidences of grace. The Antinomian says,—But I do not require evidences; I can live without them. This is unreasonable. Do you see yonder clock? That is the evidence of the time of day. The hour would be precisely the same if we had not that evidence. Still, we find the clock of great use. So we say, good works are the best evidence of spiritual life in the soul. Is it not written, "We know that we have passed from death unto life, because we love the brethren?" Loving the brethren is a good work. Again, "If any man abide in me, he shall bring forth fruit." Fruits of righteousness are good works, and they are evidence that we abide in Christ. If I am living in sin day by day, what right have I to conclude I am a child of God? I beseech you, brethren, "adorn the doctrine of God our Savior in all things."

[Completion of this sermon follows under Philemon chapter.]

Philemon

PHILEMON

1 Paul, a prisoner of Jesus Christ, and Timothy our brother, unto Philemon our dearly beloved, and fellowlaborer,

2 And to our beloved Apphia, and Archippus our fellowsoldier, and to the church in thy house:

3 Grace to you, and peace, from God our Father and the Lord Jesus Christ.

4 I thank my God, making mention of thee always in my prayers,

5 Hearing of thy love and faith, which thou hast toward the Lord Jesus, and toward all saints;

6 That the communication of thy faith may become effectual by the acknowledging of every good thing which is in you in Christ Jesus.

7 For we have great joy and consolation in thy love, because the bowels of the saints are refreshed by thee, brother.

8 Wherefore, though I might be much bold in Christ to enjoin thee that which is convenient,

9 Yet for love's sake I rather beseech thee, being such an one as Paul the aged, and now also a prisoner of Jesus Christ.

10 I beseech thee for my son Onesimus, whom I have begotten in my bonds:

11 Which in time past was to thee unprofitable, but now profitable to thee and to me:

12 Whom I have sent again: thou therefore receive him, that is, mine own bowels:

13 Whom I would have retained with me, that in thy stead he might have ministered unto me in the bonds of the gospel:

14 But without thy mind would I do nothing; that thy benefit should not be as it were of necessity, but willingly.

15 For perhaps he therefore departed for a season, that thou shouldest receive him for ever;

16 Not now as a servant, but above a servant, a brother beloved, specially to me, but how much more unto thee, both in the flesh, and in the Lord?

17 If thou count me therefore a partner, receive him as myself.

18 If he hath wronged thee, or oweth thee ought, put that on mine account;

19 I Paul have written it with mine own hand, I will repay it: albeit I do not say to thee how thou owest unto me even thine own self besides.

20 Yea, brother, let me have joy of thee in the Lord: refresh my bowels in the Lord.

21 Having confidence in thy obedience I wrote unto thee, knowing that thou wilt also do more than I say.

ONESIMUS, a servant to Philemon, an eminent person in Colosse, ran away from his master to Rome. Here he was converted to Christianity by St. Paul, who sent him back to his master with this letter. It seems, Philemon not only pardoned, but gave him his liberty; seeing Ignatius makes mention of him, as succeeding Timotheus at Ephesus.

PHILEMON

1. This single epistle infinitely transcends all the wisdom of the world. And it gives us a specimen how Christians ought to treat of secular affairs from higher principles. Paul a prisoner of Christ – To whom, as such, Philemon could deny nothing. And Timotheus – This was written before the second epistle to Timothy, ver. xxii.

2. To Apphia – His wife, to whom also the business in part belonged. And the church in thy house – The Christians who meet there.

5. Hearing – Probably from Onesimus.

6. I pray that the communication of thy faith may become effectual – That is, that thy faith may be effectually communicated to others, who see and acknowledge thy piety and charity.

7. The saints – To whom Philemon's house was open, verse ii.

8. I might be bold in Christ – Through the authority he hath given me.

9. Yet out of love I rather entreat thee – In how handsome a manner does the apostle just hint, and immediately drop, the consideration of his power to command, and tenderly entreat Philemon to hearken to his friend, his aged friend, and now prisoner for Christ! With what endearment, in the next verse, does he call Onesimus his son, before he names his name! And as soon as he had mentioned it, with what fine address does he just touch on his former faults, and instantly pass on to the happy change that was now made upon him! So disposing Philemon to attend to his request, and the motives wherewith he was going to enforce it.

10. Whom I have begotten in my bonds – The son of my age.

11. Now profitable – None should be expected to be a good servant before he is a good man. He manifestly alludes to his name, Onesimus, which signifies profitable.

12. Receive him, that is, my own bowels – Whom I love as my own soul. Such is the natural affection of a father in Christ toward his spiritual children.

13. To serve me in thy stead – To do those services for me which thou, if present, wouldest gladly have done thyself.

14. That thy benefit might not be by constraint – For Philemon could not have refused it.

15. God might permit him to be separated (a soft word) for a season, that thou mightest have him for ever – Both on earth and in heaven.

16. In the flesh – As a dutiful servant. In the Lord – As a fellow-Christian.

17. If thou accountest me a partner – So that thy things are mine, and mine are thine.

MATTHEW HENRY

Philemon was an inhabitant of Colosse, a person of some note and wealth, and a convert under the ministry of St. Paul. Onesimus was the slave of Philemon: having run away from his master, he went to Rome, where he was converted to the Christian faith, by the word as set forth by Paul, who kept him till his conduct proved the truth and sincerity of his conversion. He wished to repair the injury he had done to his master, but fearing the punishment his offense deserved might be inflicted, he entreated the apostle to write to Philemon. And St. Paul seems nowhere to reason more beautifully, or to entreat more forcibly, than in this epistle.

The apostle's joy and praise for Philemon's steady faith in the Lord Jesus, and love to all the saints. (1-7)
He recommends Onesimus as one who would make rich amends for the misconduct of which he had been guilty; and on behalf of whom the apostle promises to make up any loss Philemon had sustained. (8-22)
Salutations and a blessing. (23-25)

1-7 Faith in Christ, and love to him, should unite saints more closely than any outward relation can unite the people of the world. Paul in his private prayers was particular in remembering his friends. We must remember Christian friends much and often, as their cases may need, bearing them in our thoughts, and upon our hearts, before our God. Different sentiments and ways in what is not essential, must not make difference of affection, as to the truth. He inquired concerning his friends, as to the truth, growth, and fruitfulness of their graces, their faith in Christ, and love to him, and to all the saints. The good which Philemon did, was matter of joy and comfort to him and others, who therefore desired that he would continue and abound in good fruits, more and more, to God's honor.

8-14 It does not lower any one to condescend, and sometimes even to beseech, where, in strictness of right, we might command: the apostle argues from love, rather than authority, in behalf of one converted through his means; and this was Onesimus. In allusion to that name, which signifies "profitable," the apostle allows that in time past he had been unprofitable to Philemon, but hastens to mention the change by which he had become profitable. Unholy persons are unprofitable; they answer not the great end of their being. But what happy changes conversion makes! of evil, good; of unprofitable, useful. Religious servants are treasures in a family. Such will make conscience of their time and trusts, and manage all they can for the best. No prospect of usefulness should lead any to

CHARLES H. SPURGEON

[Continuation of sermon, "Good works," Titus 2:14, from Titus chapter.]

IV. Thus have I told you the use of good works. Now just a moment or two to tell you that the religion which we profess in this place, and which we preach, is CALCULATED TO PRODUCE GOOD WORKS IN THE CHILD OF GOD.

Some say that what is called Calvinism, which is an alias for the true gospel, is calculated to lead men into sin. Now, we will refute that, just by reminding them, that the holiest people in the world have been those who professed the doctrine which we hold. If you ask who in the dark ages were the great moral lights of the world, the answer will be, such as Athanasius, Ambrose, Chrysostom; and then coming lower still, such men as Wickliffe, Jerome of Prague, and Calvin; and every one of these held the doctrines which we love to proclaim. And just let me remind you, there never were better men in the world than the Puritans, and every one of them held fast the truth we love. I happened to find in a book the other day a statement which pleased me so much, that I thought I would read it to you. The writer says, "The Puritans were the most resolved Protestants in the nation; zealous Calvinists; warm and affectionate preachers. They were the most pious and devout people in the land; men of prayer in secret and in public, as well as in their families. Their manner of devotion was fervent and solemn, depending on the assistance of the Divine Spirit. They had a profound reverence for the holy name of God, and were great enemies not only to profane swearing, but to foolish talking and jesting. They were strict observers of the Lord's day, spending the whole of it in public and private devotion and charity. It was the distinguishing mark of a Puritan, in these times, to see him going to church twice a day, with his Bible under his arm; and while others were at plays and interludes, at revels, or walking in the fields, or at the diversions of bowling, fencing, &c., on the eve of the Sabbath, these with their families were employed in reading the Scriptures, singing psalms, repeating sermons, catechizing their children, and prayer. Nor was this the work only of the Lord's day, but they had their hours of family devotion in the week days; they were circumspect, as to all excess in eating and drinking, apparel, and lawful diversions; being frugal, industrious, exact in their dealings, and solicitous to give every one his own." That is a noble testimony to puritanical truth and the power of the gospel. But I have one, which I think will please you, in another part of the book. A learned Infidel says of the modern Calvinists and Jansenists, that "When compared with their antagonists, they have excelled, in no small degree, in the most rigid and respectable virtues; that they have been an

22 But withal prepare me also a lodging: for I trust that through your prayers I shall be given unto you.

23
 There salute thee Epaphras, my fellowprisoner in Christ Jesus;

24 Marcus, Aristarchus, Demas, Lucas, my fellowlaborers.

25 The grace of our Lord Jesus Christ be with your spirit. Amen.

19. I will repay it – If thou requirest it. Not to say, that then owest me thyself – It cannot be expressed, how great our obligation is to those who have gained our souls to Christ. Beside – Receiving Onesimus.

20. Refresh my bowels in Christ – Give me the most exquisite and Christian pleasure.

22. Given to you – Restored to liberty.

neglect their obligations, or to fail in obedience to superiors.

15-22 When we speak of the nature of any sin or offense against God, the evil of it is not to be lessened; but in a penitent sinner, as God covers it, so must we. Such changed characters often become a blessing to all among whom they reside. Christianity does not do away our duties to others, but directs to the right doing of them. True penitents will be open in owning their faults, as doubtless Onesimus had been to Paul, upon his being awakened and brought to repentance; especially in cases of injury done to others. The communion of saints does not destroy distinction of property. This passage is an instance of that being imputed to one, which is contracted by another; and of one becoming answerable for another, by a voluntary engagement, that he might be freed from the punishment due to his crimes, according to the doctrine that Christ of his own will bore the punishment of our sins, that we might receive the reward of his righteousness. Philemon was Paul's son in the faith, yet he entreated him as a brother. Onesimus was a poor slave, yet Paul besought for him as if seeking some great thing for himself. Christians should do what may give joy to the hearts of one another. From the world they expect trouble; they should find comfort and joy in one another. When any of our mercies are taken away, our trust and hope must be in God. We must diligently use the means, and if no other should be at hand, abound in prayer.

23-25 Never have believers found more enjoyment of God, than when suffering together for him. Grace is the best wish for ourselves and others; with this the apostle begins and ends. All grace is from Christ; he purchased, and he bestows it. Let us do that now, which we should do at the last breath. Then men are ready to renounce the world, and to prefer the least portion of grace and faith before a kingdom.

honor to their own age, and the best model for imitation to every age succeeding." Only think of an infidel speaking like that. I think it was an infidel that said, "Go the Arminians to hear about good works; but go to the Calvinists to see them exhibited." And even Dr. Priestly, who was a Unitarian, admits that, "They who hold the doctrines of grace, have less apparent conformity to the world, and more of a principle of real religion, than his own followers: and that they who, from a principle of religion, ascribe more to God and less to man than others, have the greatest elevation of piety."

And just now, as the Unitarians are bringing up all their great men—so great that we never heard their names to this day—and endeavoring to do all they can in London, to bring people to Unitarianism, we would just tell them this fact. Dr. Priestly ascribes the coolness of Unitarianism to their becoming more indifferent to religious doctrine—and accounts for the fact of their chapels not being well attended, by saying that Unitarians have a very slight attachment to their religious doctrines. What a mercy! for if they continued to hold them, they would inevitably be lost. A man who denies the divinity of Christ is sure to be lost. It is idle for them to talk of their being Christians; they might as well talk of being holy angels. The best proof I can give you of the holy tendency of our doctrines is this great fact, viz.:—That in every age those who have held the doctrines of grace have exhibited in their lives a holy walk and conversation.

What more can we say, then? We hope we have proved our points to all honest and consistent men. We only send you away, ye hypocrites, with this ringing in your ears, "Except ye have the spirit of Christ, ye are none of his." Except ye live like Christ, ye shall not be with Christ at last; if your spirit be not sanctified in this world, you will not find that God will sanctify you when you come before his throne. But you, poor sinners, who have no holiness of your own, and no good works at all; I know you have not any, because you are not a child of God. Do you feel that you have not? Come then, and Christ will give you some: he will give you himself. If you believe on the Lord Jesus, he will wash you from all your sins, give you a new heart, and henceforth your life shall be holy, your conduct shall be consistent, he shall keep you to the end, and you shall most assuredly be saved. God bless this testimony to any such as are living in sin, that they may be reclaimed from it; for Christ's sake! Amen.

Hebrews

HEBREWS 1

1 God, who at sundry times and in divers manners spake in time past unto the fathers by the prophets,

2 Hath in these last days spoken unto us by his Son, whom he hath appointed heir of all things, by whom also he made the worlds;

3 Who being the brightness of his glory, and the express image of his person, and upholding all things by the word of his power, when he had by himself purged our sins, sat down on the right hand of the Majesty on high;

4 Being made so much better than the angels, as he hath by inheritance obtained a more excellent name than they.

5 For unto which of the angels said he at any time, Thou art my Son, this day have I begotten thee? And again, I will be to him a Father, and he shall be to me a Son?

6 And again, when he bringeth in the firstbegotten into the world, he saith, And let all the angels of God worship him.

7 And of the angels he saith, Who maketh his angels spirits, and his ministers a flame of fire.

8 But unto the Son he saith, Thy throne, O God, is for ever and ever: a scepter of righteousness is the scepter of thy kingdom.

9 Thou hast loved righteousness, and hated iniquity; therefore God, even thy God, hath anointed thee with the oil of gladness above thy fellows.

10 And, Thou, Lord, in the beginning hast laid the foundation of the earth; and the heavens are the works of thine hands:

11 They shall perish; but thou remainest; and they all shall wax old as doth a garment;

12 And as a vesture shalt thou fold them up, and they shall be changed: but thou art the same, and thy years shall not fail.

13 But to which of the angels said he at any time, Sit on my right hand, until I make thine enemies thy footstool?

14 Are they not all ministering spirits, sent forth to minister for them who shall be heirs of salvation?

THE EPISTLE TO THE HEBREWS: IT is agreed by the general tenor of antiquity that this epistle was written by St. Paul, whose other epistles were sent to the Gentile converts; this only to the Hebrews. But this improper inscription was added by some later hand. It was sent to the Jewish Hellenist Christians, dispersed through various countries. St. Paul's method and style are easily observed therein. He places, as usual, the proposition and division before the treatise, chap. ii, 17; he subjoins the exhortatory to the doctrinal part, quotes the same scriptures, chap. i, 6; ii, 8; x, 30, 38, 6; and uses the same expressions as elsewhere. But why does he not prefix his name, which, it is plain from chap. xiii, 19 was dear to them to whom he wrote? Because he prefixes no inscription, in which, if at all, the name would have been mentioned. The ardor of his spirit carries aim directly upon his subject, (just like St. John in his First Epistle,) and throws back his usual salutation and thanksgiving to the conclusion. This epistle of St. Paul, and both those of St. Peter, (one may add, that of St. James and of St. Jude also,) were written both to the same persons, dispersed through Pontus, Galatia, and other countries, and nearly at the same time. St. Paul suffered at Rome, three years before the destruction of Jerusalem. Therefore this epistle likewise, was written while the temple was standing. St. Peter wrote a little before his martyrdom, and refers to the epistles of St. Paul; this in particular. The scope of it is, to confirm their faith in Christ; and this he does by demonstrating his glory. All the parts of it are full of the most earnest and pointed admonitions and exhortations; and they go on in one tenor, the particle therefore everywhere connecting the doctrine and the use.

HEBREWS 1

1. God, who at sundry times – The creation was revealed in the time of Adam; the last judgment, in the time of Enoch: and so at various times, and in various degrees, more explicit knowledge was given. In divers manners – In visions, in dreams, and by Revelations of various kinds. Both these are opposed to one entire and perfect Revelation which he has made to us by Jesus Christ. The very number of the prophets showed that they prophesied only "in part." Of old – There were no prophets for a large tract of time before Christ came, that the great Prophet might be the more earnestly expected. Spake – A part is put for the whole; implying every kind of divine communication. By the prophets – The mention of whom is a virtual declaration that the apostle received the whole Old Testament, and was not about to advance any doctrine in contradiction to it. Hath spoken in these last times – Intimating that no other Revelation is to be expected. Spoken – All things, and in the most perfect manner. By his Son – Alone. The Son spake by the apostles. The majesty of the Son of God is proposed,

1. Absolutely, by the very name of Son, verse 1, and by three glorious predicates, – "whom he hath appointed," "by whom he made," who "sat down;" whereby he is described from the beginning to the consummation of all things, ver. 2, 3.

2. Comparatively to angels, ver. 4.

The proof of this proposition immediately follows: the name of Son being proved, ver. 5; his being "heir of all things," ver. 6-9; his making the worlds, ver. 10-12; his sitting at God's right hand, ver. 13, &c.

2. Whom he hath appointed heir of all things – After the name of Son, his inheritance is mentioned. God appointed him the heir long before he made the worlds, Eph. iii, 11; Prov. viii, 22, &c. The Son is the firstborn, born before all things: the heir is a term relating to the creation which followed, ver. 6. By whom he also made the worlds – Therefore the Son was before all worlds. His glory reaches from everlasting to everlasting, though God spake by him to us

MATTHEW HENRY

CHARLES H. SPURGEON

This epistle shows Christ as the end, foundation, body, and truth of the figures of the law, which of themselves were no virtue for the soul. The great truth set forth in this epistle is that Jesus of Nazareth is the true God. The unconverted Jews used many arguments to draw their converted brethren from the Christian faith. They represented the law of Moses as superior to the Christian dispensation, and spoke against every thing connected with the Savior. The apostle, therefore, shows the superiority of Jesus of Nazareth, as the Son of God, and the benefits from his sufferings and death as the sacrifice for sin, so that the Christian religion is much more excellent and perfect than that of Moses. And the principal design seems to be, to bring the converted Hebrews forward in the knowledge of the gospel, and thus to establish them in the Christian faith, and to prevent their turning from it, against which they are earnestly warned. But while it contains many things suitable to the Hebrews of early times, it also contains many which can never cease to interest the church of God; for the knowledge of Jesus Christ is the very marrow and kernel of all the Scriptures. The ceremonial law is full of Christ, and all the gospel is full of Christ; the blessed lines of both Testaments meet in him; and how they both agree and sweetly unite in Jesus Christ, is the chief object of the epistle to the Hebrews to discover.

HEBREWS 1

The surpassing dignity of the Son of God in his Divine person, and in his creating and mediatorial work. (1-3)

And in his superiority to all the holy angels. (4-14)

1-3 God spake to his ancient people at sundry times, through successive generations, and in divers manners, as he thought proper; sometimes by personal directions, sometimes by dreams, sometimes by visions, sometimes by Divine influences on the minds of the prophets. The gospel revelation is excellent above the former; in that it is a revelation which God has made by his Son. In beholding the power, wisdom, and goodness of the Lord Jesus Christ, we behold the power, wisdom, and goodness of the Father, Joh 14:7; the fullness of the Godhead dwells, not typically, or in a figure, but really, in him. When, on the fall of man, the world was breaking to pieces under the wrath and curse of God, the Son of God, undertaking the work of redemption, sustained it by his almighty power and goodness. From the glory of the person and office of Christ, we proceed to the glory of his grace. The glory of his person and nature, gave to his sufferings such merit as was a full satisfaction to the honor of God, who suffered an infinite injury and affront by the sins of men.

4-14 Many Jews had a superstitious or idolatrous

FINAL PERSEVERANCE
Sermon number 75 delivered on March 23, 1856, at New Park Street Chapel, Southwark.

"For it is impossible for those who were once enlightened, and have tasted of the heavenly gift, and were made partakers of the Holy Ghost, and have tasted the good word of God, and the powers of the world to come, If they shall fall away, to renew them again unto repentance; seeing they crucify to themselves the Son of God afresh, and put him to an open shame."—Hebrews 6:4-6.

THERE are some spots in Europe which have been the scenes of frequent warfare, as for instance, the kingdom of Belgium, which might be called the battle field of Europe. War has raged over the whole of Europe, but in some unhappy spots, battle after battle has been fought. So there is scarce a passage of Scripture which has not been disputed between the enemies of truth and the upholders of it; but this passage, with one or two others, has been the special subject of attack. This is one of the texts which have been trodden under the feet of controversy; and there are opinions upon it as adverse as the poles, some asserting that it means one thing, and some declaring that it means another. We think that some of them approach somewhat near the truth; but others of them desperately err from the mind of the Spirit. We come to this passage ourselves with the intention to read it with the simplicity of a child, and whatever we find therein to state it; and if it may not seem to agree with something we have hitherto held, we are prepared to cast away every doctrine of our own, rather than one passage of Scripture.

Looking at the scope of the whole passage, it appears to us that the Apostle wished to push the disciples on. There is a tendency in the human mind to stop short of the heavenly mark. As soon as ever we have attained to the first principles of religion, have passed through baptism, and understand the resurrection of the dead, there is a tendency in us to sit still; to say, "I have passed from death unto life; here I may take my stand and rest;" whereas, the Christian life was intended not to be a sitting still, but a race, a perpetual motion. The Apostle, therefore endeavors to urge the disciples forward, and make them run with diligence the heavenly race, looking unto Jesus. He tells them that it is not enough to have on a certain day, passed through a glorious change—to have experienced at a certain time, a wonderful operation of the Spirit; but he teaches them it is absolutely necessary that they should have the Spirit all

HEBREWS 2

1 Therefore we ought to give the more earnest heed to the things which we have heard, lest at any time we should let them slip.

2 For if the word spoken by angels was stedfast, and every transgression and disobedience received a just recompense of reward;

3 How shall we escape, if we neglect so great salvation; which at the first began to be spoken by the Lord, and was confirmed unto us by them that heard him;

4 God also bearing them witness, both with signs and wonders, and with divers miracles, and gifts of the Holy Ghost, according to his own will?

5 For unto the angels hath he not put in subjection the world to come, whereof we speak.

6 But one in a certain place testified, saying, What is man, that thou art mindful of him? or the son of man, that thou visitest him?

7 Thou madest him a little lower than the angels; thou crownedst him with glory and honor, and didst set him over the works of thy hands:

8 Thou hast put all things in subjection under his feet. For in that he put all in subjection under him, he left nothing that is not put under him. But now we see not yet all things put under him.

9 But we see Jesus, who was made a little lower than the angels for the suffering of death, crowned with glory and honor; that he by the grace of God should taste death for every man.

10 For it became him, for whom are all things, and by whom are all things, in bringing many sons unto glory, to make the captain of their salvation perfect through sufferings.

11 For both he that sanctifieth and they who are sanctified are all of one: for which cause he is not ashamed to call them brethren;

12 Saying, I will declare thy name unto my brethren, in the midst of the church will I sing praise unto thee.

13 And again, I will put my trust in him. And again, Behold I and

only "in these last days."

3. Who sat down – The third of these glorious predicates, with which three other particulars are interwoven, which are mentioned likewise, and in the same order, Colossians i, 15, 17, 20. Who, being – The glory which he received in his exaltation at the right hand of the Father no angel was capable of; but the Son alone, who likewise enjoyed it long before. The brightness of his glory – Glory is the nature of God revealed in its brightness. The express image – Or stamp. Whatever the Father is, is exhibited in the Son, as a seal in the stamp on wax. Of his person – Or substance. The word denotes the unchangeable perpetuity of divine life and power. And sustaining all things – Visible and invisible, in being. By the word of his power – That is, by his powerful word. When he had by himself – Without any Mosaic rites or ceremonies. Purged our sins – In order to which it was necessary he should for a time divest himself of his glory. In this chapter St. Paul describes his glory chiefly as he is the Son of God; afterwards, ver. 6, &c., the glory of the man Christ Jesus. He speaks, indeed, briefly of the former before his humiliation, but copiously after his exaltation; as from hence the glory he had from eternity began to be evidently seen. Both his purging our sins, and sitting on the right hand of God, are largely treated of in the seven following chapters. Sat down – The priests stood while they ministered: sitting, therefore, denotes the consummation of his sacrifice. This word, sat down, contains the scope, the theme, and the sum, of the epistle.

4. This verse has two clauses, the latter of which is treated of, ver. 5; the former, ver. 13. Such transpositions are also found in the other epistles of St. Paul, but in none so frequently as in this. The Jewish doctors were peculiarly fond of this figure, and used it much in all their writings. The apostle therefore, becoming all things to all men, here follows the same method. All the inspired writers were readier in all the figures of speech than the most experienced orators. Being – By his exaltation, after he had been lower than them, chap. ii, 9. So much higher than the angels – It was extremely proper to observe this, because the Jews gloried in their law, as it was delivered by the ministration of angels. How much more may we glory in the gospel, which was given, not by the ministry of angels, but of the very Son of God! As he hath by inheritance a more excellent name – Because he is the Son of God, he inherits that name, in right whereof he inherits all things. His inheriting that name is more ancient than all worlds; his inheriting all things, as ancient as all things. Than they – This denotes an immense pre-eminence. The angels do not inherit all things, but are themselves a portion of the Son's inheritance, whom they worship as their Lord.

5. Thou art my Son – God of God, Light of Light. This day have I begotten thee – I have begotten thee from eternity, which, by its unalterable permanency of duration, is one continued, unsuccessive day. I will be to him a Father, and he shall be to me a Son – I will own myself to be his Father, and him to be my Son, by eminent tokens of my peculiar love The former clause relates to his natural Sonship, by an eternal, inconceivable generation; the other, to his Father's acknowledgment and treatment of him as his incarnate Son. Indeed this promise related immediately to Solomon, but in a far higher sense to the Messiah. Psalm ii, 7; 2 Sam. vii, 14.

6. And again – That is, in another scripture. He – God. Saith, when he bringeth in his first-begotten – This appellation includes that of Son, together with the rights of primogeniture, which the first-begotten Son of God enjoys, in a manner not communicable to any creature. Into the world – Namely, at his incarnation. He saith, Let all the angels of God worship him – So much higher was he, when in his lowest estate, than the highest angel. Psalm xcvii, 7.

7. Who maketh his angels – This implies, they are only creatures, whereas the Son is eternal, ver. 8; and the Creator himself, ver. 10. Spirits and a flame of fire – Which intimates not only their office, but also their nature; which is excellent indeed, the metaphor being taken from the most swift, subtle, and efficacious

MATTHEW HENRY

CHARLES H. SPURGEON

respect for angels, because they had received the law and other tidings of the Divine will by their ministry. They looked upon them as mediators between God and men, and some went so far as to pay them a kind of religious homage or worship. Thus it was necessary that the apostle should insist, not only on Christ's being the Creator of all things, and therefore of angels themselves, but as being the risen and exalted Messiah in human nature, to whom angels, authorities, and powers are made subject. To prove this, several passages are brought from the Old Testament. On comparing what God there says of the angels, with what he says to Christ, the inferiority of the angels to Christ plainly appears. Here is the office of the angels; they are God's ministers or servants, to do his pleasure. But, how much greater things are said of Christ by the Father! And let us own and honor him as God; for if he had not been God, he had never done the Mediator's work, and had never worn the Mediator's crown. It is declared how Christ was qualified for the office of Mediator, and how he was confirmed in it: he has the name Messiah from his being anointed. Only as Man he has his fellows, and as anointed with the Holy Spirit; but he is above all prophets, priests, and kings, that ever were employed in the service of God on earth. Another passage of Scripture, Ps 102:25-27, is recited, in which the Almighty power of the Lord Jesus Christ is declared, both in creating the world and in changing it. Christ will fold up this world as a garment, not to be abused any longer, not to be used as it has been. As a sovereign, when his garments of state are folded and put away, is a sovereign still, so our Lord, when he has laid aside the earth and heavens like a vesture, shall be still the same. Let us not then set our hearts upon that which is not what we take it to be, and will not be what it now is. Sin has made a great change in the world for the worse, and Christ will make a great change in it for the better. Let the thoughts of this make us watchful, diligent, and desirous of that better world. The Savior has done much to make all men his friends, yet he has enemies. But they shall be made his footstool, by humble submission, or by utter destruction. Christ shall go on conquering and to conquer. The most exalted angels are but ministering spirits, mere servants of Christ, to execute his commands. The saints, at present, are heirs, not yet come into possession. The angels minister to them in opposing the malice and power of evil spirits, in protecting and keeping their bodies, instructing and comforting their souls, under Christ and the Holy Ghost. Angels shall gather all the saints together at the last day, when all whose hearts and hopes are set upon perishing treasures and fading glories, will be driven from Christ's presence into everlasting misery.

their lives—that they should, as long as they live, be progressing in the truth of God. In order to make them persevere, if possible, he shows them that if they do not, they must, most certainly be lost; for there is no other salvation but that which God has already bestowed on them, and if that does not keep them, carry them forward, and present them spotless before God, there cannot be any other. For it is impossible, he says, if ye be once enlightened, and then fall away, that ye should ever be renewed again unto repentance.

We shall, this morning, answer one or two questions. The first question will be, Who are the people here spoken? Are they true Christians or not? Secondly, What is meant by falling away? And thirdly, What is intended, when it is asserted, that it is impossible to renew them to repentance?

I. First, then, we answer the question, WHO ARE THE PEOPLE HERE SPOKEN OF? If you read Dr. Gill, Dr. Owen, and almost all the eminent Calvinistic writers, they all of them assert that these persons are not Christians. They say, that enough is said here to represent a man who is a Christian externally, but not enough to give the portrait of a true believer. Now, it strikes me they would not have said this if they had had some doctrine to uphold; for a child, reading this passage, would say, that the persons intended by it must be Christians. If the Holy Spirit intended to describe Christians, I do not see that he could have used more explicit terms than there are here. How can a man be said to be enlightened, and to taste of the heavenly gift, and to be made partaker of the Holy Ghost, without being a child of God? With all deference to these learned doctors, and I admire and love them all, I humbly conceive that they allowed their judgments to be a little warped when they said that; and I think I shall be able to show that none but true believers are here described.

First, they are spoken of as having been once enlightened. This refers to the enlightening influence of God's Spirit, poured into the soul at the time of conviction, when man is enlightened with regard to his spiritual state, shown how evil and bitter a thing it is to sin against God, made to feel how utterly powerless he is to rise from the grave of his corruption, and is further enlightened to see, that "by the deeds of the law shall no flesh living be justified," and to behold Christ on the cross, as the sinner's only hope. The first work of grace is to enlighten the soul. By nature we are entirely dark; the Spirit, like a lamp, sheds light into the dark heart, revealing its corruption, displaying its sad state

the children which God hath given me.

14 Forasmuch then as the children are partakers of flesh and blood, he also himself likewise took part of the same; that through death he might destroy him that had the power of death, that is, the devil;

15 And deliver them who through fear of death were all their lifetime subject to bondage.

16 For verily he took not on him the nature of angels; but he took on him the seed of Abraham.

17 Wherefore in all things it behoved him to be made like unto his brethren, that he might be a merciful and faithful high priest in things pertaining to God, to make reconciliation for the sins of the people.

18 For in that he himself hath suffered being tempted, he is able to succor them that are tempted.

HEBREWS 3

1 Wherefore, holy brethren, partakers of the heavenly calling, consider the Apostle and High Priest of our profession, Christ Jesus;

2 Who was faithful to him that appointed him, as also Moses was faithful in all his house.

3 For this man was counted worthy of more glory than Moses, inasmuch as he who hath builded the house hath more honor than the house.

4 For every house is builded by some man; but he that built all things is God.

5 And Moses verily was faithful in all his house, as a servant, for a testimony of those things which were to be spoken after;

6 But Christ as a son over his own house; whose house are we, if we hold fast the confidence and the rejoicing of the hope firm unto the end.

7 Wherefore (as the Holy Ghost saith, To day if ye will hear his voice,

8 Harden not your hearts, as in the provocation, in the day of temptation in the wilderness:

9 When your fathers tempted me, proved me, and saw my works forty years.

10 Wherefore I was grieved with

things on earth; but nevertheless infinitely below the majesty of the Son. Psalm civ, 4.

8. O God – God, in the singular number, is never in scripture used absolutely of any but the supreme God. Thy reign, of which the scepter is the ensign, is full of justice and equity. Psalm xlv, 6, 7.

9. Thou hast loved righteousness and hated iniquity – Thou art infinitely pure and holy. Therefore God – Who, as thou art Mediator, is thy God. Hath anointed thee with the oil of gladness – With the Holy Ghost, the fountain of joy. Above thy fellows – Above all the children of men.

10. Thou – The same to whom the discourse is addressed in the preceding verse. Psalm cii, 25, 26.

12. As a mantle – With all ease. They shall be changed – Into new heavens and a new earth. But thou art eternally the same.

13. Psalm cx, 1.

14. Are they not all – Though of various orders. Ministering spirits, sent forth – Ministering before God, sent forth to men. To attend on them – In numerous offices of protection, care, and kindness. Who – Having patiently continued in well doing, shall inherit everlasting salvation.

HEBREWS 2

In this and the two following chapters the apostle subjoins an exhortation, answering each head of the preceding chapter.

1. Lest we should let them slip – As water out of a leaky vessel. So the Greek word properly signifies.

2. In giving the law, God spoke by angels; but in proclaiming the gospel, by his Son. Steadfast – Firm and valid. Every transgression – Commission of sin. Every disobedience – Omission of duty.

3. So great a salvation – A deliverance from so great wickedness and misery, into so great holiness and happiness. This was first spoken of (before he came it was not known) by him who is the Lord – of angels as well as men. And was confirmed to us – Of this age, even every article of it. By them that had heard him – And had been themselves also both eye-witnesses and ministers of the word.

4. By signs and wonders – While he lived. And various miracles and distributions of the Holy Ghost – Miraculous gifts, distributed after his exaltation. According to his will – Not theirs who received them.

5. This verse contains a proof of the third; the greater the salvation is, and the more glorious the Lord whom we despise, the greater will be our punishment. God hath not subjected the world to come – That is, the dispensation of the Messiah; which being to succeed the Mosaic was usually styled by the Jews, the world to come, although it is still in great measure to come .Whereof we now speak – Of which I am now speaking. In this last great dispensation the Son alone presides.

6. What is man – To the vast expanse of heaven, to the moon and the stars which thou hast ordained! This psalm seems to have been composed by David, in a clear, moonshine, and starlight night, while he was contemplating the wonderful fabric of heaven; because in his magnificent description of its luminaries, he takes no notice of the sun, the most glorious of them all. The words here cited concerning dominion were doubtless in some sense applicable to Adam; although in their complete and highest sense, they belong to none but the second Adam. Or the son of man, that thou visitest him – The sense rises: we are mindful of him that is absent; but to visit, denotes the care of a present God. Psalm viii, 4.

7. Thou hast made him – Adam. A little lower than the angels – The Hebrew is, a little lower than (that is, next to) God. Such was man as he came out of the hands of his Creator: it seems, the highest of all created beings. But these words

HEBREWS 2

The duty of steadfastly adhering to Christ and his gospel. (1-4)

His sufferings are no objection against his pre-eminence. (5-9)

The reason of his sufferings, and the fitness of them. (10-13)

Christ's taking the nature of man, and not his taking the nature of angels, was necessary to his priestly office. (14-18)

1-4 Christ being proved to be superior to the angels, this doctrine is applied. Our minds and memories are like a leaky vessel, they do not, without much care, retain what is poured into them. This proceeds from the corruption of our nature, temptations, worldly cares, and pleasures. Sinning against the gospel is neglect of this great salvation; it is a contempt of the saving grace of God in Christ, making light of it, not caring for it, not regarding either the worth of gospel grace, or the want of it, and our undone state without it. The Lord's judgments under the gospel dispensation are chiefly spiritual, but are on that account the more to be dreaded. Here is an appeal to the consciences of sinners. Even partial neglects will not escape rebukes; they often bring darkness on the souls they do not finally ruin. The setting forth the gospel was continued and confirmed by those who heard Christ, by the evangelists and apostles, who were witnesses of what Jesus Christ began both to do and to teach; and by the gifts of the Holy Ghost, qualified for the work to which they were called. And all this according to God's own will.

5-9 Neither the state in which the church is at present, nor its more completely restored state, when the prince of this world shall be cast out, and the kingdoms of the earth become the kingdom of Christ, is left to the government of the angels: Christ will take to him his great power, and will reign. And what is the moving cause of all the kindness God shows to men in giving Christ for them and to them? it is the grace of God. As a reward of Christ's humiliation in suffering death, he has unlimited dominion over all things; thus this ancient scripture was fulfilled in him.

10-13 Whatever the proud, carnal, and unbelieving may imagine or object, the spiritual mind will see peculiar glory in the cross of Christ, and be satisfied that it became him, who in all things displays his own perfections in bringing many sons to glory, to make the Author of their salvation perfect through sufferings. His way to the crown was by the cross, and so must that of his people be. Christ sanctifies; he has purchased and sent the sanctifying Spirit: the Spirit sanctifies as the Spirit of Christ. True believers are sanctified, endowed with holy principles and powers, set apart to high and holy uses and purposes. Christ and believers are all of one heavenly Father, who is

of destitution, and, in due time, revealing also Jesus Christ, so that in his light we may see light. I cannot consider a man truly enlightened unless he is a child of God. Does not the term indicate a person taught of God? It is not the whole of Christian experience; but is it not a part?

Having enlightened us, as the text says, the next thing that God grants to us is a taste of the heavenly gift, by which we understand, the heavenly gift of salvation, including the pardon of sin, justification by the imputed righteousness of Jesus Christ, regeneration by the Holy Ghost, and all those gifts and graces, which in the earlier dawn of spiritual life convey salvation. All true believers have tasted of the heavenly gift. It is not enough for a man to be enlightened; the light may glare upon his eyeballs, and yet he may die; he must taste, as well as see that the Lord is good. It is not enough to see that I am corrupt; I must taste that Christ is able to remove my corruption. It is not enough for me to know that he is the only Savior; I must taste of his flesh and of his blood, and have a vital union with him. We do think that when a man has been enlightened and has had an experience of grace, he is a Christian; and whatever those great divines might hold, we cannot think that the Holy Spirit would describe an unregenerate man as having been enlightened, and as having tasted of the heavenly gift. No, my brethren, if I have tasted of the heavenly gift, then that heavenly gift is mine; if I have had ever so short an experience of my Savior's love, I am one of his; if he has brought me into the green pastures, and made me taste of the still waters and the tender grass, I need not fear as to whether I am really a child of God.

Then the Apostle gives a further description, a higher state of grace: sanctification by participation of the Holy Ghost. It is a peculiar privilege to believers, after their first tasting of the heavenly gift, to be made partakers of the Holy Ghost. He is an indwelling Spirit; he dwells in the hearts, and souls, and minds of men; he makes this mortal flesh his home; he makes our soul his palace, and there he rests; and we do assert (and we think, on the authority of Scripture), that no man can be a partaker of the Holy Ghost, and yet be unregenerate. Where the Holy Ghost dwells there must be life; and if I have participation with the Holy Ghost, and fellowship with him, then I may rest assured that my salvation has been purchased by the blood of the Savior. Thou need'st not fear, beloved; if thou has the Holy Ghost, thou hast that which ensures thy salvation; if thou, by an inward communion, canst participate in his Spirit, and if by a perpetual indwelling the Holy Ghost rests in thee, thou art not only a Christian,

that generation, and said, They do alway err in their heart; and they have not known my ways.

11 So I sware in my wrath, They shall not enter into my rest.)

12 Take heed, brethren, lest there be in any of you an evil heart of unbelief, in departing from the living God.

13 But exhort one another daily, while it is called To day; lest any of you be hardened through the deceitfulness of sin.

14 For we are made partakers of Christ, if we hold the beginning of our confidence stedfast unto the end;

15 While it is said, To day if ye will hear his voice, harden not your hearts, as in the provocation.

16 For some, when they had heard, did provoke: howbeit not all that came out of Egypt by Moses.

17 But with whom was he grieved forty years? was it not with them that had sinned, whose carcasses fell in the wilderness?

18 And to whom sware he that they should not enter into his rest, but to them that believed not?

19 So we see that they could not enter in because of unbelief.

HEBREWS 4

1 Let us therefore fear, lest, a promise being left us of entering into his rest, any of you should seem to come short of it.

2 For unto us was the gospel preached, as well as unto them: but the word preached did not profit them, not being mixed with faith in them that heard it.

3 For we which have believed do enter into rest, as he said, As I have sworn in my wrath, if they shall enter into my rest: although the works were finished from the foundation of the world.

4 For he spake in a certain place of the seventh day on this wise, And God did rest the seventh day from all his works.

5 And in this place again, If they shall enter into my rest.

6 Seeing therefore it remaineth that some must enter therein, and they to whom it was first

are also in a farther sense, as the apostle here shows, applicable to the Son of God. It should be remembered that the apostles constantly cited the Septuagint translation, very frequently without any variation. It was not their business, in writing to the Jews, who at that time had it in high esteem, to amend or alter this, which would of consequence have occasioned disputes without end.

8. Now this putting all things under him, implies that there is nothing that is not put under him. But it is plain, this is not done now, with regard to man in general.

9. It is done only with regard to Jesus, God-Man, who is now crowned with glory and honor – As a reward for his having suffered death. He was made a little lower than the angels – Who cannot either suffer or die. That by the grace of God, he might taste death – An expression denoting both the reality of his death, and the shortness of its continuance. For every man – That ever was or will be born into the world.

11. For – They are nearly related to each other. He that sanctifieth – Christ, chap. xiii, 12. And all they that are sanctified – That are brought to God; that draw near or come to him, which are synonymous terms. Are all of one – Partakers of one nature, from one parent, Adam.

12. I will declare thy name to my brethren – Christ declares the name of God, gracious and merciful, plenteous in goodness and truth, to all who believe, that they also may praise him. In the midst of the church will I sing praise unto thee – As the precentor of the choir. This he did literally, in the midst of his apostles, on the night before his passion. And as it means, in a more general sense, setting forth the praise of God, he has done it in the church by his word and his Spirit; he still does, and will do it throughout all generations. Psalm xxii, 22.

13. And again – As one that has communion with his brethren in sufferings, as well as in nature, he says, I will put my trust in him – To carry me through them all. And again – With a like acknowledgment of his near relation to them, as younger brethren, who were yet but in their childhood, he presents all believers to God, saying, Behold I and the children whom thou hast given me. Isaiah viii, 17, 18.

14. Since then these children partake of flesh and blood – Of human nature with all its infirmities. He also in like manner took part of the same; that through his own death he might destroy the tyranny of him that had, by God's permission, the power of death with regard to the ungodly. Death is the devil's servant and sergeant, delivering to him those whom he seizes in sin. That is, the devil – The power was manifest to all; but who exerted it, they saw not.

15. And deliver them, as many as through fear of death were all their lifetime, till then, subject to bondage – Every man who fears death is subject to bondage; is in a slavish, uncomfortable state. And every man fears death, more or less, who knows not Christ: death is unwelcome to him, if he knows what death is. But he delivers all true believers from this bondage.

16. For verily he taketh not hold of angels – He does not take their nature upon him. But he taketh hold of the seed of Abraham – He takes human nature upon him. St. Paul says the seed of Abraham, rather than the seed of Adam, because to Abraham was the promise made.

17. Wherefore it behoved him – It was highly fit and proper, yea, necessary, in order to his design of redeeming them. To be made in all things – That essentially pertain to human nature, and in all sufferings and temptations. Like his brethren – This is a recapitulation of all that goes before: the sum of all that follows is added immediately. That he might be a merciful and faithful High Priest – Merciful toward sinners; faithful toward God. A priest or high priest is one who has a right of approaching God, and of bringing others to him. Faithful is treated of, chap. iii, 2, &c., with its use; merciful, chap. iv, 14, &c., with the use also; High Priest, chap. v, 4, &c., chap. vii, 1, &c. The use is added from chap. x, 19. In things pertaining to God, to expiate the sins of the people – Offering

MATTHEW HENRY

CHARLES H. SPURGEON

God. They are brought into relation with Christ. But the words, his not being ashamed to call them brethren, express the high superiority of Christ to the human nature. This is shown from three texts of Scripture. See Ps 22:22; 18:2; Isa 8:18.

14-18 The angels fell, and remained without hope or help. Christ never designed to be the Savior of the fallen angels, therefore he did not take their nature; and the nature of angels could not be an atoning sacrifice for the sin of man. Here is a price paid, enough for all, and suitable to all, for it was in our nature. Here the wonderful love of God appeared, that, when Christ knew what he must suffer in our nature, and how he must die in it, yet he readily took it upon him. And this atonement made way for his people's deliverance from Satan's bondage, and for the pardon of their sins through faith. Let those who dread death, and strive to get the better of their terrors, no longer attempt to outbrave or to stifle them, no longer grow careless or wicked through despair. Let them not expect help from the world, or human devices; but let them seek pardon, peace, grace, and a lively hope of heaven, by faith in him who died and rose again, that thus they may rise above the fear of death. The remembrance of his own sorrows and temptations, makes Christ mindful of the trials of his people, and ready to help them. He is ready and willing to succor those who are tempted, and seek him. He became man, and was tempted, that he might be every way qualified to succor his people, seeing that he had passed through the same temptations himself, but continued perfectly free from sin.

HEBREWS 3

The superior worth and dignity of Christ above Moses is shown. (1-6)

The Hebrews are warned of the sin and danger of unbelief. (7-13)

And of necessity of faith in Christ, and of steadfastly following him. (14-19)

1-6 Christ is to be considered as the Apostle of our profession, the Messenger sent by God to men, the great Revealer of that faith which we profess to hold, and of that hope which we profess to have. As Christ, the Messiah, anointed for the office both of Apostle and High Priest. As Jesus, our Savior, our Healer, the great Physician of souls. Consider him thus. Consider what he is in himself, what he is to us, and what he will be to us hereafter and forever. Close and serious thoughts of Christ bring us to know more of him. The Jews had a high opinion of the faithfulness of Moses, yet his faithfulness was but a type of Christ's. Christ was the Master of this house, of his church, his people, as well as their Maker. Moses was a faithful servant; Christ, as the eternal Son of God, is rightful Owner and Sovereign Ruler of the Church.

but thou hast arrived at some maturity in and by grace. Thou hast gone beyond mere enlightenment: thou hast passed from the bare taste— thou hast attained to a positive feast, and a partaking of the Holy Ghost.

Lest there should be any mistake, however, about the persons being children of God, the Apostle goes to a further stage of grace. They "have tasted the good word of God." Now, I will venture to say there are some good Christian people here who have never "tasted the good word of God." I mean by that, that they are really converted, have tasted the heavenly gift, but have not grown so strong in grace as to know the sweetness, the richness, and fatness of the very word that saves them. They have been saved by the word, but they have not come yet to realize, and love, and feed upon the word as many others have. It is one thing for God to work a work of grace in the soul, it is quite another thing for God to show us that work; it is one thing for the word to work in us—it is another thing for us really and habitually to relish, and taste, and rejoice in that word. Some of my hearers are true Christians; but they have not got to that stage wherein they can love election, and suck it down as a sweet morsel, wherein they can take the great doctrines of grace, and feed upon them. But these people had. They had tasted the good word of God, as well as received the good gift: they had attained to such a state, that they had loved the word, had tasted, and feasted upon it. It was the man of their right hand; they had counted it sweeter than honey—ay, sweeter than the droppings of the honeycomb. They had "tasted the good word of God." I say again, if these people be not believers—who are?

And they had gone further still. They had attained the summit of piety. They had received "the powers of the world to come." Not miraculous gifts, which are denied us in these days, but all those powers with which the Holy Ghost endows a Christian. And what are they? Why, there is the power of faith, which commands even the heavens themselves to rain, and they rain, or stops the bottles of heaven, that they rain not. There is the power of prayer, which puts a ladder between earth and heaven, and bids angels walk up and down, to convey our wants to God, and bring down blessings from above. There is the power with which God girds his servant when he speaks by inspiration, which enables him to instruct others, and lead them to Jesus; and whatever other power there may be—the power of holding communion with God, or the power of patient waiting for the Son of Man—they were possessed by these indi-

preached entered not in because of unbelief:

7 Again, he limiteth a certain day, saying in David, To day, after so long a time; as it is said, To day if ye will hear his voice, harden not your hearts.

8 For if Jesus had given them rest, then would he not afterward have spoken of another day.

9 There remaineth therefore a rest to the people of God.

10 For he that is entered into his rest, he also hath ceased from his own works, as God did from his.

11 Let us labor therefore to enter into that rest, lest any man fall after the same example of unbelief.

12 For the word of God is quick, and powerful, and sharper than any twoedged sword, piercing even to the dividing asunder of soul and spirit, and of the joints and marrow, and is a discerner of the thoughts and intents of the heart.

13 Neither is there any creature that is not manifest in his sight: but all things are naked and opened unto the eyes of him with whom we have to do.

14 Seeing then that we have a great high priest, that is passed into the heavens, Jesus the Son of God, let us hold fast our profession.

15 For we have not an high priest which cannot be touched with the feeling of our infirmities; but was in all points tempted like as we are, yet without sin.

16 Let us therefore come boldly unto the throne of grace, that we may obtain mercy, and find grace to help in time of need.

HEBREWS 5

1 For every high priest taken from among men is ordained for men in things pertaining to God, that he may offer both gifts and sacrifices for sins:

2 Who can have compassion on the ignorant, and on them that are out of the way; for that he himself also is compassed with infirmity.

3 And by reason hereof he ought, as for the people, so also

up their sacrifices and prayers to God; deriving God's grace, peace, and blessings upon them.

18. For in that he hath suffered being tempted himself he is able to succor them that are tempted – That is, he has given a manifest, demonstrative proof that he is able so to do.

HEBREWS 3

1. The heavenly calling – God calls from heaven, and to heaven, by the gospel. Consider the Apostle – The messenger of God, who pleads the cause of God with us. And High Priest – Who pleads our cause with God. Both are contained in the one word Mediator. He compares Christ, as an Apostle, with Moses; as a Priest, with Aaron. Both these offices, which Moses and Aaron severally bore, he bears together, and far more eminently. Of our profession – The religion we profess.

2. His house – The church of Israel, then the peculiar family of God. Num. xii, 7.

3. He that hath builded it hath more glory than the house – Than the family itself, or any member of it.

4. Now Christ, he that built not only this house, but all things, is God – And so infinitely greater than Moses or any creature.

5. And Moses verily – Another proof of the pre-eminence of Christ above Moses. Was faithful in all his house, as a servant, for a testimony of the things which were afterwards to be spoken – That is, which was a full confirmation of the things which he afterward spake concerning Christ.

6. But Christ was faithful as a Son; whose house we are, while we hold fast, and shall be unto the end, if we hold fast our confidence in God, and glorying in his promises; our faith and hope.

7. Wherefore – Seeing he is faithful, be not ye unfaithful. Psalm xcv, 7, &c.

8. As in the provocation – When Israel provoked me by their strife and murmurings. In the day of temptation – When at the same time they tempted me, by distrusting my power and goodness. Exod. xvii, 7.

9. Where your fathers – That hard-hearted and stiff-necked generation. So little cause had their descendants to glory in them. Tempted me – Whether I could and would help them. Proved me – Put my patience to the proof, even while they saw my glorious works both of judgment and mercy, and that for forty years.

10. Wherefore – To speak after the manner of men. I was grieved – Displeased, offended with that generation, and said, They always err in their hearts – They are led astray by their stubborn will and vile affections. And – For this reason, because wickedness has blinded their understanding. They have not known my ways – By which I would have led them like a flock. Into my rest – In the promised land.

12. Take heed, lest there be in any of you – As there was in them. An evil heart of unbelief – Unbelief is the parent of all evil, and the very essence of unbelief lies in departing from God, as the living God – The fountain of all our life, holiness, happiness.

13. But, to prevent it, exhort one another, while it is called Today – This today will not last for ever. The day of life will end soon, and perhaps the day of grace yet sooner.

14. For we are made partakers of Christ – And we shall still partake of him and all his benefits, if we hold fast our faith unto the end. If – But not else; and a supposition made by the Holy Ghost is equal to the, strongest assertion. Both the sentiment and the manner of expression are the same as ver. 6.

16. Were they not all that came out of Egypt – An awful consideration! The whole elect people of God (a very few excepted) provoked God presently after their great deliverance, continued to grieve his Spirit for forty years, and per-

7-13 Days of temptation are often days of provocation. But to provoke God, when he is letting us see that we entirely depend and live upon him, is a provocation indeed. The hardening of the heart is the spring of all other sins. The sins of others, especially of our relations, should be warnings to us. All sin, especially sin committed by God's professing, privileged people, not only provokes God, but it grieves him. God is loath to destroy any in, or for their sin; he waits long to be gracious to them. But sin, long persisted in, will make God's wrath discover itself in destroying the impenitent; there is no resting under the wrath of God. "Take heed:" all who would get safe to heaven must look about them; if once we allow ourselves to distrust God, we may soon desert him. Let those that think they stand, take heed lest they fall. Since tomorrow is not ours, we must make the best improvement of this day. And there are none, even the strongest of the flock, who do not need help of other Christians. Neither are there any so low and despised, but the care of their standing in the faith, and of their safety, belongs to all. Sin has so many ways and colors, that we need more eyes than ours own.

14-19 The saints' privilege is, they are made partakers of Christ, that is, of the Spirit, the nature, graces, righteousness, and life of Christ; they are interested in all Christ is, in all he has done, or will do. The same spirit with which Christians set out in the ways of God, they should maintain unto the end. Perseverance in faith is the best evidence of the sincerity of our faith. Hearing the word often is a means of salvation, yet, if not hearkened to, it will expose more to the Divine wrath. The happiness of being partakers of Christ and his complete salvation, and the fear of God's wrath and eternal misery, should stir us up to persevere in the life of obedient faith.

HEBREWS 4

*Humble, cautious fear is urged, lest any should come
    short of the promised rest, through unbelief. (1-10)
Arguments and motives to faith and hope in our
    approaches to God. (11-16)*

1-10 The privileges we have under the gospel, are greater than any had under the law of Moses, though the same gospel for substance was preached under both Testaments. There have been in all ages many unprofitable hearers; and unbelief is at the root of all unfruitfulness under the word. Faith in the hearer is the life of the word. But it is a painful consequence of partial neglect, and of a loose and wavering profession, that they often cause men to seem to come short. Let us then give diligence, that we may have a clear entrance into the kingdom of God. As God finished his work, and then rested from it, so he will cause those who believe, to finish their work, and then to enjoy their rest. It is evident, that there is a

viduals. They were not simply children, but they were men; they were not merely alive, but they were endued with power; they were men, whose muscles were firmly set, whose bones were strong; they had become giants in grace, and had received not only the light, but the power also of the world to come. These, we say, whatever may be the meaning of the text, must have been, beyond a doubt, none other than true and real Christians.

II. And now we answer the second question, WHAT IS MEANT BY FALLING AWAY?

We must remind our friends, that there is a vast distinction between falling away and falling. It is nowhere said in Scripture, that if a man fall he cannot be renewed; on the contrary, "the righteous falleth seven times, but he riseth up again;" and however many times the child of God doth fall, the Lord still holdeth the righteous; yea, when our bones are broken, he bindeth up our bones again, and setteth us once more upon a rock. He saith, "Return, ye backsliding children of men; for I am married unto you;" and if the Christian do backslide ever so far, still Almighty mercy cries, "Return, return, return, and seek an injured Father's heart." He still calls his children back again. Falling is not falling away. Let me explain the difference; for a man who falls may behave just like a man who falls away; and yet there is a great distinction between the two. I can use no better illustration than the distinction between fainting and dying. There lies a young creature; she can scarcely breathe; she cannot herself, lift up her hand, and if lifted up by any one else, it falls. She is cold and stiff; she is faint, but not dead. There is another one, just as cold and stiff as she is, but there is this difference—she is dead. The Christian may faint, and may fall down in a faint too, and some may pick him up, and say he is dead; but he is not. If he fall, God will lift him up again; but if he fall away, God himself cannot save him. For it is impossible, if the righteous fall away, "to renew them again unto repentance."

Moreover, to fall away is not to commit sin under a temporary surprise and temptation. Abraham goes to Egypt; he is afraid that his wife will be taken away from him, and he says, "She is my sister." That was a sin under a temporary surprise—a sin, of which, by-and-by, he repented, and God forgave him. Now that is falling; but it is not falling away. Even Noah might commit a sin, which has degraded his memory even till now, and shall disgrace it to the latest time; but doubtless, Noah repented, and was saved by sovereign grace. Noah fell, but Noah did not fall away. A Christian may go

for himself, to offer for sins.

4 And no man taketh this honor unto himself, but he that is called of God, as was Aaron.

5 So also Christ glorified not himself to be made an high priest; but he that said unto him, Thou art my Son, to day have I begotten thee.

6 As he saith also in another place, Thou art a priest for ever after the order of Melchisedec.

7 Who in the days of his flesh, when he had offered up prayers and supplications with strong crying and tears unto him that was able to save him from death, and was heard in that he feared;

8 Though he were a Son, yet learned he obedience by the things which he suffered;

9 And being made perfect, he became the author of eternal salvation unto all them that obey him;

10 Called of God an high priest after the order of Melchisedec.

11 Of whom we have many things to say, and hard to be uttered, seeing ye are dull of hearing.

12 For when for the time ye ought to be teachers, ye have need that one teach you again which be the first principles of the oracles of God; and are become such as have need of milk, and not of strong meat.

13 For every one that useth milk is unskillful in the word of righteousness: for he is a babe.

14 But strong meat belongeth to them that are of full age, even those who by reason of use have their senses exercised to discern both good and evil.

HEBREWS 6

1 Therefore leaving the principles of the doctrine of Christ, let us go on unto perfection; not laying again the foundation of repentance from dead works, and of faith toward God,

2 Of the doctrine of baptisms, and of laying on of hands, and of resurrection of the dead, and of eternal judgment.

3 And this will we do, if God permit.

4 For it is impossible for those who were once enlightened, and

ished in their sin!

19. So we see they could not enter in – Though afterward they desired it.

HEBREWS 4

2. But the word which they heard did not profit them – So far from it, that it increased their damnation. It is then only when it is mixed with faith, that it exerts its saving power.

3. For we only that have believed enter into the rest – The proposition is, There remains a rest for us. This is proved, ver. 3-11, thus: That psalm mentions a rest: yet it does not mean,

1. God's rest from creating; for this was long before the time of Moses. Therefore in his time another rest was expected, of which they who then heard fell short Nor is it,

2. The rest which Israel obtained through Joshua; for the Psalmist wrote after him. Therefore it is,

3. The eternal rest in heaven.

As he said – Clearly showing that there is a farther rest than that which followed the finishing of the creation. Though the works were finished – Before: whence it is plain, God did not speak of resting from them.

4. For, long after he had rested from his works, he speaks again. Gen. ii, 2.

5. In this psalm, of a rest yet to come.

7. After so long a time – It was above four hundred years from the time of Moses and Joshua to David. As it was said before – St. Paul here refers to the text he had just cited.

8. The rest – All the rest which God had promised.

9. Therefore – Since he still speaks of another day, there must remain a farther, even an eternal, rest for the people of God.

10. For they do not yet so rest. Therefore a fuller rest remains for them.

11. Lest any one should fall – Into perdition.

12. For the word of God – Preached, ver. 2, and armed with threatenings, ver. 3. Is living and powerful – Attended with the power of the living God, and conveying either life or death to the hearers. Sharper than any two-edged sword – Penetrating the heart more than this does the body. Piercing – Quite through, and laying open. The soul and spirit, joints and marrow – The inmost recesses of the mind, which the apostle beautifully and strongly expresses by this heap of figurative words. And is a discerner – Not only of the thoughts, but also of the intentions.

13. In his sight – It is God whose word is thus "powerful:" it is God in whose sight every creature is manifest; and of this his word, working on the conscience, gives the fullest conviction. But all things are naked and opened – Plainly alluding to the sacrifices under the law which were first flayed, and then (as the Greek word literally means) cleft asunder through the neck and backbone; so that everything both without and within was exposed to open view.

14. Having therefore a great high priest – Great indeed, being the eternal Son of God, that is passed through the heavens – As the Jewish high priest passed through the veil into the holy of holies, carrying with him the blood of the sacrifices, on the yearly day of atonement; so our great high priest went once for all through the visible heavens, with the virtue of his own blood, into the immediate presence God.

15. He sympathizes with us even in our innocent infirmities, wants, weaknesses, miseries, dangers. Yet without sin – And, therefore, is indisputably able to preserve us from it in all our temptations.

16. Let us therefore come boldly – Without any doubt or fear. Unto the throne of God, our reconciled Father, even his throne of grace – Grace erected it, and reigns there, and dispenses all blessings in a way of mere, unmerited favor.

more spiritual and excellent Sabbath remaining for the people of God, than that of the seventh day, or that into which Joshua led the Jews. This rest is, a rest of grace, and comfort, and holiness, in the gospel state. And a rest in glory, where the people of God shall enjoy the end of their faith, and the object of all their desires. The rest, or sabbatism, which is the subject of the apostle's reasoning, and as to which he concludes that it remains to be enjoyed, is undoubtedly the heavenly rest, which remains to the people of God, and is opposed to a state of labor and trouble in this world. It is the rest they shall obtain when the Lord Jesus shall appear from heaven. But those who do not believe, shall never enter into this spiritual rest, either of grace here or glory hereafter. God has always declared man's rest to be in him, and his love to be the only real happiness of the soul; and faith in his promises, through his Son, to be the only way of entering that rest.

11-16 Observe the end proposed: rest spiritual and eternal; the rest of grace here, and glory hereafter; in Christ on earth, with Christ in heaven. After due and diligent labor, sweet and satisfying rest shall follow; and labor now, will make that rest more pleasant when it comes. Let us labor, and quicken each other to be diligent in duty. The Holy Scriptures are the word of God. When God sets it home by his Spirit, it convinces powerfully, converts powerfully, and comforts powerfully. It makes a soul that has long been proud, to be humble; and a perverse spirit, to be meek and obedient. Sinful habits, that are become as it were natural to the soul, and rooted deeply in it, are separated and cut off by this sword. It will discover to men their thoughts and purposes, the vileness of many, the bad principles they are moved by, the sinful ends they act to. The word will show the sinner all that is in his heart. Let us hold fast the doctrines of Christian faith in our heads, its enlivening principles in our hearts, the open profession of it in our lips, and be subject to it in our lives. Christ executed one part of his priesthood on earth, in dying for us; the other he executes in heaven, pleading the cause, and presenting the offerings of his people. In the sight of Infinite Wisdom, it was needful that the Savior of men should be one who has the fellow feeling which no being but a fellow-creature could possibly have; and therefore it was necessary he should have actual experience of all the effects of sin that could be separated from its actual guilt. God sent his own Son in the likeness of sinful flesh, Ro 8:3; but the more holy and pure he was, the more he must have been unwilling in his nature to sin, and must have had deeper impression of its evil; consequently the more must he be concerned to deliver his people from its guilt and power. We should encourage ourselves by the excellence of our High Priest, to come boldly to the throne of grace. Mercy and grace are the things we want; mercy to pardon all our sins, and grace to purify our souls.

astray once, and speedily return again; and though it is a sad, and woeful, and evil thing to be surprised into a sin, yet there is a great difference between this and the sin which would be occasioned by a total falling away from grace.

Nor can a man who commits a sin, which is not exactly a surprise, be said to fall away. I believe that some Christian men—(God forbid that we should say much of it!—let us cover the nakedness of our brother with a cloak,) but I do believe that there are some Christians who, for a period of time, have wandered into sin, and yet have not positively fallen away. There is that black case of David—a case which has puzzled thousands. Certainly for some months, David lived without making a public confession of his sin, but, doubtless, he had achings of heart, for grace had not ceased its work: there was a spark among the ashes that Nathan stirred up, which showed that David was not dead, or else the match which the prophet applied would not have caught light so readily. And so, beloved, you may have wandered into sin for a time, and gone far from God; and yet you are not the character here described, concerning whom it is said, that it is impossible you should be saved; but, wanderer though you be, you are your father's son still, and mercy cries, "Repent, repent; return unto your first husband, for then it was better with you than it is now. Return, O wanderer, return."

Again, falling away is not even a giving up of profession. Some will say, "Now there is So-and-so; he used to make a profession of Christianity, and now he denies it, and what is worse, he dares to curse and swear, and says that he never knew Christ at all. Surely he must be fallen away." My friend, he has fallen, fallen fearfully, and fallen woefully; but I remember a case in Scripture of a man who denied his Lord and Master before his own face. You remember his name; he is an old friend of yours—our friend Simon Peter! he denied him with oaths and curses, and said, "I say unto thee that I know not the man." And yet Jesus looked on Simon. He had fallen, but he had not fallen away; for, only two or three days after that, there was Peter at the tomb of his Master, running there to meet his Lord, to be one of the first to find him risen. Beloved, you may even have denied Christ by open profession, and yet if you repent there is mercy for you. Christ has not cast you away, you shall repent yet. You have not fallen away. If you had, I might not preach to you; for it is impossible for those who have fallen away to be renewed again unto repentance.

But some one says, "What is falling away?"

have tasted of the heavenly gift, and were made partakers of the Holy Ghost,

5 And have tasted the good word of God, and the powers of the world to come,

6 If they shall fall away, to renew them again unto repentance; seeing they crucify to themselves the Son of God afresh, and put him to an open shame.

7 For the earth which drinketh in the rain that cometh oft upon it, and bringeth forth herbs meet for them by whom it is dressed, receiveth blessing from God:

8 But that which beareth thorns and briers is rejected, and is nigh unto cursing; whose end is to be burned.

9 But, beloved, we are persuaded better things of you, and things that accompany salvation, though we thus speak.

10 For God is not unrighteous to forget your work and labor of love, which ye have shewed toward his name, in that ye have ministered to the saints, and do minister.

11 And we desire that every one of you do shew the same diligence to the full assurance of hope unto the end:

12 That ye be not slothful, but followers of them who through faith and patience inherit the promises.

13 For when God made promise to Abraham, because he could swear by no greater, he sware by himself,

14 Saying, Surely blessing I will bless thee, and multiplying I will multiply thee.

15 And so, after he had patiently endured, he obtained the promise.

16 For men verily swear by the greater: and an oath for confirmation is to them an end of all strife.

17 Wherein God, willing more abundantly to shew unto the heirs of promise the immutability of his counsel, confirmed it by an oath:

18 That by two immutable things, in which it was impossible for God to lie, we might have a strong consolation, who have fled for refuge to lay hold upon the hope set before us:

HEBREWS 5

1. For every high priest being taken from among men – Is, till he is taken, of the same rank with them. And is appointed – That is, is wont to be appointed. In things pertaining to God – To bring God near to men, and men to God. That he may offer both gifts – Out of things inanimate, and animal sacrifices.

2. Who can have compassion – In proportion to the offense: so the Greek word signifies. On the ignorant – Them that are in error. And the wandering – Them that are in sin. Seeing himself also is compassed with infirmity – Even with sinful infirmity; and so needs the compassion which he shows to others.

4. The apostle begins here to treat of the priesthood of Christ. The sum of what he observes concerning it is, Whatever is excellent in the Levitical priesthood is in Christ, and in a more eminent manner; and whatever is wanting in those priests is in him. And no one taketh this honor – The priesthood. To himself, but he that is called of God, as was Aaron – And his posterity, who were all of them called at one and the same time. But it is observable, Aaron did not preach at all; preaching being no part of the priestly office.

5. So also Christ glorified not himself to be an high priest – That is, did not take this honor to himself, but received it from him who said, Thou art my Son, this day have I begotten thee – Not, indeed, at the same time; for his generation was from eternity. Psalm ii, 7.

6. Psalm cx, 4.

7. The sum of the things treated of in the seventh and following chapters is contained, ver. 7-10; and in this sum is admirably comprised the process of his passion, with its inmost causes, in the very terms used by the evangelists. 8. Though he were a Son – This is interposed, lest any should be offended at all these instances of human weakness. In the garden, how frequently did he call God his Father! Matt. xxvi, 39, &c. And hence it most evidently appears that his being the Son of God did not arise merely from his resurrection. Yet learned he – The word learned, premised to the word suffered, elegantly shows how willingly he learned. He learned obedience, when be began to suffer; when he applied himself to drink that cup: obedience in suffering and dying.

9. And being perfected – By sufferings, chap. ii, 10; brought through all to glory. He became the author – The procuring and efficient cause. Of eternal salvation to all that obey him – By doing and suffering his whole will.

10. Called – The Greek word here properly signifies surnamed. His name is, "the Son of God." The Holy Ghost seems to have concealed who Melchisedec was, on purpose that he might be the more eminent type of Christ. This only we know, that he was a priest, and king of Salem, or Jerusalem.

11. Concerning whom – The apostle here begins an important digression, wherein he reproves, admonishes, and exhorts the Hebrews. We – Preachers of the gospel. Have many things to say, and hard to be explained – Though not so much from the subject-matter, as from your slothfulness in considering, and dullness in apprehending, the things of God.

12. Ye have need that one teach you again which are the first principles of religion. Accordingly these are enumerated in the first verse of the ensuing chapter. And have need of milk – The first and plainest doctrines.

13. Every one that useth milk – That neither desires, nor can digest, anything else: otherwise strong men use milk; but not milk chiefly, and much less that only. Is unexperienced in the word of righteousness – The sublimer truths of the gospel. Such are all who desire and can digest nothing but the doctrine of justification and imputed righteousness.

14. But strong meat – These sublimer truths relating to "perfection," chap. vi, 1. Belong to them of full age, who by habit – Habit here signifies strength of spiritual understanding, arising from maturity of spiritual age. By, or in consequence of, this habit they exercise themselves in these things with ease, readiness, cheerfulness, and profit.

MATTHEW HENRY

CHARLES H. SPURGEON

HEBREWS 5

The office and duty of a high priest abundantly answered in Christ. (1-10)

The Christian Hebrews reproved for their little progress in the knowledge of the gospel. (11-14)

1-10 The High Priest must be a man, a partaker of our nature. This shows that man had sinned. For God would not suffer sinful man to come to him alone. But every one is welcome to God, that comes to him by this High Priest; and as we value acceptance with God, and pardon, we must apply by faith to this our great High Priest Christ Jesus, who can intercede for those that are out of the way of truth, duty, and happiness; one who has tenderness to lead them back from the by-paths of error, sin, and misery. Those only can expect assistance from God, and acceptance with him, and his presence and blessing on them and their services, that are called of God. This is applied to Christ. In the days of his flesh, Christ made himself subject to death: he hungered: he was a tempted, suffering, dying Jesus. Christ set an example, not only to pray, but to be fervent in prayer. How many dry prayers, how few wetted with tears, do we offer up to God! He was strengthened to support the immense weight of suffering laid upon him. There is no real deliverance from death but to be carried through it. He was raised and exalted, and to him was given the power of saving all sinners to the uttermost, who come unto God through him. Christ has left us an example that we should learn humble obedience to the will of God, by all our afflictions. We need affliction, to teach us submission.

11-14 Dull hearers make the preaching of the gospel difficult, and even those who have some faith may be dull hearers, and slow to believe. Much is looked for from those to whom much is given. To be unskillful, denotes want of experience in the things of the gospel. Christian experience is a spiritual sense, taste, or relish of the goodness, sweetness, and excellence of the truths of the gospel. And no tongue can express the satisfaction which the soul receives, from a sense of Divine goodness, grace, and love to it in Christ.

HEBREWS 6

The Hebrews are urged to go forward in the doctrine of Christ, and the consequences of apostasy, or turning back, are described. (1-8)

The apostle expresses satisfaction, as to the most of them. (9,10)

And encourages them to persevere in faith and holiness. (11-20)

1-8 Every part of the truth and will of God should be set before all who profess the gospel, and be urged on their hearts and consciences. We should not be

Well, there never has been a case of it yet, and therefore I cannot describe it from observation; but I will tell you what I suppose it is. To fall away, would be for the Holy Spirit entirely to go out of a man—for his grace entirely to cease; not to lie dormant, but to cease to be—for God, who has begun a good work, to leave off doing it entirely—to take his hand completely and entirely away, and say, "There, man! I have half saved thee; now I will damn thee." That is what falling away is. It is not to sin temporarily. A child may sin against his father, and still be alive; but falling away is like cutting the child's head off clean. Not falling merely, for then our Father could pick us up, but being dashed down a precipice, where we are lost for ever. Falling away would involve God's grace changing its living nature. God's immutability becoming variable, God's faithfulness becoming changeable, and God, himself being undeified; for all these things falling away would necessitate.

III. But if a child of God could fall away, and grace could cease in a man's heart—now comes the third question—Paul says, IT IS IMPOSSIBLE FOR HIM TO BE RENEWED. What did the Apostle mean? One eminent commentator says, he meant that it would be very hard. It would be very hard, indeed, for a man who fell away, to be saved. But we reply, "My dear friend, it does not say anything about its being very hard; it says it is impossible, and we say that it would be utterly impossible, if such a case as is supposed were to happen; impossible for man, and also impossible for God; for God hath purposed that he never will grant a second salvation to save those whom the first salvation hath failed to deliver. Methinks, however, I hear some one say, "It seems to me that it is possible for some such to fall away," because it says, "It is impossible, if they shall fall away, to renew them again into repentance." Well, my friend, I will grant you your theory for a moment. You are a good Christian this morning; let us apply it to yourself, and see how you will like it. You have believed in Christ, and committed your soul to God, and you think, that in some unlucky hour you may fall entirely away. Mark you, if you come to me and tell me that you have fallen away, how would you like me to say to you, "My friend, you are as much damned as the devil in hell! for it is impossible to renew you to repentance?" "Oh! no, sir," you would say, "I will repent again and join the Church." That is just the Arminian theory all over; but it is not in God's Scripture. If you once fall away, you are as damned as any man who suffereth in the gulf for ever. And yet we have heard a man talk about people being converted three, four, and

19 Which hope we have as an anchor of the soul, both sure and stedfast, and which entereth into that within the veil;

20 Whither the forerunner is for us entered, even Jesus, made an high priest for ever after the order of Melchisedec.

HEBREWS 7

1 For this Melchisedec, king of Salem, priest of the most high God, who met Abraham returning from the slaughter of the kings, and blessed him;

2 To whom also Abraham gave a tenth part of all; first being by interpretation King of righteousness, and after that also King of Salem, which is, King of peace;

3 Without father, without mother, without descent, having neither beginning of days, nor end of life; but made like unto the Son of God; abideth a priest continually.

4 Now consider how great this man was, unto whom even the patriarch Abraham gave the tenth of the spoils.

5 And verily they that are of the sons of Levi, who receive the office of the priesthood, have a commandment to take tithes of the people according to the law, that is, of their brethren, though they come out of the loins of Abraham:

6 But he whose descent is not counted from them received tithes of Abraham, and blessed him that had the promises.

7 And without all contradiction the less is blessed of the better.

8 And here men that die receive tithes; but there he receiveth them, of whom it is witnessed that he liveth.

9 And as I may so say, Levi also, who receiveth tithes, payed tithes in Abraham.

10 For he was yet in the loins of his father, when Melchisedec met him.

11 If therefore perfection were by the Levitical priesthood, (for under it the people received the law,) what further need was there that another priest should rise after the order of Melchisedec, and not be called after the order of Aaron?

12 For the priesthood being

HEBREWS 6

1. Therefore leaving the principles of the doctrine of Christ – That is, saying no more of them for the present. Let us go on to perfection; not laying again the foundation of repentance from dead works – From open sins, the very first thing to be insisted on. And faith in God – The very next point. So St. Paul in his very first sermon at Lystra, Acts xiv, 15, "Turn from those vanities unto the living God." And when they believed, they were to be baptized with the baptism, not of the Jews, or of John, but of Christ. The next thing was, to lay hands upon them, that they might receive the Holy Ghost: after which they were more fully instructed, touching the resurrection, and the general judgment; called eternal, because the sentence then pronounced is irreversible, and the effects of it remain for ever.

3. And this we will do – We will go on to perfection; and so much the more diligently, because,

4. It is impossible for those who were once enlightened – With the light of the glorious love of God in Christ. And have tasted the heavenly gift – Remission of sins, sweeter than honey and the honeycomb. And been made partakers of the Holy Ghost – Of the witness and the fruit of the Spirit.

5. And have tasted the good word of God – Have had a relish for, and a delight in it. And the powers of the world to come – Which every one tastes, who has an hope full of immortality. Every child that is naturally born, first sees the light, then receives and tastes proper nourishment, and partakes of the things of this world. In like manner, the apostle, comparing spiritual with natural things, speaks of one born of the Spirit, as seeing the light, tasting the sweetness, and partaking of the things "of the world to come."

6. And have fallen away – Here is not a supposition, but a plain relation of fact. The apostle here describes the case of those who have cast away both the power and the form of godliness; who have lost both their faith, hope, and love, ver. 10, &c., and that willfully, chap. x, 26. Of these willfull total apostates he declares, it is impossible to renew them again to repentance, (though they were renewed once,) either to the foundation, or anything built thereon. Seeing they crucify the Son of God afresh – They use him with the utmost indignity. And put him to an open shame – Causing his glorious name to be blasphemed.

8. That which beareth thorns and briers – Only or chiefly. Is rejected – No more labor is bestowed upon it. Whose end is to be burned – As Jerusalem was shortly after.

9. But, beloved – in this one place he calls them so. He never uses this appellation – We are persuaded of you things that accompany salvation – We are persuaded you are now saved from your sins; and that ye have that faith, love, and holiness, which lead to final salvation. Though we thus speak – To warn you, lest you should fall from your present steadfastness.

10. For – Ye give plain proof of your faith and love, which the righteous God will surely reward.

11. But we desire you may show the same diligence unto the end – And therefore we thus speak. To the full assurance of hope – Which you cannot expect, if you abate your diligence. The full assurance of faith relates to present pardon; the full assurance of hope, to future glory. The former is the highest degree of divine evidence that God is reconciled to me in the Son of his love; the latter is the same degree of divine evidence (wrought in the soul by the same immediate inspiration of the Holy Ghost) of persevering grace, and of eternal glory. So much, and no more, as faith every moment "beholds with open face," so much does hope see to all eternity. But this assurance of faith and hope is not an opinion, not a bare construction of scripture, but is given immediately by the power of the Holy Ghost; and what none can have for another, but for himself only.

12. Inherited the promises – The promised rest; paradise.

13. For – Ye have abundant encouragement, seeing no stronger promise could

always speaking about outward things; these have their places and use, but often take up too much attention and time, which might be better employed. The humbled sinner who pleads guilty, and cries for mercy, can have no ground from this passage to be discouraged, whatever his conscience may accuse him of. Nor does it prove that any one who is made a new creature in Christ, ever becomes a final apostate from him. The apostle is not speaking of the falling away of mere professors, never convinced or influenced by the gospel. Such have nothing to fall away from, but an empty name, or hypocritical profession. Neither is he speaking of partial declining or backslidings. Nor are such sins meant, as Christians fall into through the strength of temptations, or the power of some worldly or fleshly lust. But the falling away here mentioned, is an open and avowed renouncing of Christ, from enmity of heart against him, his cause, and people, by men approving in their minds the deeds of his murderers, and all this after they have received the knowledge of the truth, and tasted some of its comforts. Of these it is said, that it is impossible to renew them again unto repentance. Not because the blood of Christ is not sufficient to obtain pardon for this sin; but this sin, in its very nature, is opposite to repentance and every thing that leads to it. If those who through mistaken views of this passage, as well as of their own case, fear that there is no mercy for them, would attend to the account given of the nature of this sin, that it is a total and a willing renouncing of Christ, and his cause, and joining with his enemies, it would relieve them from wrong fears.

9,10 There are things that are never separated from salvation; things that show the person to be in a state of salvation, and which will end in eternal salvation. And the things that accompany salvation, are better things than ever any dissembler or apostate enjoyed. The works of love, done for the glory of Christ, or done to his saints for Christ's sake, from time to time, as God gives occasion, are evident marks of a man's salvation; and more sure tokens of saving grace given, than the enlightening and tasting spoken of before. No love is to be reckoned as love, but working love; and no works are right works, which flow not from love to Christ.

11-20 The hope here meant, is a sure looking for good things promised, through those promises, with love, desire, and valuing of them. Hope has its degrees, as faith also. The promise of blessedness God has made to believers, is from God's eternal purpose, settled between the eternal Father, Son, and Spirit. These promises of God may safely be depended upon; for here we have two things which cannot change, the counsel and the oath of God, in which it is not possible for God to lie; it would be contrary to his nature as well as to his will. And as he cannot lie; the destruction of the unbeliever, and the salvation of

five times, and regenerated over and over again. I remember a good man (I suppose he was) pointing to a man who was walking along the street, and saying, "That man has been born again three times, to my certain knowledge." I could mention the name of the individual, but I refrain from doing so. "And I believe he will fall again," said he, "he is so much addicted to drinking, that I do not believe the grace of God will do anything for him, unless he becomes a teetotaler." Now, such men cannot read the Bible; because in case their members do positively fall away, here it is stated, as a positive fact, that it is impossible to renew them again unto repentance. But I ask my Arminian friend, does he not believe that as long as there is life there is hope? "Yes," he says:

"While the lamp holds out to burn,
The vilest sinner may return."

Well, that is not very consistent, to say this in the very next breath to that with which you tell us that there are some people who fall away, and consequently fall into such a condition, that they cannot be saved. I want to know how you make these two things fit each other; I want you to make these two doctrines agree; and until some enterprising individual will bring the north pole, and set it on the top of the south, I cannot tell how you will accomplish it. The fact is you are quite right in saying, "While there is life there is hope;" but you are wrong in saying that any individual ever did fall into such a condition, that it was impossible for him to be saved.

We come now to do two things: first, to prove the doctrine, that if a Christian fall away, he cannot be saved; and, secondly, to show its use.

If a Christian fall away—not fall, for you understand how I have explained that; but if a Christian cease to be a child of God, and if grace die out in his heart—he is then beyond the possibility of salvation, and it is impossible for him ever to be renewed. Let me show you why. First, it is utterly impossible, if you consider the work which has already broken down. When men have built bridges across streams, if they have been built of the strongest material and in the most excellent manner, and yet the foundation has been found so bad that none will stand, what do they say? Why, "We have already tried the best which engineering or architecture has taught us; the best has already failed; we know nothing that can exceed what has been tried; and we do therefore feel, that there remains no possibility of ever bridging that stream, or ever running a line of railroad across this bog, or this morass, for we have already tried what is acknowledged to be the best scheme." As the apostle says, "These people have been once

changed, there is made of necessity a change also of the law.

13 For he of whom these things are spoken pertaineth to another tribe, of which no man gave attendance at the altar.

14 For it is evident that our Lord sprang out of Juda; of which tribe Moses spake nothing concerning priesthood.

15 And it is yet far more evident: for that after the similitude of Melchisedec there ariseth another priest,

16 Who is made, not after the law of a carnal commandment, but after the power of an endless life.

17 For he testifieth, Thou art a priest for ever after the order of Melchisedec.

18 For there is verily a disannulling of the commandment going before for the weakness and unprofitableness thereof.

19 For the law made nothing perfect, but the bringing in of a better hope did; by the which we draw nigh unto God.

20 And inasmuch as not without an oath he was made priest:

21 (For those priests were made without an oath; but this with an oath by him that said unto him, The Lord sware and will not repent, Thou art a priest for ever after the order of Melchisedec:)

22 By so much was Jesus made a surety of a better testament.

23 And they truly were many priests, because they were not suffered to continue by reason of death:

24 But this man, because he continueth ever, hath an unchangeable priesthood.

25 Wherefore he is able also to save them to the uttermost that come unto God by him, seeing he ever liveth to make intercession for them.

26 For such an high priest became us, who is holy, harmless, undefiled, separate from sinners, and made higher than the heavens;

27 Who needeth not daily, as those high priests, to offer up sacrifice, first for his own sins, and then for the people's: for this he did once, when he offered up himself.

28 For the law maketh men

be made than that great promise which God made to Abraham, and in him to us.

14. Gen. xxii, 17.

15. After he had waited – Thirty years. He obtained the promise – Isaac, the pledge of all the promises.

16. Men generally swear by him who is infinitely greater than themselves, and an oath for confirmation, to confirm what is promised or asserted, usually puts an end to all contradiction. This shows that an oath taken in a religious manner is lawful even under the gospel: otherwise the apostle would never have mentioned it with so much honor, as a proper means to confirm the truth.

17. God interposed by an oath – Amazing condescension! He who is greatest of all acts as if he were a middle person; as if while he swears, he were less than himself, by whom he swears! Thou that hearest the promise, dost thou not yet believe?

18. That by two unchangeable things – His promise and his oath, in either, much more in both of which, it was impossible for God to lie, we might have strong consolation – Swallowing up all doubt and fear. Who have fled – After having been tossed by many storms. To lay hold on the hope set before us – On Christ, the object of our hope, and the glory we hope for through him.

19. Which hope in Christ we have as an anchor of the soul – Entering into heaven itself, and fixed there. Within the veil – Thus he slides back to the priesthood of Christ.

20. A forerunner used to be less in dignity than those that are to follow him. But it is not so here; for Christ who is gone before us is infinitely superior to us. What an honor is it to believers, to have so glorious a forerunner, now appearing in the presence of God for them.

HEBREWS 7

1. The sum of this chapter is, Christ, as appears from his type, Melchisedec, who was greater than Abraham himself, from whom Levi descended, has a priesthood altogether excellent, new, firm, perpetual. Gen. xiv, 18, &c.

2. Being first – According to the meaning of his own name. King of righteousness, then – According to the name of his city. King of peace – So in him, as in Christ, righteousness and peace were joined. And so they are in all that believe in him.

3. Without father, without mother, without pedigree – Recorded, without any account of his descent from any ancestors of the priestly order. Having neither beginning of days, nor end of life – Mentioned by Moses. But being – In all these respects. Made like the Son of God – Who is really without father, as to his human nature; without mother, as to his divine; and in this also, without pedigree – Neither descended from any ancestors of the priestly order. Remaineth a priest continually – Nothing is recorded of the death or successor of Melchisedec. But Christ alone does really remain without death, and without successor.

4. The greatness of Melchisedec is described in all the preceding and following particulars. But the most manifest proof of it was, that Abraham gave him tithes as to a priest of God and a superior; though he was himself a patriarch, greater than a king, and a progenitor of many kings.

5. The sons of Levi take tithes of their brethren – Sprung from Abraham as well as themselves. The Levites therefore are greater than they; but the priests are greater than the Levites, the patriarch Abraham than the priests, and Melchisedec than him.

6. He who is not from them – The Levites. Blessed – Another proof of his superiority. Even him that had the promises – That was so highly favored of God. When St. Paul speaks of Christ, he says, "the promise;" promises refer to other

MATTHEW HENRY

the believer, are alike certain. Here observe, those to whom God has given full security of happiness, have a title to the promises by inheritance. The consolations of God are strong enough to support his people under their heaviest trials. Here is a refuge for all sinners who flee to the mercy of God, through the redemption of Christ, according to the covenant of grace, laying aside all other confidences. We are in this world as a ship at sea, tossed up and down, and in danger of being cast away. We need an anchor to keep us sure and steady. Gospel hope is our anchor in the storms of this world. It is sure and steadfast, or it could not keep us so.

HEBREWS 7

A comparison between the priesthood of Melchizedec and that of Christ. (1-3)

The excellence of Christ's priesthood above the Levitical priesthood is shown. (4-10)

This is applied to Christ. (11-25)

The faith and hope of the church encouraged from this. (26-28)

1-3 Melchizedec met Abraham when returning from the rescue of Lot. His name, "King of Righteousness," doubtless suitable to his character, marked him as a type of the Messiah and his kingdom. The name of his city signified "Peace;" and as king of peace he typified Christ, the Prince of Peace, the great Reconciler of God and man. Nothing is recorded as to the beginning or end of his life; thus he typically resembled the Son of God, whose existence is from everlasting to everlasting, who had no one that was before him, and will have no one come after him, in his priesthood. Every part of Scripture honors the great King of Righteousness and Peace, our glorious High Priest and Savior; and the more we examine it, the more we shall be convinced, that the testimony of Jesus is the spirit of prophecy.

4-10 That High Priest who should afterward appear, of whom Melchizedec was a type, must be much superior to the Levitical priests. Observe Abraham's great dignity and happiness; that he had the promises. That man is rich and happy indeed, who has the promises, both of the life that now is, and of that which is to come. This honor have all those who receive the Lord Jesus. Let us go forth in our spiritual conflicts, trusting in his word and strength, ascribing our victories to his grace, and desiring to be met and blessed by him in all our ways.

11-25 The priesthood and law by which perfection could not come, are done away; a Priest is risen, and a dispensation now set up, by which true believers may be made perfect. That there is such a change is plain. The law which made the Levitical priesthood, showed that the priests were frail, dying creatures, not

CHARLES H. SPURGEON

enlightened; they have had once the influence of the Holy Spirit, revealing to them their sin: what now remains to be tried. They have been once convinced—is there anything superior to conviction?" Does the Bible promise that the poor sinner shall have anything over and above the conviction of his sin to make him sensible of it? Is there anything more powerful than the sword of the Spirit? That has not pierced the man's heart; is there anything else which will do it? Here is a man who has been under the hammer of God's law; but that has not broken his heart; can you find anything stronger? The lamp of God's spirit has already lit up the caverns of his soul: if that be not sufficient, where will you borrow another? Ask the sun, has he a lamp more bright than the illumination of the Spirit! Ask the stars, have they a light more brilliant than the light of the Holy Ghost? Creation answers no. If that fails, then there is nothing else. These people, moreover, had tasted the heavenly gift; and though they had been pardoned and justified, yet pardon through Christ and justification were not enough (on this supposition) to save them. How else can they be saved? God has cast them away; after he has failed in saving them by these, what else can deliver them? Already they have tasted of the heavenly gift: is there a greater mercy for them? Is there a brighter dress than the robe of Christ's righteousness? Is there a more efficacious bath than that "fountain filled with blood?" No. All the earth echoes, "No." If the one has failed, what else does there remain?

These persons, too, have been partakers of the Holy Ghost; if that fail, what more can we give them? If, my hearer, the Holy Ghost dwells in your soul, and that Holy Ghost does not sanctify you and keep you to the end, what else can be tried? Ask the blasphemer whether he knows a being, or dares to suppose a being superior to the Holy Spirit! Is there a being greater than Omnipotence? Is there a might greater than that which dwells in the believer's new-born heart? And if already the Holy Spirit hath failed, O, heavens! tell us where we can find aught that can excel his might? If that be ineffectual, what next is to be essayed? These people, too, had "tasted the good Word of Life;" they had loved the doctrines of grace; those doctrines had entered into their souls, and they had fed upon them. What new doctrines shall be preached to them? Prophet of ages! where whilt thou find another system of divinity? Who shall we have? Shall we raise up Moses from the tomb? shall we fetch up all the ancient seers, and bid them prophecy? If, then, there is only one doctrine that is true, and if these people have fallen away after receiving

high priests which have infirmity; but the word of the oath,
which was since the law,
maketh the Son, who is consecrated for evermore.

HEBREWS 8

1 Now of the things which we
have spoken this is the sum: We
have such an high priest, who is
set on the right hand of the
throne of the Majesty in the
heavens;
2 A minister of the sanctuary,
and of the true tabernacle, which
the Lord pitched, and not man.
3 For every high priest is
ordained to offer gifts and sacrifices: wherefore it is of necessity that this man have somewhat
also to offer.
4 For if he were on earth, he
should not be a priest, seeing
that there are priests that offer
gifts according to the law:
5 Who serve unto the example
and shadow of heavenly things,
as Moses was admonished of
God when he was about to make
the tabernacle: for, See, saith he,
that thou make all things
according to the pattern shewed
to thee in the mount.
6 But now hath he obtained a
more excellent ministry, by how
much also he is the mediator of
a better covenant, which was
established upon better promises.
7 For if that first covenant had
been faultless, then should no
place have been sought for the
second.
8 For finding fault with them, he
saith, Behold, the days come,
saith the Lord, when I will make
a new covenant with the house
of Israel and with the house of
Judah:
9 Not according to the covenant
that I made with their fathers in
the day when I took them by the
hand to lead them out of the land
of Egypt; because they continued not in my covenant, and I
regarded them not, saith the
Lord.
10 For this is the covenant that I
will make with the house of Israel
after those days, saith the Lord; I
will put my laws into their mind,
and write them in their hearts:
and I will be to them a God, and

blessings also.
7. The less is blessed – Authoritatively, of the greater.
8. And here – In the Levitical priesthood. But there – In the case of
Melchisedec. He of whom it is testified that he liveth – Who is not spoken of
as one that died for another to succeed him; but is represented only as living, no
mention being made either of his birth or death.
9. And even Levi, who received tithes – Not in person, but in his successors, as
it were, paid tithes – In the person of Abraham.
11. The apostle now demonstrates that the Levitical priesthood must yield to
the priesthood of Christ, because Melchisedec, after whose order he is a priest,
　　1. Is opposed to Aaron, ver. 11-14.
　　2. Hath no end of life, ver. 15-19, but "remaineth a priest continually."
If now perfection were by the Levitical priesthood – If this perfectly answered
all God's designs and man's wants. For under it the people received the law –
Whence some might infer, that perfection was by that priesthood. What farther
need was there, that another priest – Of a new order, should be set up? From
this single consideration it is plain, that both the priesthood and the law, which
were inseparably connected, were now to give way to a better priesthood and
more excellent dispensation.
12. For – One of these cannot be changed without the other.
13. But the priesthood is manifestly changed from one order to another, and
from one tribe to another. For he of whom these things are spoken – Namely,
Jesus. Pertaineth to another tribe – That of Judah. Of which no man was suffered by the law to attend on, or minister at, the altar.
14. For it is evident that our Lord sprang out of Judah – Whatever difficulties
have arisen since, during so long a tract of time, it was then clear beyond dispute.
15. And it is still far more evident, that – Both the priesthood and the law are
changed, because the priest now raised up is not only of another tribe, but of a
quite different order.
16. Who is made – A priest. Not after the law of a carnal commandment – Not
according to the Mosaic law, which consisted chiefly of commandments that
were carnal, compared to the spirituality of the gospel. But after the power of
an endless life – Which he has in himself, as the eternal Son of God.
18. For there is implied in this new and everlasting priesthood, and in the new
dispensation connected therewith, a disannulling of the preceding commandment – An abrogation of the Mosaic law. For the weakness and unprofitableness
thereof – For its insufficiency either to justify or to sanctify.
19. For the law – Taken by itself, separate from the gospel. Made nothing perfect – Could not perfect its votaries, either in faith or love, in happiness or holiness. But the bringing in of a better hope – Of the gospel dispensation, which
gives us a better ground of confidence, does. By which we draw nigh to God –
Yea, so nigh as to be one spirit with him. And this is true perfection.
20. And – The greater solemnity wherewith he was made priest, farther proves
the superior excellency of his priesthood.
21. The Lord swear and will not repent – Hence also it appears, that his is an
unchangeable priesthood.
22. Of so much better a covenant – Unchangeable, eternal. Was Jesus made a
surety – Or mediator. The word covenant frequently occurs in the remaining
part of this epistle. The original word means either a covenant or a last will and
testament. St. Paul takes it sometimes in the former, sometimes in the latter,
sense; sometimes he includes both.
23. They were many priests – One after another.
24. He continueth for ever – In life and in his priesthood. That passeth not away
– To any successor.
25. Wherefore he is able to save to the uttermost – From all the guilt, power,

able to save their own lives, much less could they save the souls of those who came to them. But the High Priest of our profession holds his office by the power of endless life in himself; not only to keep himself alive, but to give spiritual and eternal life to all who rely upon his sacrifice and intercession. The better covenant, of which Jesus was the Surety, is not here contrasted with the covenant of works, by which every transgressor is shut up under the curse. It is distinguished from the Sinai covenant with Israel, and the legal dispensation under which the church so long remained.

26-28 Observe the description of the personal holiness of Christ. He is free from all habits or principles of sin, not having the least disposition to it in his nature. No sin dwells in him, not the least sinful inclination, though such dwells in the best of Christians. He is harmless, free from all actual transgression; he did no violence, nor was there any deceit in his mouth. He is undefiled. It is hard to keep ourselves pure, so as not to partake the guilt of other men's sins. But none need be dismayed who come to God in the name of his beloved Son.

HEBREWS 8

The excellence of Christ's priesthood above that of Aaron is shown. (1-6)

The great excellence of the new covenant above the former. (7-13)

1-6 The substance, or summary, of what had been declared was, that Christians had such a High Priest as they needed. He took upon himself human nature, appeared on earth, and there gave himself as a sacrifice to God for the sins of his people. We must not dare to approach God, or to present any thing to him, but in and through Christ, depending upon his merits and mediation; for we are accepted only in the Beloved. In all obedience and worship, we should keep close to God's word, which is the only and perfect standard. Christ is the substance and end of the law of righteousness. But the covenant here referred to, was that made with Israel as a nation, securing temporal benefits to them. The promises of all spiritual blessings, and of eternal life, revealed in the gospel, and made sure through Christ, are of infinitely greater value.

7-13 The superior excellence of the priesthood of Christ, above that of Aaron, is shown from that covenant of grace, of which Christ was Mediator. The law not only made all subject to it, liable to be condemned for the guilt of sin, but also was unable to remove that guilt, and clear the conscience from the sense and terror of it. Whereas, by the blood of Christ, a full remission of sins was provided, so that God would remember them no more. God once

that, how can they be saved?

Again, these people, according to the text, have had "the powers of the world to come." They have had power to conquer sin—power in faith, power in prayer, power of communion; with what greater power shall they be endowed? This has already failed; what next can be done? O ye angels! answer, what next! What other means remain? What else can avail, if already the great things of salvation have been defeated? What else shall now be attempted? He hath been once saved; but yet it is supposed that he is lost. How, then, can he now be saved? Is there a supplementary salvation? is there something that shall overtop Christ, and be a Christ where Jesus is defeated?

And then the apostle says, that the greatness of their sin which they would incur, if they did fall away, would put them beyond the bounds of mercy. Christ died, and by his death he made an atonement for his own murderers; he made an atonement for those sins which crucified him once; but do we read that Christ will ever die for those who crucify him twice? But the Apostle tells us that if believers do fall away, they will "crucify the Son of God afresh, and put him to an open shame." Where, then, would be an atonement for that? He has died for me; What! though the sins of all the world were on my shoulders, still they only crucified him once, and that one crucifixion has taken all those sins away; but if I crucified him again, where would I find pardon? Could heavens, could earth, could Christ himself, with bowels full of love, point me to another Christ, show to me a second Calvary, give me a second Gethsemane? Ah! no! the very guilt itself would put us beyond the pale of hope, if we were to fall away?

Again, beloved, think what it would necessitate to save such a man. Christ has died for him once, yet he has fallen away and is lost; the Spirit has regenerated him once, and that regenerating work has been of no use. God has given him a new heart (I am only speaking, of course, on the supposition of the Apostle,) he has put his law in that heart, yet he has departed from him, contrary to the promise that he should not; he has made him "like a shining light," but he did not "shine more and more unto the perfect day," he shone only unto blackness. What next? There must be a second incarnation, a second Calvary, a second Holy Ghost, a second regeneration, a second justification, although the first was finished and complete—in fact, I know not what. It would necessitate the upsetting of the whole kingdom of nature and grace, and it would, indeed, be a world turned upside down, if after the gracious Savior failed, he were to attempt the work again.

they shall be to me a people:

11 And they shall not teach every man his neighbor, and every man his brother, saying, Know the Lord: for all shall know me, from the least to the greatest.

12 For I will be merciful to their unrighteousness, and their sins and their iniquities will I remember no more.

13 In that he saith, A new covenant, he hath made the first old. Now that which decayeth and waxeth old is ready to vanish away.

HEBREWS 9

1 Then verily the first covenant had also ordinances of divine service, and a worldly sanctuary.

2 For there was a tabernacle made; the first, wherein was the candlestick, and the table, and the shewbread; which is called the sanctuary.

3 And after the second veil, the tabernacle which is called the Holiest of all;

4 Which had the golden censer, and the ark of the covenant overlaid round about with gold, wherein was the golden pot that had manna, and Aaron's rod that budded, and the tables of the covenant;

5 And over it the cherubims of glory shadowing the mercyseat; of which we cannot now speak particularly.

6 Now when these things were thus ordained, the priests went always into the first tabernacle, accomplishing the service of God.

7 But into the second went the high priest alone once every year, not without blood, which he offered for himself, and for the errors of the people:

8 The Holy Ghost this signifying, that the way into the holiest of all was not yet made manifest, while as the first tabernacle was yet standing:

9 Which was a figure for the time then present, in which were offered both gifts and sacrifices, that could not make him that did the service perfect, as pertaining to the conscience;

10 Which stood only in meats and drinks, and divers washings,

root, and consequence of sin. Them who come – By faith. To God through him – As their priest. Seeing he ever liveth to make intercession – That is, he ever lives and intercedes. He died once; he intercedes perpetually.

26. For such an high priest suited us – Unholy, mischievous, defiled sinners: a blessed paradox! Holy – With respect to God. Harmless – With respect to men. Undefiled – With any sin in himself. Separated from sinners – As well as free from sin. And so he was when he left the world. And made – Even in his human nature. Higher than the heavens – And all their inhabitants.

27. Who needeth not to offer up sacrifices daily – That is, on every yearly day of expiation; for he offered once for all: not for his own sins, for he then offered up himself "without spot to God."

28. The law maketh men high priests that have infirmity – That are both weak, mortal, and sinful. But the oath which was since the law – Namely, in the time of David. Maketh the son, who is consecrated for ever – Who being now free, both from sin and death, from natural and moral infirmity, remaineth a priest for ever.

HEBREWS 8

1. We have such an high priest – Having finished his description of the type in Melchisedec, the apostle begins to treat directly of the excellency of Christ's priesthood, beyond the Levitical. Who is set down – Having finished his oblation. At the right hand of the Majesty – Of God.

2. A minister – Who represents his own sacrifice, as the high priest did the blood of those sacrifices once a year. Of the sanctuary – Heaven, typified by the holy of holies. And of the true tabernacle – Perhaps his human nature, of which the old tabernacle was a type. Which the Lord hath fixed – Forever. Not man – As Moses fixed the tabernacle.

4. But if he were on earth – If his priesthood terminated here. He could not be a priest – At all, consistently with the Jewish institutions. There being other priests – To whom alone this office is allotted.

5. Who serve – The temple, which was not yet destroyed. After the pattern and shadow of heavenly things – Of spiritual, evangelical worship, and of everlasting glory. The pattern – Somewhat like the strokes penciled out upon a piece of fine linen, which exhibit the figures of leaves and flowers, but have not yet received their splendid colors and curious shades. And shadow – Or shadowy representation, which gives you some dim and imperfect idea of the body, but not the fine features, not the distinguishing air; none of those living graces which adorn the real person. Yet both the pattern and shadow lead our minds to something nobler than themselves: the pattern, to that holiness and glory which complete it; the shadow, to that which occasions it. Exod. xxv, 40.

6. And now he hath obtained a more excellent ministry – His priesthood as much excels theirs, as the promises of the gospel (whereof he is a surety) excels those of the law. These better promises are specified, ver. 10, xi, those in the law were mostly temporal promises.

7. For if the first had been faultless – If that dispensation had answered all God's designs and man's wants, if it had not been weak and unprofitable, unable to make anything perfect, no place would have been for a second.

8. But there is; for finding fault with them – Who were under the old covenant he saith, I make a new covenant with the house of Israel – With all the Israel of God, in all ages and nations. It is new in many respects, though not as to the substance of it:

1. Being ratified by the death of Christ.

2. Freed from those burdensome rites and ceremonies.

3. Containing a more full and clear account of spiritual religion.

4. Attended with larger influences of the Spirit.

wrote his laws to his people, now he will write his laws in them; he will give them understanding to know and to believe his laws; he will give them memories to retain them; he will give them hearts to love them, courage to profess them, and power to put them in practice. This is the foundation of the covenant; and when this is laid, duty will be done wisely, sincerely, readily, easily, resolutely, constantly, and with comfort. A plentiful outpouring of the Spirit of God will make the ministration of the gospel so effectual, that there shall be a mighty increase and spreading of Christian knowledge in persons of all sorts.

HEBREWS 9

The Jewish tabernacle and its utensils. (1-5)
Their use and meaning. (6-10)
These fulfilled in Christ. (11-22)
The necessity, superior dignity, and power of his priesthood and sacrifice. (23-28)

1-5 The apostle shows to the Hebrews the typical reference of their ceremonies to Christ. The tabernacle was a movable temple, shadowing forth the unsettled state of the church upon earth, and the human nature of the Lord Jesus Christ, in whom the fullness of the Godhead dwelt bodily. The typical meaning of these things has been shown in former remarks, and the ordinances and articles of the Mosaic covenant point out Christ as our Light, and as the Bread of life to our souls; and remind us of his Divine Person, his holy priesthood, perfect righteousness, and all-prevailing intercession. Thus was the Lord Jesus Christ, all and in all, from the beginning. And as interpreted by the gospel, these things are a glorious representation of the wisdom of God, and confirm faith in him who was prefigured by them.

6-10 The apostle goes on to speak of the Old Testament services. Christ, having undertaken to be our High Priest, could not enter into heaven till he had shed his blood for us; and none of us can enter, either into God's gracious presence here, or his glorious presence hereafter, but by the blood of Jesus. Sins are errors, great errors, both in judgment and practice; and who can understand all his errors? They leave guilt upon the conscience, not to be washed away but by the blood of Christ. We must plead this blood on earth, while he is pleading it for us in heaven. A few believers, under the Divine teaching, saw something of the way of access to God, of communion with him, and of admission into heaven through the promised Redeemer, but the Israelites in general looked no further than the outward forms. These could not take away the defilement or dominion of sin. They could neither discharge the debts, nor resolve the doubts, of him who did the service. Gospel times are, and should be, times of reformation, of clearer light as to

If you read the 7th verse, you will see that the Apostle calls nature in to his assistance. He says, "The earth which drinketh in the rain that cometh oft upon it, and bringeth forth herbs meet for them by whom it is dressed, receiveth blessing from God: But that which beareth thorns and briars is rejected, and is nigh unto cursing; whose end is to be burned." Look! there is a field; the rain comes on it, and it brings forth good fruit. Well, then, there is God's blessing on it. But there is according to your supposition, another field, on which the same rain descends, which the same dew moistens; it has been plowed and harrowed, as well as the other, and the husbandman has exercised all his craft upon it, and yet it is not fertile. Well, if the rain of heaven did not fertilize it, what next? Already all the arts of agriculture have been tried, every implement has been worn out on its surface, and yet it has been of no avail. What next? There remains nothing but that it shall be burnt and cursed—given up like the desert of Sahara, and resigned to destruction. So, my hearer, could it be possible that grace could work in thee, and then not affect thy salvation—that the influence of Divine grace could come down, like rain from heaven, and yet return unto God void, there could not be any hope for thee, for thou wouldst be "nigh unto cursing," and thine end would be "to be burned."

There is one idea which has occurred to us. It has struck us as a singular thing, that our friends should hold that men can be converted, made into new creatures, then fall away and be converted again. I am an old creature by nature; God creates me into a new thing, he makes me a new creature. I cannot go back into an old creature, for I cannot be uncreated. But yet, supposing that new creatureship of mine is not good enough to carry me to heaven. What is to come after that? Must there be something above a new creature—a new, new creature. Really, my friends, we have got into the country of Dreamland; but we were forced to follow our opponents into that region of absurdity, for we do not know how else to deal with them.

And one thought more. There is nothing in Scripture which teaches us that there is any salvation, save the one salvation of Jesus Christ—nothing that tells us of any other power, super-excellent and surpassing the power of the Holy Spirit. These things have already been tried on the man, and yet, according to the supposition, they have failed, for he has fallen away. Now, God has never revealed a supplementary salvation for men on whom one salvation has had no effect; and until we are pointed to one scripture which declares this, we will still main-

and carnal ordinances, imposed on them until the time of reformation.

11 But Christ being come an high priest of good things to come, by a greater and more perfect tabernacle, not made with hands, that is to say, not of this building;

12 Neither by the blood of goats and calves, but by his own blood he entered in once into the holy place, having obtained eternal redemption for us.

13 For if the blood of bulls and of goats, and the ashes of an heifer sprinkling the unclean, sanctifieth to the purifying of the flesh:

14 How much more shall the blood of Christ, who through the eternal Spirit offered himself without spot to God, purge your conscience from dead works to serve the living God?

15 And for this cause he is the mediator of the new testament, that by means of death, for the redemption of the transgressions that were under the first testament, they which are called might receive the promise of eternal inheritance.

16 For where a testament is, there must also of necessity be the death of the testator.

17 For a testament is of force after men are dead: otherwise it is of no strength at all while the testator liveth.

18 Whereupon neither the first testament was dedicated without blood.

19 For when Moses had spoken every precept to all the people according to the law, he took the blood of calves and of goats, with water, and scarlet wool, and hyssop, and sprinkled both the book, and all the people,

20 Saying, This is the blood of the testament which God hath enjoined unto you.

21 Moreover he sprinkled with blood both the tabernacle, and all the vessels of the ministry.

22 And almost all things are by the law purged with blood; and without shedding of blood is no remission.

23 It was therefore necessary that the patterns of things in the heavens should be purified with these; but the heavenly things

5. Extended to all men. And,

6. Never to be abolished. Jer. xxxi, 31, &c.

9. When I took them by the hand – With the care and tenderness of a parent. And just while this was fresh in their memory, they obeyed; but presently after they shook off the yoke. They continued not in my covenant, and I regarded them not – So that covenant was soon broken in pieces.

10. This is the covenant I will make after those days – After the Mosaic dispensation is abolished. I will put my laws in their minds – I will open their eyes, and enlighten their understanding, to see the true, full, spiritual meaning thereof. And write them on their hearts – So that they shall inwardly experience whatever I have commanded. And I will be to them a God – Their all-sufficient portion, and exceeding great reward. And they shall be to me a people – My treasure, my beloved, loving, and obedient children.

11. And they who are under this covenant (though in other respects they will have need to teach each other to their lives' end, yet) shall not need to teach every one his brother, saying, Know the Lord; for they shall all know me – All real Christians. From the least to the greatest – In this order the saving knowledge of God ever did and ever will proceed; not first to the greatest, and then to the least. But "the Lord shall save the tents," the poorest, "of Judah first, that the glory of the house of David," the royal seed, "and the glory of the inhabitants of Jerusalem," the nobles and the rich citizens, "do not magnify themselves," Zech. xii, 7.

12. For I will justify them, which is the root of all true knowledge of God. This, therefore, is God's method. First, a sinner is pardoned: then he knows God, as gracious and merciful; then God's laws are written on his heart: he is God's, and God is his.

13. In saying, A new covenant, he hath antiquated the first – Hath shown that it is disannulled, and out of date. Now that which is antiquated is ready to vanish away – As it did quickly after, when the temple was destroyed.

HEBREWS 9

1. The first covenant had ordinances of outward worship, and a worldly – a visible, material sanctuary, or tabernacle. Of this sanctuary he treats, ver. 2-5. Of those ordinances, ver. 6-10.

2. The first – The outward tabernacle. In which was the candlestick, and the table – The showbread, shown continually before God and all the people, consisting of twelve loaves, according to the number of the tribes, was placed on this table in two rows, six upon one another in each row. This candlestick and bread seem to have typified the light and life which are more largely dispensed under the gospel by him who is the Light of the world, and the Bread of life.

3. The second veil divided the holy place from the most holy, as the first veil did the holy place from the courts.

4. Having the golden censer – Used by the high priest only, on the great day of atonement. And the ark, or chest, of the covenant – So called from the tables of the covenant contained therein. Wherein was the manna – The monument of God's care over Israel. And Aaron's rod – The monument of the regular priesthood. And the tables of the covenant – The two tables of stone, on which the ten commandments were written by the finger of God the most venerable monument of all.

5. And over it were the cherubim of glory – Over which the glory of God used to appear. Some suppose each of these had four faces, and so represented the Three-One God, with the manhood assumed by the Second Person. With outspread wings shadowing the mercy-seat – Which was a lid or plate of gold, covering the ark.

all things needful to be known, and of greater love, causing us to bear ill-will to none, but good-will to all. We have greater freedom, both of spirit and speech, in the gospel, and greater obligations to a more holy living.

11-14 All good things past, present, and to come, were and are founded upon the priestly office of Christ, and come to us from thence. Our High Priest entered into heaven once for all, and has obtained eternal redemption. The Holy Ghost further signified and showed that the Old Testament sacrifices only freed the outward man from ceremonial uncleanness, and fitted him for some outward privileges. What gave such power to the blood of Christ? It was Christ's offering himself without any sinful stain in his nature or life. This cleanses the most guilty conscience from dead, or deadly, works to serve the living God; from sinful works, such as pollute the soul, as dead bodies did the persons of the Jews who touched them; while the grace that seals pardon, new-creates the polluted soul. Nothing more destroys the faith of the gospel, than by any means to weaken the direct power of the blood of Christ.

15-22 The solemn transactions between God and man, are sometimes called a covenant, here a testament, which is a willing deed of a person, bestowing legacies on such persons as are described, and it only takes effect upon his death. Thus Christ died, not only to obtain the blessings of salvation for us, but to give power to the disposal of them. All, by sin, were become guilty before God, had forfeited every thing that is good; but God, willing to show the greatness of his mercy, proclaimed a covenant of grace.

23-28 It is evident that the sacrifices of Christ are infinitely better than those of the law, which could neither procure pardon for sin, nor impart power against it. Sin would still have been upon us, and have had dominion over us; but Jesus Christ, by one sacrifice, has destroyed the works of the devil, that believers may be made righteous, holy, and happy. As no wisdom, learning, virtue, wealth, or power, can keep one of the human race from death, so nothing can deliver a sinner from being condemned at the day of judgment, except the atoning sacrifice of Christ; nor will one be saved from eternal punishment who despises or neglects this great salvation.

HEBREWS 10

The insufficiency of sacrifices for taking away sin. The necessity and power of the sacrifice of Christ for that purpose. (1-18)

An argument for holy boldness in the believer's access to God through Jesus Christ. And for steadfastness in faith, and mutual love and duty. (19-25)

The danger of apostasy. (26-31)

tain that the doctrine of the text is this: that if grace be ineffectual, if grace does not keep a man, then there is nothing left but that he must be damned. And what is that but to say, only going a little round about, that grace will do it? So that these words, instead of militating against the Calvinistic doctrine of final perseverance, form one of the finest proofs of it that could be afforded.

And now, lastly, we come to improve this doctrine. If Christians can fall away, and cease to be Christians, they cannot be renewed again to repentance. "But," says one, "You say they cannot fall away." What is the use of putting this "if" in, like a bugbear to frighten children, or like a ghost that can have no existence? My learned friend, "Who art thou that repliest against God?" If God has put it in, he has put it in for wise reasons and for excellent purposes. Let me show you why. First, O Christian, it is put in to keep thee from falling away. God preserves his children from falling away; but he keeps them by the use of means; and one of these is, the terrors of the law, showing them what would happen if they were to fall away. There is a deep precipice: what is the best way to keep any one from going down there? Why, to tell him that if he did he would inevitably be dashed to pieces. In some old castle there is a deep cellar, where there is a vast amount of fixed air and gas, which would kill anybody who went down. What does the guide say? "If you go down you will never come up alive." Who thinks of going down? The very fact of the guide telling us what the consequences would be, keeps us from it. Our friend puts away from us a cup of arsenic; he does not want us to drink it, but he says, "If you drink it, it will kill you." Does he suppose for a moment that we should drink it. No; he tells us the consequences, and he is sure we will not do it. So God says, "My child, if you fall over this precipice you will be dashed to pieces." What does the child do? He says, "Father, keep me; hold thou me up, and I shall be safe." It leads the believer to greater dependence on God, to a holy fear and caution, because he knows that if he were to fall away he could not be renewed, and he stands far away from that great gulf, because he know that if he were to fall into it there would be no salvation for him. If I thought as the Arminian thinks, that I might fall away, and then return again, I should pretty often fall away, for sinful flesh and blood would think it very nice to fall away, and be a sinner, and go and see the play at the theater, or get drunk, and then come back to the Church, and be received again as a dear brother who had fallen away for a little while. No doubt the minister would say, "Our

themselves with better sacrifices than these.

24 For Christ is not entered into the holy places made with hands, which are the figures of the true; but into heaven itself, now to appear in the presence of God for us:

25 Nor yet that he should offer himself often, as the high priest entereth into the holy place every year with blood of others;

26 For then must he often have suffered since the foundation of the world: but now once in the end of the world hath he appeared to put away sin by the sacrifice of himself.

27 And as it is appointed unto men once to die, but after this the judgment:

28 So Christ was once offered to bear the sins of many; and unto them that look for him shall he appear the second time without sin unto salvation.

HEBREWS 10

1 For the law having a shadow of good things to come, and not the very image of the things, can never with those sacrifices which they offered year by year continually make the comers thereunto perfect.

2 For then would they not have ceased to be offered? because that the worshipers once purged should have had no more conscience of sins.

3 But in those sacrifices there is a remembrance again made of sins every year.

4 For it is not possible that the blood of bulls and of goats should take away sins.

5 Wherefore when he cometh into the world, he saith, Sacrifice and offering thou wouldest not, but a body hast thou prepared me:

6 In burnt offerings and sacrifices for sin thou hast had no pleasure.

7 Then said I, Lo, I come (in the volume of the book it is written of me,) to do thy will, O God.

8 Above when he said, Sacrifice and offering and burnt offerings and offering for sin thou wouldest not, neither hadst pleasure therein; which are offered by the law;

6. Always – Every day. Accomplishing their services – Lighting the lamps, changing the showbread, burning incense, and sprinkling the blood of the sin offerings.

7. Errors – That is, sins of ignorance, to which only those atonements extended.

8. The Holy Ghost evidently showing – By this token. That the way into the holiest – Into heaven. Was not made manifest – Not so clearly revealed. While the first tabernacle, and its service, were still subsisting – And remaining in force.

9. Which – Tabernacle, with all its furniture and services. Is a figure – Or type, of good things to come. Which cannot perfect the worshiper – Neither the priest nor him who brought the offering. As to his conscience – So that he should be no longer conscious of the guilt or power of sin. Observe, the temple was as yet standing.

10. They could not so perfect him, with all their train of precepts relating to meats and drinks, and carnal, gross, external ordinances; and were therefore imposed only till the time of reformation – Till Christ came.

11. An high priest of good things to come – Described, ver. 15. Entered through a greater, that is, a more noble, and perfect tabernacle – Namely, his own body. Not of this creation – Not framed by man, as that tabernacle was.

12. The holy place – Heaven. For us – All that believe.

13. If the ashes of an heifer – Consumed by fire as a sin-offering, being sprinkled on them who were legally unclean. Purified the flesh – Removed that legal uncleanness, and re-admitted them to the temple and the congregation. Num. xix, 17, 18, 19.

14. How much more shall the blood of Christ – The merit of all his sufferings. Who through the eternal Spirit – The work of redemption being the work of the whole Trinity. Neither is the Second Person alone concerned even in the amazing condescension that was needful to complete it. The Father delivers up the kingdom to the Son; and the Holy Ghost becomes the gift of the Messiah, being, as it were, sent according to his good pleasure. Offered himself – Infinitely more precious than any created victim, and that without spot to God. Purge our conscience – Our inmost soul. From dead works – From all the inward and outward works of the devil, which spring from spiritual death in the soul, and lead to death everlasting. To serve the living God – In the life of faith, in perfect love and spotless holiness.

16. I say by means of death; for where such a covenant is, there must be the death of him by whom it is confirmed – Seeing it is by his death that the benefits of it are purchased. It seems beneath the dignity of the apostle to play upon the ambiguity of the Greek word, as the common translation supposes him to do.

17. After he is dead – Neither this, nor after men are dead is a literal translation of the words. It is a very perplexed passage.

18. Whence neither was the first – The Jewish covenant, originally transacted without the blood of an appointed sacrifice.

19. He took the blood of calves – Or heifers. And of goats, with water, and scarlet wool, and hyssop – All these circumstances are not particularly mentioned in that chapter of Exodus, but are supposed to be already known from other passages of Moses. And the book itself – Which contained all he had said. And sprinkled all the people – Who were near him. The blood was mixed with water to prevent its growing too stiff for sprinkling; perhaps also to typify that blood and water, John xix, 34. Exod. xxiv, 7, 8.

20. Saying, This is the blood of the covenant which God hath enjoined me to deliver unto you – By this it is established. Exod. xxiv, 8.

21. And in like manner he ordered the tabernacle – When it was made, and all its vessels, to be sprinkled with blood once a year.

MATTHEW HENRY

CHARLES H. SPURGEON

The sufferings of believers, and encouragement to maintain their holy profession. (32-39)

1-10 The apostle having shown that the tabernacle, and ordinances of the covenant of Sinai, were only emblems and types of the gospel, concludes that the sacrifices the high priests offered continually, could not make the worshipers perfect, with respect to pardon, and the purifying of their consciences. But when "God manifested in the flesh," became the sacrifice, and his death upon the accursed tree the ransom, then the Sufferer being of infinite worth, his free-will sufferings were of infinite value. The atoning sacrifice must be one capable of consenting, and must of his own will place himself in the sinner's stead: Christ did so. The fountain of all that Christ has done for his people, is the sovereign will and grace of God. The righteousness brought in, and the sacrifice once offered by Christ, are of eternal power, and his salvation shall never be done away.

11-18 Under the new covenant, or gospel dispensation, full and final pardon is to be had. This makes a vast difference between the new covenant and the old one. Under the old, sacrifices must be often repeated, and after all, only pardon as to this world was to be obtained by them. Under the new, one Sacrifice is enough to procure for all nations and ages, spiritual pardon, or being freed from punishment in the world to come. Well might this be called a new covenant.

19-25 The apostle having closed the first part of the epistle, the doctrine is applied to practical purposes. As believers had an open way to the presence of God, it became them to use this privilege. The way and means by which Christians enjoy such privileges, is by the blood of Jesus, by the merit of that blood which he offered up as an atoning sacrifice. The agreement of infinite holiness with pardoning mercy, was not clearly understood till the human nature of Christ, the Son of God, was wounded and bruised for our sins. Our way to heaven is by a crucified Savior; his death is to us the way of life, and to those who believe this, he will be precious. They must draw near to God; it would be contempt of Christ, still to keep at a distance. Their bodies were to be washed with pure water, alluding to the cleansings directed under the law: thus the use of water in baptism, was to remind Christians that their conduct should be pure and holy. While they derived comfort and grace from their reconciled Father to their own souls, they would adorn the doctrine of God their Savior in all things. Believers are to consider how they can be of service to each other, especially stirring up each other to the more vigorous and abundant exercise of love, and the practice of good works. The communion of saints is a great help and privilege, and a means of steadfastness and perseverance.

brother Charles is a little unstable at times." A little unstable! He does not know anything about grace; for grace engenders a holy caution, because we feel that if we were not preserved by Divine power we should perish. We tell our friend to put oil in his lamp, that it may continue to burn! Does that imply that it will be allowed to go out? No, God will give him oil to pour into the lamp continually. Like John Bunyan's figure; there was a fire, and he saw a man pouring water upon it. "Now," says the Preacher, "don't you see that fire would go out, that water is calculated to put it out, and if it does, it will never be lighted again;" but God does not permit that! for there is a man behind the wall who is pouring oil on the fire; and we have cause for gratitude in the fact, that if the oil were not put in by a heavenly hand, we should inevitably be driven to destruction. Take care, then Christian, for this is a caution.

It is to excite our gratitude. Suppose you say to your little boy, "Don't you know Tommy, if I were not to give you your dinner and your supper you would die? There is nobody else to give Tommy dinner and supper." What then? The child does not think that you are not going to give him his dinner and supper; he knows you will, and he is grateful to you for them. The chemist tells us, that if there were no oxygen mixed with the air, animals would die. Do you suppose that there will be no oxygen, and therefore we shall die? No, he only teaches you the great wisdom of God, in having mixed the gases in their proper proportions. Says one of the old astronomers, "There is great wisdom in God, that he has put the sun exactly at a right distance—not so far away that we should be frozen to death, and not so near that we should be scorched." He says, "If the sun were a million miles nearer to us we should be scorched to death." Does the man suppose that the sun will be a million miles nearer, and, therefore, we shall be scorched to death? He says, "If the sun were a million miles farther off we should be frozen to death." Does he mean that the sun will be a million miles farther off, and therefore we shall be frozen to death? Not at all. Yet it is quite a rational way of speaking, to show us how grateful we should be to God. So says the Apostle. Christian! if thou shouldst fall away, thou couldst never be renewed unto repentance. Thank thy Lord, then, that he keeps thee.

"See a stone that hangs in air; see a spark in ocean live;
Kept alive with death so near; I to God the glory give."

There is a cup of sin which would damn thy soul, O Christian. Oh! what grace is that which holds thy arm, and will not let thee drink it? There

9 Then said he, Lo, I come to do thy will, O God. He taketh away the first, that he may establish the second.

10 By the which will we are sanctified through the offering of the body of Jesus Christ once for all.

11 And every priest standeth daily ministering and offering oftentimes the same sacrifices, which can never take away sins:

12 But this man, after he had offered one sacrifice for sins for ever, sat down on the right hand of God;

13 From henceforth expecting till his enemies be made his footstool.

14 For by one offering he hath perfected for ever them that are sanctified.

15 Whereof the Holy Ghost also is a witness to us: for after that he had said before,

16 This is the covenant that I will make with them after those days, saith the Lord, I will put my laws into their hearts, and in their minds will I write them;

17 And their sins and iniquities will I remember no more.

18 Now where remission of these is, there is no more offering for sin.

19 Having therefore, brethren, boldness to enter into the holiest by the blood of Jesus,

20 By a new and living way, which he hath consecrated for us, through the veil, that is to say, his flesh;

21 And having an high priest over the house of God;

22 And having our hearts sprinkled from an evil conscience, and our bodies washed with pure water.

23 Let us hold fast the profession of our faith without wavering; (for he is faithful that promised;)

24 And let us consider one another to provoke unto love and to good works:

25 Not forsaking the assembling of ourselves together, as the manner of some is; but exhorting one another: and so much the more, as ye see the day approaching.

26 For if we sin willfully after that we have received the

22. And almost all things – For some were purified by water or fire. Are according to the law purified with blood – Offered or sprinkled. And according to the law, there is no forgiveness of sins without shedding of blood – All this pointed to the blood of Christ effectually cleansing from all sin, and intimated, there can be no purification from it by any other means.

23. Therefore – That is, it plainly appears from what has been said. It was necessary – According to the appointment of God. That the tabernacle and all its utensils, which were patterns, shadowy representations, of things in heaven, should be purified by these – Sacrifices and sprinklings. But the heavenly things themselves – Our heaven-born spirits: what more this may mean we know not yet. By better sacrifices than these – That is, by a better sacrifice, which is here opposed to all the legal sacrifices, and is expressed in the plural, because it includes the signification of them all, and is of so much more eminent virtue.

24. For Christ did not enter into the holy place made with hands – He never went into the holy of holies at Jerusalem, the figure of the true tabernacle in heaven, chap. viii, 2. But into heaven itself, to appear in the presence of God for us – As our glorious high priest and powerful intercessor.

27. After this, the judgment – Of the great day. At the moment of death every man's final state is determined. But there is not a word in scripture of a particular judgment immediately after death.

28. Christ having once died to bear the sins – The punishment due to them. Of many – Even as many as are born into the world. Will appear the second time – When he comes to judgment. Without sin – Not as he did before, bearing on himself the sins of many, but to bestow everlasting salvation.

HEBREWS 10

1. From all that has been said it appears, that the law, the Mosaic dispensation, being a bare, unsubstantial shadow of good things to come, of the gospel blessings, and not the substantial, solid image of them, can never with the same kind of sacrifices, though continually repeated, make the comers thereunto perfect, either as to justification or sanctification. How is it possible, that any who consider this should suppose the attainments of David, or any who were under that dispensation, to be the proper measure of gospel holiness; and that Christian experience is to rise no higher than Jewish?

2. They who had been once perfectly purged, would have been no longer conscious either of the guilt or power of their sins.

3. There is a public commemoration of the sins both of the last and of all the preceding years; a clear proof that the guilt thereof is not perfectly purged away.

4. It is impossible the blood of goats should take away sins – Either the guilt or the power of them.

5. When he cometh into the world – In the fortieth psalm the Messiah's coming into the world is represented. It is said, into the world, not into the tabernacle, chap. ix, 1; because all the world is interested in his sacrifice. A body hast thou prepared for me – That I may offer up myself. Psalm xl, 6, &c.

7. In the volume of the book – In this very psalm it is written of me. Accordingly I come to do thy will – By the sacrifice of myself.

8. Above when he said, Sacrifice thou hast not chosen – That is, when the Psalmist pronounced those words in his name.

9. Then said he – In that very instant he subjoined. Lo, I come to do Thy will – To offer a more acceptable sacrifice; and by this very act he taketh away the legal, that he may establish the evangelical, dispensation.

10. By which will – Of God, done and suffered by Christ. We are sanctified – Cleansed from guilt, and consecrated to God.

11. Every priest standeth – As a servant in an humble posture.

12. But he – The virtue of whose one sacrifice remains for ever. Sat down – As

26-31 The exhortations against apostasy and to perseverance, are urged by many strong reasons. The sin here mentioned is a total and final falling away, when men, with a full and fixed will and resolution, despise and reject Christ, the only Savior; despise and resist the Spirit, the only Sanctifier; and despise and renounce the gospel, the only way of salvation, and the words of eternal life. Of this destruction God gives some notorious sinners, while on earth, a fearful foreboding in their consciences, with despair of being able to endure or to escape it. But what punishment can be sorer than to die without mercy? We answer, to die by mercy, by the mercy and grace which they have despised. How dreadful is the case, when not only the justice of God, but his abused grace and mercy call for vengeance!

32-39 Many and various afflictions united against the early Christians, and they had a great conflict. The Christian spirit is not a selfish spirit; it puts us upon pitying others, visiting them, helping them, and pleading for them. All things here are but shadows. The happiness of the saints in heaven will last forever; enemies can never take it away as earthly goods. This will make rich amends for all we may lose and suffer here. The greatest part of the saints' happiness, as yet, is in promise. It is a trial of the patience of Christians, to be content to live after their work is done, and to stay for their reward till God's time to give it is come. He will soon come to them at death, to end all their sufferings, and to give them a crown of life. The Christian's present conflict may be sharp, but will be soon over. God never is pleased with the formal profession and outward duties and services of such as do not persevere; but he beholds them with great displeasure.

HEBREWS 11

The nature and power of faith described. (1-3)
It is set forth by instances from Abel to Noah. (4-7)
By Abraham and his descendants. (8-19)
By Jacob, Joseph, Moses, the Israelites, and Rahab. (20-31)
By other Old Testament believers. (32-38)
The better state of believers under the gospel. (39,40)

1-3 Faith always has been the mark of God's servants, from the beginning of the world. Where the principle is planted by the regenerating Spirit of God, it will cause the truth to be received, concerning justification by the sufferings and merits of Christ. And the same things that are the object of our hope, are the object of our faith. It is a firm persuasion and expectation, that God will perform all he has promised to us in Christ. This persuasion gives the soul to enjoy those things now; it gives them a subsistence or reality in the soul, by the first fruits and foretastes of them. Faith proves to the mind, the reality of things

thou art, at this hour, like the bird-catcher of St. Kilda, thou art being drawn to heaven by a single rope; if that hand which holds thee let thee go, if that rope which grasps thee do but break, thou art dashed on the rocks of damnation. Lift up thine heart to God, then, and bless him that his arm is not wearied, and is never shortened that it cannot save. Lord Kenmure, when he was dying, said to Rutherford. "Man! my name is written on Christ's hand, and I see it! that is bold talk, man, but I see it!" Then, if that be the case, his hand must be severed from his body before my name can be taken from him; and if it be engraved on his heart, his heart must be rent out before they can rend my name out.

Hold on, then, and trust believer! thou hast "an anchor of the soul, both sure and steadfast, which entereth within the veil." The winds are bellowing, the tempests howling; should the cable slip, or thine anchor break, thou art lost. See those rocks, on which myriads are driving, and thou art wrecked there if grace leave thee; see those depths, in which the skeletons of sailors sleep, and thou art there, if that anchor fail thee. It would be impossible to moor thee again, if once that anchor broke; for other anchor there is none, other salvation there can be none, and if that one fail thee, it is impossible that thou ever shouldst be saved. Therefore thank God that thou hast an anchor that cannot fail, and then loudly sing—

"How can I sink with such a prop,
As my eternal God,
Who bears the earth's huge pillars up?
And spreads the heavens abroad?"
How can I die, when Jesus lives,
Who rose and left the dead?
Pardon and grace my soul receives,
From my exalted head."

RAHAB'S FAITH

Sermon number 119 delivered on Sabbath Morning, March 1, 1857, by C.H. Spurgeon at The Music Hall, Royal Surrey Gardens.

"By faith the harlot Rahab perished not with them that believed not, when she had received the spies with peace."—Hebrews 11:31.

I. In the first place, this woman's faith was SAVING FAITH. All the other persons mentioned here were doubtless saved by faith; but I do not find it specially remarked concerning any of them that they perished not through their faith; while it is particularly said of this woman, that she was delivered amid the general destruction of Jericho purely and only through her faith. And, without doubt, her salvation was not

knowledge of the truth, there remaineth no more sacrifice for sins,

27 But a certain fearful looking for of judgment and fiery indignation, which shall devour the adversaries.

28 He that despised Moses' law died without mercy under two or three witnesses:

29 Of how much sorer punishment, suppose ye, shall he be thought worthy, who hath trodden under foot the Son of God, and hath counted the blood of the covenant, wherewith he was sanctified, an unholy thing, and hath done despite unto the Spirit of grace?

30 For we know him that hath said, Vengeance belongeth unto me, I will recompense, saith the Lord. And again, The Lord shall judge his people.

31 It is a fearful thing to fall into the hands of the living God.

32 But call to remembrance the former days, in which, after ye were illuminated, ye endured a great fight of afflictions;

33 Partly, whilst ye were made a gazingstock both by reproaches and afflictions; and partly, whilst ye became companions of them that were so used.

34 For ye had compassion of me in my bonds, and took joyfully the spoiling of your goods, knowing in yourselves that ye have in heaven a better and an enduring substance.

35 Cast not away therefore your confidence, which hath great recompense of reward.

36 For ye have need of patience, that, after ye have done the will of God, ye might receive the promise.

37 For yet a little while, and he that shall come will come, and will not tarry.

38 Now the just shall live by faith: but if any man draw back, my soul shall have no pleasure in him.

39 But we are not of them who draw back unto perdition; but of them that believe to the saving of the soul.

HEBREWS 11

1 Now faith is the substance of things hoped for, the evidence of

a son, in majesty and honor.

13. Psalm cx, 1.

14. He hath perfected them for ever – That is, has done all that was needful in order to their full reconciliation with God.

15. In this and the three following verses, the apostle winds up his argument concerning the excellency and perfection of the priesthood and sacrifice of Christ. He had proved this before by a quotation from Jeremiah; which he here repeats, describing the new covenant as now completely ratified, and all the blessings of it secured to us by the one offering of Christ, which renders all other expiatory sacrifices, and any repetition of his own, utterly needless.

16. Jer. xxxi, 33, &c.

19. Having finished the doctrinal part of his epistle, the apostle now proceeds to exhortation deduced from what has been treated of chap. v, 4, which he begins by a brief recapitulation. Having therefore liberty to enter,

20. By a living way – The way of faith, whereby we live indeed. Which he hath consecrated – Prepared, dedicated, and established for us. Through the veil, that is, his flesh – As by rending the veil in the temple, the holy of holies became visible and accessible; so by wounding the body of Christ, the God of heaven was manifested, and the way to heaven opened.

22. Let us draw near – To God. With a true heart – In godly sincerity. Having our hearts sprinkled from an evil conscience – So as to condemn us no longer. And our bodies washed with pure water – All our conversation spotless and holy, which is far more acceptable to God than all the legal sprinklings and washings.

23. The profession of our hope – The hope which we professed at our baptism.

25. Not forsaking the assembling ourselves – In public or private worship. As the manner of some is – Either through fear of persecution, or from a vain imagination that they were above external ordinances. But exhorting one another – To faith, love, and good works. And so much the more, as ye see the day approaching – The great day is ever in your eye.

26. For when we – Any of us Christians. Sin willfully – By total apostasy from God, termed "drawing back," ver. 38. After having received the experimental knowledge of the gospel truth, there remaineth no more sacrifice for sins – None but that which we obstinately reject.

28. He that, in capital cases, despised (presumptuously transgressed) the law of Moses died without mercy – Without any delay or mitigation of his punishment.

29. Of how much sorer punishment is he worthy, who – By willfull, total apostasy. It does not appear that this passage refers to any other sin. Hath, as it were, trodden underfoot the Son of God – A lawgiver far more honorable than Moses. And counted the blood wherewith the better covenant was established, an unholy, a common, worthless thing. By which he hath been sanctified – Therefore Christ died for him also, and he was at least justified once. And done despite to the Spirit of grace – By rejecting all his motions.

30. The Lord will judge his people – Yea, far more rigorously than the heathens, if they rebel against him. Deut. xxxii, 35, &c.

31. To fall into the hands – Of his avenging justice.

32. Enlightened – With the knowledge of God and of his truth.

34. For ye sympathized with all your suffering brethren, and with me in particular; and received joyfully the loss of your own goods.

35. Cast not away therefore this your confidence – Your faith and hope; which none can deprive you of but yourselves.

36. The promise – Perfect love; eternal life.

37. He that cometh – To reward every man according to his works.

38. Now the just – The justified person. Shall live – In God's favor, a spiritual and holy life. By faith – As long as he retains that gift of God. But if he draw

MATTHEW HENRY

CHARLES H. SPURGEON

that cannot be seen by the bodily eye. It is a full approval of all God has revealed, as holy, just, and good. This view of faith is explained by many examples of persons in former times, who obtained a good report, or an honorable character in the word of God. Faith was the principle of their holy obedience, remarkable services, and patient sufferings.

4-7 Here follow some illustrious examples of faith from the Old Testament. Abel brought a sacrifice of atonement from the firstlings of the flock, acknowledging himself a sinner who deserved to die, and only hoping for mercy through the great Sacrifice. Cain's proud rage and enmity against the accepted worshiper of God, led to the awful effects the same principles have produced in every age; the cruel persecution, and even murder of believers. By faith Abel, being dead, yet speaketh; he left an instructive and speaking example. Enoch was translated, or removed, that he should not see death; God took him into heaven, as Christ will do the saints who shall be alive at his second coming. We cannot come to God, unless we believe that he is what he has revealed himself to be in the Scripture. Those who would find God, must seek him with all their heart. Noah's faith influenced his practice; it moved him to prepare an ark. His faith condemned the unbelief of others; and his obedience condemned their contempt and rebellion. Good examples either convert sinners or condemn them. This shows how believers, being warned of God to flee from the wrath to come, are moved with fear, take refuge in Christ, and become heirs of the righteousness of faith.

8-19 We are often called to leave worldly connexions, interests, and comforts. If heirs of Abraham's faith, we shall obey and go forth, though not knowing what may befall us; and we shall be found in the way of duty, looking for the performance of God's promises. The trial of Abraham's faith was, that he simply and fully obeyed the call of God. Sarah received the promise as the promise of God; being convinced of that, she truly judged that he both could and would perform it. Many, who have a part in the promises, do not soon receive the things promised. Faith can lay hold of blessings at a great distance; can make them present; can love them and rejoice in them, though strangers; as saints, whose home is heaven; as pilgrims, traveling toward their home. By faith, they overcome the terrors of death, and bid a cheerful farewell to this world, and to all the comforts and crosses of it. And those once truly and savingly called out of a sinful state, have no mind to return into it. All true believers desire the heavenly inheritance; and the stronger faith is, the more fervent those desires will be. Notwithstanding their meanness by nature, their vileness by sin, and the poverty of their outward condition, God is not ashamed to be called the God of all true believers; such is his mercy, such is his love

merely of a temporal nature, not merely a deliverance of her body from the sword, but redemption of her soul from hell. O! what a mighty thing faith is, when it saves the soul from going down to the pit! So mighty is the ever-rushing torrent of sin, that no arm but that which is as strong as Deity can ever stop the sinner from being hurried down to the gulf of black despair, and, when nearing that gulf, so impetuous is the torrent of divine wrath, that nothing can snatch the soul from perdition but an atonement which is as divine as God himself. Yet faith is the instrument of accomplishing the whole work. It delivers the sinner from the stream of sin, and so, laying hold upon the omnipotence of the Spirit, it rescues him from that great whirlpool of destruction into which his soul was being hurried. What a great thing it is to save a soul! You can never know how great it is unless you have stood in the capacity of a savior to other men. You heroic man who, yesterday, when the house was burning, climbed the creaking stair-case, and, almost suffocated by the smoke, entered an upper chamber, snatched a babe from its bed and a woman from the window, bore them both down in his arms, and saved them at the peril of his own life, he can tell you what a great thing it is to save a fellow-creature. Yon noble-hearted youth who, yesterday, sprang into the river, at the hazard of himself, and snatched a drowning man from death, he felt, when he stood upon the shore, what a great thing it was to save life. Ah! but you can not tell what a great thing it is to save a soul. It is only our Lord Jesus Christ who can tell you that, for he is the only one who has ever been the Savior of sinners. And remember, you can only know how great a thing faith is by knowing the infinite value of the salvation of a soul. "Now, by faith, the harlot Rahab was delivered." That she was really saved in a gospel sense as well as temporally, seems to me to be proved from her reception of the spies which was an emblem of the entrance of the word into her heart, and her hanging out of the scarlet thread was an evidence of faith, not unaptly picturing faith in the blood of Jesus the Redeemer. But who can measure the length and breadth of that word—salvation. Ah! it was a mighty deed which faith accomplished when he bore her off in safety. Poor sinner! take comfort. The same faith which saved Rahab can save thee. Art thou literally one of Rahab's sisters in guilt? She was saved, and so mayest thou be, if God shall grant thee repentance. Woman! art thou loathsome to thyself? Dost thou stand at this moment in this assembly, and say, "I am ashamed to be here; I know I have no right to stand among people who are chaste and hon-

things not seen.

2 For by it the elders obtained a good report.

3 Through faith we understand that the worlds were framed by the word of God, so that things which are seen were not made of things which do appear.

4 By faith Abel offered unto God a more excellent sacrifice than Cain, by which he obtained witness that he was righteous, God testifying of his gifts: and by it he being dead yet speaketh.

5 By faith Enoch was translated that he should not see death; and was not found, because God had translated him: for before his translation he had this testimony, that he pleased God.

6 But without faith it is impossible to please him: for he that cometh to God must believe that he is, and that he is a rewarder of them that diligently seek him.

7 By faith Noah, being warned of God of things not seen as yet, moved with fear, prepared an ark to the saving of his house; by the which he condemned the world, and became heir of the righteousness which is by faith.

8 By faith Abraham, when he was called to go out into a place which he should after receive for an inheritance, obeyed; and he went out, not knowing whither he went.

9 By faith he sojourned in the land of promise, as in a strange country, dwelling in tabernacles with Isaac and Jacob, the heirs with him of the same promise:

10 For he looked for a city which hath foundations, whose builder and maker is God.

11 Through faith also Sara herself received strength to conceive seed, and was delivered of a child when she was past age, because she judged him faithful who had promised.

12 Therefore sprang there even of one, and him as good as dead, so many as the stars of the sky in multitude, and as the sand which is by the sea shore innumerable.

13 These all died in faith, not having received the promises, but having seen them afar off, and were persuaded of them, and embraced them, and confessed that they were strangers

back – If he make shipwreck of his faith. My soul hath no pleasure in him – That is, I abhor him; I cast him off. Hab. ii, 3, &c.

39. We are not of them who draw back to perdition – Like him mentioned ver. 38. But of them that believe – To the end, so as to attain eternal life.

HEBREWS 11

1. The definition of faith given in this verse, and exemplified in the various instances following, undoubtedly includes justifying faith, but not directly as justifying. For faith justifies only as it refers to, and depends on, Christ. But here is no mention of him as the object of faith; and in several of the instances that follow, no notice is taken of him or his salvation, but only of temporal blessings obtained by faith. And yet they may all be considered as evidences of the power of justifying faith in Christ, and of its extensive exercise in a course of steady obedience amidst difficulties and dangers of every kind. Now faith is the subsistence of things hoped for, the evidence or conviction of things not seen – Things hoped for are not so extensive as things not seen. The former are only things future and joyful to us; the latter are either future, past, or present, and those either good or evil, whether to us or others. The subsistence of things hoped for – Giving a kind of present subsistence to the good things which God has promised: the divine supernatural evidence exhibited to, the conviction hereby produced in, a believer of things not seen, whether past, future, or spiritual; particularly of God and the things of God.

2. By it the elders – Our forefathers. This chapter is a kind of summary of the Old Testament, in which the apostle comprises the designs, labors, sojourning, expectations, temptations, martyrdoms of the ancients. The former of them had a long exercise of their patience; the latter suffered shorter but sharper trials. Obtained a good testimony – A most comprehensive word. God gave a testimony, not only of them but to them: and they received his testimony as if it had been the things themselves of which he testified, ver. 4, 5, 39. Hence they also gave testimony to others, and others testified of them.

3. By faith we understand that the worlds – Heaven and earth and all things in them, visible and invisible. Where made – Formed, fashioned, and finished. By the word – The sole command of God, without any instrument or preceding matter. And as creation is the foundation and specimen of the whole divine economy, so faith in the creation is the foundation and specimen of all faith. So that things which are seen – As the sun, earth, stars. Were made of things which do not appear – Out of the dark, unapparent chaos, Gen. i, 2. And this very chaos was created by the divine power; for before it was thus created it had no existence in nature.

4. By faith – In the future Redeemer. Abel offered a more excellent sacrifice – The firstlings of his flock, implying both a confession of what his own sins deserved, and a desire of sharing in the great atonement. Than Cain – Whose offering testified no such faith, but a bare acknowledgment of God the Creator. By which faith he obtained both righteousness and a testimony of it: God testifying – Visibly that his gifts were accepted; probably by sending fire from heaven to consume his sacrifice, a token that justice seized on the sacrifice instead of the sinner who offered it. And by it – By this faith. Being dead, he yet speaketh – That a sinner is accepted only through faith in the great sacrifice.

5. Enoch was not any longer found among men, though perhaps they sought for him as they did for Elijah, 2 Kings ii, 17. He had this testimony – From God in his own conscience.

6. But without faith – Even some divine faith in God, it is impossible to please him. For he that cometh to God – in prayer, or another act of worship, must believe that he is.

7. Noah being warned of things not seen as yet – Of the future deluge. Moved

to them. Let them never be ashamed of being called his people, nor of any of those who are truly so, how much soever despised in the world. Above all, let them take care that they are not a shame and reproach to their God. The greatest trial and act of faith upon record is, Abraham's offering up Isaac, Ge 22:2. There, every word shows a trial. It is our duty to reason down our doubts and fears, by looking, as Abraham did, to the Almighty power of God.

20-31 Isaac blessed Jacob and Esau, concerning things to come. Things present are not the best things; no man knoweth love or hatred by having them or wanting them. Jacob lived by faith, and he died by faith, and in faith. Though the grace of faith is of use always through our whole lives, it is especially so when we come to die. Faith has a great work to do at last, to help the believer to die to the Lord, so as to honor him, by patience, hope, and joy. Joseph was tried by temptations to sin, by persecution for keeping his integrity; and he was tried by honors and power in the court of Pharaoh, yet his faith carried him through. It is a great mercy to be free from wicked laws and edicts; but when we are not so, we must use all lawful means for our security. In this faith of Moses' parents there was a mixture of unbelief, but God was pleased to overlook it. Faith gives strength against the sinful, slavish fear of men; it sets God before the soul, shows the vanity of the creature, and that all must give way to the will and power of God. The pleasures of sin are, and will be, but short; they must end either in speedy repentance or in speedy ruin. The pleasures of this world are for the most part the pleasures of sin; they are always so when we cannot enjoy them without deserting God and his people. Suffering is to be chosen rather than sin; there being more evil in the least sin, than there can be in the greatest suffering. God's people are, and always have been, a reproached people. Christ accounts himself reproached in their reproaches; and thus they become greater riches than the treasures of the richest empire in the world. Moses made his choice when ripe for judgment and enjoyment, able to know what he did, and why he did it. It is needful for persons to be seriously religious; to despise the world, when most capable of relishing and enjoying it. Believers may and ought to have respect to the recompense of reward. By faith we may be fully sure of God's providence, and of his gracious and powerful presence with us. Such a sight of God will enable believers to keep on to the end, whatever they may meet in the way. It is not owing to our own righteousness, or best performances, that we are saved from the wrath of God; but to the blood of Christ, and his imputed righteousness. True faith makes sin bitter to the soul, even while it receives the pardon and atonement. All our spiritual privileges on earth, should quicken us in our way to heaven. The Lord will make even Babylon fall before the faith of his people, and

est?" I bid thee still remain; yea, come again and make this thy Sabbath house of prayer. Thou art no intruder! Thou art welcome! For thou hast a sacred right to the courts of mercy. Thou hast a sacred right; for here sinners are invited, and thou art such. Believe in Christ, and thou, like Rahab, shalt not perish with the disobedient, but even thou shalt be saved.

II. But mark, Rahab's faith was a SINGULAR FAITH. The city of Jericho was about to be attacked; within its walls there were hosts of people of all classes and characters, and they knew right well that if their city should be sacked and stormed they would all be put to death; but yet, strange to say, there was not one of them who repented of sin, or who even asked for mercy, except this woman who had been a harlot. She, and she alone was delivered, a solitary one among a multitude. Now, have you ever felt that it is a very hard thing to have a singular faith? It is the easiest thing in the world to believe as every body else believes, but the difficulty is to believe a thing alone, when no one else thinks as you think; to be the solitary champion of a righteous cause when the enemy mustereth his thousands to the battle. Now, this was the faith of Rahab. She had not one who felt as she did, who could enter into her feelings and realize the value of her faith. She stood alone. O! it is a noble thing to be the lonely follower of despised truth. There be some who could tell you a tale of standing up alone. There have been days when the world poured continually a river of infamy and calumny against them, but they stemmed the torrent, and, by continued grace, made strong in weakness, they held their own until the current turned, and they, in their success, were praised and applauded by the very men who sneered before. Then did the world accord them the name of "great." But where lay their greatness? Why, in this, that they stood as firm in the storm as they stood in the calm—that they were as content to serve God alone as they were to run by fifties. To be good we must be singular. Christians must swim against the stream. Dead fish always float down the stream, but the living fish forces its way against the current. Now, worldly religious men will go just as every body else goes. That is nothing. The thing is to stand alone. Like Elijah, when he said, "I only am left and they seek my life;" to feel in one's self that we believe as firmly as if a thousand witnesses stood up by our side. O! there is no great right in a man, no strong-minded right, unless he dares to be singular. Why, the most of you are as afraid as you ever can be to go out of the fashions, and you spend more money than you

and pilgrims on the earth.

14 For they that say such things declare plainly that they seek a country.

15 And truly, if they had been mindful of that country from whence they came out, they might have had opportunity to have returned.

16 But now they desire a better country, that is, an heavenly: wherefore God is not ashamed to be called their God: for he hath prepared for them a city.

17 By faith Abraham, when he was tried, offered up Isaac: and he that had received the promises offered up his only begotten son,

18 Of whom it was said, That in Isaac shall thy seed be called:

19 Accounting that God was able to raise him up, even from the dead; from whence also he received him in a figure.

20 By faith Isaac blessed Jacob and Esau concerning things to come.

21 By faith Jacob, when he was a dying, blessed both the sons of Joseph; and worshipped, leaning upon the top of his staff.

22 By faith Joseph, when he died, made mention of the departing of the children of Israel; and gave commandment concerning his bones.

23 By faith Moses, when he was born, was hid three months of his parents, because they saw he was a proper child; and they were not afraid of the king's commandment.

24 By faith Moses, when he was come to years, refused to be called the son of Pharaoh's daughter;

25 Choosing rather to suffer affliction with the people of God, than to enjoy the pleasures of sin for a season;

26 Esteeming the reproach of Christ greater riches than the treasures in Egypt: for he had respect unto the recompense of the reward.

27 By faith he forsook Egypt, not fearing the wrath of the king: for he endured, as seeing him who is invisible.

28 Through faith he kept the passover, and the sprinkling of blood, lest he that destroyed the firstborn should touch them.

with fear, prepared an ark, by which open testimony he condemned the world – Who neither believed nor feared.

8. Gen. xii, 1-4.

9. By faith he sojourned in the land of promise – The promise was made before, Gen. xii, 7. Dwelling in tents – As a sojourner. With Isaac and Jacob – Who by the same manner of living showed the same faith. Jacob was born fifteen years before the death of Abraham. The joint heirs of the same promise – Having all the same interest therein. Isaac did not receive this inheritance from Abraham, nor Jacob from Isaac, but all of them from God. Gen. xvii, 8.

10. He looked for a city which hath foundations – Whereas a tent has none. Whose builder and former is God – Of which God is the sole contriver, former, and finisher.

11. Sarah also herself – Though at first she laughed at the promise, Gen. xviii, 12. Gen. xxi, 2.

12. As it were dead – Till his strength was supernaturally restored, which continued for many years after.

13. All these – Mentioned ver. 7-11. Died in faith – In death faith acts most vigorously. Not having received the promises – The promised blessings. Embraced – As one does a dear friend when he meets him.

14. They who speak thus show plainly that they seek their own country – That they keep in view, and long for, their native home.

15. If they had been mindful of – Their earthly country, Ur of the Chaldeans, they might have easily returned.

16. But they desire a better country, that is, an heavenly – This is a full convincing proof that the patriarchs had a Revelation and a promise of eternal glory in heaven. Therefore God is not ashamed to be called their God: seeing he hath prepared for them a city – Worthy of God to give.

17. By faith Abraham – When God made that glorious trial of him. Offered up Isaac – The will being accepted as if he had actually done it. Yea, he that had received the promises – Particularly that grand promise, "In Isaac shall thy seed be called." Offered up – This very son; the only one he had by Sarah. Gen. xxii, 1,&c.

18. In Isaac shall thy seed be called – From him shall the blessed seed spring. Gen. xxi, 12.

19. Accounting that God was able even to raise him from the dead – Though there had not been any instance of this in the world. From whence also – To speak in a figurative way. He did receive him – Afterwards, snatched from the jaws of death.

20. Blessed – Gen. xxvii, 27, 39; prophetically foretold the particular blessings they should partake of. Jacob and Esau – Preferring the elder before the younger.

21. Jacob when dying – That is, when near death. Bowing down on the top of his staff – As he sat on the side of his bed. Gen. xlviii, 16; Gen. xlvii, 31.

22. Concerning his bones – To be carried into the land of promise.

23. They saw – Doubtless with a divine presage of things to come.

24. Refused to be called – Any longer.

26. The reproach of Christ – That which he bore for believing in the Messiah to come, and acting accordingly. For he looked off – From all those perishing treasures, and beyond all those temporal hardships. Unto the recompense of reward – Not to an inheritance in Canaan; he had no warrant from God to look for this, nor did he ever attain it; but what his believing ancestors looked for, – a future state of happiness in heaven.

27. By faith he left Egypt – Taking all the Israelites with him. Not then fearing the wrath of the king – As he did many years before, Exod. ii, 14. Exod. xiv, 15, &c.

28. The pouring out of the blood – Of the paschal lamb, which was sprinkled on the door-posts, lest the destroying angel should touch the Israelites. Exod.

when he has some great thing to do for them, he raises up great and strong faith in them. A true believer is desirous, not only to be in covenant with God, but in communion with the people of God; and is willing to fare as they fare. By her works Rahab declared herself to be just. That she was not justified by her works appears plainly; because the work she did was faulty in the manner, and not perfectly good, therefore it could not be answerable to the perfect justice or righteousness of God.

32-38 After all our searches into the Scriptures, there is more to be learned from them. We should be pleased to think, how great the number of believers was under the Old Testament, and how strong their faith, though the objects of it were not then so fully made known as now. And we should lament that now, in gospel times, when the rule of faith is more clear and perfect, the number of believers should be so small, and their faith so weak. It is the excellence of the grace of faith, that, while it helps men to do great things, like Gideon, it keeps from high and great thoughts of themselves. Faith, like Barak's, has recourse unto God in all dangers and difficulties, and then makes grateful returns to God for all mercies and deliverances. By faith, the servants of God shall overcome even the roaring lion that goeth about seeking whom he may devour. The believer's faith endures to the end, and, in dying, gives him victory over death and all his deadly enemies, like Samson. The grace of God often fixes upon very undeserving and ill-deserving persons, to do great things for them and by them. But the grace of faith, wherever it is, will put men upon acknowledging God in all their ways, as Jephthah. It will make men bold and courageous in a good cause. Few ever met with greater trials, few ever showed more lively faith, than David, and he has left a testimony as to the trials and acts of faith, in the book of Psalms, which has been, and ever will be, of great value to the people of God. Those are likely to grow up to be distinguished for faith, who begin betimes, like Samuel, to exercise it. And faith will enable a man to serve God and his generation, in whatever way he may be employed. The interests and powers of kings and kingdoms, are often opposed to God and his people; but God can easily subdue all that set themselves against him. It is a greater honor and happiness to work righteousness than to work miracles. By faith we have comfort of the promises; and by faith we are prepared to wait for the promises, and in due time to receive them. And though we do not hope to have our dead relatives or friends restored to life in this world, yet faith will support under the loss of them, and direct to the hope of a better resurrection. Shall we be most amazed at the wickedness of human nature, that it is capable of such awful cruelties to fellow-creatures, or at the excellence of Divine grace, that is able to bear up the faithful under such cruelties, and to carry them safely

ought because you think you must be respectable. You dare not move in opposition to your brethren and sisters in the circle in which you move; and therefore you involve yourselves in difficulties. You are blindfolded by the rich fabric of fashion, and therefore many a wrong thing is tolerated because it is customary. But a strong-minded man is one who does not try to be singular, but who dares to be singular, when he knows that to be singular is to be right. Now, Rahab's faith, sinner as she was, had this glory, this crown about its head, that she stood alone, faithful among the faithless found.

III. Furthermore, this woman's faith was A STABLE FAITH, which stood firm in the midst of trouble, I have heard of a church clergyman who was once waited upon by his church warden, after a long time of drought, and was requested to put up the prayer for rain. "Well," said he, "my good man, I will offer it, but it's not a bit of use while the wind is in the east, I'm sure." There are many who have that kind of faith: they believe just so far as probabilities go with them, but when the promise and the probability part, then they follow the probability and part with the promise. They say, "The thing is likely, therefore I believe it." But that is no faith, it is sight. True faith exclaims, "The thing is unlikely, yet I believe it." This is real faith. Faith is to say, that "mountains, when in darkness hidden, are as real as in day." Faith is to look through that cloud, not with the eye of sight, which seeth naught, but with the eye of faith, which seeth every thing, and to say, "I trust him when I can not trace him; I tread the sea as firmly as I would the rock; I walk as securely in the tempest as in the sunshine, and lay myself to rest upon the surging billows of the ocean as contentedly as upon my bed." The faith of Rahab was the right sort of faith, for it was firm and enduring.

I will just have a little talk with Rahab this morning, as I suppose old Unbelief did commune with her. Now, my good woman, don't you see the absurdity of this thing? Why, the people of Israel are on the other side of Jordan, and there is no bridge: how are they to get over? Of course they must go up higher toward the fords; and then Jericho will be for a long time secure. They will take other cities before coming to Jericho; and, besides, the Canaanites are mighty, and the Israelites are only a parcel of slaves; they will soon be cut in pieces, and there will be an end of them; therefore, do not harbor these spies. Why put your life in jeopardy for such an improbability? "Ah," says she, "I do not care about the Jordan; my faith can believe across the Jordan, or else it were only a

29 By faith they passed through the Red sea as by dry land: which the Egyptians assaying to do were drowned.

30 By faith the walls of Jericho fell down, after they were compassed about seven days.

31 By faith the harlot Rahab perished not with them that believed not, when she had received the spies with peace.

32 And what shall I more say? for the time would fail me to tell of Gedeon, and of Barak, and of Samson, and of Jephthae; of David also, and Samuel, and of the prophets:

33 Who through faith subdued kingdoms, wrought righteousness, obtained promises, stopped the mouths of lions,

34 Quenched the violence of fire, escaped the edge of the sword, out of weakness were made strong, waxed valiant in fight, turned to flight the armies of the aliens.

35 Women received their dead raised to life again: and others were tortured, not accepting deliverance; that they might obtain a better resurrection:

36 And others had trial of cruel mockings and scourgings, yea, moreover of bonds and imprisonment:

37 They were stoned, they were sawn asunder, were tempted, were slain with the sword: they wandered in sheepskins and goatskins; being destitute, afflicted, tormented;

38 (Of whom the world was not worthy:) they wandered in deserts, and in mountains, and in dens and caves of the earth.

39 And these all, having obtained a good report through faith, received not the promise:

40 God having provided some better thing for us, that they without us should not be made perfect.

HEBREWS 12

1 Wherefore seeing we also are compassed about with so great a cloud of witnesses, let us lay aside every weight, and the sin which doth so easily beset us, and let us run with patience the race that is set before us,

2 Looking unto Jesus the author

xii, 12-18.

29. They – Moses, Aaron, and the Israelites. Passed the Red Sea – It washed the borders of Edom, which signifies red. Thus far the examples are cited from Genesis and Exodus; those that follow are from the former and the latter Prophets.

30. By the faith of Joshua.

31. Rahab – Though formerly one not of the fairest character.

32. After Samuel, the prophets are properly mentioned. David also was a prophet; but he was a king too. The prophets – Elijah, Elisha, &c., including likewise the believers who lived with them.

33, 34. David, in particular, subdued kingdoms. Samuel (not excluding the rest) wrought righteousness. The prophets, in general, obtained promises, both for themselves, and to deliver to others. Prophets also stopped the mouths of lions, as Daniel; and quenched the violence of fire, as Shadrach, Meshach, and Abednego. To these examples, whence the nature of faith clearly appears, those more ancient ones are subjoined, (by a transposition, and in an inverted order,) which receive light from these. Jephthah escaped the edge of the sword; Samson out of weakness was made strong; Barak became valiant in fight; Gideon put to flight armies of the aliens. Faith animates to the most heroic enterprises, both civil and military. Faith overcomes all impediments; effects the greatest things; attains to the very best; and inverts, by its miraculous power the very course of nature. 2 Sam. viii, 1,&c.; 1 Sam. viii, 9,&c.; 1 Sam. xiii, 3,&c.; Dan. vi, 22; Dan. iii, 27; Jude xii, 3; Jude xv, 19,&c.; Jude xvi, 28,&c.; Jude iv, 14,&c.; Jude vii, 21.

35. Women – Naturally weak. Received their dead – Children. Others were tortured – From those who acted great things the apostle rises higher, to those who showed the power of faith by suffering. Not accepting deliverance – On sinful terms. That they might obtain a better resurrection – An higher reward, seeing the greater their sufferings the greater would be their glory. 1 Kings xvii, 22; 2 Kings iv, 35.

36. And others – The apostle seems here to pass on to recent examples.

37. They were sawn asunder – As, according to the tradition of the Jews, Isaiah was by Manasseh. Were tempted – Torments and death are mentioned alternately. Every way; by threatenings, reproaches, tortures, the variety of which cannot be expressed; and again by promises and allurements.

38. Of whom the world was not worthy – It did not deserve so great a blessing. They wandered – Being driven out from men.

39. And all these – Though they obtained a good testimony, ver. 2, yet did not receive the great promise, the heavenly inheritance.

40. God having provided some better thing for us – Namely, everlasting glory. That they might not be perfected without us – That is, that we might all be perfected together in heaven.

HEBREWS 12

1. Wherefore, being encompassed with a cloud – A great multitude, tending upward with a holy swiftness. Of witnesses – Of the power of faith. Let us lay aside every weight – As all who run a race take care to do. Let us throw off whatever weighs us down, or damps the vigor of our Soul. And the sin which easily besetteth us – As doth the sin of our constitution, the sin of our education, the sin of our profession.

2. Looking – From all other things. To Jesus – As the wounded Israelites to the brazen serpent. Our crucified Lord was prefigured by the lifting up of this; our guilt, by the stings of the fiery serpents; and our faith, by their looking up to the miraculous remedy. The author and finisher of our faith – Who begins it in us, carries it on, and perfects it. Who for the joy that was set before him – Patiently

through all? What a difference between God's judgment of a saint, and man's judgment! The world is not worthy of those scorned, persecuted saints, whom their persecutors reckon unworthy to live. They are not worthy of their company, example, counsel, or other benefits. For they know not what a saint is, nor the worth of a saint, nor how to use him; they hate, and drive such away, as they do the offer of Christ and his grace.

39,40 The world considers that the righteous are not worthy to live in the world, and God declares the world is not worthy of them. Though the righteous and the worldlings widely differ in their judgment, they agree in this, it is not fit that good men should have their rest in this world. Therefore God receives them out of it. The apostle tells the Hebrews, that God had provided some better things for them, therefore they might be sure that he expected as good things from them. As our advantages, with the better things God has provided for us, are so much beyond theirs, so should our obedience of faith, patience of hope, and labor of love, be greater. And unless we get true faith as these believers had, they will rise up to condemn us at the last day.

HEBREWS 12

An exhortation to be constant and persevere. The example of Christ is set forth, and the gracious design of God in all the sufferings believers endured. (1-11)
Peace and holiness are recommended, with cautions against despising spiritual blessings. (12-17)
The New Testament dispensation shown to be much more excellent than the Old. (18-29)

1-11 The persevering obedience of faith in Christ, was the race set before the Hebrews, wherein they must either win the crown of glory, or have everlasting misery for their portion; and it is set before us. By the sin that does so easily beset us, understand that sin to which we are most prone, or to which we are most exposed, from habit, age, or circumstances. This is a most important exhortation; for while a man's darling sin, be it what it will, remains unsubdued, it will hinder him from running the Christian race, as it takes from him every motive for running, and gives power to every discouragement. When weary and faint in their minds, let them recollect that the holy Jesus suffered, to save them from eternal misery. By steadfastly looking to Jesus, their thoughts would strengthen holy affections, and keep under their carnal desires. Let us then frequently consider him. What are our little trials to his agonies, or even to our deserts? What are they to the sufferings of many others? There is a proneness in believers to grow weary, and to faint under trials and afflictions; this is from the imperfection of grace and the remains of

dry-land faith." By-and-by, they march through the Jordan dry shod, and then Faith gets firmer confidence. "Ah!" says she, secretly within herself, what she would willingly have said to her neighbors, "will you not now believe? will you not now sue for mercy?" "No," they say; "the walls of Jericho are strong; can the feeble host resist us? And lo on the morrow the troops are out, and what do they do? They simply blow a number of rams' horns; her neighbors say, "Why, Rahab, you do not mean to say you believe now? They are mad." The people just go round the city, and all hold their tongues, except the few priests blowing rams' horns. "Why, it is ridiculous. It were quite a new thing in warfare to hear of men taking a city by blowing rams' horns." That was the first day; probably the next day Rahab thought they would come with scaling-ladders and mount the walls; but no, rams' horns again, up to the seventh day; and this woman kept the scarlet thread in the window all the time, kept her father and mother, and brothers and sisters in the house, and would not let them go out; and on the seventh day, when the people made a great shout, the wall of the city fell flat to the ground; but her faith overcame her womanly timidity, and she remained within, although the wall was tumbling to the ground. Rahab's house stood alone upon the wall, a solitary fragment amid a universal wreck, and she and her household were all saved. Now would you have thought that such a rich plant would grow in such poor soil—that strong faith could grow in such a sinful heart as that of Rahab? Ah! but here it is that God exercises his great husbandry. "My Father is the husbandman," said Christ. Any husbandman can get a good crop out of good soil; but God is the husbandman who can grow cedars on rocks, who can not only put the hyssop upon the wall, but put the oak there too, and make the greatest faith spring up in the most unlikely position. All glory to his grace! the great sinner may become great in faith. "Be of good cheer, then, sinner! If Christ should make thee repent, thou hast no need to think that thou shalt be the least in the family. O! no; thy name may yet be written among the mightiest of the mighty, and thou mayest stand as a memorable and triumphant instance of the power of faith.

IV. This woman's faith was A SELF-DENYING FAITH. She dared to risk her life for the sake of the spies. She knew that if they were found in her house she would be put to death; but though she was so weak as to do a sinful deed to preserve them, yet she was so strong that she would run the risk of being put to death to save

and finisher of our faith; who for the joy that was set before him endured the cross, despising the shame, and is set down at the right hand of the throne of God.

3 For consider him that endured such contradiction of sinners against himself, lest ye be wearied and faint in your minds.

4 Ye have not yet resisted unto blood, striving against sin.

5 And ye have forgotten the exhortation which speaketh unto you as unto children, My son, despise not thou the chastening of the Lord, nor faint when thou art rebuked of him:

6 For whom the Lord loveth he chasteneth, and scourgeth every son whom he receiveth.

7 If ye endure chastening, God dealeth with you as with sons; for what son is he whom the father chasteneth not?

8 But if ye be without chastisement, whereof all are partakers, then are ye bastards, and not sons.

9 Furthermore we have had fathers of our flesh which corrected us, and we gave them reverence: shall we not much rather be in subjection unto the Father of spirits, and live?

10 For they verily for a few days chastened us after their own pleasure; but he for our profit, that we might be partakers of his holiness.

11 Now no chastening for the present seemeth to be joyous, but grievous: nevertheless afterward it yieldeth the peaceable fruit of righteousness unto them which are exercised thereby.

12 Wherefore lift up the hands which hang down, and the feeble knees;

13 And make straight paths for your feet, lest that which is lame be turned out of the way; but let it rather be healed.

14 Follow peace with all men, and holiness, without which no man shall see the Lord:

15 Looking diligently lest any man fail of the grace of God; lest any root of bitterness springing up trouble you, and thereby many be defiled;

16 Lest there be any fornicator, or profane person, as Esau, who for one morsel of meat sold his birthright.

and willingly endured the cross, with all the pains annexed thereto. And is set down – Where there is fullness of joy.

3. Consider – Draw the comparison and think. The Lord bore all this; and shall his servants bear nothing? Him that endured such contradiction from sinners – Such enmity and opposition of every kind. Lest ye be weary – Dull and languid, and so actually faint in your course.

4. Unto blood – Unto wounds and death.

5. And yet ye seem already to have forgotten the exhortation – Wherein God speaketh to you with the utmost tenderness. Despise not thou the chastening of the Lord – Do not slight or make little of it; do not impute any affliction to chance or second causes but see and revere the hand of God in it. Neither faint when thou art rebuked of him – But endure it patiently and fruitfully. Prov. iii, 11, &c.

6. For – All springs from love; therefore neither despise nor faint.

7. Whom his father chasteneth not – When he offends.

8. Of which all sons are partakers – More or less.

9. And we reverenced them – We neither despised nor fainted under their correction. Shall we not much rather – Submit with reverence and meekness – To the Father of spirits – That we may live with him for ever. Perhaps these expressions, fathers of our flesh, and Father of spirits, intimate that our earthly fathers are only the parents of our bodies, our souls not being originally derived from them, but all created by the immediate power of God; perhaps, at the beginning of the world.

10. For they verily for a few days – How few are even all our days on earth! Chastened us as they thought good – Though frequently they erred therein, by too much either of indulgence or severity. But he always, unquestionably, for our profit, that we may be partakers of his holiness – That is, of himself and his glorious image.

11. Now all chastening – Whether from our earthly or heavenly Father – Is for the present grievous, yet it yieldeth the peaceable fruit of righteousness – Holiness and happiness. To them that are exercised thereby – That receive this exercise as from God, and improve it according to his will.

12. Wherefore lift up the hands – Whether your own or your brethren's. That hang down – Unable to continue the combat. And the feeble knees – Unable to continue the race. Isaiah xxxv, 3.

13. And make straight paths both for your own and for their feet – Remove every hindrance, every offense. That the lame – They who are weak, scarce able to walk. Be not turned out of the way – Of faith and holiness.

14. Follow peace with all men – This second branch of the exhortation concerns our neighbors; the third, God. And holiness – The not following after all holiness, is the direct way to fall into sin of every kind.

15. Looking diligently, lest any one – If he do not lift up the hands that hang down. Fall from the grace of God: lest any root of bitterness – Of envy, anger, suspicion. Springing up – Destroy the sweet peace; lest any, not following after holiness, fall into fornication or profaneness. In general, any corruption, either in doctrine or practice, is a root of bitterness, and may pollute many.

16. Esau was profane for so slighting the blessing which went along with the birth-right.

17. He was rejected – He could not obtain it. For he found no place for repentance – There was no room for any such repentance as would regain what he had lost. Though he sought it – The blessing of the birth-right. Diligently with tears – He sought too late. Let us use the present time.

18. For – A strong reason this why they ought the more to regard the whole exhortation drawn from the priesthood of Christ: because both salvation and vengeance are now nearer at hand. Ye are not come to the mountain that could be touched – That was of an earthy, material nature.

corruption. Christians should not faint under their trials. Though their enemies and persecutors may be instruments to inflict sufferings, yet they are Divine chastisements; their heavenly Father has his hand in all, and his wise end to answer by all. They must not make light of afflictions, and be without feeling under them, for they are the hand and rod of God, and are his rebukes for sin. They must not despond and sink under trials, nor fret and repine, but bear up with faith and patience. God may let others alone in their sins, but he will correct sin in his own children. In this he acts as becomes a father. Our earthly parents sometimes may chasten us, to gratify their passion, rather than to reform our manners. But the Father of our souls never willingly grieves nor afflicts his children. It is always for our profit. Our whole life here is a state of childhood, and imperfect as to spiritual things; therefore we must submit to the discipline of such a state. When we come to a perfect state, we shall be fully reconciled to all God's chastisement of us now. God's correction is not condemnation; the chastening may be borne with patience, and greatly promote holiness. Let us then learn to consider the afflictions brought on us by the malice of men, as corrections sent by our wise and gracious Father, for our spiritual good.

12-17 A burden of affliction is apt to make the Christian's hands hang down, and his knees grow feeble, to dispirit him and discourage him; but against this he must strive, that he may better run his spiritual race and course. Faith and patience enable believers to follow peace and holiness, as a man follows his calling constantly, diligently, and with pleasure. Peace with men, of all sects and parties, will be favorable to our pursuit of holiness. But peace and holiness go together; there can be not right peace without holiness. Where persons fail of having the true grace of God, corruption will prevail and break forth; beware lest any unmortified lust in the heart, which seems to be dead, should spring up, to trouble and disturb the whole body. Falling away from Christ is the fruit of preferring the delights of the flesh, to the blessing of God, and the heavenly inheritance, as Esau did. But sinners will not always have such mean thoughts of the Divine blessing and inheritance as they now have. It agrees with the profane man's disposition, to desire the blessing, yet to despise the means whereby the blessing is to be gained. But God will neither sever the means from the blessing, nor join the blessing with the satisfying of man's lusts. God's mercy and blessing were never sought carefully and not obtained.

18-29 Mount Sinai, on which the Jewish church state was formed, was a mount such as might be touched, though forbidden to be so, a place that could be felt; so the Mosaic dispensation was much in outward and earthly things. The gospel state is kind and conde-

these two men. It is some thing to be able to deny ourselves. An American once said, "I have got a good religion; it's the right sort of religion; I do not know that it costs me a cent a year; and yet I believe I am as truly a religious man as anybody." "Ah!" said one who heard it, "the Lord have mercy on your miserable stingy soul, for if you had been saved you would not have been content with a cent a year"—a halfpenny per annum! I hazard this assertion, that there is nothing in the faith of that man who does not exercise self-denial. If we never give any thing to Christ's cause, work for Christ, deny ourselves for Christ, the root of the matter is not in us.

This woman, poor sinner as she was, would deny herself. She brought her life, even as that other woman, who was a sinner, brought the alabaster box of precious ointment, and broke it on the head of Christ.

V. Not to detain you too long, another point very briefly. This woman's faith was A SYMPATHIZING FAITH. She did not believe for herself only; she desired mercy for her relations. Said she, "I want to be saved, but that very desire makes me want to have my father saved, and my mother saved, and my brother saved, and my sister saved." I know a man who walks seven miles every Sabbath to hear the gospel preached in a certain place—a place where they preach the gospel. You know that very particular, superfine sort—the gospel, a gospel, the spirit of which consists in bad temper, carnal security, arrogance, and a seared conscience. But this man was one day met by a friend, who said to him, "Where is your wife?" "Wife?" said he to him. "What! does she not come with you?" "O! no", said the man; "she never goes anywhere." "Well, but," said he, "don't you try to get her to go, and the children?" "No; the fact of it is, I think, if I look to myself that is quite enough." "Well," said the other, "and you believe that you are God's elect, do you?" "Yes." "Well, then," said the other, "I don't think you are, because you are worse than a heathen man and a publican, for you don't care for your own household; therefore I don't think you give much evidence of being God's elect, for they love their fellow-creatures." So sure as our faith is real, it will want to bring others in. You will say, "You want to make proselytes." Yes; and you will reply, that Christ said to the Pharisees, "Ye compass sea and land to make one proselyte." Yes, and Christ did not find fault with them for doing so; what he found fault with them for was this—"When ye have found him ye make him tenfold more the child of hell than yourselves."

17 For ye know how that afterward, when he would have inherited the blessing, he was rejected: for he found no place of repentance, though he sought it carefully with tears.

18 For ye are not come unto the mount that might be touched, and that burned with fire, nor unto blackness, and darkness, and tempest,

19 And the sound of a trumpet, and the voice of words; which voice they that heard intreated that the word should not be spoken to them any more:

20 (For they could not endure that which was commanded, And if so much as a beast touch the mountain, it shall be stoned, or thrust through with a dart:

21 And so terrible was the sight, that Moses said, I exceedingly fear and quake:)

22 But ye are come unto mount Sion, and unto the city of the living God, the heavenly Jerusalem, and to an innumerable company of angels,

23 To the general assembly and church of the firstborn, which are written in heaven, and to God the Judge of all, and to the spirits of just men made perfect,

24 And to Jesus the mediator of the new covenant, and to the blood of sprinkling, that speaketh better things than that of Abel.

25 See that ye refuse not him that speaketh. For if they escaped not who refused him that spake on earth, much more shall not we escape, if we turn away from him that speaketh from heaven:

26 Whose voice then shook the earth: but now he hath promised, saying, Yet once more I shake not the earth only, but also heaven.

27 And this word, Yet once more, signifieth the removing of those things that are shaken, as of things that are made, that those things which cannot be shaken may remain.

28 Wherefore we receiving a kingdom which cannot be moved, let us have grace, whereby we may serve God acceptably with reverence and godly fear:

29 For our God is a consuming fire.

19. The sound of a trumpet – Formed, without doubt, by the ministry of angels, and preparatory to the words, that is, the Ten Commandments, which were uttered with a loud voice, Deut. v, 22.

20. For they could not bear – The terror which seized them, when they heard those words proclaimed, If even a beast, &c. Exod. xix, 12, &c.

21. Even Moses – Though admitted to so near an intercourse with God, who "spake to him as a man speaketh to his friend." At other times he acted as a mediator between God and the people. But while the ten words were pronounced, he stood as one of the hearers, Exod. xix, 25; Exod. xx, 19.

22. But ye – Who believe in Christ. Are come – The apostle does not here speak of their coming to the church militant, but of that glorious privilege of New Testament believers, their communion with the church triumphant. But this is far more apparent to the eyes of celestial spirits than to ours which are yet veiled. St. Paul here shows an excellent knowledge of the heavenly economy, worthy of him who had been caught up into the third heaven. To mount Sion – A spiritual mountain. To the city of the living God, the heavenly Jerusalem – All these glorious titles belong to the New Testament church. And to an innumerable company – Including all that are afterwards mentioned.

23. To the general assembly – The word properly signifies a stated convention on some festival occasion. And church – The whole body of true believers, whether on earth or in paradise. Of the first-born – The first-born of Israel were enrolled by Moses; but these are enrolled in heaven, as citizens there. It is observable, that in this beautiful gradation, these first-born are placed nearer to God than the angels. See Jam i, 18. And to God the Judge of all – Propitious to you, adverse to your enemies. And to the spirits – The separate souls. Of just men – It seems to mean, of New Testament believers. The number of these, being not yet large, is mentioned distinct from the innumerable company of just men whom their Judge hath acquitted. These are now made perfect in an higher sense than any who are still alive. Accordingly, St. Paul, while yet on earth, denies that he was thus made perfect, Phil. iii, 12.

24. To Jesus, the mediator – Through whom they had been perfected. And to the blood of sprinkling – To all the virtue of his precious blood shed for you, whereby ye are sprinkled from an evil conscience. This blood of sprinkling was the foundation of our Lord's mediatorial office. Here the gradation is at the highest point. Which speaketh better things than that of Abel – Which cried for vengeance.

25. Refuse not – By unbelief. Him that speaketh – And whose speaking even now is a prelude to the final scene. The same voice which spake both by the law and in the gospel, when heard from heaven, will shake heaven and earth. For if they escaped not – His vengeance. Much more shall not we – Those of us who turn from him that speaketh from heaven – That is, who came from heaven to speak to us.

26. Whose voice then shook the earth – When he spoke from mount Sinai. But now – With regard to his next speaking. He hath promised – It is a joyful promise to the saints, though dreadful to the wicked. Yet once more I will shake, not only the earth, but also the heaven – These words may refer in a lower sense to the dissolution of the Jewish church and state; but in their full sense they undoubtedly look much farther, even to the end of all things. This universal shaking began at the first coming of Christ. It will be consummated at his second coming. Haggai ii, 6.

27. The things which are shaken – Namely, heaven and earth. As being made – And consequently liable to change. That the things which are not shaken may remain – Even "the new heavens and the new earth," Rev. xxi, 1.

28. Therefore let us, receiving – By willing and joyful faith. A kingdom – More glorious than the present heaven and earth. Hold fast the grace, whereby we may serve God – In every thought, word, and work. With reverence – Literally,

MATTHEW HENRY

CHARLES H. SPURGEON

scending, suited to our weak frame. Under the gospel all may come with boldness to God's presence. But the most holy must despair, if judged by the holy law given from Sinai, without a Savior. The gospel church is called Mount Zion; there believers have clearer views of heaven, and more heavenly tempers of soul. All the children of God are heirs, and every one has the privileges of the first-born. Let a soul be supposed to join that glorious assembly and church above, that is yet unacquainted with God, still carnally-minded, loving this present world and state of things, looking back to it with a lingering eye, full of pride and guile, filled with lusts; such a soul would seem to have mistaken its way, place, state, and company. It would be uneasy to itself and all about it. Christ is the Mediator of this new covenant, between God and man, to bring them together in this covenant; to keep them together; to plead with God for us, and to plead with us for God; and at length to bring God and his people together in heaven. This covenant is made firm by the blood of Christ sprinkled upon our consciences, as the blood of the sacrifice was sprinkled upon the altar and the victim. This blood of Christ speaks in behalf of sinners; it pleads not for vengeance, but for mercy. See then that you refuse not his gracious call and offered salvation. See that you do not refuse him who speaketh from heaven, with infinite tenderness and love; for how can those escape, who turn from God in unbelief or apostasy, while he so graciously beseeches them to be reconciled, and to receive his everlasting favor! God's dealing with men under the gospel, in a way of grace, assures us, that he will deal with the despisers of the gospel, in a way of judgment. We cannot worship God acceptably, unless we worship him with reverence and godly fear. Only the grace of God enables us to worship God aright. God is the same just and righteous God under the gospel as under the law. The inheritance of believers is secured to them; and all things pertaining to salvation are freely given in answer to prayer. Let us seek for grace, that we may serve God with reverence and godly fear.

HEBREWS 13

1-6 The design of Christ in giving himself for us, is, that he may purchase to himself a peculiar people, zealous of good works; and true religion is the strongest bond of friendship. Here are earnest exhor-

Unless we desire others to taste the benefits we have enjoyed, we are either inhuman monsters or outrageous hypocrites; I think the last is most likely. But this woman was so strong in faith that all her family were saved from destruction. Young woman! you have a father, and he hates the Savior. O! pray for him. Mother! you have a son: he scoffs at Christ. Cry out to God for him. Ay, my friends—young people like myself—we little know what we owe to the prayers of our parents. I feel that I shall never be able sufficiently to bless God for a praying mother. I thought it was a great nuisance to be had in at such a time to pray, and more especially to be made to cry, as my mother used to make me cry. I would have laughed at the idea of any body else talking to me about these things; but when she prayed, and said, "Lord, save my son Charles," and then was overcome, and could not get any further for crying, you could not help crying too; you could not help feeling; it was of no use trying to stand against it. Ah! and there you are young man! Your mother is dying, and one thing which makes her death-bed bitter is, that you scoff God and hate Christ. O! it is the last stage of impiety, when a man can think lightly of a mother's feelings. I would hope there are none such here, but that those of you who have been so blessed, as to have been begotten and brought forth by pious men and women may take this into consideration—that to perish with a mother's prayers is to perish fearfully; for if a mother's prayers do not bring us to Christ, they are like drops of oil dropped into the flames of hell that will make them burn more fiercely upon the soul for ever and ever. Take heed of rushing to perdition over your mother's prayers!

There is an old woman weeping—do you know why? I believe she has sons too, and she loves them. I met with a little incident in company, the other day, after preaching. There was a little boy at the corner of the table, and his father asked him, "Why does your father love you, John?" Said the dear little lad, very prettily, "Because I'm a good boy." "Yes." said the father, "he would not love you if you were not a good boy." I turned to the good father and remarked that I was not quite sure about the truth of the last remark, for I believed he would love him if he were ever so bad. "Well," he said, "I think I should." And said a minister at the table, "I had an instance of that yesterday. I stepped into the house of a woman who had a son transported for life, and she was as full of her son Richard as if be had been prime minister, or had been her most faithful and dutiful son." Well, young man, will you kick against love like that—love that will bear your kicks,

HEBREWS 13

1 Let brotherly love continue.
2 Be not forgetful to entertain strangers: for thereby some have entertained angels unawares.
3 Remember them that are in bonds, as bound with them; and them which suffer adversity, as being yourselves also in the body.
4 Marriage is honorable in all, and the bed undefiled: but whoremongers and adulterers God will judge.
5 Let your conversation be without covetousness; and be content with such things as ye have: for he hath said, I will never leave thee, nor forsake thee.
6 So that we may boldly say, The Lord is my helper, and I will not fear what man shall do unto me.
7 Remember them which have the rule over you, who have spoken unto you the word of God: whose faith follow, considering the end of their conversation.
8 Jesus Christ the same yesterday, and to day, and for ever.
9 Be not carried about with divers and strange doctrines. For it is a good thing that the heart be established with grace; not with meats, which have not profited them that have been occupied therein.
10 We have an altar, whereof they have no right to eat which serve the tabernacle.
11 For the bodies of those beasts, whose blood is brought into the sanctuary by the high priest for sin, are burned without the camp.
12 Wherefore Jesus also, that he might sanctify the people with his own blood, suffered without the gate.
13 Let us go forth therefore unto him without the camp, bearing his reproach.
14 For here have we no continuing city, but we seek one to come.
15 By him therefore let us offer the sacrifice of praise to God continually, that is, the fruit of our lips giving thanks to his name.
16 But to do good and to communicate forget not: for with such sacrifices God is well pleased.

with shame. Arising from a deep consciousness of our own unworthiness. And godly fear – A tender, jealous fear of offending, arising from a sense of the gracious majesty of God.

29. For our God is a consuming fire – in the strictness of his justice, and purity of his holiness.

HEBREWS 13

1. Brotherly love is explained in the following verses.

2. Some – Abraham and Lot. Have entertained angels unawares – So may an unknown guest, even now, be of more worth than he appears, and may have angels attending him, though unseen. Gen. xviii, 2; Gen. xix, 1.

3. Remember – In your prayers, and by your help. Them that are in bonds, as being bound with them – Seeing ye are members one of another. And them that suffer, as being yourselves in the body – And consequently liable to the same.

4. Marriage is honorable in, or for all sorts of men, clergy as well as laity: though the Romanists teach otherwise. And the bed undefiled – Consistent with the highest purity; though many spiritual writers, so called, say it is only licensed whoredom. But whoremongers and adulterers God will judge – Though they frequently escape the sentence of men.

5. He – God. Hath said – To all believers, in saying it to Jacob, Joshua, and Solomon. Gen. xxviii, 15; Josh. i, 5; 1 Chr xxviii, 20.

6. Psalm cxviii, 6.

7. Remember them – Who are now with God, considering the happy end of their conversation on earth.

8. Men may die; but Jesus Christ, yea, and his gospel, is the same from everlasting to everlasting.

9. Be not carried about with various doctrines – Which differ from that one faith in our one unchangeable Lord. Strange – To the ears and hearts of all that abide in him. For it is good – It is both honorable before God and pleasant and profitable That the heart be established with grace – Springing from faith in Christ. Not with meats – Jewish ceremonies, which indeed can never establish the heart.

10. On the former part of this verse, the fifteenth and sixteenth depend; on the latter, the intermediate verses. We have an altar – The cross of Christ. Whereof they have no right to eat – To partake of the benefits which we receive therefrom. Who serve the tabernacle – Who adhere to the Mosaic law.

11. For – According to their own law, the sin-offerings were wholly consumed, and no Jew ever ate thereof. But Christ was a sin-offering. Therefore they cannot feed upon him, as we do, who are freed from the Mosaic law.

12. Wherefore Jesus also – Exactly answering those typical sin-offerings. Suffered without the gate – Of Jerusalem, which answered to the old camp of Israel. That he might sanctify – Reconcile and consecrate to God. The people – Who believe in him. By his own blood – Not those shadowy sacrifices, which are now of no farther use.

13. Let us then go forth without the camp – Out of the Jewish dispensation. Bearing his reproach – All manner of shame, obloquy, and contempt for his sake.

14. For we have here – On earth. No continuing city – All things here are but for a moment; and Jerusalem itself was just then on the point of being destroyed.

15. The sacrifice – The altar is mentioned, ver. 10; now the sacrifices:
    1. Praise;
    2. Beneficence; with both of which God is well pleased.

17. Obey them that have the rule over you – The word implies also, that lead or guide you; namely, in truth and holiness. And submit yourselves – Give up

MATTHEW HENRY

CHARLES H. SPURGEON

tations to several Christian duties, especially contentment. The sin opposed to this grace and duty is covetousness, an over-eager desire for the wealth of this world, with envy of those who have more than ourselves. Having treasures in heaven, we may be content with mean things here. Those who cannot be so, would not be content though God raised their condition. Adam was in paradise, yet not contented; some angels in heaven were not contented; but the apostle Paul, though abased and empty, had learned in every state, in any state, to be content. Christians have reason to be contented with their present lot. This promise contains the sum and substance of all the promises; "I will never, no, never leave thee, no, never forsake thee." In the original there are no less than five negatives put together, to confirm the promise: the true believer shall have the gracious presence of God with him, in life, at death, and for ever. Men can do nothing against God, and God can make all that men do against his people, to turn to their good.

7-15 The instructions and examples of ministers, who honorably and comfortably closed their testimony, should be particularly remembered by survivors. And though their ministers were some dead, others dying, yet the great Head and High Priest of the church, the Bishop of their souls, ever lives, and is ever the same. Christ is the same in the Old Testament day, as in the gospel day, and will be so to his people forever, equally merciful, powerful, and all sufficient. Still he fills the hungry, encourages the trembling, and welcomes repenting sinners: still he rejects the proud and self-righteous, abhors mere profession, and teaches all whom he saves, to love righteousness, and to hate iniquity. Believers should seek to have their hearts established in simple dependence on free grace, by the Holy Spirit, which would comfort their hearts, and render them proof against delusion. Christ is both our Altar and our Sacrifice; he sanctifies the gift. The Lord's supper is the feast of the gospel Passover. Having showed that keeping to the Levitical law would, according to its own rules, keep men from the Christian altar, the apostle adds, Let us go forth therefore unto him without the camp; go forth from the ceremonial law, from sin, from the world, and from ourselves. Living by faith in Christ, set apart to God through his blood, let us willingly separate from this evil world. Sin, sinners, nor death, will not suffer us to continue long here; therefore let us go forth now by faith and seek in Christ the rest and peace which this world cannot afford us. Let us bring our sacrifices to this altar, and to this our High Priest, and offer them up by him. The sacrifice of praise to God, we should offer always. In this are worship and prayer, as well as thanksgiving.

16-21 We must, according to our power, give to the necessities of the souls and bodies of men: God will accept these offerings with pleasure, and will accept

and will not turn round against you, but love you straight on still? But perhaps that woman—I saw her weep just now—had a mother, who has gone long ago, and she was married to a brutal husband, and at last left a poor widow; she calls to mind the days of her childhood, when the big Bible was brought out and read around the hearth, and "Our Father which art in heaven" was their nightly prayer. Now, perhaps, God is beginning some good thing in her heart. O! that he would bring her now, though seventy years of age, to love the Savior! Then would she have the beginning of life over again in her last days, which will be made her best days.

VI. One more head, and then we have done. Rahab's faith was a SANCTIFYING FAITH. Did Rahab continue a harlot after she had faith? No, no, she did not. I do not believe she was a harlot at the time the men went to her house, though the name still stuck to her, as such ill names will; but I am sure she was not afterward, for Salmon the prince of Judah married her, and her name is put down among the ancestors of our Lord Jesus Christ. She became after that a woman eminent for piety walking in the fear of God. Now, you may have a dead faith which will ruin your soul. The faith that will save you is a faith which sanctifies. "Ah!" says the drunkard, "I like the gospel, sir; I believe in Christ;" then he will go over to the Blue Lion tonight, and get drunk. Sir, that is not the believing in Christ that is of any use. "Yes," says another, "I believe in Christ;" and when he gets outside he will begin to talk lightly, frothy words, perhaps lascivious ones, and sin as before. Sir, you speak falsely; you do not believe in Christ. That faith which saves the soul is a real faith, and a real faith sanctifies men. It makes them say, "Lord, thou hast forgiven me my sins; I will sin no more. Thou hast been so merciful to me, I will renounce my guilt; so kindly hast thou treated me, so lovingly hast thou embraced me, Lord, I will serve thee till I die; and if thou wilt give me grace, and help me so to be, I will be as holy as thou art." You can not have faith, and yet live in sin. To believe is to be holy. The two things must go together. That faith is a dead faith, a corrupt faith, which lives in sin that grace may abound. Rahab was a sanctified woman. O that God might sanctify some that are here! The world has been trying all manner of processes to reform men: there is but one thing that ever will reform them, and that is, faith in the preached gospel. But in this age preaching is much despised. You read the newspaper; you read the book; you hear the lecturer; you sit and listen to the pretty essayist; but where is the preacher?

17 Obey them that have the rule over you, and submit yourselves: for they watch for your souls, as they that must give account, that they may do it with joy, and not with grief: for that is unprofitable for you.

18 Pray for us: for we trust we have a good conscience, in all things willing to live honestly.

19 But I beseech you the rather to do this, that I may be restored to you the sooner.

20 Now the God of peace, that brought again from the dead our Lord Jesus, that great shepherd of the sheep, through the blood of the everlasting covenant,

21 Make you perfect in every good work to do his will, working in you that which is wellpleasing in his sight, through Jesus Christ; to whom be glory for ever and ever. Amen.

22 And I beseech you, brethren, suffer the word of exhortation: for I have written a letter unto you in few words.

23 Know ye that our brother Timothy is set at liberty; with whom, if he come shortly, I will see you.

24 Salute all them that have the rule over you, and all the saints. They of Italy salute you.

25 Grace be with you all. Amen.

(not your conscience or judgment, but) your own will, in all things purely indifferent. For they watch over your souls – With all zeal and diligence, they guard and caution you against all danger. As they that must give account – To the great Shepherd, for every part of their behavior toward you. How vigilant then ought every pastor to be! How careful of every soul committed to his charge! That they may do this – Watch over you. With joy and not with groans – He is not a good shepherd, who does not either rejoice over them, or groan for them. The groans of other creatures are heard: how much more shall these come up in the ears of God! Whoever answers this character of a Christian pastor may undoubtedly demand this obedience.

20. The everlasting covenant – The Christian covenant, which is not temporary, like the Jewish, but designed to remain for ever. By the application of that blood, by which this covenant was established, may he make you, in every respect, inwardly and outwardly holy!

22. Suffer the word of exhortation – Addressed to you in this letter, which, though longer than my usual letters, is yet contained in few words, considering the copiousness of the subject.

23. If he come – To me.

25. Grace be with you all – St. Paul's usual benediction. God apply it to our hearts!

and bless the offerers through Christ. The apostle then states what is their duty to living ministers; to obey and submit to them, so far as is agreeable to the mind and will of God, made known in his word. Christians must not think themselves too wise, too good, or too great, to learn. The people must search the Scriptures, and so far as the ministers teach according to that rule, they ought to receive their instructions as the word of God, which works in those that believe. It is the interest of hearers, that the account their ministers give of them may be with joy, and not with grief. Faithful ministers deliver their own souls, but the ruin of a fruitless and faithless people will be upon their own heads. The more earnestly the people pray for their ministers, the more benefit they may expect from their ministry. A good conscience has respect to all God's commands, and all our duty. Those who have this good conscience, yet need the prayers of others. When ministers come to a people who pray for them, they come with greater satisfaction to themselves, and success to the people. We should seek all our mercies by prayer. God is the God of peace, fully reconciled to believers; who has made a way for peace and reconciliation between himself and sinners, and who loves peace on earth, especially in his churches. He is the Author of spiritual peace in the hearts and consciences of his people. How firm a covenant is that which has its foundation in the blood of the Son of God!

22-25 So bad are men, and even believers, through the remainders of their corruption, that when the most important, comfortable doctrine is delivered to them for their own good, and that with the most convincing evidence, there is need of earnest entreaty and exhortation that they would bear it, and not fall out with it, neglect it, or reject it. It is good to have the law of holy love and kindness written in the hearts of Christians, one towards another. Religion teaches men true civility and good breeding. It is not ill tempered or uncourteous. Let the favor of God be toward you, and his grace continually working in you, and with you, bringing forth the fruits of holiness, as the first fruits of glory.

Preaching is not taking out a manuscript sermon, asking God to direct your heart, and then reading pages prepared beforehand. That is reading—not preaching. There is a good tale told of an old man whose minister used to read. The minister called to see him, and said, "What are you doing John?" "Why, I'm prophesying, sir." "Prophesying; how is that? You mean you are reading the prophecies?" "No, I don't; I'm prophesying; for you read preaching, and call it preaching, and I read prophecies, and, on the same rule, that is prophesying." And the man was not far from right. We want to have more outspoken, downright utterances of truth and appeals to the conscience, and until we get these, we shall never see any very great and lasting reforms. But by the preaching of God's word, foolishness though it seem to some, harlots are reformed, thieves are made honest, and the worst of men brought to the Savior. Again let me affectionately give the invitation to the vilest of men, if so they feel themselves to be,

"Come, ye needy, come and welcome,
God's fine bounty glorify:
True belief and true repentance—
Every grace that brings us nigh—
Without money,
Come to Jesus Christ and buy."

Your sins will be forgiven, your transgressions cast away, and you shall henceforth go and sin no more, God having renewed you, and he will keep you even to the end. May God give his blessing, for Jesus sake! Amen.

James

JAMES 1

1 James, a servant of God and of the Lord Jesus Christ, to the twelve tribes which are scattered abroad, greeting.

2 My brethren, count it all joy when ye fall into divers temptations;

3 Knowing this, that the trying of your faith worketh patience.

4 But let patience have her perfect work, that ye may be perfect and entire, wanting nothing.

5 If any of you lack wisdom, let him ask of God, that giveth to all men liberally, and upbraideth not; and it shall be given him.

6 But let him ask in faith, nothing wavering. For he that wavereth is like a wave of the sea driven with the wind and tossed.

7 For let not that man think that he shall receive any thing of the Lord.

8 A double minded man is unstable in all his ways.

9 Let the brother of low degree rejoice in that he is exalted:

10 But the rich, in that he is made low: because as the flower of the grass he shall pass away.

11 For the sun is no sooner risen with a burning heat, but it withereth the grass, and the flower thereof falleth, and the grace of the fashion of it perisheth: so also shall the rich man fade away in his ways.

12 Blessed is the man that endureth temptation: for when he is tried, he shall receive the crown of life, which the Lord hath promised to them that love him.

13 Let no man say when he is tempted, I am tempted of God: for God cannot be tempted with evil, neither tempteth he any man:

14 But every man is tempted, when he is drawn away of his own lust, and enticed.

15 Then when lust hath conceived, it bringeth forth sin: and sin, when it is finished, bringeth forth death.

16 Do not err, my beloved brethren.

17 Every good gift and every perfect gift is from above, and cometh down from the Father of lights, with whom is no variable-

THIS is supposed to have been written by James the son of Alpheus the brother (or kinsman) of our Lord. It is called a General Epistle, because written not to a particular person or church, but to all the converted Israelites. Herein the apostle reproves that Antinomian spirit, which had even then infected many, who had perverted the glorious doctrine of justification by faith into an occasion of licentiousness. He likewise comforts the true believers under their sufferings, and reminds them of the judgments that were approaching.

JAMES 1

1. A servant of Jesus Christ – Whose name the apostle mentions but once more in the whole epistle, chap. ii, 1. And not at all in his whole discourse, Acts xv, 14, &c.; or Acts xxi, 20-25. It might have seemed, if he mentioned him often, that he did it out of vanity, as being the brother of the Lord. To the twelve tribes – Of Israel; that is, those of them that believe. Which are scattered abroad – In various countries. Ten of the tribes were scattered ever since the reign of Hosea; and great part of the rest were now dispersed through the Roman empire: as was foretold, Deut. xxviii, 25. Greeting – That is, all blessings, temporal and eternal.

2. My brethren, count it all joy – Which is the highest degree of patience, and contains all the rest. When ye fall into divers temptations – That is, trials.

4. Let patience have its perfect work – Give it full scope, under whatever trials befall you. That ye may be perfect and entire – Adorned with every Christian grace. And wanting nothing – Which God requires in you.

5. If any want – The connection between the first and following verses, both here and in the fourth chapter, will be easily discerned by him who reads them, while he is suffering wrongfully. He will then readily perceive, why the apostle mentions all those various affections of the mind. Wisdom – To understand, whence and why temptations come, and how they are to be improved. Patience is in every pious man already. Let him exercise this, and ask for wisdom. The sum of wisdom, both in the temptation of poverty and of riches, is described in the ninth and tenth verses. Who giveth to all – That ask aright. And upbraideth not – Either with their past wickedness, or present unworthiness.

6. But let him ask in faith – A firm confidence in God. St. James also both begins and ends with faith, chap. v, 15; the hindrances of which he removes in the middle part of his epistle. He that doubteth is like a wave of the sea – Yea, such are all who have not asked and obtained wisdom. Driven with the wind – From without. And tossed – From within, by his own unstableness.

8. A double minded man – Who has, as it were, two souls; whose heart is not simply given up to God. Is unstable – Being without the true wisdom; perpetually disagrees both with himself and others, chap. iii, 16.

9. Let the brother – St James does not give this appellation to the rich. Of low degree – Poor and tempted. Rejoice – The most effectual remedy against double mindedness. In that he is exalted – To be a child of God, and an heir of glory.

10. But the rich, in that he is made low – Is humbled by a deep sense of his true condition. Because as the flower – Beautiful, but transient. He shall pass away – Into eternity.

11. For the sun arose and withered the grass – There is an unspeakable beauty and elegance, both in the comparison itself, and in the very manner of expressing it, intimating both the certainty and the suddenness of the event. So shall the rich fade away in his ways – In the midst of his various pleasures and employments.

12. Happy is the man that endureth temptation – Trials of various kinds. He shall receive the crown – That fadeth not away. Which the Lord hath promised to them that love him – And his enduring proves his love. For it is love only that "endureth all things."

This epistle of James is one of the most instructive writings in the New Testament. Being chiefly directed against particular errors at that time brought in among the Jewish Christians, it does not contain the same full doctrinal statements as the other epistles, but it presents an admirable summary of the practical duties of all believers. The leading truths of Christianity are set forth throughout; and on attentive consideration, it will be found entirely to agree with St. Paul's statements concerning grace and justification, while it abounds with earnest exhortations to the patience of hope and obedience of faith and love, interspersed with warnings, reproofs, and encouragements, according to the characters addressed. The truths laid down are very serious, and necessary to be maintained; and the rules for practice ought to be observed in all times. In Christ there are no dead and sapless branches, faith is not an idle grace; wherever it is, it brings forth fruit in works.

JAMES 1

How to apply to God under troubles, and how to behave in prosperous and in adverse circumstances. (1-11)
To look upon all evil as proceeding from ourselves, and all good from God. (12-18)
The duty of watching against a rash temper, and of receiving the word of God with meekness. (19-21)
And of living according thereto. (22-25)
The difference between vain pretenses and real religion. (26,27)

1-11 Christianity teaches men to be joyful under troubles: such exercises are sent from God's love; and trials in the way of duty will brighten our graces now, and our crown at last. Let us take care, in times of trial, that patience, and not passion, is set to work in us: whatever is said or done, let patience have the saying and doing of it. When the work of patience is complete, it will furnish all that is necessary for our Christian race and warfare. We should not pray so much for the removal of affliction, as for wisdom to make a right use of it. And who does not want wisdom to guide him under trials, both in regulating his own spirit, and in managing his affairs? Here is something in answer to every discouraging turn of the mind, when we go to God under a sense of our own weakness and folly. If, after all, any should say, This may be the case with some, but I fear I shall not succeed, the promise is, To any that asketh, it shall be given. A mind that has single and prevailing regard to its spiritual and eternal interest, and that keeps steady in its purposes for God, will grow wise by afflictions, will continue fervent in devotion, and rise above trials and oppositions. When our faith and spirits rise and fall with second causes, there will be unsteadiness in our words and actions. This may not always expose men to contempt in the world, but such ways cannot please God. No condition of life is such as to hinder rejoicing in God. Those of low degree may rejoice, if they are exalted to be rich in faith and heirs of the kingdom of God; and the rich may rejoice in humbling providences, that lead to a humble and lowly disposition of mind. Worldly wealth is a withering thing.

GOD'S WILL ABOUT THE FUTURE
Sermon number 2242 intended for Reading on February 7th, 1892, at the Metropolitan Tabernacle, Newington.

"Go to now, ye that say, to day or to morrow we will go into such a city, and continue there a year, and buy and sell, and get gain: whereas ye know not what shall be on the morrow. For what is your life? It is even a vapor, that appeareth for a little time, and then vanisheth away. For that ye ought to say, If the Lord will, we shall live, and do this or that. But now ye rejoice in your boastings: all such rejoicing is evil. Therefore to him that knoweth to do good, and doeth it not, to him it is sin."—James 4:13-17.

I. To begin with, it will need but few words to convince you that COUNTING ON THE FUTURE IS FOLLY. The apostle says, "Go to now!" as if he meant, "you are acting absurdly. See how ridiculous your conduct is." "Go to now, ye that say, Today or tomorrow we will do such and such a thing." There is almost a touch of sarcasm in the words. The fact of frail, feeble man so proudly ordering his own life and forgetting God seems to the apostle James so preposterous that he scarcely deems it worth while to argue the point, he only says "Go to now!"

Let us first look at the form of this folly, and notice what it was that these people said when they were counting on the future. The text is very full of suggestions upon this matter.

They evidently thought everything was at their own disposal. They said "We will go, we will continue, we will buy, we will sell, we will get gain." But it is not foolish for a man to feel that he can do as he likes, and that everything will fall out as he desires; that he can both propose and dispose, and has not to ask God's consent at all? He makes up his mind, and he determines to do just what his mind suggests. Is it so, O man, that thy life is self governed? Is there not, after all, One greater than thyself? Is there not a higher power that can speed thee or stop thee? If thou dost not know this, thou hast not yet learned the first letter of the alphabet of wisdom. May God teach thee that everything is not at your disposal;

ness, neither shadow of turning.

18 Of his own will begat he us with the word of truth, that we should be a kind of firstfruits of his creatures.

19 Wherefore, my beloved brethren, let every man be swift to hear, slow to speak, slow to wrath:

20 For the wrath of man worketh not the righteousness of God.

21 Wherefore lay apart all filthiness and superfluity of naughtiness, and receive with meekness the engrafted word, which is able to save your souls.

22 But be ye doers of the word, and not hearers only, deceiving your own selves.

23 For if any be a hearer of the word, and not a doer, he is like unto a man beholding his natural face in a glass:

24 For he beholdeth himself, and goeth his way, and straightway forgetteth what manner of man he was.

25 But whoso looketh into the perfect law of liberty, and continueth therein, he being not a forgetful hearer, but a doer of the work, this man shall be blessed in his deed.

26 If any man among you seem to be religious, and bridleth not his tongue, but deceiveth his own heart, this man's religion is vain.

27 Pure religion and undefiled before God and the Father is this, To visit the fatherless and widows in their affliction, and to keep himself unspotted from the world.

JAMES 2

1 My brethren, have not the faith of our Lord Jesus Christ, the Lord of glory, with respect of persons.

2 For if there come unto your assembly a man with a gold ring, in goodly apparel, and there come in also a poor man in vile raiment;

3 And ye have respect to him that weareth the gay clothing, and say unto him, Sit thou here in a good place; and say to the poor, Stand thou there, or sit here under my footstool:

4 Are ye not then partial in

13. But let no man who is tempted – To sin. Say, I am tempted of God – God thus tempteth no man.

14. Every man is tempted, when – In the beginning of the temptation. He is drawn away – Drawn out of God, his strong refuge. By his own desire – We are therefore to look for the cause of every sin, in, not out of ourselves. Even the injections of the devil cannot hurt before we make them our own. And every one has desires arising from his own constitution, tempers, habits, and way of life. And enticed – In the progress of the temptation, catching at the bait: so the original word signifies.

15. Then desire having conceived – By our own will joining therewith. Bringeth forth actual sin – It doth not follow that the desire itself is not sin. He that begets a man is himself a man. And sin being perfected – Grown up to maturity, which it quickly does. Bringeth forth death – Sin is born big with death.

16. Do not err – It is a grievous error to ascribe the evil and not the good which we receive to God.

17. No evil, but every good gift – Whatever tends to holiness. And every perfect gift – Whatever tends to glory. Descendeth from the Father of lights – The appellation of Father is here used with peculiar propriety. It follows, "he begat us." He is the Father of all light, material or spiritual, in the kingdom of grace and of glory. With whom is no variableness – No change in his understanding. Or shadow of turning – in his will. He infallibly discerns all good and evil; and invariably loves one, and hates the other. There is, in both the Greek words, a metaphor taken from the stars, particularly proper where the Father of lights is mentioned. Both are applicable to any celestial body, which has a daily vicissitude of day and night, and sometimes longer days, sometimes longer nights. In God is nothing of this kind. He is mere light. If there is any such vicissitude, it is in ourselves, not in him.

18. Of his own will – Most loving, most free, most pure, just opposite to our evil desire, ver. 15. Begat he us – Who believe. By the word of truth – The true word, emphatically so termed; the gospel. That we might be a kind of first-fruits of his creatures – Christians are the chief and most excellent of his visible creatures; and sanctify the rest. Yet he says, A kind of – For Christ alone is absolutely the first-fruits.

19. Let every man be swift to hear – This is treated of from ver. 21 to the end of the next chapter. Slow to speak – Which is treated of in the third chapter. Slow to wrath – Neither murmuring at God, nor angry at his neighbor. This is treated of in the third, and throughout the fourth and fifth chapters.

20. The righteousness of God here includes all duties prescribed by him, and pleasing to him.

21. Therefore laying aside – As a dirty garment. All the filthiness and superfluity of wickedness – For however specious or necessary it may appear to worldly wisdom, all wickedness is both vile, hateful, contemptible, and really superfluous. Every reasonable end may be effectually answered without any kind or degree of it. Lay this, every known sin, aside, or all your hearing is vain. With meekness – Constant evenness and serenity of mind. Receive – Into your ears, your heart, your life. The word – Of the gospel. Ingrafted – In believers, by regeneration, ver. 18 and by habit, Heb. v, 14. Which is able to save your souls – The hope of salvation nourishes meekness.

23. Beholding his face in a glass – How exactly does the scripture glass show a man the face of his soul!

24. He beheld himself, and went away – To other business. And forgot – But such forgetting does not excuse.

25. But he that looketh diligently – Not with a transient glance, but bending down, fixing his eyes, and searching all to the bottom. Into the perfect law – Of love as established by faith. St. James here guards us against misunderstanding what St. Paul says concerning the "yoke and bondage of the law." He who keeps

12-18 It is not every man who suffers, that is blessed; but he who with patience and constancy goes through all difficulties in the way of duty. Afflictions cannot make us miserable, if it be not our own fault. The tried Christian shall be a crowned one. The crown of life is promised to all who have the love of God reigning in their hearts. Every soul that truly loves God, shall have its trials in this world fully recompensed in that world above, where love is made perfect. The commands of God, and the dealings of his providence, try men's hearts, and show the dispositions which prevail in them. But nothing sinful in the heart or conduct can be ascribed to God. He is not the author of the dross, though his fiery trial exposes it. Those who lay the blame of sin, either upon their constitution, or upon their condition in the world, or pretend they cannot keep from sinning, wrong God as if he were the author of sin. Afflictions, as sent by God, are designed to draw out our graces, but not our corruptions. The origin of evil and temptation is in our own hearts. Stop the beginnings of sin, or all the evils that follow must be wholly charged upon us. God has no pleasure in the death of men, as he has no hand in their sin; but both sin and misery are owing to themselves. As the sun is the same in nature and influences, though the earth and clouds, often coming between, make it seem to us to vary, so God is unchangeable, and our changes and shadows are not from any changes or alterations in him. What the sun is in nature, God is in grace, providence, and glory; and infinitely more.

19-21 Instead of blaming God under our trials, let us open our ears and hearts to learn what he teaches by them. And if men would govern their tongues, they must govern their passions. The worst thing we can bring to any dispute, is anger. Here is an exhortation to lay apart, and to cast off as a filthy garment, all sinful practices. This must reach to sins of thought and affection, as well as of speech and practice; to every thing corrupt and sinful. We must yield ourselves to the word of God, with humble and teachable minds. Being willing to hear of our faults, taking it not only patiently, but thankfully. It is the design of the word of God to make us wise to salvation; and those who propose any mean or low ends in attending upon it, dishonor the gospel, and disappoint their own souls.

22-25 If we heard a sermon every day of the week, and an angel from heaven were the preacher, yet, if we rested in hearing only, it would never bring us to heaven. Mere hearers are self-deceivers; and self-deceit will be found the worst deceit at last. If we flatter ourselves, it is our own fault; the truth, as it is in Jesus, flatters no man. Let the word of truth be carefully attended to, and it will set before us the corruption of our nature, the disorders of our hearts and lives; and it will tell us plainly what we are. Our sins are the spots the law discovers: Christ's blood is the laver the gospel shows. But in vain do we hear God's word, and look into the gospel glass, if we go away, and forget our spots, instead of washing them off; and forget our remedy, instead of applying to it. This is the case with those who do not hear the word as they ought. In hearing the word, we look into it for counsel and direction, and when we study it, it turns to our spiritual life. Those who keep in the law and word of God, are, and shall be, blessed in all their ways. His gracious recompense hereafter, would be connected with his present peace and comfort.

but that the Lord reigneth, the Lord sitteth King for ever and ever!

Notice, that these people, while they thought everything was at their disposal, used everything for worldly objects. What did they say? Did they determine with each other "We will today or tomorrow do such and such a thing for the glory of God, and for the extension of his kingdom"? Oh, no, there was not a word about God in it, from beginning to end! Therein they are only too truly the type of the bulk of men today. They said, "We will buy; then we will carry our goods to another market at a little distance; we will sell at a profit, and so we will get gain." Their first and their last thoughts were of the earth earthy, and their one idea seemed to be that they might get sufficient to make them feel that they were rich and increased in goods. That was the highest ambition upon their minds. Are there not many who are living just in that way now? They think that they can map our their own life; and the one object of their efforts seems to be to buy and sell, and get gain; or else to obtain honor, or to enjoy pleasure. Their heart rises not into the serene air of heaven; they are still groveling here below.

Having looked at the form of this folly of counting on the future, let us speak a little on the folly itself. It is a great folly to build hopes on that which may never come. It is unwise to count your chickens before they are hatched; it is madness to risk everything on the unsubstantial future.

Besides, the folly is seen in the fact of the frailty of our lives, and the brevity of them. "What is your life? It is even a vapor, that appeareth for a little time." That cloud upon the mountain—you see it as you rise in the morning; you have scarcely dressed yourself before all trace of it has gone. Here in our streets, the other night, we came to worship through a thick fog, and found it here even in the house of prayer. But while we worshiped, there came a breath of wind; and on our way home a stranger would not have thought that London had been, but a few hours before, so dark with dirty mist; it had all disappeared. Life is even as a vapor. Sometimes these vapors, especially at the time of sunset, are exceedingly bril-

yourselves, and are become judges of evil thoughts?

5   Hearken, my beloved brethren, Hath not God chosen the poor of this world rich in faith, and heirs of the kingdom which he hath promised to them that love him?

6   But ye have despised the poor. Do not rich men oppress you, and draw you before the judgment seats?

7   Do not they blaspheme that worthy name by the which ye are called?

8   If ye fulfill the royal law according to the scripture, Thou shalt love thy neighbor as thyself, ye do well:

9   But if ye have respect to persons, ye commit sin, and are convinced of the law as transgressors.

10   For whosoever shall keep the whole law, and yet offend in one point, he is guilty of all.

11   For he that said, Do not commit adultery, said also, Do not kill. Now if thou commit no adultery, yet if thou kill, thou art become a transgressor of the law.

12   So speak ye, and so do, as they that shall be judged by the law of liberty.

13   For he shall have judgment without mercy, that hath shewed no mercy; and mercy rejoiceth against judgment.

14   What doth it profit, my brethren, though a man say he hath faith, and have not works? can faith save him?

15   If a brother or sister be naked, and destitute of daily food,

16   And one of you say unto them, Depart in peace, be ye warmed and filled; notwithstanding ye give them not those things which are needful to the body; what doth it profit?

17   Even so faith, if it hath not works, is dead, being alone.

18   Yea, a man may say, Thou hast faith, and I have works: shew me thy faith without thy works, and I will shew thee my faith by my works.

19   Thou believest that there is one God; thou doest well: the devils also believe, and tremble.

20   But wilt thou know, O vain man, that faith without works is dead?

the law of love is free, John viii, 31, &c. He that does not, is not free, but a slave to sin, and a criminal before God, ver. 10. And continueth therein – Not like him who forgot it, and went away. This man – There is a peculiar force in the repetition of the word. Shall be happy – Not barely in hearing, but doing the will of God.

26. If any one be ever so religious – Exact in the outward offices of religion. And bridleth not his tongue – From backbiting, tale bearing, evil speaking, he only deceiveth his own heart, if he fancies he has any true religion at all.

27. The only true religion in the sight of God, is this, to visit – With counsel, comfort, and relief. The fatherless and widows – Those who need it most. In their affliction – In their most helpless and hopeless state. And to keep himself unspotted from the world – From the maxims, tempers, and customs of it. But this cannot be done, till we have given our hearts to God, and love our neighbor as ourselves.

JAMES 2

1. My brethren – The equality of Christians, intimated by this name, is the ground of the admonition. Hold not the faith of our common Lord, the Lord of glory – Of which glory all who believe in him partake. With respect of persons – That is, honor none merely for being rich; despise none merely for being poor.

2. With gold rings – Which were not then so common as now.

3. Ye look upon him – With respect.

4. Ye distinguish not – To which the most respect is due, to the poor or to the rich. But are become evil-reasoning judges – You reason ill, and so judge wrong: for fine apparel is no proof of worth in him that wears it.

5. Hearken – As if he had said, Stay, consider, ye that judge thus. Does not the presumption lie rather in favor of the poor man? Hath not God chosen the poor – That is, are not they whom God hath chosen, generally speaking, poor in this world? who yet are rich in faith, and heirs of the kingdom – Consequently, the most honorable of men: and those whom God so highly honors, ought not ye to honor likewise?

6. Do not the rich often oppress you – By open violence; often drag you – Under color of law.

7. Do not they blaspheme that worthy name – Of God and of Christ. The apostle speaks chiefly of rich heathens: but are Christians, so called, a whit behind them?

8. If ye fulfill the royal law – The supreme law of the great King which is love; and that to every man, poor as well as rich, ye do well. Lev. xix, 18.

9. Being convicted – By that very law. Exod. xxiii, 3.

10. Whosoever keepeth the whole law, except in one point, he is guilty of all – Is as liable to condemnation as if he had offended in every point.

11. For it is the same authority which establishes every commandment.

12. So speak and act – In all things. As they that shall be judged – Without respect of persons. By the law of liberty – The gospel; the law of universal love, which alone is perfect freedom. For their transgressions of this, both in word and deed, the wicked shall be condemned; and according to their works, done in obedience to this, the righteous will be rewarded.

13. Judgment without mercy shall be to him – In that day. Who hath showed no mercy – To his poor brethren. But the mercy of God to believers, answering to that which they have shown, will then glory over judgment.

14. From chap. i, 22, the apostle has been enforcing Christian practice. He now applies to those who neglect this, under the pretense of faith. St. Paul had taught that "a man is justified by faith without the works of the law." This some began already to wrest to their own destruction. Wherefore St. James, purposely

26,27 When men take more pains to seem religious than really to be so, it is a sign their religion is in vain. The not bridling the tongue, readiness to speak of the faults of others, or to lessen their wisdom and piety, are signs of a vain religion. The man who has a slandering tongue, cannot have a truly humble, gracious heart. False religious may be known by their impurity and uncharitableness. True religion teaches us to do every thing as in the presence of God. An unspotted life must go with unfeigned love and charity. Our true religion is equal to the measure in which these things have place in our hearts and conduct. And let us remember, that nothing avails in Christ Jesus, but faith that worketh by love, purifies the heart, subdues carnal lusts, and obeys God's commands.

JAMES 2

All professions of faith are vain, if not producing love and justice to others. (1-13)

The necessity of good works to prove the sincerity of faith, which otherwise will be of no more advantage than the faith of devils. (14-26)

1-13 Those who profess faith in Christ as the Lord of glory, must not respect persons on account of mere outward circumstances and appearances, in a manner not agreeing with their profession of being disciples of the lowly Jesus. St. James does not here encourage rudeness or disorder: civil respect must be paid; but never such as to influence the proceedings of Christians in disposing of the offices of the church of Christ, or in passing the censures of the church, or in any matter of religion. Questioning ourselves is of great use in every part of the holy life. Let us be more frequent in this, and in every thing take occasion to discourse with our souls. As places of worship cannot be built or maintained without expense, it may be proper that those who contribute thereto should be accommodated accordingly; but were all persons more spiritually minded, the poor would be treated with more attention than usually is the case in worshiping congregations. A lowly state is most favorable for inward peace and for growth in holiness. God would give to all believers riches and honors of this world, if these would do them good, seeing that he has chosen them to be rich in faith, and made them heirs of his kingdom, which he promised to bestow on all who love him. Consider how often riches lead to vice and mischief, and what great reproaches are thrown upon God and religion, by men of wealth, power, and worldly greatness; and it will make this sin appear very sinful and foolish. The Scripture gives as a law, to love our neighbor as ourselves. This law is a royal law, it comes from the King of kings; and if Christians act unjustly, they are convicted by the law as transgressors. To think that our good deeds will atone for our bad deeds, plainly puts us upon looking for another atonement. According to the covenant of works, one breach of any one command brings a man under condemnation, from which no obedience, past, present, or future, can deliver him. This shows us the happiness of those that are in Christ. We may serve him without slavish fear.

14-26 Those are wrong who put a mere notional belief of the

liant. Such is our life. It may sometimes be very bright and glorious; but still it is only like a painted cloud, and very soon the cloud and the color on it are alike gone. We cannot reckon upon the clouds, their laws are so variable, and their conditions so obscure. Such also is our life.

Why, then, is it, that we are always counting upon what we are going to do? How is it that, instead of living in the eternal future, where we might deal with certainties, we continue to live in the more immediate future, where there can be nothing but uncertainties? Why do we choose to build upon clouds, and pile our palaces on vapor, to see them melt away, as aforetime they have often melted, instead of by faith getting where there is no failure, where God is all in all, and his sure promises make the foundations of eternal mansions? Oh! I would say with my strongest emphasis: Do not reckon upon the future. Young people, I would whisper this in your ears; Do not discount the days to come. Old men, whispering is not enough for you, I would say, with a voice of thunder: Count not on distant years; in the course of nature, your days must be few. Live in the present; live unto God; trust him now, and serve him now; for very soon your life on earth will be over.

We thus see that counting on the future is folly.

II. Secondly, IGNORANCE OF THE FUTURE IS A MATTER OF FACT. Whatever we may say about what we mean to do, we do not know anything about the future. The apostle, by the Spirit, speaks truly when he says, "Ye know not what shall be on the morrow." Whether it will come to us laden with sickness or health, prosperity or adversity, we cannot tell. To-morrow may mark the end of our life; possibly even the end of the age. Our ignorance of the future is certainly a fact.

Only God knows the future. All things are present to him; there is no past and no future to his all-seeing eyes. He dwells in the present tense evermore as the great I AM. He knows what will be on the morrow, and he alone knows. The whole course of the universe lies before him, like an open map. Men do not know what a day

21 Was not Abraham our father justified by works, when he had offered Isaac his son upon the altar?

22 Seest thou how faith wrought with his works, and by works was faith made perfect?

23 And the scripture was fulfilled which saith, Abraham believed God, and it was imputed unto him for righteousness: and he was called the Friend of God.

24 Ye see then how that by works a man is justified, and not by faith only.

25 Likewise also was not Rahab the harlot justified by works, when she had received the messengers, and had sent them out another way?

26 For as the body without the spirit is dead, so faith without works is dead also.

JAMES 3

1 My brethren, be not many masters, knowing that we shall receive the greater condemnation.

2 For in many things we offend all. If any man offend not in word, the same is a perfect man, and able also to bridle the whole body.

3 Behold, we put bits in the horses' mouths, that they may obey us; and we turn about their whole body.

4 Behold also the ships, which though they be so great, and are driven of fierce winds, yet are they turned about with a very small helm, whithersoever the governor listeth.

5 Even so the tongue is a little member, and boasteth great things. Behold, how great a matter a little fire kindleth!

6 And the tongue is a fire, a world of iniquity: so is the tongue among our members, that it defileth the whole body, and setteth on fire the course of nature; and it is set on fire of hell.

7 For every kind of beasts, and of birds, and of serpents, and of things in the sea, is tamed, and hath been tamed of mankind:

8 But the tongue can no man tame; it is an unruly evil, full of deadly poison.

repeating (ver. 21, 23, 25) the same phrases, testimonies, and examples, which St. Paul had used, Rom. iv, 3, Heb. xi, 17, 31, refutes not the doctrine of St. Paul, but the error of those who abused it. There is, therefore, no contradiction between the apostles: they both delivered the truth of God, but in a different manner, as having to do with different kinds of men. On another occasion St. James himself pleaded the cause of faith, Acts xv, 13-21; and St. Paul himself strenuously pleads for works, particularly in his latter epistles. This verse is a summary of what follows. What profiteth it? is enlarged on, ver. 15-17; though a man say, ver. 18, 19; can that faith save him? ver. 20. It is not, though he have faith; but, though he say he have faith. Here, therefore, true, living faith is meant: but in other parts of the argument the apostle speaks of a dead, imaginary faith. He does not, therefore, teach that true faith can, but that it cannot, subsist without works: nor does he oppose faith to works; but that empty name of faith, to real faith working by love. Can that faith "which is without works" save him? No more than it can profit his neighbor.

17. So likewise that faith which hath not works is a mere dead, empty notion; of no more profit to him that hath it, than the bidding the naked be clothed is to him.

18. But one – Who judges better. Will say – To such a vain talker. Show me, if thou canst, thy faith without thy works.

19. Thou believest there is one God – I allow this: but this proves only that thou hast the same faith with the devils. Nay, they not only believe, but tremble – At the dreadful expectation of eternal torments. So far is that faith from either justifying or saving them that have it.

20. But art thou willing to know – Indeed thou art not: thou wouldest fain be ignorant of it. O empty man – Empty of all goodness. That the faith which is without works is dead – And so is not properly faith, as a dead carcass is not a man.

21. Was not Abraham justified by works – St. Paul says he was justified by faith, Rom. iv, 2, &c.: yet St. James does not contradict him; for he does not speak of the same justification. St. Paul speaks of that which Abraham received many years before Isaac was born, Gen. xv, 6. St. James, of that which he did not receive till he had offered up Isaac on the altar. He was justified, therefore, in St. Paul's sense, (that is, accounted righteous,) by faith, antecedent to his works. He was justified in St. James's sense, (that is, made righteous,) by works, consequent to his faith. So that St. James's justification by works is the fruit of St Paul's justification by faith.

22. Thou seest that faith – For by faith Abraham offered him, Heb. xi, 17. Wrought together with his works – Therefore faith has one energy and operation; works, another: and the energy and operation of faith are before works, and together with them. Works do not give life to faith, but faith begets works, and then is perfected by them. And by works was faith made perfect – Here St. James fixes the sense wherein he uses the word justified; so that no shadow of contradiction remains between his assertion and St. Paul's. Abraham returned from that sacrifice perfected in faith, and far higher in the favor of God. Faith hath not its being from works, (for it is before them,) but its perfection. That vigor of faith which begets works is then excited and increased thereby, as the natural heat of the body begets motion, whereby itself is then excited and increased. See 1 John iii, 22.

23. And the scripture – Which was afterwards written. Was hereby eminently fulfilled, Abraham believed God, and it was imputed to him for righteousness – This was twice fulfilled, – when Abraham first believed, and when he offered up Isaac. St. Paul speaks of the former fulfilling; St. James, of the latter. And he was called the Friend of God – Both by his posterity, 2 Chron. xx, 7; and by God himself, Isaiah xli, 8, so pleasing to God were the works be wrought in faith. Gen. xv, 6.

gospel for the whole of evangelical religion, as many now do. No doubt, true faith alone, whereby men have part in Christ's righteousness, atonement, and grace, saves their souls; but it produces holy fruits, and is shown to be real by its effect on their works; while mere assent to any form of doctrine, or mere historical belief of any facts, wholly differs from this saving faith. A bare profession may gain the good opinion of pious people; and it may procure, in some cases, worldly good things; but what profit will it be, for any to gain the whole world, and to lose their souls? Can this faith save him? All things should be accounted profitable or unprofitable to us, as they tend to forward or hinder the salvation of our souls. This place of Scripture plainly shows that an opinion, or assent to the gospel, without works, is not faith. There is no way to show we really believe in Christ, but by being diligent in good works, from gospel motives, and for gospel purposes. Men may boast to others, and be conceited of that which they really have not. There is not only to be assent in faith, but consent; not only an assent to the truth of the word, but a consent to take Christ. True believing is not an act of the understanding only, but a work of the whole heart. That a justifying faith cannot be without works, is shown from two examples, Abraham and Rahab. Abraham believed God, and it was reckoned unto him for righteousness. Faith, producing such works, advanced him to peculiar favors. We see then, ver. 24, how that by works a man is justified, not by a bare opinion or profession, or believing without obeying; but by having such faith as produces good works. And to have to deny his own reason, affections, and interests, is an action fit to try a believer. Observe here, the wonderful power of faith in changing sinners. Rahab's conduct proved her faith to be living, or having power; it showed that she believed with her heart, not merely by an assent of the understanding. Let us then take heed, for the best works, without faith, are dead; they want root and principle. By faith any thing we do is really good; as done in obedience to God, and aiming at his acceptance: the root is as though it were dead, when there is no fruit. Faith is the root, good works are the fruits; and we must see to it that we have both.

JAMES 3

Cautions against proud behavior, and the mischief of an unruly tongue. (1-12)

The excellence of heavenly wisdom, in opposition to that which is worldly. (13-18)

1-12 We are taught to dread an unruly tongue, as one of the greatest evils. The affairs of mankind are thrown into confusion by the tongues of men. Every age of the world, and every condition of life, private or public, affords examples of this. Hell has more to do in promoting the fire of the tongue than men generally think; and whenever men's tongues are employed in sinful ways, they are set on fire of hell. No man can tame the tongue without Divine grace and assistance. The apostle does not represent it as impossible, but as extremely difficult. Other sins decay with age, this many times gets worse; we grow more froward and fretful, as natural strength decays, and the days come on in which we have no pleasure. When other sins

may bring forth, but Jehovah knows the end from the beginning. There are two great certainties about things that shall come to pass—one is that God knows, and the other is that we do not know.

As the knowledge of the future is hidden from us, we ought not to pry into it. It is perilous, it is wicked, to attempt to lift even a corner of the veil that hides us from things to come. Search into the things that are revealed in Holy Scripture, and know them, as far as you can; but be not so foolish as to think that any man or woman can tell you what is to happen on the morrow; and do not think so much of your own judgment and foresight as to say, "That is clear, I can predict that." Never prophesy until after the event, and then, or course, you cannot prophesy; therefore never attempt to prophesy at all. You know not what shall be on the morrow, and you ought not to make any unhallowed attempt to obtain the knowledge. Let the doom of King Saul on Mount Gilboa warn you against such a terrible course.

Further, we are benefited by our ignorance of the future. It is hidden from us for our good. Suppose a certain man is to be very happy by-and-by. If he knows it, he will be discontented till the happy hour arrives. Suppose another man is to have great sorrow very soon. It is well that he does not know it, for now he can enjoy the present good. If we could have all our lives written in a book, with everything that was to happen to us recorded therein, and if the hand of Destiny should give us the book, we should be wise not to read it, but to put it by, and say:—

"My God, I would not long to see
My fate with curious eyes,
What gloomy lines are writ for me,
Or what bright lines arise."

It is sufficient that our heavenly Father knows; and his knowledge may well content us. Knowledge is not wisdom. His is wisest who does not wish to know what God has not revealed. Here, surely, ignorance is bliss: it would be folly to be wise.

We ought, for every reason, to be thankful that we do not know the future; but, at any rate, we can clearly see that to count on it is folly, and that ignorance of it is a matter of fact.

9 Therewith bless we God, even the Father; and therewith curse we men, which are made after the similitude of God.

10 Out of the same mouth proceedeth blessing and cursing. My brethren, these things ought not so to be.

11 Doth a fountain send forth at the same place sweet water and bitter?

12 Can the fig tree, my brethren, bear olive berries? either a vine, figs? so can no fountain both yield salt water and fresh.

13 Who is a wise man and endued with knowledge among you? let him shew out of a good conversation his works with meekness of wisdom.

14 But if ye have bitter envying and strife in your hearts, glory not, and lie not against the truth.

15 This wisdom descendeth not from above, but is earthly, sensual, devilish.

16 For where envying and strife is, there is confusion and every evil work.

17 But the wisdom that is from above is first pure, then peaceable, gentle, and easy to be intreated, full of mercy and good fruits, without partiality, and without hypocrisy.

18 And the fruit of righteousness is sown in peace of them that make peace.

JAMES 4

1 From whence come wars and fightings among you? come they not hence, even of your lusts that war in your members?

2 Ye lust, and have not: ye kill, and desire to have, and cannot obtain: ye fight and war, yet ye have not, because ye ask not.

3 Ye ask, and receive not, because ye ask amiss, that ye may consume it upon your lusts.

4 Ye adulterers and adulteresses, know ye not that the friendship of the world is enmity with God? whosoever therefore will be a friend of the world is the enemy of God.

5 Do ye think that the scripture saith in vain, The spirit that dwelleth in us lusteth to envy?

6 But he giveth more grace. Wherefore he saith, God

24. Ye see then that a man is justified by works, and not by faith only – St. Paul, on the other hand, declares, "A man is justified by faith," and not by works, Rom. iii, 28. And yet there is no contradiction between the apostles: because,

1. They do not speak of the same faith: St. Paul speaking of living faith; St. James here, of dead faith.

2. They do not speak of the same works: St. Paul speaking of works antecedent to faith; St. James, of works subsequent to it.

25. After Abraham, the father of the Jews, the apostle cites Rahab, a woman, and a sinner of the Gentiles; to show, that in every nation and sex true faith produces works, and is perfected by them; that is, by the grace of God working in the believer, while he is showing his faith by his works.

JAMES 3

1. Be not many teachers – Let no more of you take this upon you than God thrusts out; seeing it is so hard not to offend in speaking much. Knowing that we – That all who thrust themselves into the office. Shall receive greater condemnation – For more offenses. St. James here, as in several of the following verses, by a common figure of speech, includes himself: we shall receive, – we offend, – we put bits, – we curse – None of which, as common sense shows, are to be interpreted either of him or of the other apostles.

2. The same is able to bridle the whole body – That is, the whole man. And doubtless some are able to do this, and so are in this sense perfect.

3. We – That is, men.

5. Boasteth great things – Hath great influence.

6. A world of iniquity – Containing an immense quantity of all manner of wickedness. It defileth – As fire by its smoke. The whole body – The whole man. And setteth on fire the course of nature – All the passions, every wheel of his soul.

7. Every kind – The expression perhaps is not to be taken strictly. Reptiles – That is, creeping things.

8. But no man can tame the tongue – Of another; no, nor his own, without peculiar help from God.

9. Men made after the likeness of God – Indeed we have now lost this likeness; yet there remains from thence an indelible nobleness, which we ought to reverence both in ourselves and others.

13. Let him show his wisdom as well as his faith by his works; not by words only.

14. If ye have bitter zeal – True Christian zeal is only the flame of love. Even in your hearts – Though it went no farther. Do not lie against the truth – As if such zeal could consist with heavenly wisdom.

15. This wisdom – Which is consistent with such zeal. Is earthly – Not heavenly; not from the Father of Lights. Animal – Not spiritual; not from the Spirit of God. Devilish – Not the gift of Christ, but such as Satan breathes into the soul.

17. But the wisdom from above is first pure – From all that is earthly, natural, devilish. Then peaceable – True peace attending purity, it is quiet, inoffensive. Gentle – Soft, mild, yielding, not rigid. Easy to be entreated – To be persuaded, or convinced; not stubborn, sour, or morose. Full of good fruits – Both in the heart and in the life, two of which are immediately specified. Without partiality – Loving all, without respect of persons; embracing all good things, rejecting all evil. And without dissimulation – Frank, open.

18. And the principle productive of this righteousness is sown, like good seed, in the peace of a believer's mind, and brings forth a plentiful harvest of happiness, (which is the proper fruit of righteousness,) for them that make peace – That labor to promote this pure and holy peace among all men.

are tamed and subdued by the infirmities of age, the spirit often grows more tart, nature being drawn down to the dregs, and the words used become more passionate. That man's tongue confutes itself, which at one time pretends to adore the perfections of God, and to refer all things to him; and at another time condemns even good men, if they do not use the same words and expressions. True religion will not admit of contradictions: how many sins would be prevented, if men would always be consistent!

13-18 These verses show the difference between men's pretending to be wise, and their being really so. He who thinks well, or he who talks well, is not wise in the sense of the Scripture, if he does not live and act well. True wisdom may be known by the meekness of the spirit and temper. Those who live in malice, envy, and contention, live in confusion; and are liable to be provoked and hurried to any evil work. Such wisdom comes not down from above, but springs up from earthly principles, acts on earthly motives, and is intent on serving earthly purposes. Those who are lifted up with such wisdom, described by the apostle James, is near to the Christian love, described by the apostle Paul; and both are so described that every man may fully prove the reality of his attainments in them. It has no disguise or deceit. It cannot fall in with those managements the world counts wise, which are crafty and guileful; but it is sincere, and open, and steady, and uniform, and consistent with itself. May the purity, peace, gentleness, teachableness, and mercy shown in all our actions, and the fruits of righteousness abounding in our lives, prove that God has bestowed upon us this excellent gift.

JAMES 4

Here are cautions against corrupt affections, and love of this world, which is enmity to God. (1-10)
Exhortations to undertake no affairs of life, without constant regard to the will and providence of God. (11-17)

1-10 Since all wars and fightings come from the corruptions of our own hearts, it is right to mortify those lusts that war in the members. Worldly and fleshly lusts are distempers, which will not allow content or satisfaction. Sinful desires and affections stop prayer, and the working of our desires toward God. And let us beware that we do not abuse or misuse the mercies received, by the disposition of the heart when prayers are granted. When men ask of God prosperity, they often ask with wrong aims and intentions. If we thus seek the things of this world, it is just in God to deny them. Unbelieving and cold desires beg denials; and we may be sure that when prayers are rather the language of lusts than of graces, they will return empty. Here is a decided warning to avoid all criminal friendships with this world. Worldly-mindedness is enmity to God. An enemy may be reconciled, but "enmity" never can be reconciled. A man may have a large portion in things of this life, and yet be kept in the love of God; but he who sets his heart upon the world, who will conform to it rather than lose its friendship, is an enemy to God. So that any one who resolves at all events to be upon friendly terms with the world, must be

III. Thirdly, RECOGNITION OF GOD WITH REGARD TO THE FUTURE IS TRUE WISDOM. What says our text? "For that ye ought to say, if the Lord will, we shall live, and do this, or that." I do not think that we need always, in every letter and in every handbill, put "If the Lord will"; yet I wish that we oftener used those very words. The fashionable way is to put it in Latin, and even then to abbreviate it, and use only the consonants, "D.V.," to express it. You know, it is a fine thing when you can put your religion into Latin, and make it very short. Then nobody knows what you mean by it; or, if they do, they can praise your scholarship, and admire your humility. I do not care about those letters "D.V." I rather like what Fuller says when he describes himself as writing in the letter such passages as "God willing," or "God lending me life." He says, "I observe, Lord, that I can scarcely hold my hand from encircling these words in parenthesis, as if they were not essential to the sentence, but may as well be left out as put in. Whereas, indeed, they are not only of the commission at large, but so of the quorum, that without them all the rest is nothing; wherefore hereafter, I will write these words freely and fairly, without any enclosure about them. Let critics censure it for bad grammar, I am sure it is good divinity." So he quaintly puts the matter. Still, whether you write, "If the Lord will," or not, always let it be clearly understood; and let it be conspicuous in all your arrangements that you recognize that God is over all, and that you are under his control. When you say, "I will do this or that," always add, in thought if not in word, "If the Lord will." No harm can come to you if you bow to God's sovereign sway.

We should recognize God in the affairs of the future, because, first, there is a divine will which governs all things. I believe that nothing happens apart from divine determination and decree; even the little things in life are not overlooked by the all-seeing eye. "The very hairs of your head are numbered." The station of a rush by the river is as fixed and foreknown as the station of a king, and the chaff from the hand of the winnower is steered as much as the stars in their courses. All things are under regulation, and have

resisteth the proud, but giveth grace unto the humble.

7 Submit yourselves therefore to God. Resist the devil, and he will flee from you.

8 Draw nigh to God, and he will draw nigh to you. Cleanse your hands, ye sinners; and purify your hearts, ye double minded.

9 Be afflicted, and mourn, and weep: let your laughter be turned to mourning, and your joy to heaviness.

10 Humble yourselves in the sight of the Lord, and he shall lift you up.

11 Speak not evil one of another, brethren. He that speaketh evil of his brother, and judgeth his brother, speaketh evil of the law, and judgeth the law: but if thou judge the law, thou art not a doer of the law, but a judge.

12 There is one lawgiver, who is able to save and to destroy: who art thou that judgest another?

13 Go to now, ye that say, To day or to morrow we will go into such a city, and continue there a year, and buy and sell, and get gain:

14 Whereas ye know not what shall be on the morrow. For what is your life? It is even a vapor, that appeareth for a little time, and then vanisheth away.

15 For that ye ought to say, If the Lord will, we shall live, and do this, or that.

16 But now ye rejoice in your boastings: all such rejoicing is evil.

17 Therefore to him that knoweth to do good, and doeth it not, to him it is sin.

JAMES 5

1 Go to now, ye rich men, weep and howl for your miseries that shall come upon you.

2 Your riches are corrupted, and your garments are motheaten.

3 Your gold and silver is cankered; and the rust of them shall be a witness against you, and shall eat your flesh as it were fire. Ye have heaped treasure together for the last days.

4 Behold, the hire of the laborers who have reaped down your fields, which is of you kept back by fraud, crieth: and the cries of them which have reaped are

JAMES 4

1. From whence come wars and fightings – Quarrels and wars among you, quite opposite to this peace? Is it not from your pleasures – Your desires of earthly pleasures. Which war – Against your souls. In your members – Here is the first seat of the war. Hence proceeds the war of man with man, king with king, nation with nation.

2. Ye kill – In your heart, for "he that hateth his brother is a murderer." Ye fight and war – That is, furiously strive and contend. Ye ask not – And no marvel; for a man full of evil desire, of envy or hatred, cannot pray.

3. But if ye do ask, ye receive not, because ye ask amiss – That is, from a wrong motive.

4. Ye adulterers and adulteresses – Who have broken your faith with God, your rightful spouse. Know ye not that the friendship or love of the world – The desire of the flesh, the desire of the eye, and the pride of life, or courting the favor of worldly men, is enmity against God? Whosoever desireth to be a friend of the world – Whosoever seeks either the happiness or favor of it, does thereby constitute himself an enemy of God; and can he expect to obtain anything of him?

5. Do you think that the scripture saith in vain – Without good ground. St. James seems to refer to many, not any one particular scripture. The spirit of love that dwelleth in all believers lusteth against envy – Gal. v, 17; is directly opposite to all those unloving tempers which necessarily flow from the friendship of the world.

6. But he giveth greater grace – To all who shun those tempers. Therefore it – The scripture. Saith, God resisteth the proud – And pride is the great root of all unkind affections. Prov. iii, 34.

7. Therefore by humbly submitting yourselves to God, resist the devil – The father of pride and envy.

8. Then draw nigh to God in prayer, and he will draw nigh unto you, will hear you; which that nothing may hinder, cleanse your hands – Cease from doing evil. And purify your hearts – From all spiritual adultery. Be no more double minded, vainly endeavoring to serve both God and mammon.

9. Be afflicted – For your past unfaithfulness to God.

11. Speak not evil one of another – This is a grand hindrance of peace. O who is sufficiently aware of it! He that speaketh evil of another does in effect speak evil of the law, which so strongly prohibits it. Thou art not a doer of the law, but a judge – Of it; thou settest thyself above, and as it were condemnest, it.

12. There is one lawgiver that is able – To execute the sentence he denounces. But who art thou – A poor, weak, dying worm.

13. Come now, ye that say – As peremptorily as if your life were in your own hands.

15. Instead of your saying – That is, whereas ye ought to say.

17. Therefore to him that knoweth to do good and doeth it not – That knows what is right, and does not practice it. To him it is sin – This knowledge does not prevent, but increase, his condemnation.

the enemy of God. Did then the Jews, or the loose professors of Christianity, think the Scripture spake in vain against this worldly-mindedness? or does the Holy Spirit who dwells in all Christians, or the new nature which he creates, produce such fruit? Natural corruption shows itself by envying. The spirit of the world teaches us to lay up, or lay out for ourselves, according to our own fancies; God the Holy Spirit teaches us to be willing to do good to all about us, as we are able. The grace of God will correct and cure the spirit by nature in us; and where he gives grace, he gives another spirit than that of the world. The proud resist God: in their understanding they resist the truths of God; in their will they resist the laws of God; in their passions they resist the providence of God; therefore, no wonder that God resists the proud. Submit your understanding to the truth of God; submit your wills to the will of his precept, the will of his providence. Submit yourselves to God, for he is ready to do you good. If we yield to temptations, the devil will continually follow us; but if we put on the whole Armor of God, and stand out against him, he will leave us. Let sinners then submit to God, and seek his grace and favor; resisting the devil. All sin must be wept over; here, in godly sorrow, or, hereafter, in eternal misery. And the Lord will not refuse to comfort one who really mourns for sin, or to exalt one who humbles himself before him.

11-17 Our lips must be governed by the law of kindness, as well as truth and justice. Christians are brethren. And to break God's commands, is to speak evil of them, and to judge them, as if they laid too great a restraint upon us. We have the law of God, which is a rule to all; let us not presume to set up our own notions and opinions as a rule to those about us, and let us be careful that we be not condemned of the Lord. "Go to now," is a call to any one to consider his conduct as being wrong. How apt worldly and contriving men are to leave God out of their plans! How vain it is to look for any thing good without God's blessing and guidance! The frailty, shortness, and uncertainty of life, ought to check the vanity and presumptuous confidence of all projects for futurity. We can fix the hour and minute of the sun's rising and setting tomorrow, but we cannot fix the certain time of a vapor being scattered. So short, unreal, and fading is human life, and all the prosperity or enjoyment that attends it; though bliss or woe forever must be according to our conduct during this fleeting moment. We are always to depend on the will of God. Our times are not in our own hands, but at the disposal of God. Our heads may be filled with cares and contrivances for ourselves, or our families, or our friends; but Providence often throws our plans into confusion. All we design, and all we do, should be with submissive dependence on God. It is foolish, and it is hurtful, to boast of worldly things and aspiring projects; it will bring great disappointment, and will prove destruction in the end. Omissions are sins which will be brought into judgment, as well as commissions. He that does not the good he knows should be done, as well as he who does the evil he knows should not be done, will be condemned.

an appointed place in God's plan; and nothings happens, after all, but what he permits or ordains. Knowing that, we will not always say, "If the Lord will;" yet we will always feel it. Whatever our purposes may be, there is a higher power which we must ever acknowledge; and there is an omnipotent purpose, before which we must bow in lowliest reverence, saying, "If the Lord will."

May this be your resolve, then; let this clause, "if the Lord will," be written across your life, and let us all set ourselves to the recognition of God in the future. It is a grand thing to be able to say, "Wherever I go, and whatever happens to me, I belong to God; and I can say that God will prepare my way as well when I am old and gray-headed as he did when I was a boy. He shall guide me all the way to my everlasting mansion in glory; he was the guide of my youth, he shall be the guide of my old age. I will leave everything to him, all the way from earth to heaven; and I will be content to live only a day at a time; and my happy song shall be—

"So for tomorrow and its need
I do not pray,
But keep me, guide me, hold me, Lord,
Just for today."

IV. And now, fourthly, BOASTINGS ABOUT THE FUTURE ARE EVIL. "But now ye rejoice in your boastings: all such rejoicing is evil." I will not say much upon this point, but briefly ask you to notice the various ways in which men boast about the future.

One man says, about a certain matter, "I will do it, I have made up my mind," and he thinks, "You cannot turn me. I am a man who, when he has once put his foot down, is not to be shifted from his place." Then he laughs, and prides himself upon the strength of his will; but his boasting is sheer arrogance. Yet he rejoices in it, and the Word of God is true of such a one: "All such rejoicing is evil."

Another man says, "I shall do it, the thing is certain;" and when a difficulty is suggested, he answers, "Tut, do not tell me about my proposing and God's disposing; I will propose, and I will also dispose; I do not see any difficulty. I shall carry it out, I tell you. I shall suc-

entered into the ears of the Lord of sabaoth.

5 Ye have lived in pleasure on the earth, and been wanton; ye have nourished your hearts, as in a day of slaughter.

6 Ye have condemned and killed the just; and he doth not resist you.

7 Be patient therefore, brethren, unto the coming of the Lord. Behold, the husbandman waiteth for the precious fruit of the earth, and hath long patience for it, until he receive the early and latter rain.

8 Be ye also patient; stablish your hearts: for the coming of the Lord draweth nigh.

9 Grudge not one against another, brethren, lest ye be condemned: behold, the judge standeth before the door.

10 Take, my brethren, the prophets, who have spoken in the name of the Lord, for an example of suffering affliction, and of patience.

11 Behold, we count them happy which endure. Ye have heard of the patience of Job, and have seen the end of the Lord; that the Lord is very pitiful, and of tender mercy.

12 But above all things, my brethren, swear not, neither by heaven, neither by the earth, neither by any other oath: but let your yea be yea; and your nay, nay; lest ye fall into condemnation.

13 Is any among you afflicted? let him pray. Is any merry? let him sing psalms.

14 Is any sick among you? let him call for the elders of the church; and let them pray over him, anointing him with oil in the name of the Lord:

15 And the prayer of faith shall save the sick, and the Lord shall raise him up; and if he have committed sins, they shall be forgiven him.

16 Confess your faults one to another, and pray one for another, that ye may be healed. The effectual fervent prayer of a righteous man availeth much.

17 Elias was a man subject to like passions as we are, and he prayed earnestly that it might not rain: and it rained not on the earth by the space of three

JAMES 5

1. Come now, ye rich – The apostle does not speak this so much for the sake of the rich themselves, as of the poor children of God, who were then groaning under their cruel oppression. Weep and howl for your miseries which are coming upon you – Quickly and unexpectedly. This was written not long before the siege of Jerusalem; during which, as well as after it, huge calamities came on the Jewish nation, not only in Judea, but through distant countries. And as these were an awful prelude of that wrath which was to fall upon them in the world to come, so this may likewise refer to the final vengeance which will then be executed on the impenitent.

2. The riches of the ancients consisted much in large stores of corn, and of costly apparel.

3. The canker of them – Your perishing stores and moth-eaten garments. Will be a testimony against you – Of your having buried those talents in the earth, instead of improving them according to your Lord's will. And will eat your flesh as fire – Will occasion you as great torment as if fire were consuming your flesh. Ye have laid up treasure in the last days – When it is too late; when you have no time to enjoy them.

4. The hire of your laborers crieth – Those sins chiefly cry to God concerning which human laws are silent. Such are luxury, unchastity, and various kinds of injustice. The laborers themselves also cry to God, who is just coming to avenge their cause. Of sabaoth – Of hosts, or armies.

5. Ye have cherished your hearts – Have indulged yourselves to the uttermost. As in a day of sacrifice – Which were solemn feast-days among the Jews.

6. Ye have killed the just – Many just men; in particular, "that Just One," Acts iii, 14. They afterwards killed James, surnamed the Just, the writer of this epistle. He doth not resist you – And therefore you are secure. But the Lord cometh quickly, ver. 8.

7. The husbandman waiteth for the precious fruit – Which will recompense his labor and patience. Till he receives the former rain – Immediately after sowing. And the latter – Before the harvest.

8. Stablish your hearts – In faith and patience. For the coming of the Lord – To destroy Jerusalem. Is nigh – And so is his last coming to the eye of a believer.

9. Murmur not one against another – Have patience also with each other. The judge standeth before the door – Hearing every word, marking every thought.

10. Take the prophets for an example – Once persecuted like you, even for speaking in the name of the Lord. The very men that gloried in having prophets yet could not bear their message: nor did either their holiness or their high commission screen them from suffering.

11. We count them happy that endured – That suffered patiently. The more they once suffered, the greater is their present happiness. Ye have seen the end of the Lord – The end which the Lord gave him.

12. Swear not – However provoked. The Jews were notoriously guilty of common swearing, though not so much by God himself as by some of his creatures. The apostle here particularly forbids these oaths, as well as all swearing in common conversation. It is very observable, how solemnly the apostle introduces this command: above all things, swear not – As if he had said, Whatever you forget, do not forget this. This abundantly demonstrates the horrible iniquity of the crime. But he does not forbid the taking a solemn oath before a magistrate. Let your yea be yea; and your nay, nay – Use no higher asseverations in common discourse; and let your word stand firm. Whatever ye say, take care to make it good.

14. Having anointed him with oil – This single conspicuous gift, which Christ committed to his apostles, Mark vi, 13, remained in the church long after the other miraculous gifts were withdrawn. Indeed, it seems to have been designed to remain always; and St. James directs the elders, who were the most, if not the

JAMES 5

The judgments of God denounced against rich unbelievers.
(1-6)

Exhortation to patience and meekness under tribulations.
(7-11)

Cautions against rash swearing. Prayer recommended in afflic-
tive and prosperous circumstances. Christians to confess
their faults to each other. (12-18)

The happiness of being the means of the conversion of a sinner.
(19,20)

1-6 Public troubles are most grievous to those who live in
pleasure, and are secure and sensual, though all ranks suffer
deeply at such times. All idolized treasures will soon perish,
except as they will rise up in judgment against their possessors. Take heed of defrauding and oppressing; and avoid the
very appearance of it. God does not forbid us to use lawful
pleasures; but to live in pleasure, especially sinful pleasure, is
a provoking sin. Is it no harm for people to unfit themselves for
minding the concerns of their souls, by indulging bodily
appetites? The just may be condemned and killed; but when
such suffer by oppressors, this is marked by God. Above all
their other crimes, the Jews had condemned and crucified
that Just One who had come among them, even Jesus Christ
the righteous.

7-11 Consider him that waits for a crop of corn; and will not
you wait for a crown of glory? If you should be called to wait
longer than the husbandman, is not there something more
worth waiting for? In every sense the coming of the Lord drew
nigh, and all his people's losses, hardships, and sufferings,
would be repaid. Men count time long, because they measure
it by their own lives; but all time is as nothing to God; it is as a
moment. To short-lived creatures a few years seem an age;
but Scripture, measuring all things by the existence of God,
reckons thousands of years but so many days. God brought
about things in Job's case, so as plainly to prove that he is very
pitiful and of tender mercy. This did not appear during his
troubles, but was seen in the event, and believers now will find
a happy end to their trials. Let us serve our God, and bear our
trials, as those who believe that the end will crown all. Our
eternal happiness is safe if we trust to him: all else is mere
vanity, which soon will be done with forever.

12-18 The sin of swearing is condemned; but how many
make light of common profane swearing! Such swearing
expressly throws contempt upon God's name and authority.
This sin brings neither gain, nor pleasure, nor reputation, but
is showing enmity to God without occasion and without
advantage. It shows a man to be an enemy to God, however
he pretends to call himself by his name, or sometimes joins in
acts of worship. But the Lord will not hold him guiltless that
taketh his name in vain. In a day of affliction nothing is more
seasonable than prayer. The spirit is then most humble, and
the heart is broken and tender. It is necessary to exercise faith
and hope under afflictions; and prayer is the appointed means
for obtaining and increasing these graces. Observe, that the
saving of the sick is not ascribed to the anointing with oil, but
to prayer. In a time of sickness it is not cold and formal prayer

ceed." Then he laughs in his foolish
pride, and rejoices in his proud folly. All
such rejoicings are evil. They are foolish; but, what is worse, they are wicked.
Do I address myself to any who have no
notion about heaven or the world to
come, but who feel that they are perfect masters of this world, and, therefore talk in the manner I have
indicated, and rejoice as they think
how great they are? To such I will
earnestly say, "All such rejoicing is evil."

I heard a third man say, "I can do it.
I feel quite competent." To him the
message is the same, his boasting is
evil. Though he thinks of himself,
"Whatever comes in my way, I am
always ready for it," he is greatly mistaken, and errs grievously. I have often
been in the company of a gentleman of
this sort, but only for a very little while;
for I have generally got away from him
as soon as I could. He knows a thing or
two. He has got the great secret that so
many are seeking in vain. All of you
ordinary people, he just snuffs you out.
If you had more sense, and could do as
he does—well, then, you could be as
well off as he is. Poor man! "Nobody
needs to be poor," says he. "Nobody
needs to be poor. I was poor a little
while; but I made up my mind that I
would not remain poor. I fought my
own way, and I could begin again with
a crust, and work myself up." You will
notice his frequent use of the capital I,
but ah, dear sir, God has thunder-bolts
for these great I's! They offend him;
they are a smoke in his nostrils. Pride is
one of the things which his soul hates.
No man should speak in such a strain:
"All such rejoicing is evil."

V. That brings me to my last and most
practical point, which is this: THE USING
OF THE PRESENT IS OUR DUTY.
"Therefore to him that knoweth good,
and doeth it not, to him it is sin." I take
this text with its context. It means that
he who knows what he ought to do,
and does not do it at once, to him it is
sin. The text does not refer to men who
live in guilty knowledge of duty, and
neglect it; its message is to men who
know the present duty, and who think
that they will do it by-and-by.

It is sinful to defer obedience to the
gospel. "He that knoweth to do good,
and doeth it not, to him it is sin." Do

years and six months.

18 And he prayed again, and the heaven gave rain, and the earth brought forth her fruit.

19 Brethren, if any of you do err from the truth, and one convert him;

20 Let him know, that he which converteth the sinner from the error of his way shall save a soul from death, and shall hide a multitude of sins.

only, gifted men, to administer it. This was the whole process of physic in the Christian church, till it was lost through unbelief. That novel invention among the Romanists, extreme unction, practiced not for cure, but where life is despaired of, bears no manner of resemblance to this.

15. And the prayer offered in faith shall save the sick – From his sickness; and if any sin be the occasion of his sickness, it shall be forgiven him.

16. Confess your faults – Whether ye are sick or in health. To one another – He does not say, to the elders: this may, or may not, be done; for it is nowhere commanded. We may confess them to any who can pray in faith: he will then know how to pray for us, and be more stirred up so to do. And pray one for another, that ye may be healed – Of all your spiritual diseases.

17. Elijah was a man of like passions – Naturally as weak and sinful as we are. And he prayed – When idolatry covered the land.

18. He prayed again – When idolatry was abolished.

19. As if he had said, I have now warned you of those sins to which you are most liable; and, in all these respects, watch not only over yourselves, but every one over his brother also. Labor, in particular, to recover those that are fallen. If any one err from the truth – Practically, by sin.

20. He shall save a soul – Of how much more value than the body! ver. 14. And hide a multitude of sins – Which shall no more, how many soever they are, be remembered to his condemnation.

that is effectual, but the prayer of faith.

The great thing we should beg of God for ourselves and others in the time of sickness is, the pardon of sin. Let nothing be done to encourage any to delay, under the mistaken fancy that a confession, a prayer, a minister's absolution and exhortation, or the sacrament, will set all right at last, where the duties of a godly life have been disregarded. To acknowledge our faults to each other, will tend greatly to peace and brotherly love. And when a righteous person, a true believer, justified in Christ, and by his grace walking before God in holy obedience, presents an effectual fervent prayer, wrought in his heart by the power of the Holy Spirit, raising holy affections and believing expectations and so leading earnestly to plead the promises of God at his mercy seat, it avails much. The power of prayer is proved from the history of Elijah. In prayer we must not look to the merit of man, but to the grace of God. It is not enough to say a prayer, but we must pray in prayer. Thoughts must be fixed, desires must be firm and ardent, and graces exercised. This instance of the power of prayer, encourages every Christian to be earnest in prayer. God never says to any of the seed of Jacob, Seek my face in vain. Where there may not be so much of miracle in God's answering our prayers, yet there may be as much of grace.

19,20 It is no mark of a wise or holy man, to boast of being free from error, or to refuse to acknowledge an error. And there is some doctrinal mistake at the bottom of every practical mistake. There is no one habitually bad, but upon some bad principle. This is conversion; to turn a sinner from the error of his ways, not merely from one party to another, or from one notion and way of thinking to another. There is no way effectually and finally to hide sin, but forsaking it. Many sins are hindered in the party converted; many also may be so in others whom he may influence. The salvation of one soul is of infinitely greater importance than preserving the lives of multitudes, or promoting the welfare of a whole people. Let us in our several stations keep these things in mind, sparing no pains in God's service, and the event will prove that our labor is not in vain in the Lord. For six thousand years he has been multiplying pardons, and yet his free grace is not tired nor grown weary. Certainly Divine mercy is an ocean that is ever full and ever flowing. May the Lord give us a part in this abundant mercy, through the blood of Christ, and the sanctification of the Spirit.

you say, "I am going to repent"? Your duty is to repent now. "I am going to believe," do you say? The command of Christ is, "Believe now." "After I have believed," says one, "I shall wait a long time before I make any profession." Another says, "I am a believer, and I shall be baptized some day." But as baptism is according to the will of the Lord, you have no more right to postpone it than you have to postpone being honest or sober. All the commands of God to the characters to whom they are given come as a present demand. Obey them now. And if anyone here, knowing that God bids him to believe, refuses to believe, but says that he hopes to trust Christ one of these days, Let me read him this: "To him that knoweth to do good, and doeth it not,"—this word is in the present tense,—"to him it is sin."

I am conscious of having spoken but very feebly and imperfectly; but, you know, my heart is heavy because of this sore trial which has come upon us through the stroke that has fallen on our beloved deacon, William Olney; and when the heart is so sad, the brain cannot be very lively. May God bless this word, for Jesus' sake! Amen.

1 Peter

2 Peter

1 PETER 1

1 Peter, an apostle of Jesus Christ, to the strangers scattered throughout Pontus, Galatia, Cappadocia, Asia, and Bithynia,

2 Elect according to the foreknowledge of God the Father, through sanctification of the Spirit, unto obedience and sprinkling of the blood of Jesus Christ: Grace unto you, and peace, be multiplied.

3 Blessed be the God and Father of our Lord Jesus Christ, which according to his abundant mercy hath begotten us again unto a lively hope by the resurrection of Jesus Christ from the dead,

4 To an inheritance incorruptible, and undefiled, and that fadeth not away, reserved in heaven for you,

5 Who are kept by the power of God through faith unto salvation ready to be revealed in the last time.

6 Wherein ye greatly rejoice, though now for a season, if need be, ye are in heaviness through manifold temptations:

7 That the trial of your faith, being much more precious than of gold that perisheth, though it be tried with fire, might be found unto praise and honor and glory at the appearing of Jesus Christ:

8 Whom having not seen, ye love; in whom, though now ye see him not, yet believing, ye rejoice with joy unspeakable and full of glory:

9 Receiving the end of your faith, even the salvation of your souls.

10 Of which salvation the prophets have inquired and searched diligently, who prophesied of the grace that should come unto you:

11 Searching what, or what manner of time the Spirit of Christ which was in them did signify, when it testified beforehand the sufferings of Christ, and the glory that should follow.

12 Unto whom it was revealed, that not unto themselves, but unto us they did minister the things, which are now reported unto you by them that have preached the gospel unto you

THERE is a wonderful weightiness, and yet liveliness and sweetness, in the epistles of St. Peter. His design in both is, to stir up the minds of those to whom he writes, by way of remembrance, 2 Pet. iii, 1, and to guard them, not only against error, but also against doubting, chap. v, 12. This he does by reminding them of that glorious grace which God had vouchsafed them through the gospel, by which believers are inflamed to bring forth the fruits of faith, hope, love, and patience.

1 PETER 1

1. To the sojourners – Upon earth, the Christians, chiefly those of Jewish extraction. Scattered – Long ago driven out of their own land. Those scattered by the persecution mentioned Acts viii, 1, were scattered only through Judea and Samaria, though afterwards some of them traveled to Phenice, Cyprus, and Antioch. Through Pontus, Galatia, Cappadocia, Asia, and Bithynia – He names these five provinces in the order wherein they occurred to him, writing from the east. All these countries lie in the Lesser Asia. The Asia here distinguished from the other provinces is that which was usually called the Proconsular Asia being a Roman province.

2. According to the foreknowledge of God – Speaking after the manner of men. Strictly speaking, there is no foreknowledge, no more than afterknowledge, with God: but all things are known to him as present from eternity to eternity. This is therefore no other than an instance of the divine condescension to our low capacities. Elect – By the free love and almighty power of God taken out of, separated from, the world. Election, in the scripture sense, is God's doing anything that our merit or power have no part in. The true predestination, or foreappointment of God is,

   1. He that believeth shall be saved from the guilt and power of sin.

   2. He that endureth to the end shall be saved eternally.

   3. They who receive the precious gift of faith, thereby become the sons of God; and, being sons, they shall receive the Spirit of holiness to walk as Christ also walked.

Throughout every part of this appointment of God, promise and duty go hand in hand. All is free gift; and yet such is the gift, that the final issue depends on our future obedience to the heavenly call. But other predestination than this, either to life or death eternal, the scripture knows not of. Moreover, it is,

   1. Cruel respect of persons; an unjust regard of one, and an unjust disregard of another. It is mere creature partiality, and not infinite justice.

   2. It is not plain scripture doctrine, if true; but rather, inconsistent with the express written word, that speaks of God's universal offers of grace; his invitations, promises, threatenings, being all general.

   3. We are bid to choose life, and reprehended for not doing it.

   4. It is inconsistent with a state of probation in those that must be saved or must be lost.

   5. It is of fatal consequence; all men being ready, on very slight grounds, to fancy themselves of the elect number.

3. Blessed be the God and Father of our Lord Jesus Christ – His Father, with respect to his divine nature; his God, with respect to his human. Who hath regenerated us to a living hope – An hope which implies true spiritual life, which revives the heart, and makes the soul lively and vigorous. By the resurrection of Christ – Which is not only a pledge of ours, but a part of the purchase price. It has also a close connection with our rising from spiritual death, that as he liveth, so shall we live with him. He was acknowledged to be the Christ, but usually called Jesus till his resurrection; then he was also called Christ.

MATTHEW HENRY

The same great doctrines, as in St. Paul's epistles, are here applied to the same practical purposes. And this epistle is remarkable for the sweetness, gentleness, and humble love, with which it is written. It gives a short, and yet a very clear summary, both of the consolations and the instructions needful for the encouragement and direction of a Christian in his journey to heaven, raising his thoughts and desires to that happiness, and strengthening him against all opposition in the way, both from corruption within, and temptations and afflictions without.

1 PETER 1

The apostle blesses God for his special benefits through Christ.
(1-9)
Salvation by Christ foretold in ancient prophecy. (10-12)
All are exhorted to holy conversation. (13-16)
Such as is suitable to their principles, privileges, and obligations. (17-25)

1-9 This epistle is addressed to believers in general, who are strangers in every city or country where they live, and are scattered through the nations. These are to ascribe their salvation to the electing love of the Father, the redemption of the Son, and the sanctification of the Holy Ghost; and so to give glory to one God in three Persons, into whose name they had been baptized. Hope, in the world's phrase, refers only to an uncertain good, for all worldly hopes are tottering, built upon sand, and the worldling's hopes of heaven are blind and groundless conjectures. But the hope of the sons of the living God is a living hope; not only as to its object, but as to its effect also. It enlivens and comforts in all distresses, enables to meet and get over all difficulties. Mercy is the spring of all this; yea, great mercy and manifold mercy. And this well-grounded hope of salvation, is an active and living principle of obedience in the soul of the believer. The matter of a Christian's joy, is the remembrance of the happiness laid up for him. It is incorruptible, it cannot come to nothing, it is an estate that cannot be spent. Also undefiled; this signifies its purity and perfection. And it fadeth not; is not sometimes more or less pleasant, but ever the same, still like itself. All possessions here are stained with defects and failings; still something is wanting: fair houses have sad cares flying about the gilded and ceiled roofs; soft beds and full tables, are often with sick bodies and uneasy stomachs. All possessions are stained with sin, either in getting or in using them. How ready we are to turn the things we possess into occasions and instruments of sin, and to think there is no liberty or delight in their use, without abusing them! Worldly possessions are uncertain and soon pass away, like the flowers and plants of the field. That must be of the greatest worth, which is laid up in the highest and best place, in heaven. Happy are those whose hearts the Holy Spirit sets on this inheritance. God not only gives his people grace, but preserves them unto glory.

10-12 Jesus Christ was the main subject of the prophets' studies. Their inquiry into the sufferings of Christ and the glories that should follow, would lead to a view of the whole gospel, the sum whereof is, That Christ Jesus was delivered

CHARLES H. SPURGEON

THE NEW NATURE
Sermon number 398 delivered on Sunday Morning, June the 30th, 1861 at the Metropolitan Tabernacle, Newington.

"Being born again, not of corruptible seed, but of incorruptible, by the word of God, which liveth and abideth for over. For all flesh is as grass, and all the glory of man as the flower of grass. The grass withereth, and the flower thereof falleth away: but the word of the Lord endureth for ever. And this is the word which by the gospel is preached unto you."—1 Peter 1:23-25.

In the text there are three points which, I think, will well repay our very serious attention. The apostle brings out, first of all, a comparison and a contrast between the two births, for each life hath its own birth. Then he brings out a contrast between the manifest existence of the two lives; and then lastly, between the glory of the two lives, for each life hath its glory, but the glory of the spiritual life far excelleth the glory of the natural.

I. First, then, the apostle Peter draws A COMPARISON AND CONTRAST BETWEEN THE TWO BIRTHS WHICH ARE THE DOORWAYS OF THE TWO LIVES.

First, we have said that every life is prefaced by its birth. It is so naturally— we are born; it is so spiritually—we are born again. Except a man be born he cannot enter into the kingdom of nature; except a man be born again he cannot enter into the kingdom of heaven. Birth is the lowly gateway by which we enter into life, and the lofty portal by which we are admitted into the kingdom of heaven.

Now there is a comparison between the two births; in both there is a solemn mystery. I have read, I have even heard sermons, in which the minister seemed to me rather to play the part of a physician than of a divine, exposing and explaining the mysteries of our natural birth, across which both God in nature and the good man in delicacy must ever throw a veil. It is a hallowed thing to be born, as surely as it is a solemnity to die. Birthdays and deathdays are days of awe. Birth is very frequently used in Scripture as one of the most graphic pic-

with the Holy Ghost sent down from heaven; which things the angels desire to look into.

13 Wherefore gird up the loins of your mind, be sober, and hope to the end for the grace that is to be brought unto you at the revelation of Jesus Christ;

14 As obedient children, not fashioning yourselves according to the former lusts in your ignorance:

15 But as he which hath called you is holy, so be ye holy in all manner of conversation;

16 Because it is written, Be ye holy; for I am holy.

17 And if ye call on the Father, who without respect of persons judgeth according to every man's work, pass the time of your sojourning here in fear:

18 Forasmuch as ye know that ye were not redeemed with corruptible things, as silver and gold, from your vain conversation received by tradition from your fathers;

19 But with the precious blood of Christ, as of a lamb without blemish and without spot:

20 Who verily was foreordained before the foundation of the world, but was manifest in these last times for you,

21 Who by him do believe in God, that raised him up from the dead, and gave him glory; that your faith and hope might be in God.

22 Seeing ye have purified your souls in obeying the truth through the Spirit unto unfeigned love of the brethren, see that ye love one another with a pure heart fervently:

23 Being born again, not of corruptible seed, but of incorruptible, by the word of God, which liveth and abideth for ever.

24 For all flesh is as grass, and all the glory of man as the flower of grass. The grass withereth, and the flower thereof falleth away:

25 But the word of the Lord endureth for ever. And this is the word which by the gospel is preached unto you.

1 PETER 2

1 Wherefore laying aside all malice, and all guile, and

4. To an inheritance – For if we are sons, then heirs. Incorruptible – Not like earthly treasures. Undefiled – Pure and holy, incapable of being itself defiled, or of being enjoyed by any polluted soul. And that fadeth not away – That never decays in its value, sweetness, or beauty, like all the enjoyments of this world, like the garlands of leaves or flowers, with which the ancient conquerors were wont to be crowned. Reserved in heaven for you – Who "by patient continuance in well doing, seek for glory and honor and immortality."

5. Who are kept – The inheritance is reserved; the heirs are kept for it. By the power of God – Which worketh all in all, which guards us against all our enemies. Through faith – Through which alone salvation is both received and retained. Ready to be revealed – That revelation is made in the last day. It was more and more ready to be revealed, ever since Christ came.

6. Wherein – That is, in being so kept. Ye even now greatly rejoice, though now for a little while – Such is our whole life, compared to eternity. If need be – For it is not always needful. If God sees it to be the best means for your spiritual profit. Ye are in heaviness – Or sorrow; but not in darkness; for they still retained both faith, 1 Pet. i, 5, hope, and love; yea, at this very time were rejoicing with joy unspeakable, 1 Pet. i, 8.

7. That the trial of your faith – That is, your faith which is tried. Which is much more precious than gold – For gold, though it bear the fire, yet will perish with the world. May be found – Though it doth not yet appear. Unto praise – From God himself. And honor – From men and angels. And glory – Assigned by the great Judge.

8. Having not seen – In the flesh.

9. Receiving – Now already. Salvation – From all sin into all holiness, which is the qualification for, the forerunner and pledge of, eternal salvation.

10. Of which salvation – So far beyond all that was experienced under the Jewish dispensation. The very prophets who prophesied long ago of the grace of God toward you – Of his abundant, overflowing grace to be bestowed on believers under the Christian dispensation. Inquired – Were earnestly inquisitive. And searched diligently – Like miners searching after precious ore, after the meaning of the prophecies which they delivered.

11. Searching what time – What particular period. And what manner of time – By what marks to be distinguished. The glories that were to follow – His sufferings; namely, the glory of his resurrection, ascension, exaltation, and the effusion of his Spirit; the glory of the last judgment, and of his eternal kingdom; and also the glories of his grace in the hearts and lives of Christians.

12. To whom – So searching. It was revealed, that not for themselves, but for us they ministered – They did not so much by those predictions serve themselves, or that generation, as they did us, who now enjoy what they saw afar off. With the Holy Ghost sent down from heaven – Confirmed by the inward, powerful testimony of the Holy Ghost, as well as the mighty effusion of his miraculous gifts. Which things angels desire to look into – A beautiful gradation; prophets, righteous men, kings, desired to see and hear what Christ did and taught. What the Holy Ghost taught concerning Christ the very angels long to know.

13. Wherefore – Having such encouragement. Gird up the loins of your mind – As persons in the eastern countries were wont, in traveling or running, to gird up their long garments, so gather ye up all your thoughts and affections, and keep your mind always disencumbered and prepared to run the race which is set before you. Be watchful – As servants that wait for their Lord. And hope to the end – Maintain a full expectation of all the grace – The blessings flowing from the free favor of God. Which shall be brought to you at the final revelation of Jesus Christ – And which are now brought to you by the revelation of Christ in you.

14. Your desires – Which ye had while ye were ignorant of God.

16. Lev. xi, 44.

for our offenses, and raised again for our justification. God is pleased to answer our necessities rather than our requests. The doctrine of the prophets, and that of the apostles, exactly agree, as coming from the same Spirit of God. The gospel is the ministration of the Spirit; its success depends upon his operation and blessing. Let us then search diligently those Scriptures which contain the doctrines of salvation.

13-16 As the traveler, the racer, the warrior, and the laborer, gathered in their long and loose garments, that they might be ready in their business, so let Christians do by their minds and affections. Be sober, be watchful against all spiritual dangers and enemies, and be temperate in all behavior. Be sober-minded in opinion, as well as in practice, and humble in your judgment of yourselves. A strong and perfect trust in the grace of God, is agreeable with best endeavors in our duty. Holiness is the desire and duty of every Christian. It must be in all affairs, in every condition, and towards all people. We must especially watch and pray against the sins to which we are inclined. The written word of God is the surest rule of a Christian's life, and by this rule we are commanded to be holy every way. God makes those holy whom he saves.

17-25 Holy confidence in God as a Father, and awful fear of him as a Judge, agree together; and to regard God always as a Judge, makes him dear to us as a Father. If believers do evil, God will visit them with corrections. Then, let Christians not doubt God's faithfulness to his promises, nor give way to enslaving dread of his wrath, but let them reverence his holiness. The fearless professor is defenseless, and Satan takes him captive at his will; the desponding professor has no heart to avail himself of his advantages, and is easily brought to surrender. The price paid for man's redemption was the precious blood of Christ. Not only openly wicked, but unprofitable conversation is highly dangerous, though it may plead custom. It is folly to resolve, I will live and die in such a way, because my forefathers did so. God had purposes of special favor toward his people, long before he made manifest such grace unto them. But the clearness of light, the supports of faith, the power of ordinances, are all much greater since Christ came upon earth, than they were before. The comfort is, that being by faith made one with Christ, his present glory is an assurance that where he is we shall be also, Joh 14:3. The soul must be purified, before it can give up its own desires and indulgences. And the word of God planted in the heart by the Holy Ghost, is a means of spiritual life, stirring up to our duty, working a total change in the dispositions and affections of the soul, till it brings to eternal life. In contrast with the excellence of the renewed spiritual man, as born again, observe the vanity of the natural man. In his life, and in his fall, he is like grass, the flower of grass, which soon withers and dies away. We should hear, and thus receive and love, the holy, living word, and rather hazard all than lose it; and we must banish all other things from the place due to it. We should lodge it in our hearts as our only treasures here, and the certain pledge of the treasure of glory laid up for believers in heaven.

tures of solemn mystery. Into this, no man may idly pry, and Science herself, when she has dared to look within the veil, has turned back awestricken, from those "lower parts of the earth" in which David declares us to be "curiously wrought." Greater still is the mystery of the new birth. That we are born again we know, but how, we cannot tell. How the Spirit of God openeth upon the mind, how it is that he renews the faculties and imparts fresh desires by which those faculties should be guided, how it is that he enlightens the understanding, subdues the will, purifies the intellect, reverses the desire, lifts up the hope, and puts the fear in its right channel, we cannot tell, we must leave this among the secret things which belong unto God. The Holy Ghost worketh, but the manner of his operation is not to be comprehended. "The wind bloweth where it listeth, and thou hearest the sound thereof, but thou canst not tell whence it cometh nor whither it goeth, so is every one that is born of the Spirit." Oh! my hearers, have you felt this mystery? Explain it you cannot, nor can I, nor ought we to attempt an explanation, for where God is silent it is perhaps profanity, and certainly impertinence for us to speak. The two births then are alike in their solemn mystery.

But, then, we know this much of our natural birth, that in birth there is a life created. Yonder infant is beginning his being, another creature has lifted up its feeble cry to heaven, another mortal has come to tread this theater of action, to breathe, to live, to die. And so in the new birth, there is an absolute creation, we are made new creatures in Christ Jesus, there is another spirit born to pray, to believe in Christ, to love him here, and to rejoice in him hereafter. As no one doubts but that birth is the manifestation of a creation, so let no one doubt but that regeneration is the manifestation of a creation of God, as divine, as much beyond the power of man, as the creation of the human mind itself.

But we know also that in birth there is not only a life created, but a life communicated. Each child hath its parent. The very flowers trace themselves back to a parental seed. We spring, not from our own loins, we are not self-created, there is a life communicated. We have

hypocrisies, and envies, and all evil speakings,

2 As newborn babes, desire the sincere milk of the word, that ye may grow thereby:

3 If so be ye have tasted that the Lord is gracious.

4 To whom coming, as unto a living stone, disallowed indeed of men, but chosen of God, and precious,

5 Ye also, as lively stones, are built up a spiritual house, an holy priesthood, to offer up spiritual sacrifices, acceptable to God by Jesus Christ.

6 Wherefore also it is contained in the scripture, Behold, I lay in Sion a chief corner stone, elect, precious: and he that believeth on him shall not be confounded.

7 Unto you therefore which believe he is precious: but unto them which be disobedient, the stone which the builders disallowed, the same is made the head of the corner,

8 And a stone of stumbling, and a rock of offense, even to them which stumble at the word, being disobedient: whereunto also they were appointed.

9 But ye are a chosen generation, a royal priesthood, an holy nation, a peculiar people; that ye should shew forth the praises of him who hath called you out of darkness into his marvelous light:

10 Which in time past were not a people, but are now the people of God: which had not obtained mercy, but now have obtained mercy.

11 Dearly beloved, I beseech you as strangers and pilgrims, abstain from fleshly lusts, which war against the soul;

12 Having your conversation honest among the Gentiles: that, whereas they speak against you as evildoers, they may by your good works, which they shall behold, glorify God in the day of visitation.

13 Submit yourselves to every ordinance of man for the Lord's sake: whether it be to the king, as supreme;

14 Or unto governors, as unto them that are sent by him for the punishment of evildoers, and for the praise of them that do well.

17. Who judgeth according to every man's work – According to the tenor of his life and conversation. Pass the time of your sojourning – Your short abode on earth. In humble, loving fear – The proper companion and guard of hope.

18. Your vain conversation – Your foolish, sinful way of life.

19. Without blemish – In himself. Without spot – From the world.

21. Who through him believe – For all our faith and hope proceed from the power of his resurrection. In God that raised Jesus, and gave him glory – At his ascension. Without Christ we should only dread God; whereas through him we believe, hope, and love.

22. Having purified your souls by obeying the truth through the Spirit, who bestows upon you freely, both obedience and purity of heart, and unfeigned love of the brethren, go on to still higher degrees of love. Love one another fervently – With the most strong and tender affection; and yet with a pure heart – Pure from any spot of unholy desire or inordinate passion.

23. Which liveth – Is full of divine virtue. And abideth the same for ever.

24. All flesh – Every human creature is transient and withering as grass. And all the glory of it – His wisdom, strength, wealth, righteousness. As the flower – The most short-lived part of it. The grass – That is, man. The flower – That is, his glory. Is fallen off – As it were, while we are speaking. Isaiah xl, 6, &c.

1 PETER 2

1. Wherefore laying aside – As inconsistent with that pure love. All dissimulation – Which is the outward expression of guile in the heart.

2. Desire – Always, as earnestly as new born babes do, chap. i, 3. The milk of the word – That word of God which nourishes the soul as milk does the body, and which is sincere, pure from all guile, so that none are deceived who cleave to it. That you may grow thereby – In faith, love, holiness, unto the full stature of Christ.

3. Since ye have tasted – Sweetly and experimentally known.

4. To whom coming – By faith. As unto a living stone – Living from eternity; alive from the dead. There is a wonderful beauty and energy in these expressions, which describe Christ as a spiritual foundation, solid, firm, durable; and believers as a building erected upon it, in preference to that temple which the Jews accounted their highest glory. And St. Peter speaking of him thus, shows he did not judge himself, but Christ, to be the rock on which the church was built. Rejected indeed by men – Even at this day, not only by Jews, Turks, heathens, infidels; but by all Christians, so called, who live in sin, or who hope to be saved by their own works. But chosen of God – From all eternity, to be the foundation of his church. And precious – In himself, in the sight of God, and in the eyes of all believers.

5. Ye – Believers. As living stones – Alive to God through him. Are built up – In union with each other. A spiritual house – Being spiritual yourselves, and an habitation of God through the Spirit. An holy priesthood – Consecrated to God, and "holy as he is holy." To offer up – Your souls and bodies, with all your thoughts, words, and actions, as spiritual sacrifices to God.

6. He that believeth shall not be confounded – In time or in eternity. Isaiah xxvii, 16.

7. To them who believe, he is become the head of the corner – The chief corner stone, on which the whole building rests. Unbelievers too will at length find him such to their sorrow, Matt. xxi, 44; Psalm cxviii, 22.

8. Who stumble, whereunto also they were appointed – They who believe not, stumble, and fall, and perish for ever; God having appointed from all eternity, "he that believeth not shall be damned."

9. But ye – Who believe in Christ. Are – In a higher sense than ever the Jews were. A chosen or elect race, a royal priesthood – "Kings and priests unto God,"

MATTHEW HENRY

CHARLES H. SPURGEON

1 PETER 2

A temper suitable to the Christian character as born again, is recommended. (1-10)
Holy conversation among the Gentiles directed. (11,12)
Subjects exhorted to pay all proper obedience to their civil governors. (13-17)
Also servants to their masters, and all to be patient, according to the example of the suffering Savior. (18-25)

1-10 Evil-speaking is a sign of malice and guile in the heart; and hinders our profiting by the word of God. A new life needs suitable food. Infants desire milk, and make the best endeavors for it which they are able to do; such must be a Christian's desires after the word of God. Our Lord Jesus Christ is very merciful to us miserable sinners; and he has a fullness of grace. But even the best of God's servants, in this life, have only a taste of the consolations of God. Christ is called a Stone, to teach his servants that he is their protection and security, the foundation on which they are built. He is precious in the excellence of his nature, the dignity of his office, and the glory of his services. All true believers are a holy priesthood; sacred to God, serviceable to others, endowed with heavenly gifts and graces. But the most spiritual sacrifices of the best in prayer and praise are not acceptable, except through Jesus Christ. Christ is the chief Corner stone, that unites the whole number of believers into one everlasting temple, and bears the weight of the whole fabric. Elected, or chosen, for a foundation that is everlasting. Precious beyond compare, by all that can give worth. To be built on Christ means, to believe in him; but in this many deceive themselves, they consider not what it is, nor the necessity of it, to partake of the salvation he has wrought. Though the frame of the world were falling to pieces, that man who is built on this foundation may hear it without fear. He shall not be confounded. The believing soul makes haste to Christ, but it never finds cause to hasten from him. All true Christians are a chosen generation; they make one family, a people distinct from the world: of another spirit, principle, and practice; which they could never be, if they were not chosen in Christ to be such, and sanctified by his Spirit. Their first state is a state of gross darkness, but they are called out of darkness into a state of joy, pleasure, and prosperity; that they should show forth the praises of the Lord by their profession of his truth, and their good conduct. How vast their obligations to him who has made them his people, and has shown mercy to them! To be without this mercy is a woeful state, though a man have all worldly enjoyments.

11,12 Even the best of men, the chosen generation, the people of God, need to be exhorted to keep from the worst sins. And fleshly lusts are most destructive to man's soul. It is a sore judgment to be given up to them. There is a day of visitation coming, wherein God may call to repentance by his word and his grace; then many will glorify God, and the holy lives of his people will have promoted the happy change.

13-17 A Christian conversation must be honest; which it cannot be, if there is not a just and careful discharge of all relative duties: the apostle here treats of these distinctly. Regard to those duties is the will of God, consequently, the Christian's

links between the son and the father, and back till we come to father Adam. So in regeneration there is a life, not merely created, but communicated, even the very life of God, who hath begotten us again unto a lively hope. As truly as the father lives in the child, so truly doth the very life and nature of God live in every Swiss born heir of heaven. We are as certainly partakers of the divine nature by the new birth as we were partakers of the human nature by the old birth: so far the comparison holds good.

Equally certain is it, that in the natural and in the spiritual birth there is life entailed. There are certain propensities which we inherit, from which this side the grave we shall not be free. Our temperament brave or gay, our passions slow or hasty, our propensities sensual or aspiring, our faculties contracted or expansive are to a great measure an entailed inheritance as much linked to our future portion as are wings to an eagle or a shed to a snail. No doubt much of our history is born within us, and the infant hath within himself germ of his future actions. If I may so speak, there are those qualities, that composition and disposition of nature which will naturally, if circumstances assist, work out in full development certain results. So is it with us when we are born again: a heavenly nature is entailed upon us. We cannot but be holy; the new nature cannot but serve God, it must, it will pant to be nearer to Christ, and more like him. It hath aspirations which time cannot satisfy, desires which earth cannot surfeit, longings which heaven itself alone can gratify. There is a life entailed upon us in the moment when we pass from death unto life in the solemn mystery of regeneration.

In the old birth, and in the new birth also, a life is also brought forth which is complete in all its parts and only needs to be developed. Yon infant in the cradle shall never have another limb, or another eye. Its limb hardens, it grows, it gathers strength, its brain also enlarges its sphere, but the faculties are there already, they are not implanted afterward. Verily, so is it in the new-born child of God. Faith love, hope, and every grace are there the moment he believes in Christ. They grow 'tis true, but they were all there in the instant of

KING JAMES VERSION   JOHN WESLEY

15 For so is the will of God, that with well doing ye may put to silence the ignorance of foolish men:

16 As free, and not using your liberty for a cloke of maliciousness, but as the servants of God.

17 Honor all men. Love the brotherhood. Fear God. Honor the king.

18 Servants, be subject to your masters with all fear; not only to the good and gentle, but also to the froward.

19 For this is thankworthy, if a man for conscience toward God endure grief, suffering wrongfully.

20 For what glory is it, if, when ye be buffeted for your faults, ye shall take it patiently? but if, when ye do well, and suffer for it, ye take it patiently, this is acceptable with God.

21 For even hereunto were ye called: because Christ also suffered for us, leaving us an example, that ye should follow his steps:

22 Who did no sin, neither was guile found in his mouth:

23 Who, when he was reviled, reviled not again; when he suffered, he threatened not; but committed himself to him that judgeth righteously:

24 Who his own self bare our sins in his own body on the tree, that we, being dead to sins, should live unto righteousness: by whose stripes ye were healed.

25 For ye were as sheep going astray; but are now returned unto the Shepherd and Bishop of your souls.

1 PETER 3

1 Likewise, ye wives, be in subjection to your own husbands; that, if any obey not the word, they also may without the word be won by the conversation of the wives;

2 While they behold your chaste conversation coupled with fear.

3 Whose adorning let it not be that outward adorning of plaiting the hair, and of wearing of gold, or of putting on of apparel;

4 But let it be the hidden man of the heart, in that which is not

Rev. i, 6. As princes, ye have power with God, and victory over sin, the world, and the devil: as priests, ye are consecrated to God, for offering spiritual sacrifices. Ye Christians are as one holy nation, under Christ your King. A purchased people – Who are his peculiar property. That ye may show forth – By your whole behavior, to all mankind. The virtues – The excellent glory, the mercy, wisdom, and power of him, Christ, who hath called you out of the darkness of ignorance, error, sin, and misery.

10. Who in time past were not a people – Much less the people of God; but scattered individuals of many nations. The former part of the verse particularly respects the Gentiles; the latter, the Jews.

11. Here begins the exhortation drawn from the second motive. Sojourners: pilgrims – The first word properly means, those who are in a strange house; the second, those who are in a strange country. You sojourn in the body; you are pilgrims in this world. Abstain from desires of anything in this house, or in this country.

12. Honest – Not barely unblamable, but virtuous in every respect. But our language sinks under the force, beauty, and copiousness of the original expressions. That they by your good works which they shall behold – See with their own eyes. May glorify God – By owning his grace in you, and following your example. In the day of visitation – The time when he shall give them fresh offers of his mercy.

13. Submit yourselves to every ordinance of man – To every secular power. Instrumentally these are ordained by men; but originally all their power is from God.

14. Or to subordinate governors, or magistrates.

15. The ignorance – Of them who blame you, because they do not know you: a strong motive to pity them.

16. As free – Yet obeying governors, for God's sake.

17. Honor all men – As being made in the image of God, bought by his Son, and designed for his kingdom. Honor the king – Pay him all that regard both in affection and action which the laws of God and man require.

18. Servants – Literally, household servants. With all fear – Of offending them or God. Not only to the good – Tender, kind. And gentle – Mild, easily forgiving.

19. For conscience toward God – From a pure desire of pleasing him. Grief – Severe treatment.

21. Hereunto are ye – Christians. Called – To suffer wrongfully. Leaving you an example – When he went to God. That ye might follow his steps – Of innocence and patience.

22, 23. In all these instances the example of Christ is peculiarly adapted to the state of servants, who easily slide either into sin or guile, reviling their fellow servants, or threatening them, the natural result of anger without power. He committed himself to him that judgeth righteously – The only solid ground of patience in affliction. Isaiah liii, 4, 6, 7, 9.

24. Who himself bore our sins – That is, the punishment due to them. In his afflicted, torn, dying body on the tree – The cross, whereon chiefly slaves or servants were wont to suffer. That we being dead to sin – Wholly delivered both from the guilt and power of it: indeed, without an atonement first made for the guilt, we could never have been delivered from the power. Might live to righteousness – Which is one only. The sins we had committed, and he bore, were manifold.

25. The bishop – The kind observer, inspector, or overseer of your souls.

1 PETER 3

1. If any – He speaks tenderly. Won – Gained over to Christ.

2. Joined with a loving fear of displeasing them.

duty, and the way to silence the base slanders of ignorant and foolish men. Christians must endeavor, in all relations, to behave aright, that they do not make their liberty a cloak or covering for any wickedness, or for the neglect of duty; but they must remember that they are servants of God.

18-25 Servants in those days generally were slaves, and had heathen masters, who often used them cruelly; yet the apostle directs them to be subject to the masters placed over them by Providence, with a fear to dishonor or offend God. And not only to those pleased with reasonable service, but to the severe, and those angry without cause. The sinful misconduct of one relation, does not justify sinful behavior in the other; the servant is bound to do his duty, though the master may be sinfully froward and perverse. But masters should be meek and gentle to their servants and inferiors. What glory or distinction could it be, for professed Christians to be patient when corrected for their faults? But if when they behaved well they were ill treated by proud and passionate heathen masters, yet bore it without peevish complaints, or purposes of revenge, and persevered in their duty, this would be acceptable to God as a distinguishing effect of his grace, and would be rewarded by him. Christ's death was designed not only for an example of patience under sufferings, but he bore our sins; he bore the punishment of them, and thereby satisfied Divine justice. Hereby he takes them away from us. The fruits of Christ's sufferings are the death of sin, and a new holy life of righteousness; for both which we have an example, and powerful motives, and ability to perform also, from the death and resurrection of Christ. And our justification; Christ was bruised and crucified as a sacrifice for our sins, and by his stripes the diseases of our souls are cured. Here is man's sin; he goes astray; it is his own act. His misery; he goes astray from the pasture, from the Shepherd, and from the flock, and so exposes himself to dangers without number.

1 PETER 3

The duties of wives and husbands. (1-7)
Christians exhorted to agree. (8-13)
And encouraged to patience under persecutions for righteousness' sake, considering that Christ suffered patiently. (14-22)

1-7 The wife must discharge her duty to her own husband, though he obey not the word. We daily see how narrowly evil men watch the ways and lives of professors of religion. Putting on of apparel is not forbidden, but vanity and costliness in ornament. Religious people should take care that all their behavior answers to their profession. But how few know the right measure and bounds of those two necessaries of life, food and raiment! Unless poverty is our carver, and cuts us short, there is scarcely any one who does not desire something beyond what is good for us. Far more are beholden to the lowliness of their state, than the lowliness of their mind; and many will not be so bounded, but lavish their time and money upon trifles. The apostle directs Christian females to put on something not corruptible, that beautifies the soul, even the graces of God's Holy Spirit. A true Christian's chief care lies in right ordering his own spirit. This will do more to

regeneration. The babe in grace who is just now born to God, hath every part of the spiritual man, it only needs to grow till he becomes a perfect man in Christ Jesus.

Thus far, you perceive, that the two births have a very close resemblance to one another. I pray you, now that I have introduced the subject, do not turn from it till you have thought of the reality of the new birth, as you must of the reality of the first. You were not here if you had not been born, you shall never be in heaven unless you are born again, you had not been able today to hear, or think, or see, if you had not been born. You are not today able to pray or to believe in Christ, unless you are born again. The enjoyments of this world you could never have known, if it had not been for birth, the saved delight of God you do not know today, and you never shall know unless you be born again. Do not look upon regeneration as though it were a fancy or a fiction. I do assure you, my hearers, it is as real as is the natural birth; for spiritual is not the same as fanciful, but the spiritual is as real as even nature itself. To be born again is as much a matter of fact to be realized, to be discerned, and to be discovered, as to be born for the first time into this vale of tears.

But now comes the contrast—"being born not of corruptible seed, but of incorruptible." Herein lieth the contrast between the two. That child which has just experienced the first birth has been made partaker of corruptible seed. The depravity of his parent lieth sleeping within him. Could he speak, he might say so. David did,—"Behold, I was born in sin and shaped in iniquity." He receiveth the evil virus which was first infused into us by the fall. Not so, however, is it when we are born again. No sin is then sown within us. This sin of the old flesh remains but there is no sin in the newborn nature, it cannot sin because it is born of God himself; it is as impossible for that new nature to sin as for the Deity itself to be defiled. It is a part of the divine nature—a spark struck off from the very heart of light and life, and dead or dark it cannot be, because it would be contrary to its nature to be either the one or the other. Oh, what a difference! In the first birth—born to sin, in the next—born to holiness; in the

corruptible, even the ornament of a meek and quiet spirit, which is in the sight of God of great price.

5 For after this manner in the old time the holy women also, who trusted in God, adorned themselves, being in subjection unto their own husbands:

6 Even as Sara obeyed Abraham, calling him lord: whose daughters ye are, as long as ye do well, and are not afraid with any amazement.

7 Likewise, ye husbands, dwell with them according to knowledge, giving honor unto the wife, as unto the weaker vessel, and as being heirs together of the grace of life; that your prayers be not hindered.

8 Finally, be ye all of one mind, having compassion one of another, love as brethren, be pitiful, be courteous:

9 Not rendering evil for evil, or railing for railing: but contrariwise blessing; knowing that ye are thereunto called, that ye should inherit a blessing.

10 For he that will love life, and see good days, let him refrain his tongue from evil, and his lips that they speak no guile:

11 Let him eschew evil, and do good; let him seek peace, and ensue it.

12 For the eyes of the Lord are over the righteous, and his ears are open unto their prayers: but the face of the Lord is against them that do evil.

13 And who is he that will harm you, if ye be followers of that which is good?

14 But and if ye suffer for righteousness' sake, happy are ye: and be not afraid of their terror, neither be troubled;

15 But sanctify the Lord God in your hearts: and be ready always to give an answer to every man that asketh you a reason of the hope that is in you with meekness and fear:

16 Having a good conscience; that, whereas they speak evil of you, as of evildoers, they may be ashamed that falsely accuse your good conversation in Christ.

17 For it is better, if the will of God be so, that ye suffer for well doing, than for evil doing.

3. Three things are here expressly forbidden: curling the hair, wearing gold, (by way of ornament,) and putting on costly or gay apparel. These, therefore, ought never to be allowed, much less defended, by Christians.

4. The hidden man of the heart – Complete inward holiness, which implies a meek and quiet spirit. A meek spirit gives no trouble willingly to any: a quiet spirit bears all wrongs without being troubled. In the sight of God – Who looks at the heart. All superfluity of dress contributes more to pride and anger than is generally supposed. The apostle seems to have his eye to this by substituting meekness and quietness in the room of the ornaments he forbids. "I do not regard these things," is often said by those whose hearts are wrapped up in them: but offer to take them away, and you touch the very idol of their soul. Some, indeed only dress elegantly that they may be looked on; that is, they squander away their Lord's talent to gain applause: thus making sin to beget sin, and then plead one in excuse of the other.

5. The adorning of those holy women, who trusted in God, and therefore did not act thus from servile fear, was,

1. Their meek subjection to their husbands:

2. Their quiet spirit, "not afraid," or amazed: and

3. Their unblamable behavior, "doing" all things "well."

6. Whose children ye are – In a spiritual as well as natural sense, and entitled to the same inheritance, while ye discharge your conjugal duties, not out of fear, but for conscience' sake. Gen. xviii, 12.

7. Dwell with the woman according to knowledge – Knowing they are weak, and therefore to be used with all tenderness. Yet do not despise them for this, but give them honor – Both in heart, in word, and in action; as those who are called to be joint-heirs of that eternal life which ye and they hope to receive by the free grace of God. That your prayers be not hindered – On the one part or the other. All sin hinders prayer; particularly anger. Anything at which we are angry is never more apt to come into our mind than when we are at prayer; and those who do not forgive will find no forgiveness from God.

8. Finally – This part of the epistle reaches to chap. iv, 11. The apostle seems to have added the rest afterwards. Sympathizing – Rejoicing and sorrowing together. Love all believers as brethren. Be pitiful – Toward the afflicted. Be courteous – To all men. Courtesy is such a behavior toward equals and inferiors as shows respect mixed with love.

9. Ye are called to inherit a blessing – Therefore their railing cannot hurt you; and, by blessing them, you imitate God, who blesses you.

10. For he that desireth to love life, and to see good days – That would make life amiable and desirable. Psalm xxxiv, 12, &c.

11. Let him seek – To live peaceably with all men. And pursue it – Even when it seems to flee from him.

12. The eyes of the Lord are over the righteous – For good. Anger appears in the whole face; love, chiefly in the eyes.

13. Who is he that will harm you – None can.

14. But if ye should suffer – This is no harm to you, but a good. Fear ye not their fear – The very words of the Septuagint, Isaiah viii, 12, 13. Let not that fear be in you which the wicked feel.

15. But sanctify the Lord God in your hearts – Have an holy fear, and a full trust in his wise providence. The hope – Of eternal life. With meekness – For anger would hurt your cause as well as your soul. And fear – A filial fear of offending God, and a jealousy over yourselves, lest ye speak amiss.

16. Having a good conscience – So much the more beware of anger, to which the very consciousness of your innocence may betray you. Join with a good conscience meekness and fear, and you obtain a complete victory. Your good conversation in Christ – That is, which flows from faith in him.

17. It is infinitely better, if it be the will of God, ye should suffer. His permis-

MATTHEW HENRY   CHARLES H. SPURGEON

fix the affections, and excite the esteem of a husband, than studied ornaments or fashionable apparel, attended by a froward and quarrelsome temper. Christians ought to do their duty to one another, from a willing mind, and in obedience to the command of God. Wives should be subject to their husbands, not from dread and amazement, but from desire to do well, and please God. The husband's duty to the wife implies giving due respect unto her, and maintaining her authority, protecting her, and placing trust in her. They are heirs together of all the blessings of this life and that which is to come, and should live peaceably one with another. Prayer sweetens their converse.

8-13 Though Christians cannot always be exactly of the same mind, yet they should have compassion one of another, and love as brethren. If any man desires to live comfortably on earth, or to possess eternal life in heaven, he must bridle his tongue from wicked, abusive, or deceitful words. He must forsake and keep far from evil actions, do all the good he can, and seek peace with all men. For God, all wise and everywhere present, watches over the righteous, and takes care of them. None could or should harm those who copied the example of Christ, who is perfect goodness, and did good to others as his followers.

14-22 We sanctify God before others, when our conduct invites and encourages them to glorify and honor him. What was the ground and reason of their hope? We should be able to defend our religion with meekness, in the fear of God. There is no room for any other fears where this great fear is; it disturbs not. The conscience is good, when it does its office well. That person is in a sad condition on whom sin and suffering meet: sin makes suffering extreme, comfortless, and destructive. Surely it is better to suffer for well doing than for evil doing, whatever our natural impatience at times may suggest. The example of Christ is an argument for patience under sufferings. In the case of our Lord's suffering, he that knew no sin, suffered instead of those who knew no righteousness. The blessed end and design of our Lord's sufferings were, to reconcile us to God, and to bring us to eternal glory. He was put to death in respect of his human nature, but was quickened and raised by the power of the Holy Spirit. If Christ could not be freed from sufferings, why should Christians think to be so? God takes exact notice of the means and advantages people in all ages have had. As to the old world, Christ sent his Spirit; gave warning by Noah. But though the patience of God waits long, it will cease at last. And the spirits of disobedient sinners, as soon as they are out of their bodies, are committed to the prison of hell, where those that despised Noah's warning now are, and from whence there is no redemption. Noah's salvation in the ark upon the water, which carried him above the floods, set forth the salvation of all true believers. That temporal salvation by the ark was a type of the eternal salvation of believers by baptism of the Holy Spirit. To prevent mistakes, the apostle declares what he means by saving baptism; not the outward ceremony of washing with water, which, in itself, does no more than put away the filth of the flesh, but that baptism, of which the baptismal water formed the sign. Not the outward ordinance, but

first—partakers of corruption, in the next—heirs of incorruption in the first—depravity, in the second—perfection. What broader contrast could there be! What should make us more thoroughly long for this new birth than the glorious fact that we are by its means consciously lifted up from the ruins of the fall, and made perfect in Christ Jesus.

In the birth of the flesh too, what dread uncertainties attend it! What shall become of yonder child? It may live to curse the day in which it was born, as did the poor troubled patriarch of old. What sorrow may drive its plowshares along its yet unwrinkled brow? Ah! child, thou shalt be gray-headed one day, but ere that comes thou shalt have felt a thousand storms beating about thine heart and head. Little dost thou know thy destiny, but assuredly thou shalt be of few days and full of trouble. Not so in the regeneration, we shall never rue the day in which we are born again, never look back upon that with sorrow, but always with ecstasy and delight, for we are ushered then, not into the hovel of humanity, but into the palace of Deity. We are not then born into a valley of tears, but into an inheritance in the Canaan of God.

That child too, so fondly the object of its mother's love may one day vex or break its parent's heart. Are not children doubtful mercies? Bring they not with them sad forebodings of what they yet may be? Alas for the pretty prattlers who have grown up to be convicted criminals! But blessed be God, they who are sons of God shalt never break their father's heart. Their new nature shall be worthy of him that gave it existence. They shall live to honor him, they shall die to be perfectly like him, and shall rise to glorify him for ever. We have sometimes said that God has a very naughty family, but surely the naughtiness is in the old Adam nature, and not in Jehovah's gracious work. There is no naughtiness in the new creature. In that new creature there is no taint of sin. God's child as descended from his loins, can never sin. The new nature which God hath put into it doth never wander, doth never transgress. It were not the new nature if it did, it were not God's offspring, if it fall, for that which cometh of God is like Him, holy, pure, and undefiled, separate from sin. In this

18 For Christ also hath once suffered for sins, the just for the unjust, that he might bring us to God, being put to death in the flesh, but quickened by the Spirit:

19 By which also he went and preached unto the spirits in prison;

20 Which sometime were disobedient, when once the longsuffering of God waited in the days of Noah, while the ark was a preparing, wherein few, that is, eight souls were saved by water.

21 The like figure whereunto even baptism doth also now save us (not the putting away of the filth of the flesh, but the answer of a good conscience toward God,) by the resurrection of Jesus Christ:

22 Who is gone into heaven, and is on the right hand of God; angels and authorities and powers being made subject unto him.

1 PETER 4

1 Forasmuch then as Christ hath suffered for us in the flesh, arm yourselves likewise with the same mind: for he that hath suffered in the flesh hath ceased from sin;

2 That he no longer should live the rest of his time in the flesh to the lusts of men, but to the will of God.

3 For the time past of our life may suffice us to have wrought the will of the Gentiles, when we walked in lasciviousness, lusts, excess of wine, revelings, banquetings, and abominable idolatries:

4 Wherein they think it strange that ye run not with them to the same excess of riot, speaking evil of you:

5 Who shall give account to him that is ready to judge the quick and the dead.

6 For for this cause was the gospel preached also to them that are dead, that they might be judged according to men in the flesh, but live according to God in the spirit.

7 But the end of all things is at hand: be ye therefore sober, and watch unto prayer.

sive will appears from his providence.

18. For – This is undoubtedly best, whereby we are most conformed to Christ. Now Christ suffered once – To suffer no more. For sins – Not his own, but ours. The just for the unjust – The word signifies, not only them who have wronged their neighbors, but those who have transgressed any of the commands of God; as the preceding word, just, denotes a person who has fulfilled, not barely social duties, but all kind of righteousness.

19. By which Spirit he preached – Through the ministry of Noah. To the spirits in prison – The unholy men before the flood, who were then reserved by the justice of God, as in a prison, till he executed the sentence upon them all; and are now also reserved to the judgment of the great day.

20. When the longsuffering of God waited – For an hundred and twenty years; all the time the ark was preparing: during which Noah warned them all to flee from the wrath to come.

21. The antitype whereof – The thing typified by the ark, even baptism, now saveth us – That is, through the water of baptism we are saved from the sin which overwhelms the world as a flood: not, indeed, the bare outward sign, but the inward grace; a divine consciousness that both our persons and our actions are accepted through him who died and rose again for us.

22. Angels and authorities and powers – That is, all orders both of angels and men.

1 PETER 4

1. Arm yourselves with the same mind – Which will be Armor of proof against all your enemies. For he that hath suffered in the flesh – That hath so suffered as to be thereby made inwardly and truly conformable to the sufferings of Christ. Hath ceased from sin – Is delivered from it.

2. That ye may no longer live in the flesh – Even in this mortal body. To the desires of men – Either your own or those of others. These are various; but the will of God is one.

3. Revelings, banquetings – Have these words any meaning now? They had, seventeen hundred years ago. Then the former meant, meetings to eat; meetings, the direct end of which was, to please the taste: the latter, meetings to drink: both of which Christians then ranked with abominable idolatries.

4. The same – As ye did once. Speaking evil of you – As proud, singular, silly, wicked and the like.

5. Who shall give account – Of this, as well as all their other ways. To him who is ready – So faith represents him now.

6. For to this end was the gospel preached – Ever since it was given to Adam. To them that are now dead – In their several generations. That they might be judged – That though they were judged. In the flesh according to the manner of men – With rash, unrighteous judgment. They might live according to the will and word of God, in the Spirit; the soul renewed after his image.

7. But the end of all things – And so of their wrongs, and your sufferings. Is at hand: be ye therefore sober, and watch unto prayer – Temperance helps watchfulness, and both of them help prayer. Watch, that ye may pray; and pray, that ye may watch.

8. Love covereth a multitude of sins – Yea, "love covereth all things." He that loves another, covers his faults, how many soever they be. He turns away his own eyes from them; and, as far as is possible, hides them from others. And he continually prays that all the sinner's iniquities may be forgiven and his sins covered. Meantime the God of love measures to him with the same measure into his bosom.

9. One to another – Ye that are of different towns or countries. Without murmuring – With all cheerfulness. Prov. x, 12.

MATTHEW HENRY   CHARLES H. SPURGEON

when a man, by the regeneration of the Spirit, was enabled to repent and profess faith, and purpose a new life, uprightly, and as in the presence of God. Let us beware that we rest not upon outward forms. Let us learn to look on the ordinances of God spiritually, and to inquire after the spiritual effect and working of them on our consciences. We would willingly have all religion reduced to outward things. But many who were baptized, and constantly attended the ordinances, have remained without Christ, died in their sins, and are now past recovery. Rest not then till thou art cleansed by the Spirit of Christ and the blood of Christ. His resurrection from the dead is that whereby we are assured of purifying and peace.

1 PETER 4

The consideration of Christ's sufferings is urged for purity and holiness. (1-6)

And the approaching end of the Jewish state, as a reason for sobriety, watchfulness, and prayer. (7-11)

Believers encouraged to rejoice and glory in reproaches and sufferings for Christ, and to commit their souls to the care of a faithful God. (12-19)

1-6 The strongest and best arguments against sin, are taken from the sufferings of Christ. He died to destroy sin; and though he cheerfully submitted to the worst sufferings, yet he never gave way to the least sin. Temptations could not prevail, were it not for man's own corruption; but true Christians make the will of God, not their own lust or desires, the rule of their lives and actions. And true conversion makes a marvelous change in the heart and life. It alters the mind, judgment, affections, and conversation. When a man is truly converted, it is very grievous to him to think how the time past of his life has been spent. One sin draws on another. Six sins are here mentioned which have dependence one upon another. It is a Christian's duty, not only to keep from gross wickedness, but also from things that lead to sin, or appear evil. The gospel had been preached to those since dead, who by the proud and carnal judgment of wicked men were condemned as evildoers, some even suffering death. But being quickened to Divine life by the Holy Spirit, they lived to God as his devoted servants. Let not believers care, though the world scorns and reproaches them.

7-11 The destruction of the Jewish church and nation, foretold by our Savior, was very near. And the speedy approach of death and judgment concerns all, to which these words naturally lead our minds. Our approaching end, is a powerful argument to make us sober in all worldly matters, and earnest in religion. There are so many things amiss in all, that unless love covers, excuses, and forgives in others, the mistakes and faults for which every one needs the forbearance of others, Satan will prevail to stir up divisions and discords. But we are not to suppose that charity will cover or make amends for the sins of those who exercise it, so as to induce God to forgive them. The nature of a Christian's work, which is high work and hard work, the goodness of the Master, and the excellence of the reward, all require that our endeavors should be serious and earnest. And in all the duties and services of life, we

indeed lieth a strange difference. We know not to what that first nature tendeth, who can tell what bitterness it shall bring forth? But we know whither the new nature tendeth, for it ripeneth towards the perfect image of him that created us in Christ Jesus.

Perhaps without my endeavoring to enlarge further you could yourselves muse upon this theme. It remains but for me upon this first head to return with earnestness to that point upon which I fear the greatest difficulty lies— the realization of this birth—for we repeat it, we are speaking of a fact and not a dream, a reality and not metaphor.

Some tell you that the child is regenerated when the drops fall from priestly fingers. My brethren, a more fond and foul delusion was never perpetrated upon earth. Rome itself did never discourse upon a wilder error than this. Dream not of it. O think not that it is so. "Except a man be born again he cannot see the kingdom of God." The Lord himself addresses this sentence not to an infant but to a full-grown man. Nicodemus—one who was circumcised according to the Jewish law, but who yet, though he had received the seal of that covenant, needed as a man to be born again. We all without exception must know this change. Your life may have been moral, but it will not suffice. The most moralized human nature can never attain to the divine nature. You may cleanse and purge the fruit of the first birth, but still the inevitable decree demands the second birth for all. If from your youth up you have been so trained that you have scarcely known the vices of the people; so tended, hedged in, and kept from contamination with sin, that you have not known temptation, yet you must be born again, and this birth, I repeat it, must be as much a fact, as true, as real, and as sure as was that first birth in which you were ushered into this world. What do you know of this, my hearer? What do you know of this? It is a thing you cannot perform for yourself. You cannot regenerate yourself any more than you could cause yourself to be born. It is a matter out of the range of human power; it is supernatural, it is divine. Have you partaken of it? Do not merely look back to some hour in which you felt mysterious feel-

KING JAMES VERSION

JOHN WESLEY

8 And above all things have fervent charity among yourselves: for charity shall cover the multitude of sins.

9 Use hospitality one to another without grudging.

10 As every man hath received the gift, even so minister the same one to another, as good stewards of the manifold grace of God.

11 If any man speak, let him speak as the oracles of God; if any man minister, let him do it as of the ability which God giveth: that God in all things may be glorified through Jesus Christ, to whom be praise and dominion for ever and ever. Amen.

12 Beloved, think it not strange concerning the fiery trial which is to try you, as though some strange thing happened unto you:

13 But rejoice, inasmuch as ye are partakers of Christ's sufferings; that, when his glory shall be revealed, ye may be glad also with exceeding joy.

14 If ye be reproached for the name of Christ, happy are ye; for the spirit of glory and of God resteth upon you: on their part he is evil spoken of, but on your part he is glorified.

15 But let none of you suffer as a murderer, or as a thief, or as an evildoer, or as a busybody in other men's matters.

16 Yet if any man suffer as a Christian, let him not be ashamed; but let him glorify God on this behalf.

17 For the time is come that judgment must begin at the house of God: and if it first begin at us, what shall the end be of them that obey not the gospel of God?

18 And if the righteous scarcely be saved, where shall the ungodly and the sinner appear?

19 Wherefore let them that suffer according to the will of God commit the keeping of their souls to him in well doing, as unto a faithful Creator.

1 PETER 5

1 The elders which are among you I exhort, who am also an elder, and a witness of the suf-

10. As every one hath received a gift – Spiritual or temporal, ordinary or extraordinary, although the latter seems primarily intended. So minister it one to another – Employ it for the common good. As good stewards of the manifold grace of God – The talents wherewith his free love has intrusted you.

11. If any man speak, let him – In his whole conversation, public and private. Speak as the oracles of God – Let all his words be according to this pattern, both as to matter and manner, more especially in public. By this mark we may always know who are, so far, the true or false prophets. The oracles of God teach that men should repent, believe, obey.

12. Wonder not at the burning which is among you – This is the literal meaning of the expression. It seems to include both martyrdom itself, which so frequently was by fire, and all the other sufferings joined with, or previous to, it; which is permitted by the wisdom of God for your trial. Be not surprised at this.

13. But as ye partake of the sufferings of Christ, ver. 1 – While ye suffer for his sake, rejoice in hope of more abundant glory. For the measure of glory answers the measure of suffering; and much more abundantly.

14. If ye are reproached for Christ – Reproaches and cruel mockings were always one part of their sufferings. The Spirit of glory and of God resteth upon you – The same Spirit which was upon Christ, Luke iv, 18. He is here termed, the Spirit of glory, conquering all reproach and shame, and the Spirit of God, whose Son, Jesus Christ is. On their part he is blasphemed, but on your part he is glorified – That is, while they are blaspheming Christ, you glorify him in the midst of your sufferings, ver. 16.

15. Let none of you deservedly suffer, as an evildoer – In any kind.

16. Let him glorify God – Who giveth him the honor so to suffer, and so great a reward for suffering.

17. The time is come for judgment to begin at the house of God – God first visits his church, and that both in justice and mercy. What shall the end be of them that obey not the gospel – How terribly will he visit them! The judgments which are milder at the beginning, grow more and more severe. But good men, having already sustained their part, are only spectators of the miseries of the wicked.

18. If the righteous scarcely be saved – Escape with the utmost difficulty. Where shall the ungodly – The man who knows not God. And the open sinner appear – In that day of vengeance. The salvation here primarily spoken of is of a temporal nature. But we may apply the words to eternal things, and then they are still more awful. Prov. xi, 31.

19. Let them that suffer according to the will of God – Both for a good cause, and in a right spirit. Commit to him their souls – (Whatever becomes of the body) as a sacred deposit. In well doing – Be this your care, to do and suffer well: He will take care of the rest. As unto a faithful Creator – In whose truth, love, and power, ye may safely trust.

1 PETER 5

1. I who am a fellow-elder – So the first though not the head of the apostles appositely and modestly styles himself. And a witness of the sufferings of Christ – Having seen him suffer, and now suffering for him.

2. Feed the flock – Both by doctrine and discipline. Not by constraint – Unwillingly, as a burden. Not for filthy gain – Which, if it be the motive of acting, is filthy beyond expression. O consider this, ye that leave one flock and go to another, merely because there is more gain, a large salary! Is it not astonishing that men can see no harm in this? that it is not only practiced, but avowed, all over the nation?

3. Neither as lording over the heritage – Behaving in a haughty, domineering manner, as though you had dominion over their conscience. The word translated heritage, is, literally, the portions. There is one flock under the one chief

MATTHEW HENRY   CHARLES H. SPURGEON

should aim at the glory of God as our chief end. He is a miserable, unsettled wretch, who cleaves to himself, and forgets God; is only perplexed about his credit, and gain, and base ends, which are often broken, and which, when he attains, both he and they must shortly perish together. But he who has given up himself and his all to God, may say confidently that the Lord is his portion; and nothing but glory through Christ Jesus, is solid and lasting; that abideth for ever.

12-19 By patience and fortitude in suffering, by dependence on the promises of God, and keeping to the word the Holy Spirit hath revealed, the Holy Spirit is glorified; but by the contempt and reproaches cast upon believers, he is evil spoken of, and is blasphemed. One would think such cautions as these were needless to Christians. But their enemies falsely charged them with foul crimes. And even the best of men need to be warned against the worst of sins. There is no comfort in sufferings, when we bring them upon ourselves by our own sin and folly. A time of universal calamity was at hand, as foretold by our Savior, Mt 24:9,10. And if such things befall in this life, how awful will the day of judgment be! It is true that the righteous are scarcely saved; even those who endeavor to walk uprightly in the ways of God. This does not mean that the purpose and performance of God are uncertain, but only the great difficulties and hard encounters in the way; that they go through so many temptations and tribulations, so many fightings without and fears within. Yet all outward difficulties would be as nothing, were it not for lusts and corruptions within. These are the worst clogs and troubles. And if the way of the righteous be so hard, then how hard shall be the end of the ungodly sinner, who walks in sin with delight, and thinks the righteous is a fool for all his pains! The only way to keep the soul well, is, to commit it to God by prayer, and patient perseverance in well doing. He will overrule all to the final advantage of the believer.

1 PETER 5

Elders exhorted and encouraged. (1-4)
Younger Christians are to submit to their elders, and to yield with humility and patience to God, and to be sober, watchful, and steadfast in faith. (5-9)
Prayers for their growth and establishment. (10-14)

1-4 The apostle Peter does not command, but exhorts. He does not claim power to rule over all pastors and churches. It was the peculiar honor of Peter and a few more, to be witnesses of Christ's sufferings; but it is the privilege of all true Christians to partake of the glory that shall be revealed. These poor, dispersed, suffering Christians, were the flock of God, redeemed to God by the great Shepherd, living in holy love and communion, according to the will of God. They are also dignified with the title of God's heritage or clergy; his peculiar lot, chosen for his own people, to enjoy his special favor, and to do him special service. Christ is the chief Shepherd of the whole flock and heritage of God. And all faithful ministers will receive a crown of unfading glory, infinitely better and more honorable than all the authority, wealth, and pleasure of the world.

ings. No, but judge by the fruits. Have your fears and hopes changed places? Do you love the things you once hated, and hate the things you once loved? Are old things passed away? Have all things become new? Christian brethren, I put the query to you as well as to the rest. It is so easy to be deceived here. We shall find it no trifle to be born again. It is a solemn, it is a momentous matter. Let us not take it for granted because we have given up drunkenness that we are therefore converted, because we do not swear, because now we attend a place of worship. There is more wanted than this. Do not think you are saved because you have some good feelings, some good thoughts. There is more required than this—ye must be born again. And oh, Christian parents, train up your children in the fear of God, but do not be content with your training—they must be born again. And Christian husbands, and Christian wives, be not satisfied with merely praying that your partner's characters may become moral and honest; ask that something may be done for them which they cannot do for themselves. And you, philanthropists, who think that building new cottages, using fresh plans for drainage, teaching the poor economy, will be the means of emparadising the world; I pray you go further than such schemes as these. You must change the heart. It is but little use to alter the outward till you have renewed the inward. It is not the bark of the tree that is wrong so much as the sap. It is not the skin—it is the blood—nay, deeper than the blood—the very essence of the nature must be altered. The man must be as much made anew as if he never had an existence. Nay, a greater miracle than this, these most be two miracles combined—the old things must pass away, and new things must be created by the Holy Ghost. I tremble while I speak upon this theme, lest I, your minister, should know in theory but not in experience a mystery so sublime as this. What shall we do but together offer a prayer like this—"O God, if we be not regenerate let us know the worst of our state, and if we be, let us never cease to plead and pray for others till they too shall be renewed by the Holy Ghost." That which is born of the flesh is flesh; its best endeavors go no higher than flesh, and the flesh

ferings of Christ, and also a partaker of the glory that shall be revealed:

2 Feed the flock of God which is among you, taking the oversight thereof, not by constraint, but willingly; not for filthy lucre, but of a ready mind;

3 Neither as being lords over God's heritage, but being ensamples to the flock.

4 And when the chief Shepherd shall appear, ye shall receive a crown of glory that fadeth not away.

5 Likewise, ye younger, submit yourselves unto the elder. Yea, all of you be subject one to another, and be clothed with humility: for God resisteth the proud, and giveth grace to the humble.

6 Humble yourselves therefore under the mighty hand of God, that he may exalt you in due time:

7 Casting all your care upon him; for he careth for you.

8 Be sober, be vigilant; because your adversary the devil, as a roaring lion, walketh about, seeking whom he may devour:

9 Whom resist stedfast in the faith, knowing that the same afflictions are accomplished in your brethren that are in the world.

10 But the God of all grace, who hath called us unto his eternal glory by Christ Jesus, after that ye have suffered a while, make you perfect, stablish, strengthen, settle you.

11
To him be glory and dominion for ever and ever. Amen.

12 By Silvanus, a faithful brother unto you, as I suppose, I have written briefly, exhorting, and testifying that this is the true grace of God wherein ye stand.

13 The church that is at Babylon, elected together with you, saluteth you; and so doth Marcus my son.

14 Greet ye one another with a kiss of charity. Peace be with you all that are in Christ Jesus. Amen.

Shepherd; but many portions of this, under many pastors. But being examples to the flock – This procures the most ready and free obedience.

5. Ye younger, be subject to the elder – In years. And be all – Elder or younger. Subject to each other – Let every one be ready, upon all occasions, to give up his own will. Be clothed with humility – Bind it on, (so the word signifies,) so that no force may be able to tear it from you. James iv, 6; Prov. iii, 34.

6. The hand of God – Is in all troubles.

7. Casting all your care upon him – In every want or pressure.

8. But in the mean time watch. There is a close connection between this, and the duly casting our care upon him. How deeply had St. Peter himself suffered for want of watching! Be vigilant – As if he had said, Awake, and keep awake. Sleep no more: be this your care. As a roaring lion – Full of rage. Seeking – With all subtlety likewise. Whom he may devour or swallow up – Both soul and body.

9. Be the more steadfast, as ye know the same kind of afflictions are accomplished in – That is, suffered by, your brethren, till the measure allotted them is filled up.

10. Now the God of all grace – By which alone the whole work is begun, continued, and finished in your soul. After ye have suffered a while – A very little while compared with eternity. Himself – Ye have only to watch and resist the devil: the rest God will perform. Perfect – That no defect may remain. Stablish – That nothing may overthrow you. Strengthen – That ye may conquer all adverse power. And settle you – As an house upon a rock. So the apostle, being converted, does now "strengthen his brethren."

12. As I suppose – As I judge, upon good grounds, though not by immediate inspiration. I have written – That is, sent my letter by him. Adding my testimony – To that which ye before heard from Paul, that this is the true gospel of the grace of God.

13. The church that is at Babylon – Near which St. Peter probably was, when he wrote this epistle. Elected together with you – Partaking of the same faith with you. Mark – It seems the evangelist. My son – Probably converted by St. Peter. And he had occasionally served him, "as a son in the gospel."

MATTHEW HENRY

CHARLES H. SPURGEON

5-9 Humility preserves peace and order in all Christian churches and societies; pride disturbs them. Where God gives grace to be humble, he will give wisdom, faith, and holiness. To be humble, and subject to our reconciled God, will bring greater comfort to the soul than the gratification of pride and ambition. But it is to be in due time; not in thy fancied time, but God's own wisely appointed time. Does he wait, and wilt not thou? What difficulties will not the firm belief of his wisdom, power, and goodness get over! Then be humble under his hand. Cast "all your care;" personal cares, family cares, cares for the present, and cares for the future, for yourselves, for others, for the church, on God. These are burdensome, and often very sinful, when they arise from unbelief and distrust, when they torture and distract the mind, unfit us for duties, and hinder our delight in the service of God. The remedy is, to cast our care upon God, and leave every event to his wise and gracious disposal. Firm belief that the Divine will and counsels are right, calms the spirit of a man. Truly the godly too often forget this, and fret themselves to no purpose. Refer all to God's disposal. The golden mines of all spiritual comfort and good are wholly his, and the Spirit itself. Then, will he not furnish what is fit for us, if we humbly attend on him, and lay the care of providing for us, upon his wisdom and love? The whole design of Satan is to devour and destroy souls. He always is contriving whom he may ensnare to eternal ruin. Our duty plainly is, to be sober; to govern both the outward and the inward man by the rules of temperance. To be vigilant; suspicious of constant danger from this spiritual enemy, watchful and diligent to prevent his designs. Be steadfast, or solid, by faith. A man cannot fight upon a quagmire, there is no standing without firm ground to tread upon; this faith alone furnishes. It lifts the soul to the firm advanced ground of the promises, and fixes it there. The consideration of what others suffer, is proper to encourage us to bear our share in any affliction; and in whatever form Satan assaults us, or by whatever means, we may know that our brethren experience the same.

10-14 In conclusion, the apostle prays to God for them, as the God of all grace. Perfect implies their progress towards perfection. Stablish imports the curing of our natural lightness and inconstancy. Strengthen has respect to the growth of graces, especially where weakest and lowest. Settle signifies to fix upon a sure foundation, and may refer to him who is the Foundation and Strength of believers. These expressions show that perseverance and progress in grace are first to be sought after by every Christian. The power of these doctrines on the hearts, and the fruits in the lives, showed who are partakers of the grace of God. The cherishing and increase of Christian love, and of affection one to another, is no matter of empty compliment, but the stamp and badge of Jesus Christ on his followers. Others may have a false peace for a time, and wicked men may wish for it to themselves and to one another; but theirs is a vain hope, and will come to nought. All solid peace is founded on Christ, and flows from him.

cannot inherit the kingdom of God. That which is born of the Spirit alone is spirit, and only the Spirit can enter into spiritual things, inherit the spiritual portion which God has provided for his people. I have thus passed through the somewhat delicate and extremely difficult task of bringing out the apostle's meaning—the comparison between the two births, which are the door-steps of the two lives.

II. I now come to the second point—THE MANIFEST DIFFERENCE OF THE TWO LIVES RESULTING FROM THE TWO BIRTHS.

Brethren, look around you. To what shall we compare this immense assembly? As I look upon the many colors, and the varied faces, even if it were not in the text, I am certain that a meadow thickly besprinkled with flowers would rise up before my imagination. Look at the mass of people gathered together, and doth it not remind you of the field in its full summer glory, when the kingcups, daisies, clovers, and grass blooms, are sunning themselves in countless varieties of beauty? Ay, but not only in the poet's eye is there a resemblance, but in the mind of God, and in the experience of man. "All flesh is grass;" all that is born of the first birth, if we compare it to grass in poetry, may be compared to it also in fact, from the frailty and shortness of its existence. We passed the meadows but a month ago, and they were moved in verdant billows by the breeze like waves of ocean when they are softly stirred with the evening gale. We looked upon the whole scene, and it was exceeding fair. We passed it yesterday and the mower's scythe had cut asunder beauty from its roots, and there it lay in heaps ready to be gathered when fully dry. The grass is cut down so soon, but if it stood, it would wither, and handfuls of dust would take the place of the green and colored leaves, for doth not the grass wither and the flowers thereof fall avidly? Such is mortal life. We are not living, brethren, we are dying.

[Completion of this sermon follows under 2 Peter chapter.]

KING JAMES VERSION   JOHN WESLEY

2 PETER 1

1 Simon Peter, a servant and an apostle of Jesus Christ, to them that have obtained like precious faith with us through the righteousness of God and our Savior Jesus Christ:

2 Grace and peace be multiplied unto you through the knowledge of God, and of Jesus our Lord,

3 According as his divine power hath given unto us all things that pertain unto life and godliness, through the knowledge of him that hath called us to glory and virtue:

4 Whereby are given unto us exceeding great and precious promises: that by these ye might be partakers of the divine nature, having escaped the corruption that is in the world through lust.

5 And beside this, giving all diligence, add to your faith virtue; and to virtue knowledge;

6 And to knowledge temperance; and to temperance patience; and to patience godliness;

7 And to godliness brotherly kindness; and to brotherly kindness charity.

8 For if these things be in you, and abound, they make you that ye shall neither be barren nor unfruitful in the knowledge of our Lord Jesus Christ.

9 But he that lacketh these things is blind, and cannot see afar off, and hath forgotten that he was purged from his old sins.

10 Wherefore the rather, brethren, give diligence to make your calling and election sure: for if ye do these things, ye shall never fall:

11 For so an entrance shall be ministered unto you abundantly into the everlasting kingdom of our Lord and Savior Jesus Christ.

12 Wherefore I will not be negligent to put you always in remembrance of these things, though ye know them, and be established in the present truth.

13 Yea, I think it meet, as long as I am in this tabernacle, to stir you up by putting you in remembrance;

14 Knowing that shortly I must put off this my tabernacle, even

2 PETER 1

1. To them that have obtained – Not by their own works, but by the free grace of God. Like precious faith with us – The apostles. The faith of those who have not seen, being equally precious with that of those who saw our Lord in the flesh. Through the righteousness – Both active and passive. Of our God and Savior – It is this alone by which the justice of God is satisfied, and for the sake of which he gives this precious faith.

2. Through the divine, experimental knowledge of God and of Christ.

3. As his divine power has given us all things – There is a wonderful cheerfulness in this exordium, which begins with the exhortation itself. That pertain to life and godliness – To the present, natural life, and to the continuance and increase of spiritual life. Through that divine knowledge of him – Of Christ. Who hath called us by – His own glorious power, to eternal glory, as the end; by Christian virtue or fortitude, as the means.

4. Through which – Glory and fortitude. He hath given us exceeding great, and inconceivably precious promises – Both the promises and the things promised, which follow in their due season, that, sustained and encouraged by the promises, we may obtain all that he has promised. That, having escaped the manifold corruption which is in the world – From that fruitful fountain, evil desire. Ye may become partakers of the divine nature – Being renewed in the image of God, and having communion with them, so as to dwell in God and God in you.

5. For this very reason – Because God hath given you so great blessings. Giving all diligence – It is a very uncommon word which we render giving. It literally signifies, bringing in by the by, or over and above: implying, that good works the work; yet not unless we are diligent.

6. And to your knowledge temperance; and to your temperance patience – Bear and forbear; sustain and abstain; deny yourself and take up your cross daily. The more knowledge you have, the more renounce your own will; indulge yourself the less. "Knowledge puffeth up," and the great boasters of knowledge (the Gnostics) were those that "turned the grace of God into wantonness." But see that your knowledge be attended with temperance. Christian temperance implies the voluntary abstaining from all pleasure which does not lead to God. It extends to all things inward and outward: the due government of every thought, as well as affection. "It is using the world," so to use all outward, and so to restrain all inward things, that they may become a means of what is spiritual; a scaling ladder to ascend to what is above. Intemperance is to abuse the world. He that uses anything below, looking no higher, and getting no farther, is intemperate. He that uses the creature only so as to attain to more of the Creator, is alone temperate, and walks as Christ himself walked. And to patience godliness – Its proper support: a continual sense of God's presence and providence, and a filial fear of, and confidence in, him; otherwise your patience may be pride, surliness, stoicism; but not Christianity.

7. And to godliness brotherly kindness – No sullenness, sternness, moroseness: "sour godliness," so called, is of the devil. Of Christian godliness it may always be said, "Mild, sweet, serene, and tender is her mood, Nor grave with sternness, nor with lightness free: Against example resolutely good, Fervent in zeal, and warm in charity." And to brotherly kindness love – The pure and perfect love of God and of all mankind. The apostle here makes an advance upon the preceding article, brotherly kindness, which seems only to relate to the love of Christians toward one another.

8. For these being really in you – Added to your faith. And abounding – Increasing more and more, otherwise we fall short. Make you neither slothful nor unfruitful – Do not suffer you to be faint in your mind, or without fruit in your lives. If there is less faithfulness, less care and watchfulness, since we were pardoned, than there was before, and less diligence, less outward obedience, than when we were seeking remission of sin, we are both slothful and unfruit-

This epistle clearly is connected with the former epistle of Peter. The apostle having stated the blessings to which God has called Christians, exhorts those who had received these precious gifts, to endeavor to improve in graces and virtues. They are urged to this from the wickedness of false teachers. They are guarded against impostors and scoffers, by disproving their false assertions, ch. 3:1-7, and by showing why the great day of Christ's coming was delayed, with a description of its awful circumstances and consequences; and suitable exhortations to diligence and holiness are given.

2 PETER 1

Exhortations to add the exercise of various other graces to faith. (1-11)

The apostle looks forward to his approaching decease. (12-15)

And confirms the truth of the gospel, relating to Christ's appearing to judgment. (16-21)

1-11 Faith unites the weak believer to Christ, as really as it does the strong one, and purifies the heart of one as truly as of another; and every sincere believer is by his faith justified in the sight of God. Faith worketh godliness, and produces effects which no other grace in the soul can do. In Christ all fullness dwells, and pardon, peace, grace, and knowledge, and new principles, are thus given through the Holy Spirit. The promises to those who are partakers of a Divine nature, will cause us to inquire whether we are really renewed in the spirit of our minds; let us turn all these promises into prayers for the transforming and purifying grace of the Holy Spirit. The believer must add knowledge to his virtue, increasing acquaintance with the whole truth and will of God. We must add temperance to knowledge; moderation about worldly things; and add to temperance, patience, or cheerful submission to the will of God. Tribulation worketh patience, whereby we bear all calamities and crosses with silence and submission. To patience we must add godliness: this includes the holy affections and dispositions found in the true worshiper of God; with tender affection to all fellow Christians, who are children of the same Father, servants of the same Master, members of the same family, travelers to the same country, heirs of the same inheritance. Wherefore let Christians labor to attain assurance of their calling, and of their election, by believing and well-doing; and thus carefully to endeavor, is a firm argument of the grace and mercy of God, upholding them so that they shall not utterly fall. Those who are diligent in the work of religion, shall have a triumphant entrance into that everlasting kingdom where Christ reigns, and they shall reign with him forever and ever; and it is in the practice of every good work that we are to expect entrance to heaven.

[Continuation of sermon, "The New Nature", 1 Peter 1:23-25, from 1 Peter chapter.]

Our pulse is "beating funeral marches to the tomb." The sand runs down from the upper bulb of the glass, and it is emptying fast. Death is written upon every brow. Man, know that thou art mortal, for thou all art born of woman. Thy first birth gave thee life and death together. Thou dost only breathe awhile to keep thee from the jaws of the grave, when that breath is spent, into the dust of death thou fallest there and then. Everything, especially during the last few weeks, has taught us the frailty of human life. The senator who guided the affairs of nations and beheld the rise of a free kingdom, lived not to see it fully organized, but expired with many a weighty secret unspoken. The judge who has sentenced many, receives his own sentence at the last. From this earth, since last we met together, master-minds have been taken away, and even the monarch on his throne has owned the monarchy of Death. How many of the masses too have fallen, and have been carried to their long home! There have been funerals, some of them funerals of honored men who perished doing their Master's will in saving human life, and alas, there have been unmoored burials of others who did the will of Satan, and have inherited the flame. There have been deaths abundant on the right hand and on the left, and well have Peter's words been proved—"All flesh is grass, and all the glory thereof is as the flower of the field; the grass withereth, and the flower thereof falleth away."

Now, brethren, let us look at the other side of the question. The second birth gave us a nature too—Will that also die? Is it like grass, and its glory like the flower of the field? No, most certainly not. The first nature dies because the seed was corruptible. But the second nature was not created by corruptible seed, but with incorruptible, even the Word of God into which God has infused his own life, so that it quickens us by the Spirit. That incorruptible word produces an incorruptible life. The child of God in his new nature never dies. He can never see death. Christ, who is in him, is the immortality and the life. "He that liveth and believeth in Christ shall never die." And yet again, "Though he were dead yet shall he live." When we are born again, we receive a nature which is indestructible by accident, which is not to be consumed by fire, drowned by river, weakened by old age, or smitten down by blast of pestilence; a nature invulnerable to poison; a nature which shall not be destroyed by the sword; a nature which can never die till the God that gave it

as our Lord Jesus Christ hath shewed me.

15 Moreover I will endeavor that ye may be able after my decease to have these things always in remembrance.

16 For we have not followed cunningly devised fables, when we made known unto you the power and coming of our Lord Jesus Christ, but were eyewitnesses of his majesty.

17 For he received from God the Father honor and glory, when there came such a voice to him from the excellent glory, This is my beloved Son, in whom I am well pleased.

18 And this voice which came from heaven we heard, when we were with him in the holy mount.

19 We have also a more sure word of prophecy; whereunto ye do well that ye take heed, as unto a light that shineth in a dark place, until the day dawn, and the day star arise in your hearts:

20 Knowing this first, that no prophecy of the scripture is of any private interpretation.

21 For the prophecy came not in old time by the will of man: but holy men of God spake as they were moved by the Holy Ghost.

2 PETER 2

1 But there were false prophets also among the people, even as there shall be false teachers among you, who privily shall bring in damnable heresies, even denying the Lord that bought them, and bring upon themselves swift destruction.

2 And many shall follow their pernicious ways; by reason of whom the way of truth shall be evil spoken of.

3 And through covetousness shall they with feigned words make merchandise of you: whose judgment now of a long time lingereth not, and their damnation slumbereth not.

4 For if God spared not the angels that sinned, but cast them down to hell, and delivered them into chains of darkness, to be reserved unto judgment;

ful in the knowledge of Christ, that is, in the faith, which then cannot work by love.

9. But he that wanteth these – That does not add them to his faith. Is blind – The eyes of his understanding are again closed. He cannot see God, or his pardoning love. He has lost the evidence of things not seen.

10. Wherefore – Considering the miserable state of these apostates. Brethren – St. Peter nowhere uses this appellation in either of his epistles, but in this important exhortation. Be the more diligent – By courage, knowledge, temperance, &c. To make your calling and election firm – God hath called you by his word and his Spirit; he hath elected you, separated you from the world, through sanctification of the Spirit. O cast not away these inestimable benefits! If ye are thus diligent to make your election firm, ye shall never finally fall.

11. For if ye do so, an entrance shall be ministered to you abundantly into the everlasting kingdom – Ye shall go in full triumph to glory.

12. Wherefore – Since everlasting destruction attends your sloth, everlasting glory your diligence, I will not neglect always to remind you of these things – Therefore he wrote another, so soon after the former, epistle. Though ye are established in the present truth – That truth which I am now declaring.

13. In this tabernacle – Or tent. How short is our abode in the body! How easily does a believer pass out of it!

14. Even as the Lord Jesus showed me – In the manner which had been foretold, John xxi, 18, &c. It is not improbable, he had also showed him that the time was now drawing nigh.

15. That ye may be able – By having this epistle among you.

16. These things are worthy to be always had in remembrance. For they are not cunningly devised fables – Like those common among the heathens. While we made known to you the power and coming – That is, the powerful coming of Christ in glory.

17. For he received divine honor and inexpressible glory – Shining from heaven above the brightness of the sun. When there came such a voice from the excellent glory – That is, from God the Father. Matt. xvii, 5.

18. And we – Peter, James, and John. St. John was still alive. Being with him in the holy mount – Made so by that glorious manifestation, as mount Horeb was of old, Exod. iii, 4, 5.

19. And we – St. Peter here speaks in the name of all Christians. Have the word of prophecy – The words of Moses, Isaiah, and all the prophets, are one and the same word, every way consistent with itself. St. Peter does not cite any particular passage, but speaks of their entire testimony. More confirmed – By that display of his glorious majesty. To which word ye do well that ye take heed, as to a lamp which shone in a dark place – Wherein there was neither light nor window. Such anciently was the whole world, except that little spot where this lamp shone. Till the day should dawn – Till the full light of the gospel should break through the darkness. As is the difference between the light of a lamp and that of the day, such is that between the light of the Old Testament and of the New. And the morning star – Jesus Christ, Rev. xxii, 16. Arise in your hearts – Be revealed in you.

20. Ye do well, as knowing this, that no scripture prophecy is of private interpretation – It is not any man's own word. It is God, not the prophet himself, who thereby interprets things till then unknown.

21. For prophecy came not of old by the will of man – Of any mere man whatever. But the holy men of God – Devoted to him, and set apart by him for that purpose, spake and wrote. Being moved – Literally, carried. They were purely passive therein.

MATTHEW HENRY

CHARLES H. SPURGEON

12-15 We must be established in the belief of the truth, that we may not be shaken by every wind of doctrine; and especially in the truth necessary for us to know in our day, what belongs to our peace, and what is opposed in our time. The body is but a tabernacle, or tent, of the soul. It is a mean and movable dwelling. The nearness of death makes the apostle diligent in the business of life. Nothing can so give composure in the prospect, or in the hour, of death, as to know that we have faithfully and simply followed the Lord Jesus, and sought his glory. Those who fear the Lord, talk of his loving-kindness. This is the way to spread the knowledge of the Lord; and by the written word, they are enabled to do this.

16-21 The gospel is no weak thing, but comes in power, Ro 1:16. The law sets before us our wretched state by sin, but there it leaves us. It discovers our disease, but does not make known the cure. It is the sight of Jesus crucified, in the gospel, that heals the soul. Try to dissuade the covetous worldling from his greediness, one ounce of gold weighs down all reasons. Offer to stay a furious man from anger by arguments, he has not patience to hear them. Try to detain the licentious, one smile is stronger with him than all reason. But come with the gospel, and urge them with the precious blood of Jesus Christ, shed to save their souls from hell, and to satisfy for their sins, and this is that powerful pleading which makes good men confess that their hearts burn within them, and bad men, even an Agrippa, to say they are almost persuaded to be Christians, Ac 26:28. God is well pleased with Christ, and with us in him. This is the Messiah who was promised, through whom all who believe in him shall be accepted and saved. The truth and reality of the gospel also are foretold by the prophets and penmen of the Old Testament, who spake and wrote under influence, and according to the direction of the Spirit of God. How firm and sure should our faith be, who have such a firm and sure word to rest upon! When the light of the Scripture is darted into the blind mind and dark understanding, by the Holy Spirit of God, it is like the daybreak that advances, and diffuses itself through the whole soul, till it makes perfect day. As the Scripture is the revelation of the mind and will of God, every man ought to search it, to understand the sense and meaning. The Christian knows that book to be the word of God, in which he tastes a sweetness, and feels a power, and sees a glory, truly divine. And the prophecies already fulfilled in the person and salvation of Christ, and in the great concerns of the church and the world, form an unanswerable proof of the truth of Christianity. The Holy Ghost inspired holy men to speak and write. He so assisted and directed them in delivering what they had received from him, that they clearly expressed what they made known. So that the Scriptures are to be accounted the words of the Holy Ghost, and all the plainness and simplicity, all the power and all the pro-

should himself expire and Deity die out. Think of this, my brethren, and surely you will find reason to rejoice. But perhaps, you ask me, why it is the new nature can never die? I am sure the text teaches it never can. "But not of corruptible seed, but of incorruptible, even of the Word of God which liveth and abideth for ever." If that does not teach that the spiritual nature which is given us by the new birth never dies, it does not teach anything at all; and if it does teach that, where goes Arminian doctrine of falling from grace; where go your Arminian fears of perishing after all? But let me show you why it is that this nature never dies. First, from the fact of its nature. It is in itself incorruptible. Every like produces in like. Man, dying man, produces dying man; God, eternal God, produces everlasting nature when he begets again unto a lively hope, by the resurrection of Christ from the dead. "As is the earthy, such are they also that are earthy:" the earthy dies, we who are earthy die too. "As is the heavenly, such are they also that are heavenly," the heavenly never dies, and if we are born as the heavenly, the heavenly nature dieth neither. "The first Adam was made a living soul." We are made living souls too, but that soul at last is separated from the body. "The second Adam is made a quickening spirit," and that spirit is not only alive but quickening. Do you not perceive it?—the first was a quickened soul—quickened, receiving life for a season; the second is a quickening spirit, giving out life, rather than receiving it; like that angel whom some poet pictures, who perpetually shot forth sparklers of fire, having within himself an undying flame, the fountain of perpetual floods of light and heat. So is it with the new nature within us, it is not merely a quickened thing which may die, but a quickening thing which cannot die, being similar to Christ the quickening Spirit. But then, more than this, the new nature cannot die, because the Holy Spirit perpetually supplies it with life. "He giveth more grace"—grace upon grace. You know the apostle puts it thus: "If when we were enemies we were reconciled to God by the death of his Son, much more being reconciled we shall be saved by his life." Is not the Holy Spirit the divine agent by whom the life of Christ is infused into us? Now, the life-floods which the Holy Spirit sends into us, co-work with the immortality of the new-born spirit, and so doubly preserve the eternity of our bliss. But then, again, we are in vital union with Christ, and to suppose that the new nature could die out, were to imagine that a member of Christ would die, that a finger, a hand, an arm, could rot from the person of Jesus, that he could be maimed and divided. Doth not the apostle say, "Is Christ divided?"

5 And spared not the old world, but saved Noah the eighth person, a preacher of righteousness, bringing in the flood upon the world of the ungodly;

6 And turning the cities of Sodom and Gomorrha into ashes condemned them with an overthrow, making them an ensample unto those that after should live ungodly;

7 And delivered just Lot, vexed with the filthy conversation of the wicked:

8 (For that righteous man dwelling among them, in seeing and hearing, vexed his righteous soul from day to day with their unlawful deeds;)

9 The Lord knoweth how to deliver the godly out of temptations, and to reserve the unjust unto the day of judgment to be punished:

10 But chiefly them that walk after the flesh in the lust of uncleanness, and despise government. Presumptuous are they, selfwilled, they are not afraid to speak evil of dignities.

11 Whereas angels, which are greater in power and might, bring not railing accusation against them before the Lord.

12 But these, as natural brute beasts, made to be taken and destroyed, speak evil of the things that they understand not; and shall utterly perish in their own corruption;

13 And shall receive the reward of unrighteousness, as they that count it pleasure to riot in the day time. Spots they are and blemishes, sporting themselves with their own deceivings while they feast with you;

14 Having eyes full of adultery, and that cannot cease from sin; beguiling unstable souls: an heart they have exercised with covetous practices; cursed children:

15 Which have forsaken the right way, and are gone astray, following the way of Balaam the son of Bosor, who loved the wages of unrighteousness;

16 But was rebuked for his iniquity: the dumb ass speaking with man's voice forbad the madness of the prophet.

17 These are wells without water, clouds that are carried

2 PETER 2

1. But there were false prophets also – As well as true. Among the people – Of Israel. Those that spake even the truth, when God had not sent them; and also those that were truly sent of him, and yet corrupted or softened their message, were false prophets. As there shall be false – As well as true. Teachers among you, who will privately bring in – Into the church. Destructive heresies – They first, by denying the Lord, introduced destructive heresies, that is, divisions; or they occasioned first these divisions, and then were given up to a reprobate mind, even to deny the Lord that bought them. Either the heresies are the effect of denying the Lord, or the denying the Lord was the consequence of the heresies. Even denying – Both by their doctrine and their works. The Lord that bought them – With his own blood. Yet these very men perish everlastingly. Therefore Christ bought even them that perish.

2. The way of truth will be evil spoken of – By those who blend all false and true Christians together.

3. They will make merchandise of you – Only use you to gain by you, as merchants do their wares. Whose judgment now of a long time lingereth not – Was long ago determined, and will be executed speedily. All sinners are adjudged to destruction; and God's punishing some proves he will punish the rest.

4. Cast them down to hell – The bottomless pit, a place of unknown misery. Delivered them – Like condemned criminals to safe custody, as if bound with the strongest chains in a dungeon of darkness, to be reserved unto the judgment of the great day. Though still those chains do not hinder their often walking up and down seeking whom they may devour.

5. And spared not the old, the antediluvian, world, but he preserved Noah the eighth person – that is, Noah and seven others, a preacher as well as practicer, of righteousness. Bringing a flood on the world of the ungodly – Whose numbers stood them in no stead.

9. It plainly appears, from these instances, that the Lord knoweth, hath both wisdom and power and will, to deliver the godly out of all temptations, and to punish the ungodly.

10. Chiefly them that walk after the flesh – Corrupt nature; particularly in the lust of uncleanness. And despise government – The authority of their governors. Dignities – Persons in authority.

11. Whereas angels – When they appear before the Lord, Job i, 6; Job ii, 1, to give an account of what they have seen and done on the earth.

12. Savage as brute beasts – Several of which in the present disordered state of the world, seem born to be taken and destroyed.

13. They count it pleasure to riot in the day time – They glory in doing it in the face of the sun. They are spots in themselves, blemishes to any church. Sporting themselves with their own deceivings – Making a jest of those whom they deceive and even jesting while they are deceiving their own souls.

15. The way of Balaam the son of Bosor – So the Chaldeans pronounced what the Jews termed Beor; namely, the way of covetousness. Who loved – Earnestly desired, though he did not dare to take, the reward of unrighteousness – The money which Balak would have given him for cursing Israel.

16. The beast – Though naturally dumb.

17. Fountains and clouds promise water: so do these promise, but do not perform.

18. They ensnare in the desires of the flesh – Allowing them to gratify some unholy desire. Those who were before entirely escaped from the spirit, custom, and company of them that live in error – In sin.

19. While they promise them liberty – From needless restraints and scruples; from the bondage of the law. Themselves are slaves of corruption – Even sin, the vilest of all bondage.

20. For if after they – Who are thus ensnared. Have escaped the pollutions of

priety of the words and expressions, come from God. Mix faith with what you find in the Scriptures, and esteem and reverence the Bible as a book written by holy men, taught by the Holy Ghost.

2 PETER 2

Believers are cautioned against false teachers, and the certainty of their punishment shown from examples. (1-9)

An account of these seducers, as exceedingly wicked. (10-16)

But as making high pretenses to liberty and purity. (17-22)

1-9 Though the way of error is a hurtful way, many are always ready to walk therein. Let us take care we give no occasion to the enemy to blaspheme the holy name whereby we are called, or to speak evil of the way of salvation by Jesus Christ, who is the Way, the Truth, and the Life. These seducers used feigned words, they deceived the hearts of their followers. Such are condemned already, and the wrath of God abides upon them. God's usual method of proceeding is shown by examples. Angels were cast down from all their glory and dignity, for their disobedience. If creatures sin, even in heaven, they must suffer in hell. Sin is the work of darkness, and darkness is the wages of sin. See how God dealt with the old world. The number of offenders no more procures favor, than their quality. If the sin be universal, the punishment shall likewise extend to all. If in a fruitful soil the people abound in sin, God can at once turn a fruitful land into barrenness, and a well-watered country into ashes. No plans or politics can keep off judgments from a sinful people. He who keeps fire and water from hurting his people, Isa 43:2, can make either destroy his enemies; they are never safe. When God sends destruction on the ungodly, he commands deliverance for the righteous. In bad company we cannot but get either guilt or grief. Let the sins of others be troubles to us. Yet it is possible for the children of the Lord, living among the most profane, to retain their integrity; there being more power in the grace of Christ, and his dwelling in them, than in the temptations of Satan, or the example of the wicked, with all their terrors or allurements. In our intentions and inclinations to commit sin, we meet with strange hindrances, if we mark them. When we intend mischief, God sends many stops to hinder us, as if to say, Take heed what you do. His wisdom and power will surely effect the purposes of his love, and the engagements of his truth; while wicked men often escape suffering here, because they are kept to the day of judgment, to be punished with the devil and his angels.

10-16 Impure seducers and their abandoned followers, give themselves up to their own fleshly minds. Refusing to bring every thought to the obedience of

And was it not written, "Not a bone of him shall be broken?" and how were this true, if we were broken from him, or rolled from his body? My brethren, we receive the divine sap through Christ the stem; that divine sap keeps us alive but more the very fact that we are joined to Christ preserves our life, "Because I live ye shall live also." The new life cannot die, because God is pledged to keep it alive. "I give unto my sheep eternal life, and they shall never perish, neither shall any pluck them out of my hand." "My Father which gave them me is greater than all, and none shall pluck them out of my Father's hand." And yet again, "The water which I shall give him shall be in him a well of water, springing up unto everlasting life." And yet again, "He that believeth in me shall never hunger and never thirst." And so might we repeat multitudes of passages where the divine promise engages omnipotence and divine wisdom, to preserve the new life. So then, let us gather these all up in one. As a man born of the flesh, I shall die, as a new man born of the Spirit, I shall never die. Thou, O flesh, the offspring of flesh thou shalt see corruption. Thou, O spirit, new-created spirit, offspring of the Lord corruption thou shalt never see. With our glorious Covenant Head we may exclaim "Thou wilt not leave my soul in hell, nor wilt thou suffer thine holy one to see corruption." I shall die, yet never die. My life shall flee, yet never flee. I shall pass away, and yet abide; I shall be carried to the tomb, and yet, soaring upward, the tomb can ne'er contain the quickened Spirit. Oh, children of God, I know not any subject that ought more thoroughly to lift you out of yourselves than this. Now let the divine nature live in you; come, put down the animal for a moment, put down the mere mental faculty; let the living spark blaze up; come, let the divine element, the new-born nature that God has given to you, let that now speak, and let its voice be praise; let it look up and let it breathe its own atmosphere, the heaven of God, in which it shall shortly rejoice. O God, our Father, help us to walk not after the flesh, but after the Spirit, seeing that we have by thine own self been quickened to an immortal life.

III. I now come to the last, and perhaps the most interesting point of all. THE GLORY OF THE TWO NATURES IS CONTRASTED. Every nature has its glory. Brethren, look at the field again. There is not only the grass but there is the flower which is the glory of the field. Sometimes many colored hues begem the pastures with beauty. Now, the painted flower is the glory of the verdant field. It comes up later than the grass, and it dies sooner, for the grass is up a

KING JAMES VERSION

with a tempest; to whom the mist of darkness is reserved for ever.

18 For when they speak great swelling words of vanity, they allure through the lusts of the flesh, through much wantonness, those that were clean escaped from them who live in error.

19 While they promise them liberty, they themselves are the servants of corruption: for of whom a man is overcome, of the same is he brought in bondage.

20 For if after they have escaped the pollutions of the world through the knowledge of the Lord and Savior Jesus Christ, they are again entangled therein, and overcome, the latter end is worse with them than the beginning.

21 For it had been better for them not to have known the way of righteousness, than, after they have known it, to turn from the holy commandment delivered unto them.

22 But it is happened unto them according to the true proverb, The dog is turned to his own vomit again; and the sow that was washed to her wallowing in the mire.

2 PETER 3

1 This second epistle, beloved, I now write unto you; in both which I stir up your pure minds by way of remembrance:

2 That ye may be mindful of the words which were spoken before by the holy prophets, and of the commandment of us the apostles of the Lord and Savior:

3 Knowing this first, that there shall come in the last days scoffers, walking after their own lusts,

4 And saying, Where is the promise of his coming? for since the fathers fell asleep, all things continue as they were from the beginning of the creation.

5 For this they willingly are ignorant of, that by the word of God the heavens were of old, and the earth standing out of the water and in the water:

6 Whereby the world that then

JOHN WESLEY

the world – The sins which pollute all who know not God. Through the knowledge of Christ – That is, through faith in him, chap. i, 3. They are again entangled therein, and overcome, their last state is worse than the first – More inexcusable, and causing a greater damnation.

21. The commandment – The whole law of God, once not only delivered to their ears, but written in their hearts.

22. The dog, the sow – Such are all men in the sight of God before they receive his grace, and after they have made shipwreck of the faith. Prov. xxvi, 11.

2 PETER 3

2, 3. Be the more mindful thereof, because ye know scoffers will come first – Before the Lord comes. Walking after their own evil desires – Here is the origin of the error, the root of libertinism. Do we not see this eminently fulfilled?

4. Saying, Where is the promise of his coming – To judgment (They do not even deign to name him.) We see no sign of any such thing. For ever since the fathers – Our first ancestors. Fell asleep, all things – Heaven. water, earth. Continue as they were from the beginning of the creation – Without any such material change as might make us believe they will ever end.

5. For this they are willingly ignorant of – They do not care to know or consider. That by the almighty word of God – Which bounds the duration of all things, so that it cannot be either longer or shorter. Of old – Before the flood. The aerial heavens were, and the earth – Not as it is now, but standing out of the water and in the water – Perhaps the interior globe of earth was fixed in the midst of the great deep, the abyss of water; the shell or exterior globe standing out of the water, covering the great deep. This, or some other great and manifest difference between the original and present constitution of the terraqueous globe, seems then to have been so generally known, that St. Peter charges their ignorance of it totally upon their willfulness.

6. Through which – Heaven and earth, the windows of heaven being opened, and the fountains of the great deep broken up. The world that then was – The whole antediluvian race. Being overflowed with water, perished – And the heavens and earth themselves, though they did not perish, yet underwent a great change. So little ground have these scoffers for saying that all things continue as they were from the creation.

7. But the heavens and the earth, that are now – Since the flood. Are reserved unto fire at the day wherein God will judge the world, and punish the ungodly with everlasting destruction.

8. But be not ye ignorant – Whatever they are. Of this one thing – Which casts much light on the point in hand. That one day is with the Lord as a thousand years, and a thousand years as one day – Moses had said, Psalm xc, 4, "A thousand years in thy sight are as one day;" which St. Peter applies with regard to the last day, so as to denote both his eternity, whereby he exceeds all measure of time in his essence and in his operation; his knowledge, to which all things past or to come are present every moment; his power, which needs no long delay, in order to bring its work to perfection; and his longsuffering, which excludes all impatience of expectation, and desire of making haste. One day is with the Lord as a thousand years – That is, in one day, in one moment he can do the work of a thousand years. Therefore he "is not slow:" he is always equally ready to fulfill his promise. And a thousand years are as one day – That is, no delay is long to God. A thousand years are as one day to the eternal God.

9. The Lord is not slow – As if the time fixed for it were past. Concerning his promise – Which shall surely be fulfilled in its season. But is longsuffering towards us – Children of men. Not willing that any soul, which he hath made should perish.

10. But the day of the Lord will come as a thief – Suddenly, unexpectedly. In

Christ, they act against God's righteous precepts. They walk after the flesh, they go on in sinful courses, and increase to greater degrees of impurity and wickedness. They also despise those whom God has set in authority over them, and requires them to honor. Outward temporal good things are the wages sinners expect and promise themselves. And none have more cause to tremble, than those who are bold to gratify their sinful lusts, by presuming on the Divine grace and mercy. Many such there have been, and are, who speak lightly of the restraints of God's law, and deem themselves freed from obligations to obey it. Let Christians stand at a distance from such.

17-22 The word of truth is the water of life, which refreshes the souls that receive it; but deceivers spread and promote error, and are set forth as empty, because there is no truth in them. As clouds hinder the light of the sun, so do these darken counsel by words wherein there is no truth. Seeing that these men increase darkness in this world, it is very just that the mist of darkness should be their portion in the next. In the midst of their talk of liberty, these men are the vilest slaves; their own lusts gain a complete victory over them, and they are actually in bondage. When men are entangled, they are easily overcome; therefore Christians should keep close to the word of God, and watch against all who seek to bewilder them. A state of apostasy is worse than a state of ignorance. To bring an evil report upon the good way of God, and a false charge against the way of truth, must expose to the heaviest condemnation. How dreadful is the state here described! Yet though such a case is deplorable, it is not utterly hopeless; the leper may be made clean, and even the dead may be raised. Is thy backsliding a grief to thee? Believe in the Lord Jesus, and thou shalt be saved.

2 PETER 3

The design here is to remind of Christ's final coming to judgment. (1-4)

He will appear unexpectedly, when the present frame of nature will be dissolved by fire. (5-10)

From thence is inferred the need for holiness, and steadfastness in the faith. (11-18)

1-4 The purified minds of Christians are to be stirred up, that they may be active and lively in the work of holiness. There will be scoffers in the last days, under the gospel, men who make light of sin, and mock at salvation by Jesus Christ. One very principal article of our faith refers to what only has a promise to rest upon, and scoffers will attack it till our Lord is come. They will not believe that he will come. Because they see no changes, therefore they fear not God, Ps 55:19. What he never has done, they fancy he never can do, or never will do.

long while before the flower blooms, and when the flower is dead, the stalk of the grass still retains vitality. It is precisely so with us. Our nature has its glory, but that glory does not arrive for years. The babe has not yet the glory of full manhood, and when that glory does come, it dies before our nature dies, for "they that look out of the windows are darkened, the grinders cease because they are few." The man loses his glory and becomes a tottering imbecile before life becomes extinct. The flower comes up last and dies first, our glory comes last and dies first, too. O flesh! O flesh! what contempt is passed upon thee! Thy very existence is frail and feeble, but thy glory more frail and feeble still. It grows but late and then it dies, alas how soon! But what is the glory of the flesh? Give me your attention for a moment while I tell you briefly. In some, the glory of the flesh is BEAUTY. Their face is fair to look upon, and as the handiwork of the Great Worker, it should be admired. When a person becometh vain of it, beauty becomes shame; but to have well-proportioned features is, doubtless, no mean endowment. There is a glory in the beauty of the flesh, but how late it is developed, and how soon it fades! How soon do the cheeks become hollow! how frequently does the complexion grow sallow, and the bright eyes are dimmed, and the comely visage is marred! A part, too, of the glory of the flesh is physical strength. To be a strong man, to have the bones well set and the muscles well braced,—to have good muscular vigor is no small thing. Many men take delight in the legs of a man, and in the strength of his arm. Well, as God made him, he is a wonderful creature, and 'twere wrong for us not to admire the masterpiece of God. But how late does muscular strength arrive! There are the days of infancy, and there are the days of youth, when as yet the strong man is but feeble; and then, when he has had his little hey-day of strength, how doth the stalwart frame begin to rock and reel! and the rotting teeth and the whitened hair show that death has begun to claim the heriot clay, and will soon take possession of it for himself. "The glory thereof falleth away." To others, the glory of the flesh lies rather in the mind. They have eloquence, they can so speak as to enchant the ears of the multitude. The bees of eloquence have made their hives between the lips of the orator, and honey distils with every word. Yes, but how late is this a coming! How many years before the child speaks articulately, and before the young man is able to deliver himself with courage! And then, how soon it goes!—till, mumbling from between his toothless jaws, the poor man would speak the words of wisdom, but the lips

was, being overflowed with water, perished:

7 But the heavens and the earth, which are now, by the same word are kept in store, reserved unto fire against the day of judgment and perdition of ungodly men.

8 But, beloved, be not ignorant of this one thing, that one day is with the Lord as a thousand years, and a thousand years as one day.

9 The Lord is not slack concerning his promise, as some men count slackness; but is longsuffering to us-ward, not willing that any should perish, but that all should come to repentance.

10 But the day of the Lord will come as a thief in the night; in the which the heavens shall pass away with a great noise, and the elements shall melt with fervent heat, the earth also and the works that are therein shall be burned up.

11 Seeing then that all these things shall be dissolved, what manner of persons ought ye to be in all holy conversation and godliness,

12 Looking for and hasting unto the coming of the day of God, wherein the heavens being on fire shall be dissolved, and the elements shall melt with fervent heat?

13 Nevertheless we, according to his promise, look for new heavens and a new earth, wherein dwelleth righteousness.

14 Wherefore, beloved, seeing that ye look for such things, be diligent that ye may be found of him in peace, without spot, and blameless.

15 And account that the longsuffering of our Lord is salvation; even as our beloved brother Paul also according to the wisdom given unto him hath written unto you;

16 As also in all his epistles, speaking in them of these things; in which are some things hard to be understood, which they that are unlearned and unstable wrest, as they do also the other scriptures, unto their own destruction.

which the heavens shall pass away with a great noise – Surprisingly expressed by the very sound of the original word. The elements shall melt with fervent heat – The elements seem to mean, the sun, moon, and stars; not the four, commonly so called; for air and water cannot melt, and the earth is mentioned immediately after. The earth and all the works – Whether of nature or art. That are therein shall be burned up – And has not God already abundantly provided for this?

1. By the stores of subterranean fire which are so frequently bursting out at Etna, Vesuvius, Hecla, and many other burning mountains.

2. By the ethereal (vulgarly called electrical) fire, diffused through the whole globe; which, if the secret chain that now binds it up were loosed, would immediately dissolve the whole frame of nature.

3. By comets, one of which, if it touch the earth in its course toward the sun, must needs strike it into that abyss of fire; if in its return from the sun, when it is heated, as a great man computes, two thousand times hotter than a red-hot cannonball, it must destroy all vegetables and animals long before their contact, and soon after burn it up.

11. Seeing then that all these things are dissolved – To the eye of faith it appears as done already. All these things – Mentioned before; all that are included in that scriptural expression, "the heavens and the earth;" that is, the universe. On the fourth day God made the stars, Gen. i, 16, which will be dissolved together with the earth. They are deceived, therefore, who restrain either the history of the creation, or this description of the destruction, of the world to the earth and lower heavens; imagining the stars to be more ancient than the earth, and to survive it. Both the dissolution and renovation are ascribed, not to the one heaven which surrounds the earth, but to the heavens in general, ver. 10, 13, without any restriction or limitation. What persons ought ye to be in all holy conversation – With men. And godliness – Toward your Creator.

12. Hastening on – As it were by your earnest desires and fervent prayers. The coming of the day of God – Many myriads of days he grants to men: one, the last, is the day of God himself.

13. We look for new heavens and a new earth – Raised as it were out of the ashes of the old; we look for an entire new state of things. Wherein dwelleth righteousness – Only righteous spirits. How great a mystery!

14. Labor that whenever he cometh ye may be found in peace – May meet him without terror, being sprinkled with his blood, and sanctified by his Spirit, so as to be without spot and blameless. Isaiah lxv, 17; Isaiah lxvi, 22.

15. And account the longsuffering of the Lord salvation – Not only designed to lead men to repentance, but actually conducing thereto: a precious means of saving many more souls. As our beloved brother Paul also hath written to you – This refers not only to the single sentence preceding, but to all that went before. St. Paul had written to the same effect concerning the end of the world, in several parts of his epistles, and particularly in his Epistle to the Hebrews. Rom. ii, 4.

16. As also in all his epistles – St. Peter wrote this a little before his own and St. Paul's martyrdom. St. Paul therefore had now written all his epistles; and even from this expression we may learn that St. Peter had read them all, perhaps sent to him by St. Paul himself. Nor was he at all disgusted by what St. Paul had written concerning him in the Epistle to the Galatians. Speaking of these things – Namely, of the coming of our Lord, delayed through his longsuffering, and of the circumstances preceding and accompanying it. Which things the unlearned – They who are not taught of God. And the unstable – Wavering, double-minded, unsettled men. Wrest – As though Christ would not come. As they do also the other scriptures – Therefore St Paul's writings were now part of the scriptures. To their own destruction – But that some use the scriptures ill, is no reason why others should not use them at all.

5-10 Had these scoffers considered the dreadful vengeance with which God swept away a whole world of ungodly men at once, surely they would not have scoffed at his threatening an equally terrible judgment. The heavens and the earth which now are, by the same word, it is declared, will be destroyed by fire. This is as sure to come, as the truth and the power of God can make it. Christians are here taught and established in the truth of the coming of the Lord. Though, in the account of men, there is a vast difference between one day and a thousand years, yet, in the account of God, there is no difference. All things past, present, and future, are ever before him: the delay of a thousand years cannot be so much to him, as putting off any thing for a day or for an hour is to us. If men have no knowledge or belief of the eternal God, they will be very apt to think him such as themselves. How hard is it to form any thoughts of eternity! What men count slackness, is long-suffering, and that to us-ward; it is giving more time to his own people, to advance in knowledge and holiness, and in the exercise of faith and patience, to abound in good works, doing and suffering what they are called to, that they may bring glory to God. Settle therefore in your hearts that you shall certainly be called to give an account of all things done in the body, whether good or evil. And let a humble and diligent walking before God, and a frequent judging of yourselves, show a firm belief of the future judgment, though many live as if they were never to give any account at all. This day will come, when men are secure, and have no expectation of the day of the Lord. The stately palaces, and all the desirable things in which people given over to living for the world seek and place their happiness, shall be burned up; all sorts of creatures God has made, and all the works of men, must pass through the fire, which shall be a consuming fire to all that sin has brought into the world, though a refining fire to the works of God's hand. What will become of us, if we set our affections on this earth, and make it our portion, seeing all these things shall be burned up? Therefore make sure of happiness beyond this visible world.

11-18 From the doctrine of Christ's second coming, we are exhorted to purity and godliness. This is the effect of real knowledge. Very exact and universal holiness is enjoined, not resting in any low measure or degree. True Christians look for new heavens and a new earth; freed from the vanity to which things present are subject, and the sin they are polluted with. Those only who are clothed with the righteousness of Christ, and sanctified by the Holy Ghost, shall be admitted to dwell in this holy place. He is faithful, who has promised. Those, whose sins are pardoned, and their peace made with God, are the only safe and happy people; therefore follow after peace, and that with all men; follow after holiness as well as peace. Never expect to be found at that day of God in peace,

of age deny him utterance. Or, let the glory be wisdom. There is a man whose glory is his masterly power over others. He can foresee and look further than other men, he can match craft by craft: he is so wise that his fellows put confidence in him. This is the glory of the flesh; how late is it in coming!—from the puking child, what a distance up to the wise man! And then how soon it is gone! How often, while yet the man himself in his flesh is in vigor has the mind shewn symptoms of decay! Well, take what ye will to be the glory of the flesh, I will still pronounce over it "Vanity of vanities, all is vanity." If the flesh be frail, the glory of the flesh is frailer still, if the grass wither, certainly the flower of the grass withereth before it.

But is this true of the new nature? Brethren, is this true of that which was implanted at the second birth? I have just shown you, I think, that the existence of the new nature is eternal, because it was not born of corruptible seed, but of incorruptible. I have tried to show that it can never perish and can never die. But your unbelief suggests, "Perhaps its glory may." No, its glory never can. And what is the glory of the new-born nature? Why, its glory first of all is beauty. But what is its beauty? It is to be like the Lord Jesus. We are, when we shall see him as he is, to be like him. But that beauty shall never fade, eternity itself shall not hollow the cheeks of this seraphic comeliness, nor dim the brilliant eye of this celestial radiance. We shall be like Christ, but the likeness shall ne'er be marred by time, nor consumed by decay. I said just now that the glory of the flesh consisted sometimes in its strength, so does the glory of the Spirit consist in its vigor, but then it is a force that never shall be expended. The strength of the new-born nature is the Holy Ghost himself, and while Deity remains omnipotent, our new nature shall go on increasing in vigor till we come first to the stature of perfect men in Christ Jesus, and next come to be glorified men standing before his throne. The flower of the new nature you cannot see much of yet, you see through a glass darkly. That flower of glory consists perhaps, too, in eloquence. "Eloquence," say you, "how can that be?" I said the glory of the old nature might be eloquence, so with the new, but this is the eloquence—"Abba Father." This is an eloquence you can use now. It is one which when you cannot speak a word which might move an audience, shall still remain upon your tongue to move the courts of heaven. You shall be able to say, "Abba Father," in the very pangs of death, and waking from your beds of dust and silent clay, more eloquent still you shall cry, "Hallelujah," you shall join the eternal chorus, swell the divine symphony of cherubim and

17 Ye therefore, beloved, seeing ye know these things before, beware lest ye also, being led away with the error of the wicked, fall from your own stedfastness.

18 But grow in grace, and in the knowledge of our Lord and Savior Jesus Christ. To him be glory both now and for ever. Amen.

18. But grow in grace – That is, in every Christian temper. There may be, for a time, grace without growth; as there may be natural life without growth. But such sickly life, of soul or body, will end in death, and every day draw closer to it. Health is the means of both natural and spiritual growth. If the remaining evil of our fallen nature be not daily mortified, it will, like an evil humor in the body, destroy the whole man. But "if ye through the Spirit do mortify the deeds of the body," (only so far as we do this,) "ye shall live" the life of faith, holiness, happiness. The end and design of grace being purchased and bestowed on us, is to destroy the image of the earthy, and restore us to that of the heavenly. And so far as it does this, it truly profits us; and also makes way for more of the heavenly gift, that we may at last be filled with all the fullness of God. The strength and well-being of a Christian depend on what his soul feeds on, as the health of the body depends on whatever we make our daily food. If we feed on what is according to our nature, we grow; if not, we pine away and die. The soul is of the nature of God, and nothing but what is according to his holiness can agree with it. Sin, of every kind, starves the soul, and makes it consume away. Let us not try to invert the order of God in his new creation: we shall only deceive ourselves. It is easy to forsake the will of God, and follow our own; but this will bring leanness into the soul. It is easy to satisfy ourselves without being possessed of the holiness and happiness of the gospel. It is easy to call these frames and feelings, and then to oppose faith to one and Christ to the other. Frames (allowing the expression) are no other than heavenly tempers, "the mind that was in Christ." Feelings are the divine consolations of the Holy Ghost shed abroad in the heart of him that truly believes. And wherever faith is, and wherever Christ is, there are these blessed frames and feelings. If they are not in us, it is a sure sign that though the wilderness became a pool, the pool is become a wilderness again. And in the knowledge of Christ – That is, in faith, the root of all. To him be the glory to the day of eternity – An expression naturally flowing from that sense which the apostle had felt in his soul throughout this whole chapter. Eternity is a day without night, without interruption, without end.

if you are lazy and idle in this your day, in which we must finish the work given us to do. Only the diligent Christian will be the happy Christian in the day of the Lord. Our Lord will suddenly come to us, or shortly call us to him; and shall he find us idle? Learn to make a right use of the patience of our Lord, who as yet delays his coming. Proud, carnal, and corrupt men, seek to wrest some things into a seeming agreement with their wicked doctrines. But this is no reason why St. Paul's epistles, or any other part of the Scriptures, should be laid aside; for men, left to themselves, pervert every gift of God. Then let us seek to have our minds prepared for receiving things hard to be understood, by putting in practice things which are more easy to be understood. But there must be self-denial and suspicion of ourselves, and submission to the authority of Christ Jesus, before we can heartily receive all the truths of the gospel, therefore we are in great danger of rejecting the truth. And whatever opinions and thoughts of men are not according to the law of God, and warranted by it, the believer disclaims and abhors. Those who are led away by error, fall from their own steadfastness. And that we may avoid being led away, we must seek to grow in all grace, in faith, and virtue, and knowledge. Labor to know Christ more clearly, and more fully; to know him so as to be more like him, and to love him better. This is the knowledge of Christ, which the apostle Paul reached after, and desired to attain; and those who taste this effect of the knowledge of the Lord and Savior Jesus Christ, will, upon receiving such grace from him, give thanks and praise him, and join in ascribing glory to him now, in the full assurance of doing the same hereafter, for ever.

seraphim, and through eternity your glory shall never part awry. And then, if wisdom be glory, your wisdom, the wisdom which you inherit in the new nature, which is none other than Christ's who is made of God unto us, wisdom shall never fade, in fact it shall grow, for there you shall know even as you are known. While here you see through a glass darkly, there you shall see face to face. You sip the brook today, you shall bathe in the ocean tomorrow; you see afar off now, you shall lie in the arms of wisdom by-and-bye; for the glory of the Spirit never dies, but throughout eternity expanding, enlarging, blazing, glorifying itself through God, it shall go on never, never to fail. Brethren, whatever it may be which you are expecting as the glory of your new nature, you have not yet an idea of what it will be. "Eye hath not seen, nor ear heard, the things which God hath prepared for them that love him." But though he hath revealed them unto us by his Spirit, yet, I fear we have not fully learned them. However, we will say of this glory, whatever it may be, it is incorruptible, undefiled, and it fadeth not away. The only question we have to ask, and with that we wish, is—are we born again? Brethren, it is impossible for you to possess the existence of the new life without the new birth, and the glory of the new birth you cannot know without the new heart. I say—are you born again? Do not stand up and say, "I am a Churchman, I was baptized and confirmed." That you may be, and yet not be born again. Do not say, "I am a Baptist, I have professed my faith and was immersed." That you may be, and not be born again. Do not say, "I am of Christian parents." That you may be, and yet be an heir of wrath, even as others. Are you born again? Oh! souls, may God the Holy Ghost reveal Christ to you, and when you come to see Christ with the tearful eyes of a penitential faith, then be it known unto you that you are born again and that you have passed from death unto life, "He that believeth and is baptized shall be saved, he that believeth not shall be damned." God help you to believe!

1 John

2 John

3 John

KING JAMES VERSION

JOHN WESLEY

1 JOHN 1

1 That which was from the beginning, which we have heard, which we have seen with our eyes, which we have looked upon, and our hands have handled, of the Word of life;

2 (For the life was manifested, and we have seen it, and bear witness, and shew unto you that eternal life, which was with the Father, and was manifested unto us;)

3 That which we have seen and heard declare we unto you, that ye also may have fellowship with us: and truly our fellowship is with the Father, and with his Son Jesus Christ.

4 And these things write we unto you, that your joy may be full.

5 This then is the message which we have heard of him, and declare unto you, that God is light, and in him is no darkness at all.

6 If we say that we have fellowship with him, and walk in darkness, we lie, and do not the truth:

7 But if we walk in the light, as he is in the light, we have fellowship one with another, and the blood of Jesus Christ his Son cleanseth us from all sin.

8 If we say that we have no sin, we deceive ourselves, and the truth is not in us.

9 If we confess our sins, he is faithful and just to forgive us our sins, and to cleanse us from all unrighteousness.

10 If we say that we have not sinned, we make him a liar, and his word is not in us.

1 JOHN 2

1 My little children, these things write I unto you, that ye sin not. And if any man sin, we have an advocate with the Father, Jesus Christ the righteous:

2 And he is the propitiation for our sins: and not for ours only, but also for the sins of the whole world.

3 And hereby we do know that we know him, if we keep his commandments.

4 He that saith, I know him, and keepeth not his commandments, is a liar, and the truth is not in him.

THE great similitude, or rather sameness, both of spirit and expression, which runs through St. John's Gospel and all his epistles, is a clear evidence of their being written by the same person. In this epistle he speaks not to any particular church, but to all the Christians of that age; and in them to the whole Christian church in all succeeding ages. Some have apprehended that it is not easy to discern the scope and method of this epistle. But if we examine it with simplicity, these may readily be discovered. St. John in this letter, or rather tract, (for he was present with part of those to whom he wrote,) has this apparent aim, to confirm the happy and holy communion of the faithful with God and Christ, by describing the marks of that blessed state.

1 JOHN 1

1. That which was – Here means, He which was the Word himself; afterwards it means, that which they had heard from him. Which was – Namely, with the Father, ver. 2, before he was manifested. From the beginning – This phrase is sometimes used in a limited sense; but here it properly means from eternity, being equivalent with, "in the beginning," John i, 1. That which we – The apostles. Have not only heard, but seen with our eyes, which we have beheld – Attentively considered on various occasions. Of the Word of life – He is termed the Word, John i, 1; the Life, John i, 4; as he is the living Word of God, who, with the Father and the Spirit, is the fountain of life to all creatures, particularly of spiritual and eternal life.

2. For the life – The living Word. Was manifested – In the flesh, to our very senses. And we testify and declare – We testify by declaring, by preaching, and writing, 1 John i, 3, 4. Preaching lays the foundation, 1 John i, 5-10, writing builds there on. To you – Who have not seen. The eternal life – Which always was, and afterward appeared to us. This is mentioned in the beginning of the epistle. In the end of it is mentioned the same eternal life, which we shall always enjoy.

3. That which we have seen and heard – Of him and from him. Declare we to you – For this end. That ye also may have fellowship with us – May enjoy the same fellowship which we enjoy. And truly our fellowship – Whereby he is in us and we in him. Is with the Father and with the son – Of the Holy Ghost he speaks afterwards.

4. That your joy may be full – So our Lord also, John xv, 11; xvi, 22. There is a joy of hope, a joy of faith, and a joy of love. Here the joy of faith is directly intended. It is a concise expression. Your joy – That is, your faith and the joy arising from it: but it likewise implies the joy of hope and love.

5. And this is the sum of the message which we have heard of him – The Son of God. That God is light – The light of wisdom, love, holiness, glory. What light is to the natural eye, that God is to the spiritual eye. And in him is no darkness at all – No contrary principle. He is pure, unmixed light.

6. If we say – Either with our tongue, or in our heart, if we endeavor to persuade either ourselves or others. We have fellowship with him, while we walk, either inwardly or outwardly, in darkness – In sin of any kind. We do not the truth – Our actions prove, that the truth is not in us.

7. But if we walk in the light – In all holiness. As God is (a deeper word than walk, and more worthy of God) in the light, then we may truly say, we have fellowship one with another – We who have seen, and you who have not seen, do alike enjoy that fellowship with God. The imitation of God being the only sure proof of our having fellowship with him. And the blood of Jesus Christ his Son – With the grace purchased thereby. Cleanseth us from all sin – Both original and actual, taking away all the guilt and all the power.

8. If we say – Any child of man, before his blood has cleansed us. We have no sin – To be cleansed from, instead of confessing our sins, 1 John i, 9, the truth is not in us – Neither in our mouth nor in our heart.

MATTHEW HENRY

This epistle is a discourse upon the principles of Christianity, in doctrine and practice. The design appears to be, to refute and guard against erroneous and unholy tenets, principles, and practices, especially such as would lower the Godhead of Christ, and the reality and power of his sufferings and death, as an atoning sacrifice; and against the assertion that believers being saved by grace, are not required to obey the commandments. This epistle also stirs up all who profess to know God, to have communion with him, and to believe in him, and that they walk in holiness, not in sin, showing that a mere outward profession is nothing, without the evidence of a holy life and conduct. It also helps forward and excites real Christians to communion with God and the Lord Jesus Christ, to constancy in the true faith, and to purity of life.

1 JOHN 1

The apostle prefaces his epistle to believers in general, with evident testimonies to Christ, for promoting their happiness and joy. (1-4)
The necessity of a life of holiness, in order to communion with God, is shown. (5-10)

1-4 That essential Good, that uncreated Excellence, which had been from the beginning, from eternity, as equal with the Father, and which at length appeared in human nature for the salvation of sinners, was the great subject concerning which the apostle wrote to his brethren. The apostles had seen him while they witnessed his wisdom and holiness, his miracles, and love and mercy, during some years, till they saw him crucified for sinners, and afterwards risen from the dead. They touched him, so as to have full proof of his resurrection. This Divine Person, the Word of life, the Word of God, appeared in human nature, that he might be the Author and Giver of eternal life to mankind, through the redemption of his blood, and the influence of his new-creating Spirit. The apostles declared what they had seen and heard, that believers might share their comforts and everlasting advantages. They had free access to God the Father. They had a happy experience of the truth in their souls, and showed its excellence in their lives. This communion of believers with the Father and the Son, is begun and kept up by the influences of the Holy Spirit. The benefits Christ bestows, are not like the scanty possessions of the world, causing jealousies in others; but the joy and happiness of communion with God is all-sufficient, so that any number may partake of it; and all who are warranted to say, that truly their fellowship is with the Father, will desire to lead others to partake of the same blessedness.

5-10 A message from the Lord Jesus, the Word of life, the eternal Word, we should all gladly receive. The great God should be represented to this dark world, as pure and perfect light. As this is the nature of God, his doctrines and precepts must be such. And as his perfect happiness cannot be separated from his perfect holiness, so our happiness will be in proportion to our being made holy. To walk in darkness, is to live and act against religion. God holds no heavenly fellowship or intercourse with unholy souls. There is no truth in their profession; their practice shows its folly and falsehood. The eternal

CHARLES H. SPURGEON

LOVE'S LOGIC
Sermon number 1008 delivered on Lord's-day Morning, August 27th, 1871, at the Metropolitan Tabernacle, Newington.

"We love him because he first loved us."—1 John 4:19.

I. At the outset we will consider THE INDISPENSABLE NECESSITY OF LOVE TO GOD IN THE HEART.

There are some graces which in their vigor are not absolutely essential to the bare existence of spiritual life, though very important for its healthy growth; but love to God must be in the heart, or else there is no grace there whatever. If any man love not God, he is not a renewed man. Love to God is a mark which is always set upon Christ's sheep, and never set upon any others. In enlarging upon this most important truth, I would call your attention to the connection of the text. You will find in the seventh verse of this chapter, that love to God is set down as being a necessary mark of the new birth. "Every one that loveth is born of God, and knoweth God." I have no right, therefore, to believe that I am a regenerated person unless my heart truly and sincerely loves God. It is vain for me, if I love not God, to quote the register which records an ecclesiastical ceremony, and say that this regenerated me; it certainly did no such thing, or the sure result would have followed. If I have been regenerated I may not be perfect, but this one thing I can say, "Lord thou knowest all things, thou knowest that I love thee." When by believing we receive the privilege to become the sons of God, we receive also the nature of sons, and with filial love we cry, "Abba, Father." There is no exception to this rule; if a man loves not God, neither is he born of God. Show me a fire without heat, then show me regeneration that does not produce love to God; for as the sun must give forth its light, so must a soul that has been created anew by divine grace display its nature by sincere affection towards God. "Ye must be born again," but ye are not born again unless ye love God. How indispensable, then, is love to God.

In the eighth verse we are told also that love to God is a mark of our know-

5 But whoso keepeth his word, in him verily is the love of God perfected: hereby know we that we are in him.

6 He that saith he abideth in him ought himself also so to walk, even as he walked.

7 Brethren, I write no new commandment unto you, but an old commandment which ye had from the beginning. The old commandment is the word which ye have heard from the beginning.

8 Again, a new commandment I write unto you, which thing is true in him and in you: because the darkness is past, and the true light now shineth.

9 He that saith he is in the light, and hateth his brother, is in darkness even until now.

10 He that loveth his brother abideth in the light, and there is none occasion of stumbling in him.

11 But he that hateth his brother is in darkness, and walketh in darkness, and knoweth not whither he goeth, because that darkness hath blinded his eyes.

12 I write unto you, little children, because your sins are forgiven you for his name's sake.

13 I write unto you, fathers, because ye have known him that is from the beginning. I write unto you, young men, because ye have overcome the wicked one. I write unto you, little children, because ye have known the Father.

14 I have written unto you, fathers, because ye have known him that is from the beginning. I have written unto you, young men, because ye are strong, and the word of God abideth in you, and ye have overcome the wicked one.

15 Love not the world, neither the things that are in the world. If any man love the world, the love of the Father is not in him.

16 For all that is in the world, the lust of the flesh, and the lust of the eyes, and the pride of life, is not of the Father, but is of the world.

17 And the world passeth away, and the lust thereof: but he that doeth the will of God abideth for ever.

18 Little children, it is the last

9. But if with a penitent and believing heart, we confess our sins, he is faithful – Because he had promised this blessing, by the unanimous voice of all his prophets. Just – Surely then he will punish: no; for this very reason he will pardon. This may seem strange; but upon the evangelical principle of atonement and redemption, it is undoubtedly true; because, when the debt is paid, or the purchase made, it is the part of equity to cancel the bond, and consign over the purchased possession. Both to forgive us our sins – To take away all the guilt of them. And to cleanse us from all unrighteousness – To purify our souls from every kind and every degree of it.

10. Yet still we are to retain, even to our lives' end, a deep sense of our past sins. Still if we say, we have not sinned, we make him a liar – Who saith, all have sinned. And his word is not in us – We do not receive it; we give it no place in our hearts.

1 JOHN 2

1. My beloved children – So the apostle frequently addresses the whole body of Christians. It is a term of tenderness and endearment, used by our Lord himself to his disciples, John xiii, 33.

2. And he is the propitiation – The atoning sacrifice by which the wrath of God is appeased. For our sins – Who believe. And not for ours only, but also for the sins of the whole world – Just as wide as sin extends, the propitiation extends also.

3. And hereby we know that we truly and savingly know him – As he is the advocate, the righteous, the propitiation. If we keep his commandments – Particularly those of faith and love.

5. But whoso keepeth his word – His commandments. Verily in him the love of God – Reconciled to us through Christ. Is perfected – Is perfectly known. Hereby – By our keeping his word. We know that we are in him – So is the tree known by its fruits. To "know him," to be "in him," to "abide in him," are nearly synonymous terms; only with a gradation; knowledge, communion, constancy.

6. He that saith he abideth in him – which implies a durable state; a constant, lasting knowledge of, and communion with, him. Ought himself – Otherwise they are vain words. So to walk, even as he walked – In the world. As he, are words that frequently occur in this epistle. Believers having their hearts full of him, easily supply his name.

7. When I speak of keeping his word, I write not a new commandment – I do not speak of any new one. But the old commandment, which ye had – Even from your forefathers.

8. Again, I do write a new commandment to you – Namely, with regard to loving one another.

9. He that saith he is in the light – In Christ, united to him. And hateth his brother – The very name shows the love due to him. Is in darkness until now – Void of Christ, and of all true light.

10. He that loveth his brother – For Christ's sake. Abideth in the light – Of God. And there is no occasion of stumbling in him – Whereas he that hates his brother is an occasion of stumbling to himself. He stumbles against himself, and against all things within and without; while he that loves his brother, has a free, disencumbered journey.

11. He that hateth his brother – And he must hate, if he does not love him: there is no medium. Is in darkness – In sin, perplexity, entanglement. He walketh in darkness, and knoweth not that he is in the high road to hell.

12. I have written to you, beloved children – Thus St. John bespeaks all to whom he writes. But from the thirteenth to the twenty-seventh verse, he divides them particularly into "fathers," "young men," and "little children." Because your sins are forgiven you – As if he had said, This is the sum of what I have now written.

Life, the eternal Son, put on flesh and blood, and died to wash us from our sins in his own blood, and procures for us the sacred influences by which sin is to be subdued more and more, till it is quite done away. While the necessity of a holy walk is insisted upon, as the effect and evidence of the knowledge of God in Christ Jesus, the opposite error of self-righteous pride is guarded against with equal care. All who walk near to God, in holiness and righteousness, are sensible that their best days and duties are mixed with sin. God has given testimony to the sinfulness of the world, by providing a sufficient, effectual Sacrifice for sin, needed in all ages; and the sinfulness of believers themselves is shown, by requiring them continually to confess their sins, and to apply by faith to the blood of that Sacrifice.

1 JOHN 2

The apostle directs to the atonement of Christ for help against sinful infirmities. (1,2)

The effects of saving knowledge in producing obedience, and love to the brethren. (3-11)

Christians addressed as little children, young men, and fathers. (12-14)

All are cautioned against the love of this world, and against errors. (15-23)

They are encouraged to stand fast in faith and holiness. (24-29)

1,2 We have an Advocate with the Father; one who has undertaken, and is fully able, to plead in behalf of every one who applies for pardon and salvation in his name, depending on his pleading for them. He is ''Jesus,'' the Savior, and ''Christ,'' the Messiah, the Anointed. He alone is ''the Righteous One,'' who received his nature pure from sin, and as our Surety perfectly obeyed the law of God, and so fulfilled all righteousness. All men, in every land, and through successive generations, are invited to come to God through this all-sufficient atonement, and by this new and living way. The gospel, when rightly understood and received, sets the heart against all sin, and stops the allowed practice of it; at the same time it gives blessed relief to the wounded consciences of those who have sinned.

3-11 What knowledge of Christ can that be, which sees not that he is most worthy of our entire obedience? And a disobedient life shows there is neither religion nor honesty in the professor. The love of God is perfected in him that keeps his commandments. God's grace in him attains its true mark, and produces its sovereign effect as far as may be in this world, and this is man's regeneration; though never absolutely perfect here. Yet this observing Christ's commands, has holiness and excellency which, if universal, would make the earth resemble heaven itself. The command to love one another had been in force from the beginning of the world; but it might be called a new command as given to Christians. It was new in them, as their situation was new in respect of its motives, rules, and obligations. And those who walk in hatred and enmity to believers, remain in a dark state. Christian love teaches us to value our brother's soul, and to dread every thing hurtful to his purity and peace.

ing God. True knowledge is essential to salvation. God does not save us in the dark. He is our "light and our salvation." We are renewed in knowledge after the image of him that created us. Now, "he that loveth not knoweth not God, for God is love." All you have ever been taught from the pulpit, all you have ever studied from the Scriptures, all you have ever gathered from the learned, all you have collected from the libraries, all this is no knowledge of God at all unless you love God; for in true religion, to love and to know God are synonymous terms. Without love you remain in ignorance still, ignorance of the most unhappy and ruinous kind. All attainments are transitory, if love be not as a salt to preserve them; tongues must cease and knowledge must vanish away; love alone abides for ever. This love you must have or be a fool for ever. All the children of the true Zion are taught of the Lord, but you are not taught of God unless you love God. See then that to be devoid of love to God is to be devoid of all true knowledge of God, and so of all salvation.

II. You see the indispensable importance of love to God: let us now learn THE SOURCE AND SPRING OF TRUE LOVE TO GOD. "We love him because he first loved us." Love to God, wherever it really exists, has been created in the bosom by a belief of God's love to us. No man loves God till he knows that God loves him; and every believer loves God for this reason first and chiefly, that God loves him. He has seen himself to be unworthy of divine favor, yet he has believed God's love in the gift of his dear Son, and he has accepted the atonement that Christ has made as a proof of God's love, and now being satisfied of the divine affection towards him, he of necessity loves God.

Observe, then, that love to God does not begin in the heart from any disinterested admiration of the nature of God. I believe that, after we have loved God because he first loved us, we may so grow in grace as to love God for what he is. I suppose it is possible for us to be the subjects of a state of heart in which our love spends itself upon the loveliness of God in his own person: we may come to love him because he is so wise, so powerful, so good, so patient,

time: and as ye have heard that antichrist shall come, even now are there many antichrists; whereby we know that it is the last time.

19 They went out from us, but they were not of us; for if they had been of us, they would no doubt have continued with us: but they went out, that they might be made manifest that they were not all of us.

20 But ye have an unction from the Holy One, and ye know all things.

21 I have not written unto you because ye know not the truth, but because ye know it, and that no lie is of the truth.

22 Who is a liar but he that denieth that Jesus is the Christ? He is antichrist, that denieth the Father and the Son.

23 Whosoever denieth the Son, the same hath not the Father: (but) he that acknowledgeth the Son hath the Father also.

24 Let that therefore abide in you, which ye have heard from the beginning. If that which ye have heard from the beginning shall remain in you, ye also shall continue in the Son, and in the Father.

25 And this is the promise that he hath promised us, even eternal life.

26 These things have I written unto you concerning them that seduce you.

27 But the anointing which ye have received of him abideth in you, and ye need not that any man teach you: but as the same anointing teacheth you of all things, and is truth, and is no lie, and even as it hath taught you, ye shall abide in him.

28 And now, little children, abide in him; that, when he shall appear, we may have confidence, and not be ashamed before him at his coming.

29 If ye know that he is righteous, ye know that every one that doeth righteousness is born of him.

1 JOHN 3

1 Behold, what manner of love the Father hath bestowed upon us, that we should be called the sons of God: therefore the world

He then proceeds to other things, which are built upon this foundation.

13. The address to spiritual fathers, young men, and little children is first proposed in this verse, wherein he says, I write to you, fathers: I write to you, young men: I write to you, little children: and then enlarged upon; in doing which he says, "I have written to you, fathers," 1 John ii, 14. "I have written to you, young men," 1 John ii, 14-17. "I have written to you, little children," 1 John ii, 18-27.

14. I have written to you, fathers – As if he had said, Observe well what I but now wrote. He speaks very briefly and modestly to these, who needed not much to be said to them, as having that deep acquaintance with God which comprises all necessary knowledge. Young men, ye are strong – In faith. And the word of God abideth in you – Deeply rooted in your hearts, whereby ye have often foiled your great adversary.

15. To you all, whether fathers, young men, or little children, I say, Love not the world – Pursue your victory by overcoming the world. If any man love the world – Seek happiness in visible things, he does not love God.

16. The desire of the flesh – Of the pleasure of the outward senses, whether of the taste, smell, or touch. The desire of the eye – Of the pleasures of imagination, to which the eye chiefly is subservient; of that internal sense whereby we relish whatever is grand, new, or beautiful. The pride of life – All that pomp in clothes, houses, furniture, equipage, manner of living, which generally procure honor from the bulk of mankind, and so gratify pride and vanity. It therefore directly includes the desire of praise, and, remotely, covetousness. All these desires are not from God, but from the prince of this world.

17. The world passeth away, and the desire thereof – That is, all that can gratify those desires passeth away with it. But he that doeth the will of God – That loves God, not the world. Abideth – In the enjoyment of what he loves, for ever.

18. Little children, it is the last time – The last dispensation of grace, that which is to continue to the end of time, is begun. Ye have heard that antichrist cometh – Under the term antichrist, or the spirit of antichrist, he includes all false teachers and enemies to the truth; yea, whatever doctrines or men are contrary to Christ. It seems to have been long after this that the name of antichrist was appropriated to that grand adversary of Christ, the man of sin, 2 Thess. ii, 3. Antichrist, in St. John's sense, that is, antichristianism, has been spreading from his time till now; and will do so, till that great adversary arises, and is destroyed by Christ's coming.

19. They were not of us – When they went; their hearts were before departed from God, otherwise, they would have continued with us: but they went out, that they might be made manifest – That is, this was made manifest by their going out.

20. But ye have an anointing – A chrism; perhaps so termed in opposition to the name of antichrist; an inward teaching from the Holy Ghost, whereby ye know all things – Necessary for your preservation from these seducers, and for your eternal salvation. St. John here but just touches upon the Holy Ghost, of whom he speaks more largely, chap. iii, 24; iv, 13; v, 6.

21. I have written – Namely, 1 John ii, 13. To you because ye know the truth – That is, to confirm you in the knowledge ye have already. Ye know that no lie is of the truth – That all the doctrines of these antichrists are irreconcilable to it.

22. Who is that liar – Who is guilty of that lying, but he who denies that truth which is the sum of all Christianity? That Jesus is the Christ; that he is the Son of God; that he came in the flesh, is one undivided truth, and he that denies any part of this, in effect denies the whole. He is antichrist – And the spirit of antichrist, who in denying the Son denies the Father also.

23. Whosoever denieth the eternal Son of God, he hath not communion with the Father; but he that truly and believingly acknowledges the Son, hath communion with the Father also.

24. If that truth concerning the Father and the Son, which ye have heard from

12-14 As Christians have their peculiar states, so they have peculiar duties; but there are precepts and obedience common to all, particularly mutual love, and contempt of the world. The youngest sincere disciple is pardoned: the communion of saints is attended with the forgiveness of sins. Those of the longest standing in Christ's school need further advice and instruction. Even fathers must be written unto, and preached unto; none are too old to learn. But especially young men in Christ Jesus, though they are arrived at strength of spirit and sound sense, and have successfully resisted first trials and temptations, breaking off bad habits and connexions, and entered in at the strait gate of true conversion. The different descriptions of Christians are again addressed. Children in Christ know that God is their Father; it is wisdom. Those advanced believers, who know him that was from the beginning, before this world was made, may well be led thereby to give up this world. It will be the glory of young persons to be strong in Christ, and his grace. By the word of God they overcome the wicked one.

15-17 The things of the world may be desired and possessed for the uses and purposes which God intended, and they are to be used by his grace, and to his glory; but believers must not seek or value them for those purposes to which sin abuses them. The world draws the heart from God; and the more the love of the world prevails, the more the love of God decays. The things of the world are classed according to the three ruling inclinations of depraved nature. 1. The lust of the flesh, of the body: wrong desires of the heart, the appetite of indulging all things that excite and inflame sensual pleasures. 2. The lust of the eyes: the eyes are delighted with riches and rich possessions; this is the lust of covetousness. 3. The pride of life: a vain man craves the grandeur and pomp of a vainglorious life; this includes thirst after honor and applause. The things of the world quickly fade and die away; desire itself will ere long fail and cease, but holy affection is not like the lust that passes away. The love of God shall never fail.

18-23 Every man is an antichrist, who denies the Person, or any of the offices of Christ; and in denying the Son, he denies the Father also, and has no part in his favor while he rejects his great salvation. Let this prophecy that seducers would rise in the Christian world, keep us from being seduced. The church knows not well who are its true members, and who are not, but thus true Christians were proved, and rendered more watchful and humble. True Christians are anointed ones; their name expresses this: they are anointed with grace, with gifts and spiritual privileges, by the Holy Spirit of grace. The great and most hurtful lies that the father of lies spreads in the world, usually are falsehoods and errors relating to the person of Christ. The unction from the Holy One, alone can keep us from delusions. While we judge favorably of all who trust in Christ as the Divine Savior, and obey his word, and seek to live in union with them, let us pity and pray for those who deny the Godhead of Christ, or his atonement, and the new-creating work of the Holy Ghost. Let us protest against such antichristian doctrine, and keep from them as much as we may.

24-29 The truth of Christ, abiding in us, is a means to sever

so everything that is loveable. This may be produced within us as the ripe fruit of maturity in the divine life, but it is never the first spring and fountain of the grace of love in any man's heart. Even the apostle John, the man who had looked within the veil and seen the excellent glory beyond any other man, and who had leaned his head upon the bosom of the Lord, and had seen the Lord's holiness, and marked the inimitable beauty of the character of the incarnate God, even John does not say, "We love him because we admire him," but "We love him because he first loved us." For see, brethren, if this kind of love which I have mentioned, which is called the love of disinterested admiration, were required of a sinner, I do not see how he could readily render it. There are two gentlemen of equal rank in society, and the one is not at all obliged to the other; now, they, standing on an equality, can easily feel a disinterested admiration of each other's characters, and a consequent disinterested affection; but I, a poor sinner, by nature sunk in the mire, full of everything that is evil, condemned, guilty of death, so that my only desert is to be cast into hell, am under such obligations to my Savior and my God, that it would be idle for me to talk about a disinterested affection for him, since I owe to him my life, my all. Besides, until I catch the gleams of his mercy and his loving-kindness to the guilty, his holy, just, and righteous character are not loveable to me, I dread the purity which condemns my defilement, and shudder at the justice which will consume me for my sin. Do not, O seeker, trouble your heart with nice distinctions about disinterested love, but be you content with the beloved disciple to love Christ because he first loved you.

"I know that safe with him remains,
Protected by his power,
What I've committed to his hands
Till the decisive hour:"

And in proportion as I am thus scripturally confident, and rest in my Lord, will my love to him engross all my heart, and, consecrate my life to the Redeemer's glory.

Beloved, I desire to make this very clear, that to feel love to God we must tread along the road of faith. Truly, this

knoweth us not, because it knew him not.

2 Beloved, now are we the sons of God, and it doth not yet appear what we shall be: but we know that, when he shall appear, we shall be like him; for we shall see him as he is.

3 And every man that hath this hope in him purifieth himself, even as he is pure.

4 Whosoever committeth sin transgresseth also the law: for sin is the transgression of the law.

5 And ye know that he was manifested to take away our sins; and in him is no sin.

6 Whosoever abideth in him sinneth not: whosoever sinneth hath not seen him, neither known him.

7 Little children, let no man deceive you: he that doeth righteousness is righteous, even as he is righteous.

8 He that committeth sin is of the devil; for the devil sinneth from the beginning. For this purpose the Son of God was manifested, that he might destroy the works of the devil.

9 Whosoever is born of God doth not commit sin; for his seed remaineth in him: and he cannot sin, because he is born of God.

10 In this the children of God are manifest, and the children of the devil: whosoever doeth not righteousness is not of God, neither he that loveth not his brother.

11 For this is the message that ye heard from the beginning, that we should love one another.

12 Not as Cain, who was of that wicked one, and slew his brother. And wherefore slew he him? Because his own works were evil, and his brother's righteous.

13 Marvel not, my brethren, if the world hate you.

14 We know that we have passed from death unto life, because we love the brethren. He that loveth not his brother abideth in death.

15 Whosoever hateth his brother is a murderer: and ye know that no murderer hath eternal life abiding in him.

16 Hereby perceive we the love of God, because he laid down

the beginning, abide fixed and rooted in you, ye also shall abide in that happy communion with the Son and the Father.

25. He – The Son. Hath promised us – If we abide in him.

26. These things – From 1 John ii, 21. I have written to you – St. John, according to his custom, begins and ends with the same form, and having finished a kind of parenthesis, 1 John ii, 20-26, continues, ii, 27, what he said in the twentieth verse, concerning them that would seduce you.

27. Ye need not that any should teach you, save as that anointing teacheth you – Which is always the same, always consistent with itself. But this does not exclude our need of being taught by them who partake of the same anointing.

28. And now, beloved children – Having finished his address to each, he now returns to all in general. Abide in him, that we – A modest expression. May not be ashamed before him at his coming – O how will ye, Jews, Socinians, nominal Christians, be ashamed in that day!

29. Every one – And none else. Who practiceth righteousness – From a believing, loving heart. Is born of him – For all his children are like himself.

1 JOHN 3

1. That we should be called – That is, should be, the children of God. Therefore the world knoweth us not – They know not what to make of us. We are a mystery to them.

2. It doth not yet appear – Even to ourselves. What we shall be – It is something ineffable, which will raise the children of God to be, in a manner, as God himself. But we know, in general, that when he, the Son of God, shall appear, we shall be like him – The glory of God penetrating our inmost substance. For we shall see him as he is – Manifestly, without a veil. And that sight will transform us into the same likeness.

3. And every one that hath this hope in him – In God.

4. Whosoever committeth sin – Thereby transgresseth the holy, just, and good law of God, and so sets his authority at nought; for this is implied in the very nature of sin.

5. And ye know that he – Christ. Was manifested – That he came into the world for this very purpose. To take away our sins – To destroy them all, root and branch, and leave none remaining. And in him is no sin – So that he could not suffer on his own account, but to make us as himself.

6. Whosoever abideth in communion with him, by loving faith, sinneth not – While he so abideth. Whosoever sinneth certainly seeth him not – The loving eye of his soul is not then fixed upon God; neither doth he then experimentally know him – Whatever he did in time past.

7. Let no one deceive you – Let none persuade you that any man is righteous but he that uniformly practices righteousness; he alone is righteous, after the example of his Lord.

8. He that committeth sin is a child of the devil; for the devil sinneth from the beginning – That is, was the first sinner in the universe, and has continued to sin ever since. The Son of God was manifested to destroy the works of the devil – All sin. And will he not perform this in all that trust in him?

9. Whosoever is born of God – By living faith, whereby God is continually breathing spiritual life into his soul, and his soul is continually breathing out love and prayer to God, doth not commit sin. For the divine seed of loving faith abideth in him; and, so long as it doth, he cannot sin, because he is born of God – Is inwardly and universally changed.

10. Neither he that loveth not his brother – Here is the transition from the general proposition to one particular.

12. Who was of the wicked one – Who showed he was a child of the devil by killing his brother. And wherefore slew he him – For any fault? No, but just the

from sin, and unites us to the Son of God, Joh 15:3,4. What value should we put upon gospel truth! Thereby the promise of eternal life is made sure. The promise God makes, is suitable to his own greatness, power, and goodness; it is eternal life. The Spirit of truth will not lie; and he teaches all things in the present dispensation, all things necessary to our knowledge of God in Christ, and their glory in the gospel. The apostle repeats the kind words, "little children;" which denotes his affection. He would persuade by love. Gospel privileges oblige to gospel duties; and those anointed by the Lord Jesus abide with him. The new spiritual nature is from the Lord Christ. He that is constant to the practice of religion in trying times, shows that he is born from above, from the Lord Christ.

1 JOHN 3

The apostle admires the love of God in making believers his children. (1,2)

The purifying influence of the hope of seeing Christ, and the danger of pretending to this, and living in sin. (3-10)

Love to the brethren is the character of real Christians. (11-15)

That love described by its acting. (16-21)

The advantage of faith, love, and obedience. (22-24)

1,2 Little does the world know of the happiness of the real followers of Christ. Little does the world think that these poor, humble, despised ones, are favorites of God, and will dwell in heaven. Let the followers of Christ be content with hard fare here, since they are in a land of strangers, where their Lord was so badly treated before them. The sons of God must walk by faith, and live by hope. They may well wait in faith, hope, and earnest desire, for the revelation of the Lord Jesus. The sons of God will be known, and be made manifest by likeness to their Head. They shall be transformed into the same image, by their view of him.

3-10 The sons of God know that their Lord is of purer eyes than to allow any thing unholy and impure to dwell with him. It is the hope of hypocrites, not of the sons of God, that makes allowance for gratifying impure desires and lusts. May we be followers of him as his dear children, thus show our sense of his unspeakable mercy, and express that obedient, grateful, humble mind which becomes us. Sin is the rejecting the Divine law. In him, that is, in Christ, was no sin. All the sinless weaknesses that were consequences of the fall, he took; that is, all those infirmities of mind or body which subject man to suffering, and expose him to temptation. But our moral infirmities, our proneness to sin, he had not. He that abides in Christ, continues not in the practice of sin. Renouncing sin is the great proof of spiritual union with, continuance in, and saving knowledge of the Lord Christ.

11-15 We should love the Lord Jesus, value his love, and therefore love all our brethren in Christ. This love is the special fruit of our faith, and a certain sign of our being born again. But none who rightly know the heart of man, can wonder at the contempt and enmity of ungodly people against the children of God. We know that we are passed from death to life: we may know it by the evidences of our faith in Christ, of

is not a hard or perilous way but one prepared by infinite wisdom. It is a road suitable for sinners, and indeed saints must come that way too. If thou wouldst love God, do not look within thee to see whether this grace or that be as it ought to be, but look to thy God, and read his eternal love his boundless love, his costly love, which gave Christ for thee; then shall thy love drink in fresh life and vigor.

Remember wherever there is love to God in the soul it is an argument that God loves that soul. I recollect meeting once with a Christian woman who said she knew she loved God, but, she was afraid God did not love her. That is a fear so preposterous that it ought never to occur to anybody. You would not love God in deed and in truth unless he had shed abroad his love in your heart in a measure. But on the other hand, our not loving God is not a conclusive argument that God does not love us; else might the sinner be afraid to come to God. O loveless sinner, with heart unquickened and chill, the voice of God calls even thee to Christ. Even to the dead in sin, his voice saith "Live." Whilst thou art yet polluted in thy blood, cast out in the open field, to the loathing of thy person, the Lord of mercy passes by, and says "Live." His mighty sovereignty comes forth dressed in robes of love, and he touches the unloveable, the loveless, the depraved, degraded sinner, at enmity with God,—he touches thee in all thine alienation and he lifts thee out of it and makes thee to love him, not for thine own sake, but for his name sake and for his mercy sake. Thou hadst no love at all to him, but all the love lay in him alone; and therefore he began to bless thee, and will continue to bless thee world without end, if thou art a believer in Jesus. In the bosom of the Eternal are the deep springs of all love.

III. This leads us, in the third place, to consider for a moment THE REVIVAL OF OUR LOVE. It is sadly probable that there are in this house some who once loved God very earnestly, but now they have declined and become grievously indifferent; God's love to us never changes, but ours too often sinks to a low ebb. Perhaps some of you have become so cold in your affections, that

his life for us: and we ought to lay down our lives for the brethren.

17 But whoso hath this world's good, and seeth his brother have need, and shutteth up his bowels of compassion from him, how dwelleth the love of God in him?

18 My little children, let us not love in word, neither in tongue; but in deed and in truth.

19 And hereby we know that we are of the truth, and shall assure our hearts before him.

20 For if our heart condemn us, God is greater than our heart, and knoweth all things.

21 Beloved, if our heart condemn us not, then have we confidence toward God.

22 And whatsoever we ask, we receive of him, because we keep his commandments, and do those things that are pleasing in his sight.

23 And this is his commandment, That we should believe on the name of his Son Jesus Christ, and love one another, as he gave us commandment.

24 And he that keepeth his commandments dwelleth in him, and he in him. And hereby we know that he abideth in us, by the Spirit which he hath given us.

1 JOHN 4

1 Beloved, believe not every spirit, but try the spirits whether they are of God: because many false prophets are gone out into the world.

2 Hereby know ye the Spirit of God: Every spirit that confesseth that Jesus Christ is come in the flesh is of God:

3 And every spirit that confesseth not that Jesus Christ is come in the flesh is not of God: and this is that spirit of antichrist, whereof ye have heard that it should come; and even now already is it in the world.

4 Ye are of God, little children, and have overcome them: because greater is he that is in you, than he that is in the world.

5 They are of the world: therefore speak they of the world, and the world heareth them.

reverse; for his goodness.

13. Marvel not if the world hate you – For the same cause.

14. We know – As if he had said, We ourselves could not love our brethren, unless we were passed from spiritual death to life, that is, born of God. He that loveth not his brother abideth in death – That is, is not born of God. And he that is not born of God, cannot love his brother.

15. He, I say, abideth in spiritual death, is void of the life of God. For whosoever hateth his brother, and there is no medium between loving and hating him, is, in God's account, a murderer: every degree of hatred being a degree of the same temper which moved Cain to murder his brother. And no murderer hath eternal life abiding in him – But every loving believer hath. For love is the beginning of eternal life. It is the same, in substance, with glory.

16. The word God is not in the original.

17. But whoso hath this world's good – Worldly substance, far less valuable than life. And seeth his brother have need – The very sight of want knocks at the door of the spectator's heart. And shutteth up – Whether asked or not. His bowels of compassion from him, how dwelleth the love of God in him – Certainly not at all, however he may talk, 1 John iii, 18, of loving God.

18. Not in word – Only. But in deed – In action: not in tongue by empty professions, but in truth.

19. And hereby we know – We have a farther proof by this real, operative love. That we are of the truth – That we have true faith, that we are true children of God. And shall assure our hearts before him – Shall enjoy the assurance of his favor, and the "testimony of a good conscience toward God." The heart, in St. John's language, is the conscience. The word conscience is not found in his writings.

20. For if we have not this testimony, if in anything our heart, our own conscience, condemn us, much more does God, who is greater than our heart – An infinitely holier and a more impartial Judge. And knoweth all things – So that there is no hope of hiding it from him.

21. If our heart condemn us not – If our conscience, duly enlightened by the word and Spirit of God, and comparing all our thoughts, words, and works with that word, pronounce that they agree therewith. Then have we confidence toward God – Not only our consciousness of his favor continues and increases, but we have a full persuasion, that whatsoever we ask we shall receive of him.

23. And this is his commandment – All his commandments in one word. That we should believe and love – in the manner and degree which he hath taught. This is the greatest and most important command that ever issued from the throne of glory. If this be neglected, no other can be kept: if this be observed, all others are easy.

24. And he that keepeth his commandments – That thus believes and loves. Abideth in him, and God in him: and hereby we know that he abideth in us, by the Spirit which he hath given us – Which witnesses with our spirits that we are his children, and brings forth his fruits of peace, love, holiness. This is the transition to the treating of the Holy Spirit which immediately follows.

1 JOHN 4

1. Believe not every spirit – Whereby any teacher is actuated. But try the spirits – By the rule which follows. We are to try all spirits by the written word: "To the law and to the testimony!" If any man speak not according to these, the spirit which actuates him is not of God.

2. Every spirit – Or teacher. Which confesseth – Both with heart and voice. Jesus Christ, who is come in the flesh, is of God – This his coming presupposes, contains, and draws after it, the whole doctrine of Christ.

3. Ye have heard – From our Lord and us, that it cometh.

MATTHEW HENRY

which love to our brethren is one. It is not zeal for a party in the common religion, or affection for those who are of the same name and sentiments with ourselves. The life of grace in the heart of a regenerate person, is the beginning and first principle of a life of glory, whereof they must be destitute who hate their brother in their hearts.

16-21 Here is the condescension, the miracle, the mystery of Divine love, that God would redeem the church with his own blood. Surely we should love those whom God has loved, and so loved. The Holy Spirit, grieved at selfishness, will leave the selfish heart without comfort, and full of darkness and terror. By what can it be known that a man has a true sense of the love of Christ for perishing sinners, or that the love of God has been planted in his heart by the Holy Spirit, if the love of the world and its good overcomes the feelings of compassion to a perishing brother? Every instance of this selfishness must weaken the evidences of a man's conversion; when habitual and allowed, it must decide against him. If conscience condemn us in known sin, or the neglect of known duty, God does so too. Let conscience therefore be well informed, be heard, and diligently attended to.

22-24 When believers had confidence towards God, through the Spirit of adoption, and by faith in the great High Priest, they might ask what they would of their reconciled Father. They would receive it, if good for them. And as good-will to men was proclaimed from heaven, so good-will to men, particularly to the brethren, must be in the hearts of those who go to God and heaven. He who thus follows Christ, dwells in him as his ark, refuge, and rest, and in the Father through him. This union between Christ and the souls of believers, is by the Spirit he has given them. A man may believe that God is gracious before he knows it; yet when faith has laid hold on the promises, it sets reason to work. This Spirit of God works a change; in all true Christians it changes from the power of Satan to the power of God.

1 JOHN 4
Believers cautioned against giving heed to every one that pretends to the Spirit. (1-6)
Brotherly love enforced. (7-21)

1-6 Christians who are well acquainted with the Scriptures, may, in humble dependence on Divine teaching, discern those who set forth doctrines according to the apostles, and those who contradict them. The sum of revealed religion is in the doctrine concerning Christ, his person and office. The false teachers spake of the world according to its maxims and tastes, so as not to offend carnal men. The world approved them, they made rapid progress, and had many followers such as themselves; the world will love its own, and its own will love it. The true doctrine as to the Savior's person, as leading men from the world to God, is a mark of the spirit of truth in opposition to the spirit of error.

7-13 The Spirit of God is the Spirit of love. He that does not love the image of God in his people, has no saving knowledge

CHARLES H. SPURGEON

it is difficult to be sure that you ever did love God at all. It may be that your life has become lax, so as to deserve the censure of the Church. You are a backslider and you are in a dangerous condition; yet, if there be indeed spiritual life in you, you will wish to return. You have gone astray like a lost sheep, but your prayer is, "seek thy servant, for I do not forget thy commandments." Now, note well, that the cause which originated your love is the same which must restore it. You went to Christ as a sinner at first, and your first act was to believe the love of God to you when there was nothing in you that evidenced it. Go the same way again. Do not stop, my dear brother, to pump up love out of the dry well within yourself! Do not think it possible that love will come at your bidding. If a man would give all the substance of his house for love, it would utterly be contemned. Think of the Lord's unchanging grace, and you will feel the spring-time of love returning to your soul. Still doth the Lord reserve mercy for the sinful, still he waiteth to be gracious; he is as willing to receive you now that you have played the prodigal, as he was to have retained you at home in the bosom of his love. Many considerations ought to aid you, a backslider, to believe more in the love of God than ever you did. For think what love it must be that can invite you still to return, you, who after knowing so much have sinned against light and knowledge; you, who after having experienced so much, have given the lie to your profession. He might justly have cut you down, for you have cumbered the ground long enough. Surely, when Israel went astray from God, it was a clear proof to her of Jehovah's love when he graciously said, "They say if a man put away his wife, or she go from him, and become another man's, shall he return to her again?" Why, the answer in every bosom is "No !" Who would love a wife who had so polluted herself? But thus saith the Lord, "Thou hast played the harlot with many lovers, yet return unto me." What matchless love is this. Hear yet more of these gracious words, which you will find in the third chapter of Jeremiah's prophecy. "Go and proclaim these words toward the north, and say,

6 We are of God: he that knoweth God heareth us; he that is not of God heareth not us. Hereby know we the spirit of truth, and the spirit of error.

7 Beloved, let us love one another: for love is of God; and every one that loveth is born of God, and knoweth God.

8 He that loveth not knoweth not God; for God is love.

9 In this was manifested the love of God toward us, because that God sent his only begotten Son into the world, that we might live through him.

10 Herein is love, not that we loved God, but that he loved us, and sent his Son to be the propitiation for our sins.

11 Beloved, if God so loved us, we ought also to love one another.

12 No man hath seen God at any time. If we love one another, God dwelleth in us, and his love is perfected in us.

13 Hereby know we that we dwell in him, and he in us, because he hath given us of his Spirit.

14 And we have seen and do testify that the Father sent the Son to be the Savior of the world.

15 Whosoever shall confess that Jesus is the Son of God, God dwelleth in him, and he in God.

16 And we have known and believed the love that God hath to us. God is love; and he that dwelleth in love dwelleth in God, and God in him.

17 Herein is our love made perfect, that we may have boldness in the day of judgment: because as he is, so are we in this world.

18 There is no fear in love; but perfect love casteth out fear: because fear hath torment. He that feareth is not made perfect in love.

19 We love him, because he first loved us.

20 If a man say, I love God, and hateth his brother, he is a liar: for he that loveth not his brother whom he hath seen, how can he love God whom he hath not seen?

21 And this commandment have we from him, That he who loveth God love his brother also.

4. Ye have overcome these seducers, because greater is the Spirit of Christ that is in you than the spirit of antichrist that is in the world.

5. They – Those false prophets. Are of the world – Of the number of those that know not God. Therefore speak they of the world – From the same principle, wisdom, spirit; and, of consequence, the world heareth them – With approbation.

6. We – Apostles. Are of God – Immediately taught, and sent by him. Hereby we know – From what is said, 1 John iv, 2-6.

7. Let us love one another – From the doctrine he has just been defending he draws this exhortation. It is by the Spirit that the love of God is shed abroad in our hearts. Every one that truly loveth God and his neighbor is born of God.

8. God is love – This little sentence brought St. John more sweetness, even in the time he was writing it, than the whole world can bring.

12. If we love one another, God abideth in us – This is treated of, 1 John iv, 13-16. And his love is perfected – Has its full effect. In us – This is treated of, 1 John iv, 17-19.

14. And in consequence of this we have seen and testify that the Father sent the Son – These are the foundation and the criteria of our abiding in God and God in us, the communion of the Spirit, and the confession of the Son.

15. Whosoever shall, from a principle of loving faith, openly confess in the face of all opposition and danger, that Jesus is the Son of God, God abideth in him.

16. And we know and believe – By the same Spirit, the love that God hath to us.

17. Hereby – That is, by this communion with God. Is our love made perfect; that we may – That is, so that we shall have boldness in the day of judgment – When all the stout-hearted shall tremble. Because as he – Christ. Is – All love. So are we – Who are fathers in Christ, even in this world.

18. There is no fear in love – No slavish fear can be where love reigns. But perfect, adult love casteth out slavish fear: because such fear hath torment – And so is inconsistent with the happiness of love. A natural man has neither fear nor love; one that is awakened, fear without love; a babe in Christ, love and fear; a father in Christ, love without fear.

19. We love him, because he first loved us – This is the sum of all religion, the genuine model of Christianity. None can say more: why should any one say less, or less intelligibly?

20. Whom he hath seen – Who is daily presented to his senses, to raise his esteem, and move his kindness or compassion toward him.

21. And this commandment have we from him – Both God and Christ. That he who loveth God love his brother – Every one, whatever his opinions or mode of worship be, purely because he is the child, and bears the image, of God. Bigotry is properly the want of this pure and universal love. A bigot only loves those who embrace his opinions, and receive his way of worship; and he loves them for that, and not for Christ's sake.

1 JOHN 5

1. The scope and sum of this whole paragraph appears from the conclusion of it, 1 John v, xiii, "These things have I written to you who believe, that ye may know that ye who believe have eternal life." So faith is the first and last point with St. John also. Every one who loveth – God that begat loveth him also that is begotten of him – Hath a natural affection to all his brethren.

2. Hereby we know – This is a plain proof. That we love the children of God – As his children.

3. For this is the love of God – The only sure proof of it. That we keep his commandments: and his commandments are not grievous – To any that are born of God.

4. For whatsoever – This expression implies the most unlimited universality. Is

of God. For it is God's nature to be kind, and to give happiness. The law of God is love; and all would have been perfectly happy, had all obeyed it. The provision of the gospel, for the forgiveness of sin, and the salvation of sinners, consistently with God's glory and justice, shows that God is love. Mystery and darkness rest upon many things yet. God has so shown himself to be love, that we cannot come short of eternal happiness, unless through unbelief and impenitence, although strict justice would condemn us to hopeless misery, because we break our Creator's laws. None of our words or thoughts can do justice to the free, astonishing love of a holy God towards sinners, who could not profit or harm him, whom he might justly crush in a moment, and whose deserving of his vengeance was shown in the method by which they were saved, though he could by his almighty Word have created other worlds, with more perfect beings, if he had seen fit.

14-21 The Father sent the Son, he willed his coming into this world. The apostle attests this. And whosoever shall confess that Jesus is the Son of God, God dwelleth in him, and he in God. This confession includes faith in the heart as the foundation; makes acknowledgment with the mouth to the glory of God and Christ, and profession in the life and conduct, against the flatteries and frowns of the world. There must be a day of universal judgment. Happy those who shall have holy boldness before the Judge at that day; knowing he is their Friend and Advocate! Happy those who have holy boldness in the prospect of that day, who look and wait for it, and for the Judge's appearance!

1 JOHN 5

Brotherly love is the effect of the new birth, which makes obedience to all God's commandments pleasant. (1-5)
Reference to witnesses agreeing to prove that Jesus, the Son of God, is the true Messiah. (6-8)
The satisfaction the believer has about Christ, and eternal life through him. (9-12)
The assurance of God's hearing and answering prayer. (13-17)
The happy condition of true believers, and a charge to renounce all idolatry. (18-21)

1-5 True love for the people of God, may be distinguished from natural kindness or party attachments, by its being united with the love of God, and obedience to his commands. The same Holy Spirit that taught the love, will have taught obedience also; and that man cannot truly love the children of God, who, by habit, commits sin or neglects known duty. As God's commands are holy, just, and good rules of liberty and happiness, so those who are born of God and love him, do not count them grievous, but lament that they cannot serve him more perfectly. Self-denial is required, but true Christians have a principle which carries them above all hindrances. Though the conflict often is sharp, and the regenerate may be cast down, yet he will rise up and renew his combat with resolution. But all, except believers in Christ, are enslaved in some respect or other, to the customs, opinions, or interests of the world. Faith is the cause of victory, the means, the instrument, the spiritual Armor by which we overcome. In and by faith we

Return, thou backsliding Israel, saith the Lord; and I will not cause mine anger to fall upon you: for I am merciful, saith the Lord, and I will not keep anger for ever." "Turn, O backsliding children, saith the Lord, for I am married unto you: and I will take you, one of a city, and two of a family, and I will bring you to Zion." "Return, ye backsliding children, and I will heal your backslidings." Can you hear these words without emotion? Backslider! I pray thee take the wings of God's love to fly back to be with him. But I hear you enquiring, Will he still receive me? Shall I be once more—

"To the Father's bosom pressed,
Once again a child confessed."

It shall be so. Does he not declare that he is God and changes not, and therefore you are not consumed? Rekindled are the flames of love in the backslider's bosom when he feels all this to be true; he cries, "Behold, we come to thee for thou art the Lord our God." I pray you, then, any of you who are conscious of gross derelictions of duty, and wanderings of heart, do not ask Moses to lead you back to Christ, he knows the way to Sinai's flames, but not to Calvary's pardoning blood. Go to Christ himself at once. If you go to the law and begin to judge yourself, if you get the notion that you are to undergo a sort of spiritual quarantine, that you must pass through a mental purgatory before you may renew your faith in the Savior, you are mistaken. Come just as you are, bad as you are, hardened, cold, dead as you feel yourselves to be, come even so, and believe in the boundless love of God in Christ Jesus. Then shall come the deep repentance; then shall come the brokenness of heart; then shall come the holy jealousy, the sacred hatred of sin, and the refining of the soul from all her dross; then, indeed, all good things shall come to restore your soul, and lead you in the paths of righteousness. Do not look for these first; that would be looking for the effects before the cause. The great cause of love in the restored backslider must still be the love of God to him, to whom he clings with a faith that dares not let go its hold.

"But," saith one, "I think it is very dangerous to tell the backslider to believe in God's love, surely it will be

1 JOHN 5

1 Whosoever believeth that Jesus is the Christ is born of God: and every one that loveth him that begat loveth him also that is begotten of him.

2 By this we know that we love the children of God, when we love God, and keep his commandments.

3 For this is the love of God, that we keep his commandments: and his commandments are not grievous.

4 For whatsoever is born of God overcometh the world: and this is the victory that overcometh the world, even our faith.

5 Who is he that overcometh the world, but he that believeth that Jesus is the Son of God?

6 This is he that came by water and blood, even Jesus Christ; not by water only, but by water and blood. And it is the Spirit that beareth witness, because the Spirit is truth.

7 For there are three that bear record in heaven, the Father, the Word, and the Holy Ghost: and these three are one.

8 And there are three that bear witness in earth, the spirit, and the water, and the blood: and these three agree in one.

9 If we receive the witness of men, the witness of God is greater: for this is the witness of God which he hath testified of his Son.

10 He that believeth on the Son of God hath the witness in himself: he that believeth not God hath made him a liar; because he believeth not the record that God gave of his Son.

11 And this is the record, that God hath given to us eternal life, and this life is in his Son.

12 He that hath the Son hath life; and he that hath not the Son of God hath not life.

13 These things have I written unto you that believe on the name of the Son of God; that ye may know that ye have eternal life, and that ye may believe on the name of the Son of God.

14 And this is the confidence that we have in him, that, if we ask any thing according to his will, he heareth us:

15 And if we know that he hear us, whatsoever we ask, we

born of God overcometh the world – Conquers whatever it can lay in the way, either to allure or fright the children of God from keeping his commandments. And this is the victory – The grand means of overcoming. Even our faith – Seeing all things are possible to him that believeth.

5. Who is he that overcometh the world – That is superior to all worldly care, desire, fear? Every believer, and none else.

6. This is he – St. John here shows the immovable foundation of that faith that Jesus is the Son of God; not only the testimony of man, but the firm, indubitable testimony of God.

7. The Spirit – In the word, confirmed by miracles. The water – Of baptism, wherein we are dedicated to the Son, (with the Father and Spirit,) typifying his spotless purity, and the inward purifying of our nature. And the blood – Represented in the Lord's supper, and applied to the consciences of believers. And these three harmoniously agree in one – In bearing the same testimony, – that Jesus Christ is the divine, the complete, the only Savior of the world.

8. And there are three that testify in heaven – The testimony of the Spirit, the water, and the blood, is by an eminent gradation corroborated by three, who give a still greater testimony. The Father – Who clearly testified of the Son, both at his baptism and at his transfiguration. The Word – Who testified of himself on many occasions, while he was on earth; and again, with still greater solemnity, after his ascension into heaven, Rev. i, 5; Rev. xix, 13. And the Spirit – Whose testimony was added chiefly after his glorification, chap. ii, 27; John xv, 26; Acts v, 32; Rom. viii, 16. And these three are one – Even as those two, the Father and the Son, are one, John x, 30. Nothing can separate the Spirit from the Father and the Son. If he were not one with the Father and the Son, the apostle ought to have said, The Father and the Word, who are one, and the Spirit, are two. But this is contrary to the whole tenor of Revelation. It remains that these three are one. They are one in essence, in knowledge, in will, and in their testimony. It is observable, the three in the one verse are opposed, not conjointly, but severally, to the three in the other: as if he had said, Not only the Spirit testifies, but also the Father, John v, 37; not only the water, but also the Word, John iii, 11, John x, 41; not only the blood, but also the Holy Ghost, John xv, 26, &c. It must now appear, to every reasonable man, how absolutely necessary the eighth verse is 8. St. John could not think of the testimony of the Spirit, and water, and blood, and subjoin, "The testimony of God is greater," without thinking also of the testimony of the Son and Holy Ghost; yea, and mentioning it in so solemn an enumeration. Nor can any possible reason be devised, why, without three testifying in heaven, he should enumerate three, and no more, who testify on earth. The testimony of all is given on earth, not in heaven; but they who testify are part on earth, part in heaven. The witnesses who are on earth testify chiefly concerning his abode on earth, though not excluding his state of exaltation: the witnesses who are in heaven testify chiefly concerning his glory at God's right hand, though not excluding his state of humiliation. The seventh verse, therefore, with the sixth, contains a recapitulation of the whole economy of Christ, from his baptism to Pentecost; the eighth, the sum of the divine economy, from the time of his exaltation.

9. If we receive the testimony of men – As we do continually, and must do in a thousand instances. The testimony of God is greater – Of higher authority, and much more worthy to be received; namely, this very testimony which God the Father, together with the Word and the Spirit, hath testified of the Son, as the Savior of the world.

10. He that believeth on the Son of God hath the testimony – The dear evidence of this, in himself: he that believeth not God, in this, hath made him a liar; because he supposes that to be false which God has expressly testified.

11. And this is the sum of that testimony, that God hath given us a title to, and the real beginning of, eternal life; and that this is purchased by, and treasured up

MATTHEW HENRY

CHARLES H. SPURGEON

cleave to Christ, in contempt of, and in opposition to the world.

6-8 We are inwardly and outwardly defiled; inwardly, by the power and pollution of sin in our nature. For our cleansing there is in and by Christ Jesus, the washing of regeneration and the renewing of the Holy Ghost. Some think that the two sacraments are here meant: baptism with water, as the outward sign of regeneration, and purifying from the pollution of sin by the Holy Spirit; and the Lord's supper, as the outward sign of the shedding Christ's blood, and the receiving him by faith for pardon and justification. Both these ways of cleansing were represented in the old ceremonial sacrifices and cleansings. This water and blood include all that is necessary to our salvation. By the water, our souls are washed and purified for heaven and the habitation of saints in light. By the blood, we are justified, reconciled, and presented righteous to God. By the blood, the curse of the law being satisfied, the purifying Spirit is obtained for the internal cleansing of our natures. The water, as well as the blood, came out of the side of the sacrificed Redeemer. He loved the church, and gave himself for it, that he might sanctify and cleanse it with the washing of water by the word; that he might present it to himself a glorious church, Eph 5:25-27. This was done in and by the Spirit of God, according to the Savior's declaration. He is the Spirit of God, and cannot lie. Three had borne witness to these doctrines concerning the person and the salvation of Christ. The Father, repeatedly, by a voice from heaven declared that Jesus was his beloved Son. The Word declared that he and the Father were One, and that whoever had seen him had seen the Father. And the Holy Ghost, who descended from heaven and rested on Christ at his baptism; who had borne witness to him by all the prophets; and gave testimony to his resurrection and mediatorial office, by the gift of miraculous powers to the apostles. But whether this passage be cited or not, the doctrine of the Trinity in Unity stands equally firm and certain. To the doctrine taught by the apostles, respecting the person and salvation of Christ, there were three testimonies. 1. The Holy Spirit. We come into the world with a corrupt, carnal disposition, which is enmity to God. This being done away by the regeneration and new creating of souls by the Holy Spirit, is a testimony to the Savior. 2. The water: this sets forth the Savior's purity and purifying power. The actual and active purity and holiness of his disciples are represented by baptism. 3. The blood which he shed: and this was our ransom, this testifies for Jesus Christ; it sealed up and finished the sacrifices of the Old Testament. The benefits procured by his blood, prove that he is the Savior of the world. No wonder if he that rejects this evidence is judged a blasphemer of the Spirit of God. These three witnesses are for one and the same purpose; they agree in one and the same thing.

9-12 Nothing can be more absurd than the conduct of those who doubt as to the truth of Christianity, while in the common affairs of life they do not hesitate to proceed on human testimony, and would deem any one out of his senses who declined to do so. The real Christian has seen his guilt and misery, and his need of such a Savior. He has seen the suitableness of such a Savior to all his spiritual wants and cir-

gross presumption for him so to believe." It is never presumptuous for a man to believe the truth: whether a statement be comfortable or uncomfortable, the presumption does not lie in the matter itself: but in its untruthfulness. I say again, it is never presumptuous to believe the truth. And this is the truth, that the Lord loves his prodigal sons still, and his stray sheep still, and he will devise means to bring his banished back again, that they perish not. "If any man sin, we have an advocate with the Father, Jesus Christ the righteous."

Remember here that the motive power which draws back the backslider again, is the cord of love, the band of a man, which makes him feel he must go back to God with weeping and repentance, because God loves him still. What man among you this morning hath a son who has disobeyed him and gone from him, and is living in drunkenness, and in all manner of lust? If you have in anger told him, so that he doubts it not, that you have struck his name out of your family, and will not regard him as a child any longer, do you think that your severity will induce him to return to you in love? Far from it. But suppose instead thereof, you still assure him that you love him; that there is always a place at your table for him, and a bed in your house for him, ay, and better still, a warm place in your heart for him; suppose he sees your tears and hears your prayers for him, will not this draw him? Yes, indeed, if he be a son. It is even thus between thy God and thee, O backslider. Hear ye the Lord as he argues thy case within his own heart. "My people are bent to backsliding from me; though they called them to the most High, none at all would exalt him. How shall I give thee up, Ephraim? how shall I deliver thee, Israel? how shall I make thee as Admah? how shall I set thee as Zeboim? mine heart is turned within me, my repentings are kindled together. I will not execute the fierceness of mine anger, I will not return to destroy Ephraim; for I am God, and not man." Surely, if anything will draw you back, this will. "Ah!" saith the wandering son, "my dear father loves me still. I will arise and go to him. I will not vex so tender a heart. I will be his loving son

know that we have the petitions that we desired of him.

16 If any man see his brother sin a sin which is not unto death, he shall ask, and he shall give him life for them that sin not unto death. There is a sin unto death: I do not say that he shall pray for it.

17 All unrighteousness is sin: and there is a sin not unto death.

18 We know that whosoever is born of God sinneth not; but he that is begotten of God keepeth himself, and that wicked one toucheth him not.

19 And we know that we are of God, and the whole world lieth in wickedness.

20 And we know that the Son of God is come, and hath given us an understanding, that we may know him that is true, and we are in him that is true, even in his Son Jesus Christ. This is the true God, and eternal life.

21 Little children, keep yourselves from idols. Amen.

in, his Son, who has all the springs and the fullness of it in himself, to communicate to his body, the church, first in grace and then in glory.

12. It plainly follows, he that hath the Son – Living and reigning in him by faith. Hath this life; he that hath not the Son of God hath not this life – Hath no part or lot therein. In the former clause, the apostle says simply, the Son; because believers know him: in the latter, the Son of God; that unbelievers may know how great a blessing they fall short of.

13. These things have I written – In the introduction, chap. i, 4, he said, I write: now, in the close, I have written. That ye may know – With a fuller and stronger assurance, that ye have eternal life.

14. And we – Who believe. Have this farther confidence in him, that he heareth – That is, favorably regards, whatever prayer we offer in faith, according to his revealed will.

15. We have – Faith anticipates the blessings. The petitions which we asked of him – Even before the event. And when the event comes, we know it comes in answer to our prayer.

16. This extends to things of the greatest importance. If any one see his brother – That is. any man. Sin a sin which is not unto death – That is, any sin but total apostasy from both the power and form of godliness. Let him ask, and God will give him life – Pardon and spiritual life, for that sinner. There is a sin unto death: I do not say that he shall pray for that – That is, let him not pray for it. A sin unto death may likewise mean, one which God has determined to punish with death.

17. All deviation from perfect holiness is sin; but all sin is not unpardonable.

18. Yet this gives us no encouragement to sin: on the contrary, it is an indisputable truth, he that is born of God – That sees and loves God. Sinneth not – So long as that loving faith abides in him, he neither speaks nor does anything which God hath forbidden. He keepeth himself – Watching unto prayer. And, while he does this, the wicked one toucheth him not – So as to hurt him.

19. We know that we are children of God – By the witness and the fruit of his Spirit, chap. iii, 24. But the whole world – All who have not his Spirit, not only is "touched" by him, but by idolatry, fraud, violence lasciviousness, impiety, all manner of wickedness. Lieth in the wicked one – Void of life, void of sense. In this short expression the horrible state of the world is painted in the most lively colors; a comment on which we have in the actions, conversations, contracts, quarrels, and friendships of worldly men.

20. And we know – By all these infallible proofs. That the Son of God is come – Into the world. And he hath given us a spiritual understanding, that we may know him, the true one – "The faithful and true witness." And we are in the true one – As branches in the vine, even in Jesus Christ, the eternal Son of God. This Jesus is the only living and true God, together with the Father and the Spirit, and the original fountain of eternal life. So the beginning and the end of the epistle agree.

21. Keep yourselves from idols – From all worship of false gods, from all worship of images or of any creature, and from every inward idol; from loving, desiring, fearing anything more than God. Seek all help and defense from evil, all happiness in the true God alone.

cumstances. He has found and felt the power of the word and doctrine of Christ, humbling, healing, quickening, and comforting his soul. He has a new disposition, and new delights, and is not the man that he formerly was. Yet he finds still a conflict with himself, with sin, with the flesh, the world, and wicked powers. But he finds such strength from faith in Christ, that he can overcome the world, and travel on towards a better. Such assurance has the gospel believer: he has a witness in himself, which puts the matter out of doubt with him, except in hours of darkness or conflict; but he cannot be argued out of his belief in the leading truths of the gospel.

13-17 Upon all this evidence, it is but right that we believe on the name of the Son of God. Believers have eternal life in the covenant of the gospel. Then let us thankfully receive the record of Scripture. Always abounding in the work of the Lord, knowing that our labor is not in vain in the Lord. The Lord Christ invites us to come to him in all circumstances, with our supplications and requests, notwithstanding the sin that besets us. Our prayers must always be offered in submission to the will of God. In some things they are speedily answered; in others they are granted in the best manner, though not as requested. We ought to pray for others, as well as for ourselves. There are sins that war against spiritual life in the soul, and the life above. We cannot pray that the sins of the impenitent and unbelieving should, while they are such, be forgiven them; or that mercy, which supposes the forgiveness of sins, should be granted to them, while they willfully continue such. But we may pray for their repentance, for their being enriched with faith in Christ, and thereupon for all other saving mercies.

18-21 All mankind are divided into two parties or dominions; that which belongs to God, and that which belongs to the wicked one. True believers belong to God: they are of God, and from him, and to him, and for him; while the rest, by far the greater number, are in the power of the wicked one; they do his works, and support his cause. This general declaration includes all unbelievers, whatever their profession, station, or situation, or by whatever name they may be called. The Son leads believers to the Father, and they are in the love and favor of both; in union with both, by the indwelling and working of the Holy Spirit. Happy are those to whom it is given to know that the Son of God is come, and to have a heart to trust in and rely on him that is true! May this be our privilege; we shall thus be kept from all idols and false doctrines, and from the idolatrous love of worldly objects, and be kept by the power of God, through faith, unto eternal salvation. To this living and true God, be glory and dominion forever and ever. Amen.

again. God does not say to you prodigals, who once professed his name, "I have unchilded you, I have cast you away," but he says, "I love you still; and for my name's sake will I restrain my wrath that I cut you not off." Come to your offended Father, and you shall find that he has not repented of his love, but will embrace you still.

IV. Time fails, but I must speak for a little, time or no time, upon the fourth point—THE PERFECTING OF OUR LOVE TO GOD.

Beloved, there are few of us who know much of the deeps of the love of God; our love is shallow; ah, how shallow! Love to God is like a great mountain. The majority of travelers view it from afar, or traverse the valley at its base: a few climb to a halting place on one of its elevated spurs, whence they see a portion of its sublimities: here and there an adventurous traveler climbs a minor peak, and views glacier and alp at closer range; fewest of all are those who scale the topmost pinnacle and tread the virgin snow. So in the Church of God. Every Christian abides under the shadow of divine love: a few enjoy and return that love to a remarkable degree: but there are few in this age, sadly few, who reach to seraphic love, who ascend into the hill of the Lord, to stand where the eagle's eye hath not seen, and walk the path which the lion's welp hath never trodden, the high places of complete consecration and ardent self-consuming love. Now, mark you, it may be difficult to ascend so high, but there is one sure route. It is not the track of his works, nor the path of his own actions, but this, "We love him because he first loved us." John and the apostles confessed that thus they attained their love. For the highest love that ever glowed in human bosom there was no source but this—God first loved that man. Do you not see how this is? The knowledge that God loves me casts out my tormenting dread of God: and when this is expelled, there is room for abounding love to God.

[Continuation of this sermon follows under 2 John chapter.]

2 JOHN

1 The elder unto the elect lady and her children, whom I love in the truth; and not I only, but also all they that have known the truth;

2 For the truth's sake, which dwelleth in us, and shall be with us for ever.

3 Grace be with you, mercy, and peace, from God the Father, and from the Lord Jesus Christ, the Son of the Father, in truth and love.

4 I rejoiced greatly that I found of thy children walking in truth, as we have received a commandment from the Father.

5 And now I beseech thee, lady, not as though I wrote a new commandment unto thee, but that which we had from the beginning, that we love one another.

6 And this is love, that we walk after his commandments. This is the commandment, That, as ye have heard from the beginning, ye should walk in it.

7 For many deceivers are entered into the world, who confess not that Jesus Christ is come in the flesh. This is a deceiver and an antichrist.

8 Look to yourselves, that we lose not those things which we have wrought, but that we receive a full reward.

9 Whosoever transgresseth, and abideth not in the doctrine of Christ, hath not God. He that abideth in the doctrine of Christ, he hath both the Father and the Son.

10 If there come any unto you, and bring not this doctrine, receive him not into your house, neither bid him God speed:

11 For he that biddeth him God speed is partaker of his evil deeds.

12 Having many things to write unto you, I would not write with paper and ink: but I trust to come unto you, and speak face to face, that our joy may be full.

13 The children of thy elect sister greet thee. Amen.

This epistle was written to some Christian matron, and her religious children.

2 JOHN

1. The elder – An appellation suited to a familiar letter, but upon a weighty subject. To the elect – That is, Christian. Cyria is undoubtedly a proper name, both here and in ver. 5; for it was not then usual to apply the title of lady to any but the Roman empress; neither would such a manner of speaking have been suitable to the simplicity and dignity of the apostle.

2. For the truth's sake, which abideth in us – As a living principle of faith and holiness.

3. Grace takes away guilt; mercy, misery: peace implies the abiding in grace and mercy. It includes the testimony of God's Spirit, both that we are his children, and that all our ways are acceptable to him. This is the very foretaste of heaven itself, where it is perfected. In truth and love – Or, faith and love, as St. Paul speaks. Faith and truth are here synonymous terms.

4. I found of thy children – Probably in their aunt's house, ver. 13. Walking in the truth – In faith and love.

5. That which we had from the beginning – Of our Lord's ministry. Indeed it was, in some sense, from the beginning of the world. That we may love one another – More abundantly.

6. And this is the proof of true love, universal obedience built on the love of God. This – Love. Is the great commandment which ye have heard from the beginning – Of our preaching.

7. Carefully keep what ye have heard from the beginning, for many seducers are entered into the world, who confess not Jesus Christ that came in the flesh – Who disbelieve either his prophetic, or priestly, or kingly office. Whosoever does this is the seducer – From God. And the antichrist – Fighting against Christ.

8. That we lose not the things which we have wrought – Which every apostate does. But receive a full reward – Having fully employed all our talents to the glory of him that gave them. Here again the apostle modestly transfers it to himself.

9. Receive this as a certain rule: Whosoever transgresseth – Any law of God. Hath not God – For his Father and his God. He that abideth in the doctrine of Christ – Believing and obeying it. He hath both the Father and the Son – For his God.

10. If any came to you – Either as a teacher or a brother. And bring not this doctrine – That is, advance anything contrary to it. Receive him not into your house – As either a teacher or a brother – Neither bid him God speed – Give him no encouragement therein.

11. For he that bideth him God speed – That gives him any encouragement, is accessory to his evil deeds.

12. Having many things to write, I was not minded to write now – Only of these, which were then peculiarly needful.

13. The children of thy elect or Christian sister – Absent, if not dead, when the apostle wrote this.

MATTHEW HENRY   CHARLES H. SPURGEON

This epistle is like an abridgement of the first; it touch-es, in few words, on the same points. The elect lady is commended for her virtuous and religious education of her children; is exhorted to abide in the doctrine of Christ, to persevere in the truth, and carefully to avoid the delusions of false teachers. But chiefly the apostle beseeches her to practice the great commandment of Christian love and charity.

2 JOHN

The apostle salutes the elect lady and her children. (1-3)
Express his joy in their faith and love. (4-6)
Cautions them against deceivers. (7-11)
And concludes. (12,13)

1-3 Religion turns compliments into real expressions of respect and love. An old disciple is honorable; an old apostle and leader of disciples is more so. The letter is to a noble Christian matron, and her children; it is well that the gospel should get among such: some noble persons are called. Families are to be encouraged and directed in their love and duties at home. Those who love truth and piety in themselves, should love it in oth-ers; and the Christians loved this lady, not for her rank, but for her holiness.

4-6 It is good to be trained to early religion; and chil-dren may be beloved for their parents' sake. It gave great joy to the apostle to see children treading in their parents' steps, and likely in their turn to support the gospel. May God bless such families more and more, and raise up many to copy their example. How pleas-ing the contrast to numbers who spread irreligion, infi-delity, and vice, among their children! Our walk is true, our converse right, when according to the word of God. This commandment of mutual Christian love, may be said to be a new one, in respect of its being declared by the Lord Christ; yet, as to the matter, it is old. And this is love to our own souls, that we obey the Divine commands.

7-11 The deceiver and his deceit are described: he brings some error concerning the person or office of the Lord Jesus. Such a one is a deceiver and an antichrist; he deludes souls, and undermines the glory and kingdom of the Lord Christ. Let us not think it strange, that there are deceivers and opposers of the Lord Christ's name and dignity now, for there were such, even in the apostles' times. The more deceivers and deceits abound, the more watchful the disciples must be. Sad it is, that splendid attainments in the school of Christ, should ever be lost. The way to gain the full reward is, to abide true to Christ, and constant in religion to the end.

12,13 The apostle refers many things to a personal meeting. Pen and ink were means of strengthening and comforting others; but to see each other is more so. The communion of saints should be maintained by all methods; and should tend to mutual joy. In communion with them we find much of our present joy, and look for-ward to happiness forever.

**[Continuation of sermon, "Love's Logic",
1 John 4:19, from 1 John chapter.]**

As fear goes out, love comes in at the other door. So the more faith in God the more room there is for soul-filling love.

Again, strong faith in God's love brings great enjoyment; our heart is glad, our soul is satisfied with marrow and fatness when we know that the whole heart of God beats towards us as forcibly as if we were the only creatures he had ever made, and his whole heart were wrapt up in us. This deep enjoyment creates the flaming love of which I have just now spoken.

If the ardent love of some saints often takes the shape of admiration of God, this arises from their familiarity with God, and this famil-iarity they never would have indulged in, unless they had known that he was their friend. A man could not speak to God as to a friend, unless he knew the love that God hath toward him. The more true his knowledge and the more sure, the more close his fellowship.

Brethren beloved, if you know that God has loved you, then you will feel grateful; every doubt will diminish your gratitude, but every grain of faith will increase it. Then as we advance in grace, love to God in our soul will excite desire after him. Those we love we long to be with; we count the hours that separate us; no place so happy as that in which we enjoy their society. Hence love to God produces a desire to be with him; a desire to be like him, a longing to be with him eternally in heaven, and this breaks us away from worldliness; this keeps us from idolatry, and thus has a most blessedly sanctifying effect upon us, producing that elevated character which is now so rare, but which wherever it exists is powerful for the good of the church and for the glory of God. Oh that we had many in this church who had reached the highest platform of piety. Would God we had a band of men full of faith and of the Holy Ghost; strong in the Lord and in the power of his might. It may help those who aspire to mount high in grace, if they keep in mind that every step they climb they must use the ladder which Jacob saw. The love of God to us is the only way to climb to the love of God.

And now I must spend a minute in putting the truth of my text to the test. I want you not to listen to me so much as to listen to your own hearts, and to God's word, a minute, if you are believers. What is it we have been talking about? It is God's love to us. Get the thought into your head a minute:

**[Completion of this sermon follows under
3 John chapter.]**

3 JOHN

1 The elder unto the wellbeloved Gaius, whom I love in the truth.

2 Beloved, I wish above all things that thou mayest prosper and be in health, even as thy soul prospereth.

3 For I rejoiced greatly, when the brethren came and testified of the truth that is in thee, even as thou walkest in the truth.

4 I have no greater joy than to hear that my children walk in truth.

5 Beloved, thou doest faithfully whatsoever thou doest to the brethren, and to strangers;

6 Which have borne witness of thy charity before the church: whom if thou bring forward on their journey after a godly sort, thou shalt do well:

7 Because that for his name's sake they went forth, taking nothing of the Gentiles.

8 We therefore ought to receive such, that we might be fellowhelpers to the truth.

9 I wrote unto the church: but Diotrephes, who loveth to have the preeminence among them, receiveth us not.

10 Wherefore, if I come, I will remember his deeds which he doeth, prating against us with malicious words: and not content therewith, neither doth he himself receive the brethren, and forbiddeth them that would, and casteth them out of the church.

11 Beloved, follow not that which is evil, but that which is good. He that doeth good is of God: but he that doeth evil hath not seen God.

12 Demetrius hath good report of all men, and of the truth itself: yea, and we also bear record; and ye know that our record is true.

13 I had many things to write, but I will not with ink and pen write unto thee:

14 But I trust I shall shortly see thee, and we shall speak face to face. Peace be to thee. Our friends salute thee. Greet the friends by name.

3 JOHN

1. Caius was probably that Caius of Corinth whom St. Paul mentions, Rom. xvi, 23. If so, either he was removed from Achaia into Asia, or St. John sent this letter to Corinth.

3. For – I know thou usest all thy talents to his glory. The truth that is in thee – The true faith and love.

4. I have no greater joy than this – Such is the spirit of every true Christian pastor. To hear that my children walk in the truth – Caius probably was converted by St. Paul. Therefore when St. John speaks of him, with other believers, as his children, it may be considered as the tender style of paternal love, whoever were the instruments of their conversion. And his using this appellation, when writing under the character of the elder, has its peculiar beauty.

5. Faithfully – Uprightly and sincerely.

6. Who have testified of thy love before the church – The congregation with whom I now reside. Whom if thou send forward on their journey – Supplied with what is needful. Thou shalt do well – How tenderly does the apostle enjoin this!

7. They went forth – To preach the gospel.

8. To receive – With all kindness. The truth – Which they preach.

9. I wrote to the church – Probably that to which they came. But Diotrephes – Perhaps the pastor of it. Who loveth to have the preeminence among them – To govern all things according to his own will. Receiveth us not – Neither them nor me. So did the mystery of iniquity already work!

10. He prateth against us – Both them and me, thereby endeavoring to excuse himself.

11. Follow not that which is evil – In Diotrephes. But that which is good – In Demetrius. He hath not seen God – Is a stranger to him.

12. And from the truth itself – That is, what they testify is the very truth. Yea, we also bear testimony – I and they that are with me.

14. Salute the friends by name – That is, in the same manner as if I had named them one by one. The word friend does not often occur in the New Testament, being swallowed up in the more endearing one of brother.

This epistle is addressed to a converted Gentile. The scope is to commend his steadfastness in the faith, and his hospitality, especially to the ministers of Christ.

3 JOHN

The apostle commends Gaius for piety and hospitality. (1-8)

Cautions him against siding with Diotrephes, who was a turbulent spirit; but recommends Demetrius as a man of excellent character. (9-12)

He hopes soon to see Gaius. (13,14)

1-8 Those who are beloved of Christ, will love the brethren for his sake. Soul prosperity is the greatest blessing on this side of heaven. Grace and health are rich companions. Grace will employ health. A rich soul may be lodged in a weak body; and grace must then be exercised in submitting to such a dispensation. But we may wish and pray that those who have prosperous souls, may have healthful bodies; that their grace may shine where there is still more room for activity. How many professors there are, about whom the apostle's words must be reversed, and we must earnestly wish and pray that their souls might prosper, as their health and circumstances do! True faith will work by love. A good report is due from those who receive good; they could not but testify to the church, what they found and felt. Good men will rejoice in the soul prosperity of others; and they are glad to hear of the grace and goodness of others. And as it is a joy to good parents, it will be a joy to good ministers, to see their people adorn their profession. Gaius overlooked petty differences among serious Christians, and freely helped all who bore the image, and did the work of Christ.

9-12 Both the heart and mouth must be watched. The temper and spirit of Diotrephes was full of pride and ambition. It is bad not to do good ourselves; but it is worse to hinder those who would do good. Those cautions and counsels are most likely to be accepted, which are seasoned with love. Follow that which is good, for he that doeth good, as delighting therein, is born of God. Evilworkers vainly pretend or boast acquaintance with God.

13,14 Here is the character of Demetrius. A name in the gospel, or a good report in the churches, is better than worldly honor. Few are well spoken of by all; and sometimes it is ill to be so. Happy those whose spirit and conduct commend them before God and men. We must be ready to bear our testimony to them; and it is well when those who commend, can appeal to the consciences of such as know most of those who are commended. A personal conversation together often spares time and trouble, and mistakes which rise from letters; and good Christians may well be glad to see one another. The blessing is, Peace be to you; all happiness attend you. Those may well salute and greet one another on earth, who hope to live together in heaven. By associating with and copying the example of such Christians, we shall have peace within, and live at peace with the brethren; our communications with the Lord's people on earth will be pleasing, and we shall be numbered with them in glory everlasting.

[Continuation of sermon, "Love's Logic", 1 John 4:19, from 2 John chapter.]

"God loves me"—not merely bears with me, thinks of me, feeds me, but loves me. Oh, it is a very sweet thing to feel that we have the love of a dear wife, or a kind husband; and there is much sweetness in the love of a fond child, or a tender mother; but to think that God loves me, this is infinitely better! Who is it that loves you? God, the Maker of heaven and earth, the Almighty, All in all, does he love me? Even he? If all men, and all angels, and all the living creatures that are before the throne loved me, it were nothing to this—the Infinite loves me! And who is it that he loves? Me. The text saith, "us." "We love him because he first loved us." But this is the personal point—he loves me, an insignificant nobody, full of sin—who deserved to be in hell; who loves him so little in return—God loves me. Beloved believer, does not this melt you? Does not this fire your soul? I know it does if it is really believed. It must. And how did he love me? He loved me so that he gave up his only begotten Son for me, to be nailed to the tree, and made to bleed and die. And what will come of it? Why, because he loved me and forgave me,—I am on the way to heaven, and within a few months, perhaps days, I shall see his face and sing his praises. He loved me before I was born; before a star begun to shine he loved me, and he has never ceased to do so all these years. When I have sinned he has loved me; when I have forgotten him he has loved me; and when in the days of my sin I cursed him, yet still he loved me; and he will love me when my knees tremble, and my hair is gray with age, "even to hoar hairs" he will bear and carry his servant; and he will love me when the world is on a blaze, and love me for ever, and for ever. Oh, chew the cud of this blessed thought; roll it under your tongue as a dainty morsel; sit down this afternoon, if you have leisure, and think of nothing but this—his great love wherewith he loves you; and if you do not feel your heart bubbling with a good matter, if you do not feel your soul yearning towards God, and heaving big with strong emotions of love to God, then I am much mistaken. This is so powerful a truth, and you are so constituted as a Christian as to be wrought upon by this truth, that if it be believed and felt, the consequence must be that you will love him because he first loved you. God bless you, brethren and sisters, for Christ's sake. Amen.

Jude

JUDE

1 Jude, the servant of Jesus Christ, and brother of James, to them that are sanctified by God the Father, and preserved in Jesus Christ, and called:

2 Mercy unto you, and peace, and love, be multiplied.

3 Beloved, when I gave all diligence to write unto you of the common salvation, it was needful for me to write unto you, and exhort you that ye should earnestly contend for the faith which was once delivered unto the saints.

4 For there are certain men crept in unawares, who were before of old ordained to this condemnation, ungodly men, turning the grace of our God into lasciviousness, and denying the only Lord God, and our Lord Jesus Christ.

5 I will therefore put you in remembrance, though ye once knew this, how that the Lord, having saved the people out of the land of Egypt, afterward destroyed them that believed not.

6 And the angels which kept not their first estate, but left their own habitation, he hath reserved in everlasting chains under darkness unto the judgment of the great day.

7 Even as Sodom and Gomorrha, and the cities about them in like manner, giving themselves over to fornication, and going after strange flesh, are set forth for an example, suffering the vengeance of eternal fire.

8 Likewise also these filthy dreamers defile the flesh, despise dominion, and speak evil of dignities.

9 Yet Michael the archangel, when contending with the devil he disputed about the body of Moses, durst not bring against him a railing accusation, but said, The Lord rebuke thee.

10 But these speak evil of those things which they know not: but what they know naturally, as brute beasts, in those things

This epistle greatly resembles the second of St. Peter, which St. Jude seems to have had in view while he wrote. That was written but a very little before his death; and hence we may gather that St. Jude lived some time after it, and saw that grievous declension in the church which St. Peter had foretold. But he passes over some things mentioned by St. Peter, repeats some in different expressions and with a different view, and adds others; clearly evidencing thereby the wisdom of God which rested upon him. Thus St. Peter cites and confirms St. Paul's writings, and is himself cited and confirmed by St. Jude.

JUDE

1. Jude, a servant of Jesus Christ – The highest glory which any, either angel or man, can aspire to. The word servant, under the old covenant, was adapted to the spirit of fear and bondage that clave to that dispensation. But when the time appointed of the Father was come, for the sending of his Son to redeem them that were under the law, the word servant (used by the apostles concerning themselves and all the children of God) signified one that, having the Spirit of adoption, is made free by the Son of God. His being a servant is the fruit and perfection of his being a son. And whenever the throne of God and of the Lamb shall be in the new Jerusalem, then will it be indeed that "his servants shall serve him," Rev. xxii, 3. The brother of James – St. James was the more eminent, usually styled, "the brother of the Lord." To them that are beloved – The conclusion, ver. 21, exactly answers the introduction. And preserved through Jesus Christ – So both the spring and the accomplishment of salvation are pointed out. This is premised, lest any of them should be discouraged by the terrible things which are afterwards mentioned. And called – To receive the whole blessing of God, in time and eternity.

3. When I gave all diligence to write to you of the common salvation – Designed for all, and enjoyed by all believers. Here the design of the epistle is expressed; the end of which exactly answers the beginning. It was needful to exhort you to contend earnestly – Yet humbly, meekly, and lovingly; otherwise your contention will only hurt your cause, if not destroy your soul. For the faith – All the fundamental truths. Once delivered – By God, to remain unvaried for ever.

4. There are certain men crept in, who were of old described before – Even as early as Enoch; of whom it was foretold, that by their willfull sins they would incur this condemnation. Turning the grace of God – Revealed in the gospel. Into lasciviousness – Into an occasion of more abandoned wickedness.

5. He afterwards destroyed – The far greater part of that very people whom he had once saved. Let none therefore presume upon past mercies, as if he was now out of danger.

6. And the angels, who kept not their first dignity – Once assigned them under the Son of God. But voluntarily left their own habitation – Then properly their own, by the free gift of God. He reserved – Delivered to be kept. In everlasting chains under darkness – O how unlike their own habitation! When these fallen angels came out of the hands of God, they were holy; else God made that which was evil: and being holy, they were beloved of God; else he hated the image of his own spotless purity. But now he loves them no more; they are doomed to endless destruction. (for if he loved them still, he would love what is sinful:) and both his former love, and his present righteous and eternal displeasure towards the same work of his own hands, are because he changeth not; because he invariably loveth righteousness, and hateth iniquity. 2 Pet. ii, 4.

7. The cities which gave themselves over to fornication – The word here means, unnatural lusts. Are set forth as an example, suffering the vengeance of eternal fire – That is, the vengeance which they suffered is an example or a type of eternal fire.

This epistle is addressed to all believers in the gospel. Its design appears to be to guard believers against the false teachers who had begun to creep into the Christian church, and to scatter dangerous tenets, by attempting to lower all Christianity into a merely nominal belief and outward profession of the gospel. Having thus denied the obligations of personal holiness, they taught their disciples to live in sinful courses, at the same time flattering them with the hope of eternal life. The vile character of these seducers is shown, and their sentence is denounced, and the epistle concludes with warnings, admonitions, and counsels to believers.

JUDE

The apostle exhorts to steadfastness in the faith. (1-4)

The danger of being infected by false professors, and the dreadful punishment which shall be inflicted on them and their followers. (5-7)

An awful description of these seducers and their deplorable end. (8-16)

Believers cautioned against being surprised at such deceivers arising among them. (17-23)

The epistle ends with an encouraging doxology, or words of praise. (24,25)

1-4 Christians are called out of the world, from the evil spirit and temper of it; called above the world, to higher and better things, to heaven, things unseen and eternal; called from sin to Christ, from vanity to seriousness, from uncleanness to holiness; and this according to the Divine purpose and grace. If sanctified and glorified, all the honor and glory must be ascribed to God, and to him alone. As it is God who begins the work of grace in the souls of men, so it is he who carries it on, and perfects it. Let us not trust in ourselves, nor in our stock of grace already received, but in him, and in him alone. The mercy of God is the spring and fountain of all the good we have or hope for; mercy, not only to the miserable, but to the guilty. Next to mercy is peace, which we have from the sense of having obtained mercy. From peace springs love; Christ's love to us, our love to him, and our brotherly love to one another. The apostle prays, not that Christians may be content with a little; but that their souls and societies may be full of these things. None are shut out from gospel offers and invitations, but those who obstinately and wickedly shut themselves out. But the application is to all believers, and only to such. It is to the weak as well as to the strong. Those who have received the doctrine of this common salvation, must contend for it, earnestly, not furiously. Lying for the truth is bad; scolding for it is not better. Those who have received the truth must contend for it, as the apostles did; by suffering with patience and courage for it, not by making others suffer if they will not embrace every notion we call faith, or important.

5-7 Outward privileges, profession, and apparent conversion, could not secure those from the vengeance of God, who turned aside in unbelief and disobedience. The destruction of the unbelieving Israelites in the wilderness, shows that none ought to presume on their privileges. They had miracles as their daily bread; yet even they perished in unbelief. A great

THE HOLY SPIRIT AND THE ONE CHURCH
Sermon number 167 delivered on December 13, 1857, at the Music Hall, Royal Surrey Gardens.

"These be they who separate themselves, sensual, having not the Spirit."—Jude 1:19.

I. First, our text suggests AN INQUIRY—Have we the Spirit? This is an inquiry so important, that the philosopher may well suspend all his investigations to find an answer to this question on his own personal account. All the great debates of politics, all the most engrossing subjects of human discussion, may well stop today, and give us pause to ask ourselves the solemn question—"Have I the Spirit?" For this question does not deal with any externals of religion, but it deals with religion in its most vital point. He that hath the Spirit, although he be wrong in fifty things, being right in this, is saved; he that hath not the Spirit, be he never so orthodox, be his creed as correct as Scripture – ay and in his morals outwardly as pure as the law, is still unsaved; he is destitute of the essential part of salvation—the Spirit of God dwelling in him.

The first work of the Spirit in the heart is a work during which the Spirit is compared to the wind. You remember that when our Savior spoke to Nicodemus he represented the first work of the Spirit in the heart as being like the wind, "which bloweth where it listeth;" "even so;" saith he, "is every one that is born of the Spirit." Now you know that the wind is a most mysterious thing; and although there be certain definitions of it which pretend to be explanations of the phenomenon, yet they certainly leave the great question of how the wind blows, and what is the cause of its blowing in a certain direction, where it was before. Breath within us, wind without us, all motions of air, are to us mysterious. And the renewing work of the Spirit in the heart is exceedingly mysterious. It is possible that at this moment the Spirit of God may be breathing into some of the thousand hearts before me; yet it would be blasphemous if any one should ask, "Which way went the Spirit from God to such a heart? How

they corrupt themselves.

11 Woe unto them! for they have gone in the way of Cain, and ran greedily after the error of Balaam for reward, and perished in the gainsaying of Core.

12 These are spots in your feasts of charity, when they feast with you, feeding themselves without fear: clouds they are without water, carried about of winds; trees whose fruit withereth, without fruit, twice dead, plucked up by the roots;

13 Raging waves of the sea, foaming out their own shame; wandering stars, to whom is reserved the blackness of darkness for ever.

14 And Enoch also, the seventh from Adam, prophesied of these, saying, Behold, the Lord cometh with ten thousands of his saints,

15 To execute judgment upon all, and to convince all that are ungodly among them of all their ungodly deeds which they have ungodly committed, and of all their hard speeches which ungodly sinners have spoken against him.

16 These are murmurers, complainers, walking after their own lusts; and their mouth speaketh great swelling words, having men's persons in admiration because of advantage.

17 But, beloved, remember ye the words which were spoken before of the apostles of our Lord Jesus Christ;

18 How that they told you there should be mockers in the last time, who should walk after their own ungodly lusts.

19 These be they who separate themselves, sensual, having not the Spirit.

20 But ye, beloved, building up yourselves on your most holy faith, praying in the Holy Ghost,

21 Keep yourselves in the love of God, looking for the mercy of our Lord Jesus Christ unto eternal life.

22 And of some have compassion, making a difference:

23 And others save with fear,

8. In like manner these dreamers – Sleeping and dreaming all their lives. Despise authority – Those that are invested with it by Christ, and made by him the overseers of his flock. Rail at dignities – The apostle does not seem to speak of worldly dignities. These they had "in admiration for the sake of gain," ver. 16; but those holy men, who for the purity of their lives, the soundness of their doctrine, and the greatness of their labors in the work of the ministry, were truly honorable before God and all good men; and who were grossly vilified by those who turned the grace of God into lasciviousness. Probably they were the impure followers of Simon Magus, the same with the Gnostics and Nicolaitans, Rev. ii, 15. 2 Pet. ii, 10.

9. Yet Michael – It does not appear whether St. Jude learned this by any Revelation or from ancient tradition. It suffices, that these things were not only true, but acknowledged as such by them to whom he wrote. The archangel – This word occurs but once more in the sacred writings, 1 Thess. iv, 16. So that whether there be one archangel only, or more, it is not possible for us to determine. When he disputed with the devil – At what time we know not. Concerning the body of Moses – Possibly the devil would have discovered the place where it was buried, which God for wise reasons had concealed. Durst not bring even against him a railing accusation – Though so far beneath him in every respect. But simply said, (so great was his modesty!) The Lord rebuke thee – I leave thee to the Judge of all.

10. But these – Without all shame. Rail at the things of God which they know not – Neither can know, having no spiritual senses. And the natural things, which they know – By their natural senses, they abuse into occasions of sin.

11. Woe unto them – Of all the apostles St. Jude alone, and that in this single place, denounces a woe. St. Peter, to the same effect, pronounces them "cursed children." For they have gone in the way of Cain – The murderer. And ran greedily – Literally, have been poured out, like a torrent without banks. After the error of Balaam – The covetous false prophet. And perished in the gainsaying of Korah – Vengeance has overtaken them as it did Korah, rising up against those whom God had sent.

12. These are spots – Blemishes. In your feasts of love – Anciently observed in all the churches. Feeding themselves without fear – Without any fear of God, or jealousy over themselves. Twice dead – In sin, first by nature, and afterwards by apostasy. Plucked up by the roots – And so incapable of ever reviving.

13. Wandering stars – Literally, planets, which shine for a time, but have no light in themselves, and will be soon cast into utter darkness. Thus the apostle illustrates their desperate wickedness by comparisons drawn from the air, earth, sea, and heavens.

14. And of these also – As well as the antediluvian sinners. Enoch – So early was the prophecy referred to, ver. 4. The seventh from Adam – There were only five of the fathers between Adam and Enoch, 1 Chron. i, 1-3. The first coming of Christ was revealed to Adam; his second, glorious coming, to Enoch; and the seventh from Adam foretold the things which will conclude the seventh age of the world. St. Jude might know this either from some ancient book, or tradition, or immediate Revelation. Behold – As if it were already done, the Lord cometh!

15. To execute judgment – Enoch herein looked beyond the flood. Upon all – Sinners, in general. And to convict all the ungodly, in particular, of all the grievous things which ungodly sinners (a sinner is bad; but the ungodly who sin without fear are worse) have spoken against him, ver. 8, 10, though they might not think, all those speeches were against him.

16. These are murmurers – Against men. Complainers – Literally, complainers of their fate, against God. Walking – With regard to themselves. After their own foolish and mischievous desires. Having men's persons in admiration for the sake of gain – Admiring and commending them only for what they can get.

number of the angels were not pleased with the stations God allotted to them; pride was the main and direct cause or occasion of their fall. The fallen angels are kept to the judgment of the great day; and shall fallen men escape it? Surely not. Consider this in due time. The destruction of Sodom is a loud warning to all, to take heed of, and flee from fleshly lusts that war against the soul, 1Pe 2:11. God is the same holy, just, pure Being now, as then. Stand in awe, therefore, and sin not, Ps 4:4. Let us not rest in anything that does not make the soul subject to the obedience of Christ; for nothing but the renewal of our souls to the Divine image by the Holy Spirit, can keep us from being destroyed among the enemies of God.

8-16 False teachers are dreamers; they greatly defile and grievously wound the soul. These teachers are of a disturbed mind and a seditious spirit; forgetting that the powers that be, are ordained of God, Ro 13:1. As to the contest about the body of Moses, it appears that Satan wished to make the place of his burial known to the Israelites, in order to tempt them to worship him, but he was prevented, and vented his rage in desperate blasphemy. This should remind all who dispute never to bring railing charges. Also learn hence, that we ought to defend those whom God owns. It is hard, if not impossible, to find any enemies to the Christian religion, who did not, and do not, live in open or secret contradiction to the principles of natural religion. Such are here compared to brute beasts, though they often boast of themselves as the wisest of mankind. They corrupt themselves in the things most open and plain. The fault lies, not in their understandings, but in their depraved wills, and their disordered appetites and affections. It is a great reproach, though unjust to religion, when those who profess it are opposed to it in heart and life. The Lord will remedy this in his time and way; not in men's blind way of plucking up the wheat with the tares. It is sad when men begin in the Spirit, and end in the flesh. Twice dead; they had been once dead in their natural, fallen state; but now they are dead again by the evident proofs of their hypocrisy. Dead trees, why cumber they the ground! Away with them to the fire. Raging waves are a terror to sailing passengers; but when they get into port, the noise and terror are ended. False teachers are to expect the worst punishments in this world and in that to come. They glare like meteors, or falling stars, and then sink into the blackness of darkness forever. We have no mention of the prophecy of Enoch in any other part or place of Scripture; yet one plain text of Scripture, proves any point we are to believe. We find from this, that Christ's coming to judge was prophesied of, as early as the times before the flood. The Lord cometh: what a glorious time will that be! Notice how often the word "ungodly" is repeated. Many now do not at all refer to the terms godly, or ungodly, unless it be to mock at even the words; but it is not so in the language taught us by the Holy Ghost. Hard speeches of one another, especially if ill grounded, will certainly come into account at the day of judgment. These evil men and seducers are angry at every thing that happens, and never pleased with their own state and condition. Their will and their fancy, are their only rule and law. Those who please their sinful appetites, are most prone to yield to ungovernable passions. The men of God, from the beginning of the world, have declared the doom denounced on them.

entered it there?" And it would be foolish for a person who is under the operation of the Spirit to ask how it operates: thou knowest not where is the storehouse of the thunder; thou knowest not where the clouds are balanced; neither canst thou know how the Spirit goeth forth from the Most High and enters into the heart of man. It may be, that during a sermon two men are listening to the same truth; one of them hears as attentively as the other and remembers as much of it; the other is melted to tears or moved with solemn thoughts; but the one though equally attentive, sees nothing in the sermon, except, maybe, certain important truths well set forth; as for the other, his heart is broken within him and his soul is melted. Ask me how it is that the same truth has an effect upon the one, and not upon his fellow: I reply, because the mysterious Spirit of the living God goes with the truth to one heart and not to the other. The one only feels the force of truth, and that may be strong enough to make him tremble, like Felix; but the other feels the Spirit going with the truth, and that renews the man, regenerates him, and causes him to pass into that gracious condition which is called the state of salvation. This change takes place instantaneously. It is as miraculous a change as any miracle of which we read in Scripture.

II. Thus, I have tried to help you to answer the first question—the inquiry, Have we received the Spirit? And this brings me to the CAUTION. He that has not received the Spirit is said to be sensual. Oh, what a gulf there is between the least Christian and the greatest moralist! What a wide distinction there is between the greatest professor destitute of grace, and the least of God's believers who has grace in his heart. As great a difference as there is between light and darkness, between death and life, between heaven and hell, is there between a saint and a sinner; for mark, my text says, in no very polite phrase, that if we have not the Spirit we are sensual. "Sensual!" says one; "well, I am not converted man—I don't pretend to be; but I am not sensual." Well, friend, and it is very likely that you are not—not in the common acceptation

pulling them out of the fire; hating even the garment spotted by the flesh.

24 Now unto him that is able to keep you from falling, and to present you faultless before the presence of his glory with exceeding joy,

25 To the only wise God our Savior, be glory and majesty, dominion and power, both now and ever. Amen.

17. By the apostles – He does not exempt himself from the number of apostles. For in the next verse he says, they told you, not us.

19. These are they who separate themselves, sensual, not having the Spirit – Having natural senses and understanding only, not the Spirit of God; otherwise they could not separate. For that it is a sin, and a very heinous one, "to separate from the church," is out of all question. But then it should be observed,

1. That by the church is meant a body of living Christians, who are "an habitation of God through the Spirit:"

2. That by separating is understood, renouncing all religious intercourse with them; no longer joining with them in solemn prayer, or the other public offices of religion: and,

3. That we have no more authority from scripture to call even this schism, than to call it murder.

20. But ye, beloved, not separating, but building yourselves up in your most holy faith – Than which none can be more holy in itself, or more conducive to the most refined and exalted holiness. Praying through the Holy Spirit – Who alone is able to build you up, as he alone laid the foundation. In this and the following verse St. Jude mentions the Father, Son, and Spirit, together with faith, love, and hope.

21. By these means, through his grace, keep yourselves in the love of God, and in the confident expectation of that eternal life which is purchased for you, and conferred upon you, through the mere mercy of our Lord Jesus Christ.

22. Meantime watch over others, as well as yourselves, and give them such help as their various needs require. For instance,

1. Some, that are wavering in judgment, staggered by others' or by their own evil reasoning, endeavor more deeply to convince of the whole truth as it is in Jesus.

2. Some snatch, with a swift and strong hand, out of the fire of sin and temptation.

3. On others show compassion in a milder and gentler way; though still with a jealous fear, lest yourselves be infected with the disease you endeavor to cure.

See, therefore, that while you love the sinners, ye retain the utmost abhorrence of their sins, and of any the least degree of, or approach to, them.

24. Now to him who alone is able to keep them from falling – Into any of these errors or sins. And to present them faultless in the presence of his glory – That is, in his own presence, when he shall be revealed in all his glory. Please see Notes at Matt. i, 1.

MATTHEW HENRY

17-23 Sensual men separate from Christ, and his church, and join themselves to the devil, the world, and the flesh, by ungodly and sinful practices. That is infinitely worse than to separate from any branch of the visible church on account of opinions, or modes and circumstances of outward government or worship. Sensual men have not the spirit of holiness, which whoever has not, does not belong to Christ. The grace of faith is most holy, as it works by love, purifies the heart, and overcomes the world, by which it is distinguished from a false and dead faith. Our prayers are most likely to prevail, when we pray in the Holy Ghost, under his guidance and influence, according to the rule of his word, with faith, fervency, and earnestness; this is praying in the Holy Ghost. And a believing expectation of eternal life will arm us against the snares of sin: lively faith in this blessed hope will help us to mortify our lusts. We must watch over one another; faithfully, yet prudently reprove each other, and set a good example to all about us. This must be done with compassion, making a difference between the weak and the willfull. Some we must treat with tenderness. Others save with fear; urging the terrors of the Lord. All endeavors must be joined with decided abhorrence of crimes, and care be taken to avoid whatever led to, or was connected with fellowship with them, in works of darkness, keeping far from what is, or appears to be evil.

24,25 God is able, and as willing as able, to keep us from falling, and to present us faultless before the presence of his glory. Not as those who never have been faulty, but as those who, but for God's mercy, and a Savior's sufferings and merits, might most justly have been condemned long ago. All sincere believers were given him of the Father; and of all so given him he has lost none, nor will lose any one. Now, our faults fill us with fears, doubts, and sorrows; but the Redeemer has undertaken for his people, that they shall be presented faultless. Where there is no sin, there will be no sorrow; where there is the perfection of holiness, there will be the perfection of joy. Let us more often look up to him who is able to keep us from falling, to improve as well as maintain the work he has wrought in us, till we shall be presented blameless before the presence of his glory. Then shall our hearts know a joy beyond what earth can afford; then shall God also rejoice over us, and the joy of our compassionate Savior be completed. To him who has so wisely formed the scheme, and will faithfully and perfectly accomplish it, be glory and majesty, dominion and power, both now and for ever. Amen.

of the term sensual; but understand that this word, in the Greek, really means what an English word like this would mean, if we had such a one—soulish. We have not such a word—we want such a one. There is a great distinction between mere animals and men, because man hath a soul, and the mere animal hath none. There is another distinction between mere men and a converted man. The converted man hath the Spirit—the unconverted man hath none; he is a soulish man—not a spiritual man; he has got no further than mere nature and has no inheritance in the spiritual kingdom of grace. Strange it is that soulish and sensual should after all mean the same! Friend, thou hast not the Spirit. Then thou art nothing better—be thou what thou art, or whatsoever thou mayest be—than the fall of Adam left thee. That is to say, thou art a fallen creature, having only capacities to live here in sin, and to live for ever in torment; but thou hast not the capacity to live in heaven at all, for thou hast no Spirit; and therefore thou art unable to know or enjoy spiritual things. And mark you, a man may be in this state, and be a sensual man, and yet he may have all the virtues that could grace a Christian; but with all these, if he has not the Spirit, he has got not an inch further than where Adam's fall left him—that is, condemned and under the curse. Ay, and he may attend to religion with all his might—he may take the sacrament, and be baptized, and may be the most devout professor; but if he hath not the Spirit he hath not started a solitary inch from where he was, for he is still in "the bonds of iniquity," a lost soul.

I may have said some rough things this morning, but I am not given much to cutting and trimming, and I do not suppose I shall begin to learn that art now. If the thing is untrue, it is with you to reject it; if it be true, at your own peril reject what God stamps with divine authority. May the blessing of the Father, the Son, and the Holy Spirit rest upon the one church of Israel's one Jehovah. Amen and Amen.

Revelation

REVELATION 1

1 The Revelation of Jesus Christ, which God gave unto him, to shew unto his servants things which must shortly come to pass; and he sent and signified it by his angel unto his servant John:

2 Who bare record of the word of God, and of the testimony of Jesus Christ, and of all things that he saw.

3 Blessed is he that readeth, and they that hear the words of this prophecy, and keep those things which are written therein: for the time is at hand.

4 John to the seven churches which are in Asia: Grace be unto you, and peace, from him which is, and which was, and which is to come; and from the seven Spirits which are before his throne;

5 And from Jesus Christ, who is the faithful witness, and the first begotten of the dead, and the prince of the kings of the earth. Unto him that loved us, and washed us from our sins in his own blood,

6 And hath made us kings and priests unto God and his Father; to him be glory and dominion for ever and ever. Amen.

7 Behold, he cometh with clouds; and every eye shall see him, and they also which pierced him: and all kindreds of the earth shall wail because of him. Even so, Amen.

8 I am Alpha and Omega, the beginning and the ending, saith the Lord, which is, and which was, and which is to come, the Almighty.

9 I John, who also am your brother, and companion in tribulation, and in the kingdom and patience of Jesus Christ, was in the isle that is called Patmos, for the word of God, and for the testimony of Jesus Christ.

10 I was in the Spirit on the Lord's day, and heard behind me a great voice, as of a trumpet,

11 Saying, I am Alpha and Omega, the first and the last: and, What thou seest, write in a book, and send it unto the seven churches which are in Asia; unto Ephesus, and unto

IT is scarce possible for any that either love or fear God not to feel their hearts extremely affected in seriously reading either the beginning or the latter part of the Revelation. These, it is evident, we cannot consider too much; but the intermediate parts I did not study at all for many years; as utterly despairing of understanding them, after the fruitless attempts of so many wise and good men: and perhaps I should have lived and died in this sentiment, had I not seen the works of the great Bengelius. But these revived my hopes of understanding even the prophecies of this book; at least many of them in some good degree: for perhaps some will not be opened but in eternity. Let us, however, bless God for the measure of light we may enjoy, and improve it to his glory. The following notes are mostly those of that excellent man; a few of which are taken from his Gnomon Novi Testamenti, but far more from his Ekklarte Offenbarung, which is a full and regular comment on the Revelation. Every part of this I do not undertake to defend. But none should condemn him without reading his proofs at large. It did not suit my design to insert these: they are above the capacity of ordinary readers. Nor had I room to insert the entire translation of a book which contains near twelve hundred pages. All I can do is, partly to translate, partly abridge, the most necessary of his observations; allowing myself the liberty to alter some of them, and to add a few notes where he is not full. His text, it may be observed, I have taken almost throughout, which I apprehend he has abundantly defended both in the Gnomon itself, and in his Apparatus and Crisis in Apocalypse. Yet I by no means pretend to understand or explain all that is contained in this mysterious book. I only offer what help I can to the serious inquirer, and shall rejoice if any be moved thereby more carefully to read and more deeply to consider the words of this prophecy. Blessed is he that does this with a single eye. His labor shall not be in vain.

REVELATION 1

1. The Revelation – Properly so called; for things covered before are here revealed, or unveiled. No prophecy in the Old Testament has this title; it was reserved for this alone in the New. It is, as it were, a manifesto, wherein the Heir of all things declares that all power is given him in heaven and earth, and that he will in the end gloriously exercise that power, maugre all the opposition of all his enemies. Of Jesus Christ – Not of "John the Divine," a title added in latter ages. 2. Who hath testified – In the following book. The word of God – Given directly by God. And the testimony of Jesus – Which he hath left us, as the faithful and true witness. Whatsoever things he saw – In such a manner as was a full confirmation of the divine original of this book.

3. Happy is he that readeth, and they that hear, the words of this prophecy – Some have miserably handled this book. Hence others are afraid to touch it; and, while they desire to know all things else, reject only the knowledge of those which God hath shown. They inquire after anything rather than this; as if it were written, "Happy is he that doth not read this prophecy." Nay, but happy is he that readeth, and they that hear, and keep the words thereof – Especially at this time, when so considerable a part of them is on the point of being fulfilled.

4. John – The dedication of this book is contained in the fourth, fifth, and sixth verses; but the whole Revelation is a kind of letter. To the seven churches which are in Asia – That part of the Lesser Asia which was then a Roman province. There had been several other churches planted here; but it seems these were now the most eminent; and it was among these that St. John had labored most during his abode in Asia. In these cities there were many Jews. Such of them as believed in each were joined with the Gentile believers in one church. Grace be unto you, and peace – The favor of God, with all temporal and eternal blessings. From him who is, and who was, and who cometh, or, who is to come – A wonderful translation of the great name JEHOVAH: he was of old, he is now, he

MATTHEW HENRY

CHARLES H. SPURGEON

The Book of the Revelation of St. John consists of two principal divisions. 1. Relates to "the things which are," that is, the then present state of the church, and contains the epistle of John to the seven churches, and his account of the appearance of the Lord Jesus, and his direction to the apostle to write what he beheld, ch. 1:9-20. Also the addresses or epistles to seven churches of Asia. These, doubtless, had reference to the state of the respective churches, as they then existed, but contain excellent precepts and exhortations, commendations and reproofs, promises and threatenings, suitable to instruct the Christian church at all times. 2. Contains a prophecy of "the things which shall be hereafter," and describes the future state of the church, from the time when the apostle beheld the visions here recorded. It is intended for our spiritual improvement; to warn the careless sinner, point out the way of salvation to the awakened inquirer, build up the weak believer, comfort the afflicted and tempted Christian, and, we may especially add, to strengthen the martyr of Christ, under the cruel persecutions and sufferings inflicted by Satan and his followers.

REVELATION 1

Divine origin, the design, and the importance of this book. (1-3)

The apostle John salutes the seven churches of Asia. (4-8)

Declares when, where, and how, the revelation was made to him. (9-11)

His vision, in which he saw Christ appear. (12-20)

1-3 This book is the Revelation of Jesus Christ; the whole Bible is so; for all revelation comes through Christ, and all relates to him. Its principal subject is to discover the purposes of God concerning the affairs of the church, and of the nations as connected therewith, to the end of the world. These events would surely come to pass; and they would begin to come to pass very shortly. Though Christ is himself God, and has light and life in himself, yet, as Mediator between God and man, he receives instructions from the Father. To him we owe the knowledge of what we are to expect from God, and what he expects from us. The subject of this revelation was, the things that must shortly come to pass. On all who read or hear the words of the prophecy, a blessing is pronounced. Those are well employed who search the Bible. It is not enough that we read and hear, but we must keep the things that are written, in our memories, in our minds, in our affections, and in practice, and we shall be blessed in the deed. Even the mysteries and difficulties of this book are united with discoveries

DECLENSION FROM FIRST LOVE

Sermon number 217 delivered on September 26, 1858, at New Park Street Chapel, Southwark.

"Nevertheless I have somewhat against thee, because thou hast left thy first love."—Revelation 2:4.

IT IS A GREAT THING to have as much said in our commendation as was said concerning the church at Ephesus. Just read what "Jesus Christ, who is the faithful witness," said of them—"I know thy works, and thy labor, and thy patience, and how thou canst not bear them which are evil: and thou hast tried them which say they are apostles, and are not, and hast found them liars: and hast borne, and hast patience, and for my name's sake hast labored, and hast not fainted." Oh, my dear brothers and sisters, we may feel devoutly thankful if we can humbly, but honestly say, that this commendation applies to us. Happy the man whose works are known and accepted of Christ. He is no idle Christian, he has practical godliness; he seeks by works of piety to obey God's whole law, by works of charity to manifest his love to the brotherhood, and by works of devotion to show his attachment to the cause of his Master. "I know thy works." Alas! some of you cannot get so far as that. Jesus Christ himself can bear no witness to your works, for you have not done any. You are Christians by profession, but you are not Christians as to your practice. I say again, happy is that man to whom Christ can say, "I know thy works." It is a commendation worth a world to have as much as that said of us. But further, Christ said, "and thy labor." This is more still. Many Christians have works, but only few Christians have labor. There were many preachers in Whitfield's day that had works, but Whitfield had labor. He toiled and travailed for souls. He was "in labors more abundant." Many were they in the apostle's days who did works for Christ; but pre-eminently the apostle Paul did labor for souls. It is not work merely, it is anxious work; it is casting forth the whole strength, and exercising all the energies for Christ. Could the Lord Jesus say as much as that of you—"I know thy labor"? No. He might say, "I know thy loitering; I know thy laziness; I know thy shirking of the work; I know thy boasting of what little thou dost; I know thine ambition to be thought something of , when thou art nothing." But ah! friends, it is more than most of us dare to hope that Christ could say, "I know thy labor."

I. First, WHAT WAS OUR FIRST LOVE? Oh, let us go back—it is not many years with some of us. We are but youngsters in God's ways, and it is not so long with any of you that you will have very great difficulty in reckoning it. Then if you are Christians, those days were so happy that your memory will never forget them, and therefore you can easily return to that

Smyrna, and unto Pergamos, and unto Thyatira, and unto Sardis, and unto Philadelphia, and unto Laodicea.

12 And I turned to see the voice that spake with me. And being turned, I saw seven golden candlesticks;

13 And in the midst of the seven candlesticks one like unto the Son of man, clothed with a garment down to the foot, and girt about the paps with a golden girdle.

14 His head and his hairs were white like wool, as white as snow; and his eyes were as a flame of fire;

15 And his feet like unto fine brass, as if they burned in a furnace; and his voice as the sound of many waters.

16 And he had in his right hand seven stars: and out of his mouth went a sharp twoedged sword: and his countenance was as the sun shineth in his strength.

17 And when I saw him, I fell at his feet as dead. And he laid his right hand upon me, saying unto me, Fear not; I am the first and the last:

18 I am he that liveth, and was dead; and, behold, I am alive for evermore, Amen; and have the keys of hell and of death.

19 Write the things which thou hast seen, and the things which are, and the things which shall be hereafter;

20 The mystery of the seven stars which thou sawest in my right hand, and the seven golden candlesticks. The seven stars are the angels of the seven churches: and the seven candlesticks which thou sawest are the seven churches.

REVELATION 2

1 Unto the angel of the church of Ephesus write; These things saith he that holdeth the seven stars in his right hand, who walketh in the midst of the seven golden candlesticks;

2 I know thy works, and thy labor, and thy patience, and how thou canst not bear them which are evil: and thou hast tried them which say they are apostles, and are not, and hast

cometh; that is, will be for ever. And from the seven spirits which are before his throne – Christ is he who "hath the seven spirits of God." "The seven lamps which burn before the throne are the seven spirits of God." "The lamb hath seven horns and seven eyes, which are the seven spirits of God." Seven was a sacred number in the Jewish church: but it did not always imply a precise number.

5. And from Jesus Christ, the faithful witness, the first begotten from the dead, and the prince of the kings of the earth – Three glorious appellations are here given him, and in their proper order. He was the faithful witness of the whole will of God before his death, and in death, and remains such in glory. He rose from the dead, as "the first fruits of them that slept;" and now hath all power both in heaven and earth. He is here styled a prince: but by and by he hears his title of king; yea, "King of kings, and Lord of lords." This phrase, the kings of the earth, signifies their power and multitude, and also the nature of their kingdom. It became the Divine Majesty to call them kings with a limitation; especially in this manifesto from his heavenly kingdom; for no creature, much less a sinful man, can bear the title of king in an absolute sense before the eyes of God.

6. To him that loveth us, and, out of that free, abundant love, hath washed us from the guilt and power of our sins with his own blood, and hath made us kings – Partakers of his present, and heirs of his eternal, kingdom. And priests unto his God and Father – To whom we continually offer ourselves, an holy, living sacrifice. To him be the glory – For his love and redemption. And the might – Whereby he governs all things.

7. Behold – In this and the next verse is the proposition, and the summary of the whole book. He cometh – Jesus Christ. Throughout this book, whenever it is said, He cometh, it means his glorious coming. The preparation for this began at the destruction of Jerusalem, and more particularly at the time of writing this book; and goes on, without any interruption, till that grand event is accomplished.

8. I am the Alpha and the Omega, saith the Lord God – Alpha is the first, Omega, the last, letter in the Greek alphabet. Let his enemies boast and rage ever so much in the intermediate time, yet the Lord God is both the Alpha, or beginning, and the Omega, or end, of all things. God is the beginning, as he is the Author and Creator of all things, and as he proposes, declares, and promises so great things: he is the end, as he brings all the things which are here revealed to a complete and glorious conclusion. Again, the beginning and end of a thing is in scripture styled the whole thing. Therefore God is the Alpha and the Omega, the beginning and the end; that is, one who is all things, and always the same.

9. I John – The instruction and preparation of the apostle for the work are described from the ninth to the twentieth verse. Your brother – In the common faith. And companion in the affliction – For the same persecution which carried him to Patmos drove them into Asia. This book peculiarly belongs to those who are under the cross. It was given to a banished man; and men in affliction understand and relish it most.

10. I was in the Spirit – That is, in a trance, a prophetic vision; so overwhelmed with the power, and filled with the light, of the Holy Spirit, as to be insensible of outward things, and wholly taken up with spiritual and divine. What follows is one single, connected vision, which St. John saw in one day; and therefore he that would understand it should carry his thought straight on through the whole, without interruption.

11. Saying, What thou seest – And hearest. He both saw and heard. This command extends to the whole book. All the books of the New Testament were written by the will of God; but none were so expressly commanded to be written. In a book – So all the Revelation is but one book: nor did the letter to the angel of each church belong to him or his church only; but the whole book was sent to them all. To the churches – Hereafter named; and through them to all churches,

of God, suited to impress the mind with awe, and to purify the soul of the reader, though he may not discern the prophetic meaning. No part of Scripture more fully states the gospel, and warns against the evil of sin.

4-8 There can be no true peace, where there is not true grace; and where grace goeth before, peace will follow. This blessing is in the name of God, of the Holy Trinity, it is an act of adoration. The Father is first named; he is described as the Jehovah who is, and who was, and who is to come, eternal, unchangeable. The Holy Spirit is called the seven spirits, the perfect Spirit of God, in whom there is a diversity of gifts and operations. The Lord Jesus Christ was from eternity, a Witness to all the counsels of God. He is the First-born from the dead, who will by his own power raise up his people. He is the Prince of the kings of the earth; by him their counsels are overruled, and to him they are accountable. Sin leaves a stain of guilt and pollution upon the soul. Nothing can fetch out this stain but the blood of Christ; and Christ shed his own blood to satisfy Divine justice, and purchase pardon and purity for his people. Christ has made believers kings and priests to God and his Father. As such they overcome the world, mortify sin, govern their own spirits, resist Satan, prevail with God in prayer, and shall judge the world. He has made them priests, given them access to God, enabled them to offer spiritual and acceptable sacrifices, and for these favors they are bound to ascribe to him dominion and glory forever. He will judge the world. Attention is called to that great day when all will see the wisdom and happiness of the friends of Christ, and the madness and misery of his enemies. Let us think frequently upon the second coming of Christ. He shall come, to the terror of those who wound and crucify him by apostasy; he shall come, to the astonishment of the whole world of the ungodly. He is the Beginning and the End; all things are from him and for him; he is the Almighty; the same eternal and unchanged One. And if we would be numbered with his saints in glory everlasting, we must now willing submit to him, receive him, and honor him as a Savior, who we believe will come to be our Judge. Alas, that there should be many, who would wish never to die, and that there should not be a day of judgment!

9-11 It was the apostle's comfort that he did not suffer as an evildoer, but for the testimony of Jesus, for bearing witness to Christ as the Immanuel, the Savior; and the Spirit of glory and of God rested upon this persecuted apostle. The day and time when he had this vision was the Lord's day, the Christian Sabbath, the first day of

first bright spot in your history. Oh, what love was that which I had to my Savior the first time he forgave my sins. I remember it. You remember each for yourselves, I dare say, that happy hour when the Lord appeared to us, bleeding on his cross, when he seemed to say, and did say in our hearts, "I am thy salvation; I have blotted out like a cloud thine iniquities, and like a thick cloud thy sins." Oh, how I loved him! Passing all loves except his own was that love which I felt for him then. If beside the door of the place in which I met with him there had been a stake of blazing faggots, I would have stood upon them without chains; glad to give my flesh, and blood, and bones, to be ashes that should testify my love to him. Had he asked me then to give all my substance to the poor, I would have given all and thought myself to be amazingly rich in having beggared myself for his name's sake. Had he commanded me then to preach in the midst of all his foes, I could have said:—

> "There's not a lamb amongst thy flock
> I would disdain to feed,
> There's not a foe before whose face
> I'd fear thy cause to plead."

I could realize then the language of Rutherford, when he said, being full of love to Christ, once upon a time, in the dungeon of Aberdeen—"Oh, my Lord, if there were a broad hell betwixt me and thee, if I could not get at thee except by wading through it, I would not think twice but I would plunge through it all, if I might embrace thee and call thee mine."

Now it is that first love that you and I must confess I am afraid we have in a measure lost. Let us just see whether we have it. When we first loved the Savior how earnest we were; there was not a single thing in the Bible, that we did not think most precious; there was not one command of his that we did not think to be like fine gold and choice silver. Never were the doors of his house open without our being there. If there were a prayer meeting at any hour in the day we were there. Some said of us that we had no patience, we would do too much and expose our bodies too frequently—but we never thought of that "Do yourself no harm," was spoken in our ears; but we would have done anything then. Why there are some of you who cannot walk to the Music Hall on a morning, it is too far. When you first joined the church, you would have walked twice as far. There are some of you who cannot be at the prayer meeting—business will not permit; yet when you were first baptized, there was never a prayer meeting from which you were absent. It is the loss of your first love that makes you seek the comfort of your bodies instead of the prosperity of your souls. Many have been the young Christians who have joined this church, and old ones too, and I have said to them, "Well, have you got a ticket for a seat?" "No, sir." "Well, what will you do? Have you got a preference ticket?" "No, I cannot get one; but I do not mind

found them liars:

3 And hast borne, and hast patience, and for my name's sake hast labored, and hast not fainted.

4 Nevertheless I have somewhat against thee, because thou hast left thy first love.

5 Remember therefore from whence thou art fallen, and repent, and do the first works; or else I will come unto thee quickly, and will remove thy candlestick out of his place, except thou repent.

6 But this thou hast, that thou hatest the deeds of the Nicolaitans, which I also hate.

7 He that hath an ear, let him hear what the Spirit saith unto the churches; To him that overcometh will I give to eat of the tree of life, which is in the midst of the paradise of God.

8 And unto the angel of the church in Smyrna write; These things saith the first and the last, which was dead, and is alive;

9 I know thy works, and tribulation, and poverty, (but thou art rich) and I know the blasphemy of them which say they are Jews, and are not, but are the synagogue of Satan.

10 Fear none of those things which thou shalt suffer: behold, the devil shall cast some of you into prison, that ye may be tried; and ye shall have tribulation ten days: be thou faithful unto death, and I will give thee a crown of life.

11 He that hath an ear, let him hear what the Spirit saith unto the churches; He that overcometh shall not be hurt of the second death.

12 And to the angel of the church in Pergamos write; These things saith he which hath the sharp sword with two edges;

13 I know thy works, and where thou dwellest, even where Satan's seat is: and thou holdest fast my name, and hast not denied my faith, even in those days wherein Antipas was my faithful martyr, who was slain among you, where Satan dwelleth.

14 But I have a few things against thee, because thou

in all ages and nations.

12, 13. And I turned to see the voice – That is, to see him whose voice it was. And being turned, I saw – It seems, the vision presented itself gradually. First he heard a voice; and, upon looking behind, he saw the golden candlesticks, and then, in the midst of the candlesticks, which were placed in a circle, he saw one like a son of man – That is, in an human form. As a man likewise our Lord doubtless appears in heaven: though not exactly in this symbolical manner, wherein he presents himself as the head of his church. He next observed that our Lord was clothed with a garment down to the foot, and girt with a golden girdle – Such the Jewish high priests wore. But both of them are here marks of royal dignity likewise.

14. His head and his hair – That is, the hair of his head, not his whole head. Were white as white wool – Like the Ancient of Days, represented in Daniel's vision, Dan. vii, 9. Wool is commonly supposed to be an emblem of eternity. As snow – Betokening his spotless purity. And his eyes as a flame of fire – Piercing through all things; a token of his omniscience.

15. And his feet like fine brass – Denoting his stability and strength. As if they burned in a furnace – As if having been melted and refined, they were still red hot. And his voice – To the comfort of his friends, and the terror of his enemies. As the voice of many waters – Roaring aloud, and bearing down all before them.

16. And he had in his right hand seven stars – In token of his favor and powerful protection. And out of his mouth went a sharp two-edged sword – Signifying his justice and righteous anger, continually pointed against his enemies as a sword; sharp, to stab; two-edged, to hew. And his countenance was as the sun shineth in his strength – Without any mist or cloud.

17. And I fell at his feet as dead – Human nature not being able to sustain so glorious an appearance. Thus was he prepared (like Daniel of old, whom he peculiarly resembles) for receiving so weighty a prophecy.

18. And he that liveth – Another peculiar title of God. And I have the keys of death and of hades – That is, the invisible world. In the intermediate state, the body abides in death, the soul in hades. Christ hath the keys of, that is, the power over, both; killing or quickening of the body, and disposing of the soul, as it pleaseth him. He gave St. Peter the keys of the kingdom of heaven; but not the keys of death or of hades. How comes then his supposed successor at Rome by the keys of purgatory? From the preceding description, mostly, are taken the titles given to Christ in the following letters, particularly the four first.

19. Write the things which thou hast seen – This day: which accordingly are written, ver. 11-18. And which are – The instructions relating to the present state of the seven churches. These are written, ver. 20-chap. iii, 22. And which shall be hereafter – To the end of the world; written, chap. iv, 1, &c.

20. Write first the mystery – The mysterious meaning of the seven stars – St. John knew better than we do, in how many respects these stars were a proper emblem of those angels: how nearly they resembled each other, and how far they differed in magnitude, brightness, and in other circumstances.

REVELATION 2

1. Write – So Christ dictated to him every word. These things saith he who holdeth the seven stars in his right hand – Such is his mighty power! Such his favor to them and care over them, that they may indeed shine as stars, both by purity of doctrine and holiness of life! Who walketh – According to his promise, "I am with you always, even to the end of the world." In the midst of the golden candlesticks – Beholding all their works and thoughts, and ready to "remove the candlestick out of its place," if any, being warned, will not repent. Perhaps here is likewise an allusion to the office of the priests in dressing the lamps, which was to keep them always burning before the Lord.

the week, observed in remembrance of the resurrection of Christ. Let us who call him "Our Lord," honor him on his own day. The name shows how this sacred day should be observed; the Lord's day should be wholly devoted to the Lord, and none of its hours employed in a sensual, worldly manner, or in amusements. He was in a serious, heavenly, spiritual frame, under the gracious influences of the Spirit of God. Those who would enjoy communion with God on the Lord's day, must seek to draw their thoughts and affections from earthly things. And if believers are kept on the Lord's holy day, from public ordinances and the communion of saints, by necessity and not by choice, they may look for comfort in meditation and secret duties, from the influences of the Spirit; and by hearing the voice and contemplating the glory of their beloved Savior, from whose gracious words and power no confinement or outward circumstances can separate them. An alarm was given as with the sound of the trumpet, and then the apostle heard the voice of Christ.

12-20 The churches receive their light from Christ and the gospel, and hold it forth to others. They are golden candlesticks; they should be precious and pure; not only the ministers, but the members of the churches; their light should so shine before men, as to engage others to give glory to God. And the apostle saw as though the Lord Jesus Christ appeared in the midst of the golden candlesticks. He is with his churches always, to the end of the world, filling them with light, and life, and love. He was clothed with a robe down to the feet, perhaps representing his righteousness and priesthood, as Mediator. This vest was girt with a golden girdle, which may denote how precious are his love and affection for his people. His head and hairs white like wool and as snow, may signify his majesty, purity, and eternity. His eyes as a flame of fire, may represent his knowledge of the secrets of all hearts, and of the most distant events. His feet like fine brass burning in a furnace, may denote the firmness of his appointments, and the excellence of his proceedings. His voice as the sound of many waters, may represent the power of his word, to remove or to destroy. The seven stars were emblems of the ministers of the seven churches to which the apostle was ordered to write, and whom Christ upheld and directed. The sword represented his justice, and his word, piercing to the dividing asunder of soul and spirit, Heb 4:12. His countenance was like the sun, when it shines clearly and powerfully; its strength too bright and dazzling for mortal eyes to behold. The apostle was overpowered with the greatness of the luster and glory in which Christ appeared. We may

standing in the crowd an hour, or two hours. I will come at five o'clock so that I can get in. Sometimes I don't get in, sir; but even then I feel that I have done what I ought to do in attempting to get in." "Well," but I have said, "you live five miles off, and there is coming and going back twice a day—you cannot do it." "Oh, sir," they have said "I can do it; I feel so much the blessedness of the Sabbath and so much enjoyment of the presence of the Savior." I have smiled at them; I could understand it, but I have not felt it necessary to caution them—and now their love is cool enough. That first love does not last half so long as we could wish. Some of you stand convicted even here; you have not that blazing love, that burning love, that ridiculous love as the worldling would call it, which is after all the love to be most coveted and desired. No, you have lost your first love in that respect. Again, how obedient you used to be. If you saw a commandment, that was enough for you—you did it. But now you see a commandment, and you see profit on the other side; and how often do you dally with the profit and choose the temptation, instead of yielding an unsullied obedience to Christ.

Again, how happy you used to be in the ways of God. Your love was of that happy character that you could sing all day long; but now your religion has lost its luster, the gold has become dim; you know that when you come to the Sacramental table, you often come there without enjoying it. There was a time when every bitter thing was sweet; whenever you heard the Word, it was all precious to you. Now you can grumble at the minister. Alas! the minister has many faults, but the question is, whether there has not been a greater change in you than there has been in him. Many are there who say, "I do not hear Mr. So-and-so as I used to,"—when the fault lies in their own ears. Oh, brethren, when we live near to Christ, and are in our first love, it is amazing what a little it takes to make a good preacher for us. Why, I confess I have heard a poor illiterate Primitive Methodist preach the gospel, and I felt as if I could jump for joy all the while I was listening to him, and yet he never gave me a new thought or a pretty expression, nor one figure that I could remember, but he talked about Christ; and even his common things were to my hungry spirit like dainty meats. And I have to acknowledge, and, perhaps, you have to acknowledge the same—that I have heard sermons from which I ought to have profited, but I have been thinking on the man's style, or some little mistakes in grammar. When I might have been holding fellowships with Christ in and through the ministry, I have, instead thereof, been getting abroad in my thoughts even to the ends of the earth. And what is the reason for this, but that I have lost my first love.

Again: when we were in our first love, what would we do for Christ; now how little will we do. Some of the actions which we performed when we were young Christians, but just converted, when we

hast there them that hold the doctrine of Balaam, who taught Balac to cast a stumblingblock before the children of Israel, to eat things sacrificed unto idols, and to commit fornication.

15 So hast thou also them that hold the doctrine of the Nicolaitans, which thing I hate.

16 Repent; or else I will come unto thee quickly, and will fight against them with the sword of my mouth.

17 He that hath an ear, let him hear what the Spirit saith unto the churches; To him that overcometh will I give to eat of the hidden manna, and will give him a white stone, and in the stone a new name written, which no man knoweth saving he that receiveth it.

18 And unto the angel of the church in Thyatira write; These things saith the Son of God, who hath his eyes like unto a flame of fire, and his feet are like fine brass;

19 I know thy works, and charity, and service, and faith, and thy patience, and thy works; and the last to be more than the first.

20 Notwithstanding I have a few things against thee, because thou sufferest that woman Jezebel, which calleth herself a prophetess, to teach and to seduce my servants to commit fornication, and to eat things sacrificed unto idols.

21 And I gave her space to repent of her fornication; and she repented not.

22 Behold, I will cast her into a bed, and them that commit adultery with her into great tribulation, except they repent of their deeds.

23 And I will kill her children with death; and all the churches shall know that I am he which searcheth the reins and hearts: and I will give unto every one of you according to your works.

24 But unto you I say, and unto the rest in Thyatira, as many as have not this doctrine, and which have not known the depths of Satan, as they speak; I will put upon you none other burden.

25 But that which ye have

2. I know – Jesus knows all the good and all the evil, which his servants and his enemies suffer and do. Weighty word, "I know," how dreadful will it one day sound to the wicked, how sweet to the righteous! The churches and their angels must have been astonished, to find their several states so exactly described, even in the absence of the apostle, and could not but acknowledge the all-seeing eye of Christ and of his Spirit. With regard to us, to every one of us also he saith, "I know thy works." Happy is he that conceives less good of himself, than Christ knows concerning him.

4. But I have against thee, that thou hast left thy first love – That love for which all that church was so eminent when St. Paul wrote his epistle to them. He need not have left this. He might have retained it entire to the end. And he did retain it in part, or there could not have remained so much of what was commendable in him. But he had not kept, as he might have done, the first tender love in its vigor and warmth. Reader, hast thou?

5. It is not possible for any to recover the first love, but by taking these three steps,

   1. Remember:

   2. Repent:

   3. Do the first works.

Remember from whence thou art fallen – From what degree of faith, love, holiness, though perhaps insensibly. And repent – Which in the very lowest sense implies a deep and lively conviction of thy fall.

6. But thou hast this – Divine grace seeks whatever may help him that is fallen to recover his standing. That thou hatest the works of the Nicolaitans – Probably so called from Nicolas, one of the seven deacons, Acts vi, 5. Their doctrines and lives were equally corrupt. They allowed the most abominable lewdness and adulteries, as well as sacrificing to idols; all which they placed among things indifferent, and pleaded for as branches of Christian liberty.

7. He that hath an ear, let him hear – Every man, whoever can hear at all, ought carefully to hear this. What the Spirit saith – In these great and precious promises. To the churches – And in them to every one that overcometh; that goeth on from faith and by faith to full victory over the world, and the flesh, and the devil. In these seven letters twelve promises are contained, which are an extract of all the promises of God.

8. These things saith the first and the last, who was dead and is alive – How directly does this description tend to confirm him against the fear of death! verses 10, 11. Even with the comfort wherewith St. John himself was comforted, chap. i, 17, 18, shall the angel of this church be comforted.

9. I know thy affliction and poverty – A poor prerogative in the eyes of the world! The angel at Philadelphia likewise had in their sight but "a little strength." And yet these two were the most honorable of all in the eyes of the Lord. But thou art rich – In faith and love, of more value than all the kingdoms of the earth. Who say they are Jews – God's own people. And are not – They are not Jews inwardly, not circumcized in heart. But a synagogue of Satan – Who, like them, was a liar and a murderer from the beginning.

10. The first and last words of this verse are particularly directed to the minister; whence we may gather, that his suffering and the affliction of the church were at the same time, and of the same continuance. Fear none of those things which thou art about to suffer – Probably by means of the false Jews. Behold – This intimates the nearness of the affliction.

11. The second death – The lake of fire, the portion of the fearful, who do not overcome, chap. xxi, 8.

12. The sword – With which I will cut off the impenitent, verse 16.

13. Where the throne of Satan is – Pergamos was above measure given to idolatry: so Satan had his throne and full residence there. Thou holdest fast my name – Openly and resolutely confessing me before men. Even in the days wherein

MATTHEW HENRY

CHARLES H. SPURGEON

well be contented to walk by faith, while here upon earth. The Lord Jesus spake words of comfort; Fear not. Words of instruction; telling who thus appeared. And his Divine nature; the First and the Last. His former sufferings; I was dead: the very same whom his disciples saw upon the cross. His resurrection and life; I have conquered death, and am partaker of endless life. His office and authority; sovereign dominion in and over the invisible world, as the Judge of all, from whose sentence there is no appeal. Let us listen to the voice of Christ, and receive the tokens of his love, for what can he withhold from those for whose sins he has died? May we then obey his word, and give up ourselves wholly to him who directs all things aright.

REVELATION 2

Epistles to the churches in Asia, with warnings and encouragements,
To the church at Ephesus; (1-7)
To the church at Smyrna; (8-11)
To the church at Pergamos; (12-17)
To the church at Thyatira. (18-29)

1-7 These churches were in such different states as to purity of doctrine and the power of godliness, that the words of Christ to them will always suit the cases of other churches, and professors. Christ knows and observes their state; though in heaven, yet he walks in the midst of his churches on earth, observing what is wrong in them, and what they want. The church of Ephesus is commended for diligence in duty. Christ keeps an account of every hour's work his servants do for him, and their labor shall not be in vain in the Lord. But it is not enough that we are diligent; there must be bearing patience, and there must be waiting patience. And though we must show all meekness to all men, yet we must show just zeal against their sins. The sin Christ charged this church with, is, not the having left and forsaken the object of love, but having lost the fervent degree of it that at first appeared. Christ is displeased with his people, when he sees them grow remiss and cold toward him. Surely this mention in Scripture, of Christians forsaking their first love, reproves those who speak of it with carelessness, and thus try to excuse indifference and sloth in themselves and others; our Savior considers this indifference as sinful. They must repent: they must be grieved and ashamed for their sinful declining, and humbly confess it in the sight of God. They must endeavor to recover their first zeal, tenderness, and seriousness, and must pray as earnestly, and watch as diligently, as when they first set out in the ways of God. If the presence of Christ's grace and Spirit is slighted,

look back upon them, seem to have been wild and like idle tales. You remember when you were a lad and first came to Christ, you had a half-sovereign in your pocket; it was the only one you had, and you met with some poor saint and gave it all away. You did not regret that you had done it, your only regret was that you had not a great deal more, for you would have given all. You recollected that something was wanted for the cause of Christ. Oh! we could give anything away when we first loved the Savior. If there was a preaching to be held five miles off, and we could walk with the lay-preacher to be a little comfort to him in the darkness, we were off. If there was a Sunday-school, however early it might be, we would be up, so that we might be present. Unheard-of feats, things that we now look back upon with surprise, we could perform them. Why cannot we do them now? Do you know there are some people who always live upon what they have been. I speak very plainly now. There is a brother in this church who may take it to himself; I hope he will. It is not very many years ago since he said to me, when I asked him why he did not do something—"Well, I have done my share; I used to do this, and I have done the other; I have done so-and-so." Oh, may the Lord deliver him, and all of us, from living on "has beens!" It will never do to say we have done a thing. Suppose, for a solitary moment, the world should say, "I have turned round; I will stand still." Let the sea say, "I have been ebbing and flowing, lo! these many years; I will ebb and flow no more." Let the sun say, "I have been shining, and I have been rising and setting so many days; I have done this enough to earn me a goodly name; I will stand still;" and let the moon wrap herself up in veils of darkness, and say, "I have illuminated many a night, and I have lighted many a weary traveler across the moors; I will shut up my lamp and be dark forever." Brethren, when you and I cease to labor, let us cease to live. God has no intention to let us live a useless life. But mark this; when we leave our first works, there is no question about having lost our first love; that is sure. If there be strength remaining, if there be still power mentally and physically, if we cease from our office, if we abstain from our labors, there is no solution of this question which an honest conscience will accept, except this, "Thou hast lost thy first love, and, therefore, thou hast neglected thy first works." Ah! we were all so very ready to make excuses for ourselves. Many a preacher has retired from the ministry, long before he had any need to do so. He has married a rich wife. Somebody has left him a little money, and he can do without it. He was growing weak in the ways of God, or else he would have said,

"My body with my charge lay down,
And cease at once to work and live."

And let any man here present who was a Sunday-school teacher and who has left it, who was a tract

already hold fast till I come.

26 And he that overcometh, and keepeth my works unto the end, to him will I give power over the nations:

27 And he shall rule them with a rod of iron; as the vessels of a potter shall they be broken to shivers: even as I received of my Father.

28 And I will give him the morning star.

29 He that hath an ear, let him hear what the Spirit saith unto the churches.

REVELATION 3

1 And unto the angel of the church in Sardis write; These things saith he that hath the seven Spirits of God, and the seven stars; I know thy works, that thou hast a name that thou livest, and art dead.

2 Be watchful, and strengthen the things which remain, that are ready to die: for I have not found thy works perfect before God.

3 Remember therefore how thou hast received and heard, and hold fast, and repent. If therefore thou shalt not watch, I will come on thee as a thief, and thou shalt not know what hour I will come upon thee.

4 Thou hast a few names even in Sardis which have not defiled their garments; and they shall walk with me in white: for they are worthy.

5 He that overcometh, the same shall be clothed in white raiment; and I will not blot out his name out of the book of life, but I will confess his name before my Father, and before his angels.

6 He that hath an ear, let him hear what the Spirit saith unto the churches.

7 And to the angel of the church in Philadelphia write; These things saith he that is holy, he that is true, he that hath the key of David, he that openeth, and no man shutteth; and shutteth, and no man openeth;

8 I know thy works: behold, I have set before thee an open door, and no man can shut it: for thou hast a little strength,

Antipas – Martyred under Domitian. Was my faithful witness – Happy is he to whom Jesus, the faithful and true witness, giveth such a testimony!

14. But thou hast there – Whom thou oughtest to have immediately cast out from the flock. Them that hold the doctrine of Balaam – Doctrine nearly resembling his. Who taught Balak – And the rest of the Moabites. To cast a stumbling block before the sons of Israel – They are generally termed, the children, but here, the sons, of Israel, in opposition to the daughters of Moab, by whom Balaam enticed them to fornication and idolatry. To eat things sacrificed to idols – Which, in so idolatrous a city as Pergamos, was in the highest degree hurtful to Christianity. And to commit fornication – Which was constantly joined with the idol-worship of the heathens.

15. In like manner thou also – As well as the angel at Ephesus. Hast them that hold the doctrine of the Nicolaitans – And thou sufferest them to remain in the flock.

16. If not, I come to thee – who wilt not wholly escape when I punish them. And will fight with them – Not with the Nicolaitans, who are mentioned only by the by, but the followers of Balaam. With the sword of my mouth – With my just and fierce displeasure. Balaam himself was first withstood by the angel of the Lord with "his sword drawn," Num. xxii, 23, and afterwards "slain with the sword," Num. xxxi, 8.

17. To him that overcometh – And eateth not of those sacrifices. Will I give of the hidden manna – Described, John vi. The new name answers to this: it is now "hid with Christ in God." The Jewish manna was kept in the ancient ark of the covenant. The heavenly ark of the covenant appears under the trumpet of the seventh angel, chap. xi, 19, where also the hidden manna is mentioned again. It seems properly to mean, the full, glorious, everlasting fruition of God. And I will give him a white stone – The ancients, on many occasions, gave their votes in judgment by small stones; by black, they condemned; by white ones they acquitted. Sometimes also they wrote on small smooth stones. Here may be an allusion to both. And a new name – So Jacob, after his victory, gained the new name of Israel. Wouldest thou know what thy new name will be? The way to this is plain, overcome. Till then all thy inquiries are vain. Thou wilt then read it on the white stone.

18. And to the angel of the church at Thyatira – Where the faithful were but a little flock. These things saith the Son of God – See how great he is, who appeared "like a son of man!" chap. i, 13. Who hath eyes as a flame of fire – "Searching the reins and the heart," verse 23. And feet like fine brass – Denoting his immense strength. Job comprises both these, his wisdom to discern whatever is amiss, and his power to avenge it, in one sentence, Job xlii, 2, "No thought is hidden from him, and he can do all things."

19. I know thy love – How different a character is this from that of the angel of the church at Ephesus! The latter could not bear the wicked, and hated the works of the Nicolaitans; but had left his first love and first works. The former retained his first love, and had more and more works, but did bear the wicked, did not withstand them with becoming vehemence. Mixed characters both; yet the latter, not the former, is reproved for his fall, and commanded to repent. And faith, and thy service, and patience – Love is shown, exercised, and improved by serving God and our neighbor; so is faith by patience and good works.

20. But thou sufferest that woman Jezebel – who ought not to teach at all, 1 Tim. ii, 12. To teach and seduce my servants – At Pergamos were many followers of Balaam; at Thyatira, one grand deceiver. Many of the ancients have delivered, that this was the wife of the pastor himself. Jezebel of old led the people of God to open idolatry. This Jezebel, fitly called by her name, from the resemblance between their works, led them to partake in the idolatry of the heathens. This she seems to have done by first enticing them to fornication, just as Balaam did: whereas at Pergamos they were first enticed to idolatry, and afterwards to fornication.

MATTHEW HENRY

CHARLES H. SPURGEON

we may expect the presence of his displeasure. Encouraging mention is made of what was good among them. Indifference as to truth and error, good and evil, may be called charity and meekness, but it is not so; and it is displeasing to Christ. The Christian life is a warfare against sin, Satan, the world, and the flesh. We must never yield to our spiritual enemies, and then we shall have a glorious triumph and reward. All who persevere, shall derive from Christ, as the Tree of life, perfection and confirmation in holiness and happiness, not in the earthly paradise, but in the heavenly. This is a figurative expression, taken from the account of the garden of Eden, denoting the pure, satisfactory, and eternal joys of heaven; and the looking forward to them in this world, by faith, communion with Christ, and the consolations of the Holy Spirit. Believers, take your wrestling life here, and expect and look for a quiet life hereafter; but not till then: the word of God never promises quietness and complete freedom from conflict here.

8-11 Our Lord Jesus is the First, for by him were all things made; he was before all things, with God, and is God himself. He is the Last, for he will be the Judge of all. As this First and Last, who was dead and is alive, is the believer's Brother and Friend, he must be rich in the deepest poverty, honorable amidst the lowest abasement, and happy under the heaviest tribulation, like the church of Smyrna. Many who are rich as to this world, are poor as to the next; and some who are poor outwardly, are inwardly rich; rich in faith, in good works, rich in privileges, rich in gifts, rich in hope. Where there is spiritual plenty, outward poverty may be well borne; and when God's people are made poor as to this life, for the sake of Christ and a good conscience, he makes all up to them in spiritual riches. Christ arms against coming troubles. Fear none of these things; not only forbid slavish fear, but subdue it, furnishing the soul with strength and courage. It should be to try them, not to destroy them. Observe, the sureness of the reward; "I will give thee:" they shall have the reward from Christ's own hand. Also, how suitable it is; "a crown of life:" the life worn out in his service, or laid down in his cause, shall be rewarded with a much better life, which shall be eternal. The second death is unspeakably worse than the first death, both in the agonies of it, and as it is eternal death: it is indeed awful to die, and to be always dying. If a man is kept from the second death and wrath to come, he may patiently endure whatever he meets with in this world.

12-17 The word of God is a sword, able to slay both sin and sinners. It turns and cuts every way;

distributor and who has given it up, who was active in the way of God but is now idle, stand tonight before the bar of his conscience, and say whether he be not guilty of this charge which I bring against him, that he has lost his first love.

I need not stop to say also, that this may be detected in the closet as well as in our daily life; for when first love is lost, there is a want of that prayerfulness which we have. I remember the day I was up at three o'clock in the morning. Till six, I spent in prayer, wrestling with God. Then I had to walk some eight miles, and started off and walked to the baptism. Why, prayer was a delight to me then. My duties at that time kept me occupied pretty well from five o'clock in the morning till ten at night, and I had not a moment for retirement, yet I would be up at four o'clock to pray; and though I feel very sleepy now-a-days, and I feel that I could not be up to pray, it was not so then, when I was in my first love. Somehow or other, I never lacked time then. If I did not get it early in the morning, I got it late at night. I was compelled to have time for prayer with God; and what prayer it was! I had no need then to groan because I could not pray; for love, being fervent, I had sweet liberty at the throne of grace. But when first love departs, we begin to think that ten minutes will do for prayer, instead of an hour, and we read a verse or two in the morning, whereas we used to read a portion, but never used to go into the world without getting some marrow and fatness. Now, business has so increased, that we must get into bed as soon as we can; we have not time to pray. And then at dinner time, we used to have a little time for communion; that is dropped. And then on the Sabbath-day, we used to make it a custom to pray to God when we got home from his house, for just five minutes before dinner, so that what we heard we might profit by; that is dropped. And some of you that are present were in the habit of retiring for prayer when you went home; your wives have told that story; the messengers have heard it when they have called at your houses, when they have asked the wife—"What is your husband?" "Ah!" she has said, "he is a godly man; he cannot come home to his breakfast but he must slip upstairs alone. I know what he is doing—he is praying." Then when he is at table, he often says—"Mary, I have had a difficulty today, we must go and have a word or two of prayer together." And some of you could not take a walk without prayer, you were so fond of it you could not have too much of it. Now where is it? You know more than you did; you have grown older; you have grown richer, perhaps. You have grown wiser in some respects; but you might give up all you have got, to go back to

"Those peaceful hours you once enjoyed,
How sweet their memory still!"
Oh, what would you give if you could fill
"That aching void,

and hast kept my word, and hast not denied my name.

9 Behold, I will make them of the synagogue of Satan, which say they are Jews, and are not, but do lie; behold, I will make them to come and worship before thy feet, and to know that I have loved thee.

10 Because thou hast kept the word of my patience, I also will keep thee from the hour of temptation, which shall come upon all the world, to try them that dwell upon the earth.

11 Behold, I come quickly: hold that fast which thou hast, that no man take thy crown.

12 Him that overcometh will I make a pillar in the temple of my God, and he shall go no more out: and I will write upon him the name of my God, and the name of the city of my God, which is new Jerusalem, which cometh down out of heaven from my God: and I will write upon him my new name.

13 He that hath an ear, let him hear what the Spirit saith unto the churches.

14 And unto the angel of the church of the Laodiceans write; These things saith the Amen, the faithful and true witness, the beginning of the creation of God;

15 I know thy works, that thou art neither cold nor hot: I would thou wert cold or hot.

16 So then because thou art lukewarm, and neither cold nor hot, I will spue thee out of my mouth.

17 Because thou sayest, I am rich, and increased with goods, and have need of nothing; and knowest not that thou art wretched, and miserable, and poor, and blind, and naked:

18 I counsel thee to buy of me gold tried in the fire, that thou mayest be rich; and white raiment, that thou mayest be clothed, and that the shame of thy nakedness do not appear; and anoint thine eyes with eyesalve, that thou mayest see.

19 As many as I love, I rebuke and chasten: be zealous therefore, and repent.

20 Behold, I stand at the door, and knock: if any man hear my voice, and open the door, I will

21. And I gave her time to repent – So great is the power of Christ! But she will not repent – So, though repentance is the gift of God, man may refuse it; God will not compel.

22. I will cast her into a bed – Into great affliction – And them that commit either carnal or spiritual adultery with her, unless they repent – She had her time before. Of her works – Those to which she had enticed them and which she had committed with them. It is observable, the angel of the church at Thyatira was only blamed for suffering her. This fault ceased when God took vengeance on her. Therefore he is not expressly exhorted to repent, though it is implied.

23. And I will kill her children – Those which she hath born in adultery, and them whom she hath seduced. With death – This expression denotes death by the plague, or by some manifest stroke of God's hand. Probably the remarkable vengeance taken on her children was the token of the certainty of all the rest. And all the churches – To which thou now writest. Shall know that I search the reins – The desires. And hearts – Thoughts.

24. But I say to you who do not hold this doctrine – Of Jezebel. Who have not known the depths of Satan – O happy ignorance! As they speak – That were continually boasting of the deep things which they taught. Our Lord owns they were deep, even deep as hell: for they were the very depths of Satan. Were these the same of which Martin Luther speaks? It is well if there are not some of his countrymen now in England who know them too well! I will lay upon you no other burden – Than that you have already suffered from Jezebel and her adherents.

25. What ye – Both the angel and the church have.

26. By works – Those which I have commanded. To him will I give power over the nations – That is, I will give him to share with me in that glorious victory which the Father hath promised me over all the nations who as yet resist me, Psalm ii, 8, 9.

27. And he shall rule them – That is, shall share with me when I do this. With a rod of iron – With irresistible power, employed on those only who will not otherwise submit; who will hereby be dashed in pieces – Totally conquered.

28. I will give him the morning star – Thou, O Jesus, art the morning star! O give thyself to me! Then will I desire no sun, only thee, who art the sun also. He whom this star enlightens has always morning and no evening. The duties and promises here answer each other; the valiant conqueror has power over the stubborn nations. And he that, after having conquered his enemies, keeps the works of Christ to the end, shall have the morning star, – an unspeakable brightness and peaceable dominion in him.

REVELATION 3

1. The seven spirits of God – The Holy Spirit, from whom alone all spiritual life and strength proceed. And the seven stars – which are subordinate to him. Thou hast a name that thou livest – A fair reputation, a goodly outside appearance. But that Spirit seeth through all things, and every empty appearance vanishes before him.

2. The things which remain – In thy soul; knowledge of the truth, good desires, and convictions. Which were ready to die – Wherever pride, indolence, or levity revives, all the fruits of the Spirit are ready to die.

3. Remember how – Humbly, zealously, seriously. Thou didst receive the grace of God once, and hear – His word. And hold fast – The grace thou hast received. And repent – According to the word thou hast heard.

4. Yet thou hast a few names – That is, persons. But though few, they had not separated themselves from the rest; otherwise, the angel of Sardis would not have had them. Yet it was no virtue of his, that they were unspotted; whereas it was his fault that they were but few. Who have not defiled their garments – Either by spotting themselves, or by partaking of other men's sins. They shall walk with

but the believer need not fear this sword; yet this confidence cannot be supported without steady obedience. As our Lord notices all the advantages and opportunities we have for duty in the places where we dwell, so he notices our temptations and discouragements from the same causes. In a situation of trials, the church of Pergamos had not denied the faith, either by open apostasy, or by giving way so as to avoid the cross. Christ commends their steadfastness, but reproves their sinful failures. A wrong view of gospel doctrine and Christian liberty, was a root of bitterness from which evil practices grew. Repentance is the duty of churches and bodies of men, as well as of particular persons; those who sin together, should repent together. Here is the promise of favor to those that overcome. The influences and comforts of the Spirit of Christ, come down from heaven into the soul, for its support. This is hidden from the rest of the world. The new name is the name of adoption; when the Holy Spirit shows his own work in the believer's soul, this new name and its real import are understood by him.

18-29 Even when the Lord knows the works of his people to be wrought in love, faith, zeal, and patience; yet if his eyes, which are as a flame of fire, observe them committing or allowing what is evil, he will rebuke, correct, or punish them. Here is praise of the ministry and people of Thyatira, by One who knew the principles from which they acted. They grew wiser and better. All Christians should earnestly desire that their last works may be their best works. Yet this church connived at some wicked seducers. God is known by the judgments he executes; and by this upon seducers, he shows his certain knowledge of the hearts of men, of their principles, designs, frame, and temper. Encouragement is given to those who kept themselves pure and undefiled. It is dangerous to despise the mystery of God, and as dangerous to receive the mysteries of Satan. Let us beware of the depths of Satan, of which those who know the least are the most happy. How tender Christ is of his faithful servants! He lays nothing upon his servants but what is for their good. There is promise of an ample reward to the persevering, victorious believer; also knowledge and wisdom, suitable to their power and dominion. Christ brings day with him into the soul, the light of grace and of glory, in the presence and enjoyment of him their Lord and Savior. After every victory let us follow up our advantage against the enemy, that we may overcome and keep the works of Christ to the end.

The world can never fill,"
but which only the same love that you had at first, can ever fully satisfy!

II. And now, beloved, WHERE DID YOU AND I LOSE OUR FIRST LOVE, if we have lost it? Let each one speak for himself, or rather, let me speak for each.

Have you not lost your first love in the world some of you? You used to have that little shop once, you had not very much business; well, you had enough, and a little to spare. However, there was a good turn came in business; you took two shops, and you are getting on very well. Is it not marvelous, that when you grew richer and had more business, you began to have less grace?

Oh, friends, it is a very serious thing to grow rich. Of all the temptations to which God's children are exposed it is the worst, because it is one that they do not dread, and therefore it is the more subtle temptation. You know a traveler if he is going a journey, takes a staff with him, it is a help to him; but suppose he is covetous, and says, "I will have a hundred of these sticks," that will be no help to him at all; he has only got a load to carry, and it stops his progress instead of assisting him. But I do believe there are many Christians that lived near to God, when they were living on a pound a week, that might give up their yearly incomes with the greatest joy, if they could have now the same contentment, the same peace of mind, the same nearness of access to God, that they had in times of poverty. Ah, too much of the world is a bad thing for any man! I question very much whether a man ought not sometimes to stop, and say, "There is an opportunity of doing more trade, but it will require the whole of my time, and I must give up that hour I have set apart for prayer; I will not do the trade at all; I have enough, and therefore let it go. I would rather do trade with heaven than trade with earth."

Again: do you not think also that perhaps you may have lost your first love by getting too much with worldly people? When you were in your first love, no company suited you but the godly; but now you have got a young man that you talk with, who talks a great deal more about frivolity, and gives you a great deal more of the froth and scum of levity, than he ever gives you of solid godliness. Once you were surrounded by those that fear the Lord, but now you dwell in the tents of "Freedom," where you hear little but cursing. But, friends, he that carrieth coals in his bosom must be burned; and he that hath ill companions cannot but be injured. Seek, then, to have godly friends, that thou mayest maintain thy first love.

But another reason. Do you not think that perhaps you have forgotten how much you owe to Christ? There is one thing, that I feel from experience I am compelled to do very often, viz., to go back to where I first started:—

come in to him, and will sup with him, and he with me.

21 To him that overcometh will I grant to sit with me in my throne, even as I also overcame, and am set down with my Father in his throne.

22 He that hath an ear, let him hear what the Spirit saith unto the churches.

REVELATION 4

1 After this I looked, and, behold, a door was opened in heaven: and the first voice which I heard was as it were of a trumpet talking with me; which said, Come up hither, and I will shew thee things which must be hereafter.

2 And immediately I was in the spirit: and, behold, a throne was set in heaven, and one sat on the throne.

3 And he that sat was to look upon like a jasper and a sardine stone: and there was a rainbow round about the throne, in sight like unto an emerald.

4 And round about the throne were four and twenty seats: and upon the seats I saw four and twenty elders sitting, clothed in white raiment; and they had on their heads crowns of gold.

5 And out of the throne proceeded lightnings and thunderings and voices: and there were seven lamps of fire burning before the throne, which are the seven Spirits of God.

6 And before the throne there was a sea of glass like unto crystal: and in the midst of the throne, and round about the throne, were four beasts full of eyes before and behind.

7 And the first beast was like a lion, and the second beast like a calf, and the third beast had a face as a man, and the fourth beast was like a flying eagle.

8 And the four beasts had each of them six wings about him; and they were full of eyes within: and they rest not day and night, saying, Holy, holy, holy, Lord God Almighty, which was, and is, and is to come.

9 And when those beasts give glory and honor and thanks to him that sat on the throne, who

me in white – in joy; in perfect holiness; in glory. They are worthy – A few good among many bad are doubly acceptable to God. O how much happier is this worthiness than that mentioned, chap. xvi, 6.

5. He shall be clothed in white raiment – The color of victory, joy, and triumph. And I will not blot his name out of the book of life – Like that of the angel of the church at Sardis: but he shall live for ever. I will confess his name – As one of my faithful servants and soldiers.

7. The holy one, the true one – Two great and glorious names. He that hath the key of David – A master of a family, or a prince, has one or more keys, wherewith he can open and shut all the doors of his house or palace. So had David a key, a token of right and sovereignty, which was afterward adjudged to Eliakim, Isaiah xxii, 22. Much more has Christ, the Son of David, the key of the spiritual city of David, the New Jerusalem; the supreme right, power, and authority, as in his own house. He openeth this to all that overcome, and none shutteth: he shutteth it against all the fearful, and none openeth. Likewise when he openeth a door on earth for his works or his servants, none can shut; and when he shutteth against whatever would hurt or defile, none can open.

8. I have given before thee an opened door – To enter into the joy of thy Lord; and, meantime, to go on unhindered in every good work. Thou hast a little strength – But little outward human strength; a little, poor, mean, despicable company. Yet thou hast kept my word – Both in judgment and practice.

9. Behold, I – who have all power; and they must then comply. I will make them come and bow down before thy feet – Pay thee the lowest homage. And know – At length, that all depends on my love, and that thou hast a place therein. O how often does the judgment of the people turn quite round, when the Lord looketh upon them! Job xlii, 7, &c.

10. Because thou hast kept the word of my patience – The word of Christ is indeed a word of patience. I also will keep thee – O happy exemption from that spreading calamity! From the hour of temptation – So that thou shalt not enter into temptation; but it shall pass over thee. The hour denotes the short time of its continuance; that is, at any one place. At every one it was very sharp, though short; wherein the great tempter was not idle, chap. ii, 10. Which hour shall come upon the whole earth – The whole Roman empire. It went over the Christians, and over the Jews and heathens; though in a very different manner. This was the time of the persecution under the seemingly virtuous emperor Trajan. The two preceding persecutions were under those monsters, Nero and Domitian; but Trajan was so admired for his goodness, and his persecution was of such a nature, that it was a temptation indeed, and did thoroughly try them that dwelt upon the earth.

11. Thy crown – Which is ready for thee, if thou endure to the end.

12. I will make him a pillar in the temple of my God – I will fix him as beautiful, as useful, and as immovable as a pillar in the church of God. And he shall go out no more – But shall be holy and happy for ever. And I will write upon him the name of my God – So that the nature and image of God shall appear visibly upon him. And the name of the city of my God – Giving him a title to dwell in the New Jerusalem. And my new name – A share in that joy which I entered into, after overcoming all my enemies.

14. To the angel of the church at Ladies – For these St. Paul had had a great concern, Colossians ii, 1. These things saith the Amen – That is, the True One, the God of truth. The beginning – The Author, Prince, and Ruler. Of the creation of God – Of all creatures; the beginning, or Author, by whom God made them all.

15. I know thy works – Thy disposition and behavior, though thou knowest it not thyself. That thou art neither cold – An utter stranger to the things of God, having no care or thought about them. Nor hot – As boiling water: so ought we to be penetrated and heated by the fire of love. O that thou wert – This wish of our Lord plainly implies that he does not work on us irresistibly, as the fire does

REVELATION 3

Epistle to the church at Sardis. (1-6)
Epistle to the church at Philadelphia. (7-13)
Epistle to the church at Laodicea. (14-22)

1-6. The Lord Jesus is he that hath the Holy Spirit with all his powers, graces, and operations. Hypocrisy, and lamentable decay in religion, are sins charged upon Sardis, by One who knew that church well, and all her works. Outward things appeared well to men, but there was only the form of godliness, not the power; a name to live, not a principle of life. There was great deadness in their souls, and in their services; numbers were wholly hypocrites, others were in a disordered and lifeless state. Our Lord called upon them to be watchful against their enemies, and to be active and earnest in their duties; and to endeavor, in dependence on the grace of the Holy Spirit, to revive and strengthen the faith and spiritual affections of those yet alive to God, though in a declining state. Whenever we are off our watch, we lose ground. Thy works are hollow and empty; prayers are not filled up with holy desires, alms-deeds not filled up with true charity, Sabbaths not filled up with suitable devotion of soul to God. There are not inward affections suitable to outward acts and expressions; when the spirit is wanting, the form cannot long remain. In seeking a revival in our own souls, or the souls of others, it is needful to compare what we profess with the manner in which we go on, that we may be humbled and quickened to hold fast that which remains. Christ enforces his counsel with a dreadful threatening if it should be despised. Yet our blessed Lord does not leave this sinful people without some encouragement. He makes honorable mention of the faithful remnant in Sardis, he makes a gracious promise to them. He that overcometh shall be clothed in white raiment; the purity of grace shall be rewarded with the perfect purity of glory. Christ has his book of life, a register of all who shall inherit eternal life; the book of remembrance of all who live to God, and keep up the life and power of godliness in evil times. Christ will bring forward this book of life, and show the names of the faithful, before God, and all the angels, at the great day.

7-13 The same Lord Jesus has the key of government and authority in and over the church. He opens a door of opportunity to his churches; he opens a door of utterance to his ministers; he opens a door of entrance, opens the heart. He shuts the door of heaven against the foolish, who sleep away their day of grace; and against the workers of iniquity, how vain and confident soever they may be. The church in Philadelphia is

"I, the chief of sinners am,
But Jesus died for me."

You and I get talking about our being saints; we know our election, we rejoice in our calling, we go on to sanctification; and we forget the hole of the pit whence we were digged. Ah, remember my brother, thou art nothing now but a sinner saved through grace; remember what thou wouldst have been, if the Lord had left thee. And surely, then, by going back continually to first principles, and to the great foundation stone, the cross of Christ, thou wilt be led to go back to thy first love.

Dost thou not think, again, that thou hast lost thy first love by neglecting communion with Christ? Now preacher, preach honestly, and preach at thyself. Has there not been, sometimes, this temptation to do a great deal for Christ, but not to live a great deal with Christ? One of my besetting sins, I feel, is this. If there is anything to be done actively for Christ, I instinctively prefer the active exercise to the passive quiet of his presence. There are some of you, perhaps, that are attending a Sunday school, who would be more profitably employed to your own souls if you were spending that hour in communion with Christ. Perhaps, too, you attend the means so often, that you have no time in secret to improve what you gain in the means. Mrs. Bury once said, that if "all the twelve apostles were preaching in a certain town, and we could have the privilege of hearing them preach, yet if they kept us out of our closets, and led us to neglect prayer, better for us never to have heard their names, than to have gone to listen to them." We shall never love Christ much except we live near to him. Love to Christ is dependent on our nearness to him. It is just like the planets and the sun. Why are some of the planets cold? Why do they move at so slow a rate? Simply because they are so far from the sun: put them where the planet Mercury is, and they will be in a boiling heat, and spin round the sun in rapid orbits. So, beloved, if we live near to Christ, we cannot help loving him: the heart that is near Jesus must be full of his love. But when we live days and weeks and months without personal intercourse, without real fellowship, how can we maintain love towards a stranger? He must be a friend, and we must stick close to him, as he sticks close to us—closer than a brother; or else, we shall never have our first love.

There are a thousand reasons that I might have given, but I leave each of you to search your hearts, to find out why you have lost, each of you, your first love.

III. Now, dear friends, just give me all your attention for a moment, while I earnestly beseech and implore of you to SEEK TO GET YOUR FIRST LOVE RESTORED. Shall I tell you why? Brother, though thou be a child of God, if thou hast lost thy first love, there is some trouble near at hand. "Whom the Lord loveth, he

liveth for ever and ever,

10 The four and twenty elders fall down before him that sat on the throne, and worship him that liveth for ever and ever, and cast their crowns before the throne, saying,

11 Thou art worthy, O Lord, to receive glory and honor and power: for thou hast created all things, and for thy pleasure they are and were created.

REVELATION 5

1 And I saw in the right hand of him that sat on the throne a book written within and on the backside, sealed with seven seals.

2 And I saw a strong angel proclaiming with a loud voice, Who is worthy to open the book, and to loose the seals thereof?

3 And no man in heaven, nor in earth, neither under the earth, was able to open the book, neither to look thereon.

4 And I wept much, because no man was found worthy to open and to read the book, neither to look thereon.

5 And one of the elders saith unto me, Weep not: behold, the Lion of the tribe of Juda, the Root of David, hath prevailed to open the book, and to loose the seven seals thereof.

6 And I beheld, and, lo, in the midst of the throne and of the four beasts, and in the midst of the elders, stood a Lamb as it had been slain, having seven horns and seven eyes, which are the seven Spirits of God sent forth into all the earth.

7 And he came and took the book out of the right hand of him that sat upon the throne.

8 And when he had taken the book, the four beasts and four and twenty elders fell down before the Lamb, having every one of them harps, and golden vials full of odors, which are the prayers of saints.

9 And they sung a new song, saying, Thou art worthy to take the book, and to open the seals thereof: for thou wast slain, and hast redeemed us to God by thy blood out of every kindred, and tongue, and people, and nation;

10 And hast made us unto our

on the water which it heats. Cold or hot – Even if thou wert cold, without any thought or profession of religion, there would be more hope of thy recovery.

16. So because thou art lukewarm – The effect of lukewarm water is well known. I am about to spew thee out of my mouth – I will utterly cast thee from me; that is, unless thou repent.

17. Because thou sayest – Therefore "I counsel thee," &c. I am rich – In gifts and grace, as well as worldly goods. And knowest not that thou art – In God's account, wretched and pitiable.

18. I counsel thee – who art poor, and blind, and naked. To buy of me – Without money or price. Gold purified in the fire – True, living faith, which is purified in the furnace of affliction. And white raiment – True holiness. And eye salve – Spiritual illumination; the "unction of the Holy One," which teacheth all things.

19. Whomsoever I love – Even thee, thou poor Laodicean! O how much has his unwearied love to do! I rebuke – For what is past. And chasten – That they may amend for the time to come.

20. I stand at the door, and knock – Even at this instant; while he is speaking this word. If any man open – Willingly receive me. I will sup with him – Refreshing him with my graces and gifts, and delighting myself in what I have given. And he with me – In life everlasting.

21. I will give him to sit with me on my throne – In unspeakable happiness and glory. Elsewhere, heaven itself is termed the throne of God: but this throne is in heaven.

22. He that hath an ear, let him hear, &c. – This stands in the three former letters before the promise; in the four latter, after it; clearly dividing the seven into two parts; the first containing three, the last, four letters. The titles given our Lord in the three former letters peculiarly respect his power after his resurrection and ascension, particularly over his church; those in the four latter, his divine glory, and unity with the Father and the Holy Spirit. Again, this word being placed before the promises in the three former letters, excludes the false apostles at Ephesus, the false Jews at Smyrna, and the partakers with the heathens at Pergamos, from having any share therein. In the four latter, being placed after them, it leaves the promises immediately joined with Christ's address to the angel of the church, to show that the fulfilling of these was near; whereas the others reach beyond the end of the world. It should be observed, that the overcoming, or victory, (to which alone these peculiar promises are annexed,) is not the ordinary victory obtained by every believer; but a special victory over great and peculiar temptations, by those that are strong in faith.

REVELATION 4

We are now entering upon the main prophecy. The whole Revelation may be divided thus: The first, second, and third chapters contain the introduction; The fourth and fifth, the proposition; The sixth, seventh, eighth, and ninth describe things which are already fulfilled; The tenth to the fourteenth, things which are now fulfilling; The fifteenth to the nineteenth, things which will be fulfilled shortly; The twentieth, twenty-first, and twenty-second, things at a greater distance.

1. After these things – As if he had said, After I had written these letters from the mouth of the Lord. By the particle and, the several parts of this prophecy are usually connected: by the expression, after these things, they are distinguished from each other, chap. vii, 9; xix, 1. By that expression, and after these things, they are distinguished, and yet connected, chap. vii, 1; xv, 5; xviii, 1. St. John always saw and heard, and then immediately wrote down one part after another: and one part is constantly divided from another by some one of these expressions.

2. And immediately I was in the spirit – Even in an higher degree than before, chap. i, 10. And, behold, a throne was set in heaven – St. John is to write "things

commended; yet with a gentle reproof. Although Christ accepts a little strength, yet believers must not rest satisfied in a little, but strive to grow in grace, to be strong in faith, giving glory to God. Christ can discover this his favor to his people, so that their enemies shall be forced to acknowledge it. This, by the grace of Christ, will soften their enemies, and make them desire to be admitted into communion with his people. Christ promises preserving grace in the most trying times, as the reward of past faithfulness; To him that hath shall be given. Those who keep the gospel in a time of peace, shall be kept by Christ in an hour of temptation; and the same Divine grace that has made them fruitful in times of peace, will make them faithful in times of persecution. Christ promises a glorious reward to the victorious believer. He shall be a monumental pillar in the temple of God; a monument of the free and powerful grace of God; a monument that shall never be defaced or removed. On this pillar shall be written the new name of Christ; by this will appear, under whom the believer fought the good fight, and came off victorious.

14-22 Laodicea was the last and worst of the seven churches of Asia. Here our Lord Jesus styles himself, "The Amen;" one steady and unchangeable in all his purposes and promises. If religion is worth anything, it is worth every thing. Christ expects men should be in earnest. How many professors of gospel doctrine are neither hot nor cold; except as they are indifferent in needful matters, and hot and fiery in disputes about things of lesser moment! A severe punishment is threatened. They would give a false opinion of Christianity, as if it were an unholy religion; while others would conclude it could afford no real satisfaction, otherwise its professors would not have been heartless in it, or so ready to seek pleasure or happiness from the world. One cause of this indifference and inconsistency in religion is, self-conceit and self-delusion; "Because thou sayest." What a difference between their thoughts of themselves, and the thoughts Christ had of them! How careful should we be not to cheat our owns souls! There are many in hell, who once thought themselves far in the way to heaven. Let us beg of God that we may not be left to flatter and deceive ourselves. Professors grow proud, as they become carnal and formal. Their state was wretched in itself. They were poor; really poor, when they said and thought they were rich. They could not see their state, nor their way, nor their danger, yet they thought they saw it. They had not the garment of justification, nor sanctification: they were exposed to sin and shame; their rags that would defile them. They were naked, without house or

chasteneth," and he is sure to chasten thee when thou sinnest. It is calm with you to night, is it? Oh! but dread that calm, there is a tempest lowering. Sin is the harbinger of tempest: read the history of David. All David's life, in all his troubles, even in the rocks of the wild goats, and in the caves of Engedi, he was the happiest of men till he lost his first love; and from the day when his lustful eye was fixed upon Bathsheba, even to the last, he went with broken bones sorrowing to his grave. It was one long string of afflictions: take heed it be not so with thee. "Ah, but," you say, "I shall not sin as David did." Brother, you cannot tell: if you have lost your first love, what should hinder you but that you should lose your first purity? Love and purity go together. He that loveth is pure; he that loveth little shall find his purity decrease, until it becomes marred and polluted. I should not like to see you, my dear friends, tried and troubled: I do weep with them that weep. If there be a child of yours sick, and I hear of it, I can say honestly, I do feel something like a father to your children, and as a father to you. If you have sufferings and afflictions, and I know them, I desire to feel for you, and spread your griefs before the throne of God. Oh, I do not want my heavenly Father to take the rod out to you all; but he will do it, if you fall from your first love. As sure as ever he is a Father, he will let you have the rod if your love cools. Bastards may escape the rod. If you are only base-born professors you may go happily along; but the true-born child of God, when his love declines, must and shall smart for it.

There is yet another thing, my dear friends, if we lose our first love—what will the world say of us if we lose our first love? I must put this, not for our name's sake, but for God's dear name's sake. O what will the world say of us? There was a time, and it is not gone yet, when men must point at this church, and say of it, "There is a church, that is like a bright oasis in the midst of a desert, a spot of light in the midst of darkness." Our prayer meetings were prayer meetings indeed, the congregations were as attentive as they were numerous. Oh, how you did drink in the words; how your eyes flashed with a living fire, whenever the name of Christ was mentioned! And what, if in a little time it shall be said, "Ah, that church is quite as sleepy as any other; look at them when the minister preaches, why they can sleep under him, they do not seem to care for the truth. Look at the Spurgeonites, they are just as cold and careless as others; they used to be called the most pugnacious people in the world, for they were always ready to defend their Master's name and their Master's truth, and they got that name in consequence, but now you may swear in their presence and they will not rebuke you: how near these people once used to live to God and his house, they were always there; look at their prayer meetings, they would fill their seats as full at a prayer meeting as at an ordinary service; now they are all gone back."

God kings and priests: and we shall reign on the earth.

11 And I beheld, and I heard the voice of many angels round about the throne and the beasts and the elders: and the number of them was ten thousand times ten thousand, and thousands of thousands;

12 Saying with a loud voice, Worthy is the Lamb that was slain to receive power, and riches, and wisdom, and strength, and honor, and glory, and blessing.

13 And every creature which is in heaven, and on the earth, and under the earth, and such as are in the sea, and all that are in them, heard I saying, Blessing, and honor, and glory, and power, be unto him that sitteth upon the throne, and unto the Lamb for ever and ever.

14 And the four beasts said, Amen. And the four and twenty elders fell down and worshiped him that liveth for ever and ever.

REVELATION 6

1 And I saw when the Lamb opened one of the seals, and I heard, as it were the noise of thunder, one of the four beasts saying, Come and see.

2 And I saw, and behold a white horse: and he that sat on him had a bow; and a crown was given unto him: and he went forth conquering, and to conquer.

3 And when he had opened the second seal, I heard the second beast say, Come and see.

4 And there went out another horse that was red: and power was given to him that sat thereon to take peace from the earth, and that they should kill one another: and there was given unto him a great sword.

5 And when he had opened the third seal, I heard the third beast say, Come and see. And I beheld, and lo a black horse; and he that sat on him had a pair of balances in his hand.

6 And I heard a voice in the midst of the four beasts say, A measure of wheat for a penny, and three measures of barley for a penny; and see thou hurt

which shall be;" and, in order thereto, he is here shown, after an heavenly manner, how whatever "shall be," whether good or bad, flows out of invisible fountains; and how, after it is done on the visible theater of the world and the church, it flows back again into the invisible world, as its proper and final scope.

3. And he that sat was in appearance – Shone with a visible luster, like that of sparkling precious stones, such as those which were of old on the high priest's breastplate, and those placed as the foundations of the new Jerusalem, chap. xxi, 19, 20. If there is anything emblematical in the colors of these stones, possibly the jasper, which is transparent and of a glittering white, with an intermixture of beautiful colors, may be a symbol of God's purity, with various other perfections, which shine in all his dispensations. The sardine stone, of a blood-red color, may be an emblem of his justice, and the vengeance he was about to execute on his enemies. An emerald, being green, may betoken favor to the good; a rainbow, the everlasting covenant. See Gen. ix, 9. And this being round about the whole breadth of the throne, fixed the distance of those who stood or sat round it.

4. And round about the throne – In a circle, are four and twenty thrones, and on the thrones four and twenty elders – The most holy of all the former ages, Isaiah xxiv, 23; Heb. xii, 1; representing the whole body of the saints. Sitting – In general; but falling down when they worship. Clothed in white raiment – This and their golden crowns show, that they had already finished their course and taken their place among the citizens of heaven. They are never termed souls, and hence it is probable that they had glorified bodies already. Compare Matt. xxvii, 52.

5. And out of the throne go forth lightnings – Which affect the sight. Voices – Which affect the hearing. Thunderings – Which cause the whole body to tremble. Weak men account all this terrible; but to the inhabitants of heaven it is a mere source of joy and pleasure, mixed with reverence to the Divine Majesty. Even to the saints on earth these convey light and protection; but to their enemies, terror and destruction.

6. And before the throne is a sea as of glass, like crystal – Wide and deep, pure and clear, transparent and still. Both the "seven lamps of fire" and this sea are before the throne; and both may mean "the seven spirits of God," the Holy Ghost; whose powers and operations are frequently represented both under the emblem of fire and of water.

7. And the first – Just such were the four cherubim in Ezekiel, who supported the moving throne of God; whereas each of those that overshadowed the mercy-seat in the holy of holies had all these four faces: whence a late great man supposes them to have been emblematic of the Trinity, and the incarnation of the second Person. A flying eagle – That is, with wings expanded.

8. Each of them hath six wings – As had each of the seraphim in Isaiah's vision. "Two covered his face," in token of humility and reverence: "two his feet," perhaps in token of readiness and diligence for executing divine commissions. Round about and within they are full of eyes. Round about – To see everything which is farther off from the throne than they are themselves. And within – On the inner part of the circle which they make with one another.

9, 10. And when the living creatures give glory; the elders fall down – That is, as often as the living creatures give glory, immediately the elders fall down. The expression implies, that they did so at the same instant, and that they both did this frequently. The living creatures do not say directly, "Holy, holy, holy art thou;" but only bend a little, out of deep reverence, and say, "Holy, holy, holy is the Lord." But the elders, when they are fallen down, may say, "Worthy art thou, O Lord our God."

11. Worthy art thou to receive – This he receives not only when he is thus praised, but also when he destroys his enemies and glorifies himself anew. The glory and the honor and the power – Answering the thrice-holy of the living creatures, verse 9. For thou hast created all things – Creation is the ground of all

harbor, for they were without God, in whom alone the soul of man can find rest and safety. Good counsel was given by Christ to this sinful people. Happy those who take his counsel, for all others must perish in their sins. Christ lets them know where they might have true riches, and how they might have them. Some things must be parted with, but nothing valuable; and it is only to make room for receiving true riches. Part with sin and self-confidence, that you may be filled with his hidden treasure. They must receive from Christ the white raiment he purchased and provided for them; his own imputed righteousness for justification, and the garments of holiness and sanctification. Let them give themselves up to his word and Spirit, and their eyes shall be opened to see their way and their end. Let us examine ourselves by the rule of his word, and pray earnestly for the teaching of his Holy Spirit, to take away our pride, prejudices, and worldly lusts. Sinners ought to take the rebukes of God's word and rod, as tokens of his love to their souls. Christ stood without; knocking, by the dealings of his providence, the warnings and teaching of his word, and the influences of his Spirit. Christ still graciously, by his word and Spirit, comes to the door of the hearts of sinners. Those who open to him shall enjoy his presence. If what he finds would make but a poor feast, what he brings will supply a rich one. He will give fresh supplies of graces and comforts. In the conclusion is a promise to the overcoming believer. Christ himself had temptations and conflicts; he overcame them all, and was more than a conqueror. Those made like to Christ in his trials, shall be made like to him in glory. All is closed with the general demand of attention. And these counsels, while suited to the churches to which they were addressed, are deeply interesting to all men.

REVELATION 4

A vision of God, as on his glorious throne, around which were twenty-four elders and four living creatures. (1-8)

Whose songs, and those of the holy angels, the apostle heard. (9-11)

1-8 After the Lord Jesus had instructed the apostle to write to the churches "the things that are," there was another vision. The apostle saw a throne set in heaven, an emblem of the universal dominion of Jehovah. He saw a glorious One upon the throne, not described by human features, so as to be represented by a likeness or image, but only by his surpassing brightness. These seem emblems of the excellence of the Divine nature, and of God's awful justice. The

"Ah," says the world, "just what I said; the fact is, it was a mere spasm, a little spiritual excitement, and it has all gone down." And the worldling says, "Ah, ah, so would I have it, so would I have it!" I was reading only the other day of an account of my ceasing to be popular; it was said my chapel was now nearly empty, that nobody went to it: and I was exceedingly amused and interested. "Well, if it come to that," I said, "I shall not grieve or cry very much; but if it is said the church has left its zeal and first love, that is enough to break any honest pastor's heart." Let the chaff go, but if the wheat remain we have comfort. Let those who are the outer-court worshipers cease to hear, what signifieth? let them turn aside, but O, ye soldiers of the Cross, if ye turn your backs in the day of battle, where shall I hide my head? what shall I say for the great name of my Master, or for the honor of his gospel? It is our boast and joy, that the old-fashioned doctrine has been revived in these days, and that the truth that Calvin preached, that Paul preached, and that Jesus preached, is still mighty to save, and far surpasses in power all the neologies and new-fangled notions of the present time. But what will the heretic say, when he sees it is all over? "Ah," he will say, "that old truth urged on by the fanaticism of a foolish young man, did wake the people a little; but it lacked marrow and strength, and it all died away!" Will ye thus dishonor your Lord and Master, ye children of the heavenly king? I beseech you do not so—but endeavor to receive again as a rich gift of the Spirit your first love.

And now, once again, dear friends, there is a thought that ought to make each of us feel alarmed, if we have lost our first love. May not this question arise in our hearts—Was I ever a child of God at all? Oh, my God, must I ask myself this question? Yes, I will. Are there not many of whom it is said, they went out from us because they were not of us; for if they had been of us, doubtless they would have continued with us? Are there not some whose goodness is as the morning cloud and as the early dew—may that not have been my case? I am speaking for you all. Put the question—may I not have been impressed under a certain sermon, and may not that impression have been a mere carnal excitement? May it not have been that I thought I repented but did not really repent? May it not have been the case, that I got a hope somewhere but had not a right to it? And I never had the loving faith that unites me to the Lamb of God. And may it not have been that I only thought I had love to Christ, and never had it, for if I really had love to Christ should I be as I now am? See how far I have come down! May I not keep on going down until my end shall be perdition, and the never-dying worm, and the fire unquenchable? Many have gone from heights of a profession to the depths of damnation, and may not I be the same? May it not be true of me that I am as a wandering star for whom is reserved blackness of darkness for

not the oil and the wine.

7 And when he had opened the fourth seal, I heard the voice of the fourth beast say, Come and see.

8 And I looked, and behold a pale horse: and his name that sat on him was Death, and Hell followed with him. And power was given unto them over the fourth part of the earth, to kill with sword, and with hunger, and with death, and with the beasts of the earth.

9 And when he had opened the fifth seal, I saw under the altar the souls of them that were slain for the word of God, and for the testimony which they held:

10 And they cried with a loud voice, saying, How long, O Lord, holy and true, dost thou not judge and avenge our blood on them that dwell on the earth?

11 And white robes were given unto every one of them; and it was said unto them, that they should rest yet for a little season, until their fellowservants also and their brethren, that should be killed as they were, should be fulfilled.

12 And I beheld when he had opened the sixth seal, and, lo, there was a great earthquake; and the sun became black as sackcloth of hair, and the moon became as blood;

13 And the stars of heaven fell unto the earth, even as a fig tree casteth her untimely figs, when she is shaken of a mighty wind.

14 And the heaven departed as a scroll when it is rolled together; and every mountain and island were moved out of their places.

15 And the kings of the earth, and the great men, and the rich men, and the chief captains, and the mighty men, and every bondman, and every free man, hid themselves in the dens and in the rocks of the mountains;

16 And said to the mountains and rocks, Fall on us, and hide us from the face of him that sitteth on the throne, and from the wrath of the Lamb:

17 For the great day of his wrath is come; and who shall be able to stand?

the works of God: therefore, for this, as well as for his other works, will he be praised to all eternity. And through thy will they were – They began to be. It is to the free, gracious and powerfully-working will of him who cannot possibly need anything that all things owe their first existence. And are created – That is, continue in being ever since they were created.

REVELATION 5

1. And I saw – This is a continuation of the same narrative. In the right hand – The emblem of his all-ruling power. He held it openly, in order to give it to him that was worthy. It is scarce needful to observe, that there is not in heaven any real book of parchment or paper or that Christ does not really stand there, in the shape of a lion or of a lamb.

2. And I saw a strong angel – This proclamation to every creature was too great for a man to make, and yet not becoming the Lamb himself. It was therefore made by an angel, and one of uncommon eminence.

3. And none – No creature; no, not Mary herself. In heaven, or in earth, neither under the earth – That is, none in the universe. For these are the three great regions into which the whole creation is divided. Was able to open the book – To declare the counsels of God. Nor to look thereon – So as to understand any part of it.

4. And I wept much – A weeping which sprung from greatness of mind. The tenderness of heart which he always had appeared more clearly now he was out of his own power. The Revelation was not written without tears; neither without tears will it be understood. How far are they from the temper of St. John who inquire after anything rather than the contents of this book! yea, who applaud their own clemency if they excuse those that do inquire into them!

5. And one of the elders – Probably one of those who rose with Christ, and afterwards ascended into heaven. Perhaps one of the patriarchs. Some think it was Jacob, from whose prophecy the name of Lion is given him, Gen. xlix, 9. The Lion of the tribe of Judah – The victorious prince who is, like a lion, able to tear all his enemies in pieces. The root of David – As God, the root and source of David's family, Isaiah xi, 1, 10. Hath prevailed to open the book – Hath overcome all obstructions, and obtained the honor to disclose the divine counsels.

6. And I saw – First, Christ in or on the midst of the throne; secondly, the four living creatures making the inner circle round him; and, thirdly, the four and twenty elders making a larger circle round him and them.

7. And he came – Here was "Ask of me," Psalm ii, 8, fulfilled in the most glorious manner. And took – it is one state of exaltation that reaches from our Lord's ascension to his coming in glory. Yet this state admits of various degrees. At his ascension, "angels, and principalities, and powers were subjected to him." Ten days after, he received from the Father and sent the Holy Ghost. And now he took the book out of the right hand of him that sat upon the throne – who gave it him as a signal of his delivering to him all power in heaven and earth. He received it, in token of his being both able and willing to fulfill all that was written therein.

8. And when he took the book, the four living creatures fell down – Now is homage done to the Lamb by every creature. These, together with the elders, make the beginning; and afterward, chap. v, 14, the conclusion. They are together surrounded with a multitude of angels, chap. v, 11, and together sing the new song, as they had before praised God together, chap. iv, 8, &c. Having every one – The elders, not the living creatures. An harp – Which was one of the chief instruments used for thanksgiving in the temple service: a fit emblem of the melody of their hearts. And golden phials – Cups or censers. Full of incense, which are the prayers of the saints – Not of the elders themselves, but of the other saints still

MATTHEW HENRY

CHARLES H. SPURGEON

rainbow is a fit emblem of that covenant of promise which God has made with Christ, as the Head of the church, and with all his people in him. The prevailing color was a pleasant green, showing the reviving and refreshing nature of the new covenant. Four-and-twenty seats around the throne, were filled with four-and-twenty elders, representing, probably, the whole church of God. Their sitting denotes honor, rest, and satisfaction; their sitting about the throne signifies nearness to God, the sight and enjoyment they have of him. They were clothed in white raiment; the imputed righteousness of the saints and their holiness: they had on their heads crowns of gold, signifying the glory they have with him. Lightning and voices came from the throne; the awful declarations God makes to his church, of his sovereign will and pleasure. Seven lamps of fire were burning before the throne; the gifts, graces, and operations of the Spirit of God in the churches of Christ, dispensed according to the will and pleasure of him who sits upon the throne. In the gospel church, the laver for purification is the blood of the Lord Jesus Christ, which cleanses from all sin. In this all must be washed, to be admitted into the gracious presence of God on earth, and his glorious presence in heaven. The apostle saw four living creatures, between the throne and the circle of the elders, standing between God and the people. These seem to signify the true ministers of the gospel, because of their place between God and the people. This also is shown by the description given, denoting wisdom, courage, diligence, and discretion, and the affections by which they mount up toward heaven.

9-11 All true believers wholly ascribe their redemption and conversion, their present privileges and future hopes, to the eternal and most holy God. Thus rise the forever harmonious, thankful songs of the redeemed in heaven. Would we on earth do like them, let our praises be constant, not interrupted; united, not divided; thankful, not cold and formal; humble, not self-confident.

REVELATION 5

A book sealed with seven seals, which could be opened by none but Christ, who took the book to open it. (1-7)

Upon which all honor is ascribed to him, as worthy to open it. (8-14)

1-7 The apostle saw in the hand of him that sat upon the throne, a roll of parchments in the form usual in those times, and sealed with seven seals. This represented the secret purposes of God

ever? May I not have shone brightly in the midst of the church for a little while, and yet may I not be one of those poor foolish virgins who took no oil in my vessel with my lamp, and therefore my lamp will go out? Let me think, if I go on as I am, it is impossible for me to stop, if I am going downwards I may go on going downwards. And O my God, if I go on backsliding for another year—who knows where I may have backslidden to? Perhaps into some gross sin. Prevent, prevent it by thy grace! Perhaps I may backslide totally. If I am a child of God I know I cannot do that. But still, may it not happen that I only thought I was a child of God, and may I not so far go back that at last my very name to live shall go because I always have been dead? Oh! how dreadful it is to think and to see in our church, members who turn out to be dead members! If I could weep tears of blood, they would not express the emotion that I ought to feel, and that you ought to feel, when you think there are some among us that are dead branches of a living vine. Our deacons find that there is much of unsoundness in our members. I grieve to think that because we cannot see all our members, there are many who have backslidden. There is one who says, "I joined the church, it is true, but I never was converted. I made a profession of being converted, but I was not, and now I take no delight in the things of God. I am moral, I attend the house of prayer, but I am not converted. My name may be taken off the books; I am not a godly man." There are others among you who perhaps have gone even further than that—have gone into sin, and yet I may not know it. It may not come to my ears in so large a church as this. Oh! I beseech you, my dear friends, by him that liveth and was dead, let not your good be evil spoken of, by losing your first love.

Are there some among you that are professing religion, and not possessing it? Oh, give up your profession, or else get the truth and sell it not. Go home, each of you, and cast yourselves on your faces before God, and ask him to search you, and try you, and know your ways, and see if there be any evil way in you, and pray that he may lead you in the way everlasting. And if hitherto you have only professed, but have not possessed, seek ye the Lord while he may be found, and call ye upon him while he is near. Ye are warned, each one of you; you are solemnly told to search yourselves and make short work of it. And if any of you be hypocrites, at God's great day, guilty as I may be in many respects, there is one thing I am clear of—I have not shunned to declare the whole counsel of God. I do not believe that any people in the world shall be damned more terribly than you shall if you perish; for of this thing I have not shunned to speak—the great evil of making a profession without being sound at heart. No, I have even gone so near to personality, that I could not have gone further without mentioning your names. And rest assured, God's grace being with me, neither

REVELATION 7

1 And after these things I saw four angels standing on the four corners of the earth, holding the four winds of the earth, that the wind should not blow on the earth, nor on the sea, nor on any tree.

2　And I saw another angel ascending from the east, having the seal of the living God: and he cried with a loud voice to the four angels, to whom it was given to hurt the earth and the sea,

3　Saying, Hurt not the earth, neither the sea, nor the trees, till we have sealed the servants of our God in their foreheads.

4　And I heard the number of them which were sealed: and there were sealed an hundred and forty and four thousand of all the tribes of the children of Israel.

5　Of the tribe of Juda were sealed twelve thousand. Of the tribe of Reuben were sealed twelve thousand. Of the tribe of Gad were sealed twelve thousand.

6　Of the tribe of Aser were sealed twelve thousand. Of the tribe of Nepthalim were sealed twelve thousand. Of the tribe of Manasses were sealed twelve thousand.

7　Of the tribe of Simeon were sealed twelve thousand. Of the tribe of Levi were sealed twelve thousand. Of the tribe of Issachar were sealed twelve thousand.

8　Of the tribe of Zabulon were sealed twelve thousand. Of the tribe of Joseph were sealed twelve thousand. Of the tribe of Benjamin were sealed twelve thousand.

9　After this I beheld, and, lo, a great multitude, which no man could number, of all nations, and kindreds, and people, and tongues, stood before the throne, and before the Lamb, clothed with white robes, and palms in their hands;

10　And cried with a loud voice, saying, Salvation to our God which sitteth upon the throne, and unto the Lamb.

11　And all the angels stood round about the throne, and about the elders and the four

upon earth, whose prayers were thus emblematically represented in heaven.

9. And they sing a new song – One which neither they nor any other had sung before. Thou hast redeemed us – So the living creatures also were of the number of the redeemed. This does not so much refer to the act of redemption, which was long before, as to the fruit of it; and so more directly to those who had finished their course, "who were redeemed from the earth," ver. 1, out of every tribe, and tongue, and people, and nation – That is, out of all mankind.

10. And hast made them – The redeemed. So they speak of themselves also in the third person, out of deep self-abasement. They shall reign over the earth – The new earth: herewith agree the golden crowns of the elders. The reign of the saints in general follows, under the trumpet of the seventh angel; particularly after the first resurrection, as also in eternity, chap. xi, 18; xv, 7; xx, 4; xxii, 5; Dan. vii, 27; Psalm xlix, 14.

11. And I saw – The many angels. And heard – The voice and the number of them. Round about the elders – So forming the third circle. It is remarkable, that men are represented through this whole vision as nearer to God than any of the angels. And the number of them was – At least two hundred millions, and two millions over. And yet these were but a part of the holy angels. Afterward, chap. vii, 11, St. John heard them all.

12. Worthy is the Lamb – The elders said, ver. 9, "Worthy art thou." They were more nearly allied to him than the angels. To receive the power, &c. – This sevenfold applause answers the seven seals, of which the four former describe all visible, the latter all invisible, things, made subject to the Lamb. And every one of these seven words bears a resemblance to the seal which it answers.

13. And every creature – In the whole universe, good or bad. In the heaven, on the earth, under the earth, on the sea – With these four regions of the world, agrees the fourfold word of praise. What is in heaven, says blessing; what is on earth, honor; what is under the earth, glory; what is on the sea, strength; is unto him. This praise from all creatures begins before the opening of the first seal; but it continues from that time to eternity, according to the capacity of each.

REVELATION 6

1. I heard one – That is, the first. Of the living creatures – Who looks forward toward the east.

2. And I saw, and behold a white horse, and he that sat on him had a bow – This color, and the bow shooting arrows afar off, betoken victory, triumph, prosperity, enlargement of empire, and dominion over many people.

3. And when he had opened the second seal, I heard the second living creature – Who looked toward the west. Saying, Come – At each seal it was necessary to turn toward that quarter of the world which it more immediately concerned.

4. There went forth another horse that was red – A color suitable to bloodshed.

5. And when he had opened the third seal, I heard the third living creature – Toward the south. Saying, Come. And behold a black horse – A fit emblem of mourning and distress; particularly of black famine, as the ancient poets term it. And he that sat on him had a pair of scales in his hand – When there is great plenty, men scarce think it worth their while to weigh and measure everything, Gen. xli, 49. But when there is scarcity, they are obliged to deliver them out by measure and weight, Ezek. iv, 16. Accordingly, these scales signify scarcity. They serve also for a token, that all the fruits of the earth, and consequently the whole heavens, with their courses and influences; that all the seasons of the year, with whatsoever they produce, in nature or states, are subject to Christ. Accordingly his hand is wonderful, not only in wars and victories, but likewise in the whole course of nature.

6. And I heard a voice – It seems, from God himself. Saying – To the horseman, "Hitherto shalt thou come, and no farther." Let there be a measure of wheat for

about to be revealed. The designs and methods of Divine Providence, toward the church and the world, are stated, fixed, and made a matter of record. The counsels of God are altogether hidden from the eye and understanding of the creature. The several parts are not unsealed and opened at once, but after each other, till the whole mystery of God's counsel and conduct is finished in the world. The creatures cannot open it, nor read it; the Lord only can do so. Those who see most of God, are most desirous to see more; and those who have seen his glory, desire to know his will. But even good men may be too eager and hasty to look into the mysteries of the Divine conduct. Such desires, if not soon answered, turn to grief and sorrow. If John wept much because he could not look into the book of God's decrees, what reason have many to shed floods of tears for their ignorance of the gospel of Christ! of that on which everlasting salvation depends! We need not weep that we cannot foresee future events respecting ourselves in this world; the eager expectation of future prospects, or the foresight of future calamities, would alike unfit us for present duties and conflicts, or render our prosperous days distressing. Yet we may desire to learn, from the promises and prophecies of Scripture, what will be the final event to believers and to the church; and the Incarnate Son has prevailed, that we should learn all that we need to know. Christ stands as Mediator between God and both ministers and people. He is called a Lion, but he appears as a Lamb slain. He appears with the marks of his sufferings, to show that he pleads for us in heaven, in virtue of his satisfaction. He appears as a Lamb, having seven horns and seven eyes; perfect power to execute all the will of God, and perfect wisdom to understand it, and to do it in the most effectual manner. The Father put the book of his eternal counsels into the hand of Christ, and Christ readily and gladly took it into his hand; for he delights to make known the will of his Father; and the Holy Spirit is given by him to reveal the truth and will of God.

8-14 It is matter of joy to all the world, to see that God deals with men in grace and mercy through the Redeemer. He governs the world, not merely as a Creator, but as our Savior. The harps were instruments of praise; the vials were full of odors, or incense, which signify the prayers of the saints: prayer and praise should always go together. Christ has redeemed his people from the bondage of sin, guilt, and Satan. He has not only purchased liberty for them, but the highest honor and preferment; he made them kings and priests; kings, to rule over their own spirits, and to overcome the world, and the evil one; and he

you nor myself shall be spared in the pulpit in any personal sin that I may observe in any one of you. But oh, do let us be sincere! May the Lord sooner split this church till only a tenth of you remain, than ever suffer you to be multiplied a hundred-fold unless you be multiplied with the living in Zion, and with the holy flock that the Lord himself hath ordained, and will keep unto the end. To-morrow morning, we shall meet together and pray, that we may have our first love restored; and I hope many of you will be found there to seek again the love which you have almost lost.

And as for you that never had that love at all, the Lord breathe it upon you now for the love of Jesus. Amen.

AN EARNEST WARNING ABOUT BEING LUKEWARM
Sermon number 1185 delivered on July 26th, 1874, at the Metropolitan Tabernacle, Newington.
Reading: Revelation 3:14-21.

No Scripture ever wears out. The epistle to the church of Laodicea is not an old letter which may be put into the waste basket and be forgotten; upon its page still glow the words, "He that hath an ear, let him hear what the Spirit saith unto the churches." This Scripture was not meant to instruct the Laodiceans only, it has a wider aim. The actual church of Laodicea has passed away, but other Laodiceas still exist—indeed, they are sadly multiplied in our day, and it has ever been the tendency of human nature, however inflamed with the love of God, gradually to chill into lukewarmness. The letter to the Laodiceans is above all others the epistle for the present times.

I should judge that the church at Laodicea was once in a very fervent and healthy condition. Paul wrote a letter to it which did not claim inspiration, and therefore its loss does not render the Scriptures incomplete, for Paul may have written scores of other letters besides. Paul also mentions the church at Laodicea in his letter to the church at Colosse; he was, therefore, well acquainted with it, and as he does not utter a word of censure with regard to it, we may infer that the church was at that time in a sound state. In process of time it degenerated, and cooling down from its former ardor it became careless, lax, and indifferent. Perhaps its best men were dead, perhaps its wealth seduced it into worldliness, possibly its freedom from persecution engendered carnal ease, or neglect of prayer made it gradually backslide; but in any case it declined till it was neither cold nor hot. Lest we should ever get into such a state, and lest we should be in that state now, I pray that my discourse may come with power to the hearts of all present, but especially to the consciences of the members of my own church. May God grant that it may tend to the arousing of us all.

beasts, and fell before the throne on their faces, and worshiped God,

12 Saying, Amen: Blessing, and glory, and wisdom, and thanksgiving, and honor, and power, and might, be unto our God for ever and ever. Amen.

13 And one of the elders answered, saying unto me, What are these which are arrayed in white robes? and whence came they?

14 And I said unto him, Sir, thou knowest. And he said to me, These are they which came out of great tribulation, and have washed their robes, and made them white in the blood of the Lamb.

15 Therefore are they before the throne of God, and serve him day and night in his temple: and he that sitteth on the throne shall dwell among them.

16 They shall hunger no more, neither thirst any more; neither shall the sun light on them, nor any heat.

17 For the Lamb which is in the midst of the throne shall feed them, and shall lead them unto living fountains of waters: and God shall wipe away all tears from their eyes.

REVELATION 8

1 And when he had opened the seventh seal, there was silence in heaven about the space of half an hour.

2 And I saw the seven angels which stood before God; and to them were given seven trumpets.

3 And another angel came and stood at the altar, having a golden censer; and there was given unto him much incense, that he should offer it with the prayers of all saints upon the golden altar which was before the throne.

4 And the smoke of the incense, which came with the prayers of the saints, ascended up before God out of the angel's hand.

5 And the angel took the censer, and filled it with fire of the altar, and cast it into the earth: and there were voices, and thunderings, and light-

a penny – The word translated measure, was a Grecian measure, nearly equal to our quart. This was the daily allowance of a slave. The Roman penny, as much as a laborer then earned in a day, was about seven pence halfpenny English.

7. I heard the voice of the fourth living creature – Toward the north.

8. And I saw, and behold a pale horse – Suitable to pale death, his rider. And hades – The representative of the state of separate souls. Followeth even with him – The four first seals concern living men. Death therefore is properly introduced. Hades is only occasionally mentioned as a companion of death. So the fourth seal reaches to the borders of things invisible, which are comprised in the three last seals. And power was given to him over the fourth part of the earth – What came single and in a lower degree before, comes now together, and much more severely.

9. And when he opened the fifth seal – As the four former seals, so the three latter, have a close connection with each other. These all refer to the invisible world; the fifth, to the happy dead, particularly the martyrs; the sixth, to the unhappy; the seventh, to the angels, especially those to whom the trumpets are given. And I saw – Not only the church warring under Christ, and the world warring under Satan; but also the invisible hosts, both of heaven and hell, are described in this book.

10. And they cried – This cry did not begin now, but under the first Roman persecution.

11. And there was given to every one a white robe – An emblem of innocence, joy, and victory, in token of honor and favorable acceptance.

12. And I saw – This sixth seal seems particularly to point out God's judgment on the wicked departed. St. John saw how the end of the world was even then set before those unhappy spirits. This representation might be made to them, without anything of it being perceived upon earth. The like representation is made in heaven, chap. xi, 18. And there was a great earthquake – Or shaking, not of the earth only, but the heavens. This is a farther description of the representation made to those unhappy souls.

13. And the stars fell to, or towards, the earth – Yea, and so they surely will, let astronomers fix their magnitude as they please. As a fig tree casteth its untimely figs, when it is shaken by a mighty wind – How sublimely is the violence of that shaking expressed by this comparison!

14. And the heavens departed as a book that is rolled together – When the scripture compares some very great with a little thing, the majesty and omnipotence of God, before whom great things are little, is highly exalted. Every mountain and island – What a mountain is to the land, that an island is to the sea.

15. And the kings of the earth – They who had been so in their day. And the great men and chief captains – The generals and nobles. Hid themselves – So far as in them lay. In the rocks of the mountains – There are also rocks on the plains; but they were rocks on high, which they besought to fall upon them.

16. To the mountains and the rocks – Which were tottering already.

REVELATION 7

1. And after these things – What follows is a preparation for the seventh seal, which is the weightiest of all. It is connected with the sixth by the particle and; whereas what is added, verse 9, stands free and unconnected. I saw four angels – Probably evil ones. They have their employ with the four first trumpets, as have other evil angels with the three last; namely, the angel of the abyss, the four bound in the Euphrates, and Satan himself. These four angels would willingly have brought on all the calamities that follow without delay.

2. And I saw another (a good) angel ascending from the east – The plagues begin in the east; so does the sealing. Having the seal of the only living and true God: and he cried with a loud voice to the four angels – Who were hasting to execute

MATTHEW HENRY

CHARLES H. SPURGEON

makes them priests; giving them access to himself, and liberty to offer up spiritual sacrifices. What words can more fully declare that Christ is, and ought to be worshiped, equally with the Father, by all creatures, to all eternity! Happy those who shall adore and praise in heaven, and who shall for ever bless the Lamb, who delivered and set them apart for himself by his blood. How worthy art thou, O God, Father, Son, and Holy Ghost, of our highest praises! All creatures should proclaim thy greatness, and adore thy majesty.

REVELATION 6

The opening of the seals; The first, second, third, and fourth. (1-8)
The fifth. (9-11)
The sixth. (12-17)

1-8 Christ, the Lamb, opens the first seal: observe what appeared. A rider on a white horse. By the going forth of this white horse, a time of peace, or the early progress of the Christian religion, seems to be intended; its going forth in purity, at the time when its heavenly Founder sent his apostles to teach all nations, adding, Lo! I am with you alway, even to the end of the world. The Divine religion goes out crowned, having the Divine favor resting upon it, armed spiritually against its foes, and destined to be victorious in the end. On opening the second seal, a red horse appeared; this signifies desolating judgments. The sword of war and persecution is a dreadful judgment; it takes away peace from the earth, one of the greatest blessings; and men who should love one another, and help one another, are set upon killing one another. Such scenes also followed the pure age of early Christianity, when, neglectful of charity and the bond of peace, the Christian leaders, divided among themselves, appealed to the sword, and entangled themselves in guilt. On opening the third seal, a black horse appeared; a color denoting mourning and woe, darkness and ignorance. He that sat on it had a yoke in his hand. Attempts were made to put a yoke of superstitious observances on the disciples. As the stream of Christianity flowed further from its pure fountain, it became more and more corrupt. During the progress of this black horse, the necessaries of life should be at excessive prices, and the more costly things should not be hurt. According to prophetic language, these articles signified that food of religious knowledge, by which the souls of men are sustained unto everlasting life; such we are invited to buy, Isa 55:1. But when the dark clouds of ignorance and superstition, denoted by the black horse, spread

I. My first point will be THE STATE INTO WHICH CHURCHES ARE VERY APT TO FALL. A church may fall into a condition far other than that for which it has a repute. It may be famous for zeal and yet be lethargic. The address of our Lord begins, "I know thy works," as much as to say, "Nobody else knows you. Men think better of you than you deserve. You do not know yourselves, you think your works to be excellent; but I know them to be very different." Jesus views with searching eyes all the works of his church. The public can only read reports, but Jesus sees for himself. He knows what is done, and how it is done, and why it is done. He judges a church not merely by her external activities, but by her internal pieties; he searches the heart, and tries the reins of the children of men. He is not deceived by glitter; he tests all things, and values only that gold which will endure the fire. Our opinion of ourselves and Christ's opinion of us may be very different, and it is a very sad thing when it is so. It will be melancholy indeed if we stand out as a church notable for earnestness and distinguished for success, and yet are not really fervent in spirit, or eager in soul-winning. A lack of vital energy where there seems to be most strength put forth, a lack of real love to Jesus where apparently there is the greatest devotedness to him, are sad signs of fearful degeneracy. Churches are very apt to put the best goods into the window, very apt to make a fair show in the flesh, and like men of the world, they try to make a fine figure upon a very slender estate. Great reputations have often but slender foundations, and lovers of the truth lament that it should be so. Not only is it true of churches, but of every one of us as individuals, that often our reputation is in advance of our deserts. Men often live on their former credit, and trade upon their past characters, having still a name to live, though they are indeed dead. To be slandered is a dire affliction, but it is, upon the whole, a less evil than to be thought better than we are; in the one case we have a promise to comfort us, in the second we are in danger of self-conceit. I speak as unto wise men, judge ye how far this may apply to us.

The condition described in our text is, secondly, one of mournful indifference and carelessness. They were not cold, but they were not hot; they were not infidels, yet they were not earnest believers; they did not oppose the gospel, neither did they defend it; they were not working mischief, neither were they doing any great good; they were not disreputable in moral character, but they were not distinguished for holiness; they were not irreligious, but they were not enthusiastic in piety nor eminent for zeal: they were what the world calls "Moderates," they were of the Broad-church school, they were neither bigots nor Puritans, they were prudent and avoided fanaticism, respectable and averse to excitement. Good things were maintained among them, but they did not make too much of them; they had prayer-meetings,

nings, and an earthquake.

6 And the seven angels which had the seven trumpets prepared themselves to sound.

7 The first angel sounded, and there followed hail and fire mingled with blood, and they were cast upon the earth: and the third part of trees was burnt up, and all green grass was burnt up.

8 And the second angel sounded, and as it were a great mountain burning with fire was cast into the sea: and the third part of the sea became blood;

9 And the third part of the creatures which were in the sea, and had life, died; and the third part of the ships were destroyed.

10 And the third angel sounded, and there fell a great star from heaven, burning as it were a lamp, and it fell upon the third part of the rivers, and upon the fountains of waters;

11 And the name of the star is called Wormwood: and the third part of the waters became wormwood; and many men died of the waters, because they were made bitter.

12 And the fourth angel sounded, and the third part of the sun was smitten, and the third part of the moon, and the third part of the stars; so as the third part of them was darkened, and the day shone not for a third part of it, and the night likewise.

13 And I beheld, and heard an angel flying through the midst of heaven, saying with a loud voice, Woe, woe, woe, to the inhabiters of the earth by reason of the other voices of the trumpet of the three angels, which are yet to sound!

REVELATION 9

1 And the fifth angel sounded, and I saw a star fall from heaven unto the earth: and to him was given the key of the bottomless pit.

2 And he opened the bottomless pit; and there arose a smoke out of the pit, as the smoke of a great furnace; and the sun and the air were darkened by reason of the smoke of the pit.

their charge. To whom it was given to hurt the earth and the sea – First, and afterwards "the trees."

3. Hurt not the earth, till we – Other angels were joined in commission with him. Have sealed the servants of our God on their foreheads – Secured the servants of God of the twelve tribes from the impending calamities; whereby they shall be as clearly distinguished from the rest, as if they were visibly marked on their foreheads.

4. Of the children of Israel – To these will afterwards be joined a multitude out of all nations. But it may be observed, this is not the number of all the Israelites who are saved from Abraham or Moses to the end of all things; but only of those who were secured from the plagues which were then ready to fall on the earth. It seems as if this book had, in many places, a special view to the people of Israel.

5. Judah is mentioned first, in respect of the kingdom, and of the Messiah sprung therefrom.

7. After the Levitical ceremonies were abolished, Levi was again on a level with his brethren.

8. Of the tribe of Joseph – Or Ephraim; perhaps not mentioned by name, as having been, with Daniel, the most idolatrous of all the tribes. It is farther observable of Daniel, that it was very early reduced to a single family; which family itself seems to have been cut off in war, before the time of Ezra; for in the Chronicles, where the posterity of the patriarchs is recited, Daniel is wholly omitted.

9. A great multitude – Of those who had happily finished their course. Such multitudes are afterwards described, and still higher degrees of glory which they attain after a sharp fight and magnificent victory, chap. xiv, 1; xv, 2; xix, 1; xx, 4.

10. Salvation to our God – Who hath saved us from all evil into all the happiness of heaven. The salvation for which they praise God is described, verse 15; that for which they praise the Lamb, verse 14; and both, in the sixteenth and seventeenth verses.

11. And all the angels stood – In waiting. Round about the throne, and the elders and the four living creatures – That is, the living creatures, next the throne; the elders, round these; and the angels, round them both. And they fell on their faces – So do the elders, once only, chap. xi, 16. The heavenly ceremonial has its fixed order and measure.

12. Amen – With this word all the angels confirm the words of the "great multitude;" but they likewise carry the praise much higher. The blessing, and the glory, and the wisdom, and the thanksgiving, and the honor, and the power, and the strength, be unto our God for ever and ever – Before the Lamb began to open the seven seals, a sevenfold hymn of praise was brought him by many angels, chap. v, 12. Now he is upon opening the last seal, and the seven angels are going to receive seven trumpets, in order to make the kingdoms of the world subject to God. All the angels give sevenfold praise to God.

13. And one of the elders – What stands, verses 13-17, might have immediately followed the tenth verse; but that the praise of the angels, which was at the same time with that of the "great multitude," came in between. Answered – He answered St. John's desire to know, not any words that he spoke.

14. My Lord – Or, my master; a common term of respect. So Zechariah, likewise, bespeaks the angel, Zech. i, 9; iv, 4; vi, 4. Thou knowest – That is, I know not; but thou dost. These are they – Not martyrs; for these are not such a multitude as no man can number. But as all the angels appear here, so do all the souls of the righteous who had lived from the beginning of the world. Who come – He does not say, who did come; but, who come now also: to whom, likewise, pertain all who will come hereafter. Out of great affliction – Of various kinds, wisely and graciously allotted by God to all his children. And have washed their robes – From all guilt. And made them white – In all holiness. By the blood of the Lamb – Which not only cleanses, but adorns us also.

MATTHEW HENRY

CHARLES H. SPURGEON

over the Christian world, the knowledge and practice of true religion became scarce. When a people loathe their spiritual food, God may justly deprive them of their daily bread. The famine of bread is a terrible judgment; but the famine of the word is more so. Upon opening the fourth seal, another horse appeared, of a pale color. The rider was Death, the king of terrors. The attendants, or followers of this king of terrors, hell, a state of eternal misery to all who die in their sins; and in times of general destruction, multitudes go down unprepared into the pit. The period of the fourth seal is one of great slaughter and devastation, destroying whatever may tend to make life happy, making ravages on the spiritual lives of men. Thus the mystery of iniquity was completed, and its power extended both over the lives and consciences of men. The exact times of these four seals cannot be ascertained, for the changes were gradual. God gave them power, that is, those instruments of his anger, or those judgments: all public calamities are at his command; they only go forth when God sends them, and no further than he permits.

9-11 The sight the apostle beheld at the opening the fifth seal was very affecting. He saw the souls of the martyrs under the altar; at the foot of the altar in heaven, at the feet of Christ. Persecutors can only kill the body; after that there is no more they can do; the soul lives. God has provided a good place in the better world, for those who are faithful unto death. It is not their own death, but the sacrifice of Christ, that gives them entrance into heaven. The cause in which they suffered, was for the word of God; the best any man can lay down his life for; faith in God's word, and the unshaken confession of that faith. They commit their cause to him to whom vengeance belongs. The Lord is the comforter of his afflicted servants, and precious is their blood in his sight. As the measure of the sin of persecutors is filling up, so is the number of the persecuted, martyred servants of Christ. When this is fulfilled, God will send tribulation to those who trouble them, and unbroken happiness and rest to those that are troubled.

12-17 When the sixth seal was opened, there was a great earthquake. The foundations of churches and states would be terribly shaken. Such bold figurative descriptions of great changes abound in the prophecies of Scripture; for these events are emblems, and declare the end of the world and the day of judgment. Dread and terror would seize on all sorts of men. Neither grandeur, riches, valor, nor strength, can support men at that time. They would be glad to be no more seen; yea, to have no longer any

but there were few present, for they liked quiet evenings at home: when more attended the meetings they were still very dull, for they did their praying very deliberately and were afraid of being too excited. They were content to have all things done decently and in order, but vigor and zeal they considered to be vulgar. Such churches have schools, Bible-classes, preaching rooms, and all sorts of agencies; but they might as well be without them, for no energy is displayed and no good comes of them. They have deacons and elders who are excellent pillars of the church, if the chief quality of pillars be to stand still, and exhibit no motion or emotion. They have ministers who may be the angels of the churches, but if so, they have their wings closely clipped, for they do not fly very far in preaching the everlasting gospel, and they certainly are not flames of fire: they may be shining lights of eloquence, but they certainly are not burning lights of grace, setting men's hearts on fire. In such communities everything is done in a half-hearted, listless, dead-and-alive way, as if it did not matter much whether it was done or not. It makes one's flesh creep to see how sluggishly they move: I long for a knife to cut their red tape to pieces, and for a whip to lay about their shoulders to make them bestir themselves. Things are respectably done, the rich families are not offended, the skeptical party is conciliated, and the good people are not quite alienated: things are made pleasant all round. The right things are done, but as to doing them with all your might, and soul, and strength, a Laodicean church has no notion of what that means. They are not so cold as to abandon their work, or to give up their meetings for prayer, or to reject the gospel; if they did so, then they could be convinced of their error and brought to repentance; but on the other hand they are neither hot for the truth, nor hot for conversions, nor hot for holiness, they are not fiery enough to burn the stubble of sin, nor zealous enough to make Satan angry, nor fervent enough to make a living sacrifice of themselves upon the altar of their God. They are "neither cold nor hot."

This is a horrible state, because it is one which in a church wearing a good repute renders that reputation a lie. When other churches are saying, "See how they prosper! see what they do for God!" Jesus sees that the church is doing his work in a slovenly, make-believe manner, and he considers justly that it is deceiving its friends. If the world recognizes such a people as being very distinctly an old-fashioned puritanical church, and yet there is unholy living among them, and careless walking, and a deficiency of real piety, prayer, liberality, and zeal, then the world itself is being deceived, and that too in the worst way, because it is led to judge falsely concerning Christianity, for it lays all these faults upon the back of religion, and cries out, "It is all a farce! The thing is a mere pretense! Christians are all hypocrites!" I fear there are churches of this sort. God grant we

3 And there came out of the smoke locusts upon the earth: and unto them was given power, as the scorpions of the earth have power.

4 And it was commanded them that they should not hurt the grass of the earth, neither any green thing, neither any tree; but only those men which have not the seal of God in their foreheads.

5 And to them it was given that they should not kill them, but that they should be tormented five months: and their torment was as the torment of a scorpion, when he striketh a man.

6 And in those days shall men seek death, and shall not find it; and shall desire to die, and death shall flee from them.

7 And the shapes of the locusts were like unto horses prepared unto battle; and on their heads were as it were crowns like gold, and their faces were as the faces of men.

8 And they had hair as the hair of women, and their teeth were as the teeth of lions.

9 And they had breastplates, as it were breastplates of iron; and the sound of their wings was as the sound of chariots of many horses running to battle.

10 And they had tails like unto scorpions, and there were stings in their tails: and their power was to hurt men five months.

11 And they had a king over them, which is the angel of the bottomless pit, whose name in the Hebrew tongue is Abaddon, but in the Greek tongue hath his name Apollyon.

12 One woe is past; and, behold, there come two woes more hereafter.

13 And the sixth angel sounded, and I heard a voice from the four horns of the golden altar which is before God,

14 Saying to the sixth angel which had the trumpet, Loose the four angels which are bound in the great river Euphrates.

15 And the four angels were loosed, which were prepared for an hour, and a day, and a month, and a year, for to slay the third part of men.

15. Therefore – Because they came out of great affliction, and have washed their robes in his blood. Are they before the throne – It seems, even nearer than the angels. And serve him day and night – Speaking after the manner of men; that is, continually. In his temple – Which is in heaven. And he shall have his tent over them – Shall spread his glory over them as a covering.

16. Neither shall the sun light on them – For God is there their sun. Nor any painful heat, or inclemency of seasons.

17. For the Lamb will feed them – With eternal peace and joy; so that they shall hunger no more. And will lead them to living fountains of water – The comforts of the Holy Ghost; so that they shall thirst no more. Neither shall they suffer or grieve any more; for God "will wipe away all tears from their eyes."

REVELATION 8

1. And when he had opened the seventh seal, there was silence in heaven – Such a silence is mentioned but in this one place. It was uncommon, and highly observable: for praise is sounding in heaven day and night. In particular, immediately before this silence, all the angels, and before them the innumerable multitude, had been crying with a loud voice; and now all is still at once: there is an universal pause. Hereby the seventh seal is very remarkably distinguished from the six preceding. This silence before God shows that those who were round about him were expecting, with the deepest reverence, the great things which the Divine Majesty would farther open and order. Immediately after, the seven trumpets are heard, and a sound more august than ever. Silence is only a preparation: the grand point is, the sounding the trumpets to the praise of God. About half an hour – To St. John, in the vision, it might seem a common half hour.

2. And I saw – The seven trumpets belong to the seventh seal, as do the seven phials to the seventh trumpet. This should be carefully remembered, that we may not confound together the times which follow each other.

3. And – In the second verse, the "trumpets were given" to the seven angels; and in the sixth, they "prepared to sound." But between these, the incense of this angel and the prayers of the saints are mentioned; the interposing of which shows, that the prayers of the saints and the trumpets of the angels go together: and these prayers, with the effects of them, may well be supposed to extend through all the seven.

4. And the smoke of the incense came up before God, with the prayers of the saints – A token that both were accepted.

5. And there were thunderings, and lightnings, and voices, and an earthquake – These, especially when attended with fire, are emblems of God's dreadful judgments, which are immediately to follow.

6. And the seven angels prepared themselves to sound – That each, when it should come to his turn, might sound without delay. But while they do sound, they still stand before God.

7. And the first sounded – And every angel continued to sound, till all which his trumpet brought was fulfilled and till the next began. There are intervals between the three woes, but not between the four first trumpets.

8. And the second angel sounded, and as it were a great mountain burning with fire was cast into the sea – By the sea, particularly as it is here opposed to the earth, we may understand the west, or Europe; and chiefly the middle parts of it, the vast Roman empire.

9. And the third part of the creatures that were in the sea – That is, of all sorts of men, of every station and degree. Died – By those merciless invaders. And the third part of the ships were destroyed – It is a frequent thing to resemble a state or republic to a ship, wherein many people are embarked together, and share in the same dangers. And how many states were utterly destroyed by those inhuman conquerors!

being. Though Christ be a Lamb, he can be angry, and the wrath of the Lamb is exceedingly dreadful; for if the Redeemer himself, who appeases the wrath of God, be our enemy, where shall we find a friend to plead for us? As men have their day of opportunity, and their seasons of grace, so God has his day of righteous wrath. It seems that the overthrow of the paganism of the Roman empire is here meant. The idolaters are described as hiding themselves in their dens and secret caves, and vainly seeking to escape ruin. In such a day, when the signs of the times show those who believe in God's word, that the King of kings is approaching, Christians are called to a decided course, and to a bold confession of Christ and his truth before their fellowmen. Whatever they may have to endure, the short contempt of man is to be borne, rather than that shame which is everlasting.

REVELATION 7

A pause between two great periods. (1-3)
The peace, happiness, and safety of the saints, as signified by an angel's sealing 144,000. (4-8)
A song of praise. (9-12)
The blessedness and glory of those that suffered martyrdom for Christ. (13-17)

1-8 In the figurative language of Scripture, the blowing of the four winds together, means a dreadful and general destruction. But the destruction is delayed. Seals were used to mark for each person his own possessions. This mark is the witness of the Holy Ghost, printed in the hearts of believers. And the Lord would not suffer his people to be afflicted before they were marked, that they might be prepared against all conflicts. And, observe, of those who are thus sealed by the Spirit, the seal must be on the forehead, plainly to be seen alike by friends and foes, but not by the believer himself, except as he looks steadfastly in the glass of God's word. The number of those who were sealed, may be understood to stand for the remnant of people which God reserved. Though the church of God is but a little flock, in comparison with the wicked world, yet it is a society really large, and to be still more enlarged. Here the universal church is figured under the type of Israel.

9-12 The first fruits of Christ having led the way, the Gentiles converted later follow, and ascribe their salvation to God and the Redeemer, with triumph. In acts of religious worship we come nigh to God, and must come by Christ; the throne of God could not be approached by sinners, were it not for a Mediator. They were clothed with the robes of justification, holiness,

may not be numbered with them!

In this state of the church there is much self-glorification, for Laodicea said, "I am rich and increased with goods, and have need of nothing." The members say, "Everything goes on well, what more do we want? All is right with us." This makes such a condition very hopeless, because reproofs and rebukes fall without power, where the party rebuked can reply, "We do not deserve your censures, such warnings are not meant for us." If you stand up in the pulpit and talk to sleepy churches, as I pretty frequently do, and speak very plainly, they often have the honesty to say, "There is a good deal of truth in what the man has said:" but if I speak to another church, which really is half asleep, but which thinks itself to be quite a model of diligence, then the rebuke glides off like oil down a slab of marble, and no result comes of it. Men are less likely to repent when they are in the middle passage between hot and cold, than if they were in the worst extremes of sin. If they were like Saul of Tarsus, enemies of God, they might be converted; but if, like Gamaliel, they are neither opposed nor favoring, they will probably remain as they are till they die. The gospel converts a sincerely superstitious Luther, but Erasmus, with his pliant spirit, flippant, and full of levity, remains unmoved. There is more hope of warming the cold than the lukewarm.

When churches get into the condition of half-hearted faith, tolerating the gospel, but having a sweet tooth for error, they do far more mischief to their age than downright heretics.

It is harder a great deal to work for Jesus with a church which is lukewarm than it would be to begin without a church. Give me a dozen earnest spirits and put me down anywhere in London, and by God's good help we will soon cause the wilderness and the solitary place to rejoice; but give me the whole lot of you, half-hearted, undecided, and unconcerned, what can I do? You will only be a drag upon a man's zeal and earnestness. Five thousand members of a church all lukewarm will be five thousand impediments, but a dozen earnest, passionate spirits, determined that Christ shall be glorified and souls won, must be more than conquerors; in their very weakness and fewness will reside capacities for being the more largely blessed of God. Better nothing than lukewarmness.

Alas, this state of lukewarmness is so congenial with human nature that it is hard to fetch men from it. Cold makes us shiver, and great heat causes us pain, but a tepid bath is comfort itself. Such a temperature suits human nature. The world is always at peace with a lukewarm church, and such a church is always pleased with itself. Not too worldly,—no! We have our limits! There are certain amusements which of course a Christian must give up, but we will go quite up to the line, for why are we to be miserable? We are not to be so greedy as to be called miserly,

16 And the number of the army of the horsemen were two hundred thousand thousand: and I heard the number of them.

17 And thus I saw the horses in the vision, and them that sat on them, having breastplates of fire, and of jacinth, and brimstone: and the heads of the horses were as the heads of lions; and out of their mouths issued fire and smoke and brimstone.

18 By these three was the third part of men killed, by the fire, and by the smoke, and by the brimstone, which issued out of their mouths.

19 For their power is in their mouth, and in their tails: for their tails were like unto serpents, and had heads, and with them they do hurt.

20 And the rest of the men which were not killed by these plagues yet repented not of the works of their hands, that they should not worship devils, and idols of gold, and silver, and brass, and stone, and of wood: which neither can see, nor hear, nor walk:

21 Neither repented they of their murders, nor of their sorceries, nor of their fornication, nor of their thefts.

REVELATION 10

1 And I saw another mighty angel come down from heaven, clothed with a cloud: and a rainbow was upon his head, and his face was as it were the sun, and his feet as pillars of fire:

2 And he had in his hand a little book open: and he set his right foot upon the sea, and his left foot on the earth,

3 And cried with a loud voice, as when a lion roareth: and when he had cried, seven thunders uttered their voices.

4 And when the seven thunders had uttered their voices, I was about to write: and I heard a voice from heaven saying unto me, Seal up those things which the seven thunders uttered, and write them not.

5 And the angel which I saw stand upon the sea and upon the earth lifted up his hand to heaven,

10. And the third angel sounded, and there fell from heaven a great star, and it fell on the third part of the rivers – It seems Africa is meant by the rivers; (with which this burning part of the world abounds in an especial manner;) Egypt in particular, which the Nile overflows every year far and wide.

11. And the name of the star is called Wormwood – The unparalleled bitterness both of Arius himself and of his followers show the exact propriety of his title. And the third part of the waters became wormwood – A very considerable part of Africa was infected with the same bitter doctrine and Spirit. And many men (though not a third part of them) died – By the cruelty of the Arians.

12. And the fourth angel sounded, and the third part of the sun was smitten – Or struck. After the emperor Theodosius died, and the empire was divided into the eastern and the western, the barbarous nations poured in as a flood.

13. And I saw, and heard an angel flying – Between the trumpets of the fourth and fifth angel. In the midst of heaven – The three woes stretch themselves over the earth from Persia eastward, beyond Italy, westward; all which space had been filled with the gospel by the apostles.

REVELATION 9

1. And the fifth angel sounded, and I saw a star – Far different from that mentioned, chap. viii, 11. This star belongs to the invisible world. The third woe is occasioned by the dragon cast out of heaven; the second takes place at the loosing of the four angels who were bound in the Euphrates. The first is here brought by the angel of the abyss, which is opened by this star, or holy angel. Falling to the earth – Coming swiftly and with great force. And to him was given – when he was come. The key of the bottomless pit – A deep and hideous prison; but different from "the lake of fire."

2. And the sun and the air were darkened – A figurative expression, denoting heavy affliction. This smoke occasioned more and more such darkness over the Jews in Persia.

3. And out of the smoke – Not out of the bottomless pit, but from the smoke which issued thence. There went forth locusts – A known emblem of a numerous, hostile, hurtful people.

4. And it was commanded them – By the secret power of God. Not to hurt the grass, neither any green thing, nor any tree – Neither those of low, middling, or high degree, but only such of them as were not sealed – Principally the unbelieving Israelites. But many who were called Christians suffered with them.

5. Not to kill them – Very few of them were killed: in general, they were imprisoned and variously tormented.

6. The men – That is, the men who are so tormented.

7. And the appearances – This description suits a people neither thoroughly civilized, nor entirely savage; and such were the Persians of that age. Of the locusts are like horses – With their riders. The Persians excelled in horsemanship. And on their heads are as it were crowns – Turbans. And their faces are as the faces of men – Friendly and agreeable.

8. And they had hair as the hair of women – All the Persians of old gloried in long hair. And their teeth were as the teeth of lions – Breaking and tearing all things in pieces.

9. And the noise of their wings was as the noise of chariots of many horses – With their war-chariots, drawn by many horses, they, as it were, flew to and fro.

10. And they have tails like scorpions – That is, each tail is like a scorpion, not like the tail of a scorpion. To hurt the unsealed men five months – Five prophetic months; that is, seventy-nine common years. So long did these calamities last.

11. And they have over them a king – One by whom they are peculiarly directed and governed. His name is Abaddon – Both this and Apollyon signify a destroyer. By this he is distinguished from the dragon, whose proper name is Satan.

and victory; and they had palms in their hands, as conquerors used to appear in their triumphs. Such a glorious appearance will the faithful servants of God make at last, when they have fought the good fight of faith, and finished their course. With a loud voice they gave to God and the Lamb the praise of the great salvation. Those who enjoy eternal happiness must and will bless both the Father and the Son; they will do it publicly, and with fervor. We see what is the work of heaven, and we ought to begin it now, to have our hearts much in it, and to long for that world where our praises, as well as our happiness, will be made perfect.

13-17 Faithful Christians deserve our notice and respect; we should mark the upright. Those who would gain knowledge, must not be ashamed to seek instruction from any who can give it. The way to heaven is through many tribulations; but tribulation, how great soever, shall not separate us from the love of God. Tribulation makes heaven more welcome and more glorious. It is not the blood of the martyrs, but the blood of the Lamb, that can wash away sin, and make the soul pure and clean in the sight of God; other bloodstains, this is the only blood that makes the robes of the saints white and clean. They are happy in their employment; heaven is a state of service, though not of suffering; it is a state of rest, but not of sloth; it is a praising, delightful rest. They have had sorrows, and shed many tears on account of sin and affliction; but God himself, with his own gracious hand, will wipe those tears away. He deals with them as a tender father. This should support the Christian under all his troubles. As all the redeemed owe their happiness wholly to sovereign mercy; so the work and worship of God their Savior is their element; his presence and favor complete their happiness, nor can they conceive of any other joy. To him may all his people come; from him they receive every needed grace; and to him let them offer all praise and glory.

REVELATION 8

The seventh seal is opened and seven angels appear with seven trumpets, ready to proclaim the purposes of God. (1,2)

Another angel casts fire on the earth, which produces terrible storms of vengeance. (3-5)

The seven angels prepare to sound their trumpets. (6)

Four sound them. (7-12)

Another angel denounces greater woes to come. (13)

1-6 The seventh seal is opened. There was pro-

but we will give as little as we can to the cause. We will not be altogether absent from the house of God, but we will go as seldom as we can. We will not altogether forsake the poor people to whom we belong, but we will also go to the world's church, so as to get admission into better society, and find fashionable friends for our children. How much of this there is abroad! Compromise is the order of the day. Thousands try to hold with the hare and run with the hounds, they are for God and Mammon, Christ and Belial, truth and error, and so are "neither hot nor cold." Do I speak somewhat strongly? Not so strongly as my Master, for he says, "I will spew thee out of my mouth." He is nauseated with such conduct, it sickens him, and he will not endure it. In an earnest, honest, fervent heart nausea is created when we fall in with men who dare not give up their profession, and yet will not live up to it; who cannot altogether forsake the work of God, but yet do it in a sluggard's manner, trifling with that which ought to be done in the best style for so good a Lord and so gracious a Savior. Many a church has fallen into a condition of indifference, and when it does so it generally becomes the haunt of worldly professors, a refuge for people who want an easy religion, which enables them to enjoy the pleasures of sin and the honors of piety at the same time; where things are free and easy, where you are not expected to do much, or give much, or pray much, or to be very religious; where the minister is not so precise as the old school divines, a more liberal people, of broad views, free-thinking and free-acting, where there is full tolerance for sin, and no demand for vital godliness. Such churches applaud cleverness in a preacher; as for his doctrine, that is of small consequence, and his love to Christ and zeal for souls are very secondary. He is a clever fellow, and can speak well, and that suffices. This style of things is all too common, yet we are expected to hold our tongue, for the people are very respectable. The Lord grant that we may be kept clear of such respectability!

We have already said that this condition of indifference is attended with perfect self-complacency. The people who ought to be mourning are rejoicing, and where they should hang out signals of distress they are flaunting the banners of triumph. "We are rich, we are adding to our numbers, enlarging our schools, and growing on all sides; we have need of nothing. What can a church require that we have not in abundance?" Yet their spiritual needs are terrible. This is a sad state for a church to be in. Spiritually poor and proud. A church crying out to God because it feels itself in a backsliding state; a church mourning its deficiency, a church pining and panting to do more for Christ, a church burning with zeal for God, and therefore quite discontented with what it has been able to do; this is the church which God will bless: but that which writes itself down as a model for others, is very probably grossly mistaken and is in

6 And sware by him that liveth for ever and ever, who created heaven, and the things that therein are, and the earth, and the things that therein are, and the sea, and the things which are therein, that there should be time no longer:

7 But in the days of the voice of the seventh angel, when he shall begin to sound, the mystery of God should be finished, as he hath declared to his servants the prophets.

8 And the voice which I heard from heaven spake unto me again, and said, Go and take the little book which is open in the hand of the angel which standeth upon the sea and upon the earth.

9 And I went unto the angel, and said unto him, Give me the little book. And he said unto me, Take it, and eat it up; and it shall make thy belly bitter, but it shall be in thy mouth sweet as honey.

10 And I took the little book out of the angel's hand, and ate it up; and it was in my mouth sweet as honey: and as soon as I had eaten it, my belly was bitter.

11 And he said unto me, Thou must prophesy again before many peoples, and nations, and tongues, and kings.

REVELATION 11

1 And there was given me a reed like unto a rod: and the angel stood, saying, Rise, and measure the temple of God, and the altar, and them that worship therein.

2 But the court which is without the temple leave out, and measure it not; for it is given unto the Gentiles: and the holy city shall they tread under foot forty and two months.

3 And I will give power unto my two witnesses, and they shall prophesy a thousand two hundred and threescore days, clothed in sackcloth.

4 These are the two olive trees, and the two candlesticks standing before the God of the earth.

5 And if any man will hurt

12. One woe is past; behold, there come yet two woes after these things – The Persian power, under which was the first woe, was now broken by the Saracens: from this time the first pause made a wide way for the two succeeding woes.

13. And the sixth angel sounded – Under this angel goes forth the second woe. And I heard a voice from the four corners of the golden altar – This golden altar is the heavenly pattern of the Levitical altar of incense. This voice signified that the execution of the wrath of God, mentioned verses 20, 21, should, at no intercession, be delayed any longer.

14. Loose the four angels – To go every way; to the four quarters. These were evil angels, or they would not have been bound. Why, or how long, they were bound we know not.

15. And the four angels were loosed, who were prepared – By loosing them, as well as by their strength and rage. To kill the third part of men – That is, an immense number of them. For the hour, and day, and month, and year – All this agrees with the slaughter which the Saracens made for a long time after Mahomet's death.

16. And the number of the horsemen was two hundred millions – Not that so many were ever brought into the field at once, but (if we understand the expression literally) in the course of "the hour, and day, and month, and year." So neither were "the third part of men killed" at once, but during that course of years.

17. And thus I saw the horses and them that sat on them in the vision – St. John seems to add these words, in the vision, to intimate that we are not to take this description just according to the letter. Having breastplates of fire – Fiery red. And hyacinth – Dun blue. And brimstone – A faint yellow. Of the same color with the fire and smoke and brimstone, which go out of the mouths of their horses. And the heads of their horses are as the heads of lions – That is, fierce and terrible. And out of their mouth goeth fire and smoke and brimstone – This figurative expression may denote the consuming, blinding, all-piercing rage, fierceness, and force of these horsemen.

18. By these three – Which were inseparably joined. Were the third part of men – In the countries they over-ran. Killed – Omar alone, in eleven years and a half, took thirty-six thousand cities or forts. How many men must be killed therein!

19. For the power of these horses is in their mouths, and in their tails – Their riders fight retreating as well as advancing: so that their rear is as terrible as their front. For their tails are like serpents, having heads – Not like the tails of serpents only. They may be fitly compared to the amphisbena, a kind of serpent, which has a short tail, not unlike a head from which it throws out its poison as if it had two heads.

20. And the rest of the men who were not killed – Whom the Saracens did not destroy.

21. Neither repented of their murders, nor of their sorceries – Whoever reads the histories of the seventh, eighth, and ninth centuries, will find numberless instances of all these in every part of the Christian world. But though God cut off so many of these scandals to the Christian name, yet the rest went on in the same course. Some of them, however, might repent under the plagues which follow.

REVELATION 10

1. And I saw another mighty angel – Another from that "mighty angel," mentioned, chap. v, 2; yet he was a created angel; for he did not swear by himself, verse 6. Clothed with a cloud – In token of his high dignity. And a rainbow upon his head – A lovely token of the divine favor. And yet it is not too glorious for a creature: the woman, chap. xii, 1, is described more glorious still. And his face as the sun – Nor is this too much for a creature: for all the righteous "shall shine forth as the sun," Matt. xiii, 43. And his feet as pillars of fire – Bright as flame.

MATTHEW HENRY

CHARLES H. SPURGEON

found silence in heaven for a space; all was quiet in the church, for whenever the church on earth cries through oppression, that cry reaches up to heaven; or it is a silence of expectation. Trumpets were given to the angels, who were to sound them. The Lord Jesus is the High Priest of the church, having a golden censer, and much incense, fullness of merit in his own glorious person. Would that men studied to know the fullness that is in Christ, and endeavored to be acquainted with his excellency. Would that they were truly persuaded that Christ has such an office as that of Intercessor, which he now performs with deep sympathy. No prayer, thus recommended, was ever denied hearing and acceptance. These prayers, thus accepted in heaven, produced great changes upon earth. The Christian worship and religion, pure and heavenly in its origin and nature, when sent down to earth and conflicting with the passions and worldly projects of sinful men, produced remarkable tumults, here set forth in prophetical language, as our Lord himself declared, Lu 12:49.

7-13 The first angel sounded the first trumpet, and there followed hail and fire mingled with blood. A storm of heresies, a mixture of dreadful errors falling on the church, or a tempest of destruction. The second angel sounded, and a great mountain, burning with fire, was cast into the sea; and the third part of the sea became blood. By this mountain some understand leaders of the persecutions; others, Rome sacked by the Goths and Vandals, with great slaughter and cruelty. The third angel sounded, and there fell a star from heaven. Some take this to be an eminent governor; others take it to be some person in power who corrupted the churches of Christ. The doctrines of the gospel, the springs of spiritual life, comfort, and vigor, to the souls of men, are corrupted and made bitter by the mixture of dangerous errors, so that the souls of men find ruin where they sought refreshment. The fourth angel sounded, and darkness fell upon the great lights of heaven, that give light to the world, the sun, and the moon, and the stars. The guides and governors are placed higher than the people, and are to dispense light, and kind influences to them. Where the gospel comes to a people, and has not proper effects on their hearts and lives, it is followed with dreadful judgments. God gives alarm by the written word, by ministers, by men's own consciences, and by the signs of the times; so that if people are surprised, it is their own fault. The anger of God makes all comforts bitter, and even life itself burdensome. But God, in this world, sets bounds to the most terrible judgments. Corruption of doctrine and worship in the church are great judgments, and also are

a sad plight. This church, which was so rich in its own esteem, was utterly bankrupt in the sight of the Lord. It had no real joy in the Lord; it had mistaken its joy in itself for that. It had no real beauty of holiness upon it; it had mistaken its formal worship and fine building and harmonious singing for that. It had no deep understanding of the truth and no wealth of vital godliness, it had mistaken carnal wisdom and outward profession for those precious things. It was poor in secret prayer, which is the strength of any church; it was destitute of communion with Christ, which is the very life blood of religion; but it had the outward semblance of these blessings, and walked in a vain show. There are churches which are poor as Lazarus as to true religion, and yet are clothed in scarlet and fare sumptuously every day upon the mere form of godliness. Spiritual leanness exists side by side with vain-glory. Contentment as to worldly goods makes men rich, but contentment with our spiritual condition is the index of poverty.

Once more, this church of Laodicea had fallen into a condition which had chased away its Lord. The text tells us that Jesus said, "I stand at the door and knock." That is not the position which our Lord occupies in reference to a truly flourishing church. If we are walking aright with him, he is in the midst of the church, dwelling there, and revealing himself to his people. His presence makes our worship to be full of spirituality and life; he meets his servants at the table, and there spreads them a feast upon his body and his blood; it is he who puts power and energy into all our church-action, and causes the word to sound out from our midst. True saints abide in Jesus and he in them. Oh, brethren, when the Lord is in a church, it is a happy church, a holy church, a mighty church, and a triumphant church; but we may grieve him till he will say, "I will go and return to my place, until they acknowledge their offense and seek my face." Oh, you that know my Lord, and have power with him, entreat him not to go away from us. He can see much about us as a people which grieves his Holy Spirit, much about any one of us to provoke him to anger. Hold him, I pray you, and do not let him go, or if he be gone, bring him again to his mother's house, into the chamber of her that bare him, where, with holy violence, we will detain him and say, "Abide with us, for thou art life and joy, and all in all to us as a church. Ichabod is written across our house if thou be gone, for thy presence is our glory and thy absence will be our shame." Churches may become like the temple when the glory of the Lord had left the holy place, because the image of jealousy was set up and the house was defiled. What a solemn warning is that which is contained in Jeremiah 7:12-15, "But go ye now unto my place which was in Shiloh, where I set my name at the first, and see what I did to it for the wickedness of my people Israel. And now, because ye have done all these works, saith the Lord, and I spake unto you, ris-

them, fire proceedeth out of their mouth, and devoureth their enemies: and if any man will hurt them, he must in this manner be killed.

6 These have power to shut heaven, that it rain not in the days of their prophecy: and have power over waters to turn them to blood, and to smite the earth with all plagues, as often as they will.

7 And when they shall have finished their testimony, the beast that ascendeth out of the bottomless pit shall make war against them, and shall overcome them, and kill them.

8 And their dead bodies shall lie in the street of the great city, which spiritually is called Sodom and Egypt, where also our Lord was crucified.

9 And they of the people and kindreds and tongues and nations shall see their dead bodies three days and an half, and shall not suffer their dead bodies to be put in graves.

10 And they that dwell upon the earth shall rejoice over them, and make merry, and shall send gifts one to another; because these two prophets tormented them that dwelt on the earth.

11 And after three days and an half the Spirit of life from God entered into them, and they stood upon their feet; and great fear fell upon them which saw them.

12 And they heard a great voice from heaven saying unto them, Come up hither. And they ascended up to heaven in a cloud; and their enemies beheld them.

13 And the same hour was there a great earthquake, and the tenth part of the city fell, and in the earthquake were slain of men seven thousand: and the remnant were affrighted, and gave glory to the God of heaven.

14 The second woe is past; and, behold, the third woe cometh quickly.

15 And the seventh angel sounded; and there were great voices in heaven, saying, The kingdoms of this world are become the kingdoms of our

2. And he had in his hand – His left hand: he swore with his right.

3. And he cried – Uttering the words set down, verse 6. And while he cried, or was crying – At the same instant. Seven thunders uttered their voices – In distinct words, each after the other. Those who spoke these words were glorious, heavenly powers, whose voice was as the loudest thunder.

4. And I heard a voice from heaven – Doubtless from him who had at first commanded him to write, and who presently commands him to take the book; namely, Jesus Christ. Seal up those things which the seven thunders have uttered, and write them not – These are the only things of all which he heard that he is commanded to keep secret: so something peculiarly secret was revealed to the beloved John, besides all the secrets that are written in this book. At the same time we are prevented from inquiring what it was which these thunders uttered: suffice that we may know all the contents of the opened book, and of the oath of the angel.

5. And the angel – This manifestation of things to come under the trumpet of the seventh angel hath a twofold introduction: first, the angel speaks for God, verse 7; then Christ speaks for himself, chap. xi, 3. The angel appeals to the prophets of former times; Christ, to his own two witnesses.

6. And swear – The six preceding trumpets pass without any such solemnity. It is the trumpet of the seventh angel alone which is confirmed by so high an oath. By him that liveth for ever and ever – Before whom a thousand years are but a day.

7. But in the days of the voice of the seventh angel – Who sounded not only at the beginning of those days, but from the beginning to the end. The mystery of God shall be fulfilled – It is said, chap. xvii, 17, "The word of God shall be fulfilled." The word of God is fulfilled by the destruction of the beast; the mystery, by the removal of the dragon.

8. And – what follows from this verse to chap. xi, 13, runs parallel with the oath of the angel, and with "the fulfilling of the mystery of God," as it follows under the trumpet of the seventh angel; what is said, verse 11, concerning St. John's "prophesying again," is unfolded immediately after; what is said, verse 7, concerning "the fulfilling the mystery of God," is unfolded, chap. xi, 15-19 and in the following chapters.

9. Eat it up – The like was commanded to Ezekiel. This was an emblem of thoroughly considering and digesting it. And it will make thy belly bitter, but it will be sweet as honey in thy mouth – The sweetness betokens the many good things which follow, chap. xi, 1, 15, &c.; the bitterness, the evils which succeed under the third woe.

11. Thou must prophesy again – Of the mystery of God; of which the ancient prophets had prophesied before. And he did prophesy, by "measuring the temple," chap. xi, 1; as a prophecy may be delivered either by words or actions.

REVELATION 11

In this chapter is shown how it will fare with "the holy city," till the mystery of God is fulfilled; in the twelfth, what will befall the woman, who is delivered of the man-child; in the thirteenth, how it will be with the kingdom of Christ, while the "two beasts" are in the height of their power.

1. And there was given me – By Christ, as appears from the third verse. And he said, Arise – Probably he was sitting to write.

2. But the court which is without the temple – The old temple had a court in the open air, for the heathens who worshiped the God of Israel. Cast out – Of thy account. And measure it not – As not being holy. In so high a degree. And they shall tread – Inhabit. The holy city – Jerusalem, Matt. iv, 5. So they began to do, before St. John wrote. And it has been trodden almost ever since by the Romans, Persians, Saracens, and Turks. But that severe kind of treading which is

the usual causes and tokens of other judgments coming on a people. Before the other three trumpets were sounded, there was solemn warning how terrible the calamities would be that should follow. If lesser judgments do not take effect the church and the world must expect greater; and when God comes to punish the world, the inhabitants shall tremble before him. Let sinners take warning to flee from the wrath to come; let believers learn to value and to be thankful for their privileges; and let them patiently continue in well doing.

REVELATION 9

The fifth trumpet is followed by a representation of another star as falling from heaven and opening the bottomless pit, out of which come swarms of locusts. (1-12)

The sixth trumpet is followed by the loosing of four angels bound in the great river Euphrates. (13-21)

1-12 Upon sounding the fifth trumpet, a star fell from heaven to the earth. Having ceased to be a minister of Christ, he who is represented by this star becomes the minister of the devil; and lets loose the powers of hell against the churches of Christ. On the opening of the bottomless pit, there arose a great smoke. The devil carries on his designs by blinding the eyes of men, by putting out light and knowledge, and promoting ignorance and error. Out of this smoke there came a swarm of locusts, emblems of the devil's agents, who promote superstition, idolatry, error, and cruelty. The trees and the grass, the true believers, whether young or more advanced, should be untouched. But a secret poison and infection in the soul, should rob many others of purity, and afterwards of peace. The locusts had no power to hurt those who had the seal of God. God's all-powerful, distinguishing grace will keep his people from total and final apostasy. The power is limited to a short season; but it would be very sharp. In such events the faithful share the common calamity, but from the pestilence of error they might and would be safe. We collect from Scripture, that such errors were to try and prove the Christians, 1Co 11:19. And early writers plainly refer this to the first great host of corrupters who overspread the Christian church.

13-21 The sixth angel sounded, and here the power of the Turks seems the subject. Their time is limited. They not only slew in war, but brought a poisonous and ruinous religion. The antichristian generation repented not under these dreadful judgments. From this sixth trumpet learn that

ing up early and speaking, but ye heard not; and I called you, but ye answered not; therefore I will do unto this house, which is called by my name, wherein ye trust, and unto the place which I gave to you and to your fathers, as I have done to Shiloh. And I will cast you out of my sight, as I have cast out all your brethren, even the whole seed of Ephraim."

II. Now let us consider, secondly, THE DANGER OF SUCH A STATE. The great danger is, first, to be rejected of Christ. He puts it, "I will spew thee out of my mouth,"—as disgusting him, and causing him nausea. Then the church must first be in his mouth, or else it could not be spewed from it. What does this mean? Churches are in Christ's mouth in several ways, they are used by him as his testimony to the world; he speaks to the world through their lives and ministries. He does as good as say, "O sinners, if ye would see what my religion can do, see here a godly people banded together in my fear and love, walking in peace and holiness." He speaks powerfully by them, and makes the world see and know that there is a true power in the gospel of the grace of God. But when the church becomes neither cold nor hot he does not speak by her, she is no witness for him. When God is with a church the minister's words come out of Christ's mouth. "Out of his mouth went a two-edged sword," says John in the Revelation, and that "two-edged sword" is the gospel which we preach. When God is with a people they speak with divine power to the world, but if we grow lukewarm Christ says, "Their teachers shall not profit, for I have not sent them, neither am I with them. Their word shall be as water spilt on the ground, or as the whistling of the wind." This is a dreadful thing. Better far for me to die than to be spewed out of Christ's mouth.

Then he also ceases to plead for such a church. Christ's special intercession is not for all men, for he says of his people, "I pray for them: I pray not for the world, but for them which thou hast given me." I do not think Christ ever prays for the church of Rome— what would he pray for, but her total overthrow? Other churches are nearing the same fate; they are not clear in his truth or honest in obedience to his word: they follow their own devices, they are lukewarm. But there are churches for which he is pleading, for he has said, "For Zion's sake will I not hold my peace, and for Jerusalem's sake I will not rest, until the righteousness thereof go forth as brightness, and the salvation thereof as a lamp that burneth." Mighty are his pleadings for those he really loves, and countless are the blessings which come in consequence. It will be an evil day when he casts a church out of that interceding mouth, and leaves her unrepresented before the throne because she is none of his. Do you not tremble at such a prospect? Will you not ask for grace to return to your first love? I know that the Lord Jesus will never leave off pray-

Lord, and of his Christ; and he shall reign for ever and ever.

16 And the four and twenty elders, which sat before God on their seats, fell upon their faces, and worshiped God,

17 Saying, We give thee thanks, O Lord God Almighty, which art, and wast, and art to come; because thou hast taken to thee thy great power, and hast reigned.

18 And the nations were angry, and thy wrath is come, and the time of the dead, that they should be judged, and that thou shouldest give reward unto thy servants the prophets, and to the saints, and them that fear thy name, small and great; and shouldest destroy them which destroy the earth.

19 And the temple of God was opened in heaven, and there was seen in his temple the ark of his testament: and there were lightnings, and voices, and thunderings, and an earthquake, and great hail.

REVELATION 12

1 And there appeared a great wonder in heaven; a woman clothed with the sun, and the moon under her feet, and upon her head a crown of twelve stars:

2 And she being with child cried, travailing in birth, and pained to be delivered.

3 And there appeared another wonder in heaven; and behold a great red dragon, having seven heads and ten horns, and seven crowns upon his heads.

4 And his tail drew the third part of the stars of heaven, and did cast them to the earth: and the dragon stood before the woman which was ready to be delivered, for to devour her child as soon as it was born.

5 And she brought forth a man child, who was to rule all nations with a rod of iron: and her child was caught up unto God, and to his throne.

6 And the woman fled into the wilderness, where she hath a place prepared of God, that they should feed her there a thousand two hundred and

here peculiarly spoken of, will not be till under the trumpet of the seventh angel, and toward the end of the troublous times. This will continue but forty-two common months, or twelve hundred and sixty common days; being but a small part of the non-chronos.

3. And I – Christ. Will give to my two witnesses – These seem to be two prophets; two select, eminent instruments.

4. These are the two olive trees – That is, as Zerubbabel and Joshua, the two olive trees spoken of by Zechariah, Zech. iii, 9, iv, 10, were then the two chosen instruments in God's hand, even so shall these be in their season. Being themselves full of the unction of the Holy One, they shall continually transmit the same to others also. And the two candlesticks – Burning and shining lights. Standing before the Lord of the earth – Always waiting on God, without the help of man, and asserting his right over the earth and all things therein.

5. If any would kill them – As the Israelites would have done Moses and Aaron, Num. xvi, 41. He must be killed thus – By that devouring fire.

6. These have power – And they use that power. See verse 10. To shut heaven, that it rain not in the days of their prophesying – During those "twelve hundred and sixty days." And have power over the waters – In and near Jerusalem. To turn them into blood – As Moses did those in Egypt. And to smite the earth with all plagues, as often as they will – This is not said of Moses or Elijah, or any mere man besides. And how is it possible to understand this otherwise than of two individual persons?

7. And when they shall have finished their testimony – Till then they are invincible. The wild beast – Hereafter to be described. That ascendeth – First out of the sea, chap. xiii, 1, and then out of the bottomless pit, chap. xvii, 8. Shall make war with them – It is at his last ascent, not out of the sea, but the bottomless pit, that the beast makes war upon the two witnesses. And even hereby is fixed the time of "treading the holy city," and of the "two witnesses." That time ends after the ascent of the beast out of the abyss, and yet before the fulfiling of the mystery. And shall conquer them – The fire no longer proceeding out of their mouth when they have finished their work. And kill them – These will be among the last martyrs, though not the last of all.

8. And their bodies shall be – Perhaps hanging on a cross. In the street of the great city – Of Jerusalem, a far greater city, than any other in those parts. This is described both spiritually and historically: spiritually, as it is called Sodom Isaiah i, and Egypt; on account of the same abominations abounding there, at the time of the witnesses, as did once in Egypt and Sodom. Historically: Where also their Lord was crucified – This possibly refers to the very ground where his cross stood. Constantine the Great enclosed this within the walls of the city. Perhaps on that very spot will their bodies be exposed.

9. Three days and a half – So exactly are the times set down in this prophecy. If we suppose this time began in the evening, and ended in the morning, and included (which is no way impossible) Friday, Saturday, and Sunday, the weekly festival of the Turkish people, the Jewish tribes, and the Christian tongues; then all these together, with the heathen nations, would have full leisure to gaze upon and rejoice over them.

10. And they that dwell upon the earth – Perhaps this expression may peculiarly denote earthly-minded men. Shall make merry – As did the Philistines over Samson. And send gifts to one another – Both Turks, and Jews, and heathens, and false Christians.

11. And great fear fell upon them that saw them – And now knew that God was on their side.

12. And I heard a great voice – Designed for all to hear. And they went up to heaven, and their enemies beheld them – who had not taken notice of their rising again; by which some had been convinced before.

13. And there was a great earthquake and the tenth part of the city fell – We have

God can make one enemy of the church a scourge and a plague to another. The idolatry in the remains of the eastern church and elsewhere, and the sins of professed Christians, render this prophecy and its fulfillment more wonderful. And the attentive reader of Scripture and history, may find his faith and hope strengthened by events, which in other respects fill his heart with anguish and his eyes with tears, while he sees that men who escape these plagues, repent not of their evil works, but go on with idolatries, wickedness, and cruelty, till wrath comes upon them to the utmost.

REVELATION 10

The Angel of the covenant presents a little open
*   book, which is followed with seven thunders.*
*   (1-4)*
At the end of the following prophecies, time
*   should be no more. (5-7)*
A voice directs the apostle to eat the book. (8-10)
And tells him he must prophesy further. (11)

1-7 The apostle saw another representation. The person communicating this discovery probably was our Lord and Savior Jesus Christ, or it was to show his glory. He veils his glory, which is too great for mortal eyes to behold; and throws a veil upon his dispensations. A rainbow was upon his head; our Lord is always mindful of his covenant. His awful voice was echoed by seven thunders; solemn and terrible ways of discovering the mind of God. We know not the subjects of the seven thunders, nor the reasons for suppressing them. There are great events in history, perhaps relating to the Christian church, which are not noticed in open prophecy. The final salvation of the righteous, and the final success of true religion on earth, are engaged for by the unfailing word of the Lord. Though the time may not be yet, it cannot be far distant. Very soon, as to us, time will be no more; but if we are believers, a happy eternity will follow: we shall from heaven behold and rejoice in the triumphs of Christ, and his cause on earth.

8-11 Most men feel pleasure in looking into future events, and all good men like to receive a word from God. But when this book of prophecy was thoroughly digested by the apostle, the contents would be bitter; there were things so awful and terrible, such grievous persecutions of the people of God, such desolations in the earth, that the foresight and foreknowledge of them would be painful to his mind. Let us seek to be taught by Christ, and to obey his orders; daily meditating on his word, that it may nourish our souls; and then declaring it according to our several

ing for his own elect, but for churches as corporate bodies he may cease to pray, because they become anti-Christian, or are mere human gatherings, but not elect assemblies, such as the church of God ought to be. Now this is the danger of any church if it declines from its first ardor and becomes lukewarm. "Remember therefore from whence thou art fallen, and repent, and do thy first works; or else I will come unto thee quickly, and will remove thy candlestick out of his place, except thou repent."

What is the other danger? This first comprehends all, but another evil is hinted at,—such a church will be left to its fallen condition, to become wretched,— that is to say, miserable, unhappy, divided, without the presence of God, and so without delight in the ways of God, lifeless, spiritless, dreary, desolate, full of schisms, devoid of grace, and I know not what beside, that may come under the term "wretched." Then the next word is "miserable," which might better be rendered "pitiable." Churches which once were a glory shall become a shame. Whereas men said, "The Lord has done great things for them," they shall now say, "see how low they have fallen! What a change has come over the place! What emptiness and wretchedness! What a blessing rested there for so many years, but what a contrast now!" Pity will take the place of congratulation, and scorn will follow upon admiration. Then it will be "poor" in membership, poor in effort, poor in prayer, poor in gifts and graces, poor in everything. Perhaps some rich people will be left to keep up the semblance of prosperity, but all will be empty, vain, void, Christless, lifeless. Philosophy will fill the pulpit with chaff, the church will be a mass of worldliness, the congregation an assembly of vanity. Next, they will become blind, they will not see themselves as they are, they will have no eye upon the neighborhood to do it good, no eye to the coming of Christ, no eye for his glory. They will say, "We see," and yet be blind as bats. Ultimately they will become "naked," their shame will be seen by all, they will be a proverb in everybody's mouth. "Call that a church!" says one. "Is that a church of Jesus Christ?" cries a second. Those dogs that dared not open their mouths against Israel when the Lord was there will begin to howl when he is gone, and everywhere will the sound be heard, "How are the mighty fallen, how are the weapons of war broken."

In such a case as that the church will fail of overcoming, for it is "to him that overcometh" that a seat upon Christ's throne is promised; but that church will come short of victory. It shall be written concerning it even as of the children of Ephraim, that being armed and carrying bows they turned their backs in the day of battle. "Ye did run well," says Paul to the Galatians, "what did hinder you that ye should not obey the truth?" Such a church had a grand opportunity, but it was not equal to the occasion, its members were born for a great work, but

threescore days.

7 And there was war in heaven: Michael and his angels fought against the dragon; and the dragon fought and his angels,

8 And prevailed not; neither was their place found any more in heaven.

9 And the great dragon was cast out, that old serpent, called the Devil, and Satan, which deceiveth the whole world: he was cast out into the earth, and his angels were cast out with him.

10 And I heard a loud voice saying in heaven, Now is come salvation, and strength, and the kingdom of our God, and the power of his Christ: for the accuser of our brethren is cast down, which accused them before our God day and night.

11 And they overcame him by the blood of the Lamb, and by the word of their testimony; and they loved not their lives unto the death.

12 Therefore rejoice, ye heavens, and ye that dwell in them. Woe to the inhabiters of the earth and of the sea! for the devil is come down unto you, having great wrath, because he knoweth that he hath but a short time.

13 And when the dragon saw that he was cast unto the earth, he persecuted the woman which brought forth the man child.

14 And to the woman were given two wings of a great eagle, that she might fly into the wilderness, into her place, where she is nourished for a time, and times, and half a time, from the face of the serpent.

15 And the serpent cast out of his mouth water as a flood after the woman, that he might cause her to be carried away of the flood.

16 And the earth helped the woman, and the earth opened her mouth, and swallowed up the flood which the dragon cast out of his mouth.

17 And the dragon was wroth with the woman, and went to make war with the remnant of her seed, which keep the com-

---

here an unanswerable proof that this city is not Babylon or Rome, but Jerusalem. For Babylon shall be wholly burned before the fulfilling of the mystery of God. But this city is not burned at all.

14. The second woe is past – The butchery made by the Saracens ceased about the year 847, when their power was so broken by Charles the Great that they never recovered it.

15. And the seventh angel sounded – This trumpet contains the most important and joyful events, and renders all the former trumpets matter of joy to all the inhabitants of heaven. The allusion therefore in this and all the trumpets is to those used in festal solemnities. All these seven trumpets were heard in heaven: perhaps the seventh shall once be heard on earth also, 1 Thess. iv, 16. And there were great voices – From the several citizens of heaven. At the opening of the seventh seal "there was silence in heaven;" at the sounding of the seventh trumpet, great voices. This alone is sufficient to show that the seven seals and seven trumpets do not run parallel to each other.

16. And the four and twenty elders – These shall reign over the earth, chap. v, 10. Who sit before God on their thrones – which we do not read of any angel.

17. The Almighty – He who hath all things in his power as the only Governor of them. Who is, and who was – God is frequently styled, "He who is, and who was, and who is to come" but now he is actually come, the words, "who is to come," are, as it were, swallowed up.

18. And the heathen nations were wroth – At the breaking out of the power and kingdom of God. This wrath of the heathens now rises to the highest pitch; but it meets the wrath of the Almighty, and melts away. In this verse is described both the going forth and the end of God's wrath, which together take up several ages.

19. And the temple of God – The inmost part of it. Was opened in heaven – And hereby is opened a new scene of the most momentous things, that we may see how the contents of the seventh trumpet are executed; and, notwithstanding the greatest opposition, (particularly by the third woe,) brought to a glorious conclusion.

REVELATION 12

1. And a great sign was seen in heaven – Not only by St. John, but many heavenly spectators represented in the vision. A sign means something that has an uncommon appearance, and from which we infer that some unusual thing will follow. A woman – The emblem of the church of Christ, as she is originally of Israel, though built and enlarged on all sides by the addition of heathen converts; and as she will hereafter appear, when all her "natural branches are again "grafted in." She is at present on earth; and yet, with regard to her union with Christ, may be said to be in heaven, Eph. ii, 6. Accordingly, she is described as both assaulted and defended in heaven, verses 4, 7.

2. And being with child she crieth, travailing in birth – The very pain, without any outward opposition, would constrain a woman in travail to cry out. These cries, throes, and pains to be delivered, were the painful longings, the sighs, and prayers of the saints for the coming of the kingdom of God. The woman groaned and travailed in spirit, that Christ might appear, as the Shepherd and King of all nations.

3. And behold a great red dragon – His fiery-red color denoting his disposition. Having seven heads – Implying vast wisdom. And ten horns – Perhaps on the seventh head; emblems of mighty power and strength, which he still retained. And seven diadems on his heads – Not properly crowns, but costly bindings, such as kings anciently wore; for, though fallen, he was a great potentate still, even "the prince of this world."

4. And his tail – His falsehood and subtlety. Draweth – As a train. The third part – A very large number. Of the stars of heaven – The Christians and their teach-

stations. The sweetness of such contemplations will often be mingled with bitterness, while we compare the Scriptures with the state of the world and the church, or even with that of our own hearts.

REVELATION 11

The state of the church is represented under the figure of a temple measured. (1,2)

Two witnesses prophesy in sackcloth. (3-6)

They are slain, after which they arise and ascend to heaven. (7-13)

Under the seventh trumpet, all antichristian powers are to be destroyed and there will be a glorious state of Christ's kingdom upon earth. (14-19)

1,2 This prophetical passage about measuring the temple seems to refer to Ezekiel's vision. The design of this measuring seems to be the preservation of the church in times of public danger; or for its trial, or for its reformation. The worshipers must be measured; whether they make God's glory their end, and his word their rule, in all their acts of worship. Those in the outer court, worship in a false manner, or with dissembling hearts, and will be found among his enemies. God will have a temple and an altar in the world, till the end of time. He looks strictly to his temple. The holy city, the visible church, is trodden under foot; is filled with idolaters, infidels, and hypocrites. But the desolations of the church are limited, and she shall be delivered out of all her troubles.

3-13 In the time of treading down, God kept his faithful witnesses to attest the truth of his word and worship, and the excellence of his ways, The number of these witnesses is small, yet enough. They prophesy in sackcloth. It shows their afflicted, persecuted state, and deep sorrow for the abominations against which they protested. They are supported during their great and hard work, till it is done. When they had prophesied in sackcloth the greatest part of 1260 years, antichrist, the great instrument of the devil, would war against them, with force and violence for a time. Determined rebels against the light rejoice, as on some happy event, when they can silence, drive to a distance, or destroy the faithful servants of Christ, whose doctrine and conduct torment them. It does not appear that the term is yet expired, and the witnesses are not at present exposed to endure such terrible outward sufferings as in former times; but such things may again happen, and there is abundant cause to prophesy in sackcloth, on account of the state of religion. The depressed state of real Christianity may

inasmuch as they were unfaithful, God put them aside and used other means. He raised up in their midst a flaming testimony for the gospel, and the light thereof was cast athwart the ocean, and gladdened the nations, but the people were not worthy of it, or true to it, and therefore he took the candlestick out of its place, and left them in darkness. May God prevent such an evil from coming upon us: but such is the danger to all churches if they degenerate into listless indifference.

III. Thirdly, I have to speak of THE REMEDIES WHICH THE LORD EMPLOYS. I do earnestly pray that what I say may come home to all here, especially to every one of the members of this church, for it has come very much home to me, and caused great searching of heart in my own soul, and yet I do not think I am the least zealous among you. I beseech you to judge yourselves, that you be not judged. Do not ask me if I mean anything personal. I am personal in the most emphatic sense. I speak of you and to you in the plainest way. Some of you show plain symptoms of being lukewarm, and God forbid that I should flatter you, or be unfaithful to you. I am aiming at personality, and I earnestly want each beloved brother and sister here to take home each affectionate rebuke. And you who come from other churches, whether in America or elsewhere, you want arousing quite as much as we do, your churches are not better than ours, some of them are not so good, and I speak to you also, for you need to be stirred up to nobler things.

Note, then, the first remedy. Jesus gives a clear discovery as to the church's true state. He says to it— "Thou art lukewarm, thou art wretched and miserable, and poor, and blind, and naked." I rejoice to see people willing to know the truth, but most men do not wish to know it, and this is an ill sign. When a man tells you that he has not looked at his ledger, or day-book, or held a stock-taking for this twelvemonths, you know whereabouts he is, and you say to your manager, "Have you an account with him? Then keep it as close as you can." When a man dares not know the worst about his case, it is certainly a bad one, but he that is right before God is thankful to be told what he is and where he is. Now, some of you know the faults of other people, and in watching this church you have observed weak points in many places,—have you wept over them? Have you prayed over them? If not, you have not watched as you should do for the good of your brethren and sisters, and, perhaps, have allowed evils to grow which ought to have been rooted up: you have been silent when you should have kindly and earnestly spoken to the offenders, or made your own example a warning to them. Do not judge your brother, but judge yourself: if you have any severity, use it on your own conduct and heart. We must pray the Lord to use this remedy, and make us know just where we are. We

mandments of God, and have the testimony of Jesus Christ.

REVELATION 13

1 And I stood upon the sand of the sea, and saw a beast rise up out of the sea, having seven heads and ten horns, and upon his horns ten crowns, and upon his heads the name of blasphemy.

2 And the beast which I saw was like unto a leopard, and his feet were as the feet of a bear, and his mouth as the mouth of a lion: and the dragon gave him his power, and his seat, and great authority.

3 And I saw one of his heads as it were wounded to death; and his deadly wound was healed: and all the world wondered after the beast.

4 And they worshiped the dragon which gave power unto the beast: and they worshiped the beast, saying, Who is like unto the beast? who is able to make war with him?

5 And there was given unto him a mouth speaking great things and blasphemies; and power was given unto him to continue forty and two months.

6 And he opened his mouth in blasphemy against God, to blaspheme his name, and his tabernacle, and them that dwell in heaven.

7 And it was given unto him to make war with the saints, and to overcome them: and power was given him over all kindreds, and tongues, and nations.

8 And all that dwell upon the earth shall worship him, whose names are not written in the book of life of the Lamb slain from the foundation of the world.

9 If any man have an ear, let him hear.

10 He that leadeth into captivity shall go into captivity: he that killeth with the sword must be killed with the sword. Here is the patience and the faith of the saints.

11 And I beheld another beast coming up out of the earth; and he had two horns like a lamb, and he spake as a dragon.

ers, who before sat in heavenly places with Christ Jesus. And casteth them to the earth – Utterly deprives them of all those heavenly blessings.

5. And she brought forth a man child – Even Christ, considered not in his person, but in his kingdom. In the ninth age, many nations with their princes were added to the Christian church. Who was to rule all nations – When his time is come. And her child – Which was already in heaven, as were the woman and the dragon. Was caught up to God – Taken utterly out of his reach.

6. And the woman fled into the wilderness – This wilderness is undoubtedly on earth, where the woman also herself is now supposed to be. It betokens that part of the earth where, after having brought forth, she found a new abode. And this must be in Europe; as Asia and Africa were wholly in the hands of the Turks and Saracens; and in a part of it where the woman had not been before. In this wilderness, God had already prepared a place; that is, made it safe and convenient for her.

7. And there was war in heaven – Here Satan makes his grand opposition to the kingdom of God; but an end is now put to his accusing the saints before God. The cause goes against him, verses 10, 11, and Michael executes the sentence. That Michael is a created angel, appears from his not daring, in disputing with Satan, Jude 9, to bring a railing accusation; but only saying, "The Lord rebuke thee." And this modesty is implied in his very name; for Michael signifies, "Who is like God?" which implies also his deep reverence toward God, and distance from all self-exaltation. Satan would be like God: the very name of Michael asks, "Who is like God?" Not Satan; not the highest archangel. It is he likewise that is afterward employed to seize, bind, and imprison that proud spirit.

8. And he prevailed not – The dragon himself is principally mentioned; but his angels, likewise, are to be understood. Neither was this place found any more in heaven – So till now he had a place in heaven. How deep a mystery is this! One may compare this with Luke x, 18; Eph. ii, 2; iv, 8; vi, 12.

9. And the great dragon was cast out – It is not yet said, unto the earth – He was cast out of heaven; and at this the inhabitants of heaven rejoice. He is termed the great dragon, as appearing here in that shape, to intimate his poisonous and cruel disposition. The ancient serpent – In allusion to his deceiving Eve in that form. Dragons are a kind of large serpent. Who is called the Devil and Satan – These are words of exactly the same meaning; only the former is Greek; the latter, Hebrew; denoting the grand adversary of all the saints, whether Jews or Gentiles.

10. Now is come – Hence it is evident that all this chapter belongs to the trumpet of the seventh angel. In the eleventh chapter, from the fifteenth to the eighteenth verse, are proposed the contents of this extensive trumpet; the execution of which is copiously described in this and the following chapters. The salvation – Of the saints. The might – Whereby the enemy is cast out. The kingdom – Here the majesty of God is shown. And the power of his Christ – Which he will exert against the beast; and when he also is taken away, then will the kingdom be ascribed to Christ himself, chap. xix, 16; xx, 4. The accuser of our brethren – So long as they remained on earth. This great voice, therefore, was the voice of men only. Who accused them before our God day and night – Amazing malice of Satan, and patience of God!

11. And they have overcome him – Carried the cause against him. By the blood of the Lamb – Which cleanses the soul from all sin, and so leaves no room for accusing. And by the word of their testimony – The word of God, which they believed and testified, even unto death.

12. Woe to the earth and the sea – This is the fourth and last denunciation of the third woe, the most grievous of all. The first was only, the second chiefly, on the earth, Asia; the third, both on the earth and the sea, Europe.

13. And when the dragon saw – That he could no longer accuse the saints in heaven, he turned his wrath to do all possible mischief on earth. He persecuted the woman – The ancient persecutions of the church were mentioned, chap. i,

MATTHEW HENRY

CHARLES H. SPURGEON

relate only to the western church. The Spirit of life from God, quickens dead souls, and shall quicken the dead bodies of his people, and his dying interest in the world. The revival of God's work and witnesses, will strike terror into the souls of his enemies. Where there is guilt, there is fear; and a persecuting spirit, though cruel, is a cowardly spirit. It will be no small part of the punishment of persecutors, both in this world, and at the great day, that they see the faithful servants of God honored and advanced. The Lord's witnesses must not be weary of suffering and service, nor hastily grasp at the reward; but must stay till their Master calls them. The consequence of their being thus exalted was a mighty shock and convulsion in the antichristian empire. Events alone can show the meaning of this. But whenever God's work and witnesses revive, the devil's work and witnesses fall before him. And that the slaying of the witnesses is future, appears to be probable.

14-19 Before the sounding of the seventh and last trumpet, there is the usual demand of attention. The saints and angels in heaven know the right of our God and Savior to rule over all the world. But the nations met God's wrath with their own anger. It was a time in which he was beginning to reward his people's faithful services, and sufferings; and their enemies fretted against God, and so increased their guilt, and hastened their destruction. By the opening the temple of God in heaven, may be meant, that there was a more free communication between heaven and earth; prayer and praises more freely and frequently going up, graces and blessings plentifully coming down. But it rather seems to refer to the church of God on earth. In the reign of antichrist, God's law was laid aside, and made void by traditions and decrees; the Scriptures were locked up from the people, but now they are brought to the view of all. This, like the ark, is a token of the presence of God returned to his people, and his favor toward them in Jesus Christ, as the Propitiation for their sins. The great blessing of the Reformation was attended with very awful providences; as by terrible things in righteousness God answered the prayers presented in his holy temple now opened.

REVELATION 12

A description of the church of Christ and of Satan, under the figures of a woman and of a great red dragon. (1-6)

Michael and his angels fight against the devil and his angels, who are defeated. (7-12)

The dragon persecutes the church. (13,14)

His vain endeavors to destroy her, He renews his war against her seed. (14-17)

shall never get right as long as we are confident that we are so already. Self-complacency is the death of repentance.

Our Lord's next remedy is gracious counsel. He says, "I counsel thee to buy of me gold tried in the fire." Does not that strike you as being very like the passage in Isaiah, "Come ye, buy, and eat; yea, come, buy wine and milk without money and without price"? It is so, and it teaches us that one remedy for lukewarmness is to begin again just as we began at first. We were at a high temperature at our first conversion. What joy, what peace, what delight, what comfort, what enthusiasm we had when first we knew the Lord! We bought gold of him then for nothing, let us go and buy again at the same price.

If religion has not been genuine with us till now, or if we have been adding to it great lumps of shining stuff which we thought was gold and was not, let us now go to the heavenly mint and buy gold tried in the fire, that we may be really rich. Come, let us begin again, each one of us. Inasmuch as we may have thought we were clothed and yet we were naked, let us hasten to him again, and at his own price, which is no price, procure the robe which he has wrought of his own righteousness, and that goodly raiment of his Spirit, which will clothe us with the beauty of the Lord. If, moreover, we have come to be rather dim in the eye, and no longer look up to God and see his face, and have no bright vision of the glory to be revealed, and cannot look on sinners with weeping eyes, as we once did, let us go to Jesus for the eye-salve, just as we went when we were stone blind at first, and the Lord will open our eyes again, and we shall behold him in clear vision as in days gone by. The word from Jesus is, "Come near to me, I pray you, my brethren. If you have wandered from me, return; if you have been cold to me I am not cold to you, my heart is the same to you as ever, come back to me, my brethren. Confess your evil deeds, receive my forgiveness, and henceforth let your hearts burn towards me, for I love you still and will supply all your needs." That is good counsel, let us take it.

Now comes a third remedy, sharp and cutting, but sent in love, namely, rebukes and chastenings. Christ will have his favored church walk with great care, and if she will not follow him fully by being shown wherein she has erred, and will not repent when kindly counseled, he then betakes himself to some sharper means. "As many as I love I rebuke and chasten." The word here used for "love" is a very choice one; it is one which signifies an intense personal affection. Now, there are some churches which Christ loves very specially, favoring them above others, doing more for them than for others, and giving them more prosperity; they are the darlings of his heart, his Benjamins. Now, it is a very solemn thing to be dearly loved by God. It is a privilege to be coveted, but mark you, the man who is so honored occu-

12 And he exerciseth all the power of the first beast before him, and causeth the earth and them which dwell therein to worship the first beast, whose deadly wound was healed.

13 And he doeth great wonders, so that he maketh fire come down from heaven on the earth in the sight of men,

14 And deceiveth them that dwell on the earth by the means of those miracles which he had power to do in the sight of the beast; saying to them that dwell on the earth, that they should make an image to the beast, which had the wound by a sword, and did live.

15 And he had power to give life unto the image of the beast, that the image of the beast should both speak, and cause that as many as would not worship the image of the beast should be killed.

16 And he causeth all, both small and great, rich and poor, free and bond, to receive a mark in their right hand, or in their foreheads:

17 And that no man might buy or sell, save he that had the mark, or the name of the beast, or the number of his name.

18 Here is wisdom. Let him that hath understanding count the number of the beast: for it is the number of a man; and his number is Six hundred threescore and six.

REVELATION 14

1 And I looked, and, lo, a Lamb stood on the mount Sion, and with him an hundred forty and four thousand, having his Father's name written in their foreheads.

2 And I heard a voice from heaven, as the voice of many waters, and as the voice of a great thunder: and I heard the voice of harpers harping with their harps:

3 And they sung as it were a new song before the throne, and before the four beasts, and the elders: and no man could learn that song but the hundred and forty and four thousand, which were redeemed from the earth.

9, ii, 10, vii, 14; but this persecution came after her flight, verse 6, just at the beginning of the third woe.

14. And there were given to the woman the two wings of the great eagle, that she might fly into the wilderness to her place – Eagles are the usual symbols of great potentates. So Ezek. xvii, 3, by "a great eagle', means the king of Babylon. Here the great eagle is the Roman empire; the two wings, the eastern and western branches of it.

15. Water is an emblem of a great people; this water, of the Turks in particular. About the year 1060 they overran the Christian part of Asia. Afterward, they poured into Europe, and spread farther and farther, till they had overflowed many nations.

16. But the earth helped the woman – The powers of the earth; and indeed she needed help through this whole period.

17. And the dragon was wroth – Anew, because he could not cause her to be carried away by the stream. And he went forth – Into other lands. To make war with the rest of her seed – Real Christians, living under heathen or Turkish governors.

MATTHEW HENRY   CHARLES H. SPURGEON

1-6 The church, under the emblem of a woman, the mother of believers, was seen by the apostle in vision, in heaven. She was clothed with the sun, justified, sanctified, and shining by union with Christ, the Sun of Righteousness. The moon was under her feet; she was superior to the reflected and feebler light of the revelation made by Moses. Having on her head a crown of twelve stars; the doctrine of the gospel, preached by the twelve apostles, is a crown of glory to all true believers. As in pain to bring forth a holy family; desirous that the conviction of sinners might end in their conversion. A dragon is a known emblem of Satan, and his chief agents, or those who govern for him on earth, at that time the pagan empire of Rome, the city built upon seven hills. As having ten horns, divided into ten kingdoms. Having seven crowns, representing seven forms of government. As drawing with his tail a third part of the stars in heaven, and casting them down to the earth; persecuting and seducing the ministers and teachers. As watchful to crush the Christian religion; but in spite of the opposition of enemies, the church brought forth a manly issue of true and faithful professors, in whom Christ was truly formed anew; even the mystery of Christ, that Son of God who should rule the nations, and in whose right his members partake the same glory. This blessed offspring was protected of God.

7-11 The attempts of the dragon proved unsuccessful against the church, and fatal to his own interests. The seat of this war was in heaven; in the church of Christ, the kingdom of heaven on earth. The parties were Christ, the great Angel of the covenant, and his faithful followers; and Satan and his instruments. The strength of the church is in having the Lord Jesus for the Captain of their salvation. Pagan idolatry, which was the worship of devils, was cast out of the empire by the spreading of Christianity. The salvation and strength of the church, are only to be ascribed to the King and Head of the church. The conquered enemy hates the presence of God, yet he is willing to appear there, to accuse the people of God. Let us take heed that we give him no cause to accuse us; and that, when we have sinned, we go before the Lord, condemn ourselves, and commit our cause to Christ as our Advocate. The servants of God overcame Satan by the blood of the Lamb, as the cause. By the word of their testimony: the powerful preaching of the gospel is mighty, through God, to pull down strong holds. By their courage and patience in sufferings: they loved not their lives so well but they could lay them down in Christ's cause. These were the warriors and the weapons by which Christianity overthrew the power of pagan idolatry; and if

pies a position of great delicacy. The Lord thy God is a jealous God, and he is most jealous where he shows most love. The Lord lets some men escape scot free for awhile after doing many evil things, but if they had been his own elect he would have visited them with stripes long before. He is very jealous of those whom he has chosen to lean upon his bosom and to be his familiar friends. Your servant may do many things which could not be thought of by your child or your wife; and so is it with many who profess to be servants of God—they live a very lax life, and they do not seem to be chastened for it, but if they were the Lord's own peculiarly beloved ones he would not endure such conduct from them. Now mark this, if the Lord exalts a church, and gives it a special blessing, he expects more of it, more care of his honor, and more zeal for his glory than he does of any other church; and when he does not find it, what will happen? Why, because of his very love he will rebuke it with hard sermons, sharp words, and sore smitings of conscience. If these do not arouse it he will take down the rod and deal out chastenings. Do you know how the Lord chastens churches? Paul says, "For this cause some are sickly among you, and many sleep." Bodily sickness is often sent in discipline upon churches, and losses, and crosses, and troubles are sent among the members, and sometimes leanness in the pulpit, breakings out of heresy and divisions in the pew, and lack of success in all church work. All these are smitings with the rod. It is very sad, but sometimes that rod does not fall on that part of the church which does the wrong. Sometimes God may take the best in the church, and chasten them for the wrong of others. You say, "How can that be right?" Why, because they are the kind of people who will be most benefited by it. If a vine wants the knife, it is not the branch that bears very little fruit which is trimmed, but the branch which bears much fruit is purged because it is worth purging. In their case the chastening is a blessing and a token of love. Sorrow is often brought upon Christians by the sins of their fellow-members, and many an aching heart there is in this world that I know of, of brethren and sisters who love the Lord and want to see souls converted, but they can only sigh and cry because nothing is done. Perhaps they have a minister who does not believe the gospel, and they have fellow-members who do not care whether the minister believes it or not, they are all asleep together except those few zealous souls who besiege the throne of grace day and night, and they are the ones who bear the burden of the lukewarm church. Oh, if the chastening comes here, whoever bears it, may the whole body be the better for it, and may we never rest till the church begins to glow with the sacred fire of God, and boil with enthusiastic desire for his glory.

The last remedy, however, is the best of all to my mind. I love it best and desire to make it my food when it is not my medicine. The best remedy for

KING JAMES VERSION　　　JOHN WESLEY

4 These are they which were not defiled with women; for they are virgins. These are they which follow the Lamb whithersoever he goeth. These were redeemed from among men, being the firstfruits unto God and to the Lamb.

5 And in their mouth was found no guile: for they are without fault before the throne of God.

6 And I saw another angel fly in the midst of heaven, having the everlasting gospel to preach unto them that dwell on the earth, and to every nation, and kindred, and tongue, and people,

7 Saying with a loud voice, Fear God, and give glory to him; for the hour of his judgment is come: and worship him that made heaven, and earth, and the sea, and the fountains of waters.

8 And there followed another angel, saying, Babylon is fallen, is fallen, that great city, because she made all nations drink of the wine of the wrath of her fornication.

9 And the third angel followed them, saying with a loud voice, If any man worship the beast and his image, and receive his mark in his forehead, or in his hand,

10 The same shall drink of the wine of the wrath of God, which is poured out without mixture into the cup of his indignation; and he shall be tormented with fire and brimstone in the presence of the holy angels, and in the presence of the Lamb:

11

And the smoke of their torment ascendeth up for ever and ever: and they have no rest day nor night, who worship the beast and his image, and whosoever receiveth the mark of his name.

12 Here is the patience of the saints: here are they that keep the commandments of God, and the faith of Jesus.

13 And I heard a voice from heaven saying unto me, Write, Blessed are the dead which die in the Lord from henceforth: Yea, saith the Spirit, that they may rest from their labors; and their works do follow them.

14 And I looked, and behold a

REVELATION 13

1. And I stood on the sand of the sea – This also was in the vision. And I saw – Soon after the woman flew away. A wild beast coming up – He comes up twice; first from the sea, then from the abyss. He comes from the sea before the seven phials; "the great whore" comes after them

2. The three first beasts in Daniel are like "a leopard," "a bear," and "a lion." In all parts, except his feet and mouth, this beast was like a leopard or female panther; which is fierce as a lion or bear, but is also swift and subtle.

3. And I saw one – Or the first. Of his heads as it were wounded – So it appeared as soon as ever it rose. The beast is first described more generally, then more particularly, both in this and in the seventeenth chapter. The particular description here respects the former parts; there, the latter parts of his duration: only that some circumstances relating to the former are repeated in chap. xvii, 1-18. This deadly wound was given him on his first head by the sword, verse 14; that is, by the bloody resistance of the secular potentates.

4. And they worshiped the dragon – Even in worshiping the beast, although they knew it not. And worshiped the wild beast – Paying him such honor as was not paid to any merely secular potentate. That very title, "Our most holy Lord," was never given to any other monarch on earth. Saying, Who is like the wild beast – "Who is like him?" is a peculiar attribute of God; but that this is constantly attributed to the beast, the books of all his adherents show.

5. And there was given him – By the dragon, through the permission of God. A mouth speaking great things and blasphemy – The same is said of the little horn on the fourth beast in Daniel

7. And it was given him – That is, God permitted him.

8. And all that dwell upon the earth will worship him – All will be carried away by the torrent, but the little flock of true believers. The name of these only is written in the Lamb's book of life. And if any even of these "make shipwreck of the faith," he will blot them "out of his book;" although they were written therein from (that is, before) the foundation of the world, chap. xvii, 8.

9. If any one have an ear, let him hear – It was said before, "He that hath an ear, let him hear." This expression, if any, seems to imply, that scarce will any that hath an ear be found. Let him hear – With all attention the following warning, and the whole description of the beast.

10. If any man leadeth into captivity – God will in due time repay the followers of the beast in their own kind. Meanwhile, here is the patience and faithfulness of the saints exercised: their patience, by enduring captivity or imprisonment; their faithfulness, by resisting unto blood.

11. And I saw another wild beast – So he is once termed to show his fierceness and strength, but in all other places, "the false prophet." He comes to confirm the kingdom of the first beast. Coming up – After the other had long exercised his authority. Out of the earth – Out of Asia. But he is not yet come, though he cannot be far off for he is to appear at the end of the forty-two months of the first beast. And he had two horns like a lamb – A mild, innocent appearance. But he spake like a dragon – Venomous, fiery, dreadful. So do those who are zealous for the beast.

12. And he exerciseth all the authority of the first wild beast – Described in the second, fourth, fifth, and seventh verses. Before him – For they are both together. Whose deadly wound was healed – More thoroughly healed by means of the second beast.

13. He maketh fire – Real fire. To come down – By the power of the devil.

14. Before the wild beast – Whose usurped majesty is confirmed by these wonders. Saying to them – As if it were from God. To make an image to the wild beast – Like that of Nebuchadnezzar, whether of gold, silver, or stone.

17. That no man might buy or sell – Such edicts have been published long since against the poor Vaudois. The second beast will enforce the receiving this mark

MATTHEW HENRY

CHARLES H. SPURGEON

Christians had continued to fight with these weapons, and such as these, their victories would have been more numerous and glorious, and the effects more lasting. The redeemed overcame by a simple reliance on the blood of Christ, as the only ground of their hopes. In this we must be like them. We must not blend any thing else with this.

12-17 The church and all her friends might well be called to praise God for deliverance from pagan persecution, though other troubles awaited her. The wilderness is a desolate place, and full of serpents and scorpions, uncomfortable and destitute of provisions; yet a place of safety, as well as where one might be alone. But being thus retired could not protect the woman. The flood of water is explained by many to mean the invasions of barbarians, by which the western empire was overwhelmed; for the heathen encouraged their attacks, in the hope of destroying Christianity. But ungodly men, for their worldly interests, protected the church amidst these tumults, and the overthrow of the empire did not help the cause of idolatry. Or, this may be meant of a flood of error, by which the church of God was in danger of being overwhelmed and carried away. The devil, defeated in his designs upon the church, turns his rage against persons and places. Being faithful to God and Christ, in doctrine, worship, and practice, exposes to the rage of Satan; and will do so till the last enemy shall be destroyed.

REVELATION 13

A wild beast rises out of the sea, to whom the dragon gives his power. (1-10)
Another beast, which has two horns like a lamb, but speaks as a dragon. (11-15)
It obliges all to worship its image, and receive its mark, as persons devoted to it. (16-18)

1-10 The apostle, standing on the shore, saw a savage beast rise out of the sea; a tyrannical, idolatrous, persecuting power, springing up out of the troubles which took place. It was a frightful monster! It appears to mean that worldly, oppressing dominion, which for many ages, even from the times of the Babylonish captivity, had been hostile to the church. The first beast then began to oppress and persecute the righteous for righteousness' sake, but they suffered most under the fourth beast of Daniel, (the Roman empire,) which has afflicted the saints with many cruel persecutions. The source of its power was the dragon. It was set up by the devil, and supported by him. The wounding the head may be the abolishing pagan idolatry; and the

backsliding churches is more communion with Christ. "Behold," saith he, "I stand at the door and knock." I have known this text preached upon to sinners numbers of times as though Christ knocked at their door and they had to open it, and so on. The preacher has never managed to keep to free grace for this reason, that the text was not meant to be so used, and if men will ride a text the wrong way, it will not go. This text belongs to the church of God, not to the unconverted. It is addressed to the Laodicean church. There is Christ outside the church, driven there by her unkindness, but he has not gone far away, he loves his church too much to leave her altogether, he longs to come back, and therefore he waits at the doorpost. He knows that the church will never be restored till he comes back, and he desires to bless her, and so he stands waiting, knocking and knocking, again and again; he does not merely knock once, but he stands knocking by earnest sermons, by providences, by impressions upon the conscience, by the quickenings of his Holy Spirit; and while he knocks he speaks, he uses all means to awaken his church. Most condescendingly and graciously does he do this, for having threatened to spew her out of his mouth, he might have said, "I will get me gone; and I will never come back again to thee," that would have been natural and just; but how gracious he is when, having expressed his disgust he says, "Disgusted as I am with your condition, I do not wish to leave you; I have taken my presence from you, but I love you, and therefore I knock at your door, and wish to be received into your heart. I will not force myself upon you, I want you voluntarily to open the door to me." Christ's presence in a church is always a very tender thing. He never is there against the will of the church, it cannot be, for he lives in his people's wills and hearts, and "worketh in them to will and to do of his own good pleasure." He does not break bolt and bar and come in as he often does into a sinner's heart, carrying the soul by storm, because the man is dead in sin, and Christ must do it all, or the sinner will perish; but he is here speaking to living men and women, who ought also to be loving men and women, and he says, "I wish to be among you, open the door to me." We ought to open the door at once, and say, "Come in, good Lord, we grieve to think we should ever have put thee outside that door at all."

And then see what promises he gives. He says he will come and sup with us. Now, in the East, the supper was the best meal of the day, it was the same as our dinner; so that we may say that Christ will come and dine with us. He will give us a rich feast, for he himself is the daintiest and most plenteous of all feasts for perishing souls. He will come and sup with us, that is, we shall be the host and entertain him: but then he adds, "and he with me," that is, he will be the host and guest by turns. We will give him of our best, but poor fare is that, too poor for him, and

white cloud, and upon the cloud one sat like unto the Son of man, having on his head a golden crown, and in his hand a sharp sickle.

15 And another angel came out of the temple, crying with a loud voice to him that sat on the cloud, Thrust in thy sickle, and reap: for the time is come for thee to reap; for the harvest of the earth is ripe.

16 And he that sat on the cloud thrust in his sickle on the earth; and the earth was reaped.

17 And another angel came out of the temple which is in heaven, he also having a sharp sickle.

18 And another angel came out from the altar, which had power over fire; and cried with a loud cry to him that had the sharp sickle, saying, Thrust in thy sharp sickle, and gather the clusters of the vine of the earth; for her grapes are fully ripe.

19 And the angel thrust in his sickle into the earth, and gathered the vine of the earth, and cast it into the great winepress of the wrath of God.

20 And the winepress was trodden without the city, and blood came out of the winepress, even unto the horse bridles, by the space of a thousand and six hundred furlongs.

REVELATION 15

1 And I saw another sign in heaven, great and marvelous, seven angels having the seven last plagues; for in them is filled up the wrath of God.

2 And I saw as it were a sea of glass mingled with fire: and them that had gotten the victory over the beast, and over his image, and over his mark, and over the number of his name, stand on the sea of glass, having the harps of God.

3 And they sing the song of Moses the servant of God, and the song of the Lamb, saying, Great and marvelous are thy works, Lord God Almighty; just and true are thy ways, thou King of saints.

4 Who shall not fear thee, O Lord, and glorify thy name? for

under the severest penalties.

18. Here is the wisdom – To be exercised. "The patience of the saints" availed against the power of the first beast: the wisdom God giveth them will avail against the subtlety of the second. Let him that hath understanding – Which is a gift of God, subservient to that wisdom. Count the number of the wild beast – Surely none can be blamed for attempting to obey this command. For it is the number of a man – A number of such years as are common among men. And his number is six hundred and sixty-six years – So long shall he endure from his first appearing.

REVELATION 14

1. And I saw on mount Sion – The heavenly Sion. An hundred forty-four thousand – Either those out of all mankind who had been the most eminently holy, or the most holy out of the twelve tribes of Israel the same that were mentioned, chap. vii, 4, and perhaps also, chap. xvi, 2. But they were then in the world, and were sealed in their foreheads, to preserve them from the plagues that were to follow. They are now in safety, and have the name of the Lamb and of his Father written on their foreheads, as being the redeemed of God and of the Lamb, his now unalienable property. This prophecy often introduces the inhabitants of heaven as a kind of chorus with great propriety and elegance. The church above, making suitable reflections on the grand events which are foretold in this book, greatly serves to raise the attention of real Christians, and to teach the high concern they have in them. Thus is the church on earth instructed, animated, and encouraged, by the sentiments temper, and devotion of the church in heaven.

2. And I heard a sound out of heaven – Sounding clearer and clearer: first, at a distance, as the sound of many waters or thunders; and afterwards, being nearer, it was as of harpers harping on their harps. It sounded vocally and instrumentally at once.

3. And they – The hundred forty-four thousand – Sing a new song – And none could learn that song – To sing and play it in the same manner. But the hundred forty-four thousand who were redeemed from the earth – From among men; from all sin.

4. These are they who had not been defiled with women – It seems that the deepest defilement, and the most alluring temptation, is put for every other. They are virgins – Unspotted souls; such as have preserved universal purity. These are they who follow the Lamb – Who are nearest to him. This is not their character, but their reward. First fruits – Of the glorified spirits. Who is ambitious to be of this number?

5. And in their mouth there was found no guile – Part for the whole. Nothing untrue, unkind, unholy. They are without fault – Having preserved inviolate a virgin purity both of soul and body.

6. And I saw another angel – A second is mentioned, verse 8; a third, verse 9. These three denote great messengers of God with their assistants; three men who bring messages from God to men. The first exhorts to the fear and worship of God; the second proclaims the fall of Babylon; the third gives warning concerning the beast. Happy are they who make the right use of these divine messages! Flying – Going on swiftly. In the midst of heaven – Breadthways. Having an everlasting gospel – Not the gospel, properly so called; but a gospel, or joyful message, which was to have an influence on all ages. To preach to every nation, and tribe, and tongue, and people – Both to Jew and Gentile, even as far as the authority of the beast had extended.

7. Fear God and give glory to him; for the hour of his judgment is come – The joyful message is properly this, that the hour of God's judgment is come. And hence is that admonition drawn, Fear God and give glory to him.

8. And another angel followed, saying, Babylon is fallen – With the overthrow

MATTHEW HENRY

CHARLES H. SPURGEON

healing of the wound, introducing popish idolatry, the same in substance, only in a new dress, but which as effectually answers the devil's design. The world admired its power, policy and success. They paid honor and subjection to the devil and his instruments. It exercised infernal power and policy, requiring men to render that honor to creatures which belongs to God alone. Yet the devil's power and success are limited. Christ has a chosen remnant, redeemed by his blood, recorded in his book, sealed by his Spirit; and though the devil and antichrist may overcome the body, and take away the natural life, they cannot conquer the soul, nor prevail with true believers to forsake their Savior, and join his enemies. Perseverance in the faith of the gospel and true worship of God, in this great hour of trial and temptation, which would deceive all but the elect, is the character of those registered in the book of life. This powerful motive and encouragement to constancy, is the great design of the whole Revelation.

11-18 Those who understand the first beast to denote a worldly power, take the second to be also a persecuting and assumed power, which acts under the disguise of religion, and of charity to the souls of men. It is a spiritual dominion, professing to be derived from Christ, and exercised at first in a gentle manner, but soon spake like the dragon. Its speech betrayed it; for it gives forth those false doctrines and cruel decrees, which show it to belong to the dragon, and not to the Lamb. It exercised all the power of the former beast. It pursues the same design, to draw men from worshiping the true God, and to subject the souls of men to the will and control of men. The second beast has carried on its designs, by methods whereby men should be deceived to worship the former beast, in the new shape, or likeness made for it. By lying wonders, pretended miracles. And by severe censures. Also by allowing none to enjoy natural or civil rights, who will not worship that beast which is the image of the pagan beast. It is made a qualification for buying and selling, as well as for places of profit and trust, that they oblige themselves to use all their interest, power, and endeavor, to forward the dominion of the beast, which is meant by receiving his mark. To make an image to the beast, whose deadly wound was healed, would be to give form and power to his worship, or to require obedience to his commands. To worship the image of the beast, implies being subject to those things which stamp the character of the picture, and render it the image of the beast. The number of the beast is given, so as to show the infinite wisdom of God, and to exercise the wisdom of men. The

yet he will partake of it. Then he shall be host, and we will be guest, and oh, how we will feast on what he gives! Christ comes, and brings the supper with him, and all we do is to find the room. The Master says to us, "Where is the guest chamber?" and then he makes ready and spreads his royal table. Now, if these be the terms on which we are to have a feast together, we will most willingly fling open the doors of our hearts and say, "Come in, good Lord." He says to you, "Children, have you any meat?" and if you are obliged to say, "No, Lord," he will come in unto you none the less readily, for there are the fish, the net is ready to break, it is so full, and here are more upon the coals ready. I warrant you, if we sup with him, we shall be lukewarm no longer. The men who live where Jesus is soon feel their hearts burning. It is said of a piece of scented clay by the old Persian moralist that the clay was taken up and questioned. "How camest thou to smell so sweetly, being nothing but common clay?" and it replied, "I laid for many a year in the sweet society of a rose, until at last I drank in its perfume;" and we may say to every warm-hearted Christian, "How calmest thou so warm?" and his answer will be, "My heart bubbled up with a good matter, for I speak of the things which I have made touching the King. I have been with Jesus, and I have learned of him."

Now, brethren and sisters, what can I say to move you to take this last medicine? I can only say, take it, not only because of the good it will do you, but because of the sweetness of it. I have heard say of some persons that they were pledged not to take wine except as a medicine, but then they were very pleased when they were ill: and so if this be the medicine, "I will come and sup with him, and he with me," we may willingly confess our need of so delicious a remedy. Need I press it on you? May I not rather urge each brother as soon as he gets home today to see whether he cannot enter into fellowship with Jesus? and may the Spirit of God help him!

This is my closing word, there is something for us to do in this matter. We must examine ourselves, and we must confess the fault if we have declined in grace. And then we must not talk about setting the church right, we must pray for grace each one for himself, for the text does not say, "If the church will open the door," but "If any man hear my voice and open the door." It must be done by individuals: the church will only get right by each man getting right. Oh, that we might get back into an earnest zeal for our Lord's love and service, and we shall only do so by listening to his rebukes, and then falling into his arms, clasping him once again, and saying, "My Lord and my God." That healed Thomas, did it not? Putting his fingers into the print of the nails, putting his hand into the side, that cured him. Poor, unbelieving, staggering Thomas only had to do that and he became one of the strongest of believers, and said, "My Lord and my God." You will love your Lord

thou only art holy: for all nations shall come and worship before thee; for thy judgments are made manifest.

5 And after that I looked, and, behold, the temple of the tabernacle of the testimony in heaven was opened:

6 And the seven angels came out of the temple, having the seven plagues, clothed in pure and white linen, and having their breasts girded with golden girdles.

7 And one of the four beasts gave unto the seven angels seven golden vials full of the wrath of God, who liveth for ever and ever.

8 And the temple was filled with smoke from the glory of God, and from his power; and no man was able to enter into the temple, till the seven plagues of the seven angels were fulfilled.

REVELATION 16

1 And I heard a great voice out of the temple saying to the seven angels, Go your ways, and pour out the vials of the wrath of God upon the earth.

2 And the first went, and poured out his vial upon the earth; and there fell a noisome and grievous sore upon the men which had the mark of the beast, and upon them which worshiped his image.

3 And the second angel poured out his vial upon the sea; and it became as the blood of a dead man: and every living soul died in the sea.

4 And the third angel poured out his vial upon the rivers and fountains of waters; and they became blood.

5 And I heard the angel of the waters say, Thou art righteous, O Lord, which art, and wast, and shalt be, because thou hast judged thus.

6 For they have shed the blood of saints and prophets, and thou hast given them blood to drink; for they are worthy.

7 And I heard another out of the altar say, Even so, Lord God Almighty, true and righteous are thy judgments.

8 And the fourth angel poured

of Babylon, that of all the enemies of Christ, and, consequently, happier times, are connected. Babylon the great – So the city of Rome is called upon many accounts. Babylon was magnificent, strong, proud, powerful. So is Rome also. Babylon was first, Rome afterwards, the residence of the emperors of the world. What Babylon was to Israel of old, Roman hath been both to the literal and spiritual "Israel of God."

9. And a third angel followed – At no great distance of time. Saying, If any one worship the wild beast – This worship consists, partly in an inward submission, a persuasion that all who are subject to Christ must be subject to the beast or they cannot receive the influences of divine grace, or, as their expression is, there is no salvation out of their church; partly in a suitable outward reverence to the beast himself, and consequently to his image.

10. He shall drink – With Babylon, chap. xvi, 19. And shall be tormented – With the beast, chap. xx, 10. In all the scripture there is not another so terrible threatening as this. And God by this greater fear arms his servants against the fear of the beast. The wrath of God, which is poured unmixed – Without any mixture of mercy; without hope. Into the cup of his indignation – And is no real anger implied in all this? O what will not even wise men assert, to serve an hypothesis!

11. And the smoke – From the fire and brimstone wherein they are tormented. Ascendeth for ever and ever – God grant thou and I may never try the strict, literal eternity of this torment!

12. Here is the patience of the saints – Seen, in suffering all things rather than receive this mark. Who keep the commandments of God – The character of all true saints; and particularly the great command to believe in Jesus.

13. And I heard a voice – This is most seasonably heard when the beast is in his highest power and fury. Out of heaven – Probably from a departed saint. Write – He was at first commanded to write the whole book. Whenever this is repeated it denotes something peculiarly observable. Happy are the dead – From henceforth particularly:

1. Because they escape the approaching calamities:
2. Because they already enjoy so near an approach to glory.

Who die in the Lord – In the faith of the Lord Jesus. For they rest – No pain, no purgatory follows; but pure, unmixed happiness. From their labors – And the more laborious their life was, the sweeter is their rest. How different this state from that of those, verse 11, who "have no rest day or night!" Reader, which wilt thou choose? Their works – Each one's peculiar works. Follow – or accompany them; that is, the fruit of their works. Their works do not go before to procure them admittance into the mansions of joy; but they follow them when admitted.

14. In the following verses, under the emblem of an harvest and a vintage, are signified two general visitations; first, many good men are taken from the earth by the harvest; then many sinners during the vintage. The latter is altogether a penal visitation; the former seems to be altogether gracious. Here is no reference in either to the day of judgment, but to a season which cannot be far off. And I saw a white cloud – An emblem of mercy. And on the cloud sat one like a son of man – An angel in an human shape, sent by Christ, the Lord both of the vintage and of the harvest. Having a golden crown on his head – In token of his high dignity. And a sharp sickle in his hand – The sharper the welcome to the righteous.

15. And another angel came out of the temple – "Which is in heaven," verse 17. Out of which came the judgments of God in the appointed seasons.

16. Crying – By the command of God. Thrust in thy sickle, for the harvest is ripe – This implies an high degree of holiness in those good men, and an earnest desire to be with God.

18. And another angel from the altar – Of burnt offering; from whence the martyrs had cried for vengeance. Who had power over fire – As "the angel of the

MATTHEW HENRY

CHARLES H. SPURGEON

number is the number of a man, computed after the usual manner among men, and it is 666. What or who is intended by this, remains a mystery. To almost every religious dispute this number has yet been applied, and it may reasonably be doubted whether the meaning has yet been discovered. But he who has wisdom and understanding, will see that all the enemies of God are numbered and marked out for destruction; that the term of their power will soon expire, and that all nations shall submit to our King of righteousness and peace.

REVELATION 14

Those faithful to Christ celebrate the praises of God. (1-5)

Three angels; one proclaiming the everlasting gospel; another, the downfall of Babylon; and a third, the dreadful wrath of God on the worshipers of the beast. The blessedness of those who die in the Lord. (6-13)

A vision of Christ with a sickle, and of a harvest ripe for cutting down. (14-16)

The emblem of a vintage fully ripe, trodden in the winepress of God's wrath. (17-20)

1-5 Mount Sion is the gospel church. Christ is with his church, and in the midst of her in all her troubles, therefore she is not consumed. His presence secures perseverance. His people appear honorably. They have the name of God written in their foreheads; they make a bold and open profession of their faith in God and Christ, and this is followed by suitable acting. There were persons in the darkest times, who ventured and laid down their lives for the worship and truth of the gospel of Christ. They kept themselves clean from the wicked abominations of the followers of antichrist. Their hearts were right with God; and they were freely pardoned in Christ; he is glorified in them, and they in him. May it be our prayer, our endeavor, our ambition, to be found in this honorable company. Those who are really sanctified and justified are meant here, for no hypocrite, however plausible, can be accounted to be without fault before God.

6-13 The progress of the Reformation appears to be here set forth. The four proclamations are plain in their meaning; that all Christians may be encouraged, in the time of trial, to be faithful to their Lord. The gospel is the great means whereby men are brought to fear God, and to give glory to him. The preaching of the everlasting gospel shakes the foundations of antichrist in the world, and hastens its downfall. If any persist in being subject to the beast, and in promoting his cause, they must expect to be forever miserable

till your soul is as coals of juniper if you will daily commune with him. Come close to him, and once getting close to him, never go away from him any more. The Lord bless you, dear brethren, the Lord bless you in this thing.

HEAVENLY WORSHIP

Sermon number 110 delivered on December 28th, 1856, at the Music Hall, Royal Surrey Gardens.
Reading: Revelation 14:1-3.

THIS morning I shall endeavor to show you, first of all, the object of heavenly worship—the Lamb in the midst of the throne; in the next place we shall look at the worshipers themselves, and note their manner and their character; in the third place we shall listen to hear their song, for we may almost hear it; it is like "the noise of many waters and like great thunder;" and then we shall close by noting, that it is a new song which they sing, and by endeavoring to mention one or two reasons why it must necessarily be so.

I. In the first place, then, we wish to take a view of THE OBJECT OF HEAVENLY WORSHIP. The divine John was privileged to look within the gates of pearl; and on turning round to tell us what he saw—observe how he begins—he saith not, "I saw streets of gold or walls of jasper;" he saith not, "I saw crowns, marked their luster, and saw the wearers." That he shall notice afterwards. But he begins by saying, "I looked, and, lo, a Lamb!" To teach us that the very first and chief object of attraction in the heavenly state is "the Lamb of God which taketh away the sins of the world." Nothing else attracted the Apostle's attention so much as the person of that Divine Being, who is the Lord God, our most blessed Redeemer: "I looked, and, lo a Lamb!" Beloved, if we were allowed to look within the veil which parts us from the world of spirits, we should see, first of all, the person of our Lord Jesus. If now we could go where the immortal spirits "day without night circle the throne rejoicing," we should see each of them with their faces turned in one direction; and if we should step up to one of the blessed spirits, and say, "O bright immortal, why are thine eyes fixed? What is it that absorbs thee quite, and wraps thee up in vision?" He, without deigning to give an answer, would simply point to the center of the sacred circle, and lo, we should see a Lamb in the midst of the throne. They have not yet ceased to admire his beauty, and marvel at his wonders and adore his person.

He is the theme of song and the subject of observation of all the glorified spirits and of all the angels in paradise. "I looked, and, lo, a Lamb!"

Christian, here is joy for thee; thou hast looked, and thou hast seen the Lamb. Through thy tearful eyes thou hast seen the Lamb taking away thy sins.

out his vial upon the sun; and power was given unto him to scorch men with fire.

9 And men were scorched with great heat, and blasphemed the name of God, which hath power over these plagues: and they repented not to give him glory.

10 And the fifth angel poured out his vial upon the seat of the beast; and his kingdom was full of darkness; and they gnawed their tongues for pain,

11 And blasphemed the God of heaven because of their pains and their sores, and repented not of their deeds.

12 And the sixth angel poured out his vial upon the great river Euphrates; and the water thereof was dried up, that the way of the kings of the east might be prepared.

13 And I saw three unclean spirits like frogs come out of the mouth of the dragon, and out of the mouth of the beast, and out of the mouth of the false prophet.

14 For they are the spirits of devils, working miracles, which go forth unto the kings of the earth and of the whole world, to gather them to the battle of that great day of God Almighty.

15 Behold, I come as a thief. Blessed is he that watcheth, and keepeth his garments, lest he walk naked, and they see his shame.

16 And he gathered them together into a place called in the Hebrew tongue Armageddon.

17 And the seventh angel poured out his vial into the air; and there came a great voice out of the temple of heaven, from the throne, saying, It is done.

18 And there were voices, and thunders, and lightnings; and there was a great earthquake, such as was not since men were upon the earth, so mighty an earthquake, and so great.

19 And the great city was divided into three parts, and the cities of the nations fell: and great Babylon came in remembrance before God, to give unto her the cup of the wine of the fierceness of his wrath.

waters," chap. xvi, 5, had over water. Cried, saying, Lop off the clusters of the vine of the earth – All the wicked are considered as constituting one body.

20. And the winepress was trodden – By the Son of God, chap. xix, 15. Without the city – Jerusalem. They to whom St. John writes, when a man said, "The city," immediately understood this. And blood came out of the winepress, even to the horses' bridles – So deep at its first flowing from the winepress! One thousand six hundred furlongs – So far! at least two hundred miles, through the whole land of Palestine.

REVELATION 15

1. And I saw seven holy angels having the seven last plagues – Before they had the phials, which were as instruments whereby those plagues were to be conveyed. They are termed the last, because by them the wrath of God is fulfilled – Hitherto. God had born his enemies with much longsuffering; but now his wrath goes forth to the uttermost, pouring plagues on the earth from one end to the other, and round its whole circumference. But, even after these plagues, the holy wrath of God against his other enemies does not cease, chap. xx, 15.

2. The song was sung while the angels were coming out, with their plagues, who are therefore mentioned both before and after it, verses 1-6. And I saw as it were a sea of glass mingled with fire – It was before "clear as crystal," chap. iv, 6, but now mingled with fire, which devours the adversaries. And them that gained, or were gaining, the victory over the wild beast – More of whom were yet to come. The mark of the beast, the mark of his name, and the number of his name, seem to mean here nearly the same thing. Standing at the sea of glass – Which was before the throne. Having the harps of God – Given by him, and appropriated to his praise.

3. And they sing the song of Moses – So called, partly from its near agreement, with the words of that song which he sung after passing the Red Sea, Exod. xv, 11, and of that which he taught the children of Israel a little before his death, Deut. xxxii, 3, 4. But chiefly because Moses was the minister and representative of the Jewish church, as Christ is of the church universal. Therefore it is also termed the sons of the Lamb.

5. After these things the temple of the tabernacle of the testimony – The holiest of all. Was opened – Disclosing a new theater for the coming forth of the judgments of God now made manifest.

6. And the seven angels came out of the temple – As having received their instructions from the oracle of God himself. St. John saw them in heaven, verse 1, before they went into the temple. They appeared in habits like those the high priest wore when he went into the most holy place to consult the oracle. In this was the visible testimony of God's presence. Clothed in pure white linen – Linen is the habit of service and attendance. Pure – unspotted, unsullied. White – Or bright and shining, which implies much more than bare innocence. And having their breasts girt with golden girdles – In token of their high dignity and glorious rest.

7. And one of the four living creatures gave the seven angels – After they were come out of the temple. Seven golden phials – Or bowls. The Greek word signifies vessels broader at the top than at the bottom. Full of the wrath of God, who liveth for ever and ever – A circumstance which adds greatly to the dreadfulness of his wrath.

8. And the temple was filled with smoke – The cloud of glory was the visible manifestation of God's presence in the tabernacle and temple. It was a sign of protection at erecting the tabernacle and at the dedication of the temple. But in the judgment of Korah the glory of the Lord appeared, when he and his companions were swallowed up by the earth. So proper is the emblem of smoke from the glory of God, or from the cloud of glory, to express the execution of judg-

in soul and body. The believer is to venture or suffer any thing in obeying the commandments of God, and professing the faith of Jesus. May God bestow this patience upon us. Observe the description of those that are and shall be blessed: such as die in the Lord; die in the cause of Christ, in a state of union with Christ; such as are found in Christ when death comes. They rest from all sin, temptation, sorrow, and persecution; for there the wicked cease from troubling, there the weary are at rest. Their works follow them: do not go before as their title, or purchase, but follow them as proofs of their having lived and died in the Lord: the remembrance of them will be pleasant, and the reward far above all their services and sufferings. This is made sure by the testimony of the Spirit, witnessing with their spirits, and the written word.

14-20 Warnings and judgments not having produced reformation, the sins of the nations are filled up, and they become ripe for judgments, represented by a harvest, an emblem which is used to signify the gathering of the righteous, when ripe for heaven, by the mercy of God. The harvest time is when the corn is ripe; when the believers are ripe for heaven, then the wheat of the earth shall be gathered into Christ's garner. And by a vintage. The enemies of Christ and his church are not destroyed, till by their sin they are ripe for ruin, and then he will spare them no longer. The winepress is the wrath of God, some terrible calamity, probably the sword, shedding the blood of the wicked. The patience of God towards sinners, is the greatest miracle in the world; but, though lasting, it will not be everlasting; and ripeness in sin is a sure proof of judgment at hand.

REVELATION 15

A song of praise is sung by the church. (1-4)
Seven angels with the seven plagues; and to them
one of the living creatures gives seven golden
vials full of the wrath of God. (5-8)

1-4 Seven angels appeared in heaven; prepared to finish the destruction of antichrist. As the measure of Babylon's sins was filled up, it finds the full measure of Divine wrath. While believers stand in this world, in times of trouble, as upon a sea of glass mingled with fire, they may look forward to their final deliverance, while new mercies call forth new hymns of praise. The more we know of God's wonderful works, the more we shall praise his greatness as the Lord God Almighty, the Creator and Ruler of all worlds; but his title of Emmanuel, the King of saints, will make him dear to us. Who that considers the

Rejoice, then! In a little while, when thine eyes shall have been wiped from tears, thou wilt see the same Lamb exalted on his throne. It is the joy of the heart to hold daily fellowship and communion with Jesus; thou shalt have the same joy in heaven; "there shalt thou see him as he is, and thou shalt be like him." Thou shalt enjoy the constant vision of his presence, and thou shalt dwell with him for aye. "I looked, and, lo, a Lamb!" Why, that Lamb is heaven itself; for as good Rutherford says, "Heaven and Christ are the same things; to be with Christ is to be in heaven, and to be in heaven is to be with Christ." And he very sweetly says in one of his letters, wrapped up in love to Christ. "Oh! my Lord Christ, if I could be in heaven without thee, it would be a hell; and if I could be in hell, and have thee still, it would be a heaven to me, for thou art all the heaven I want." It is true, is it not Christian? Does not thy soul say so?

All thou needest to make thee blessed, supremely blessed, is "to be with Christ, which is far better."

And now observe the figure under which Christ is represented in heaven. "I looked, and, lo, a Lamb." Now, you know Jesus, in Scripture, is often represented as a lion: he is so to his enemies, for he devoureth them, and teareth them to pieces. "Beware, ye that forget God, lest he tear you in pieces, and there be none to deliver."

Why should Christ in heaven choose to appear under the figure of a lamb, and not in some other of his glorious characters? We reply, because it was as a lamb that Jesus fought and conquered, and, therefore as a lamb he appears in heaven. I have read of certain military commanders, when they were conquerors, that on the anniversary of their victory they would never wear anything but the garment in which they fought. On that memorable day they say, "Nay, take away the robes; I will wear the garment which has been embroidered with the saber-cut, and garnished with the shot that hath riddled it; I will wear no other garb but that in which I fought and conquered." It seems as if the same feeling possessed the breast of Christ. "As a Lamb," saith he, "I died, and worsted hell; as a Lamb I have redeemed my people, and therefore as a Lamb I will appear in paradise."

But, perhaps, there is another reason; it is to encourage us to come to him in prayer. Ah, believer, we need not be afraid to come to Christ, for he is a Lamb. To a lion-Christ we need fear to come; but the Lamb-Christ!—oh, little children, were ye ever afraid of lambs? Oh, children of the living God, should ye ever fail to tell your griefs and sorrows into the breast of one who is a Lamb? Ah, let us come boldly to the throne of the heavenly grace, seeing a Lamb sits upon it. One of the things which tend very much to spoil prayer-meetings is the fact that our brethren do not pray boldly. They would practice reverence, as truly they ought, but they should remember that the highest reverence is consistent with true familiarity.

20 And every island fled away, and the mountains were not found.

21 And there fell upon men a great hail out of heaven, every stone about the weight of a talent: and men blasphemed God because of the plague of the hail; for the plague thereof was exceeding great.

REVELATION 17

1 And there came one of the seven angels which had the seven vials, and talked with me, saying unto me, Come hither; I will shew unto thee the judgment of the great whore that sitteth upon many waters:

2 With whom the kings of the earth have committed fornication, and the inhabitants of the earth have been made drunk with the wine of her fornication.

3 So he carried me away in the spirit into the wilderness: and I saw a woman sit upon a scarlet colored beast, full of names of blasphemy, having seven heads and ten horns.

4 And the woman was arrayed in purple and scarlet color, and decked with gold and precious stones and pearls, having a golden cup in her hand full of abominations and filthiness of her fornication:

5 And upon her forehead was a name written, MYSTERY, BABYLON THE GREAT, THE MOTHER OF HARLOTS AND ABOMINATIONS OF THE EARTH.

6 And I saw the woman drunken with the blood of the saints, and with the blood of the martyrs of Jesus: and when I saw her, I wondered with great admiration.

7 And the angel said unto me, Wherefore didst thou marvel? I will tell thee the mystery of the woman, and of the beast that carrieth her, which hath the seven heads and ten horns.

8 The beast that thou sawest was, and is not; and shall ascend out of the bottomless pit, and go into perdition: and they that dwell on the earth shall wonder, whose names were not written in the book of life from the foundation of the world, when they behold the

ment, as well as to be a sign of favor. Both proceed from the power of God, and in both he is glorified. And none – Not even of those who ordinarily stood before God. Could go into the temple – That is, into the inmost part of it. Till the seven plagues of the seven angels were fulfilled – Which did not take up a long time, like the seven trumpets, but swiftly followed each other.

REVELATION 16

1. Pour out the seven phials – The epistles to the seven churches are divided into three and four: the seven seals, and so the trumpets and phials, into four and three. The trumpets gradually, and in a long tract of time, overthrow the kingdom of the world: the phials destroy chiefly the beast and his followers, with a swift and impetuous force. The four first affect the earth, the sea, the rivers, the sun; the rest fall elsewhere, and are much more terrible.

2. And the first went – So the second, third, &c., without adding angel, to denote the utmost swiftness; of which this also is a token, that there is no period of time mentioned in the pouring out of each phial. They have a great resemblance to the plagues of Egypt, which the Hebrews generally suppose to have been a month distant from each other. Perhaps so may the phials; but they are all yet to come. And poured out his phial upon the earth – Literally taken. And there came a grievous ulcer – As in Egypt, Exod. ix, 10, 11. On the men who had the mark of the wild beast – All of them, and them only. All those plagues seem to be described in proper, not figurative, words.

3. The second poured out his phial upon the sea – As opposed to the dry land. And it become blood, as of a dead man – Thick, congealed, and putrid. And every living soul – Men, beasts, and fishes, whether on or in the sea, died.

4. The third poured out his phial on the rivers and fountains of water – Which were over all the earth. And they became blood – So that none could drink thereof.

5. The Gracious one – So he is styled when his judgments are abroad, and that with a peculiar propriety. In the beginning of the book he is termed "The Almighty." In the time of his patience, he is praised for his power, which otherwise might then be less regarded. In the time of his taking vengeance, for his mercy. Of his power there could then be no doubt.

6. Thou hast given then, blood to drink – Men do not drink out of the sea, but out of fountains and rivers. Therefore this is fitly added here. They are worthy – Is subjoined with a beautiful abruptness.

7. Yea – Answering the angel of the waters, and affirming of God's judgments in general, what he had said of one particular judgment.

8. The fourth poured out his phial upon the sun – Which was likewise affected by the fourth trumpet. There is also a plain resemblance between the first, second, and third phials, and the first, second, and third trumpet. And it was given him – The angel. To scorch the men – Who had the mark of the beast. With fire – As well as with the beams of the sun. So these four phials affected earth, water, fire, and air.

9. And the men blasphemed God, who had power over these plagues – They could not but acknowledge the hand of God, yet did they harden themselves against him.

10. The four first phials are closely connected together; the fifth concerns the throne of the beast, the sixth the Mahometans, the seventh chiefly the heathens. The four first phials and the four first trumpets go round the whole earth; the three last phials and the three last trumpets go lengthways over the earth in a straight line. The fifth poured out his phial upon the throne of the wild beast – It is not said, "on the beast and his throne." Perhaps the sea will then be vacant. And his kingdom was darkened – With a lasting, not a transient, darkness. However the beast as yet has his kingdom. Afterward the woman sits upon the

power of God's wrath, the value of his favor, or the glory of his holiness, would refuse to fear and honor him alone? His praise is above heaven and earth.

5-8 In the judgments God executes upon antichrist and his followers, he fulfills the prophecies and promises of his word. These angels are prepared for their work, clothed with pure and white linen, their breasts girded with golden girdles, representing the holiness, and righteousness, and excellence of these dealings with men. They are ministers of Divine justice, and do every thing in a pure and holy manner. They were armed with the wrath of God against his enemies. Even the meanest creature, when armed with the anger of God, will be too hard for any man in the world. The angels received the vials from one of the four living creatures, one of the ministers of the true church, as in answer to the prayers of the ministers and people of God. Antichrist could not be destroyed without a great shock to all the world, and even the people of God would be in trouble and confusion while the great work was doing. The greatest deliverances of the church are brought about by awful and astonishing steps of Providence; and the happy state of the true church will not begin till obstinate enemies shall be destroyed, and lukewarm or formal Christians are purified. Then, whatever is against Scripture being purged away, the whole church shall be spiritual, and the whole being brought to purity, unity, and spirituality, shall be firmly established.

REVELATION 16

The first vial is poured out on the earth, the second on the sea, the third on the rivers and fountains. (1-7)

The fourth on the sun, the fifth on the seat of the beast. (8-11)

The sixth on the great river Euphrates. (12-16)

And the seventh on the air, when shall follow the destruction of all antichristian enemies. (17-21)

1-7 We are to pray that the will of God may be done on earth as it is done in heaven. Here is a succession of terrible judgments of Providence; and there seems to be an allusion to several of the plagues of Egypt. The sins were alike, and so were the punishments. The vials refer to the seven trumpets, which represented the rise of antichrist; and the fall of the enemies of the church shall bear some resemblance to their rise. All things throughout their earth, their air, their sea, their rivers, their cities, all are condemned to ruin, all accursed for the wickedness

No man more reverent than Luther; no man more fully carried out for the passage, "He talked with his Maker as a man talketh with his friend." We may be as reverent as the angels, and yet we may be as familiar as children in Christ Jesus. Now, our friends, when they pray, very frequently say the same thing every time. They are Dissenters; they cannot bear the Prayer Book; they think that forms of prayer are bad, but they always use their own form of prayer notwithstanding; as much as if they were to say that the bishop's form would not do, but their own they must always use. But a form of prayer being wrong, is as much wrong when I make it as when the bishop makes it; I am as much out of order in using what I compose myself continually and constantly, as I am when I am using one that has been composed for me; perhaps far more so, as it is not likely to be one-half so good. If our friends, however, would lay aside the form into which they grow, and break up the stereotyped plates with which they print their prayers so often, they might come boldly to the throne of God, and need never fear to do so; for he whom they address is represented in heaven under the figure of a Lamb, to teach us to come close to him, and tell him all our wants, believing that he will not disdain to hear them.

And you will further notice that this Lamb is said to stand. Standing is the posture of triumph. The Father said to Christ, "Sit thou on my throne, till I make thine enemies thy footstool." It is done; they are his footstool, and here he is said to stand erect, like a victor over all his enemies. Many a time the Savior knelt in prayer; once he hung upon the cross; but when the great scene of our text shall be fully wrought out, he shall stand erect, as more than conqueror, through his own majestic might. "I looked, and, lo, a Lamb stood on the Mount Sion." Oh, if we could rend the veil—if now we were privileged to see within it—there is no sight would so enthrall us as the simple sight of the Lamb in the midst of the throne. My dear brethren and sisters in Christ Jesus, would it not be all the sight you would ever wish to see, if you could once behold him whom your soul loveth? Would it not be a heaven to you, if it were carried out in your experience—"Mine eye shall see him, and not another's?" Would you want anything else to make you happy but continually to see him?

And if a single glimpse of him on earth affords you profound delight; it must be, indeed, a very sea of bliss, and an abyss of paradise, without a bottom or a shore, to see him as he is; to be lost in his splendors, as the stars are lost in the sunlight, and to hold fellowship with him, as did John the beloved, when he leaned his head upon his bosom. And this shall be thy lot, to see the Lamb in the midst of the throne.

II. The second point is, THE WORSHIPERS, WHO ARE THEY? Turn to the text, and you will note, first of all, their numbers—"I looked, and, lo, a Lamb stood on

beast that was, and is not, and yet is.

9 And here is the mind which hath wisdom. The seven heads are seven mountains, on which the woman sitteth.

10 And there are seven kings: five are fallen, and one is, and the other is not yet come; and when he cometh, he must continue a short space.

11 And the beast that was, and is not, even he is the eighth, and is of the seven, and goeth into perdition.

12 And the ten horns which thou sawest are ten kings, which have received no kingdom as yet; but receive power as kings one hour with the beast.

13 These have one mind, and shall give their power and strength unto the beast.

14 These shall make war with the Lamb, and the Lamb shall overcome them: for he is Lord of lords, and King of kings: and they that are with him are called, and chosen, and faithful.

15 And he saith unto me, The waters which thou sawest, where the whore sitteth, are peoples, and multitudes, and nations, and tongues.

16 And the ten horns which thou sawest upon the beast, these shall hate the whore, and shall make her desolate and naked, and shall eat her flesh, and burn her with fire.

17 For God hath put in their hearts to fulfill his will, and to agree, and give their kingdom unto the beast, until the words of God shall be fulfilled.

18 And the woman which thou sawest is that great city, which reigneth over the kings of the earth.

REVELATION 18

1 And after these things I saw another angel come down from heaven, having great power; and the earth was lightened with his glory.

2 And he cried mightily with a strong voice, saying, Babylon the great is fallen, is fallen, and is become the habitation of devils, and the hold of every foul spirit, and a cage of every

beast; and then it is said, "The wild beast is not," chap. xvii, 3, 7, 8.

11. And they – His followers. Gnawed their tongues – Out of furious impatience. Because of their pains and because of their ulcers – Now mentioned together, and in the plural number, to signify that they were greatly heightened and multiplied.

12. And the sixth poured out his phial upon the great river Euphrates – Affected also by the sixth trumpet. And the water of it – And of all the rivers that flow into it. Was dried up – The far greater part of the Turkish empire lies on this side the Euphrates.

13. Out of the mouth of the dragon, the wild beast, and the false prophet – It seems, the dragon fights chiefly against God; the beast, against Christ; the false prophet, against the Spirit of truth; and that the three unclean spirits which come from them, and exactly resemble them, endeavor to blacken the works of creation, of redemption, and of sanctification. The false prophet – So is the second beast frequently named, after the kingdom of the first is darkened; for he can then no longer prevail by main strength, and so works by lies and deceit. Mahomet was first a false prophet, and afterwards a powerful prince: but this beast was first powerful as a prince; afterwards a false prophet, a teacher of lies. Like frogs – Whose abode is in fens, marshes, and other unclean places. To the kings of the whole world – Both Mahometan and pagan. To gather them – To the assistance of their three principals.

15. Behold, I come as a thief – Suddenly, unexpectedly. Observe the beautiful abruptness. I – Jesus Christ. Hear him. Happy is he that watched – Looking continually for him that "cometh quickly." And keepeth on his garments – Which men use to put off when they sleep. Lest he walk naked, and they see his shame – Lest he lose the graces which he takes no care to keep, and others see his sin and punishment.

16. And they gathered them together to Armageddon – Macedon, or Megiddo, is frequently mentioned in the Old Testament. Armageddon signifies the city or the mountain of Megiddo; to which the valley of Megiddo adjoined. This was a place well known in ancient times for many memorable occurrences; in particular, the slaughter of the kings of Canaan, related, Judg. v, 19. Here the narrative breaks off. It is resumed, chap. xix, 19.

17. And the seventh poured out his phial upon the air – Which encompasses the whole earth. This is the most weighty phial of all, and seems to take up more time than any of the preceding. It is done – What was commanded, verse 1. The phials are poured out.

18. A great earthquake, such as had not been since men were upon the earth – It was therefore a literal, not figurative, earthquake.

19. And the great city – Namely, Jerusalem, here opposed to the heathen cities in general, and in particular to Rome. And the cities of the nations fell – Were utterly overthrown. And Babylon was remembered before God – He did not forget the vengeance which was due to her, though the execution of it was delayed.

20. Every island and mountain was "moved out of its place," chap. vi, 14; but here they all flee away. What a change must this make in the face of the terraqueous globe! And yet the end of the world is not come.

21. And a great hail falleth out of heaven – From which there was no defense. From the earthquake men would fly into the fields; but here also they are met by the hail: nor were they secure if they returned into the houses, when each hailstone weighed sixty pounds.

REVELATION 17

1. And there came one of the seven angels, saying, Come hither – This relation concerning the great whore, and that concerning the wife of the Lamb, chap. xxi, 9, 10, have the same introduction, in token of the exact opposition between

MATTHEW HENRY

CHARLES H. SPURGEON

of that people. No wonder that angels, who witness or execute the Divine vengeance on the obstinate haters of God, of Christ, and of holiness, praise his justice and truth; and adore his awful judgments, when he brings upon cruel persecutors the tortures they made his saints and prophets suffer.

8-11 The heart of man is so desperately wicked, that the most severe miseries never will bring any to repent, without the special grace of God. Hell itself is filled with blasphemies; and those are ignorant of the history of human nature, of the Bible, and of their own hearts, who do not know that the more men suffer, and the more plainly they see the hand of God in their sufferings, the more furiously they often rage against him. Let sinners now seek repentance from Christ, and the grace of the Holy Spirit, or they will have the anguish and horror of an unhumbled, impenitent, and desperate heart; thus adding to their guilt and misery through all eternity. Darkness is opposed to wisdom and knowledge, and forebodes the confusion and folly of the idolaters and followers of the beast. It is opposed to pleasure and joy, and signifies anguish and vexation of spirit.

12-16 This probably shows the destruction of the Turkish power, and of idolatry, and that a way will be made for the return of the Jews. Or, take it for Rome, as mystical Babylon, the name of Babylon being put for Rome, which was meant, but was not then to be directly named. When Rome is destroyed, her river and merchandise must suffer with her. And perhaps a way will be opened for the eastern nations to come into the church of Christ. The great dragon will collect all his forces, to make one desperate struggle before all be lost. God warns of this great trial, to engage his people to prepare for it. These will be times of great temptation; therefore Christ, by his apostle, calls on his professed servants to expect his sudden coming, and to watch that they might not be put to shame, as apostates or hypocrites. However Christians differ, as to their views of the times and seasons of events yet to be brought to pass, on this one point all are agreed, Jesus Christ, the Lord of glory, will suddenly come again to judge the world. To those living near to Christ, it is an object of joyful hope and expectation, and delay is not desired by them.

17-21 The seventh and last angel poured forth his vial, and the downfall of Babylon was finished. The church triumphant in heaven saw it and rejoiced; the church in conflict on earth saw it and became triumphant. God remembered

the Mount Sion, and with him an hundred forty and four thousand." This is a certain number put for an uncertain—I mean uncertain to us, though not uncertain to God. It is a vast number, put for that "multitude which no man can number," who shall stand before the throne of God. Now, here is something not very pleasant to my friend Bigot yonder. Note the number of those who are to be saved; they are said to be a great number, even a "hundred forty and four thousand," which is but a unit put for the vast innumerable multitude who are to be gathered home. Why, my friend, there are so many as that belonging to your church. You believe that none will be saved but those who hear your minister, and believe your creed; I do not think you could find one hundred and forty-four thousand anywhere. You will have to enlarge your heart I think; you must take in a few more, and not be so inclined to shut out the Lord's people, because you cannot agree with them. I do abhor from my heart that continual whining of some men about their own little church as the "remnant"—the "few that are to be saved." They are always dwelling upon strait gates and narrow ways, and upon what they conceive to be a truth, that but few shall enter heaven. Why, my friends, I believe there will be more in heaven than in hell. If you ask me why I think so, I answer, because Christ, in everything, is to "have the pre-eminence," and I cannot conceive how he could have the pre-eminence if there are to be more in the dominions of Satan than in paradise. Moreover, it is said there is to be a multitude that no man can number in heaven; I have never read that there is to be a multitude that no man can number in hell. But I rejoice to know that the souls of all infants, as soon as they die, speed their way to paradise. Think what a multitude there is of them! And then there are the just, and the redeemed of all nations and kindreds up till now; and there are better times coming, when the religion of Christ shall be universal; when he shall reign from pole to pole with illimitable sway; when kingdoms shall bow before him, and nations be born in a day; and in the thousand years of the great millennial state there will be enough saved to make up all the deficiencies of the thousands of years that have gone before. Christ shall have the pre-eminence at last; his train shall be far larger than that which shall attend the chariots of the grim monarch of hell. Christ shall be master everywhere, and his praise sounded in every land. One hundred and forty-four thousand were observed, the types and representatives of a far larger number who are ultimately to be saved.

But notice, whilst the number is very large, how very certain it is. By turning over the leaves of your Bible to a previous chapter of this book, you will see that at the 4th verse it is written, that one hundred and forty-four thousand were sealed; and now we find there are one hundred and forty-four thousand

unclean and hateful bird.

3 For all nations have drunk of the wine of the wrath of her fornication, and the kings of the earth have committed fornication with her, and the merchants of the earth are waxed rich through the abundance of her delicacies.

4 And I heard another voice from heaven, saying, Come out of her, my people, that ye be not partakers of her sins, and that ye receive not of her plagues.

5 For her sins have reached unto heaven, and God hath remembered her iniquities.

6 Reward her even as she rewarded you, and double unto her double according to her works: in the cup which she hath filled fill to her double.

7 How much she hath glorified herself, and lived deliciously, so much torment and sorrow give her: for she saith in her heart, I sit a queen, and am no widow, and shall see no sorrow.

8 Therefore shall her plagues come in one day, death, and mourning, and famine; and she shall be utterly burned with fire: for strong is the Lord God who judgeth her.

9 And the kings of the earth, who have committed fornication and lived deliciously with her, shall bewail her, and lament for her, when they shall see the smoke of her burning,

10 Standing afar off for the fear of her torment, saying, Alas, alas, that great city Babylon, that mighty city! for in one hour is thy judgment come.

11 And the merchants of the earth shall weep and mourn over her; for no man buyeth their merchandise any more:

12 The merchandise of gold, and silver, and precious stones, and of pearls, and fine linen, and purple, and silk, and scarlet, and all thyine wood, and all manner vessels of ivory, and all manner vessels of most precious wood, and of brass, and iron, and marble,

13 And cinnamon, and odors, and ointments, and frankincense, and wine, and oil, and fine flour, and wheat, and beasts, and sheep, and horses, and chariots, and slaves, and

them. I will show thee the judgment of the great whore — Which is now circumstantially described. That sitteth as a queen — In pomp, power, ease, and luxury. Upon many waters — Many people and nations, verse 15.

2. With whom the kings of the earth — Both ancient and modern, for many ages. Have committed fornication — By partaking of her idolatry and various wickedness. And the inhabitants of the earth — The common people. Have been made drunk with the wine of her fornication — No wine can more thoroughly intoxicate those who drink it, than false zeal does the followers of the great whore.

3. And he carried me away — In the vision. Into a wilderness — The campagna di Romansa, the country round about Rome, is now a wilderness, compared to what it was once. And I saw a woman — Both the scripture and other writers frequently represent a city under this emblem. Sitting upon a scarlet wild beast — The same which is described in the thirteenth chapter.

4. And the woman was arrayed — With the utmost pomp and magnificence. In purple and scarlet — These were the colors of the imperial habit: the purple, in times of peace; and the scarlet, in times of war. Having in her hand a golden cup — Like the ancient Babylon, Jer. li, 7. Full of abominations — The most abominable doctrines as well as practices.

5. And on her forehead a name written — Whereas the saints have the name of God and the Lamb on their foreheads.

6. And I saw the woman drunk with the blood of the saints — So that Rome may well be called, "The slaughter-house of the martyrs." She hath shed much Christian blood in every age; but at length she is even drunk with it, at the time to which this vision refers. The witnesses of Jesus — The preachers of his word. And I wondered exceedingly — At her cruelty and the patience of God.

7. I will tell thee the mystery — The hidden meaning of this.

8. The beast which thou sawest (namely, verse 3) was, &c. This is a very observable and punctual description of the beast.

9. Here is the mind that hath wisdom — Only those who are wise will understand this. The seven heads are seven hills.

10. And they are seven kings — Anciently there were royal palaces on all the seven Roman hills.

11. And the wild beast that was, and is not, even he is the eighth — When the time of his not being is over. The beast consists, as it were, of eight parts. The seven heads are seven of them; and the eighth is his whole body, or the beast himself. Yet the beast himself, though he is in a sense termed the eighth, is of the seven, yea, contains them all.

12. The ten horns are ten kings — It is nowhere said that these horns are on the beast, or on his heads. And he is said to have them, not as he is one of the seven, but as he is the eighth. They are ten secular potentates, contemporary with, not succeeding, each other, who receive authority as kings with the beast, probably in some convention, which, after a very short space, they will deliver up to the beast. Because of their short continuance, only authority as kings, not a kingdom, is ascribed to them. While they retain this authority together with the beast, he will be stronger than ever before; but far stronger still, when their power is also transferred to him.

13. In the thirteenth and fourteenth verses is summed up what is afterwards mentioned, concerning the horns and the beast, in this and the two following chapters. These have one mind, and give — They all, with one consent, give their warlike power and royal authority to the wild beast.

14. These — Kings with the beast. He is Lord of lords — Rightful sovereign of all, and ruling all things well. And King of kings — As a king he fights with and conquers all his enemies. And they that are with him — Beholding his victory, are such as were, while in the body, called, by his word and Spirit. And chosen — Taken out of the world, when they were enabled to believe in him. And faithful — Unto death.

the great and wicked city; though for some time he seemed to have forgotten her idolatry and cruelty. All that was most secure was carried away by the ruin. Men blasphemed: the greatest judgments that can befall men, will not bring to repentance without the grace of God. To be hardened against God, by his righteous judgments, is a certain token of sure and utter destruction.

REVELATION 17

One of the angels who had the vials, explains the meaning of the former vision of the antichristian beast that was to reign 1260 years, and then to be destroyed. (1-6)

And interprets the mystery of the woman, and the beast that had seven heads and ten horns. (7-18)

1-6 Rome clearly appears to be meant in this chapter. Pagan Rome subdued and ruled with military power, not by art and flatteries. She left the nations in general to their ancient usages and worship. But it is well known that by crafty and politic management, with all kinds of deceit of unrighteousness, papal Rome has obtained and kept her rule over kings and nations. Here were allurements of worldly honor and riches, pomp and pride, suited to sensual and worldly minds. Prosperity, pomp, and splendor, feed the pride and lusts of the human heart, but are no security against the Divine vengeance. The golden cup represents the allurements, and delusions, by which this mystical Babylon has obtained and kept her influence, and seduced others to join her abominations. She is named, from her infamous practices, a mother of harlots; training them up to idolatry and all sorts of wickedness. She filled herself with the blood of the saints and martyrs of Jesus. She intoxicated herself with it; and it was so pleasant to her, that she never was satisfied. We cannot but wonder at the oceans of Christian blood shed by men called Christians; yet when we consider these prophecies, these awful deeds testify to the truth of the gospel. And let all beware of a splendid, gainful, or fashionable religion. Let us avoid the mysteries of iniquity, and study diligently the great mystery of godliness, that we may learn humility and gratitude from the example of Christ. The more we seek to resemble him, the less we shall be liable to be deceived by antichrist.

7-14 The beast on which the woman sat was, and is not, and yet is. It was a seat of idolatry and persecution, and is not; not in the ancient form, which was pagan: yet it is; it is truly the seat of idolatry and tyranny, though of another sort and

saved; not 143,999, and 144,001, but exactly the number that are sealed. Now, my friends may not like what I am going to say; but if they do not like it, their quarrel is with God's Bible, not with me. There will be just as many in heaven as are sealed by God— just as many as Christ did purchase with his blood; all of them, and no more and no less. There will be just as many there as were quickened to life by the Holy Spirit, and were, "born again, not of blood, nor of the will of the flesh, nor of the will of man, but of God." "Ah," some say, "there is that abominable doctrine of election." Exactly so, if it be abominable; but you will never be able to cut it out of the Bible. You may hate it, and gnash and grind your teeth against it; but, remember, we can trace the pedigree of this doctrine, even apart from Scripture, to the time of the apostles. Church of England ministers and members, you have no right to differ from me on the doctrine of election, if you are what you profess by your own Articles. You who love the old Puritans, you have no right to quarrel with me; for where will you find a Puritan who was not a strong Calvinist? You who love the fathers, you cannot differ from me. What say you of Augustine? Was he not, in his day, called a great and mighty teacher of grace? And I even turn to Roman Catholics, and, with all the errors of their system, I remind them that even in their body have been found those who have held that doctrine, and, though long persecuted for it, have never been expelled the church. I refer to the Jansenists. But, above all, I challenge every man who reads his Bible to say that that doctrine is not there. What saith the 9th of Romans? "The children being not yet born, neither having done any good or evil, that the purpose of God according to election might stand, not of works, but of him that calleth: It was said unto her, The elder shall serve the younger." And then it goes on to say to the carping objector— "Nay, but, O man, who art thou that repliest against God? Shall the thing formed say to him that formed it, Why hast thou made me thus? Hath not the potter power over the clay, of the same lump to make one vessel unto honor, and another unto dishonor?" But enough on this subject.

One hundred and forty-four thousand, we say, is a certain number made to represent the certainty of the salvation of all God's elect, believing people. Now, some say that this doctrine has a tendency to discourage men from coming to Christ. Well, you say so; but I have never seen it, and blessed be God I have never proved it so. I have preached this doctrine ever since I began to preach; but I can say this,—ye shall not (and I am now become a fool in glorying) ye shall not find among those who have not preached the doctrine, one who has been the instrument of turning more harlots, more drunkards, and more sinners of every class, from the error of their ways, than I have, by the simple preaching of the doctrine of free grace; and, while this has been

souls of men.

14 And the fruits that thy soul lusted after are departed from thee, and all things which were dainty and goodly are departed from thee, and thou shalt find them no more at all.

15 The merchants of these things, which were made rich by her, shall stand afar off for the fear of her torment, weeping and wailing,

16 And saying, Alas, alas, that great city, that was clothed in fine linen, and purple, and scarlet, and decked with gold, and precious stones, and pearls!

17 For in one hour so great riches is come to nought. And every shipmaster, and all the company in ships, and sailors, and as many as trade by sea, stood afar off,

18 And cried when they saw the smoke of her burning, saying, What city is like unto this great city!

19 And they cast dust on their heads, and cried, weeping and wailing, saying, Alas, alas, that great city, wherein were made rich all that had ships in the sea by reason of her costliness! for in one hour is she made desolate.

20 Rejoice over her, thou heaven, and ye holy apostles and prophets; for God hath avenged you on her.

21 And a mighty angel took up a stone like a great millstone, and cast it into the sea, saying, Thus with violence shall that great city Babylon be thrown down, and shall be found no more at all.

22 And the voice of harpers, and musicians, and of pipers, and trumpeters, shall be heard no more at all in thee; and no craftsman, of whatsoever craft he be, shall be found any more in thee; and the sound of a millstone shall be heard no more at all in thee;

23 And the light of a candle shall shine no more at all in thee; and the voice of the bridegroom and of the bride shall be heard no more at all in thee: for thy merchants were the great men of the earth; for by thy sorceries were all nations deceived.

15. People, and multitudes, and nations, and tongues – It is not said tribes: for Israel hath nothing to do with Rome in particular.

16. And shall eat her flesh – Devour her immense riches.

17. For God hath put it into their heart – Which indeed no less than almighty power could have effected. To execute his sentence – till the words of God – Touching the overthrow of all his enemies, should be fulfilled.

18. The woman is the great city, which reigneth – Namely, while the beast "is not," and the woman "sitteth upon him."

REVELATION 18

1. And I saw another angel coming down out of heaven – Termed another, with respect to him who "came down out of heaven," chap. x, 1. And the earth was enlightened with his glory – To make his coming more conspicuous. If such be the luster of the servant, what images can display the majesty of the Lord, who has "thousand thousands" of those glorious attendants "ministering to him, and ten thousand times ten thousand standing before him?"

2. And he cried, Babylon is fallen – This fall was mentioned before, chap. xiv, 8; but is now declared at large.

4. And I heard another voice – Of Christ, whose people, secretly scattered even there, are warned of her approaching destruction. That ye be not partakers of her sins – That is, of the fruits of them.

5. Even to heaven – An expression which implies the highest guilt.

6. Reward her – This God speaks to the executioners of his vengeance. Even as she hath rewarded – Others; in particular, the saints of God. And give her double – This, according to the Hebrew idiom, implies only a full retaliation.

7. As much as she hath glorified herself – By pride, and pomp, and arrogant boasting. And lived deliciously – In all kinds of elegance, luxury, and wantonness. So much torment give her – Proportioning the punishment to the sin. Because she saith in her heart – As did ancient Babylon, Isai xlvii, 8, 9. I sit – Her usual style. Hence those expressions, "The chair, the seat of Rome: he sat so many years." As a queen – Over many kings, "mistress of all churches; the supreme; the infallible; the only spouse of Christ; out of which there is no salvation." And am no widow – But the spouse of Christ. And shall see no sorrow – From the death of my children, or any other calamity; for God himself will defend "the church."

8. Therefore – as both the natural and judicial consequence of this proud security. Shall her plagues come – The death of her children, with an incapacity of bearing more. Sorrow – of every kind. And famine – In the room of luxurious plenty: the very things from which she imagined herself to be most safe. For strong is the Lord God who judgeth her – Against whom therefore all her strength, great as it is, will not avail.

10. Thou strong city – Rome was anciently termed by its inhabitants, Valentia, that is, strong. And the word Rome itself, in Greek, signifies strength. This name was given it by the Greek strangers.

12. Merchandise of gold, &c. – Almost all these are still in use at Rome, both in their idolatrous service, and in common life. Fine linen – The sort of it mentioned in the original is exceeding costly. Thyine wood – A sweet-smelling wood not unlike citron, used in adorning magnificent palaces. Vessels of most precious wood – Ebony, in particular, which is often mentioned with ivory: the one excelling in whiteness, the other in blackness; and both in uncommon smoothness.

13. Cinnamon – A shrub whose wood is a fine perfume. And beasts – Cows and oxen. And of chariots – a purely Latin word is here inserted in the Greek. This St. John undoubtedly used on purpose, in describing the luxury of Rome. And of bodies – A common term for slaves. And souls of men – For these also are

form. It would deceive into stupid and blind submission all the inhabitants of the earth within its influence, except the remnant of the elect. This beast was seven heads, seven mountains, the seven hills on which Rome stands; and seven kings, seven sorts of government. Five were gone by when this prophecy was written; one was then in being; the other was yet to come. This beast, directed by the papacy, makes an eighth governor, and sets up idolatry again. It had ten horns, which are said to be ten kings who had as yet no kingdoms; they should not rise up till the Roman empire was broken; but should for a time be very zealous in her interest. Christ must reign till all enemies be put under his feet. The reason of the victory is, that he is the King of kings, and Lord of lords. He has supreme dominion and power over all things; all the powers of earth and hell are subject to his control. His followers are called to this warfare, are fitted for it, and will be faithful in it.

15-18 God so ruled the hearts of these kings, by his power over them, and by his providence, that they did those things, without intending it, which he purposed and foretold. They shall see their folly, and how they have been bewitched and enslaved by the harlot, and be made instruments in her destruction. She was that great city which reigned over the kings of the earth, when John had this vision; and every one knows Rome to be that city. Believers will be received to the glory of the Lord, when wicked men will be destroyed in a most awful manner; their joining together in sin, will be turned to hatred and rage, and they will eagerly assist in tormenting each other. But the Lord's portion is his people; his counsel shall stand, and he will do all his pleasure, to his glory, and the happiness of all his servants.

REVELATION 18

Another angel from heaven proclaims the fall of mystical Babylon. (1-3)
A voice from heaven admonishes the people of God, lest they partake of her plagues. (4-8)
The lamentations over her. (9-19)
The church called upon to rejoice in her utter ruin. (20-24)

1-8 The downfall and destruction of the mystical Babylon are determined in the counsels of God. Another angel comes from heaven. This seems to be Christ himself, coming to destroy his enemies, and to shed abroad the light of his gospel through all nations. The wickedness of this Babylon was very great; she had forsaken the true God, and set up idols, and had drawn all sorts of men into spiritual adultery, and by her

so, I hold that no argument can be brought to prove that it has a tendency to discourage sinners, or bolster them up in sin. We hold, as the Bible says, that all the elect, and those only, shall be saved; all who go to Christ are elect. So that if any of you have in your heart a desire after heaven and after Christ; if you carry out that desire in sincere and earnest prayer, and are born again, you may as certainly conclude your election as you can conclude that you are alive. You must have been chosen of God before the foundation of the world, or you would never have done any of these things, seeing they are the fruits of election.

But why should it keep any one from going to Christ? "Because," says one, "if I go to Christ I may not be elect." No, sir, if you go, you prove that you are elect. "But," says another, "I am afraid to go, in case I should not be elect." Say as an old woman once said, "If there were only three persons elected, I would try to be one of them; and since he said, 'He that believeth shall be saved,' I would challenge God on his promise, and try if he would break it." No, come to Christ; and if you do so, beyond a doubt you are God's elect from the foundation of the world; and therefore this grace has been given to you. But why should it discourage you? Suppose there are a number of sick folk here, and a large hospital has been built. There is put up over the door, "All persons who come shall be taken in:" at the same time it is known that there is a person inside the hospital, who is so wise that he knows all who will come, and has written down the names of all who will come in a book, so that, when they come, those who open the doors will only say, "How marvelously wise our Master was, to know the names of those who would come." Is there anything dispiriting in that? You would go, and you would have all the more confidence in that man's wisdom, because he was able to know before that they were going. "Ah, but," you say, "it was ordained that some should come." Well, to give you another illustration; suppose there is a rule that there always must be a thousand persons, or a very large number in the hospital. You say, "When I go perhaps they will take me in, and perhaps they will not." "But," says someone, "there is a rule that there must be a thousand in: somehow or other they must make up that number of beds, and have that number of patients in the hospital." You say, "Then why should not I be among the thousand; and have not I the encouragement that whosoever goes shall not be cast out? And have I not again the encouragement, that if they will not go, they must be fetched in somehow or other; for the number must be made up; so it is determined and so it is decreed." You would therefore have a double encouragement, instead of half a one; and you would go with confidence, and say, "They must take me in, because they say they will take all in that come; and on the other hand, they must take me in,

24 And in her was found the blood of prophets, and of saints, and of all that were slain upon the earth.

REVELATION 19

1 And after these things I heard a great voice of much people in heaven, saying, Alleluia; Salvation, and glory, and honor, and power, unto the Lord our God:

2 For true and righteous are his judgments: for he hath judged the great whore, which did corrupt the earth with her fornication, and hath avenged the blood of his servants at her hand.

3 And again they said, Alleluia. And her smoke rose up for ever and ever.

4 And the four and twenty elders and the four beasts fell down and worshipped God that sat on the throne, saying, Amen; Alleluia.

5 And a voice came out of the throne, saying, Praise our God, all ye his servants, and ye that fear him, both small and great.

6 And I heard as it were the voice of a great multitude, and as the voice of many waters, and as the voice of mighty thunderings, saying, Alleluia: for the Lord God omnipotent reigneth.

7 Let us be glad and rejoice, and give honor to him: for the marriage of the Lamb is come, and his wife hath made herself ready.

8 And to her was granted that she should be arrayed in fine linen, clean and white: for the fine linen is the righteousness of saints.

9 And he saith unto me, Write, Blessed are they which are called unto the marriage supper of the Lamb. And he saith unto me, These are the true sayings of God.

10 And I fell at his feet to worship him. And he said unto me, See thou do it not: I am thy fellowservant, and of thy brethren that have the testimony of Jesus: worship God: for the testimony of Jesus is the spirit of prophecy.

continually bought and sold at Rome. And this of all others is the most gainful merchandise to the Roman traffickers.

14. And the fruits – From what was imported they proceed to the domestic delicates of Rome; none of which is in greater request there, than the particular sort which is here mentioned. The word properly signifies, pears, peaches, nectarines, and all of the apple and plum kinds. And all things that are dainty – To the taste. And splendid – To the sight; as clothes, buildings, furniture.

19. And they cast dust on their heads – As mourners. Most of the expressions here used in describing the downfall of Babylon are taken from Ezekiel's description of the downfall of Tyre, Ezek. xxvi, 1 – Ezek. xxviii, 19.

20. Rejoice over her, thou heaven – That is, all the inhabitants of it; and more especially, ye saints; and among the saints still more eminently, ye apostles and prophets.

21. And a mighty angel took up a stone, and threw it into the sea – By a like emblem Jeremiah foreshowed the fall of the Chaldean Babylon, Jer. li, 63, 64.

22. And the voice of harpers – Players on stringed instruments. And musicians – Skillful singers in particular.

23. For thy merchants were the great men of the earth – A circumstance which was in itself indifferent, and yet led them into pride, luxury, and numberless other sins.

24. And in her was found the blood of the prophets and saints – The same angel speaks still, yet he does not say "in thee," but in her, now so sunk as not to hear these last words. And of all that had been slain – Even before she was built. See Matt. xxiii, 35.

REVELATION 19

1. I heard a loud voice of a great multitude – Whose blood the great whore had shed. Saying, Hallelujah – This Hebrew word signifies, Praise ye Jah, or Him that is. God named himself to Moses, EHEIEH, that is, I will be, Exod. iii, 14; and at the same time, "Jehovah," that is, "He that is, and was, and is to come:" during the trumpet of the seventh angel, he is styled, "He that is and was," chap. xvi, 5; and not "He that is to come;" because his long-expected coming is under this trumpet actually present. At length he is styled, "Jah," "He that is;" the past together with the future being swallowed up in the present, the former things being no more mentioned, for the greatness of those that now are.

2. For true and righteous are his judgments – Thus is the cry of the souls under the altar changed into a song of praise.

4. And the four and twenty elders, and the four living creatures fell down – The living creatures are nearer the throne than the elders. Accordingly they are mentioned before them, with the praise they render to God, chap. iv, 9, 10; v, 8, 14; inasmuch as there the praise moves from the center to the circumference. But here, when God's judgments are fulfilled, it moves back from the circumference to the center. Here, therefore, the four and twenty elders are named before the living creatures.

5. And a voice came forth from the throne – Probably from the four living creatures, saying, Praise our God – The occasion and matter of this song of praise follow immediately after, verses 6, &c.; God was praised before, for his judgment of the great whore, verses 1-4. Now for that which follows it: for that the Lord God, the Almighty, takes the kingdom to himself, and avenges himself on the rest of his enemies. Were all these inhabitants of heaven mistaken? If not, there is real, yea, and terrible anger in God.

6. And I heard the voice of a great multitude. So all his servants did praise him. The Almighty reigneth – More eminently and gloriously than ever before.

7. The marriage of the Lamb is come – Is near at hand, to be solemnized speedily. What this implies, none of "the spirits of just men," even in paradise, yet

MATTHEW HENRY   CHARLES H. SPURGEON

wealth and luxury kept them in her interest. The spiritual merchandise, by which multitudes have wickedly lived in wealth, by the sins and follies of mankind, seems principally intended. Fair warning is given to all that expect mercy from God, that they should not only come out of this Babylon, but assist in her destruction. God may have a people even in Babylon. But God's people shall be called out of Babylon, and called effectually, while those that partake with wicked men in their sins, must receive of their plagues.

9-19 The mourners had shared Babylon's sensual pleasures, and gained by her wealth and trade. The kings of the earth, whom she flattered into idolatry, allowing them to be tyrannical over their subjects, while obedient to her; and the merchants, those who trafficked for her indulgences, pardons, and honors; these mourn. Babylon's friends partook her sinful pleasures and profits, but are not willing to share her plagues. The spirit of antichrist is a worldly spirit, and that sorrow is a mere worldly sorrow; they do not lament for the anger of God, but for the loss of outward comforts. The magnificence and riches of the ungodly will avail them nothing, but will render the vengeance harder to be borne. The spiritual merchandise is here alluded to, when not only slaves, but the souls of men, are mentioned as articles of commerce, to the destroying the souls of millions. Nor has this been peculiar to the Roman antichrist, and only her guilt. But let prosperous traders learn, with all their gains, to get the unsearchable riches of Christ; otherwise; even in this life, they may have to mourn that riches make to themselves wings and fly away, and that all the fruits their souls lusted after, are departed from them. Death, at any rate, will soon end their commerce, and all the riches of the ungodly will be exchanged, not only for the coffin and the worm, but for the fire that cannot be quenched.

20-24 That which is matter of rejoicing to the servants of God on earth, is matter of rejoicing to the angels in heaven. The apostles, who are honored and daily worshiped at Rome in an idolatrous manner, will rejoice in her fall. The fall of Babylon was an act of God's justice. And because it was a final ruin, this enemy should never molest them any more; of this they were assured by a sign. Let us take warning from the things which brought others to destruction, and let us set our affections on things above, when we consider the changeable nature of earthly things.

because they must have a certain number: that number is not made up, and why should not I be one?" Oh, never doubt about election; believe in Christ, and then rejoice in election; do not fret about it till you have believed in Christ.

"I looked, and, lo, a Lamb stood on the Mount Sion, and with him an hundred forty and four thousand." And who were these people, "having his Father's name written in their foreheads?" Not Bs for "Baptists," not Ws for "Wesleyans," not Es for "Established Church:" they had their Father's name and nobody else's. What a deal of fuss is made on earth about our distinctions! We think such a deal about belonging to this denomination, and the other. Why, if you were to go to heaven's gates, and ask if they had any Baptists there, the angel would only look at you, and not answer you; if you were to ask if they had any Wesleyans, or members of the Established Church, he would say, "Nothing of the sort;" but if you were to ask him whether they had any Christians there, "Ay," he would say, "an abundance of them: they are all one now—all called by one name; the old brand has been obliterated, and now they have not the name of this man or the other; they have the name of God, even their Father, stamped on their brow." Learn then dear friends, whatever the connection to which you belong, to be charitable to your brethren, and kind to them, seeing that, after all, the name you now hold here will be forgotten in heaven, and only your Father's name will be there known.

One more remark here, and we will turn from the worshipers to listen to their song. It is said of all these worshipers that they learned the song before they went there. At the end of the third verse it is said, "No man could learn that song but the hundred and forty and four thousand, which were redeemed from the earth." Brethren, we must begin heaven's song here below, or else we shall never sing it above. The choristers of heaven have all had rehearsals upon earth, before they sing in that orchestra. You think that, die when you may, you will go to heaven, without being prepared. Nay, sir; heaven is a prepared place for a prepared people, and unless you are "made meet to be partakers of the inheritance of the saints in light," you can never stand there among them. If you were in heaven without a new heart and a right spirit, you would be glad enough to get out of it; for heaven, unless a man is heavenly himself, would be worse than hell. A man who is unrenewed and unregenerate going to heaven would be miserable there. There would be a song— he could not join in it; there would be a constant hallelujah, but he would not know a note: and besides, he would be in the presence of the Almighty, even in the presence of the God he hates, and how could he be happy there? No, sirs; ye must learn the song of paradise here, or else ye can never sing it.

You must learn to feel that "sweeter sounds than

11 And I saw heaven opened, and behold a white horse; and he that sat upon him was called Faithful and True, and in righteousness he doth judge and make war.

12 His eyes were as a flame of fire, and on his head were many crowns; and he had a name written, that no man knew, but he himself.

13 And he was clothed with a vesture dipped in blood: and his name is called The Word of God.

14 And the armies which were in heaven followed him upon white horses, clothed in fine linen, white and clean.

15 And out of his mouth goeth a sharp sword, that with it he should smite the nations: and he shall rule them with a rod of iron: and he treadeth the wine-press of the fierceness and wrath of Almighty God.

16 And he hath on his vesture and on his thigh a name written, KING OF KINGS, AND LORD OF LORDS.

17 And I saw an angel standing in the sun; and he cried with a loud voice, saying to all the fowls that fly in the midst of heaven, Come and gather yourselves together unto the supper of the great God;

18 That ye may eat the flesh of kings, and the flesh of captains, and the flesh of mighty men, and the flesh of horses, and of them that sit on them, and the flesh of all men, both free and bond, both small and great.

19 And I saw the beast, and the kings of the earth, and their armies, gathered together to make war against him that sat on the horse, and against his army.

20 And the beast was taken, and with him the false prophet that wrought miracles before him, with which he deceived them that had received the mark of the beast, and them that worshiped his image. These both were cast alive into a lake of fire burning with brimstone.

21 And the remnant were slain with the sword of him that sat upon the horse, which sword proceeded out of his mouth:

know. O what things are those which are yet behind! And what purity of heart should there be, to meditate upon them! And his wife hath made herself ready – Even upon earth; but in a far higher sense, in that world. After a time allowed for this, the new Jerusalem comes down, both made ready and adorned, chap. xxi, 2.

8. And it is given to her – By God. The bride is all holy men, the whole invisible church. To be arrayed in fine linen, white and clean – This is an emblem of the righteousness of the saints – Both of their justification and sanctification.

9. And he – The angel, saith to me, Write – St. John seems to have been so amazed at these glorious sights, that he needeth to be reminded of this. Happy are they who are invited to the marriage supper of the Lamb – Called to glory.

10. And I fell before his feet to worship him – It seems, mistaking him for the angel of the covenant. But he saith, See thou do it not – In the original, it is only, See not, with a beautiful abruptness. To pray to or worship the highest creature is flat idolatry. I am thy fellow servant and of thy brethren that have the testimony of Jesus – I am now employed as your fellow servant, to testify of the Lord Jesus, by the same Spirit which inspired the prophets of old.

11. And I saw the heaven opened – This is a new and peculiar opening of it, in order to show the magnificent expedition of Christ and his attendants, against his great adversary. And behold a white horse – Many little regarded Christ, when he came meek, "riding upon an ass;" but what will they say, when he goes forth upon his white horse, with the sword of his mouth? White – Such as generals use in solemn triumph. And he that sitteth on him, called Faithful – In performing all his promises. And True – In executing all his threatenings. And in righteousness – With the utmost justice. He judgeth and maketh war – Often the sentence and execution go together.

12. And his eyes were as a flame of fire – They were said to be as or like a flame of fire, before, chap. i, 14; an emblem of his omniscience. And upon his head are many diadems – For he is king of all nations. And he hath a name written, which none knoweth but himself – As God he is incomprehensible to every creature.

13. And he is clothed in a vesture dipped in blood – The blood of the enemies he hath already conquered. Isaiah lxiii, 1, &c.

15. And he shall rule them – Who are not slain by his sword. With a rod of iron – That is, if they will not submit to his golden scepter. And he treadeth the wine press of the wrath of God – That is, he executes his judgments on the ungodly. This ruler of the nations was born (or appeared as such) immediately after the seventh angel began to sound. He now appears, not as a child, but as a victorious warrior.

16. And he hath on his vesture and on his thigh – That is, on the part of his vesture which is upon his thigh. A name written – It was usual of old, for great personages in the eastern countries, to have magnificent titles affixed to their garments.

17. Gather yourselves together to the great supper of God – As to a great feast, which the vengeance of God will soon provide; a strongly figurative expression, (taken from Ezek. xxxix, 17,) denoting the vastness of the ensuing slaughter.

19. And I saw the kings of the earth – The ten kings mentioned chap. xvii, 12; who had now drawn the other kings of the earth to them, whether Popish, Mahometan, or pagan. Gathered together to make war with him that sat upon the horse – All beings, good and evil, visible and invisible, will be concerned in this grand contest. See Zech. xiv, 1, &c.

20. The false prophet, who had wrought the miracles before him – And therefore shared in his punishment; these two ungodly men were cast alive – Without undergoing bodily death. Into the lake of fire – And that before the devil himself, chap. xx, 10. Here is the last of the beast.

21. Here is a most magnificent description of the overthrow of the beast and his adherents. It has, in particular, one exquisite beauty; that, after exhibiting the two

REVELATION 19

The church in heaven and that on earth triumph,
and praise the Lord for his righteous judg-
ments. (1-10)
A vision of Christ going forth to destroy the beast
and his armies. (11-21)

1-10 Praising God for what we have, is praying for what is yet further to be done for us. There is harmony between the angels and the saints in this triumphant song. Christ is the Bridegroom of his ransomed church. This second union will be completed in heaven; but the beginning of the glorious millennium (by which is meant a reign of Christ, or a state of happiness, for a thousand years on earth) may be considered as the cele-bration of his espousals on earth. Then the church of Christ, being purified from errors, divi-sions, and corruptions, in doctrine, discipline, worship, and practice, will be made ready to be publicly owned by him as his delight and his beloved. The church appeared; not in the gay, gaudy dress of the mother of harlots, but in fine linen, clean and white. In the robes of Christ's righteousness, imputed for justification, and imparted for sanctification. The promises of the gospel, the true sayings of God, opened, applied, and sealed by the Spirit of God, in holy ordinances, are the marriage-feast. This seems to refer to the abundant grace and consolation Christians will receive in the happy days which are to come. The apostle offered honor to the angel. The angel refused it. He directed the apostle to the true and only object of religious worship; to worship God, and him alone. This plainly condemns the practice of those who wor-ship the elements of bread and wine, and saints, and angels; and of those who do not believe that Christ is truly and by nature God, yet pay him a sort of worship. They stand convicted of idolatry by a messenger from heaven. These are the true sayings of God; of him who is to be worshiped, as one with the Father and the Holy Spirit.

11-21 Christ, the glorious Head of the church, is described as on a white horse, the emblem of justice and holiness. He has many crowns, for he is King of kings, and Lord of lords. He is arrayed in a vesture dipped in his own blood, by which he purchased his power as Mediator; and in the blood of his enemies, over whom he always pre-vails. His name is "The Word of God;" a name none fully knows but himself; only this we know, that this Word was God manifest in the flesh; but his perfections cannot be fully understood by any creature. Angels and saints follow, and are like Christ in their Armor of purity and right-eousness. The threatenings of the written word he is going to execute on his enemies. The

music knows mingle in your Savior's name," or else you can never chant the hallelujahs of the blest before the throne of the great "I AM." Take that thought, whatever else you forget; treasure it up in your memory, and ask grace of God that you may here be taught to sing the heavenly song, that after-wards in the land of the hereafter, in the home of the beautified, you may continually chant the high praises of him that loved you.

III. And now we come to the third and most interest-ing point, namely, THE LISTENING TO THEIR SONG. "I heard a voice from heaven, as the voice of many waters, and as the voice of a great thunder: and I heard the voice of harpers harping with their harps;" singing—how loud and yet how sweet!

First, then, singing how loud! It is said to be "like the voice of many waters." Have you never heard the sea roar, and the fullness thereof? Have you never walked by the sea-side, when the waves were singing, and when every little pebble-stone did turn chorister, to make up music to the Lord God of hosts? And have you never in time of storm beheld the sea, with its hundred hands, clapping them in gladsome adoration of the Most High? Have you never heard the sea roar out his praise, when the winds were holding carnival—perhaps singing the dirge of mariners, wrecked far out on the stormy deep, but far more likely exalting God with their hoarse voice, and praising him who makes a thousand fleets sweep over them in safety, and writes his furrows on their own youthful brow? Have you never heard the rumbling and booming of ocean on the shore, when it has been lashed into fury and has been driven upon the cliffs? If you have, you have a faint idea of the melody of heaven. It was "as the voice of many waters." But do not suppose that it is the whole of the idea. It is not the voice of one ocean, but the voice of many, that is needed to give you an idea of the melodies of heaven. You are to suppose ocean piled upon ocean, sea upon sea,—the Pacific piled upon the Atlantic, the Arctic upon that, the Antarctic higher still, and so ocean upon ocean, all lashed to fury, and all sounding with a mighty voice the praise of God. Such is the singing of heaven. Or if the illus-tration fails to strike, take another. We have men-tioned here two or three times the mighty falls of Niagara. They can be heard at a tremendous dis-tance, so awful is their sound. Now, suppose water-falls dashing upon waterfalls, cataracts upon cataracts, Niagaras upon Niagaras, each of them sounding forth their mighty voices, and you have got some idea of the singing of paradise. "I heard a voice like the voice of many waters." Can you not hear it? Ah! if our ears were opened we might almost cast the song. I have thought sometimes that the voice of the Aeolian harp, when it has swollen out grandly, was almost like an echo of the songs of those who sing before the throne; and on the summer eve,

and all the fowls were filled with their flesh.

REVELATION 20

1 And I saw an angel come down from heaven, having the key of the bottomless pit and a great chain in his hand.

2 And he laid hold on the dragon, that old serpent, which is the Devil, and Satan, and bound him a thousand years,

3 And cast him into the bottomless pit, and shut him up, and set a seal upon him, that he should deceive the nations no more, till the thousand years should be fulfilled: and after that he must be loosed a little season.

4 And I saw thrones, and they sat upon them, and judgment was given unto them: and I saw the souls of them that were beheaded for the witness of Jesus, and for the word of God, and which had not worshiped the beast, neither his image, neither had received his mark upon their foreheads, or in their hands; and they lived and reigned with Christ a thousand years.

5 But the rest of the dead lived not again until the thousand years were finished. This is the first resurrection.

6 Blessed and holy is he that hath part in the first resurrection: on such the second death hath no power, but they shall be priests of God and of Christ, and shall reign with him a thousand years.

7 And when the thousand years are expired, Satan shall be loosed out of his prison,

8 And shall go out to deceive the nations which are in the four quarters of the earth, Gog and Magog, to gather them together to battle: the number of whom is as the sand of the sea.

9 And they went up on the breadth of the earth, and compassed the camp of the saints about, and the beloved city: and fire came down from God out of heaven, and devoured them.

10 And the devil that deceived them was cast into the lake of fire and brimstone, where the

opposite armies, and all the apparatus for a battle, verses 11-19; then follows immediately, verse 20, the account of the victory, without one word of an engagement or fighting. Here is the most exact propriety; for what struggle can there be between omnipotence, and the power of all the creation united against it! Every description must have fallen short of this admirable silence.

REVELATION 20

1. And I saw an angel decending out of heaven – Coming down with a commission from God. Jesus Christ himself overthrew the beast: the proud dragon shall be bound by an angel; even as he and his angels were cast out of heaven by Michael and his angels. Having the key of the bottomless pit – Mentioned before, chap. ix, 1. And a great chain in his hand – The angel of the bottomless pit was shut up therein before the beginning of the first woe. But it is now first that Satan, after he had occasioned the third woe, is both chained and shut up.

2. And he laid hold on the dragon – With whom undoubtedly his angels were now cast into the bottomless pit, as well as finally "into everlasting fire," Matt. xxv, 41. And bound him a thousand years – That these thousand do not precede, or run parallel with, but wholly follow, the times of the beast, may manifestly appear,

1. From the series of the whole book, representing one continued chain of events.

2. From the circumstances which precede. The woman's bringing forth is followed by the casting of the dragon out of heaven to the earth. With this is connected the third woe, whereby the dragon through, and with, the beast, rages horribly. At the conclusion of the third woe the beast is overthrown and cast into "the lake of fire." At the same time the other grand enemy, the dragon, shall be bound and shut up.

3. These thousand years bring a new, full, and lasting immunity from all outward and inward evils, the authors of which are now removed, and an affluence of all blessings. But such time the church has never yet seen. Therefore it is still to come.

4. These thousand years are followed by the last times of the world, the letting loose of Satan, who gathers together Gog and Magog, and is thrown to the beast and false prophet "in the lake of fire." Now Satan's accusing the saints in heaven, his rage on earth, his imprisonment in the abyss, his seducing Gog and Magog, and being cast into the lake of fire, evidently succeed each other.

5. What occurs from chap. xx, 11 – chap. xxii, 5, manifestly follows the things related in the nineteenth chapter. The thousand years came between; whereas if they were past, neither the beginning nor the end of them would fall within this period. In a short time those who assert that they are now at hand will appear to have spoken the truth. Meantime let every man consider what kind of happiness he expects therein. The danger does not lie in maintaining that the thousand years are yet to come; but in interpreting them, whether past or to come, in a gross and carnal sense. The doctrine of the Son of God is a mystery. So is his cross; and so is his glory. In all these he is a sign that is spoken against. Happy they who believe and confess him in all!

3. And set a seal upon him – How far these expressions are to be taken literally, how far figuratively only, who can tell? That he might deceive the nations no more – One benefit only is here expressed, as resulting from the confinement of Satan. But how many and great blessings are implied! For the grand enemy being removed, the kingdom of God holds on its uninterrupted course among the nations; and the great mystery of God, so long foretold, is at length fulfilled; namely, when the beast is destroyed and Satan bound.

4. And I saw thrones – Such as are promised the apostles, Matt. xix, 28; Luke xxii, 30. And they – Namely, the saints, whom St. John saw at the same time,

MATTHEW HENRY

CHARLES H. SPURGEON

ensigns of his authority are his name; asserting his authority and power, warning the most powerful princes to submit, or they must fall before him. The powers of earth and hell make their utmost effort. These verses declare important events, foretold by the prophets. These persons were not excused because they did what their leaders bade them. How vain will be the plea of many sinners at the great day! We followed our guides; we did as we saw others do! God has given a rule to walk by, in his word; neither the example of the most, nor of the chief, must influence us contrary thereto: if we do as the most do, we must go where the most go, even into the burning lake.

REVELATION 20

Satan is bound for a thousand years. (1-3)
The first resurrection; those are blessed that have part therein. (4-6)
Satan loosed. Gog and Magog. (7-10)
The last and general resurrection. (11-15)

1-3 Here is a vision, showing by a figure the restraints laid on Satan himself. Christ, with Almighty power, will keep the devil from deceiving mankind as he has hitherto done. He never wants power and instruments to break the power of Satan. Christ shuts by his power, and seals by his authority. The church shall have a time of peace and prosperity, but all her trials are not yet over.

4-6 Here is an account of the reign of the saints, for the same space of time as Satan is bound. Those who suffer with Christ, shall reign with him in his spiritual and heavenly kingdom, in conformity to him in his wisdom, righteousness, and holiness: this is called the first resurrection, with which none but those who serve Christ, and suffer for him, shall be favored. The happiness of these servants of God is declared. None can be blessed but those that are holy; and all that are holy shall be blessed. We know something of what the first death is, and it is very awful; but we know not what this second death is. It must be much more dreadful; it is the death of the soul, eternal separation from God. May we never know what it is: those who have been made partakers of a spiritual resurrection, are saved from the power of the second death. We may expect that a thousand years will follow the destruction of the antichristian, idolatrous, persecuting powers, during which pure Christianity, in doctrine, worship, and holiness, will be made known over all the earth. By the all-powerful working of the Holy Spirit, fallen man will be new created; and faith and holiness will as certainly prevail, as

when the wind has come in gentle zephyrs through the forest, you might almost think it was the floating of some stray notes that had lost their way among the harps of heaven, and come down to us, to give us some faint foretaste of that song which hymns out in mighty peals before the throne of the Most High. But why so loud? The answer is, because there are so many there to sing. Nothing is more grand than the singing of multitudes.

And, indeed, there is something very grand in the singing of multitudes. I remember hearing 12,000 sing on one occasion in the open air. Some of our friends were then present, when we concluded our service with that glorious hallelujah. Have you ever forgotten it? It was indeed a mighty sound; it seemed to make heaven itself ring again. Think, then, what must be the voice of those who stand on the boundless plains of heaven, and with all their might shout, "Glory and honor and power and dominion unto him that sitteth on the throne, and to the Lamb for ever and ever."

One reason, however, why the song is so loud is a very simple one, namely, because all those who are there think themselves bound to sing the loudest of all.

And every saint will join that sonnet, and each one lift up his heart to God, then how mighty must be the strain of praise that will rise up to the throne of the glorious God our Father!

But note next, while it was a loud voice, how sweet it was. Noise is not music. There may be "a voice like many waters," and yet no music. It was sweet as well as loud; for John says, "I heard the voice of harpers harping with their harps." Perhaps the sweetest of all instruments is the harp. There are others which give forth sounds more grand and noble, but the harp is the sweetest of all instruments. I have sometimes sat to hear a skillful harper, till I could say, "I could sit and hear myself away," whilst with skillful fingers he touched the chords gently, and brought forth strains of melody which flowed like liquid silver, or like sounding honey into one's soul. Sweet, sweet beyond sweetness; words can scarcely tell how sweet the melody. Such is the music of heaven. No jarring notes there, no discord, but all one glorious harmonious song. You will not be there, formalist, to spoil the tune; nor you, hypocrite, to mar the melody; there will be all those there whose hearts are right with God, and therefore the strain will be one great harmonious whole, without a discord.

IV. We now close with a remark upon the last point: WHY IS THE SONG SAID TO BE A NEW SONG? But one remark here. It will be a new song, because the saints were never in such a position before as they will be when they sing this new song. They are in heaven now; but the scene of our text is something more than heaven. It refers to the time when all the

beast and the false prophet are, and shall be tormented day and night for ever and ever.

11 And I saw a great white throne, and him that sat on it, from whose face the earth and the heaven fled away; and there was found no place for them.

12 And I saw the dead, small and great, stand before God; and the books were opened: and another book was opened, which is the book of life: and the dead were judged out of those things which were written in the books, according to their works.

13 And the sea gave up the dead which were in it; and death and hell delivered up the dead which were in them: and they were judged every man according to their works.

14 And death and hell were cast into the lake of fire. This is the second death.

15 And whosoever was not found written in the book of life was cast into the lake of fire.

REVELATION 21

1 And I saw a new heaven and a new earth: for the first heaven and the first earth were passed away; and there was no more sea.

2 And I John saw the holy city, new Jerusalem, coming down from God out of heaven, prepared as a bride adorned for her husband.

3 And I heard a great voice out of heaven saying, Behold, the tabernacle of God is with men, and he will dwell with them, and they shall be his people, and God himself shall be with them, and be their God.

4 And God shall wipe away all tears from their eyes; and there shall be no more death, neither sorrow, nor crying, neither shall there be any more pain: for the former things are passed away.

5 And he that sat upon the throne said, Behold, I make all things new. And he said unto me, Write: for these words are true and faithful.

6 And he said unto me, It is done. I am Alpha and Omega, the beginning and the end. I will

Dan. vii, 22, sat upon them; and Judgment was given to them. 1 Cor. vi, 2.

5. The rest of the dead lived not till the thousand years – Mentioned, verse 4. Were ended – The thousand years during which Satan is bound both begin and end much sooner. The small time, and the second thousand years, begin at the same point, immediately after the first thousand. But neither the beginning of the first nor of the second thousand will be known to the men upon earth, as both the imprisonment of Satan and his loosing are transacted in the invisible world. By observing these two distinct thousand years, many difficulties are avoided. There is room enough for the fulfilling of all the prophecies, and those which before seemed to clash are reconciled; particularly those which speak, on the one hand, of a most flourishing state of the church as yet to come; and, on the other, of the fatal security of men in the last days of the world.

6. They shall be priests of God and of Christ – Therefore Christ is God. And shall reign with him – With Christ, a thousand years.

7. And when the former thousand years are fulfilled, Satan shall be loosed out of his prison – At the same time that the first resurrection begins. There is a great resemblance between this passage and chap. xii, 12. At the casting out of the dragon, there was joy in heaven, but there was woe upon earth: so at the loosing of Satan, the saints begin to reign with Christ; but the nations on earth are deceived.

8. And shall go forth to deceive the nations in the four corners of the earth – (That is, in all the earth) the more diligently, as he hath been so long restrained, and knoweth he hath but a small time. Gog and Magog – Magog, the second son of Japhet, is the father of the innumerable northern nations toward the east. The prince of these nations, of which the bulk of that army will consist, is termed Gog by Ezekiel also, Ezek. xxxviii, 2. Both Gog and Magog signify high or lifted up; a name well suiting both the prince and people. When that fierce leader of many nations shall appear, then will his own name be known. To gather them – Both Gog and his armies. Of Gog, little more is said, as being soon mingled with the rest in the common slaughter. The Revelation speaks of this the more briefly, because it had been so particularly described by Ezekiel. Whose number is as the sand of the sea – Immensely numerous: a proverbial expression.

9. And they went up on the breadth of the earth, or the land – Filling the whole breadth of it. And surrounded the camp of the saints – Perhaps the Gentile church, dwelling round about Jerusalem. And the beloved city – So termed, likewise, Ecclesiasticus xxiv, 11.

10. And they – All these. Shall be tormented day and night – That is, without any intermission. Strictly speaking, there is only night there: no day, no sun, no hope!

11. And I saw – A representation of that great day of the Lord. A great white throne – How great, who can say? White with the glory of God, of him that sat upon it, – Jesus Christ. The apostle does not attempt to describe him here; only adds that circumstance, far above all description, From whose face the earth and the heaven fled away – Probably both the aerial and the starry heaven; which "shall pass away with a great noise." And there was found no place for them – But they were wholly dissolved, the very "elements melting with fervent heat." It is not said, they were thrown into great commotions, but they fled entirely away; not, they started from their foundations, but they "fell into dissolution;" not, they removed to a distant place, but there was found no place for them; they ceased to exist; they were no more. And all this, not at the strict command of the Lord Jesus; not at his awful presence, or before his fiery indignation; but at the bare presence of his Majesty, sitting with severe but adorable dignity on his throne.

12. And I saw the dead, great and small – Of every age and condition. This includes, also, those who undergo a change equivalent to death, 1 Cor. xv, 51. And the books – Human judges have their books written with pen and ink: how

unbelief and unholiness now do. We may easily perceive what a variety of dreadful pains, diseases, and other calamities would cease, if all men were true and consistent Christians. All the evils of public and private contests would be ended, and happiness of every kind largely increased. Every man would try to lighten suffering, instead of adding to the sorrows around him. It is our duty to pray for the promised glorious days, and to do every thing in our public and private stations which can prepare for them.

7-10 While this world lasts, Satan's power in it will not be wholly destroyed, though it may be limited and lessened. No sooner is Satan let loose, than he again begins deceiving the nations, and stirring them up to make war with the saints and servants of God. It would be well if the servants and ministers of Christ were as active and persevering in doing good, as his enemies in doing mischief. God will fight this last and decisive battle for his people, that the victory may be complete, and the glory be to himself.

11-15 After the events just foretold, the end will speedily come; and there is no mention of any thing else, before the appearing of Christ to judge the world. This will be the great day: the Judge, the Lord Jesus Christ, will then put on majesty and terror. The persons to be judged are the dead, small and great; young and old, low and high, poor and rich. None are so mean, but they have some talents to account for; and none so great, as to avoid having to account for them. Not only those alive at the coming of Christ, but all the dead. There is a book of remembrance both for good and bad: and the book of the sinner's conscience, though formerly secret, will then be opened. Every man will recollect all his past actions, though he had long forgotten many of them. Another book shall be opened, the book of the Scriptures, the rule of life; it represents the Lord's knowledge of his people, and his declaring their repentance, faith, and good works; showing the blessings of the new covenant. By their works men shall be justified or condemned; he will try their principles by their practices. Those justified and acquitted by the gospel, shall be justified and acquitted by the Judge, and shall enter into eternal life, having nothing more to fear from death, or hell, or wicked men; for these are all destroyed together. This is the second death; it is the final separation of sinners from God. Let it be our great concern to see whether our Bibles justify or condemn us now; for Christ will judge the secrets of all men according to the gospel. Who shall dwell with devouring flames?

chosen race shall meet around the throne, when the last battle shall have been fought, and the last warrior shall have gained his crown. It is not now that they are thus singing, but it is in the glorious time to come, when all the hundred and forty and four thousand—or rather, the number typified by that number—will be all safely housed and all secure. I can conceive the period. Time was—eternity now reigns. The voice of God exclaims, "Are my beloved all safe?" The angel flies through paradise and returns with this message, "Yea, they are." "Is Fearful safe? Is Feeble-mind safe? Is Ready-to-Halt safe? Is Despondency safe?" "Yes, O king, they are," says he. "Shut-to the gates," says the Almighty, "they have been open night and day; shut them to now." Then, when all of them shall be there, then will be the time when the shout shall be louder than many waters, and the song shall begin which will never end. There is a story told in the history of brave Oliver Cromwell, which I use here to illustrate this new song. Cromwell and his Ironsides before they went to battle bowed the knee in prayer, and asked for God's help. Then, with their Bibles in their breasts, and their swords in their hands—a strange and unjustifiable mixture, but which their ignorance must excuse—they cried, "The Lord of hosts is with us, the God of Jacob is our refuge;" and rushing to battle they sang—They had to fight up hill for a long time, but at last the enemy fled. The Ironsides were about to pursue them and win the booty, when the stern harsh voice of Cromwell was heard—"Halt! halt! now the victory is won, before you rush to the spoil return thanks to God;" and they sang some such song as this—"Sing unto the Lord, for he has gotten us the victory! Sing unto the Lord." It was said to have been one of the most majestic sights in that strange, yet good man's history. (I say that word without blushing, for good he was.) For a time the hills seemed to leap, whilst the vast multitude, turning from the slain, still stained with blood, lifted up their hearts to God. We say, again, it was a strange sight, yet a glad one. But how great shall be that sight, when Christ shall be seen as a conqueror, and when all his warriors, fighting side by side with him, shall see the dragon beaten in pieces beneath their feet. Lo, their enemies are fled; they were driven like thin clouds before a Biscay gale. They are all gone, death is vanquished, Satan is cast into the lake of fire, and here stands the King himself, crowned with many crowns, the victor of the victors. And in the moment of exaltation the Redeemer will say, "Come let us sing unto the Lord;" and then, louder than the shout of many waters, they shall sing, "Hallelujah! the Lord God Omnipotent reigneth." Ah! that will be the full carrying out of the great scene! My feeble words cannot depict it. I send you away with this simple question, "Shall you be there to see the conqueror crowned?" Have you "a good hope through grace" that you shall? If so, be glad; if not, go to your

give unto him that is athirst of the fountain of the water of life freely.

7 He that overcometh shall inherit all things; and I will be his God, and he shall be my son.

8 But the fearful, and unbelieving, and the abominable, and murderers, and whoremongers, and sorcerers, and idolaters, and all liars, shall have their part in the lake which burneth with fire and brimstone: which is the second death.

9 And there came unto me one of the seven angels which had the seven vials full of the seven last plagues, and talked with me, saying, Come hither, I will shew thee the bride, the Lamb's wife.

10 And he carried me away in the spirit to a great and high mountain, and shewed me that great city, the holy Jerusalem, descending out of heaven from God,

11 Having the glory of God: and her light was like unto a stone most precious, even like a jasper stone, clear as crystal;

12 And had a wall great and high, and had twelve gates, and at the gates twelve angels, and names written thereon, which are the names of the twelve tribes of the children of Israel:

13 On the east three gates; on the north three gates; on the south three gates; and on the west three gates.

14 And the wall of the city had twelve foundations, and in them the names of the twelve apostles of the Lamb.

15 And he that talked with me had a golden reed to measure the city, and the gates thereof, and the wall thereof.

16 And the city lieth foursquare, and the length is as large as the breadth: and he measured the city with the reed, twelve thousand furlongs. The length and the breadth and the height of it are equal.

17 And he measured the wall thereof, an hundred and forty and four cubits, according to the measure of a man, that is, of the angel.

18 And the building of the wall of it was of jasper: and the city

different is the nature of these books! Were opened – O how many hidden things will then come to light; and how many will have quite another appearance than they had before in the sight of men!

13. Death and hades gave up the dead that were in them – Death gave up all the bodies of men; and hades, the receptacle of separate souls, gave them up, to be re-united to their bodies.

14. And death and hades were cast into the lake of fire – That is, were abolished for ever; for neither the righteous nor the wicked were to die any more: their souls and bodies were no more to be separated. Consequently, neither death nor hades could any more have a being.

REVELATION 21

1. And I saw – So it runs, chap. xix, 11, xx, 1, 4, 11, in a succession. All these several representations follow one another in order: so the vision reaches into eternity. A new heaven and a new earth – After the resurrection and general judgment. St. John is not now describing a flourishing state of the church, but a new and eternal state of all things.

2. And I saw the holy city – The new heaven, the new earth, and the new Jerusalem, are closely connected. This city is wholly new, belonging not to this world, not to the millennium, but to eternity. This appears from the series of the vision, the magnificence of the description, and the opposition of this city to the second death, chap. xx, 11, 12; xxi, 1, 2, 5, 8, 9; xxii, 5. Coming down – In the very act of descending.

3. They shall be his people, and God himself shall be with them, and be their God – So shall the covenant between God and his people be executed in the most glorious manner.

4. And death shall be no more – This is a full proof that this whole description belongs not to time, but eternity. Neither shall sorrow, or crying, or pain, be any more: for the former things are gone away – Under the former heaven, and upon the former earth, there was death and sorrow, crying and pain; all which occasioned many tears: but now pain and sorrow are fled away, and the saints have everlasting life and joy.

5. And he that sat upon the throne said – Not to St. John only. From the first mention of "him that sat upon the throne," chap. iv, 2, this is the first speech which is expressly ascribed to him. And he – The angel. Saith to me, Write – As follows. These sayings are faithful and true – This includes all that went before. The apostle seems again to have ceased writing, being overcome with ecstasy at the voice of him that spake.

6. And he – That sat upon the throne. Said to me, It is done – All that the prophets had spoken; all that was spoken, chap. iv, 1. We read this expression twice in this prophecy: first, chap. xvi, 17, at the fulfilling of the wrath of God; and here, at the making all things new. I am the Alpha and the Omega, the beginning and the end – The latter explains the former: the Everlasting. I will give to him that thirsteth – The Lamb saith the same, chap. xxii, 17.

7. He that overcometh – Which is more than, "he that thirsteth." Shall inherit these things – Which I have made new. I will be his God, and he shall be my son – Both in the Hebrew and Greek language, in which the scriptures were written, what we translate shall and will are one and the same word. The only difference consists in an English translation, or in the want of knowledge in him that interprets what he does not understand.

8. But the fearful and unbelieving – Who, through want of courage and faith, do not overcome. And abominable – That is, sodomites. And whoremongers, and sorcerers, and idolaters – These three sins generally went together; their part is in the lake.

9. And there came one of the seven angels that had the seven phials – Whereby

MATTHEW HENRY

CHARLES H. SPURGEON

REVELATION 21

A new heaven, and new earth: the new Jerusalem where God dwells, and banishes all sorrow from his people. (1-8)

Its heavenly origin, glory, and secure defense. (9-21)

Its perfect happiness, as enlightened with the presence of God and the Lamb, and in the free access of multitudes, made holy. (22-27)

1-8 The new heaven and the new earth will not be separate from each other; the earth of the saints, their glorified, bodies, will be heavenly. The old world, with all its troubles and tumults, will have passed away. There will be no sea; this aptly represents freedom from conflicting passions, temptations, troubles, changes, and alarms; from whatever can divide or interrupt the communion of saints. This new Jerusalem is the church of God in its new and perfect state, the church triumphant. Its blessedness came wholly from God, and depends on him. The presence of God with his people in heaven, will not be interrupted as it is on earth, he will dwell with them continually. All effects of former trouble shall be done away. They have often been in tears, by reason of sin, of affliction, of the calamities of the church; but no signs, no remembrance of former sorrows shall remain. Christ makes all things new. If we are willing and desirous that the gracious Redeemer should make all things new in order hearts and nature, he will make all things new in respect of our situation, till he has brought us to enjoy complete happiness. See the certainty of the promise. God gives his titles, Alpha and Omega, the Beginning and the End, as a pledge for the full performance. Sensual and sinful pleasures are muddy and poisoned waters; and the best earthly comforts are like the scanty supplies of a cistern; when idolized, they become broken cisterns, and yield only vexation. But the joys which Christ imparts are like waters springing from a fountain, pure, refreshing, abundant, and eternal. The sanctifying consolations of the Holy Spirit prepare for heavenly happiness; they are streams which flow for us in the wilderness. The fearful durst not meet the difficulties of religion, their slavish fear came from their unbelief; but those who were so dastardly as not to dare to take up the cross of Christ, were yet so desperate as to run into abominable wickedness. The agonies and terrors of the first death will lead to the far greater terrors and agonies of eternal death.

9-21 God has various employments for his holy angels. Sometimes they sound the trumpet of Divine Providence, and warn a careless world; sometimes they discover things of a heavenly

houses, fall on your knees, and pray to God to save you from that terrible place which must certainly be your portion, instead of that great heaven of which I preach, unless you turn to God with full purpose of heart.

A NEW CREATION

Sermon number 3467 published on Thursday, July 15th, 1915. Delivered at the Metropolitan Tabernacle, Newington.

He that sat upon the throne said, Behold I make all things new.—Revelation 21:5.

I. A NEW CREATION.

I make. That is a divine word. I make all things. That, also, is divine. I make all things new. This our Lord Jesus Christ has done upon the greatest scale. We must view his purpose. It is the purpose and intention of the Lord Jesus to make this world entirely new. You recollect how it was made at first—pure and perfect. It sang with its sister-spheres the song of joy and reverence. It was a fair world, full of everything that was lovely, beautiful, happy, holy. And if we might be permitted to dream for a moment of what it would have been if it had continued as God created it, one might fancy what a blessed world it would be at this moment. Had it possessed a teeming population like its present one, and if, one by one, those godly ones had been caught away, like Elijah, without knowing death, to be succeeded by pious descendants—oh! what a blessed world it would have been! A world where every man would have been a priest, and every house a temple, every garment a vestment, and every meal a sacrifice, and every place holiness to the Lord, for the tabernacle of God would have been among them, and God himself would have dwelt among them! What songs would have hailed the rising of the sun—the birds of paradise caroling on every hill and in every dale their Maker's praise! What songs would have ushered in the stillness of the night! Ay, and angels, hovering over this fair world, would oft have heard the strain of joy breaking the silence of midnight, as glad and pure hearts beheld the eyes of the Creator beaming down upon them from the stars which stud the vault of heaven. But there came a serpent, and his craft spoiled it all. He whispered into the ears of a mother Eve; she fell, and we fell with her, and what a world this now is! If a man walks about in it with his eyes open, he will see it to be a horrible sphere. I do not mean that its rivers, its lakes, its valleys, its mountains are repulsive. Nay, it is a world fit for angels, naturally; but it is a horrible world morally. As I walked the other day down the streets of Paris, and saw the soldiers with their pretty dresses, and the knives and forks which they carried with them to carve men and make a meal for death, I could not

was pure gold, like unto clear glass.

19 And the foundations of the wall of the city were garnished with all manner of precious stones. The first foundation was jasper; the second, sapphire; the third, a chalcedony; the fourth, an emerald;

20 The fifth, sardonyx; the sixth, sardius; the seventh, chrysolite; the eighth, beryl; the ninth, a topaz; the tenth, a chrysoprasus; the eleventh, a jacinth; the twelfth, an amethyst.

21 And the twelve gates were twelve pearls; every several gate was of one pearl: and the street of the city was pure gold, as it were transparent glass.

22

And I saw no temple therein: for the Lord God Almighty and the Lamb are the temple of it.

23 And the city had no need of the sun, neither of the moon, to shine in it: for the glory of God did lighten it, and the Lamb is the light thereof.

24 And the nations of them which are saved shall walk in the light of it: and the kings of the earth do bring their glory and honor into it.

25 And the gates of it shall not be shut at all by day: for there shall be no night there.

26 And they shall bring the glory and honor of the nations into it.

27 And there shall in no wise enter into it any thing that defileth, neither whatsoever worketh abomination, or maketh a lie: but they which are written in the Lamb's book of life.

REVELATION 22

1 And he shewed me a pure river of water of life, clear as crystal, proceeding out of the throne of God and of the Lamb.

2 In the midst of the street of it, and on either side of the river, was there the tree of life, which bare twelve manner of fruits, and yielded her fruit every month: and the leaves of the tree were for the healing of the nations.

3 And there shall be no more

room had been made for the kingdom of God. Saying, Come, I will show thee the bride – The same angel had before showed him Babylon, chap. xvii, 1, which is directly opposed to the new Jerusalem.

10. And he carried me away in the spirit – The same expression as before, chap. xvii, 3. And showed me the holy city Jerusalem – The old city is now forgotten, so that this is no longer termed the new, but absolutely Jerusalem.

11. Having the glory of God – For her light, verse 23, Isaiah xl, 1, 2, Zech. ii, 5. Her window – There was only one, which ran all round the city. The light did not come in from without through this for the glory of God is within the city. But it shines out from within to a great distance, verses 23, 24.

12. Twelve angels – Still waiting upon the heirs of salvation.

14. And the wall of the city had twelve foundations, and on them the names of the twelve apostles of the Lamb – Figuratively showing that the inhabitants of the city had built only on that faith which the apostles once delivered to the saints.

15. And he measured the city, twelve thousand furlongs – Not in circumference, but on each of the four sides. Jerusalem was thirty-three furlongs in circumference; Alexandria thirty in length, ten in breadth. Nineveh is reported to have been four hundred furlongs round; Babylon four hundred and eighty. But what inconsiderable villages were all these compared to the new Jerusalem!

18. And the building of the wall was jasper – That is, the wall was built of jasper. And the city – The houses, was of pure gold.

19. And the foundations were adorned with precious stones – That is, beautifully made of them. The precious stones on the high priest's breastplate of judgment were a proper emblem to express the happiness of God's church in his presence with them, and in the blessing of his protection.

20. A sardonyx is red streaked with white; a sardius, of a deep red; a chrysolite, of a deep yellow; a beryl, sea-green; a topaz, pale yellow; a chrysoprase is greenish and transparent, with gold specks; a jacinth, of a red purple; an amethyst, violet purple.

22. The Lord God and the Lamb are the temple of it – He fills the new heaven and the new earth. He surrounds the city and sanctifies it, and all that are therein. He is "all in all."

23. The glory of God – Infinitely brighter than the shining of the sun.

24. And the nations – The whole verse is taken from Isaiah lx, 3. Shall walk by the light thereof – Which throws itself outward from the city far and near. And the kings of the earth – Those of them who have a part there. Bring their glory into it – Not their old glory, which is now abolished; but such as becomes the new earth, and receives an immense addition by their entrance into the city.

26. And they shall bring the glory of the nations into it – It seems, a select part of each nation; that is, all which can contribute to make this city honorable and glorious shall be found in it; as if all that was rich and precious throughout the world was brought into one city.

27. Common – That is, unholy. But those who are written in the Lamb's book of life – True, holy, persevering believers. This blessedness is enjoyed by those only; and, as such, they are registered among them who are to inherit eternal life.

REVELATION 22

1. And he showed me a river of the water of life – The ever fresh and fruitful effluence of the Holy Ghost. See Ezek. xlvii, 1-12; where also the trees are mentioned which "bear fruit every month," that is, perpetually. Proceeding out of the throne of God, and of the Lamb – "All that the Father hath," saith the Son of God, "is mine;" even the throne of his glory.

2. In the midst of the street – Here is the paradise of God, mentioned, chap. ii, 7. Is the tree of life – Not one tree only, but many. Every month – That is, in

MATTHEW HENRY

CHARLES H. SPURGEON

nature of the heirs of salvation. Those who would have clear views of heaven, must get as near to heaven as they can, on the mount of meditation and faith. The subject of the vision is the church of God in a perfect, triumphant state, shining in its luster; glorious in relation to Christ; which shows that the happiness of heaven consists in intercourse with God, and in conformity to him. The change of emblems from a bride to a city, shows that we are only to take general ideas from this description. The wall is for security. Heaven is a safe state; those who are there, are separated and secured from all evils and enemies. This city is vast; here is room for all the people of God. The foundation of the wall; the promise and power of God, and the purchase of Christ, are the strong foundations of the safety and happiness of the church. These foundations are set forth by twelve sorts of precious stones, denoting the variety and excellence of the doctrines of the gospel, or of the graces of the Holy Spirit, or the personal excellences of the Lord Jesus Christ. Heaven has gates; there is a free admission to all that are sanctified; they shall not find themselves shut out. These gates were all of pearls. Christ is the Pearl of great price, and he is our Way to God. The street of the city was pure gold, like transparent glass. The saints in heaven tread gold under foot. The saints are there at rest, yet it is not a state of sleep and idleness; they have communion, not only with God, but with one another. All these glories but faintly represent heaven.

22-27 Perfect and direct communion with God, will more than supply the place of gospel institutions. And what words can more fully express the union and co-equality of the Son with the Father, in the Godhead? What a dismal world would this be, if it were not for the light of the sun! What is there in heaven that supplies its place? The glory of God lightens that city, and the Lamb is the Light thereof. God in Christ will be an everlasting Fountain of knowledge and joy to the saints in heaven. There is no night, therefore no need of shutting the gates; all is at peace and secure. The whole shows us that we should be more and more led to think of heaven as filled with the glory of God, and enlightened by the presence of the Lord Jesus. Nothing sinful or unclean, idolatrous, or false and deceitful, can enter. All the inhabitants are made perfect in holiness. Now the saints feel a sad mixture of corruption, which hinders them in the service of God, and interrupts their communion with him; but, at their entrance into the holy of holies, they are washed in the laver of Christ's blood, and presented to the Father without spot. None are admitted into heaven who work abominations. It is free from

help thinking—this is a pretty world, this is. Only let one man lift his finger, and a hundred thousand men are ready to meet a hundred thousand other men, all intent upon doing—what? Why, upon cutting each other's throats, upon tearing out each other's bleeding hearts, and wading up to their knees in each other's gore, till the ditches be full of blood, horses and men all mingled, and left to be food for dogs and for carrion crows. And then the victors on either side in the fray, return, and beat the drums, and sound the trumpets, and say, Glory! glory! see what we have done. Devils could not be worse than men when their passions are let loose. Dogs would scarce tear each other as men do. Men of intellect sit down, and put their fingers to their foreheads, racking their brains to find out new ways of using gunpowder, and shot, and shell, so as to be able to blow twenty thousand souls into eternity as easily as twenty might be massacred by present appliances. And he is considered a clever man, a patriot, a benefactor of his own nation, who, by dint of genius, can discover some new way of destroying his fellow creatures. Oh! it is a horrible world, appalling to think of. When God looks at it, I wonder he does not stamp it out, just as you and I do a spark of coal that flies upon our carpet from the fire. It is a dreadful world. But Jesus Christ, who knew that we should never make this world much better, let us do what we would with it, designed from the very first to make a new world of it. Truly, truly, this seems to me to be a glorious purpose. To make a world is something wonderful, but to make a world new is something more wonderful still.

II. ADORE THIS GREAT REGENERATOR.

He says, Behold I make all things new. Behold him! He is a man dressed in the common garments of the poor! He hath no form nor comeliness, and when you shall see him there is no beauty in him that you should desire him. He has come to make the world new. He has no soldiery, no book of laws, no new philosophy. He had come to make the world new, and to do this he has brought with him—what? Why, himself. He spends a life of weariness and sorrow amongst those who despise him, and if you want to know first and foremost how he makes all things new, you must see him sweating great drops of blood in the garden—that is the blood of the new world which he is pouring forth! You must see him bound, scourged, spat upon, led to the accursed tree. While God's wrath for sin is yet unspent, the world cannot be new; but when that wrath on account of sin is all poured upon the head of the great Substitute, then the world stands in a new relation to God, and it can be a new world. See the Savior then, in groans and pangs which cannot be described, bearing the curse of God, for he made him to be sin for us, though he knew no sin. The curse fell on him, as it is written, Cursed is every one

curse: but the throne of God and of the Lamb shall be in it; and his servants shall serve him:

4 And they shall see his face; and his name shall be in their foreheads.

5 And there shall be no night there; and they need no candle, neither light of the sun; for the Lord God giveth them light: and they shall reign for ever and ever.

6 And he said unto me, These sayings are faithful and true: and the Lord God of the holy prophets sent his angel to shew unto his servants the things which must shortly be done.

7 Behold, I come quickly: blessed is he that keepeth the sayings of the prophecy of this book.

8 And I John saw these things, and heard them. And when I had heard and seen, I fell down to worship before the feet of the angel which shewed me these things.

9 Then saith he unto me, See thou do it not: for I am thy fellowservant, and of thy brethren the prophets, and of them which keep the sayings of this book: worship God.

10 And he saith unto me, Seal not the sayings of the prophecy of this book: for the time is at hand.

11 He that is unjust, let him be unjust still: and he which is filthy, let him be filthy still: and he that is righteous, let him be righteous still: and he that is holy, let him be holy still.

12 And, behold, I come quickly; and my reward is with me, to give every man according as his work shall be.

13 I am Alpha and Omega, the beginning and the end, the first and the last.

14 Blessed are they that do his commandments, that they may have right to the tree of life, and may enter in through the gates into the city.

15 For without are dogs, and sorcerers, and whoremongers, and murderers, and idolaters, and whosoever loveth and maketh a lie.

16 I Jesus have sent mine angel to testify unto you these

inexpressible abundance. The variety, likewise, as well as the abundance of the fruits of the Spirit, may be intimated thereby. And the leaves are for the healing of the nations – For the continuing their health, not the restoring it; for no sickness is there.

3. And there shall be no more curse – But pure life and blessing; every effect of the displeasure of God for sin being now totally removed. But the throne of God and the Lamb shall be in it – That is, the glorious presence and reign of God. And his servants – The highest honor in the universe. Shalt worship him – The noblest employment.

4. And shall see his face – Which was not granted to Moses. They shall have the nearest access to, and thence the highest resemblance of, him. This is the highest expression in the language of scripture to denote the most perfect happiness of the heavenly state, 1 John iii, 2. And his name shall be on their foreheads – Each of them shall be openly acknowledged as God's own property, and his glorious nature most visibly shine forth in them.

5. And they shall reign for ever and ever – What encouragement is this to the patience and faithfulness of the saints, that, whatever their sufferings are, they will work out for them "an eternal weight of glory!" Thus ends the doctrine of this Revelation, in the everlasting happiness of all the faithful. The mysterious ways of Providence are cleared up, and all things issue in an eternal Sabbath, an everlasting state of perfect peace and happiness, reserved for all who endure to the end.

6. And he said to me – Here begins the conclusion of the book, exactly agreeing with the introduction, (particularly verses 6, 7, 10, with chap. i, 1, 3,) and giving light to the whole book, as this book does to the whole scripture. These sayings are faithful and true – All the things which you have heard and seen shall be faithfully accomplished in their order, and are infallibly true. The Lord, the God of the holy prophets – Who inspired and authorized them of old. Hath now sent me his angel, to show his servants – By thee. The things which must be done shortly – Which will begin to be performed immediately.

7. Behold, I come quickly – Saith our Lord himself, to accomplish these things. Happy is he that keepeth – Without adding or diminishing, verses 18, 19, the words of this book.

8. I fell down to worship at the feet of the angel – The very same words which occur, chap. xix, 10. The reproof of the angel, likewise, See thou do it not, for I am thy fellow servant, is expressed in the very same terms as before. May it not be the very same incident which is here related again? Is not this far more probable, than that the apostle would commit a fault again, of which he had been so solemnly warned before?

9. See thou do it not – The expression in the original is short and elliptical, as is usual in showing vehement aversion.

10. And he saith to me – After a little pause. Seal not the sayings of this book – Conceal them not, like the things that are sealed up. The time is nigh – Wherein they shall begin to take place.

11. He that is unrighteous – As if he had said, The final judgment is at hand; after which the condition of all mankind will admit of no change for ever. Unrighteous – Unjustified. Filthy – Unsanctified, unholy.

12. I – Jesus Christ. Come quickly – To judge the world. And my reward is with me – The rewards which I assign both to the righteous and the wicked are given at my coming. To give to every man according as his work – His whole inward and outward behavior shall be.

13. I am the Alpha and the Omega, the first and the last – Who exist from everlasting to everlasting. How clear, incontestable a proof, does our Lord here give of his divine glory!

14. Happy are they that do his commandments – His, who saith, I come – He speaks of himself. That they may have right – Through his gracious covenant. To

MATTHEW HENRY

CHARLES H. SPURGEON

hypocrites, such as make lies. As nothing unclean can enter heaven, let us be stirred up by these glimpses of heavenly things, to use all diligence, and to perfect holiness in the fear of God.

REVELATION 22

A description of the heavenly state, under the figures of the water and the tree of life, and of the throne of God and the Lamb. (1-5)

The truth and certain fulfilling of all the prophetic visions. The Holy Spirit, and the bride, the church, invite, and say, Come. (6-19)

The closing blessing. (20,21)

1-5 All streams of earthly comfort are muddy; but these are clear, and refreshing. They give life, and preserve life, to those who drink of them, and thus they will flow for evermore. These point to the quickening and sanctifying influences of the Holy Spirit, as given to sinners through Christ. The Holy Spirit, proceeding from the Father and the Son, applies this salvation to our souls by his new-creating love and power. The trees of life are fed by the pure waters of the river that comes from the throne of God. The presence of God in heaven, is the health and happiness of the saints. This tree was an emblem of Christ, and of all the blessings of his salvation; and the leaves for the healing of the nations, mean that his favor and presence supply all good to the inhabitants of that blessed world. The devil has no power there; he cannot draw the saints from serving God, nor can he disturb them in the service of God. God and the Lamb are here spoken of as one. Service there shall be not only freedom, but honor and dominion. There will be no night; no affliction or dejection, no pause in service or enjoyment: no diversions or pleasures or man's inventing will there be wanted. How different all this from gross and merely human views of heavenly happiness, even those which refer to pleasures of the mind!

6-19 The Lord Jesus spake by the angel, solemnly confirming the contents of this book, particularly of this last vision. He is the Lord God faithful and true. Also by his messengers; the holy angels showed them to holy men of God. They are things that must shortly be done; Christ will come quickly, and put all things out of doubt. And by the integrity of that angel who had been the apostle's interpreter. He refused to accept religious worship from John, and reproved him for offering it. This presents another testimony against idolatrous worship of saints and angels. God calls every one to witness to the declarations here made. This book, thus kept open, will have effect upon men; the filthy and unjust will be

that hangeth on a tree. It pleased the Father to bruise him; he hath put him to grief; he hath made his soul to be an offering for sin. That dolorous pain, then, of the Master was the world's new-making. It was then and there that the world was born again. No mother's pangs, when she brought forth a man-child, were such as those of Christ when he brought forth the new creation. It was there in the travail of his soul—did you ever catch that idea, the travail of his soul—it was there that the new world was born! Behold I make all things new is a mysterious voice from the broken heart of a dying Savior. From the empty tomb, as he rises, I hear it come in silvery notes, Behold I make all things new. You must trace the birth of the new creation up to the grave of our Lord Jesus Christ, to the place where the cross stood, and where his body lay.

III. BEHOLD AND BELIEVE.

Behold, the Lord Jesus is now enthroned in heaven. He it is who makes all things new. Is not this what some of you here present deeply need. If you look within, yourselves will see much to disgust and alarm you. Peradventure, you dare not take stock of yourselves now; you dare not consider where you are, nor what you are, nor whither you are bound. To speak candidly, you say, I want reforming. Very likely, but you want a great deal more than mere reformation. I have heard of a being who used habitually to swear, God mend me! Somebody said, Better make a new one. That is the case with full many of you. You are saying, Well, I will turn over a new leaf. You had better shut the book up altogether, and never turn over any more leaves, for all the pages are alike bad. Oh! well, says one, I shall try if I cannot alter. I wish you would try God's altering of you, instead of altering yourselves. Well, but surely, surely, I may wash and be clean; I will try to make myself as clean as possible Yes, yes, that is all very well; but what if you have a corpse in the house. I would have you make it clean, yet that will not make it live. However much you may wash it, it is corrupt still. You may reform yourselves as much as ever you please, all your reformation will be futile; you need more, a great deal more than that. The fact is, you must be made new. Nothing less will do; you must be made new; you must be born again. Ah! says one, if I could be made new, there might be a chance for me. Well now, Christ looks down from this throne in heaven, and he says, Behold I will make all things new. Yes, you say, but he will not make me new. Why not? Does he not say, I make all things new? But my heart is as hard as a rock, say you. Well, but he says, I will make all things new, so he can give you a new heart. Oh! but I am so very stubborn. Aye, aye, but he makes all things new, and he can make you as tender and sensitive as a little child. Oftentimes a gray-headed sinner has looked back to his childhood, and remembered the time when he used to sing his little

things in the churches. I am the root and the offspring of David, and the bright and morning star.

17 And the Spirit and the bride say, Come. And let him that heareth say, Come. And let him that is athirst come. And whosoever will, let him take the water of life freely.

18 For I testify unto every man that heareth the words of the prophecy of this book, If any man shall add unto these things, God shall add unto him the plagues that are written in this book:

19 And if any man shall take away from the words of the book of this prophecy, God shall take away his part out of the book of life, and out of the holy city, and from the things which are written in this book.

20 He which testifieth these things saith, Surely I come quickly. Amen. Even so, come, Lord Jesus. The grace of our Lord Jesus Christ be with you all. Amen.

the tree of life – To all the blessings signified by it. When Adam broke his commandment, he was driven from the tree of life. They who keep his commandments shall eat thereof.

15. Without are dogs – The sentence in the original is abrupt, as expressing abhorrence. The gates are ever open; but not for dogs; fierce and rapacious men.

16. I Jesus have sent my angel to testify these things – Primarily. To you – The seven angels of the churches; then to those churches – and afterwards to all other churches in succeeding ages. I – as God. Am the root – And source of David's family and kingdom; as man, am descended from his loins. "I am the star out of Jacob," Num. xxiv, 17; like the bright morning star, who put an end to the night of ignorance, sin, and sorrow, and usher in an eternal day of light, purity, and joy.

17. The Spirit and the bride – The Spirit of adoption in the bride, in the heart of every true believer. Say – With earnest desire and expectation. Come – And accomplish all the words of this prophecy. And let him that thirsteth, come – Here they also who are farther off are invited. And whosoever will, let him take the water of life – He may partake of my spiritual and unspeakable blessings, as freely as he makes use of the most common refreshments; as freely as he drinks of the running stream.

18, 19. I testify to every one, &c. – From the fullness of his heart, the apostle utters this testimony, this weighty admonition, not only to the churches of Asia, but to all who should ever hear this book. He that adds, all the plagues shall be added to him; he that takes from it, all the blessings shall be taken from him; and, doubtless, this guilt is incurred by all those who lay hindrances in the way of the faithful, which prevent them from hearing their Lord's "I come," and answering, "Come, Lord Jesus." This may likewise be considered as an awful sanction, given to the whole New Testament; in like manner as Moses guarded the law, Deut. iv, 2, and Deut. xii, 32; and as God himself did, Mal. iv, 4, in closing the canon of the Old Testament.

20. He that testifieth these things – Even all that is contained in this book. Saith – For the encouragement of the church in all her afflictions. Yea – Answering the call of the Spirit and the bride. I come quickly – To destroy all her enemies, and establish her in a state of perfect and everlasting happiness. The apostle expresses his earnest desire and hope of this, by answering, Amen. Come, Lord Jesus!

21. The grace – The free love. Of the Lord Jesus – And all its fruits. Be with all – Who thus long for his appearing!

MATTHEW HENRY

CHARLES H. SPURGEON

more so, but it will confirm, strengthen, and further sanctify those who are upright with God. Never let us think that a dead or disobedient faith will save us, for the First and the Last has declared that those alone are blessed who do his commandments. It is a book that shuts out from heaven all wicked and unrighteous persons, particularly those who love and make lies, therefore cannot itself be a lie. There is no middle place or condition. Jesus, who is the Spirit of prophecy, has given his churches this morning-light of prophecy, to assure them of the light of the perfect day approaching. All is confirmed by an open and general invitation to mankind, to come and partake freely of the promises and of the privileges of the gospel. The Spirit, by the sacred word, and by convictions and influence in the sinner's conscience, says, Come to Christ for salvation; and the bride, or the whole church, on earth and in heaven, says, Come and share our happiness. Lest any should hesitate, it is added, Let whosoever will, or, is willing, come and take of the water of life freely. May every one who hears or reads these words, desire at once to accept the gracious invitation. All are condemned who should dare to corrupt or change the word of God, either by adding to it, or taking from it.

20,21 After discovering these things to his people on earth, Christ seems to take leave of them, and return to heaven; but he assures them it shall not be long before he comes again. And while we are busy in the duties of our different stations of life; whatever labors may try us, whatever difficulties may surround us, whatever sorrows may press us down, let us with pleasure hear our Lord proclaiming, Behold, I come quickly; I come to put an end to the labor and suffering of my servants. I come, and my reward of grace is with me, to recompense, with royal bounty, every work of faith and labor of love. I come to receive my faithful, persevering people to myself, to dwell forever in that blissful world. Amen, even so, come, Lord Jesus. A blessing closes the whole. By the grace of Christ we must be kept in joyful expectation of his glory, fitted for it, and preserved to it; and his glorious appearance will be joyful to those who partake of his grace and favor here. Let all add, Amen. Let us earnestly thirst after greater measures of the gracious influences of the blessed Jesus in our souls, and his gracious presence with us, till glory has made perfect his grace toward us. Glory be to the Father, and to the Son, and to the Holy Ghost; as it was in the beginning, is now, and ever shall be, world without end. Amen.

hymn at his mother's knee, and he has said, "Ah! I have been in many strange places since then, and my heart has got seared and hard; I wish I could get back to what I was then!" Well, you can, you can. Christ can bring you there. Nay, he can bring you to something better than you ever were when those golden ringlets hung so plentifully about that pretty little head of yours, for you were not so innocent then as you now think you were. Christ can make you really pure in heart; he can make you a new creature, so that you shall be converted and become as a little child. Oh! say you, how can I get it? How can I prepare myself for him? You do not want to prepare yourself for him. Go to him just as you are; trust him to do it, and he will do it. That is faith, you know—trust, dependence. Canst thou believe that Christ can save thee? Oh! thou canst believe that; well now, wilt thou trust him to save thee? Wilt thou trust him to deliver thee from thy drunkenness, from thine angry temper, thy pride, thy love of self, thy lusts? Dost thou desire to be a new creature in Christ Jesus? If so, that very desire must have come from heaven. I could fain hope that he has already begun the good work in you, and he that begins it will carry it on. Do not be afraid, however bad thy character, or however vicious thy disposition. "Behold," says Christ, "I make all things new." What a wonder it is that a man should ever have a new heart!

We will not entertain any more doubt about Christ's power to save. Rather, by God's grace, may we henceforth believe more in him, and, according to our faith, so shall it be done unto us. If we can only trust him for those of our friends whose faults seem to us few and light, our little trust will reap little reward; but if we can go with strong faith in a great God, and bring great sinners in our arms, and put them down before this mighty Regenerator of men, and say, "Lord, if thou wilt thou canst make them new; and if we will never cease the pleading till we get the blessing, then we shall see ever-accumulating illustrations of the fact that Jesus makes all things new;" and calling up the witnesses of his redeeming power, we shall cry in the ears of a drowsy Church and an incredulous world, "Behold, behold, behold! He makes all things new." The Lord give us eyes to see it. Amen.